THE LAW
of
REAL PROPERTY

BY

THE RT. HON. SIR ROBERT MEGARRY,
M.A., LL.D. (Cantab.), Hon.LL.D. (Hull, Nottingham,
The Law Society of Upper Canada, and London),
Hon. D.U. (Essex), F.B.A.
*A Bencher of Lincoln's Inn; an Honorary Fellow of Trinity Hall, Cambridge;
formerly the Vice-Chancellor of the Supreme Court*

AND

SIR WILLIAM WADE,
Q.C., M.A., LL.D. Hon. Litt.D. (Cantab.), F.B.A.
*Formerly the Master of Gonville and Caius College, Cambridge;
formerly Rouse Ball Professor of English Law in the
University of Cambridge and Professor of English Law in the
University of Oxford; Honorary Bencher of Lincoln's Inn*

EIGHTH EDITION

BY

CHARLES HARPUM
LL.D. (Cantab.)
*A Barrister and Bencher of Lincoln's Inn;
Emeritus Fellow of Downing College,
Cambridge; a former Law Commissioner 1994–2001*

STUART BRIDGE
M.A. (Cantab.)
*One of Her Majesty's Circuit Judges; Bencher of the Middle Temple;
Life Fellow of Queens' College, Cambridge; Law Commissioner
for England and Wales 2001–2008*

and

MARTIN DIXON
M.A. (Oxon.); Ph.D. (Cantab.)
*Fellow of Queens' College, Cambridge;
Reader in the Law of Real Property, University of Cambridge*

LONDON
SWEET & MAXWELL
2012

EET & MAXWELL

 THOMSON REUTERS

First Edition	- - - -	1957
Second Impression	- -	1958
Second Edition	- - - -	1959
Second Impression	- -	1964
Third Edition	- - - -	1966
Second Impression	- -	1971
Fourth Edition	- - - -	1975
Second Impression	- -	1979
Third Impression	- -	1982
Fifth Edition	- - - -	1984
Sixth Edition	- - - -	2000
Seventh Edition	- - - -	2008
Eighth Edition	- - - -	2012

Published in 2012 by Sweet & Maxwell, 100 Avenue Road, London NW3 3PF
part of Thomson Reuters (Professional) UK Limited
(Registered in England & Wales, company No 1679046.
Registered Office and address for service:
Aldgate House, 33 Aldgate High Street, London EC3N 1DL)

Typeset by Interactive Sciences Ltd, Gloucester
Printed and bound by CPI Group (UK) Ltd, Croydon, CR0 4YY

*For further information on our products and services, visit www.sweetandmaxwell.co.uk

No natural forests were destroyed to make this product;
only farmed timber was used and re-planted.

A CIP catalogue record for this book is available from the British Library.

Paperback ISBN 978-041-402329-1
Hardback ISBN 978-041-404596-5

Thomson Reuters and the Thomson Reuters logo are trademarks of Thomson Reuters.
Sweet & Maxwell ® is a registered trademark of Thomson Reuters (Professional) UK
Limited.

PREFACE

In this eighth edition, *Megarry & Wade* returns to the pattern it followed in the 1970s of appearing every four years. The most striking features of the last four years have been as follows.

First, the law on perpetuities and has been prospectively eliminated except in relation to trusts and wills by the Perpetuities and Accumulations Act 2009 and even there its role is now simply a restraining one. Accumulations are for almost all purposes now gone. Chapter 9 has been substantially rewritten to reflect these striking developments.

Second, the major legislative development that was considered in the seventh edition of the work, the Land Registration Act 2002, has now been the subject of a number of important judicial decisions, many on appeal from the adjudicator, in which it has been explored and illuminated (see Chapters 7 and 35).

Third, there have been a crop of important decisions from the highest appellate court, which, since the last edition, has become the Supreme Court. These decisions include two on proprietary estoppel, the first time that this doctrine has been considered at this level for over a century (see Chapter 16). There have also been important recent Supreme Court decisions on leases for lives (considered in Chapter 17) and on the downward extent of land ownership (see Chapter 3). The Supreme Court has perhaps been rather less successful in its latest attempt to clarify the rights of unmarried cohabitants (see Chapter 11).

Fourth, the Human Rights Act 1998 has begun to make itself felt rather more in relation to property law than it had previously (see Chapters 1 and 22).

The law is stated as of December 1, 2011.

S.B.

M.J.D.

C.H.

Queens' College,
Cambridge

Falcon Chambers,
London

January 16, 2012

PREFACE TO THE FIRST EDITION

This is a book in which we have attempted to state the English law of real property within a reasonable compass and in a form which will be both intelligible to students and helpful to practitioners. In some other spheres, the claims of student and practitioner are barely reconcilable, but here we are fortunate in our subject. In the main, the English law of real property rests on the logical development of clear principles, and it is these principles that throughout we have sought to emphasise. There are indeed certain passages in this book which are addressed solely or mainly to the student, and a number of details which, though important to the practitioner, need trouble none save the more zealous students; but for the most part it is our hope to have achieved a work of dual utility.

The book is founded on pre-war manuscript from which *A Manual of the Law of Real Property* has already been drawn. As first conceived, the task was to revise and bring the manuscript up to date; in the outcome most, but by no means all, of that manuscript has found its way into this book, while at the same time much new material has been interwoven with it. For unlike the manuscript and the *Manual*, this is a work of joint authorship, with all the mutual aid that flows from the application of a second mind to that was conceived and in the main executed as a complete entity. Instead of dividing up the subject-matter and each writing the text of part, nearly all of this book has been covered by each of us in close detail, often more than once. It would be too much to hope that even this time-consuming process has extirpated all error, but we hope that the result will be thought to have justified the effort. In addition to this, other factors have combined to delay publication, including our geographical separation, the press of other claims upon our time, difficulties in resolving how much of the original manuscript to omit, and the troubles of the printing industry in 1956. The printers' skill has, however, enabled us to keep the text under constant revision, and although the vicissitudes of publication have made it difficult to ensure that the whole of the text has been brought up to the same date, we hope that in general the law will be found to have been accurately stated down to the beginning of 1957, with such later additions as the state of the proofs admitted.

The publication of this work completes the original scheme for two books of a common design but different scope. Those who in student days have become familiar with the *Manual* should be able to turn with ease to the greater amplitude of this book; and the similarity of design will, we hope, not only assist teachers of law in their tasks, but also make it possible for future editions of the *Manual* to become a little slimmer.

Finally, we have the pleasure of giving thanks where thanks are due. Some of our obligations are general and distributed; we are grateful to many of those whom we have severally sought to teach, for they have themselves taught us more than they are ever likely to realise. Other gratitude is more specific. The publishers and printers have earned more praise than even they are accustomed to; it would be wrong if we did not mention specifically the printers' skill and publishers' generosity which made it possible for the work to proceed when the manuscript and galley proofs had reached a condition more deplorable than any we had seen before. Mr I. Goldsmith also gave invaluable help with the manuscript at that stage, Mr P. V. Baker read the proofs, and Mr R. Higgins prepared the table of cases and table of statutes. To all of them we are grateful.

LINCOLN'S INN,   R. E. M.
New Year's Day, 1957   H. W. R. W.

THE LAW OF REAL PROPERTY

CONTENTS

APPENDIX

TABLE OF CASES

xv

Table of Cases

TABLE OF STATUTES

COMMONWEALTH STATUTES

ALPHABETICAL LIST OF STATUTES

This list will enable any statute to be found in the chronological Table of Statutes

TABLE OF STATUTORY INSTRUMENTS

GLOSSARY

[The object of this glossary is to provide a ready source of reference to the meanings of some of the more troublesome technical expressions used in the text. For the most part, brief but not necessarily exhaustive definitions have been given, with references to the paragraphs of the text where further information can be obtained and the terms may be seen in their context. Where the text contains a convenient collection and explanation of a number of contrasting terms, a simple reference to the appropriate pages is given instead of setting out the definition.]

Absolute: not conditional or determinable (in relation to an estate) (6–013).
Abstract of title: an epitome of documents and facts showing ownership (8–028).
Ademption: failure of a testamentary gift, e.g. by the testator ceasing to own the property (14–086).
Administrators: persons authorised to administer the estate of an intestate (14–139); compare Executors.
Advancement: gift by parent or husband to provide for child or wife (11–015).
Advowson: a right of presenting a clergyman to a vacant benefice (31–007).
Alienation: the act of disposing of or transferring property.
Ante-nuptial: before marriage.
Appendant: attached to land by operation of law (27–066); compare Appurtenant.
Approvement: appropriation of portion of manorial waste free from rights of common.
Appurtenant: attached to land by act of parties (27–065); compare Appendant.
Assent: an assurance by personal representatives vesting property in the person entitled (14–141).
Assignment: a disposition or transfer, usually of a lease.
Assurance: a disposition or transfer.
Assured tenancy: a residential tenancy with limited statutory protection as to rent and possession (22–081).

Base fee: a fee simple produced by partially barring an entail (3–075).
Beneficial owner: a person entitled for his own benefit and not, e.g., as trustee.
Beneficiaries: those entitled to benefit under a trust or will.
Bona vacantia: goods without an owner.

Caution against first registration: a mechanism by which a person with an interest in unregistered land can ensure that he is informed of an application to register the title (7–045).
Cestui que trust: a beneficiary under a trust.
Cestui que vie: a person for whose life an estate *pur autre vie* lasts (3–087).
Charge: an incumbrance securing the payment of money.
Chattel real: a leasehold interest (1–012).
Codicil: a supplementary will (14–015).
Collaterals: blood relations who are neither ancestors nor descendants.
Commonhold: a form of registered freehold that can be used where the property forms part of an estate or building and there are shared common parts (33–003).
Commorientes: persons dying at the same time (14–064).
Condition precedent: a condition which must be fulfilled before a disposition can take effect (3–056).
Condition subsequent: a condition which may defeat a gift after it has taken effect (3–056).
Consolidation: a requirement that a mortgagor shall not redeem one mortgage without another (25–055).
Constructive: inferred or implied (8–017, 11–017).
Contingent: operative only upon an uncertain event (9–001): compare Vested.
Conversion: a change in the nature of property, either actually or notionally (10–009).
Conveyance: an instrument (other than a will) transferring property.
Copyhold: a form of tenure peculiar to manors prior to 1926 (2–013).
Corporeal: admitting of physical possession (27–001).

Covenant: a promise contained in a deed.

Deed: a document signed, sealed and delivered.
Deed poll: a deed with only one party (8–037); compare Indenture.
Defeasance: the determination of an interest on a specified event.
Demise: a transfer, usually by the grant of a lease.
Determine: terminate, come to an end.
Devise: a gift of real property by will.
Disentail: to bar an entail (3–080).
Disseisin: dispossession; see Seisin.
Distrain, distress: the lawful extrajudicial seizure of chattels to enforce a right, e.g. to the payment of rent, now abolished.
Dominant tenement: land to which the benefit of a right is attached (27–005); compare Servient tenement.

Easement: a right over land for the benefit of other land, such as a right of way (27–003 et seq.).
Ejectment: obsolete action for recovery of land (4–018).
Emblements: growing crops which an outgoing tenant may take (3–105).
En ventre sa mere: conceived but not born.
Enfranchise: the statutory right of certain lessees to purchase the fee simple (22–193).
Entail: an estate or interest descending only to issue of the grantee.
Equitable easement: a right over land operating in equity only (8–080).
Equities: equitable rights.
Equity of redemption: the sum of a mortgagor's rights in the mortgaged property (24–017).
Escheat: a lord's right to ownerless realty (2–010).
Escrow: a document which upon delivery will become a deed.
Estate: 1. the *quantum* of an interest in land (2–005): compare Tenure.
        2. an area of land (2–005).
        3. the whole of the property owned by a deceased person (14–123).
Estate contract: a contract for the sale or lease of land (5–025, 8–075).
Estate rentcharge: a rentcharge created for certain purposes of management (31–019).
Estoppel: prohibition of a party from denying facts which he has led another to assume to be true (16–002).
Estovers: wood which a tenant may take for domestic and other purposes (3–097).
Execute: to perform or complete, e.g. a deed.
Executors: persons appointed by a testator to administer his estate (14–138); compare Administrators.

Fee: base (3–075), conditional (3–056), determinable (3–054), simple (3–008), tail (3–008).
Fee farm rent: a rentcharge payable in lieu of purchase money (6–013, 31–017).
Fine: 1. a collusive action partially barring an entail (3–076); compare Recovery.
      2. a premium or a lump sum payment, e.g. for the grant of a lease.
Foreclosure: proceedings by a mortgagee which free mortgaged property from the equity of redemption (25–006).
Franchise: royal right granted to a subject, e.g. to hold a market (31–013).
Freehold: 1. free tenure (2–007, 2–020).
          2. an estate of uncertain maximum duration (3–003).

General equitable charge: an equitable charge of a legal estate not protected by a deposit of title deeds (8–074).
Good consideration: natural love and affection for near relatives (8–008).

Hereditaments: inheritable rights in property (27–001).
Heriot: the best beast of a deceased tenant, to which the lord of the manor was entitled (2–028).

In esse: in existence (opposed to *in posse,* not in existence) (20–052).
In gross: existing independently of a dominant tenement.

Incorporeal: not admitting of physical possession (27–001).
Incumbrance: a liability burdening property.
Indenture: a deed between two or more parties (8–037); compare Deed poll.
Injunction: an order of a court restraining a breach of obligation, or commanding performance.
Instrument: a legal document.
Interesse termini: the rights of a lessee before entry (17–079).
Intestacy: the failure to dispose of property by will.

Jus accrescendi: right of survivorship (13–003).
Jus tertii: a third party's title (4–010).

Lapse: the failure of a gift, especially by the beneficiary predeceasing the testator (14–055).
Legal memory: any time later than the accession of Richard I in 1189 (28–059).
Letters of administration: an authorisation to persons to administer the estate of a deceased person
    (14–139).
Licence: a permission, e.g. to enter on land (34–001).
Lien: a form of security for unpaid money (24–002).
Limitation of actions: statutory barring of rights of action after a period of years (35–003).
Limitation, words of: words delimiting the estate granted to some person previously mentioned
    (3–023); compare Purchase, words of.
Limited owner: an owner with an estate less than a fee simple.
Lis pendens: a pending action (8–064).

Mesne: intermediate, middle (2–003).
Minor: a person under 18 years of age.
Mortgage: transfer of property as security for a loan (24–001).

Notice: 1. knowledge or imputed knowledge (8–005, 8–015 et seq.).
          2. A form of entry to protect a proprietary interest in registered land, which may be an
             agreed notice or a unilateral notice (7–070, 7–073, 7–074).
Nuncupative: oral (of wills) (14–052).

Overreach: to transfer rights from land to the purchase-money paid therefor (6–052 et seq.).
Overriding interest: an interest in registered land which binds the proprietor without being entered
    on the register (7–008, 7028, 7–086).

Parol: word of mouth.
Particular estate: an estate less than a fee simple (9–009).
Periodic tenancy: tenancy from year to year, month to month, etc. (17–064, 17–070).
Perpetuity: undue remoteness of a future gift; excessive inalienability (9–012).
Personal chattels: (14–109).
Personal representatives: executors or administrators (14–138).
Possibility of reverter: the grantor's right to the land if a determinable fee determines.
Powers: an authority given to a person to dispose of property which is not his, general (9–111),
    special (9–111).
Prescription: the acquisition of easements or profits by long user (28–043, 35–002).
Privity of contract: the relation between parties to a contract (20–003).
Privity of estate: the relation of landlord and tenant (20–004).
Probate: the formal confirmation of a will, granted by the court to an executor (14–124).
Profit à prendre: right to take something from another's land (27–055).
Protected tenancy: a contractual tenancy fully protected by the Rent Acts (22–134).
Protector of the settlement: the person able to control the barring of an entail (3–080).
Puisne mortgage: a legal mortgage not protected by a deposit of title deeds (8–072, 26–027).
Pur autre vie: for the life of another person (3–087).
Purchase, words of: words conferring an interest on the person they mention (3–023); compare
    Limitation, words of.

Recovery: a collusive action completely barring an entail (3–073); compare Fine, 1.

Rectification: 1. The correction of a written instrument that does not correctly record what the parties agreed (15–122).
    2. The alteration of the register of title to correct a mistake which prejudicially affects the title of the registered proprietor (7–132).

Regulated tenancy: a protected or statutory tenancy (22–131).

Release: waiver of some right or interest without transfer of possession.

Remainder: the interest of a grantee subject to a prior particular estate (9–008).

Rent: fee farm rent (6–013, 31–017), ground rent (15–046), rack rent (15–046), rentcharge (31–014).

Restriction: an entry in the register of title regulating the circumstances in which a disposition of a registered estate or charge may be the subject of an entry in the register (7–077).

Restrictive covenant: a covenant restricting the use of land (5–026, 32–032).

Resulting: returning to the grantor, or remaining in him, by implication of law or equity (11–009).

Reversion: the interest remaining in a grantor after granting a particular estate (9–008).

Riparian owner: the owner of land adjoining a watercourse (3–047).

Root of title: a document from which ownership is traced (15–078).

Seignory: the rights of a feudal lord.

Seisin: the possession of land by a freeholder (3–018).

Servient tenement: land burdened by a right such as an easement (27–005); compare Dominant tenement.

Settlement: provisions for persons in succession (or the instruments making such provisions) (Appendix, A-032).

Severance: the conversion of a joint tenancy into a tenancy in common (13–036).

Severance, words of: words showing that property is to pass in distinct shares (13–017).

Socage: freehold tenure (2–004).

Specialty: a contract by deed.

Squatter: a person wrongfully occupying land and claiming title to it.

Statutory owner: persons with the powers of a tenant for life (10–016).

Statutory tenant: a person holding over under the Rent Acts (22–132).

Statutory trusts: certain trusts imposed by statute (11–004), especially— 1. the trust of land under co-ownership (13–051). 2. the trusts for issue on intestacy (14–119).

Subinfeudation: alienation by creating a new tenure (2–014).

Sub-mortgage: a mortgage of a mortgage (25–146).

Sui juris: "of his own right," i.e. subject to no disability.

Surrender: the transfer of an interest (e.g. for life, or for years) to the person next entitled to the property (18–083).

Survivorship: a surviving joint tenant's right to the whole land (13–003).

Tabula in naufragio: "a plank in a shipwreck" (a form of tacking mortgages) (26–051).

Tacking: extension of a mortgagee's security to cover a later loan (26–050).

Tenement: property held by a tenant.

Tenure: the set of conditions upon which a tenant holds land (2–004); compare Estate, 1.

Term of years: a period with a defined minimum for which a tenant holds land (6–018).

Time immemorial: the time of the accession of Richard I in 1189 (28–059).

Title: the evidence of a person's right to property, or the right itself.

Trust: bare (12–008), completely constituted (11–003), constructive (11–017), express (11–005), implied (11–009), incompletely constituted (11–033), resulting (11–013), secret (11–043).

Trust corporation: one of certain companies with a large paid-up capital, or one of certain officials (Appendix, A-098).

Trust of land: any trust of property which consists of or includes land, whether the interests under that trust are successive, concurrent or otherwise (12–002).

Undivided share: the interest of a tenant in common (13–010).

User: use, enjoyment (Note: *not* the person who uses).

Vested: unconditionally owned (9–001); compare Contingent.

Vesting assent (Appendix, A-005), declaration (11–068), deed (Appendix, A-004).

Voluntary conveyance: a conveyance not made for valuable consideration.

Volunteer: a person who takes under a disposition without having given valuable consideration.

Waiver: abandonment of a legal right.

Waste: ameliorating (3–092), equitable (3–095), permissive (3–093), voluntary (3–094).

CHAPTER 1

INTRODUCTION

Section 1. Real Property in Perspective

English real property law has tended to have an unenviable reputation for its **1–001** complexity. Until comparatively recently, that reputation was thoroughly deserved, but that is no longer the case. For more than 150 years, the objective of reformers has been to make dealings in land as simple as dealings in stocks and shares.[1] As a result of the statutory reforms of real property law,[2] particularly those in 1925[3] and since, the process of dealing in land has been simplified so much that this objective is now close to realisation. About three fifths of all the land in England and Wales is now registered at HM Land Registry,[4] and the titles are computerised and publicly accessible on the internet. Mortgages can be created electronically,[5] and it seems likely that the electronic transfer of title to land will be possible in the not too distant future.[6]

Although the content of the law of real property is increasingly statutory, it is, however, in no sense a statutory code. It is therefore still essential to have an understanding of the substratum of common law and equitable principles

---

[1] For the beginnings of the process and the first proposals for the registration of title to land, see J. S. Anderson, *Lawyers and the Making of English Land Law 1832–1940,* (Clarendon Press, 1992), pp. 63 et seq.

[2] The process began with the Conveyancing Act 1881.

[3] Usually referred to as "the 1925 property legislation". For a brief explanation, see below, para.1–016.

[4] See below, para.7–001.

[5] See below, para.7–161.

[6] The legislative framework for the introduction of electronic conveyancing now exists: see below, paras 7–157 et seq. Since July 1996, securities on the London and Dublin Stock Exchanges have been traded electronically under the CREST system. Gilt-edged securities are also traded electronically.

upon which the statutory framework has been overlaid,[7] together with some grasp of the way in which the subject has developed historically.[8]

1–002   **Scope of the subject.** It is not easy to distinguish accurately between real property and conveyancing. In general, the former is static, and the latter dynamic. Real property deals with the rights and liabilities of land owners, whereas conveyancing is concerned with how rights in land may be created and transferred. The two inevitably overlap and there is no scientific dividing line between them. In reality, real property and conveyancing are not so much separate (but closely related) subjects, but two parts of the one subject of land law.[9]

The material in this book has been arranged in such a way as to minimise the amount of repetition and preliminary explanation. Those topics that can be understood in isolation have been treated in the later chapters. However the main principles are explained first, because they constantly interact. They are not easy to grasp on initial acquaintance. This is due in part to their historical origins and partly to the technical language which is a feature of the subject. The glossary of terms which precedes this chapter may be helpful in relation to the latter.

The purpose of this Chapter is threefold. First, it provides a brief guide to the subjects that are examined in this book. Secondly, it gives an idea of the nature of real property and introduces a number of the most important technical terms. Finally, it introduces those aspects of the law on human rights that are most likely to affect the law of real property.

1–003   After this introductory chapter, Chapters 2 and 3 give an account of tenures and estates respectively. *Tenure* means the holding of land on certain terms and conditions. It refers to the *manner* in which the law allows a person to hold land. Points of tenure are extremely rare in practice today[10]; but historically tenure was the fundamental doctrine of land law. It is therefore examined first. *Estates* are of much greater importance in both theory and practice. The term "estate" refers to the duration of a landowner's interest. He may hold his land in fee simple, i.e. as absolute owner; or he may hold it for a limited interest—for his life or under a lease for a period of years.[11] He will then be said to have an estate in fee simple, or for life, or for a term of years, as the case may be. Chapter 3 explains the classification and nature of the various estates, and the rules for their creation, Chapter 4, *Possession of Land*, provides an analysis of the nature of estate ownership and the fundamental importance of possession in the law of real property.

---

[7] As registered title has gradually become the norm, some of the best-known features of this underlying framework—particularly the difference between legal and equitable interests (explained in Ch.4)—have declined in importance.

[8] For an outline of the main statutory developments affecting land law, see below, paras 1–016—1–017.

[9] Ch.15 provides an introduction to conveyancing law.

[10] They tend to arise principally in relation to the Crown's rights to land.

[11] One of the three limited forms of estate, the entail, can no longer be created as a result of recent legislation: see below, para.3–031.

Chapter 5, *Law and Equity,* contains the fundamental doctrine which has given a peculiar dual character to English land law. "Law" and "equity" are used in a technical sense. They correspond to the two systems of justice, "common law" and "equity", which were administered in separate courts until 1875. The character of the law of property has been significantly influenced by their interaction. Equity mitigated the rigour of the ancient common law in the interests of justice and at the expense of tradition and formality. Although the two systems have been administered together for over 120 years, interests in land are still classified as "legal" or "equitable" with consequences that are still important, though much less so than formerly. This is a typical example of a distinction that can only be understood historically, but which nonetheless underpins the 1925 property legislation. In Chapter 6, *The Legislative Transformation of the Law of Real Property and the Protection of Estates and Interests,* there is a description of how statute has transformed and developed the law of real property both in 1925 and subsequently. Its underlying theme is how legal estates and equitable interests are protected. It explains the reduction of legal estates to two by the Law of Property Act 1925, the protection of land charges, the development of registration of title, and the extension of overreaching. It considers whether it is possible to create new equitable interests and how personal rights may affect third parties through the law of torts and the imposition of constructive trusts.

Chapter 7, *Registration of Title,* gives a detailed account of the system of **1–004** registered title under which a computerised official register of title is rapidly replacing the cumbersome practice of examining title deeds. The whole of England and Wales has been subject to compulsory registration since December 1, 1990, and the range of dealings with unregistered land to which the requirement of compulsory registration applies has been extended so that most dispositions of unregistered land must now be completed by registering the title. As the registered system is now the predominant one, it is considered before the older unregistered system, which it replaces. Chapter 8, *Unregistered Conveyancing: Titles and Incumbrances,* explains the workings of the principles of common law and equity where title is unregistered. The two systems combined to shape the practice of buying and selling land and to protect a variety of subsidiary interests over it such as mortgages and restrictive covenants. These rules were modified by a statutory requirement that a number of subsidiary rights should be registered if they were to bind third parties. This traditional system of conveyancing is rapidly disappearing and is being replaced by the system of registered title mentioned above.

Chapter 9, *Perpetuities and Accumulations* is concerned with future interests. If A gives land to B for life and, after B's death, to C in fee simple, C has a future interest for the period of B's life. There are limits to the future interests which the law allows. In particular the period of time during which they can take effect is limited by the rule against perpetuities, reformed (but not in all respects improved) by the Perpetuities and Accumulations Act 1964 and then substantially limited by the Perpetuities and Accumulations Act 2009. Its near relation, the rule against accumulations, prevented income from being added to capital for an excessive period, but has been prospectively abolished from April 6, 2010.

1–005 The next four chapters are concerned with trusts in the law of real property. Chapter 10 explains the ways in which trusts have been employed in relation to real property both in the past and now. Chapter 11 describes how trusts of land are created whether expressly or otherwise, and it examines the constitution of trusts and the formalities required to create a trust. It also introduces the law relating to trustees.

Chapter 12 is concerned with trusts of land and the Trusts of Land and Appointment of Trustees Act 1996. After 1996, a unitary system of trusts of land replaced the previous tri-partite structure of settlements (which were concerned with successive interests in land and were governed by the Settled Land Act 1925), trusts for sale and bare trusts (which were regulated to varying degrees by the Law of Property Act 1925). It ceased to be possible to create settlements under the Settled Land Act 1925 after 1996, though existing ones continued. The trust of land, as its name suggests, applies to all types of trusts of land, whether the interests are successive or otherwise. Apart from Settled Land Act settlements created before 1997, virtually all other trusts (whenever created) are now trusts of land and subject to the provisions of the Trusts of Land and Appointment of Trustees Act 1996. The elaborate rules governing the transfer and management of settled land are now found in the Appendix to this book.

In Chapter 13, *Co-ownership,* the subject of concurrent (rather than successive) interests in land is considered. Such interests are very common and they arise, for example, where X and Y are entitled to a particular piece of land in equal shares. The share of each is merely a part interest in the whole. The device of the trust of land is employed in virtually all cases of co-ownership as a means of giving effect to the rights of the owners.

1–006 Chapter 14, *Wills and Intestacy,* describes the legal machinery for succession on death, both in the case where a person dies leaving a will of his property and in the case where he does not. This is followed in Chapter 15, *Contracts of Sale,* by an account of the rules governing the formation and effect of agreements to sell land. This chapter provides a general introduction to the law of conveyancing. Chapter 16, *Proprietary Estoppel,* explains the operation of this ancient doctrine, now much used in relation to informal dealings with land. If an owner of land in some way leads another person to believe that he has or will enjoy some right or benefit over that property, and that person acts to his detriment in that belief, an "equity" is said to arise in favour of the claimant. The court may give effect to that "equity" by granting the claimant some right or redress that is appropriate in the circumstances, whether over the land or otherwise.

1–007 The next five chapters are devoted to leases and tenancies which explain the general law of landlord and tenant, the most litigated area of land law. Chapter 17, *The Nature of Leases and their Creation,* is concerned with the characteristics of leases, both as contracts and as interests in land, how they differ from licences, the different types of leases and tenancies, and how they are created.

Chapter 18, *The Determination of Leases*, explains the nine different ways in which a lease may be brought to an end. Chapter 19, *Common Obligations of Landlord and Tenant*, examines some of the principal obligations of landlord and tenant. There is an explanation of the obligations implied by law in the absence of express provision and of the position of the parties under a lease that contains the so-called "usual covenants".[12] The final part of the chapter looks at the position of certain covenants that are commonly found in leases, such as the covenants to pay rent, and not to assign, underlet or part with possession without the landlord's consent. Chapter 20 is *Leasehold Covenants*. A covenant is a promise made by deed usually in a conveyance or a lease. Most covenants in leases are capable of binding successors in title. The rules which govern the transmission of the benefit and the burden of such covenants differ according to whether the lease was granted before 1996 (when they are a complex amalgam of ancient common law and more modern statute) or after 1995 (when the rules are contained in the Landlord and Tenant (Covenants) Act 1995). Chapter 21, *Leasehold Conveyancing*, explains the particular rules of arises conveyancing that apply to the grant and assignment of leases. The general principles of landlord and tenant do not apply to all types of leases. In fact, Parliament has, for many years, regulated different types of tenancies. In Chapter 22, *Security of Tenure*, there is an account of these special statutory provisions which specific kinds of tenancy, e.g. tenancies of houses and flats, tenancies of shops and offices, and tenancies of farms and farmland. These controls, which are a statutory system of their own and merit a book to themselves, have in fact been substantially relaxed over the last 20 years. Chapter 23, *Fixtures*, examines how the law determines whether something that has been attached to land has become part of the land for the purposes of the law and whether, if it has, a person with a limited interest in the land may remove it when his interest terminates. It is not specifically an aspect of the law relating to landlord and tenant, but, in practice, it most commonly arises in that context. It is therefore treated at this stage of the book.

The next three chapters are concerned with mortgages. A mortgage is a **1–008** conveyance of land for the purpose of securing a loan of money, under which the lender is given power to sell the land or take various other steps in relation to it if the debt, or the interest upon it, is not paid when due. Chapter 24 explains the nature of mortgages and how they are created. Chapter 25 is account of the rights of the parties under a mortgage or charge over land. Chapter 26 addresses the difficulty subject of the priority of competing mortgages and charges over land.

There are then five chapters which are devoted to what are called incorporeal hereditaments. These comprise a class of rights over land, some of them rather curious. The best-known and most important are easements and profits à prendre. An easement is a right over a neighbour's land, such as a right of way or a right of light. A profit is similar, except that it is a right to remove

[12] For the meaning of the word "covenant", see below.

something from the land, such as a right to work gravel, to graze animals, or to take game or fish. Chapter 27 explains the nature of easements and profits. The ways in which they are created is addressed in Chapter 28, and the means by which they may be extinguished are set out in Chapter 29. Chapter 30 surveys some of the species of easements and profits and their particular characteristics. Chapter 31, *Other Incorporeal Hereditaments*, deals with the other miscellany of rights that are also classified as incorporeal hereditaments, such as rentcharges (most of which will be phased out in 2037 under the Rentcharges Act 1977), what is left of the law on tithes, and franchises.

1–009   Chapter 32, *Freehold Covenants,* explains the principles that apply to covenants affecting freehold (as opposed to leasehold) land. The principles differ markedly from those which apply to leasehold covenants. Only the burden of a negative or *restrictive* covenant, such as a covenant not to use a house for business purposes, can pass on the sale of the land affected by it so as to bind the person into whose hands it has come. Although restrictive covenants were part of the law of contract, they have developed into a doctrine of property. Because it is not possible for the burden of positive covenants to bind the covenantor's successors in title,[13] Parliament has intervened, and has, in the Commonhold and Leasehold Reform Act 2002, introduced a new system of freehold ownership called commonhold, under which it is possible to set up schemes in which the burden of such covenants will be reciprocally binding on properties within the scheme. This is explained in Chapter 33, though it is, in practice, virtually never used. Licences are mere permission to go on to or use land belonging to another. Although there were attempts to transform them into property rights, this transformation was abruptly reversed. In Chapter 34, *Licences*, there is an account of the nature of licences, the different ways in which they may be created, and how they may be terminated. The chapter also examines the statutory right of spouses and civil partners to occupy the common home.

1–010   The last part of the book deals with certain miscellaneous (but not unimportant) subjects. In Chapter 35, *Adverse Possession and Limitation,* an explanation is given as to how a squatter can become the owner of unregistered land by (in most cases) 12 years' occupation of it. The much more limited application of adverse possession in relation to registered land, introduced by the Land Registration Act 2002, is also explained. Finally, Chapter 36, *Disabilities,* examines the position of those, such as minors and mental patients, who are less able to dispose of land than other people. In particular, this considers the effect of the Mental Capacity Act 2005.

Section 2. Meaning of "Real Property"

1–011 In common with so many expressions in English law, the explanation of the term "real property" is historical.

---

[13] Though a number of devices exist which, in practice, enable the burden of positive covenants to run with the covenantor's land.

In early law, property was deemed "real" if the courts would restore to a dispossessed owner the thing itself, the *"res"*, and not merely give compensation for the loss. Thus if X forcibly evicted Y from his freehold land, Y could bring a "real" action by which he could obtain an order from the court that X should return the land to him.[14] But if X took Y's sword or glove from him, he could bring only a personal action which gave X the choice of either returning the article to Y or paying him its value. In consequence a distinction was made between real property (or "realty"), which could be specifically recovered, and personal property (or "personalty"), which could not. In making this distinction, English law follows the natural division between immovables (i.e. land) and movables, but with one important exception. In general, all interests in land are real property, except leaseholds (or "terms of years") which are classified as personalty.

This peculiar exception initially arose because leases fell outside the feudal **1–012** system of landholding by tenure. Originally leases were treated as personal business arrangements under which one party allowed the other the use of his land for a rent.[15] Such personal contracts did not create rights in the land itself which could attract feudal status. Leases helped to supply a useful form of investment at a time when there was little other. Money either might be employed in buying land and letting it out on lease in order to obtain income from the capital, or in buying a lease for a lump sum which could be recovered with interest out of the produce of the land. Such commercial transactions were more in the sphere of money than of land. The classification of lease-holds as personal property was discovered to be advantageous. Leases were immune from feudal burdens and could be bequeathed by will before wills of freeholds were allowed.[16] In this way the illogical position continued until it became too well settled to alter.

Leaseholds are still, therefore, personalty in law. However, having been recognised so long as interests in land and not only contractual rights,[17] they have been classed under the paradoxical heading of "chattels real". "Chattels" indicates their personal nature,[18] "real" shows their connection with the land.[19]

Although strictly speaking a book on real property should exclude lease- **1–013** holds, it has long been usual to include them, and this course is adopted here.

The legislation of 1925 abolished many of the remaining differences between the legal principles applicable to realty and personalty respectively. For example, before 1926, if a person died intestate (i.e. without a will), all his realty passed to his heir, while his personalty was divided between certain of

---

[14] For real actions, see below, paras 4–014 et seq.
[15] Below, para.3–009.
[16] Below, para.3–010.
[17] Below, para.3–015.
[18] Cattle were the most important chattels in early days, hence the name.
[19] See *Smith v Baker* (1737) 1 Atk. 386 at 385; *Ridout v Pain* (1747) 3 Atk. 486 at 492, per Lord Hardwicke L.C. (*"extradictions* out of the real").

his relatives. After 1925, however, realty and personalty both pass on intestacy to certain relatives. Nevertheless, the distinction may still sometimes be relevant.

Real property is subclassified into corporeal and incorporeal hereditaments,[20] though this classification is of little practical importance. "Hereditament" indicates property which descended to the heir on intestacy before 1926, i.e. realty as opposed to personalty. Corporeal hereditaments are lands, buildings, minerals, trees and all other things which are part of or are fixed to land. They are the physical matter over which ownership is exercised. By contrast, incorporeal hereditaments are not things at all, but rights. Certain rights were classified as real property, so that on intestacy before 1926 they also descended to the heir, rather than to the relatives entitled to personalty. The most important incorporeal hereditaments are easements and profits,[21] but there are others also.[22]

Section 3. The Basis of the Law of Real Property

1–014   **1. Common law, equity and statute.** The origin of the law of real property is the origin of the common law itself.[23] In this context, "common law" means the law which was applied to the country as a whole by the king's ordinary courts, as opposed to the local feudal and customary laws which varied from place to place and were administered in each locality free from central control until the middle of the 12th century. The centralised judicial system established in the two centuries after the Norman Conquest—particularly in the region of Henry II—resulted in a body of new and uniform rules, although some of the old customs survived in the form of local variations of common law.[24]

The new rules were laid down and developed by the decisions of the judges in particular cases. Centralised records were kept and a systematic body of doctrine began to develop. "Common law" came to mean the ordinary judge-made law of the three central royal courts.[25] This was then contrasted with statute. Statutory reform of the land law was by no means unknown or insignificant. For example, the Acts of Edward I had a significant effect on the development of real property and one of them necessarily remains in force today.[26] With time, these statutes came to be regarded as of a piece with the judge-made rules, and the "common law" might, in a suitable context, include

---

[20] See further, below, para.27–001.
[21] See above, para.1–008, and below, Ch.27. Rentcharges (below, para.31–014), though formerly important, are in the process of being phased out with some material exceptions.
[22] See below, Ch.31.
[23] See below, paras 4–015 et seq.
[24] The local courts continued to function, but their jurisdiction came to be limited to small claims, particularly in relation to minor wrongs.
[25] The King's Bench, Common Pleas and Exchequer.
[26] Statute *Quia Emptores* 1290, below, para.2–015.

these ancient statutes, for the purposes of contrast with more modern parliamentary legislation.

A third force entered the field in the form of equity. As shall be explained,[27] **1–015** certain interests in land were not protected by the courts of common law but were protected by the Chancellor, the royal official who dispensed the Crown's residuary powers of redressing wrong. It was the Chancellor who first compelled trustees to carry out their trusts. He also devised remedies for cases where, owing to non-compliance with some formality, the result at common law would not have been equitable. In this context "common law" came to be contrasted with "equity" as well as with statute. Rights which the common law would recognise and enforce were known as rights at common law, or simply as "legal rights". Rights enforced by the Chancellor, but not at common law, were called rights in equity, or "equitable rights". As the name implies, the Chancellor proceeded on grounds of equity or good conscience. He would grant special remedies where the justice of the case required some tempering of the rigour of common law. In the course of time, equity developed into a separate branch of the legal system. It profoundly modified the common law of real property. The special characteristics of equitable rights led to the fundamental distinction between legal and equitable interests in land which was adopted as the foundation of the reforms of 1925 in relation to land with unregistered title. Although common law and equity are distinct concepts, there is a modern trend to minimise these distinctions and, in relation to the registration of title in particular, the distinction is of little importance.

2. Statutory reform. The statutory reform of the law of real property began **1–016** in the 19th century, particularly in the periods 1832–45 and 1881–90. However, the most significant changes to the law were made between 1922 and 1925. There were two stages in this legislation. First, by the Law of Property Act 1922, and the Law of Property (Amendment) Act 1924, the necessary changes in the law were made.[28] Secondly, these Acts were for the most part repealed before they could come into force, and were replaced by a series of Acts passed in 1925. The Acts of 1925 consolidated both the changes made by the Acts of 1922 and 1924 together with much of the law laid down by earlier statutes (particularly those of 1881–90), which were also repealed and replaced by the new legislation. The resulting body of law was broken down into six consolidating Acts:

(i) the Settled Land Act 1925;

(ii) the Trustee Act 1925;

(iii) the Law of Property Act 1925;

(iv) the Land Registration Act 1925;

---

[27] Below, para.5–003 et seq.
[28] It should be noted that the 1924 Act made a number of amendments to the 1922 Act.

(v) the Land Charges Act 1925; and

(vi) the Administration of Estates Act 1925.

These Acts, together with those unrepealed parts of the 1922 and 1924 Acts, constitute "the 1925 property legislation" and were all brought into force on January 1, 1926.

1–017   The form of the legislation can sometimes affect its construction. Because the 1925 Acts are consolidation Acts, they are presumed not to alter the pre-existing law more than their wording necessarily requires. Where the Acts of 1922 and 1924 left the old law unchanged, the presumption is that the Acts of 1925 did not alter it either.[29] But where the Acts of 1922 or 1924 changed the previous law, the presumption is only that the Acts of 1925 have not further modified it.[30] It is therefore sometimes necessary to have recourse to the repealed parts of the Acts of 1922 and 1924 to resolve obscurities in the Acts of 1925.[31]

Since 1925 there has been a steady flow of legislation which, until recently, has been of a piecemeal character for carrying out particular reforms. Over the last few years, however, more sweeping changes have taken place. As a result, very significant parts of the 1925 legislation have now been replaced, either in whole[32] or in part,[33] or at least prospectively.[34] The main statutes are:

- the Law of Property (Amendment) Act 1926;

- the Perpetuities and Accumulations Act 1964;

- the Law of Property (Joint Tenants) Act 1964;

- the Land Registration and Land Charges Act 1971[35];

- the Land Charges Act 1972[36];

- the Local Land Charges Act 1975;

- the Rentcharges Act 1977;

- the Charging Orders Act 1979;

---

[29] See, e.g. *Beswick v Beswick* [1968] A.C. 58 (LPA 1925 s.56); and see *Re Eichholz* [1959] Ch. 708 (especially at 726, 727), where the presumption was stated but misapplied; see (1960) 76 L.Q.R. 197 (R.E.M.); *Lloyds Bank Ltd v Marcan* [1973] 1 W.L.R. 339 at 344 (affirmed at 1387); *Re Dodwell & Co Ltd's Trust* [1979] Ch. 301 at 308 (LPA 1925, s.164).
[30] See *Grey v IRC* [1960] A.C. 1 (LPA 1925, s.53); *Re Turner's W.T.* [1937] Ch. 15 (TA. 1925, s.31).
[31] See, e.g. *State Bank of India v Sood* [1997] Ch. 276 at 287.
[32] Such as LRA 1925, which was repealed and replaced by LRA 2002.
[33] Such as TA 1925 Pt I, repealed and replaced by TA 2000
[34] Such as SLA 1925, which now applies only to settlements in existence before 1997: see TLATA 1996 ss.1, 2. Similarly, PAA 1964 only applies to dispositions made before April 6, 2010: see PAA 1964 s.15(5A).
[35] Repealed by LRA 2002.
[36] Another consolidating Act, which replaced LCA 1925.

- the Land Registration Acts 1986, 1988 1997[37];

- the Reverter of Sites Act 1987;

- the Law of Property (Miscellaneous Provisions) Acts 1989 and 1994;

- the Access to Neighbouring Land Act 1992;

- the Landlord and Tenant (Covenants) Act 1995;

- the Trusts of Land and Appointment of Trustees Act 1996;

- the Trustee Delegation Act 1999;

- the Trustee Act 2000;

- the Land Registration Act 2002[38];

- the Commonhold and Leasehold Reform Act 2002;

- the Perpetuities and Accumulations Act 2009; and

- the Mortgage Repossessions (Protection of Tenants etc) Act 2010.

Section 4. The Law in Action

To conclude this introduction, it may be helpful to give an example of a typical transaction involving land, namely a sale of a house. The situation envisaged is that V (the vendor) has agreed to sell his house to P (the purchaser) and that their solicitors (or licensed conveyancers) proceed to make the legal arrangements.[39]   **1–018**

Before the parties bind themselves by contract to the transaction, they will usually have to attend to a number of preliminary matters. First, P will commonly purchase the house with the aid of a mortgage and will therefore need to ensure that the necessary financial arrangements are in place. Secondly, it is good practice for P to have the property surveyed. It is for the purchaser to satisfy himself as to the physical state of the property. Thirdly, P's solicitor or licensed conveyancer will almost always investigate V's title in advance of the exchange of contracts.[40] This is explained below.

The parties then enter into a contract by which V agrees to sell and P agrees to buy the house.[41] That contract must be made in writing and must contain all the terms agreed by the parties. Either the contract must be contained in   **1–019**

---

[37] Repealed in whole or part by LRA 2002.

[38] Which repealed virtually all previous legislation on land registration, including most of LRA 1986, 1988 and 1997, mentioned above.

[39] See further below, Ch.15.

[40] This might not be possible where there is a sale by auction.

[41] Commonly the sale will be one of a chain of sales. Thus P may be selling his house and V may be purchasing another. The exchange of all of the contracts in the chain is usually synchronised by telephone in accordance with a practice devised by The Law Society.

one document and signed by both parties or, where contracts are exchanged (as commonly happens), each party must sign one part which is then given to, or held to the order of, the other. The contract does not transfer the full legal ownership from V to P.[42] In the normal case, where the title is registered, V must execute a transfer of the land to P. Title will pass to P when that transfer has been submitted to HM Land Registry for registration, and P registered as owner of the land.[43] P will in turn pay V the purchase price. This final exchange of the transfer for money is called completion. Although the exchange of contracts and completion sometimes occur on the same day, there is normally an interval of a week or two between the two stages.

P will not wish to part with his money without making sure that he will receive what V contracted to sell him, so he (or rather his solicitor) will investigate V's title. If V's title is registered, there is unlikely to be any doubt as to his entitlement to convey the land. Although P will wish to be sure that he is not (for example) merely a tenant who has only a leasehold interest to sell, and that there are no other restrictions on his powers of disposition, all of that will be apparent from the register. There may very occasionally be situations where V does not in fact own the land of which he is the registered proprietor. For example, he may have been registered as the owner by mistake and some third party is the true owner and is also registered as proprietor of the same land.

1–020   A far more common source of trouble is incumbrances. V's property may be subject to easements, such as rights to light or rights of way acquired by neighbours, or to restrictive covenants which prevent any occupant from using it in a particular way, for instance, as a shop or for business. V may have mortgaged it as security for a loan, so that the creditor has rights in the land which must be protected. V is required to disclose to P prior to contract any incumbrances that will not be discharged on completion[44] and which are not apparent on an inspection of the land. An inspection of the register will reveal the existence of many incumbrances, but there are some which will bind a purchaser even though they are not protected by registration, such as certain easements and the proprietary rights of persons in actual occupation. If before completion P discovers an incumbrance that V ought to have disclosed, he will be entitled to terminate the contract and recover damages from V.

Where P purchases the property with the aid of a mortgage from a bank or other lending institution, both the transfer of title and the mortgage[45] take effect simultaneously. P will then be able to occupy the house so long as he keeps up the payments due under the loan. The creditor is given an immediate

---

[42] In some continental legal systems the two steps are elided.

[43] Registration vests the legal title and has effect from the time when the application for registration is made: see LRA 2002 s.74; below, para.7–114. Where the title has not been registered, V executes a deed of conveyance to P. This transfers the legal title to P at once. However, P must apply to have the title registered at the Land Registry within two months: see below, para.7–019.

[44] In practice, where there is a mortgage, the property will not be sold unless the mortgage will be discharged out of the proceeds of sale.

[45] Known as a "registered charge" where the title to the land is registered.

and indefeasible interest in the land as security against non-payment. Until he has repaid the loan, P's position is not unlike that of a tenant, but one who pays mortgage interest instead of rent.

Section 5. Human Rights and Property Law

1. The Human Rights Act 1998. On October 2, 2000, the Human Rights   **1–021**
Act 1998 came into force. The Act is intended to "give further effect to rights and freedoms guaranteed under the European Convention on Human Rights".[46] Its central concept is that of "Convention Rights", which comprise the rights and freedoms set out in s.1 of the Convention.[47] The Act necessarily has an impact on the law of real property. This is because at least two articles of the Convention can be engaged where there are disputes about land, namely art.8 (right to respect for private and family life)[48] and, above all, art.1 of the First Protocol (protection of property).[49] What follows can only be the barest introduction to a complex and far-reaching subject.[50] It is, however, a matter that may arise in a dispute concerning land, which is why it must be considered at the beginning of this book.

Under s.2 of the Act, a court or tribunal determining a question which has   **1–022**
arisen in connection with a Convention right, must take into account (amongst other things) the decisions and opinions of the European Court of Human Rights at Strasbourg. While a court in this country is not bound by the Strasbourg court, it must have very good reasons for departing from it.[51] Furthermore, by s.3, primary and subordinate legislation[52] must be read and given effect in a way which is compatible with the Convention Rights, so far as it is possible to do so.[53] That is not an application of the ordinary principles of statutory interpretation. Even if the provision in question is unambiguous, a court or tribunal may have to give it a meaning different from that which Parliament intended.[54] However, the meaning given to the provision "must be

---

[46] Preamble. The Convention was already treated as relevant by the courts in a number of respects: see Lord Bingham of Cornhill, *Hansard*, HL, Vol.573, cols.1465–1467 (July 3, 1996).

[47] HRA 1998 s.1. The relevant Articles of the ECHR are set out in HRA 1998, Sch.1: s.1(3).

[48] Below, para.1–030.

[49] Below, para.1–024.

[50] Reference should be made to specialist treatments of the subject, notably, T. Allen, *Property and the Human Rights Act 1998* (Oxford: Hart Publishing, 2005).

[51] *Ofulue v Bossert* [2008] EWCA Civ 7 at [32]; [2009] Ch. 1 at 14 (not considered on appeal: [2009] UKHL 16; [2009] A.C. 990). A court might depart from the Strasbourg court, e.g. if it was satisfied that it had misunderstood English domestic law: *Ofulue v Bossert* [2008] EWCA Civ 7 at [32]; [2009] Ch. 1 at 14. See too *Kay v Lambeth LBC* [2006] UKHL 10 at [28]; [2006] 2 A.C. 465 at 490, 491.

[52] The terms are defined by HRA 1998 s.21.

[53] HRA 1998 s.3. For a list of the decisions in which HRA 1998 s.3 had been applied, see *Ghaidan v Godin-Mendoza* [2004] UKHL 557, [2004] 2 A.C. 557 at 580; Appendix to the opinion of Lord Steyn.

[54] See *Ghaidan v Godin-Mendoza* [2004] UKHL 557 at [29], [30]; [2004] 2 A.C. 557 at 571.

compatible with the underlying thrust of the legislation being construed".[55] One consequence of this requirement is that a court may be compelled to depart from an earlier decision that would otherwise be binding upon it as a matter of precedent.[56] Interpretation under s.3 has been described as "the prime remedial remedy".[57] Under s.4, if a court is satisfied that a provision of primary legislation is incompatible with a Convention right, it may so declare,[58] but it must nonetheless apply the provision in that particular dispute.[59] It is clear that "resort to s.4 must always be an exceptional course", and there is "a strong rebuttable presumption in favour of an interpretation consistent with Convention Rights".[60]

1–023   It is provided by s.6 of the Act that, subject to certain exceptions,[61] it is unlawful for a public authority to act[62] in a way which is incompatible with Convention rights. The Act creates a new cause of action in respect of such unlawfulness.[63] "Public authority" includes:

(i) a court or tribunal[64]; and

(ii) any person certain of whose functions are of a public nature.[65] In relation to a particular act, such a person is not a public authority if the nature of the act is private;

but does not include either House of Parliament.[66]

---

[55] *Ghaidan v Godin-Mendoza*, above, at [33]; 572, per Lord Nicholls. See too Lord Rodger at [124]; 602. In that case, which concerned a statutory succession to a protected tenancy under the Rent Act 1977, a provision of that Act which permitted a person who was living with the original tenant "as his or her wife or husband" was interpreted to include a stable and monogamous same-sex relationship, to avoid contravening ECHR, Art.14 (prohibition of discrimination).

[56] See, e.g. *Beaulane Properties Ltd v Palmer* [2005] EWHC 817 (Ch); [2006] Ch.79, the decision in which was incompatible with *J A Pye (Oxford) Ltd v Graham* [2002] UKHL 30 at [44], [45]; [2003] 1 A.C. 419 at 437, 438. The decision in *Beaulane* was itself incorrect in the light of the subsequent decision of the Grand Chamber in *J A Pye (Oxford) Ltd v UK*, Appl. No.44302/02 (2007), and has been disapproved: see *Ofulue v Bossert* [2008] EWCA Civ 7 at [49]; [2009] Ch. 1 at 20.

[57] *Ghaidan v Godin-Mendoza*, above, at [50]; 577; per Lord Steyn. For examples of the application of HRA 1998 s.3 in the sphere of property law, see *PW & Co v Milton Gate Investments Ltd* [2003] EWHC 1994 (Ch); [2004] Ch. 142, interpreting LPA 1925 ss.141, 142; below, para.20–063.; *Barca Mears* [2004] EWHC 2170 (Ch); [2005] 2 F.L.R. 1; and *Donohoe v Ingram* [2006] EWHC 282 (Ch); [2006] 2 F.L.R. 1084; interpreting IA 1986 s.335A; below, para.13–072.

[58] HRA 1998 s.4(2). For the approach to be adopted by a court in exercising this role, see *Wilson v First County Trust Ltd (No.2)* [2003] UKHL 40 at [61] et seq.; [2004] 1 A.C. 816 at 842 et seq.

[59] HRA 1998 s.4(6).

[60] *Ghaidan v Godin-Mendoza*, above, at [50]; 577; per Lord Steyn.

[61] See HRA 1998 s.6(2).

[62] "Act" includes a failure to act: HRA 1998 s.6(6).

[63] See HRA 1998 ss.7–9.

[64] HRA 1998 s.6(3)(a).

[65] HRA 1998 s.6(3)(b). In relation to a particular act, such a person is not a public authority if the nature of the act is private: see s.6(5).

[66] HRA 1998 s.6(4).

Accordingly, there are two categories of public authority.[67] First, there are "core" public authorities, that is, persons or bodies all of whose functions are of a public nature. In relation to such bodies s.6 could apply to all their activities. Secondly, there are "hybrid" public authorities, certain of whose functions are of a public nature. With such a body, it is necessary to make an assessment both of the functions of the body as a whole (to ascertain whether it is a public authority at all), and of the particular act in issue. It has been held that a parochial church council is not a public authority for these purposes, when it enforces an ancient liability imposed on some landowners, called lay rectors, to pay for the repair of the chancel of certain pre-Reformation parish churches.[68] Such an act "is no more a public act than is the enforcement of a restrictive covenant of which church land has the benefit".[69]

It is significant that the courts are public authorities. In addition to their duties under s.3 of the Act to interpret legislation in a way that is compatible with convention rights,[70] they must also apply and develop the common law in a way that is compatible with Convention rights. Because they cannot lawfully act in a way that is incompatible with such rights, they are bound to depart from earlier decisions that are incompatible with Convention rights, but which would otherwise be binding upon them as a matter of precedent.

2. Protection of Property

(a) Article 1 of the First Protocol. It is provided by Article 1 of the First **1–024**
Protocol of the Convention that:

> "Every natural or legal person is entitled to the peaceful enjoyment of his possessions No one shall be deprived of his possessions except in the public interest and subject to the conditions provided for by law and by the general principles of international law. The preceding provisions shall not, however, in any way impair the right of a State to enforce such laws as it deems necessary to control the use of property in accordance with the general interest or to secure the payment of taxes or other contributions or penalties."

The Court of Human Rights has frequently stated that the Article comprises three distinct but related rules[71]:

> (i) a general principle of peaceful enjoyment of property: in substance it guarantees the right of property

---

[67] See *Aston Cantlow and Wilmcote with Billesley PCC v Wallbank* [2003] UKHL 37; [2004] 1 A.C. 546.

[68] See *Aston Cantlow and Wilmcote with Billesley PCC v Wallbank*, above; and see below, para.31–009.

[69] *Aston Cantlow and Wilmcote with Billesley PCC v Wallbank*, above, at [16]; 556, per Lord Nicholls.

[70] Above, para.1–022.

[71] The analysis was first made in *Sporrong and Lönnroth v Sweden*, Series A No.52 (1983), at [61].

(ii) a rule that is concerned with the deprivation of possessions and which subjects it to certain conditions; and

(iii) a rule that recognises that the Contracting States are entitled to control the use of property in accordance with the general interest, by enforcing such laws as they deem necessary for the purpose.

Rules (ii) and (iii) are concerned with particular instances of interference with the right to peaceful enjoyment of property and are to be construed in the light of the general principle in (i).[72] There may be cases which fall within neither (ii) nor (iii), but which fall within (i), as where particular planning restrictions on property imposed an excessive burden on the owner that did not strike a fair balance between the demands of the general interest of the community and the requirements of the protection of the individual's fundamental rights.[73]

1–025   *(b) "Possessions".* Article 1 of the First Protocol refers to both "possessions" and to "property". "Possessions" has an autonomous meaning, and is not restricted to chattels or other tangible property.[74] It includes, e.g. contractual rights in relation to property,[75] and it may include "claims, in respect of which the applicant can argue that he or she has at least a 'legitimate expectation' of obtaining effective enjoyment of a property right".[76] Thus while the autonomous concept does not extend to rights that are unknown in the national law, it may include known "rights" which turn out to be invalid, such as the grant of an option by a local authority that was *ultra vires*.[77] The right to peaceful enjoyment of "possessions" does not "extend to grant relief from liabilities incurred in accordance with the civil law", as where a person purchases land with knowledge of an incumbrance that affects that property.[78]

1–026   *(c) Deprivation and control.* Article 1 of the First Protocol is concerned to protect property against the activities of the state.[79] It draws a distinction between the deprivation of possessions and the control of property.

---

[72] *James v UK*, Series A No.98 (1986), at [37].
[73] *Sporrong and Lönnroth v Sweden*, above, at [69].
[74] *Gasus Dosier and Fordertechnik GmbH v Netherlands*, Series A No.306–B (1995), at [53].
[75] *Wilson v First County Trust Ltd (No.2)* [2003] UKHL 40; [2004] 1 A.C. 816. It will include rights in property that are regulated by contract, such as the right of a member of an unincorporated association to a share in the assets of the association: see *Hanchett-Stamford v Att Gen* [2008] EWHC 330 (Ch) at [47], [48]; [2009] Ch. 173 at 188, 189. See below, para.13–094.
[76] *J A Pye (Oxford) Ltd v UK*, Appl. No.44302/02 (2007), at [61].
[77] *Stretch v UK*, No.44277/98 (2003), the sequel to *Stretch v West Dorset DC* (1997) 77 P & CR 342. cf. *Wilson v First County Trust Ltd (No.2)* [2003] UKHL 40 at [168]; [2004] 1 A.C. 816 at 872.
[78] *Aston Cantlow and Wilmcote with Billesley PCC v Wallbank* [2003] UKHL 37 at [91]; [2004] 1 A.C. 546 at 579, per Lord Hobhouse. See too at [71], [133], 134]; at 572, 590.
[79] *Bramelid and Malmström v Sweden* (1982) 5 E.H.R.R. 249, 255.

(1) DEPRIVATION. The state may take property, if the public interest so **1–027** requires, on payment of compensation.[80] A taking of property without compensation will normally infringe Article 1,[81] and is treated as justifiable only in exceptional circumstances.[82] Compensation terms are material to whether the legislation in dispute strikes a fair balance between the interests at stake and in particular, whether it imposes a disproportionate burden on the person deprived of his property.[83] Article 1 does not guarantee a right to full compensation in all circumstances: legitimate objectives of public interest (e.g. to achieve greater social justice) may call for less than reimbursement of full market value.[84]

Deprivation may not in fact involve a taking by the state for the benefit of the state.[85] It may, for example, occur under redistributive legislation, where one private citizen is required to transfer his property to another, as under legislation which enables tenants holding under long leases to acquire the freehold reversion from their landlords.[86] Furthermore, "what is not an actual expropriation may amount to what one might call a *de facto* expropriation".[87] A case which may appear to be a case of the control of the use of property may in fact be one of deprivation.[88] Conversely, some cases of apparent deprivation of property are, when analysed, cases of control: loss of ownership of possessions will not always be characterised as deprivation.[89] A striking example concerns the law on adverse possession that applied to registered land before the Land Registration Act 2002 came into force.[90] The Grand Chamber of the Court of Human Rights held that the relevant statutory provisions[91] "were part of the general land law, and were concerned to regulate, amongst other things, limitation periods in the context of the use and ownership of land as between individuals" and this was a control of land and

---

[80] See *R. (Alconbury Ltd) v Secretary of State for the Environment, Transport and the Regions* [2001] UKHL 23 at [72]; [2003] 2 A.C. 295 at 325.
[81] See *R. (Trailer and Marina (Leven) Ltd) v Secretary of State for the Environment, Food and Rural Affairs* [2004] EWCA Civ 1580 at [42]; [2005] 1 W.L.R. 1267 at 1277.
[82] *James v UK*, Series A No.98 (1986), at [54].
[83] *James v UK*, above, at [54].
[84] *Lithgow v UK*, Series A No.102 (1986) at [121]. For a case where art.1 of the First Protocol was infringed because of the inflexibility of the assessment of compensation (which was below market value), see *Papachelas v Greece* (2000) 30 E.H.R.R. 923.
[85] See *J A Pye (Oxford) Ltd v UK*, Appl. No.44302/02 (2007), at [57]: the UK Government was responsible "for legislation which is activated as a result of the interactions of private individuals". See too at [65].
[86] See *James v UK*, Series A No.98 (1986), where the Leasehold Reform Act 1967 was unsuccessfully challenged. See below, para.22–197.
[87] *R. (Trailer and Marina (Leven) Ltd) v Secretary of State for the Environment, Food and Rural Affairs* [2004] EWCA Civ 1580 at [47]; [2005] 1 W.L.R. 1267 at 1278, per Neuberger L.J.
[88] As in *Papamichalopoulos v Greece*, Series A No.260-B (1993), where the Greek Navy unlawfully occupied and built a naval base upon the applicant's land.
[89] *J A Pye (Oxford) Ltd v UK*, Appl. No.44302/02 (2007), at [64].
[90] See below, para.35–001. For the principles now applicable to adverse possession of registered land, see below, paras 35–070 et seq.
[91] LRA 1925 s.75; LA 1980 s.17.

not a deprivation of possessions within Article 1 of the First Protocol.[92] There is no deprivation for the purposes of the Article where a person's right is subject from the outset to some restriction or qualification that is now being enforced against him.[93]

1–028   Even where the deprivation of possessions is adequately compensated, it will contravene Article 1 of the First Protocol unless it can be shown to be in the public interest, which is expressly required by the Article. Thus "a deprivation of property effected for no reason other than to confer a private benefit on a private party cannot be 'in the public interest'".[94] However, to meet the requirement, it is not necessary:

> "that the transferred property should be put into use for the general public or that the community generally, or even a substantial proportion of it, should directly benefit from the taking. The taking of property in pursuance of a policy calculated to enhance social justice within the community can properly be described as being 'in the public interest'".[95]

As part of the requirement that the deprivation is in the public interest, it must be shown to satisfy the requirement of proportionality. There must be "a reasonable relationship of proportionality between the means employed and the aim sought to be realised",[96] and this requires that a fair balance must be struck "between the general interest of the community and the requirements and the requirements of the protection of the individual's fundamental rights".[97] In making this determination, the Court of Human rights accords national bodies a wide "margin of appreciation". The Court of Human Rights has accepted that the notion of "public interest" is necessarily extensive.

> "In particular . . . the decision to enact laws expropriating property will commonly involve consideration of political, economic and social issues on which opinions within a democratic society may reasonably differ widely. The Court, finding it natural that the margin of appreciation available to the legislature in implementing social and economic policies should be a wide one, will respect the legislature's judgment as to what is 'in the public interest' unless that judgment be manifestly without reasonable foundation".[98]

---

[92] *J A Pye (Oxford) Ltd v UK,* Appl. No.44302/02 (2007), at [66]; [2007] Conv. 552 (M.J.D.).
[93] *Wilson v First County Trust Ltd (No.2)* [2003] UKHL 40 at [106]; [2004] 1 A.C. 816 at 854.
[94] *James v UK,* Series A No.98 (1986), at [40].
[95] *James v UK,* Series A No.98 (1986), at [41].
[96] *James v UK,* Series A No.98 (1986), at [50].
[97] *Sporrong and Lönnroth v Sweden* Series A No.52 (1983), at [69]. cf. para.1–024, above.
[98] *James v UK,* Series A No.98 (1986), at [46]. But cf. *Immobiliare Saffi v Italy* (2000) 30 E.H.R.R. 756, where it was suggested that the margin of appreciation was wider in relation to "matters such as housing, which plays a central role in the welfare and economic policies of modern societies": see [49].

It has been recognised that:

> "by conceding a margin of appreciation to each national system, the court has recognised that the Convention, as a living system, does not need to be applied uniformly by all states but may vary in its application according to local needs and conditions".[99]

The doctrine of the margin of appreciation is not available to domestic courts applying the Convention. However, where the Strasbourg Court has held that a matter falls within a contracting state's margin of appreciation, the English court should "consider whether the domestic rule serves a legitimate aim and is proportionate (according the appropriate degree of respect to the decision-maker in domestic law) but that it should find that the law is Convention-compliant if those tests are satisfied".[100] Where the Strasbourg court has itself already carried out this exercise, its decision should be followed and applied by the English court.[101]

(2) CONTROL. Where the intervention complained of is characterised as **1–029** control of property rather than as a deprivation of possessions the situation is as follows.

(i) Whether or not there has been an infringement of Article 1 of the First Protocol depends upon whether there has been a reasonable relationship of proportionality between the means employed and the aim sought to be realised.[102] That is the same balancing exercise that has to be performed in a case of deprivation.

(ii) Certain interferences are expressly permitted by Article 1, namely:

> "the right of a State to enforce such laws as it deems necessary to control the use of property in accordance with the general interest or to secure the payment of taxes or other contributions or penalties."[103]

(iii) There is normally no requirement for the payment of compensation in cases where the legislation in issue restricts the use of property.[104] Provided that state could properly take the view that the

---

[99] *R. v D.P.P. Ex p. Kebiline* [2000] 2 A.C. 326 at 380, per Lord Hope.
[100] *Ofulue v Bossert* [2008] EWCA Civ 7 at [37]; [2009] Ch. 1 at 16, per Arden L.J.
[101] *Ofulue v Bossert*, above, at [37]; at 16.
[102] *Jacobsson v Sweden*, Series A No.163 (1990) at [55].
[103] See *R. (Trailer and Marina (Leven) Ltd) v Secretary of State for the Environment, Food and Rural Affairs* [2004] EWCA Civ 1580 at [51]; [2005] 1 W.L.R. 1267 at 1279, 1280.
[104] See, e.g. *Mellacher v Austria*, Series A No.169 (1990) (rent restriction legislation).

benefit to the community outweighs the detriment to the individual, a fair balance will have been struck without the need to compensate the person affected.[105]

1–030 **3. Right to respect for private and family life.** Article 8(1) of the Convention provides that "Everyone has the right to respect for his private and family life, his home and his correspondence". That is qualified by Article 8(2), which provides that:

> "There shall be no interference by a public authority with the exercise of this right except such as is in accordance with the law and is necessary in a democratic society in the interests of national security, public safety or the economic well-being of the country, for the prevention of disorder or crime, for the protection of health or morals, or for the protection of the rights and freedoms of others."

Article 8, which can cover a very wide spectrum of personal interests, has been raised on a number of occasions in relation to claims concerning land and in particular in connection with attempts to evict persons from their homes. "Home" has an autonomous meaning that includes not just a private residence, but also business premises and a person's office.[106] Article 8 is concerned to protect a person's home "as a place where he is entitled to be free from arbitrary interference by public authorities" and it is, therefore, part of the obligation imposed on contracting states to protect a person's right to privacy as distinct from his right to the peaceful enjoyment of his possessions, which is protected under Article 1 of the First Protocol.[107] As regards Article 8(2), an interference will be considered "necessary in a democratic society" for a legitimate aim if it answers a "pressing social need" and, in particular, if it is proportionate to the legitimate aim pursued.[108] The more serious the interference with the applicant's rights, the greater will be the reasons of public interest that are required to justify the state's conduct. The margin of appreciation will be correspondingly narrowed.[109] It should be noted that Article 8(2) is concerned not just with questions of substantive law, but also with procedure.[110]

---

[105] *R. (Trailer and Marina (Leven) Ltd) v Secretary of State for the Environment, Food and Rural Affairs* [2004] EWCA Civ 1580; [2005] 1 W.L.R. 1267. For a case of control of use where interference was disproportionate, see *Chassagnou v France* (2000) 29 E.H.R.R. 615 (control of hunting rights).

[106] *Niemietz v Germany* (1992) 16 E.H.R.R. 97 at [29]–[31]. It does not include land over which a landowner permits persons to engage in sport or hunting, which are essentially public and not private activities: see *R. (Countryside Alliance) v Att Gen* [2007] UKHL 52; [2008] A.C. 719.

[107] *Harrow LBC v Qazi* [2003] UKHL 43 at [50]; [2004] 1 A.C. 983 at 1004, per Lord Hope, applying *Marckx v Belgium*, Series A No.31 (1979) at [31].

[108] *Connors v UK*, Appl. No.66746/01 (2004) at [81].

[109] *Connors v UK*, above, at [86].

[110] *Kay v Lambeth LBC* [2006] UKHL 10 at [68]; [2006] 2 A.C. 465 at 504.

The applicability of Article 8 has arisen most acutely in proceedings for **1–031** possession, brought by a public authority, where the applicant has no proprietary or contractual right to remain in his home, whether because his tenancy or licence to occupy the land has terminated, or because he is a trespasser. In such cases, the Court of Human Rights insists that, to avoid a violation of Article 8, there must be procedural safeguards, which require the evicting authority to establish proper justification for the serious interference with his rights.[111] This matter is explained below in Chapter 22.[112] The Supreme Court has declined follow earlier decisions of the House of Lords in order to comply with the interpretation given to Article 8 by the Court of Human Rights.[113]

---

[111] *Connors v UK*, above, at [95].
[112] See paras 22–075—22–078.
[113] See *Manchester CC v Pinnock* [2010] UKSC 45; [2010] 3 W.L.R. 1441; *Hounslow LBC v Powell* [2011] UKSC 8; [2011] 2 W.L.R. 287.

CHAPTER 2

TENURES AND ESTATES

Part 1

INTRODUCTION

2–001   **1. Crown ownership.** Although in practice land is commonly, and correctly, described as owned by its various proprietors, English land law still retains its original basis, that all land in England is owned by the Crown. A small part of that land is in the Crown's own occupation and such land has been described in a recent statute as "demesne land".[1] The rest is occupied by tenants holding either directly or indirectly from the Crown. In England all land is held of a lord,[2] and allodial land (i.e. land owned independently and not "held of" some lord) is unknown.

2–002   **2. Feudal structure.** This unusually perfect feudal structure was imposed after the Norman Conquest. William I regarded the whole of England as his by conquest. To reward his followers and those of the English who submitted to him, he granted and confirmed certain lands to be held of him as overlord.[3] These lands were granted not by way of an out-and-out transfer, but to be held from the Crown upon certain conditions. Thus, Blackacre might have been granted to X on the terms that he did homage and swore fealty, and that he provided five armed horsemen to fight for the Crown for 40 days in each year. Whiteacre might have been granted to Y on condition that he supported the King's train in his coronation. X and Y might each in turn grant land to other

---

[1] See LRA 2002 ss.79–81, 132(1), (2). This terminology is adopted in this work. Prior to LRA 2002, there was no generally accepted term for the land held in possession by the Crown as paramount feudal lord.

[2] Expressed by the maxim, *"nulle terre sans seigneur"*: P. & M. i, p.232; H.E.L. ii, p.199; Co.Litt. p.1b; *Doe d. Hayne v Redfern* (1810) 12 East 96 at 103; *Att Gen of Ontario v Mercer* (1883) 8 App.Cas. 767 at 772.

[3] Williams R.P. p.12.

persons to hold of them in return for services, and these others might repeat the process.

3. Services. In this way the feudal pyramid was constructed from the top   2–003
downwards, with the King at the apex and the actual occupants of the land at the base. In the middle were persons who both rendered and received services, much in the same way as a modern leasehold tenant who has sublet the property. In days when land and its produce constituted nearly the whole tangible wealth of a country, it was more usual to secure the performance of services by the grant of land in return for those services than it was to secure them by payment. The whole social organisation was based on landholding in return for service, and for most purposes, such as military service and taxation, government was carried on by devolving upon each lord the control of his immediate tenants. The King need look only to his "tenants in chief", they in their turn to their immediate dependants, and so on downwards if there were further steps in the scale.

Tenants in chief were those who held directly of the King. There were about 1,500 of them in 1086, at the time of Domesday Book. Those who in fact occupied the land were called tenants in demesne. Those who stood between the King and tenants in demesne were called mesne lords or mesnes (mesne, pronounced "mean", meaning intermediate). The King was lord paramount. The status of lordship, including the right to receive the tenant's services, was called seignory.

4. Tenure. Feudal services became to a certain extent standardised. Thus   2–004
there was one set of services (which included the provision of armed horse-men for battle) which became known as knight's service, and there was another set (which included the performance of some honourable service for the King in person) which was known as grand sergeanty. Each of these sets of services was known as a *tenure*, because it showed upon what terms the land was held (*tenere*, to hold).[4] The commonest type of tenure was that known as socage, which was a residual category of free tenure that was neither military nor spiritual.

5. Estates. Whatever the tenure, the land might be held for different periods   2–005
of time. It might be granted for life (for so long as the tenant lived), in tail (for so long as the tenant or any of his descendants lived), or in fee simple (for so long as the tenant or any of his heirs, whether descendants or not, were alive).[5] Each of these interests was known as an *estate*, a word derived from *status*.[6] Thus the Crown might grant land to A for an estate in fee simple, and A in turn might grant it to B for life. In this situation, both the Crown and A retained

[4] Co.Litt. p.la.
[5] Leaseholds (which are now estates): see below, para.3–015) fell outside the feudal system, since in early times they were not considered to be estates but merely personal contracts. See Challis pp.63, 64, above, para.1–012 and below, para.3–009.
[6] H.E.L. ii, pp.351, 352; Williams R.P. pp.7, 8.

interests in the land. A person might hold land for one or more estates, yet this was only a qualified form of ownership.

The largest estate in land, the fee simple, has come more and more to resemble absolute ownership, and its proprietor is commonly called the owner of the land. This is because the tenurial relationship is now so slender that it can be ignored for practical purposes. However, even today, it is in one sense true to say that all land in England is vested in the Crown. A subject can hold it only as tenant. When we say "X owns Blackacre in fee simple", we really mean "X holds Blackacre of Y (his lord) by the tenure of fee and common socage for an estate in fee simple". But the difference in practice is negligible and the full formula is, therefore, not used. It should be noted that both in popular speech and in legal parlance the word "estate" is often used in other senses, for example, as a description of an area of land (as in "The Blackacre estate is to be sold"), or as a general term meaning property (as in "the deceased's net estate"). The context will usually leave little doubt about which sense is intended.

2–006   **6. Fundamental doctrine.** There are thus two fundamental doctrines in the law of real property:

> (i) the doctrine of tenures: all land is held of the Crown, either directly or indirectly, in one or other of the various tenures; and

> (ii) the doctrine of estates: land held in tenure is also held for an estate, that is to say for some period of time.

In short, tenure is concerned with the terms upon which land is held. The estate determines for how long.

Part 2

TYPES OF TENURE

2–007   There were three main types of tenure at common law.[7] The classification was based upon the services that the tenant was obliged to perform for his lord. The incidents of each of the forms of tenure differed.

First, there were three forms of free tenure:

> (i) Tenures in Chivalry (or Military Tenures): these were grand sergeanty and knight's service.

> (ii) Tenures in Socage: these were the less exalted tenures of petty sergeanty and socage.

---

[7] See S. F. C. Milsom, *Historical Foundations of the Common Law* 2nd edn (Oxford, OUP, 1981) Ch.5; A.W.B. Simpson, *A History of the Land Law* 2nd edn (Oxford, OUP, 1986) Ch.1.

(iii) Spiritual Tenures: these were frankalmoign[8] and divine service.[9]

Secondly, there were unfree tenures. The great unfree tenure was villeinage, later called copyhold. There was also a variety known as customary freehold. Generally speaking, free tenure was the tenure of landed proprietors and independent farmers, whereas unfree tenure was the tenure of common labourers. Some aspects of unfree tenure retain some significance.

Thirdly, there were certain miscellaneous tenures that did not conveniently fit into the scheme explained above. These included a form of knight service called "homage ancestral" and the "manors of ancient demesne" (manors which belonged to the Crown in 1066).

Leasehold tenure, the one form of tenure which remains familiar today, played no part in this scheme. It stood outside the feudal system, having developed relatively late. It has to be treated as a separate subject, both historically and legally.[10]

It is necessary to give a brief account of some of the aspects of the operation of tenures because, remarkably, aspects of the doctrine have survived into the 21st century and can still create difficulties.

1. General characteristics of feudal tenure

First, each form of tenure required the tenant to perform certain services in exchange for the land that had been granted to him. For example, a tenant who held by knight service was originally required to provide his lord with a fixed number of fully armed horsemen for 40 days each year. In time most services were commuted for a money payment. **2–008**

Second, there were certain other "incidents" that attached to each form of tenure. For example, a lord might require an incoming tenant to pay a "relief". The amount of this relief depended upon the type of tenure. Thus the relief payable for land held in military tenure was one year's value of the land, whereas in relation to land held in socage tenure, it was one year's rent and was payable only where an annual money rent was reserved. One of the most valuable rights in relation to land held in military tenure was wardship. Wardship was the lord's right to manage for his own profit the lands of a tenant who left as his heir a male under 21 or a female under 14.[11] **2–009**

Third, when an estate determined, the land "escheated" to the lord of whom the tenant held was entitled to the land. In other words, the immediate lord was entitled to the land by virtue of his own estate. The commonest cause of escheat was where the tenant died without heirs. It also occurred where the **2–010**

---

[8] Frankalmoign or "free alms" arose where land was granted to an ecclesiastical corporation where no specific services were reserved and no fealty was demanded. For a recent discussion of frankalmoign, see *Crown Estate Commissioners v Roberts* [2008] EWHC 1302 (Ch); [2008] 2 E.G.L.R. 165.

[9] This arose where land was granted in return for specific spiritual services, such as the saying of a mass on specified days or occasions.

[10] See below, para.17–002.

[11] Or 16, if she had not married before the land descended to her.

tenant was convicted of a felony and sentenced to death. Although the circumstances in which land may escheat are now limited, it does still occur and can give rise to considerable practical difficulties.[12] If a tenant was attainted of high treason, his land was forfeited to the Crown under the royal prerogative.

2. Unfree tenure and its legacy

2–011   The greatest surviving legacy of the doctrine of tenures is in relation to land formerly held in unfree tenure. A large proportion of England after the Conquest was held in villein tenure, and most agricultural labour was done by villein tenants.[13] This tenure was closely connected with that important feudal unit, the manor. A manor usually consisted of:

   (i) the lord's demesne, comprising the manor house and the cultivable land which the lord himself occupied

   (ii) the land held by tenants, in either free or unfree tenure; and

   (iii) the waste land of the manor, on which the tenants could pasture their beasts.[14]

These constituent elements of a manor are still significant for the purposes of certain legislation.[15]

2–012   There was in time a fundamental change in the status of unfree tenure. At first, the villein tenant was literally a tenant "at the will of the lord".[16] The lord could at any time evict him. The King's courts would not protect him, and he could not sue his lord in the manor court. However, although his tenure was precarious in theory, it came in practice to be protected. Customs arose in each manor that tenants should not lose their lands unless they had done some act which was recognised as meriting forfeiture. The "custom of the manor" became the recognised "law" of the manor court. Although there was no means of enforcing it against the lord, he normally observed it.[17] The villein was therefore said to hold "at the will of the lord and according to the custom of the manor". In practice the second condition was the more important, though only the first was recognised by the common law.

2–013   From the 15th century onwards, the royal courts, beginning with the Court of Chancery, began to protect tenants of villein land against their lords. In time, the villein tenant came to hold his land "at the will of the lord according

---

[12] See below, para.2–023.

[13] H.E.L. iii, p.198; *Heydon's Case* (1584) 3 Co.Rep. 7a at 8b.

[14] For the manor, see P. & M. i, pp.594 et seq.; H.E.L. ii, pp.375 et seq.; iii, pp.32, 33, 491, 492; *Hampshire CC v Milburn* [1992] 1 A.C. 325 at 338; *Crown Estate Commissioners v Roberts* [2008] EWHC 1302 (Ch) at [9]–[11]; [2008] 2 E.G.L.R. 165 at 167.

[15] See LPA 1925 s.193; *ADM Milling Ltd v Tewkesbury TC* [2011] EWHC 595 (Ch); [2011] 3 W.L.R. 674; below para.28–034; and see; CRA 1965 s.22(1)(b); below, para.27–050. CRA 1965 will be repealed when the Commons Act 2006 is brought fully into force.

[16] P. & M. i, p.360.

[17] P. & M., i, pp.361, 376, 377.

to the custom of the manor",[18] not only by custom but at law as well. Everything was regulated by the custom of the particular manor in question, which, when proved, would be enforceable at common law. This change was marked by a change in name: "tenure in villeinage" became known as "tenure by copy of the court roll" or "copyhold", and the term "villein" was reserved for the few remaining persons whose status was still unfree.[19] The name "copyhold" was derived from the manner in which such land was conveyed. In the case of free tenures (after 1290) a conveyance could be made without reference to the lord.[20] Copyholds, however, could be transferred only by a process of surrender and admittance made in the lord's court. The transaction was recorded on the court rolls and the transferee had a copy of the entry to prove his title. He therefore held "by copy of the court roll". By the end of the 16th century the legal position of the copyholder had become substantially settled. Copyhold lost its taint of servility, and became merely a form—indeed, one of the commonest forms—of tenure. Since rents could not be increased as the value of money fell, copyhold lands became valuable inheritances to their tenants, and permanently ceased to be a source of much profit to their lords.[21]

Certain rights enjoyed by the lord in relation to copyhold land have retained some significance. In particular, the ownership of all timber and minerals was vested in the lord.[22] However, as they were in the possession of the tenant, it was a trespass for the lord to enter to take them without the tenant's consent [23] Both these rules were subject to any custom to the contrary, but in the absence of any such custom, the trees and minerals could not be dealt with except by agreement between lord and tenant.[24]

Part 3

REDUCTION IN THE NUMBER OF TENURES

Section 1. Prohibition of New Tenures After 1290

1. Before 1290

In early times there was no theoretical limit to the number of intervening   2–014
tenures between the King and the tenant in occupation of the land. A new rung
could always be added at the bottom of the feudal ladder by the creation of a

---

[18] *Brown's Case* (1581) 4 Co.Rep. 21a.
[19] H.E.L. iii, p.206.
[20] Below, para.2–015.
[21] H.E.L. iii, p.212.
[22] *Eardley v Earl Granville* (1876) 3 Ch.D. 826 at 832. For this reason, it was not worthwhile for copyhold tenants to cultivate timber.
[23] *Bourne v Taylor* (1808) 10 East 189 (minerals); *Whitechurch v Holworthy* (1815) 4 M. & S. 340 (trees).
[24] *Commissioners of Inland Revenue v Joicey (No.2)* [1913] 2 K.B. 580 at 586.

further tenure. This process was called subinfeudation. It was popular in an age where land was almost the only form of capital wealth. At that time, the seller of land preferred to take payment in the form of a continuing right to rent or services charged on the land. For example, the King might grant to A, A might grant to B and B might grant to C. A and B would then be mesne lords.[25] The system was, however, cumbersome. Furthermore, it became common for B to subinfeudate to C for cash, reserving only nominal services. If, therefore, the land were held in military tenure and B died leaving an infant heir, A's wardship would be valueless. All he would receive would be the right to receive C's nominal services. The logic of subinfeudation was that land should be granted in return for genuine and not nominal services.[26]

The alternative to subinfeudation was substitution. B might grant to C not by creating a new tenure but by allowing C to step into his shoes so that C became, and B ceased to be, tenant of A. There were however drawbacks if A could be compelled to take C for his tenant at B's instance. The personal qualities of C might be material while the feudal bond retained its personal character. Nevertheless, it appears to have become the general rule in the 13th century that tenants could alienate by substitution without their lords' consent.

2. The Statute *Quia Emptores* 1290

2–015　　*(a) The statute.* Magna Carta 1217, c.39, had attempted to meet the lords' objections by prohibiting alienations which left insufficient security for the services. But dissatisfaction continued until the matter was resolved by the statute *Quia Emptores* 1290.[27] The effect of this was as follows.

   (i) Alienation by subinfeudation was prohibited (c.1).

  (ii) All free tenants were authorised to alienate the whole or part of their land by substitution, without the lord's consent, the new tenant to hold by the same services as the old (c.1).

 (iii) On alienation of part of the land by substitution, the feudal services were to be apportioned (c.2).

 (iv) The statute applied only to grants in fee simple (c.3).

---

[25] See above, para.2–003.

[26] See S. F. C. Milsom, *Historical Foundations of the Common Law*, pp.110–118.

[27] The first chapter of the statute can be stated in abbreviated form as follows: "Whereas purchasers of lands and tenements have many times heretofore entered into their fees, to be holden in fee of their feoffors and not of the chief lords of the fees, whereby the said chief lords have many times lost their escheats, marriages and wardships; which things seemed very hard and extreme unto those lords and other great men: our lord the king has granted, provided and ordained that henceforth it shall be lawful for every freeman to sell at his own pleasure his lands and tenements, or part of them; so nevertheless that the feoffee shall hold the same lands or tenements of the chief lord of the same fee, by such service and customs as his feoffor held before." For the historical and legal background to the statute, see S. F. C. Milsom, *Historical Foundations of the Common Law*, p.113; J. M. W. Bean, *The Decline of English Feudalism* (Manchester, The University Press 1968), p.79.

(b) Effect of the statute. Given the developing practice of making disposi-   2–016
tions of land for money rather than services, *Quia Emptores* was probably
inevitable.[28] Its effect was that, thereafter, no new tenures in fee simple could
be created except by the Crown. Existing tenures could be freely transferred
from hand to hand, and they could be extinguished as before by escheat or
forfeiture.[29] The network of tenures could therefore no longer grow. It could
only contract. Every conveyance of land in fee simple by a subject after 1290
was bound to be an out-and-out transfer and could not create the relationship
of lord and tenant between the parties.[30] On such a conveyance no services
could be reserved. Any rights reserved, such as a rent, had to be rights existing
independently of the relationship of lord and tenant.

(c) Limits of statute. Since the statute did not mention the Crown either   2–017
expressly or by necessary implication, the Crown was not bound by it.[31]
Indeed, had the statute bound the Crown it would have had strange consequences. If the Crown had been prohibited from making infeudatory grants it
would have meant that, if it wished to make a disposition of land which it held
in demesne, it would have had to transfer the land to the transferee as
allodium, with no prospect of escheat or forfeiture.[32] In fact it was clear that
the statute did not prevent the Crown from granting land to be held of the
Crown. However, the Tenures Abolition Act 1660 provided that such grants
could be made only in common socage.[33] One consequence of the fact that the
Statute did not bind the Crown was that the statute conferred no right of free
alienation upon tenants in chief.[34]

(d) Effect today. Quia Emptores 1290 is still in force today. While the   2–018
wholly archaic doctrine of tenures remains, it cannot be repealed. The statute
operates every time that a conveyance in fee simple is executed, automatically
shifting the status of tenant from grantor to grantee. It ensures that all land
held by a subject is held in tenure of the Crown either directly or indirectly.
The lord of the fee is the successor in title to the person who was lord in 1290,
because no change in the tenure can have occurred since then. It is exceptionally rare for records of a mesne lordship to have been preserved for so long,
except in the case of manors where mesne tenure remained of importance until

---

[28] See above, para.2–014.

[29] For escheat and forfeiture, see above, para.2–010.

[30] It was in fact some time before subinfeudation ceased in practice, though the reasons for this
delay are unclear: see J. M. Kaye, *Medieval English Conveyances* (Cambridge University Press
2009), pp.83–85.

[31] Litt. 140. See H.E.L. iii, p.84, i, p.473. Tenants in chief were prevented from subinfeudating:
Re Holliday [1922] 2 Ch. 698.

[32] There is no concept of allodial land in England and Wales: see above, para.2–001.

[33] s 4. For this statute, see below, para.2–019.

[34] An Ordinance of 1256 forbidding them to alienate without a royal licence remained
effective. However, in 1327 tenants in chief were given a right of free alienation, subject only to
the payment of a reasonable fine in some cases: 1 Edw. 3. St. 2, cc.12, 13, 1327; cf, 34 Edw. 3,
c.15, 1360, confirming alienations made before 1272. The Tenures Abolition Act 1660 abolished
this fine: s.1.

1925 and later.[35] Other cases are governed by the presumption that, if no mesne lord appears, the land is held directly of the Crown.[36] Innumerable mesne lordships came to be forgotten as, with the passage of time and the inflation of the currency, the ancient services or commutation rents ceased to be worth collecting. After 1290 the feudal pyramid began to crumble. The number of mesne lordships could not be increased, evidence of existing mesne lordships gradually disappeared with the passing of time, and so most land came to be held directly from the Crown.

Section 2. The Tenures Abolition Act 1660

2–019   The system of landholding in return for services fell into decay long before the most onerous incidents of tenure were legally abolished. The Crown assiduously preserved the incidents of military tenure, such as wardships, for the sake of revenue.[37] However, following the restoration of the monarchy, the Tenures Abolition Act 1660 converted all tenures into free and common socage[38] with the exception of frankalmoign (which became obsolete in any event)[39] and copyhold. Nearly all burdensome incidents were abolished for all land of free tenure. Escheat and forfeiture survived as the only important incidents of free tenure.

Section 3. The 1925 Legislation

A. Tenures

2–020   **1. Before 1926.** From 1645 until 1926 there was in effect a dual system of tenure. Almost all land was either socage (often called freehold) or copyhold. The methods of conveying freehold land were quite different from those applicable to copyhold. Although copyhold had the great merit that the books of the manor were a register of title,[40] it had disadvantages. Its peculiar mode of conveyance (surrender and admittance) made it impossible to convey freeholds and copyholds by a single deed. It was subject both to customary incidents which might vary from manor to manor and also the lord's rights to timber and minerals. Accordingly provision was made by statute for the enfranchisement of copyholds, i.e. the conversion of land of copyhold tenure into freehold. This was initially to enable copyhold to be enfranchised by

---

[35] See below, para.2–020.
[36] Williams R.P. p.58; Challis p.33; and see *Re Lowe's WT* [1973] 1 W.L.R. 882.
[37] Bl.Comm. ii, pp.69, 76.
[38] See *Crown Estate Commissioners v Roberts* [2008] EWHC 1302 (Ch) at [75]; [2008] 2 E.G.L.R. 165 at 172.
[39] It was finally abolished by AEA 1925 Sch.2 Pt I.
[40] Freehold titles had mostly to be proved in the traditional way by investigating past transactions recorded in the title deeds: below, para.15–069.

agreement between the lord and tenant.[41] Later statutes allowed proceedings to be brought by a lord or a tenant to secure compulsory enfranchisement.[42]

2. After 1925. By the Law of Property Act 1922 (which took effect at the **2–021** beginning of 1926) all copyhold land was converted into land of freehold tenure.[43] The way in which freehold and copyhold incidents were dealt with is explained below. A new system of intestate succession was introduced whereby all special customs of descent were superseded.[44] The result was that, as from the beginning of 1926 (when these provisions all took effect), all land has been held in freehold, the modern name for free and common socage.

B. Incidents

1. Freehold. Of the surviving feudal incidents that existed in relation to **2–022** freehold, escheat on the death of the tenant intestate and without heirs was often the one valuable right of the lord still in existence in 1925. In most cases it was impossible for the mesne lord to prove his lordship, because freeholders could alienate their land without reference to the lord. There might, therefore, have been no event for many years by which he might have marked his lordship. The Administration of Estates Act 1925 abolished this form of escheat and provided that if a person died leaving property not disposed of by will, that property should pass to the Crown[45] in default of any of the limited class of relatives set out in the Act.[46] Escheat for felony no longer existed in 1925. It was abolished by the Forfeiture Act 1870, together with the Crown's prerogative right of forfeiture for high treason.

Although the two principal forms of escheat ceased to exist, escheat was not **2–023** abolished. It will occur whenever a freehold estate determines. Escheat is a principle, inseparable from tenure, which ensures that land will never be without an owner.[47] If there is no tenant of the land and no mesne lord, it will return to the Crown. The circumstances in which a freehold may determine so that the land escheats include the following, of which the first two occur regularly:

> (i) where a landowner's trustee in bankruptcy (if he is an individual) or liquidator (if it is a corporation) exercises his statutory power[48] to disclaim the land[49];

---

[41] Copyhold Acts of 1841, 1843 and 1844.
[42] Copyhold Acts of 1852, 1858 and 1887 (consolidated in the Copyhold Act 1894).
[43] s.128 and Sch. 12, para.(1).
[44] AEA 1925 s.45(1) Sch. 2, Pt 1; see below, paras 14–104 et seq.
[45] Or, as the case may be, the Duchy of Lancaster or Cornwall.
[46] ss.45, 46; and see Crown Estate Act 1961 s.8(3). See below, paras 14–124, 14–128.
[47] See *Ho Young v Bess* [1995] 1 W.L.R. 350 at 355.
[48] IA 1986 ss.315 and 178 respectively.
[49] See *Scmlla Properties Ltd v Gesso Properties (B.V.I.) Ltd* [1995] B.C.C. 793 (the leading modern case, which contains a perceptive and illuminating discussion of the issues). See too *British General Insurance Co Ltd v Att Gen* [1945] L.J.N.C.C.R. 113, discussed (1946) 62 L.Q.R. 223 (R.E.M.); and also (1931) 75 S.J. 843 (T.C. Williams).

(ii) where a company's property has vested in the Crown (in the person of the Treasury Solicitor)[50] as *bona vacantia* because the company has been dissolved,[51] and the Crown has exercised its statutory right to disclaim[52];

(iii) where the Crown made an infeudatory grant of a freehold subject to restrictions as to the user of the land that are enforceable by a right of entry, and that right of entry has been exercised.[53]

Escheat takes place automatically, and the freehold is extinguished.[54]

2–024   On the dissolution of a company governed by the Companies Acts, statute vests its property in the Crown, in the person of the Treasury Solicitor,[55] as *bona vacantia*.[56] Although in those circumstances, the Crown may disclaim the freehold,[57] this has a "boomerang effect",[58] because the land then escheats to a different part of the Crown, the Crown Estate.[59] Although it has been suggested that, in consequence, it is not easy to discern the reason for these provisions so far as they relate to freeholds,[60] there is a reason for it. Although it has never been finally determined whether the Treasury Solicitor is liable for onerous property that passes to him as *bona vacantia*, it is commonly assumed that he may be.[61] By disclaiming the property, the Treasury Solicitor protects himself from any such liability, because the property is deemed never to have vested in him.[62] By contrast, where property has been disclaimed by the Treasury Solicitor and has vested in the Crown Estate, the Crown Estate incurs no liability in respect of it unless it takes possession of, or exercises control over, the property.[63] The practical consequence is that where an escheat of a freehold occurs, the Crown Estate takes no action in relation to

---

[50] Or, depending where the land may be, in the Crown in right of the Duchy of Lancaster or in the Duke of Cornwall.

[51] See Companies Act 2006 s.1012.

[52] For this right to disclaim and its operation, see Companies Act 2006 ss.1013, 1014; and see *Cromwell Developments Ltd v Godfrey* [1998] 2 E.G.L.R. 62 at 66. Under Companies Act 2006 s.1013(3), the Treasury Solicitor must normally disclaim within three years of receiving notice of the vesting.

[53] See the Crown Estates Act 1961 s.3(8), which permits such grants.

[54] *Scmlla Properties Lid v Gesso Properties (B.V.I.) Ltd* [1995] B.C.C. 793. It is clear from that case, that escheat applies as much to registered land as it does to unregistered: ibid., at 802.

[55] Or Duchy of Lancaster or Duke of Cornwall.

[56] Companies Act 2006 s.1012.

[57] Companies Act 2006 ss.1013, 1014.

[58] *Scmlla Properties Ltd v Gesso Properties (B.V.I.) Ltd* [1995] B.C.C. 793 at 805, per Burnton, Q.C.

[59] Or, as the case may be, the Duchy of Lancaster or Duke of Cornwall. For the Crown Estate, see the Crown Estate Act 1961.

[60] *Scmlla Properties Ltd v Gesso Properties (B.V.I.) Ltd* [1995] B.C.C. 793 at 805. See too (1954) 70 L.Q.R. 25 (D.W. Elliott).

[61] See, e.g. *Toff v McDowell* (1993) 69 P. & C.R. 535, where it was assumed without argument that, where a freehold reversion on a lease vested in the Crown as *bona vacantia*, the Crown was subject to the burden of the covenants of that lease.

[62] Companies Act 2006 s.1014(1).

[63] See *Halsbury's Laws of England*, vol.12(1), p.89, para.234.

the land unless and until a person seeks to acquire the property from it.[64] It will not, therefore, sell just part of the land, or grant rights over it.[65]

Where the corporation dissolved is not governed by the Companies Acts, **2–025** there will be an escheat of its real property.[66] Leases owned by such a corporation, on the other hand, will pass to the Crown under the Crown's prerogative right to *bona vacantia*, i.e. personal property without an owner.[67] Escheat does not determine any subordinate interest in the land in question, such as a mortgage or lease. The Crown takes the land subject to such rights.[68]

It sometimes happens that a company or corporation is dissolved at a time when it held land on trust for a third party. Formerly, the Crown was not bound by trusts (even though it was bound by incumbrances), but the harshness of this rule was ameliorated by statute.[69] The position today is that the trust beneficiaries will, in practice, seek a vesting order,[70] and this is so whether the land has passed to the Treasury Solicitor as *bona vacantia* or to the Crown Estate by escheat.[71]

2. Copyhold. In the case of copyholds, the incidents were in most cases still **2–026** fully effective in 1925. The Law of Property Act 1922 divided them into three classes.

(a) Those abolished forthwith.[72] As soon as the Act came into force (on **2–027** January 1, 1926), the following incidents were abolished subject to a single payment of compensation[73]:

    (i) forfeiture for alienation in freehold (i.e. for purporting to convey the land as freehold) or without licence;

---

[64] cf. *Hackney LBC v Crown Estate Commissioners* (1995) 72 P. & C.R. 233.

[65] This point arises quite commonly in practice.

[66] *Re Wells* [1933] Ch. 29 at 54, approving Challis p.467; *Re Strathblaine Estates Ltd* [1948] Ch. 228. Previously it had been doubtful whether there was escheat, or reverter to the donor: Co.Litt. 13b; Preston ii, p.50; Challis pp.65, 66, 226; (1933) 49 L.Q.R. 160 (Sir W. S. Holdsworth), 240 (F. E. Farrer); (1935) 51 L.Q.R. 347 (M. W. Hughes), 361 (F. E. Farrer). See also below, para.9–101.

[67] *Re Wells*, above (equitable interest in leaseholds).

[68] *Att Gen of Ontario v Mercer* (1883) 8 App. Cas. 767 at 772; *Scmlla Properties Ltd v Gesso Properties (B.V.I.) Ltd* [1995] B.C.C. 793 at 806–808.

[69] Crown Lands Act 1819 s.1.

[70] See TA 1925 s.44; *Re Strathblaine Estates Ltd* [1948] Ch. 228. Where there has been an escheat, following the dissolution of a corporation, the court can by order create a corresponding estate and vest it in the person who would have been entitled to the estate had it not determined: LPA 1925 s.181(1). Although s.181 is inapplicable where a person claims an interest under a trust (see *Re Strathblaine Estates Ltd* [1948] Ch. 228 at 231), such an order was made to the grantee of an option who had complied with the terms of that option: see *UBS Global Asset Management (UK) Ltd v Crown Estate Commissioners* Unreported June 9, 2011 (Chancery Division).

[71] Whether right or wrong, this convenient practice is invariably followed. The Attorney General is joined as the defendant to the action.

[72] Sch.12 para.(1).

[73] Sch.13 Pt II para.13, as amended by LPAmA 1924 Sch.2 para.4(3), and LPAmA 1926 Sch. (usually 20% of the annual value of the land).

(ii) fealty and customary suits and services;

(iii) escheat for want of heirs[74]; and

(iv) special customs of descent (e.g. gavelkind and borough English),
dower, freebench (the usual name for dower in copyhold land) and
curtesy.

2–028   *(b) Those preserved until 1936.*[75] This class automatically disappeared after
December 31, 1935, unless previously extinguished either voluntarily or
compulsorily. Until 1936 the parties could extinguish them at any time
voluntarily, or either party could serve a notice on the other requiring the
amount of compensation to be ascertained.[76] Immediately on service of the
notice the incidents ceased, and compensation became payable as fixed by the
Minister of Agriculture according to a scale.

So long as any incidents in this class existed, no conveyance of the land
would pass the legal estate unless it was produced to the steward of the manor
within six months and indorsed by him with a certificate that all payments due
on the transfer had been duly made. This provision was necessary since the
land, being freehold, became transferable without reference to the lord, and
thus the lord might not know that there had been a conveyance entitling him
to a fine or some other payment.

Even though the incidents ceased at the end of 1935 (and thus production
of a conveyance made after 1935 was unnecessary), the lord was enabled to
claim compensation, originally up to 1941, and later, by a war-time extension,
up to the end of October 1950.[77]

The incidents in this class were as follows:

(i) quit rents, chief rents and other similar payments;

(ii) fines, reliefs, heriots and dues (including fees payable to
stewards);

(iii) forfeitures other than for alienation in freehold or without licence;
and

(iv) timber rights.

2–029   *(c) Those preserved indefinitely.*[78] The rights and liabilities, which continue
indefinitely unless abolished by written agreement between lord and tenant,
are as follows:

[74] In *British General Insurance Co. Ltd v Att Gen* [1945] L.J.N.C.C.R. 113 at 125, it was said
that all kinds of escheat were abolished for enfranchised land by LPA 1922 Sch.12 para.(1)(c).
But the more natural interpretation is that escheat is excluded only where the Crown takes as *bona
vacantia* under the AEA 1925 (replacing Pt VIII of the LPA 1922).
[75] LPA 1922 ss.128, 129, 138, 140, Sch.13, Pt II.
[76] In order to give the tenant time to raise the money the lord was prohibited from serving a
notice until 1931: LPA 1922 s.138(1)(b).
[77] Postponement of Enactments (Miscellaneous Provisions) Act 1939 s.3; SI 1949/836.
[78] LPA 1922 ss.128(2), 138, Sch.12, paras (4)–(6).

(i) any rights of the lord or tenant to mines and minerals[79];

(ii) any rights of the lord in respect of fairs, markets and sporting;

(iii) any tenant's rights of common (e.g. to pasture beasts on the waste land of the manor)[80]; and

(iv) any liability of lord or tenant for the upkeep of dykes, ditches, sea walls, bridges, and the like.

Only by the existence of these rights and duties is land which was formally copyhold now distinguishable from other land as regards the conditions of tenure. In practice, the existence of such rights has become important because, if they are to be protected for the future against purchasers of the land which is affected by them, they must be registered before October 13, 2013.[81]

Lordships of manors continue to exist, representing mesne tenure between the Crown and the freeholders. Since they carry the right to the manorial records, there is a market for them for historical or antiquarian purposes.[82] Often they also carry the right to hold a court baron and sometimes also a court leet, though in nearly all cases such courts have lost all legal jurisdiction.[83] There is an increasing interest in manorial titles because they may carry with them corporeal land.[84]

Part 4

TENURE AND OWNERSHIP TODAY

There is only one feudal tenure left today, namely socage, now called freehold. Feudal incidents have in practice disappeared,[85] except for land formerly held in grant sergeanty, petty sergeanty or copyhold, where some traces of the former tenure remain. Except in the case of land formerly copyhold, mesne lordships are nearly all untraceable, for it is many years since there were any enforceable rights to preserve evidence of the relationship of lord and tenant; **2–030**

---

[79] "Mines" is a more comprehensive term than "minerals", because it relates not only to the minerals but also to the passages in the mine: *Batten Pooll v Kennedy* [1907] 1 Ch. 256. For the meaning of "minerals", see *Earl of Lonsdale v Att Gen* [1982] 1 W.L.R. 887 at 924, 925.

[80] A statutory scheme for registration of these rights was introduced in 1965: see CRA 1965, which is in the process of replacement by the Commons Act 2006: see below, para.27–051.

[81] LRA 2002, s.117. See below, paras 7–031, 7–088.

[82] Some may carry land with them as well: see below, para.7–017.

[83] Various obsolete jurisdictions were extinguished by AJA 1977 s.23 and Sch.4, as recommended by Law Com. No.72 (1976). For courts leet, see H.E.L. i, p.135.

[84] See LPA 1925 s.62(3). For LPA 1925 s.62, see below, para.28–027. cf. *Commission for New Towns v J. J. Gallagher Ltd* [2002] EWHC 2668 (Ch), at [63]–[65]; [2003] 2 P. & C.R. 24 at 42.

[85] For a Crown grant in 1913 of Canadian land in socage in fee simple subject to rent service (a royalty), see *Att Gen for Alberta v Huggard Assets Ltd* [1953] A.C. 420. In principle there is nothing to prevent the Crown reserving services upon such grants.

consequently the courts are ready to act on the presumption that the land is held directly of the Crown, e.g. for the purposes of escheat.[86]

Yet despite the sweeping changes made by statute, "the fundamental principles of the law of ownership of land remain the same as before the legislation of 1925. Land is still the object of feudal tenure; the Sovereign remains the lord paramount of all the land within the realm; every parcel of land is still held of some lord . . . and the greatest interest which any subject can have in land is still an estate in fee simple and no more".[87] The title "tenant in fee simple" is still the technically correct description of the person who is popularly regarded as the owner of land, and every conveyance in fee simple substitutes the new tenant for the old as provided by the statute *Quia Emptores* 1290. Nevertheless, as will be seen, for all practical purposes ownership in fee simple "differs from the absolute dominion of a chattel in nothing except the physical indestructibility of its subject".[88] Our law has preferred to suppress one by one the practical consequences of tenure rather than to strike at the root of the theory of tenure itself. It remains possible, therefore, that in rare cases not covered by the statutory reforms recourse may have to be had to the feudal principles which still underlie our land law.[89]

The one field in which rules derived from tenure remain of practical importance is, paradoxically, leasehold ("landlord and tenant"). Leasehold developed independently of the feudal system, and although it became a genuine tenure, it was never part of the network of tenures which connected land ownership with the Crown. It forms a separate branch of the law which in due course will be explained at length.[90]

For practical purposes, therefore, the law of tenure is no longer of assistance in solving problems about rights over land. The owner in fee simple is regarded as absolute owner, and the fundamentals of his title depend on principles which have nothing to do with tenure. The basis of land ownership is the system of estates, which is the subject of the following chapter. The final part of that chapter will elucidate what ownership really means in modern land law.

---

[86] See, e.g. *Re Lowe's WT* [1973] 1 W.L.R. 882 at 886.

[87] Cyprian Williams, "The fundamental principles of the present law of ownership of land" (1931) 75 S.J. 848.

[88] Challis p.218; and see below, para.3–035, but compare para.3–001, fn.2.

[89] e.g. in cases of escheat: above, para.2–023.

[90] See below, Ch.17.

ESTATES

Part 1

CLASSIFICATION

The term "estate", as has been explained,[1] indicates an interest in land of some particular duration. The purpose of this chapter is to consider the different kinds of estate, i.e. the various possible interests in land classified according to their duration. **3–001**

It is the doctrine of estates, coupled with the permanence of land as opposed to destructible chattels, which makes the law relating to land so much more complex than the law governing chattels.[2] At common law it can in general be said that only two distinct legal rights can exist at the same time in chattels, namely, possession and ownership. If A lends his watch to B, the ownership of the watch remains vested in A, while B has possession of it. But in the case of land, a large number of legal rights could and still can exist at the same time. Thus the position of Blackacre today may be that A is entitled to the land for life, B to a life interest in remainder (i.e. after A's death), and C to the fee simple in remainder. At the same time, D may own a lease for 99 years, subject to a sub-lease in favour of E for 21 years, and the land may be subject to a mortgage in favour of F, a profit à prendre in favour of G, easements such as rights of way in favour of H, J and K, and so on indefinitely. Before 1926 all these estates and interests could exist as legal rights. Some, but not all, can exist as legal rights today.

In the case of a chattel, ownership is absolute. It is either owned outright by one person (or by several persons jointly or in common with each other) or it is not owned at all. However there is in law, at least in theory, no absolute ownership of land. The land is held in tenure and there is a presumption that **3–002**

---

[1] Above, para.2–005.
[2] Land is not always indestructible, e.g. an upper floor of a house: below, para.3–035.

it is held directly of the Crown.[3] It may so be held for various different estates, i.e. for a greater or less period of time. In popular speech one may refer to X's ownership of Blackacre; but technically one should speak of X holding Blackacre for an estate in fee simple in socage tenure or for a term of years, and subject perhaps to easements, mortgages, and the like, which give other people limited rights of property in the land. Land law, therefore, has to concern itself with many varieties of qualified ownership.

3–003   The system of estates is of vital importance, but since it was radically amended in 1925, the past tense will be used in much of the discussion. The present law can be understood only by reference to the old.

Estates were divided into two classes:

1. freehold estates; and

2. leasehold estates.

It should be noted that "freehold" here has nothing to do with freehold (or socage) tenure. The word "freehold" is sometimes used to express the quality of the tenure, and sometimes the quantity of the estate. "Freehold" is normally used by the man in the street as combining these senses. Thus when an estate agent advertises "a desirable freehold residence", he is referring to a fee simple estate in land of freehold tenure.

Section 1. Estates of Freehold

3–004   **1. The three estates.** There were three estates of freehold:

(i) fee simple;

(ii) fee tail; and

(iii) life estate.[4]

The fee simple and the life estate have always existed in English law. The fee tail was introduced by statute in 1285, but can no longer be created. Before considering the estates in any detail a brief account of each must be given.

3–005   *(a) Fee simple.* Originally this was an estate which endured for so long as the original tenant or any of his heirs (blood relations, and their heirs, and so on)[5] survived. Thus at first a fee simple would terminate if the original tenant

---

[3] See *Re Lowe's W.T.* [1973] 1 W.L.R. 882 at 886, per Russell L.J., where "the theoretical possibility" of an escheat to a mesne lord was considered to be "so remote that it may be wholly ignored". See above, Ch.2.
[4] Co.Litt. p.43b.
[5] For the exact meaning of "heir" see the 5th edition of this work at p.540.

died without leaving any descendants or collateral blood relations (e.g. brothers or cousins), even if before his death the land had been conveyed to another tenant who was still alive.[6] However, by 1306, it was settled that where a tenant in fee simple alienated the land, the fee simple would continue as long as there were heirs of the new tenant, and so on, irrespective of any failure of the original tenant's heirs.[7] From that time onwards a fee simple was virtually perpetual. It would terminate only if the tenant for the time being died leaving no heir, when it would escheat to his lord.[8]

(b) Fee tail. This was an estate which continued for so long as the original **3–006** tenant or any of his lineal descendants survived. Thus if the original tenant died leaving no relatives except a brother, a fee simple would continue, but a fee tail would come to an end. The terms "fee tail", "estate tail", "entail" and "entailed interest" are often used interchangeably; but "fee tail" was the correct expression for a legal entail,[9] and "entailed interest" was usually reserved for an equitable entail.[10]

(c) Life estate. As its name indicates, this lasted for life only. The name **3–007** "life estate" usually indicated that the measuring life was that of the tenant himself, e.g. when the grant was to A for life. The form of life estate where the measuring life was that of some person was known as an estate *"pur autre vie"* (for the life of another), e.g. to A for so long as B lives.

2. "Freehold". A common feature of all estates of freehold was that the **3–008** duration of the estate, though limited, was uncertain. Nobody could say when the death would occur of a particular person and all his future heirs, or of a person and all his descendants, or of a person alone. Nor was it certain that the duration would be perpetual. The estate was always liable to determine if some event occurred. In the case of the fee simple and the fee tail, the word "fee" denoted (i) that the estate was an estate of inheritance, i.e. an estate which, on the death of the tenant, was capable of descending to his heir[11]; and (ii) that the estate was one which might continue for ever).[12] The words "simple" and "tail" distinguished the classes of heirs who could inherit. A fee simple descended to the heirs general, including collaterals.[13] A fee tail descended to heirs special, i.e. to lineal descendants only.

A life estate, on the other hand, was not a fee. It was not an estate of inheritance and it could not continue for ever. On the death of the tenant an

---

[6] H.E.L. iii, p.106; P. & M. ii, p.14.
[7] YB. 33–35 Edw. 1 (R.S.) 362; H.E.L. iii, pp.106, 107.
[8] Above, para.2–010.
[9] Challis p.60. A legal entail can no longer exist: below, para.6–009.
[10] Below, para.6–012.
[11] Litt. pp.1, 9; Preston i, p.262; Challis p.218. After 1925, the concept of heir has been virtually obsolete: see below, paras 14–104 and 14–131—14–133.
[12] Preston i, pp.419, 480.
[13] Preston i, p.428. Formerly the word "simple" also signified "absolute", as opposed to "conditional"; Co.Litt. p.1b; Challis p.218; below, para.3–052, fn.243.

ordinary life estate determined, and an estate *pur autre vie* did not descend to the tenant's heir, but passed under the special rules of occupancy.[14] Life estates were sometimes called "mere freeholds" or simply "freeholds", as opposed to "freeholds of inheritance".[15]

Each estate of freehold could exist in a number of varied forms which will be considered in due course.

Section 2. Leaseholds

3–009   **1. Nature of leases.** At first, the three estates of freehold were the sole estates recognised by law. The only other lawful right to the possession of land was known as a tenancy at will, under which the tenant could be ejected at any time, and which therefore gave him no estate at all.[16] Terms of years grew up outside this system of estates. Originally they were regarded not as property (as object of ownership) but as personal contracts binding only on the parties. The leaseholder was not fully protected against other persons until the end of the 15th century, and the nature of the remedy (the action of ejectment) marked off leaseholds from the other estates.[17] When they became fully protected by the law of property they became estates,[18] but it was too late for them to be classified with the others.

3–010   **2. "Less than freehold".** Leaseholds have long been denominated "estates less than freehold", and in theory they are inferior.

> "In law the duration of a term is immaterial, and a term for 21 years is as great an estate as one for 21,000 years. The distinction is between a chattel interest, which is a term for years, and a freehold interest. A freehold interest of the smallest duration is greater in the contemplation of law than the longest term."[19]

Nevertheless, their inferiority exists only in history and in theory. A rent-free lease for 3,000 years may be as secure and as valuable as any freehold estate.[20] It is true that the early attitude towards leases led to their being classified as personal and not as real property, and that this distinction, which is still law, remains of some importance.[21] It is also true that, before 1926, leasehold property could not be entailed or granted by deed for life.[22] On the other hand, leases in early times had the important advantage that, since they were

---

[14] For the special rules of occupancy, see the 5th edition of this work at pp.93—94.
[15] Co.Litt. p.266b, n.1; Preston i, p.214; Challis p.99.
[16] Below, para.3–014.
[17] Below, paras 4–018 et seq.; H.E.L. iii, pp.213–217; iv, p.486.
[18] Litt. p.58.
[19] *Re Russell Road Purchase-Moneys* (1871) L.R. 12 Eq. 78 at 84, per Malins V.C.
[20] cf. below, para.24–020, in regard to mortgages.
[21] Above, para.1–012.
[22] Below, para.3–079.

personalty, they could be devised, while wills of freehold land were not allowed before 1540.[23]

3. Categories of leaseholds. Today the various forms of leasehold estates are of the first importance. Their distinguishing characteristic, by contrast with freehold estates, is that their maximum duration is fixed in time. The principal categories, which are dealt with more fully later, are as follows.[24]   **3–011**

(a) Fixed term of certain duration. The tenant may hold the land of a fixed term of certain duration,[25] as under a lease for 99 years.[26] The possibility of the term being curtailed (e.g. by forfeiture for non-payment of rent) under some provision to this effect in the lease does not affect the basic conception, which is one of certainty of duration in the absence of steps being taken for extension or curtailment. A lease for "99 years if X so long lives" also fell under this head. It was not an estate of freehold,[27] because although X would probably die before the 99 years had run, the maximum duration of the lease was fixed. Even if there was no chance of X outliving the 99 years, so that the duration of the lease would be the same as an estate granted "to X for life", as a matter of law the former was leasehold and the latter freehold. Partly as a result of the intervention of statute, such leases are very rare today.[28]   **3–012**

(b) Fixed term with duration capable of being rendered certain. A lease of land "to A from year to year", with no other provision as to its duration, will continue indefinitely unless either landlord or tenant takes some step to determine it. However, either party can give half a year's notice to determine it at the end of a year of the tenancy, and thus ensure its determination on a fixed date. "The term continues until determined as if both parties made a new agreement at the end of each year for a new term for the ensuing year."[29] At any given moment, therefore, the tenant's estate has a fixed term set to it, though it may later be extended if no notice is given. The same applies to quarterly, monthly, weekly and other periodical tenancies. A term of years accompanied by an option for either party to renew the lease is, on similar principles, regarded as a lease for a term certain.   **3–013**

---

[23] The Statute of Wills 1540 made it possible to leave land by will.
[24] Below, paras 17–001 et seq.
[25] Bracton Bk. iv, c. 28, f. 207; Preston i, p.203.
[26] A purported lease of uncertain duration is void: see, *Berrisford v Mexfield Housing Co-operative Ltd* [2011] UKSC 52 at [33]–[37]. Because of the principle that a lease must be granted for a term of certain duration, it has been said that "The concept of a permanent lease is almost a contradiction in terms": *The Raphael Fishing Company Ltd v The State of Mauritius* [2008] UKPC 43 at [68], per Lord Neuberger. See too, below, para.17–003.
[27] Cru.Dig. i, p.47.
[28] Below, para.17–113.
[29] *Prudential Assurance Co Ltd v London Residuary Body* [1992] 2 A.C. 386 at 394, per Lord Templeman. See below, para.17–079.

3–014   *(c) Tenancies at will and at sufferance.* Tenancies at will and tenancies at sufferance,[30] which are generally treated as part of the law relating to leasehold estates,[31] require special explanation,[32] as they are "unlike any other tenancy".[33] A tenancy at will is a tenancy which may continue indefinitely or may be determined by either party at any time.[34] This involves tenure[35] (i.e. a relationship of landlord and tenant) but no definite estate,[36] because there is no defined duration of the interest. The tenant has nothing which he can alienate.[37] T holds of L, but not for any appointed period. This resembles the earliest type of precarious tenure (*precarium*), which perhaps existed before estates were granted at all.[38]

A tenancy at sufferance arises where a tenancy has terminated but the tenant "holds over" (i.e. remains in possession) without the landlord's assent or dissent.[39] Such a tenant differs from a trespasser only in that his original entry was not wrongful and the landlord must re-enter before he can sue for trespass.[40] His "estate" in the land[41] is no true estate, and there is no real tenure.[42] The "tenancy" seems to have originated as a pretext to prevent the occupation being regarded as "adverse possession", which in time could bar the landlord's title altogether.[43] The old rules as to adverse possession have long disappeared,[44] and this "tenancy" might be permitted to go with them. Neither tenancies at will nor tenancies at sufferance, therefore, need be classified as additions to the catalogue of estates. If they are excluded, the classification can be simplified into freeholds and leaseholds.

3–015   **4. Leasehold tenure and estates.** In early times, when leaseholds were regarded as mere contractual rights to occupy land,[45] they were hardly estates at all. However, in time, when the law came to give them full protection as proprietary interests,[46] they were added to the list of recognised legal estates. They always remained outside the feudal system of land-holding, but when they became a new type of estate it was impossible to deny that they were also

---

[30] For these interests, see below, paras 17–100, 17–105.
[31] Preston i, pp.25, 28, 29, etc., speaks of an "estate at will" cf. Co. Litt. p.55a, n.3; Bl.Comm. ii, p.144; Cru.Dig. i, p.242; Tudor L.C. p.11.
[32] And see below, paras 17–100 et seq.
[33] *Wheeler v Mercer* [1957] A.C. 416 at 427, per Viscount Simonds.
[34] Below, para.17–104.
[35] Litt. p.460; Co.Litt. p.270b, fn.1.
[36] Litt. p.68 ("no certain nor sure estate"); cf. Litt. p.132.
[37] Bl.Comm. ii, p.144.
[38] Bracton Bk. ii, c. 9, f. 27 (Digby, 178); Co.Litt. pp.55a, 266b, fn.1; Bl.Comm. ii, p.55.
[39] See below, para.17–105.
[40] See Co.Litt. pp.57b, 270b, fn.1; *Land v Sykes* [1992] 1 E.G.L.R. 1 at 4.
[41] So called: Cru.Dig. i, p.249; Tudor L.C. p.7.
[42] See Co.Litt. p.270b, fn.1.
[43] *Remon v City of London Real Property Co Ltd* [19211 1 K.B. 49 at 58: Tudor L.C. p.9.
[44] Below, para.35–016.
[45] Above, para.3–009.
[46] Below, para.4–019.

a new type of tenure. Every tenant must hold by tenure of some sort if he is to hold an estate at all.[47]

This position has been recognised since the time of Littleton[48] (c. 1480), and is still recognised today. Tenure is essential between landlord and tenant,[49] and leaseholds are within the statutory term[50] "land of any tenure".[51] By a paradox of history the relationship of landlord and tenant, which was originally no tenure at all, is now the only tenure which has any practical importance. It is non-feudal tenure and was not, of course, affected by the statute *Quia Emptores* 1290, which applies only to fees simple,[52] and so does not prevent the grant of sub-leases. The one remaining feudal tenure, socage, has been shorn of all the incidents of any consequence, whereas in the case of leaseholds a valuable rent (called *rent-service* because of the tenure[53]) is nearly always payable, and the lord, although now to be deprived of his tenurial remedy of distress,[54] usually has power to determine the lease if the tenant does not fulfil his obligations. In all these ways it appears that leases imply tenure. A lease is still personalty, as opposed to realty, but the most important differences to which this technicality gave rise have now been abolished.[55]

5. Interests in leaseholds. At common law a freehold estate could not be **3–016** created out of a leasehold estate, for the obvious reason that a disposition by a leaseholder was only a disposition of personalty and he could give no seisin. The estates of freehold were peculiar to the land law and there was no corresponding system for personalty. But when other methods of conveyance not dependent upon seisin were introduced (for example, wills and trusts), these technical difficulties were overcome. Thus, if A held Blackacre for a term of 200 years, at common law he could not effectively assign the lease to X for life with remainder to Y absolutely. This would merely give the whole lease to X outright.[56] Because limited estates in personalty could not be created, a limited gift was an absolute gift. But when, in due course, wills and settlements by way of trust were invented, A could carry out his design by employing one or other of the new kinds of disposition. Even when a trust was

---

[47] Above, para.2–007.

[48] Litt. 132, saying that a tenant for years owes fealty to his landlord because of the tenure subsisting between them. Cf. the doctrine of denial of title, below, para.18–007; and see *Abidogun v Frolan Health Care Limited* [2001] EWCA Civ 1821; [2002] L. & T.R. 16.

[49] *Milmo v Carreras* [1946] KB. 306 at 310, 311; *Parc Battersea Ltd v Hutchinson* [1999] 2 E.G.L.R. 33, at 34, 35.

[50] LPA 1925 s.205(1)(ix).

[51] *Re Brooker* [1926] W.N. 93; *Re Berton* [1939] Ch. 200 at 203; cf. Hood & Challis p.333; below, para.17–002.

[52] Above, para.2–015.

[53] Below, para.19–062.

[54] Tribunals, Courts and Enforcement Act 2007, s.71; but see below, paras 19–061 et seq.

[55] Below, para.14–076.

[56] *Woodcock v Woodcock* (1600) Cro.Eliz. 795; *Anon* (1552) 1 Dy. 74a; *North v Butts* (1557) 2 Dy. 139b at 140b; "The gift of a term (like any other chattel) for an hour was good for ever"; *Wright d. Plowden v Cartwright* (1757) 1 Burr. 282 at 284, per Lord Mansfield C.J.

employed, however, it was impossible to create an entailed interest in personalty. It was only after 1925 that leasehold property could be entailed.[57] After 1996, it has not been possible to create an entail of either real or personal property.[58]

Section 3. Remainders and Reversions

3–017   An estate in land may exist in one of three different ways: in possession, in remainder or in reversion.[59] An estate in possession gives an immediate right to possession and enjoyment of the land. Estates in remainder or reversion, on the other hand, are future interests, and in the mean time some other person is usually entitled in possession. "Remainder" signifies a future gift to some person not previously entitled to the land. "Reversion" signifies the residue of an owner's interest after he has granted away some lesser estate in possession to some other person.[60]

Reversions and remainders are fully treated in Chapter 9, but at this point the general meaning of the terms may be made clear by examples. If A owns land in fee simple, and makes a grant "to B for life and thereafter to C in fee simple", B has a life estate in possession and so long as that estate continues C has a fee simple estate in remainder. When B dies, C has the fee simple in possession. A, having granted away his whole interest, has nothing. But if A had granted the land "to B for life and thereafter to C for life (or in tail)", B would have had a life estate in possession, C would have had a life estate (or estate tail) in remainder, and A would have retained the fee simple in reversion. So too, if A had merely granted the land "to B for life", A would have had the fee simple in reversion while B had his life estate in possession. A reversion will therefore be found in every case where the owner has made a grant which does not exhaust the whole of his own interest.[61]

Similarly, if A wishes to grant his land to B for life and thereafter to C in fee simple, and does so by single deed, C's estate is a remainder. But if the transaction is carried out in two steps by two successive grants, C's estate is a reversion, because he has acquired the reversion which was left in A after his initial grant to B. If A grants to B a lease, A is likewise said to retain the reversion; and if B grants a sub-lease to C both A and B have reversions. In the eye of the law a lease is always a lesser estate than a freehold,[62] so that if a tenant for life grants a lease for 100 years (for example) he retains a life estate in reversion expectant upon the lease.

---

[57] Below, para.3–079.
[58] TLATA 1996 Sch.1, para.5; below, para.3–031.
[59] Bl.Comm. ii, p.163.
[60] "Reversion, reversio, commeth of the Latine word *revertor,* and signifieth a returning againe": Co.Litt. p.142h.
[61] See below, para.9–008.
[62] Above, para.3–010.

Section 4. Seisin

1. Meaning of seisin. One very important distinction between freeholders **3–018** and leaseholders was that only a freeholder had seisin. Seisin has nothing to do with the word "seizing", with its implication of violence. To medieval lawyers, as Maitland said, it suggested the very opposite-peace and quiet.[63] A man who was put in seisin of land was "set" there and continued to "sit" there.[64] Seisin thus denotes quiet possession of land,[65] but of a particular kind. Although at first the term was applied to the possession of a leaseholder as well as that of a freeholder,[66] during the 15th century it became confined to those who held an estate of freehold.[67] A leaseholder merely had possession; his landlord, as the freeholder, was seised.[68] As it was essential that someone should always have seisin,[69] it followed that a freeholder remained seised even after he had granted a term of years and given up physical possession of the land. Receipt of rent was evidence of seisin,[70] but a mere right to recover possession was not by itself seisin.[71] Further, only land of freehold tenure carried seisin with it. A copyholder could not be seised, even if he held a fee simple.[72] In that case, seisin was in the lord of the manor.

2. Elements of seisin. From this it will be seen that a person was seised **3–019** only if:

    (i) he held an estate in freehold,

    (ii) the land was of freehold tenure, and

    (iii) either he had physical possession of the land, or a leaseholder or copyholder held the land from him.

Seisin, therefore, was a word which reflected the historical differences between the two main types of tenure and estates. It meant possession of land, disregarding those interests (leaseholds and copyholds) which the King's courts did not at first protect as property.[73] However, the attribution of seisin to lords of manors and landlords, who did not have possession, made it difficult to define seisin concisely. "Possession by a freeholder" embodies the fundamental idea.

---

[63] P & M. ii, p.30. Originally seisin had a specific feudal meaning, namely the possession of a tenant with his lord's authority: S.F.C. Milsom, *Historical Foundations of the Common Law* 2nd edn (Oxford: OUP, 1981), p.120.
[64] P & M. ii, p.30.
[65] Co.Litt. p.153a; *Brediman's Case* (1607) 6 Co.Rep. 56b at 57b.
[66] Williams, *Seisin,* p.4.
[67] Maitland, Coll.Pp. i, p.359; Challis p.99.
[68] Litt. p.324; Co.Litt. pp.17a, 200b.
[69] See below, para.3–020.
[70] See *De Grey v Richardson* (1747) 3 Atk. 469 at 472.
[71] *Leach v Jay* (1878) 9 Ch D 42.
[72] Preston i, pp.212, 213.
[73] See below, para.4–019.

3–020   **3. Nature of seisin.** Seisin was a characteristic product of the feudal system, and the three following rules help to explain its nature.

> (i) Someone had always to be seised. The person seised was the person against whom any default of feudal services had to be enforced,[74] and if seisin could be in abeyance the feudal system could not work. The common law abhorred an abeyance of seisin.[75]

> (ii) The person seised must be a person with a status in the feudal scale, i.e. a person who held in free tenure for an estate of freehold. The person at the bottom of the scale was seised of the land. A mesne lord was seised of a seignory, i.e. the right to the tenant's services.[76]

> (iii) Seisin was a fact, not a right. If A, a freeholder, was dispossessed by B, B acquired seisin and A was disseised. A could, of course, recover the land from B, and be put back into seisin. But until he did so B claimed the freehold and, having actual possession, was seised in the eye of the law.

3–021   **4. Significance of seisin.** Seisin is no longer important, because the distinctions which gave it its peculiar meaning no longer exist.[77] However, it was the key to many of the mysteries of land law before the statutory reforms of the 1830s and later. Before those reforms, it was in general the person seised—and he alone—who could exercise an owner's rights over the land. It did not matter whether his seisin was rightful or wrongful, or subject to the right of some other person to recover the land. Only the person seised could convey, for only he could give livery of seisin. Only the heir of the person seised could succeed to the land at that person's death. The fact of seisin, irrespective of the strength of the title of the person seised, used to be of far greater technical importance than it is today.[78] Thus, for example, the rule set out in the previous paragraph that there could be no abeyance of seisin because there had to be someone to perform the tenant's feudal services, is meaningless when the concept of feudal services is obsolete. Possession is still, of course, of great importance, and it is possession, not seisin, that the law now protects.[79] It is seldom if ever necessary to distinguish it from seisin.

---

[74] Above, para.2–014.

[75] For this principle and for exceptional cases, some common law and some statutory, see Challis pp.100, 101; CA 1881 s.30; *Re Pilling's Trusts* (1884) 26 Ch D 432 at 433.

[76] P. & M. ii, pp.38, 39.

[77] For a recent example, see *Roberts v Swangrove Estates Ltd* [2008] EWCA Civ 98; [2008] Ch. 459, where the Court of Appeal rejected the contention that the Crown could not disseise a subject, and held that it could acquire title by adverse possession in the same manner as any other person.

[78] H.E.L. iii, pp.91, 92. For discussion of seisin, possession and ownership, see below, paras 4–001 et seq.

[79] See below, Ch.4.

Part 2

ESTATES OF FREEHOLD

The two main branches of the law concerning estates of freehold relate to: **3–022**

(1) the words required to create each of the estates, and

(2) the characteristics of each estate.

The first of these is now, in practice, of little practical importance. It should be noted that after 1996 it has not been possible to create an entail, though existing entails remain unaffected.[80]

Section 1. Words of Limitation

1. Meaning. In a conveyance inter vivos (i.e. a transfer of land between **3–023** living persons) or in a will, the "words of limitation" are the words which limit (i.e. define or mark out) the estate to be taken. They do not confer an estate on any person. The estate is conferred by "words of purchase".[81] In this technical sense a "purchaser" is a person who takes property by grant (e.g. by gift or sale) and not by operation of law (e.g. by intestacy[82]). In a conveyance today "to A in fee simple", the words "in fee simple" are words of limitation, because they "measure out the quantity of estate"[83] that A is to have, and the words "to A" are words of purchase that actually confer the estate on A.

2. Inter vivos. At common law, a freehold estate of inheritance[84] could be **3–024** created in a conveyance inter vivos only by a phrase that included the word "heirs".[85] An attempt to grant a freehold estate in other terms (as "to A", or "to A in fee simple") gave A merely a life estate.[86] This incongruous rule survived until 1925, with only a minor mitigation in 1881.

3. In wills. In the case of gifts by will, the attitude of the courts was **3–025** different. Conveyances inter vivos were originally accompanied by a solemn ceremony using a precise form of words. Later, as conveyances became more complex, professional assistance was usually sought. For these reasons and because any flaw in the transaction could normally be rectified if the grantor was still alive, such conveyances were construed strictly. Most wills of land

---

[80] Below, para.3–031.
[81] For this distinction, see Fearne pp.79, 80.
[82] Below, para.14–104.
[83] *Goodright v Wright* (1717) 1 P.Wms. 397, per Parker C.J.
[84] i.e. a fee simple or a fee tail.
[85] Litt. 1; Co.Litt. 20a. Even analogous expressions such as "relatives", "issue", "descendants", "assigns", "for ever", or "in tail" were ineffective.
[86] Litt. 1; Co.Litt. 20a.

were first enforced by the Court of Chancery, which looked to the intent of any transaction rather than the form. When the Statute of Wills 1540 first compelled common law courts to give effect to wills, they followed the same practice of liberal construction.[87] Wills were often home-made, and since they were operative only on the testator's death, mistakes could not be rectified.[88] Effect would therefore be given to the testator's intention provided that it was clear.[89] Strict words of limitation were not required.

The position today is set out below, taking the fee simple, fee tail and life estate in turn and dealing separately under each head with conveyances inter vivos and wills. Little need now be said about the law before 1926, which is seldom likely to arise in practice.[90]

A. Words of Limitation for a Fee Simple

I. CONVEYANCES INTER VIVOS

3–026 After 1925 there has been no necessity for words of limitation to create a fee simple. A conveyance made by deed after 1925, whether to a natural person or to a corporation aggregate,[91] without words of limitation,

> "shall pass to the grantee the fee simple or other the whole interest which the grantor had power to convey in such land unless a contrary intention appears in the conveyance".[92]

The same is true of a conveyance to a corporation sole by its corporate designation. It is no longer necessary, as it was prior to 1926,[93] to indicate a

---

[87] See below, para.14–071.

[88] Testators' "ignorance and simplicity demands a favourable interpretation of their words": *Paramour v Yardley* (1579) 2 Plowd. 539 at 540, in argument; cf *Newis v Lark* (1571) 2 Plowd. 403 at 413.

[89] *Throckmerton v Tracy* (1555) 1 Plowd. 145 at 162, 163; Perkins, s.555.

[90] For a more detailed treatment of the law before 1926, see the 6th edition of this work at paras 3–026—3–040.

[91] Corporations are legal persons, distinct from the individuals who represent them. This artificial personality may be created by royal charter, or by some rule of law. Corporations are usually classified as of two kinds, aggregate and sole. A corporation aggregate is made up of two or more individuals acting under a corporate name, e.g. the mayor and corporation of a borough, a dean and chapter, or a limited company. A corporation sole consists of a single individual holding an office, which has a perpetual succession. Few corporations sole are known to the law: examples are (at common law) a bishop, a parson; and (by statute) the Treasury Solicitor and the Secretary of State for Defence. Although there are cases in which the Crown has been recognised to be a corporation sole: see e.g. Bl.Comm. i, 469; *Att Gen v Kohler* (1861) 9 H.L.C. 654 at 671; *Re Mason* [1928] Ch. 385 at 401, these cases may not be the final word on the subject. Although in previous editions of this work, the decision of the House of Lords in *Town Investments Ltd v Department of the Environment* [1978] A.C. 359 was criticised for casting doubt on the matter (see too (1992) 108 L.Q.R. 173; (1992) 142 N.L.J. 1315 at 1317 (H.W.R.W.)), the status of the Crown is not clear. It has been held that "at least for some purposes, the Crown has a legal personality. It can be appropriately described as a corporation sole or a corporation aggregate . . . The Crown can hold property and enter into contracts": *Re M* [1994] 1 A.C. 377 at 424, per Lord Woolf. The Crown may in fact be *sui generis*.

[92] LPA 1925 s.60(1).

[93] See the sixth edition of this work at para.3–029.

grant to a corporation sole as such by using the word "successors".[94] In practice, the words "in fee simple" are often inserted in conveyances of unregistered land to make it clear that there is no contrary intention.[95] In transfers of registered land no words of limitation are employed. The form of transfer defines the property by reference to its registered title (which is in respect of a particular estate, whether freehold or leasehold) and the transferor transfers the property so defined to the transferee.[96]

<h3 style="text-align:center">II. GIFTS BY WILL</h3>

The rule applicable to conveyances inter vivos after 1925 has applied to devises by will which took effect after 1837. By the Wills Act 1837,[97] any devise of land passes the fee simple or other the whole interest of which the testator has power to dispose unless a contrary intention is apparent from the will. Accordingly, contrary to the rule prior to 1838,[98] a devise "to A" passes the fee simple unless a contrary intention is shown.[99] **3–027**

B. Words of Limitation for a Fee Tail

I. CONVEYANCES INTER VIVOS

At common law, to create a fee tail, it was necessary to use the word "heirs" followed by some words of procreation, i.e. words which confined "heirs" to descendants of the original grantee,[100] e.g. "to X and the heirs of his body". An entail was an interest that could pass only to lineal descendants of the original grantee, who were known as "heirs special".[101] By the addition of suitable words an entail could be further restricted so that it descended only to a particular class of descendants.[102] Thus, for example, where land was granted "to A and the heirs male of his body", this created what was called a tail male, and only those male descendants of A who could trace an unbroken descent from him through males could inherit.[103] In addition, a **3–028**

---

[94] LPA 1925 s.60(2). A conveyance by both personal and corporate designations, e.g. "to A, Bishop of Ely", is now more ambiguous than previously, since in most cases under the previous law the necessary words of limitation made it clear whether there was a grant to A in his private capacity or as corporation sole.

[95] There was formerly an important conveyancing reason for including these words: see the sixth edition of this work at para.5–048.

[96] See Form TR1, below, para.7–149.

[97] s.28. The Act applies to any will made or confirmed after 1837: s.34.

[98] See the sixth edition of this work at para.3–031.

[99] The rule applies to the transfer of existing interests and not to the creation of new ones to which the old rule still applies: *Nicholls v Hawkes* (1853) 10 Hare 342. In practice this can seldom occur now; e.g. it is only in very rare cases that a perpetual rentcharge can be granted: below, para.31–018. A grant of such a rentcharge "to A" by will takes effect as grant for A's lifetime in the absence of contrary intention.

[100] Preston ii, 477, 478.

[101] See *Doe d. Littledale v Smeddle* (1818) 2 B. & Ald. 1 26: *Galley v Barrington* (1824) 2 Bing. 387.

[102] See Challis 294. Where the class of descendants was unrestricted, the entail was called a tail general.

[103] It was also possible to create a tail female, where corresponding rules applied.

"special tail" could be created, confining the heirs entitled to those descended from a specified spouse, such as "to A and the heirs of his body begotten upon Mary", when only issue of A and Mary could inherit. The restrictions could be combined, as where land was granted "to X and the heirs female of his body begotten upon Elizabeth". This was an example of a special tail female.

3–029 In a conveyance "to A and the heirs of his body", the words following A's name were words of limitation and not purchase. They conferred no estate on A's heir presumptive or heir apparent but merely a *spes successionis*. However, a conveyance of land "to the heirs of the body of A", made after A's death, gave a fee tail to the heir of A's body.[104]

3–030 After 1881, it became possible to create a fee tail by using the words "in tail" as an alternative to "heirs" plus words of procreation.[105] Thus "to X in tail" would create a fee tail, and "to A in tail male" created a tail male. These rules were preserved by the Law of Property Act 1925[106] and the law thus remained unchanged. The policy of the Act of 1925 was to maintain the strict rules for limitation of entails. In this way, entails could not arise unintentionally but had to be deliberately created.

3–031 **3. No entails can be created after 1996.** Entails became virtually obsolete and their prospective abolition was recommended by the Law Commission,[107] which Parliament implemented. Under the Trusts of Land and Appointment of Trustees Act 1996,[108] where after 1996 a person purports by an instrument[109] to grant to another an entailed interest in real or personal property, the instrument operates not to create an entail, but as a declaration that the property is held absolutely for the person to whom the interest was granted. If a person purports by an instrument to declare himself to be a tenant in tail of real or personal property, the instrument is not effective to create an entailed interest.[110] Thus, for example, if A purports to create a settlement of Blackacre under which B is to be a tenant in tail,[111] B will be absolutely entitled to the property. Similarly if A declares himself trustee of Whiteacre for B for life, thereafter to himself in tail, the attempt to create an entail in reversion will be ineffective and A will have a fee simple in reversion instead. The Act has no effect on entails created before 1997.[112]

---

[104] *Mandeville's Case* (1328) YB. 2 Edw. 3, Hil. pl. 1 and 2; Co.Litt. 26b.
[105] CA 1881 s.51.
[106] ss.60(4)(b), (c); 130(1), now repealed by TLATA 1996 s.25(2), Sch.4.
[107] (1989) Law Com. No.181, para.16.1.
[108] Sch.1, para.5. The Act came into force on January 1, 1997.
[109] An entail, whether of real or personal property, could only be created by an instrument: see LPA 1925 ss.130(6), 205(l)(xxvi); SLA 1925 ss.1, 117(1)(xxiv).
[110] It has been suggested, apparently seriously, that entails may have survived their apparent demise in TLATA 1996 and that they can and should still be created: see Histed, "Finally Barring the Entail"(2000) 116 L.Q.R. 445; Pascoe, "Solicitors: Be bold—create entailed interests" [2001] Conv. 396. It is most unlikely that any court would hold that an entail could be created after 1996. Nor, given how easy it is to bar an entail (see below, para.3–080, 3–081), is it clear why anyone would now wish to create one.
[111] Whether in possession or in reversion.
[112] Although this is not explicitly stated in the Act, it is implicit: cf. TLATA 1996 s.2.

II. GIFTS BY WILL

The rule before 1926 was that any words showing an intention to create an **3–032** entail were sufficient in a will, even if no technical expressions were used.[113] The Law of Property Act 1925[114] made the rules for the creation of entails more rigid than before. It laid down that informal expressions would no longer suffice to create an entail by will, but that expressions that would have been effective to create an entail in a deed before 1926 must be employed. This reflected the policy already mentioned and made the creation of an entail a matter of technical words rather than a matter of intention. The same rules therefore applied to both deeds and wills, but in contrast to the position of the fee simple, it was the restrictive rules applicable to deeds rather than the more liberal rules for wills that were extended.

Special provision was made for expressions that could formerly have created an entail in a will but could no longer do so.[115] Such expressions, in both deeds and wills, and for both realty and personalty, operated to create "absolute, fee simple or other interests corresponding to those which, if the property affected had been personal estate, would have been created therein by similar expressions before [1926]".[116] The effect of this provision was (and is likely to remain) uncertain. It has been the subject of some comment[117] but no reported decision. It is at least clear that no entail could arise in such cases because personalty could not be entailed before 1926.[118]

The prohibition on the creation of entails after 1996 applies as much to wills as it does to any other form of instrument. The effect of a purported grant of an entail by will is therefore to confer on the grantee an absolute interest in the property.

C. *Words of Limitation for a Life Estate*

I. CONVEYANCES INTER VIVOS

A life estate was created before 1926 either by words showing an intention to **3–033** create a life estate, such as "to A for life", or by using expressions insufficient to create a fee simple of fee tail, such as "to A", or "to A for ever". The rule that a life estate was created by such imperfect expressions has already been explained.[119] A tenancy for an indefinite period more than from year to year was usually construed as a tenancy for life.[120]

After 1925, a fee simple (or the whole of the interest the grantor has power to convey, if it is less than a fee simple) passes unless a contrary intention is

---

[113] e.g. "to A and his seed": Co.Litt. 9b; "to A and his descendants": *Re Sleeman* [1929] W.N. 16; "to A and his issue": *Slater v Dangerfield* (1846) 15 M. & W. 263 at 272. See Preston ii, 534 et seq.

[114] s.130(1).

[115] LPA 1925 s.130(2).

[116] LPA 1925 s.130(2).

[117] See (1936) 6 C.L.J. 67; (1949) 9 C.L.J. 185 (S.J. Bailey), and contrast (1945) 9 C.L.J. 46 (REM.).

[118] Below, para.3–079.

[119] Above, para.3–024.

[120] *Re Coleman's Estate* [1907] 1 I.R. 488 at 492.

shown.[121] Thus in order to create a life interest words showing an intention to do so must normally be used, e.g. "to A for life".

II. WILLS

3–034   Before the Wills Act 1837 a devise passed only a life estate unless an intention to create a fee simple or fee tail was shown.[122] It has been explained that, by section 28 of that Act the fee simple passes unless a contrary intention is shown.[123] The rule for wills therefore anticipated the modern rule for deeds, and they are now the same. Some words of limitation are therefore equally necessary in order to create a life interest by will.

Section 2. Nature of the Estates of Freehold

A. The Fee Simple

3–035   The fee simple is the most substantial estate which can exist in land.[124] Although strictly speaking it is still held in tenure and therefore falls short of absolute ownership, in practice it is absolute ownership,[125] because nearly all traces of the old feudal burdens have disappeared. "A tenant in fee simple enjoys all the advantages of absolute ownership, except the form".[126] His powers of "enjoying, using and abusing" his land are indeed limited in many ways by statute and by the rights of his neighbours, but they are not limited by any inherent narrowness in the concept of property in land. A fee simple may exist in an upper storey of a building, separately from the rest,[127] though such "flying freeholds" give rise to practical problems in relation to maintenance and support.[128] A fee simple may even also be made movable, so as

---

[121] Above, para.3–026.

[122] Above, para.3–027.

[123] Above, para.3–027. For a recent example, see *Charles v Barzey* [2002] UKPC 68; [2003] 1 W.L.R. 437: a devise by which a person could use premises for as long as he wished gave the devisee a life interest.

[124] Litt. 11; Williams R.P. 6.

[125] See Challis 218.

[126] 75 S.J. 843 (T.C. Williams). To Joshua Williams' statement that "the first thing the student has to do is to get rid of the idea of absolute ownership", Maitland added "and the next thing the student has to do is painfully to reacquire it": Maitland, Coll. Pp. i, p.196.

[127] "A man may have an inheritance in an upper chamber though the lower buildings and soil be in another": Co.Litt. 48b. There have long been flying freeholds in New Square, Lincoln's Inn, which statute regulated: see Lincoln's Inn Act 1860; (1977) 41 Conv. (N.S.) 11 (M. Vitoria). See too *Sovmots Investments Ltd v Secretary of State for the Environment* [1979] A.C. 114, e.g. at 179, 184. For a claim to a "subterranean flying freehold" see *Grigsby v Melville* [1974] 1 W.L.R. 80 at 83, per Russell L.J.

[128] Maintenance and support cannot be dealt with by covenant, because the burden of a positive covenant does not run with freehold land: see *Rhone v Stephens* [1994] 2 A.C. 310: see below, para.32–017. For the future, these difficulties can be overcome by creating a commonhold: see below, Ch.33. Where there is a flying freehold, one freeholder may be liable in nuisance or negligence for failing to repair the property if that failure causes loss to the other. However, each party may have to bear the cost of such repairs to the extent that each benefits from them: see *Abbahall Ltd v Smee* [2003] EWCA Civ 1831; [2003] 1 W.L.R. 1472 (where the flying freehold had been acquired by adverse possession: see *Mount Carmel Investments Ltd v Peter Thurlow Ltd* [1988] 1 W.L.R. 1078).

to shift from plot to plot within a defined area,[129] or so as to vary with changes of a boundary such as the foreshore.[130]

Pre-eminent among a fee simple owner's rights are his right of alienation (the right to transfer to another the whole or any part of his interest in the land) and his right to everything in, on, or over the land. These will be considered in turn, and will be followed by a discussion of the various types of fee simple.

I. RIGHT OF ALIENATION

In general, the owner of a fee simple may dispose of his estate in whatever way he thinks fit, either by will or inter vivos, although this has not always been so.[131] This freedom of disposition is subject to certain qualifications: **3–036**

(a) Where a person fails to make reasonable financial provision on death for a spouse, civil partner, former spouse or civil partner, or for certain other categories of near relatives or dependants, an application may be made by that person to the court to require the deceased's estate to make such provision.[132]

(b) There are prohibitions on sexual, racial and disability discrimination in making dispositions of land.[133]

(c) It is common for a person to enter into contractual restrictions on his power to dispose of land. For example, many mortgages contain provisions by which, until the mortgage is redeemed, the mortgagor may not make any disposition of the mortgaged premises without the prior consent of the mortgagee.[134]

II. RIGHT TO EVERYTHING IN, ON OR OVER THE LAND

1. General rule. There is an ancient maxim: *cujus est solum, ejus est usque*   **3–037**
ad coelum et ad inferos,[135] meaning that the owner of the soil is presumed to own everything "up to the sky and down to the centre of the earth".[136]

---

[129] *Weldon v Bridgewater* (1595) Cro. Eliz. 421; Co.Litt. 4a, 48b; 1 Preston 258; Challis, 54. In earlier times such estates were commonly held in the open fields, strips being allotted annually in rotation. Examples may still be found, e.g. a fee simple in such part of a specified area as may be allocated in an annual drawing of lots (the "lot meadows" at Yarnton, Oxfordshire): see (1936) 1 Conv. (N.S.) 53 (F.E. Farrer); (1978) 122 S.J. 723 (W.A. Greene); [1982] Conv. 208 (R.E. Annand).

[130] *Baxendale v Instow Parish Council* [1982] Ch. 14.

[131] See the 6th edition of this work at paras 3–043—3–044.

[132] See IPFDA 1975 (as amended); below, paras 14–004 et seq.

[133] See Sex Discrimination Act 1975 ss.30—32; Race Relations Act 1976 ss.21—24; Disability Discrimination Act 1995 (as amended) ss.22—24, 24G—24L.

[134] For mortgages, see below, Ch.24.

[135] *Mitchell v Moseley* [1914] 1 Ch. 438 at 450.

[136] "A colourful phrase often upon the lips of lawyers since it was first coined by Accursius in Bologna in the 13th Century": *Bernstein of Leigh (Baron) v Skyviews & General Ltd* [1978] Q.B. 479 at 485, per Griffiths J. And see *Corbett v Hill* (1870) L.R. 9 Eq. 671 at 673; *Wandsworth Board of Works v United Telephone Co* (1884) 13 Q.B.D. 904 at 915 ("fanciful phrases").

Although "this brocard" has been criticised,[137] the presumption remains firmly part of English law "encapsulating, in simple language, a proposition of law which has commanded general acceptance".[138] Above the surface, the development of powered flight has made it impossible to apply the brocard literally.[139] An owner's rights in the airspace above his land extend only to such height as is necessary for the ordinary use and enjoyment of the land and structures upon it.[140] As regards rights beneath the surface land, the brocard applies,[141] and the owner is presumed to own the minerals beneath.[142] For practical purposes, the rights downwards are unlimited: "there must obviously be some stopping point, as one reaches the point at which physical features such as pressure and temperature render the concept of the strata belonging to anybody so absurd as to be not worth arguing about".[143] As to the land itself, the owner in fee simple is prima facie in possession of, and therefore entitled to, any chattel which is not the property of any known person which is found under or attached to his land,[144] e.g. in a field[145] or in the bed of a canal.[146] This rule also applies to any unattached chattel found on the land if, but only if, before the chattel is found, the owner has manifested an intention to exercise control over things which may be upon the land.[147] Otherwise the finder is prima facie entitled as against the landowner, though not against the true owner of the chattel, if any.[148] All of these rules are now qualified by the provisions of the Treasure Act 1996 which is explained later.[149]

---

[137] *Commissioner for Railways v Valuer-General* [1974] A.C. 328 at 351, per Lord Wilberforce.

[138] *Bocardo SA v Star Energy UK Onshore Ltd* [2010] UKSC 35 at [26]; [2011] 1 A.C. 380 at 398, per Lord Hope D.P.S.C.

[139] *Bocardo SA v Star Energy UK Onshore Ltd* [2010] UKSC 35; at [20]; [2011] 1 A.C. 380 at 396.

[140] *Bernstein of Leigh (Baron) v Skyviews & General Ltd*, supra (aircraft taking photographs: no trespass). However, the upward extent of a landowner's ownership of the air column is substantial. Thus it is well settled that "a party is not entitled to swing his crane over neighbouring land without the consent of the neighbouring owner": *London & Manchester Assurance Co Ltd v O. & H. Construction Ltd* [1989] 2 E.G.L.R. 185 at 186, per Harman J. See too *Anchor Brewhouse Developments Ltd v Berkley House (Docklands Developments) Ltd* [1987] 2 E.G.L.R. 173 (oversailing tower cranes); *Laiqat v Majid* [2005] EWHC 1305 (QB) (extractor fan protruding into the claimant's airspace). See further below, para.3–043.

[141] *Bocardo SA v Star Energy UK Onshore Ltd* [2010] UKSC 35; at [27]; [2011] 1 A.C. 380 at 399.

[142] See below, para.3–044.

[143] *Bocardo SA v Star Energy UK Onshore Ltd* [2010] UKSC 35; at [27]; [2011] 1 A.C. 380 at 399, per Lord Hope D.P.S.C.

[144] *Elwes v Brigg Gas Co* (1886) 33 Ch D 562 (prehistoric boat excavated by tenant held property of landlord); *South Staffordshire Water Co v Sharman* [1896] 2 Q.B. 44 (gold rings found by workmen in pool held property of landowner); *Waverley Borough Council v Fletcher* [1996] Q.B. 334 (medieval gold brooch excavated by member of the public using metal detector in recreation ground); [1996] Conv. 216 (J. Stevens).

[145] *Att Gen of the Duchy of Lancaster v G.E. Overton (Farms) Ltd* [1982] Ch. 277.

[146] *R. v Rowe* (1859) 28 L.J.M.C. 128.

[147] *Parker v British Airways Board* [1982] Q.B. 1004 (gold bracelet found in airport lounge; no claim by owner: finder entitled). Trespassers cannot claim as finders.

[148] *Bridges v Hawkesworth* (1851) 15 Jur. 1079; *Hannah v Peel* [1945] K.B. 509; see Goodhart, *Essays in Jurisprudence and the Common Law*, 75–90.

[149] Below, para.3–045.

The owner is also entitled to land added by gradual accretion, as where his territory is extended by deposits caused by currents in the sea or in a lake or by the action of winds, or even by human action, provided that it is not the deliberate action of the claimant himself.[150] Conversely the owner may lose part of his land from erosion, sometimes called avulsion or diluvion, brought about by similar causes. The doctrine of accretion requires that the process should be gradual and imperceptible, but the fact that movement could occasionally be detected by an observer may not be fatal. Where the land affected is subject to a lease, the tenant obtains the benefit of the accretion and the terms of the lease apply to it. But a conveyance or lease of land may be so worded as to exclude accretions or movements of boundaries altogether.[151] Sudden accretions of substantial size belong to the Crown, as also do islands which arise in the sea.[152] The foreshore (the land between high and low water[153]) is the property of the Crown, unless the Crown has parted with its rights in any particular place.[154]

An owner can, if he wishes, divide his land horizontally or in any other way. **3–038** He can dispose of minerals under the surface, or the top floor of a building,[155] so as to make them separate properties. But unless some contrary intention is shown[156] a grant will normally pass the owner's whole interest in the space above and below the land, so that, for example, a lease will give the tenant the right to the airspace above the land let.[157]

The owner may in general use his property in the natural course of user in any way he thinks fit,[158] though this principle has been significantly qualified by developments in the law of nuisance and negligence.[159] Formerly, it had been held that a landowner might waste or despoil his land as he pleased, and was not liable merely because he neglected it.[160] However, the courts now impose "a measured duty of care" on a landowner, which arises if he knows or is presumed to know of a defect or condition giving rise to a hazard on his

---

[150] *Southern Centre of Theosophy Inc v South Australia* [1982] A.C. 706, containing a full discussion of the authorities including Bracton bk. 2, ch. 2, f.9; Bl. Comm. ii, 262; *R. v Lord Yarborough* (1828) 2 Bli. (N.S.) 147; *Att Gen v M'Carthy* [1911] 2 I.R. 260; *Att Gen of Southern Nigeria v John Holt & Co (Liverpool) Ltd* [1915] A.C. 599.

[151] As in *Baxendale v Instow Parish Council* [1982] Ch. 14 (conveyance of foreshore). Where title is registered, any agreement which modifies the operation of accretion and diluvion must be registered: LRA 2002 s.61(2); LRR 2003 r.123. See below, para.7–118.

[152] Bl. Comm. ii, 262, discussing also (at 261) islands which arise in rivers.

[153] On the meaning of "the low water line", see *Anderson v Alnwick DC* [1993] 1 W.L.R. 1156.

[154] *Att Gen v Emerson* [1891] A.C. 649 at 653.

[155] Above, para.3–035; and see LPA 1925 s.205(1)(ix).

[156] *Truckell v Stock* [1957] 1 W.L.R. 161.

[157] *Kelsen v Imperial Tobacco Co. (of Great Britain and Ireland) Ltd* [1957] 2 Q.B. 334; *Grigsby v Melville* [1974] 1 W.L.R. 80; *Davies v Yadegar* [1990] E.G.L.R. 71; *Haines v Florensa* [1990] 1 E.G.L.R. 73. It has been held that there is no such presumption where the lease is of, or includes, a roof: *Rosebery Ltd v Rocklee Ltd* [2011] EWHC (Ch) B1; [2011] L. & T.R. 21.

[158] *Wilson v Waddell* (1876) 2 App. Cas. 95 at 99; (1895) 11 L.Q.R. 225 (T.C. Williams).

[159] See, e.g. *Holbeck Hall Hotel Ltd v Scarborough BC* [2000] Q.B. 836; *Abbahall Ltd v Smee* [2002] EWCA Civ 1831; [2003] 1 W.L.R. 1472.

[160] *Giles v Walker* (1890) 24 Q.B.D. 656 (thistles); *Brady v Warren* [1900] 2 I.R. 632 (rabbits).

land[161] and foresees as a reasonable person that the defect or hazard will, if not remedied, cause damage to a neighbour's land.[162] He is then under a duty "to do that which is reasonable in all the circumstances . . . to prevent or minimise the known risk of damage or injury" to his neighbour or to his property.[163] What is reasonable depends upon that landowner's individual circumstances.[164]

A freehold owner can sue for damages or seek injunctions against those who commit trespass or nuisance.[165] It sometimes happens that a landowner wishes to undertake works on his property that can be carried out only by going on to his neighbour's land. If the neighbour refuses his consent, the landowner may apply to the court for an "access order" to enable him to do works that are reasonably necessary for the preservation of all or any part of his land. This will be granted only if those works cannot be carried out (or would be substantially more difficult to carry out) without entry on to the neighbour's land.[166]

3–039   **2. Qualifications.** The freedom of the freehold owner is qualified in many ways.

3–040   *(a) Other rights over his land.* He is naturally subject to such rights as others have over his land, such as rights of way, the rights of tenants under leases, and the rights of mortgagees.

3–041   *(b) Statute.* It was said more than 70 years ago that, "the fundamental assumption of modern statute law is that the landowner holds his land for the

---

[161] Which may be natural or man-made, e.g. an unstable mound of earth (*Leakey v National Trust* [1980] Q.B. 485), or flowing water in a man-made watercourse (*Green v Lord Somerleyton* [2003] EWCA Civ 198; [2004] 1 P. & C.R. 520).

[162] *Holbeck Hall Hotel Ltd v Scarborough BC* [2000] Q.B. 836 at 856. Where he owns a flying freehold, his neighbour's land may include the land beneath his own: see *Abbahall Ltd v Smee* [2002] EWCA Civ 1831 at [13]; [2003] 1 W.L.R. 1472 at 1475.

[163] *Leakey v National Trust* [1980] Q.B. 485 at 524, per Megaw L.J. See too *Abbahall Ltd v Smee* [2002] EWCA Civ 1831 at [25]; [2003] 1 W.L.R. 1472 at 1479; and *Lambert v Barratt Homes Ltd (Manchester Division)* [2010] EWCA Civ 681; [2010] 2 E.G.L.R. 59.

[164] *Goldman v Hargrave* [1967] 1 A.C. 645 at 663 (liability for spread of fire); *Lambert v Barratt Homes Ltd (Manchester Division)* [2010] EWCA Civ 681; [2010] 2 E.G.L.R. 59 (landowner aware that naturally draining water from his land was causing damage to an owner of lower land).

[165] In relation to damages, even after parting with the land; *G.U.S. Property Management Ltd v Littlewoods Mail Order Stores Ltd* 1982 S.C. 157 at 177 (HL) Abatement by means of self-redress can only be employed in simple cases (such as lopping branches that overhang from a neighbour's tree) or in cases or urgency: *Burton v Winters* [1993] 1 W.L.R. 1077 at 1080 et seq; *Chamberlain v Lindon* [1998] 1 W.L.R. 1252 at 1260 et seq; *Macnab v Richardson* [2008] EWCA Civ 1631; [2009] 3 E.G.L.R. 1. For abatement in relation to the exercise of easements and profits, see below, paras 29–004, 29–006.

[166] Access to Neighbouring Land Act 1992, considered below, para.30–036. For the Party Walls, etc., Act 1996, see below, para.30–041. Prior to the Access to Neighbouring Land Act 1992, a landowner could be injuncted if he trespassed on his neighbour's land in order to carry out essential works to his own property: see *Trenberth (John) Ltd v National Westminster Bank Ltd* (1979) 39 P. & C.R. 104.

public good".[167] Since the last quarter of the 19th century, there has been much legislation imposing restrictions and liabilities on landowners in the public interest and subjecting them to control by public authorities.

These statutes are of great importance but they do not, generally speaking, affect the principles of the law of real property. They restrict the liberties of great numbers of landowners and so many affect, among other things, the prices at which they can sell their land and the terms of sale. But the substance of the various possible transactions in land is not thereby altered: sales, settlements, leases, mortgages, and so on, continue as before.[168] These statutes form a body of regulatory or administrative law, which stands apart from property law.

The statutes that provide protection for tenants are dealt with concisely in this book,[169] as are the Leasehold Reform Act 1967 and the Leasehold Reform, Housing and Urban Development Act 1993.[170] These Acts provide a mechanism by which certain categories of tenant are able to purchase the freehold from their landlords for their own private purposes and without payment of full compensation. This book does not treat the statutes that regulate housing,[171] public health,[172] planning,[173] or compulsory purchase.[174]

(c) Liability in tort. A landowner may be liable in tort for injuries caused to **3–042** third parties by acts and omissions, e.g. if he withdraws support to which his neighbour is entitled,[175] or if water in a reservoir escapes,[176] or if a lamp projecting over a highway gets into a dangerous state of repair and injuries a passer-by.[177] In the same way he may be liable for nuisance. The following are examples—

    (a) Where he makes an unusual and excessive collection of manure which attracts flies and causes a smell.[178]

---

[167] (1936) 49 Harv.L.R. 426 at p.436 (W. I. Jennings).

[168] But statutory controls may be relevant to such transactions, e.g. a contract to sell land may be made conditional upon obtaining planning permission: see below para.15–008.

[169] Below, Ch.22.

[170] See below, para.22–214.

[171] See the Housing Acts 1985, 1988, 1996 and 2004, the Local Government and Housing Act 1989 and the Homelessness Act 2002.

[172] See the Public Health Acts 1875 to 1961, Building Act 1984, Environmental Protection Act 1990 and Housing Act 2004.

[173] See Town and Country Planning Act 1990.

[174] The principal statutes are the Acquisition of Land Act 1981, Compulsory Purchase Act 1965, Land Compensation Acts 1961 and 1973, Planning and Compensation Act 1991 and Planning and Compulsory Purchase Act 2004.

[175] See below, para.27–027.

[176] *Rylands v Fletcher* (1868) L.R. 3 H.L. 330; and see Reservoirs Act 1975 (as amended by Water Act 2003 and Flood and Water Management Act 2010). cf. *Transco Plc v Stockport MBC* [2003] UKHL 61; [2004] 2 A.C. 1 (no liability in relation to a piped supply of water to a block of flats, where the pipe fractured and caused the collapse of an embankment supporting a gas main). The rule in *Rylands v Fletcher* does not apply if the harm suffered by the claimant was not reasonably foreseeable: see *Cambridge Water Co v Eastern Counties Leather Plc* [1994] 2 A.C. 264.

[177] *Tarry v Ashton* (1876) 1 Q.B.D. 314.

[178] *Bland v Yates* (1914) 58 S.J. 612.

(b) Where he permits go-kart racing on his land that causes excessive noise.[179]

(c) Where he fails to take reasonable steps to prevent the incursion of tree roots into neighbouring land.[180]

(d) Where he is the owner of a flying freehold, and he fails to carry out repairs to the property and the property beneath his suffers damage in consequence.[181]

(e) Where he demolishes a property but fails to take steps to support and to provide weatherproofing for an adjacent property.[182]

A neighbour who suffers loss in consequence of the nuisance may recover the reasonable remedial expenditure that he has incurred.[183]

3–043   *(d) Airspace.* The owner's rights over the airspace above his land and buildings are limited to the height necessary for their ordinary use and enjoyment.[184] Within this limit, he can take proceedings for trespass, and often also for nuisance, if his airspace is invaded by a tree, a crane, a cornice, an extractor fan, or telephone wires,[185] or if projectiles are fired over it.[186] Damages may be claimed for any injury, but the most important remedy is an injunction to prevent the wrong continuing. A landowner has a prima facie right to a prohibitory injunction to restrain any trespass on his land whether or not the trespass harms him.[187] It will be granted almost invariably for a violation of his airspace,[188] and refused only in exceptional circumstances.[189]

---

[179] *Tetley v Chitty* [1986] 1 All E.R. 663.

[180] *Delaware Mansions Ltd v Westminster CC* [2001] UKHL 55; [2002] 1 A.C. 321; *L E Jones (Insurance Brokers) Ltd v Portsmouth CC* [2002] EWCA Civ 1723; [2003] 1 W.L.R. 427.

[181] *Abbahall Ltd v Smee* [2002] EWCA Civ 1831; [2003] 1 W.L.R. 1472.

[182] *Rees v Skerrett* [2001] EWCA Civ 760; [2001] 1 W.L.R. 1541.

[183] *Delaware Mansions Ltd v Westminster CC* [2001] UKHL 55; [2002] 1 A.C. 321; *Abbahall Ltd v Smee* [2002] EWCA Civ 1831 at [25]; [2003] 1 W.L.R. 1472 at 1478.

[184] Above, para.3–037.

[185] *Fay v Prentice* (1845) 1 C.B. 828 at 835; *Lemmon v Webb* [1895] A.C. I; *Gifford v Dent* [1926] W.N. 336; 71 S.J. 83; *Kelsen v Imperial Tobacco Co (of Great Britain and Ireland) Ltd* [1957] 2 Q.B. 334; *Anchor Brewhouse Developments Ltd v Berkley House (Docklands Developments) Ltd* [19871 2 E.G.L.R. 173; *London & Manchester Assurance Co Ltd v O. & H. Construction Ltd* [1989] 2 E.G.L.R. 185; *Laiqat v Majid* [2005] EWHC 1305 (QB).

[186] *Clifton v Viscount Bury* (1887) 4 T.L.R. 8.

[187] *Patel v W.H. Smith (Eziot) Ltd* [1987] 1 W.L.R. 853; *Anchor Brewhouse Developments Ltd v Berkley House (Docklands Developments) Ltd* [1987] 2 E.G.L.R. 173; and see *Lovett v Fairclough* (1990) 61 P. & CR. 385 at 403 (trespass by casting a fishing line from Scotland into England).

[188] *Trenberth (John) Ltd v National Westminster Bank Ltd* (1979) 39 P. & CR. 104 (erection of scaffolding).

[189] *Behrens v Richards* [1905] 2 Ch. 614; *Patel v W.H. Smith (Eziot) Ltd*, supra, at 859, 863; *Gooden v Ketley* [1996] E.G.C.S. 47; *Anchor Brewhouse Developments Ltd v Berkley House (Docklands Developments) Ltd*, supra, at 177. Where a landowner seeks a mandatory injunction requiring his neighbour to remove part of a structure that intrudes into his airspace, relief is never granted as a matter of course: see, e.g. *Tollemache & Cobbold Breweries Ltd v Reynolds* [1983] 2 E.G.L.R. 158 (protruding eaves: injunction refused).

In such a case the court will not grant an injunction and then suspend its operation.[190]

Aircraft enjoy a wide dispensation under the Civil Aviation Act 1982,[191] which provides that no action shall lie in respect of trespass or nuisance by reason only of the flight of aircraft over property at a height which is reasonable under the circumstances, provided the proper regulations are observed.

(e) Minerals. Although prima facie a tenant in fee simple is entitled to all **3–044** mines and minerals[192] under his land,[193] this is subject to some exceptions. Thus at common law, as modified by statute, the Crown is entitled to all gold and silver in gold and silver mines[194]; and under the Petroleum Act 1998 petroleum existing in its natural condition in strata is vested in the Crown.[195] Under the Coal Act 1938 all interests in coal (except interests arising under a coal mining lease) were vested in the Coal Commission in return for compensation. These interests (including coal-mining leases) were vested subsequently in the National Coal Board,[196] then in the British Coal Corporation,[197] and finally, (following the privatisation of the coal industry) in the Coal Authority.[198] That body has extensive powers to license coal-mining operations.[199]

(f) Treasure. Under the Treasure Act 1996,[200] all treasure is vested in the **3–045** Crown or its franchisee.[201] The old law on treasure trove was abolished.[202] Treasure is elaborately defined[203] and includes:

---

[190] *Jaggard v Sawyer* [1995] 1 W.L.R. 269, disapproving *Woollerton & Wilson Ltd v Richard Costain Ltd* [1970] 1 W.L.R. 411 (where an injunction was suspended in such circumstances).

[191] s.76(1), replacing earlier legislation. See *Bernstein of Leigh (Baron) v Skyviews & General Ltd* [1978] Q.B. 479 (aircraft taking photographs protected).

[192] For the meaning of "mines and minerals" in a lease, see *Lonsdale (Earl) v Att Gen* [1982] 1 W.L.R. 887 (on the facts, oil and natural gas not included); and see *Coleman v Ibstock Brick Ltd* [2008] EWCA Civ 73 at [10].

[193] *Mitchell v Mosley* [1941] 1 Ch. 438 at 450; *Bocardo SA v Star Energy UK Onshore Ltd* [2010] UKSC 35 at [10]; [2011] 1 A.C. 380 at 392.

[194] *The Case of Mines* [1568] 1 Plowd. 310; Royal Mines Acts 1688, 1693; and see *Att Gen v Morgan* [1891] 1 Ch. 432.

[195] ss.1, 2. The Act consolidates earlier legislation. On the previous and related legislation see *Lonsdale (Earl) v Att Gen*, above.

[196] Coal Nationalisation Act 1946.

[197] Coal Industry Act 1987.

[198] Coal Industry Act 1994 ss.7, 8. The Authority is not the servant or agent of the Crown and does not enjoy any status, immunity or privilege of the Crown: s.1(5).

[199] Coal Industry Act 1994 Pt II.

[200] See (1996) 146 N.L.J. 1346 (C. MacMillan); [1997] Conv. 273 (J. Marston and L. Ross). The Act provides a more rational system for the preservation of historical artefacts than the law of treasure trove, a royal prerogative of profit that was never intended for that purpose. The Act was brought into force on September 27, 1997: SI 1997/1977. For the Code of Practice made under Treasure Act 1996 s.11, see [1998] Conv. 252 (J. Marston and L. Ross).

[201] s.4. For the franchisee, see s.5.

[202] s.4(3).

[203] ss.1, 3.

(a) certain coin and other objects[204] at least 300 years old when found;

(b) any object at least 200 years old when found and of a class designated by the Secretary of State[205] as being of outstanding historical, archaeological or cultural importance;

(c) any object which before the Act came into force would have been treasure trove[206]; or

(d) an object found with any of (a)–(c).

The title that vests in the Crown or its franchisee is however subject to any prior interests or rights in the property.[207] A person who finds an object which he believes or has reasonable grounds for believing is treasure must notify the coroner for the district in which the object was found within 14 days of the day either on which he finds the object or on which he first believes or has reason to believe the object is treasure.[208]

3–046   *(g) Wild animals.* Wild animals cannot be owned.[209] However, a landowner has what is sometimes called a "qualified property" in them, consisting of the exclusive right to catch, kill and appropriate the animals on his land, unless they are protected by law; and as soon as the animals are killed, they fall into the ownership of the landowner, even if killed by a trespasser.[210]

3–047   *(h) Water.* A landowner has no property in water which either percolates through his land[211] or flows through it in a defined channel.[212] In the case of percolating water, at common law the landowner could draw any or all of it off without regard to the claims of neighbouring owners[213]; but now, by statute, he normally cannot do so without a licence granted by a river authority unless the water is taken for the domestic purposes of his household.[214]

---

[204] The objects and the coin (unless one of at least 10) must have a content of at least 10% by weight gold or silver.

[205] See Treasure Act 1996 s.2.

[206] For the old law of treasure trove, see the 5th edition of this work at p.64.

[207] Treasure Act 1996 s.4(2).

[208] Treasure Act 1996 s.8.

[209] *The Case of Swans* (1592) 7 Co.Rep. 15b at 17b.

[210] *Blades v Higgs* (1865) 11 H.L.C. 621; *R. v Townley* (1871) L.R. 1 C.C.R. 315.

[211] *Ballard v Tomlinson* (1885) 29 Ch D 115 at 121. Where the water percolates from higher to lower ground, the owner of the lower property is under no obligation to receive it and may erect barriers to pen it back, provided that, in so doing, he does not act unreasonably: *Home Brewery Co Ltd v William Davis & Co (Leicester) Ltd* [1987] Q.B. 339. Cf. *Palmer v Bowman* [2000] 1 W.L.R. 842 at 855, where the Court of Appeal found it unnecessary to decide whether that conclusion was correct.

[212] *Mason v Hill* (1833) 5 B. & Ad. 1 at 24. See generally W Howarth, *Wisdom's Law of Watercourses* (6th edn) (Crayford: Shaws & Sons Ltd, 2011).

[213] *Chasemore v Richards* (1859) 7 H.L.C. 349; *Langbrook Properties Ltd v Surrey CC* [1970] 1 W.L.R. 161; *Thomas v Gulf Oil Refining Ltd* (1979) 123 S.J. 787; and see *Bradford Corpn v Pickles* [1895] A.C. 587; *Stephens v Anglian Water Authority* [1987] 1 W.L.R. 1381.

[214] Water Resources Act 1991 (as amended by Water Act 2003), ss.24, 24A, 27, 27A.

In the case of water flowing through a defined channel, even at common law the riparian owner (the owner of the land through which the water flows) could not always take all the water[215]; but he has certain valuable rights.

(1) FISHING. As part of his natural right of ownership,[216] he has the sole right **3–048** to fish in the water.[217] Except in tidal waters,[218] the public has no right of fishing even if there is a public right of navigation.[219] For although a public right of navigation on a river may be acquired in much the same way as a public right of way over land can be acquired,[220] this no more entitles the public to fish in the stream than a right of way entitles the public to shoot on the highway[221]: the public's right is merely a right of passage.

(2) FLOW. He is entitled to the flow of water through the land unaltered in **3–049** volume or quantity,[222] subject to ordinary and reasonable use by the upper riparian owners,[223] though he has no right to object to the level of the water being lowered unless this causes damage or a nuisance.[224] He is bound by corresponding obligations to the lower riparian owners.[225]

(3) ABSTRACTION. The ordinary and reasonable use, which at common law **3–050** a riparian owner was entitled to make of the water flowing through his land, was—

> (i) the right to take and use all water necessary for ordinary pur-
> poses[226] connected with his riparian tenement (such as for water-
> ing his cattle[227] or for domestic purposes,[228] or, possibly, in some

[215] As to the right to divert water, see (1958) 74 J Q.R. 361 (D.R. Derham).
[216] See *Cooper v Phibbs* (1867) L.R. 2 H.L. 149 at 165.
[217] *Eckroyd v Coulthard* [1898] 2 Ch. 358 at 366.
[218] *Malcomson v O'Dea* (1863) 10 H.L.C. 593; *Alfred F Beckett Ltd v Lyons* [1967] Ch. 449 (coal on sea shore). The right to fish in tidal waters includes the ancillary right to dig for bait, provided that the taking of bait is directly related to an actual or intended exercise of the right to fish: *Anderson v Alnwick DC* [1993] 1 W.L.R. 1156 at 1166 et seq. See too *Adair v National Trust* [1998] N.I. 33 (public right to fish extends to the collection of shellfish on the exposed foreshore when the tide is out).
[219] *Pearce v Scotcher* (1882) 9 Q.B.D. 162; *Blount v Layard* [1891] 2 Ch. 681 at 689, 690.
[220] Below, para.27–028. The Rights of Way Act 1932 s.1 (now replaced in an amended form by the Highways Act 1980 s.31), does not apply to public rights of navigation: *Att Gen ex re. Yorkshire Derwent Trust Ltd v Brotherton* [1992] 1 A.C. 425; below, para.27–038.
[221] *Smith v Andrews* [1891] 2 Ch. 678 a 695, 696. But local inhabitants may sometimes acquire fishing rights: below, para.27–049.
[222] See *Scott-Whitehead v N.C.B.* (1985) 53 P. & CR. 263; [1987] Conv. 368 (S. Tromans).
[223] See *John Young & Co v The Bankier Distillery Co* [1893] A.C. 691 at 698.
[224] *Tate & Lyle Industries Ltd v Greater London Council* [1983] 2 A.C. 509 (ferry terminals caused silting at plaintiffs' jetty: claim of riparian right failed, but claim for special damage for public nuisance succeeded).
[225] The right to drain naturally occurring water on to another's land is an incident of ownership of the higher land and cannot exist as an easement: *Palmer v Bowman* [2000] 1 W.L.R. 842. There can be an easement of drainage in relation to water contained by dykes on the higher land: *Green v Lord Somerleyton* [2003] EWCA Civ 198; [2004] 1 P. & C.R. 520. See below, para.27–031.
[226] *Miner v Gilmour* (1858) 12 Moo.P.C. 131 at 156.
[227] *McCartney v Londonderry and Lough Swilly Ry* [1904] A.C. 301 at 306.
[228] *Kensit v Great Eastern Ry* (1883) 23 Ch D 566 at 574.

manufacturing districts, for manufacturing purposes[229]), even though this completely exhausted the stream[230]; and

(ii) the right to use the water for extraordinary purposes connected with his riparian tenement, provided the use was reasonable[231] and the water was restored substantially undiminished in volume and unaltered in character.[232] Such purposes included irrigation[233] and (in all districts[234]) manufacturing purposes,[235] such as for cooling apparatus.[236] The amount by which the flow might be diminished was a question of degree in each case.[237]

Statute has severely curtailed these rights, so that in most cases a riparian owner cannot take any water without a licence granted by a water authority. The two main exceptions are where the water is taken for use on a holding comprising the riparian land and any other land held with it, and the use is for either—

(i) the domestic purposes of the occupier's household, or

(ii) agricultural purposes other than "spray irrigation" (i.e. watering land by jets or sprays from hoses and the like).

If a licence is granted, it constitutes a defence to any action (e.g. by a lower riparian owner) in respect of the abstraction of any water in accordance with it.[238]

3–051   Apart from these rights a riparian owner cannot take water from a stream at all; thus without statutory authority a waterworks company owning land on the bank of a stream cannot take water to supply a neighbouring town.[239] The owner of only one bank of a non-tidal stream is prima facie entitled to exercise

---

[229] See *Todmorton v Ormerod Joint Stock Mill Co Ltd* (1883) 11 Q.B.D. 155 at 168. *Sed quaere:* such a rule would enable an upper riparian owner, by starting a factory on his land, to take all the water previously enjoyed by factories lower down; and compare *McIndoe v Jutland Flat (Waipori) Gold Mining Co Ltd* (1893) 12 N.Z.L.R. 226 at 238. See generally (1959) 22 M.L.R. 35 (A.H. Hudson).

[230] *McCartney v Londonderry and Lough Swilly Ry,* above, at 307.

[231] See *Sharp v Wilson, Rotheray & Co* (1905) 93 L.T. 155.

[232] *McCartney v Londonderry and Lough Swilly Ry,* supra, at 307; *Rugby Joint Water Board v Walters* [19671 Ch. 397 (spray irrigation).

[233] See *Embrey v Owen* (1851) 6 Exch. 353; *Rugby Joint Water Board v Walters*, above.

[234] Semble, despite the language in *Elinhurst v Spencer* (1849) 2 Mac. & G. 45 at 50.

[235] *Swindon Waterworks Co Ltd v Wilts and Berks Canal Navigation Co* (1875) L.R. 7 H.L. 697 at 704.

[236] *Kensit v Great Eastern Ry* (1883) 23 Ch D 566.

[237] *Embrey v Owen,* above, at 372.

[238] Water Resources Act 1991 (as amended by the Water Act 2003), ss.24, 24A, 27, 27A, 48, 70. See *Cargill v Gotts* [1981] 1 W.L.R. 441; (1981) 97 L.Q.R. 382 (P. Jackson). Drought restrictions may also be imposed under the provisions of Pt II, Chap. III of the Act.

[239] See *Swindon Waterworks Co Ltd v Wilts and Berks Canal Navigation Co* (1875) L.R. 7 H.L. 697.

riparian rights up to the middle of the stream.[240] But when the waters are tidal, prima facie the Crown is entitled to the foreshore (i.e. the land between ordinary high and low water marks) and there are no private riparian rights,[241] though it is possible for them to be created.[242]

III. TYPES OF FEE SIMPLE

A fee simple may be absolute or modified; a modified fee simple (sometimes called a modified fee) is any fee simple except a fee simple absolute. There are three main types of fee simple.[243]

3–052

1. Fee simple absolute. This is the type most frequently encountered in practice, and is an estate which continues indefinitely. "Fee" and "simple" have already been explained. "Absolute" means perpetual, i.e. not determinable by any special event.[244]

3–053

2. Determinable fee. A determinable fee is a fee simple which will automatically determine on the occurrence of some specified event which may never occur.[245] If the event is bound to happen at some time, the estate created is not a determinable fee; because it is said to be an essential characteristic of every fee that it may possibly last for ever.[246] Thus a grant "to A until the death of B" gives A a life estate *pur autre vie*,[247] but a grant to X "as long as the church of St Paul shall stand", creates a determinable fee simple.[248] In the latter case, X's estate may continue for ever, but if the specified state of affairs comes about, the fee determines and the land reverts to the original grantor or his estate. The grantor's interest is called a possibility of reverter, i.e. a

3–054

---

[240] *Micklethwait v Newlay Bridge Co* (1886) 33 Ch D 133. Where a person owns an island in the river, the riparian owner is presumptively entitled to exercise riparian rights up to the middle of the channel between the bank and the island: *Great Torrington Commons Conservators v Moore Stevens* [1904] 1 Ch. 347.

[241] Above, para.3–037.

[242] *Gann v Free Fishers of Whitstable* (1865) 11 H.L.C. 192; *Loose v Castleton* (1978) 41 P. & C.R. 19; below, para.27–072.

[243] "Fee simple" has sometimes been used to mean "fee simple absolute" only: Co.Litt. 1b; Preston i, 428–431; Challis 438; but here the term is used in its wider and more usual sense. And "fee" by itself is sometimes used for "fee simple absolute": see Litt. 293; Challis 438.

[244] See below, paras 6–013—6–016.

[245] Preston i, 419, 431, 479; Challis 251. It should be noted that, "land conveyed for a particular purpose does not automatically revert to the grantor when the land ceases to be used for the purpose for which it was conveyed. Even though land be conveyed for a particular purpose, in the absence of express provision to the contrary it is taken to be conveyed in fee simple absolute and not for a determinable fee": *Blanchfield v Att Gen of Trinidad and Tobago* [2002] UKPC 1, at [15], per Lord Millett (land compulsorily acquired by the Crown to be used as a US naval base did not revert to the original landowners, when the lease of the naval base was surrendered).

[246] Challis 251.

[247] Challis 252; Litt. 740. Compare *Vernon v Gatacre* (1564) 3 Dy. 253a; *Gawen v Raintes* (1600) Cro.Eliz. 804.

[248] *Walsingham's Case* (1573) 2 Plowd. 547 at 557; and see *Idle v Cook* (1705) 1 P.Wms. 70 at 75 ("so long as such a tree stands"); see also the catalogue of examples given by Challis, 225–260.

possibility of having an estate at a future time.[249] If the occurrence of the determining event becomes impossible, the possibility of reverter is destroyed and the fee simple becomes absolute, e.g. if land is given "to A until B marries" and B dies a bachelor.[250]

3–055   It has been suggested that the Statute *Quia Emptores* 1290 made it impossible to create determinable fees at common law[251] but there are dicta,[252] assumptions[253] and a decision[254] to the contrary, and the suggestion seems unsound in principle.[255] In any case, whatever doubts there may be about determinable fees created by direct grant (which are rarely encountered in practice), it has long been generally accepted that such fees can be created by means of trusts.[256]

3–056   **3. A fee simple upon condition.**[257] Akin to but distinct from a determinable fee is a fee simple which has some condition attached to it by which the estate given to the grantee may be cut short. A grant of land "to X in fee simple on condition that he does not marry Y", for example, will give X a fee simple, which is liable to forfeiture if the forbidden marriage takes place. This type of condition is sometimes called a condition subsequent, in order to distinguish it from a condition precedent relating to the beginning of the estate, e.g. "to x in fee simple when he reaches 21".[258]

The difference between a determinable fee and a fee simple defeasible by condition subsequent is not always easy to discern.[259] The essential distinction is that the determining event in a determinable fee itself sets the limit for the estate first granted. A condition subsequent, on the other hand, is an independent clause added to a limitation of a complete fee simple absolute which operates so as to defeat it. Thus a devise to a school in fee simple "until it ceases to publish its accounts" creates a determinable fee, whereas a devise to the school in fee simple "on condition that the accounts are published annually" creates a fee simple defeasible by condition subsequent.[260] Words

---

[249] Preston i, 441; Fearne 381 ; Challis 83; and see *Re Rowhook Mission Hall, Horsham* [1985] Ch. 62 at 74.

[250] Preston i, 440; Challis 254; and see *Re Leach* [19121 2 Ch. 422 at 429.

[251] See the authorities cited in *Hopper v Corporation of Liverpool* (1944) 88 S.J. 213 and *Third Report of Real Property Commissioners* (1832) 36; Marsden, *Perpetuities,* 71; Sweet's note in Challis 439.

[252] See Challis 251–262, 437–439; 23 Col.L.R. 207 (R.R.B. Powell).

[253] See *Re Leach* [1912] 2 Ch. 422; contrast *Re Chardon* [1928] Ch. 464 at 469, treating the question as open.

[254] *Hopper v Corporation of Liverpool,* supra, analysed in 1945 Conv.Y.B. 203 and noted at (1946) 62 L.Q.R. 222 (REM.). See also *Re Rowhook Mission Hall, Horsham* [1985] Ch. 62 at 74.

[255] See Morris and Leach, 209, 210.

[256] An example, once common, was the usual provision of a marriage settlement whereby the settlor granted land to himself until the solemnisation of the marriage.

[257] Commonly called a conditional fee. But there has been much confusion of language over determinable and conditional fees. "Conditional fee" was often used for both (see, e.g. Challis 261, 262), and "determinable fee" may cover both: SLA 1925 s.117(1)(iv).

[258] Conditions precedent are explained later: see below, para.9–105.

[259] See *Re Moore* (1888) 39 Ch D 116.

[260] *Re Da Costa* [1912] 1 Ch. 337.

such as "while", "during", "as long as", "until" and so on are apt for the creation of a determinable fee,[261] whereas words which form a separate clause of defeasance, such as "provided that", "on condition that", "but if", or "if it happen that", operate as a condition subsequent.[262]

The distinction is therefore really one of words.[263] The determining event **3–057** can be incorporated into the limitation in such a way as to create either a determinable fee or a fee simple defeasible by condition subsequent, which-ever the grantor wishes. The estate is determinable if the words limit the maximum period of time that it can endure. The limitation marks its bounds or compass. If the words define the event that will, if it happens, cut short the estate before it attains its boundary, they take effect as a condition.[264]

The distinction has been called "little short of disgraceful to our jurispru-dence".[265] It is sometimes a fine one, but it is important, since there are differences between the two forms of fee. These are set out here, although this requires a number of references to later parts of the book.

(a) *Determination.* A determinable fee automatically determines when the **3–058** specified event occurs,[266] for the natural limits of its existence have been reached and the land reverts to the grantor or, if the grantor is dead, to the person entitled under his will or intestacy.[267] A fee simple upon condition merely gives the grantor (or whoever is entitled to his interest in the land, if the grantor is dead)[268] a right to enter and determine the estate when the event occurs.[269] Unless and until entry is made, the fee simple continues.[270] The *possibility of reverter* after a determinable fee therefore operates automat-ically. The *right of entry* arising on a breach of condition is exercisable at the option of the grantor or his successor. These two special rights must be carefully distinguished.[271]

As a condition subsequent thus gives rise to a right of forfeiture, the courts continue it strictly, and require precise wording; such a condition is void unless it can be seen precisely and distinctly from the moment of its creation

---

[261] *Newis v Lark* (1571) 2 Plowd. 403 at 413; *Mary Portington's Case* (1613) 10 Co.Rep. 35b at 4tb; Challis 252.

[262] *Mary Portington's Case*, supra, at 42a; Litt. 328–330; Shep. 121; and see *Sifton v Sifton* [1938] A.C. 656 at 677. Technically such words reserve a right of entry (below, para.6–027) to the grantor. This is a reservation out of the grant, which is quite distinct from a limitation. cf *Brandon v Robinson* (1811) 18 Ves. 429 at 432, 433.

[263] *Dean v Dean* [1891] 3 Ch. 150 at 155.

[264] Preston i, 49; see *Re Moore*, above.

[265] *Re King's Trusts* (1892) 29 L.R.Ir. 401 at 410. per Porter M.R.

[266] Co.Litt. 214b; Challis 252; *Newis v Lark*, supra; *Mary Portington's Case*, above, at 42a.

[267] As to the transferability of possibilities of reverter and rights of entry, see below, para.3–068.

[268] See below, para.3–068.

[269] Litt. 331; Co.Litt. 214b; Challis 208, 261.

[270] *Matthew Manning's Case* (1609) 8 Co.Rep. 94b at 95b; Challis 219; *Re Evan's Contract* [1920] 2 Ch. 469 at 472.

[271] Here again, however, there is confusion of terminology, Challis (76 fn., 228) uses "possibil-ity of reverter" as meaning "right of entry".

what events will cause a forfeiture.[272] Thus conditions subsequent requiring a donee to "continue to reside in Canada",[273] or prohibiting marriage with a person "not of Jewish parentage and of the Jewish faith",[274] have been held insufficiently precise, and so void. But a condition of defeasance if the donee should "be or become a Roman Catholic" has been upheld, as creating no uncertainty.[275] The question is one of certainty of concept and not ease of application, so that a sufficiently certain condition is not invalidated merely by possible difficulties in ascertaining whether events have occurred which give rise to a forfeiture.[276]

3–059   These strict rules do not, however, apply to a condition precedent: in order to qualify, the claimant need only show that, whatever its possible uncertainty in other cases, he at least has complied with it.[277] A condition against marriage with "a person professing the Jewish faith" may thus be valid as a condition of entitlement but void as a condition of forfeiture.[278]

The court may grant relief against forfeiture where the object of a condition subsequent is to secure the payment of money or the performance of covenants, provided that the breach is not wilful and the default is made good.[279] This equitable jurisdiction, well established in the fields of leases[280] and mortgages,[281] may occasionally be invoked in other cases, but only where a person seeks to claim back his own property. Relief will not be given where, by reason of the forfeiture, a party has to forgo a right to make a contractual claim or is prevented from using property to which he had a mere contractual right.[282]

3–060   *(b) Remoteness.* Under the rules against remoteness a right of entry was void at common law if it might possibly arise at too distant a date. It follows that in such a case a condition subsequent had no effect and the fee simple

---

[272] *Clavering v Ellison* (1859) 7 H.L.C. 707; *Fraser v Canterbury Diocesan Board of Finance (No.2)* [2005] UKHL 65 at [45]; [2006] 1 A.C. 377 at 392; *Nathan v Leonard* [2002] EWHC 1701 (Ch) at [17]—[20]; [2003] 1 W.L.R 827 at 834—5. A court will however try to uphold the validity of a gift, particularly if it is contained in a will. It will therefore admit evidence as to the meaning which a testator attached to particular words: *Re Tepper's W.T.* [1987] Ch. 358 (condition of defeasance if a recipient married "outside the Jewish faith").

[273] *Sifton v Sifton* [1938] A.C. 656; cf *Re Coghlan* [1963] I.R. 246.

[274] *Clayton v Ramsden* [1943] A.C. 320; *Re Tarnpolsk* [1958] 1 W.L.R. 1157; *Re Krawitz* [1959] 1 W.L.R. 1192.

[275] *Blathwayt v Baron Cawley* [1976] A.C. 397.

[276] *Re Gape* [1952] Ch. 743.

[277] *Re Allen* [1953] Ch. 810; *Re Abrahams' WT* [1969] 1 Ch. 463.

[278] *Re Abrahams' W.T.*, supra; *Re Tepper's W.T.*, supra. See likewise *Re Tuck's S.T.* [1978] Ch. 49, where Lord Denning M.R. criticised both the distinctions explained above, and held that the problem could be solved by a clause empowering some other person (such as the Chief Rabbi) to decide disputes. For further criticisms see (1977) 8 Sydney L.R. 400 (P. Butt); (1982) 98 L.Q.R. 551 (C.T. Emery).

[279] See *Shiloh Spinners Ltd v Harding* [1973] A.C. 691. cf *Sport Internationaal Bussum B V v Inter-Footwear Ltd* [1984] 1 W.L.R. 776.

[280] Below, para.18–033.

[281] Below, para.24–017.

[282] *UK Housing Alliance (North West) Ltd v Francis* [2010] EWCA Civ 117 at [11]; [2010] 3 All E.R. 519 at 524.

became absolute.[283] But a determinable limitation could not last beyond the limiting event, no matter how far in the future that event might lie; and this was so even if the possibility of reverter was void for remoteness.[284] Statute has now modified this rule.[285]

(c) Existence at law. It is probable that a determinable fee cannot exist as a legal estate after 1925, apart from statutory exceptions, but that a fee simple subject to a condition subsequent can do so.[286]   **3–061**

(d) Flexibility. Determinable fees are less hampered by restrictions on the events on which they may be made to determine. Conditions subsequent are more jealously regarded by the law and are more readily held to be void (so making the fee simple absolute) as being contrary to public policy. The law of conditions is a large subject and its rules apply to all kinds of dispositions, including trusts, and not only to the rights of entry at common law with which we are here concerned. The following general rules can be deduced from the authorities.   **3–062**

(1) ALIENATION. The condition must not take away the power of alienation. One of the incidents of ownership is the right to sell or otherwise dispose of the property.[287] A condition[288] against alienation is said to be repugnant to this right, and contrary to public policy,[289] if is substantially takes away the tenant's power of alienation; and such conditions are void. Examples are conditions prohibiting—   **3–063**

> alienation at any time[290];
> alienation during a person's life[291];
> alienation to anyone except X[292];
> alienation to anyone except a brother of the donee[293]; or
> alienation by mortgage[294] or by will.[295]

The question is, however, one of degree, and it is possible for some kinds of "partial restraint" to be valid. An example, well known but much criticised,

---

[283] *Sifton v Sifton* [1938] A.C. 656.
[284] Below, para.9–099.
[285] Below, paras 9–102, 9–103.
[286] Below, para.6–014.
[287] Litt. 360. Above, para.2–015 (Statute *Quia Emptores* 1290). But see the position in relation to trusts of land: below, para.12–019.
[288] But not a mere contract or covenant, where breach gives rise to a claim for damages but not to forfeiture of the estate: *Caldy Manor Estate Ltd v Farrell* [1974] 1 W.L.R. 1303.
[289] (1917) 33 L.Q.R. 11 (E. Jenks).
[290] Co.Litt. 223a; *Hood v Oglander* (1865) 34 Beav 513 at 522.
[291] *Re Rosher* (1884) 26 Ch D 801; *Corbett v Corbett* (1888) 14 P.D. 7.
[292] *Re Cockerill* [1929] 2 Ch. 131; *Attwater v Attwater* (1853) 18 Beav. 330; cf *Re Elliott* [1896] 2 Ch. 353 (condition that part of proceeds of sale should be paid to X held void).
[293] *Re Brown* [1954] Ch. 39 (holding that the doctrine extends to personalty, e.g. to a share under a trust for sale).
[294] *Ware v Cann* (1830) 10 B. & C. 433.
[295] *Re Jones* [1898] 1 Ch. 438; *Re Dunstan* [1918] 2 Ch. 304.

is given by a case where land was devised to A "on the condition that he never sells it out of the family". The condition was held valid on the grounds that it did not prohibit any form of alienation except sale, it did not prohibit sales to members of the family, and it bound only A and not subsequent owners of the land.[296] And a condition that land should not be disposed of except to four sisters or their children has been upheld.[297] But it would not be safe to treat these decisions as examples of the court's normal attitude to restraints on alienation.

3–064   Entails[298] and life interests[299] are, in principle, equally protected against such restraints. But in the case of life interests the court is much more willing to find that what appears to be a conditional limitation is intended to be determinable,[300] which makes an important difference.[301] Thus provisos for forfeiture of a life interest upon any attempt at alienation, or upon bankruptcy, are generally upheld.[302]

3–065   (2) COURSE OF LAW. The condition must not be directed against a course of devolution prescribed by law. A condition rendering a fee simple liable to be defeated if the tenant dies intestate,[303] becomes bankrupt,[304] or has the estate seized in execution,[305] is void; for on each of these events the law prescribes that a fee simple shall devolve in a particular way, and this course of devolution cannot be altered by condition.[306]

3–066   (3) PUBLIC POLICY. The condition must not be illegal, immoral or otherwise contrary to public policy. The condition most frequently encountered under this head is a condition in restraint of marriage. Partial restraints, for example, prohibiting marriage with a Papist,[307] or a Scotsman,[308] or a person who had been a domestic servant,[309] have been held good.[310] But total restraints (or

---

[296] *Re Macleay* (1875) L.R. 20 Eq. 186 (Jessel M.R.). Contrast *Re Rosher, supra; Re McDonnell* [1965] I.R. 354; Gray, *Restraints on the Alienation of Property,* 2nd edn (Boston: Boston Book Co), 28, 43; Jarman 1480. And see discussion by Harman J. in *Re Brown, supra. Re Macleay* was distinguished in *Re Brown* by the fact that in the latter case the permitted class was small and was bound to diminish. See also (1917) 33 L.Q.R. 236, 342 (Sweet); (1954) 70 L.Q.R. 15 (REM.); and see *Petrofina (Gt Britain) Ltd v Martin* [1965] Ch. 1073 at 1097 (not reversed on appeal, [1966] Ch. 146).
[297] *Doe d. Gill v Pearson* (1805) 6 East 173.
[298] See below, para.3–076.
[299] *Brandon v Robinson* (1811) 18 Ves. 429; *Rochford v Hackman* (1852) 9 Hare 475 at 480.
[300] *Rochford v Hackman, supra,* at 480, 482; *Hurst v Hurst* (1882) 21 Ch D 278 at 283.
[301] This has been explained above, para.3–058.
[302] See Jarman 1485, 1496; Lewin, 5–119—5–126. The common "protective trusts" set out in TA 1925 s.33 include a determinable life interest.
[303] *Re Dixon* [1903] 2 Ch. 458.
[304] *Re Machu* (1882) 21 Ch D 838.
[305] *Re Dugdale* (1888) 38 Ch D 176 at 182.
[306] *Holmes v Godson* (1856) 8 De G.M. & G. 152.
[307] *Duggan v Kelly* (1847) 10 Ir.Eq.R. 295.
[308] *Perrin v Lyon* (1807) 9 East 170.
[309] *Jenner v Turner* (1880) 16 Ch D 188.
[310] And see *Greene v Kirkwood* [1895] 1 I.R. 130; but such gifts should be closely scrutinised for sufficient certainty; see above, para.3–058.

restraints which are virtually total, e.g. against marrying a person who has not freehold property worth £500 per annum[311]) are void unless the intent is not primarily to restrain marriage but simply to provide for the donee until marriage,[312] or unless the donee has already been married once.[313] A condition giving a wife an incentive to cease to cohabit with her husband is bad.[314]

Other conditions which are contrary to public policy, and therefore void, are conditions requiring the donee to acquire a dukedom[315] (as being a title which then carried with it legislative rights), or forbidding entry into the naval or military services,[316] or the undertaking of any public office.[317] A donee may be forbidden to dispute a will, but such a condition is void if drawn so widely as to disable the donee from protecting his rights.[318] A condition may forbid a change of religion,[319] but only in the case of an adult: for otherwise it conflicts with the parent's duty to provide proper religious instruction for his child.[320] A condition that X should not be allowed to set foot on the property has been held good.[321]

(4) DETERMINABLE FEES. A determinable fee, on the other hand, is not so **3–067** strictly confined,[322] "if the gift is until marriage, and no longer, there is nothing to carry the gift beyond the marriage".[323] A devise of freeholds on trust for X "until he shall assign charge or otherwise dispose of the same or some part thereof or become bankrupt . . . or do something whereby the said annual income or some part thereof would become payable to or vested in some other person" has been held to give X a determinable fee.[324] On any of

---

[311] *Keily v Monck* (1795) 3 Ridg.P.C. 205.

[312] See *Jones v Jones* (1876) 1 Q.B.D. 279; *Re Hewett* [1918] 1 Ch. 458 (personalty). The rules as to personalty are "proverbially difficult": *Re Hewett* [1918] 1 Ch. 458 at 463, per Younger J. Partial restraints are treated as intended merely *in terrorem* (and so void in law) unless enforced by a gift over or a clear clause of revocation. See *Re Whitting* [1905] 1 Ch. 96; *Re Hanlon* [1933] Ch. 254.

[313] *Newton v Marsden* (1862) 2 J. & H. 356 (woman); *Allan v Jackson* (1875) 1 Ch D 399 (man).

[314] *Wilkinson v Wilkinson* (1871) L.R. 12 Eq. 604 (life estate); *Re Johnson's W.T.* [1967] Ch. 387.

[315] *Egerton v Brownlow* (1853) 4 H.L.C. 1 (fee tail); contrast *Re Wallace* [1920] 2 Ch. 274 (the "barren title" of baronet).

[316] See *Re Beard* [1908] 1 Ch. 383.

[317] *Re Edgar* [1939] 1 All E.R. 635.

[318] *Cooke v Turner* (1846) 15 M. & W. 727; *Re Boulter* [1922] 1 Ch. 75; *Nathan v Leonard* [2002] EWHC 1701 (Ch) at [17]—[20]; [2003] 1 W.L.R 827 at 834—5.

[319] *Hodgson v Halford* (1879) 11 Ch D 959 (life estate). Public policy in relation to religious discrimination may be changing: see *Blathwayt v Baron Cawley* [1976] A.C. 397 at 425, 426 (above, paras 3–058—3–059). cf *Re Remnant's S.T.* [1970] Ch. 560.

[320] *Re Borwick* [1933] Ch. 657 (personalty); *Re Tegg* [1936] 2 All E.R. 878 (personalty).

[321] *Re Talbot-Ponsonby* [1937] 4 All E.R. 309.

[322] *Brandon v Robinson* (1811) 18 Ves. 429 at 432, 433; *Re Wilkinson* [1926] Ch. 842 at 847.

[323] *Morley v Rennoldson* (1843) 2 Hare 570 at 580, per Wigram V.C.; and see *Leong v Chye* [1955] A.C. 648 at 660.

[324] *Re Leach* [1912] 2 Ch. 422; Jenks (1917) 33 L.Q.R. 14. *Re Machu* (1882) 21 Ch D 838 does not conflict with this, since the fee simple was subject to a condition, and was not a determinable fee; Challis 261.

the events occurring X's estate would determine; if he died before any of them occurred, the fee simple would become absolute, for it ceases to be possible for any of them to occur.[325] But although a fee may thus be made determinable on alienation or on bankruptcy or on similar events, a limitation would probably be void if it were contrary to public policy for the fee to be determinable on the stated event, e.g. if the event were the return to her husband of a wife who was separated from him.[326] In such a case the whole gift fails, for there is no proper limitation; whereas a corresponding conditional gift would become absolute, since the fee is properly limited even though the condition fails.[327]

3–068   (e) *Alienability of the expectant interest.* At common law a right of entry and a possibility of reverter were descendible but not alienable inter vivos, because they were not themselves estates but merely special rights incident to other estates.[328] Nor did they become devisable by the Statute of Wills 1540. But rights of entry for condition broken were made devisable in 1837[329] and alienable inter vivos in 1845.[330] Since 1925 they may also be made exercisable by any person,[331] not merely by the grantor or his successors in title, so that they may be given to some other person at the moment of their creation. It has been held that a possibility of reverter is devisable,[332] and, in principle, it should also be assignable.[333]

3–069   **4. Nature of modified fees.** The owner of a modified fee has the same rights over the land as the owner of a fee simple absolute: thus the common law refused to restrain him from committing acts of waste,[334] such as opening and working mines. Equity, on the other hand, intervened to prevent the commission of equitable waste, i.e. acts of wanton destruction,[335] although the owner of a fee simple absolute is under no such restraint; for where there is a modified fee, there is some other person interested in expectancy whose interest may need protecting.

---

[325] *Re Leach* [1912] 2 Ch. 422 at 429.
[326] cf. *Re Moore* (1888) 39 Ch D 116 (life interest in personalty determinable on wife returning to husband; held void).
[327] Co.Litt. 206a, b; *Re Greenwood* [1903] 1 Ch. 749; cf. *Sifton v Sifton* [1938] A.C. 656.
[328] Co.Litt. 201 a, fn.1; Challis 76n.
[329] Wills Act 1837 s.3; *Pemberton v Barnes* [1899] 1 Ch. 544.
[330] RPA 1845 s.6; LPA 1925 s.4(2); Wolst. & C. i, 60.
[331] LPA 1925 s.4(3).
[332] *Bath and Wells Diocesan Board of Finance v Jenkins* [2002] EWHC 218 (Ch); [2003] Ch. 89, construing Wills Act 1837 s.3.
[333] As a "future equitable interest" under LPA 1925 s.4(2), which in any case is not exclusive of any interest of any kind. Only if "interest" is made synonymous with "estate" is there any difficulty in fitting possibilities into it. The only possibility specifically included is "a possibility coupled with an interest", which does not include a possibility of reverter: Challis 76n.
[334] Challis 262; *Lewis Bowless Case* (1615) 11 Co.Rep. 79b at 81a. For waste, see below, para.3–090.
[335] Williams R.P. 414; *Re Hanbury's S.E.* [1913] 2 Ch. 357 at 365.

At common law the owner of a modified fee could not convey a fee simple absolute but merely a fee liable to determination, for a man cannot convey more than he has.[336] But these interests now fall within the statute law dealing with settlements and trusts of land, so that they are now subject to the statutory powers of making sales and other dispositions.[337] A modified fee may, moreover, become enlarged into a fee simple absolute, e.g. by the determining event becoming impossible.[338]

B. The Fee Tail

I. HISTORY

1. Origins: the Statute *De Donis Conditionalibus* 1285. There are few fee tails now in existence and, as already explained, none can now be created.[339] Only a brief account will therefore be given of the history of the entail.[340] Its hallmark was a limitation to a person and the heirs *of his body,* restricting inheritance to his lineal descendants, as opposed to the collateral relations who could inherit the fee simple if there were no issue.[341] The fee tail was not created by, but was the consequence of, the Statute *De Donis Conditionalibus* 1285.[342] Prior to that statute, two types of fee simple were employed to make provision respectively for daughters by way of marriage-gifts[343] and for younger sons. The intention in making such gifts was to ensure that the land would revert to the settlor or his heir on any failure of issue. However, a marriage-gift became absolute after three generations and could then be freely alienated. The gift to a younger son came to be regarded as a fee simple granted conditionally upon the birth of issue: once a child was born, the fee became absolute and the son could then alienate the land.[344] The Statute was passed in response to a baronial petition[345] to give settlors more secure control of the land which they had settled. It provided that in the case of these conditional gifts, the will of the donor should be observed according to the form expressed in the deed of gift. Notwithstanding any alienation by the donee, the land would descend to his issue on his death and would revert to

3–070

---

[336] Preston i, 435, 436.
[337] Below, paras 12–016; Appendix, paras A–032—A–034.
[338] Above, para.3–058.
[339] Above, para.3–031.
[340] For fuller accounts, see S.F.C. Milsom, *Historical Foundations of the Common Law* (2nd ed), Ch.8; J. H. Baker, *An Introduction to English Legal History* 4th edn (Oxford: OUP, 2002) at pp.269—289; J. Biancalana, *The Fee Tail and the Common Recovery in Medieval England 1176—1502* (Cambridge: Cambridge University Press, 2001).
[341] Above, para.3–008.
[342] Statute of Westminster II, 1285, c.1.
[343] Known as the *maritagium.*
[344] See Milsom, *Historical Foundations of the Common Law* at pp.171–173; Baker, *An Introduction to English Legal History* at pp.272—273.
[345] For this petition, see J. H. Baker and S. F. C. Milsom, *Sources of English Legal History,* p.48.

the donor when the donee and all his issue were dead.[346] Although the statute by its terms merely modified the rules relating to conditional fees, this modification was so important that the estate was thereafter renamed "fee tail" or "estate tail". For all practical purposes it was a new estate.[347]

3–071   A fee tail, unlike a fee simple, was followed by a reversion or remainder.[348] On the failure of the donee's lineal issue the land would still belong to the original donor in fee simple. The fee tail was a lesser estate that did not exhaust his interest. Alternatively he could also alienate this reversionary interest and thereby make someone else entitled by way of remainder. The tenant in tail by contrast had in substance only a life estate. If he alienated the land it was recoverable after his death by the heir to the fee tail or (if he died without issue) by the reversioner or remainderman. The Statute therefore gave to landowners what the common law had always denied to them: the power to create a virtually inalienable estate. It "established a general perpetuity by Act of Parliament",[349] and for some 200 years this "common grievance of the realm"[350] continued. However in the 15th century the courts, with their accustomed hostility to restraints upon alienation, began to countenance devices by which the Statute could be frustrated.[351]

3–072   **2. Fee tail barrable by recovery or fine.** Two devices were successful, namely the common recovery and the fine. Each involved an ingenious abuse of an action at law, and each took advantage of the binding effect of a judgment of the court. It is necessary here only to explain in the barest outline how each worked.[352]

3–073   *(a) The common recovery.* By 1472,[353] it was recognised that a tenant in tail in possession could "bar" the entail by means of a collusive action known as a "common recovery". To ensure that the claims of the tenant in tail's heirs and any reversioner or remainderman were barred, there were two elements in this process.

[346] The statute provided for a writ of "formedon in the descender" to enable the donee's issue to claim the land. Reversioners and remaindermen were already protected by writs of formedon in the reverter and formedon in the remainder; H.E.L. iii, 18; P. & M. ii, 28; (1940) 7 C.L.J. 238 (W. H. Humphreys); (1944) 8 C.L.J. 275, fn.9 (S. J. Bailey); and occasionally a formedon in the descender had been used before in the statute in cases where a tenant in tail died seised and his heir entitled under the entail was not also the heir general; (1956) 72 L.Q.R. 391 (S. F. C. Milsom). "Formedon" is from *"forma doni"*.
[347] See *Willion v Berkley* (1561) 1 Plowd. 223 at 248; H.E.L. ii, 350.
[348] Challis 298.
[349] *Mildmay's Case* (1605) 6 Co.Rep. 40a. It has been described as a "juridical monster"; Milsom, *Historical Foundations of the Common Law* at p.177.
[350] Bl.Comm. ii, 116 (where the many inconveniences of entails are bewailed).
[351] H.E.L. iii, 118, 119.
[352] For a fuller account, see A. W. B. Simpson, *A History of the Land Law* 2nd edn (Oxford: OUP, 1986), Ch.6.
[353] *Taltarum's Case* (1472) YB. 12 Edw. 4, Mich., fo. 14b, pl. 16, fo. 19a, pl. 25; 13 Edw. 4, Mich., fo. 1a. pl. 1. A full translation of the record and reports is in Kiralfy, *Source Book of English Law* (London: Sweet & Maxwell, 1957) pp. 86–89 (where the name of the case appears as *Talcarn's Case*, or in the modern style, *Hunt v Smyth*); and there is an account of the case in Challis 309.

(i) An accomplice of the tenant in tail would bring an action claiming the fee simple on the basis of a wholly spurious title. The tenant in tail would not contest this suit, but would submit to it, allowing the accomplice to "recover" it. That barred the tenant in tail and his issue.

(ii) In order to bar the reversioner or remainderman, the tenant in tail would in those proceedings "vouch to warranty" some third party. When one person conveyed land to another, he would "warrant" the grantee in his holding.[354] By virtue of this warranty, the grantor agreed to provide the grantee with lands of equivalent value[355] if his title turned out to be bad. In the collusive recovery, the vouchee to warranty would in fact be a landless man of straw[356] and he would always default.

The effect of this subterfuge was that the accomplice acquired the fee simple absolute. The other claimants were barred and left to console themselves with a valueless judgment.[357] The accomplice then either reconveyed the land to the tenant in tail, or paid him the purchase price if he was himself to buy it. The entail had been turned into a fee simple. **3–074**

The common recovery could only be brought against the person seised. It could not therefore be employed against a tenant in tail in remainder unless the freeholder in possession would collaborate.[358] It was this limitation that the second device, the fine, was designed to circumvent.

(b) The fine. A fine was a final compromise of litigation that was entered in the court's records to show the terms on which, with the court's leave, the action was discontinued.[359] The practice of "levying a fine" pre-dated the common recovery. It was commonly employed in early times as a method of conveyancing because of its sanctity as a compromise approved by the court and registered in the court records.[360] The Statute expressly prohibited the barring of entails by fines.[361] However it was held in the Exchequer Chamber that the law had been changed by virtue of the Statute of Fines 1489, which dealt with fines generally, and that a fine would bar the issue in tail.[362] The effect of this decision was subsequently confirmed by statute in 1540.[363] **3–075**

---

[354] This warranty was the predecessor of the modern covenants for title; below, para.7–151.
[355] Known as "*escambium*" or "*excambium*". For the workings of *escambium*, see J. M. Kaye, *Medieval English Conveyances* (Cambridge: Cambridge University Press, 2009), pp.301—318.
[356] He was in practice the common crier of the Court of Common Pleas who was paid four pence for his services; Baker, *An Introduction to English Legal History*, at p.282.
[357] *Capel's Case* (1593) 1 Co.Rep. 6lb; *Cholmley's Case* (1597) 2 Co.Rep. 50a at 52a.
[358] Challis, 310; Cru.Dig. v, 274; Williams R.P. 106.
[359] Williams R.P. 73n; H.E.L. iii, 236 et seq.
[360] Williams R.P. 73n; H.E.L. iii, 236 et seq. See too C.A.F. Meekings, *The 1235 Surrey Eyre* (1979) 31 Surrey Record Society at p.43.
[361] Statute of Westminster II, c.1, s.4.
[362] *Anon* (1527) 1 Dy. 2b. Blackstone saw the statute as a covert attempt by "that politic prince, King Henry VII" to provide a means of barring entails; Bl.Comm. ii, 354.
[363] Statute of Fines; 32 Hen.8, c.36.

Although the fine could be levied without the concurrence of the tenant in possession, it suffered from one serious disadvantage. It barred the rights of the issue in tail but did not bar the owner of the subsequent remainder, reversion or other estate.[364] The estate produced by a fine was known as a "base fee", which was in effect a determinable fee simple. It endured for as long as the entail would have continued if it had been barred, and determined when the entail would have ended.[365]

3–076 To suppress still further the inconveniences of the Statute *De Donis Conditionalibus,* the judges created a rule that the power to suffer recoveries and levy fines was an inseparable incident of every entail. Any attempt to hamper this power in any way was void.[366] It followed therefore that the interests of issue in tail, remaindermen and reversioners were in fact wholly precarious, precisely contrary to the provisions of the Statute.

Although by the 18th century fines and recoveries had become purely formal, they remained dilatory, complicated and expensive. However the barring of entails had come to play a vital part in the system of family settlements.[367] Simpler methods of barring entails were therefore provided by the Fines and Recoveries Act 1833,[368] which was designed to produce almost exactly the same results as the earlier law. As it is still in force today, its provisions are considered with the present law.

II. RIGHTS OF A TENANT IN TAIL

3–077 Apart from the peculiar law about alienation a tenant in tail had all the rights of enjoyment of a fee simple owner. He was not liable for waste of any kind, and he could therefore cut timber, open mines or pull down buildings as he pleased,[369] even if some statute restrained him from barring the entail.[370] A statute of 1540 empowered him to grant leases binding on his issue (but not remaindermen or reversioners) for terms of not more than 21 years or a period of three lives.[371] This power remained until superseded by the new law of settlements in the nineteenth century.[372]

III. PRESENT LAW

3–078 **1. Existence only in equity.** After 1925 it was not possible for an entail to exist as a legal estate.[373] The significance of this is explained in Chapter 6. All

[364] *Margaret Podger's Case* (1613) 9 Co.Rep. 104a.
[365] On base fees see Challis 325 et seq.
[366] See Fearne 256 et seq., where the authorities are collected.
[367] See below, 10–005.
[368] This statute was drafted by the eminent conveyancer Peter Brodie, who was also one of the Real Property Commissioners. It was highly regarded by many, though some considered that he could have achieved its effect more directly; see J. S. Anderson. *Lawyers and the Making of English Land Law 1832–1940,* (Oxford University Press, 1992) p.7.
[369] Williams R.P. 114, 198; *Lord Glenorchy v Bosvilie* (1733) Ca.t.Talb. 3 at 16 (not liable for equitable waste).
[370] *Att Gen v Duke of Marlborough* (1813) 3 Madd. 498.
[371] 32 Hen. 8, c. 28; and see *Att Gen v Duke of Marlborough,* above, at 532.
[372] See below, paras 10–005 et seq.
[373] LPA 1925 s. 1; below, para.6–008.

entails exist as equitable interests behind trusts. This means that the legal estate must be vested in some trustees or trustee (who may be the tenant in tail himself) on trust for the person entitled in tail and everyone else interested in the land. This does not alter anyone's rights of enjoyment: only the bare legal ownership is affected.[374] Similarly a "base fee" can no longer exist as a legal estate but only as an equitable interest in the nature of a base fee.

2. Personalty entailable. In the period after 1925 and before 1997 any 3–079 property, real or personal, could be entailed. Before 1926 this had not been the case.

> (i) Statute *De Donis* 1285 applied only to "tenements", i.e. property held in tenure, real property.[375]

> (ii) An entail could only subsist in a hereditament, i.e. land which was heritable. Thus life estates (which were not inheritable) and lease-holds (which were personalty) could not be entailed.[376]

A purported grant of personalty in tail before 1926 (whether by deed or will) gave the grantee absolute ownership of the property.[377]

After 1925 and before 1997, entails could be created in personalty. All the rules applying to entails of realty (e.g. as to words of limitation and barring) applied equally to entails of personalty.[378] It was expressly provided however that if personalty was directed "to be enjoyed or held with, or upon trusts corresponding to trusts affecting" land which was already held in tail, this was sufficient to entail the personalty,[379] provided that the exact wording was used.[380]

3. Barring the entail

(a) Barring inter vivos: the Fines and Recoveries Act 1833.[381] The Act 3–080 provides that an entail can be barred by any assurance (i.e. any conveyance or other transfer) which a fee simple owner can employ, except a will. Such a disentailing assurance passes a fee simple to the transferee. Although an

---

[374] The correct title for an entail is now "entailed interest" rather than "estate tail" or "fee tail"; it is no longer a legal estate for which the land itself is held.

[375] Challis 43, 47, 61.

[376] *Leventhorpe v Ashbie* (1635) 1 Roll.Abr. 831, pl. 1; *Leonard Lovie's Case* (1614) 10 Co.Rep. 78a; Co.Litt. 20a, n.5.

[377] Norton, *Deeds*, 376 (deed); *Dawson v Small* (1874) 9 Ch. App. 651 (will); and see *Portman v Viscount Portman* [1922] 2 A.C. 473. A gift using informal words, such as "to A and his issue" or "to A and his descendants", usually gave the property to A and such of his issue or descendants as were alive at the relevant date; *Re Hammond* [1924] 2 Ch. 276.

[378] LPA 1925 s.130(1) (repealed, TLATA 1996 Sch.4). An entail of personalty had to be made by instrument: see LPA 1925 ss.130(6); 205(1)(xxvi); SLA 1925 ss.1, 117(1)(xxiv).

[379] LPA 1925 s.130(3) (repealed, TLATA 1996 Sch.4).

[380] *Re Jones* [1934] Ch. 315 at 321.

[381] The Act remains in force "in regard to dealings with entailed interests as equitable interests"; LPAmA 1924 Sch.9, para.4.

entailed interest is nowadays always equitable, any disentailing assurance must be made or evidenced by deed.[382] A mere declaration that the entail is barred will not suffice because it is not an "assurance" as the Act requires.[383]

A disentailing assurance is unlikely to be made nowadays on an inter vivos disposition of the land. As entails operate only in equity, it is no longer necessary to bar the entail in order to convey the legal fee simple.[384] When a tenant in tail in possession wishes to bar the entail, he will usually convey his entailed interest to trustees by way of disentailing assurance. They will then reconvey the resulting equitable fee simple back to him.[385] Although in principle a tenant in tail could now execute a disentailing assurance in his own favour,[386] this is not the practice.[387]

If a tenant in tail in remainder wishes to execute a disentailing assurance that will bar the entail, he must obtain the consent of the "protector of the settlement".[388] The protector is normally the person who is entitled to the land in possession.[389] Any disentailing assurance executed without his concurrence will create only a base fee.[390] The interests of the issue in tail will be barred, but not those of the remainderman or reversioner. Base fees are rarely if ever encountered nowadays.

3–081   *(b) Barring by will.* By virtue of s.176 of the Law of Property Act 1925, a tenant in tail can now bar his entail by will, and thus dispose of the fee simple or any other estate. This power is subject to a number of limitations.

(a)   It applies only to entails in possession: there is no power to bar an entail in remainder by will, even if the protector consents.

(b)   The tenant in tail must be of full age.

(c)   The will must be either executed after 1925 or confirmed by a codicil executed after 1925.

(d)   The will must refer specifically either to—

(i)   the property (e.g. "Blackacre"),[391] or

---

[382] FRA 1833 ss.15, 40. In general a disposition of an equitable interest can be made in writing without a deed: LPA 1925 s.53(1)(c); below, para.11–044.

[383] A declaration of trust will suffice: *Carter v Carter* [1896] 1 Ch. 162.

[384] Entailed interests usually took effect under a settlement made under the SLA 1925: below, Appendix, A–033. Under such a settlement, the legal estate and the powers of disposition of the settled land are vested in the life tenant.

[385] For a precedent, see Prideaux, Vol. iii, 415.

[386] A disentailing assurance is a "conveyance": LPA 1925 s.205(l)(ii). Since 1925, it has been possible for a person to convey land to himself: LPA 1925 s.72(3). This subsection is particularly intended to cover conveyances by a person in one capacity to himself in another: *Rye v Rye* [1962] A.C. 496 at 511, 514.

[387] See the doubt raised in Wolst. & C. i, 151.

[388] FRA 1833 s.34.

[389] FRA 1833 s.22. This follows the position that existed prior to 1833.

[390] FRA 1833 s.34.

[391] See *Acheson v Russell* [1951] Ch. 67 ("all other my estate and interest" in the property held sufficiently specific).

(ii) the instrument under which it was acquired (e.g. "all the property to which I succeeded under Uncle Harry's will"), or
(iii) entails generally (e.g. "all property to which I am entitled in tail").

This power extends to all entailed property, whether real or personal, whenever the entail was created.

(c) Unbarrable entails. It became a rule, as has been seen, that it was **3–082** impossible to create an unbarrable entail, and that any attempt to restrain the tenant from barring was ineffective.[392] This rule was not affected by the Fines and Recoveries Act 1833.[393] Despite this general rule there are certain entails which cannot be barred, e.g. those made unbarrable by Act of Parliament.[394] Furthermore there are certain persons who are unable to bar an entail, such as persons who lack capacity[395] and bankrupts.[396]

3. Descent. The old law of inheritance still applies to entails. They could **3–083** not exist if it did not.[397] However on the death of a tenant in tail, the entail (if unbarred) descends according to the *general* law that was in force before 1926. Special customs such as gavelkind (that applied in Kent) are therefore excluded.[398]

C. The Life Estate

After 1925 an interest in land for life can no longer exist as a legal estate but **3–084** only as an equitable interest.[399] In general, the law of life estates set out below appears to apply equally to the corresponding life interests after 1925; at all events, this is assumed in practice.[400]

I. TYPES OF LIFE ESTATE

The two types of life estate were the ordinary life estate for the life of the **3–085** tenant and the estate *pur autre vie*.

---

[392] Above, para.3–075.
[393] See *Dawkins v Lord Penrhyn* (1878) 4 App.Cas. 51 at 64.
[394] These include the entails given by reward to the first Duke of Marlborough (6 Anne, c.6, 1706, s.5; 6 Anne, c.7, 1706, s.4) and the first Duke of Wellington (54 Geo. 3, c.161, 1814, s.28). cf *Hambro v Duke of Marlborough* [1994] Ch. 158; below, Appendix, A-071.
[395] But the entail may be barred by an order of the Court of Protection or by a deputy appointed by the Court pursuant to the Mental Capacity Act 2005, s.16.
[396] The power to bar an entail vests instead in the bankrupt's trustee in bankruptcy: IA 1986 s.314(1); Sch.5 Pt II para.13.
[397] AEA 1925 s.45(2). For an explanation of the old rules of inheritance, see the 5th edition of this work at p.532.
[398] LPA 1925 s.130(4); *Re Higham* [1937] 2 All E.R. 17.
[399] LPA 1925 s.1; below, para.6–009.
[400] See, e.g. *Re Harker's W.T.* [1938] Ch. 323.

3–086   **1. Estate for the life of the tenant.** This arose either by express limitation, as by a grant "to A for life"[401], or, prior to 1926, by operation of law in certain circumstances, as where, under the old laws of succession, a widower or a widow became entitled to a life estate (curtesy and dower).[402]

3–087   **2. Estate *pur autre vie*.** An estate *pur autre vie* was an estate which was granted for the life of someone other than the tenant. The person whose life measured the duration of the estate was called the "*cestui que vie*". More than one *cestui que vie* could be named, and the estate could be limited either for the longest or for the shortest (i.e. for the joint lives) of such persons.[403] An estate *pur autre vie* could arise either—

(i) by the owner of life estate assigning it to another person. As nobody can give what they do not have,[404] the assignor could create no interest which would last longer than his own life;

(ii) by express grant, e.g. "to A for the life of X".

Where land is granted to A for the life of B and A predeceases B, A's interest passes like any other property to his personal representatives, who hold it in trust for the persons entitled under his will.[405]

3–088   Both types of life estate could be made determinable or subject to conditions subsequent.[406] Limitations of this kind were often found in settlements, for example, where a life interest was given to a wife, if she should survive her husband, "during her widowhood" or to a man "until he may become bankrupt". The principles governing such determinable or conditional life interests were probably[407] the same as those governing the corresponding types of fee simple.[408]

II. POSITION OF A TENANT FOR LIFE AT COMMON LAW

3–089   A tenant for life at common law was subject to important restrictions imposed by the law of waste (particularly as to timber and minerals), and by the rules relating to emblements and fixtures. These rules still apply to the modern equitable life interests.[409]

---

[401] Above, para.3–007.

[402] For curtesy and dower, see the 5th edition of this work at p.543.

[403] Challis 356.

[404] Commonly expressed in Latin: *"nemo dat quad non habet"*.

[405] AEA 1925 s. 45(l)(a). For the position prior to 1926, see the 6th edition of this work at para.3–095.

[406] Co.Litt. 42a; *Brandon v Robinson* (181 1) 18 Ves. 429; and see *Re Evans's Contract* [1920] 2 Ch. 469. See also above, para.3–058.

[407] In *Re Machu* (1882) 21 Ch D 838 at 842 the possibility of determinable interests being subject to special rules was raised but not decided.

[408] Above, paras 3–052 et seq.

[409] This was assumed in *Re Harker's W.T.* [19381 Ch. 323, but criticised at (1938) 2 Conv.(N.S.) 233 (H. Potter).

Waste

1. Function. "Waste", it has been said, " is a somewhat archaic subject, **3–090** now seldom mentioned".[410] It can arise in other connections, notably in the law of landlord and tenant,[411] but it is most suitably considered in relation to life interests, where it is applicable both to ordinary life interests and to interests *pur autre vie*.[412] Liability for waste is tortious in character.[413] Its object is to prevent a limited owner, such as a tenant for life or years, despoiling the land to the prejudice of those in reversion or remainder. Their remedy is to bring an action for damages or to apply for an injunction[414]; and if the tenant for life has profited from the waste (e.g. by cutting timber), he may be made liable for the money received from the sale, or an account.[415]

2. Nature. Technically, waste consists of any act which alters the nature of **3–091** the land, whether for the better or for the worse, e.g. the conversion of arable land into a woodland or vice versa.[416] Four types of waste must be considered: ameliorating, permissive, voluntary and equitable.[417]

(a) Ameliorating waste. Alterations which improve the land, such as con- **3–092** verting dilapidated store buildings into dwellings[418] or a farm into a market-garden,[419] constitute what is paradoxically termed ameliorating waste. Claims for this type of waste find little favour in the courts unless the whole character of the property has been changed. Where improvements have been made, an action for damages will fail because no damage has been suffered, and an injunction will be awarded only if the court thinks fit.[420]

(b) Permissive waste. This is failure to do that which ought to be done, as **3–093** by the non-repair of buildings[421] or sea or river walls,[422] or the failure to clean

---

[410] *Mancetter Developments Ltd v Garmanson Ltd* [1986] Q.B. 1212 at 1218, per Dillon L.J.

[411] It is seldom of importance in dealings between landlord and tenant nowadays because actions in respect of disrepair are usually brought on the covenant to repair: *Mancetter Developments Ltd v Garmanson Ltd*, above, at pp.1218, 1223. See below, para.19–110.

[412] See *Edward Seymor's Case* (1612) 10 Co.Rep. 95b at 98a.

[413] *Mancetter Developments Ltd v Garmanson Ltd*, above, at 1219, 1222, 1223.

[414] *Woodhouse v Walker* (1880) 5 Q.B.D. 404 (damages); *Lowndes v Norton* (1864) 33 L.J.Ch. 583 (injunction).

[415] *Seagram v Knight* (1867) 2 Ch. App. 628 at 632; *Dashwood v Magniac* [1891] 3 Ch. 306.

[416] Co.Litt. 53a, b; *Lord Darcy v Askwith* (1618) Rob. 234; but see *Jones v Chappell* (1875) L.R. 20 Eq. 539.

[417] For the common law rules about waste, see (1950) 13 Conv.(N.S.) 278 (M.E. Bathurst).

[418] *Doherty v Allman* (1878) 3 App.Cas. 709; and see *Hyman v Rose* [1912] A.C. 623 (chapel into cinema).

[419] *Meux v Cobley* [1892] 2 Ch. 253; cf. *Jones v Chappell* (1875) L.R. 20 Eq. 539 (erection of buildings).

[420] *Doherty v Allman, supra; Re Mcintosh and Pontypridd Improvements Co Ltd* (1891) 61 L.J.Q.B. 164.

[421] Co.Litt. 53a; *Powys v Blagrave* (1854) 4 De G.M. & G. 448.

[422] *Anon.* (1564) Moo.K.B. 62; *Griffith's Case* (1564) Moo.K.B. 69.

out a ditch or moat so as to prevent foundations becoming rotten.[423] But mere non-cultivation of land is not permissive waste.[424] A tenant for life is not liable for permissive waste unless an obligation to repair is imposed upon him by the terms of the limitation under which he holds.[425] This obligation is as rare in life tenancies as it is common in tenancies for years.

3–094   *(c) Voluntary waste.* This is doing that which ought not to be done. "The committing of any spoil or destruction in houses, lands, etc., by tenants, to the damage of the heir, or of him in reversion or remainder"[426] is voluntary waste. Examples of voluntary waste include:

 (i) removal of fixtures that are not tenant's fixtures[427];

 (ii) removal of tenant's fixtures without making good any damage so caused[428];

 (iii) opening and working a mine in the land[429] (but not merely working a mine already open[430]); and

 (iv) cutting timber.[431]

Timber consists of oak, ash and elm trees which are at least 20 years old and not too old to have a reasonable quantity of usable wood in them.[432] Other trees may rank as timber by local custom, e.g. beech in Buckinghamshire, willow in Hampshire and birch in Yorkshire and Cumberland[433]; and custom may also prescribe some qualification other than an age of 20 years for the trees to be considered timber, e.g. an age of 24 years or a specified girth.[434]

A tenant for life is liable for voluntary waste[435] unless his interest was granted to him by an instrument[436] exempting him from liability for voluntary waste, e.g. a grant "without impeachment of waste".[437] Where there is such

---

[423] *Sticklehorne v Hatchman* (1586) Owen 43.
[424] *Hutton v Warren* (1836) 1 M. & W. 466 at 472.
[425] *Re Cartwright* (1889) 41 Ch D 532.
[426] Bacon's *Abridgement* (7th edn), viii, 379; and see *Mancetter Developments Ltd v Garmanson Ltd* [19861 Q.B. 1212 at 1218, 1221.
[427] *Mancetter Developments Ltd v Garmanson Ltd*, supra, at 1218. For tenant's fixtures, see below, paras 23–010 et seq.
[428] *Mancetter Developments Ltd v Garmanson Ltd*, above; *Wessex Reserve Forces and Cadets Association v White* [2005] EWHC 983 (QB) at [70]; [2005] 3 E.G.L.R. 124 at 133. There is no liability for minimal damage: *Re De Falbe* [1901] Ch. 523 at 542.
[429] *Saunders's Case* (1599) 5 Co.Rep. 12A; *Campbell v Wardlaw* (1883) 8 App.Cas. 641.
[430] *Dashwood v Magniac* 189 113 Ch. 306 at 360.
[431] *Honywood v Honywood* (1874) L.R. 18 Eq. 306.
[432] *Honywood v Honywood*, above at 309.
[433] *Aubrey v Fisher* (1809) 10 East 446 (Bucks); Cru.Dig. i, 117 (Hants); *Countess of Cumberland's Case* (1610) Moo.K.B. 812 (Yorks.); *Pinder v Spencer* (1617) Noy 30 (Cumb.)
[434] *Honywood v Honywood*, above, at 309.
[435] *Pardoe v Pardoe* (1900) 82 L.T. 547; *Re Ridge* (1885) 31 Ch D 504 at 507; H.E.L. iii, 121, 122. As to a tenant for life of leaseholds, see *Re Parry and Hopkin* [1900] 1 Ch. 160; *Re Field* [1925] Ch. 636.
[436] See *Dowman's Case* (1583) 9 Co.Rep. 1a at 10b.
[437] *Lewis Bowles's Case* (1616) 11 Co.Rep. 79b at 82b; *Waldo v Waldo* (1841) 12 Sim. 107.

an exemption the tenant is said to be "unimpeachable of waste"; otherwise he is said to be "impeachable of waste". Thus if nothing is said about waste, the tenant is impeachable; in practice, however, he is often made unimpeachable.

(d) *Equitable waste.* Even where a tenant for life is unimpeachable of **3–095** waste, it is considered to be inequitable for him to ruin the property by acts of wanton destruction. To prevent this the equitable remedy of an injunction[438] will be granted. "Equitable waste is that which a prudent man would not do in the management of his own property."[439] The term applies to acts such as stripping a house of all its lead, iron, glass, doors, boards, etc., to the value of £3,000,[440] or pulling down houses,[441] or cutting timber planted with the object of providing ornament or shelter[442] (whether or not in fact it does provide it[443]), unless this is necessary for the preservation of part of the timber.[444] These acts are, of course, also voluntary waste, but are not relevant as such where the tenant is unimpeachable. Equitable waste therefore is a peculiarly flagrant branch of voluntary waste, which the ordinary dispensation from waste will not excuse.

There is one exception to the general rule that a tenant for life is liable for equitable waste even though he was granted his interest without impeachment of waste. He will not be liable if it expressly appears from the document that confers his interest upon him that he is to have the right to commit equitable waste as well as voluntary waste.[445]

Timber and minerals

Although largely governed by the general law of waste, the rights of a tenant **3–096** for life with regard to timber and minerals are so important as to merit separate treatment.

1. Timber

(a) *Estovers.* Whether impeachable of waste or not, a tenant for life can take **3–097** reasonable estovers (or botes) from the land. These consist of wood and timber taken as:

    (i) house-bote, for repairing the house or burning in it;

    (ii) plough-bote, for making and repairing agricultural implements; and

---

[438] Below, para.5–015.
[439] *Turner v Wright* (1860) 2 De G.F. & J. 234 at 243, per Lord Campbell, L.C.
[440] *Vane v Lord Barnard* (1716) 2 Vern. 738.
[441] *Williams v Day* (1680) 2 Ch.Ca. 32.
[442] *Marker v Marker* (1851) 9 Hare 1.
[443] *Weld -Blundell v Wolseley* [1903] 2 Ch. 664.
[444] *Baker v Sebright* (1879) 13 Ch D 179.
[445] LPA 1925 s.135; *Micklethwait v Micklethwait* (1857) 1 De G. & J. 504 at 524.

(iii) hay-bote, for repairing fences.[446]

The tenant's right to house-bote does not entitle him to cut down timber in excess of his present needs in order to use it for any repairs which become necessary in the future. nor does it authorise him to sell the timber, even if he employs the proceeds in repairs, or the timber proves unfit for repairs.[447]

3–098   *(h) Timber estate.* If the land is a timber estate (an estate cultivated mainly for the produce of saleable timber which is cut periodically[448]), the tenant can cut and sell timber according to the rules of proper estate management even if he is impeachable of waste. The reason fir this rule is that the timber properly cut on such an estate is part of the annual fruits of the land rather than part of the inheritance.[449]

3–099   *(c) Timber planted for ornament or shelter.* As has been seen,[450] it is equitable waste to cut timber planted for ornament or shelter, and only a tenant unimpeachable of equitable waste is permitted to do this.

3–100   *(d) Trees.* A tenant for life, even if he is impeachable of waste, may cut dotards (dead trees not fit for use as timber) and all trees which are not timber, e.g. in most cases larches or willows.[451] But there are a number of exceptions to this. It is voluntary waste to cut trees which would be timber but for their immaturity (unless the cutting is necessary to thin them out and so allow proper development)[452] or to cut fruit trees in a garden or orchard.[453] Further, it is voluntary waste to cut wood which a prudent man would not cut, such as willows which help to hold a river bank together[454]; and it may be equitable waste to cut trees planted for ornament or shelter, or to grub up an entire wood.[455]

3–101   *(e) Normal rules.* Subject to the above special rules, the position is that a tenant for life who is unimpeachable of waste may cut and sell timber and keep all the proceeds.[456] But if the tenant is impeachable of waste, his only

---

[446] Co.Litt. 4lb, 53b; Tudor L.C. 147.
[447] *Gorges v Stanfield* (1597) Cro.Eliz. 593; *Simmons v Norton* (1831) 7 Bing. 640; Co.Litt. 53b.
[448] *Honywood v Honywood* (1874) L.R. 18 Eq. 306 at 309, 310, where "merely" is used in place of "mainly".
[449] *Honywood v Honywood*, above, at 309, 310; *Dashwood v Magniac* [1891] 3 Ch. 306; *Re Trevor-Batye* [1912] 2 Ch. 339.
[450] Above, para.3–095.
[451] *Herlakenden's Case* (1589) 4 Co.Rep. 62a at 63b; *Phillipps v Smith* (1845) 14 M. & W. 589: *Honywood v Honywood*, above; *Re Harker's W.T.* [1938] Ch. 323.
[452] *Phillipps v Smith*, supra, at 594; *Bagot v Bagot* (1863) 32 Beav. 509 at 518; *Earl Cowley v Wellesey* (1866) L.R. 1 Eq. 656.
[453] Co.Litt. 53a; *Kaye v Banks* (1770) Dick. 431.
[454] *Stripping's Case* (1621) Winch 15.
[455] *Lord Tamworth v Lord Ferrers* (1801) 6 Ves. 419; *Aston v Aston* (1749) 1 Ves.Sen. 264 at 265.
[456] *Lewis Bowles's Case* (1615) 11 Co.Rep. 79b; Cru.Dig. i, 127.

right to cut timber is that given to him by statute, subject to prescribed conditions.[457]

(f) Ownership of severed timber. Standing trees are part of the land and do **3–102** not belong to the tenant for life until properly cut by him. Therefore if the land is sold with the trees standing, the life tenant cannot claim any share of the price even though he could lawfully have cut them.[458] The rule at common law was that severed trees belonged to the life tenant if he had the right to sever them, whether they had been felled by him, by a stranger, or by an act of God (such as a storm).[459] If he was not entitled to sever them, they belonged to the owner of the next vested estate or interest of inheritance.[460] Life estates can now exist only in equity and the equitable rules are less stringent. A court of equity has sometimes been willing to declare the proceeds of timber wrong- fully cut to be part of the settled property, to be held for the benefit of all parties other than the wrongdoer.[461] The tenant for life may also be allowed to take the income if the court would have authorised the cutting.[462]

2. Minerals. The mineral rights of a tenant for life depend on two factors, **3–103** namely, whether the mine was already open when his tenancy began, and whether he is impeachable of waste.

A tenant for life may work a mine and take all the proceeds unless: **3–104**

(i) he is impeachable of waste, and

(ii) the mine was not open when his tenancy began.

Where both these conditions are satisfied, he cannot work the mine at all, for to open and work an unopened mine is voluntary waste.[463] But it is not waste to continue working a mine already open[464] even if new pits are made on different parts of the same plot of land to pursue the same or a new vein, for the grantor, by opening or allowing the opening of the mines, has shown an

---

[457] SLA 1925 s.66, applicable only to settled land. This is one of the many statutory powers of a tenant for life under the settled land legislation. See notes in Wolst. & C. iii, 145. Subject to minor exceptions, it has not been possible to create settlements after 1996: see TLATA 1996 s.2.

[458] *Re Llewellin* (1887) 37 Ch D 317; *Re Londesborough* [1923] 1 Ch. 500.

[459] *Anon.* (1729) Mos. 237 at 238; *Lewis Bowles's Case*, above, at 84a.

[460] *Paget's Case* (1593) 5 Co.Rep. 76b; *Bewick v Whitfield* (1734) 3 P.Wms. 267; *Honywood v Honywood* (1874) L.R. 18 Eq. 306; but see *Tooker v Annesley* (1832) 5 Sim. 235 at 240.

[461] *Lushington v Boldero* (1851) 15 Beav. 1; *Honywood v Honywood*, supra; Tudor L.C. 155.

[462] *Tooker v Annesley*, supra; *Waldo v Waldo* (1835) 7 Sim. 261; (1841) 12 Sim. 107; *Bateman v Hotchkin (No. 2)* (1862) 31 Beav. 486; compare *Re Harrison Trusts* (1884) 28 Ch D 220 at 228 (larches: trust for sale).

[463] Above, para.3–094. As to the meaning of "open', see *Greville-Nugent v Mackenzie* [1900] A.C. 83; *Re Morgan* [1914] 1 Ch. 910 at 919, 920; *Elias Snowdon Slate Quarries Co* (1879) 4 App.Cas. 454 at 465.

[464] *Viner v Vaughan* (1840) 2 Beav. 466 at 469.

intent that the minerals should be treated as part of the profits of the land.[465] Minerals improperly mined are dealt with in the same way as timber wrongfully cut.[466]

In relation to settlements, the Settled Land Act 1925 contains powers authorising a tenant for life to grant mining leases in certain circumstances.[467]

Emblements and fixtures

3–105   A tenant for life cannot foresee the date on which his estate will determine. In order to encourage him to cultivate his land by assuring him of the fruits of his labour, the law gives him a right to emblements (growing crops).[468] This means that the tenant's personal representatives, or in the case of an estate *pur autre vie* the tenant himself,[469] may enter the land after the life estate has determined and reap the crops which the tenant has sown.[470] This applies only to cultivated crops such as corn, hemp, and flax, and not to things such as fruit trees and timber; and it extends only to the crops actually sown by the tenant for life[471] and growing at the determination of the tenancy.[472] Where the end of the tenancy is brought about by the tenant's own act (e.g. where a life estate is granted to a widow until remarriage and she remarries) there is no right to emblements.[473]

Prima facie any fixtures attached to the land by a tenant for life must be left after his death for the person next entitled to the land; but trade fixtures and ornamental and domestic fixtures are excepted. This is explained in greater detail later.[474]

---

[465] *Re Hall* [1916] 2 Ch. 488 at 493; *Spencer v Scurr* (1862) 31 Beav. 334; cf. *Re Ridge* (1885) 31 Ch. 504 at 508 and contrast *Re Maynard* [1899] 2 Ch. 347.
[466] *Re Barrington* (1886) 33 Ch D 523 at 527; above.
[467] See SLA 1925 ss. 4l, 42, 45–47. See the sixth edition of this work at para.3–113.
[468] *Graves v Weld* (1833) 5 B. & Ad. 105 at 107.
[469] *Kelly v Webber* (1860) 3 L.T. 124.
[470] Co.Litt. 55b.
[471] *Grantham v Hawley* (1615) Hob. 132.
[472] *Graves v Weld*, above, at 119.
[473] *Oland's Case* (1602) 5 Co.Rep. 1 16a; Williams R.P. 135.
[474] Below, para.23–019.

CHAPTER 4

POSSESSION OF LAND

Part 1

OWNERSHIP, POSSESSION AND TITLE

1. Estate ownership. It has been explained that ownership in its fullest **4–001** sense means that the owner holds the land in tenure for an estate in fee simple absolute.[1] Tenure is an unimportant element in this formula of ownership: the vital element is the estate. The nature of estate ownership will to a large extent have become obvious from the preceding chapter. But the picture is not complete without some investigation of the theory of ownership which was developed by the common law, under which "absolute ownership" turns out to contain an unexpected measure of relativity.

Normally, but not invariably,[2] the title to an estate in land at common law is derivative. This is because the fee simple absolute is usually obtained by some kind of transfer from its previous owner, either by conveyance inter vivos or under his will or through the law of intestate succession. He can transmit no greater estate than he owned himself; and since the same was necessarily true of his own predecessors in title, the fee simple absolute which he owned must have had a continuous history going back to the year 1189, the limit of legal memory,[3] or perhaps more accurately, at least since the statute *Quia Emptores* 1290, which prohibited subinfeudation and thereby required free tenants to make substitutionary grants.[4] It is true that in earlier times the law allowed "tortious assurances" under which a tenant in tail or for life could convey a fee simple, due to the almost magical efficacy of the ancient forms of conveyance, feoffments, fines and recoveries. But all such possibilities were finally terminated in 1845.[5] From then on, unless otherwise provided by

[1] See above, para.3–005.
[2] For an exception to the normal rule, see below, para.4–003.
[3] For this see below, para.28–059.
[4] See above, paras 2–015, 2–016.
[5] RPA 1845 s.4, providing simply that a feoffment "shall not have any tortious operation". From then on all forms of conveyance were "innocent", i.e. subject to the *nemo dat* rule. Fines and recoveries had been abolished in 1833; see above, para.3–076.

statute, there was at common law no exception to the principle *nemo dat quod non habet*: no one can convey what he does not own. It is possible, as will be seen in the next chapter, for a purchaser to take a title free from some incumbrance which was binding on the vendor, so that in one sense he may obtain more than the vendor had himself.[6] However, as regards the vendor's own estate in the land, the principle is fundamental.

4–002   There is a clear contrast between ownership at common law and registered ownership under the system of registration of title. Under that system the estate of the registered proprietor is determined by what is shown on the register rather than by the estate of his predecessor. This is because registration confers title.[7] Even a registered title is to some extent derivative. This is because, if a person is mistakenly registered as proprietor of land which in fact belonged to another, the register may in certain circumstances be altered to correct the error.[8] However, in principle, the registered system is not governed by the maxim *nemo dat quod non habet*, which for centuries dominated conveyancing at common law.

4–003   **2. Possessory title.** Title to land at common law is not always derivative. It is possible for an entirely fresh title to be created, conferring a new fee simple estate. This occurs where land is acquired by adverse possession under what is now the Limitation Act 1980.[9] All that is relevant at this point is that under that Act, as under its predecessors back to 1833,[10] the remedy and title of a dispossessed owner of unregistered land are normally extinguished after the land has been in adverse possession for 12 years.[11] The Act does not transfer the dispossessed owner's estate to the adverse possessor. It merely extinguishes the earlier title, leaving the adverse possessor free from any claims under it. He then has a new and independent freehold title,[12] based upon his own possession.[13] Here, therefore, is an example of a non-derivative title, based primarily on the fact of possession, but protected by statute against the former owner. An investigation of this phenomenon, and of its history, will explain the essential nature of title, the strong links between possession and ownership, and the legal foundations of the fee simple estate.[14]

4–004   By way of example, if S (squatter) wrongfully takes possession of land belonging to O (owner), O immediately acquires a right of action against S for

---

[6] See below, paras 5–011—5–013.
[7] See below, paras 7–115 et seq.
[8] See below, paras 4–013, fn.54, 7–001.
[9] For details, see below. For adverse possession and limitation, see Ch.35.
[10] The present law of limitation originated in RPLA 1833, which swept away the complexities of the previous law: see *J A Pye (Oxford) Ltd v Graham* [2002] UKHL 30 at [33]—[38]; [2003] 1 A.C. 419 at 433—435.
[11] See LA 1980 ss.15, 17.
[12] See below, para.4–008.
[13] The position in relation to registered land was and is different. For the operation of adverse possession under LRA 1925, see the 6th edition of this work at para.6–116. For the attenuated role of adverse possession under LRA 2002, see below, para.35–070.
[14] See generally, M. Wonnacott, *Possession of Land* (2006).

recovery of the land.[15] If O takes no action, in 12 years (normally) his right of action becomes barred and his title extinguished by limitation. S can no longer be disturbed by O, and as against the rest of the world S is protected by the fact of his possession. Possession by itself gives a good title against all the world, except someone having a better legal right to possession.[16]

This last proposition is fundamental to the concept of title to land. If the occupier's possession is disturbed, for example by trespass or nuisance, he can sue on the strength of his possession and does not have to prove his title. It follows that the person disturbing the occupier's possession cannot attack his title, if he admits his possession; in the language of pleading, a defendant sued for trespass in such a case cannot plead *jus tertii* (that the land belongs to some third party, not to the claimant[17]). As against a defendant having no title to the land, the occupier's possession is in itself a title.[18] But if the defendant himself lays claim to the land by a title of his own, he may of course plead his own title and so put the claimant's title in issue. He is then alleging a title not in a third party but in himself.[19] Accordingly he may show title in a third party if he himself claims through the third party, e.g. as purchaser, tenant or licensee.[20]

3. History

(a) *Proprietary and possessory actions.* This essentially possessory charac- **4–005**
ter of title to land is a product of historical evolution and, in particular, of the old forms of action. For some time after the middle of the 12th century there

---

[15] O may re-enter, but if resisted he may be guilty of an offence under the Criminal Law Act 1977. O will therefore be put to an action if S refuses to give up possession, though CPR rr.55.20—55.28 provides a speedy means of recovering it by means of an interim possession order: see below, para.4–028.

[16] *Asher v Whitlock* (1865) L.R. 1 Q.B.1. This is the leading decision on the principle in modern times. H enclosed manorial land, and died in 1860 leaving the land by his will to his widow for life or until remarriage, remainder to his daughter in fee simple. The widow remarried, and two years after her death in 1863 the daughter's heir successfully claimed the land from the husband. The reason was that the heir had succeeded to H's possessory rights, and that these were good against the husband since his was a later possession. The lord of the manor was not a party to the proceedings, and it was not shown that his title was barred; and see *Perry v Clissold* [1907] A.C. 73

[17] "It is well settled that in an action of trespass a defendant may not set up a *jus tertii*. He may set up a title in himself, or show that he acted on the authority of the real owner, but he cannot set up a mere *jus tertii*": *Nicholls v Ely Beet Sugar Factory (No.1)* [1931] 2 Ch. 84 at 86, per Farwell J. cf. *Lall v Lall* [1965] 1 W.L.R. 1249.

[18] It is however essential that possession should be taken. In *Marsden v Miller* (1992) 64 P. & CR. 239, two neighbours each made use of a piece of land of unknown ownership. One of them then erected a fence around the strip that was removed by the other within 24 hours. The erection of the fence in those circumstances was not such an assumption of control of the land by the former that he could bring trespass proceedings against his neighbour.

[19] See fn.17 above.

[20] "If possession be shown, the defendant is not at liberty to set up the title of a third party unless he justifies what he has done under a licence from such third party": *Lord Fitzhardinge v Purcell* [1908] 2 Ch. 139 at 145, per Parker J.

were (at least in name) both proprietary and possessory actions, the former asserting title and the latter asserting possessory rights.[21] Thus if S disseised O of a piece of land, O could recover the land by a possessory action, showing merely the fact of dispossession. But this did not prejudice the question of title, and if S claimed title he might still recover the land again from O by a proprietary action. Originally the possessory actions were speedy and temporary remedies introduced in the king's courts for the purpose of preserving the peace and preventing forcible dispossessions, whether rightful or wrongful. But they were extended so fast and so far that they soon came to cover almost all claims, and superseded the ancient proprietary actions which lay only in the feudal courts.[22]

4–006   *(b) Title based on seisin.* Title to land therefore depended on the better right to possession (seisin) rather than vice versa. The concept of ownership was never really disentangled from that of possession.[23] As between two rival claimants, the land belonged to the one who could lay claim to the earlier and therefore the better seisin, whether that seisin was his own or that of some person to whose rights he had succeeded, e.g. as heir or feoffee. Seisin was thus the root of all titles. When in the seventeenth century the action of ejectment[24] had been perfected as a general action for the recovery of land, it shifted the basis of title from the technical seisin of feudal law to the simple fact of possession.[25] This was because the action of ejectment was a form of trespass action, which lay for a wrongful disturbance of possession, whereas the older possessory actions belonged to the family of the "real actions" which were peculiar to real property and were available only for claims based on seisin.[26]

---

[21] See below, paras 4–014—4–017. Even the proprietary ("droitural") actions had a strong possessory flavour: Litt. p.478; H.E.L. iii, pp.89, 90: Lightwood, *Possession of Land*, pp.71–75.

[22] H.E.L. iii, pp.8–14; see below, para.4–016. For the feudal origin of the possessory actions, see S. F. C. Milsom, *Historical Foundations of the Common Law*, Ch.6.

[23] H.E.L. ii, pp.88 et seq., and above, para.3–018, for the pre-eminence of seisin in medieval law. An owner disseised had a mere right of entry or action, which at common law was not assignable; he could not convey (being unable to deliver seisin); neither curtesy nor dower could be taken at his death; his death without heirs caused no escheat. Rights of entry did not become assignable at law until the RPA 1845; above, para.3–068.

[24] See below, para.4–018.

[25] In *Doe d. Crisp v Barber* (1788) 2 T.R. 749 and *Doe d. Carter v Barnard* (1849) 13 Q.B. 945 it was laid down that mere possession (i.e. possession unaccompanied by any other interest) would not support an action of ejectment. But this doctrine was wrong: see *Asher v Whitlock*, above, *Perry v Clissold* [1907] A.C. 73 at 79, 80; *Hawdon v Khan* (1920) 20 SR. (N.S.W.) 703 at 707, 712; *Allen v Roughley* (1955) 94 C.L.R. 98, noted in [1956] C.L.J. 177 (H.W.R.W.); *Oxford Meat Co Pty Ltd v McDonald* [1963] SR. (N.S.W.) 423; *Nair Service Society Ltd v K.C. Alexander AIR* 1968 S.C. 1 165; *Spark v Whale Three Minute Car Wash (Cremorne Junction) Pty Ltd* (1970) 92 W.N. (N.S.W.) 1087; *Marsden v Miller* (1992) 64 P. & CR. 239 at 242–243; Lightwood, *Time Limit on Actions*, pp.120–126; and see *Davison v Gent* (1857) 1 H. & N. 744. The shift towards mere possession as the basis of title was further assisted by the RPLA 1833: see Lightwood, *Possession of Land*, pp.123, 124.

[26] For ejectment, see below, para.4–018.

(c) Possession as a root of title. The real actions were abolished in 1833[27] **4–007**
and the action of ejectment in 1852.[28] However, the substantive law is still that
developed from the action of ejectment,[29] so that it remains true that, in
relation to unregistered land, possession is a root of title.[30] Any distinction
between seisin and possession as the basis of title is obscured by the well-
established rule that possession of land, if exclusive of other claimants[31] and
not otherwise explained, is evidence of seisin in fee simple.[32] Possession by
a tenant or an agent is obviously no foundation for a title against the landlord
or the principal, because the possession is not adverse. Where the possession
is truly adverse, there is little merit today in preserving for this purpose any
distinction between seisin and possession. It is possession that forms the
recognised root of title.[33] Ownership, as between two rival claimants, is the
better right to possession.

"Possession is a legal concept which depends on the performance of overt
acts, and not on intention".[34] It requires an appropriate degree of physical
control of the land and it must be a single and exclusive possession, though

[27] RPLA 1833, s.36.
[28] CLPA 1852, s.3.
[29] See *Bristow v Cormican* (1878) 3 App.Cas. 641 at 661. At one time an order for possession
could not be made in *ex parte* proceedings. However since the introduction in 1970 of summary
possession proceedings (now found at CPR Pt.55; below, para.4–026), the courts have been
willing in wholly exceptional cases to make such an order where there is a real danger to life, limb
or property: *Re Milward and Sons Ltd* (1980, unreported). Once an order for possession has been
made the consequent writ or warrant of possession (CPR Sch.1, RSC Ord.45, rr.3, 12; Form 66;
Sch.2, CCR Ord.26, r.17, Form N49) operates in rem. A writ for possession requires the
enforcement officer (formerly it was the sheriff, but see Courts Act 2003, s.99; Sch.7) to enter the
land and "cause" the claimant "to have possession of it" (Form 66). A warrant for possession is
directed to bailiff who is "required to give possession of the land to the claimant": Form N49. The
writ or warrant thus takes effect against all persons there, whether or not they were defendants:
R. v Wandsworth County Court, Ex p. Wandsworth LBC [1975] 1 W.L.R. 1314. If after entry by
the enforcement officer the defendant wrongfully resumes possession, the plaintiff may seek a
writ of restitution to restore him to possession. This can be enforced even if there are new
unlawful occupiers who have come on to the land since the original writ was issued: *Wiltshire CC
v Frazer (No.2)* [1986] 1 W.L.R. 109.
[30] See (1940) 56 L.Q.R. 376, where in a valuable article A.D. Hargreaves maintained that seisin
is still the basis; see esp. the summary at 397.
[31] Where the alleged trespasser is not a claimant (i.e. where he is merely disputing the
plaintiff's actual possession), the plaintiff need show only slight evidence of possession: *Wuta-
Ofei v Danquah* [1961] 1 W.L.R. 1238; and acts of possession are strengthened by a claim of
right: *Fowley Marine (Emsworth) Ltd v Gafford* [1968] 2 Q.B. 618 (exclusive possession of tidal
creek successfully shown); *Ocean Estates Ltd v Pinder* [1969] 2 A.C. 19 (acts of possession
strengthened by documentary title); and see below, para.35–016.
[32] *Peaceable d. Uncle v Watson* (1811) 4 Taunt. 16 at 17; *Jayne v Price* (1814) 5 Taunt. 326;
Jones v Smith (1841) 1 Hare 43 at 60; *Re Atkinson & Horsell's Contract* [1912] 2 Ch. 1 at 9;
Lightwood, *Possession of Land*, 114–121; (1940) 56 L.Q.R. 376 at 381, 382 (A.D.
Hargreaves).
[33] See Lightwood, *Possession of Land*, 124, 126; Pollock & Wright, *Possession*, pp.93–96; *Re
Atkinson & Horsell's Contract* [1912] 2 Ch. 1 at 9.
[34] *Simpson v Fergus* (1999) 79 P. & C.R. 398 at 402, per Robert Walker L.J. Intention *is*
relevant where a squatter claims to have acquired title by adverse possession, but this is additional
to his showing factual possession of the land: see below, para.35–016. There is no difference as
to quality of possession that is required (i) to maintain an action of trespass against an intruder;
and (ii) to found a claim based upon adverse possession: see *Powell v McFarlane* (1977) 38 P.
& C.R. 452 at 469.

there can be a single possession exercised by or on behalf of several persons jointly.[35] What is an appropriate degree of physical control will depend upon the nature of the land and the purposes for which it might be used.[36]

4. Titles relative

4–008   *(a) Relativity of titles.* "At common law . . . there is no such concept as an 'absolute' title. Where questions of title to land arise in litigation the court is concerned only with the relative strengths of the titles proved by the rival claimants. If party A can prove a better title than party B he is entitled to succeed notwithstanding that C may have a better title than A, if C is neither a party to the action nor a person by whose authority B is in possession or occupation of the land."[37]

Some examples will illustrate this fundamental doctrine and the right and wrong occasions for the plea of *jus tertii*. If last year S dispossessed O of land which had hitherto belonged to O, and O is taking no action, there are now two incompatible titles to the land. As between O and S, O is the owner, because he can recover the land by bringing an action. However, as between S and the rest of the world (except O and persons claiming through him) S is owner, for he is in possession and that is equivalent to ownership as against all persons who have no better right.[38] Thus S can sue strangers for trespass or nuisance, just as O could before.[39] Furthermore, S can convey the land, or make any other disposition which an owner can make.[40] If S dies, the land will pass under his will or intestacy.[41] But all such rights derived through S are subject to O's (or his successor in title's) paramount right to recover the land. S's possession at once gives him all the rights and powers of ownership, at

---

[35] *J A Pye (Oxford) Ltd v Graham* [2002] UKHL 30 at [41]; [2003] 1 A.C. 419 at 436.

[36] *Lord Advocate v Lord Lovat* (1880) 5 App.Cas. 273 at 288; *Powell v McFarlane* (1977) 38 P. & C.R. 452 at 470, 471.

[37] *Ocean Estates Ltd v Pinder* [1969] 2 A.C. 19 at 24, 25, per Lord Diplock. See too *Wells v Pilling PC* [2009] EWHC 556 (Ch) at [7]; [2009] 2 E.G.L.R. 29 at 30.

[38] *Doe d. Hughes v Dyeball* (1829) Moo. & M. 346; 3 C. & P. 610 (one year's possession held a good title as against a stranger); *Doe d. Humphrey v Martin* (1841) Car. & M. 32; *Asher v Whitlock* (1865) L.R. 1 Q.B. 1 (above, para.4–004).

[39] *Graham v Peat* (1801) 1 East 244; *Chambers v Donaldson* (1809) 11 East 65; *Nicholls v Ely Beet Sugar Factory (No.1)* [1931] 2 Ch. 84 at 86; *Hunter v Canary Wharf Ltd* [1997] A.C. 655 at 703; *Pemberton v Southwark LBC* [2000] 1 W.L.R. 1672 ("tolerated trespasser" holding over after termination of secure tenancy could sue the freeholder for cockroach infestation). See below, para.29–003. Similarly if A supports his house on B's land (having no right), he cannot sue if B removes the support, but he can sue if C does: *Jeffries v Williams* (1850) 5 Exch. 792 at 800; and see *Laing v Whaley* (1858) 3 H. & N. 675. Again, if A uses B's road for access to his house he cannot sue if B obstructs the road, but he can if C does: *Beckett v Midland Ry* (1867) L.R. 3 C.P. 82 at 103. But contrast below, para.29–003.

[40] See Litt. pp.472, 474, 476, 477. But compare *R. v Edwards* [1978] Crim.L.R. 49, where a squatter was convicted of obtaining by deception. She had received rent from a tenant to whom she had let part of the property. The court considered that she was never more than a trespasser and that "the one thing she was not entitled to do was to let". It is not apparent why she should not have had the power to let or why the Crown was able to rely on the *jus tertii*.

[41] Litt. 385 (intestacy); *Asher v Whitlock* (1865) L.R. 1 Q.B. 1 (will and intestacy: two stages of devolution); *Allen v Roughley* (1955) 94 C.L.R. 98 (will).

least for the purposes of the civil law.[42] S has, in fact, a legal estate, a fee simple absolute in possession.[43] But so also has O, until such time as his title is extinguished by limitation.

(b) The better title. There is thus no absurdity in speaking of two or more **4–009** adverse estates in the land, for their validity is relative. If O allows his title to become barred by lapse of time, S's title becomes the better, and S then becomes " absolute owner". But if O brings his action within the time allowed, he can successfully assert his better title based on his prior possession; as against O, S's legal estate is nothing.[44]

(c) Jus tertii. It has been explained that third parties who have themselves **4–010** no title cannot exploit the relative weakness of S's title by pleading *jus tertii*. If X (a stranger) takes possession of the land from S, S or his successors can recover it within the limitation period and X cannot plead that the land is not in fact S's but O's.[45] This is self-evident, for otherwise anyone could help himself to the land.[46] If X claims the land, he must do so on the strength of some title of his own, not on the weakness of S's.[47]

On the other hand, suppose that, while S is still in undisturbed possession, O dies and by his will leaves all his land to X. If X acts in time he can obtain the land by asserting O's superior title. But here S, who is in possession, can compel X to prove his title, and if X's title, as derived from O, is subject to a *jus tertii* then S can plead it. If, for example, S can prove that O revoked the will in favour of X by a later will in favour of Y, S can plead that the land is not X's but Y's; and therefore, since Y's title shows X to be a mere stranger, S's possession is a good title against X. This again is self-evident, for otherwise S would have no protection against anyone purporting to claim through O. S can plead *jus tertii* against O himself if O has conveyed or demised the land to Z, for then the right to possession can be shown to be in

---

[42] cf. *R. v Edwards*, supra.

[43] *Rosenberg v Cook* (1881) 8 Q.B.D. 162 at 165; *Central London Commercial Estates Ltd v Kato Kagaku Ltd* [1998] 4 All E.R. 948 at 951. The old maxim was that a wrongdoer could not qualify his wrong, i.e. he was taken to claim the largest possible interest: Co.Litt. p.27la. "For a disseisor, abator, intruder, usurper, etc., have a fee simple, but it is not a lawful fee": Co.Litt. p.2a; and see Co.Litt. p.297a; Litt. pp.519, 520; Williams, *Seisin*, p.7, cited with approval by Dixon J. in *Wheeler v Baldwin* (1934) 52 C.L.R. 609 at 632; *Leach v Jay* (1878) 9 Ch D 42 at 44, 45; *Spark v Meers* [1971] 2 N.S.W.L.R. 1 at 12. Thus if S is a leasehold tenant his encroachments are presumed to enure to the benefit of his landlord: below, paras 28–056, 35–027. See also below, para.35–059. For the context of modern legislation, see (1964) 80 L.Q.R. 63 (B. Rudden).

[44] "When any man is disseised, the disseisor has only the naked possession, because the disseisee may enter and evict him; but against all other persons the disseisor has a right, and in this respect only can be said to have the right of possession, for in respect to the disseisee he has no right at all": Gilbert, *Tenures,* p.21, cited in Butler's note to Co.Litt. p.238a.

[45] *Asher v Whitlock* (1865) L.R. 1 Q.B. 1, above, para.4–003; *Spark v Whale Three Minute Car Wash (Cremorne Junction) Pty Ltd* (1970) 92 W.N. (N.S.W.) 1087.

[46] "Can it be at the mere will of any stranger to disturb the person in possession?": *Asher v Whitlock* (1865) L.R. 1 Q.B. 1 at 6, per Cockburn C.J.

[47] *Martin d. Tregonwell v Strachan* (1743) 5 T.R. 107n., affd. (1744) Willes 444; *Roe d. Haldane v Harvey* (1769) 4 Burr. 2484; *Bristow v Cormican* (1878) 3 App.Cas. 641 at 661.

Z, not in O.[48] It is only the title behind O's original possession that S is not allowed to dispute.[49]

4–011   Where one party has obtained possession by permission of the other, he naturally cannot use that possession to support a plea of *jus tertii* against that other. This explains why a tenant or licensee is estopped from denying the title of his lessor or licensor.[50]

Sometimes neither party may be able to show possession in fact, and the question then is which of them can show possession in law, i.e. the better right to possession. This is a straight contest of documentary titles, and either can defend an action of trespass by showing that the plaintiff is not the true owner.[51]

4–012   5. Ownership. Although the person with the best ascertained right to possession is often called the "absolute owner", it is clear from the foregoing analysis that English law knows no abstract ownership, as opposed to the right to recover possession, unless perhaps the Crown's universal seignorial rights should be so classified.[52] O may be "owner" of Blackacre, but it is always theoretically possible for someone to come forward and prove a better title, as by proving that he owns the reversion on a long term of years which has now expired, or by finding a lost will which alters the devolution of the property.

4–013   This "possessory ownership" is well illustrated by the ordinary procedure for proving title to a purchaser of unregistered land.[53]

> "The standing proof that English law regards, and has always regarded, Possession as a substantive root of title, is the standing usage of English lawyers and landowners. With very few exceptions, there is only one way in which an apparent owner of English land who is minded to deal with it can show his right so to do; and that way is to show that he and those

---

[48] *Roe d. Haldane v Harvey* (1769) 4 Burr. 2484 (the defendant, being in possession, proved that the plaintiff Haldane had conveyed the land to another person, and so had no title); *Doe d. Wawn v Horn* (1838) 3 M. & W. 333 (defendant in possession proved that plaintiff had demised the land, so the proper plaintiff was the tenant); *Culley v Doe d. Taylerson* (1840) 3 Per. & D. 539 at 552, 557 (defendant in possession proved that plaintiff's claim as heir to A was bad because A had devised the land to B); cf. *Doe d. Lloyd v Passingham* (1827) 6 B. & C. 305 (defendant in possession proved that legal estate was outstanding in a trustee). The many cases in which actions of ejectment failed for want of the immediate legal title are in fact cases of *jus tertii* properly pleaded. For modern examples see above, para.4–006, fn.26, and *Wirral BC v Smith* (1982) 43 P. & CR. 312.

[49] "Possession gives the defendant a right against every man who cannot show a good title": *Roe d. Haldane v Harvey* (1769) 4 Burr. 2484 at 2487, per Lord Mansfield C.J. See [1956] C.L.J. 177 (H.W.R.W.). For the same principle applied to personalty (a motor car), see *Wilson v Lombank Ltd* [1963] 1 W.L.R. 1294.

[50] See below, para.17–125.

[51] *Lord Fitzhardinge v Purcell* [19081 2 Ch. 139 at 145.

[52] For the Crown's seignorial rights, see above, para.2–001.

[53] See below, paras 15–074 et seq.

through whom he claims have possessed the land for a time sufficient to exclude any reasonable probability of a superior adverse claim."[54]

It is by limitation that any such superior claim will have been excluded. Adverse possession and limitation together are therefore the foundations of a good title. If this is understood, the nature of a title acquired by limitation becomes plain. Where title is unregistered there is no "parliamentary conveyance"[55] from the one party to the other; one title is extinguished altogether and a new one arises. The new title is, however, subject to the rights of third parties, whether legal or equitable,[56] unless they too have been barred by limitation.[57]

Part 2

ACTIONS FOR THE RECOVERY OF LAND

The substantive law of real property has been deeply marked by the remedies 4–014 which the law has provided, at various periods of history, for the recovery of land. This part gives short account of the way in which these remedies have influenced the character of real property law and the concept of title. The law developed on the principle *ubi remedium, ibi jus*: rights result from remedies. The story begins with the ancient real actions and ends with modern reforms.

Section 1. The Real Actions

1. The writ of right. The real actions began as remedies to enforce feudal 4–015 customs.[58] Originally feudal lords were sovereign in their own courts baron. If they chose to depart from the customs of their courts, e.g. as to inheritance of a tenant's fee, no redress was available to the disappointed claimant. The

---

[54] Pollock and Wright, *Possession*, pp. 94–5. Even under the system of registration of title (below, Ch.7) titles are still relative, though to a lesser extent. If A claims that B has been registered by mistake because A has a better title to the land, A can apply to have the register altered: see below, para.7–133. However, even if A proves that B was registered by mistake, the register may not be altered, and A may be left to his claim for indemnity against the Land Registry.

[55] This expression attained some currency (see *Scott v Nixon* (1843) 3 Dr. & War. 388 at 407; *Doe d. Jukes v Sumner* (1845) 14 M. & W. 39 at 42; and see *Dawkins v Lord Penrhvn* (1877) 6 Ch D 318 at 323), but it is now established that it is erroneous: see *Tichborne v Weir* (1892) 67 L.T. 735; *Re Atkinson & Horsell's Contract* [1912] 2 Ch. 1 at 9. Thus the possessor is not entitled to any right that depends on the making of a grant, e.g. a way of necessity: *Wilkes v Greenway* (1890) 6 T.L.R. 449. For such easements, see below, para.28–013.

[56] Below, paras 5–013 and 35–055.

[57] Below, paras 35–024, 35–025.

[58] For an authoritative modern treatment of these actions, see S. F. C. Milsom, *Historical Foundations of the Common Law*, Ch.6. For more detail, see S. F. C. Milsom, *The Legal Framework of English Feudalism* (Cambridge University Press).

first attempt by the Crown to meet this grievance was by the writ of right. This commanded the lord to "do full right" to the claimant, with the threat that if he did not, the sheriff would.[59] As the lord was often unable to grant the land to the claimant, because he had accepted another's homage for it,[60] the action was transferred to the county court,[61] where it was originally tried by battle. In or about 1179, Henry II introduced a new procedure, the Grand Assize, by which the defendant could claim trial before royal justices.[62] Various forms of the writ were in time adapted to different cases, including claims to incorporeal hereditaments. Procedure was extremely cumbersome, with numerous pretexts for making essoins (excuses for non-appearance and other defaults) and other dilatory pleas.

The writ of right developed at a time when land was heritable but not freely alienable. The only effective method of alienating land in the 12th century was by subinfeudation, rather than, as now, by substitution.[63]

4–016   **2. The possessory assizes.** In origin, the four possessory assizes, like the writ of right, were intended to provide speedy remedies against lords who departed from the customs of their feudal courts. They were tried by royal justices with a jury. Two of the assizes must be mentioned.[64] The first is the assize of *mort d'ancestor*,[65] which in origin was probably intended to prevent feudal lords from taking a deceased tenant's land into their own hands and then excluding the heir until he agreed to pay an exorbitant relief.[66] It enabled the heir to recover the land from the lord swiftly and leave the appropriate relief to subsequent agreement. The other is *novel disseisin*. The wording of the writ suggests that it originally provided a means by which a tenant could recover his land when it had been taken from him by his feudal lord without proper observance of his feudal customs, as for example in a dispute (real or contrived) about services due from the tenant.[67]

In time, particularly after the statute *Quia Emptores* 1290 had prohibited alienation by subinfeudation,[68] these assizes came to be used against third

---

[59] For the form of writ see *Glanvill* (ed. G. D. G. Hall), I, 6 (p. 5); J. H. Baker, *An Introduction to English Legal History* (4th ed), p.539. The writ emerged in the mid-twelfth century.

[60] The person who had given homage was the notional defendant to the action, and was known as "the tenant". The real defendant was, however, often the lord, because if the claimant succeeded, the lord could be compelled to find other land for the ousted tenant (*escambium*). By taking his homage the lord undertook to protect the tenant in his holding.

[61] By a process called "*tolt*".

[62] Either in eyre or on special commission. The action was transferred from the county court by writ of *pone*.

[63] Above, para.2–014.

[64] The others were *darrein presentment*, which was to resolve disputes as to the right to present to a living, and *utrum*, which was to determine whether land had been given in free alms to the church, without feudal service to the lord.

[65] Introduced by the Assize of Northampton 1176, c.4. For specimen writs, see *Glanvill*, XIII, 3 (p. 150); J. H. Baker, *An Introduction to English Legal History*, p.543.

[66] S. F. C. Milsom, *Historical Foundations of the Common Law*, p.135. For reliefs, see above, para.2–009.

[67] S. F. C. Milsom, *Historical Foundations of the Common Law*, p.140. For specimen writs, see *Glanvill*, XIII, 33 (p.167); J. H. Baker, *An Introduction to English Legal History*, p.545.

[68] Above, para.2–015.

parties who had wrongly taken the land than against lords who had abused their feudal rights. The actions therefore came to protect possession, whether rightful or wrongful.

Novel disseisin, as its name implies, was intended at first to be a speedy remedy. But no new limitation date was prescribed after the Statute of Westminster I of 1275 appointed the year 1242, at the same time as it appointed the year 1189 for the writ of right and other purposes.[69] Thus the action lost its "novel" aspect and became merely one form of proprietary action for trying title.[70]

3. Writs of entry. The writs of entry were developed in the 13th century as   **4–017**
a means by which lords could recover land from tenants "who had been admitted under earlier grants which were either invalid or no longer availed them".[71] These writs eventually covered many cases for which the older actions were not adapted.[72] Their common feature was that the plaintiff claiming the land averred that the defendant or his predecessor in title "had no entry thereto save through some wrongful act or event. This put in issue that act or event alone, and not the whole title. The Statute of Marlbridge 1267 allowed writs of entry "in the post", in which the defendant's wrongful title, if complicated, did not have to be pleaded precisely, but it was enough to claim that he came in after (post) the wrongful act or event.[73] This rounded off the system of the real actions, which would then meet any case. But they became a "hopeless tangle"[74] and better remedies were therefore badly needed. Indeed, for a while, freeholders resorted to the action of trespass when seeking to recover land, even though it was not a real action but gave only a remedy in damages.[75]

All the real actions were in essence demands for seisin, and could not therefore be used by leaseholders or copyholders.[76]

Section 2. The Action of Ejectment

1. Origin. The action of ejectment[77] was originally invented for the protec-   **4–018**
tion of leaseholders, but was later extended to copyholders also.[78] Since it was

---

[69] D. W. Sutherland, *The Assize of Novel Disseisin* (1973), p.139.

[70] D. W. Sutherland, *The Assize of Novel Disseisin*, at pp.153 et seq.; S. F. C. Milsom, *Historical Foundations of the Common Law*, p.157.

[71] J. H. Baker, *An Introduction to English Legal History*, p.234. For a specimen writ, see ibid., p.541.

[72] For some of the advantages enjoyed by such writs over the writ of right, see D. W. Sutherland, *The Assize of Novel Disseisin*, p.82.

[73] Maitland, *Forms of Action*, p.42.

[74] Maitland, *Forms of Action*, p.43.

[75] See D. W. Sutherland, *The Assize of Novel Disseisin*, Ch.V.

[76] See above, para.3–018; S. F. C. Milsom, *Historical Foundations of the Common Law*, Ch.7; A. W. B. Simpson, *A History of the Land Law* (2nd ed), pp. 71–77; Ch.7.

[77] For the action of ejectment, see A. W. B. Simpson, *A History of the Land Law*, Ch.7; Bl. Comm. iii, p.200, and appendix No. II.

[78] *Melwich v Luter* (1588) 4 Co.Rep. 26a; H.E.L. iii, p.209; vii, p.9.

a species of the action of trespass (its proper title was "trespass in ejectment"), it belonged to a group of actions which were of later invention than
the real actions, and were free from most of their archaisms. It was therefore
pressed into service by freeholders as well, at a period when the real actions
had become intolerable. This was done with the aid of John Doe and Richard
Roe and some elaborate legal fictions.

4–019   **2. Recovery of leaseholds.** As leases grew in popularity, it became necessary to protect tenants by some better remedy than a mere action of trespass
for damages. The action *Quaere ejecit infra terminum*, introduced about 1235,
did allow a tenant to recover his land specifically, but it was held to be
confined to actions against the lessor and his successors.[79] It was not until the
second half of the 15th century that the common law courts, fearing competition from the specific remedies available in the Chancery, abandoned their
scruples and allowed a leaseholder to recover his land specifically from any
wrongful claimant.[80] By awarding a writ of possession to a leaseholder, and
by strengthening the remedy in other ways, a personal action of trespass was
"licked into the form of a real action".[81] The result was the action of trespass
in ejectment,[82] or, for short, "ejectment". Once the leaseholder was able to
recover his land from all comers, it could no longer be denied that he had an
estate in the land (a right in rem), or that he held it in tenure.

4–020   **3. Procedure.** By 1600, a century after its invention, ejectment was in
common use by freeholders; and by about 1650 its form for this purpose had
been perfected.[83] A full description need not be given, but the essence of the
action was that the nominal plaintiff was John Doe, asserting that he was
tenant of the true plaintiff and that he (Doe) had entered upon the land and had
thence been ejected by Richard Roe. In the perfected form of the action Doe
and Roe were imaginary characters, Roe being known as "the casual ejector".
The first real step in the proceedings was that the plaintiff's solicitor sent to
the defendant the declaration (or statement of claim) in Doe's action against
Roe, under cover of a letter advising the defendant to apply for leave to defend
the action in Roe's place and ending "otherwise I shall suffer judgment to be
entered against me and you will be turned out of possession. Your loving
friend, Richard Roe".[84] It was then essential for the true defendant to appear
as such, but the court would allow him to do so only if he confessed the lease,
entry and ouster: that is to say, if he undertook not to dispute any of the

---

[79] H.E.L. iii, p.214; A. W. B. Simpson, *A History of the Land Law*, p.74.
[80] Bl.Comm. iii, p.200; H.E.L. vii, p.8, n.7. Specific restitution in ejectment was finally allowed
in 1499, after a period of uncertainty: H.E.L. iii, p.216; A. W. B. Simpson, *A History of the Land
Law*, p. 144.
[81] *Goodtitle v Tombs* (1770) 3 Wils. KB. 118 at 120 per Wilmot C.J. For details see H.E.L. vii,
p.13.
[82] Its Latin title was a trespass *de ejectione firmae*.
[83] For details, see H.E.L. vii, p.10.
[84] The common forms of these documents are printed in Sutton, *Personal Actions at Common
Law* (London: Butterworth & Co, 1929), pp.53, 54, and in Bl.Comm. iii, appendix, No. II.

fictitious allegations. Thus, when the action came to trial, the only question left was whether Doe had a good claim to the land, and this was merely the question whether the plaintiff, as Doe's lessor, had a better title than the defendant. The action was then entitled Doe d. A v B, meaning Doe on the demise of A v B.[85]

4. Limitations. This piece of make-believe rapidly put the real actions out   **4–021**
of business. But it did not supplant them completely. In the first place, ejectment was subject to a 20-year period of limitation; but longer periods were appointed for the real actions, so that after 20 years a plaintiff might find that only a real action was open to him.[86] Second, ejectment was also barred if the plaintiff had lost his right of entry upon the land, for then he had no title to grant an effective lease in possession to Doe; and there were certain occasions when, for technical reasons derived from the medieval law, a right of entry was "tolled" (taken away), and all that remained was a right of action.[87] In those cases the plaintiff would be driven to fall back on the real actions, for although he had a title, he could not sue in ejectment. These cases, like novel disseisin in its early days, provide examples of a wrongful possessor being protected against the true owner. Thirdly, ejectment would not lie for incorporeal hereditaments such as advowsons, where the fictions of lease, entry and ouster broke down.[88]

5. Titles relative. The theory that the action of ejectment introduced a new   **4–022**
concept of "ownership" into English law, in the sense that a plaintiff had to prove a title that was absolutely good rather than one that was relatively better than the defendant's, was a fallacy. The issue in ejectment was a purely relative one, and the relativity of all titles, which all depend in the last resort upon possession, has already been explained.[89] Far from requiring a plaintiff to prove absolute ownership, the action of ejectment preserved the conception of relative titles which had been part of English law from the time of the writ of right, while at the same time avoiding the difficulties which surrounded the real actions. What it did was to shift the basis of title from the feudal concept of seisin to the modern concept of adverse possession.

Section 3. Statutory Reforms

1. Abolition of real actions. It has already been explained that the real   **4–023**
actions were abolished by the Real Property Limitation Act 1833.[90] The only

---

[85] The plaintiff could, however, use any names he pleased, and sometimes the casual ejector was named as the defendant; thus cases were tendentiously entitled *Fairclaim d. Fowler v Shamtitle* (1762) 3 Burr. 1290 and *Goodtitle d. Pye v Badtitle* (1800) 8 T.R. 638.
[86] H.E.L. vii, pp.20, 22.
[87] H.E.L. vii, pp.20, 22; Lightwood, *Possession of Land*, p.44; Co.Litt. pp.237a, 325a. The old law was very complex.
[88] H.E.L. vii, p.21.
[89] Above, para.4–008.
[90] RLPA 1833 s.36, naming the various actions. See above, para.4–007.

exceptions were the old actions for dower and advowsons, for which there were no satisfactory substitutes.[91] At the same time the old rules about "tolling" rights of entry were abolished.[92] Thus the action of ejectment was left without competitors. The action itself underwent no reform, and Doe and Roe still had to play their old parts in actions by freeholders.

4–024   **2. Abolition of forms of action.** Finally the Common Law Procedure Act 1852 abolished the forms of action in general and ejectment in particular.[93] Thereafter a plaintiff merely had to institute his action for the recovery of land by pleading his claim to it in ordinary language. But this did not bring about any change in the substantive law: an action for the recovery of land would meet with the same success or failure as an action of ejectment would have done before the Act. Similarly, when new rules of court were introduced by the Judicature Acts 1873–1875,[94] the new procedure made no change in the substantive law relating to titles. But the amalgamation of legal and equitable jurisdiction[95] meant that the same form of proceedings could be used to assert either a legal or an equitable title,[96] thus consummating a reform which Lord Mansfield had unsuccessfully attempted in the 18th century, when the action of ejectment was confined to claims at law.[97]

3. Modern law

4–025   *(a) Title to land.* The law of title to land remains as it was in the latter days of the action of ejectment. An action for recovery of land is still in essence an action of trespass. However, as is explained below, the scope of the action has recently been widened.

(b) Remedies

4–026   (1) SUMMARY POSSESSION PROCEEDINGS. Under Part 55 of the Civil Procedure Rules[98] there are two swift remedies against a person who occupies land without the consent of a person who has a right to possession of them. It has been held that these remedies are available not only to an estate owner (whether or not he is in possession of the land), but also to a licensee, whether he is in possession or merely has a contractual right to possession, even

---

[91] RPLA 1833 s.36. These exceptions were abolished by the Common Law Procedure Act 1860 ss.26, 27; this was the final disappearance of real actions.

[92] RPLA 1833 s.39.

[93] CLPA 1852 ss.168—221.

[94] Judicature Act 1873, Sched. There is now one code of procedure governing both the High Court and the county court: see the Civil Procedure Rules, made pursuant to the Civil Procedure Act 1997 s.1.

[95] Above, para.5–017.

[96] See *General Finance Mortgage and Discount Co v Liberator Permanent Benefit Building Society* (1878) 10 Ch D 15 at 24; *Antrim County Land Building and Investment Co Ltd v Steward* [1904] 2 I.R. 357; cf. below, para.25–024.

[97] H.E.L. vii, p.19, 23. See, e.g. *Doe d. Lloyd v Passingham* (1827) 6 B. & C. 305; *Doe d. Butler v Lard Kensington* (1846) 8 Q.B. 429 at 449; *Cole on Ejectment*, pp.66, 287.

[98] Replacing RSC Ord.113 and CCR Ord.24.

though he could not have brought ejectment under the old law.[99] A mere contractual right of access is not, however, sufficient.[100] The result is striking. Not only will possession be protected against all save those who have a better right to possess the land, but the mere right to possess will also be, even where the person having that right has no estate in or title to the land.[101] This extension of the remedy demonstrates the courts' unwillingness to be fettered "by the arcane and archaic rules relating to ejectment", and it has been suggested that the law "should develop and adapt to accommodate a claim by anyone entitled to use and control, effectively amounting to possession of the land in question".[102] The two swift remedies are as follows.

First, the claimant may issue a claim form seeking possession even if he cannot discover the names of the squatters.[103] The court may make an order for possession a specified number of clear days[104] after it has been served.[105] On proof of the case, the court must make the order.[106] There is no power to suspend its operation[107] (and this principle is unaffected by the Human Rights Act 1998[108]), though the court has a discretion to grant a stay of execution if the defendant seeks to appeal.[109] This procedure is not available against a tenant holding over after the determination of his tenancy,[110] though the position of an unlawful subtenant is unclear.[111] It may however be used to eject a licensee whose licence has expired.[112] An order for possession may be

4–027

---

[99] *Manchester Airport Plc v Dutton* [2000] Q.B. 133 (licensees who had been granted the right to occupy a wood to carry out work preparatory to the extension of an airport runway could bring proceedings against environmental protesters who had set up camps in the wood); *Alamo Housing Co-operative Ltd v Meredith* [2003] EWCA 495; [2004] L.G.R. 81 (former tenant in possession with a continuing obligation to landlord to obtain vacant possession from the former subtenants could take possession proceedings against the subtenants). cf. *Hill v Tupper* (1863) 2 H. & C. 121 at 127, 128 (licensee of canal had no right of action against third parties for infringement of his rights under the licence, and could only sue with the consent and in the name of the canal company, below, para.27–010).

[100] *Countryside Residential (North Thames) Ltd v Tugwell* (2000) 81 P & CR 10.

[101] cf. above, para.4–004.

[102] *Mayor of London v Hall* [2010] EWCA Civ 817 at [27]; [2011] 1 W.L.R. 504 at 516, per Lord Neuberger M.R.

[103] See CPR rr.55.3(4), 55.6.

[104] Five for residential property and two for other land: CPR r.55.5.

[105] Possession cases should normally be commenced in the county court unless there is a reason for bringing it in the High Court: CPR r.55.2.

[106] At the date set for the hearing, the court will either decide the claim (if there is no defence) or give case management directions for its further conduct: CPR r.55.8.

[107] *McPhail v Persons, Names Unknown* [1973] Ch. 447; *Swordheath Properties Ltd v Floydd* [1978] 1 W.L.R. 550. The power to postpone the giving up of possession in cases of exceptional hardship in HA 1980 s.89 (below, paras 22–098; 22–170), does not apply to trespassers: see *Boyland & Son Ltd v Rand* [2006] EWCA Civ 1860; [2007] H.L.R.369.

[108] *Kay v Lambeth LBC* [2006] UKHL 10 at [110], [174], [192], [206]; [2006] 2 A.C. 465 at 517, 534, 537, 541 (discussing ECHR, Art.8). But see below, para.22–076.

[109] *Bibby v Partap* [1996] 1 W.L.R. 931 (decided on provisions in Trinidad and Tobago that were the same as then applied in England and Wales); *Admiral Taverns (Cygnet) Ltd v Daniel* [2009] EWCA Civ 1501; [2009] 1 W.L.R. 2192.

[110] CPR r.55.5.

[111] Under RSC O113, the procedure was available against such a subtenant: see *Moore Properties (Ilford) Ltd v McKeon* [1976] 1 W.L.R. 1278. However, the definition of "a possession claim against trespassers" in CPR r.55.1((b), excludes a claim against a subtenant.

[112] *Greater London Council v Jenkins* [1975] 1 W.L.R. 155.

obtained which authorises the enforcement officer to evict all persons found on the premises, whether bound by the judgment or not.[113] The order may extend to the whole of the premises, even though only part of them had been wrongfully occupied.[114] However, the court will not make an order in relation to other premises on which there has not yet been any trespass, though it may grant a *quia timet* injunction to prevent any threatened trespass on such other land.[115]

4–028   The second remedy available against squatters is an interim possession order.[116] This is a particularly expeditious form of summary proceedings that is enforced by criminal sanctions.[117] A squatter who fails to leave within 24 hours of the order, or who re-enters as a trespasser within a year thereafter, commits a criminal offence.[118]

4–029   (2) MESNE PROFITS. As against a trespasser, the owner, or a person in possession or having a contractual[119] or statutory[120] right to possession, may claim damages for the trespass. In making such a claim for "mesne profits", as it is traditionally called,[121] the owner may elect to seek either restitution of the benefit which the defendant has received or damages for the loss he has suffered.[122]

> (i) Usually the owner will claim compensation for having been deprived of the use and occupation of the land. This is assessed according to the current open market value of the land, normally

---

[113] *R. v Wandsworth County Court, Ex p. Wandsworth LBC* [1975] 1 W.L.R. 1314; *Wiltshire County Council v Frazer* (1983) 47 P. & CR. 69; above, para.4–007. See too *Secretary of State for the Environment, Food v Rural Affairs v Meier* [2009] UKSC 11 at [6], [36], [76]; [2009] 1 W.L.R. 2780 at 2784, 2791, 2801.

[114] *University of Essex v Djemal* [1980] 1 W.L.R. 1301 (sit-in students); *Wiltshire County Council v Frazer* (1983) 47 P. & CR. 69 ("new age travellers" who parked their caravans on, but without obstructing, an ancient highway); *Secretary of State for the Environment, Food v Rural Affairs v Meier* [2009] UKSC 11 at [7], [24], [97]; [2009] 1 W.L.R. 2780 at 2784, 2788, 2807. Lord Neuberger M.R. left open the correctness of the *Djemal* case: see [2009] UKSC 11 at [71]; [2009] 1 W.L.R. 2780 at 2800.

[115] *Secretary of State for the Environment, Food v Rural Affairs v Meier* [2009] UKSC 11; [2009] 1 W.L.R. 2780; overruling *Ministry of Agriculture, Fisheries and Food v Heyman* (1989) 59 P. & CR. 48 and *Secretary of State for the Environment, Food and Rural Affairs v Drury* [2004] 1 W.L.R. 1906.

[116] This order was first introduced in 1995, and the provisions are now found in CPR rr.55.20—55.28. It only lies against a person who has throughout been a trespasser and not against one who holds over after lawful occupation. Furthermore, the claimant must have had an immediate right to possession at the time of the claim and throughout the period of unlawful possession of which he complains.

[117] See Criminal Justice and Public Order Act 1994 ss.75, 76.

[118] See Criminal Justice and Public Order Act 1994 s.76(2)–(4).

[119] See *Manchester Airport Plc v Dutton* [2000] Q.B. 133; above, para.4–026.

[120] See *Mayor of London v Hall* [2011] EWCA Civ 817; [2011] 1 W.L.R. 504.

[121] See *Goodtitle v Tombs* (1770) 3 Wils. KB. 118, per Wilmot C.J.

[122] *Ministry of Defence v Ashman* (1993) 66 P. & CR. 195; *Ministry of Defence v Thompson* [1993] 2 E.G.L.R. 107; *Dean and Chapter of Canterbury Cathedral v Whitbread Plc* (1995) 72 P. & CR. 9 at 16. The two forms of claim are mutually exclusive: *Ministry of Defence v Ashman*, above, at 201. For fuller consideration of the issues raised by these cases: see, e.g. (1994) 110 L.Q.R. 420 (E. Cooke); (1996) 112 L.Q.R. 39 (P. Watts).

the ordinary letting value.[123] The landowner is entitled to this sum "whether or not he can show that he would have let the property to anybody else, and whether or not he would have used the property himself".[124] Although this claim is distinct from the claim for compensation for use and occupation which lies where there is some kind of tenancy between the parties, as explained later,[125] there may be no practical distinction between the two.[126]

(ii) A landowner may seek restitution for the benefit received by the defendant where he cannot claim the ordinary letting value, because, e.g. the property is not available for letting on the open market.[127]

The court may make an interim award to the owner in respect of:

(i) mesne profits;

(ii) use and occupation (where a tenant holds over)[128]; or

(iii) rent

where it is certain that he will be entitled under one or other of these heads at the end of the proceedings.[129]

In addition to mesne profits, the landowner may, in the usual way, recover any other losses that he has suffered in consequence of the trespass. For example, where the trespasser has erected a wall on the land or laid tarmac on a path over it, the landowner can claim the cost of the removal of the wall or tarmac.[130]

---

[123] *Clifton Securities Ltd v Huntley* [1948] 2 All E.R. 283; *Swordheath Properties Ltd v Tabet* [1979] 1 W.L.R. 285; *Lewisham LBC v Masterson* (1999) 80 P. & C.R. 117. For a discussion of this so-called "user principle" in assessing damages, see *Stoke-on-Trent City Council v W & J. Wass Ltd* [1988] 1 W.L.R. 1406. The sum may be less than the open market value, as where the defendant remained on the premises involuntarily and had previously paid a rent that was less than the open market rent: see *Ministry of Defence v Ashman* (1993) 66 P. & CR. 195.

[124] *Inverugie Investments Ltd v Hackett* [1995] 1 W.L.R. 713 at 717, per Lord Lloyd (tenant's claim for mesne profits against his trespassing landlord in respect of loss-making hotel).

[125] Below, para.17–105.

[126] *Dean and Chapter of Canterbury Cathedral v Whitbread Plc* (1995) 72 P. & CR. 9 at 16.

[127] As in *Ministry of Defence v Ashman* (1993) 66 P. & CR. 195; *Ministry of Defence v Thompson* [1993] 2 E.G.L.R. 107 (property available only to members of the armed services).

[128] Below, para.17–105.

[129] CPR Pt 25, r. 7(d). See *Old Grovebury Manor Farm Ltd v W Seymour Plant Sales & Hire Ltd* [1979] 1 W.L.R. 263.

[130] See *Field Common Ltd v Elmbridge BC* [2008] EWHC 2079 (Ch) at [29]; [2009] 1 P. & C.R. 1 at 9.

CHAPTER 5

LAW AND EQUITY

Part 1

GENERAL PRINCIPLES

5–001   A fundamental distinction in the law of real property is that between legal and equitable interests in land. This was a product of the history of the courts. The judges in the courts of common law were concerned with legal interests, the Chancellor in his Court of Chancery with equitable interests. Although these rival jurisdictions were amalgamated in 1873, the dual system which they produced remains firmly embedded in the law. The importance of the distinction has been much reduced by the 1925 and subsequent legislation, particularly in relation to the system of registered title.[1]

Section 1. The Historical Basis of Equity

1. Common law: the writ system

5–002   *(a) The writs.* In order to commence an action in any of the common law courts (King's Bench, Common Pleas and Exchequer) normally a writ had first to be issued under the seal of the Chancellor, the keeper of the Great Seal. Each different kind of action had its own writ, often with its own special procedure.[2] If an heir was claiming land from a dispossessor after his father's death, the action had to be started by a writ of *mort d'ancestor*; if he was the grandfather of the heir, a writ of *aiel* had to be used, and if he was the great-grandfather, a writ of *besaiel*.[3] No action could succeed unless the correct writ was chosen.[4] There was, therefore, a strictly *formulary* legal system: a plaintiff would succeed only if some writ provided a formula to fit his case.

---

[1] Registered title is now governed by LRA 2002: see below, Ch.7.
[2] Maitland, *Forms of Action,* p.2; J. H. Baker, *An Introduction to English Legal History,* p.53. For a discussion of actions for the recovery of land, see above paras 4.014 and following.
[3] Maitland, *Forms of Action,* p.31.
[4] Maitland, *Forms of Action,* p.4; H.E.L. ix, p.245.

England was no exception to the rule that in early law justice was dominated by procedure.[5]

(b) New writs. At first new writs were invented with comparative freedom   **5–003** for cases not covered by existing writs, though some were disallowed by the courts.[6] They were severely restricted by the Provisions of Oxford 1258, in which the Chancellor swore that he would seal no new form of writ without the command of the King and his Council.[7] But the Statute of Westminster II, 1285, provided in the famous Chapter 24, *In Consimili Casu,* that the clerks in Chancery should have a limited power to invent new writs. If there already existed one writ, and in a like case (*in consimili casu*), falling under like law and requiring like remedy, there was none, the clerks in Chancery might make a suitable writ, or else refer the matter to the next Parliament. The result, nevertheless, was to stunt the growth of the writ system,[8] and to leave many cases without remedy.

2. Petitions to the King and Chancellor. Suitors therefore turned to the   **5–004** King, as the fountain of justice. Their petitions were heard by the King's Council, of which the Chancellor was an important member.[9] After the reign of Edward III petitions were often addressed to the Chancellor alone, and in this way he acquired a regular and expanding judicial business. At first the decisions upon the petitions were made either in the name of the King's Council or else with the advice of the serjeants and judges. During the course of the 15th century the Chancellor began to make decrees on his own authority, and his decrees thereafter became frequent.[10]

3. The Court of Chancery

(a) The Chancellor. In this way there gradually came into existence a Court   **5–005** of Chancery in which the Chancellor, acting independently of the King's Council, sat as a judge administering a system of justice called equity.[11]

---

[5] Maine, *Early Law and Custom,* p.389; Maitland, *Forms of Action,* pp.1, 6.

[6] Maitland, *Forms of Action,* 41.

[7] Maitland, *Forms of Action,* pp.41, 46, 51; H.E.L. i, p.398.

[8] There was a widespread belief from the sixteenth century onwards that this statute was the origin of the action on the case: [1971] C.L.J. 213 at 217 (J.H. Baker). In fact very few new writs were created under the statute and all were concerned with real property: (1931) 31 Columbia L.R. 778 (T.F.T. Plucknett). It is now known that the action on the case derived from certain types of trespass action: S.F.C. Milsom, *Historical Foundations of the Common Law,* Ch.11.

[9] H.E.L. i, p.400.

[10] See (1969) 42 *Bulletin of the Institute of Historical Research* 129; (1970) 86 L.Q.R. 84 (M.E. Avery). For early reports of decisions by the Chancellor, see *Cardinal Beaufort's Case* (1453), J.H. Baker and S.F.C. Milsom, *Sources of English Legal History,* p.95; *Anon.* (1467), J.H. Baker and S.F.C. Milsom, *Sources of English Legal History,* p.98.

[11] The Chancery was not the only court which exercised an equity jurisdiction. Not only were there a number of local conciliar courts with an equity jurisdiction during the Tudor and Stuart period (see J.H. Baker, *An Introduction to English Legal History,* p.121), but the Court of Exchequer had an equity side until 1842 (see W.H. Bryson. *The Equity Side of Exchequer* (1975)); and in the Law Journal Reports there was a separate series of Exchequer Equity reports. cf. *Billson v Residential Apartments Ltd* [1992] 1 A.C. 494 at 512, where Browne-Wilkinson V.C. said that it had not been explained "how, in 1816, the Court of Exchequer came to be ruling upon equitable doctrines".

Although prior to the appointment of Sir Thomas More in 1529 the Chancellor had sometimes been a layman, he was usually a senior clergyman. After the 1550s, however, a lawyer was normally appointed.[12] Equity, which had varied with the ideas of each Chancellor, began with Lord Ellesmere (1596–1617) to develop into a code of principles, and the work of Lord Nottingham (1673–1682) in systematising the rules earned him the title of the Father of Equity.[13] When Lord Eldon retired in 1827 the rules of equity were as well settled as those of the common law; a *"rigor aequitatis"* had developed, and he could safely say

> "nothing would inflict on me greater pain, in quitting this place, than the recollection that I had done anything to justify the reproach that the equity of this court varies like the Chancellor's foot".[14]

But equity, although it followed the inevitable course towards fixity and dogma, remained in general a more modern and flexible system than the common law. Originally it provided the means, needed in every legal system, of adapting general rules to particular cases, and this character was never entirely lost.

5–006 (b) *A court of conscience.* In the course of time various subsidiary officials were appointed to assist the Chancellor, a system of appeals grew up, and finally in 1875 the Chancery system was merged with the common law courts to form the present Supreme Court of Judicature.[15] In short, the practice of petitioning the King for justice in exceptional cases gradually opened the way to a supplementary system of law administered regularly by a court, but by a court quite different and separate from the courts of common law. The latter decided cases according to the strict common law rules, and with much fondness for technicality. Chancery, on the other hand, deliberately mitigated the rigour of the common law, tempering its rules to the needs of particular cases on principles which seemed just and equitable to generations of Chancellors, and technical pleas were usually unsuccessful. The common law courts were mainly concerned with enforcing the strict rights of the parties regardless of their merits, whereas Chancery was a court of conscience where remedies would be withheld from a party guilty of sharp practice or any kind of unconscionable conduct.

5–007 (c) *Conflict.* The decrees of the Chancellor would often, therefore, conflict with judgments obtained at common law. A party who had lost his case because of some trickery or accident, for example, could obtain in Chancery

---

[12] J. H. Baker, *An Introduction to English Legal History*, 108.

[13] *Kemp v Kemp* (1801) 5 Ves. 849 at 858.

[14] *Gee v Pritchard* (1818) 2 Swans. 402 at 414. Selden had complained (*Table Talk*, p.31b) that equity varied with the conscience of each Chancellor, and that this was as absurd as making the measurement known as a foot vary with each Chancellor's foot.

[15] Below, para.5–017. For the reorganisation of the Court of Chancery in the 19th century, see H.E.L. i, pp.442 et seq.

an injunction forbidding his opponent to execute the common law judgment. This power to interrupt the common law process was used so often that this type of injunction was called a "common injunction". The Chancellor's jurisdiction to issue it was clearly established after the decision of James I in the celebrated dispute between Coke C.J. and Lord Ellesmere L.C.[16]

(d) Equity acts in personam. A peculiarity of equity was that it acted in **5–008** personam, *"on the person"*. The Chancellor's ultimate sanction was to imprison for contempt anyone who disobeyed his decree. He could not, as could the common law courts, award damages enforceable by a sheriff's execution against the defendant's property. But he could decree that the defendant should pay a sum of money, and imprison him if he would not, or that he should do or abstain from doing something on pain of imprisonment for disobedience.[17]

Section 2. The Nature of Equitable Rights

1. Legal and equitable ownership. The essential difference between legal **5–009** and equitable rights is best understood by comparing absolute ownership with trusts. Trusts were not enforceable at common law but only by the Chancellor.[18] If land was conveyed to A in fee simple upon trust for B in fee simple, the common law courts regarded A as absolute owner and would not recognise any rights in B. But the Chancellor would enforce trusts, as matters of conscience, and compel A to hold the land on B's behalf and to allow B to enjoy it. In such a case A is the "legal owner", B is the "equitable owner". The land is vested in A, but since he is trustee of it he is not the beneficial owner: he has only the "bare legal estate", and the beneficial interest belongs to B.

Legal ownership confers rights in rem, rights of property in the land itself, which can be enforced against anyone. Equitable ownership conferred at first only a right in personam, a right to compel the trustee personally to perform his trust. But what should happen if the trustee died or disposed of the land? Trusts would have been hopelessly insecure if means had not been found to protect them from such events.

2. Extent of enforcement. The Chancellors solved this problem by extend- **5–010** ing the categories of persons upon whom performance of the trust would be enjoined. As case followed case the extensions became very wide. In 1465 it was laid down that a trust would be enforced against anyone who took a

---

[16] It often said that the dispute was resolved in *Earl of Oxford's Case* (1615) 1 Ch.Rep. 1, but this was not in fact the case: see (1969) 4 *Irish Jurist,* 368 (J. H. Baker). For the legal background to the dispute, see (1976) 20 *American Journal of Legal History* 192 (C. M. Gray).

[17] Maitland, *Equity,* p.9; H.E.L. i, p.458.

[18] For the history of trusts, see S. F. C. Milsom, *Historical Foundations of the Common Law,* p.233.

conveyance of the land *with notice of the trust.*[19] In 1483 the Chancellor said that he would enforce a trust against the trustee's heir.[20] In 1522 it was said that a trust would be enforced against anyone to whom the land had been conveyed as a gift.[21] It was later decided that others such as the executors and execution creditors of the trustees would be bound by the trust.[22]

5–011   **3. The purchaser without notice.** Two equitable principles explain these developments. First, a person who takes the land without giving value in exchange (such as an heir, executor or donee) must take it with all its burdens, equitable as well as legal: trusts bind volunteers. Secondly, even a person who has given value will be bound if before he obtained the land he knew of the trust: trusts bind all who take with notice. Both these principles are summed up in the cardinal maxim in which is expressed the true difference between legal and equitable rights:

> "Legal rights are good against all the world; equitable rights are good against all persons except a bona fide purchaser of a legal estate for value without notice, and those claiming under such a purchaser."[23]

Such as purchaser is often referred to, somewhat inappropriately, as "equity's darling".[24]

5–012   **4. Equitable interests.** This rule runs right though the law of property and it has been called "the polar star of equity".[25] Its detailed anatomy will be investigated later,[26] and it will be shown that it now has only a residual role in relation to dealings with unregistered land and none in relation to registered land. Its general meaning is that equitable rights advanced almost to the status of legal rights, but not quite. Equity always stopped short of enforcing a trust against a person who had bought the land from the legal owner in genuine ignorance of the existence of the trust. An equitable owner was therefore never quite in the impregnable position of a legal owner: he never had an absolutely indefeasible title. But the rules relating to notice and the system of conveyancing founded upon them protected equitable interests, as we shall see, for nearly all practical purposes, so that for the sake of their other advantages they were very much used. They became much more than rights in personam against trustees. They were a new species of property right, in

---

[19] YB. 5 Edw. 4, Mich. pl. 16.
[20] YB. 22 Edw. 4, Pasch. pl. 18.
[21] YB. 14 Hen. 8, Mich. pl. 5, to. 7. See *Chudleigh's Case* (1595) 1 Co.Rep. 113b at 122b.
[22] For accounts of these developments, see Maitland, *Equity,* p.112; and A. W. B. Simpson, *A History of the Land Law* (2nd ed), p.179.
[23] Maitland, *Equity,* pp.114, 115; cf. LPA 1925 s.2(5). Where the title to land is registered, the doctrine of notice has no role to play: see below, paras 6–046, 7–064, 8–006.
[24] Maitland, *Coll. Pp.,* iii, p.350. The appellation is inappropriate because if the defence of bona fide purchase is established, an encumbrance will have been defeated and the proper working of the system of conveyancing will have failed.
[25] *Stanhope v Earl Verney* (1761) 2 Eden 81 at 85, per Lord Henley L.C.
[26] See below, para.8–005.

reality rights in rem.[27] However, they were exceptional because of their peculiar infirmity: they would be lost if the legal title came to a bona fide purchaser without notice. They are therefore commonly called "equitable interests" *(sc.* in property); for "equity has modelled them into the shape and quality of real estates".[28]

5. Persons bound. The wide, proprietary character of equitable interests is shown by the present form of the fundamental rule. Instead of enumerating all the classes of persons bound in addition to trustees themselves, the rule lays down in the first place that equities bind *all* persons, and then gives a single but very important exception. This change of form marks an increase in scope. In 1905 the question arose whether a squatter (a person who had obtained title to land by long occupation uncontested by the previous owner[29]) was bound by an equitable interest created by the previous owner. A squatter was not among the classes of persons held liable in the line of cases which led to the rule. But he was not a purchaser for value; and the rule was so well established in its wide form that there was no difficulty in deciding that the squatter was bound.[30]

5–013

This special characteristic of equitable rights may be made clearer by an illustration. Suppose that in 1920[31] A was legal owner of Blackacre, holding it upon trust for B absolutely, and that Blackacre was subject to a legal lease to a tenant T, to a legal right of way owned by R, to a legal mortgage in favour of L and an equitable mortgage[32] in favour of E. If in 1921 A succeeded in selling Blackacre to a purchaser P who had no notice of any of the other interests, P's position would be as follows. On taking a conveyance of the legal estate he would still be bound by T's lease, R's right of way and L's legal mortgage, since these belong to the class of legal estates and interests which bind all comers. But B's trust and E's equitable mortgage would be defeated by the purchase of the legal estate without notice: B and E would lose their rights over the land, and their only remedies would be against A personally.

---

[27] Maitland laid stress on the personal nature of equitable rights, for historical and other good reasons: *Equity,* pp.23, 29, 107, 117. If by rights in rem is meant (as normally) rights enforceable against third parties generally, as opposed to rights in personam which are enforceable only against specified persons (e.g. contractual rights), then equitable rights to property are unquestionably rights in rem, though somewhat different from legal rights to property.

[28] *Burgess v Wheate* (1759) 1 Eden 177 at 249, per Henley L.K.

[29] See above, para.3–117; below, para.21–001.

[30] *Re Nisbet and Potts' Contract* [1906] 1 Ch. 386 (squatter held liable to restrictive covenant); followed in *Ashe v Hogan* [1920] 1 I.R. 159. Contrast *Bolling v Hobday* (1882) 31 W.R. 9 (squatter held free from trust for sale), and see 51 S.J. 141, 155 (T. C. Williams). LA 1980 s.18 (below, para.35–038) makes provision for land held upon trust which alters the principle in *Bolling v Hobday.* The difficulty which was felt was that a squatter acquired a new legal estate (below, para.35–055), and not the legal estate which was subject to the trust. But in reality it is the land, not the estate, which is affected.

[31] This date is chosen because, if created after 1925, the equitable mortgage would probably have been registrable: see below, para.26–025.

[32] A less formal type of mortgage: below, para.24–041.

Section 3. Equitable Remedies

5–014   **1. Discretionary nature of equitable remedies.** A further distinction between law and equity lay in the matter of remedies. In general, if a legal right was infringed, the person injured was entitled as of right to a legal remedy, either an order for the recovery of his land or damages. Thus, if A trespassed on X's land X had a legal right to sue him for damages and, on proving his case, he was entitled to damages as of right. If the trespass was trivial the damages might be nominal (e.g. £2) or contemptuous (e.g. 1p) and X might be ordered to pay the costs; but he had a right to judgment. A plaintiff seeking an equitable remedy, on the other hand, had no right to anything at all; equitable remedies were discretionary, and even if the plaintiff proved his case, equity might refuse to give him any assistance if, for example, his claim was trivial or it would be inconvenient or unconscionable to grant an equitable remedy. This discretion was exercised not arbitrarily according to the whim of the judge but "judicially", according to settled principles, so that a plaintiff could succeed in equity only if, in addition to a right having been infringed, there was no equitable principle which prevented him from being granted a remedy.[33]

5–015   **2. The remedies.** The principal remedies given by equity were specific performance (an order to a person to carry out his obligations) and injunction (an order to a person to refrain from doing some act in the future or, more rarely, to put right something already done). These remedies were evolved from the forms of decree acting in personam. Equity would also make orders for money payments either where no remedy existed at law, as, for example, where a trustee had dissipated trust moneys, or as an adjunct to equitable relief.[34] It would on occasions even award damages, although the limits of the jurisdiction were ill-defined.[35] The Court of Chancery was finally given a statutory power to award damages by the Chancery Amendment Act 1858. That Act provided that, in any case where the Chancery had power to entertain an application for an injunction or specific performance, it could award damages either in addition to or in substitution for such injunction or specific performance.[36] This did not alter the rule that equitable remedies were discretionary, nor did it enable the court to award damages in all cases. The Chancery could award damages only where it had jurisdiction to grant specific performance or an injunction, and in no other case.[37]

---

[33] Snell, *Equity,* paras 15–04—15–14.

[34] For example, specific performance with compensation: [1981] C.L.J. 48 (C.H.); and damages when relief was granted against a penalty of forfeiture: S. Goldstein, ed., *Equity and Contemporary Legal Developments* (C.H.), p. 829.

[35] See (1992) 108 L.Q.R. 652 (P. McDermott).

[36] The provision is now found in the Senior Courts Act 1981 s.50.

[37] *Lavery v Pursell* (1889) 39 Ch D 508; *Proctor v Bayley* (1889) 42 Ch D 390: *Wroth v Tyler* [1974] Ch. 30; *Johnson v Agnew* [1980] A.C. 367 at 400; *Jaggard v Sawyer* [1995] 1 W.L.R. 269; below, para.15–118; Wh. & T. ii. 399 et seq.; [1975] C.L.J. 224 (J. A. Jolowicz); [1977] C.L.J. 369 (P. H. Pettit); [1981] Conv. 286 (T. Ingman and J. Wakefield). The measure of damages is the same as at common law: *Johnson v Agnew* [1980] A.C. 367 at 400; *Att Gen v Blake* [2001] 1 A.C. 268 at 281.

In the same way that the Chancery was originally unable to give the legal remedy of damages, the common law courts were unable to give the equitable remedies of specific performance and injunction. Consequently a plaintiff who wanted, say, damages for past trespasses, and an injunction to restrain future trespasses, formerly had to take proceedings both in one of the common law courts and in Chancery.

3. Relationship with law. The manner in which the courts of common law 5–016 and of Chancery used to operate side by side, with mutually exclusive but complementary jurisdictions, cannot here be explained at length.[38] But it may be illustrated by the fourfold classification of the jurisdiction in equity. This comprised:

(i) the exclusive jurisdiction, dealing with matters which the common law totally ignored, such as trusts;

(ii) the concurrent jurisdiction, where equity offered remedies better suited to some cases than damages at common law, as, for example, specific performance of contracts for the sale of land, and injunctions against trespass or breach of covenant;

(iii) the auxiliary jurisdiction, where equity assisted common law procedure, for example, by decrees for discovery of documents; and

(iv) the overriding jurisdiction, interrupting common law process in the manner already explained.[39]

In all these ways equity supplied or corrected deficiencies of the common law. But until 1875 equity was administered in its own separate court. To put an end to multiplicity of proceedings where both legal and equitable issues arose in the same case was one of the principal objects of the Judicature Acts 1873 and 1875.

Section 4. The Judicature Acts: Union of the Courts of Law and Equity

1. Union of courts. By the Judicature Act 1873[40] the superior courts of law 5–017 and equity were united into one Supreme Court, now known as the Senior

---

[38] Maitland, *Equity,* p.17; Ashburner, *Equity* (2nd edn), p.10; Snell, *Equity,* paras 1–15—1–17.
[39] Above, para.5–007. This classification of equitable jurisdictions was rendered obsolete by the Judicature Act 1873.
[40] This came into force on November 1, 1875 (Supreme Court of Judicature (Commencement) Act 1874 s.2). The Judicature Acts 1873 and 1875 were replaced by the JA 1925, now in turn replaced by what was first enacted as the Supreme Court Act 1981, but with the creation of the United Kingdom Supreme Court, has been renamed the Senior Courts Act 1981: see Constitutional Reform Act 2005 s.59; Sch.11, Pt.1, para.1(1).

Courts, divided into a High Court and Court of Appeal. All parts of the Supreme Court were given full jurisdiction both in law and in equity without any distinction of subject-matter. For convenience the High Court was divided into five Divisions, each of which had certain matters assigned to it. In 1880,[41] the Common Pleas Division and Exchequer Division were merged into the Queen's Bench Division. In 1972, the Probate, Divorce and Admiralty Division was re-named the Family Division,[42] with some adjustments of jurisdiction. There are now three Divisions of the Senior Courts[43]:

    (i) the Chancery Division,

    (ii) the Queen's Bench Division,[44] and

    (iii) the Family Division.

5–018   **2. Jurisdiction of Divisions.** It is important to notice that these are only divisions of one court, the High Court, and not separate courts having distinct jurisdiction.[45] Each Division of the High Court has the same jurisdiction and can enforce both legal and equitable rights and give both legal and equitable remedies. This means that it is no longer necessary to go to two separate courts to enforce legal and equitable rights or to obtain legal and equitable remedies. If a point of equity arises in an action in the Queen's Bench Division, for example, the court can deal with it; and it will not be fatal to an action if it is started in the wrong Division, for the case may be transferred to the proper Division if it is not decided in the Division in which it was started.[46] The allocation of business between the three Divisions cannot therefore affect any question of law: it is so arranged merely for administrative convenience.

5–019   **3. Law and equity still distinct.** Law and equity nevertheless remain distinct.[47] The two bodies of law have not been altered, although they are now both administered by the same court.[48] A legal right is still enforceable against a purchaser of a legal estate without notice, while an equitable right is not (in the rare cases where the doctrine of notice is still applicable). Equitable rights are still enforceable only by equitable remedies, subject to the statutory jurisdiction to award damages in addition to or in substitution for an injunction or a decree of specific performance. The so-called "fusion of law and equity" has not in fact altered the substance of any person's rights, duties or

---

[41] Order in Council of December 16, 1880, made under JA 1873 s.32.
[42] AJA 1970.
[43] Senior Courts Act 1981 s.5.
[44] There are a number of specialist subdivisions within the Queen's Bench, which include the Administrative Court, the Commercial Court, and the Technology and Construction Court.
[45] *Serrao v Noel* (1885) 15 Q.B.D. 549 at 558.
[46] Senior Courts Act 1981 s.65; and see s.61(3) and *Practice Direction* [1973] 1 W.L.R. 627.
[47] *Salt v Cooper* (1880) 16 Ch D 544 at 549.
[48] *Clements v Matthews* (1883) 11 Q.B.D. 808 at 814.

remedies: it has altered only the courts which enforce them. The reform was therefore primarily a reform of procedure, providing new judicial machinery for the enforcement of the settled rules of law and equity.[49] An equitable owner can bring proceedings to assert his title and recover land in the same way as a legal owner, whereas previously only a legal owner could use the action at law for the recovery of land.[50]

4. Conflict. The continuing distinction between the two systems is emphas-   **5–020** ised by the provision that where there is any conflict or variance between the rules of law and those of equity, the rules of equity shall prevail.[51] This effectively preserves the established relationship between law and equity, by which equitable principles can modify common law rules. Before the Judicature Acts equity asserted itself, when in conflict with common law, by the overriding jurisdiction and the common injunction.[52] The Judicature Acts abolished both this special machinery and the need for it. In practice, of course, these cases of conflict were not fought out because of equity's acknowledged right to the last word. Common law and equity have been harmoniously administered side by side for centuries.

Much therefore still depends upon the division between legal and equitable interests. Our property law is as much founded upon it now as it was before the Judicature Acts. The Court of Chancery is a ghost, but like many other English legal ghosts, its influence can be felt on every side.

Part 2

EQUITABLE RIGHTS BEFORE 1926

Equitable rights may be divided into two classes: those modelled upon   **5–021** common law rights; and those invented by equity independently. In this part there is an explanation of the development of the best-known equitable rights. The means by which equitable rights and interests are now protected is explained in later chapters.

1. "Equity follows the law". The device of the trust brought into being a   **5–022** large family of equitable interests closely corresponding to the analogous legal estates. The legal fee simple could, for example, be held by trustees upon trust for A for life with remainder to B in tail with remainder to C in fee simple; or upon trust for A for 99 years; or upon trust for A until he should die or

---

[49] See *United Scientific Holdings Ltd v Burnley BC* [1978] A.C. 904 at 925, 945, emphasising the extent of fusion. Contrast (1954) 70 L.Q.R. 326 at 327 (Sir R. Evershed); (1977) 93 L.Q.R. 529 (P.V. Baker).

[50] This is recognised by, e.g. LA 1980 s.18(1); below, para.35–038. For actions for the recovery of possession of land, see above, paras 4–014 et seq.

[51] JA 1873 s.25(11), now SCA 1981 s.49(l). For a leading illustration, see below, para.17–048; and see generally Snell, *Equity,* paras 1–23—1–25.

[52] Above, para.5–007.

become bankrupt. Equitable life interests, entails, leases, reversions and remainders, and any other interest corresponding to an interest recognised at common law, could thus be created under trusts. The maxim was "Equity follows the law".[53]

This was carried to great lengths. An equitable fee simple, for example, descended on intestacy to the heirs general, an equitable entail descended to the heirs of the body. Even the common law's mysterious methods of barring entails[54] were adopted in due course, so that there were equitable fines and recoveries.[55] And for the creation of this type of equitable interest equity adopted many of the common law rules as to words of limitation. It is true that there were exceptions, as mentioned below. "But", as a great authority wrote:

> "the cases, where the analogy fails, are not numerous; and there scarcely is a rule of law or equity, of a more ancient origin, or which admits of fewer exceptions, than the rule, that equity followeth the law".[56]

5–023   **2. Equity corrects the law.** Equity did not, of course, follow the law in matters where it was concerned to amend it. The maxim means rather that equity was content to adopt much common law doctrine without modification for the purpose of developing the trust. In particular the fundamental rules as to the possible estates, devolution on intestacy and words of limitation were followed respectfully.[57]

5–024   **3. New equitable interests.** Quite apart from those equitable interests which corresponded in a general way with the comparable common law estates, equity devised certain interests in land which had no common law equivalents. These were therefore additions made by equity to the limited number of interests in land which the law permits.[58] They were few in number, for the law was slow to extend the species of property rights (rights in rem) which could be created by private transactions.[59] Personal rights and duties of almost any kind can be created by contract as rights in personam. But rights in rem, binding not only the parties but other persons generally, can exist only in the form approved by the law and not in any novel form desired by the parties creating them. Yet equity did make possible certain dispositions of property which were impossible at common law. Some of these could exist

---

[53] Snell, *Equity*, paras 5–05—5–07.
[54] Above, paras 3–072 et seq.
[55] *Kirkham v Smith* (1749) Amb. 518; Bayley, *Fines and Recoveries* (London: Butterworth, 1828) p.254.
[56] Co.Litt. p.290b, fn.1 (xvi) by Butler.
[57] Even in these regions however there were exceptions: see the 5th edition of this work at p.120.
[58] Called "nondescript equities" by Challis p.183.
[59] It is appears that it is no longer possible to create novel equitable rights in land: see LPA 1925 s.4(1); below, para.6–064; and see *Hanchett-Stamford v Attorney General* [2008] EWHC 330 (Ch) at [31]; [2009] Ch. 173 at 183.

only under trusts, where the interests affected were equitable in any case; these included executory interests[60] (which by statute became capable of existing at law[61]), and life interests, remainders and reversions (but not entails) in leaseholds and other personalty.[62] But apart from trusts of the ordinary kind, equity introduced three important new interests in property: estate contracts, restrictive covenants, and the mortgagor's equity of redemption. These property rights, which are distinct from "mere equities",[63] require brief explanation.

(a) *Estate contracts.* Equity would decree specific performance of certain **5–025** contracts which were remediable only by damages at common law. Of these the most important were contracts for the sale or lease of land, now called estate contracts.[64] A purchaser under contract to buy land had therefore at common law only a right to damages if his vendor broke the contract. But in equity he had a right to compel his vendor to convey the land itself. This right to specific performance of the contract created a right in the land, a species of equitable property right. Therefore, if A agreed to sell land to B, but instead later sold and conveyed it to C, B could recover the land from C if C had notice of B's contract when he obtained the land. B was equitable owner from the time of the contract, and could enforce his equitable right to the land against anyone except a bona fide purchaser of a legal estate without notice of the contract.

(b) *Restrictive covenants.* A landowner selling a plot of land will often wish **5–026** to restrict its use if he has other land adjoining. He may make his purchaser contract accordingly, but a simple contract will bind only the parties and not other future owners. Equity allowed covenants restrictive of the use of land (for example, covenants not to build, or not to use the property otherwise than as a private dwelling) to run with the land[65] so as to bind all future owners except a bona fide purchaser of a legal estate without notice of the covenant. The benefit of such a covenant, belonging to the original vendor, was thus a new kind of property right created by equity.

(c) *Mortgagor's equity of redemption.* If A conveyed his land to B as **5–027** security for a loan, equity would allow A at any time, after repayment of the loan fell due, and despite any contrary provisions in the mortgage, to recover his land by paying to B what was due to him under the loan. This was the equitable right to redeem. Taken together with the other rights of the mortgagor, the mortgagor thus had an "equity of redemption", which was in effect ownership of the property subject to the rights of the mortgagee.[66] A could so

---

[60] Above, para.5–023; and see the 5th edition of this work at p.1179.
[61] See the 5th edition of this work at p.1179.
[62] Above, para.3–016; and see the 5th edition of this work at pp.815, 1169.
[63] See below, para.8–012.
[64] For fuller explanation, see below, paras 8–075, 15–050.
[65] For fuller explanation, see below, para.32–030. The leading case was *Tulk v Moxhay* (1848) 2 Ph. 774; below, para.32–033.
[66] For fuller explanation, see below, para.24–017.

recover the land not only from B but from anyone to whom B had conveyed it, saving only a bona fide purchaser of a legal estate without notice of the mortgage. Equity thus gave the mortgagor a right of property which was valuable if, as is usual, the land was worth more than the amount of the debt.

5–028   **4. Separation of legal and equitable interests.** Often the legal estate in land carries with it the beneficial interest, and no separate equitable interest exists.[67] If Blackacre is merely conveyed to X in fee simple, X takes it beneficially, for his own enjoyment.[68] But although in the case of a beneficial legal owner there is no need to consider separately the legal and equitable estate in land, in other cases this is the only way to arrive at a proper understanding of the law. The ability of the beneficial owner of a legal estate to separate the equitable from the legal interest, so that the legal owner becomes a mere trustee for the equitable owner, is one of the fundamentals of English law.[69] The way in which equity sometimes protects a person's rights in property without conferring any equitable interest in it upon him is considered further on.[70]

---

[67] See *Selby v Aston* (1797) 3 Ves. 339.
[68] See *Sammes's Case* (1609) 13 Co.Rep. 54 at 56; Co.Litt. p.23a; *Commissioner of Stamp Duties (Queensland) v Livingston* [1965] A.C. 694 at 712.
[69] See *Abbot v Burton* (1708) 1 Mod. 181 at 182; Challis p.385.
[70] See below, paras 6–068, 14–147.

CHAPTER 6

THE LEGISLATIVE TRANSFORMATION OF THE LAW OF REAL
PROPERTY AND THE PROTECTION OF ESTATES AND INTERESTS

It has been explained that the modern law of real property owes its present **6–001** structure primarily to statute.[1] Although much of the legislation dates back to the great reforms of 1925, there have been other very significant developments more recently, especially in relation to land registration. This chapter explains some of the main landmarks of the statutory reform of land law and, in particular, the way in which the legislation has attempted to protect legal estates and equitable interests and, at the same time, to simplify and expedite the conveyancing process by which land is transferred and estates in and rights over land are created. There is also a brief consideration of the ways in which both common law and equity have developed remedies to protect interests in land.

The following issues are addressed: **6–002**

(i) the reduction of legal estate to two by the Law of Property Act 1925;

(ii) the protection of certain equitable interests by registration in the register of land charges pursuant to the Land Charges Act 1972 (replacing the Land Charges Act 1972);

(iii) the extension of registration of title by the Land Registration Acts of 1925 and 2002;

(iv) the extension of overreaching provisions by the Law of Property Act 1925;

---

[1] See above, paras 1–016, 1–017.

(v) the effect of sale on legal and equitable rights;

(vi) whether it is possible to create new equitable interests; and

(vii) personal rights which may affect third parties.

Part 1

THE REDUCTION OF LEGAL ESTATES TO TWO

Section 1. The General Scheme

6–003   The property legislation of 1925 radically altered the system of legal and equitable interests in order to simplify the law, to protect purchasers from interests of which they had no notice, and at the same time to protect equitable owners.

6–004   **1. Two estates.** The scheme of the Acts was to provide that after 1925 only two kinds of legal estate could exist, the fee simple absolute in possession and the lease. Apart from leases, therefore, all interests derived out of the fee simple had thereafter to be equitable. Accordingly all of the following were and can only be equitable interests:

(i) life interests;

(ii) entails (which can no longer be created)[2];

(iii) the remainders or reversions expectant upon a life estate or entail, even if that estate is in fee simple;

(iv) determinable fees; and

(v) base fees.

6–005   **2. The indivisible fee.** Conveyancing is greatly facilitated by this uniform system of allowing life and other interests to exist only behind trusts of the legal estate. Before 1926 it was always possible for a fee simple owner to make a settlement by which the legal estate was split up into portions. If a settlor settled land on A for life with remainder to B in fee simple, there would be no immediate fee simple owner during A's life. The absolute owner had temporarily disappeared. The scheme introduced by the 1925 legislation ensures that he can never disappear. The legal estate, the fee simple absolute in possession, cannot be split up into derivative interests. Derivative interests can be created only as trusts of the fee simple, which itself remains inviolate. Therefore in conveyancing the title to the fee simple will now always have a

---

[2] TLATA 1996 Sch.1 para.5; above, para.3–031.

continuous history. It cannot be lost among the fragments of life or other lesser interests.

3. Leases. Leases may still exist as legal estates, but they stand on a different footing from the interests mentioned above. A lease is generally a business transaction for which the mechanism of trusts is inapposite. Leases as legal estates were no serious danger to purchasers since the possession of the tenant was usually self-evident. Leases therefore may, and ordinarily do, still take effect as legal estates.   **6–006**

4. "Family" and "commercial" interests. The key to the present arrange-   **6–007**
ment of legal and equitable interests is the distinction between what may very loosely be described as "family" and "commercial" transactions.[3] Life interests and determinable fees, for example, are typically found in family settlements made by deed or will. To these the machinery of a trust is natural and convenient. The legislation makes all such interests equitable, under trusts of the legal estate. By contrast, leases, easements, profits and similar interests (often generically called incumbrances) are generally granted for money or other valuable consideration on a commercial basis. For these the machinery of a trust is out of place. The purchaser expects a legal estate and, as will be seen, the scheme of the Act ensures that he may still get one.

5. Section 1. Section 1 of the Law of Property Act 1925, must now be   **6–008**
looked at more closely. The terms of the first three subsections of this section are as follows.

> "1.—(1) The only estates in land which are capable of subsisting or of being conveyed or created at law are—
>
>> (a) An estate in fee simple absolute in possession
>> (b) A term of years absolute.
>
> (2) The only interests or charges in or over land which are capable of subsisting or of being conveyed or created at law are—
>
>> (a) An easement, right, or privilege in or over land for an interest equivalent to an estate in fee simple absolute in possession or a term of years absolute
>> (b) A rentcharge in possession issuing out of or charged on land being either perpetual or for a term of years absolute
>> (c) A charge by way of legal mortgage
>> (d) [Land tax, tithe rentcharge,[4]] and any other similar charge on land which is not created by an instrument

---

[3] These terms must not be interpreted literally. Trusts are often set up nowadays for purposes which are unconnected with the family. Equally, there are some "commercial" interests, which are concerned solely with family rights, such as a spouse's matrimonial home rights under the Family Law Act 1996: below, para.34–022.

[4] These four words have been repealed: see below, para.6–026.

(e) Rights of entry exercisable over or in respect of a legal term of years absolute, or annexed, for any purpose, to a legal rentcharge.

(3) All other estates, interests, and charges in or over land take effect as equitable interests."

6–009   **6. Existence at law.** Section 1 does not provide that the estates and interests mentioned in subsections (1) and (2) are *necessarily* legal, but merely that they alone *can* be legal. For example, a life interest or a determinable fee cannot be legal estates because they are not included in s.1. On the other hand, a lease for a term of years is included in s.1 and so may exist either as a legal estate, as it normally does, or as an equitable interest under a trust. A leasehold is "land" for the purposes of the Act.[5] This means that a life interest in leasehold land must be equitable, because it is governed by s.1(1).

6–010   **7. Incidents.** The incidents of equitable interests are in general similar to those attaching to corresponding legal estates before 1926. Thus the position of a tenant for life as regards waste seems to have remained unchanged despite the conversion of his legal life estate into an equitable life interest at the beginning of 1926. There is no express provision on this point but "equity follows the law".[6]

6–011   **8. Rights over other land.** The general scheme of the section is to deal with the legal rights of ownership in the land itself in subsection (1), and with legal rights over the land of another in subsection (2). Subsection (2) contains an important list of charges or incumbrances which can still be legal and of which purchasers must therefore still beware. This list is modelled on the traditional definition of real property,[7] which includes not only physical land (corporeal hereditaments) but also certain rights over land such as easements, profits (covered by subsection (2)(a)) and rentcharges (incorporeal hereditaments).[8] Any of these, being real property, can be held for any estate or interest known to the law.[9] For this reason they are included within the meaning of "land" for the purposes of the Law of Property Act 1925.[10] A rentcharge, for example, can be held in fee simple, for a term of years, or for life. In the first two cases, but not in the third, it may still be a legal incumbrance, either under subsection (1) as "land" held for a permissible legal estate, or in its own rights under subsection (2)(b). There are other incorporeal hereditaments which rank as real property in our law and which may be held for either of the two possible legal estates although they are not mentioned in subsection (2), such as an advowson (the right to present a

---

[5] Above, para.3–015.
[6] Above, para.5–022.
[7] See above, para.1–013.
[8] For incorporeal hereditaments, see above, para.1–008; below, para.27–001.
[9] Below, para.27–002.
[10] LPA 1925 s.205(1)(ix).

clergyman to a living).[11] These curiously assorted interests all fall within the statutory definition of "land" mentioned above.

9. Estates and interests. It will be noted that the rights mentioned in **6–012** subsection (1) are called legal *estates* and those mentioned in subsection (2) are called legal *interests or charges*. This is a convenient distinction between rights over a person's own land and rights over the land of another, but both types of rights are referred to in the Act as "legal estates", and have the same incidents attached to them as attached to legal estates before 1926.[12] The title of "estate owner" is given to the owner of a legal estate.[13] After 1925 equitable rights in land have been called equitable interests. The name "estate" is reserved for legal rights.

The various legal estates and interests must now be examined more closely.

Section 2. The Estates and Interests

1(a). "Fee simple absolute in possession". The meaning of *"fee simple"* **6–013** has already been considered.[14]

"Absolute" is used in its accustomed sense to distinguish a fee simple which will continue for ever[15] from a modified fee, such as a determinable fee or a base fee.[16] The policy of the Act requires that any such interest, being less than a fee simple absolute, should take effect only in equity, under a trust of the legal estate. A fee simple defeasible by condition subsequent would also necessarily be equitable but for the Law of Property (Amendment) Act 1926.[17] By this Act an amendment was made to meet an unforeseen difficulty connected with rentcharges. In some parts of the country, particularly Manchester and the north, it has been a common practice to sell a fee simple not for a capital sum, but for an income in the form of a perpetual rentcharge (an annual sum charged on the land).[18] Rentcharges of this kind are commonly called "fee farm rents". A scheme for their commutation and extinguishment was enacted in 1977, but this will not be completed until 2037.[19]

The remedies for non-payment of a rentcharge include a right to enter on **6–014** the land temporarily to collect rents and profits.[20] Further, in a number of cases an express right of re-entry is reserved by the conveyance, entitling the

---

[11] Below, para.31–007. Advowsons are no longer "land" for the purposes of the registration of title under what is now LRA 2002: see Patronage (Benefices) Measure 1986 s.6.

[12] LPA 1925 s.1(4).

[13] LPA 1925 s.1(4).

[14] Above, para.3–005.

[15] See *Edward Seymor's Case* (1612) 10 Co.Rep. 95b at 97b.

[16] Above, para.3–052.

[17] Sch.

[18] For rentcharges, see below, paras 6–021; 31–014.

[19] See below, para.31–014.

[20] Below, para.31–030.

grantor to enter and determine the fee simple and thus regain his old estate if any payment is a specified number of days in arrear. The reservation of a right of re-entry clearly made the fee simple less than absolute. The concern that the fee would therefore be equitable prompted the enactment of the Schedule to the Law of Property (Amendment) Act 1926, which added a clause to the Law of Property Act 1925, s.7(1). This provided that "a fee simple subject to a legal or equitable right of entry or re-entry is for the purposes of this Act a fee simple absolute". In consequence, a fee simple is a legal estate even though it is subject to a right of entry. The exception is widely drawn so that it affects all conditional fees. This is because the effect of a condition subsequent annexed to the fee simple is to give rise to a right of re-entry exercisable on breach of the condition, and until this right of re-entry is exercised, the fee simple continues.[21] Consequently, by virtue of the Amendment Act any fee simple defeasible by condition subsequent appears able to rank as a legal estate if limited to take effect as such, even though it is far from being "absolute" in the ordinary sense of the word.[22]

Two other statutory exceptions to the meaning of *absolute* are to be found in s.7 of the Law of Property Act 1925. These relate to fees simple liable to be divested by statute, and to the property of corporations.

6–015

(i) By subsection (1)[23] a fee simple may be absolute for the purposes of the Act although liable to be divested "by virtue of the Land Clauses Acts, or any similar statute".[24] Such Acts provide that land granted or acquired for various public purposes shall re-vest in the grantor, his successors, or some other person if the purpose is not carried out, or if use for that purpose ceases in the future. Thus a highway authority, in which the surface of the highway is vested until the land ceases to be used as a highway, has a legal estate.[25] The exception contained in s.7 used to be considerably wider. As originally drafted, it also included cases of divestment under certain statutes where land had been conveyed to trustees for the purpose of providing a school, museum, church or chapel, and the building ceased to be required for that purpose.[26] There was a conflict of authority as to whether the legal estate vested in the

---

[21] Above, para.3–056.

[22] It is now clear that any fee simple that was absolute by virtue of s.7(1) of the Law of Property Act 1925 could not create a settlement under SLA 1925, see SLA 1925 s.1(1)(ii)(c) (as amended by TLATA 1996 s.25(1); Sch.3, para.2); below, Appendix, A–033.

[23] As amended by Reverter of Sites Act 1987 s.8(3), Sch.

[24] See, e.g. *Re Cawston's Conveyance* [1940] Ch. 27; *Pickin v British Railways Board* [1974] A.C. 765.

[25] *Tithe Redemption Commission v Runcorn UDC* [1954] Ch. 383, holding the Local Government Act 1929 to be a "similar statute".

[26] The relevant statutes were the School Sites Act 1841, the Literary and Scientific Institutions Act 1854 and the Places of Worship Act 1873.

revertee[27] or whether the trustees held it on a bare trust for him.[28] In the former case, if the trustees remained in adverse possession for 12 years after the building ceased to be used for its original purpose the rights of the revertee would be barred under the Limitation Act 1980, but in the latter case they would not.[29] However, the Reverter of Sites Act 1987 provides that trustees hold the legal estate on trust for the revertee, with a power to sell the land, but without the need to consult him.[30] They may therefore sell the land even if they cannot ascertain his identity. If it proves impossible for the trustees to find the revertee,[31] they may apply to the Charity Commissioners to have both his interest extinguished and a scheme drawn up for the property to be applied for other charitable purposes.[32]

(ii) By subsection (2) similar provision is made for a fee simple vested in a corporation. A fee simple, which is liable to determine by reason of the dissolution of the corporation, is a fee simple absolute for the purposes of the Act.[33]   **6–016**

The three exceptions made by s.7 (as amended) are, of course, exceptions only for the purposes of the Act, that is to say, for the purpose of allowing those interests to be legal estates. Section 7 does not alter the conditions attached to them.

"*In possession*" means that the estate must be immediate, and not in remainder or reversion.[34] Remainders and reversions are equitable interests, taking effect behind a trust of the legal estate. But, in order to prevent temporary interests such as leases from disturbing the legal ownership, "possession" is defined so as to include not only physical possession of the land but also the receipt of rents and profits or the right to receive them, if any.[35]   **6–017**

---

[27] This will be the persons entitled to the estate of the original grantor: see *Fraser v Canterbury Diocesan Board of Finance (No.1)* [2001] Ch. 669. That case was subsequently disapproved but not on that point: see *Fraser v Canterbury Diocesan Board of Finance (No.2)* [2005] UKHL 65; [2006] 1 A.C. 377. See too *Bath & Wells Diocesan Board of Finance v Jenkinson* [2002] EWHC 218 (Ch) at [78], [79]; [2002] 2 P. & C.R. 350 at 367.

[28] *Re Clayton's Deed Poll* [1980] Ch. 99 favoured the latter view, but Nourse J. declined to follow it in *Re Rowhook Mission Hall, Horsham* [1985] Ch. 62, preferring the former: see (1984) 100 L.Q.R. 527 (C. E. Evans).

[29] Below, para.35–039.

[30] s.1 (as amended by TLATA 1996 Sch.2, para.6). But for the amendments made by the 1996 Act, the revertee, as a beneficiary under a trust of land, would have had a right to be consulted about any sale, and might have been entitled to occupy the land: see TLATA 1996 ss.11, 12; below, paras 12–026 et seq. Quite apart from the practical difficulties that this would have created, it often takes some time to determine who is entitled to the land.

[31] For the steps which the trustees must take to find the revertee, see s.3.

[32] s.2.

[33] This situation could arise in relation to land in England and Wales which is owned by a corporation, such as an overseas company, which is not subject to the Companies Acts. See above, para.2–025.

[34] See *District Bank Ltd v Webb* [1958] 1 W.L.R. 148.

[35] LPA 1925 s.205(1)(xix): and see s.95(4).

Thus fee simple is still "in possession" even though the owner has granted a lease, because he is entitled to the rent reserved by the lease, and even if the land has also been mortgaged, for he is entitled to the rents and profits, if any, in excess of any interest payable to the mortgagee.[36] But if land has been granted "to A for life, remainder to B in fee simple", the interests of both A and B are necessarily equitable, for a life interest cannot be legal and B's fee simple is not in possession. These words therefore mean that future estates of freehold cannot be legal.[37]

6–018   **1(b). "Term of years absolute".** A term of years absolute is a lease which creates in interest in land.[38] *"Term of years"* is defined as including a term of less than a year, or for a year or years and a fraction of a year, or from year to year.[39] It means any term for any period having a fixed and certain maximum duration.[40] Thus in addition to a tenancy for a specified number of years (e.g. "to X for 99 years"), such tenancies as a yearly tenancy or a weekly tenancy are "terms of years" within the definition. In law the term is considered to be for a period of a year or a week respectively. Although in practice such terms continue to run on until determined, the parties are notionally treated as making a new agreement for a fresh term at the end of every period.[41] However, a lease "for the life of X" cannot exist as a legal estate, because it is limited by the uncertain duration of X's life and not by a term of years.[42]

Tenancies at will and at sufferance are perhaps best regarded as not being estates or interests within the meaning of the Act, but as being bare tenure and mere occupation respectively.[43] If this view is legitimate it avoids the absurdity of turning these special types of tenancy into equitable interests. It would be strange if a fee simple owner became trustee for a tenant for years holding over after expiry of the lease, and stranger still if he became trustee for his tenant at sufferance, holding over without his consent.

6–019   *"Absolute".* This word is not used in this context in any intelligible sense, because it is provided that a term of years may be absolute even though it is:

> "liable to determination by notice, re-entry, operation of law, or by a provision for cesser on redemption, or in any other event (other than the

---

[36] Below, para.25–026.

[37] For a very limited exception, see Welsh Church (Burial Grounds) Act 1945 s.1(2).

[38] It is possible to grant a lease that does not create an interest in land, and such a lease is not a term of years: see *Bruton v London & Quadrant Housing Trust* [2000] 1 A.C. 406; below, para.17–001.

[39] LPA 1925 s.205(1)(xxvii); below, para.17–001; for an analogy cf. Litt. 67. See also *Re Land and Premises at Liss, Hants* [1971] Ch. 986 at 990. cf. *E.W.P. Ltd v Moore* [1992] Q.B. 460.

[40] *Prudential Assurance Co Ltd v London Residuary Body* [1992] 2 A.C. 386; *Berrisford v Mexfield Housing Co-operative Ltd* [2011] UKSC 52.

[41] *Prudential Assurance Co Ltd v London Residuary Body* [1992] 2 A.C. 386 at 394.

[42] For terms of years determinable on life, see below, para.17–113.

[43] Above, para.3–014; below, para.17–100.

dropping of a life, or the determination of a determinable life interest)".[44]

This means that a term of years may be absolute even if it contains a clause enabling either party to determine it by giving notice,[45] or if it provides (as is almost always the case) that the landlord may recover the land if the rent is not paid or a covenant is broken.[46] "Operation of law" is illustrated by a proviso for cesser on redemption in relation to a mortgage by demise of unregistered land.[47]

It will be apparent from this that, by the express provisions of the Act, a term of years absolute may consist of a tenancy which is neither a "term of years" nor "absolute" according to the natural meaning of the words, e.g. a monthly tenancy liable to be forfeited for non-payment of rent.

It should be noted that, unlike a fee simple absolute, a term of years absolute may be a legal estate even though not "in possession". A lease granted now but to commence in five years' time may thus be legal, although there is a limit to the length of time which may elapse between the grant of a lease and the commencement of the term.[48] There is no limit to the length of a term of years absolute: terms of 3,000 years were common in the case of mortgages by demise.[49] However, there is no such thing as a lease in perpetuity, because that is not a "term" at all.[50]

2(a). "An easement, right, or privilege in or over land for an interest 6–020 equivalent to an estate in fee simple absolute in possession or a term of years absolute". This head includes both easements and profits à prendre.[51] An easement confers the right to use the land of another in some way, or to prevent it from being used for certain purposes. Thus rights of way, rights of water and rights of light may exist as easements. A profit à prendre gives the right to take something from the land of another, e.g. peat, fish or wood. "Right or privilege" means only rights in property known to the law, such as profits or other incorporeal hereditaments[52] (not being rentcharges, which are separately dealt with next). Rights such as a franchise to wrecks[53] or treasure trove[54] can thus apparently still exist at law. Under this head rights can be legal only if they are held for interests equivalent to one of the two legal

---

[44] LPA 1925 s.205(1)(xxvii).

[45] Consider *Simons v Associated Furnishers Ltd* [1931] 1 Ch. 379.

[46] See below, para.18–006.

[47] Below, para.24–020.

[48] Below, para.17–074.

[49] Below, para.24–020. Mortgages by demise are, in practice, obsolete, and cannot be created where the title is registered: see below, para.7–050.

[50] Below, paras 17–003, 17–065 et seq.

[51] For these interests, see below, paras 27–006 et seq.

[52] See below, para.27–001.

[53] *R. v Forty-Nine Casks of Brandy* (1836) 3 Hagg.Adm. 257.

[54] *Att Gen v Trustees of the British Museum* [1903] 2 Ch. 598 at 612. For franchises, see below, para.31–013. Treasure trove has now been abolished: see above, para.3–045.

estates; thus a right of way for 21 years may be legal but a right of way for life must be equitable.

6–021   **2(b). "A rentcharge in possession issuing out of or charged on land being either perpetual or for a term of years absolute".** A "rentcharge" is a right which, independently of any lease or mortgage, gives the owner the right to a periodical sum of money secured on land, as where the fee simple owner of Blackacre charges the land with a payment of £50 per annum to X.[55] The rentcharge is a burden on the land since the free-holder is personally liable to pay it, and if payment is in arrear the beneficiary has a right of entry on the land.[56] With certain exceptions,[57] as from July 22, 1977, no new rentcharge can be created; and most existing rentcharges will be extinguished 60 years later, i.e. on July 22, 2037.[58]

6–022   *"In possession"*. Under the subsection a rentcharge to start at a date subsequent to that on which it is granted cannot be legal, whether it is perpetual or for a term of years absolute. But the Law of Property (Entailed Interests) Act 1932[59] provided that a rentcharge was "in possession" notwithstanding that the payments were limited to commence or accrue at a date subsequent to its creation, unless the rentcharge was limited to take effect in remainder after or expectant on the failure or determination of some other interest.

6–023   *"Issuing out of or charged on land"*. "Land" includes another rentcharge.[60] Thus if P charged his fee simple estate in Blackacre with the payment to Q of £100 per annum in perpetuity, Q could create a legal rentcharge of £50 per annum in favour of R, charged on his rentcharge of £100.

6–024   *"Being either perpetual or for a term of years absolute"*. "Perpetual" is used here in place of "fee simple absolute" used in 2(a) above, but there seems to be no practical importance in this difference of wording.

6–025   **2(c). "A charge by way of legal mortgage".** This is fully explained later.[61] It is the usual method of creating a legal mortgage after 1925, and is similar in effect to the now-obsolete form of mortgage made by grant of a long term of years. This type of interest in land was created by the Law of Property Act 1925.[62]

---

[55] For rentcharges, see below, para.31–014.
[56] Below, para.31–030.
[57] Of which the most significant are estate rentcharges: see Rentcharges Act 1977 s.2(3)(c), (4), (5); below, para.31–019; and see *Orchard Trading Estate Management Ltd v Johnson Security Ltd* [2002] EWCA Civ 406; [2002] 2 E.G.I.R. 1.
[58] Rentcharges Act 1977 ss.2, 3; below, para.31–018.
[59] s.2. The Act takes its name from another matter.
[60] LPA 1925 ss.122, 205(1)(ix); below, para.31–032.
[61] Below, para.24–025.
[62] It has its origin in the Land Transfer Act 1875, which applied only to registered land.

2(d). "[Land tax, tithe rentcharge], and any other similar charge on   6–026
land which is not created by an instrument". This group comprises periodical payments with which land is burdened by law and not by some conveyance or other voluntary act of parties. "Instrument" is so defined as to exclude
statute[63] and the charges covered in this group are statutory. In fact the three
main charges that fell within this paragraph, land tax, tithe rentcharge and tithe
redemption annuity, have all been abolished[64] and the first four words, brack-
eted above, have been repealed.[65] The unrepealed remnant still has some
effect, even though it is no longer grammatical and lacks any point of
reference for "similar".

2(e). "Rights of entry exercisable over or in respect of a legal term of   6–027
years absolute, or annexed, for any purpose, to a legal rentcharge". It has
already been explained that a legal term of years absolute is usually made
subject to the right of the landlord to re-enter if the tenant fails to pay rent or
comply with the covenants [66] It has been said that the right of entry "is what
gives value and substance" to the freehold reversion.[67] A right of entry is
itself an interest in land[68] and in the cases mentioned it may still be a legal
right. The statutory language appears to be wide enough to cover any right of
entry affecting a legal lease. However, it has been held that the scheme of the
Act requires the right to be merely equitable if it is created on the assignment
of the lease (rather than, as normally, on its grant), and it is limited to an
uncertain period instead of being perpetual or for a term of years.[69]
    A right of entry or re-entry is often attached to a legal rentcharge in order
to secure the due payment of the rent.

Concurrent legal estates. Any number of legal estates may exist con-   6–028
currently in the same piece of land.[70] Thus A may have the legal fee simple
in Blackacre, subject to a legal mortgage in favour of B, a legal rentcharge in
favour of C, a legal lease in favour of D, and so on. The legal fee simple is
often referred to as *the* legal estate because of its paramount importance. Legal
leases, mortgages, rentcharges, easements and the like are regarded as incumbrances upon it.

---

[63] LPA 1925 s.205(1)(viii).
    [64] See Finance Act 1963 Pt V, Sched. 14 (land tax); Tithe Act 1936 s.1 (tithe rentcharge);
Finance Act 1977 s.56 (tithe redemption annuity).
    [65] Tithe Act 1936 s.48, Sched. 9 (tithe rentcharge); Finance Act 1963 s.73, Sched. 14 (land
tax).
    [66] Above, para.6–019.
    [67] *Cowan v Department of Health* [1992] Ch. 286 at 295, per Mummery J.
    [68] *Cowan v Department of Health*, above, at 295. For the alienability of a right of entry, see
above, para.3–068.
    [69] *Shiloh Spinners Ltd v Harding* [1973] A.C. 691. The exercise of such a right will not put an
end to the lease, but there is no reason in principle or in the language of the Act why this should
matter.
    [70] LPA 1925 s.1(5).

Part 2

THE PROTECTION OF ESTATES AND INTERESTS

Section 1. Extension of System of Registration of Charges for Unregistered Land

6–029   **1. Registration.** The most serious concern in transactions in land is the possibility that some interest may not be discovered by an intending purchaser or other disponee prior to the disposition. If the interest is legal an innocent purchaser will find himself bound by it. If the interest is equitable, its owner may lose it to a purchaser without notice. Registration of interests, particularly of those which are least likely to appear in a routine investigation of title, is one obvious solution to such problems. It was in limited use before 1926, but it was greatly extended by the 1925 legislation.[71] By the Land Charges Act 1925, which has since been replaced by the Land Charges Act 1972, many important interests became registrable, and for the first time, registration of land charges became a fundamental part of the general system of unregistered conveyancing.

Under this system of registration the substance of the doctrine of notice was virtually abandoned. Notice has a residual role only where the 1972 Act does not apply. If the right in issue is registrable, the question is whether it is registered rather than whether the purchaser knows or should have known of it.

As part of the explanation of the general strategy of the 1925 reforms, the elements of the system of registration of land charges are briefly set out below. A detailed explanation of the system is given in Chapter 8.[72]

6–030   **2. Principles of registration.** The two cardinal principles of the registration of land charges are:

(i) failure to register makes the interest *void against a purchaser*[73]; and

(ii) registration is deemed to constitute *actual notice to all persons for all purposes* connected with the land.[74]

It is a corollary of (i) that if an interest is registrable but unregistered a purchaser is unaffected by notice obtained through other channels. Even though he knew of the interest, he will take free from it.[75] The doctrine of

[71] See the sixth edition of this work at para.4–056.
[72] See below, paras 8–061 et seq.
[73] See LCA 1972 s.4; below, para.8–093.
[74] LPA 1925 s.198.
[75] By LPA 1925 s.199(1)(i), a purchaser is not to be prejudicially affected by notice of any registrable land charge which is void against him for want of registration. The purchaser will take free of the unregistered incumbrance even though the incumbrancer is in possession of the land: below, para.8–095. Because notice is irrelevant, the ancient rule that the fact of possession constitutes notice of the rights of the possessor (below, para.8–020) does not apply.

notice thus exists in name only. It has been mechanised by statute. The test is now the state of the register, not the state of the purchaser's mind. This system cannot be translated into terms of the equitable rules about a purchaser without notice. It is a separate system and this can be shown by two examples.

First, certain legal rights[76] are registrable, and if not registered are void **6–031** against a purchaser. Registration thus deprives these legal rights of some of the security against purchasers which they formerly enjoyed. This cannot be explained by reference to the doctrine of notice, which had no application to legal rights.

Secondly, under the rules of equity a purchaser without notice took free **6–032** from equities if he gave *value* and acquired a *legal estate.* An unregistered right is in some cases void against a purchaser if he gave *value* and acquired *any estate, legal or equitable,* and in other cases void against a purchaser only if he gave *money or money 's worth* and acquired a *legal estate.*[77]

3. Unregistered interests. In cases not covered by the provisions as to **6–033** registration the ordinary legal and equitable rules still apply. Where an equitable interest is registrable but has not been registered the position is as follows.

(i) It will be binding on any person who takes the land by way of gift

(ii) A charge which is void for non-registration only as against a purchaser of the legal estate for money or money's worth, will not necessarily bind any other type of purchaser. If the legal estate is conveyed to a person in consideration of marriage, he will take free of the charge if he has no notice of it.[78]

The legislation is concerned with the protection of purchasers, and registrable interests remain valid for all other purposes despite non-registration.

4. Summary. The position created by the extension of registration is **6–034** therefore best described as follows.

(i) Most legal rights are not registrable; these continue to be good against the whole world.

(ii) Some equitable rights are not registrable; these continue to be good against the whole world except a bona fide purchaser for value of a legal estate without notice or someone claiming through such a person.

---

[76] Below, para.6–036.
[77] LCA 1972 s.4, below, para.8–093.
[78] Below, para.8–093.

(iii) A few legal rights and many equitable rights are registrable. If these are not registered, they will be void for non-registration against certain purchasers, irrespective of any question of notice. If they are registered, they bind every purchaser, again irrespective of notice. Whether they are legal or equitable no longer makes any difference.

6–035   **5. Classification of rights.** The following is a summary of the most important rights which are registrable after 1925. These rights are not self-explanatory but they will be dealt with in detail later.[79]

(a) Legal interests

6–036   (i) A charge on land imposed by certain statutes such as the Agricultural Holdings Act 1986.

(ii) A puisne mortgage, defined as a legal mortgage not protected by a deposit of title deeds. This covers most second, third or later legal mortgages.

(iii) An Inland Revenue charge for inheritance tax.[80]

(b) Equitable interests

6–037   (i) A limited owner's charge. This includes a charge on land acquired by some limited owner, such as a tenant for life, who pays out of his own pocket capital transfer tax (e.g. on the death of the previous owner) which should have been borne by the estate. Security for the debt from the estate to the tenant for life is provided by the charge.

(ii) A general equitable charge, defined as an equitable charge which affects a legal estate in land but does not arise under a trust and is not secured by a deposit of title deeds. This class covers many equitable mortgages and annuities. It is a residuary class into which equitable interests may fall if not registrable under other heads.

(iii) An estate contract,[81] defined as a contract to convey or create a legal estate. This includes every contract for the sale or lease of a legal estate.

(iv) A restrictive covenant,[82] provided that it is made after 1925 and is not made between lessor and lessee.

(v) An equitable easement, or similar right, provided that it is created after 1925. An easement held for life would be an example, but in practice few easements fall within this category.

[79] Below, paras 8–063 et seq.
[80] Below, para.8–078.
[81] Above, para.5–025.
[82] Above, para.5–026.

6. Operation of the system. There is no uniting legal thread that links the   **6–038** categories of interest that may be protected as land charges. However, the following points may be noted.

(i) Interests of a "family" type found under settlements and trusts of land are not registrable. These are sufficiently protected by the mechanism of overreaching which is explained below.[83]

(ii) Mortgages have special peculiarities, particularly in the device of protection by a deposit of title deeds. This protection makes registration unnecessary and explains the reservations as to title deeds in (a)(ii) and (b)(ii) above.

(iii) Registrable interests are a miscellaneous collection because they comprise only such interests as are not sufficiently protected by other means. Registration has been introduced only where it was thought necessary to strengthen the weak points of the existing system of conveyancing, not as a comprehensive system. Thus there is no presumption that equitable interests which cannot be overreached (as explained below) are registrable.[84]

Section 2. Registration of Title

1. Registration of title and its development. The system of unregistered   **6–039** conveyancing is being rapidly replaced by registration of title under the Land Registration Act 2002. Under the system of registered title, which is explained in Chapter 7, not only are third party rights over land recorded on the register, but the title is itself registered. When registered land is sold, the legal title to the land does not pass to the purchaser when the vendor executes the transfer (which is the equivalent of a deed of conveyance in unregistered conveyancing) but only when that transfer is registered.[85] So powerful is the effect of registration that it will vest the legal title in the registered proprietor even if the transfer to him was void, e.g., because it was a forgery.[86] A registered proprietor has no document of title[87]: the register alone is conclusive as to the state of the title.[88] The register may be altered in certain circumstances, and in particular to correct a mistake.[89] However, a registered proprietor who suffers

---

[83] See paras 6–057 et seq.
[84] See *Shiloh Spinners Ltd v Harding* [1973] A.C. 691. Examples which fall into neither category include an equitable right of entry (below, para.8–080); and an equity arising by estoppel (below, Ch.16).
[85] LRA 2002 s.27(1); below, para.7–053.
[86] LRA 2002 s.58(1); below, para.7–117.
[87] Although there is a power by rules to make provision for the issue of a land certificate to a registered proprietor (as happened prior to LRA 2002), it has not been exercised: cf. LRA 2002 Sch.10, para.4.
[88] The register is kept in computerised form.
[89] See LRA 2002 Sch.4; below, para.7–133.

loss in consequence is entitled to an indemnity from the Land Registry.[90] The register is an open public document,[91] which can be accessed online. It is therefore possible for any internet user, on payment of a fee, to download a copy of a registered title and the accompanying title plan.

6–040   Registration of title has a long history.[92] The first territory in the British Empire to adopt it was South Australia, where it was introduced by Sir Robert Torrens in 1858.[93] The "Torrens system" has been followed in many other countries, but it differs in many respects from the system eventually adopted in England.[94] Torrens' objective was to "escape from the grievous yoke of the English property"[95] by making radical changes in it. The English policy, on the other hand, was to simplify the machinery of conveyancing without altering the substantive rules of law. Neither of these policies was wholly successful, but the two systems remained distinct.[96]

The introduction of registration of title in England and Wales was a protracted affair. The first serious proposals for title registration were made in the 1840s,[97] and the first legislation was enacted in 1862.[98] The legislation was not a success and the registry was little used. Not only was registration not compulsory, but it was only possible to register a title that was in all respects sound.[99] The Land Transfer Act 1875 laid the foundations of the modern development of registration of title.[100] However, registration of title under the Act was voluntary. Few titles were registered until the Land Transfer Act 1897 made registration of title compulsory on certain dealings with land in the County of London.[101] The Land Transfer Acts of 1875 and 1897 were amended by the Law of Property Act 1922 and were then consolidated in the Land Registration Act 1925.[102] The 1925 Act introduced effective compulsory registration on an area by area basis, but even then its implementation was

---

[90] See LRA 2002 Sch.8, below, para.7–140.

[91] LRA 2002 s.66; below, paras 7–002, 7–120.

[92] For a full account, see J. S. Anderson, *Lawyers and the Making of English Land Law 1832–1940*. See too Ruoff & Roper, 1.003–1.006; A. W. B. Simpson. *A History of the Land Law*, pp.280–283.

[93] S. Rowton Simpson, *Land Law and Registration*, p.68.

[94] The differences between the two systems have been diminished by LRA 2002.

[95] Torrens, *South Australian Registration of Title* (1859), p.44.

[96] Contrasting features of the Torrens system are that boundaries are officially surveyed ("guaranteed boundaries"), rectification and indemnity are less freely available and there are no overriding interests (overriding interests are explained below, at paras 6–044, 7–008).

[97] J. S. Anderson, *Lawyers and the Making of English Land Law 1832–1940*, pp.63–73.

[98] Land Registry Act 1862.

[99] The title had to be what the Court of Chancery would have regarded as a good marketable title, which was at that time a remarkably difficult standard to achieve.

[100] It relaxed the requirement of a marketable title as a pre-condition for registration.

[101] Under this Act it became possible for the first time for registration to be made compulsory in a county by Order in Council. Compulsory registration could not be introduced, however, if the county council voted to oppose it at a meeting attended by two-thirds of its members: Land Transfer Act 1897 s.20.

[102] There were Land Registration Acts in 1936, 1966, 1986, 1988 and 1997. There was also further provision in the Land Registration and Land Charges Act 1971. The legislation was supplemented by the substantial LRR 1925.

postponed for 10 years.[103] The areas were gradually extended, until finally in December 1990, the whole of England and Wales was subject to compulsory registration.[104] In areas of compulsory registration (and now, therefore, in the whole of England Wales), specified dispositions of unregistered land were required to be registered. The number of dispositions that triggered compulsory first registration was also extended.[105] The position today is that any disposition

The Land Registration Act 2002,[106] which came into force on October 13, **6–041**
2003, repealed and replaced all the earlier legislation. It has made fundamental changes to the law governing the registration of title. It creates the framework for dematerialised electronic conveyancing under which dispositions of registered land will be made and registered simultaneously.[107] It contains a statutory code of priorities that is different from that applicable to unregistered land. The Act reflects the principles underlying title registration and, in particular, the principle that registration and not possession is the basis of title.[108] It has abandoned any notion, once current, that title registration is mere machinery. The substantive law applicable to land with registered title is now very different from that which applies to unregistered land.[109] The stated objective of the Act is to create a register which is a complete and accurate a reflection of the state of the title at any given time, so that it is possible to investigate title on-line, with the absolute minimum of additional enquiries and inspections.[110]

A person may be registered with his own title as the proprietor of a freehold estate, a lease granted for more than seven years,[111] a rentcharge, and a profit à prendre in gross.[112]

2. Principles of registration. As indicated in the previous paragraph, the **6–042**
principles for determining the priority of interests in registered land are completely different from those that apply to unregistered land. The general principle is, as might be expected, that the priority of an interest depends upon

---

[103] LRA 1925 s.120. Even after the 10-year period had elapsed, the Lord Chancellor might be compelled by a county council or local law society to hold a public inquiry into whether compulsory registration should be introduced into a particular county: LRA 1925 s.122. By January 1, 1937, only Eastbourne, Hastings and Middlesex had joined London as areas of compulsory registration.

[104] See below, para.7–001.

[105] See LRA 1997 s.1. For the dispositions that now trigger the requirement of compulsory first registration, see LRA 2002 s.4; below, para.7–014.

[106] Which implemented recommendations from the Law Commission and the Land Registry, see (2001) Law Com. No.271; below, para.7–003.

[107] See below, para.7–157.

[108] See below, Ch.35. The law on the adverse possession of registered land is now quite different from the law applicable to unregistered land.

[109] See below, para.7–001.

[110] See (2001) Law Com. No.271 at para.1.5.

[111] Some leases granted for seven years or less must also be registered: see below, para.7–014.

[112] LRA 2002 s.3(1); below, para.7–010. For profits à prendre in gross, see below, para.27–071.

the date of its creation: the first in time of creation prevails.[113] That is subject to a significant exception.[114] A purchaser of registered land for valuable consideration takes it subject only to:

(i) An interest protected in the register either as a registered charge or by means of an entry called a "notice";

(ii) An unregistered interest that falls within a statutory list, often called an "overriding interest" (though that is not a term employed by the Land Registration Act 2002);

(iii) An interest that is excepted from the effect of registration[115]; and

(iv) In the case of a disposition of a leasehold estate, where the burden of the interest is incident to the estate.[116]

6–043   Most incumbrances affecting registered land should be registered. Legal charges are protected as registered charges.[117] Other incumbrances on land, whether legal or equitable, are protected by the entry of a notice,[118] though some interests cannot be so protected.[119] In particular, interests under trusts of land and settlements cannot be protected by notice.[120] The correct form of protection for such interests is the entry of a restriction, to ensure that the interests of beneficiaries under such rights are "overreached".[121] Overreaching is explained below.[122]

6–044   There are some interests which are protected even though they are not registered. Under the Land Registration Act 1925 these were called "overriding interests", and although that term is not employed in the Land Registration Act 2002, there continue to be such interests, though the number of scope of these either has or will be reduced under the provisions of the 2002 Act.[123] The reasons for such interests are partly historical and partly pragmatic. They can be troublesome because they conflict with the policy of the Act to create

---

[113] LRA 2002 s.28; below, para.7–060.

[114] See LRA 2002 ss.29, 30; below, paras 7–061—7–063.

[115] There are various gradations of registered title: see below, paras 7–023 et seq. Most proprietors are registered with absolute title and there are no interests excepted from the effect of such registration. However, there are other gradations, such as good leasehold title (where the superior title to leasehold property is not registered or deduced) and possessory title (where the first registered proprietor's title was based upon possession and not upon a deduction of a paper title), where there are exceptions from the effect of registration.

[116] This covers the case where the lease contains a covenant restrictive of the user of the property demised. Contrary to the normal rule, such covenants are not registrable as such, because they are a term of the lease: see LRA 2002 s.33(c).

[117] LRA 2002 s.27(2)(f); Sch.2, Pt.2; below, para.7–057.

[118] LRA 2002 s.32; below, para.7–070.

[119] LRA 2002 s.33; see below, para.7–070.

[120] LRA 2002 s.33(a).

[121] LRA 2002 s.42(1)(b); below, para.7–078.

[122] See paras 6–057 et seq.

[123] See below, paras 7–086 et seq.

a conclusive register,[124] and thereby add to the burden of inquiry on the disponee prior to a disposition. The interests include the following:

(i) A lease granted for a term not exceeding seven years unless it was required to be registered at the time when it was granted[125];

(ii) Subject to significant exceptions that are explained later, an unregistered interest belonging at the time of the disposition to a person in actual occupation[126];

(iii) A limited class of legal easements and profits à prendre[127]; and

(iv) Local land charges.[128]

A number of miscellaneous interests will lose their overriding status on October 13, 2003, and should therefore be registered before then.[129]

3. The effects of non-registration. Certain dispositions of registered land **6–045** are required to be completed by registration,[130] and operate only in equity until they are registered in the manner provided by the Land Registration Act 2002.[131] If there is a subsequent registered disposition for valuable consideration that is then registered, that subsequent disposition will take priority over the prior disposition that has not been completed by registration.[132] In many cases, in consequence of that priority, the subsequent disposition will override the earlier one,[133] unless the prior interest happens to fall within one of the categories of overriding interest and is therefore protected as such.

As regards other interests in registered land that constitute an incumbrance, such as restrictive covenants, estate contracts or equitable charges, but which have not been protected by the entry of a notice, these will not bind a purchaser of a registered estate for valuable consideration whose disposition is registered, unless the interest is protected as an overriding interest, as it may sometimes be.[134]

---

[124] See above, para.6–041.

[125] LRA 2002 Sch.3, para.1

[126] LRA 2002 Sch.3, para.2; below, paras 7–089—7–097.

[127] LRA 2002 Sch.3, para.3; below, paras 7–098—7–100.

[128] LRA 2002 Sch.3, para.6; below, paras 7–030, 7–087.

[129] See LRA 2002 s.117; below, para.7–088.

[130] For those dispositions, see LRA 2002 s.27(2); below, paras 7–053, 7–054. Such registered dispositions consist of the grant or transfer of a legal estate, such as the grant of a lease or easement of or over registered land, or the transfer of a registered freehold.

[131] LRA 2002 s.27(1); below, para.7–053.

[132] LRA 2002 ss.29, 30; above, para.6–042.

[133] Thus if a registered proprietor charges his property, but the chargee fails to register it, and the proprietor then makes a subsequent registered disposition of the property, the subsequent disponee will take free of the unregistered charge.

[134] An example would be where a lessee in actual occupation under a lease had the benefit of an option to renew the lease, but had not protected it by a notice. If the freehold reversion was sold, and the purchaser was registered as proprietor, the unregistered option would bind him because it was an unregistered interest of a person in actual occupation: cf. para.6–044.

6–046   **4. The irrelevance of the doctrine of notice.** The doctrine of notice has no place in registered conveyancing, whether under the Land Registration Act 1925,[135] or under the Land Registration Act 2002, which makes specific provision for the application of principles of notice in three cases, and therefore necessarily excludes it in all others.[136] "The only kind of notice recognised is by entry on the register."[137] If a right is capable of registration but has not been registered, it will not bind a purchaser for valuable consideration unless it takes effect as an overriding interest.

Section 3. Extension of Overreaching Provisions

1. Methods of holding land on trust

6–047   *(a) Introduction.* Land may be held on trust by trustees in a number of different ways:

> (i) for persons who are entitled to the land successively, as where A by his will leaves property to his widow, B, for life and after her death to his children;

> (ii) for persons who are concurrently entitled to the land, as where land is held for A and B jointly; or

> (iii) for A absolutely, a type of trust known as a "bare trust".

6–048   *(b) Successive interests.* Prior to 1997,[138] successive interests in land might take effect either as settled land (often called a "strict settlement"[139]) or under a trust for sale. In a strict settlement (which was governed by the Settled Land Act 1925), the land itself was given to the beneficiaries, e.g. "to A for life with remainder to B in fee simple".[140] In a trust for sale the land was given to trustees who were instructed to sell it, invest the proceeds of sale, and hold the trust fund, perhaps again for A for life with remainder to B absolutely.

Whether the land was held in strict settlement or on trust for sale, the land could be sold. From the moment of sale the trusts attached to the proceeds of sale and not to the land. The trusts were said to be *overreached*, i.e. transferred from the land to the purchase-money. The land was in either case freed from

---

[135] " . . . the doctrine of purchaser for value without notice has no application to registered land": *Barclays Bank Plc v Boulter* [1998] 1 W.L.R. 1 at 11 per Mummery L.J.

[136] See below, para.7–064.

[137] *Williams & Glyn's Bank Ltd v Boland* [1981] A.C. 487 at 504, per Lord Wilberforce; below, para.8–006.

[138] When TLATA 1996 came into force.

[139] The term "strict settlement" primarily meant a marriage settlement in the usual form. However, in the absence of a better term it was often used to describe any settlement, in whatever form, that fell within the Settled Land Acts.

[140] The Settled Land Act settlement was the traditional means employed by settlors who wished to keep land in the family. The provisions of the Settled Land Act 1925 ensured that such land was not inalienable, even though it was held in settlement.

the trusts by the sale and the purchaser took the full beneficial interest in the land.[141]

After 1996, no further settlements can be created under the Settled Land Act 1925, though existing ones continue to be governed by its provisions.[142] When a settlor or testator now creates successive interests in land, they take effect under a trust of land,[143] the effect of which is briefly explained below. Although it remains possible to create trusts for sale of land expressly, and certain consequences still follow from so doing,[144] there will usually be no reason to do so. This is because:

(i) all trusts for sale—whether created before 1997 or after 1996—take effect as trusts of land[145]; and

(ii) there is implied into every trust for sale, despite any provision to the contrary in the disposition creating it, a power for the trustees to postpone sale.[146]

(c) Concurrent interests. Before 1997, concurrent interests in land usually took effect behind a trust for sale,[147] express or implied. Land might be conveyed to A and B to hold on an express trust for sale for C and D jointly or in common,[148] or it might simply be conveyed to A and B jointly or in common. In the latter case, there was a trust for sale implied by statute[149] and A and B held the property on a trust for themselves as joint tenants or tenants in common. The trustees had a duty to sell, but in the absence of a contrary intention, this was coupled with an implied power to postpone sale,[150] which in practice was commonly exercised. Since 1996, concurrent interests in land, whenever created, take effect behind trusts of land.[151]   **6–049**

(d) Bare trusts. A bare trust arises where a trustee is to hold or manage the land for the sole benefit of one beneficiary who is of full age.[152] The trustee is, in effect, a nominee, who holds the land at the direction of the beneficiary. Before 1997, such trusts took effect neither as settlements under the Settled Land Act 1925 nor (in the absence of an express provision) as trusts for sale. There was some uncertainty as to the powers of a bare trustee and whether   **6–050**

---

[141] For overreaching, see below.
[142] TLATA 1996 s.2(1).
[143] TLATA 1996 s.1.
[144] Below, para.12–005.
[145] TLATA 1996 s.1(2).
[146] TLATA 1996 s.4(1). The trustees are under no liability if, in the exercise of their discretion, they choose to postpone sale of the land for an indefinite period: see s.4(1).
[147] Concurrent interests could sometimes arise under Settled Land Act settlements, as where two persons were entitled to land for their joint lives: below, para.13–090.
[148] For the differences between joint tenancies and tenancies in common, see below, Ch.13.
[149] LPA 1925 ss.34 and 36; below, para.13–090. Those sections have now been amended by TLATA 1996 Sch. 2, paras 3, 4.
[150] LPA 1925 s.25, repealed by TLATA 1996 Sch.4.
[151] TLATA 1996 s.1. See below.
[152] For a fuller consideration of the nature of bare trusts, see below, para.12–008.

such a trustee could ever make a disposition of the land which would overreach the interest under the trust.[153] These uncertainties no longer exist. Bare trusts, whenever created, now take effect as trusts of land.[154]

6–051   **2. Trusts of land.** Any trust of property which consists of or includes land is a trust of land except for settled land (which is confined to settlements created prior to 1997) and land to which the Universities and College Estates Act 1925 applies.[155] Trustees of land hold the property on trust for the beneficiaries and are under no obligation to sell it. For the purposes of exercising their functions as trustees, they have in relation to the land held in trust all the powers of an absolute owner.[156] Provided that certain conditions are satisfied, trustees of land may make a disposition that will overreach all interests under the trust.[157] The details of trusts of land are fully explained later.[158]

6–052   **3. Overreaching.** Overreaching is the necessary corollary of a trust or power of disposition.[159] The term is nowadays understood in two distinct senses.

6–053   *(a) Subordination of one interest to another.* In its traditional meaning,[160] overreaching is the process whereby existing proprietary interests, whether legal or equitable, are subordinated to or "overridden" by[161] some later interest or estate created pursuant to a trust or power.[162] Thus under a mortgage, a mortgagor in possession has a statutory power to grant certain leases of the land. If he grants such a lease, it will bind the mortgagee, thereby subordinating the mortgagee's interest to the lessee's and so overreaching it, without transferring it to other property.[163] A mortgagee in possession has a similar power to grant certain leases which will bind the mortgagor's interest in the land, and so overreach that interest.[164] Overreaching in this broad sense was well-known by the early years of the 19th century.[165]

---

[153] See below, para.12–008.
[154] TLATA 1996 s.1(2).
[155] TLATA 1996 s.1.
[156] TLATA 1996 s.6(1). The instrument creating the trust may provide that this provision should not apply: TLATA 1996 s.8(1).
[157] Below, para.12–036.
[158] Below, Chs 11 and 12.
[159] Sugden, *Powers,* 483; *State Bank of India v Sood* [1997] Ch. 276.
[160] See Sugden, *Powers,* 482, 483; [1987] Conv. 451 at 453 (W. J. Swadling). This meaning has now been accepted by the Court of Appeal: *State Bank of India v Sood*, above.
[161] Prior to 1926 at least, the terms "overreach" and "override" were often used interchangeably: see Farwell, *Powers,* 581. An interest in unregistered land can probably be overridden however (but not overreached) in cases where the disposition is not within the powers of the grantor, but where the purchaser takes in good faith and without notice of the irregularity: cf. *State Bank of India v Sood* [1997] Ch. 276 at 281.
[162] [1990] C.L.J. 277 (C.H.).
[163] See below, paras 6–056, 25–073.
[164] See below, paras 6–056, 25–073.
[165] See e.g. *Wheate v Hall* (1809) 17 Ves. 80 at 86.

(b) Transfer of an interest in property to its proceeds. Overreaching has **6–054** tended to be used in a narrower sense to mean the process by which an interest in land is transferred from the land to the purchase money or other property acquired in exchange for it, leaving the land free from that interest. Thus where, under a settlement created before 1997, land is settled on A for life, with remainder to B in fee simple, A has a statutory power to sell the land (in fee simple), and when he does so, B's interest will be transferred from the land to the purchase money.[166] It is clear, however, that even in the context of dispositions of land held in trust, there has been a reversion to the wider traditional understanding of overreaching. Thus where trustees for sale mortgaged a property in consideration of an existing indebtedness, the interests of the beneficiaries were overreached by that mortgage and thereafter bound the equity of redemption.[167]

The draftsman of the 1925 property legislation placed statutory restrictions on the circumstances in which interests under both trusts for sale[168] and strict settlements could be overreached, thereby providing greater protection for the beneficiaries.[169] Overreaching applies to trusts of both registered and unregistered land,[170] and to all types of property, not merely land.

Interests under both trusts of land and strict settlements may all be overreached if the disposition is one which is within the powers of the trustees,[171] whether those powers are conferred by statute or by the trust itself.[172] Overreaching is therefore a valuable means of preventing interests of the "family" type from inconveniencing purchasers. It is inappropriate for rights of a "commercial" character such as estate contracts or restrictive covenants which cannot readily be converted into money.[173] Their protection is necessarily by registration because they are intended to endure despite changes in the ownership of the land burdened by them.

4. Extent of overreaching. Overreaching, like registration, can be applied, **6–055** and has been applied, to legal interests as well as to certain types of equitable

---

[166] See below, Appendix, A–094—A–100. In such a situation, B's interest can be said to be both "overreached and overridden": see *City of London Building Society v Flegg* [1988] A.C. 73, 74, per Lord Templeman (a case concerned with an overreaching disposition by trustees for sale).

[167] *State Bank of India v Sood* [1997] Ch. 276.

[168] Which are now trusts of land.

[169] Below, Appendix, A–098 et seq.

[170] See in relation to LRA 1925 *City of London Building Society* v *Flegg,* above; and LRA 1925 s.58(3). As regards the present law, see LRA 2002 ss.42(1)(b); 44.

[171] For the limits on the dispositive powers of life tenants under a strict settlement, see below, Appendix, A–005. Trustees of land will normally have in relation to the land subject to the trust all the powers of an absolute owner, so that all dispositions will be within their powers: see below, para.12–016.

[172] For a more detailed treatment of the overreaching provisions applicable to trusts of land and strict settlements, see below, para.12–036; Appendix A–093.

[173] See *Birmingham Midshires Mortgage Services Ltd v Sabherwal* (1999) 80 P. & C.R. 256; [2000] Conv.267 (M.J.D.); (2000) 116 LQR 341 (C.H.); *Sommer v Sweet* [2005] EWCA Civ 227 at [26]. Both cases concerned an equity by estoppel (see below, Ch.16). In the former case, effect would be given to the equity by means of a beneficial interest under a trust of land and in the latter by an easement. The former could be overreached, but the latter could not.

interests. Before 1926 the rights of beneficiaries under a settlement might be either legal (if the legal estate had been conveyed to them) or equitable (if it had been conveyed to trustees on trust from them). In either case the rights could be overreached:

(i) under an express power contained in the settlement, or

(ii) under the Settled Land Act 1882.

Since 1925 no legal life estate, entail or remainder is possible. A power to overreach legal estates under settlements is therefore no longer needed. However, overreaching is now far more important than it was prior to 1926 because of the statutory extension of what are now trusts of land[174] to certain situations where they did not exist before, e.g. under an intestacy, or in the case of concurrent interests.[175]

6–056   **5. Other overreaching conveyances.** Although settlements and trusts of land are the most important sources of overreaching conveyances, they are not the only sources. Thus, if X has mortgaged his land to M, and then fails to keep up the payments due, M has a statutory power to sell the land free from X's equitable right to redeem it. X's rights will then be transferred to the purchase-money in M's hands, for M is a trustee for X of any surplus after paying off the mortgage debt.[176] Again, a conveyance by the personal representatives of a deceased person will overreach the claims of the beneficiaries under the will or intestacy; the purchaser gets a clear title, and the beneficiaries are satisfied out of the purchase-money.[177] A list of overreaching conveyances is to be found in s.2(1) of the Law of Property Act 1925,[178] though it is not comprehensive. This section and others in the 1925 property legislation[179] regulate the manner in which overreaching can take place in those situations specifically listed in s.2(1), but they do not preclude it in other cases.[180] Thus mortgagors or mortgagees, if in possession, have statutory powers to grant leases which will overreach both the rights of the other party, and those of other prior parties.[181]

In general, it is only equitable rights that need now to be overreached. There are, however, a few exceptional cases where there is a statutory power to overreach legal rights. These include:

---

[174] What were trusts for sale prior to 1997.
[175] See below, paras 13–051 (concurrent interests), 14–104 (intestacy). See too para.12–014.
[176] Below, para.25–020.
[177] Below, para.14–142.
[178] As amended by TLATA 1996 Sch.3, para.4.
[179] See, e.g. SLA 1925 s.94(1).
[180] This is clear from the history of the 1925 property legislation: [1990] C.L.J. 277, 287–304 (C.H.). What is now LPA 1925 s.2(l) differs markedly from its precursor, LPA 1922 s.3(2). See *State Bank of India v Sood* [1997] Ch. 276 at 287.
[181] LPA 1925 s.99; below, para.25–073.

(i) a mortgagee's power to overreach the mortgagor's legal estate on sale[182];

(ii) a mortgagor's right to grant a lease that is binding on the mortgagee[183]; and

(iii) a mortgagee's corresponding right to grant a lease that is binding on the mortgagor.[184]

Section 4. Effect of a Sale on Legal and Equitable Rights

The operation of the provisions set out above on a sale of land subject to legal and equitable rights may be summarised and illustrated as follows. 6–057

1. Summary

(a) Where the title is unregistered.

The purchaser takes subject to all legal rights.

Exceptions: He takes free from:

(i) the few legal rights which are void against him for want of registration; and

(ii) the few legal rights which are overreached

(2) The purchaser takes subject to all equitable rights. 6–058

Exceptions: He takes free from:

(i) equitable rights which are void against him for want of registration: notice is irrelevant;

(ii) the many equitable rights which are overreached, e.g. under a settlement or trust of land: notice is irrelevant; and

(iii) unregistrable and non-overreachable equitable rights in respect of which he can show either that he is a bona fide purchaser of a legal estate for value without notice, or else that he claims through such a person.

(b) Where the title is registered. The purchaser takes subject to all entries on 6–059
the register, any overriding interests and any rights excluded from registration
by reason of the class of title, but free from all other rights. Notice is

---

[182] LPA ss.101, 103, 104; below, para.25–016.
[183] LPA 1925 s.99; below, para.25–073.
[184] LPA 1925 s.99; below, para.25–073.

irrelevant. It is immaterial for this purpose whether a right is legal or equitable.

6–060   **2. Example.** An example may be of assistance in understanding the above summary. A has bought land from trustees of land, and at the time of the sale the land was subject to:

(i) the rights of the beneficiaries under the trust of land,

(ii) a restrictive covenant imposed before 1926,

(iii) a binding contract of sale made by the trustees with X shortly before they offered the land to A (an estate contract), and

(iv) a lease to Y (a legal estate).

A's position is as follows.

(a) Where the title is unregistered.

6–061   (i) A is not bound by the rights of the beneficiaries (class (2)(ii) above).

(ii) He is bound by the pre-1926 restrictive covenant only if he had notice of it at the time of completing his purchase (class (2)(iii) above).

(iii) He is bound to give up the land to X, the earlier purchaser, only if X registered his estate contract before A completed his purchase (class (2)(i) above).

(iv) He is in any event bound by the lease.

(b) Where the title is registered.

6–062   (i) A is not bound by the rights of the beneficiaries: they will be overreached in the same way as when the title is unregistered.

(ii) He is bound by the pre-1926 restrictive covenant only if it was protected by an appropriate entry on the register.[185]

(iii) He is bound to give up the land to X, the earlier purchaser, only if X either protected his estate contract by an entry on the register before A was registered as proprietor of the land, or was for some reason in actual occupation of the land at the time of A's purchase so that the right was an overriding interest.

(iv) He is bound by the lease either because it is protected by an entry on the register or because it takes effect as an overriding interest.

---

[185] In practice, such an entry would have been made at the time when the title was first registered or not at all.

3. Legal and equitable rights. The classical doctrine that legal rights bind   **6–063**
all the world while equitable rights do not bind a bona fide purchaser of a legal
estate without notice is now of only residual importance in dealings with
unregistered land. It has no role to play in the scheme of registered conveyancing. Indeed where title is registered the difference between legal and
equitable rights is now much diminished. Where title is registered, whether a
right is legal or equitable is relevant only to the remedies that exist to enforce
that right and to the nature of any entry that is made on the register to protect
the right.

Section 5. New Equitable Interests?

It is often said that the category of equitable interests is not closed and that   **6–064**
new ones may therefore be created.[186] However this ignores the Delphic
proviso to s.4(1) of the Law of Property Act 1925 by which:

> "after the commencement of this Act (and save as hereinafter expressly
> enacted), an equitable interest in land shall only be capable of being
> validly created in any case in which an equivalent equitable interest in
> property real or personal could have been validly created before such
> commencement".

This proviso has tended to be overlooked and although it has never been the
subject of any detailed judicially consideration.[187] it has been assumed that it
precludes There appear to be three elements in it.

(i) It makes it clear that equitable interests in land can be created in
any case in which such interests could have existed in real or
personal property prior to 1926.[188] It is therefore one of the
provisions of the 1925 legislation that assimilate the rules applicable to real and personal property.

(ii) That general rule is subject to the qualification that some interests
cannot be created after 1925 because of certain provisions of the
Law of Property Act 1925 itself.[189]

---

[186] Harman J. is reputed to have said that "Equity is not presumed to be of an age past
childbearing", but was unable to recall the context: see Megarry, *Miscellany-at-Law* (1955), p.
142; *A Second Miscellany-at-Law* (1973), p. 293. See too *Pennine Raceway Ltd v Kirklees
Metropolitan BC* [1983] QB 382 at 392. cf. *Western Fish Products Ltd v Penwith DC* (1978)
[1981] 2 All E.R. 204 at 218, where Megaw L.J. observed that "the system of equity has become
a very precise one. The creation of new rights and remedies is a matter for Parliament, not the
judges".

[187] cf. *E. R. Ives Investment Ltd v High* [1967] 2 QB 379 at 395; and see (1937) 59 L.Q.R. 259
at 260 (C. V. Davidge); but see *Hatchett-Stamford v Att. Gen.* [2008] EWHC 330 (Ch) at [31];
[2009] Ch. 173 at 183, 184.

[188] Wolst. & C. i. 60.

[189] There were a number of such provisions: see, e.g. LPA 1925 s.130(2) (now repealed; above,
para.3–032).

(iii) It appears to preclude the creation of novel forms of equitable interest after 1925. This would seem to follow from the use in the proviso of the word "only".[190]

6–065   It is this third element that is the most important, and the history of the proviso tends to confirm that it was intended to have this effect.[191] In its final form, the draftsman's scheme for the protection of equitable interests in unregistered land appears to have been based on the assumption that, as far as possible, all equitable interests should be either overreachable or registrable as land charges, and that the doctrine of notice should pay only a residual role.[192] The draftsman did not lay down a general rule that all equitable rights over land which were incapable of being overreached should be registrable. Instead he specifically listed the charges that could be registered in the Land Charges Act 1925.[193] The creation of new equitable interests would necessarily defeat the draftsman's purpose because it would increase the number of rights which would depend for their protection on the doctrine of notice. No new kinds of equitable interest have in fact been created since 1925.[194] However it has become clear that the list of registrable rights is incomplete. A number of equitable rights have arisen that do not fall within it and these are therefore protected by the doctrine of notice.[195] It may be noted that the practical objection to the creation of new types of equitable interest does not apply where the title is registered. The burden of any interest affecting a registered estate can be protected by the entry of a notice in the register.[196]

Section 6. Personal Rights which May Affect Third Parties

6–066   Although legislation would probably now be required to create new equitable proprietary interests, rights of a purely personal character affecting land may sometimes be enforced indirectly by or against third parties either under the law of tort or by means of a constructive trust. The availability of such remedies is most likely to be important where the right in issue is:

(i) a mere licence[197]; or

---

[190] This was assumed to be the case in *Hanchett-Stamford v Attorney-General* [2008] EWHC 330 (Ch) at [31]; [2009] Ch. 173 at 183–184.

[191] See J. S. Anderson, *Lawyers and the Making of English Land Law 1832–1940*, at p. 309. LPA 1925 s.4 was first introduced by the LPAmA 1924, together with both the final version of the overreaching provisions and the extension of the system of registration of land charges.

[192] He originally intended that all equitable interests should be overreachable, whether of a family or of a commercial character: J. S. Anderson, op. cit., at 296.

[193] Now replaced by LCA 1972.

[194] Though there have been unsuccessful attempts to do so: below, paras 34–017 (contractual licences), 34–022 (deserted wife's equity). If it had been cited, the proviso might have provided another ground for rejecting the deserted wife's equity.

[195] Below, paras 8–080, 8–081.

[196] LRA 2002 s.32.

[197] It seems probable that licences are merely personal rights which do not create interests in land: below, Ch.34.

(ii) a property right which is not binding on a purchaser of the land because it has not been registered.[198]

Formerly, it also arose in the context of contractual rights, as where A sold land to B expressly subject to C's contractual licence from A to use that property. The rule of privity of contract meant that C could not enforce the contract between A and B. Such cases should now be rare, following the enactment of the Contracts (Rights of Third Parties) Act 1999,[199] because it is open to parties to make their contract enforceable by a third party.

1. Remedies in tort. It is increasingly common for litigants to have **6–067** recourse to the so-called economic torts, such as inducing breach of contract, causing loss by unlawful means[200] and conspiracy,[201] in relation to dealings with land. Thus, by way of example, there is no doubt that "on ordinary principles" the tort of wrongful interference with a contract is applicable to contracts concerning land.[202] The tort is committed when C deliberately procures an act which, as a matter of law or construction, is a breach of a contract made between A and B.[203] There must be a breach of contract: merely preventing or hindering performance is not sufficient.[204] For C to be liable, "actual knowledge of the breach, and the intention that the breach be committed, must be established".[205] For these purposes, wilful blindness is treated as actual knowledge.[206] Constructive notice of the agreement,[207] or honest doubts as to its existence or validity,[208] are not enough.

---

[198] Below, paras 7–053 (registered land); 8–091 (unregistered land).

[199] For a discussion of the Act, which implemented the recommendations in (1996) Law Com. No.242, see *Avraamides v Colwill* [2006] EWCA Civ 1533; and see further below, para. 11–022.

[200] For the elements of this tort, see *OBG Ltd v Allan* [2007] UKHL 21 at [47], [51]; [2008] A.C. 1 at 31–33; *Thames Valley Housing Association Ltd v Elegant Homes (Guernsey) Ltd* [2011] EWHC 1288 (Ch) at [102], [103]. It is a tort of primary liability: *OBG Ltd v Allan* [2007] UKHL 21 at [8]; [2008] A.C. 1 at. 20–21. For a case where such a claim failed, see *Meretz Investments NV v ACP Ltd* [2007] EWCA Civ 1303; [2008] Ch. 244.

[201] As regards conspiracy, see *Midland Bank Trust Co Ltd v Green (No.3)* [1982] Ch. 529; *Hemingway Securities Ltd v Dunraven Ltd* [1995] 1 E.G.L.R. 61 at 62.

[202] *Binions v Evans* [1972] Ch. 359 at 371, per Megaw L.J. See too *Sefton v Tophams Ltd* [1965] Ch. 1140 at 1160–1162, 1187.

[203] *OBG Ltd v Allan* [2007] UKHL 21 at [39]; [2008] A.C. 1 at 29. For the essentials of the tort, see *OBG Ltd v Allan* [2007] UKHL 21 at [39]–[44]; 29–31; *Thames Valley Housing Association Ltd v Elegant Homes (Guernsey) Ltd* [2011] EWHC 1288 (Ch) at [101].

[204] *OBG Ltd v Allan* [2007] UKHL 21 at [44]; [2008] A.C. 1 at 30–31. There is no tort where D knowingly deprives A of his claim to a remedy against C for interference with A's contract with B: *Law Debenture Trust Corporation v Ural Caspian Oil Corporation Ltd* [1995] Ch. 152. But cf. (1995) 111 L.Q.R. 400 (P. Cane).

[205] *Crestfort Ltd v Tesco Stores Ltd* [2005] EWHC 805 (Ch) at [60]; [2005] 3 E.G.L.R. 25 at 32, per Lightman J.

[206] *Emerald Construction Ltd v Lowthian* [1966] 1 W.L.R. 691 at 700, 701; *OBG Ltd v Allan* [2007] UKHL 21 at [40]; [2008] A.C. 1 at 29–30.

[207] *Swiss Bank Corporation v Lloyds Bank Ltd* [1979] Ch. 548 at 575 (reversed on other grounds [1982] A.C. 584).

[208] *Smith v Morrison* [1974] 1 W.L.R. 659 at 677, 678.

In one remarkable case,[209] B Ltd, which owned a garage, covenanted that it would buy petrol only from A, and that if it sold the garage, it would obtain a similar covenant from the purchaser. A " solus agreement" of this kind is personal to the parties to it and does not create a property right. C Ltd acquired the shares in B Ltd. procured the transfer of the garage to one of its subsidiary companies in order to defeat the solus tie, and started to sell petrol from a different supplier. Even though the subsidiary had been registered as proprietor of the garage, the court granted a mandatory injunction in interlocutory proceedings requiring it to reconvey the property to B Ltd.[210] In this way, a mere contractual right was enforced against a third party who had brought about its breach.

In another case,[211] B granted A a contractual licence to live in a cottage for her lifetime. B then sold the cottage to C expressly subject to A's rights. C attempted to evict A. One ground for dismissing C's claim, was that it amounted to an interference with B's contractual rights with A. In effect therefore, C was held to be bound by B's licence.

Justification may be a defence.[212] In particular, C may plead that his conduct was justified by some equal or superior right.[213] Thus if A contracted to sell Blackacre to C, and then subsequently contracted to sell it to B, C would be entitled to require A to fulfil his contract even though he knew that he would thereby procure a breach of A's contract with B.[214] Similarly, if A had mortgaged his land to C, C could exercise his paramount power of sale even though in so doing he might bring about a breach of some contract relating to the land which A had made with B and of which C was aware.[215] It is less clear whether C would be justified in interfering in a contract just because it was not binding on him for want of registration. There is some authority which suggests that he would.[216] However, in another case, C was held liable in the tort of conspiracy where land was transferred to her by B in

---

[209] *Esso Petroleum Co Ltd v Kingswood Motors (Addlestone) Ltd* [1974] Q.B. 142. Although the case has been criticised: see (1977) 41 Conv. (N.S.) 318 (R. J. Smith), not only has it been repeatedly applied (see *Hemingway Securities Ltd v Dunraven Ltd* [1995] 1 E.G.L.R. 61; *Test Valley BC v Minilec Engineering Ltd* [2005] 2 E.G.L.R. 113), but its correctness was not doubted by the Court of Appeal in *Law Debenture Trust Corporation v Ural Caspian Oil Corporation Ltd*, above.

[210] *À fortiori*, A could have obtained an injunction restraining the transfer of the property to the subsidiary if he had acted sooner: cf. *Smith v Morrison,* above. See too *Hemingway Securities Ltd v Dunraven Ltd* [1995] 1 E.G.L.R. 61; below, para.18–053; [1995] Conv. 416 (P. Luxton and M. Wilkie), where a tenant sublet without the landlord's consent in breach of covenant. The subtenant was considered to have induced or assisted that breach and was ordered to surrender the sublease. For a similar case, see *Crestfort Ltd v Tesco Stores Ltd* [2005] EWHC 805 (Ch); [2005] 3 E.G.L.R. 25.

[211] *Binions v Evans* [1972] Ch. 359.

[212] See, e.g., *Meretz Investments NV v ACP Ltd* [2007] EWCA Civ 1303 at [142]; [2008] Ch. 244 at 282–283.

[213] *Read v Friendly Society of Operative Stonemasons* [1902] 2 KB. 88 at 96, 97.

[214] *Pritchard v Briggs* [1980] Ch. 338 at 415.

[215] *Edwin Hill v First National Finance Corporation Plc* [1989] 1 W.L.R. 225 at 229. Cf. *Meretz Investments NV v ACP Ltd* [2007] EWCA Civ 1303; [2008] Ch. 244. For a mortgagee's power of sale, see below, para.25–013.

[216] cf. *Miles v Bull (No.2)* [1969] 3 All E.R. 1585 at 1590.

order to defeat A's unregistered option to purchase it.[217] This was so even though C took the land free of the option.[218]

2. Constructive trusts.[219] In certain circumstances, if B grants A a right **6–068** over his land and then transfers the property to C expressly subject to that right, the court may impose a constructive trust on C, requiring him to give effect to the right, even though it is not binding on him as a matter of property law.[220] In such a case, the court imposes a new liability on C rather than holding him bound by an existing interest.[221] It will do so only if it would be unconscionable for him to deny A the right.[222] If there is no contract between A and B, no tortious remedy is likely to be available to A and a constructive trust of this kind may provide the only possible form of relief.[223]

---

[217] *Midland Bank Trust Co Ltd Green (No.3)* [1982] Ch. 529 (where the point was not expressly argued). Justification is a defence to the tort of conspiracy: *Crofter Hand Woven Harris Tweed Co Ltd v Veitch* [1942] A.C. 435 at 476.
[218] *Midland Bank Trust Co Ltd v Green* [1981] A.C. 513; below, para.8–095.
[219] Below, paras 11–017 et seq.
[220] e.g. because it is a personal right such as a licence or is a property right which is void against C for non-registration.
[221] *IDC Group Ltd v Clark* [1992] 1 E.G.L.R. 187 at 190.
[222] *IDC Group Ltd v Clark* [1992] 1 E.G.L.R. 187 at 190; *Ashburn Anstalt v Arnold* [1989] Ch. 1 at 22, 25; *Lloyd v Dugdale* [2001] EWCA Civ 1754 at [50]–[52]; [2002] 2 P. & C.R. 167 at 181–183.
[223] In some cases, A may be able to enforce a contract between B and C for his benefit pursuant to the Contracts (Rights of Third Parties) Act 1999; see below, para.11–022.

CHAPTER 7

REGISTRATION OF TITLE

Part 1

INTRODUCTION

7–001　**1. The nature of land registration.** Registration of title is a fundamental departure from the traditional system by which the title is deduced historically. Instead the register records the title to the property that has been registered,[1] providing a statement of the title as it stands at any given time.[2] This makes it unnecessary for a purchaser of registered land to investigate title by examination of the abstract of title and title deeds, as he would on the purchase of unregistered land. Prior to the introduction of compulsory first registration, this process of investigation had to be repeated in full by every subsequent purchaser. Where title is registered, a purchaser investigates title by searching the register: the register is the title.[3] The purchaser can discover from the register whether the seller has power to sell the land.[4] The register also discloses many important incumbrances, though in relation to a diminishing number of other incumbrances,[5] the purchaser must make investigations in much the same way as in the case of unregistered land.

---

[1] See further below, para.7–113.

[2] It is possible to discover the history of a title on application to the Land Registry, to the extent that it is held in electronic form: see below, para.7–123.

[3] Formerly, the registered proprietor was given a land certificate, which had to be produced in certain circumstances. However, this practice has been abolished since LRA 2002 came into force. Although there is a power to make provision for such certificates by rules (see LRA 2002 Sch.10 para.4), it has not been exercised. Accordingly, such certificates are now irrelevant.

[4] The register tells him who owns the legal estate and he can assume that the owner's powers of disposition are unfettered in the absence of any entry to the contrary in the register: see below, paras 7–049 et seq.

[5] For unregistered interests which override registered dispositions: see below, paras 7–008, 7–086.

The differences between the system of registered title and the traditional system are substantive and do not merely affect the machinery of conveyancing. They include the following:

(i) Registration vests the legal title in the registered proprietor, whether or not there has been a valid transfer to him.[6]

(ii) The system of registered title abandons the principle that no one can pass a better title than he has (*nemo dat quod non habet*),[7] and substitutes for it a principle of qualified indefeasibility of the registered title.[8] The register can be altered, but the circumstances in which this may happen are limited.[9]

(iii) The system of priorities for registered land is entirely statutory and is completely different from the rules applicable to unregistered land.[10]

(iv) A registered title is guaranteed by the State in the sense that, where there is a mistake in the register and a person suffers loss in consequence, the Land Registry will indemnify that person for his loss.[11]

The whole of England and Wales has been subject to compulsory registration since December 1, 1990.[12] This means that where there is a disposition of unregistered land that triggers compulsory registration, the title must be registered.[13] At present about 60 per cent of the land area of England and Wales has been registered. Much of the unregistered land is rural because most urban land has been registered on the occurrence of a triggering disposition.

2. Open register.[14] Prior to December 3, 1990, the land register was not **7–002** open to public inspection,[15] though an Index Map could (and still can) be searched by the public.[16] From this index it is possible to determine whether any particular parcel of land has been registered. The secrecy of the land

---

[6] See below, para.7–117.
[7] See above, para.4–001.
[8] See below, paras 7–131 et seq.
[9] See below, paras 7–133 et seq.
[10] See below, para.7–060.
[11] See below, paras 7–140 et seq.
[12] SI 1989/1347.
[13] See below, paras 7–013, 7–018—7–020.
[14] See Ruoff & Roper, 4.009.
[15] In general no person could inspect the register without the authority of the registered proprietor.
[16] See LRA 2002 s.68; LRR 2003 rr.10, 145.

registration system was much criticised, and the Law Commission recommended that the register should be open to public inspection.[17] That recommendation was implemented by the Land Registration Act 1988, which was brought into force on December 3, 1990.[18]

Until the Land Registration Act 2002 came into force on October 13, 2003,[19] any person might, subject to prescribed conditions and on payment of a fee, inspect and make copies of and extracts from both entries in the register and documents referred to in the register which were in the custody of the registrar (other than leases or charges or copies of leases or charges).[20] Other documents in the custody of the registrar (i.e. leases and charges and documents not referred to on the register) might be inspected as of right in certain prescribed cases,[21] and at his discretion in all other instances.[22]

The Land Registration Act 2002 further extended the open register. A person may now inspect and make copies of, or any part of, among other things, the register of title and any document which is referred to in the register and kept by the registrar (including leases and charges).[23] This is, however, subject to certain exceptions, which are explained later.[24]

The open nature of the register is not merely notional. It is no longer necessary to make an application to the Land Registry for a copy of the register. The register of title is kept in computerised form and is now available for inspection via the Land Registry website on payment of a fee to the Land Registry. However, it is still necessary to apply to the Land Registry for an official copy of the register, either by paper application[25] or online.[26] A copy downloaded from the Land Register Online website is not an official copy.

7–003   **3. The Land Registration Act 2002.** It has been explained that the Land Registration Act 2002, and the rules made under it, replaced all earlier legislation on land registration, and in particular the Land Registration Act 1925 and the Land Registration Rules 1925.[27] The 2002 Act enacted the joint recommendations of the Law Commission and the Land Registry.[28] One of the principal functions of the 2002 Act was to provide the legislative framework for the introduction of electronic conveyancing. Electronic conveyancing is to

[17] (1986) Law Com. No.148.

[18] By SI 1990/1359.

[19] There were in fact four commencement orders: SI 2003/935, SI 2003/1028, SI 2003/1612 and SI 2003/1725. The last order brought the Act into force as regards dealings with land and repealed all previous legislation.

[20] LRA 1925 s.112(1) (substituted by LRA 1988).

[21] LRA 1925 s.112(2)(a) (substituted by LRA 1988). The special cases concerned criminal proceedings, receivership and insolvency.

[22] LRA 1925 s.112(2)(b) (substituted by LRA 1988).

[23] LRA 2002 s.66(1)(a), (b).

[24] LRA 2002 s.66(2), LRR 2003 Pt 13; below, para.7–121.

[25] Using Form OC1 for a copy of the register and Form OC2 for a copy of any document referred to in the register: see LRR 2003 rr.134, 135.

[26] See LRPG 11.

[27] See above, para.6–041.

[28] See (2001) Law Com. No.271. There was a prior consultative report: (1998) Law Com. No.254.

be introduced gradually. The first pilot schemes for aspects of such a system have been launched. An eventual consequence of the introduction of electronic conveyancing is that it will become impossible to make a disposition of registered land except by simultaneously registering it.[29] It will therefore be registration that confers title, thereby creating a system of title by registration rather than merely the registration of title.[30]

The changes made by the Land Registration Act 2002 are so substantial that authorities on the previous law are unlikely to provide much assistance, except in those comparatively rare cases where the legislation has not changed. In interpreting the Act, guidance may be obtained from the joint reports of the Law Commission and Land Registry which preceded it.[31] The Land Registry has also published an extensive series of Practice Guides.[32]

Rules have been made pursuant to the Act,[33] in particular the Land Registration Rules 2003, but also others dealing with, e.g. adjudication[34] and fees. The power to make land registration rules,[35] which are rules that explain how land registration is conducted, is exercisable by the Lord Chancellor with the advice and assistance of the Rules Committee.[36] The Rules Committee comprises a judge of the Chancery Division of the High Court, and persons nominated by specified interested bodies (such as the General Council of the Bar and the Council of the Law Society).[37]

4. Basic concepts. The Land Registration Act 2002 employs the following concepts either by name or in substance. **7–004**

(a) Registrable estates. The Act provides that certain legal estates may be registered with their own titles.[38] Although the Act does not use the term, these are for convenience referred to as registrable estates.[39] When a registrable estate has been registered, it is called a registered estate.[40] **7 005**

(b) Registrable dispositions. Certain dispositions of a registered estate must be registered if they are to take effect at law and not merely in equity. These **7–006**

---

[29] LRA 2002 s.93; below, para.7–163.

[30] See (2001) Law Com. No.271, para.1.10. cf. *Creque v Penn* [2007] UKPC 44 at [13].

[31] See (1998) Law Com. No.254 (consultative report) and (2001) Law Com. No.271 (final report). Recourse to such reports is "both appropriate and permissible": *Yaxley v Gotts* [2000] Ch. 162 at 182, per Clarke L.J.

[32] These are available on the Internet from *www.landreg.gov.uk* (under Forms, Guides and Publications).

[33] The rule-making powers are found throughout LRA 2002. There are in addition some general rule-making powers in LRA 2002 Sch.10.

[34] See LRRAR 2003 and APPR 2003.

[35] Defined by LRA 2002 s.132(1). Not all rules made pursuant to LRA 2002 are land registration rules.

[36] LRA 2002 s.127(1).

[37] LRA 2002 s.127(2).

[38] "Legal estate" has the same meaning as in LPA 1925: LRA 2002 s.132(1). See above, para.6–012; and LPA 1925 s.1(4).

[39] Registered estates do not include registered charges (which do not have their own title on the register): see LRA 2002 s.132(1).

[40] LRA 2002 s.132(1).

are called registrable dispositions.[41] They are transfers of the legal estate or the creation of legal estates, interests or charges. The Act prescribes the registration requirements for such dispositions.[42]

7–007   *(c) Protection of interests.* There are three methods of protecting interests in land by means of an entry in the register:

(i) Legal charges are protected by entry in the register as registered charges.[43] They do not have their own titles, but the name of the proprietor of the charge is recorded in the register.[44]

(ii) The burden of many (but not all) interests may be protected by the entry of a notice,[45] which may be either an agreed or a unilateral notice.[46] Both cautions against dealings and inhibitions, which were forms of protection available under the Land Registration Act 1925,[47] were prospectively abolished by the Land Registration Act 2002.[48]

(iii) A restriction may be entered which regulates the circumstances in which a disposition of a registered estate or charge may be the subject of an entry in the register.[49] Restrictions may be used for a wide range of purposes. They are the only means of protecting interests under a trust of land or a settlement and are entered to ensure that such interests are overreached on any disposition of the land affected.[50]

7–008   *(d) Overriding interests.* These are estates, rights and interests which are not protected in the register in any way, but which nonetheless override first registration or, as the case may be, a disposition of a registered estate.[51] The interests which override first registration are more extensive than those which override a registered disposition.[52] Unlike the Land Registration Act 1925, the Land Registration Act 2002 does not use the term "overriding interests" as such,[53] but retains the concept.[54] The range of overriding interests is narrower than it was under the Land Registration Act 1925,[55] and will become narrower

---

[41] LRA 2002 ss.27, 132(1).
[42] LRA 2002 s.27(4), Sch.2.
[43] LRA 2002 ss.27(2)(f), 132(1).
[44] LRA 2002 Sch.2, para.8.
[45] LRA 2002 s.32.
[46] LRA 2002 s.34.
[47] See respectively LRA 1925 ss.54 and 57.
[48] For the transitional provisions, see LRA 2002 s.134; Sch.12 paras 1–4.
[49] LRA 2002 s.40.
[50] See LRA 2002 ss.33(a), 42(1)(b).
[51] LRA 2002 Sch.1 and Sch.3.
[52] See below, para.7–086.
[53] For overriding interests under LRA 1925, see s.3(xvi) of that Act.
[54] The term "overriding interest" appears in LRR 2003 rr.28, 57.
[55] See LRA 2002 Sch.3; below, paras 7–086 et seq.

still as certain interests cease to be overriding on October 13, 2013.[56] Overriding interests are an obstacle to achieving a conclusive register, which is one of the principal objectives of the Land Registration Act 2002.[57] Accordingly, the Act contains a number of provisions for eliminating them as far as possible.

Part 2

FIRST REGISTRATION

1. Voluntary and compulsory first registration. The Land Registration   **7–009**
Act 2002 makes provision for:

(a) the voluntary first registration of an unregistered legal estate by a landowner; and

(b) the compulsory first registration of an unregistered legal estate where any one of a number of specified triggering events occurs in relation to that estate.[58]

(a) Voluntary first registration. A person who owns or is entitled to have   **7–010**
vested in him[59] any of the following unregistered estates may apply to be registered as proprietor of that estate with its own title:

(a) a freehold estate in land;

(b) a lease granted for a term of which more than seven years are unexpired[60];

(c) a discontinuous lease of any duration[61];

(d) a rentcharge that is either perpetual or for a term of years of which more than seven years are unexpired;

(e) a franchise (such as a right to hold a market) granted for an interest equivalent to a fee simple absolute in possession or a term of years of which more than seven years are unexpired; and

---

[56] See below, paras 7–030, 7–031, 7–087, 7–088.

[57] For this objective, see above, para.6–041; and see (2001) Law Com. No.271, paras 2.24–2.25, 8.1.

[58] See generally LRPG 1.

[59] Such as a beneficiary under a bare trust, but not a person who has contracted to buy the land: LRA 2002 s.3(6).

[60] Typically, this will be a lease that was granted for 21 years or less before LRA 2002 came into force, and which was not, at that time, registrable. If, in relation to the same land, a person holds a lease in possession and a lease in reversion that is to take effect in possession on, or within one month of the end of the lease in possession, they are treated as creating one continuous term for the purposes of LRA 2002 s.3: see s.3(7).

[61] A typical example of a discontinuous lease is a timeshare lease under which the lessee is entitled to occupy the property for a series of discontinuous periods.

(f) a profit à prendre in gross (such as a right to fish or shoot game) granted for an interest equivalent to a fee simple absolute in possession or a term of years of which more than seven years are unexpired.[62]

Two classes of lease are not voluntarily registrable:

(i) A "PPP lease",[63] as defined by the Greater London Authority Act 1999.[64] Such leases, which have been granted for terms of 30 years, relate to underground railways, stations and other installations. It was thought that the difficulties of mapping the demised premises would make registration impractical.

(ii) A term of years created in favour of a mortgagee under a mortgage by demise,[65] where there is a subsisting right of redemption.[66] The term of years is simply a mechanism for mortgaging the land.[67]

7–011   There are three changes in the estates that can be registered in comparison with the previous law.

(i) It is now possible to register profits à prendre in gross with their own titles. There was no such provision in the Land Registration Act 1925.

(ii) The length of lease that may be registered has been significantly reduced. Under the Land Registration Act 1925, it was only possible to register voluntarily an unregistered lease if it had more than 21 years unexpired.[68]

(iii) Under the Land Registration Act 1925, the owner of a manor could register it with its own title.[69] That is no longer possible under the Land Registration Act 2002, which intentionally makes no provision for their registration.[70] However, the Act applies to dealings with manors that had been registered before it came into force.[71] It is possible for the registered proprietor of a manor to apply to the registrar to have the title removed from the register.[72]

---

[62] LRA 2002 s.3(1)–(4). For rentcharges, see below, para.31–014, for franchises, see below, para.31–013 and for profits à prendre in gross, see below, para.27–001 and 27–068.

[63] See LRA 2002 s.90(1). "PPP" is short for "public–private partnership".

[64] See s.218; LRA 2002 s.90(6).

[65] See LPA 1925 ss.85(1), 86(1), below, para.24–020.

[66] LRA 2002 s.3(4).

[67] For mortgages by demise and sub-demise, see below, para.24–020.

[68] See LRA 1925 s.8(1)(a).

[69] See the definition of "land" in LRA 1925 s.3(viii), which included a manor, and LRR 1925 rr.50, 51. Manors are an incorporeal hereditament. For the nature of such rights after 1925, see above, para.2–029.

[70] See (2001) Law Com. No.271, para.3.21.

[71] See below, para.7–054.

[72] LRA 2002 s.119.

Special provision is made by the Land Registration Act 2002 to deal with **7–012**
the voluntary registration of certain Crown land. Because only an *estate* in
land may be registered with its own title, the Crown was unable to register the
land that was held by Her Majesty in demesne as sovereign or lord paramount.[73] The most significant holding of demesne land is the foreshore.[74]
Under the Act, Her Majesty may grant an estate in fee simple absolute in
possession to Herself in order to make an application for the voluntary
registration of that estate under the provisions explained above.[75]

(b) Compulsory first registration. The compulsory registration of unregis- **7–013**
tered legal estates under the Land Registration Act 1925 was triggered by
particular dispositions of unregistered land.[76] The transactions involving
unregistered land that required registration were considerably extended by the
Land Registration Act 1997[77] with effect from April 1, 1998.[78] The Land
Registration Act 2002 has further extended the triggers, notably in relation to
leases. In particular, all leases granted for a term of more than seven years out
of an unregistered estate in land must now be registered. Under the Land
Registration Act 1925, compulsory registration applied to leases granted for
more than 21 years.[79] The reason for the extension was to ensure that most
business leases were registered: the average length of such leases has fallen
steadily.[80] Furthermore, as explained below, the Land Registration Act 2002
contains a power to add additional triggers to compulsory registration,[81] and
that power has been exercised to add three further triggers with effect from
April 6, 2009.[82]

(1) DISPOSITIONS REQUIRING REGISTRATION. The dispositions of unregistered **7–014**
land that are required to be registered fall into four categories.[83]

(a) Certain transfers and grants of or out of an unregistered legal estate
which is either a freehold or a lease of which more than seven years

---

[73] Defined by LRA 2002 s.132(1), as land belonging to Her Majesty in right of the Crown
which is not held for an estate in fee simple absolute in possession. This is qualified to exclude
freehold land that has escheated to the Crown but where there has been no act of entry or
management by the Crown: see LRA 2002 s.132(2).

[74] Because the foreshore is usually vested in the Crown (whether as such or in right of the
Duchy of Lancaster) or in the Duke of Cornwall, the registrar must notify the appropriate officer
if there is any application for the first registration of foreshore: see LRR 2003 r.31. In some cases,
the registrar must notify the Port of London authority, which, by statute, is the owner of much (but
not all) of the foreshore of the tidal reaches of the River Thames. For the history, see the Preamble
to the Thames Conservancy Act 1857 (20 & 21 Vict., c.clxvii).

[75] LRA 2002 s.79(1), (2). It was thought that, at common law, Her Majesty could not have
granted Herself a fee simple out of demesne land: see (2001) Law Com. No.271, para.11.9.

[76] See LRA 1925 s.123 (as originally enacted).

[77] Implementing the recommendations in (1995) Law Com. No.235, which was published
jointly by HM Land Registry and the Law Commission.

[78] See LRA 1997 s.1, substituting and inserting respectively LRA 1925 ss.123, 123A. The new
triggers were brought into force by SI 1997/3036.

[79] See LRA 1925 s.123(1) (as substituted).

[80] See (2001) Law Com. No.271, para.2.6.

[81] LRA 2002 s.5; below, para.7–016.

[82] Land Registration Act 2002 (Amendment) Order 2008; SI 2008/2872.

[83] See LRA 2002 s.4.

are unexpired at the date of the disposition, whether made for valuable or other consideration,[84] by way of gift, or pursuant to an order of the court,[85] namely:

(i) a transfer of the freehold estate in land, other than a transfer by operation of law[86];

(ii) a transfer of a leasehold estate in land,[87] other than a transfer by operation of law,[88] the assignment of a mortgage term,[89] or the assignment or surrender of a lease to the owner of the immediate reversion where the term is to merge in that reversion.[90]

The relevant transfers in (i) and (ii) include:

(a) a transfer to give effect to a partition of land subject to a trust of land[91];

(b) a transfer by a deed that appoints, or has effect as if it appointed, a new trustee[92] or is made in consequence of the appointment of a new trustee[93]; or

(c) a transfer by a vesting order[94] that is consequential on the appointment of a new trustee.[95]

(iii) the grant of a lease for a term of years absolute of more than seven years from the date of the grant, other than the grant of a mortgage term[96]; and

(iv) the grant of a term of years absolute of any duration that is to take effect in possession after the end of a period of three months beginning with the date of the grant.[97] The reason for requiring the registration of such reversionary leases is the difficulty of otherwise discovering their existence.[98]

---

[84] This includes a conveyance of property with a negative value (such as an assignment of a lease for what is sometimes called a "reverse premium"): LRA 2002 s.4(6). "Valuable consideration" does not include marriage consideration or a nominal consideration in money: LRA 2002 s.132(1).

[85] An example of a transfer in pursuance of an order of the court would be where a court made a property adjustment order on a divorce under which one former spouse was required to transfer the unregistered matrimonial home to the other.

[86] LRA 2002 s.4(1)(a)(i), (iii), (2)(a), (3). An example of a transfer by operation of law is where a landowner dies, and his land vests in the executors of his will.

[87] LRA 2002 s.4(1)(a)(i), (iii), (2)(b).

[88] LRA 2002 s.4(3).

[89] LRA 2002 s.4(4)(a).

[90] LRA 2002 s.4(4)(b). For the extinguishment of leases by merger, see below, para.18–090.

[91] LRA 2002 s.4(1)(a)(iii) (added by Land Registration Act 2002 (Amendment) Order 2008).

[92] See Charities Act 1993 s.83.

[93] LRA 2002 s.4(1)(aa)(i) (added by Land Registration Act 2002 (Amendment) Order 2008).

[94] Under TA 1925 s.44; below, para.11–069.

[95] LRA 2002 s.4(1)(aa)(ii) (added by Land Registration Act 2002 (Amendment) Order 2008).

[96] LRA 2002 s.4(1)(c), (5).

[97] LRA 2002 s.4(1)(d).

[98] See (2001) Law Com. No.271, para.3.32. For reversionary leases, see below, para.17–077.

For these purposes, a transfer or grant by way of gift includes a transfer or grant for the purpose of:

(i) constituting a trust, other than a bare trust in favour of the settlor[99]; or

(ii) transferring the bare legal title to a beneficiary under a trust who has become absolutely entitled, except where the trust was a bare trust under which the settlor retained the entire beneficial interest.[100]

The reason for the exceptions is that there is no gift where a person vests land in nominees for himself, and where those nominees then re-convey that land to him.

(b) Certain transfers and grants in connection with a secure tenant's right to buy under Pt V of the Housing Act 1985.[101] These are as follows:

(i) where a secure tenant has a right to buy under the Housing Act 1985, the reversion is unregistered, and it is sold to a private sector landlord, the transfer of the reversion must be registered[102]: this is part of the means by which the tenant's right to buy is preserved;

(ii) where a secure tenant has a right to buy under the Housing Act 1985, and the landlord grants a lease of the reversion to a private sector landlord, the title to the lease must be registered, whatever the duration of that lease[103]; and

(iii) where a lease is granted to a secure tenant pursuant to the statutory right to buy provisions, the title to that lease must be registered, whatever its duration.[104]

(c) Any disposition that is made by way of an assent[105] (including a vesting assent[106]) of a freehold estate or of a lease having more than seven years to run on the date of the disposition.[107] This means that where such estates pass on death, whether of an absolute owner or of a tenant for life under the Settled Land Act 1925, the title will be subject to compulsory registration.

---

[99] LRA 2002 s.4(7)(a). Thus a transfer by A of unregistered land to B and C to hold on trust for D and E will trigger the requirement of compulsory registration.

[100] LRA 2002 s.4(7)(b). Thus a transfer of unregistered land by A to B and C to hold on trust for A will not trigger the requirement of compulsory registration.

[101] See below, para.22–180.

[102] LRA 2002 s.4(1)(b), replicating HA 1985 Sch.9A para.2(1).

[103] LRA 2002 s.4(1)(f), replicating HA 1985 Sch.9A para.2(1).

[104] LRA 2002 s.4(1)(e), replacing in part HA 1985 s.154.

[105] For assents, see below, paras 14–141 et seq.

[106] "Vesting assent" has the same meaning as in SLA 1925: see LRA 2002 s.4(9) and SLA 1925 s.117(1)(xxxi). The application to registered land of SLA 1925 is dealt with by rules: see LRA 2002 s.89; LRR 2003 Sch.7. See below, para.7–112.

[107] LRA 2002 s.4(1)(a)(ii), (2).

(d)　In certain cases where there is a legal mortgage of a freehold estate or of a lease having more than seven years to run at the date of the mortgage, there is a requirement to register the estate which is mortgaged. This will be the case where the mortgage takes effect on its creation as a mortgage that is to be protected by a deposit of documents of title relating to the mortgaged estate, and is a first legal mortgage which ranks in priority ahead of any other mortgages (if any) affecting the mortgaged estate.[108] Thus if the owner of an unregistered freehold executes a first legal mortgage over the property, the requirement of compulsory registration applies to the freehold title.

7–015　The provisions on compulsory first registration apply to a grant by Her Majesty out of demesne land of:

(a)　an estate in fee simple absolute in possession otherwise than to Herself by way of voluntary first registration[109];

(b)　an estate in land for a term of years absolute of more than seven years from the date of the grant, that is made for valuable consideration, by way of gift[110] or in pursuance of an order of any court.[111]

These provisions do not apply to the grant of an estate in mines and minerals held apart from the surface.[112]

7–016　As has been mentioned,[113] there is a power, exercisable by statutory instrument, and after consultation, by which the Lord Chancellor may add to the relevant events that trigger compulsory registration.[114] A relevant event for these purposes is an event relating to an unregistered legal estate, which is an estate in land, a rentcharge, a franchise or a profit à prendre in gross.[115] The power could not therefore be employed to introduce compulsory registration of title in other circumstances. This power, which has already been exercised once,[116] is likely to be utilised to reduce still further the length of registrable leases to those granted for more than three years.[117]

---

[108] LRA 2002 s.4(1)(g), (8).

[109] LRA 2002 s.80(1)(a). There is no requirement that the grant should be made for valuable consideration, by way of gift or in pursuance of an order of the court. For the voluntary first registration of a freehold estate granted out of demesne land, see above, para.7–012.

[110] A gift includes a grant for the purposes of constituting a trust under which Her Majesty does not retain the entire beneficial interest: LRA 2002 s.80(2).

[111] LRA 2002 s.80(1)(b).

[112] LRA 2002 s.80(3).

[113] Above, para.7–013.

[114] LRA 2002 s.5(1), (4). The power cannot be exercised to require the registration of an estate granted to a mortgagee, in other words, the lease that is granted under a mortgage by demise or sub-demise: see LRA 2002 s.5(3). There is a similar power to extend triggers for compulsory registration in relation to events relating to demesne land: LRA 2002 s.80(4).

[115] LRA 2002 s.5(2).

[116] See above, paras 7–013, 7–014.

[117] (2001) Law Com. No.271, para.3.17.

Although the Land Registration Act 2002 does not contain provisions to compel the registration of all remaining unregistered land, it is one of the strategic objectives of the Land Registry to bring about the completion of the register.

(2) DISPOSITIONS THAT ARE NOT REQUIRED TO BE REGISTERED. The dispositions   **7–017**
of unregistered land that do not fall within the requirement of compulsory registration[118] include the following:

   (a)   a transfer of land to a nominee or by that nominee to the transferor: the transfer is made neither as a gift nor for any consideration[119];

   (b)   the surrender of a lease which merges in the immediate reversion[120];

   (c)   the grant of an incorporeal hereditament, such as an easement or a profit à prendre)[121]; and

   (e)   a transfer of mines and minerals held apart from the surface.[122]

One exception that existed under the previous law, namely a conveyance of corporeal hereditaments which were part of a manor (such as the demesne lands of the manor) and were included in the sale of the manor as such,[123] was not replicated in the Land Registration Act 1925.[124] Under the general words that are implied on a conveyance of a manor,[125] there passes with the manor, amongst other things, "all pastures, feedings, wastes, warrens, commons, mines, minerals, quarries, furzes, trees, woods, underwoods, coppices, and the ground and soil thereof". Although the authorities on the general words implied on a conveyance other than of a manor have suggested that they do not pass corporeal land,[126] the words used in relation to a conveyance of a manor suggest that, if the manor does include any corporeal land within the description in those general words, that land will pass with the manor. If that is correct,[127] the the requirement of registration will apply to a conveyance of

---

[118] Including those that are expressly excluded from it by statute.

[119] LRA 2002 s.4(7).

[120] LRA 2002 s.4(4)(b).

[121] Under LRA 1925 s.123(3)(a), incorporeal hereditaments were expressly excluded. While there is no such express exclusion in LRA 2002, the creation of such interests is not included in the list of triggering dispositions. A profit à prendre in gross may be voluntarily registered: see above, para.7–010.

[122] LRA 2002 s.4(9).

[123] See LRA 1925 s.123(3)(c). The reason for this exception was, apparently, that as the manor (meaning the incorporeal lordship of the manor) was itself not subject to compulsory registration, nor should a sale of the lands of the manor together with the lordship.

[124] See (2001) Law Com. No.271, para.3.23.

[125] See LPA 1925 s.62(3). For the implied grant of easements and profits under LPA 1925 s.62(1), see below, paras 28–027 et seq.

[126] See *Commission for New Towns v J J Gallagher Ltd* [2003] EWHC 2668 (Ch) at [58]–[68]; [2003] 2 P. & C.R. 24 at 40–43.

[127] The point often arises in practice, but there appears to be no reported decision on the point. cf. *Crown Estate Commissioners v Roberts* [2008] EWHC 1302 (Ch) at [144]; [2008] 2 E.G.L.R. 165 at 178 (where the issue concerned rights rather than corporeal land).

a manor that does in fact comprise unregistered land of the description falling within the general words even if the parcels clause of the conveyance is silent.

7–018   (3) THE DUTY TO REGISTER AND THE EFFECT OF NON-REGISTRATION. Where the requirement of registration applies, there is a statutory duty on the responsible estate owner (or his successor in title) to apply to the registrar to be registered as the proprietor of the registrable estate before the end of the period of registration.[128]

> (a) Where the requirement of registration is triggered by the creation of a legal mortgage,[129] the registrable estate is the estate charged by the mortgage and the responsible estate owner is the transferee or grantee of that estate.[130] As there is a danger that the mortgagor may fail to apply for registration, the mortgagee is also given power to apply for registration of the estate, whether or not the mortgagor consents.[131]
>
> (b) In all other cases, the registrable estate is the estate which is transferred or granted, and the responsible estate owner is the transferee or grantee of that estate.[132]

The period for registration is two months beginning with the date of the triggering event, or such longer period as the registrar may provide.[133] An interested person[134] may apply to the registrar for an extension to the period for registration. If the registrar is satisfied that there is good reason for extending the period, he may by order provide for the period of registration to end on such later date as he may specify in that order.[135]

7–019   The first registration of dispositions is "compulsory" because there is a statutory sanction for non-compliance with the requirement of registration. If a disposition that triggers the requirement of registration is not registered within the period of registration (whether that period is two months or any period extended by order of the registrar), that disposition becomes void as regards the transfer, grant or creation of a *legal* estate.[136] In the case of the

---

[128] LRA 2002 s.6(1).

[129] See LRA 2002 s.4(1)(g); above para.7–014(d).

[130] LRA 2002 s.6(2). The registrar must enter the mortgagee as the proprietor of the legal charge if he is satisfied as to that person's entitlement: LRR 2003 r.22.

[131] LRA 2002 s.6(6); LRR 2003 r.21.

[132] LRA 2002 s.6(3).

[133] LRA 2002 s.6(4).

[134] Which might be the estate owner, or where registration is required because the land has been mortgaged, the mortgagee.

[135] LRA 2002 s.6(5).

[136] LRA 2002 s.7(1). Although the effect of this subsection makes the fee simple determinable, the possibility of reverter to which it gives rise is to be disregarded for the purposes of determining whether a fee simple is a fee simple absolute: LRA 2002 s.7(4). For determinable fees, see above, para.3–054.

transfer of a qualifying estate, other than on the appointment of a new trustee, the legal estate reverts to the transferor, who holds it on a bare trust for the transferee.[137] Where the transfer arises on the appointment of a new trustee, the legal estate reverts to the person in whom it was vested immediately before the transfer.[138] In the case of a grant of a lease or the creation of a legal mortgage, the disposition has effect as a contract made for valuable consideration to grant the lease or create the mortgage.[139] If an application for first registration is made, but is cancelled, e.g. because the purchaser fails to answer a requisition raised by the registrar,[140] the effect is as if no application had been made, and the statutory sanction applies.[141] Even if the disposition of a legal estate has become void under this provision, it will be treated as not having done so if the registrar then makes an order extending the period for registration.[142]

In those rare cases where a disposition becomes void for non-registration, but no order for extending time is made by the registrar, there are the following consequences: **7–020**

(a) The interest of the transferee, grantee or mortgagee is at risk if there is a further disposition of the legal estate by the disponor. In those cases where the disposition takes effect as a notional estate contract, it should be registered as a land charge,[143] but in practice is unlikely to be. If it is not registered, it will not bind any purchaser of the legal estate for money or money's worth.[144]

(b) The disposition has to be made again.[145] The transferee, grantee or mortgagor is liable to the other party for all the costs of and incidental to that replication, and is liable to indemnify the other party in respect of any liability reasonably incurred by him because of the failure to comply with the requirement of registration.[146]

(4) DISPOSITIONS PENDING FIRST REGISTRATION. Where there has been a disposition of unregistered land to which the requirement of registration applies, and there is then a dealing with the legal estate before that disposition **7–021**

---

[137] LRA 2002 s.7(2)(a).
[138] LRA 2002 s.7(2)(aa).
[139] LRA 2002 s.7(2)(b). Because the disposition is deemed to take effect as a contract, it is immaterial that it did not comply with the formal requirements for a contract for the sale of an interest in land contained in LP(MP)A 1989 s.2 (below, para.15–014).
[140] See LRR 2003 r.16.
[141] *Sainsbury's Supermarket Ltd v Olympia Homes Ltd* [2005] EWHC 1235 at [67]–[71]; [2006] 1 P. & C.R. 289 at 317–318.
[142] LRA 2002 s.7(3).
[143] Under LCA 1972 s.2(4)(iv); below, para.8–075.
[144] LCA 1972 s.4(6); below, para.8–093.
[145] That disposition will itself be subject to the requirement of registration within the period for registration prescribed by LRA 2002 s.6(4).
[146] LRA 2002 s.8.

has been registered, the Land Registration Act 2002 applies to that dealing as if it had taken place after the date of first registration of that estate.[147]

7–022   **2. Applications for first registration.** The procedure for applications to the registrar for first registration is prescribed by rules, which provide details as to the forms to be used and the documents that must be submitted in making the application.[148] There is a duty on the applicant to disclose most, but not all, overriding interests which affect the estate to be registered, of which the applicant has actual knowledge, to ensure that they are noted in the register.[149] The duty does not extend to interests which cannot be noted in the register,[150] or to certain other interests, such as public rights,[151] local land charges (which are registered in local registers),[152] and certain leases with less than one year to run on the date of the application.[153]

In examining a title on an application for first registration, the registrar may make searches and enquiries and give notices to other persons, direct that searches and enquiries be made by the applicant, and advertise the application.[154] If there is an objection to the application[155] which is not groundless and cannot be disposed of by agreement, the registrar must refer the matter for resolution to the adjudicator,[156] who determines disputed applications to the registrar.[157] If there is no objection to the application, but the registrar refuses to register land either at all or with a particular class of title,[158] there is no dispute that can be referred to the adjudicator or any right of appeal from the registrar's decision.[159] The only remedy for a party who is aggrieved by the

---

[147] LRR 2003 r.38(1); LRA 2002 Sch.10 para.1. If more than one disposition is made prior to first registration, difficult issues of priority can arise, because the provisions of LRA 2002 cannot apply in their entirety: see Harpum & Bignell, 2–24.

[148] See LRA 2002 s.14; LRR 2003 rr.13–20 (general provisions on applications); and rr.21–38 (first registration); Ruoff & Roper, Ch.9 and LRPG 1, LRPG 2.

[149] LRA 2002 s.71(a); LRR 2003 r.28. This is part of the strategy of reducing the number and scope of overriding interests: cf. above, para.7–008; and below, para.7–101.

[150] See LRA 2002 ss.33 and 90(4); below, para.7–070.

[151] For public rights, see below, para.27–032.

[152] For local land charges, see below, para.8–107.

[153] LRR 2003 r.28(2).

[154] LRR 2003 r.30.

[155] This will usually be by a person who has lodged a caution against first registration. These cautions are explained below at paras 7–044 and following.

[156] LRA 2002 s.73(5)–(7).

[157] For the office and functions of the adjudicator, see below, para.7–130. The adjudicator may direct one of the parties to commence court proceedings instead, or one of the parties may decide to do so.

[158] This will happen where the registrar is not satisfied as to the applicant's proof of title. It happens typically where there is an application based upon adverse possession, where the registrar considers that the applicant has not proved his entitlement. For the different classes of title, see below, para.7–023.

[159] There is a right to appeal from the registrar to the county court in two specific cases, namely where he requires the production of documents for the purposes of proceedings before him (see LRA 2002 s.75) and where he makes an order about costs in relation to any proceedings before him (see LRA 2002 s.76). There is no right of appeal in any other case.

decision is to make an application for judicial review.[160] This is also the case whenever there is a decision by the registrar in the exercise of his discretion where there has been no application.

3. The effect of first registration. When an applicant applies for the first registration of an estate, it may be because he is seeking voluntary first registration or because there has been a disposition of unregistered land that triggered the requirement of registration. In the latter case, any issues of priority will necessarily have been determined on the conveyance that triggered first registration by the rules applicable to unregistered land.[161] With one exception,[162] first registration has no effect on priorities, but is intended to reflect the state of the title when the application for first registration was made. The effect of first registration depends upon the class of title with which the land is registered.[163] There are four classes of title with which an applicant for registration may be registered:

7–023

    (i) absolute;

    (ii) qualified;

    (iii) possessory; or

    (iv) good leasehold.

The first three of these apply to both freehold and leasehold titles. The fourth applies only to leasehold titles.[164]

(a) Absolute title. A person may be registered with an absolute title to freehold land if he has a good holding title,[165] that is one which the registrar considers to be such as a willing buyer could properly be advised by a competent professional adviser to accept.[166] A defect in title is not a bar to registration with an absolute title, provided that the registrar considers that it will not cause the holding under it to be disturbed.[167] A person may be registered with an absolute title to leasehold land provided that the registrar is satisfied that the applicant has a good holding title in the same way as with a freehold title, and also that he approves the lessor's title to grant the lease.[168]

7–024

---

[160] See *Quigly v Chief Land Registrar* [1993] 1 W.L.R. 1435 at pp.1438, 1439; and see *Diep v Land Registry* [2010] EWHC 3315 (Admin) (where the application failed). For a summary of the grounds upon which judicial review may be sought, see *Council of Civil Service Unions v Minister for the Civil Service* [1985] A.C. 374, at pp.410, 411.

[161] These are explained below in Ch.8.

[162] See below, para.7–026(c).

[163] Application for first registration is made using Form FR1: see LRR 2003 r.23(1). The applicant is required to state in his application the class of title that he seeks.

[164] See LRA 2002 ss.9(1), 10(1).

[165] For the gradations of title, see below, para.15–075.

[166] LRA 2002 s.9(2)

[167] LRA 2002 s.9(3).

[168] LRA 2002 s.10(2).

This means that the lessor's title, if unregistered, will have to be deduced to the registrar.[169]

7–025   Where a person is registered with an absolute freehold or leasehold title, the estate is vested in the proprietor[170] together with all interests subsisting for the benefit of the estate.[171] The registrar will make any entry in relation to the benefit of mines and minerals where he is satisfied that they are included in the title.[172] However, the necessary evidence is seldom available.

7–026   The registered estate is vested in the first registered proprietor subject to certain interests. Whether the registered proprietor holds the land for himself alone or as a trustee, it will be vested in him subject to the following interests. The first three apply to both freehold and leasehold titles, but the fourth applies only to leaseholds.[173] They are:

   (a)   interests which are the subject of an entry in the register in relation to the estate;

   (b)   unregistered interests which override first registration;

   (c)   interests acquired under the Limitation Act 1980 of which the proprietor has notice; and

   (d)   in relation to leasehold property, implied and express covenants, obligations and liabilities incident to the estate.

7–027   (1) INTERESTS WHICH ARE THE SUBJECT OF AN ENTRY IN THE REGISTER IN RELATION TO THE ESTATE.[174] When the title is first registered, the registrar must enter a notice in the register of the burdens that appear from his examination of the title to affect the registered estate.[175] He must also register any mortgagee as proprietor of a registered charge affecting the estate.[176] If it is apparent that the registered proprietor's powers are limited in some way, he may enter a restriction to reflect that limitation.[177] If, by mistake, a burden affecting the title is not entered in the register, the incumbrancer affected may

---

[169] If the lease is one that triggers compulsory registration and is granted pursuant to a contract for lease, the lessee is entitled to require the lessor to deduce the freehold title, unless the contact otherwise provides: see LPA 1925 s.44(1), (4A), (11). See para.21–005 below.

[170] Registration vests both legal and beneficial title even if the conveyance to the first registered proprietor was invalid: see below, para.7–116.

[171] LRA 2002 ss.11(3), 12(3).

[172] LRR 2003 r.32. If he is satisfied that the minerals are *excluded*, he must also make an appropriate note in the register: r.32.

[173] See LRA 2002 ss.11(4) (freeholds), 12(4) (leaseholds).

[174] LRA 2002 ss.11(4)(a), 12(4)(b).

[175] See LRR 2003 rr.28(4), 35.

[176] See LRR 2003 rr.22, 34 and 38. Those rules cover three cases, namely, (i) where the creation of a first legal mortgage triggers the requirement of registration; (ii) the voluntary first registration of land that is subject to a legal mortgage (see too LRA 2002 s.13(b)); and (iii) the creation of a legal mortgage after the disposition of the legal estate that triggered the requirement of registration, but before registration had taken place (see above, para.7–021).

[177] LRA 2002 s.42(1)(a). The registrar must give notice of such an entry to the proprietor of the registered estate: LRA 2002 s.42(3).

seek the alteration of the register to correct that mistake under principles that are explained later in this chapter.[178]

(2) UNREGISTERED INTERESTS THAT OVERRIDE FIRST REGISTRATION.[179] It has **7–028** been explained that there are certain unregistered interests which nonetheless bind the first registered proprietor.[180] The number of overriding interests that affect a property on first registration should diminish as a result of the Land Registration Act 2002. As explained above, an applicant for first registration must disclose to the registrar most overriding interests affecting the estate to be registered of which he has actual knowledge.[181] These interests will be noted in the register and will not then be overriding.

The unregistered interests that override first registration are not identical to **7–029** those that override a disposition of registered land.[182] This is because, as explained above, subject to one exception, first registration does not affect priorities, which are previously determined by the operation of the rules of unregistered conveyancing.[183] It follows that matters which may be relevant to whether an interest can override a disposition of registered land, such as whether the disponee made enquiry of persons in actual occupation, are irrelevant on first registration.[184]

There are now 14 unregistered interests which override first **7–030** registration.[185]

(a) Any lease granted for a term of seven years or less which is not required to be registered.[186] This reflects the requirements of compulsory registration. A lease that is not required to be registered (or was not when it was granted[187]), takes effect as an overriding interest.

(b) An interest belonging to a person in actual occupation, so far as relating to land of which he is in actual occupation, except for an interest under a settlement under the Settled Land Act 1925.[188] This provision is narrower than its equivalent in the Land Registration Act 1925[189]:

---

[178] See below, paras 7–133 et seq.
[179] LRA 2002 ss.11(4)(b), 12(4)(c). See Ruoff & Roper, Ch.10; LRPG 15.
[180] See above, para.7–008.
[181] See above, para.7–022.
[182] For these, see LRA 2002 Sch.3; below, para.7–087.
[183] See above, para.7–023.
[184] This must have been true under the equivalent provisions of LRA 1925 s.70(1), but it was not made explicit.
[185] See LRA 2002 Sch.1; s.90(5). There was a 15th for a transitional period of three years after LRA 2002 came into force: see LRA 2002 Sch.12, para.7; below, para.7–032.
[186] LRA 2002 Sch.1 para.1; Sch.12 para.12. For the leases that are required to be registered even if granted for seven years or less, see LRA 2002 s.4(1)(d), (e) and (f), above, para. 7–014(a)(iv) and (b)(ii), (iii).
[187] In other words, any lease granted for 21 years or less prior to October 13, 2003: see LRA 2002 Sch.12 para.12.
[188] LRA 2002 Sch.1 para.2. See further below, paras 7–089 and following.
[189] See LRA 1925 s.70(1)(g); and paras 6–047—6–063 of the sixth edition of this work.

(i) It is no longer possible to protect an interest affecting the whole of the land within a registered title by the occupation of part only of that land.[190]

(ii) It no longer protects those who are not in actual occupation but merely in receipt of the rents and profits from the land.[191]

The rights of persons in actual occupation are considered more fully in the context of unregistered interests which override registered dispositions.[192] Certain rights cannot be protected by actual occupation.[193]

(c) A legal easement or profit à prendre.[194] The only easements and profits that can override first registration are those which are legal, and not those that are merely equitable. In practice, the easements and profits that are likely to be overriding are those that were acquired by implied grant or reservation or by prescription, because these will not be apparent from the paper title and may not be known to the applicant for first registration.[195]

(d) A customary right.[196] Customary rights are rights which are enjoyed by members of a local community but not by the public at large. They must be of ancient origin, strictly since the beginning of legal memory in 1189, but that will be presumed from long user in the absence of proof of a later origin.[197]

(e) A public right.[198] Public rights are rights exercisable over land by any person under the general law. The best-known examples are the right to use a public highway and the rights to fish and navigate over the foreshore. In relation to highways, both the public right to use the highway and the highway authority's ownership of the surface of the highway, are public rights.[199]

(f) A local land charge.[200] Local land charges are recorded in registers held by local authorities pursuant to the Local Land Charges Act 1975. They are concerned with charges and restrictions imposed

---

[190] Reversing the effect of *Ferrishurst Ltd v Wallcite Ltd* [1999] Ch. 355: see the sixth edition of this work at para.6–055; and below, para.7–090.

[191] See the sixth edition of this work at paras 6–048, 6–056.

[192] See below, paras 7–089 et seq.

[193] See below, para.7–097.

[194] LRA 2002 Sch.1 para.3. For the nature of easements and profits, see below, Ch.27.

[195] For a more detailed treatment in the context of unregistered interests that override registered dispositions, see below, paras 7–098 et seq.

[196] LRA 2002 Sch.1 para.4. For customary rights, see below, para.27–049.

[197] Examples include a custom for local fishermen to moor their vessels on the foreshore: *Attorney General v Wright* [1897] 2 Q.B. 318, or to dry their nets on private land: *Mercer v Denne* [1905] 2 Ch. 538.

[198] LRA 2002 Sch.1 para.5. For public rights, see below, para.27–032.

[199] *Secretary of State for the Environment, Transport and the Regions v Baylis* (2000) 80 P. & C.R. 324.

[200] LRA 2002 Sch.1 para.6. For local land charges, see below, para.8–107.

under statutory authority by public authorities. Because they are subject to a separate registration regime, such charges take effect according to that regime and override first registration.

(g) Certain mineral rights.[201] There are three classes of mineral rights which override first registration.

(i) Any interest in any coal or coal mine, the rights attached to any such interest, and certain other rights under the Coal Industry Act 1994.[202] It would, in practice, be difficult to register such rights because of their uncertain extent and such rights cannot be noted in the register.[203]

(ii) In the case of land to which title was registered before 1898, rights to mines and minerals (and incidental rights) created before 1898.[204] The reason why such rights are overriding is because the existence of such rights was not usually recorded on the register.

(iii) In the case of land to which title was registered between 1898 and 1925 inclusive, rights to mines and minerals (and incidental rights) created before the date of registration of the title.[205] The reason is the same as for (ii).

(h) A franchise.[206] A franchise is a grant to a subject by the Crown of a privilege that forms part of the royal prerogative.[207] Such franchises include the right to hold a fair or market, and a right of wreck. Some franchises relate to specific land, such as a right to hold a fair on Blackacre.[208] The right constitutes an encumbrance on that land and is called an "affecting franchise" in the Land Registration Rules 2003.[209] Other franchises are more general, as where there is a right to hold a market in a particular locality.[210] These are not encumbrances on any specific land and are called "relating franchises" in the Rules.[211] Although franchises are voluntarily registrable with their own titles, a franchise that is neither registered with its own title nor (in the case of an affecting franchise) noted against the land affected by it, takes effect as an overriding interest.

[201] LRA 2002 Sch.1 paras 7–9.
[202] LRA 2002 Sch.1 para.7.
[203] See LRA 2002 s.33(e); below, para.7–070. There is, however, a system of coal mining searches, provided by the Coal Authority, that indicate whether mining has been or is likely in future to be conducted on the land.
[204] LRA 2002 Sch.1 para.8. The Land Transfer Act 1897, which amended the Land Transfer Act 1875, came into force on January 1, 1898.
[205] LRA 2002 Sch.1 para.9.
[206] LRA 2002 Sch.1 para.10.
[207] See below, para.31–013.
[208] As in *Wyld v Silver* [1963] Ch. 243.
[209] See LRR 2003 r.217(1).
[210] As in *Attorney General v Horner* (1884) 14 Q.B.D. 245.
[211] See LRR 2003 r.217(1).

(i) A manorial right.[212] It has been explained that only a handful of manorial rights remain after 1925,[213] of which the lord's rights to mines and minerals[214] and the lord's sporting rights are the most important. These rights may be protected by a notice in the register of the land which they burden, but if they are not, they will be overriding interests.

(j) What is commonly called a Crown rent.[215] This is a right to rent which was reserved to the Crown on the granting of any freehold estate (whether or not the right is still vested in the Crown). Although obscure, these rights do still exist.[216]

(k) A non-statutory right in respect of an embankment or sea or river wall.[217] This is an obscure form of liability that may affect a person who owns land adjacent to the sea or a river. Such a landowner is not liable at common law to maintain or repair sea walls or river banks. However, such liability may have arisen by prescription, by grant, pursuant to a covenant that is supported by a rentcharge, by custom, or by tenure.[218]

(l) What is generally called a corn rent,[219] but is technically a right to payment in lieu of tithe. It is a liability to make a payment under an Act of Parliament, other than one of the Tithe Acts, out of or charged upon any land in commutation of tithes.[220] It is very rare, but still survives. Although the sums are normally small, this is not always the case.

(m) A right in respect of a church chancel.[221] This liability,[222] which has been described as "anachronistic, even capricious",[223] requires the

---

[212] LRA 2002 Sch.1 para.11.

[213] See above, para.2–029.

[214] For the curious nature of the lord's rights in the absence of any custom of the manor to the contrary, see above, para.2–013.

[215] LRA 2002 Sch.1 para.12.

[216] See (2001) Law Com. No.271, para.8–43.

[217] LRA 2002 Sch.1 para.13.

[218] See (1998) Law Com. No.258, para.5.39.

[219] LRA 2002 Sch.1 para.14.

[220] See (2001) Law Com. No.271, para.8.46.

[221] LRA 2002 Sch.1 para.16 (inserted by Land Registration Act 2002 (Transitional Provisions) (No 2) Order 2003). When LRA 2002 was enacted, chancel repair liability had been held to contravene the ECHR: see *Aston Cantlow and Wilmcote with Billesley PCC v Wallbank* [2001] EWCA Civ 713; [2002] Ch. 51. That decision was reversed by the House of Lords: [2003] UKHL 37; [2004] 1 A.C. 546. As chancel repair liability had been an overriding interest under LRA 1925 s.70(1)(c), it was considered necessary to insert it into LRA 2002. The insertion was made pursuant to LRA 2002 s.134(1) (power for the Lord Chancellor to make transitional provisions). There must be some doubt as to the *vires* for the order.

[222] See below, para.31–008.

[223] *Aston Cantlow and Wilmcote with Billesley PCC v Wallbank* [2003] UKHL 37 at [2]; [2004] 1 A.C. 546 at 553, per Lord Nicholls of Birkenhead.

owner of certain land which was formerly glebe land, to pay for repairs to the chancel of the parish church.[224]

(n) A PPP lease.[225] The nature of these leases has been explained.[226] They are incapable of any form of substantive registration[227] and therefore take effect as overriding interests.

Of those overriding interests, (h) to (m) will cease to be overriding on October 13, 2013.[228] Such interests may be protected by an application to lodge a caution against first registration and no fee is payable in respect of such an entry prior to October 13, 2013.[229]   **7–031**

(3) INTERESTS ACQUIRED UNDER THE LIMITATION ACT 1980 OF WHICH THE PROPRIETOR HAS NOTICE.[230] Where a squatter has acquired title to all or part of the land which is the subject of first registration, the first registered proprietor takes the land subject to the squatter's rights if, but only if, he has notice of them at the time of registration. This is the one situation in which first registration can affect priorities. It is also one of the very rare instances in the Land Registration Act 2002 where the doctrine of notice has any application. It was intended to deal with a case where a squatter had acquired title to unregistered land by adverse possession, had then left the land, and the former paper owner had then resumed possession. If, less than 12 years after the former paper owner had retaken possession of the land,[231] he sold it to a purchaser, there would be nothing to indicate to that purchaser that that former paper owner did not own the land. He would still retain the title deeds and he would be in occupation of the land.[232] In those circumstances, the first registered proprietor would take free of the squatter's estate on first registration. The date on which notice of the squatter's rights is relevant is the date of registration, not the date of the conveyance of the land.   **7–032**

For a transitional period of three years after the Land Registration Act 2002 came into force, this provision was, in effect, suspended. This is because, for that period, rights acquired by adverse possession prior to the coming into force of the Act were overriding interests.[233]

---

[224] The land would have been formerly owned by the rector, who was obliged to repair the chancel of the parish church, the parishioners having responsibility for the repair of the nave. When many rectories were sold into private hands following the dissolution of the monasteries, the liability passed to the "lay rectors" or "lay impropriators". See *Aston Cantlow and Wilmcote with Billesley PCC v Wallbank* [2003] UKHL 37 at [97]–[103]; [2004] 1 A.C. 546 at pp.580–582.

[225] LRA 2002 s.90(5).

[226] See above, para.7–010.

[227] LRA 2002 s.90.

[228] LRA 2002 s.117(1).

[229] LRA 2002 s.117(2). For cautions against first registration, see below, para.7–044.

[230] LRA 2002 s.11(4)(c), 12(4)(d).

[231] So that the squatter's title would not have been barred by the former paper owner's adverse possession.

[232] See (2001) Law Com. No.271, at para.3.46.

[233] LRA 2002 Sch.12 para.7.

7–033   (4) IN THE CASE OF A LEASEHOLD ESTATE, THE IMPLIED AND EXPRESS COVE-
NANTS, OBLIGATIONS AND LIABILITIES INCIDENT TO THE ESTATE.[234] In addition to
the three matters mentioned above, which apply to the first registered proprietor of both a freehold and a leasehold estate with absolute title, the first
registered proprietor of a leasehold takes it subject to the implied and express
covenants, obligations and liabilities incident to the estate. The burdens in
question must be:

(a)   proprietary rights so that they will include only those covenants that
create proprietary interests, typically restrictive covenants; and

(b)   "incident to" the estate registered, and will therefore include the
burden of a landlord's right of re-entry for breach of covenant.[235]

In practice neither restrictive covenants nor rights of entry contained in leases
are registrable.[236] Each will be apparent from the documents comprising the
lease.

7–034   The first registered proprietor may not be entitled to the land for his own
benefit or not exclusively for his own benefit, as where he holds it on trust,[237]
or perhaps subject to an equity arising in favour of a third party by reason of
proprietary estoppel.[238] In such circumstances, as between the proprietor and
the persons beneficially entitled to the estate, the estate is vested the proprietor
subject to such of the their interests of which he has notice.[239] Were it not for
this exception a fiduciary owner might, on first registration, claim to take the
land free from the beneficial interests affecting the land.

7–035   *(b) Qualified title.* Qualified title is rare and it is not a class of title for which
application will be made. The effect of registration with a qualified title is the
same as registration with an absolute title, except that it does not affect the
enforcement of an estate, right or interest that is excepted from the effect of
registration.[240] Examples of when the registrar is likely to register land with
a qualified title include:

(a)   where the applicant has deduced a root of title that is less than 15
years old[241]; or

(b)   where, at some stage, a disposition of the land was made in breach
of trust in circumstances in which the title might still be
challenged.[242]

---

[234] LRA 2002 s.12(4)(a). cf. LRA 1925 s.9(a), which was similarly worded.
[235] cf. LPA 1925 ss.141(1), (below, paras 20–060 and following, 20–079).
[236] See below, paras 7–070 (restrictive covenants); 7–054 (rights of entry).
[237] See Chs 10–13.
[238] See Ch.16. This is especially so because of the close interconnection between constructive
trusts and proprietary estoppel in cohabitation cases: see below, paras 11–032; 16–036.
[239] LRA 2002 ss.11(5), 12(5).
[240] LRA 2002 ss.11(6), 12(7).
[241] For the root of title in unregistered conveyancing, see below, paras 15–074—15–081.
[242] See Ruoff & Roper, 6.005.

(c) Possessory title. The registrar may register a person with possessory title **7–036**
if he is of opinion that two conditions are satisfied.[243] The first is that the
person is either in actual possession of the land, or in receipt of the rents and
profits of the land, by virtue of the freehold or leasehold estate. The second is
that there is no other title with which he may be registered.[244] It is doubtful
whether a squatter who is in adverse possession but has not barred the estate
of the paper owner would satisfy the first requirement.[245] Although he is in
possession and, by virtue of his adverse possession has a legal estate in fee
simple,[246] he is not in possession by virtue of that estate but vice versa. In any
event, it is unlikely that the registrar would exercise his discretion to register
a person with a possessory title in favour of a squatter who could not adduce
evidence supporting his claim to have acquired title by adverse possession.

Registration with possessory title has the same effect as registration with an **7–037**
absolute title, except that it does not affect the enforcement of any estate, right
or interest that is adverse to, or in derogation of, the proprietor's title, if that
estate, right or interest subsisted at the time of first registration or was then
capable of arising.[247] For example, in a case where the applicant was registered with a possessory freehold title and it subsequently transpired that the
applicant only had a leasehold estate, the holder of the freehold reversion
would be entitled to assert his estate when the applicant's lease expired.
Similarly, if the land registered with possessory title was subject to restrictive
covenants that had been created by a previous paper owner of the land, but had
not been registered on the squatter's application for first registration because
the paper title was not deduced, those covenants could still be enforced against
the applicant.

(d) Good leasehold title. A person may be registered with a good leasehold **7–038**
title if the registrar considers it to be such as a willing buyer could properly
be advised by a competent professional adviser to accept.[248] As with an
absolute title, it must therefore be a good holding title.[249] A lessee will be
registered with a good leasehold title rather than an absolute title where the
registrar is not able to approve the lessor's title to grant the lease.[250] Registration with a good leasehold title has the same effect as registration with an
absolute title, except that it does not affect the enforcement of any estate, right
or interest affecting, or in derogation of, the title of the lessor to grant the

---

[243] LRA 2002 ss.9(5), 10(6).
[244] In deciding this question, the registrar "is entitled to take a cautious—even an ultra
cautious—view of the position so as to avoid putting public funds at risk": *Diep v Land Registry*
[2010] EWHC 3315 (Admin) at [18], per Mitting J.
[245] For adverse possession of unregistered land, see below, para.35–014.
[246] See above, para.4–008.
[247] LRA 2002 ss.11(7), 12(8).
[248] LRA 2002 s.10(3).
[249] LRA 2002 s.10(4); see above, para.7–024.
[250] See LRA 2002 s.10(2); above, para.7–024. Under a contract to grant a lease, where the grant
of the lease will trigger the requirement of registration, the grantee can require the lessor to
deduce his title in the absence of a provision in the contract: see LPA 1925 s.44(4A); below,
para.21–005.

lease.[251] If, for example, the lessor had no title to the land which he had purported to lease, the registration of the lease with a good leasehold title would not prevent the true owner from evicting the lessee.

7–039   **4. Upgrading titles.** The registrar can upgrade a title in certain circumstances.[252] He may upgrade:

(a)   a possessory or qualified freehold to an absolute title if he is satisfied as to the title[253];

(b)   a good leasehold title to an absolute title if he is satisfied as to the superior title[254];

(c)   a possessory or qualified leasehold title to good leasehold title if he is satisfied as to the title to the estate[255];

(d)   a possessory or qualified leasehold title to an absolute title if he is satisfied both as to the title to the estate and as to the superior title[256];

(e)   a freehold title registered for more than 12 years with possessory title to an absolute title if he is satisfied that the proprietor is in possession of the land (in the sense explained below)[257]; and

(f)   a leasehold title registered for more than 12 years with possessory title to a good leasehold title if he is satisfied that the proprietor is in possession of the land (in the sense explained below).[258]

In determining whether he is satisfied as to any title, the registrar must apply the same standards as he would on an application for first registration.[259] The registrar may upgrade a title on his own volition or on application by the registered proprietor, by a person entitled to be registered as proprietor, or by a person interested in a derivative registered estate, such as a lessee.[260]

7–040   For the purposes of the provisions set out in the previous paragraph, a proprietor, X, will be regarded as being possession of the land in three circumstances.[261]

(a)   where the land is physically in X's possession[262];

---

[251] LRA 2002 s.12(6).
[252] LRA 2002 s.62.
[253] LRA 2002 s.62(1).
[254] LRA 2002 s.62(2).
[255] LRA 2002 s.62(3)(a).
[256] LRA 2002 s.62(3)(b).
[257] LRA 2002 s.62(4). See para.7–040.
[258] LRA 2002 s.62(5). See para.7–040.
[259] LRA 2002 s.62(8). For the relevant standards under LRA 2002 ss.9, 10; see above, para.7–024.
[260] LRA 2002 s.62(7). For the requirements of any application, see LRR 2003 r.124.
[261] See further below, para.7–135.
[262] LRA 2002 s.131(1).

(b) where the land is physically in the possession of Y, a person who is entitled to be registered as proprietor[263];

(c) where the land is treated as being in X's possession. That will be so where:

    (i) X is the landlord and the land is in the physical possession of the tenant, Z;

    (ii) X is a mortgagor and the land is in the physical possession of the mortgagee, Z;

    (iii) X has granted a licence of the land, which is in the possession of the licensee, Z; and

    (iv) X is a trustee of land, which is in the physical possession of a beneficiary, Z.[264]

In each of these four cases, X will not only be treated as being in possession where Z is in physical possession, but also where Z is deemed to be in physical possession,[265] as, for example, where in (i), a tenant, Z, has sub-let, or in (ii) where a mortgagee, Z, has exercised his power of leasing.[266]

The registrar cannot exercise any of the powers set out above[267] if there is **7–041** outstanding any claim that is adverse to the title of the registered proprietor, where that claim is made by virtue of an estate, right or interest whose enforceability is preserved by virtue of the existing entry about the class of title.[268] For example, if a person had been registered with possessory title based upon 12 years' adverse possession of previously unregistered land, and there is an outstanding claim that the land is subject to restrictive covenants that were binding on the former paper owner,[269] that issue must be resolved before the owner's title can be upgraded to an absolute title, even though the proprietor has been registered for more than 12 years.

The registrar's power to upgrade a possessory title after 12 years[270] is **7–042** indirectly linked to the 12-year limitation period for the recovery of possession of land.[271] Although, the Limitation Act 1980 no longer applies to adverse possession of registered estates,[272] it continues to apply to any paper title against which the first registered proprietor may have adversely possessed, because any prior estate is excluded from the effect of registration with

---

[263] LRA 2002 s.131(1).

[264] LRA 2002 s.131(2).

[265] LRA 2002 s.131(2).

[266] See LPA 1925 s.99(2); below, para.25–074.

[267] See para.7–039.

[268] LRA 2002 s.62(6).

[269] See above, para.7–037. A squatter is bound by restrictive covenants affecting the land: see *Re Nisbet & Potts' Contract* [1906] 1 Ch 386; below, para.35–036.

[270] LRA 2002 ss.62(4), (5); above, para.7–039. There is a power for the Lord Chancellor to change this period by order: see LRA 2002 s.62(9).

[271] See LA 1980 s.15(2); below, para.35–007.

[272] See LRA 2002 s.96; below, para.35–071.

a possessory title.[273] Although a person should only be registered with possessory title if he satisfies the registrar that he has barred the rights of any paper owner (in other words, after a period of 12 years' adverse possession), the requirement that a possessory title can only be upgraded 12 years after that registration provides a reasonable (though not absolute) assurance that the proprietor's title would thereafter be unlikely to be challenged.[274] Once upgraded, the title cannot thereafter be challenged,[275] and any person who suffers loss by reason of the upgrading of a title is entitled to be indemnified by the registrar.[276]

7–043　　　Where a title to a registered freehold or leasehold estate is upgraded to absolute, the proprietor ceases to hold the estate subject to any estate, right or interest whose enforceability was preserved by virtue of the previous entry about the class of title.[277] Thus, for example, if the title had previously been possessory, the proprietor would no longer be subject to any adverse estates, rights or interests that subsisted at the time of first registration. The same principle applied where the title to a registered leasehold title is upgraded to good leasehold.[278] However, the upgrading does not affect or prejudice the enforcement of any estate, right or interest affecting or in derogation of, the title of the lessor to grant the lease.[279]

7–044　　　**5. Cautions against first registration.** Cautions against first registration are the mechanism by which a person who claims an interest in unregistered land can ensure that he is notified of any application for the first registration of that land and can then object to that registration unless his rights are appropriately protected in the register.[280] Cautions against first registration were retained by the Land Registration Act 2002,[281] but in a form that is significantly different from previously. Under the Land Registration Act 2002, the registrar is required to keep a separate register of cautions against first registration, which comprises an individual caution register for each caution against the registration of title to an unregistered estate.[282]

---

[273] LRA 2002 ss.11(7), 12(8); above, para.7–037.

[274] The rights of the owner of the estate against which adverse possession was taken will be barred. There is always a risk that that estate was not a freehold, but a leasehold estate, so that time will only run against the freehold reversioner once the leasehold estate has determined. Only then does the right of action accrue: see LA 1980 Sch.1 para.4; *Chung Ping Kwan v Lam Island Development Co Ltd* [1997] A.C. 38, 46; below, para.35–026.

[275] See below, para.7–043.

[276] See LRA 2002 Sch.8 para.1(2)(a); below, para.7–140.

[277] LRA 2002 s.63(1).

[278] LRA 2002 s.63(2).

[279] LRA 2002 s.63(2).

[280] If a person has an interest that is registrable as a land charge, it should be so registered in any event, because otherwise it may be defeated by a purchaser of the land affected prior to first registration. First registration merely gives effect to and reflects the effect of any conveyance which may trigger it: se above, para.7–029. For land charges, see below, para.8–062.

[281] The Act abolished cautions against dealings. For cautions against first registration, see LRPG 3.

[282] LRA 2002 s.19. For the form and arrangement of the cautions register, see LRR 203 rr.40, 41. For searches of the cautions register, see below, para.7–120. Under LRA 1925, details of cautions were recorded on a "caution title".

Subject to one important qualification, cautions may be lodged by the **7–045**
owner of a qualifying estate or by a person who is entitled to an interest
affecting such a qualifying estate.[283] For these purposes, a qualifying estate is
a legal estate which relates to the land to which the caution relates and is an
estate in land, a rentcharge, a franchise, or a profit à prendre in gross.[284] For
example, a person who had the benefit of an easement, an option, a restrictive
covenant or a charging order over a parcel of unregistered land could lodge a
caution in relation to that interest. A person who claimed to be a beneficiary
under a trust of land could also lodge a caution so as to ensure that, on first
registration, an appropriate restriction was entered in the register.[285]

The Land Registration Act 2002 introduced an important qualification on
the power to lodge cautions. It is no longer possible to lodge a caution against
the first registration of:

(a) a freehold estate by the owner of that estate; or

(b) a leasehold estate, granted for a term of which more than seven years
     are unexpired, by the owner of that estate[286]; or

(c) a superior reversionary title (whether freehold or leasehold) by the
     owner of a leasehold estate granted for a term of which more than
     seven years are unexpired.[287]

These limitations are intended to ensure that if a person owns a legal estate
that can be registered with its own title, he protects it by registering the title
to it.[288] Lodging a caution is an inferior form of protection. It is merely a
procedural device. It has no effect on the validity or priority of the cautioner's
interest in the legal estate to which the caution relates.[289] In particular, it will
not protect a landowner against adverse possession of his land, whereas
registration of that land can now do so.[290]

---

[283] LRA 2002 s.15(1). Application is to the registrar: LRA 2002 s.15(4). It is made on Form
CT1: see LRR 2003 r.42. The "cautioner" for the purposes of the Act is the person shown as such
in the cautions register, who will either be the person who lodged the caution, or the person who
claims that the whole of the interest that entitled the original cautioner to lodge the caution has
vested in him by operation of law as successor to the cautioner: see LRA 2002 s.22; LRR 2003
rr.51, 52.

[284] LRA 2002 s.15(2). As regards demesne land, LRA 2002 s.15 applies as if that land were
held by Her Majesty for an unregistered estate in fee simple absolute in possession: LRA 2002
s.81.

[285] For restrictions, see below, para.7–077.

[286] There is power for the Lord Chancellor to alter the length of lease by order: see LRA 2002
s.118(1)(c). It is likely that, in due course, the period will be reduced so as to apply to leases
having more than 3 years unexpired.

[287] LRA 2002 s.15(3). This provision applies only to applications made on or after October 13,
2005: see LRA 2002 s.134(2); Sch.12 para.14(1).

[288] See (2001) Law Com. No.271, para.3.58. If a lease has been registered but the freehold has
not, the existence of the lease should become apparent on the first registration of the freehold from
the Index Map (see above, para.7–002).

[289] LRA 2002 s.16(3).

[290] See below, para.35–070.

7–046   If there is an application for the first registration of land to which a caution relates, the registrar must give the cautioner notice of the application and of his right to object to it.[291] The registrar may not determine the application for first registration until the end of the period prescribed by rules, unless the cautioner has objected before then or indicated that he does not intend to object.[292] A person must not exercise his right to lodge a caution against first registration without reasonable cause.[293] Breach of this duty is actionable in damages.[294] In practice this is an important safeguard and it is explained more fully below.[295]

7–047   A caution may be withdrawn or cancelled.

> (a) The cautioner may *withdraw* a caution against first registration by application to the registrar.[296]

> (b) Both the owner of the legal estate to which the caution relates, and the owner of a derivative legal estate, may apply[297] to the registrar to *cancel* the caution.[298] The registrar must give the cautioner notice of the application.[299] If the cautioner does not object to the application within the period prescribed by rules,[300] the registrar must cancel the registration of the caution.[301] Contrary to the general rule that any person may object to an application,[302] only the cautioner may object to an application to cancel the caution.[303]

7–048   The cautions register may be altered by the court or by the registrar for the purposes of correcting a mistake or bringing the register up to date.[304] These powers are analogous to the powers of the court and registrar to alter the register of title.[305] Where the registrar alters the register under these powers, he may pay such amount as he thinks fit in respect of costs reasonably

---

[291] LRA 2002 s.16(1).
[292] LRA 2002 s.16(2). The prescribed period is 15 business days after the date of the issue of the notice: see LRR 2003 r.53. For business days, see LRR 2003 r.216.
[293] LRA 2002 s.77(1).
[294] LRA 2002 s.77(2).
[295] See para.7–076.
[296] LRA 2002 s.17. The application is on Form WCT: LRR 2003 r.43.
[297] Application is made on form CCT: LRR 2003 r.44.
[298] LRA 2002 s.18(1); LRR 2003 r.45(a). Where the land to which the caution relates is demesne land, both Her Majesty and the owner of a legal estate affecting the demesne land, may apply to cancel the caution: LRR 2003 r.45(b). In general, a person who consented to the lodging of the caution or his successor in title by operation of law, may not apply to cancel a caution: see LRA 2002 s.18(2). He may only do so if the relevant interest has come to an end, or if the original consent was vitiated by fraud, misrepresentation, mistake, undue influence or duress: LRR 2003 r.46. For consent to a caution, see LRR 2003 r.47.
[299] LRA 2002 s.18(3).
[300] The period is 15 business days: LRR 2003 r.53.
[301] LRA 2002 s.18(4).
[302] See LRA 2002 s.73(1).
[303] LRA 2002 s.73(2); LRR 2003 r.52.
[304] LRA 2002 ss.20(1), 21(1).
[305] See below, paras 7–132 et seq.

incurred by a person in connection with the alteration.[306] In certain circumstances either the court must direct the registrar to alter the cautions register or, if there is an application to the registrar, he must alter the register.[307] This will be so where the court decides or the registrar is satisfied that:

(a) the cautioner does not own the relevant interest or owns only part of it; or

(b) the relevant interest does not exist in whole or part, or has come to an end, wholly or in part.

Part 3

DEALINGS WITH REGISTERED LAND

Section 1. Powers of Disposition

A landowner may not have unrestricted powers to dispose of his land, either **7–049** because his powers are limited either by statute, or, where the landowner is a corporation, by its public documents. Although under the Land Registration Act 1925 it was assumed that a registered proprietor had unfettered powers of disposition in the absence of any entry to the contrary in the register,[308] the position was not clear from the Act itself and there was authority that appeared to be against that view.[309] The matter is important, because if a registered proprietor makes a disposition that he has no power to make, the disponee's title could be vulnerable, notwithstanding its registration. The Land Registration Act 2002 therefore introduced the concept of "owner's powers".[310] Subject to the qualifications explained below,[311] these may be exercised by the person who is, or is entitled to be registered as, the proprietor of a registered estate or a registered charge.[312] The concept of owner's powers also provides protection for disponees. In the absence of any entry in the register restricting the disponor's powers, the disponee's title cannot be challenged on the ground that the disponor had no power to make the disposition. The registration of the disposition cannot therefore be a mistake that is capable of rectification.[313]

The scope of owner's powers depends upon whether the owner is the **7–050** proprietor of a registered estate or of a registered charge.

In the case of a registered estate, "owner's powers" consist of:

---

[306] LRA 2002 s.21(3).
[307] LRR 2003 rr.48, 49.
[308] *State Bank of India v Sood* [1997] Ch. 276 at 284.
[309] *Hounslow LBC v Hare* (1990) 24 H.L.R. 9. See (2001) Law Com. No.271, para.4.3.
[310] LRA 2002 s.23.
[311] See paras 7–051, 7–052.
[312] LRA 2002 s.24.
[313] For rectification, see below, para.7–132.

(i) a power to make a disposition of any kind permitted by the general law in relation to an interest of that description other than a mortgage by demise or sub-demise; and

(ii) a power to charge the estate at law with the payment of money.[314]

In relation to a registered charge, "owner's powers" comprise:

(i) a power to make a disposition of any kind permitted by the general law in relation to an interest of that description other than a legal sub-mortgage[315]; and

(ii) a power to charge at law with the payment of money indebtedness secured by the registered charge.[316]

As regards these provisions:

(i) The dispositions permitted by the general law are necessarily subject to the limitations or pre-conditions that are imposed on such dispositions by the general law.[317]

(ii) The provisions that restrict the means of creating charges and sub-charges are intended to simplify the law. Mortgages by demise or sub-demise are in practice obsolete, and this is recognised in the prohibition of their creation.[318] In consequence, a registered proprietor must either mortgage his land by means of a charge by way of legal mortgage[319] or by charging the land with the payment of money.[320] When a legal charge, created by a registrable disposition, is registered, it takes effect as a charge by deed by way of legal mortgage.[321]

(iii) Under the Land Registration Act 2002, the only way in which a legal chargee can create a sub-charge (in other words a charge over

---

[314] LRA 2002 s.23(1).

[315] A legal sub-mortgage means a transfer by way of mortgage, a sub-mortgage by sub-demise, and a charge by way of legal mortgage: LRA 2002 s.23(3).

[316] LRA 2002 s.23(2).

[317] e.g., if trustees of land are to make a conveyance that overreaches the trusts, the purchaser must pay the proceeds to the trustees, of whom there must be at least two unless there is a single trustee which is a trust corporation: see above, para.6–054; and below, para.12–037. Another example is the inability of a legal chargee to exercise his power of sale unless that power has arisen: see below, para.25–013.

[318] See (2001) Law Com. No.271, para.4.7.

[319] For the charge by way of legal mortgage, see below, para.24–025.

[320] The Land Registry's non-compulsory Form CH1 uses the latter formula, which derives from LRA 1925 s.25(1)(a).

[321] LRA 2002 s.51.

the indebtedness secured by his legal charge) is to charge that indebtedness with the payment of money.[322]

To protect disponees of registered land, the Land Registration Act 2002 **7–051** provides that a person's right to exercise owner's powers in relation to a registered estate or charge is to be taken to be free from any limitation affecting the validity of a disposition,[323] except in relation to a limitation on those powers that is reflected by an entry in the register[324] or imposed by, or under, the Act.[325] The effect of these provisions is that a disponee of registered land is entitled to assume that the disponor has the power to make the disposition to him, unless there is something in the register that places a limit on his powers. In this way the disponee's title cannot be questioned if it transpires that the disponor did not have power to make the particular disposition. This protection is limited to that purpose and does not affect the lawfulness of the disposition.[326] This means that if, for example, trustees sold land without obtaining the consent of a beneficiary, which was required under the trust, but where there was no restriction in the register to indicate the need for consent, the purchaser's title could not be challenged. The trustees would still have committed a breach of trust and would be liable for that breach. There might be circumstances where, although the disponee's title could not be challenged, he might be personally implicated in the breach of trust and be accountable in equity for the knowing receipt of property transferred in breach of trust.[327]

The Land Registration Act 2002 imposes limitations on how registrable **7–052** dispositions of registered land may be made. A registrable disposition of a registered estate or charge only has effect if it complies with any requirements as to form and content contained in rules,[328] and the rules duly make such

---

[322] For sub-charges, see below, para.25–148; and see *Credit & Mercantile Plc v Marks* [2004] EWCA Civ 568; [2005] Ch. 81.

[323] LRA 2002 s.26(1). It has been held by the Adjudicator that this does not include a case where a person has been registered as proprietor by mistake: it is concerned with fetters on an owner's powers: see *Ajibade v Bank of Scotland Plc* (2008) REF/2006/163 and 174.

[324] As by a restriction or notice. It is not entirely clear what is meant by the words "reflected by an entry in the register". A legal charge over a registered estate will necessarily be registered and it will commonly exclude the mortgagor's statutory power of leasing (see LPA 1925 s.99(1); below, para.25–071. As the charge is registered and, if inspected, would reveal the exclusion, the limitation on the owner's powers is ascertainable from the register. Since June 19, 2006, where a lease that is granted out of land that is subject to a legal charge, is submitted for registration, and the chargee's consent to the lease is not lodged with it, the Land Registry will make an entry in the register of the lease to the effect that its registration is subject to any rights that may have arisen by reason of the absence of chargee's consent, unless the lease was authorised under LPA 1925 s.99.

[325] LRA 2002 s.26(2). For an example of a limitation imposed by LRA 2002, see s.25(1); below, para.7–052.

[326] LRA 2002 s.26(3).

[327] For the principles of knowing receipt, see, e.g., *Bank of Credit and Commerce International (Overseas) Ltd v Akindele* [2001] Ch. 437.

[328] LRA 2002 s.25(1). The power to prescribe the form and content of dispositions can be extended to dispositions other than registrable dispositions: LRA 2002 s.25(2).

provision.[329] This differs from the position under the Land Registration Act 1925 and the rules made under it. Under the previous legislation, although there were prescribed forms for many types of disposition, registered charges could be in any form,[330] and in practice, there were no prescribed forms for leases. By contrast, there is now a voluntary form of application to register a charge,[331] and, since June 19, 2006, most registrable leases are "prescribed clauses leases", which must begin with the "required wording".[332]

Section 2. Registrable Dispositions

7–053　　**1. The dispositions that must be registered.** Where an estate, or a charge over that estate, has been registered, certain dispositions of or out of that estate or charge are themselves required to be registered.[333] The provisions governing such registrable dispositions differ from the triggers for the compulsory registration of dispositions of unregistered land[334] both as to the range of dispositions that are included and as to the consequences of non-registration. If a disposition of a registered estate or a registered charge is required to be completed by registration, it does not operate at law, but merely in equity, until the relevant registration requirements are met.[335] Until it is registered, a registrable disposition is vulnerable and may, in certain circumstances, be defeated by a subsequent registrable disposition made for valuable consideration and registered.[336] The registration requirements for registrable dispositions are prescribed.[337]

7–054　　*(a) Registrable dispositions of a registered estate.* The following dispositions of a registered estate must be registered:

> (a) A transfer of that estate, including a transfer by operation of law, other than a transfer on the death or bankruptcy of an individual proprietor, or a transfer on the dissolution of a corporate proprietor.[338]

> (b) The grant of a lease for a term of years absolute of more than seven years from the date of the grant.[339] There is a power for the Lord

---

[329] See LRR 2003 rr.58, 58A, 59, 60, 103, 116.
[330] LRA 1925 s.25(2).
[331] LRR 2003 r.103; Form CH1.
[332] LRR 2003 r.58A. The "required wording" is set out in LRR 2003 Sch.1A. The purpose of the prescribed clauses at the beginning of the lease is to ensure that all the matters that should be recorded in the register are set out in a standard form. See below, para.7–059.
[333] See above, para.7–006.
[334] See above, paras 7–013—7–015.
[335] LRA 2002 s.27(1).
[336] LRA 2002 ss.29(1), 30(1); see below, para.7–061.
[337] LRA 2002 s.27(4); Sch.2; below, para.7–057.
[338] LRA 2002 ss.27(2)(a), (5)(a), (5)(b). For the registration of transfers by operation of law, see LRR 2003 r.161.
[339] LRA 2002 s.27(2)(b)(i).

Chancellor to substitute a different term,[340] and it is anticipated that, in due course, leases granted for a term of more than three years will be made registrable dispositions.[341]

(c) The grant of a lease of any duration that is to take effect in possession after the end of a period of three months beginning with the date of the grant.[342]

(d) The grant of a lease of any duration under which the right to possession is discontinuous.[343] All such leases are registrable because of the difficulty of discovering their existence.

(e) The grant of a lease of any duration to a secure tenant pursuant to the statutory right to buy provisions of Part V of the Housing Act 1985.[344]

(f) The grant of a lease of any duration by a private sector landlord to a former secure tenant pursuant to the latter's preserved right to buy under s.171A of the Housing Act 1985.[345]

(g) Where the registered estate is a franchise or a manor, the grant of a lease of any duration of that franchise or manor.[346] Such leases will be very rare. The reason why they are registrable regardless of duration is because of the difficulty of otherwise discovering them.

(h) The express grant or reservation of a legal easement, right or privilege, whatever the duration of that right.[347] For these purposes, an express grant does not include a grant as a result of the operation of s.62 of the Law of Property Act 1925.[348] Furthermore, the grant of rights of common, which must be registered under Pt 1 of the Commons Act 2006, and which can only be made expressly,[349] are not registrable under the Land Registration Act 2002.[350] One consequence of this provision is that easements granted in leases for terms that are not registrable will be separately registrable, as where X grants Y a lease of part of his property for five years together with a right of way over X's retained land. The lease is not registrable,

---

[340] LRA 2002 s.118(d).
[341] See (2001) Law Com. No.271, para.3.17.
[342] LRA 2002 s.27(2)(b)(ii).
[343] LRA 2002 s.27(2)(b)(iii).
[344] LRA 2002 s.27(2)(b)(iv).
[345] LRA 2002 s.27(2)(b)(v).
[346] LRA 2002 s.27(2)(c).
[347] LRA 2002 s.27(2)(d).
[348] LRA 2002 s.27(7). For LPA 1925 s.62, see below, paras 28–027 and following.
[349] For the creation of rights of common, see Commons Act 2006 s.6; below, para.27–061.
[350] LRA 2002 s.27(2)(d).

but the easement is. The reason for requiring the registration of all such easements is that they may not be readily discoverable.[351]

(i) The express grant or reservation of a rentcharge issuing out of or charged on land, that is either perpetual or for a term of years absolute, or a legal right of entry annexed for any purpose to a legal rentcharge.[352] The circumstances in which rentcharges can now be created are very limited due to the Rentcharges Act 1977.[353] Rights of entry in a legal lease[354] are not required to be registered.[355]

(j) The grant of a legal charge.[356] In one situation, the creation of a legal charge does not have to be registered when it is created, namely where the charge arises by operation of law, under statutory powers, and is registrable as a local land charge.[357] In those circumstances, the charge takes effect as an unregistered interest that overrides a registered disposition and will therefore bind any person who acquires the land.[358] However, the charge cannot be realised until it is registered.[359] Registration is required, because it should not be possible for a person to dispose of registered land unless it is apparent from the register that he has powers of disposition over that land.[360]

7–055   Special provision is made for PPP leases relating to transport in London,[361] the nature of which have been explained.[362] Neither the grant of a PPP lease,[363] nor the grant of an easement right or privilege for the benefit of such a lease, is a registrable disposition.[364]

7–056   *(b) Registrable dispositions of a registered charge.* The following dispositions of a registered charge must be registered:

(a) a transfer of that charge; and

---

[351] As explained above at (b), it is likely that the length of leases that must be registered will in due course be reduced to terms of more than three years.

[352] LRA 2002 s.27(2)(e). In some rentcharges, the owner of the rentcharge reserves a right of entry over the land subject to the rentcharge, in the event of the failure to pay the rent or to perform the covenants supported by the rentcharge.

[353] See below, para.31–018. In practice, only estate rentcharges under Rentcharges Act 1977 s.2(3)(c), are now created: see below, paras 31–019; 32–021.

[354] See above, para.6–027.

[355] See LRA 2002 s.27(4); Sch.2 paras 7(1), (3); LRR 2003 r.77.

[356] LRA 2002 s.27(2)(f).

[357] LRA 2002 s.27(5)(c).

[358] See LRA 2002 Sch.3 para.6; below, para.7–087.

[359] LRA 2002 s.55. See too LRR 2003 r.104.

[360] See (2001) Law Com. No.271, para.7.42.

[361] LRA 2002 s.90.

[362] Above, para.7–010.

[363] As defined by Greater London Authority Act 1999 s.218: see LRA 2002 s.90(6).

[364] LRA 2002 s.90(3).

(b) the grant of a sub-charge.[365]

2. The registration requirements

(a) Registrable dispositions of a registered estate. The prescribed registra-   **7–057**
tion requirements for registrable dispositions of a registered estate are as
follows.[366]

(a) Where there is a transfer of the whole or part of a registered estate,
the transferee, or his successor in title, must be registered as the
proprietor.[367]

(b) Where there is the grant of a lease, the grantee, or his successor in
title, must be registered as the proprietor of the lease, and a notice
of the lease must be entered in the register of the superior title.[368]

(c) Where there is a lease of a franchise or manor for a term of more
than seven years from the date of the grant, the grantee, or his
successor in title, must be registered as the proprietor of the lease,
and a notice of the lease must be entered in the register of the
franchise or manor.[369] In the case of a lease of franchise or manor for
a term of seven years or less from the date of the grant, a notice of
the lease must be entered in the register of that franchise or
manor.[370]

(d) Where there is a disposition under which a legal rentcharge or a
profit à prendre in gross is created for an interest equivalent to a fee
simple absolute in possession or for a term of years absolute of more
than seven years,[371] the grantee, or his successor in title, must be
entered in the register as the proprietor of the interest created and
notice must be entered in the register of the title subject to the
rentcharge or profit.[372] By contrast, if a legal rentcharge or a profit
à prendre in gross is created for a term of seven years or less, and
cannot, therefore, be registered with its own title, a notice must be
entered in the register of the title subject to that rentcharge or
profit.[373]

---

[365] LRA 2002 s.27(3).
[366] LRA 2002 s.27(4); Sch.2 Pt.1.
[367] LRA 2002 Sch.2 para.2(1). Where the transfer is of part only, the registrar is required to
make certain entries in the registers of both the title out of which the transfer was made and the
title of the part transferred: LRA 2002 Sch.2 para.2(2); LRR 2003 r.72.
[368] LRA 2002 Sch.2 para.3.
[369] LRA 2002 Sch.2 para.4.
[370] LRA 2002 Sch.2 para.5.
[371] Both these interests are capable of being created with their own registered titles: see LRA
2002 s.3; above, para.7–010.
[372] LRA 2002 Sch.2 para.6.
[373] LRA 2002 Sch.2 para.7(1), (2)(a).

(e) Where there is a disposition by which a legal easement, right or privilege (other than a profit à prendre in gross) is granted or reserved, a notice must be entered in the register of the title of the servient tenement and if the dominant tenement is registered, the proprietor must be registered in that register as the proprietor of the easement, right or privilege.[374] In this way, both the benefit and the burden of the easement, right or privilege are registered.

(f) Where there is a disposition by which a legal right of entry is annexed for any purpose to a legal rentcharge, a notice must be entered in the register of the title subject to that right of entry, and the proprietor of the rentcharge must be entered in the register of the rentcharge as the proprietor of the right of entry.[375] Once again, in this way, both the benefit and burden of the interest are registered. As has been explained, the registrar does not register the benefit and burden of a right of entry contained in a lease.[376]

(g) In the case where a legal charge is created, the chargee, or his successor in title, must be entered in the register of the estate charged as the proprietor of the charge.[377] A legal charge does not have a separate title.

There is a general provision in the Land Registration Act 2002 by which, where there is a registrable disposition of a registered estate, other than a transfer of that estate or the creation of registered charge over it, and a person is entered in the register as proprietor of the interest in question, the registrar must enter a notice in the register in respect of that interest.[378]

7–058   *(b) Registrable dispositions of a registered charge.*[379] The prescribed registration requirements for registrable dispositions of a registered charge are that:

(a) Where the charge is transferred, the transferee or his successor in title, must be entered in the register of the property charged as the proprietor of the charge.[380]

(b) Where the chargee creates a sub-charge, the sub-chargee, or his successor in title, must be registered in the register of the property charged as the proprietor of the sub-charge.[381]

---

[374] LRA 2002 Sch.2 para.7(1), (2). See too s.59(1).
[375] LRA 2002 Sch.2 para.7(1), (2).
[376] See above, para.7–054(i).
[377] LRA 2002 Sch.2 para.8. See too, s.59(2).
[378] LRA 2002 s.38.
[379] LRA 2002 s.27(4); Sch.2 Pt.2.
[380] LRA 2002 Sch.2 para.10.
[381] LRA 2002 Sch.2 para.11. The entry of the person in the register as the proprietor of the sub-charge on a registered charge must be made in relation to that charge: s.59(3).

3. Applications for registration. As has been explained, the form and **7–059**
content of applications to register registrable dispositions is prescribed by
rules.[382] The disponee will have to make an application to the Land Registry
in the correct manner[383] and must submit with the application the instrument
of transfer or grant, and any other relevant documents.[384]

There are a number of prescribed forms of transfer depending upon the
nature of the transaction.[385] There are, for example, different forms of transfer
for:

> (i) a transfer of part of a title to a registered estate by the owner[386] or
> under a power of sale[387];
>
> (ii) a transfer of the whole of the title by the owner[388] or under a power
> of sale[389];
>
> (iii) an assent of part[390] or of the whole of a registered title[391]; and
>
> (iv) a transfer[392] or an assent of a charge.[393]

An example of a transfer of the whole of the title to a registered estate is given
later in this chapter.[394]

As regards registrable leases granted on or after June 19, 2006, which are
called prescribed clauses leases,[395] these must now begin with the required
wording that is prescribed by rules.[396] The registrar must make entries in the
register to record certain matters disclosed by the required wording.[397] There
is a form for the creation of a legal charge, but its use is voluntary.[398] The
Registry will also accept the lender's own form of charge.[399] There are no
prescribed forms of grant for other registrable dispositions. The relevant deed
must be submitted with the application for registration.

---

[382] Above, para.7–052. The relevant requirements are found in LRR 2003 Pt.6.

[383] It will generally be on Form AP1 (application to change the register), which is the form that
must be used if no other form of application is prescribed: LRR 2003 r.13.

[384] When making an application to register a registrable disposition, the applicant must also
provide information about certain unregistered interests affecting the registered estate: LRA 2002
s.71(b). This is explained later: see below, para.7–101.

[385] LRR 2003 rr.58 (transfer of a registered estate), 116 (transfer of a registered estate). For
guidance on the appropriate transfer form in less straightforward transactions, see LRPG 21.

[386] Form TP1.

[387] Form TP2.

[388] Form TR1.

[389] Form TR2.

[390] Form AS3.

[391] Form AS1.

[392] Form TR3.

[393] Form AS2.

[394] See below, para.7–149.

[395] See above, para.7–052.

[396] LRR 2003 r.58A; Sch.1A.

[397] LRR 2003 r.72A.

[398] Form CH1; LRR 2003 r.104.

[399] LRPG 29, para.4.

Section 3. The Priority of Competing Interests

7–060   **1. The basic rule.** Where title is registered, the principles that determine the priority of competing interests are now entirely statutory, and not as under the Land Registration Act 1925, a mixture of common law and statute.[400] The basic rule is that the priority of an interest affecting a registered estate or charge is not affected by a disposition of the estate or charge.[401] It makes no difference for the purposes of this rule whether the interest or disposition is registered.[402] The effect of this rule is that the date of the creation of an interest determines its priority: the first of the competing interests to be created has priority.

7–061   **2. Registered dispositions made for valuable consideration.** The basic rule is subject to an important exception.[403] If a registrable disposition of a registered estate is made for valuable consideration and then completed by registration,[404] a prior interest affecting the estate whose priority was not protected at the time of registration[405] is postponed to the interest under the disposition.[406] In other words, the interest created or transferred by the registered disposition takes priority over the prior unprotected interest.[407] This principle is extended to the grant of leases out of a registered estate that are not registrable dispositions.[408] The grant of the lease is treated as if it were a registrable disposition that was registered at the time of the grant.[409]

The same rule applies in relation to a disposition of a registered charge made for valuable consideration. The interest acquired by the disponee takes priority to any interest affecting the charge whose priority was not protected at the date on which it was registered.[410]

For this rule to apply, there must be a registered disposition. A purported disposition which is of no legal effect, such as a forged transfer, will not

---

[400] See the sixth edition of this work at para.6–095.

[401] LRA 2002 s.28(1). References in the Act to an interest affecting an estate or charge are a reference to an adverse right affecting the title to the estate or charge: LRA 2002 s.132(3)(b).

[402] LRA 2002 s.28(2).

[403] The exception is analogous to LRA 1925 ss.20, 23, under the previous law.

[404] The onus of proving a disposition was made for valuable consideration rests upon the party asserting it. If the onus is not discharged, the basic rule applies: *Halifax Plc v Curry Popeck* [2008] EWHC 1692 Ch at [46].

[405] An entry in the register has effect from the time of the making of an application to register the disposition: LRA 2002 s.74; below, para.7–114.

[406] LRA 2002 s.29(1).

[407] Although the provisions operate to postpone unprotected interests to registered dispositions for valuable consideration, the practical effect is to destroy them *as against that subsequent disponee* and in respect of his estate or interest: see Ruoff & Roper, 15.039. The unprotected interest may not be defeated as against other estates or interests. Thus if a lessee took free of an unprotected interest, that interest might continue to bind the freehold reversion.

[408] In other words, leases granted for 7 years or less, which are not otherwise required to be registered.

[409] LRA 2002 s.29(4).

[410] LRA 2002 s.30(1).

constitute a registered disposition.[411] This is so even though, in consequence of the invalid disposition, the donee is mistakenly registered as proprietor. That proprietor will therefore take subject to *all* interests affecting the registered estate at the time of registration, whether or not they are protected (as explained below).[412]

For these purposes, the priority of an interest will be protected in the following circumstances:

7-062

(i) In any case, if the interest:

    (a) is a registered charge;

    (b) is the subject of a notice in the register;

    (c) is an unregistered interest that falls within any of the paragraphs of Sch.3 to the Land Registration Act 2002, and which thereby overrides a registered disposition[413]; or

    (d) appears from the register to be excepted from the effect of registration, as for example, where the registered estate is registered with possessory title, so that any estate, right or interest that subsisted at the date of first registration was unaffected by that registration[414]; and

(ii) in the case of a disposition of a leasehold estate (or of a charge which relates to a leasehold estate), if the burden of the interest is incident to the estate.[415] In other property legislation, the words "incident to" always refer to the benefit or burden of covenants, conditions, and rights of re-entry.[416] The protected interests (which must be proprietary interests) would therefore appear to be the burden of rights of re-entry and of covenants[417] that create proprietary rights.[418]

Two examples will illustrate the workings of these provisions.

7-063

    (a) X, the proprietor of a registered freehold estate, grants Y an option to purchase the land, which Y fails to protect by a notice. X then

---

[411] *Malory Enterprises Ltd v Cheshire Homes (UK) Ltd* [2002] EWCA Civ 151 at [65]; [2002] Ch. 216 at 232, a case on LRA 1925 s.20, but the reasoning must apply to dispositions under LRA 2002. For the effect of registration, see below, para.7–116.

[412] This will be important if the register is not rectified against the proprietor, despite the fact that the purported disposition under which he was registered was a nullity. For alteration of the register, see below, para.7–132.

[413] For these interests, see below, para.7–086. If an interest was formerly an overriding interest but was then protected in the register and, for some reason, that entry was deleted from the register, the interest will not resume its status as an overriding interest: see LRA 2002 ss.29(3), 30(3).

[414] LRA 2002 ss.29(2)(a) (registered estates); 30(2)(a) (registered charges).

[415] LRA 2002 s.29(2)(b) (registered estates); 30(2)(b) (registered charges). cf. above, para.7–033.

[416] See, e.g., LPA 1925 ss.77(5), 141(1), 142(1); L & TCA 1995 ss.3(1), 4(a).

[417] Which would generally be restrictive covenants.

[418] This accords with the corresponding provision in LRA 1925 s.23(1)(a).

contracts to sell the land to Z and enters a notice in the register in respect of his estate contract. Before X can complete the sale to Z, Y exercises his option and seeks specific performance against X. Z also seeks to enforce his contract against X. Y will be successful and will obtain specific performance in his favour. When the sale is completed pursuant to the court's decree, and Y is registered as proprietor, he will be entitled to have Z's notice removed from the register, because Y's option, being first in time, had priority over Z's estate contract, and its registration is irrelevant.

(b) If in the previous example, X had completed the sale of the land to Z prior to Y exercising the option, and when Z had been registered as proprietor, Y had not protected his option by entering a notice, Z would take free of Y's option. Although the option initially had priority over Z's estate contract, Z was a purchaser of the registered estate for valuable consideration and, as the option was unprotected at the date when Z was registered as proprietor, Y's priority was defeated by Z.

7–064   Questions of knowledge, notice or good faith are irrelevant to the statutory rules of priority, subject to one exception mentioned below.[419] As has been mentioned, concepts of knowledge and notice have very little role to play under the Land Registration Act 2002,[420] and this is consistent with the principles of title registration, which substitute registration for notice. Knowledge, notice or good faith are relevant only where the legislation makes it explicit.[421]

The principle set out above is subject to one qualification. It has already been explained that, even though a disponee may take free of a proprietary right under the priority rules applicable to registered land, he may still incur personal liability in law or equity.[422] However, although a disposition knowingly made by both parties in fraud of a third party can be set aside, it is not fraud to take a disposition with knowledge of a third party claim or of an unprotected interest.[423]

7–065   **3. Special cases.** There are a number of special provisions that affect the priority of particular types of interest.

7–066   First, the effect of a disposition of a registered estate or charge on a charge for unpaid inheritance tax[424] is to be determined in accordance with the

---

[419] See para.7–066.
[420] See above, para.7–032; and see *Chaudhary v Yavuz* [2011] EWCA Civ 1314 at [20].
[421] For those cases, see LRA 2002 ss.11(4)(c), 12(4)(d) (above, para.7–032); s.31 (below, para.7–066); and s.86(5) (below, para.7–111). LRA 2002 contains no definition of "purchaser". The word is only used in relation to other statutory provisions: see LRA 2002 ss.31, 91(8).
[422] See above, paras 6–066 and following.
[423] *Mehra v Mehra* [2008] 3 E.G.L.R. 153 at 159 (County Court); (2001) Law Com. No.271, para.5.16.
[424] See Inheritance Tax Act 1984 s.237.

relevant provisions of the Inheritance Tax Act 1984[425] and not by an application of the general principles of priority set out above.[426] If such a charge has not been registered, a disponee will take free of it only if he was a purchaser in good faith for money or money's worth. There is also a special rule applicable to dispositions by a registered proprietor who has been adjudged bankrupt.[427] This is explained below.[428]

Second, the status of three types of interest is either clarified or changed in a way that may affect the priority of that interest.

7–067

(a) At common law, a right of pre-emption,[429] unlike an option, does not create an interest in land from the date of the grant of the right, but may become an interest in land at some later date, when the right of pre-emption is triggered.[430] The precise date and circumstances in which an equitable interest in land will arise depends upon the terms of the right of pre-emption.[431] The common law position has created considerable practical difficulty and it is therefore provided that a right of pre-emption, created on or after October 13, 2003[432] in relation to registered land, has effect from the time of creation as an interest capable of binding successors in title (subject to the rules about the effect of dispositions on priority).[433] Accordingly, a right of pre-emption created on or after the Land Registration Act 2002 came into force, is a proprietary right from its inception and can be protected accordingly.

(b) The principles of proprietary estoppel are explained in Chapter 16. Where an equity arises by estoppel,[434] that equity entitles the person in whose favour it has arisen to seek relief from the court. Once the court decides how to give effect to that equity, any proprietary right that arises under the court's order (such as an easement) can be protected in the register in the appropriate way. However, it may be necessary to determine the status of that equity after it has arisen, but before a court has been asked to give effect to it, as where the owner

---

[425] Inheritance Tax Act 1984 ss.237(6), 238.

[426] LRA 2002 s.31.

[427] LRA 2002 s.86(5).

[428] See para.7–111.

[429] A distinction has been drawn between a right of pre-emption, where the grantee has the right to purchase at a fixed price (or at a price that is not chosen by the grantor) before the grantor is free to sell to anyone else, and a right of first refusal, where the grantee has the first right to refuse an offer to purchase at the price at which the grantor is willing to sell: see *Bircham & Co Nominees (No 2) Ltd v Worrell Holdings Ltd* [2001] 3 E.G.L.R. 83, at 87. However, the statutory references to rights of pre-emption in LPA 1925 s.186; LCA 1972 s.2(4)(iv); and LRA 2002 s.115(1) should, in principle, include both.

[430] *Pritchard v Briggs* [1980] Ch. 338.

[431] See the analysis in *Speciality Shops Ltd v Yorkshire and Metropolitan Estates Ltd* [2003] 2 P. & C.R. 410, 416–7; and see below, para.15–062.

[432] When LRA 2002 came into force.

[433] LRA 2002 s.115.

[434] See below, para.16–001.

of the land affected by the equity has disposed of it, so that the question arises as to whether that equity is merely personal or whether it creates a proprietary right that could bind the purchaser of the land.[435] The preponderance of authority favours the view that an equity arising by estoppel is a proprietary right and, as such, capable of binding third parties.[436] This view has been endorsed by the Land Registration Act 2002. It declares that, for the avoidance of doubt, in relation to registered land, an equity by estoppel has effect from the time the equity arises as an interest capable of binding successors in title (subject to the rules about the effect of dispositions on priority).[437]

(c) There is a category of equitable rights that fall short of being equitable interests in land and which are known as mere equities.[438] These are explained in detail later.[439] The common characteristic of mere equities is that they are a claim to discretionary equitable relief in relation to property and they include a right to have an instrument, such as a transfer, set aside on grounds of fraud or undue influence, and a right to have a document, such as a lease, rectified to correct a mutual mistake.[440] Because they are regarded as something less than an equitable interest, in the context of unregistered land, it has been held in the context of unregistered land that they can be defeated by a purchaser of either a legal or equitable interest without notice of the mere equity.[441] As has been explained, concepts of notice have no place in the principles of priority that apply to registered land. In relation to registered land, prior to the Land Registration Act 2002, mere equities were treated as proprietary rights.[442] The Act provides that, for the avoidance of doubt, in relation to registered land, a mere equity has effect from the time the equity arises as an interest capable of binding successors in title (subject to the rules about the effect of dispositions on priority).[443] The effect, therefore, is that mere equities are treated in the same way as any other interest in registered land for the purposes of priority and are subject to the rules set out above.[444] There are no

---

[435] See further, below, para.16–030.
[436] See especially *Singh v Sandhu* Unreported, May 4, 1995 (Court of Appeal), and the review of the authorities in *Locabail (UK) Ltd v Bayfield Properties Ltd* Unreported, March 9, 1999 (Chancery Division) at [26]–[32].
[437] LRA 2002 s.116; below, para.16–029.
[438] See (2001) Law Com. No.271, paras 5.32–5.36.
[439] See para.8–012.
[440] An equity arising by estoppel may be such a mere equity.
[441] See, e.g. *Mid-Glamorgan County Council v Ogwr BC* (1993) 68 P. & C.R. 1 at 9.
[442] See *Nurdin & Peacock Plc v D B Ramsden & Co Ltd* [1999] 1 E.G.L.R. 119.
[443] LRA 2002 s.116.
[444] See paras 7–060—7–062.

special rules applicable to them as there are where title is unregistered.

Third, as regards the priority of registered charges on the same registered **7–068** estate or the same registered charge, the charges are taken to rank as between themselves in the order shown in the register.[445] This principle operates in conjunction with the principles of priority explained above.[446] For example, if X, the proprietor of a registered estate, charges his land by way of legal charge to Y, and then creates a further legal charge in favour of Z:

(i) If Y registers his legal charge before X creates the further charge in favour of Z, Y's charge will necessarily have priority over Z's, and Z will take subject to it. The order in which the charges appear in the register will therefore be Y's and then Z's.

(ii) If Y fails to register his legal charge before X creates the further charge in favour of Z, that of itself will not affect the priority of the two charges: the basic rule applies.[447] However, if Z then registers his charge, before Y has registered his, Z's charge will take priority to Y's unprotected charge, because it is a registrable disposition for valuable consideration.[448] If Y subsequently registers his charge, the order in which the charges will appear in the register will therefore be Z's and then Y's.

The rules of priority for competing charges set out above are subject to two exceptions. First, the registered chargees can agree to alter the priority of their respective charges.[449] Secondly, there are some statutory charges which purport to take priority over existing registered charges.[450] The registrar is required to notify the proprietor of any registered charge or charge protected by notice of the creation of the statutory charge.[451] The registrar must make an entry in the register showing the priority of the statutory charge.[452] Without such provisions, an existing chargee might make further advances to the registered chargee[453] in ignorance of the fact that the priority of his charge had been subordinated to the statutory charge. Indemnity is payable for any loss suffered by reason of a breach of this duty.[454]

---

[445] LRA 2002 s.48; LRR 2003 r.101.
[446] Paras 7–060—7–062.
[447] LRA 2002 s.28; above, para.7–060.
[448] LRA 2002 s.29; above, para.7–061.
[449] LRR 2003 r.102.
[450] See, e.g., a charge in favour of the Legal Services Commission: see Access to Justice Act 1999 s.10(7).
[451] LRA 2002 s.50; LRR 2003 r.106.
[452] LRR 2003 r.105.
[453] For further advances, see below, para.7 103.
[454] See below, para.7–140.

Section 4. Notices and Restrictions

7–069   **1. Introduction.** The Land Registration Act 2002 simplified the means of protecting interests in registered land. In place of the four methods of protection that had previously existed, namely, notices, cautions against dealings, restrictions and inhibitions,[455] there are now just notices and restrictions. The Act contained transitional provisions which dealt with the effect of existing entries in the register when the Act came into force.[456]

If a registered estate or charge is subject to some form of incumbrance (other than a registered charge), that is intended to be capable of binding any owner of the land, such as an easement, a restrictive covenant, an option or a lien, the appropriate form of protection is a notice. To fill the vacuum that would otherwise have been left by the abolition of cautions against dealings, the Land Registration Act 2002 created two different types of notice, agreed and unilateral notices. The latter can be entered in the register on application by a person claiming an interest without the consent of the proprietor of the registered estate or charge affected by it. If that interest is valid, the notice will protect its priority, something which a caution against dealings did not do. The registered proprietor can apply to cancel a unilateral notice, if he considers that it should not have been entered.

By contrast with a notice, a restriction does not directly protect the priority of an interest, though it may have that effect indirectly. Where there is a restriction in the register, it prevents the registration of any disposition of a registered estate or charge except in accordance with the terms of that restriction. It is an appropriate entry where an owner of a registered estate or charge has limited powers of disposition.[457] It also provides a means of ensuring that overreaching requirements are met on a disposal of land held in trust.

2. Notices

7–070   *(a) The nature of a notice.* A notice is an entry in the register in respect of the burden of an interest which affects a registered estate or charge.[458] The entry of the notice is made in relation to the registered estate or charge affected by that interest.[459] The fact that a notice has been entered does not necessarily mean that the interest is valid. However, if it is valid, the entry of the notice protects the interest for the purposes of the rules on priority.[460]

---

[455] See the sixth edition of this work at paras 6–079—6–093.

[456] See LRA 2002 Sch.12, para.2. Thus, LRA 1925 ss.55, 56, continue to govern cautions notwithstanding their repeal (see too LRR 2003 rr.218–223), notices take effect as agreed notices under LRA 2002, and restrictions and inhibitions take effect as restrictions under LRA 2002.

[457] This is important, given the concept of "owner's powers" that is explained above at para.7–050.

[458] LRA 2002 s.32(1).

[459] LRA 2002 s.32(2).

[460] LRA 2002 s.32(3). For the rules on priority, see above, paras 7–060—7–062.

Although there is no list of interests that can be protected by the entry of a notice:

(i) The registrar is required to enter a notice of the burden of a registrable disposition of a registered estate, other than a transfer of that estate or the creation of registered charge[461]; and

(ii) There is a list of interests, in relation to which it is not possible to enter a notice.[462] These excluded interests are:

(a) An interest under either a trust of land or a settlement under the Settled Land Act 1925.[463] Such interests are overreachable and should be protected by the entry of an appropriate restriction.[464]

(b) A leasehold estate granted for a term of three years or less from the date of grant and which is not required to be registered.[465] The prohibition on the noting of leases does not extend to all leases that cannot be registered with their own titles. It is possible to enter a notice in respect of the burden of any lease granted for more than three years.[466]

(c) A restrictive covenant made between lessor and lessee, so far as it relates to the demised premises.[467] Restrictive covenants in leases are not noted, because they will normally be apparent from the lease itself.[468] This exception is narrower than the equivalent provision in the previous legislation, by which it was not possible to note any restrictive covenant between lessor and lessee, even if it related to property other than that demised.[469]

(d) An interest which is capable of being registered under Pt 1 of the Commons Act 2006.[470] The rights of common to which this refers, are registrable only under that Act and cannot be registered in the register of title.[471]

---

[461] LRA 2002 s.38; above, para.7–057.
[462] LRA 2002 s.33. Most, but not all of these, are similar to the exclusions under LRA 1925.
[463] LRA 2002 s.33(a).
[464] See below, paras 7–078, 7–081.
[465] LRA 2002 s.33(b).
[466] This might be done, e.g. where the lease had the benefit of an easement over the landlord's property, which would have to be noted, regardless of the length of the grant: see above, para.7–054(h).
[467] LRA 2002 s.33(c).
[468] See too LRA 2002 s.29(2)(b); above, para.7–062(b).
[469] LRA 1925 s.50(1). This gave rise to difficulties: see *Oceanic Village Ltd v United Attractions Ltd* [2000] Ch. 234, at pp.252–4.
[470] LRA 2002 s.33(d). Pt 1 of Commons Act 2006, replaced the Commons Registration Act 1965.
[471] See Commons Act 2006 s.3(7).

(e) An interest in any coal or coal mine, the rights attached to any such interest and the rights of any person under certain provisions of the Coal Industry Act 1994.[472] The prohibition on noting interests in coal or coal mines is carried forward from the previous legislation[473] and reflects the practical difficulty of identifying the location of such rights.

(f) A PPP lease.[474] These leases have been explained.[475] They are incapable of any form of registration.

7–071 Notices may or must be entered in the register by the registrar in certain circumstances. For example, as already explained, he is required to note some registrable dispositions of a registered estate.[476] Another case where the registrar may enter a notice in respect of that interest is where it appears to him that a registered estate is subject to an unregistered overriding interest that falls within Sch.1 of the Act,[477] and is not excluded by the provisions set out above.[478]

7–072 Alternatively, a notice may be entered upon application to the registrar by:

(i) the person who claims to be entitled to the benefit of an interest affecting a registered estate or charge that can be protected by a notice[479]; or

(ii) the registered proprietor or the person entitled to be registered as proprietor of the registered estate or charge affected by the interest.[480]

An application for a notice may (and sometimes must) be for an agreed notice, or it may be for a unilateral notice.

7–073 *(b) Agreed notices.* An agreed notice is very similar to a notice entered under the previous legislation,[481] and is normally employed to protect interests which are not disputed. An application for an agreed notice can only be approved by the registrar if it is made by or with the consent of the registered

---

[472] LRA 2002 s.33(d). The provisions of the Coal Industry Act 1994 are ss.8, 49 and 51.
[473] See LRA 1925 s.70(4).
[474] LRA 2002 s.90(4).
[475] See above, para.7–010.
[476] LRA 2002 s.38; above, paras 7–057, 7–080.
[477] See above, paras 7–028—7–030.
[478] LRA 2002 s.37(1). He must give notice to the registered proprietor (unless he has applied for or consented to the entry) and to the person who appears to him to have the benefit of an interest (unless he applied for or consented to the entry, or no address for service on him is set out in the register): LRA 2002 s.37(2); LRR 2003 r.89. For interests that cannot be noted, see LRA 2002 s.33; above, para.7–080(b).
[479] LRA 2002 s.34(1). It will not be capable of protection by notice if it is excluded by LRA 2002 s.33; above, para.7–080(b).
[480] LRA 2002 s.34(3), (4).
[481] Which are treated as agreed notices: LRA 2002 Sch.12 para.2(1).

proprietor or the person entitled to be registered as proprietor, or if the registrar is satisfied as to the validity of the applicant's claim.[482] In practice, if the registered proprietor does not consent, the applicant is likely to register a unilateral notice, rather than trying to persuade the registrar that his claim is valid. This is because the evidential burden in relation to the latter is more demanding.[483] As regards certain types of interest, rules provide that an applicant must apply for an agreed rather than a unilateral notice.[484] This gives these rights greater protection. The registered proprietor cannot apply for their cancellation (as he could if they were protected by a unilateral notice[485]), and they can only be removed on an application to alter the register if the interest protected by the notice no longer subsists, so that the register should be brought up to date, or if the entry of the notice was a mistake, as where the person who applied to register the notice did not have the rights which he claimed.[486]

The form and content of an application for an agreed notice are prescribed.[487] The notice entered in the register must identify the registered estate or charge affected and, if only part of a registered estate is affected it must clearly identify that part.[488] It must also give details of the interest protected.[489] An example would be "(9 October 2006) Contract for sale dated 29 September 2006 in favour of Ruth White".[490]

The only circumstance in which an agreed notice can be cancelled is if the interest which it protects has determined. There is no specific cancellation provision in the Land Registration Act 2002, because the Act makes specific provision for updating the register and removing superfluous entries,[491] though rules make provision for applications to cancel agreed notices.[492]

(c) Unilateral notices. A person who claims to have the benefit of an **7–074** interest affecting a registered estate or charge may apply for the entry of a unilateral notice.[493] The registrar does not have to be satisfied of the validity of the applicant's claim (as he must be with an agreed notice), merely that the interest claimed is one that can be protected by a notice. Details of the interest must be given in a statutory declaration by the applicant or a certificate by his

---

[482] LRA 2002 s.34(3).

[483] See LRPG 19, para.3.4.2.

[484] LRR 2003 r.80. These include a home rights notice under FLA 1996, an inheritance tax notice, a notice in respect of an order under the Access to Neighbouring Land Act 1994, notice of a variation of a lease by a leasehold valuation tribunal under LTA 1987 s.38, or a notice in respect of a public or customary right. For the special provisions as to home rights under FLA 1996, see LRR 2003 r.82. These provisions follow the previous law: see LRA 1925 ss.49(1), 64(5)–(7) (as amended); FLA 1996 s.31(10).

[485] See below, para.7–084.

[486] For alteration of the register, see below, para.7–132.

[487] See LRR 2003 r.81. Application is on Form AN1.

[488] LRR 2003 r.84(2).

[489] LRR 2003 r.84(3).

[490] See LRPG 19, para.3.3.2. The date is the date on which the notice is taken to be entered in the register: LRR 2003 r.20.

[491] See LRA 2002 Sch.4 para.5(b), (d); below, para.7–133.

[492] LRR 2003 r.87. Application is on Form CN1.

[493] Application is on Form UN1: LRR 2003 r.83.

conveyancer.[494] The application does not require the consent of the registered proprietor, though the registrar must give notice of the entry to him.[495] A unilateral notice in the register must indicate that it is such a notice and identify the beneficiary of the notice.[496] As was formerly the case with cautions against dealings, the register entry will not, however, specify the exact nature of the interest which it protects.[497] An example would be "(9 October 2006) UNILATERAL NOTICE in respect of an agreement dated 29 September 2006, made between Stephen Black and Ruth White." It would also give the name and address of Ruth White as the beneficiary.[498]

The beneficiary of a unilateral notice[499] may apply to the registrar for the removal of a unilateral notice.[500]

By their nature, unilateral notices have the potential for abuse. Doubtful or spurious entries could be made to frustrate a disposition or to extract a payment from the registered proprietor. However, there are a number of safeguards which are intended to deter or frustrate such practices.

7–075 First, the registered proprietor (or a person entitled to be registered as proprietor) may apply for the cancellation of the unilateral notice.[501] The registrar must notify the beneficiary of that application and that the notice will be cancelled if he fails to object to it.[502] If the beneficiary exercises his right to object to the application,[503] that objection will be dealt with in accordance with the procedure for disputed applications.[504] If the beneficiary of a unilateral notice fails to object within the prescribed period,[505] the registrar must cancel the notice.[506]

7–076 Second, a person is under a duty not to apply for the entry of a notice or restriction without reasonable cause, and may be liable in damages for breach of statutory duty if he does so.[507] Because of that statutory duty a court may order a person to withdraw an application to enter a unilateral notice,[508] and

---

[494] See Form UN1.

[495] LRA 2002 s.35(1).

[496] LRA 2002 s.35(2).

[497] Because of the vague nature of the entry in the register, cautions were often entered not as a hostile form of entry but in order to protect commercially sensitive transactions. It was considered that this practice should be carried through to unilateral notices: see (2001) Law Com. No.271, para.6.26.

[498] See LRPG 19, para.3.3.3.

[499] Or, as the case may be, his personal representatives (if he is dead) or his trustee in bankruptcy (if he is insolvent): see LRA 2002 s.35(3); LRR 2003 r.85(2).

[500] LRA 2002 s.35(3); LRR 2003 r.85. Application is made on Form UN2.

[501] LRA 2002 s.36(1).

[502] LRA 2002 s.36(2).

[503] LRA 2002 s.73(3).

[504] See LRA 2002 s.73(5)–(8); below, para.7–129. It is a breach of statutory duty for a person to object to an application without reasonable cause (so that the person might be liable in damages): LRA 2002 ss.77(1)(c), (2).

[505] 15 business days: LRR 2003 r.86(3).

[506] LRA 2002 s.36(3).

[507] LRA 2002 ss.77(1)(b), (2). If a person has a reasonably arguable case, his conduct will not breach the statutory duty: *Fitzroy Developments Ltd v Fitzrovia Properties Ltd* [2011] EWHC 1849 (Ch) at [144].

[508] See *Loubatières v Mornington Estates (UK) Ltd* [2004] EWHC 825 (Ch).

could, presumably, order the cancellation of a notice that had been entered in the register. In practice, if, as often happens, a registered proprietor seeks the removal of a unilateral notice as a matter of urgency (usually because a sale is pending), he may apply to the High Court, acting in its inherent jurisdiction, to seek the vacation of that notice.[509] The court has a wide inherent jurisdiction[510] to order the vacation of any entry in the register,[511] and it was often used in the past in relation to cautions against dealings.[512] Although the point has been left open,[513] there is nothing in the Land Registration Act 2002 that takes away this useful jurisdiction. It is commonly exercised speedily on an interim application, without awaiting the trial of any action, thereby preventing the entry from improperly inhibiting dealings with the land. Where the registration is only arguably correct, an interim application to vacate the entry will usually be dismissed only on terms. The party who opposes vacation will normally be required to give an undertaking to pay the landowner damages if at trial it is held that the entry was wrongly made.[514] It has never been determined whether the county court has any similar jurisdiction,[515] but as it was created by statute it cannot have an inherent jurisdiction.

3. Restrictions

(a) *The nature of restrictions.* A restriction is an entry in the register **7–077** regulating the circumstances in which a disposition of a registered estate or charge may be the subject of an entry in the register.[516] The range of restrictions is therefore very wide, and this is necessarily so because of the variety of situations where a restriction may be required. At one extreme, a restriction may prevent any dealings with a registered estate or charge,[517] whether indefinitely, for a specified period, or until the occurrence of an event.[518] At the other, it might merely prevent the registration of a particular

---

[509] See *Donnelly v Weighbridge Construction Ltd* [2006] EWHC 348 (TCC), where the inherent jurisdiction was exercised to order the vacation of a unilateral notice.

[510] *Heywood v B.D.C. Properties Ltd (No.2)* [1964] 1 W.L.R. 267; *Calgary and Edmonton Land Co Ltd v Dobinson* [1974] Ch. 102.

[511] This applies not just to the Land Register but also to charges in relation to unregistered land in the Land Charges Register: see below, para.8–106.

[512] *Rawlplug Co Ltd v Kamvale Properties Ltd* (1968) 20 P. & CR. 32; *Calgary & Edmonton Land Co Ltd v Discount Bank (Overseas) Ltd* [1971] 1 W.L.R. 81; *Lester v Burgess* (1973) 26 P. & C.R. 536; *Calgary & Edmonton Land Co Ltd v Dobinson* [1974] Ch. 102; *Alpenstow Ltd v Regalian Properties Plc* [1985] 1 W.L.R. 721; *Clowes Developments (UK) Ltd v Mulchinock* [1998] 1 W.L.R. 42.

[513] See *Red River UK Ltd v Sheikh* [2007] EWHC 1038 (Ch) at [9]–[12].

[514] See *Tucker v Hutchinson* (1987) 54 P. & C.R. 106 at 112; *Godfrey v Torpey* [2006] EWHC 1423 (Ch) at [12]–[14].

[515] The point was left open in *Crawford v Clarke* Unreported, July 23, 1999 Court of Appeal, but see the earlier hearing in the same case (1999) 78 P. & C.R. D35 at D36 ("there is plainly an arguable case that the county court had no jurisdiction to grant the relief sought", per Chadwick L.J.).

[516] LRA 2002 s.40(1).

[517] LRA 2002 s 40(2)(a)

[518] LRA 2002 s.40(2)(b).

disposition without notice having first been given to, or the consent obtained of a named individual.[519]

Where a restriction is entered in the register, no entry in respect of a disposition to which the restriction applies may be made in the register except in accordance with the terms of the restriction.[520] However, the registrar, on the application of a person who appears to him to have a sufficient interest in the restriction,[521] may by order disapply the restriction in relation to a specified disposition or to dispositions of a specified kind, or he may provide that a restriction has effect in relation to a particular disposition or kinds of disposition with specified modifications.[522] If, for example, a disposition could only be made with the consent of a person who could not be found, the registrar might dispense with the requirement, if satisfied that the disposition should be made.

7–078　　*(b) Where the registrar may enter a restriction.* The registrar may enter a restriction in the register if it appears to him necessary or desirable to do so for any of the following three purposes.[523]

The first is to prevent invalidity or unlawfulness in relation to dispositions of a registered estate or charge. For example, if a public body or a corporation has limited powers, the registrar may enter a restriction to reflect those limitations. This is important because a registered proprietor is presumed to have owner's powers in the absence of any entry to the contrary in the register.[524] Another example would be where trustees of land are required to obtain the consent of a beneficiary before making a disposition of the land. If consent were not obtained, the disposition would be a breach of trust and so unlawful.

The second purpose is to secure that interests, which are capable of being overreached on a disposition of a registered estate or charge, are overreached. The nature of overreaching has been explained.[525] Where there is a trust of land, a disposition of that land will not overreach the trust unless the proceeds are paid to or by the direction of at least two trustees except where the trustee is a trust corporation.[526] There is a standard form of restriction to ensure that there can be no disposition by a sole registered proprietor unless authorised by the court.[527]

---

[519] LRA 2002 s.40(3).

[520] LRA 2002 s.41(1).

[521] LRA 2002 s.41(3). Application is on Form RX2. For the requirements, see LRR 2003 r.96; Ruoff & Roper, 44.019.

[522] LRA 2002 s.41(2).

[523] LRA 2002 s.42(1). In other words, there are two requirements, namely, that one of the three purposes must exist and it must be necessary or desirable to enter the restriction in those circumstances: see *Jayasinghe v Liyange* [2010] EWHC 265 (Ch) at [16]; [2010] 1 W.L.R. 2106 at 2111.

[524] See LRA 2002 s.23; above, para.7–050.

[525] Above, paras 6–052 et seq.

[526] LPA 1925 s.27(2); below, para.12–037.

[527] See LRR 2003 Sch.4 Form A. The entry of such a restriction is in fact mandatory in certain cases: see below, para.7–081.

The third purpose is to protect a right or claim in relation to a registered estate or charge.[528] An example might be where A has contributed funds towards the cost of purchasing a property and claims an interest in the property under a resulting or constructive trust.[529] Specific provision is made to enable a person, who is entitled to the benefit of a charging order relating to an interest under a trust, to enter a restriction to protect that charging order.[530] Because the charge applies only to a beneficial interest, any disposition of the land is likely to overreach that interest, so that the chargee's claim will lie against the proceeds of sale. It is therefore necessary to have a mechanism for notifying the chargee of any pending disposition. Unfortunately the prescribed form of restriction is useless, because it merely requires that no disposition of the registered estate or charge is to be registered unless the disponee (or his conveyancer) certifies that written notice was given to the person with the benefit of the charging order.[531] As this can be done after the disposition, this effectively deprives the chargee of any effective means of securing payment from the proceeds.[532]

As regards the protection of rights and claims, it is provided that a restriction cannot be entered for the purpose of protecting the priority of an interest which is, or could be, protected by the entry of a notice.[533] However, there may be cases where it may be appropriate to enter either or both a restriction and a notice. For example, a right of pre-emption may be protected by a notice, to ensure that it binds any purchaser of the land affected,[534] but it might also be the subject of a restriction, by which no disposition could be registered without the written consent of the grantee of the right.[535]

A restriction may be entered on application to the registrar[536] or by the **7–079** registrar on his own initiative, though in the latter case, he must notify the registered proprietor of the entry in the register.[537] A person may apply to the registrar for the entry of a restriction if he either is, or has the consent of, the registered proprietor of the estate or charge in question or is entitled to be registered as proprietor,[538] or if he otherwise has (or is to be regarded as

---

[528] It is clear from *Jayasinghe v Liyange* [2010] EWHC 265 (Ch); [2010] 1 W.L.R. 2106

[529] For such trusts, see below, paras 11–009 et seq.

[530] LRA 2002 s.42(3).

[531] See LRR 2003 r.93(k); Sch.4 Form K.

[532] Given the widespread criticism, the failure to amend Form K is incomprehensible. It is common for a chargee to apply for a non-standard restriction when obtaining a charging order.

[533] LRA 2002 s.42(2).

[534] For the status of rights of pre-emption in registered land under LRA 2002, see above, para.7–067. A right of pre-emption granted over registered land after LRA 2002 came into force has effect as an interest in land (see LRA 2002 s.115) and can be protected by a notice: see LRA 2002 s.32(1); above, para.7–060.

[535] See LRR 2003 Sch.4 Form N.

[536] The form of application is prescribed by rules: see LRR 2003 r.92, and is usually made on Form RX1. However, in relation to prescribed clauses leases granted on or after June 19, 2006, an application for a standard form of restriction (see below) can be made by completing Clause LR13 of the required wording (see LRR 2003 Sch.1A): see Ruoff & Roper, 44.008.03.

[537] LRA 2002 s.42(3). The registrar's decision can only be challenged by way of judicial review.

[538] LRA 2002 s.43(1)(a), (b).

having) a sufficient interest in the making of the entry.[539] A person may have a sufficient interest for these purposes without having or claiming a proprietary interest in the registered estate.[540] As regards the form of restriction, many have been prescribed by rule, and these are known as standard form restrictions.[541] If a person applies for a restriction that is not in a standard form, the registrar may only approve the application if it appears to him that the terms of the proposed restriction are reasonable and that its application would be straightforward and not an unreasonable burden on him.[542]

Where there is an application to enter a restriction, the registrar must give notice both of the application and of the right to object to it to the registered proprietor of the relevant estate or charge,[543] except where the application is made by or with the consent of the registered proprietor or of a person entitled to be registered as proprietor,[544] or the restriction is one that is required to be entered.[545] There are circumstances in which a person must apply for the entry of a restriction.[546] Furthermore, the court or registrar may make an order that requires the entry of a restriction.

Where notice has been given, the registrar cannot determine the application until the time for making an objection[547] has expired, unless before that time, the person notified has either exercised his right to object or given the registrar notice that he does not intend to do so.[548] If there is an objection, it will be dealt with in accordance with the usual procedure.[549]

7–080   *(c) Where a restriction must be entered.* In certain circumstances a restriction must be entered.

7–081   First, the registrar is required to enter a restriction in two circumstances:

(i) Where he enters two or more persons in the register as the proprietor of a registered estate, he must enter such restrictions as are prescribed by rules for the purpose of securing the overreaching of any overreachable interests on any disposition.[550] There is one prescribed form of restriction,[551] which has already been explained.[552]

---

[539] LRA 2002 ss.43(1)(c), (2)(c). Pursuant to LRA 2002 s.43(2)(c), rules have prescribed what are presently 23 classes of persons who are to be regarded as having a sufficient interest for these purposes: see LRR 2003 r.93. This does not preclude persons not within that list from satisfying the registrar that they have in fact a sufficient interest.

[540] *Republic of Croatia v Republic of Serbia* [2009] EWHC 1559 (Ch) at [46] and following; [2010] Ch. 200 at 214 and following.

[541] LRA 2002 s.42(2)(d); LRR 2003 rr.91, 91A and Sch.4 (there are presently 41 such forms). See Ruoff & Roper, 44.009.

[542] LRA 2002 s.43(3).

[543] LRA 2002 s.45(1) ("notifiable applications").

[544] LRA 2002 s.45(3)(a).

[545] LRA 2002 s.45(3)(b), (c).

[546] See below, paras 7–080 et seq.

[547] 15 business days: LRR 2003 r.197(2).

[548] LRA 2002 s.45(2).

[549] LRA 2002 s.73; below, para.7–129.

[550] LRA 2002 s.44(1).

[551] LRR 2003 r.95(2); Sch.4 Form A.

[552] See above, para.7–078.

(ii) Under certain statutes (including the Land Registration Act 2002) the registrar is required to enter a restriction and these must be in the form prescribed by rules.[553]

Second, there is a power under the Act to make rules requiring that an **7–082** application for a restriction should be made. Under the rules, there is a duty to apply for a restriction in certain cases where land is held upon a trust of land, and the restriction is necessary either to ensure that on any disposition of the land the trusts are overreached, or because the trustees have limited dispositive powers.[554] In certain circumstances, a charity or the official custodian for charities is required to apply for a restriction.[555]

(d) Where the court may order the entry of a restriction. The court has **7–083** power to make an order requiring the registrar to enter a restriction in the register where it appears to the court to be necessary or desirable to do so for the purpose of protecting a right or claim in relation to a registered estate or charge.[556] As with the registrar,[557] the court cannot order the entry of a restriction for the purpose of protecting an interest which is, or could be, the subject of a notice.[558] However, as has been explained, there may be cases where the entry of both a notice and a restriction in relation to a particular interest may be appropriate.[559] The court has power to direct that the restriction has overriding priority.[560] As explained below, where an intending purchaser has made a priority search of the register, no entry can be made during the priority period, and this way the purchaser can register the purchase with priority over any application for registration made during that period.[561] If an application for a restriction is made to the court during the currency of a period of priority protection, the purchaser will have priority over that restriction[562] unless the court orders that it is to have overriding priority.[563] Given the potentially serious consequences of making such an order, the court may make it subject to such terms and conditions as it thinks fit.[564] It is likely to require the applicant to undertake to indemnify any person, who acts in good

---

[553] LRA 2002 s.44(2). An example under LRA 2002, is the entry of a bankruptcy restriction: see LRA 2002 s.86(2); LRR 2003 r.166. As regards other statutes, see LRR 2003 r.95(2).

[554] See LRR 2003 rr.94(1)–(5), (7).

[555] LRR 2003 rr.94(8), 176(2), (3), 178(2).

[556] LRA 2002 s.46(1). The standard forms of restriction that a court is likely to order are LRR 2003 Sch.4, Forms AA—HH (freezing orders, restraint orders and interim receiving orders). A standard form restriction in respect of a freezing order may, by preventing any disposition, restrict a registered proprietor more than is justified by the terms of the freezing order: see *Perry v Princess International Sales & Services Ltd* [2005] EWHC 2042 (Comm) at [32]–[35].

[557] Above, para.7–078.

[558] LRA 2002 s.46(2).

[559] Above, para.7–078.

[560] LRA 2002 s.46(3). Where it makes such an order, the applicant should apply to the registrar for the entry of the restriction, using Form AP1 rather than RX1: see LRR 2003 rr.13, 92(8); Ruoff & Roper, 44.020.

[561] LRA 2002 s.72; below, para.7–125.

[562] LRA 2002 s.72(2).

[563] LRA 2002 ss.46(3), 72(4).

[564] LRA 2002 s.46(5).

faith, and who suffers loss in consequence of the court's order. Where a restriction with overriding priority is made, the entry in the register must make this fact clear.[565] Where the official search with priority preceded the application for a restriction and that restriction was ordered during the priority period, the registrar must give notice of the entry to the person who applied for it (or his conveyancer or agent), unless he is satisfied that such notice is unnecessary.[566]

7–084   *(e) Withdrawal and cancellation of restrictions.* A person may apply to the registrar for the withdrawal of a restriction as provided by rules.[567] Where the restriction was mandatory, e.g. to give effect to an order of the court or because it was required by statute to be entered, no application can be made to withdraw it.[568] In any other case, it can only be withdrawn with the consent of:

> (i) all persons who appear to the registrar to have an interest in the restriction;
>
> (ii) any person whose consent is required under the terms of the restriction;
>
> (iii) any person to whom notice must be given under the terms of the restriction; and
>
> (iv) any specified person whose certificate is required to be given under the terms of the restriction.[569]

A person may apply to the registrar to cancel a restriction. The application must be accompanied by evidence to satisfy the registrar that the restriction is no longer required. The registrar must cancel the restriction if he is so satisfied.[570]

The registrar may cancel a restriction. He is specifically empowered to do so when registering a disposition in relation to a restriction that was entered to protect an interest, right or claim arising under a trust of land if the registered estate is no longer subject to such a trust.[571] However, he may cancel a restriction in exercise of his general powers to bring the register up to date and remove superfluous entries,[572] if he is satisfied that the entry no longer applies.[573]

7–085   **4. Pending land actions, writs, orders and deeds of arrangement.** Where title to land is unregistered, specific provision is made in the Land Charges

---

[565] LRR 2003 r.100(1).
[566] LRR 2003 r.100(2).
[567] LRA 2002 s.47. Application is on Form RX4: see LRR 2003 r.98(1).
[568] LRR 2003 r.98(3).
[569] LRR 2003 r.98(2).
[570] LRR 2003 r.97. Application is on Form RX3.
[571] LRR 2003 r.99.
[572] See LRA 2002 Sch.4 paras 5(b), (c).
[573] See Ruoff & Roper, 44.017.

Act 1972[574] for the registration as land charges of pending land actions, writs, orders and deeds of arrangement.[575] Under the Land Registration Act 1925, these matters could only be protected by the entry of a caution against dealings, namely pending land actions, writs, orders and deeds of arrangement.[576] As the Land Registration Act 2002 abolished cautions against dealings, it was necessary to make specific provision for the protection of such interests.

The four matters are as follows:

(i) a pending land action, which is any action or proceeding pending in court relating to land or any interest in or charge on land[577];

(ii) a writ or order affecting land issued or made by any court for the purpose of enforcing a judgment or recognisance[578];

(iii) an order appointing a receiver or sequestrator[579]; and

(iv) a deed of arrangement.[580]

All four are treated as interests affecting an estate or charge for the purposes of the Act,[581] though none can be overriding interests.[582] Although the fact that they are regarded as interests would suggest that each of the four matters could be protected by the entry of a notice,[583] it is expressly provided that neither an order appointing a receiver or sequestrator nor a deed of arrangement can be.[584] Accordingly, they can only be protected by means of a restriction. As regards a pending land action and a writ or order affecting land, the appropriate entry will normally be a notice, to ensure that any purchaser of the land should be bound by the action or order. However, it is possible that there may be occasions where this is not appropriate.[585] Thus, for example, if a person claimed that the registered proprietor of land held it on a bare trust for him, those proceedings would be an action relating to land, and so a pending land action.[586] It would not be possible to protect those proceedings

---

[574] Which replaced LCA 1925.
[575] See LCA 1972 ss.5–7; below, paras 8–064—8–067.
[576] See LRA 1925 s.59.
[577] LRA 2002 s.87(1)(a), referring to the definition of pending land action in LCA 1972 s.17(1). For pending land actions, see below, para.8–064. See, e.g., *Donnelly v Weighbridge Construction Ltd* [2006] EWHC 348 (TCC) (claim to a lien was a pending land action).
[578] LRA 2002 s.87(1)(b), referring to LCA 1972 s.6(1)(a).
[579] LRA 2002 s.87(1)(c).
[580] LRA 2002 s.87(1)(d). For deeds of arrangement, see below, para.8–067.
[581] See LRA 2002 s.87(1).
[582] LRA 2002 s.87(3).
[583] See LRA 2002 s.32(1); above, para.7–070.
[584] LRA 2002 s.87(2). The reasons are as follows. An order appointing a receiver or sequestrator of land may create an interest in land, but it will not always do so. A deed of arrangement is analogous to a bankruptcy order. As a bankruptcy order is protected by a restriction (LRA 2002 s.86(4); below, para.7–110), the same should protect a deed of arrangement.
[585] Proceedings brought to claim a beneficial interest *as a tenant in common* under a trust of land are not a pending land action: see below, para.8–064.
[586] For bare trusts, see above, para.6–050.

by the entry of a notice, because no notice may be entered in respect of an interest under a trust of land.[587] Accordingly, a restriction would have to be entered to ensure that any interest that might be established was overreached.[588]

Section 5. Unregistered Interests which override Registered Dispositions

7–086   **1. Introduction.** The unregistered interests which override first registration and the reasons for them have already been explained.[589] It has also been explained that a registrable disposition for valuable consideration takes effect subject to those unregistered interests that override a registered disposition which are listed in Sch.3 to the Land Registration Act 2002.[590]

7–087   The unregistered interests that override a registered disposition are not identical to those which override first registration.[591] The following categories are, however, the same, and no further comment is needed upon them:

    (i) a customary right[592];

    (ii) a public right[593];

    (iii) a local land charge[594];

    (iv) certain mineral rights[595];

    (v) a franchise[596];

    (vi) a manorial right[597];

    (vii) a right to rent which was reserved to the Crown on the granting of any freehold estate (whether or not the right is still vested in the Crown)[598];

    (viii) a non-statutory right in respect of an embankment or sea or river wall[599];

    (ix) a right to payment in lieu of tithe[600]; and

---

[587] LRA 2002 s.33(a)(i); above, para.7–070.
[588] cf. above, para.7–078.
[589] Above, paras 7–028 et seq.
[590] Above, para.7–062.
[591] For the unregistered interests which override first registration, see above, para.7–030.
[592] LRA 2002 Sch.3 para.4.
[593] LRA 2002 Sch.3 para.5.
[594] LRA 2002 Sch.3 para.6.
[595] LRA 2002 Sch.3 paras 7–9.
[596] LRA 2002 Sch.3 para.10.
[597] LRA 2002 Sch.3 para.11.
[598] LRA 2002 Sch.3 para.12.
[599] LRA 2002 Sch.3 para.13.
[600] LRA 2002 Sch.3 para.14.

(x) a right in respect of a church chancel.[601]

The unregistered leases that override a registered disposition are virtually the same as those which override first registration,[602] though the wording is not identical. A lease granted for a term not exceeding seven years will override a registered disposition unless it was required to be registered at the time when it was granted.[603]

Of these interests, those numbered (v)–(x) will cease to have overriding **7–088** status as of October 13, 2013,[604] as with the same classes of unregistered interest that override first registration.[605] Those who have the benefit of such rights should therefore protect them by the entry of a notice by that date. No fee is payable for such registration.[606] It is an important part of the policy of the Land Registration Act 2002 to reduce the scope and impact of overriding interests.[607]

2. Interests of persons in actual occupation

(a) The principle. The rights of persons in actual occupation constituted **7–089** both the most sweeping and the most often litigated category of overriding interests under the Land Registration Act 1925.[608] The purpose of this category of overriding interests was unclear under the 1925 Act and difficult cases arose where actual occupation was not readily discoverable.[609] There was tension between the view that actual occupation should protect a right whether or not it was discoverable,[610] and the fact that the physical presence of a person in actual occupation should be such as to put any purchaser upon inquiry.[611] The Land Registration Act 2002 significantly limits the circumstances in which the unregistered rights of persons in actual occupation can override a registered disposition.[612] It also clarifies the reasons of this class of interests.

The fundamental principle under the 2002 Act remains the same as it did under the Land Registration Act 1925 (as that Act had been interpreted). An

---

[601] LRA 2002 Sch.3 para.16.

[602] See above, para.7–030.

[603] LRA 2002 Sch.2 para.1.

[604] LRA 2002 s.117.

[605] Above, para.7–031.

[606] LRA 2002 s.117(2).

[607] See Law Com. No.271, paras 2.24–2.25, 8.1.

[608] See LRA 1925 s.70(1)(g); and see the sixth edition of this work at paras 6–047 et seq.

[609] See, e.g., *Lloyds Bank Plc v Rosset* [1989] Ch. 350 (which was decided on appeal on another ground: see [1991] 1 A.C. 107).

[610] Which appears to have been the original justification for this class of overriding interests: see (1998) Law Com. 154, para.5.57.

[611] See *Malory Enterprises Ltd v Cheshire Homes Ltd* [2002] EWCA Civ 151 at [81]; [2002] Ch. 216 at 236. LRA 1925 s.70(1)(g) provided by way of an exception to the protection of the rights of a person in actual occupation, that such rights were not overriding if inquiry was made of the person and his rights were not revealed. As Mustill L.J. explained in *Lloyds Bank Plc v Rosset* [1989] Ch. 350 at 397, the reference to inquiry "would be meaningless if actual occupier embraced those whose existence it would be impractical to detect".

[612] See Law Com. No.271, paras 8.53–8.64.

unregistered interest belonging at the time of the disposition to a person in actual occupation overrides a registered disposition.[613] However, this is subject to a number of important qualifications, which are set out below.

7–090 *(b) Only applicable to land in actual occupation.* The occupant's interest is protected "so far as relating to land of which he is in actual occupation".[614] Prior to the 2002 Act it had been held that a person who was in actual occupation of part of a parcel of land might thereby protect an unregistered interest which he had in the whole.[615] This placed an unreasonable burden of inquiry on a purchaser and one that was more extensive than would have been the case had the title been unregistered.[616] The Act reversed that decision and a person can only protect his unregistered interest in relation to land of which he is in actual occupation.

7–091 *(c) No protection for an interest under a settlement.* The Land Registration Act 2002 retains the principle of its predecessor[617] that an interest under a settlement under the Settled Land Act 1925 cannot be protected by the actual occupation of the beneficiary.[618] After 1996, such settlements could no longer be created,[619] and any interests under such settlements should have been protected by an appropriate restriction.[620]

7–092 *(d) Interest not disclosed on inquiry.* An unregistered interest of a person of whom inquiry was made before the disposition and who failed to disclose the right when he could reasonably have been expected to do so will not override a registered disposition.[621] The effect of this provision is to create an estoppel against the person with the interest. The same principle applied under the Land Registration Act 1925.[622]

Any inquiry must be directed to the occupier, for "reliance upon the untrue *ipse dixit* of the vendor will not suffice".[623] It was held in relation to the Land Registration Act 1925, that no inquiry could be made of children, who were not regarded as being in actual occupation in any event.[624] However, it is

---

[613] LRA 2002 Sch.3 para.2. It will be noted that it is the date of *disposition* that is relevant, not the date of the registration of that disposition. This is because of the so-called "registration gap": see below, para.7–150. Cf. LRA 2002 ss.29(1), 30(1); above, para.7–061. Although it has been suggested, obiter, by Lewison J. that, from the wording of para.2, actual occupation may also be required at the date of registration of the relevant disposition (see *Thompson v Foy* [2009] EWHC 1076 (Ch) at [122]–[126]; [2010] 1 P. & C.R. 308 at 349), it is clear that this was not Parliament's intention: see (1998) Law Com. No.254, para.5.113; and (2001) Law Com. No.271, para.8.54. See too *In the matter of the North East Property Buyers Litigation* [2010] EWHC 2991 (Ch) at [46]; and see below, para.7–150.

[614] LRA 2002 Sch.3 para.2.

[615] *Ferrishurst Ltd v Wallcite Ltd* [1999] Ch. 355.

[616] See (2001) Law Com. No.271, para.8.57.

[617] See LRA 1925 s.86(2).

[618] LRA 2002 Sch.3 para.2(a).

[619] See TLATA 1996 s.2(1) (subject to minor exceptions: see s.2(2)).

[620] See LRR 2003 Sch.7 para.7.

[621] LRR 2002 Sch.3 para.2(b).

[622] LRA 1925 s.70(1)(g): see above, para.7–089.

[623] *Hodgson v Marks* [1971] Ch. 892 at 932, per Russell L.J.

[624] *Hypo-Mortgage Services Ltd v Robinson* [1997] 2 F.C.R. 422; below, para.7–096.

unclear what a purchaser should do in the case of an occupier who is unable to understand any inquiry by reason of his mental incapacity.[625]

(e) Occupation not apparent. The 2002 Act created a new limitation on the **7–093** unregistered interests which could override a registered disposition. To fall within this limitation, two conditions must be met.[626]

The first is that the interest belongs to a person whose *occupation* would not have been obvious on a reasonably careful inspection of the land at the time of the disposition. The condition is concerned with whether the *occupation* and not the interest is obvious. It is not enough that the occupation could have been discovered on reasonable inquiry. It must be obvious.[627]

The second condition is that the *interest* is one of which the disponee does not have actual knowledge at the time of the disposition. Thus, even if a person's occupation is not obvious, his unregistered interest will still override a registered disposition if the disponee had actual knowledge of the interest. It is not enough that the disponee could have discovered the interest on reasonable inquiry. He must actually know of it at the time of the disposition. Although it has been held that the disponee has actual knowledge of an interest if he has "actual knowledge of the facts which give rise to the alleged interest"[628] that is neither what the 2002 Act says, nor what Parliament intended.[629] What is required is "real knowledge" of the existence of the interest.[630]

In practice, once an intending disponee knows that a person is in actual occupation of the relevant land, he will normally make inquiry of such person as to his interest (if any) in the land, unless the disponee is to be given vacant possession on completion of the disposition (when he has remedies against the seller if it is not[631]). The rights of persons in actual occupation are normally an issue, therefore, in cases where a registered estate is charged rather than sold.

(f) Reversionary leases. It is not possible to protect by occupation a **7–094** reversionary lease of land that has not yet taken effect. It has been explained

---

[625] The point would have arisen in *Link Lending Ltd v Bustard* [2010] EWCA Civ 424; [2010] 2 E.G.L.R. 55 had inquiries been made.

[626] LRA 2002 Sch.2 para.2(c).

[627] "It is the visible signs of occupation which have to be obvious on inspection": *Thomas v Clydesdale Bank Plc* [2010] EWHC 2755 (QB) at [40], per Ramsey J., though on the facts of that case that conclusion was highly questionable (intermittent presence of builders, interior designer and project manager). There is a parallel with the duty of a seller of land to disclose to the intending purchaser defects in title that are latent, that is, which are not obvious on a reasonable inspection of the land: see below, para.15–070.

[628] *Thomas v Clydesdale Bank Plc* [2010] EWHC 2755 (QB) at [49], per Ramsey J. The case arose on an application to set aside a judgment under CPR r.39.3(3), where the test is only whether the applicant has a reasonable prospect of success at trial. Ramsey J. may therefore have preferred to leave the matter for resolution at trial.

[629] Once again, the principle in the 2002 Act was drawn by analogy from a rule of conveyancing law, namely that a seller does not have to disclose a defect in title of which the purchaser actually knows: see below, para.15–070; and see (2001) Law Com. No.271 at para.8.62.

[630] See *Mehra v Mehra* [2008] 3 E.G.L.R. 153 at 162, [122], per Judge Marshall.

[631] See below, paras 15–089 et seq.

that a lease granted for *any* duration out of registered land, which is to take effect in possession more than three months after the date of the grant, is a registrable disposition.[632] A situation could arise where:

(a) a registered proprietor grants a reversionary lease to take effect more than three months after the making of the grant;

(b) that reversionary lease is not registered;

(c) the person having the benefit of that reversionary lease enters into possession before the date on which the lease is to take effect; and

(d) the registered proprietor makes a disposition of his registered estate before the reversionary lease takes effect.

In those circumstances, the interest of the person who is to be the lessee will not override the registered disposition.[633] Such cases will be rare.

7–095　　　*(g) Actual occupation not receipt of rents and profits.* It has already been explained in relation to first registration that a person who is not in actual occupation but merely in receipt of the rents and profits from the land can no longer protect his unregistered interest by that receipt.[634] The same is true in relation to registered dispositions. There are transitional provisions, which preserve the overriding status of a person whose unregistered interest was protected by reason of the receipt of rents and profits immediately before the 2002 Act came into force.[635] That protection ends if the holder of the interest ceases to receive rents and profits.[636]

7–096　　　*(h) The meaning of "actual occupation".* The meaning of "actual occupation" under the Land Registration Act 1925 was considered many times. Those authorities must now be read subject to the provisions of the 2002 Act. Whether or not a person is in actual occupation of land is a question of fact[637] that depends upon the nature and state of the property in question,[638] and the courts have been unwilling to "lay down a code or catalogue of situations" in which such occupation will be established.[639] "'Occupation' is a concept

---

[632] LRA 2002 s.27(2)(b)(ii); above, para.7–054.

[633] LRA 2002 Sch.2 para.2(d).

[634] See above, para.7–030.

[635] See LRA 2002 Sch.12 para.8.

[636] LRA 2002 Sch.12 para.8. If, e.g. X, the holder of the residue of an unregistered lease, had granted a sublease before the 2002 Act came into force, his interest would be protected as an overriding interest unless and until the sublease was terminated.

[637] *Williams & Glyn's Bank Ltd v Boland* [1981] A.C. at 504, 506, 511.

[638] *Malory Enterprises Ltd v Cheshire Homes Ltd* [2002] EWCA Civ 151 at [80]; [2002] Ch. 216 at 236.

[639] *Hodgson v Marks* [1971] Ch. 892 at 932, per Russell L.J.

which may have different connotations according to the nature and purpose of the property which is claimed to be occupied."[640] Although the matter is ultimately one of fact, the cases provide some guidance.[641]

First, there has to be some physical presence (and not merely some legal entitlement to occupy),[642] but this does not mean that the person claiming the overriding interest must reside or work on the premises.[643] It was held that it was possible to be in actual occupation of a garage by parking a car in it regularly,[644] though depositing garden debris and maintaining a compost heap on land did not amount to actual occupation.[645] In some cases, the distinction between possession and occupation has not always been clearly drawn.[646] Where a person is not physically present on the land, it will usually be necessary to show that his occupation was "manifested and accompanied by a continuing intention to occupy".[647] In such a case:

"the degree of permanence and continuity of presence of the person concerned, the intentions and wishes of that person, the length of absence from the property and the reason for it and the nature of the property and personal circumstances of the person are among the relevant factors".[648]

Second, occupation does not necessarily require the personal presence of the person claiming the right.[649] An employee, agent or a contractor (such as a caretaker or a builder) who is specifically employed for a purpose that

[640] *Abbey National BS v Cann* [1991] 1 A.C. 56 at 93, per Lord Oliver. See too *Lloyds Bank Plc v Rosset* [1989] Ch. 350 at 377, 394 (on appeal [1991] 1 A.C. 107, where no question on LRA 1925 s.70(1)(g) arose).

[641] See the summary in *Thompson v Foy* [2009] EWHC 1076 (Ch) at [127]; [2010] 1 P. & C.R. 308 at 350; approved in *Link Lending Ltd v Bustard* [2010] EWCA Civ 424 at [31]; [2010] 2 E.G.L.R. 55 at 58.

[642] *Williams & Glyn's Bank Ltd v Boland*, above, at 505. It is thought that the suggestion that a lodger is not a person in actual occupation (*Hodgson v Marks*, above, at 932) would not be followed.

[643] *Lloyds Bank Plc v Rosset* [1989] Ch. 350 at 377.

[644] *Kling v Keston Properties Ltd* (1983) 49 P. & C.R. 212 at 219 (where the car was trapped in the garage due to the defendant's conduct, but where the result would probably have been the same if the garage had been used for its ordinary purpose). See too *Re Boyle's Claim* [1961] 1 W.L.R. 339 at 345 (person in actual occupation of a garage but not of a hedge). cf. *Epps v Esso Petroleum Co Ltd* [1973] 1 W.L.R. 1071 at 1079, 1080 (no actual occupation where a car was parked on an open strip of land).

[645] *Bhullar v McArdle* [2001] EWCA Civ 510 at [35]; (2001) 82 P. & C.R. 481 at 488.

[646] cf. *Malory Enterprises Ltd v Cheshire Homes Ltd* [2002] EWCA Civ 151 at [82]; [2002] Ch. 216 at 236, 237 (steps to secure derelict land treated as acts of actual occupation, *sed quaere*).

[647] *Thompson v Foy* [2009] EWHC 1076 (Ch) at [127]; [2010] 1 P. & C.R. 308 at 350, per Lewison J. See *Link Lending Ltd v Bustard* [2010] EWCA Civ 424; [2010] 2 E.G.L.R. 55 (person with severe medical condition in a care home was still in actual occupation of her house).

[648] *Link Lending Ltd v Bustard* [2010] EWCA Civ 424 at [27]; [2010] 2 E.G.L.R. 55 at 57, per Mummery L.J. cf. *Mehra v Mehra* [2008] 3 E.G.L.R. 153 at 163, [116].

[649] *Abbey National BS v Cann* [1991] 1 A.C. 56 at 93; *Thompson v Foy* [2009] EWHC 1076 (Ch) at [127]; [2010] 1 P. & C.R. 308 at 350.

entails his being in occupation, can occupy on behalf of his employer.[650] However, occupation by a licensee for his own purposes (rather than for the person claiming the right) will not suffice.[651] Difficult questions are less likely to arise now that actual occupation must be obvious on a reasonably careful inspection of the land.[652]

Third, actual occupation involves some degree of permanence and continuity.[653] Mere fleeting presence, as where a prospective purchaser or tenant is allowed on to the premises to plan decorations, measure for furnishings, or undertake acts preparatory to moving in, will not suffice.[654] If a person normally resides or works in a property, he will not cease to be in actual occupation merely because he is temporarily absent (as where he spends a period in hospital[655] or goes abroad for some time), even if he is away on a regular and repeated basis,[656] at least if there is some evidence of his presence on the land, such as his furniture or belongings.[657] That evidence must now be such that the person's actual occupation is obvious, as explained above. There are practical difficulties for an intending disponee in relation to possible occupants who are absent, because he cannot make inquiry of them, and may be unable to ascertain their status or rights.[658]

Fourth, a person can be in actual occupation of land simultaneously with another,[659] including the seller or mortgagor whose disposition of the land has put the occupier's rights in issue.[660] In those cases where occupation is shared

---

[650] *Strand Securities Ltd v Caswell* [1965] Ch. 958 at 981, 984; *Lloyds Bank Plc v Rosset*, above, at 377, 397; *Abbey National BS v Cann*, above, at 93. It is controversial whether a person can be in actual occupation when he is not himself present on the premises but is employing builders to carry out work on them. In *Lloyds Bank Plc v Rosset*, above, Nicholls and Purchas L.JJ. held that he could, but cf. Mustill L.J. at 397 et seq. But see now *Thomas v Clydesdale Bank Plc* [2010] EWHC 2755 (QB).

[651] *Strand Securities Ltd v Caswell*, above, at 984; *Lloyds Bank Plc v Rosset*, above, at 405.

[652] See above, para.7–093.

[653] *Abbey National BS v Cann*, above, at 93.

[654] *Abbey National BS v Cann*, above, at 93, 94. Similarly, a builder who comes on to the premises to carry out renovation work is not himself thereby in actual occupation: *Canadian Imperial Bank of Commerce v Bell* (1991) 64 P. & C.R. 48 at 51. cf. *Malory Enterprises Ltd v Cheshire Homes Ltd* [2002] EWCA Civ 151 at [82]; [2002] Ch. 216 at 236, 237, where, in relation to derelict land, acts such as boarding up windows and fencing the site to keep trespassers out, and using the land for storage, sufficed to show actual occupation.

[655] In *Link Lending Ltd v Bustard* [2010] EWCA Civ 424; [2010] 2 E.G.L.R. 55, the defendant was held to be in actual occupation even though she had been in a residential home for over a year, was incapable of safely living in her house, and had visited it only briefly on supervised visits.

[656] *Kingsnorth Finance Ltd v Tizard* [1986] 1 W.L.R. 783 at 788 (wife separated from husband, but visited the house every day to look after the children).

[657] *Chhokar v Chhokar* [1984] F.L.R. 313 at 317. See too in the analogous context of what is now F.L.A. 1996 s.30, *Hoggett v Hoggett* (1979) 39 P. & C.R. 121 at 127, 128; below, para.34–024. Actual occupation will not be established merely because a person keeps some of his furniture on the property: *Strand Securities Ltd v Caswell*, above, at 985; *Thompson v Foy* [2009] EWHC 1076 (Ch) at [127]; [2010] 1 P. & C.R. 308 at 350.

[658] See above, para.7–092.

[659] Although possession is single and exclusive, occupation can be shared: see *Lloyd v Dugdale* [2001] EWCA Civ 1754 at [43]; [2002] 2 P. & C.R. 167 at 180.

[660] *Williams & Glyn's Bank Ltd v Boland* [1981] A.C. 487 at 505; *Lloyds Bank Plc v Rosset*, above, at 394.

with the seller or mortgagor, the occupier's presence need not be inconsistent with or adverse to his.[661] Inquiry must therefore be directed to any adult members of his family (and indeed to anyone else) who happens to be in occupation with him.[662] The view once current, that a wife's occupation could be attributed to her husband,[663] has long been discredited.[664] However, notwithstanding this rejection, it has been held that children are not in actual occupation in their own right, but merely "as shadows of occupation of their parents".[665]

Finally, a right to use is not a right to occupy. Accordingly, a right that is, or is akin to, an easement, such as a right to use a staircase to gain access to a property, is not a right of a person in actual occupation.[665a]

(h) Protects only proprietary rights. A person can only protect a proprietary **7–097** interest by his actual occupation,[666] though whether or not a person has a proprietary right can sometimes give rise to difficult questions.[667] An interest is an adverse right affecting the title to any estate or charge.[668] It does not, therefore, include a personal right such as a contractual licence[669] or a positive covenant.[670] As has been explained, it will, however, include a right of pre-emption, an equity arising by estoppel and a mere equity.[671]

Both under the 2002 Act, and under other statutes, there are certain rights and interests which cannot be protected as overriding interests by reason of a person's actual occupation. Examples under the 2002 Act include pending land actions, writs, orders and deeds of arrangement,[672] and former overriding interests which were the subject of a notice in the register, but where, for some reason (such as a mistake) that notice has been deleted from the register.[673] As regards other statutes, examples include[674] a spouse or civil partner's home rights under the Family Law Act 1996,[675] the rights of a leaseholder who has

---

[661] *Williams & Glyn's Bank Ltd v Boland*, above, at 505, 506, 511.

[662] *Williams & Glyn's Bank Ltd v Boland*, at 508.

[663] See *Caunce v Caunce* [1969] 1 W.L.R. 440; *Bird v Syme-Thomson* [1979] 1 W.L.R. 440.

[664] *Williams & Glyn's Bank Ltd Boland*, above, at 505, 506, 511. At 505, Lord Wilberforce described such a view as "heavily obsolete".

[665] *Hypo-Mortgage Services Ltd v Robinson* [1997] 2 F.C.R. 422 at 426, per Nourse L.J. (applying *Bird v Syme-Thomson*, above). cf. [1998] Fam. Law 349 (E. Cooke).

[665a] *Chaudhary v Yavuz* [2011] EWCA Civ 1314 at [27]–[33]. The circumstances in which an easement can be an overriding interest are much more limited under LRA 2002 than was the case under LRA 1925: see below, para.7–098.

[666] LRA 2002 Sch.3 para.2.

[667] See, e.g., *In the matter of the North East Property Buyers Litigation* [2010] EWHC 2991 (Ch), not following *Redstone Mortgages Plc v Welch* [2009] 3 E.G.L.R. 71 (County Court); *Thompson v Foy* [2009] EWHC 1076 (Ch) at [134]–[138]; [2010] 1 P. & C.R. 308 at 351–353.

[668] LRA 2002 s.132(3)(b).

[669] See below, para.34–016.

[670] See below, para.32–017.

[671] See above, para.7–067.

[672] LRA 2002 s.87(3); above, para.7–085.

[673] LRA 2002 ss.29(3), 30(3); above, para.7–062. In other words, once an overriding interest has been noted in the register, it can never be an overriding interest again.

[674] See Ruoff & Roper, 10.023.

[675] FLA 1996. s.31(10)(b); below, para.34–025.

given notice of his intention to acquire the freehold or an extended lease,[676] the rights conferred on a person under an access order made under the Access to Neighbouring Land Act 1992[677] and a right to call for an overriding lease under the Landlord and Tenant (Covenants) Act 1995.[678]

7–098   **3. Easements and profits à prendre.** Under the Land Registration Act 1925,[679] most easements and profits à prendre could exist as overriding interests, even if expressly granted or reserved.[680] However, the 2002 Act has significantly restricted the circumstances in which an unregistered easement or profit can override a registered disposition.[681] There are transitional provisions by which any easements and profits à prendre that were overriding interests when the Act came into force retain that status.[682]

Two main principles underlie the provisions of the Act[683]:

(i) Rights expressly granted or reserved should be registered.

(ii) Purchasers should be protected against rights that are difficult to discover. Easements and profits can create serious conveyancing problems because the person who has the benefit of them does not lose them merely because they have not been used for many years.[684] They may in consequence be undiscoverable.

7–099   *(a) The easement or profit must be legal.* Only an unregistered legal easement or profit à prendre can override a registered disposition.[685] The consequences are as follows:

(i) No easement or profit which is expressly granted or reserved after the 2002 Act came into force, but which has not been registered, can override a registered disposition. This is because such a grant or reservation operates only in equity until it is registered.[686]

(ii) The only easements and profits that can be legal are those that arise by implied grant or reservation[687] or by prescription.[688]

---

[676] LRA 1967 s.5(5); LRHUDA 1993 s.97(1).
[677] Access to Neighbouring Land Act 1992 s.5(5); below, para.30–038.
[678] L & TCA 1995 s.20(6); below, para.20–027.
[679] See LRA 1925 s.70(1)(a).
[680] See *Celsteel Ltd v Alton House Holdings Ltd* [1985] 1 W.L.R. 204; *Thatcher v Douglas* (1996) 146 N.L.J. 204; and the sixth edition of this work at para.6–042.
[681] LRA 2002 Sch.3 para.3.
[682] LRA 2002 Sch.12 para.9.
[683] See (2001) Law Com. No.271, paras 8.68–8.72.
[684] In one case non-user of a right of way for 175 years did not constitute abandonment: see *Benn v Hardinge* (1992) 66 P. & C.R. 246; below, para.29–009.
[685] LRA 2002 Sch.3 para.3(1).
[686] LRA 2002 s.27(1); above, para.7–053.
[687] See below, paras 28–012 et seq.
[688] See below, paras 28–043 et seq.

(b) The classes of legal easement and profits which can override a regis- **7–100**
tered disposition. A legal easement or profit à prendre will only override a
registered disposition if it falls within one of four categories.[689]

The first category is a legal easement or profit which is registered as a right
of common under Pt 1 of the Commons Act 2006.[690] It has been explained that
such rights cannot be protected by a notice.[691] They are protected instead
under the separate system of registration applicable to rights of common in
what is now Pt 1 of the Commons Act 2006.[692]

The second category is a legal easement or profit à prendre which is within
the actual knowledge of the disponee.[693] A seller of land does not have to
disclose to an intending buyer an easement or profit of which the buyer
actually knows.[694] If the disponee knows of an unregistered legal easement or
profit when the disposition is made to him, there is no injustice if it binds
him.

The third category is a legal easement or profit à prendre which would have
been obvious on a reasonably careful inspection of the land over which the
easement or profit is exercisable.[695] A seller of land does not have to disclose
to an intending buyer an easement or profit which is obvious on a reasonable
inspection of the land, because such a right is not a latent defect in title.[696] As
it is for a purchaser to ascertain for himself whether such a right exists, there
is no reason why he should not be bound by such an easement.

The fourth category, which will only be relevant in cases where none of the
other three categories is applicable, is where the person entitled to the
easement or profit proves that it has been exercised in the period of one year
ending with the day of disposition.[697] The purpose of this provision is to
protect easements and profits which are not readily apparent, but which are in
regular usage, such as rights of drainage. A seller of land may not always be
aware that his neighbour has rights of drainage under his land, and will not,
therefore, disclose those rights to an intending purchaser. However, there
would be serious consequences for the neighbour if a purchaser were to take
free of those rights so that he could block off the drains.[698]

The practical effect of these provisions is that purchasers will take free of
dormant easements that are unregistered and not obvious. The onus is therefore on those who have the benefit of such rights to register them.

---

[689] What follows states the effect of LRA 2002 Sch.3 para.3, which is couched negatively in
terms of which unregistered legal easements and profits will *not* override a registered
disposition.
[690] LRA 2002 Sch.3 para.3(1).
[691] LRA 2002 s.33(d); above, para.7
[692] Replacing Commons Registration Act 1965.
[693] LRA 2002 Sch.3 para.3(1)(a).
[694] See below, paras 15–070, 15–083.
[695] LRA 2002 Sch.3 para.3(1)(b).
[696] See below, para.15–070.
[697] LRA 2002 Sch.3 para.3(2).
[698] This is not likely to be a problem for some years, because of the transitional provisions
explained above at para.7–098.

7–101   **4. Registering unregistered interests that override registered dispositions.** It has been explained that one of the objectives of the Land Registration
Act 2002 is, in time, to create a register that is conclusive, so far as it can be,
and that the reduction in the number and scope of overriding interests is
necessary to achieve that objective.[699] One method of reduction is to ensure
that they are brought on to the register. On an application to register a
registrable disposition, the applicant must provide the registrar with information about such overriding interests that affect the estate to be registered as are
specified in rules.[700] The registrar may then note them in the register.[701] The
obligation of disclosure only extends to overriding interests of which the
applicant actually knows,[702] and there are certain overriding interests that do
not have to be disclosed because they will not be noted in the register. These
include those interests that cannot be noted in the register[703] (such as an
interest under a trust of land), public rights (such as public rights of way) and
local land charges (which are registered in a separate register).[704]

Section 6. Charges

7–102   **1. Introduction.** A number of points have already been explained about
charges and sub-charges of registered land under the Land Registration Act
2002, including:

> (i) the restrictions on the types of charge and sub-charge that may now
> be created over a registered estate or charge[705]; and

> (ii) the rules for determining the priority of competing registered
> charges.[706]

Certain other matters require consideration.[707]

7–103   **2. Tacking and further advances.** Tacking is the process by which a
mortgagee who makes a further secured advance to the borrower may obtain
priority over an intervening charge.[708] The Land Registration Act 2002 recast
the law on tacking further advances, both by codifying the existing practice of
lenders and by introducing a new method of tacking.[709] The proprietor of a

---

[699] See above, para.7–008.
[700] LRA 2002 s.71(b); LRR 2003 r.57. See above, para.7–022.
[701] LRR 2003 r.57(5). See too the registrar's power to note overriding interests: LRA 2002 s.37;
above, para.7–071.
[702] LRR 2003 r.57(1).
[703] See LRA 2002 ss.33, 90(4); above, para.7–070.
[704] LRR 2003 r.57(2). For local land charges and their registration, see below, para.8–107.
[705] Above, para.7–050.
[706] Above, para.7–068.
[707] For the discharge of charges, see below, para.7–137.
[708] See further below, paras 26–056 et seq.
[709] LRA 2002 s.49; (2001) Law Com. No.271, paras 7.18–7.36.

registered charge may make a further advance on the security of a charge that will rank in priority to a subsequent charge if:

(i) the proprietor has not received from the subsequent chargee notice of the creation of that subsequent charge[710];

(ii) the further advance is made in pursuance of an obligation and that obligation was entered in the register at the time of the creation of the subsequent charge[711]; or

(iii) the parties to the prior charge have agreed a maximum amount for which the charge is security and at the time of the subsequent charge the agreement was entered in the register[712]; or

(iv) the subsequent chargee agrees.[713]

Of these methods, (ii) codified the practice of lenders, and (iii) was completely new.

3. The powers of a registered chargee and sub-chargee. All charges   **7–104** created by a registrable disposition of a registered estate take effect as a charge by deed by way of legal mortgage.[714] The powers of chargee to make a disposition of that charge have already been explained.[715] The 2002 Act also makes provision for the protection of purchasers from a chargee who makes a disposition of the property charged. Subject to any entry to the contrary in the register, the proprietor of a registered charge is taken to have, in relation to the property subject to the charge, the powers of disposition conferred by law on the owner of a legal charge.[716] However, this provision merely prevents the title of the disponee being called into question. It does not affect the lawfulness of the disposition.[717] The registered proprietor of a sub-charge has, in relation to the property subject to the principal charge or any intermediate charge, the same powers as the sub-chargor.[718]

4. Realisation of a chargee's security. The 2002 Act makes provision for   **7–105** two matters which concern the realisation of a chargee's security.

---

[710] LRA 2002 s.49(1). Notice is treated as having been received at the time when it ought to have been received: LRA 2002 s.49(2), and that time is prescribed by rules: see LRR 2003 r.107.

[711] LRA 2002 s.49(3). For application to register the obligation, which must be on Form CH2, see LRR 2003 r.108.

[712] LRA 2002 s.49(4). For application to register the agreement, which must be on Form CH3, see LRR 2003 r.109.

[713] LRA 2002 s.49(6); LRR 2003 r.102; and see above, para.7–068.

[714] LRA 2002 s.51. See below, paras 24–027, 24–034.

[715] See above, para.7–050.

[716] LRA 2002 s.52(1). For those powers, see below, paras 25–005 et seq.

[717] LRA 2002 s.52(2).

[718] LRA 2002 s.53. It has been held that the mere existence of a sub-charge does not divest the sub-chargor of the right to possession: see *Credit & Mercantile Plc v Marks* [2005] Ch. 81. See below, paras 25–024 (mortgagee's right to possession), 25–149 (powers of sub-mortgagee).

First, where a registered chargee exercises his power of sale and, after discharging the charge and the properly incurred costs, charges and expenses incident to the sale, there is a surplus, he holds that surplus on trust for any subsequent incumbrancer, or if there is none, for the registered proprietor of the land.[719] The chargee is taken to have notice of anything in the register immediately before the disposition on sale.[720] This means that the chargee must search the register immediately before the sale to ascertain whether there is any other registered charge in the register or any notice of an equitable charge. He will then know to whom he must pay any surplus.

Second, some local land charges have to be registered in order to enforce them. Local land charges are not normally registrable in the register of title[721] and override both first registration and any registered disposition.[722] However, where the local land charge creates a charge over land for the payment of money,[723] that charge cannot be realised until it is registered as a registered charge.[724] It should be clear from the register that a person has dispositive powers over registered land.[725]

7–106   **5. Consolidation of charges.** A mortgagor who has more than one mortgage with the lender may redeem one of the charges without having to redeem them all unless a contrary intention is expressed in one or more of the mortgages.[726] A mortgagee may, however, reserve a right to consolidate the charges so that he can require the mortgagor to redeem all the mortgages and not just one or some of them.[727] The consolidation of registered charges is permitted, but the chargee should apply to the registrar for an appropriate entry in the register.[728]

Section 7. Special Cases

7–107   **1. Introduction.** There are a number of special cases for which the 2002 Act makes provision of which four should be mentioned briefly, namely:

(i) the Crown;

(ii) devolution on the death of a registered proprietor;

(iii) the effect of the bankruptcy of a registered proprietor; and

---

[719] LPA 1925 s.105; below, para.25–020.
[720] LRA 2002 s.54.
[721] They are registrable in the local land charges register: see below, para.8–107.
[722] The creation of a legal charge which is a local land charge is not required to be registered: see LRA 2002 s.27(5)(c); above, para.7–054.
[723] See, e.g., Public Health Act 1936 s.291; Prevention of Damage by Pests Act 1949 s.7; *Hackney LBC v Crown Estate Commissioners* (1995) 72 P. & C.R. 233.
[724] LRA 2002 s.55.
[725] (2001) Law Com. No.271, para.7.42.
[726] See LPA 1925 s.93(1); below, para.25–057.
[727] For consolidation, see below, paras 25–055 et seq.
[728] See LRA 2002 s.57; LRR 2003 r.110. Application is on Form CC: LRR 2003 r.110(2).

(iv) settlements under the Settled Land Act 1925.

2. The Crown. It has been explained that the Act provides a mechanism by **7–108** which demesne land can for the first time be registered: Her Majesty grants to Herself a freehold estate, which is then registered.[729] The Act also makes provision for what is, in effect, the converse case where a registered freehold estate escheats. It has been explained that an escheat occurs whenever a freehold estate comes to an end.[730] In those circumstances, the feudal lord of whom the estate was held becomes entitled to the land. In the absence of proof of any mesne lordship, that feudal lord is presumed to be the Crown or (in the relevant parts of the country) the Duchy of Lancaster or Cornwall.[731] It has also been explained that where an escheat occurs, the subordinate interests that affected the former freehold are not determined.[732]

Formerly, if a registered freehold escheated, the title was removed from the register because the estate no longer existed, and this remains the practice on the determination of an estate other than a freehold estate.[733] However, although this practice was logical, it was undesirable that the title to land, having once been registered, should be removed from the register, particularly as the incumbrances which affected the former freehold would continue. The practice has changed under the 2002 Act. Where a registered freehold determines, the title may remain on the register, but the registrar may enter a note of the fact that the estate has determined both in the register of that title and in the register of any inferior affected registered title.[734] The title will remain on the register in that state until either:

(i) the original freehold revives (as where a dissolved company is restored to the register[735]), in which case the entry in the register as to the escheat will be removed; or

(ii) the Crown grants a new freehold estate, when the old title will be closed and a new title opened. Subsisting incumbrances recorded in the register of the former title are carried across to the new one.

3. Devolution on the death of a registered proprietor. Although transfers **7–109** of a registered estate or charge that take effect by operation of law are normally required to be registered, this is subject to certain exceptions.[736] One exception is that, on the death of a registered proprietor, his estate or charge

---

[729] See above, para.7–012.
[730] See above, para.2–023.
[731] See above, para.2–018.
[732] See above, para.2–025.
[733] LRR 2003 r.79.
[734] LRA 2002 s.82; LRR 2003 r.173(1). Where the registrar is in doubt as to whether the estate has escheated, the register must contain a statement to that effect: LRR 2003 r.173(2).
[735] cf. Companies Act 2006 s.1024, and see LRPG 35, para.7.5.1.
[736] LRA 2002 s.27(5); above, para.7–054.

will pass to his executors on death or to his administrators on the grant of letters of administration, without the need to register them as proprietors. Although the deceased's personal representatives may apply to be registered,[737] it is not necessary for them to do so in order to make a disposition of the registered estate or charge. However, an application to register a transfer from personal representatives who were not registered proprietors has to be accompanied by the original grant of probate or letters of administration.[738] Devolution on death is considered more fully below.[739]

7–110   **4. The effect of the bankruptcy of a registered proprietor.** Another exception to the general rule that transfers of a registered estate or charge by operation of law must be registered is in relation to bankruptcy. The statutory provisions are intended to ensure that any registered estate or charge of the bankrupt is dealt with in accordance with the provisions of the Insolvency Act 1986. The steps taken on bankruptcy, so far as they affect registered land, are briefly as follows.[740]

(i) When a petition in bankruptcy is presented, the petition is registered as a pending action under the Land Charges Act 1972.[741] As soon as practicable thereafter, the registrar must enter in the register of title in relation to any registered estate or charge which appears to him to be affected, a notice in respect of that pending action.[742] That notice will continue in force until either a restriction is entered as explained in (ii) or the trustee in bankruptcy is registered as proprietor.[743]

(ii) A bankruptcy order is made by which the registered proprietor is adjudicated bankrupt.[744] Again, this is initially registered under the

---

[737] Personal representatives may apply to be registered: LRR 2003 r.163.

[738] LRR 2003 r.162(1). Provided any restriction is complied with, the registrar is required to assume that the personal representatives are acting correctly and within their powers, whether or not he knows the terms of the deceased's will: LRR 2003 r.162(2).

[739] See para.14–128.

[740] See LRA 2002 s.86.

[741] LCA 1972 s.5(1)(b), (3)(b). The registrar controls both the Land Charges Department and the Land Registry: see LCA 1972 ss.1(1), 17(1). There is an obligation on the court to notify the Chief Land Registrar of the petition: see Insolvency Rules 1986 r.6.13; 1986/1925. Breach of that obligation does not give rise to a private right of action either at common law or for breach of statutory duty: *St John Poulton's Trustee in Bankruptcy v Ministry of Justice* [2010] EWCA Civ 392; [2011] Ch. 1.

[742] LRA 2002 s.86(2). The words "appears to him" are significant. The registrar may not always be sure whether the bankrupt is the same person as a person of the same name who is registered as proprietor of an estate or charge. Unusually, the notice is entered in the proprietorship register of the registered estate and not the charges register: see LRR 2003 rr.8(1)(e), 165(1). It is entered in the charges register in relation to any registered charge belonging to the bankrupt: LRR 2003 r.165(1). For the divisions of the register, see below, para.7–113.

[743] LRA 2002 s.86(3).

[744] IA 1986 ss.274(3)(b), 278(a).

Land Charges Act 1972, this time as a bankruptcy order.[745] As soon as practicable thereafter, the registrar must enter a bankruptcy restriction in relation to any registered estate or charge which appears to him to be affected by the order.[746] The restriction prevents any disposition of the registered estate or charge until the trustee in bankruptcy is registered as proprietor of it.[747]

(iii) The making of a bankruptcy order will be followed by the appointment of a trustee in bankruptcy unless it is annulled or discharged in the interim.[748] Once appointed, the trustee is entitled to be registered as proprietor in place of the bankrupt, provided that he produces the bankruptcy order; his certificate of appointment; and a certificate signed by him that the registered estate or charge is comprised in the bankrupt's estate.[749]

Generally, a disposition by a person who has been adjudged bankrupt is void.[750] However, where the proprietor of a registered estate or charge is adjudged bankrupt, the title of his trustee in bankruptcy is void against a person to whom a registrable disposition of the estate or charge is made, if the following conditions are met[751]: **7–111**

(i) the disposition is made for valuable consideration[752] and the registration requirements are met[753];

(ii) the disponee acts in good faith;

(iii) at the time of the disposition:

(1) no notice or restriction is entered in the register in relation to the registered estate or charge under the provisions explained in the previous paragraph[754]; and
(2) the disponee has no notice of the bankruptcy petition or the adjudication.

---

[745] LCA 1972 s.6(1)(c).

[746] LRA 2002 s.86(4); LRR 2003 r.166.

[747] LRR 2003 r.166(1).

[748] *Re Palmer* [1994] Ch. 316 at 324; and see LRR 2003 r.167.

[749] LRR 2003 r.168. For the procedure where a trustee in bankruptcy vacates his office, see LRR 2003 r.169.

[750] IA 1986 s.284(1).

[751] LRA 2002 s.86(5). See para.7–066 above.

[752] Valuable consideration does not include marriage consideration or a nominal consideration in money: LRA 2002 s.132(1).

[753] LRA 2002 s.86(6). For the registration requirements, see LRA 2002 Sch.2, above, paras 7–057, 7–058.

[754] If the bankruptcy restriction is entered after the registrable disposition has been made but before the disposition is registered, the title of the trustee in bankruptcy is not avoided under LRA 2002 s.86(5): see *Pick v Chief Land Registrar* [2011] EWHC 206 (Ch).

This is one of the rare occasions in which the concepts of good faith and the doctrine of notice apply to dispositions of registered land.[755] In this regard, the 2002 Act follows the 1925 Act.[756]

7–112   **5. Settled Land.** Settlements under the Settled Land Act 1925 are explained in the Appendix to this work. After 1996 it ceased to be possible to create new settlements.[757] Settlements of registered land are not dealt with specifically by the 2002 Act, but by rules made under it.[758] Among other things, these rules:

> (i) require the settled land to be registered in the name of the tenant for life[759];
>
> (ii) prescribe the forms of restriction that are required and when there is a duty to apply for them[760];
>
> (iii) prescribe the form of transfer of registered land into an existing settlement[761];
>
> (iv) prescribe the steps that must be taken if land ceases to be settled during the lifetime of the life tenant[762]; and
>
> (v) prescribe the form of transfer where a settlement continues after the death of the tenant for life.[763]

Part 4

REGISTRATION AND THE REGISTERS

1. The registers and indices

7–113   *(a) The registers.* The registrar is required to keep two registers, the register of title[764] and the register of cautions against first registration.[765] The latter has been explained,[766] though it is necessary to refer to aspects of it in this Part,

---

[755] See above, para.7–064.
[756] See LRA 1925 s.61(6). Cf. IA 1986 s.284(4), which applies to a narrower situation that LRA 2002 s.86(5).
[757] TLATA 1996 s.2
[758] LRA 2002 s.89; LRR 2003 r.186; Sch.7.
[759] LRR 2003 Sch.7 para.1.
[760] LRR 2003 Sch.7 paras 2, 3, 5, 7.
[761] LRR 2003 Sch.7 paras 4, 6.
[762] LRR 2003 Sch.7 paras 8, 9.
[763] LRR 2003, Sch.7, para.12.
[764] LRA 2002 s.1.
[765] LRA 2002 s.19.
[766] See above, para.7–044.

e.g. in relation to inspections of the register.[767] As regards the former, the details of how it is arranged and kept are found in rules.[768]

The register of title may be kept in electronic or paper form,[769] though in practice it is now the former. Each individual register has a title number and consists of three parts,[770] namely:

(i) The property register, which contains a description of the registered estate and which must refer to a title plan, based on the Ordnance Survey map.[771] It contains other details, such as the benefit of easements.[772]

(ii) The proprietorship register, which contains details of the class of title, the name of the registered proprietor, an address for service, any restrictions, and certain other matters.[773]

(iii) The charges register, which is the converse of the property register in that it records the incumbrances that effect a registered estate, such as registered charges and interests protected by notice.[774]

The provisions for inspecting the register of title and the cautions register are explained below.[775]

(b) The indices. The registrar is required to keep three indices. **7–114**
The first is the index.[776] This comprises two parts, the index map and an index of relating franchises and manors. From the index map it is possible to ascertain in relation to any parcel of land:

(i) whether there is any pending application either for first registration of a registered estate or for a caution against the first registration of such an estate;

(ii) whether there is any registered estate relating to that parcel and if so, the title number; and

(iii) whether there is any caution against first registration relating to that parcel and if so, the title number.[777]

---

[767] See below, para.7–120.
[768] LRA 2002 s.1(2); LRR 2003 Pt 1.
[769] LRR 2003 r.2.
[770] LRR 2003 r.4.
[771] For boundaries, see below, para.7–118.
[772] LRR 2003 r.5. The property register of a leasehold title must contain other prescribed information: see LRR 203 r.6.
[773] LRR 2003 r.8.
[774] LRR 2003 r.9.
[775] See para.7–120.
[776] LRA 2002 s.68; LRR 2003.
[777] LRR 2003 r.10(1)(a).

Manors, and some franchises, which are called "relating franchises" in the rules,[778] do not constitute an incumbrance on land. The index of relating franchises and manors provides a verbal description of:

(i) any pending application either for the first registration, or for a caution against first registration, of a relating franchise[779];

(ii) registered relating franchises and manors;

(iii) cautions against the first registration of a relating franchise.[780]

Both the index map and the index of relating franchises may be searched.[781] In practice, a search of the index map should always be made by an intending purchaser of unregistered land, particularly because it will reveal whether there are any cautions against the first registration of the land to be purchased.[782] The intending purchaser may then search the cautions register.

The second of the indices is the index of proprietors' names.[783] This records the name of the registered proprietor of every registered estate and registered charge, together with the title number. There is a limited right to search the index,[784] though the court may authorise a search in other cases.[785]

The third of the indices is the day list.[786] This records the date and time of every pending application. This is necessary to determine the priority of competing applications. Registration has effect from the time of the making of the application to register an unregistered legal estate (in the case of first registration) or to register a registrable disposition.[787] In general, and subject to exceptions, an application is taken to be made at the time of the day that notice of it is entered in the day list.[788]

2. The effect of registration

7–115 *(a) Introduction.* It has been explained that it is registration that vests legal title in the proprietor of a registered estate.[789] It is necessary to consider the effect of registration where the instrument, which purported to make the disposition, is for some reason void, e.g. because it was a forgery or because, by some mistake, a landowner purported to dispose of land which he had

---

[778] For relating franchises, see above, para.7–030.

[779] It is not longer possible to apply for the registration of a manor: see above, para.7–011.

[780] LRR 2003 r.10(1)(b).

[781] See LRR 2003 rr.145 (index map), 146 (index of relating franchises and manors).

[782] See Ruoff & Roper, 30.001.

[783] LRR 2003 r.11.

[784] LRR 2003 r.11(3), (4).

[785] *Parkinson v Hawthorne* [2008] EWHC 3499 (Ch); [2009] 1 W.L.R. 1665 (judgment creditor authorised to search).

[786] LRR 2003 r.12.

[787] LRA 2002 s.74.

[788] LRR 2003 r.15.

[789] Above, paras 7–025, (first registration), 7–053 (registrable disposition).

previously conveyed. The position under the Land Registration Act 1925 was, apparently, that:

(i) First registration vested the legal and beneficial title to the land in the first registered proprietor even if he had no title to it.[790]

(ii) Where title was already registered and there was a purported disposition of the registered estate that was a nullity, only the bare legal title vested in the registered proprietor,[791] who held it on a bare trust for the person who would otherwise have been the owner of the land.[792]

The position under the Land Registration Act 2002, which is significantly different in its drafting, is as follows.

(b) First registration. The effect of first registration has been explained.[793]   **7–116**
The provisions of the 2002 Act are only explicable if registration of a person as first registered proprietor vests in him both legal and beneficial title. The Act provides that where a person is registered as first registered proprietor with absolute title the estate is vested in him together with all interests subsisting for the benefit of the estate.[794] However, if that person is not entitled to the estate for his own benefit (as where he holds on trust for another), or not entitled solely for his own benefit (as where he holds on trust for himself and one or more other persons), then, as between himself and the persons beneficially entitled to the estate, the estate is vested in him subject to such of their interests of which he has notice.[795] This provision would be unnecessary if it had been intended that first registration should vest only the bare legal title in a person who was not the beneficial owner.

If, therefore, A is registered as the first registered proprietor of land in circumstances where he had no title to it, he will be both the legal and beneficial owner of that land. Because A has been registered as proprietor by mistake, the person who would otherwise be the owner should seek the alteration of the register, under the provisions explained below,[796] and will either be registered as proprietor in place of A, or will receive an indemnity from the registrar for the loss of his land.[797]

---

[790] Cf. LRA 1925 s.5.

[791] Cf. LRA 2002 s.69.

[792] *Malory Enterprises Ltd v Cheshire Homes (UK) Ltd* [2002] EWCA Civ 151 at [64], [65]; [2002] Ch. 216 at 232. The reasoning is unsatisfactory: see "Registered Land—A Law Unto Itself?" (C.H.) in J. Getzler (ed.) *Rationalizing Property, Equity and Trusts: Essays in Honour of Edward Burn* 1st edn (Oxford: OUP, 2003); and compare [2002] EWCA Civ 151 at [65]; [2002] Ch. 216 at 232 with *Hesketh v Willis Cruisers Ltd* (1968) 19 P. & C.R. 573 at 579–580.

[793] See above, paras 7–023 et seq.

[794] LRA 2002 ss.11(3) (freehold), 12(3) (leasehold).

[795] LRA 2002 ss.11(5) (freehold), 12(5) (leasehold).

[796] See paras 7–132 et seq.

[797] For the provisions on indemnity, see below, paras 7–140 et seq.

7–117   *(c) Registration as proprietor of a registered estate.* Where a person is registered as the proprietor of a registered legal estate, the legal estate is deemed to be vested in him, even if it would not otherwise be so.[798] This provision applies to a legal estate, which, as defined, includes not just freehold and leasehold estates in land, but all those interests or charges in or over land that can subsist at law.[799] Where a person has been mistakenly registered as the proprietor of a legal estate, by reason of a void transfer or other disposition, the legal and beneficial title to the legal estate must vest in that person. If the void disposition had been the grant of a legal charge or an easement, it would make no sense to say that the chargee or grantee had merely the bare legal title to that legal estate.

7–118   **3. Boundaries.** Unless a boundary has been determined, all boundaries that are shown in the register of title are general boundaries,[800] and do not determine the exact line of the boundary.[801] The general boundary will extend to cases where there is a presumption of ownership, as where the owner of land adjacent to a non-tidal river or a road is rebuttably presumed to own the bed of the river or the soil under the highway to the mid-point.[802] By reason of the general boundaries rule, such land is within the registered title although not shown on the title plan.[803] This was clear prior to the Land Registration Act 2002,[804] and it is not thought that the 2002 Act has changed the position.[805] It is, however, possible to have an exact boundary determined and the rules make detailed provision for the procedure for determining boundaries

---

[798] LRA 2002 s.58(1). This is subject to one necessary exception: where the entry is made in pursuance of a registrable disposition in relation to which some other registration requirement remains to be met, the registration is incomplete, the disposition operates in equity only (see LRA 2002 s.27(1); above, para.7–053), and the legal title does not vest until the requirements are met: LRA 2002 s.58(2). For the registration requirements, see LRA 2002 s.27(4); Sch.4; above, paras 7–057, 7–058. If, e.g., A granted B an easement over A's registered freehold, and, B is registered as proprietor of the easement in the register of the dominant tenement, that easement does not take effect as a legal easement until the burden of that easement is noted in the register of A's registered freehold: see LRA 2002 Sch.2, para.7; above, para.7–057.

[799] See LRA 2002 s.132(1), which refers to the definition in LPA 1925 s.205(1)(x) ("the estates, interests and charges, in or over land (subsisting or created at law) which are by this Act authorised to subsist or to be created as legal estates", namely, those estates listed in LPA 1925 s.1; above, paras 6–008 et seq).

[800] LRA 2002 s.60(1). The matter was previously dealt with by rules: see LRR 1925 r.278. The courts do not accept that there is any limit in relation to the amount of land that may fall within the scope of a general boundary. It depends upon all the circumstances and, in particular, the quantity of land abutting the boundary: *Drake v Fripp* [2011] EWCA Civ 1279 at [20]; [2012] P. & C.R. 67 at 76.

[801] LRA 2002 s.60(2). The general boundaries rule applies only to the *filed* plan and does not enable the registrar or the court to alter any *transfer* plan: see *Chadwick v Abbotswood Properties Ltd* [2004] EWHC 1058 (Ch) at [59]; [2005] 1 P & CR 139 at 153.

[802] For this presumption, which is a strong one, see, e.g., *London Land Tax Commissioners v Central London Rly Co* [1913] AC 364. Where a person owns land adjacent to a river towpath, he is presumed to own both the towpath and half the width of the river: see *Thames Conservators v Kent* [1918] 2 KB 272.

[803] *Hesketh v Willis Cruisers Ltd* (1968) 19 P. & C.R. 573 at 575, 579; *Frazer v Martin* [2009] EWHC 2692 (Ch); [2010] 1 P. & C.R. 268.

[804] See LRR 1925 r.278; *Hesketh v Willis Cruisers Ltd* (1968) 19 P. & C.R. 573.

[805] See (2001) Law Com. No.271 at para.9.11.

whether on application to the registrar, or by the registrar on his own initiative.[806]

The principles of accretion and diluvion have been explained.[807] The fact that a registered estate in land is shown in the register as having a particular boundary does not affect the operation of accretion or diluvion.[808] Where either occurs, the filed plan in the register of title will necessarily have to be amended to bring the register up to date.[809] Where the parties enter into an agreement as to the operation of accretion and diluvion, as by excluding it,[810] that agreement must be registered.[811]

4. The use of the register to record defects in title. There may be   **7–119**
occasions where a registered estate becomes liable to determination, as for example, where it is subject to a rentcharge, the rentcharge owner has a right to re-enter in the event of a failure to pay the rentcharge, and the owner of the estate subject to the rentcharge has failed to pay the rentcharge.[812] If it appears to the registrar that a right to determine a registered estate is exercisable, he may enter the fact in the register.[813] This power is subject to rules,[814] and the rules imply that it will be exercised on application to the registrar (though there is no reason why the registrar should not exercise the power of his own volition).[815] The registrar must give notice of the application to the registered proprietor of both the estate and any registered charge over it.[816] Certain specified persons may apply to registrar for the removal of the entry.[817]

5. Inspecting the registers and obtaining copies of the registers and   **7–120**
documents. The open nature of the register of title has been explained.[818] Any person may inspect and make copies of, or of any part of:

    (i) the register of title;

    (ii) any document kept by the registrar which is referred to in the register of title: this was an extension of the law because prior to the 2002 Act it was not normally possible to obtain copies of leases and charges[819];

---

[806] See LRA 2002 ss.60(3), (4); LRR 2003 rr.118–122. See LRPG 40, para.3.3 for a detailed explanation.

[807] See above, para.3–037.

[808] LRA 2002 s.62(1).

[809] For the power of the registrar to update the register, see LRA 2002 Sch.4 para.5, below, para.7–137.

[810] See, e.g., *Baxendale v Instow Parish Council* [1982] Ch. 14.

[811] LRA 2002 s.61(2); LRR 2003 r.123.

[812] For rentcharges, see above, para.6–021; and below, para.31–014.

[813] LRA 2002 s.64(1). The entry is made in the property register of the title: see LRR 2003 r.125(1).

[814] LRA 2002 s.64(2).

[815] See LRR 2003 r.125(2).

[816] LRR 2003 r.125(4).

[817] LRR 2003 r.125(5).

[818] See above, para.7–002.

[819] See LRA 1925 s.112(1)(b).

(iii) any other document kept by the registrar which relates to an application to him; or

(iv) the register of cautions against first registration.[820]

It is possible to obtain an official copy[821] of any of the four matters listed above.[822] It is admissible to the same extent as the original.[823]

7–121   The statutory right, explained in the previous paragraph, is subject to rules, which may provide exceptions to the right and impose conditions on its exercise.[824] Under the rules that have been made, a person may apply to the registrar to designate a relevant document an exempt information document if he claims that the document contains prejudicial information.[825] Provided that the registrar is satisfied that the applicant's claim is not groundless, he must designate the document an exempt information document.[826] A person who thereafter applies for a copy of the document will only be entitled to see the edited version of the document, which excludes the allegedly prejudicial material. It is possible for a person to apply to see the full document, and in certain circumstances, the registrar must provide a copy.[827] The person who applied to have a document designated as an exempt information document may apply to have the designation removed.[828]

7–122   **6. Conclusiveness of filed copies.** As between the parties to certain dispositions of registered land:

(i) where an entry in the register relating to a registered estate refers to a document kept by the registrar; and

(ii) that document is not an original;

the document kept by the registrar is to be taken to be correct and to contain all material parts of the original document.[829] This presumption applies as between the parties to a registrable disposition, to the grant of an interest out of registered land that cannot be registered (e.g., a lease for a term of seven years or less), and to the disposition of such an unregistrable interest.[830] No party to the disposition can require the production of the original document.[831] However, no party to the disposition can be affected by any provision of the

---

[820] LRA 2002 s.66(1). For applications to inspect and copy, see LRR 2003 r.133.
[821] Under the LRA 1925, an official copy was called an "office copy".
[822] LRA 2002 s.67. For applications for an official copy, see LRR 2003 rr.134, 135.
[823] LRA 2002 s.67(1).
[824] LRA 2002 s.66(2).
[825] LRR 2003 r.136(1). "Prejudicial information" is defined in LRR 2003 r.131: it is material that could cause unwarranted harm or distress to the applicant or another, or material which is commercially sensitive (e.g., details of a turnover rent in a lease).
[826] LRR 2003 r.136(2).
[827] See LRR 2003 r.137.
[828] LRR 2003 r.138.
[829] LRA 2002 s.120(1), (2).
[830] LRA 2002 s.120(1).
[831] LRA 2002 s.120(3).

original document that is not contained in the document kept by the registrar.[832] There is a right to indemnity for any person who suffers loss by reason of a mistake in a document kept by the registrar which is not an original and is referred to in the register.[833]

7. Historical information. The register records the title as it stands at any **7–123** given time. It does not provide a history of the title. Sometimes it is necessary to ascertain the history of the title.[834] The registrar often does hold records that show the history of the title. It is possible to apply to the registrar for information about the history of a registered title.[835] This takes the form of an application for a copy of a particular edition of the register for a specified date, and it may relate to an existing title or to a title that has been closed.[836] Provided that the registrar is keeping in electronic form an edition of the registered title for the day specified in the application he must issue a copy of the relevant edition(s).[837]

8. Official searches and priority protection. One of the problems that **7–124** exist in relation to registered conveyancing is the hiatus between the completion of a disposition and its subsequent registration. A disponee can only apply to register a disposition after that disposition has been made. There is a risk that third party rights might be created in the course of this so-called "registration gap".[838] To overcome these difficulties, there is a system by which, where there is a proposed disposition for valuable consideration that is either a registrable disposition or a disposition that will trigger first registration, the disponee can protect the priority of the intended disposition in his favour pending its completion and registration. The 2002 Act creates a principle of priority protection,[839] which is at present triggered by an application for an official search of the register with priority[840] (an official search may be made with or without priority[841]).

If an intending disponee of registered land for valuable consideration makes **7–125** a valid official search with priority,[842] that gives him a period of priority

---

[832] LRA 2002 s.120(4).
[833] LRA 2002 Sch.8 para.1(1)(e); below, para.7–140.
[834] For example, if the property is subject to an easement, and it is suspected that the easement may have been extinguished because the dominant and servient tenements were formerly in common ownership. See below, para.29–014.
[835] LRA 2002 s.69.
[836] LRR 2003 r.144.
[837] LRR 2003 r.144(3).
[838] See further below, para.7–150.
[839] LRA 2002 s.72.
[840] LRA 2002 s.70.
[841] See LRR 2003 rr.147, 151. For official searches without priority, see below, para.7–127.
[842] For the application for such a search (which can be made both in relation to a disposition that will trigger first registration and where there is a proposed disposition of a registered estate), see LRR 2003 r.147. The application is taken to have been made when it is entered on the day list: see LRR 2003 r.148. An official certificate of search with priority must be issued by the registrar if the application is in order: LRR 2003 r.149.

protection[843] in which to complete the disposition and then to apply to register it.[844] Any application to change the register made during that priority period is postponed until the end of the period, thereby protecting the priority of the protected disposition if it is registered within the period.[845] There may be a pending disposition of registered estate and also a further disposition which is dependent upon that prior disposition (as where a property is to be purchased with the aid of a mortgage). In those circumstances, if an official search with priority is made by the disponee under the pending dependent disposition, but not under the primary disposition, the priority protection extends to the prior disposition upon which the subsequent disposition is dependent.[846]

If there are two or more official search certificates with priority, the general rule is that their priority is determined according to the time of their entry in the day list.[847] This is subject to one exception. Where there is a pending disposition of registered estate and a further dependent disposition of that registered estate and both intending disponees make an official search with priority, the registrar must assume (unless the contrary appears) that the prior disposition has priority over the dependent disposition.[848]

At present, the only basis upon which priority protection can be obtained is by making an official search with priority,[849] and it is only available to an intending disponee under a registrable disposition for valuable considera-tion.[850] There is power to make rules for priority periods to apply where a contract to make a registrable disposition is noted in the register.[851] There are no such rules at present and none are likely to be made until electronic conveyancing has been introduced.[852]

7–126   In two circumstances, the intending disponee will not obtain priority protec-tion. The first is where there is an earlier protected application.[853] The second is where a court has ordered the registrar to enter a restriction in the register and has made a direction that the entry is to have overriding priority.[854]

7–127   Any person may apply for an official search without priority[855]: he need not be an intending disponee. Provided that the application is in order, the

---

[843] The priority period is normally 30 business days: LRR 2003 r.131.

[844] LRA 2002 s.72(1), (2), (6)(a).

[845] LRA 2002 s.72(2); LRR 2003 r.148.

[846] LRR 2003 r.151. The same rule applies in relation to a pending application for first registration: LRR 2003 r.152.

[847] LRR 2003 r.153(1).

[848] LRR 2003 r.153(2).

[849] LRA 2002 s.72(6)(a).

[850] See LRR 2003 r.147(1), and see the definitions of "protectable disposition" and "pur-chaser" in LRR 2003 r.131.

[851] LRA 2002 s.72(6)(b).

[852] As regards electronic conveyancing, there is power to require a contract to make a registrable disposition to be made electronically and simultaneously registered: see LRA 2002 s.93.

[853] LRA 2002 s.72(3).

[854] LRA 2002 s.72(4). For the court's power to order that a restriction be entered in the register and that it should have overriding priority, see LRA 2002 s.46; above, para.7–083.

[855] See LRR 2003 r.155.

registrar must issue an official search certificate.[856] There are many reasons why a person who was not an intending disponee might wish to make such a search, e.g., a chargee, which had exercised its power of sale and held a surplus after discharge of its charge and the expenses of the sale. That surplus must be paid to the person next entitled to it.[857] As has been explained,[858] the chargee is taken to have notice of anything in the register immediately before the disposition on sale,[859] and must therefore search the register immediately before the sale to ascertain whether there is any other charge affecting the property, in order to know for whom he holds the surplus.

9. Outline applications. As indicated above, the system of priority protec- **7–128** tion operates only in relation to a disposition for valuable consideration. There is a limited system for protecting the priority of applications to register other forms of disposition by means of an outline application.[860] It can only be used in relation to a right, interest or matter that is in existence at the time of the application and it cannot be used for:

   (i) an application which could be protected by an official search with priority;

  (ii) an application for first registration;

 (iii) an application for a caution against first registration or in respect of the cautions register;

 (iv) an application dealing with part only of the land comprised in a registered title; or

  (v) certain other applications.[861]

Examples of where it might be employed would include any voluntary transfer of the whole of a registered estate, including an assent, and applications for notices or restrictions.

The way the procedure works is that an outline application is made in accordance with rules and this gives the applicant a reserved period of four business days in which to submit the application, which then takes its priority from the outline application.[862]

10. Objections to applications. Anyone may object to any application to **7–129** the registrar.[863] This is subject to two exceptions:

---

[856] LRR 2003 r.156.
[857] LPA 1925 s.105.
[858] See above, para.7–105.
[859] LRA 2002 s.54.
[860] LRR 2003 r.54.
[861] LRR 2003 r.54(2). The applications in (v) are applications under LRR 2003 Pt.13, which include applications for official copies, in relation to exempt information documents, for historical information and for official searches.
[862] This summarises the effect of LRR 2003 r.54.
[863] LRA 2002 s.73(1). For the procedure, see LRR 2003 r.19.

(i) The only persons who can object to an application to cancel a caution against first registration[864] are the person who lodged the caution and the person for the time being shown as the cautioner in the cautions register.[865]

(ii) The only persons who can object to an application to cancel a unilateral notice[866] are the person shown in the register as the beneficiary of the notice and a person who is entitled to be registered as the beneficiary of such a notice.[867]

Where an objection is made to an application, unless the registrar is satisfied that the objection is groundless,[868] he must give notice of the objection to the applicant and may not determine the application until the objection has been disposed of.[869] If it is not possible to dispose of the objection by agreement, the registrar must refer the matter to the adjudicator for resolution.[870]

7–130   **11. The adjudicator.** The Lord Chancellor must appoint an adjudicator.[871] His jurisdiction is limited.[872] His functions are:

(i) to determine disputes referred to him out of an objection to an application,[873] which includes a power to give effect to any equity arising by estoppel[874];

(ii) once electronic conveyancing is operative,[875] to hear appeals in relation to network access agreements[876]; and

(iii) to rectify or set aside certain documents, namely:

(a) an instrument by which a registrable disposition is made;
(b) an instrument which creates an interest that may be the subject of a notice in the register;
(c) a contract to make a disposition in paragraphs (a) or (b);
(d) an instrument which transfers an interest which is the subject of a notice in the register.[877]

---

[864] For such applications, see LRA 2002 s.18; above, para.7–047.
[865] LRA 2002 s.73(2); LRR 2003 r.52.
[866] For such applications, see LRA 2002 s.36, above, para.7–075.
[867] LRA 2002 s.73(3); LRR 2003 r.86(7).
[868] LRA 2002 s.73(6).
[869] LRA 2002 s.73(5); and see The Land Registration (Referral to the Adjudicator to HM Land Registry) Rules 2003; SI 2003/2114.
[870] LRA 2002 s.73(7).
[871] LRA 2002 s.107(1). There is not only an adjudicator, but there are also three full-time deputy adjudicators and a substantial number of part-time deputy adjudicators.
[872] See LRA 2002 s.108.
[873] LRA 2002 s.108(1)(a); above, para.7–129.
[874] See LRA 2002 s.110(4). For proprietary estoppel, see below, Ch.16.
[875] For electronic conveyancing, see below, para.7–157.
[876] LRA 2002 s.108(1)(b); Sch.5 para.4; below para.7–160.
[877] LRA 2002 s.108(2), (3). The purpose of this power was to obviate the need for and expense of an application to the High Court: see (2001) Law Com. No.271, para.16.9. The registrar has a power to correct clerical errors in any application or accompanying document: see LRR 2003 r.130.

Any order made by the adjudicator has the same effect as an order for rectification by the High Court.[878] This means, e.g., that rectification relates back to the time when the instrument was executed.[879]

Where a disputed application is referred to the adjudicator he may, instead of determining the matter himself, direct a party to the proceedings to commence proceedings for the purpose of obtaining the court's decision on the matter.[880] If the adjudicator does not make such a direction, he must decide the case himself. If either party wishes to withdraw from the dispute, the adjudicator has a discretion whether to terminate the reference or proceed to a determination on the merits.[881] The practice and procedure before the adjudicator are prescribed by rules.[882] An appeal lies from the adjudicator's decision to the High Court,[883] but permission to appeal is required.[884] The appeal takes the form of a rehearing and not a review.[885] Because the court may make any order that the adjudicator could have made, it may retrospectively reinstate any application that the adjudicator had cancelled, though it will not ordinarily do so if third party rights had supervened, as this would re-arrange the scheme of priorities provided for in the 2002 Act.[886]

Part 5

INDEFEASIBILITY

1. The core principles. The register of title, like the cautions register,[887]   **7–131** can be altered, either by the court or by the registrar. The main grounds for so doing are:

(i) to bring it up to date; or

(ii) to correct a mistake in it.

The first of these is an essential feature of any system of title registration. If the register is to be an accurate reflection of the title to the land, it must be kept up-to-date. As regards the second, the powers of the registrar and the court are tempered by a principle of qualified indefeasibility. The circumstances in

---

[878] LRA 2002 s.108(4).

[879] See (2001) Law Com. No.271, para.16.10.

[880] LRA 2002 s.110(1). See *Jayasinghe v Liyange* [2010] EWHC 265 (Ch) at [29]–[33]; [2010] 1 W.L.R. 2106 at 2113, 2114.

[881] *Chief Land Registrar v Silkstone* [2011] EWCA Civ 801; [2011] 41 E.G. 116.

[882] LRA 2002 s.109; The Adjudicator to Her Majesty's Land Registry (Practice and Procedure) Rules 2003; SI 2003/2171 (as amended). See Ruoff & Roper, Ch.48.

[883] LRA 2002 s.111.

[884] See CPR PD 52 para.23.8B. Presumably, this requirement has been imposed under Access to Justice Act 1999 s.54(1). It is not found in LRA 2002.

[885] *Starglass Properties Ltd v Dudgeon* [2006] All E.R. (D) 203 (Feb).

[886] *Chief Land Registrar v Franks* [2011] EWCA Civ 772; [2011] 40 E.G. 102.

[887] See above, para.7–048.

which the register can be rectified against certain classes of registered proprietor are limited. If the register is altered to correct a mistake and that alteration prejudicially affects the title of the registered proprietor, he is entitled to an indemnity for any loss that he suffers. Conversely, if the register is not altered, a person suffering loss by reason of the mistake will also be entitled to an indemnity for that loss. There is, therefore, a State guarantee of title, so that the registered proprietor and those dealing with him may rely upon his title being as it appears on the register, and will normally be able to claim compensation if it is not.

2. Alteration of the register

7–132   *(a) The meaning of rectification.* Under the Land Registration Act 1925, any alteration of the register to correct a mistake was referred to as "rectification".[888] The Land Registration Act 2002 has a more limited definition of rectification. It is an alteration which involves the correction of a mistake and prejudicially affects the title of a registered proprietor.[889]

(b) Alteration pursuant to a court order

7–133   (1) THE GROUNDS FOR ALTERING THE REGISTER. The court may make an order for alteration of the register for three reasons.[890] Only in relation to the first of them could the alteration constitute rectification for the purposes of the Act, and even then, it will not do so in every case.

The first is to correct a mistake.[891] What constitutes a mistake is widely interpreted and is not confined top any particular kind of mistake.[892] It is suggested therefore that there will be a mistake whenever the registrar would have done something different had he known the true facts at the time at which he made or deleted the relevant entry in the register, as by:

(i)   making an entry in the register that he would not have made or would not have made in the form in which it was made;

(ii) deleting an entry which he would not have deleted; or

(iii) failing to make an entry in the register which he would otherwise have made.

Examples of mistakes include the following:

---

[888] The term was wider than that: it included alteration of the register to give effect to a decision of the court as to substantive property rights and in cases of consent: see LRA 1925 s.82(1).

[889] LRA 2002 Sch.4 para.1. The title will not be prejudicially affected (1) where it is altered to give effect to an overriding interest, because it was already subject to that interest: see (2001) Law Com. No.271, para.10.16; or (2) by the substitution of one general boundary with a more accurate one: see *Strachey v Ramage* [2008] EWCA Civ 384 at [45]–[47]; (2009) 1 P. & C.R. 154 at 169, 170; *Drake v Fripp* [2011] EWCA Civ 1279 at [22]; [2012] 1 P. & C.R. 67 at 77.

[890] LRA 2002 Sch.4 para.2(1).

[891] LRA 2002 Sch.4 para.2(1)(a).

[892] *Baxter v Mannion* [2011] EWCA Civ 120; [2011] 1 W.L.R. 1594. The same was true under LRA 1925 s.82(1)(h): see *Chowood Ltd v Lyall (No.2)* [1930] 2 Ch. 156 at 168.

(i) Where a person has been registered as proprietor pursuant to a void disposition, such as a forged transfer, or where the transfer was of land which the seller had already sold.[893]

(ii) Where a person has been registered pursuant to a void disposition, any subsequent disposition by such a registered proprietor.[894]

(iii) Where a person has been registered as proprietor of land to which a squatter had previously barred his rights by his adverse possession.[895]

(iv) Where a person was registered as proprietor on the basis of his adverse possession, when he had not in fact been in adverse possession for the requisite period.[896]

(v) Where on first registration a person was registered as proprietor of the freehold and it subsequently transpires that he held under a long lease.

(vi) Where a person has been registered as the proprietor of land that in fact belonged to another person because the plan annexed to a conveyance was inaccurate and incorporated neighbouring land.

(vii) Where, at the time of first registration, the property was subject to an incumbrance, such as a land charge, and that incumbrance was omitted from the register on first registration.

(viii) Where an incumbrance is entered in the register in error, e.g. where it was spent, invalid or non-existent.

(ix) Where an entry in the register is deleted in error.

The second circumstance in which the court may order the alteration of the register is for the purpose of bringing it up to date.[897] This will normally occur because, in the course of litigation, the court determines the substantive rights of the parties to a dispute, e.g. where it decides that one of the parties has some estate, right or interest in or over the land of the other, and the register must

---

[893] There is no mistake where the registrar registers a transfer that was voidable but had not been avoided at the date of registration.

[894] Although this point has not been definitively decided by any court, the text reflects the approach now adopted by the Adjudicator: see *Knight's Construction (March) Ltd v Roberto Mac Ltd* [2011] 2 E.G.L.R. 123 (reviewing the authorities); and it is consistent with the previous law. Under LRA 1925 if X, whose title to registered land was merely voidable, charged registered land in favour of Y before his title was avoided, a court would not order rectification of the register against Y, even if it set aside the disposition to X: *Norwich and Peterborough Building Society v Steed* [1993] Ch. 116. However, if the purported disposition to X was wholly void, the court had a discretion to order rectification against Y: *Argyle Building Society v Hammond* (1985) 49 P. & C.R. 148.

[895] For an example under LRA 1925, see *Chowood Ltd v Lyall (No.2)* [1930] 2 Ch. 156.

[896] *Baxter v Mannion* [2011] EWCA Civ 120; [2011] 1 W.L.R. 1594.

[897] LRA 2002 Sch.4 para.2(1)(b).

therefore be altered to reflect this outcome. Such a case can never be one of rectification, but of alteration: there is no alteration because of any mistake.

The third ground upon which the court may order the alteration of the register is to give effect to an estate, right or interest that has been excepted from the effect of registration.[898] Where a title is registered with good leasehold, qualified or possessory title, the registration takes effect subject to the rights excepted from the effect of registration.[899]

When the court does make an order for the alteration of the register, its order, when served on the registrar, imposes upon him a statutory duty to give effect to it.[900]

7–134   (2) THE EXERCISE OF DISCRETION. The 2002 Act distinguishes between an alteration of the register that is rectification and one that is not.

Where, in any proceedings, the court has the power to make an order for the alteration of the register and it decides that one of the three grounds for altering the register exists, it must make order for the alteration of the register unless there are exceptional circumstances which justify its not doing so.[901] This principle does not apply where the alteration would amount to rectification.[902]

7–135   Where the court decides that there is a mistake in the register, but that an alteration of the register would amount to rectification (because it will prejudicially affect the title of a registered proprietor[903]), there is a significant restriction upon its power to order rectification in one situation.[904] That is where the proprietor is in possession of the land affected. The circumstances in which a proprietor will be regarded as being in possession have been explained,[905] and they are where the land is:

(i) physically in the registered proprietor's possession[906];

---

[898] LRA 2002 Sch.4 para.2(1)(c).

[899] See LRA 2002 ss.11(6), (7) and 12(6), (7), (8); above, paras 7–035—7–038.

[900] LRA 2002 Sch.4 para.2(2) and see para.4(b), (c). The order must state the title number of the title affected and the alteration to be made, and must direct the registrar to make the alteration: LRR 2003 r.127(1). Service on the registrar must be made by making an application for the registrar to give effect to the order (using Form AP1), accompanied by the order: LRR 2003 r.127(2).

[901] LRA 2002 Sch.4 para.4(a); LRR 2003 r.126. In practice the adjudicator adopts a similar approach when dealing with a disputed application: see e.g., *Derbyshire CC v Fallon* [2007] EWHC 1326 (Ch); [2007] 3 E.G.L.R. 44, where the exceptional circumstances included the fact that person had built on land mistakenly included in his title.

[902] LRA 2002 Sch.4 para.4(a); LRR 2003 r.126.

[903] See above, para.7–132.

[904] See LRA 2002 Sch.4 para.3.

[905] See above, para.7–040; and see LRA 2002 s.131.

[906] LRA 2002 s.131(1). The requirement that the land should be physically in his possession means that there is no place for the rebuttable presumption, applied in relation to LRA 1925, that a proprietor is in possession of the land comprised in the registered title: see *Kingsalton Ltd v Thames Water Developments Ltd* [2001] EWCA Civ 20 at [21], [23], [51]; [2002] 1 P. & C.R. 184 at 191, 197.

(ii) physically in the possession of some other person who is entitled to be registered as proprietor[907]; and

(iii) treated as being in the registered proprietor's possession in certain specified situations, e.g. where the land is in the possession of his tenant or licensee.[908]

Where the proprietor is in possession for these purposes, the court may not order the rectification of the register unless:

(i) the proprietor consents;

(ii) the proprietor has by fraud or lack of proper care caused or substantially contributed to the mistake; or

(iii) it would for any other reason be unjust for the alteration not to be made.[909]

It is for the party seeking rectification to prove the exception.[910] As regards (ii), it is not necessary that the proprietor has caused the mistake in the sense that, but for his conduct, the mistake would not have occurred. It is enough that his conduct, although not the only cause, substantially contributed to the mistake.[911] Grounds (ii) and (iii) will generally be determined according to the facts and through the exercise of discretion rather than on precedent.[912] The effect of the indemnity provisions[913] may be relevant to the exercise of discretion,[914] and this is particularly so under the 2002 Act, where rectification and indemnity are intended to be correlatives.[915] Another circumstance that may be relevant is that the proprietor in possession is the first registered

---

[907] LRA 2002 s.131(1).

[908] LRA 2002 s.131(2),

[909] LRA 2002 Sch.4 para.3(2).

[910] *Sainsbury's Supermarkets Ltd v Olympia Homes Ltd* [2005] EWHC 1235 (Ch) at [90]; [2006] 1 P. & C.R. 289 at 326. See [2005] Conv. 447 (M.J.D.).

[911] See *Prestige Properties Ltd v Scottish Provident Institution* [2002] EWHC 330 (Ch) at [36]; [2003] Ch. 1 at 15 (a decision on the indemnity provisions in LRA 1925 s.83). It is not enough that the proprietor caused or contributed to the registration (rather than the mistake): *Sainsbury's Supermarkets Ltd v Olympia Homes Ltd* [2005] EWHC 1235 (Ch) at [86]; [2006] 1 P. & C.R. 289 at 323.

[912] Thus, e.g., in *James Hay Pension Trustees Ltd v Cooper Estates Ltd* [2005] EWHC 36 (Ch), the court ordered rectification of a transfer, which included land that the parties had not intended to be sold. There was in consequence a mistake in the register because the rectification of the transfer related back to the time that it was executed (see *Earl of Malmesbury v Countess of Malmesbury* (1862) 31 Beav. 407 at 418). Rectification of the register was ordered because the defendant was "the accidental owner of a small parcel of land which it never intended to acquire and which is of no use to it save as a means of extracting a ransom payment": [2005] EWHC 36 (Ch) at [41], per Hart J.

[913] See LRA 2002 Sch.8; below, paras 7–140 et seq.

[914] See *Epps v Esso Petroleum Co Ltd* [1973] 1 W.L.R. 1071 at 1081 et seq. The contrary was held in *Nouri v Marvi* [2006] 1 E.G.L.R. 71, also a case on LRA 1925 s.82(3), but *Epps* was not cited.

[915] Rectification is an alteration of the register that prejudicially affects the title of a registered proprietor: LRA 2002 Sch.4 para.1; above, para.7–132.

proprietor and an incumbrance affecting the property has been mistakenly omitted from his title on first registration. Even though the first registered proprietor may not be to blame for the omission, he benefits if the register is not rectified because the effect of first registration means that he takes free of the incumbrance.[916] This can work hardship in the exceptional cases where the incumbrancer is unable to recover indemnity, as where he had the right to mines and minerals.[917]

Where the court can order rectification of the register, whether because the proprietor is not in possession or, if he is, because one of the exceptions mentioned above is established, the court must order rectification of the register unless there are exceptional circumstances which justify its not doing so.[918]

7–136   (3) THE EFFECT OF RECTIFICATION. The powers relating to rectification extend to changing for the future the priority of any interest affecting the registered estate or charge concerned.[919] Because the effect of rectification is therefore prospective from the date of the order,[920] where the court orders rectification of the register:

(i)   It affects the proprietor of the registered estate or charge from the time that rectification is ordered.[921]

(ii) It affects the priority of any interest affecting the registered estate or charge concerned that is created or arises after rectification is ordered.

(iii) It does not affect the priority of derivative estates and interests that were created between the time of the mistake and the order for rectification.[922]

7–137   *(c) Alteration by the registrar.* There are four grounds upon which the registrar may alter the register.[923] The first three grounds are the same as those upon which the court may order the alteration of the register, namely, (i) for the purposes of correcting a mistake; (ii) bringing the register up to date; and

---

[916] See LRA 2002 s.11; above, para.7–026.

[917] LRA 2002 Sch.8 para.2; below, para.7–141. A court might be required to rectify the register on such facts by HRA 1998 s.3, in order to comply with Article 1 of Protocol 1 of ECHR (deprivation of property); cf. *Kingsalton Ltd v Thames Water Developments Ltd* [2001] EWCA Civ 20 at [30], [45]; [2002] 1 P. & C.R. 184 at 193, 196.

[918] LRA 2002 Sch.2 para.3(3).

[919] LRA 2002 Sch.4 para.8.

[920] Retrospective rectification would do violence to the integrity of the register and therefore, in this respect, rectification of the register differs from rectification of an instrument, which is retrospective to the making of the instrument: see above, para.7–135, fn.912. The better view is that the law was the same under LRA 1925: see the judgment of Arden L.J. in *Malory Enterprises Ltd v Cheshire Homes Ltd* [2002] EWCA Civ 151 at [71]–[79]; [2002] Ch. 216 at 233–236. cf. Clarke and Schiemann L.JJ., at [87], [89]; p. 238.

[921] *Sainsbury's Supermarkets Ltd v Olympia Homes Ltd* [2005] EWHC 1235 (Ch) at [96]; [2006] 1 P. & C.R. 289 at 328.

[922] *Sainsbury's Supermarkets Ltd v Olympia Homes Ltd* [2005] EWHC 1235 (Ch) at [96]; [2006] 1 P. & C.R. 289 at 328.

[923] LRA 2002 Sch.4 para.5.

(iii) giving effect to any estate, right, or interest excepted from the effect of registration.[924] The fourth ground, which overlaps with the second, is for the purpose of removing a superfluous entry.[925] This is an important power, which enables the registrar, whether on application or of his own volition, to remove spent entries in the register, as where a lease or charge has determined. It is essential that the registrar should have this power if the register is to be an accurate reflection of the title at any given time.[926] There are a number of provisions in the Land Registration Rules 2003 which are concerned with the removal of spent entries, either on application or otherwise. Specific provision is made in relation to applications to the registrar on the determination of registered estates (other than freeholds),[927] certain notices,[928] and registered charges.[929] There is also a general provision applicable in all other cases, where there is either an application by the registrar to alter the register,[930] or the registrar is considering altering the register without an application having been made.[931] In such circumstances, the registrar is normally required to give notice of the proposed alteration to the registered proprietor of the registered estate, the registered proprietor of any registered charge, and any person who appears to the registrar to have the benefit of a notice.[932] If there is an application to alter the register and some person objects to that application, the usual provisions as to disputed applications will apply.[933] Where the registrar alters the register of his own volition without an application, his decision to do so can only be challenged by judicial review.[934]

The principles that govern rectification by the court, including the limita- **7–138** tions on rectification where there is a registered proprietor in possession,[935] apply equally to rectification by the registrar.[936] However, no rules have been made as to when the registrar *must* exercise his power to alter the register in cases that do not amount to rectification of the register.[937]

---

[924] LRA 2002 Sch.4 para.5(a)–(c).

[925] LRA 200 Sch.4 para.5(d).

[926] See above, para.6–041.

[927] LRR 2003 r.79.

[928] LRR 2003 r.87; above, 7–073.

[929] LRR 2003 rr.114, 115. The registrar requires proof of discharge whether on Form DS1 or electronically by means of an "ED" (electronic discharge), together with an application to alter the register: LRR 2003 rr.114, 115. However, there is provision by which the registrar may accept and act on proof of satisfaction of a charge without application: LRR 2003 r.114(4). This is important: one element of electronic conveyancing is an ED without any application to the registrar. The lender's computer sends notification of the discharge of the charge to the registry's computer and the charge is then automatically removed from the register: see LRPG 31 at Part 7. This practice is only possible because the registrar has authority under LRA 2002 Sch.4 para.5, to alter the register to bring it up to date and remove spent entries without the need for an application.

[930] For the evidence required, see LRR 2003 r.129.

[931] LRR 2003 r.128.

[932] LRR 2003 r.128(2).

[933] See above, para.7–129.

[934] See above, para.7–022.

[935] See above, para.7–135.

[936] LRA 2002 Sch.4 para.6.

[937] For the power to make such rules, see LRA 2002 Sch.4 para.7(a). For the rules made in relation to alteration by the court, see above, para.7–134.

Where the register is altered in a case not involving rectification, the registrar has a power to pay costs in such amount as he thinks fit in respect of any costs or expenses reasonably incurred by a person in connection with the alteration,[938] as where a person incurs costs in investigating whether an entry in the register is spent. The registrar may make such a payment if the costs and expenses had to be incurred urgently and it was not reasonably practicable to apply for his consent.[939] He may also give retrospective approval for costs and expenses already incurred.[940]

7–139 *(d) Standing to seek alteration.* There is no statutory provision as to who may make an application to the court or to the registrar to alter the register. It might therefore be expected that any person may make such an application, whether or not they have any direct interest in the matter, just as any person may object to an application (subject to two exceptions).[941] While it has been assumed that a person must have an interest in order to make such an application,[942] the adjudicator has taken a contrary view,[943] and it is suggested that that is the correct position. Although there is no express statutory duty to act reasonably in making an application to alter the register[944]:

(i) in the case of an application to the court, it has ample case management powers to strike out proceedings which are brought without reasonable cause[945]; and

(ii) in the case of an application to the registrar, the registered proprietor (or indeed any other person) could object to the application in the usual way.[946]

3. Indemnity

7–140 *(a) Entitlement.* A person is entitled to be indemnified by the registrar if he suffers loss by reason of any of the following.[947]

(i) The rectification of the register.[948] This is the commonest situation in which indemnity is paid. As explained above, rectification is an alteration that entails the correction of a mistake and prejudicially

---

[938] LRA 2002 Sch.4 para.9(1). This power was new in the LRA 2002.
[939] LRA 2002 Sch.4 para.9(2)(a).
[940] LRA 2002 Sch.4 para.9(2)(b).
[941] LRA 2002 s.73; above, para.7–129.
[942] *Wells v Pilling Parish Council* [2008] EWHC 556 (Ch); [2008] 2 E.G.L.R. 29. The only issue in that case was whether the issue of standing was a matter of public or private law. Lewison J. held that it was a matter of private law, it being common ground that in those circumstances standing to apply was required.
[943] *Burton v Walker* (2009) REF/2007/1124 at [23] and following, distinguishing *Wells v Pilling Parish Council.*
[944] cf. LRA 2002 s.77; above, paras 7–046, 7–075, 7–076.
[945] See CPR Pt 3.4.
[946] LRA 2002 s.73; above, para.7–129.
[947] LRA 2002 Sch.8 para.1(1).
[948] LRA 2002 Sch.8 para.1(1)(a).

affects the title of a registered proprietor.[949] There are two special cases where a person is treated as having suffered loss by reason of rectification of the register:

(a) Where he suffers loss by reason of the upgrading of a title.[950]

(b) Where the register is rectified against a proprietor of a registered estate or charge claiming in good faith under a forged disposition. He is treated as having suffered loss by reason of rectification as if the disposition had not been forged.[951] If it were not for this provision, the registered proprietor would recover no indemnity. Because a forged disposition is a nullity, he would not be regarded as suffering loss.[952]

(ii) A mistake whose correction would involve rectification of the register.[953] If the register is rectified and a person suffers loss by reason of that rectification, that loss is recoverable under the previous paragraph. If, however, the register is not rectified, the person who is the victim of the mistake is likely to suffer loss and, if so, is entitled to an indemnity under this paragraph. Even if the register is rectified in favour of an applicant, he may still suffer loss because rectification is prospective and does not affect rights and interests created in the period between the mistake and its rectification.[954] For example, if a registered charge in the register is deleted in error and a further charge is then created and registered, the first chargee will lose its priority even if the charge is subsequently restored to the register. No indemnity is payable under this paragraph until a decision has been made as to whether the register should be altered to correct the mistake. The loss is determined in the light of that decision.[955]

(iii) A mistake in an official search.[956]

(iv) A mistake in an official copy.[957]

(v) A mistake in a document kept by the registrar which is not an original and is referred to in the register.[958]

---

[949] LRA 2002 Sch.4 para.1: see para.7–132.

[950] LRA 2002 Sch.8 para.1(2)(a). For the upgrading of titles, see LRA 2002 s.62; above, paras 7–039 et seq.

[951] LRA 2002 Sch.8 para.1(2)(b).

[952] See *Att Gen v Odell* [1906] 2 Ch. 47 (reversed by LRA 1925 s.83(4)).

[953] LRA 2002 Sch.8 para.1(1)(b).

[954] See LRA 2002 Sch.4 para.8; above, para.7–136. For a case where loss was suffered in this situation under LRA 1925 see *Freer v Unwins Ltd* [1976] Ch. 288.

[955] LRA 2002 Sch.8 para.1(3).

[956] LRA 2002 Sch.8 para.1(1)(c). Official searches have been explained above, para.7–124.

[957] LRA 2002 Sch.8 para.1(1)(d). For official copies, see above, para.7–120.

[958] LRA 2002 Sch.8 para.1(1)(e). See above, para.7–122.

(vi) The loss or destruction of a document lodged at the registry for inspection or safe custody.[959]

(vii) A mistake in the cautions register.[960]

(viii) A failure by the registrar to give notice of the creation of an overriding statutory charge to the proprietor of any registered charge or charge protected by notice in relation to the registered estate affected.[961]

A "mistake" for the purposes of these provisions includes something mistakenly omitted as well as something mistakenly included.[962] Rectification has the meaning already explained, namely, an alteration which involves the correction of a mistake and prejudicially affects the title of a registered proprietor.[963] A person suffers loss by reason of one of the factors set out above, if the error was an effective cause of the loss, even if it was not the principal or sole effective cause of the loss.[964]

Application for an indemnity may be made by way of a letter to the registrar[965] or to the court. A court may determine any question as to whether the claimant is entitled to an indemnity or the amount of any such indemnity.[966] In practice, issues of indemnity will often arise out of an application to rectify the register, whether before the court or the adjudicator, and will be addressed as part of the resolution of that issue.

For the purposes of the Limitation Act 1980, the right to an indemnity is a simple contract debt, and the cause of action arises at the time when the claimant knows, or but for his own default might have known of the existence of his claim.[967] Accordingly, it will be barred six years from that date.[968]

7–141   On first registration it may be difficult for the registrar to ascertain whether the mines and minerals have been severed from the land, or whether the land is former copyhold where, on enfranchisement, the lord's right to the minerals were reserved.[969] Because of these difficulties,[970] no indemnity is payable on

---

[959] LRA 2002 Sch.8 para.1(1)(f).

[960] LRA 2002 Sch.8 para.1(1)(g). For the cautions register, see above, para.7–044.

[961] LRA 2002 Sch.8 para.1(1)(h). For the registrar's duty to give notification of such overriding statutory charges, see LRA 2002 s.50; above, para.7–068.

[962] LRA 2002 Sch.8 para.11(1).

[963] LRA 2002 Sch.8 para.11(2). See above, para.7–132.

[964] *Prestige Properties Ltd v Scottish Provident Institution* [2002] EWHC 330 (Ch) at [35], [36]; [2003] Ch. 1 at 14–15. See too *Dean v Dean* (2000) 80 P. & C.R. 457.

[965] There is no prescribed form of application. See LRPG 39, para.5.2, explaining the information that should be given in the letter.

[966] LRA 2002 Sch.8 para.7(1). A successful applicant is presumptively entitled to the costs of any such application on an indemnity basis rather than on the standard basis: see *Prestige Properties Ltd v Scottish Provident Institution* [2002] EWHC 330 (Ch) at [73], [74]; [2003] Ch. 1 at 28. See further below, para.7–144.

[967] LRA 2002 Sch.8 para.8.

[968] See LA 1980 s.5.

[969] For the reservation of mines ands minerals on the enfranchisement of copyhold, see above, 2–029.

[970] See (2001) Law Com. No.271, para.10.39.

account of, or the existence of any right to work or get, any mines or minerals, unless it is noted in the register to the registered title that the registered estate concerned includes the mines or minerals.[971]

(b) Measure. The award of an indemnity is the means by which a registered **7–142** title is state guaranteed.[972] The measure of indemnity flows from its nature:

(i) It is an *indemnity* and it is payable for the loss that the person suffers "by reason of" any of the factors set out above.[973] This entitles him to recover both direct and consequential losses.[974]

(ii) Interest is payable on that loss,[975] at the rate for court judgment debts,[976] from the time when it occurs until the payment of indemnity.[977]

(iii) Where an indemnity is payable in respect of the loss of an estate, interest or charge:

    (a) Where the register is rectified,[978] the measure of indemnity is its value immediately before the rectification of the register, but as if there were to be no rectification.[979] Interest is payable on that sum from the date of rectification until payment.[980]

    (b) Where, however, the mistake is one whose correction would involve rectification of the register,[981] the measure is the value of the estate, interest or charge at the time when the mistake which caused the loss was made.[982] Interest is payable from the date when loss was suffered by reason of the mistake, until the payment of indemnity.[983]

(iv) There is no statutory limit on the recovery of indemnity in any case where the loss suffered is not of an estate, interest or charge.[984]

The claimant's entitlement to costs is explained below.[985]

---

[971] LRA 2002 Sch.8 para.2. cf. para.7–135, above.

[972] See above, para.7–001.

[973] LRA 2002 Sch.8 para.1: see para.7–140.

[974] See (2001) Law Com. No.271, para.10.41.

[975] LRA 2002 Sch.8 para.9; LRR 2003 r.195(1).

[976] LRR 2003 r.195(3).

[977] LRR 2003 r.195(2).

[978] That is in a case within LRA 2002 Sch.8 para.1(1)(a); above para.7–140.

[979] LRA 2002 Sch.8 para.6(a).

[980] LRA 2002 Sch.8 para.9; LRR 2003 rr.195(1), (2)(a), (3).

[981] That is in a case within LRA 2002 Sch.8 para.1(1)(b); above para.7–140.

[982] LRA 2002 Sch.8 para.6(b). For the reasons why this is the relevant date, see (2001) Law Com. No.271, para.10.43

[983] LRA 2002 Sch.8 para.9; LRR 2003 rr.195(1), (2)(b), (3).

[984] *Prestige Properties Ltd v Scottish Provident Institution* [2002] EWHC 330 (Ch) at [36]; [2003] Ch. 1 at 15.

[985] See para.7–144.

7–143   No indemnity is payable on account of any loss suffered by a claimant in two circumstances:

(i) Where that loss was suffered wholly or partly as a result of his own fraud.[986] Any fraud on the part of the claimant that was an effective cause of his loss will bar his claim.

(ii) Where the claimant's loss was suffered wholly as a result of his lack of proper care.[987] For this bar to indemnity to apply, the claimant's lack of proper care must have been the sole cause of his loss.[988]

By contrast, where loss is suffered by a claimant partly as a result of his own lack of proper care, any indemnity payable to him will be reduced to such extent as is fair having regard to his share of responsibility for the loss.[989] This means that the amount of any indemnity will be reduced where the claimant (or his agent)[990] was contributorily negligent in relation either to the occurrence of the loss or in mitigating or limiting that loss.[991] The relevant conduct will normally be that of the claimant's conveyancer, and the care to be expected of the claimant may be judged by reference to the ordinary duty of care owed by a conveyancer in the conveyancing transaction in question.[992]

These limitations on the right to indemnity apply not only to the claimant's own fraud or lack of proper care, but also to that of a person from whom he derived title other than under a disposition for valuable consideration.[993]

7–144   *(c) Costs.* The right to indemnity includes a right to recover costs and expenses, but only if they were reasonably incurred by the claimant with the consent of the registrar,[994] unless:

(i) the costs or expenses had to be incurred urgently and it was not reasonably practicable to apply for the registrar's consent[995]; or

---

[986] LRA 2002 Sch.8 para.5(1)(a).

[987] LRA 2002 Sch.8 para.5(1)(b).

[988] *Dean v Dean* (2000) 80 P. & C.R. 457. Asking whether the loss would have been suffered "but for" the claimant's negligent conduct will rarely be helpful, because it will not establish that the claimant's lack of care was the sole effective cause of his loss: see 462 and 464–5.

[989] LRA 2002 Sch.8 para.5(2).

[990] But not a third party. It is the claimant's "*own* lack of proper care" that is relevant: see *Prestige Properties Ltd v Scottish Provident Institution* [2002] EWHC 330 (Ch) at [36]; [2003] Ch. 1 at 15.

[991] *Prestige Properties Ltd v Scottish Provident Institution* [2002] EWHC 330 (Ch) at [36]; [2003] Ch. 1 at 15.

[992] *Prestige Properties Ltd v Scottish Provident Institution* [2002] EWHC 330 (Ch) at [36]; [2003] Ch. 1 at 16.

[993] LRA 2002 Sch.8 para.5(3).

[994] LRA 2002 Sch.8 para.3(1). This requirement will be met if the registrar gives his retrospective consent after costs and expenses have been incurred: LRA 2002 Sch.8 para.3(3).

[995] LRA 2002 Sch.8 para.3(2).

(ii) the claimant applied to the court to determine his entitlement to an indemnity.[996]

Even if no indemnity is otherwise payable, the registrar has a power to pay such costs and expenses reasonably incurred by the claimant with the consent of the registrar in connection with a claim to indemnity.[997] The registrar may make such a payment in respect of costs or expenses which had to be incurred urgently and where it was not reasonably practicable to apply for his consent.[998] The sort of circumstances in which it will be appropriate for the registrar to make such payment would be where a claimant had to incur costs and expenses in determining whether there had been a mistake entitling him to indemnity.[999]

(d) Rights of recourse. Where an indemnity is paid (which includes any **7–145** payment of interest[1000]), the registrar is given certain rights of recourse against those whose conduct may have led to the payment.

First, he is entitled to recover the amount paid from any person who caused or substantially contributed to the loss by his fraud.[1001]

Second, for the purpose of recovering the amount paid he is entitled to enforce any right of action (of whatever nature and however arising) which the claimant would have been entitled to enforce had the indemnity not been paid.[1002] If, for example, the successful claimant could have sued his solicitor for negligence in such circumstances, the registrar may sue the solicitor for that negligence. The registrar's position is analogous to that of an insurer who is subrogated to the assured's rights of action against a tortfeasor.

Third, where the register has been rectified, the registrar is entitled to enforce any right of action (of whatever nature and however arising) which the person in whose favour the register has been rectified would have been entitled to enforce had it not been rectified.[1003] This right goes beyond any right of subrogation that an insurer would have. It means, for example, that if rectification is ordered in favour of A because of the negligence of A's solicitor, and indemnity is paid to the other party to the transaction, B, who suffers loss by reason of that rectification, the registrar can recover the amount of that indemnity from A's solicitor, even though B might not have been able to do so, because A's solicitor owed B no duty of care.[1004]

---

[996] LRA 2002 Sch.8 Para.7(2). For applications to the court, see above, para.7–140.

[997] LRA 2002 Sch.8 para.4(1). This requirement will be met if the registrar gives his retrospective consent after costs and expenses have been incurred: LRA 2002 Sch.8 para.4(2)(b).

[998] LRA 2002 Sch.8 para.4(2)(a).

[999] See (2001) Law Com. No.271, para.10.46.

[1000] LRA 2002 Sch.8 para.10(3).

[1001] LRA 2002 Sch.8 para.10(1)(a).

[1002] LRA 2002 Sch.8 para.10(1)(b), (2)(a).

[1003] LRA 2002 Sch.8 para.10(1)(b), (2)(b).

[1004] See (2001) Law Com. No.271, para.10.52.

Part 6

CONVEYANCING

7–146   **1. Introduction.** The register of title and the system of title registration have transformed the way in which conveyancing is conducted and there will be further fundamental changes as the introduction of electronic conveyancing proceeds. In this Part, the course of a typical conveyancing transaction involving a registered title is followed to show the significance of the register at the various stages in the conveyancing process.

7–147   **2. Contract.** Where the parties have contracted to sell a property, it is possible for the purchaser to protect the estate contract by entering an agreed or unilateral notice.[1005] In practice, it is only contracts that may last for some time, such as options, rights of pre-emption and conditional contracts, which are so protected. Instead, as has been explained, a purchaser will protect his position pending completion by a priority search of the register.[1006]

7–148   **3. Proving title.** Because of the open register,[1007] there are no longer any provisions as to how a seller of registered land has to prove his title.[1008] Although there is a power to make rules with respect to proof of title or perfection of title, that power has not been exercised. It is therefore a matter of contract between the parties as to the proof of title that a purchaser will require.[1009] The seller must deduce title in the manner agreed.

It is the register that proves a seller's title and it also shows the incumbrances to which that title is subject, except for those unregistered interests which override a registered disposition.

7–149   **4. The transfer.** A specimen form of transfer is set out below. Two points may be noted about that form. First, Box 9 refers to the covenants for title, which are explained below.[1010] Second, although in Box 10, provision is made for a declaration of trust, the making of such a declaration, although highly desirable, is not mandatory.[1011]

[1005] See above, paras 7–073, 7–074.
[1006] See above, para.7–125.
[1007] See above, para.7–002.
[1008] As there were previously under LRA 1925 s.110.
[1009] cf. Standard Conditions of Sale (4th edn), c.4.1.1, 4.1.2, by which the seller must provide the buyer with official copies of the register and of any document referred to in it that is kept by the registrar.
[1010] See para.7–151.
[1011] By LRA 2002 s.78, the registrar is not to be affected with notice of a trust. cf. *Stack v Dowden* [2007] UKHL 17 at [52]; [2007] 2 A.C. 432 at 453.

Land Registry
Transfer of whole of registered title(s)

If you need more room than is provided for in a panel, and your software allows, you can expand any panel in the form. Alternatively use continuation sheet CS and attach it to this form.

Leave blank if not yet registered.	1	Title number(s) of the property:
Insert address including postcode (if any) or other description of the property, for example 'land adjoining 2 Acacia Avenue'.	2	Property:
	3	Date:
Give full name(s).	4	Transferor:
Complete as appropriate where the transferor is a company.		For UK incorporated companies/LLPs Registered number of company or limited liability partnership including any prefix: For overseas companies (a) Territory of incorporation: (b) Registered number in the United Kingdom including any prefix:
Give full name(s).	5	Transferee for entry in the register:
Complete as appropriate where the transferee is a company. Also, for an overseas company, unless an arrangement with Land Registry exists, lodge either a certificate in Form 7 in Schedule 3 to the Land Registration Rules 2003 or a certified copy of the constitution in English or Welsh, or other evidence permitted by rule 183 of the Land Registration Rules 2003.		For UK incorporated companies/LLPs Registered number of company or limited liability partnership including any prefix: For overseas companies (a) Territory of incorporation: (b) Registered number in the United Kingdom including any prefix:
Each transferee may give up to three addresses for service, one of which must be a postal address whether or not in the UK (including the postcode, if any). The others can be any combination of a postal address, a UK DX box number or an electronic address.	6	Transferee's intended address(es) for service for entry in the register:
	7	The transferor transfers the property to the transferee

Place 'X' in the appropriate box. State the currency unit if other than sterling. If none of the boxes apply, insert an appropriate memorandum in panel 11.

8   Consideration

☐ The transferor has received from the transferee for the property the following sum (in words and figures):

☐ The transfer is not for money or anything that has a monetary value

☐ Insert other receipt as appropriate:

Place 'X' in any box that applies.

Add any modifications.

9   The transferor transfers with

☐ full title guarantee

☐ limited title guarantee

Where the transferee is more than one person, place 'X' in the appropriate box.

10   Declaration of trust. The transferee is more than one person and

☐ they are to hold the property on trust for themselves as joint tenants

☐ they are to hold the property on trust for themselves as tenants in common in equal shares

Complete as necessary.

☐ they are to hold the property on trust:

Insert here any required or permitted statement, certificate or application and any agreed covenants, declarations and so on.

11   Additional provisions

The transferor must execute this transfer as a deed using the space opposite. If there is more than one transferor, all must execute. Forms of execution are given in Schedule 9 to the Land Registration Rules 2003. If the transfer contains transferee's covenants or declarations or contains an application by the transferee (such as for a restriction), it must also be executed by the transferee.

12 Execution

WARNING
If you dishonestly enter information or make a statement that you know is, or might be, untrue or misleading, and intend by doing so to make a gain for yourself or another person, or to cause loss or the risk of loss to another person, you may commit the offence of fraud under section 1 of the Fraud Act 2006, the maximum penalty for which is 10 years' imprisonment or an unlimited fine, or both.

Failure to complete this form with proper care may result in a loss of protection under the Land Registration Act 2002 if, as a result, a mistake is made in the register.

Under section 66 of the Land Registration Act 2002 most documents (including this form) kept by the registrar relating to an application to the registrar or referred to in the register are open to public inspection and copying. If you believe a document contains prejudicial information, you may apply for that part of the document to be made exempt using Form EX1, under rule 136 of the Land Registration Rules 2003.

© Crown copyright (ref: LR/HO) 07/09

7–150   **5. The "registration gap".** As between the parties, the transfer, or indeed
any registrable disposition, takes effect from the date that it is executed.[1012]
However, as has been explained, registration has effect from the time of the
making of the application to register a registrable disposition.[1013] There is,
accordingly, a hiatus between the disposition and its registration.[1014] The
existence of this so-called "registration gap" leads to difficulties.

One particular concern was that during the period between the making of a
disposition and its registration, a person might be allowed into actual occupation and might be granted an interest in land by the disponor which might then
bind the disponee.[1015] This was overcome by judicial decision,[1016] and the
result is incorporated in the provisions of the Land Registration Act 2002.
Although the date at which an interest must be protected if it is not to be
overridden by a registered disposition for valuable consideration is the date at
which that disposition is registered,[1017] the date at which a person must both
own the relevant interest and be in actual occupation is the date of the
disposition.[1018]

It is however possible that a disponor could terminate a registered estate or
interest after the disposition was made but before it was registered. In one
case, after a lessee had assigned a registered leasehold, but before the assignee
had been registered as proprietor, the assignor purported to determine the lease
under a break clause that was personal to the assignor. It was held that the
lease had been determined.[1019]

In many cases, because the disponee will be entitled to the particular estate
or interest in equity pending registration,[1020] he will have the same rights as
if he had been registered.[1021] For example, where a registered freeholder has
assigned the reversion on a lease, the assignee of the reversion was entitled to
forfeit the lease by peaceable re-entry, even though it had not yet been
registered as proprietor of the freehold.[1022]

[1012] "Once the transfer . . . has been executed the die has been cast": *Lloyds Bank Plc v Rosset*
[1989] Ch. 350 at 372, per Nicholls L.J. (on appeal) [1991] 1 A.C. 107). See too *Abbey National
B.S. v Cann* [1991] 1 A.C. 56 at 84.

[1013] LRA 2002 s.74; above, para.7–114. There are no direct sanctions to compel the expeditious
registration of a registrable disposition (cf. compulsory first registration, above, para.7–019).
However, until the registration requirements are met, the disposition takes effect in equity only:
see LRA 2002 s.27(1); above, para.7–053.

[1014] See above, para.7–124.

[1015] See the discussion in relation to overriding interests under LRA 1925 in (1998) Law Com.
No.254, para.5–112.

[1016] See *Abbey National B.S. v Cann* [1991] 1 A.C. 56.

[1017] See LRA 2002 ss.29(1), 30(1); above, para.7–061.

[1018] LRA 2002 Sch.3 para.2; above, para.7–089.

[1019] *Brown & Root Technology Ltd v Sun Alliance and London Assurance Co Ltd* [2001] Ch.
733. The case turned primarily on the terms of the lease.

[1020] See LRA 2002 s.27(1); above, para.7–053.

[1021] Indeed, LRA 2002 contains a number of provisions which apply equally to a person who
is entitled to be registered as to a registered proprietor: see, e.g., LRA 2002 s.24(b) (exercise of
owner's powers); s.34(3)(a) (application for an agreed notice); s.36(1)(b) (application to cancel a
unilateral notice); s.43(1) (application for a restriction); s.62(7)(b) (application to upgrade title);
s.131(1) (definition of proprietor in possession).

[1022] *Scribes West Ltd v Relsa Anstalt (No.3)* [2004] EWCA Civ 1744; [2005] 1 W.L.R.
1847.

When electronic conveyancing is introduced, the registration gap will disappear because dispositions will be simultaneously registered.[1023]

6. Covenants for title

(a) The nature of covenants for title. In box 10 of the Transfer set out above,[1024] the words "with full title guarantee" are important and their effect must be explained in detail. They imply covenants for title on the part of the seller, which are the nearest thing to a guarantee that the purchaser receives from the seller.[1025] The remedy for their breach is damages and they are the principal (and often only) remedy available to a purchaser of land after completion of a sale, if it subsequently transpires that there was some defect in the seller's title. The present law is found in the Law of Property (Miscellaneous Provisions) Act 1994, which implemented in amended form recommendations made by the Law Commission.[1026] It applies to conveyances made after June 1995.[1027]

7–151

(b) When the covenants will be implied. Under the 1994 Act, covenants for title may be implied into any instrument made after June 1995, effecting or purporting to effect a disposition of property, whether or not for valuable consideration.[1028] For these purposes, "disposition" expressly includes the grant of a lease,[1029] but it will also include, e.g. the grant of an easement. The new covenants (unlike the old) may therefore apply where a landlord grants a lease.[1030] They may also apply to dispositions of property other than land, including assignments of choses in action.[1031] Covenants for title will be implied only if the disposition is expressed to be made with either full or limited title guarantee.[1032] These are a matter for negotiation between the parties to the disposition. They are not a consequence of the capacity of the person making the disposition. A feature of the covenants implied by the 1994 Act is that they are expressed in plain and straightforward language, in contrast to the position prior to July 1995.[1033]

7–152

[1023] LRA 2002 s.93; below, para.7–163.

[1024] para.7–149.

[1025] As has been explained, a seller is under an obligation to deduce a title in accordance with the terms of the contract of sale: see above, para.7–148. This obligation, like most others under the contract, is merged in the deed of conveyance and no action lies for its breach thereafter: see generally *Knight Sugar Co Ltd v The Alberta Railway & Irrigation Co* [1938] 1 All E.R. 266 at 269. For the doctrine of merger, see below, para.15–100.

[1026] See (1991) Law Com. No.199.

[1027] For an account of the law applicable to covenants implied in conveyances executed before July 1, 1995, see the sixth edition of this work at paras 5–048—5–065.

[1028] LP(MP)A 1994 s.1(2).

[1029] LP(MP)A 1994 s.1(4).

[1030] See below, para.19–018.

[1031] LP(MP)A 1994 s.1(4).

[1032] LP(MP)A 1994 s.1(2). For the Welsh equivalents, see s.8(4). See box 9 of Form TR1, above, at para.7–149.

[1033] For the terms of the covenants implied before July 1995, see LPA 1925 Sch.2 (now repealed).

7–153   *(c) The covenants: full title guarantee.* Where a disposition is made with full title guarantee, the person making the disposition[1034] impliedly covenants[1035] that:

> (i) he has the right[1036] to dispose of the property as he purports to[1037];
>
> (ii) he will at his own cost do all that he reasonably can to give the disponee the title he purports to give[1038];
>
> (iii) the property is free from all charges, incumbrances and third party rights other than those of which the disponor neither knew nor could reasonably be expected to know[1039]; and
>
> (iv) where the disposition is of a leasehold, the lease is subsisting at the time of the disposition and that there are no subsisting breaches of the tenant's obligations that would render the lease liable to forfeiture.[1040]

As regards (i), (iii) and (iv), the disponor is not liable for:

> (a) any matter to which the disposition is expressly made subject[1041];
>
> (b) anything actually known by the disponee or which was a necessary consequence of facts of which he actually knew[1042]; and
>
> (c) where there is a disposition of an interest, the title which is registered under the Land Registration Act 2002, in addition to (a) and (b), anything which at the time of the disposition was entered in relation to that interest in the register of title under that Act.[1043]

[1034] Where a disposition is expressed to be made at the direction of a person (as where a nominee conveys at the direction of the beneficial owner, or a vendor conveys to a third party at the direction of the purchaser), the implied covenants apply to him as if he were the person making the disposition: LP(MP)A 1994 s.8(3).

[1035] LP(MP)A 1994 s.1(2)(a).

[1036] With the concurrence of any other person conveying the property.

[1037] LP(MP)A 1994 s.2(1).

[1038] LP(MP)A 1994 s.2(1). Where, as will now usually be the case, a disposition of unregistered land is required to be registered, this obligation requires the disponor to give all reasonable assistance to establish to the satisfaction of the Chief Land Registrar the right of the disponee to be registered as proprietor of the land: LP(MP)A 1994 s.2(2)(b).

[1039] LP(MP)A 1994 s.3(1). There is no liability under this covenant in respect of liabilities and third party rights imposed by statute which are merely potential (such as a power for a body compulsorily to acquire property), or which are imposed in relation to property generally (such as a liability to pay council tax): LP(MP)A 1994 s.3(2).

[1040] LP(MP)A 1994 s.4(1).

[1041] LP(MP)A 1994 s.6(1).

[1042] LP(MP)A 1994 s.6(2). cf. *Yandle & Sons v Sutton* [1922] 2 Ch. 199 at 210; below, para.15–070 (from which this provision is derived). In determining the disponee's actual knowledge, LPA 1925 s.198 (deemed notice by virtue of registration as a land charge: below, para.8–085) is disregarded: LP(MP)A 1994 s.6(3).

[1043] LP(MP)A 1994 s.6(4) (as substituted).

In the case of the disposition of an existing legal estate:

(1) Where the title is already registered, there is a presumption that the disposition is of the whole of that interest.[1044]

(2) Where the title is unregistered, then subject to the terms of the instrument, it is presumed that, if the property is a leasehold, the disponor purports to dispose of the unexpired portion of the lease. In any other case, the presumption is that the property disposed of is the fee simple.[1045]

Where the disposition is a mortgage either of property subject to rentcharge, **7–154** or of a lease, the mortgagor impliedly covenants, in addition to the covenants set out above, that he will fully and promptly observe and perform all the obligations:

(v) imposed by the rentcharge that are enforceable by the owner of it as such; or (as the case may be)

(vi) under the lease that are imposed on him in his capacity as tenant.[1046]

The operation of any of the implied covenants may be either limited or extended by a term of the instrument making the disposition,[1047] and in practice often is.

(d) The covenants: limited title guarantee. Where a disposition is made with **7–155** limited title guarantee, the position is the same as where full title guarantee is given, subject to one important exception. To the extent that they are applicable, the disponee impliedly enters into covenants (i), (ii) and (iv)–(vi) set out in the two preceding paragraphs, but not (iii).[1048] He covenants instead that he has not, since the last disposition for value, either charged or incumbered the property by means of any charge or incumbrance which subsists at the time when the disposition is made, or allowed the property to become charged or incumbered in that way,[1049] and that he is not aware that anyone else has done so.[1050]

The covenants implied by the 1994 Act do not include a covenant for quiet enjoyment, as did the covenants in conveyances prior to July 1995. The Law Commission considered that such a covenant was inappropriate, because it did not relate to the title to the property but to the enjoyment of the land

---

[1044] LP(MP)A 1994 s.2(3)(a).
[1045] LP(MP)A 1994 s.2(3)(b). In many case, the disposition will trigger compulsory registration of the title.
[1046] LP(MP)A 1994 s.5.
[1047] LP(MP)A 1994 s.8(1).
[1048] LP(MP)A 1994 s.1(2)(b).
[1049] e.g. by allowing a third party to acquire title to part of the land by adverse possession.
[1050] LP(MP)A 1994 s.3(3).

granted.[1051] If a vendor retained land adjoining the part which he had sold, the objective of the covenant for quiet enjoyment could be better achieved by the use of restrictive covenants. In practice, covenants for quiet enjoyment are rarely enforced except by tenants against their landlords.[1052] A covenant for quiet enjoyment is (and continues to be) implied at common law on the grant of a lease.[1053]

7–156   *(e) The enforceability of the covenants.* The benefit of the new covenants runs with the disponee's estate or interest in the land.[1054] They may therefore be enforced by any person in whom that estate or interest (in whole or in part) is for the time being vested.[1055] As regards the burden of the covenant, the disponor's liability is absolute. It is not limited (as it had been in covenants implied in conveyances before July 1995) to the conduct of certain persons for whom he is held responsible.[1056] The disponor's liability is therefore more extensive than under the old covenants, and this was undoubtedly the objective of the legislation.

Of the six covenants, set out above, under which a disponor may be liable,[1057] (i),[1058] (iii)[1059] and (iv)[1060] will necessarily be broken (if at all) at the time of the disposition and the right to sue on them will expire 12 years thereafter.[1061] That is not the case in relation to the other covenants. For example, breach of covenant (ii)[1062] would not occur until the disponor had refused to take the necessary steps to give the disponee the title which he had purported to give. The limitation period would run from that date.

7. Electronic conveyancing

7–157   *(a) Introduction.* The Land Registration Act 2002 created the framework for the introduction of a system of paperless conveyancing, in which all the main stages of a conveyancing transaction will be conducted electronically. Most of the detail of electronic conveyancing either is or will be contained in rules.[1063] The Act creates the necessary structure for the system and embodies its fundamental concepts. The provisions consist of just five sections[1064] and

---

[1051] (1991) Law Com. No.199, para.4.33.

[1052] See (1991) Law Com. No.199, para.4–35.

[1053] See below, para.19–003.

[1054] LP(MP)A 1994 s.7 (a provision added in the course of the passage of the legislation through Parliament under an amendment proposed by Lord Brightman). cf. (1991) Law Com. No.199, para.4.9.

[1055] LP(MP)A 1994 s.7.

[1056] See the 6th edition of this work at paras 5–054, 5–062, 5–063.

[1057] Above, paras 7–153, 7–154.

[1058] Power to dispose.

[1059] Freedom from incumbrances.

[1060] Lease subsisting and not liable to forfeiture.

[1061] The limitation period is 12 years, because the covenants are made by deed: see LA 1980 s.8; below, para.35–006.

[1062] Further assurance.

[1063] For the rule-making powers, see LRA 2002 ss.91(2)(c), (3)(d), (7); 93(1); 95; Sch.5, paras 1–3, and 5. The rules to date are the Land Registration (Network Access) Rules 2008 (S1 2008/1748) and the Land Registration (Electronic Conveyancing) Rules 2008 (SI 2008/1750).

[1064] See LRA 2002 ss.91–95.

one schedule.[1065] The most important features of the legislation are the powers conferred on the Lord Chancellor to make rules to require that specified dispositions of registered land can only be conducted by means of a document in electronic form, and that that document, when it takes effect, is simultaneously registered.[1066] The registrar is empowered to make provision for a system of electronic settlement.[1067] The actual process of making the disposition and registering it will be carried out by conveyancers who have been authorised to do so by the registrar.[1068] Electronic conveyancing is being introduced incrementally, though the Land Registry has recently announced that proposals for the introduction of electronic transfers have been postponed.[1069] The main features of the system of electronic conveyancing created by the Act are as follows.

(b) The Land Registry Network. The Act authorises the registrar to provide, **7–158** or arrange for the provision of, an electronic communications network for the purposes of electronic conveyancing.[1070] Access to this network is made available to a person who is not a member of the land registry by means of a network access agreement.[1071] It is envisaged that different property professionals, such as solicitors, licensed conveyancers, estate agents and mortgage lenders, will be able to enter into such agreements on meeting specified criteria.[1072] An agreement may authorise access for one or more of the following purposes:

    (i) the communication, posting or retrieval of information;

    (ii) the making of changes to the register of title or cautions register;

    (iii) the issue of official certificates of search;

    (iv) the issue of official copies; or

    (v) such other conveyancing purposes as the registrar thinks fit.[1073]

Furthermore, in accordance with rules, the registrar may confer authority to carry out his functions by means of such network access agreements.[1074] Such

---

[1065] See LRA 2002 Sch.5.

[1066] LRA 2002 s.93. See below, para.7–163.

[1067] LRA 2002 s.94. In other words, provision will be made to ensure that all the monies for the purchase are transferred electronically.

[1068] Though provision will be made for those who wish to carry out their own conveyancing: see LRA 2002 Sch.5 para.7.

[1069] See the Land Registry's *Report on Responses to E-Conveyancing Secondary Legislation Part 3* (2011).

[1070] LRA 2002 s.92(1).

[1071] LRA 2002 Sch.5 paras 1, 2; Land Registration (Network Access) Rules 2008.

[1072] The criteria are laid down by rules and the registrar is required to enter into a network access agreement with an applicant who meets those criteria: LRA 2002 Sch.5 para.1(4); Land Registration (Network Access) Rules 2008 r.4.

[1073] LRA 2002 Sch.5 para.1(2). Under the Land Registration (Network Access) Rules 2008 there are three grades of network access: see r.3.

[1074] LRA 2002 Sch.5 para.1(3).

agreements may therefore be used to authorise conveyancers to carry out the process of registration, though the present rules do not extend to registration except in relation to electronic charges.[1075] The terms on which access to the land registry network may be authorised may include requirements to ensure that the network is employed for specified transactions, thereby ensuring that they must be carried out electronically.[1076] Furthermore, it is a term of such an agreement that transactions are carried out in accordance with network transaction rules.[1077] Such rules will explain "how to go about network transactions",[1078] which include provision about the procedure to be followed and the supply of information.[1079]

7–159   Obligations under a network access agreement override any obligation that the person authorised might owe, e.g., in his professional capacity.[1080] Thus, even if a solicitor's client did not want a transaction carried out electronically, the solicitor would be bound nonetheless to carry it out electronically. It is envisaged that when electronic conveyancing is introduced, electronic documents may be authenticated by a client's solicitor or licensed conveyancer. A conveyancer has no implied authority to sign a document on behalf of his client and can do so only if he has the actual authority of his client.[1081] Standard forms of authority will be employed to ensure that a conveyancer does in fact have actual authority to authenticate an electronic document. The Act creates a presumption of authority where a person authorised under a network access agreement uses the network for the purpose of making a disposition or contract on behalf of his client.[1082] The presumption applies where the agent authenticates the electronic disposition or contract as agent and the document contains a statement that he is acting under the authority of his principal.[1083]

7–160   A person who has access to the network granted by a network access agreement may terminate the agreement at any time by notice to the registrar.[1084] There is also power for the registrar to terminate a network access agreement. The details are in rules.[1085] Those rules empower the registrar to terminate network access agreements if a person:

    (i) fails to comply with the terms of the agreement;

    (ii) ceases to be a person with whom the registrar would be required to enter into a network access agreement conferring the authority which the agreement confers; or

---

[1075] See the Land Registration (Electronic Conveyancing) Rules 2008.
[1076] LRA 2002 Sch.5 para.2(1), (2).
[1077] LRA 2002 Sch.5 para.2(3).
[1078] LRA 2002 Sch.5 para.5(1).
[1079] LRA 2002 Sch.5 para.5(2). This could include a requirement about the disclosure of overriding interests under LRA 2002 s.71; above, para.7–101.
[1080] LRA 2002 Sch.5 para.6; Land Registration (Network Access) Rules 2008 r.6.
[1081] See below, para.15–041.
[1082] LRA 2002 Sch.5 para.8(a).
[1083] LRA 2002 Sch.5 para.8(b).
[1084] LRA 2002 Sch.5 para.3(1).
[1085] LRA 2002 Sch.5 para.3(2).

(iii) does not comply with conditions prescribed by rules.[1086]

A person aggrieved by the registrar with respect to entry into, or termination of, a network access agreement may appeal against the decision to the adjudicator.[1087]

(c) Formal requirements. The Land Registration Act 2002 creates new **7–161** formal requirements for the authentication of electronic documents in place of the traditional requirements of writing or the use of a deed.[1088] The new formal requirements apply to dispositions of registered land or interests in registered land. They do not apply to contracts to make dispositions, but provision could be made for these under other statutory provisions.[1089] The formalities in the 2002 Act apply to a document in electronic form that has three characteristics.[1090]

First,[1091] it must purport to effect a disposition of:

(i) a registered estate or charge[1092];

(ii) an interest which is the subject of a notice in the register; or

(iii) unregistered land, which triggers the requirement of compulsory first registration.[1093]

The second of these categories is novel because it envisages that the principles of registration of title will be extended to dispositions of merely equitable interests, e.g. an assignment of the benefit of an option or of an equitable charge.[1094]

Second, the disposition must of a kind specified by rules.[1095] This is consistent with the incremental introduction of electronic conveyancing, so that, for example, it might be provided initially that only registered charges are to be effected electronically.

Third,[1096] each of the following conditions must be met:

(i) The document must make provision for the time and date when it is to take effect. As regards the formal requirements for the

---

[1086] LRA 2002 Sch.5 para.3(3).

[1087] LRA 2002 Sch.5 para.4. See above, para.7–130.

[1088] LRA 2002 s.91. The relevant statutory provisions are found in LP(MP)A 1989 s.1 (deeds: below, para.8–049 et seq.) and LPA 1925 s.53 (written dispositions: below, para.11–044).

[1089] See Electronic Communications Act 2000 s.8. A draft Order in respect of contracts for the sale of land which were to be made electronically was issued for consultation in March 2001, but to date, no Order has been made.

[1090] See LRA 2002 s.91(1)–(3).

[1091] See LRA 2002 s.91(2). For the grant of electronic charges, which is the only form of electronic disposition of land so far introduced, see Land Registration (Electronic Conveyancing) Rules 2008; and Ruoff & Roper, 19.015.

[1092] For such dispositions, see above, paras 7–054, 7–056.

[1093] For these dispositions, see above, para.7–014.

[1094] See too, LRA 2002 s.93(1); below, para.7–163.

[1095] LRA 2002 s.91(2).

[1096] See LRA 2002 s.91(3).

disposition of land other than by electronic means, there are well-known principles and practices for determining when deeds of conveyance take effect.[1097] It was therefore necessary for there to be some equivalent in relation to electronic conveyancing.

(ii) The document has the electronic signature of each person by whom it purports to be authenticated.[1098] There are a variety of different methods of authenticating electronic documents, such as "public" or "dual key" cryptography.

(iii) Each electronic signature must be certified.[1099] Certification is the means by which a person's electronic signature is verified as his. It is not enough that a document purports to be authenticated by X unless the other party to the transaction can be confident that it is indeed X who has authenticated the document. Hence the need for certification.

(iv) The document must comply with such other conditions as rules may provide. The purpose of this provision is to enable other conditions, e.g. as to a specified level of security, to be prescribed from time to time.

7–162   An electronic document that meets the requirements set out in the previous paragraph is deemed to have certain effects.

(i) It is to be regarded as being in writing and signed by each individual, and sealed by each corporation, whose electronic signature it has.[1100]

(ii) It is to be regarded for the purposes of any enactment as a deed.[1101] This has a double significance. First, the statutory formality provisions applicable to dispositions are not disapplied. Instead, the electronic document is deemed to satisfy them. Secondly, although in those cases where a deed is required by any enactment an electronic document will be deemed to be a deed, such a document will not be a deed for any other purpose. This is important because there is a common law rule that an agent can only be given authority to execute a deed by deed.[1102] That rule does not apply to

---

[1097] See below, para.8–038.

[1098] As explained above, at least initially, it is likely that electronic documents will be authenticated by a party's conveyancer: see para.7–159.

[1099] For the meaning of "signature" and "certification" in this context, see Electronic Communications Act 2000 s.7(2), (3): LRA 2002 s.91(10).

[1100] LRA 2002 s.91(4). If a an electronic instrument purports to be authenticated by a company under CA 2006 s.44(2), the instrument is deemed to have been duly executed by the company under CA 2006 s.44(5): see LRA 2002 s.91(9) (as amended).

[1101] LRA 2002 s.91(5).

[1102] See *Powell v London and Provincial Bank* [1893] 2 Ch. 555 at 563.

the authentication of electronic documents because they are not deemed to be deeds for the purposes of the common law.[1103]

(iii) If the electronic document is authenticated by a person as agent, the document is to be regarded for the purposes of any enactment as authenticated by him under the written authority of his principal.[1104] This means that the other party to the disposition cannot require the agent to produce his written authority. The provision does not deem the agent to have authority where he had none at all. It merely deems him, for the purposes of the relevant enactment, to have authenticated the electronic document under his principal's written authority.[1105]

(iv) If an assignment of an interest is made electronically under this provision, notice of that assignment may also be given electronically in accordance with rules,[1106] and will then be regarded for the purposes of any enactment as given in writing.[1107]

(d) Making electronic conveyancing compulsory. There is power in relation **7–163**
to certain transactions to require that they be carried out by means of a document in electronic form and that, when the document has effect, it is electronically communicated to the registrar and complies with the registration requirements.[1108] In this way, electronic dispositions will be registered at the same time as they take effect, thereby eliminating the registration gap.[1109]

The transactions are as follows:

(i) a disposition of a registered estate or charge[1110] that has been specified in rules;

(ii) a disposition of an interest which is the subject of a notice in the register[1111] that has been specified in rules;

(iii) a contract to make a disposition in (i) or (ii).[1112]

The relevant registration requirements are:

[1103] See (2001) Law Com. No.271, para.13.20.
[1104] LRA 2002 s.91(6). For an example of a statutory requirement that an agent be authorised in writing, see, e.g., LPA 1925 s.53(1)(a) (disposition of an interest in land).
[1105] cf. para.7–159 above, where there is a presumption of authority to overcome an agent's lack of implied authority.
[1106] These have yet to be made.
[1107] LRA 2002 s.91(7). For legal assignments in writing of choses in action, see LPA 1925 s.136; below, para.32–010.
[1108] LRA 2002 s.93(2).
[1109] See above, para.7–150.
[1110] In relation to a registered charge, "disposition" includes the postponement of that charge.
[1111] Such as an option or an equitable charge.
[1112] See LRA 2002 s.93(1), (2).

(a) As regards registrable dispositions, those set out in Schedule 2 of the Land Registration Act 2002.[1113]

(b) In the case of any other disposition, or a contract, such requirements as rules may provide.[1114]

The introduction of compulsory electronic conveyancing, where the disposition is simultaneously registered, will in time create a system where the priority of an interest will be determined by the date of its registration, because that is the date of its creation.[1115] Furthermore, because it will be impossible to create many interests without registering them, the number of overriding interests that can exist will necessarily diminish. The register will therefore become a much more accurate record of the title than it is at present. This accords with the fundamental objective of the Land Registration Act 2002, to make the register as complete and accurate a record of the state of the title at any given time as it can be.[1116]

[1113] LRA 2002 s.93(3)(a). For those requirements, see above, para.7–057. Where a disposition falls within LRA 2002 s.93, LRA 2002 s.27(1) (above, para.7–053) does not apply: LRA 2002 s.93(4).

[1114] LRA 2002 s.93(3)(b). No such rules have yet been made. The Lord Chancellor is under a duty to consult before making rules under s.93: see LRA 2002 s.93(5).

[1115] cf. LRA 2002 s.28(1); above, para.7–060.

[1116] See (2001) Law Com. No.271, para.1.5; above, para.6–041.

CHAPTER 8

UNREGISTERED CONVEYANCING: TITLES AND INCUMBRANCES

Part 1

THE UNREGISTERED SYSTEM IN DECLINE

Unregistered conveyancing is applicable where the title is not yet registered or cannot be registered.[1] It is the traditional practice of investigating the title to land on sale, so as to make certain that the purchaser really does become owner and does not find himself burdened with unsuspected liabilities. This practice, developed and refined over the centuries, eventually became unduly troublesome, despite the reforms of 1925. The system of registered convey ancing, which is now predominant, has been explained in Chapter 7. Many dispositions of unregistered land now trigger the requirement of compulsory first registration.[2] However, an understanding of unregistered conveyancing is still important. Not only do the principles demonstrate the working and interaction of legal and equitable interests in their classic form and in the context of everyday transactions but also they continue to apply to dispositions of unregistered land which do not trigger the requirement of compulsory registration.[3] Indeed, they are also applicable to the grant of most leases for a term of seven years or less, and to the assignment of an unregistered lease where seven years or less of the term are unexpired, whether or not the reversionary title is registered.[4]

8–001

    The central dilemma of land law is how to reconcile security of title with ease of transfer. The law permits a wide variety of incumbrances and charges such as leases, easements, restrictive covenants, estate contracts and mortgages, as already explained in outline. The owners of these interests are

8–002

[1] Above, para.6–039.
[2] See above, para.7–014.
[3] See above, para.7–017.
[4] See above, paras 7–014, 7–054.

concerned that the land should not be transferred in any manner which might defeat them. A purchaser of the land, on the other hand, is concerned that he should not be bound by any interest not fully known to him in advance. The solution adopted in 1925 in relation to unregistered conveyancing was to require the registration of those third party interests which were likely to be the most elusive. Prior to that time, the protection of incumbrances had been achieved by imposing a high duty of care upon the purchaser. He was expected to make full and detailed investigation of his vendor's title so that, barring accidents, he would be bound to find out all the facts. The law's principal instrument for this purpose was the equitable doctrine of notice.

8–003   Legal estates and interests would of course bind the purchaser in any event, and for them he had to inquire at his peril. But many equitable incumbrances could exist, and from them he would be safe only if he could show that he was a bona fide purchaser of a legal estate without notice. It was in order that he might, if necessary, be in a position to defend himself with this plea that he would undertake the elaborate inquiries required by the old system. These inquiries had to be repeated upon every purchase, so that the same title might be investigated again and again at quite short intervals, wasteful of effort though that was. Before Parliament came to his assistance with statutory reforms, a purchaser investigating title often had to make elaborate investigations into family settlements, joint ownership and other complexities, with the result that the intricacies of conveyancing became an obstacle to the ready marketability of land.

8–004   The reformers of 1925 put their faith primarily in a modification of the old system of conveyancing. This was achieved, as already described, by the reorganisation of legal and equitable interests, by the system of overreaching, and by the extended use of registration of land charges. By these means it was given a further lease of life.[5] At the same time, provision was made for its progressive replacement by registration of title that was explained in the previous Chapter. Although these two radically different systems still operate side by side, they are both based on the same general structure of estates and interests, though not on the same underlying principles.[6] The detailed rules about leases, mortgages, easements, settlements and so forth are in general similar under both systems, subject to some significant exceptions. Those exceptions have become much more pronounced since the enactment of the Land Registration Act 2002. It was the intention of that Act that the principles applicable to registered conveyancing should reflect the nature and potential of a system of registration of title even if the result was very different from the position where title was unregistered.[7]

Unregistered conveyancing as it has operated since 1925 is comprised of three disparate elements:

[5] See (1977) 40 M.L.R. 505 (A. Offer); and J. S. Anderson, *Lawyers and the Making of English Land Law 1832–1940.*

[6] Unregistered title is ultimately based upon possession, whereas registered title rests upon the fact of registration. See below, para.35–001.

[7] See (1998) Law Com. No.258, at para.1.6.

1. The doctrine of the purchaser without notice.

2. The procedure followed on a sale of land and of the form and effect of the conveyance.

3. The system of registration of land charges.

Part 2

THE PURCHASER WITHOUT NOTICE

It is a fundamental rule that a purchaser of a legal estate for value without notice is "an absolute, unqualified, unanswerable defence"[8] against the claims of any prior equitable owner or incumbrancer. The onus of proof lies on the person putting forward this plea.[9] It is a single plea, and is not sufficiently made out by proving purchase for value and leaving it to the plaintiff to prove notice if he can.[10] The scope of the rule is explained, and then its elements are analysed. **8–005**

1. The Scope of the Rule. Subject to very limited statutory exceptions that have been explained,[11] the doctrine of notice has no role to play in registered conveyancing.[12] In unregistered conveyancing, notice will continue to be relevant in two situations. The first is in relation to those dispositions for value of unregistered land that are not required to be completed by registration.[13] In practice this is likely to be confined to: **8–006**

 (i) the grant of leases for 7 years or less; and

 (ii) the assignment or mortgage of existing unregistered leases land having 7 years or less to run.

The second situation is on application for first registration following a conveyance that is required to be registered.[14] The issue of whether the purchaser (or some person through whom he derived title) took free of a right over the land because he was a bona fide purchaser will have to be determined by the

---

[8] *Pilcher* v *Rawlins* (1872) 7 Ch. App. 259 at 269, James L.J.

[9] *Re Nisbett and Potty Contract* [1906] 1 Ch. 386 at 404, 409, 410; *Barclays Bank Plc v Boulter* [1998] 1 W.L.R. 1 at 8.

[10] *Re Nisbett and Potts' Contract* [1905] 1 Ch. 391 at 402 (on appeal, [1906] 1 Ch. 386); *Wilkes v Spooner* [1911] 2 KB. 473 at 486.

[11] See LRA 2002 ss.11(4)(c), 12(4)(d) (above, para.7–032); s.31 (above, para.7–066); and s.86(5) (above, para.7–111).

[12] Above, para.7–064.

[13] Above, para.7–017.

[14] For the dispositions of unregistered land that trigger compulsory first registration, see above, para.7–014.

registrar when he registers the title because it will affect the entries he makes on the register. In general, on first registration, issues of priority are settled according to the principles of unregistered conveyancing.[15]

8–007   **2. Bona fide.** The purchaser must act in good faith. Any sharp practice or unconscionable conduct may forfeit the privileges of a purchaser in the eyes of equity in accordance with general principles. But although good faith is traditionally mentioned as "a separate test which may have to be passed even though absence of notice is proved",[16] there are no clear examples of it operating independently in that way.[17] It therefore serves mainly to emphasise that the purchaser must be innocent as to notice, and this is considered in detail below.

8–008   **3. Purchaser for value.** The words "for value" are included to show that value must have been given, because "purchaser" in its technical sense does not necessarily imply this.[18] "Value" does not necessarily mean full value.[19] It means any consideration in money, money's worth (e.g. other land, or stocks and shares, or services) or marriage.[20] "Money's worth" extends to all forms of non-monetary consideration in the sense used in the law of contract, but it also includes the satisfaction of an existing debt.[21] "Marriage", how-ever, extends only to a future marriage. An ante-nuptial agreement (i.e. a promise made in consideration of future marriage) is deemed to have been made for value as regards both the spouses and the issue of the marriage.[22] However, a promise made in respect of a past marriage (a post-nuptial agreement) is not.[23] "Good consideration" (the natural love and affection which a person has for his near relatives) is unimportant and does not amount to value.[24] "Purchaser" is not confined to someone who acquires a fee simple; it includes, for example, mortgagees and lessees, who are purchasers to the extent of their interests.[25]

If the purchase is for money consideration, the purchaser must actually pay all the money before receiving notice of the equitable interest. If such notice is received before the money is paid, no obligation or security for its payment

---

[15] First registration can affect priorities to a limited extent: see, e.g. above, para.7–032.

[16] *Midland Bank Trust Co Ltd v Green* [1981] A.C. 513 at 528, per Lord Wilberforce.

[17] Though it is easy to imagine such cases, e.g. if a purchaser induced a vendor by fraud or coercion to sell land to him at an undervalue.

[18] cf. above, para.3–023.

[19] *Basset v Nosworthy* (1673) Rep.t.Finch 102; Wh. & T. ii, 138, 140.

[20] See, e.g. *Wormald v Maitland* (1866) 35 L.J.Ch. 69 at 73; *Salih v Atchi* [1961] A.C. 778.

[21] *Thorndike v Hunt* (1859) 3 De G. & i. 563; Maitland, *Equity,* 134; (1943) 59 L.Q.R. 208 (R.E.M.).

[22] *Att Gen v Jacobs Smith* [1895] 2 Q.B. 341.

[23] Wh. & T. ii, 791.

[24] *Goodright d. Humphreys v Moses* (1774) 2 Wm.B1. 1019.

[25] *Goodright d. Humphreys v Moses* (1774) 2 Wm.B1. 1019; *Brace v Duchess of Marlborough* (1728) 2 P.Wms. 491; *Re King's Leasehold Estates* (1873) L.R. 16 Eq. 521 at 525.

will be enforceable.[26] The mere execution of a conveyance of a legal estate before notice is received, without payment of the money, will not suffice.[27]

4. Of a legal estate. This element is most important. The immunity from **8–009** equities enjoyed by the purchaser without notice is founded on equity's deference to the legal estate. "As courts of equity break in upon the common law, when necessity and conscience require it, still they allow superior force and strength to a legal title to estates."[28] The legal owner cannot be challenged by merely equitable claimants unless he is a volunteer or has notice.

A purchaser of an equitable interest, even without notice, is in an entirely different position.[29] If A and B hold land on trust for X, and X sells his equitable interest to Y, Y takes subject to any other prior equitable interests there may be in the land, whether or not he has notice of them. The owner of an equitable interest can prima facie convey only what is vested in him, so that if part of his equitable interest has already been conveyed away, a subsequent purchaser can take only so much of it as remains.[30] The rule is therefore that where the equities are equal (but only where they are equal), the first in time prevails.[31] It is only acquisition of the legal estate for value and without notice which will reverse the natural order of priority. An illustration is provided by a case where land held upon trust was fraudulently mortgaged first to legal and later to equitable mortgagees, none of whom had notice of the trust. It was held that the legal mortgagee took priority over the beneficiaries under the trust, but that the equitable mortgagees did not.[32]

The purchaser must have the legal estate properly vested in him (by a **8–010** conveyance[33]) before he will be safe. If he has paid the purchase-money, but then gets notice of a prior equitable interest before the purchase is completed by the conveyance of the legal estate, he will take subject to the equity.[34] But this does not apply to a subsequent equitable interest. A purchaser who takes a conveyance of the legal estate with notice of an equitable interest created after he contracted to buy the land takes free from it; for his equitable interest

---

[26] *Tourville v Naish* (1734) 3 P.Wms. 307; *Taylor Barnard v Tozer* [1984] 1 E.G.L.R. 21 at 22; Wh. & T. ii, 140.

[27] *Story v Windsor* (1743) 2 Atk. 630. For the converse case, see below, para.8–010.

[28] *Wortley v Birkhead* (1754) 2 Ves.Sen. 571 at 574, per Lord Hardwicke L.C.; and see *Pilcher v Rawlins* (1872) 72 Ch.App. 259 at 268, 269; *L. & S. W. Ry v Gomm* (1882) 20 Ch D 562 at 586.

[29] *Phillips v Phillips* (1862) 4 De G.F. & J. 208.

[30] See *Phillips v Phillips,* above, at 215.

[31] Snell, *Equity,* para.4–047.

[32] *Cave v Cave* (1880) 15 Ch D 639.

[33] But an imperfect conveyance operating by estoppel may suffice: *Sharpe v Foy* (1868) 4 Ch. App. 35.

[34] *Wigg v Wigg* (1739) 1 Atk. 382 at 384. For this rule as applied to mortgages, see *Saunders v Dehew* (1692) 2 Vern. 271; *Allen v Knight* (1846) 5 Hare 272, affirmed 16 L.J.Ch. 370; *Mumford v Stohwasser* (1874) L.R. 18 Eq. 556; cf. *McCarthy & Stone Ltd v Julian S. Hodge & Co Ltd* [1971] 1 W.L.R. 1547 (equity registered before legal estate vested in mortgagee). In *Mumford v Stohwasser,* the *obiter dicta* of Jessel M.R. at 562–563 are not clear.

under the contract[35] has priority over the later equity, and the conveyance merely carries out the contract.[36]

The rule that the purchaser must take a legal estate before receiving notice is subject to two qualifications, or perhaps three.

8–011   *(a) Superior right to legal estate.* A purchaser without notice who acquires only an equitable interest can defeat a prior equity if his equitable interest gives him a superior right to the legal estate. This rule is thus consistent with the principle that the legal estate must prevail. The simplest example is where the purchaser procures a conveyance not to himself but to some person who is trustee for him, and neither purchaser nor trustee has notice of the equity at the time of the conveyance.[37]

This exception does not alter the general rule that a purchaser of an equitable interest who purchases it from the owner of the legal estate, but does not obtain the legal estate, is bound by all previous equitable interests affecting the land, whether or not he has notice of them. Nor is a superior right to a legal estate any shield against the legal estate itself. A purchaser of a legal estate without notice of a prior equitable interest takes free from it in accordance with the basic rule, even though the equitable interest conferred an equitable right to call for a legal estate.[38] Thus, if A holds land upon trust to convey the legal estate to B, but then wrongfully conveys it to C, a purchaser without notice, C's title, of course, prevails.

8–012   *(b) Mere equities.* A purchaser without notice does not have to take a legal estate in order to take free from a "mere equity", i.e. an equitable right that falls short of an equitable interest in land.[39] There are a number of such "equities", arising out of special forms of equitable relief which the court will normally enforce against successors in title. Examples are the right of a party to a deed to have the deed set aside on account of fraud[40] or undue influence[41] and the right to have a document rectified for mutual mistake,[42] as where a lease stated the rent to be £130 but £230 was the figure to which the parties

---

[35] See above, para.4–025.

[36] An example similar in principle is *Barclays Bank Ltd v Bird* [1954] Ch. 274.

[37] *Stanhope v Earl Verney* (1761) 2 Eden 81; "the *cestuy que trust* and trustees are one": see at 85, per Lord Henley L.C.

[38] *Garnham v Skipper* (1885) 55 L.J.Ch. 263; 53 L.T. 940 (contract to grant legal mortgage to A followed by grant of legal mortgage to B. B, having no notice, prevailed).

[39] *Phillips v Phillips* (1862) 4 De G.F. & J. 208 at 218; *Westminster Bank Ltd v Lee* [1956] Ch. 7; *Mid-Glamorgan County Council v Ogwr BC* (1993) 68 P. & CR. 1 at 9. But see D. O'Sullivan "The Rule in *Phillips v Phillips*" (2002) 118 L.Q.R. 296.

[40] *Bowen v Evans* (1844) 1 Jo. & Lat. 178 at 263, 264; *Phillips Phillips,* above; *Ernest Vivian* (1863) 33 L.J.Ch. 513; *Latec Investments Ltd v Hotel Terrigal Pty Ltd* (1965) 1 13 C.L.R. 265; and see *Cloutte v Storey* [1911] 1 Ch. 18 at 24, 25. For settling aside conveyances, see below, para.8–054.

[41] *Bainbrigge v Browne* (1881) 18 Ch D 188 (charge of equitable interest, executed under undue influence, held binding only upon volunteers and purchasers with notice, and so not upon chargee who took without notice; but the case contains no mention of "mere equities" or of the importance of the legal estate).

[42] See, e.g. *Blacklocks v J.B. Developments (Godalming) Ltd* [19821 Ch. 183; *Taylor Barnard v Tozer* [1984] 1 E.G.L.R. 21 at 22. For rectification, see below, para.15–122.

had in fact agreed.[43] The right of a mortgagor to reopen a foreclosure is probably in the same category.[44] On the other hand the rights of beneficiaries under a trust,[45] and a vendor's lien for unpaid purchase-money,[46] are equitable interests in land as opposed to mere equities; thus they will obey the general rule and bind a purchaser without notice unless he obtains the legal estate. The same is presumably true of estate contracts and restrictive covenants.[47]

The courts have not explained precisely where the dividing line between **8–013** equitable interests and mere equities lies.[48] All that can be said is that mere equities which may affect a purchaser are essentially rights which are ancillary to or dependent upon some interest in the land which that purchaser takes.[49] There is thus a parallel with the ordinary rule relating to the purchaser of a legal estate without notice. Just as that purchaser takes the estate free from any equitable interests which affect it (and *à fortiori* any mere equities), so a purchaser of an equitable interest takes it free from any mere equities affecting it of which he has no notice.[50]

Underlying the whole subject is the principle that it is only *where the equities are equal* that the first in time prevails[51]; and sometimes the balance between competing equities may be too delicate to be settled by rigid rules. Even an equitable interest may lose priority to a later equity if there has been negligence or fraud on the part of the equitable owner.[52] A "mere equity" has the additional weakness that it is more at the discretion of the court; and the court may be reluctant to exercise its discretion against an innocent purchaser without notice, even though he does not have the legal estate, and even though the person entitled to the earlier equity cannot be accused of misconduct.[53]

---

[43] *Garrard v Frankel* (1862) 30 Beav. 445 (which must now be read subject to the doubts expressed upon it in *Riverlate Properties Ltd v Paul* [1975] Ch. 133; below, para.15 122). *Smith v Jones* [1954] 2 All E.R. 823 is evidently a case of a purchaser of a legal estate without notice: the report in [1954] 1 W.L.R. 1089 is not clear on the point.

[44] For this right, see below, para.25–012.

[45] *Cave v Cave* (1880) 15 Ch D 639; cf. *Re Vernon, Ewens & Co* (1886) 33 Ch D 402.

[46] *Mackreth v Symmons* (1808) 15 Ves. 329; *Rice v Rice* (1853) 2 Drew. 73; *Kettlewell v Watson* (1882) 21 Ch D 685 at 711 (on appeal, (1884) 26 Ch D 501); *Cave v Cave* (1880) 15 Ch D 639 at 648, 649. For this lien, see below, paras 15–055; 24–003.

[47] *National Provincial Bank Ltd v Ainsworth* [1965] A.C. 1 175 at 1238, per Lord Upjohn.

[48] It is unlikely to matter much for the future. Where title is registered, as is now usually the case, mere equities are treated in the same manner as any other interest in land: see LRA 2002 s.116(b); above, para.7–067(c).

[49] *National Provincial Bank Ltd v Ainsworth* [1965] A.C. 1 175 at 1238. The benefit of a mere equity passes with the land that it affects under the "all estate" clause (LPA 1925 s.63(1)): *Boots the Chemist Ltd v Street* [1983] 2 E.G.L.R. 51. See too *Berkeley Leisure Group Ltd v Williamson* [1996] E.G.C.S. 18. For the "all estate" clause, see below, para.8–044.

[50] See (1955) 71 L.Q.R. 481, 482 (R.E.M.), approved in *National Provincial Bank Ltd v Ainsworth*, above, at 1238, per Lord Upjohn.

[51] *Rice v Rice*, above, contains a classic discussion of this principle by Kindersley V.C.

[52] *Rice v Rice*, above (lien of unpaid vendor postponed to equitable mortgage because vendor had signed receipt for the purchase-money); *Re King's Settlement* [1931] 2 Ch. 294. And even a legal estate may lose its priority for similar reasons: see the cases on mortgages cited below, para.26–010.

[53] See [1955] C.L.J. at 160 (H.W.R.W.); (1955) 19 Conv.(N.S.) 343 (F. R. Crane); (1957) 21 Conv.(N.S.) at 201 (V. T. H. Delany); (1976) 40 Conv.(N.S.) 209 (A. R. Everton).

8–014   *(c) Subsequent acquisition of legal estate.* A purchaser of an equitable interest who pays the purchase-money without notice of a prior equity has been held to be protected if he later acquires a legal estate, even with notice, provided it is not conveyed to him in breach of trust.[54] However, this supposed exception may be merely a corollary of the general rule. For if the legal estate is subject to a prior equity inconsistent with the purchaser's title, it will necessarily be a breach of trust to convey it to him,[55] whether or not the facts are known to the person conveying it. If the prior equity is consistent with the purchaser's title, as where it is a mere incumbrance such as a restrictive covenant, the "breach of trust" exception probably does not apply at all. This is because it is founded on rules devised for competing mortgages,[56] which are wholly inapplicable to consistent titles. Those rules were abolished as regards mortgages in 1925,[57] being "technical and not satisfactory".[58] They would be best abandoned altogether.

8–015   **5. Without notice.** There are three kinds of notice.

8–016   *(a) Actual notice.* "Knowledge and notice are different things".[59] A person may be regarded as having notice of a fact not because he knows it, but because for legal purposes he is to be taken to know it.[60] In practice, however, this distinction is not always observed.[61] The term "actual notice" has been used to cover a number of different situations:

(i) A person is commonly said to have "actual notice" of a fact of

---

[54] *Bailey v Barnes* [1894] 1 Ch. 25 at 36; cf. *Powell v London and Provincial Bank* [1893] 1 Ch. 610, affirmed [1893] 2 Ch. 555. In *Bailey v Barnes* property subject to equitable claims by creditors was first mortgaged to A (legal estate) and then sold to B (equity of redemption). Neither A (it seems) nor B had notice. B later got notice, paid off A and acquired the legal estate. *Held,* the equity did not bind B. As A, it seems, had no notice himself, B, as A's successor in title, would not in any case have been bound: below, para.8–025. But the Court of Appeal invoked the principle of tacking mortgages (below, para.26–050), though this seems inapplicable to the facts since the legal estate was from the first subject to the equity and not paramount to it, as was requisite for tacking: below, para.26–055. The same difficulty arises in *McCarthy & Stone Ltd v Julian S. Hodge & Co Ltd* [1971] 1 W.L.R. 1547, although there the purchaser had constructive notice at the outset and therefore failed. See *Macmillan Inc v Bishopsgate Investment Trust Plc* [1995] 1 W.L.R. 978 at 1002–1005.

[55] See *Mumford v Stohwasser* (1874) L.R. 18 Eq. 566; *McCarthy & Stone Ltd v Julian S. Hodge & Co Ltd,* above (breach of trust no mortgage land already subject to contract of sale).

[56] Explained below, para.26–050.

[57] LPA 1925 s.94(3); below, para.26–064. Apparently the provision applies only to mortgages: *McCarthy & Stone Ltd v Julian S. Hodge & Co Ltd,* above, at 1556; contrast (1957) 21 Conv.(N.S.) at 196 (V. H. T. Delany).

[58] *Bailey v Barnes* [1894] 1 Ch. 25 at 36.

[59] *MCP Pension Trustees Ltd v Aon Pension Trustees Ltd* [2010] EWCA Civ 377, at [17]; [2011] 3 W.L.R. 455 at 462, per Elias L.J.

[60] *Ashburner's Principles of Equity,* (2nd edn) (Butterworth & Co, 1933) 59. See too *Rignall Developments Ltd v Halil* [1988] Ch. 190, at 200–202; and below, para.8–085.

[61] Though in certain contexts it can be of considerable importance: see below, paras 8–085; 15–084.

which he has subjective knowledge, regardless of how that knowledge was acquired.[62]

(ii) A person who is provided with the means to know a fact, but does not avail himself of that means, will have actual notice of that fact. Thus, if a person is supplied with a document in a conveyancing transaction, but does not read it, he will still have actual notice of its contents.[63]

(iii) If a person has actual notice of a fact, he will continue to have such notice even if he subsequently forgets that fact because "it is quite impossible to say that notice lapses with memory".[64]

(iv) By statute a number of rights have become registrable in the Land Charges Register, and it has been provided that registration of such rights constitutes actual notice.[65] This subject is considered below.[66]

(b) Constructive notice

(1) DUTY OF DILIGENCE. Equitable interests would have been entirely inse-   **8–017**
cure if it had been made easy for purchasers to acquire the legal estate without notice, as by merely asking no questions. Accordingly the Court of Chancery insisted that purchasers should inquire about equitable interests with no less diligence than about legal interests, which they could ignore only at their own peril. The motto of English conveyancing is *caveat emptor*[67]: the risk of incumbrances is on the purchaser, who must satisfy himself by a full investigation of title before completing his purchase.[68] However, the *caveat emptor* principle has long been tempered by the obligation imposed on a vendor of land at common law to disclose latent defects in his title before he contracts to sell it.[69]

---

[62] *Lloyd v Banks* (1868) 3 Ch. App. 488. He is not however regarded as having notice of facts which have come to his ears only in the form of vague rumours: *Barnhart v Greenshields* (1853) 9 Moo. P.C. 18 at 36, explained in *Reeves v Pope* [1914] 2 K.B. 284.

[63] *Eagle Trust Plc v SBC Securities Ltd* [1993] 1 W.L.R. 484 at 494. See too below, para.8–020.

[64] *MCP Pension Trustees Ltd v Aon Pension Trustees Ltd* [2010] EWCA Civ 377, at [18]; [2011] 3 W.L.R. 455 at 462, per Elias L.J. See too *Rignall Developments Ltd v Halil* [1988] Ch. 190 at 201–202; *Eagle Trust Plc v SBC Securities Ltd* [1993] 1 W.L.R. 484 at 494; *Polly Peck International Plc v Nadir (No.2)* [1992] 4 All E.R. 769 at 781.

[65] LPA 1925 s.198(1). A person may be fixed with actual notice of a land charge by reason of this subsection even though he could not have discovered its existence: below, para.8–088; and see *Eagle Trust Plc v SBC Securities Ltd, above,* at 494.

[66] Below, para.8–085.

[67] Let a purchaser beware.

[68] It should be noted however that the courts have frequently warned against the extension of the doctrine of constructive notice into commercial transactions unconnected with dispositions of land: see, e.g. *Eagle Trust Plc v SBC Securities Ltd* [1993] 1 W.L.R. 484 at 504–506.

[69] See below, para.15–070.

8–018   (2) STANDARD REQUIRED. By the doctrine of constructive notice equity adopted a similar principle and adapted itself to the ordinary conveyancing practice. A purchaser would be able to plead absence of notice only if he had made all usual and proper inquiries, and had still found nothing to indicate the equitable interest.[70] If he fell short of this standard he could not plead that he had no notice of rights which proper diligence would have discovered. Of these he was said to have "constructive notice". A purchaser accordingly has constructive notice of a fact if he:

(i) had actual notice that there was some incumbrance and a proper inquiry would have revealed what it was; or

(ii) deliberately abstained from inquiry in an attempt to avoid having notice; or

(iii) omitted by carelessness or for any other reason to make an inquiry which a purchaser acting on skilled advice ought to make and which would have revealed the incumbrance.[71]

A purchaser's ordinary duties fall into two main categories: inspection of the land, and investigation of the vendor's title.

8–019   (3) INSPECTION OF LAND. A purchaser is expected to inspect the land and make inquiry as to anything which appears inconsistent with the title offered by the vendor.

It is an ancient rule that the fact of possession constitutes notice of the rights of the possessor.[72] Two reasons have been given for this. First, occupation of the premises by a person whose presence is inconsistent with the vendor's title places any purchaser on inquiry as to the occupier's rights.[73] Secondly, and in the alternative, it is said that as possession is prima facie evidence of title,[74] a purchaser is deemed to have notice of the rights of any person in possession.[75] There is an important distinction between these two explanations. If the latter is correct, a purchaser will have notice of the rights of the possessor, even though his possession is not immediately apparent.[76] Modern authority tends to confirm the latter view.[77] A purchaser should therefore:

---

[70] *Bailey v Barnes*; LPA 1925 s.199(1)(ii).
[71] See *Jones v Smith* (1841) 1 Hare 43 at 55; *Kemmis v Kemmis* [1988] 1 W.L.R. 1307; Snell, *Equity*, para.4–033; Maitland, *Equity*, 118, 119.
[72] See [1990] C.L.J. 277 at 315–320 (C.H.).
[73] *Barnhart v Greenshields* (1853) 9 Moo. P.C. 18 at 32.
[74] *Jones v Smith* (1841) 1 Hare 43 at 60; above, para.4–007.
[75] *Holmes v Powell* (1856) 8 De G.M. & G. 572 at 580, 581. This is in accordance with the protection which the law gives to persons in possession: above, para.4–008. It is clear that a person may be in possession of land even though he is not in occupation of it, e.g. where the land consists of fields or woodland.
[76] *Holmes v Powell*, above, at 581.
[77] *Kingsnorth Finance Co Ltd v Tizard* [1986] 1 W.L.R. 783.

(i) ascertain whether there is anybody in possession or occupation of the land apart from the vendor, at least if there are any circumstances from which a reasonable person might infer this[78]; and

(ii) make inquiry of any such person.[79]

The mere fact that there is on the land a person, such as a spouse, whose presence is not inconsistent with that of the vendor does not obviate the need for the purchaser to make inquiry of them.[80] The old view to the contrary has now been discredited.[81] If, for example, a husband is sole legal owner of land, but his wife has an equitable interest in the property by reason of some contribution to the cost of its acquisition, any purchaser will be bound by her interest unless it was not disclosed after proper inquiry by her.[82] There may of course be circumstances in which a person in possession of land is estopped from asserting any interest in it.[83]

Occupation by a tenant is notice of the interest of the tenant,[84] the terms of **8–020** his tenancy[85] and his other rights,[86] though not of any right not apparent from the lease, such as a right to have it rectified[87] on account of a mistake. However, a purchaser is under no duty to find out to whom a tenant pays rent or otherwise to investigate the tenant's title, so that failure to make such inquiries does not give him constructive notice of any rights of the tenant's landlord, who may be a different person from the vendor.[88]

Notice resulting from occupation extends in general to all equitable rights which the occupier may have in the land.[89] Notice that property is subject to

[78] *Kingsnorth Finance Co Ltd v Tizard* [1986] 1 W.L.R. 783. The case has been criticised for imposing an excessive burden of inquiry on any purchaser: All E.R. Rev. 1986, 181–184 (P. J. Clarke); [1986] Conv. 283 (M. P. Thompson). It is, however, in accordance with earlier authority. In practice, the first of these inquiries will usually be necessary only where the vendor is mortgaging the property. If he is leasing the land or assigning an existing lease, the purchaser will not complete unless vacant possession can be given. See *Northern Bank Ltd v Henry* [1981] I.R. 1 at 9, 10.

[79] The purchaser should make inquiry of the occupier or possessor personally, since "the untrue *ipse dixit* of the vendor will not suffice": *Hodgson v Marks* [1971] Ch. 892 at 932, per Russell L.J. Although that was a decision on registered land, the rules for unregistered land were also set out.

[80] *Kingsnorth Finance Co Ltd Tizard,* above.

[81] See *Williams & Glyn's Bank Ltd v Boland* [1981] A.C. 487, a case on registered land, in which earlier authorities on unregistered land such as *Caunce v Caunce* [1969] 1 W.L.R. 286 were disapproved.

[82] *Kingsnorth Finance Co Ltd Tizard,* above. For interests obtained by contribution, see below, para.11–016.

[83] For example, an agent who negotiates a sale or mortgage on behalf of his principal impliedly represents to the purchaser that the property is free from any undisclosed interest of the agent's: *Midland Bank Ltd v Farmpride Hatcheries Ltd* [1981] 2 E.G.L.R. 147 (directors residing in their company's property).

[84] *Daniels v Davison* (1809) 16 Ves. 249; *Allen v Anthony* (1816) 1 Mer. 282; *Mumford v Stohwasser* (1874) L.R. 18 Eq. 556; *Hunt v Luck* [1902] 1 Ch. 428; *Ramlal v Chaitlal* [2003] UKPC 12 at [30]; [2004] 1 P. & C.R. 1 at 11.

[85] *Taylor v Stibbert* (1794) 2 Ves. Jun. 437.

[86] *Barnhart v Greenshields* (1853) 9 Moo. P.C. 18.

[87] *Smith v Jones* [1954] 1 W.L.R. 1089.

[88] *Hunt v Luck,* above.

[89] *Jones v Smith* (1841) 1 Hare 43; *Barnhart v Greenshields,* above.

trusts is notice of all the trusts to which it is subject in the hands of the trustees[90] and notice of the existence of a document that might be expected to be relevant[91] is notice of its contents.[92]

8–021   (4) INVESTIGATION OF TITLE. A purchaser has constructive notice of all rights which he would have discovered[93] had he investigated the vendor's title to the land for the period allowed by law in ordinary cases where the parties make no special agreement as to length of title. Investigation of title means the examination of documents relating to transactions in the land during the period immediately prior to the purchase.[94] This period used by convention to be at least 60 years, but by the Vendor and Purchaser Act 1874 it was reduced to at least 40 years, and by the Law of Property Act 1925 to at least 30 years. Under the Law of Property Act 1969 it is now at least 15 years.[95] The period is "at least" 15 years, because the purchaser can require proof of a good root of title which is at least 15 years old, and see all subsequent documents which trace the dealing with the property.[96] A good root of title may be, for example, a conveyance or a mortgage, provided that it offers a clear starting point for the title. To do this it must be a document which deals with the whole legal and equitable interest in the land, describes the property adequately, and contains nothing to throw any doubt on the title.[97]

8–022   For example, if the title consists of a series of conveyances respectively 5, 14, 25 and 48 years old, as well as older deeds, a purchaser is entitled to production of the conveyance 25 years old and all subsequent conveyances. If in fact he fails to investigate the title at all,[98] or else investigates it for only part of this period (e.g. because he has agreed to accept a shorter title, or to make no objection to some dubious transaction),[99] he is fixed with constructive notice of everything that he would have discovered had he investigated the whole title for the full statutory period. A purchaser is not concerned with transactions prior to the root of title. He may be affected by notice if he actually investigates them or inquires about them, but not otherwise.[100] A purchaser who, having notice of relevant title deeds, inquires for them, and is met with a reasonable excuse for their non-production is (by an exceptional rule) free from notice of their contents.[101] But this does not alter the rule as to

---

[90] *Perham v Kempster* [1907] 1 Ch. 373.

[91] *Re Valletort Sanitary Steam Laundry Co* [1903] 2 Ch. 654; Snell, *Equity,* para.4–030.

[92] *Bisco v Earl of Banbury* (1676) 1 Ch. Ca. 287.

[93] See *Carter v Williams* (1870) L.R. 9 Eq. 678.

[94] For a fuller account of proof of title, see below, para.15–074.

[95] LPA 1969 s.23. See below, para.15–077, for these periods. For the interrelationship between periods of limitation and the period for which title has to be investigated, see [1985] Conv. 272 (M. Dockray).

[96] Below, paras 15–077—15–078.

[97] Below, paras 15–077—15–078.

[98] *Worthington v Morgan* (1849) 16 Sim. 547.

[99] *Re Cox & Neve's Contract* [1891] 2 Ch. 109 at 117, 118; *Re Nisbett and Potts'* Contract [1906] 1 Ch. 386.

[100] Below, para.15–080.

[101] *Hewitt v Loosemore* (1851) 9 Hare 449 at 458; *Espin v Pemberton* (1859) 3 De G. & J. 547; Williams, V. & P 309, criticised below, para.26–013.

notice by failing to inquire at all[102] even if an inquiry would probably have been met by some false but apparently reasonable excuse.[103]

(c) Imputed notice. If a purchaser employs an agent, such as a solicitor, any **8–023** actual or constructive[104] notice which the agent receives is imputed to the purchaser.[105] The basis of this doctrine is that a person who empowers an agent to act for him is not allowed to plead ignorance of his agent's dealings.[106] Thus where a solicitor discovered an equitable mortgage on the title and was deceived by a forged receipt into believing that the mortgage had been discharged, the purchaser had imputed notice of the mortgage and was bound by it.[107] Since solicitors are usually employed to investigate title this branch of the doctrine of notice is essential. But, in order to check its extension, it is confined by statute to notice which the agent acquires acting as such in the same transaction.[108] Where the same solicitor acts for both parties, there is a conflict of authority as to whether any notice that he acquires will be imputed to both parties.[109] The older cases tended to favour the view that it would,[110] but in more recent decisions, the courts have held that what the solicitor learns when acting for one party, he does not learn while acting as agent for the other.[111] Notice will not be imputed to a party just because the solicitor knows that another member of his firm acted for the other party in an earlier transaction, unless the facts are so compelling as to put him on inquiry.[112] Nor will a purchaser be fixed with notice if he employed the vendor's solicitor not generally but merely to draw up the conveyance.[113] Because imputed notice rests upon a person's presumed knowledge of his

---

[102] *Peto v Hammond* (1861) 30 Beav. 495.

[103] *Jones v Williams* (1857) 24 Beav. 47.

[104] *Re The Alms Corn Charity* [1901] 2 Ch. 750.

[105] In a conveyancing transaction, a solicitor has authority to receive communications for his client from the other party. It is his duty to pass them on to his principal. Even if this does not happen, then in the absence of fraud by the agent, the client will be estopped from denying that he received the information: *Strover v Harrington* [1988] Ch. 390 at 409, 410.

[106] Williams, V. & P. 306.

[107] *Jared v Clements* [1903] 1 Ch. 428.

[108] LPA 1925 s.199(1)(ii)(b); replacing CA. 1882, s.3(1)(ii); *Thorne v Marsh* [1895] A.C. 495 at 501.

[109] A party could certainly plead that he purchased without notice if the solicitor had entered into a conspiracy with the vendor to conceal something from the purchaser: *Sharpe v Foy* (1868) 4 Ch.App. 35; *Cave v Cave* (1880) 15 Ch D 639.

[110] *Dryden v Frost* (1838) 3 My. & Cr. 670; *Meyer v Chartres* (1918) 34 T.L.R. 589; and see *Kennedy v Green* (1834) 3 My. & Cr. 699; *Lloyds Bank Ltd v Marcan* [1973] 1 W.L.R. 339 at 348 (affd. [1973] 1 W.L.R. 1387); but see *Bateman v Hunt* [1904] 2 K.B. 530.

[111] *Halifax Mortgage Services Ltd v Stepsky* [1996] Ch. 207; *Birmingham Midshires Mortgage Services v Mahal* (1996) 73 P. & CR. D7; *Barclays Bank Plc v Thomson* [1997] 4 All E.R. 816 at 828, 829; *National Westminster Bank Plc v Beaton* (1997) 30 H.L.R. 99; *Leamington Spa B.S. v Verdi* (1997) 75 P. & CR. D16; below, para.25–131. In each of these cases, a solicitor acting for a creditor also gave advice in an independent capacity to a surety prior to her agreeing to guarantee her husband's debts. The earlier authorities were not cited, but some of them pre-date what is now LPA 1925 s.199(1)(ii)(b).

[112] *B v B (P Ltd Intervening) (No.2)* [1995] 1 F.L.R. 374; [1995] Fam. Law 244 (S. Cretney).

[113] *Kettlewell v Watson* (1882) 21 Ch D 685; (1884) 26 Ch D 639.

agent's dealings, an exception also arises where the agent deliberately defrauds the principal.[114]

8–024   *(d) Extent of doctrine of notice.* The tendency of the Court of Chancery was constantly to extend and refine the doctrines of constructive and imputed notice. So much property was held under trusts and other equitable dispositions that the frequent appearance of the bona fide purchaser of the legal estate without notice would have been intolerable. Equity's ambition was to eliminate him, so far as possible, by ensuring that it should be almost impossible to escape notice of any equity properly created and recorded. In so far as he could be excluded, equitable rights were as secure as legal rights. Equity's policy was in the main successful, as may be judged from the rarity and abstruseness of the cases in which the defence of purchaser without notice has been made out. Even today, when the doctrine of notice has such a limited role to play, there are still situations in which it can pose a threat to a purchaser.[115]

The Conveyancing Act 1882 is regarded as closing the period in which the rules relating to notice were widely extended. Apart from the change in the law about imputed notice, mentioned above, the Act merely stated that a purchaser should not be affected by notice unless he had failed to make "such inquiries and inspections as ought reasonably to have been made by him".[116] This, it has been said, "really does no more than state the law as it was before, but its negative form shows that a restriction rather than an extension of the doctrine of notice was intended by the legislature[117]."

8–025   **6. Successor in title.** The protection of the doctrine of purchaser without notice also extends to any purchaser claiming through such a purchaser,[118] even though he took with notice of the equity.[119] Similarly, a mere volunteer, if he claims through a purchaser without notice, can presumably claim freedom from the equity, because the principle is that once a legal estate has passed into the hands of a purchaser without notice of the equity, that equity ceases to be enforceable against that estate, and cannot be revived.[120] Unless this were so, the owner of the equity could, by widely advertising his claim, make it difficult for the purchaser without notice to dispose of the land for the price that he gave for it.[121]

The only qualification to this rule is based on the principle that a man cannot take advantage of his own wrong. If a trustee disposes of trust property

---

[114] Williams V. & P., 306, 307.

[115] Most notably where A, the sole legal owner of unregistered land, holds the property on trust for himself and B, and then mortgages it: see below, para.13–106.

[116] s.3(1)(i), replaced by LPA 1925 s.199(1)(ii). See Maitland, *Equity,* 120, 121.

[117] *Bailey v Barnes* [1894] 1 Ch. 25 at 35, per Lindley L.J.; and see *Caunce v Caunce* [1969] 1 W.L.R. 286 at 293. cf. *Northern Bank Ltd v Henry* [1981] I.R. 1 at 15–17.

[118] *Sweet v Southcote* (1786) 2 Bro. CC. 66; *Wilkes v Spooner* [1911] 2 KB. 473; Wh. & T. ii, 110.

[119] See, e.g. *Harrison v Forth* (1695) Prec. Ch. 51; *Wilkes v Spooner,* above.

[120] Maitland, *Equity,* p.117.

[121] Maitland, *Equity,* p.117.

to a purchaser without notice, and later reacquires the property, he will again hold it subject to the trusts, and not free from them.[122]

Part 3

CONVEYANCING PRACTICE

The procedure followed on an ordinary sale of unregistered land will now be   **8–026** described in outline, together with some details about the form and effect of the conveyance. Almost all conveyances of unregistered land must now be completed by registration.[123] However, in such circumstances, the sale is still conducted according to the principles of unregistered conveyancing. It is only when the land has been conveyed that an application for registration of the title can be made. All the conveyancing documents (including the conveyance itself) must then accompany that application.[124]

Section 1. From Contract to Completion

1. The contract. First of all the parties will have made a contract in writing.   **8–027** Contracts for the sale of land are subject to many rules both as to formalities and as to their effect, but this subject is largely unaffected by the differences between registered and unregistered conveyancing, and is therefore treated independently in Chapter 15.

Standard conveyancing practice commonly follows the National Conveyancing Protocol, which was first introduced by The Law Society in 1990.[125] The Protocol provides a code of practice that is appropriate for sales of domestic property by private treaty (rather than by auction) and has been introduced in order to streamline such transactions. Quite apart from this Protocol, it has long been normal to incorporate into contracts for the sale of land standard sets of conditions of sale which regulate the conduct of the transaction. There is now one principal set, the Standard Conditions of Sale.[126] In practice, whether the National Protocol is used or not, much of the legal work associated with the purchase of land is nowadays conducted before contract.

Prior to the exchange of written contracts, a purchaser will normally search the local land charges register[127] and will make certain other inquiries of the

---

[122] *Re Stapleford Colliery Co* (1880) 14 Ch D 432 at 445; *Gordon v Holland* (1913) 82 L.J.P.C. 81; and contrast *Piggott v Stratton* (1859) 1 De G.F. & J. 33 with *Wilkes v Spooner*, above.

[123] See above, para.7–014.

[124] LRR 2003 r.24. Application is made in Form FR1: LRR 2003 r.23.

[125] The 5th edition of the Protocol appeared in 2004. The Protocol sets out the steps which a vendor of land should take to provide the purchaser with as much information as possible at the commencement of the transaction. Use of the Protocol is entirely voluntary.

[126] 4th edn, 2003. There is also a set of Standard Commercial Property Conditions (2nd edn, 2004).

[127] For local land charges, see below, para.8–107.

relevant local authorities[128] on matters not registrable as local land charges.[129] Where the National Protocol is not employed, he will submit to the vendor a series of written inquiries before contract that are intended to clear up doubts concerning the state of the property. Such inquiries are now much more limited in their scope than was formerly the case, and are confined to matters not otherwise readily ascertainable.[130] They are unnecessary where the National Protocol is employed, because the vendor will supply the purchaser with the information by means of a completed questionnaire.[131]

8–028   **2. Delivery of the abstract or epitome of title.** The vendor is under an obligation to prove that he has a good title. Whether the title is deduced before or after contracts have been exchanged, the first stage in this process is for the vendor (V) to deliver to the purchaser (P) either an abstract of title or an epitome of title.[132] The traditional abstract of title consists in part of an epitome of the various documents,[133] and in part of a recital of the relevant events, such as births, deaths and marriages, which affect the title. The abstract starts with a good root of title and traces the devolution of the property down to V. Thus a very simple abstract might consist of:

>   (i) an epitome of a conveyance by A to B;
>
>   (ii) a recital of B's death;
>
>   (iii) a recital of probate of B's will being granted to X and Y;
>
>   (iv) an epitome of the assent by X and Y in favour of V.

In practice, epitomes of title are normally used in place of the traditional abstract (though a previous abstract may be included in the epitome). An epitome consists of a chronological index of all the material documents, events, etc, that would otherwise be included in the abstract, together with photocopies of the documents.

8–029   **3. Consideration of abstract or epitome.** P then peruses the abstract or epitome of title, considers the validity of the title shown, and, in the case of an abstract, checks it against V's title deeds, grants of probate, and other papers which prove the statements made in the abstract.

---

[128] It will not always be possible to make such inquiries, e.g. if the property is purchased at auction.

[129] Such inquiries relate to matters such as roads, sewers, drains, and, above all, planning.

[130] Following guidelines given by the Conveyancing Standing Committee of the Law Commission: *Preliminary Enquiries: House Purchase. A Practice Recommendation* (1987).

[131] The vendor's solicitor will send the purchaser's solicitor a package of documents containing all the necessary information about both the title and the property, other than matters covered by local searches.

[132] This is part of the package provided under the National Protocol.

[133] Abstracts conventionally employ a form of shorthand.

4. Requisitions on title. P's examination of the abstract or epitome usually **8–030** discloses a number of points upon which he requires further information. This further explanation is obtained by means of "requisitions on title", a series of written questions which P delivers to V. Requisitions usually consist of a mixture of requests for information genuinely needed (e.g. as to the date of a death not revealed by the abstract, or as to some incumbrance which the abstract mentions but does not explain), statements of the obvious (e.g. that V, having agreed to sell free from incumbrances, must discharge the mortgage or obtain the concurrence of his mortgagee to the sale of the property free from the mortgage), and general inquiries designed to make V commit himself to a definite statement (e.g. whether there are any incumbrances other than those specifically mentioned). In addition to dealing with matters disclosed in the abstract of title, requisitions cover most or all of the points raised in inquiries before contract.

5. Replies to requisitions. V then answers the requisitions within the **8–031** agreed time; if his answers are unsatisfactory on any point, P may make further requisitions.

6. Draft conveyance. P next prepares a draft conveyance in the form which **8–032** he thinks it should take. He sends this draft to V for his approval; V makes any alterations he considers necessary, returns it to P, who makes any further amendments, and so on until the conveyance is agreed. P then prepares an engrossment (fair copy) of the conveyance and sends it to V for execution.

7. Searches. As explained above, a search of the Register of Local Land **8–033** Charges will normally be undertaken by P prior to contract.[134] P will also search the Land Charges Register.[135] For the reasons explained later, such a search can only be made by P after V has deduced his title.[136]

8. Completion. Completion then takes place. Traditionally this took place **8–034** at the office of V's solicitor, but in practice completions are normally made by post in accordance with The Law Society's Code for Completion. V delivers to P the conveyance duly executed. It is only if P is entering into some obligation towards V, as by binding himself to observe restrictive covenants, that P will have to execute the conveyance as well, though even if he does not do so he will still be bound by the covenants if he takes possession under the deed.[137] In addition to receiving the conveyance, P is entitled to receive the title deeds. This is more than a contractual right, for the owner of land has a

---

[134] See para.8–027.
[135] For land charges, see below, paras 8–062 et seq.
[136] See below, para.8–086. Where the National Protocol is employed, the vendor will conduct the searches of the Land Charges Register. For searches of the Land Charges Register and the Register of Local Land Charges, see below, paras 8–102, 8–107.
[137] Litt. 374; Dart, V. & P 507; and see below, para.32–025.

right to the title deeds under a general rule.[138] However, V may retain any deed which:

(i) relates to other land retained by him; or

(ii) creates a trust which is still subsisting; or

(iii) relates to the appointment or discharge of trustees of a subsisting trust.[139]

If V retains any deeds, he must give P an acknowledgement of P's right to production of the deeds and, unless V is a mortgagee or trustee of the land, an undertaking for their safe custody.[140] In return, P pays V the purchase-money either in cash or by banker's draft. The exact amount due is settled by the "completion statement" which apportions the outgoings up to the day of completion. It is for the purchaser to have the conveyance duly stamped, which is usually done after completion. Most conveyances will now require registration under the Land Registration Act 1925.[141]

Section 2. The Conveyance

A. Precedent of a Conveyance

8–035

Commencement and date.

THIS CONVEYANCE is made the 1st day of June, 2011,

Parties.

BETWEEN William Walton of No. 1 Smith Street Oldham in the County of Lancashire Composer (hereinafter called "the vendor") of the one part and Michael Tippett of No. 2 Brown Street Oxted in the County of Surrey Musician (hereinafter called "the purchaser") of the other part

---

[138] Co. Litt. 6a ("the purchaser shall have all the charters, deeds and evidences, as incident to the lands . . . for the evidences are, as it were, the sinews of the land".); *Harrington v Price* (1832) 3 B. & Ad. 170; *Loosemore v Radford* (1842) 9 M. & W. 657; cf. *Re Knight's Question* [1958] Ch. 381. And see Halsbury, (4th edn), vol. 39(2), para.87, where special rules as to tenants for life, mortgagees, etc., are stated.

[139] LPA 1925 s.45(9).

[140] As to the effect of such acknowledgements and undertakings see LPA 1925 s.64, and notes thereto in Wolst. & C. The benefit of these covenants runs with the land at common law (below, para.32–011), the burden runs with the deeds by LPA 1925 s.64(2), (9).

[141] See LRA 2002 s.4; above, para.7–014.

WHEREAS—

Recitals.

(1) The vendor is the estate owner in respect of the fee simple of the property hereby assured for his own use and benefit absolutely free from incumbrances

(2) The vendor has agreed with the purchaser to sell to him the said property free from incumbrances for the price of £100,000

Testatum.
Consideration.

NOW THIS DEED WITNESSETH that in consideration of the sum of £200,000 now paid by the purchaser to the vendor (the receipt whereof the vendor acknowledges) the vendor hereby conveys to the purchaser

Parcels.

ALL THAT messuage or dwelling house with the yard gardens offices and outbuildings thereto belonging known as 15 Britten Road Aldeburgh in the County of Suffolk which premises are more particularly delineated and coloured pink on the plan annexed hereto

Habendum.

TO HOLD the same unto the purchaser in fee simple

Covenants for title

THE PROPERTY is conveyed with full title guarantee

Testimonium.

IN WITNESS WHEREOF the parties to these presents have hereunto set their hands the day and year first written above

Attestation Clause

Signed as a deed by the
vendor in the presence
of John Ireland clerk to   WILLIAM WALTON
Argue and Phibbs solicitors

JOHN IRELAND

B. Details of the Conveyance

In the very simple form of conveyance set out above, the following matters **8–036** should be noticed. The titles refer to the side-notes to its various parts.

1. Commencement. The old practice was for the initial words to be "This **8–037** Indenture". An indenture was a deed made in two counterparts, each having an indented or irregular edge. The deed was written out twice on a single sheet of parchment, which was then severed by cutting it with an irregular edge; the two halves of the parchment thus formed two separate deeds which could be fitted together to show their genuineness. This contrasted with a "deed poll", a deed to which there was only one party, which at the top had been polled, or shaved even.[142] The modern practice is for the commencement to describe the general nature of the document, e.g. "This Conveyance", or "This Mortgage".[143]

8–038   **2. Date.** Whatever date is in fact inserted in the conveyance, the document when executed[144] takes effect from the date upon which it was delivered by the parties to it.[145] A deed which has been executed but not delivered is ineffective.[146] Delivery is effected formally by doing some act showing that the deed is intended to be operative. When a company executes a deed in accordance with the provisions of the Companies Act 2006, it is presumed to be delivered upon its being executed, unless a contrary intention is proved.[147] By contrast, where a corporation aggregate which is not a company executes a deed, there will be no such presumption.[148] A deed may be delivered in escrow, i.e. delivered on the condition that it is not to become operative until some stated event occurs,[149] in which case it takes effect as soon as the event occurs; it is not revocable in the meantime.[150] Usually a vendor of land will execute the conveyance some days before completion. It had become the practice for him to deliver it to his solicitor in escrow, the condition being the completion of the purchase by the purchaser; and delivery on this condition will be inferred without proof.[151] The deed then took effect when the solicitor delivered it to the purchaser (or his solicitor) on completion; but the grantee's title, as against the grantor but not third parties, appeared to operate from the date of the earlier delivery in escrow.[152] This practice developed because of the old rule that a deed was itself required to authorise an agent to deliver a

---

[142] Norton, *Deeds,* 27

[143] See LPA 1925 s.57.

[144] The different methods of executing a deed are considered below, para.8–049. Since July 31, 1990 a seal has not been required for a deed executed by an individual or by a company: below, paras 8–050, 8–051.

[145] Norton, *Deeds,* 189; *Bentray Investments Ltd v Venner Time Switches Ltd* [1985] 1 E.G.L.R. 39 at 43.

[146] Co.Litt. 35b, 171b; Norton, *Deeds,* 10.

[147] Companies Act 2006 s.46.

[148] *Longman v Viscount Chelsea* (1989) 58 P. & CR. 189 at 199, rejecting the view that LPA 1925 s.74(1) created a presumption of delivery on the execution of a deed by a corporation aggregate.

[149] Norton, *Deeds,* 18 et seq. For useful summaries of the law, see *Bank of Scotland Plc v King* [2007] EWHC 2747 (Ch) at [49]–[53]; [2008] 1 E.G.L.R. 65 at 69, 70; *Silver Queen Maritime Ltd v Persia Petroleum Services Plc* [2010] EWHC 2867 (QB) at [107] et seq.

[150] *Beesly v Hallwood Estates Ltd* [1961] Ch. 105; *Kingston v Ambrian Investment Co Ltd* [1975] 1 W.L.R. 161; *Venetian Glass Gallery Ltd v Next Properties Ltd* [1989] 2 E.G.L.R. 42.

[151] *Glessing v Green* [1975] 1 W.L.R. 863; *Bentray Investments Ltd v Venner Time Switches Ltd* [1985] 1 E.G.L.R. 39. cf. *Longman v Viscount Chelsea* (1989) 58 P. & CR. 189 where it was held on such facts that there had been no delivery in escrow because the parties had negotiated "subject to the completion of the lease".

[152] Preston, Abstracts, iii, 65; *Alan Estates Ltd v W.G. Stores Ltd* [1982] Ch. 511, a case on a lease in which opinions in the Court of Appeal were divided.

deed.[153] That rule has now been abrogated,[154] and in the course of or in connection with a transaction a solicitor or licensed conveyancer is conclusively presumed in favour of a purchaser to have authority to deliver the deed.[155] In the light of this, when a vendor gives his solicitor an executed conveyance in advance of completion, he should no longer be regarded as delivering it in escrow. The most natural interpretation of his conduct is that he is authorising his solicitor to deliver the deed on completion.

3. Parties. If any other person is an essential party to the transaction, such **8–039** as a mortgagee who is releasing the property from his mortgage, he will be included as a party.

4. Recitals. These are of two types: **8–040**

    (a) *Narrative recitals,* which deal with such matters as how the vendor became entitled to the land; and

    (b) *Introductory recitals,* which explains how and why the existing state of affairs is to be altered, e.g. that the parties have agreed on the sale of the property.

These recitals can create estoppels. For example, the common form of recital of ownership set out above will estop the vendor from denying that he owns the legal estate. If at the time of the conveyance he does not own the legal estate but later acquires it, it will in effect pass to the purchaser under the doctrine of "feeding the estoppel" (explained elsewhere[156]) as against the vendor and persons claiming through him.[157]

5. Testatum. This is the beginning of the operative part of the conveyance. **8–041** Since the Law of Property (Miscellaneous Provisions) Act 1989 came into force on July 31, 1990, the testatum has acquired added importance. An instrument will not now be a deed unless it is clear on its face[158] that it is intended to be so by the person making or the parties to it.[159] Two obvious methods are for the instrument to describe itself as a deed or to be signed as a deed.[160] The words of the testatum, "Now this deed witnesseth . . . " meet this requirement.

---

[153] Co.Litt, 52a; *Powell v London and Provincial Bank* [1893] 2 Ch. 555.

[154] LP(MP)A 1989 s.1(1)(c).

[155] LP(MP)A 1989 s.1(5) (as amended by The Regulatory Reform (Execution of Deeds and Documents) Order 2005; 2005 SI/1906). It need no longer be a conveyancing transaction.

[156] Below, para.17–098.

[157] *Cumberland Court (Brighton) Ltd v Taylor* [1964] Ch. 29.

[158] It is not enough that the instrument was intended to be a formal one with legal effect: see *HSBC Trust Co (UK) Ltd v Quinn* [2007] EWHC 1543 (Ch) at [49]–[51].

[159] LP(MP)A 1989 s.1(2)(a). An instrument shall not be taken to make it clear on its face that it is intended to be a deed merely because it is executed under seal: LP(MP)A 1989 s.1(2A) (inserted by The Regulatory Reform (Execution of Deeds and Documents) Order 2005; SI 2005/1906).

[160] LP(MP)A 1989 s.1(2)(a). Other methods may of course be used.

8–042   6. Consideration. The consideration is stated to show *(inter alia)* that the transaction is not a voluntary one.[161]

8–043   7. Receipt clause. This is inserted to save a separate receipt being given. A solicitor who produces a conveyance containing such a clause which has been executed by the vendor thereby shows the purchaser that he has authority from the vendor to receive the purchase-money.[162]

8–044   8. Operative words. These effect the actual conveyance of the property. Formerly they included an "all estate clause" declaring that the conveyance passed the whole estate, title and interest which the vendor had in the land or had power to convey. But statute has rendered that superfluous by providing that every conveyance shall have this effect unless a contrary intention is expressed in it.[163] If the vendor purports to convey as legal owner but proves only to have an equitable interest, that interest will accordingly pass to the purchaser.[164]

8–045   9. Parcels. This is the description of the property. Description by reference to an annexed plan is a common alternative, but is not essential if an accurate verbal description can be given.[165] Very often a conveyance both describes the property verbally and also includes a plan. In that case it is advisable to provide that one or other shall prevail in case of inconsistency. For example, if the plan is expressed to be included "for the purposes of facilitating identification only" the verbal description will prevail.[166] However, if the property is said to be "more particularly described in the plan", then the plan will prevail.[167] If the verbal description is insufficient, as by failing to indicate

---

[161] See below, paras 8–057, 11–011.

[162] LPA 1925 s.69.

[163] LPA 1925 s.63. For the scope of this section and its interrelationship with LPA 1925 s.62 (below, para.28–027), see *Harbour Estates Ltd v HSBC Bank Plc* [2004] EWHC 1714 (Ch); [2005] Ch. 194.

[164] *Thellusson v Liddard* [1900] 2 Ch. 635. A legal charge by husband and wife as co-owners, which is ineffective at law because her signature is forged, nevertheless creates an equitable charge on his beneficial interest (*First National Securities Ltd v Hegarty* [1985] Q.B. 850 at 854; *Ahmed v Kendrick* (1987) 56 P. & CR. 120; *First National Bank Plc v Achampong* [2003] EWCA Civ 487; [2003] 2 P & CR D33).

[165] *Re Sharman's Contract* [1936] Ch. 755. The parcels clause must itself be construed in the context of the conveyance as a whole: see *Strachey v Ramage* [2008] EWCA Civ 384 at [36]; [2008] 2 P. & C.R.154 at 166.

[166] See *Hopgood v Brown* [1955] 1 W.L.R. 213; *Johnson v Shaw* [2003] EWCA Civ 894 at [35]; [2004] 1 P. & C.R. 123 at 133.

[167] *Eastwood v Ashton* [1915] A.C. 900; for other examples, see Lord Sumner's speech at 914 and Norton on *Deeds*; 237, 238, 243; and see *Wallington v Townsend* [1939] 2 All E.R. 225. See, however, *Truckell v Stock* [1957] 1 W.L.R. 161, and contrast *Grigsby v Melville* [1974] 1 W.L.R. 80. If both phrases are used, they are "mutually stultifying": *Neilson v Poole* (1968) 20 P. & CR. 909 at 916, per Megarry J. See Alan *Wibberley Buildings Ltd v Insley* [1999] 1 W.L.R. 894 at 899.

a boundary, the court may have recourse to the plan, even though it is "by way of identification only".[168] In such a case, the court adopts an objective test. Taking into account the surrounding circumstances, including the topography,[169] the language of the conveyance, and the representation of the plan, what would the reasonable lay person think that they were buying?[170]

A common defect of conveyances is that boundaries are inadequately defined.[171] In that case extrinsic evidence is admissible to establish the true intent of the parties, which may be clear from other documents, such as auction particulars.[172] That extrinsic evidence may include the subsequent conduct of the parties to the conveyance.[173] But if the location of boundaries is clear from the conveyance, neither extrinsic evidence nor any presumptions can be used to contradict it, save only in proceedings for rectification.[174] These are general rules which also apply to other obscurities in the definition of the land or of the interest granted.[175]

The conveyance will pass all fixtures without mention, because they are part of the land and pass with it.[176] But it will not pass removable chattels such as movable greenhouses.[177] The purchaser is entitled on completion to all fixtures attached to the land at the date of the contract.[178]

10. Habendum. This shows that the purchaser is to hold the land for his own benefit and not upon trust for a third party. It also contains the usual

8–046

---

[168] *Wigginton & Milner Ltd v Winster Engineering Ltd* [1978] 1 W.L.R. 1462; and see *Hatfield v Moss* [1988] 2 E.G.L.R. 58; *Targett v Ferguson* (1996) 72 P. & C.R. 106; *Affleck v Shorefield Holidays Ltd* [1997] E.G.C.S. 159.

[169] See *Alan Wibberley Buildings Ltd v Insley* [1999] 1 W.L.R. 894 at 896; *Cook v J.D. Weatherspoon Plc* [2006] EWCA Civ 330 at [11]; [2006] 2 P. & C.R. 326 at 329; *Strachey v Ramage* [2008] EWCA Civ 384 at [37]; [2008] 2 P. & C.R.154 at 167.

[170] *Toplis v Green*, Unreported February 14, 1992 CA); *Targett v Ferguson*, above, at 114; *Chadwick v Abbotswood Properties Ltd* [2004] EWHC 1058 (Ch) at [44]; [2005] 1 P. & C.R. 139 at 150.

[171] It is particularly undesirable to use small-scale plans taken from Ordnance Survey maps: *Mayer v Hurr* (1983) 49 P. & CR. 56; *Clarke v O'Keefe* (1997) 80 P. & CR. 126 (where the inadequacy of the plan justified the admission of extrinsic evidence to identify the boundary).

[172] *Scarfe v Adams* [1981] 1 All E.R. 843. See too *Spall v Owen* (1981) 44 P. & CR. 36; *Mayer v Hurr*, above; and *Re St Clement's Leigh-on-Sea* [1988] 1 W.L.R. 720.

[173] *Watcham v Attorney General of East Africa Protectorate* [1919] A.C. 533; *Ali v Lane* [2006] EWCA Civ 1532; [2007] 1 E.G.L.R. 71; *Haycocks v Neville* [2007] EWCA Civ 28 at [31]; [2007] 1 E.G.L.R. 78 at 81; *Bradford v James* [2008] EWCA Civ 837 at [29]; *Piper v Wakeford* [2008] EWCA Civ 1378.

[174] *Scarfe v Adams*, above, at 851; *Clarke v O'Keefe*, above; cf. *Alan Wibberley Buildings Ltd v Insley* [1999] 1 W.L.R. 894, where the so-called "hedge and ditch" presumption overrode the wording of a conveyance which defined the boundary by reference to an Ordnance Survey map, but where the two properties separated by that boundary had never been in common ownership.

[175] *Scarfe v Adams*, above; *Spall v Owen*, above.

[176] Although LPA 1925 s.62, expressly includes "building, erections, fixtures", fixtures would pass as part of the land even if s.62 were expressly excluded.

[177] *H. E. Dibble Ltd v Moore* [1970] 2 Q.B. 181; *Deen v Andrews* (1985) 52 P. & CR. 17; below, para.23–021.

[178] For discussion of fixtures, see below, Ch.23.

words of limitation.[179] It is followed by the acknowledgement and under-taking where these are to be included.[180]

8–047   11. Covenants for title. The words "with full title guarantee" imply covenants for title.[181] These have already been explained.[182]

8–048   12. Testimonium, and

8–049   13. Attestation clause. At common law, a deed had to be sealed.[183] The method of attestation that must now be employed depends upon the legal status of the party who is making the deed. As regards the execution of deeds by companies incorporated under the Companies Acts, the matter is now governed by Part 4 of the Companies Act 2006.[184]

8–050   *(a) Individuals.* A seal is no longer required for the valid execution of a deed by an individual.[185] To be a deed, an instrument must be signed either by the maker in the presence of an attesting witness, or at the maker's direction in his presence and in the presence of two attesting witnesses.[186]

8–051   *(b) Companies.* A company may execute a deed by affixing its common seal.[187] However, a company need not have a common seal,[188] and the deed will be validly executed if, instead, it is signed on behalf of the company by two authorised signatories or by a by a director of the company in the presence of a witness who attests the signature[189] and is expressed to be executed by the company.[190] For these purposes, the authorised signatories are:

(i) Every director of the company; and

---

[179] Above, para.3–023.
[180] Above, para.8–034.
[181] See LP(MP)A 1994 s.2.
[182] See above, paras 7–151 et seq.
[183] *Goddard's Case* (1584) 2 Co. Rep. 4b at 5a. The two other essentials of a deed were that it should be written on paper or parchment and delivered. The requirement of paper or parchment has been abrogated by LP(MP)A 1989 s.1(1)(a). There is now no restriction on the substance upon which a deed may be written.
[184] For the law as it was between July 31, 1990 and September 14, 2005, see the sixth edition of this work at paras 5–073—5–075. The law was altered with effect from September 15, 2005, by The Regulatory Reform (Execution of Deeds and Documents) Order 2005; SI 2005/1906, which amended LPA 1925 s.74, Companies Act 1985 s.36A, and LP(MP)A 1989 s.1. That Order implemented the recommendations in (1998) Law Com. No.253. The provisions relating to companies were then further changed when the relevant provisions of Pt 4 of the Companies Act 2006 were brought into force on April 6, 2008.
[185] LP(MP)A 1989 s.1(1)(b).
[186] LP(MP)A 1989 s.1(3). For these purposes, the signing of a document "includes making one's mark on the instrument": s.1(4)(b). Where the makers of the deed did not sign it in the presence of the attesting witness, but later delivered the deed, they were estopped from disputing its validity: *Shah v Shah* [2001] EWCA Civ 527; [2002] Q.B. 35.
[187] Companies Act 2006 s.44(1)(b).
[188] Companies Act 2006 s.45(1).
[189] Companies Act 2006 ss.44(2), 46(1).
[190] Companies Act 2006 s.44(4).

(ii) In the case of either a private company with a secretary or a public company, the secretary or any joint secretary of the company.[191]

In favour of a purchaser in good faith for valuable consideration, a document signed as set out above is deemed to have been duly executed by the company.[192] Where a document is to be signed by a person on behalf of more than one company, it is not duly signed by that person for the purposes of this section unless he signs it separately in each capacity.[193] However, a person may sign by one signature both on his own behalf and on behalf of a company which is also a party to that document.[194]

(c) Other corporations aggregate. A deed which is made by a corporation **8–052** aggregate that is not a company within the Companies Act 2006, such as a Cambridge college, must be sealed with the corporation's common seal. In practice, that sealing is likely to be attested by either:

(i) "two members of the board of directors, council or other governing body of the corporation"; or

(ii) "its clerk, secretary or other permanent officer or his deputy, and a member of the board of directors".

This is because if the deed is so sealed, it raises a presumption of due execution in favour of a purchaser.[195] However, it does not dispense with the requirement for delivery of the deed.[196]

(d) Corporations sole. The common law requirement of sealing still applies **8–053** to a deed executed by a corporation sole.[197]

C. Setting Aside and Modification of Conveyances

An executed conveyance may be avoided, set aside or modified by the court[198] **8–054** in various cases of fraud, undue influence, or mistake; and where this occurs

---

[191] Companies Act 2006 s.44(3). Cf. Companies Act 1985 s.36A(4), applicable prior to April 6, 2008, under which the authorised signatories were a director and the secretary of the company, or two company directors.

[192] Companies Act 2006 s.44(5). "Purchaser" includes a lessee, mortgagee, or other person who for valuable consideration acquires an interest in property: Companies Act 2006 s.44(5).

[193] Companies Act 2006 s.44(6).

[194] *Williams v Redcard Ltd* [2011] EWCA Civ 466.

[195] LPA 1925 s.74(1) (as amended by The Regulatory Reform (Execution of Deeds and Documents) Order 2005; 2005 SI/1906).

[196] *Bolton MBC v Torkington* [2003] EWCA Civ 1634; [2004] Ch. 66.

[197] None of the statutory provisions which now regulate attestation apply to corporations sole. LP(MP)A 1989 s.1 expressly does not: s.1(10). LPA 1925 s.74(1) applies only to a corporation aggregate. The Companies Act 2006 ss.44 and 46 applies only to companies formed or registered under that Act, and to companies that existed when the Act came into force: Companies Act 2006 s.1. There is, however, power to extend its provisions to unregistered companies: see Companies Act 2006 s.1043 (not yet in force). That power is likely to be exercised (as it was under the equivalent provision of the Companies Act 1985).

[198] For minors' dispositions, see below, para.36–012.

the court may order the document to be delivered up for cancellation.[199] The jurisdiction is either equitable or statutory. In either case the conveyance is not void but voidable. Where the jurisdiction is equitable, the right to set aside the instrument is a mere equity.[200] If therefore the property comes into the hands of an innocent purchaser (including a purchaser of an equitable interest[201]) without notice of the vitiating facts, his title will be unimpeachable. If the right is statutory, provision is normally made for the protection of purchasers. The extent of that protection depends upon the wording of the statute and may override the proprietary principles that would otherwise apply.[202]

8–055   **1. Misrepresentation.** The court has an inherent jurisdiction to set aside a conveyance induced by fraudulent misrepresentation,[203] and may also set aside a conveyance induced by innocent misrepresentation under the Misrepresentation Act 1967.[204]

8–056   **2. Conveyances made with intent to defraud creditors.** Where, after December, 28 1986, a transaction (including a conveyance[205]) was entered into at an undervalue and was made for the purpose of putting assets beyond the reach of the creditors of the transferor[206] or otherwise prejudicing them, the court has a power to make such order as it thinks fit for restoring the position to what it would have been had the transaction not been entered into, and for protecting the interests of persons who are victims of the transaction.[207] No order will be made against a purchaser in good faith who acquires

[199] See Snell, *Equity*, para.14–007.

[200] Above, para.8–012.

[201] Above, para.8–012.

[202] This point is of some importance. Where title to land is registered, the wording of the statute may be such that a transaction may be set aside against a purchaser with notice, even though under the provisions of LRA 2002, he would otherwise take free of the claimant's right: *Kemmis v Kemmis* [1988] 1 W.L.R. 1307 (a case on MCA 1973 s.37).

[203] See, e.g. *Brownlie v Campbell* (1880) 5 App. Cas. 925 at 937; below, para.15–112. For the position of a co-owner who is induced by the fraud of the other to agree to a mortgage of the property, see below, para.25–120.

[204] s.1(b). This reverses the former common law rule: see *Angel v Jay* [1911] 1 K.B. 666; below, para.15–112.

[205] IA 1986 s.425(1).

[206] See, e.g. *Midland Bank Plc v Wyatt* [1995] 1 F.L.R. 696 (declaration of trust of matrimonial home to safeguard it from commercial risk, not to benefit daughters).

[207] IA 1986 ss.423–425; see Snell, *Equity*, para.22–054. A transaction is at an undervalue if it is a gift or a transaction in consideration of marriage or the formation of a civil partnership or for a value that is significantly less than that of the property transferred: IA 1986 s.423(1) (as amended by the Civil Partnerships Act 2004 Sch.27, para.121); *Re M C Bacon Ltd* [1990] B.C.L.C. 324 at 340; *Jones v National Westminster Bank Plc* [2001] EWCA Civ 1541 at [24]–[29]; [2002] 1 P & CR D20. See, e.g. *Re Kumar* [1993] 1 W.L.R. 224 (transfer to co-owner on assumption of sole liability on a joint mortgage a transfer at an undervalue); *Agricultural Mortgage Corporation Plc v Woodward* [1995] 1 B.C.L.C. 1; *Barclays Bank Plc v Eustice* [1995] 1 W.L.R. 1238 (grants of tenancies which had a greater surrender value that the consideration given for them). cf. *Pinewood Joinery v Starelm Properties Ltd* [1994] 2 B.C.L.C. 412 (transfer for £1 of property worth £0.75 million but mortgaged for £2.65 million not at an undervalue); *Chen v Delaney* [2010] EWHC 6 (Ch); [2010] 1 E.G.L.R. 21 (sale and leaseback not a transaction at an undervalue). Any consideration received by the company for the transaction, even if it was from some third party, will be taken into account in determining whether the transaction was at an undervalue: see *Phillips v Brewin Dolphin Bell Lawrie* Ltd [2001] UKHL 2 at [20]; [2001] 1

any interest in property for value and without notice of the relevant circumstances.[208]

3. Voluntary conveyances made with intent to defraud a subsequent 8–057
purchaser. Every voluntary disposition of land made with intent to defraud a subsequent purchaser is by statute voidable at the instance of that purchaser.[209] A subsequent conveyance for value is not per se evidence of fraudulent intent.[210]

4. Conveyances made at an undervalue by a person subsequently 8–058
declared bankrupt or by a company which becomes insolvent. Where an individual is adjudged bankrupt and has "at the relevant time" entered into a transaction with any person at an undervalue,[211] his trustee in bankruptcy may apply to the court for such order as it thinks fit for restoring the position to what it would have been had the transaction not been entered into.[212] The "relevant time" means any time within the five years preceding the presentation of the bankruptcy petition.[213] However, if the transaction was entered into between two and five years prior to that petition, the transaction will be set aside only if the individual was insolvent at the time or became so in consequence of the transaction.[214] The court can make an order against someone other than the transferee.[215] However, it will not make an order against a purchaser who in good faith and for value acquired any interest in property that was formerly the bankrupt's from anybody other than the bankrupt.[216] There are analogous provisions which apply to transactions by a company which goes into liquidation or against which an administration order is made.[217]

W.L.R. 143 at 150. For those who may apply to have the transaction set aside, see IA 1986 s.424. For the orders which the court may make, see IA 1986 s.425(1). The court's powers are not limited to setting the transaction aside, but to restoring and protecting so far as is practicable: see *Chohan v Saggar* [1994] 1 B.C.L.C. 706.

[208] IA 1986 s.452(2).

[209] LPA 1925 s.173(1). See generally Snell, *Equity,* para.20–063.

[210] LPA 1925 s.173(2).

[211] A property adjustment order made under Matrimonial Causes Act 1973 s.24, is not a transaction at an undervalue, as the transferee is to be regarded as having given consideration equivalent to the value of the property being transferred: *Hill v Haines* [2007] EWCA Civ 1284; [2008] Ch. 412.

[212] IA 1986 ss.339, 342 (as amended by Insolvency (No.2) Act 1994 s.2, and Civil Partnerships Act 2004 Sch.27, para.121). The meaning of "undervalue" in s.339 is the same as in IA 1986 s.423 (above): s.339(3). The Insolvency (No.2) Act 1994 was enacted to remedy perceived drafting errors in IA 1986 ss.241 and 342.

[213] IA 1986 s.341(1).

[214] IA 1986 s.341(2). See s.341(3) for the definition of insolvency.

[215] IA 1986 s.342(1).

[216] IA 1986 s.342(2) (as amended by the Insolvency (No.2) Act 1994 s.2). For the circumstances in which such a purchaser will be rebuttably presumed to have acquired an interest from such a third party otherwise than in good faith, see IA 1986 s.342(2A), (4), (5) (inserted by the Insolvency (No.2) Act 1994 s.2).

[217] IA 1986 ss.238, 240, 241 (as amended by the Insolvency (No.2) Act 1994 s.1). A transaction is at an undervalue for these purposes if it is a gift, or for a value that is significantly less than that of the property transferred: IA 1986 s.238(4).

8–059   5. Conveyances made to defeat a claim for financial relief by a spouse or civil partner. The court may set aside any disposition made with the intention of defeating a claim for financial relief by a spouse in matrimonial proceedings,[218] or by a civil partner.[219] However, the court will not do so in favour of a purchaser for valuable consideration (other than marriage or formation of a civil partnership, as the case may be) who acted in good faith and without notice of any intention on the part of the transferor to defeat the claim of the spouse[220] or civil partner.[221]

8–060   6. Conveyances induced by undue influence or unconscionability.[222] Conveyances made under undue influence may be set aside under the court's equitable jurisdiction.[223] Two elements must be proved by the party seeking relief before undue influence is established:

(i) there must be a relationship capable of giving rise to the necessary influence; and

(ii) that influence arising from that relationship must have been abused.[224]

The relationship may either be presumed or proved.[225] There are a number of well-known categories of relationship, such as doctor and patient and solicitor and client, where it is presumed.[226] Those categories do not include husband and wife or banker and customer.[227] However, the existence of the necessary relationship of confidence may be proved as a fact in any particular case,[228] if one party has reposed a sufficient degree of trust and confidence in the

---

[218] MCA 1973 s.37(2). "Disposition" includes a conveyance: s.37(6). The concept of "defeating a claim" is widely defined: s.37(1). The presentation of a petition for bankruptcy by a spouse does not fall within s.37: *Woodley v Woodley (No.2)* [1994] 1 W.L.R. 1167. For a full discussion of these provisions, see *Kemmis v Kemmis* [1988] 1 W.L.R. 1307 and *Sherry v Sherry* [1991] 1 F.L.R. 307.

[219] Civil Partnerships Act 2004 Sch.5, paras 74, 75.

[220] MCA 1973 s.37(4). "Notice" in this context includes "constructive notice": *Kemmis v Kemmis* [1988] 1 W.L.R. 1307. cf. Inheritance (Provision for Family and Dependants) Act 1975 s.10, below, para.14–004.

[221] Civil Partnerships Act 2004 Sch.5, para.75(3).

[222] See Sir K. Lewison, "Under the Influence", [2011] R.L.R. (pending).

[223] See, e.g. *Cheese v Thomas* [1994] 1 W.L.R. 129; *Langton v Langton* [1995] 3 F.C.R. 521; and below, para.25–120.

[224] *Royal Bank of Scotland Plc v Etridge* [2001] UKHL 44 at [6]–[12]; [2002] 2 A.C. 773 at 794–796; *National Commercial Bank (Jamaica) Ltd v Hew* [2003] UKPC 51 at [30].

[225] *Royal Bank of Scotland Plc v Etridge* [2001] UKHL 44 at [13]; [2002] 2 A.C. 773 at 796; *National Commercial Bank (Jamaica) Ltd v Hew* [2003] UKPC 51 at [31].

[226] *National Commercial Bank (Jamaica) Ltd v Hew* [2003] UKPC 51 at [31].

[227] *Bank of Montreal v Stuart* [1911] A.C. 120 (husband and wife); *National Westminster Bank Plc v Morgan* [1985] A.C. 686 (banker and customer).

[228] Including that of husband and wife: *Barclays Bank Plc v O'Brien* [1994] 1 A.C. 180 at 190; wife and husband: *Simpson v Simpson* [1992] 1 F.L.R. 601 (husband dependent on wife through age and infirmity); employer and employee: *Steeples v Lea* [1998] 1 F.L.R. 138; and banker and customer: *National Westminster Bank Plc v Morgan* [1985] A.C. 686 at 708; *Petrou v Woodstead Finance Ltd* [1986] F.L.R. 158 at 169, 170 (where the banker acquires "a dominating influence" over the customer).

other.[229] Whatever the nature of the relationship of confidence, a court will only intervene where the influence arising from it has been abused.[230]

Where a person proves a relationship of confidence and the transaction is a disadvantageous one that cannot reasonably be explained by the relationship, undue influence will be established unless the other party adduces satisfactory evidence to the contrary.[231]

There is a developing jurisdiction under which the court may set aside a conveyance on grounds of unconscionability.[232] Furthermore, as will be seen,[233] in some cases conveyances may be rectified, set aside or modified for mutual mistake.

Part 4

REGISTRATION OF LAND CHARGES

The system of registration *of title* was explained in the previous chapter. **8–061** The system of unregistered conveyancing is reinforced by a much more limited system for the registration *of land charges*.[234]

Section 1. Land Charges

The object of the registration of land charges is to simplify traditional **8–062** conveyancing by eliminating the doctrine of notice and the elaborate inquiries which it necessitated. If the incumbrance is registrable and duly registered, its owner is protected and the purchaser can ascertain it without trouble. If it is not registered, the purchaser takes free from it and the owner's rights against the land are defeated. The mechanics of the system have some serious defects.[235]

---

[229] *Goldsworthy v Brickell* [1987] Ch. 378 a t 401. Whether or not this is so is an issue of fact: compare *Avon Finance Co Ltd v Bridger* [1985] 2 All E.R. 281 with *Forsdike v Forsdike* (1997) 74 P. & CR. D4 (both cases involving a son and an elder parent: undue influence was established in the former but not the latter).

[230] *Royal Bank of Scotland Plc v Etridge* [2001] UKHL 44 at [93]; [2002] 2 A.C. 773 at 816; *National Commercial Bank (Jamaica) Ltd v Hew* [2003] UKPC 51 at [33], [34].

[231] *Royal Bank of Scotland Plc v Etridge* [2001] UKHL 44 at [14], [21]–[26]; [2002] 2 A.C. 773 at 796, 798–799; *"R" v Attorney-General for England and Wales* [2003] UKPC 22 at [22].

[232] See *Boustany v Pigott* (1993) 69 P. & CR. 298 (where the Privy Council set aside a lease on this ground). Unconscionability is subsuming some of the older grounds of relief (such as purchase from a poor and ignorant person, as in *Fry v Lane* (1888) 40 Ch D 312). See [1995] L.M.C.L.Q. 538 (N. Bamforth).

[233] Below, para.15–122.

[234] There was an older system of registration, the registration of deeds. This was introduced by statute in Yorkshire and Middlesex in the early 18th century, but suffered from serious drawbacks. The Middlesex and the Yorkshire Deeds Registers were closed in 1940 and 1976 respectively.

[235] For the history of the land charges system prior to LCA 1925, see the sixth edition of this work at para.5–086.

Two different classes of registers are in operation: the central Land Charges Register and the various Local Land Charges Registers.

Section 2. Land Charges Register

A. Registrable Interests

8–063   The legislation governing land charges, initially found in the Land Charges Act 1925, has now been consolidated, with later amendments, in the Land Charges Act 1972,[236] and references in this chapter are to the latter Act. The Land Charges Rules 1974[237] regulate the procedure, and prescribe the contents of the registers and the forms.

The five registers[238] under the Act are kept in the Land Charges Department of the Land Registry at Plymouth, and searches can now be carried out electronically. One of the five registers—the annuities register—is now obsolete, and will not be considered. Of the remainder—land charges, pending actions; writs and orders; deeds of arrangement—the most important is land charges, which will be considered last.

In relation to the registers of pending actions and writs and orders, registration must be "in the name of the estate owner or other person whose estate or interest is intended to be affected".[239] Deeds of arrangement are registered in the name of the debtor.[240] Land charges can only be registered in the name of the estate owner.[241] Registration is accordingly an adverse entry against the owner for the time being of the burdened land, recording the interest claimed and the name of the claimant. There is no investigation or guarantee of the claim by the registrar. All that the applicant need do is fill in a form with the necessary particulars and submit it in the appropriate registry, either electronically or by post.

8–064   **1. Pending actions.** The register of pending actions contains pending actions, and petitions in bankruptcy.[242] A "pending land action" (often called by its old name of *lis pendens*) is " any action or proceeding pending in court relating to land or any interest in or charge on land".[243] The words "relating

---

[236] Except as regards local land charges: below, para.8–107.
[237] SI 1974/1286 (as amended).
[238] As required by LCA 1972 s.1.
[239] LCA 1972 ss.5(4), 6(2).
[240] LCA 1972 s.7(1).
[241] LCA 1972 ss.3(1), 5(4); and see below, paras 8–076, 8–086.
[242] LCA 1972 s.5.
[243] LCA 1972 s.17(1). It is expressly provided by statute that certain applications to the court are pending land actions for these purposes. The relevant applications are for: (i) a restraint order to prohibit dealings with property in connection with certain criminal proceedings (see Proceeds of Crime Act 2002 s.47(1)(b); Drug Trafficking Act 1994 s.26(12)(b)); (ii) an access order under the Access to Neighbouring Land Act 1992 (LCA 1972 s.6(1)(d), inserted by Access to Neighbouring Land Act 1992 s.5(6); and see below, para.18–227); (iii) an acquisition order under LTA 1987 s.28(5); and (iv) a vesting order under LRHUDA s.97(2)(b). See Ruoff & Roper, 42–022.

to land" are of wide and indefinite meaning, but in this context they mean that the claim must affect the title to the land by asserting some claim to it or to some proprietary right over it.[244] They do not, however, include the following claims:

(i) to prevent the land from being sold until some matter has been dealt with[245];

(ii) to a declaration that no contract affecting the land exists[246];

(iii) by a creditor in a company's liquidation[247];

(iv) for damages for breach of a repairing covenant in a lease[248];

(v) to enforce a contractual right to enter upon a neighbour's land to erect a fence[249]; or

(vi) for a sum of money and a charge on the land if the claim succeeds.[250]

Prior to 1997, a claim to share in the proceeds of sale of land held on trust for sale was not a pending land action: because of the doctrine of conversion, such a share was not regarded as an interest in land, but in the notional proceeds of sale.[251] However, trusts for sale are now included within the definition of a trust of land,[252] and the doctrine of conversion has been retrospectively abolished.[253] Notwithstanding this change, it remains the case that a claim to an undivided share in land cannot be registered as a pending land action.[254]

---

[244] As in *Whittingham v Whittingham* [1979] Fam. 9 (wife's claim to house in divorce proceedings); *Greenhi Builders Ltd v Allen* [1979] 1 W.L.R. 156 (claim to easement); *Selim Ltd v Bickenhall Engineering Ltd* [1981] 1 W.L.R. 1318 (application for leave to bring proceedings under Leasehold Property (Repairs) Act 1938); *Godfrey v Torpey* [2006] EWHC 1423 (Ch) (claim by A that A's creditor, B, was the owner of property which had been vested in the name of C). A claim for a property adjustment order in matrimonial proceedings will be registrable even though the land has not been specifically identified in those proceedings but only in the application for registration: *Perez-Adamson v Perez-Rivas* [1987] Fam. 89.
[245] *Calgary and Edmonton Land Co Ltd v Dobinson* [1974] Ch. 102.
[246] *Heywood v BDC Properties Ltd (No.2)* [1964] 1 W.L.R. 971.
[247] *Calgary and Edmonton Land Co Ltd v Dobinson*, above.
[248] *Regan & Blackburn Ltd v Rogers* [1985] 1 W.L.R. 870; *13–20 Embankment Gardens Ltd v Coote* (1997) 74 P. & CR. D6.
[249] *Albany Construction Co Ltd v Cunningham* [2004] EWHC 3392 (Ch).
[250] *Haslemere Estates Ltd v Baker* [1982] 1 W.L.R. 1109.
[251] See *Taylor v Taylor* [1968] 1 W.L.R. 378, where a wife claimed beneficial co-ownership of the home but sought an order for sale and a share of the proceeds. For the former doctrine of conversion, see below, para.12–006.
[252] TLATA 1996 s.1(2).
[253] TLATA 1996 s.3(1), (3).
[254] The definition of "land" in LCA 1972 s.17(1) still excludes "an undivided share in land" (i.e. an interest under a tenancy in common). Prior to 1997, the reason for this exclusion was the now-abolished doctrine of conversion. Elsewhere in the property legislation, the exclusion of undivided shares from the definition of land was removed by TLATA 1996. It was decided to retain it in the legislation on land charges to ensure that claims concerning beneficial interests were kept off the title.

"If they were made registrable as land charges the effect would be to bring onto the Land Charges Register orders affecting only beneficial interests, which under normal conveyancing procedure now take effect only behind a trust, and do not appear on the title to the land".[255]

There are other types of claim by beneficiaries under trust of land that *will* be registrable as pending land actions.[256]

8–065   The court has a wide discretion to order the removal of an unjustified entry.[257] Registration ensures that if the owner disposes of the land before the action is decided the new owner will be bound by the claim.[258] For equitable claims, registration has the advantage of ensuring that third parties have notice, and for legal and equitable claims alike it avoids the penalties of non-registration.[259]

Registration lasts for five years. If the case has not then been decided, registration may be renewed for successive periods of five years.[260]

8–066   **2. Writs and orders affecting land.** The register of writs and orders is for writs and orders *enforcing* judgments and orders of the court. It does not include writs employed to *commence* an action relating to land which come under the head of pending land actions. The chief items are as follows.[261]

> (i) Writs or orders affecting land issued or made by a court for the purpose of enforcing a judgment or recognisance, e.g. an order of the court charging the land of a judgment debtor with payment of the money due,[262] or an access order.[263] No writ or order affecting an interest under a trust of land may be registered in this register.[264] Nor is a freezing injunction registrable, because it merely prevents a litigant from disposing of his assets pending the trial of some claim against him.[265]

---

[255] *Perry v Phoenix Assurance Plc* [1988] 1 W.L.R. 940 at 945, per Browne-Wilkinson V.C. That case was concerned with the registration of a writ or order under LCA 1972 s.6; see below.

[256] A claim for an order relating to the exercise of the powers by trustee under TLATA 1996 s.14 (below, paras 12–021, 13–064), would be registrable if it was an action or proceeding pending in court relating to land or any interest in or charge on land, e.g. a claim to be entitled to occupy the premises under TLATA 1996 s.12.

[257] See below.

[258] If registered, the charge will bind a purchaser even if he had no express notice of the action: *Perez-Adamson v Perez-Rivas* [1987] Fam. 89; and see LCA 1972 s.5(7).

[259] See below, para.8–106.

[260] LCA 1972 s.8.

[261] LCA 1972 s.6.

[262] Charging Orders Act 1979.

[263] LCA 1972 s.6(1)(d), inserted by Access to Neighbouring Land Act 1992 s.5(1). For these orders, see below, paras 30–036 et seq.

[264] LCA 1972 s.6(1A), inserted by TLATA 1996 s.25(1), Sched. 3, para.12(1), (3). This restriction preserves the rule that charging orders over an undivided share in land are incapable of registration: see *Perry v Phoenix Assurance Plc* [1988] 1 W.L.R. 940, above.

[265] *Stockler v Fourways Estates Ltd* [1984] 1 W.L.R. 25. For freezing injunctions, see CPR 25.1(1)(f). These were previously known as *Mareva* injunctions after *Mareva Compania Naviera S.A. v International Bulk Carriers S.A.* [1975] 2 L1.Rep. 509, which first sanctioned their use.

(ii) An order appointing a receiver or sequestrator of land.[266]

(iii) A bankruptcy order, whether or not the bankrupt's estate is known to include land.[267]

Registration remains effective for five years, but may be renewed for successive periods of five years.[268]

3. Deeds of arrangement. The Deeds of Arrangement Act 1914 elabo-   **8–067**
rately defines deeds of arrangement, and the definition applies to this register.[269] For the present purpose a deed of arrangement may be taken as any document whereby control over a debtor's property is given for the benefit of his creditors generally, or, if he is insolvent, for the benefit of three or more of his creditors. A common example arises when a debtor, seeking to avoid bankruptcy, assigns all his property to a trustee for all his creditors.

Registration is effective for five years and may be renewed for successive periods of five years.[270] The registration may he effected by the trustee of the deed or by any creditor assenting to or taking the benefit of the deed.[271]

4. Land charges. This is the most important register. Land charges are   **8–068**
divided into six classes, A, B, C, D, E and F.[272] The most important classes, D and C, are sub-divided.

Class A consists of charges imposed on land by some statute, but which   **8–069**
comes into existence only when some person makes an application. Thus, where a landlord who is not entitled to land for his own benefit (such as a life tenant under the Settled Land Act 1925), has to pay compensation to an agricultural tenant or a tenant holding under a farm business tenancy, the landlord is entitled to a charge on the land for the amount of such compensation.[273] A Class A charge should be registered as soon as it arises.[274]

Class B consists of charges which are similar to those in Class A except that   **8–070**
they are not created on the application of any person, but are imposed automatically by statute.[275] Most charges thus imposed appear to be local land charges, and as these are registrable in a separate register, few charges are registrable in Class B. An example is a charge on land recovered or preserved for an assisted litigant under the Access to Justice Act 1999 in respect of legal

---

[266] Such an order may be registered even though the receivership does not create an interest in land: *Clayhope Properties Ltd v Evans* [1986] 1 W.L.R. 1223 (receiver appointed because of a landlord's failure to observe a repairing covenant: below, para.19–127).
[267] LCA 1972 s.6(1)(c), as substituted by IA 1985 s.235(1), Sch.8, para.21.
[268] LCA 1972 s.8.
[269] LCA 1972 ss.7, 17(1).
[270] LCA 1972 s.8.
[271] LCA 1972 s.7(1).
[272] LCA 1972 s.2.
[273] AHA 1986 s.86(1)–(3) (such a charge requires an application to the Minister of Agriculture, Fisheries and Food); ATA 1995 s.33(2) (no ministerial consent required).
[274] LCA 1972 s.4(2).
[275] LCA 1972 s.2(3).

services funded by the Legal Services Commission.[276] Such a charge should be registered as soon as it is created.[277]

8–071   *Class C* land charges are divided into four categories.[278]

8–072   C (i): A PUISNE MORTGAGE. This is a legal mortgage not protected by a deposit of documents relating to the legal estate affected.

8–073   C (ii): A LIMITED OWNER'S CHARGE. This is an equitable charge which a tenant for life or statutory owner acquires under any statute by discharging inheritance tax or other liabilities,[279] and to which the statute gives special priority. Thus on the death of a tenant for life of settled land, inheritance tax must be paid. If a succeeding tenant for life finds the money out of his own pocket instead of leaving the burden on the settled property itself, he is entitled to a charge on the land in the same way as if he had lent money to the estate on mortgage.[280] Such a charge arises automatically[281] and, being equitable,[282] is registrable in Class C (ii).[283]

8–074   C (iii): A GENERAL EQUITABLE CHARGE. This is any equitable charge on land which:

(i)   is not included in any other class of land charge;

(ii) is not secured by a deposit of documents relating to the legal estate affected[284]; and

(iii) does not arise, or affect an interest arising, under a trust of land or settlement.[285]

This is a residuary class which catches equitable charges not registrable elsewhere. It includes equitable annuities, e.g. rentcharges for life, if created after 1925,[286] and equitable mortgages of a legal estate if not protected by a deposit of title deeds[287] and if not limited owner's charges. It also includes an unpaid vendor's lien.[288] It specifically excludes a charge given by way of

---

[276] Access to Justice Act 1999 s.10(7).

[277] LCA 1972 s.4(5).

[278] LCA 1972 s.2(4).

[279] If a tenant for life pays off a mortgage on the settled property he may keep it alive and enforce his rights as mortgagee: *Lord Gifford v Lord Fitzhardinge* [1899] 2 Ch. 32; see below, para.25–102.

[280] Inheritance Tax Act 1984 s.212(2).

[281] *Lord Advocate v Countess of Moray* [1905] A.C. 531 at 539.

[282] LPA 1925 s.1(3).

[283] LCA 1972 s.2(4)(ii) as amended by the Inheritance Tax Act 1984 s.276, Sch.8, para.3.

[284] This excludes "protected" mortgages of a legal estate as explained below, para.26–025.

[285] LCA 1972 s.2(4), as amended by TLATA 1996 s.25(1), Sch.3, para.12(1), (2).

[286] Annuities created prior to 1926 were registrable under the now obsolete register of annuities: see above, para.8–063.

[287] Equitable mortgages protected by a deposit of title deeds can now only take effect if there is a binding contract to create a mortgage: see *United Bank of Kuwait Plc v Sahib* [1997] Ch. 107; below, paras 15–051, 24–041.

[288] *Uziell-Hamilton v Keen* (1971) 22 P. & CR. 655. See [1997] Conv. 336 at 342 (D. G. Barnsley).

indemnity against rents equitably apportioned or charged exclusively on land in exoneration of other land and against the breach or non-observance of covenants or conditions.[289] Equitable mortgages of an equitable interest under a settlement or a trust of land are excluded, as they are overreached on a conveyance to a purchaser, and therefore no question of enforcing them against him can arise.[290] The same applies to other charges on the proceeds of sale of land, as opposed to charges on the land itself, such as an agreement to share the proceeds of sale,[291] or an estate agent's charge on them for commission.[292]

C (iv): AN ESTATE CONTRACT. This is a "contract by an estate owner" (i.e. the **8–075** owner of a legal estate[293]) "or by a person entitled at the date of the contract to have a legal estate conveyed to him to convey or create a legal estate". The contract must be made in writing, contain all the terms expressly agreed and be signed by both parties.[294] A notice to treat served under a compulsory purchase order is not a contract and cannot be registered.[295] The definition expressly includes "a contract conferring either expressly or by statutory implication a valid option to purchase, a right of pre-emption or any other like right".[296] The definition applies both to ordinary contracts for the sale, sub-sale,[297] lease,[298] or mortgage[299] of a legal estate, whether unconditional or conditional,[300] and also to unilateral contracts such as an option to renew a lease,[301] to purchase the reversion,[302] or to require a tenant to surrender his lease instead of assigning it.[303] However, it does not apply to such contracts

---

[289] LP(Am)A 1926 Sch.

[290] Below, paras 12–036 et seq. And Appendix, A–093 et seq, where it is also explained how a number of land charges (including general equitable charges) may be overreached even though created prior to the trust for sale or settlement.

[291] *Thomas v Rose* [1968] 1 W.L.R. 1797.

[292] *Georgiades v Edward Wolfe & Co Ltd* [1965] Ch. 487.

[293] LCA 1972 s.17(1); LPA 1925 s.205(1)(v); above.

[294] LP(MP)A 1989 s.2, below, para.15–014.

[295] *Capital Investments Ltd v Wednesfield UDC* [1965] Ch. 774.

[296] For options as interests in land, see below, para.15–014.

[297] i.e. a resale by a purchaser before the land has been conveyed to him. cf. *Barrett v Hilton Developments Ltd* [1975] Ch. 237; below, para.8–076.

[298] See *Blamires v Bradford Corporation* [1964] Ch. 585, where a testamentary option to occupy land for life at a rent had been exercised.

[299] Equitable mortgages by deposit of title deeds can only take effect as contracts to grant a mortgage: see *United Bank of Kuwait Plc v Sahib* [1997] Ch. 107; below, paras 15–015, 24–041. It has not been decided whether such mortgages are required to be registered as estate contracts. Although the wording of LCA 1972 s.2(4) suggests that they should, in principle this seems unnecessary: see below, para.26–029.

[300] At any rate if the condition is extraneous to the parties themselves (*Haslemere Estates Ltd v Baker* [1982] 1 W.L.R. 1109), and probably if it is not: see *Williams v Burlington Investments Ltd* (1977) 121 S.J. 424 (agreement to grant mortgage of unsold land on demand).

[301] *Phillips v Mobil Oil Co Ltd* [1989] 1 W.L.R. 888; and see *Markfaith Investment Ltd v Chiap Hua Flashlights Ltd* [1991] 2 A.C. 43. As a matter of literal interpretation, this seems correct, though the practical need to register such covenants is not apparent: see [1990] Conv. 168 and 250 (J. Howell). An assignee of the reversion prior to 1926 would have been bound by such a covenant regardless of notice because it touched and concerned the land: below, para.20–040. The requirement of registration may have been due to a mistake in drafting: below, para.8–096.

[302] *Midland Bank Trust Co Ltd v Green* [1981] A.C. 513; below, para.8–095.

[303] *Greene v Church Commissioners for England* [1974] Ch. 467.

at one remove (i.e. a contract authorising an agent to make such a contract),[304] nor to a contract to sell an interest under a trust of land,[305] nor to a boundary agreement unless it clearly involves the transfer of land.[306] Registration of a right of pre-emption is held, anomalously, to take effect only from the time when the right becomes exercisable.[307] Where an option which has been registered is then exercised, it is unnecessary to register additionally the resultant contract of sale.[308]

8–076   If V contracts to sell land to P, who then contracts to sell it to Q, it is against V, the estate owner,[309] and not P. that Q must register his estate contract. Registration against P will not be effective even if P later acquires the legal estate.[310] This is a trap for sub-purchasers, who often will not know that the sub-vendor is not an estate owner. But when a yearly tenant agreed that if he acquired the freehold he would grant his sub-tenant a lease for 10 years, the contract was somewhat surprisingly held to be registrable as an estate contract because even though the tenant had only a hope of acquiring the freehold, his yearly tenancy made him an estate owner.[311]

It has also been held that a contract by a landowner with an agent to convey the land to such persons as the agent should direct is registrable.[312] Yet here it seems that the contract created no specifically enforceable rights in the land, for the agent's interest was merely financial, and damages would have been an adequate remedy.

There are certain rights which, by statute, are registrable as if they were contracts, namely:

    (i) a tenant's notice to purchase the freehold or take an extended lease under the Leasehold Reform Act 1967[313];

    (ii) certain notices given under the Leasehold Reform, Housing and Urban Development Act 1993[314]; and

---

[304] *Thomas v Rose* [1968] 1 W.L.R. 1797.

[305] It is not a contract "to convey or create a legal estate" within LCA 1972 s.2(4): cf. *Re Rayleigh Weir Stadium* [1954] 1 W.L.R. 786.

[306] *Neilson v Poole* (1969) 20 P. & CR. 909; *Joyce v Rigolli* [2004] EWCA Civ 79; [2004] 1 P. & C.R. D55.

[307] *Pritchard v Briggs* [1980] Ch. 339, below, para.15–065. The position of rights of pre-emption in relation to registered land is now different: see above, para.7–067.

[308] *Armstrong and Holmes Ltd v Holmes* [1993] 1 W.L.R. 1482.

[309] LCA 1972 ss.3(1), 17(1). Contrast s.5(4), which is not confined to estate owners: above, para.8–063.

[310] *Barrett v Hilton Developments Ltd* [1975] Ch. 237, a decision strengthened by the contrast mentioned in the preceding note; *Property Discount Corporation Ltd v Lyon Group Ltd* [1981] 1 W.L.R. 300.

[311] *Sharp v Coates* [1949] 1 KB. 285. A legal estate in *other* land is of course irrelevant: see at 294. Such a contract should be registered against the freeholder: above, para.8–063.

[312] *Turley v Mackay* [1944] Ch. 37, questioned in *Thomas v Rose*, above; and see *Re Rayleigh Weir Stadium*, above, at 791.

[313] Leasehold Reform Act 1967 s.5(5); below, para.22–205.

[314] LRHUDA 1993 s.97(1).

(iii) a request for an overriding lease under the Landlord and Tenant (Covenants) Act 1995.[315]

Class D land charges are divided into three categories.[316] **8–077**

D (i): INLAND REVENUE CHARGES. These are statutory charges in favour of **8–078** the Board of Inland Revenue which arise automatically when inheritance tax is unpaid.[317] Inheritance tax is levied primarily on the estate of a deceased person but a liability to tax may also arise on certain gifts made inter vivos. Where the charge affects land it is registrable under this head,[318] but in practice this precaution is rarely taken.

D (ii): RESTRICTIVE COVENANTS. Under this head any covenant or agreement **8–079** restrictive of the user of land[319] may be registered provided it:

(i) was entered into after 1925, and

(ii) is not "between a lessor and a lessee".

Thus restrictive covenants in leases are never registrable, even where they relate not to the land demised but to adjoining land of the lessor.[320] The normal rules as to privity of contract and privity of estate apply and where there is neither of these the question is one of notice.[321] Similarly restrictive covenants made before 1926 still depend upon the doctrine of notice for their effect against purchasers, since they are enforceable against everyone except a purchaser for value of a legal estate without notice.

D (iii): EQUITABLE EASEMENTS. Any "easement, right or privilege over or **8–080** affecting land" is registrable under this head, provided:

(i) it is merely equitable, and

(ii) it was created or arose after 1925.

An example would be an easement granted after 1925 merely by contract, or only for life).[322]

---

[315] L & TCA 1995 s.20(6); below, para.20–029.
[316] LCA 1972 s.2(5).
[317] Inheritance Tax Act 1984 s.237.
[318] LCA 1972 s.2(5), as amended by the Inheritance Tax Act 1984 s.276, Sched. 8, para.3(1). Inheritance tax was introduced by the Finance Act 1986. The Capital Transfer Tax Act 1984 was renamed the Inheritance Tax Act by the Finance Act 1986 s.100(1)(b).
[319] A covenant will be a restrictive covenant if it restricts the purposes for which the land may be used, its development, or the buildings which may be constructed upon it: see *Langevad v Chiswick Quay Freeholds Ltd* [1999] 1 E.G.L.R. 61 at 62. A covenant which restricts alienation is not a restrictive covenant: see *University of East London Higher Education Corpn v Barking and Dagenham LBC* [2004] EWHC 2710 (Ch) at [28]; [2005] Ch. 354 at 365.
[320] *Darstone Ltd v Cleveland Petroleum Co Ltd* [1969] 1 W.L.R. 1807.
[321] Below, para.20–004.
[322] Below, para.28–003.

Much trouble has been caused both by the vagueness of this definition and by the injustice of applying it to informal arrangements, such as agreements between neighbours as to rights of way, which the dominant owner omits to register. These defects have caused the Court of Appeal to hold, at one extreme, that it does not include an equitable right of way arising by acquiescence or estoppel,[323] and, at the other extreme, that it includes the whole residue of equitable proprietary rights capable of binding a purchaser. The latter decision was reversed by the House of Lords, which held that the definition should be given "its plain prima facie meaning".[324] This meaning, though not precisely explained, is evidently narrow. It would appear to be confined to rights in the nature of easements and profits.[325] Accordingly the House of Lords held that it does not extend to an equitable right of entry.[326] Nor does it extend to a right to remove fixtures at the end of a lease,[327] or to the interest of public authority requisitioning land under Defence Regulations.

8–081   The courts have therefore rejected the contention[328] that the policy of 1925 was to require registration of all equitable interests in land which were not protected by deposit of title deeds and not overreachable.[329] An example of an unregistrable interest that is not overreachable is an equity arising by estoppel.[330] The defects of the legislation are now so obvious that the advantage lies in giving it the narrowest possible scope.

8–082   *Class E* consists of annuities created before 1926 but not registered until after 1925. They are, in practice, obsolete.[331]

8–083   *Class F* consists of charges affecting any land by virtue of Part IV of the Family Law Act 1996.[332] These "home rights"[333] are explained later.[334]

8–084   *Companies.* Most charges on land created by a company for securing money (including a charge created by a deposit of title deeds[335]) require registration within 21 days in the Companies Register maintained under the

---

[323] *E.R. Ives Investment Ltd v High* [1967] 2 Q.B. 379, holding that the equitable grounds on which the purchaser (with notice) was bound were unaffected by the Land Charges Act 1925: see below, para.16–006. For a discussion of this very difficult case, see (1995) 58 M.L.R. 637 at 643 (G. Battersby).

[324] *Shiloh Spinners Ltd v Harding* [1973] A.C. 691 at 721, per Lord Wilberforce; and see *Poster v Slough Estates Ltd* [1968] 1 W.L.R. 1515 at 1520, 1521.

[325] See (1937) 53 L.Q.R. 259 (C. V. Davidge); (1948) 12 Conv.(n.s.) 202 (J. F. Gamer); [1986] Conv. 31 (M. P. Thompson). cf. LPA 1925 s.1(2)(a); above, para.6–020.

[326] *Shiloh Spinners Ltd v Harding,* above.

[327] *Poster v Slough Estates Ltd,* above.

[328] *Lewisham Borough Council v Maloney* [1948] 1 K.B. 50.

[329] The policy for registered land is quite different: see above, para.7–064.

[330] Below, Ch.16.

[331] Prior to 1926, they would have been registered in the old register of annuities: see above, para.8–063.

[332] As amended by the Civil Partnerships Act 2004.

[333] FLA 1996 s.30(2).

[334] Below, para.34–023.

[335] *Re Wallis & Simmonds (Builders) Ltd* [1974] 1 W.L.R. 391. To be enforceable, such charges must now be binding contracts to mortgage: see below, paras 15–015, 24–041.

Companies Act 2006.[336] For floating charges this suffices in place of registration in the Land Charges Register, and has the same effect.[337] For other charges, this suffices if the charge was created before 1970[338] but otherwise the charge requires registration on both registers. The two systems of registration do not fit together neatly, and so it has proved necessary to adopt the cumbersome system of double registration.[339]

B. Effects of Registration and Non-Registration

1. Effect of registration

(a) *Actual notice.* By the Law of Property Act 1925,[340] registration under **8–085** the Land Charges Act of any instrument or matter required or authorised to be registered under the Act[341] is deemed to constitute actual notice of the interest registered "to all persons and for all purposes[342] connected with the land affected, as from the date of registration or other prescribed date and so long as the registration continues in force". There are exceptions to this rule,[343] but in general it prevents any person claiming to be a purchaser without notice of a registered interest.

(b) *Names register.;* Registration is effected against the name of the estate **8–086** owner at the time.[344] An error in the name registered (or in the description of the property) does not invalidate the registration if the name or description given may fairly be called a version of the true name (e.g. "Frank" or "Francis") or description; but a person who makes an official search in the correct name and description is protected even if it fails to reveal the entry.[345]

---

[336] s.870.
[337] LCA 1972 s.3(7), as amended by the Companies Consolidation (Consequential Provisions) Act 1985 s.30, Sched. 2; see *Re Molton Finance Ltd* [1968] Ch. 325.
[338] Even if the company's name differed from the estate owner's and did not appear on the title, thereby creating a trap: *Property Discount Corporation Ltd v Lyon Group Ltd* [1981] 1 W.L.R. 300.
[339] See [1982] Conv. 43 (D. M. Hare and T. Flanagan). In relation to registered land, there is power for the Lord Chancellor to make rules for the transmission of applications for the registration of charges that must also be registered in the Companies Register: see LRA 2002 s.121. To date no rules have been made.
[340] s.198.
[341] Thus registration of a covenant in a lease, or of any other non-registrable interest, is nugatory.
[342] These words mean "for all purposes for *which notice is material,* that is to say for the purpose of the enforcement of third parties' rights against the land affected": *Rignall Developments Ltd v Halil* [1988] Ch. 190 at 202, per Millett J. "Notice" has a technical meaning that is not synonymous with "knowledge": above, para.8–016. Thus a person who is deemed to have actual notice of a matter under s.198 will not thereby have the *mens rea* for the commission of a criminal offence *(Wrekin D.C. v Shah* (1985) 150 J.P. 22), nor lose a right to rescind for misrepresentation in respect to that matter: *Coles v White City (Manchester) Greyhound Association Ltd* (1928) 45 T.L.R. 125 at 127, affirmed at 230. A purchaser may terminate a contract for the sale of land on grounds of non-disclosure of a land charge even though he has actual notice of it under s.198: *Rignall Developments Ltd v Halil,* above: see below, para.15–084.
[343] Below, paras 25–053, 26–067.
[344] See LCA 1972 ss.3(1), 17(1); Land Charges Rules 1974 r.5, Sch.1.
[345] *Oak Co-operative B.S. v Blackburn* [1968] Ch. 730; for searches, see below, para.8–102.

This system of registration against names is seriously defective from the point of view of a purchaser. There is no map or plan enabling him to search against the land itself.[346] He must search against the names of all previous owners of the land, as ascertained from the title deeds and he must describe the property in accordance with the title.[347] The rights most likely to concern a purchaser, namely Classes C and D, only became registrable after 1925, but in the course of time the cost of searches may become considerable. It has been said that "this system will end in chaos if it is perpetuated",[348] and that "it is obvious that such a register must in time sink under its own weight".[349] Trouble can be saved if each purchaser preserves the certificate of the search which he made when purchasing the land, and then hands on the certificate with the title deeds so that subsequent owners can rely upon it (which in practice occurs). However, there is no means of enforcing this practice.

8–087   A further difficulty formerly arose where the estate owner died before the land charge had been registered. Because the charge had to be registered "in the name of the estate owner whose estate is intended to be affected",[350] it was questionable whether registration could validly be made in the deceased's name.[351] To resolve this difficulty, the Law Commission recommended that such registration after death should be effective,[352] and this has been implemented.[353] It is now provided in relation respectively to the registers of land charges, of pending actions, and of writs and orders affecting land, that where a person has died and at the time of his death:

(i)   a land charge had been created; or

(ii) there was a pending land action; or

(iii) there was a writ or order affecting land

that would, apart from his death, have been registrable against his name, it may be so registered notwithstanding his death.[354]

8–088   *(c) Names behind the root of title.* In 1955, when 30 years had elapsed since 1925, the time arrived when the names of persons against whom charges were registered might lie behind the root of title; and this possibility became much

---

[346] See *Horrill v Cooper*, CA February 29, 2000, shortly reported at (2000) 80 P & CR D16, at D17. See the transcript at [19] (approving the text of this paragraph in the sixth edition) and [39] (quoted at 80 P & CR D17).

[347] *Horrill v Cooper*, above.

[348] (1940) 56 L.Q.R. 373 (D. W. Logan); and see Sir J. Stewart-Wallace, *Principles of Land Registration* (1937) pp. 83–84.

[349] (1931) 75 S.J. 807. For an account of the mechanism, see *Oak Co-operative B.S. v Blackburn*, above.

[350] LCA 1972 s.3(1).

[351] Because he was no longer the estate owner: see generally [1979] Conv. 249 (A. M. Prichard).

[352] (1989) Law Com. No.184, para.2.7.

[353] By LP(MP)A 1994 s.15

[354] See respectively LCA 1972 ss.3(1A), 5(4A), 6(2A) (as inserted).

more serious in 1969 when the period for title was reduced to 15 years.[355] A purchaser may be unable to discover the relevant names, but none the less he will be deemed to have actual notice of the charges because they are in fact registered. A problem of this kind had already arisen in the case of leases, owing to an intending tenant's inability to inspect the freehold title or a superior leasehold title.[356] These are grave difficulties, and a Committee[357] which studied them despaired of finding any satisfactory solution except by abandoning name registration and pressing on with the registration of title throughout the country. "We are the inheritors of a transitory system which was bound to disclose this defect after 30 years, and it seems too late to disclaim our inheritance."[358]

(d) Compensation scheme. In 1969 a palliative was provided in the form of **8–089** financial compensation at public expense for purchasers affected by undiscoverable land charges.[359] The compensation is recoverable by action in the High Court against the Chief Land Registrar.[360] There are two main requirements. First, at the date of completion (which must be after 1969) neither the purchaser nor any agent of his, acting as such in the transaction, must have had any "actual knowledge" of the charge; and for this purpose, contrary to the general rule, registration is to be disregarded.[361] Secondly, the charge must be registered against the name of an owner of an estate in the land who was not, as such, a party to any transaction in the relevant title, or concerned in any event in it.[362] The "relevant title" means the full title as under an open contract, together with any additional title contracted to be shown; and if a document in the title expressly provided that it was to take effect subject to some registrable interest (e.g. a restrictive covenant), the title includes the transaction creating that interest.[363] The scheme avoids the problem of leases by excluding grants and mortgages of leases derived out of the freehold; but, with no apparent logic, it extends to sub-leases,[364] and it extends generally to sales, exchanges, mortgages and compulsory purchases.

---

[355] Below, para.15–077.

[356] This is explained below, para.21–005.

[357] Report of the Committee on Land Charges 1956 (Cmd. 9825), discussed in [1956] C.L.J. 215 (H.W.R.W.).

[358] Report of the Committee on Land Charges, above, at 8.

[359] LPA 1969 s.25, implementing recommendations made in (1969) Law Com. No.18.

[360] LPA 1969 s.25(4), (6).

[361] LPA 1969 s.25(1), (2), (11).

[362] LPA 1969 s.25(1). The wording of this section could create a difficulty in one situation. Suppose a charge was registered against the name of a landowner, Joan Smith. She subsequently changed her name by deed poll or marriage to Joan Jones. She then conveyed the land to a purchaser. If at some future date that conveyance became the root of title in a conveyancing transaction, could the purchaser claim an indemnity if he failed to discover the land charge registered against Joan Smith? The wording of the section suggests that he could not.

[363] LPA 1969 s.25(3), (10). Where compensation has been so claimed, the registrar may make additions or alterations to the registers and index so as to facilitate disclosure: S1 1970/136.

[364] LPA 1969 s.25(9). It appears that a sub-lessee can claim compensation for, e.g. a registered restrictive covenant on the freehold title but that a lessee cannot. This discrimination seems inexplicable.

The compensation scheme has to date generated very few claims,[365] and may not have been strictly necessary. This is because of the practice of carrying forward with the title deeds the results of previous searches of the land charges register, thereby overcoming the difficulty of discovering the names of the owners of the land prior to the root of title.[366]

8–090   *(e) Transactions on the title.* Name registration is not only inherently defective; it has also been applied too widely. Its utility is greatest where it brings to a purchaser' s notice, and so also protects, some equitable incumbrance which the purchaser might otherwise miss when investigating title, such as a prior contract for sale to another person (an estate contract).[367] But where the transaction normally appears or is mentioned in the title deeds, as for example does a restrictive covenant in a conveyance or an option in a lease, there is no risk of the purchaser overlooking it; yet there is a considerable risk of its owner failing to register it, so that it will be defeated by a purchase of a legal estate. To require registration in such cases merely creates insecurity of property. The difficulties in requiring registration of equitable easements have already been noted.[368]

These unsuitable requirements have been aggravated by errors of drafting. Registration was not intended to apply to covenants in leases, including options to renew the lease or to purchase the reversion, since all such obligations are self-evident from the lease itself; and the Law of Property Act 1922 provided accordingly.[369] But when the saving clause was transposed to the Law of Property Act 1925 it remained confined to "this Part of this Act" although "this Part" no longer contained the provisions about registration, as the corresponding part of the Act of 1922 had done.[370] The legal profession, misguided by the author of the legislation himself,[371] acted on the assumption that options in leases were exempt from registration until this was shown to be wrong.[372]

2. Effect of non-registration

8–091   *(a) Persons affected.* It is only as against third parties, i.e. successors in title, that non-registration may invalidate a registrable interest. Failure to register is immaterial as between the original parties to the transaction, e.g. as

---

[365] See the sixth edition of this work at para.5–113.

[366] See above, para.8–086, where it is pointed out that there is no legal sanction to enforce this practice.

[367] Curiously enough, it is the practice of some solicitors not to register ordinary contracts of sale, though they are ideally suited for protection by a names register.

[368] Above, para.8–080.

[369] LPA 1922 s.28(4), expressly providing that no registration of any land charge should be necessary. LP(Am)A 1924, Sch.3, Pt II, para.4, amended this into the defective form of LPA 1925 s.6.

[370] For another mistake of this kind, see below, para.8–096.

[371] Wolst & C., 12th edn, i, 246, explaining that, "the lease is the charter of the title". See *Taylors Fashions Ltd v Liverpool Victoria Trustees Co Ltd* [1982] Q.B. 133 at 143.

[372] In *Beesly v Hallwood Estates Ltd* [1960] 1 W.L.R. 549. That decision has since been approved by the Court of Appeal: *Phillips v Mobil Oil Co Ltd* [1989] 1 W.L.R. 888.

between the vendor and the purchaser under an estate contract, or as between the covenantor and the covenantee in the case of a restrictive covenant. A registrable transaction, even though not registered, remains valid in every respect except as against certain purchasers.[373]

(b) Categories of purchaser. If a registrable incumbrance is not registered, **8–092** the consequences fall into two main categories:

> (i) the incumbrance may be void against a purchaser for value of any interest in the land; or
>
> (ii) the incumbrance may be void against a purchaser for money or money's worth of a legal estate in the land.

One difference between (i) and (ii) is that a purchaser of an equitable interest is protected in case (i) but not in case (ii); and a purchaser of an equitable interest does not come within (ii) even if the legal estate which is subject to the incumbrance is specifically declared to be held in trust for him.[374] Another difference is that marriage is "value" but is not "money or money's worth",[375] so that in the case of land settled by an ante-nuptial marriage settlement, the spouses and issue will be protected in case (i) but not in case (ii). In both cases "purchaser" has an extended meaning and includes a lessee, mortgagee or other person taking an interest in land for value.[376] The crucial time in every case is the completion of the transaction, i.e. the actual transfer of the legal estate or the equitable interest, as the case may be[377] subsequent registration cannot impose any burden on the purchaser.

(c) Effect. The effect of non-registration may be summarised as follows. **8–093**

> (i) In general, whichever register is concerned, failure to register any registrable matter in the appropriate register[378] makes it void against a purchaser for value of any interest in the land.[379]
>
> (ii) But in the case of a post-1925 estate contract, restrictive covenant, equitable easement or inland revenue charge[380] (i.e. charges within

---

[373] *Lloyds Bank Plc v Carrick* [1996] 4 All E.R. 630 at 642. Thus on a compulsory acquisition the statutory right to compensation is not prejudiced by non-registration: *Blamires v Bradford Corporation* [1964] Ch. 585.

[374] *McCarthy & Stone Ltd v Julian S. Hodge & Co Ltd* [1971] 1 W.L.R. 1547. See above, para.8–014.

[375] Above, para.8–008.

[376] LCA 1972 s.17(1).

[377] LCA 1972 s.4, makes unregistered land charges void unless registered "before the completion of the purchase". The corresponding provisions for other registers are less specific, but "purchaser" means a person who "takes" an interest for value (s.17(1)), so that the moment of taking is presumably the critical moment.

[378] i.e. under LCA 1972: *Kitney v M.E.P.C. Ltd* [1977] 1 W.L.R. 981 (entry in Middlesex deeds register insufficient).

[379] LCA 1972 ss.4–7.

[380] In the case of inland revenue charges the purchaser must be in good faith and nominal consideration does not count: Inheritance Tax Act 1984 ss.238, 272. This provides that such a charge, if unregistered, and so void against a purchaser, is attached to the proceeds of sale, so that it is not destroyed but overreached.

Class C(iv) or Class D) non-registration makes it void against a purchaser of a legal estate for money or money's worth.[381]

(iii) Bankruptcy petitions (registrable as pending actions) and the title of the trustees in bankruptcy under bankruptcy orders (registrable as writs and orders) are void only against a bona fide purchaser of a legal estate for money or money's worth.[382]

(iv) Any other pending land action is void against a purchaser for value of any interest in the land, unless he has express notice of it.[383]

Where an interest is void for non-registration, any right that depends upon or is a consequence of that interest will also be void. Thus, where a purchaser under an unregistered estate contract had paid the entire price, so that the vendor held it on a bare trust for her, a subsequent legal mortgagee took free not only of her estate contract but her interest under the bare trust as well.[384]

8–094   *(d) Exclusion of the doctrine of notice.* It should be noted that with the comparatively unimportant exception of (iv) above, the equitable doctrine of notice is wholly excluded. Under the Land Charges Act 1972[385] the purchaser is not required to act in good faith, except under (iii) above: the unregistered interest is simply void against him. He does not need to rely upon the provision (seemingly redundant) of the Law of Property Act 1925[386] that he is not to be prejudiced by notice of any interest which is void against him under the Land Charges Acts, which in any case is narrower in scope since under that Act good faith is necessary.[387] In the result, therefore, it is immaterial that the purchaser was not diligent in investigating title[388] or had actual

---

[381] LCA 1972 s.4(6). It does not follow that an unregistered charge in this category will necessarily be valid as against any other form of purchaser. It could be defeated by a bona fide purchaser of a legal estate made in consideration of marriage who had no notice of the charge: see above, para.6–033

[382] LCA 1972 ss.5(8), 6(5), as amended by IA 1985 s.235, Sch.8, para.21, and Sch.10, Pt III.

[383] LCA 1972 s.5(7). This does not prevent a fresh action being brought against the purchaser if there is some charge or interest which is enforceable against him.

[384] *Lloyds Bank Plc v Carrick* [1996] 4 All E.R. 630; criticised (1996) 112 L.Q.R. 549 (P. Ferguson). For the bare trust which arises where a purchaser has paid the whole purchase price, see below, para.15–056.

[385] s.17(1) defines "purchaser" as "any person (including a mortgagee or lessee) who, for valuable consideration, takes any interest in land or in a charge on land". "Valuable consideration" may, in this context, include nominal consideration: see *Midland Bank Trust Co Ltd v Green* [1981] A.C. 513 at 532.

[386] s.199(1).

[387] s.205(1)(xxi) defines "purchaser" as "a purchaser in good faith for valuable consideration . . . " except in Part I of the Act, not here relevant. "Nominal consideration" is, however, expressly excluded. Nominal consideration is a sum that "can be mentioned as consideration but is not necessarily paid": *Midland Bank Trust Co Ltd v Green* [1981] A.C. 513 at 532, per Lord Wilberforce. cf. *Nurdin & Peacock Plc v D. B. Ramsden & Co Ltd* [1999] 1 E.G.L.R. 119 at 123.

[388] In *Sharp v Coates* [1949] 1 K.B. 285 (above, para.8–076), the owner of the defeated interest was in possession, so that the purchaser had at least constructive notice of it.

knowledge of the interest,[389] or deliberately intended to defeat it,[390] or that the owner of the interest was in possession of the land.[391] It has even been held that where land is granted expressly subject to another person's interest, the grantee is not subject to that interest if it is registrable but unregistered.[392] It is possible that in that situation, the court would now in appropriate circumstances impose a constructive trust upon the grantee,[393] though it will not do so merely because a conveyance is made "subject to" an unregistered land charge. If such a trust can be imposed at all, it will only be where the circumstances make it unconscionable for the grantee to refuse to give effect to the unregistered charge.[394] It is possible also, in special circumstances, for a party to be estopped from asserting that an unregistered charge is ineffective.[395] But in general the penalties for non-registration are inexorable.

(e) A notable illustration. The rigour of these rules is exemplified by **8–095** *Midland Bank Trust Co Ltd v Green.*[396] In this case a husband and wife arranged a collusive sale for the purpose of defeating a land charge which they knew to be unregistered. The husband had granted to his son, who occupied a farm as his tenant, a 10-year option to purchase the farm at a price of £22,500. Wishing to revoke the option six years later, and ascertaining that it was unregistered, he conveyed the farm, then worth about £40,000, to his wife for £500. The House of Lords held that the wife took the farm free from the option. It was held that the conveyance to the wife was a genuine sale to a purchaser for money or money's worth; that a party was entitled to take deliberate advantage of non-registration; and that the clear words of the Land Charges Act 1972 could not be qualified by any requirement of good faith. That requirement was conspicuously absent from the definition of "purchaser" in the Land Charges Act 1972,[397] in contrast with the definition in the

---

[389] *Coventry Permanent Economic B.S. v Jones* [1951] 1 All E.R. 901 at 904: *Hollington Bros. Ltd v Rhodes* [1951] 2 T.L.R. 691 at 696; and see above, para.6–030.

[390] *Midland Bank Trust Co Ltd v Green* [1981] A.C. 513, below, para.8–095.

[391] *Hollington Bros Ltd v Rhodes*, above. The opinion to the contrary in *Bendall v McWhirter* [1952] 2 Q.B. 466 at 483 must be regarded as erroneous, being based on LPA 1925 s.14, which is inapplicable, as explained below. See (1952) 68 L.Q.R. at 384, 385 (REM); *Westminster Bank Ltd v Lee* [1956] Ch. 7 at 21.

[392] *Hollington Bros Ltd v Rhodes* [1951] 2 T.L.R. 691 (assignee of leasehold "subject to . . . such leases and tenancies as may affect the premises" held free from prior agreement for an underlease to another person who had taken possession but had not registered an estate contract): *Markfaith Investment Ltd v Chiap Hua Flashlights Ltd* [1991] 2 A.C. 43.

[393] *Ashburn Anstalt v Arnold* [1989] Ch. 1 at 22–26; *Lloyd v Dugdale* [2001] EWCA Civ 1754 at [50]–[52]; [2002] 2 P. & C.R. 167 at 181–183. When it applies, the Contracts (Rights of Third Parties) Act 1999 may make recourse to constructive trusts unnecessary.

[394] *Ashburn Anstalt v Arnold*, above, at 25. In the *Hollington* case, above, at 696, Harman J. said: "I do not see how that which is void and which is not to prejudice the purchaser can be validated by some equitable doctrine". See too *Markfaith Investment Ltd v Chiap Hua Flashlights Ltd*, above, where on facts "indistinguishable" from the *Hollington* case, the Privy Council did not consider the possibility of imposing a constructive trust.

[395] As in *Taylors Fashions Ltd v Liverpool Victoria Trustees Co Ltd* [1982] Q.B. 133. He may also be bound if he fails to plead non-registration when sued: *Balchin v Buckle* (1982) 126 S.J. 412.

[396] [1981] A.C. 513.

[397] See fn.385, above.

Law of Property Act 1925,[398] the presumed reason being to eliminate the necessity of inquiring into the purchaser's motives and state of mind where there is a failure to register. Lord Wilberforce said that the terms of the Land Charges Act 1972 were clear and definite, that the Act was intended to provide a simple and understandable system for the protection of title to land, and that to read it down or gloss it would destroy its usefulness.[399] The answer to any complaint of injustice is that the Act provides a simple and effective protection: registration.

Although as a matter of property law, a purchaser may take free of an unregistered land charge, the person whose interested has been defeated may have other remedies. For example:

(i) Following *Midland Bank Trust Co Ltd v Green*, the son's executors brought proceedings for conspiracy against his parents[400] and against his solicitors for negligence.[401]

(ii) In other cases, where land has been conveyed to a company controlled by the transferor in order to defeat an unregistered estate contract, the court has decreed specific performance of the estate contract against the transferor and required it to procure a transfer from the company which it controlled.[402]

8–096   *(f) Persons in possession or occupation.* In one important respect the policy of 1925 appears to have been made more rigorous than intended. Where the owner of the interest is in occupation of the land the obvious fact of his occupation ought to protect his rights against any later purchaser, just as under the doctrine of notice.[403] In the case of land with registered title that principle was respected by the Land Registration Act 1925, and in a more restricted form by the Land Registration Act 2002, under which the proprietary rights of a person in actual occupation are an overriding interest in many circumstances, and as such will bind a purchaser although unregistered.[404] In the case of unregistered titles it was apparently also intended that actual occupation or possession should give protection, since the Law of Property Act 1922[405] provided:

"This Part of this Act shall not prejudicially affect the interest of any person in possession or in actual occupation of land to which he may be entitled in virtue of such possession or occupation."

[398] See fn.387, above.
[399] *Midland Bank Trust Co Ltd v Green*, above, at 528.
[400] *Midland Bank Trust Co Ltd v Green (No.3)* [1982] Ch. 529; above, para.6–067.
[401] *Midland Bank Trust Co Ltd v Hett, Stubbs & Kemp* [1979] Ch. 384.
[402] *Jones v Lipman* [1962] 1 W.L.R. 832; *Coles v Samuel Smith Old Brewery (Tadcaster)(an unlimited company)* [2007] EWCA Civ 1461; [2008] 2 E.G.L.R. 159.
[403] Above, para.8–019.
[404] See above, paras 7–089 et seq.
[405] s.33. The wording was not very apt for this purpose, but probably sufficient. It read as if its primary purpose may have been to prevent the interests of adverse possessors from being turned into equitable interests.

The same part of the Act of 1922 contained the amendments extending the scheme for the registration of land charges.[406] But when that Act was later broken up into the 1925 legislation, and the provisions for registration were moved to the Land Charges Act 1925, the section quoted was carried without amendment into Part I of the Law of Property Act 1925.[407] In that position it has little if any effect since it can no longer govern the provisions about registration. So it may be due to a drafting error that the interest of a person in actual occupation can be defeated by a later purchase.[408]

(h) No duty to register. Although in his own interests the owner of a **8–097** registrable land charge obviously ought to register it, he is under no duty to anyone else to do so. This has an effect on the measure of damages for breach of contract. If V contracts to sell land to P, who fails to register the estate contract, and V conveys the land to X in breach of contract, P can recover full damages from V (or the full amount paid by X to V[409]), even though P, had he registered, could have enforced his equitable interest against X and so would have suffered no loss.[410]

3. Companies. If a charge registrable in the Companies Register[411] is not **8–098** duly registered there within 21 days of its creation, it is, in addition to any consequences of not being registered in the Land Charges Register, void as a security as against the liquidator and all creditors of the company, and the money becomes immediately payable.[412]

4. Unregistrable interests. Unregistrable equitable interests, e.g. pre-1926 **8–099** restrictive covenants and pre-1926 equitable mortgages where there is either a deposit of title deeds or there has been no transfer since 1925, are still governed by the old doctrine of notice.

C. Differences Between Class C and Class D Land Charges

1. Date of creation. The main difference between Class C and Class D land **8–100** charges is that a Class C land charge can be registered if it is either created or

---

[406] s.14 and Sch.7.
[407] s.14.
[408] See (1977) 41 Conv.(N.S.) 415 at 419; [1990] C.L.J. 277 at 315–320 (C.H.); [1982] Conv. 213 (M. Friend and J. Newton). The point was left open in *Lloyds Bank Plc v Carrick* [1996] 4 All E.R. 630 at 642, but Morritt L.J. observed that "what is now s.14 of the Law of Property Act 1925 does not achieve for unregistered land that which s.70(l)(g) of the Land Registration Act 1925 achieves for registered land". The relevant provision in registered land is now LRA 2002 Sch.3, para.2.
[409] *Lake v Bayliss* [1974] 1 W.L.R. 1073 (since V is a qualified trustee for P: below, para.15–053).
[410] *Wright v Dean* [1948] Ch. 686 (unregistered option for tenant to purchase freehold): *Hollington Bros Ltd v Rhodes* [1951] 2 T.L.R. 691 (unregistered contract to grant underlease). See [1956] C.L.J. 227, fn.57 (H.W.R.W.).
[411] See above, para.8–084.
[412] Companies Act 2006 s.874; *Capital Finance Co Ltd v Stokes* [1969] 1 Ch. 261. Delay in registration will be cured by the registrar's certificate of registration: *Re CL Nye Ltd* [1971] Ch. 442. His decision in this regard is not subject to judicial review: Companies Act 2006 s.869; *R. v Registrar of Companies, Ex p. Central Bank of India* [1986] Q.B. 1114.

transferred after 1925, but a Class D land charge can be registered only if it is created after 1925.[413]

8–101   2. Non-registration. A further difference between Class C and Class D land charges is the effect of non-registration considered above.[414] This, however, is a qualified distinction, since estate contracts (Class C(iv)) created after 1925 fall into the same category for this purpose as Class D.[415]

D. Operation of the Register

8–102   1. Searches. The means by which an intending purchaser of land can discover registrable incumbrances is by a search.[416] This may be made in person,[417] but it is advisable to obtain an official search.[418] An official certificate of search has three advantages.

   (i)   It is conclusive in favour of a purchaser or intending purchaser,[419] provided that his application correctly specified the persons[420] and the land[421] it therefore frees him from any liability in respect of rights which it fails to disclose.[422] The correct name is that which appears on the title deeds.[423]

   (ii) It protects a solicitor or trustee who makes the official search from liability for any error in the certificate.[424]

   (iii) It provides protection against incumbrances registered in the interval between search and completion.[425] If a purchaser completes his transaction before the expiration of the 15th day after the date of the certificate[426] (excluding days when the registry is not open to the public), he is not affected by any entry made after the date of the certificate and before completion, unless it is made pursuant to

[413] LCA 1972 s.4(6), (7).
[414] Above, para.8–093.
[415] Above, para.8–093.
[416] See generally, LRPG63, Pt.4.
[417] LCA 1972 s.9. "Anyone who nowadays is foolish enough to search personally deserves what he gets": *Oak Co-operative B.S. v Blackburn* [1968] Ch. 730 at 743; per Russell L.J.
[418] LCA 1972 s.10, providing also for enquiry by telephone. Inquiry may also be made both by fax (see Land Charges (Amendment) Rules 1990 (S1 1990/485)) and, for those who have direct access as Business e-service users, by direct computer link: see Land Charges (Amendment) Rules 1995 (SI 1995/1355).
[419] LCA 1972 s.10(4). cf. *Re C.L. Nye Ltd* [1971] Ch. 442.
[420] A trivial error may be fatal: *Oak Co-operative B.S. v Blackburn* 119681 Ch. 730 (Francis Davis Blackburn specified by mistake for Francis David Blackburn: purchaser not protected); and see above, para.8–086.
[421] *Du Sautoy v Simes* [1967] Ch. 1 146; the application must give "no reasonable scope for misunderstanding" in the Registry: see at 1168. See too *Horrill v Cooper* (2000) 80 P & CR D16 at D17.
[422] See *Stock v Wanstead and Woodford BC* [1962] 2 Q.B. 469 (local land charges).
[423] *Standard Property Investment Plc v British Plastics Federation* (1985) 53 P. & CR. 25.
[424] LCA 1972 s.12.
[425] LCA 1972 s.11(5), (6).
[426] Defined by Land Charges Rules 1974 r.17(2).

a priority notice[427] entered on the register on or before the date of the certificate.[428]

If the official certificate of search mistakenly fails to mention an incum- **8–103** brance duly registered before the purchaser's search, the owner of the incumbrance is unjustly deprived of his rights over the land, since the certificate is conclusive. Parliament made no provision for compensation, but the court will award damages for negligence against the public authority responsible,[429] which in the case of the central register is the Crown.

A single search is effective for all divisions of all registers.

2. Priority notices. Special provision had to be made to provide for a rapid **8–104** sequence of transactions, such as the creation of a restrictive covenant followed immediately by the creation of a mortgage before there has been time to register the covenant. Thus, if V is selling land to P, who is raising the purchase-money by means of a loan on mortgage from M, and is to enter into a restrictive covenant with V, the conveyance from V to P creating the restrictive covenant will be simultaneous with the creation of the mortgage by P to M, which enables P to pay V. In such a case, V's restrictive covenant could not be registered before the simultaneous execution of the mortgage, and so it will be void against M, a purchaser for money or money's worth of a legal estate, unless V has availed himself of the machinery of the priority notice. To do this he must give a priority notice to the registrar at least 15 days before the creation of the restrictive covenant, and then, if he registers his charge within 30 days of the entry of the priority notice in the register, the registration dates back to the moment of the creation of the restrictive covenant, i.e. to the execution of the conveyance from V to P.[430] Days on which the registry is not open to the public are again excluded in the computation of these periods. The requirement of 15 days' advance notice is to allow the expiry of the 15 days' period of protection given to those who made official searches before the priority notice was lodged.[431] Priority notices are not, of course, confined to restrictive covenants, but apply to all charges governed by the Land Charges Act 1972.

Where another charge is created simultaneously with a charge which is **8–105** protected by a priority notice, and that other charge is subject to or dependent

---

[427] Below, para.8–104.
[428] LCA 1972 s.11(5), (6).
[429] *Ministry of Housing and Local Government v Sharp* [1970] 2 Q.B. 223 (damages awarded against local authority for overlooking entry on register of local land charges); *Coats Patons (Retail) Ltd v Birmingham Corporation* (1971) 69 L.G.R. 356 (exemption clause ineffective). cf. LCA 1972 s.10(6) (enacted after the *Sharp* decision), which provides that in the absence of fraud nobody employed in the registry is liable for any loss suffered by reason of any discrepancy between the particulars stated in the certificate as being those for which the search was being made and those in the request for a search, or in any communication of the result of a search except in a certificate. If the clerk cannot be personally liable for his negligence, presumably his employers cannot be liable vicariously. For local land charges: below, para.8–107.
[430] LCA 1972 s.11; Land Charges Rules 1974 (SI 1974/1286), rr.4, 7, 8.
[431] See above, para.8–102.

on the protected charge, the other charge is deemed to have been created after the protected charge.[432] Thus time is notionally allowed for the priority notice to operate.

8–106   **3. Vacation of registration.** The court has a wide jurisdiction, both statutory[433] and inherent,[434] to order the vacation of any registration, i.e. that the entry be removed from the register. The owner of the land affected thus has a means of clearing off an unjustified blot on his title, e.g. where an estate contract is registered against him but the contract never existed,[435] or has been terminated.[436] In a proper case this power will be exercised speedily on motion, and with a certain robustness,[437] without awaiting the trial of any action, thereby preventing the entry from improperly inhibiting dealings with the land. Where the registration is only arguably correct, a motion to vacate the entry will usually be dismissed only on terms. The party seeking vacation will normally be required to give an undertaking to pay the landowner damages if at trial it is held that the entry was wrongly made.[438]

Section 3. Local Land Charges Registers

8–107   **1. The registers.** In addition to the registers kept by the Land Charges Department of the Land Registry, registers of local land charges are kept in London, by each London borough (or the City of London), and elsewhere by each district council.[439] These registers were introduced by the Land Charges Act 1925 and were reorganised by the Local Land Charges Act 1975, which came into force on August 1, 1977.[440] Their purpose is to enable purchasers to discover the numerous charges and restrictions which public authorities, both central and local, may impose upon land under statutory powers, for

[432] LCA 1972 s.11(4). For an example, see Wolst & C. ii, 102.
[433] LCA 1972 s.1(6). See *Northern Developments (Holdings) Ltd v U.D.T Securities Ltd* [1976] I W.L.R. 1230 (entries of pending land actions vacated).
[434] *Heywood v B.D.C. Properties Ltd (No.2)* [1964] 1 W.L.R. 267; *Calgary and Edmonton Land Co Ltd v Dobinson* [1974] Ch. 102; but see *Norman v Hardy* [1974] 1 W.L.R. 1048, not followed in *Northern Developments (Holdings) Ltd v U.D.T Securities Ltd,* above. See too, above, para.7–076 (removal of entries in the register of title). It is thought that only the High Court has such an inherent jurisdiction, and that the county court does not: above, para.7–076.
[435] *Heywood v B.D.C. Properties Ltd (No.2),* above: and see *Rawlplug Co Ltd v Kamvale Properties Ltd* (1968) 20 P. & CR. 32 at 40.
[436] *Hooker v Wyle* [1974] 1 W.L.R. 235.
[437] *Rawlplug Co Ltd v Kamvale Properties Ltd,* above.
[438] See *Tucker v Hutchinson* (1987) 54 P. & CR. 106 at 112 where the Court of Appeal expressed a preference for *Northern Developments (Holdings) Ltd v U.D.T Securities Ltd,* above, over *Norman v Hardy,* above.
[439] LLCA 1975, replacing the Land Charges Act 1925 s.15 and other legislation: Local Land Charges Rules 1977 (S1 1977/985) amended by the Local Land Charges (Amendment) Rules 1978 (SI 1978/1638), 1989 (SI 1989/951) and 2003 (SI 2003/2502). See generally Report of Law Commission on Local Land Charges, (1974) Law Com. No.62, on which the Act of 1975 was based; J. E. Boothroyd, *Garner's Local Land Charges* 14th edn (London: Sweet & Maxwell, 2010).
[440] SI 1977/984.

example under the legislation governing public health, housing, highways and town and country planning. These liabilities may be of great importance, particularly since statutory charges may have overriding effect and prevail over pre-existing incumbrances such as mortgages.[441] Local land charges, almost without exception,[442] are governmental in character, as contrasted with ordinary land charges, which are mostly matters of private right.[443]

The machinery of local registration has an important advantage over that **8–108** operated centrally at the Land Registry in that the charges are registered against the land itself and not against the owner of it.[444] Thus a series of searches against successive owners is unnecessary, and there are no problems of discovering names. Since these registers are public, a purchaser can and normally does search the registers (which are public) before contract.[445]

In other respects, and subject to certain requirements of the statutory rules, the local authority may keep the register in such form as it thinks fit. In particular, it need not be kept in documentary form, so that it may be kept by computer.[446] The same applies to the index to the register which the local authority must also keep.

It is important to note that the system of local land charges applies as much to registered land as it does to unregistered. Where title to the land is registered, local land charges still have to be registered in local authority registers as they are seldom registrable at the Land Registry.[447]

2. Registration of charges. Local land charges are not registrable under the **8–109** Land Charges Act 1972.[448] This is necessary because the effects of non-registration differ.[449]

The Act of 1975 gives local land charges a wide definition which is then cut down by exclusions.[450] The definition, briefly summarised, comprises any charge acquired by a local authority, water authority or new town development corporation under public health or highways legislation "or any similar charge acquired by a local authority under any other Act", if binding on

---

[441] See *Westminster City Council v Haymarket Publishing Ltd* [1981] 1 W.L.R. 677 (rating surcharge on unoccupied premises, registered as local land charge, held to prevail over prior mortgage).

[442] For one exception see below, para.28–101 (notice in lieu of obstruction of light).

[443] Though inland revenue charges are an exception: above, para.8–078.

[444] Registration must be "by reference to the land affected": LLCA 1975 s.5(3); and it must show the situation and extent of the land: Local Land Charges Rules 1977 (SI 1977/985), r.6.

[445] A vendor is in fact obliged to disclose to the purchaser prior to the contract those local land charges which amount to latent defects in title (as many will): below, para.15–070. The view to the contrary expressed obiter in *Re Forsey and Hollebone's Contract* [1927] 2 Ch. 379 (below, para.15–084) has at last been disapproved: *Rignall Developments Ltd v Halil* [1988] Ch. 190. A purchaser will not always be able to search the register prior to contract, e.g. if he buys at auction.

[446] Local Government (Miscellaneous Provisions) Act 1982 s.34, amending the LLCA 1975.

[447] Such charges take effect as overriding interests: LRA 2002 Sch.1, para.6, Sch.3, para.6; above, paras 7–030, 7–087.

[448] LLCA 1975 s.17, amending LCA 1972.

[449] Below, para.8–111.

[450] ss.1, 2.

successive owners of the land affected; positive or negative obligations or restrictions imposed or enforceable by ministers, government departments or local authorities, if binding on successors[451] and any other matter expressly made a local land charge by statute or regulation. Among the exclusions are covenants or agreements between lessor and lessee; restrictions which bind successive owners because made for the benefit of the authority's land (thus excluding ordinary restrictive covenants, which are registrable as land charges); restrictions in by-laws; conditions in planning permissions granted before August 1977; and forestry dedication covenants.

8–110   The great majority of local land charges are expressly declared to be such by some statute.[452] Examples are charges recoverable to local authorities for works required for drainage and sewerage works, for repairing or demolishing dangerous buildings, for cleansing filthy premises or for providing dustbins; charges levied for the making up of roads or for coast protection works; numerous items under the town and country planning legislation, including enforcement notices, tree preservation orders, building preservation notices, conditions in planning permissions granted after July 1977, and potential claims for repayment of compensation money paid on refusal of planning permission, in case permission should later be given.[453] A few compulsory purchase orders are expressly made local land charges,[454] but in general compulsory purchase orders do not appear to be registrable. One particular species of local land charge is a "general charge" which may be registered by a local authority which has incurred expenditure which will in due course give rise to a local land charge in their favour, thus protecting their claim in advance.[455]

8–111   **3. Non-registration.** Formerly, failure to register a local land charge had an effect similar to that of failure to register an ordinary land charge: the charge was void against a purchaser for money or money's worth of a legal estate in the land affected who completed his purchase before the charge was registered.[456]

The Local Land Charges Act 1975 made a significant change. Failure to register no longer affects the enforceability of the charge, but a purchaser suffering loss when the charge is enforced[457] is entitled to compensation.[458]

---

[451] The terms of s.1(1)(d) ("any positive obligation affecting land enforceable by a Minister of the Crown, government department or local authority under any covenant or agreement") would seem to include ordinary contracts of purchase or options enforceable by the authority. Positive covenants may be binding on successors under local Acts of Parliament: see (1974) Law Com. No.62, para.87.

[452] For a table of these, see Halsbury (4th edn), vol. 26, para.674.

[453] See *Ministry of Housing and Local Government v Sharp* [1970] 2 Q.B. 223; above, para.8–103.

[454] e.g. under the New Towns Act 1981 s.12.

[455] LLCA 1975 s.6.

[456] LCA 1925 s.15(1).

[457] But, in the absence of enforcement, not for other loss suffered because the charge was not registered: see *Pound v Ashford BC* [2003] EWHC 1088 (Ch); [2004] 1 P. & C.R. 12.

[458] LLCA 1975 s.10.

The present rule expresses the principle that charges imposed in the public interest ought to be enforced, but that compensation should be paid by public authorities who fail to give warning of them.[459] The right to compensation is conditional on a proper search, whether personal or official, having been made with negative results. Compensation is payable in all cases by the authority maintaining the register, but that authority can recover it from the authority which ought to have registered it, if the loss is due to their default.[460] Compensation is also payable where an official search fails to disclose an existing local land charge, whether registered or not.[461] Entitlement to compensation is equivalent to an action in tort.[462] Although compensation will normally be assessed at the date when the land is purchased, it may be assessed at a later date if the normal date would cause manifest injustice to the claimant.[463]

There are facilities for personal and official searches, with due provision for **8–112** computerised registers, which are generally similar to those of the Land Charges Act 1972, except that priority notices are not available, and searches do not give a period of protection.[464] The court has power to order the cancellation of the registration of a local land charge.[465]

---

[459] There is a statutory duty to register: s.5.

[460] s.10(4), (5).

[461] s.10(1)(b). Contrast land charges: above, para.8–103.

[462] *Smith v South Gloucestershire District Council* [2002] EWCA Civ 1131 at [10]; [2002] 3 E.G.L.R. 1 at 2.

[463] *Smith v South Gloucestershire District Council*, above.

[464] These procedures proved unsuitable for local land charges and were discontinued: see (1974) Law Com No.62, para.70.

[465] LLCA 1975 s.5(5).

CHAPTER 9

PERPETUITIES AND ACCUMULATIONS

Part 1

VESTED AND CONTINGENT FUTURE INTERESTS

9–001 **1. Classification of future interests.** This chapter is concerned with future interests in land, that is, interests which confer a right to the enjoyment of the land at a future time, such as a right to land by way of remainder after the death of a living person. The Chapter begins with an explanation of the nature of future interests. That is followed by a consideration of the limits to the future interests that the law allows. Those limits are imposed by three rules, namely, the rule against perpetuities, the rule against perpetual trusts and the rule against excessive accumulations of income. These rules are mix of common law and statute.

In relation to future interests, there is a fundamental distinction between vested and contingent remainders, which is particularly important in relation to the subject of perpetuities. "Perpetuities" are contingent interests which may take effect at too remote a date in the future. Any future interest may be either vested or contingent, and vested interests may be either "vested in interest" or "vested in possession" An interest is "vested in possession" when it gives the right of present enjoyment.[1] Of course, it is not then a future interest. If it is vested in interest but not in possession (for which situation the term "vested" is ordinarily used by itself) it is a "future interest", since the right of enjoyment is postponed. However, it is also an already subsisting right in property vested in its owner: it is a present right to future enjoyment.[2] By contrast with a vested interest, a contingent interest is one which will give no

---

[1] See Fearne, *Contingent Remainders*, 2. Fearne's treatise (10th edn, 1844, with notes by Butler) is the classic work on the whole subject of future interests. The other leading works are *Gray on Perpetuities* (4th edn, 1942); Morris and Leach, *The Rule against Perpetuities* (2nd edn, 1962; supp. 1964); Maudsley, *The Modern Law of Perpetuities* (Butterworths, 1979).

[2] Fearne p.2.

right at all unless or until some future event happens. If land is transferred to trustees to hold on trust for A, B and C, all of whom are living persons, as follows:

> "to A for life, remainder to B for life, remainder to C in fee simple if he survives B",

A's interest is vested in possession, B's is vested in interest but not in possession (a vested remainder) and C's is contingent. If B dies first, C's remainder will vest; and on A's death it will fall into possession.

2. Conditions of vesting. A remainder is vested if two requirements are   **9–002**
satisfied:

(i) the person or persons entitled to it must be ascertained[3]; and

(ii) it must be ready to take effect in possession forthwith, and be prevented from doing so only by the existence of some prior interest or interests.[4]

If either requirement is not satisfied, the remainder is contingent.

In relation to the example given in the previous paragraph:

> "to A for life, remainder to B for life, remainder to C in fee simple if he survives B",

it has been explained that B's interest is vested and C's is contingent. Neither interest is vested in possession, because A has the only interest which is vested both in interest and in possession. C's interest is bound to remain contingent during B's life, even if A is already dead. This is because it depends not only upon the determination of B's life interest but upon the further contingency of C outliving B. B's interest is vested because, if A's life interest were to terminate forthwith, an ascertained person, B, is already entitled to the land, subject only to A's prior interest. Even if A is aged 23 and B is 97, so that it is improbable that B's interest will ever vest in possession, B nevertheless has a vested interest[5]; for an interest may be vested even if there is no certainty of it taking effect in possession at any time,[6] otherwise no future life interest or entail could be vested.[7] If, prior to 1997, land was given to X in tail, remainder to Y in fee simple, Y's remainder is vested, not because X's entail is bound to determine at some time (because this is not the case[8]) but because Y has

---

[3] Fearne 9: *Re Legh's S.T.* [1938] Ch. 39 at 52.
[4] cf. Fearne 3–9, 216; Gray, ss.101, 108; (1913) 29 L.Q.R. 290 (H.T. Tiffany).
[5] Fearne 216.
[6] *Smith d. Dormer v Packhurst* (1740) 3 Atk. 135.
[7] Fearne 216.
[8] *Contra*, Smith, *Executory Interests*, p.67 (this work forms Vol. ii of the 10th edn of Fearne, *Contingent Remainders*, above).

been at once *invested* with the fee simple, subject only to X's entail.[9] On the other hand, an interest is not necessarily vested because it is bound to take effect at some time. For example, if property is given:

"to A and B for their joint lives, with remainder to the survivor",

the death of one before the other is bound to occur at some time.[10] However, since it is uncertain which will be the survivor, the remainder is contingent, whether the remainder is in fee simple[11] or for life.[12]

9–003   Other examples of contingent interests occur where there is a gift to the heir of a living person (for until that person dies, his heir cannot be ascertained),[13] or where although the gift is in favour of a specified person, it is made contingent upon some event occurring, e.g.:

"to A upon attaining 25 or marrying",[14] or
"to B if he returns to England".[15]

In such cases, the interests of A and B are contingent until the event occurs, at which point they become vested.[16]

There are no restrictions on the kinds of conditions to which gifts can be made subject, provided that they do not offend against public policy[17] or against the rules explained in this chapter.

9–004   **3. Concealed vestings and contingencies.** It is in most cases obvious whether or not a remainder is made subject to a contingency; but there are some apparently conditional phrases which do not create legal contingencies, and some apparently unconditional remainders which are nevertheless contingent. For example, a limitation made prior to 1997[18]:

"To A in tail, but if A's issue should at any time fail then to B in fee simple",

would have given B a vested remainder, for the phrase beginning "but if" adds no contingency other than the inevitable possibility that A's entail may come to its natural end; it can be read as being merely the equivalent of

---

[9] Hawkins & Ryder 282. Entails can no longer be created: above, para.3–031.
[10] See below, para.14–064, as to LPA 1925 s.184, which deals with the ascertainment of the survivor in doubtful cases.
[11] *Biggot v Smyth* (1628) Cro.Car. 102; *Quarm v Quarm* [1892] 1 Q.B. 184.
[12] *Whitby v Von Luedecke* [1906] 1 Ch. 783; *Re Legh's S.T.* [1938] Ch. 39.
[13] Challis 75. cf. below, para.14–133.
[14] *Leake v Robinson* (1817) 2 Mer. 363.
[15] *Re Arbib and Class's Contract* [1891] 1 Ch. 601.
[16] Preston i, 88.
[17] See above, para.3–066.
[18] Entails cannot be created after 1996: see above, para.3–031.

"subject to the prior interest".[19] The limitation in effect is simply to A in tail with remainder to B in fee simple, giving B a vested remainder. Similarly a limitation:

> "To A (a bachelor) for life, remainder to his eldest son for life, but in default of such issue then to B in fee simple",

gives B a vested remainder. This is because the contingency expressed is merely the non- existence of a preceding life interest on the failure of which B stands ready to take.[20] But if the gift had been:

> "To A (a bachelor) for life, remainder to his eldest son (if any) in fee simple, remainder to B in fee simple",

B's remainder would have been contingent, for there was a rule that no interest which followed a contingent fee simple could be vested.[21] This was because although a grantor can create any number of successive life interests (limited interests) and vest them in living persons, he can part with the fee simple (an absolute interest) only once. Any two limitations of the fee simple are not therefore successive but alternative, and if one is contingent the other must depend on the converse contingency.[22] For somewhat similar reasons a gift which follows a determinable or conditional fee simple is regarded as contingent, as for example B's interest in a limitation:

> "To A in fee simple until he ceases to reside in the family home, remainder to B in fee simple."[23]

4. Size of beneficiary's interest. An interest may be vested even though the size of the beneficiary's interest is not finally ascertained. For example, where land is devised:

9–005

> "to A for life, remainder to all his children who shall attain the age of 21 years",

each child obtains a vested interest on attaining his majority[24]; but these vested interests are liable to open to let in each child who subsequently attains

---

[19] See *Maddison v Chapman* (1858) 4 K. & J. 709 at 719 (affd. (1859) 3 De G. & J. 536); *Permanent Trustee Co of New South Wales Ltd v d'Apice* (1968) 118 C.L.R. 105.

[20] For the effect of expressions such as "in default of such issue", see *White v Summers* [1908] 2 Ch. 256 at 271 et seq.

[21] *Loddington v Kime* (1697) 1 Ld.Raym. 203; 1 Salk. 199; Fearne 225, 374–377; Gray, s.112, who is hesitant. The rule is disputed by Hayes, *Limitations*, pp. 81 et seq.; (1913) 29 L.Q.R. 296 (H.T. Tiffany). But the authorities in favour of the rule seem sufficient, and its principle seems sound.

[22] See 1 Ld.Raym. at p. 208.

[23] Gray, s.114, fn.3.

[24] *Brackenbury v Gibbons* (1876) 2 Ch D 417 at 419; *Randoll v Doe d. Roake* (1817) 5 Dow 202.

full age.[25] Thus if X and Y are the only children who have attained their majority, they each have a vested interest in one-half of the property, but that interest may later be partially divested in favour of subsequent children.[26] The divesting affects only the *quantum* of the interest vested in each beneficiary.[27] When Z becomes 21, the shares of X and Y in the land each falls to one-third and Z has the other third; and so on for the other children.[28] X and Y can dispose of their vested shares either inter vivos or by will,[29] although even in the hands of the transferee the shares will be liable to be diminished if other children attain full age. However, any child of A who dies under 21 has no interest in the property at all.[30] This is because the contingent interest which he had while alive has failed to vest.

9–006   **5. Vested interest subject to divesting.** A remainder may also be vested and yet subject to a possibility of its being divested, not only partially but completely. For example, if land is held in trust for A for life, remainder to such of A's issue as A shall appoint, and in default of appointment among all A's children in equal shares, the remainders to the children in equal shares are vested, subject to being divested to the extent of any appointment made by A.[31] In cases of doubt the law favours early vesting. Every interest is construed as being vested forthwith if that is possible, and if not, it is treated as becoming vested as soon as possible.[32]

9–007   **6. Assignability.** It is with reference to the fact that such interests will vest, if at all, in the future that vested and contingent remainders are classed as future interests. In one sense a vested remainder is an existing interest, and therefore not future. And in one sense a contingent remainder is future, but is not an interest: it is only a possibility that an interest may arise if some contingency happens. Contingent remainders were regarded in this manner by the common law,[33] and were therefore inalienable by conveyance.[34] This was because there was no subsisting estate which could be granted. However,

---

[25] *Re Lechmere and Lloyd* (1881) 18 Ch D 524 at 529; *Baldwin v Rogers* (1853) 3 De G.M. & G. 649 at 657.

[26] *Cattlin v Brown* (1853) 11 Hare 372 at 379; *Holmes v Prescott* (1864) 10 Jur. (N.S.) 507 at 510.

[27] *Matthews v Temple* (1699) Comb. 467; *Stanley v Wise* (1788) 1 Cox Eq. 432 at 433.

[28] *Doe d. Comberbach v Perryn* (1789) 3 T.R. 484 at 493, 495.

[29] *Oppenheim v Henry* (1853) 10 Hare 441. For the alienability of contingent interests, see below, para.9–007.

[30] *Rhodes v Whitehead* (1865) 2 Dr. & Sm. 532.

[31] *Cunningham v Moody* (1748) 1 Ves.Sen. 174; *Doe d. Willis v Martin* (1790) 4 T.R. 39; *Lambert v Thwaites* (1866) L.R. 2 Eq. 151; *Re Master's Settlement* [1911] 1 Ch. 321; Fearne 226 et seq.; Farwell, *Powers*, 310 et seq.; Challis 75. For a classification of vested remainders, see *Restatement of the Law of Property*, para.157.

[32] Smith, *Executory Interests*, 73; Hawkins & Ryder 302; Jarman 1365 et seq.

[33] Challis 76, 77; Williams R.P. 398, 400.

[34] *Lampets Case* (1612) 10 Co. Rep. 46b. But they could be released, i.e. waived in favour of the holder of a prior vested estate (*Lampets Case*); and until the FRA 1833, they could to some extent be alienated by fine or recovery operating by estoppel: Fearne 365, 366; Cru.Dig. ii, 333; Williams R.P. 398.

exceptionally, they could pass by inheritance,[35] e.g. where a parcel of land, Whiteacre, was limited to A in tail, but if A should inherit Blackacre, then to B and his heirs. If B died, and A then inherited Blackacre, B's heir would take Whiteacre.[36] Courts of equity would enforce assignments of contingent remainders[37] by compelling the assignor to convey the property to the assignee when it fell into possession.[38] In this way, contingent remainders could in practice be sold. Statutes gave further assistance. By a liberal interpretation of the Statute of Wills 1540, it was held that contingent interests could be devised[39]; and this was confirmed by the Wills Act 1837.[40] Finally, by the Real Property Act 1845,[41] they became fully alienable at law. Although a right does not necessarily become an interest in land merely because statute has made it alienable, it now seems proper to regard such contingent interests as interests in land rather than mere possibilities; but the difference between vested and contingent interests is of course unaffected. Where the contingency is as to the person entitled, as in the case of a limitation to the heir of a living person,[42] or the survivor of two living persons,[43] there is still no transmissible interest vested in anyone.[44]

Part 2

REVERSIONS

1. Nature of reversions. So far the nature of reversions and remainders has been explained only briefly.[45] A reversion is such part of a grantor's interest as is not disposed of by his grant. A remainder is such part as is disposed of, provided that it is postponed to some estate in possession created at the same time. Thus if a tenant in fee simple grants a life interest, the fee simple which he retains is a reversion. His estate in fee simple in possession has become a fee simple in reversion. If, on the other hand, he creates a lesser estate and by the same instrument disposes of some or all of the residue of his estate to one or more other persons, the interests of those other persons are not reversions but remainders. In the case of a reversion, the land reverts to the grantor when the lesser estate determines. In the case of a remainder, it remains away from

9–008

---

[35] *Weale v Lower* (1672) Pollexf. 54; *Goodright d. Larmer v Searle* (1756) 2 Wils.K.B. 29.
[36] Fearne 364 et seq.; Challis 76n.
[37] *Wright v Wright* (1750) 1 Ves.Sen. 409; *Crofts v Middleton* (1856) 8 De G.M. & G. 192.
[38] Fearne 548 et seq.
[39] *Jones v Roe d. Perry* (1789) 3 T.R. 88; Fearne 368 (discussing earlier authorities to the contrary, e.g. *Bishop v Fountaine* (1695) 3 Lev. 427).
[40] s.3.
[41] s.6, now replaced by LPA 1925 s.4(2).
[42] Fearne 371.
[43] *Doe d. Calkin v Tomkinson* (1813) 2 M. & S. 165.
[44] *Re Cresswell* (1883) 24 Ch D 102 at 107.
[45] Above, para.3–017.

him for the benefit of some third party.[46] It follows that while there may be many remainders created out of one estate, there can be but one reversion. Thus, if X, a tenant in fee simple, granted land:

"to A for life, remainder to B for life, remainder to C for life",

he retained the reversion in fee simple, and yet had created two remainders, namely, those of B and C. It will be seen that a reversion arises by operation of law, a remainder by act of parties.[47] If, in the above example, X then grants away his own interest to Y, Y does not obtain an interest in remainder, but a transfer of X's reversion. A reversion therefore need not necessarily be owned by the person who created the antecedent estate.

9–009   Estates less than a fee simple, and upon which therefore remainders or reversions (or both) are expectant, are called "particular estates",[48] for such an estate is given for a particular portion of time,[49] and is only a part (*or particula*[50]) of the fee simple. But no fee simple could be a particular estate, even if it was a determinable fee.[51] Future interests expectant on a conditional or determinable fee simple, such as a right of entry or a possibility of reverter, are neither reversions nor remainders, for they exist independently of any estate in their owners. There has been a disposal of the fee simple, and there is therefore nothing left of the grantor's estate, even though the fee simple granted is made determinable or subject to conditions. These special interests are best treated in connection with the special types of fee simple to which they attach,[52] and they may here be left out of account.

9–010   **2. All reversions are vested.** From its very nature it follows that a reversion is a vested interest.[53] It is the remnant of an estate which has never passed away from the grantor, and he or (if he is dead) his representatives stand ready to receive the land as soon as the particular estate determines. According to feudal principles, moreover, a freehold reversioner on a term of years has an estate which is vested not only in interest but also in possession, for the grant of a lease does not deprive a grantor of seisin.[54] He therefore has what is properly called a freehold in possession subject to the term.[55] From this point of view a reversion on a lease is not a reversion or, indeed, a future interest

---

[46] See the discussions by Maitland at (1890) 6 L.Q.R. 25 and S.S., Vol. 17, p. xxxviii. In the text, "reversion" is always employed in its correct sense, although in practice the terms "reversions" or "reversionary interests" are often loosely applied to remainders as well as reversions.

[47] Williams R.P. 362.

[48] Preston, *Conveyancing*, iii, 169.

[49] Preston, *Conveyancing*, iii, 169.

[50] Williams R.P. 361.

[51] Preston, i, 91.

[52] Above, para.3–052; below, para.9–089.

[53] Cru.Dig. ii, 336; Challis 67.

[54] Challis 233; see *De Grey v Richardson* (1747) 3 Atk. 469 at 472.

[55] Challis 100.

at all.[56] This technicality is a relic of the ancient doctrine that leases were not even estates and were to be disregarded for feudal purposes.[57] However, as has been explained, leases have long since achieved the status of estates, and it is therefore both correct and a matter of ordinary usage to speak of a landlord's reversion.[58] Although seisin as such is no longer of any importance, a landlord's reversion is still an ambiguous interest. As explained above, it is regarded as being an estate in possession for the purposes of the Law of Property Act 1925.[59]

3. Reversions after 1925. Before 1926 a reversion might be legal or **9–011** equitable, depending on the estate out of which it was created. After 1925 a reversion upon an entail or life estate is necessarily equitable.[60] Even if it is a fee simple absolute it is not in possession. A reversion upon a term of years, however, can still exist as a legal estate because:

(i) if the owner of a legal fee simple absolute in possession grants a lease, his estate remains a legal estate; for "possession" for this purpose is defined by statute so as to include the right to receive the rents and profits, if any[61]; and

(ii) if the owner of a legal term of years absolute grants a sublease, there is nothing in this to render his estate any the less legal; any number of legal estates can exist concurrently in the same land.[62]

Part 3

PERPETUITIES

Section 1. Introduction

1. Policy against perpetuities. It has commonly been the ambition of **9–012** landowners to dictate to posterity how their land is to devolve in the future, and so to fetter the powers of alienation of those to whom they may give it.[63] It has always been the purpose of the courts, as a matter of public policy, to confine such settlements within narrow limits and to frustrate them when they attempt to reach too far into the future. It has already been explained how the

---

[56] *Wakefield & Barnsley Union Bank Ltd v Yates* [1916] 1 Ch. 452 at 460.
[57] Above, para.3–015.
[58] Challis 80.
[59] Above, para.6–017.
[60] LPA 1925 s.1(1), (3).
[61] LPA 1925 s.205(1)(xix); above, para.6–017.
[62] LPA 1925 s.1(5); above, para.6–028.
[63] *"Te teneam moriens* [thee may I grasp when dying] is the dying lord's apostrophe to his manor, for which he is forging these fetters, that seem, by restricting the dominion of others, to extend his own": Jarman, *Wills* (1st edn), i. 196.

courts in time circumvented the designs of the barons who had obtained by the Statute *De Donis* 1285 the power to create an inalienable estate tail.[64] For similar reasons the courts later laid down that all unduly remote future interests were void as "perpetuities". As Lord Nottingham L.C. observed in 1681:

> "the law hath so long laboured to defeat perpetuities, that now it is become a sufficient reason of itself against any settlement to say it tends to a perpetuity . . . such perpetuities fight against God, by affecting a stability which human providence can never attain to, and are utterly against the reason and policy of the common law".[65]

9–013 **2. Rules against perpetuities.** All types of future interests have therefore been made subject to important rules limiting the period for which a settlor can exercise control over property. A settlor cannot render property inalienable for ever, nor can he settle it so that it may vest an inordinate number of years in the future. The following rules must be distinguished.

> (i) The rules of common law which governed contingent remainders and executory interests. Those rules finally became obsolete in 1926.[66]
>
> (ii) The rule in *Whitby v Mitchell*,[67] sometimes called the old rule against perpetuities, or the rule against double possibilities. That rule was abolished in 1925.[68]
>
> (iii) The rule against perpetuities. This is sometimes referred to as the modern rule against perpetuities to distinguish it from the rule in *Whitby v Mitchell*.
>
> (iv) The rule against inalienability or perpetual trusts.
>
> (v) The rule against accumulations.

Rules (iii), (iv) and (v) are still applicable to varying degrees and are explained in this chapter. However, in relation to dispositions made after April 5, 2010,[69] the circumstances in which rule (iii) can apply have been restricted and rule (v) is abolished, except in relation to charitable trusts.

9–014 **3. Origin of the rules.** The old contingent remainder rules were of medieval origin, and were later complicated by the invention of executory interests under the Statute of Uses 1535 and the Statute of Wills 1540. The rule in

---

[64] Above, paras 3–071, 3–072.
[65] *Duke of Norfolk's Case* (1681) 2 Swans. 454 at 460.
[66] See Appendix 4 of the 5th edition of this work.
[67] (1890) 44 Ch D 85.
[68] See Appendix 4 of the 5th edition of this work.
[69] When PAA 2009 came into force.

Whitby v Mitchell dated from the 16th century, but its scope was uncertain and was complicated by technicalities of the old law of future interests. A clearer and more comprehensive rule was needed, and this was eventually evolved in the form known as the modern rule against perpetuities. Its general outline first emerged in 1685, when the House of Lords settled the great legal controversy which arose in the *Duke of Norfolk's Case*.[70] The new principle was that the vesting of an interest must not be capable of exceeding a period based upon an existing lifetime. It was developed step by step[71] until it reached its final form in 1833.[72] The rule against inalienability is also based on decided cases of respectable antiquity. The rule against accumulations, on the other hand, now prospectively abolished in most cases, had a statutory and comparatively modern origin, the Accumulations Act 1800.

Section 2. The Rule against Perpetuities

A. History

1. Origin. The combined effect of the Statute of Uses 1535 and the Statute **9–015** of Wills 1540 was to bring into existence a whole new family of future interests which were free from the strict rules which governed remainders at common law. These "executory interests" were contrary to the law's policy against perpetuities, since they could be used to make gifts take effect at remote future dates. In this way the ultimate ownership and right of alienation of the fee simple absolute might be put into abeyance for a long time. A comprehensive rule was needed to keep all such interests within reasonable limits, while at the same time enabling landowning families to retain their land in their families from generation to generation. The rule eventually devised allowed settlors to leave the ultimate ownership uncertain for a maximum period of one subsisting lifetime (which is invariably referred to as a life in being) and a further 21 years. This rule was modelled upon the period for which the power of alienation could normally be restrained in settlements operating at common law.[73] Land could be settled upon A for life with remainder to his son in tail, so that the maximum period which could elapse before the entail could effectively be barred was A's lifetime plus the son's minority, i.e. 21 years.

2. Development. It was many years before the rule was finally settled.[74] In **9–016** 1662 the limitation of a term of years to several living persons in succession

---

[70] (1681) 2 Swans 454: (1685) 3 Ch.Ca. 1; H.E.L. vii, 223–225. The development of the modern rule is explained in H.E.L. vii, 215–238.

[71] H.E.L. vii, 226. 227; below, para.9–015.

[72] *Cadell v Palmer* (1833) 1 Cl & F 372 (also a decision of the House of Lords).

[73] See *Long v Blackall* (1797) 7 T.R. 100 at 102; Hargrave, p. 518; Butler's notes to Co.Litt. 20(a), note (5); Fearne 444, 566.

[74] See H.E.L. vii, 215 et seq.; Morris & Leach, Ch.1 (dealing both with the history of the rule and its general place in the legal system); (1977) 126 U. Penn L.R. 19 (G. L. Haskins, discussing the historical, social and legal background).

was held good[75]; and, in 1678, so was an executory devise which might not have vested until the expiration of a lifetime plus 21 years.[76] But the rule became firmly established only by later stages. *The Duke of Norfolk's Case*[77] in 1685 settled beyond doubt that a shifting use that was bound to take effect, if at all, during a life in being was valid. In 1697 a life in being plus one year was held valid[78]; and in 1736 this was extended to a life in being plus a minority, i.e. plus a maximum period of 21 years.[79]

In 1797 it was settled that a child *en ventre sa mere* (conceived but not born) might be treated as a life in being,[80] thus extending the period by a possible further nine months. By then it had also become accepted that the period of 21 years after the life in being also might be extended to cover a further period of gestation if it existed.[81] In 1805 it was finally settled that the lives in being might be chosen at random and be unconnected with the property.[82] In 1833 the rule was completed by the decision of the House of Lords in *Cadell v Palmer*[83] that the period of 21 years was an absolute period without reference to any minority, but that the periods of gestation could be added only if in fact gestation existed. These two last decisions show that the analogy with common law limitations was not followed very far.

Although originally, the function of the rule was to ensure that land was freely alienable, that is no longer a concern.[83a] Its purpose now is to:

"strike a balance between on the one hand the freedom of the present generation and, on the other, that of future generations to deal as they wish with property in which they have interests".[83b]

9–017   **3. Reform.** The invention of this rule provided a general solution to the problem of perpetuity. Subject to a few exceptions the courts applied it to all contingent interests in property, whether in realty or personalty and whether created by deed, will, contract or otherwise. It is a striking example of wholly new law created judicially. It was amended in minor respects by the Law of Property Act 1925, and then much more extensively by the Perpetuities and Accumulations Act 1964,[84] an act that, while saving many gifts that would

---

[75] *Goring v Bickerstaffe* (1662) Pollexf. 31.
[76] *Taylor d. Smith v Biddall* (1678) 2 Mod. 289.
[77] (1685) 3 Ch.Ca. 1.
[78] *Lloyd v Carew* (1697) Show. P.C. 137.
[79] *Stephens v Stephens* (1736) Ca.t.Talb. 228.
[80] *Long v Blackall* (1797) 7 T.R. 100.
[81] Lewis, *Perpetuity*, p.149. These extensions were assisted by a statute of 1698 (10 Will. 3, c.22; Ruff. 10 & 11 Will. 3, c.16) which enacted that a child born after the father's death should be deemed to be born in his lifetime for purposes of succession: Lewis, *Perpetuity*, p.149.
[82] *Thellusson v Woodford* (1805) 11 Ves. 112.
[83] (1833) 1 Cl. & F. 372.
[83a] Generally land is freely alienable, because trustees of land have the powers of an absolute owner: see TLATA 1996 s.6(1); below, para.12–016. It is however possible to place fetters on such powers: see TLATA 1996 s.8; below, para.12–019.
[83b] The so-called "Dead Hand Rationale": (1981) 97 L.Q.R. 593 at 594 (R. Deech).
[84] For the PAA 1964 see Elphinstone, *Perpetuities and Accumulations Act 1964*; Morris & Leach, 1964 Supp.; Maudsley, *The Modern Law of Perpetuities*.

otherwise have been void at common law, did so at the price of making the law needlessly complex.

There has now been further reform of a more radical kind. The Perpetuities and Accumulations Act 2009, which came into force on April 6, 2010, and which implemented recommendations from the Law Commission,[85] creates a single mandatory perpetuity period of 125 years and restricts the application of the rule against perpetuities to interests arising under wills and trusts. However, subject to one exception that is explained later,[86] the 2009 Act is only prospective in effect and does not affect dispositions of land made before April 6, 2010.[87] These remain subject to the previous law.

The trend of modern legislation both in this country and elsewhere is to prolong the period in which a gift may vest,[88] thereby achieving more exactly the settlor's objectives. Thus, in the Cayman Islands, a 150-year perpetuity period has been adopted.[89] In many states in the United States of America, the rule against perpetuities has been abolished altogether and this has brought in its wake, so-called perpetual "dynasty trusts".[90] Within the Commonwealth, both Manitoba[91] and Bermuda[92] have also abolished the rule.

Prior to the enactment of the Perpetuities and Accumulations Act 2009, statutory reform in this country had proceeded by building on the old law, though that approach was abandoned by the 2009 Act. Because of the legislative approach that had been adopted, it is regrettably necessary to understand the old law, as it still governs:

(i) Future interests which take effect under dispositions made prior to July 16, 1964 (when the Perpetuities and Accumulations Act 1964 came into force), though these will now be rare; and

(ii) Future interests which were created after July 15, 1964 and before April 6, 2010, because the provisions of the Perpetuities and Accumulations Act 1964 generally apply only where a disposition would fail under the old law.[93]

---

[85] (1998) Law Com. No.251.

[86] See below, para.9–051.

[87] PAA 2009 s.15(1).

[88] By the principle of "wait and see": below, para.9–030. See (1984) 4 O.J.L.S. 454 at 459 (R. Deech).

[89] Cayman Islands Perpetuities Law (1999 Revision).

[90] See (2006) 27 Cardozo L.R. 2465 (M. M. Schanzenbach and R. H. Sitkoff). The rule against perpetuities had been abolished in 21 states by the end of 2005: 27 Cardozo L.R. 2465. There must be serious doubts as to whether dynasty trusts will prove to be administratively workable. For a critical view of the American perpetual trust movement, which is entirely tax driven, see (2011) 127 L.Q.R. 423 (L.W. Waggoner).

[91] Perpetuities and Accumulations Act 1983 (SM. 1982–83, c.43); (1984) 4 O.J.L.S. 454 (R. Deech).

[92] Perpetuities and Accumulations Act 2009 (Bermuda 2009, c.23). The abolition does not extend to trusts of land, which are subject to a 100-year perpetuity period: see s.3(1) and Perpetuities and Accumulations Act 1989 (Bermuda 1989, c.60), s.3(1).

[93] Subject to two exceptions explained below at para.9–018, PAA 1964 does not apply to instruments taking effect on or after April 6, 2010: see PAA 1964 s.15(5A), inserted by PAA 2009 s.16.

B. Statement of the Rule

9–018 The rule in its classical form, as it existed before the Perpetuities and Accumulations Act 1964, can be summarised in two propositions.[94]

    (i) Any future interest in any property, real or personal,[95] is void from the outset if it may possibly vest after the perpetuity period has expired.

    (ii) The perpetuity period consists of any life or lives in being[96] together with a further period of 21 years[97] and any period of gestation.

The Perpetuities and Accumulations Act 1964[98] introduced two important modifications.

    (i) Instead of being void because it might possibly vest outside the perpetuity period, the interest was void only where it had to so vest, if it was to vest at all. This is the so-called "wait and see" principle.

    (ii) The perpetuity period could, alternatively, be a fixed period not exceeding 80 years if the settlor chose to use it.

The introduction of the principle of "wait and see" altered the character and application of the rule fundamentally. The 1964 Act (as it will be called) applied to interests arising under instruments[99] which took effect after July 15, 1964, but before April 6, 2010.

The Perpetuities and Accumulations Act 2009[100] has gone further.

    (i) It restricts the types of disposition to which the rule against perpetuities can apply. Many dispositions of property made after the Act came into force will not be subject to the rule against perpetuities at all.

---

[94] For the classical definitions, see *Re Thompson* [1906] 2 Ch. 199 at 202; Gray, s.201; Morris & Leach 1; Lewis, *Perpetuity*, p.164.

[95] Marsden, *Perpetuities*, 4; Morris & Leach 12.

[96] *Lord Dungannon v Smith* (1846) 12 Cl. & F. 546 at 563.

[97] This is unaffected by the reduction of the age of majority to 18 under the Family Law Reform Act 1969 (below, para.36–002).

[98] The Act was based on the Fourth Report of the Law Reform Committee, Cmnd. 18 (1956) which was first acted on in Western Australia: see the Law Reform (Property, Perpetuities and Succession) Act 1962, of that State, now replaced by the Property Law Act 1969 Pt xi. The Perpetuities Act (Northern Ireland) 1966 avoided some of the drafting defects of the English Act.

[99] See *Re Holt's Settlement* [1969] 1 Ch. 100 at 120 (order of court under the Variation of Trusts Act 1958 was an "instrument" for this purpose).

[100] PAA 2009 was passed using a new form of Parliamentary procedure, employing a Special Public Bill Committee. There is much useful material in the proceedings of the Committee: see HL Paper 127.

(ii) It has introduced one mandatory perpetuity period of 125 years which applies regardless of the terms of the relevant instrument.[101]

(iii) The principle of "wait and see" applies for that 125-year period.[102]

As has been explained, the 2009 Act (as it will be called) applies, with two exceptions, to instruments taking effect on or after April 6, 2010. The 2009 Act does not apply (and the 1964 Act continues to apply) in relation to:

(i) a will executed before April 6, 2010, even though the testator dies on or after that date[103]; and

(ii) an instrument made in exercise of a special power of appointment on or after April 6, 2010, where the instrument creating that special power took effect before that date.[104] The nature of special powers of appointment is explained later.[105]

The following discussion accordingly deals separately with:

(i) the rule at common law,[106] and

(ii) the rule as amended by statute;

but in discussing the elements of the rule the corresponding common law and statutory principles will be treated together so far as possible.

There is some doubt as to whether the rule against perpetuities applies to the Crown,[107] though in principle it should. There are legislative provisions which pre-suppose that the rule applies to the Crown. Thus:

9-019

(i) the Crown was stated to be bound by the 1964 Act, without any qualification[108]; and

(ii) the Crown is authorised by statute to make dispositions that, prior to April 6, 2010, would otherwise have been void for perpetuity.[109]

---

[101] See below, para.9–065.
[102] See below, para.9–067.
[103] PAA 2009 s.15(1)(a); and see PAA 1964 s.15(5A)(a) (inserted by PAA 2009 s.16).
[104] PAA 2009 s.15(1)(b); and see PAA 1964 s.15(5A)(b) (inserted by PAA 2009 s.16).
[105] See below, paras 9–120—9–122.
[106] The phrase "at common law" is used to describe the rule as unamended by statute.
[107] See *Cooper v Stuart* (1889) 14 App. Cas. 286 at 290.
[108] PAA 1964 s.15(7).
[109] Crown Estate Act 1961 s.3(8) (disposal of land on condition with a right of re-entry for breach: the right of re-entry is not subject to the rule against perpetuities). See below, para.9–108. Under PAA 2009, rights of re-entry in respect of a legal estate where there is no trust are no longer subject to the rule against perpetuities: see below, paras 9–029, 9–110.

The 2009 Act is more guarded. It provides that the Act does not extend the application of the rule against perpetuities in relation to the Crown, but, subject to that, it binds the Crown.[110]

1. The meaning of "vest"

9–020   *(a) Vest in interest.* The rule does not require that an interest should be incapable of vesting in possession after the period has run, but only that it should be incapable of becoming vested *in interest* outside the period.[111] This distinction has already been explained.[112] Thus, at common law,[113] if land was devised on trust for X for life with remainder to his first and other sons successively for life, the limitations were valid even if X was a bachelor at the time of the gift. Each of X's sons obtained a vested interest at birth. These interests were not invalidated by the fact that some of the sons might not be entitled to possession of the property until after the period had run. It was therefore immaterial that, if X was a bachelor at the time of the gift and his eldest son outlived him by 50 years, the interest of the second son would not vest in possession until 29 years after the perpetuity period had expired.[114] The same principle does of course apply to cases where there is a fixed perpetuity period, whether under the 1964 Act or the 2009 Act.

9–021   *(b) Test.* For the purposes of the perpetuity rule, however, an interest will rank as vested only if it satisfies a particularly stringent test. The two usual requirements[115] must be satisfied:

(i) the person or persons entitled must be ascertained; and

(ii) the interest must be ready to take effect in possession forthwith, subject only to any prior interests.

There is also a third requirement:

(iii) the size of the benefit must be known.

The importance of this third requirement will be explained in connection with class gifts, which are discussed below. If there is any possibility that a person's share of the property given may vary according to some future event, the whole gift will fail for remoteness if that event might possibly happen

---

[110] PAA 2009 s.17.
[111] *Evans v Walker* (1876) 3 Ch D 211.
[112] Above, para.9–001.
[113] In other words, where the relevant perpetuity period was a life in being and 21 years and not 80 years, as it might have been under PAA 1964, or 125 years, as it must be under PAA 2009.
[114] *Re Hargreaves* (1890) 43 Ch D 401.
[115] Above, paras 9–002, 9–003.

outside the perpetuity period.[116] Thus, for example, in a gift "to such of A's grandchildren as attain 21", where A was alive at the date of the gift and none of his grandchildren had yet come of age, the whole gift would fail under the perpetuity rule at common law. This was so, even as regards any grand-children of A who were alive at the date of the gift, and so were bound to attain 21 (if at all) during their own lifetimes.[117] Until it was known exactly how many grandchildren would ultimately attain 21, the size of each grand-child's interest would necessarily remain uncertain, and its final determination might well occur outside the perpetuity period. In other words, the possibility that the size of a person's share might vary is treated as a contingency (as indeed it is[118]) for perpetuity purposes.

If the size of a person's interest is known, it is immaterial that its amount **9–022** or value may fluctuate. Thus, for example, an annuity or rentcharge was not void for perpetuity merely because it was made to vary with the total rent and outgoings of a house[119] or its rating assessment,[120] and this variation might occur outside the period. However, it was otherwise if the annuity or ren-tcharge might not arise until the perpetuity period had expired.[121]

(c) Leaning towards vesting. As has already been explained,[122] in doubtful **9–023** cases, the court leans in favour of vesting. A natural inclination to save gifts from the perpetuity rule has sometimes led to fine distinctions. For example, a bequest to an unborn person "at 21", or "when he attains 21", is clearly contingent.[123] But it has been held that "to B, to be paid at 21" gave B an immediately vested interest, with a postponed right of enjoyment.[124] It has also been held that "to A at 21, but if A dies under that age, to B" gave A a vested interest, subject to being divested in favour of B if the contingency occurred.[125] In this class of case the words of contingency were treated as governing the gift to B but not the gift to A. For the future, given the existence of a 125-year perpetuity period under the 2009 Act, it seems unlikely that such issues will arise.

---

[116] *Jee v Audley* (1787) 1 Cox Eq. 324; *Leake v Robinson* (1817) 2 Mer. 363; *Cattlin v Brown* (1853) 11 Hare 372; *Pearks v Moseley* (1880) 5 App.Cas. 714; *Re Whiteford* [1915] 1 Ch. 347 at 352. See Morris & Leach, p.38.

[117] cf. *Boreham v Bignall* (1850) 8 Hare. 131.

[118] Gray, s.110.1 and note.

[119] *Re Cassel* [1926] Ch. 358.

[120] *Beachway Management Ltd v Wisewell* [1971] Ch. 610.

[121] *Re Whiteford* [1915] 1 Ch. 347; *Re Johnson's S. T.* [1943] Ch. 341 (trust to make up unborn beneficiary's income to a given amount). A discretionary trust would similarly fail at common law: below, para.9–105.

[122] Above, para.9–006. See *Duffield v Duffield* (1829) 3 Bli (N.S.) 260 at 331; *Re Petrie* [1962] Ch. 355 (realisation of estate: executor's year taken).

[123] *Stapleton v Cheales* (1711) Prec.Ch. 317; *Hanson v Graham* (1801) 6 Ves. 239; cf. *Re Blackwell* [1926] Ch. 223 ("upon attaining 21").

[124] *Re Couturier* [1907] 1 Ch. 470.

[125] *Phipps v Ackers* (1842) 9 Cl. & F. 583; *Re Heath* [1936] Ch. 259; *Re Mallinson's Trusts* [1974] 1 W.L.R. 1120. See Jarman 1388 et seq. for a variety of special cases, in particular as to the effect of an ultimate gift over on the construction of the prior gift. See also Morris & Leach 44.

(d) Interests within the rule

9–024   (1) THE POSITION AT COMMON LAW AND UNDER THE 1964 ACT. At common law
and under the 1964 Act, the rule against perpetuities applied to all types of
proprietary interests.[126] Thus, for example, an easement in fee simple to use
all drains "hereafter to pass" under the grantor's adjacent land was void for
perpetuity at common law because it might first arise in favour of a successor
in title to the grant at an indefinitely future date.[127]

There are certain exceptions to the rule against perpetuities that apply to
dispositions that were made prior to April 6, 2010. These are explained
later.[128]

9–025   (2) THE POSITION UNDER THE 2009 ACT. The position under the 2009 Act is
quite different. The rule against perpetuities only applies in the five circumstances set out in s.1 of the Act and not otherwise. In this way the rule is
confined to dispositions of property that are made by, or arise under, a will or
trust. The intention was to exclude the operation of the rule against perpetuities in relation to essentially "commercial" transactions arising from freely
negotiated bargains,[129] and to confine it to the situations for which the rule
was first created.[130] The five situations were the rule applies under the 2009
Act are set out in the following paragraphs. Although each of the five
situations is defined by reference to interests created by "an instrument", this
is taken to include a case where provision is made in relation to property to
which the Act would apply if it was contained in an instrument.[131] The
obvious case is an oral declaration of trust of personalty, which is valid and
enforceable even though it is not evidenced in writing.[132]

9–026   The first situation is where an instrument limits property in trust so as to
create successive estates and interests. The rule against perpetuities applies to
the estates and interests so created.[133] Thus, where a trust (whether created
inter vivos or by will) limits property to A for life, thereafter to B for life,
thereafter to C absolutely, the rule will apply to the interests of B and C, which
will be valid only if they vest within the 125-year perpetuity period.

This circumstance expressly includes two cases:

---

[126] For the limited perpetuity period applicable to options under PAA 1964 s.9(2), see below,
para.9–135.
[127] *Dunn v Blackdown Properties Ltd* [1961] Ch. 433. See too *Re Beechwood Homes Ltd's
Application* [1994] 2 E.G.L.R. 178 at 179; *Shrewsbury v Adam* [2005] EWCA Civ 1006 at [43];
[2006] 1 P. & C.R. 474 at 483–4 (grant of rights of way over roads to be constructed); *Magrath
v Parkside Hotels Ltd* [2011] EWHC 143 (Ch) (right to exercise a right of fire escape over
existing or future staircases: *sed quaere*). cf *S.E. Ry v Associated Portland Cement Manufacturers
(1900) Ltd* [1910] 1 Ch. 12; *Sharpe v Durrant* (1911) 55 S.J. 423; *Smith v Colbourne* [1914] 2
Ch. 533.
[128] See below, paras 9–137—9–145.
[129] See (1998) Law Com. No.251 at para.7.22.
[130] See (1998) Law Com. No.251 at para.7.21.
[131] PAA 2009 s.19.
[132] See below, para.11–036.
[133] PAA 2009 s.1(2).

(i) The first is where an estate or interest in land arises under a right of reverter on the determination of a determinable fee,[134] as, for example, where land is granted to the University of X until it shall no longer be used for the purposes of that University. The rule applies to the right of reverter that will operate should the determining event occur.[135]

(ii) The second is the analogous case in relation to property other than land, where there is a resulting trust that arises on the determination of a determinable interest, as where trustees hold a sculpture on trust for the Y Art Gallery until the Gallery shall cease to exhibit it. The rule applies to the interest arising under the resulting trust should the Gallery remove the sculpture from display.[136]

The second situation is where an instrument limits property in trust so as to **9–027** create an estate or interest which is subject to a condition precedent, but which is not one of successive estates or interests falling within the first situation mentioned above. The rule against perpetuities applies to the estate or interest so created.[137] Thus, for example, where a testator devises Blackacre to "my first grandson to become a solicitor", the rule against perpetuities applies to that contingent interest, which will fail if it does not vest within the perpetuity period.

The third situation is where an instrument limits property in trust so as to **9–028** create an estate or interest subject to a condition subsequent. The rule against perpetuities applies to:

(i) the right of re-entry in the case of land; and

(ii) the equivalent right in the case of property other than land

that becomes exercisable if the condition is broken.[138] If, for example, Blackacre is held in trust for the benefit of the XYZ Institute, on condition that it shall be used solely for the purposes of the Institute, the rule against perpetuities applies to the right of re-entry that can be exercised if Blackacre ceases to be used in accordance with the condition.

It should be noted that the rule only applies where the interest subject to the **9–029** condition subsequent arises under the terms of a trust instrument. A fee simple subject to a legal or equitable right of entry or re-entry can exist at law.[139] Although rights of entry affecting a legal estate created before April 6, 2010 are subject to the rule against perpetuities,[140] the rule no longer applies to such

---

[134] For determinable fees, see above, para.3–054.
[135] PAA 2009 s.1(7)(a).
[136] PAA 2009 s.1(7)(b).
[137] PAA 2009 s.1(3).
[138] PAA 2009 s.1(4).
[139] LPA 1925 s.7(1); above, para.6–014.
[140] LPA 1925 s.4(3).

rights created after April 5, 2010.[141] Accordingly, it is now possible to create a legal fee simple subject to a right of re-entry that can exist in perpetuity. By way of example, if A sells Blackacre to B, and B enters into positive covenants with A and his successors in title, those covenants could be made indirectly enforceable in perpetuity by reserving a perpetual right of re-entry in the event of any breach. This is so even though, as is explained later, the burden of positive covenants does not run with any land which may be burdened by them.[142] Prior to April 6, 2010, this device could be used only for the duration of the perpetuity period.[143]

9–030   The fourth situation is concerned with the obscure doctrine of executory bequests. Although after 1925 it has only been possible to create successive interests in land under a trust, it may still be possible to create successive legal interests in chattels by will without a trust, though there appears to be no authority on this point.[144] Prior to 1926, it was settled that such bequests were subject to the rule against perpetuities.[145] Under the 2009 Act, the rule against perpetuities applies where a will limits personal property so as to create successive interests under the doctrine of executory bequests.[146] If, say, a picture were bequeathed successively to A for life, thereafter to B for life and then to C absolutely, the rule against perpetuities would apply to the successive interests of B and C, just as it would if the interests had been created under a trust.

9–031   The fifth situation concerns powers of appointment.[147] If an instrument creates a power of appointment, the rule against perpetuities applies to the power.[148] The manner in which the rule applies to such powers is explained later.[149]

There are exceptions to the application of the rule against perpetuities under the 2009 Act. These are explained later.[150]

9–032   Important categories of future interests, such as rights of entry, contracts to create interests in land at a future date, options and future easements, which are created on or after April 6, 2010, are no longer subject to the rule against perpetuities. Where the rule does not apply, future interests may be created either in perpetuity or for any period of time that the parties may agree. In many cases, particularly in relation to options, the parties will be well-advised to limit the duration of the agreement because of the potentially adverse effect

---

[141] PAA 2009 ss.1(9), 21, amending LPA 1925 s.4(3).

[142] See below, para.32–017.

[143] See *Shiloh Spinners Ltd v Harding* [1973] A.C. 691; below, para.32–022.

[144] See (1998) Law Com. No.251 at para.7.31, n.50.

[145] See *Re Backhouse* [1921] 2 Ch. 51, criticised below at para.9–091. cf. *Re Hubbard's W.T.* [1963] Ch. 275 at 290.

[146] PAA 2009 s.1(5).

[147] For the nature of a power of appointment, see below, para.9–116. For the meaning of powers of appointment for the purposes of the 2009 Act, see PAA 2009 ss.11, 20(2), (3); below, para.9–121.

[148] PAA 2009 s.1(6).

[149] See below, para.9–122.

[150] See below, paras 9–139, 9–144, 9–146.

that such interests can have on the value and marketability of the land. However, the matter is entirely one for the parties.

2. No "wait and see" at common law

(a) Possibilities. The cardinal doctrine of the rule at common law was that **9–033** everything depended upon possibilities, not probabilities or actual events.[151] Every interest had to be considered at the time when the instrument creating it took effect. Thus a deed had to be considered at the time when it is executed and a will at the moment of the testator's death.[152] If at the relevant moment there was the slightest possibility that the perpetuity period might be exceeded,[153] the limitation was void *ab initio*, even if it was most improbable that this would in fact happen and even if, as events turned out, it did not.[154] For example, if property was given:

"to the first son of A who may marry",

the gift failed at common law if A was alive and had no married son at the time of the gift. This is because the following sequence of events was possible:

(i) all existing sons of A might die unmarried;

(ii) A might then have another son (not a life in being at the time of the gift);

(iii) A might then die;

iv) A's last-born son might marry more than 21 years after the death of A, the last surviving life in being.

This possibility might have been extremely remote, as where a son of A was to be married within the next week, or where A was a woman past the age of child-bearing. However, the degree of improbability was immaterial.[155]

(b) Impossibility. Even where it could be proved that the birth of further **9–034** children was a physical impossibility, the rule at common law maintained the same disregard for the facts of life.[156] But it respected the legal proprieties,

---

[151] Morris & Leach 70.

[152] *Vanderplank v King* (1843) 3 Hare 1 at 17; *Re Mervin* [1891] 3 Ch. 197 at 204: Lewis, *Perpetuity*, 171. Supp. 64; Gray, s.231; Morris & Leach 56.

[153] Ambiguity might be resolved in favour of validity: see *Re Deeley's Settlement* [1974] Ch. 454.

[154] This sentence was approved in *Re Watson's S.T.* [1959] 1 W.L.R. 732 at 739.

[155] For a clear modern statement of the position at common law, see *Air Jamaica Ltd v Charlton* [1999] 1 W.L.R. 1399 at 1408.

[156] *Jee v Audley* (1787) 1 Cox Eq. 324; *Re Dawson* (1888) 39 Ch D 155; *Re Deloitte* [1926] Ch. 56; *Figg v Clarke* [1997] 1 W.L.R. 603. For reforms made by PAA 1964, see below, para.9–043. In the Irish Republic the courts have rejected the doctrine as absurd: *Exham v Beamish* [1939] I.R. 336.

and so would disregard what can only be done in breach of trust.[157] In one case[158] the gift was made:

> "to such of the grandchildren of G, living at the testatrix's death or born within five years thereafter, who should attain 21 or being female marry under that age".

The perpetuity period could have been exceeded only if a child of G born after the testatrix's death (and so not a life in being) had had a child within the prescribed period of five years after the testatrix's death. This was rejected as being not merely physically but legally impossible: no legitimate child can be born to a person under the age of 16.[159] Accordingly, the gift was good.

9–035 Considerable care was therefore necessary to detect any possibility, however remote and in whatever improbable circumstances, that a gift might transgress the rule. Thus a gift of property to certain persons "if the minerals under the said farm should be worked" offended the perpetuity rule and was void because of the possibility that the minerals would first be worked outside the perpetuity period.[160]

9–036 *(c) Gifts which might never vest.* It was immaterial that the gift might never vest at all. The question was whether, if it did vest, it was capable of vesting outside the period. A gift to the first son of X, a bachelor, might never vest at all, because X might never have a son. But this possibility did not render the gift void for perpetuity. The gift was incapable of vesting outside the perpetuity period. If X did have a son, the son must be born or conceived during X's lifetime[161] and X was a life in being. The rule required, therefore, that the gift shall be bound to vest, *if it vested at all*, within the perpetuity period.

To this rule against "wait and see" there were two special exceptions which are considered below under the respective headings of "alternative contingencies" and "powers of appointment".[162]

9–037 *(d) Express clauses.* A gift which would otherwise be too remote could be validated by the insertion of an express clause confining its vesting to the proper period. Thus a gift by a testator to such of his issue as should be living when certain gravel pits become exhausted was void as it stood, even if it was highly probable that the pits would be worked out in five or six years.[163] The

---

[157] *Re Atkins W.T.* [1974] 1 W.L.R. 761 (postponing sale).
[158] *Re Gaite's W.T.* [1949] 1 All E.R. 459.
[159] Marriage Act 1949 s.2, invalidating any marriage by a person under the age of 16. The law admits the physical impossibility of child-bearing for other purposes: see e.g. *Re Widdow's Trusts* (1871) L.R. 11 Eq. 408; *Re Millner's Estate* (1872) L.R. 14 Eq. 245; *Re White* [1901] 1 Ch. 570; *Re Tennant's Settlement* [1959] Ir.Jur.Rep. 76; *Re Westminster Bank Ltd's Declaration of Trusts* [1963] 1 W.L.R. 820; *Re Pettifor's W.T.* [1966] 1 W.L.R. 778; and contrast *Croxton v May* (1878) 9 Ch D 388.
[160] *Thomas v Thomas* (1902) 87 L.T. 58.
[161] cf. Human Fertilisation and Embryology Act 1990 s.28 (as amended) (definition of "father").
[162] Below, paras 9–095, 9–127.
[163] *Re Wood* [1894] 3 Ch. 381.

gift would have been valid, however, if had been worded "to such of my issue as shall be living 21 years after my death or when the gravel pits are exhausted, whichever first happens"[164] or "to such of my children and grandchildren as shall be living when the gravel pits are exhausted, provided that no grandchild aged 21 or over shall participate". However, a clause seeking to confine the vesting within the period had to do so explicitly. Thus the addition of words, which provided that the vesting should be postponed only "so far as the rules of law and equity will permit", would not validate a void gift,[165] though "within the limitations prescribed by law" might have sufficed.[166]

3. "Wait and see" under the 1964 Act

(a) Operation of the rule. The absolute certainty required by the rule at common law was convenient in that it enabled the validity of contingent gifts to be determined at the outset. But this convenience was bought at too high a price. The rule defeated many gifts which might well have vested within the permitted period, and which in any case could have been validated by an express clause of the kind mentioned in the previous paragraph. In order to stop this "slaughter of the innocents",[167] the 1964 Act introduced the principle of "wait and see". The Act provided that a gift was to fail only if and when "it becomes established that the vesting must occur, if at all, after the end of the perpetuity period"; and until that time arrived the Act required the disposition to be treated as if it were not subject to the rule.[168] Corresponding provision was made for powers and rights (for example, an option[169]) which did not so much "vest" as become exercisable in the future, and accordingly any power, option or other right was to be void for perpetuity only if and so far as it was not fully exercised within the period.[170] Thus the principle extended to all classes of proprietary interests, powers and rights. But it had two limitations:

9–038

(i) it applied only to instruments taking effect after July 15, 1964 (which will not often matter now)[171]; and

(ii) it applied only to dispositions which would be void at common law.

In a case to which the 1964 Act applies, in other words, where there was a disposition that was made on or after July 16, 1964 and before April 6, 2010,

---

[164] See (1938) 51 Harv.L.R. 638 at 645 (W.B. Leach).

[165] *Portman v Viscount Portman* [1922] A.C. 473.

[166] *Re Vaux* [1939] Ch. 465, on which see *IRC v Williams* 1969] 1 W.L.R. 1197; and contrast *Re Abrahams' W.T.* [1969] 1 Ch. 463.

[167] Leach (1952) 68 L.Q.R. 35.

[168] s.3(1).

[169] For options, etc., see below, para.9–134.

[170] PAA 1964 s.3(2), (3).

[171] As has been explained, PAA 1964 does not apply to instruments taking effect on or after April 6, 2010, which are subject instead to the PAA 2009: see above, para.9–018.

the first step is always to apply the rule at common law. It is only if the gift fails to satisfy the rule at common law that it will fall within the scope of the 1964 Act. Instead of replacing the old rule, the Act merely supplemented it by coming to the rescue when needed, but not otherwise. Unfortunately, this means that old common law rules cannot be laid to rest, but continue to have a role in any case where the 1964 Act applies.

9–039   *(b) Impossibility of vesting in time.* Under the 1964 Act, a gift which would be void for perpetuity at common law, is void only if and when circumstances make it clear that it can only vest outside the perpetuity period. If circumstances make this clear at the outset, the gift is void from the beginning. In other cases its validity depends on later events which actually happen, and not on events which might happen, as at common law. Thus where land was devised by a will made prior to April 6, 2010[172]:

> "to A's first son to marry",

and A was a bachelor at the testator's death, it is clear that the gift would be void at common law. It is equally clear that the first son to marry might be a son who married in A's lifetime or within 21 years of A's death. The Act therefore allowed those who must administer A's estate to wait and see whether this happened. If it did (or does), the gift is good. However, if A died before any of his sons had married, and none of them married during the next 21 years, it then "becomes established" that the gift was incapable of vesting within the perpetuity period, and thereupon it failed or fails. In effect, it operated like a gift "to A's first son to marry before the expiration of 21 years from A's death", which of course was valid at common law, and involved a similar period of waiting to see whether any son of A became entitled. Had A died before the testator, the gift would in any case have been valid at common law, and the Act would have no application.

9–040   Similarly, in the case of a gift to such of the testator's issue as were alive when certain gravel pits became exhausted,[173] the gift would be valid if the pits were exhausted within 21 years of the death of the survivor of those of the issue who were alive at the testator's death. In the case of a grant of the right to use all drains "hereafter to pass" under certain land, the grant would be valid in respect of all drains constructed within 21 years of the death of the survivor of the grantor and the grantee.[174]

In all these cases it will be seen that the perpetuity periods that were made available by the 1964 Act were such as the donor could himself have validly used at common law, had he been well advised. The change to "wait and see" was in one sense merely a reframing of the gift so as to give it the best possible chance of satisfying the rule at common law.

[172] See above, para.9–018.
[173] cf. above, para.9–037.
[174] This is under s.3(3). cf. above, para.9–024. For explanation of the choice of lives in being, which is governed by PAA 1964, see below, para.9–055.

(c) Relation to other rules. Where other provisions of the 1964 Act　**9–041** (explained later) may save a gift to which that Act applies by reducing an excessive age, or by excluding members of a class, or by accelerating vesting during the life of a surviving spouse, the Act requires the "wait and see" rule to be applied first.[175] These other provisions come into play only if and when it becomes apparent that "wait and see" by itself will not save the gift. The order of priority of these various gift-saving provisions is therefore "first wait and see". This embodies the policy that the gift should be given every opportunity to take effect as the donor intended, and that only as a last resort should his dispositions be modified by statute.

(d) Maintenance and advancement. While the validity of a gift remains in　**9–042** suspense under the "wait and see" provisions trustees have their usual powers of maintenance and advancement, which enable them to use income and capital for the benefit of contingent beneficiaries, subject to certain restrictions.[176] It if turns out that a contingent beneficiary who has been assisted in this way fails to qualify for the gift, e.g. by failing to attain 21 or marry, the validity of the trustees' action is unaffected.[177] It is therefore possible for a substantial part of a gift to be used for the benefit of someone who never becomes entitled to take, at the expense of the one who does become entitled.

(e) Future parenthood. The 1964 Act created statutory presumptions as to　**9–043** "future parenthood" to remedy the absurdities which can occur under the rule at common law.[178] Where the gift was made after July 15, 1964 and before April 6, 2010, the 1964 Act requires it to be presumed that:

(i) a male can have a child at the age of 14 years or over, but not under that age; and

(ii) a female can have a child at the age of 12 years or over but not under that age, or over the age of 55 years.[179]

However, these presumptions are rebuttable. Evidence may be given to show that a living person will or will not be able to have a child at the time in question.[180] Thus, medical evidence of a person's incapacity may be given, and may be contradicted by evidence of capacity.

The above provisions apply only where a perpetuity question arises "in any proceedings", meaning legal proceedings.[181] If necessary, a declaratory judgment can be sought.[182] Once the question is decided, the decision will govern any future proceedings concerning the same gift for perpetuity purposes.[183]

---

[175] This is the effect of the opening words of s.3, excluding ss.4 and 5.
[176] TA 1925 ss.31, 32.
[177] PAA 1964 s.3(1). See (1964) 80 L.Q.R. at 494 (Morris and Wade).
[178] Above, para.9–034.
[179] s.2(1)(a).
[180] s.2(1)(b).
[181] s.2(1).
[182] CPR 40.20.
[183] s.2(3).

9–044   For the purposes of the 1964 Act, "having a child" extends not only to natural birth but to "adoption, legitimation or other means".[184] It is obviously possible that a child may be legitimated or adopted after the date of the gift by a woman over 55, thus falsifying the statutory presumption. To deal with this, and also with any cases of births inconsistent with the statutory ages or evidence of incapacity, the High Court is given discretion by the 1964 Act to make such order as it thinks fit for placing the persons interested in the property, so far as may be just, in the position they would have held had the statutory provisions not been applied.[185] The Act therefore contemplates the possibility that it may not be right to order full restitution by those who had previously taken the property, or expected to take it.

9–045   The rules on future parenthood have no application under the 2009 Act, which dispenses with the concept of lives in being and adopts a 125-year perpetuity period instead.[186] The discussion below of lives in being at common law and under the 1964 Act has no relevance therefore to dispositions which are made after April 5, 2010.

4. Lives in being at common law

9–046   *(a) Relevant lives.* Any living person or persons might be used as lives in being, since for a gift to be valid at common law it was only necessary to demonstrate that it must necessarily vest, if at all, within the period of a (meaning "any") life in being plus 21 years. In the literal sense, everyone alive at the time of the gift was a life in being.[187] Nevertheless, the only lives in being which could be of assistance for the purposes of the perpetuity rule were those which in some way or other could govern the time when the gift was to vest. The only lives worth considering were therefore those which were implicated in the contingency upon which the vesting had been made to depend.[188]

9–047   *(b) Lives mentioned in gift.* It follows that the life or lives in being had to be mentioned in the gift either expressly or by implication. In the great majority of cases the only lives which could possibly be of use were those of the persons expressly mentioned in the gift. Any or all of them might be used to demonstrate, if possible, that the gift was bound to vest, if at all, within the permitted period. There was therefore no difficulty in ascertaining the relevant lives. Sometimes lives which were relevant to the period of vesting were brought in by implication, without express mention. If a testator gave property to such of his grandchildren as attained the age of 21, his children's lives clearly helped to confine the period of time within which the gift could vest. Accordingly, his children could be taken as lives in being. They were all

---

[184] s.2(4). For the right of such children to take, see below, para.14–073.
[185] PAA 1964 s.2(2).
[186] See further below, para.9–065.
[187] See *Pownall v Graham* (1863) 33 Beav. 242 at 246, 247.
[188] cf. Morris & Leach 62.

bound to have been born[189] by the time of the testator's death, and a gift to grandchildren presupposed the existence of children. The gift was therefore good,[190] because no grandchild could take longer than 21 years from its parent's death to reach the age of 21. But a gift to the grandchildren of a living person was bad,[191] unless the class was restricted in some way, e.g. to those living at the death of a life in being.[192] This was because the living person might have another child after the date of the gift and then, more than 21 years after all those alive at the date of the gift had died, that child might have a child.

Consequently, everyone who: **9–048**

    (i) was alive at the time of the gift, and

    (ii) was mentioned in it either expressly or by implication

was considered as a possible life in being. It did not follow that everyone so mentioned *would* be an effective life in being, because the life of the person in question might have no connection with the contingency which governed the vesting and thus set no limit to the time within which it must occur. If A granted B the right in fee simple "to use all drains hereafter to pass under Blackacre", both A and B were mentioned in the gift, but neither of their lives had any bearing on the fact that no such drain might be built until long after the perpetuity period, when some successor of B might claim to use it. The gift was therefore void.[193] For similar reasons all persons not mentioned in the gift had to be ignored, since the length or shortness of their lives could have no bearing on the vesting of the gift.

(c) Time for ascertaining lives. The perpetuity period commenced: **9–049**

    (i) In the case of gifts made inter vivos, the date of the instrument; and

    (ii) In the case of wills, the date of the testator's death.

It was that time when the facts had to be ascertained. A person had to be alive at that moment in order to be a life in being.[194]

(d) Choice of lives. For a person to be a life in being for the purposes of the rule, it was unnecessary that he should receive any benefit from the gift or that **9–050**

---

[189] Or about to be born: see below, para.9–057; Morris & Leach 65.
[190] Gray, ss.220, 370; cf. *Blagrove v Hancock* (1848) 16 Sim. 371 (where, however, the excessive age of 25 was specified); *Re Lodwig* [1916] 2 Ch. 26.
[191] *Seaman v Wood* (1856) 22 Beav. 591 at 594.
[192] *Wetherell v Wetherell* (1863) 1 De G.J. & S. 134 at 139, 140.
[193] *Dunn v Blackdown Properties Ltd* [1961] Ch. 433; above, para.9–024.
[194] See above, para.9–033.

he should be related in any special way to the beneficiaries.[195] Nor was there any restriction upon the number of lives selected provided that it was reasonably possible to ascertain who they were, "for let the lives be never so many, there must be a survivor, and so it is but the length of that life".[196]

> "If a term be limited to one for life, with twenty several remainders for lives to other persons successively, who are all alive and in being, so that all the candles are lighted together, this is good enough."[197]

For example, gifts by a testator to such of his descendants as were living:

> (i) 21 years after the death of the last survivor of the members of a given school living at the testator's death[198]; or

> (ii) 20 years after the death of the last survivor of all the lineal descendants of Queen Victoria living at the testator's death[199];

were held to be valid. In the latter case the testator died in 1926, when there were 120 lives in being and it was reasonably possible to follow the duration of their lives. To avoid the risk that the limitation might be void for uncertainty because of the difficulties of identifying the large number of measuring lives in such a case,[200] it was the practice to use the measuring life of a recently deceased monarch. The clearest possible case of uncertainty occurred where a testatrix chose the period "until 21 years from the death of the last survivor of all persons who shall be living at my death".[201]

The lives had to be human lives, and not the lives of animals.[202]

9–051   Because of the difficulties mentioned in the previous paragraph, the 2009 Act makes provision for cases where:

> (i) property is limited in trust by an instrument taking effect, or in the case of a will, executed, before April 6, 2010[203];

---

[195] *Cadell v Palmer* (1833) 1 Cl. & F. 372. This was said to be a mistaken doctrine (*Cole v Sewell* (1848) 2 H.L.C. 186 at 233), and Lewis, *Perpetuity*, p.167, calls it "a flagrant abuse of the spirit of the Rule". But the law had generally been supposed to be thus for some time (see, e.g. *Goodman v Goodright* (1759) 2 Burr. 873 at 879); and it was settled beyond question by *Cadell v Palmer*.

[196] *Scatterwood v Edge* (1697) 1 Salk. 229. ("The candles were all lighted at once", as Twisden J. used to say: see *Love v Wyndham* (1670) 1 Mod. 50 at 54).

[197] *Howard v Duke of Norfolk* (1681) 2 Swans 454 at 458, per Lord Nottingham L.C. And see *Low v Burron* (1734) 3 P. Wms. 262 at 265; *Robinson v Hardcastle* (1786) 2 Bro.C.C. 22 at 30; *Thellusson v Woodford* (1805) 11 Ves. 112 at 136.

[198] *Pownall v Graham* (1863) 33 Beav. 242 at 245, 247.

[199] *Re Villar* [1929] 1 Ch. 243.

[200] As to which, see *Re Villar, Public Trustee v Villar* [1929] 1 Ch. 243; and *Re Leverhulme (No.2)* [1943] 2 All E.R. 274.

[201] *Re Moore* [1901] 1 Ch. 936.

[202] For remarks on this, see *Re Kelly* [1932] I.R. 255 at 260, 261. *Re Dean* (1889) 41 Ch D 552 is probably incorrect on this point. See Gray, s.896, and below, para.9–143, fn.544. See also below, para.9–150, as to the necessity for a beneficiary able to enforce the trust.

[203] See PAA 2009 s.15(2). The procedure explained in this paragraph does not apply if the trusts were exhausted before April 6, 2010 or if, before then, the property became held on trust for charitable purposes by way of a final disposition of the property: PAA 2009 s.15(3).

(ii) the instrument specifies a perpetuity period by reference to the lives of persons in being when the trust was created; and

(iii) the trustees believe that it is difficult or not reasonably practicable for them to ascertain whether the lives have ended and therefore, whether the perpetuity period has terminated.[204]

In those circumstances, if the trustees execute a deed stating that belief and that the relevant provision of the 2009 Act applies,[205] the instrument takes effect as if it specified a perpetuity period of 100 years.[206] The rule against perpetuities has effect as if the only perpetuity period applicable to the instrument were 100 years.[207] The deed, which is irrevocable,[208] becomes subject to certain provisions of the 2009 Act[209] in place of the provisions of the 1964 Act which would otherwise have applied.[210]

5. Alternative fixed period under the 1964 Act. "Royal lives clauses", of the type discussed above,[211] were much used as a draftsman's device for providing a long perpetuity period when required for any purpose under the rule at common law.[212] In order to provide a more straightforward substitute the 1964 Act made available an alternative perpetuity period consisting of a fixed period of years not exceeding 80.[213] Although this period was to be "specified in that behalf" in the instrument,[214] it probably sufficed if, without expressly stating it to be the perpetuity period, the limitation specified a period of years within which vesting had to occur.[215]   **9–052**

Nothing in the 1964 Act affected the validity of an ordinary "royal lives clause" or similar perpetuity clause where the gift had to vest, if at all, within the specified period.

6. Lives in being under the 1964 Act

(a) Effect of the introduction of "wait and see". It is questionable whether the introduction of the "wait and see" principle required any special provision to be made restricting the persons who could be used as lives in being. The policy of the "wait and see" provisions of the 1964 Act was not to alter the   **9–053**

---

[204] PAA 2009 s.12(1).
[205] The relevant provision is PAA 2009 s.12(2).
[206] PAA 2009 s.12(2)(a).
[207] PAA 2009 s.12(2)(b).
[208] PAA 2009 s.12(3).
[209] PAA 2009 s.12(2)(c). The provisions are PAA 2009 ss.6–11.
[210] PAA 2009 s.12(2)(d). The provisions disapplied are PAA 1964 ss.1–12.
[211] See para 9–050.
[212] e.g. to confine a discretionary trust within legal limits. See Fourth Report of the Law Reform Committee, 1956, Cmnd. 18, p.6.
[213] s.1. A period "from the date of my death to the 1st day of January 2020", which was specified as the perpetuity period in a will, was held to fall within this section: *Re Green's W.T.* [1985] 3 All E.R. 455.
[214] PAA 1964 s.1(1).
[215] See the previous edition of this work at para.9–042.

length of the perpetuity period,[216] but to provide that gifts shall be valid if they do in fact vest within it rather than be void if they might by possibility vest outside it. The perpetuity period itself remained unchanged, and the lives in being which determined the period in any given case ought likewise to have remained unchanged. This was assumed (correctly, it is suggested) by the Law Reform Committee when they recommended the change to "wait and see".[217]

The use of statutory lives made the law needlessly complicated and was the subject of widespread criticism.[218]

9–054   *(b) Conditions for the use of statutory lives in being.* It is only for the purpose of its "wait and see" provisions that the 1964 Act defined the lives in being.[219] A gift which was valid at common law (e.g. one confined by a conventional "royal lives clause") was unaffected. Where the donor had chosen the alternative of appointing a fixed statutory perpetuity period, of course no lives in being could be used.[220]

In all other cases where "wait and see" applied, the Act provided that the perpetuity period should be determined by reference to the lives of certain categories of persons and no others. The definition was therefore both imperative and exclusive. The persons concerned had, of course, to be in being at the relevant time. In addition, they had to satisfy two requirements:

(i) they had to be ascertainable at the commencement of the perpetuity period; and

(ii) if a "description of persons", they had not to be so numerous as to render it impracticable to ascertain the date of death of the survivor.[221]

The second of these requirements conformed with the rule at common law, as already explained.[222] The first requirement was new, and was a restriction of the rule at common law. For example, in a gift by will:

"to A's first grandchild to marry a woman born before my death" (A being alive at the testator's death),

the gift was presumably valid at common law because it would have to vest during the lifetime of the potential wife, who was by definition a life in being. It did not matter that the wife is not ascertainable at the commencement of the perpetuity period, i.e. at the testator's death. But in cases where the "wait and

[216] Except by introducing the alternative fixed period under s.1, above.
[217] Fourth Report, Cmnd. 18 (1956), paras 17, 18.
[218] For these criticisms, see the previous edition of this work at paras 9–044—9–045.
[219] PAA 1964 s.3(4).
[220] PAA 1964 s.3(4).
[221] s.3(4); see *Re Thomas Meadows & Co Ltd* [1971] Ch. 278.
[222] See above, para.9–050.

see" provisions of the Act applied, such a life could not be used, because it was unascertainable at the outset.

(c) Statutory categories of lives in being. Where the conditions mentioned **9–055** above were satisfied, the 1964 Act provided that four categories of lives in being were to be used.[223] If none of these were in fact available, the perpetuity period for "wait and see" purposes was 21 years only.[224] The four statutory categories were as follows.[225]

(1) THE DONOR: "the person by whom the disposition was made". **9–056**

(2) A DONEE: "a person to whom or in whose favour the disposition was **9–057** made, that is to say:

> (i) in the case of a disposition to a class of persons, any member or potential member of the class;
>
> (ii) in the case of an individual disposition to a person taking only on certain conditions being satisfied, any person as to whom some of the conditions are satisfied and the remainder may in time be satisfied";
>
> (iii) and (iv) (these concern special powers of appointment, discussed separately below);
>
> (v) "in the case of any power, option or other right, the person on whom the right is conferred".

(3) A DONEE'S PARENT OR GRANDPARENT: "a person having a child or **9–058** grandchild within sub-paragraphs (i) or (iv) of paragraph (b) above, or any of whose children or grandchildren, if subsequently born, would by virtue of his or her descent fall within those sub-paragraphs".

(4) THE OWNER OF A PRIOR INTEREST: "any person on the failure or determi- **9–059** nation of whose prior interest the disposition is limited to take effect".[226]

(d) "The disposition". Each of these categories was defined in relation to **9–060** "the disposition"[227]; and it is plain from the Act that each distinct gift counted as a distinct disposition. Thus, in a gift by will:

> "To A's first son to marry, and, in default of any son of A marrying, then to B's first son to marry" (A and B being alive and without married sons at the testator's death),

---

[223] s.3(5).
[224] s.3(4)(b).
[225] s.3(5).
[226] See *Re Thomas Meadows & Co Ltd* [1971] Ch. 278.
[227] Registration of a member of a pension scheme could be "the disposition": *Re Thomas Meadows & Co Ltd*, above.

there were two separate dispositions. Any son of A alive at the testator's death was a life in being under (b) for the purposes of the first gift, and under (d) for the purposes of the second gift. Any such son of B was a life in being under (b) for the purposes of the second gift, but not a life in being at all for the purposes of the first gift. A was also a life in being under (c) for the purposes of the first gift, but not the second; and B was a life in being under (c) for the purposes of the second gift, but not the first. The scheme was thus both more complicated and more restrictive than that under the rule at common law. At common law royal lives, or any other lives, could be specified by the settlor. But such lives were useless for statutory "wait and see" purposes.

A class gift was a single "disposition" to which the Act applied as explained below.[228]

9–061　　*(e) Comparison with common law lives.* There were many situations in which the statutory rules diverged from the principle of the rule at common law for no apparent reason. However, in general, the 1964 Act allowed a greater number of lives in being to be used than could be used at common law. The Act was more restrictive than the common law in two situations:

> (i) where a life in being was not an ascertainable person at the time of the gift; and
>
> (ii) where there was a gift over and the donee dies more than 21 years before the gift is to vest.

9–062　　**7. Perpetuity period without lives in being.** If no lives in being were available, the perpetuity period was 21 years only. This was the case both at common law[229] and under the 1964 Act,[230] unless, of course, the alternative statutory perpetuity period (not exceeding 80 years)[231] had been used.[232]

9–063　　**8. Children *en ventre sa mere*.** For the purpose of the perpetuity rule, a child *en ventre sa mere*[233] was treated as if it had been born,[234] even if the child did not benefit from the gift.[235] Two cases could arise.

> (i) A child might be *en ventre sa mere* at the beginning of the period, i.e. at the time of the gift. In this case the child was treated as a life

---

[228] Below, para.9–077.

[229] Marsden 34.

[230] s.3(4)(b). This applied only in cases of "wait and see". In other cases the Act left the common law unchanged.

[231] Above, para.9–051.

[232] The position is different under PAA 2009, where there is a single perpetuity period of 125 years: see s.5, below, para.9–065.

[233] "In simple English it is an unborn child inside the mother's womb": *Royal College of Nursing v Dept of Health and Social Security* [1981] A.C. 800 at 802, per Lord Denning M.R. On the perpetuity aspects of delayed posthumous births by means of sperm banks or other devices, see (1979) 53 A.L.J. 311 (C. Sappideen).

[234] *Thellusson v Woodford* (1805) 11 Ves. 112 at 141.

[235] *Re Wilmer's Trusts* [1903] 2 Ch. 411.

in being.[236] Thus if a testator gave property for life to the child which the wife was expecting, with remainder contingent upon certain circumstances existing at that child's death, or bound to occur within 21 years thereof, the remainder was good, for the contingency had to be resolved within the permissible period.[237]

(ii) A child might be *en ventre sa mere* during the period. In this case the period was extended so far as was necessary to include the period of gestation.[238] Thus if property was given to the first of A's sons to reach 21 years, the gift was valid even if A's only son was unborn at A's death. The perpetuity period in such a case was A's lifetime plus the period of gestation and 21 years.

It will be seen from this that two periods of gestation might arise in the same case.[239] In those circumstances both were allowed.[240]

These rules did not allow the addition of any period or periods of nine months or so for all cases. They applied only where gestation actually existed, and where the date of the subsequent birth affected the period chosen.[241]

These rules were not changed by the 1964 Act. They have no application to cases under the 2009 Act, where there is a 125-year perpetuity period.[242]

9. "Surviving spouse" conditions. Donors often made gifts to such chil- **9–064** dren as might be living at the death of their last-surviving parent. Such gifts often failed at common law where one parent was not a life in being, and so the 1964 Act made special provision to avert this problem. Where a gift was made by will:

> "to A (a bachelor) for life, with remainder to any wife of A for life, with remainder to such of their children as survive them both",

the remainder to the children was void at common law if A was alive at the same time of the gift.[243] But if the gift was made after July 15, 1964, the 1964 Act saved the remainder to the children. It provided that, subject to the "wait and see" rule:

> "where a disposition is limited by reference to the time of death of the survivor of a person in being at the commencement of the perpetuity period and any spouse of that person, and that time has not arrived at the

[236] *Thellusson v Woodford*, above, at 143; *Re Wilmer's Trusts*, above, at 421.

[237] *Long v Blackall* (1797) 7 T.R. 100.

[238] Gray, s.221; Morris and Leach 65; Jarman 305, 306.

[239] In exceptional cases, there might even be three periods of gestation: see *Smith v Farr* (1838) 3 Y. & C. Ex. 328; Gray, s.222.

[240] *Thellusson v Woodford* (1805) 11 Ves. 112 at 143, 149, 150. See, by way of example, *Gulliver v Wickett* (1745) 1 Wils.K.B. 105.

[241] *Cadell v Palmer* (1833) 1 Cl. & F. 372 at 421, 422.

[242] See below, para 9–065.

[243] Above, para.9–033.

end of the perpetuity period, the disposition shall be treated for all purposes, where to do so would save it from being void for remoteness, as if it had instead been limited by reference to the time immediately before the end of that period".[244]

In such cases, therefore, under the "wait and see" rule no change in the time of vesting was required if the survivor of the parents in fact died within the perpetuity period (A's lifetime plus 21 years). But if A's widow survived him for 21 years, the "wait and see" rule could do no more, and the Act then converted the gift into a gift to the children then living, even if some of them predeceased the widow and so fell outside the class which the testator intended to benefit.

These issues do not arise where:

(i) A fixed perpetuity period not exceeding 80 years is specified in a disposition subject to the 1964 Act; or

(ii) A disposition is subject to the 2009 Act which is subject to the fixed 125-year perpetuity period specified by that Act.

10. The fixed perpetuity period under the 2009 Act

9–065   *(a) A single mandatory perpetuity period.* As has been mentioned, the 2009 Act has introduced a single fixed perpetuity period of 125 years.[245] This period must apply,[246] and any specification of a perpetuity period in the relevant instrument is ineffective.[247] The old common law perpetuity period of a life in being and 21 years is wholly irrelevant in relation to dispositions made after April 5, 2010.

9–066   *(b) The commencement of the perpetuity period.* Subject to certain exceptions in relation to powers of appointment and pension schemes, which are explained later,[248] the perpetuity period starts when the relevant instrument takes effect.[249] A will takes effect at the testator's death.[250]

9–067   **11. "Wait and see" under the 2009 Act.** Under the 2009 Act, the principle of "wait and see" applies to those estates, interests, rights and powers that are still subject to the rule against perpetuities.[251] Thus, in the case of the vesting of an estate or interest, a disposition made after April 5, 2010 is not void merely because it might vest outside the 125-year statutory perpetuity

---

[244] PAA 1964 s.5.
[245] PAA 2009 s.5(1); above, para.9–018.
[246] For the instruments to which PAA 2009 applies, see above, paras 9–018, and 9–026— 9–031. PAA 2009 does not apply to a special power of appointment created after April 5, 2010, but pursuant to an instrument made before April 6, 2010: see below, para.9–122.
[247] PAA 2009 s.5(2).
[248] See below, paras 9–122, and 9–145.
[249] PAA 2009 s.6(1).
[250] PAA 2009 s.20(6).
[251] PAA 2009 s.7.

period.[252] Until such time, if any, as it becomes established that the vesting must occur outside that perpetuity period, the estate or interest is treated as if it were not subject to the rule against perpetuities.[253] There are corresponding provisions in relation to the exercise of other rights and powers that are subject to the rule against perpetuities.[254]

12. Class gifts

(a) At common law

(1) NATURE OF CLASS GIFTS. A class gift is a gift of property to all who come **9–068** within some description. The fact that some of the individuals are named does not deprive the gift of its characteristic as a class gift, provided it is a gift to the body as a whole.[255] The property is divisible in shares which vary according to the number of persons in the class.[256] Thus gifts of property:

"to my children who shall live to be 25",[257] or

"to all the nephews and nieces of my late husband who were living at his death, except A and B",[258] or "to my children A, B, C, D, and E, and such of my children hereafter to be born as shall attain the age of 21 years or marry",[259] or

"to A, B, C, D and E if living",[260]

are class gifts. The essence of the matter in each case is the intention that if one member of the class is subtracted the shares of the others will be increased. But gifts of property to be equally divided between:

"the five daughters of X",[261] or

"my nine children",[262]

or a gift of £5,000:

---

[252] PAA 2009 s.7(1).
[253] PAA 2009 s.7(2)(a). The validity of anything done prior to that time, as by the exercise of powers of maintenance or advancement, is not affected: PAA 2009 s.7(2)(b).
[254] PAA 2009 ss.7(3)–(6).
[255] *Sammut v Manzi* [2008] UKPC 58 at [31]; [2009] 1 W.L.R. 1834 at 1844.
[256] See Gray, s.369n.; *Pearks v Moseley* (1880) 5 App.Cas. 714 at 723; *Kingsbury v Walter* [1901] A.C. 187 at 192; Jarman 341, 348.
[257] *Boreham v Bignall* (1850) 8 Hare 131.
[258] *Dimond v Bostock* (1875) 10 Ch.App. 358.
[259] *Re Jackson* (1883) 25 Ch D 162.
[260] *Re Hornby* (1859) 7 W.R. 729.
[261] *Re Smith's Trusts* (1878) 9 Ch D 117
[262] *Re Stansfield* (1880) 15 Ch D 84.

"to each of my daughters",[263]

are not class gifts, for a distinct one-fifth or one-ninth share or the sum of £5,000 is given to each child, exactly as if he or she had been named.[264] These shares cannot vary according to the number of the recipients. It is therefore necessary to distinguish class gifts, where the ultimate shares are at first uncertain in amount, from groups of independent gifts, where the shares are quantified from the beginning.

9–069   (2) APPLICATION OF RULE. At common law the perpetuity rule applied to class gifts in the following way. If a single member of the class might possibly take a vested interest outside the period, the whole gift failed, even as regards those members of the class who had already satisfied any required contingency.[265] A class gift could not be good as to part and void as to the rest.[266] Until the total number of members of the class had been ascertained, it could not be said what share any member of the class would take, and this state of affairs would continue so long as it was possible for any alteration in the number to be made. Commonly the offending possibility was that the number might be increased; but the possibility that it might be decreased was equally fatal. Even though in such a case the minimum amount of each share was fixed within the period, the whole gift was void if the shares could be augmented by an event which was too remote.[267] However, a gift to a class as joint tenants, if it otherwise complied with the rule, was not invalidated merely because the joint tenancy gave a right of survivorship[268] which might operate outside the period.[269]

9–070   (3) GIFTS NOT SEVERABLE. At common law class gifts were not severable, since it was the essence of the rule that any taint of remoteness affected the whole class. However, what appeared at first sight to be a gift to a class might in fact be two gifts to separate classes, so that the first might be valid even if the second was void. If the size of the shares given to members of a class could not be affected by some further contingent gift which was too remote, the class gift might stand although the further gift could not.[270]

---

[263] *Wilkinson v Duncan* (1861) 30 Beav.111; *Rogers v Mutch* (1878) 10 Ch D 25.

[264] Similarly, a gift to "each child that may be born to either of the children of either of my brothers": *Storrs v Benbow* (1853) 3 De G.M. & G. 390.

[265] Thus even a vested share could fail for perpetuity, for although vested in the ordinary sense it is not vested in the special perpetuity sense (above, para.9–020): *Leake v Robinson* (1817) 2 Mer. 363. See criticism of this rule by Leach in (1938) 51 Harv. L.R. 1328, and (1952) 68 L.Q.R. 35 at 50; Morris & Leach, 125; *Re Drummond* [1988] 1 W.L.R. 233 at 240, 241.

[266] *Pearks v Moseley* (1880) 5 App.Cas. 714 at 723; *Re Lord's Settlement* [1947] 2 All E.R. 685; *Re Hooper's S.T.* [1948] Ch. 586.

[267] *Smith v Smith* (1870) 5 Ch.App. 342; *Hale v Hale* (1876) 3 Ch D 643; *Re Hooper's* S.T. [1948] Ch. 586.

[268] For joint tenancy and survivorship, see below, para.13–003.

[269] See *Re Roberts* (1881) 19 Ch D 520; Gray, s.232.1.

[270] For examples, the previous edition of this work at para.9–061.

(4) 1964 ACT. The 1964 Act mitigated the severity of the common law rule **9–071** as applied to class gifts[271] and the 2009 Act also contains saving provisions.[272] However, before the two Acts are explained, it is necessary to examine the judge-made rules which govern the closing of classes. These rules are an essential part of the common law as to class gifts. They must therefore be applied before it can be determined whether the 1964 Act is applicable in relation to dispositions made before April 6, 2010. Although the common law is irrelevant when applying dispositions that are subject to fixed-term perpetuity periods, whether under the 1964 Act or the 2009 Act, these judge-made class-closing rules still apply to such dispositions.

(b) Rules of construction as to closing of classes

(1) THE RULE IN ANDREWS V PARTINGTON. For the sake of convenience the **9–072** courts have laid down the rule, often called the Rule in *Andrews v Partington*,[273] that a numerically uncertain class of beneficiaries normally closes when the first member becomes entitled to claim his share.[274] If this were not so, it would be impossible to give him his portion without waiting until there could be no more members of the class. The settlor is therefore presumed to have intended that the class should close as soon as the first share vests in possession.[275] No one born subsequently can enter the class, but any potential member of it already born is included. By closing the class against those born later, the maximum number of shares is fixed and the first taker can receive his share.[276]

(2) OPERATION. If the gift is contingent, e.g. upon the members of the class **9–073** attaining 21, the class will close when the first member attains 21, if he is then entitled in possession. Any others who are then in existence but under age will take their shares if they attain 21. However, any not yet born will be excluded, so that the minimum size of the shares may be fixed. If such a gift is preceded by a life interest, the class will not close until the death of the tenant for life at the earliest, since no share can vest in possession before then. If there is then no member aged 21, the class will remain open until there is such a member, whereupon it will close, so as to exclude any person then unborn.[277] For no obvious reason there is an exception where the members of the class are to take vested interests at birth, and no member exists at the time when the

---

[271] See below, paras 9–077, 9–078, and 9–081—9–086.
[272] See below para.9–079.
[273] (1791) 3 Bro.C.C. 401.
[274] See below, para.14–088, where this rule is further explained. For valuable accounts of it for the purposes of the perpetuity rule, see Morris & Leach 109 et seq.; (1954) 70 L.Q.R. 61 (J.H.C. Morris, dealing especially with the perpetuity rule); [1958] C.L.J. 39 (S.J. Bailey, dealing especially with the rule against accumulations). See also the discussions of the rule in two cases not concerned with perpetuities, *Re Bleckly* [1951] Ch. 740; and *Re Tom's Settlement* [1987] 1 W.L.R. 1021.
[275] *Barrington v Tristram* (1801) 6 Ves. 345 at 348; Jarman 1660, 1671.
[276] If any other potential member of the class dies without having become entitled, those who do become entitled will receive accrued shares in addition.
[277] Below, para.14–092; *Re Bleckly* [1951] Ch. 740.

property is available for distribution. In such cases the class remains open indefinitely, *i.e.* no special rule applies.[278]

9–074   (3) EXAMPLES. In relation to dispositions made before the 2009 Act came into force on April 6, 2010, this doctrine is important because, by limiting a class, it might save a gift which at common law would otherwise be void for perpetuity.[279] Some examples will explain its operation in the context of the common law.

> (i) Devise "to all A's grandchildren", where A is living at the testator's death and has a living grandchild. The class closes at once, since one share is already vested in possession, and includes only grandchildren who are already lives in being.[280] Therefore the gift, which would otherwise be void for perpetuity, is saved. But if A had no grandchildren living at the testator's death, the gift would fail,[281] for the class might remain open beyond the perpetuity period.

> (ii) Devise "to A for life, with remainder to all the grandchildren of B in equal shares", where B is living at the testator's death. Here the class will close at A's death, if a grandchild is born to B before that moment.[282] But the perpetuity rule at common law will not allow the will trustees to wait and see whether this happens. The matter must be settled on the facts as they stand at the testator's death. Therefore if B has a grandchild living at the testator's death, the remainder is saved; for one share has vested, and even if that grandchild dies before A, someone will be entitled (by succession) to call for that share at A's death.[283] However, if B has no grandchild living at the testator's death, the remainder fails. There is then no certainty that the class will close at A's death, since no grandchild will necessarily be born in A's lifetime.

> (iii) If the gifts to the grandchildren in the above examples had been contingent on some further event (e.g. on attaining 21 or previously marrying), it would have been necessary for a grandchild to have fulfilled the condition before the testator's death in order to save the class gift. This again follows from the requirements of the perpetuity rule at common law. Were it not for the perpetuity rule the class could remain open until the first grandchild reached 21 or

---

[278] *Shepherd v Ingram* (1764) Amb. 448; (1954) 70 L.Q.R. 66, 67 (J.H.C. Morris).

[279] See *Picken v Matthews* (1878) 10 Ch.D. 264. In cases where the 1964 Act is applicable, and there is no fixed perpetuity period under s.1 of that Act, it is necessary to ascertain first whether the disposition is valid at common law: see above, para.9–038.

[280] cf. *Warren v Johnson* (1673) 2 Rep.Ch. 69.

[281] Jarman 1683; (1954) 70 L.Q.R. 66 (J.H.C. Morris); *Shepherd v Ingram* (1764) Amb. 448. This would be the exceptional case where the special rule does not apply. But even if it did, the gift would be equally void for perpetuity.

[282] *Ayton v Ayton* (1787) 1 Cox Eq. 327; (1954) 70 L.Q.R. at 67 (J.H.C. Morris).

[283] *Re Chartres* [1927] 1 Ch. 466.

married, or (in example (ii)) until the life tenant died, whichever was the later.

(4) INTENTION. The doctrine applies both to deeds[284] and wills, but is most **9–075** commonly encountered in relation to the construction of wills, and it is explained more generally in that context below.[285] Because it is a rule of construction, it will yield to any expression of contrary intention. If, therefore, it is apparent from the document that the draftsman has specifically considered the date on which the class is to close, the rule will be excluded.[286] But expressions like "all or any", and "born or to be born", may not by themselves prevent the class being prematurely closed for the sake of convenience, at least where the gift is to take effect in the future.[287] Where the language is ambiguous and one interpretation makes the gift void for perpetuity, the court may prefer the interpretation which will save the gift.[288] There are certain other class gifts which, even though outside the rule of construction, have been construed as confining the gift to those living at the testator's death.[289]

(5) CLASS CLOSING DURING THE PERIOD OF "WAIT AND SEE".[290] A question **9–076** that has not been addressed in any decision hitherto is whether the rule in *Andrews v Partington* will be applied to a gift that is void at common law during the "wait and see" period under the 1964 Act. An example would be a gift by will:

"to A's grandchildren who attain 25",

where at the date of the testator's death A is alive and there is just one grandchild aged 24. If the rule applies, and the grandchild lives for one more year, he can call for the distribution to him of the trust property. If it does not, the trustees will have to wait until the end of the perpetuity period before making a distribution. The only logical reason why the rule should not apply is because it is implicitly excluded by the provisions for class reduction that are contained in the 1964 Act.[291] However the function of these statutory provisions is quite different from the class closing rules at common law. Class closing enables class gifts to vest at the earliest possible date, whereas the

---

[284] *Re Knapp's Settlement* [1895] 1 Ch. 91.
[285] Below, para.14–088.
[286] *Re Tom's Settlement* [1987] 1 W.L.R. 1021 at 1026.
[287] See below, para.14–088.
[288] *Pearks v Moseley* (1880) 5 App.Cas. 714 at 719; *Re Mortimer* [1905] 2 Ch. 502 at 506; *Re Hume* [1912] 1 Ch. 693; *Re Deeley's Settlement* [1974] Ch. 454.
[289] See, e.g. *Elliott v Elliott* (1841) 12 Sim. 276 (to the children of A at 22); *Re Coppard's Estate* (1887) 35 Ch D 350 (similar, but at 25); see also *Re Barker* (1905) 92 L.T. 831 at 834; *Wetherell v Wetherell* (1863) 1 De G.J. & S. 134; *Re Powell* [1898] 1 Ch. 227 (gift to grandchildren of a living person held valid). In principle these decisions are doubtful: see Jarman 1676; Gray, ss.634–642; Morris & Leach 113, 250.
[290] See Maudsley, *The Modern Law of Perpetuities* 145; [1988] Conv. 339 (P. Sparkes and R. Snape).
[291] Considered below, para.9–077.

class reduction rules may save such a gift at the end of the period of wait and
see if it would otherwise fail for perpetuity.[292]

9–077   *(c) Class-reduction under the 1964 Acts.* Even where a class gift was made
after July 15, 1964 and before April 6, 2010, so as to be subject to the 1964
Act, it is necessary to construe it first, taking account of the class-closing rules
where applicable, and then to determine whether it is valid or void at common
law. If it is valid, the Act will not apply. But if it would be void, the Act will
save some or all of it, if that can be done by eliminating offending members
of the class. The principle that a class gift cannot be partially good and
partially bad was abandoned in the 1964 Act, and it is thus no longer true that
any taint of remoteness affects the whole class.

The Act provides that where the inclusion of potential members of a
class[293] would cause the disposition to fail for remoteness, those persons shall,
unless their exclusion would exhaust the class, be deemed for all the purposes
of the disposition to be excluded.[294] This provision comes into play whenever
it "becomes apparent" that inclusion of the potential members would be
fatal.[295] But, following its policy of allowing the donor's intentions to take
effect if possible, the Act requires the "wait and see" rule to be applied first.
Only if that fails to save the gift will the question of class-reduction
arise.[296]

The following gift by will may be taken by way of example:

"to all the children of A who marry".

9–078   If A has predeceased the testator, the gift is valid at common law and the
Act does not apply. If A survives the testator, so that the gift would be void
at common law, the "wait and see" rule protects the whole class so long as
any member may marry within the perpetuity period (the lifetimes of A, and
of any children of A born before the testator's death, plus 21 years). If all A's
children marry within this period, there is no question of excluding members
of the class. But if at the end of the period unmarried children of A are living,
it then becomes apparent that the whole class gift would be void at common
law, even as modified by "wait and see". Thereupon the Act excludes those
unmarried children, provided that they are not the only members of the class,
thus saving the gift to the other members. The practical effect of these two
rules ("wait and see" and class-reduction) is that the Act treats a class gift as
a gift to those members of the class who do in fact comply with the perpetuity
rule.

---

[292] [1988] Conv. 339, above, at 344.

[293] For the purposes of the 1964 Act, a person is treated as a member of a class if in his case
all the conditions identifying a member of the class are satisfied, and as a potential member of a
class if in his case some only of the conditions are satisfied, but there is a possibility that the
remainder will in time be satisfied: PAA 1964 s.15(3).

[294] PAA 1964 s.4(4).

[295] PAA 1964 s.4(4).

[296] Above, para.9–041.

The 1964 Act makes special provision for cases where class-reduction has to be combined with age-reduction.[297] This is explained below.[298]

(d) Class reduction under the 2009 Act. The 2009 Act contains similar class **9–079** reduction provisions in relation to dispositions made after April 5, 2010. They apply if it is apparent at the time when an instrument takes effect or becomes so later that the inclusion of persons as potential member of a class[299] would cause an estate or interest to become void for remoteness.[300] From the time when it becomes apparent those persons are treated as excluded from the class unless their exclusion would exhaust the class.[301]

As with the 1964 Act, the class reduction provisions of the 2009 Act apply only after the application of the "wait and see" rule.[302] However, because the 2009 Act has a fixed perpetuity period that is not linked to age, it does not contain any age-reduction provisions.[303]

13. Reduction of excessive ages. At common law gifts frequently failed **9–080** because they were made contingent upon the beneficiary attaining an age greater than 21. Thus property might be given:

"to the first of A's children to attain the age of 25".

In certain circumstances the gift would be good. This would be so if A was dead at the time of the gift. He could therefore have no further children and since every possible claimant was a life in being, the gift would be valid.[304] Even if A was then alive, the gift would be valid if one of his children was already aged 25 or over, so that the gift would vest at once.[305] But if A was alive and no child had attained the age of 25, the gift was bad.[306] This was so even if a child had attained the age of 24, because there was no certainty that he would not die before his 25th birthday. It was therefore possible that a child born after the date of the gift and shortly before the death of A might be the first child to reach the age of 25.[307]

Both the Law of Property Act 1925 and the 1964 Act contain provisions for substituting lower ages in such cases, so that the gift may comply with the perpetuity rule. The provisions of the Law of Property Act 1925 only apply to instruments which took effect before July 16, 1964, and those of the 1964 Act

---

[297] s.4(3).
[298] See, para.9–086.
[299] PAA 2009 s.8(4) explains the circumstances in which a person is treated as a member or a potential member of a class. They are the same as under PAA 1964 s.15(3), above, para.9–077.
[300] PAA 2009 s.8(1).
[301] PAA 2009 s.8(2).
[302] See PAA 2009 s.8(3).
[303] See (1998) Law Com. No.251, para.8.29.
[304] *Southern v Wollaston* (No.2) (1852) 16 Beav.276.
[305] *Picken v Matthews* (1878) 10 Ch D 264.
[306] *Merlin v Blagrave* (1858) 25 Beav.125.
[307] See e.g. *Re Finch* (1881) 17 Ch D 211, where the child was 19.

to instruments which took effect after July 15, 1964 and before April 6, 2010.[308] As there will be few cases in which s.163 of the Law of Property Act 1925 is now relevant, reference should be made to the previous edition of this work where those are explained.[309]

9–081 The 1964 Act replaced and prospectively repealed the Law of Property Act 1925, s.163, by an amended provision.[310]

9–082 (1) CONDITIONS. Where it applies, the 1964 Act provides for age-reduction where the following conditions are all satisfied:

    (i) the instrument took effect after July 15, 1964;

    (ii) the disposition is not saved by the "wait and see" rule[311];

    (iii) "the disposition is limited by reference to the attainment by any person or persons of a specified age exceeding 21 years"; and

    (iv) it is apparent when the disposition is made, or becomes apparent later:

        (1) that the disposition would otherwise be void for remoteness, but

        (2) that it would not be thus void if the specified age had been 21 years.

In such cases the disposition is treated for all purposes as if, in place of the age specified, there had been specified the nearest age which would prevent the disposition from being void for remoteness.[312]

9–083 (2) EXAMPLES. Thus in the case of a gift by will to which the 1964 Act applies:

    "to the first of A's children to attain the age of 25",

where A is alive and unmarried at the testator's death, it is necessary to wait and see whether a child of A in fact attains 25 during A's lifetime or within 21 years of A's death. If so, the child will take at 25. But if at A's death his only child is aged three, it is apparent that the child cannot take at age 25 within the perpetuity period. The qualifying age is therefore reduced to 24, being the nearest age at which the gift could be good. If A left three children aged three, two and one at A's death, the problem is more difficult. Is the qualifying age first to be reduced to 24, and then successively to 23 and 22 in case the two elder children die prematurely? Or is there to be a single reduction to 22, so as to eliminate perpetuity trouble once and for all? Since

---

[308] See below, para.9–081.
[309] See paras 9–071, 9–072 and 9–077 of the previous edition of this work.
[310] PAA 1964 ss.4(6), 15(5).
[311] For this principle, see above, para.9–038.
[312] PAA 1964 s.4(1).

the 1964 Act requires reduction to the nearest age which prevents the gift being void, and since it intends that "wait and see" shall continue to operate, the former solution may be right. In that case no reduction is required if the eldest child is aged six or more at A's death, unless and until that child dies under 25. A case can, however, be made for a once-for-all reduction to an age which will protect all the children.[313]

The same dilemma arises where the gift is to a class, as in a gift by will: **9–084**

> "to all A's children who attain the age of 25".

If, say, A is alive at the testator's death but dies 10 years later, leaving children aged three, two and one, there is a stronger case for once-for-all reduction to 22. Although 24 would be the nearest age at which "wait and see" could continue, it would require the assumption that the younger children might die, leaving only the eldest child to take. However, the gift is to the children as a class. If it is to be preserved as such, there should be a reduction to an age which will protect them all. Here again a case can be made for the alternative solution, i.e. for age-reduction by stages.[314]

(3) DIFFERENTIAL AGES. The 1964 Act also makes provision for differential **9–085** ages, as, for example, in a gift to which it applies:

> "to all the children of A who being sons attain 25 or being daughters attain 30".

Where the conditions for the application of the 1964 Act, mentioned above, are satisfied, the effect is to reduce each such age so far as it is necessary to save the gift.[315]

(4) CLASS-REDUCTION. The 1964 Act allows age-reduction to be combined **9–086** with class-reduction, where this would save a gift which neither form of reduction would by itself be able to save. An example is a gift by will to which that Act applies:

> "to such of A's children as attain 25 together with such children as attain 25 of any children of A who may die under 25".[316]

If A is unmarried at the time of the gift, and at his death his only two children are aged three and one, it is plain that no grandchildren can attain 25 within the perpetuity period, even if their qualifying age is reduced to 21. The grandchildren are therefore excluded from the class, and the qualifying age for A's children is then reduced as already explained.[317]

---

[313] See [1969] C.L.J. 286 (M.J. Prichard).
[314] See [1969] C.L.J. 286 at 290.
[315] PAA 1964 s.4(2).
[316] For this form of gift, see above, para.9–070.
[317] PAA 1964 s.4(3).

An age-reduction under the 1964 Act will both save and accelerate a remainder or gift over limited to take effect upon the failure of the gift to the first beneficiary. For example, in a gift "to the first of A's children to attain 25, but if no such child attains 25 then to the eldest of B's children living at the date of B's death", the section will validate the first part of the gift and thereby also save the gift over in case all A's children die in infancy.

9–087   **14. Gifts which follow void gifts.** The general rule is that where there are successive limitations in one instrument of gift, the perpetuity rule must be applied to each limitation separately. Thus if there is a gift:

> "to A for life, remainder to his eldest son for life, remainder to B's eldest grandson in fee simple"

there are three distinct gifts, each of which must by itself pass the test of the rule. Where all the gifts are valid, no difficulty arises. But where one of the gifts is void, this may sometimes invalidate another gift. The rules are as follows.

9–088   *(a) No limitation is void merely because it is followed by a void limitation.*[318] A gift "to A for life" standing by itself is clearly good, and it is not invalidated merely because a limitation which infringes the rule is added, e.g. "to A for life, remainder to the first of his descendants to marry a Latvian". In such a case A takes a life interest and, after his death, the property reverts to the grantor or, if the grantor is dead, passes under his will or intestacy.[319]

9–089   *(b) At common law a limitation which was subsequent to and dependent upon a void limitation was itself void, even though it would itself have to vest (if at all) within the perpetuity period.*[320]

9–090   (1) THE RULE. A limitation was not void merely because it followed a void limitation. It was invalidated by the rule only if, in addition to following the void limitation, it was also dependent upon it. A "dependent" limitation for this purpose was one intended to take effect only if the prior gift did, or (as the case may be) did not, itself take effect. By contrast, an independent limitation was one intended to take effect in any case, whether the prior gift took effect or not.[321] The vesting of a dependent limitation therefore remained uncertain until the fate of the prior gift could be seen. An independent

---

[318] *Garland v Brown* (1864) 10 L.T. 292. But see *Re Abraham's W.T.* [1969] I Ch. 463, where valid and void limitations were so intermixed as to vitiate the whole settlement.

[319] *Stuart v Cockerell* (1870) 5 Ch.App. 713.

[320] *Proctor v Bishop of Bath and Wells* (1794) 2 Hy.B1. 358; *Re Abbott* [1893] 1 Ch. 54 at 57; *Re Hubbard's W.T.* [1963] Ch. 275; *Re Leek* [1967] Ch. 1061.

[321] J.H.C. Morris in (1950) 10 C.L.J. 392 criticised the rule about "dependent" gifts as meaningless. But its principle seemed clear from the authorities cited below and from the initial classification of contingent remainders by Fearne 5. See also Morris & Leach 173; (1950) 14 Conv. (N.S.) 148 (A.K.R. Kiralfy).

limitation vested (in interest) at its own separate time, and the fate of the prior gift, to which it was subject, affected only the date at which it finally took effect in possession. It follows that:

> (i) a gift made "subject to" a prior void gift would often nevertheless be independent of it as regards the all-important moment of vesting[322]; and

> (ii) where the prior void gift was a gift in fee simple, the subsequent gift would always be dependent, since it had to be contingent upon the prior gift failing.[323]

If, for example, a testator devised property in fee simple:

> "to the first of X's sons to become a clergyman, but if X has no such son, to Y for life",

and when the testator died X was alive, the first part of the gift was clearly void at common law. This is because the required event might occur more than 21 years after the death of lives in being. The gift to Y was, equally clearly, subsequent to and dependent upon this void limitation. Its vesting depended entirely upon the gift to X's son not taking effect. It therefore made no difference that it was itself bound to vest (if at all) within Y's lifetime and so within the perpetuity period.[324]

(2) CLASSES OF LIMITATION. Limitations, which followed void limitations, **9–091** could be divided into three classes for the purposes of the rule against perpetuities at common law.

> (i) *Vested*. These were always safe from the perpetuity rule.[325] Example: gift to A for life, remainder for life to A's first son to marry, remainder to B in fee simple. If A is alive and has no married son at the time of the gift, the second gift is void; but the remainder to B is valid, for since it is ready to take effect in possession at any time, whether the prior interests determine naturally or fail, it must be vested from the beginning.[326]

---

[322] See *Re Canning's W.T.* [1936] Ch. 309.

[323] As explained above, para.9–004.

[324] *Proctor v Bishop of Bath and Wells* (1794) 2 Hy.B1. 358. See also *Re Hubbard's W.T.* [1963] Ch. 275; *Re Buckton's S.T.* [1964] Ch. 497 (good examples of the settled rules); contrast *Re Robinson* [1963] 1 W.L.R. 628; and see (1964) 80 L.Q.R. 323 (R.E.M.).

[325] See *Re Allan* [1958] 1 W.L.R. 220. So far as *Re Backhouse* [1921] 2 Ch. 51 invalidated vested interests, it was probably wrong in principle and contrary to authorities cited under the next class: see Morris & Leach 175–179.

[326] *Lewis v Waters* (1805) 6 East 336; *Re Hubbard's W.T.* [1963] Ch. 275; Fearne 222; Jarman 366. To the same class belong cases where there is a void appointment and a vested gift in default of appointment: Jarman 364. cf. (1944) 60 L.Q.R. 297, 298 (R.E.M.).

(ii) *Contingent, but independent.* This class would be valid if its own contingency did not infringe the perpetuity rule, and it would make no difference that some prior gift failed for perpetuity.[327] Example: gift to A for life, remainder for life to A's first son to marry, remainder in fee simple to B (an infant) at 21. Here again, unless A already had a married son, the first remainder would be void. But B's remainder was still valid, for the only contingency was that B should attain 21, an event which had nothing to do with the possible events which made the prior gift void.

(iii) *Contingent, but dependent.* In this case the ulterior gift failed, even though itself bound to vest (if at all) within the perpetuity period.[328] Example: gift to A for life, remainder in fee simple to A's first son to marry, but if there was no such son then remainder to B for life. Here, unless A already had a married son, both remainders were void. B's remainder, although itself confined to the period of a life in being (B), was a contingent interest, for it followed a gift in fee simple[329]; and the contingency was that no son of A should marry. Since B's remainder depended upon precisely the converse contingency to that which invalidated the prior gift, it was dependent upon that gift not taking effect and was therefore void. It would make no difference if the words "but if there is no such son" were omitted, since the contingency which they expressed was inherent in any gift which followed a gift in fee simple.[330] If the final remainder had been to B in fee simple, it would have failed on its own account, quite apart from its dependence on the prior gift, for there would have been nothing to confine it within the perpetuity period. The contingency itself was unduly remote, since some successor in title to B could have taken at a distant time in the future.[331]

9–092   (3) CONSTRUCTION. The dependence or independence of a gift was a question of construction. It was governed by the donor's intention so far as it can be ascertained from the terms of the gift.[332]

---

[327] *Re Abbott* [1893] 1 Ch. 54; *Re Canning's W.T.* [1936] Ch. 309; *Re Coleman* [1936] Ch. 528; *Re Hubbard's W.T.,* above.

[328] *Re Thatcher* (1859) 26 Beav.365 at 369; *Re Hewitt's Settlement* [1915] 1 Ch. 810; *Re Ramadge* [1919] 1 I.R. 205; *Re Hubbard's W.T.,* above.

[329] As explained above, para.9–004.

[330] *Proctor v Bishop of Bath and Wells* (1794) 2 Hy.Bl. 358; *Palmer v Holford* (1828) 4 Russ. 403 (decided on this ground alone without mention of "dependence"); cf. The remarks of Jessel M.R. in *Miles v Harford* (1879) 12 Ch D 691 at 703. *Re Mill's Declaration of Trust* [1950] 1 All E.R. 789, [1950] 2 All E.R. 292 was a case of this type, although the judgments proceeded upon the alternative (but logically posterior) ground that the ultimate gift was dependent. For the rule under which B's successors can take, see Jarman 1342.

[331] See previous footnote.

[332] For further discussion, see the previous edition of this work at para.9–084.

(c) *Where the 1964 Act applies, a gift cannot fail merely because it is* **9–093**
dependent upon a prior void gift. If the gift was made after July 15, 1964 and
before April 6, 2010, so that it is governed by the 1964 Act, it will not fail
merely because it is "ulterior to and dependent upon" another gift which is
void.[333] Where the Act applies, therefore, all the complications of the law
about dependent gifts disappear. Each distinct gift must stand or fall by itself,
and the perpetuity rule must be applied to each in isolation.

It is also provided that the vesting of an interest shall not be prevented from
being accelerated on the failure of a prior interest merely because the failure
is caused by remoteness.[334] However, any contingency specifically applicable
to the ulterior gift must, of course, be fulfilled before it can vest.[335] These rules
under the 1964 Act operate *ab initio*, and are not dependent upon the "wait
and see" rule.

(d) *The position under the 2009 Act.* The 2009 Act follows the 1964 Act **9–094**
and provides, in relation to gifts made after April 5, 2010, that:

(i) An estate or interest is not void for remoteness only because it is
ulterior to and dependent upon an estate or interest which is so
void[336]; and

(ii) The vesting of an estate or interest is not prevented from being
accelerated merely because a prior estate fails by reason of
remoteness.[337]

15. Alternative contingencies

(a) *"Wait and see" at common law.* Where a gift expressed two alternative **9–095**
contingencies upon which the property might vest, and one contingency was
too remote and one was not, the gift was good at common law if in fact the
valid contingency occurred.[338] This was one of the rare occasions when even
the common law would allow "wait and see".[339] Thus in one case[340] a testator
gave property to his grandchildren and issue of his grandchildren living:

"on the decease of my last surviving child or on the death of the last
surviving widow or widower of my children as the case may be whichever shall last happen".

---

[333] PAA 1964 s.6.
[334] PAA 1964 s.6.
[335] *Re Edwards' W.T.* [19481 Ch. 440; *Re Allan* [1958] 1 W.L.R. 220; *Re Hubbard's W.T.* [1963]
Ch. 275.
[336] PAA 2009 s.9(1).
[337] PAA 2009 s.9(2).
[338] *Longhead d. Hopkins v Phelps* (1770) 2 Wm.Bl. 704; *Hodgson v Halford* (1879) 11 Ch D
959.
[339] For the other case, see below para.9–127 (powers of appointment).
[340] *Re Curryer's W.T.* [1938] Ch. 952.

It was held that this gift did not necessarily infringe the perpetuity rule as it stood, and that if in fact one of the testator's children outlived all the other children and their spouses, the gift would be valid. There were two alternatives:

(i) that one of the testator's children (a life in being) would be the last survivor, or

(ii) that the spouse of one of the testator's children (not necessarily a life in being) would be the last survivor.

If the former alternative actually occurred, the gift did not infringe the rule. If the latter in fact occurred, it did, and must fail. Whether it was to fail or not could only be told by events.

9–096   *(b) Implicit alternatives.* This beneficial principle applied only if the two alternative contingencies were expressed in the gift.[341] If only one contingency was expressed in the gift and that might be too remote, the gift failed even if there were in fact two contingencies. Thus in one case,[342] only one contingency was expressed, namely, that if no son of A became a clergyman, B should be entitled. In fact, two contingencies were implicit in the gift, namely:

(i) A might leave no son; this would be known at A's death, which would be within the period;

(ii) A might leave one or more sons, who might become clergymen more than 21 years after A's death, which would be outside the period.

Nevertheless, the gift to B was void *ab initio*, for the only contingency expressed was a void one. Had the gift over been worded:

"but if no son of A shall become a clergyman, or if A shall leave no son, to B in fee simple",

the gift to B would have been valid if A had died leaving no son, i.e. if the valid contingency had occurred.[343]

9–097   *(c) 1964 Act.* The 1964 Act did not change this rule. However, where the Act applies, the "wait and see" rule operates in its normal way if the unduly remote contingency occurs or if only one contingency is expressed. In the example in (a), above,[344] the "surviving spouse" rule[345] might also assist.

---

[341] *Re Harvey* (1888) 39 Ch D 289; *Re Bence* [1891] 3 Ch. 242.
[342] *Proctor v Bishop of Bath and Wells* (1794) 2 Hy.Bl. 353; see above, paras 9–088, 9–089.
[343] *Miles v Harford* (1879) 12 Ch D 691 at p.703.
[344] para.9–095.
[345] Above, para.9–064.

(d) 2009 Act. The rule is also unaffected by the 2009 Act, which will apply **9–098**
to gifts made after April 5, 2010. However, as with the 1964 Act, the "wait
and see" principle applies in the usual way.

16. Determinable and conditional interests

(a) Determinable interests[346]

(1) THE RULE AT COMMON LAW.   **9–099**

> "The rule against perpetuities is not dealing with the duration of interests
> but with their commencement, and so long as the interest vests within
> lives in being and 21 years it does not matter how long that interest
> lasts".[347]

That is to say, the perpetuity rule does not invalidate a limitation merely
because it provides that an interest shall cease at some future date outside the
perpetuity period. Accordingly where property is given to an unborn
person:

> "for life or until she becomes a member of the Roman Catholic
> Church",[348]

or:

> "for life or until marriage",[349]

the specified event may occur outside the perpetuity period but at common
law the limitation is nevertheless valid. The better view is that it is immaterial
that the determinable interest is a fee simple and the event on which it will
determine may not happen for centuries,[350] *e.g.* where property is conveyed to
the X Co Ltd in fee simple until the premises are used otherwise than as a
biscuit factory, or to trustees "for so long as the premises are used for the
purpose of a public library".[351] In certain circumstances these interests may
cease at any time in the future, and the perpetuity rule will not prolong
them.

(2) POSSIBILITY OF REVERTER. The grantor's possibility of reverter was, it   **9–100**
seems, exempt from the perpetuity rule at common law, and so always able to

---

[346] For these, see above, para.3–054.
[347] *Re Chardon* [1928] Ch. 464 at 468, per Romer J.; see Gray, ss.41, 603.9.
[348] *Wainwright v Miller* [1897] 2 Ch. 255.
[349] *Re Gage* [1898] 1 Ch. 498. And see *Re Randell* (1888) 38 Ch.D. 213; *Re Blunt's Trusts*
[1904] 2 Ch. 767.
[350] See *Att Gen v Pyle* (1738) 1 Atk. 435; *Boughton v James* (1844) 1 Coll.C.C. 26 at 46;
Tiffany, *Real Property*, 603.
[351] *Hopper v Corporation of Liverpool* (1944) 88 S.J. 213; above, para.3–055.

take effect. On the face of it this was anomalous.[352] A possibility of reverter was not a reversion (and so vested) but a "bare possibility" that an interest might vest in the future,[353] and so necessarily contingent.[354] Because it was a potential fetter on property, such an interest ought to have been subject to the perpetuity rule,[355] and in one case (of a conveyance inter vivos before 1926) it was held that it was.[356] However, the weight of authority indicated that there could be a valid reverter or resulting trust[357] after an interest which terminated, even where an express gift after that interest would be void for perpetuity.[358]

9–101   (3) RESULTING TRUSTS. After 1925, a determinable interest could only take effect in equity so that any possibility of reverter was thereafter equitable. The equitable doctrine was that any beneficial interest of which the settlor failed to dispose remained in him under a resulting trust,[359] and that this interest was vested *ab initio* even if it was uncertain when, if ever, it would become effective.[360]

9–102   (4) 1964 ACT. In cases of dispositions made after July 15, 1964 and before April 6, 2010, the 1964 Act applied the perpetuity rule to possibilities of reverter and resulting trusts arising on the termination of any other determinable interest in property.[361] The anomaly of their exemption at common law was thereby removed. The preceding determinable interest was made absolute in cases where the possibility of reverter or resulting trust failed.[362] If during the period when the 1964 Act applied, a testator left property to an orphans' home for so long as it existed, with a gift over to A in case the prior gift terminated, the first step was to apply the "wait and see" rule. If the orphans' home ceased to exist within 21 years (there are no lives in being), A could take. But after the 21 years neither A nor the testator's successors could take, and the property belonged to the home absolutely.[363]

---

[352] See *Minster Square Ltd v Radyne (Overseas) Ltd* [1997] P.L.S.C.S. 340.

[353] Above, para.3–054.

[354] Jarman 289; Tudor L.C. 702; cf. Challis 76n, classifying possibilities as one degree more remote than contingent remainders, since there is merely a chance that upon a certain contingency an interest may arise; and cf. above, para.3–054. Gray, ss.113, 312, maintained that they are vested interests, though a "vested possibility" seems a contradiction in terms.

[355] See Fourth Report of the Law Reform Committee (1956, Cmnd. 18), para.39.

[356] *Hopper v Corporation of Liverpool* (1944) 88 S.J. 213 (Vice-Chancellor of Lancaster); see (1946) 62 L.Q.R. 222 (R.E.M.); 1945 Conv. YB. 203; (1957) 21 Conv. (N.S.) 213 (P. H. Pettit).

[357] For resulting trusts, see below, para.11–009.

[358] For illustrations, see the previous edition of this work at para.9–090.

[359] Below, para.11–009.

[360] *Re Cooper's Conveyance Trusts* [1956] 1 W.L.R. 1096; cf. *Gibson v South American Stores (Gath and Chaves) Ltd* [1950] Ch. 177. For a fuller consideration of the position prior to the 1964 Act, see the previous edition of this work at para.9–091.

[361] PAA 1964 s.12.

[362] PAA 1964 s.12.

[363] In *Minster Square Ltd v Radyne (Overseas) Ltd* [1997] P.L.S.C.S. 340, PAA 1964 s.12 was applied to an easement that was granted subject to the possibility of its determination in certain events. When those events did not occur within 21 years, the grantor's right, equivalent to a possibility of reverter, became void for perpetuity and the easement became absolute.

The 1964 Act achieved this result by requiring the possibility of reverter or resulting trust to be treated as if it were a condition subsequent created by a separate disposition.[364] Conditions subsequent are discussed below. The rules for determinable and conditional interests were in this way assimilated.

(5) 2009 ACT. As regards dispositions made after April 5, 2010, the same rule   **9–103** applies as under the 1964 Act. If an interest arising on the determination of a determinable fee simple is void for remoteness, the determinable fee simple becomes absolute.[365] Similarly, if an interest arising under a resulting trust on the determination of a determinable interest is void for remoteness, that determinable interest becomes absolute.[366]

(b) *Conditional interests.* A condition may be either precedent or   **9–104** subsequent.[367]

(1) CONDITIONS PRECEDENT. A condition precedent is one which must be   **9–105** fulfilled before the beneficiary is entitled to a vested interest. It is to conditions of this type that the perpetuity rule most commonly applies, and many examples have already been given, such as "to A at 21", and "to A if he survives B". A less obvious but similar type of case is a discretionary trust, as where land is given to trustees upon trust to apply the rents and profits for the benefit of an unborn person in the trustees' absolute discretion. Since the trustees need not necessarily pay the beneficiary any particular sum within the perpetuity period, at common law the whole gift would fail.[368] This is because no ascertainable interest would ever vest at all, even if, by reason of the terms of the trust, the beneficiary would have to be born within the period. Some decision by the trustees would be a condition precedent to every payment.

(2) 1964 ACT. Where the 1964 Act applies, conditions precedent are subject   **9–106** to the "wait and see" principle. For the purposes of the Act discretionary trusts rank as powers of appointment,[369] which are discussed below.

(3) 2009 ACT. Under the 2009 Act, the rule against perpetuities applies where   **9–107** an instrument, made after April 5, 2010, limits property in trust so as to create an estate that is subject to a condition precedent, whether or not there are also successive interests.[370] The principle of "wait and see" applies to such conditions.[371] As under the 1964 Act, discretionary trusts are treated as powers of appointment.[372]

---

[364] PAA 1964 s.12(1).
[365] PAA 2009 s.10(1).
[366] PAA 2009 s.10(2).
[367] Above, para.3–056.
[368] *Re Blew* [1906] 1 Ch. 624; *Re Coleman* [1936] Ch. 528; *Re Leek* [1967] Ch. 1061; above, para.9–021, fn.118: and see, e.g. *Pickford v Brown* (1856) 2 K. & J. 426.
[369] PAA 1964 s.15(2). See below, para.9–118.
[370] PAA 2009 ss.1(2) and (3); above, paras 9–026 and 9–027.
[371] PAA 2009 s 7; above, para.9–067.
[372] PAA 2009 s.20(2).

9–108   (4) CONDITIONS SUBSEQUENT. A condition subsequent, as already explained,[373] is one which authorises the grantor or his representatives to determine an existing interest. A gift of land to trustees in fee simple:

> "on condition that it shall always be used for the purposes of a hospital only"

gives the grantor and his successors in title a right of re-entry if the condition is broken. At common law, if such a condition infringed the perpetuity rule the right of re-entry was void, because it was contingent.[374] The interest which it was intended to defeat was not invalidated.[375] It became instead an absolute interest, since the condition subsequent could defeat it only if re-entry was actually made,[376] and that was impossible because the right of re-entry was void. In relation to dispositions made before April 6, 2010, the rule against perpetuities applied to a legal right of re-entry even where the land was not held in trust.[377]

By way of illustration of the operation of the above rules, if there was a valid gift by a testator to his grandchildren followed by a provision for the forfeiture of the interest of any grandchild who forsook the Jewish faith or married outside that faith, the provision might not take effect until the perpetuity period had run. It was accordingly void at common law, and could neither carry the property to any other person[378] nor determine the interests of the grandchildren, despite any intention to do so.[379] The grandchildren accordingly took absolute interests.

In contrast to an estate or interest subject to a condition subsequent, a determinable interest determines automatically at common law, as explained above, whether the possibility of reverter is void or not.[380]

9–109   (5) 1964 ACT. Apart from the introduction of the "wait and see" principle, the 1964 Act did not change these rules. As already explained,[381] the 1964 Act extended the law governing conditions subsequent so that it also governed possibilities of reverter and resulting trusts.

---

[373] Above, para.3–056.

[374] *Re the Trustees of Hollis' Hospital and Hague's Contract* [1889] 2 Ch. 440; *Re Da Costa* [1912] 1 Ch. 337; *Re Macleay* (1875) L.R. 20 Eq. 186; *Dunn v Flood* (1883) 25 Ch D 629; 28 Ch D 586 at 592; *Imperial Tobacco Co Ltd v Wilmott* [1964] 1 W.L.R. 902.

[375] *Blease v Burgh* (1840) 2 Beav.221; *Ring v Hardwick* (1840) 2 Beav.352.

[376] Above, para.3–058.

[377] See LPA 1925 s.4(3) (proviso), which was repealed by PAA 2009: see below, para.9–110.

[378] *Re Brown and Sibly's Contract* (1876) 3 Ch D 156; *Re Spitzel's W.T.* [1939] 2 All E.R. 266; *Re Pratt's S.T.* [1943] Ch. 356.

[379] *Re Pratt's S.T.* [1943] Ch. 356, confirming Jarman (now p.1425); and see *Harding v Nott* (1857) 7 E. & B. 650. If a gift over is void some reason other than perpetuity, then if such an intention appears the condition may defeat the first gift even though the gift over is void: *Doe d. Blomfield v Eyre* (1848) 5 C.B. 713.

[380] For this distinction generally, see above, paras 3–056, 3–057; for its application in this context, see *Re Talbot* [1933] Ch. 895 and cases there cited.

[381] Above, para.9–102.

(6) 2009 ACT. Under the 2009 Act, the rule against perpetuities expressly **9–110** applies to an instrument, made after April 5, 2010, which limits property in trust so as to create a condition subsequent. Any right of re-entry exercisable in relation to land if the condition is broken is subject to the rule, as is any equivalent right exercisable in the case of property other than land if the condition is broken.[382] However, as has been explained, because the rule only applies in the cases set out in s.1 of the 2009 Act, it will no longer be applicable to a right of re-entry where a legal estate is subject to a condition subsequent but where no trust arises.[383] The operation of the rule against perpetuities is subject to "wait and see". If a condition subsequent is broken, a right of re-entry (or equivalent right exercisable in the case of property other than land) that is then exercisable is only to be treated as void for remoteness if and in so far as it is not fully exercised within the perpetuity period.[384]

17. Powers and duties

(a) Powers, duties and trusts generally

(1) PERPETUITY RULE APPLIES. Trusts often authorise persons to do things **9–111** which they would otherwise have no legal ability to do. Such provisions create powers.

The exercise of a power creates or alters an interest, and accordingly it was the general rule at common law that a power which was exercisable outside the perpetuity period was void. A power given to trustees to lease[385] or to sell,[386] which might be exercisable during the lifetime of an unborn person, was therefore void *ab initio* at common law. The same principle necessarily also applied to duties, because a duty to do something includes a power to do it. Accordingly, a trust to sell which might be exercised outside the perpetuity period was void at common law, even though it might be for the benefit of living persons whose equitable interests in the property vest at once and so are valid.[387] However, it was unnecessary to set a separate time-limit to trusts and powers if they were incidental to an interest which would ensure that their exercise could only be within the perpetuity period,[388] as for example where powers were given to a tenant for life who was a life in being. Where a power of sale was limited to come into existence at the end of a life in being, the court might find an intention in the will or settlement that the power should be exercised, if at all, within a reasonable period. Since 21 years was more than

---

[382] PAA 2009 s.1(4).

[383] See above, para.9–029. In consequence, the proviso to LPA 1925 s.4(3) (above, para.9–109) has been repealed: see PAA 2009 s.1(9).

[384] PAA 2009 ss.7(3), (4).

[385] *Re Allott* [1924] 2 Ch. 498 (power exercisable during the lifetime of an unborn person and so void); *Air Jamaica Ltd v Charlton* [1999] 1 W.L.R. 1399 at 1408, 1409.

[386] *Re Daveron* [1893] 3 Ch. 421 (trust to sell in 49 years' time held void); *Goodier v Johnson* (1881) 18 Ch D 441 at 446 (trust to sell during the lifetime of an unborn person held void); *Re Wood* [1894] 3 Ch. 381 (trust to sell gravel pits when they were worked out held void).

[387] *Goodier v Edmunds* [1893] 3 Ch. 455 at 461; and see preceding note.

[388] *Peters v Lewes & East Grinstead Ry* (1881) 18 Ch D 429 at 433, 434; *Re Wills' W.T.* [1959] Ch. 1; cf. *Pilkington v I.R.C.* [1964] A.C. 612.

a reasonable period for this purpose, such a power was held valid.[389] It was also held that a trust to sell at the "expiration" of a term of 21 years arose at the same moment as the expiration of the term, and so did not exceed the perpetuity period.[390]

9–112   (2) STATUTORY POWERS. The perpetuity rule might also apply to statutory powers. Many powers which used to be conferred on trustees and beneficiaries by lengthy clauses in settlements are now, for the sake of convenience, implied by statute. For example, trustees have statutory power to advance capital to a potential beneficiary.[391] If they do so by making a settlement on him and his children, this is analogous to a power of appointment and therefore subject to the special perpetuity rules discussed below.[392] Statutory powers of sale, leasing and management, on the other hand, which Parliament intends all owners to have as a matter of policy and which themselves create no beneficial interest, have not been subjected to the rule. Trustees of land, who normally have the powers of a beneficial owner, may exercise them at any time.[393] This is so regardless of when the trust was created.

9–113   (3) 1964 ACT. The 1964 Act extended its "wait and see" principle to powers. In a case governed by the 1964 Act, a power is no longer void merely because it might be exercised outside the perpetuity period. It will be void only to the extent that it is not in fact fully exercised during the period.[394] The person on whom the power is conferred counts as a life in being.[395] These rules have already been explained.[396] Similarly other provisions of the Act, for example for reducing excessive ages, may apply to grants of powers in the same way as to other grants. Presumably all these provisions also extend to duties, for the reasons given in the previous paragraph, although duties do not so easily fit within the statutory words "any power, option or other right".[397]

9–114   (4) ADMINISTRATIVE POWERS. The 1964 Act also provided that the perpetuity rule should not invalidate a power conferred on trustees or other persons to dispose of property for full consideration or to do any other act in the administration (as opposed to the distribution) of any property.[398] The 1964 Act thereby made a distinction between administrative (or ancillary) powers and beneficial powers. A power to sell or let for full value, or to make or vary investments, is accordingly exempted from the perpetuity rule, but a power to

---

[389] See *Peters v Lewes & East Grinstead Ry*, above, at 434; *Re Lord Sudeley and Baines & Co* [1894] 1 Ch. 334; and as to construction of powers, Jarman 319.
[390] *English v Cliff* [1914] 2 Ch. 376.
[391] TA 1925 s.32.
[392] *Pilkington v I.R.C.* [1964] 1 Ch. 612; *Re Abraham's W.T.* [1969] 1 Ch. 463.
[393] Below, para.12–016.
[394] PAA 1964 s.3(3).
[395] PAA 1964 s.3(5)(b)(v).
[396] Above, paras 9–038, 9–055.
[397] See PAA 1964 s.3(5)(b)(v).
[398] PAA 1964 s.8(1).

sell at an undervalue is not, because it contains an element of gift.[399] The Act also protected powers to pay reasonable remuneration for services, e.g. those of trustees or agents.[400] Furthermore, and exceptionally, the Act protected these various powers if they are exercised after July 15, 1964, even if the instrument conferring them took effect before that date.[401] This reflected the opinion that the application of the perpetuity rule to such powers was a mistake.[402]

(5) 2009 ACT. Under the 2009 Act, the only powers to which the rule against perpetuities applies are powers of appointment.[403] These are defined to include a discretionary power to create or transfer a beneficial interest in property without the provision of valuable consideration.[404] They are explained below.[405] **9–115**

(b) Powers of appointment and analogous powers

(1) CLASSIFICATION. The powers which most frequently have to be con- sidered in relation to the perpetuity rule are powers of appointment. A power of appointment is a power for the person to whom it is given ("the donee of the power") to appoint property to such persons ("the objects of the power") as he may select. The power is known as a "special power" if the donee's choice is restricted to a limited class of objects, such as X's children, and as a "general power" if his choice is unrestricted. Special powers are very common in settlements, as where land is given: **9–116**

> "to A for life, and after his death to such of his surviving children in such shares as he may by deed or will appoint".

The distinction between general and special powers is important because special powers to some extent restrict disposal of the property, so that the perpetuity rule applies to their exercise, whereas general powers do not, and are therefore unobjectionable.

The rules explained below also apply in principle to powers which are analogous to powers of appointment, such as a trustee's power of advance- ment, even if statutory,[406] and a discretionary trust.[407] Any power to create or

---

[399] In practice, the dispositive powers of trustees of land are generally statutory, and are the same as those of an absolute owner (see TLATA 1996 s.6; below, para.12–016). A power to dispose of trust property at an undervalue would have to be express, because otherwise any disposition would be a breach of trust: see *Buttle v Saunders* [1950] 2 All E.R. 193. For trustees' investment powers, which are, once again, those of an absolute owner, see TA 2000 s.3.

[400] PAA 1964 s.8(1). For the statutory power for trustees to remunerate their agents and themselves, see TA 2000 Pt.V.

[401] PAA 1964 ss.8(2), 15(5).

[402] See Law Reform Committee *Fourth Report of the Law Reform Committee* (HMSO 1956), Cmnd.18, para.34, comparing the rule to an unruly dog wandering into the wrong places.

[403] PAA 2009 s.1(6); above, para.9–031.

[404] PAA 2009 s.20(2).

[405] See paras 9–120 et seq.

[406] *Pilkington v IRC*, above.

[407] Above, para.9–112.

alter a beneficial interest deriving from a settlor by way of gift will fall within these rules.

9–117   (2) GENERAL OR SPECIAL. For the purposes of the application of the perpetuity rule at common law, a power to appoint with the consent of X was a special power,[408] unless the court could find grounds for holding that the donee was in substance the owner of the property and free to deal with it at will.[409] A power exercisable jointly by two or more persons had also been held to be special,[410] and probably a power for the donee to appoint to anyone except himself would also have been held to be special.[411] On the other hand, a power for the donee to appoint to himself or anyone else except X,[412] or to a class of people including himself,[413] would probably have been held to be general. In a case where the donee might at once appoint to himself he could, by doing so, obtain unfettered powers of disposition. An unrestricted power to appoint by will only was the subject of a distinction. It was held to be special for the purpose of deciding the validity of the power,[414] but general for the purpose of determining the validity of the appointment.[415] This was because such a power fettered the property during the donee's life but left him an unrestricted choice in his will.

9–118   (3) 1964 ACT. The 1964 Act in effect confirmed the above distinctions in cases where it applies, and provided for the resolution of doubtful cases. For the purposes of the rule against perpetuities a power of appointment is to be treated as a special power under the 1964 Act unless it satisfies two conditions:

   (i) it is expressed to be exercisable by one person only; and

   (ii) it empowers the donee to transfer the whole property to himself immediately at all times when he is himself of full age and capacity without the consent of any other person or compliance with any other condition (not being a mere formal condition as to its mode of exercise).[416]

These conditions determine the character of the power from the outset. If a power is exercisable by A and B jointly, or by A with the consent of B, the

---

[408] *Re Watts* [1931] 2 Ch. 302.

[409] *Re Duke* [1921] 1 Ch. 34; *Re Phillips* [1931] 1 Ch. 347.

[410] *Re Churston Settled Estate* [1954] Ch. 334 (criticised at (1955) 71 L.Q.R. 242 (A.H. Droop); supported by Morris & Leach 137); *Re Earl of Coventry's Indentures* [1974] Ch. 77.

[411] See *Re Park* [1932] 1 Ch. 500; (1937) 1 Conv. (N.S.) 198 (F. E. Farrer).

[412] Consider *Platt v Routh* (1841) 3 Beav.257; affirmed sub nom. *Drake v Att Gen* (1843) 10 Cl. & F. 257; and see (1932) 48 L.Q.R. 475 (H.P.). Compare *Re Triffitt's Settlement* [1958] Ch. 852 at 860, 861 (exclusion of two persons, and requirement of consent of trustees: a special power for perpetuity purposes).

[413] cf. *Re Penrose* [1933] Ch. 793.

[414] *Wollaston v King* (1868) L.R. 8 Eq. 165; *Morgan v Gronow* (1873) L.R. 16 Eq. 1.

[415] *Rous v Jackson* (1885) 29 Ch D 521; *Re Flower* (1885) 55 L.J.Ch. 200.

[416] PAA 1964 s.7.

subsequent death of B will not make it a general power for the purposes of the Act. As regards powers exercisable by will only, the Act confirmed the previous case-law by providing that for the purpose of applying the perpetuity rule to an appointment made under such a power, the power shall be treated as general if it would have been so treated had it been exercisable by deed.[417]

(4) EXERCISE OF SPECIAL POWERS UNDER THE 1964 ACT. In general, the 1964 Act applies to powers of appointment (including for this purpose discretionary trusts[418]) in the same way as it applies to other transactions. The conferring of a power and the exercise of a power are both "dispositions" within the meaning of the 1964 Act.[419] The "wait and see" principle applies, and both the donee and the objects or potential objects of the power may count as lives in being.[420] However, there are two special provisions. **9–119**

> (i) In the case of a special power (as determined according to the rules set out above, whenever it was created), the 1964 Act applies only when both the creation and the exercise of the power were under instruments taking effect after July 15, 1964.[421] The governing date is therefore the date of the original settlement, not the date of the exercise of the special power. This will not often matter now.

> (ii) The alternative fixed perpetuity period (not exceeding 80 years) could not be used in the exercise of a special power.[422] But it could be used in the creation of a special power, and in that case it will of course govern the exercise of the power also. In other words, the alternative fixed period could apply to a special power only if it was specified in the original settlement. If it was not so specified, the donee of the power cannot prolong the perpetuity period by invoking it.

(5) 2009 ACT. As has been explained the rule against perpetuities applies to an instrument which creates a power of appointment.[423] Like the 1964 Act, the 2009 Act distinguishes between special and general powers, but in a more elaborate way. The objective is however much the same. A general power is tantamount to ownership and is therefore not subject to the rule against perpetuities. **9–120**

The principles for determining whether the power is general or special for the purposes of the application of the rule against perpetuities under the 2009 Act are as follows. **9–121**

---

[417] PAA 1964 s.7.
[418] PAA 1964 s.15(2) includes any discretionary power to transfer a beneficial interest without valuable consideration.
[419] PAA 1964 s.15(2).
[420] PAA 1964 ss.3(2), (3), (5)(b)(iii)–(v).
[421] PAA 1964 s.15(5).
[422] PAA 1964 s.1(2).
[423] PAA 2009 s.1(6); above, para.9–031.

(i) A power will be a special power unless the instrument creating it expresses it to be exercisable by one person. This principle applies whether the power of appointment is exercisable by will or otherwise.[424]

(ii) A power that is exercisable other than by will (even if it is also exercisable by will) will be a special power unless at all times during its currency, the donee, being of full age and capacity, can immediately transfer the whole of the interest governed by the power to himself without the consent of any other person or compliance with any other condition (ignoring a formal condition as to the mode of its exercise).[425]

(iii) A power that is exercisable by will (even if it is also exercisable otherwise than by will) will be a special power unless the donee can exercise it so as to transfer the whole of the estate or interest governed by the power to his personal representatives.[426]

(iv) If a power is exercisable by will or otherwise and it falls within either (ii) or (iii) above, but not both, it will be a special power.[427]

9–122   (6) EXERCISE OF SPECIAL POWERS UNDER THE 2009 ACT. It has been explained that, in general, the perpetuity period under the 2009 Act starts when the relevant instrument takes effect.[428] However, where an instrument, which is subject to the rule against perpetuities, because:

(i) it limits property in trust so to as to create successive interests[429]; or

(ii) it creates an estate or interest which is subject to a condition precedent[430] or subsequent[431];

is made in the exercise of a special power of appointment, the perpetuity period starts when the instrument creating the power takes effect.[432] This is subject to an exception in relation to a nomination of benefits under a pension scheme which is explained later.[433] The provisions of the 2009 Act do not apply to an instrument made in the exercise of a special power of appointment,

---

[424] PAA 2009 ss.11(1), (2)(a), (3), (4)(a).
[425] PAA 2009 ss.11(1), (2)(b).
[426] PAA 2009 s.11(3), (4)(b).
[427] PAA 2009 s.11(5), (6).
[428] PAA 2009 s.6(1); above, para.9–066.
[429] Under PAA 2009 s.1(2); above, para.9–026.
[430] Under PAA 2009 s.1(3); above, para.9–027.
[431] Under PAA 2009 s.1(4); above, para.9–028.
[432] PAA 2009 s.6(2).
[433] PAA 2009 s.6(3). See below, para.9–145.

where the instrument creating that special power was made prior to April 6, 2010, even if the special power is exercised on or after that date.[434]

(c) Application of the rule to powers of appointment. The application of the **9–123** perpetuity rule to powers of appointment can best be understood by dealing separately with the two questions:

> (i) Does the power itself infringe the rule?
>
> (ii) If it does not, does the appointment made under the power infringe the rule?

(1) VALIDITY OF THE POWER

(i) A special power. The position in relation to special powers of appoint- **9–124** ment is as follows.

> (i) COMMON LAW. At common law, a special power of appointment was subject to the ordinary rule relating to powers. It was therefore void if it could be exercised outside the period. Time ran from the date when the instrument creating the power took effect.[435] Thus, if the donee of the power would not necessarily be ascertained within the period (if at all)[436] or was capable of exercising the power when the period has expired,[437] it was bad. However, a power given exclusively to a person living when it was created could never be void for remoteness,[438] unless it allowed only appointments that would necessarily be void.[439] If a power complied with these conditions, it was not invalidated merely because an appointment might be made under it which offended the rule.[440]
>
> (ii) 1964 ACT. If the power was created by an instrument taking effect after July 15, 1964 and before April 6, 2010, it will not be void *ab initio* merely because it could be exercised outside the perpetuity period. The "wait and see" principle of the 1964 Act applies, and the power will be void only in so far as it is not in fact fully exercised within the period.[441]
>
> (iii) 2009 ACT. As regards an instrument which takes effect after April 5, 2010, the position is the same as under the 1964 Act. Even if a special power can be exercised outside the perpetuity period, the

---

[434] PAA 2009 s.15(1)(b); and see PAA 1964 s.15(5A)(b), inserted by PAA 2009 s.16.
[435] *Re De Sommery* [1912] 2 Ch. 622; *Re Watson's S.T.* [1959] 1 W.L.R. 732.
[436] See *Re Hargreaves* (1890) 43 Ch D 401.
[437] *Re Abbott* [1893] 1 Ch. 54 (power exercisable by the survivor of X and her husband: X might have married someone not born when the power was given, and so it was void).
[438] Jarman 329.
[439] *Bristow v Boothby* (1826) 2 Sim. & St. 465; Gray, § 476.
[440] *Slark v Dakyns* (1874) 10 Ch.App. 35.
[441] PAA 1964 s.3(3).

principle of "wait and see" applies, and the power must be treated as void for remoteness only if and so far as it is not fully exercised within the perpetuity period.[442]

If a power is void for remoteness, whether at common law or under the 1964 or 2009 Acts, a gift in default of appointment (e.g. "but if no appointment shall be made, to X and Y equally") is not thereby invalidated. Provided it does not itself infringe the rule, it is valid.[443]

9–125   *(ii) A general power.* For the purposes of the perpetuity rule, whether at common law or under the 1964 and 2009 Acts, a general power to appoint by deed or will is so nearly equivalent to absolute ownership that the time and manner of its exercise are irrelevant.[444] It is the time at which the power is acquired that is relevant and the perpetuity rule is satisfied if the power must be acquired (if at all) within the period.[445] The circumstances in which a power was regarded as a special power at common law, and when it is regarded as a special power under the 1964 and 2009 Acts have been explained above.[446]

Under the 1964 Act, the "wait and see" principle applies in the usual way, so that a general power is not void merely because it might be acquired at too remote a time. It is valid unless and until it becomes established that it will not be exercisable within the perpetuity period.[447]

Similarly, under the 2009 Act, a general power of appointment will be treated as valid until such time (if any) that it becomes established that the power will not be exercisable within the perpetuity period.[448]

9–126   (2) VALIDITY OF APPOINTMENTS MADE UNDER A VALID POWER. Obviously, if the power itself is void, no valid appointment can be made under it. But even if the power is valid, an appointment made under it may nevertheless be too remote.

9–127   *(i) A special power.* In the case of a special power of appointment, the property is fettered from the moment the power is created. If an appointment is made, it will carry the property to one or more persons designated by the original settlor who is in reality the true donor. The perpetuity period therefore starts to run from the creation of the power.[449] But, as has been seen,[450] the

---

[442] PAA 2009 ss.7(3), (4).
[443] *Re Abbott* [1893] 1 Ch. 54. Such gifts may be vested: above. para.9–002.
[444] See *Re Fane* [1913] 1 Ch. 404 at 413; PAA 1964 s.7; PAA 2009 s.11.
[445] *Bray v Hammersley* (1830) 3 Sim. 513; 2 Cl. & F. 453.
[446] See paras 9–117 (common law), 9–118 (1964 Act) and 9–121 (2009 Act).
[447] PAA 1964 s.3(2).
[448] PAA 2009 ss.7(5), (6).
[449] *Re Brown and Sibley's Contract* (1876) 3 Ch D 156; *Re Thompson* [1906] 2 Ch. 199 (common law); PAA 2009 s.6(2). See above, paras 9–119 and 9–122.
[450] Above, para.9–125.

mere fact that the power authorises the making of an appointment which may be too remote does not invalidate it. Until the appointment is in fact made, it cannot be said whether it is too remote. Even at common law, therefore, the principle seems to have been to wait and see.[451]

(ii) A general power. In considering the applicability of the rule against perpetuities to an appointment that has been made under a general power of appointment, the law recognises that a general power of appointment is tantamount to absolute ownership: prior to the exercise of the power of appointment, the property is unfettered and the donee of the power is able to deal with it as he wishes. In consequence, the position at common law was that the perpetuity period did not begin to run until the date of the appointment.[452] This was so even if the power was exercisable by deed only[453] or by will only.[454] Thus, for the purposes of the perpetuity rule there was no difference between the exercise of a general power and a conveyance by an absolute owner. **9–128**

The position under the 1964 and 2009 Acts is the same. Where a general power of appointment has been exercised, the perpetuity period applicable to the disposition made pursuant to it,[455] commences with that exercise.[456]

The difference between appointments under general and special powers may therefore be summarised as follows. In both cases, the relevant facts are those existing at the time of the appointment; but the time from which the perpetuity period runs, and at which the lives in being must be ascertained, is the creation of the power in the case of a special power, and the exercise of the power in the case of a general power.

18. Contractual interests, obligations, covenants and options. The perpetuity rule was devised in order to control interests in property, not mere personal obligations. However, contracts relating to property may themselves create proprietary rights. These were subject to the rule against perpetuities and the 1964 Act made important changes in relation to such contracts. The application of the rule against perpetuities to essentially commercial transactions was a constant source of practical difficulty and a trap for the unwary. In relation to contracts relating to land made after April 5, 2010, the rule against perpetuities has no further application.[457] **9–129**

---

[451] *Re Witty* [1913] 2 Ch. 666 at 673, per Cozens-Hardy M.R. For the operation of the perpetuity rule at common law in relation to a special power, see the previous edition of this work at paras 9–110, 9–111.

[452] *Re Thompson* [1906] 2 Ch. 199 at 202.

[453] Consider *Re Phillips* [1931] 1 Ch. 347.

[454] Above, para.9–117. Contrast the rule as to the power itself, above para.9–125.

[455] Under the 2009 Act, that disposition must itself be one that is subject to the rule against perpetuities: see PAA 2009 s.1, above, paras 9–025—9–031.

[456] This follows from PAA 1964 s.15(5) (in the case of the 1964 Act) and from PAA 2009 ss.5(1), (2) (in the case of the 2009 Act).

[457] This follows from PAA 2009 s.1. See above, para.9–032.

(a) Personal obligations (at common law)

9–130   (1) CONTRAST WITH PROPRIETARY INTERESTS. The perpetuity rule was never applied to mere personal obligations created by contract, e.g. to pay money,[458] or to buy stone exclusively from a particular quarry.[459] The rule was directed against the tying up of property by the grant of interests in it which might vest at too remote a date. In this context "interests" meant rights of property, enforceable against other persons generally according to the principles governing legal and equitable interests.[460] Contracts, on the other hand, primarily create personal obligations between the contracting parties. Therefore, between the parties themselves (and their respective personal representatives, who can sue and be sued on a deceased person's contract), the rule against perpetuities, in its classical common law form, had no application.[461] A contracting party might be made liable on any contingency, however remote, so that, e.g. an option given by one corporation to another in (say) 1800 or 1950 might remain enforceable forever.[462]

9–131   (2) SPECIFIC PERFORMANCE. It made no difference that the contract was specifically enforceable (as for example a contract for the sale of land), and thus gave one party a right to obtain specific property. The rights of the parties between themselves were personal as well as proprietary, and "specific performance is merely an equitable mode of enforcing a personal obligation with which the rule against perpetuities has nothing to do".[463] If the vendor, for instance, had parted with the land contracted to be sold, it was useless to decree specific performance against him when he could no longer perform his obligations. The property itself, therefore, was not fettered by the vendor's obligations in so far as they were personal to him. "The real answer to the argument founded on the inconvenience of tying up land is that the action upon the covenant sounds in damages only unless the defendant has still got the land to which the covenant relates."[464]

9–132   (3) ASSIGNMENT. Since it is the general rule that the benefit, but not the burden, of a contract is assignable,[465] it was always the case that an assignee of a contractual right could enforce it against the original promisor personally,

---

[458] *Walsh v HM Sec of State for India* (1863) 10 H.L.C. 367; *Witham v Vane* (1883) reported in Challis 440; *Borland's Trustee v Steel Brothers & Co Ltd* [1901] 1 Ch. 279; see Challis 440.

[459] *Keppell v Bailey* (1834) 2 My. & K. 517 at 527; *South Eastern Ry v Associated Portland Cement Manufacturers (1900) Ltd* [1901] 1 Ch. 12 (allowing landowner to make a tunnel under adjoining land); see 54 S.J. 471, 501; *Sharpe v Durrant* (1911) 55 S.J. 423; [1911] W.N. 158 (allowing landowner to make crossings over a tramway); (1911) 27 L.Q.R. 151; Challis 184.

[460] The true character of equitable interests as rights in rem clearly emerges here: see above, para.5–012.

[461] Challis 184n. But restrictive covenants create property rights: see above, para.5–026.

[462] Challis 184n.

[463] *Hutton v Watling* [1948] Ch. 26 at 36, per Jenkins J.

[464] *South Eastern Ry v Associated Portland Cement Manufacturers (1900) Ltd* [1910] 1 Ch. 12 at 34, per Farwell L.J.

[465] cf. below, para.17–061.

or his estate if he was dead, at any time, regardless of the perpetuity rule.[466] However, the assignment itself, which was proprietary in nature and so resembled a conveyance rather than a contract, had to take effect within the perpetuity period, running from the date when it was made.[467]

(b) Proprietary interests (at common law)

(1) PERSONAL AND PROPRIETARY RIGHTS. Many contracts create not only **9–133** personal obligations but interests in property as well. Contracts for the sale or lease of land, if specifically enforceable, are binding as equitable interests (estate contracts) not only upon the original promisor but also upon his successors in title, subject to the reservations which must always be remembered.[468] Against such successors in title, who are not parties to the contract, the contract can be enforced only in so far as it creates an interest in land, a right in rem; and to this element of it the perpetuity rule applied.[469] At common law, therefore, although a contract creating an interest in property which might arise outside the perpetuity period was valid as against the original promisor, or his estate, at the suit of anyone entitled to the benefit of it, it was void as against third parties. It is probable that a firm contract (as opposed to a mere option) for sale "in 25 years' time" would also have been void against a third party, because the purchaser's equitable interest, though it arose at once,[470] could not be truly vested until the time had expired.[471]

(2) OPTIONS. The contracts which most commonly produce contingent **9–134** interests in property, capable of arising after an extended period of time, are options.[472] At common law these had to obey the rules set out above, and since the time for exercising the option usually had no connection with lives in being (unless, for example, a "royal lives clause" was used), the perpetuity period was normally 21 years only.

Options are commonly found in leases. They may take the form of an option to purchase the reversion (i.e. the freehold, or some superior lease) or to renew the lease. Options to purchase the reversion were also subject to the common law rules explained above.[473] However, options to renew a lease

---

[466] *South Eastern Ry v Associated Portland Cement Manufacturers (1900) Ltd* [1910] 1 Ch. 12.

[467] Gray, §329, fn.1. Thus an assignment of a contract that was to take effect on the occurrence of a contingency was subject to the perpetuity rule.

[468] Above, paras 5–009 et seq. As to estate contracts, see above, para.5–025; below, paras 15–051 et seq.

[469] *L. & S.W. Ry v Gomm* (1882) 20 Ch D 562; *Woodall v Clifton* [1905] 2 Ch. 257; *Worthing Corpn v Heather* [1906] 2 Ch. 532. And see the illuminating judgment of Jenkins J. in *Hutton v Watling* [1948] Ch. 26, not challenged on this point on appeal: [1948] Ch. 398.

[470] Below, para.15–052.

[471] See Gray, § 330, fn.2. Ordinary contracts for sale were safe because even if no date was fixed for completion there was an implied term that completion shall take place within a reasonable time.

[472] For options see below, para.15–062.

[473] *Woodall v Clifton* [1905] 2 Ch. 257; *Coronation Street Industrial Properties Ltd v Ingall Industries Plc* [1989] 1 W.L.R. 304 at 307.

enjoyed a special exemption from the perpetuity rule.[474] This was because options to renew a lease, unlike options to purchase a freehold, were among the recognised leasehold covenants which "run with the land",[475] and if long leases were to be allowed, this class of covenant had, in general, to be allowed to run with them. However, statute has provided that a contract to renew a lease for more than 60 years is void.[476]

9–135   *(c) Statutory changes.* The 1964 Act made three changes in the law in the case of instruments taking effect after July 15, 1964 and before April 6, 2010.

(i) Subject to one exception, an option to acquire for value any interest in land was subject to a perpetuity period of 21 years only.[477] No period based on lives in being and no alternative fixed statutory period could be used. The "wait and see" principle also applied.[478] As against a successor in title of the person who gave the option, therefore, the option was valid for 21 years from the date of the instrument creating it (assuming that it was duly registered) and thereafter was void. Certain rights of pre-emption conferred on public or local authorities in respect of land devoted to religious purposes, which ceases to be used as such, were exempted from the application of this rule.[479]

(ii) A contract or other disposition inter vivos which created an interest in property was void even between the original contracting parties whenever it would have been void for remoteness as against a third party.[480]

(iii) The perpetuity rule did not apply to an option for a lessee (whether under a lease or an agreement for a lease) to purchase the freehold or a superior leasehold reversion, provided that it was exercisable only by the lessee or his successors in title and that it ceased to be exercisable not later than one year after the end of the lease.[481]

---

[474] "The rule against perpetuities does not apply to a covenant which touches and concerns the land": *Coronation Street Industrial Properties Ltd v Ingall Industries Plc* [1989] 1 W.L.R. 304 at 307, per Lord Templeman. See too *L. & S.W. Ry v Gomm* (1882) 20 Ch D 562 at 579; *Woodall v Clifton*, above, at 265, 268; *Weg Motors Ltd v Hales* [1962] Ch. 49; Gray § 230.
[475] Below, para.20–040; *Muller v Trafford* [1901] 1 Ch. 54 at 61. This in itself was somewhat anomalous.
[476] Below, para.17–122.
[477] PAA 1964 s.9(2).
[478] PAA 1964 s.3(1), (3).
[479] PAA 1964 s.3(1), (3).
[480] PAA 1964 s.10. The language of this provision was curious. See (1964) 80 L.Q.R. 486 at 525.
[481] PAA 1964 s.9(1). For the rationale behind this, see the previous edition of this work at para.9–120, and the Fourth Report of the Law Reform Committee, Cmnd. 18, 1956, paras 35–38.

Changes (i) and (ii) above did not fit together neatly, because (i) was **9–136** confined to options relating to land whereas (ii) operated more widely.[482] None of the rules set out above, whether at common law or under the 1964 Act, has any application to contracts made after April 5, 2010.[483]

C. Exceptions to the Perpetuity Rule

There are certain exceptions to the perpetuity rule at common law and **9–137** under the 1964 and 2009 Acts.[484] The ones that are likely to be encountered are set out below.[485]

1. Certain gifts to charities. The general rule is that a gift to a charity[486] **9–138** is subject to the rule in the same way as any other gift.[487] If there was a gift to a private person with a gift over to a charity, the gift over was void for perpetuity at common law if it was capable of vesting outside the period.[488] Where the gift was subject to the provisions of the 1964 Act or the 2009 Act, the principle of "wait and see" applies to the gift over for the relevant perpetuity period.[489] But if there is a gift to one charity followed by a gift over to another charity on a certain event, the gift over is not void merely because the event may occur outside the perpetuity period.[490] Thus where property was given to Charity A with a proviso that it shall go to Charity B if Charity A failed to keep the testator's tomb in repair, the gift over was valid at common law.[491] To this extent alone charities were exempted from the rule against perpetuities.[492] This exception would not save a gift to a natural person merely because it was preceded by a gift to charity.[493]

The 2009 Act expressly preserves the exception set out in the previous **9–139** paragraph in relation to dispositions under the Act which remain subject to the

---

[482] For illustrations, see the previous edition of this work at paras 9–121—9–122.

[483] See above, para.9–130.

[484] Under the 2009 Act, the application of the rule, as set out in PAA 2009 s.1, is expressly subject to the exceptions listed in s.2 (explained below) and any further exceptions that may be created under s.3 (below, para.9–147): see PAA 2009 s.1(8).

[485] For the exemption from the rule of limitations after entails, see the previous edition of this work at paras 9–123—9–126.

[486] For charities, see below, para.36–028.

[487] *Chamberlayne v Brockett* (1872) 8 Ch.App. 206 at 21 1; *Re Bowen* [1893] 2 Ch. 49 1 at 494; dicta to the contrary (e.g. *Goodman v The Mayor and Free Burgesses of the Borough of Saltash* (1882) 2 App.Cas. 633 at 650; *Re St Stephen, Coleman Street* (1888) 39 Ch D 492 at 501; *Re Rymer* [1895] 1 Ch. 19 at 25) are concerned with "inalienability" (below, para.9–147) rather than "perpetuity".

[488] *Att Gen v Gill* (1726) 2 P. Wms. 369; *Re Johnson's Trusts* (1866) L.R. 2 Eq. 716; and see *Re Bushnell* [1975] 1 W.L.R. 1596.

[489] See PAA 1964 s.3(1); PAA 2009 s.7.

[490] *Christ's Hospital v Grainger* (1849) 1 Mac. & G. 460.

[491] *Re Tyler* [1891] 3 Ch. 252 (doubted in *RSPCA of N.S.W. v Benevolent Society of N.S.W.* (1960) 102 C.L.R. 629); contrast *Re Dalziel* [19431 Ch. 277. This is so even if the maintenance of the tomb will leave no surplus for Charity A: *Re Davies* [1915] 1 Ch. 543. The gift to Charity A was also valid, even though it might continue indefinitely: see above, para.9–099.

[492] For their exception from the rule against inalienability, see below, para.9–161.

[493] *Re Bowen* [1893] 2 Ch. 491.

rule against perpetuities. It is provided that the rule against perpetuities does not apply where either:

> (i) Charity B becomes entitled to property on the determination of a determinable interest vested in Charity A[494]; or

> (ii) property is given to Charity A subject to a condition subsequent, and Charity B is entitled to the property should the condition be satisfied.[495]

9–140   **2. Certain contracts and covenants.** As has been explained, under the 2009 Act, the rule against perpetuities does not apply to contracts made after April 5, 2010.[496] As regards contracts made before April 6, 2010, the position is as follows.

> (i) *Personal obligations.* The exemption of personal obligations that were created by contract or covenant, and the changes made by the 1964 Act, have already been explained.[497]

> (ii) *Options in leases.* The exemptions that were allowed for options to renew leases (at common law) and for options to acquire the reversion (under the 1964 Act) have also already been explained.[498]

> (iii) *Restrictive covenants.* A restrictive covenant (whether affecting freehold or leasehold land) creates an equitable interest in the land,[499] which is enforceable against future occupiers at any distance in time. It was never subject to the perpetuity rule, because a future breach of the covenant did not bring about the vesting of any interest in the land.[500] This was not, therefore, a genuine exception.

9–141   **3. Forfeiture of leases and enforcement of rentcharges.** Leases often contain a forfeiture clause, by which the tenant agrees that if at any time he breaks the terms of the lease the landlord may re-enter and put an end to the lease.[501] This contingent liability to re-entry runs with the land demised and

---

[494] PAA 2009 ss.2(1), (2).
[495] PAA 2009 s.2(3).
[496] See above, paras 9–130, 9–137.
[497] Above, paras 9–130 et seq.
[498] Above, paras 9–130 et seq.
[499] Above, para.5–026, below, para.32–030 et seq.
[500] *Mackenzie v Childers* (1889) 43 Ch D 265 at 279; *Marten v Flight Refuelling Ltd* [1962] Ch. 115 at 136; Gray, § 280.
[501] See below, para.18–012.

is a proprietary interest.[502] However, because it is a recognised incident of leases it is exempt from the perpetuity rule.[503]

For similar reasons statutory exemption was given in 1925 to certain rights of entry reserved to secure the payment of rentcharges, whether such rights were given by contract or by statute.[504] For any rentcharges created after July 15, 1964 and before April 6, 2009,[505] the exemption was extended to all powers and remedies for enforcing rentcharges.[506] Under the 2009 Act, the rule against perpetuities could not apply to rentcharges in any event.[507] The statutory exemptions mentioned above are spent and have therefore been repealed or disapplied for the future.[508]

4. Mortgages. "The rule has never been applied to mortgages". Accordingly, a clause postponing the mortgagor's right to redeem the property was not invalid merely because the right was postponed for longer than the perpetuity period.[509]   **9–142**

5. Right of survivorship. As already mentioned,[510] a joint tenant's right of survivorship[511] is exempt from the rule against perpetuities,[512] because it can always be destroyed by severance by the other joint tenant.   **9–143**

6. Pension schemes. Under the 2009 Act, the rule against perpetuities does not apply to an interest or right arising under any of: **9–144**

   (i) an occupational pension scheme;

   (ii) a personal pension scheme;

   (iii) a public service pension scheme.[513]

The exemption is wider than was the case prior to the 2009 Act.[514] However, the exception mentioned above does not apply if the interest or right arises

---

[502] LPA 1925 s.1(2)(e); above, para.6–027.
[503] *Re Tyrrell's Estate* [1907] 1 I.R. 292 at 298; Gray, § 303; Challis 186 and see *Re Garde Browne* [1911] 1 I.R. 205 at 210; *Woodall v Clifton* [1905] 2 Ch. 257 at 279.
[504] LPA 1925 s.121(6) (contrast the proviso to s.4(3)); below, para.31–031. Both the proviso to s.4(3) and s.121(6) LPA 1925 were repealed by PAA 2009: see ss.1(9) and 4(a).
[505] Subject to limited exceptions, of which the most important is estate rentcharges, it ceased to be possible to create new rentcharges after August 21, 1977: see below, para.31–018.
[506] PAA 1964 ss.11(1), 15(5); see (1964) 80 L.Q.R. 486 at 528.
[507] They are not listed in PAA 2009 s.1, as being subject to the rule against perpetuities.
[508] See PAA 2009 s.4(a) (which repeals LPA 1925 s.121(6) and s.16 (which inserts PAA 1964 s.15(5A)).
[509] *Knightsbridge Estates Trust Ltd v Byrne* [1939] Ch. 441 at 463, per Greene M.R. (affirmed on another ground, [1940] A.C. 613).
[510] Above, para.9–069.
[511] Below, para.13–003.
[512] *Re Roberts* (1881) 19 Ch D 520; Gray § 232.1.
[513] PAA 2009 ss.2(4), 20(4). These three categories of pension scheme are defined by reference to Pension Schemes Act 1993 ss.1 and 181: see PAA 2009 s.20(5).
[514] See Pension Schemes Act 1993 s.163, repealed by PAA 2009 s.4(c).

under an instrument which either nominates benefits under the scheme, or is made in exercise of a power of advancement arising under the scheme.[515] These remain subject to the rule.[516] Furthermore, the perpetuity period applicable to such instruments commences when the member concerned becomes a member of the pension scheme.[517]

9–145 **7. Miscellaneous.** The Law of Property Act 1925[518] set out a list of certain special rights that were exempted from the perpetuities rule. These rights related to rentcharges,[519] minerals, timber, and repair or maintenance of land, building, sewers, and other things. The general effect of the exemptions was to enable rights which were merely ancillary to other valid interests to be exercised outside the perpetuity period.[520]

Under the 2009 Act, the rule against perpetuities no longer applies to any of the matters which were previously exempted from it by the Law of Property Act 1925, and that provision has therefore been repealed.[521]

9–146 **8. Power to specify exceptions.** The 2009 Act contains a power whereby the Lord Chancellor may by order provide that the rule against perpetuities shall not apply either to cases of a specified description or if specified conditions are fulfilled.[522] In this way, further exceptions may be made to the rule without the need for primary legislation.

Section 3. The Rule against Inalienability

1. "Perpetual trusts"

9–147 *(a) The principle.* It is a fundamental principle of English law that property must not be rendered inalienable.[523] It is therefore necessary to prohibit not only indefeasible future interests which are unduly remote, but immediate gifts which are subject to some permanent restraint upon alienation. The two principles are often confused, but need to be considered separately. Restraints upon alienation attached to direct gifts of property are generally invalid on

---

[515] PAA 2009 s.2(5).
[516] PAA 2009 s.1.
[517] See PAA 2009 ss.6(3), (4). In this respect, nominations and the exercise of advancement differ from special powers of appointment, which have been explained above at para.9–122.
[518] s.162.
[519] See also above, para.9–142.
[520] *Dunn v Blackdown Properties Ltd* [1961] Ch. 433; *Magrath v Parkside Hotels Ltd* [2011] EWHC 143 (Ch). cf. above, para.9–024.
[521] PAA 2009 s.4(b).
[522] PAA 2009 s.3.
[523] cf. above, para.3–063 (conditions in restraint of alienation); and see *Carne v Long* (1860) 2 De G.F. & J. 75 at 80. But see below, para.12–019.

their face, as repugnant to the interest granted.[524] But if a trust is employed, the donor's intention may be that the capital shall be held indefinitely, or that some beneficial interest given to a club or other permanent institution shall continue indefinitely so that it is, in effect, inalienable. The rule now to be explained is therefore sometimes also called "the rule against perpetual trusts",[525] although the rule against such trusts is only part of a wider rule against inalienability.

(b) Trusts for non-charitable purposes. The trusts in question are the **9–148** so-called non-charitable purpose trusts, by which the trust property is to be applied to promote some particular purpose rather than to benefit some individual or a class. Such trusts have been held void for two reasons.

(1) PERPETUAL DURATION. Where the trust is for purposes, the ordinary **9–149** perpetuity rule cannot prevent the property from being tied up indefinitely, since there are no individual beneficiaries in whom successive interests are to vest. Such trusts will however fail if they may be of perpetual duration.[526] However, although property cannot be rendered inalienable for ever, or for a period to which no clear and definite limit is set,[527] it seems that alienation may be validly restricted for a period which cannot exceed a life or lives in being at the time of the gift, and further 21 years.[528] This period is borrowed from the rule against perpetuities,[529] and as under that rule, the lives must probably be human lives.[530] A purpose trust "for so long as the law permits" will be valid for a period of 21 years.[531]

In cases involving purpose trusts, it would seem desirable that a settlor should be able to specify a perpetuity period of a fixed number of years whether greater or less than 21 and unconnected with any lives in being. However, both the 1964 Act and the 2009 Act expressly refrained from making any change in the law where property is to be applied for purposes.[532] In relation to the 1964 Act, this was generally thought to preclude the employment of the fixed perpetuity period provided for by the Act, but some doubts were raised due to the wording of that Act.[533] The 2009 Act "does not affect the rule of law which limits the duration of non-charitable purpose

---

[524] See above, para.3–063.

[525] See Gray, § 909.1.

[526] *Leahy v Att Gen for N.S.W.* [1959] A.C. 457; *Re Bushnell* [19751 1 W.L.R. 1596 at 1602. The "wait and see" provisions of PAA 1964 and PAA 2009 do not apply to purpose trusts: PAA 2004 s.15(4); PAA 2009 s.18. Charitable trusts may be and often are of perpetual duration.

[527] *Kennedy v Kennedy* [1914] A.C. 215; *Re Wightwick's W.T.* [1950] Ch. 260.

[528] See *Thellusson v Woodford* (1805) 11 Ves. 112 at 135, 146; *Came v Long* (1860) 2 De G.F. & J. 75 at 80; *Re Dean* (1889) 41 Ch D 552 at 557. See too *Re Denley's Trust Deed* [1969] 1 Ch. 373.

[529] Above, para.9–018.

[530] *Re Dean* (1889) 41 Ch D 552 (upholding a trust for dogs and horses for their lives) is probably wrong; see above, para.9–050.

[531] *Pirbright v Salwey* [1896] W.N. 86; *Re Hooper* [1932] 1 Ch. 38.

[532] PAA 1964 s.15(4); PAA 2009 s.18.

[533] See Maudsley, *The Modern Law of Perpetuities* 177.

trusts".[534] That must preclude any attempt to apply the Act's 125-year perpetuity period to non-charitable purpose trusts.[535]

9–150 (2) UNENFORCEABILITY. Even if a valid perpetuity period has been specified, a purpose trust may be held to be void because there is no one who can enforce it and because the court cannot control its execution.[536] This is the so-called "beneficiary principle". The rule that such trusts are invalid is applied inflexibly. Even if the trustees are willing to carry out a purpose trust, it will fail because of the court's inability to control its performance.[537] Although this rule has often been criticised, there is a good reason for it. "It is not possible to contemplate with equanimity the creation of large funds devoted to non-charitable purposes which no court and no department of state can control, or in the case of maladministration reform".[538]

9–151 *(c) Cases in which non-charitable purposes have been upheld.* In a number of cases trusts for non-charitable purposes have been upheld. These have been described as "concessions to human weakness or sentiment",[539] "when Homer has nodded", which will not be extended.[540] These cases fall into three main categories of which the first two are anomalous, whereas the third is consistent with principle.

9–152 (1) TRUSTS FOR TOMBS AND MONUMENTS. A trust to erect a tomb or funerary monument will be valid provided that the executors or trustees are willing to carry out the wishes of the testator or settlor.[541] However a trust for the upkeep of a grave or monument will be valid only if it is confined to a perpetuity period.[542] It is now provided by statute that a burial or local authority may enter into an agreement with any person on payment of a sum of money to maintain a grave, tombstone or other memorial for a period of up to 99 years.[543]

---

[534] PAA 2009 s.18.

[535] See the Explanatory Notes to PAA 2009, at para.78.

[536] *Morice v Bishop of Durham* (1804) 9 Ves. 399; (1805) 10 Ves. 522; *Re Astor's S.T.* [1952] Ch. 534; *Re Endacott* [1960] Ch. 232. This rule applies only to non-charitable purpose trusts: trusts for charitable purposes are enforceable by the Attorney General.

[537] *Re Shaw* [1957] 1 W.L.R. 729 at 745.

[538] *Re Astor's S.T.* [1952] Ch. 534 at 542, per Roxburgh J. See too *R. v District Auditor, Ex p. West Yorkshire Metropolitan County Council* [1986] R.V.R. 24; [1986] C.L.J. 391 (C.H.). For a possible solution to this problem, see the Bermudan Trusts (Special Provisions) Act 1989.

[539] *Re Astor's S.T.* [1952] Ch. 534 at 547.

[540] *Re Endacott* [1960] Ch. 232 at 250. Some of the exceptional cases are clearly incorrect, see e.g. *Re Thompson* [1934] Ch. 342 (trust for the furtherance of fox-hunting, where the validity of the gift was not challenged by the remainderman).

[541] *Trimmer v Danby* (1856) 25 L.J.Ch. 424 (bequest by the painter Turner for the erection of a monument to his own memory in St Paul's Cathedral "among those of my brothers in art"). The monument need not be for the testator himself: *Mussett v Bingle* [1876] W.N. 170 (bequest for a monument to the testator's wife's first husband).

[542] *Mussett v Bingle* [1876] W.N. 170; *Re Hooper* [1932] 1 Ch. 38. If such trusts are set up in perpetuity they will be void: *Rickard v Robson* (1862) 31 Beav.244; *Yeap Cheah Neo v Ong Cheng Neo* (1875) L.R. 6 P.C. 381.

[543] Parish Councils and Burial Authorities (Miscellaneous Provisions) Act 1970 s.1.

(2) TRUSTS FOR THE UPKEEP OF ANIMALS. There is some authority which **9–153** suggests that trusts for the maintenance of animals may be validly created. The authority for this supposed exception is very weak,[544] and some of the cases can be better explained in other ways.[545]

(3) PURPOSE TRUSTS FOR THE BENEFIT OF A PERSON OR PERSONS. A trust for **9–154** a purpose which benefits directly or indirectly a person or persons will be valid provided that it is confined to a perpetuity period.[546] Such trusts do not offend the beneficiary principle because any person who benefits, although having no beneficial interest in the property, has *locus standi* to enforce the trust.[547] If the purpose for which the trust was set up comes to an end, the property passes on a resulting trust to the settlor or donor.[548] It does not become the absolute property of those who have benefited from the trust.[549]

(d) Cases in which gifts for purposes are interpreted as absolute gifts. In **9–155** some situations a gift that is expressed to be for a purpose will be construed as an outright gift to a person. The rule, which is one of construction of the instrument creating the gift, applies where the primary reason for the gift is to benefit a named individual and the expressed purpose is merely the motive for making it.[550] Even if the purpose is fulfilled or cannot be carried out, the donee takes absolutely.[551] It is often difficult to distinguish gifts of this kind from trusts for purposes which benefit persons directly or indirectly (considered above).[552]

(e) Gifts to unincorporated associations. An unincorporated association, **9–156** such as a club or society, consists of two or more persons contractually bound together for common purposes other than for business, each having mutual duties and obligations, in an organisation having rules regulating such matters as membership and control of funds.[553] Such a body is regarded in law as no more than the aggregate of its members.[554] At one time it was thought that a gift to an unincorporated association could be valid only if it took effect as a

---

[544] *Re Dean* (1889) 41 Ch D 552 (the testator left his horses and hounds to his trustees with an annuity for up to 50 years for the maintenance of the animals). See above, para.9–050.

[545] See, e.g. *Pettingall v Pettingall* (1842) 11 L.J.Ch. 176 (gift of £50 per annum to an executor conditional upon his maintaining out of it the testator's favourite black mare).

[546] *Re Sanderson's Trust* (1854) 3 K. & J. 497; *Re the Trusts of the Abbott Fund* [1900] 2 Ch. 326; *Re Denley's Trust Deed* [1969] 1 Ch. 373. See too *Re Northern Developments Holdings Ltd* (Unreported October 6, 1978, Megarry V.C.); *Carreras Rothermans Ltd v Freeman Mathews Treasure Ltd* [1985] Ch. 207 at 223.

[547] *Re Denley's Trust Deed,* above (trust of sports ground for use by employees of a company).

[548] *Re the Trusts of the Abbott Fund,* above (fund subscribed for the upkeep of two deaf and dumb ladies; surplus returned to the subscribers on the death of the ladies).

[549] *Re Sanderson's Trust,* above.

[550] *Re Sanderson's Trust,* above, at 503; *Re Andrew's Trust* [1905] 2 Ch. 48; *Re Lipinski's W.T.* [1976] Ch. 235; *Re Osoba* [1979] 1 W.L.R. 247.

[551] e.g. *Re Osoba* (gift to daughter for her training "up to university grade" held to be an absolute one).

[552] Compare *Re the Trusts of the Abbott Fund,* above, with *Re Andrew's Trust,* above.

[553] *Conservative and Unionist Central Office v Burrell* [19821 1 W.L.R. 522 at 525.

[554] *Leahy v Att Gen for N.S.W.* [1959] A.C. 457 at 477.

gift to the then members as joint tenants or as tenants in common. If it was in the nature of an endowment, it was void for perpetuity.[555] Neither of these alternatives was satisfactory and such gifts are now wherever possible construed as a gift to the members of the association subject to their contractual rights *inter se*.[556] Provided that the rules do not prevent the distribution of the association's assents amongst its members on dissolution,[557] the gift will be valid.[558]

Where an inter vivos gift is made for the purposes of a more amorphous body that is not an unincorporated association, the person who receives it on behalf of that body undertakes to apply it for those purposes as agent for the contributor.[559] It is unclear whether a gift of this kind could be validly made by will, because an agency could not be set up at the moment of death.[560]

9–157   **2. Protective trusts.** Another form of limitation that can offend against the rule against inalienability is the protective trust.[561] This may be created by directing any life or lesser interest to be held "on protective trusts" thereby incorporating statutory forms of trust,[562] or by setting out express trusts. Such trusts provide for the income to be paid to the principal beneficiary during his life (or lesser period) under a determinable limitation, i.e. until he attempts any alienation, or any other event occurs whereby he might be deprived of any of the income; and thereafter the property is held on discretionary trusts for a number of persons, including the principal beneficiary.

If such a trust is created in favour of, for example, an unborn child of a living person, to vest at birth, it seems that at common law it is partly valid and partly void. On the principle that the perpetuity rule is not concerned with the determination of interests,[563] the determinable interest will duly terminate whenever the specified event occurs, even if it is outside the perpetuity period. However, because the discretionary trust might arise at too remote a date, it was void at common law. Where either the 1964 Act or the 2009 Act applies, the result will be different. If the determinable interest in fact outlasts the

---

[555] *Leahy v Att Gen for N.S.W.* [1959] A.C. 457 at 478.

[556] *Neville Estates Ltd v Madden* [1962] Ch. 832 at 849; *Re Recher's W.T.* [1972] Ch. 526; *Conservative and Unionist Central Office v Burrell* [1982] 1 W.L.R. 522 at 529; *News Group Newspapers Ltd v S.O.G.A.T 1982* [1986] I.C.R. 716; *Re Horley Town Football Club* [2006] EWHC 2386 (Ch); *Hanchett-Stamford v Att Gen* [2009] Ch. 173; [2007] Conv. 274 (P. Luxton). A gift expressed to be for a purpose that is for the benefit of the members of the association will also be construed in this manner: *Re Lipinski's W.T.* [1976] Ch. 235. See below, para.13–094.

[557] Including the last surviving member: see *Hanchett-Stamford v Att Gen* [2009] Ch. 173.

[558] *Re Recher's W.T.,* above. Even if the rules as they stand do preclude the members from dividing the assets amongst themselves, the gift should be valid provided that the rules can be changed by the association. For the position where the rules are controlled by an outside body, see *Re Grant's W.T.* [19801 1 W.L.R. 360. cf. *Re Horley Town Football Club* [2006] EWHC 2386 (Ch) at [117].

[559] *Conservative and Unionist Central Office v Burrell,* above.

[560] In *Conservative and Unionist Central Office v Burrell* [1982] 1 W.L.R. 522 at 530, Brightman L.J. considered that the answer to this problem was "not difficult to find" but unfortunately all commentators have failed to do so.

[561] See generally Snell, *Equity,* paras 22–006 et seq.

[562] See TA 1925 s.33.

[563] Above, para.9–099.

perpetuity period, it will become absolute and the discretionary trust will be void.[564] If the interest determines during the perpetuity period, the discretionary trust will be valid up to the end of the perpetuity period, but thereafter void.[565]

3. Capital and income

(a) Inalienable capital. If the beneficial interest, i.e. the right to the income, **9–158** is itself free from any trust or restraint and so is freely assignable, it does not matter that the capital may be vested inalienably in trustees. Thus, a life interest in a trust fund may be given to an unborn person, provided of course that it must vest within the perpetuity period, even though the capital of the fund must be held by the trustees until the beneficiary's death, which may be after the end of the perpetuity period.[566] The same principle has been applied even to the case of a determinable interest in the income of a trust fund,[567] analogous to a determinable fee in real property, where the capital might have remained in the hands of the trustees for ever.

(b) Alienable income. If this is correct it would seem that a gift to trustees **9–159** upon trust "to apply the income to the upkeep of my grave" is bad, since both capital and income are tied up indefinitely by the trust.[568] However, a trust "to pay the income to X during such time as my grave is properly tended" is good, because X can dispose of his determinable interest in the income without any breach of trust. The fact that the capital is to be held upon trust meanwhile is not material. This is because the person able to dispose of the income and the persons entitled on the determination of the interest could at any time combine and put an end to the trust.[569]

(c) Settled land and land held on a trust of land. From the enactment of the **9–160** Settled Land Act 1882 until 1997,[570] land held upon trust for limited interests was alienable, and it was only a beneficial interest in land which could be made inalienable. This remains the case in relation to land that was settled prior to 1997. However, where land is held on a trust of land, it is now open to a settlor to restrict or exclude the trustees' powers of disposition.[571] In this

---

[564] Above, paras 9–102 (1964 Act), 9–103 (2009 Act).

[565] In other words, the principle of "wait and see" is applied: see PAA 1964 s.3(3); and PAA 2009 s.7. Under both Acts, discretionary trusts are treated as powers of appointment: see PAA 1964 s.15(2) (above, para.9–106); and PAA 2009 s.20(2) (above, para.9–107).

[566] *Wainwright v Miller* [1897] 2 Ch. 255; *Re Gage* [1898] 1 Ch. 498.

[567] *Re Chardon* [1928] Ch. 464, followed in *Re Chambers' W.T.* [1950] Ch. 267. If the determining event is so vague that the time of its happening could never be proved by evidence, the capital is perpetually tied up and the gift is void: *Re Wightwick's W.T.* [1950] Ch. 260 (abolition of vivisection by law "in the United Kingdom of Great Britain and Ireland, on the continent of Europe and elsewhere").

[568] See, e.g. *Re Dalziel* [1943] Ch. 277.

[569] *Re Chardon* [1928] Ch. 464 at 470; *Re Wightwick's W.T.* [1950] Ch. 260 at 264, 265; *Re Chambers' W.T.* [1950] Ch. 267.

[570] When TLATA 1996 came into force: below, para.12–002.

[571] TLATA 1996 s.8(1); below, para.12–019.

way, it is possible that land may be made inalienable for the duration of the trust.[572]

9–161   **4. Exemption of charities.** Charities are exempt from the rule against inalienability; no gift for charitable purposes is void merely because it renders property inalienable in perpetuity.[573] Were this not so it would be virtually impossible to make gifts to charity, since the income, if not also the capital, would almost always be confined by some trust for use for the purposes of the charity only.

Part 4

ACCUMULATIONS

9–162   The rule against excessive accumulations, which is explained below, has been abolished in relation to instruments taking made after April 5, 2010,[574] subject to a minor exception.[575] It applies to instruments taking effect prior to April 6, 2010, and resembles the rule against inalienability in that it is directed against remoteness of control over property, whether or not vested in a beneficiary, rather than against remoteness of vesting.

The principle at common law was that accumulations of income could validly be directed only for so long as property might validly be rendered inalienable.[576] These two restrictions therefore originally went hand in hand. However, they parted company when the Accumulations Act 1800 drastically cut down the period allowed for accumulation, without affecting the rest of the law about inalienability. The Act was the sequel to the famous case of *Thellusson v Woodford*.[577] The "Thellusson Act", as it was often called, was stigmatised by Lord Cranworth L.C. as being "one perhaps of the most ill-drawn Acts to be found in our statute book".[578] Mr Thellusson had by his will directed that the income of his property should be accumulated at compound interest during the lives of his sons, grandsons and great-grandchildren living at his death, and that on the death of the survivor the accumulated fund should be divided among certain of his descendants. Because this direction was confined to lives in being, it was held to be valid. However, as it was

---

[572] But see below, para.12–019.

[573] *Chamberlayne v Brockett* (1872) 8 Ch.App. 206 at 211. A charitable trust established in 1585 was upheld in *Att Gen v Webster* (1875) L.R. 20 Eq. 483.

[574] PAA 2009 ss.13, 15(1). Wills executed prior to April 6, 2010 remain subject to the previous law: PAA 2009 s.15(1)(a); as do instruments made in exercise of a special power of appointment if the instrument creating the power took effect before that date: PAA 2009 s.15(1)(b).

[575] PAA 2009 s.14; below, para.9–171.

[576] See *Thellusson v Woodford* (1799) 4 Ves. 227 at 317, 318, 338, 339; (1805) 11 Ves. 112 at 146, 147.

[577] (1799) 4 Ves. 227; (1805) 11 Ves. 112. See the discussion of Thellusson and his will at (1974) 118 S.J. 544, 560.

[578] *Tench v Cheese* (1855) 6 De G.M. & G. 453 at 460 per Lord Cranworth L.C.; and see *Edwards v Tuck* (1853) 3 De G.M. & G. 40 at 55 ("Lord Loughborough's Act").

calculated that the accumulated fund would probably amount to many millions of pounds,[579] Parliament intervened to prevent other testators or settlors afflicting their successors with compulsory hoarding upon this scale.[580]

The common law rule was that a direction to accumulate was valid if it was confined to the perpetuity period,[581] so that in theory Mr Thellusson might have effectively directed accumulation for a further 21 years. However, at that time, the principle that an extra 21 years is always available had not been firmly settled.[582] The normal perpetuity period was therefore considered to be excessively long in the case of accumulations, and the statutory rules cut it down severely.

Few other jurisdictions adopted a rule against excessive accumulations even though most have a rule against perpetuities. Not only are the assumptions that underlie the rule questionable, but also the operation of the rule restricting accumulations is needlessly complicated and its application can be capricious. It has caused considerable difficulty in the administration of many trusts, especially pension trusts. As mentioned above, all of the statutory restrictions on accumulations that are explained below have been repealed in relation to instruments made after April 5, 2010,[583] but continue to apply to instruments made prior to April 6, 2010.[584]

A. The Statutory Periods

1. The periods. The law applicable to instruments made before April 6, 2010, is contained in the Law of Property Act 1925[585] and the 1964 Act. If the disposition took effect before July 16, 1964, so that only the 1925 Act applied to it, accumulation of income could not be directed by any person,[586] either expressly or impliedly,[587] for longer than one (not more[588]) of the following periods.

   (i) The life of the grantor or settlor.

9–163

---

[579] Challis 201; Marsden 321. Under favourable circumstances less than £750,000 might have produced over £100,000,000 by the end of the period. In fact, owing to mismanagement and the costs of litigation, the fund actually accumulated was comparatively small: H.E.L. vii, 230; and see (1965) 62 L.S.Gaz. 613; (1970) 21 N.I.L.Q. 131 (G. W. Keeton); (1994) 45 N.I.L.Q. 13 (P. Polden).

[580] *See Re Earl of Berkeley* [1968] Ch. 744 at 780, approving this statement.

[581] *Harrison v Harrison* (1786) cited 4 Ves. 338; *Wilson v Wilson* (1851) 1 Sim. (N.S.) 288 at 298; Marsden 314; Challis 201.

[582] Above, para.9–016; Challis 201.

[583] PAA 2009 ss.13, 15(1). The provisions repealed are LPA 1925, ss.164–166; and PAA 1964 s.13.

[584] Including both wills and instruments made in exercise of a special power of appointment if the instrument creating the power took effect before April 6, 2010.

[585] LPA 1925, ss.164–166 (replacing with amendments the Accumulations Acts 1800 and 1892).

[586] This means a natural person not a corporation: *Re Dodwell & Co Ltd's Trust* [1979] Ch. 301, holding that the Act of 1800 was framed in terms of natural persons only and that LPA 1925, being a consolidating Act, did not alter the law.

[587] *See Re Rochford's S.T.* [1965] Ch. 111.

[588] *Re Errington* (1897) 76 L.T. 616.

(ii) 21 years from the death of the grantor, settlor or testator.

(iii) The minority or respective minorities only of any person or persons living or *en ventre sa mere* at the death of the grantor, settlor or testator.

(iv) The minority or respective minorities only of any person or persons who, under the limitations of the instrument directing accumulation, would for the time being, if of full age, be entitled to the income directed to be accumulated.[589]

The 1964 Act added two further periods in the case of dispositions taking effect after July 15, 1964 and before April 6, 2009.

(v) 21 years from the making of the disposition.

(vi) The minority or respective minorities of any person or persons in being at that date.[590]

In other words, where the 1964 Act applies, it allows periods (ii) and (iii) to run from the date of a settlement inter vivos, as well as from the death of the settlor. Previously it appeared arbitrary that those periods could run only from the date of death.[591]

9–164   **2. Choice of periods.** The question which period has been chosen in any particular case is one of construction.[592] The first two periods cause little difficulty. As regards the first, it is the only period of a life available for accumulation, and it must be the life of the grantor or settlor himself and not of some other person.[593] The second period is a fixed term of years which starts to run at the beginning of the day after the testator's death and expires at the end of the 21st anniversary of his death.[594] Thus if a testator directed accumulation to start at the end of an interval after his death and to continue for 21 years, he would have exceeded the second period.[595]

9–165   **3. The periods of minorities.** The third, fourth and sixth periods are all minorities. Minority now ends at the age of 18.[596] But this does not affect the validity of directions for accumulation in dispositions made before 1970 with reference to the earlier period of minority ending at 21.[597]

---

[589] LPA 1925 s.164(1).
[590] PAA 1964 s.13.
[591] See e.g. *Re Bourne's S.T.* [1946] 1 All E.R. 411 at 415, 416; *Jagger v Jagger* (1883) 25 Ch D 729 at 733.
[592] *Jagger v Jagger* (1883) 25 Ch D 729; see e.g. *Re Watt's W.T.* [1936] 2 All E.R. 1555.
[593] *Re Lady Rosslyn's Trust* (1848) 16 Sim. 391.
[594] *Gorst v Lowndes* (1841) 11 Sim. 434; *Att Gen v Poulden* (1844) 3 Hare 555.
[595] *Webb v Webb* (1840) 2 Beav.493.
[596] Family Law Reform Act 1969 s.1. The Act does not change the second and fifth periods of 21 years but only the meaning of "minority", "infancy", "full age" and similar expressions.
[597] Family Law Reform Act 1969 Sch.3, para.7; SI 1969/1140.

The third period and (where it applies) the sixth period differ from the fourth period in the following respects.

(a) Living minors. The third and sixth periods are confined to the minorities **9–166** of persons alive or *en ventre sa mere* at the death of the settlor or at the date of the settlement, as the case may be. The fourth period is not confined in this way.[598]

(b) Beneficiaries. The third and sixth periods are not confined to the **9–167** minorities of those who are prospectively entitled to any benefit under the gift, whereas the fourth period is confined to the minorities of those who can say "but for my minority I should be entitled to the income which is being accumulated".[599]

(c) Successive minorities. The third and sixth periods can never exceed a **9–168** single minority, because even if accumulation is directed during a large number of minorities, the period is in effect merely the longest of these minorities. Nor can any accumulation continue under them for longer than the second period, except where a child is *en ventre sa mere* at the relevant time. Under the fourth period, on the other hand, accumulation is possible during the minorities of persons unborn at the time of the gift.[600] These minorities may be successive, because any beneficiary's interest may be made subject to accumulation during his own minority.[601]

(d) Purchase of land. Where accumulation is directed for the sole[602] **9–169** purpose of purchasing land, only the fourth period may be selected.[603] But this restriction does not apply to accumulations to be held as capital money under the Settled Land Act 1925.[604]

4. Application of rules. These rules apply whether the limitations were **9–170** contained in a deed or a will,[605] whether the accumulation is at simple or compound interest,[606] whether there is a positive direction or a mere power to accumulate,[607] and whether the whole or any part of the income of a fund is to be accumulated.[608]

---

[598] See *Sidney v Wilmer* (1863) 4 De.G.J. & S. 84.

[599] See *Jagger v Jagger* (1883) 25 Ch D 729 at 733, as corrected in *Re Cattell* [1914] 1 Ch. 177 at 189.

[600] See *Re Cattell,* above, at 189.

[601] For successive accumulations, see the previous edition of this work at para.9–159.

[602] *Re Knapp* [1929] 1 Ch. 341.

[603] LPA 1925 s.166(1).

[604] LPA 1925 s.166(2).

[605] *Re Lady Rosslyn's Trust* (1848) 16 Sim. 391.

[606] *Re Hawkins* [1916] 2 Ch. 570 at 577; *Re Garside* [1919] 1 Ch. 132 at 137; and see PAA 1964 s.13(2).

[607] *Re Robb* [1953] Ch. 459; *Baird v Lord Advocate* [1979] A.C. 666; PAA 1964 s.13(2).

[608] *Re Travis* [1900] 2 Ch. 541 (surplus income).

9–171   **5. Restrictions on accumulations under the 2009 Act.** As has been explained, the 2009 Act has abolished the rule against excessive accumulations in relation to instruments made after April 5, 2010, by repealing the statutory provisions that imposed the rule.[609]

In relation to trusts for charitable purposes, the 2009 Act imposes one restriction upon the otherwise unfettered power of trustees to accumulate.[610] If an instrument to which the 2009 Act applies, provides for property to be held on trust for charitable purposes, and imposes a duty or confers power upon the trustees to accumulate for more than 21 years, that duty or power ceases at the end of 21 years from the day when it commenced,[611] unless the instrument provides for the power or duty to terminate on the death of the settlor or of one of the settlors, determined by name or by the order of their deaths.[612] If charity trustees wish to accumulate for more than the 21-year statutory period, they must obtain the consent of the court or the Charity Commission for England and Wales.[613]

B. Excessive Accumulation

9–172   **1. Exceeding perpetuity period.** If the period for which accumulation is directed may possibly exceed the perpetuity period, the direction to accumulate is totally void.[614] This is the original common law rule, and it applies to instruments made before April 6, 2010. This applies even to accumulations for the benefit of charities.[615]

The 1964 Act appears to have left this rule of common law unaltered. Although it might have been expected that the "wait and see" principle would be applied, the Act contained no such provision.[616]

2. Exceeding accumulation period

9–173   *(a) Excess void.* If the period for which accumulation is directed cannot exceed the perpetuity period but exceeds the relevant accumulation period, the direction to accumulate is good *pro tanto* and only the excess over the appropriate accumulation period is void.[617] The statutory provisions merely cut down the wider powers permitted by common law.[618]

---

[609] Above, para.9–162.

[610] PAA 2009 s.14.

[611] PAA 2009 ss.14(1), (3), (4).

[612] PAA 2009 s.14(5).

[613] PAA 2009 s.14(2).

[614] *Marshall v Holloway* (1820) 2 Swans. 432; *Boughton v James* (1844) 1 Coll.C.C. 26 at 45.

[615] *Martin v Maugham* (1844) 14 Sim. 230.

[616] PAA 1964 s.3(1) applies only where an interest may vest too remotely. Remote vesting was not the basis of the rule against accumulations: above, para.9–162. For fuller discussion, see para.9–162 of the previous edition of this work.

[617] Challis 202, 203; *Griffiths v Vere* (1803) 9 Ves. 127; *Eyre v Marsden* (1838) 2 Keen 564 (affirmed 4 My. & Cr. 231).

[618] *Leake v Robinson* (1817) 2 Mer. 363 at 389.

As has been explained above, in the one case under the 2009 Act where a restriction is placed upon trustees' powers to accumulate—where the trust is a charitable trust—the Act adopts the same approach.[619] Any power or duty to accumulate is good for 21 years and thereafter void.

(b) Appropriate period. In determining the appropriate period, the starting **9–174** point is to ascertain which of the periods the testator or settlor seemingly had in mind,[620] if, indeed, he had any in mind.[621] Thus, where accumulation is directed by a deed made inter vivos for the lifetime of someone other than the settlor, accumulation takes place during the first of the periods, i.e. during the period common to the lives of the settlor and the named person.[622] However, the first period is clearly inapplicable to accumulations directed by will, and in a case such as the above arising under a will, the second period is the most appropriate. Accumulation will therefore take place for 21 years from the testator's death if the named person so long lives.[623] The second period is also the most appropriate where a will has directed accumulation for a period of years,[624] or, until X is 25,[625] or from the time Y remarries until her death,[626] or from the death of either A or B until the death of the survivor,[627] or, in some cases, during an inappropriate minority.[628] In each of these cases, if accumulation is still continuing 21 years after the death of the settlor or testator, it must cease forthwith even if it has been proceeding for only a short period, e.g. two years.[629]

(c) Minorities. If property was given by will to all the children of X (a living **9–175** person) who attain their majority, and accumulation of the whole fund is directed while any child of X is a minor:

(i) The first two periods are clearly not intended.

(ii) The fourth is not appropriate, because the accumulation is directed to continue for as long as any child is a minor even if some of the children are of full age. Even though the latter children are of full age, they are not entitled to the income to be accumulated within the wording of the fourth period.

---

[619] PAA 2009 s.14; above, para.9–171.

[620] The question is determined "by reference to the language employed and the facts of the case": *Re Watt's W.T.* [1936] 2 All E.R. 1555 at 1562, per Bennett J.

[621] See *Re Ransome* [1957] Ch. 348 at 361.

[622] *Re Lady Rosslyn's Trust* (1848) 16 Sim. 391.

[623] *Griffiths v Vere* (1803) 9 Ves. 127; *Talbot v Jevers* (1875) L.R. 20 Eq. 255 (for A's life or such portion of it as the rules of law will permit).

[624] *Longdon v Simson* (1806) 12 Ves. 295 at 298.

[625] *Crawley v Crawley* (1835) 7 Sim. 427; and see *Carey's Trustees v Rose* 1957 S.C. 252 (trust for unborn person on attaining full age).

[626] *Weatherall v Thornburgh* (1878) 8 Ch D 261.

[627] *Webb v Webb* (1840) 2 Beav.493.

[628] *Re Ransome* [1957] Ch. 348.

[629] *Shaw v Rhodes* (1836) 1 My. & Cr. 135.

(iii) The third period is the most appropriate. So far as it is exceeded the direction is void; accumulation will therefore cease as soon as all children living at the testator's death are of full age.[630]

9–176 *(d) The 1964 Act.* In the case of settlements made inter vivos after July 15, 1964 but before April 6, 2010, the fifth or sixth periods may be appropriate.

C. Surplus Income

1. Person entitled

9–177 *(a) Under the 1925 and 1964 Acts.* Where a direction to accumulate is void, either wholly or partially, the income so released passes to the persons who would have been entitled had no such accumulation been directed.[631] Thus if a beneficiary is entitled in possession to the enjoyment of the property or to its income, subject only to an excessive trust for accumulation, that beneficiary will be entitled to any income not validly accumulated.[632] For example, where property is given by will to X, subject to a direction that the income exceeding a certain figure is to be accumulated during X's life for the benefit of Y, the accumulation must cease 21 years after the testator's death and the surplus income will go to X.[633] Where there is no such person, as, for example, if X is given a mere annuity of a certain sum and excessive accumulation of the surplus is directed, the surplus after 21 years reverts to the settlor or his estate,[634] or in the case of a will may pass under a residuary gift,[635] or, in default, go to the persons entitled on intestacy.[636]

9–178 *(b) Under the 2009 Act.* It has been explained that, where trustees of a charitable trust may or must accumulate income, the 2009 Act normally restricts the duration of that power or duty to 21 years.[637] After the termination of the power or duty, the income to which the duty or power would otherwise have applied, must either go to the person who would have been entitled to it, or be applied for the purposes for which it would have had to be applied, if there had been no duty or power to accumulate.[638]

9–179 **2. No acceleration.** There is no acceleration of subsequent interests.[639] Thus a remainderman whose interest is not to fall into possession until the

---

[630] *Re Watt's W.T.* [1936] 2 All E.R. 1555.
[631] LPA 1925 s.164(1); *Green v Gascoyne* (1865) 4 De G.J. & S. 565; *Beard v Shadler* [2011] EWHC 114 (Ch).
[632] *Combe v Hughes* (1865) 2 De G.J. & S. 657.
[633] *Trickey v Trickey* (1832) 3 My. & K. 560.
[634] *Re O'Hagen* [1932] W.N. 188.
[635] *O'Neill v Lucas* (1838) 2 Keen 3 13; *Ellis v Maxwell* (1841) 3 Beav.587; *Re Ransome* [1957] Ch. 348. The income is treated as income of the residue, not as capital, as between tenant for life and remainderman: *Morgan v Morgan* (1851) 4 De G. & Sm. 164; *Re Garside* [1919] 1 Ch. 132; and see [1979] Conv. 423 (J. G. Riddall).
[636] *Mathews v Keble* (1868) 3 Ch.App. 691; *Re Walpole* [1933] Ch. 431.
[637] PAA 2009 s.14; above, para.9–171.
[638] PAA 2009 s.14(6).
[639] *Green v Gascoyne* (1865) 4 De G.J. & S. 565 at 569; see *Re Parry* (1889) 60 L.T. 489.

dcath of a life annuitant cannot claim surplus income arising before the annuitant's death.[640] The statutory rules do not alter any disposition made by the testator except his direction to accumulate.[641]

D. The Rule in Saunders v Vautier[642]

1. The rule. Under this rule a beneficiary of full age who has an absolute, **9–180** vested and indefeasible interest in property may at any time, notwithstanding any direction to accumulate, require the transfer of the property to him and terminate any accumulation. A person may do as he likes with his own, and the court will not enforce a mere restraint on his enjoyment of the property if that restraint cannot benefit any other person.[643] Thus if property is given absolutely to A, aged 10, with a direction to accumulate the income for his benefit until he is 24, A can demand payment of both the original property and the accumulations as soon as he is of full age.[644]

2. Operation. The rule applies equally where a number of adult bene- **9–181** ficiaries seeking to put an end to an accumulation together comprise every person who has any vested or contingent interest in the property[645]; and it applics to charitics.[646] But it will not apply if there is a gift to a class of persons[647] or charities[648] not yet determined. This remained true, at common law, even if an increase in the class was most improbable, e.g. dependant on a woman of 65 having another child.[649] But the 1964 Act applies its presumptions as to "future parenthood", already explained,[650] in cases where the disposition took effect after July 15, 1964 but before April 6, 2010.[651] An accumulation cannot be terminated at the sole request of a beneficiary whose interest is future, contingent or in any way limited, because in all such cases there are bound to be other persons interested in the accumulation, either actually or potentially.[652] Where the rule in *Saunders v Vautier* does apply, it makes any trust for accumulation precarious. As regards trusts created prior to

---

[640] See *Weatherall v Thornburgh* (1878) 8 Ch D 261 at 269, 271, 272; *Berry v Geen* [1938] A.C. 575; *Re Robb* [1953] Ch. 459.

[641] *Eyre v Marsden* (1838) 2 Keen. 564 at 574, affirmed 4 My. & Cr. 231.

[642] (1841) 4 Beav.1 15, affirmed Cr. & Ph. 240.

[643] See *Gosling v Gosling* (1859) Johns. 265 at 272.

[644] *Josselyn v Josselyn* (1837) 9 Sim. 63.

[645] See *Berry v Geen* [1938] A.C. 575 at 582.

[646] *Wharton v Masterman* [1895] A.C. 186.

[647] *Green v Gascoyne* (1865) 4 De G.J. & S. 565.

[648] *Re Jefferies* [1936] 2 All E.R. 626; there is no such entity as "charity": *Re Jefferies*.

[649] *Re Deloitte* [1926] Ch. 56.

[650] Above, para.9–043.

[651] PAA 1964 s.14.

[652] See *Eyre v Marsden* (1839) 4 My. & Cr. 23 1; *M'Donald v Bryce* (1838) 2 Keen 276. As to determination of an accumulation of surplus income subject to an annuity (which may raise difficult questions as to the precise rights of the annuitant, who may have an interest in the accumulation if a deficiency of income in any year may be made up out of the accumulated fund), see *Re Travis* [1900] 2 Ch. 541 at 548; *Wharton v Masterman* [1895] A.C. 186; *Harbin v Masterman* [1896] 1 Ch. 351; *Berry v Geen* [1938] A.C. 575; *Re Coller's Deed Trusts* [1939] Ch. 277.

April 6, 2010, this is so, whether or not the trust to accumulate is confined to one of the permitted periods.[653]

E. Exceptions from the Rule against Accumulations

9–182   Where the rule against excessive accumulations applies,[654] it is subject to the following exceptions.

9–183   **1. Payment of debts:** a provision for accumulation for the payment of the debts of any person.[655] By the terms of the Act this exception includes an accumulation directed for the payment of any debts, whether of the settlor or testator, or any other person.[656] Indeed, an accumulation for the payment of the debts of the settlor or testator is valid even if it may exceed the perpetuity period.[657] Such a direction can cause little mischief, because the creditors may terminate the accumulation at any time by demanding payment.[658] However, an accumulation to pay the debts of any other person (though not the National Debt[659]) must be confined within the perpetuity period.[660]

The exception extends only to debts deriving from an existing source of obligation.[661] The accumulation must be directed bona fide for their payment.[662] Subject to this, the exception may extend both to existing and to contingent debts,[663] as where the object of the accumulation is to discharge a mortgage[664] or to provide for liability under a leasehold covenant not yet broken.[665]

9–184   **2. Portions:** a provision for accumulation for raising portions for any issue of the grantor, settlor or testator or any person to whom an interest is limited under the settlement.[666] Because this is a statutory exception from the rule against accumulations only, such accumulations must be confined to the perpetuity period.[667]

---

[653] *Wharton v Masterman* [1895] A.C. 186 at 200.

[654] As explained, subject to one limited exception there are no restrictions on powers or duties to accumulate in most instruments which take effect on or after April 6, 2010: see above, para.9–162.

[655] LPA 1925 s.164(2)(i).

[656] *Viscount Barrington v Liddell* (1852) 2 De G.M. & G. 480 at 497, 498.

[657] *Lord Southampton v Marquis of Hertford* (1813) 2 V & B. 54 at 65; *Bateman v Hotchkin* (1847) 10 Beav.426.

[658] Gray, § 676.

[659] Superannuation and other Trust Funds (Validation) Act 1927 s.9.

[660] See *Viscount Barrington v Liddell* (1852) 2 De G.M. & G. 480 at 498; Marsden 344.

[661] *Re Rochford's S.T.* [1965] Ch. 111 (accumulation for paying estate duty on deaths of living persons not exempted).

[662] *Mathews v Keble* (1868) 3 Ch.App. 691 at 697.

[663] *Varlo v Faden* (1859) 1 De. G.F. & J. 211 at 224, 225.

[664] *Bateman v Hotchkin* (1847) 10 Beav.426 at 433.

[665] *Re Hurlbatt* [1910] 2 Ch. 553.

[666] LPA 1925 s.164(2)(ii).

[667] For a fuller treatment of this exception, see the previous edition of this work at para.9–173.

3. Timber or wood: a provision for accumulation of the produce of timber   **9–185**
or wood.[668] Although expressly excepted from the statutory accumulation
rules, such a direction will be void if it can exceed the perpetuity period.[669]

4. Minority: accumulations made during a minority under the general law   **9–186**
or any statutory power.[670] While the person entitled to any trust property is a
minor, a statutory power is given to the trustees to apply the income for his
maintenance with duty to accumulate the residue of the income.[671] The period
of such accumulation is to be disregarded when determining the period for
which accumulations are permitted.[672] Thus if a testator directs accumulation
for 21 years after his death and the beneficiary at the end of this period is a
minor, the accumulations both for the 21 years and during the minority are
valid.[673]

5. Maintenance of property: a provision for maintaining property at its   **9–187**
present value.[674] If the property is of a wasting nature, it may be kept up out
of income. This is not "accumulation" within the meaning of the Law of
Property Act 1925, because the property is never augmented, even though
income is added to capital.[675] This head is accordingly not a true exception to
the rule but merely a case in which there is no real accumulation. Thus
directions made prior to April 6, 2010 to devote surplus income to maintaining
buildings in a proper state of repair[676] (as distinct from building new
houses[677]), or to apply a fixed annual sum to keep up a "sinking fund"
insurance policy to replace the capital lost by the expiry of leaseholds,[678] are
outside the statutory rules against accumulations.[679] However, an accumulation for replacing the capital lost in payment of estate duty is not within this
exception, at any rate if it extends to more than a reasonable proportion of the
income.[680]

Dispositions falling within this exception are confined to the perpetuity
period.[681]

---

[668] LPA 1925 s.164(2)(iii). This exception is said to be due to the need for naval timber in 1800:
Marsden, *Perpetuities*, p.346, who also cites Pepys's dictum that "timber is an excrescence of the
earth, provided by God for the payment of debts".
[669] *Ferrand v Wilson* (1845) 4 Hare 344.
[670] LPA 1925 s.165.
[671] TA 1925 s.31. They had to do so in any case, unless otherwise empowered, owing to the
inability of a minor to give a binding receipt (as to minor's disabilities, see below. para.36–002.
A married minor may now give a valid receipt under LPA 1925 s.21.
[672] LPA 1925 s.165.
[673] *Re Maher* [1928] Ch. 88.
[674] *Re Gardiner* [1901] 1 Ch. 697 at 699, 700.
[675] *Re Gardiner* [1901] 1 Ch. 697 at 699, 700. *A fortiori* if surplus income is not added to
capital but is merely retained to meet possible future deficiencies of income for paying annuities:
Re Earl of Berkeley [1968] Ch. 744.
[676] *Vine v Raleigh* [1891] 2 Ch. 13; *Re Mason* [1891] 3 Ch. 467.
[677] *Vine v Raleigh* [1891] 2 Ch. 13 at 26.
[678] *Re Gardiner* [1901] 1 Ch. 697.
[679] For other examples, see *Bassil v Lister* (1851) 9 Hare 177 at 184.
[680] *Re Rochford's S.T* [1965] Ch. 111
[681] *Curtis v Lukin* (1842) 5 Beav.147.

9–188   **6. Certain commercial contracts:** transactions which cannot fairly be described as settlements or dispositions. The Law of Property Act 1925 merely provided that no person might "settle or dispose"[682] of property in breach of the restrictions against accumulations, and there are many commercial transactions involving accumulation which are not properly within these terms, e.g. partnership agreements providing for the accumulation of certain profits,[683] certain policies of life insurance,[684] investment trusts which capitalise part of their income[685] and the statutory trusts upon which certain service charges must be held.[686] Such transactions, and provisions for making payments (e.g. of premiums) in respect of them, were accordingly always outside the rule; and most of them also fell outside the perpetuity rule as being mere personal obligations sounding in contract.[687]

---

[682] LPA 1925 s.164(1).
[683] See *Bassil v Lister* (1851) 9 Hare 177 at 184.
[684] *Bassil v Lister* (1851) 9 Hare 177 at 184.
[685] *Re A.E.G. Unit Trust (Managers) Ltd's Deed* [1957] Ch. 415.
[686] *Retirement Care Group Ltd v HMRC* (2007) SP00607 at [20] (Special Commissioners). For the statutory trusts, see LTA 1987 s.42; below, para.19–088.
[687] See above, para.9–130.

THE USE OF TRUSTS IN THE LAW OF REAL PROPERTY

This chapter examines the use of the trust in the law of real property. It serves **10–001** as an introduction to the material considered in the following chapters: the express and implied creation of trusts of land (Chapter 11); the operation of the Trusts of Land and Appointment of Trustees Act 1996 (Chapter 12); and the law of concurrent co-ownership (Chapter 13). There is also a link with the Appendix, which contains an examination of settlements regulated by the Settled Land Act 1925, being those created after 1925 and before 1997.

There is a long history of the use of the trust in the law of real property, but **10–002** it has always played a central role in relation to the creation and operation of successive and concurrent co-ownership interests. Traditionally, the trust has been the tool through which a settlor can ensure that land devolves in succession to named individuals or a class of individuals,[1] often members of his family, or through which two or more people can enjoy simultaneously the fruits of land ownership, be that possession or investment income. In serving these needs, the trust is no less important today, albeit that there is the added attraction that the trust can also be used to minimise fiscal liability, ring-fence assets and facilitate the full economic exploitation of property rights through securitisation and asset backed securities. Much of this law is outside the scope of the present work. This role of this chapter is to introduce the legal framework and background for the analysis to follow.

Successive and concurrent co-ownership. The law concerning the use of **10–003** the trust in the law of successive and concurrent co-ownership of land has never been static, and this chapter will examine some of the history of the subject in order to better explain the present law. The present law is found in the Trusts of Land and Appointment of Trustees Act 1996 and this represented

---

[1] Subject to questions of perpetuity, which were once of considerable importance, but whose impact is much reduced by the Perpetuities and Accumulations Act 2009, see below Ch.9.

a significant break with the past by introducing a unitary system of trusts of land to govern both successive and concurrent co-ownership. This Act is considered in detail in Chapter 12, but the "trust of land" that it establishes in fact built on concepts and ideas already known to the law, especially the trust for sale of land[2] which could be used for both concurrent and successive co-ownership until 1997.

Part 1

Section 1. Settlements and trusts for sale prior to 1926

10–004   Traditionally, the word "settlement" has been employed in a general sense for all kinds of arrangements by which property was given to particular persons in succession. If A by his will left property to B for life with remainder to C in fee simple, that was a simple type of settlement. Whenever a donor created a limited interest (an interest less than a fee simple absolute) there was usually a settlement, since someone would or might be entitled in succession after the limited interest.[3] The essence of a settlement was a series of interests created by a single gift, whether by deed or will. Almost all of the examples given in the chapter on perpetuities were also examples of settlements and the question under the old law of perpetuities was whether certain remainders and other rights could exist at all.[4] The more elaborate types of settlement, such as the old-fashioned marriage settlement,[5] were the product of the settlor's desire to keep his land in the family and to make appropriate provision for the various members of the family who would not inherit the land itself. Such transactions had long ago become fiscally disadvantageous and were very uncommon by the time that settlements were prospectively abolished by the Trusts of Land and Appointment of Trustees Act 1996.

In the course of time, two distinct methods of settling land had come into general use: the strict settlement and the trust for sale. The term "strict settlement" was an appropriate description of the complicated type of family settlement which flourished before statute intervened, but in essence the term "settlement" came to be used in a special sense to mean any settlement which was *not* made by way of trust for sale.

Section 2. The strict settlement before 1926

10–005   **1. Evils of settlements.**[6] The classical strict settlement was devised to preserve a family estate intact through succeeding generations. In its simplest

---

[2] See below, para.10–007.

[3] Leases were an exception, and did not normally give rise to settlements: below, para.A–044.

[4] See Ch.9 and the changes made by the Perpetuities and Accumulations Act 2009.

[5] See the fifth edition of this work at p.411.

[6] For a fuller account, see the fifth edition of this work at p.312; and B. English and J. Saville, *Strict Settlement: A Guide for Historians* (Hull, Hull University Press, 1983), Ch.1.

form, a testator granted the land to A (his eldest son) for life, with remainder to A's eldest son in tail.[7] The settlement would also commonly contain provision for other members of the family[8] which was usually raised by mortgaging the land, thereby burdening the property with debt. A's eldest son could not alienate the land until he came of age, when he might bar the entail. If A were still alive, his consent to the barring was required, otherwise the son could create no more than a base fee. In practice, this consent would not be forthcoming and, as the son usually needed ready money, he would come to an agreement with A. A would grant his son some immediate share (perhaps an annual income) in return for the resettlement of the land on A for life, remainder to the son for life, remainder to the son's eldest son in tail.

So long as this process of settlement and resettlement continued, no person of full age ever had more than a life estate in the land. The life tenant could alienate his own life interest but had no power to sell or lease the land. In general, any improvements to the land had to be met out of his own pocket. Although extensive powers of management and even of sale might be conferred by the settlement, the practice was not universal. In the absence of such powers, the land might be rendered both unmanageable and inalienable. During the course of the 19th century, the fetters were gradually removed from settled land by a series of statutes. These culminated in the Settled Land Act 1882.[9]

2. The Settled Land Act 1882. The general scheme of the Settled Land Act 1882[10] was to give the tenant for life under the settlement wide powers of dealing with the land free from the trusts of the settlement without the consent of the other beneficiaries, or application to the court, just as if he were the owner in fee simple. The rights of beneficiaries were protected in the case of a sale by shifting the settlement from the land to the purchase-money, which had to be paid to the trustees or into court. The purchaser would have no concern with the trusts of the settlement. The main features of the Act were as follows.   **10–006**

   (i) It applied to any land or estate or interest in land, which under any document stood for the time being limited to, or in trust for, any persons by way of succession.[11] It was immaterial whether the interests were legal or equitable.

---

[7] Further more restrictive limitations would have violated the perpetuity rules: above, paras 9–015, 9–111.

[8] e.g. annuities for widows ("jointures") and lump sums for younger children ("portions").

[9] At this point, we should note also that, prior to 1926, the legal estate in settled land might either be split up between beneficiaries or vested in trustees according to the way in which the settlement was made. For an excellent account of the changes in the law of settled land, see A. Underhill's lecture, printed in *A Century of Law Reform* (1901), pp.281–297, and *Select Essays in Anglo-American Legal History* (1909) III, pp.674–686.

[10] There is a full account of the Act in the fifth edition of this work at pp.317–324.

[11] SLA 1882 s.2. It also applied to land held by, or in trust for, infants; SLA 1882 s.59.

(ii) Wide powers of sale, exchange, leasing, mortgaging and otherwise dealing with the land were given to the tenant for life or other limited owner in possession.[12] In exercising those powers, the life tenant was deemed to be in the position of a trustee and was required to "have regard to the interests of all parties entitled under the settlement".[13]

(iii) Although additional powers could be conferred on the life tenant by the settlement, any provision in it which purported to take away or cut down his statutory powers, either directly or indirectly, was void.[14]

(iv) There was an elaborate definition of the persons who were to be the trustees of the settlement.[15] Normally they consisted of the persons expressly appointed as trustees. Although the legal estate might in certain circumstances be vested in them,[16] they had no real control over the land. Their main function was to receive and hold any capital, e.g. when land was sold.

(v) When the life tenant exercised his powers, and the settled land was for example sold, the rights of the beneficiaries were overreached (i.e. transferred from the land to the proceeds of sale), provided that the money was paid to the trustees (of whom there had to be not less than two), or into court.[17] It was immaterial for these purposes whether the legal estate was vested in the life tenant or in the trustees. Capital money in the hands of the trustees (which had to be invested in the manner provided for by the Act[18]) was treated as if it were the land "for all purposes of disposition, transmission, and devolution".[19] It made no difference that the purchaser had notice of the interests under the settlement. The statute provided that they were to be overreached, whether they were legal or equitable.[20]

Section 3. Trusts for sale

10–007   **1. Objects of trusts for sale.** A trust for sale was a trust which directed the trustees to sell the trust property, invest the proceeds, and hold the resulting

---

[12] SLA 1882 ss.3(i), 3(iii), 6, 18, and 2(5) respectively.
[13] SLA 1882 s.53.
[14] SLA 1882 s.51.
[15] SLA 1882 s.2(8); SLA 1890 s.16.
[16] This depended upon how the settlement was created.
[17] SLA 1882 ss.20, 22(1), 39(1).
[18] SLA 1882 s.21.
[19] SLA 1882 s.22(5).
[20] SLA 1882 s.20(2).

fund upon the trusts declared by the settlor.[21] Its objects and operation were therefore quite different from those of a strict settlement. Instead of aiming to preserve a family estate intact, as did the old strict settlement, the trust for sale set out by treating the property as potential money. Dividing it among the family was therefore easy, and there was the convenience that a mixed fund of land and personalty could be disposed of under the same set of trusts. This form of settlement was ideal for settling fortunes made in commerce, and for this reason, trusts for sale were sometimes called "traders' settlements".[22] They were of more recent origin than strict settlements, but reflected the importance of the merchant in the wider economy as compared to the landed gentry.[23]

2. Position pending sale. In a trust for sale, the legal estate was vested in **10–008** the trustees upon trust to sell the land and hold the income until sale and the proceeds thereafter upon specified trusts for the beneficiaries. The trustees were usually given power to postpone sale in their discretion, and to manage the land until sale. It followed that the trustees did not have to sell until market conditions were suitable. Often the consent of the beneficiaries entitled in possession was made a prerequisite to a sale, and in the meantime they could usually have the benefit of the property itself if they wished, whether by living in a house, or by enjoying the rents if it was let. The purchase-money arising on a sale was usually directed to be invested in stocks, shares and other securities,[24] and then held upon trusts for the members of the family. These trusts would often provide for life interests, widows' annuities, remainders to children, and so on, in much the same way as a strict settlement. There was one significant difference however: until 1926 no entail could be created under a trust for sale but only under a settlement.[25]

3. The doctrine of conversion. The effect of creating a trust for sale was **10–009** that even before sale the rights of beneficiaries were for certain purposes deemed to be rights in personalty. Equity treated as done that which ought to be done.[26] As soon as there was a binding obligation to sell, the interests of the beneficiaries were notionally converted into the money into which the land was destined to be converted. This was the equitable doctrine of conversion. Although its consequences were often followed out logically (there could, for example, be no entail under a trust for sale made before 1926 because

---

[21] It is still possible to create a trust for sale: TLATA 1996, s.1(2). However, it takes effect as a trust of land. There will therefore be little point in creating such a trust now. cf. below, para.12–005.

[22] For other situations in which trusts for sale were employed, see (1984) 100 L.Q.R. 86 at 87 (J. S. Anderson).

[23] See the fifth edition of this work at p.314.

[24] See Davidson, *Precedents in Conveyancing*, 3rd edn, III, pp.711, 712, 868.

[25] See below.

[26] See, e.g. *Lechmere v Earl of Carlisle* (1733) 3 P. Wms. 211 at 215; *Guidot v Guidot* (1745) 3 Atk. 254 at 256.

personalty was not entailable[27]) it was never an absolute rule to be applied in all circumstances.[28] The doctrine was a source of considerable difficulty and has now been abolished with retrospective effect.[29]

10–010   **4. The Settled Land Acts 1882 and 1884 and trusts for sale.** The Settled Land Act 1882 applied to land held upon trust for sale for the benefit of a person with a life or other limited interest.[30] The apparent effect was that all the powers, including that of sale, belonged to the life beneficiary and not to the trustees. The courts interpreted the legislation very narrowly,[31] and consternation among conveyancers led to a change in the law in the Settled Land Act 1884.[32] This provided that in the case of trusts for sale, the tenant for life should be unable to exercise the powers of the Act of 1882 without an order of the court, and that until such an order was made, the trustees could sell without the consent of the tenant for life.[33] A purchaser could safely deal with the trustees for sale unless such an order had been registered as a *lis pendens* (pending action).[34]

Although the Act of 1884 restored the trustees' power of sale it did not equip them with other powers of management (e.g. of leasing) which they might need if sale was postponed. Nor was this the only disadvantage of trusts for sale: they were unsatisfactory from a conveyancer's point of view.[35] In consequence, the practice developed towards the end of the 19th century of keeping trusts off the face of the title by making the trustees appear as absolute owners.[36] The device did not prove to be wholly successful.[37]

10–011   **5. Trust for sale or power of sale.** After the Act of 1884 it was essential for conveyancing purposes to distinguish between a trust for sale and other forms of settlement. If there was a trust for sale and no order of the court had been made, a purchaser could get a good title only from the trustees. In any other case he could obtain a good title only from the tenant for life. The distinction was not always a clear one. A mere power of sale given to trustees was not a trust for sale: there had to be an imperative obligation upon the trustees to sell and not merely a discretionary power. But trusts and powers

---

[27] Above, para.10–008.

[28] For a review of the substantial and often contradictory body of authority, see (1984) 100 L.Q.R. 86 (J. S. Anderson).

[29] See TLATA 1996 s.3(1), (3), subject to certain exceptions: TLATA 1996 ss.3(2), 18(3); below, para.12–006.

[30] s.63. This section was not included in the original Bill but was added during the passage through Parliament: 27 S.J. 113; 28 S.J. 703.

[31] See *Taylor v Poncia* (1884) 25 Ch D 646.

[32] s.7.

[33] SLA 1884 s.6(1).

[34] SLA 1884 s.7(vi).

[35] For example, the beneficiaries might have elected to take the land as land, so that the trustees could no longer sell. For this and other drawbacks, see J. S. Anderson, *Lawyers and the Making of English Land Law 1832–1940*, pp.269–273; and [1990] C.L.J. 277 at 283–286 (C.H.).

[36] See, e.g. *Re Chafer and Randall's Contract* [1916] 2 Ch. 258; *Re Soden and Alexandery Contract* [1918] 2 Ch. 258.

[37] J. S. Anderson, op. cit. p.271.

often shade into one another, and a trust to sell with a power to postpone sale had to be distinguished from a trust to retain with a power to sell; even words such as "upon trust to sell" might not create a trust for sale if from the context it was clear that a mere power was intended.[38] A trust "to retain or sell the land" was a borderline case: it might or might not be construed as a trust for sale, depending upon whether the general intention of the settlement was that the land should be sold[39] or that it should be retained as land.[40] In such a case it would be unclear to a purchaser who was entitled to sell the land: trustee (trust for sale) or tenant for life (all other cases).

6. Bare trusts. The Settled Land Acts never applied to a trust where one or more persons of full age were entitled in possession absolutely and there was no element of succession, whether there was a trust for sale or not.[41] Thus a conveyance "to A in fee simple in trust for B in fee simple" created a bare trust which was not within the Acts.[42] Bare trusts long remained outside the provisions of the 1925 property legislation which governed trusts for sale and settled land. However, after 1996, they take effect as a trust of land whenever created.[43]

10–012

Part 2

Section 1. The Settled Land Act 1925

The Settled Land Act 1925 continued the policy of the Act of 1882, making certain extensions and alterations to the statutory powers. In substance the position of a tenant for life was little changed. The powers contained in the 1882 Act (as amended) were repeated in the Act of 1925. However, as part of the wider design of the 1925 legislation to improve the system of conveyancing, important changes were made in the legal machinery by which settlements were made and settled land was disposed of. It should be emphasised that, subject to certain minor exceptions,[44] it has not been possible to create new settlements after 1996.[45] References to settlements under the 1925 Act are therefore to settlements created after 1925 but before 1997. A detailed analysis of the operation of the Settled Land Act 1925 is to be found in the Appendix. The following sections will consider only the principal attributes of settlements governed by the Settled Land Act 1925.

10–013

---

[38] *Re Hotchkys* (1886) 32 Ch D 408; *Re Newbould* (1913) 110 L.T. 6.
[39] *Re Johnson* [1915] 1 Ch. 435; and see *Re Crisp* (1907) 95 L.T. 865.
[40] *Re Whitey Settlement* [1930] 1 Ch. 179.
[41] See e.g. *Re Earle and Webster's Contract* (1883) 24 Ch D 144.
[42] See, e.g. *Re British Land Co and Allen's Contract* (1900) 44 S.J. 593.
[43] TLATA 1996 s.1(2).
[44] Below, para.12–002.
[45] TLATA 1996, s.2(1), (2).

Section 2. Principal Alterations Made by the Settled Land Act 1925

A. *Trusts for Sale were Excluded from the Act*

10–014   Land subject to "an immediate binding trust for sale"[46] was expressly excluded from the definition of settled land.[47] If a trust for sale arose, the Settled Land Act 1925 could not apply, even if the land was previously settled.[48]

B. *The Legal Estate was Normally in the Tenant for Life*

10–015   Before 1926 the legal estate in settled land was either vested in trustees or split between the beneficiaries. This depended on how the settlement was made.[49] In either case, the tenant for life was able to deal with it by his statutory powers. After 1925, apart from the exception stated below, the whole legal estate will always have been vested in the tenant for life; and that legal estate will usually have been a fee simple absolute in possession.[50] However, this estate has been given to the tenant for life not for his personal benefit (because he is a trustee of it, as he is of the other statutory privileges[51]) but to make the system of conveyancing more logical. Instead of being endowed with a power to sell or administer a legal fee simple which was held by the trustees, the tenant for life has been given the legal fee simple itself. But since he must be prevented from taking advantage of it except for proper purposes, his powers as fee simple owner are still restricted.[52] The result of these changes is to make it easier to trace the title to the legal estate (where it is unregistered), thereby improving the position of a purchaser.[53] Where a settlement was made after 1925, the legal estate had to be conveyed to the life tenant, unless, of course, it was already vested in him,[54] as where the owner of property settled it upon himself as tenant for life, with remainders over ("with remainders over" is a concise way of referring to the remainders following the life interest without setting them out in detail).

10–016   Any tenant for life under the Settled Land Act 1925 is therefore not only a trustee of the statutory powers, as he was before 1926, but is also a trustee of

---

[46] SLA 1925 s.117(1)(xxx), referring to LPA 1925 s.205(1)(xxix). The meaning of this phrase gave rise to some difficulty: see the fifth edition of this work at p.386.

[47] SLA 1925 s.1(7), added by LP(Am)A 1926, Sch. For a detailed account of trusts for sale (which were governed by LPA 1925), see the fifth edition of this work at p.385. See too below, para.10–020.

[48] e.g. where land was left to A for life thereafter to trustees for sale. The land ceased to be settled on A's death.

[49] Above, para.10–006.

[50] Above, para.6–008. Other interests in land (e.g. leaseholds) could also be settled, but they were less common.

[51] Below, Appendix, para.A–056.

[52] Below, Appendix, para.A–026.

[53] Below, Appendix, paras A–015 et seq.

[54] SLA 1925 s.4(2).

the legal estate. Both the powers[55] and the estate[56] are vested in him for himself and the other beneficiaries under the settlement. The tenant for life's trusteeship is however a "highly interested" one.[57] On the one hand, he must have regard to the interests of all parties under the settlement. The court can therefore intervene if he seeks to sell at a price well below the value of the property,[58] or effect any transaction which, although within his powers, will prejudice other beneficiaries.[59] Furthermore, any exercise of his powers which is not made bona fide will be restrained even though it may cause no pecuniary loss.[60] Against this, however, the tenant for life's fiduciary position is necessarily qualified by the fact that he is also a beneficiary, so that "he can legitimately exercise his powers with some, but not, of course, an exclusive, regard for his own personal interests, wishes and tastes".[61] The inherent conflict of interest in the tenant for life's position is one of the principal reasons why settlements were prospectively abolished by the Trusts of Land and Appointment of Trustees Act 1996.[62]

There are two cases in which the legal and statutory powers under a settlement are not vested in the tenant for life, but in the "statutory owner". They are as discussed below. Note, however, that under these provisions, the legal estate is never vested in the trustees of the settlement *as such*, but only in some other capacity, such as statutory owner,[63] or special personal representatives.[64]

1. Tenant for life a minor. A legal estate cannot be vested in a minor after   **10–017**
1925[65] and it would be undesirable to give him the statutory powers. Consequently where the person who would otherwise be the tenant for life is a minor, the legal estate and the statutory powers are vested in the "statutory owner" who is:

(i) any personal representative in whom the land is vested, providing no vesting instrument[66] has been executed[67]; but otherwise,

---

[55] SLA 1925 s.107(1).

[56] SLA 1925 s.16(1); see *Re Boston's W.T.* [1956] Ch. 395 (esp. at 405); (1956) 72 L.Q.R. 328 (R.E.M.). For the power of a tenant for life to acquire the settled land or part of it, see below, Appendix, para.A–007.

[57] *Re Earl of Stamford and Warrington* [1916] 1 Ch. 404 at 420, per Younger J.

[58] *Wheelwright v Walker (No.1)* (1883) 23 Ch D 752 at 762.

[59] See *Hampden v Earl of Buckinghamshire* [1893] 2 Ch. 531 at 544; and by way of example, *Re Earl Somers* (1895) 11 T.L.R. 567 (life tenant, who was a total abstainer, restrained from leasing a public house on terms that no intoxicating liquor should be sold there).

[60] *Middlemas v Stevens* [1901] 1 Ch. 574; and see *Dowager Duchess of Sutherland v Duke of Sutherland* [1893] 3 Ch. 169.

[61] *Re Boston's W.T.* [1956] Ch. 395 at 405, per Vaisey J.; and see (1956) 72 L.Q.R. 327 (R.E.M.). See too *Cardigan v Curzon-Howe* (1885) 30 Ch D 531 at 540.

[62] Below, para.12–003.

[63] Below

[64] Below, Appendix, para.A–019.

[65] LPA 1925 s.1(6); below, para.36–003.

[66] Below, para.10–019.

[67] Such cases will now be rare. It used to arise, e.g. where the settlement had been made by the will of a testator who had just died.

(ii) the trustees of the settlement.[68]

10–018   **2. No tenant for life**. Although there is usually a tenant for life, there are situations where there is not, e.g. where the first life interest is not to begin until marriage, or until after a period of accumulation. In such cases, the provisions of the 1925 Act are designed to ensure that the land can always be dealt with,[69] and preserve the principle that the legal estate and the managerial powers should not be separated. Thus, where under a settlement there is no tenant for life,[70] the legal estate and statutory powers are vested in the "statutory owner", who is:

(i) any person of full age upon whom the settlement expressly confers the powers[71]; but if there is none,

(ii) the trustees of the settlement.[72]

C. All Settlements Had to be Made by Two Documents

10–019   Before 1926 a settlement was usually made by one document. If the settlement was made by will, the will constituted the settlement. A settlement inter vivos was made by deed. This considerably complicated conveyancing transactions.[73] The Settled Land Act 1925 met these difficulties by adopting what had long been the practice of conveyancers in cases of trust for sale made inter vivos.[74] That practice was to draw two separate deeds (each referring to the other): a conveyance to the trustees upon trust to sell, and a trust instrument declaring the trusts of the proceeds of sale. When the land was sold, the purchaser took the conveyance and the trustees retained the trust instrument.

The two documents made necessary by the Act were a vesting instrument (or, where the title was registered, a transfer in lieu of a vesting instrument),[75] and a trust instrument.[76] The vesting instrument contained all the information to which a purchaser was entitled. The trust instrument set out the details of the settlement and any purchaser would not normally be concerned with them.

---

[68] SLA 1925 ss.26 (powers) and 117(xxvi); SLA 1925 s.4(2). Where a personal representative is the statutory owner, he must follow the directions of the trustees of the settlement: SLA 1925 s.26(2).
[69] Which was not always the case prior to 1926: see, e.g. *Re Home's S.E.* (1888) 39 Ch D 84; *Re Astor* [1922] 1 Ch. 364.
[70] See below, Appendix, para.A–048.
[71] See, e.g. *Re Craven SE* [1926] Ch. 985; *Re Norton* [1929] 1 Ch. 84.
[72] SLA 1925 ss.23 (powers) and 117(xxvi) (definition); SLA 1925 s.4(2). For a further case of a statutory owner, see SLA 1925 s.23(2).
[73] See the fifth edition of this work at p.327.
[74] See J. M. Lightwood (1927) 3 C.L.J. 62, 63; S. J. Bailey (1942) 8 C.L.J. 43, 44.
[75] Below, Appendix, para.A–006.
[76] SLA 1925 ss.4(1), 6, 8(1).

The trusts are said to be "behind the curtain" formed by the vesting instrument, and the purchaser is not entitled to look behind the curtain.[77] These provisions are examined in greater detail in the Appendix.

Part 3

TRUSTS FOR SALE AFTER 1925 AND BEFORE 1997

1. The nature of a trust for sale. Prior to 1997, the alternative method of **10–020** creating a settlement of land was by means of a trust for sale. Such a trust was also used to govern concurrent co-ownership of land. The nature of a trust for sale has already been explained.[78] Such trusts were subject to provisions of the Law of Property Act 1925, and a number of these have been amended by the TLATA 1996, so that they apply with necessary modifications to the new "trust of land".[79] It has been explained that, in respect of successive interest, trusts for sale and settlements under the Settled Land Act 1925 were mutually exclusive.[80] If there was an immediate binding trust for sale,[81] there could be no settlement.[82] The main distinction between trusts for sale (in relation to either successive or concurrent co-ownership) and settlements was that under a trust for sale all powers of dealing with the land were vested in the trustees, whereas under a settlement they were given to the tenant for life.

2. Species of trust for sale. A trust for sale could arise either expressly, **10–021** where land was deliberately limited on trust for sale, or by operation of statute.

Where trusts for sale were expressly created inter vivos, it was the invariable practice to employ two documents[83]:

(i) a conveyance or, where the land was registered, a transfer, to the trustees on trust for sale; and

(ii) a trust instrument.

A purchaser was not concerned to see the trust instrument, and it was irrelevant that he had notice of the trust. When the trustees exercised their powers of disposition, the trusts were overreached, provided any capital monies were paid to the trustees, of whom there had to be at least two, except where the trustee was a trust corporation.[84] Testamentary trusts for sale were

---

[77] SLA 1925 s.110(2); but in four cases a purchaser is concerned to see the trust instrument: see below, Appendix, paras A–010, A–014.

[78] Above, para.10–007.

[79] See below para.12–002.

[80] Above, para.10–014.

[81] LPA 1925 s.205(1)(xxix) (as originally enacted). See the fifth edition of this work at p.386.

[82] 83 SLA 1925 s.1(7).

[83] It was not a legal necessity.

[84] LPA 1925 s.27(2) (this subsection has since been amended to apply to trusts of land). For overreaching, see below.

also created by two documents, the will and the written assent. The will operated as the trust instrument and a purchaser from the trustees for sale was not concerned to see it. The written assent took effect as a conveyance from the deceased's personal representatives which vested the legal estate in the trustees for sale.[85]

A trust for sale also was a convenient device for liquidating and distributing property, and it was employed by statute in a number of cases. In these situations, a trust of land is now imposed[86] and the provisions are considered in detail in the context of such trusts.[87] For example, where the trust for sale arose because land was conveyed to two or more persons for their concurrent enjoyment, it was rare for two instruments to be used because the conveyance itself triggered the imposition of the statutory trust for sale under LPA 1925 ss.34 and 35 (and now a trust of land: s.5 TLATA 1996). In this case, being the normal case of family joint-ownership, the trust arose by operation of statute.

3. Position of trustees for sale

10–022   *(a) Power to postpone sale.* Unless a contrary intention appeared, trustees for sale had an implied power to postpone sale and were not liable even if they did so indefinitely.[88] However, if they refused to sell, the court had power to order a sale at the instance of any person interested, and could make such order as it thought fit.[89] It was the trustees' duty to sell the property unless they unanimously agreed to exercise the power to postpone sale.[90] Nevertheless, many trusts for sale were created with the intention that the land should be retained for specific purposes,[91] and the courts took this into account when a sale was sought. They might in their discretion decline to order a sale. This practice has now been given statutory effect in relation to trusts of land.[92]

10–023   *(b) Other powers of trustees for sale.* Trustees for sale had all the powers of a tenant for life *and* the trustees of the settlement under the Settled Land Act 1925.[93] Pending sale, they could (for example) lease or mortgage the land

---

[85] An assent was necessary even if the trustees for sale and the personal representatives were the same persons: see below, para.11–129.

[86] See TLATA 1996 s.5(1).

[87] Below, para.12–014.

[88] LPA 1925 s.25 (now repealed).

[89] LPA 1925 s.30 (now repealed).

[90] See *Re Mayo* [1943] Ch. 302. As an exception to the general rule, charity trustees do not have to be unanimous, but may act by a majority.

[91] e.g. where a property was purchased jointly as a family home.

[92] See TLATA 1996 ss.14, 15; below, paras 12–021 et seq.

[93] LPA 1925 s.28(1) (now repealed). These included the powers of management conferred by SLA 1925 s.102, during a minority, even though no minority in fact existed. If land previously settled became subject to a trust for sale, the trustees had any additional powers conferred by the settlement on the tenant for life or trustees of the settlement: LPA 1925 s.28(1). For a fuller account, see the fifth edition of this work at p.392. The application of the provisions of the Settled Land Act 1925 to trusts for sale was not always easy: cf. *State Bank of India v Sood* [1997] Ch. 276 at 282.

in the same circumstances as a tenant for life under a settlement might have done.[94] Provided that they did not, by selling all the land, cease to be trustees for sale,[95] they could purchase further land with any proceeds of sale in their hands.[96] It was implicit in the Law of Property Act 1925 that a settlor or testator might make the sale by trustees subject to their obtaining the prior consent of one or more persons.[97]

(c) *Application of income.* Unless there was a contrary provision in the trust   **10–024**
for sale, the income from the land until sale was to be applied in the same way as the investments representing the proceeds of sale would be applied.[98]

(d) *Curtailment of powers.* The extent to which it was possible to curtail the   **10–025**
powers of trustees for sale was uncertain. It has been explained above that a trust to sell could be made subject to the prior consent of one or more persons. There was authority which suggested that, in consequence, it was possible to make land held on trust for sale inalienable, despite the obvious paradox of the result. In one case, a testator had directed that the trustees for sale were to sell certain land only with the consent of X. X was a contingent remainderman who was to benefit only if the land was unsold at the death of the life beneficiary.[99] X's consent to a sale was unobtainable for obvious reasons. The question whether the court would dispense with it, or what would happen to X's interest if it did, was not raised.

Apart from the question of consents, it was probably the case that the powers of the trustees for sale could not be cut down[100] except where a particular power was, by statute, expressly subject to a contrary intention.[101] There was no provision corresponding to s.106 of the Settled Land Act 1925.[102] However, it was arguable that that section was imported together with the Settled Land Act powers by s.28 of the Law of Property Act 1925.[103]

4. Position of beneficiaries

(a) *Powers in trustees.* Subject to one qualification explained below, all   **10–026**
powers of disposition and management were vested in the trustees for sale and not in the beneficiary or beneficiaries who were entitled to an immediate life interest in possession. Such persons either received the net income or they

---

[94] See below, Appendix, paras A–059, A–064.
[95] LPA 1925 s.205(1)(xxix) (as originally enacted); *Re Wakeman* [1945] Ch. 177.
[96] LPA 1925 s.28(1); SLA 1925, s.73(1)(xi); *Re Wellsted's WT* [1949] Ch. 296.
[97] LPA 1925 s.28(1). If the consent of more than two persons was required, a bona fide purchaser for value was protected if the consent of any two was obtained: LPA 1925 s.26 (now repealed).
[98] LPA 1925 s.28(2) (now repealed). This was subject to keeping down the cost of repairs and insurance and other outgoings.
[99] *Re Inns* [1947] Ch. 576 at 582.
[100] This followed from the apparently mandatory wording of LPA 1925 s.28(1) (trustees "shall have all" Settled Land Act powers). See the fifth edition of this work at p.395.
[101] e.g. the power to postpone sale: see LPA 1925 s.25(1); above, para.10–022.
[102] Below, Appendix, para.A–082.
[103] cf. the argument in *Re Davies' WT* [1932] 1 Ch. 530 at 532, 533; and see the fifth edition of this work at p.395.

might enjoy the property in specie by occupying it pending any sale.[104] Indeed, trusts for sale were often created with the express intention that the beneficiary entitled in possession should occupy the land.

10–027　　*(b) Delegation.* Although all the powers were vested in the trustees for sale, they might revocably and in writing delegate certain of them to the person of full age[105] who for the time being was beneficially entitled in possession to the net rents and profits of the land for his life or any less period.[106] The powers which could be delegated were the powers of, and incidental to, leasing, accepting surrenders of leases and management.[107] The powers delegated had to be exercised in the name of and on behalf of the trustees.[108] Liability for misuse of the power rested with the person exercising it, who was deemed to be in the position of a trustee.[109]

10–028　　*(c) Consultation.* In relation to the exercise of all their powers, the trustees were required:

> (i) so far as was practicable, to consult the persons of full age for the time being beneficially interested in possession in the rents and profits of the land; and
>
> (ii) so far as consistent with the general interests of the trust, to give effect to their wishes, or the wishes of the majority in terms of value.[110]

This provision was confined to trusts for sale which were either created by statute or showed an intention that the provision was to apply. This had the effect of excluding most express trusts for sale from its ambit. In any case, a purchaser was not concerned to see that the trustees had complied with this requirement,[111] though a beneficiary could restrain a trustee who sought to breach it.[112]

5. The doctrine of conversion

10–029　　*(a) The nature and purpose of the doctrine.* Reference has already been made to one aspect of the doctrine of conversion[113] and the difficulties to which it gave rise.[114] It was long settled that where land was directed to be

---

[104] See *City of London BS v Flegg* [1988] A.C. 54 at 81.
[105] Other than an annuitant.
[106] LPA 1925 s.29(1) (s.29 has now been repealed).
[107] LPA 1925.
[108] LPA 1925 s.29(2).
[109] LPA 1925 s.29(3).
[110] LPA 1925 s.26(3) (as amended by LP(Am)A 1926, Sch.) (now repealed).
[111] LPA 1925.
[112] *Wailer v Waller* [1967] 1 W.L.R. 451.
[113] For another aspect of the doctrine of conversion, see below, para.12–053 (vendor becomes trustee for purchaser).
[114] Above para.10–009.

sold, it was considered in equity to be money.[115] This doctrine turned on "the maxim that Equity considers to have been done what ought to have been done pursuant to the trust".[116] Even if there was a power to invest the proceeds of sale in the purchase of other land, then unless the settlement otherwise provided, that land was held on trust for sale[117] and so treated as money. Correspondingly, if money was directed to be laid out for the purchase of land, it was thereafter treated as land.[118] A trust to sell land and purchase other land with the proceeds of sale worked a double conversion, so that the interests of the beneficiaries remained land throughout.[119] Conversion operated from the date on which the trust for sale was created, which was the date either of the conveyance to the trustees for sale, or of the death of the testator if it arose by will.[120] The doctrine of conversion apparently rested on the principle that it would be wrong that the precise moment at which the trustees carried out their administrative duty of selling should determine whether the rights of the beneficiaries were realty or personalty, especially where a delay in selling might be due to a breach of trust.[121]

(b) Criticisms of the doctrine of conversion

(1) THE RIGHTS OF THE BENEFICIARIES PENDING SALE. If the doctrine of **10–030** conversion was strictly applied, then no person could have any beneficial interest in the land held on trust pending sale.[122] Yet it was obvious that a beneficiary had such an interest in the sense that, until sale, the land was held for his benefit.[123] This paradox was long appreciated[124] and the courts were unwilling to press the doctrine so far. It was therefore accepted on a number of occasions that pending sale, the beneficiary's interest was an interest in land.[125] This was especially so in cases where a statutory trust for sale was imposed in cases of co-ownership.[126]

It was sometimes said that the doctrine of conversion was essential to ensure that the interests of the beneficiaries were overreached on any sale.[127]

---

[115] *Fletcher v Ashburner* (1779) 1 Bro.C.C. 497.

[116] *Re Walker* [1908] 2 Ch. 705 at 712, per Parker J.

[117] LPA 1925 s.32 (now repealed).

[118] Wh. & T. 1, 301; *Re Scarth* (1879) 10 Ch D 499.

[119] See Wh. & T. 1, 309.

[120] *Clarke v Franklin* (1858) 4 K. & J. 257; *Re Lord Grimthorpe* [1908] 1 Ch. 666. Where the title to the land was registered it was uncertain whether conversion operated from the execution of the transfer in favour of the trustees for sale or from their registration as proprietors.

[121] *Re Richerson* [1892] 1 Ch. 379 at 383; Maitland, *Equity*, 277.

[122] It was not easy to accept that "all beneficial interest in a parcel of land evaporates (in nubibus?)": see [1979] C.L.J. 251 at 253 (M. J. Prichard).

[123] *Irani Finance Ltd v Singh* [1971] Ch. 59 at 68.

[124] "The equitable interest in that estate must have resided somewhere": *Pearson v Lane* (1809) 17 Ves. 101 at 104, per Grant MR.

[125] *Franks v Bollans* (1867) 37 L.J.Ch. 148 at 158. See too the same case on appeal: (1868) 3 Ch.App. 717 at 718, 719.

[126] See *Williams & Glyn's Bank Ltd v Boland* [1979] Ch. 312 at 329; [1981] A.C. 487 at 507.

[127] *Irani Finance Ltd v Singh*, above, at 80; *City of London Building Society v Flegg* [1988] A.C. 54 at 82. These remarks could not be readily reconciled with the decision in *Williams & Glyn's Bank Ltd v Boland*, above. See [1987] Conv. 451 at 455 (W. J. Swadling); [1988] Conv. 108 at 117 (M. P. Thompson). For overreaching, see below, para.12–035.

However this view must be regarded as questionable[128] for the following reasons:

(i) It is now settled that "overreaching is the process whereby existing interests are subordinated to a later interest or estate created pursuant to a trust or power".[129] A disposition under a mere power of sale would therefore have overreached interests under a trust, just as much as a disposition under a trust for sale.[130] This was so even though the doctrine of conversion had no application to *powers* of sale.[131]

(ii) The doctrine of conversion was usually relevant to determine whether beneficial interests under a trust for sale of land were to be regarded as interests in land or in personalty. Overreaching however has no necessary connection with trusts of land. Trustees who have a trust or power of sale can overreach the beneficial interests whatever the nature of the trust property. Thus if trustees sell shares, the equitable interests in them will be overreached and will attach instead to the proceeds of sale.[132]

(iii) When overreaching occurs, the trusts are transferred from the original subject-matter of the trust to the actual proceeds of the sale. By contrast, the effect of the doctrine of conversion was that the beneficial interests of those entitled under a trust for sale of land were regarded as interests in the notional proceeds of sale from the date of the creation of the trust: the doctrine did not turn "sovereigns into acres, or vice versa".[133]

10–031   (2) APPLICATION UNINTENDED. In many cases, the application of the doctrine of conversion did not accord with the intention of the settlor. Trusts for sale were developed in the nineteenth century as a conveyancing device to enable trust property to be sold without the consent of the beneficiaries. Although the same result could be achieved by conferring on the trustees a mere power of sale, any purchaser would in such a case have had to investigate whether the power was exercisable.[134] The mandatory obligation to sell under a trust for sale, coupled as it often was with a power to postpone,[135] was in many cases therefore no more than a fiction intended to achieve a conveyancing purpose.

[128] See [1979] C.L.J. 251 at 253 (M. J. Prichard); (1984) 100 L.Q.R. 86 at 109 (J. S. Anderson) [1990] C.L.J. 277 at 278 (C.H.).

[129] *State Bank of India v Sood* [1997] Ch. 276 at 281, per Peter Gibson L.J.

[130] See, e.g. *Wheate v Hall* (1809) 17 Ves. 80 at 86; Sugden, *Powers*, p.482; Farwell, *Powers*, p.581.

[131] See, e.g. Farwell, *Powers*, p.617; Wh. & T. 1, 306.

[132] See R. Nolan [2002] C.L.J. 169 suggesting overreaching as an explanation of the decision in *Vandervell v IRC* [1967] 2 A.C. 291, an infamous case involving a trust of shares and disputed dispositions.

[133] *Chandler v Pocock* (1880) 15 Ch D 491 at 496, per Jessel M.R.

[134] See (1984) 100 L.Q.R. 86 at 89 (J. S. Anderson).

[135] See above, para.10–022.

The doctrine of conversion which it necessarily triggered must frequently have been an unintended and unwanted consequence. It is also clear that the imposition of a statutory trust for sale in all cases where there was a legal tenancy in common in existence at the beginning of 1926[136] had the unfortunate effect of frustrating the intentions of a number of testators who failed to amend their wills after the enactment of the Law of Property Act 1925.[137] The courts nevertheless insisted that the doctrine had to be applied.[138]

(3) APPLICATION UNCERTAIN. The doctrine of conversion was never applied as an absolute rule in all cases where land was held on trust for sale, nor was its application consistent.[139] For example: **10–032**

    (i) there was a sharp divergence of judicial opinion as to whether the doctrine should always be applied to the beneficial interest of a co-owner under a statutory trust for sale[140] or only where it was essential to the working of the 1925 property legislation[141]; and

    (ii) there was a series of cases in which a court had to consider whether a beneficiary under a trust for sale was to be regarded as having an interest in land for the purposes of a particular statute.[142]

To overcome the latter point, it became the practice for new statutes to deal expressly with their application to interests under a trust for sale.[143]

[136] LPA 1925 Sch.1, Pt IV. For discussion of the transitional provisions, see the fifth edition of this work at p. 447. Of course, a legal tenancy in common can no longer exist, below para.13–034.
[137] See *Re Price* [1928] Ch. 579; *Re Kempthorne* [1930] 1 Ch. 268; *Re Newman* [1930] 2 Ch. 409. cf. *Re Warren* [1932] 1 Ch. 42.
[138] *Re Newman*, above, at 417.
[139] [1990] Conv. 12 at 22 (R. J. Smith). For the historical background to the doctrine, see (1984) 100 L.Q.R. 86 (J. S. Anderson). For the later authorities, see [1978] Conv. 194 (H. Forrest); [1986] Conv. 415 (J. Warburton).
[140] See, e.g. *Harman v Glencross* [1986] Fam. 81 at 94, 95.
[141] See, e.g. *Williams Glyn's Bank Ltd v Boland* [1979] Ch. 312 at 336, where Ormrod L.J. described the imposition of a trust for sale in such a case as a "legal fiction". One way in which the courts attempted to resolve this uncertainty was by having regard to the purpose for which the trust was set up: see *Barclay v Barclay* [1970] 2 Q.B. 677; [1971] C.L.J. 44 (M. J. Prichard).
[142] Thus a beneficiary under a trust for sale had a sufficient interest in land to register a caution under the previous system of land registration (LRA 1925 s.54(1) as was; *Elias v Mitchell* [1972] Ch. 652); to constitute an overriding interest (LRA 1925 s.70(1)(g) as was; *Williams & Glyn's Bank Ltd v Boland* [1981] A.C. 487); for his equitable interest to pass under the "all estate clause" (LPA 1925 s.63(1); *Ahmed v Kendrick* (1987) 56 P. & C.R. 120); for any contract to sell his interest to require written evidence (LPA 1925 s.40 (since repealed); see *Cooper v Critchley* [1955] Ch. 431); and to constitute a "beneficial interest in real estate" (AEA 1925 s.51(2); *Re Bradshaw* [1950] Ch. 582. cf. *Re Donkin* [1948] Ch. 74); but not to register a charging order as a writ or order affecting land (LCA 1972 s.6; see *Perry v Phoenix Assurance Plc* [1988] 1 W.L.R. 940); or to register as a *lis pendens* a claim to a share of the proceeds of sale of the property held on trust (LCA 1972 s.5 (replacing LCA 1925 s.2); *Taylor v Taylor* [1968] 1 W.L.R. 378). There is no doubt about the status of such an interest after TLATA 1996, below para.12–006.
[143] See, e.g. Limitation Act 1980, s.38(1); LP(MP)A 1989 s.2 (in each case as originally enacted: both have since been amended by TLATA 1996); Charging Orders Act 1979 s.2 (which did not require amendment by TLATA 1996).

10–033   **6. Protection of purchasers.** For the protection of any purchaser from the trustees for sale, a trust for sale once created was deemed to subsist until the land had been conveyed either to the beneficiaries themselves or to some other person under their direction.[144]

Part 4

TRUSTS OF LAND AFTER JANUARY 1, 1997

10–034   The Trusts of Land and Appointment of Trustees Act 1996, which came into force on January 1, 1997 introduced a unitary system of trusts of land and abolished the threefold division between settlements, trusts for sale and bare trusts. A trust of land today is any trust of property which consists of or includes land,[145] and includes an express, implied, resulting or constructive trust, a trust for sale and a bare trust. The TLATA 1996 is also applicable to trusts created or arising before 1997, save for land that was settled land prior to 1997 or land which is subject to the Universities and College Estates Act 1925.[146] This means that trusts for sale (whether express or implied) and bare trusts that were in existence on January 1, 1997, automatically became trusts of land[147] and all new trusts which include or consists of land must be trusts of land governed by TLATA 1996. It is impossible to create new settlements. Generally, the "trust of land" follows the model of the trust for sale and both the legal estate in the land and all the powers of disposition and management are vested in the trustees of land. TLATA 1996 and its regulation of the trust of land are considered in detail in Chapter 12.

---

[144] LPA 1925 s.23 (now repealed). This was to meet the difficulty that if all the beneficiaries were of full age and capacity, they could put an end to the trust for sale by electing to have the land retained. This might have turned the land into settled land.

[145] TLATA 1996, s.1(1).

[146] TLATA 1996, s.1(3).

[147] TLATA 1996, s.19(2).

CHAPTER 11

CREATING TRUSTS OF LAND

TRUSTS OF LAND

This chapter considers the various ways in which trusts of land may arise. It **11–001** will consider express, resulting and constructive trusts and includes an analysis of *Stack v Dowden*[1] and *Jones v Kernott*[2] where the House of Lords and the Supreme Court respectively, restated the law of implied trusts (at least in so far as they affect land used for residential purposes) to reflect the realities of modern living. In addition, certain formality issues are considered, particularly the rules concerning completely and incompletely constituted trusts and the formalities required for the creation of a trust and the transfer of an equitable interest. There is a connection here with principles of proprietary estoppel, for that doctrine in some circumstances operates as an antidote to an otherwise fatal lack of formality.[3] To conclude the chapter, there is a discussion of the role of the trustees of trusts of land and this has a connection with the material on the analysis of the Trusts of Land and Appointment of Trustees Act 1996 (TLATA) considered in Chapter 12.

The nature of trusts (and incidentally of powers) has already been briefly discussed in connection with settlements.[4] Much of the law of trusts is more appropriate to books on equity than to a book on real property, and this chapter will focus on matters of most concern to land law.

---

[1] [2007] UKHL 17, [2007] AC 432.
[2] [2011] UKSC 53. See also *Abbott v Abbott* [2007] UKPC 53 where Baroness Hale gave the Advice of the Privy Council on the same issue.
[3] Ch.16.
[4] Above, para.10–011.

Part 1

CLASSIFICATION AND TYPES OF TRUST

A. *Conveyancing Classification*

11–002   From the point of view of a conveyancer, land held in trust is either settled land or held under a trust of land. As is explained, with effect from January 1, 1996 it is no longer possible to create settled land.[5] Wherever land becomes subject to a trust thereafter, there is a trust of land for the purposes of the Trusts of Land and Appointment of Trustees Act 1996. This is so whether the interests of the beneficiaries under that trust are successive, concurrent or absolute.[6]

B. *Judicial Classification*

11–003   The courts have established a general classification of trusts as statutory, express, implied or resulting, and constructive trusts. This is not the only classification, nor are all the categories clearly defined or mutually exclusive. The terminology is not used consistently, particularly in relation to implied, resulting and constructive trusts. The nomenclature is to some extent a matter of convenience and not decisive of substantive matters.[7]

11–004   **1. Trusts imposed by statute.** Various trusts are imposed by statute. Some are expressly described as "statutory trusts", as with trusts for certain relations on an intestacy.[8] Others, although not given this name, are nevertheless trusts imposed by statute, e.g. the trusts which are:

    (a)   imposed on the property of an intestate[9];

    (b)   imposed on property which trustees have obtained by foreclosure[10]; or

    (c)   created by an attempt to convey a legal estate in land to a minor.[11]

11–005   **2. Express trusts.** These are trusts declared by a settlor. To create an express trust, the "three certainties" of a trust must be present, i.e. imperative words, certainty of subject-matter, and certainty of objects.[12]

---

[5] Above, para.10–034 and below para.12–002.
[6] i.e. where there is a bare trust.
[7] See Snell, *Equity*, Chs 10 and 21.
[8] AEA 1925 ss.46, 47; below, para.14–002.
[9] AEA 1925 s.33 (as amended); below, para.14–089.
[10] LPA 1925 s.31 (as amended by TLATA 1996 s.5(1); Sch.2 para.1); below, para.12–007.
[11] TLATA 1996 s.2(6); Sch.1 paras 1, 2; below, para.12–004; below, para.36–006.
[12] *Knight v Knight* (1840) 3 Beav. 148 at 173; (1940) 2 M.L.R. 20 (Glanville Williams).

(a) Imperative words. The settlor must indicate that a trust is intended. **11–006** Although at one time words expressing a request (known as precatory words), such as "in the full confidence", "recommending" or "my dying request", were construed as creating a trust,[13] that is no longer so.[14] Under the present law such words create no trust unless the instrument as a whole shows an intention that they should.[15] Where the words are not imperative, the donee holds the property beneficially free from any trust.[16]

(b) Certainty of subject-matter. Both the property to be vested in the trustees **11–007** and the beneficial interest to be taken by each beneficiary must be defined with sufficient certainty. If there is no certainty as to what is conveyed to the trustees, the entire transaction is ineffective, e.g. if a testator purports to leave "the bulk of my property" to trustees.[17] Examples of uncertainty of beneficial interest occur where defined property is given to X on trust that he should leave to A and B "the bulk" of it[18] or "such parts of my estate as he shall not have sold or disposed of".[19] In such cases the donee holds the property beneficially free from any trust,[20] unless it is clear that the whole of the property was to be held on trust and the only uncertainty is which part was intended for each beneficiary. In that case the donee will hold on a resulting trust for the settlor.[21]

(c) Certainty of objects.[22] The objects (i.e. the persons or purposes intended **11–008** to benefit by the trust) must be defined with sufficient certainty. Where there

---

[13] See, e.g. *Harding v Glyn* (1739) 1 Atk. 469; Wh. & T. ii, 285.

[14] Sometimes, this is clearly expressed. In *Suggitt v Suggitt* [2011] EWHC 903 (Ch), a testamentary estoppel case, (see Ch 16), the testator stated that "AND I EXPRESS THE WISH (without imposing a trust) that if at anytime my son John Michael Suggitt shall in the absolute opinion of Caroline show himself capable of working on and managing my farmland that she shall transfer my farmland to him". John, specifically denied the benefit of a trust, successfully established a claim in estoppel.

[15] See *Re Adams and the Kensington Vestry* (1884) 27 Ch D 394 at 410; *Re Williams* [1897] 2 Ch. 12; *Cominsky v Bowring-Hanbury* [1905] A.C. 84; *Re Johnson* [1939] 2 All E.R. 458.

[16] See, e.g. *McCormick v Grogan* (1869) L.R. 4 H.L. 82.

[17] *Palmer v Simmonds* (1854) 2 Drew. 221; contrast *Bromley v Tryon* [1952] A.C. 265. Where a settlor purports to create a trust of an undefined part of a homogenous mass, there is some authority that a distinction is to be drawn between tangible and intangible property. A purported declaration of trust of "20 cases of my 80 cases of wine" will fail for uncertainty. The quality of the different cases may vary, so that it is essential to segregate the property: *Re London Wine Co (Shippers) Ltd* (1975) [1986] P.C.C. 121. A declaration of trust of "50 of my 950 shares in X. Co. Ltd" has been held to be valid however, because no such segregation was required: *Hunter v Moss* [1994] 1 W.L.R. 452. That decision has been strongly criticised: see (1994) 110 L.Q.R. 335 (D. J. Hayton). It is difficult to reconcile with *Re Goldcorp Exchange Ltd* [1995] 1 A.C. 74, but *Holland v Newbury* (1998) BCC 567 (a transfer would not be void for uncertainty simply by virtue of the fact that numbers of the particular shares to be transferred out of a larger bulk were not given) does not regard *Hunter* as *per incuriam* or wrongly decided.

[18] *Palmer v Simmonds*, above.

[19] *Re Jones* [1898] 1 Ch. 438; but see *Re Thomson's Estate* (1879) 13 Ch D 144; *Re Sanford* [1901] 1 Ch. 939. As to executory trusts, see below, para.11–033.

[20] See, e.g. *Fox v Fox* (1859) 27 Beav. 301.

[21] See, e.g. *Boyce v Boyce* (1849) 16 Sim. 476; cf. *Re Clarke* [1923] 2 Ch. 407.

[22] See (1982) 98 L.Q.R. 551 (C. T. Emery).

is a fixed trust for the benefit of individuals, it must be possible to draw up a complete list of the objects.[23] Where there is a discretionary trust (i.e. a trust to distribute the property coupled with a power to select which member or members of a class of objects should benefit),[24] it must be possible to say with certainty whether any given individual is or is not a member of the class of objects.[25] A trust for "my old friends" is uncertain as to the concept of who are to be regarded as the donor's "old friends", and so is void.[26] Subject to certain exceptions,[27] trusts for pure purposes that are not exclusively charitable are void.[28] This is sometimes explained on the grounds that such purposes are too vague to be executed.[29] However, non-charitable purpose trusts fail not so much because of uncertainty as to their objects, but because there is no beneficiary who can enforce them, and in some cases at least, because they may be perpetual.[30] A trust for charitable purposes will not fail for uncertainty since the Crown in some cases and the court in others will direct a suitable mode of application.[31] If a trust is void for uncertainty of objects, there is a resulting trust for the settlor.[32]

11–009 **3. Implied or resulting trusts.** An implied or resulting trust[33] is said to exist where, on a conveyance of property, a trust arises by operation of equity.[34] However, the basis for such trusts is the presumed intention[35] of the settlor or of the parties whose conduct leads to their creation. They are not imposed by law.[36] The presumption of a resulting trust can be rebutted by evidence of any intention that is inconsistent with such a trust and not merely

---

[23] *IRC v Broadway Cottages Trust* [1955] Ch. 20 at 29; *Re Gulbenkian's Settlements* [1970] A.C. 508 at 524.

[24] Discretionary trusts of land are uncommon but do occasionally occur: see, e.g. *Leahy v Att Gen (NSW)* [1959] A.C. 457.

[25] *McPhail v Doulton* [1971] A.C. 424.

[26] *Brown v Gould* [1972] Ch. 53 at 57.

[27] Considered above, paras 9–141—9–147.

[28] See, e.g. *Chichester Diocesan Fund v Simpson* [1944] A.C. 341 (a trust for "charitable or benevolent" objects held void because not all benevolent objects are charitable).

[29] See, e.g. *Farley v Westminster Bank* [1939] A.C. 430 at 433 (trust for the churchwardens of St. Cuthbert's Church "for parish work" held to be void because the purpose was not charitable).

[30] Above, paras 9–148, 9–14, 9–150.

[31] *Morice v Bishop of Durham* (1804) 9 Ves. 399 at 405.

[32] See, e.g. *Kendall v Granger* (1842) 5 Beav. 300; *Re Carville* [1937] 4 All E.R. 464.

[33] The terms are generally treated as synonymous. In practice, the term "implied trust" is little used now, and such trusts are invariably referred to as "resulting trusts".

[34] See generally, R. Chambers, *Resulting Trusts* (Oxford, Clarendon Press, 1997). cf. *Explaining Resulting Trusts* (2008) 124 LQR 72 (W. Swadling).

[35] In *Jones v Kernott* [2011] UKSC 53, Lord Walker and Lady in their joint opinion take the view that resulting trusts are "presumed", but arise by imputed intention, at para.29. This occurs in the context of an explanation about why it is not inappropriate to "impute" an intention to the parties in some cases of joint-ownership of land, below, para.11–029.

[36] See *Westdeutsche Landesbank Girozentrale v Islington LBC* [1996] A.C. 669 at 708, disapproving suggestions to the contrary in *Re Vandervell's Trusts (No.2)* [1974] Ch. 269 at 289. See also *Air Jamaica v Charlton* (PC Appeal No.27 of 1998), (1999) 1 W.L.R. 1399, per Lord Millett as to the type of intention required and below para.11–010.

evidence that there was an intention to make a gift.[37] A number of these trusts are of importance in land law.

(a) Trusts not exhaustive. Where a disposition of property is made by the **11–010** owner, and all or part of the equitable interest is not effectively disposed of, there is normally a resulting trust for the owner. If the property is conveyed expressly on trust, e.g. "to X on trust", there is no difficulty. A trustee can take no benefit from the fact that the declared trusts do not exhaust the beneficial interest. To the extent that the beneficial interest is not disposed of, it results to the grantor.[38] Thus, if G conveys property to X on trust for a beneficiary who is dead, there is a resulting trust of the entire beneficial interest in favour of G.[39] The rule that there is a resulting trust in such circumstances can be rebutted by evidence:

(i) that the trustee was intended to take beneficially[40]; or

(ii) that the settlor had expressly or by necessary implication abandoned any interest in the property: the undisposed of interest will then pass to the Crown as bona vacantia.[41]

One particular example of this type of resulting trust arises where a trust is made for some specific purpose, and later that purpose wholly fails. In such a case, there is a resulting trust for the party who paid for or provided the property: the trusts declared do not exhaust the whole beneficial interests.[42] Thus, where A and B, intending marriage, contribute equally and buy a house as joint tenants, but later decide not to marry, there will be a resulting trust in their favour as tenants in common in equal shares, so that there will be no right of survivorship.[43]

---

[37] *Westdeutsche Landesbank Girozentrale v Islington LBC*, above, at 708; (1996) 16 L.S. 110 (W. Swadling). cf. [1996] R.L.R. 3 (P. Birks). In some case, it seems that the presumption should not be made at all: "The time has come to make it clear, in line with *Stack v Dowden* (see also *Abbott v Abbott* [2007] UKPC 53, [2007] 2 All E.R. 432), that in the case of the purchase of a house or flat in joint names for joint occupation by a married or unmarried couple, where both are responsible for any mortgage, there is no presumption of a resulting trust arising from their having contributed to the deposit (or indeed the rest of the purchase) in unequal shares", *Jones v Kernott*, above at para.25 per Lord Walker and Lady Hale.

[38] See *Merchant Taylors' Co v Att Gen* (1871) 6 Ch.App. 512 at 518.

[39] *Re Tilt* (1896) 74 L.T. 163.

[40] See, e.g. *Smith v Cooke* [1891] A.C. 297.

[41] *West Sussex Constabulary's Widows, Children and Benevolent (1930) Fund Trusts* [1971] Ch. 1; *Westdeutsche Landesbank Girozentrale v Islington LBC*, above, at 708. In *Air Jamaica*, above, where the property did not fall as *bona vacantia*, Lord Millet notes that a resulting trust "responds to the absence of any intention [of the transferor] to pass a beneficial interest to the recipient" and thus it can arise "even where the transferor positively wished to part with the beneficial interest" at p.16. As a matter of evidence, a resulting trust would be difficult to rebut on this basis and the Crown less likely to take property as bona vacantia.

[42] See *Westdeutsche Landesbank Girozentrale v Islington LBC*, above, at 715, criticising the reasoning (but not the result) in *Re Ames' Settlement* [1946] Ch. 217.

[43] *Burgess v Rawnsley* [1975] Ch. 429. If the contributions are unequal, the shares will be in proportion to them. This reasoning probably survives the rejection of the "proportionate share" resulting trust in *Jones v Kernott*, above fn.37, because in cases such as this the intentions of the parties have failed ab initio rather than after a period of joint occupation for joint purposes.

11–011   *(b) Voluntary conveyance.* Where before 1926 property was conveyed without any consideration, but not expressly on trust, difficult questions could arise. Resulting uses and resulting trusts must be distinguished, for after the Statute of Uses 1535 a resulting use would be executed by the statute and so carry the legal estate back to the grantor, whereas a resulting trust was purely equitable, so that the grantor would continue to hold the legal estate as trustee for the grantor.

11–012   (1) RESULTING USES. Before 1535 it had been settled that on a voluntary conveyance in fee simple by A to B in which no use was expressed, there was a presumption of a resulting use to the grantor of the whole estate granted.[44] If it appeared that a gift was intended, as where a use was expressed in the conveyance (e.g. in favour of B), that of course prevented a resulting use from being implied. A resulting use was also excluded if the conveyance was made either for valuable consideration (even if nominal[45]) or for good consideration, e.g. the "natural love and affection" that indicated a genuine gift if B was a near relation of A.[46] If B held of A in tenure, that also sufficed, so that no resulting use arose on a grant in tail, for life or for years.[47]

11–013   (2) RESULTING TRUSTS. After the Statute of Uses 1535 a resulting use was executed by the Statute, with the result that such a conveyance was totally ineffective, and A was regarded as holding the same estate as before.[48] When trusts later came into use and a grant "unto and to the use of B" became a common form merely for the purpose of vesting the legal estate in B, whether or not upon further trusts, it was arguable that a voluntary grant in such terms raised a resulting trust in equity for the grantor, by analogy with the old doctrine of resulting uses. But, rather curiously, this question was never settled. The old authorities seem to show that a resulting trust would arise if circumstances pointed to the conclusion that the grantee was not intended to take beneficially,[49] but that in the absence of such evidence the grantee would take for his own use.[50] Unlike resulting uses, resulting trusts were not excluded merely by the presence of a nominal consideration.[51] In practice it would nearly always be made clear whether a voluntary conveyance was

---

[44] H.E.L. iv, p.424; *Beckwith's Case* (1589) 2 Co.Rep. 56b at 58a; *Armstrong d. Neve v Wolsey* (1755) 2 Wils.K.B. 19; Sanders, *Uses*, i, 60, 97, 365; Williams R.P. pp.185, 186; Norton, *Deeds*, 410.

[45] *Case of Sutton's Hospital* (1612) 10 Co.Rep. la.

[46] See Sanders, *Uses*, ii, 98–100; above, para.8–008.

[47] H.E.L. iv, p.429. The statute Quia Emptores 1290 prevented tenure arising between grantor and grantee on grants in fee simple (above, paras 2–015, 2–016), but not on grants of lesser estates.

[48] See the authorities cited above, and *Godbold v Freestone* (1694) 3 Lev. 406 at 407; *Harris v Bishop of Lincoln* (1723) 2 P. Wms. 135; Preston, *Conveyancing*, ii, p.487.

[49] *Duke of Norfolk v Browne* (1697) Prec.Ch. 80; *R. v Williams* (1735) Bunb. 342.

[50] *Lloyd v Spillet* (1740) 2 Atk. 148; *Young v Peachy* (1741) 2 Atk. 254. Lord Hardwicke was clearly of opinion that there was no imperative rule demanding a resulting trust.

[51] See *Hayes v Kingdome* (1681) 1 Vern. 33 at 34; *Sculthorp v Burgess* (1790) 1 Ves. Jun. 91 at 92.

intended as a gift or not, so that the point was never squarely raised in a modern case.[52]

(3) AFTER 1925. The Law of Property Act 1925 has disposed of the difficulty **11–014** in the case of conveyances executed after 1925. Since uses can no longer be executed and so turned into legal estates, the old form of conveyance "unto and to the use of A" is now obsolete. A conveyance simply "to A" now suffices. Nevertheless, where this formula was used in a voluntary conveyance a resulting use would still have arisen in equity, and take effect as a trust, for the repeal of the Statute of Uses does not alter the equitable principle under which the use resulted. However, this is now prevented by the statutory provision that "in a voluntary conveyance a resulting trust shall not be implied merely by reason that the property is not expressed to be conveyed for the use or benefit of the grantee".[53] Since in a voluntary grant made after 1925 "to A for his own benefit" the last four words would undoubtedly rebut a resulting trust, it follows that a resulting trust cannot now arise merely from the omission of any such formula in a grant made simply "to A", with no indication whether or not A was intended to take for his own benefit. Of course, where there is evidence that A was to take as trustee for the grantor, there will be a resulting trust to that effect.[54]

(4) ADVANCEMENT. One class of case was always outside the doctrine of **11–015** resulting trusts. Where the grantee was the wife[55] or child of the grantor there was a contrary presumption ("the presumption of advancement") that a beneficial gift was intended.[56] But other relationships (e.g. where the grantee

[52] Though see the remarks of Jessel M.R. in *Strong v Bird* (1874) L.R. 18 Eq. 315 at 318; and (in the opposite sense) of James L.J. in *Fowkes v Pascoe* (1875) 10 Ch.App. 343 at 348. The authorities are collected in the editorial note to Maitland, *Equity*, 1936 edn, 330. Text-writers conflicted equally freely on the question: see Wh. & T. ii, 762. A resulting trust was favoured by Maitland, *Equity*, 77; Williams R.P. p.194; Lewin 131; and opposed by Sanders, *Uses*, i, 365; Ashburner, *Equity*, 107.
[53] LPA 1925 s.60(3), (4). cf. *Tinsley v Milligan* [1994] 1 A.C. 340 at 371; R. Chambers, *Resulting Trusts*, 14–19.
[54] *Hodgson v Marks* [1971] Ch. 892, admitting evidence of oral agreement not indicated in the grant.
[55] Or (probably) a fiancée: see *Moate v Moate* [1948] 2 All E.R. 486 at 487 (though it may be conditional on the parties' subsequently marrying). In any event, it has been suggested that the presumption applies in such a case by virtue of the Law Reform (Miscellaneous Provisions) Act 1970, s.2(1), though whether conditionally or unconditionally is uncertain: see *Mossop v Mossop* [1989] Fam. 77 at 82.
[56] It is uncertain whether there is any presumption of advancement when a mother contributes towards the cost of a property purchased by her son or daughter: *Bennet v Bennet* (1878–79) LR 10 Ch D 474 Ch; Snell, above, 23–07; *Sekhon v Alissa* [1989] 2 F.L.R. 94. It was held applicable in *Close Invoice Finance Ltd v Abaowa* [2010] EWHC 1920 (QB) doubting *Bennet*, with support from *Nelson v Nelson* (1995) 184 C.L.R. 538 in the High Court of Australia. In *Jones v Kernott*, above, Lord Walker and Lady Hale assume that the presumption of advancement does not apply from a mother to her children, at para.24. Note, the presumption was rebutted in *Abaowa* given that it is now weak—*Lavelle v Lavelle* [2004] EWCA Civ 223, (2004) 2 FCR 418. Indeed, it has been suggested that even if the presumption survives between husband and wife, it will seldom be decisive if other evidence is available: *Pettitt v Pettitt* [1970] A.C. 777 at 811; *Gissing v Gissing* [1971] A.C. 886 at 907. cf. *McHardy & Sons v Warren* [1994] 2 F.L.R. 338, where a husband paid his earnings into a joint bank account, from which the mortgage on the house was

was husband or nephew of the grantor) raised no such presumption.[57] The presumption could always be rebutted by evidence that the wife or child was not intended to take beneficially.[58] The presumption of advancement and, in particular the relationships that give rise to it, are wholly out of date and may lead to arbitrary results.[59] However, that does not mean it has no role to play even in the 21st century.[60] The presumption of advancement will be abolished prospectively if section 199 of the Equality Act 2010 is brought into force.[61]

11–016	*(c) Purchase with another's money: presumed resulting trusts.* Where land is conveyed to one person, but the purchase-money[62] is provided by another as purchaser,[63] there is presumed to be a resulting trust in favour of the person providing the purchase-money. If V conveys land to P, A being the real purchaser and as such providing the purchase-money, prima facie P holds on a resulting trust for A.[64] Similarly, if A provides part of the purchase-money,[65] provided this is at the time of purchase,[66] he acquires a proportionate share in equity.[67] Nevertheless these are only presumptions, and will not apply in the following cases.

paid. Although the house was in his name alone, it was held that the repayments could be regarded as made jointly. See [1994] Fam. Law 567 (J. Dewar).

[57] The presumption does not apply as between man and mistress: see *Lawson v Coombes* [1999] 2 W.L.R. 720 at 726, 729. The point had been left open in *Cantor v Cox* [1976] 2 E.G.L.R. 105.

[58] *Stock v McAvoy* (1875) L.R. 15 Eq. 55; *Gross v French* [1976] 1 E.G.L.R. 129 (money provided by mother for daughter's house but without intent to make daughter owner); *Sekhon v Alissa*, above (a similar situation); *Simpson v Simpson* [1992] 1 F.L.R. 601 (transfer of property to a wife by a husband who was seriously ill, simply as a matter of convenience).

[59] See, e.g. *Trends in Contemporary Trust Law* (ed. A. J. Oakley), p.33 (J. D. Davies); and below.

[60] In *Antoni v Antoni*, [2007] UKPC 10, the Privy Council held, on an appeal from the Commonwealth of the Bahamas, that the presumption, "a construct of equity", was a rebuttable evidentiary presumption whose "relevance and importance" the trial judge had overlooked. If effective, it would bar the converse presumption of resulting trust, per Lord Scott at para.20. cf. *Laskar v Laskar* [2008] EWCA Civ 347; (2008) 7 EG 142 (CS).

[61] Much of the Act came into force on 1 October 2010 and further provisions on 1 April 2011. These do not include section 199.

[62] For these purposes, borrowed money is equated to a cash contribution: *Crisp v Mullings* [1976] 2 E.G.L.R. 103; *Marsh v Von Sternberg* [1986] 1 F.L.R. 526; *Springette v Defoe* [1992] 2 F.L.R 388 (but note the disapproval of *Springette* in *Stack*, above at p.457. So too is a discount under the "right to buy" legislation (below, para.22–180), *Springette v Defoe*, above, but this can be rebutted, *Ashe v Mumford*, *Times*, November 15, 2000.

[63] And not, for example, as mortgagee.

[64] *Dyer v Dyer* (1788) 2 Cox Eq. 92.

[65] It has been held that no interest is acquired from the payment of rent under a tenancy, because this purchases no asset but merely pays for the use of the property: *Savage v Dunningham* [1974] Ch. 181. This reasoning is open to doubt because the consideration paid under a lease, whether rent or premium, purchases an estate in land: *Malayan Credit Ltd v Jack Chia-MPH Ltd* [1986] A.C. 549 at 560. Perhaps the point is that it does not purchase the superior estate of the landlord.

[66] *Curley v Parkes* [2004] EWCA Civ 1515, (2005) Conv. 79 (M.J.D.).

[67] *Wray v Steele* (1814) 2 V. & B. 388; *Gissing v Gissing* [1971] A.C. 886 at 897; *Heseltine v Heseltine* [1971] 1 W.L.R. 342 (money provided by wife); *Dewar v Dewar* [1975] 1 W.L.R. 1532 (money provided by brother); *Close Invoice Finance Ltd v Abaowa*, above (deposit provided by mother).

(i) Where they are rebutted by evidence that P was intended to benefit, A's money being in effect a gift or loan to P.[68]

(ii) Where they are rebutted by the presumption of advancement which arises if P is the wife or child of A.[69]

(iii) Where a family home is held jointly, but the equitable interests are undeclared, the Supreme Court has held in *Jones v Kernott* that the "time has come to make it clear, in line with *Stack v Dowden* (see also *Abbott v Abbott* [2007] UKPC 53, [2007] 2 All E.R. 432), that in the case of the purchase of a house or flat in joint names for joint occupation by a married or unmarried couple, where both are responsible for any mortgage, there is no presumption of a resulting trust arising from their having contributed to the deposit (or indeed the rest of the purchase) in unequal shares".[70] In such cases, the size of the beneficial interests is to be determined by reference to the presumption that "equity follows the law" or the inferred or imputed common intention of the parties.[71]

It has been explained that the presumption of advancement is itself rebuttable by evidence of contrary intention.[72] This has given rise to some difficulty where A has transferred property to B for some illegal purpose. In a controversial decision, *Tinsley v Milligan*,[73] the House of Lords held that a claim to a beneficial interest under a presumed resulting trust, made by a person who has contributed to the price, would not fail merely because the property was acquired in the course of an illegal transaction. "A party to an illegality can recover by virtue of a legal or equitable property interest if, but only if, he can establish his title without relying on his own illegality."[74] In that case, two female lovers, A and B, purchased land which was conveyed to B alone to facilitate a social security fraud to which they were both parties. This was held not to bar A's claim to an equitable interest in the property under a presumed resulting trust. A necessary consequence of the decision is that, in a case

---

[68] e.g. *Fowkes v Pascoe* (1875) 10 Ch.App. 343; *Standing v Bowring* (1885) 31 Ch D 282; *Dewar v Dewar*, above (gift from mother), not mentioning the presumption of advancement. In *Westdeutsche Landesbank Girozentrale v Islington LBC* [1996] A.C. 669 at 708, Lord Browne-Wilkinson accepted that the presumption of a resulting trust could be rebutted "by evidence of any intention inconsistent with such trust, not only by evidence of an intention to make a gift". See (1996) 16 L.S. 110 (W. Swadling).

[69] Above. In *Ashe*, above, the presumption was rebutted because the entire transaction was a sham. In similar vein, see *Painter v Hutchinson* [2007] EWHC 758 (Ch).

[70] *Jones v Kernott*, above at para.25 per Lord Walker and Lady Hale.

[71] *Jones v Kernott*, above.

[72] Above, para.11–015.

[73] [1994] 1 A.C. 340. See (1994) 110 L.Q.R. 3 (R. A. Buckley); (1995) 111 L.Q.R. 135 (N. Enonchong). For the very different approach adopted in Australia, see *Nelson v Nelson* above; (1996) 112 L.Q.R. 386 (F. D. Rose); [1996] R.L.R. 78 (N. Enonchong).

[74] *Tinsley v Milligan*, above, at 375, per Lord Browne-Wilkinson. See too *Rowan v Dann* (1991) 64 P. & C.R. 202 at 209 (decided before *Tinsley v Milligan* had been heard by the House of Lords). Evidence of illegality may be given, however, to rebut a spurious defence by the party resisting the claim: see *Silverwood v Silverwood* (1997) 74 P. & C.R. 453.

where the presumption of advancement applies, A will only be able to rebut the presumption of gift in favour of B by relying on the underlying illegality. His claim will therefore fail.[75] Because the relationships to which the presumption of advancement applies have not evolved in line with changing social conditions, this leads to arbitrary results. Thus where A is a male, he will be able to recover property transferred for an illegal purpose to his mistress,[76] but not if it is made to his wife[77] or son.[78] By contrast, where A is female, she should, in principle, succeed in recovering property transferred to her husband to further an illegal design.[79] The presumption of advancement does not apply to a transfer by a wife to her husband,[80] and she would not, therefore, have to rely on the illegality of the act. The present law has been judicially criticised,[81] and the courts have devised one means of ameliorating its potentially mischievous effects. It has been held that a person may recover property even if he has to lead evidence of an illegal purpose, provided that he withdrew from that purpose before it was wholly or partially executed.[82] The Law Commission has recommended that the courts should be given a structured discretion to deal with illegal transactions, thereby overcoming the difficulties explained above.[83]

11–017   **4. Constructive trusts.** There is no accepted definition of a constructive trust[84] and no single principle which unites the circumstances in which it may be imposed. It is a residual category of trusts. A constructive trustee is subject to some aspect of an express trustee's liability, but not necessarily to all his

---

[75] *Tinsley v Milligan*, above, at 375.

[76] *Lawson v Coombes* [1999] 2 W.L.R. 720 (property transferred to defeat any ancillary relief proceedings brought by A's wife), disapproving *Cantor v Cox* [19761 2 E.G.L.R. 105 (in which A's claim failed on grounds of illegality).

[77] *Tinker v Tinker* [1970] P. 136 (property conveyed by a husband to his wife to keep it out of the hands of his creditors in case he should go bankrupt). But see *In the matter of Stephen Edwards* sub nom *Bessie Edwards v Crown Prosecution Service (Proceeds of Crime Unit)* [2011] EWHC 1688 (Admin) where Cranston J held that the presumption of an equitable joint-tenancy flowing from a legal joint-tenancy was rebutted (under *Stack*) in the husband's favour because much of the proceeds were derived from crime. The result was that the wife had a smaller share and the husband (and hence recovery of proceeds of crime) a greater share. Neither *Tinsley* nor *Tinker* appear to have been cited and perhaps *Tinker* may be distinguished because the property purchase was not in order to facilitate an illegal purpose, but using assets derived from such.

[78] *Chettiar v Chettiar* [1962] A.C. 294 at 302 (transfer to son disguised as a sale to circumvent regulations which restricted rubber planting).

[79] There is no authority directly in point.

[80] See, e.g. *Mercier v Mercier* [1903] 2 Ch. 98.

[81] See *Tribe v Tribe* [1996] Ch. 107 at 118, 134; *Silverwood v Silverwood* (1997) 74 P. & CR. 453 at 458.

[82] *Tribe v Tribe*, above. The court declined to define the limits of this "doctrine of the *locus poenitentiae*", but did comment that "genuine repentance" was not required: *Tribe v Tribe* at 135, per Millett L.J. See [1996] C.L.J. 23 (G. Virgo). See also *Painter v Hutchinson*, above.

[83] *The illegality defence*, (2010) Law Com No 320, following the provisional recommendations of the consultation paper, (1999) Law Com. CP No.154. See *The illegality defence: turning back the clock* [2010] 74 Conv. 282 (Paul S Davies).

[84] Snell, *Equity*, Ch.21.

fiduciary obligations.[85] English law tends to treat constructive trusts as "institutional".[86] The trust "arises by operation of law as from the date of the circumstances which give rise to it: the function of the court is merely to declare that such trust has arisen in the past".[87] In some other jurisdictions the courts will impose a "remedial constructive trust". This is "a judicial remedy giving rise to an enforceable equitable obligation", the retrospectivity of which is a matter for the court's discretion.[88] It remains to be seen whether English law will develop remedial constructive trusts.[89] It appears not to be a prerequisite to liability that the trustee should ever have received any property.[90] A constructive trustee may be personally liable to account for any improper gain which he has made or for any loss which his acts or omissions have caused, or in appropriate circumstances, he may hold specific property in his hands on trust. There are a number of well-known situations in which a constructive trust is imposed.

(a) *Where there is an existing fiduciary relationship.* If by virtue of his position a trustee or other fiduciary obtains any valuable interest in the trust property for himself, the general rule is that he holds it on a constructive trust for the beneficiaries.[91] An example is where a trustee of a lease either obtains a renewal for his own benefit[92] or acquires the freehold reversion.[93]   **11–018**

(b) *Where a stranger intermeddles in a trust.*[94] A constructive trust will be imposed on a person who in some way intermeddles in a trust where: **11–019**

---

[85] *Lonrho Plc v Fayed (No.2)* [1992] 1 W.L.R. 1 at 12. See (1997) 1 E.I..R. 437 (C.H.). cf. [1999] C.L.J. 294 (L. Smith).

[86] See *Re Polly Peck International Plc (No.2)* [1998] 3 All E.R. 812 at 823–827.

[87] *Westdeutsche Landesbank Girozentrale v Islington LBC* [1996] A.C. 669 at 714, per Lord Browne-Wilkinson. See also *Air Jamaica v Charlton*, above.

[88] *Westdeutsche Landesbank Girozentrale v Islington LBC*, above. See too *Halifax BS v Thomas* [1996] Ch. 217 at 229.

[89] See the adoption of a remedial constructive trust by Lord Scott in *Thorner v Major* [2009] 1WLR 776 at 784 for this "has been recognised at least since *Gissing v Gissing* [1971] A.C. 886". This will surprise many, as will his view that many estoppel cases are "more comfortably viewed as constructive trust cases", id. In *Clarke v Meadus*, [2010] EWHC 3117 (Ch), Warren J noted that a remedial constructive trust was a "juridical beast which English case law has set its face against", at para.82, but concluded that the concept was not precluded by *Stack v Dowden* above and was merely a different route to the same result as that achieved by proprietary estoppel, at para.83. For differing views on the remedial constructive trust, contrast *The Frontiers of Liability*, edited by P. B. H. Birks (Oxford: OUP, 1994), vol.ii, 165 (D. W. M. Waters); with (1998) 12 T.L.I. 202 (P. B. H. Birks).

[90] *Selangor United Rubber Estates Ltd v Cradock (No.3)* [1969] 1 W.L.R. 1555 at 1582; *Royal Brunei Airlines Sdn. Bhd. v Tan* [1995] 2 A.C. 378, at 382. But cf. *Westdeutsche Landesbank Girozentrale v Islington LBC* [1996] A.C. 669 at 705 (treating cases of dishonest assistance in a breach of trust as the only instances where a person might be liable without receipt of trust property: *sed quaere*).

[91] *Bray v Ford* [1896] A.C. 44 at 51.

[92] *Keech v Sandford* (1726) Sel.Ca.t.King 61; cf. *Re Morgan* (1881) 18 Ch D 93. See generally Snell, *Equity*, 246.

[93] *Protheroe v Protheroe* [1968] 1 W.L.R. 519.

[94] See (1986) 102 L.Q.R. 114, 267; (C.H.); (1991) 107 L.Q.R. 71 at 80 (Sir Peter Millett); *The Frontiers of Liability* (ed. P. B. H. Birks), Vol. i, 9 (C.H.); (1996) 112 L.Q.R. 56 (5. Gardner).

(i) he acts as a trustee although not so appointed and commits a breach of trust[95];

(ii) he dishonestly procures or assists in a breach of trust[96]; or

(iii) he receives trust property transferred to him in breach of trust, with sufficient knowledge that it is trust property and of the breach.[97]

11–020   *(c) Where parties enter into an agreement to make mutual wills.* If A and B agree to leave their property to the survivor for life with remainder to X, and make mutual wills accordingly, the survivor will hold the property on trust for X, so that he will be unable to defeat X's expectations by revoking his will.[98] In this case the constructive trust solves the problem of allowing a third party to sue on a contract.

11–021   *(d) Where a vendor contracts to sell land to a purchaser.* Where a vendor enters into a specifically enforceable contract to sell land, he is regarded for certain purposes as a trustee of the property for the purchaser.[99] The vendor's fiduciary obligations may be regarded as based upon a constructive trust.

[95] e.g. *Pearce v Pearce* (1856) 25 L.J.Ch. 893.

[96] *Royal Brunei Airlines Sdn. Bhd. v Tan*, above (disapproving *Barnes v Addy* (1874) 9 Ch.App. 244); (1995) 111 L.Q.R. 545 (C.H.); [1995] C.L.J. 505 (R. Nolan). See too *Twinsectra Ltd v Yardley* (2002) 2 A.C. 164; *Dubai Aluminium Company Limited v Salaam* [2002] 2 A.C. 366; and *Barlow Clowes International Ltd (In Liquidation) v Eurotrust International Ltd* (2005) UKPC 37, (2006) 1 W.L.R. 1476; (2007) Conv. 168 (D. Ryan); It is questionable whether this form of accessory liability, which is the equitable equivalent of the tort of inducing a breach of contract, should be characterised as a form of constructive trusteeship at all, nor in *Tan* did the Privy Council do so. In *Dubai*, Lord Millett makes this point, at para.141, but accepts that the defendant may be liable to account as if he were a constructive trustee. This is the formulation adopted in *Statek Corp v Alford* [2008] EWHC 32 (Ch).

[97] The degree of knowledge or notice required for liability is whether the recipient's state of knowledge made it unconscionable for him to retain the benefit of the receipt, *Bank of Credit and Commerce International (Overseas Ltd) v Akindele* (2001) Ch 437; (2004) L.M.C.L.Q 421 (R. Stevens), but this may not resolve the uncertainty expressed in *Polly Peck international Plc v Nadir (No.2)* [1992] 4 All E.R. 769 at 777. In *Att Gen of Zambia v Meer Care & Desai* [2007] EWHC 952 (Ch), the eleventh defendant was liable for knowing receipt because he had "constructive knowledge" of the breach. It is arguable that such liability should be regarded as restitutionary and not imposed because of the recipient's wrongdoing: *Royal Brunei Airlines Sdn. Bhd. v Tan*, above, at 386. For the view that liability is strict but subject to the defences of change of position and bona fide purchase, see [1989] L.M.C.L.Q. 296 (P. B. H. Birks). This form of liability can apply to a recipient of land: *Cowan de Groot Properties Ltd v Eagle Trust Plc* [1992] 4 All E.R. 700 at 759–760; *Eagle Trust Plc v S.B.C. Securities Ltd* [1993] 1 W.L.R. 484 at 503–504.

[98] *Dufour v Pereira* (1769) Dick. 419; *Re Oldham* [1925] Ch. 75; *Re Hagger* [1930] 2 Ch. 190; *Re Green* [1951] Ch. 148; *Re Cleaver* [1981] 1 W.L.R. 939; *Re Dale* [1994] Ch. 31; Snell, *Equity*, 190. For there to be a valid mutual will, there must be a contract between the parties: see *Re Dale*, above; *Re Goodchild* [1997] 1 W.L.R. 1216, applied *Charles v Fraser* [2010] EWHC 2154 (Ch). If, subsequent to the mutual wills agreement, the first testator to die is shown to have altered his will so that it no longer conforms to the mutual wills agreement, the agreement is terminated: *Re Hobley, The Times*, May 23, 1997. In *Olins v Walters* [2007] EWHC 3060 (Ch), Norris J. found that the doctrine of mutual wills was "anomalous and unprincipled", at para.8, echoing Rimer L.J. in the interlocutory appeal in the case.

[99] Below, para.15–052. See *Lysaght v Edwards* (1876) 2 Ch D 499; A. J. Oakley, *Constructive Trusts* (3rd edn), p.282.

(e) Where it would be inequitable for a landowner to deny a claimant an **11–022**
interest in land. Where a person acquires land in circumstances in which it
would be inequitable to deny the claimant an interest in the property, a
constructive trust will be imposed upon him.[100] Such trusts have been imposed
upon a purchaser who:

    (i) reneged on an informal promise to allow the vendor to remain in
        a cottage rent-free[101]; and

    (ii) repudiated a contract, not otherwise binding on him, to which a
        conveyance to him was expressly made subject and which he had
        undertaken to respect.[102]

It is however clear that a constructive trust will not be imposed on a purchaser
merely because he acquires the land "subject to" some third party right that
would not otherwise bind him. Such a trust will be created only "where there
are very special circumstances showing that the transferee of the property
undertook a new liability to give effect to provisions for the benefit of third
parties",[103] so that his conscience was affected.[104] The "heresy"[105] that the
grantor of an irrevocable contractual licence would in all cases become
subject to a constructive trust for the benefit of the licensee, regardless of
whether his conduct was unconscionable,[106] has now been rejected.[107] Even
then, there must, be a serious doubt as to the correctness of the remaining
cases which do allow a constructive trust. They suggest that a constructive

---

[100] *Gissing v Gissing* [1971] A.C. 886 at 905; *Ashburn Anstalt v Arnold* [1989] Ch. 1 at 22.

[101] *Bannister v Bannister* [1948] 2 All E.R. 133. See also *Collings v Lee* (2001) 2 All E.R. 332
where the new land owner never paid the purchase price, this being part of a scheme to defraud
the transferors of the registered title.

[102] *Lyus v Prowsa Developments Ltd* [1982] 1 W.L.R. 1044; [1983] C.L.J. 54 (C.H.). See too
Binions v Evans [1972] Ch. 359 at 368. The possibility of a constructive trust does not appear to
have been argued in either *Hollington Brothers Ltd v Rhodes* [1951] 2 T.L.R. 691 or *Markfaith
investment Ltd v Chiap Hua Flashlights Ltd* [1991] 2 A.C. 43. See above, para.8–094.

[103] *IDC Group Ltd v Clark* [1992] 1 E.G.L.R. 187 at 190, per Browne-Wilkinson V.C.; not
questioned on appeal: (1992) 65 P. & C.R. 179.

[104] *Ashburn Anstalt v Arnold*, above, at 25; *IDC Group Ltd v Clark*, above, at 189. No
constructive trust will be imposed therefore if the vendor has sold "subject to" the right merely
in order to satisfy his duty to disclose any incumbrances known to him. In *Lloyd v Dugdale*,
[2001] EWCA Civ 1754: (2001) 48 EG 129 (CS), where the claim failed, the Court of Appeal
made it clear that the purchaser must, in effect, be accepting some new liability—and this would
be difficult to establish. *Lloyd* was approved and applied in *Chaudhary v Yavuz* [2011] EWCA Civ
1314 where it was also made clear that incorporation of the Standard Conditions of Sale did not
mean that a purchaser took land "subject to" pre-existing obligations. What mattered was
registration under the LRA 2002.

[105] *IDC Group Ltd v Clark*, above, at 189, per Browne-Wilkinson V.C.

[106] *DHN Food Distributors Ltd v Tower Hamlets BC* [1976] 1 W.L.R. 852.

[107] *Ashburn Anstalt v Arnold*, above, at 22, 24; *Canadian Imperial Bank of Commerce v Bello*
(1991) 64 P. & C.R. 48 at 51. Both decisions remain good authority on this point although they
have been overruled on another: *Prudential Assurance Co Ltd v London Residuary Body* [1992]
2 A.C. 386. See too, *Lloyd v Dugdale*, above, where Sir Christopher Slade was explicit that
"notwithstanding some previous authority suggesting the contrary, a contractual licence is not to
be treated as creating a proprietary interest in land so as to bind third parties who acquire the land
with notice of it, on this account alone", at para.52.

trust can be employed to impose on the trustee the burden of an encumbrance over land[108] rather than one of the incidents of trusteeship, which has been the invariable characteristic of a constructive trust hitherto.[109] As such, they pose a threat to the security of title to land by providing a means of circumventing the policy which underlies the registration of title. The Contracts (Rights of Third Parties) Act 1999 offers a solution, although it is not used widely. Under the Act, a person who is not a party to a contract will normally be able to enforce it if there is an express term to that effect, or if the contract purports to confer a benefit on him.[110]

A more conventional example of this type of constructive trust is sufficiently important to merit separate treatment.

11–023   *(f) Where a party has acted to his or her detriment in reliance upon a common intention that he or she will acquire an interest in a property,*[111] *(or an enlarged share in property already co-owned.*[112]*)* It frequently happens that land is purchased in A's name alone, but B claims an interest in the property by reason either of some contribution direct or indirect to its acquisition or from having made some improvement to it. To succeed, B will have to demonstrate:

> (i) a common intention that both parties should have a beneficial interest in the property; and
>
> (ii) that B acted to his (or as is commonly the case, her[113]) detriment on the basis of that common intention so that it would be inequitable for A to deny B an interest.[114]

The House of Lords has now classified this trust as constructive,[115] and have made it clear that this concept is preferable to using a resulting trust in cases where the property is used by a couple for residential purposes,[116] but not others.[117] However, there may well be situations where it is indistinguishable

---

[108] Such as the burden of an option in *Lyus v Prowsa Developments Ltd*, above; or a licence in *Ashburn Anstalt v Arnold*, above (where the claim in fact failed).

[109] See (1997) 1 E.L.R. 437 at 451 (C.H.); R. J. Smith, *Property Law* 5th edn, p.458. See also [2000] Conv. 398 (S.B.) where it is argued that principles of wrongful interference or assumption of responsibility offer a better solution.

[110] See below, para.11–035.

[111] See [1990] Conv. 370 (D. J. Hayton).

[112] See below para.11–030.

[113] For a case where B was described by Slade L.J. as "a kept man", see *Thomas v Fuller-Brown* [1988] 1 F.L.R. 237. For a case where A and B were female lovers, see *Tinsley v Milligan* [1994] 1 A.C. 340.

[114] *Gissing v Gissing* [1971] A.C. 886 at 905; *Grant v Edwards* [1986] Ch. 638 at 654.

[115] *Lloyds Bank Plc v Rosset* [1991] 1 A.C. 107 at 132.

[116] *Stack v Dowden*, above at 447, per Lord Walker, a matter disputed by Lord Neuberger, at 465 in that case. In *Abbott v Abbott*, above, Baroness Hale (who gave the extensive judgment in *Stack*), confirmed this approach, at para.4. In *Jones v Kernott*, Lord Walker and Lady Hale made it clear that a resulting trust was inappropriate, above 11–016.

[117] In *Laskar v Laskar* above, a resulting trust was used to determine the precise shares of each party when the property had been purchased by mother and daughter as an investment, and this is not doubted in *Jones v Kernott*. It is open to a claimant to adduce evidence that a resulting trust more accurately reflects the parties intentions, *Jones v Kernott* at para.25.

from a presumed resulting trust.[118] This will be the case where B's detrimental act consists of a contribution to the cost of acquiring the property and the common intention of A and B is that B's interest should be commensurate with his contribution.[119] Neither form of trust will arise if B's contribution is by way of gift or loan.[120]

The existence of this form of constructive trust is important because there **11–024** is in this country no special doctrine of "family assets", whether in relation to married or merely cohabiting parties.[121] While some jurisdictions, such as California, recognise a common law claim for "palimony" between cohabitants,[122] "English law recognises neither the term nor the obligation to which it gives effect".[123] The trust was initially developed in disputes between spouses on the breakdown of marriage, though it is now seldom necessary to have recourse to it in such circumstances.[124] There is a broad statutory jurisdiction under the Matrimonial Causes Act 1973 to make property adjustment orders either when a court grants a decree of divorce, nullity or judicial separation, or at any time thereafter.[125] A similar jurisdiction exists in relation to the breakdown of a civil partnership.[126] Such constructive trusts have, however been relevant in a domestic context[127]:

    (i) on the death of a spouse, in deciding what property passes with his or her estate[128];

[118] Lord Walker in *Stack*, at para.28 noted "[w]hether the trust should be regarded as a resulting trust or a constructive trust may seem a distinctly academic enquiry". This may not be so when it comes to quantification of shares, see para.11–028.

[119] *McFarlane v McFarlane* [1972] NI. 59 at 67; *Tinsley v Milligan*, above, at 371 ("a development of the old law of resulting trusts", per Lord Browne-Wilkinson). cf. *Midland Bank Plc v Cooke* [1995] 4 All E.R. 562. Lord Neuberger noted in *Stack*, at para.106, that the result in *Oxley v Hiscock* [2005] Fam. 211 (which he regarded as rightly decided), would have been dictated by a resulting trust analysis, despite being considered by the Court of Appeal as a mater of constructive trust.

[120] See in relation to constructive trusts *Spence v Brown* (1988) 18 Fam. Law 291 (contribution by mother by way of loan to extension to daughter's house). In determining whether a payment was a loan the courts will look to the substance of what happened rather than as to how the parties described the transaction: *Risch v McFee* [1991] 1 F.L.R. 105; *Stokes v Anderson* [1991] 1 F.L.R. 391 (in each case a "loan" was found in fact to be a cash contribution). See [1991] Fam. Law 311 (S. M. Cretney).

[121] See *Pettitt v Pettitt* [1970] A.C. 777 at 795, 801, 810, 817, 820; *Gissing v Gissing* [1971] A.C. 886 at 899, 904, in relation to spouses. As regards cohabitants, see *Walker v Hall* [1984] F.L.R. 126 at 135; *Grant v Edwards* [1986] Ch. 638 at 651; *Windeler v Whitehall* [1990] 2 F.L.R. 505 at 506, 513 (where Millett J. spoke of "some kind of erroneous belief in a doctrine of community of property without benefit of clergy").

[122] See, *Marvin v Marvin* 557 P.2d. 957 (1976).

[123] *Windeler v Whitehall*, above, at 506, per Millett J.

[124] Although it may be decisive in other common law jurisdictions without equivalent matrimonial jurisdiction, *Abbott v Abbott*, above.

[125] s.24. On remarriage, a party loses the right to obtain such an order: s.28(3) (as amended by the Matrimonial and Family Proceedings Act 1984 s.5).

[126] Civil Partnership Act 2004 Sch.5, esp. Pt 2.

[127] It has been accepted by the Privy Council that such a trust may also arise in a commercial transaction See *Austin v Keele* (1987) 72 A.L.R. 579 where the claim failed on the facts.

[128] The surviving spouse may have a claim against the deceased's estate under the Inheritance (Provision for Family and Dependants) Acts 1975: below, para.14–004.

   (ii) on the insolvency of a spouse, in determining what property is available for his or her creditors[129];

   (iii) where co-owners (whether married, in civil partnership or otherwise) mortgage land and the mortgage is held not to be binding on one of them,[130] in determining the extent of the interest that is bound by the mortgage[131];

   (iv) in cases between unmarried cohabitants, whether engaged or not,[132] and whether on the breakdown of their relationship[133] or on death[134] or insolvency of one of the parties; and

   (v) in cases concerning other family members, particularly parent and child.[135]

11–025   (1) COMMON INTENTION.[136] It is now clear that common intention is relevant both as to whether a party has an interest in the property and to the quantum of that share if he does.[137] The latter is considered below.[138]

The common intention that both A and B should have a beneficial interest in the property[139] despite it being in the sole name of one only, may arise by inference, by express agreement or possibly by imputation, although whether imputation is permitted when the claimant seeks to establish an interest for the first time is uncertain.[140]

A common intention will be inferred in two situations, being cases where it can be "deduced objectively from their conduct".[141] In other words, there must be evidence from which the court may reasonably infer that the parties actually had a common intention, even though they did not articulate it as such. Thus, positive evidence that the parties did not have such an intention

---

[129] *Midland Bank Plc v Dobson* [1986] 1 F.L.R. 171; *Lloyds Bank Plc v Rosset* [1991] 1 A.C. 107; *Segal v Pasram*, Ch D (Bankruptcy Court) June 7, 2007, No.478 of 2000, a post-*Stack* decision.

[130] e.g. because his consent to it was obtained as a result of the fraud or undue influence: see *Barclays Bank Plc v O'Brien* [1994] 1 A.C. 180; para.25–118.

[131] *Midland Bank Plc v Cooke* [1995] 4 All E.R. 562.

[132] Where engaged couples break off their engagement, "any rule of law relating to the rights of husbands and wives in relation to property in which either or both has or have an interest" applies equally to them: Law Reform (Miscellaneous Provisions) Act 1970 s.2(1). However, it has been held that this does not include the property adjustment provisions of M.C.A. 1973: *Mossop v Mossop* [1989] Fam. 77.

[133] *Eves v Eves* [1975] 1 W.L.R. 1338; *Grant v Edwards* [1986] Ch. 638; *Stack v Dowden*, above, *Jones v Kernott* above.

[134] *Layton v Martin* [1986] 2 F.L.R. 227 (where the claim in fact failed). Again, the survivor may have a claim against the deceased's estate under the Inheritance (Provision for Family and Dependants) Acts 1975: below, para.14–004.

[135] *Ritchie v Ritchie*, 21/8/07, Case NoLS70535.

[136] See [1992] Fam. Law 72 (P. J. Clarke). cf. (1996) 16 L.S. 325 (N. Glover and P. Todd).

[137] *Jones v Kernott*, above, *Stack v Dowden*, above. See also, *Oxley v Hiscock*, above; *Midland Bank Plc v Cooke* [1995] 4 All E.R. 562; *Clough v Killey* (1996) 72 P. & C.R. D22.

[138] Below, para.11–028.

[139] The intention must relate to a specific property: *Layton v Martin* [1986] 2 F.L.R. 227 at 237.

[140] As opposed to assisting in its quantification.

[141] *Jones v Kernott*, above, at para. per Lord Walker and Lady Hale at para.51(3).

will defeat the inference.[142] The first case is where B contributes directly to the purchase price, whether by a cash contribution or its equivalent, or by paying mortgage instalments.[143] Secondly, in response to changing social and economic conditions, it is now clear that the common intention may be inferred from the parties' whole course of conduct in relation to the property.[144] This second approach has generated criticism,[145] not least because it offers little predictability nor certainty for third parties.[146] However, it now is established.[147]

In cases, where a common intention as to beneficial ownership cannot be inferred (and there is no express agreement[148]), the question arises whether such an intention can be imputed. An imputed intention is one "which is attributed to the parties, even though no such actual intention can be deduced from their actions and statements, and even though they had no such intention. Imputation involves concluding what the parties would have intended, whereas inference involves concluding what they did intend."[149] In *Stack v Dowden* both Lord Walker and Baroness Hale[150] seem content with the possibility of imputing an intention, although Lord Neuberger disagrees.[151] In *Jones v Kernott*, Lord Walker and Lady Hale identify circumstances when it might be possible to impute an intention, but these concern quantification of interests rather than acquisition of interests,[152] and although the difference in

[142] What is needed is evidence of the absence of a common intention, not merely the absence of evidence that they had one. cf. *Midland Bank v Cooke* [1995] 4 All E.R. 562.

[143] *Grant v Edwards*, above, at 647; *Lloyds Bank Plc v Rosset* [1991] 1 A.C. 107 at 132. The contributions are taken as evidence of the parties' intentions: *Grant v Edwards*, above, at 655. A discount on a sale to a sitting tenant has been treated as equivalent to a direct contribution: *Marsh v Von Sternberg* [1986] 1 F.L.R. 26; *Evans v Hayward* [1995] 2 F.L.R. 511. The court may be willing to infer a common intention from a wedding present or loan made to a married couple: *McHardy & Sons v Warren* [1994] 2 F.L.R. 338; *Midland Bank Plc v Cooke* [1995] 4 All E.R. 562; *Halifax BS v Brown* [1996] 1 F.L.R. 103. cf. [1994] Fam. Law 567 (J. Dewar).

[144] *Stack v Dowden* above at 455, per Baroness Hale (with whom Lord Walker, Lord Hoffmann and Lord Hope agreed), confirmed in *Abbott v Abbott*, above at para.6 per Baroness Hale. In *Stack*, Lord Walker regarded Lord Bridge's narrow approach in *Rosset* (which would admit of only the first means of establishing inferred common intention) as not taking full account of the views expressed in *Gissing v Gissing* [1971] A.C. 886, esp. at 896 and 909.

[145] (2007) 123 L.Q.R 511 (W. Swadling); [2007] Conv. 352 et seq. (M.J.D; M.Pawlowski).

[146] The actual result in *Stack* relied heavily on the parties' financial contributions, rather than their whole course of dealings in relation to the property. So too *Hiscock v Oxley*, above. In *Abbott*, the new approach was more to the fore, the Advice emphasising the joint nature of the parties' dealings with each other and the property, but again financial commitments played a large part, above, at paras 18 et seq. In *Morris v Morris* [2008] EWCA Civ 257, the Court of Appeal noted that conduct did not *necessarily* prove a common intention and that a court should be cautious before making such an inference on conduct alone.

[147] See *Stack v Dowden* above at p.459 (para.69) where Baroness Hale indicates the factors that are to be taken into account. Although not in point in the case, the approach is confirmed by *Jones v Kernott*, above at paras 15 and 51.

[148] On which see below

[149] Per Lord Neuberger, *Stack v Dowden* above at p.472. This is quoted, without disapproval as to the definition by Lord Walker and Lady Hale in *Jones v Kernott*, above at para.26.

[150] *Stack v Dowden*, above at p.447 and p.455 respectively

[151] *Stack v Dowden*, above at p.472.

[152] "[W]here it is clear that the beneficial interests are to be shared, but it is impossible to divine a common intention as to the proportions in which they are to be shared", at para.31. See also para.51. See also Lord Collins at para.60.

practice may rarely be decisive, and the tenor of both *Stack* and *Kernott* is in favour of permitting imputed intention, it is not unarguable that an imputed intention cannot support the acquisition of an interest rather than determine its quantification.[153]

In all other cases, which may now be few in the light of the expanded circumstances in which a common intention can be inferred (or imputed), express agreement will have to be proved.[154] In three situations in particular, there is authority that B's interest is entirely dependent upon proof of such express agreement. However, there is every possibility that the need for express agreement in these cases might now be redundant because of the possibility of finding an inferred intention under the "whole course of dealings" approach.

(i) Where, on the acquisition of the property, B has contributed to the purchase price but A and B have agreed that B should have a greater or lesser share than would otherwise be presumed from the size of B's contribution.[155] In the absence of express agreement, the normal principles of presumed resulting trust could apply, but not "in the case of the purchase of a house or flat in joint names for joint occupation by a married or unmarried couple"[156] when the inferred/imputed intention approach applies.

(ii) Where B has contributed indirectly to the acquisition of the property by undertaking household expenditure which A would otherwise have had to meet.[157] There can be no presumed resulting trust in respect of such indirect contributions (irrespective of the view taken in *Jones v Kernott*[158]), and much will depend on whether a common intention can be inferred or imputed in such cases. That now seems likely.

(iii) Where B has carried out some improvement to the property (other than work of a trivial kind).[159] The general rule is that where B voluntarily spends money on improving property which belongs either to A alone or to A and B, he or she acquires no interest or increased interest in the property in the absence of express agreement.[160] There is a statutory exception to this rule which applies

---

[153] As is pointed out in *Jones v Kernott*, above at paras 17 and 51, the nature of the enquiry is very different.

[154] *Lloyds Bank Plc v Rosset*, above, at 133; *Burns v Burns* [1984] Ch. 317. But see *Morris v Morris*, above.

[155] *Re Densham* [1975] 1 W.L.R. 1519; *Lloyds Bank Plc v Rosset*, above, at 132; *Drake v Whipp* [1996] 1 F.L.R. 826; *Clough v Killey* (1996) 72 P. & C.R. D22.

[156] *Jones v Kernott*, above, para.25, per Lord Walker and Lady Hale; above para.11–016.

[157] *Grant v Edwards* [1986] Ch. 638.

[158] Above

[159] *Eves v Eves* [1975] 1 W.L.R. 1338; *Ungurian v Lesnoff* [1990] Ch. 206. Improvements which are "so trifling as to be almost de minimis" will be discounted: *Lloyds Bank Plc v Rosset* [1991] 1 A.C. 107 at 131, per Lord Bridge; *Windeler v Whitehall* [1990] 2 F.L.R. 505 at 514.

[160] *Pettitt v Pettitt* [1970] A.C. 777 at 818; *Thomas v Fuller-Brown* [1988] 1 F.L.R. 237 at 240; *Harwood v Harwood* [1991] 2 F.L.R. 274 at 294.

both to spouses (and by extension to engaged couples) and to civil partners. The Matrimonial Proceedings and Property Act 1970[161] has "declared" that substantial contributions in money or money's worth by a husband or wife to the improvement of real or personal property[162] belonging beneficially to either or both of them are to entitle the contributor to such share as was agreed or, in default, "as may seem in all the circumstances just". It is clear from the section that the contributing spouse acquires a beneficial interest or an enlarged beneficial interest in the property.[163] A trust of land is presumably imposed to give effect to the spouse's interest in the same way as if it arose under a constructive trust by reason of common intention.[164] Again, such improvements now may easily generate an inferred or imputed common intention.

Where express common intention is essential to establish a beneficial interest, it must be founded on evidence of "express discussions between the partners, however imperfectly remembered and however imprecise their terms may have been".[165] In determining from such evidence whether there is a common intention, a court will draw the inferences that a reasonable person would have drawn at the relevant time.[166] Such an intention is sufficiently established if A induces B to believe that B will have an interest in the property, even if A does not in fact so intend.[167] Assertions by the parties as to their common intentions which are unsupported by contemporaneous evidence will be treated with caution where they are raised in order to defeat a claim by a creditor.[168]

---

[161] s 37, extended to engaged couples as explained above, para.11–024. This provision, being declaratory, is retrospective: *Davis v Vale* [1971] 1 W.L.R. 1022. It reverses *Pettitt v Pettitt*, above, where the House of Lords held that improvements made by the husband did not entitle him to a share since no agreement to that effect existed at the time of the improvement. See also Civil Partnership Act 2004 s.65.

[162] See *Harnett v Harnett* [1973] Fam. 156 at 167 (contributions must be identifiable with relevant improvements: not discussed on appeal, [1974] 1 W.L.R. 219); *Re Nicholson* [1974] 1 W.L.R. 476; *Samuels' Trustee v Samuels* (1973) 233 E.G. 149 (£227 held substantial contribution; Act gives wife no rights against husband's trustee in bankruptcy in respect of below-bankruptcy contributions).

[163] If prior to the improvement the parties are beneficial joint tenants, the operation of the section will presumably sever the joint tenancy, below, para.13–041.

[164] Considered below, para.11–027.

[165] *Lloyds Bank Plc v Rosset* [1991] 1 A.C. 107 at 132, per Lord Bridge. See too *Hammond v Mitchell* [1991] 1 W.L.R. 1127 at 1139 where Waite J. observed that, "the tenderest exchanges of a common law courtship may assume an unforeseen significance many years later when they are brought under equity's microscope".

[166] *Gissing v Gissing* [1971] A.C. 886 at 906; *Burns v Burns* [1984] Ch. 317 at 336. The subsequent conduct of the parties cannot affect what was originally agreed in the absence of an express or implied variation: *Marsh v Von Sternberg* [1986] 1 F.L.R. 526 at 533.

[167] *Eves v Eves* [1975] 1 W.L.R. 1338; *Grant v Edwards* [1986] Ch. 638. In each of those cases, A provided a specious excuse why the land should not be conveyed to A and B jointly. See too *Lloyds Bank Plc v Rosset*, above, at 133. cf. (1990) 106 L.Q.R. 539 (J. D. Davies); (1991) 54 M.L.R. 126 (S. Gardner).

[168] *Midland Bank Plc v Dobson* [1986] 1 F.L.R. 171 at 174.

11–026   (2) DETRIMENTAL RELIANCE. A constructive trust "does not come into being merely from a gratuitous intention to transfer or create a beneficial interest",[169] because such an intention would amount to an unenforceable declaration of trust.[170] B must have acted to his detriment in reliance upon the parties' common intention[171] and in the reasonable expectation that he would thereby acquire an interest in the property.[172] It is this detriment that takes the trust outside the formal requirements normally applicable to declarations of trusts of land.[173] The acts of detrimental reliance must amount to "an irrevocable change of legal position"[174] and be of a kind upon which B could not reasonably have been expected to embark unless he or she was to have an interest in the property.[175] B will therefore acquire no interest if the acts are ones which he or she would have undertaken in any event. In consequence, the performance of normal domestic duties will not suffice.[176] The extent to which acts unrelated to the acquisition or improvement of the property will satisfy the requirement of detriment has not been finally determined.[177] The House of Lords has held that a payment by B to reduce the overdraft of a company that had purchased a property used by A and B as their matrimonial home was not referable to its acquisition.[178] However, where A promised B that he would provide her with a home for the rest of her life, and in reliance upon this B abandoned her flat and a promising academic career in Poland, those acts were considered to be a sufficient detriment to justify the imposition of a constructive trust.[179] Recent cases, including *Jones v Kernott*, have tended not to comment on the role of detriment in crystallising the constructive trust, but instead focus on factors which establish the common intention, possibly because such factors might also constitute the necessary detriment.

11–027   (3) THE NATURE OF THE TRUST. Although a constructive trust of this kind commonly crystallises at the time when the property is acquired, this need not

---

[169] *Austin v Keele* (1987) 72 A.L.R. 579 at 587, per Lord Oliver.

[170] *Gissing v Gissing*, above, at 905; *Midland Bank Plc v Dobson*, above, at 175. For the formalities required for the creation of trusts, see below, para.11–037.

[171] The detrimental acts must be referable to that common intention: *Grant v Edwards*, above, at 653; *Austin v Keele*, above, at 588.

[172] *Gissing v Gissing*, above, at 905.

[173] For these, see LPA 1925 s.53(1)(b); below, para.11–037.

[174] *Austin v Keele*, above, at 588, per Lord Oliver.

[175] *Grant v Edwards*, above, at 650.

[176] This is so whether B is A's spouse (*Midland Bank Plc v Dobson* [1986] 1 F.L.R. 171, where there was express common intention) or not (*Burns v Burns* [1984] Ch. 317, where there was no such intention).

[177] Compare *Grant v Edwards*, above, at 656 (where Browne-Wilkinson V.C. expressly left the question open), with *Layton v Martin* [1986] 2 F.L.R. 227 at 237 (where Scott J. suggested that "contributions to the acquisition or preservation of specific property" were essential). In cases of inferred common intention the detriment must always be referable to the acquisition of the property: *Winkworth v Edward Baron Development Co Ltd* [1986] 1 W.L.R. 1512 at 1515; *Windeler v Whitehall* [1990] 2 F.L.R. 505 at 514.

[178] *Winkworth v Edward Baron Development Co Ltd*, above.

[179] *Ungurian v Lesnoff* [1990] Ch. 206; [1990] C.L.J. 25 (M. Oldham). In that case, the facts of which are remarkable, the defendant also carried out substantial improvements to the property. See too *Maharaj v Chand* [1986] A.C. 898 at 907; *Chun v Ho* [2002] EWCA Civ, (2003) 1 F.L.R. 23.

be so. It may arise subsequently, as where B either improves A's property or discharges the mortgage on it some years after its acquisition.[180]

The trust will give effect to the common intention of the parties, whether express, inferred or imputed. After 1996, this will normally mean that A (whether alone or jointly with B) holds the property on a trust of land for himself and B as beneficial joint tenants or tenants in common.[181] There may however be occasions where the parties have expressly agreed that B should be able to live in the house for the rest of his or her lifetime. In such cases, A may hold the property on a trust of land for B for his lifetime. Prior to 1997, it had been held that in such circumstances a settlement under the Settled Land Act 1925 might be created,[182] of which B was the life tenant.[183] However, after 1996, no new settlements can be created.[184]

(4) QUANTIFYING THE BENEFICIAL INTEREST.[185] Although the shares of the **11–028** parties may be determined at the time of the express or implied agreement between them, the valuation of those shares takes place on the dissolution of the trust.[186] The trust terminates when the parties' interests are realised (whether on sale or when one party purchases the interest of the other),[187] not as was once thought on the date when the parties separated.[188]

Where the parties have expressly agreed the shares in which they are to hold, that will normally be conclusive,[189] and a court will depart from it only if there is good cause to do so.[190] One possibility is that one party may be able to rely on proprietary estoppel to vary the expressly agreed shares, even if that agreement was in writing.[191] In the absence of such agreement, the position is

---

[180] *Bernard v Josephs* [1982] Ch. 391 at 404; *Grant v Edwards* [1986] Ch. 638 at 651; *Austin v Keele* (1987) 72 A.L.R. 579 at 587; *Harwood v Harwood* [1991] 2 F.L.R. 274 at 294; *Lloyds Bank Plc v Rosset* [1991] 1 A.C. 107 at 132.

[181] See e.g. *Lloyds Bank Plc v Rosset* [1989] Ch. 350 (reversed [1991] 1 A.C. 107, but not so as to affect this point).

[182] There must be a "settlement" within SLA 1925 s.1: see *Griffiths v Williams* [1978] 2 E.G.L.R. 121. This requirement has been overlooked, see below, Appendix para.A–040.

[183] *Ungurian v Lesnoff*, above. See too *Bannister v Bannister* [1948] 2 All E.R. 133; *Binions v Evans* [1972] Ch. 359; below, Appendix para.A–040. If the title was registered, the finding that B had a life estate could have unfortunate consequences. An interest under a settlement could not have taken effect as an overriding interest: LRA 1925 s.86(2) as was. The same position obtains under the LRA 2002 Sch.1 para.2; Sch.3 para.2(a).

[184] TLATA 1996 s.2; above, para.10–034.

[185] See (1991) 11 O.J.L.S. 39 (P. Sparkes).

[186] *Cowcher v Cowcher* [1972] 1 W.L.R. 425 at 432; *Marsh v Von Sternberg* [1986] 1 F.L.R. 526 at 533.

[187] *Gordon v Douce* [1983] 1 W.L.R. 563; *Walker v Hall* [1988] F.L.R. 126; *Turton v Turton* [1988] Ch. 542.

[188] *Hall v Hall* (1981) 3 F.L.R. 379; *Bernard v Josephs*, above, at 399. This view was illogical because once B acquired an interest in the property it was indefeasible unless and until he or she expressly assigned it: *Brykiert v Jones* (1981) 2 F.L.R. 373; *Turton v Turton*, above, at 552.

[189] *Pettitt v Pettitt* [1970] A.C. 777 at 813; *Lloyds Bank Plc v Rosset* [1991] 1 A.C. 107 at 132; *Savill v Goodall* [1993] 1 F.L.R. 755; *Clough v Killey* (1996) 72 P. & C.R. D22. This is analogous to the position where the conveyance expressly declares what the respective interests of the parties are to be. This will normally (but not always) be conclusive: *Goodman v Gallant* [1986] Fam. 106.

[190] *Clough v Killey* (1996) 72 P. & C.R. D22 at D24.

[191] *Clarke v Meadus* [2010] EWHC 3117 (Ch)

less clear, and there has been a shift in judicial practice from quantification that is determined by reference to the parties' contributions to one that depends upon the common intentions of the parties as deduced from all relevant circumstances.[192] Such a common intention may be express, inferred, and sometimes imputed.[193]

11–028.1   *(i) By reference to contributions.* Until recently, the court looked at the contributions made by the parties to determine their shares.[194] However, this approach is now frowned upon, to the point that reliance on it may be impossible,[195] in respect of property purchased by a couple for their joint occupation as a family home.[196] In such cases, the court must look to the common intention of the parties—inferred or imputed—rather than a contribution driven resulting trust approach. However, such an approach is not ruled out in cases where property was purchased for commercial purposes[197] or perhaps where the domestic partners are also business partners.[198]

In those cases where the share can be determined by reference to contributions, the task is to find out how much of the total outlay had been contributed by each, whether directly, or by the assumption of mortgage commitments. The parties' beneficial interests would then be proportionate to their financial contributions.[199] For these purposes, a mortgage advance was considered to be the same as a cash payment.[200] However, the amount of capital repaid would necessarily affect the valuation of the parties' respective shares when they came to be realised on sale.[201] Where A and B had contributed to the mortgage successively, no distinction was drawn between payments of interest and capital in determining the respective shares of the parties *inter se.*[202] Although the quantification of the parties' interests from their contributions was not carried out "as a strict mathematical exercise", it was only in the last resort

---

[192] *Stack v Dowden*, above.

[193] *Jones v Kernott*, above, per Lord Walker and Lady Hale, with whom Lord Collins agreed expressly.

[194] *Crisp v Mullings* [1976] 2 E.G.L.R. 103; *Walker v Hall* [1984] F.L.R. 126; *Young v Young* [1984] F.L.R. 375; *Springette v Defoe* [1992] 2 F.L.R. 388; *Huntingford v Hobbs* [1993] 1 F.L.R. 736.

[195] Reliance on it "would be rare in a domestic context", *Jones v Kernott*, above at para.31 per Lord Walker and Lady Hale.

[196] *Jones v Kernott*, above para.25. Above para.11–016. This echoes *Stack v Dowden* where it was made clear that the cases cited above—*Walker v Hall, Springette v Defoe, Huntingford v Hobbs*—should not be followed in the domestic context, at p.457.

[197] *Laskar v Laskar*, above

[198] *Jones v Kernott*, above at para.31 per Lord Walker and Lady Hale.

[199] *Walker v Hall*, above, at 130.

[200] *Marsh v Von Sternberg* [1986] 1 F.L.R. 526 at 533; *Harwood v Harwood* [1991] 2 F.L.R. 274 at 292; *Huntingford v Hobbs*, above, at 745.

[201] See, e.g. *Re Densham* [1975] 1 W.L.R. 1519.

[202] *Passee v Passee* [1988] 1 F.L.R. 263 at 267. This is material for instalment mortgages, where, as in that case, the initial payments are largely of interest. There is no authority for an interest only mortgage under which B pays the interest on the loan and A the premiums on the endowment policy. In principle both premium and interest should be regarded globally as mortgage repayments and it should be irrelevant that, strictly speaking, B made no payments towards the capital cost of acquiring the property.

that the court should "abandon the attempt in favour of applying the presumption of equality".[203] In cases where B's interest arose from an improvement that he or she had made to the property,[204] there was some authority which suggested that B's share would be quantified by having regard to the amount by which the improvement enhanced the value of the property at the time when it was made.[205]

(ii) By reference to common intention. More recent authorities suggest a **11–029** different approach. Where the court infers (or possibly imputes) a common intention that the contributor should have an interest in the property, whether that arises by direct contribution or on the basis of the parties entire course of conduct, it may then have regard to the whole course of conduct between the parties to determine the actual shares of the parties.[206] The task is to determine the parties' common intention as to the shares they should have. This common intention may, and usually will be, inferred—in other words, it will arise from an objective assessment deduced from all of their conduct.[207] However, in those cases where it is clear that the parties intended to share the beneficial interest, but it is impossible to infer a common intention as to the size of each of their shares, then it is permissible to impute such an intention. When an intention is imputed, the essence is to ensure that "each is entitled to that share which the court considers fair having regard to the whole course of dealing between them in relation to the property".[208] This approach, save perhaps the use of imputation, does in fact accord with a number of earlier authorities[209] which suggested that the common intention as to the extent of a claimant's beneficial interest did not have to be ascertained "once and for all at the date of its acquisition."[210] In both *Stack*[211] and *Abbott*,[212] the court approved the

---

[203] *Bernard v Josephs* [1982] Ch. 391 at 404, per Griffiths L.J. See too *Gissing v Gissing* [1971] A.C. 886 at 908. Where B's contributions are of an indirect character, the presumption of equal division may be the only possible solution.

[204] Whether by a constructive trust or under the Matrimonial Proceedings and Property Act 1970 s.37.

[205] *Re Nicholson* [1974] 1 W.L.R. 476 (decided under the Matrimonial Proceedings and Property Act 1970 s.37).

[206] *Jones v Kernott* above; *Oxley v Hiscock*, per Chadwick L.J. at para.69 ((2007) Conv. 14 (J. Mee); (2005) 17 C.F.L.Q. 259 (G. Battersby); (2004) Conv. 496 (M. Thompson); (2005) Conv. 79 (M.J.D.)), approved in *Stack v Dowden* above at para.61; (2007) Conv. 354 (M. Pawlowski) (2007) CLJ 517 (D. Fox and A. Cloherty); (2007) L.Q.R. 511 (W. Swadling). See too *Midland Bank Plc v Cooke* [1995] 4 All E.R. 562; (1996) 112 L.Q.R. 378 (S. Gardner); [1996] C.L.J. 194 (M. Oldham); (1996) 8 C.F.L.Q. 261 (G. Battersby); [1996] Fam. Law 298 (D. Wragg); [1997] Conv. 66 (M. J. D.). See too *Drake v Whipp* [1996] I F.L.R. 826; [1997] Conv. 467 (A. Dunn). For the position where the property was conveyed initially to both parties, but the equitable interest was left undeclared, see below para.11–030.

[207] *Jones v Kernott*, above at para.51 per Lord Walker and Lady Hale.

[208] *Oxley v Hiscock* [2005] Fam 211, para.69 per Chadwick L.J., approved and cited in *Jones v Kernott*, above at para.51 per Lord Walker and Lady Hale.

[209] See especially *Gissing v Gissing*, above, at 909; *Stokes v Anderson* [1991] 1 F.L.R. 391 at 400.

[210] *Stokes v Anderson*, above, at 399, per Nourse L.J.

[211] Above at para.61.

[212] Above at para.6.

approach presented by the Law Commission in its discussion paper on *Sharing Homes*[213] that:

> "If the question really is one of the parties' 'common intention', we believe that there is much to be said for adopting what has been called a 'holistic approach' to quantification, undertaking a survey of the whole course of dealing between the parties and taking account of all conduct which throws light on the question what shares were intended."[214]

Thus, in *Jones v Kernott*, the Supreme Court approved a quantification of the shares in the former family home that rested on an examination of the parties conduct over an extended period of time since it was originally purchased with the result that one was entitled to 10 per cent and the other 90 per cent.[215] In another case, a wife contributed half of the deposit on the common home, which was vested in the husband's name. Although she made no further financial contributions to the cost of acquiring the property, the court held that, having regard to the course of dealings between the parties, the wife was entitled to a half share in the property.[216] The result of approaching quantification in this way is that a person who has made a small monetary contribution may end up with a substantial share in the property on the basis of the parties' common intention, although there is no reason to depart from reliance on monetary contributions if that would produce a fair result.[217] Thus, there is now symmetry between how an interest arises and how a share is quantified—it depends on the common intention of the parties, either express, inferred or imputed.

11–030   *(iii) Where legal title is held jointly: generally.* The previous sections have discussed the situation where the claimant owns neither the legal nor equitable title, but makes a case based on implied trusts both as to the existence of an equitable share and then its size. If successful, the sole owner then holds the land on trust of land for himself and the claimant as tenants in common in the shares as determined. In fact, however, these were not the facts of *Stack v Dowden* nor *Jones v Kernott*, for in both cases the parties were joint registered

---

[213] (2002), Law Com. No.278.

[214] At para.4.27.

[215] *Jones* and *Stack* both involved property conveyed into joint names, so there was no dispute about whether one party had an interest at all. While Lord Walker and Lady Hale in *Jones* recognise that this may cause differences in result (as in a single owner case the burden falls on the claimant to establish an interest in the first place), the principles to be applied are the same, *Jones v Kernott*, above at para.51.

[216] *Midland Bank Plc v Cooke*, above. Had her share been determined according to her contribution, she would have had a mere 6.47% interest in the property. The fact that the parties were married was a significant factor: see at 576. cf. *Drake v Whipp*, above, where the parties were not married and the claimant, whose monetary contribution was 19.4%, was awarded a one-third share.

[217] As in *Stack* and *Oxley*.

proprietors, holding the land (as they must[218]) as joint tenants at law but in some undeclared manner. Of course, in many cases of joint legal ownership, the nature and extent of the beneficial interests will have been declared at the time of purchase, either in the trust instrument, by separate written agreement or as a consequence of completion of Land Registry forms at the time of registration.[219] This will be conclusive.[220] Where the equitable ownership is not expressly declared, the following principles apply.

(i) The starting point is that "equity follows the law" and thus (absent some special circumstance[221]), the parties are to be taken as joint-tenants in equity,[222] with the consequence that severance on relationship breakdown or other circumstance[223] results in equal shares.[224] This is a presumption not to be lightly dismissed because, according to *Jones v Kernott*, it is how both parties are likely to see their relationship developing and because evidence of an agreement as to any other share is likely to be misremembered and tainted by ill-will.[225] Although not mentioned in *Jones v Kernott*, another compelling reason for not departing from the presumption of equitable joint-tenancy, which does not require an analysis of the parties conduct over periods of time, is that this is what the parties have done by becoming joint-registered proprie-tors without declaring equitable shares. The law must assume— especially in property matters—that people say what they mean and are intending to be bound by the formal documents they have executed. It is not clear why a later change of mind, or a failure to understand the effect of formally executed documents, *of itself* justifies varying the equitable ownership.

(ii) However, this presumption can be displaced by showing that the parties had a different common intention when the property was

---

[218] LPA 1925 s.1(6), below para.13–051.

[219] See para.13–026.

[220] *Stack*, above, at para.49 and see *Goodman v Gallant* [1986] Fam. 106, although this can be "affected by proprietary estoppel", per Baroness Hale at para.49 and is what occurred in *Clarke v Meadus*, above. This will be rare, for it requires one of the parties to the express declaration to have led the other to believe, unconscionably, that they will not rely on that declaration as evidence of equitable ownership. See generally Ch.16 below.

[221] For example, that the property was an investment property to which the right of survivorship would not normally attach, *Laskar v Laskar*, above; or that the purchase money had been provided in unequal portions at the time of purchase, *Dyer v Dyer*, above. See also *Malayan Credit Ltd v Jack Chia-MPH Ltd* [1986] 1 A.C. 549.

[222] *Jones v Kernott* above at para.51, per Lord Walker and Lady Hale.

[223] e.g. bankruptcy, see *Segal v Pasram*, above.

[224] *Goodman v Gallant*, above.

[225] *Jones v Kernott* above at para.51, per Lord walker and Lady Hale. See also, Baroness Hale in *Stack v Dowden* that "It cannot be the case that all the hundreds of thousands, if not millions, of transfers into joint names using the old forms are vulnerable to challenge in the courts simply because it is likely that the owners contributed unequally to their purchase", ibid at p.458.

first acquired or that they formed a different common intention at a later date.[226]

(iii) This displacing common intention may be express, inferred ("deduced objectively from their conduct"[227]) or imputed (where there is no "direct evidence or by inference what their actual intention was as to the shares"[228]). If express or inferred, the court should give effect to the intention actually discovered. If imputed, each should have that share which the court considers fair having regard to the whole course of dealing between them and the property.[229]

Thus, in *Stack*, Ms Dowden sought to depart from the presumption that equity follows the law on the basis that it did not reflect the reality of the parties' true intentions. Baroness Hale accepted that it was possible to establish non-equal shares,[230] despite the absence of an express declaration of trust or the recognised special cases, but only where the claimant could prove a contrary intention and that this was likely to arise only in exceptional cases.[231] Such an exceptional case, though not considered in *Stack*, was *Abbey National Plc v Stringer*[232] where one of the two legal owners was held to have the entire equitable interest in the property, thus defeating entirely the mortgagee's security.[233] The difficulty is, of course, to identify those cases that are "exceptional" so as to justify departing from the normal presumption of an equitable joint-tenancy, bearing in mind that "strong feelings are aroused when couples split up"[234] In *Jones v Kernott*, the Supreme Court again found that there was an inferred common intention that the property should not be held equally in equity, but the evidence is less compelling than in *Stack*.[235] Clearly, context is everything.

11–031   *(iv) Where legal title is held jointly: factors raising an inferred common intention as to shares, and factors relevant to imputing an intention.* The factors from which we may infer a displacing common intention, or in reference to which the court might impute a common intention, will vary from

---

[226] *Jones v Kernott* above at para.51, per Lord walker and Lady Hale.

[227] Id.

[228] Id.

[229] Id.

[230] Thus indicating that the parties were not joint-tenants in equity.

[231] *Stack*, above, para.68.

[232] [2006] EWCA Civ 338, [2006] 2 P. & C.R. DG15, CA (Civ Div).

[233] The claimant's consent to the mortgage was vitiated by undue influence; (2006) Conv. 577 (M.J.D.).

[234] *Stack*, above, para.68.

[235] Much seemed to revolve around Mr Jones cashing in an insurance policy (not related to the disputed property), in order that he be able to acquire another property in which to live after quitting the property in dispute, also suggesting that there was an agreement that he did not have to make payments in respect of the disputed property. Lord Walker and Lady Hale note that the trial judge "did not go into detail", at para.48, but nevertheless felt able to draw the necessary inference. Imputation was, therefore, not required.

case to case. In *Stack,* Baroness Hale gives the following examples, explicitly approved in *Jones v Kernott.*[236]

> "Many more factors than financial contributions may be relevant to divining the parties' true intentions. These include: any advice or discussions at the time of the transfer which cast light upon their intentions then; the reasons why the home was acquired in their joint names; the reasons why (if it be the case) the survivor was authorised to give a receipt for the capital moneys; the purpose for which the home was acquired; the nature of the parties' relationship; whether they had children for whom they both had responsibility to provide a home; how the purchase was financed, both initially and subsequently; how the parties arranged their finances, whether separately or together or a bit of both; how they discharged the outgoings on the property and their other household expenses. When a couple are joint owners of the home and jointly liable for the mortgage, the inferences to be drawn from who pays for what may be very different from the inferences to be drawn when only one is owner of the home. The arithmetical calculation of how much was paid by each is also likely to be less important. It will be easier to draw the inference that they intended that each should contribute as much to the household as they reasonably could and that they would share the eventual benefit or burden equally. The parties' individual characters and personalities may also be a factor in deciding where their true intentions lay. In the cohabitation context, mercenary considerations may be more to the fore than they would be in marriage, but it should not be assumed that they always take pride of place over natural love and affection. At the end of the day, having taken all this into account, cases in which the joint legal owners are to be taken to have intended that their beneficial interests should be different from their legal interests will be very unusual."[237]

This is an extensive set of criteria, and there must be concerns that, even though it will be "very unusual" to depart from the presumption of equitable joint-tenancy, in fact these criteria give the court a wide discretion in the matter. Neither is the issue confined to couples in a relationship sharing the family home, for in *Ritchie v Ritchie*[238] the trial judge had no hesitation in extending the *Stack* analysis to property held by mother and son, and so quantified the shares unequally in favour of the former. Nor are the consequences confined only to the legal owners themselves: *Segal v Pasram*[239] (where the presumption was not displaced) illustrates how the matter will be relevant on the bankruptcy of one of the legal owners and may affect the position of creditors; and *Abbey National v Stringer* demonstrates that not

---

[236] *Jones v Kernott* above at para.51, per Lord Walker and Lady Hale.
[237] *Stack v Dowden* above at 459 (para.69).
[238] Above.
[239] Above.

even third parties will always be protected from uncertain equitable ownership by their ability to overreach by paying capital monies to two trustees.[240]

11–032   (5) COMPARISON WITH PROPRIETARY ESTOPPEL.[241] There are close parallels between constructive trusts which arise from the parties' common intention and the doctrine of proprietary estoppel.[242] By that doctrine, if A, by his conduct, encourages B to believe that he has some right in relation to A's property, and B acts in some way to his detriment in reliance upon that belief, an equity arises in B's favour to which the court may give effect in the manner and to the extent that it considers appropriate.[243] In this way B may acquire a proprietary interest in, or right over, A's property.[244] Although these parallels have often been acknowledged,[245] the two doctrines at present remain distinct,[246] and although the differences between them are not substantial, it seems they are to remain so.[247]

It is often said that constructive trusts depend upon proof of some bilateral consensus between the parties, whereas estoppel will be established if B unilaterally acts to his detriment on the basis of some express or implied representation by A. However, a representation by A that leads B to believe that he will acquire an interest in the property may be evidence of express common intention.[248] Where a constructive trust is alleged, B must prove that he acted in reliance upon the common understanding with A.[249] However, where the basis of B's claim is proprietary estoppel, he will be presumed to

---

[240] Undue influence vitiated the consent of one of the legal owners who, having been held to own 100 per cent of the equity, found her "share" completely unencumbered. The lender, despite having searched the title register and conduct a proper overreaching disposition, was left with no security at all.

[241] See [1990] Conv. 370 at 371 (D. J. Hayton) (1993) 109 L.Q.R. 1 14 (P. Ferguson); and below, para.13–036.

[242] Proprietary estoppel is considered, below, para.16–001.

[243] See, e.g. *Crabb v Arun DC* [1976] Ch. 179 at 193; *Jennings v Rice* [2002] EWCA Civ 159.

[244] e.g. *Chaudhary v Yavuz* [2011] EWCA Civ 1314, an easement by estoppel.

[245] *Grant v Edwards* [1986] Ch. 638 at 656; *Re Basham* [1986] 1 W.L.R. 1498 at 1504; *Austin v Keele* (1987) 72 A.L.R. 579 at 587; *Lloyds Bank Plc v Rosset* [1991] 1 A.C. 107 at 132; *Yaxley v Gott* [1999] E.G.C.S. 92.

[246] *Stokes v Anderson*, above, at 399. See too *Maharaj v Chand* [1986] A.C. 898 at 908. Because of the close similarities between them, constructive trust and proprietary estoppel will nowadays often be pleaded in the alternative.

[247] In *Stack*, above at para.37, Lord Walker comments that "in *Oxley v Hiscock* Chadwick L.J. considered the conceptual basis of the developing law in this area, and briefly discussed proprietary estoppel, a suggestion first put forward by Sir Nicolas Browne-Wilkinson V.C. in *Grant v Edwards* [1986] Ch. 638, 656. I have myself given some encouragement to this approach (*Yaxley v Gotts* [2000] Ch. 162,177) but I have to say that I am now rather less enthusiastic about the notion that proprietary estoppel and 'common interest' constructive trusts can or should be completely assimilated. Proprietary estoppel typically consists of asserting an equitable claim against the conscience of the 'true' owner. The claim is a 'mere equity'. It is to be satisfied by the minimum award necessary to do justice (*Crabb v Arun District Council* [1976] Ch 179, 198), which may sometimes lead to no more than a monetary award. A 'common intention' constructive trust, by contrast, is identifying the true beneficial owner or owners, and the size of their beneficial interests." For a contrary view, see *Clarke v Meadus*, above and above para.11–017, especially if the constructive trust can be regarded as "remedial".

[248] *Gissing v Gissing*, above, at 905; *Lloyds Bank Plc v Rosset*, above, at 133.

[249] *Grant v Edwards*, above, at 652; *Lloyds Bank Plc v Rosset*, above, at 131.

have acted in reliance on A's representation if a reasonable person would have done so.[250] Where a constructive trust arises, the claimant acquires a beneficial interest in the property at the time when he acts to his detriment.[251] In a case of proprietary estoppel, the claimant's detrimental reliance raises only an inchoate "equity" in his favour.[252] The precise nature of the claimant's right remains in limbo until the court determines how best to give effect to it, although the equity itself is proprietary.[253] Although the court will often grant the claimant the interest that he was intended to have, it is not bound to do so and has a discretion as to how the equity should be satisfied.[254] Indeed, the circumstances may make it inappropriate for the claimant to be granted any interest in the property.[255] An interest arising under a constructive trust is undoubtedly a proprietary right which is capable of binding a third party. Although an equity arising by estoppel enjoys the same status, the successful claimant is not certain to be awarded an interest in the land at all, let alone a beneficial share. It is however clear in relation both to constructive trusts arising out of common intention and to proprietary estoppel that B's claim may be defeated if it is tainted by unlawful or inequitable conduct.[256]

5. Other classifications: completely and incompletely constituted trusts.   **11–033**
In addition to the main classification considered above, equity classified trusts in other ways. One of these must be considered here,[257] namely the distinction between completely and incompletely constituted trusts. A trust is completely constituted as soon as the trust property is vested in the trustee. Until this has been done, it is incompletely constituted. The usual example of an incompletely constituted trust is where a settlor covenants with trustees to transfer to them property which he may acquire in the future.

---

[250] *Greasley v Cooke* [1980] 1 W.L.R. 1306. Of course, reliance may be absent on the facts, *Powell v Benney* [2007] EWCA Civ 1283.

[251] *Turton v Turton* [1988] Ch. 542 at 555; *Grant v Edwards*, above, at 651, 652. The quantum of the claimant's interest will not necessarily be determined at that time: see above, para.11–029.

[252] *Griffiths v Williams* [1978] 2 E.G.L.R. 121 at 122.

[253] At least for registered title, LRA 2002 s.116.

[254] *Burrows v Sharp* (1989) 23 H.L.R. 82 at 92; *Jennings v Rice* [2002] EWCA Civ 159.

[255] *Dodsworth v Dodsworth* (1973) 228 E.G. 1115 (court ordered reimbursement of expenditure); *Jennings v Rice* [2002] EWCA Civ 159 (payment of a lump sum).

[256] See as regards constructive trusts, *Winkworth v Edward Baron Development Co Ltd* [1986] 1 W.L.R. 1512 at 1516 (B had acted in breach of her duties as a director of a company and could not claim a beneficial interest in its property in priority to its creditors); and in relation to estoppel, *J. Willis & Son v Willis* [1986] 1 E.G.L.R. 62 (false claims submitted by B as to his expenditure on the property).

[257] Another distinction, formerly of some significance, is between executed and executory trusts. An executory trust is one which calls for the execution of some further instrument for the purpose of defining the beneficial interests exactly. For example, at one time marriage articles often provided that certain property belonging to one of the parties should be settled upon them and their children. The property was at once subject to a valid trust, but until the settlement was duly executed the trust was executory. The importance of the distinction between executed and executory trusts lies in the more liberal manner in which executory trusts are construed for some purposes: see, e.g. below, para.13–030.

11–034   *(a) Completely constituted trusts.* A trust may be completely constituted in one of two circumstances[258]:

>   (i) Where the trust property is vested in the trustees upon the required trusts.

>   (ii) Where "a present irrevocable declaration of trust" is made by the settlor.[259] It is not essential that the settlor should use the words "I declare myself a trustee", but he must do something equivalent to this. Thus, where a man cohabiting with a woman authorised her to draw on his bank account and said repeatedly "the money is as much yours as mine", a declaration of trust was found as to a half share of the money.[260]

Although words of direct gift have occasionally been construed as declarations of trust,[261] it is now generally regarded as well established that an imperfect attempt to transfer property to a volunteer[262] (a person who gives no valuable consideration) or to trustees for a volunteer[263] will not be construed as a declaration of trust. Nor will the court compel the settlor to perfect his attempted transfer in proceedings brought by the volunteer, for "there is no equity in this court to perfect an imperfect gift",[264] save perhaps where it would be unconscionable for the transfer to fail.[265] Thus if A owns leasehold property and, wishing to give it to E, endorses on the lease "This deed and all thereto belonging I give to E from this time forth", neither this endorsement nor the delivery of the lease to E's mother on his behalf (E being an infant) will give E any beneficial interest in the lease. The legal term of years has not been vested in E or his mother, because a deed is required for this,[266] and A's words will not be construed as a declaration of trust.[267]

11–035   *(b) Volunteers.* The importance of the distinction between a completely and incompletely constituted trust lies in the fact that if a trust is completely constituted, it can be enforced by the beneficiaries even if they are volunteers.[268] By contrast, if the trust is incompletely constituted, it will be enforced

---

[258] *Milroy v Lord* (1862) 4 De G.E & J. 264 at 274; *Richards v Delbridge* (1874) L.R. Eq. 11 at 14.

[259] *Re Cozens* [1913] 2 Ch. 478 at 486. There is no power of revocation unless it is expressly reserved: *Re Bowden* [1936] Ch. 71.

[260] *Paul v Constance* [1977] 1 W.L.R. 527. See too *Vandenberg v Palmer* (1858) 4 K. & J. 204.

[261] See, e.g. *Richardson v Richardson* (1867) L.R. 3 Eq. 686; and see *Bowman v Secular Society Ltd* [1917] A.C. 406 at 436, 437.

[262] *Jones v Lock* (1865) 1 Ch. App. 25; *Re Swinburne* [1926] Ch. 38.

[263] *Jeffreys v Jeffreys* (1841) Cr. & Ph. 138; cf. *Re Wale* [1956] 1 W.L.R. 1346.

[264] *Milroy v Lord* (1862) 4 De G.E. & J. 264 at 274, per Turner L.J.

[265] *Pennington v Waine* [2002] 1 W.L.R. 2075; [2003] Conv. 192 (M. Halliwell). The result is controversial, for it cannot be unconscionable simply because the transferor's intentions have been thwarted by a rule of law or equity about formality.

[266] Below, para.17–034.

[267] *Richards v Delbridge* (1874) L.R. 18 Eq. 11.

[268] *Paul v Paul* (1882) 20 Ch D 742.

at the suit of beneficiaries who gave valuable consideration[269] (including those regarded as "within the marriage consideration" under a marriage settlement[270]) but cannot be enforced by volunteers.[271] The difference may be compared with the familiar distinction between grants and contracts at common law. A grant by deed at once vests the property in the grantee, whether or not he gave consideration for it. A contract to make a grant in the future will be enforceable only if supported by valuable consideration. It is therefore in the context of an incompletely constituted trust that the maxim "equity will not assist a volunteer" is applicable. Completely constituted trusts are, of course, enforceable at the suit of volunteer beneficiaries.

In the context of covenants to settle property, the distinction between completely and incompletely constituted trusts would disappear if use were made of the Contracts (Rights of Third Parties) Act.[272] This enables a person who is not a party to a contract to enforce it if there is an express term to that effect, or if the contract purports to confer a benefit on him.[273]

Part 2

FORMALITIES REQUIRED FOR THE CREATION OF A TRUST

A. Pure Personalty

An enforceable trust of pure personalty can be validly created by word of **11–036** mouth, whether the owner is declaring himself a trustee of the property or is transferring it to a third party on trust for the beneficiaries.[274]

B. Land

1. The general rule. Trusts of land must be evidenced in writing. Before **11–037** 1677 a trust of land could be created orally. Thereafter, first by the Statute of Frauds 1677,[275] and after 1925 by the Law of Property Act 1925,[276] a "declaration of trust respecting any land or any interest therein must be manifested and proved by some writing signed by some person who is able to

---

[269] *Pullan v Koe* [1913] 1 Ch. 9. If they do so, other beneficiaries who are volunteers may also enforce it. *Davenport v Bishopp* (1843) 2 Y. & CCC. 451; (1846) 1 Ph. 698.

[270] Above, para.8–008.

[271] *Re Plumptre's Marriage Settlement* [1910] 1 Ch. 609; *Re Pryce* [1917] 1 Ch. 234. But see (1975) 91 L.Q.R. 236 (I. U. Barton) and (1976) 92 L.Q.R. 236 (R. P. Meagher and I. R. E Lehane), criticising *Re Pryce* and decisions following it on the ground that there may be a completely constituted trust of the benefit of the covenant. For the intention necessary to create a trust of the benefit of a covenant, see (1982) 98 L.Q.R. 17 (J. D. Feltham).

[272] The Act implements (with some modifications) the recommendations of the Law Commission: see (1996) Law Com. No.242.

[273] The contract will not be enforceable by the third party, even if it is made for his benefit, if on a proper construction of the contract it appears that the parties did not intend it to be enforceable by him.

[274] e.g. *Harris v Truman* (1881) 7 QBD 340 at 356.

[275] ss.7, 8.

[276] s.53(1)(b), (2).

declare such trust or by his will".[277] The chief points to note on this provision are as follows.

11–038   *(a) "Any land".* This includes leaseholds.[278]

11–039   *(b) Evidenced.* It is settled that the statutory words "manifested and proved" merely require that the trust should be evidenced by writing.[279] The declaration need not be made in writing.[280] It suffices if an oral declaration is supported by some signed acknowledgement or declaration[281] in existence when the action is begun,[282] such as a letter[283] or a recital in a deed,[284] even if this was made some time after the trust was declared.[285] The writing must show not only that there is a trust but also what its terms are.[286]

A trust will never be void for lack of written evidence, but merely unenforceable. It follows that where A transfers property to B who orally agrees to hold it on trust for C, C cannot enforce the trust. However, the trust is not void, and B will not therefore hold it on a resulting trust for A.[287] B will take the property beneficially (because the trust cannot be enforced against him) unless (as would generally be the case in such circumstances) he is estopped from relying on the lack of writing because it would be fraud for him to do so.[288]

11–040   *(c) "Some person who is able to declare such trust".* This means the owner of the beneficial interest, so that if a trust is declared of an equitable interest under an existing trust, the writing must be signed by the beneficiary. The signatures of the trustees are not sufficient.[289]

11–041   *(d) "Or by his will".* These words allow even an informal will (if valid as such[290]) to suffice.

2. Exceptions to the general rule. To these requirements there are two important exceptions.

---

[277] Most wills are required to be in writing, but some may be oral: see below, para.14–039.
[278] See *Forster v Hale* (1798) 3 Yes. 696; affirmed 5 Yes. 308.
[279] This is an exception to the general rule that writing is required for the creation or disposition of an interest in land: LPA 1925 s.53(1)(a).
[280] *Randall v Morgan* (1805) 12 Yes. 67 at 74.
[281] See *Ambrose v Ambrose* (1717) 1 P.Wms. 321.
[282] See *Forster v Hale*, above.
[283] *Morton v Tewart* (1842) 2 Y. & C.C.C. 67; *Childers v Childers* (1857) 1 De G. & I. 482.
[284] See *Deg v Deg* (1727) 2 P.Wms. 412; and see *Re Holland* [1902] 2 Ch. 360.
[285] *Rochefoucauld v Boustead* [1897] 1 Ch. 196 at 206; and see *Barkworth v Young* (1856) 4 Drew. 1.
[286] *Smith v Matthews* (1861) 19 Beav. 330.
[287] The contrary is suggested in *Hodgson v Marks* [1971] Ch. 892 at 933. However that case is best explained as one where it would have been fraudulent for B to rely on LPA 1925 s.53(l)(b): see *Hodgson v Marks* at 908, 909.
[288] Below, para.11–043.
[289] *Tierney v Wood* (1854) 19 Beav. 330; *Kronheim v Johnson* (1877) 7 Ch D 60.
[290] See below, para.14–048.

(a) Resulting, implied or constructive trusts. The requirements do not apply **11–042** to the creation or operation of resulting, implied or constructive trusts.[291] Thus, for example, if land is conveyed to A in circumstances where A and B have contributed to the purchase price, B will not be precluded from enforcing the trust in his favour because of the lack of written evidence of it.

(b) Where it would be fraud for the trustee to rely on the absence of writing. **11–043** The court will not permit a statute to be used as an engine of fraud.[292] "It is a fraud on the part of a person to whom land is conveyed, to deny the trust and claim the land himself. Consequently, notwithstanding the statute, it is competent for a person claiming land conveyed to another to prove by parol evidence that it was so conveyed upon trust for the claimant, and that the grantee, knowing the facts, is denying the trust and relying upon the form of conveyance and the statute, in order to keep the land himself."[293]

It is on this principle that secret trusts are enforced.[294] If a testator informs X of his intention to leave property to X to be held on trust for Y, and X acquiesces, whether expressly or by silence, this trust will be enforced even though it is not contained in the will or evidenced by writing.[295] This applies whether the trust is:

(i) half secret, i.e. where the will discloses that the property is held upon trust without disclosing the beneficiary (e.g. "to X upon trusts which I have already communicated to him")[296]; or

(ii) fully secret, i.e. where the gift is apparently beneficial (e.g. "to X absolutely").[297]

However, in the case of fully secret trusts it suffices if the trusts are communicated at any time before the testator's death.[298] In relation to half secret trusts, there is some rather unsatisfactory authority for saying that the trusts must

---

[291] LPA 1925 s.53(2) (replacing Statute of Frauds 1677 s.8).

[292] *Stickland v Arlidge* (1804) 9 Yes. 516; *Lincoln v Wright* (1859) 4 De G. & I. 16; *Re Duke of Marlborough* [1894] 2 Ch. 133; *McGillycuddy of the Reeks v Joy* [1959] I.R. 189; *Gilmurray v Corr* [1978] N.I. 99; cf. *Hodgson v Marks*, above, at 933. The ambit of this doctrine is uncertain: compare [1984] C.L.J. 306; [1988] Conv. 267 (T. G. Youdan); with [1987] Conv. 246 (I. D. Feltham).

[293] *Rochefoucauld v Boustead* [1897] 1 Ch. 196 at 206, per Lindley L.J.; and see *Haigh v Kaye* (1872) 7 Ch.App. 469 at 474; *Du Boulay v Raggett* (1988) 58 P. & C.R. 138 at 150.

[294] See Snell, *Equity*, 108 et seq.; *Drakeford v Wilks* (1747) 3 Atk. 539.

[295] *Jones v Badley* (1868) 3 Ch.App. 262; *Re Maddock* [1902] 2 Ch. 220; *Re Falkiner* [1924] 1 Ch. 88.

[296] *Blackwell v Blackwell* [1929] A.C. 318; *Re Colin Cooper* [1939] Ch. 811.

[297] *Re Boyes* (1884) 26 Ch D 531. As to the position where only one of several beneficiaries is told of the trust, see *Re Stead* [1900] 1 Ch. 237 at 241, on which see (1972) 88 L.Q.R. 225 (B. Perrins).

[298] *Moss v Cooper* (1861) 1 I. & H. 352. The trust is destroyed if the trustee predeceases the testator (*Re Maddock* [1902] 2 Ch. 220 at 231) but not if the beneficiary does so: *Re Gardner (No.2)* [1923] 2 Ch. 230 (*sed quaere*: it is not apparent how a trust can be constituted in favour of a dead person: cf. para.11–010.

have been declared to and agreed by X before or at the time of making the will,[299] and that the will must show this to be the case.[300]

Part 3

FORMALITIES REQUIRED FOR THE TRANSFER OF AN INTEREST UNDER A TRUST

11–044   **1. General rule: dispositions must be made in writing.** By the Law of Property Act 1925, "a disposition of an equitable interest or trust subsisting at the time of the disposition, must be in writing signed by the person disposing of the same, or by his agent thereunto lawfully authorised in writing or by will".[301] This provision differs significantly from the Statute of Frauds 1677,[302] from which it derives.[303] The Statute of Frauds applied only to "grants and assignments" of equitable interests, whereas the present provision is broader and applies to any "disposition".[304] Furthermore, the requirements of the Law of Property Act 1925 do not affect the creation or operation of resulting, implied or constructive trusts.[305] There was no such qualification in the Statute of Frauds.[306] The following points should be noted.

11–045   *(a) "Disposition".* "Disposition" is given a very wide meaning.[307] It includes oral instructions given by a beneficiary to a bare trustee for him to hold the property on trust for other persons,[308] but not instructions to the trustee to transfer both the legal and equitable interests together to others.[309]

11–046   *(b) "In writing".* An oral disposition supported by evidence of it is not enough. Unlike the rule for the creation of trusts,[310] the rule here requires the

---

[299] *Johnson v Ball* (1851) 5 De G. & Sm. 85; *Blackwell v Blackwell* [1929] A.C. 318 at 339; *Re Colin Cooper* [1939] Ch. 811.

[300] *Re Keen* [1937] Ch. 236.

[301] s.53(1)(c). See [1979] Conv. 17 (G. Battersby); (1984) 47 M.L.R. 385 (B. Green).

[302] s.9. Previously an oral assignment was valid.

[303] The wording was changed by the Law of Property (Amendment) Act 1924 Sch.3 Pt II para.15. The changes may not have been intended: see S. Anderson, *Lawyers and the Making of English Land Law 1832–1940*, p.311.

[304] *Grey v IRC* [1960] A.C. 1.

[305] s.53(2), above, para.11–042.

[306] s.8 of that Act (the nearest equivalent to LPA 1925 s.53(2)) qualified s.7, but not s.9.

[307] "The wide meaning that it would seem to have in normal everyday usage": *Grey v IRC* [1958] Ch. 690 at 722, per Ormerod L.J. The broad definition of "disposition" found in LPA 1925 s.205(1)(ii) has not always been applied in cases on s.53(1)(c): see *Re Paradise Motor Co Ltd* [1968] 1 W.L.R. 1125. cf. *Grey v IRC*, above, at 719.

[308] *Grey v IRC* [1960] A.C. 1; see (1960) 76 L.Q.R. 197 (REM).

[309] *Vandervell v IRC* [1967] 2 A.C. 291.

[310] Above, para.11–037.

disposition itself to be written,[311] and is thus not a mere rule of evidence.[312]

(c) "Signed by the person disposing of the same or by his agent thereunto **11–047** *lawfully authorised in writing".* The disposition must be made by or on behalf of the person having the equitable interest. If a person is divested of his equitable interest through the exercise of a power, that exercise does not fall within the formal requirements of the Law of Property Act 1925 and need not be made in writing.[313] The fact that a disposition may be made by an agent should be contrasted with:

(i) the rule for the creation of a trust of land, where the signature of an agent is not enough[314]; and

(ii) the rule for contracts for the disposition of land, where the signature of an agent suffices even if his authority was given only by word of mouth.[315]

(d) The rule applies to pure personalty as well as land. Although a trust of **11–048** pure personalty is enforceable even if it is not evidenced in writing,[316] once the trust has been created, a disposition of any interest under it is void unless it is in writing.[317]

2. Exception: resulting, implied or constructive trusts. As mentioned **11–049** above,[318] the requirement that a disposition of an equitable interest must be made in writing does not apply where that disposition is brought about through the creation or operation of a resulting, implied or constructive trust.[319] The reason for this exception is not apparent and it has led to curious results. It has been held that a specifically enforceable contract to transfer an equitable interest in circumstances where the transferee has furnished the consideration creates a constructive trust in favour of the transferee. This vests

---

[311] See *Re Tyler* [1967] 1 W.L.R. 1269.

[312] There is an obvious parallel with the requirement that a legal estate can only be transferred by deed. It ensures that where A makes a disposition of his equitable interest to B, B can prove his title to that interest to the trustees. This may be important because of the rule in *Dearle v Hall* (1828) 3 Russ. 1; below, para.26–015.

[313] See *Re Vandervell's Trusts (No.2)* [1974] Ch. 269, where A, a bare trustee holding on trust for B, had power to declare trusts in favour of C and was held to have done. Although this is probably the most plausible explanation of this difficult case, it may be doubted whether on the facts A's conduct did amount to a declaration of new trusts: see (1975) 38 M.L.R. 557 (J. W. Harris).

[314] Above, para.11–040.

[315] Below, para.15–041.

[316] Above, para.11–036.

[317] See *Oughtred v IRC* [1960] A.C. 206, and the notes of the draftsman in Wolst. & C., 12th edn, p.321. If LPA 1925 s.53(1)(c) were confined to dispositions of equitable interests in land it would be otiose: see s.53(1)(a).

[318] Above, para.11–042.

[319] LPA 1925 s.53(2).

the equitable interest in him, without the need for writing.[320] It is not clear why the need for a written disposition of an equitable interest should be obviated simply because the agreement to make it is specifically enforceable and the purchaser has paid the price or met his reciprocal obligations.

Part 4

TRUSTEES

Section 1. Appointment of Trustees

A. *Original Appointment*

11–050   **1. Appointment.** Trustees are usually appointed by the settlor when creating the trust. If he neither makes an appointment nor makes any provision for one, the court may appoint trustees.[321] Once the trust has been created, the settlor has no power to make an appointment unless he has reserved such a power. A person appointed trustee need not accept the trust[322] even if he had agreed to do so before it was created,[323] provided he disclaims the trust before he has accepted it either expressly or by acting as trustee.[324] A disclaimer is void if it relates only to part of the trusts.[325] It should preferably be express but it may be inferred from conduct.[326] Although the presumption is in favour of acceptance, a person appointed a trustee who is completely inactive in relation to the trust for a long period (e.g. for more than 25 years) may be held thereby to have disclaimed the trust.[327] Disclaimer operates retrospectively to divest the person appointed both of his office and the trust property.[328]

11–051   **2. Maximum number.** Subject to one exception,[329] no more than four trustees of settled land or land held on a trust of land can be appointed, whether the title is unregistered or registered.[330] Thus, if more than four are named as trustees, the first four named who are able and willing to act become

---

[320] *Neville v Wilson* [1997] Ch. 144; [1996] C.L.J. 436 (R. Nolan); [1996] Conv. 368 (M. P. Thompson). See also *Oughtred v IRC* [1960] A.C. 206.

[321] e.g. *Re Smirthwaite* (1871) U.R. 11 Eq. 251.

[322] *Robinson v Pett* (1734) 3 P.Wms. 249 at 251.

[323] See *Doyle v Blake* (1804) 2 Sch. & Lef. 231 at 239 (executor).

[324] *Conyngham v Conyngham* (1750) 1 Yes.Sen. 522; *Noble v Meymott* (1851) 14 Beav. 471.

[325] *Re Lord and Fullerton's Contract* [1896] 1 Ch. 228.

[326] *Stacey v Elph* (1833) 1 My. & K. 195. This is so even for freehold land: *Re Gordon* (1877) 6 Ch D 531 and *Re Birchall* (1889) 40 Ch D 436, ignoring doubts expressed in *Re Ellison's Trusts* (1856) 2 Jur. (N.S.) 62.

[327] *Jago v Jago* (1893) 68 UT. 654; *Re Clout and Frewer's Contract* [1924] 2 Ch. 230.

[328] *Peppercorn v Wayman* (1852) 2 De G. & Sm. 230; *Re Martinez' Trusts* (1870) 22 L.T. 403.

[329] Below.

[330] TA 1925 s.34(2) (as amended by TLATA 1996 s.25(1), Sch.3 para.3); below, Appendix para.A–091, para.13–085.

trustees to the exclusion of the others.[331] However, these provisions apply only to private trusts of land.[332] In general there is no limit to the number of trustees of either:

(i) land held on trust for charitable, ecclesiastical or public purposes[333]; or

(ii) pure personalty.[334]

3. Minimum number. There is no minimum number of trustees even in the case of land.[335] However, whether the land is settled or held on a trust of land, then notwithstanding any contrary provision, a sole trustee cannot give a valid receipt for capital money unless that trustee is a trust corporation.[336] This restriction, however, does not affect the right of a sole personal representative acting as such to give valid receipts for purchase-money,[337] e.g. where a sole administrator sells under the trust which is imposed on all the property of an intestate.[338]

11–052

B. Replacement

Even if there are properly appointed trustees when the trust is created, it may later become necessary to appoint new trustees, e.g. owing to the death of trustees. The events upon which new trustees can be appointed may be specified in the trust instrument. This is not usual however, and reliance is normally placed on certain statutory provisions. The principal provisions are found in the Trustee Act 1925, but these have been supplemented by Part II of the Trusts of Land and Appointment of Trustees Act 1996. These provisions of the 1996 Act owe little to the Law Commission from whose report the remainder of the Act derives, but were for the most part introduced by amendment during the passage of the legislation through Parliament.[339] Part II of the 1996 Act applies to all trusts and not merely to trusts of land.[340]

11–053

---

[331] TA 1925 s.34(2) (as amended by TLATA 1996 s.25(1), Sch.3 para.3); below, Appendix para.A–091, para.13–085.

[332] TA 1925 s.34(3).

[333] TA 1925 s.34(3).

[334] See Lewin 163.

[335] See *Re Myhill* [1928] Ch. 100; *Re Wight & Best's Brewery Co Ltd's Contract* [1929] W.N. 11; UPA 1925 s.27(2) (as substituted by UP(Am)A 1926 s.7; Sch; and amended by TLATA 1996 s.25(1), Sch.3 para.4).

[336] SLA 1925 s.18(1); LPA 1925 s.27(2) (as amended); below, Appendix para.A–098, para.12–037.

[337] SLA 1925 s.18(1); LPA 1925 s.27(2) (as amended); below, Appendix para.A–098, para.12–037.

[338] By AEA 1925 s.33 (as amended by TLATA 1925 s.5(1), Sch.2 para.5); below, para.14–008.

[339] Mainly at the behest of the Law Society.

[340] cf. (1989) Law Com. No.181, paras 9.1, 9.2; draft Bill, cl. 18 (under which TA 1925 s.36 would have been amended, rather than having free-standing provisions as in TLATA 1996 Pt II).

1. Replacement under the Trustee Act 1925

11–054   *(a) Power to appoint.* By the Trustee Act 1925,[341] a new trustee or trustees[342] may be appointed if a trustee:

   (i) is dead (and this includes a person nominated trustee by a will who predeceases the testator[343]); or

   (ii) remains outside the United Kingdom for a continuous[344] period exceeding 12 months; or

   (iii) desires to be discharged from all or any of his trusts or powers; or

   (iv) refuses to act (e.g. if he disclaims[345]); or

   (v) is unfit to act (e.g. if he is bankrupt[346]); or

   (vi) is incapable of acting, as by mental disorder,[347] or age and infirmity,[348] or, in the case of a corporation, by dissolution[349]; or

   (vii) is a minor[350]; or

   (viii) is removed under a power in the trust instrument.[351]

This provision applies notwithstanding any express provision specifying when new trustees may be appointed[352] unless a contrary intention is shown.[353]

11–055   *(b) Method of appointment.* The appointment must be made in writing[354] and must be made:

   (i) by the person or persons[355] nominated by the trust instrument for the purpose of appointing trustees, i.e. nominated generally[356] and

---

[341] s.36(1).

[342] Including Settled Land Act trustees: see *Re Dark* [1954] Ch. 291.

[343] TA 1925 s.36(8).

[344] See *Re Walker* [1901] 1 Ch. 259 (continuity broken by return for a week).

[345] *Re Birchall* (1889) 40 Ch D 436.

[346] *Re Roche* (1842) 2 Dr. & War. 287 at 289; *Re Hopkins* (1881) 19 Ch D 61 at 63.

[347] *Re East* (1873) 8 Ch.App. 735; *Re Blake* [1887] W.N. 173.

[348] *Re Lemann's Trusts* (1883) 22 Ch D 633.

[349] TA 1925 s.36(3).

[350] An implied, resulting or constructive trust may make a minor a trustee, though he cannot be appointed one: below, para.11–061.

[351] TA 1925 s.36(2).

[352] See *Re Wheeler and De Rochow* [1896] 1 Ch. 315.

[353] TA 1925 s.69(2).

[354] But the last surviving trustee cannot appoint by his will: *Re Parker's Trusts* [1894] Ch. 1.

[355] In the absence of a contrary intention, the power does not pass to the survivor of two or more nominees, unless the property is vested in them (see *Re Bacon* [1907] 1 Ch. 475; *Re Harding* [1923] 1 Ch. 183; Farwell, *Powers*, pp.514, 515) or they are trustees and hold the power as such: TA 1925 s.18(l); see *Re Smith* [1904] 1 Ch. 139.

[356] *Re Walker & Hughes' Contract* (1883) 24 Ch D 698.

not merely in certain stated events[357]; in default of there being any such person able and willing to act (as where the person nominated cannot be found,[358] or disagrees[359]), the appointment may be made,

(ii) by the "surviving or continuing trustees or trustee", a term which includes a trustee who is retiring or refuses to act[360] but not a trustee removed against his will[361]; or if there is no such trustee,

(iii) by the personal representatives of the last remaining (or sole[362]) trustee[363]; or, finally, if there is no such person,[364] or it is doubtful,[365]

(iv) by the court.[366]

(c) Who may be appointed. It is expressly provided that the person making **11–056** the appointment may appoint himself.[367] Even if he appoints a person whom the court would not normally[368] appoint, such as a beneficiary,[369] or the solicitor to the trustees or beneficiaries,[370] the appointment will not as a result be rendered invalid. However, the appointment of a minor as a trustee, whether of realty or personalty, is void.[371]

2. Replacement under the Trusts of Land and Appointment of Trustees Act 1996

(a) Power to appoint. The Trusts of Land and Appointment of Trustees Act **11–057** 1996 confers two distinct but limited powers to appoint trustees as a replacement for all or some of the existing trustees. What connects them, is that they are exercisable by the beneficiaries under the trust, but only in circumstances in which those beneficiaries could have terminated the trust. The powers may

---

[357] *Re Wheeler and De Rochow* [1896] 1 Ch. 315; *Re Sichel's Settlements* [1916] 1 Ch. 358.
[358] *Cradock v Witham* [1895] W.N. 75.
[359] *Re Sheppard's S.T.* [1953] Ch. 59.
[360] TA 1925 s.36(8).
[361] *Re Stoneham S.T.* [1953] Ch. 59.
[362] *Re Shafto's Trusts* (1885) 29 Ch D 247; but see *Nicholson v Field* [1893] 2 Ch. 511.
[363] TA 1925 s.36(1).
[364] See *Re Higginbottom* [1892] 3 Ch. 132.
[365] See *Re May's W.T.* [1941] Ch. 109 (trustee in enemy territory).
[366] TA 1925 s.41. For the principles guiding the court, see *Re Tempest* (1866) 1 Ch.App. 485; *Re Northcliffe's Settlements* [1937] 3 All E.R. 804.
[367] TA 1925 s.36(1); contrast s.36(6); below, para.11–063.
[368] For exceptional cases, see, e.g. *Re Clissold* (1864) 10 U.T. 642; *Re Marquis of Ailesbury and Lord Iveagh* [1893] 2 Ch. 345.
[369] *Forster v Abraham* (1874) L.R. 17 Eq. 351 (tenant for life); cf. below, Appendix para.A–050.
[370] *Re Coode* (1913) 108 U.T. 94.
[371] LPA 1925 s.20.

be excluded by a provision to that effect in the disposition creating the trust.[372]

11–058   (1) RETIREMENT AND REPLACEMENT AT THE BEHEST OF THE BENEFICIARIES. The first power is exercisable only where two conditions are satisfied:

(i) There is no person nominated for the purpose of appointing new trustees by the instrument, if any, creating the trust.[373] Where the trust instrument conferred a power of appointment on X who is now dead, there will be no person nominated and the condition will be satisfied. It will be otherwise, however, if X is alive but lacks capacity.[374]

(ii) The beneficiaries under the trust are of full age and capacity and (taken together) are absolutely entitled to the property subject to the trust.[375] As such, they are able to determine the trust and to require the trustees to transfer the trust property to them or at their direction.[376]

The beneficiaries may then do either or both of the following:

(i) direct one or more of the trustees to retire[377]; and

(ii) direct the trustee or trustees for the time being (or if there are none, the personal representatives of the last person who was a trustee) to appoint by writing to be trustee or trustees the person or persons specified.[378]

In the latter case, the Act, by necessary implication, confers on the person or persons directed a power to appoint new trustees. In the limited circumstances in which it is exercisable, the effect of this statutory power is to reverse the rule that beneficiaries cannot direct trustees as to the exercise of their power to appoint new trustees.[379]

---

[372] TLATA 1996 s.2l(5). For trusts in existence when the Act came into force, there is a power for the settlor (or if more than one, such of the settlors as are alive and of full capacity) to execute a deed (which is irrevocable) providing that the powers shall not apply: TLATA 1996 s.21(6), (7).

[373] TLATA 1996 s.19(1)(a). A settlor or testator who wishes to exclude the power may readily do so by nominating the persons who may appoint new trustees.

[374] The suggestion made in C. Whitehouse and N. Hassall, *The Trusts of Land and Appointment of Trustees Act 1996* (Butterworths Law, 1997) para.2.143, that the condition is satisfied if X lacks capacity is not justified by the wording of TLATA 1996 s.19(1)(a). cf. TLATA 1996 s.20(1)(b); below.

[375] TLATA 1996 s.19(l)(b).

[376] Under the rule in *Saunders v Vautier* (1841) 4 Beav. 115; above, para.9–169.

[377] Certain pre-conditions must be met before the trustee is obliged to retire. In particular, reasonable arrangements must be made for the protection of any rights he may have in connection with the trust (e.g. a right to be reimbursed for expenditure) and there must be at least two trustees or a trust corporation to perform the trust: TLATA 1996 s.19(3).

[378] TLATA 1996 s.19(2).

[379] See *Re Brockbank* [1948] Ch. 206.

(2) REPLACEMENT OF AN INCAPABLE TRUSTEE. The second power may be **11–059**
exercised where:

    (i) a trustee is incapable by reason of mental disorder of exercising his
        functions as trustee;

    (ii) there is no person who is both entitled to appoint a new trustee
        under the provisions of the Trustee Act 1925 explained above,[380]
        and is willing and able to do so; and

    (iii) the beneficiaries under the trust are of full age and capacity and
        (taken together) are absolutely entitled to the property subject to
        the trust.[381]

Where these circumstances occur, the beneficiaries may give a written direction to the person who can act on behalf of the incapable trustee[382] to appoint
by writing the persons or persons specified in the direction to be the new
trustee or trustees.[383] Once again, the Act impliedly confers on the person
directed a power to appoint a new trustee.

(b) Method of appointment. In exercising the power, the beneficiaries may   **11–060**
either give a joint direction, or each give a separate direction which specifies
the appointment and retirement of the same person or persons.[384] Both the
direction and the subsequent appointment must be made in writing,[385] though
in practice a deed is likely to be employed for the latter.[386]

(c) Who may be appointed. There are no restrictions on who may be   **11–061**
appointed as trustees, so that the beneficiaries may appoint one or more of
their own number. There is, however, a general requirement that where there
is a trust both of land and of the proceeds of sale of land, the same persons
must be appointed as trustees of both, even though the appointments are
required to be made by separate instruments.[387] This requirement also applies
to the powers conferred by the 1996 Act.[388]

3. Number. Where a single trustee was originally appointed, the appoint-   **11–062**
ment of a single trustee in his place is valid.[389] In the case of settled land or
land held on a trust of land, a sole trustee (not being a trust corporation) cannot

---

[380] s.36; above, para.11–054.
[381] TLATA 1996 s.20(1).
[382] Namely, a receiver, a person acting under an enduring or lasting power of attorney (below,
para.36–026), or a person authorised for the purpose by the authority having jurisdiction under Pt
VII of the Mental Health Act 1983 (below, para.36–024): TLATA 1996 s.20(2).
[383] TLATA 1996 s.20(2).
[384] TLATA 1996 s.21(1), (2).
[385] TLATA 1996 ss.19(2), 20(2).
[386] See TA 1925 s.40; below, para.11–068.
[387] TA 1925 s.35(1) (as substituted by TLATA 1996 s.25(1); Sch.3 para.3); LPA 1925 s.24 (as
substituted by TLATA 1996 s.25(1); Sch.3 para.4).
[388] TLATA 1996 s.21(4).
[389] TA 1925 s.37(1)(c).

be appointed under the statutory power if, after his appointment, he would be unable to give receipts for capital money,[390] as would be the case if there were no other trustee. There is never any obligation to appoint more than two trustees even if originally more than two were appointed.[391] The appointment may increase the number of trustees, provided that, in the case of settled land or land held on a trust of land, the number is not increased above four.[392] A separate set of trustees may be appointed for any part of the trust property held on distinct trusts.[393] The restrictions on the numbers of trustees apply whether appointment is made under the Trustee Act 1925 or the Trusts of Land and Appointment of Trustees Act 1996.[394]

C. Additional Trustees

11–063 Even though no occasion has arisen for the appointment of new trustees, if there are not more than three trustees, one or more additional trustees may be appointed, provided that the effect of the appointment is not to increase the number above four.[395] The appointment must be made by the same persons and in the same way as an appointment of new trustees,[396] except that there is no provision for an appointment by the personal representatives of the last remaining trustees, or for the appointor to appoint himself.[397]

Section 2. Retirement and Removal of Trustees

11–064 **1. Retirement.** A trustee may retire:

> (i) if another trustee is appointed in his place[398];
>
> (ii) if no new trustee is being appointed in his place, provided that after his discharge there will be left either two or more persons or a trust corporation to act in the trust.[399] The retirement is effected by a deed declaring the trustee's desire to retire. This is executed by the retiring trustee, the continuing trustees and the person entitled to

---

[390] TA 1925 s.37(2). Even before the enactment of this provision, it was well established that a sole surviving trustee who, on retiring, appointed one trustee to succeed him rather than two, committed a breach of trust: *Hume v Hulme* (1833) 2 My. & K. 682; *Barnes v Addy* (1873) 28 L.T. 398 (argued but not clearly decided on appeal: see (1874) 9 Ch.App. 244 at 250, 253).

[391] TA 1925 s.37(1)(c) (as amended by TLATA 1996 s.25(1), Sch.3 para.3).

[392] TA 1925 s.37(1)(a).

[393] TA 1925 s.37(1)(b).

[394] TLATA 1996 s.19(5).

[395] TA 1925 s.36(6) (as amended by TLATA 1996 s.25(1); Sch.3 para.3). The limit is not confined to trusts of land.

[396] TA 1925 s.36(6). After 1999, it is possible for a person acting under a registered power of attorney to appoint an additional trustee: see TA 1925, s.36(6A) (inserted by the Trustee Delegation Act 1999 s.8).

[397] *Re Powers S.T.* [1951] Ch. 1074. This is an accident of drafting: see (1952) 68 L.Q.R. 19 (REM).

[398] Above, para.11–054.

[399] TA 1925 s.39(1) (as amended by TLATA 1996 s.25(1); Sch.3 para.3).

appoint new trustees, all of whom must concur in the retirement[400];

(iii) if authorised to do so by an express power in the trust instrument[401];

(iv) with the consent of all the beneficiaries if they are all of full age and capacity and between them absolutely entitled to the trust property[402]; and

(v) with the leave of the court.[403] This method should be employed only in cases of difficulty,[404] for if the trustee applies to the court without good cause he may have to pay his own costs.[405]

2. Removal. A trustee may be removed: **11–065**

(a) under the statutory powers to appoint new trustees considered above[406];

(b) under any express power to do so contained in the trust instrument[407];

(c) under the court's inherent jurisdiction to remove a trustee where it is necessary for the safety of the trust property or the welfare of the beneficiaries. Examples include:

  (i) where the trustee has been inactive for a long period[408];
  (ii) where his interests conflict with those of the beneficiaries[409]; or
  (iii) where there has been friction with the beneficiaries on the mode of administering the trust.[410]

Section 3. Vesting of Trust Property

Some trustees have no property vested in them, as is normally the case with   **11–066**
trustees of settled land.[411] In such cases, no question of the devolution of trust

---

[400] TA 1925 s. 39(1).

[401] e.g. *Lord Camoys v Best* (1854) 19 Beav. 414.

[402] cf. *Wilkinson v Parry* (1828) 4 Russ. 272 at 276.

[403] *Forshaw v Higginson* (1855) 20 Beav. 485; *Gardiner v Downes* (1856) 22 Beav. 395.

[404] See *Re Stokes' Trusts* (1872) L.R. 13 Eq. 333; *Re Chetwynd's Settlement* [1902] 1 Ch. 692.

[405] *Howard v Rhodes* (1837) 1 Keen 581; *Porter v Watts* (1852) 21 L.J.Ch. 211.

[406] See TA 1925 s.36 (above, para.11–054); TLATA 1996 ss.19, 20 (above, paras 11–058, 11–059).

[407] e.g. *London and County Banking Co v Goddard* [1897] 1 Ch. 642.

[408] *Reid v Hadley* (1885) 2 T.L.R. 12.

[409] *Passingham v Sherborn* (1849) 9 Beav. 424.

[410] *Letterstedt v Broers* (1884) 9 App.Cas. 371.

[411] Below, Appendix para.A–092.

property arises. But where property is vested in trustees, questions of the transfer of the trust property arise on their death, retirement or removal, or on the appointment of new trustees.

A. On Death

11–067 Trustees are always made joint tenants or joint owners of the trust property, whether it is real or personal. The advantage of this is that on the death of one trustee the estate or interest vested in him passes to the surviving trustees by the doctrine of survivorship.[412] Where a sole surviving trustee dies, any estate or interest held by him on trust vests in his personal representatives notwithstanding any provision in his will.[413] Until new trustees are appointed, the personal representatives may exercise any power or trust exercisable by the former trustee,[414] without being obliged to do so.[415]

B. On Appointment of New Trustees

11–068 **1. Vesting declaration.** On an appointment of new trustees, the trust property has to be vested in the new trustees jointly with any continuing trustees. By the Trustee Act 1925,[416] if an appointment of new trustees is made by deed, a declaration therein by the appointor that the property shall vest in the trustees ("a vesting declaration") is sufficient to vest the property in them. Such a vesting declaration is implied in the absence of an express provision to the contrary.[417] It should be noted that these provisions apply even if the trust property is not vested in the appointor. He has a statutory power to transfer what he has not got.[418] Thus where A and B are trustees and X has the power to appoint new trustees, if A dies and X appoints C a trustee in his place, the deed of appointment will vest the trust property in B and C jointly.

11–069 **2. Exceptions.** In certain cases, however, the trust property cannot be transferred by a vesting declaration, either express or implied. These cases are when the property consists of:

(a) the benefit of a mortgage over land to secure trust money[419];

(b) land held under a lease with a provision against assigning or disposing of the land without consent, unless:

---

[412] Above, para.13–003. Powers given to the trustees jointly also pass to the survivors: TA 1925 s.18(1).

[413] AEA 1925 s.1.

[414] TA 1925 s.18(2): see *Re Waidanis* [1908] 1 Ch. 123; (1977) 41 Conv. (N.S.) 432 (P. W. Smith). Two or more personal representatives of a sole trustee may give valid receipts for capital money: see Wolst. & C. iv. 21.

[415] See *Re Ridley* [1904] 2 Ch. 774; *Re Benett* [1906] 1 Ch. 216.

[416] TA 1925 s.40(1)(a).

[417] TA 1925 s.40(1)(b). The danger that an express declaration might be defective in form is met by TA 1925 s.40(3).

[418] See LPA 1925 s.9(1).

[419] TA 1925 s.40(4)(a). Land conveyed on trust to secure debentures or debenture stock will vest in the new trustee under TA s.40(1): s.40(4)(a).

     (i) the requisite consent has been obtained; or

     (ii) the vesting declaration would not be a breach of covenant or give rise to a forfeiture[420];

  (c) any share, stock or other property which is transferable only in books kept by a company or other body, or in a way directed by statute[421]; or

  (d) land of registered title.

In these excepted cases, the trust property must be transferred by the method appropriate to the subject-matter, e.g. in the case of shares, by a duly registered transfer. The reason for (c) is apparent when the normal mode of transfer of such property is considered; (a) is included to avoid bringing the trusts on to the title,[422] for otherwise when the borrower sought to repay the loan, he would have to investigate the trust documents to see that he was paying the right persons; and (b) is included to avoid accidental breaches of the terms of the lease.[423] Where the trust property consists of registered land, the new trustee must be registered as a proprietor of the land.[424]

The court has a wide jurisdiction to make vesting orders where this is desirable.[425]

C. On Retirement or Removal

Where a trustee retires or is discharged from a trust without a new trustee   **11–070** being appointed, and the transaction is effected by deed, the trust property can be divested from the former trustee and vested solely in the continuing trustees by means of a vesting declaration.[426] This applies only if the deed is executed by the retiring trustee, the continuing trustees and any person with power to appoint new trustees.[427] There are the same exceptions in the case of vesting declarations on the appointment of new trustees.[428] This special provision is necessary since the right of survivorship operates only on death and not on retirement.

Section 4. Procedure in the Case of Settled Land and Trusts of Land

A. Where the Title is Unregistered

1. One instrument. Although it is undesirable, an express trust of land may   **11–071** be created by only one instrument. In this case, where a new trustee is

---

[420] TA 1925 s.40(4)(b).
[421] TA 1925 s.40(4)(c).
[422] Lewin 435.
[423] Wolst. & C. iv. 67.
[424] Below, para.11–074.
[425] TA 1925 ss.44–56.
[426] TA 1925 s.40(2)(a). s.40(2) has been amended by TLATA 1996 s.25(1), Sch.3 para.3.
[427] Such a vesting declaration is now implied: TA 1925 s.40(2)(b).
[428] See above.

appointed, the appointment may be made by a single document. This may be merely in writing, but it should be made by deed so that the legal estate may be vested in the new and continuing trustees by virtue of the Trustee Act 1925,[429] thus avoiding the necessity of a separate conveyance. In addition, a memorandum must be endorsed on or annexed to the instrument creating the trust of land, stating the names of those who are the trustees after the appointment is made,[430] and not merely the names of the new trustees.

11–072   **2. Two instruments.** Normally, however, an express trust of land is created by two documents.[431] In this case, and in the case of settled land, the procedure is more complicated. There must be[432]:

> (i) an instrument to go with the conveyance on a trust of land or the vesting instrument;
>
> (ii) an appointment to go with the trust instrument; or
>
> (iii) an endorsement of the conveyance on a trust of land or on the vesting instrument stating the names of those who are the trustees after the appointment.

11–073   In the case of settled land, the first document must be a deed. However, it merely states who are the trustees. In the case of a trust of land, it may be merely in writing, but, as before, should be by deed in order to take advantage of s.40 of the Trustee Act 1925. In either case it effects the actual appointment of the persons named in it as trustees of land. A similar procedure applies if a trustee of settled land is discharged without a new trustee being appointed.[433] The second document, both for settled land and trusts of land, is an appointment which may be made either in writing or by deed.

B. Where the Title is Registered

11–074   **1. Trusts of land.** Because the trustees will be registered as proprietors of any registered land held upon a trust of land, any new trustee must also be so registered. This may be done in various ways.[434] First, the existing trustees as registered proprietors may execute a transfer in the usual form in favour of all the new trustees.[435] Secondly, they may submit the deed of appointment to the

---

[429] s.40; above, para.11–068.
[430] TA 1925 s.35(3) (substituted by TLATA 1996 s.25(l); Sch.3 para.3).
[431] Below, para.12–012.
[432] TA 1925 s.35 (as amended by TLATA 1996 s.25(l); Sch.3 para.3); SLA 1925 s.35(l); cf. above, para.10–024.
[433] SLA 1925 s.35(1): there is no corresponding provision for trusts of land.
[434] Ruoff & Roper, 37.011.
[435] Form TR1 is appropriate, together with AP1.

registrar.[436] This is deemed to be a conveyance of the land,[437] to which the registrar must give effect by means of the proper entry on the register.[438] Thirdly, appointment by the court under s.41 of the Trustee Act 1925 is to be treated as a registrable disposition and must be registered to take effect.[439] An application for alteration of the register for the removal of a deceased joint-trustee may also be made.[440]

2. Settled land. Where the title to settled land is registered, any new trustees of the settlement will be appointed by deed in the usual way. An application is then made to modify the existing restriction on the register[441] by substituting the names of the new and continuing trustees.[442]

11–075

---

[436] A deed of appointment might actually be required if one of the existing trustee-proprietors has remained out of the UK for 12 months, or refuses to at, or is incapable of acting, a transfer per se might not be effective.

[437] TA 1925 s.40(5). The persons making the declaration are deemed to be parties to the conveyance.

[438] Form AP1, together with the deed and evidence that the appointment was properly made, LRR 2003 rr.161(3), 203.

[439] LRA 2002 s.27(5). Form AP1 and the court order should be lodged, LRR 2003 rr.13, 161(1).

[440] LRR 2003 r.164. Form AP1 and the death certificate should be lodged.

[441] Being a Form G restriction.

[442] Ruoff & Roper 37.016.02. Form AP1 should be used. The application should be made by the life tenant, the previous trustees and the new and continuing trustees, being the person interested in the restriction which needs amendment.

THE TRUSTS OF LAND AND APPOINTMENT OF TRUSTEES ACT 1996

12–001   As we have seen,[1] the trust was adapted and developed by the 1925 property legislation in order to govern co-owned land. The principal reason for this was to enhance and ensure the free alienability of land while at the same time offering a measure of protection for those beneficially interested in it, either as to use, or more likely in terms of its capital value. At the time of the 1925 property legislation, co-ownership of land did not normally arise because of a desire for joint-ownership of the family home in the modern sense, but rather as a device for the management of a major asset for the benefit of a number of persons, often but not exclusively the extended family. Possession was not as important as income generation and capital preservation. The original scheme of the 1925 legislation reflects this, as well as the fact that co-ownership almost always arose as a result of the deliberate and express creation of a trust for clearly defined objectives, rather than as a consequence of modern living.

The material in this chapter builds on the material considered in Chapter 10, "The Use of Trusts in the Law of Real Property". That chapter considered the use of the trust for sale in the period after 1925 and before the entry into force of the Trusts of Land and Appointment of Trustees Act 1996[2] (known as the TLATA 1996). An appreciation of the trust for sale is necessary in order to understand the scheme of the TLATA 1996 as it governs co-owned land today.

TRUSTS OF LAND

12–002   **1. The nature of a trust of land.** It has already been explained that the Trusts of Land and Appointment of Trustees Act 1996, which came into force on January 1, 1997, introduced a unitary system of trusts of land.[3] The threefold division between settlements, trusts for sale and bare trusts has gone. Subject to two exceptions, explained below, a trust of land is any trust of

---

[1] Above, Ch.10.
[2] On January 1, 1997.
[3] Above, paras 10–001, 10–034. For commentaries on the Act, see [1997] Conv. 401 (A. J. Oakley); 411 (N. Hopkins); (1998) 61 M.L.R. 56 (L. M. Clements).

property which consists of or includes land.[4] It therefore applies irrespective of the category of trust, and includes:

    (i) an express, implied, resulting or constructive trust of land;

    (ii) an expressly or impliedly created trust for sale of land whenever created; and

    (iii) a bare trust of land.[5]

The trust of land in general follows the model of the trust for sale. Both the legal estate in the land and all the powers of disposition and management are vested in the trustees of land.[6] Where, as will usually be the case, the title to the land is registered, it will be registered in the names of the trustees.[7] As a consequence of such registration, the trustees have full owner's powers and may deal with the land as if they were absolute owners, unless the contrary is stipulated in the register.[8] Without such a limitation, properly entered on the register,[9] a disponee is not to be concerned with any limitation on the trustees powers contained in the trust instrument (unless the limitation is imposed by the LRA 2002 itself).[10] Consequently, a disponee can deal safely with the trustees without having to investigate the trust instrument or be concerned that it might contain something which would otherwise invalidate the disposition.[11]

The TLATA 1996 is also applicable to trusts created or arising before 1997.[12] As a result, trusts for sale (whether express or implied) and bare trusts

---

[4] TLATA 1996 s.1(1). A mixed trust of land and personalty will therefore be a trust of land. However, it is only in relation to the land so held that the trustees of land have the powers conferred by the Act: TLATA 1996 s.6(1), below, para.12–015.

[5] TLATA 1996 s.1(2). It appears to have been assumed that where a person grants another a limited interest (as where A grants B an interest in Blackacre for life), only the limited interest takes effect under the trust of land, and that the reversion to the settlor does not: see LPA 1925 s.2(1A) (inserted by TLATA 1996 s.25(1) Sch.3 para.4), which provides that such reversionary interests will be overreached as if they were an interest under the trust of land. The provision is puzzling: it is difficult to see how an equitable reversion can exist other than under a trust of land. The provision was introduced on the basis of an analogy with SLA 1925 s.1(4) (which is derived from SLA 1882 s.2(2)). However, the analogy is very questionable. As a settlement had to be created by an instrument (SLA 1925 s.1(1)), it was necessary to make provision for a reversion that was not specifically dealt with by the instrument which created the limited interest. No such need exists in relation to a trust of land which can be created in certain circumstances without any instrument.

[6] Subject to their power to delegate any of their functions to one or more beneficiaries: TLATA 1996 s.9; below, para.12–024. For the analogous but more limited powers of delegation that were conferred on trustees for sale, see above, para.10–022.

[7] See Ruoff & Roper 37–005 et seq.

[8] LRA 2002 ss.23, 24.

[9] For example, by the entry of a restriction.

[10] LRA 2002 s.26.

[11] Of course, the disponee might not acquire priority over subsisting beneficial interests if overreaching does not occur, but this is not due to a limitation in the trustee's powers, but is a natural consequence of the priority rule found in LRA 2002 s.29.

[12] TLATA 1996 s.1(2). Many (but not all) of the provisions of the Act of 1996 apply to personal representatives: TLATA 1996 s.18(1); see below, para.12–035.

that were in existence on January 1, 1997, automatically became trusts of land.[13] The two exceptional situations in which the Act does not apply are:

(i) in relation to land which was settled land prior to 1997; and

(ii) as regards land which is subject to the Universities and College Estates Act 1925.[14]

12–003　　**2. The reasons for the introduction of trusts of land.** Trusts of land were introduced on the recommendation of the Law Commission.[15] Amongst the principal defects in the law identified by the Law Commission which their introduction was intended to remedy were the following[16]:

(i) The continuation of a dual system of settlements and trusts for sale was considered to be unnecessary. One particular difficulty was that successive interests in land created a settlement under the Settled Land Act 1925 unless a trust for sale was expressly imposed. This often led to the creation of inadvertent settlements and this could cause conveyancing difficulties for purchasers where the existence of the settlement was not appreciated.[17]

(ii) A number of specific difficulties existed in relation to settled land, of which three examples may be given. The first was its complexity. The second was the inadequate (and uncertain) protection that was given to purchasers where a life tenant made an unauthorised disposition.[18] The third was the conflict of interest inherent in the position of the tenant for life. He was both a beneficiary and a trustee for the other beneficiaries, but the courts were in practice remarkably indulgent to such life tenants and did not treat them like ordinary trustees.[19] In reality, this meant that tenants for life were able to give preference to their own personal interests and their trusteeship was often descriptive rather than substantive.

---

[13] TLATA 1996 s.192); and see s.4. There are however some differences between those trusts of land which were created before 1997 and those created after 1996: see, e.g. below, para.12–026.

[14] TLATA 1996 s.1(3). The Universities and College Estates Act 1925, applies to certain universities and colleges (Oxford, Cambridge and Durham Universities and their respective colleges, and Eton and Winchester Colleges), and lays down a distinct code of rules applicable to dealings with land subject to it. It was considered preferable for those rules to continue to apply rather than imposing a trust of land governed by TLATA. This also avoided difficult and complex consequential repeals and amendments.

[15] See (1989) Law Com. No.181; [1990] Conv. 12 (R. J. Smith). The Bill attached to the Law Commission's Report differed substantially from the one that was eventually introduced and enacted. cf. [1996] Conv. 411 (N. Hopkins).

[16] They are summarised in Law Com. No.181; para.1.3.

[17] cf. paras A–039 et seq.

[18] Above.

[19] See, e.g. *Re Thornhill's Settlement* [1941] Ch. 24 (below, para.A–088); *England v Public Trustee* (1968) 112 S.J. 70.

(iii) There were also a number of specific problems in relation to trusts for sale. The primary obligation of the trustees to sell was inconsistent with the expectations of the trustees and beneficiaries in the most common circumstance in which a trust for sale arose.[20] The application of the doctrine of conversion had become particularly uncertain and unsatisfactory and there were perceived to be uncertainties as to the rights of occupation of a tenant in common.[21]

(iv) Bare trusts were anomalous and were neither settlements nor trusts for sale. There was also uncertainty as to the ability to overreach such trusts.[22]

In addition to these defects a number of others have been identified, of which two may be mentioned. The first was that the statutory powers given to tenants for life and trustees of the settlement under the Settled Land Act 1925 (and therefore sometimes also to trustees for sale) were "notoriously restrictive" and had "come to be seen as inappropriate for modern conditions".[23] This was particularly important in relation to charitable trusts.[24] The second was that a tenant for life under the Settled Land Act 1925, unlike any other person in a position of trusteeship, was born to the role and could not be readily removed or replaced if he turned out to be unsuitable.[25]

3. Trusts of land in cases which would formerly have created a settle- **12–004** **ment.** As has been explained,[26] subject to two exceptions, it is not possible to create any new settlements for the purposes of the Settled Land Act 1925.[27] Specific provision is made for certain situations arising after 1996 which, prior to 1997, would have created a settlement.[28] Two of these situations, namely where land is held either in trust for a minor[29] or on charitable, ecclesiastical

---

[20] See Martin Dixon "To sell or not to sell: that is the question: the irony of the Trusts of Land and Appointment of Trustees Act 1996" (2011) 70 CLJ 579.

[21] See above, para.10–029, for conversion. See below, para.13–026 for questions concerning occupation.

[22] cf. below, para.12–009.

[23] See [1998] Conv. 246 (C. Jessel). This was in fact touched upon by the Law Commission: (1989) Law Com. No.181, para.1.5. The Commission's principal reasons for widening the powers of trustees of land were to give them the greatest flexibility and to make the law simpler: (1989) Law Com. No.181 para.10.5.

[24] Prior to 1997, in the absence of any extension of their powers by the court or by the Charity Commission, charity trustees had, in relation to any land held in trust, the powers of the tenant for life and the trustees of the settlement under the SLA 1925 s.29; below, Appendix paras A–014, A–055. Such trusts now take effect as trusts of land, and the trustees therefore have the beneficial owner powers of such trustees: see below, para.36–029. For the powers of trustees of land, see below, para.12–015.

[25] See, e.g. *Hambros v Duke of Marlborough* [1994] Ch. 158, below, Appendix para.A–071; and S. Bright and J. Dewar, *Land Law: Themes and Perspectives*, 151 at 171 (Ch). Although there are ways of dealing with this problem in the case of settled land (see below, Appendix para.A–055, they are likely to be employed only in extreme cases.

[26] Below, Appendix para.A–054.

[27] TLATA 1996 s.2(1), (2).

[28] TLATA 1996 s.2(6); Sch.1.

[29] TLATA 1996 Sch.1 paras 1, 2.

or public trusts,[30] are fully explained in a later chapter.[31] A third situation is where, by an instrument, land becomes charged either voluntarily or in consideration of marriage, by way of family arrangement, whether immediately or after an interval, with the payment of:

(i) a rentcharge for the life of a person or a shorter period; or

(ii) capital, annual or periodical sums for the benefit of a person.

This instrument now takes effect as a trust of land and operates as a declaration that the land is held in trust for giving effect to the charge.[32]

4. Trusts for sale as trusts of land

12–005   *(a) Express trusts for sale take effect as trusts of land.* Although a trust for sale may still be created expressly,[33] it takes effect as a trust of land. Furthermore, the Act provides in relation to any trust for sale, whenever made, that there is an implied power (which overrides any contrary provision in the disposition creating the trust) for the trustees to postpone sale, and that they are not liable in any way for indefinitely postponing sale in the exercise of their discretion.[34] It remains the case, however, that express trustees for sale are under a duty to sell. Consequently, unless they are charity trustees,[35] they must be unanimous in exercising the power to postpone.[36] However, any person who is a trustee or who has an interest in property subject to a trust of land might in such circumstances apply to the court to stop the sale.[37] The fact that the settlor has expressly imposed a trust for sale—and therefore imposed a duty to sell—is a consideration that the court will take into account in making its decision on any such application. This is explained more fully later.[38]

---

[30] TLATA 1996 para.4.

[31] Ch.20.

[32] TLATA 1996 Sch.1 para.3. cf. SLA 1925 s.1(1)(v); below, Appendix para.A–037.

[33] Trusts for sale cannot arise impliedly after 1996, because of amendments to the legislation by which any implied trusts take effect as trusts of land: below, para.12–011. The definition of "trust for sale" in LPA 1925 s.205(1)(xxix) has been amended by TLATA 1996 s.25(2); Sch.4. It is now "an immediate trust for sale" (i.e. not a trust to sell at some future date) and not, as formerly, "an immediate binding trust for sale": cf. above, para.10–020; and see the 5th edition of this work at p.386.

[34] TLATA 1996 s.4(1), (2). Any liability incurred by trustees prior to 1997 is, however, unaffected: TLATA 1996 s.4(3).

[35] Who may act by majority: see, e.g. *Perry v Shipway* (1859) 1 Giff. 1 at 9; *Re Whiteley* [1910] 1 Ch. 600 at 607, 608.

[36] See (1997) 1 13 L.Q.R. 207 at 208 (P. H. Pettit). In this regard, express trustees for sale differ from other trustees of land, who have a power to sell the land, and must therefore be unanimous in its exercise: below, para.12–016.

[37] TLATA 1996 ss.14, 15; below, paras 13–064 et seq.

[38] Below, paras 12–021 et seq.

(b) Abolition of the doctrine of conversion. The Act abolishes those aspects **12–006**
of the doctrine of conversion[39] by which:

(i) a beneficial interest in land held on a trust for sale was regarded as
an interest in personalty; and

(ii) a beneficial interest in personal property held on trust for sale to
purchase land was regarded as an interest in land.[40]

The abolition of the doctrine in (ii), necessarily means that it is also abolished
where a settlor directs that a sum of money (rather than personalty that must
first be sold and converted into money) shall be applied in the purchase of
land.[41] Because of the introduction of the trust of land, the effect of abolishing
these aspects of the doctrine is likely to be comparatively limited. It will be
relevant—that is, the abolition will bite—only in respect of trusts for sale that
were in existence when the Trusts of Land and Appointment of Trustees Act
1996 was brought into force on January 1, 1997, or which are expressly
created after that date. The latter are unlikely to be common. This is because
where there is a trust of land (not being an express trust for sale), there is no
duty to sell and so conversion would have been irrelevant even if the doctrine
had not been abolished.

A number of the provisions of the Act confer rights on a beneficiary who
is "beneficially entitled to an interest in possession in land subject to the
trust".[42] As a result of the abolition of the doctrine of conversion, all beneficiaries entitled in possession under a trust of land—including any trust for
sale—will have the rights conferred by these provisions.[43]

There are two exceptions to the abolition of the doctrine of conversion **12–007**
which necessarily will be short-lived. Where a person died before 1997, the
doctrine of conversion continues to apply to:

(i) any trust created by that person's will[44]; or

---

[39] Above, para.10–029.

[40] TLATA 1996 s.3(1). The criticism of the side note to the section in (1997) 1 13 L.Q.R. 207
at 209 (P. H. Pettit) appears to be based on a misconception: see S. Bright and J. Dewar (eds),
Land Law: Themes and Perspectives (Oxford: OUP, 1998), 151 at 173 (Ch).

[41] The suggestion to the contrary in (1996) 10 T.L.I. 97 (P. Matthews) is plainly erroneous: see
S. Bright and J. Dewar (eds), *Land Law: Themes and Perspectives*, 151 at 173 (Ch).

[42] See, e.g. ss.9 (below, para.12–024), 11 (below, para.12–026), 12 (below, para.12–027). An
annuitant is not beneficially entitled to an interest in possession: TLATA 1996 s.22(3). Nor, in
principle, is the object of a discretionary trust, as he merely has a right to be considered by the
trustees and to compel due administration of the trust. For a different view, see C. Whitehouse and
N. Hassall, *The Trust of Land and Appointment of Trustees Act 1996* (Butterworths),
para.2.168.

[43] The suggestion in [1996] *Current Law Statutes* 47–15 (P. Kenny) that beneficiaries under
trusts for sale do not have such rights would defeat one of the main reasons for abolishing the
doctrine of conversion. cf. (1989) Law Com. No.181, para.13.6. It has been rejected by most other
commentators: see, e.g. [1998] C.L.J. 123, 131 (D. G. Barnsley).

[44] TLATA 1996 s.3(2).

(ii) the deceased's personal representatives in the administration of his estate (whether he died testate or intestate).[45]

As regards the first of these exceptions, a testator who had died before the 1996 Act came into force would necessarily have made his dispositions on the basis of the previous law. To have applied the abolition of the doctrine of conversion to those dispositions retrospectively, thereby altering their effect, would have defeated the testator's intentions and so caused injustice. The second exception covers the case of personal representatives who, at the time when the Act came into force, were treating the deceased's beneficial interest under a trust for sale as personalty for the purposes of its devolution (as they were bound to do).

Of the statutory repeals and amendments consequent upon the abolition of the doctrine of conversion, two require specific mention. First, prior to 1997, where trustees of personalty or of land held upon trust for sale had a power to invest money in land, they held any such land on trust for sale unless the settlement otherwise provided.[46] This preserved the character of the investment as personalty. That provision is now repealed as regards land purchased after 1996, whatever the date of the instrument creating the trust.[47] The trustees will hold such land on a trust of land. This is simply a corollary of the definition of a trust of land as one which consists of or includes land.[48] Secondly, where trustees lend money on mortgage and the property becomes vested in them free from the right of repayment (e.g. by foreclosure[49]), it is provided that the trustees hold that land on trust:

(i) to apply the income from it in the same manner as the interest paid on the mortgage debt would have been applicable; and

(ii) if the property is sold, to apply the proceeds of sale in the same manner as the repayment of the mortgage debt would have been applicable.[50]

This provision ensures that the character of the money advanced by the trustees as personalty is not affected by the fortuitous circumstance that the mortgagor's interest in the property is extinguished.

5. Bare trusts as trusts of land

12–008   *(a) The nature of a bare trust.* A bare trust is a trust to hold or manage the land for the sole benefit of one beneficiary who is of full age. Such a trust is

---

[45] TLATA 1996 s.18(3).
[46] LPA 1925 s.32.
[47] TLATA 1996 s.5(1); Sch.2 para.2.
[48] TLATA 1996 S.J.; above, para.12–002.
[49] Below, para.25–006. Such cases will now be extremely rare.
[50] LPA 1925 s.31 (as amended by TLATA 1996 s.5(I); Sch.2, para.1). cf. below, Appendix para.A–011.

called a bare, or simple, trust.[51] It arises when the nature of the trust is not prescribed by the settlor but is left to the ordinary rules of law, as where T purchases land with money provided by Z,[52] or X conveys land "to T in fee simple on trust for Z in fee simple".

Where there is a bare trust T, the trustee, must obey Z's instructions about the disposition of the land.[53] Z may therefore call for an outright conveyance to him. It is pointless to keep the legal and equitable interests separated where only one person is entitled to the whole beneficial interest. This is equally true if the trustees are expressly given duties to perform, e.g. to sell, or to accumulate the income, provided that all such duties are for the benefit of one person only, and that person is of full age. This is the basis of the rule in *Saunders v Vautier*.[54]

(b) *The uncertain position of bare trusts prior to 1997.* Prior to 1997, there **12–009** was some uncertainty both as to the powers of disposition that a bare trustee of land had, and (consequent upon this) whether he could make an over-reaching conveyance.[55] Prior to the 1925 legislation, a bare trustee of land had no power of sale and therefore could only convey good title to the property with the concurrence of the beneficiary.[56] After 1925 and before 1997, the extent of a bare trustee's powers was not clearly settled. However, it appears to have depended on whether the title to the land was registered or unregistered. If a bare trustee was registered as proprietor of the trust property, the Land Registration Act 1925 (as was then applicable) conferred on him all the powers of disposition of an absolute owner unless a restriction had been entered on the register.[57] By contrast, a bare trustee of unregistered land had no powers of disposition prior to 1961. The Trustee Investments Act 1961, however, conferred on all trustees (including a bare trustee of land) a power to sell the trust property in the absence of an expression of contrary intention in the instrument creating the trust.[58] However, although a bare trustee might

---

[51] cf. above, para.10–012. The authorities provide only limited guidance as to the meaning of "bare trust", a term which has been described as "ambiguous": *Christie v Ovington* (1875) 1 Ch D 278 at 281, per Hall V.C. The expression was used in a number of statutes, e.g. FRA 1833 s.27, but the meaning given to it varied from statute to statute: see *Re Blandy Jenkins' Estate* [19171 1 Ch. 46 and *Herdegen v Federal Commissioner of Taxation* (1988) 84 A.L.R. 271 at 281.

[52] See *Dyer v Dyer* (1788) 2 Cox Eq. 92 at 93; *Finch v Finch* (1808) 15 Ves. 43 at 50.

[53] Lewin; Williams R.P. p.191; *Herdegen v Federal Commissioner of Taxation*, above, at 281, 282.

[54] (1841) 4 Beav. 115; Cr. & Ph. 240; above, para.9–180.

[55] Overreaching occurs when a disposition is made pursuant to a trust or power: below, para.12–036.

[56] *Lee v Soames* (1888) 34 W.R. 884.

[57] LRA 1925 ss.18, 21 and 25 (now repealed); [1990] C.L.J. 277 at 310 (C.H.). This remains the position under the LRA 2002 above para.7–050. The register is a public document and the beneficiary may therefore choose not to enter a restriction so as to avoid disclosing the existence of his interest in the property.

[58] s.1(1) provides that "a trustee may invest any property in his hands, whether at the time in a state of investment or not . . . ". This gives the trustee power to sell in order to invest (*Re Pratt's W.T.* [1943] Ch. 326), and the words "any property" in place of "any trust fund" (TA 1925 s.1(1)) extended the power to land. See [1990] C.L.J. 277 at 303 (Ch). The change in the law was probably inadvertent.

by exercising his powers have passed a good title to a purchaser, he was personally liable for breach of trust if he acted contrary to the beneficiary's wishes. In principle, if a bare trustee did have a power of sale, such a sale ought to have overreached the interest of the beneficiary on payment to one trustee alone.[59] However, the contrary was assumed, and the point was never settled.[60]

12–010   *(c) Effect as trusts of land.* By bringing bare trusts (including those in existence when the Trusts of Land and Appointment of Trustees Act 1996 came into force) within the scope of trusts of land, these uncertainties have been resolved. Both the powers of trustees of land, and the circumstances in which a disposition by trustees of land will overreach the interests of the beneficiaries are explained below and necessarily apply to bare trusts.[61]

12–011   **6. Species of trust of land.** A trust of land may arise:

    (a) expressly, where land is deliberately limited on a trust of land;

    (b) impliedly, where through the doctrines of equity there is an implied, resulting or constructive trust; or

    (c) by operation of statute.[62]

12–012   *(a) Express trusts of land.* It has already been explained that, prior to 1997, express trusts for sale were invariably created by two documents:

    (i) in the case of an inter vivos trust, a conveyance or transfer to the trustees and a trust instrument[63]; and

    (ii) where the trust was testamentary, the will and a written assent to the trustees for sale.[64]

The same practice now applies to the express creation of trusts of land. In particular, where the title to the land to be held in trust is unregistered and comprises a freehold or a lease having more than seven years to run, the assent, conveyance or assignment to the trustees, must be registered within two months. This is because the requirement of compulsory registration now applies to such assents, and to conveyances or assignments if made for valuable or other consideration (as in the case of a marriage settlement) or by

---

[59] For overreaching, see below, para.12–036. Payment to two trustees was only required in relation to trusts for sale and settlements: see TA 1925 s.14(1) (as originally enacted).

[60] See *Hodgson v Marks* [1971] Ch. 892.

[61] Below, paras 12–015 (powers); 12–036 (overreaching).

[62] See TLATA 1996 s.5.

[63] The use of two documents was a matter of practice rather than legal necessity.

[64] Above, para.10–021.

way of gift.[65] In order that the Registrar may determine whether to enter a restriction limiting the powers of the trustees, but not for any other purpose,[66] the application for first registration should set out some detail of the trusts on which the land is held.[67] There is the opportunity to indicate the nature of the equitable ownership (whether joint-tenant or tenant in common and in what shares; whether held for an unincorporated association)[68] and this should be completed as appropriate. The nature of the trusts will not appear on the register, but will serve as a written memorandum and will be conclusive as to the interests of the transferees.[69] These provisions in effect ensure that, in the case of an inter vivos trust, the application for registration satisfies the requirement of a trust instrument.[70]

Where the trust arises by will, the personal representatives must make a written assent in favour of the trustees of land even if they are the same persons as the personal representatives.[71] Where the assent was made prior to April 1998 and the title to the land is unregistered, a purchaser from the trustees of land may be entitled to require production of such an assent to prove that they had ceased to act as personal representatives if they sell as trustees of land,[72] though not if they sell as personal representatives.[73] However, as explained above, if the title to the land is required to be registered, this difficulty should not arise.

Where the land to be subject to the express trust is already registered, the title should be transferred to the trustees in the usual way using the normal Land Registry forms. No special forms are required to establish the trust, but it may be appropriate to make entries against the title by way of restriction to safeguard the position of the beneficiaries.[74] As has always been the case, an express trust of land is required to be manifested and proved by some writing signed by a person who is able to declare the trust,[75] although on a transfer of registered title to trustees the relevant Land Registry Forms can fulfil this role if the trusts are made explicit. If they are not, and in all other cases, for example where a registered proprietor declares themselves trustee, some written memorandum is essential.

---

[65] LRA 2002 s.4. See above para.7–014.

[66] In particular, *not* to give the Registrar notice of the trusts, LRA 2002 s.78.

[67] On the relevant transfer forms and Form FR1.

[68] In the section of the forms titled "Declaration of Trust".

[69] Subject to rectification for fraud etc., *Goodman v Gallant* [1986] 1 All E.R. 311.

[70] A trust of land may be declared orally, but it is unenforceable in the absence of written evidence: see LPA 1925 s.53(1)(b); below, para.11–037. In the case of first registration the owners of the land (or their agent) must execute the application for registration. In the case of a transfer or assent of registered land, both the transferors and the transferees must execute the instrument.

[71] *Re Yerburgh* [1928] W.N. 208; *Re King's W.T.* [1964] Ch. 542; below, para.14–146; cf. *Re Cugny's W.T.* [1931] 1 Ch. 305.

[72] See *Re Hodge* [1940] Ch. 260 at 264. cf. *Re King's W.T.*, above.

[73] See AEA 1925 s.36(4); *Eaton v Dames* [1894] W.N. 32; *Re Ponder* [1921] 2 Ch. 59; *Re Pitt* (1928) 44 T.L.R. 371; J.M.L. 87 L.J. News. 372.

[74] Above and see Ruoff and Roper, para.37.006.

[75] LPA 1925 s.53(1)(b)

12–013   *(b) Implied, resulting and constructive trusts.* The circumstances in which implied, resulting and constructive trusts arise or are imposed have already been explained.[76] It is provided that such trusts now take effect as trusts of land.[77] This avoids the difficulties that sometimes occurred in the past:

> (i) when successive interests arose under a constructive trust and were held to create a settlement under the Settled Land Act 1925[78]; and

> (ii) when concurrent interests arose which did not fall within the statutory provisions which imposed a trust for sale in many but not all cases of co-ownership.[79]

The trustee or trustees will be the person or persons in whom the legal estate is vested and who, for registered title, will be the registered proprietor or proprietors.

12–014   *(c) Statutory trusts of land.* A statutory trust is imposed in a number of circumstances, though the reasons for its imposition differ.[80] The situations are as follows:

> (i) Where a person dies intestate, his personal representatives hold all his property, both real and personal, on trust with a power to sell it.[81] Personal representatives must have power to sell the deceased's property to enable them to meet his debts and any expenses, and to distribute what remains of the estate.

> (ii) If two or more persons are entitled to land as joint tenants or tenants in common, a trust of land is normally imposed by the Law of Property Act 1925[82] (as amended by the Trusts of Land and Appointment of Trustees Act 1996[83]). This is explained more fully

---

[76] Above, paras 11–009, 11–017.

[77] TLATA 1996 s.1(2)(a). A constructive trust which created a settlement under the Settled Land Act 1925 prior to 1997 is unaffected by this provision: TLATA 1996 s.1(3). All other implied, resulting and constructive trusts take effect as trusts of land whenever created: TLATA 1996 s.1(2)(b).

[78] Below, Appendix para.A–041.

[79] Below, para.13–053.

[80] The situations in which a trust is imposed are the same as those where a trust for sale was imposed prior to 1997: above, para.12–021.

[81] AEA 1925 s.33 (as amended by TLATA 1996 s.5(1); Sch.2 para.5); below, para.14–105. To the extent that the property is land, there is a trust of land and the personal representatives necessarily have a power of sale: see TLATA 1996 s.6(1); below, paras 12–015, 12–016. The reference to a power of sale is included to avoid any uncertainty in relation to the deceased's personalty.

[82] ss.34 (tenancy in common), 36 (joint tenancy).

[83] Sch.2 paras 3 (tenancy in common), 4 (joint tenancy).

later.[84] The use of a trust facilitates both conveyancing and the management of the co-owned property.[85]

(iii) Where land reverts to the grantor's estate under the Reverter of Sites Act 1987,[86] the trustees have a statutory power to sell the land even before they have identified the person or persons entitled to the proceeds.[87] In practice it is often desirable that the land should be sold before the identity of those entitled is established. This can take some time, as many of the grants were made in the 19th century.

7. Position of trustees of land

(a) Powers of trustees of land. It has already been explained that trusts of **12–015** land follow the model of trusts for sale, rather than that of settlements, in that both the legal estate in the land and the powers of disposition and management are vested in the trustees.[88] Section 6 of the Trusts of Land and Appointment of Trustees Act 1996 confers on trustees of land:

(i) in relation to the land, all the powers of an absolute owner (subject to certain limitations)[89];

(ii) a power to convey land to the beneficiaries where they are absolutely entitled to it[90]; and

(iii) a power to purchase land.[91]

Each of these powers is explained in more detail below.[92] They are all, however, subject to the following restrictions.

(a) The trustees must have regard to the rights of the beneficiaries when exercising them.[93]

---

[84] Below, para.13–051.

[85] Below, para.13–031. In practice, where the land is to be registered in the name of two or more persons (as will usually be the case), there will often be a statement in the transfer or application for first registration as to the express trusts on which the land is held. Most cases of co-ownership will therefore take effect as express rather than statutory trusts.

[86] Above, para.6–015. The Act applies to conveyances made for the purposes of providing a school, museum, church or chapel, where the building has ceased to be required for that purpose. See, e.g. *Fraser v Canterbury Diocesan Board of Finance* [2007] EWHC 1590 (Ch), (2007) 28 E.G. 121 (CS).

[87] Reverter of Sites Act 1987 s.1 (as amended by TLATA 1996 Sch.2 para.6). The position of the trustees is analogous to that of personal representatives in a case of intestacy in that they do not have to consult the beneficiaries of the trust before exercising the power to sell the land. See above, para.6–015.

[88] Above, para.10–034.

[89] s.6(1).

[90] s.6(2).

[91] s.6(3), (4).

[92] For the trustees' power of partition under s.7; see below, para.13–101.

[93] s.6(5). This is likely to be of particular relevance where trustees exercise their power to purchase land for occupation by a beneficiary.

(b) The powers cannot be exercised by the trustees in contravention of, or of an order made in pursuance of, any other enactment or any rules of law or equity.[94] Thus the trustees are not authorised to act in a breach of trust[95] or to engage in conduct that would in some other way contravene their fiduciary obligations.[96] Nor may they delegate any functions which, as trustees, they could not otherwise delegate.[97]

(c) Where trustees are authorised by any statutory provision[98] to act subject to any restriction, limitation or condition, they cannot exercise the powers given to them by the 1996 Act in any way that it is prevented by those restrictions, limitations or conditions.[99] For example, if trustees of land are minded to exercise their power to invest in the purchase of land, they must first comply with the obligations imposed on all trustees by the Trustee Act 2000 when choosing investments.[100]

12–016   (1) TRUSTEES HAVE ALL THE POWERS OF A BENEFICIAL OWNER. Prior to 1997, because of the inadequacy of the statutory powers conferred on trustees for sale,[101] it had for some time been the practice of conveyancers, when drafting an express trust for sale, to confer on the trustees all the powers of a beneficial owner. This practice has now been adopted in the Trusts of Land and Appointment of Trustees Act 1996. It provides that, for the purposes of exercising their functions as trustees, the trustees of land have in relation to

---

[94] TLATA 1996 s.6(6). The reference to an "order" includes an order of the court or of the Charity Commissioner: TLATA 1996 s.6(7).

[95] One consequence of this limitation is that certain trustees, such as constructive or resulting trustees of land, or nominees who hold land on a bare trust, will not normally be able to make any disposition of the trust property except to or with the concurrence of the beneficiary under the trust. This is because any other disposition would be a breach of trust. Such trusts do not necessarily have all the incidents normally associated with the relationship of trustee and beneficiary: cf. *Berkley v Poulett* [1977] 1 E.G.L.R. 86 at 93; *Target Holdings Ltd v Redferns* [1996] A.C. 421 at 434–436. For the protection of purchasers, see below, paras 12–030 et seq.

[96] An obvious example is the rule that a trustee cannot sell trust property to himself. Such a sale can be set aside at the behest of the beneficiaries, and it seems a purchaser/mortgagee from the trustee may not obtain good title even if there appears to have been overreaching, *HSBC Bank Plc v Dyche* [2009] EWHC 2954 (Ch); [2010] B.P.I.R. 138; but note the criticism of this, [2011] 74 Conv. 1 (MJD) and [2011] 74 Conv. 169 (N. Gravells). There is strong authority (despite *Dyche*) that such a sale is not a breach of trust: see *Tito v Waddell (No.2)* [1977] Ch. 106 at 248. cf. para.A–079.

[97] See generally Trustee Act 2000. In summary, trustees may delegate ministerial acts, but not their fiduciary powers, such as the power to sell the land. For a detailed consideration of when trustees may delegate their functions, see (1999) Law Com. No.260, Pt IV, which led to the Trustee Act 2000.

[98] Other than TLATA 1996 s.6.

[99] TLATA 1996 s.6(8).

[100] See TA 2000, Pt II and Pt III. Thus the trustees should, e.g. have regard both to the need for diversification of investments so far as that was appropriate to the circumstances of the trust, and to the suitability of the proposed investment.

[101] Trustees for sale had all the powers of the tenant for life and the trustees of the settlement under the Settled Land Act 1925: LPA 1925 s.28(1) (now repealed). See above, para.10–023.

the land subject to the trust all the powers of an absolute owner.[102] But, these powers are not as sweeping as they might at first sight appear to be. In addition to the limitations on the exercise of the powers of trustees of land explained above, there are several important restrictions on these specific powers.

(i) They are given to the trustees only for the purposes of exercising their functions as trustees. They are therefore conferred on the trustees in a fiduciary capacity and must be exercised in the best interests of the trust.[103]

(ii) They are applicable only in relation to the land held in trust. This is so even though a trust of land is a trust of property which comprises or includes land,[104] and may therefore also include personalty. Thus, while the trustees may (for example) insure the land held in trust against fire or other risks, they cannot insure against any liabilities that they may themselves incur in their capacity as trustees.[105] Furthermore, once the trustees have sold all the land, they cease to have the powers conferred by the 1996 Act, except where it otherwise provides,[106] or where they purchase more land and thereupon become trustees of land once again.[107]

(iii) Subject to certain exceptions, trustees of land[108] are under a duty, in exercising any function in relation to the land, to consult the beneficiaries (so far as is practicable) and to give effect to their wishes (to the extent that it is consistent with the general interest of the trust.[109] This obligation is explained later.[110]

The most important of the powers which are conferred on trustees of land is that of sale. This is most likely to be an issue where land is held on trust for beneficiaries with concurrent interests, and it is therefore considered more fully in that context.[111] However, it should be noted here that, in the absence of an express trust for sale,[112] trustees of land will have a mere power of sale

---

[102] s.6(1). It should be noted that the Act distinguishes between the trustees' "functions" and their "powers". The former includes the entirety of the trustees' powers and obligations and is therefore much wider than the latter. This distinction, which has been overlooked by some commentators, is of some importance: see below, para.12–023.

[103] *Cowan v Scargill* [1985] Ch. 270 at 286, 287. See too *Harries v The Church Commissioners for England* [1992] 1 W.L.R. 1241 at 1246.

[104] TLATA 1996 s.1(1).

[105] The extent of trustees' powers to insure trust property (other than where it is held on a trust of land) was remarkably uncertain. However, see now TA 2000 s.34, substituting a new TA 1925 s.19 and which provides a new general power to insure *any* trust property.

[106] cf. TLATA 1996 s.17.

[107] Below, para.12–018.

[108] Other than personal representatives: s.18(1); below, para.12–035.

[109] TLATA 1996 s.11.

[110] Below, para.12–026.

[111] Below, para.13–064.

[112] After 1996, there will be a trust for sale only (i) where it was already in existence when TLATA 1996 was brought into force on January 1, 1997; or (ii) where it was expressly created thereafter: above, para.12–005.

which, like all powers, can be exercised only by a unanimous decision of the trustees[113] or pursuant to an order of the court.[114]

Although the powers of trustees of land are substantially wider than were those of trustees for sale prior to 1997, it appears, however, that in one minor respect they may be narrower.[115] Amongst the powers conferred on trustees for sale were certain powers of an altruistic character[116] such as a power to grant land for public and charitable purposes,[117] and to sell or lease land for small dwellings and small holdings at less than the best consideration or rent that might be obtained.[118] As trustees have no power to give away trust assets or dispose of them at an undervalue in the absence of express authorisation, it would seem that they can no longer make dispositions of this character.[119]

12–017   (2) TRUSTEES MAY REQUIRE BENEFICIARIES TO TAKE A CONVEYANCE OF THE LAND. The 1996 Act makes provision for the case where each of the beneficiaries is of full age and capacity and is absolutely entitled either to all or to some particular parcel of the land held on a trust of land. In such a case, the trustees are entitled to convey the land to the beneficiaries, even though they are not required by them to do so.[120] Thus where land is held on trust for A for life, thereafter to B, C and D equally, and A dies, the trustees may convey the land to B, C and D provided that they are of full age and capacity, whether or not the beneficiaries ask them to do so. The object of the provision is to enable the trust to be carried out (whether in whole or part) and the trustees discharged.[121] For that reason, the trustees may exercise this power without the need to consult the beneficiaries.[122] Furthermore, the beneficiaries are required to do whatever is necessary to secure that the land vests in them,[123] and if they fail to do so, the court may make an order requiring them to do so.[124]

This statutory power is confined to cases where there are two or more beneficiaries. In such circumstances, although the trustees convey the land to

---

[113] Exceptionally, charity trustees may act by a majority: above para.12–005. Where a periodic tenancy is vested in two or more joint tenants, the determination of the tenancy is not considered to be the exercise of a power, and can be effected by just one of them. Such an act is not a breach of trust and not a "function relating to" the land within s.11 TLATA 1996: see *Crawley BC v Ure* [1996] Q.B. 13 and *Brackley v Notting Hill Housing Trust* [2001] EWCA Civ 601, (2001) 35 EG 106; see below, para.13–006.

[114] Under TLATA 1996 s.14; below, para.12–021.

[115] See [1998] Conv. 246 (C. Jessel).

[116] See below, Appendix paras A–058, A–074.

[117] SLA 1925 s.55.

[118] SLA 1925 s.57.

[119] For the future, settlors can of course expressly grant the necessary powers if they are minded to do so.

[120] TLATA 1996 s.6(2).

[121] cf. (1989) Law Com. No.181, para.14.3.

[122] Below.

[123] e.g. by registering the transfer to them (even if the land is unregistered, the transfer will now trigger the requirement of compulsory registration: see LRA 2002 s.4).

[124] TLATA 1996 s.6(2).

persons who are absolutely entitled, the land will remain subject to a trust of land. The provision enables them to transfer their trusteeship (and the obligations that go with it) to the beneficiaries. By contrast, where trustees convey land to a sole beneficiary who is absolutely entitled to it, the trust terminates, and the trustees need no express authority to make the conveyance.

(3) TRUSTEES MAY PURCHASE LAND. Trustees of land have a power to **12–018** purchase a legal estate in any land in England and Wales.[125] This power, which applies to trustees not only of land but of the proceeds of sale of land,[126] may be exercised to purchase land:

(a) by way of investment;

(b) for occupation by any beneficiary; or

(c) for any other reason.[127]

This is an extension of the powers of trustees holding land. Prior to 1997, trustees for sale could invest or otherwise apply capital money in the purchase of either freehold land or leasehold land held for a term of at least 60 years.[128] However, if the trustees sold all the land held on trust for sale, they ceased to be trustees for sale, and as trustees of personalty no longer had this power.[129] The present power applies to freeholds and to leaseholds of any duration.[130] It is couched in wide terms to avoid the difficulties that have in the past arisen

---

[125] TLATA 1996 s.6(3). The restriction of this power reflects the fact that trusts are not universally recognised and enforced by other states under their conflict of laws rules. cf. Recognition of Trusts Act 1987, which implements the Hague Convention on the Law Applicable to Trusts and on Their Recognition. Even where the Convention has been incorporated by a state into its domestic law, it contains wide "let out" provisions, e.g. to protect marital property rights and rights of succession: see Arts 15, 16.

[126] TLATA 1996 s.17(1). For these purposes, "proceeds of sale" include any proceeds of a disposition of land held in trust (including settled land), or any property representing any such proceeds: TLATA 1996 s.17(3). Thus, if all the land which was held in a Settled Land Act settlement was sold, so that the settlement ceased (see TLATA 1996 s.2(4); above, para.A–025), the trustees would have the power to purchase land conferred by TLATA 1996 s.6(3). If land remains settled land notwithstanding the sale of part of the property, the trustees of the settlement do not have these powers, but only those conferred by the Settled Land Act 1925: TLATA 1996 s.17(5).

[127] TLATA 1996 s.6(4). An example of (c) might be where trustees purchased land for a beneficiary to be used for the purposes of his business.

[128] LPA 1925 s.28(1) (now repealed); SLA 1925 s.73(1)(xi). In the case of settled land, the trustees of the settlement continue to have this power. The power is one either to invest or otherwise apply capital money and these are distinct: see *Re Duke of Marlborough's Settlement* (1886) 32 Ch D 1. The power to apply capital money may be employed to purchase a residence for a beneficiary (whether or not that constitutes an investment). See below.

[129] Above, para.10–023. In the absence of express provision in the trust instrument, trustees of personalty (except trustees of a pension trust who have the same powers of investment as a beneficial owner: Pensions Act 1995 s.34(1)) now have the general powers of investment under the TA 2000 and this includes the power to invest in the purchase of land.

[130] See (1989) Law Com. No.181, para.10.8.

because of the narrow interpretation given to express powers to purchase land.[131] In exercising this power, the trustees are once again under an obligation to consult the beneficiaries so far as is practicable.[132]

(b) Curtailment of powers

12–019   (1) EXCLUSION AND RESTRICTION OF POWERS. The powers conferred on trustees of land by the Trusts of Land and Appointment of Trustees Act 1996 may be restricted or wholly excluded by an express provision in the disposition creating the trust[133] except:

(i) where the property is held on charitable, ecclesiastical or public trusts[134];

(ii) where the provision purports to exclude or modify the implied power to postpone sale where trustees of land hold the property on trust for sale[135];

(iii) where any enactment prohibits or restricts any such provision excluding or restricting the power[136]; or

(iv) in relation to the requirement that consent be obtained to the exercise of any such power, unless this is permitted by any enactment.[137]

The effect of these provisions is that a careful settlor may now create a trust of land under which the property may be made inalienable for the duration of the trust.[138] Where the title to the land held in trust is registered,[139] there is an

---

[131] An express power for trustees merely to "invest" in the purchase of land has been held not to authorise the trustees to purchase a residence for a beneficiary: see *Re Power* [1947] Ch. 572; *Re Peacenik's EST* [1964] 1 W.L.R. 720 at 723. This narrow view of what constitutes an investment has been criticised: (1947) 63 L.Q.R. 421 (REM). More recently, it has been held that occupation by a beneficiary is no more than a method of enjoying in specie the rents and profits of the land: *City of Landon BS v Flegg* [1988] A.C. 54 at 83. See (1997) Law Com. CE No.146, Pt VIII.

[132] TLATA 1996 s.11; below, para.12–026.

[133] TLATA 1996 s.8(1). See too, in relation to trustees' powers of partition (under TLATA 1996 s.7), below, para.13–101. The term "disposition" is widely defined: see LPA 1925 s.205(1)(ii) (which is applicable: see TLATA 1996 s.23(2)).

[134] TLATA 1996 s.8(3). The reason for this exception (which was introduced by amendment during the passage of the legislation through Parliament) is that trustees must administer a charitable trust as effectively as possible to achieve its objects. This might not be possible if their powers could be excluded or constrained.

[135] TLATA 1996 s.4(1); above, para.12–005.

[136] TLATA 1996 s.8(4).

[137] TLATA 1996 s.8(4). The reasons for this are explained below, para.12–020.

[138] See Ch.9 for the impact of the rule against perpetuities.

[139] Any transfer of unregistered land to trustees of land will have to be registered: see LRA 2002 s.4.

obligation to apply for an appropriate restriction to be entered on the register reflecting the exclusion or restriction of the trustees' powers.[140]

The ability of a settlor to restrict the trustees' powers stands in sharp contrast to the position in relation to settled land, where the powers conferred on a tenant for life or statutory owner could not in any way be excluded or restricted.[141] It has been explained that the extent to which it was possible to curtail the powers of trustees for sale was uncertain, but that there appeared to be ways by which it might be achieved.[142] Furthermore, the courts developed a doctrine by which they would not order a sale of land held on trust for sale where the purposes for which the land was acquired still subsisted, even though the trustees were not unanimous in exercising the power to postpone sale.[143] Although this doctrine was most commonly applied in the context of the family home, it was also employed for other purposes, e.g. to preserve land from development.[144]

The Law Commission gave little indication as to why it recommended that settlors should have a virtually unfettered freedom to restrict the powers of trustees of land,[145] although this freedom does provide a counterpoise for the much wider powers that trustees of land now enjoy. It gives settlors greater flexibility to make arrangements that are effective to achieve their wishes.[146] A settlor can (for example) provide both for the retention within the family of an ancestral home or estate and for its maintenance.[147] However, it seems unlikely that many settlors will attempt to create trusts which so restrict the trustees' powers that the evils once associated with settlements are revived.[148] But, if they do, the trustees (or beneficiaries) may not be without remedy.[149] It seems probable that the court has power under the Trusts of Land and Appointment of Trustees Act 1996 to override the restrictions imposed by the settlor to the extent that it is necessary to enable the trustees to exercise their functions.[150] This is explained later.[151] Even if this is not the case, where in the management or administration of any trust property, any disposition is in the court's opinion expedient, but cannot be effected by reason of the absence of

[140] LRR 2003 r.94(4) and (5), for a standard Form B restriction. A beneficiary may also apply for such a restriction, LRA 2002 s.43(1)(c), LRR 2003 r.93(c).

[141] SLA 1925 s.106; below, Appendix para.A–082.

[142] By making the remainderman's interest contingent on the property not being sold and then requiring his consent to its sale: above, para.10–025.

[143] See above, para.10–022; and below, para.13–064.

[144] *Re Buchanan-Wollaston's Conveyance* [1939] Ch. 738.

[145] cf. (1989) Law Com. No.181 para.10.10. A condition which takes away an absolute owner's right to alienate the property is normally void as being contrary to public policy, because the right of disposition is an incident of such ownership (see above, para.3–031. However, this principle may not apply in its full force to property held by trustees in cases where the restraints on alienation are intended by the settlor to preserve the property for the enjoyment of the beneficiaries.

[146] This was not always possible when creating a settlement under the Settled Land Act 1925 because of the prohibition on fettering powers contained in SLA 1925 s.106.

[147] cf. *Raikes v Lygon* [1988] 1 W.L.R. 281; below, Appendix para.A–071.

[148] See above, para.10–005; cf. [1990] Conv. 12 at 16 (R. J. Smith).

[149] See [1997] Conv. 263 (G. Watt); and see below, para.12–023.

[150] TLATA 1996 s.14(1), (2); below, para.12–021.

[151] Below, para.12–023.

any power, it may give the trustees the necessary power, either generally or in the particular instance.[152]

12–020   (2) CONSENTS. If the disposition creating a trust of land makes provision requiring any consent to be obtained to the exercise of any power conferred by the Trusts of Land and Appointment of Trustees Act 1996,[153] the power may not be exercised without that consent[154] except where any enactment prohibits or restricts such control.[155] Where such a consent requirement exists in relation to a trust of registered land,[156] an application should be made to register an appropriate restriction.[157] The court has power under the Act to relieve trustees of their obligation to obtain the consent of any person.[158] This is explained below.[159]

12–021   (3) POWERS OF THE COURT. Prior to 1997, where there was a trust for sale and either:

(i) the trustees refused to sell or to exercise any of their other powers; or

(ii) any requisite consent could not be obtained

any person interested[160] might apply to the court for an order giving effect to the proposed transaction, and the court had power to make such order as it

---

[152] TA 1925 s.57. It has never been decided whether the court could confer on trustees a power which the settlor had expressly excluded, but where its absence was disadvantageous to the trust. However, there seems to be no reason to restrict "the absence of any power" to cases where none was conferred. cf. *Re Cockerell's S.T.* [1956] Ch. 372, where the court sanctioned a sale, even though the settlor had provided that a sale should take place only at a later date.

[153] s.6; above, para.12–015.

[154] TLATA 1996 s.8(2). For the protection of purchasers, see TLATA 1996 s.10; below, para.12–030.

[155] TLATA 1996 s.8(4). This exception, which was added by amendment during the passage of the legislation through Parliament, arose out of a concern about pension schemes. cf. Pensions Act 1995 s.35(4), which prohibits the restriction of the investment powers of pension trustees by reference to the consent of the employer.

[156] Including land which is required to be registered on its transfer to the trustees of land: see LRA 1925 s.123 (as substituted by LRA 1997).

[157] LRA 2002 s.43(1). A Form N restriction would be used. However, where the trust instrument does not itself impose a consent requirement, an application by a beneficiary for a Form N restriction requiring their consent will be refused, *Coleman v Bryant* [2007] All E.R. (D) 101 (Jul). See para.12–019.

[158] TLATA 1996 s.14(1), (2).

[159] Below.

[160] This term was widely interpreted. It included (i) a trustee for sale (whether or not he was also a beneficiary): *Re Buchanan-Wollaston's Conveyance* [1939] Ch. 738; *Re Mayo* [1943] Ch. 302; (ii) a beneficiary under the trust for sale: e.g. *Jones v Challenger* [1961] 1 Q.B. 176; (iii) a trustee in bankruptcy of such a beneficiary: *Re Solomon* [1967] Ch. 573 at 586; (iv) a receiver appointed by way of equitable execution to enforce a judgment debt against a beneficiary: *Levermore v Levermore* [1979] 1 W.L.R. 1277; (v) a judgment creditor who had obtained a charging order against a beneficiary: *First National Securities Ltd v Hegerty* [1985] Q.B. 850 at 867; *Midland Bank Plc v Pike* [1988] 2 All E.R. 434; *Lloyds Bank Plc v Byrne* [1993] 1 F.L.R. 369 at 370; and (vi) a secured creditor, such as a mortgagee, even if his mortgage was not binding on all the beneficiaries under the trust for sale: *Kingsnorth Finance Co Ltd v Tizard* [1986] 1 W.L.R. 783 at 795.

thought fit.[161] A considerable body of authority grew up around this provision, particularly in the context of land which was in co-ownership.

The Trusts of Land and Appointment of Trustees Act 1996 contains somewhat similar but wider provisions that are derived in part from the practice that evolved in relation to trusts for sale.[162] The intention of the legislation was that the court should have power to intervene "in any dispute relating to a trust of land",[163] other than as to the appointment or removal of trustees.[164] On an application[165] by any person who is either a trustee of land or has an interest[166] in any property[167] which is subject to either a trust of land[168] or a trust of the proceeds of sale of land,[169] the court is given discretion to make such an order as it thinks fit in relation to two matters:

(i) the exercise by the trustees of any of their functions,[170] which expressly includes an order to relieve the trustees of the obligation to obtain the consent of, or to consult, any person in connection with the exercise of any of their functions[171]; and

(ii) the nature or extent of a person's interest in property subject to the trust, which it may declare.[172]

In relation to (i), the power to relieve the trustees of the obligation to obtain a necessary consent to the exercise of some function should, in principle, apply not only where there are practical difficulties in obtaining such consent (as where the relevant person cannot be found), but also where it has been refused.[173] As regards (ii), the element of discretion is intelligible only if it is confined to a decision by the court whether or not to make a declaration as to

---

[161] LPA 1925 s.30(i) (now repealed).

[162] TLATA 1996 ss.14, 15. cf. (1989) Law Com. No.181 paras 12.1–12.13.

[163] (1989) Law Com. No.181 para.12.6.

[164] TLATA 1996 s.14(3). For the appointment and removal of trustees, see below paras 11–050, 11–065.

[165] Whether that application is made before 1997 or after 1996: TLATA 1996 s.14(4).

[166] The expression "interest in property" is to be widely interpreted (as was the equivalent expression in LPA 1925 s.30, above). It would probably include an object of a discretionary trust (who has the right to compel the proper administration of the trust).

[167] Including personal property.

[168] TLATA 1996 s.14(1).

[169] TLATA 1996 s.17(2). For the meaning of a trust of the proceeds of sale of land, see TLATA 1996 s.17(3)–(6).

[170] TLATA 1996 s.14(2)(a).

[171] For the obligation of trustees to consult certain beneficiaries in the exercise of any of their functions, see TLATA 1996 s.11; below para.12–026.

[172] TLATA 1996 s.14(2)(b).

[173] This was the case in relation to trusts for sale under the different wording of LPA 1925 s.30: *Re Beale's* S.T. [1932] 2 Ch. 15. The Draft Bill in (1989) Law Com. No.181 did not specifically mention the issue of consents in its equivalent provision. Although it was added when the Bill was redrafted by the Law Commission, there is no reason to think that there was any intention to change the law. Cases seeking to dispense with required consents are rare, simply because so few trusts of land incorporate such a requirement and HM Land Registry will not register a restriction requiring the consent of some named person unless such an obligation is express, above para.12–020.

a person's proprietary rights.[174] It seems improbable that the court originally was intended to have discretion to vary such rights and the cases proceed on the basis that the court is declaring existing entitlements, rather than varying them.[175]

12–022   In exercising its discretion, the matters to which the court is required to have regard include the following:

(a) the intentions of the person or persons (if any) who created the trust

(b) the purposes for which the property subject to the trust is held

(c) the welfare of any minor who occupies or might reasonably be expected to occupy any land subject to the trust as his home; and

(d) the interests of any secured creditor of any beneficiary.[176]

It should be emphasised both that this list is not an exhaustive one,[177] and that the relevant factors will sometimes conflict, so that the court will have to decide which is to prevail. The court is also required to have regard to certain additional factors in relation to particular functions. First, it must have regard to the circumstances and wishes of any beneficiaries of full age who are entitled to an interest in possession in property[178] subject to the trust or (in case of dispute) of the majority (according to the value of their combined interests).[179] This applies to all applications except those relating to the exercise by the trustees of their powers either:

(i) to convey land to beneficiaries who are absolutely entitled to it[180]; or

---

[174] Compare the provision as originally drafted by the Law Commission, which seems preferable: see (1989) Law Com. No.181, Draft Bill, cl. 6.

[175] Of course, the element of discretion now involved in the "declaration" of entitlement under a constructive trust may make this distinction illusory, see the decision under s.14 in *Stack v Dowden* (2007) 2 W.L.R. 831 which can easily be seen as the court varying entitlements established at the time of acquisition rather than declaring those entitlements, above para.11–023. In *Borivoje Prazic v Penelope Prazic* (2006) 2 F.L.R. 1128, the Court of Appeal refused an application under s.14 to determine beneficial interests because the property was subject to divorce proceedings abroad. This applies the general principle that "as the decision of the House of Lords in *White v White* makes plain, issues between a husband and a wife are to be determined within the four corners of the Matrimonial Causes Act and on the application of the statutory criteria there set out", per Thorpe L.J. at para.25. However, the Court had no doubt that it could in an appropriate case "determine" the beneficial interests of the parties under a s.14 application and this now seems to be accepted. See also *Hiscock v Oxley* [2004] 3 W.L.R. 715 (under the rubric of a claim via constructive trust) and *Chun v Ho* (2003) 1 F.L.R. 23 (in the context of a claim in proprietary estoppel).

[176] TLATA 1996 s.l5(1). The section is inapplicable where a trustee in bankruptcy applies for an order for sale under TLATA 1996 s.14: TLATA 1996 s.15(4). see IA 1986 s.335A; below para.13–070.

[177] *White v White* [2003] EWCA Civ 924, [2004] 2 F.L.R. 321.

[178] Whether land or personalty.

[179] TLATA 1996 s.15(3).

[180] See TLATA 1996 s.6(2); above, para.12–017.

(ii) to exclude a beneficiary from occupation of any land held in trust.[181]

Secondly, on an application relating to the exercise of the power to exclude a beneficiary from occupation of any land held in trust,[182] the court must have regard to the circumstances and wishes of each of the beneficiaries who is (or apart from any previous exercise by the trustees of those powers would be) entitled to occupy the land.[183]

Most issues relating to the exercise of the court's discretion are likely to **12–023** arise in relation to property which is in co-ownership, and they are discussed in that context.[184] However, one matter, already mentioned,[185] must be considered here. This is whether the court may, in the exercise of its statutory discretion, override an express exclusion by the settlor[186] of all or some of the powers conferred on the trustees by the Trusts of Land and Appointment of Trustees Act 1996. It is suggested that there are at least three reasons why it can.

(i) The court is authorised to make an order "relating to the exercise of the trustees of any of their *functions*".[187] Trustees' functions comprise the totality of their powers and obligations,[188] including their paramount duty to act in the best interests of the beneficiaries and to further the purposes of the trust,[189] and their duty to maintain an even hand between life tenant and remainderman.[190] The exclusion of all or some of the trustees' powers will not therefore deprive them of all of their functions and, in particular, it will not affect their fundamental duties.[191] They should therefore be able to seek the assistance of the court to the extent that the exclusion impedes their performance of any such duty.

(ii) The settlor's intentions are merely one factor which the court must take into account on an application for an order, and may be outweighed by others.[192]

(iii) The court is expressly empowered to override any requirement imposed by the settlor that a particular consent be obtained in

---

[181] See TLATA 1996 s.13. This is explained, below, para.12–029.
[182] Below, para.12–029.
[183] TLATA 1996 s.15(2).
[184] Below, para.13–064.
[185] Above, para.12–019.
[186] Under TLATA 1996 s.8.
[187] TLATA 1996 s.14(2)(a).
[188] Above, para.12–016.
[189] See *Cowan v Scargill* [1985] Ch. 270 at 286, 287; *Harries v The Church Commissioners for England* [1992] 1 W.L.R. 1241 at 1246; above, para.12–016.
[190] See P. D. Finn, *Fiduciary Obligations*, Ch.13.
[191] This point is overlooked in [1997] Conv. 263, 266 (G. Watt).
[192] TLATA 1996 s.15(1); above, para.12–022.

connection with the exercise of any function.[193] This is closely analogous to the present issue, and there is no obvious reason for adopting a different approach in relation to each.

The example may be given of a settlor who created a trust of land but excluded the trustees' powers to sell, lease or charge the land held in trust. His intention was to ensure the retention of the property in his family for the duration of the trust. If he failed to make proper provision for the maintenance and upkeep of the estate, so that it fell into disrepair, an application by the trustees to the court for power to sell, lease or charge part of the land to the extent necessary to maintain as much of the estate as possible should in principle succeed.

8. Position of beneficiaries

12–024   *(a) Delegation of functions.* It has been explained that, under the Settled Land Act 1925, where land is settled:

(i) the powers of disposition and management are normally vested in the tenant for life[194];

(ii) most such powers are exercisable on notice to the trustees of the settlement,[195] but that some require the consent of the trustees or an order of the court[196]; and

(iii) any attempt to confer such powers on the trustees of the settlement instead is ineffective.[197]

By contrast, where land was held on trust for sale prior to 1997, the powers of disposition and management were vested in the trustees for sale, subject to a limited power to delegate revocably the exercise of certain powers to the adult beneficiary who was entitled in possession to the net rents and profits of the land.[198]

The Trusts of Land and Appointment of Trustees Act 1996 adopts a middle course between these two positions.[199] Where property is held on a trust of land, all powers and other functions in relation to a trust of land are vested in the trustees.[200] However, they are given authority to delegate for any period or

---

[193] TLATA 1996 s.14(2)(a); above, para.12–021.
[194] Below, Appendix para.A–055.
[195] Below, Appendix para.A–057.
[196] Below, Appendix para.A–066.
[197] Below, Appendix para.A–080.
[198] LPA 1925 s.29 (now repealed); above, para.10–027. Any such delegation made before 1997 is unaffected by the repeal of LPA 1925 s.29 or the provisions of TLATA 1996: see TLATA 1996 s.9(9).
[199] One reason for the prospective abolition of settled land was the inherent conflict of interest in the position of the tenant for life, who is both a beneficiary and a trustee for the other beneficiaries: above, para.12–003.
[200] Above, para.12–002.

indefinitely[201] *any* of their functions as trustees which relate to the land.[202] This power can only be exercised by a power of attorney[203] given by all the trustees jointly in favour of one or more beneficiaries who are beneficially entitled to an interest in possession in land subject to the trust.[204] Because trustees' powers must be exercised unanimously, the power of attorney:

(i) may be revoked at any time by any one or more of the trustees[205];

(ii) will be revoked by the appointment of a new trustee: in such circumstances, the power must be exercised afresh by all the trustees jointly[206]; but

(iii) will not be revoked where a person ceases to be a trustee whether on death or otherwise: in such a case, the unanimity of the remaining trustees is not affected.[207]

Should a beneficiary to whom the functions are delegated cease to be a person beneficially entitled to an interest in possession in land subject to the trust,[208] the power is revoked if the functions were delegated to him alone. If they were delegated to two or more beneficiaries jointly, they will be revoked only if each of the beneficiaries ceases to be entitled. Otherwise the functions remain exercisable by the remaining beneficiary or beneficiaries. Where the functions were delegated severally, the power is revoked only as regards the beneficiary whose interest has ceased.[209]

Beneficiaries to whom functions have been delegated are subject to the **12–025** same duties and liabilities as trustees in relation to their exercise,[210] although a beneficiary to whom some function has been delegated, is not required either

---

[201] See TLATA 1996 s.9(5).

[202] TLATA 1996 s.9(1). This power is separate and distinct from the trustees' powers to delegate collectively certain of their functions to an agent or nominee (see TA 2000 Pt IV), and the power of an individual trustee to delegate all of his trusts, powers and discretions under TA 1925 s.25. The latter form of delegation can only be made for a period of up to one year: TA 1925 s.25(1). It should be noted that TLATA 1996 s.9 underwent substantial amendment during its passage through Parliament, mainly because of concerns raised by the Law Society.

[203] Which cannot be an enduring power of attorney within the Enduring Powers of Attorney Act 1985 (now repealed) or a lasting power of attorney under the Mental Capacity Act 2005: TLATA 1996 s.9(6) (as amended by Sch.6 para.42 Mental Capacity Act 2005). This is because such a power of attorney is irrevocable once the donor has lost capacity: see Enduring Powers of Attorney Act 1985 s.2 and s.13 Mental Capacity Act 2005. For the revocability of a power of attorney given under TLATA 1996 s.9(1); see below. No new enduring powers of attorney can be created, but existing powers are preserved and integrated into the scheme of the Mental Capacity Act 2005.

[204] TLATA 1996 s.9(1), (3). An annuitant is not such a beneficiary: TLATA 1996 s.22(3).

[205] TLATA 1996 s.9(3). This will not be the case where the power is expressed to be irrevocable and is given by way of security: TLATA 1996 s.22(3).

[206] TLATA 1996.

[207] TLATA 1996.

[208] As where the beneficiary has a determinable interest and the determining event occurs.

[209] TLATA 1996 s.9(4).

[210] TLATA 1996 s.9(7).

to obtain the consent of the trustees or to notify them of his intention to exercise it.[211] They are not, however, regarded as trustees for any other purposes, and in particular:

  (a) they have no power to sub-delegate those functions[212]; and

  (b) if they make a disposition of the trust property, in order to overreach the trusts, any capital money must be paid to the trustees of the land and not to them.[213]

Where trustees have exercised the power to delegate some or all of their functions to one or more beneficiaries, they are jointly and severally liable for the acts or defaults of any such beneficiary in exercising the function if, and only if, the trustees did not exercise reasonable care in deciding to delegate it.[214] This provision, which was the result of an amendment made during the passage of the Trusts of Land and Appointment of Trustees Act 1996 through Parliament,[215] has been criticised because it apparently imposes no duty on the trustees to keep under review a beneficiary's exercise of any function once a delegation has been made.[216] However, trustees are under a paramount duty to act in the best interests of the trust,[217] and it seems likely that they would be in breach of that duty if they failed to revoke a power of attorney once it became apparent that a beneficiary was abusing the functions that had been delegated to him.[218]

It may happen that the trustees delegate their functions under the Act and either that delegation is subsequently revoked or it transpires that the person to whom they purported to delegate, X, was not in fact beneficially entitled to an interest in possession in land subject to the trust, so that the delegation is invalid. X may have dealt with or disposed of that land. There is statutory protection for third parties in the following situations.

  (i) Where the delegation has been revoked, and a person, Y, then deals with X without knowledge of the revocation, the transaction is

---

[211] Compare the position of a tenant for life of settled land: below, Appendix paras A–057, A–066.

[212] This is because the reason for allowing trustees to delegate a function to a beneficiary is that he (and not some agent) should exercise it. Contrast the position of a tenant for life under the Settled Land Act 1925. As a trustee he may employ agents whenever a trustee might under TA 2000 Pt IV. He may also delegate all his trusts and discretions by power of attorney under TA 1925 s.25.

[213] TLATA 1996 s.9(7). For overreaching, see below, para.12–036.

[214] TLATA 1996 s.9(8).

[215] As originally drafted, trustees would have been vicariously liable for the acts and defaults of the beneficiary to whom the functions had been delegated, whether or not they had acted with reasonable care. The change was made because of opposition to the provision from the Law Society.

[216] See [1997] Conv. 372 (A. Kenny). cf. (1999) Law Com. No.260, pp.125, 134, 135.

[217] Above, paras 12–016, 12–023.

[218] In other words they would be in breach of their own *primary* duty, rather than *vicariously* liable for the defaults of the beneficiary. TLATA 1996 s.9(8) is concerned only with the latter form of liability.

treated as being as valid as it would have been if the delegation had not been revoked.[219]

(ii) Where the delegation was made to the wrong person, and Y deals in good faith with X without knowledge of the mistake, X is deemed to be a person to whom the functions could be delegated.[220]

(iii) Where in any subsequent transaction between Y and a purchaser, Z, Z's interest depends on the validity of the earlier transaction between X and Y, there is a conclusive presumption that Y did not know of the revocation or that the delegation to X was mistaken if, within three months after the completion of the purchase Y makes a statutory declaration to that effect,[221] or, in the case of a revocation,[222] if the transaction between X and Y took place within 12 months of the date of the delegation.[223]

(b) Consultation. Prior to 1997, where land was held on trust for sale, **12–026** trustees for sale were under a limited statutory duty to consult the beneficiaries entitled in possession when exercising their powers. This applied only where the trust for sale was created by statute or showed an intention that the provision was to apply.[224]

The Trusts of Land and Appointment of Trustees Act 1996 imposes a much wider duty of consultation on trustees of land, which applies in relation to the exercise of any function relating to land subject to the trust[225] (with one minor exception[226]). The trustees must:

(i) so far as practicable, consult the beneficiaries of full age who are beneficially entitled to an interest in possession in the land; and

(ii) so far as consistent with the general interest of the trust, give effect to the wishes of those beneficiaries, or the wishes of the majority according to the value of their combined interests.[227]

This obligation applies to all trusts of land created after 1996 except where the disposition provides to the contrary,[228] or where the trust arises under a will

---

[219] Powers of Attorney Act 1971 s.5(2).
[220] TLATA 1996 s.9(2).
[221] Powers of Attorney Act 1971 s.5(4)(b); TLATA 1996 s.9(2). In relation to registered land, see too LRR 2003 1925 rr.61, 62, 63. Ruoff & Roper 13.006.05 et seq.
[222] Z will in practice require Y to make such a statutory declaration. cf. LRR 2003 r.62(2).
[223] Powers of Attorney Act 1971 s.5(4)(a). In relation to registered land, see too LRR 2003 r.62, Ruoff & Roper, 13.006.07 et seq.
[224] LPA 1925 s.26(3) (as amended by LP(Am)A 1926 Sch.); above, para.10–028.
[225] TLATA 1996 s.11.
[226] It does not apply to the power to convey land to beneficiaries who are absolutely entitled to it under s.6(2): see TLATA 1996 s.11(2)(c); below, Appendix para.A–022.
[227] TLATA 1996 s 11(1)
[228] Thereby reversing the position that existed in relation to trusts for sale prior to 1997.

made before 1997 (even if the testator dies after 1996).[229] As regards any trust that was created before 1997 by a disposition,[230] the duty to consult does not apply[231] unless provision that it should is made by a deed executed by the settlor who is of full age and capacity, or where more than one person created the trust, such of them as are alive and of full capacity.[232] It should be noted that this does produce a substantive difference between:

> (i) those trusts that were created before 1997 but which now take effect as trusts of land; and
>
> (ii) trusts of land created after 1996.[233]

As regards the former, the trustees are now under no obligation to consult the beneficiaries about the exercise of their powers, even in relation to those trusts where, prior to 1997, such a duty existed.[234] However, on any application relating to the exercise by the trustees of their functions,[235] the courts must take into account the wishes of the beneficiaries of full age who are entitled to an interest in possession in the property held in trust.[236] In practice therefore, trustees are well advised to consult such beneficiaries—whether or not they are obliged to do so—in order to minimise the risk that one of them may make an application to the court.

(c) The right to occupy

12–027   (1) BACKGROUND. Prior to 1997, where land was held in trust, the rights of those entitled in possession to occupy the land (assuming that it was both suitable for that purpose and available) were as follows.

(i) Settled land. A tenant for life (or person having the powers of a tenant for life) was entitled to occupy the land as an incident of the legal ownership that was vested in him.

(ii) Trust for sale: successive interests. Where there were successive interests under an express trust for sale, it was a matter for the trustees' discretion whether the beneficiary having the life interest should be permitted to occupy the land.[237]

---

[229] TLATA 1996 s.11(2).

[230] Or after 1996 by reference to such a trust, e.g. through the exercise of a power of appointment contained in a trust made before 1997.

[231] TLATA 1996 s.11(3).

[232] TLATA 1996. The deed importing such a duty to consult is irrevocable: TLATA 1996 s.11(4).

[233] This distinction arose as a result of an amendment made during the passage of the Bill through Parliament at the prompting of the Law Society. The concern was that to impose a requirement of consultation on all trusts might run counter to the intentions of the settlor. However, for reasons explained below, this amendment is unlikely to have much practical effect.

[234] LPA 1925 s.26(3) was repealed by TLATA 1996 s.25(2), Sch.4, without any saving to cover this situation. This was probably due to an oversight.

[235] TLATA 1996 s.14, above, para.12–021.

[236] TLATA 1996 s.15(3); above, para.12–022.

[237] *Re Bagot's Settlement* [1894] 1 Ch. 177.

(iii) Trusts for sale: concurrent interests. Although there had been some uncertainty as to the rights of co-owners entitled in possession under a trust for sale,[238] it had been settled that in the absence of some indicator to the contrary,[239] they would normally have a right to occupy the land pending sale.[240]

(iv) Bare trust. A beneficiary under a bare trust was entitled to occupy the land because the trustees held the land as nominees to his order.

After 1996, in relation to trusts of land,[241] the Trusts of Land and Appointment of Trustees Act 1996 confers a statutory right of occupation in the circumstances explained below. This right was conferred for two reasons. First, there was thought to be some uncertainty as to the powers of trustees for sale to allow beneficiaries into occupation.[242] Secondly, there was a concern that although trustees of land would have the powers of an absolute owner,[243] it might not be a proper exercise of that power to allow beneficiaries into occupation.[244]

(2) THE RIGHT. The Trusts of Land and Appointment of Trustees Act 1996 **12–028** confers a statutory right on a beneficiary who is beneficially entitled to an interest in possession in land to occupy the land at any time.[245] This right continues only so long as certain conditions are satisfied.

    (i) The purposes of the trust must at the time include the making available of the land for occupation either by him specifically or by the beneficiaries (whether in general or of some class of which he is a member).[246] If this is not the case, there is still a right of occupation if the land is in fact held by trustees so as to be available for the beneficiary's occupation.[247]

    (ii) There is no right to occupy land which is at the time either unavailable[248] or unsuitable for occupation by him.[249]

---

[238] cf. (1955) 19 Conv. (N.S.) 146 (F. R. Crane); (1966) 82 L.Q.R. 29 at 33 (REM).

[239] e.g. the terms of an express trust (which commonly place the matter at the discretion of the trustees), or the purpose for which the trust was created.

[240] *City of London BS v Flegg* [1988] A.C. 54 at 81; below, para.13–062.

[241] Which include all trusts for sale and bare trusts that were in existence when the Act came into force.

[242] See (1989) Law Com. No.181, para.13.2.

[243] TLATA 1996 s.6(l); above, para.12–016.

[244] (1989) Law Com. No.181, para.13.2. This was presumably because of the decision in *Re Power* [1947] Ch. 572; above, para.12–018.

[245] TLATA 1996 s.12(1).

[246] TLATA 1996 s.12(1)(a).

[247] TLATA 1996 s.12(1)(b).

[248] As where the trustees had already let it pursuant to the exercise of their powers of disposition after due consultation with the beneficiaries.

[249] TLATA 1996 s.12(2), as where a beneficiary sought to occupy a farm when he had no farming experience: see [1996] Conv. 411 at 419 (N. Hopkins). cf. [1990] Conv. 12 at 18 (R. J. Smith).

If at any stage these conditions cease to be satisfied—as where land has ceased to be suitable for a beneficiary who is occupying it—the occupation *may* be terminated by the trustees. The beneficiary's right is also subordinated to the trustees' power, explained below, to exclude or restrict it where two or more beneficiaries are entitled to occupy the land.[250] Furthermore, the trustees may from time to time impose reasonable conditions on the beneficiary in relation to his occupation.[251] These may include a requirement that:

(i) he pay any outgoings or expenses in respect of the land, such as meeting the costs of repairs and decoration; and

(ii) he assume any other obligation in relation to the land or to some activity that is (or is to be) carried out on the land, such as obtaining planning permission for a particular purpose, or making changes to the property so that it is fit to be used as a home.[252]

The Act is not explicit as to whether this qualified statutory right to occupy the land is additional to any common law right to occupy the land that the *beneficiary* might otherwise have, or whether it has wholly replaced it.[253] If, however, the scheme laid down in the Act is to be effective, and in particular, if trustees are to be able to exercise their powers (explained below) to exclude or restrict the right of a beneficiary to occupy the land, then the common law rights must be superseded. This will only be the case in relation to a beneficiary who is beneficially entitled to an interest in possession in land, but who has no other rights. Thus where that beneficiary also holds the legal estate as trustee (as will commonly be the case where the land is held in co-ownership[254]), he has a right at common law to occupy the land by reason of his joint legal ownership of it.[255] There is nothing in the Act to remove that right. Similarly, trustees who hold land as nominees on a bare trust cannot, in practice, impose conditions on the beneficiary's occupancy, because they must act at his direction.

12–029   (3) EXCLUSION OR RESTRICTION OF THE RIGHT TO OCCUPY. Where only one beneficiary has a statutory right to occupy the land,[256] the trustees have no power to exclude or restrict that right.[257] However, where two or more beneficiaries are entitled to occupy the land, the trustees may exclude or restrict the entitlement of any one or more (but not all) of them.[258] Any

---

[250] TLATA 1996 s.12(3).
[251] TLATA 1996 s.13(3). For the factors which the trustees are to take into account in deciding whether or not to impose conditions, see TLATA 1996 s.13(4); below, para.12–029.
[252] TLATA 1996 s.13(5).
[253] See [1998] C.L.J. 123 (D. G. Barnsley).
[254] For the imposition of a trust of land in cases of co-ownership, see below, para.13–051.
[255] cf. below, paras 13–005, 13–062.
[256] i.e. where TLATA 1996 s.12(1) is satisfied, and s.12(2) is inapplicable.
[257] This follows from TLATA 1996 ss.12, 13(1).
[258] TLATA 1996 s.13(l).

exclusion or restriction must not be unreasonable.[259] Equally, as explained above, the trustees are entitled to impose reasonable conditions on *any* beneficiary in relation to his occupation under the statutory right, and this is so even if he is the only beneficiary with such a right (so that no issue arises of excluding any other beneficiary).[260] Like all powers, the power to exclude or restrict the right to occupy must be exercised by the trustees unanimously.[261]

In exercising the powers to exclude or restrict beneficiaries, or to impose conditions on an occupying beneficiary, the matters to which the trustees are required to have regard include the intentions of the settlor (or settlors), the purposes for which the land is held and the circumstances and wishes of each of the beneficiaries who has a statutory right to occupy the land.[262] It should be emphasised that the settlor's intentions are merely one factor that the trustees must consider, and will not necessarily be decisive.

The conditions which the trustees may impose[263] on an occupying beneficiary, where they have exercised their power to exclude one or more other beneficiaries, include a requirement that:

(i) he makes payment by way of compensation to the beneficiary whose entitlement has been excluded or restricted[264]; or

(ii) he forgoes any payment or other benefit to which he would otherwise be entitled under the trust so as to benefit the excluded or restricted beneficiary.[265]

The Act gives protection to any beneficiary with a statutory right of occupation, and also to any other person occupying the land with him, such as a spouse, partner or relative. It provides that the powers given to exclude or restrict a beneficiary from occupation or to impose conditions on a beneficiary in occupation may not be exercised either so as to prevent *any* person[266] who is in occupation from continuing to occupy the land, or in a manner likely to result in any such person ceasing to occupy the land, unless he either consents or the court has given its approval.[267] It should be noted that, although the beneficiary's occupation cannot be terminated directly or indirectly through the power to exclude, restrict or impose conditions, the trustees are entitled to terminate that occupation if the beneficiary ceases to have a *right* to occupy

---

[259] TLATA 1996 s.13(2).

[260] TLATA 1996 s.13(3).

[261] Above, para.12–016.

[262] TLATA 1996 s.13(4).

[263] Under TLATA 1996 s.13(3); above. As explained, such conditions must be reasonable.

[264] It should be noted that trustees have a power but no duty to require this. cf. below, para.13–063.

[265] TLATA 1996 s.13(6).

[266] And not just a person entitled to occupy under TLATA 1996 s.12.

[267] TLATA 1996 s.13(7). In giving or withholding its approval, the matters to which the court will have regard include those set out in TLATA 1996 s.13(4), above. see TLATA 1996 s.13(8).

the land. This may be either because he ceases to be beneficially entitled to an interest in possession of the land,[268] or because the conditions upon which that right depends[269] are no longer satisfied.

9. Protection of purchasers

12–030   *(a) Consent requirements.* It has been explained that a settlor may impose a requirement that the consent of one or more persons be obtained by the trustees of land to the exercise of all or some of their functions.[270] Where such requirements are imposed in relation to land held on charitable, ecclesiastical or public trusts, any purchaser must ensure that all requisite consents are obtained,[271] irrespective of how many may be required.[272] But, in relation to all other trusts of land, if the consent of more than two persons is required, a purchaser is protected if he obtains the consent of any two of them.[273] However, this provision operates only for the protection of a purchaser. The trustees will be guilty of a breach of trust if they do not obtain all the stipulated consents. In favour of a purchaser, the consent of a minor is not required to any disposition, but where the trust expresses such a requirement, the trustees must obtain the consent of either a parent who has parental responsibility for the child[274] or a guardian of his.[275] Where the consent of a mental patient is required, it may be given by a receiver appointed on his behalf by the Court of Protection[276] or by an attorney acting under an enduring or lasting power of attorney.[277]

12–031   *(b) Other cases: unregistered land.* The Trusts of Land and Appointment of Trustees Act 1996 contains a number of provisions which are intended to provide protection for purchasers of unregistered land that is or has been subject to a trust of land.[278]

12–032   (1) FAILURE TO COMPLY WITH STATUTORY REQUIREMENTS. The Act makes provision for the protection of purchasers without actual notice that the trustees have in some way contravened certain of its requirements. "Actual notice" is not defined, but the context suggests that it means something which either the purchaser or his agent actually knows.[279] In these cases, although a

---

[268] As where he has a determinable interest, and the determining event occurs.
[269] TLATA 1996 s.12(1); above, para.12–028.
[270] Above, para.12–020.
[271] Except those of any minor: see below.
[272] TLATA 1996 s.10(2). There was a similar requirement prior to 1997: see SLA 1925 s.29(1) (now repealed).
[273] TLATA 1996 s.10(1) (replicating the effect of LPA 1925 s.26(1) which applied to trusts for sale prior to 1997: see above, para.10–023.
[274] See Children Act 1989 ss.2, 3.
[275] TLATA 1996 s.10(3).
[276] Below, para.36–022.
[277] Below, paras 36–026, 36–027.
[278] TLATA 1996 s.16. For the protection of those who either deal with, or whose title depends upon an earlier dealing with, a person to whom trustees have delegated all or some of their functions under TLATA 1996 s.9, see above, para.12–025.
[279] cf. [1998] Conv. 168 at 177, 178 (G. Ferris and G. Battersby).

purchaser will be protected, the trustees will be accountable to the beneficiaries for any loss caused by their breach of trust. The provisions may be
summarised as follows:

(a) A purchaser is not concerned to see that the trustees of land have, in
    exercising their powers or functions, complied with their obligations
    to have regard to the rights of the beneficiaries, or to consult them
    and to give effect to their wishes.[280] It seems to be clear from this
    that these obligations are personal to the trustees and do not affect
    the land as such.[281]

(b) Where trustees[282] convey land to a purchaser in contravention either
    of some other enactment or rule of law or equity,[283] or of some
    statutory restriction or limitation on the exercise of their powers,[284]
    the conveyance is not invalidated where that purchaser had no actual
    notice of the contravention.[285] An example would be where all the
    beneficiaries under a trust, being of full age and capacity and
    collectively absolutely entitled to the land, instructed the trustees to
    convey the land to them jointly,[286] but where the trustees sold the
    land to a purchaser instead. The purchaser would obtain a good title
    unless he knew of the trustees' breach of trust.

(c) Where the powers of trustees have been expressly limited,[287] it is the
    duty of the trustees to bring it to the notice of any purchaser.
    However, if they make a conveyance that does not comply with that
    limitation to a purchaser who has no actual notice of it, the convey-
    ance is not invalidated.[288] If, therefore, the trust instrument excluded
    the trustees' power to mortgage the land held in trust, but the
    trustees nonetheless did so, the mortgage would be valid, provided
    that the mortgagee did not know of the restriction on the trustees'
    powers. This provision does not apply where the land is held on
    charitable, ecclesiastical or public trusts,[289] because the powers

---

[280] TLATA 1996 s.16(1). For these obligations, see respectively, TLATA 1996 ss.6(5), 11(1),
above, paras 12–015, 12–026). See too in relation to obtaining the consent of beneficiaries to
partition under TLATA 1996 s.7(3), below, para.13–101.

[281] Contrast the requirement that trustees obtain any consent to the exercise of any power:
TLATA 1996 s.8(2); above, para.12–020.

[282] Other than trustees of land which is held on charitable, ecclesiastical or public trusts:
TLATA 1996 s.16(6). See below, para.36–028.

[283] TLATA 1996 s.6(6); above, para.12–015.

[284] TLATA 1996 s.6(8); above, para.12–015.

[285] TLATA 1996 s.16(2).

[286] As they are entitled to do under the rule in *Saunders v Vautier* (1841) 4 Beav 115; Cr. &
Ph. 240; above, para.9–169.

[287] TLATA 1996 s.8; above, para.12–019.

[288] TLATA 1996 s.16(3). The reason for imposing this positive obligation is to preserve the
curtain principle and keep the trust instrument off the title. A conveyance will be invalidated only
if a purchaser has actual notice of the limitation and not merely constructive notice. He is not
expected to investigate the trust instrument: see (1989) Law Com. No.181, para.10–010.

[289] TLATA 1996 s.16(6). See below, para.36–028.

conferred by the 1996 Act on the trustees of such trusts cannot be limited.[290]

12–033   (1) DEED OF DISCHARGE. In relation to settled land, where the settlement comes to an end, the trustees should execute a deed of discharge to indicate this fact.[291] There was no equivalent provision in relation to land held on trust for sale prior to 1997.[292] However, the Trusts of Land and Appointment of Trustees Act 1996 has introduced such a requirement in relation to trusts of land.[293] Where trustees of land convey land to those of full age and capacity whom they believe to be absolutely entitled to the land under the trust, they must execute a deed of discharge declaring that they are discharged from the trust in relation to that land.[294]

It is provided that a subsequent purchaser of the land to which the deed of discharge relates[295] is entitled to assume that, as from its date, the land was no longer subject to the trust of land, unless the purchaser or registrar has actual notice that the trustees were mistaken in their belief that the land was conveyed to beneficiaries of full age and capacity who were absolutely entitled to the land under the trust.[296] For the future, this protection will be of most importance to the registrar on an application for first registration rather than to subsequent purchasers.[297] This is because any conveyance of unregistered land by trustees on the termination of the trust to those absolutely entitled must be completed by registration.[298]

12–034   *(c) Other cases: registered land.* The provisions explained above have no application where the title to the land acquired by the purchaser is registered,[299] as they are not needed.[300] "In registered conveyancing it is fundamental that any registered proprietor can exercise all or any powers of disposition unless some entry on the register exists to curtail or remove those powers."[301] Where there is a trust of land and the title is registered, the Land

---

[290] TLATA 1996 s.8(3).

[291] See SLA 1925 s.17; below, Appendix para.A–020.

[292] cf. LPA 1925 s.23 (now repealed); above, para.10–033.

[293] Implementing the recommendation in (1989) Law Com. No.181, paras 14.1–14.3.

[294] TLATA 1996 s.16(4). If they fail to do so, the court may make an order requiring them to do so.

[295] TLATA 1996 s.16(5).

[296] For registered title see Ruoff & Roper, 37.011.02 on the discharge of restrictions protecting the trust.

[297] In relation to registered land, if the registrar does have actual notice that the trustees were mistaken, one of two things may happen. First, the registrar will be entitled to refuse to register the transfer. Secondly, if he does register the transfer notwithstanding his actual notice of the mistake, there may be a ground for seeking rectification of the register: see LRA 2002 Sch.4, above, para.7–132.

[298] LRA 2002 s.4.

[299] TLATA 1996 s.16(7). For the background to this provision, see (1989) Law Com. No.181, para.10.10.

[300] LRA 2002 s.23. For the disputed view that this was not the case under the LRA 1925 (which, as the authors admit, would have very serious consequences), see [1998] Conv. 168 (G. Ferris and G. Battersby).

[301] *State Bank of India v Sood* [1997] Ch. 276 at 284, per Peter Gibson L.J in reference to the LRA 1925 . This is now reflected in LRA 2002 ss.23, 26. Above para.7–049.

Registration Act 2002 requires or permits[302] the entry on the register of restrictions as may be either prescribed or expedient, for the protection of those beneficially interested in the land held on trust or the exercise of the trustees' powers. If, therefore, the trustees' powers or functions can only be exercised with the consent of some specified person, or have been limited in some way by the instrument creating the trust, the trustees should apply for the entry of a restriction on the register to reflect this.[303] Any disposition made by the trustees must be in accordance with these restrictions.[304] A purchaser is not concerned with any limitations on the powers of trustees that are not protected on the register.[305] When the trust comes to an end and the trustees transfer the land to the person beneficially entitled to it, they should apply to the registrar to remove any such restrictions.[306] The transferee can then deal with the land as beneficial owner.

10. Application to personal representatives. Subject to certain excep- **12–035** tions, the provisions of the Trusts of Land and Appointment of Trustees Act 1996 relating to trustees of land, apply equally to personal representatives.[307] However, this is without prejudice to their functions for the purposes of administration,[308] and it is also subject to appropriate modifications.[309] By way of exception,[310] personal representatives (unlike trustees of land) are not obliged to obtain any consents to any disposition[311] or to consult with

---

[302] LRA 2002 s.44(1), Registrar required to enter a Form A restriction in certain circumstances. Under LRR 2003 r.94(1), a trustee must apply for a restriction where a trust arises not as the result of a registrable disposition or where there is a change such as severance of an equitable joint-tenancy, or where their powers are limited, see Ruoff & Roper 37.008. A beneficiary may apply for a restriction, e.g. to ensure capital monies are paid to two trustees, LRA 2002 s.43(1)(c).

[303] LRA 2002 s.44(1). A form N restriction may be used to ensure compliance with an express consent requirement, above para.7–077. A Form C restriction may be used to reflect any limitations on the powers of personal representatives.

[304] No provision is made for the entry of restrictions in relation to the trustees' obligations to have regard to the rights of the beneficiaries, or to consult them and to give effect to their wishes. As explained above, para.12–032, where title is unregistered, these obligations are treated as purely personal to the beneficiaries and do not create rights that are capable of binding purchasers.

[305] LRA 2002 ss.23, 26. It is arguable that there may be situations in which a purchaser, either knowing or (probably) being put upon inquiry that the trustees of land have transferred registered land to him in breach of trust, acquires a good title to it (there being no adverse entry on the register), but is nonetheless personally liable in equity to the beneficiaries for what is commonly called "knowing receipt" of trust property: see below, para.11–019. But note the doubts expressed in M. Conaglen and A. Goymour "Knowing Receipt and Registered Land", Chapter 5, in C. Mitchell (ed.), *Constructive and Resulting Trusts* (Oxford: Hart, 2010). See also the suggestion in *HSBC Bank Plc v Dyche* that a transfer in breach of trust may not overreach and give good title to the purchaser, even if there are two trustees, above para.12–015.

[306] See LRA 2002 Sch.4 para.5. Ruoff & Roper, 37–011.02.

[307] TLATA 1996 s.18(1). One exception of a transitional nature has already been explained: where a person died before 1997, the doctrine of conversion continues to apply to personal representatives in the administration of his estate: TLATA 1996 s.18(3); above, para.12–007.

[308] TLATA 1996 s.18(1).

[309] Including the substitution of (i) references to persons interested in the due administration of the estate for references to beneficiaries; and (ii) references to the will for references to the disposition creating the trust: TLATA 1996 s.18(2).

[310] TLATA 1996 s.18(1).

[311] See TLATA 1996 s.10; above, paras 12–020, 12–030.

beneficiaries in relation to the exercise of their powers.[312] Nor is there any power for a person who has an interest in property to apply to the court for an order.[313]

OVERREACHING UNDER A TRUST OF LAND

12–036   **1. Overreaching.** Where trustees of land either sell the land or make some other disposition of the property, and in consequence capital money is paid to them by the purchaser, the rights of the beneficiaries are transferred from the land to those proceeds. It has already been explained that overreaching is, and has always been, the necessary corollary of the exercise of a trust or power to sell or to make some other disposition.[314] For this reason, the Trusts of Land and Appointment of Trustees Act 1996 makes no express provision for overreaching to take place on dispositions made by trustees of land under their powers.[315]

12–037   **2. Position of purchaser.** A proper disposition under a trust of land is automatically effective to overreach the rights of the beneficiaries under it, so that the purchaser is not concerned with them. These rights are necessarily equitable. Trustees of land have no power to overreach either legal estates[316] or rights already existing when the trust of land was created.[317] The purchaser's immunity from the rights of the beneficiaries depends, however, upon the sale being made in accordance with the law and the terms of the trust.[318] The Law of Property Act 1925 requires that, notwithstanding anything to the contrary in the trust of land or of any trust affecting the proceeds of sale of the land if sold,[319] the proceeds of sale or other capital money, "shall not be paid to or applied by the direction of fewer than two persons as trustees, except

---

[312] TLATA 1996 s.11; above, para.12–026.

[313] TLATA 1996 s.14; above, para.12–021.

[314] See *State Bank of India v Sood* [1997] Ch. 276 at 281; Sugden, *Powers*, 482; above, paras 6–052, 12–036.

[315] Nor was there any express provision in LPA 1925 in relation to trusts for sale prior to 1997. It was implicit in LPA 1925 s.28(1) (now repealed) that overreaching took place in relation to capital money arising from the exercise by the trustees of their powers. Unless expressly restricted by the trust, trustees of land have, in relation to the land, all the powers of an absolute owner: TLATA 1996 s.6(1); above, para.12–016.

[316] Unlike mortgagees exercising their paramount power of sale: see below, para.25–022.

[317] Except in the special case of an *ad hoc* trust of land: see the fifth edition of this work at p.407. Such *ad hoc* trusts have seldom (if ever) been used.

[318] If a disposition is made in accordance with the statutory requirements governing overreaching, but contrary to the terms of the trust (i.e. there is a breach of trust), the position in unregistered land is as explained above, para.12–032. With registered title, the registered proprietors have all the powers of an absolute owner, unless the contrary is expressed on the register, and this might be thought to protect the purchaser provided that the statutory requirements for overreaching have been met, absent an entry on the register, even if there is a breach of trust in executing the disposition. The contrary has been argued, and disputed: [1998] 62 Conv. 168. (G. Ferris and G. Battersby); [2000] 64 Conv. 267 (MJD); [2001] 65 Conv. 221 (G. Ferris and G. Battersby); [2007] 71 Conv. 120 (N. Jackson) and see above para.12–015.

[319] But see *Re Wight & Best's Brewery Co Ltd's Contract* [1929] W.N. 11.

where the trustee is a trust corporation".[320] There is no provision for payment into court. Where no capital money arises (e.g. on the grant of a lease without a fine[321]) it is unnecessary to have more than one trustee.[322] Furthermore, a sole personal representative, acting as such, may give a valid receipt even for capital money.[323]

Where two or more persons apply to be registered as proprietors of registered land then, unless they are beneficial joint tenants,[324] a restriction must be entered on the register. This provides that no disposition by a sole proprietor (other than a trust corporation) under which capital money arises shall be registered except under an order of the registrar or of the court.[325]

The Law of Property Act 1925 omits to say what will happen if these statutory directions are not obeyed. The existence of a trust of land will not always appear from the title deeds or the register, as where a house stands in the husband's sole name but was bought partly with the wife's money, so that she owns a share under a statutory trust of land.[326] It is now clear however that in such circumstances (i.e., where there is but one trustee) the wife's (or any other con-owner's) interest will not be overreached. Where the title is unregistered, the purchaser will obtain a good title only if he is a bona fide purchaser of a legal estate without notice of the trust.[327] If the wife (or other co-owner) is in possession or occupation of the land, a purchaser is likely to be fixed with notice of her interest.[328] In the usual case where the title is registered, the purchaser will take the land free of any interest unless the equitable owner is in actual occupation so that she has an overriding interest.[329]

However, where the capital money is paid to at least two trustees or to a trust corporation, the interests of the beneficiaries will be overreached even though those beneficiaries may be in occupation of the land and may never have been consulted by the trustees.[330] The same is true where trustees of land

---

[320] LPA 1925 ss.2(1)(ii), 27(2), as amended by LP(Am)A 1926 Sch.; and TLATA 1996 s.25(1), Sch.3, para.4.

[321] See *Re Myhill* [1928] Ch. 100.

[322] LPA 1925 s.27(2), as amended by LP(Am)A 1926 Sch; and TLATA 1996 s.25(1), Sch.3 para.4.

[323] LPA 1925 s.27(2).

[324] Where A and B hold the land on trust for themselves as beneficial joint tenants and A dies, the trust of land terminates and B can pass a good title: below, para.13–055.

[325] Standard From A restriction, LRA s.44(1)

[326] See para.11–016. The proprietor and trustee should apply to enter a From A restriction in such a case, LRR 2003 r.94(1). To avoid the difficulties which these implied trusts create, it is now common for land to be conveyed to either spouses or civil partners jointly. This does not prevent a trust when the claim springs from circumstances arising after one party has purchased the property and their partner joins them at a later date.

[327] *Williams & Glyn's Bank Ltd v Boland* [1979] Ch. 312 at 330; *Kingsnorth Finance Co Ltd v Tizard* [1986] 1 W.L.R. 783. See too *City of London Building Society v Flegg* [1988] A.C. 54 at 83. The purchaser will then be required to first register the title (LRA 2002 s.4) and, at first registration, will be bound because of LRA ss.11 and 12 and Sch.1 para.2. See above Ch.7.

[328] See above, para.8–019.

[329] LRA 2002 s.29 and Sch.3 para.2. See *Williams & Glyn's Bank Ltd v Boland* [1981] A.C. 487. See above, para.7–086.

[330] *City of London Building Society v Flegg*, above. For the trustees' duty to consult the beneficiaries, see TLATA 1996 s.11, above, para.12–026. See too TLATA 1996 s.16(1); above, para.12–032.

mortgage the land held in trust as security for existing and future liabilities.[331]

12–038   **3. Proposals for reform.** In 1989 the Law Commission proposed that a conveyance of the legal estate in land by trustees for sale (as they then were) should not overreach the interest of any beneficiary of full age and capacity who had a right to occupy the property and who was in actual occupation of it at the date of the conveyance, unless that person expressly or impliedly consented.[332] At present there is no such general requirement of consent and, as explained above, this can on occasions cause considerable hardship to the equitable owners.[333] The Commission's proposals were criticised because they went further than was necessary to protect beneficiaries while increasing the burden of inquiries which would have to be made by purchasers.[334] A sale or lease of trust property will in practice require the concurrence of any beneficiary who is in occupation, because without his agreement the trustees cannot convey with vacant possession. It is in relation to mortgages of the property that the interests of beneficiaries most require protection.[335] The Government decided not to implement the Law Commission's proposals because they were not widely supported. There is now no realistic prospect of a change to the overreaching machinery, and no evidence that reform is believed to be necessary.

[331] *State Bank of India v Sood* [1997] Ch. 276.

[332] (1989) Law Com. No.188, para.4.15. For criticism, see [1990] C.L.J. 277 at 328 (C.H.).

[333] *City of London Building Society v Flegg*, above; *Birmingham Midshires Mortgage Services Ltd v Sabherwal* CCRTF 1999/0734/B3; *State Bank of India v Sood* above; above, para.12–037.

[334] [1990] C.L.J. 277 at 328 (C.H.). See too J. S. Anderson, *Lawyers and the Making of English Land Law*, 332.

[335] cf. *State Bank of India v Sood*; above, at 290.

CO-OWNERSHIP

Some consideration already has been given to the law of co-ownership. **13–001** This has been in the context of trusts of land generally[1] and the legislative scheme governing their operation now found in the Trusts of Land and Appointment of Trustees Act 1996.[2] As discussed, this Act applies to both successive and concurrent co-ownership. Successive co-ownership under the Settled Land Act 1925 is now described in the Appendix, being of mainly historical interest.[3] Of much more importance in modern land law is where two or more persons are entitled to the simultaneous enjoyment of land. This may include couples in a relationship occupying the family home, property purchased as an investment, commercial business property or, indeed, land held for any purpose where there is more than one person seeking to enjoy the present rights of ownership. This is concurrent co-ownership and forms the subject matter of this chapter.

Two types of such ownership are of primary importance:

(1) joint tenancy; and

(2) tenancy in common.[4]

When used in this context the title "tenancy" means simply co-ownership, and has nothing to do with leases. The terms "co-ownership" and "concurrent

---

[1] Chs 10 and 11.
[2] Ch.12
[3] See also Ch.10.
[4] Two further types of co-ownership used to exist, coparcenary and tenancy by entireties. These are now virtually extinct and need not be considered. See the fifth edition of this work at pp.456 (coparcenary) and 460 (tenancy by entireties).

interests" may each be used to indicate any of the forms of co-ownership discussed in this chapter.

Part 1

JOINT TENANCY AND TENANCY IN COMMON

Section 1. Nature of the Tenancies

A. *Joint Tenancy*

13–002   "A gift of lands to two or more persons in joint tenancy is such a gift as imparts to them, with respect to all other persons than themselves, the properties of one single owner."[5] Although as between themselves joint tenants have separate rights, as against everyone else they are in the position of a single owner.[6] The intimate nature of joint tenancy is shown by its two principal features, the right of survivorship and the "four unities".

13–003   **1. The right of survivorship.** This is, above all others, the distinguishing feature of a joint tenancy.[7] On the death of one joint tenant, his interest in the land passes to the other joint tenants by the right of survivorship (*jus accrescendi*). This process continues until there is one survivor, who then holds the land as sole owner.[8] A joint tenancy cannot pass under the will[9] or intestacy[10] of a joint tenant. In each case the right of survivorship takes precedence. It is often said therefore that each joint tenant holds nothing by himself and yet holds the whole together with the other.[11] Whether he takes everything or nothing depends upon whether or not he is the last joint tenant to survive.[12]

At common law, if there could be no right of survivorship there could be no joint tenancy. A corporation could not therefore be a joint tenant because it could never die.[13] A conveyance to a corporation jointly with another corporation or individual made the grantees tenants in common.[14] However, by statute, a corporation can now acquire and hold any property in joint tenancy

---

[5] Williams P.R. 143.

[6] Williams P.R. 145; *Hammersmith & Fulham LBC v Monk* [1992] 1 A.C. 478 at 492.

[7] Preston, *Abstracts*, ii, p.57.

[8] Litt. p.280; Co.Litt. p.181a; Preston, *Abstracts*, ii, p.57.

[9] Litt. p.287; Co.Litt. p.185b ("*jus accrescendi praefertur ultimae voluntati*"); *Swift d. Neale v Roberts* (1764) 3 Burr. 1488; *Gould v Kemp* (1834) 2 My. & K. 304 at 309.

[10] cf. AEA 1925 ss.1(1), 3(4).

[11] Co.Litt. p.186a.

[12] Where there is a doubt as to who has survived (e.g. where all the joint tenants die in an accident), statute usually resolves the question who is deemed to be the survivor: LPA 1925 s.184; below, para.14–055.

[13] Litt. p.297; Bl.Comm. ii, p.184; Williams R.P. p.331; *Bennett v Holbech* (1671) 2 Wms.Saund. 317, 319; *Law Guarantee & Trust Society Ltd v Bank of England* (1890) 24 QBD 406 at 411.

[14] *Fisher v Wigg* (1700) 1 Ld. Raym. 622 at 627; Litt. p.296; Co.Litt. p.189b; Cru.Dig. ii, p.372.

in the same manner as if it were an individual.[15] Trustees are always made joint tenants because of the convenience of the trust property passing automatically by the right of survivorship to the other trustees when one trustee dies. If trustees were made tenants in common, a conveyance of the trust property to the surviving trustees by the personal representatives of the deceased trustee would have been necessary. In contrast, the right of survivorship of a joint tenancy is often unsuitable for beneficial owners (though perhaps not for two people in a stable relationship) because it introduces an element of chance. However, it is ideal for trustees.

The right of survivorship does not mean that a joint tenant cannot dispose of his interest in the land independently. He has full power of alienation inter vivos, though if, for example, he conveys his interest, he destroys the joint tenancy by severance and turns his interest into a tenancy in common. But he must act in his lifetime, for a joint tenancy cannot be severed by will.[16] These rules are explained later.[17]

2. The four unities must be present. The four unities of a joint tenancy are the unities of possession, interest, title and time.[18]   **13–004**

(a) Unity of possession. Unity of possession is common to all forms of co-ownership. At common law, each co-owner is as much entitled to possession of any part of the land as the others.[19] He cannot point to any part of the land as his own to the exclusion of the others; if he could, there would be separate ownership and not co-ownership. This doctrine has led to difficulties where one joint tenant (for example) occupies the whole property, or takes the whole of the rents and profits, to the exclusion of the others. No one co-owner (whether a joint tenant or a tenant in common) has a better right to the property than another, so that an action for trespass or for rent or for money had and received or an account will not normally lie.[20] But destruction of part of the subject-matter (e.g. by removing soil) is actionable in damages.[21] There is also an equitable jurisdiction to compel a co-owner (whether a joint tenant or a tenant in common[22]) to pay a due proportion of an occupation rent if it   **13–005**

---

[15] Bodies Corporate (Joint Tenancy) Act 1899; see *In b. Martin* (1904) 90 L.T. 264; *Re Thompson's S.T.* [1905] 1 Ch. 229. This provision became necessary when banks and other corporations began to act as trustees.

[16] *Carr v Isard* LTL 29/8/2007.

[17] Below, paras 13–036 et seq.

[18] This analysis appears to have been first made by Blackstone, Comm. ii, 180–182, but it is disparaged by Challis p.367, as having a "captivating appearance of symmetry and exactness" rather than any practical utility; yet see Preston, *Abstracts*, ii, p.62. It has been accepted in the House of Lords: *AG Securities v Vaughan* [1990] 1 A.C. 417 at 472, 474.

[19] Litt. p.288; Bl.Comm. ii, p.182; *Wiseman v Simpson* [1988] 1 W.L.R. 35 at 42. In the case of co-ownership in remainder (e.g. where land was limited to A for life with remainder to B and C in fee simple) there was a potential unity of possession.

[20] *M'Mahon v Burchell* (1846) 2 Ph. 127; *Kennedy v De Trafford* [1897] A.C. 180 at 190; *Jones v Jones* [1977] 1 W.L.R. 438; Co.Litt. p.200b.

[21] *Wilkinson v Haygarth* (1847) 12 Q.B. 837; and see *Martyn v Knowilys* (1799) 8 T.R. 145 (cutting trees).

[22] *Re Pavlou* [1993] 1 W.L.R. 1046.

is necessary to do equity between the parties.[23] Until recently, the court only decreed such an occupation rent where one co-owner had excluded or evicted the other, as where one co-owner left the home after the breakdown of the relationship and under threats of violence.[24] However, it will now be willing to order such a payment in any case where a marriage or relationship breaks down and one of the parties leaves the home.[25] Furthermore, a co-owner who has received more than his share can be compelled by the other to account for the surplus. Formerly this was under a statute of 1705, since repealed, which gave the co-owner an action of account.[26] However, since 1925 this obligation to account arises out of the trust that is now imposed in most cases of joint tenancy.[27] If the joint tenants hold the legal estate, they are trustees for, and therefore accountable to, one another. If the legal estate is vested in others (e.g. a testator's personal representatives), they are beneficiaries under a trust and a court may hold them accountable inter se in administering the trust.

The position under the common law has, however, been modified by the Trusts of Land and Appointment of Trustees Act 1996 (TLATA) which, while not interfering with the common law conception of unity of possession, has invested the court with a statutory jurisdiction to regulate occupation of co-owned land and a discretion to order payments from one co-owner to another.[28]

13–006   *(b) Unity of interest.* The interest of each joint tenant is the same in extent, nature and duration, for in theory of law they hold just one estate. This has important consequences:

> (i) Although in theory of law each joint tenant has the whole of the property, the rents and profits of the land are to be divided equally between them.
>
> (ii) There can be no joint tenancy between those with interests of a different nature, e.g. a freeholder and a tenant for years, a tenant in possession and tenant in remainder, or a tenant with a vested

---

[23] *Dennis v McDonald* [1982] Fam. 63; *Re Pavlou*, above. See too *Ali v Hussein* (1974) 231 E.G. 372; *Bernard v Josephs* [1982] Ch. 391. cf. *Stott v Radcliffe* (1982) 126 S.J. 310; *Lloyds Bank Plc v Byrne* [1993] 1 F.L.R. 369 at 374. For a survey of the old equitable practice, see *Dennis v McDonald*, above, at pp.68–71. For the court's jurisdiction to grant an occupation order in matrimonial proceedings, see FLA 1996 s.33; below, para.34–024.

[24] As in *Dennis v McDonald*, above; *Ali v Hussein*, above.

[25] *Re Pavlou*, above, at 1050. It is otherwise if the departure was voluntary.

[26] 4 & 5 Anne, see *Henderson v Eason* (1851) 17 Q.B. 701. The statute was repealed by LP(Am)A 1924 Sch.10.

[27] Below, paras 13–051—13–053. For equitable accounting between co-owners, see below, para.13–073, where it is considered whether the statutory jurisdiction under TLATA 1996 (below) has superseded equitable accounting.

[28] For the statutory right of a beneficiary beneficially entitled to an interest in possession under a trust of land to occupy the land held in trust and for the trustees' power to exclude or restrict that occupation, and to order payments, see TLATA 1996 ss.12, 13; above, para.12–027; below, para.13–062.

interest and a tenant with a contingent interest.[29] But personal disability (e.g. if a person is a minor or a mental patient) is not inconsistent with a joint tenancy.[30]

(iii) There can be no joint tenancy between those whose interests are similar but of different duration. Thus before 1926 a tenant in fee simple and a tenant in tail both owned freeholds but the differing durations of the estates prevented them from being held in joint tenancy.[31]

(iv) Any legal act, e.g. a conveyance or lease of the land, or a surrender of a lease,[32] or the exercise of a break clause,[33] or the giving of a notice,[34] requires the participation of all the joint tenants. They cannot be effected by one joint tenant alone because he does not by himself have the whole estate.[35] But exceptions are found in the cases of personal representatives[36] and of the determination of periodic tenancies (e.g. weekly or monthly tenancies), which are determinable on the usual notice[37] given by one of joint landlords[38] or one of joint tenants.[39] A periodic tenancy continues only so long as it is the will of both parties that it should continue,[40] and there is a notional renewal of the term at the end of each period[41] which

---

[29] *Kenworthy v Ward* (1853) 11 Hare 196 at 198, 199; *M'Gregor v M'Gregor* (1859) 1 De G.E. & J. 63 at 74; *Ruck v Barwise* (1865) 2 Dr. & Sm. 510 at 512. See, e.g. *Woodgate v Unwin* (1831) 4 Sim. 129 (gift to class on attaining 21 cannot create joint tenancy, for some interests would be vested and some contingent: *Ruck v Barwise*, above, at 512); cf. *M'Gregor v M'Gregor* above, at 74, showing that the interpretation put on *Woodgate v Unwin*, above, in *Booth v Arlington* (1857) 3 Jur. (N.S.) 835 at 837 is unsound. See also Tudor L.C. 275.

[30] *Re Gardner* [1924] 2 Ch. 243 at 251.

[31] Bl.Comm. ii, p 181

[32] *Leek and Moorlands BS v Clark* [1952] 2 Q.B. 788.

[33] *Hounslow LBC v Pilling* [1993] 1 W.L.R. 1242. See too *Osei-Bonsu v Wandsworth LBC* [1999] 1 W.L.R. 101.

[34] *Newman v Keedwell* (1977) 35 P. & C.R. 393 (a statutory counter-notice under the Agricultural Holdings Act 1948).

[35] Bl.Comm. ii, p.183. This rule has assumed some importance in more recent cases. Thus in *Thames Guaranty Ltd v Campbell* [1985] Q.B. 210, a contract by one joint tenant to grant a mortgage was effective to bind only his own beneficial interest. The lender sought specific performance but it was refused because of the probable hardship to the other joint tenant, the borrower's wife. In *Ahmed v Kendrick* (1987) 56 P. & C.R. 120, one joint tenant forged the signature of the other on a registered transfer. Only the equitable interest of the party making the transfer passed to the purchaser. Below, para.13–039.

[36] See below, para.14–148.

[37] See below, para.17–082.

[38] *Doe d. Aslin v Summersett* (1830) 1 B. & Ad. 135; *Parsons v Parsons* [1983] 1 W.L.R. 1390. The criticism of these cases in [1983] Conv. 194 (F. Webb) has been rejected by the Court of Appeal: *Hammersmith & Fulham LBC v Monk* [1991] 1 E.G.L.R. 263 (affirmed on appeal: [1992] 1 A.C. 478).

[39] *Greenwich LBC v McGrady* (1982) 46 P. & C.R. 223; *Hammersmith & Fulham LBC v Monk* [1992] 1 A.C. 478; *Newham LBC v Hill* (1998) 76 P. & C.R. D24. See [1992] Conv. 279 (S. Goulding).

[40] *Hammersmith & Fulham LBC v Monk* [1991] 1 E.G.L.R. 263 at 269; [1992] 1 A.C. 478 at 484; *AG. Securities v Vaughan* [1990] 1 A.C. 417 at 473.

[41] *Prudential Assurance Co Ltd v London Residuary Body* [1992] 2 A.C. 386 at 394.

requires the consent of all the parties.[42] A co-owner who gives
notice without the consent of the others does not commit a breach
of the trust that applies in cases of co-ownership[43] because the
interest which is subject to the trust would in any event terminate
at the end of the period of the notice.[44] The notice does not
therefore operate as a disposition of the property and does not need
the consent of all of the joint tenants.[45]

Unity of interest must apply to the estate which is held jointly; but if that
requirement is satisfied, it does not matter that one joint tenant has a further
and separate interest in the same property.[46] A conveyance "to A and B as
joint tenants for lives, remainder to B in fee simple" would make A and B
joint tenants for life despite the remainder to B.[47]

13–007   *(c) Unity of title.* Each joint tenant must claim his title to the land under the
same act or document.[48] This requirement is satisfied if all the tenants
acquired their rights by the same conveyance[49] or if they simultaneously took
possession of land and acquired title to it by adverse possession.[50]

13–008   *(d) Unity of time.* The interest of each tenant must vest at the same time.[51]
This does not necessarily follow from unity of title. For example, if before
1926, land was conveyed "to A for life, remainder to the heirs of B and C",
and B and C died at different times in A's lifetime, B's heirs and C's heirs
took the fee simple in remainder as tenants in common. The heirs could not
take as joint tenants, for although there was unity of title there was no unity
of time.[52]

---

[42] *Hammersmith & Fulham LBC v Monk*, above. For telling criticism of this result, see (1992)
108 L.Q.R. 375 (J. Dewar); [1998] Fam. Law 590 (S. Cretney: "One moment you have an
apparently secure tenancy; the next minute it has disappeared by the unilateral (and secret) action
of your former partner of which you know nothing"). cf. *Hounslow LBC v Pilling* [1993] 1
W.L.R. 1242 at 1246, 1247.

[43] *Crawley BC v Ure* [1996] Q.B. 13. See too *Harrow LBC v Johnstone* [1997] 1 W.L.R. 459
(issue of notice not a breach of an ouster order). For the trust of land in cases of co-ownership,
see below, para.13–051.

[44] *Hammersmith & Fulham LBC v Monk*, above, at 490.

[45] *Newlon Housing Trust v Alsulaimen* [1999] 1 A.C. 313 (MCA 1973 s.37(2)(b)).

[46] Burton's *Compendium*, 245.

[47] Co.Litt. pp.182a, b, 184a; *Wiscot's Case* (1599) 2 Co.Rep. 60b; *Quarm v Quarm* [1892] 1
Q.B. 184. Litt. p.285 and Co.Litt. p.188a, which speak of joint tenants, one for life and one in fee,
must be understood to refer to this situation.

[48] Litt. p.278; Co.Litt. pp.189a, 299b; Bl.Comm. ii, p.181; AG *Securities v Vaughan*, above, at
435, 474. Two documents, executed by each of two co-owners, might be regarded as a single title
if the purpose was to artificially exclude a joint-tenancy and thereby perpetrate a sham, *Antoniades v Villiers* [1990] 1 A 417.

[49] Cru.Dig. ii, p.367.

[50] Litt. p.278; *Ward v Ward* (1871) 6 Ch.App. 789; below, para.35–016.

[51] Bl.Comm. ii, p.181; *AG Securities v Vaughan*, above, at 436, 474. For "vest" (in interest),
see above, para.9–001.

[52] Co.Litt. p.188a; Bl.Comm. ii, p.181.

B. Tenancy in Common

A tenancy in common differs significantly from a joint tenancy. **13–009**

1. The tenants hold in undivided shares. Unlike joint tenants, tenants in **13–010**
common hold in undivided shares. Each tenant in common has a distinct share
in property which has not yet been divided among the co-tenants.[53] Thus
tenants in common have quite separate interests. The only fact which brings
them into co-ownership is that they both have shares in a single property
which has not yet been divided among them. While the tenancy in common
lasts, no one can say which of them owns any particular parcel of land.

2. There is no right of survivorship. The size of each tenant's share is **13–011**
fixed once and for all and is not affected by the death of one of his com-
panions. When a tenant in common dies, his interest passes under his will or
intestacy, for his undivided share is his to dispose of as he wishes.[54] But rights
equivalent to survivorship may be given by express limitation.[55]

The absence of the right of survivorship can create anomalies. Where a
husband and wife are beneficial joint tenants and one of the spouses dies
intestate, the survivor will acquire the property by right of survivorship and
will in addition be entitled to a statutory legacy.[56] If, however, the home is
owned by the spouses as tenants in common,[57] the survivor will receive only
the statutory legacy, although he may require the personal representatives to
apply this sum towards the acquisition of the deceased's interest in the
property.[58] Although the Law Commission recommended a change in the law
so that a surviving spouse should in all cases receive the whole estate of the
first to die,[59] the government rejected the proposal.[60]

3. Only the unity of possession is essential. Although the four unities of **13–012**
a joint tenancy may be present in a tenancy in common, the only unity which
is essential is the unity of possession.[61] In particular, it should be noted that
the unity of interest may be absent and the tenants may hold unequal interests,
so that one tenant in common may be entitled to a one-fifth share and the other
to four-fifths, or one may be entitled for life and another in fee simple.[62]

---

[53] *Fisher v Wiggs* (1700) 12 Mod. 296 at 302; *Re King's Theatre, Sunderland* [1929] 1 Ch. 483
at 488.
[54] Challis p.368.
[55] See *Doe d. Borwell v Abey* (1813) 1 M. & S. 428; *Haddesley v Adams* (1856) 22 Beav. 266;
Taafe v Conmee (1862) 10 H.L.C. 64.
[56] AEA 1925 s.46; SI 1993/2906; below, para.14–089.
[57] Even if the spouses had once been joint tenants, a tenancy in common may have been created
by the unilateral act of the first spouse to die: below, para.13–038.
[58] Below, para.14–098.
[59] (1989) Law Com. No.187.
[60] The Law Commission's proposals were criticised on the ground that the code of intestate
distribution is already generous to a surviving spouse: S. M. Cretney and J. M. Masson, *Principles
of Family Law* (6th edn), 203. See too [1990] Conv. 358 (R. Kerridge).
[61] Co.Litt. p.189a; Cru.Dig. ii, p.399.
[62] Challis p.370; Williams R.P. p.148; Bl Comm. ii, p.191; and see *Sturton v Richardson* (1844)
10 M. & W. 17.

Section 2. Estates in which the Tenancies could Exist

13–013   In general, before 1926, joint tenancies and tenancies in common could exist at law or in equity (i.e. as legal estates or as equitable interests), and in possession or in remainder, in any of the estates of freehold or in leasehold.[63] Thus if land was given to A and B as joint tenants for their lives, they enjoyed it jointly for their joint lives, and the survivor enjoyed the whole for the rest of his life,[64] whereas an interest given simply for their joint lives would end as soon as one died.[65] If A and B were made tenants in common for life, the survivor would retain his original share and no more,[66] the deceased's share having passed to the remainderman. Where X and Y were joint tenants for the life of X, if X survived he became sole tenant of the whole for the rest of his life, whereas if Y were the survivor he took nothing. The estate which he acquired by survivorship was one which determined at the moment he received it.[67] After 1925 the position is substantially the same except that a tenancy in common can no longer exist at law. This is explained below.[68] Further, since life estates and entails can exist only in equity,[69] even a joint tenancy in such interests must also be equitable.

Section 3. Creation of the Tenancies

13–014   The key to a proper understanding of joint tenancies and tenancies in common is always to consider the legal estate separately from the equitable interest. Thus A and B may be legal joint tenants but equitable tenants in common; that is to say, A and B hold the legal estate jointly upon trust for themselves as tenants in common. Their rights of enjoyment, therefore, are the rights of tenants in common, not the rights of joint tenants. The effect of A's death on the legal joint tenancy is that B is solely entitled. However, A's equitable interest (his undivided share) passes under his will or intestacy. The result is that B holds the legal estate on trust for himself as to his share, and for A's personal representatives as to A's share.

The methods of creating joint tenancies and tenancies in common must now be considered. These are the primary rules of common law and equity, on which the statutory reforms of 1925 were later superimposed. Note also that it is always possible for a joint tenant to turn his beneficial interest into a

---

[63] Williams R.P. p.143. As to periodic tenancies, see above, para.13–006.
[64] *Moffat v Burnie* (1853) 18 Beav. 211; *Jones v Jones* (1881) 44 L.T. 642 at 644.
[65] *Re Legh's S.T.* [1938] Ch. 39.
[66] Co.Litt p.191a; Preston, *Abstracts*, ii, p.63.
[67] Challis p.366.
[68] Below, para.13–034.
[69] Above, para.6–004. It ceased to be possible to create entails after 1996: above, para.3–031.

tenancy in common by effecting a severance. The manner in which this may be done is explained later.[70]

I. AT LAW

Prior to 1926 there was an ancient presumption that where the legal title to property was vested in two or more persons they were joint tenants and not tenants in common.[71] Joint tenancy had been advantageous to both feudal lords and tenants before feudal tenures were abolished.[72] It was also preferred by conveyancers who had to investigate title. Joint tenants held by a single title, whereas the title of every tenant in common had to be separately examined.[73] If a joint tenant died, there was one less tenant but still one title. If however a tenant in common died and devised his share equally between his 12 children, that would increase the titles that had to be investigated before the property could be sold as a whole.

13–015

Because of the presumption in favour of a joint tenancy, a conveyance of land before 1926 to two or more persons created a joint tenancy of the legal estate unless either:

(i) one of the unities was absent; or

(ii) words of severance were employed.

Since 1925 joint tenancy has been the *only* form of co-ownership of a legal estate.[74] However in either of the two situations noted above (absence of unties or words of severance) an equitable tenancy in common will now be created instead. The common law rules are therefore still applicable in a different context and must be considered.

1. Absence of unities. The four unities have already been considered. If there is unity of possession but one or more of the other unities is missing, the parties take as tenants in common. If there is no unity of possession, the parties take as separate owners.

13–016

2. Words of severance

(a) Express words. Any words in the grant which show that the tenants are each to take a distinct share in the property amount to words of severance and

13–017

---

[70] Below, para.13–036. Since 1925, it has only been possible to sever a joint tenancy in equity: below, para.13–036.

[71] *Campbell v Campbell* (1792) 4 Bro.C.C. 15; *Morley v Bird* (1798) 3 Ves. 628; *Corbett d. Clymer v Nicholls* (1851) 2 L.M. & P. 87 at 89. "The law loves not fractions of estates, nor to divide and multiply tenures": *Fisher v Wigg* (1700) 1 Salk. 391 at 392, per Holt C.J.

[72] See the 5th edition of this work at p.424. For the abolition of feudal tenures, see above, para.2–019.

[73] See *Bruerton's Case* (1594) 6 Co.Rep. p.la; *Fisher v Wigg* (1700) 1 P.Wms. 14 at 21; *Garland v Jekyll* (1824) 2 Bing. 273.

[74] Below, para.13–034.

thus create a tenancy in common.[75] Words which have been held to have this effect include:

"in equal shares"[76]
"share and share alike"[77]
"to be divided between"[78]
"to be distributed amongst them in joint and equal proportions"[79]
"equally"[80]
"between"[81]
"amongst"[82]
"respectively".[83]

13–018 *(b) Other provisions.* Even if there are no clear words of severance, the gift taken as a whole may show that a tenancy in common is intended.[84] Two examples may be given. First, it has been held that certain provisions for the use of capital or income or both for the maintenance and advancement of those concerned created a tenancy in common.[85] For example, if under a settlement on children containing such provisions, an advance was made to one child, it could not have been done unless the child was tenant in common and so had a distinct share.[86] Secondly, a bequest to A and B on condition that they should pay the testator's widow an annuity "in equal shares" has been

---

[75] See *Robertson v Fraser* (1871) 6 Ch.App. 696 at 699. Decisions on particular expressions (other than those given in the text) are *Marryat v Townley* (1748) 1 Ves.Sen. 102 ("respective ages") *Sutcliffe v Howard* (1868) 38 L.J.Ch. 472 ("respective lives"); *Re Atkinson* [1892] 3 Ch. 52 ("respective heirs"); *Sheppard v Gibbons* (1742) 2 Atk. 441 ("severally"); *Halton v Finch* (1841) 4 Beav. 186 ("each"); *Liddard v Liddard* (1860) 28 Beav. 266 and *Robertson v Fraser* (1871) 6 Ch.App. 696 ("participate"). At one time stronger words were required in deeds than in wills, and in law than in equity, but these differences gradually decreased: see Saunders, *Uses*, i, 130.

[76] *Payne v Webb* (1874) L.R. 19 Eq. 26.

[77] *Heathe v Heathe* (1740) 2 Atk. 121; and see *James v Collins* (1627) Het. 29 ("part and part alike"). Contrast *Re Schofield* [1918] 2 Ch. 64 (mere reference to "share" insufficient).

[78] (1750) 1 Ves.Sen. 542; cf. *Askeman v Burrows* (1814) 3 V. & B. 54 (personally). For similar expressions, see *Fisher v Wigg* (1700) 1 P.Wms. 14; *Goodtitle d. Hood v Stokes* (1753) 1 Wils.K.B. 341; *Bridge v Yates* (1842) 12 Sim. 645; *Lucas v Goldsmid* (1861) 29 Beav. 657.

[79] *Ettricke v Ettricke* (1767) Amb. 656.

[80] *Lewen v Dodd* (1595) Cro.Eliz. 443; *Lewen v Cox* (1599) Cro.Eliz. 695; *Denn d. Gaskin v Gaskin* (1777) 2 Cowp. 657; *Right d. Compton v Compton* (1808) 9 East 267 at 276.

[81] *Lashbrook v Cock* (1816) 2 Mer. 70. But "all and every" (introducing members of a class, e.g. children) were not normally words of severance: *Stratton v Best* (1787) 2 Bro.C.C. 233; *Binning v Binning* (1895) 13 R. 654; but contrast *Re Grove's Trusts* (1862) 3 Gif. 575.

[82] *Richardson v Richardson* (1845) 14 Sim. 526.

[83] *Stephens v Hide* (1734) Ca.t.Talb.27.

[84] See, e.g. *Ryves v Ryves* (1871) L.R. 11 Eq. 539; *Surtees v Surtees* (1871) L.R. 12 Eq. 400.

[85] *Re Ward* [1920] 1 Ch. 334; *Bennett v Houldsworth* (1911) 104 L.T. 304; *Re Dunn* [1916] 1 Ch. 97.

[86] *L'Estrange v L'Estrange* [1902] 1 I.R. 467; cf. *Twigg v Twigg* [1933] I.R. 65. Since 1925 there has been an implied statutory power of advancement: TA 1925 s.32. This is applicable to land held upon a trust of land but not to settled land: TA 1925 s.32(2); *Re Stimpson's Trusts* [1931] 2 Ch. 77. However the power can be exercised only in favour of a person "entitled to the capital of the trust property or of any share thereof". It would probably not be applicable therefore where land was held on trust for joint tenants.

held to create a tenancy in common, since the testator was presumed to have intended that the gift should correspond to the obligation.[87]

(c) Words negativing a tenancy in common. Expressions which by them- **13–019**
selves might create a tenancy in common can be negatived by words showing a clear intention to create a joint tenancy.[88] Contradictory expression such as "jointly and severally" or "as joint tenants in common in equal shares" are nowadays normally resolved by construing the document[89] and without recourse to the quaint rule that the first word prevailed in a deed, but the last in a will.[90]

(d) Special cases. Mention may be made of two special situations. First, **13–020**
under a testamentary gift to a vague class, such as the testator's "relations", the court can sometimes save the gift from uncertainty by restricting the class to those who would take on an intestacy.[91] The class will then take as joint tenants, not as tenants in common in the statutory shares, unless by an express reference to the statutes governing intestacy or otherwise the testator has shown a contrary intention.[92] Secondly, under a substitutionary gift, as where a gift to children in equal shares provides that children of a deceased child are to take that child's share, prima facie those substituted will take as joint tenants unless there are further words of severance; for in a gift to a compound class, compound words of severance are usually required.[93]

II. IN EQUITY

Unlike the common law, equity did not favour joint tenancy.[94] Equity often **13–021**
did not follow the law where it was merely feudal in character, and equity in this case was more concerned to achieve fairness than to simplify the tasks of conveyancers. Equity therefore preferred the certainty and equality of a tenancy in common to the chance of "all or nothing" which arose from the right of survivorship.[95] "Equity leans against joint tenants and favours tenancies in common." This maxim meant that a tenancy in common would exist in equity not only in those cases where it would have existed at law, but also

---

[87] *Re North* [1952] Ch. 397.
[88] See cases collected in Halsbury 4th edn, Vol. 50 (revised edn), para.627.
[89] *Martin v Martin* (1987) 54 P. & C.R. 238 ("beneficial joint tenants in common in equal shares" held to create a tenancy in common), cf. *Joyce v Barker Bros (Builders) Ltd* (1980) 40 P. & C.R. 512 (where identical words were held to create a joint tenancy: see [1988] Conv. 57 (J. E. Martin).
[90] *Slingby's Case* (1587) 5 Co.Rep. 18b at 19a (deed); *Perkins v Bayton* (1781) 1 Bro.C.C. 118 (will); contrast *Cookson v Bingham* (1853) 17 Beav. 262, 3 De G.M. & G. 668 (will: contrary intention). For this rule, see below, para.14–070.
[91] See below, para.14–064.
[92] *Re Ganloser's WT* [1952] Ch. 30; and see *Re Kilvert* [1957] Ch. 388; *Re Pulton's WT* [1987] 1 W.L.R. 795.
[93] *Re Brooke* [1953] 1 W.L.R. 439; Jarman 1792, 1797; but see *Re Froy* [1938] Ch. 566.
[94] *Burgess v Rawnsley* [1975] Ch. 429 at 438, per Lord Denning M.R.; and see *Gould v Kemp* (1834) 2 My. & K. 304 at 309.
[95] "Survivorship is looked upon as odious in equity": *R. v Williams* (1735) Bunb. 342 at 343, *per cur*; and see *Re Woolley* [1903] 2 Ch. 206 at 211.

in certain other cases where an intention to create a tenancy in common *ought* to be presumed. There are several such special cases, in all of which persons who were joint tenants at law were compelled by equity to hold the legal estate upon trust for themselves as equitable tenants in common. These rules, which have not been altered by the 1925 legislation, remain applicable and are stated in their present form.[96] A tenancy in common which arises in one of these ways is classified as a resulting or constructive trust.[97]

1. Purchase-money provided in unequal shares

13–022   *(a) The presumptions.* If two or more persons together purchase property and provide the money in equal shares they are presumed in equity to be joint tenants.[98] However if their contributions are unequal, the purchasers are presumed to take beneficially as tenants in common in shares proportionate to the sums advanced.[99] Thus if A contributes one-third and B two-thirds of the price, they are presumed to be equitable tenants in common as to one-third and two-thirds respectively. Although this distinction has been criticised,[100] it is long established.[101]

13–023   *(b) Rebutting the presumptions.* Each of these two presumptions can be rebutted by evidence of contrary intention, whether from the surrounding circumstances,[102] by proof of express agreement between the parties, or from the wording of the conveyance or transfer of the property to the co-owners.

13–024   (1) SURROUNDING CIRCUMSTANCES. There are many situations in which these presumptions have been rebutted by evidence or surrounding circumstances. For example, where T devised a mortgage by will to A and B as tenants in common, and A and B then purchased the mortgagor's equity of redemption, they were held to be tenants in common of the property even though each had half the price. The purchase was considered to flow from the devise.[103]

A tenancy in common is also established when a court exercises its discretion, based on the course of the parties' conduct in relation to the land, to quantify the shares of co-owners who have not expressly declared their beneficial interests. This is explained below in the context of the creation of

---

[96] The list of such special situations is not closed: *Malayan Credit Ltd v Jack Chia-MPH Ltd* [1986] A.C. 549 at 560.

[97] See above, paras 11–009, 11–017.

[98] *Aveling v Knipe* (1815) 19 Ves. 441 at 445; *Robinson v Preston* (1858) 4 K. & J. 505 at 510; *Harrison v Barton* (1860) 1 J. & H. 287 at 292.

[99] *Lake v Gibson* (1729) 1 Eq.Ca.Abr. 290 at 291; *Robinson v Preston*, above, at 510; *Bull v Bull* [1955] 1 Q.B. 234; *Ulrich v Ulrich* [1968] 1 W.L.R. 180 at 185; *Crisp v Mullings* [1976] 2 E.G.L.R. 103; and see *Bernard v Joseph* [1982] Ch. 391. It seems that originally a tenancy in common would be presumed only if the contributions were unequal and that fact was recited in the conveyance to the purchasers: Sugden, V. & P. 698; [1982] Conv. 213 at 214 (M. Friend and J. Newton); [1990] C.L.J. 297 at 298 (C.H.).

[100] *Jackson v Jackson* (1804) 9 Ves. 591 at 604n.

[101] Page Wood V.C. described it as "settled" in *Robinson v Preston*, above, at 510.

[102] *Edwards v Fashion* (1712) Prec. Ch. 332; *Harrison v Barton*, above.

[103] *Edwards v Fashion*, above.

trusts of land[104] and arises from the decision in *Stack v Dowden*.[105] Save where there is quantification on the basis of *Stack v Dowden*, the tenancy in common will arise at the moment of acquisition, for had the parties originally been joint-tenants, their later actions in seeking to establish the size of their "own" share would have operated to sever the joint-tenancy to equal shares[106]—and this is usually what one party wishes to avoid.[107]

(2) EXPRESS AGREEMENT. The presumption (whether of joint tenancy or **13–025** tenancy in common) which arises from the contributions made by the parties to the cost of acquiring the land will be rebutted by proof of an express agreement between them that they should hold the property in some other way. Thus if A and B make unequal contributions to the initial purchase price, the presumption of a tenancy in common will be rebutted if the parties have expressly agreed that they should hold the property as beneficial joint tenants.[108]

(3) THE WORDING OF THE CONVEYANCE OR TRANSFER. The mere fact that the **13–026** legal title to the property is conveyed "to A and B jointly" does not rebut the equitable presumption of a tenancy in common because it is silent as to their beneficial interest.[109] However, as a general rule, where the conveyance expressly declares not only in whom the legal title is to vest but also how the beneficial interests are to be held, a court will give effect to that trust.[110] This is subject to two exceptions. The first is where the trust is either set aside on grounds of fraud or mistake or rectified.[111] The second is where the purchasers did not assent to the terms of the declaration.[112] Thus in one case land was conveyed to A and B as joint tenants beneficially, but without the approbation of C and D who had contributed a substantial part of the purchase price. C and D were held to be equitable tenants in common of the property in proportion to their contributions notwithstanding the declaration.[113]

Many of the difficulties that have previously arisen are now obviated because of the introduction of new Land Registry forms under the Land

---

[104] See para.11–028.

[105] [2007] 2 A.C. 432. See too *Jones v Kernott* [2011] UKSC 53.

[106] *Goodman v Gallant* [1986] 2 W.L.R. 236.

[107] See below (severance).

[108] *Re Densham* [1975] 1 W.L.R. 1519. A common but uncommunicated intention between the parties will not suffice; *Springette v Defoe* [1992] 1 F.L.R. 388 probably remains good authority on this point—see *Jones v Kernott* above. See above, para.11–025.

[109] *Pettitt v Pettitt* [1970] A.C. 777 at 813; *Crisp v Mullings*, above; *Walker v Hall* [1984] F.L.R. 126 at 133; *Huntingford v Hobbs* [1993] 1 F.L.R. 736 at 744.

[110] *Pettitt v Pettitt* above, at 813; *Gissing v Gissing* [1971] A.C. at 905; *Pink v Lawrence* (1977) 36 P. & C.R. 98 at 101; *Goodman v Gallant* [1986] Fam. 106; *Turton v Turton* [1988] Ch. 542 at 553; *Huntingford v Hobbs*, above, at 753. A party seeking rectification must prove that the terms of the conveyance did not record the true intentions of the parties: see *Roy v Roy* (1991) [1996] 1 F.L.R. 541.

[111] *Pettitt v Pettitt*, above, at 813; *Pink v Lawrence* (1977) 36 P. & C.R. 98 at 101.

[112] The parties may have assented to the declaration in the conveyance even if they did not execute the instrument: Re *Gorman* [1990] 1 W.L.R. 616, not following *Robinson v Robinson* [1977] 1 E.G.L.R. 80.

[113] *City of London BS v Flegg* [1988] A.C. 54 at 70.

Registration Act 2002.[114] The relevant forms allow the applicants for registration to set out any declaration of trust affecting the land where it is to vest in joint proprietors.[115] The form should state whether the transferees or recipients hold on trust for themselves either as joint tenants or as tenants in common; or, if neither of these, on what trusts.[116] In the case of an assent or transfer of registered land, the instrument must be executed by all necessary parties.[117] Where the application is for first registration, the person lodging the application must confirm that he has authority to do so. In the absence of some vitiating factor, the terms of the assent, transfer or application for registration will be conclusive as to the trusts declared.

13–027   (c) *Failure of purpose.* If the property was acquired for a common purpose which later fails, there is an equitable tenancy in common even where the contributions were equal.[118]

13–028   **2. Loan on mortgage.** Where two or more persons advance money on mortgage, whether in equal or unequal shares, equity presumes a tenancy in common in the land between the mortgagees.[119] "If two people join in lending money upon a mortgage, equity says, it could not be the intention that the interest in that should survive. Though they take a joint security, each means to lend his own and take back his own."[120] "It is obvious, however, that this proposition cannot be put higher than a presumption capable of being rebutted."[121]

13–029   **3. Partnership assets and property acquired for business purposes.** Where partners acquire land as part of their partnership assets, they are presumed to hold it as beneficial tenants in common.[122] It was an ancient rule

---

[114] See Ruoff and Roper 37.006.

[115] For example, FR1 for first registration and TR1 for a transfer of whole. Most dispositions of unregistered freehold land or of leaseholds with more than seven years to run must now be completed by registration: see LRA 2002 s.4.

[116] See *Harwood v Harwood* [1991] 2 F.L.R. 275 and *Huntingford v Hobbs* [1993] 1 F.L.R. 736 for examples of the difficulties that can arise when incorrect forms are used. These were decisions under the LRA 1925 (repealed).

[117] i.e. both the transferors and transferees.

[118] *Burgess v Rawnsley* [1975] Ch. 429 (though in that case there was no such failure). See too *Ulrich v Ulrich* [1968] 1 W.L.R. 180 at 185. For this type of trust see above, para.11–010.

[119] *Petty v Styward* (1632) 1 Ch.Rep. 57; *Rigden v Vallier* (1751) 2 Ves.Sen. 252 at 258; *Vickers v Cowell* (1839) 1 Beav. 529. For a doubt as to the logic of this rule see *Harrison v Barton* (1860) 1 J. & H. 287 at 292.

[120] *Morley v Bird* (1798) 3 Ves. 628 at 631, per Arden M.R.

[121] *Steeds v Steeds* (1889) 22 QBD 537 at 541, per Wills J. It should be noted that the "joint account clause" which was normally inserted in a mortgage to make the mortgagees appear as joint tenants to the outside world, and so simplify the mechanism of discharging the mortgage did not affect this presumption of a tenancy in common in the relationship of mortgagees *inter se: Re Jackson* (1887) 34 Ch D 732. Such a clause is now implied, see LPA 1925 s.111.

[122] *Jeffreys v Small* (1683) 1 Vern. 217; *Lake v Gibson* (1729) 1 Eq.Ca.Abr. 290; *Lake v Craddock* (1732) 3 P.Wms 158; Sugden, V. & P. 698.

that the right of survivorship had no place in business.[123] The rule extends to any joint undertaking carried on with a view to profit, even if there is no formal partnership between the parties,[124] and even if the property has not been purchased but acquired by inheritance by the persons who use it for business.[125] Thus where premises are held by two joint tenants at law for their individual business purposes, they will be tenants in common in equity.[126] Although the partners must hold the legal estate as joint tenants, in equity they are presumed to be entitled in undivided shares.[127] On the death of a partner, the surviving partners (or whoever holds the legal estate) will be compelled to hold the legal estate on trust for those entitled to the property of a deceased partner as to his share.[128]

The presumption of a tenancy in common may however be rebutted by evidence of contrary intention. Thus if property is conveyed to two or more persons as beneficial joint tenants, that declaration will be conclusive in the absence of any grounds for rectification.[129]

4. Contracts and executory trusts. It sometimes happens that a prelimi-   **13–030**
nary contract or declaration of trust is required to be perfected by the execution of a proper deed of settlement. An example that was formerly common was a contract to execute a marriage settlement upon certain terms known as marriage articles. In construing such articles and other executory transactions[130] the court would readily find that gifts to classes, e.g. to the children of the marriage, were intended to give each child a separate share for his own family, even though the appropriate words of severance were absent, and decree accordingly. "Joint tenancy as a provision for the children of a marriage, is an inconvenient mode of settlement, because during their minorities, no use can be made of their portions for their advancement, as the joint

---

[123] *Hammond v Jethro* (1611) 2 Brownl. & Golds. 97 at 99; *Buckley v Barber* (1851) 6 Exch. 164 at 179. The rule *"jus accrescendi inter mercatores pro beneficium commercii locum non ha bet"* (Co.Litt. p.182a) was applied at law as regards the chattels of merchants and manufacturers: *Buckley v Barber*, above; but not to land: cf. Partnership Act 1890 s.20(2). See Lindley and Banks, *Partnership*, 17th edn (London: Sweet & Maxwell, 1995), 18–62, 19–14.

[124] *Lake v Gibson*, above; *Lyster v Dolland* (1792) 1 Ves.Jun. 431; *Dale v Hamilton* (1846) 5 Hare 369; (1847) 2 Ph. 266; *Darby v Darby* (1856) 3 Drew 495; Re *Hulton* (1890) 62 L.T. 200. Contrast *Ward v Ward* (1871) 6 Ch.App. 789 (farming jointly but not as partners).

[125] *Jackson v Jackson* (1804) 9 Ves. 591; cf. *Morris v Barrett* (1829) 3 Y. & J. 384.

[126] *Malayan Credit Ltd v Jack Chia-MPH Ltd* [1986] A.C. 549.

[127] *Re Fuller's Contract* [1933] Ch. 652. After 1925 and before 1997, the legal estate was held upon a statutory trust for sale. After 1996, it has been held on a trust of land: see below, para.13–051. For the nature of a partner's equitable interest in the partnership property see *Rodriguez v Speyer Brothers* [1919] A.C. 59 at 68; *Burdett-Coutts v L.R.C.* [1960] 1 W.L.R. 1027; Lindley and Banks, *Partnership*, above, 19–03, 19–04.

[128] *Elliott v Brown* (1791) 3 Swans. 489; Re *Ryan* (1868) 3 Ir.R.Eq. 222 at 232; *Wray v Wray* [1905] 2 Ch. 349; Partnership Act 1890 s.20(2).

[129] *Barton v Morris* [1985] 1 W.L.R. 1257 (mere inclusion of such property in partnership accounts for tax purposes held to be irrelevant).

[130] See, e.g. *Synge v Hales* (1814) 2 Ball & B. 499; *Mayn v Mayn* (1867) L.R. 5 Eq. 150; compare *Re Bellasis' Trust* (1871) L.R. 12 Eq. 218.

tenancy cannot be severed."[131] This was not a case where equity enforced a tenancy in common on persons who were joint tenants at law. It was simply an example of the rule that contracts are construed so as to give effect to the true intention of the parties. But the question normally fell to the Chancery side since the remedy sought would be a decree for the execution of a proper settlement by deed, i.e. a decree for specific performance.[132]

III. THE EFFECT OF THE 1925 AND SUBSEQUENT LEGISLATION

13–031   The mechanisms for the co-ownership of land have been affected both by the 1925 property legislation and the Trusts of Land and Appointment of Trustees Act 1996. Under the law as it stood before 1926, joint tenancy was clearly the convenient form of co-ownership for non-beneficial owners such as trustees, since the right of survivorship prevented the property from becoming entangled with the personal affairs of a deceased trustee. But for beneficial owners, tenancy in common was almost always preferable, so that the share of each co-owner would devolve or be disposable just like his other property, free from the right of survivorship.

1. The practical drawbacks of the tenancy in common[133]

13–032   *(a) Investigation of titles.* The tenancy in common was a source of great inconvenience in conveyancing. Whether the tenancy was legal or equitable, a purchaser who bought the land as a whole parcel was compelled to investigate the titles of all the tenant in common co-owners. Since there was no unity of title, the titles to all the separate shares had to be scrutinised and pieced together.

13–033   *(b) Management of land.* Even where there was no difficulty in deducing title to land held by tenants in common, its management often proved troublesome. Thus if a freehold was held in common and the property was leased to tenants, it was necessary to obtain the agreement of all the co-owners (as landlords) to the execution of any improvements or repairs.

In order to eliminate such difficulties, four substantial changes were made by the Law of Property Act 1925. These were:

(i) the abolition of legal tenancies in common;

(ii) the abolition of the right to sever a legal joint tenancy;

(iii) the imposition of a trust for sale in most cases of co-ownership; and

---

[131] *Taggart v Taggart* (1803) 1 Sch. & Lef. 84 at 88, per Lord Redesdale L.C. There is now an implied statutory power of advancement where land is held upon a trust of land though not where it is settled: TA 1925 s.32. However, it may not apply to beneficial joint tenants: above, para.13–018.

[132] For this remedy, see below, para.15–115.

[133] See J. S. Anderson, *Lawyers and the Making of English Land Law 1832–1940*, pp.286–290.

(iv) the conferment of powers of disposition and management on those trustees.

The imposition originally of a trust for sale—and its replacement after 1995 by the trust of land—is considered later,[134] but the abolition of legal tenancies in common and of the right to sever a legal joint tenancy must now be explained.

2. The abolition of legal tenancies in common. Even if there are clear **13–034** words of severance, after 1925 the legal estate cannot be held as a tenancy in common.[135] A tenancy in common can now exist only in equity; at law the only form of co-ownership possible after 1925 is a joint tenancy. Thus a conveyance today "to A, B and C in fee simple as tenants in common" (all being of full age) will vest the legal estate in A, B and C as joint tenants, although in equity they will be tenants in common.[136] If any of the co-owners is a minor, he cannot hold a legal estate in land.[137] Therefore if A is a minor, he will be co-owner in equity but the legal estate will vest in B and C alone.[138] B and C will be trustees for A, B and C. If A, B and C are all minors, the legal estate remains in the grantor who holds it on trust for the minors.[139]

3. The abolition of the right to sever a legal joint tenancy. A legal joint **13–035** tenancy cannot be severed after 1925.[140] This rule is a necessary counterpart of the rule that a legal tenancy in common cannot be created. It does not prevent one joint tenant from releasing his interest to the others, nor does it affect the right to sever a joint tenancy in equity.[141] Severance of a joint tenancy in equity is now the only circumstance where severance is possible.

Section 4. The Right of Severance

A. *Severance in equity*

The common law mitigated the uncertainty of the right of survivorship by **13–036** enabling a joint tenant to destroy the joint tenancy by severance. In this way it became a tenancy in common. "Severance" is normally used to describe the process whereby a joint tenancy is converted into a tenancy in common.[142] No

---

[134] Below, para.13–051.
[135] LPA 1925 ss.1(6), 34(1), 36(2); SLA 1925 s.36(4).
[136] LPA 1925 s.34(2).
[137] LPA 1925 s.1(6).
[138] TLATA 1996 Sch.1 para.1(2); below, para.36–006.
[139] See TLATA 1996 s.2(6); Sch.1 para.1(1); Ruoff & Roper 13.005.01.
[140] LPA 1925 s.36(2).
[141] LPA 1925 s.36(2).
[142] Strictly it also includes partition. See below, para.13–099. For proposals as to how the law on severance might be reformed, see [1995] Conv. 105 (L. Tee). Any reform would be controversial.

joint tenant owns any distinct share in the land, but each has a potential share equal in size to that of the others.[143] The size depends on the number of joint tenants at the time in question. Thus if there are five, each has the right to sever his joint tenancy and become a tenant in common of one undivided fifth share. If one joint tenant dies before severance, each of the survivors has a potential quarter share and so on. It is no bar to severance that the joint tenants are husband and wife.[144]

Where land is conveyed to two or more persons as joint tenants beneficially, each will share equally on severance even though they may have contributed unequally to the purchase price.[145] It may however be possible for a trust to declare expressly that the beneficial interests of two or more parties should those of joint tenants unless and until severed, but that in the event of severance their interests should be in some specified shares other than equal shares.[146] So also a written notice to server, signed by both parties, might indicate severance to unequal shares.[147]

Before 1926, a joint tenancy could be severed both at law and in equity,[148] but as explained above, this is now possible only in equity. Since 1925, a joint tenancy may be severed in equity in the following ways:

> (i) in the same manner as a joint tenancy of personal estate could have been severed prior to 1926[149];
>
> (ii) by notice in writing to the other joint tenants[150];
>
> (iii) by the act of some third party;
>
> (iv) by the acquisition of another estate in the land; and

---

[143] *Goodman v Gallant* [1986] Fam. 106 at 118, 119.

[144] *Bedson v Bedson* [1965] 2 Q.B. 666 at 690; *Radziej v Radziej* [1967] 1 W.L.R. 659; *Re Draper's Conveyance* [1969] 1 Ch. 486; *Harris v Goddard* [1983] 1 W.L.R. 1203 at 1208. The contrary view was expressed in *Bedson v Bedson*, above, at 678, apparently on the basis of LPA 1925 s.36(1), (3). But the subsections seem to provide no support: see (1966) 82 L.Q.R. 29 (REM).

[145] *Goodman v Gallant*, above, at 117.

[146] *Goodman v Gallant*, above, at 119.

[147] In *Singla (Trustee in Bankruptcy for Brown) v Brown* [2007] EWHC 405 (Ch), [2008] 2 W.L.R. 283, it was held that a written notice to sever to shares of 99%:1%, endorsed by the recipient, was in effect a transfer of 49% from one former joint tenant to the other. This seems unduly complex, but it brought the severance within s.339 Insolvency Act 1986 as a potential transaction at an undervalue prior to bankruptcy, albeit that the judge then decided to exercise his discretion against ordering the transaction's undoing. For written notice to sever, see below para.13–044.

[148] The rules of severance prior to 1926 are explained in the previous edition of this work at pp.430 et seq. The old common law methods of severance must be treated with some caution because the equitable rules which now apply lean against joint tenancies: see *Burgess v Rawnsley* [1975] Ch. 429 at 438.

[149] LPA 1925 s.36(2). However, "the methods of severance of a joint tenancy in personal estate before 1926 were precisely the same as the methods of severance of a joint tenancy in real estate": *Nielson-Jones v Fedden* [1975] Ch. 222 at 229, per Walton J. cf. [1975] C.L.J. 28 at 29 (M. J. Pritchard).

[150] LPA 1925 s.36(2).

(v) by homicide.

Each of these must now be considered.

1. Methods of severance recognised in equity before 1926. In *Williams v* **13–037**
Hensman,[151] Page Wood V.C. listed the three methods by which a joint
tenancy of personal estate[152] could be severed before 1926:

    (i) "an act of any one of the persons interested operating upon his
       own share";

    (ii) "by mutual agreement"; or

    (iii) "by any course of dealing sufficient to intimate that the interests of
        all were mutually treated as constituting a tenancy in common".

If any one of these methods is established, the joint tenancy will be severed
in equity. The onus of proof rests on the party asserting that severance has
occurred.[153]

(a) An act operating upon the share of any one of the joint tenants. At **13–038**
common law, the ability to alienate property was favoured above the right of
survivorship.[154] If therefore a joint tenant alienates his beneficial interest inter
vivos, his joint tenancy is severed.[155] The person to whom the interest is
assigned takes it as a tenant in common with the other joint tenants, because
he has no unity of title with them.[156] Any severance must take place during the
lifetime of the joint tenant. A joint tenant "cannot make a will of what he
holds in jointure",[157] nor can a will sever a joint tenancy.[158]

(1) TOTAL ALIENATION. If A, B and C are beneficial joint tenants and A **13–039**
assigns his interest to X,[159] X will become tenant in common as to one-third
with B and C as to two-thirds, but B and C will remain joint tenants of those
two-thirds as between themselves.[160] If B then dies, C alone profits by the

---

[151] (1861) 1 J. & H. 546 at 557. This statement of the law is always treated as authoritative:
Burgess v Rawnsley, above, at 438; *Harris v Goddard*, above, at 1209; *Hunter v Babbage* [1994]
2 FL.R. 806 at 811; *Re Palmer* [1994] Ch. 316 at 341.

[152] Personal estate included leaseholds: above, para.1–013.

[153] *Re Denny* (1947) 177 L.T. 291 at 293; *Greenfield v Greenfield* (1979) 38 P. & C.R. 570 at
578.

[154] *"Alienato rei praefertur jur accrescendi"*: Co.Litt. p.185a. In equity the rule was the same:
Patriche v Powlett (1740) 2 Atk. 54 at 55.

[155] *Re Wilks* [1891] 3 Ch. 59 at 61.

[156] Litt. p.292; Williams R.P. p.147.

[157] *Swift d. Neale v Roberts* (1764) 3 Burr. 1488 at 1496, per Lord Mansfield. Because of the
operation of the right of survivorship he has nothing to leave by will: *Gould v Kemp* (1834) 2 My.
& K. 304 at 309; above, para.13–003.

[158] Cru.Dig. ii, p.382. *Aliter* a mutual wills agreement; below, para.13–039. See also, *Carr v
Isard*, above.

[159] An assignment or any other disposition of an equitable interest must be made in writing
signed by the person disposing of that interest: LPA 1925 s.53(1)(c): see above, para.11–044.

[160] If A had assigned his interest to B, B, like X, would hold A's one-third share as a tenant in
common. B's acquisition of A's share would have no effect on his joint tenancy with C of the
remaining two-thirds: Litt. pp.304, 312, *Wright v Gibbons* (1949) 78 C.L.R. 313 at 324, 332.

right of survivorship, X and C being left as tenants in common as to one-third and two-thirds respectively.[161]

If one joint tenant forges the signatures of the others on a purported conveyance of the property, that conveyance will not transfer the legal estate, but is effective to pass the forger's beneficial interest to the purchaser, thereby severing the joint tenancy.[162] It has been held that, where the joint tenant and the purchaser act in concert, the transaction is a sham and has no effect on the joint tenancy.[163] However, it is questionable whether such a transaction can in law be regarded as a sham, as the parties plainly did intend it to have legal consequences.[164] It has long been settled that a contract by one joint tenant to sell his interest effects a severance in equity provided that the contract is specifically enforceable.[165] If, therefore, a joint tenant contracts to sell his interest to X, this causes a severance in equity. The trustees will therefore hold the legal estate subject to X's equitable right to share as tenant in common.[166] It is for this reason that severance was brought about by a covenant in marriage articles or a marriage settlement to settle property held in joint tenancy.[167] Similarly a mutual wills agreement between two joint tenants will sever the joint tenancy.[168] A declaration of trust by one joint tenant of his interest in favour of a third party will also sever the joint tenancy as regards that share.[169]

13–040   (2) PARTIAL ALIENATION. Although at common law the right to alienate was preferred to the right of survivorship, the right of survivorship took precedence over mere encumbrances.[170] The distinction lay between acts which were inconsistent with the right of survivorship and those which were not. Thus a rentcharge could be satisfied out of one joint tenant's share of the rents

[161] See *Philpott v Dobbinson* (1829) 3 Moo. & P. 320 at 330; *Denne d. Bowyer v Judge* (1809) 11 East 288; *Williams v Hensman*, above.

[162] LPA 1925 s.63(1); *Ahmed v Kendrick* (1987) 56 P. & C.R. 120; *Abbey National Plc v Moss* (1993) 26 H.L.R. 249; *Bankers Trust Co v Namdar* [1997] E.G.C.S. 20. See below, para.13–105.

[163] *Penn v Bristol & West BS* [1995] 2 F.L.R. 938 (not considered on appeal: [1997] 1 W.L.R. 1356).

[164] See [1996] Fam. Law 28 at 29 (S. Cretney).

[165] *Brown v Raindle* (1796) 3 Ves. 256 at 257; *Re Hewett* [1894] 1 Ch. 362 at 367; *Burgess v Rawnsley* [1975] Ch. 429 at 443. However no severance occurs if all the joint tenants contract to sell their interests: *Re Hayes' Estate* [1920] 1 I.R. 207.

[166] Such a contract constitutes the vendor a constructive trustee of the equitable interest for the purchaser: see *Neville v Wilson* [1997] Ch. 144. Once the purchaser has paid the consideration, the vendor will in any event have no equity which he can assert against him: *Rose v Watson* (1864) 33 L.J.Ch. 385.

[167] *Caldwell v Fellowes* (1870) L.R. 9 Eq. 410; *Baillie v Treherne* (1881) 17 Ch D 388; *Burnaby v Equitable Reversionary Interest Society* (1885) 28 Ch D 416. In *Re Hewett*, above, it was held that an aptly worded covenant would sever a joint tenancy in property subsequently acquired.

[168] *Re Wilford's Estate* (1879) 11 Ch D 267; *In b. Heys* [1914] P. 192; above, para.11–020. In England, there must be a contract between the parties before the mutual wills doctrine will operate. In other jurisdictions the requirements are less exacting: cf. *Szabo v Boros* (1967) 64 D.L.R. (2d) 48.

[169] See *Re Mee* (1971) 23 D.L.R. (3d) 491; *Re Sorensen and Sorensen* (1977) 90 D.L.R. (3d) 26.

[170] "*Jus accrescendi praefertur oneribus*": Litt. p.289; Co.Litt. p.185a.

and profits[171] without disturbing the joint tenancy. These distinctions may no longer be strictly applied now that the equitable rules for the severance of interests in personalty prevail.[172] The trend of modern decisions is to treat any partial alienation by a joint tenant as a severance if it can be regarded as an act operating on his share. Thus the following dispositions by a joint tenant have all been held to effect a severance:

(i) the execution of a mortgage or charge over his interest[173];

(ii) a specifically enforceable contract to grant a charge over his interest[174]; and

(iii) a purported mortgage over the entire property where he has forged the signatures of the other joint tenants.[175]

Although the point is not free from doubt, both principle and judicial opinion suggest that a lease for years granted by one or more (but not all[176]) of the joint tenants will effect a severance of the joint tenancy[177] not just for the duration of the lease but thereafter.[178] A lease for years confers a right to possession of some particular share of the land for a fixed period, and this right arises by a separate title.[179]

By contrast, where a joint tenant creates an encumbrance such as an easement or profit, no estate or interest passes to the grantee. Such a grant destroys none of the four unities and provided that it does not interfere with

---

[171] Above, para.13–006.

[172] cf. *Burgess v Rawsley*, above, at 438.

[173] *York v Stone* (1709) 1 Salk. 158; *Williams v Hensman* (1861) 1 J. & H. 546 at 558; *Re Pollard's Estate* (1863) 3 De G.J. 7 S. 541 at 558; *Re Sharer* (1912) 57 S.J. 60. Before 1926, the execution of a mortgage severed the joint tenancy because it involved an outright transfer of the joint tenant's interest to the mortgagee: see *Lyons v Lyons* [1967] V.R. 169 at 173. In Australia, it has been held that a mortgage under the Torrens system of title registration does not sever a joint tenancy. It operates as a mere security without any transfer or grant of an interest to the mortgagee: *Lyons v Lyons*, above.

[174] See *Thames Guaranty Ltd v Campbell* [1985] Q.B. 210 (where specific performance was in fact refused because of the prejudice it would have caused to the other joint tenant).

[175] *First National Securities Ltd v Hegerty* [1985] Q.B. 850; *Edwards v Lloyds TSB Bank* [2004] EWHC 1745 (Ch). cf. *Rogers v Resi-Statewide Corporation Ltd* (1991) 105 A.L.R. 145 at 150.

[176] See *Palmer v Rich* [1897] 1 Ch. 134.

[177] *Clerk v Clerk* (1694) 2 Vern. 323; *Gould v Kemp* (1834) My. & K. 304 at 310; *Cowper v Fletcher* (1865) 6 B. & S. 464 at 472; *Re Armstrong* [1920] 1 J.R. 239. Contra, *Harbin v Loby* (1629) Noy 157 at 158; Co.Litt. p.185a; Preston, *Abstracts*, ii, p.58; Challis p.367n. For a full discussion of the authorities, see *Frieze v Unger* [1960] V.R. 230 at 241 et seq.

[178] This was certainly the case where a joint tenant of a lease granted an underlease, whether to a stranger (*Sym's Case* (1584) Cro. Eliz. 33; *Connolly v Connolly* (1866) 17 fr.Ch.R. 208 at 233) or to one of his fellow joint tenants (*Pleadal's Case* (1579) 2 Leon. 159; and see Co.Litt. p.192a). But a lease for life granted by one joint tenant to another does not effect a severance: *Re Sorensen and Sorensen*, above.

[179] It has been settled that the rights of a lessee were unaffected by the death of a joint tenant who granted him the lease: *Anon* (1560) 2 Dy. 187a; *Harbin v Barton* (1595) Moo.K.B. 395; *Whitlock v Horton* (1605) Cro.Jac. p.91; *Lampit v Starkey* (1612) 2 Brownl. & Golds. 172 at 175; *Smallman v Agbrow* (1617) Cro.Jac p 417; Litt. p.289. See too *Frieze v Unger*, above, at 244.

the rights of the other joint tenants (and in particular, the right to possession) the joint tenancy will not be severed.[180]

13–041   (3) OTHER SITUATIONS. Alienation is not the only way in which a joint tenant may act upon his own share so as to sever the joint tenancy. Severance may also occur if he enlarges his beneficial interest. Thus where a husband and wife are beneficial joint tenants of the matrimonial home and one of them substantially improves the property, that party's share in the property will thereby be enlarged in the absence of any express or implied agreement to the contrary between them.[181]

It has been suggested that a mere declaration to sever by one joint tenant will effect a severance under this head.[182] However the better view is that such an act is insufficient and that this method of severance is successful only where a joint tenant alienates his interest, or in some other way acts so that there is a change in his equitable interest in the property.[183]

13–042   *(b) Mutual agreement.* A joint tenancy can be severed by the mutual agreement of all[184] the joint tenants.[185] Originally such an agreement had to amount to an enforceable contract,[186] so that this form of severance was simply an example of joint tenants acting upon their own share. Furthermore, any such agreement would be invalid if any of the joint tenants lacked capacity.[187] However severance by mutual agreement is now acknowledged to be a distinct category of severance and it is no longer necessary that the agreement should be enforceable as a contract.[188]

---

[180] Litt. p.286; Co.Litt. p.185a; *Lyons v Lyons*, above, at 174; *Hedley v Roberts* [1977] V.R. 282 at 286–289.

[181] Matrimonial Proceedings and Property Act 1970 s.37; above, para.11–025. This is a potential trap of some seriousness. Many couples own their homes as beneficial joint tenants, with the intention that the survivor takes the property. If one of them substantially improves the property, the tenancy may be severed without either of them realising it, thereby defeating the parties' intentions. Following *Stack v Dowden*, [2007] 2 A.C. 432, it is likely that this will occur also with unmarried couples, given that the size of each co-owner's "share" may be determined by reference to the whole course of dealing between the couple after they have acquired the property, above para.11–028.

[182] *Hawkesley v May* [1956] 1 Q.B. 304 at 313; *Re Draper's Conveyance* [1969] 1 Ch. 486 at 491.

[183] *Harris v Goddard* [1983] 1 W.L.R. 1203 at 1209; *Corin v Patton* (1990) 169 C.L.R. 540 at 547, 548, 584.

[184] Agreement between some but not all of the joint tenants will not suffice: *Wright v Gibbons* (1949) 78 C.L.R. 313 at 322.

[185] It is not necessary that all should agree to sever their interests. Thus if A, B and C are joint tenants, the three may agree that A should sever his joint tenancy, leaving B and C as joint tenants *inter se.*

[186] *Frewen v Relfe* (1787) 2 Bro.C.C. 220; *Wilson v Bell* (1843) 5 Ir.Eq.R. 501 at 507; *Kingsford v Ball* (1852) 2 Giff. App. i; *Re Wilford's Estate* (1879) 11 Ch D 267 at 269; Cru.Dig. ii, p.389; and see *Lyons v Lyons*, above at 171.

[187] *Re Wilks* [1891] 3 Ch. 59 at 62 (the joint tenants were minors).

[188] *Burgess v Rawnsley* [1975] Ch. 429 at 444, 446; *Hunter v Babbage* [1994] 2 F.L.R. 806 at 812; *Davis v Smith*, November 23, 2011. See [1975] C.L.J. 28 at 30 (M.J. Pritchard). See also *Wallbank v Price* [2007] EWHC 3001 (Ch), [2008] Family Law 318, where a written agreement severed the joint-tenancy.

(c) Course of dealing. Severance by a course of dealing depends upon **13–043** inferences drawn from conduct where there is no express act of severance. To fall within this head of severance there must be "a course of dealing by which the shares of all the parties to the contest have been affected".[189] For this reason, a unilateral statement of an intention to sever by one joint tenant, whether communicated to the other joint tenants or not, will not constitute a course of dealing,[190] though a written notice to the other joint tenants may sever for reasons considered shortly.[191] Although it is not necessary that the joint tenants should have reached a concluded agreement,[192] the acts and dealings with the property must indicate an intention by them that they should hold in common.[193] Thus periodic distributions of property amongst joint tenants[194] or the apportionment of the profits of trade amongst the joint owners of a business[195] on the assumption that they are tenants in common,[196] has been held to constitute such a course of dealing. However inconclusive negotiations by one joint tenant to purchase the interest of the other,[197] or a mere agreement in principle to do so but without any final commitment will not suffice.[198] Where a house is jointly owned, the mere conversion of it into two self-contained maisonettes,[199] or its inclusion in partnership accounts purely for tax purposes[200] will not amount to a sufficient course of dealing to effect a severance.

2. By notice in writing. A method of unilateral severance by notice in **13–044** writing was introduced by the 1925 legislation.[201] It is provided that:

"where a legal estate (not being settled land) is vested in joint tenants beneficially, and any tenant desires to sever the joint tenancy in equity, he

---

[189] *Williams v Hensman* (1861) 1 J. & H. 546 at 558, per Page Wood V.C. (emphasis added).

[190] *Burgess v Rawnsley*, above at 448. The suggestion to the contrary at 439 cannot be supported: see [1976] C.L.J. 20 at 23 (D.J. Hayton). See too *Harris v Goddard*, above, at 1209; *Gore v Carpenter* (1990) 60 P. & C.R. 456 at 462.

[191] LPA 1925 s.36(2), below. A mere verbal notice per se can never effect a severance: *Burgess v Rawnsley*, above, at 448 but it may be evidence of a mutual agreement, see *Davis v Smith* above.

[192] *Burgess v Rawnsley*, above: *Greenfield v Greenfield* (1979) 38 P. & C.R. 570 at 577.

[193] *Wilson v Bell* (1843) 5 Ir.Eq.R. 501 at 507.

[194] *Wilson v Bell*, above, Re *Denny* (1947) 177 L.T. 291. There is, however, no severance where the rents of jointly-owned properties are used as a common fund for the maintenance of the joint tenants: *Palmer v Rich* [1897] 1 Ch. 134 at 143.

[195] *Jackson v Jackson* (1804) 9 Ves. 591.

[196] *Hunter v Babbage* [1994] 2 F.L.R. 806 at 812.

[197] *McDowell v Hirschfield Lipson & Rumney* [1992] 2 F.L.R. 126.

[198] *Gore v Carpenter*, above.

[199] *Greenfield v Greenfield*, above.

[200] *Barton v Morris* [1985] 1 W.L.R. 1257.

[201] The suggestion in *Burgess v Rawnsley*, above, at 439, 444, that severance by written notice was effective in the case of personalty before 1926 is incorrect; cf. *Burgess v Rawnsley*, above, at 447; and see *Re Wilks* [1891] 3 Ch. 59; *Harris v Goddard*, above, at 1209; *Hunter v Babbage*, above, at 814, 815. See [1976] CLJ 20 (D. Hayton).

shall give to the other joint tenants a notice in writing[202] of such desire".[203]

The wording of this provision suggests that there are significant limitations on this power to sever. First, it applies only to notices in writing given inter vivos. There is still no power to sever by will. Secondly, and for no obvious reason, it has no application to settled land, nor to personal property[204] other than leaseholds.[205] Thirdly, because the legal estate must be "vested in joint tenants beneficially", it would seem to apply only where the legal and beneficial joint tenants are one and the same. On a strict construction of the section, this method of severance would not therefore be available where A and B held the legal estate on trust either for A, B and C as joint tenants, or for X and Y as joint tenants. It is possible, however, to construe the statutory words so as to give them a wider meaning and include cases where there is not complete symmetry between the legal and beneficial owners. This would seem to be more in accordance with the purpose behind permitting unilateral severance by written notice.[206]

The notice in writing need not be in any particular form. A writ or originating summons commencing legal proceedings or an affidavit sworn in those proceedings may suffice,[207] but only if the relief sought would necessarily entail a severance of the joint tenancy. Furthermore, it is essential that the notice should seek an immediate severance and not one at some time in the future.[208] Therefore although a prayer in a divorce petition that the matrimonial home should be sold and the proceeds divided equally will satisfy the requirements of the section,[209] a prayer for the court to grant a property adjustment order at some future time will not.[210] A mere proposal to sever made in the course of negotiations will not constitute a notice within the section.[211]

---

[202] See LPA 1925 s.196; *Re Berkeley Road, N.W. 9* [1971] Ch. 648 (notice duly posted in accordance with s.196 but not received, held effective); *Kinch v Bullard* [1999] 1 W.L.R. 423 (wife intercepted and destroyed notice served on her husband on her behalf after it had been delivered, because his death appeared imminent: the notice was held to be effective as it complied with s.196). See also *Quigley v Masterson* [2011] EWHC 2529 (Ch) where "give" was interpreted broadly, so as to effect a severance.

[203] LPA 1925 s.36(2), proviso.

[204] This latter limitation has been criticised: *Nielson-Jones v Fedden* [1975] Ch. 222 at 229; *Burgess v Rawnsley*, above at 447.

[205] Leaseholds fall within s.36(2): LPA 1925 ss.1(1), 205(1)(x).

[206] This aspect s.36(2) has received little judicial attention, but a restrictive interpretation serves no purpose.

[207] *Burgess v Rawnsley*, above, at 447; *Quigley v Masterson* [2011] EWHC 2529 (Ch)—application to Court of Protection.

[208] *Harris v Goddard*, above.

[209] *Re Draper's Conveyance* [1969] 1 Ch. 486, as explained in *Harris v Goddard*, above.

[210] *Harris v Goddard*, above; *Hunter v Babbage* [1994] 2 F.L.R. 806 at 818. See MCA 1973 s.24. A property adjustment order would not necessarily involve severance of the joint tenancy.

[211] *Gore v Carpenter* (1990) 60 P. & C.R. 456.

3. By the act of a third party. In a number of circumstances the interest **13–045** of a joint tenant will be severed not by his deliberate act but by some form of involuntary alienation.

(a) On the bankruptcy of the joint tenant. It has long been settled that where **13–046** a joint tenant is adjudicated bankrupt, the joint tenancy will be severed when his property is vested in his trustee in bankruptcy.[212] That vesting operates as an involuntary form of alienation. Since the enactment of the Insolvency Act 1986,[213] there has been some uncertainty as to the date upon which severance occurs. At common law, where a person was adjudicated bankrupt, the bankruptcy was deemed to relate back to the commission by him of an act of bankruptcy.[214] It followed that if a joint tenant committed an act of bankruptcy and then died before he had been adjudicated bankrupt, the joint tenancy would be regarded as having been severed prior to his death.[215] The same rule applied under the Bankruptcy Act 1914.[216] Under the Insolvency Act 1986, however, the bankrupt is no longer divested of his property on the making of the bankruptcy order. Instead, his estate (which comprises all property belonging to or vested in him at the commencement of the bankruptcy[217]) vests in the trustee in bankruptcy immediately on the latter's appointment.[218] This will usually occur some time after the making of the bankruptcy order.[219] Although the official receiver acts as the receiver of the bankrupt's estate in the interim,[220] he acquires no title to the property.[221] Consequently, it is uncertain whether severance takes place at the time of the bankruptcy order or only on the appointment of the trustee in bankruptcy, although in one case it was assumed to occur at the earlier date.[222] The point will be material if A owned property jointly with B, and either A or B died after a bankruptcy order had been made against A but before a trustee had been appointed. If A dies before any bankruptcy order is made, but where an insolvency administration order is subsequently made against his estate,[223] that order relates back to A's death. It has no effect on the joint tenancy therefore and B takes the property by survivorship.[224]

---

[212] *Morgan v Marquis* (1853) 9 Ex. 145 at 147; *Bedson v Bedson* [1965] 2 Q.B. 666 at 690; *Re Rushton* [1972] Ch. 197 at 203; *Re Gorman* [1990] 1 W.L.R. 616 at 620.

[213] The Act came into force on December 29, 1986.

[214] See, e.g. *Cooper v Chitty* (1755) 1 Burr. 20, 31, 32; *Smith v Stokes* (1801) 1 East 363, 367. Both the concept of an act of bankruptcy and the relation back to the trustee's title were abolished by IA 1986: see Re *Dennis* [1996] Ch. 80 at 88.

[215] *Smith v Stokes*, above.

[216] *Re Dennis*, above.

[217] s.283(1).

[218] s.306(1).

[219] cf. IA 1986 ss.287, 293.

[220] IA 1986 s.287.

[221] The bankrupt is however under a duty to deliver up possession of his estate to him: IA 1986 s.291.

[222] *Re Pavlou* [1993] 1 W.L.R. 1046 at 1048. See however [1993] Fam. Law 196; [1995] All E.R. Rev. 292 (S.M. Cretney) and [1995] C.L.J. 52 at 59 (L. Tee).

[223] Under the Administration of Insolvent Estates of Deceased Persons Order. SI 1986/1999.

[224] *Re Palmer* [1994] Ch. 316; [1995] C.L.J. 52 (L. Tee); [1995] Conv. 68 (M. Haley).

13–047   *(b) Other cases.* Other situations in which a joint tenancy may be severed
by the act of a third party include:

> (i) the imposition of a charging order in respect of a money judgment
>   against one joint tenant[225]; and

> (ii) the imposition of a charge in favour of the Legal Aid Fund under
>   the Legal Aid Act 1988.[226]

13–048   **4. By acquisition of another estate in the land.** It was never fatal to a joint
tenancy that one of the joint tenants was *initially* given some further estate in
the land in addition to his joint tenancy.[227] However at common law prior to
the Judicature Act 1873, the *subsequent* acquisition of some further estate in
the land by a legal joint tenant destroyed the unity of interest and severed the
joint tenancy.[228] Thus if land was limited to A, B and C as joint tenants for
life, with remainder to C in fee simple, the mere existence of C's fee simple
remainder did not destroy his joint tenancy for life. However, if A acquired
C's fee simple, A's life estate merged in the fee simple and severed his joint
tenancy for life.[229] So also if land were held by X for life with remainder to
Y and Z in fee simple as joint tenants, and X conveyed his life estate to Y, the
joint tenancy was severed.[230] If X had instead surrendered his life estate to Y,
this would have extinguished it, and so Y and Z would have benefited from
their joint tenancy taking effect in possession.[231]

The basis of this form of severance was the doctrine of merger[232]: "whenever a greater estate and a less coincide and meet in one and the same person,
without any intermediate estate, the less is immediately . . . sunk or drowned
in the greater."[233] Although the operation of the doctrine at law was automatic, equity by contrast leaned against merger.[234] The intention of the person
in whom the interests coalesced determined whether merger occurred.[235] In
the absence of evidence of intention, there would be no merger if it was in the
interests of the party or consistent with his duty that merger should not take
place.[236] Since 1873, the equitable rules of merger have prevailed.[237] As
severance of a joint tenancy by the acquisition of another estate operates only
if merger takes place, it is no longer automatic, but depends upon the intention

---

[225] Charging Orders Act 1979 ss.2(1), (2); 3(4); *Midland Bank Plc v Pike* [1988] 2 All E.R.
434. See below, para.13–074.
[226] s.16(6); *Bedson v Bedson* [1965] 2 Q.B. 666 at 691.
[227] Above, para.13–006.
[228] *Morgan's Case* (t. Eliz. 1) 2 And. 202; *Wiscot's Case* (1599) 2 Co.Rep. p.60b.
[229] *Morgan's Case* (t. Eliz. 1) 2 And. 202; *Wiscot's Case* (1599) 2 Co.Rep. p.60b.
[230] Co.Litt. p.183a; Preston *Conveyancing*, iii, p.24.
[231] See below, para.18–083.
[232] See below, para.18–090.
[233] 2 Bl.Comm. p.177.
[234] *Chambers v Kingham* (1878) 10 Ch D 743, 745.
[235] *Forbes v Moffatt* (1811) 18 Ves. 384 at 390.
[236] *Re Fletcher* [1917] 1 Ch. 339 at 341.
[237] JA 1873 s.25(4). See now LPA 1925 s.185.

of the party who acquires the estate.[238] There is little authority on when a joint tenancy will now be held to have been severed by the operation of the doctrine of merger.[239] In principle however, the acquisition by one equitable joint tenant of the legal estate as trustee should not, without more, sever the joint tenancy.[240]

5. Homicide. One consequence of the rule that no one may benefit in law **13–049** from his own crime,[241] is that, in general, if one joint tenant criminally kills another, the killer cannot take any beneficial interest by survivorship. This rule of public policy, commonly known as the "forfeiture rule", applies to cases of deliberate and intentional homicide, whether the killing is murder, manslaughter or aiding and abetting a suicide.[242] It has not been conclusively settled in England whether the application of the rule causes the automatic severance of the joint tenancy or whether a constructive trust is imposed to prevent the killer from obtaining any benefit from his crime.[243] Where there are just two joint tenants the answer will be the same on either view. Thus if A and B hold the legal estate on trust for themselves as joint tenants, and A murders B, the legal estate will vest by survivorship in A alone but upon trust for himself and B's estate as equitable tenants in common in equal shares.[244] However, if there is a third joint tenant, C, the two different approaches lead to different results. The legal estate will necessarily vest in A and C jointly. If severance is automatic they will hold it upon trust for A, B's estate and C as tenants in common in equal shares. If a constructive trust is imposed they will hold it for C as to one-third and for A and C as joint tenants as to the remaining two-thirds.[245]

The court now has a statutory power[246] to modify the application of the forfeiture rule in cases where a person has unlawfully killed[247] another (other than where he has been convicted of murder[248]). It may do so only if it is satisfied that, having regard to the conduct of the offender and of the deceased

---

[238] See (1990) 41 N.I.L.Q. 359 (A. Dowling).

[239] cf. *Nielson-Jones v Fedden* [1975] Ch. 222 at 228.

[240] The decision to the contrary in *Conolly v Conolly* (1867) I.R. 1 Eq. 376 is unlikely to be followed in England.

[241] e.g. *in b. Hall* [1914] P.1. See the general survey by T.G. Youdan (1973) 89 L.Q.R. 235; and see below, para.14–069.

[242] *Dunbar v Plant* [1998] Ch. 412; [1998] C.L.J. 31 (S.B.).

[243] The remarks in *Re K* [1985] Ch. 85 at 100, suggest that severance is automatic. In Australia, however, the courts impose a constructive trust instead, and there are persuasive reasons for preferring this latter view: see *Rasmanis v Jurewitsch* (1969) 70 S.R. (N.S.W.) 407; *Public Trustee v Evans* (1985) 2 N.S.W. L.R. 188; *Re Stone* [1989] 1 Qd.R. 351.

[244] *Re K*, above, at 100; *Re Stone*, above, at 352–353.

[245] *Rasmanis v Jurewitsch*, above at 411–412. See (1974) 37 M.L.R. 481 at 488–492 (T.K. Earnshaw and P.J. Pace); M. Cope, *Constructive Trusts* (Law Book Company of Australasia, 1992) 561–56.

[246] Forfeiture Act 1982 s.2(1); see below, para.14–059.

[247] The forfeiture rule may apply even if a person has been acquitted of a charge of murder or manslaughter provided that in civil proceedings the court is satisfied on the balance of probabilities that he was guilty of a killing that fell within the scope of the rule: *Gray v Barr* [1971] 2 Q.B. 554; *Public Trustee v Evans*, above, at 190.

[248] Forfeiture Act 1982 s.5.

and to such other circumstances as may appear material to it, the justice of the case so requires.[249] In exercise of this power, the court may hold that the right of survivorship applies, notwithstanding that one joint tenant killed another.[250]

B. Devolution of the legal estate

13–050 Where a joint tenancy is severed, the co-owner does not cease to be a joint tenant and trustee of the legal estate if that was his position before severance took place. He can divest himself of the legal estate only by retiring from the trust, or by releasing his interest in the legal estate to the other tenants of it. Where the legal title to unregistered land is vested in joint tenants beneficially, and one of them severs his joint tenancy, he should ensure that a memorandum of severance is indorsed on, or annexed to, the conveyance which vested the legal estate in the co-owners. This will ensure that his interest is protected if there is subsequently a conveyance of the legal estate by a sole surviving joint tenant. This is explained later.[251]

Section 5. The Imposition of a Statutory Trust in Cases of Co-ownership

A. The imposition of a statutory trust of land

13–051 The conversion of tenancies in common into equitable interests would not by itself have simplified the investigation of title. Where the title was unregistered a purchaser would have had notice of the trusts. It was therefore essential to provide overreaching machinery, so that it would be necessary for any purchaser to investigate only the title to the legal estate. Prior to 1997, this was achieved by imposing a statutory trust for sale upon land conveyed to or held by or on behalf of two or more persons beneficially, whether as tenants in common or joint tenants.[252] After 1996, a trust of land is imposed instead in the same circumstances, and all existing trusts for sale have become trusts of land.[253] The trust is imposed whether the co-owners are given interests in the land itself or in the income from it.[254] In the following cases, therefore, the legal estate is subject to a statutory trust of land[255]:

> (i) a conveyance or devise to A and B jointly (i.e. as beneficial joint tenants);

---

[249] Forfeiture Act 1982 s.2(2).
[250] Forfeiture Act 1982 s.2(4)(b); *Re K* [1985] Ch. 85; affirmed [1986] Ch. 180.
[251] See below, paras 13–056 et seq.
[252] This states the combined effect of LPA 1925 ss.34 and 36 (as they had been interpreted), which dealt with the various cases. The machinery is described in more detail below.
[253] TLATA 1996 s.1 above, para.12–002. See LPA 1925 ss.34, 36 (as amended by TLATA 1996 s.5(1); Sch.2).
[254] *Re House* [1929] 2 Ch. 166.
[255] LPA 1925 s.36(1) (as amended by TLATA 1996 s.5(1); Sch.2).

(ii) a conveyance[256] or devise[257] to A and B as tenants in common; and

(iii) a conveyance or devise to X and Y jointly upon trust for A and B either jointly or in common (or upon trust to pay the income to A and B jointly or in common).[258]

In the case of a devise it should be noted that the legal estate vests not in any of the persons named, but in the testator's personal representatives,[259] who therefore become trustees of land. Since they automatically hold the deceased's property on trust to give effect to the will, there is no point in creating another set of trustees. There are special provisions for settled land, which are discussed in the Appendix, being now largely of historical interest.[260]

The Law of Property Act 1925 had been interpreted in such a way that a **13–052** trust of land[261] is imposed in all cases of beneficial co-ownership.[262] In the case of joint beneficial interests this is effected in a straightforward way[263] by s.36(1).[264] In the case of beneficial interests in common the position is more difficult. Section 34(1) provides that "an undivided share in land shall not be capable of being created except as provided by the Settled Land Act 1925 or as hereinafter mentioned".[265] The draftsman appears to have contemplated that a tenancy in common could be created in just four situations:

(i) where settled land comes to be held "on trust for persons entitled in possession under a trust instrument in undivided shares"[266];

(ii) where land "is expressed to be conveyed to any persons in undivided shares"[267];

(iii) where land is devised or bequeathed "to two or more persons in undivided shares"[268]; and

---

[256] LPA 1925 s.34(2) (as amended by TLATA 1996 s.5(1); Sch.2).

[257] LPA 1925 s.34(3) (as amended by TLATA 1996 ss.5(1), 25(2); Schs 2, 4).

[258] *Re House*, above (devise upon trust for tenants in common held to fall within LPA 1925 s.34(3)). The same presumably applies to a conveyance which will then fall within s.34(2), but it is not clear whether the legal estate vests in X and Y or in A and B. The case is even more difficult, on the wording of s.34(2), where there is a conveyance to X (alone) upon trust for A and B in common. Beneficial joint tenancy is clearly dealt with by s.36: the legal estate vests in the trustee or trustees.

[259] LPA 1925 s.34(3) (as amended by TLATA 1996 ss.5(1), 25(2); Schs 2, 4).

[260] See also para.10–013. No new settlements may be created after 1997: see above, para.12–002.

[261] And before 1997, a trust for sale.

[262] *Williams & Glyn's Bank Ltd v Boland* [1981] A.C. 487 at 503; *City of London BS v Flegg* [1988] A.C. 54 at 77.

[263] See however, 62 L.J.News. 437; 64 L.J.News. 66.

[264] As amended by TLATA 1996 s.5(i); Sch.2.

[265] See too SLA 1925 s.36(4) (as amended by TLATA 1996 s.25(i); Sch.3). For comment on these provisions, see (1963) 27 Conv. (N.S.) 51 at 53–54 (B. Rudden); [1982] Conv. 213 (M. Friend and J. Newton); [1986] Conv. 379; [1987] Conv. 451 at 454–457; (W. J. Swadling); C.L.J. 277 at 297–302 (C.H.).

[266] SLA 1925 s.36(i); below, para.13–090.

[267] LPA 1925 s.34(2) (see now, as amended by TLATA 1996 s.5(1); Sch.2).

[268] LPA 1925 s.34(3) (see now, as amended by TLATA 1996 ss.5(i), 25(2); Schs 2, 4).

(iv) where land is conveyed to trustees to hold on an express trust of land[269] for two or more persons as tenants in common.[270]

If a tenancy in common is created in one of these ways, it will be apparent on the face of the title (if unregistered) that the land is held upon a trust of land. A purchaser will therefore know that any purchase monies must be paid to at least two trustees if the beneficial interests are to be overreached.[271] It is therefore at least possible that the draftsman meant what he said in s.34(1) and intended that a tenancy in common should only be created in one of the four ways outlined above.[272] The fundamental weakness of his scheme however is that he failed to provide what was to happen in cases of non-compliance.

13–053   There are in fact a number of situations that fall outside the various provisions, though some of these could not have been foreseen in 1925.[273] The following are amongst the most important[274]:

(i) a conveyance to A and B as joint tenants, where equity presumes them to take as beneficial tenants in common, e.g. because they are partners, or contribute purchase-money in unequal shares[275];

(ii) a conveyance to X, purchasing as trustee for A and B who are equitable owners in common of the purchase money;

(iii) a declaration by A, as sole owner, that he holds on trust for himself and B in equal shares[276];

---

[269] Prior to 1997, an express trust for sale.

[270] This is not explicitly covered by the Law of Property Act 1925, but cf. LPA 1922 Sch.3 paras 2(6), (7). See too LPA 1925 s.3(1)(b) (repealed by TLATA 1996 s.25(2); Sch.4); 73 L.J.News 355 (J. M. Lightwood); [1990] C.L.J. 277 at 299 (C.H.).

[271] LPA 1925 s.27(2) (as amended by LP (Am)A 1926, Sch.; TLATA 1996 s.25(1); Sch.3). Prior to 1997, the fact that land was held on trust for sale was also relevant because the powers of the trustees were restricted: see LPA 1925 s.28(1) (now repealed). By contrast, trustees of land have the powers of an absolute owner: see TLATA 1996 s.6(i); above, para.12–016.

[272] See [1982] Conv. 213 (M. Friend and J. Newton); [1990] C.L.J. 277 at 298 (C.H.). cf. J.S. Anderson, *Lawyers and the Making of English Land Law 1832–1940*, pp.330–331.

[273] See (1944) 9 Conv. (N.S.) 37 et seq. For difficulties in applying the provisions to leases, see (1989) 18 *Anglo-American Law Review* 151 (P. Sparkes).

[274] A situation that was a possible cause of difficulty prior to 1997 was a conveyance to A (a minor) and B (an adult) as tenants in common: see the fifth edition of this work at p.438. If they were joint tenants, LPA 1925 s.19(2) (repealed by TLATA 1996 s.25(2); Sch.4) covered the case. It *may* have been wide enough to include tenants in common: see [1990] C.L.J. 277 at 300 (C.H.). For conveyances after 1996 there is no difficulty: see TLATA 1996 s.2(6); Sch.1 para.1(2).

[275] Above para.13–022. This situation does not fall within LPA 1925 s.34(2), because the land is not expressed to be conveyed to A and B in undivided shares. In two such cases (of purchasers contributing unequally) different solutions have been found: that the case falls within LPA 1925 s.36(1), which governs beneficial joint tenancy (*Re Buchanan-Wollaston's Conveyance* [1939] Ch. 217 at 222; [1939] Ch. 738 at 744); and that SLA 1925 s.36(4) governs any case of tenancy in common not otherwise provided for (*Bull v Bull* [1955] 1 Q.B. 234; *City of London BS v Flegg* [1988] A.C. 54 at 77). cf. [1990] C.L.J. 277 at 298–301 (C.H.).

[276] See, e.g. *Re Hind* [1933] Ch. 208; *Jones v Jones* [1972] 1 W.L.R. 1269.

(iv) where a spouse acquires a share or an enhanced share in the matrimonial home by virtue of substantial improvement which he has made to the property subsequent to its acquisition[277]; and

(v) where A acquires a beneficial interest under a constructive trust in property belonging to B because he acted to his detriment in reliance on the parties' common intention that he should have such a share.[278]

The courts found a way of escape in s.36(4) of the Settled Land Act 1925[279] which provides that an undivided share in land cannot be created "except under a trust instrument or under the Law of Property Act 1925 and shall then only take effect behind a trust of land"[280] Plainly this provision is not well framed to remedy the deficiencies of the Law of Property Act 1925. But to employ it for that purpose is probably a better course than to extend the incomplete provisions of that Act by straining their language.[281] It is perhaps surprising that the opportunity was not taken in the Trusts of Land and Appointment of Trustees Act 1996 to rectify the position formally.

Most dispositions of either a freehold or a leasehold (having more than seven years to run), or the grant of lease for more than seven years, to two or more persons as tenants in common will now have to be completed by registration, whether or not the title is already registered.[282] The trusts upon which the land is to be held must be set out in the application for first registration (if the title is unregistered) or in the transfer or assent (if title is already registered).[283] Where the transferees are tenants in common in equity, the last survivor of them will be unable to give a valid receipt for capital money arising on any disposition of the land.[284] In those circumstances a restriction will be entered on the register by which no disposition by a sole proprietor of the land under which capital money arises is to be registered except under an order of the registrar or of the court.[285]

The imposition of a statutory trust of land in all cases where there is tenancy **13–054** in common is not without its hazards. The existence of the trust may not be apparent on the face of the title. A person who appears to be an absolute owner may turn out to be a trustee of land. Unless a co-trustee is appointed, he will

---

[277] Matrimonial Proceedings and Property Act 1970 s.37. Following *Stack v Dowden* [2007] 2 A.C. 432, equitable principles raise the same possibility for unmarried partners. See above para.11–025.

[278] Above, para.11–023. For a case where the court, in giving effect to an equity by estoppel, declared that A held land upon trust for sale for A and B equally, see *Holiday Inns v Broadhead* (1974) 232 E.G. 951, 1087. For proprietary estoppel, see below, Ch.16.

[279] As now amended by TLATA 1996 s.25(1); Sch.3.

[280] See *Bull v Bull*, above, at 237; *City of London BS v Flegg*, above, at 77.

[281] The solution adopted in *Re Buchanan-Wollaston's Conveyance*, above, is at the expense of the word "beneficially" in LPA 1925 s.36(1).

[282] See LRA 2002 s.4.

[283] See above Ruoff & Roper 37.006 and also 12–011 and 13–026.

[284] The survivor of beneficial joint tenants would be able to give such a valid receipt.

[285] Form A restriction, see Ruoff & Roper 37.007. LRA 2002 s.44(1), LRR 2003 r.95(2)(a). See also LRR 2003 r.94(1) for additional situations where the restriction should be entered.

be unable to make an overreaching conveyance. The difficulties which may result from this have been explained.[286]

Provided that these difficulties can be overcome, the advantages of employing the device of a trust are two-fold.[287] First, it keeps the beneficial interests of the co-owners off the title. A purchaser is not concerned with the beneficial interests in the land, but only with the legal estate vested in the trustees of land. Provided that he pays his purchase-money to trustees of land who are either two or more in number or a trust corporation, he takes free from the rights of the beneficiaries.[288] It will not matter to the purchaser whether there are three or 30 people entitled, or whether they are joint tenants or tenants in common.[289] Secondly, the imposition of a trust makes it much easier to administer property that is owned by more than four co-owners. As has been explained, the trustees are, in exercising their functions, obliged to consult the beneficiaries of full age who are entitled to an interest in possession in the land and, so far as consistent with the general interest of the trust, to give effect to the wishes of the majority (according to the value of the combined interests).[290] However:

> (i) such functions can be exercised without the concurrence of all such beneficiaries[291];
>
> (ii) the court may relieve the trustees of the need to obtain consents if, e.g. the beneficiaries cannot readily be contacted[292]; and
>
> (iii) the trustees' overriding concern is to act in the general interest of the trust.[293]

B. Determination of the statutory trust of land

13–055   **1. Union in sole tenant.** Once all the legal and equitable interests in the property have finally vested in one person (e.g. where A, B and C were beneficial joint tenants in fee simple and B and C have died), there can no longer be an effective trust and the statutory trust of land therefore ceases.[294] In the example given, A can sell as sole owner and take the purchase-

---

[286] See above, para.12–037; para.13–031.

[287] English law is unique in having adopted the trust as a device to give effect to co-ownership: see J.S. Anderson "The 1925 Property Legislation: Setting Contexts" in S. Bright and J. Dewar eds, *Land Law: Themes and Perspectives*, 107.

[288] For this overreaching machinery, see above, para.12–037.

[289] The statutory machinery has to apply to a joint tenancy because, as has been explained (see above, para.13–036) a joint tenancy may be severed, and a purchaser must be absolved from inquiring whether this has happened. See below, paras 13–056, 13–057.

[290] TLATA 1996 s.11; above, para.12–026.

[291] As was required prior to 1926: see above, paras 13–032, 13–033.

[292] TLATA 1996 s.14(2); above, para.12–021.

[293] TLATA 1996 s.11(1)(b).

[294] *Re Cook* [1948] Ch. 212.

money.[295] Nothing in the Law of Property Act 1925 affects the right of a survivor of joint tenants who is solely and beneficially interested to deal with his legal estate as if it were not held on a trust of land.[296] A surviving joint tenant does not therefore have to go through the pointless procedure of appointing another trustee of a trust under which he is the sole beneficiary.

2. Investigation of title: unregistered land

(a) The situation prior to 1964. Prior to 1964, a particular problem existed **13–056** for a purchaser of unregistered land. He could not tell whether a vendor, who was the surviving owner of the legal estate, was also solely entitled in equity unless he investigated the beneficial interests. A beneficial joint tenancy, for example, might have been turned into a tenancy in common[297] by some act or event not shown in the title to the legal estate, and perhaps not even known to the vendor, so that A, in the above example, might turn out to be a trustee of land for himself and some other person claiming through B or C. Even in this case the purchaser, if he had made all due inquiries and found no evidence of a tenancy in common, could probably plead that he was a bona fide purchaser of the legal estate for value without notice of the outstanding equitable interest.[298] But no purchaser wishes to be driven to that plea. There was also the practical problem of what proof of a negative (non-severance) could be given.

(b) Statements under the Act of 1964. The above situation violated the **13–057** principle of the 1925 legislation that the purchaser should not be concerned with beneficial interests.[299] It was remedied by the Law of Property (Joint Tenants) Act 1964,[300] though the legislation itself creates a number of problems.[301] This short statute provides that, in favour of a purchaser of a legal estate, a survivor of two or more joint tenants shall "be deemed to be solely and beneficially interested if the conveyance includes a statement that he is so interested".[302] Thus the purchaser of the legal estate will take it without notice of any severance and will defeat the equitable title of any owner of a severed

---

[295] For the protection of purchasers, see above, para.12–003. Where title is registered, any purchaser from A can rely on the absence of any restriction against a disposition by a sole proprietor of the kind that should have been entered if A, B and C had been beneficial tenants in common:); above, para.13–053.

[296] LPA 1925 s.36(2) (as amended by LP(Am)A 1926 s.7, Sch.; TLATA 1996 s.5(1); Sch.2 para.4).

[297] i.e. severed, e.g. by a sale of a share: above, paras 13–038, 13–039.

[298] *Williams & Glyn's Bank Ltd v Boland* [1979] Ch. 312 at 330, 334.

[299] Purchasers often had to be advised to obtain the appointment of another trustee to join the vendor in receiving the purchase money, in case the land was still held on trust: see 219 L.T.News 217.

[300] The legislation was retrospective. It was deemed to have come into force on January 1, 1926: s.2. It was a Private Member's Bill introduced by Sir Barnett Janner MP with the express intention of making it unnecessary for a surviving joint tenant to have to appoint a second trustee when he wished to sell the land.

[301] See M. P. Thompson, *Barnsley's Conveyancing Law and Practice*, 4th edn (Oxford: OUP, 1996), p.316; and below.

[302] s.1(1) (as amended by LP(MP)A 1994 s.21; Schs 1, 2).

share. Where the survivor has himself died, his personal representatives are given corresponding powers.[303]

13–058   *(c) The exclusion of the Act.* The Act of 1964 does not apply if, before the date of the conveyance by the survivor, a memorandum of severance is indorsed on or annexed to the conveyance which vested the legal estate in the joint tenants. The memorandum must be signed by one or all of them and record the severance on a specified date.[304] Nor does the Act apply where, before the same date, a bankruptcy order has been registered[305] so as to affect the purchaser with actual notice of it,[306] or where the title to the land is registered.[307]

13–059   *(d) Severance.* The Act of 1964 provides more convenient conveyancing machinery in the normal case where there has been no severance. But where there has been a severance, which may be unknown to the survivor, the title of the owner of the severed share will be imperilled unless he attaches a memorandum of severance to the document of title. The Act gives him no power to insist upon this, but his powers as co-owner probably suffice. Nor does the Act say what is to happen where the vendor conveys on the basis that he is solely and beneficially interested but the purchaser has notice that there has been severance. On its face, the Act even then protects the purchaser, and this appears to have been Parliament's intention.[308] If this is so, the Act has made the rights of the beneficiaries more vulnerable to fraud than they were hitherto.[309] It is possible that a court would not allow a purchaser to take advantage of the Act in circumstances where he knew of or was a party to the vendor's inequitable conduct.[310]

13–060   **3. Investigation of title: registered land.** It has already been explained that where registered land is transferred to co-owners they are required to state in the transfer the trusts upon which they hold the land.[311] If they hold on trust such that the survivor cannot give a valid receipt for capital money on a disposition of the land, a restriction must be entered on the register to that effect.[312] If a beneficial joint tenant of registered land subsequently severs the joint tenancy, he should ensure that a restriction is then placed upon the register to indicate that the survivor can no longer give a valid receipt for capital money.[313] The Law of Property (Joint Tenants) Act 1964 has no

---

[303] s.1(2). See [1977] Conv. 423 (P.W. Smith).
[304] s.1(i).
[305] Under LCA 1972; above, para.8–066.
[306] s.1(1), as amended by IA 1985 s.235(1), Sch.8 para.13.
[307] See below.
[308] See (1966) 30 Conv. (N.S.) 27 at 28 (P. Jackson).
[309] M. P. Thompson, *Barnsley's Conveyancing Law and Practice*, 4th edn, p.316; and below.
[310] cf. the judicial restriction of the provision protecting purchasers from mortgagees: below, para.25–016.
[311] Above, paras 13–026, 13–053.
[312] The form A restriction.
[313] The form A restriction, Ruoff & Roper 37.008.

application to registered land.[314] This is because those who promoted the Act apparently assumed that if there was no restriction on the register, any purchaser from a surviving joint tenant would obtain a good title even if severance had in fact taken place. It is now clear that this assumption is not always correct. An interest under a trust of land can be an overriding interest if it is supported by discoverable actual occupation.[315] If therefore severance took place, and one of the tenants in common died, leaving his share by will to some person who was in occupation of the land, any purchaser of the land from the survivor who completed without being given vacant possession,[316] would take the land subject to the beneficial interest of that occupier unless he had made enquiries of that person and he failed to disclose his rights when it was reasonable to do so.[317] A purchaser is not normally at risk if he purchases with vacant possession.

C. Operation of the statutory trust

The working of the statutory trust imposed by the Trusts of Land and **13–061** Appointment of Trustees Act 1996 as it applies to cases of co-ownership must now be explained.[318] In relation to many aspects of the law, it is necessary to consider the position prior to 1997 when a trust for sale rather than a trust of land was imposed in such cases. This will make clear the changes that the 1996 Act has brought about. Furthermore, although the statutory provisions prior to 1997 differ significantly from those which now apply, the case law that developed in relation to them is likely to remain relevant as regards some parts of the current law.

1. Rights of beneficiaries

(a) The right to occupy. Prior to 1997 beneficial co-owners of land had a **13–062** common law right of occupation pending sale.[319] Before 1926 they had been entitled to occupy the land themselves,[320] and it was eventually settled that the imposition of the statutory trust for sale, which was primarily a conveyancing device, did not deprive them of this right.[321] Occupation of the premises by a beneficiary was no more than the enjoyment in specie of the rents and profits of the land to which he was entitled,[322] and was not a separate and severable

---

[314] s.3.
[315] LRA 2002 s.29 and Sch.3 para.2; *Williams & Glyn's Bank Ltd v Boland* [1981] A.C. 487; above, para.7–089.
[316] Typically a mortgagee.
[317] LRA 2002 s.29 and Sch.3 para.2(b).
[318] The Act as a whole is examined in detail in Ch.12.
[319] *City of London BS v Flegg* [1988] A.C. 54 at 71, 81 cf. *Barclay v Barclay* [1970] 1 Q.B. 677.
[320] Above, para.13–005. See [1998] C.L.J. 123 at 127 (D.G. Barnsley).
[321] *Bull v Bull* [1955] 1 Q.B. 234, approved in *Williams & Glyn's Bank Ltd v Boland* [1981] A.C. 487; and see *Cook & Cook* [1962] P. 235; *IRC v Lloyds Private Banking Ltd* [1998] 2 F.C.R. 41 at 49.
[322] *City of London BS v Flegg*, above, at 81.

right.[323] The interests of the beneficiaries could therefore be overreached in the usual way on a disposition by the trustees for sale.[324]

It has been explained that after 1997, where land is held on a trust of land, a beneficiary who is beneficially entitled to an interest in possession in land, has a statutory right to occupy it,[325] subject to the trustees' powers to exclude or restrict that right in certain circumstances.[326] This statutory right is unlikely to be in issue in the common case of co-ownership where the legal and beneficial owners of the land are one and the same. In such a situation, the co-owners' right to possession is simply a concomitant of their ownership of the legal estate,[327] and the unity of possession to which all co-owners are entitled at common law.[328]

The statutory right of occupation given to beneficiaries has been criticised on the ground that it has reduced the rights that beneficial co-owners had hitherto enjoyed.[329] This is because the right:

> (i) depends upon the purposes of the trust and the availability and suitability of the land for occupation[330]; and

> (ii) is subject to the trustees' power to exclude or restrict the beneficiary's right of occupation.[331]

13–063   It has been suggested that, in consequence, an equitable co-owner no longer enjoys unity of possession as that concept has hitherto been understood.[332] This may be more apparent than real. First, as indicated above, where a person is both a legal and beneficial co-owner, his right to occupy cannot be restricted or excluded without his consent or a court order. This is because he is a trustee, and the power to restrict or exclude must be exercised unanimously.[333] Secondly, even where a beneficiary's entitlement to occupy the land does depend upon the Act, it is suggested that any exercise by the trustees of their power of exclusion will normally be on terms that he is compensated by the beneficiaries who remain in occupation.[334] To deny a beneficiary who is entitled in possession both the right to receive the rents and profits of the land and the right to enjoy it in specie by occupation is likely to be regarded as unreasonable in the absence of some compelling circumstance.[335] Notwithstanding the criticisms of the statutory power to exclude a co-owner (whether

---

[323] *City of London BS v Flegg*, above, at 81.
[324] *City of London BS v Flegg*, above, and see above, para.12–037.
[325] TLATA 1996 s.12; above, para.12–027.
[326] TLATA 1996 s.13; above, para.12–028.
[327] Above, para.12–027.
[328] Above, para.13–005.
[329] See [1998] C.L.J. 123 (D. G. Barnsley).
[330] TLATA 1996 s.12(1), (2); above, para.12–027.
[331] TLATA 1996 s.13; above, para.12–028.
[332] [1998] C.L.J. 123 at 137 (D. G. Barnsley).
[333] See above, para.12–016.
[334] Under TLATA 1996 s.13(6). A beneficiary who is already in occupation can only be excluded by his consent or by court order: s.13(7). See above, para.12–028.
[335] cf. TLATA 1996 s.13(2); above, para.12–028.

or not on terms), its availability has a significant advantage. It gives the court greater flexibility in the case where the relationship between co-owners has come to an end, and one of them has applied for an order for sale.[336] In practice, it is in this situation that the power is most likely to be employed.

(b) Disputes between co-owners. Many disputes between co-owners of land **13–064** arise on the termination of the relationship or arrangement between the parties, where one of them wishes to have the property sold but the other does not. The relevant provisions of the Trusts of Land and Appointment of Trustees Act 1996 have already been explained,[337] but their application to such disputes requires more detailed consideration. It will be recalled that under these provisions:

    (i) a trustee of land; and

    (ii) any person who has an interest in any property which is subject to either a trust of land or a trust of the proceeds of sale of land

may apply to the court, which may make such an order as it thinks fit in relation to the exercise by the trustees of any of their functions.[338] It may, for example, direct or restrain a sale or other disposition by the trustees, or relieve the trustees of the necessity of obtaining any consent to a disposition that would otherwise be needed by them.[339]

Prior to 1997, the courts evolved a number of principles as to how they would exercise their discretion in disputes under the equivalent but narrower provision that was applicable where land was held on trust for sale.[340] The matters to which the court is required to have regard in exercising its discretion under the 1996 Act[341] are intended to be a consolidation and rationalisation of those principles.[342] Although the authorities on the law prior to 1997 will therefore continue to provide guidance,[343] the outcome will not in all cases be the same as it would have been under the previous law. This is because the legislation is much more specific as to the matters which a court is required to take into account on such an application[344] and because the trustees are no longer under a duty to sell should they not agree to postpone sale.[345] Six of these matters are expressly mentioned, of which two have

---

[336] Under TLATA 1996 s.14; below.
[337] ss.14, 15; above, paras 12–021 et seq.
[338] TLATA 1996 ss.14(1), (2), 17(2)–(6).
[339] TLATA 1996 s.14(2); *Abbey National Mortgages Plc v Powell* (1999) 78 P. & C.R. D16.
[340] LPA 1925 s.30; now repealed.
[341] TLATA 1996 s.15(1); below; and see above, para.12–022.
[342] See (1989) Law Com. No.181, para.12.9.
[343] See *TSB Bank Plc v Marshall* [1998] 3 E.G.L.R. 100 at 102; [1998] Fam. Law 596 at 597 (R. Bailey-Harris).
[344] TLATA 1996 s.15(1).
[345] *Mortgage Corporation Ltd v Shaire* [2001] 3 W.L.R. 639; (2000) 64 Conv. 315 (S. Pascoe). See "To sell or not to sell: that is the question: the irony of the Trusts of Land and Appointment of Trustees Act 1996" (2011) 70 C.L.J. 579 (M.J.D.). See also "Equitable Co-ownership: Proprietary Rights in Name Only?" in *Modern Studies in Property Law*, Vol. 4, ed. E. Cooke (Oxford: Hart Publishing, 2006) (M.J.D.).

already been discussed.[346] The remaining four are considered in detail below.[347] It has been explained[348] that this list is not exhaustive, and that in a given situation not only may there be other considerations, but two or more of the matters specifically listed may conflict, and the court will therefore have to decide which is to be given the greater weight. It should be noted that these factors must be taken into account in all cases, regardless of who the applicant may be, including where the applicant does not have proprietary priority over those wishing to resist sale,[349] except where a trustee in bankruptcy applies for an order.[350] Rather different principles then govern the application.[351]

13–065   (1) THE INTENTIONS OF THE PERSON WHO CREATED THE TRUST. This is most likely to be relevant in cases where the trust has been expressly created, and the intentions of the settlor may be discernable. There seems no reason why the settlor should not indicate his intentions in the trust instrument expressly or by necessary implication.[352] Thus one reason why a settlor may choose to create an express trust for sale after 1996,[353] is because he wishes to make it clear that the trustees should sell the land.[354] Where two or more people created the trust, "intention" means a common intention (not each party's current competing intention) and also an intention that was held at the time the trust was created.[355]

13–066   (2) THE PURPOSES FOR WHICH THE PROPERTY SUBJECT TO THE TRUST IS HELD. Prior to 1997, it had long been the practice on an application for sale by a co-owner[356] for the court to have regard to the underlying purpose of the trust.[357] The court considered whether the object of the trust was indeed to sell

---

[346] See TLATA 1996 ss.15(2) (views of beneficiaries entitled to occupy on an application relating to the trustees' power to exclude or restrict the right to occupy), 15(3) (circumstances and wishes of the beneficiaries of full age entitled to an interest in possession); above, para.12–022.

[347] TLATA 1996 s.15(1).

[348] Above, para.12–022.

[349] e.g. because a co-owner has an overriding interest after a failure to overreach, *Bank of Ireland Home Mortgages Ltd v Bell*, (2001) 2 F.L.R. 809; (2002) 66 Conv. 61 (R. Probert). This is not strictly a dispute between the co-owners, but a mortgagee has power to apply under TLATA s.14, above para.13–064. Although a non-priority secured creditor undoubtedly may apply for, and the court undoubtedly has the power to order, a sale (the priority co-owner being paid first out of the proceeds of sale), it is arguable that the court does not give sufficient weight to the fact that the creditor lacks priority: above.

[350] TLATA 1996 s.15(4).

[351] Below, para.13–070.

[352] See *Olszanecki v Hillocks* [2002] EWHC 1997 (Ch) where the proven intention of one (now deceased) co-owner was to allow the other to remain in occupation and so sale was refused when requested by the deceased co-owner's heir.

[353] cf. above, para.12–005.

[354] cf. *Barclay v Barclay* [1970] 2 Q.B. 677.

[355] *White v White* [2003] EWCA Civ 924, [2004] 2 F.L.R. 321.

[356] The same was true where the co-owner was a trustee who sought an order for possession: *Bull v Bull* [1955] 1 Q.B. 234.

[357] *Re Buchanan-Wollaston's Conveyance* [1939] Ch. 738; *Jones v Challenger* [1961] 1 Q.B. 176; *Re Evers' Trust* [1980] 1 W.L.R. 1327; *Harris v Harris* (1995) 72 P. & C.R. 408.

the land[358] or to retain it for some secondary or collateral purpose.[359] This practice has now been made statutory. Once again, there seems no reason why a settlor should not set out the purposes of the trust expressly when he creates it.

The cases decided prior to 1997 on trusts for sale provide guidance as to what, in the absence of any express statement, constitutes a purpose and when it is at an end.[360] Many of them arose on the separation of married or unmarried couples. Where there were no children, the underlying purpose of the trust was regarded as the provision of a home for the parties while the relationship subsisted.[361] Neither party had a right to demand a sale until the termination of the relationship.[362] Even when the parties had separated, the court would decline to order a sale in appropriate circumstances,[363] or it might order a sale on terms.[364] This practice continues under s.14, and a sale may be postponed until a future date chosen by reference to a special interest of the occupying co-owner.[365] The power remains to refuse a sale indefinitely, especially if one co-owner has assured the other on relationship breakdown that she would not be evicted without her consent.[366] It is clear, therefore, that the outcome of an application for sale under s.14 is heavily dependant on the facts,[367] with no paramount obligation to sell.[368] Under the previous law,[369] the court had no power to act unless it made an order for sale.[370] However, it might have indicated that it would order a sale unless the party in occupation agreed to make some financial adjustment in favour of the other, e.g. by offering to pay an occupation rent pending an eventual sale.[371] After 1996, the court's powers are wider and it can act directly to achieve such a result. It may make any order relating to the exercise by the trustees of any of their functions as it thinks fit.[372] It could (for example) make an order for sale to take effect

---

[358] Because it was a trust *for sale*.

[359] *Jones v Challenger*, above, *Barclay v Barclay*, above.

[360] The issue is one of fact; see, e.g. *Harris v Harris*, above.

[361] *Jones v Challenger*, above, at 182; *Bernard v Josephs* [1982] Ch. 391 at 405.

[362] *Jones v Challenger*, above, at 182. Where the parties are married, the relationship may be regarded as terminated even if there has been no divorce: *Rawlings v Rawlings* [1964] P. 398 at 418, 419.

[363] *Bedson v Bedson* [1965] 2 Q.B. 66; *Hayward v Hayward* [1976] 1 E.G.L.R. 46 (no sale at behest of deserting spouse).

[364] *Ali v Hussein* (1974) 231 E.G. 372 (occupying co-owner given opportunity to buy out the other).

[365] *Chun v Ho* [2002] EWCA Civ 1075, sale postponed until a fixed time by when the occupying co-owner would have finished her studies.

[366] *Holman v Howes* [2007] EWCA Civ 877.

[367] See, e.g. *Smith v Smith*, [2009] EWCA Civ 1297; [2010] 1 F.L.R. 1402 where the fact that the home was larger than the party resisting sale could possibly require, when combined with the fact that it had been purchased originally as a family home, was sufficient to justify an order for sale on relationship breakdown.

[368] *Oke v Rideout* [1998] C.L.Y. 4876, sale refused.

[369] i.e. where there had been an application to the court under LPA 1925 s.30.

[370] *Bernard v Josephs*, above, at 410. See too *Dennis v McDonald* [1982] Fam. 63 at 73, 74.

[371] *Bernard v Josephs*, above, at 410. See too *Dennis v McDonald* [1982] Fam. 63 at 73, 74. See (1982) 98 L.Q.R. 519 (F. Webb); [1984] Conv. 103 (M. P. Thompson).

[372] TLATA 1996 s.14(2).

at some future date, and, in the interim, exclude one of the co-owners on terms that the other compensate him.[373]

13–067 Because the court must have regard to the purpose for which the trust was created, a co-owner's right to a sale may be restricted by agreement or by his conduct.[374] If a trustee-beneficiary has covenanted to sell only with another co-owner's consent, the court will not normally assist him to break his contract by forcing a sale against the other co-owner's wishes.[375] Similarly where one co-owner has been induced to move house and contribute to the purchase of a new home in reliance on an assurance that he could remain there, the other co-owner is unlikely to obtain an order for sale.[376] It should be noted, however, that as the purpose for which the property is held is now just one of the factors that a court is required to take into account in exercising its discretion, there might be circumstances where the other factors outweighed the purpose, notwithstanding the objecting co-owner's personal circumstances or conduct.[377]

Where the co-owners are married, or in civil partnership, and the relationship comes to an end on divorce or dissolution, any application for sale should be heard by the court that is dealing with any application for ancillary relief.[378] The court then has extensive discretionary powers and may make a property adjustment order.[379] In practice it will be the exercise of those powers that is determinative.[380]

---

[373] See TLATA 1996 s.13(6). In *Stack v Dowden*, [2007] 2 A.C. 432, the House of Lords (by majority) refused Mr Stack's request for compensation under this section on the ground that he would not be kept out of his money for long. Lord Neuberger, dissenting on this point, felt that although the case for compensation was weak under the statutory criteria, on balance the factors listed in s.14 leaned towards an award, in particular that a payment would not compromise the interests of the children. The other factors were neutral or irrelevant. He was bolstered in this view by the fact that the parties had already agreed a payment, which was now disputed by Ms Dowden.

[374] *Holman v Howes*, above.

[375] *Re Buchanan-Wollaston's Conveyance*, above.

[376] *Charlton v Lester* [1976] 1 E.G.L.R. 131; *Jones v Jones* [1977] 1 W.L.R. 438.

[377] This might occur where, e.g. a creditor of one of the co-owners is seeking a sale and the court takes the view that the creditor should not be kept out of its money, *Putnam & Sons v Taylor* [2009] EWHC 317 (Ch).

[378] *Williams v Williams* [1976] Ch. 278. At p.286, Roskill L.J. suggested that, "nowadays it is desirable that applications should be made under all the relevant sections of all the modern legislation". However, an application under TLATA is not precluded in such circumstances, and may be granted, *Smith v Smith* [2009].

[379] Matrimonial Causes Act 1973 (as amended by the Matrimonial Homes and Property Act 1981 and the Matrimonial and Family Proceedings Act 1984), ss.24, 24A, 25, 25A (s.24A expressly confers a power of sale, but only when the court has made an order for financial provision of a property adjustment order: see *Wicks v Wicks* [1999] Fam. 65 at 80). See *Harman v Glencross* [1986] Fam. 81 at 96. The existence of these statutory powers influenced the manner in which the discretion to order a sale under LPA 1925 s.30 was exercised in cases where MCA 1973 was inapplicable, as where the parties either chose not to divorce or were not married: see *Re Evers' Trust* [1980] 1 W.L.R. 1327 at 1332, 1333; *Dennis v McDonald*, above, at 73, 74; *Bernard v Josephs* [1982] Ch. 391 at 410; [1984] Conv. 103 (M. P. Thompson). For civil partnership see CPA 2004 ss.65–72.

[380] As explained above, para.12–021, it seems unlikely that TLATA 1996 s.14(2) confers on the court any specific power to vary beneficial interests under a trust of land, although in determining the share of those interests under the rubric in *Stack*, above, the court may come very close to doing that.

(3) THE WELFARE OF ANY MINOR WHO OCCUPIES OR MIGHT REASONABLY BE **13–068** EXPECTED TO OCCUPY ANY LAND SUBJECT TO THE TRUST AS HIS HOME. Prior to 1997, in cases where the co-owners were either married or lived together as man and wife, there was some uncertainty as to the relevance of any children in determining both the purpose of the trust and whether, on the termination of the couple's relationship, that purpose had come to an end. In some cases it was held that the purpose of the trust was to provide a family home. A sale would not be ordered therefore merely because the relationship between the parents had terminated, but only when accommodation was no longer required for the children.[381] In other cases the court took the view that as the children were not beneficiaries under the trust for sale, their interests could only be taken into account incidentally as a factor which affected the equities between the two co-owners.[382] This uncertainty has now been resolved by the 1996 Act. In an application made under the Act for an order of sale, the court must take into account the welfare of any minor.[383]

As already explained, where the co-owners are married or in civil partnership and the issue of sale arises on divorce, it is likely to be subsumed in any order which the court makes for ancillary relief under the Matrimonial Causes Act 1973 or Civil Partnership Act 2004. In such proceedings,[384] the court will take into account the welfare of any child who is a minor.[385] Where the co-owners are not married, provision of a home for a child may be obtained in one of two ways, namely under the Children Act 1989 or under the Trusts of Land and Appointment of Trustees Act 1996.[386] Under the Children Act 1989, the court has power to make an order requiring one parent to transfer property either to the other or to the child for the benefit of that child, or to create a settlement for the benefit of that child.[387] However, there are constraints on the court when exercising its discretion in such a case. Commonly it will be the mother who is seeking an order. However, where the parents are

---

[381] *Williams v Williams* [1976] Ch. 278; *Re Evers' Trust*, above. See too *Rawlings v Rawlings* [1964] P. 398 at 419.

[382] *Burke v Burke* [1974] 1 W.L.R. 1063; *Re Densham* [1975] 1 W.L.R. 1519 at 1531; *Re Bailey* [1977] 1 W.L.R. 278; *Re Holliday* [1981] Ch. 405 at 417. For attempts to reconcile the authorities, see *Cousins v Dzosens, The Times*, December 12, 1981; *Chhokar v Chhokar* [1984] F.L.R. 313 at 327 (where Cumming-Bruce L.J. suggested that, "as a matter of common sense, the arrangements made by the court should take proper account of the need of the children for accommodation").

[383] And in considering whether to make an order for compensation, *Stack*, above, per Lord Neuberger.

[384] There is little practice yet in relation to civil partnership.

[385] MCA 1973 s.25(3) (substituted by the Matrimonial and Family Proceedings Act 1984 s.3). See CPA 2004 s.72 and Sch.5 which makes provision for civil partners corresponding to that available under the MCA 1973.

[386] In practice, applications may be made under both Acts. See [1998] Fam. Law 349 at 350 et seq. (E. Cooke). An application will probably be made under the provisions of the Children Act 1989 alone only where the applicant has no interest in the property.

[387] s.15; Sch.1. These provisions are applicable where the parents are married and in some cases where they are unmarried. Where the parents are unmarried, a claim under the Children Act 1989 will lie only against the biological parent of the child and not against a step-parent even if he treats the child as a child of the family: see *J v J (A Minor: Property Transfer)* [1993] 2 F.L.R. 56. The provision is amended to incorporate civil partnerships, CPA 2004 s.78.

unmarried, she has no right to be supported by the other, and in the absence of any interest in the property, "no right in herself to have even a roof over her head".[388] There is therefore a concern that the court's order may be seen to confer a "windfall" on her.[389] The court is likely to peg the duration of such orders in favour of the children to the period required for their education. Thereafter the property reverts to the father, because the children cease to have any continuing claim on him.[390] Where the mother is a co-owner and seeks an order under the Trusts of Land and Appointment of Trustees Act 1996, she does so on her own behalf, rather than on behalf of the children (as is the case under the Children Act 1989). On such an application, the court will have regard to all circumstances, including the interests of the children. In practice, it seems likely that, in many such cases, the court will make an order postponing any sale of the family home during the period of the children's minority, and perhaps not until their education is finished (if that is later).[391] The proceeds of sale will then be split between the parents according to their interests.

13–069   (4) THE INTERESTS OF ANY SECURED CREDITOR OF ANY BENEFICIARY.[392] Prior to 1997, where a secured creditor of a co-owner applied for a sale of property,[393] the principle that the court applied was the same as in cases of insolvency.[394] That principle, explained more fully below,[395] was that the voice of the creditor would normally prevail and a sale would be ordered in the absence of exceptional circumstances.[396] This was held to apply:

(i) where a creditor obtained a charging order[397] against the beneficial interest of a co-owner[398];

(ii) where a creditor had a mortgage over a property with a registered

---

[388] *T v S* (Financial Provision for Children) [1994] 2 F.L.R. 883 at 890, per Johnson J.

[389] *T v S* (Financial Provision for Children) [1994] 2 F.L.R. 883 at 890, per Johnson J. cf. *Pearson v Franklin* [1994] 1 W.L.R. 370 at 375, 376.

[390] *T v S* (Financial Provision for Children), above, at 891. See too *A v A* (A Minor: Financial Provision) [1994] 1 F.L.R. 657.

[391] cf. *Martin-Sklan v White* [2006] EWHC 3313 (Ch), an application in relation to bankruptcy (below) where there were other factors supporting a postponement.

[392] See (1985) 5 O.J.L.S. 132 (N. P. Gravells); [1995] J.B.L. 384 (S. Cooper). These must now be read subject to TLATA 1996 ss.14, 15.

[393] Under LPA 1925 s.30. As now with TLATA 1996 s.14, an application would be necessary only if the secured creditor was *not* a mortgagee with priority over all the co-owners. With such priority, a mortgagee may sell in exercise of their paramount power of sale.

[394] See *Lloyds Bank Plc v Byrne* [1993] 1 F.L.R. 369; *Zandfarid v B.C.C.I. International SA* [1996] 1 W.L.R. 1420, 1429.

[395] Below, para.13–071.

[396] For a case in which the circumstances were exceptional, see *Halifax Mortgage Services Ltd v Muirhead* (1997) 76 P. & C.R. 418 (charge in favour of the creditor had not been executed by the debtor, but had been altered by the creditor's solicitors).

[397] Charging Orders Act 1979 s.2; below, para.13–076.

[398] *Lloyds Bank Plc v Byrne*, above; *Barclays Bank Plc v Hendricks* [1996] 1 F.L.R. 258.

title, but that charge was subject to the overriding interest of a co-owner[399];

(iii) where one co-owner forged the signature of the other on a mortgage of the property which they owned, so that it was binding only on the beneficial interest of the forger[400]; and

(iv) where although both co-owners had executed a mortgage in favour of a creditor, it was rescinded as against one of them because it had been induced by the fraud or undue influence of the other.[401]

Although, it was not certain whether these principles would still apply after 1996, the (relatively scarce) evidence is that the courts prefer to take a broadly similar view. First, although the interests of any secured creditor of any beneficiary are just one factor that a court is now required to take into account on an application for an order under s.14 of the Trusts of Land and Appointment of Trustees Act 1996,[402] they appear to continue to carry considerable weight.[403] Generally, when a secured creditor applies for a sale, the court does "not consider it is right to put off the evil day indefinitely and effectively keep the claimant out of its money with no prospect of any recovery in the near future".[404] Secondly, where such an application is made by the trustee of a bankrupt's estate, those factors do not apply.[405] Although this makes it clear that the analogy with bankruptcy need not be applied, and that a much more flexible approach is available when a secured creditor's interests are in issue,[406] this has not yet been fully argued.[407] Neither has there been full

---

[399] *Bank of Baroda v Dhillon* [1998] 1 F.L.R. 324. In such circumstances, the creditor could not have obtained an order for possession against the beneficiary having an overriding interest: see *Williams & Glyn's Bank Ltd v Boland* [1981] A.C. 487; *Kemmis v Kemmis* [1988] 1 W.L.R. 1307.

[400] *Bankers Trust Co v Namdar* [1997] E.G.C.S. 20; [1996] Conv. 371 (A. Dunn); above, para.13–039.

[401] *Zandfarid v B.C.C.I. International SA*, above, at 1428–1430. See below, para.25–120.

[402] Under TLATA 1996 s.15(1).

[403] *Bank of Ireland Home Mortgages Ltd v Bell* (2001) 2 All E.R. (Comm) 920; *First National Bank Plc v Achampong* (2003), Case No. B2/2002/1986; *TSB Bank v Marshall* (1998) 2 F.L.R. 769. But contrast *Edwards v Lloyds TSB* [2004] EWHC 1745 (Ch); *Mortgage Corp Ltd v Shaire* [2001] 3 W.L.R. 639 and *Alliance & Leicester Plc v Slayford* [2001] 1 All E.R. (Comm) 1 where a sale was refused or postponed. See also *Pritchard Englefield v Steinberg* [2004] EWHC 1908 (Ch), where a sale was also ordered but it is not clear whether (or why) the co-owner had priority over the chargee.

[404] *Putnam & Sons v Taylor* [2009] EWHC 317 (Ch) at para. 36. But note the more lenient view taken in *Close Invoice Finance v Pile* [2008] EWHC 1580 (Ch), where the s.15 factors were relevant by analogy (the case was under CPR r.73.10(1) as both co-owners were subject to the charging order) and the judge was persuaded to order an 18 month postponement of sale.

[405] TLATA 1996 s.15(4). The application is then governed by IA 1986 s.335A (as inserted by TLATA 1996 s.25(1); Sch.3); below, para.13–070.

[406] In at least one case prior to 1997 the court did adopt a more flexible approach: see *Abbey National Plc v Moss* (1993) 26 H.L.R. 249. This case was criticised at the time because it could not be reconciled with earlier authorities: see [1994] Fam. Law 255 (S. M. Cretney).

[407] In *Alliance & Leicester Plc v Slayford*, above, sale was refused after an application under TLATA s.14 (the mortgagee not having priority over a co-owner), so the secured creditor proceeded to make the mortgagor bankrupt on his personal covenant to pay. Although the mortgagee thereby released its security, the chances of a sale were greatly enhanced and with it the prospect of recovering at least some money while finally bringing the saga to a conclusion.

consideration of whether it is appropriate, save in exceptional circumstances, to order sale in favour of a non-priority mortgagee who could have taken simple steps to secure priority (and thereby a power of sale as of right) at the time the mortgage was executed.[408]

(c) Bankruptcy of a co-owner

13–070 (1) APPLICATIONS TO THE COURT. Where a co-owner of land is bankrupt, his trustee in bankruptcy will commonly wish to obtain a sale of the property.[409] In deciding whether or not to exercise his powers, the trustee must not favour the interests of a secured creditor over the unsecured, but must act in the best interests of the bankrupt's estate.[410] Any application by him for an order relating to the exercise by trustees of land of any of their functions[411] must be made to the court having jurisdiction in relation to the bankruptcy.[412] The provisions of the Trusts of Land and Appointment of Trustees Act 1996, explained above,[413] which specify the matters which the court is to take into account in all other such applications[414] are excluded.[415] Instead the court is required to make such order as it thinks just and reasonable having regard to the interests of the bankrupt's creditors[416] and all the circumstances of the

See also *National Westminster Bank v Rushmer* [2010] EWHC 554 (Ch), [2010] 2 F.L.R. 362; *Hameed v Qayum* [2009] EWCA Civ. 352, [2009] 2 F.L.R. 962.

[408] Above para.13–064.

[409] Under the Insolvency Act 1986 s.283A, inserted by the Enterprise Act 2002 s.262, a bankrupt's dwelling-house (which includes an interest in such a house) which at the date of the bankruptcy was the sole or principal residence of: (a) the bankrupt, (b) the bankrupt's spouse, or (c) a former spouse of the bankrupt will cease to be part of the bankrupt's estate and will vest in the bankrupt at the end of three years beginning with the date of the bankruptcy, unless the interest has been realised or a possession order or an order for sale has been applied for. The trustee in bankruptcy may apply for orders extending this time limit. The effect, and intention, is that steps should be taken quickly to realise the bankrupt's assets, including applying for an order for sale.

[410] *Re Ng* [1998] 2 F.L.R. 386. The courts view with disfavour applications for sale by a trustee in bankruptcy where the principal creditor is a mortgagee which has chosen not to enforce its security, e.g. to avoid bad publicity, as in *Re Ng*. However, trustees in bankruptcy will be assumed to be the best judges of what is in the interests of the creditors in the absence of evidence that they acted to the contrary: *Judd v Brown* [1999] 1 F.L.R. 1191 at 1198.

[411] Under TLATA 1996 s.14.

[412] IA 1986 s.335A(1) (inserted by TLATA 1996 s.25(1), Sch.3). For the background to the legislation, see (1991) 107 L.Q.R. 177 (S. M. Cretney) (dealing with the precursor to the present provisions).

[413] Above, paras 13–064, 13–069.

[414] TLATA 1996 s.15.

[415] TLATA 1996 s.15(4). Prior to 1997, it had been suggested that the principle which applied in cases of bankruptcy was not in fact a special one, but was merely an application of the general rule that the court would look to the underlying purpose of the trust in considering whether to order a sale. Where property was acquired for the purpose of joint occupation that purpose came to an end when the interest of one of the co-owners vested in his trustee in bankruptcy: *Abbey National Plc v Moss* (1993) 26 H.L.R. 249 at 257 (criticised [1994] Fam. Law 255 (S. M. Cretney)). However, this was open to question. The purpose for which the co-owners acquired the property was considered to be irrelevant in relation to the trustee in bankruptcy because it was *res inter alios acta*: *Re Solomon* [1967] Ch. 573 at 589; *Re Holliday* [1981] Ch. 405 at 419; *Re Citro* [1991] Ch. 142 at 157. By virtue of TLATA 1996 s.15(4), this latter view necessarily prevails.

[416] Whether secured or unsecured: see *Judd v Brown*, above, at 1197. Even if there is unlikely to be any surplus on any sale to meet the claims of the creditors after discharging the expenses of the bankruptcy, a sale may still be justified. It is in the interests of the creditors that those

case other than the needs of the bankrupt.[417] Furthermore, where the application is made in respect of land which includes a dwelling-house which is or
has been the home of the bankrupt or his spouse or former spouse,[418] the court
must, in addition to these factors, have regard to:

> (i) the conduct of the spouse or former spouse, to the extent that it
>   contributed to the bankruptcy;
>
> (ii) the needs[419] and financial resources of the spouse or former
>   spouse; and
>
> (iii) the needs of any children.[420]

When the trustee in bankruptcy's application is made more than one year from
the date on which the property vested in the trustee in bankruptcy, the court
is required to assume, unless the circumstances of the case are exceptional,
that the interests of the bankrupt's creditors outweigh all other
considerations.[421]

(2) THE EXERCISE OF DISCRETION. These statutory provisions are essentially **13–071**
a codification of the rules previously applied at common law. The principle
underlying them is the same, namely, that in a case of insolvency a sale of the
land should be ordered by the court[422] in the absence of exceptional circumstances, even in the common case where the co-owners are spouses or
partners.[423] "A person must discharge his liabilities before there is any room
for being generous."[424]

(3) EXCEPTIONAL CIRCUMSTANCES. Where exceptional circumstances exist, **13–072**
the court may either refuse a sale altogether[425] or postpone it.[426] What
constitutes an exceptional circumstance is a question of fact in any given case
as to which the court will not lay down a list.[427] But, exceptional means
something "which is out of the ordinary course, or unusual, or special, or

expenses should, so far as possible, be discharged out of the bankrupt's assets: see *Trustee of the
Estate of Bowe v Bowe* (1994) [1998] 2 F.L.R. 439.

[417] IA 1986 s.335A(2)(a), (c). The "needs" of the bankrupt is to be interpreted widely, so the
court must exclude from consideration the psychological, emotional and medical needs of the
bankrupt as well as their financial needs, *Everitt v Budhram* [2009] EWHC 1219 (Ch), [2010] Ch.
170.

[418] The provision does not therefore apply to an unmarried couple: *Re Citro* [1991] Ch. 142 at
159.

[419] Also to be interpreted widely, *Everitt v Budhram* above.

[420] IA 1986 s.335A(2)(b). Also to be interpreted widely, *Everitt v Budhram* above.

[421] IA 1986 s.335A(3).

[422] Subject only to a short period of suspension to enable the bankrupt and his family to arrange
their affairs: *Re Lowrie* [1981] 3 All E.R. 353 at 355.

[423] See *Re Citro* [1991] Ch. 142 (the leading modern authority in which the earlier decisions
were reviewed). cf. (1991) 107 L.Q.R. 177 (S. M. Cretney); [1991] C.L.J. 45 (J. C. Hall).

[424] *Re Bailey* [1977] 1 W.L.R. 278 at 283, per Walton J.

[425] As in *Judd v Brown* [1998] 2 F.L.R. 360.

[426] As in *Re Raval* [1998] 2 F.L.R. 718.

[427] *Claughton v Charalambous* [1999] 1 F.L.R. 740 at 744.

uncommon. To be exceptional a circumstance need not be unique, unprece-
dented or very rare; but it cannot be one that is regularly, or routinely, or
normally encountered."[428] It was once argued that failure to consider carefully
whether there were any exceptional circumstances, by simply presuming a
sale after one year's grace, might involve contravention of art.8 of the
European Convention on Human Rights.[429] However, while it may true that an
automatic order for sale would raise concerns about compatibility with the
European Convention,[430] clearly it would also be contrary to the explicit
injunction of the Insolvency Act itself to consider a range of circumstances,
including exceptional ones. It is now established that the provisions of the Act
are compatible with the Convention, including the preference for sale after
one year, absent exceptional circumstances.[431]

The following are examples of exceptional circumstances which have either
arisen, or have been suggested:

    (i) where the bankrupt's spouse was seriously ill[432];

   (ii) where a house had been specially adapted for a handicapped
       child[433] or spouse;

  (iii) where the bankrupt was bankrupt on his own petition, was not
       being pressed by creditors, and the property was occupied by his
       former wife and his children[434];

  (iv) the need for the children to have a stable support network when
       their mother was an alcoholic and there was enough equity in the
       property even if a sale was delayed[435]; and

   (v) inordinate delay by the trustee[436] but not if this is neither inordi-
       nate nor disproportionate.[437]

---

[428] *Hosking v Michaelides* [2006] B.P.I.R. 1192, in reference to the IA s.336 (applicable where
the spouse has occupation rights under the Family Law Act 1986) which employs the same
concept.

[429] *Barca v Mears* (2005) 2 F.L.R. 1; (2005) Conv. 161 (M.J.D.).

[430] Especially post *Manchester City Council v Pinnock (No.2)* [2011] UKSC 6, [2011] 2
W.L.R. 220. Above para.???

[431] *Jackson v Bell* [2001] EWCA Civ 387; *Nicholls v Lan* [2006] EWHC 1255 (Ch); [2007] 1
F.L.R. 744; *Foyle v Turner* [2007] B.P.I.R. 24; *Turner v Avis* [2009] 1 F.L.R. 74.

[432] *Judd v Brown*, above; *Re Raval*, above; *Claughton v Charalambous*, *Everitt v Budhram*
above. See also *Re Bremner* [1999] B.P.I.R. 185, a case under IA 1986 s.336.

[433] *Re Bailey*, above, at 284; *Claughton v Charalambous*, above, at 744.

[434] *Re Holliday* [1981] Ch. 405, a decision described as being "very much against the run of
the recent authorities": *Harman v Glencross* [1986] Fam. 81 at 95, per Balcombe L.J. See too *Re
Citro*, above, at 157.

[435] *Martin-Sklan v White* [2006] EWHC 3313 (Ch). a case applying an equivalent test under IA
1986 s.337. There is no difference in the meaning of exceptional circumstances between the
various provisions of the IA 1986, *Hosking v Michaelides*, *Everitt v Budhram* above.

[436] *The Official Receiver for Northern Ireland v Rooney* [2009] B.P.I.R. 536, applying the
equivalent provision in Northern Ireland.

[437] *Foyle v Turner*; *Turner v Avis* above, where delay did not constitute an exceptional
circumstance. The provisions of the Enterprise Act 2002 are likely to make this ground otiose,
above para.13–070.

However, the court is unlikely to regard as exceptional the displacement of the bankrupt's wife and of any children, or her inability to buy a comparable home elsewhere.[438] Such circumstances are "the melancholy consequences of debt and improvidence with which every civilised society has been familiar".[439] Likewise, it is not an exceptional circumstance justifying postponement of sale that a bankrupt's creditors would still be repaid in full with statutory interest if the sale of the family home which he jointly owned with his former partner were to be delayed[440] or that a child attends a special school close to the property.[441] In *Nicholls v Lan*,[442] it appears that the mental and physical health of the co-owner resisting sale was regarded as an exceptional circumstance,[443] but that after balancing the interests of the creditors, an order for sale remained the most appropriate exercise of the jurisdiction. It is clear in this case that the trial judge did indeed balance the interests of the parties as required by the statute and the Convention, and that the appeal court was not prepared to disturb his findings. Thus, even the existence of exceptional circumstances will not necessarily mean a postponement of sale: a balance still needs to be weighed.

(d) Equitable accounting after sale.[444] Where property held on a trust of **13–073** land is sold following an application to the court under s.14 of the Trusts of Land and Appointment of Trustees Act 1996, it is often necessary to settle accounts between the co-owners (or if one of them is insolvent, his trustee in bankruptcy). This may be for one of three reasons. First, one of the co-owners may have left the property some time before the sale, and the party who remained may be held liable to pay an occupation rent for the period thereafter.[445] Secondly, one of the co-owners may have expended money on improvements to the premises. Neither party can take the benefit of an increase in the value of the property without making an allowance for what has been expended by the other in order to obtain it.[446] Credit will be given for the actual expenditure or for the amount by which the improvement has increased the value of the property, whichever is the lesser.[447] Thirdly, one of the parties may have paid the whole or a disproportionate part of the mortgage instalments. Credit will always be given for the capital element in such payments.

---

[438] *Re Citro*, above. For discussion see (1992) 55 M.L.R. 284 (D. Brown). See also *Re Karia* [2006] above.

[439] *Re Citro*, above, at 157, per Nourse L.J. See too *Re Lowrie* [1981] 3 All E.R. 353 at 356.

[440] *Donohoe v Ingram*, above.

[441] *Barca v Mears*, above. However, the educational difficulties were not severe and it was not clear that the child would have to change schools.

[442] [2007] 1 F.L.R. 744.

[443] Above, at para.43, 45.

[444] See [1995] Conv. 391 (E. Cooke); and below, para.13–101.

[445] *Re Pavlou* [1993] 1 W.L.R. 1046; above para.13–005. *Rahnema v Rahbari* [2008] 2 P. & C.R. DG5.

[446] *Leigh v Dickeson* (1884) 15 QBD 60 at 65, 67. This rule has its origin in equity practice in a partition suit.

[447] *Re Pavlou*, above, at 1049, cf. *Bernard v Josephs* [1982] Ch. 391 at 405, 408 (credit given for actual expenditure without reference to the increase in value of the property).

The interest element is often treated as being equal to an occupation rent and so disregarded.[448] This is not a rule of law however and the parties are entitled to insist that the occupation rent and the mortgage interest should each be separately calculated and that any difference between the two should be brought into account.[449]

In *Stack v Dowden*,[450] Baroness Hale noted that the statutory powers under TLATA 1996 s.13[451] have:

> "replaced the old doctrines of equitable accounting under which a beneficiary who remained in occupation might be required to pay an occupation rent to a beneficiary who was excluded from the property".

In *Murphy v Gooch*,[452] the Court of Appeal took the view that equitable accounting was no more than:

> "a body of (non-binding) guidelines or rules of convenience aimed at achieving justice between the co-owners. The thrust of these guidelines was that, where it is just to do so, co-owners may be given credit for monies paid and expenditure incurred on the jointly owned property, a co-owner in sole occupation of property may be charged with or required to give credit to his co-owner for an occupation rent and these credits may be offset against each other."[453]

As such, and following the dictum in *Stack*, the statutory principles must be applied in preference to "equitable accounting".

Note, however, while it is certain that there is overlap between the statutory jurisdiction and the equitable principles, and that the result may often be the same irrespective of what mechanism is employed,[454] there is no suggestion in TLATA 1996 that the equitable doctrine has in fact been abrogated.

13–074   **2. Charging orders.** Although charging orders are a form of security over property for the payment of a sum of money and therefore more properly belong in a chapter on mortgages, it is convenient to treat them in some detail here. This is because the most difficult issues in relation to such orders arise

---

[448] *Suttill v Graham* [1977] 1 W.L.R. 819. However, if one party has been ousted by the other, the fact that the remaining co-owner has paid all the mortgage instalments after that ouster will be disregarded and no credit will be given to him for paying the ousted party's share: *Cracknell v Cracknell* [1971] P. 356; *Shinh v Shinh* [1977] 1 All E.R. 97. cf. above, para.13–005.

[449] *Re Gorman* [1990] 1 W.L.R. 616 at 626; *Re Pavlou*, above, at 1051.

[450] Above, at para.94.

[451] Above, paras 12–027, 12–028.

[452] [2007] EWCA Civ 603, (2007) 2 F.L.R. 934.

[453] *Murphy v Gooch*, above, at para.10 per Lightman J.

[454] "Indeed, it may be that it would be a rare case when the equitable and statutory principles would produce a different result", *Murphy v Gooch*, above, at para.12.

in connection with land held upon trust.[455] These cannot be understood without an explanation of the system of charging orders.

(a) The nature of a charging order. Under the Charging Orders Act 1979,[456] **13–075**
a discretionary power is conferred on the court[457] to impose a charging order on the property of a debtor (including any land or interest in land which he owns[458]) to secure payment of any sum of money that is or will become payable under a judgment.[459] In deciding whether or not to make a charging order the court is required to consider all the circumstances of the case and, in particular, any evidence before it as to the personal circumstances of the debtor, and whether any other creditor of the debtor would be likely to be unduly prejudiced by the making of the order.[460] A charging order, when granted, has the same effect as if it were an equitable charge created by the debtor by writing under hand.[461] As such it may be enforced either by a sale of the property or by the appointment of a receiver.[462]

(b) Application to land held upon trust. Formerly the court could make a **13–076**
charging order on "any land or interest in land".[463] However these words were held not to include the interest of a beneficiary under a trust for sale, which by a strict application of the doctrine of conversion, was considered to be in the proceeds of sale and not in the land itself.[464] By contrast, where A and B held land on trust for themselves as joint tenants and a judgment was obtained against them jointly, a charging order could be imposed on the legal estate in the property.[465] This unsatisfactory situation was remedied by the Charging Orders Act 1979, and the doctrine of conversion has, in any event, been retrospectively abolished.[466] A charging order may now be imposed on:

(i) land or any interest in land which is held by the debtor beneficially[467];

---

[455] Prior to the abolition of the doctrine of conversion by TLATA 1996 s.3(1) (above, para.12–006), there were a number of difficulties in relation to charging orders and interests under a trust for sale: see below, para.13–076.

[456] The Act gives effect to the recommendations of the Law Commission: (1976) Law Com. No.74. It replaces AJA 1956 s.35, which itself replaced LPA 1925 s.195. Charging orders on land were first introduced by the Judgments Act 1838 s.13. See *Irani Finance Ltd v Singh* [1971] Ch. 59 at 76–78; (1984) 100 L.Q.R. 86 at 90–93 (J.S. Anderson).

[457] For the appropriate court, see the Charging Orders Act 1979 s.1(2).

[458] Charging Orders Act 1979 s.2; considered below.

[459] Charging Orders Act 1979 s.1. Charging orders may also be made in certain criminal proceedings: see the Criminal Justice Act 1988; Drug Trafficking Act 1994.

[460] Charging Orders Act 1979 s.1(5).

[461] Charging Orders Act 1979 s.3(4); *First National Securities Ltd v Hegerty* [1985] Q.B. 850 at 863.

[462] *Midland Bank Plc v Pike* [1988] 2 All E.R. 434 at 435.

[463] AJA 1956 s.35.

[464] *Irani Finance Ltd v Singh*, above, criticised [1971] C.L.J. 46 (M. J. Pritchard); (1971) 34 M.L.R. 441(S. M. Cretney); and see above, para.10–030.

[465] *National Westminster Bank Ltd v Allen* [1971] 2 Q.B. 718.

[466] TLATA 1996 s.3(1); above, para.12–006.

[467] Charging Orders Act 1979 s.2(1)(a)(i). A charging order over property held on trust should not be made under this paragraph: *Clark v Chief Land Registrar* [1993] Ch. 294 at 305 (on appeal, [1994] Ch. 370).

(ii) any interest of the debtor's under any trust of land[468];

(iii) land held on trust where the judgment is against the trustee as such[469];

(iv) land held on a bare trust for the debtor[470]; or

(v) land held on trust for two or more debtors who together hold the whole beneficial interest under the trust unencumbered and for their own benefit.[471]

The Land Charges Act 1972 and the Land Registration Act 2002 apply to charging orders as they apply to other writs or orders for the purpose of enforcing judgments.[472] In the case of land with unregistered title, a charging order can be registered as a land charge only if it is a "writ or order affecting land".[473] A charging order made against the interest of a beneficiary under a trust of land cannot be registered in this way.[474] Where the title is registered, a judgment creditor may enter a notice when the charging order relates to the legal title.[475] Where the charging order relates to a beneficial interest under a trust of land, it should be protected by the entry of a restriction.[476] However, where the charging order would in the case of unregistered land have been registrable as a land charge, it may now be protected by the entry of a notice rather than by a caution.[477]

13–077   *(c) Procedure.*[478] On an application for a charging order by a judgment creditor (which is invariably made without notice) the court may make an interim order. The court will direct that a copy of any such order be served on the judgment debtor, and, where it relates to an interest under a trust, on some or all of the trustees. It may direct that a copy should also be served on any other creditor of the debtor or on any other interested person. The matter is then adjourned for further consideration inter partes. In those proceedings, the court may make the charging order final (with or without modifications[479]) or discharge it. The court may however order the postponement of the execution

---

[468] Charging Orders Act 1979 s.2(1)(a)(ii).

[469] Charging Orders Act 1979 s.2(1)(b)(i).

[470] Charging Orders Act 1979 s.2(1)(b)(ii).

[471] Charging Orders Act 1979 s.2(1)(b)(iii). This paragraph is intended to cover the situation that arose in *National Westminster Bank Ltd v Allen*, above.

[472] Charging Orders Act 1979 s.3(2).

[473] LCA 1972 s.6(1)(a).

[474] LCA 1972 s.6(1A) (inserted by TLATA 1996 s.25(1), Sch.3). This is logical. As beneficial interests under trusts of land are not themselves registrable as land charges but are protected by overreaching, charging orders which bind such interests should be treated in the same manner. cf. *Perry v Phoenix Assurance Plc* [1988] 1 W.L.R. 940; [1989] Conv. 133 (N.S. Price).

[475] Charging Orders Act 1979 s.3(2).

[476] Ruoff & Roper, 44.009.15.

[477] LRR 2003 Rule 93(k).

[478] See generally CPR Part 73 and Practice Direction 73. See too *Roberts Petroleum Ltd v Bernard Kenny Ltd* [1983] 2 A.C. 192 at 204.

[479] The court may attach conditions to the order: Charging Orders Act 1979 s.3(1).

of the order.[480] Although the jurisdiction to grant a charging order is discretionary:

> "a judgment creditor is in general entitled to enforce a money judgement which he has lawfully obtained against a judgment debtor by all or any of the means of execution prescribed by the relevant rules of court".[481]

The burden of showing cause why an interim charging order should not be made absolute rests on the judgment debtor.[482] The court may decline to make the order final because of events which have occurred subsequent to the interim order, such as supervening insolvency of the debtor,[483] or the sale of the property to a purchaser who acquired it without notice of the order.[484]

The judgment debtor or any person interested in any property to which the charging order relates may apply to the court at any time to have the order discharged or varied.[485] Where a charging order is imposed on the beneficial interest of one co-owner, the other is a person interested for these purposes.[486] This is because a creditor will normally enforce such a charging order by an application to the court for the sale of the property under s.14 of the Trusts of Land and Appointment of Trustees Act 1996.[487] Although the co-owner whose interest is not affected by the charging order would be entitled to his share of the proceeds of any sale, he will commonly not wish to see the property sold.

(d) Charging orders and the family home. Where a creditor seeks a charging order against the beneficial interest of a co-owner, the court has a discretion not only whether to make the order absolute,[488] but if it does, whether to order an immediate sale to enforce the charge.[489] The exercise of this discretion has caused some difficulty where two people are joint owners of the family home and a charging order is sought against the one of their beneficial interests.[490] **13–078**

---

[480] The court may attach conditions to the order: Charging Orders Act 1979 s.3(1); *Austin-Fell v Austin-Fell* [1990] Fam. 172.

[481] *Roberts Petroleum Ltd v Bernard Kenny Ltd* [1982] 1 W.L.R. 301 at 307, per Lord Brandon. The House of Lords affirmed this principle but reversed the decision on appeal: [1983] 2 A.C. 192. See *First National Securities Ltd v Hegerty* [1985] Q.B. 850 at 866, 867.

[482] *Roberts Petroleum Ltd v Bernard Kenny Ltd* [1982] 1 W.L.R. 301 at 307.

[483] *Roberts Petroleum Ltd v Bernard Kenny Ltd* [1983] 2 A.C. 192 (where the debtor was a company which went into liquidation).

[484] *Howell v Montey* (1990) 61 P. & C.R. 18.

[485] Charging Orders Act 1979 s.3(5). Presumably such an application would have to be made before the order was executed.

[486] *Harman v Glencross* [1986] Fam. 81.

[487] Above, paras 13–064, 13–069.

[488] Charging Orders Act 1979 ss.1(5), 3(1).

[489] TLATA 1996 ss.14, 15; above, para.13–069; *First National Securities Ltd v Hegerty*, above, at 856 (a case on LPA 1925 s.30).

[490] For discussion see [1985] Conv. 129 (P. F. Smith); (1985) 5 O.J.L.S. 132 (N. P. Gravells); [1986] Conv. 218 (J. Warburton); [1989] Fam. Law 438; [1993] Fam. Law 184 (S. M. Cretney). These must now be read subject to TLATA 1996 ss.14, 15 and the same considerations would apply if the roles were reversed or the couple were civil partners.

13–079   (1) WHERE NO DIVORCE OR SIMILAR PROCEEDINGS ARE PENDING BETWEEN THE PARTIES. Prior to 1997, where no divorce proceedings were pending between the parties and there were no exceptional circumstances, the court normally exercised its discretion in favour of the creditor both in making the charging order absolute[491] and in ordering an immediate sale of the property (subject only to a short postponement) on an application by the creditor under the now repealed s.30 of the Law of Property Act 1925.[492] As explained above, this may no longer be the case on an application under s.14 of the Trusts of Land and Appointment of Trustees Act 1996, although the matter is not settled.[493] The interests of any secured creditor are now only one factor that the court is directed to consider even in the absence of exceptional circumstances, but there is authority which indicates that this is a powerful factor.[494]

13–080   (2) WHERE DIVORCE PROCEEDINGS ARE PENDING BETWEEN THE PARTIES.[495] Where divorce proceedings are pending, the court normally directs that the charging order application should be transferred to the Family Division so that both sets of proceedings can be heard together.[496] Even prior to 1997, the court would normally prefer the claims of the wife and any children over those of the husband's creditor[497] and would usually make the charging order absolute but postpone its enforcement until any children of the marriage had reached a specified age.[498] In exceptional circumstances the court might even make a property adjustment order transferring the husband's interest in the home to the wife, which would necessarily defeat any charging order obtained by a creditor.[499] The position is not different after 1996[500] especially as a court need not order a sale almost as a matter of course on the application of a secured creditor.[501]

---

[491] *First National Securities Ltd v Hegerty*, above.

[492] *Lloyds Bank Plc v Byrne* [1993] 1 F.L.R. 369; above, para.13–069. Most of the cases concern spouses, but the same principles apply to unmarried cohabitants and civil partners. Indeed, it would not be different in principle if the co-owners were in no emotional relationship, save that there is likely to be less reason to postpone sale.

[493] Above, paras 13–068, 13–069. The cases do not treat a creditor with a charging order over co-owned land any differently from a secured creditor under a mortgage. For whether they should, see *To sell or not to sell* (M.J.D.) above fn.345.

[494] Above, para.13–072.

[495] It seems clear that the same principles would apply to dissolution of a civil partnership.

[496] *Harman v Glencross* [1986] Fam. 81.

[497] This was controversial: for a different view see *First National Securities Ltd v Hegerty*, above at 868, per Stephenson L.J. ("the court should not use its powers under Pt II of the Matrimonial Causes Act 1973 to override the claims of a creditor seeking security for a debt by a charging order").

[498] *Harman v Glencross*, above, at 99, 104; *Austin-Fell v Austin-Fell*, above. For the form of such a *Mesher* order see *Mesher v Mesher* (1973) [1980] 1 All E.R. 126. Sale is commonly postponed until the children reach the age of 17 or 18.

[499] This was in fact the situation in *Harman v Glencross*, above. If the husband is subsequently adjudged bankrupt such a transfer may be challenged as a transaction at an undervalue or as a preference: IA 1986 ss.339, 340. But see *Re Abbott* [1983] Ch. 45; *Harman v Glencross*, above, at 97.

[500] Above 13–078.

[501] See above, para.13–069.

3. Proposals for reform. It has been explained that the law governing   **13–081**
co-ownership has been reformed as a result of the introduction of the trust of
land and the abolition of the doctrine of conversion as it applied to trusts for
sale.[502] Mention should be made of certain earlier proposals for reform made
by the Law Commission, none of which has been implemented.

(a) Statutory co-ownership of the matrimonial home. In 1978 the Commis-   **13–082**
sion recommended that there should be a statutory scheme of co-ownership of
the matrimonial home by which married couples would automatically have an
equitable half share in the property.[503] A Bill to implement the proposals[504]
was introduced into Parliament in 1979 but failed to complete all its stages. In
1988 the Law Commission proposed a more limited reform. It recommended
that the purchase of property by one or both spouses for their joint use or
benefit should give rise to joint ownership of that property subject to a
contrary intention on the part of the purchasing spouse, known to the other
spouse,[505] but this was not accepted by the Government.

(b) The rights of cohabitants. After extensive consultation,[506] the Law   **13–083**
Commission has produced proposals for property adjustment legislation for
eligible unmarried cohabitants.[507] It would not apply to married couples or
civil partners because jurisdiction already exists for these cases.[508] The proposed scheme does not envisaged mandatory co-ownership of the family
home, nor presumptions of such, but instead favours a structured discretion
for property adjustment for certain types of unmarried cohabitants, provided
they are in a lawful intimate relationship.[509] There would be eligibility
thresholds based on the length of the relationship[510] and the ability to opt out.
Parliament would have to decide whether the scheme applied only to those
eligible unmarried cohabitants with children, or where no children were
involved.

The discretion would be structured to re-balance the cohabitants' position
on relationship breakdown in the light of what they brought to the relationship, and what they gained or forwent because of it. The discretion would not
be unlimited and wide-ranging in the sense of that enjoyed on the breakdown
of marriage or civil partnership because mere cohabitation, even for the

---

[502] Above, paras 12–003 et seq.

[503] (1978) Law Com. No.86. For criticism see (1978) 94 L.Q.R. 26 (A.A.S. Zuckerman), but
cf. [1983] J.S.W.L. 67 (A. Evans).

[504] Matrimonial Homes (Co-Ownership) Bill (introduced by Lord Simon of Glaisdale).

[505] (1988) Law Com. No.175.

[506] See Law Commission Consultation Paper No.179, *Cohabitation: The Financial Consequences of Relationship Breakdown* 2006.

[507] Report No.307 of July 31, 2007, *Cohabitation: The Financial Consequences of Relationship
Breakdown.*

[508] Above para.13–068.

[509] Thus co-habitation by extended families (e.g. parents and children) and others would be
outside the jurisdiction. The proposed scheme is seen as a response to relationship breakdown (as
the title makes clear) rather than a measure concerning co-ownership per se.

[510] The proposals are not firm in this regard, the Commission proposing a threshold of between
two and five years. As this is not simply a legal question, the Law Commission suggest that
Parliament decide. The Government has indicated that implementation will be postponed until the
impact of similar legislation in Scotland is assessed.

necessary period of time, would not entitle the applicant to financial relief. Applicants would have to demonstrate that they were eligible for financial relief by establishing "qualifying contributions" to the parties' relationship (not necessarily the property itself) and relief would be available where the applicant could show an economic disadvantage, or where the respondent retained a benefit, as a result of the applicant's contributions to the relationship. At present, there is no indication that these proposals will be enacted.

13–084   *(c) Registration of the rights of co-owners.* In 1982, in response to the conveyancing problems which arose out of the decision of the House of Lords in *Williams & Glyn's Bank Ltd v Boland*,[511] and by way of an addendum to its earlier proposals,[512] the Commission put forward a hybrid scheme by which the rights of co-owners would be both registrable and overreachable. Under this scheme, it would have remained the case that the beneficial interests of any co-owner would have been overreached if a purchaser paid the purchase money to the trustees (of whom there would have to be not less than two) or to a trust corporation. However if the purchaser had failed to comply with these requirements and paid the purchase money to just one trustee, he would not have been bound by the interests of the beneficiaries unless they had been registered either as land charges (where the title was unregistered) or by notice on the register (where the title was registered).[513] It was also proposed that the consent of both spouses would have been required to any disposition of the matrimonial home. These proposals were much criticised and were abandoned.[514] A more limited version of the Law Commission's scheme, which would have required co-owners other than spouses to register their beneficial interests to protect them against purchasers in cases where there was only one trustee for sale, was introduced into Parliament in 1985 but withdrawn.[515]

D. The Vesting of the Legal Estate

13–085   The various provisions which impose the statutory trust of land also limit the number of the trustees in accordance with the principle that in settlements and trusts of land there shall not be more than four trustees.[516] The rules are as follows.

1. Unregistered land

13–086   *(a) Tenancies in common.* A conveyance of land to trustees of land on trust for tenants in common is subject to the general rule which limits the number

---

[511] [1981] A.C. 487. See above, paras 7–089, 8–019.

[512] (1978) Law Com. No.86, above.

[513] (1982) Law Com. No.115. A new category of land charge, Class G, was proposed. For land charges, see above, para.8–062. For the LRA 2002 see para.7–070.

[514] See [1982] Conv. 393 (J.T. Farrand); [1983] J.S.W.L. 67 (A. Evans); (1987) Law Com. No.158, para.2.7. For the view that, although these proposals were rejected, the courts have since their publication "been pursuing a policy which is in many respects very similar to that of the Commission", see [1993] Fam. Law 231 (J. Dewar).

[515] Land Registration and Law of Property Bill. See (1987) Law Com. No.158, para.1.3.

[516] There is no restriction on the number of trustees who may hold land on trust for charitable, ecclesiastical or public purposes: see TA 1925 s.34(3).

of trustees of land to four.[517] If the conveyance is made to the tenants in common themselves, and they are of full age, it operates as a conveyance "to the grantees, or if there are more than four grantees, to the first four named in the conveyance, as joint tenants in trust for the persons interested in the land"[518] A gift of land by will to, or on trust for[519] tenants in common operates as a gift to the testator's personal representatives in trust for the persons interested in the land.[520] The number of personal representatives cannot exceed four.[521]

(b) Joint tenancies. There are no provisions dealing expressly with the **13–087** number of persons in whom the legal estate can be vested when two or more persons are beneficially entitled as joint tenants.[522] But the trust of land arising in such cases is subject to the general provision that in a disposition of land on trust of land the number of trustees shall not exceed four, and "where more than four persons are named as such trustees, the first four named (who are willing and able to act) shall alone be the trustees".[523] In the case of a devise to joint tenants, the general rules against more than four personal representatives[524] or trustees of land[525] prevent the legal estate from vesting in or being conveyed to more than four persons.

2. Registered land. Where registered land is subject to a trust of land, the **13–088** land is registered in the names of the trustees.[526] The statutory restrictions affecting the number of persons entitled to hold land on a trust of land apply as much to registered land as they do where the title is unregistered.[527]

E. The Operation of the Present Law

An example illustrating the present position may be useful. **13–089**

    (i) In 1998 X purported to convey land to A, B, C, D and E in fee simple. All were of full age. The legal estate vested in A, B, C and D on trust. In equity, A, B, C, D and E were tenants in common if

---

[517] TA 1925 s.34(2) (as amended by TLATA 1996 s.25(2); Sch.3 para.3); above, para.11–051.

[518] LPA 1925 s.34(2) (as amended by TLATA 1996 s.5(1), Sch.2 para.3).

[519] *House* [1929] 2 Ch. 166.

[520] LPA 1925 s.34(3) (as amended by TLATA 1996 ss.5(1), 25(2); Sch.2 para.3; Sch.4).

[521] Supreme Court Act 1981 s.1 14(1); below, para.14–133.

[522] But see LPA 1925 s.36(1) (as amended by TLATA 1996 s.5(1), Sch.2 para.4). This may be intended to apply the mechanism set out in LPA 1925 s.34(2), (3) to land held for beneficial joint tenants.

[523] TA 1925 s.34(2) (as amended by TLATA 1996 s.25(2); Sch.3 para.3). The language is obviously designed to fit express trusts of land and is not very apt for statutory trusts, where no persons are "named as . . . trustees". However it seems probable that it would be held applicable.

[524] Below, para.14–149.

[525] TA 1925 s.34(2) (as amended by TLATA 1996 s.25(2); Sch.3 para.3); above, para.11–051.

[526] Ruoff & Roper 37.005.

[527] TA 1925 s.34; above, para.11–051.

there were words of severance or if it was one of equity's special cases, but otherwise joint tenants.

(ii) If they were joint tenants and A died, B, C and D would then hold the legal estate on trust for B, C, D and E as joint tenants. E would not automatically fill the vacancy at law, but could, of course, be appointed a new trustee in place of A.

(iii) If B afterwards sold his interest to P, then B, C and D would continue to hold the legal estate, but on trust for P as tenant in common of a quarter and C, D and E as joint tenants of three-quarters.

(iv) If C then severed his share by agreement[528] with D and E, the legal estate would remain in B, C and D as before, on trust for P and C as tenants in common of one-quarter each, and D and E as joint tenants of half.

(v) On D's death, B and C would hold on trust for P, C and E as tenants in common as to one-quarter, one-quarter and one-half respectively.

Section 6. Position of Settled Land

13–090   Settled land is dealt with in the Appendix.[529] A brief summary is given here of how co-ownership applied to settled land.

A. *Joint Tenancy*

If two or more persons of full age are entitled to settled land[530] as joint tenants (but not as tenants in common[531]) they together constitute the tenant for life,[532] even, it seems, if they are more than four in number. If any of them are minors, such one or more of them as for the time being is or are of full age constitute the tenant for life.[533] If they are all minors, the legal estate and statutory powers are vested in the statutory owner[534] until one of them is of full age.[535] The land therefore remains settled land, and there is no trust of land.[536]

---

[528] Severance by notice maybe impossible if LPA 1925 s.36(2) is strictly construed, for the legal estate is not vested in all the joint tenants beneficially: see above, para.13–044.

[529] Appendix paras A–001 et seq.

[530] No new settlements can be created after 1996: see above, para.10–034.

[531] Prior to 1926, it was possible for two or more tenants in common to be the tenant for life: see SLA 1882 s.2(6).

[532] SLA 1925 s.19(2). One joint tenant for life cannot force the other to sell: above, Appendix para.A–055.

[533] SLA 1925 s.19(3).

[534] Above, para.10–017.

[535] SLA 1925 s.26(4), (5).

[536] cf. LPA 1925 s.36(1) (as amended by TLATA 1996 s.5(1); Sch.2 para.4); *Re Gaul and Houlston's Contract* [1928] Ch. 689.

B. Tenancy in Common

1. Trust of land. The scheme of the 1925 legislation was that whenever two **13–091** or more tenants in common became entitled in possession, the land could not be settled land and had to be held upon trust for sale. After 1996, a trust of land is imposed instead of a trust for sale.[537] Therefore if A and B are tenants in common for life, the land cannot be settled land but is held on a trust of land.[538] The same is true where, prior to 1997, land was devised to A for life and after his death to his children in equal shares. During A's life the land is settled land but on his death it ceases to be so.

In these situations the person or persons, whoever they may be, in whom the legal estate is vested will hold it upon a trust of land.[539] Any former Settled Land Act trustees are empowered to require the legal estate to be conveyed to them if it is not already vested in them. Although the settlement is superseded by the statutory trust of land, it is appropriate that the same trustees should be able to act, if they wish, in the new trust. If they do, they will hold the land in trust for the persons interested in the land.[540]

2. Devolution on death. A consequential difficulty arises in tracing the **13–092** devolution of the legal estate on death. We have seen how, in a settlement made prior to 1997 upon A for life with remainder to B in fee simple, the legal estate devolves at A's death upon A's ordinary personal representatives, since the settlement no longer exists.[541] In a settlement on A for life with remainder to his children in equal shares the same rule applies in the first instance. But then (paradoxical as it may seem[542]) s.36 of the Settled Land Act 1925 is also held to apply, so that the trustees of the settlement (which *ex hypothesi* no longer exists) may call upon A's personal representatives to convey the land to them. If they are the same persons, they should assent in favour of themselves as trustees of land.[543] In any case, the land is held on a trust of land, and is not settled land for any purpose other than the interpretation of s.36.

A similar procedure should presumably be followed in cases where land would, apart from s.36, continue to be settled, e.g. where the limitations in an instrument made prior to 1997 are to A for life, remainder to his children as tenants in common for life, remainder to B in fee simple. On A's death, if he leaves children, the land becomes subject to a trust of land, and the former

---

[537] TLATA 1996 s.1; above, paras 12–002, 12–005.

[538] SLA 1925 s.36(1), (2) (as amended by TLATA 1996 s.25(1), Sch.3 para.2). For the difficulties of construction of s.36(1), see the 5th edition of this work at p.452.

[539] SLA 1925 s.36(1), (2) (as amended by TLATA 1996 s.25(1), Sch.3 para.2).

[540] SLA 1925 s.36(2), (6) (as amended or substituted by TLATA 1996 s.25(1), Sch.3 para.2).

[541] Below, Appendix para.A–018.

[542] See 71 L.J.News. 179.

[543] *Re Cugny's W.T.* [1931] 1 Ch. 305. Despite the dictum at p.309, this should be an ordinary assent, and not a vesting assent; and Appendix para.A–023.

trustees of the settlement will have to call for the legal estate since it will have vested in A's ordinary personal representatives.[544]

13–093   **3. Registered land.** The provisions of s.36 of the Settled Land Act 1925 apply as much to registered land as they do where the title is unregistered, and the mechanics are dealt with by Land Registration Rules.[545] The former trustees of the settlement may require that the property be transferred to them. That transfer should contain a restriction that, except under an order of the registrar, no disposition is to be registered unless authorised by the Settled Land Act 1925, and except where the sole proprietor is a trust corporation, no disposition under which capital money arises is to be registered unless the money is paid to at least two proprietors.[546]

Section 7. The Special Position of Unincorporated Associations

13–094   **1. Nature of an unincorporated association.** An unincorporated association (such as a club or society) is a body of "two or more persons bound together for one or more common purposes, not being business purposes, by mutual undertakings, each having mutual duties and obligations, in an organisation which has rules which identify in whom control of it and its funds rests and upon what terms and which can be joined or left at will".[547] It is now accepted that a body cannot be an unincorporated association unless there is a contractual bond between the members,[548] although at one time it seems to have been assumed that there was no such requirement and that a grouping of persons together for a common purpose was sufficient.[549] It is often said that an unincorporated association is not in law a separate entity but merely the aggregate of its members,[550] but this is not reflected in the manner in which such associations are now taken to hold their property.

2. Method of property holding

13–095   *(a) The traditional view.* The legal title to the property of an unincorporated association is usually vested in its officers as trustees. At one time it was thought that the only way in which the trustees could hold the property was on trust for the persons who were members at the time it was acquired, either

---

[544] Below, Appendix para.A–018.
[545] LRR 2003 Sch.7.
[546] LRR 2003 Sch.7, restrictions G, H or I as appropriate. See Ruoff & Roper, 37.013, 37.014.
[547] *Conservative and Unionist Central Office v Burrell* [1982] 1 W.L.R. 522 at 525, per Lawton L.J.; see above para.9–146.
[548] *Conservative and Unionist Central Office v Burrell*, above at 525.
[549] cf. *Leahy v Att Gen for New South Wales* [1959] A.C. 457 at 486 (order of nuns assumed to be an unincorporated association).
[550] *Leahy v Att Gen for New South Wales*, above, at 477.

as joint tenants or as tenants in common.[551] The consequences of this view were inconvenient. If strictly applied, it meant that any member:

(i) could at any stage demand to sever his share of the association's property;

(ii) would retain his share of that property after leaving the association, unless he assigned it in writing to the other members[552];

(iii) could leave his share by will on his death if he was a tenant in common; and

(iv) would only have an interest in those assets of the association which were acquired during the period of his membership.

In practice these rules were unworkable and were disregarded.

(b) Property holding based upon contract. In order to escape from these **13–096** difficulties, the courts developed a new form of property holding by unincorporated associations.[553] It is now accepted that the trustees of such an association hold its property on trust for the members not as joint tenants or as tenants in common, but "subject to their respective contractual rights and liabilities towards one another as members of the association".[554] A characteristic of this novel form of property holding is that a member cannot sever his share.[555] It will accrue to the other members on his death or resignation, even though they may include persons who joined the association after it had acquired the property in question.[556] The interest passes without the need for the member to make any written or (as the case may be) testamentary disposition. The nature of the rights of a member of such an association has never been explained,[557] although the last surviving member is entitled to take the remaining property absolutely.[558]

This form of property holding was evolved in a series of decisions concerning the validity of gifts to unincorporated associations. However, its implications are not confined to that issue. One consequence is that on the dissolution

---

[551] *Leahy v Att Gen for New South Wales*, above, at 477, Any attempt to create an endowment for an unincorporated association will be void as a non-charitable purpose trust: *Re Grant's W.T.* [1980] 1 W.L.R. 360; above, para.9–174.

[552] LPA 1925 s.53(i)(c); above, para.11–044.

[553] cf. *Walker v Hall* [1984] F.L.R. 126 at 135, per Lawton L.J. denying, obiter, that there was any "special law relating to property used in common by . . . members of a club".

[554] *Neville Estates Ltd v Madden* [1962] Ch. 832 at 849, per Cross J. See too *Re Recher's W.T.* [1972] Ch. 526; *Universe Tankships Inc of Monrovia v IT WE* [1981] I.C.R. 129 at 156–159; *Conservative and Unionist Central Office v Burrell*, above, at 529; *News Group Newspapers Ltd v S.O.G.A.T 1982* [1986] I.C.R. 716; *In the Matter of Horley Town Football Club* [2006] EWCH 2386 (Ch).

[555] "The individual members would only have any realisable rights in the property if and when the club was dissolved": *Abbatt v Treasury Solicitor* [1969] 1 W.L.R. 1575 at 1583, per Lord Denning MR.

[556] *Neville Estates Ltd v Madden*, above, at 849.

[557] One view is that it is akin to the rights of a person entitled under the unadministered estate of a deceased person. These are explained, below, para.14–130.

[558] *Hanchett-Stamford v HM Attorney General* [2008] EWHC 330 (Ch); [2009] Ch 173.

of such an association,[559] its assets will commonly be distributed amongst the persons who are then members, in accordance with the rules of the society.[560]

13–097   *(c) Conveyancing implications.* It used to be the practice for land to be conveyed to the officers of an unincorporated association on an express trust for sale for the members of the society for the time being.[561] It is now more usual for the property to be held upon a trust of land for the members of the association according to it rules, to be dealt with by the trustees as directed by the managing committee of the society. As the property is not held for the members as joint tenants or as tenants in common, the provisions of the Law of Property Act 1925 which deal with the creation of such tenancies[562] have no application. Where the title to the land is registered, it is the practice to register the trustees as proprietors, but with a restriction that no disposition of the land shall be registered unless authorised by the rules of the association.[563]

Section 8. Determination of Joint Tenancies and Tenancies in Common

13–098   Joint tenancies and tenancies in common may de determined by partition or by union in a sole tenant. As already explained, joint tenancies may also be determined by severance, which converts them into tenancies in common.[564]

A. Partition

13–099   **1. Voluntary partition.** Joint tenants and tenants in common can always make a voluntary partition of the land if all agree.[565] Their co-ownership comes to an end by each of them becoming sole tenant of the piece of land allotted to him. This voluntary partition must be effected by deed.[566]

13–100   **2. Compulsory partition.** Although at common law there was no right to compel a partition,[567] the Partition Acts of 1539 and 1540[568] conferred a

---

[559] For the circumstances in which an unincorporated association may be dissolved, see *Re GKN Bolts & Nuts Ltd (Automotive Division) Birmingham Works Sports and Social Club* [1982] 1 W.L.R. 774.

[560] *Re Sick and Funeral Society* [1973] Ch. 51. Difficult questions may arise on such a dissolution: see *Davis v Richards & Wallington Industries Ltd* [1990] 1 W.L.R. 1511 at 1538 et seq; [1992] Conv. 41 (S. Gardner).

[561] See *Abbatt v Treasury Solicitor* [1969] 1 W.L.R. 1575. This method is still sometimes employed: see *Encyclopaedia of Forms and Precedents* 5th edn, (London: Butterworths Law, 1994) Vol.7, p.351. The trust for sale would now take effect as a trust of land.

[562] ss.34, 36, above, paras 13–051 et seq.

[563] See Ruoff & Roper, 44.009.22.

[564] Above, para.13–036.

[565] Litt. pp.290, 318.

[566] LPA 1925 ss.52(1), 205(1)(ii).

[567] Litt. pp.290, 318. For a fuller account of the history of partition, see the previous edition of this work at p.454.

[568] 31 Hen. 8, c. 1 (estates of inheritance); 32 Hen. 8, c. 32 (estates for life or years). The procedure was improved by the Partition Act 1697 (8 & 9 Will. 3, c. 31).

statutory right for joint tenants and tenants in common to do so.[569] One tenant was entitled to insist upon a partition[570] however inconvenient it might be.[571]

3. Sale. It was not until the Partition Act 1868[572] that the court was **13–101** empowered to decree a sale instead of partition, an order which might be highly desirable where, for example, the cost of partition proceedings would exceed the value of the property,[573] or where a single house had to be partitioned into thirds, and the owner of two-thirds was given all the chimneys and fireplaces and the only stairs.[574]

The Partition Acts were repealed[575] and replaced in turn by a statutory power for trustees for sale to partition land with the consent of the beneficiaries.[576] After 1996, trustees of land have had similar powers under the Trusts of Land and Appointment of Trustees Act 1996. Where beneficiaries of full age are absolutely entitled in undivided shares to land subject to the trust,[577] the trustees of land have a power to partition all or part of it.[578] They may provide (by way of mortgage or otherwise) for the payment of any equality money.[579] Where trustees exercise their power, they should convey the partitioned land to those entitled whether absolutely or, where the person entitled is a trustee, on trust.[580]

The power to partition can only be exercised with the prior consent of each of those beneficiaries.[581] If the trustees or any of the beneficiaries refuse to consent, any trustee or any person who has an interest in the property subject to the trust of land, may apply to the court for an order under the powers already explained.[582] The court may make such order as it thinks fit,[583] including an order to partition or sell the land.[584]

---

[569] See fn.(2) to Co.Litt. p.169a.

[570] *Parker v Gerard* (1754) Amb. 236.

[571] *Warner v Baynes* (1750) Amb. 589; *Baring v Nash* (1813) 1 V. & B. 551 at 554.

[572] As amended by the Partition Act 1876. See *Pemberton v Barnes* (1871) 6 Ch.App. 685; *Powell v Powell* (1874) 10 Ch.App. 130; *Drinkwater v Ratcliffe* (1875) L.R. 20 Eq. 528.

[573] See *Griffies v Griffies* (1863) 11 W.R. 943.

[574] See *Turner v Morgan* (1803) 8 Ves. 143, 11 Ves. 157n.

[575] For a retrospective account see [1982] Conv. 415 (R. Cock).

[576] See LPA 1925 s.28(3) (repealed by TLATA 1996 s.25(2); Sch.4).

[577] This includes the situation where the person absolutely entitled is a trustee or personal representative, who holds the interest on trust for some other person or persons: TLATA 1996 s.22(1).

[578] TLATA 1996 s.7(i). The power may either be expressly excluded by a provision in the disposition creating the trust of land, or made subject to the requirement that it be exercised subject to the trustees obtaining some consent: TLATA 1996 s.8(1), (2). cf. above, para.12–019.

[579] TLATA 1996 s.7(1).

[580] TLATA 1996 s.7(2). The property transferred may be subject to any mortgage created for raising equality money: ibid. If that share is affected by an incumbrance, the trustees may either give effect to it or provide for its discharge as they think fit: TLATA 1996 s.7(4).

[581] TLATA 1996 s.7(3).

[582] TLATA 1996 s.14(1), (2); above, paras 12–021, 13–064.

[583] TLATA 1996 s 14(2).

[584] See *Rodway v Landy* (2001) Ch. 703.

On a partition of the property, it will often be necessary for accounts to be taken between the former co-owners in the same way as if there were a sale.[585] The guiding principle in such equitable accounting is that neither party can take the benefit of any increase in the value of the property without making an allowance for what has been expended by the other in order to obtain it.[586]

B. Union in a Sole Tenant

13–102   **1. Union.** Joint tenancies and tenancies in common may be determined if the whole of the land becomes vested in a single beneficial owner. Thus where one of two surviving joint tenants dies, the other becomes sole tenant by right of survivorship and the joint tenancy is at an end. Similarly if one joint tenant or tenant in common acquires the interests of all of the other tenants, e.g. by purchasing them, the co-ownership is at an end.[587]

13–103   **2. Release.** Because in theory each joint tenant is seised of the whole of the land, the appropriate way for one joint tenant to transfer his rights to another joint tenant before 1926 was by deed of release, which operated to extinguish his interest.[588] Although it has been retrospectively provided that one co-owner can convey to another by grant,[589] the power of a joint tenant to release his interest has been preserved,[590] so that a joint tenant may still release his legal estate or equitable interest (or both) to his fellow joint tenants. A release resembles a conveyance (and differs from a surrender[591]) in that it benefits only the person in whose favour it is made. Thus if A, B and C are beneficial joint tenants and A releases his beneficial interest to B, B alone acquires A's one-third share as equitable tenant in common. He remains joint tenant with C as to the other two-thirds.[592] Any purported disclaimer to which the other joint tenants are parties will be construed as a release.[593] A tenant in common, on the other hand, cannot release his share to the other tenants for a "release supposes the party to have the thing in demand".[594] As a tenancy in common can only exist in equity,[595] he will therefore have to assign his interest in writing to the other tenants.[596]

13–104   **3. Sale.** Co-ownership in land is also extinguished if the land is duly sold to a purchaser by trustees of land under their powers of disposition.[597] The

---

[585] *Re Pavlou* [1993] 1 W.L.R. 1046 at 1048; above, para.13–073.

[586] *Re Pavlou*, above, at 1048. See [1995] Conv. 391 (E. Cooke).

[587] See, e.g. *Burton v Camden LBC* [1998] 1 F.L.R. 681.

[588] Co.Litt. pp.9b, 200b; Preston, *Abstracts*, ii, p.61; Cru.Dig. ii, p.382.

[589] LPA 1925 s.72(4). Prior to 1926 such a grant was inoperative but was construed as a release: *Eustace v Scawen* (1624) Co.Jac. 696; *Chester v Willans* (1670)2 Wms. Saund. 96; Halsbury Vol. 39, para.530.

[590] LPA 1925 s.36(2). See *Burton v Camden LBC*, above, at 684.

[591] See above, para.13–048.

[592] See above, para.13–035; Litt. pp.304, 305; Co.Litt. p.193a.

[593] *Re Schär* [1951] Ch. 280.

[594] Co.Litt. p.193a, n.(1).

[595] LPA 1925 s.1(6).

[596] See LPA 1925 s.53(1)(c).

[597] See TLATA 1996 s.6(1); above, para.12–016.

interests of the co-owners are overreached and attach instead to the proceeds of sale.[598]

Section 9. The Conveyancing Implications of Implied Co-ownership

The imposition of a trust of land in cases of co-ownership may cause   **13–105**
conveyancing difficulties[599] where the interest of one of the co-owners arises informally, as under a constructive trust.[600] In such cases, proprietary rights are created without any written or registrable transaction and there will be no indication of their existence on the title. Without making intimate inquiries, a purchaser from one cohabitant will have no means of knowing whether resulting, constructive or statutory trusts exist in favour of another and whether he should comply with the requirements governing the disposition of land held on a trust of land.[601] The judicial reluctance to require such enquiries[602] was reversed in 1980, when the "easy-going practice of dispensing with enquiries as to occupation beyond that of the vendor" was held by the House of Lords to be inadequate.[603] The potential conveyancing difficulties are usually overcome by requiring any cohabitant either to be joined as a party to the conveyance or to sign a waiver of his or her rights in the property.[604] Neither of these methods has proved infallible. In some cases, A has forged B's signature on the conveyance or transfer, so that no legal estate has passed but only A's beneficial interest.[605] In others, A has procured B's signature to a conveyance or waiver by fraud or undue influence in circumstances in which the purchaser has been unable to rely on the instrument.[606]

There have been few cases of sales or leases in which a purchaser has taken   **13–106**
subject to the rights of a beneficiary, and those which have arisen have been characterised by unusual facts.[607] Property is normally sold or let with vacant possession, and in consequence any dispute between the cohabitants as to whether the land should be sold will usually have been resolved prior to

---

[598] See above, para.12–036.
[599] See [1990] C.L.J. 277 at 312 (C.H.); [1993] Fam. Law 231 (I. Dewar).
[600] para.11–023.
[601] Above, para.12–037.
[602] See *Caunce v Caunce* [1969] 1 W.L.R. 286.
[603] *Williams & Glyn's Bank Ltd v Boland* [1981] A.C. 487 at 508, per Lord Wilberforce. cf. how this matter is dealt with under the Land Registration Act 2002 Sch.3 para.2, above, para.7–089.
[604] But compare LPA 1925 s.42.
[605] See, e.g. *Ahmed v Kendrick* (1987) 56 P. & C.R. 120; above, paras 8–044, 13–039.
[606] See, e.g. *Barclays Bank Plc v O'Brien* [1994] 1 A.C. 180; below, para.25–118. Normally the transaction has been a mortgage or the provision of some other form of security.
[607] See *Hodgson v Marks* [1971] Ch. 892 (vacant possession was not to be given on completion); *Chhokar v Chhokar* [1984] F.L.R. 313 (husband connived with purchaser to defeat wife's rights while she was in a maternity hospital); and *Ahmed v Kendrick*, above (husband forged wife's name on the transfer after she had ceased to live with him).

completion. In practice, conveyancing difficulties have most commonly arisen where A has mortgaged a property in which B already has an interest.[608] Where the monies advanced are paid to A alone, B's interest is not over-reached.[609] In those circumstances, the mortgage will not have priority to B:

(i) if A's title was unregistered and the mortgagee had notice of B's interest[610]; or

(ii) if A's title was registered and B's interest achieved priority as an unregistered interest which overrides because he was in actual occupation of the land.[611]

By contrast, the mortgage will take priority over B's interest if B was either involved in the process of securing the mortgage or must have known that a mortgage would be necessary to finance the balance of the purchase price.[612] In such circumstances he or she will be taken to have impliedly consented to the charge, and will be estopped from asserting his interest.[613] If A subsequently re-mortgages the property for a larger sum without B's consent, B's interest will be subordinated to the new mortgage but only to the extent of the original charge which it replaces. In one case this was explained as an extension of the estoppel principle set out above.[614] However, in a later case the same answer was reached on the more orthodox (and, it is suggested, preferable) basis that the second mortgagee was subrogated to the rights of the first.[615]

13–107   The constructive trust based upon the common intentions of the parties has not only given rise to conveyancing difficulties,[616] but has proved to be an unsatisfactory method of adjusting property rights between cohabitants on the

---

[608] Where A mortgages the property at the time of acquisition, B will not gain priority over the mortgagee merely because he or she contributes to the purchase price. The transfer of the legal estate to A and the mortgage are regarded as taking place simultaneously, so that there is no moment of time in which B could gain priority: *Abbey National BS v Cann* [1991] 1 A.C. 56; below, para.17–102.

[609] Above, para.12–037.

[610] *Kingsnorth Finance Co Ltd v Tizard* [1986] 1 W.L.R. 783; above, para.8–019.

[611] *Williams & Glyn's Bank Ltd v Boland*, above; para.25–118.

[612] *Abbey National BS v Cann*, above, at 95.

[613] *Bristol and West BS v Henning* [1985] 1 W.L.R. 778; *Paddington BS v Mendelsohn* (1985) 50 P. & C.R. 244; *Skipton BS v Clayton* (1993) 66 P. & C.R. 223 at 229; (1996) 8 C.EL.Q. 261 at 266 (G. Battersby). This will be so, even though the mortgage is in fact for a sum greater than that to which B had agreed: *Abbey National BS v Cann*, above.

[614] *Equity & Law Home Loans Ltd v Prestidge* [1992] 1 W.L.R. 137. Although the decision has been criticised (see [1992] C.L.I. 223 (M.J.D.); [1992] Conv. 206 (M. P. Thompson)), the result, if not the reasoning, seems correct: see (1992) 108 L.Q.R. 371 (R. J. Smith).

[615] *Castle Phillips Finance v Piddington* [1995] 1 F.L.R. 783. cf. *Bankers Trust Co v Namdar* [1997] E.G.C.S. 20.

[616] See [1987] Conv. 93 (J. Eekelaar); (1990) 106 L.Q.R. 539 (J. D. Davies); (1993) 109 L.Q.R. 263 (S. Gardner).

breakdown of their relationship.[617] The more closely the relationship resembles marriage, the less likely it is that there will have been a common understanding that the non-owning partner should have an interest in the shared home.[618] In some jurisdictions, a statutory power exists to adjust property rights between unmarried cohabitants on the termination of their relationship in a manner similar to that applicable to spouses in this country.[619] On the recommendation of the Scottish Law Commission, such a power has been introduced in Scotland,[620] and this has been followed by recommendations in relation to England and Wales, but not implementation in the foreseeable future.[621] It has also been suggested that constructive trusts based upon common intention are unnecessary and that the law would be better served if they were subsumed "within the more flexible doctrine of proprietary estoppel",[622] but this may be untenable and unnecessary after the decision in *Stack v Dowden*.[623]

---

[617] For judicial criticism, see *Burns v Burns* [1984] Ch. 317 at 332, 345. Where A and B cohabit and B dies, A may be in a stronger position than if their relationship had terminated inter vivos. This will be so where (i) A and B lived together in the same household for two years as if they were husband and wife; or (ii) A was partly or wholly maintained by B: see the Inheritance (Provision for Family and Dependants) Act 1975, s.1(1)(ba) (as inserted by the Law Reform (Succession) Act 1995, s.2), (e), below, para.14–005; and (1982) 2 O.J.L.S. 277 (C.H.).

[618] "A woman's place is often still in the home, but if she stays there, she will acquire no interest in it": [1987] Conv. 93 at 94 (J. Eekelaar).

[619] See, e.g. the New South Wales De Facto Relationships Act 1984; [1992] Fam. Law 72 at 76 (P. J. Clarke).

[620] Scottish Law Com. No.135 (1992). See Family Law Act (Scotland) 2002.

[621] Above para.13–083.

[622] [1987] Conv. 93 at 101 (J. Eekelaar). See too [1990] Conv. 370 (D. J. Hayton).

[623] Above para.11–023.

WILLS AND INTESTACY

14–001 This chapter summarises the law of succession with particular reference to its application to real property. It considers first the extent to which English law respects the principle of testamentary freedom. It then goes on to examine the nature of a will, the formalities to be satisfied in order to make, revoke or revive wills, the operation of wills and the basic principles of construction which are applied. It then considers the rules of intestacy, which apply where a person dies leaving property undisposed of. Finally, the means whereby legal estates devolve on death are dealt with.

Section 1. Freedom of Testation

14–002 **1. Historical development.** For some while after the Norman Conquest it was possible for a man to dispose of both his realty and his personalty by will. At first his powers of disposition over personalty were confined to a fixed proportion, his widow and children being entitled to the rest.[1] During the 14th century this restriction disappeared in nearly all parts of the country. However, in some places it survived until the 17th and 18th centuries, the last case being that of London, where it was abolished in 1725.[2] Realty, on the other hand, could at first be freely devised, but by the end of the 13th century all power of testamentary disposition had disappeared except in the case of local

---

[1] P. & M. iif, p.348; H.E.L. iii, p.550. The fraction varied locally; often he was free to dispose of only a third if he left a widow and children, but a half if he left either a widow or children but not both.

[2] 11 Geo. I c. 18 1724 ss.17, 18; and see H.E.L., iii, p.552.

customs. But this restriction was soon evaded by means of uses[3] and the general belief that the Statute of Uses 1535 had abolished this indirect power of testamentary disposition[4] provoked such an outcry that the Statute of Wills 1540[5] authorised the devise of all socage land and two-thirds of land held by knight service.[6] When the Tenures Abolition Act 1660 converted all land held by knight service into land of socage tenure, all land became devisable. But this power extended only to estates in fee simple: land held in tail could not be disposed of by will before the Law of Property Act 1925[7]; and land held *pur autre vie* did not become devisable until the Statute of Frauds was enacted in 1677.[8] Copyhold land was not within the Statute of Wills 1540, and devises were effected by the testator in his lifetime making a surrender to the uses of his will.[9] If the testator was a joint tenant, this had the incidental effect of severing the joint tenancy.[10] But by Preston's Act 1815[11] a devise without a previous surrender was rendered effective, and the Wills Act 1837 applied to copyholds as well as to lands of other tenures. It is this latter Act, as amended, which governs wills of all property, real or personal, today.

2. Statutory restrictions on freedom of testation

(a) Inheritance (Family Provision) Act 1938. From the 14th century until 1939 there was, in general, no restriction upon a testator's power to dispose of property as he thought fit. He was under no obligation to provide for his family or dependants. The Inheritance (Family Provision) Act 1938 gave the court a limited power to modify the effect of a will in certain cases, and the Intestates' Estates Act 1952 gave the court power to modify the rules of succession on intestacy. Those powers were later extended by the Family Provision Act 1966 and the Family Law Reform Act 1969.[12]   **14–003**

(b) Inheritance (Provision for Family and Dependants) Act 1975[13]

(1) PROVISION UNDER THE ACT. The legislation explained above was replaced by the Inheritance (Provision for Family and Dependants) Act 1975, which   **14–004**

---

[3] For the Statute of Uses, see the fifth edition of this work, Appendix 3.
[4] This belief was probably unfounded: see 94 S.S. at p.203 (J. H. Baker); and (1941) 7 C.L.J. 354 (R.E.M.).
[5] As explained by the Statute of Wills 1542.
[6] See A. W. B. Simpson, *A History of the Land Law*, 2nd edn (Oxford, OUP), p.191.
[7] Above, para.3–081.
[8] s.12.
[9] Scriven 146.
[10] *Porter v Porter* (1605) Cro.Jac. 100; *Gale v Gale* (1789) 2 Cox Eq. 136; *Edwards v Champion* (1847) 1 De G. & Sm. 75; (1853) 3 De G. M. & G. 202; and see above, paras 13–003, 13–036 et seq.
[11] 55 Geo. 3 c.192.
[12] For details of this legislation, see the fifth edition of this work at p.500.
[13] For more detailed surveys, see J. Mason, R. Bailey-Harris and R. Probert, *Cretney's Principles of Family Law*, 8th edn, pp.214–229; *Theobald on Wills*, 17th edn, Ch.13; Francis, *Inheritance Act Claims: Law, Practice and Procedure* (London: Jordans).

conferred wider powers.[14] Its principal objects were to improve the provision for a surviving spouse, no longer confining it to maintenance; to include all children of the deceased even though not under a disability, together with non-relatives who were treated as children of the family or else were dependant on the deceased; and to extend the court's power to make orders. It is not the purpose of the Act "to provide legacies or rewards for meritorious conduct",[15] nor does it confer power on the court "to reform the deceased's dispositions or those which statute makes of his estate to accord with what the court itself might have thought would be sensible if it had been in the deceased's position".[16] The Law Commission has recently published a Report on the law of intestacy and family provision which makes a number of recommendations for reform and appends two draft Bills to give effect to them.[17] Reference will be made to these recommendations in the following text.

14–005   (2) APPLICANTS. The persons for whom provision may now be made by the court are any of the following, provided that the deceased died after March 31, 1976 and was then domiciled in England and Wales[18]:

(a)   the spouse or civil partner of the deceased[19];

(b)   a former spouse or civil partner of the deceased who has not formed a subsequent marriage or civil partnership[20];

(c)   a cohabitant of the deceased, that is a person who, during the whole of the two-year period ending immediately before the death, was

---

[14] As recommended by the Law Commission ((1974) Law Com. No.61). In view of the substantial changes made in the 1975 Act, decisions on the 1938 Act as to the exercise of the court's powers provide little guidance and must be approached with caution: *Moody v Stevenson* [1992] Ch. 486 at 502; cf. *Re Coventry* [1980] Ch. 461 at 474.

[15] *Re Coventry*, above, at 474, per Oliver J.

[16] *Re Coventry*, above, at 475.

[17] Law Com. No.331, *Intestacy and Family Provision Claims on Death* (2011); see also prior Consultation Paper, Law Com. CP No.191 (2009).

[18] I(PFD)A 1975 s.1, as amended by Civil Partnership Act 2004 s.71 Sch.4 para.15. For domicile, see *Agulian v Cyganik* [2006] EWCA Civ 129; [2006] W.T.L.R. 565; *Holliday v Musa* [2010] EWCA Civ 335; [2010] 2 F.L.R. 702 (illustrating the difficulties of proving that the deceased's domicile of origin had been displaced by domicile of choice). For law reform proposals, see Law Com. No.331, paras 7.11 et seq.

[19] This includes a wife by a polygamous marriage (*Re Sehota* [1978] 1 W.L.R. 1506) as well as a person who had in good faith entered into a void marriage or formed a void civil partnership with the deceased, provided that the marriage or civil partnership had not been dissolved or annulled during the deceased's lifetime and that the person had not formed a subsequent marriage or civil partnership: I(PFD)A 1975 ss.25(4), 25(4A), as amended by Civil Partnership Act 2004 s.71 Sch.4 para.27.

[20] Orders are made routinely in proceedings for divorce, etc removing the right to claim provision in the event of the former spouse or civil partner's death: see I(PFD)A 1975 ss.15, 15ZA, latter as inserted by Civil Partnership Act 2004 s.71 Sch.4 para.21. Even where no such order has been made, a former spouse who has already obtained ancillary relief is unlikely to be successful in a family provision claim: see e.g. *Re Fullard* [1982] Fam. 42; *Cameron v Treasury Solicitor* [1996] 2 F.L.R. 716; *Barrass v Harding* [2001] 1 F.L.R. 138.

living in the same household as the deceased, either as the husband or wife or as the civil partner of the deceased[21];

(d) a child of the deceased[22];

(e) any other person who, although not a child of the deceased, has been treated by the deceased as a child of the family in relation to any marriage or civil partnership to which the deceased was at any time a party[23];

(f) any other person (not otherwise entitled to claim) who was being maintained wholly or partly by the deceased immediately before the death.[24]

(3) CRITERIA. The Act sets out in detail the matters to which the court is to have regard in exercising its jurisdiction, such as the financial resources and needs[25] and any physical or mental disability of the applicant or applicants and

14–006

---

[21] Added by Law Reform (Succession) Act 1995 s.2. A cohabitant may only claim as such where the deceased died after 1995. In deciding whether a couple are living together as husband and wife, the court "should not ignore the multifarious nature of marital relationships", and the relationship need not be a sexual one: *Re Watson* [1999] 1 F.L.R. 878 at 883, per Neuberger J; *Baynes v Hedger* [2008] EWHC 1587 (Ch); [2008] 2 F.L.R. 1805; *Lindop v Agus* [2009] EWHC 1795 (Ch); [2010] 1 F.L.R. 631. On whether they cohabited "immediately before" the death of the deceased, the court should look at "the settled state of affairs during the relationship" and not merely "the immediate de facto situation prevailing before the deceased's death": *Gully v Dix* [2005] EWCA Civ 221 at [15]; [2004] 1 W.L.R. 1399 at 1404, per Judge Weeks Q.C., as approved by the Court of Appeal. It is immaterial that the applicant's presence in the country was unlawful: *Witkowska v Kaminski* [2006] EWHC 1940 (Ch); [2007] 1 F.L.R. 1547. For law reform proposals, see Law Com. No.331, paras 8.144 et seq.

[22] This includes an illegitimate child and a child *en ventre sa mere* at the death of the deceased: I(PFD)A 1975 s.25(1). An adopted person is to be treated in law as if born as the child of the adopter or adopters: Adoption and Children Act 2002 s.67(1). If a child of the deceased is therefore adopted by someone else before family provision proceedings are commenced, the right to make a claim will be lost: *Re Collins* [1990] Fam. 56.

[23] It has been suggested, but never decided, that treatment of the claimant as a child of the family by the deceased even *before* the marriage ceremony would suffice: *Re Callaghan* [1985] Fam. 1 at 6. To fall within this paragraph, it is necessary that the deceased "has, as wife or husband (or widow or widower) under the relevant marriage, expressly or impliedly, assumed the position of a parent towards the applicant, with the attendant responsibilities and privileges of that relationship": *Re Leach* [1986] Ch. 226 at 237, per Slade L.J. For law reform proposals, see Law Com. No.331, paras 6.27 et seq.

[24] See Ross [2010] Fam. Law 490. The applicant will be treated as having been maintained by the deceased only if the deceased was making a substantial contribution in money or money's worth (otherwise than for full valuable consideration) towards the applicant's reasonable needs: I(PFD)A 1975 s.1(3). This requires the court to balance the reciprocal benefits conferred by the deceased and the applicant upon each other: *Jelley v Iliffe* [1981] Fam. 128 at 141; *Bishop v Plumley* [1991] 1 W.L.R. 582 at 587. Although it must appear that the deceased had assumed responsibility for maintaining the applicant, this will be presumed from the mere fact that the applicant was being maintained by the deceased: *Jelley v Iliffe*, above; *Baynes v Hedger* [2009] EWCA Civ 374; [2009] 2 F.L.R. 767. The words "immediately before the death of the deceased" are not construed literally, but "refer to the general arrangements for maintenance subsisting at the time of death": *Jelley v Iliffe*, above, at 141, per Griffiths L.J. For law reform proposals, see Law Com. No.331, paras 6.43 et seq.

[25] "Financial resources" are widely defined to include earning capacity; and in considering "financial needs" the court must take account of the person's financial obligations and responsibilities: I(PFD)A 1975, s.3(6).

any beneficiaries of the estate.[26] Although the list is apparently open-ended,[27] certain additional factors are required to be taken into account in relation to applications in specific classes.[28] The ground of application must be that the deceased's will or the law of intestacy, or both in combination, do not make "reasonable financial provision" for the applicant.[29]

14–007   In the case of a spouse or civil partner in class (a), "reasonable financial provision" means such provision as it would be reasonable in all the circumstances for a spouse or civil partner to receive, whether or not that provision is required for the applicant's maintenance.[30] In addition to the age of the applicant, the duration of the marriage or civil partnership and the contribution made by the applicant to the welfare of the deceased's family (including any contribution made by looking after the home or caring for the family), the court is required to have regard to the provision which the applicant might reasonably have expected to receive if on the day of the deceased's death the marriage or civil partnership, instead of being terminated by death, had been terminated by divorce or dissolution.[31]

14–008   In the case of all other applicants, "reasonable financial provision" means such provision as it would be reasonable in all the circumstances for the applicant to receive for his maintenance.[32] Although the Act does not define maintenance, it has been held to connote "only those payments which will directly or indirectly enable the applicant in the future to discharge the cost of his daily living at whatever standard of living is appropriate to him."[33] It must not be given too limited a meaning: "it does not mean just enough to enable a person to get by; on the other hand, it does not mean anything which may be regarded as reasonably desirable for his general benefit or welfare."[34] There is no threshold requirement that an adult applicant, such as a child of the deceased, who is in employment show a moral claim or some other special

---

[26] I(PFD)A 1975 s.3(1).

[27] It includes "any other matter, including the conduct of the applicant or any other person, which in the circumstances of the case the court may consider relevant": I(PFD)A 1975 s.3(1)(g).

[28] I(PFD)A 1975 s.3(2), (2A), (3) and (4).

[29] I(PFD)A 1975 s.2. The court is required to take into account the facts as known at the hearing: s.3(5). Changes in circumstances (such as an increase or decrease in the size of the deceased's estate since his death) may, therefore, be relevant: *Re Hancock* [1998] 2 F.L.R. 346.

[30] I(PFD)A 1975 s.1(2)(a), (aa), as amended by Civil Partnership Act 2004 s.71 Sch.4 para.15.

[31] I(PFD)A 1975 s.3(2), as amended by Civil Partnership Act 2004 s.71; Sch.4 para.17. This "divorce analogy" is only one element that the court will take into account, and should not be given undue prominence: *Re Besterman* [1984] Ch. 458; *Re Krubert* [1997] Ch. 97; *Baker v Baker* [2008] EWHC 977 (Ch); [2008] 2 F.L.R. 1956; cf. *Moody v Stevenson* [1992] Ch. 486. It is not applicable where a decree of judicial separation, or separation order, was in force, and the separation was continuing, at the date of death. See also *Cunliffe v Fielden* [2005] EWCA Civ 1508; [2006] Ch. 361 (where the Court of Appeal considered the effect on the 1975 Act jurisdiction of the House of Lords decision in *White v White* [2001] 1 A.C. 596 on ancillary relief on divorce); and *Iqbal v Ahmed* [2011] EWCA Civ 900; [2011] W.T.L.R. 1351. For law reform proposals, see Law Com. No.331, paras 2.141 et seq.

[32] I(PFD)A 1975 s.1(2)(b).

[33] *Re Dennis* [1981] 2 All E.R. 140 at 145, per Browne-Wilkinson J.

[34] *Re Coventry* [1980] Ch. 461 at 485, per Goff L.J.

circumstance before an application may succeed, but the court is likely to treat such claims without more with a degree of scepticism.[35]

(4) APPLICATIONS. Application has to be made within six months of the first grant of representation,[36] but the court may extend the time.[37] A claim under the Act is personal to the applicant and will be extinguished by his death if no order has been made in his lifetime.[38]   **14–009**

(5) POWERS OF THE COURT. The court has wide discretion to order provision to be made for the applicant from the deceased's net estate by way of lump sum or periodical payments, transfer or settlement of specific property or of property to be acquired, or variation of a pre-existing marriage or civil partnership settlement.[39] The order may contain such consequential or supplementary provisions as the court thinks necessary or expedient.[40] It may direct the setting aside of a capital sum to produce periodical payments, thus allowing the rest of the estate to be distributed.[41] There are extensive powers for later variation or discharge of orders for periodical payments, and for interim orders giving immediate financial assistance pending final decision of the case.[42] In addition, there are anti-avoidance provisions under which the court may order payments or transfers to be made by recipients of certain dispositions made by the deceased within six years before death for less than full valuable consideration and with intent to defeat the Act; and similarly for contracts to leave property by will, if made for insufficient consideration and with similar intent.[43]   **14–010**

(6) NET ESTATE. The deceased's net estate, out of which the provision has to be made, is defined[44] so as to include property over which he had a general power of appointment at the time of his death; property ordered to be recovered under the anti-avoidance provisions mentioned above; property   **14–011**

---

[35] *Re Hancock* [1998] 2 F.L.R. 346 at 351; *Re Pearce* [1998] 2 F.L.R. 705 at 710; *Espinosa v Bourke* [1999] 1 F.L.R. 747 at 755; *Ilott v Mitson* [2011] EWCA Civ 346; [2011] W.T.L.R. 779; cf. *Re Jennings* [1994] Ch. 286 at 295. The Law Commission has considered whether the current approach towards adult children is too harsh but has decided not to recommend reform: Law Com. CP No.191, paras 5.7 et seq.; Law Com. No.331, paras 6.2 et seq.

[36] The grant of representation must be a valid one. If a grant is revoked and a new grant made, time runs from the date of the latter grant: *Re Freeman* [1984] 1 W.L.R. 1419. No application under the 1975 Act will be entertained unless a grant of representation has been made: *Re McBroom* [1992] 2 F.L.R. 49.

[37] I(PFD)A 1975 s.4. See *Re Salmon* [1981] Ch. 167 (extension of four and a half months refused, since estate had been distributed without warning of impending 1975 Act claim); cf. where no prejudice to beneficiaries of estate: *Stock v Brown* [1994] 1 F.L.R. 840 (leave granted over six years after grant); *McNulty v McNulty* [2002] EWHC 123 (Ch); [2002] W.T.L.R. 737 (over three years).

[38] *Whytte v Ticehurst* [1986] Fam. 64.

[39] I(PFD)A 1975 s.2. See (1986) 102 L.Q.R. 445 (J.G. Miller). The court currently has no power to order pension sharing under this jurisdiction; the Law Commission does not recommend reform of this position: Law Com. No.331, paras 7.99 et seq.

[40] I(PFD)A 1975 s.2(4).

[41] I(PFD)A 1975 s.2(3).

[42] I(PFD)A 1975 ss.6, 5.

[43] I(PFD)A 1975 ss.10, 11. See *Re Dawkins* [1986] 2 F.L.R. 360.

[44] I(PFD)A 1975 s.25(1).

passing by statutory nomination[45] or by *donatio mortis causa*[46]; and the deceased's severable share under any beneficial joint tenancy, if the court so orders.[47]

Section 2. Nature of a Will

14–012   A will is an instrument that both contains and is made with the intention that it should be a revocable ambulatory disposition of the maker's property which is to take effect on death.[48] A document can be a will only if it is made with immediate testamentary intent. Its operation may be made subject to an express condition. However, if it transpires that an apparently unconditional will was in fact subject to some condition that was expressed externally, it will be void (and cannot be admitted to probate) as the testator lacked the requisite *animus testandi* at the time when it was executed.[49]

14–013   **1. A will is ambulatory.** Until the death of the testator a will has no effect at all,[50] but operates as a mere declaration of his intention, which may be changed from time to time. For this reason, a will is said to be "ambulatory". This distinguishes a will from a conveyance, settlement or other dealing inter vivos, which operates at once or at some fixed time.[51] A will is also ambulatory in that, subject to a contrary intention being expressed, it "speaks from death", i.e. it is capable of disposing of all property owned by the testator at his death, even if acquired after the date of the will.[52]

14–014   **2. A will is revocable.** Notwithstanding any declaration in the will itself or any other document, a will can be revoked at any time.[53] A binding contract not to revoke a will does not prevent its revocation,[54] though it gives a right of action for damages against the testator's estate if the will is revoked.[55] Such a contract will usually be construed as confined to acts of revocation performed as such, and not to the revocation that usually results automatically

---

[45] See below, para.14–018.

[46] For such gifts in contemplation of death, see below, para.14–100.

[47] I(PFD)A 1975 s.9; see, e.g. *Jessop v Jessop* [1992] 1 F.L.R. 591. In this case, the application must be made within six months of the grant of representation, and there is no judicial power to extend time; see reform proposals in Law Com. No.331, paras 7.11 et seq. For valuation of share, see *Dingmar v Dingmar* [2006] EWCA Civ 942; [2007] Ch. 109; see reform proposals in Law Com. No.331, paras 7.86 et seq.

[48] *Re Berger* [1990] Ch. 118 at 129 and 132.

[49] *Corbett v Newey* [1998] Ch. 57 (deceased intended her will to be effective only when certain gifts of land had been completed, but these conditions were not expressed in the will).

[50] *Re Baroness Llanover* [1903] 2 Ch. 330 at 335; *Re Thompson* [1906] 2 Ch. 199 at 205.

[51] See Jarman 26. But a will may, as soon as made, rank as a "disposition" for certain statutory purposes: see *Re Gilpin* [1954] Ch. 1, and contrast *Berkeley v Berkeley* [1946] A.C. 555 ("provision"), noted (1946) 62 L.Q.R. 340 (REM).

[52] Wills Act 1837 s.24.

[53] *Vynior's Case* (1609) 8 Co. Rep. p.8lb.

[54] *In b. Heys* [1914] P. 192.

[55] *Synge v Synge* [1894] 1 Q.B. 466.

from entry into marriage or civil partnership[56]; and even if the contract is wide enough to extend to marriage, it will be valid only so far as it is not in restraint of marriage.[57] In the case of land,[58] or where an implied trust arises from an agreement to make mutual wills,[59] the effect of a contract not to revoke the will is that the person to whom the assets have passed may be compelled to hold these on trust in accordance with the terms of the contract.[60]

3. Codicils. A codicil is similar to a will and is governed by the same rules. **14–015** A testamentary document is usually called a codicil if it is supplementary to a will and adds to, varies or revokes provisions in the will: if it is an independent instrument, it is called a will. Although sometimes indorsed on a will, a codicil may be a separate document, and can stand by itself even if the will to which it is supplementary is revoked.[61] Codicils are construed in such a way as to disturb the provisions of a will no more than is absolutely necessary to give effect to the codicil.[62]

4. Capacity. A testator must be mentally capable of making a will, that is **14–016** to say, he must understand the nature of the act and its effects, as well as the extent of the property of which he is disposing, and he must be able to comprehend and appreciate the claims to which he ought to give effect.[63] It follows that:

> "no disorder of the mind shall poison his affections, pervert his sense of right, or prevent the exercise of his natural faculties—that no insane delusion shall influence his will in disposing of his property and bring about a disposal of it which, if the mind had been sound, would not have been made."[64]

[56] *Re Marsland* [1939] Ch. 820; for revocation by marriage or civil partnership, see below, para.14–038.
[57] *Robinson v Ommanney* (1883) 23 Ch D 285; for restraint of marriage, see above, para.3–066.
[58] i.e. where the contract creates an equitable interest: see above, para.5–025; *Goylmer v Paddiston* (1670) 2 Ventr. 353; and see fn.61, below.
[59] Above, para.11–020.
[60] *Dufour v Pereira* (1769) Dick. 419 and cases cited above, para.11–020. Where title to the land is registered, a contract to devise may be protected by entry of a notice on the register: LRA 2002 s.32, above. Where title to the land is unregistered, the purchaser of a legal estate without notice, or against whom the contract is void for want of registration, will take free from it: see above, paras 8–002, 8–093. Yet *quaere* whether a contract to devise is an estate contract within the meaning of the LCA 1972. For the statutory definition, see above, para.8–075.
[61] *Black v Jobling* (1869) L.R. 1 P. & D. 685; *In b. Savage* (1870) L.R. 2 P. & D. 78.
[62] *Doe d. Hearle v Hicks* (1832) 1 Cl. & F. 20; Jarman 194.
[63] *Banks v Goodfellow* (1870) L.R. 5 Q.B. 549; *Sharp v Adam* [2006] EWCA Civ 449; [2006] W.T.L.R. 1059. The statutory test of capacity contained in the Mental Disorder Act 2005 is generally considered not to apply to the issue of testamentary capacity: see *Scammell v Farmer* [2008] EWHC 1100 (Ch); [2008] W.T.L.R. 1261; *Re Key* [2010] EWHC 408 (Ch); [2010] 1 W.L.R. 2020 at [94].
[64] *Banks v Goodfellow*, above, at 565 per Cockburn C.J. This specific element is "as much concerned with mood as with cognition": *Sharp v Adam*, above, at [93] per May L.J. It is therefore now possible to challenge testamentary capacity on the basis of the inadequacy of the testator's decision-making powers rather than merely the testator's failures of comprehension: *Re Key*, above (testator's bereavement at loss of wife following marriage of 65 years).

The legal burden of proof of testamentary capacity rests on the person who is seeking to prove the will.[65] However, capacity will be presumed if the will has been duly executed and is rational on its face; in such circumstances, the evidential burden shifts onto the person who is seeking to challenge the will to raise real doubt as to the testator's capacity.[66] There is a "golden rule" —although it is a rule of good practice, not a rule of law[67]—that, where an elderly and infirm testator makes a will, the execution should be witnessed by a medical practitioner who satisfies himself as to the testator's capacity and records his findings in writing.[68] Compliance with this rule does not guarantee the grant of probate, but highly persuasive evidence would be required for a person to succeed in contesting the will on the basis of incapacity.[69] Even where a testator does not have testamentary capacity at the time of execution, it will be sufficient if at that time he understood that he was executing a will for which he had given prior instructions.[70]

14–017   **5. Knowledge and approval.** The testator must "know and approve" of the contents of his will at the time of execution.[71] Once the testator's capacity is proved, and it is proved that the will was executed duly complying with the statutory formalities, knowledge and approval are to be presumed.[72] However, if circumstances surrounding execution raise a suspicion that the will did not truly represent the testator's intentions, knowledge and approval must be affirmatively proved on the balance of probabilities. This doctrine of "suspicious circumstances" applies in particular where the person who has prepared the will, or who has suggested its terms, takes a substantial benefit under it.[73] Suspicion may be aroused in various degrees,[74] and the greater the degree of suspicion, the more difficult it will be to remove.[75] It is not always necessary or advisable for the court to analyse the issue of knowledge and approval in two stages, in particular where the single issue is whether the testator appreciated the contents of the will at the time of execution.[76] In the event that the court is satisfied of the testator's knowledge and approval, it remains open to those challenging the will to argue that it was made as a result of the undue

---

[65] *Sharp v Adam*, above, at [73].

[66] *Re Key*, above, at [97].

[67] *Sharp v Adam*, above, at [27]; *Re Key*, above, at [6].

[68] *Kenward v Adams*, *The Times*, November 29, 1975.

[69] *Sharp v Adam*, above, at [27].

[70] *Parker v Felgate* (1883) L.R. 8 P.D. 171; *Perrins v Holland* [2010] EWCA Civ 840; [2011] 2 All E.R. 174.

[71] *Morrell v Morrell* (1882) 7 P.D. 68 at 70.

[72] *Barry v Butlin* (1838) 2 Moo. P.C. 480, 484; *Hoff v Atherton* [2004] EWCA Civ 1554; [2005] W.T.L.R. 99.

[73] *Wintle v Nye* [1959] 1 W.L.R. 284; *Fuller v Strum* [2001] EWCA Civ 1879; [2002] 1 W.L.R. 1097; *Sherrington v Sherrington* [2005] EWCA Civ 326; [2005] W.T.L.R. 587; *Boudh v Bodh* [2007] EWCA Civ 1019; [2008] W.T.L.R. 411.

[74] *Fuller v Strum*, above, at [33].

[75] *Wintle v Nye*, above, at 291.

[76] *Gill v RSPCA* [2010] EWCA Civ 1430; [2011] 3 W.L.R. 85 at [22] and [64].

influence[77] or fraud[78] of another person.[79] The burden of proving these matters will rest on those who are asserting them.[80]

6. Age. No will made by a person under 18 years is valid,[81] except in the **14–018** special cases of privilege (soldiers, sailors, marines and airmen) explained later.[82] However, minors of 16 years or more have statutory power to make nominations of certain property (e.g. money in savings banks) to take effect on death.[83]

Section 3. The Formalities of a Will[84]

A. History

The Statute of Wills 1540[85] required a will of realty to be made in writing, **14–019** although it was unnecessary for it to be signed by the testator, or witnessed. Wills of personalty could be made by word of mouth. The Statute of Frauds 1677[86] required all wills of realty[87] not only to be in writing but also to be signed by the testator (or by some person in his presence and by his direction) and attested in his presence by at least three credible witnesses. The statute also laid down such stringent requirements for nuncupative (i.e. oral) wills of personalty over £30[88] that thereafter wills of personalty were usually made in writing. Written wills of personalty required no witnesses and did not need to be signed by the testator if written or acknowledged by him.[89] The Wills Act 1837 repealed these provisions as regards all wills made after 1837[90] and substituted a uniform code for both realty and personalty. The rules have been amended several times, and in particular the Administration of Justice Act 1982 has made important changes.

---

[77] This requires proof of coercion of the testator such that he does something that he does not desire to do: *Wingrove v Wingrove* (1885) 11 P.D. 81; see statement of principles in *Edwards v Edwards* [2007] EWHC 1119 (Ch); [2007] W.T.L.R. 1387 at [47], followed in *Cowderoy v Cranfield* [2011] EWHC 1616 (Ch); [2011] W.T.L.R. 1699.

[78] *Wilkinson v Joughin* (1866) L.R. 2 Eq. 319; *Re Posner* [1953] P. 277.

[79] *Tyrrell v Painton* [1894] P. 151 at 157; *Gill v RSPCA*, above, at [13].

[80] *Parfitt v Lawless* (1872) 2 P. & D. 462; *Craig v Lamoureux* [1920] A.C. 349.

[81] Wills Act 1837 s.7, as amended by Family Law Reform Act 1969 s.3(1).

[82] Below, para.14–048.

[83] See Williams, Mortimer & Sunnucks, *Executors, Administrators and Probate*, 18th edn, (London: Sweet & Maxwell, 2000), para.9–07; Administration of Estates (Small Payments) Act 1965 (and SI 1984/539, raising the maximum amount for nominations to £5,000).

[84] See generally *Theobald on Wills*, 17th edn, Chs 3–9.

[85] s.1. This did not affect customary wills: Rob. Gav. 299.

[86] s.5. This expressly applied to land devisable by custom, e.g. gavelkind.

[87] Leaseholds and copyholds were not within the statute (Cru.Dig. vi, p.69).

[88] ss.19, 20.

[89] See H.E.L. iii, p.538; Bailey, *Wills*, 21, 22.

[90] ss.2, 34.

B. Formal Wills

I. EXECUTION

14–020 The provision which governs the formal requirements for the execution of a will made by a testator dying after December 31, 1982, is s.9 of the Wills Act 1837, as reformulated with amendments by the Administration of Justice Act 1982.[91] It is as follows:

> "No will shall be valid unless—
>
> (a) it is in writing, and signed by the testator, or by some other person in his presence and by his direction; and
> (b) it appears that the testator intended by his signature to give effect to the will; and
> (c) the signature is made or acknowledged by the testator in the presence of two or more witnesses present at the same time; and
> (d) each witness either—
>
> > (i) attests and signs the will; or
> > (ii) acknowledges his signature,
>
> in the presence of the testator (but not necessarily in the presence of any other witness),
>
> but no form of attestation shall be necessary."[92]

14–021   **1. Writing.** The will must be in writing. Any form of writing, printing, typewriting and the like may be employed,[93] or a combination of these, e.g. a printed form completed in manuscript[94]; but pencil writing on a will made in ink is presumed to be merely deliberative, and will be excluded from probate unless it appears to be intended to be operative.[95] No special form of words need be used: all that is required is an intelligible document[96] which indicates an *animus testandi* (intention to make a will).[97]

14–022   **2. Signature by testator.** The will must be signed by the testator, or by someone else in his presence and by his direction.[98] The testator's signature

---

[91] s.17. This section was enacted in response to recommendations of the Law Reform Committee in *The Making and Revocation of Wills*, Cmnd. 7902 (1980).

[92] The major changes to the Wills Act 1837 s.9, as originally enacted, are paras (b) and (d)(ii) and the omission of the requirement that the testator's signature be "at the foot or end" of the will.

[93] See, e.g. *In b. Usborne* (1909) 25 T.L.R. 519.

[94] *In b. Moore* [1892] P. 378.

[95] *In b. Adams* (1872) L.R. 2 P. & D. 367.

[96] e.g. *Thorn v Dickens* [1906] W.N. 54 (entire will consisting of words "all for mother").

[97] In *Re Meynell* [1949] W.N. 273 probate was granted of written instructions to a solicitor, which had been duly witnessed because of fears that the testator might die suddenly. Where these formalities are observed there is a strong presumption of *animus testandi*.

[98] Wills Act 1837 s.9.

may be made in any way, provided there is an intention to execute the will. Thus initials,[99] a stamped name,[100] a mark[101] (even if the testator could write[102]), or a signature in a former[103] or assumed[104] name all suffice.[105] But a seal is not enough for the will must be signed, and sealing is not signing;[106] nor is a photocopied signature sufficient.[107] Similar principles apply to signature by someone on behalf of the testator. Thus signature of his own name instead of that of the testator is sufficient.[108] But it is essential that the signature should be made in the testator's presence and authorised by him, either expressly or by implication.[109] The testator must have intended by his signature to give effect to the will.[110] A signature in the normal place at the end of the will obviously fulfils this requirement, but questions may arise where the signature is in an abnormal place, as explained below.

3. Position of signature. Under the Act of 1837 the signature had to be at **14–023** the "foot or end" of the will,[111] a provision that was the subject both of legislative amendment and considerable litigation.[112] The Act of 1982, as set out above, has now abolished the rule about the position of the testator's signature where he dies after 1982. The signature may now be placed in any position in the will,[113] provided that it appears that it is intended to give effect to it, and is not, for example, merely an indication that the document is the testator's property. Normally the testator will sign the instrument only after it has been written. However, the time at which the signature is appended is immaterial when the writing and signing of the will are all part of one operation.[114]

[99] *In b. Savory* (1851) 15 Jur. 1042.
[100] *Jenkins v Gaisford* (1863) 3 Sw. & Tr. 93.
[101] e.g. a thumb-mark: *In b. Finn* (1936) 53 T.L.R. 153.
[102] *Baker v Dening* (1838) 8 A. & E. 94.
[103] *In b. Glover* (1847) 11 Jur. 1022.
[104] *In b. Redding* (1850) 2 Rob. Ecc. 339.
[105] And see *In b. Chalcraft* [1948] P. 222 (testatrix too ill to complete more than part of her surname: held valid); *In b. Cook* [1960] 1 W.L.R. 353 ("your loving Mother": held valid).
[106] *Wright v Wakeford* (1811) 17 Ves. 454.
[107] *Lim v Thompson* [2009] EWHC 3341 (Ch); [2010] W.T.L.R. 661.
[108] *In b. Clark* (1839) 2 Curt. 329.
[109] *In b. Marshall* (1866) 13 L.T. 643; *Barrett v Bem* [2011] EWHC 1247 (Ch); [2011] W.T.L.R. 1117.
[110] Wills Act 1837 s.9(b), applying to deaths after 1982, above, para.14–020. It must be *by the act of signing* that the testator intended to give effect to the will, and not e.g. by presenting to witnesses a previously executed will which the testator had subsequently amended but had not re-signed: *Re White* [1991] Ch. 1 at 9. Where a testator by mistake signed a "mirror" will prepared for his spouse, it could not be said that he intended to give effect to that will: *Marley v Rawlings* [2011] EWHC 161 (Ch); [2011] 1 W.L.R. 2146.
[111] Wills Act 1837 s.9. Formerly the signature might be anywhere in the will (*Lemoyne v Stanley* (1681) 3 Lev. 1), and a holograph will (i.e. one made in the testator's own handwriting) might be effective even if unsigned: *In b. Cosser* (1848) 1 Rob. Ecc. 633.
[112] For the law as it stood prior to 1983, see the fifth edition of this work at p.507.
[113] See *Wood v Smith* [1993] Ch. 90 (opening words of will, "My Will by Percy Winterbone of 150, High Street, Margate", a sufficient signature); *Weatherhill v Pearce* [1995] 1 W.L.R. 592 (attestation clause, "Signed by the said testator Doris Weatherhill . . . ", a sufficient signature); [1995] Conv. 256 (S. Grattan).
[114] *Re White* [1991] Ch. 1 at 8; *Wood v Smith*, above.

14–024   Effect will be given to dispositions contained in a document which has not been executed as a will if the document is incorporated in a will. For this to be the case:

>   (i) the will must clearly[115] identify the document to be incorporated[116];
>
>   (ii) the will must refer to the document as being already in existence[117] and not as one subsequently to be made[118]; and
>
>   (iii) the document must in fact be in existence when the will[119] (or a codicil confirming it[120]) is executed.

14–025   **4. Presence of witnesses.** The testator must make the whole[121] of the signature (or acknowledge it) in the presence of two witnesses present at the same time.[122] Whether the signature to the will is made by the testator or by someone in his presence and by his direction, there is no need for witnesses to be present at the time of the signature if they are present when the testator subsequently makes a proper acknowledgment[123] of the signature. But either the signature or the acknowledgment must be made in the simultaneous presence of two witnesses. An express acknowledgment is desirable but not essential[124]; a gesture by the testator may suffice,[125] and an acknowledgment by a third party is effective if it can be shown that it should be taken to be the acknowledgment of the testator.[126] It is immaterial if the witnesses do not know that the document is a will[127]; it suffices if they see the testator write something (even if they do not know that it is his signature)[128] or if he asks them to sign a document on which they see his signature,[129] or could have seen it if they had looked.[130] But there is no signature in the presence of a witness if, although in the room, he had no knowledge that the testator was

---

[115] But see *In b. Saxton* [1939] 2 All E.R. 418.

[116] *In b. Garnett* [1894] P. 90.

[117] *In b. Sutherland* (1866) L.R. 1 P. & D. 198.

[118] *University College of North Wales v Taylor* [1908] P. 140.

[119] *Singleton v Tomlinson* (1878) 3 App.Cas. 404.

[120] *In b. Hunt* (1853) 2 Rob. Ecc. 622. But the will, speaking from the date of the codicil, must here refer to the document as existing (*In b. Truro* (1866) L.R. 1 P. & D. 201); it is not enough that in fact the document was made before the codicil: *In b. Smart* [1902] P. 238.

[121] *Re Colling* [1972] 1 W.L.R. 1440.

[122] Wills Act 1837 s.9.

[123] See *Re Groffman* [1969] 1 W.L.R. 733 (will in testator's pocket: no sufficient acknowledgement).

[124] Except where the testator is acknowledging a signature made by someone else on his behalf: see *In b. Summers* (1850) 14 Jur. 791.

[125] *In b. Davies* (1850) 2 Rob. Ecc. 337.

[126] *Inglesant v Inglesant* (1874) L.R. 3 P. & D. 172; but see *Morritt v Douglas* (1872) L.R. 3 P. & D. 1.

[127] *Daintree v Fasulo* (1888) 13 P.D. 102; *In b. Benjamin* (1934) 150 L.T. 417.

[128] *Smith v Smith* (1866) L.R. 1 P. & D. 143.

[129] *Fischer v Popham* (1875) L.R. 3 P. & D. 246; and see *Brown v Skirrow* [1902] P. 3 at 5.

[130] *In b. Gunston* (1882) 7 P.D. 102 (see at 108); but not if the signature is covered up.

writing; a man cannot be a witness to an act of which he is unconscious.[131] Similarly, a blind person cannot witness a will.[132] It is desirable but not essential[133] that the witnesses should be of full age and sound intelligence.

5. Signature by witnesses. The witnesses must then sign in the presence of **14–026** the testator.[134] No form of attestation is necessary,[135] although a proper attestation clause showing that the will has been executed in accordance with the statutory requirements will facilitate the grant of probate.[136] All that is necessary is that after the testator's signature has been made or acknowledged[137] in the joint presence of two witnesses, they should sign their names in the testator's presence.[138] It suffices that the testator knew that they were signing,[139] and either saw them sign,[140] or could have seen them if he had wished,[141] or if he had not been blind.[142] There is no need for the witnesses to sign in each other's presence,[143] although this is both usual and desirable. They may sign by a mark[144] or initials,[145] and the position of their signatures is immaterial, provided they are made with intent to attest the operative[146] signature of the testator.[147]

Under the Act of 1837 there was no provision allowing a witness to **14–027** acknowledge his signature. Thus, if the testator signed in the presence of A, who signed his name, and then B was called in and both the testator and A acknowledged their signature to B, who then signed, probate was refused.[148] But this difficulty has been removed (in the case of testators dying after 1982) by the provision that a witness may acknowledge his signature "in the

---

[131] *Brown v Skirrow* [1902] P. 3.

[132] *In b. Gibson* [1949] P. 434.

[133] Wills Act 1837 s.14; Jarman 143, 144; *Smith v Thompson* (1931) 146 L.T. 14 (effective attestation by infant).

[134] Wills Act 1837 s.9. The testator must be mentally as well as physically present, but latitude is allowed if a proper signature in the presence of witnesses has already been made: *In b. Chalcraft* [1948] P. 222 (testatrix losing consciousness after signature and during attestation: will held valid).

[135] Wills Act 1837 s.9; and see *In b. Colver* (1889) 60 L.T. 368 (will executed in form of a deed held valid); *In b. Denning* [1958] 1 W.L.R. 462 (mere presence of two other signatures).

[136] *Re Papillon* [2006] EWHC 3419 (Ch); [2008] W.T.L.R. 269 at [22].

[137] See *Couser v Couser* [1996] 1 W.L.R. 1301.

[138] *Kayll v Rawlinson* [2010] EWHC 1269 (Ch); [2010] W.T.L.R. 1443.

[139] *Jenner v Finch* (1879) 5 P.D. 106.

[140] e.g. *Casson v Dade* (1781) I Bro. C.C. 99 (view from carriage of witness signing in attorney's office).

[141] *In b. Trimnell* (1865) 11 Jur. (N.S.) 248.

[142] *In b. Piercy* (1845) 1 Rob. Ecc. 278.

[143] *In b. Webb* (1855) Dea. & Sw. 1.

[144] *In b. Amiss* (1849) 2 Rob. Ecc. 116. But a seal does not suffice: *In b. Byrd* (1842) 3 Curt. 117.

[145] *In b. Streatley* [1891] P. 172.

[146] *Phipps v Hale* (1874) L.R. 3 P. & D. 166.

[147] *In b. Braddock* (1876) 1 P.D. 433 (witnesses to codicil signed on will to which it was pinned: held valid); *In b. Streatley*, above.

[148] As in *Wyatt v Berry* [1893] P. 5; *Re Colling* [1972] 1 W.L.R. 1440.

presence of the testator (but not necessarily in the presence of any other witness)".[149]

14–028   **6. International wills.** Any will that complies with Arts 2 to 5 of the Annex to the Convention on International Wills 1973 is valid as regards form, irrespective of the place where it is made, of the locality of the assets and of the nationality, domicile or residence of the testator.[150] The requirements of those Articles are generally similar to those of English law, but in addition the will is required to be acknowledged before "a person authorised to act in connection with international wills" who must attach to the will a certificate in the form of Art.10 certifying compliance with the formalities. The ordinary rules as to revocation are unaffected.

II. ALTERATIONS

14–029   "No obliteration, interlineation, or other alteration made in any will after the execution thereof[151] shall be valid or have any effect, except so far as the words or effect of the will before such alteration shall not be apparent, unless such alteration shall be executed in like manner as hereinbefore is required for the execution of the will . . . ".[152]

The same section of the Act goes on to provide that the signatures of the testator and the witnesses may be written either opposite or near to the alteration (e.g. in the margin) or else at the foot or end of, or opposite to a memorandum referring to the alteration. Signature by means of initials suffices.[153] A codicil confirming a will gives effect to any alterations of the will existing at the date of the codicil,[154] unless the codicil shows that the testator was treating the will as being unaltered.[155]

14–030   An obliteration or erasure of part of a will, even though unattested, has the effect of revoking that part in so far as it makes it impossible to read ("not apparent"), provided that there was an intention to revoke.[156] The same applies to the pasting of paper over part of a will,[157] provided the words are not decipherable by any natural means, such as by the use of magnifying glasses or by holding the will up to the light.[158] The court will not permit

---

[149] AJA 1982 s.17, quoted above, para.14–020.
[150] AJA 1982 s.27 Sch.2 (setting out the Annex).
[151] See *In b. Campbell* [1954] 1 W.L.R. 516 (interlineation prior to execution).
[152] Wills Act 1837 s.21. It is not enough that the witnesses attest the amendments to the will if the testator does not sign them or re-execute the will: *Re White* [1991] Ch. 1.
[153] *In b. Blewitt* (1880) 5 P.D. 116.
[154] *In b. Hall* (1871) L.R. 2 P. & D. 256 at 257, 258.
[155] *Re Hay* [1904] 1 Ch. 317 (unattested deletion of three legacies in will; codicil revoked one legacy: held, the other two stood).
[156] *Townley v Watson* (1844) 3 Curt. 761. For revocation by destruction, see below, para.14–034.
[157] *In b. Horsford* (1874) L.R. 3 P. & D. 211.
[158] *Ffinch v Combe* [1894] P. 191; *In b. Brasier* [1899] P. 36.

physical interference with the will, as by using chemicals[159] or removing paper pasted over the words[160]; for they must be "apparent" on the will as it stands. Similarly, they are not "apparent" if they can be read only by making some other document, such as an infra-red photograph.[161] But intention to revoke is always necessary, and where paper is pasted over the amounts of legacies, but not the names of the recipients, the intention is evidently to revoke only by substituting new amounts. The doctrine of conditional revocation (explained below)[162] may then come to the rescue, so that the original amounts are unrevoked and can be proved by any means, including infra-red photography.[163]

III. REVOCATION

A will or codicil may be revoked by another will or codicil, by destruction, or by entry into marriage or civil partnership; and revocation may be conditional.   **14–031**

1. By another will or codicil. A revocation clause expressly revoking all former wills is effective,[164] provided it is contained in a document[165] executed with the proper formalities.[166] This is so even if the testator had been misled as to the effect of the clause,[167] but not if the testator did not know of its presence.[168] A misapprehension may, however, admit the doctrine of conditional revocation, explained below.[169] A will is not revoked merely because a later will begins (as is usual) "This is the last will and testament" of the testator, or some similar phrase.[170]   **14–032**

A will is revoked by implication if a later will is executed which merely repeats the former will[171] or is inconsistent with it[172]; but if the repetition or inconsistency is merely partial, those parts of the former will which are not   **14–033**

---

[159] *Ffinch v Combe*, above, at 193.

[160] *In b. Horsford*, above. Where words illegible in 1874 had gradually become legible, they were admitted to probate in 1894: *Ffinch v Combe*, above; and see *In b. Gilbert* [1893] P. 183 for removal of paper in order to ascertain whether an earlier will had been revoked, for the obliteration of the revoking words would not revive it: below, para.14–045.

[161] *In b. Itter* [1950] P. 130.

[162] Below, para.14–042.

[163] *In b. Itter*, above.

[164] Including, in the absence of special circumstances (*Smith v Thompson* (1931) 146 L.T. 14), the exercise of any power of appointment made thereby: *Re Kingdon* (1886) 32 Ch D 604; *Lowthorpe-Lutwidge v Lowthorpe-Lutwidge* [1935] P. 151.

[165] See *Re Spracklan's Estate* [1938] 2 All E.R. 345 (duly executed letter directing destruction of will in recipient's custody held effective).

[166] Wills Act 1837 s.20.

[167] *Collins v Elstone* [1893] P. 1; *Re Horrocks* [1939] P. 198 at 216; but see *Re Phelan* [1972] Fam. 33.

[168] *In b. Oswald* (1874) L.R. 3 P. & D. 162; *In b. Moore* [1892] P. 378.

[169] Below, para.14–042.

[170] *Simpson v Foxon* [1907] P. 54.

[171] *Re Hawksley's Settlement* [1934] Ch. 384 at 397 et seq.

[172] *In b. Bryan* [1907] P. 125.

repeated in the later will or inconsistent with it remain effective.[173] Any number of testamentary documents may be read together, each being effective except so far as subsequently varied or revoked. The sum total constitutes the testator's will.[174]

14–034   **2. By destruction.** A will is revoked "by the burning, tearing, or otherwise destroying the same by the testator, or by some person in his presence and by his direction, with the intention of revoking the same".[175] There are thus two elements: an act of destruction, together with an intention to revoke (*animus revocandi*).

14–035   *(a) Act of destruction.* It is not necessary that the will should be completely destroyed; there must, however, be some burning, tearing or other destruction of the whole will or some essential part of it, as by cutting off[176] or obliterating[177] the signature of the testator[178] or the witnesses.[179] It is not enough for the testator to draw a line through part of the will, indorse it "all these are revoked" and kick it into the corner.[180] Destruction of part of a will normally revokes that part alone,[181] unless the part destroyed is so important as to lead to the conclusion that the rest cannot be intended to stand alone.[182] Destruction by someone other than the testator is ineffective unless carried out both in his presence[183] and by his direction[184]; the testator cannot ratify an unauthorised destruction.[185]

14–036   If a will has been destroyed without being revoked (e.g. because an *animus revocandi* was lacking), it is proved by means of a draft or copy, or even by oral evidence.[186] A will kept in the testator's possession but which cannot be found at the testator's death is presumed to have been destroyed by him *animo*

---

[173] *Lemage v Goodban* (1865) L.R. 1 P. & D. 57.

[174] *In b. Fenwick* (1867) L.R. 1 P. & D. 319; cf. *Townsend v Moore* [1905] P. 66 (two inconsistent wills of uncertain priority: probate refused to each); *Re Robinson* [1930] 2 Ch. 332 (no revocation by ineffective disposition).

[175] Wills Act 1837 s.20.

[176] *In b. Gullan* (1858) 1 Sw. & Tr. 23.

[177] *In b. Morton* (1887) 12 P.D. 141; contrast *In b. Godfrey* (1893) 69 L.T. 22 (signature remaining legible). The courts apply the same test in cases involving the Wills Act 1837 s.20 as they do in cases of alteration under s.21 (para.14–029, above). If the signature is still "apparent", the will is taken to have been revoked: *Re Adams* [1990] Ch. 601.

[178] *In b. Gullan*, above.

[179] *Williams v Tyley* (1858) John. 530.

[180] *Cheese v Lovejoy* (1858) 2 P.D. 251.

[181] See *In b. Woodward* (1871) L.R. 2 P. & D. 206 (seven or eight lines out of a will written on seven sheets); *In b. Nunn* (1936) 105 L.J.P. 57 (part of will cut out and remaining parts stitched together; partial revocation only); *Re Everest* [1975] Fam. 44 (similar).

[182] *Leonard v Leonard* [1902] P. 243 (two out of five sheets destroyed).

[183] *In b. Dadds* (1857) Dea. & Sw. 290; *In b. De Kremer* (1965) 110 S.J. 18 (solicitor burnt will on client's telephone instructions).

[184] *Gill v Gill* [1909] P. 157.

[185] *Gill v Gill*, above.

[186] *In b. Dadds*, above (copy); *Sugden v Lord St Leonards* (1876) 1 P.D. 154 (oral evidence of a beneficiary: the leading case on this subject); *Mills v Millward* (1889) 15 P.D. 20 (affidavit by executor); *Re Webb* [1964] 1 W.L.R. 509.

revocandi and cannot be proved[187] unless the presumption is rebutted by evidence of non-revocation.[188]

(b) Intent to revoke. The testator must have an *animus revocandi* at the time **14–037** of the destruction. If a will is intentionally torn up by a testator who is drunk[189] or believes the will to be ineffective,[190] it is not revoked, for an intent to destroy the document is no substitute for the requisite intent to revoke the will.[191] "All the destroying in the world without intention will not revoke a will, nor all the intention in the world without destroying: there must be the two."[192]

3. By marriage or civil partnership. Marriage automatically revokes all **14–038** wills made by the parties to the marriage.[193] This is so even where the marriage is voidable and is later annulled.[194] The same rule applies in relation to civil partnerships.[195] However, there are two important exceptions.

(a) Certain appointments. A disposition in a will under a power of appoint- **14–039** ment is not revoked by the testator's subsequent marriage or civil partnership unless, in default of appointment, the property would pass to his personal representatives.[196] The general intention of this provision is that if the testator's new "family" will get the property even if the will is revoked, there is no harm in allowing the marriage or civil partnership to revoke it. But if in default of appointment the property would pass out of the "family", as defined by the rules of intestacy, or only partly to that family,[197] the will is allowed to stand so far as it exercises the power of appointment, though the rest of the will is revoked.[198]

(b) Will in expectation of marriage or civil partnership. Where it appears **14–040** from the will that at the time it was made the testator was expecting to be married to, or to form a civil partnership with, a particular person and that the testator intended that the will should not be revoked by the marriage or civil partnership, the will is not revoked by the marriage or civil partnership.[199] If the testator's intention relates to a particular disposition only in the will, that disposition is not revoked, nor is the remainder of the will, unless it appears

---

[187] *Eckersley v Platt* (1866) L.R. 1 P. & D. 281; *Allan v Morrison* [1900] A.C. 604.
[188] *Sugden v Lord St Leonards*, above; *Re Zielinski* [2007] W.T.L.R. 1655.
[189] *In b. Brassington* [1902] P. 1.
[190] *In b. Thornton* (1889) 14 P.D. 82; cf. *In b. Southerden* [1925] P. 177 at 185.
[191] See *Giles v Warren* (1872) L.R. 2 P. & D. 401.
[192] *Cheese v Lovejoy* (1877) 2 P.D. 251 at 253, per James L.J.
[193] Wills Act 1837 s.18, as substituted by AJA 1982 s.18 (for wills made after 1982).
[194] *Re Roberts* [1978] 1 W.L.R. 653.
[195] Wills Act 1837 s.18B, inserted by Civil Partnership Act 2004 s.71 Sch.4 para.2.
[196] Wills Act 1837 s.18(2).
[197] See *In b. McVicar* (1869) L.R. 1 P. & D. 671; *Re Paul* [1921] 2 Ch. 1.
[198] *In b. Russell* (1890) 15 P.D. 111; see also *In b. Gilligan* [1950] P. 32 at 38, which contains a helpful explanation of the enactment; (1951) 67 L.Q.R. 351 (J.D.B. Mitchell).
[199] Wills Act 1837 s.18(3); Wills Act 1837 s.18B(3), as inserted by Civil Partnership Act 2004 s.71 Sch.4 para.2; see, e.g. *Court v Despallieres* [2009] EWHC 3340 (Ch), [2010] W.T.L.R. 437.

from the will that the testator intended the marriage or civil partnership to revoke the remainder.[200]

14–041   *(c) Dissolution of marriage or civil partnership.* Since 1982, the dissolution or annulment of the testator's marriage subsequent to the execution of the will has affected gifts and appointments to the testator's former spouse unless the will showed a contrary intention. If the testator died after 1982 but before 1996, the will took effect as if any appointment of the former spouse as executor or trustee had been omitted and there was a deemed lapse of any devise or bequest to the former spouse.[201] However, this gave rise to anomalous results, and the law was changed with prospective effect.[202] If the testator dies after 1995, and the testator's marriage or civil partnership is dissolved or annulled subsequent to the execution of the will, then except in so far as a contrary intention appears by the will, provisions appointing executors or trustees, if they appoint the former spouse or civil partner, shall take effect, and any property devised or bequeathed to the former spouse or civil partner shall pass, as if that person had died on the day of dissolution or annulment.[203] It follows that a gift in an unrevoked will to X should the testatrix's husband predecease her, will now take effect in favour of X if the parties are divorced before the testatrix's death, even though her former husband is still alive at that time.

14–042   **4. Conditional revocation.** Revocation of a will may be conditional, in which case the will remains unrevoked until the condition has been fulfilled.[204] One particular kind of conditional revocation is known as dependent relative revocation.[205] If revocation is relative to another will and intended to be dependent upon the validity of that will, the revocation is ineffective unless that other will takes effect. Four examples may be given.

14–043   *(a) Destruction.* If a will is destroyed by a testator who is about to make a new will, and the evidence shows that he intended to revoke the old will only in order to make way for a new one, the old will remains valid if the new will

---

[200] Wills Act 1837 s.18(4); Wills Act 1837 s.18B(4), inserted by Civil Partnership Act 2004 s.71, Sch.4 para.2. These provisions reverse the effect of *Re Coleman* [1976] Ch. 1.

[201] Wills Act 1837 s.18A(1)(b), as inserted by AJA 1982 s.18(2).

[202] *Re Sinclair* [1985] Ch. 446, where a husband's will left his estate to his wife, and if she predeceased him, to a charity. When, following their divorce, the husband predeceased his former wife without having revoked his will, his estate passed on intestacy and not to the charity. Reform was recommended by the Law Commission in Law Com. No.217, and implemented by the Law Reform (Succession) Act 1995, s.3.

[203] Wills Act 1837 s.18A, as amended by Law Reform (Succession) Act 1995 s.3; Wills Act 1837 s.18C, as inserted by Civil Partnership Act 2004 s.71 Sch.4 para.2.

[204] e.g. *In b. Southerden* [1925] P. 177 (will destroyed in mistaken belief that testator's widow would take all his property on his intestacy; held, not revoked); cf. *Campbell v French* (1797) 3 Ves. 321 (mistaken belief that legatee was dead); *In b. Greenstreet* (1930) 74 S.J. 188.

[205] A title "somewhat overloaded with unnecessary polysyllables. The resounding adjectives add very little, as it seems to me, to any clear idea of what is meant. The whole matter can be quite simply expressed by the word 'conditional' ": *In b. Hope Brown* [1942] P. 136 at 138, per Langton J.

is never executed.[206] No special declaration of intention is necessary, since the court will readily infer it from the fact that a new will was contemplated.[207] But if the evidence indicates an intention to revoke the will in any event, the fact that a new will was contemplated does not prevent the revocation from taking effect.[208]

(b) Revival. If Will No.1 is revoked by Will No.2, the revocation of Will No.2 is not sufficient to revive Will No.1,[209] so that if the testator revokes Will No.2 in the mistaken belief that he is thereby reviving Will No.1, the doctrine of dependent relative revocation applies and the revocation of Will No.2 is ineffective.[210]   **14–044**

(c) Obliterations.[211] If a testator obliterates a legacy and by unattested writing substitutes a new legacy,[212] or pastes over the amount of a legacy an unattested slip of paper bearing a new amount,[213] the old legacy remains effective if the court is satisfied that it was revoked only on the erroneous supposition that the new legacy would be effective.   **14–045**

(d) Gifts to attesting witnesses.[214] The doctrine also applies where a testator executes a will which expressly revokes an earlier one and each will contains a gift in similar terms to X who attests the second will. Under the Wills Act 1837[215] the legacy in the second will to X will be void if the first will is revoked in its entirety. In those circumstances the gift in the first will remains effective because the testator did not intend it to be invalidated by the execution of the second.[216]   **14–046**

IV. REVIVAL

A will revoked by destruction *animo revocandi* can never be revived.[217] Any other will can be revived, but only by re-execution with the proper formalities   **14–047**

---

[206] *Onions v Tyrer* (1716) 2 Vern. 742; *Dixon v Solicitor to the Treasury* [1905] P. 42 (testator gave instructions for new will, tore off his signature from old will and died before new will completed: old will admitted to probate); *In b. Hope Brown*, above (new will incomplete by reason of omission of names of beneficiaries: both old and new wills admitted to probate); *In b. Bromham* [1952] 1 All E.R. 110 (will mutilated with intention (never completed) of making a new will: old will admitted to probate); *In b. Cocke* [1960] 1 W.L.R. 491; cf. *Re Feis* [1964] Ch. 106. For a full review of the authorities, see *Re Finnemore* [1991] 1 W.L.R. 793.

[207] *Re Jones* [1976] Ch. 200.

[208] *Re Jones*, above.

[209] For revival, see below, para.14–047.

[210] *Powell v Powell* (1866) L.R. 1 P. & D. 209; *In b. Bridgewater* [1965] 1 W.L.R. 416 (letter by testator admissible evidence both of destruction and of his intent).

[211] For obliterations, see above, para.14–030.

[212] *In b. Horsford* (1874) L.R. 3 P. & D. 211; *In b. McCabe* (1873) L.R. 3 P. & D. 94 (substitution of different legatee); *Sturton v Whellock* (1883) 52 L.J.P. 29 (gifts to grandchildren at 21: "one" obliterated and unattested "five" substituted); cf. *In b. Hope Brown*, above.

[213] *In b. Itter* [1950] P. 130 (new amounts signed but not attested).

[214] Below, para.14–066.

[215] s.15.

[216] *In b. Crannis* (1978) 122 S.J. 489; *Re Finnemore*, above.

[217] *Rogers v Goodenough* (1862) 2 Sw. & Tr. 342; *In b. Reade* [1902] P. 75.

or by a codicil showing an intention to revive it.[218] If a will has been revoked by a subsequent will, the first will is thus not revived merely by the revocation of the later will.[219] If a will is first partially revoked, then wholly revoked, and then revived, the revival does not extend to the part partially revoked unless an intention to this effect is shown.[220]

C. Informal Wills

14–048   A long-standing dispensation from the rules of formality is confirmed by the Wills Act 1837 in the following words:

> "Provided always . . . that any soldier being in actual military service, or any mariner or seaman being at sea, may dispose of his personal estate as he might have done before the making of this Act."[221]

Under this privilege completely informal dispositions are permitted, even by minors, and it has since been extended to realty as well as personalty.[222] The underlying doctrine, borrowed from Roman law,[223] is that a soldier or sailor may at times be *inops consilii*, cut off from skilled advice and help; but the privilege is not lost merely because such advice and help is available, nor are the rules of Roman law incorporated.[224]

I. PRIVILEGED TESTATORS

14–049   **1. A soldier in actual military service.** It is not enough that the testator was in an army; he must have been "in actual military service" when he made the will. This phrase means active service in the armed forces in connection with hostilities including insurrection,[225] whether past, present or believed to be imminent in the future; and it is to be interpreted liberally.[226] A soldier is deemed to be in actual military service from the moment he received mobilisation orders[227] until the full conclusion of the operations,[228] which may last for many years beyond the end of hostilities.[229] Thus the privilege extends to

---

[218] Wills Act 1837 s.22, see *Goldie v Adam* [1938] P. 85; *In b. Davis* [1952] P. 279 (revival by duly attested inscription on envelope containing will; intention to revive inferred from facts); *Re Pearson* [1963] 1 W.L.R. 1358 (revival of will containing revocation clause revokes later will).

[219] *In b. Hodgkinson* [1893] P. 339. The law was otherwise before 1838: *Usticke v Bawden* (1824) 2 Add. 116.

[220] Wills Act 1837 s.22.

[221] s.11, replacing Statute of Frauds 1677 s.22, which was in similar terms. Before 1677 anyone might make an informal will of personalty: above, para.14–019.

[222] Wills (Soldiers and Sailors) Act 1918 s.3; see below, para.14–054.

[223] *Drummond v Parish* (1843) 3 Curt. 522 at 531.

[224] *Re Booth* [1926] P. 118; *Re Wingham* [1949] P. 187.

[225] *Re Jones* [1981] Fam. 7 (soldier shot by "clandestine assassins and arsonists" in Northern Ireland).

[226] *Re Wingham* [1949] P. 187 at 196 (an airman undergoing training in Canada held to be privileged.)

[227] *Gattward v Knee* [1902] P. 99; *Re Booth* [1926] P. 118.

[228] *Re Limond* [1915] 2 Ch. 240.

[229] *Re Colman* [1958] 1 W.L.R. 457.

an escort for those delimiting a frontier after fighting is over,[230] and to a member of an army of occupation, even though fighting ended nine years earlier,[231] but not to a wounded soldier in a London hospital.[232]

"Soldier" includes both officers and other ranks, an army nurse,[233] and a member of the Air Force[234]; and in the Second World War it included members of the Women's Auxiliary Air Force,[235] Auxiliary Transport Service, and Home Guard.[236]

2. A mariner or seaman at sea. This includes both members of the Royal **14–050** Navy[237] and merchant seamen; it has been held to extend to a typist employed on a liner.[238] It includes an admiral directing naval operations on a river,[239] and a master mariner in his ship lying in the Thames before starting on her voyage.[240] A seaman on shore leave is deemed to be at sea, if he is a member of a ship's crew[241] or has received orders to join a ship.[242] It makes no difference that his ship is in dock for refitting[243] or is permanently stationed in harbour,[244] provided that he has not been paid off. The seaman need not be serving with, or engaged to join, a British registered ship, provided that he is domiciled in the U.K.[245]

3. A member of Her Majesty's Naval or Marine Forces so circum- **14–051** **stanced that, had he been a soldier, he would have been in actual military** **service.**[246] This enables a member of the navy or marines who has been called up to make an informal will even though he has not joined his ship.[247]

II. EXTENT OF THE PRIVILEGE

A testator within one of the above categories may make (or revoke) a will **14–052** even if he is a minor,[248] and, whatever his age, he may make or revoke a will

---

[230] *Re Limond*, above.

[231] *Re Colman*, above (British army in Germany).

[232] *In b. Grey* [1922] P. 140.

[233] *In b. Stanley* [1916] P. 192.

[234] Wills (Soldiers and Sailors) Act 1918 s.5.

[235] *In b. Rowson* [1944] 2 All E.R. 36.

[236] *Re Wingham* [1949] P. 187 at 196.

[237] The statutory restrictions on informal dispositions of wages, prize money, etc., by seamen in the Navy and Marines were repealed by the Navy and Marines (Wills) Act 1953.

[238] *In b. Hale* [1915] 2 I.R. 362.

[239] *In b. Austen* (1853) 2 Rob.Ecc. 611.

[240] *In b. Patterson* (1898) 79 L.T. 123.

[241] *In b. Newland* [1952] P. 71.

[242] *In b. Wilson* [1952] P. 92; *Re Servoz-Gavin* [2009] EWHC 3168 (Ch); [2011] Ch. 162; cf. *Re Rapley* [1983] 1 W.L.R. 1069 (no orders received).

[243] *In b. Newland*, above.

[244] *In b. M'Murdo* (1867) L.R. 1 P. & D. 540; *In b. Anderson* [1916] P. 49 at 52.

[245] *Re Servoz-Gavin*, above.

[246] Wills (Soldiers and Sailors) Act 1918 s.2.

[247] See *In b. Anderson* [1916] P. 49 at 52; *In b. Yates* [1919] P. 93.

[248] Wills (Soldiers and Sailors) Act 1918 s.1 (declaratory, removing doubts raised by *Re Wernher* [1918] 1 Ch. 339), as amended by Family Law Reform Act 1969 s.3(1) (reduction of age of majority from 21 to 18). This is contrary to the usual rule: see above, para.14–018.

informally. The will may be in writing, with or without witnesses or signature, or it may be nuncupative, i.e. oral. Thus farewell words spoken at a railway station may constitute a valid will.[249] The testator need not know that he is making a will, provided he gives deliberate expression to his wishes as to the destination of his property on his death.[250] Those entitled to make informal wills are also entitled to revoke a will, even if it has been made formally, in an informal manner, as by an unattested letter to a relative asking that the will should be burned, "for I have already cancelled it".[251] Marriage (and now, presumably, civil partnership) also effects revocation.[252]

14–053   A will made in compliance with the above conditions remains valid indefinitely unless revoked. This is so even after the military or other service is over[253]; but thereafter any revocation must be formal. It formerly seemed that a minor was unable to revoke the will save by marriage, but in 1969 a general power of revocation was conferred.[254]

14–054   The statutory privileges at first applied only to wills of personalty,[255] but they were extended to realty by the Wills (Soldiers and Sailors) Act 1918.[256] However, as regards any testator who is a minor there seems to be ground for supposing that the latter enactment may have been unintentionally frustrated by the Administration of Estates Act 1925,[257] except in the case of a minor who is married or registers a civil partnership or dies leaving issue, or devises of interests *pur autre vie*. The Act of 1918 allows a guardian for the testator's infant children to be appointed by a privileged will.[258]

Section 4. Operation of Wills

A. Lapse

I. GENERAL RULE

14–055   A legacy or bequest (i.e. a testamentary gift of personalty) or a devise (i.e. a testamentary gift of realty) is said to lapse if the beneficiary dies before the testator.[259] In such a case, unless a contrary intention is shown, the gift fails

---

[249] *In b. Yates* [1919] P. 93.

[250] *Re Stable* [1919] P. 7 ("If I stop a bullet, everything of mine will be yours"); *In b. Spicer* [1949] P. 441; *Re Servoz-Gavin*, above. Contrast *In b. Donner* (1917) 34 T.L.R. 138 (soldier told, incorrectly, that on intestacy his mother would get all his property: "That is just what I want. I want my mother to have everything": held no will but rather a reason for making no will); similarly *In b. Knibbs* [1962] 1 W.L.R. 852.

[251] *In b. Gossage* [1921] P. 194.

[252] *In b. Wardrop* [1917] P. 54.

[253] *Re Booth* [1926] P. 118 (over 40 years); and see *In b. Coleman* [1920] 2 I.R. 352.

[254] Family Law Reform Act 1969 s.3(3).

[255] Wills Act 1837 s.11.

[256] s.3, giving power to dispose of real estate in England and Ireland.

[257] s.51(3) (as amended by TLATA 1996 Sch.3 para.6(4)): see below, para.36–015.

[258] s.4, reversing *In b. Tollemache* [1917] P. 246.

[259] The term "lapse" is also sometimes applied to the failure of gifts through events which occur after the testator's death, such as failure to satisfy a contingency: see, e.g. *Smell v Dee* (1707) 2 Salk. 415; *Re Parker* [1901] 1 Ch. 408; *Re Fox's Estate* [1937] 4 All E.R. 664; and see above, para.14–041.

and the property comprised in it falls into residue,[260] which means that it passes under any general or residuary gift in the will, such as "all the rest of my property I leave to X". If there is no residuary gift, or if the gift which lapses is itself a gift of all or part of the residue, there is a partial intestacy and the property passes to the persons entitled on intestacy.[261] A special case of statutory lapse is where a gift to a spouse or civil partner lapses as a consequence of the testator's marriage or civil partnership being dissolved, annulled or declared void.[262]

II. EXCLUSION OF THE GENERAL RULE

The general rule as to lapse is excluded in four cases, though one of these is now obsolete. **14–056**

1. Moral obligation. A legacy which is not mere bounty but is intended to **14–057**
satisfy some moral obligation recognised by the testator, whether legally enforceable or not, is outside the doctrine of lapse, so that even if the legatee predeceases the testator the legacy can be claimed by the legatee's personal representatives.[263] A legacy bequeathed in order to pay a debt barred by lapse of time[264] or by the bankruptcy law,[265] or intended to pay the debts of someone for whom the testator felt morally responsible[266] may thus be saved from lapse.

2. Gifts to issue. Subject to contrary intention appearing in the will, where **14–058**
a testator who dies after 1982[267] makes a gift to his child or remoter descendant and that child or descendant predeceases him, leaving issue who survive him, the gift is to "take effect" as a gift to the issue directly, and the issue take in equal shares *per stirpes*.[268] A child or descendant *en ventre sa mere* at the testator's death and born alive thereafter is to be treated as having survived him.[269] Whether a child is legitimate or not is now immaterial.[270]

3. Class gifts. A class gift,[271] e.g. "to all my children", is normally **14–059**
construed as a gift only to those members of the class who are living at the

---

[260] Wills Act 1837 s.25. Previously the same rule applied to personalty, but realty passed to the heir: *Wright v Hall* (1724) Fort. 182.
[261] *Ackroyd v Smithson* (1780) 1 Bro.C.C. 503; *Re Forrest* [1931] 1 Ch. 162; *Re Midgley* [1955] Ch. 576.
[262] Above, para.14–041.
[263] *Stevens v King* [1904] 2 Ch. 30; but see *Theobald on Wills* (17th edn, 2010), para.22–006.
[264] *Williamson v Naylor* (1838) 3 Y. & C.Ex. 208.
[265] *Re Sowerby's Trusts* (1856) 2 K. & J. 630.
[266] *Re Leach* [1948] Ch. 232 (bequest to pay son's debts).
[267] For the position of a testator dying before 1983, see the fifth edition of this work at p.519.
[268] Wills Act 1837 s.33, as inserted by AJA 1982 s.19. For *per stirpes*, see below, para.14–120.
[269] Wills Act 1837 s.33(4)(b).
[270] Wills Act 1837 s.33(4)(a).
[271] For class gifts, see above, para.9–068.

testator's death. There is then no question of lapse in the case of a child who predeceases the testator, since nothing was ever given to him. However, subject to contrary intention appearing in the will, where a testator who dies after 1982[272] makes a class gift to his children or remoter descendants, the class will include the issue of a deceased member of the class who are living at the testator's death.[273] The issue take in equal shares *per stirpes*.[274] Illegitimacy is disregarded, and children conceived before the testator's death but born alive after it are treated as being alive then.[275]

14–060   **4. Entails.** Under the Wills Act 1837 s.32, subject to any contrary intention in the will, there was no lapse if property was given to a person in tail and he predeceased the testator, leaving issue living at the testator's death capable of inheriting under the entail. In that case the gift took effect as if the legatee or devisee had died immediately after the testator. After 1996, entails can no longer be created and this provision has, therefore, been repealed.[276]

14–061   **5. Exceptions.** In two cases the above provisions of the Wills Act 1837[277] do not apply so as to prevent a lapse.

14–062   *(a) Appointments under special powers.* The Act does not apply to an appointment by will under a special power,[278] for it is confined to cases where there is a "devise or bequest" of property. It does, however, apply to appointments under general powers,[279] for the property is then construed as devisable by the appointor.[280]

14–063   *(b) Interests terminable on donee's death and certain contingent gifts.* Formerly the Act expressly excluded gifts of any estate or interest determinable at or before the testator's death, such as a gift of a mere life interest or in joint tenancy. This exclusion no longer appears in the Act, but it is unlikely that the position has changed. It seems improbable that issue of the donee of a life interest could contend that the gift should take effect as a bequest to him for his life.[281] The gift of a mere life interest is likely to be held to show a contrary intention, since it clearly indicates that after the death of the donee the gift is not intended to take effect at all. In any case the gift may fail as being a gift for the life of the father, "take effect" meaning merely "operate".[282] For similar reasons, it is thought that a bequest "to X as and when he

---

[272] For the position of a testator dying before 1983, see the fifth edition of this work at p.521.

[273] Wills Act 1837 s.33(2).

[274] Wills Act 1837 s.33(3); see below, para.14–104.

[275] Wills Act 1837 s.33(4).

[276] TLATA 1996 s.25(2) Sch.4. For the abolition of entails see above, para.3–031.

[277] s.33, as substituted by AJA 1982 s.19; see paras 14–058 and 14–059 above. Except as indicated, the position was the same for testators who died prior to 1983.

[278] *Holyland v Lewin* (1884) 26 Ch D 266.

[279] *Eccles v Cheyne* (1856) 2 K. & J. 676.

[280] Wills Act 1837 s.27; below, para.14–095.

[281] This question cannot arise in respect of gifts made by a testator who died before 1983: see the fifth edition of this work at p.521.

[282] *Re Butler* [1918] 1 I.R. 394.

is 25", where X predeceased the testator aged 20 leaving issue, would not take effect as a gift to the issue.[283]

III. COMMORIENTES

Where a devisee or legatee dies at nearly the same time as the testator, it is necessary to determine which of them survived the other in order to know whether the gift lapsed. Similar questions between *commorientes* (those dying together) arise on intestacy and in respect of joint tenancies. Before 1926 there was no means of settling the question if there was no evidence of the order of deaths. The estate of neither person could therefore benefit from that of the other. The Law of Property Act 1925 resolves this problem for deaths occurring after 1925 by providing that where it is uncertain which survived the other, for all purposes affecting the title to property the younger shall be deemed to have survived the elder, subject to any order of the court.[284] The section applies equally to cases of simple uncertainty, as where one of the parties is on a ship which founders with all hands on an uncertain date and the other dies at home during that period, and to common disasters, such as practically simultaneous deaths in an air-raid,[285] or deaths in an unknown sequence in a common shipwreck.[286] However, it does not apply where one person is merely presumed to have died because he disappeared over seven years before the other died.[287]

14–064

This rule is modified as between spouses and civil partners if one of them dies intestate.[288] Further, for the purposes of inheritance tax the old rule has been restored, and the deceased are deemed to have died simultaneously.[289] It is still prudent to insert a survivorship clause in a will, making gifts by a husband to his wife conditional upon her surviving him for (say) a month.[290] Then if both are killed in an accident with all their issue and the wife actually or notionally survives the husband for a short while, the husband's property will pass to (for example) his own parents rather than to his wife's parents.

14–065

B. Gifts to Witnesses

1. No benefit for witness. The Wills Act[291] provides that where a beneficiary, or his spouse or civil partner, has attested the will, the gift to that

14–066

---

[283] For the situation where the testator died before 1983, see the fifth edition of this work at p.521.

[284] s.184. These words probably do not confer any general discretion on the court, e.g. to avoid hardship, but merely indicate that the statutory presumption is rebuttable: see *Re Lindop* [1942] Ch. 377 at 382 (but the point was reserved in *Hickman v Peacey* [1945] A.C. 304 at 337).

[285] *Hickman v Peacey* [1945] A.C. 304, the majority of the House of Lords rejecting the argument that the section is inapplicable where the deaths may have been simultaneous.

[286] *Re Rowland* [1963] Ch. 1.

[287] *Re Albert* [1967] V.R. 875.

[288] See below, para.14–117.

[289] Inheritance Tax Act 1984 ss.4(2), 54(4). This point used to be important in the days of capital transfer tax, but is no longer so. Even if LPA 1925 s.184 did apply, there would be no second charge to tax on the death of the notional survivor: Inheritance Tax Act 1984 s.141.

[290] For the statutory survivorship clause that applies in cases of intestacy, see AEA 1925 s.46(2A); below, para.14–118.

[291] s.15, as amended by Civil Partnership Act 2004 s.71 Sch.4 para.3.

beneficiary shall be "utterly null and void". Formerly this rule applied even if there were two other witnesses to the will, so that the beneficiary's signature was superfluous.[292] But where the testator has died after May 29, 1968, the attestations of any beneficiaries (or their spouses) are for this purpose to be disregarded if without them the will is duly executed.[293] Thus if one of the three attesting witnesses is a legatee, the legacy is good; if two of them are legatees, both legacies fail.

14–067   **2. Limits.** The limits of the rule should be noticed:

   (i) It does not apply if no witnesses at all were necessary for the validity of the will, such as the will of a soldier in actual military service.[294]

   (ii) It does not apply to a person who signs the will not as a witness but on the testator's behalf[294a] or merely to show that he agrees with the contents of the will.[295]

   (iii) A beneficiary who marries a witness (or becomes their civil partner) after the execution of the will is not disabled from claiming under it.[296]

   (iv) The rule does not apply to gifts to a person as trustee.[297] But the trustee cannot himself benefit; thus a solicitor trustee who attested the will cannot charge professional fees, although expressly so empowered by the will,[298] unless he is not appointed trustee until after the will has been executed.[299]

   (v) The rule does not apply if the gift is made or confirmed by any will or codicil not attested by the beneficiary.[300] Thus if there is a gift by will confirmed by codicil, a beneficiary who witnesses only one document is entitled to the gift since he can claim under the other document. This is so even where the residuary legatee under a will attested a codicil which, by revoking certain legacies, would swell the residue.[301]

   (vi) The rule has no application where the testator leaves a gift to a legatee as secret trustee, and the will is witnessed by a beneficiary

---

[292] *In b. Bravda* [1968] 1 W.L.R. 479.
[293] Wills Act 1968 s.1.
[294] *Re Limond* [1915] 2 Ch. 240.
[294a] *Barrett v Bem* [2011] EWHC 1247 (Ch); [2011] W.T.L.R. 1117 (beneficiary signing will at the testator's direction to comply with Wills Act 1837 s.9(a)).
[295] *Kitcat v King* [1930] P. 266; cf. *In b. Bravda* [1968] 1 W.L.R. 479.
[296] *Thorpe v Bestwick* (1881) 6 QBD 311.
[297] *Cresswell v Cresswell* (1868) L.R. 6 Eq. 69; *Re Ray's W.T.* [1936] Ch. 520 (prior to testatrix's death witness becomes Abbess to whom property is given on trust: gift effective).
[298] *Re Pooley* (1888) 40 Ch D 1.
[299] *Re Royce's W.T.* [1959] Ch. 626.
[300] *Re Marcus* (1887) 56 L.J.Ch. 830; *Re Trotter* [1899] 1 Ch. 764.
[301] *Gurney v Gurney* (1855) 3 Drew. 208.

under that trust. The witness takes under the trust and not the will.[302]

(vii) In certain circumstances a gift to a legatee (or his spouse or civil partner) who witnesses a will may be saved by the doctrine of dependant relative revocation, if there was a gift in similar terms to the same legatee in a previous will.[303]

3. Limited interests. The effect of the rule in the case of a limited interest is to accelerate the subsequent interests. Thus if property is given to A for life, with remainder to B, the effect of A attesting the will is that B is entitled to the property as soon as the testator dies.[304] Similarly if property is given to X, Y and Z as joint tenants, and X attests the will, Y and Z are entitled to the whole of the property[305]; had they been tenants in common, X's third would have fallen into residue and passed on intestacy.[306] **14–068**

C. Murder or Manslaughter of Testator[307]

The common law recognises, as part of a wider rule of public policy, that "no person can obtain, or enforce, any rights resulting to him from his own crime."[308] It follows that a person who is convicted[309] of a deliberate and intentional killing can take no benefit under the will or intestacy of his victim.[310] This is so whether the killing was in law murder, manslaughter, or aiding and abetting a suicide, and whether or not it involved acts or threats of violence.[311] Thus a killer's prospective share under his victim's intestacy devolves as if he did not exist, e.g. on his brothers and sisters, and not on the Crown.[312] There may however be great injustice in imposing what may be a severe civil sanction on a person who has either been acquitted, or whose **14–069**

---

[302] *Re Young* [1951] Ch. 344. For secret trusts, see above, para.11–043.

[303] See *Re Finnemore* [1991] 1 W.L.R. 793, above, para.14–043.

[304] *Jull v Jacobs* (1876) 3 Ch D 703. Contrast *Re Doland's W.T.* [1970] Ch. 267 (substitutional or dependent gift falls with offending gift).

[305] *Young v Davies* (1863) 2 Dr. & Sm. 167.

[306] *Hoare v Osborne* (1864) 33 L.J.Ch. 586.

[307] See (1990) 10 O.J.L.S. 289 (S. M. Cretney); S. M. Cretney, *Law, Law Reform and the Family* (Oxford: OUP, 1999), p.73.

[308] *In b. Crippen* [1911] P. 108 at 112, per Evans P. Although this general rule has often been affirmed (see, e.g. *Davitt v Titcumb* [1990] Ch. 110), it is not now applied inflexibly. cf. Forfeiture Act 1982 s.1(1).

[309] The rule may apply even if a person has been acquitted of a charge of murder or manslaughter, provided that in civil proceedings the court is satisfied on the balance of probabilities that he was guilty of a killing that fell within the scope of the rule: *Gray v Barr* [1971] 2 Q.B. 554.

[310] The so-called "forfeiture rule": *In b. Hall* [1914] P. 1 (will: manslaughter); *Re Sigsworth* [1935] Ch. 89 (intestacy: murder). For the application of this rule to joint tenancies, see above, para.13–049.

[311] *Dunbar v Plant* [1998] Ch. 412 (suicide pact); [1998] C.L.J. 31 (S.B.); *Dalton v Latham* [2003] EWHC 796 (Ch); [2003] W.T.L.R. 687 (manslaughter by reason of diminished responsibility); *Re Land* [2006] EWHC 2069 (Ch); [2007] 1 W.L.R. 1009 (gross negligence manslaughter).

[312] *Re Callaway* [1956] Ch. 559.

moral culpability is limited.[313] These considerations prompted the further relaxation of the rule by statute. Under the terms of the Forfeiture Act 1982,[314] the court now has power to modify the rule in all cases of unlawful killing,[315] except where a person has been convicted of murder.[316] It may do so if it is satisfied that the justice of the case so requires,[317] e.g. in cases where the unlawful killing involves little moral blame.[318] The discretion will normally be exercised in cases of suicide pacts.[319] The forfeiture rule no longer precludes applications under the Inheritance (Provision for Family and Dependants) Act 1975[320] or the Matrimonial Causes Act 1973, or applications for social security benefits.[321]

Section 5. Construction of Wills

14–070   The construction of wills is a vast and difficult subject[322] of which only a few of the more important rules can be mentioned here.[323]

A. General Rule

14–071   **1. Ascertaining intention.** The cardinal rule of construction is that effect must be given to the intention of the testator as expressed in the will, the words being given their natural meaning. The will alone must be looked at,

---

[313] e.g. a "battered wife" who has endured years of torment at the hands of her husband and is put on probation for his manslaughter: *Re K* [1985] Ch. 85.

[314] The Act began as a Private Member's Bill: (1990) 10 O.J.L.S. 289 (S. M. Cretney).

[315] s.2. Application to the court must be made within three months of any conviction for an offence of which an unlawful killing is an element: s.2(3). The court has no discretion to extend time: *Re Land* [2006] EWHC 2069 (Ch); [2007] 1 W.L.R. 1009 at [10].

[316] s.5.

[317] This does not empower the court to "do justice between the parties": *Dunbar v Plant*, above, at 427. Phillips L.J. considered that the discretion under the Act should be exercised where the forfeiture rule appeared to "conflict with the ends of justice": *Dunbar v Plant* at 436.

[318] s.2(2). See *Re K* [1985] Ch. 85; [1986] Ch. 180: *Re S* [1996] 1 W.L.R. 235.

[319] *Dunbar v Plant*, above, at 438.

[320] See, e.g. *Re Land*, above.

[321] s.3. This means that the court may make an order under the Act of 1975 where the forfeiture rule is the sole reason for the claimant failing to obtain reasonable provision: *Re Land*, above, not following the anomalous decision in *Re Royse* [1985] Ch. 22. If the claimant does not apply for relief under the Forfeiture Act 1982 within three months of conviction, he may still apply for provision under the Act of 1975, seeking an extension of time within that statute if necessary: see *Re Land*, above.

[322] "Wills and the construction of them do more perplex a man, than any other learning": *Roberts v Roberts* (1613) 2 Bulstr. 123 at 130, per Coke C.J. Lord Eldon L.C. began one judgment: "Having had doubts upon this Will for 20 years . . . ": *Earl of Radnor v Shafto* (1805) 11 Ves. 448 at 453; but see R. Megarry, *Miscellany-at-Law: A Diversion for Lawyers and Others* 1st edn (London: Sweet & Maxwell, 1955), p.244. For a discussion of more liberal approaches to interpretation of wills, see Kerridge and Rivers (2000) 116 L.Q.R. 287.

[323] See for detailed treatment of the subject *Hawkins on the Construction of Wills*, edited by R. Kerridge 2nd Revised edn (London: Sweet & Maxwell, 2000).

and, in general,[324] no evidence can be received to contradict the meaning of the words used in the will. "The will must be in writing, and the only question is, what is the meaning of the words used in that writing."[325]

The words of the will must normally be given their natural meaning, or the most appropriate of their several natural meanings, except so far as that leads to absurdities or inconsistencies. But there is nothing to prevent words from being construed in some special sense if the will clearly shows that they are used in that sense; and in recent years the courts have been readier to accept that the testator may have used words otherwise than in accordance with their "strict" meaning. Thus "money", in its strict legal meaning, comprises only cash and debts due, but a bequest in a home-made will of "all moneys of which I die possessed" may be construed as including stocks and shares and personal property generally.[326] The court may invoke what is sometimes known as the "dictionary principle": the testator, by showing in the will that he has used a word in a particular sense, has made his own dictionary for the purposes of the will.[327]

2. Illegitimate children. It was a settled rule that "children" was to be interpreted as meaning "legitimate children".[328] Virtually all vestiges of this rule have now been removed by statute and illegitimate children are treated in almost all respects in the same way as those who are legitimate. In any will or codicil made after 1969, references to any relationship between two persons shall be construed without regard to whether or not the parents of either of them, or the parents of any person through whom the relationship is deduced, have or had been married to each other at any time.[329] This is subject to the contrary intention appearing.[330] The use of the word "heir" or of any expression which prior to 1997 was used to create an entailed interest does not show a contrary intention if it is contained in any disposition of property made on or after April 4, 1988.[331]   **14–072**

3. Adopted children. In the case of adopted children, if the adoption preceded the testator's death, the adopted children are treated as "children" of   **14–073**

---

[324] Contrast *Re Jones's W.T.* [1965] Ch. 1124 and *Re Jebb* [1966] Ch. 666 (cases on "contrary intention").

[325] *Grey v Pearson* (1857) 6 H.L.C. 61 at 106, per Lord Wensleydale.

[326] *Perrin v Morgan* [1943] A.C. 399.

[327] *Hill v Crook* (1873) L.R. 6 HL 265 at 285.

[328] *Wilkinson v Adam* (1813) 1 V. & B. 422 at 462.

[329] Family Law Reform Act 1987 ss.1, 19, replacing the Family Law Reform Act 1969 s.15. The 1987 Act followed two Law Commission Reports: Law Com. Nos 118 and 157. See generally [1988] Conv. 410 (J. G. Miller). On the rights of legitimated children, see the Legitimacy Act 1976 ss.5, 6.

[330] See above fn.329.

[331] Family Law Reform Act 1987 s.19(2). Prior to that date the rule had been otherwise: Family Law Reform Act 1969 s.15(2). The devolution of property along with a title of honour is unaffected by the 1987 Act: s.19(4). Entails cannot be created after 1996: see above, para.3–031.

the adopter for purposes of dispositions of property,[332] unless a contrary intention appears from the will or the surrounding circumstances.[333]

14–074   **4. Mistakes and inept language.** Where the testator's intention is sufficiently clear from the will itself the court may be able to omit or supply words inserted or omitted by mischance.[334] The court may also strike out words if it is shown (e.g. from a draft) that the effect of the version signed by the testator was not known to and approved by him.[335] But this rule extends only to the deletion of words, not to their insertion. Vague expressions such as "X's relations" or "X's successors" may be construed as references to the persons who would be entitled on X's intestacy, so as to save the gift from being void for uncertainty.[336] Meaningless and incongruous expressions may sometimes be disregarded.[337] Statute now allows extrinsic evidence, including evidence of the testator's intention, to be admitted to assist in the interpretation of any part of the will that is meaningless.[338]

14–075   Prior to 1983 the doctrine of rectification of mistakes in legal documents did not apply to wills,[339] and the court would not insert missing provisions, even where caused by mere miscopying of a draft[340] or by failing to provide for some obvious contingency.[341] But where the testator dies after 1982, the court has been given a limited statutory power to rectify his will if it is satisfied that it fails to carry out his intentions in consequence of a clerical error[342] or of a failure to understand his instructions.[343] Application must be made within six months from the date on which representation was first taken out, unless the court permits an extension of time.[344] After that six month period has elapsed, the personal representatives may distribute the estate without liability, regardless of the possibility of a later application being

---

[332] Adoption and Children Act 2002 ss.69, 70.

[333] *Re Jones's W.T.* [1965] Ch. 1124 (statement by testator admitted in evidence); *Re Brinkley's W.T.* [1968] Ch. 407.

[334] See, e.g. *Re Riley's W.T.* [1962] 1 W.L.R. 344; *Re Morris* [1971] P. 62; *Re Phelan* [1972] Fam. 33 (revocation clause omitted).

[335] *Re Reynette-James* [1976] 1 W.L.R. 161.

[336] *Rowland v Gorsuch* (1789) 2 Cox Eq. 187; *Re Gansloser's W.T.* [1952] Ch. 30; *Re Kilvert* [1957] Ch. 388. As to the share taken, see above, para.13–020.

[337] *Re Macandrew's W.T.* [1964] Ch. 704.

[338] AJA 1982 s.21, as recommended by the Law Reform Committee, Cmnd. 5301 (1973).

[339] For rectification generally see below, para.15–122.

[340] *Re Reynette-James*, above.

[341] *Re Hammersley* [1965] Ch. 481.

[342] AJA 1982 s.20(1)(a), as recommended by the Law Reform Committee, fn.338 above. A "clerical error" includes "an error made in the process of recording the intended words of the testator in the drafting or transcription of his will": *Wordingham v Royal Exchange Trust Co Ltd* [1992] Ch. 412 at 419, per Evans-Lombe, Q.C. (failure by solicitor to include exercise of a power of appointment in will: rectification ordered). It is not however confined to errors of transcription but also includes the case where the will contains a provision which is not in accordance with the testator's wishes: *Re Segelman* [1996] Ch. 171; *Marley v Rawlings* [2011] EWHC 161 (Ch); [2011] 1 W.L.R. 2146.

[343] AJA 1982 s.20(1)(b). See *Re Segelman*, above, at 180.

[344] AJA 1982 s.20(2); *Gerling v Gerling* [2010] EWHC 3661 (Ch); [2011] W.T.L.R. 1029.

permitted, though without prejudice to any power to recover assets by virtue of the court's order.[345]

B. Extrinsic Evidence

The general rule is that only the words of the will may be considered. **14–076** Extrinsic evidence of the testator's intention (i.e. evidence not gathered from the will itself) is normally inadmissible. But the rule is subject to qualifications, and its rigour has been mitigated by statute.

1. Surrounding circumstances. Evidence of facts and circumstances exist- **14–077** ing when the will was made is always admissible in order to explain its terms. "You may place yourself, so to speak, in [the testator's] armchair."[346] Thus extrinsic evidence is admissible to show that certain words had a peculiar meaning to the testator by the custom of the district or the usage of the class of persons to which he belonged,[347] or that a description was mistaken, in which case the testator's true intention is carried out; *falsa demonstratio non nocet* (a mistake in description does no harm).[348] Where the testator is under a misapprehension as to what he owns, however, the court is not at liberty to alter the language so as to make the gift apply to an altogether different asset, even though it may be satisfied that he would have done so had he appreciated the position.[349] Nicknames,[350] or symbols used by the testator in his trade,[351] may be explained by evidence; thus it may be shown that a gift for "mother" was intended for the testator's wife, whom he always described thus.[352]

2. Equivocations

(a) Ambiguity. Evidence of the testator's intention has always been admis- **14–078** sible to explain an equivocation. There is said to be an equivocation or ambiguity in a will when there is a description of a person or thing which can apply equally well to two or more persons or things. Thus if a testator devises his close (enclosed land) "in the occupation of W" and he has two such closes, there is an equivocation.[353] By statute,[354] extrinsic evidence, including

---

[345] AJA 1982 s.20(3).

[346] *Boyes v Cook* (1880) 14 Ch D 53 at 56, per James L.J.; but the testator is not to be assumed to have a well-stocked law library: *Re Follett* [1955] 1 W.L.R. 429; (1955) 71 L.Q.R. 17, 326 (REM).

[347] *Shore v Wilson* (1842) 9 Cl. & F. 355 at 498 et seq.

[348] See, e.g. *Re Ray* [1916] 1 Ch. 461; *Re Price* [1932] 2 Ch. 54; *Re Posner* [1953] P. 277 (bequest to "my wife R" upheld although R was not the testator's wife).

[349] *Re Lewis's W.T.* [1985] 1 W.L.R. 102 (gift of farm and stock did not refer to the testator's majority shareholding in the farm). See too *Re Tetsall* [1961] 1 W.L.R. 938.

[350] *Re Ofner* [1909] 1 Ch. 60.

[351] *Kell v Charmer* (1856) 23 Beav. 195 (jeweller's bequest of "the sum of i.x.x." which was the trade symbol for £100).

[352] *Thorn v Dickens* [1906] W.N. 54 (the entire will was "all for mother").

[353] *Richardson v Watson* (1833) 4 B. & Ad. 787.

[354] AJA 1982 s.21, as recommended by the Law Reform Committee, Cmnd. 5301 (1973). This section applies to persons dying after 1982. For the problems that formerly existed, see the fifth edition of this work at p.529.

evidence of the testator's intention, is admissible in so far as the language used in any part of his will is meaningless or is ambiguous on the face of it. The same applies also in so far as evidence, other than evidence of the testator's intention, shows that the language used in any part of his will is ambiguous in the light of surrounding circumstances.[355]

14–079   *(b) Effect of extrinsic evidence.* Once extrinsic evidence of the testator's intention is admitted, it will be given effect even if it shows that someone apparently outside the scope of the gift was intended to take. Thus, in one case[356] a testatrix gave part of her property "to my nephew Arthur Murphy". She had three nephews of that name and extrinsic evidence was admitted to explain this ambiguity. The evidence admitted showed that the testatrix intended to benefit an illegitimate nephew called Arthur Murphy, and it was held that he took to the exclusion of the two legitimate nephews. Had there been only one legitimate and one illegitimate nephew, there would have been no ambiguity, for "nephew" prima facie meant "legitimate nephew"; consequently no extrinsic evidence would have been admitted and the legitimate nephew would have taken.[357]

14–080   *(c) Uncertainty.* If extrinsic evidence fails to resolve an ambiguity, the gift is void for uncertainty.[358] The same applies where the description is on the face of it indefinite, e.g. a gift by a testator "to one of the sons of X", X having at the time several sons.[359]

C. Contradictions

14–081   **1. Inconsistency.** Extrinsic evidence is not admissible to explain a contradiction in a will, e.g. a gift of "one hundred pounds (£500) to X". In such a case, the quaint[360] rule is that the second expression prevails over the first[361] since it is the latest in the testator's mind. This contrasts with a deed, where the former of two inconsistent expressions prevails, for what has once been done cannot be undone.[362] Before resorting to such a rule of thumb, however, the court tries to reconcile the two provisions in some way.[363]

14–082   A prevalent form of contradiction is where the testator makes inconsistent gifts to his wife and children, as by saying "I leave everything to my wife and then it shall be for our children". Where the testator dies after 1982 there is

---

[355] AJA 1982 s.21; see *Re Williams* [1985] 1 W.L.R. 905.
[356] *Re Jackson* [1933] Ch. 237.
[357] *Re Fish* [1894] 2 Ch. 83.
[358] *Richardson v Watson*, above, where the evidence showed that in fact the testator intended both closes to pass.
[359] *Strode v Russel* (1708) 2 Vern. 621 at 624, 625; cf. *Dowset v Sweet* (1753) Amb. 175.
[360] See above, para.13–019.
[361] *Perkins v Baynton* (1781) 1 Bro.C.C. 118; *Re Hammond* [1938] 3 All E.R. 308 (refusing to apply the rule for commercial documents that the words control the figures).
[362] *Doe d. Leicester v Biggs* (1809) 2 Taunt. 109 at 113; *Forbes v Git* [1922] 1 A.C. 256 at 259; cf. above, para.13–019.
[363] See *Wallop v Darby* (1611) Yelv. 209 (gift to X in tail, followed by a separate gift of the same property to Y in fee simple: held, Y took a remainder after X's entail); *Fyfe v Irwin* [1939] 2 All E.R. 271 at 281.

now a statutory solution: a gift to a spouse in terms which in themselves would give an absolute interest is to take effect as an absolute gift, notwithstanding any purported gift to the testator's issue in the same instrument.[364]

2. The rule in *Lassence v Tierney*. A long-standing rule for the construction of a certain type of contradictory gift is the rule in *Lassence v Tierney*.[365] This applies to deeds as well as to wills,[366] and to realty as well as to personalty.[367] This rule has been stated as follows:

14–083

> "If you find an absolute gift to a legatee in the first instance, and trusts are engrafted or imposed on that absolute interest which fail, either from lapse or invalidity or any other reason, then the absolute gift takes effect so far as the trusts have failed to the exclusion of the residuary legatee or next of kin as the case may be."[368]

Thus, if there is a gift to X of a fee simple or an absolute interest in personalty, and later in the will[369] or in a codicil[370] there is a direction that the property given to X shall be held for X for life with remainder to his children, if the gift to the children fails, whether partly[371] or wholly (e.g. through there being no children[372] or through the perpetuity rule being infringed[373]), the gift of the fee simple or absolute interest to X takes effect instead of the property passing under a residuary gift or as on intestacy.[374] For the rule to apply, there must be an initial absolute gift which is subsequently cut down[375]; one continuous limitation containing both gift and restrictions will normally not bring the doctrine into play,[376] nor will a gift in which the names of the beneficiaries are immediately followed by the words "subject to the provisions hereinafter contained".[377]

---

[364] AJA 1982 s.22; *Harrison v Gibson* [2005] EWHC 2957 (Ch); [2006] 1 W.L.R. 1212. A similar provision applies to civil partners: Civil Partnership Act 2004 s.71 Sch.4 para.5. For criticism of these provisions, see N. Lowe and G. Douglas, *Bromley's Family Law*, 10th edn (Oxford: OUP, 2006), p.1094.

[365] (1849) 1 Mac. & G. 551.

[366] *Re Gatti's Voluntary S.T.* [1936] 2 All E.R. 1489; *Att Gen v Lloyds Bank Ltd* [1935] A.C. 382.

[367] *Moryoseph v Moryoseph* [1920] 2 Ch. 33.

[368] *Hancock v Watson* [1902] A.C. 14 at 22, per Lord Davey.

[369] *Hulme v Hulme* (1839) 9 Sim. 644.

[370] *Norman v Kynaston* (1861) 3 De G.F. & J. 29.

[371] *Re Coleman* [1936] Ch. 528. See also *Re Litt* [1946] Ch. 154; *Re Atkinson's W.T.* [1957] Ch. 117.

[372] *Watkins v Weston* (1863) 3 De G.J. & S. 434.

[373] *Ring v Hardwick* (1840) 2 Beav. 352.

[374] *Whittell v Dunin* (1820) 2 Jac. & W. 279.

[375] See, e.g. *Re Burton's S.T.* [1955] Ch. 348, on the distinction between a true gift and mere administrative direction.

[376] *Re Payne* [1927] 2 Ch. 1.

[377] *Re Cohen's W.T.* [1936] 1 All E.R. 103.

D. A Will Speaks from Death

14–084   A will speaks from death. There are two aspects of this rule. First, it is applied by statute to property. Secondly, the courts have applied it to certain persons.

I. AS TO PROPERTY

14–085   It has already been explained that a will is ambulatory.[378] By the Wills Act 1837,[379] a will, unless it shows a contrary intention:

> (i) speaks from death; and

> (ii) takes effect as if it had been executed immediately before the testator's death

as regards all property comprised in it. This means that a will is capable of disposing of all property owned by the testator at his death even if he acquired it after making his will. Thus, a gift of "my shares in the Great Western Railway Company" includes not only those owned when the will was made, but those acquired subsequently[380]; and a devise of "all the lands of which I am seised" carries with it land acquired after the will was made,[381] together with all fixtures attached to the land, even if they were affixed after the will was made.[382]

14–086   This rule applies to all generic descriptions (i.e. descriptions of a class of objects which may increase or decrease[383]) and is not confined to general or residual gifts[384]; but it has no application to a gift of a specific object existing at the date of the will.[385] Thus if a testator makes a will giving "my piano" to X and subsequently sells that piano and buys another, X has no claim to it,[386] unless the will is confirmed by a codicil made after the purchase.[387] The bequest is said to have been adeemed, meaning that the gift has failed because the specified property ceased to exist, or ceased to belong to the testator, between the date of his will and his death.[388] Ademption will also occur if before his death the testator contracts to sell the property,[389] or if an option to

---

[378] Above, para.14–013.

[379] s.24; see *Re Bancroft* [1928] Ch. 577.

[380] *Trinder v Trinder* (1866) L.R. 1 Eq. 695; contrast *Re Tetsall* [1961] 1 W.L.R. 938 ("my 750 shares").

[381] *Doe d. York v Walker* (1844) 12 M. & W. 591.

[382] For fixtures, see below, Ch.23.

[383] *Re Slater* [1906] 2 Ch. 480 at 485. See *All Souls College v Coddrington* (1719) 1 P.Wms. 597 (bequest of library "now in the custody" of X includes after-added books).

[384] *Re Ord* (1879) 12 Ch D 22 at 25.

[385] *Emuss v Smith* (1848) 2 De G. & Sm. 722 at 733, 736.

[386] *Re Sikes* [1927] 1 Ch. 364.

[387] *Re Reeves* [1928] Ch. 351.

[388] See Bailey, *Wills*, 109, 113; cf. *Re Heilbronner* [1953] 1 W.L.R. 1254 and see above, para.14–013.

[389] *Re Edwards* [1958] Ch. 168.

purchase which he granted before his death is subsequently exercised.[390] In each such case the specific asset had become a mere right to receive the purchase price.

1. Class gifts

(a) The problem of distribution. Class gifts[391] are construed on the ordinary principle that the testator's intention shall govern the persons who are to take.[392] But a special problem arises where one member of the class becomes qualified to take before the maximum number of members can be fixed. Suppose, for example, that the testator leaves property "to all my grand-children who attain 21 in equal shares". As soon as a grandchild attains 21 he becomes entitled to a share. But to how much? If all future grandchildren are to be included, nothing can safely be paid out to him until all the parents, uncles and aunts are dead, so that the maximum number of shares is known. The essence of the problem, therefore, is an inconsistency in the testator's directions: *all* are to *take*, yet each is to take rather than have to await the completion of the class.

14–087

(b) The rule in Andrews v Partington. In order to expedite the distribution of the property, the courts have adopted the rule, already discussed in relation to the rule against perpetuities,[393] known as the rule in *Andrews v Parting-ton*.[394] This rule cuts down the class by confining it to persons in existence when the first capital[395] share becomes payable.[396] The interests of after-born members of the class are sacrificed for the purpose of fixing the maximum number of shares. Because this is unfair to them, the rule "has been repeatedly attacked over the two hundred years or so that it has survived",[397] and it has artificial limits. It may be generally stated as follows[398]:

14–088

---

[390] *Lawes v Bennett* (1785) 1 Cox Eq. 167; *Re Isaacs* [1894] 3 Ch. 506; *Re Carrington* [1932] 1 Ch. 1; *Re Rose* [1949] Ch. 78.

[391] For definition, see above, para.9–068.

[392] Thus a gift, after a life interest to X (a spinster), to X's issue who attain 21 may be confined to issue born before X's death, without the aid of the rule in *Andrews v Partington* (below): *Re Cockle's W.T.* [1967] Ch. 690.

[393] Above, para.9–072.

[394] (1791) 3 Bro.C.C. 401. It applies to both realty and personalty (see *Re Canney's Trust* (1910) 101 L.T. 905) and to settlements as well as wills: see *Re Knapp's Settlement* [1895] 1 Ch. 91; *Re Wernher's S.T.* [1961] 1 W.L.R. 136.

[395] The rule will not therefore apply to gifts of income only, e.g. for joint lives: *Re Stephens* [1904] 1 Ch. 322 (also holding that the closing of the class may be postponed by a period of accumulation of income); *Re Ward* [1965] Ch. 856 (discretionary trusts). But it is not excluded because land is held upon trust for sale and sale is postponed: *Re Edmondson's W.T.* [1972] 1 W.L.R. 183.

[396] *Re Emmet's Estate* (1880) 13 Ch D 484.

[397] *Re Harker's W.T.* [1969] 1 W.L.R. 1124 at 1127, per Goff J.

[398] The best general account of the rule and its various refinements is that given by J. H. C. Morris (1954) 70 L.Q.R. 61 et seq., where he also deals with its effect on the operation of the perpetuity rule (already considered, above, para.9–072); and see Jarman, 1660 et seq. Helpful statements of the rule will be found in *Re Chartres* [1927] 1 Ch. 466 at 471 and in [1958] C.L.J. 39 (S. J. Bailey).

A class closes when the first member becomes entitled in possession; but where the shares of its members are to vest at birth, it will remain open indefinitely unless a member was born before the testator's death or before the end of some intermediate limitation. All persons born after the closing of the class are excluded from it.

The artificial element is the exception in the case of shares which vest at birth and not on some later contingency such as attainment of full age or marriage.

14–089   This is a rule of convenience for resolving the testator's contradictory directions.[399] He can therefore exclude it by expressing a contrary intention,[400] so that the contradiction disappears. He may exclude it by implication, as by giving trustees a power of advancement under which they can pay out presumptive shares.[401] For such an implication "the standard is high" and there must be "an inescapable incompatibility" with the operation of the rule.[402] Consequently the rule will not normally be excluded by expressions such as "all", "all and every", or "all or any"[403]; and if the class gift is in remainder or in the future even expressions like "born or to be born" may be taken as referring to persons born between the testator's death and the falling into possession of the remainder.[404] But the words "whenever born" have been held to exclude the rule, being emphatic and expressly unlimited as to time.[405]

14–090   *(c) Examples.* The operation of the rule is best explained by examples.

>   (i) Devise "to all my sisters". Sisters alive at the testator's death take, and any sisters born afterwards are excluded. But if no sister was alive at the testator's death, the exception applies and any sister born subsequently can take.[406] Similarly a devise "to all A's children" or "to all my grandchildren" will benefit only those born before the testator's death, unless no member of the class has by then been born.[407] If only one member of the class was born before the testator's death, he or she takes the whole.

[399] *Re Emmet's Estate*, above, at 490; *Re Stephens* [1904] 1 Ch. 322 at 328; *Re Chartres*, above, at 474; [1958] C.L.J. 39 at 42 (S. J. Bailey); cf. *Re Drummond* [1988] 1 W.L.R. 234 at 242, where the rule was described as a rule of construction rather than of convenience.

[400] *Scott v Earl of Scarborough* (1838) 1 Beav. 154 ("now born or who shall hereafter be born"); *Hodson v Micklethwaite* (1854) 2 Drew. 294; *Re Ransome* [1957] Ch. 348; *Re Tom's Settlement* [1987] 1 W.L.R. 1021 ("each minor specified beneficiary who shall be living" at a specified date).

[401] *Re Henderson* [1969] 1 W.L.R. 651.

[402] *Re Clifford's S.T.* [1981] Ch. 63 at 67, per Megarry V-C.

[403] See *Re Emmet's Estate* (1880) 13 Ch D 484; *Re Edmondson's W.T.* [1972] 1 W.L.R. 183 at 187.

[404] *Scott v Earl of Scarborough*, above, at 168; *Re Chapman's S.T.* [1977] 1 W.L.R. 1163.

[405] *Re Edmondson's W.T.*, above.

[406] *Weld v Bradbury* (1715) 2 Vern. 705.

[407] See *Re Chartres*, above. Provided that the gift vests at once, it makes no difference that there are special trusts during minority: *Re Manners* [1955] 1 W.L.R. 1096.

(ii) Devise "to all my grandchildren who attain 21". The class closes **14–091**
when the first grandchild attains 21,[408] whether or not he was born
before the testator's death. When the class closes, all grandchildren
then alive are included in it: those under 21 will obtain their shares
on attaining 21; if any of them dies under 21, his potential share is
divided among those who reach 21. Even if there is no grandchild
alive at the testator's death, the class will nevertheless close when
the first grandchild attains 21 (since the shares were not to vest at
birth).[409] There is however some doubt on this last point.[410]

(iii) Devise "to A for life, remainder to all his grandchildren who attain **14–092**
21". Here the class closes at A's death, if by then any grandchild
who survived the testator, or was born after his death, has attained
21.[411] As any such grandchild's interest will have vested, it will
make no difference if he has predeceased A, for someone will be
entitled to take his share under his will or intestacy,[412] and so the
class must close. If at A's death there are no grandchildren,[413] or
only infant grandchildren,[414] the class closes when the first of them
attains 21.[415]

Where the remainders are accelerated by the premature determination of the prior life interest (e.g. by disclaimer or release[416]) and
a remainderman is already qualified to take, the rule will not apply
unless, it seems, the limitation is one to which the rule would in
any case apply. Thus if the gift is to A for life with remainder to
his children who attain 21, no remainderman could be born after
A's death, and so the premature determination of A's life interest
will not bring within the rule a limitation which otherwise would
stand outside it.[417] But had the remainder been to A's *grandchildren* who attain 21, the rule would apply to the limitation so as
to exclude some remaindermen, as explained above, and so it has
been held also to apply if A's life interest is prematurely determined.[418] Yet it seems contrary to principle for the class to be
closed as a result of a disposition not made by the testator, and for

---

[408] *Andrews v Partington* (1791) 3 Bro.C.C. 401; *Re Deloitte* [1919] 1 Ch. 209; *Re Chartres*,
above. If a grandchild has attained 21 before the testator's death, the class closes at once: *Picken
v Matthews* (1878) 10 Ch D 264.
[409] *Pearse v Catton* (1839) 1 Beav. 352; and see *Re Bleckly* [1951] Ch. 740 at 749.
[410] See Morris (1954) 70 L.Q.R. 61 at 68, 69.
[411] *Re Emmet's Estate* (1880) 13 Ch D 484; *Re Knapp's Settlement* [1895] 1 Ch. 91 at 96.
[412] *Greenwood v Greenwood* [1939] 2 All E.R. 150.
[413] *Re Bleckly* [1951] Ch. 740.
[414] See authorities cited in fn.411, above.
[415] Similarly on a gift of a reversionary interest the class remains open until the reversion falls
into possession: *Walker v Shore* (1808) 15 Ves. 122.
[416] See [1958] C.L.J. 39 (S. J. Bailey); [1973] C.L.J. 246 (A. M. Prichard).
[417] *Re Kebty-Fletcher's W.T.* [1969] 1 Ch. 339; *Re Harker's W.T.* [1969] 1 W.L.R. 1124.
[418] *Re Davies* [1957] 1 W.L.R. 922, as explained in *Re Harker's W.T.*, above.

the rule to be open to manipulation at the expense of the unborn.[419]

14–093   *(d) Individual gifts.* An even more drastic rule of convenience is applied where there is not one gift divisible among a class, but a series of gifts to each member of a class, for example, a gift of £100 to each of the children of X who attains 21. Here the class closes at the testator's death, and if X has then no living child the gift fails altogether.[420] The object of this rule is to enable the personal representatives to deal with the residue by fixing the maximum number of legacies at once. But the testator may exclude the rule by a sufficiently clear direction, and it will not be applied unless the circumstances require it.[421]

14–094   **2. Gifts to individuals.** In the case of gifts to existing individuals, the date of the will, and not the date of the testator's death, is normally the relevant time. Thus a gift "to the eldest son of my sister", there being such a son living at the date of the will, is a gift to him personally; if he dies before the testator, the gift lapses and the eldest son at the testator's death has no claim.[422] Similarly, a bequest "to Lord Sherborne" is a gift to the holder of the title at the date of the will.[423] But like all rules of construction, this yields to a contrary intention, and a legacy "to the Lord Mayor of London for the time being" operates as a gift to the person holding that office at the testator's death,[424] while a gift "to the Mayor of Lowestoft for the benefit of poor and needy fishermen of Lowestoft" takes effect as a gift to the Mayor of Lowestoft for the time being, on the stated trusts, and not as a gift to a particular person who is Mayor at a particular time.[425]

E. Exercise of Powers of Appointment

14–095   A general devise or bequest (e.g. "I give all my property to X") operates to exercise a general power of appointment unless a contrary intention (and not merely an absence of intention[426]) is shown by the will,[427] or unless the general power is expressed to be exercisable only in some special way, e.g. by referring to the power[428] or the property.[429] On the other hand, a special power (which for this purpose includes a power, commonly known as a hybrid

---

[419] See generally *Re Harker's W.T.*, above.
[420] *Rogers v Mutch* (1878) 10 Ch D 25; *Re Bellville* [1941] Ch. 414.
[421] *Re Bellville*, above. Presumably, therefore, if the residue is not distributable until some future date, e.g. after a life interest, all persons living at that date will be admitted.
[422] *Amyot v Dwarris* [1904] A.C. 268.
[423] *Re Whorwood* (1887) 34 Ch D 446.
[424] *Re Daniels* (1918) 87 L.J.Ch. 661.
[425] *Re Pipe* (1937) 106 L.J.Ch. 252.
[426] *Re Thirlwell* [1958] Ch. 146; (1958) 74 L.Q.R. 21 (REM).
[427] Wills Act 1837 s.27; see, e.g. *Re Lawry* [1938] Ch. 318.
[428] *Phillips v Cayley* (1889) 43 Ch D 222; contrast *Re Lane* [1908] 2 Ch. 581 (reference to "any power" which the testator might have held sufficient).
[429] *Re Phillips* (1889) 41 Ch D 417.

power, to appoint to "anyone except X")[430] is not exercised by a general bequest or devise unless the will shows a contrary intention, as by referring expressly to the power or to the property.[431]

F. "To A, but if He Die Without Issue, to B"

Where a gift is made "to A, but if he die without issue, to B", it has been **14–096** provided by statute that the gift over to B becomes void as soon as any issue of A attains majority.[432] This did not apply where, in a will taking effect before 1997, an entail was given to A. It is not, however, excluded merely because A's "children" are specified instead of his "issue".[433] Where it applies, A's interest thus becomes absolute either if any issue attains full age (even if none survives A) or if A dies leaving any issue (even if none attains full age).

G. "To A and his children": The Rule in Wild's Case

1. Before 1926. Under the rule in *Wild's Case*[434] the effect of a devise "to **14–097** A and his children" depended upon the facts existing when the will was made. Its peculiarity was that it continued to obey the old principle that the time of making the will was the significant time, even after the modern rule that the will speaks from death was adopted for other forms of gift.[435]

(i) If A had no children when the will was made, he took an estate tail, even if children had been born before the testator's death. "Children" was construed as a word of limitation, for the only way in which the testator could have intended to benefit A's children under an immediate gift was by their being entitled to succeed under A's entail.[436] Yet by barring the entail, A could of course prevent his children from taking anything.

(ii) If A had children living (and not merely *en ventre sa mere*[437]) when the will was made, the word "children" was treated as a word of purchase and A took jointly with all his children living at the testator's death, in accordance with the usual rules for class gifts.

---

[430] *Re Byron's Settlement* [1891] 3 Ch. 474.
[431] See *Re Ackerley* [1913] 1 Ch. 510; compare *Re Beresford's W.T.* [1938] 3 All E.R. 566 (mere use of "I appoint . . . " not enough).
[432] LPA 1925 s.134, amended by the Family Law Reform Act 1969 s.1(3) and Sch.1. This has been the rule for land since 1882 and for all property since 1925. For the law prior to 1882, see the fifth edition of this work at p.536.
[433] *Re Booth* [1900] 1 Ch. 768.
[434] (1599) 6 Co.Rep. 16b at 17a, 17b.
[435] See (1936) 6 C.L.J. 67 at 78 (S.B.).
[436] *Wild's Case*, above, at 17a.
[437] *Roper v Roper* (1867) L.R. 3 C.P. 32.

14–098　　**2. After 1925.**

(i) If no children were living at the date of the will, then prior to 1997, A could not take an entail because it could not be created by informal words after 1925.[438] In such a case a fee simple interest passed and A was, it seems, solely entitled to it, even if children were born after the will was made but before the testator died.[439] However, it may have been that A took a life interest, with remainder to his children in fee simple.[440] Although after 1996 A cannot take an entail because it can no longer be created at all, the result should be the same.

(ii) The second branch of the rule has not been affected. As before, A takes jointly with all his children living at the testator's death.[441]

H. The Meaning of "Land"

14–099　A gift of "land" has always included freeholds,[442] though before the Wills Act 1837 it did not include leaseholds unless the testator had no freeholds[443] or showed an intention to include leaseholds.[444] Since the Act, "land" has included leaseholds unless a contrary intention appears in the will.[445] But a gift of "real estate" does not[446] include leaseholds, unless the testator had no freeholds.[447]

Section 6. Gifts in Contemplation of Death

14–100　　**1. Nature of a *donatio mortis causa*.**[448] Although in general it is not possible for a person to dispose of his property after his death except by an instrument that complies with the Wills Act 1837, there is an ancient and anomalous exception to this, the *donatio mortis causa*, which derives from the civil law.[449] It has been described as a gift "of an amphibious nature, being a

---

[438] Above, para.3–032.
[439] LPA 1925 s.130(2) (repealed by TLATA 1996 s.25(2) Sch.4); see (1956) 5 C.L.J. 46 (R.E.M.).
[440] See (1936) 6 C.L.J. 67 at 80; (1946) 9 C.L.J. 185 (S.B.).
[441] See sources cited at fn.440 above.
[442] *Thompson v Lady Lawley* (1800) 2 B. & P. 303.
[443] *Rose v Bartlett* (1631) Cro.Car. 292.
[444] *Hobson v Blackburn* (1833) 1 My. & K. 571.
[445] Wills Act 1837 s.26.
[446] *Butler v Butler* (1884) 28 Ch D 66.
[447] *Re Holt* [1921] 2 Ch. 17.
[448] See generally *Snell's Equity*, 32nd edn (2010), paras 24–016 et seq; Williams, Mortimer and Sunnucks, *Executors, Administrators and Probate*, 19th edn (London: Sweet & Maxwell, 2008), Ch.43.
[449] See the leading case *Ward v Turner* (1752) 2 Ves. Sen. 431; and Bl.Comm. ii, p.514. For a statement of the civil law and a contrast with the position in Roman law, see J. Domat, *The Civil Law in its Natural Order*, Pt II, 4.2.1.3.

gift which is neither entirely inter vivos nor testamentary".[450] It is a contingent gift made in contemplation of death that is recoverable by the donor if death does not in fact occur at that time.[451]

2. The essential elements of a *donatio mortis causa*. A *donatio mortis*   **14–101**
causa will be valid only if three conditions are satisfied[452]:

  (i) The gift must be made in contemplation, although not necessarily in expectation, of impending death: this means "not the possibility of death at some time or other, but death within the near future, what may be called death for some reason believed to be impending".[453]

  (ii) The gift must be made upon condition that it is absolute and perfected only on the donor's death, being revocable until that event occurs and ineffective if it does not.

  (iii) There must be delivery of the subject matter of the gift, or the essential indicia of title thereto, which amounts to a parting with dominion and not mere physical possession over the subject matter of the gift.[454]

3. The operation of a *donatio mortis causa*. If the donor effectively   **14–102**
transferred title to the donee, e.g. by delivery, the gift becomes unconditional on the donor's death and no further step is needed to perfect it. If the donor recovers or revokes the gift, the donee will then hold the property on trust for him.[455] If the act of delivery is not sufficient to transfer the title to the donee, the donor's personal representatives hold the property on trust for him and can be compelled to transfer it to him.[456] The trust is one which is "raised by operation of law",[457] that is to say a constructive trust.[458]

**4. The property which may be the subject matter of a *donatio mortis*   14–103
causa.** Prior to 1991, it had always been assumed[459] that it was not possible

---

[450] *Re Beaumont* [1902] 1 Ch. 889 at 892, per Buckley J. The phrase comes from Story's *Equity Jurisprudence*, para.606.
[451] *Delgoffe v Fader* [1939] Ch. 922 at 927.
[452] *Sen v Headley* [1991] Ch. 425 at 431.
[453] *Re Craven's Estate* [1937] Ch. 423 at 426, per Farwell J. Gifts made by persons who are seriously ill (*Cain v Moon* [1896] 2 Q.B. 283); who have had an accident (*Birch v Treasury Solicitor* [1951] Ch. 298); or who are about to have surgery (*Re Craven's Estate*, above), are obvious examples. It does not matter that the donor's death results from a cause other than that contemplated: *Wilkes v Allington* [1931] 2 Ch. 104.
[454] *Birch v Treasury Solicitor*, above (gift of deposits at various banks: donee given the pass books); *Woodard v Woodard* [1992] R.T.R. 35 (gift of car: one set of keys given to donee).
[455] *Staniland v Willott* (1852) 3 Mac. & G. 664.
[456] *Re Beaumont*, above, at 893.
[457] *Duffield v Elwes* (1827) 1 Bli.(N.S.) 497 at 543.
[458] *Sen v Headley*, above, at 439.
[459] On the authority of certain remarks by Lord Eldon in *Duffield v Elwes*, above, at 535–543 (HL).

to make a *donatio mortis causa* of land[460] but only of certain types of personalty.[461] However in *Sen v Headley*,[462] while accepting that the doctrine of gifts in contemplation of death was anomalous, the Court of Appeal saw no reason why there should be anomalous exceptions to it. In that case transfer of the keys of a box which contained the title deeds was considered to satisfy the requirements of delivery. The trust raised by the gift was a constructive trust which was immune from the formal requirements normally applicable to trusts of land.[463]

Section 7. The Rules of Intestacy

14–104   The rules relating to intestacy must now be explained. If the deceased dies wholly intestate, leaving no effective will, these rules govern the devolution of all his property. If he dies partly testate and partly intestate, the rules apply to all the property which does not pass under his will, unless the will directs otherwise.[464] Before 1926 realty and personalty descended differently. All the realty vested in the heir; the personalty devolved through the personal representatives upon the next-of-kin. If a widower died intestate leaving three sons and four daughters, the eldest son was the heir and took all the realty, but all seven children shared the personalty equally. In the case of deaths occurring after 1925, both realty and personalty devolve in the same way under a statutory code of intestacy; and for those dying after 1952, the Intestates' Estates Act 1952, as amended, has made some important modifications to the code. It is no longer necessary to consider the rules for the devolution of realty or personalty before 1926.[465] The rules relating to realty will govern certain rare situations, but those concerning personalty seldom arise.[466]

A. The Present Rules of Intestacy

14–105   Under the Administration of Estates Act 1925,[467] all property, whether real or personal, is held on trust by the deceased's personal representatives with power to sell it.[468] Out of any ready money of the deceased and any money

---

[460] In *Duffield v Elwes*, above, it was held that it was possible to make a *donatio mortis causa* of a mortgage of land which was in equity a mere security for money.

[461] The types of personal property that may or may not be the subject of a *donatio mortis causa* follow from the requirement that for there to be a valid gift there must be delivery of the property or of some indicia of title: see *Snell's Equity*, 32nd edn (2010), para.24–020.

[462] [1991] Ch. 425. For differing views on the case see [1991] C.L.J. 404 (J. W. A. Thornely); [1991] Conv. 307 (M. Halliwell); and (1992) 43 N.I.L.Q. 35 (P. Sparkes).

[463] LPA 1925 s.53(2); see above, para.11–042.

[464] A will providing only that nothing shall go to X excludes X from benefit under the intestacy rules: *Re Wynn* [1984] 1 W.L.R. 237.

[465] For these rules, see the fifth edition of this work at pp.540 et seq.

[466] Below, paras 14–130 et seq.

[467] s.33(1) (as amended by TLATA 1996 Sch.2 para.5).

[468] This trust will apply to all those assets which fall to be administered according to English law under its conflict of laws rules (such as immovable property in England), even if the deceased died domiciled abroad. The consequences of this can be unfortunate: *Re Collens* [1986] Ch. 505.

arising from the disposition of any other part of his estate (after payment of costs) the personal representatives must pay all funeral, testamentary and administration expenses, debts and other liabilities, and set aside a fund to meet the pecuniary legacies (if any) bequeathed by the deceased's will.[469] The residue must then be distributed to the persons beneficially entitled under the intestacy. The rules for ascertaining these persons are stated as amended by the Intestates' Estates Act 1952. The Act of 1925 is still the primary Act, but the Act of 1952 made important amendments, in particular by increasing the rights of a surviving spouse. Following statutory recognition of civil partnerships, civil partners have been given equivalent rights to widows and widowers on intestacy.[470]

1. The surviving spouse or civil partner. Surviving spouses (whether **14–106** widows or widowers) and civil partners have equal rights. But the extent of these rights varies greatly depending upon the other relatives who survive the intestate. In the following summary[471] "specified relatives" means parent, brother or sister of the whole blood, or issue of a brother or sister of the whole blood. "Issue" is used in its normal meaning, as including children, grandchildren, or remoter descendants, but references to "leaving issue" and "leaving no issue" refer only to issue who attain an absolutely vested interest.[472]

(a) No issue and no specified relative. If the intestate leaves no issue and no **14–107** specified relative, the surviving spouse or civil partner takes the whole residuary estate absolutely.

(b) Issue. If the intestate leaves issue (whether or not there are any specified **14–108** relatives), the surviving spouse or civil partner takes the following interests.

(1) THE "PERSONAL CHATTELS" ABSOLUTELY. These are elaborately **14–109** defined.[473] They include furniture, horses, cars, plate, books, jewellery, wines and "articles of household or personal use or ornament", but exclude chattels used at the date of the intestate's death for business purposes, money and securities for money. Roughly speaking, the phrase includes everything that goes to make a home (though not the house itself), and more besides, such as a small yacht used for family purposes,[474] and a stamp collection kept as a hobby.[475] The phrase thus has a meaning quite distinct from "personalty" or "personal property".

[469] AEA 1925 s.33(2) (as amended by TLATA 1996 Sch.2 para.5).
[470] Civil Partnership Act 2004 s.71 and Sch.4 paras 7–12.
[471] For full details see the Intestates' Estates Act 1952 s.1(2), and the table therein contained. The effect of the amendments on AEA 1925 ss.46–49, may conveniently be seen from Sch.1 to the IEA 1952. These provisions must be read subject to the amendments made by the Law Reform (Succession) Act 1995 s.1, as regards persons dying intestate after 1995, and by the Civil Partnership Act 2004 Sch.4 paras 7–12.
[472] AEA 1925 s.47(2)(b), (c); see below, para.14–121.
[473] AEA 1925 s.55(1)(x).
[474] *Re Chaplin* [1950] Ch. 507.
[475] *Re Reynolds' W.T.* [1966] 1 W.L.R. 19; see (1966) 82 L.Q.R. 18 (R.E.M.). See also *Re Crispin's W.T.* [1975] Ch. 245 (collection of clocks and watches worth £50,000 included).

14–110   (2) £250,000 ABSOLUTELY free of taxes payable on death and costs, together with interest at the rate of 6 per cent per annum from the date of death until payment.[476] This is colloquially referred to as the statutory legacy. Both the £250,000 and the interest on it are charged on the residuary estate and are therefore payable out of capital,[477] but the interest is *primarily* payable out of income.[478]

14–111   (3) A LIFE INTEREST in half of the residuary estate. Provision is made whereby the surviving spouse or civil partner may call upon the personal representatives to purchase the life interest for a lump sum[479] (ascertained as prescribed by statutory order),[480] thus enabling the estate to be distributed forthwith. This right may be exercised only within 12 months of the first grant of representation, unless the court extends the time limit for special reasons,[481] and it is exercisable only in so far as the property is in possession.[482] A written notice must be served on the personal representatives.[483] If the surviving spouse or civil partner is the sole personal representative, the right is effective only if written notice is given to the Senior Registrar of the Family Division of the High Court.[484]

14–112   *(c) No issue but specified relatives.* If the intestate leaves no issue, but one or more of the specified relatives, the surviving spouse or civil partner takes:

    (i) the "personal chattels" absolutely (as above);

    (ii) £450,000 absolutely (as above);

    (iii) half of the residuary estate absolutely.[485]

These provisions are subject to a number of rules.

14–113   (1) INCREASE OF STATUTORY LEGACIES. The Lord Chancellor may by order increase the sums mentioned above of £250,000 and £450,000.[486] In 1952 they were respectively £5,000 and £20,000, and they have since been increased in stages.[487]

---

[476] The rate of interest is as specified by order of the Lord Chancellor under AEA 1925 s.47A(3A), (3B), added by AJA 1977 s.28(3); see SI 1977/1491, as amended by SI 1983/1374.

[477] *Re Saunders* [1929] 1 Ch. 674.

[478] AEA 1925 s.46(4).

[479] AEA 1925 s.47A(1), added by IEA 1952 s.2.

[480] AEA 1925 s.47A(3A), (3B), added by AJA 1977 s.28(3); SI 1977/1491.

[481] AEA 1925 s.47A(5); see e.g. *Morley-Clarke v Brooks* [2011] W.T.L.R. 297.

[482] AEA 1925 s.47A(3).

[483] AEA 1925 s.47A(6).

[484] AEA 1925 s.47A(7) (as amended by the Senior Courts Act 1981).

[485] AEA 1925 s.46(1)(i), as amended by IEA 1952 s.1.

[486] Family Provision Act 1966 s.1.

[487] The fixed sums were increased by the Family Provision Act 1966 and the Family Provision (Intestate Succession) Orders of 1972, 1981, 1987, 1993 and 2009: see respectively SI 1972/916, SI 1981/255, SI 1987/799, SI 1993/2906 and SI 2009/135. The governing provision is now the 2009 Order, which applies where the intestate died on or after February 1, 2009.

(2) APPROPRIATION OF HOME. The surviving spouse or civil partner has a **14–114** special right to have appropriated to him or her any dwelling-house forming part of the residuary estate in which he or she was resident at the intestate's death.[488] The spouse or civil partner may require the personal representatives (even if he or she is one of them[489]) to appropriate the house, at a proper valuation, as part of the property to which he or she is entitled absolutely[490]; and the right must be exercised within 12 months of the first grant of representation.[491] It applies to whatever interest the intestate had in the house, but it does not apply in the case of a leasehold which would expire or be determinable by notice within two years of the intestate's death.[492] The right to call for an appropriation does not, however, give the spouse or civil partner an equitable interest in the house, or any right to retain possession of it.[493] If the house is worth more than the spouse's or civil partner's absolute interest (that is £250,000 where there are issue and no personal chattels), the spouse or civil partner may pay the balance in cash.[494]

(3) PARTIAL INTESTACY. These rules apply equally to partial intestacies. The **14–115** former rule by which the sum received as a statutory legacy[495] under the intestacy was diminished by the value of any beneficial interest which the surviving spouse took under the deceased's will,[496] does not apply as regards persons dying after 1995.[497]

(4) SEPARATION. If spouses are separated by a judicial separation order and **14–116** the separation is continuing, the property of either of them who dies intestate will devolve as if the other were already dead.[498] A similar provision applies to civil partners who are subject to a separation order.[499]

(5) COMMORIENTES. If spouses or civil partners die in circumstances which **14–117** make it uncertain which survived the other (a phrase which is held to cover simultaneous deaths)[500] the statutory presumption that the younger survived the elder[501] is modified for the purposes of applying the rules of intestate succession. It is now always to be presumed that the spouse or civil partner predeceased the intestate,[502] and so takes no benefit as a *surviving* spouse or

---

[488] IEA 1952 s.5 and Sch.2.

[489] IEA 1952 Sch.2 para.5(1).

[490] IEA 1952 Sch.2 para.1(1); *Re Collins* [1975] 1 W.L.R. 309 (valuation to be at time of appropriation).

[491] IEA 1952 Sch.2 para.3(1).

[492] IEA 1952 Sch.2 para.1(2).

[493] *Lall v Lall* [1965] 1 W.L.R. 1249.

[494] IEA 1952 Sch.2, para.5(2); *Re Phelps* [1980] Ch. 275.

[495] i.e. £250,000 or £450,000.

[496] See AEA 1925 ss.49(1)(a), (1)(aa), (2), (3). For this rule, see the fifth edition of this work at p.551.

[497] Law Reform (Succession) Act 1995, s.1(2)(b), implementing a recommendation in Law Com. No.187 (1989), para.55.

[498] Matrimonial Causes Act 1973 s.18(2).

[499] Civil Partnership Act 2004 s.57.

[500] *Hickman v Peacey* [1945] A.C. 304, above, para.14–064.

[501] LPA 1925 s.184; above, para.14–064.

[502] AEA 1925 s.46(3).

civil partner. Thus, if H (husband, aged 60) and W (wife, aged 50) are simultaneously killed in an accident and both die intestate, in distributing H's property W will be presumed to have predeceased H and so will have no rights in his intestacy, although she will be deemed to have survived him for other purposes. In distributing W's property, however, H will be presumed to have predeceased W,[503] and the same presumption will hold good for other purposes. It is only in the case of spouses or civil partners that the normal presumption (of the younger person's survival) is modified: if H and his son are simultaneously killed, both intestate, the son can take under H's intestacy; but H cannot take under his son's, for H is presumed to have died first.

14–118   (6) SURVIVAL BY 28 DAYS. In the case of a person dying intestate after 1995, the spouse or civil partner can only take if he or she survives the deceased for a period of 28 days beginning with the day on which the intestate died.[504]

14–119   **2. The issue.** Subject to the rights of the surviving spouse or civil partner, if any, the property is held on special statutory trusts for the surviving issue.[505] Under these trusts the property is held upon trust for all the children of the deceased living at his death in equal shares, but qualified as follows.

14–120   *(a) Subject to representation*, i.e. subject to the rule that surviving issue of a deceased child stand in his shoes and take his share[506]; descent is thus *per stirpes*.

14–121   *(b) Subject to the rule that no issue attains a vested interest until he is 18 years old or married or a civil partner.*[507] This means that if a minor dies without having married or having formed a civil partnership, the property must be dealt with from that moment as if the minor had never existed.[508] Thus if X dies leaving a widow and infant son, the widow takes a life interest in half the residue. If the son dies before either marrying or attaining his majority, the widow forthwith takes either all or half the residue absolutely, just as if there had been no issue.

14–122   *(c) Subject to hotchpot.* For deaths after 1995, the elaborate rules as to hotchpot are abolished.[509] However, in relation to deaths prior to 1996,[510] the following must be brought into account:

[503] This is by the operation of LPA 1925 s.184; IEA 1952 s.1(4) does not apply, since it is confined to cases where the LPA 1925 would otherwise require the spouse to have survived the intestate.
[504] AEA 1925 s.46(2A) (inserted by the Law Reform (Succession) Act 1995, s.1(1)), implementing recommendations in (1989) Law Com. No.187, paras 56, 57. The Law Commission had recommended a survival period of 14 days, but this was increased to 28 days by Parliament. It is common for wills to contain an express survivorship clause having a similar effect.
[505] AEA 1925 ss.46(1)(i), (ii), 47.
[506] AEA 1925 s.47(1)(i).
[507] AEA 1925 s.47 (as amended by Family Law Reform Act 1969 s.3(2) and Civil Partnership 2004 s.71; Sch.4 para.8).
[508] AEA 1925 s.47(2).
[509] Law Reform (Succession) Act 1995 s.1(2), implementing recommendations in Law Com. No.187 (1989), para.55.
[510] For an account of these rules, see the fifth edition of this work at p.553.

(i) any money or property received by any children of the deceased by way of advancement or upon marriage; or

(ii) in the case of a partial intestacy, any benefit received under the deceased's will by any children or remoter issue.[511]

3. The other relatives. If no issue attains a vested interest, then, subject to any claim of a surviving spouse or civil partner, the relatives of the deceased are entitled in the following order; any member of one class who takes a vested interest excludes all members of subsequent classes.   **14–123**

(i) The parents of the deceased are entitled in equal shares absolutely[512]; if one is dead, the survivor is entitled absolutely.[513]

(ii) The brothers and sisters of the whole blood, on the statutory trusts.[514] A division may be made here, for at this point the "specified relatives" end. Those included in the foregoing classes may take an interest even though the intestate left a surviving spouse; those in the subsequent classes[515] cannot.

(iii) The brothers and sisters of the half blood, on the statutory trusts.

(iv) The grandparents, if more than one in equal shares.

(v) The uncles and aunts of the whole blood, on the statutory trusts.

(vi) The uncles and aunts of the half blood, on the statutory trusts.

4. The Crown. Finally, in the event of none of the above surviving the intestate, the Crown (or the Duchy of Lancaster or Duke of Cornwall) takes the estate as *bona vacantia* in lieu of any right to escheat.[516]   **14–124**

A number of points arise on the foregoing list.

(1) STATUTORY TRUSTS. The statutory trusts for the brothers, sisters, uncles and aunts are the same as those for the issue.[517] Thus deceased brothers, sisters, uncles and aunts are represented by their surviving descendants (e.g. nephews, nieces and cousins of the intestate),[518] and their interests in every case are contingent upon their attaining full age, marrying or forming a civil partnership. "Uncles" and "aunts" include only blood relations; an aunt's husband, although bearing the courtesy title of uncle, has no claim.   **14–125**

---

[511] AEA 1925 ss.47(1)(iii); 49(1)(a), (2), (3).
[512] AEA 1925 s.46(1)(iii).
[513] AEA 1925 s.46(1)(iv).
[514] AEA 1925 s.46(1)(v).
[515] ibid.
[516] AEA 1925 s.46(1)(vi).
[517] AEA 1925 s.47(3).
[518] AEA 1925 s.47(5), added by IEA 1952. This contains a slip in drafting which appears to exclude the descendants unless one of the brothers, uncles, etc., also survives: but this is to be ignored: *Re Lockwood* [1958] Ch. 231; see (1958) 74 L.Q.R. 25 (R.E.M.).

14–126   (2) ILLEGITIMATE CHILDREN. As regards any person who dies on or after April 4, 1988, the status of illegitimacy either of the deceased himself or of any other person is irrelevant for the purposes of entitlement on intestacy. An illegitimate child is equated to one who was born legitimate.[519] However for these purposes there is a rebuttable presumption that the father of an illegitimate person (and those related to that person solely through his father) predeceased him.[520] Where the intestate died after 1969 but before April 4, 1988, an illegitimate child was treated as legitimate for the purposes of the rules of intestate succession only as regards his parents.[521] No disabilities attach to persons legitimated by the subsequent marriage of their parents.[522]

14–127   (3) ADOPTED CHILDREN. Adopted children are treated as children of their adoptive parents, provided that the death occurred after the adoption.[523]

14–128   (4) CROWN DISCRETION. The Crown usually modifies its strict rights by making provision for dependants of the deceased, whether related to him or not, and for others for whom he might reasonably have been expected to make provision. This purely discretionary power, which the Act confirms,[524] is made all the more necessary by the increased prospects of the Crown of succeeding to property of an intestate.

14–129   (5) EXECUTOR'S CLAIM. On a partial intestacy the executor cannot take undisposed of property beneficially unless an intention to this effect is shown by the will[525]; this rule now applies to an executor both as against the Crown and as against the statutory next-of-kin.

B. Survivals of the Old Rules

I. THE HEIR

14–130 In the case of all persons dying after 1925 the foregoing rules supersede the old rules relating to intestacy. But in the case of realty the old general law of descent still has to be applied in three cases.

14–131   **1. Mental patient.** If the deceased was a mental patient of full age at the end of 1925 and dies without having recovered testamentary capacity, any

---

[519] Family Law Reform Act 1987 ss.1, 18, replacing Family Law Reform Act 1969 s.14. See [1988] Conv. 410 (J. G. Miller).

[520] Family Law Reform Act 1987 s.18(2).

[521] Family Law Reform Act 1969 s.14. The rule that an illegitimate child could not succeed to an entail was however preserved by that section.

[522] Legitimacy Act 1976 s.5(3). There is an exception in relation to the descent of titles of honour: Legitimacy Act 1976 Sch.1 para.4.

[523] Adoption and Children Act 2002 s.67. Adoption does not affect the descent of any title of honour or of any property that devolves with that title: Adoption and Children Act 2002 s.71(1).

[524] AEA 1925 s.46(1)(vi). For the practice, see N. D. Ing, *Bona Vacantia* (London: Butterworth, 1971) Ch.10. Since 2002, the Treasury Solicitor has published its policy for making grants to those whom the deceased might reasonably have been expected to benefit: see *http://www.bona vacantia.gov.uk* for details.

[525] AEA 1925 s.49(1)(b). See *Re Skeats* [1936] Ch. 683.

realty as to which he died intestate descends according to the general law in force before 1926.[526]

2. Entail. An entail not disposed of by the will of the deceased[527] descends   **14–132**
in accordance with the general law in force before 1926.[528] Since entails were
to be preserved, this could only be done by preserving their peculiar rules of
devolution.[529] There was one statutory amendment to these rules that applied
to any entail arising under either an inter vivos disposition or a will made after
April 3, 1988. In the absence of an expression of contrary intention in the
instrument which created it, such an entail is not limited (as were entails
created prior to that date) to legitimate issue.[530] Such a contrary intention was
not implied from the use of the words "heirs" or "in tail".[531]

3. Limitation to heir. If property is limited after 1925, whether inter vivos   **14–133**
or by will, to the heir of a deceased person, the "heir" is ascertained according
to the general law in force before 1926.[532] This is not a case of descent on
intestacy, for the heir takes as purchaser.

II. PERSONALTY

In the case of personalty, the old rules never apply to deaths occurring after   **14–134**
1925.[533] These rules still retain some of their importance, however, particularly in showing title to leaseholds, and in the practice of reversion
conveyancing.

C. Reform of the Law

In 1989, the Law Commission published a Report criticising the existing law   **14–135**
and making recommendations for its reform.[534] Its principal recommendation,
that the surviving spouse should in all cases receive the whole estate, was not
accepted by Government, although some of its subsidiary recommendations
were implemented by the Law Reform (Succession) Act 1995. Following
further criticism of the current law,[535] emanating from a consultation exercise
on the appropriate level of the statutory legacy payable to the intestate's
surviving spouse, the Ministry of Justice asked the Law Commission to
review the law of intestacy and family provision. A Consultation Paper was

---

[526] AEA 1925 s.51(2).
[527] Above, para.3–081.
[528] LPA 1925 s.130(4); AEA 1925 ss.45(2), 51(4).
[529] As a result of the Trusts of Land and Appointment of Trustees Act 1996, it ceased to be possible to create new entails after 1996: see above, para.3–031.
[530] See Family Law Reform Act 1987 ss.1(1), 19(1), (2).
[531] Family Law Reform Act 1987 s.19(2).
[532] LPA 1925 s.132; AEA 1925 s.51(1). By the former section the heir appears to take only an equitable interest, even in the (highly unlikely) event of an immediate conveyance by deed.
[533] AEA 1925 s.45(1).
[534] Law Com. No 187, Distribution on Intestacy (1989); see S.M. Cretney, *Law, Law Reform and the Family* (1999), p.246.
[535] Kerridge (2007) 71 Conv. 47.

published in October 2009,[536] and a final Report was published in December 2011.[537]

14–136 The 2011 Report recommends that where a person dies intestate survived by a spouse or civil partner, but no children, the surviving spouse or civil partner should obtain the whole estate.[538] This recommendation differs from the principal recommendation of the 1989 Report which would have applied this rule in all cases. The 2011 Report further recommends that where a person dies leaving children as well as a spouse or civil partner, the surviving spouse or civil partner should receive the personal chattels, a statutory legacy and one half of the balance of the estate, thereby dispensing with the practical difficulties caused by the conferment of a life interest.[539] It also recommends a means of regulating the up-dating of the statutory legacy to ensure that it keeps pace with inflation and a simplification of the definition of personal chattels.[540] No recommendation for reform is made in relation to other relatives of the intestate. However, the 2011 Report does recommend that cohabitants who have lived in the same household as the intestate (as his or her spouse or civil partner) for the five years preceding the death should have the same entitlement on intestacy as a surviving spouse.[540a]

Section 8. Devolution of Legal Estates

14–137 **1. Vesting of property.** Hitherto we have examined only the beneficial devolution of property on death. We must now turn to the machinery by which the property becomes vested in those beneficially entitled. The general rule today is that all property first vests in the personal representatives of the deceased, who in due course transfer to the beneficiaries any of the property not required in the due administration of the estate, e.g. for payment of debts. In this context, "estate" is used not in the technical sense of an estate in land, but as a collective expression for the sum total of the assets and liabilities of the deceased.

14–138 **2. Executors.** "Personal representatives" is a phrase which includes both executors and administrators. If a person makes a will, he may (but need not) appoint one or more persons to be his executor or executors, with the duty of paying debts, taxes and funeral expenses, and ultimately of distributing the

---

[536] Law Com. CP No.191, Intestacy and Family Provision Claims on Death (2009).
[537] Law Com. No.331, Intestacy and Family Provision Claims on Death (2011).
[538] Law Com. No.331, paras 2.15 et seq.
[539] Law Com. No.331, paras 2.27 et seq.
[540] Law Com. No 331, paras 2.114 et seq.; paras 2.96 et seq.
[540a] Law Com. No.331, Pt 8. Where the couple had a child together who was living with them at the date of the intestate's death, the period is reduced to two years: Law Com. No.331, paras 8.89 et seq. No entitlement is recommended where the intestate leaves a surviving spouse or civil partner, although in such circumstances the cohabitant may be able to bring a claim for family provision under the Inheritance (Provision for Family and Dependants) Act 1975: Law Com. No.331, paras 8.64 et seq.; and see above, para.14–005.

estate to those entitled. The executor derives his powers from the will, although he must obtain confirmation of his position by "proving the will", i.e. obtaining a grant of probate from the court.[541] If a sole or only surviving executor who has obtained probate dies having himself appointed an executor, the latter, on proving the original executor's will, becomes executor of the original testator also. This "chain of representation" may be continued indefinitely until broken by failure to appoint an executor, or failure of an executor to obtain a grant of probate.[542]

3. Administrators. If a person dies without having appointed an executor, or if none of the executors he has appointed is able and willing to act, application must be made to the court by some person or persons interested in the estate for "letters of administration" appointing an administrator or administrators. The duties of an administrator are substantially the same as those of an executor. If the deceased left no will, simple administration is granted; if he left a will, administration with the will annexed (formerly "*cum testamento annexo*") is granted.[543] The grant may be limited in any way the court thinks fit,[544] e.g. it may endure only during the minority of the sole executor).[545] There is no "chain of representation" for administrators. If a sole or last surviving administrator dies without completing the administration of the estate, application must be made for a grant of administration *de bonis non administratis* (more shortly, *de bonis non*), which is a grant "in respect of the goods left unadministered".

Applications for grants both of probate and of letters of administration are regulated by the Non-Contentious Probate Rules 1987 (as amended).[546]

4. Vesting of property. Prior to 1897 a deceased's personal estate (including his leaseholds) devolved on his personal representatives, but his realty passed directly to his heir (on an intestacy) or to his devisee (under any will). Under the Land Transfer Act 1897, all property, whether real or personal, vested in the deceased's personal representatives.[547] The Administration of Estates Act 1925 substantially repeated the provisions of that Act. In the case of deaths after 1925, all land owned by the deceased, including leaseholds[548] and Crown lands,[549] vests in the personal representatives,[550] with the following exceptions:

14–139

14–140

---

[541] See, e.g. *Chetty v Chetty* [1916] 1 A.C. 603; *Bainbridge v IRC* [1955] 1 W.L.R. 1329 at 1335; *Biles v Caesar* [1957] 1 W.L.R. 156; *Re Crowhurst Park* [1974] 1 W.L.R. 583.
[542] AEA 1925 s.7, replacing 25 Edw. 3, St. 5, c. 5, 1351. For criticism, see (1980) 77 *Law Society's Gazette* 265 (A. V. Barker).
[543] Senior Courts Act 1981 s.119.
[544] Senior Courts Act 1981 s.113.
[545] Senior Courts Act 1981 s.118.
[546] SI 1987/2024 as amended by SI 1991/1876 and SI 1991/2684.
[547] For an account of the law before 1926 see the fifth edition of this work at pp.559–561.
[548] AEA 1925 s.3(1).
[549] AEA 1925 s.57; e.g. land passing as *bona vacantia*. The LTA 1897, did not bind the Crown, so that land escheating to the Crown did not vest in the personal representatives: *In b. Hartley* [1899] P. 40.
[550] AEA 1925 s.1(1).

(i) entails, unless disposed of by the deceased's will[551];

(ii) property to which the deceased was entitled as a joint tenant[552];

(iii) property to which the deceased was entitled as corporation sole[553]; and

(iv) interests which ceased on the death of the deceased, such as an interest for his life.[554]

Property subject to a general power of appointment exercised by the will of the deceased passes to his personal representatives.[555] On an intestacy, or where there are no executors to administer a will, the deceased's real and personal estate vests initially in the Public Trustee,[556] pending a grant of representation.[557]

5. Assents

14–141   *(a) Unregistered land.* If A dies leaving land, the title to which is unregistered, to B, and B wishes to sell the land to C, B establishes his title by proving:

(i) the grant of representation to certain persons as A's personal representatives; and

(ii) an assent or conveyance by those persons as personal representatives in favour of B.[558]

Where the assent or conveyance is made after March 1998, it triggers the requirement of compulsory registration[559] and should be registered within two

---

[551] AEA 1925 s.3(3).

[552] AEA 1925 s.3(4).

[553] AEA 1925 s.3(5).

[554] AEA 1925 s.1(1).

[555] AEA 1925 s.3(2).

[556] Compare the situation where there are executors. The property vests in them at the moment of death and the grant of probate confirms their right to act: above, para.14–138.

[557] AEA 1925 s.9 (as substituted by LP(MP)A 1994 s.14(1)), implementing a recommendation in (1989) Law Com. No.184, para.2.23. Before July 1995, when this provision was brought into force, the deceased's property vested in the Probate Judge, who was the President of the Family Division: see AEA 1925 s.55(1)(xv) (now repealed; cf. the fifth edition of this work at p.560.). The change to the Public Trustee (which was retrospective: see LP(MP)A 1994 s.14(2)) was made because the President was not a corporation sole and obvious difficulties were foreseen should the President die in office. See Law Com. No.184, para.2.22; [1995] Conv. 476, 479 (L. Clements). For the functions of the Public Trustee in relation to the service of notices and documents concerning a deceased's estate, see LP(MP)A 1994 s.19; and SI 1995/1330. Prior to the Act of 1994, service of any notice in respect of an intestate's property before any grant of administration had been made, had to be on the President of the Family Division: see, e.g. *Edwards v Strong* [1994] E.G.C.S. 182.

[558] Before 1926 B also had to prove A's will, showing that he was beneficially entitled.

[559] LRA 2002 s.4(1)(a)(ii). The registration requirement was introduced by LRA 1997 s.1.

months.[560] In order to secure registration, the personal representatives must satisfy the registrar that the assent or conveyance has been correctly made.[561]

There will, however, be many cases where an assent of unregistered land **14–142** was made prior to April 1998. In such cases the grant of probate[562] and the written assent[563] are essential documents of title. If the land is subsequently sold the assent has the effect of overreaching the equitable interests declared by the will.[564] In other words, a bona fide purchaser for value[565] from a devisee is not concerned with the terms of the will: he is concerned only to see that the legal estate has devolved upon the personal representatives, and that they have in turn vested it by assent or conveyance in the vendor.[566] Unless the purchaser has evidence to the contrary,[567] he cannot require the will to be disclosed[568]; and even if the assent is in favour of the wrong person the purchaser is protected, for the assent passes the legal estate,[569] and the purchaser will have no notice of the beneficiary's claim.[570] Interests arising under wills are therefore now kept off the title to the legal estate, just as are beneficial interests arising under trusts for sale and settlements.

(b) Registered land. Where the title is registered, B will have to show **14–143** merely that he is registered as proprietor. When a sole registered proprietor dies, his personal representatives may on production of the grant of probate or letters of administration either secure their own registration, or transfer the land in favour of a purchaser or to the person entitled under the will or on intestacy. On the death of the registered proprietor, his estate immediately devolves on his personal representatives whether or not any reference to this appears on the register.[571] Once there has been a grant of probate or letters of administration, the personal representatives may apply to become registered proprietors, but they are not obliged to do so.[572] If the personal representatives are registered as proprietors, the registrar may enter a restriction against their

---

[560] LRA 2002 ss. 6(1), (4).

[561] The registrar may require production not only of title deeds proving the deceased's title to the legal estate, but also of a copy of the deceased's will: *Ruoff & Roper, Registered Conveyancing* (London: Sweet & Maxwell), para.9–017.

[562] *Re Miller and Pickersgill's Contract* [1931] 1 Ch. 511 at 514. The same applies to letters of administration. Grants of representation, being orders of the court, cannot be invalidated against purchasers on account of lack of jurisdiction, or the absence of any consent, even though there was notice of the defect: LPA 1925 s.204; *Hewson v Shelley* [1914] 2 Ch. 13; *Re Bridgett and Hayes' Contract* [1928] Ch. 163.

[563] AEA 1925 s.36(2), (4); Williams V. & P. 281, n. (g).

[564] AEA 1925 s.39(1)(ii), giving personal representatives the overreaching powers of trustees of land (for which see above, para.12–036); but a sole personal representative can receive purchase money: LPA 1925 s.27(2), as amended by LP(Am)A 1926 Sch.

[565] AEA 1925 s.55(1)(xviii).

[566] AEA 1925 s.36(7).

[567] *Re Duce and Boots Cash Chemists (Southern) Ltd's Contract* [1937] Ch. 642.

[568] AEA 1925 s.36(7).

[569] AEA 1925 s.36(4).

[570] See also below, paras 15–078, 15–079.

[571] Above, para.7–109.

[572] LRR 2003 r.163.

title in order to prevent any disposition which is inconsistent with the terms of the will or with the law relating to intestacy.[573]

14–144 Even if the personal representatives are not registered as proprietors, they may still make a disposition of the deceased's registered estate. They can do this by applying to the registrar to alter the register to bring it up to date by registering as its proprietor the person entitled to the estate or the purchaser.[574] The registrar is under no duty to investigate why the disposition is being made, and he must assume that the personal representatives are acting correctly and within their powers.[575] Responsibility for proper administration of the deceased's estate in accordance with the terms of the will and the intestacy rules falls upon the deceased's personal representatives and is of no concern to the registrar.[576]

14–145 *(c) Precautions.* Two supplemental provisions further illustrate the functions of the grant of representation and of the personal representatives in the machinery of devolution:

> (i) The person in whose favour an assent or conveyance of a legal estate is made may require notice of it to be indorsed on the grant of probate or letters of administration.[577] In this way, the grant of representation may be made a kind of register of dispositions,[578] indicating that some specified assent or conveyance is the right one.
>
> (ii) A written statement by a personal representative that he has not disposed of a legal estate is sufficient evidence to a purchaser that no previous assent or conveyance has been made, unless notice is indorsed on the grant of representation as provided above[579]; thus a purchaser can obtain from the personal representative a document which acts as a curtain over all the personal representative's acts.

Both these provisions are permissive, not mandatory; but it is always advisable to employ them.

14–146 *(d) Changes of capacity.* A personal representative is often given power to act in some other capacity, as where a will appoints X and Y both personal representatives and trustees of land. In such a case the legal estate will not vest in them as trustees of land unless as personal representatives they make a

---

[573] Ruoff & Roper, para.13–005.05. Where there is a trust of land and the trustees' powers are restricted (see TLATA 1996 s.8), the personal representatives are then required to apply for a restriction to be entered in the register: LRR 2003 r.94(4).

[574] LRR 2003 r.162.

[575] LRR 2003 r.162(2).

[576] This follows from LRR 2003 r.162(2).

[577] AEA 1925 s.36(5).

[578] See fn.562, above.

[579] AEA 1925 s.36(6).

written assent in favour of themselves as trustees of land.[580] Where the title is unregistered, an assent therefore remains an essential link in the title to the legal estate, showing that the property is no longer subject to the personal representatives' powers of administration, even where it is to remain vested in the same persons. As has been explained, any such assent made after March 1998 triggers the requirement of compulsory registration of the land.[581] Where the title is already registered, the personal representatives will either be registered in their representative capacity,[582] or they may secure their registration as trustees of land subject to the appropriate restrictions (if any).[583] The registrar is required to assume that they are acting correctly and within their powers.[584]

6. Ownership of assets. Although the personal representatives are in a fiduciary position, it is not right to regard them as holding only the legal estate in the assets, with the equitable interests in the beneficiaries. While the administration is being carried out, it cannot be said whether any particular asset will be needed for the payment of debts or discharge of other liabilities, and it follows that no beneficiary can assert that he has any interest in it, legal or equitable. With the exception of property specifically devised or bequeathed,[585] the personal representatives have the whole ownership, legal and equitable, of the assets vested in them and the beneficiaries have no equitable interest in those assets, whether the estate devolves by will[586] or on intestacy.[587] A beneficiary who is solely entitled under an intestacy cannot, for the purposes of a statutory right to compensation, claim to be "entitled to an interest" in a house which forms part of an unadministered estate[588]; and a surviving spouse or civil partner with the right to call for the matrimonial home to be appropriated to him or her[589] has no *locus standi* to defend an action for possession of it.[590] The rights of the beneficiaries are protected by the rule that the court will control the personal representatives and ensure that the assets are duly administered in the interests of the beneficiaries and all other persons concerned.[591] This rule means that a residuary legatee has an

14–147

---

[580] *Re King's W.T.* [1964] Ch. 542, criticised in (1964) 80 L.Q.R. 328 (R. R. A. Walker), (1964) 28 Conv. (N.S.) 298 (J. F. Garner) and (1976) 29 C.L.P. 60 (E. C. Ryder); cf. *Re Yerburgh* [1928] W.N. 208; *Re Edwards' W.T.* [1982] Ch. 30. An assent to the passing of an equitable interest requires no formality and may be inferred from conduct: *Re Edwards' W.T.*, above.

[581] See above, para.14–141.

[582] See above, paras 14–143, 14–144.

[583] LRR 2003 r.163.

[584] See above, para.14–144.

[585] *Kavanagh v Best* [1971] N.I. 89.

[586] *Commissioner of Stamp Duties (Queensland) v Livingston* [1965] A.C. 694; *Marshall v Kerr* [1995] 1 A.C. 148 at 157, 165.

[587] *Eastbourne Mutual Benefit BS v Hastings Corporation* [1965] 1 W.L.R 861.

[588] ibid.

[589] See above, para.14–114.

[590] *Lall v Lall* [1965] 1 W.L.R. 1249; and see C. Sherrin and R. Bonehill, *The Law and Practice of Intestate Succession*, 3rd edn (London: Sweet & Maxwell, 2004), para.12–005.

[591] *Commissioner of Stamp Duties (Queensland) v Livingston*, above, at 712.

immediate entitlement to future payment (at the completion of the administration of the estate) of such assets as then form the residue of the estate.[592]

14–148   **7. Powers of personal representatives.** Personal representatives have joint
and several powers over pure personalty but only joint authority in relation to
the sale or conveyance of realty (including leaseholds).[593] Personal representatives have in relation to any real estate comprised in the deceased's estate
all the powers conferred by Part I of the Trusts of Land and Appointment of
Trustees Act 1996,[594] and thus all the powers of an absolute owner.[595]
Although they should sell the property only if that is necessary for the
purposes of administration, e.g. to pay the deceased's debts, a conveyance to
a purchaser for value in good faith is not invalidated merely because he knows
that all the debts and other liabilities have been met.[596] Nor is a conveyance
to a purchaser for value in good faith invalidated merely because the probate
or letters of administration under which the personal representatives acted are
subsequently revoked.[597]

8. Number of personal representatives

14–149   *(a) Maximum.* No grant of probate or letters of administration can be made
to more than four personal representatives in respect of the same property.[598]
If more than four executors are appointed by a testator, they must decide
among themselves who shall apply for probate.

14–150   *(b) Minimum.* A sole personal representative, whether original or by survivorship, has full power to give valid receipts for capital money or any other
payments.[599] As has been explained, subject to certain exceptions, personal
representatives are in the same position as trustees of land.[600] They have the
same powers as such trustees,[601] but without their disability as to receiving
capital money severally.[602] However, where any person interested in the estate

---

[592] *Re Hemming* [2008] EWHC 2731 (Ch); [2009] Ch. 313, following *Re Leigh's W.T.* [1970]
Ch. 277.
[593] AEA 1925 s.2(2) (as amended by LP(MP)A 1994, extending the provisions of s.2(2) to
contracts to convey as well as to conveyances). The amendment implemented a recommendation
in (1989) Law Com. No.184 para.2.13. For the background to the change, see (1989) Law Com.
No.184 para.2.11; [1995] Conv. 476, 478 (L. Clements).
[594] AEA 1925 s.39 (as amended by TLATA 1996); TLATA 1996 s.18.
[595] TLATA 1996 s.6(1). For these powers, see above, para.12–016.
[596] AEA 1925 ss.36(8), 55(1)(xviii).
[597] AEA 1925 ss.37, 55(1)(xviii), retrospectively confirming *Hewson v Shelley* [1914] 2 Ch.
13.
[598] Senior Courts Act 1981 s.114(1). This is strictly construed: see *In b. Holland* (1936) 105
L.J.P. 113.
[599] LPA 1925 s.27(2) (as amended by LP(Am)A 1926 Sch.; TLATA 1996 s.25(1) Sch.3
para.4).
[600] See above, para.12–035.
[601] See TLATA 1996 s.6; above, para.12–016.
[602] See above, para.12–037.

is a minor or has a life interest in it, the court when granting administration, may not appoint a sole administrator (other than a trust corporation) unless it appears to the court to be expedient to do so.[603] A sole executor can act under such circumstances, but the court has power to appoint additional personal representatives.[604]

---

[603] Senior Courts Act 1981 s.114(2).
[604] Senior Courts Act s.114(4).

CONTRACTS OF SALE

15–001   A contract to sell or make any other disposition of any interest in land differs from other contracts in at least three main respects. First, such a contract can only be made in writing in accordance with the formalities laid down by the Law of Property (Miscellaneous Provisions) Act 1989.[1] Secondly, the usual remedy for the enforcement of such contracts is specific performance rather than the normal award of damages,[2] and this has influenced many of the rules which apply to conveyancing contracts. Thirdly, and as a consequence of this, a purchaser, even before conveyance, acquires an immediate equitable interest in the property.[3]

Contracts for the sale of land are such an integral part of the whole system of conveyancing that they have many peculiarities drawn from land law. Such contracts invariably contain express terms which are called "conditions of sale".[4] However, the common law has evolved an extensive web of rules which regulate the affairs of vendors and purchasers in the absence of such conditions. To the extent that a matter is governed by them (rather than by a condition of sale), the contract is said to be "open".[5] Although it has never been conclusively settled whether these "open contract" rules are to be regarded as rights conferred by law or as terms which will, as a matter of law,

---

[1] s.2, considered in detail, below, para.15–015.

[2] By contrast, specific performance of a contract for the sale of goods, although possible where the goods are specific or ascertained (see Sale of Goods Act 1979 s.52), is exceptional: *Re Wait* [1972] 1 Ch. 606.

[3] Above, para.5–025.

[4] "The word 'condition' is traditional rather than appropriate . . . Shortly, they are no more than the terms of the contract": *Property Bloodstock Ltd v Emerton* [1968] Ch. 94 at 118, per Danckwerts L.J.

[5] See below, para.15–047. It is very rare indeed for an entire contract to be open nowadays. For examples of such contracts, see *Pips (Leisure Productions) Ltd v Walton* (1980) 43 P. & C.R. 415; *Chaitlal v Ramlal* [2003] UKPC 12 at [22]; [2004] 1 P. & C.R. 1 at 8, 9 (sub nom. *Ramlal v Chaitlal*).

be implied in the contract,[6] they are generally regarded as the latter because damages are recoverable for their breach.[7] Between the contract and either the conveyance (where title is unregistered) or the lodging of the transfer for registration (where title is registered),[8] which are respectively the first and last formal steps in a sale of land, many questions arise which have to be decided according to the settled practices of conveyancers. The performance of a contract is thus affected in numerous ways, and there is a body of rights which are applicable only to such contracts. Three issues are considered in this chapter:

(1) the types of contract that can exist for the sale or other disposition of land;

(2) the essentials that must be satisfied for there to be a valid contract for the sale of land; and

(3) the rights and duties created by contracts relating to land.

Part 1

TYPES OF CONTRACT

There are four principal types of contract for the sale or other disposition of land: **15–002**

(1) an unconditional contract of sale;

(2) a contract that is subject to some form of condition;

(3) an option to purchase; and

(4) a right of pre-emption (including a right of first refusal).[9]

In fact, both options and rights of pre-emption may be regarded as types of conditional contract, at least for some purposes.[10] The usual form of binding

---

[6] For the suggestion that they are rights conferred by law, see *Ogilvie v Foljambe* (1817) 3 Mer. 53 at 63; *Want v Stallibrass* (1873) 8 Exch. 175 at 185. cf. *Ellis v Rogers* (1885) 29 Ch D 661 at 670, 671, where Cotton L.J. considered that they might be terms implied in the contract.

[7] If such rules were merely rights conferred by law, the only consequence of their breach might be that the party in default would be unable to enforce the contract: see (1992) 108 L.Q.R. 280 at 282, 283 (C.H.).

[8] For applications to register dispositions of registered land, see above, para.7–059.

[9] For the question whether and in what circumstances a right of pre-emption can be properly characterised as a contract for the sale or other disposition of land, see below, paras 15–061 et seq.

[10] Below, paras 15–012—15–013.

contract is unconditional. Its principal elements are treated in the course of this chapter and no more need be said of it here.

Section 1. Conditional Contracts

15–003   **1. Types of conditional contract.** There are usually said to be four types of conditional contract,[11] and it is a matter of construction, based upon the characteristics of the particular arrangement, as to the category into which the agreement falls.[12]

15–004   *(a) Condition precedent to a binding agreement.* This is an arrangement between V and P subject to a condition precedent to the making of any binding agreement at all. To describe such an arrangement as a conditional contract is a misnomer for there is no contract at all. The commonest example is an agreement "subject to contract",[13] and other phrases which have been held to have the same effect include "subject to the preparation and approval of a formal contract",[14] "subject to suitable agreements being arranged between your solicitors and mine"[15] and "subject to lease".[16] Such arrangements are of considerable importance and are considered in detail below.[17]

15–005   *(b) Unilateral contract.* In this situation, one party, A, assumes a unilateral obligation to buy property from or sell property to the other, B, on the occurrence of a certain event, which neither is obliged to bring about. Although A cannot withdraw from the contract as long as it remains conditional, B is not bound by it unless and until he elects to become so.[18] Options and rights of pre-emption are probably best regarded as examples of such contracts,[19] but because they are subject to certain special rules, they are

[11] See *Wood Preservation Ltd v Prior* [1969] 1 W.L.R 1077 at 1090. See [1982] C.L.P. 151 (A. J. Oakley); [1992] Conv. 318 (C.H.).

[12] See [1992] Conv. 318 at 319 (C.H.).

[13] *Eccles v Bryant* [1948] Ch. 93.

[14] *Wynn v Bull* (1877) 7 Ch D 29. See too *Page v Norfolk* (1894) 70 L.T. 781 ("subject to our approving a detailed contract to be entered into"). cf. *Branca v Cobarro* [1947] K.B. 854 ("This is a provisional agreement until a fully legalized agreement, drawn up by a solicitor and embodying all the conditions herewith stated, is signed", held to create an immediate binding contract); and see *Immingham Storage Co Ltd v Clear Plc* [2011] EWCA Civ 89 at [26]–[30].

[15] *Lockett v Norman-Wright* [1925] Ch. 56.

[16] Negotiations for the grant of a lease are nowadays often conducted on this basis (or indeed "subject to contract"). In such cases, the parties commonly do not enter into a formal contract to grant a lease, but proceed directly to the exchange of lease and counterpart: see *Longman v Viscount Chelsea* (1989) 58 P. & C.R. 189; *Akiens v Saloman* (1992) 65 P. & C.R. 364; *Enfield LBC v Arajah* [1995] E.G.C.S. 164. The principle of these cases will not be extended to unilateral acts, where the only question is whether or not the act has been done. Thus where a landlord agreed to the tenant making alterations to the leasehold premises subject to it entering into a formal licence agreement with the landlord, the landlord was taken to have consented: *Mount Eden Land Ltd v Prudential Assurance Co Ltd* [1997] 1 E.G.L.R. 37. See too *Next Plc v N.F.U. Mutual Insurance Co Ltd* [1997] E.G.C.S. 181.

[17] Below, para.15–010.

[18] See *Little v Courage Ltd* (1994) 70 P. & C.R. 469 at 474. Because B is not bound, it is generally impossible to imply terms into a unilateral contract.

[19] *Wood Preservation Ltd v Prior*, above, at 1090.

considered separately.[20] One form of such unilateral contracts that is sometimes found is where A agrees to sell or purchase land if B performs certain
conditions.[21]

(c) Condition precedent. This construction is appropriate where V enters **15–006**
into a bilateral contract to sell property to P subject to a condition precedent
which one or other party is obliged to bring about. Although there is a binding
contract between the parties it is not a contract for the sale of land until the
condition precedent is fulfilled.[22] Neither party can waive the condition
precedent, because the existence of the contract depends upon it.[23] For the
same reason, if the condition is void for uncertainty, the whole contract fails
ab initio.[24] Such contracts are in practice rare.[25] The only cases which are
likely to fall into this category are those where it is for some reason impossible
to enter into a contract for the sale of land unless and until some condition is
fulfilled,[26] such as a contract by V to sell land which he does not yet own, that
is contingent upon his acquiring it.[27] There is a tendency in the cases to
characterise contracts in this way when in fact they fall into the fourth
category.[28]

(d) Condition subsequent. The usual kind of conditional contract is where **15–007**
there is an immediate, binding contract for the sale of land which may be
terminated by one or (sometimes) both parties if a condition to which it is
subject is not performed.[29] The condition is one which either one or (in some
cases) both parties are obliged to perform or use their best endeavours to bring

---

[20] Below, para.15–012 (options), para.15–013 (pre-emptions).

[21] See, e.g. *Daulia Ltd v Four Millbank Nominees Ltd* [1978] Ch. 231; [1979] C.L.J. 31 (C. H.
and D. L. Jones) (A undertook to sell land to B if B attended A's premises with the deposit and
draft contract on a given date).

[22] For this reason, the doctrine of conversion (below, para.15–060) does not operate until the
condition is satisfied.

[23] [1982] C.L.P. 151 at 177 (A. J. Oakley). cf. *Ee v Kakar* (1979) 40 P. & C.R. 223, where
Walton J. held that a "condition precedent" could be waived. However, the condition was in fact
a condition subsequent: see [1981] C.L.J. 23 (A. J. Oakley). See too *Sainsbury Plc v O'Connor*
[1991] 1 W.L.R. 963 at 979, where it appears to have been assumed that a condition precedent
can be waived.

[24] *Lee-Parker v Izzet (No.2)* [1972] 1 W.L.R. 775 at 780. It has not been settled what the test
of certainty is: see [1992] Conv. 318 at 320, 321 (C.H.).

[25] Unfortunately this is not always appreciated. Thus in *Lee-Parker v Izzet (No.2)*, above, a
term that the sale was conditional upon the purchaser obtaining a satisfactory mortgage was
treated as a condition precedent. Because the condition was held to be void for uncertainty, the
contract was void *ab initio*. The Privy Council has declined to follow the decision: *Graham v
Pitkin* [1992] 1 W.L.R. 403.

[26] See *Property Bloodstock Ltd v Emerton* [1968] Ch. 94 at 116, doubting the analysis in
Aberfoyle Plantations Ltd v Cheng [1960] A.C. 115.

[27] cf. *Wylson v Dunn* (1887) 34 Ch D 569.

[28] See, e.g. *Mitcham v Magnus Homes South West Ltd* (1996) 74 P. & C.R. 235 at 243.

[29] There is authority that the doctrine of conversion (below, para.15–060) applies to such
contracts: *Gordon Hill Trust Ltd v Segall* [1941] 2 All E.R. 379. But see *Sainsbury Plc v
O'Connor* [1991] 1 W.L.R. 963 at 979; *Michaels v Harley House (Marylebone) Ltd* [1997] 1
W.L.R. 967 at 975–978 (not considered on appeal: [2000] Ch. 104).

about[30] within the time specified (or implied) in the contract[31] or implied by law.[32] If the party who is required to bring about the fulfilment of the condition fails to use his best endeavours to do so:

(i) he cannot plead its non-fulfilment as a defence to any action for specific performance brought by the other[33]; and

(ii) he will be liable to pay damages for loss of bargain if the other party does not or is unable to proceed with the sale.[34]

The contract will become unconditional in two circumstances. The first is if the condition is held to void for uncertainty.[35] The second is where the condition is waived by one party. Waiver is possible only if the condition is solely for his benefit.[36] If the performance of the condition affects both parties, as where the date for completion is linked to its fulfilment, neither party can waive it.[37] It is now clear that a court will consider the issue of waiver in deciding into which of the four categories a conditional contract falls, because only a condition subsequent is capable of waiver.[38] The party who has the benefit of a condition loses his right to waive it once the other party exercises his right to terminate the contract for non-performance of that condition.[39]

15–008   Amongst the agreements which have been held to fall within this category are contracts conditional upon the obtaining of:

(i) the landlord's consent to the assignment of the lease (where the property to be conveyed was a lease)[40]

---

[30] If neither party is obligated to perform the condition, the contract will be unilateral and therefore in the second category of conditional contracts explained above: *Re Longlands Farm* [1968] 3 All E.R. 552 at 555. cf. *Tesco Stores Ltd v William Gibson Son Ltd* (1970) 214 E.G. 835.

[31] *Jolley v Carmel Ltd* [2000] 3 E.G.L.R. 68.

[32] Below, para.15–009.

[33] *Gordon Hill Trust Ltd v Segall*, above, at 387, 388; *Yewbelle Ltd v London Green Developments Ltd* [2006] EWHC 3166 (Ch); [2007] 1 E.G.L.R. 137 (reversed on other grounds: [2007] EWCA Civ 475; [2008] 1 P. & C.R. 279).

[34] *Day v Singleton* [1899] 2 Ch. 320.

[35] cf. *Graham v Pitkin*, above, at 405, 406. See [1992] Conv. 318 at 322 (C.H.), where the possible tests of certainty are also considered.

[36] *Bennett v Fowler* (1840) 2 Beav 302; *Batten v White* (1960) 12 P. & C.R. 66; *Usanga v Bishop* (1974) 232 E.G. 835; *Balbosa v Ayoub Ali* [1990] 1 W.L.R. 914 at 919; *Graham v Pitkin*, above, at 405.

[37] *Heron Garage Properties Ltd v Moss* [1974] 1 W.L.R. 148. For other conditions which could not be waived see *Federated Homes Ltd v Turner* [1975] 1 E.G.L.R. 147 (condition that a right of access be obtained to property including land retained by the vendor); *Ganton House Investments Ltd v Corbin* [1988] 2 E.G.L.R. 69 (contract to assign lease conditional on obtaining the landlord's consent).

[38] *Graham v Pitkin*, above, at 405, 406; [1992] Conv. 318 at 321, 322 (C.H.).

[39] *Irwin v Wilson* [2011] EWHC 326 (Ch); [2011] 2 P. & C.R. 126.

[40] *Lehmann v McArthur* (1868) 3 Ch.App. 496.

(ii) the production of certain documents relating to title[41];

(iii) planning permission[42]

(iv) a satisfactory survey[43]

(v) vacant possession on completion[44]; and

(vi) a mortgage (or other finance).[45]

There is some doubt whether a contract that is expressed to be contingent upon the approval of the vendor's title by the purchaser's solicitor is a conditional contract at all. Although in some cases the provision has been treated as a condition subsequent,[46] it may do no more than express what is implied in the contract in any event,[47] namely that "the title must be investigated and approved of in the usual way, which would be by the solicitor of the purchaser".[48]

2. The time for performance. Where a conditional contract fixes a date 15–009
either for the performance of the condition or for the completion of the sale,
the condition must be performed by that date.[49] In each case, time is of the
essence and will not be extended by reference to equitable principles.[50] If a
party fails to perform the condition (whether precedent or subsequent) by the
relevant date, the other is entitled to terminate the contract. In the absence of
any factors giving rise to an estoppel, this is so even if the condition is in fact
subsequently performed before the contract is determined.[51] If no date is fixed
for completion, the condition must be fulfilled within a reasonable time
determined objectively.[52]

---

[41] *Irwin v Wilson* [2011] EWHC 326 (Ch); [2011] 2 P. & C.R. 126.

[42] *Batten v White*, above; *Heron Garage Properties Ltd v Moss*, above. cf. *Tesco Stores Ltd v William Gibson Son Ltd*, above, where the condition was construed as a unilateral contract. Sed quaere. What constitutes planning permission for the purposes of a condition is a matter of construction: see, e.g., *Smith v Royce Properties Ltd* [2001] EWCA Civ 949; [2002] 2 P. & C.R. 67; *Castlebay Ltd v Asquith Properties Ltd* [2005] EWCA Civ 1734.

[43] *Ee v Kakar* (1979) 40 P. & C.R. 223. See n.23, above.

[44] *Usanga v Bishop*, above.

[45] *Graham v Pitkin* [1992] 1 W.L.R. 403. See too *Meehan v Jones* (1982) 149 C.L.R. 571; (1983) 3 O.J.L.S. 438 (M. P. Furmston).

[46] See, e.g. *Caney v Leith* [1937] 2 All E.R. 532; *Smallman v Smallman* [1972] Fam. 25 at 32. The effect of such a condition subsequent would be that the opinion of the solicitor as to the title, if given in good faith, would be conclusive one way or the other. The matter could not be reopened by either party in court proceedings.

[47] Below, paras 15–074 et seq.

[48] *Hussey v Horne-Payne* (1879) 4 App. Cas. 311 at 322, per Lord Cairns L.C.

[49] *Aberfoyle Plantations Ltd v Cheng* [1960] A.C. 115 at 124.

[50] *Aberfoyle Plantations Ltd v Cheng*, above, at 125. For the equitable principles applicable to time stipulations in a contract for the sale of land, see, below, para.15–092.

[51] *Millers Wharf Partnership Ltd v Corinthian Column Ltd* (1990) 61 P. & C.R. 461.

[52] *Aberfoyle Plantations Ltd v Cheng*, above, at 124; *Re Longlands Farm* [1968] 3 All E.R. 552 at 556.

3. "Subject to contract"

15–010 *(a) Meaning.* When an intending purchaser agrees to buy a property by private treaty,[53] that agreement is usually made "subject to contract". Where a document or preliminary agreement is expressed to be "subject to contract", it means that the parties do not intend to be contractually bound until another document embodying all the terms of the agreement between them is signed by the parties.[54] Normally this will occur on the exchange of formal written contracts in accordance with the usual conveyancing practice,[55] though it may take place at some other time is the parties so agree.[56] Once the parties have begun negotiations "subject to contract", that qualification governs their subsequent dealings until contracts are exchanged, unless both agree expressly or by necessary implication that it should be expunged or waived.[57] It is only in "a strong and exceptional case" that the words "subject to contract" will not be given their prima facie meaning.[58] This may, however, happen where the words are meaningless, as where the contract was complete and no further agreement was intended,[59] or where a detailed agreement replacing an existing contract was clearly intended to be binding.[60] It should be noted that a binding contract for the sale of land can no longer arise from a written offer and acceptance,[61] and that the main significance of the words "subject to contract" will now be in cases where draft contracts are exchanged.[62]

Although a party to negotiations which are "subject to contract" might be able to satisfy a court that the parties had subsequently agreed to convert the document into a contract or that some form of estoppel had arisen to prevent either of them from refusing to proceed with the transaction, such cases will necessarily be rare.[63] A party cannot usually claim to have been encouraged

---

[53] For sales by auction see below, para.15–022.

[54] *Tiverton Estates Ltd v Wearwell Ltd* [1975] Ch. 146 at 159, 160. "As everybody . . . knows, that expression, when used in relation to the sale of land, means that, although the parties have reached an agreement, no legally binding contract comes into existence until the exchange of formal written contracts takes place": *Christos v Secretary of State for Transport* [2003] EWCA Civ 1073 at [34]; [2004] 1 E.G.L.R. 5 at 7, per Mummery L.J.

[55] For the exchange of contracts see below, para.15–036.

[56] *Eccles v Bryant* [1948] Ch. 93 at 105.

[57] *Sherbrooke v Dipple* (1980) 41 P. & C.R. 173; *Cohen v Nessdale Ltd* [1982] 2 All E.R. 97. See too *Henderson Group Plc v Superabbey Ltd* [1988] 2 E.G.L.R. 155 at 157; *Christos v Secretary of State for Transport* [2003] EWCA Civ 1073 at [37]; [2004] 1 E.G.L.R. 5 at 7.

[58] *Chillingworth v Esche* [1924] 1 Ch. 97 at 114, per Sargant L.J.

[59] *Michael Richards Properties Ltd v Corporation of Wardens of St. Saviour's Parish, Southwark* [1975] 3 All E.R. 416. See too *Westway Homes Ltd v Moores* (1991) 63 P. & C.R. 480 (exercise of option "subject to contract" held to be meaningless, because the terms of the contract were prescribed by the option agreement itself).

[60] *Alpenstow Ltd v Regalian Properties Plc* [1985] 1 W.L.R. 721; [1985] C.L.J. 356 (C.H.).

[61] LP(MP)A 1989 s.2; *Commission for the New Towns v Cooper (Great Britain) Ltd* [1995] Ch. 259 at 287, 294; below, para.15–037.

[62] *Commission for the New Towns v Cooper (Great Britain) Ltd*, above, at 293.

[63] *Att Gen of Hong Kong v Humphreys Estate (Queen's Gardens) Ltd* [1987] A.C. 114 at 127, 128. See too *James v Evans* [2000] 3 E.G.L.R. 1; *Edwin Shirley Productions Ltd v Workspace Management Ltd* [2001] 2 E.G.L.R. 16 at 21, [44]–[46]; *London & Regional Investments Ltd v TBI Plc* [2002] EWCA Civ 355 at [41]–[43]; *Haq v Island Homes Housing Association* [2011] EWCA Civ 805; [2011] 2 P. & C.R. 277. For proprietary estoppel, see below, Ch.16.

to act to his detriment in the course of negotiations "subject to contract".[64] If therefore he incurs expenditure in preparation for the anticipated contract, he will be unable to recover that sum if no contract is in fact concluded.[65]

(b) Effect. The effect of using the phrase "subject to contract" is that both **15–011** parties remain free to withdraw from the arrangement without incurring any legal liability.[66] If the purchaser has paid any deposit, he is entitled to its return should he decline to proceed.[67] Commonly either or both of the parties will be buying or selling another property. It has become usual to synchronise all such sales and purchases in what is known as a "chain".[68] This can be organised only if the parties are not contractually bound at the preliminary stage. Furthermore, the purchaser does not wish to be bound until he has arranged the necessary finance for the purchase and his solicitor has made the necessary inquiries before contract.[69] One consequence of the parties' freedom to withdraw at will is that the vendor may (when property prices are rising) "gazump"[70] the purchaser by threatening to sell to another buyer unless a higher price is paid. Similarly, if property prices are falling, the purchaser may threaten to pull out of the agreement unless the vendor reduces the price, an abuse known as "gazundering". A number of devices have been employed to overcome these malpractices. The best-known is a so-called "lock-out" or "exclusivity" agreement by which V, for good consideration, agrees with P that, for a specified period of time, he will not negotiate with anyone except P in relation to the sale of his property.[71] It is essential to the validity of the agreement that it should be confined to a fixed period for otherwise it will be void for uncertainty as a mere agreement to negotiate.[72] Such an agreement is merely a negative agreement not to deal with anyone other than P. It is not a contract for the sale or other disposition of an interest in land and does not therefore have to comply with the formal requirements for such contracts.[73] The primary remedy for breach of a lock-out agreement is damages and the

---

[64] Below, para.16–009.
[65] *Regalian Properties Plc v London Docklands Development Corporation* [1995] 1 W.L.R. 212; [1995] C.L.J. 243 (G. Virgo); [1995] R.L.R. 100 (E. McKendrick).
[66] In *Goding v Frazer* [1967] 1 W.L.R. 286 at 293, Sachs J. spoke of "this hybrid type of 'subject to contract' transaction, which is so often referred to as a gentleman's agreement, but which experience shows is only too often a transaction in which each side hopes the other will act like a gentleman and neither intends so to act if it is against his material interest".
[67] *Chillingworth v Esche*, above.
[68] See *Domb v Isoz* [1980] Ch. 548 at 560, 561.
[69] *Domb v Isoz*, above, at 560, 561. See above, para.8–027.
[70] Described as a "verb of doubtful etymology": *Wroth v Tyler* [1974] Ch. 30 at 55, per Megarry J.
[71] *Walford v Miles* [1992] 2 A.C. 128 at 139; (1992) 108 L.Q.R. 405 (Sir Patrick Neill); *Pitt v P.H.H. Asset Management Ltd* [1994] 1 W.L.R. 327. Unless the parties otherwise agree, a lock-out agreement will not found a claim for substantial damages or a long-term injunction: *Moroney v Isofam Investments S.A.* [1997] E.G.C.S. 178. cf. *Dandara Holdings Ltd v Co-operative Retail Services Ltd* [2004] EWHC 1476 (Ch); [2004] 2 E.G.L.R. 163.
[72] *Walford v Miles*, above, approving *Courtney Fairburn Ltd v Tolaini Brothers (Hotels) Ltd* [1975] 1 W.L.R. 297.
[73] *Pitt v P.H.H. Asset Management Ltd*, above, at 332, 334; [1993] C.L.J. 392 (C. MacMillan). cf. [1994] Conv. 58 (M. P. Thompson).

measure will be the amount which P has wasted in costs during the period of exclusivity.[74]

The conduct of conveyancing under the umbrella of "subject to contract" has arisen as a matter of custom and practice not because of any particular rule of law. It is quite unknown in Scotland where would-be purchasers submit sealed bids for the property offering both a price and terms for completion. The seller accepts the one which suits him best and the contract is then concluded. Chain sales do not exist and gazumping and gazundering are impossible. If desired, such a system could be readily adopted in England and Wales.[75]

Section 2. Options and Rights of Pre-emption

15–012   **1. Options.** An option is an undertaking by the grantor that he will sell certain property to the grantee if the latter wishes to purchase it within a specified period.[76] It may be created by a contract between the grantor and the grantee (which may stand by itself or be part of some other transaction such as a sale or lease), or it may be granted by will. It is only with the former that we are here concerned.[77] An option has been described as "a relationship sui generis".[78] It shares certain characteristics with other types of legal relationship but does not exactly correspond to any of them. First, it is "not the same juristic creature as a contract of sale",[79] because it binds only the grantor until it is exercised.[80] Secondly, it has been likened to an "irrevocable offer" to sell,[81] but it is really only from the grantee's standpoint that it can be so regarded.[82] In explaining the grantor's position, an option may be seen as analogous to a conditional contract.[83] However, the performance of the contingency lies within the sole power of the grantee[84] and the contract is not therefore "conditional" in the same sense as is a contract subject to a

---

[74] See *Tye v House* [1997] 2 E.G.L.R. 171; *Moroney v Isofam Investments S.A.* [1997] E.G.C.S. 178; *Dandara Holdings Ltd v Co-operative Retail Services Ltd* [2004] EWHC 1476 (Ch); [2004] 2 E.G.L.R. 163.

[75] See the Explanatory Guide, "House Selling the Scottish Way for England and Wales", produced by the Conveyancing Standing Committee of the Law Commission (1987).

[76] For the application of the rule against perpetuities to options see above, para.9–118.

[77] For testamentary options see M. Dray and A. Rosenthal *Barnsley's Land Options* 4th edn (London: Sweet & Maxwell, 2005), Ch.6.

[78] *Spiro v Glencrown Properties Ltd* [1991] Ch. 537 at 544, per Hoffmann J. See [1994] Conv. 483 (N. P. Gravells).

[79] *Chippenham Golf Club Trustees v North Wiltshire DC* (1991) 64 P. & C.R. 527 at 531, per Scott L.J. (power to sell did not confer a power to grant an option).

[80] For the nature of the grantor's obligations see [1984] C.L.J. 55 (S. Tromans).

[81] *Stromdale Ball Ltd v Burden* [1952] Ch. 223 at 235; *Mountford v Scott* [1975] Ch. 258 at 264; *United Scientific Holdings Ltd v Burnley BC* [1978] A.C. 904 at 945. An "irrevocable offer" has been described as "juristically a contradiction in terms", because the word "irrevocable" implies the existence of an obligation, whereas "offer" implies none: *Varty v British South Africa Co* [1965] Ch. 508 at 523, per Diplock L.J.

[82] *Spiro v Glencrown Properties Ltd*, above at 543.

[83] *Griffith v Pelton* [1958] Ch. 205 at 225.

[84] *Spiro v Glencrown Properties Ltd*, above, at 544.

condition precedent or subsequent.[85] A court will adopt a purposive analysis in any given case to decide which of these analogies is the most appropriate to apply to the issue which it must determine.[86] Thus an option has been treated as a conditional contract for the purposes of:

(i) the formalities required for a contract for the sale of an interest in land,[87] so that although the grant of the option has to comply with those requirements, its exercise does not[88]; and

(ii) registration as a land charge,[89] so that it is unnecessary to register as an estate contract the contract for sale that arises from the exercise of the option as well as the option itself.[90]

The grantor's undertaking to sell to the grantee will be enforceable even though the consideration for the option is only nominal, such as a payment of £1.[91] When the option is exercised in accordance with its terms, the original unilateral agreement, which imposed no immediate obligations on either party to do anything, is converted into a bilateral agreement that creates reciprocal rights and obligations on both parties.[92]

If the grantor of an option transfers the land in breach of the option, he will be liable in damages to the grantee.[93] The grantee may seek an injunction to restrain any such disposition.[94]

2. Rights of pre-emption. There are two forms of contract that are often described generically as rights of pre-emption, namely:　　　　　　　　**15–013**

(i) A right of first refusal, whereby the grantee has the first right to refuse an offer to purchase at the price at which the grantor is prepared to sell the land; and

(ii) A right of pre-emption, strictly so-called, where the grantee has the right to purchase the land either at a fixed price or at a price not determined by the grantor before the grantor is free to sell the land to anyone else.[95]

---

[85] For these forms of conditional contract, see above, paras 15–006, 15–007.
[86] *Spiro v Glencrown Properties Ltd*, above at 544. See too *Re Mulholland's W.T.* [1949] 1 All E.R. 460; *Chippenham Golf Club Trustees v North Wiltshire DC*, above, at 531.
[87] See LP(MP)A 1989 s.2; below, para.15–015.
[88] *Spiro v Glencrown Properties Ltd*, above; below, para.15–018.
[89] See LCA 1972 s.2(4)(iv); above, para.8–075.
[90] *Armstrong Holmes Ltd v Holmes* [1993] 1 W.L.R. 1482.
[91] *Mountford v Scott*, above.
[92] *Sudbrook Trading Estate Ltd v Eggleton* [1983] 1 A.C. 444 at 477.
[93] *Midland Bank Trust Co Ltd v Green* [1980] Ch. 590 at 611 (not considered on appeal: [1981] A.C. 513).
[94] *Mason v Schuppisser* (1899) 81 L.T. 147 at 148.
[95] See *Bircham & Co, Nominees (2) Ltd v Worrell Holdings Ltd* [2001] EWCA Civ 775 at [31]; (2001) 82 P. & C.R. 427 at 438.

Both forms are referred to as rights of pre-emption in this work.[96] Where a landowner grants a right of pre-emption, it imposes upon him for an agreed period[97] a negative obligation to refrain from selling the land, without first giving the grantee the opportunity to purchase it in preference to any other buyer. The grantor is under no obligation to sell the property, but should he decide to do so, he must first offer[98] it to the grantee, who is then free to accept or reject the proposal.[99] If the grantor decides to sell the property and offers it to the grantee, then unless the instrument creating the right of pre-emption otherwise provides,[100] that offer may be revoked before acceptance should the grantor reconsider his decision to sell.[101]

If the grantor disposes of the land without first offering it to the grantee he will be liable to the latter in damages.[102] Furthermore any such disposition can be restrained by injunction[103] and the grantor can be required to offer to sell the land to the grantee.[104]

An option differs from a right of pre-emption in that it is a standing offer that can be accepted in accordance with its terms, whereas a right of pre-emption requires the grantor to offer to sell the land to the grantee, and the grantee may either accept or reject that offer.[105] The different effects of options and rights of pre-emption are explained later.[106]

Part 2

THE ESSENTIALS OF A VALID CONTRACT

15–014   **1. Introduction.** A contract for the sale or other disposition of land made on or after September 27, 1989 is neither valid nor enforceable unless it

---

[96] There are a number of statutory references to rights of pre-emption: see, e.g., LPA 1925 s.186; LCA 1972 s.2(4)(iv); LRA 2002 s.115. There is no reason in principle why they should not apply to both rights of first refusal and rights of pre-emption in the strict sense. See above, para.7–067.

[97] The rule against perpetuities applied to rights of pre-emption created before April 6, 2010, as it did to options created before that date: PAA 1964 s.9(2); above, para.9–134. But see below, para.15–062. Options and rights of pre-emption that are created after April 5, 2010 are no longer subject to the rule against perpetuities: see above, para.9–136.

[98] Whether or not a communication from the grantor amounts to an offer is a matter of construction of that document: *Churchman v Lampon* [1990] 1 E.G.L.R. 211.

[99] See *Mackay v Wilson* (1947) 47 S.R.(N.S.W.) 315 at 325; *Pritchard v Briggs* [1980] Ch. 338 at 389, 423.

[100] As it did in *Pritchard v Briggs*, above. As to the various possibilities, see *Speciality Shops Ltd v Yorkshire and Metropolitan Estates Ltd* [2002] EWHC 2969 (Ch) at [25]–[29]; [2003] 2 P. & C.R. 410 at 416, 417.

[101] *Tuck v Baker* [1990] 1 E.G.L.R. 195.

[102] *Gardner v Coutts Co* [1968] 1 W.L.R. 173 (gift of land a breach of the right of pre-emption).

[103] *Coventry v London, Brighton South Coast Rly* (1867) L.R. 5 Eq. 104; *Manchester Ship Canal Co v Manchester Racecourse Co* [1901] 2 Ch. 37.

[104] *London South Western Rly Co v Blackmore* (1870) L.R. 4 H.L. 610; *Tiffany Investments Ltd v Bircham & Co, Nominees (2) Ltd* [2003] EWCA Civ 1759; [2004] 2 P. & C.R. 144.

[105] See *Coaten v PBS Corporation* [2006] EWHC 1781 (Ch) at [30]; [2006] 3 E.G.L.R. 43 at 45.

[106] Below, para.15–062.

complies with the requirements of s.2 of the Law of Property (Miscellaneous Provisions) Act 1989, which came into force on that date.[107] Under the law prior to that date, it was possible to have a contract that was valid but not enforceable because it did not comply with the statutory requirements of writing.[108] It is necessary to consider in detail the requirements of s.2. Although it is a comparatively recent provision, "it has given rise to a considerable amount of difficulty over its short life".[109]

Section 2 of the Law of Property (Miscellaneous Provisions) Act 1989 **15–015** implemented the recommendations of the Law Commission,[110] and imposed more stringent formal requirements for contracts for the sale or other disposition of an interest in land than had previously been required.[111] It provided that a contract for the sale or other disposition of an interest in land "can only be made in writing and only by incorporating all the terms which the parties have expressly agreed in one document or, where the contracts are exchanged, in each".[112] The terms may be incorporated in a document either by being set out in it or by reference to some other document.[113] The document incorporating the terms or, where contracts are exchanged, one of the documents incorporating them (but not necessarily the same one) must be signed by or on behalf of each party to the contract.[114]

There can no longer be a valid but unenforceable oral contract for the sale of land as was formerly the case. In consequence, the old doctrine of part performance, under which an oral contract might become enforceable if there were sufficient acts of part performance of the contract, has been abolished, because no contractual obligation exists that can be partly performed. Unless an agreement is made in writing in accordance with the provisions of the section then, subject to the possibility of rectification in certain cases,[115] it is void. One effect of this has been that it is no longer possible to create an equitable mortgage of land by the mere deposit of the title deeds with the lender.[116] To be valid, any contract to grant a mortgage must now comply with

---

[107] LP(MP)A 1989 s.5(3), (4).

[108] See LPA 1925 s.40, which was repealed by LP(MP)A 1989 s.4; Sch.2.

[109] *Courtney v Corp Ltd* [2006] EWCA Civ 518 at [1], per Arden L.J. For a withering criticism of s.2, see *North Eastern Properties Ltd v Coleman* [2010] EWCA Civ 227 at [43]; [2010] 1 W.L.R. 2715 at 2724.

[110] (1987) Law Com. No.164. The draft Bill attached to the Law Commission's Report differs significantly from the wording of the final legislation: see *Pitt v P.H.H. Asset Management Ltd* [1994] 1 W.L.R. 327 at 331; *Commission for the New Towns v Cooper (Great Britain) Ltd* [1995] Ch. 259 at 287 (below, para.15–036); *North Eastern Properties Ltd v Coleman* [2010] EWCA Civ 227 at [41]; [2010] 1 W.L.R. 2715 at 2724.

[111] See *Firstpost Homes Ltd v Johnson* [1995] 1 W.L.R. 1567 at 1571, where the main differences between the law under LP(MP)A 1989 s.2, and LPA 1925 s.40, are succinctly summarised.

[112] s.2(1).

[113] s.2(2); below, para.15–027.

[114] s.2(3); below, paras 15–039—15–041.

[115] Below, para.15–032.

[116] For this doctrine, see *Russel v Russel* (1783) 1 Bro.C.C. 269. The deposit of deed was taken both to show a contract to create a mortgage and to be part performance of that contract: *Edge v Worthington* (1786) 1 Cox Eq. 211; *Pryce v Bury* (1853) 2 Drew. 41 (affd. L.R. 16 Eq. 153n.); *Carter v Wake* (1877) 4 Ch D 605 at 606.

the requirements laid down in the Act.[117] Furthermore, where there is at its inception a valid written contract, any subsequent agreement to vary its terms which does not itself comply with s.2 will be ineffective, even if the variation would take the agreement outside the scope of the section.[118]

Because of the fundamental changes made to the law by s.2, authorities on the previous law are "not necessarily of much, if any, assistance" in interpreting the section.[119]

1. Contract for the sale or other disposition of an interest in land

15–016   *(a) Types of transaction.* Subject to certain exceptions considered below, the provisions of the Act apply to "a contract for the sale or other disposition of an interest in land".[120]

15–017   First, there must be a *contract.* Where the document, not being the grant of an option, takes the form of a mere offer to sell, without any promise by the addressee to purchase, it will not comply with the requirements of the section.[121] At the other extreme, although it applies to a contract to *make* a disposition, it does not apply to the disposition itself.[122] Thus, although a legal mortgage incorporates a contract to repay the debt secured,[123] it must be granted by deed and does not have to comply with s.2 of the 1989 Act.[124]

15–018   Secondly, that contract must for the sale or other disposition of an interest in land. "Disposition" is widely defined to include a mortgage, charge, lease or indeed any other assurance of property.[125] It will therefore apply to:

> (i) A contract to sell a freehold[126];
>
> (ii) A contract to grant, assign, or surrender a lease or sub-lease[127]

---

[117] *United Bank of Kuwait Plc v Sahib* [1997] Ch. 107; (1997) 113 L.Q.R. 533 (M. Robinson). For such contracts, see below, para.24–041. It is apparently possible to create an equitable charge by means of writing under LPA 1925 s.53(1)(a): see *Murray v Guinness*, Unreported, Lightman J., April 29, 1998, but see *Kinane v Mackie-Conteh* [2005] EWCA Civ 45 at [18].

[118] *McCausland v Duncan Lawrie Ltd* [1997] 1 W.L.R. 38; *Kilcarne Holdings Ltd v Targetfollow (Birmingham) Ltd* [2004] EWHC 2547 at [208]; *Dolphin Quays Developments Ltd v Mills* [2006] EWHC 931 at [42]–[47]; [2007] 1 P. & C.R. 201 at 209, 210. See too below, para.15–040.

[119] *Rudra v Abbey National Plc* (1998) 76 P. & C.R. 537 at 541, per Robert Walker L.J.

[120] s.2(1).

[121] *Firstpost Homes Ltd v Johnson* [1995] 1 W.L.R. 1567.

[122] "Section 2 is concerned with contracts for the creation of legal estates or interests in land, not with documents that actually create or transfer such estates or interests": *Helden v Strathmore Ltd* [2011] EWCA Civ 452 at [27]; [2011] 2 E.G.L.R. 39 at 41, per Lord Neuberger M.R.

[123] See, e.g., below, para.25–002.

[124] "A deed is a different kind of instrument from an ordinary contract; and it is not a requirement of the execution of a deed that it should comply with the requirements of section 2 of the 1989 Act": *Eagle Star Insurance Co Ltd v Green* [2001] EWCA Civ 1389 at [16], per Mummery L.J. See too *Target Holdings Ltd v Priestley* (1999) 79 P. & C.R. 305 at 316–320; and *Scottish & Newcastle Plc v Lancashire Mortgage Corpn Ltd* [2007] EWCA Civ 684 at [53].

[125] LP(MP)A 1989 s.2(6); LPA 1925 s.205(1)(ii).

[126] In principle this should, as a matter of construction, include conditional contracts, whether subject to a condition precedent or subsequent.

[127] *Commission for the New Towns v Cooper (Great Britain) Ltd* [1995] Ch. 259 (contract to surrender an underlease within s.2).

(iii) A contract to mortgage freehold or leasehold land[128];

(iv) A contract to grant an incorporeal hereditament, such as an easement or a profit à prendre[129];

(v) A contract to devise particular land by will[130];

(vi) A unilateral contract by X to enter into a contract to sell land to Y if Y performs certain acts[131]; and

(vii) The grant of an option, though not its exercise, because an option is regarded for these purposes as a conditional contract.[132]

The position both as to the grant and exercise of a right of pre-emption is much less clear. No express provision is made in s.2 for such rights any more than it is for options. It is suggested that the position should, in principle, be as follows.

(1) Where title to land is unregistered, a right of pre-emption does not create an interest in land at the time when it is granted but an equitable interest may arise subsequently when the grantor decides to sell the land.[133] The right then becomes an option to purchase the land, and the grantor must offer to sell the property to the grantee.[134] A concluded contract for the sale of land is made when that offer is accepted.[135] There are in reality therefore two contracts:

(a) the grant of a right of pre-emption; and

(b) its exercise.

As regards the former contract, the matter may depend upon whether the right of pre-emption is capable of creating an equitable

---

[128] *Eagle Star Insurance Co Ltd v Green* [2001] EWCA Civ 1389 at [15]. The mortgage itself must be granted by deed, which does not have to comply with the requirements of LP(MP)A 1989 s.2, but rather, s.1: see, at [15], [16].

[129] cf. *Webber v Lee* (1882) 9 Q.B.D. 315 (contract to grant shooting rights fell within Statute of Frauds 1677, s.4).

[130] *Taylor v Dickens* [1998] 1 F.L.R. 806 at 819. That case was disapproved in *Gillett v Holt* [2001] Ch. 201, but not on this point.

[131] *Sharif v Sadiq*: [2004] EWHC 1913 (Ch). The previous law was the same: see *Daulia Ltd v Four Millbank Nominees Ltd* [1978] Ch. 231. See too *Godden v Merthyr Tydfil Housing Association* (1997) 74 P. & C.R. D1.

[132] *Spiro v Glencrown Properties Ltd* [1991] Ch. 537; [1991] C.L.J. 236 (A. J. Oakley). See too *Chippenham Golf Club v North Wiltshire DC* (1991) 64 P. & C.R. 527 at 530, where Scott L.J. observed that "it was evident that the draftsman of this section did not take account of options". The principle in the text applies to both "call options" where, as in *Spiro v Glencrown Properties Ltd*, the grantee can call for a transfer of the property, and a "put option", where the grantor can require a person to take the land: see *Active Estates Ltd v Parness* [2002] 3 E.G.L.R. 13 at 18.

[133] Sometimes, it will not even create an interest in land at that stage, but only when the grantor has offered to sell the land and his offer is accepted by the grantee: for the possibilities, see *Speciality Shops Ltd v Yorkshire and Metropolitan Estates Ltd* [2003] EWHC 2969 (Ch) at [25]–[29]; [2003] 2 P. & C.R. 410 at 416, 417.

[134] *Pritchard v Briggs* [1980] Ch. 338 at 418, 423; *Kling v Keston Properties Ltd* (1983) 49 P. & C.R. 212 at 217.

[135] *Brown v Gould* [1972] Ch. 53 at 58.

interest in land before any offer made by the grantor is accepted. That is unsatisfactory, because it turns on fine points of construction. The latter contract is certainly a contract for the sale or other disposition of an interest in land and should therefore have to comply with the formal requirements of the Act.[136] This will not always be straightforward, because, as is explained below, an exchange of correspondence will commonly not comply with the requirements of s.2.[137] The parties will be well advised to sign one document containing all the terms of the proposed sale.

(2) As regards a right of pre-emption granted in relation to registered land after the coming into force of the Land Registration Act 2002, it has effect from the time of creation as an interest capable of binding successors in title.[138] The purpose of this provision was to avoid the difficulties as to the status of rights of pre-emption.[139] As such a right of pre-emption is treated as an interest in land from its inception, both the creation and the exercise of the right should have to comply with s.2.

15–019   Thirdly, s.2 has no application to a transaction which is not a "sale or other disposition" even though it may concern land.[140] For that reason the following transaction do not fall within it.

(i) A "sale" by a tenant to his landlord of fixtures (i.e. objects attached to land[141]) which he has a right to remove,[142] because in law this is no more than a waiver of his right to sever and take away what is legally part of the landlord's premises.[143]

(ii) A "lock-out" agreement by which a vendor agrees for a specific period *not* to sell to anyone save the purchaser.[144]

(iii) A compromise of possession proceedings between mortgagee and mortgagor.[145]

---

[136] The grant of the pre-emption is unlikely to contain all the terms of any subsequent contract of sale: *Smith v Morgan* [1971] 1 W.L.R. 803.

[137] See para.15–037.

[138] LRA 2002 s.115; above, para.7–067. LRA 2002 came into force on October 13, 2003.

[139] See (2001) Law Com. No.271 at paras 5.26–5.28.

[140] Cases under the previous law may still be relevant as to whether a contract is of this description: see *Nweze v Nwoko* [2004] EWCA Civ 379 at [34]; [2004] 2 P. & C.R. 667 at 675.

[141] See below, Ch.23.

[142] For such "tenant's fixtures" see below, paras 23–012 et seq.

[143] *Hallen v Runder* (1834) 1 Cr.M. & R. 266 at 276; *Lee v Gaskell* (1876) 1 Q.B.D. 700. The same applies to an agreement by the landlord to extend the tenant's time for removing the fixtures: *Thomas v Jennings* (1896) 66 L.J.Q.B. 5 at 8.

[144] *Pitt v P.H.H. Asset Management Ltd* [1994] 1 W.L.R. 327. For lock-out agreements see above, para.15–011.

[145] *Kumah v Osbornes* [1997] E.G.C.S. 1. For the mortgagee's right to possession, see below, para.25–024.

(iv) A boundary agreement between neighbours which is intended to delineate the boundary between the properties even though it may in fact involve a transfer of land.[146]

(v) A contract under which one party binds himself to put a property on the market and to account for part of the proceeds of sale if the property is sold.[147]

(b) Transactions excluded. The Act specifically excludes three categories of **15–020** contract from the operation of s.2.[148]

(1) SHORT LEASES. As a lease for a term not exceeding three years at the best **15–021** rent which can be reasonably obtained without taking a fine may be granted orally,[149] it is provided that a contract to grant such a lease may also be made orally.[150]

(2) SALES AT PUBLIC AUCTION. Under the previous law, a contract made in **15–022** the course of a public auction was made on the fall of the hammer, and the auctioneer had authority to sign a memorandum on behalf of both the vendor[151] and the purchaser.[152] In this way, a contract made at auction was in practice always enforceable. The 1989 Act adopts a different approach. Auction sales are excluded from the application of s.2 and there is a binding contract on the fall of the hammer even in the absence of any writing. This is to ensure that neither party can thereafter withdraw.[153]

(3) CONTRACTS REGULATED UNDER THE FINANCIAL SERVICES ACT 1986. To **15–023** avoid any possibility that a contract to sell an investment that was secured on or included an interest in land might fall within the Act,[154] it is provided that s.2 does not apply to a contract regulated under the Financial Services Act 1986.[155]

In addition to the express exclusions above, there are certain other contracts **15–024** or agreements which, on grounds of policy, do not fall within s.2 of the 1989 Act. Thus the section does not apply to the statutory contract that arises in a case of compulsory purchase where a notice to treat has been served and the

---

[146] *Joyce v Rigolli* [2004] EWCA Civ 79; [2004] 1 P. & C.R. D55. Any transfers of land pursuant to such an agreement are regarded as *de minimis*: see at [45].
[147] *Nweze v Nwoko* [2004] EWCA Civ 379; [2004] 2 P. & C.R. 667.
[148] See s.2(5).
[149] LPA 1925 s.54(2); below, para.17–034.
[150] See (1987) Law Com. No.164, para.4.10; below, para.17–037. See too *Parc Battersea Ltd v Hutchinson* [1999] 2 E.G.L.R. 33 at 36.
[151] *Beer v London Paris Hotel Co* (1875) L.R. 20 Eq. 412 at 426.
[152] *Sims v Landray* [1894] 2 Ch. 318 at 320.
[153] See (1987) Law Com. No.164, para.4.11.
[154] cf. *Driver v Broad* [1893] 1 Q.B. 744 (contract to sell debentures which were secured on the entirety of a company's property, including land, held to be within the Statute of Frauds 1677 s.4).
[155] See (1987) Law Com. No.164, para.4.12.

parties have agreed the price.[156] Another case is where, pursuant to Pt 36 of the Civil Procedure Rules, the parties have agreed the terms of settlement of litigation that will involve disposition of an interest in land. The obligation that arises from such an agreement is not primarily contractual, but is sui generis, and the court has power, if need be, to order the parties to enter into a contract that complies with s.2 of the 1989 Act.[157]

15–025   *(c) Interest in land.* "Interest in land" is defined by the 1989 Act to mean "any estate, interest or charge in or over land".[158] The following have been held to be contracts for the sale of interests in land either under the Act or its predecessor:

(i) an indivisible contract for the sale of both land and chattels[159];

(ii) a contract to sell fixtures, even when they are sold separately from the land[160];

(iii) an agreement to sell building materials from a house, which the buyer was to demolish[161]; and

(iv) a contract to sell slag and cinders which had become part of the land.[162]

The mere fact that a contract concerns land will not bring it within the ambit of the section if it is not one for the disposition of an interest in land. Thus neither a contract to grant a licence nor a contractual licence itself is within the section because a licence creates no interest in property.[163]

15–026   The Act provides no definition of "land" as such,[164] though it has been assumed to have the same meaning as it had under the previous law. There is nothing to compel such an interpretation and there is a case for departing from the earlier characterisation of what was regarded as land where that was irrational, e.g., in the case of certain growing crops. Under the previous law, there was a distinction between "those crops which, broadly speaking, are

---

[156] *Llanelec Precision Engineering Co Ltd v Neath Port Talbot County Borough Council* [2000] 3 E.G.L.R. 158. The same was true under the previous law: see *Munton v Greater London Council* [1976] 1 W.L.R. 649.

[157] *Orton v Collins* [2007] EWHC 803 (Ch); [2007] 1 W.L.R. 2953.

[158] s.2(6) (as amended by TLATA 1996, s.25(2); Sch.4, to reflect the abolition of the doctrine of conversion by s.3 of that Act: see above, para.12–006.

[159] *Wright v Robert Leonard Developments Ltd* [1994] E.G.C.S. 69 (a decision on LP(MP)A 1989 s.2); [1995] Conv. 484 (M. P. Thompson); *Kilcarne Holdings Ltd v Targetfollow (Birmingham) Ltd* [2004] EWHC 2547 at [189]. The parties are however at liberty "to hive off part of the terms of their composite bargain into a separate contract distinct from the written land contract that incorporates the rest of the terms": *Tootal Cleaning Ltd v Guinea Properties Ltd* (1992) 64 P. & C.R. 452 at 456, per Scott L.J. See (1993) 109 L.Q.R. 191 (D. Wilde); and below, para.15–034.

[160] *Jarvis v Jarvis* (1893) 63 L.J.Ch. 10 at 13.

[161] *Lavery v Pursell* (1888) 39 Ch D 508.

[162] *Morgan v Russell Sons* [1909] 1 K.B. 357.

[163] *Ashburn Anstalt v Arnold* [1989] Ch. 1; below, para.34–019.

[164] There are definitions of "disposition" and "interest in land": see LP(MP)A 1989 s.2(6).

produced in the year by the labour of the year, and crops such as fruit growing on trees, where the productive act is the planting of the trees, and where the fruit is produced by the trees year after year, primarily as the result of that initial productive act".[165] The former, which were known as *fructus industriales*, and included annual crops such as wheat, corn and potatoes, were never regarded as land but always as chattels.[166] The latter, called *fructus naturales*, such as grass, timber and fruit trees, were regarded as land unless:

   (i) they were to be severed by the vendor and not by the purchaser[167]; or

  (ii) the purchaser was bound by the contract to sever them as soon as possible.[168]

The justification for these rules was never apparent and it was suggested that the statutory requirement of a written memorandum was inapposite in such cases and should have been confined to "such interests as are known to conveyancers".[169] Now that the formal requirements for contracts for the disposition of an interest in land have been made more rigorous, there is much to be said for rejecting these old distinctions and for treating all crops as chattels for the purposes of s.2. The same may be true as regards contracts to sell fixtures which are to be severed. This is particularly so because the Sale of Goods Act 1979[170] defines "goods" as including not only "industrial growing crops" but also "things attached to or forming part of the land which are agreed to be severed before sale or under the contract of sale". This last phrase would cover *fructus naturales* and such things as building materials or fixtures if sold separately, for then there must be a severance under the contract. Although under the previous law, a contract could at one and the same time, be a contract for the sale of both land within the Law of Property Act 1925 and goods within the Sale of Goods Act 1979, such an overlap has little to commend it. A growing crop is not "land" in the plain and natural meaning of that word.

2. All the terms

(a) The terms. The written terms of the contract must incorporate "all the terms which the parties have expressly agreed".[171] It follows that there will be no valid contract if one or more of the terms agreed between the parties are

15–027

---

[165] *Saunders v Pilcher* [1949] 2 All E.R. 1097 at 1104, per Jenkins L.J.
[166] See *Duppa v Mayo* (1669) 1 Wms. Saund. 275; *Marshall v Green* (1875) 1 C.P.D. 35 at 42.
[167] *Smith v Surman* (1829) 9 B. & C. 561.
[168] *Marshall v Green*, above.
[169] *Marshall v Green*, above, at 38, per Lord Coleridge C.J.
[170] s.61(1).
[171] LP(MP)A 1989 s.2(1). There will be no contract if only the main terms are recorded: *Enfield LBC v Arajah* [1995] E.G.C.S. 164.

not incorporated in the document that they have signed,[172] as the parties had expressly agreed that the completion date should take place one week after the making of the agreement, but this was not recorded in the documents said to constitute the contract.[173] In this respect the 1989 Act was not intended to change the law materially.[174] Under the previous law, a memorandum was required to record all the terms agreed between the parties,[175] though omissions could sometimes be cured by submission to or waiver of a missing term. However, because the 1989 Act requires that all express terms must be made in writing, omissions can no longer be cured in this way, though rectification may be possible in some cases.[176]

The Act provides that the terms of the contract may be incorporated in a document either by being set out in it or by reference to some other document.[177] Prior to the 1989 Act, a document might be incorporated impliedly rather than expressly. It was enough that the documents could be connected.[178] However, the principles of joinder of documents in such cases were contrived and led to uncertainty. The requirement in the 1989 Act that any incorporation should be by reference to some other document suggests that the old rules on joinder would not be applied and that a document would only be incorporated if it were referred to expressly or by necessary implication.[179] This would achieve greater certainty and would accord better with the policy of the 1989 Act. The documents incorporated may be referred to in very general terms, for example that "there shall be incorporated into this Agreement the further terms and conditions (if any) expressly agreed and set out in the written correspondence between the parties' solicitors relating to this transaction".[180] The purpose of such a provision is to ensure that if any terms were agreed prior to contracting and those terms were not expressly included in the written contract, that omission would not invalidate the contract.[181]

There are three essential elements upon which the parties must expressly agree if there is to be a valid contract for the sale of land or of an interest in land.[182] These are:

---

[172] *Grossman v Hooper* [2001] EWCA Civ 615 at [20]; [2001] 2 E.G.L.R. 82 at 84. If there is one contract for the sale of both land and chattels, it must include the terms relating to each: *Wright v Robert Leonard Developments Ltd* [1994] E.G.C.S. 69.

[173] *Ruddick v Ormston* [2005] EWHC 2547 (Ch); [2006] 1 P. & C.R. D57.

[174] See (1987) Law Com. No.164, para.4.7.

[175] *Hawkins v Price* [1947] Ch. 645.

[176] Below, para.15–032.

[177] LP(MP)A 1989 s.2(2).

[178] See *Timmins v Moreland Street Property Co Ltd* [1958] Ch. 110 at 130; *Elias v George Sahely Co (Barbados) Ltd* [1983] 1 A.C. 646.

[179] cf. *Record v Bell* [1991] 1 W.L.R. 853 at 860, suggesting that incorporation must be express. See too *Firstpost Homes Ltd v Johnson* [1995] 1 W.L.R. 1567 at 1573. In that case a letter offering to sell land referred to an enclosed plan. It was held that the letter and the plan were not one document.

[180] *Jones v Forest Fencing Ltd* [2001] EWCA Civ 1700; [2001] P.L.S.C.S. 249. See too *Courtney v Corp Ltd* [2006] EWCA Civ 518; [2006] P.L.S.C.S. 132 ("subject to our formal terms and conditions").

[181] *Jones v Forest Fencing Ltd* [2001] EWCA Civ 1700 at [7].

[182] *Rossiter v Miller* (1878) 3 App.Cas. 1124 at 1143, 1148.

(i) the parties;

(ii) the property;

(iii) the consideration.

If these elements have been determined with sufficient certainty[183] and incorporated into the written agreement, the requirements of the Act will be satisfied. This is so even though the parties have not agreed on other terms, such as the completion date,[184] whether a deposit should be taken,[185] or whether vacant possession should be given on completion.[186] Such lacunae will be regulated by the open contract rules implied by law.[187] Indeed, even if the parties have expressly agreed what would otherwise be implied by law, its omission from the written contract is unlikely to prove fatal.[188]

(b) Certainty. "If there is an essential term which has yet to be agreed and there is no express or implied provision for its solution, the result in point of law is that there is no binding contract."[189] In accordance with this principle, the three essential elements outlined above must be defined with sufficient certainty. However, this requirement is met if they fall within the maxim *id certum est quod certum reddi potest* (that is certain which can be made certain). Furthermore, in considering whether the terms are sufficiently certain, the court construes the agreement according to the usual principles.[190] In particular, it will have regard to all the background knowledge which would reasonably have been available to the parties in the situation in which they were at the time of the contract, the so-called "factual matrix".[191] As a contract for the sale of an interest in land must now be made in writing, cases of uncertainty should be less common. Under the previous law, a memorandum evidencing the contract between the parties could be construed out of a document which had been created for a quite different purpose, such as a receipt or a letter. This is no longer possible. However, as the written contract is now intended to be a self-contained document providing "reliable uncontrovertible evidence of the existence and terms of a transaction" in order to minimise disputes,[192] the courts may insist upon a higher degree of certainty

15–028

---

[183] Below, para.15–028.

[184] Below, paras 15–092, 15–093.

[185] Below, para.15–107.

[186] Below, para.15–089.

[187] *Perry v Suffields Ltd* [1916] 2 Ch. 187. For the implication of the open contract rules, see above, para.15–032.

[188] See *Farrell v Green* (1974) 232 E.G. 587. cf. [1989] Conv. 431 at 436 (P. H. Pettit). In such circumstances, the written agreement would probably be rectified even if it did not satisfy the section: LP(MP)A 1989 s.2(4); below, para.15–032

[189] *British Bank for Foreign Trade Ltd v Novinex Ltd* [1949] 1 K.B. 623 at 629, per Denning J. (cited with approval by Cohen L.J.). Although that case was not concerned with land, the principle there stated has been applied in conveyancing cases.

[190] See *Investors Compensation Scheme Ltd v West Bromwich BS* [1998] 1 W.L.R. 896 at

[191] *Trustees of Morden College v Mayrick* [2006] EWHC 574 (Ch) at [62].

[192] (1987) Law Com. No.164, para.2.7. See too *Firstpost Homes Ltd v Johnson* [1995] 1 W.L.R. 1567.

in identifying both the parties and the property sold than was formerly the case.[193] Some of the decisions on the previous law may need to be treated with caution therefore.[194]

15–029   (1) PARTIES. It is essential that the parties (or their agents[195]) should be stated,[196] but it is not necessary to give their names, provided that they are identifiable in such a way that "their identity cannot be fairly disputed".[197] Thus references to the "proprietor",[198] "mortgagees",[199] or "trustees"[200] of the property, or to "the legal personal representatives of X"[201] were held to suffice under the old law. Although such descriptions do not exclude all uncertainty, they may be more precise than the names of those concerned, for there may be more than one person of the same name.[202] A decision that "personal representatives" (without saying of whom) was adequate, must be open to doubt however.[203]

The following descriptions by themselves[204] have been held to be too indefinite:

    (i) "the vendor"[205];

    (ii) "landlord"[206];

    (iii) "proposing lender"[207];

    (iv) "my friend"[208]; or

    (v) "my clients".[209]

---

[193] There has been a marked change of practice over the last century as to the degree of precision with which the property is described in conveyancing documents: (1994) 57 M.L.R. 361 (A. Pottage).

[194] This especially so after *Firstpost Homes Ltd v Johnson*, above.

[195] *Davies v Sweet* [1962] 2 Q.B. 300.

[196] *Williams v Lake* (1859) 2 E. & E. 349; *Williams v Byrnes* (1863) 1 Moo.P.C.(N.S.) 154 at 196; *Stokell v Niven* (1889) 61 L.T. 18.

[197] *Carr v Lynch* [1900] 1 Ch. 613 at 615, per Farwell J.; *Potter v Duffield* (1874) L.R. 18 Eq. 4 at 7; *Rossiter v Miller* (1878) 3 App.Cas. 1124 at 1147, 1153; *Goldsmith Ltd v Baxter* [1970] Ch. 85.

[198] *Sale v Lambert* (1874) L.R. 18 Eq. 1; *Rossiter v Miller*, above.

[199] *Allen Co Ltd v Whiteman* (1920) 89 L.J.Ch. 534 at 538.

[200] *Catling v King* (1877) 5 Ch D 660 at 664.

[201] *Towle v Topham* (1877) 37 L.T. 308; and see *Hood v Lord Barrington* (1868) L.R. 6 Eq. 218.

[202] See *Catling v King*, above, at 664; *Donnison v People's Cafe Co* (1881) 45 L.T. 187 at 189.

[203] *Fay v Miller Wilkins Co* [1941] Ch. 360, criticised (1941) 57 L.Q.R. 432 (R.E.M.).

[204] The circumstances may, however, narrow down the description so that they suffice: see e.g. *Commins v Scott* (1875) L.R. 20 Eq. 11; *Sidle v Bond-Cabell* (1885) 2 T.L.R. 44.

[205] *Potter v Duffield*, above.

[206] *Coombs v Wilks* [1891] 3 Ch. 77.

[207] *Pattle v Anstruther* (1893) 69 L.T. 175.

[208] *Rossiter v Miller* (1878) 3 App.Cas. 1124 at 1141.

[209] *Lovesy v Palmer* [1916] 2 Ch. 233.

Land may be sold or let by many people other than the owner of the fee simple, e.g. by tenants, mortgagees or persons having a power of sale.[210] To allow parol evidence of the identity of one of the parties would defeat the purpose of the Act.[211] Conversely, it is not enough to give the names of the parties if the contract does not indicate their capacities,[212] e.g. which is vendor and which is purchaser.[213] But where there is an agent for an undisclosed principal, a contract in the name of that agent is good and binds both him and his principal, even if the other party knows that he is merely an agent.[214]

(2) PROPERTY. In relation to the property, two matters must be certain, namely the identity of the land which is to be sold and the estate which is to be granted.   **15–030**

As regard the identity of the land, the rule prior to the enactment of the 1989 Act was that the property had to be *described* with sufficient certainty in the contract, but parol evidence could then be adduced to *identify* the land.[215] For these purposes a general description sufficed.[216] On this basis, "Mr O's house",[217] "the house in Newport",[218] "my house"[219] and even "this place"[220] were all upheld with the aid of oral evidence, as descriptions.[221] In a case of a written contract the Court of Appeal went so far as to hold that "twenty-four acres of land, freehold, at Totmonslow" could be identified by oral evidence,[222] even in the absence of "my" or "the" or any other particular. It remains to be seen whether the courts will be so willing to strain language in cases arising under the 1989 Act. Indeed, it may no longer be permissible to adduce parol evidence to identify the land.[223] Although in one case such evidence was adduced, no reference was made to the 1989 Act and its possible

---

[210] See *Donnison v People's Cafe Co*, above, at 189.

[211] See *Potter v Duffield* (1874) L.R. 18 Eq. 4 at 8; *Jarrett v Hunter* (1886) 34 Ch D 182 at 184, 185.

[212] *Stokell v Niven* (1889) 61 L.T. 18.

[213] *Vanderburgh v Spooner* (1866) L.R. 1 Ex. 316 (vendor); *Dewar v Mintoft* [1912] 2 K.B. 373 (purchaser).

[214] *Basma v Weekes* [1950] A.C. 441 (purchaser's agent); *Davies v Sweet* [1962] 2 Q.B. 300 (vendor's agent). Yet is the document the *true* contract?

[215] *Harewood v Retese* [1990] 1 W.L.R. 333 at 341. See too *Plant v Bourne* [1897] 2 Ch. 281.

[216] *Shardlow v Cotterell* (1881) 20 Ch D 90 at 96, 98 ("property purchased at £420 at Sun Inn, Pinxton" on a specified day, sufficiently certain). These cases date from a time when descriptions of the property were vague. There has been a trend towards much greater precision in such descriptions since then: (1994) 57 M.L.R. 361 at 368 (A. Pottage).

[217] *Ogilvie v Foljambe* (1817) 3 Mer. 53.

[218] *Owen v Thomas* (1843) 3 My. K. 353; and see *Bleakley v Smith* (1840) 11 Sim. 150 ("the property in Cable Street"); *Wood v Scarth* (1855) 2 K. J. 33 ("the intended new public-house at Putney").

[219] *Cowley v Watts* (1853) 17 Jur. 172.

[220] *Waldron v Jacob* (1870) 5 I.R.Eq. 131.

[221] See *Sheers v Thimbleby Son* (1897) 76 L.T. 709 at 712.

[222] *Plant v Bourne*, above. This may be justified on the basis that a vendor is presumed to be selling his own property: *Plant v Bourne* at 290.

[223] See *Rudra v Abbey National Plc* (1998) 76 P. & C.R. 537 at 541, 542.

effect.[224] However, many problems may be resolved by reference to the matrix of fact against which the parties contracted,[225] and even if the description of the land in the contract is vague, it may be sufficiently identified by a plan forming part of the agreement.[226] It has been said that:

> "the meaning to be ascribed to 'the property' in the conveyance is the meaning which it would be given by a reasonable person who knows what the parties knew at the time they contracted".[227]

It will therefore be assumed, for example, that fixtures are included unless, before the sale, the vendor tells the intending purchaser that they are no longer for sale.[228]

Problems of uncertainty may arise where a sale of land is to be completed in instalments. If the particular tracts of land that are to be conveyed on payment of each instalment are not sufficiently identifiable, as where "a proportionate part" of the land is to be transferred when each payment is made, the contract as a whole will fail for uncertainty. This is so even though the identity of the totality of the land included in the agreement is certain.[229]

A contract will not be invalidated merely because it does not state the interest which the vendor intends to pass or that it is subject to incumbrances of which the purchaser knows or which are patent.[230] Where the contract is silent, it is presumed that the vendor is selling a fee simple subject to such incumbrances.[231] A contract to grant a lease, however, must specify or provide a means of determining[232] the date on which the term is to commence[233] and

---

[224] *Freeguard v Rogers* [1999] 1 W.L.R. 375 (grant of option to purchase "the property known as 9, Graffham Close, Chichester" coupled with an erroneous Land Registry title number: extrinsic evidence admissible to show that the property comprised both a freehold house and a leasehold garage under two separate title numbers).

[225] As in *Trustees of Morden College v Mayrick* [2006] EWHC 574 (Ch) at [60]–[62]. The summary of the case at [2006] P.L.S.C.S. 70 does not cover this point. See too *Westvilla Properties Ltd v Dow Properties Ltd* [2010] EWHC 30 (Ch); [2010] 2 P. & C.R. 332.

[226] See, e.g., *Ahmed v Wingrove (No.1)* [2007] EWHC 1918 (Ch) at [12]–[14]; [2007] 1 P. & C.R. D41 at D41, D42.

[227] *Taylor v Hamer* [2002] EWCA Civ 1130 at [90]; [2003] 1 E.G.L.R. 103 at 110, per Sedley L.J. The case was not concerned with the issue of certainty but with what was included within the contract.

[228] *Taylor v Hamer*, above.

[229] *Bushwall Properties Ltd v Vortex Properties Ltd* [1976] 1 W.L.R. 591. The decision does appear unnecessarily harsh: see [1976] C.L.J. 215 (C. T. Emery). The courts are generally reluctant to hold agreements void for uncertainty: below, para.15–031. cf. *Hillreed Land Ltd v Beautridge* [1994] E.G.C.S. 55 where the grantee of an option agreed to pay £*x* an acre for all the land for which he could obtain planning permission and £*y* an acre for the rest. No planning permission having been obtained, the option was void for uncertainty.

[230] For patent incumbrances, see below, para.15–070.

[231] *Cox v Middleton* (1854) 2 Drew. 209 at 216, 217; *Timmins v Moreland Street Property Co Ltd* [1958] Ch. 110 at 118, 119.

[232] See, e.g. *Trustees of National Deposit Friendly Society v Beatties of London Ltd* [1985] 2 E.G.L.R. 59 at 61.

[233] *Blore v Sutton* (1817) 3 Mer. 237; *Cartwright v Miller* (1877) 36 L.T. 398; *Harvey v Pratt* [1965] 1 W.L.R. 1025 at 1027.

must state its duration.[234] "There must be a certain beginning and a certain ending, otherwise it is not a perfect lease, and a contract for a lease ... must contain those elements."[235] It will not be assumed that a term is to commence on the date of the agreement,[236] or when the tenant is to take possession,[237] or to begin paying rent.[238]

(3) CONSIDERATION. The contract must define with sufficient certainty the price to be paid, or, in the case of a contract to grant a lease, the rent or premium payable. The question whether the consideration has been expressed with sufficient certainty has generally arisen in the context of options to purchase land or renew a lease where the parties have attempted to retain some flexibility by postponing the determination of the price or rent until the option is exercised. Unless the parties make express provision for what is to happen in default of agreement,[239] there is a risk that such an arrangement will be regarded as a mere agreement to negotiate "which is not recognised as an enforceable contract".[240] However, the courts are reluctant to hold an instrument void for uncertainty.[241]

15–031

There are at least three types of option,[242] and an analysis of them demonstrates the various methods which the courts apply to save them from invalidity, where that is possible.

> (i) The option may provide for a price or rent "to be agreed" with no formula for quantifying the consideration. Such arrangements have been often been held to be void because they amount to mere agreements to contract.[243] However, the court may be able to imply a formula for assessment in such cases.[244] Thus in once case, an

---

[234] *Fitzmaurice v Bayley* (1860) 9 H.L.C. 78; *Clarke v Fuller* (1864) 16 C.B.(N.S.) 24. Thus an agreement to grant an underlease for the residue of the head lease "less a few days" was void for uncertainty: *Dolling v Evans* (1867) 36 L.J.Ch. 474.

[235] *Marshall v Berridge* (1881) 19 Ch D 233 at 245, per Lush L.J.

[236] *Marshall v Berridge*, above.

[237] *Edwards v Jones* (1921) 124 L.T. 740; and see *Rock Portland Cement Co Ltd v Wilson* (1882) 52 L.J.Ch. 214. Prima facie, however, a renewed lease will run from the expiration of the existing lease: see *Verlander v Codd* (1823) T.R. 352; *Wood v Aylward* (1888) 58 L.T. 667.

[238] *Humphrey v Conybeare* (1899) 80 L.T. 40. This is particularly the case today when "rent-free" periods are often allowed for tenants to fit out the premises and commence trading: see *Trustees of National Deposit Friendly Society v Beatties of London Ltd*, above at 61.

[239] As in *Miller v Lakefield Estates Ltd* (1988) 57 P. & C.R. 104; [1990] Conv. 288 at 289 (J. E. Martin).

[240] *Walford v Miles* [1992] 2 A.C. 128 at 136, per Lord Ackner.

[241] *Brown v Gould* [1972] Ch. 53 at 56. For statements of the applicable principles, see *BJ Aviation Ltd v Pool Aviation Ltd* [2002] EWCA Civ 163 at [19]–[24]; [2002] P. & C.R. 369 at 374; and *Mamidoil-Jetoil Greek Petroleum Co SA v Okta Crude Oil Refiner AD* [2001] EWCA Civ 406 at [69]; [2001] 2 Lloyd's Rep.76 at 89.

[242] *Brown v Gould*, above, at 58.

[243] *King's Motors (Oxford) Ltd v Lax* [1970] 1 W.L.R. 426.

[244] In the past, the courts would imply a term only where the contract was valid and had been partially performed, as where there was a term in a lease that for the first five years the rent should be £1,250 per annum, and thereafter at such rent as should be agreed between the parties: *Beer v Bowden* (1976) [1981] 1 W.L.R. 522n. See too *Trustees of National Deposit Friendly Society v Beatties of London Ltd* [1985] 2 E.G.L.R. 59. For such rent review clauses, see below, para.19–065.

option to renew a lease at a rent to be agreed, but not exceeding the existing rent, was upheld as valid. The court implied a term that the rent should be a fair rent agreed between the parties not exceeding the existing rent.[245] By contrast, a provision by which a lease might be renewed "subject to the renegotiation of the rent payable in no less a sum than that which shall be payable under the terms of this Agreement at this date" was held to be void as an agreement to agree. The renegotiation of the rent was a condition precedent to the renewal and, in the circumstances, this precluded the implication of any objective criteria such as fairness or reasonableness.[246] In one case of a right of pre-emption, the grantee was offered the first refusal to purchase certain land at "a figure to be agreed upon". The court implied a term that the grantor would offer to sell the land at the price at which she was willing to sell the land.[247] Although it has been suggested that the judge in that case "implied a substantial amount, perhaps too much",[248] it should be noted that a right of first refusal has been described as "the first right to refuse an offer to purchase at the price at which the grantor is willing to sell".[249] Where the parties provide some machinery for ascertaining the consideration, the courts will be very ready to imply a formula from that fact. Thus where the price is to be such as may be agreed upon by two valuers, that will necessarily imply that it should be a fair and reasonable one.[250]

(ii) The option may provide that the price is to be determined according to some stated formula, but without providing any machinery for the working out of that formula. In such a case, the court will supply whatever machinery is necessary for assessment.[251]

(iii) The option may provide both a formula and machinery for assessing the consideration.[252] If the machinery breaks down,[253] the

---

[245] *Corson v Rhuddlan BC* (1989) 69 P. & C.R. 185; [1990] Conv. 288 at 290 (J. E. Martin). The court doubted the correctness of *King's Motors (Oxford) Ltd v Lax*, above, suggesting that in that case a term could have been implied that the rent should be fair.

[246] *BJ Aviation Ltd v Pool Aviation Ltd* [2002] EWCA Civ 163; [2002] P. & C.R. 369.

[247] *Smith v Morgan* [1971] 1 W.L.R. 803.

[248] *Miller v Lakefield Estates Ltd*, above, at 198, per May L.J.

[249] *Bircham & Co, Nominees (2) Ltd v Worrell Holdings Ltd* [2001] EWCA Civ 775 at [31]; (2001) 82 P. & C.R. 427 at 438, per Chadwick L.J.

[250] *Sudbrook Trading Estates Ltd v Eggleton* [1983] 1 A.C. 444 at 477. See too *Lear v Blizzard* [1983] 3 All E.R. 662.

[251] *Brown v Gould*, above ("rent to be fixed having regard to the market value of the premises").

[252] One commonly used formula, "at a fair and reasonable market rent", has proved troublesome: see *ARC Ltd v Schonfield* [1990] 2 E.G.L.R. 52.

[253] cf. *Harben Style Ltd v Rhodes Trust* [1995] 1 E.G.L.R. 118, where the landlord refused to appoint a valuer to fix a rent under a rent review clause, because it was likely that the rent would be reduced. Under the lease the rent due prior to any review continued to be payable if no new rent was fixed. In those circumstances, the court held that there had been no failure of machinery and refused to imply any obligation on the part of the landlord to appoint a valuer.

court will supply its own, provided that it is merely subsidiary and inessential, but not where the personal qualities of the particular valuer are an essential element of the agreement.[254] Thus where a will conferred an option on the testator's son to purchase a farm "at the agricultural value thereof determined for probate purposes . . . as agreed with the district valuer" and the district valuer declined to make the valuation, the machinery was held to be an inessential element and an inquiry was directed to determine the value of the land.[255]

(c) Rectification. If there is "convincing proof"[256] that, by mistake, **15–032** either:

(i) the written "contract" does not in some way record the terms agreed between the parties, as where it either omits terms that have been agreed between the parties or contains terms that have not been agreed; or

(ii) the parts exchanged on an exchange of contracts do not in all respects correspond[257];

the court may order rectification of the contractual documents.[258] In these circumstances, there is necessarily no contract until the court makes its order because the documents do not satisfy the requirements of s.2 of the Act. The court is therefore given a discretion to declare in the order for rectification the time at which the contract shall come into being, or be deemed to have done so.[259] However, it will exercise this discretion only where the written document does not correctly record the parties' intentions. It will not do so where

---

[254] *Sudbrook Trading Estate Ltd v Eggleton*, above; (1982) 28 L.Q.R. 539 (J. Murdoch); *Royal Bank of Scotland Plc v Jennings* [1997] 1 E.G.L.R. 101. cf. *Saipem SpA v Rafidain Bank* [1994] C.L.C. 253.

[255] *Re Malpass* [1985] Ch. 42. See too *Scottish Wholefoods Collective Warehouse Ltd v Raye Investments Ltd* [1994] 1 E.G.L.R. 245 (option to sell "at the current market price" to be agreed upon between the parties not void where the parties could not agree).

[256] *Joscelyne v Nissen* [1970] 2 Q.B. 86 at 98, per Russell L.J. For a valuable statement of the criteria that must be satisfied before a court will rectify an instrument, see *Swainland Builders Ltd v Freehold Properties Ltd* [2002] EWCA Civ 560 at [33], [34]; [2002] 2 E.G.L.R. 71 at 74.

[257] *Domb v Isoz* [1980] Ch. 548 at 558 (provision concerning fixtures and fittings contained only in one of the signed parts). cf. *Harrison v Battye* [1975] 1 W.L.R. 58 at 60 (parts differed as to amount of deposit payable, but there was no evidence to justify rectification).

[258] *Domb v Isoz*, above; *Wright v Robert Leonard Developments Ltd* [1994] E.G.C.S. 69 (contract to sell a flat omitted the fixtures and fittings that were to be included; rectification was ordered to incorporate the term); [1995] J.B.L. 176 (M. Haley). Rectification is normally granted in cases of mutual mistake, but may exceptionally be given in cases where the mistake is unilateral: see below, para.15–122. cf. *Oun v Ahmad* [2008] EWHC 545 (Ch) at [44].

[259] LP(MP)A 1989 s.2(4); *Wright v Robert Leonard Developments Ltd*, above (contract deemed to have come into effect on exchange).

the parties have deliberately omitted to record certain terms and their mistake is merely as to the legal consequences of this omission.[260]

15–033   *(d) Collateral contracts.* It often happens that one party enters into a contract to sell or purchase land on the strength of some assurance by the other.[261] In such circumstances there may in fact be two contracts:

> (i) the principal contract of sale; and

> (ii) the collateral undertaking.

The consideration for the latter is the making of the principal contract. In such cases, "the collateral contract may in substance be regarded as another way of enforcing a term omitted from what purports to be a contract in writing".[262] If the collateral contract is not itself a contract for the sale or other disposition of an interest in land,[263] it will not have to comply with s.2 of the 1989 Act. Thus in one case, V's solicitor was unable to obtain official copies of the register of V's title before contracts were due to be exchanged, but gave certain undertakings as to V's title in a side letter. P exchanged contracts on the strength of those promises (which were subsequently honoured) and V was able to enforce that contract against him. The undertakings in the side letter were not terms of the main contract but were collateral to it.[264] There can be no collateral contract, in the sense explained above, if the principal contract contains a provision which acknowledges that the agreement constitutes the entire agreement between the parties.[265]

15–034   *(e) Separate agreements.* It is always open to parties to break up a composite agreement that includes a sale of land into two or more separate contracts, provided that the land contract is not made conditional upon the performance of some other expressly agreed part of the bargain.[266] One means of ensuring that this is so is by including an entire agreement clause in the land contract.[267]

---

[260] *Oun v Ahmad* [2008] EWHC 545 (Ch). The case contains an illuminating analysis of the operation both of LP(MP)A 1989 in general, and the court's power of rectification under s.2(4) in particular: see at [27] et seq.

[261] The undertaking is commonly contained in a side letter: see e.g. *Record v Bell* [1991] 1 W.L.R. 853.

[262] (1987) Law Com. No.164, para.5.7.

[263] See, e.g. *Lotteryking Ltd v AMEC Properties Ltd* [1995] 2 E.G.L.R. 13 (landlord's collateral undertaking to remedy damp did not have to comply with LP(MP)A 1989 s.2); *Johnsey Estates Ltd v Newport Marketworld Ltd* [1996] E.G.C.S. 87 (contract by A with B to guarantee lease to be granted by B to C outside s.2).

[264] *Record v Bell*, above; [1991] C.L.J. 399 (C.H.); (1992) 108 L.Q.R. 217 (R. J. Smith). There were cases of collateral contracts in similar circumstances under the previous law: *Jamieson v Kinmell Bay Land Co Ltd* (1931) 47 L.T. 593.

[265] *Inntrepreneur Pub Co v East Crown Ltd* [2000] 3 E.G.L.R. 31.The existence of an entire agreement clause is not incompatible with a agreement that is separate from and not conditional upon the principal contract: see below, para.15–034.

[266] *North Eastern Properties Ltd v Coleman* [2010] EWCA Civ 227 at [54]; [2010] 1 W.L.R. 2715 at 2727.

[267] *North Eastern Properties Ltd v Coleman* [2010] EWCA Civ 227 at [54], [83]; [2010] 1 W.L.R. 2715 at 2727, 2734.

Such separated contracts and their terms will then be regarded as discrete and not as one contract.[268] Furthermore, s.2 of the Act applies only to executory contracts. Once the parties have completed a sale of land it is irrelevant that the agreement which preceded the transfer was void because it did not comply with the section. In such circumstances, any other terms of the agreement that are not themselves a contract for the sale of land and which have not merged on completion,[269] may be enforceable. However, this will be so only where those terms are supported by consideration and can therefore be regarded as a "supplemental agreement".[270] Whether or not there are two contracts or one composite contract is a question of fact in every case.[271] However, a court will be wary of artificially dividing what is in reality a composite transaction.[272]

3. One document. The Act provides that "the document incorporating the terms or, where contracts are exchanged, one of the documents incorporating them (but not necessarily the same one) must be signed by or on behalf of each party to the contract".[273] This provision has two important effects each of which must be considered. First, it restricts the manner in which a contract for the sale of land may be made. Secondly, a valid contract will be mutually enforceable by both parties.   **15–035**

(a) Method of contracting

(1) METHODS LISTED IN THE ACT. The wording of the Act[274] suggests that there are now just two ways in which a written contract for the sale or other disposition of land may be made.   **15–036**

First, each of the parties may sign one document incorporating all the agreed terms. This method was sometimes employed under the previous law.[275] As electronic documents are treated as being made in writing,[276] there seems no reason in principle why such a document should not be in electronic form. There may be one electronic document which is signed by all the parties to it.[277]

---

[268] *Tootal Clothing Ltd v Guinea Properties Ltd* (1992) 64 P. & C.R. 452 at 456; (1993) 109 L.Q.R. 191 (D. Wilde). cf. (1993) 22 Anglo-American Law Review, 498 at 507 (M. Haley).

[269] For the doctrine of merger see below, para.15–100.

[270] *Tootal Clothing Ltd v Guinea Properties Ltd*, above, at 455, per Scott L.J. (contract by landlord to pay tenant £30,000 for shop-fitting works after completion held to be enforceable). For criticism of the case see [1993] Conv. 89 (P. Luther).

[271] *Grossman v Hooper* [2001] EWCA Civ 615 at [21], [22]; [2001] 2 E.G.L.R. 82 at 84.

[272] *Kilcarne Holdings Ltd v Targetfollow (Birmingham) Ltd* [2004] EWHC 2547 (Ch) at [189].

[273] LP(MP)A 1989 s.2(3).

[274] s.2(1), (3). These provisions differ significantly from those in the draft Bill attached to (1987) Law Com. No.164, p.24.

[275] *Smith v Mansi* [1963] 1 W.L.R. 26.

[276] See *J Pereira Fernandes SA v Mehta* [2006] EWHC 813 (Ch) at [16] [2006] 1 W.L.R. 1543 at 1548 (email satisfied requirements of Statute of Frauds 1677 s.4); *Orton v Collins* [2007] EWHC 803 (Ch); [2007] 1 W.L.R. 2953 (email offer to settle a case under CPR Pt 36).

[277] What can constitute a signature on an electronic document is considered below at para.15–039.

Secondly, the parties may exchange contracts, which has long been the "customary way" of concluding contracts for the sale of land, particularly domestic sales.[278] The essential characteristic of exchange of contracts is "that each party shall have such a document signed by the other party in his possession or control", and it occurs when each party (or more usually his solicitor or licensed conveyancer) has the contract signed by the other in his actual or constructive possession.[279] This may be brought about in one of three ways.

(i)   There may be a physical exchange of the contracts by the parties' solicitors or licensed conveyancers, usually at the offices of one of them. Exchanges of this kind are usually impracticable in cases of chain sales.[280]

(ii)   The parts may be exchanged by post. It has never been settled whether the contract is concluded at the time when the second of the two parts has been posted or only when it is received,[281] though the latter accords better with the essential characteristic of exchange of contracts outlined above. Exchange by post is inevitably uncertain and cannot achieve the synchronisation that is necessary in chain sales.

(iii) Exchange may be effected where the solicitor or licensed conveyancer for each of the parties unequivocally appropriates his client's part of the contract and holds it to the order of the other party. This forms the basis for the modern practice by which contracts are exchanged by telephone or fax. It provides the only effective method of bringing about an exchange of contracts where there is a chain of sales.[282] There are a number of different methods by which this can be done, as for example where each solicitor or licensed conveyancer, having in his possession the part of the contract signed by his client, agrees by telephone to hold it to the order of the other party.[283]

---

[278] See *Eccles v Bryant* [1948] Ch. 93 at 97, per Lord Greene M.R.

[279] *Domb v Isoz* [1980] Ch. 548 at 557, per Buckley L.J. See too *Harrison v Battye* [1995] 1 W.L.R. 58. For a detailed analysis of what constitutes an exchange of contracts, see *Commission for the New Towns v Cooper (Great Britain) Ltd* [1995] Ch. 259 at 285, 286.

[280] *Domb v Isoz*, above, at 558, 564.

[281] See *Eccles v Bryant*, above, at 97, 98, where Lord Greene M.R. left the point open. It should be recalled that the so-called "postal rule", by which an offer is deemed to be accepted when that acceptance is posted (see *Henthorn v Fraser* [1892] 3 Ch. 27 at 33), is an exception to the general principle that an acceptance must be communicated to the offeror: *Holwell Securities Ltd v Hughes* [1974] 1 W.L.R. 155; *Brinkibon Ltd v Stahag Stahl GmbH* [1983] 2 A.C. 34 at 41. Where an option can be exercised only by giving notice to the grantor, then the postal rule will not apply: *Holwell Securities Ltd v Hughes*, above.

[282] It has been described as "a practice without which contracts could not be exchanged with the maximum of safety and the minimum of delay": *Domb v Isoz*, above, at 564, per Templeman L.J.

[283] The Law Society has produced three formulae which may be adopted for exchanging contracts by telephone, telex or fax: see (1986) 83 L.S.Gaz 2139; (1989) 86/11 L.S.Gaz. 26.

The Act has not affected the well-established practice for the exchange of contracts, nor was it intended to do so.[284]

What the parties cannot do is each to sign a separate document in different terms, as where on one page of a diary one party agreed to sell a parcel of land, and on another, the other party agreed to purchase land.[285] There were two documents and not one, and there was no exchange of contracts because the two documents did not contain mutual obligations to buy and to sell.[286]

(2) CONTRACTS BY CORRESPONDENCE. The wording of the Act suggests that **15–037** no contract can arise from a mere exchange of letters between the parties unless that correspondence can be regarded as an "exchange of contracts".[287] It has indeed been held by the Court of Appeal that a simple offer and acceptance made by post or fax will not satisfy the requirements of s.2,[288] because there can be no exchange of contracts unless the parties have reached a prior written or oral agreement.[289] This was certainly not the intention of the Law Commission.[290] Although it has been suggested that Parliament may have chosen to go further than the Law Commission recommendation "and required a greater degree of formality in this very important area of the law where it is crucial that the parties know for certain when they are bound and on what terms",[291] the reasons for the changes are not known.[292]

Not only does this interpretation significantly restrict the manner in which a contract for the sale of land can be made, but it means that s.2 of the 1989 Act conflicts with the provision of the Law of Property Act 1925 which regulates contracts by correspondence and the policy that lies behind it.[293] By that provision the Lord Chancellor may from time to time prescribe and publish forms of contracts and conditions of sale which shall apply to "contracts by correspondence" unless excluded or modified by the correspondence.[294] Conditions of sale have been prescribed[295] and these regulate

---

[284] "The present practice of exchanging contracts should not be inhibited": (1987) Law Com. No.164, para 4.6.

[285] *Ruddick v Ormston* [2005] EWHC 2547 (Ch); [2006] 1 P. & C.R. D57. See too *De Serville v Argee* (2001) 82 P. & C.R. D24 at D25.

[286] *Ruddick v Ormston* [2005] EWHC 2547 (Ch) at [25]; [2006] 1 P. & C.R. D57 at D58.

[287] See *Hooper v Sherman* Unreported, November 30, 1994, CA, as explained in *Commission for the New Towns v Cooper (Great Britain) Ltd* [1995] Ch. 259 at 288, 289, 295. See too *De Serville v Argee* (2001) 82 P. & C.R. D24 at D25.

[288] *Commission for the New Towns v Cooper (Great Britain) Ltd*, above; [1995] C.L.J. 502 (A. J. Oakley).

[289] *Commission for the New Towns v Cooper (Great Britain) Ltd*, above, at 295.

[290] See (1987) Law Com. No.164, para.4.15; and contrast cl.1 of the draft Bill appended to that Report with LP(MP)A 1989 s.2.

[291] *Commission for the New Towns v Cooper (Great Britain) Ltd*, above, at 287, per Stuart-Smith L.J. See too *McCausland v Duncan Lawrie Ltd* [1997] 1 W.L.R. 38 at 44, 46, 49.

[292] It is understood that they were made when the Law Commission's Bill was redrafted in anticipation of its introduction into Parliament. The Parliamentary debates provide no clue as to why.

[293] This was acknowledged in *Commission for the New Towns v Cooper (Great Britain) Ltd*, above, at 287, 295. cf. *Hooper v Sherman*, above, where the Court of Appeal considered that it was still possible to create by correspondence a contract complying with LP(MP)A 1989 s.2. See [1995] Conv. 317 (M. P. Thompson).

[294] s.46.

[295] S.R. & O. 1925, No.779/L. 14.

matters such as the date and place of completion and the deduction of title. Their objective is "to supply the common forms for facilitating the carrying out of contracts by correspondence",[296] in order to meet the case where parties contract without taking legal advice. A "contract by correspondence" will not arise unless there has been an exchange of letters.[297] There will be no such contract where one party signs a copy of a letter already signed by the other.[298] In the light of this, it will only be in a very rare case that a contract by correspondence could now arise in a situation to which the provisions of s.2 of the 1989 Act were applicable,[299] and this seldom-used provision of the Law of Property Act 1925 appears to be largely redundant.

This restriction on the manner in which a contract for the sale of land can be made is hard to justify and is likely to cause difficulty in a number of common transactions, as where V, having granted P a right of pre-emption, offers in writing to sell the land to P. In such circumstances, a written acceptance by P of V's offer will not suffice. There will either have to be a formal exchange of contracts, or both V and P will have to sign one contract.[300]

15–038   *(b) Mutual enforceability.* There can be a valid contract only if it is signed by or on behalf of *both* parties.[301] Under the previous law, it was enough that the party to be charged had signed a memorandum, even if the claimant had not. It follows that any valid contract must now be reciprocally enforceable by both parties to it. It is no longer possible for one party to a contract to be bound by that contract in circumstances where he cannot enforce it against the other.[302]

4. Signed

15–039   *(a) Signature.* The document incorporating the terms (or one of them where contracts are exchanged) "must be signed by or on behalf of each party to the contract".[303] If A contracts with B to convey land to C, C's signature is not

---

[296] Wolst. & C. i, 405.

[297] *Stearn v Twitchell* [1985] 1 All E.R. 631; *Fischer v Toumazos* [1991] 2 E.G.L.R. 204 at 206.

[298] *Pips (Leisure Productions) Ltd v Walton* (1980) 43 P. & C.R. 415 at 416; *Fischer v Toumazos*, above, at 206.

[299] In *Commission for the New Towns v Cooper (Great Britain) Ltd* [1995] Ch. 259 at 287, 295, it was suggested that one might arise where there was a prior oral agreement between the parties and the exchange of correspondence was intended by the parties to be an "exchange of contracts". This has been criticised: see [1995] C.L.J. 502 (A. J. Oakley). A contract to grant a short lease within LPA 1925 s.54(2) could still be made by correspondence as it is outside the ambit of LP(MP)A 1989 s.2: above, para.15–021.

[300] See above, para.15–018.

[301] LP(MP)A 1989 s.2(3).

[302] See [1989] Conv. 431 at 439 (P. H. Pettit). cf. *RG Kensington Management Co Ltd v Hutchinson IDH Ltd* [2002] EWHC 1180 (Ch) at [57]; [2003] 2 P & C.R. 195 at 206.

[303] LP(MP)A 1989 s.2(3). For cases where there was no valid contract because not all parties to the agreement signed it, see *Enfield LBC v Arajah* [1995] E.G.C.S. 164 (no contract where only one of three purchasers signed solely on his own account); and *Chandler v Clark* [2002] EWCA Civ 1249; [2003] 1 P. & C.R. 239 (conditional agreement by husband to renounce his beneficial interest in favour of his wife signed by the husband only).

required because he is not a party to the contract.[304] The same must also be true where a contract, to which s.2 of the 1989 Act applies, is made for the benefit of a third party in accordance with the Contracts (Rights of Third Parties) Act 1999. The third party is necessarily not a party to that contract and may enforce it even though he has not signed it.[305]

The Act gives no guidance as to what constitutes a signature. Under the previous law, the word "signed" was given an extended meaning by the courts. Where the name of the party to be charged appeared in some part of the document[306] in some form, whether in writing, typewriting, print or otherwise,[307] there was a sufficient signature, provided that that party had shown in some way that he recognised the document as an expression of the contract.[308] However, this is no longer the law. "The purpose of section 2 is to require a clear assent to all the terms, not simply to require a signature somewhere on the document."[309] Accordingly, the word "signed" is "to have the meaning which the ordinary man would understand it to have".[310] Therefore where a person typed his name and address on a letter,[311] he was held not to have signed it.[312] It has also been that a mere initialling of alterations to a document will not suffice.[313] In principle, a faxed signature, or a signature that has been scanned and inserted into an electronic document, or a pdf copy of an actual written signature appended to an electronic document by the maker, all ought to be sufficient as, in each case, the signature authenticates the document.

(b) *Alterations.* Any alterations that are made to a concluded written **15–040** contract must themselves comply with the requirements of s.2.[314] This cannot be achieved by an exchange of letters,[315] and the parties will therefore either have to exchange identical signed copies of the variation, or they will both have to sign one document which makes the change.[316] If they did not comply

---

[304] *RG Kensington Management Co Ltd v Hutchinson IDH Ltd* [2002] EWHC 1180 (Ch) at [57]; [2003] 2 P & C.R. 195 at 206; and *Milebush Properties Ltd v Tameside MBC* [2010] EWHC 1022 (Ch) at [65]–[66]; [2010] 2 E.G.L.R. 93 at 99, not following *Jelson Ltd v Derby CC* [1999] 3 E.G.L.R. 91.

[305] See s.1 of that Act.

[306] *Caton v Caton* (1867) L.R. 2 H.L. 127 at 142.

[307] *Tourret v Cripps* (1879) 48 L.J.Ch. 567; *Halley v O'Brien* [1920] 1 I.R. 330 at 339.

[308] *Evans v Hoare* [1982] 1 Q.B. 593; *Leeman v Stocks* [1951] Ch. 941; *Bilsland v Terry* [1977] N.Z.L.R. 43.

[309] *Newell v Tarrant* [2004] EWHC 772 (Ch) at [47], per Kosmin Q.C.

[310] *Firstpost Homes Ltd v Johnson* [1995] 1 W.L.R. 1567 at 1576, per Peter Gibson L.J.

[311] That was signed by the intending vendor.

[312] *Firstpost Homes Ltd v Johnson*, above; see [1996] C.L.J. 192 (A. J. Oakely).

[313] *Newell v Tarrant* [2004] EWHC 772 (Ch) at [47], [49]; [2004] PLSCS 93. Kosmin Q.C. accepted that "as a matter of principle that a party can sign the document by writing only his initials on it, provided that it is clear that he intended to authenticate the full terms of the document": *Newell v Tarrant* at [47].

[314] *McCausland v Duncan Lawrie Ltd* [1997] 1 W.L.R. 38; [1996] Conv. 366 (M. P. Thompson).

[315] Above, para.15–037.

[316] *Campbell v Haynes* [1998] P.L.S.C.S. 86 (letter purporting to vary the date for completion and to incorporate certain conditions of sale of no effect); and see [1996] Conv. 366 at 368 (M. P. Thompson).

with s.2, the alteration will be a nullity and the original contract will remain enforceable because no binding agreement has superseded it.[317] However, the change which the parties agree may be so fundamental that it amounts to a rescission of the original contract.[318] Where one party to a contract agrees to waive a term of that contract that is exclusively for his benefit, that does not constitute a variation of the contract that must comply with s.2.[319]

In principle, an agreement to rescind a contract for the sale of land may be made orally because it is not a contract for the sale or other disposition of an interest in land within s.2.[320] Where the parties intend that the first contract for the sale of an interest in land should be rescinded and replaced by a second contract, it is by no means certain that rescission will always take place if that second contract fails to comply with s.2. The intention to rescind in such a case may be regarded as contingent upon the validity of the second contract.[321]

15–041   *(c) Agents.* The Act requires that the contract be signed "by or on behalf of" each contracting party.[322] There is no requirement that the agent should be given written authority to sign.[323] The same person may sign on behalf of both parties if has been authorised to do so by each of them.[324] Furthermore a person may, with one signature, sign on behalf of himself and on behalf of a company, of which he is a director, even though he does not expressly sign "on behalf of" the company.[325] Neither an estate agent[326] nor a solicitor[327] has implied authority to sign a contract. Such authority must be expressly given, though the principal may of course subsequently ratify any unauthorised signature.[328]

Where a firm of solicitors purported to sign a contract to sell land on behalf of a company that had not yet been incorporated, it was held that the contract was in fact made, and was for the purposes of s.2 to be signed, on behalf of

[317] *McCausland v Duncan Lawrie Ltd*, above.
[318] The test is whether the alteration goes "to the very root" of the original contract: *British Benningtons Ltd v N. W. Cachar Tea Co Ltd* [1923] A.C. 48 at 68, per Lord Sumner. See, e.g. *Ginns v Tabor* [1995] E.G.C.S. 182 (decided under the old law).
[319] *Courtney v Corp Ltd* [2006] EWCA Civ 518 at [14]; [2006] P.L.S.C.S. 132.
[320] G. H. Treitel, *The Law of Contract* 12th edn, para.5–026.
[321] See [1989] Conv. 431 at 436, 437 (P. H. Pettit).
[322] LP(MP)A 1989 s.2(3).
[323] *McLaughlin v Duffill* [2008] EWCA Civ 1627; [2010] Ch. 1. As that case made clear, a contract to sell differs in this respect from the creation or disposition of an interest in land under LPA 1925 s.53(1)(a). See too see LPA 1925 s.53(1)(c) (disposition of equitable interest); above, para.11–047.
[324] *Gavaghan v Edwards* [1961] 2 Q.B. 220.
[325] *Williams v Redcard Ltd* [2011] EWCA Civ 466; [2011] 25 E.G. 106; see above, para.8–051.
[326] *Wragg v Lovett* [1948] 2 All E.R. 968 at 969 (no authority to sign even where the estate agent is instructed to sell at a defined price). cf. *Kean v Mear* [1920] 2 Ch. 574.
[327] *Smith v Webster* (1876) 3 Ch D 49; *H. Clark (Doncaster) Ltd v Wilkinson* [1965] Ch. 694 at 702.
[328] *Maclean v Dunn* (1828) 4 Bing. 722.

the firm, and could be enforced by it, even though it had purported to contract as agent.[329]

5. Effect of non-compliance with section 2. An agreement that does not **15–042** comply with the provisions of the Act has no effect as a contract because it is void. However, the acts of the parties made pursuant to or in reliance upon such a void agreement may have legal consequences.[330] The extent of those consequences is uncertain following the decisions of the House of Lords on proprietary estoppel in *Cobbe v Yeoman's Row Management Ltd*[331] and *Thorner v Major*,[332] discussed in the next chapter,[333] even though neither case was directly concerned with s.2.[334] Those consequences fall under three possible heads, namely:

(i) proprietary estoppel[335];

(ii) constructive trust imposed to prevent unconscionable conduct[336]; and

(iii) restitution of benefits conferred.

(a) Estoppel. Section 2(5) of the 1989 Act provides expressly that nothing **15–043** in s.2 "affects the creation or operation of resulting, implied or constructive trusts".[337] The section is silent about proprietary estoppel, and it has, in consequence, been suggested that proprietary estoppel cannot "be prayed in aid in order to render enforceable an agreement that statute has declared to be void".[338] However, it has subsequently been held that "proprietary estoppel in a case involving a sale of land has survived the enactment of section 2 of the 1989 Act".[339] Nonetheless, the circumstances in which a person will be estopped from denying that an agreement is void for non-compliance with s.2 are likely to be very limited, because the policy of s.2 is "to protect the public

---

[329] *Braymist Ltd v The Wise Finance Co Ltd* [2002] EWCA Civ 127; [2002] Ch. 273. This was the result of Companies Act 1985 s.36C(1) (now Companies Act 2006 s.51).

[330] See (1987) Law Com. No.164, Pt.V; Goff & Jones, *The Law of Restitution* 7th edn, Ch.21.

[331] [2008] UKHL 55; [2008] 1 W.L.R. 1752.

[332] [2009] UKHL 18; [2009] 1 W.L.R. 776.

[333] See below, Ch.16.

[334] But see *Cobbe v Yeoman's Row Management Ltd* [2008] UKHL 55 at [29]; [2008] 1 W.L.R. 1752 at 1769; *Thorner v Major* [2009] UKHL 18 at [99]; [2009] 1 W.L.R. 776 at 804.

[335] See below, Ch.16.

[336] See above, para.11–022.

[337] LP(MP)A 1989 s.2(5).

[338] *Cobbe v Yeoman's Row Management Ltd* [2008] UKHL 55 at [29]; [2008] 1 W.L.R. 1752 at 1769, per Lord Scott.

[339] *Whittaker v Kinnear* [2011] EWHC 1479 (QB) at [30], per Bean J. The case was concerned with a collateral oral agreement, by which the defendant agreed to sell a property at an undervalue on the understanding that she could continue to live there.

by preventing parties from being bound by a contract for the disposition of an interest in land unless it has been fully documented in writing".[340]

The agreement must have all the elements of a contract so that it can be enforced as such. Accordingly, proprietary estoppel will not apply if the parties intended to enter into a formal agreement setting out the terms on which land was to be acquired or where further terms remain to be agreed.[341] Where that is not the case, a party should be able to rely upon the doctrine of proprietary estoppel only where to do so would not compromise the policy of the Act.[342] This may be so in:

> "those cases in which a supposed bargain has been so fully performed by one side, and the general circumstances of the matter are such, that it would be inequitable to disregard the claimant's expectations, and insufficient to grant him no more than a restitutionary remedy".[343]

If such substantial performance was not essential, mere preliminary acts, such as instructing a solicitor to investigate title or a surveyor to conduct a survey might lead to the enforcement of oral agreements.[344] Furthermore, without such substantial performance, the defendant's conduct is unlikely to "shock the conscience of the court",[345] which is likely to be fatal to any claim founded on proprietary estoppel.

15–044   *(b) Constructive trust.* As explained above, s.2 of the 1989 Act does not affect the creation or operation of resulting, implied or constructive trusts,[346] so that the imposition of a constructive trust to prevent unconscionable conduct[347] will not of itself contravene the policy of the Act. However, as with proprietary estoppel, a party cannot rely on this exception to enforce an informal agreement if:

(i) the parties intended to make a formal agreement setting out the terms;

(ii) further terms remained to be agreed so that the interest in the property was not clearly identified; or

(iii) the parties did not intend their agreement to be immediately binding.[348]

[340] See *Herbert v Doyle* [2010] EWCA Civ 1095 at [10]; [2011] 1 E.G.L.R. 119 at 120, per Arden L.J.

[341] *Herbert v Doyle* [2010] EWCA Civ 1095 at [57]; [2011] 1 E.G.L.R. 119 at 125.

[342] See further below, para.16–026.

[343] *Yaxley v Gotts* [2000] Ch. 162 at 180, per Robert Walker L.J.

[344] *Anderson Antiques (UK) Ltd v Anderson Wharf (Hull) Ltd* [2007] EWHC 2086 (C) at [33].

[345] *Cobbe v Yeoman's Row Management Ltd* [2008] UKHL 55 at [92]; [2008] 1 W.L.R. 1752 at 1788, per Lord Walker.

[346] LP(MP)A 1989 s.2(5) see para.15–043.

[347] See above, para.11–022.

[348] *Herbert v Doyle* [2010] EWCA Civ 1095 at [57]; [2011] E.G.L.R. 119 at 125.

This is most likely to arise in cases where the purchaser acts to his detriment in reliance on an informal agreement with the vendor that he shall acquire or have an interest in the land,[349] as where:

(a) a builder converted a property into flats on the basis of an oral agreement with the owner that he should be granted a long lease of one of them. The court imposed a constructive trust on the vendor to give effect to the transaction.[350]

(b) cohabitant A informally agreed to buy out the other cohabitant, B, for a specified sum and to assume responsibility for the mortgage. It was held that a constructive trust had arisen in favour of A, rendering it unconscionable not to permit him to enforce the oral agreement for sale.[351]

(c) Restitution. Where there is some form of agreement that does not **15–045** constitute a valid contract and one of the parties incurs expenditure in reliance upon it, he may be able to claim restitution of the benefits he has conferred. For example:

(i) an intending purchaser, who makes payments pursuant to the agreement, may be able to recover them on the basis that there has been a total failure of consideration[352];

(ii) an intending purchaser who improves the land may recover the value of the benefit conferred on the vendor if the latter freely accepts those improvements[353];

(iii) an intending purchaser, who, with vendor's encouragement, obtains planning permission for the development of the land he wishes to buy, may recover the value of his services in obtaining that planning permission[354]; or

(iv) an intending vendor who carried out works requested by the purchaser should be able to recover the cost of them.[355]

---

[349] Above, paras 11–023 et seq.

[350] *Yaxley v Gotts* [2000] Ch. 162, especially at 181, 193.

[351] *Oates v Stimson* [2006] EWCA Civ 548; [2006] P.L.S.C.S. 117. B had denied the agreement.

[352] *Cobbe v Yeoman's Row Management Ltd* [2008] UKHL 55 at [43]; [2008] 1 W.L.R. 1752 at 1774. There may be no such total failure if the purchaser has entered into possession and enjoyed the land: cf Goff & Jones, *The Law of Restitution* 7th edn, para.20–013. It is no longer an objection that the payments were made under a mistake of law: see *Kleinwort Benson Ltd v Glasgow City Council* [1999] 1 A.C. 153.

[353] *Yaxley v Gotts* [2000] Ch. 162 at 172; Goff & Jones, *The Law of Restitution* 7th edn, para.23–003.

[354] *Cobbe v Yeoman's Row Management Ltd* [2008] UKHL 55 at [40]–[44]; [2008] 1 W.L.R. 1752 at 1773, 1774.

[355] See *British Steel Corporation v Cleveland Bridge and Engineering Co Ltd* [1981] 1 All E.R. 504 at 511.

Part 3

CONTRACTS IN PRACTICE

Section 1. Cases Where it is Usual to have a Contract

15–046 Traditionally, whenever a transaction involves payment of a lump sum it has been the practice for a contract to be made first and a conveyance or transfer some time later. This is because the purchaser wishes to be sure of his bargain and yet to have time to investigate the title fully before paying his money and taking over the liabilities of ownership. Thus a formal contract is nowadays normally made on:

>   (i) a sale of a freehold;

>   (ii) the grant of a lease of a flat by the freeholder; or

>   (iii) an assignment by a tenant who holds under a lease at a ground rent (a rent representing the value of the land without the buildings on it.[356])

If, on the other hand, no capital payment is to be made, there is often no contract, e.g. on the grant or assignment of a lease at a rack rent (a rent representing the full value of the land and buildings). A mortgage, although involving a capital payment, is rarely preceded by a contract; for it is in essence an investment of money rather than a purchase of land, and it will probably be no loss to the mortgagee if the deal falls through before completion. These statements are, however, no more than generalisations and they are less true than once they were. Thus because of the widespread practice by which the purchaser investigates the vendor's title before contracts are exchanged, the time between contract and completion has steadily diminished, and it is by no means unknown for both to take place on the same day.[357] Furthermore, when a lease is granted, it is by no means uncommon to dispense with a contract and to proceed directly to the exchange of lease and counterpart even when the consideration for the lease is a premium rather than the payment of a rack rent.[358]

Section 2. Types of Contract

There are three main types of contract and something has already been said about each.

---

[356] The capital sum paid for a lease is usually called a premium.
[357] In such a case, there are good reasons why the parties still enter into a contract before completion: see below, para.15–100.
[358] See, e.g. *Longman v Viscount Chelsea* (1989) 58 P. & C.R. 189.

1. Open contracts. An open contract means a contract where only certain 15–047
terms have been expressly agreed, leaving others to be implied by the general
law. The simplest possible contract is where only the parties, property and
price are specified, e.g. where A agrees to buy Blackacre from B for
£100,000.[359] This is the most "open" contract of all and though it is unbusinesslike it is perfectly effective in law. It is implied that the vendor must show
a good title within a reasonable time and then complete the contract by the
appropriate conveyance or transfer.[360] It is for the purchaser at his own
expense to prepare the draft conveyance or transfer for the vendor to
execute.[361]

Contracts which are wholly open are in practice very rare nowadays,[362] and
they are likely to disappear because of the stricter formal requirements that
now apply to contracts for the sale of land.[363] However, the principles which
apply to open contracts form the bedrock upon which conveyancing law is
built.[364] As has already been explained, the open contract rules will regulate
the affairs of the parties to the extent that their contract does not do so
expressly.[365] The effect of these rules is considered below.[366]

2. Contracts made by correspondence. It has already been explained[367] 15–048
that in the case of "contracts by correspondence", the Law of Property Act
1925[368] provides that the Statutory Form of Conditions of Sale 1925[369] made
by the Lord Chancellor, shall govern the contract, subject to any modification
or contrary intention expressed in the correspondence. However, because
contracts by correspondence can arise only by an exchange of letters,[370] they
are seldom likely to occur in future.[371]

3. Formal contracts. The wide range of matters which have to be dealt 15–049
with between contract and completion mean that, in practice, open contracts
are not employed. A contract will invariably contain conditions of sale which
modify the open contract position,[372] and this has been the practice for two
centuries.[373] Conditions of sale—which are "merely the terms of the sale and

---

[359] Above, para.15–027.
[360] See *Chaitlal v Ramlal* [2003] UKPC 12 at [22]; [2004] 1 P. & C.R. 1 at 8, 9.
[361] Although the vendor prepares the draft contract, the purchaser bears the greater part of the
costs of a conveyancing transaction and must of course pay his own solicitor's costs.
[362] See above, para.15–001.
[363] Written contracts made in compliance with LP(MP)A 1989 s.2 are in practice likely to be
made on legal advice in most cases: above, para.15–036.
[364] Above, para.15–001.
[365] Above, para.15–001.
[366] Below, para.15 050.
[367] Above, para.15–037.
[368] s.46.
[369] S.R. & O. 1925, No.779/L. 14. For these Conditions, see Wolst & C., i, 405.
[370] *Stearn v Twitchell* [1985] 1 All E.R. 631; above, para.15–037.
[371] Above, para.15–037.
[372] See *Tweed v Mills* (1865) L.R. 1 C.P. 39 at 45; [1992] C.L.J. 263 at 281 (C.H.).
[373] For the history of such conditions see [1992] C.L.J. 263 at 264 (C.H.).

purchase"[374]—are of two types. First, there are *special* conditions which regulate the details of that particular transaction, specifying such matters as the parties, the property, the price, the giving of vacant possession and any specific incumbrances to which the sale is made subject. Secondly, the contract will usually incorporate a set of *general* conditions. These are standard form conditions which regulate a wide range of matters which are likely to arise in most conveyancing transactions. These include the payment of a deposit, the timetable for the deduction of title and (if it is not the subject of a special condition) completion,[375] the responsibility for the property pending completion and the remedies for breach of the agreement. In practice, it is common to modify the general conditions in any particular case. Although such general conditions have been described as "very much part of the small print",[376] they are given their full status as contractual terms.[377] Sets of standard conditions were first developed by local law societies in the second half of the 19th century. There is now just one set of general conditions that is normally used, the Standard Conditions of Sale.[378] Under those conditions, the general conditions apply except as varied or excluded by the special conditions.[379] In the absence of such an express provision, the court will have to resolve any such conflict by determining which condition was intended by the parties to be the dominant one.[380]

Section 3. Terms of a Contract

15–050 The following are examples of the matters usually dealt with in the special or general conditions of a formal contract for the sale of land. Most of them are explained in greater detail below.

(i)   Provision for the payment of a deposit (usually 10 per cent of the purchase-money)[381] and for the payment of interest on the purchase-money if completion is delayed.

(ii) Where the title is unregistered, the length and nature of the title to be shown by the vendor[382] and any special provisions, e.g. as to making no objection to some specified defect in title or flaw in the

---

[374] *Property Bloodstock Ltd v Emerton* [1968] Ch. 94 at 112, per Danckwerts L.J.

[375] Commonly the completion date is fixed by special condition. The general conditions provide a fall-back position.

[376] *Lyme Valley Squash Club Ltd v Newcastle under Lyme BC* [1985] 2 All E.R. 405 at 410, per Blackett-Ord V.C. cf. [1985] Conv. 243 (H. W. Wilkinson).

[377] *Squarey v Harris-Smith* (1981) 42 P. & C.R. 118 at 128.

[378] 4th edn, 2003, above, para.8–027.

[379] Standard Conditions of Sale, c.1.1.4.

[380] See [1988] Conv. 400 at 401 (C.H.). Compare *Korogluyan v Matheou* (1975) 30 P. & C.R. 309 with *Topfell Ltd v Galley Properties Ltd* [1979] 1 W.L.R. 446.

[381] For deposits, see below, para.15–107.

[382] Below, para.15–077.

evidence of title.[383] Where title is registered, the title number of the property, the class of title and copies of any documents referred to on the register.[384]

(iii) The time within which the evidence of title,[385] requisitions on title and other matters must be dealt with.

(iv) The date and place for completion of the sale.[386]

(v) Power for either party to terminate the contract because the other has failed to perform his obligations under the agreement after service of a notice to complete.[387]

Section 4. Effect of a Contract

There is great deal of law peculiar to contracts for the sale of land, but it cannot be fully explained without opening up the wider subject of conveyancing, that is, the law which is concerned with the sale and transfer of land. There is of course no precise boundary between real property and conveyancing and the two subjects inevitably overlap. Although the detailed practice of conveyancing lies outside the scope of this book, some of the borderland must be explored in order to understand the special rights and liabilities which contracts for the sale of land create. For the purposes of this chapter, the rules which apply to contracts for sale are taken to include contracts for the grant or assignment of leases except where the contrary is stated. **15–051**

A. *The Purchaser at Once Becomes Owner in Equity*

1. The purchaser as owner. If the purchaser is potentially entitled to the equitable remedy of specific performance,[388] he obtains an immediate equitable interest in the property contracted to be sold.[389] He is, or soon will be, in a position to call for it specifically. As equity "looks upon things agreed to be done as actually performed",[390] the purchaser becomes the owner in the eyes **15–052**

---

[383] Below, para.15–081.

[384] Such as restrictive covenants. cf. *Faruqi v English Real Estates Ltd* [1979] 1 W.L.R. 963, where the sale was made subject merely to "entries on the register". These related to restrictive covenants, the terms of which were unknown. The court declined to decree specific performance at the behest of the vendor because he had failed to make full and frank disclosure of the nature of the entries.

[385] Where title is unregistered, the evidence is in the form of an "abstract of title" or, more usually nowadays, an "epitome of title", see below, para.15–077. For the more common position where title is registered, see below, para.15–086.

[386] Under the Standard Conditions of Sale, this is "either at the seller's solicitor's office or at some other place which the seller reasonably specifies": c. 6.2.2. In practice, completion is often telephonic.

[387] Below, para.15–095.

[388] Above, para.5–015; below, para.15–115.

[389] Above, paras 5–025, 6–037, 8–075.

[390] *Re Cary-Elwes' Contract* [1906] 2 Ch. 143 at 149, per Swinfen Eady J.

of equity from the date of contract.[391] It is therefore irrelevant that the date for completion (when the purchaser may pay the price and take possession of the land) has not arrived.[392] The purchaser becomes owner in equity through the operation of the doctrine of conversion.[393] However, conversion will operate only if:

> (i) the contract between the parties is valid, i.e. one which is "sufficient in form and in substance, so that there is no ground whatever for setting it aside"[394]; and

> (ii) title to the land is made by the vendor or is accepted by the purchaser.[395]

The purchaser's equitable ownership is, as has been seen, a proprietary interest, enforceable against third parties, though it must be registered to protect it against purchasers.

15–053   **2. The vendor as trustee.** As between the parties to it, the contract creates a relationship of trustee and beneficiary,[396] though it is one which does not have all the incidents normally associated with a trust.[397] The vendor is said to be a trustee for the purchaser,[398] and the purchaser is regarded as the beneficial owner, at least for the purposes of disposition.[399] However, the nature of this trust must be carefully understood. Although as against third parties it creates an equitable interest,[400] the proprietary consequences between the parties themselves are limited, because the vendor retains his lien over the property for the price until it is paid.[401] It imposes obligations on the

---

[391] See *Lysaght v Edwards* (1876) 2 Ch D 499 at 506–510; Williams V. & P. 59, 545. *Aliter* if specific performance would not be granted: *Central Trust and Deposit Co v Snider* [1916] 1 A.C. 266 at 272.

[392] The purchaser does not of course become the legal owner of the land until it is conveyed to him or (where title is registered) he is registered as proprietor of it.

[393] *Lysaght v Edwards*, above, at 506.

[394] *Lysaght v Edwards*, above, at 507, per Jessel M.R.

[395] *Lysaght v Edwards*, above, at 507. In such a case conversion then operates retrospectively to the date of the contract: below, para.15–060. See A. J. Oakley, *Constructive Trusts* 3rd edn, pp.283–285. cf. (1960) 24 Conv. (N.S.) 47 (P. H. Pettit).

[396] See A. J. Oakley, *Constructive Trusts*, Ch.6.

[397] *Berkley v Poulett* [1977] 1 E.G.L.R. 86 at 93. Stamp L.J. there observed that "you may search the Trustee Act 1925 without obtaining much that is relevant to the relationship of vendor and purchaser". The nature of the vendor's trusteeship is explained below.

[398] *Lysaght v Edwards*, above, at 506.

[399] *Baldwin v Belcher* (1844) 1 Jo. & Lat. 18 at 26.

[400] Because of the doctrine of conversion, it may have consequences as regards inheritance: below, para.15–060. Furthermore, in negotiations with potential sub-purchasers, the purchaser can describe himself without misrepresentation as owner of the land: *Gordon Hill Trust Ltd v Segall* [1941] 2 All E.R. 379. Normally, it is relevant as to priority: see, e.g., *Sookraj v Samaroo* [2004] UKPC 50 at [15].

[401] "The purchaser has neither a legal nor an equitable right, as against the seller, until he pays the purchase price": *Baldwin v Belcher*, above, at 26, per Sugden L.C.; *Shaw v Foster* (1872) L.R. 5 H.L. 321 at 349; below, para.15–055.

vendor[402] and transfers the risk of damage to or destruction of the property to the purchaser.[403]

The vendor's principal obligation under this curious form of trust[404] is to manage[405] and preserve the property with the same care as is required of any other trustee.[406] "Equity imposes duties on the vendor to protect, pending completion, the interest which the purchaser acquired under the contract."[407] The duty does not go beyond that.[408] Thus, for example, a vendor was held liable when between contract and conveyance a trespasser removed a large quantity of surface soil from the land, for with reasonable vigilance he should have observed and prevented the damage.[409] However, provided that the vendor has acted with due care since the date of the contract, the purchaser cannot complain of the condition of the property which he has agreed to buy, even if (for example) a house turns out to be unfit for habitation.[410] The vendor's liability is that of a trustee in possession and ceases if the purchaser goes into possession before completion.[411]

3. Nature of trusteeship. It is necessary to distinguish the trusteeship that arises from the existence of a specifically enforceable contract between vendor and purchaser and the trust or lien that arises from a payment of some or all of the purchase price by the purchaser: **15–054**

"A purchaser who enters into a specifically enforceable contract for the sale of land acquires an equitable interest in the land and retains that

---

[402] Below.

[403] Below, para.15–057.

[404] See generally the valuable review of the law in *Englewood Properties Ltd v Patel* [2005] EWHC 188 (Ch) at [40]–[57]; [2005] 1 W.L.R. 1961 at 1971–1978.

[405] See *Earl of Egmont v Smith* (1877) 6 Ch D 468; *Abdulla v Shah* [1959] A.C. 124.

[406] *Phillips v Silvester* (1872) 8 Ch.App. 173 at 177; *Raffety v Schofield* [1897] 1 Ch. 937 at 944, 945. See [1995] Cambrian L.R. 33 (A. Dowling).

[407] *Englewood Properties Ltd v Patel*, above, at [54]; [2005] 1 W.L.R. 1961 at 1977.

[408] Although in one case, a vendor was held to be liable when, without the purchaser's knowledge, he withdrew an application for planning permission which had been made prior to contract (see *Sinclair-Hill v Sothcott* (1973) 26 P. & C.R. 490), the correctness of that case has been doubted because it "goes to the very limits of the principle" and is supportable only on the basis that the existing planning permission was part of the property which the vendor was under a duty to preserve: see *Englewood Properties Ltd v Patel*, above, at [57]; [2005] 1 W.L.R. 1961 at 1978, per Lawrence Collins J. Thus there was no breach of the duty where, between contract and completion, the vendor applied for and obtained planning permission subject to conditions to which the purchaser could reasonably have taken exception: *Englewood Properties Ltd v Patel*, above; *Heronsgate Enterprise Ltd v Harman (Chesham) Ltd* Unreported, January 21, 1993, CA; nor where a vendor failed to take covenants from neighbouring properties when he was bound by contract to a third party to do so, even though that failure exposed the purchaser to a potential damages claim from that third party: *Englewood Properties Ltd v Patel*, above.

[409] *Clarke v Ramuz* [1891] 2 Q.B. 456. See too *Phillips v Lamdin* [1949] 2 K.B. 33 (removal of door by vendor: order for specific restitution); *Davron Estates Ltd v Turnshire Ltd* (1982) 133 N.L.J. 937 (vendor liable for damage committed by squatters).

[410] *Hoskins v Woodham* [1938] 1 All E.R. 692; *Scott-Polson v Hope* (1958) 14 D.L.R. (2d) 333; cf. *Miller v Cannon Hill Estates Ltd* [1931] 2 K.B. 113 (where the general principle was accepted, but where there was either an express warranty or an implied term that a newly constructed house would be fit for habitation).

[411] *Phillips v Silvester*, above.

interest for as long as the contract remains enforceable. On making pre-completion payments on account of the price the purchaser acquires also an equitable lien on the land to secure their repayment (subject to any set-offs and the possible forfeiture of the deposit) if the contract goes off."[412]

15–055   *(a) Trusteeship arising from specifically enforceable contract.* While he remains unpaid, the vendor's trusteeship arising from a specifically enforce-able contract is of a peculiar kind,[413] because although a trustee, he has "a personal and substantial interest in the property, a right to protect that interest, and an active right to assert that interest if anything should be done in derogation of it".[414] He may occupy the land and take the rents and profits for himself up to the day fixed for handing over possession. Until the purchase price is paid he may stay in possession under his common law lien as vendor,[415] which arises at the date of contract.[416] Ordinarily both these rights will expire when the contract is completed by delivery of the conveyance or transfer, the purchase-money is paid, and the purchaser is let into possession. But if the vendor parts with possession of the land before he receives payment, he has an equitable lien on the land which entitles him, if he cannot obtain payment, to ask the court for an order for sale.[417] It has been held that an unpaid vendor's lien can arise only where the contract is one of which a court would order specific performance.[418] This limitation appears to be unjustified however, and the better view is that a valid contract between the parties is the only prerequisite.[419]

The vendor must pay all expenses properly attributable to his period of beneficial enjoyment, e.g. rates and taxes apportioned up to the date of completion, for in respect of these he has not the ordinary trustee's right of indemnity against the beneficiary.[420] Conversely he may take the benefit of

---

[412] *Sookraj v Samaroo* [2004] UKPC 50 at [15], per Lord Scott. See too [1984] C.L.J. 134 at 136–139 (C.H.).

[413] *Rayner v Preston* (1881) 18 Ch D 1 at 6. In that case Brett L.J. doubted whether the vendor was ever trustee for the purchaser: see at 11, but this goes too far. For more measured opinions, see *Berkley v Poulett* [1977] 1 E.G.L.R. 86 at 93; *Chang v Registrar of Titles* (1976) 137 C.L.R. 177 at 184, 189.

[414] *Shaw v Foster* (1872) L.R. 5 H.L. 321 at 338, per Lord Cairns.

[415] *Phillips v Silvester*, above, at 176; below, para.24–002.

[416] *Re Birmingham* [1959] Ch. 523.

[417] *Mackreth v Symmons* (1808) 15 Ves. 329; Wh. & T. ii, 848; Snell, *Equity*, para.44–010; below, para.24–003. This is an equitable interest in land (above, para.5–012), registrable as a general equitable charge where the title is unregistered (above) and as a notice where title is registered (above, paras 7–070 et seq.).The unpaid vendor's lien arises on the exchange of contracts: see *Barclays Bank Plc v Estates Commercial Ltd* [1997] 1 W.L.R. 415. See generally [1997] Conv. 336 (D. G. Barnsley).

[418] *Capital Finance Co Ltd v Stokes* [1969] 1 Ch. 261 at 278; *London Cheshire Insurance Co Ltd v Laplagrene* [1971] Ch. 499 at 514; *Re Bond Worth* [1980] Ch. 228 at 251. But see to the contrary: *Ecclesiastical Commissioners v Piney* [1899] 2 Ch. 729 (aff'd [1900] 2 Ch. 736).

[419] "The peculiar and discretionary grounds for resisting specific performance are simply not appropriate to be indiscriminately applied as criteria of exclusion": *Hewett v Court* (1983) 46 A.L.R. 87 at 105, per Deane J. See [1997] Conv. 336 at 339 (D. G. Barnsley).

[420] *Re Watford Corporation and Ware's Contract* [1943] Ch. 82; Williams V. & P. 560.

statutory compensation falling due to the "owner" before completion.[421] But broadly speaking, "as between vendor and purchaser generally the powers of the vendor to act as owner of the property, and (inter alia) to change tenants and holdings, are suspended pending completion of the purchase."[422]

(b) Trusteeship or lien arising from payment of the purchase price.[423] It has **15–056** been explained that the proprietary consequences of the trust arising from a specifically enforceable contract are in practice limited as between vendor and purchaser because of the vendor's lien for the price.[424] However, the purchaser does become in some sense the owner of the property in equity to the extent that he pays all or part of the price[425] (or furnishes other consideration[426]).[427] There is some uncertainty as to the nature of this ownership. It is often said that the purchaser has a lien over the property for the amount that he has paid,[428] but there is also authority that the vendor holds the property on trust for him,[429] and that he will hold it on a bare trust once the whole price has been paid.[430] All modern cases treat the purchaser's right as a lien. It is as if "the vendor had executed an equitable mortgage in favour of the purchaser for the amount of his deposit, interest and costs".[431] The purchaser may assert his proprietary claim not only against the land, but should the vendor sell it to some third party in breach of contract, to the proceeds of that sale as well.[432]

The lien extends not only to the sums paid by way of deposit or part purchase, but also includes other sums ancillary to the deposit, such as interest on the deposit, interest paid on the unpaid balance of the purchase money paid to the vendor, the costs of any action to recover the deposit, and, apparently, the purchaser's costs of investigating title.[433]

---

[421] *Re Hamilton-Snowball's Conveyance* [1959] Ch. 308 (compensation on derequisition).

[422] *Raffety v Schofield* [1897] 1 Ch. 937 at 945, per Romer J.

[423] See [1994] C.L.J. 263 (S. Worthington); *Interests in Goods* (eds N. Palmer and E. McKendrick), Ch.25 (J. Phillips); [1977] Conv. 336 at 350 (D. G. Barnsley); (1997) 1 E.L.R. 437 at 457 (C.H.).

[424] Above, para.15–055.

[425] Payment must be to the vendor however. There is no lien if payment is made to a stakeholder, as commonly happens with a deposit: *Combe v Lord Swaythling* [1947] Ch. 625.

[426] See *Lake v Bayliss* [1974] 1 W.L.R. 1073 (where the consideration was the withdrawal of two writs and the assumption of liabilities under a planning application).

[427] The leading case is *Rose v Watson* (1864) 33 L.J.Ch. 385 (a fuller report than 10 H.L.C. 672). See too *Wythes v Lee* (1855) 3 Drew. 396; *Middleton v Magnay* (1864) 2 H. & M. 233; *Levy v Stogdon* [1898] 1 Ch. 478; *Whitbread Co Ltd v Watt* [1902] 1 Ch. 835; *Combe v Lord Swaythling*, above; *Chattey v Farndale Holdings Inc* [1997] 1 E.G.L.R. 153.

[428] e.g. *Middleton v Magnay*, above; *Whitbread Co Ltd v Watt*, above; *Hewett v Court* (1983) 46 A.L.R. 87. The issue usually arises in connection with a claim by the purchaser to recover his deposit: below, para.15–108.

[429] *Rose v Watson*, above, at 390; *Shaw v Foster* (1872) L.R. 5 H.L. 321 at 349.

[430] *Rose v Watson*, above, at 390; *Shaw v Foster*, above, at 356; *Re Pagani* [1892] 1 Ch. 236 at 238; *Chang v Registrar of Titles* (1976) 137 C.L.R. 177 at 184, 189; *Coffey v Brunel Construction Co Ltd* [1983] I.R. 36 at 40, 43.

[431] *Cabra Estates Plc v Glendower Investments* [1992] E.G.C.S.137, per Roger Kaye QC.

[432] *Lake v Bayliss*, above.

[433] *Cabra Estates Plc v Glendower Investments*, above (this point does not appear from the case summary, but only from the transcript).

For the lien to arise there must be a valid contract between the parties[434] though it need not be specifically enforceable.[435] A purchaser can assert a lien only "where a purchase goes off by reason of some default on the part of the vendor".[436] The basis for the imposition of the lien is not wholly clear,[437] but it appears to arise out of the relationship of the parties by operation of equity[438] as a correlative of the unpaid vendor's lien.[439] The lien can be excluded expressly or impliedly by the contract between the parties.[440]

4. The risk passes

15–057   *(a) The position under open contract.* Under the trust that arises from a specifically enforceable contract, the property at once belongs to the purchaser in equity. In consequence the risk of damage or destruction to the property also passes to him as soon as conversion has operated.[441] Thus if a house has been sold and is, without the fault of the vendor, destroyed by fire before completion, the purchaser must nevertheless pay the full purchase-money and take the land as it is.[442] It is important for a purchaser of buildings to insure at once in his own name, since he undertakes the risk of accidents before he takes the property itself. He cannot take the benefit of any insurance maintained by the vendor in the vendor's name alone[443]; for insurance is normally only a personal indemnity against loss, and since the vendor is entitled to the whole purchase-money and so loses nothing he can recover nothing under his

---

[434] *Whitbread Co Ltd v Watt* [1901] 1 Ch. 911 at 915 (aff'd [1902] 1 Ch. 835); *Re Barrett Apartments Ltd* [1985] I.R. 350. The purchaser must have had a present, future or contingent right to the legal estate: *Chattey v Farndale Holdings Inc* [1997] 1 E.G.L.R. 153.

[435] *Chattey v Farndale Holdings Inc*, above; *Hewett v Court*, above. In the latter case, Deane J. explained that "an equitable lien to secure repayment of instalments of purchase price is only of real value if specific performance of the contract would not be decreed": (1983) 46 A.L.R. 87 at 106.

[436] *Cornwall v Henson* [1899] 2 Ch. 710 at 714, per Cozens-Hardy J. See too *Ridout v Fowler* [1904] 1 Ch. 658 at 663; *Hedworth v Jenwise Ltd* [1994] E.G.C.S. 133. A purchaser in default has no lien for his deposit or other part payments therefore: *Dinn v Grant* (1852) 5 De G. & Sm. 451.

[437] See (1993) 109 L.Q.R. 159 at 162 (W. M. C. Gummow).

[438] *Hewett v Court*, above, at 105.

[439] *Wythes v Lee* (1855) 3 Drew. 396 at 403.

[440] *Cabra Estates Plc v Glendower Investments* [1992] E.G.C.S.137.

[441] The risk of defects in title which arise between contract and completion remains with the vendor, however, unless the parties have agreed otherwise: see *Wroth v Tyler* [1974] Ch. 30. For defects in title, see below, para.15–080.

[442] *Paine v Meller* (1801) 6 Ves. 349; *Rayner v Preston* (1881) 18 Ch D 1. The same principle applies if between contract and completion a building is listed as being of architectural or historical importance: there is no frustration, and the purchaser must take the land: *Amalgamated Investment Property Co Ltd v John Walker Sons Ltd* [1977] 1 W.L.R. 164; or a notice of intended compulsory purchase is served on the vendor: *E. Johnson Co (Barbados) Ltd v N.S.R. Ltd* [1997] A.C. 400; below, para.15–082. The doctrine of frustration *can* apply to contracts for the sale of land: see *Wong Lai-Ying v Chinachem Investments Co Ltd* [1978] H.K.L.R. 1, where the Privy Council held that a contract to purchase an interest in a block of flats was frustrated when the building was destroyed in a landslip. In *Hildron Finance Ltd v Sunley Holdings Ltd* [2010] EWHC 1681 (Ch); [2010] 3 E.G.L.R. 1, a conditional contract to sell a caretaker's flat in a block of flats was frustrated when the tenants of the block acquired the flat when exercising their right to enfranchise the block under LRHUDA 1993.

[443] *Rayner v Preston*, above.

policy.[444] If the vendor does in fact obtain payment of the insurance money, the insurers can recover it.[445] Even if they do not, equity does not require the vendor to pay the money to the purchaser, for his qualified trusteeship extends only to the land, and not to the proceeds of a personal contract of insurance.[446]

By statute,[447] an insurance company can be required to lay out any insurance money in reinstating premises destroyed or damaged by fire at the request of a person interested. However, it now seems that this obligation may arise only where the assured was under an obligation to the person interested to reinstate the premises, as where a landlord has covenanted with a tenant to do so.[448] This is seldom likely to be the situation as between vendor and purchaser.

(b) *Insurance by the purchaser.* The position as to insurance is in practice **15–058** often regulated by conditions of sale and this is explained below. However, in the absence of any such agreement between vendor and purchaser, it is essential for the latter, if he wishes to insure the buildings, to take out insurance on his own account. In domestic conveyancing, the purchaser will in those circumstances commonly insure from the date of contract. Although this will lead to duplication of insurance by vendor and purchaser, the cost is not large because the period between contract and completion is normally short. To avoid such duplication the parties may arrange, with the consent of the insurers, for the vendor's existing insurance to be extended to cover the purchaser. Section 47 of the Law of Property Act 1925 provides that "where . . . money becomes payable" under the vendor's insurance policy in respect of damage to the property after the date of the contract, the vendor shall pay that money to the purchaser on completion. This is subject to: (a) the terms of the contract; (b) any requisite consent of the insurers; and (c) the payment by the purchaser of his share of the premium.[449] It has been assumed that, in consequence of this section, where the insurers consent to include the purchaser in the insurance, it is unnecessary to make further terms about the insurance money or premium. However, there must be a doubt as to whether the section achieves that effect. The vendor is entitled to receive from the purchaser the full contract price and will therefore suffer no personal loss if the property is damaged. It follows that on a literal interpretation of the section

---

[444] See following note.

[445] *Castellain v Preston* (1883) 11 Q.B.D. 380. Yet if the contract of insurance is framed not as an indemnity against loss but as a guarantee against fire, the vendor will be entitled to the insurance money: *Collingridge v Royal Exchange Assurance Corp.* (1877) 3 Q.B.D. 173.

[446] *Rayner v Preston* (1881) 18 Ch D 1.

[447] Fires Prevention (Metropolis) Act 1774, s.83. See *Vural Ltd v Security Archives Ltd* (1989) 60 P. & C.R. 258 at 272.

[448] *Lonsdale Thompson Ltd v Black Arrow Group Plc* [1993] Ch. 361; [1993] C.L.J. 387 (A. J. Oakley). In that case the landlord had contracted to sell the reversion before the fire and made no claim on the policy. It was held that notwithstanding the contract of sale, he had an insurable interest beyond the value of his reversion and his insurers could be required by the tenant to reinstate the premises. cf. [1989] Conv. 1 at 5 (H. W. Wilkinson).

[449] Presumably these conditions must be satisfied *before* the loss occurs.

no insurance money will become payable under the policy and the purchaser will receive nothing.[450]

15–059   *(c) Conditions of sale.* The Law Commission, after reviewing this area of the law, concluded that the law should be changed so that risk passed only on completion.[451] However, no proposals for legislation followed because the recommendation was incorporated in the Standard Conditions of Sale.[452] The relevant condition[453] provides that the vendor retains the risk of damage to or destruction of the property until completion. The purchaser may rescind the contract if at any time before then the physical state of the property makes it unusable for its purpose at the date of contract. The vendor may also rescind in such circumstances, but only if the damage is of a kind against which he could not reasonably have insured, or which it is not legally possible to make good, e.g. because of planning restrictions. The vendor is under no obligation to insure the premises and s.47 of the Law of Property Act 1925 is excluded.

15–060   **5. Conversion.** Another consequence of the change in beneficial ownership brought about by the contract is that the equitable doctrine of conversion applies.[454] If, for example, A contracts to sell land to B and then dies leaving all his land to X and all his other property to Y, Y will be entitled to the purchase-money when the contract is duly completed by the executors; for A's beneficial interest consisted of money due from B rather than of land.

15–061   **6. Specific enforceability.** The vendor's trusteeship, the passing of the risk and conversion (but not the lien or trust arising from a payment of the price) all flow from the fact that the contract is specifically enforceable. If it is not they are all excluded. For example, there might be a flaw in the vendor's title, so that the purchaser refused to complete. In that case the vendor would not be liable for negligent damage to the property, he could recover any insurance money payable for accidental damage, and the land would pass under a devise of real property.

15–062   **7. Options.** The nature of an option has already been explained.[455] It creates an immediate interest in the land, for the grantor has bound himself to enter into a contract of sale if and when the grantee exercises the option in

---

[450] This is almost certainly the case where the insurance is left in the vendor's name only, but the same conclusion would appear to follow even where the insurers have agreed to include the purchaser in the insurance: see Law Com WP No.109 (1988), paras 2.9–2.17; and *Ziel Nominees Pty Ltd v V.A.C.C. Insurance Co Ltd* (1975) 50 A.L.J.R. 106 (a case where the vendors had attempted to assign the benefit of the policy to the purchaser without the insurer's consent).

[451] (1988) Law Com WP No.109. See [1989] Conv. 1 (H. W. Wilkinson).

[452] (1990) See Law Com. No.191.

[453] What is now Standard Conditions of Sale, 4th edn, c.5.1. See (1992) 89/38 L.S.Gaz 23 (T. Aldridge).

[454] See above, paras 10–009, 10–029; Snell, *Equity*, paras 24–002—24–004; *Lysaght v Edwards* (1876) 2 Ch D 499.

[455] Above, para.15–012.

accordance with its terms.[456] In this way, the grantee obtains a specifically enforceable right to secure the land in certain conditions, and the equitable interest which arises under the option is not "altered or superseded by some other and different interest on the exercise of the option".[457]

8. Rights of pre-emption. The position in relation to rights of pre-emption and rights of first refusal is more complex. These rights differ from an ordinary option in that they entitle the holder to be offered the land on certain terms only if the owner decides to dispose of it. But this is merely an additional condition, and in principle it ought not to prevent the holder acquiring an immediate interest in the land, since here also he has secured to himself a specifically enforceable though contingent right to obtain it under a contract of sale.[458] Furthermore, the legislation of 1925 and later contains many indications that rights of pre-emption were intended to take effect as interests in land which could bind purchasers if duly registered, on a par with other forms of option. The definition of estate contract in the Land Charges Act 1972, for example, includes "a valid option to purchase, a right of pre-emption or any other like right"[459]; and the Law of Property Act 1925 provides that "all statutory and other rights of pre-emption affecting a legal estate" shall, unless released, "remain in force as equitable interests only".[460] However, the courts have not treated rights of pre-emption as a form of option but as distinct rights in themselves which may in certain circumstances create an interest in land. As regards registered land, Parliament has intervened. The law is as follows.

15–063

First, where rights of pre-emption (including rights of first refusal) have been granted on or after October 13, 2003 in relation to registered land,[461] they take effect as an interest in land from the time of their creation, and are therefore capable of binding successors in title in accordance with the rules of priority applicable to registered land.[462] This provision was intended to overcome the difficulties that had arisen in relation to the status of these rights at common law.[463] In consequence, most rights of pre-emption that are now granted will take effect as interests in land.

15–064

---

[456] See *L. S. W. Ry v Gomm* (1882) 20 Ch D 562 at 581; *Griffith v Pelton* [1958] Ch. 205 at 225; *Webb v Pollmount Ltd* [1966] Ch. 584 at 597; *McCarthy Stone Ltd v Julian S. Hodge Co Ltd* [1971] 1 W.L.R. 1547; *First National Securities Ltd v Chiltern DC* [1975] 1 W.L.R. 1075 at 1079, 1080; *Mountford v Scott* [1975] Ch. 258 (consideration nominal: specific performance granted).

[457] *Armstrong Holmes Ltd v Holmes* [1993] 1 W.L.R. 1482 at 1488, per Judge Baker.

[458] *Birmingham Canal Co v Cartwright* (1879) 11 Ch D 421.

[459] s.2(4) Class C(iv), replacing LCA 1925 s.10. For similar provisions see LPA 1925 s.2(3)(iv); S.L.A. 1925 ss.58(2), 61(2); PAA 1964 s.9(2); all clearly indicating that a right of pre-emption ranks as an interest in land.

[460] s.186.

[461] LRA 2002 came into force on October 13, 2003.

[462] LRA 2002 s.115; above, para.7–067. For the rules on priority, see above, paras 7–060 et seq.

[463] See (2001) Law Com. No.271 at paras 5.26–5.28.

15–065　　　Secondly, as regards all other rights of pre-emption (including rights of first refusal) the matter is governed by the common law. After a period of doubt, it is now settled that a right of pre-emption does not create an equitable interest at its inception, but is merely a contractual right. It differs from an option because, unlike an option, the grantee cannot require the grantor to sell the land to him. The matter lies entirely at the volition of the grantor and it is this that is said to mark out this contingency from all others.[464] A right of pre-emption may become an interest in land in some but not all cases.[465] Whether and when it becomes an interest in land depends upon the terms on which the right was granted, as the following examples illustrate:

(i) Where, on the occurrence of the triggering event (typically that the grantor of the right of pre-emption decides to sell the land), the grantor is obliged both to offer to sell the land and to keep the offer for a specified period, the grantee has an equitable interest from the making of the offer for the period during which it cannot be revoked. His position is analogous to the holder of an option.[466]

(ii) If, on the triggering event, the grantor is obliged to offer to sell the land to the grantee, but is not required to leave the offer open and can, therefore, revoke it at any time prior to acceptance,[467] the grantee does not acquire an equitable interest in land on the occurrence of the triggering event, at least so long as the grantor no longer wishes to dispose of the land.[468]

(iii) Where the grantor's obligation, when the triggering event occurs, is to offer to sell the land to the grantee at a price to be fixed by an arbitrator in default of agreement, but where either party can withdraw once the price has been determined, the grantee does not acquire an equitable interest when the triggering event happens.[469]

(iv) There may be a case where, on the occurrence of the triggering event, the grantor of the pre-emption is not obliged to offer to sell the land to the grantee, but the grantee is entitled to make an offer to buy the land. The grantee will not acquire an equitable interest in the land unless his offer is accepted. If the grantor were to refuse to sell to him, but then accepted an offer from a third party that was

---

[464] *Pritchard v Briggs* [1980] Ch. 338; at pp.389 (Goff L.J.), 418 (Templeman L.J.), 422 (Stephenson L.J.).

[465] See the valuable analysis in *Speciality Shops Ltd v Yorkshire and Metropolitan Estates Ltd* [2002] EWHC 2969 (Ch) at [25]–[29]; [2003] 2 P. & C.R. 410 at 416, 417.

[466] *Pritchard v Briggs*, above; *Bircham & Co, Nominees (2) Ltd v Worrell Holdings Ltd* [2001] EWCA Civ 775 at [34]–[36]; (2001) 82 P. & C.R. 427 at 439, 440.

[467] See *Tuck v Baker* [1990] 1 E.G.L.R. 195.

[468] *Bircham & Co, Nominees (2) Ltd v Worrell Holdings Ltd* [2001] EWCA Civ 775 at [37]; (2001) 82 P. & C.R. 427 at 440.

[469] *Dowling v Wallis* (2000) 80 P. & C.R. 362.

the same as or lower than the grantee's, the grantee's only remedy would be a claim in damages.[470]

The difficulty with rights of pre-emption at common law that follows from this analysis is that it is not possible to protect their priority even though the legislature had assumed that it was.[471]

Although a right of pre-emption implies a negative obligation on the owner not to part with the land so as to frustrate the right, it is not a restrictive covenant which could bind successors in title. This is because "a restrictive covenant is concerned with restricting the use of land, and not with restraints on alienation".[472]

B. *The Vendor must Convey the Land Described in the Contract*

1. The obligation. In the particulars of sale in the contract,[473] the vendor **15–066** must accurately describe the land which he intends to convey.[474] That description will usually encompass four matters:

    (i) the physical identity of the land[475];

    (ii) the estate to be transferred[476];

    (iii) proprietary rights which enure for the benefit of the land; and

    (iv) any incumbrances which burden the property.

A vendor who misdescribes the land in the particulars commits a breach of contract. Examples of such misdescriptions have included:

    (a) erroneous statements as to the size of the land[477];

---

[470] *Speciality Shops Ltd v Yorkshire and Metropolitan Estates Ltd* [2002] EWHC 2969 (Ch) at [28], [29]; [2003] 2 P. & C.R. 410 at 417.

[471] Above, para.15–063.

[472] *University of East London Higher Education Corpn v Barking and Dagenham LBC* [2004] EWHC 2710 (Ch) at [28]; [2005] Ch. 354 at 365, per Lightman J; *Crestfort Ltd v Tesco Stores Ltd* [2005] EWHC 805 (Ch) at [59]; [2005] 3 E.G.L.R. 25 at 31. But see *Test Valley BC v Minilec Engineering Ltd* [2005] 2 E.G.L.R. 113 at 124, [162] et seq.

[473] Although it has been said that "the proper office of the particulars is to describe the subject-matter of the contract, that of the conditions to state the terms on which it is sold" (*Torrance v Bolton* (1872) L.R. 14 Eq. 124 at 130, per Malins V.C.), the distinction between particulars and conditions of sale is one of practice rather than substance: J. T. Farrand, *Contract and Conveyance* (4th edn), p.50.

[474] *Swaisland v Dearsley* (1861) 29 Beav 430 at 436.

[475] Where title is registered, the description found in the property register is commonly adopted.

[476] A vendor is presumed to transfer the fee simple free from incumbrances unless either the contract states otherwise or the purchaser is aware that this is not the case: *Timmins v Moreland Street Property Co Ltd* [1958] Ch. 110 at 118.

[477] *Watson v Burton* [1957] 1 W.L.R. 19 (land consisting of 2,360 square yards described as consisting of 3,920 square yards); *King Brothers (Finance) Ltd v North Western British Road Services Ltd* [1986] 2 E.G.L.R. 253.

(b)   where land was registered merely with possessory title, a statement that it was "registered freehold property"[478]; and

(c)   a statement that land was leasehold when it was in fact held on an underlease,[479] but not a description of a "sub-underlease" as an underlease.[480]

Where the misdescription is substantial, the purchaser may either terminate the contract and sue the vendor for damages, or seek specific performance with compensation or damages in addition.[481] In this context, a misdescription will be substantial if the purchaser would not have entered into the contract but for it.[482] Where the misdescription is insubstantial, the vendor may specifically enforce the contract against the purchaser subject to an abatement of the price.[483] These remedies are explained later.[484]

15–067   **2. Conditions of sale.** If has long been common to include in contracts for the sale of land a condition of sale providing that in the event of any error, omission or misdescription in the particulars of sale, the purchaser shall not be able to terminate the contract, but shall complete it either with or (in some forms of the condition) without compensation.[485] However, where the misdescription is substantial in the sense explained above, the purchaser may terminate the contract and seek damages for its breach notwithstanding that the contract contains such a condition of sale.[486]

15–068   **3. Misdescription and misrepresentation.** A purchaser of land may be induced to enter into a contract because of the matters contained in the draft particulars of sale.[487] If those particulars are inaccurate, the purchaser will have remedies for both misrepresentation and breach of the subsequent contract of which the erroneous particulars become part.[488] In practice purchasers

---

[478] *Re Brine and Davies' Contract* [1935] Ch. 388 (such a description implied that the vendor had an absolute title).

[479] *Re Russ and Brown's Contract* [1934] Ch. 34. An underlease is vulnerable to forfeiture for breach of covenant by the underlessor whereas a lease can be forfeited only for the lessee's own breach.

[480] *Becker v Partridge* [1966] 2 Q.B. 155 at 170 where Danckwerts L.J. observed that "the term 'sub-underlease' is not really a conveyancing expression in current use".

[481] See [1981] C.L.J. 47 (C.H.).

[482] *Smith v Tolcher* (1828) 4 Russ. 302 at 305; *Flight v Booth* (1834) 1 Bing. (n.c.) 370 at 377; *Ridley v Oster* [1939] 1 All E.R. 618 at 622. As to whether the test of substantiality is subjective, objective, or both, see [1992] C.L.J. 263 at 274 (C.H.).

[483] Conditions of sale may however exclude the entitlement to an abatement.

[484] Below, paras 15–102, 15–105 (damages), 15–071, 15–117 (specific performance with compensation or damages).

[485] See [1992] C.L.J. 263 at 270 (C.H.). For the present version of the condition, see Standard Conditions of Sale (4th edn), c. 7.1.

[486] *Flight v Booth*, above.

[487] See e.g. *South Western General Property Co Ltd v Marton* [1982] 2 E.G.L.R. 19 (misstatement in auction particulars).

[488] A misrepresentation remains actionable even though it has become a term of the contract: Misrepresentation Act 1967 s.1(a).

often pursue their remedies for misrepresentation (which are explained below)[489] in preference to a claim for breach of contract.

C. The Vendor must show a Good Title

A vendor is under a two-fold obligation as to the title of the property which he is selling. First, he must disclose to the purchaser prior to contracting all latent defects in title save those of which the purchaser is aware.[490] Secondly, by the contractual completion date he must both have the title which he has contracted to give and be able to prove that fact. The second obligation is as important as the first because "it is a fundamental part of a vendor's obligations to prove his title".[491] It should be noted that the first of these obligations arises at the time of contracting[492] whereas the second must be satisfied at the date for completion.[493] Although the second of these obligations was established by the beginning of the 19th century, the first emerged only at the end of that century.

15–069

1. Duty to disclose latent defects

(a) The obligation. In relation to matters other than title, the general principle is *caveat emptor*: a vendor is under no obligations of disclosure to a purchaser who is bound to make proper inquiries for himself.[494] Thus, for example, a vendor is not required to tell an intending purchaser that the property to be sold was the site of a gruesome murder.[495] However in relation to title, the principle of *caveat emptor* is much qualified. A vendor is under a duty to disclose to the purchaser before contracting any latent defects in title.[496] He is under no obligation to disclose any defect in title of which the purchaser is aware[497] or which is patent, in relation to which the principle of

15–070

---

[489] Below, paras 15–104, 15–112.

[490] See (1992) 108 L.Q.R. 280 (C.H.).

[491] *Horton v Kurzke* [1971] 1 W.L.R. 769 at 772 per Goff J.

[492] *Re Haedicke and Lipski's Contract* [1901] 2 Ch. 666 at 668.

[493] "The vendor must be prepared to make out a good title on the day when a purchase is to be completed": *Cornish v Rowley* (1800) 1 Selwyn's *Nisi Prius* (13th edn), 218 and 219, per Lord Kenyon C.J. A vendor cannot serve a valid notice to complete if he has not proved his title: see *Horton v Kurzke* [1971] 1 W.L.R. 769 at 772; below, para.15–095.

[494] See, e.g., *Lowndes v Lane* (1789) 2 Cox 363; *Terrene Ltd v Nelson* [1937] 3 All E.R. 739 at 744; *Taylor v Hamer* [2002] EWCA Civ 1130 at [41]; [2003] 1 E.G.L.R. 103 at 106. A vendor may, however, be liable in the tort of deceit if he deliberately conceals structural or other physical defects in the property (as in *Gordon v Selico Co Ltd* [1986] 1 E.G.L.R. 71, where dry rot was deliberately concealed) or surreptitiously makes a material alteration to the property and then seeks to conceal it from the purchaser (as in *Taylor v Hamer* [2002] EWCA Civ 1130; [2003] 1 E.G.L.R. 103, where flagstones were removed). See below, para.15–073.

[495] *Sykes v Taylor-Rose* [2004] EWCA Civ 299; [2004] 2 P. & C.R. 579.

[496] *Reeve v Berridge* (1880) 20 Q.B.D. 523; *Re White and Smith's Contract* [1896] 1 Ch. 637; *Re Haedicke and Lipski's Contract*, above; *Molyneux v Hawtrey* [1903] 2 K.B. 487. See too *Peyman v Lanjani* [1985] Ch. 457 at 496, 497; Halsbury (4th edn reissue) Vol. 42, para.55; (1992) 108 L.Q.R. 280 at 325 et seq. (C.H.).

[497] *Re Gloag and Miller's Contract* (1883) 23 Ch D 320 at 327, *McGrory v Alderdale Estate Co Ltd* [1918] A.C. 503 at 508; below, para.15–083.

caveat emptor applies.[498] A defect is not patent merely because the purchaser has constructive notice of it.[499] It must be one "which arises either to the eye, or by necessary implication from something which is visible to the eye".[500] Thus an obvious right of way is likely to be patent,[501] but a tenancy,[502] a restrictive covenant[503] and a local land charge[504] are all latent incumbrances.[505]

The nature of the vendor's obligation to disclose latent defects prior to contract is obscure and cannot be regarded as finally settled. In some cases it has been explained on the basis that it is akin to fraud for a vendor not to reveal a defect in title of which he is aware.[506] In others, however, it is justified on the basis that the vendor's title is a matter exclusively within his knowledge and the purchaser therefore necessarily relies upon him to disclose any latent defects in it.[507] He must therefore disclose all latent defects in title, whether or not he knows of them. This may best be explained not as a pre-contractual duty of disclosure at all but as an implied term of a contract for the sale of land that the vendor has disclosed all latent defects in title.[508] The remedies available for failing to disclose latent defects in title suggest that this latter analysis is the correct one.

15–071   *(b) Remedies.* If a vendor contracts to sell land which he does not own or to which the title is bad,[509] the purchaser may at once treat the contract as repudiated and sue the vendor for damages.[510] He does not have to wait until the contractual completion date.[511] This can be justified only if the vendor is in breach of some contractual obligation that is distinct from his duty to

---

[498] *Bowles v Round* (1800) 5 Ves. 508; *Yandle & Sons v Sutton* [1922] 2 Ch. 199 at 204.
[499] *Caballero v Henty* (1874) 9 Ch.App. 447, rejecting earlier authority to the contrary. See (1992) 108 L.Q.R. 280 at 321–324 (C.H.).
[500] *Yandle & Sons v Sutton* [1922] 2 Ch. 199 at 210, per Sargant J.
[501] *Shonleigh Nominees Ltd v Att Gen* [1974] 1 W.L.R. 305 at 311, 315, 323. Not all rights of way will be patent: see *Ashburner v Sewell* [1891] 3 Ch. 405.
[502] *Caballero v Henty*, above; *Pagebar Properties Ltd v Derby Investment Holdings Ltd* [1972] 1 W.L.R. 1500.
[503] *Hone v Gakstatter* (1909) 53 S.J. 286; *Re Stone and Saville's Contract* [1963] 1 W.L.R. 163.
[504] *Rignall Developments Ltd v Halil* [1988] Ch. 190.
[505] For the meaning of "incumbrances", see below, para.15–082.
[506] *Carlish v Salt* [1906] 1 Ch. 335; *F B Entertainment Ltd v Leisure Enterprises Ltd* [1976] 2 E.G.L.R. 76 at 79; *Sakkas v Donford Ltd* (1982) 46 P. & C.R. 290 at 302.
[507] *Yandle & Sons v Sutton*, above, at 210; *Peyman v Lanjani* [1985] Ch. 457 at 496.
[508] See (1992) 108 L.Q.R. 280 at 332 (C.H.).
[509] For what constitutes a bad title, see below, para.15–075.
[510] *Bartlett v Tuchin* (1815) 1 Marsh. 586; *Roper v Coombs* (1827) 9 Dowl. & Ry. 562; *Brewer v Broadhead* (1882) 22 Ch D 105; *Lee v Soames* (1888) 36 W.R. 884; *Pips (Leisure Productions) Ltd v Walton* (1980) 43 P. & C.R. 415; *Pinekerry Ltd v Needs (Kenneth) (Contractors) Ltd* (1992) 64 P. & C.R. 245. See [1993] C.L.J. 22 (A. J. Oakley).
[511] *Forrer v Nash* (1865) 35 Beav. 167 at 171. There was a view that in such circumstances the purchaser could only "rescind in equity": *Halkett v Earl of Dudley* [1907] 1 Ch. 590; (1977) 41 Conv.(N.S.) 18 (C. T. Emery). This meant that he was no longer liable to an action for specific performance but could be sued for damages if the vendor perfected his title by the completion date. However this view was open to strong objections and has now been doubted: see *Pips (Leisure Productions) Ltd v Walton* (1980) 43 P. & C.R. 415 at 423–425; (1992) 108 L.Q.R. 280 at 301–313 (C.H.).

convey the land with a good title on the contractual completion date. There is authority which suggests that it is the vendor's failure to disclose a defect in title that constitutes that breach.[512] Where the non-disclosure relates to either an insubstantial matter or a removable defect in title, the purchaser cannot terminate the contract.[513] In such circumstances either the vendor or the purchaser may seek specific performance of the contract subject to an abatement of the price in respect of any insubstantial but irremovable defect in title.[514]

(c) *Conditions of sale.* There are two types of condition of sale upon which **15–072** vendors commonly rely in cases of non-disclosure. The first is the condition, considered above,[515] which purports to exclude the purchaser's right to terminate the contract in the event of any error, omission or misdescription in the particulars of sale. This condition will be inapplicable in cases where the non-disclosure relates to a substantial latent defect in title.[516] Secondly, a sale is often made with some general exclusion, such as "subject to any existing rights and easements of whatever nature".[517] However, it is a fundamental rule of equity that the vendor cannot rely on such a condition to cover a latent defect in title of which he knew or ought to have known,[518] as where the defect is one which he ought to have discovered when he acquired the land.[519]

(d) *Non-disclosure and misrepresentation.* Mere non-disclosure of a defect **15–073** in title does not constitute a misrepresentation.[520] However, "suppression of

---

[512] *Stevens v Adamson* (1818) 2 Stark. 422; *Peyman v Lanjani*, above, at 497.

[513] *Pips (Leisure Productions) Ltd v Walton*, above, at 424.

[514] *Dyer v Hargrave* (1805) 10 Ves. 505 at 507; *Rutherford v Acton-Adams* [1915] A.C. 866 at 869, 870; *Frasers Islington Ltd v The Hanover Trustee Co Ltd* [2010] EWHC 1514 (Ch) at [16] et seq. The circumstances may be such that a vendor may obtain specific performance subject to an abatement of the price even where full performance by him is not impossible, but could only be at a disproportionate cost, though this will always depend upon the circumstances: *Frasers Islington Ltd v The Hanover Trustee Co Ltd* [2010] EWHC 1514 (Ch) at [23] et seq. See generally [1981] C.L.J. 47 at 51; [1992] C.L.J. 263 and 270 (C.H.); and below, para.15–117. Obviously no question of abatement arises in respect of a removable defect which is discharged on or before completion.

[515] Above, para.15–067.

[516] *Re Puckett and Smith's Contract* [1902] 2 Ch. 258. Such a condition usually provides for compensation to be payable where there is an error, omission or misdescription. In cases where the non-disclosure is insubstantial, the vendor may enforce the contract subject to payment of compensation: *Re Belcham and Gawley's Contract* [1930] 1 Ch. 56.

[517] See *Heywood v Mallalieu* (1883) 25 Ch D 357. For a modern example, see Standard Conditions of Sale 4th edn, c.3.1.

[518] *Edwards v Wickwar* (1865) L.R. 1 Eq. 68 at 70; *Nottingham Patent Brick and Tile Co v Butler* (1885) 15 Q.B.D. 261 at 271; (1886) 16 Q.B.D. 778 at 786; *Re Turpin and Ahern's Contract* [1905] 1 I.R. 85 at 103; *Becker v Partridge* [1966] 2 All E.R. 266 at 271 (a fuller report than [1966] 2 Q.B. 155); *Rignall Developments Ltd v Halil* [1988] Ch. 190 at 197; *William Sindall Plc v Cambridgeshire CC* [1994] 1 W.L.R. 1016 at 1023; *Weir v Area Estates Ltd* [2010] EWCA Civ 801 at [17]–[22]; [2010] 3 E.G.L.R. 91 at 93. See [1992] C.L.J. 263 at 298–305 (C.H.). For a case that is inconsistent with this principle and must be open to doubt, see *Beyfus v Lodge* [1925] Ch. 350.

[519] *Becker v Partridge*, above.

[520] For a clear statement of the interrelationship between non-disclosure and misrepresentation, see *Atlantic Estates Plc v Ezekiel* [1991] 2 E.G.L.R. 202 at 203.

the truth may contain a suggestion of falsity",[521] and a vendor may be liable to a purchaser for misrepresentation if his failure to disclose a latent defect in title misleads the latter.[522] Thus a negative answer to a precontractual inquiry as to the existence of any boundary disputes was held to be a misrepresentation where the vendor failed to disclose a long-standing boundary dispute which he erroneously believed to have been settled.[523]

The distinction between non-disclosure and misrepresentation has not always been clearly drawn. This has happened largely because of the now discredited use of the terminology of "rescission" in cases where one party to a contract treated it as discharged by the other's breach[524] rather than confining it to situations where the contract was rescinded *ab initio* for fraud or misrepresentation.[525]

2. Duty to prove good title.

15–074   "In the absence of express stipulation to the contrary . . . , a contract for the sale of land in fee simple obliges the vendor to make a good title to the whole legal and equitable interest in the freehold free from encumbrances."[526]

This obligation is subject to two qualifications. The purchaser takes the land subject to irremovable defects in title which are either patent[527] or of which he knew when he contracted.[528] The manner in which a vendor of land discharges that obligation and proves that he has a good title to it depends upon whether the title to the property is registered or unregistered. In practice, the registered system is now the norm because, to date, about three-fifths of the total land in England and Wales has been registered.[529]

15–075   *(a) Gradations of title.* Before examining these two methods of deducing title, something must be said as to the different gradations of title.[530] These

---

[521] *McKeown v Boudard Peveril Gear Co Ltd* (1896) 74 L.T. 712 at 713, per Rigby L.J.

[522] Similar issues have arisen in relation to proof of title. Thus a condition of sale that required a purchaser to assume some fact as to the devolution of the vendor's title constituted an implied representation that the vendor knew nothing to make that fact untrue: *Re Banister* (1879) 12 Ch D 131 at 146, 147. The effect in that case was that the vendor could not rely on the condition of sale and had to prove his title in the usual way.

[523] *Walker v Boyle* [1982] 1 W.L.R. 495. The existence of a boundary dispute makes the title doubtful rather than positively bad. However, a court will not force a purchaser to buy a law suit: *Nottingham Patent Brick and Tile Co v Butler* (1886) 16 Q.B.D. 778 at 789; below, paras 15–080, 15–116.

[524] Below, para.15–106.

[525] For cases of non-disclosure where "rescission" was used in the now-discredited sense see, e.g. *Re Haedicke and Lipski's Contract* [1901] 2 Ch. 666; *Re Banister*, above; *Becker v Partridge*, above.

[526] *Leominster Properties Ltd v Broadway Finance Ltd* (1981) 42 P. & C.R. 372 at 380, per Slade J. See too *Re Ossemsley's Estates Ltd* [1937] 3 All E.R. 774 at 778.

[527] *Yandle Sons v Sutton* [1922] 2 Ch. 199 at 210; above, para.15–070.

[528] *Timmins v Moreland Street Property Co Ltd* [1958] Ch. 110 at 132; below.

[529] See above, para.7–001.

[530] See *Barclays Bank Plc v Weeks Legg Dean* [1999] Q.B. 309 at 324–326.

cannot be measured or even defined precisely but are matters of degree. A *good title* is one which is free from incumbrances and which can be proved in the manner required by law. Such a title can be forced on an unwilling purchaser[531] without the need for any special condition of sale.[532] A *good holding title* is strictly a bad title, but one which is in fact perfectly marketable. It is a title which is imperfect in some way, but the holding under which is unlikely to be challenged successfully, normally because any adverse claims have been barred by lapse of time. It has been said that such titles although bad from a conveyancer's perspective are nonetheless "good in a business man's point of view".[533] A *bad title* is anything else, and includes a situation where the vendor has no title to the property at all, or only title to some lesser estate than he contracted to sell, or where the land is subject to some substantial but undisclosed latent defect in title. A *doubtful* title is one which the vendor cannot prove with certainty to be good,[534] and which is therefore in law bad.[535] A title is not necessarily doubtful merely because a doubt is raised with regard to it. Commonly the doubt will relate to a blot which has been cured by lapse of time so that any adverse claims have been barred.[536] In such a case, a court will attempt to resolve the doubt[537] and:

"if the facts and circumstances of a case are so compelling to the mind of the court that the court concludes beyond reasonable doubt that the purchaser will not be at risk of a successful assertion against him of the incumbrance, the court should declare in favour of a good title shown".[538]

(b) Unregistered title

(1) PROOF OF TITLE. Title to unregistered land is deduced by exhibiting to the **15–076** purchaser the records of past transactions in the land, e.g. sales, mortgages and grants of probate, and by proving other relevant events such as deaths. This procedure has two main purposes: to persuade the purchaser that the vendor

---

[531] *Pyrke v Waddington* (1852) 10 Hare 1 at 8.

[532] *Re Spollon and Long's Contract* [1936] Ch. 713 at 718. It appears that a "good marketable title" is not the same as a "good title" (or "open market title"), but is one that can be forced on the purchaser under *that particular* contract: *Barclays Bank Plc v Weeks Legg Dean*, above.

[533] *Re Scott and Alvarez's Contract (No.2)* [1895] 2 Ch. 603 at 613, per Lindley L.J.

[534] See, e.g. *Nottingham Patent Brick and Tile Co v Butler* (1886) 16 Q.B.D. 778 (title depended on whether the vendor had taken free of certain restrictive covenants when he acquired the land because he was a purchaser without notice).

[535] Such a title may in the end prove to be good, but it will be treated as bad until such proof is forthcoming: see, e.g. *Rignall Developments Ltd v Halil* [1988] Ch. 190.

[536] See, e.g. *Re Atkinson and Horsell's Contract* [1912] 2 Ch. 1.

[537] See [1992] C.L.J. 263 at 291, 292 (C.H.).

[538] *M.E.P.C. Ltd v Christian-Edwards* [1981] A.C. 205 at 220, per Lord Russell of Killowen. In that case, an unfulfilled sale contract of 1912 was held to have been necessarily abandoned, and the title therefore good. It is not to be inferred from the passage quoted that a vendor must refute any doubt as to his title beyond reasonable doubt. The ordinary civil standard applies: see *Quadrini v Wine Cellar Ltd (t/a Booze Buster)* [2006] EWHC 2996 (Ch) at [83].

owns the land; and to give the purchaser his opportunity to inquire about the existence of equitable interests by which, if he made no inquiries, he would be bound. For the first purpose the vendor's title deeds are merely evidence; it is possible that owing to fraud, forgery or mistake he is not really the true owner, so that the purchaser will not obtain a good title.[539] For the second purpose the proof of title is conclusive: if the purchaser has made all reasonable inquiries and found nothing, he is safe from all equitable interests except such as are registered.[540]

For the purpose of proving title the parties may agree on as much, or as little, disclosure of documents as they wish. For the purpose of searching for equities the purchaser is required to search back for a certain period. If he fails to do so, he has constructive notice of anything he would have discovered by doing so.[541]

15–077　　(2) FIFTEEN YEARS' TITLE. If there is no agreement to the contrary, the period is now at least 15 years under the Law of Property Act 1969.[542] There are special rules in the case of leases, which are explained elsewhere.[543] The period is "at least" 15 years because the title must start from a document known as a good root of title, and it will only be by chance that such a document amongst the title deeds will be exactly 15 years old. Normally therefore only a document that is more than 15 years old will suffice.

The period for which title has to be shown has been steadily reduced over the last 120 years,[544] largely without jeopardy to purchasers. That this has occurred is attributable to two main factors. The first is the reduction in the period of limitation. In most cases, title to land will be barred by 12 years' adverse possession.[545] The second factor is the simplification of conveyancing that has followed the property legislation of 1925. It is noteworthy that although the reduction of the period of title to 15 years was accompanied by the scheme, explained earlier, for compensation purchasers affected by registered land charges which they could not discover from the title shown,[546] it is understood that very few successful claims have been made.

15–078　　(3) GOOD ROOT OF TITLE. A good root of title is a document which describes the land sufficiently to identify it, which shows a disposition of the whole legal and equitable interest contracted to be sold, and which contains nothing

---

[539] For relative titles and "true owners", see above, para.4–008.

[540] See above, paras 6–030, 8–018.

[541] Above, para.8–022.

[542] s.23.

[543] Below, para.21–005.

[544] Prior to the enactment of the Vendor and Purchaser Act 1874 s.2, title was deduced for at least 60 years according the custom of conveyancers. That Act reduced the period to 40 years, and it was further reduced to 30 years by LPA 1925 s.44(1).

[545] Below, Ch.35. There has been a direct link between the limitation period and the period for which title has to be deduced. See below, para.35–001.

[546] LPA 1969 s.25; above, para.8–089.

to throw any doubt on the title.[547] Examples of documents which commonly serve as roots of title are:

    (i) a conveyance on sale;

    (ii) a legal mortgage[548];

    (iii) an assent by a personal representative made after 1925 (after 1925 devises of land take effect not by force of the will but by force of the personal representatives' assent or conveyance,[549] which should describe the property[550]); and

    (iv) a voluntary conveyance.[551]

Examples of documents which will not serve as roots of title on a sale of the fee simple are:

    (i) a will taking effect after 1925[552];

    (ii) a lease; and

    (iii) an equitable mortgage.

A squatter's title, i.e. a title obtained by adverse possession for 12 years or more,[553] must be proved from a good root of title, by showing the full title of the person from whom the squatter took the land and then proving the adverse possession.[554] This will often be difficult, and the vendor will generally try to stipulate that the purchaser shall accept a title beginning with the adverse possession.

(4) DEDUCTION OF TITLE. Having established a good root of title of the necessary age, the vendor must then prove all the later steps in the title which lead to himself. If the land has been in his ownership for more than 15 years there may be nothing more to prove. But more probably there will have been intervening transfers on sale, death or otherwise, which are necessary links in deducing the title to be proved. Statements in documents 20 years old or more

15–079

---

[547] Williams V. & P. 124.

[548] Since 1925 a mortgage may no longer be made by a conveyance in fee simple (below, para.24–019) and such a mortgage is not therefore in law a good root of title, though it may be accepted in practice.

[549] Above, para.14–141. An assent under seal by a person with no power to make an assent takes effect as a conveyance: *Re Stirrup's Contract* [1961] 1 W.L.R. 449.

[550] See examples given in Prideaux, vol. iii, 874 et seq.

[551] *Re Marsh and Earl Granville* (1883) 24 Ch D 11 at 24. See Williams V. & P. 127.

[552] The assent is now the effective disposition of the legal estate: above, para.14–141.

[553] See above, para.4–003.

[554] *Re Atkinson and Horsell's Contract* [1912] 2 Ch. 1; Williams V. & P. 122.

are to be taken as sufficient evidence unless proved to be inaccurate.[555] If the proof is defective at any point, or if the title shown appears to be bad or doubtful,[556] the purchaser is entitled to terminate the contract on the ground that the vendor is unable to perform it.

15–080   (5) DEFECTS ANTERIOR TO THE ROOT OF TITLE. By statute, a purchaser may not make any inquiry or objection about matters anterior to the root of title.[557] This provision, which is subject to certain exceptions,[558] has the same effect as a contractual condition in similar terms would have done.[559] Because it has this status, not only can it be ousted by an contrary provision in the contract,[560] but, in accordance with the general rule of equity,[561] it cannot be relied upon by a vendor to force on the purchase a pre-root defect in title of which the vendor knew or ought to have known.[562] In general, however, the purchaser must be content with a title starting with a good root in accordance with the contract. If he discovers *aliunde* (for example, from an accidental disclosure of older documents) that the earlier title is doubtful due to some technical defect, so that it is questionable whether the vendor is really owner at all, he must nevertheless take the property with the title as it stands.[563] This is consistent with the essential function of conditions of sale, which is "to protect the vendor from inquiries which he himself may be unable to satisfy, and against objections which he cannot explain away".[564] If, however, the purchaser can prove that the title is wholly bad, as where the vendor has no title at all to the land or where the property is subject to some undisclosed but irremovable latent incumbrance of a substantial character,[565] then specific performance will not be decreed against him.[566] This is because the court will

[555] LPA 1925 s.45(6).
[556] e.g. *Re Handman and Wilcox's Contract* [1902] 1 Ch. 599 (title dependent upon purchase without notice, insufficiently proved).
[557] LPA 1925 s.45(1), replacing CA 1881 s.3(3), which confirmed earlier practice.
[558] LPA 1925 s.45(1), proviso. This entitles the purchaser to see (i) any power of attorney under which an abstracted document is executed, (ii) any document creating a subsisting incumbrance, (iii) any document creating any limitation or trust by reference to which a disposition is made by a document appearing in the abstract (which is in fact confined to dispositions by trustees which are not overreaching dispositions).
[559] LPA 1925 s.45(11); *Nottingham Patent Brick and Tile Co v Butler* (1885) 15 Q.B.D. 261 at 272 (aff'd (1886) 16 Q.B.D. 778). See J. T. Farrand, *Contract and Conveyance* 4th edn, p.99; *Barnsley's Conveyancing Law and Practice* 4th edn, pp.27, 278; [1992] C.L.J. 263 at 303 (C.H.).
[560] LPA 1925 s.45(10), proviso.
[561] Above, para.15–072.
[562] *Becker v Partridge* [1966] 2 All E.R. 266. This limitation is necessarily preserved in relation to LPA 1925 s.45(1) by s.45(11).
[563] See *Re Scott and Alvarez's Contract (No.1)* [1895] 1 Ch. 596, where specific performance was decreed, so removing the doubt expressed in *Re National Provincial Bank and Marsh* [1895] 1 Ch. 190 at 192.
[564] *Edwards v Wickwar* (1865) L.R. 1 Eq. 68 at 70, per Page Wood V.C. See too *Re Sandbach and Edmondson's Contract* [1891] 1 Ch. 99.
[565] See above, para.15–070.
[566] *Re Scott and Alvarez's Contract (No.2)* [1895] 2 Ch. 603, where fresh evidence turned a doubt as to the title into a certainty that it was bad.

not force a purchaser to take a title that will expose him to an immediate law suit.[567] However, unless the vendor knew or ought to have known of the defect, he will be able to rely upon the statutory provision that the purchaser is precluded from making any inquiry or objection as to matters before the root of title.[568] The purchaser will therefore be in breach of contract and the vendor may both forfeit his deposit[569] and sue him for damages.[570] The measure of damages will be the difference between the contract price and the market value of the land subject to the defect in title on the date on which the purchaser refuses to complete.[571] It follows therefore that the worse the vendor's title is, the greater the damages will be. The result has been acknowledged to be unsatisfactory,[572] and Parliament has attempted to ameliorate the position by providing that where a court refuses to grant specific performance, or in any action for the return of a deposit, it may, if it thinks fit, order the repayment of any deposit.[573] The weakness of this provision is that it does not bar the vendor's action against the purchaser for damages.[574] The court is therefore unlikely in practice to order the return of any deposit except in a case where its value exceeds the vendor's claim for damages.[575]

(6) AGREEMENT NOT TO INVESTIGATE. If a purchaser expressly agrees not to question the earlier title, or some intermediate step in the title to be shown under the contract, his position is similar to that outlined above in respect of pre-root defects in title. If it turns out that the vendor's title is bad owing to that part of the title into which he has agreed not to inquire: **15–081**

> (i) the vendor may rely upon the condition limiting his obligation unless he knew or ought to have known of the flaw in the title[576];

---

[567] [1895] 2 Ch. 603, at 613; *Pyrke v Waddingham* (1852) 10 Hare 1 at 8; *Re Nichols' Von Joel's Contract* [1910] 1 Ch. 43 at 46. For this rule, see [1990] C.L.J. 263 at 291 (C.H.); and below, para.15–116.

[568] LPA 1925 s.45(1), above.

[569] *Re Scott and Alvarez's Contract (No.2)*, above. For deposits, see below, para.15–107.

[570] There is no reported case in which this has occurred, but it appears to be correct in principle. Although LPA 1925 s.45(11) protects a purchaser against specific performance in any case in which it would not have been decreed in relation to a contract which contained a term similar to that found in s.45(1), it does not protect him against a damages claim: see J. T. Farrand, *Contract and Conveyance* 4th edn, p.99; *Barnsley's Conveyancing Law and Practice* 4th edn, p.278.

[571] See *Williams Bros v E. T. Agius Ltd* [1914] A.C. 510.

[572] *Re Scott and Alvarez's Contract (No.2)*, above, at 614.

[573] LPA 1925 s.49(2). Although the sub-section was apparently passed to deal with this situation (see Wolst. & C, i, 125), its application is not confined to it: see below, para.15–111.

[574] *Dimsdale Developments (South East) Ltd v De Haan* (1983) 47 P. & C.R. 1. Compare the New South Wales Conveyancing Act 1919 s.55(1), which not only gives a purchaser the right to recover his deposit in a case in which specific performance is refused against him, but relieves him of any liability under the contract "whether at law or in equity". See [1984] C.L.J. 134 at 169–171 (C.H.).

[575] As was the case in *Dimsdale Developments (South East) Ltd v De Haan*, above.

[576] *Edwards v Wickwar* (1865) L.R. 1 Eq. 68; *Else v Else* (1872) L.R. 13 Eq. 196; *Re Marsh and Earl Granville* (1883) 24 Ch D 11.

(ii) the court will not decree specific performance against the purchaser if to do so would expose him to a lawsuit[577]; and

(iii) the purchaser will be in breach of contract[578] and as such, will be
liable both to forfeit any deposit that he has paid[579] and to pay
damages to the vendor for his loss of bargain.

Thus the purchaser, by imprudently agreeing to accept the title in some respect
unproved, has in effect become the vendor's insurer.

15–082   (7) FREEDOM FROM INCUMBRANCES. It has already been explained that a
good title means a title free from all incumbrances except those which are
patent or are known to the purchaser at the time of contracting.[580] The term
"incumbrances" covers all subsisting third party rights such as leases,[581]
rentcharges, mortgages, easements and restrictive covenants.[582] It also
includes statutory liabilities, if they are not merely potential[583] or imposed on
property (or a particular class of property) generally.[584] Parliament has now
expressly endorsed this definition.[585] There is some doubt as to whether
statutory restrictions upon the user of property should be regarded as defects
in title. On some occasions they have been so treated, but in each case the
restriction placed the title at risk so that the property was liable either to
demolition or to compulsory purchase.[586] However, as the fitness of the
property for the purpose for which the purchaser intends it is generally a

---

[577] Above, para.15–080.

[578] *Re Scott and Alvarez's Contract (No.2)*, above, at 612. This is because an express condition
which prohibits the purchaser from raising objections (rather than merely exempting the vendor
from answering them) amounts to an agreement that he will take the whole risk of the title turning
out bad on account of the matters mentioned.

[579] Subject to the court's discretion under LPA 1925 s.49(2) to order its repayment: above.

[580] Above, para.15–069.

[581] Though see *District Bank Ltd v Webb* [1958] 1 W.L.R. 148. The meaning of "incumbrance"
can vary with the circumstances: see *Belvedere Court Management Ltd v Frogmore Developments
Ltd* [1997] Q.B. 858 at 877.

[582] It has been held that the service of a notice under a rent review clause in a lease is a defect
in title because it may lead to a permanent alteration in the rights of the lessor and lessee: *F B
Entertainment Ltd v Leisure Enterprises Ltd* [1976] 2 E.G.L.R. 76 at 79. However, the risk that
a landlord may operate a break clause in a lease is not a defect in title: *Aslan v Berkeley House
Properties Ltd* [1990] 2 E.G.L.R. 202.

[583] *Re Allen and Driscoll's Contract* [1904] 2 Ch. 226 (street paving); *Re Farrer and Gilbert's
Contract* [1914] 1 Ch. 125 (land improvement rentcharge not effective until resolution by local
authority); *Re Forsey and Hollebone's Contract* [1927] 2 Ch. 379 (resolution by local authority
to prepare a town planning scheme, held no incumbrance); and see *Manning v Turner* [1957] 1
W.L.R. 91 (potential liability to estate duty: termination held valid).

[584] Such as rates or local taxes: see, e.g. *Barraud v Archer* (1831) 9 L.J.Ch.(o.s.) 173 (liability
to drainage taxes).

[585] See LP(MP)A 1994 s.3(2), which was based upon this passage in the fifth edition of this
work at p.611; HL Paper 62 (Session 1993–94), p.28.

[586] *Sidney v Buddery* (1949) 1 P. & C.R. 34; *Sakkas v Donford* (1982) 46 P. & C.R. 46. It is
suggested that the principle was correctly stated in *Harris v Weaver* [1980] 2 N.Z.L.R 437 at 439,
where Chilwell J. observed that planning restrictions "are matters of quality not of title unless
they prevent the giving of title". cf. *James Macara Ltd v Barclay* [1945] K.B. 148 where a vendor
was in breach of his obligation to give vacant possession because the Crown had served a notice
of requisition in respect of the premises: see below, para.15–090.

matter for him, such restrictions will not usually be regarded as a defect in title.[587] It follows that it is the purchaser and not the vendor who bears the risk that they may be imposed between contract and completion.[588] It should be noted that even though a statutory restriction on user may not be a defect in title, it may sometimes prevent the vendor from giving vacant possession on completion.[589]

Because the vendor must convey the land free from incumbrances, the purchaser may refuse to complete if any incumbrance comes to light or arises which he has not agreed to accept, and which will bind him if he takes the land.[590] Although there is some authority which suggests that a statutory liability must be borne by a purchaser if it attaches to the property after the date of the contract, this seems wrong in principle.[591] If a liability would have been an incumbrance if it had arisen before the contract, the same should be true if it arises in the period between contract and completion.[592] If the vendor has made title in accordance with the contract but completion is then delayed for reasons for which he is not to blame, the purchaser may not object to the title on the ground of a defect in title that arose during the period of delay.[593]

A purchaser's concern is only with those incumbrances which are irremovable and will not be discharged on completion, such as restrictive covenants and easements. Although technically defects in title, incumbrances which are removable by the vendor as of right are regarded as "matters of conveyance" rather than matters of title and the vendor has until completion to secure their discharge.[594] Examples of matters of conveyance include:

---

[587] *Edler v Auerbach* [1950] 1 K.B. 359 at 374; *Hill v Harris* [1965] 2 Q.B. 601; *Gosling v Anderson* (1971) 220 E.G. 1117 (revs'd on appeal on other grounds: (1972) 223 E.G. 1743). The vendor may of course be liable for misrepresentation if prior to contracting he leads the purchaser to believe that the property may be used for the purpose intended when this is not the case: *Laurence v Lexourt Holdings Ltd* [1978] 1 W.L.R. 1128.

[588] *Amalgamated Investment Property Co Ltd v John Walker Sons Ltd* [1977] 1 W.L.R. 164 (building listed as being of architectural or historic interest). cf. *Aquis Estates Ltd v Minton* [1975] 1 W.L.R. 1452.

[589] See *Topfell Ltd v Galley Properties Ltd* [1979] 1 W.L.R. 446; below, para.15–090.

[590] Objection may be made to incumbrances created between contract and completion even though the purchaser could have protected himself against them by registering his estate contract, for he is under no duty to register: above, para.8–097.

[591] *Re Farrer and Gilbert's Contract* [1914] 1 Ch. 125; *Hillingdon Estates Co v Stonefield Estates Ltd* [1952] Ch. 627. In the former case the point was conceded. In the latter, the purchaser would have borne the risk of the liability for other reasons: see below. There is no doubt that a vendor will be in breach of his closely analogous obligation to give vacant possession if a statutory liability is imposed between contract and completion that precludes the giving of such possession: *Cook v Taylor* [1942] Ch. 349; *James Macara Ltd v Barclay* [1945] K.B. 148 (requisitioning notices); *Wroth v Tyler* [1974] Ch. 30 (wife's statutory rights of occupation).

[592] In practice the parties often agree that the purchaser should bear the cost of compliance with any statutory liabilities which may arise between contract and completion: see Standard Conditions of Sale 4th edn, c.3.1.4.

[593] *Hillingdon Estates Co v Stonefield Estates Ltd*, above; A. J. Oakley, *Constructive Trusts* 3rd edn, p.296.

[594] See, e.g. *Leominster Properties Ltd v Broadway Finance Ltd* (1981) 42 P. & C.R. 372 at 380.

(i) a mortgage that will be discharged on completion[595];

(ii) on the sale of settled land or land held upon a trust of land, the appointment of a co-trustee so that a valid receipt for the proceeds of sale can be given[596]; and

(iii) anomalously, on a sale of leasehold property, the obtaining of the landlord's licence to assign[597] where the terms of the lease require it.[598]

15–083   (8) WAIVER. A purchaser under an open contract is held to have waived his right to object to an incumbrance if (i) he knew that it was irremovable, and (ii) despite this, he contracted to purchase the property or took some other step inconsistent with his right to terminate the contract, such as entering into possession[599] or exercising some other right under the contract.[600]

15–084   (9) LAND CHARGES. A serious stumbling-block was created in 1927 by the decision in *Re Forsey and Hollebone's Contract*[601] that an irremovable land charge (e.g. a restrictive covenant created since 1925) or a local land charge, unknown to the purchaser but already registered at the time of the contract, had to be accepted under the above doctrine, since registration is by statute "deemed to constitute actual notice ... to all persons and for all purposes connected with the land affected".[602] This violated conveyancing principles, since the proper time for searching the register is between contract and completion[603]; and in any case, as regards land charges, the purchaser could not usually make a full search before contract since he would not then know

---

[595] *Leominster Properties Ltd v Broadway Finance Ltd*, above. Similarly, the concurrence of a mortgagee to a sale where the mortgage is immediately redeemable is a matter of conveyance: *Re Priestley's Contract* [1947] Ch. 469 at 477.

[596] *Hatten v Russell* (1888) 38 Ch D 334.

[597] For the covenant against assigning without the landlord's consent, see below, para.19–093.

[598] *Ellis v Rogers* (1885) 29 Ch D 661. To treat the obtaining of the licence to assign as a matter of conveyance is anomalous because the vendor cannot compel the landlord to assent to the assignment. The reason for the anomaly is a practical one. Until the tenant contracts to assign, the landlord may not know the identity of the assignee and is not therefore in a position to give or withhold his consent. In practice a contract to sell a lease that is subject to this requirement is normally made conditional upon the obtaining of the landlord's consent: see above, para.15–008.

[599] *Re Gloag and Miller's Contract* (1883) 23 Ch D 320 at 327 (where a distinction is drawn between this situation and the case where the vendor expressly contracts to give a good title free from incumbrances, or where the objection to title is removable); *Ellis v Rogers* (1888) 29 Ch D 661; *McGrory v Aldersdale Estates Co* [1918] A.C. 503; *Ezekial v Kohali* [2009] EWCA Civ 35. As to the question, raised but left unresolved in *Ellis v Rogers* (1888) 29 Ch D 661 at 671, whether the right to a good title is founded on contract or on the general law, see above, para.15–001.

[600] *Aquis Estates Ltd v Minton* [1975] 1 W.L.R. 1452.

[601] [1927] 2 Ch. 379 (Eve J.).

[602] LPA 1925, s.198(1). For notice by registration, see above, para.8–085.

[603] See *Re White and Smith's Contract* [1896] 1 Ch. 637. Until contracts have been exchanged, the purchaser has of course no right to see the vendor's title, though in practice he is usually permitted to do so.

the names of previous owners on the title.[604] Nor did the decision appear to be right in law, since willingness to waive objection to the incumbrance could hardly be imputed to a purchaser who had no knowledge of it at all. Indeed this equation of a statutory form of notice with the knowledge required for waiver has been described as "deeply suspect",[605] because it was not the purpose of the statutory notice to affect the relationship between vendors and purchasers but to protect third party rights.[606] The decision led to an inconvenient change in conveyancing practice by which purchasers were (in effect) compelled to investigate title prior to the exchange of contracts, something that was impracticable in cases of sales by auction.[607] Fortunately two developments have occurred which have restored the law to what it was thought to be before 1927. First, the Law of Property Act 1969 removed the difficulty as regards land charges (but not local land charges).[608] Any question of the purchaser's knowledge of a registered land charge is to be determined by reference to his actual knowledge[609] and without regard to the statutory "deemed" notice. Furthermore, any stipulation to the contrary, or which restricts the purchaser's remedies in respect of such a charge is void.[610] Secondly, *Re Forsey and Hollebone's Contract*[611] has probably now received its quietus as a result of a subsequent case concerned with local land charges.[612] The earlier decision was doubted and its reasoning was criticised on the grounds set out in this paragraph.[613] A purchaser will probably now take subject to a local land charge which amounts to a defect in title only when he actually knows of it at the time of contracting.

(10) EXPRESS TERMS. It is only where the contract is open as to the title that waiver can be implied from the making of the contract. If the vendor expressly contracts to show, for example, "a valid title"[614] or "a good marketable title",[615] he must carry out his promise and show a title entirely free from incumbrances. Even if the property is subject to an irremovable incumbrance which is patent or of which the purchaser knows, he is entitled to insist that

15–085

---

[604] For these and other difficulties occasioned by the decision, see *Rignall Developments Ltd v Halil* [1988] Ch. 190 at 201.

[605] *Rignall Developments Ltd v Halil*, above, at 201, per Millett J.

[606] *Rignall Developments Ltd v Halil*, above, at 202.

[607] *Rignall Developments Ltd v Halil*, above, at 201.

[608] s.24, which applies to contracts for the sale of unregistered land made after 1969. This reform was recommended by the Committee on Land Charges (1956) Cmd. 9825. For a fuller discussion, see [1954] C.L.J. 89 (H.W.R.W.); and contrast *Coles v White City (Manchester) Greyhound Association Ltd* (1928) 45 T.L.R. 125, 230, noted above, para.8–085, fn.344.

[609] Or that of his counsel, solicitor or other agent: s.24(4).

[610] s.24(2).

[611] [1927] 2 Ch. 379.

[612] *Rignall Developments Ltd v Halil*, above; [1987] Conv. 291 (C.H.). The charge was a potential liability to repay an improvement grant. For local land charges, see above, para.8–107.

[613] Millett J. chose to distinguish *Re Forsey and Hollebone's Contract* on its facts rather than refuse to follow it: [1988] Ch. 190 at 202, 203.

[614] *Re Gloag and Miller's Contract* (1883) 23 Ch D 320.

[615] *Cato v Thompson* (1882) 9 Q.B.D. 616.

the vendor should show a good title.[616] The vendor is in such circumstances obliged to find some means of removing the incumbrance by the completion date, e.g. by securing its release. But if, having discovered irremovable incumbrances, he takes some step indicating a desire to proceed (such as going into possession of the property or exercising some right conferred by the contract) without reserving his rights as to the title, this may amount to a waiver even of an express promise of a clear title.[617] The essence of the matter is that no waiver can be implied merely from the purchaser's entering into the contract if that is inconsistent with the express terms of the contract.[618]

Here again, it was held that the rule was different where the incumbrance was registered as a land charge or local land charge, and that even a sale "free from incumbrances" was made subject to incumbrances deemed to be known to the purchaser because of registration prior to the contract.[619] As explained above, this pitfall has now been removed by statute as regards land charges[620] and (probably) by judicial decision in relation to local land charges.[621]

(c) Registered title

15–086   (1) PROOF OF TITLE. Where, as is usually now the case, title is registered, the register of title is itself proof of title to the land and of all the incumbrances that affect that registered title other than overriding interests.[622] Under the Land Registration Act 2002 there are no prescriptive rules as to how a vendor must prove and/or perfect his title to registered land, although there is a power to make such rules, which has not been exercised.[623] The fundamental changes in the law and practice of registered conveyancing since the 1925 Act was enacted make prescriptive rules unnecessary.[624] The register is an open public document that can be inspected by anybody.[625] An official search which gives priority protection can be made quickly and cheaply either on-line or by post.[626] The proof of title that a purchaser may require is therefore a matter for agreement between him and the vendor.[627] Even though a vendor may produce copies of the register and any documents referred to in it to prove his title, a purchaser will invariably conduct his own official search

---

[616] *Re Gloag and Miller's Contract*, above, at 613; *McGrory v Alderdale Estate Co Ltd* [1918] A.C. 503 at 508.

[617] *Re Gloag and Miller's Contract*, above; *Aquis Estates Ltd v Minton* [1975] 1 W.L.R. 1452.

[618] *Re Gloag and Miller's Contract*, above, at 327.

[619] *Re Forsey and Hollebone's Contract* [1927] 2 Ch. 379 at 387. See [1954] C.L.J. 89, 102, 103 (H.W.R.W.)

[620] LPA 1969 s.24.

[621] *Rignall Developments Ltd v Halil* [1988] Ch. 190; above, para.15–084.

[622] See above, para.7–148.

[623] LRA 2002 Sch.10, para.2(1).

[624] See (2001) Law Com. No.271, paras 12.7, 12.8.

[625] See above, paras 7–002, 7–120.

[626] See above, paras 7–124 et seq.

[627] By Standard Conditions of Sale 4th edn, c.4.1.1, the evidence of title that must be provided by a vendor includes an official copy of the register and title plan and any document referred to in the register and kept by the registrar. In relation to residential property, the register and title plan must be included in a vendor's home information pack (above, para.15–069).

with priority before completion both to ensure that there are no new entries and to protect the priority of his purchase.[628]

(2) WHERE GROUNDS FOR ALTERATION OF THE REGISTER EXIST. In the usual case where a vendor is registered with absolute title, there is no root of title and therefore no possibility of defects anterior to the root. Accordingly, the provisions of the Law of Property Act 1925 which restrict inquiries and objections to matters lying behind the root of title[629] cannot apply.[630] One feature of registered title which has no equivalent in unregistered conveyancing is the possibility that the court or registrar may alter the register.[631] As regards proof of title, it is only those alterations that amount to rectification of the register that will concern a purchaser, in other words, where grounds exist for altering the register to correct a mistake, where that alteration would prejudicially affect the title of a registered proprietor.[632] The power to rectify the register is discretionary.[633] If a ground for rectification exists,[634] it must therefore make the title doubtful rather than positively bad because there can be no certainty that rectification will be ordered.[635] Such a title could not therefore be forced on a purchaser in the absence of full disclosure prior to contract of the matter in respect of which rectification might lie, unless it was insubstantial.

There may be certain circumstances, in which a third party has a right to be registered as proprietor, as where a squatter can demonstrate that he barred the title of the registered proprietor before the Land Registration Act 2002 came into force, and is therefore entitled to be registered as proprietor.[636] Where such circumstances exist the title will necessarily be bad.

15–087

(3) NOTICES AND LOCAL LAND CHARGES. The Land Registration Act 2002 contains no provision analogous to that found in the Law of Property Act 1925 in relation to the registration of land charges in unregistered land,[637] by which the protection of an interest in registered land by means of an agreed or unilateral notice constitutes notice to all persons for all purposes. Where an interest is protected by a notice, registration protects its priority, if valid.[638] There is therefore no prospect that a purchaser of registered land will be taken to contract with knowledge of an interest merely because it is protected by means of a notice.

15–088

---

[628] See above, paras 7–124 et seq.

[629] Above, para.15–080.

[630] LPA 1925 s.45(1) refers to the title "before the time prescribed by law": see [1992] C.L.J. 263 at 303 (C.H.).

[631] Above, paras 7–132 et seq.

[632] See LRA 2002 Sch.4 para.1; above, para.7–132.

[633] See LRA 2002 Sch.4 paras 2(1), 5.

[634] Above, paras 7–135, 7–138.

[635] In cases in which rectification is ordered, an indemnity will be payable to the proprietor if he suffers loss in consequence unless his claim is barred by lapse of time: see above, paras 7–140 et seq.

[636] LRA 2002 Sch.12 para.18(1); below, para.35–095.

[637] s.198; above, paras 8 085, 15 084.

[638] LRA 2002 s.32(3).

Local land charges take effect as overriding interests in registered land.[639] The registration of such a charge in the local land charges register therefore constitutes actual notice to all persons for all purposes under the provisions of the Law of Property Act 1925[640] whether the title is registered or unregistered. However, the erroneous nature of the decision in *Re Forsey and Hollebone's Contract*[641] has now been made plain[642] and it is unlikely that it will be followed. A purchaser of registered land will therefore be entitled to object to any local land charge constituting a defect in title which has not been disclosed prior to contract.

D. The Vendor must give Vacant Possession on Completion

15–089	(a) *The obligation.* Under an open contract, a vendor impliedly contracts to give vacant possession on completion.[643] This implication will be rebutted:

(i) by an express stipulation to the contrary[644]; or

(ii) if at the time of contracting, the property was subject to some irremovable incumbrance or other impediment to vacant possession which was either known to the purchaser or patent.[645]

The purchaser's knowledge of a removable impediment to vacant possession is irrelevant.[646] It is usual for the parties to provide expressly that vacant possession shall be given on completion (if that is to be the case).[647] Such an express provision will prevail even if, to the purchaser's knowledge, the property is not vacant at the time of contract and the impediment is an irremovable incumbrance.[648] It will be apparent that the obligation to give vacant possession is closely analogous to the vendor's obligation to convey

---

[639] LRA 2002 Sch.1 para.6; Sch.3 para.6; above, paras 7–030, 7–087.

[640] s.198. For local land charges, see above, para.8–107.

[641] [1927] 2 Ch. 379; above, para.15–084.

[642] *Rignall Developments Ltd v Halil* [1988] Ch. 190; above, para.15–084.

[643] *Cook v Taylor* [1942] 2 All E.R. 85 at 87 (a better report than [1942] Ch. 349); *Midland Bank Ltd v Farmpride Hatcheries Ltd* [1981] 2 E.G.L.R. 147 at 151. See generally [1988] Conv. 324, 400 (C.H.); [1991] Conv. 185 at 188 (D. G. Barnsley); K. Shaw, *Vacant Possession: Law and Practice* (Estates Gazette, 2010).

[644] *Midland Bank Ltd v Farmpride Hatcheries Ltd*, above at 151. cf. *Re Crosby's Contract* [1949] 1 All E.R. 830 (grant of option on terms that the grantee would accept "without objection" the vendor's title, held not to enable grantor to grant a lease prior to the exercise of the grant).

[645] *Cook v Taylor*, above, at 87. See too *Timmins v Moreland Street Property Co Ltd* [1958] Ch. 110 at 118, 119. cf. *Farrell v Green* (1974) 232 E.G. 587 at 589 (which was decided *per incuriam* on this point).

[646] Were it otherwise, a vendor could with impunity leave his chattels on the premises after completion, which he cannot do: see *Cumberland Consolidated Holdings Ltd v Ireland* [1946] K.B. 264 at 270.

[647] See Standard Conditions of Sale 4th edn, Special Condition 4.

[648] *Hissett v Reading Roofing Co Ltd* [1969] 1 W.L.R. 1757; *Sharneyford Supplies Ltd v Edge* [1987] Ch. 305 (lease of maggot farm). *A fortiori* where the impediment to vacant possession is removable: *Cumberland Consolidated Holdings Ltd v Ireland* [1946] K.B. 264.

the land free from incumbrances and is subject to similar rules,[649] and in particular, those which govern the extent to which it can be modified by conditions of sale.[650]

(b) The substance of the obligation. The meaning of "vacant possession" **15–090** can vary according to the context.[651] It has been said that the vendor will be in breach of this obligation in two situations[652]:

(i) The first is where the vendor leaves his own property on the premises, because he thereby claims a right to use the premises for his own purposes. This involves a continuing form of activity on the premises by the vendor.[653]

(ii) The second is where there is a physical impediment which substantially prevents a purchaser from obtaining the quality of possession for which he had contracted will constitute a breach of the obligation.[654] This latter obligation will be broken where, for example:

(a) The vendor leaves substantial amounts rubbish on the premises[655];

(b) There remain on the premises persons who are lawfully in possession, such as tenants or licensees[656] (but not those whose rights are less extensive, such as those who merely have a profit à prendre over the land[657]).

However, those two situations are not exhaustive. A vendor will also be in breach of his obligation to give vacant possession by reason of:

---

[649] See [1988] Conv. 324 at 331 (C.H.).

[650] See [1988] Conv. 400 (C.H.) where the authorities are discussed.

[651] *Topfell Ltd v Galley Properties Ltd* [1979] 1 W.L.R. 446 at 449.

[652] See *Cumberland Consolidated Holdings Ltd v Ireland* [1946] K.B. 264 at 270, 271; *Legal & General Assurance Society Ltd v Expeditors International (UK) Ltd* [2006] EWHC 1008 (Ch) at [36]–[41]; [2007] 1 P. & C.R. 103 at 111; *Ibrend Estates BV v NYK Logistics (UK) Ltd* [2011] EWCA Civ 683 at [42]; [2011] 36 E.G. 94 at 99.

[653] *Cumberland Consolidated Holdings Ltd v Ireland* [1946] K.B. 264 at 270; *Legal & General Assurance Society Ltd v Expeditors International (UK) Ltd* [2006] EWHC 1008 (Ch) at [36], [41]; [2007] 1 P. & C.R. 103 at 111, 112; *Ibrend Estates BV v NYK Logistics (UK) Ltd* [2011] EWCA Civ 683 at [42]; [2011] 36 E.G. 94 at 99.

[654] See *Cumberland Consolidated Holdings Ltd v Ireland* [1946] K.B. 264 at 271; *Korogluyan v Matheou* (1975) 30 P. & C.R. 309 at 316; *Legal & General Assurance Society Ltd v Expeditors International (UK) Ltd* [2006] EWHC 1008 (Ch) at [37], [42]; [2007] 1 P. & C.R. 103 at 111, 112.

[655] *Cumberland Consolidated Holdings Ltd v Ireland*, above (large quantities of rubbish including solidified cement bags left on the premises). cf. *Hynes v Vaughan* (1985) 50 P. & C.R. 444 (suggesting that outdoor rubbish may be different).

[656] *Beard v Porter* [1948] 1 K.B. 321; *Sharneyford Supplies Ltd v Edge*, above.

[657] *Horton v Kurzke* [1971] 1 W.L.R. 769 (agricultural grazing tenancy). In such circumstances the vendor may be in breach of his obligations to show a good title.

(iii) The presence on the premises of trespassers, for although the contrary has been held,[658] the better view is that it is the duty of the vendor to evict them[659]; and

(iv) Legal impediments to the enjoyment of the property such as a notice to requisition the land,[660] an order restricting the number of persons who can occupy the land,[661] or a notice to enter served as part of the process of compulsory acquisition by a local authority.[662]

Because the vendor's obligation to give vacant possession necessarily arises at the time for completion, it can be broken by a matter that arises at any time before that date whether before or after the parties contracted.[663]

15–091   *(c) Remedies.* The position of a vendor who is in breach of his obligation to give vacant possession is as follows.

(i) He will be unable to obtain specific performance of the contract of sale against the purchaser.[664] However he may have the contract specifically enforced against him by the purchaser, and have to pay compensation for the impediment to vacant possession.[665]

(ii) The purchaser may refuse to complete and may both recover any deposit that he has paid[666] and sue the vendor for damages for the loss of his bargain.[667]

(iii) If the purchaser does complete even though vacant possession is not given, he may recover as damages the sum necessary to place him in the position in which he would have been had the contract

[658] *Sheikh v O'Connor* [1987] 2 E.G.L.R. 269 (*obiter*); criticised [1988] Conv. 324 (C.H.); [1991] Conv. 185, 191, 192 (D. G. Barnsley).

[659] *Herkanaidu v Lambeth LBC* [1999] P.L.S.C.S. 291; *Cumberland Consolidated Holdings Ltd v Ireland*, above, at 271 (*obiter*).

[660] See *Cook v Taylor* [1942] 2 All E.R. 85; *James Macara Ltd v Barclay* [1945] K.B. 148 (which must be taken to have overruled *Re Winslow Hall Estates Co and United Glass Bottle Manufacturers Ltd's Contract* [1941] Ch. 503, the facts of which were identical).

[661] *Topfell Ltd v Galley Properties Ltd* [1979] 1 W.L.R. 446.

[662] *Korogluyan v Matheou* (1975) 30 P. & C.R. 309. By contrast, where the notice served as part of the process of compulsory purchase does not confer on the acquiring authority an immediate right to possession, the vendor will still be able to give vacant possession: see *Hillingdon Estates Co v Stonefield Estates Ltd* [1952] Ch. 627 at 633 (a mere notice to treat made by a local authority under its compulsory purchase powers); *E. Johnson Co (Barbados) Ltd v N.S.R. Ltd* [1997] A.C. 400 (notice of intended compulsory purchase which did not give the Crown a right to immediate possession).

[663] For cases in which the impediment to vacant possession arose between contract and completion, see *Cook v Taylor* [1942] 2 All E.R. 85; *James Macara Ltd v Barclay*, above; *Wroth v Tyler* [1974] Ch. 30.

[664] *Cook v Taylor* [1942] 2 All E.R. 85.

[665] *Topfell Ltd v Galley Properties Ltd* [1979] 1 W.L.R. 446. For specific performance with compensation, see below, para.15–118.

[666] *Cook v Taylor*, above.

[667] *Engell v Fitch* (1869) L.R. 4 Q.B. 659; *Sharneyford Supplies Ltd v Edge* [1987] Ch. 305.

been performed. Where the impediment to vacant possession is irremovable (as where the property is let to a tenant), the measure will be the difference between the purchase price and the market price of the property subject to the impediment, plus any consequential loss.[668] Where it is possible to remove the impediment, the purchaser may recover the cost of so doing.[669]

(iv) The obligation to give vacant possession remains actionable after completion and does not merge in the conveyance.[669a] However, although the purchaser can sue the vendor for damages for breach of contract, he cannot terminate the contract and have the conveyance set aside.[670]

E. Stipulations as to Time

1. The general rule

(a) The position prior to the Judicature Act 1873. At common law, time was **15–092** "of the essence of the contract".[671] If either party failed to complete on time, he was in breach and the other party could treat the contract as terminated. But in equity the position was different.[672] Although it had once been held that time could *never* be of the essence in equity,[673] this view did not prevail.[674] It came to be recognised that time might be of the essence of a contract in equity "by express stipulation between the parties,[675] by the nature of the property,[676] or by surrounding circumstances, showing the intention of the parties that the contract was to be completed within a limited time".[677] Mere delay in completion did not bar a suit for specific performance in the absence of laches,[678] unless a notice was served on the party in delay requiring him to complete within a reasonable time.[679] However, it was only in connection with specific performance that this indulgence was shown, and it did not deprive

---

[668] *Beard v Porter* [1948] 1 K.B. 321 (costs arising from purchase of another property held recoverable).

[669] *Cumberland Consolidated Holdings Ltd v Ireland* [1946] K.B. 264 (cost of removing rubbish recoverable).

[669a] See below, para.15–100.

[670] *Howard-Jones v Tate* [2011] EWCA Civ 1330, not following *Gunatunga v De Alwis* (1995) 72 P. & C.R. 161.

[671] See, e.g. *Beamish v Owens* (1846) 7 L.T.O.S. 187; *Parkin v Thorold* (1852) 16 Beav 59 at 65.

[672] For the history see *Equity and Contemporary Legal Developments* (ed. S. Goldstein), 829 at 860 (C.H.); [1992] Conv. 318 at 324 (C.H.).

[673] *Gregson v Riddle* (1784) Unreported: see *Seton v Slade* (1802) 7 Ves. 265 at 268.

[674] See *Lloyd v Collett* (1793) 4 Ves. 689.

[675] *Seton v Slade* (1802) 7 Ves. 265 at 270; *Levy v Lindo* (1817) 3 Mer. 81 at 84.

[676] Because it was of a wasting or fluctuating character: *Hudson v Temple* (1860) 30 L.J.Ch. 251 (sale of 24-year residue of lease); *XEY S.A. v Abbey Life Assurance Co Ltd* (1994) 69 P. & C.R. D5 (contract to grant six-year underlease); *Newman v Rogers* (1793) 4 Bro. C.C. 391 (sale of reversion); *Machbryde v Weeks* (1856) 22 Beav 533 (sale of lease of mines and minerals).

[677] *Roberts v Berry* (1853) 3 De G.M. G. 284 at 291, per Turner L.J.

[678] *Harrington v Wheeler* (1799) 4 Ves. 686.

[679] See *Taylor v Brown* (1839) 2 Beav 180; *Wells v Maxwell* (1863) 8 L.T. 713 at 714.

the other party of his right to claim damages for any loss occasioned by the breach.[680] Even in equity, a court might decree specific performance with compensation for loss caused by the defendant's delay.[681]

15–093 *(b) The effect of the Judicature Act 1873.* Since the Judicature Act 1873, the equitable doctrine has prevailed:

> "Stipulations in a contract, as to time or otherwise, which according to the rules of equity are not deemed to be or to have become of the essence of the contract, are also construed and have effect at law in accordance with the same rules."[682]

In the period following the Act, this provision was taken to mean that a party could not terminate a contract on the ground of delay in performance in circumstances where equity would before the Act have decreed specific performance.[683] However, it is now clear that this provision "places no ban upon further development of the rules by judicial decision".[684] In contracts for the sale of land, it remains the case that time will not be of the essence except in the circumstances outlined below.

If a vendor or purchaser fails to complete on the due date[685] he will still be in breach of contract even though time is not of the essence. The other party may therefore recover damages for any loss which he has suffered.[686] Thus, where the purchaser needed the property for professional purposes, and her practice was injured by the vendor's delay in completion, she recovered damages for this and other expenses.[687] In another case, the sales of one house by A to B and of another by B to C were due for completion on the same day. A failed to complete, causing B to default. C recovered the cost of this temporary accommodation as damages from B.[688]

---

[680] A court of equity would if need be issue a common injunction restraining proceedings at law. Prior to the Judicature Act 1873, there does not in fact appear to have been any reported example of a claim at law for damages for delay by a plaintiff against whom the defendant had obtained a decree of specific performance in Chancery.

[681] *Gedye v Duke of Montrose* (1858) 26 Beav 45.

[682] LPA 1925 s.41, replacing JA 1873 s.25(7).

[683] *Stickney v Keeble* [1915] A.C. 386 at 417.

[684] *United Scientific Holdings Ltd v Burnley BC* [1978] A.C. 904 at 927, per Lord Diplock.

[685] Where the contract is silent as to the completion date, "the law implies that completion is to take place within a reasonable time" having regard to the conveyancing steps that have to be carried out: *Johnson v Humphrey* (1946) 174 L.T. 324 at 326, per Roxburgh J; *Chaitlal v Ramlal* [2003] UKPC 12 at [22]; [2004] 1 P. & C.R. 1 at 9 (sub nom *Ramlal v Chaitlal*). This is so, even where the parties have left the date for future agreement: *Walters v Roberts* (1980) 41 P. & C.R. 210 at 216.

[686] *Raineri v Miles* [1981] A.C. 1050, approving (at 1084, 1094) the statement in the fourth edition of this book that "whether time is of the essence or not, a party who is actually injured by breach of a time stipulation can recover damages". The Standard Conditions of Sale 4th edn make provision for compensation for delay in completion caused by a default: c. 7.3. In this context, "default" means in breach of contract: *Anglo Continental Educational Group (GB) Ltd v ASN Capital Investments Ltd* [2010] EWHC 2649 (Ch) at [57]. Query whether this condition may be invalid as a penalty: cf. *Newbery v Turngiant Ltd* (1991) 63 P. & C.R 458.

[687] *Phillips v Lamdin* [1949] 2 K.B. 33.

[688] *Raineri v Miles*, above (B also recovered from A).

(c) Where time is of the essence. However, time will be regarded as the **15–094** essence in a number of circumstances. Where this is the case, the consequences of failure to perform the obligation on time will depend upon the nature of the term broken.[689] In the case where there is a failure to complete a contract for the sale of land, the party not in default may treat the contract as terminated and sue the other for damages.[690]

(1) EXPRESS PROVISION. Time will be of the essence in relation to a partic- **15–095** ular term[691] where a contractual provision makes it so expressly,[692] or where the term is a condition, as where a deposit must be paid by a particular date.[692a] Time is not normally of the essence for the completion of contracts for the sale of land under the general conditions of sale in ordinary use.[693] However, it is usual to provide in the contract that time may be made of the essence unilaterally if one party fails to complete on time by service upon him thereafter of a notice to complete.[694] No particular form is required for such a notice, but it must inform the recipient clearly and unambiguously of what he is required to do to fulfil his contractual obligations.[695] The notice once served is binding on both parties and if the party serving it is himself unable to complete on the date specified in the notice, the recipient may treat the

---

[689] See *Re Olympia York Canary Wharf Ltd (No.2)* [1993] B.C.C. 159 at 173.

[690] See, e.g. *Harold Wood Brick Co Ltd v Ferris* [1935] 2 K.B. 198; *Etzin v Reece* [2003] 1 P. & C.R. D16. In such a case, the court will not decree specific performance at the behest of the party in breach even if the delay is very slight: see *Union Eagle Ltd v Golden Achievement Ltd* [1997] A.C. 514; below, para.15–114.

[691] "There is . . . no general concept that time is of the essence of a contract as a whole: the question is whether time is of the essence of a particular term in question": *British and Commonwealth Holdings Plc v Quadrex Holdings Ltd* [1989] Q.B. 842 at 856, per Browne-Wilkinson V.C.

[692] Equivocal phrases such as "on or about" or "on or before" a certain date will probably not make time of the essence: see *Lock v Bell* [1931] 1 Ch. 35 (where time was of the essence for other reasons, but where the use of that phrase provided a "little latitude"); *James Macara Ltd v Barclay* [1945] K.B. 148 at 156.

[692a] *Samarenko v Dawn Hill House Ltd* [2011] EWCA Civ 1445.

[693] See the Standard Conditions of Sale 4th edn, c.6.1.1. It is of the essence for certain intermediate obligations, such as the raising of requisitions: see c.4.2.3.

[694] Standard Conditions of Sale 4th edn, c. 6.8. Under this condition, the party who receives the notice can be required to complete within 10 working days: c. 6.8.2. The party serving the notice may specify a longer period than the condition allows: *Delta Vale Properties Ltd v Mills* [1990] 1 W.L.R. 445. However, if he specifies a shorter period, he may himself commit a repudiatory breach of contract if he purports to terminate the contract at the end of it: *Rightside Properties Ltd v Gray* [1975] Ch. 72. Under some conditions of sale (though not under the Standard Conditions of Sale), the express provision will have a saving for any other rights and remedies that the aggrieved party might have. In those circumstances, a notice that does not comply with the terms of the condition of sale may sometimes be valid under the general law, if the period which is specifies is reasonable: see *Dimsdale Developments (South East) Ltd v De Haan* (1983) 47 P. & C.R. 1 at 10, as explained in *Country and Metropolitan Homes Surrey Ltd v Topclaim Ltd* [1996] Ch. 307 at 314, 315. See further below, para.15–098.

[695] *Delta Vale Properties Ltd v Mills*, above, at 452. Express provisions providing for notices to complete "are just as subject to the notices to the law about waiver and estoppel as any other contractual provisions": *Munro v Premier Associates Ltd* (2000) 80 P. & C.R. 439 at 446, per Park J. In that case, the purchaser, by its conduct, waived the requirement that the completion date should have passed before a notice to complete could be served.

contract as at an end.[696] It is usually provided that such a notice to complete can be served only if the server is himself "ready able and willing to complete" the contract.[697] There is a considerable (if not always consistent) body of authority as to when a party is or is not in such a position.[698] No notice can be served after specific performance has been decreed because the carrying out of the contract has by then become a matter for the court.[699]

The conditions of sale usually make express provision as to the remedies for failure to comply with a notice to complete.[700] Typically, these will involve the right to terminate the contract, to forfeit (or recover) any deposit, and to recover damages.

15–096   (2) SUBJECT-MATTER OF THE CONTRACT. Time may be of the essence of a contract because the nature of the subject-matter of the contract requires it. This will be the case for example on the sale of a wasting asset such as a leasehold,[701] or of a business such as a public-house sold as a going concern.[702] Although it has been held that time is of the essence in a contract for the sale of a house required for immediate occupation,[703] this view might not

---

[696] *Quadrangle Development and Construction Co Ltd v Jenner* [1974] 1 W.L.R. 68. cf. *Oakdown Ltd v Bernstein Co* (1984) 49 P. & C.R. 282 at 295. Although a vendor who serves a notice to complete must remain ready, able and willing to complete throughout the notice period, he is entitled to a sufficient period to set up the necessary administrative arrangements for completion. He is not required, throughout that period, to "remain posed to complete at a moment's notice in case the purchaser should suddenly turn up armed with the completion money and calling for completion": *Aero Properties Ltd v Citycrest Properties Ltd* [2002] 2 P. & C.R. 305 at 310, 311, per Blackburne J. See too *Midill (97PL) Ltd v Park Lane Estates Ltd* [2008] EWCA Civ 1227 at [25]; [2009] 1 W.L.R. 2460 at 2467.

[697] See Standard Conditions of Sale 4th edn, c.6.8.1.

[698] A party will be "ready able and willing" even though he has sent an inaccurate completion statement (*Carne v Debono* [1988] 1 W.L.R. 1107), has failed to produce a vacating receipt in respect of a discharged mortgage (*Edwards v Marshall-Lee* [1975] 2 E.G.L.R. 149), is in breach of his obligations as vendor to take reasonable care of the property (*Prosper Homes Ltd v Hambros Bank Executor Trustee Co Ltd* (1979) 39 P. & C.R. 395), being a leaseholder is a defendant to forfeiture proceedings which, as a matter of law were bound to fail (*Lambeth LBC v Vincent* [2000] 2 E.G.L.R. 73), or has substantially misdescribed the land to be sold (*Bechal v Kitsford Holdings Ltd* [1989] 1 W.L.R. 105; *sed quaere*), but not where he has failed either to deduce a good title or otherwise satisfied the purchaser as to hi title (*Horton v Kurzke* [1971] 1 W.L.R. 769 at 772; *Walia v Michael Naughton Ltd* [1985] 1 W.L.R. 1115; *Chaitlal v Ramlal* [2003] UKPC 12; [2004] 1 P. & C.R. 1), or failed to disclose a latent defect in title (*Pagebar Properties Ltd v Derby Investment Holdings Ltd* [1972] 1 W.L.R. 1500), or is unable to give vacant possession (*Eagleview Ltd v Worthgate Ltd* [1998] E.G.C.S. 119, but see to the contrary *Herkanaidu v Lambeth LBC* [1999] P.L.S.C.S. 291). See too *Clowes Developments (UK) Ltd v Mulchinock* [1998] 1 W.L.R. 42 (the validity of a notice to complete served by a developer who was alleged not to have complied with its obligations to construct roads on the estate, raised a serious issue to be tried).

[699] *Singh v Nazeer* [1979] Ch. 474; *Ahmed v Wingrove (No.2)* [2007] EWHC 1777 (Ch) at [10].

[700] See Standard Conditions of Sale 4th edn, cc.7.5 (seller's remedies); 7.6 (buyer's remedies).

[701] See, e.g. *Pips (Leisure Productions) Ltd v Walton* (1980) 43 P. & C.R. 415 (15 years to run).

[702] *Day v Luhke* (1868) L.R. 5 Eq. 336; *Lock v Bell* [1931] 1 Ch. 35. In *Coslake v Till* (1826) 1 Russ. 376, a delay of one day was held a breach.

[703] *Tilley v Thomas* (1867) 3 Ch.App. 61 at 67.

now be followed.[704] In any event, the general conditions of sale will often negative the inference that time is of the essence.[705]

(3) UNILATERAL AND CONDITIONAL CONTRACTS. Time is of the essence where **15–097** a contract is unilateral, such as an option, under which it rests with one party to take action by a certain date if the other party is to be placed under an obligation.[706] Similarly time is of the essence where a contract is made conditional upon some act being done by a fixed date, or within a reasonable time.[707]

Where a contract of sale comes about when an option is exercised, the position is the same as any other contract to buy and sell land,[708] so that time will not normally be of the essence.[709]

(4) UNREASONABLE DELAY. It remains the case that, where one party has **15–098** unreasonably delayed either in completing the contract or in performing some intermediate obligation under it,[710] the other party may terminate the contract if the breach goes to the root of the contract.[711] However, the innocent party may do this only if he has first served on the party in delay a notice specifying a reasonable period for the performance of the obligation.[712] This is because in the absence of laches a notice to complete is required to bar a claim to specific performance.[713] However it is not apparent why if a delay in performance of a contractual obligation is a breach of contract,[714] an unreasonable delay should not be regarded as a repudiatory breach.[715] A notice to complete can be served as soon as one party fails to perform the obligation on time.[716] It is not necessary to wait until the delay is unreasonable.[717] The period specified must however be reasonable, but this is judged by reference to all the

[704] *Smith v Hamilton* [1951] Ch. 174 at 179. See [1980] Conv. 238 (J. T. Farrand); *Barnsley's Conveyancing Law and Practice* 4th edn, p.424. cf. *Raineri v Miles* [1981] A.C. 1050 at 1082.
[705] See Standard Conditions of Sale 4th edn, c.6.1.1.
[706] *Finch v Underwood* (1876) 2 Ch D 310; *United Scientific Holdings Ltd v Burnley BC* [1978] A.C. 904 at 928, 945; *Di Luca v Juraise (Springs) Ltd* [1998] 2 E.G.L.R. 125. See too *Chiltern Court (Baker Street) Residents Ltd v Wallabrook Property Co Ltd* [1989] 2 E.G.L.R. 207 at 208.
[707] *Aberfoyle Plantations Ltd v Cheng* [1960] A.C. 115. For conditional contracts, see above, para.15–009.
[708] Above, para.15–092.
[709] *Ahmed v Wingrove (No.2)* [2007] EWHC 1777 (Ch) at [9].
[710] See *Behzadi v Shaftesbury Hotels Ltd* [1992] Ch. 1 (notice to vendor to deduce title).
[711] *United Scientific Holdings Ltd v Burnley BC* [1978] A.C. 904 at 946.
[712] *Graham v Pitkin* [1992] 1 W.L.R. 403 at 406. For the view that the case was decided *per incuriam* and is contrary to *Howe v Smith* (1884) 27 Ch D 89: [1994] Conv. 342; [1995] Conv. 84 (D.G. Barnsley). *Sed quaere*: see [1995] Conv. 83 (C.H.).
[713] *Graham v Pitkin*, above, at 406.
[714] *Raineri v Miles* [1981] A.C. 1050; above, para.15–093.
[715] See [1992] Conv. 318 (C.H.). cf. *United Scientific Holdings Ltd v Burnley BC*, above, at 945.
[716] *Behzadi v Shaftesbury Hotels Ltd* [1992] Ch. 1. For the view that a notice to complete can be served even *before* there has been a breach of contract, see *Bernard v Williams* (1928) 139 L.T. 22 at 25; *Phillips v Lamdin* [1949] 2 K.B. 33 at 42; [1978] Conv. 144 at 157 (C. T. Emery).
[717] *Behzadi v Shaftesbury Hotels Ltd*, above, overruling *Smith v Hamilton* [1951] Ch. 174.

circumstances.[718] If it is plain that the party in default will not complete, that period may be very short.[719]

F. Discharge of the Contract

15–099   **1. Completion.** The vendor's fundamental obligation under the contract is to convey the land, whether freehold or leasehold,[720] to the purchaser or, unless the contract otherwise provides, at the purchaser's direction.[721] The principal obligations of both parties are discharged at completion.[722] Where title is unregistered completion takes place when the title has been accepted, the conveyance executed and delivered and the purchase-money paid.[723] Where title is registered, completion probably takes place on "payment of the price against delivery of the executed transfer"[724] rather than when that transfer is registered.[725] Should any defect in title arise after completion, the purchaser must rely on the covenants for title which are implied by the conveyance or when a transfer is registered.[726] These have already been explained.[727]

A purchaser, however, may have a conveyance set aside on grounds of fraud,[728] misrepresentation[729] or common mistake.[730] If a purchaser knows of a misrepresentation but chooses nonetheless to complete the contract, he

---

[718] *MacBryde v Weeks* (1856) 22 Beav 533 at 543. In determining what is reasonable, the court ignores any difficulty that the purchaser may experience in raising the price: *British and Commonwealth Holdings Plc v Quadrex Holdings Ltd* [1989] Q.B. 842 at 860 (not following *Re Barr's Contract* [1956] Ch. 551).

[719] *Ajit v Sammy* [1967] 1 A.C. 255 (six days held reasonable where the purchase had no prospect of raising the price).

[720] For leasehold conveyancing, see below, Ch.21.

[721] See *Pittack v Naviede* [2010] EWHC 1509 (Ch) at [26]–[34]; [2011] 1 W.L.R. 1666 at 1673–1675. Although under Standard Conditions of Sale 4th edn, c.1.5, the purchaser is not entitled to assign the contract, this does not preclude a sub-sale by him: see *Pittack v Naviede* [2010] EWHC 1509 (Ch) at [45]; [2011] 1 W.L.R. 1666 at 1679.

[722] See [1991] Conv. 15, 81 and 185 (D. G. Barnsley).

[723] *Re Atkins' W.T.* [1974] 1 W.L.R. 761 and 766. Completion can take place even if part of the purchase-money is unpaid, provided that it is secured by a mortgage or charge: see [1991] Conv. 15 at 26–28; and perhaps even where it is paid by a cheque that is then dishonoured: *Redican v Nesbitt* [1924] S.C.R. 135.

[724] *Abbey National B.S. v Cann* [1991] 1 A.C. 56 at 85, per Lord Oliver.

[725] See LRA 1925 s.110(6); *Dogma Properties Ltd v Gale* (1984) 134 N.L.J. 453.

[726] Even if it transpires that the title is wholly bad, the conveyance cannot be set aside on the ground of total failure of consideration: *Clarke v Lamb* (1875) L.R. 10 C.P. 334.

[727] Above, paras 5–047, 6–102. In conveyances made after July 1, 1995, the covenants are implied only where the conveyance or transfer is made with either full or limited guarantee: see LP(MP)A 1994 ss.2, 3.

[728] *Edwards v M'Leay* (1815) G. Coop. 308; aff'd (1818) 2 Swans. 287 (vendor concealed from purchaser his lack of title to part of the land).

[729] Misrepresentation Act 1967 s.1(b). This is so even though the misrepresentation has become a term of the contract: see s.1(a). Where the misrepresentation was not fraudulent, a court may award damages in lieu of rescission: see s.2(2). For misrepresentation, see below, paras 15–104, 15–112.

[730] *Bingham v Bingham* (1748) 1 Ves. Sen. 126 (purchaser was owner of the land that the vendor purported to convey to him). See below, para.15–123.

thereby loses his right to seek rescission of the conveyance[731] but may still recover damages for negligent misrepresentation.[732]

2. Merger. On completion, many of the obligations in the contract of sale **15–100** are merged in the conveyance or transfer.[733] They are presumed to have been superseded by the new agreement embodied in the deed.[734] Thus, for example, a purchaser loses any right to claim compensation in equity for misdescription[735] or because the vendor has no title to part of the land.[736] However, the presumption of merger is rebuttable. Completion does not bring about an automatic discharge of the whole contract if there are terms which are not intended to be so discharged. Some examples may be given. First, there are certain cases where the loss caused to the claimant by the defendant's breach of contract cannot be quantified until completion has taken place. This is the situation as regards damages for delay,[737] for breach of the vendor's fiduciary obligation to manage and preserve the property between contract and completion,[738] and for failure to give vacant possession on completion.[739] Secondly, certain conditions of sale survive completion. These include a condition that compensation shall be payable for any error, omission or misdescription in the particulars of sale,[740] an option for the vendor to buy back the property from the purchaser within a specified period,[741] and an undertaking by a purchaser of a freehold reversion to indemnify the vendor against any claims brought by the tenant.[742] Thirdly, a collateral warranty does not merge on completion because it is concerned with a matter that is not covered by the conveyance.[743]

---

[731] *Campbell v Fleming* (1834) 1 Ad. & El. 40; *Gordon v Selico Co Ltd* [1986] 1 E.G.L.R. 71 at 77.

[732] Under the Misrepresentation Act 1967 s.2(1): *Production Technology Consultants Ltd v Bartlett* [1988] 1 E.G.L.R. 182.

[733] *Knight Sugar Co Ltd v Alberta Railway Irrigation Co* [1938] 1 All E.R. 266 at 269. Where title is unregistered, merger operates on the execution of the conveyance. Although merger does apply to registered land, it is not settled whether it occurs on the execution of the transfer or on registration. The former seems preferable: [1991] Conv. 15 at 24 (D. G. Barnsley).

[734] *Leggott v Barrett* (1880) 15 Ch D 306 at 311; *Re Cooper and Crondace's Contract* (1904) 90 L.T. 258 at 259; *Hissett v Reading Roofing Co Ltd* [1969] 1 W.L.R. 1757 at 1763; *International Press Centre v Norwich Union Insurance Co* (1986) 36 B.L.R. 134 at 136, 137.

[735] *Greswolde-Williams v Barneby* (1901) 83 L.T. 708. cf. *Hissett v Reading Roofing Co Ltd*, above, at 1764.

[736] *Clayton v Leech* (1889) 41 Ch D 103.

[737] *Phillips v Lamdin* [1949] 2 K.B. 33 at 42; *Raineri v Miles* [1981] A.C. 1050 at 1084.

[738] *Clarke v Ramuz* [1891] 2 Q.B. 456 at 461, 462. If the purchaser completes without objection, knowing of the breach of duty, he will be taken to have waived his right to sue: *Berkley v Poulett* [1977] 1 E.G.L.R. 86 at 93.

[739] *Hissett v Reading Roofing Co Ltd*, above, at 1763, 1764; *Gunatunga v De Alwis* (1995) 72 P. & C.R. 161.

[740] *Palmer v Johnson* (1884) 13 Q.B.D. 351. cf. *Ex p. Riches* (1883) 27 S.J. 313. See [1992] C.L.J. 263 at 275, 276 (C.H.).

[741] *Mason v Schuppisser* (1899) 81 L.T. 147.

[742] *Eagon v Dent* [1965] 3 All E.R. 334. See Standard Conditions of Sale 4th edn, c.3.3.2(e).

[743] *Lawrence v Cassel* [1930] 2 K.B. 83; *Hancock v B.W. Brazier (Anerley) Ltd* [1966] 1 W.L.R. 1317.

G. Certain Terms are Void

15–101   By the Law of Property Act 1925[744] certain terms are made void. Some are intended to protect purchasers from having bad titles foisted upon them, such as a stipulation that the purchaser shall not employ his own solicitor.[745] Others are intended to compel the use of the Acts conveyancing machinery, as by invalidating provisions which require the purchaser to pay the costs of obtaining a vesting order or of appointing trustees.[746]

H. Remedies

15–102   One or more of the following remedies will be available to a vendor or purchaser in case of dispute about the effect of the contract.

1. Action for damages

15–103   *(a) The general rule.* An action for damages is the primary remedy under the law of contract, though it is less important in relation to contracts for the sale of land than specific performance. The measure of damages is the loss to the claimant from the non-performance of the contract.[747] A vendor, for example, can recover the difference between the price agreed to be paid and the net value of the property left on his hands,[748] giving credit for any deposit paid by the purchaser.[749] A purchaser can claim for the loss of a bargain, i.e. the amount by which the net value of the property when conveyed to him at the due date would have exceeded the purchase price.[750] But the court may order such damages to be assessed at some other date where justice so requires[751]; this may be the date of the hearing if the property has risen in

---

[744] LPA 1925 ss.42, 48.

[745] s.48(1).

[746] s.42(2). One of the provisions—LPA 1925 s.42(3)—was of a transitional character and was concerned with the situation where an interest that had been a legal estate prior to 1926 could no longer subsist as such after 1925, so that the outstanding legal estate had to be got in: cf. *Weir v Area Estates Ltd* [2010] EWCA Civ 801 at [24], [25]; [2010] 3 E.G.L.R. 91 at 93, 94.

[747] *Johnson v Agnew* [1980] A.C. 367 at 400. For the circumstances in which a claimant might claim any gain that the defendant has made in consequence of the breach, see *Att Gen v Blake* [2001] 1 A.C. 268

[748] *Noble v Edwards* (1877) 5 Ch D 378. Where the vendor resells the property, he can recover both the loss on and the expenses of the resale: *Janred Properties Ltd v E.N.I.T.* [1989] 2 All E.R. 444 at 456.

[749] *Ng v Ashley King Developments Ltd* [2010] EWHC 456 (Ch); [2011] Ch. 115. For deposits, see below, para.15–107.

[750] Together with damages in respect of any special circumstances known to the vendor: *Cottrill v Steyning and Littlehampton B.S.* [1966] 1 W.L.R. 753. Thus if at the time of contracting, a vendor is unaware that the purchaser is negotiating a profitable sub-sale, and the vendor then refuses to complete, he will not be liable for the loss of that sub-sale: *Seven Seas Properties Ltd v Al-Essa (No.2)* [1993] 1 W.L.R. 1083. The purchaser need not accept an offer of repurchase by the vendor: *Strutt v Whitnell* [1975] 1 W.L.R. 870.

[751] *Johnson v Agnew*, above; *E. Johnson Co (Barbados) Ltd v N.S.R. Ltd* [1997] A.C. 400 (land compulsorily acquired between commencement of proceedings and trial). The date selected can significantly affect the quantum of damages: see *Suleman v Shahsavari* [1988] 1 W.L.R. 1181 (where in regard to a house sold for a price of £46,500, the difference between damages assessed at the breach date and those assessed at judgment was £20,000).

value meanwhile.[752] Where the purchaser claims damages for his loss of bargain he cannot in addition recover his costs, e.g. for investigation of title. If he is to be placed in the position in which he would have been had the contract been performed, he would necessarily have incurred those costs.[753]

Damages may be assessed on a "cost of cure" basis where the claimant can establish that his loss consists of or includes the cost of doing work that in breach of contract the defendant failed to do.[754] Thus where a vendor of land fails to carry out work that he contracted to do to the property prior to sale, the claimant may recover the cost of that work if either he does it himself or he can show that he intends to do so.[755] However, the court may refuse to award damages assessed on this basis if to do so would be unreasonable: the question in every case is to determine the loss that the claimant has actually suffered.[756]

(b) *Damages for misrepresentation.* Damages will be awarded against a **15–104** vendor for the tort of deceit if he induces a purchaser to contract by means of a fraudulent misrepresentation.[757] Even if the misrepresentation is not fraudulent, the vendor will be liable in damages unless he can show that he had reasonable grounds to believe and did believe up to the time of the contract that the facts represented were true.[758] It has been held that the measure of damages is the same as that for deceit.[759] According to that measure, the

---

[752] *Suleman v Shahsavari*, above. See too *Wroth v Tyler* [1974] Ch. 30; *Grant v Dawkins* [1973] 1 W.L.R. 1406. In both these decisions damages were awarded in lieu of or in addition to specific performance under what is now the Supreme Court Act 1981 s.50 (above, para.5–015). Damages under that Act are awarded on the same basis as at common law: *Johnson v Agnew*, above.

[753] See *Cullinane v British "Rema" Manufacturing Co Ltd* [1954] 1 Q.B. 292 at 308.

[754] *Tito v Waddell (No.2)* [1977] Ch. 106 at 332. See too *Radford v De Froberville* [1977] 1 W.L.R. 1262.

[755] *Dean v Ainley* [1987] 1 W.L.R. 1729.

[756] *Ruxley Electronics and Construction Ltd v Forsyth* [1996] A.C. 344.

[757] *Doyle v Olby (Ironmongers) Ltd* [1969] 2 Q.B. 158; *McMeekin v Long* [2003] 2 E.G.L.R. 81; *Doe v Skegg* [2006] P.L.S.C.S. 213.

[758] Misrepresentation Act 1967 s.2(1), making innocent misrepresentation actionable on the same basis as a fraudulent misrepresentation. The onus of proving reasonable belief rests on the defendant: *Howard Marine and Dredging Co Ltd v A. Ogden Sons (Excavations) Ltd* [1978] Q.B. 574. Although the Misrepresentation Act 1967 only applies where a person has entered into a contract after a misrepresentation, that will include the grant of a lease, even where, as is often the case, there is no prior contract: see *Northcote Housing Association v Dixon* [2001] P.L.S.C.S. 272. A lease is a contract: see below, para.17–001.

[759] *Royscot Trust Ltd v Rogerson* [1991] 2 Q.B. 297; applied in *Bridgegrove Ltd v Smith* [1997] 2 E.G.L.R. 40; *Pankhania v Hackney LBC* [2004] EWHC 323 (Ch); [2004] 1 E.G.L.R. 135. This view is based upon a questionable interpretation of the Misrepresentation Act 1967 s.2(1), by which if a defendant would be liable for damages had the misrepresentation been fraudulent, he "shall be so liable notwithstanding that the misrepresentation was not made fraudulently". These words may have been intended only to remove the bar to damages for non-fraudulent misrepresentations and not to import the same measure of damages: see (1991) 107 L.Q.R. 547 (R. Hooley). The correctness of the decision was left open in *Smith New Court Securities Ltd v Citibank N.A.* [1997] A.C. 254 at 267, 282, 283. However, it is difficult to reconcile with the long-established policy of "imposing more extensive liability on intentional wrongdoers than on merely careless defendants": see at 280, per Lord Steyn. Whether the fiction of fraud will be applied to exclude a defence of contributory negligence in an action brought under s.2(1) has not been finally settled: compare *Gran Gelato Ltd v Richcliff (Group) Ltd* [1992] Ch. 560 at 572–575 with *Alliance & Leicester B.S. v Edgestop Ltd* [1993] 1 W.L.R. 1462 at 1473–1477.

vendor is liable to pay damages for all loss suffered by the purchaser in consequence of having entered into the contract.[760] These include any difference between the price paid and the value of the land sold[761] plus any consequential loss.[762] The claimant is, however, under a duty to mitigate his loss once he has discovered the misrepresentation.[763] Where the misrepresentation has become a term of the contract, the purchaser may sue for damages for breach of contract, and the quantum of damages will be such as to place him in the position in which he would have been had the representation been true.[764] In cases where the purchaser has entered into a contract after a misrepresentation that was not fraudulent, the court or arbitrator may declare the contract subsisting[765] and award damages in lieu of rescission if it would be equitable to do so, having regard both to the nature of the misrepresentation and to the loss that would be caused to the respective parties by upholding the contract or rescinding it.[766] Such damages are assessed on a contractual basis and will not exceed the difference between the value of the property as received and its value if the representation had been true.[767]

2. Termination for breach

15–105   *(a) When termination occurs.* Although a claimant may always sue for damages for any breach of contract, he will not be entitled to treat a contract as discharged unless the breach is such as to render further performance by him purposeless.[768] This will be the case:

> "where a party indicates either expressly or implicitly that he does not intend to complete his side of the contract or where, having regard to the

---

[760] *Smith New Court Securities Ltd v Citibank N.A.*, above, at 267. See too *Cemp Properties (UK) Ltd v Dentsply Research Development Corporation* [1991] 2 E.G.L.R. 197; *William Sindall Plc v Cambridgeshire CC* [1994] 1 W.L.R. 1016 at 1037, 1043.

[761] *Cemp Properties (UK) Ltd v Dentsply Research Development Corporation*, above, at 200, 201. Although the court will normally value the land at the time when it is acquired this is not an inflexible rule, and will not be applied, e.g. if the misrepresentation continued to operate after the transaction so that the claimant was induced to retain the land, or if the circumstances were such that he was "locked in" to the property: *Smith New Court Securities Ltd v Citibank N.A.*, above, at 267.

[762] *Doyle v Olby (Ironmongers) Ltd*, above; *East v Maurer* [1991] 1 W.L.R. 461.

[763] *Smith New Court Securities Ltd v Citibank N.A.*, above, at 267, 285.

[764] *Smith Kline French Laboratories Ltd v Long* [1989] 1 W.L.R. 1 at 6.

[765] Even if the contract has already been rescinded: *William Sindall Plc v Cambridgeshire CC*, above, at 1044.

[766] Misrepresentation Act 1967 s.2(2). See *William Sindall Plc v Cambridgeshire CC*, above, at 1036–1038. For a case where the court declined to make such an award, see *Northcote Housing Association v Dixon* [2001] P.L.S.C.S. 272.

[767] *William Sindall Plc v Cambridgeshire CC*, above, at 1038, 1045. Such damages will be taken into account when assessing liability in any claim that is also made under the Misrepresentation Act 1967 s.2(1): see s.2(3).

[768] *Thompson v Corroon* (1993) 66 P. & C.R. 445 at 459. The mistaken exercise of a contractual rescission clause may not constitute a repudiatory breach of the contract. It will only be so where the party's conduct clearly shows an intention to abandon and refuse to perform the contract: see *Woodar Investment Development Ltd v Wimpey Construction UK Ltd* [1980] 1 W.L.R. 277; *Eminence Property Developments Ltd v Heaney* [2010] EWCA Civ 1168; [2010] 3 E.G.L.R. 165.

contract as a whole, the obligation which is broken is of vital importance".[769]

Once this happens, the contract is ended as regards further performance but remains alive for the awarding of damages.[770] These principles apply as much to contracts for the sale of land as they do to any other type of contract.[771] When the contract is brought to an end in this way:

(i) where the breach is by the vendor, the purchaser may sue for damages and recover any deposit or other part payments which he has paid (with interest); and

(ii) where it is the purchaser who is in breach, the vendor may forfeit any deposit and sue for damages for any loss that exceeds the value of that deposit.[772]

(b) The "rescission" heresy. Where a contract is voidable, for example on **15–106** account of misrepresentation or fraud, the injured party may rescind the contract, treating it as non-existent, and claim restitutio in integrum, i.e. to be put back into his original position, recovering any property transferred or payment made. This is commonly called rescission ab initio.[773] Where a claimant accepts a repudiation of the contract by the defendant and treats the contract as discharged, he is sometimes said to "rescind" the contract. This is not an apt term in this context, since the contract remains in force for some purposes as explained above. After much confusion both in judgments[774] and textbooks[775] on this last point, the House of Lords has made it clear that acceptance of a repudiatory breach, despite being called "rescission", does not disqualify the injured party from claiming damages, even where he has already obtained an order for specific performance if that order proves abortive.[776]

(c) Return or forfeiture of deposit

(1) NATURE OF A DEPOSIT. A deposit "is an earnest for the performance of the **15–107** contract; in the event of completion of the contract the deposit is applicable

---

[769] *Thompson v Corroon* (1993) 66 P. & C.R. 445 at 459, per Lord Lowry.

[770] *Heyman v Darwins* [1942] A.C. 356 at 379.

[771] *Johnson v Agnew* [1980] A.C. 367 at 392, 393. See too *Buckland v Farmer Moody* [1979] 1 W.L.R. 221; *Thompson v Corroon*, above.

[772] For deposits, see below, para.15–107.

[773] *Johnson v Agnew* [1980] A.C. 367 at 393. For rescission *ab initio*, see below, para.15–112.

[774] The line of erroneous decisions ran from *Henty v Schröder* (1879) 12 Ch D 666 to *Horsler v Zorro* [1975] Ch. 302.

[775] Especially Williams, V. & P. 1004, 1025 and Williams, *The Contract of Sale of Land*, 121, criticised in (1975) 91 L.Q.R. 337 (M. J. Albery), and providing "almost a perfect illustration of the dangers, well perceived by our predecessors but tending to be neglected in modern times, of placing reliance on textbook authority for an analysis of judicial decisions": *Johnson v Agnew*, above, at 395, per Lord Wilberforce.

[776] *Johnson v Agnew* [1980] A.C. 367; and see *Biggin v Minton* [1977] 1 W.L.R. 701; *Ogle v Comboyuro Pty Ltd* (1976) 136 C.L.R. 444; [1980] C.L.J. 58 (A. J. Oakley).

towards payment of the purchase price; in the event of the purchaser's failure to complete in accordance with the terms of the contract, the deposit is forfeit, equity having no power to relieve against forfeiture".[777] Although there is no obligation to pay a deposit in the absence of an express contractual provision, such a term is invariably included in a contract to sell land. Payment of a deposit is a fundamental term of the contract[778] and the vendor may treat the agreement as discharged if the purchaser fails to pay it by the date stipulated in the contract.[779] A deposit of 10 per cent of the purchase price is usually taken on the exchange of contracts.[780] It makes no difference to the function of a deposit that it is paid to a stakeholder rather than to the vendor or his agent.[781]

A vendor may forfeit a deposit if the purchaser defaults even though the amount bears no reference to his loss. Deposits are therefore an anomalous exception to the rule that such payments are unlawful as penalties.[782] A deposit that exceeds 10 per cent will be regarded as a penalty in the absence of special circumstances. It will therefore be recoverable by the purchaser in full and the vendor will be left to his remedy in damages to recover his actual loss.[783] If the vendor's loss exceeds the amount of the deposit and he claims damages for breach of contract, he must give credit for the amount of the deposit.[784]

15–108   (2) RIGHTS OF THE PARTIES. Where the purchaser terminates a contract because of a breach by the vendor, he may recover his deposit and has an equitable lien over the land agreed to be sold to secure its repayment,[785] unless it was paid to a stakeholder rather than to the vendor or his agent.[786] If the vendor terminates the contract on account of the purchaser's default, he may forfeit the deposit, even though the contract makes no express provision for so doing.[787] If that does not adequately compensate him for his loss, he may

---

[777] *Workers Trust Merchant Bank Ltd v Dojap Investments Ltd* [1993] A.C. 573 at 578, 579, per Lord Browne-Wilkinson. See too *Howe v Smith* (1884) 27 Ch D 89 at 101; *Soper v Arnold* (1889) 14 App. Cas. 429 at 435. For a full discussion of the modern law on deposits, see [1994] Conv. 41, 100 (A. J. Oakley).

[778] *Samarenko v Dawn Hill House Ltd* [2011] EWCA Civ 1445. If the purchaser fails to pay a deposit, the vendor may sue him for it regardless of his actual loss: *hhinton v Sparkes* (1868) L.R. 3 C.P. 161.

[779] *Samarenko v Dawn Hill House Ltd* [2011] EWCA Civ 1445.

[780] See Standard Conditions of Sale 4th edn, c.2.2.1. Those conditions make provision for a "travelling deposit" where the sale is part of a chain, so that the vendor may use any deposit that he receives as a deposit on the property which he is purchasing in England and Wales as his residence: see c.2.2.5, and [1994] Conv. 41 at 44 (A. J. Oakley).

[781] *Hall v Burnell* [1911] 2 Ch. 551.

[782] *Linggi Plantations Ltd v Jagatheesan* [1971] 1 M.L.J. 89 at 91.

[783] *Workers Trust Merchant Bank Ltd v Dojap Investments Ltd*, above; (1993) 109 L.Q.R. 524 (H. Beale); [1993] C.L.J. 389 (C.H.). See too [1984] C.L.J. 134 at 161–166 (C.H.).

[784] *Ng v Ashley King Developments Ltd* [2010] EWHC 456 (Ch); [2011] Ch. 115; above, para.15–103.

[785] *Whitbread Co Ltd v Watt* [1902] 1 Ch. 835; above, para.15–056. For equitable liens, see below, para.24–003.

[786] *Combe v Lord Swaythling* [1947] Ch. 625.

[787] *Ex p. Barrell* (1875) 10 Ch.App. 512 at 514.

recover any additional loss as damages.[788] However, the vendor must normally return any part payment that he has already received,[789] because such payments are usually regarded as conditional upon completion of the contract and cannot therefore be retained.[790]

(3) STAKEHOLDERS AND AGENTS. A stakeholder is a person who holds a sum **15–109** of money as agent for both parties,[791] on terms requiring him to pay it either to the person who eventually becomes entitled to it under the contract,[792] or at the joint instructions of both parties even if the event upon which the stake is held has not occurred.[793] If the sale goes off by the purchaser's fault the stakeholder must pay over the deposit to the vendor, who may retain it, unless the contract provides otherwise. If the deposit is paid to a person who is merely the vendor's agent, rather than a stakeholder, any action to recover it must be brought against the vendor,[794] and the vendor can at any time require his agent to pay over the deposit to him.[795] A stakeholder resembles a banker in that he is not accountable for any interest earned by the deposit, whereas an agent must account for it to the vendor.[796] In the absence of any contractual provision, a solicitor or an estate agent who receives a deposit from a purchaser is deemed to do so as agent for the vendor, but an auctioneer receives it as a stakeholder.[797] If an agent or a stakeholder defaults or becomes insolvent, it is the vendor and not the purchaser who must bear the loss.[798]

(4) PRE-CONTRACTUAL "DEPOSITS". Sometimes a person who has agreed to **15–110** purchase land "subject to contract" is asked to pay a pre-contractual deposit to the vendor's estate agent as an earnest of his seriousness.[799] This payment does not fulfil the ordinary function of the deposit unless and until the parties exchange contracts.[800] The purchaser can normally require its return at any

---

[788] *Icely v Grew* (1836) 6 N. & M. 467; *Shuttleworth v Clews* [1910] 1 Ch. 176.

[789] *Mayson v Clouet* [1924] A.C. 980; *Hillel v Christoforides* (1991) 63 P. & C.R. 301 at 306.

[790] *McDonald v Dennys Lascelles Ltd* (1933) 48 C.L.R. 457 at 477–479. In some cases the payments may be unconditional and therefore irrecoverable: see (1981) 97 L.Q.R. 389 (J. Beatson).

[791] He is not a trustee of the money. His liability to account for it is contractual or quasi-contractual: *Potters v Loppert* [1973] Ch. 399 at 406; *Hastingwood Property Ltd v Saunders Bearman Anselm* [1991] Ch. 114 at 123; *Rockeagle Ltd v Alsop Wilkinson* [1992] Ch. 47 at 52.

[792] *Collins v Stimson* (1883) 11 Q.B.D. 142 at 144; *Skinner v Reed's Trustee* [1967] Ch. 194. Once the event occurs on which the stake is payable, the stakeholder is not bound to retain the deposit but may pay it to the party whom he adjudges to be entitled to it. This is so even though there is a dispute between the vendor and the purchaser: *Hastingwood Property Ltd v Saunders Bearman Anselm*, above.

[793] *Rockeagle Ltd v Alsop Wilkinson*, above. The stakeholder has no lien over the deposit in such circumstances for money that is owed to him by either the vendor or the purchaser.

[794] *Ellis v Goulton* [1893] 1 Q.B. 350.

[795] *Edgell v Day* (1865) L.R. 1. C.P. 80.

[796] *Harington v Hoggart* (1830) 1 B. & Ad. 577 at 586, 587.

[797] *Tudor v Hamid* [1988] 1 E.G.L.R. 251 at 255 (solicitor); *Ojelay v Neosale Ltd* [1987] E.G.L.R. 167 at 168 (estate agent); *Harington v Hoggart*, above, at 589 (auctioneer).

[798] *Ojelay v Neosale Ltd* [1987] E.G.L.R. 167 at 168.

[799] For agreements "subject to contract" see above, para.15–010.

[800] *Chillingworth v Esche* [1924] 1 Ch. 97 at 115.

time.[801] If the agent absconds or becomes insolvent, the loss will normally fall on the purchaser. The vendor is not liable to repay the deposit because the agent will not at that stage have his authority to receive the deposit.[802]

15–111   (5) DISCRETION OF COURT. Under the Law of Property Act 1925[803] the court has discretion to order the return of a deposit in any case where specific performance is refused or the return of the deposit is claimed in an action.[804] It was the draftsman's intention that this section should apply in those cases where a vendor was unable to obtain specific performance because his title turned out to be wholly bad, but where the purchaser was in breach of contract by not completing because of a term in the contract.[805] But for this power, the purchaser would have no ground for the recovery of his deposit.[806] Although the discretion has been exercised in that situation,[807] it is not confined to it.[808] However, a deposit is intended to secure performance and if a purchaser is unable to perform his obligations, "the circumstances which make it appropriate for the court to exercise its discretion under s.49(2) in his favour must be exceptional".[809] In such a case, "the search is for something more",[810] namely "something special or exceptional to justify overriding the ordinary contractual expectations of the parties."[811]

The court's statutory discretion cannot be excluded by agreement between the parties.[812] The section confers a jurisdiction on the court which cannot be ousted by agreement between the parties.[813]

---

[801] *Chillingworth v Esche*, above. The purchaser can normally make a restitutionary claim to recover the deposit because of the failure of the expectation upon which payment was made. Where there is no such failure, the deposit will be irrecoverable: see *Sharma v Simposh Ltd* [2011] EWCA Civ 1383 (deposit paid pursuant to an oral agreement under which a property was taken off the market by the intending vendor who kept open his offer to sell at a fixed price not recoverable).

[802] *Sorrell v Finch* [1977] A.C. 728. See (1976) 92 L.Q.R. 484 (F. M. B. Reynolds).

[803] s.49(2).

[804] See [1984] C.L.J. 134 at 169 (C.H.); [1992] C.L.J. 263 at 293 (C.H.); [1994] Conv. 100 (A. J. Oakley).

[805] See Wolst. & C., i. 125 (repeating Sir Benjamin Cherry's own commentary on the subsection found in the 11th and 12th editions). cf. *Safehaven Investments Inc v Springbok Ltd* (1995) 71 P. & C.R. 59 at 70.

[806] See *Re Scott and Alvarez's Contract (No.2)* [1895] 2 Ch. 603; above, para.15–080.

[807] See, e.g. *James Macara Ltd v Barclay* [1944] 2 All E.R. 31 at 32; [1994] Conv. 100 at 101 (A. J. Oakley). In this situation, an order for repayment of the deposit may not always assist the purchaser because he remains liable damages to the vendor: above, para.15–080.

[808] *Universal Corporation v Five Ways Properties Ltd* [1979] 1 All E.R. 552 at 554.

[809] *Omar v El-Wakil* [2001] EWCA Civ 1090 at [37]; [2002] 2 P. & C.R. 36 at 46, per Arden L.J.

[810] *Bidaisee v Sampath* (1995) 46 W.I.R. 461 at 467, per Lord Nicholls (a case on the equivalent provision in Trinidad and Tobago).

[811] *Midill (97PL) Ltd v Park v Park Lane Estates Ltd* [2008] EWCA Civ 1227 at [52]; [2009] 1 W.L.R.2460 at 2475, per Carnwath L.J., adopting and applying Lord Nicholls' judgment in *Bidaisee v Sampath* (1995) 46 W.I.R. 461. Decisions on the exercise of discretion under LPA 1925 s.49(2), decided before the *Midill* case must now be treated with caution.

[812] *Aribisala v St James' Docks (Grosvenor Dock) Ltd* [2007] EWHC 1694 (Ch); [2007] 3 E.G.L.R. 39.

[813] *Aribisala v St James' Docks (Grosvenor Dock) Ltd* [2007] EWHC 1694 (Ch) at [30]–[33]; [2007] 3 E.G.L.R. 39 at 42, approving [1984] C.L.J. 134 at 175 (C.H.).

3. Rescission ab initio. Where one party has been induced to enter into a   **15–112** contract because the other has misled him[814] by some misrepresentation as to a material fact,[815] he may rescind the contract *ab initio*. In general, if a party seeks rescission, he must be able to effect restitution of what he has received under the contract.[816] Common law allowed either rescission or an action for damages if the misrepresentation was fraudulent.[817] Equity went further, and allowed rescission (but neither damages nor compensation[818]) even for inno- cent misrepresentation if it had both misled the other party and induced him to enter into the contract. Since the Judicature Act 1873, the equitable rules have prevailed.[819]

Rescission is a particularly important remedy for a purchaser.[820] If he has been induced to contract by the vendor's misrepresentation he may escape from a contract which might otherwise have bound him to complete or pay damages.[821] There were formerly two limitations on rescission for mis- representation but each has been removed by the Misrepresentation Act 1967. First, it was thought that a misrepresentation ceased to be actionable if it became a term of the subsequent contract.[822] However, a contract may now be rescinded even though the misrepresentation has become incorporated into the contract.[823] Secondly, the right to rescind for an innocent (but not a fraudulent) misrepresentation ceased on completion, and this was so even though the purchaser might have been unable to discover that he had been misled until after he had taken possession.[824] It is now provided that a person may rescind a contract, notwithstanding that it has been performed, if he would otherwise

---

[814] There will be no misrepresentation if the vendor notifies the purchaser or his solicitor that he made an erroneous statement and corrects it before contracts are exchanged: *Strover v Harrington* [1988] Ch. 390.

[815] It is enough if the misrepresentation "induces the person to whom it is made, whether solely or in conjunction with other inducements, to contract on the term on which he does contract": *Museprime Properties Ltd v Adhill Properties Ltd* (1990) 61 P. & C.R. 111 at 124, per Scott J. For the nature of a misrepresentation, see *Atlantic Estates Plc v Ezekiel* [1991] 2 E.G.L.R. 202 at 203.

[816] See G. H. Treitel, *The Law of Contract* 12th edn, para.9–094.

[817] The validity of a contract at law was not affected by an innocent misrepresentation unless there was a total failure of consideration: *Kennedy v Panama, New Zealand and Australian Royal Mail Co Ltd* (1867) L.R. 2 Q.B. 580 at 587.

[818] *Gilchester Properties Ltd v Gomm* [1948] 1 All E.R. 493 (innocent misrepresentation as to rents of the property: purchaser's remedy held to be rescission, not specific performance with abatement of the price, as to which see below, para.15–117.

[819] Above, para.5–020; *Pan Atlantic Insurance Co Ltd v Pine Top Insurance Co Ltd* [1995] 1 A.C. 501 at 543, 544.

[820] It is not available to a sub-purchaser or successor in title: *Gross v Lewis Hillman Ltd* [1970] Ch. 445.

[821] He may be able to seek specific performance with damages in addition under the Mis- representation Act 1967 s.2(1): *Topfell Ltd v Galley Properties Ltd* [1979] 1 W.L.R. 446 at 451; see [1981] C.L.J. 47 at 74 (C.H.).

[822] See *Compagnie Française de Chemin de Fer Paris–Orléans v Leeston Shipping Co* (1919) 1 Ll.L.R. 235; *Pennsylvania Shipping Co v Compagnie Nationale de Navigation* [1936] 2 All E.R. 1167.

[823] Misrepresentation Act 1967 s.1(a). On the interrelationship of remedies for misrepresenta- tion and for breach of contract in such cases, see G. H. Treitel, *The Law of Contract* 12th edn, para.9–089; [1981] C.L.J. 47 at 74 (C.H.).

[824] *Angel v Jay* [1911] 1 K.B. 666.

have been entitled to rescind without alleging fraud.[825] The Act does impose one restriction on rescission in cases of misrepresentations made otherwise than fraudulently. As already explained, the court is given a wide discretion to declare the contract subsisting and to award damages in lieu of rescission if this would be equitable, having regard (inter alia) to any loss that would be caused by upholding the contract or rescinding it.[826] The section was passed to remove the anomaly "by which a minor misrepresentation gave rise to a right of rescission whereas a warranty in the same terms would have grounded no more than a claim for modest damages".[827] Although the maxim caveat emptor has little application to defects in title,[828] it has always applied to other matters.[829] The Act substantially weakens that application so that vendors have to exercise a higher degree of caution than formerly.

15–113   The Act merely entitles the misled party "to rescind the contract", without saying what is to happen to any executed conveyance, which may be a grant but not a contract. If the right to rescind after performance is to be effective, the grant must necessarily be set aside,[830] though the court may prefer to award damages in lieu of rescission.

Clauses which restrict the vendor's liability for misrepresentation, which are often included in standard forms of contract, are effective only in so far as the vendor can show that the restriction satisfies the requirement of reasonableness in the Unfair Contract Terms Act 1977.[831] It has been held that the common clause that "no error, mis-statement or omission in any preliminary answer shall annul the sale" fails to pass this test,[832] and other common form clauses may not satisfy the requirement in the particular circumstances of a case.[833] But a vendor may protect himself against misrepresentations made by his agent by stating that the agent has no authority to make representations of any kind.[834]

---

[825] Misrepresentation Act 1967 s.1(b).

[826] Misrepresentation Act 1967 s.2(2); above, para.15–104.

[827] *William Sindall Plc v Cambridgeshire CC* [1994] 1 W.L.R. 1016 at 1038, per Hoffmann L.J.

[828] Above, para.15–070.

[829] *Haywood v Cope* (1858) 25 Beav. 140.

[830] For the court's power to do so, see above, para.8–055, below, para.15–123. It is clear from the legislative history that the Act is intended to authorise the cancellation of conveyances and leases where restitutio in integrum is possible: see 277 H.L.Deb. cols 48–53 (October 18, 1966).

[831] Misrepresentation Act 1967 s.3, as amended by the Unfair Contract Terms Act 1977 s.8. See [1984] Conv. 12 (H. W. Wilkinson); [1992] C.L.J. 263 at 266 (C.H.).

[832] *Walker v Boyle* [1982] 1 W.L.R. 495; and see *South Western General Property Co Ltd v Marton* [1982] 2 E.G.L.R. 19. cf. *Swingler v Khosla* [1991] 1 E.G.L.R. 245 at 254.

[833] See *Cleaver v Schyde Investments Ltd* [2011] EWCA Civ 929; [2011] 2 P. & C.R. 336 (SCS, c.7.1.3, which limits the power to rescind for errors and omissions only if they are fraudulent or reckless, did not on the particular facts, satisfy the requirement of reasonableness, even though it normally would).

[834] *Collins v Howell-Jones* [1981] 2 E.G.L.R. 108, approving *Overbrooke Estates Ltd v Glencombe Properties Ltd* [1974] 1 W.L.R. 1355. See too *Museprime Properties Ltd v Adhill Properties Ltd* (1990) 61 P. & C.R. 111 at 120; (1981) 97 L.Q.R. 522 (J. Murdoch).

4. Equitable relief. The court's jurisdiction (rarely exercised) to grant relief 15–114
against the consequences of a mistake is considered below in connection with
rectification.[835] Relief against a forfeiture clause may also be granted, e.g.
where instalments of purchase money are in arrear.[836] The doctrine does not
extend to granting relief by way of an order for specific performance where
the person seeking relief was in breach of an essential term of the
contract.[837]

5. Specific performance

(a) Right to specific performance. An order of the court compelling specific 15–115
performance of the contract is the remedy most commonly sought by vendors
and purchasers of land. The performance which can be compelled is the due
completion of the transaction in proper form according to the contract. This
remedy is purely equitable, and in principle is confined to cases where the
common law remedy of damages is inadequate.[838] But land is always treated
as being of unique value, so that the remedy of specific performance is
available to the purchaser as a matter of course[839]; and even though the vendor
is merely concerned to obtain the purchase-money, so that he could be
adequately compensated in damages for the purchaser's refusal to complete,
the remedy of specific performance is equally available to him. A vendor can
in fact "thrust the property down the purchaser's throat"[840]; and claims by
vendors for specific performance are common, since it is often more convenient to them to get rid of the property than to resell it and claim damages.
Specific performance is thus available to vendor and purchaser alike. However, this statement is subject to two qualifications. First, the view that was
formerly held that the remedy is available to one of the parties only if it is
available to the other (the supposed requirement of mutuality) is miscon-
ceived.[841] Secondly, the court will not decree specific performance where, at
trial, the vendor is unable to convey the land.[842] It is of the essence of the
remedy that the purchaser should obtain the land.[843]

---

[835] Below, para.15–123.

[836] *Starside Properties Ltd v Mustapha* [1974] 1 W.L.R. 816.

[837] *Union Eagle Ltd v Golden Achievement Ltd* [1997] A.C. 514 (time of the essence for
completion of the contract: specific performance refused, even though the purchaser tendered the
price 10 minutes' late). The Privy Council left open how it might deal with a situation where there
was a penalty or in which the party terminating the contract might have been unjustly enriched
by improvements made to the land by a purchaser in possession. See too *Etzin v Reece* [2003] 1
P. & C.R. D16 at D18. cf. *Legione v Hateley* (1983) 152 C.L.R. 406; *Stern v McArthur* (1988)
165 C.L.R. 489; [1984] C.L.J. 134 (C.H.); *Equity and Contemporary Legal Developments* (ed. S.
Goldstein), 829 at 863 (C.H.).

[838] However specific performance may be decreed even of agreements to create transient
interests such as a contract for a short lease or to grant a licence: *Verrall v Great Yarmouth
Borough Council* [1981] Q.B. 202.

[839] *AMEC Properties Ltd v Planning Research Systems Plc* [1992] 1 E.G.L.R. 70 at 72.

[840] *Hope v Walter* [1900] 1 Ch. 257 at 258, per Lindley L.J.

[841] *Price v Strange* [1978] Ch. 337, disapproving statements in Fry, *Specific Performance; Lyus
v Prowsa Developments Ltd* [1982] 1 W.L.R. 1044.

[842] *E. Johnson Co (Barbados) Ltd v N.S.R. Ltd* [1997] A.C. 400 at 409–411.

[843] *Re Scott and Alvarez's Contract* [1895] 2 Ch. 603 at 615.

15–116   *(b) Remedy discretionary.* Like other equitable remedies, specific performance is discretionary. However, the court's discretion is governed by settled
principles.[844] Examples of where the remedy may be refused include the
following:

>   (i) in proper cases where there is mistake or great hardship,[845] even
>   though these do not invalidate the contract at law;
>
>   (ii) where there has been delay causing injustice to the other
>   party[846];
>
>   (iii) where the vendor would be required "to embark upon difficult or
>   uncertain litigation in order to secure any requisite consent or
>   obtain vacant possession"[847];
>
>   (iv) where the property is being used for illegal purposes, which would
>   make the purchaser liable to prosecution,[848] even though on this
>   ground he has no right to terminate the contract; or
>
>   (v) where the vendor's title is doubtful but he has failed to disclose the
>   known cause of that doubt and the purchaser has agreed to accept
>   any defects that there may be.[849]

In these cases the contract will remain binding at law, so that the party in
default will be liable in damages, but equity will not assist with a decree of
specific performance. On the other hand, specific performance may be decreed

---

[844] *AMEC Properties Ltd v Planning Research Systems Plc*, above, at 72. The court's discretion
cannot be fettered by any agreement between the parties: *Quadrant Visual Communications Ltd
v Hutchison Telephone (UK) Ltd* [1993] B.C.L.C. 442 at 451.

[845] Snell *Equity*, paras 17–30, 17–045. See *Patel v Ali* [1984] Ch. 283 (personal hardship
combined with delay). The mere fact that the vendor company has been placed in receivership is
no defence to an action for specific performance: *Freevale Ltd v Metrostore (Holdings) Ltd* [1984]
Ch. 199; nor will a court take into account the effects of any such decree on the likely distribution
of the assets of an insolvent company: *AMEC Properties Ltd v Planning Research Systems Plc*,
above.

[846] See *Lazard Brothers Co Ltd v Fairfield Properties Co (Mayfair) Ltd* (1977) 121 S.J. 793,
not following *Milward v Earl of Thanet* (1801) 5 Ves. 720n.; *Easton v Brown* [1981] 3 All E.R.
278.

[847] *Wroth v Tyler* [1974] Ch. 30 at 50, per Megarry J.; *Mean Machines Ltd v Blackheath Leisure
(Carousel) Ltd* (1999) 78 P. & C.R. D36.

[848] *Hope v Walter* [1900] 1 Ch. 257.

[849] *Faruqi v English Real Estates Ltd* [1979] 1 W.L.R. 963; [1992] C.L.J. 263 at 287 (C.H.).
Where the vendor's title is bad but he knew only that it was doubtful, a purchaser who agreed to
take the land subject to any defects but does not complete will be in breach of contract. In such
a case, the court is unlikely to decree specific performance but will leave the vendor to his remedy
in damages: *Warren v Richardson* (1830) You. 1; *Re Scott and Alvarez's Contract (No.2)* [1895]
2 Ch. 603; see [1992] C.L.J. 263 at 288 (C.H.); above, para.15–080. Where the vendor has failed
to disclose a latent defect in title of which he knows or ought to have known, he cannot rely on
a condition of sale in general terms to protect himself, and will therefore be in breach of his
obligation to show a good title. The vendor will therefore be unable to obtain specific performance and will be liable to the purchaser in damages: above, paras 15–071, 15–072. For the
gradations of title, see above, para.15–075.

before the legal time for performance has arrived if there has been an anticipatory breach, e.g. by repudiation.[850]

(c) Specific performance with abatement of the price or damages. Specific **15–117** performance may be decreed in cases where the vendor is unable to convey what he contracted to sell, either because he has misdescribed the land in the particulars of sale[851] or because the property is subject to some undisclosed incumbrance.[852]

(1) THE PURCHASER'S REMEDIES. In the absence of hardship,[853] the purchaser **15–118** may always seek specific performance of the contract subject to an abatement of the price[854] for the deficiency.[855] Thus in one case, three legal tenants in common contracted to sell land, but one of them lacked capacity. The purchaser was able to obtain specific performance of the two shares that could be conveyed with compensation for the remainder.[856] The purchaser may in the alternative seek specific performance against the vendor with damages in addition.[857] The precise interrelationship between these alternative remedies is obscure.[858] Specific performance with compensation was developed by courts of equity in the 18th century, but it was only in 1858 that the Court of Chancery was given a general power to award damages in addition to a decree for specific performance.[859]

(2) THE VENDOR'S REMEDY. A vendor who was unable to convey exactly **15–119** what he had contracted to transfer had no remedy at law against a purchaser who refused to complete,[860] though this strict rule has long been ameliorated

---

[850] *Hasham v Zenab* [1960] A.C. 316. See (1960) 76 L.Q.R. 200 (R.E.M.).

[851] Above, para.15–066.

[852] Above, para.15–070.

[853] For a case of hardship see *Earl of Durham v Legard* (1865) 34 Beav 611 (no specific performance with abatement where the acreage given in the particulars of sale was nearly twice what it actually was but where the contract price had been agreed on the basis of the property's rental income not its acreage).

[854] The remedy is variously described as specific performance either with compensation or with abatement of the price. See [1981] C.L.J. 47 (C.H.).

[855] *Rutherford v Acton-Adams* [1915] A.C. 866 at 870. The decision in *Rudd v Lascelles* [1900] 1 Ch. 815, that a purchaser cannot obtain specific performance with compensation in cases where the property differs substantially from that which the vendor contracted to convey, appears to be based on an erroneous application of principles (considered below) by which in *vendor* may obtain the remedy. See [1981] C.L.J. 47 at 59 (C.H.).

[856] *Basma v Weekes* [1950] A.C. 441 (on appeal from Sierra Leone, where legal tenancies in common were still possible).

[857] See Supreme Court Act 1981 s.50; above, para.5–015.

[858] See [1981] C.L.J. 47 at 67 (C.H.). Where the purchaser seeks compensation he may be unable to recover any consequential loss. It has also been held that compensation can be recovered only up to the amount of the purchase price. For any additional sum, the purchaser must seek damages: *Grant v Dawkins* [1973] 1 W.L.R. 1406. *Sed quaere.*

[859] Chancery Amendment Act 1858 s.2; see above, para.5–015. The Court of Chancery did on occasions award damages prior to that date: see (1992) 108 L.Q.R. 652 (P. McDermott).

[860] *Tomkins v White* (1806) 3 Smith's Rep. 435. The common law rule of strict compliance was subject to the exception of matters de minimis: *Belworth v Hassell* (1815) 4 Camp. 140.

by the employment of conditions of sale.[861] In equity however a breach of contract is not necessarily a bar to relief,[862] and a vendor may seek specific performance if he can comply substantially with the agreement, subject to an abatement of the price "for any small and immaterial deficiency".[863]

15–120   *(d) Effect of a decree of specific performance.* When a decree of specific performance is made, the contract remains in force and is not merged in the judgment.[864] However, because the court is seised of the matter, it controls the working out, variation or cancellation of the order,[865] and it does so according to equitable principles.[866] It follows that neither party can act unilaterally thereafter without the leave of the court, e.g. by serving a notice to complete on the other[867] or by contracting to sell the property to a third party.[868] If the order is not complied with, the claimant may apply to the court either for its enforcement or to dissolve the order and put an end to the contract.[869] If the order is dissolved, he will then become entitled to damages.[870] He cannot claim such dissolution as of right and the court will not order it if to do so would be unjust in the circumstances then existing to the other party,[871] for equity "will not permit a party unconscionably to insist upon his legal rights".[872]

15–121   **6. Injunction.** This equitable remedy, the negative counterpart of specific performance, is rarely appropriate in cases of vendor and purchaser, but it may be useful to prevent a breach of contract, e.g. if the vendor threatens to demolish a building while he is still in possession of the property.[873]

---

[861] See in particular the condition, in use since the beginning of the 19th century, that omissions and errors in description should not annul the sale and that the purchaser should complete with or (in some forms of the condition) without compensation. The vendor will not be able to rely on such a condition where the error or omission is substantial: *Flight v Booth* (1834) 1 Bing. (N.C.) 370; above, para.15–067.

[862] "Equity does not need to expunge a breach of contract in order to award specific performance": *Raineri v Miles* [1981] A.C. 1050 at 1063, per Templeman L.J. See *Equity and Contemporary Legal Developments* (ed. S. Goldstein), p.829 at 855 (C.H.).

[863] *Rutherford v Acton-Adams*, above, at 869, 870, per Viscount Haldane; above, para.15–066. For the close interrelationship between the legal and equitable rules, see [1992] C.L.J. 263 at 270 (C.H.).

[864] *Austins of East Ham Ltd v Macey* [1941] Ch. 338 at 341; *Johnson v Agnew* [1980] A.C. 367 at 393.

[865] *Singh v Nazeer* [1979] Ch. 474 at 480, 481. It is otherwise if the parties themselves come to an agreement.

[866] *Johnson v Agnew*, above, at 399.

[867] *Singh v Nazeer*, above.

[868] *G.K.N. Distributors Ltd v Tyne Tees Fabrications Ltd* (1985) 50 P. & C.R. 403.

[869] *Johnson v Agnew*, above, at 394.

[870] *Johnson v Agnew*, above, at 399.

[871] *Johnson v Agnew*, above, at 399; *Hillel v Christoforides* (1991) 63 P. & C.R. 301. This view has been criticised: see (1980) 96 L.Q.R. 403 (M. Hetherington). However it does seem correct in principle, for the defendant may have acted to his detriment in reliance upon the decree: see (1981) 97 L.Q.R. 26 (D. Jackson).

[872] *Hillel v Christoforides* (1991) 63 P. & C.R. 301 at 304, per Millett J.

[873] Williams V. & P. 558.

7. Rectification and setting aside. These are equitable remedies based on mistake.

(a) Rectification. Rectification may be sought where the agreement that the **15–122** parties reached was not correctly recorded in their written contract by reason of a common mistake.[874] The court may then correct the mistake so that the terms of the contract accurately reproduce what the parties agreed[875]; and the court may order specific performance of the contract as so rectified, even in the same action.[876] This might be done, for example, where there was an agreement to build and let four houses but the written contract wrongly gave the number as six,[877] or where the rent agreed upon was wrongly stated.[878] The burden of proof in actions for rectification is heavy. The court requires "convincing proof" that the written words were contrary to the mutual intentions of the parties.[879] There is one qualification to the requirement of mutual mistake. A court may order rectification in a case of unilateral mistake, if:

(i) the circumstances make it inequitable to hold the mistaken party to the contract; and

(ii) the other party either knew of the mistake or turned a blind eye to it.[880]

Where the title to land is unregistered, rectification may be used to correct mistakes in a conveyance, e.g. if it gives the purchaser more land,[881] or wider

---

[874] *Domb v Isoz* [1980] Ch. 548 at 559. For the requirement that the mistake must normally be mutual, see *Riverlate Properties Ltd v Paul* [1975] Ch. 133, disapproving certain nineteenth-century authorities which suggested that a unilateral mistake might suffice. Rectification will not be ordered where there is no mistake as to the effect of the document in issue but only as to some other document: *London Regional Transport v Wimpey Group Services Ltd* [1986] 2 E.G.L.R. 41.

[875] A contract for the sale of land must be made in writing and incorporate all the terms agreed between the parties: LP(MP)A 1989 s.2(1); above, para.15–015. This does not preclude rectification if the written document does not record what the parties agreed. The court has power to specify the date when a contract comes into being in consequence of an order for rectification: LP(MP)A 1989 s.2(4); above, para.15–032.

[876] *Craddock Brothers v Hunt* [1923] 2 Ch. 136; *U.S.A. v Motor Trucks Ltd* [1924] A.C. 196. For details of the remedy, see generally Snell, *Equity*, Ch.16; *Riverlate Properties Ltd v Paul* [1975] Ch. 133.

[877] *Olley v Fisher* (1886) 34 Ch D 367.

[878] *Garrard v Frankel* (1862) 30 Beav 445; but see *Riverlate Properties Ltd v Paul*, above, at 142.

[879] *Joscelyne v Nissen* [1970] 2 Q.B. 86 at 98, per Russell L.J.; *Blacklocks v J.B. Developments (Godalming) Ltd* [1982] Ch. 183 at 191, per Mervyn Davies J.

[880] *Commission for the New Towns v Cooper (Great Britain) Ltd* [1995] Ch. 259; [1995] C.L.J. 502 (A. J. Oakley) (landlord mistakenly granted tenant a right to terminate the lease, having been misled into doing so by the tenant); *J.J. Huber Ltd v The Private DIY Co Ltd* (1995) 70 P. & C.R. D33 (mistake as to liability for rates in lease appreciated by the tenant); *Coles v William Hill Organisation Ltd* [1998] E.G.C.S. 40 (break clause included by mistake of which tenants were aware). See too *Weeds v Blaney* [1978] 2 E.G.L.R. 84; *Thomas Bates Son Ltd v Wyndham's (Lingerie) Ltd* [1981] 1 W.L.R. 505; *Kemp v Neptune Concrete Ltd* [1988] 2 E.G.L.R. 87.

[881] *Beale v Kyte* [1907] 1 Ch. 564.

rights,[882] than he was entitled to have under the contract, or if it creates a joint tenancy when a tenancy in common was intended.[883] But, because it is an equitable remedy, it will not be available where there has been long delay, or where the land affected has passed into the hands of a bona fide purchaser who had no notice of the mistake in the conveyance.[884] Since the right to rectification is a "mere equity", such a purchaser need not necessarily acquire the legal estate.[885]

Where the title to land is registered, the court or registrar has a discretionary power to alter the register in certain circumstances, and, in particular, to correct a mistake.[886] That is subject to limitations that have been explained above, in cases where the correction of the mistake would prejudicially affect the title of a registered proprietor.[887]

15–123   *(b) Setting aside for mistake.* At common law, a contract will be void if it was made under a mutual mistake that renders its subject-matter "essentially and radically different" from that which the parties believed to exist.[888] For a contract to be void for common mistake:

> (i) there must be a common assumption as to the existence of a state of affairs;

> (ii) there must be no warranty by either party that that state of affairs exists;

> (iii) the non-existence of the state of affairs must not be attributable to the fault of either party;

> (iv) the non-existence of the state of affairs must render performance of the contract impossible; and

> (v) the state of affairs may be the existence, or a vital attribute, of the consideration to be provided or circumstances which must subsist if performance of the contractual adventure is to be possible.[889]

The Court of Appeal has held that there is no equitable jurisdiction to grant rescission for common mistake in circumstances that fell short of those in

---

[882] *Clarke v Barnes* [1929] 2 Ch. 368; cf. below, para.28–042.

[883] *Re Colebrook's Conveyances* [1972] 1 W.L.R. 1397.

[884] Williams V. & P. 791; *Smith v Jones* [1954] 1 W.L.R. 1089; *Taylor Barnard Ltd v Tozer* [1984] 1 E.G.L.R. 21; cf. *Garrard v Frankel* (1862) 30 Beav 445.

[885] Above, para.8–012.

[886] LRA 2002 Sch.4 paras 2, 5; above, paras 7–133, 7–137.

[887] See above, para.7–135.

[888] *Associated Japanese Bank (International) Ltd v Credit du Nord S.A.* [1989] 1 W.L.R. 255 at 268, per Steyn J.

[889] *Great Peace Shipping Ltd v Tsavliris Salvage (International) Ltd* [2002] EWCA Civ 1407 at [76]; [2003] Q.B. 679 at 703.

which a contract was void at common law.[890] Earlier authorities which had held otherwise were decided *per incuriam*.[891]

8. Declarations by the court (Vendor and Purchaser Summons). In the 19th century, issues as to title were usually settled in specific performance proceedings, which were costly and cumbersome.[892] In a much expedited form, specific performance proceedings are once again the normal method for deciding disputes which may arise in the investigation of title (e.g. whether a good title has been shown according to the contract, or whether some incumbrance must be accepted by the purchaser). However, there are two alternative procedures available. The first is to ask the court to make a declaration. The second is the Vendor and Purchaser Summons, introduced by the Vendor and Purchaser Act 1874[893] and now authorised by the Law of Property Act 1925.[894] This is a little used summary procedure[895] designed for the decision of particular points arising between contract and conveyance. It may not be used to question the existence or validity of the contract, but only for matters arising under it.[896] The court may make such order as it thinks just. This will normally be a declaration, but it may sometimes include an order for termination of the contract and repayment of deposit and conveyancing expenses.[897] What a purchaser cannot recover are damages over and above such expenses, such as damages for delay.[898] If a party wishes for a declaration as to the validity of the contract, or any other matter outside the scope of a Vendor and Purchaser Summons (including a claim for damages for loss of bargains), he must claim it in an ordinary action.

15-124

---

[890] *Great Peace Shipping Ltd v Tsavliris Salvage (International) Ltd*, above.
[891] They were inconsistent with the decision of the House of Lords in *Bell v Lever Bros Ltd* [1932] A.C. 161.
[892] For a detailed account, see (1992) 108 L.Q.R. 280 at 292–301 (C.H.).
[893] s.9.
[894] s.49(1). See [2001] Conv. 301 (G.L.H. Griffiths).
[895] "This is nowadays a not altogether usual form of application": *Walia v Michael Naughton Ltd* [1985] 1 W.L.R. 1115 at 1116, per Judge Finlay.
[896] LPA 1925 s.49(1).
[897] *Re Hargreaves and Thompson's Contract* (1886) 32 Ch D 454. Claims for compensation are expressly within the scope of such a summons: LPA 1925 s.49(1).
[898] *Re Wilsons and Steven's Contract* [1894] 3 Ch. 546.

CHAPTER 16

PROPRIETARY ESTOPPEL

Section 1. The Nature of Proprietary Estoppel

16–001 **1. The basis of the doctrine.** Proprietary estoppel, which was once also referred to as "estoppel by acquiescence" or "estoppel by encouragement",[1] is a means by which property rights may be affected or created.[2] The term describes the equitable jurisdiction by which a court may interfere in cases where the assertion of strict legal rights is found to be unconscionable.[3] Although this jurisdiction is of ancient origin,[4] it has been much developed by the courts in recent years[5] and some of its more "archaic and arcane" features have been abandoned.[6] The flexibility of the jurisdiction is such that the

---

[1] *Taylor Fashions Ltd v Liverpool Victoria Trustees Co Ltd* [1982] Q.B. 133 fn. at 151, per Oliver J. The term "proprietary estoppel" is now the regular description: see *Gillett v Holt* [2001] Ch. 210. The term "quasi-estoppel" (*Kammins Ballrooms Co Ltd v Zenith Investments (Torquay) Ltd* [1971] A.C. 850 at 884, per Lord Diplock; *J. Willis & Son v Willis* [1986] 1 E.G.L.R. 62, per Parker L.J.), although in some senses accurate, fortunately has not become widely used.

[2] *Western Fish Products Ltd v Penwith DC* [1981] 2 All E.R. 204 at 217; *West Middlesex Golf Club Ltd v Ealing LBC* (1993) 68 P. & C.R. 461 at 478. See too [1991] Conv. 36 (G. Battersby) (a particularly important contribution to the literature on estoppel). Rights cannot be created by estoppel in favour of the general public: *CIN Properties Ltd v Rawlins* [1995] 2 E.G.L.R. 130 at 134; [1995] Conv. 332 at 336 (M. Haley).

[3] *Taylor Fashions Ltd v Liverpool Victoria Trustees Co Ltd*, above, at 147; *Gillett v Holt*, above, at 225 per Robert Walker L.J; [2001] Conv. 78 (M.P. Thompson); [2000] C.L.J. 453 (M.J.D.). See too *Ward v Kirkland* [1967] Ch. 194 at 235. For a general account of the jurisdiction in its many forms, see Snell, *Equity*, Ch.12.

[4] See, e.g. *Edlin v Battaly* (1675) 2 Lev 152; *Short v Taylor* (c.1693–1700), cited in Anon (1709) 2 Eq.Ca.Abr. 522.

[5] See especially *Gillett v Holt*, above; *Cobbe v Yeoman's Row Management Limited* [2008] 1 W.L.R. 1752; *Thorner v Major* [2009] 1 W.L.R. 776. "The doctrine is one of comparatively recent development (if not recent origin)": *Watson v Goldsbrough* [1986] 1 E.G.L.R. 265 at 267, per Browne-Wilkinson V.C. In recent cases the courts have stressed that the constituent elements of proprietary estoppel cannot be examined in watertight compartments, but are intertwined: see *Gillett v Holt*, above, at p.225, described by Lord Neuberger as a "masterly judgment", *Thorner v Major*, above at 802. Similarly, in determining how to give effect to the equity, the court looks at the whole sequence of events: see *Jennings v Rice* [2002] EWCA Civ 159 at [49]; [2003] 1 P. & C.R.100 at 114; *Suggitt v Suggitt* [2011] EWHC 903 (Ch); and see (2006) 122 L.Q.R. 492 (S. Gardner).

[6] See *Habib Bank Ltd v Habib Bank A.G. Zurich* [1981] 1 W.L.R. 1265 at 1285, per Oliver L.J.

criteria for relief can be stated only in broad terms.[7] Indeed, such is its nature that "it is important to note at the outset that the doctrine of proprietary estoppel cannot be treated as subdivided into three or four watertight compartments"[8] and that "the fundamental principle that equity is concerned to prevent unconscionable conduct permeates all the elements of the doctrine".[9]

With that in mind and without attempting to provide an exclusive definition, it is possible to summarise the essential elements of proprietary estoppel as follows.[10]

(i) An equity arises where:

    (a) the owner of land (O) induces, encourages or allows the claimant (C) to believe that he has or will enjoy some right or benefit over O's property;

    (b) in reliance upon this belief, C acts to his detriment to the knowledge of O; and

    (c) O then seeks to take unconscionable advantage of C by denying him the right or benefit which he expected to receive.[11]

(ii) This equity gives C the right to go to court to seek relief. C's claim is an equitable one and subject to the normal principles governing equitable remedies.[12]

(iii) The court has a wide discretion as to the manner in which it will give satisfy the equity in order to avoid an unconscionable result,

---

[7] The courts are unwilling to define too exactly the ambit of the doctrine: *Amalgamated Investment & Properly Co Ltd v Texas Commerce International Bank Ltd* [1982] Q.B. 84 at 103; *Taylor Fashions Ltd v Liverpool Victoria Trustees Co Ltd*, above, at 148.

[8] *Gillett v Holt*, above, at 225, per Robert Walker L.J.

[9] *Gillett v Holt*, above, at 225.

[10] The best-known statement of the principles is found in Lord Kingsdown's dissenting judgment in *Ramsden v Dyson* (1866) L.R. 1 H.L. 129 at 170 and 171, with a modern reformulation by Oliver J. in *Taylor Fashions Ltd v Liverpool Victoria Trustees Co Ltd*, above, at 151–152. See too *Rochdale Canal Co v King (No.2)* (1853) 16 Beav. 630 at 633 and 634; *Cairncross v Lorimer* (1860) 3 Macq. 827 at 829 and 830; *De Bussche v Alt* (1878) 8 Ch D 286 at 314; *Sarat Chunder Dey v Gopal Chunder Laha* (1892) L.R. 19 I.A. 203 at 215, 216; *Chalmers v Pardoe* [1963] 1 W.L.R. 677 at 681, 682; *Holiday Inns Inc v Broadhead* (1974) 232 E.G. 951 at 1087; *Crabb v Arun DC* [1976] Ch. 179 at 188; *Western Fish Products Ltd v Penwith DC*, above, at 217; *Watson v Goldsbrough*, above, at 267; *Roebuck v Mungovin* [1994] 2 A.C. 224 at 235; *John v George* (1996) 71 P. & C.R. 375 at 384.

[11] In *Lloyd v Dugdale* [2001] EWCA Civ 1754 at [26]; [2002] 2 P. & C.R. 167 at 176, Sir Christopher Slade stated that the equivalent passage in the sixth edition of this work "accurately summarised" the essential elements of proprietary estoppel.

[12] Above, para.5–014. A particularly striking example is *Murphy v Rayner* [2011] EWHC (Ch) 1, where the abuse of trust by the claimant would have caused her to forfeit all relief, if the claim had been made out. In *Suggitt v Suggitt*, above, the failure of the claimant "to come clean and make the fullest disclosure", effectively limited their remedy, at para.38 per Judge Roger Kaye QC.

having regard to all the circumstances of the case, including, but not limited to, the expectations and conduct of the parties.[13]

(iv) The relief which the court may give may be either negative, in the form of an order restraining O from asserting his legal rights, or positive, by ordering O either to grant or convey to C some estate, right or interest in or over his land, to pay C appropriate compensation, or to act in some other way.

(v) The issue in any given case is whether it would be unconscionable for O to deny that which he has allowed or encouraged C to assume to his detriment.[14] The courts no longer inquire (as once they did) whether the circumstances can be "fitted within the confines of some preconceived formula".[15]

The flexibility of proprietary estoppel, in terms both of the circumstances which may fall within its scope and the remedies that a court can give to satisfy any equity which arises, is its strength and its weakness. The court's freedom to mould the remedy to suit the circumstances precisely makes the outcome unpredictable. This is not conducive to the settlement of disputes and leads to costly litigation.[16]

Proprietary estoppel has some similarities with both common law estoppel and the now abolished equitable doctrine of part performance. Something must be said at the outset about its relationship with each of these.

16–002   **2. Relationship with common law estoppel.** It is perhaps unfortunate that proprietary estoppel should be so called. Although the equitable doctrine shares some characteristics with estoppel at common law,[17] it differs fundamentally from it.[18] Estoppel in the strict, common law sense is an aspect of the law of evidence by which a person may be precluded from denying something

---

[13] *Jennings v Rice*, above, at [56], per Robert Walker L.J. The judge emphasised that while a court would take into account both the expectations and the detriment suffered, amongst other factors, the essence of the doctrine of proprietary estoppel was to avoid an unconscionable result and to satisfy the equity.

[14] *Taylor Fashions Ltd v Liverpool Victoria Trustees Co Ltd*, above, at 151 and 152, per Oliver J. See too *Crabb v Arun DC*, above, at 195; *John v George*, above, at 143; *Nationwide Anglia BS v Ahmed* (1995) 70 P. & C.R. 381 at 390. For a discussion of unconscionability in this context, see [1995] L.M.C.L.Q. 538 at 540–542 (N. Bamforth); (2006) 26 Legal Studies 475 (N. Hopkins); *Confining and defining proprietary estoppel: the role of unconscionability* (2010) 30 Legal Studies 408 (M.J.D.).

[15] *Taylor Fashions Ltd v Liverpool Victoria Trustees Co Ltd*, above, at 151 and 152.

[16] Such litigation may turn on fine points of evidence: cf. *Wayling v Jones* (1993) 69 P. & C.R. 170; [1996] Fam. Law 89 (R. Bailey-Harris). As one of the few doctrines that may lead to the acquisition of a property right or a right to use property without formality, it is often the argument of last resort: cf. *Century (UK) Ltd SA v Clibbery* [2004] EWCH 1870 (Ch).

[17] cf. *Proctor v Bennis* (1887) 36 Ch D 740 at 765.

[18] Snell, *Equity*, Ch.10. For the relationship between proprietary and promissory estoppel, see *Chitty on Contracts* 3–160 et seq.; [1988] Conv. 346 (P.T. Evans).

that he has asserted.[19] The principle is that when A, by his words or conduct, has led B to believe in a particular state of affairs, he will not be permitted to deny that assumption once B has acted to his prejudice upon it.[20] This estoppel is purely negative in its operation. It may provide a defence but it is not a cause of action.[21] By contrast, proprietary estoppel may operate positively and found a cause of action,[22] and this has long been recognised.[23]

3. Relationship with the former doctrine of part performance. Until the **16–003** Law of Property (Miscellaneous) Provisions Act 1989 came into force, there was no requirement that a contract for the sale of an interest in land should be made in writing.[24] An oral contract was valid, but was unenforceable in the absence of either a sufficient memorandum in writing or sufficient acts of part performance.[25] The basis of the doctrine of part performance was similar to that of proprietary estoppel. It was that:

> "if one party to an agreement stands by and lets the other party incur expense or prejudice his position on the faith of the agreement being valid he will not then be allowed to turn round and assert that the agreement is unenforceable".[26]

Not only was the close kinship between the two doctrines often acknowledged in the course of the 19th century, but in some cases the two were not clearly differentiated.[27] Indeed in the present century the very existence of the doctrine of proprietary estoppel was denied and the earlier authorities were explained as examples of the doctrine of part performance.[28] Such a view was

---

[19] *London Joint Stock Bank v Macmillan* [1918] A.C. 777 at 818; *Evans v Bartlam* [1937] A.C. 473 at 484. See too *Sarat Chunder Dey v Gopal Chunder Laha*, above, at 210. The trend in later authorities was to acknowledge that it is also a substantive rule of law: *Canadian and Dominion Sugar Co Ltd v Canadian National (West Indies) Steamship Ltd* [1947] A.C. 46 at 56.

[20] *Pickard v Sears* (1837) 6 A. & E. 469 at 474; *Maclame v Gatty* [1921] 1 A.C. 376 at 386; *Moorgate Mercantile Co Ltd v Twitchings* [1976] Q.B. 225 at 241.

[21] *Seton, Laing & Co v Lafone* (1887) 19 QBD 68 at 70; *Low v Bouverie* [1891] 3 Ch. 82 at 101.

[22] *Crabb v Arun DC*, above, at 187.

[23] "The common-law doctrine of estoppel . . . is not the same as the equitable doctrine. You cannot found an action on it as you can in equity": *Williams v Pinckney* (1897) 67 L.J.Ch. 34 at 37, per Vaughan Williams L.J.

[24] For the Law of Property (Miscellaneous Provisions) Act 1989 s.2, which came into force on September 27, 1989, see above, para.15–014.

[25] LPA 1925 s.40, repealed by LP(MP)A 1989 s.4. See the fifth edition of this work at pp.571 et seq.

[26] *Steadman v Steadman* [1976] A.C. 536 at 540, per Lord Reid. For discussion, see *Yaxley v Gotts* [2000] Ch. 162 at 171–172.

[27] See, e.g. *Gregory v Mighell* (1811) 18 Ves. 328 at 333; *Dillwyn v Llewelyn* (1862) 4 De G.F. & J. 517 at 521; *Nunn v Fabian* (1865) 11 Jur. (N.S.) 868; *Ramsden v Dyson* (1866) L.R. 1 H.L. 129 at 170 and 171; *McManus v Cooke* (1887) 35 Ch D 681 at 694 et seq. This danger remains, if not in analysis at least in outcome: cf. *Kinane v Mackie-Conteh* [2005] 6 E.G. 140 (CS); [2005] EWCA Civ 45.

[28] *Ariff v Jadunath Majumdar* (1931) L.R. 58 I.A. 91 at 102; *Canadian Pacific Ry Co v R* [1931] A.C. 414 at 428 and 429. The opinion of the Privy Council was in each case given by Lord Russell of Killowen. For an attempt to run together contract and proprietary estoppel, see *Vaughan v Vaughan* [1953] 1 Q.B. 762 at 768.

inconsistent with earlier authority[29] and is now plainly untenable. The existence of a valid contract is not a prerequisite to an equity by estoppel.[30] Furthermore, it was an essential element of the doctrine of part performance that the acts relied upon should be referable to the contract.[31] There is no requirement in relation to proprietary estoppel that the detrimental acts should point to any arrangement between the parties because none may exist. The doctrine of part performance has now been abolished and contracts for the sale of any interest in land must be made in writing.[32] Despite some dicta to the contrary, this has not affected the operation of the doctrine of proprietary estoppel.[33]

Section 2. Historical Background

16–004   **1. The emergence of the doctrine.** The earliest cases of proprietary estoppel were principally concerned with two situations. The first was where C built on O's land in the mistaken belief either that it was his or that he had a right to do so,[34] as where a life tenant granted to C a lease that he had no power to grant, and the remainderman, O, knowing of the defect in title, stood by while C expended money on the premises.[35] No equity would arise if C was either aware of the defect in his title,[36] or acted to his detriment while the parties were still negotiating the terms of a formal agreement.[37]

The second situation was where C was O's tenant and was encouraged to believe either that he would be granted some renewal or extension of his term,[38] or that O would not exercise some right which he had under the

[29] See, e.g. *Forbes v Ralli* (1925) L.R. 52 I.A. 178 at 187.

[30] *Voyce v Voyce* (1991) 62 P. & C.R. 290 at 296. Indeed, in many cases estoppel is pleaded because of the absence of a valid or comprehensive contract, for example *Flowermix Ltd v Site Development (Ferndown) Ltd* Unreported, April 11, 2000, Arden J.; *Kinane v Mackie-Conteh* above, *Cobbe v Yeoman's Row Management Ltd* above; *Herbert v Doyle* [2010] EWCA Civ 1095; *Whittaker v Kinnear* [2011] EWHC 1479 (QB). For the relationship between proprietary estoppel and contract, see also para.16–034.

[31] *Maddison v Alderson* (1883) 8 App.Cas. 467 at 479; and see the fifth edition of this work at p.591.

[32] LP(MP)A 1989 s.2.

[33] *Whittaker v Kinnear* above at [30], per Bean J, following the view found in the Law Commission Report that led to LP(MP)A 1989 s.2, (1987) Law. Com. No.164 at paras 5.4 et seq. See also [2005] Conv. 247 (M.J.D); cf. *Akiens v Salomon* (1992) 65 P. & C.R. 364. For doubts see *Cobbe v Yeoman's Row Management Ltd*, above at 1769, per Lord Scott and see *Herbert v Doyle*, above, for the limitation on the operation of the doctrine in such cases. Above para.15–043.

[34] *Short v Taylor* (c.1693–1700) 2 Eq.Cas.Abr. 522 at 523; *Steed v Whitaker* (1740) Barn. C. 220; *Lord Cawdor v Lewis* (1835) 1 Y. & C.Ex. 427.

[35] *Huning v Ferrers* (1711) Gilb. Rep. 85; *Savage v Foster* (1723) 9 Mod. 35; *Stiles v Cowper* (1748) 3 Atk. 693.

[36] *Kenney v Brown* (1796) 3 Ridgw. P.C. 462 at 518, 519; *Master, etc, of Clare Hall v Harding* (1848) 6 Hare 273.

[37] *East India Co v Vincent* (1740) 2 Atk. 83.

[38] Although this principle was always accepted (see, e.g. *Nunn v Fabian* (1865) 11 Jur. (N.S.) 868; *Ramsden v Dyson* (1866) L.R. 1 H.L. 129 at 140, 141 and 170), there are few cases (if any) in which it was established. *Gregory v Mighell* (1811)18 Ves. 328, which is usually cited as illustrative, was a case of part performance.

lease.[39] Such circumstances were often alleged by C, but seldom established.[40] Although in some of these earlier cases the relief given took the negative form of an injunction to restrain ejectment proceedings at common law brought by O against C,[41] in others it was of a positive character.[42] O might be ordered to pay compensation to C for his expenditure (secured if need be by a lien over O's land),[43] to execute a conveyance in C's favour[44] or to take some other step to perfect C's title.[45]

2. The principles defined. In the middle of the 19th century, the doctrine **16–005** of proprietary estoppel was rapidly developed in a series of decisions arising out of the activities of industrial entrepreneurs.[46] The cases commonly arose out of the construction of a railway or canal by C with the consent of O, but before O had granted C the appropriate legal right over his land (whether by a conveyance of land or the grant of an easement).[47] In all of these cases the court gave effect to C's equity, usually by ordering O to make the necessary grant to C[48] on terms that C paid O an appropriate sum for the right or interest obtained. These decisions provided the foundation for the modern law of estoppel which subsequently emerged in a series of important decisions.[49] The circumstances which would give rise to an equity were clarified,[50] and it was recognised that the court had a wide discretion as to how it could most

---

[39] *Jackson v Cator* (1800) 5 Ves. 688 (tenant beautified gardens with landlord's assent; landlord could not then exercise his right to cut timber on the demised premises).

[40] *Att Gen v Baliol College, Oxford* (1744) 9 Mod. 407; *Dann v Spurner* (1802) 7 Ves. 231; *Pilling v Armitage* (1805) 12 Ves. 78; *Ramsden v Dyson*, above. The tenant sometimes alleges that the landlord is estopped from refusing to grant him a new lease. see *J.T. Developments Ltd v Quinn* (1990) 62 P. & C.R. 33 (where the claim succeeded).

[41] e.g. *Huning v Ferrers*, above; *Steed v Whitaker*, above. An injunction might also be granted to prevent O interfering with C's exercise of his right: *Cotching v Bassett* (1862) 32 Beav. 101 (alteration to ancient lights by C with O's assent; O restrained from obstructing them).

[42] See *Lord Cawdor v Lewis*, above, at 433.

[43] e.g. *Neesom v Clarkson* (1845) 4 Hare 97; *Unity Joint Stock Mutual Banking Association v King* (1858) 25 Beav. 72.

[44] e.g. *Stiles v Cowper*, above.

[45] See *Savage v Foster*, above, where O was required to levy a fine to bar his rights under an entail.

[46] The cases reveal a strong judicial sympathy for these activities.

[47] *Powell v Thomas* (1848) 6 Hare 300; *Duke of Devonshire v Eglin* (1851) 14 Beav. 530; *Duke of Beaufort v Patrick* (1853) 17 Beav. 60; *Somersetshire Coal Co v Harcourt* (1858) 2 De G. & J. 596; *Loird v Birkenhead Rly Co* (1859) Johns. 500; *Mold v Wheatcroft* (1859) 27 Beav. 510. See too *Rochdale Canal Co v King (No.2)* (1853) 16 Beav. 630 (construction of mill by C on understanding that water could be taken from O's canal); *Unity Joint Stock Mutual Banking Association v King*, above (father permitted sons to construct granaries and other buildings on his land).

[48] In one case a canal company was granted an injunction against the landowner on terms that it exercised its statutory powers of compulsory purchase to acquire the land: *Somersetshire Coal Co v Harcourt*, above.

[49] *Dillwyn v Llewelyn* (1862) 4 De G.F. & J. 517; *Ramsden v Dyson* (1866) L.R. 1 H.L. 129; *Plimmer v Mayor, etc, of Wellington* (1884) 9 App.Cas. 699. However, as will be apparent from the foregoing analysis, the suggestion that the evolution of the doctrine of proprietary estoppel "in the form in which we now know it cannot be dated before *Dillwyn v Llewelyn*" (*Sen v Headley* [1991] Ch. 425 at 439, per Nourse L.J.) is incorrect.

[50] *Ramsden v Dyson*, above, at 170 and 171.

appropriately give effect to that equity.[51] "The court must look at the circumstances in each case to decide in what way the equity can be satisfied."[52] This would commonly (but not necessarily) involve the grant of some proprietary right or interest by O to C. Relief would often be given on terms (e.g. as to payment), but the doctrine could be employed to perfect a gift.[53] The courts clearly distinguished between the equity, which arose from C's detrimental reliance, and the relief by which effect was given to it. Although a court would (if need be) protect C in his possession pending the grant of relief by the court,[54] C did not enjoy any defined property right in consequence of his equity until the court made its final order.[55] That order would be implemented by a conveyance or grant of the property right (if any) to which C was adjudged to be entitled. C could enforce his equity against both O and any person who acquired O's land with notice of it.[56] There is no suggestion in the extensive corpus of 19th century authority that proprietary estoppel was a means by which novel property rights might be created.[57] It was however recognised that in giving effect to an equity arising by estoppel, a court might declare a licence granted by O to C to be irrevocable, as where C had acted to his detriment in the belief encouraged by O that he might enjoy the premises on a permanent basis.[58]

16–006   **3. Licences by estoppel.** Although these principles concerning the origin and nature of estoppel were reaffirmed by the Privy Council as late as 1963,[59] there was an unwarranted divergence from them shortly thereafter in some, but not all,[60] cases. There were two developments of importance. First, the equity which arose by estoppel and the subsequent order of the court giving effect to it came to be confused. If the court held that C was entitled to a particular right over O's land by estoppel, C would be regarded as having acquired this right from the time at which he had acted to his detriment and not merely from the time of the court's order.[61] Thus in one case concerned

---

[51] *Dillwyn v Llewelyn*, above, at 522; *Ramsden v Dyson*, above, at 171; *Plimmer v Mayor etc, of Wellington*, above, at 713 and 714.

[52] *Plimmer v Mayor etc, of Wellington*, above, at 714, per Sir Arthur Hobhouse. The parallels with the more recent decision in *Jennings v Rice* [2002] EWCA Civ 159; [2003] 1 P. & C.R.100, are striking.

[53] C's detrimental reliance took the case out of the general principle that equity would not perfect an imperfect gift: *Dillwyn v Llewelyn*, above, at 521.

[54] *Ramsden v Dyson*, above, at 171.

[55] In some of the cases C appears to have been no more than a licensee: see e.g. *Duke of Devonshire v Eglin*, above.

[56] *Duke of Beaufort v Patrick*, above; *Plimmer v Mayor etc, of Wellington*, above.

[57] Indeed the converse appears to have been the case. If the "right" visualised by the parties was of too indefinite a character to be expressly granted, C's claim would fail: *Bankart v Tennant* (1870) L.R. 10 Eq. 141 at 148, 149.

[58] *Plimmer v Mayor, etc, of Wellington*, above. Of course, this did not mean that the licence became proprietary, merely that it was irrevocable between the parties, but see below para.16–006. For the analogous doctrine of the executed licence, see below, para.16–037.

[59] *Chalmers v Pardoe* [1963] 1 W.L.R. 677 at 683, 684.

[60] See, e.g. *Dodsworth v Dodsworth* (1973) 228 E.G. 1115.

[61] See, e.g. *Ward v Kirkland* [1967] Ch. 194 at 242 and 243. For criticism, see [1988] Conv. 346 at 352 and 353 (P. T. Evans).

with unregistered land,[62] C was held to have an "equity which amounted to an equitable easement" over O's land.[63] However, that right was not in all respects the same as an equitable easement expressly granted because it was not registrable as a land charge and depended for its protection against third parties on the doctrine of notice.[64] Secondly, the doctrine of proprietary estoppel came to be employed to protect the rights of occupation of licensees.[65] If C, a licensee, acted to his detriment in reliance on an understanding that he could remain on O's land for as long as he wished, his licence became irrevocable.[66] That right of occupation—a so-called "licence coupled with an equity"[67]—appeared to be capable of protection not only against O himself, but against any successor in title who took with notice.[68] It was immaterial whether that successor in title acquired the land before[69] or after[70] C had obtained an order of the court giving effect to his equity. In this way such "equitable licences"[71] or "licences by estoppel"[72] were in effect given the status of equitable proprietary rights.[73]

Although an equity arising by estoppel is now best regarded as a species of equitable proprietary right,[74] it is questionable whether an estoppel licence can be so regarded. There was no case prior to 1926 in which a licence made irrevocable by estoppel was held to bind a third party[75] and many of the post-1925 cases where this occurred can be explained on other grounds. As the creation of novel equitable interests after 1925 appears to have been prohibited by statute,[76] the correctness of treating an "estoppel licence" as an equitable proprietary right is in great doubt. Furthermore, not only has it now been settled that contractual licences do not create equitable interests in

---

[62] *E.R. Ives Investment Ltd v High* [1967] 2 Q.B. 379. It is difficult to distil a ratio from the case: see (1967) 31 Conv. (N.S.) 332 (FR. Crane); (1967) 30 M.L.R. 580 (H.W. Wilkinson); [1991] Conv. 36 at 39, (1995) 58 M.L.R. 637 at 643 (G. Battersby).

[63] *E.R. Ives Investment Ltd v High*, above, at 405, per Winn L.J. See too *Shiloh Spinners Ltd v Harding* [1973] A.C. 691 at 721 (where Lord Wilberforce, in discussing the earlier decision, referred to "a right by estoppel—producing an effect similar to an easement").

[64] Above, para.8–099. The case might now be explained on the basis that the equity arising by estoppel may itself, prior to satisfaction by the court, be a proprietary right which will bind a purchaser of unregistered land with notice: below, para.16–031.

[65] *Inwards v Baker* [1965] 2 Q.B. 29; *Jones v Jones* [1977] 1 W.L.R. 438; *Williams v Staite* [1979] Ch. 291; *Hussey v Palmer* [1972] 1 W.L.R. 1286. Such an approach may still persist; see *Parker v Parker* [2003] EWHC 1846 (Ch); [2003] P.L.S.C.S. 191.

[66] *Re Sharpe* [1980] 1 W.L.R. 219 at 223.

[67] *Inwards v Baker*, above, at 37, per Lord Denning M.R.

[68] *Inwards v Baker*, above, at 37, per Lord Denning M.R.

[69] *Inwards v Baker*, above, at 37, per Lord Denning M.R.

[70] *Williams v Staite*, above.

[71] *Re Sharpe*, above, at 225 per Browne-Wilkinson J.; *J. Willis & Son v Willis* [1986] 1 E.G.L.R. 62 at 63, per Parker L.J.

[72] A phrase widely used by academic writers: see, e.g. [1981] Conv. 347 (P. Todd).

[73] See [1973] C.L.J. 123 at 125 et seq. (R.J. Smith). cf. *Pascoe v Turner* [1979] 1 W.L.R. 431 at 439.

[74] Below, para.16–029. This view is supported by 19th century authority: see, e.g. *Duke of Beaufort v Patrick* (1853) 17 Beav. 60.

[75] In *Plimmer v Mayor etc, of Wellington* (1884) 9 App.Cas. 699, an equity arising by estoppel, to which effect was subsequently given by an irrevocable licence, was held binding on a statutory successor in title. For the full facts of the case, see (1883) 1 N.Z.L.R. (CA) 229

[76] LPA 1925 s.4 (1), proviso. See above, para.6–064.

land,[77] it has also been suggested that no licence of any kind may do so[78] and there is no reason to depart from this orthodox position now that the status of the equity by estoppel itself has been settled.[79] In any event, it is not obvious that a licence declared to be irrevocable by reason of estoppel should create an equitable interest in land when a contractual licence does not.[80]

Where a court is asked to give effect to an equity arising by estoppel, the fact that the claimant, C, was a licensee prior to the events giving rise to the claim should of itself be irrelevant. The question in each case should be how best to give effect to the equity that has arisen in his favour.[81] Indeed, this may result in the continuation of the claimant's licence (or the grant of one where none existed before), but the fact that the source of the claim was estoppel should not pre-determine the status of the remedy given by the court. The trend of modern decisions has been to adopt this approach[82] and this looks set to continue under s.116 of the Land Registration Act 2002.[83] Indeed, over the last decade or so there has been a reversion to the solid principles laid down in the 19th century.[84]

Section 3. The Elements of Estoppel

A. Establishing the Equity

16–007   A claimant who wishes to establish an equity arising by estoppel must satisfy the court on three matters,[85] bearing in mind that the fundamental principle is to prevent unconscionable conduct.[86]

1. Encouragement or acquiescence. The owner of the land, O must have encouraged C by words or conduct to believe that he has or will in the future

[77] *Ashburn Anstalt v Arnold* [1989] Ch. 1; below. See too *Canadian Imperial Bank of Commerce v Bello* (1991) 64 P. & C.R. 48 at 51; *I.D.C. Group Ltd v Clark* [1992] 1 E.G.L.R. 187 at 189; *Lloyd v Dugdale* [2001] EWCA Civ 1754 at [50] et seq.; [2002] 2 P. & C.R. 167, at 181 et seq.

[78] *I.D.C. Group Ltd v Clark*, above, at 189.

[79] Below, para.16–031.

[80] See (1988) 51 M.L.R. 226 (J. Hill); [1991] Conv. 36 (G. Battersby). cf. *Habermann v Koehler* (1996) 73 P. & C.R. 515.

[81] For the forms of relief which the court may give, see below, para.16–020.

[82] See, e.g. *Pascoe v Turner* [1979] 1 W.L.R. 431; *Burrows v Sharp* (1989) 23 H.L.R. 83; *Lloyd v Dugdale* above.

[83] See below, para.16–031.

[84] The starting point was the judgment of Scarman L.J. in *Crabb v Arun DC* [1976] Ch. 179 at 192 et seq. which has been widely applied since: see, e.g. *Griffiths v Williams* [1978] 2 E.G.L.R. 121; *Jones v Jones* [1977] 1 W.L.R. 438 at 443; *Pascoe v Turner* above, at 437; *Coombes v Smith* [1986] 1 W.L.R. 808 at 815; *Roebuck v Mungovin* [1994] 2 A.C. 224 at 235.

[85] While it is convenient to examine the three prerequisites for a claim as if they were separate components, they do not in fact operate in isolation and must necessarily impact on each other. "In the end the court must look at the matter in the round": *Gillett v Holt* [2001] Ch. 210 at 225, per Robert Walker L.J. See too *Gonthier v Orange Contract Scaffolding Ltd* [2002] EWCA Civ 873; [2003] P.L.C.S. 156; *Bexley LBC v Maison Maurice Ltd* [2006] EWHC 3192 (Ch); [2007] 10 E.G. 184.

[86] In *Murphy v Burrows* [2004] EWHC 1900 (Ch), despite the existence of qualifying assurances and some detriment, an overall assessment meant that "the overarching requirement of unconscionability" was not satisfied, at [33], per Richard Sheldon QC. So, "ultimately the question becomes one viewed as at the moment of crystallisation, namely, whether, looked at in

enjoy some right or benefit over O's property. The mere fact that C acts to his detriment in the expectation of acquiring rights over O's land will not raise an equity in his favour unless O has encouraged that expectation.[87] However, O cannot defeat the equity by establishing that he did not mean to encourage C if C reasonably believed that such encouragement had taken place.[88] O's conduct may be either active or passive,[89] and need not be the promise of a specific right or interest, provided it is "clear enough" in the circumstances.[90]

(a) Active encouragement. Active conduct has been held to include: **16–008**

   (i) a request that C should act in a particular manner[91];

   (ii) a written or oral assurance that C would have certain rights over O's land,[92] or a greater share of land co-owned with O[93]; and

   (iii) the giving of consent to C to undertake construction work either on O's land,[94] or on his own land in a manner which would in some way affect O.[95]

In cases of active encouragement, it is no bar to an equity arising in favour of C that he was under no misapprehension as to his rights,[96] or that either O

the round, in the circumstances that have happened, it would be unconscionable for the promise not to be kept", *Suggitt v Suggitt*, above at para.43, per Roger Kaye QC.

[87] *Att Gen v Baliol College, Oxford* (1744) 9 Mod. 407; *Kenney v Brown* (1796) 3 Ridgw. P.C. 462; *Pilling v Armitage* (1805) 12 Ves. 78; *Master, etc, of Clare Hall v Harding* (1848) 6 Hare 273; *Ramsden v Dyson* (1866) L.R. 1 H.L. 129; *Brinnand v Ewens* (1987) 19 H.L.R. 415.

[88] *Thorner v Major*, above.

[89] *Russell v Watts* (1883) 25 Ch D 559 at 576; *Plimmer v Mayor, etc, of Wellington* (1884) 9 App.Cas. 699 at 712.

[90] *Thorner v Major*, above at 794 per Lord Walker. See also *Suggitt v Suggitt*, above.

[91] e.g. *Plimmer v Mayor etc, of Wellington*, above (C constructed jetty and warehouse at O's request).

[92] e.g. *Dillwyn v Llewelyn* (1862) 4 De G.F. & I. 517 (memorandum by O that he gave his lands to C); *Michaud v City of Montreal* (1923) 129 L.T. 417 (written undertaking by O to give C certain land); *Forbes v Ralli* (1925) L.R. 52 I.A. 178 (written assurance of "permanent lease"); *Veitch v Caldicott* (1945) 173 L.T. 30 (oral assurance by trustee for creditors that he would not sell C's house); *Griffiths v Williams*, above (oral assurance by mother that daughter could live in her house for life); *Pascoe v Turner*, above (oral assurance by O to his former mistress that the house in which they lived was hers); *Gillett v Holt* above (repeated oral assurances by O that his farm and associated businesses would pass by will to C); *Jennings v Rice* [2002] EWCA Civ 159 at [49]; [2003] 1 P. & C.R. 100 at 114 (oral assurances that C would inherit O's house); *Lloyd v Dugdale*, [2001] EWCA Civ 1754; [2002] 2 P. & C.R. 167 (oral assurances as to the grant of a commercial lease, but where estoppel failed on other grounds); *Suggitt v Suggitt* above (oral assurances by O to one of his children concerning the family farm).

[93] *Clarke v Meadus* [2010] EWHC 3117 (Ch) where this possibility is admitted despite a declaration of trust settling those shares.

[94] e.g. *Ahmad Yar Khan v Secretary of State for India* (1901) L.R. 28 I.A. 211 (construction of canal with government consent).

[95] *Cotching v Bassett* (1862) 32 Beav. 101 (alteration by C to ancient lights with O's permission).

[96] *Plimmer v Mayor etc, of Wellington*, above; *Veitch v Caldicott*, above, at 34; *Ward v Kirkland* [1967] Ch. 194 at 238; *Taylor Fashions Ltd v Liverpool Victoria Trustees Co Ltd* (1979) [1982] Q.B. 133n. at 148. In many cases, C will be clear that the land belongs to O, but will be trusting an assurance as to future use or ownership of the land, see, e.g. *Cobbe v Yeoman's Row Management Ltd* above.

alone, or both O and C acted under a mistaken assumption as to their respective rights.[97]

16–009   *(b) Passive encouragement.* Passive encouragement occurs when O, an owner of land, stands by and allows C to act to his detriment knowing that he mistakenly believes that he has or will obtain an interest in or right over O's land.[98] In such a situation, "the circumstance of looking on is in many cases as strong as using terms of encouragement".[99] Thus an equity arose in C's favour where he constructed an engine shed on O's land and O both acquiesced in its construction and accepted rent for it.[100] In another case, in which a lease had been forfeited, the lessors knowingly allowed the underlessees to believe that their sub-leases were still subsisting. The underlessees having acted to their detriment in this belief, the lessors were estopped from denying the validity of the underleases.[101] Likewise, where O stands by as C converts a loft space believing, inaccurately, that it forms part of the demised premises.[102] Formerly the courts adopted defined criteria for establishing acquiescence,[103] and still sometimes do,[104] but the approach is now generally more flexible.[105] The trend of authority is that it is no longer necessary to force C's conduct "into a Procrustean bed constructed from some unalterable criteria",[106] but to consider whether in the circumstances it would be unconsciona-

---

[97] *Sarat Chunder Dey v Gopal Chunder Laha* (1892) L.R. 19 I.A. 203 at 215 and 216; *Re Eaves* [1940] Ch. 109 at 117 and 118; *Taylor Fashions Ltd v Liverpool Victoria Trustees Co Ltd*, above, at 144 et seq. (where the authorities are fully reviewed).

[98] See, e.g. *Watson v Goldsbrough* [1986] 1 E.G.L.R. 265 at 267; *Munt v Beasley* [2006] EWCA Civ 370.

[99] *Dann v Spurner* (1802) 7 Ves. 231 at 236 per Lord Eldon L.C. See too *De Bussche v Alt* (1878) 8 Ch D 286 at 314 ("quiescence under such circumstances as that assent may be reasonably inferred from it": per Thesiger L.J.); *Ward v Kirkland*, above, at 239.

[100] *Mold v Wheatcroft* (1859) 27 Beav. 510. See too *Powell v Thomas* (1848) 6 Hare 300.

[101] *Hammersmith and Fulham LBC v Top Shop Centres Ltd* [1990] Ch. 237.

[102] *Munt v Beasley*, above.

[103] The so-called "five probanda", set out by Fry J. in an unreserved judgment in *Willmott v Barber* (1880) 15 Ch D 96 at 105 and 106. See *Russell v Watts* (1883) 25 Ch D 559 at 585; *Civil Service Musical Instrument Association v Whiteman* (1899) 68 L.J.Ch. 484; *Kammins Ballrooms Co Ltd v Zenith Investments (Torquay) Ltd* [1971] A.C. 850 at 884; *Crabb v Arun DC* [1976] Ch. 179 at 194; *E. & L. Berg Homes Ltd v Grey* [1980] 1 E.G.L.R. 103 at 106; *Coombes v Smith* [1986] 1 W.L.R. 808 at 817 (where the probanda were applied erroneously in a case of active encouragement); *Blue Haven Enterprises Ltd v Tully* [2006] UKPC 17 at [22] et seq.

[104] e.g. *Matharu v Matharu* (1994) 68 P. & C.R. 93; criticised [1994] Fam. Law 625 (J. Dewar); (1995) 7 C.E.L.Q. 59 (G. Battersby); (1995) 58 M.L.R. 412 (P. Milne). See also the Privy Council decision on appeal from Jamaica in *Blue Haven Enterprises Ltd v Tully* [2006] UKPC 17 where, in denying the estoppel, it was held that the last of "five probanda" was missing. An alternative, and it is suggested better, ground for deciding in favour of O was that O had not behaved unconscionably.

[105] *Electrolux Ltd v Electrix Ltd* (1954) 71 P.R.C. 23 at 33; *Hopgood v Brown* [1955] 1 W.L.R. 213 at 223; *Shaw v Applegate* [1977] 1 W.L.R. 970 at 978; *H. P. Bulmer Ltd v J. Bollinger SA* [1977] 2 C.M.L.R. 625 at 681; *Taylor Fashions Ltd v Liverpool Victoria Trustees Co Ltd*, above, at 153 and 154; *Lloyds Bank Plc v Carrick* [1996] 4 All E.R. 630 at 640. Given the fine line between active and passive encouragement, some element of flexibility seems desirable.

[106] *Taylor Fashions Ltd v Liverpool Victoria Trustees Co Ltd*, above, at 154, per Oliver J. See also *Gonthier v Orange Contract Scaffolding Ltd* [2002] EWCA Civ 873; [2003] P.L.C.S. 156.

ble for O to insist upon his strict legal rights.[107] The one element that is clearly essential is that O's conduct should have encouraged C to act as he did. Mere inaction by O in the face of an infringement of his rights cannot therefore amount to acquiescence because it does not induce C to act.[108] In cases of passive encouragement, it is unlikely that O's conduct will be regarded as unconscionable unless he was aware of:

(i) his own proprietary rights[109];

(ii) C's expenditure[110] or other detrimental acts[111]; and

(iii) C's mistaken belief that he had or would acquire an interest in or over O's land.[112]

Where the parties are negotiating "subject to contract" or "subject to lease" there will usually be no room for estoppel.[113] The use of these conventional phrases is normally taken to negative any encouragement on O's part,[114] and may also ensure that a post-detriment withdrawal of the assurance or denial of the right is not unconscionable.[115]

---

[107] See *Ward v Kirkland*, above, at 239; *Crabb v Arun DC*, above, at 195; *Amalgamated Investment & Property Co Ltd v Texas Commerce International Bank Ltd* [1982] Q.B. 84 at 104.

[108] *Proctor v Bennis* (1887) 36 Ch D 740 at 761; *Moorgate Mercantile Co Ltd v Twitchings* [1977] A.C. 890 at 902.

[109] *Armstrong v Sheppard & Short Ltd* [1959] 2 Q.B. 384.

[110] *Swallow Securities Ltd v Isenberg* [1985] 1 E.G.L.R. 132; *Barclays Bank Plc v Zaroovabli* [1997] Ch. 321 at 330, 331.

[111] Notice of C's intention to act to his detriment will suffice: *Crabb v Arun DC*, above, at 189 and 198.

[112] "You cannot encourage a belief of which you do not have any knowledge": *Brinnand v Ewens* (1987) 19 H.L.R. 415 at 418, per Nourse L.J. (O was unaware that C, a tenant of part of a house, was undertaking repairs in the belief that he would acquire a tenancy of the whole house). See too *Barclays Bank Plc v Zaroovabli*, above, at 331. The extent of C's acts of detriment may be relevant in determining whether O must have known of C's mistake: see *Bibby v Stirling* (1998) 76 P. & C.R. D36 (construction of large greenhouse by C only compatible with a belief that he might remain on the land indefinitely).

[113] *Att Gen of Hong Kong v Humphreys Estate (Queen's Gardens) Ltd* [1987] A.C. 114; *Akiens v Salomon* (1992) 65 P. & C.R. 364 (but cf. Evans L.J., dissenting, at 372 and 373); *James v Evans* [2000] 3 E.G.L.R. 1. In *Gonthier v Orange Contract Scaffolding Ltd* [2002] EWCA Civ 873; [2003] P.L.C.S. 156 at [54], Lindsay J. noted the "considerable impediment in the way of any such claim succeeding where the qualification applies". Similarly, if a person incurs expenditure in the hope of obtaining a contract relating to land (e.g. by preparing development plans), no equity will arise: *Haslemere Estates Ltd v Baker* [1982] 1 W.L.R. 1109 at 1119. However, if such expenditure is incurred in response to an assurance that such a contract, or other advantage, will be obtained, and there is no qualification "subject to contract", then an estoppel can arise, *Whittaker v Kinnear* above; *Lloyd v Sutcliffe* [2007] EWCA Civ 153; (2007) N.P.C. 23, although care must be taken not to undermine the policy behind LP(MP)A 1989 s.2. See below, para.16–018 and above para.15–043.

[114] *Derby & Co Ltd v I.T.C. Pension Trust Ltd* [1977] 2 All E.R. 890 at 896.

[115] For a case in which an equity arose notwithstanding the use of the phrase "subject to contract", see *Salvation Army Trustee Co Ltd v West Yorkshire MCC* (1980) 41 P. & C.R. 179 but note the contrary result in *Haq v Island Homes Housing Association* [2011] EWCA Civ 805. It is possible to explain such a possibility on the ground that, notwithstanding the qualification, it might still be unconscionable for the assurance to be denied or withdrawn; for example where the qualification has itself been waived orally. See *Proprietary Estoppel and Formalities in Land Law*

16–010   *(c) Agents.* In considering whether O encouraged C to act as he did, the court will have regard not only to O's own knowledge and conduct, but also to that of any agent of his.[116] In general, that agent will be taken to have the authority which he purports to exercise.[117] If O considers that he has exceeded his instructions, he can so inform C before C acts to his detriment.[118] In cases of acquiescence, only those matters which come to the knowledge of O's agent in the course of his agency will be imputed to C.[119]

16–011   *(d) Right over property.* For an equity to arise, C must have been led to believe that he had or would obtain some right or benefit in or over O's property,[120] although it is not necessary that this should amount to a specific right or benefit.[121] However, a belief that he will acquire a right of a non-proprietary character will not suffice. Thus a local authority was not estopped from refusing C planning permission to build on his own land, because he had no expectation of acquiring rights over the property of the authority.[122] However, for these purposes the acquisition of property rights includes the release or non-enforcement by O of some right that he has over C's land, such as a covenant or easement. Thus where O had leased land to C, reserving a right to enter and cut timber, he was restrained from so doing after he had encouraged C to beautify the land by laying out gardens.[123] It was once thought that no equity can arise unless C's expectation that he will acquire some interest relates to specific property of O's,[124] but it is now clear that this

---

and the Land Registration Act 2002: A Theory of Unconscionability in Modern Studies in Property Law, Vol.2, ed. E Cooke (Hart Publishing, 2003) (M.J.D.).

[116] Thus if C acts to his detriment with the assent and co-operation of O's agent, that will be regarded as sufficient encouragement: *Rochdale Canal Co v King (No.2)* (1853) 16 Beav. 630; *Laird v Birkenhead Rly Co* (1859) Johns 500.

[117] *Crabb v Anun DC*, above, at 193.

[118] *Crabb v Anum DC*, above, at 193. In general, a lawful owner does not have to repeat his assertion of full entitlement to the land once it has been clearly made (*Blue Haven Enterprises Ltd v Tully* [2006] UKPC 17, relying on *The Master or Keeper, Fellows and Scholars of Clare Hall v Harding* (1848) 6 Hare 273 at pp.296–297) and so there is no requirement for O to remind C of the agent's limitations if C acts to his detriment after being informed of the true position by O.

[119] *Att Gen to the Prince of Wales v Collom* [1916] 2 K.B. 193 (C's expenditure made with the knowledge of O's land agent imputed to O). cf. *Swallow Securities Ltd v Isenberg*, above (porter's knowledge of C's improvement to flat not imputed to O).

[120] *Western Fish Products Ltd v Penwith DC* [1981] 2 All E.R. 204 at 217. A local authority can be estopped from denying a right of way over land it owns at the time of the encouragement or acquiesence, even if that land was acquired by compulsory purchase and the estoppel arose out of events linked to the compulsory purchase: *Bexley LBC v Maison Maurice Ltd* [2006] EWHC 3192 (Ch); [2007] 10 E.G. 184.

[121] *Thorner v Major*, above.

[122] *Western Fish Products Ltd v Penwith DC*, above. See too *Lloyds Bank Plc v Carrick* [1996] 4 All E.R. 630 at 641 (no equity arising by proprietary estoppel where O already held the land in question on a bare trust for C). However, a local authority was estopped from denying a right of way over land which it had acquired by compulsory purchase: *Bexley London BC v Maison Maurice Ltd* above.

[123] *Jackson v Cator* (1800) 5 Ves. 688. In that case it was enough for the court to grant an injunction, but in other cases it might be appropriate to require O to release the right.

[124] *Layton v Martin* [1986] 2 F.L.R. 227 at 238 (representation by O that he would provide "financial security" for his mistress, C, not sufficient). But see *Chun v Ho* [2002] EWCA Civ 1075; [2004] 1 F.L.R. 23, where, without reference to *Layton v Martin*, the Court of Appeal

requirement will be satisfied if the property is ascertainable at the critical time, as where O leads C to believe that he will inherit his residuary estate.[125] It is no bar to the equity that the property subject to it changes over time[126] and even where the property is not acquired until after C has acted to his detriment in reliance upon the expectation.[127]

(e) A promise to leave property by will or on death. Traditionally, courts **16–011.1** have approached with caution a claim of proprietary estoppel based on a promise by O to make a will in favour of C or otherwise leave specific property to C on O's death. This is because of the revocable nature of a will and the testamentary freedom it brings.[128] Nevertheless, recent cases have built upon a number of earlier isolated instances,[129] and not only are such claims now more frequent, they more frequently succeed.[130] As a matter of principle, it must be possible that O can behave so unconscionably towards C during his life that a provision in O's will (or the application of the rules on intestacy) can be overridden by a successful claim to an estoppel. The leading Court of Appeal authority suggests that it is not the revocability of testamentary dispositions and testamentary freedom per se that is important,[131] but whether, taking a broad view, the quality of the assurance and the detrimental reliance are such that repudiation of the assurance would be unconscionable in all the circumstances.[132] This was not addressed specifically when the matter came before the House of Lords in a similar case, but in allowing the

refused to disturb the trial judge's finding that a promise made by O to set up a new life with C on O's release from prison was sufficiently certain to found an estoppel.

[125] *Thorner v Major,* above, *Suggitt v Suggitt,* above; *Re Basham* [1986] 1 W.L.R. 1498 at 1510. See also *Jones v Watkins* Unreported, Court of Appeal (Civil Division) Transcript No.1200 of 1987 per Slade L.J; *Gillett v Holt,* above.

[126] "However, given that the doctrine of proprietary estoppel requires a retrospective assessment to be made, whilst the identity of the property must be certain, its extent might vary and that was something to be ascertained when the equity crystallised, when the promise or assurance falls to be performed", *Suggitt v Suggitt* at 42 per Roger Kaye QC, summarising the effect of *Thorner v Major,* above.

[127] *Wayling v Jones* (1993) 69 P. &. C.R. 170. In that case O promised to leave his hotel business by will to C. O intended the promise to apply to the hotel which he owned when he died, not the one which he owned when C began to act to his detriment and which O subsequently sold. See [1995] Conv. 409 at 411 (C. Davies).

[128] [1999] Conv. 46 (M.J.D.).

[129] *Re Basham* above, *Jones v Watkins* above; *Wayling v Jones* above.

[130] *Thorner v Major,* above. See also *Gillett v Holt,* above, where the potential testator was not dead and C successfully prevented an intended disposition under a new will; *Jennings v Rice* [2002] EWCA Civ 159; *Ottey v Grundy* [2003] EWCA Civ 1176; *Murphy v Burrows* [2004] EWHC 1900 (Ch) (principle accepted but relief refused on other grounds); *Hopper v Hopper* [2008] EWHC 228 (Ch); *Suggitt v Suggitt,* above, where the claim succeeded on (as the judge noted) noticeably less certain evidence than *Thorner.*

[131] Thus, it is largely irrelevant whether C knew that a will was revocable: see *Gillett v Holt,* above, at p.227. The decision in *Taylor v Dickens* [1998] 1 F.L.R. 806 (where C's claim of estoppel in relation to promises made by O before death was dismissed precisely because C knew the will was revocable) was criticised, ibid. (*Taylor* was compromised before an appeal could be heard). In *Lloyd v Sutcliffe* [2007] EWCA Civ 153; at [38], Wilson L.J. glossed this by explaining that, "the law requires that the promisor should make clear not that the promise cannot be revoked, but that it will not be revoked". It is suggested that, in so far as the reasoning in these cases conflict, the emphasis in *Lloyd* is to be preferred.

[132] *Gillett v Holt,* above, at p.232.

estoppel where the assurances were implied from unspecific hints and an appreciation of the general relationship between the claimant and the deceased, their Lordships endorsed the Court of Appeal's broad approach.[133] It is now also established that, by reason of estoppel, O may be prevented from disposing of his property on death, subject to the court's equitable jurisdiction to give effect to the equity in the most appropriate way.[134]

16–012   **2. Detrimental reliance.** C must have acted to his detriment in reliance upon his belief that he has or will acquire some right over O's land. In the absence of detriment, it would seldom (if ever) be unconscionable for O to insist upon his strict legal rights.[135] However, detriment "is not a narrow or technical concept".[136]

16–013   *(a) Detriment.* C must prove that he has acted to his detriment.[137] The issue of detriment "must be judged at the moment when the person who has given the assurance seeks to go back on it".[138] Detriment may take many forms, and the acts relied upon may be unconnected with either O or C's land.[139] Indeed it has been said that the categories of detriment are not closed.[140]

16–014   (1) EXPENDITURE. The most obvious examples of detriment have involved expenditure by C on O's land, as where he built a house,[141] constructed a garage wall,[142] or installed drains[143] on the property, or carried out improvements to it.[144] Expenditure by C on his own land also will suffice.[145] Thus in one case, the Salvation Army built a new hall on land which it had agreed to purchase, in reliance upon O compulsorily acquiring their existing premises.[146]

[133] *Thorner v Major*, above.

[134] Thus O's estate may be required to pay a sum of money to C, as in *Jennings v Rice* above and *Campbell v Griffin* above.

[135] *Watts v Storey* (1984) 134 N.L.J. 631, quoted with approval in *Gillett v Holt* [2001] Ch. 210 at 232.

[136] *Gillett v Holt*, above, at p.232 per Robert Walker L.J.

[137] *Stevens & Cutting Ltd v Anderson* [1990] 1 E.G.L.R. 95 at 99, not following *Greasley v Cooke* [1980] 1 W.L.R. 1306 at 1314. See too *Coombes v Smith* [1986] 1 W.L.R. 808 at 821.

[138] *Gillett v Holt* above at p.232, citing with approval the judgment of Slade L.J. in *Jones v Watkins* [1987] CAT 1200; November 26, 1987.

[139] See, e.g. *Greasley v Cooke*, above. In *Ottey v Grundy*, above, the detriment comprised services to O (comfort and care) and C's lost career opportunity and was completely unrelated to the land claimed (an apartment in Jamaica and a boat). See also *Campbell v Griffin* above (personal care services to O).

[140] *Watts v Storey*, above, per Dunn L.J.

[141] *Inwards v Baker* [1965] 2 Q.B. 29.

[142] *Hopgood v Brown* [1955] 1 W.L.R. 213.

[143] *Ward v Kirkland* [1967] Ch. 194.

[144] *Dodsworth v Dodsworth* (1973) 228 E.G. 1115; *Pascoe v Turner* [1979] 1 W.L.R. 431 (home improvements and decorations); *Watson v Goldsbrough* [1986] 1 E.G.L.R. 265 (stocking ponds with fish).

[145] *Rochdale Canal Co v King (No.2)* (1853) 16 Beav. 630 (construction of mill); *Cotching v Bassett* (1862) 32 Beav. 101 (alteration to ancient lights); *E.R. Ives Investment Ltd v High* [1967] 2 Q.B. 379 (construction of garage).

[146] *Salvation Army Trustee Co Ltd v West Yorkshire MCC* (1980) 41 P. & C.R. 179. See also *Bexley LBC v Maison Maurice Ltd* (2007) 10 E.G. 184 where the claimant constructed a roadway partly on his own land and partly on that of the local authority owner.

(2) OTHER FORMS OF DETRIMENT. There was sufficient detriment where C: **16–015**

(i) sold off part of his land in the belief that he would obtain a right of access over property belonging to O[147];

(ii) looked after O or members of O's family without payment[148];

(iii) refused employment with tied accommodation and worked unpaid for O for many years[149];

(iv) gave up career[150] or educational opportunities[151];

(v) worked for O for 40 years, for below market wages, forgoing other employment opportunities[152]; and

(vi) "positioned his whole life on the basis of the assurances given to him and reasonably believed by him".[153]

(3) COUNTERVAILING BENEFITS. In considering what detriment C has suf-   **16–016**
fered, the court will take into account any countervailing benefits that he has received from O.[154] In a number of cases, C's enjoyment of O's property rent-free has been considered to outweigh any detriment that he may have incurred, whether in expending money[155] or giving up alternative accommodation.[156] In such circumstances it is not unconscionable for O to insist upon his strict legal rights.[157] However, given that the court must make a "broad enquiry" and that detriment is "not a narrow or technical concept" it is not a matter of balancing financial gains and losses. Consequently, the fact that C may have derived considerable, permanent social and financial benefit from his relationship with O does not preclude a finding of detriment.[158]

(b) Reliance. C must have acted as he did in reliance upon O's active or   **16–017**
passive encouragement. However, such reliance will be readily inferred once

---

[147] *Crabb v Arun DC* [1976] Ch. 179.

[148] *Greasley v Cooke*, above; *Campbell v Griffin* above.

[149] *Re Basham* [1986] 1 W.L.R. 1498. See too *Wayling v Jones* (1993) 69 P. & C.R. 170.

[150] *Ottey v Grundy* above (acting); *Chun v Ho* [2002] EWCA Civ 1075; [2003] 1 FLR 23 (politics).

[151] *Gillett v Holt*, above.

[152] *Gillett v Holt*, above. See also *Thorner v Major*, above.

[153] *Suggitt v Suggitt*, above, at 59.

[154] *Watts v Storey* (1984) 134 N.L.J. 631.

[155] *Lee-Parker v Izzett (No.2)* [1972] 1 W.L.R. 775; *E. & L. Berg Homes Ltd v Grey* [1980] 1 E.G.L.R. 103; *Bostock v Bryant* (1990) 61 P. & C.R. 23; *Sledmore v Dalby* (1996) 72 P. &. C.R. 196.

[156] *Watts v Storey*, above.

[157] *Lovett v Fainclough* (1990) 61 P. & C.R. 385 at 402 and 403 (12 years' free fishing adequate compensation for modest expenditure on improvement of river bank).

[158] As in *Gillett v Holt*, above, where Mr Gillett already had achieved a degree of financial security and land ownership because of his association with Mr Holt but nevertheless was able to establish detriment sufficient to found an estoppel.

it is shown that O encouraged C and C acted to his detriment.[159] In such circumstances, the onus will be on O to show that there was no such reliance.[160] If therefore O can prove that C would have acted as he did in any event,[161] that he acted on the basis of independent advice,[162] or that his conduct was motivated by some other factor,[163] no equity will arise. Thus in one case where C left her husband and became pregnant by O, it was held that she did so out of affection for him rather than because of any expectation that she would acquire an interest in his property.[164] However, it is clear that this principle cannot be taken too far. The existence of a second, or even dominant, motive for C's actions does not preclude a finding of reliance. Thus, in at least three recent cases it was clear that C's actions were motivated by kindness, love or affection for O, but this did not prevent a finding of reliance where the active or passive encouragement of O exerted at least some influence on C.[165] It seems that in cases of estoppel, where the aim is to prevent unconscionability, the court is loath to penalise those claimants whose actions are not motivated solely by a desire to acquire O's land or some interest in it. Such an approach is understandable in family and similar relationships where equity would not want to reward only those who act for themselves in contrast to those who might act for the benefit of others. It is unlikely, however, that this generous approach can be stretched to cover more distant relationships, including those of a commercial nature, where the parties can be expected to be more astute to protect their own interests.[166] In such cases, proof by O that C had a dominant motive for his action, irrespective of reliance on O's encouragement, may be sufficient to defeat the claim of estoppel. However, O

---

[159] *Greasley v Cooke*, above, as explained in *Stevens & Cutting Ltd v Anderson* [1990] 1 E.G.L.R. 95 at 97, and *Bostock v Bryant*, above, at 31. See too *Hammersmith and Fulham LBC v Top Shop Centres Ltd* [1990] Ch. 237 at 262; *Lim v Ang* [1992] 1 W.L.R. 113 at 118; and Snell, *Equity*, Ch.10.

[160] *Grant v Edwards* [1986] Ch. 638 at 656; *Wayling v Jones* (1993) 69 P. & C.R. 170. In the latter case, C was O's homosexual partner and worked for him, receiving only pocket money and living expenses on the understanding that O would leave to C in his will the hotel that he owned. It appears that C would have acted as he did if O had made no promise at all to him, but that, the promise having been made, C would have left O had he known that he had reneged on it: *Wayling v Jones*, at 175 and 176. See (1995) 111 L.Q.R. 389 (E. Cooke).

[161] *Taylor Fashions Ltd v Liverpool Victoria Trustees Co Ltd* [1982] Q.B. 133 fn. at 155 and 156 (installation of lift by tenants 18 years before expiry of term not undertaken in reliance upon option to renew).

[162] cf. *Western Fish Products Ltd v Penwith DC* [1981] 2 All E.R. 204 at 217 (C acted in the belief that he had an existing legal right to build a factory rather than on the basis of any representation from the local planning authority).

[163] Such as natural love and affection: cf. *Re Basham*, above, at 1505 (where on the facts, C's conduct went "well beyond what was called for by natural love and affection", per Nugee, QC).

[164] *Coombes v Smith* [1986] 1 W.L.R. 808.

[165] *Campbell v Griffin*, above (normal human kindness); *Ottey v Grundy*, above (love and affection for partner); *Chun v Ho* above (love and affection for partner).

[166] cf. *Cobbe* v *Yeoman's Row Management Limited*, above.

cannot escape the equity by showing that he did not intend C to rely on the assurances: it is enough if it was reasonable for C to rely on them.[167]

3. Unconscionability. To establish an equity by estoppel, it must be uncon- **16–018** scionable for O to act in such a way as to defeat the expectation that C had been encouraged to believe that he had.[168] Absence of unconscionability is fatal to C's claim,[169] but O:

> "cannot escape an estoppel by asserting, even credibly, that his personal subjective conscience was only weakly responsive to the stimuli which others would have recognised and that he has thus failed to detect anything unconscionable in his behaviour".[170]

Unconscionability has an objective element and is not to be tested only by reference to the subjective state of O's mind.[171] It is not essential that O should also have been guilty of unconscionable conduct in permitting C to assume that he could act as he did.[172] It is O's subsequent refusal to permit C's use or enjoyment of the land that must be unconscionable. It has been explained that the requirement of unconscionability is now regarded as the essential element of proprietary estoppel.[173] But the courts will not invoke proprietary estoppel "as a general jurisdiction in equity to relieve hardship resulting from the application of the general law",[174] or merely "because justice and good conscience" seem to require it.[175] Estoppel is not a remedy for unconscionable conduct per se,[176] but "it is equally true that focussing on

---

[167] *Thorner v Major*, above. "It may be that there could be exceptional cases where, even though a person reasonably relied on a statement, it might be wrong to conclude that the statement-maker was estopped, because he could not reasonably have expected the person so to rely. However, such cases would be rare" ibid at 799 per Lord Neuberger.

[168] *Crabb v Arun DC* [1976] Ch. 179 at 195; *Taylor Fashions Ltd v Liverpool Victoria Trustees Co Ltd*, above at 151 and 152. cf. *Lloyds Bank Plc v Carrick* [1996] 4 All E.R. 630 at 641 (C's expectation that she was beneficial owner of the property she had contracted to purchase from O was defeated not by O subsequently mortgaging the property, but by C's failure to register her estate contract: *sed quaere*).

[169] *Murphy v Burrows*, above.

[170] *Gonthier v Orange Contract Scaffolding Ltd* [2003] EWCA Civ 873 at [4] per Lindsay J.

[171] *Gonthier v Orange Contract Scaffolding Ltd.*

[172] *Lim v Ang*, above, at 117.

[173] *Taylor Fashions Ltd v Liverpool Victoria Trustees Co Ltd*, above; *Gillett v Holt* above.

[174] *E. & L. Berg Homes Ltd v Grey*, above, at 108, per Ormrod L.J.

[175] *Haslemere Estates Ltd v Baker* [1982] 1 W.L.R. 1109 at 1119, per Megarry V.C. Although much criticised and perhaps wrong in the result, the point made in *Taylor v Dickens*, above, that "there is no equitable jurisdiction to hold a person to a promise simply because the court thinks it unfair, unconscionable or morally objectionable for him to go back on it. If there were such a jurisdiction, one might as well forget the law of contract and issue every civil judge with a portable palm tree" at 820, per Judge Weeks, contains a grain of truth and reflects a concern that estoppel should not be used to avoid the normal rules that govern dispositions and contracts concerning land.

[176] *Cobbe v Yeoman's Row Management Ltd*, above.

technicalities can lead to a degree of strictness inconsistent with the fundamental aims of equity".[177]

The courts have not attempted any definite list of factors that will determine
whether O's conduct is unconscionable, but have preferred to make a broad
enquiry in each case. "In the end the court must look at the matter in the
round".[178] It is, however, possible to list some of the factors that have been
considered in determining whether O's conduct was unconscionable:

(i) the relative positions of O and C[179];

(ii) the equivocal or unequivocal nature of the assurances[180];

(iii) whether the detriment was sufficiently substantial[181];

(iv) whether the proposed agreement or discussions were "subject to
contract" or "subject to lease"[182];

(v) whether the use of the land for which the original assurance was
given could still be achieved[183];

(vi) in cases where the parties have tried, but failed, to enter into a
binding contract for the disposition of an interest in land,[184] the
failed agreement may give rise to estoppel when it is unconscionable to rely on the failure. However, this will only be in exceptional
cases,[185] and it may well be only where O has expressly or
impliedly promised not to rely on the lack of formality in the
disputed transaction.[186] It would be difficult to establish the equity

---

[177] *Thorner v Major*, above at p.804 per Lord Neuberger.

[178] *Gillett v Holt* [2002] Ch. 210 at 225, per Robert Walker L.J.

[179] See *Sledmore v Dalby* (1996) 72 P. & C.R. 196 (C had lived on the property rent-free for
18 years, but his use of the premises had become minimal, whereas O had a pressing need for the
property to accommodate her).

[180] *Murphy v Burrows*, above, where this prevented an estoppel, but see *Jones v Watkins* above
where equivocal assurances were not fatal.

[181] *Gillett v Holt*, above, at pp.231–235.

[182] *Att Gen of Hong Kong v Humphreys Estate (Queen's Gardens) Ltd* [1987] A.C. 114.

[183] *Clark v Clarke* [2006] EWHC 275 (Ch), where the repudiation of the assurance by O in the
future would not be unconscionable if C could no longer use the land for the purpose for which
the assurance was made. This suggests that something which could once have been unconscionable may cease to be so if external factors intervene.

[184] e.g. *Flowermix Ltd v Site Development (Ferndown) Ltd* Lawtel LTL, April 26, 2000
(contract void for uncertainty of subject matter); *Kinane v Mackie-Conteh* [2005] EWCA Civ 45;
(2005) 6 E.G. 140 (CS) (no valid mortgage in the absence of written instrument); *Lloyd v Sutcliffe*
[2007] EWCA Civ 153; (2007) 22 E.G. 162 (negotiations were only an invitation to treat);
Whittaker v Kinnear, above (contract appeared to misrepresent the parties' bargain). But note
Cobbe v Yeoman's Row Management Ltd above (contract failed to comply with LP(MP)A 1989
s.2) where there was no estoppel because in that commercial context both parties knew, or should
have known, that a written contract was essential. Hence it was not unconscionable to insist on
such a contract.

[185] See *Herbert v Doyle*, above and above para.15–043.

[186] See *Kinane v Mackie-Conteh* above, at [28]; *Confining and defining proprietary estoppel:
the role of unconscionability* (2010) 30 Legal Studies 408 (M.J.D.); [2005] Conv. 501 (B.
McFarlane).

if the parties intended to enter into a formal agreement setting out the terms on which land was to be acquired or where further terms remain to be agreed[187]; and

(vii) whether O intended to make his assurance irrevocable.[188]

B. Bars to the Equity

No equity will arise if the owner lacks capacity at the time when the claimant is alleged to have been encouraged to act to his detriment. Thus not only can "nothing of acquiescence" be imputed to a minor,[189] but positive acts of encouragement by a person purporting to act on a minor's behalf without authority will not bind him, though he may be taken to have adopted them by his conduct when he subsequently comes of age.[190] However, where the person under a disability himself makes the representation in circumstances where his conduct amounts to fraud, an equity may arise.[191] Although an equity can be asserted against the Crown[192] or a local authority,[193] this is subject to the important limitation that a public body cannot act outside its powers.[194] Therefore no estoppel can be raised "to prevent the exercise of a statutory discretion or to prevent or excuse the performance of a statutory duty".[195] It is also the case that estoppel cannot be invoked "to render valid a transaction which the legislature, on the general grounds of public policy, has enacted to be invalid or void,"[196] e.g., an estoppel founded on illegal user. However, to determine whether this is so, the court examines the mischief at which the statute is directed.[197]

16–019

[187] *Herbert v Doyle* [2010] EWCA Civ 1095 at [57]. See also *Haq v Island Homes Housing Association*, above.

[188] *Lloyd v Sutcliffe* [2007] EWCA Civ 153 at [30]; and see above, para.16–011(e).

[189] *Duke of Leeds v Earl of Amherst* (1846) 2 Ph. 117 at 123, per Lord Cottenham L.C.

[190] *Somersetshire Coal Canal Co Ltd v Harcourt* (1858) 2 De G. & I. 596 (where O's steward purported to act on his behalf).

[191] *Savage v Foster* (1723) 9 Mod. 35 at 37; Story's *Equity Jurisprudence*, para.385.

[192] *Plimmer v Mayor, etc, of Wellington* (1884) 9 App.Cas. 699.

[193] *Crabb v Arun DC*, above; *Bexley London BC v Maison Maurice Ltd* above.

[194] *West Middlesex Golf Club Ltd v Earling LBC* (1993) 68 P. & C.R. 461 at 485.

[195] *Western Fish Products Ltd v Penwith DC* (1978) [1981] 2 All E.R. 204 at 219, per Megaw L.J. See *R v East Sussex CC Ex p. Reprotech (Pebsham) Ltd* [2003] 1 W.L.R. 348, at p.358 where Lord Hoffmann implies that the matter would be dealt with more properly in the context of legitimate expectation. See too *Yarmouth (Isle of Wight) Harbour Commissioners v Harold Hayles (Yarmouth Isle of Wight) Ltd* [2004] EWHC 3375 (Ch); *Rowland v Environment Agency* [2003] EWCA Civ 1885; [2005] Ch. 1.

[196] *Yaxley v Gotts* [2000] Ch. 162 at 181 and 182, per Clarke L.J. For the relationship of estoppel to statutory formalities for the creation of a contract concerning land, see below para.16–034.

[197] *Yaxley v Gotts*; and see below, para.16–026. An earlier decision, *Hanning v Top Deck Travel Group Ltd* (1993) 68 P. & C.R. 14 at 21, in which it was suggested that there could be no estoppel in relation to the illegal user of common land, must now be open to question. In a case where it is alleged that an easement has arisen by prescription (and prescription, like some cases of estoppel, is based upon acquiescence), illegal use is not necessarily a bar if the landowner could lawfully have authorised the conduct: see *Bakewell Management Ltd v Brandwood* [2004] UKHL 14; [2004] 2 A.C. 519, overruling *Hanning* on this point. See below, para.28–034.

C. The Form of Relief

16–020   **1. Discretionary nature of relief.** The court will look at the circumstances in each case to determine how the equity can best be satisfied,[198] and it has a wide discretion as to the order which it may make.[199] The essence of the relief is to avoid an unconscionable result.[200] This discretion is exercised according to equitable principles and:

"the court must take a principled approach and cannot exercise a completely unfettered discretion according to the individual judge's notion of what is fair in any particular case".[201]

In some cases the court has done no more than restrain O from asserting his legal rights.[202] In others it has ordered O to grant to C a right over or an interest in his land,[203] to convey the land to C either in fee simple[204] or for a term of years,[205] or to require O's personal representatives to transfer the land, or some of it, to C.[206] The court may order O to make a money payment to C by way of compensation,[207] which may be secured by a lien over O's property.[208] In a number of cases C has been granted a mere licence.[209] Relief may be and commonly is given on terms, e.g. C may be required to make

---

[198] *Plimmer v Mayor, etc, of Wellington*, above, at 714. See too *Lord Cawdor v Lewis* (1835) 1 Y. & C.Ex. 427 at 433; *Roebuck v Mungovin* [1994] 2 A.C. 224 at 235. The aim of the relief is to satisfy the equity, not to satisfy C's expectations or to compensate for his detriment, although either might actually result, *Jennings v Rice* [2003] 1 P. & C.R. 100. For an analysis of the manner in which the discretion is exercised, see (1999) 115 L.Q.R. 438 (pre-*Jennings*) and (2006) 122 L.Q.R. 492 (post-*Jennings*) (S. Gardner).

[199] *Holiday Inns Inc v Broadhead* (1974) 232 E.G. 951 at 1087; *Griffiths v Williams* [1978] 1 E.G.L.R. 121 at 122; *Burrows v Sharp* (1989) 23 H.L.R. 82 at 91.

[200] *Jennings v Rice*, above.

[201] *Jennings v Rice*, above at [43] at 112, per Robert Walker L.J. See also *Williams v Staite* [1979] Ch. 291 at 301; *J. Willis & Son v Willis* [1986] 1 E.G.L.R. 62 at 63.

[202] e.g. *Cotching v Bassett* (1862) 32 Beav. 101; *Marharaj v Chand* [1986] A.C. 898.

[203] *Crabb v Arun DC* [1976] Ch. 179 (court ordered the grant of an easement); *Holiday Inns Inc v Broadhead*, above (C granted a beneficial half share in O's property).

[204] *Dillwyn v Llewelyn* (1862) 4 De G. E. & J. 517; *Pascoe v Turner* [1979] 1 W.L.R. 431; *Voyce v Voyce* (1991) 62 P. & C.R. 290; *Durant v Heritage* [1994] E.G.C.S. 134. See too *Lim v Ang*, above (transfer of beneficial half share in property ordered).

[205] *Griffiths v Williams*, above; *Watson v Goldsbrough* [1986] 1 E.G.L.R. 265; *J. T. Developments Ltd v Quinn* (1990) 62 P. & C.R. 33.

[206] *Thorner v Major*, above; *Suggitt v Suggitt*, above.

[207] *Veitch v Caldicott* (1945) 173 L.T. 30; *Dodsworth v Dodsworth* (1973) 228 E.G. 1115; *Burrows v Sharp*, above; *Baker v Baker* [1993] 2 F.L.R. 247; *Wayling v Jones* (1993) 69 P. & C.R. 170; *Jennings v Rice*, above; *Campbell v Griffin* [2001] EWCA Civ 990. Both the reasons for awarding compensation and the quantification of the amount have varied, and will depend upon the circumstances. This may have reference to the nature of the expectation created: (see [1995] Conv. 409 (C. Davies)) but in both *Jennings* and *Campbell* the compensation was significantly less than the value of the expectation.

[208] *Unity Joint Stock Mutual Banking Association v King* (1858) 25 Beav. 72; *Burrows v Sharp*, above; *Baker v Baker*, above.

[209] *Inwards v Baker* [1965] 2 Q.B. 29; *Williams v Staite*, above; *Parker v Parker*, above. This form of relief is not without its difficulties: see above, para.16–006; and below, para.16–033.

some payment for the right which he is granted,[210] or provision may be made for the person who would be entitled in the absence of an estoppel.[211]

2. Factors relevant to the exercise of the discretion

(a) Minimum equity. In granting relief, the court will "analyse the minimum **16–021** equity to do justice" to C.[212] It will not therefore give him a greater right or interest than he believed he had or expected to receive.[213] Prior to 1997, a particular problem had arisen when C had been encouraged to believe that he could occupy O's property indefinitely. If the court had granted him an indefinite licence to reside on the property, the effect of its order might have been to create a settlement under the Settled Land Act 1925[214] of which C would have been the life tenant.[215] Because such a life tenant has extensive powers of disposition under that Act,[216] C would thereby have acquired an interest in the property that would considerably have exceeded his expectations.[217] In such circumstances it became the practice for the court to make an order that more closely corresponds to C's expectations, such as by requiring O to grant him a long lease at a nominal rent determinable on C's death.[218] Since the Trusts of Land and Appointment of Trustees Act 1996 came into force,[219] these particular difficulties no longer exist, because new settlements cannot be created.[220]

Although C's expectations provide an upper limit to the relief which may be given, the court is not bound to give effect to them in the manner which C envisaged if circumstances have changed so as to make it inappropriate, or if a more appropriate form of relief would remedy the unconscionability.[221] Thus if C has acted to his detriment in the belief that he can live with O and the parties subsequently become estranged, the court will not give C a right to reside on the premises but will find some other means of giving effect to the equity. This will commonly take the form of an order that O should pay C

---

[210] *Duke of Devonshire v Eglin* (1851) 14 Beav. 530; *Duke of Beaufort v Patrick* (1853) 17 Beav. 60; *Lim v Ang* [1992] 1 W.L.R. 113. See too *Crabb v Arun DC*, above, where C would have been required to pay O for the easement which he was granted by the court, had O's conduct not been such that C's own land had been rendered useless for a number of years. In *Cameron v Murdoch* (1986) 63 A.L.R. 575 at 596, the Privy Council gave effect to C's equity by allowing him to purchase land from O at a discount.

[211] *Suggitt v Suggitt*, above.

[212] *Crabb v Arun DC*, above, at 198, per Scarman L.J. "One has to make up one's mind how far it is necessary to go to see that [C] has not suffered any wrong": *Veitch v Caldicott*, above, at 34, per Atkinson J.

[213] *Dodsworth v Dodsworth* (1973) 228 E.G. 1115; *Watson v Goldsbrough*, above, at 267.

[214] The point is not free from doubt: see above, para.16–006.

[215] *Dodsworth v Dodsworth*, above. For there to be a settlement within SLA 1925 s.1, there must be some "instrument", but the order of the court may satisfy this requirement: *Griffiths v Williams* [1978] 1 E.G.L.R. 121 at 123. See below, Appendix, para.A–041.

[216] See below, Appendix, para.A–040.

[217] *Dodsworth v Dodsworth*, above.

[218] *Griffiths v Williams*, above.

[219] On January 1, 1997.

[220] See below, Appendix, para.10–034.

[221] *Burrows v Sharp* (1989) 23 H.L.R. 82 at 92. cf. (1984) 100 L.Q.R. 376 (S. Moriarty); *Jennings v Rice* above.

compensation for his expenditure,[222] or for the loss of the right of occupation which C expected to receive.[223] Furthermore, no relief of any kind will be given if the "right" which C claims is too indefinite to be adequately defined or granted.[224]

16–022   *(b) Conduct of the parties.*[225] "In determining the relief appropriate the court must look at the conduct of the parties as well as the extent of the equity."[226] The jurisdiction to give relief is an equitable one and the conduct of both the claimant, C, and the owner of the land, O, is relevant to its exercise.[227]

16–023   (1) CONDUCT OF THE CLAIMANT. A party seeking equitable relief must come with clean hands. Although trivial misconduct will not be fatal to his claim, the court will refuse relief if he has seriously misconducted himself,[228] as it did where C had submitted a fraudulent claim for improvements to O's property which had never been made,[229] where C had engaged in persistent and oppressive manipulation of O[230] and where C had abused a position of trust.[231]

16–024   (2) CONDUCT OF THE LANDOWNER. The conduct of the owner of the land may influence both the extent of the relief granted and the terms upon which it is given.[232] In one case the court ordered O to transfer the fee simple in a house to C rather than merely giving her a licence to live there for her lifetime. Only in this way could it adequately protect C against O, who intended to evict her from the house by any means available.[233] In a case in which C's equity was satisfied by the grant of a right of way over O's property, the court did not require C to pay anything in return because O had rendered C's land sterile for several years by its high-handed conduct.[234]

16–025   (3) MISCONDUCT AFTER THE GRANT OF RELIEF. Once a court has given effect to C's equity, his subsequent conduct will not normally affect the right which

---

[222] *Dodsworth v Dodsworth*, above; *Burrows v Sharp*, above.

[223] *Baker v Baker* [1993] 2 E.L.R. 247.

[224] *Bankart v Tennant* (1870) L.R. 10 Eq. 141 at 148 (where the alleged "right" was to take surplus water from a canal); *Willis v Hoare* (1998) 77 P. & C.R. D42 (undertaking to offer C a sub-lease without any indication of terms too uncertain). cf. *Orgee v Orgee* (1997) E.G.C.S. 152.

[225] See [1986] Conv. 406 (M. P. Thompson).

[226] *Baker v Baker* [1993] 2 F.L.R. 247 at 258, per Roch L.J.

[227] *Suggitt v Suggitt*, above

[228] *J. Willis & Son v Willis* [1986] 1 E.G.L.R. 62. See too *Williams v Staite* [1979] Ch. 291 at 301.

[229] *J. Willis & Son v Willis*, above.

[230] *Yeo v Wilson* July 27, 1998 (Chancery Division); LTL Document Ac0007193.

[231] *Murphy v Rayner*, above.

[232] *Baker v Baker*, above.

[233] *Pascoe v Turner* [1979] 1 W.L.R. 431. Could not the equity have been better satisfied by the grant of a long lease determinable on the death of C? cf. *Griffiths v Williams* [1978] 1 E.G.L.R. 121 at 123; and see [1979] Conv. 379 at 381 (F. R. Crane).

[234] *Crabb v Arun DC* [1976] Ch. 179.

he has been granted. Where C has been given some proprietary right over O's land which he then abuses, O has the usual tortious remedies of trespass and nuisance against him.[235] It has, however, been suggested that where C had been granted no more than a licence, O might be able to revoke it in a case of serious misconduct by C.[236] Even if this is the case (which is by no means certain),[237] the degree of impropriety that is required to justify the revocation of C's licence is greater than that which will bar his initial claim to relief.[238]

(c) Other bars to relief

(1) ENFORCEMENT CONTRARY TO STATUTE. The court will not give effect to **16–026** C's equity if and to the extent that to do so would contravene some statute.[239] This latter principle is subject to two qualifications. First, the court will give such relief as does not conflict with the statute even if it cannot give the more extensive rights which C might otherwise have sought.[240] As has been explained, this requires the court to examine the mischief which the statute sought to address.[241] Secondly, it is not every statutory provision that is fatal to the enforcement of an equity. If the statute merely regulates the dealings between the parties to a transaction, rather than laying down some more general rule of a public character, the court may give effect to an equity in C's favour and O may be unable to rely on the statute.[242] O may therefore be estopped from relying on the provisions of:

> (i) a registration statute which would otherwise render void for non-registration some right or interest of C's[243]; or

---

[235] *Williams v Staite*, above, at 300.

[236] *Williams v Staite*, above, at 298. See [1986] Conv. 406 at 412 et seq. (M. P. Thompson).

[237] *J. Willis & Son v Willis*, above, at 63.

[238] *J. Willis & Son v Willis*, above.

[239] *Chalmers v Pardoe* [1963] 1 W.L.R. 677 (relief refused because its grant would have contravened a prohibition on dealing with land without the consent of a statutory body); *London & Associated Investment Trust Plc v Calow* (1986) 53 P. & C.R. 340 at 354 and 355 (party not estopped from relying on a statutory provision which prohibited contracting out). cf. *Ward v Kirkland* [1967] Ch. 194 at 241, 242, where Ungoed-Thomas J., in giving effect to an equity, granted C a right which O had no capacity by statute to grant. *Sed quaere*: see (1966) 30 Conv. (N.S.) 233 at 236 (F. R. Crane).

[240] *Maharaj v Chand* [1986] A.C. 898 (C granted an injunction to restrain eviction by O even though she could not claim an interest in the property by reason of a statutory prohibition). cf. Snell, *Equity*, Ch.10, suggesting that the equity itself is barred, rather than merely the remedy.

[241] *Yaxley v Gotts* [2000] Ch. 162 at 181 and 182; above, para.16–019.

[242] There is a close parallel with the doctrine that a court will not permit a statute to be used as an instrument of fraud: see, above, para.11–043. Although the precise basis of the doctrine is controversial, one possible explanation is that it is an aspect of equitable estoppel: see *Steadman v Steadman* [1976] A.C. 536 at 540.

[243] See *Taylor Fashions Ltd v Liverpool Victoria Trustees Co Ltd* (1979) [1982] Q.B. 133n., where O was estopped from relying on LCA 1925 s.13(2) (now LCA 1972 s.4(6); above, para.8–094) when C had failed to register an estate contract as a land charge. cf. *Lyus v Prowsa Developments Ltd* [1982] 1 W.L.R. 1044 at 1054, where the doctrine that a statute cannot be used as an instrument of fraud was applied to LRA 1925 s.20(1).

(ii) a statute requiring compliance with certain formalities for contracts[244] or trusts relating to land.[245]

16–027   (4) ENFORCEMENT INEQUITABLE. Other bars to equitable relief, such as
laches, should in principle apply to C's claim. However, where C is either in
possession of O's land or exercising the right over it which he believes that he
has, mere delay will not bar his claim. In such circumstances C is not sleeping
on his rights but is relying upon his equity.[246]

D. The Nature of the Equity

16–028   **1. The characteristics of the equity.** The equity which arises by estoppel
is an equitable proprietary right to go to a court to seek relief. The court has
a wide discretion as to the manner in which it may satisfy the equity, which
may or may not involve the grant to C of a proprietary right over O's land. If
the court does order that C be granted a property right, that grant is not
retrospective, but operates only from the time of the execution of the court's
order.[247] Before the Land Registration Act 2002 was brought into force,[248]
there was controversy as to the nature of the equity,[249] both because of its
discretionary character and because it did not always lead to the grant of a
property right. There were two principal views. The first was that it was a
"mere equity", akin to a right to seek rectification or specific performance, but
of an "inchoate" character.[250] As such, it was a proprietary right, the benefit
of which passed on a transfer by C of his land,[251] and which could in
appropriate circumstances bind a third party who acquired O's land.[252] The

---

[244] LP(MP)A 1989 s.2. *Whittaker v Kinnear*, above. But see *Cobbe v Yeoman's Row Management Ltd* above and *Herbert v Doyle* above which suggest limits to the extent to which estoppel
can be used to enforce an otherwise invalid contract. cf. *Yaxley v Gotts* [2000] Ch. 162, above,
para.15–043 and below para.16–034. The suggestion in *Yaxley* that the estoppel requires a
constructive trust to shield it from the effect of s.2 (by use of s.2(5)) has not been followed
explicitly, although see *Brightlingsea Haven Ltd v Morris* [2008] EWHC 1928 (QB). Such a view
fails to recognise that estoppels are not caught by s.2 precisely because they remedy unconscionability and do not need the shield of a constructive trust or LP(MP)A 1989 s.2(5).
[245] LPA 1925 s.53(1)(b); above, para.11–043. cf. *Rochefoucauld v Boustead* [1897] 1 Ch. 196
(where the doctrine that a statute may not be used as an instrument of fraud was applied to the
precursor of this provision).
[246] *Voyce v Voyce* (1991) 62 P. & C.R. 290 at 293. cf. *Williams v Greatrex* [1957] 1 W.L.R. 31;
below, para.35–041.
[247] *Griffiths v Williams* [1978] 1 E.G.L.R. 121 at 123; *Williams v Staite* [1979] Ch. 291 at 300
and 301. See [1992] Fam. Law 72 at 75 (P. J. Clarke).
[248] On October 13, 2003.
[249] See [1992] Conv. 53 at 57 (J. E. Martin).
[250] See [1991] Conv. 15 (G. Battersby). See too (1976) 40 Conv. (N.S.) 156 at 158 (E. R. Crane)
and [1986] Conv. 406 (M. P. Thompson). For mere equities, see para.8–012.
[251] *Boots the Chemist Ltd v Street* [1983] 2 E.G.L.R. 51; above, para.8–013. There is some
authority that the benefit of an equity arising by estoppel does indeed pass automatically on a
conveyance of land: see *Brikom Investments Ltd v Carr* [1979] Q.B. 467 at 484 and 485 (where
Lord Denning M.R.'s remarks, although made in relation to promissory estoppel, were intended
to apply more generally).
[252] See below, and note *Lloyd v Dugdale* [2001] EWCA Civ 1754; [2002] 2 P. & C.R. 13, where
although the estoppel did not bind on the facts (there was no actual occupation of the burdened
land), the court had no doubt that it was capable of doing so.

second view was that the equity was a purely personal right enforceable only by C against O. This is because the "flexible claim does not seem certain or stable enough to qualify as a property interest".[253] This view was questionable and is now untenable. Although there were decisions which supported the view that an equity by estoppel was a personal right,[254] the weight of both authority and practice suggested that it was proprietary[255] and this view has now prevailed.[256]

2. The equity as a proprietary right: Land Registration 2002 s.116.   **16–029**
Section 116 of the Land Registration Act 2002 declares that "for the avoidance of doubt", in relation to registered land, both an equity by estoppel and a mere equity[257] are interests which are capable of binding successors in title.[258]

Although there has been some discussion over the precise effect of this provision,[259] it is clear that the Law Commission considered that it put the proprietary nature of the equity by estoppel beyond doubt.[260] Indeed, there is no reason to believe that the section means anything other than exactly what it says. Attempts to interpret it differently appear to be based on pre-conceived notions of what estoppel should be, rather than what the statute provides that it is.

Because an equity by estoppel has proprietary effect in the period after it has arisen but before it is satisfied, it may bind purchasers. If the equity is protected, whether by the entry of a notice or (as will usually be the case) as an overriding interest by reason of C's actual occupation,[261] any purchaser from O will be bound by C's equity, as by any other protected property right in registered land. When the court or Adjudicator[262] comes to give effect to that equity, whether against O or any purchaser from him, the relief granted

---

[253] (1990) 106 L.Q.R. 87 at 97 (D. J. Hayton); [1998] Conv. 502 (P. Critchley).

[254] See, e.g. *Ward v Kirkland* [1967] Ch. 194 at 241 and 242.

[255] *Ahmad Yar Khan v Secretary of State for India* (1901) L.R. 28 I.A. 211 at 218, per Lord Macnaghten; *Voyce v Voyce*, above, at 294, per Dillon L.J. See also *Plimmer v Mayor, etc, of Wellington* (1884) 9 App.Cas. 699 at 714. Of course, if an equity arising by estoppel is proprietary, then not only may it be binding on third parties according to the normal rules of registered or unregistered title, but, as indicated above, the benefit may be transmissible: cf. (1995) 7 C.F.L.Q. 59 at 63 (G. Battersby); [1995] Conv. 332 at 336 (M. Haley). See also *Voyce v Voyce*, above, at 293, where Dillon L.J. drew an analogy between the grant of relief in a case of estoppel and the remedy of specific performance. The analogy is a close one. Where a party seeks specific performance, the court may make the decree, award damages in lieu under the Supreme Court Act 1981 s.50, or dismiss the action. Another possible analogy is with a pending land action: see (1995) 58 M.L.R. 637 at 642 (G. Battersby).

[256] See below, para.16–029. There were in fact few cases where the status of the estoppel arose directly. In many cases, the litigation was between O and C and was concluded before O had made any disposition to a purchaser. A rare example is *Lloyd v Dugdale*, above. See also the Advice of the Privy Council in *Henry v Henry* [2010] UKPC 3.

[257] For mere equities, see above, para.8–012.

[258] See (2001) Law Com. No.271, paras 5.29–5.36; and see above, para.7–067.

[259] cf. [2003] C.L.J. 661 (B. McFarlane).

[260] (2001) Law Com. No.271, para.5.31.

[261] See above paras 7–089 et seq, especially at para.7 097.

[262] See LRA 2002 s.110(4); above, para.7–130.

may take the form of the award of a proprietary right to or over land (which should then be protected in the register of title in the appropriate way), but may also result in some non-proprietary relief, such as a monetary payment.[263] Once relief has been given, the equity is spent, and s.116 is no longer relevant. If O then sells the land, any purchaser will be bound by any property right granted by the court or Adjudicator to satisfy C's equity, provided that right has been protected.[264]

16–029.1   **3. Unregistered title.** There is no equivalent of s.116 in relation to unregistered title. Although it is perhaps conceivable that a court might take a different approach where title was unregistered, the case law prior to the Land Registration Act 2002 provides a sufficient basis for adopting the same approach.[265] Indeed, there was no suggestion prior to the 2002 Act that the position in registered and unregistered title was different and s.116 itself states that the proprietary nature of the equity by estoppel is "declared for the avoidance of doubt".

16–029.2   **4. After acquired land.** In one situation, C's equity arising by estoppel can only be a personal right against O. This is where O has not yet acquired the property in which C believes he is to have an interest.[266]

16–030   **5. Effect on third parties.** Prior to the Land Registration Act 2002, there was authority that an equity arising by estoppel was capable of binding a third party who acquired the land affected by it.[267] This is now settled,[268] but the precise circumstances in which this can occur depend upon whether title to the land is unregistered or registered.[269]

16–031   *(a) Unregistered land.* It has been held on a number of occasions that where O conveys his land, the transferee is bound by an equity which affects the property. Two reasons have been given for this.

(i) At common law, an estoppel is binding on both the parties to it and their "privies".[270] For these purposes:

---

[263] See above, para.16–020, for the different forms of relief that a court may give.

[264] For the priority of registered dispositions, see above, paras 7–060 et seq.

[265] *Ahmad Yar Khan v Secretary of State for India* (1901) L.R. 28 I.A. 211 at 218, per Lord Macnaghten.

[266] *Abbey National BS v Cann* [1991] 1 A.C. 56 at 89. See [1991] Conv. 155 at 161 (P. T. Evans). See also [2005] Conv. 14 (S. Bright and B. McFarlane).

[267] *Lloyd v Dugdale* above where C failed because they did not satisfy the priority rules of the Land Registration Act 1925 rather than because his estoppel could never bind a third party. See also *J. T. Developments Ltd v Quinn* (1990) 62 P. & C.R. 33 at 36, where purchasers for value of land did not even dispute that they were bound by an equity affecting it. See generally (1994) 14 L.S. 147 (S. Baughen).

[268] Above, para.16–029.

[269] This is what is meant in LRA 2002 s.116 by the reference to the equity being "subject to the rules about the effect of dispositions on priority". In some earlier cases, it is not apparent whether the land was registered or unregistered: see, e.g. *J. T. Developments Ltd v Quinn*, above.

[270] Co.Litt p.352a. and 352b.

"he who takes an estate under a deed, is privy in estate, and therefore never can be in a better situation than he from whom he takes it".[271]

This principle has been applied in a number of modern cases where the estoppel arose from a representation made by O,[272] but never in case of acquiescence.

(ii) In accordance with the normal rules of unregistered conveyancing,[273] an equity by estoppel is binding either on a purchaser with notice of it,[274] or on a donee irrespective of whether he has notice of it.[275]

Given the equitable nature of an equity arising by estoppel, and the confirmation of the proprietary nature of the equity in relation to registered land, the latter explanation is the better one, particularly as it can be applied whether the equity arises by representation or acquiescence.

(b) Registered land. A purchaser of registered land takes it free of all rights and interests except those which are protected by an entry on the register or which exist as unregistered interests which override.[276] By contrast, a donee takes the land subject to all prior proprietary rights which bound the transferor whether registered or not.[277] As a proprietary right,[278] an equity arising by estoppel may be protected by a notice.[279] However, an equity will seldom be so protected because the party in whose favour it arises is unlikely to appreciate the need to register his right, even assuming he realises that he has a right. An equity arising by estoppel will be protected against a purchaser in most cases therefore only if it can exist as an unregistered interest which overrides a registered disposition.[280] In practice the only relevant category is

16–032

[271] *Taylor v Needham* (1810) 2 Taunt. 278 at 283, per Mansfield C.J. This was in effect an application of the common law rule, *"nemo dat quod non habet"*.

[272] *Hopgood v Brown* [1955] 1 W.L.R. 213 at 255, 229 and 231; *Brikom Investments Ltd v Carr* [1979] Q.B. 467 at 484.

[273] Above, paras 8–005 et seq.

[274] *Duke of Beaufort v Patrick* (1853) 17 Beav. 60 at 78; *Gresham Life Assurance Society v Crowthen* [1914] 2 Ch. 219; *Inwards v Baker* [1965] 2 Q.B. 29 at 37; *E.R. Ives Investment Ltd v High* [1967] 2 Q.B. 379 at 400 and 405. In *Lloyds Bank Plc v Carrick* [1996] 4 All E.R. 630 at 642, Morritt L.J. inclined to the view that, in consequence of these earlier decisions, an equity arising by estoppel was a proprietary right. cf. *United Bank of Kuwait Plc v Sahib* [1997] Ch. 107 at 142 (denying proprietary status to an equity arising by estoppel but without consideration of the relevant authorities). An equity arising by estoppel does not fall within any of the classes of land charge and should not, therefore, be registrable as such: cf. *E.R. Ives Investment Ltd v High* [1967] 2 Q.B. 379 at 395, 400 and 405; *Shiloh Spinners Ltd v Harding* [1973] A.C. 691 at 721.

[275] *Voyce v Voyce* (1991) 62 P. & C.R. 290 at 294 and 296.

[276] LRA 2002 s.29; above, para.7–061.

[277] LRA 2002 s.28, above, para.7–060.

[278] LRA 2002 s.116; above, para.16–029.

[279] LRA 2002 s.32; above, para.7–070. Under the Land Registration Act 1925, it was the practice of the Land Registry to treat an equity arising by estoppel as a proprietary right that could be protected by a notice (LRA 1925 s.49(1)(f)) or caution (LRA 1925 s.54(1)). See the previous edition of this work at para.13–032.

[280] LRA 2002 Sch.3.

the rights of persons in actual occupation.[281] Prior to the Land Registration
Act 2002 it had been accepted on a number of occasions that an equity arising
by estoppel could be an overriding interest of this kind and this is now
confirmed by s.116 of the Act.[282]

16–033   **4. Effect after judgment.** The effect of any relief granted by a court to
satisfy an equity arising by estoppel depends upon normal property principles.
A right created by the court's order does not enjoy any special status but must
be protected in the appropriate way if it is to bind third parties.[283] If the court
orders O to grant some right, estate or interest to C, that conveyance should
be executed (and if need be registered) in the usual manner.[284] The effect of
the relief may be to give C no more than a personal right to occupy land, either
because O is restrained from evicting him,[285] or because C is granted a licence
on terms[286] or an irrevocable licence.[287] Although such a licence was once
thought to be binding on a third party with notice of it,[288] the recognition that
contractual licences do not create property rights[289] has cast serious doubt on
the correctness of this conclusion.[290] C's position as a licensee will therefore
be vulnerable against a third party purchaser. This is a factor that the court
now takes into account when giving relief. It may grant C a proprietary right
if a licence would not adequately protect his position.[291]

Section 4. Contrast with Other Forms of Relief

16–034   **1. Contract.** There is no reason why both a claim in contract and to an
equity by proprietary estoppel should not arise from the same factual mix,[292]
providing that there is sufficient evidence of unconscionability to justify

---

[281] LRA 2002 Sch.3, para.2; above, paras 7–089 et seq. What constitutes actual occupation for
these purposes is narrower than under LRA 1925 s.70(1)(g).

[282] *Lee-Parker v Izzett (No.2)* [1972] 1 W.L.R. 775 at 780; *Singh v Sandhu* Unreported May 4,
1995, CA; *Locobail (UK) Ltd v Bayfield Properties Ltd* Unreported March 9, 1999, Lawrence
Collins, QC; *Lloyd v Dugdale* [2001] EWCA Civ 1754 at [26]; [2002] 2 P. & C.R. 167. cf.
Canadian Imperial Bank of Commerce v Bello (1991) 64 P. & C.R. 48 at 52, where it was held
that a *promissory* estoppel (which confers no proprietary rights) could not be an overriding
interest. See also *Henry v Henry* above.

[283] See [1991] Conv. 36 at 38; (1995) 58 M.L.R. 637 at 641; (1995) 7 C.E.L.Q. 59 at 63 (G.
Battersby); (1994) 14 L.S. 147 (S. Baughen).

[284] See, e.g. the orders made in *Pascoe v Turner* [1979] 1 W.L.R. 431 and *Voyce v Voyce* (1991)
62 P. & C.R. 290.

[285] e.g. *Maharaj v Chand* [1986] A.C. 898.

[286] *Parker v Parker* [2003] EWHC 1846 (Ch); [2003] P.L.S.C.S. 191.

[287] e.g. *Williams v Staite* [1979] Ch. 291.

[288] *Williams v Staite*.

[289] See *Ashburn Anstalt v Arnold* [1989] Ch. 1; below, para.34–019.

[290] See above, para.16–006.

[291] *Pascoe v Turner* above, at 438 and 439. cf. *Matharu v Matharu* (1994) 68 P. & C.R. 93;
[1995] Conv. 61 at 66 (M. Welstead).

[292] See [1983] Conv. 50 (M.P. Thompson). This is subject to one significant exception. No
claim to an equity arising by estoppel will lie where a vendor holds the land in question for a
purchaser on a bare trust arising from the specifically enforceable contract of sale: *Lloyds Bank
Plc v Carrick* [1996] 4 All E.R. 630 at 641.

circumventing the need for formality in contracts concerning land.[293] However, it is clear that the existence of a valid or failed contract is not a prerequisite to an equity by estoppel and of course many cases simply do not fit a contractual model.[294] The occasions on which an estoppel may arise are varied. For example, an estoppel may arise where:

(a) there was no agreement of any kind between the parties[295];

(b) a gift was intended[296];

(c) the essentials for a valid contract were absent[297];

(d) a contract was void for uncertainty.[298] or

(e) the contract did not encapsulate the entirety of the bargain between the parties.[299]

Furthermore, should there be the possibility of a contract, the manner in which a court gives effect to an equity arising by estoppel differs substantially from the way in which it enforces a contract. A court will enforce a contract according to its terms and will award damages, assessed according to settled principles, for any breach that is committed. By contrast, where a claim is based upon estoppel:

(i) the rights of the parties are not fixed at the time when the claimant acts to his detriment, but may be varied by the court to take account of subsequent events[300];

(ii) the court has a wide discretion as to how best to give effect to the equity and is not obliged to give effect to the expectations of the

---

[293] *Whittaker v Kinnear*, above. See the limitations expressed in *Cobbe v Yeoman's Row Management Ltd* above; *Herbert v Doyle* above; *Haq v Island Homes Housing Association*, above. See above para.15–043.

[294] *Dillwyn v Llewelyn* (1862) 4 De G.F. & I. 517; *Plimmer v Mayor etc, of Wellington* (1884) 9 App.Cas. 699; *Voyce v Voyce* (1991) 62 P. & C.R. 290 at 296.

[295] This will commonly be the situation where the equity arises out of acquiescence by the party estopped: see, e.g. *Savage v Foster* (1723) 9 Mod. 35. In such cases C acts to his detriment in a mistaken belief that he has a right to act as he does, not in reliance upon some express or implied agreement with O: *Willmott v Barber* (1880) 15 Ch D 96 at 105.

[296] *Dillwyn v Llewelyn*, above; *Inwards v Baker* [1965] 2 Q.B. 29; *Voyce v Voyce*, above (equity in favour of the donee); *Baker v Baker* [1993] 2 F.L.R. 247 (equity in favour of the donor).

[297] *Crabb v Arun DC*, above; *Kinane v Mackie-Conteh* above; *Cobbe v Yeoman's Row Management Ltd* above. See (1976) 92 L.Q.R. 342 (P. J. Millett) refuting the contrary suggestion in (1976) 92 L.Q.R. 174 (P. S. Atiyah).

[298] *Holiday Inns Inc v Broadhead* (1974) 232 E.G. 951 at 1087; *Lim v Ang* [1992] 1 W.L.R. 113. See too *Ramsden v Dyson* (1866) L.R. 1 H.L. 129 at 170; *Plimmer v Mayor, etc, of Wellington* (1884) 9 App.Cas. 699 at 713; *Lee-Parker v Izzett (No.2)* [1972] 1 W.L.R. 775 at 780 and 781; *Flowermix Ltd v Site Development (Ferndown) Ltd*, above.

[299] *Whittaker v Kinnear*, above

[300] Above, para.16–021.

parties[301] because the "focus of the doctrine is on the unconscionable conduct of the defendant and its effect. It is not the same thing
as seeking to enforce the agreement"[302]; and

(iii) in those cases in which the payment of compensation is considered
to be the appropriate remedy, it does not "assess loss as though it
were awarding damages", but maintains "a more flexible approach
designed to achieve justice between the parties".[303]

16–035   **2. Presumed resulting trusts.**[304] Where a person has contributed all or
some part of the purchase price of a property:

(i) he is presumed to have a beneficial interest in that property proportionate to his contribution unless that presumption is rebutted by
evidence that he intended to make a gift or loan of the money. But
"in the case of the purchase of a house or flat in joint names for
joint occupation by a married or unmarried couple, where both are
responsible for any mortgage, there is no presumption of a resulting trust arising from their having contributed to the deposit (or
indeed the rest of the purchase) in unequal shares"[305]; and

(ii) his proportionate share under such a trust is fixed at the time when
the property is acquired.

The recognition of an equitable interest arising from such a presumed resulting trust is not formally a matter for the discretion of the court. By contrast,
where an equity by estoppel arises, the claimant's rights remain inchoate until
such time as a court, exercising an equitable discretion, decides how best to
give effect to his equity.[306] Furthermore, an equity may arise even where C has
made a gift to O.[307]

16–036   **3. Constructive trusts based on common intention.** A constructive trust
will be imposed when B acts to his detriment in reliance upon a common

---

[301] Above, para.16–020. If the court does give effect to expectations, it must explain why this
is not an indirect enforcement of an otherwise invalid contract: *Kinane v Mackie-Conteh*,
above.
[302] *Cobbe v Yeoman's Row Management Ltd*, above, at 2977 per Mummery L.J.
[303] *Baker v Baker* above at 258, per Roch L.J.
[304] For such trusts, see above, para.11–016.
[305] *Jones v Kernott* [2011] UKSC 53 at para.25 per Lady Hale and Lord Walker. This follows
criticism of the use of resulting trusts in *Stack v Dowden* [2007] UKHL 17, [2007] 2 W.L.R. 831,
Lord Neuberger disagreeing on this point. In *Abbott v Abbott*, [2007] UKPC 53, the Privy
Council, hearing an appeal from the Court of Appeal of Antigua and Barbuda, followed the
majority in *Stack*, above. But cf. *Laskar v Laskar* [2008] EWCA Civ 347; [2008] 7 E.G. 142 (CS)
where the Court of Appeal applied a resulting trust in respect of property purchased by mother
and daughter by way of an investment as well as a home.
[306] Above, para.16–028.
[307] *Baker v Baker* above (gift by C to O of purchase price of house on the understanding that
C could live there rent-free for life).

understanding that he will acquire an interest in A's property.[308] Both the close similarities and the differences between such a trust and proprietary estoppel have already been explained.[309] Such a constructive trust arises as soon as B acts to his detriment. From that moment he acquires an equitable interest in A's property. Where an equity arises by estoppel, however, the claimant C has no more than an inchoate right until the court decides how the equity should be satisfied. Relief may sometimes be given without granting C any property right over O's land.[310]

Where it is alleged that an equity has arisen by estoppel, the court will take into account countervailing benefits that C has received from O.[311] However, such benefits have not been taken into account in cases where B has alleged that a constructive trust has arisen from his detrimental reliance on a common understanding with A. For this reason, proprietary estoppel may provide a better means of doing complete justice between the parties.

4. Licences. A licence is no more than permission to do on another's land what would otherwise be a trespass.[312] It is now settled that a contractual licence does not create a proprietary interest in land, and the same is almost certainly true of other forms of licence.[313] Proprietary estoppel has no necessary connection with the law of licences. It is a means by which C may obtain relief (commonly in the form of the grant of some proprietary right) where he has acted to his detriment in reliance upon some expectation created by O. If C is in possession of O's land, an equity may arise in his favour even if he is a trespasser.[314] If C is a licensee, one form of relief which the court may give is of course to declare that his licence is thereafter irrevocable[315] or revocable only on terms or after a period of time.[316]

16–037

There is one similarity between proprietary estoppel and one aspect of the law of licences. A licence once acted upon cannot be revoked.[317] Thus if A

---

[308] Above, para.11–025.

[309] Above, para.11–032 where the differences between the two remedies are set out more fully.

[310] This is one important reason why there may be resistance to the view put forward in *Oxley v Hiscock* [2004] EWCA Civ 546 at [70] and [71]; [2005] Fam. 211 at 246–7, by Chadwick L.J. that common intention constructive trusts and proprietary estoppel should be assimilated. cf. *Stack v Dowden* [2007] UKHL 17 at [37]; [2007] 2 W.L.R. 831 at 843 (Lord Walker).

[311] Above, para.16–016.

[312] For licences, see below, Ch.34.

[313] *Ashburn Anstalt v Arnold* [1989] Ch. 1; *Canadian Imperial Bank of Commence v Bello* (1991) 64 P. & C.R. 48 at 51; *I.D.C. Group Ltd v Clark* [1992] 1 E.G.L.R. 187 at 189. See, below, para.34–019.

[314] See, e.g. *Hopgood v Brown* [1955] 1 W.L.R. 213.

[315] *Plimmer v Mayor etc, of Wellington*, above.

[316] *Parker v Parker*, above.

[317] "A licence executed is not countermandable; but only when it is executory": *Winter v Brockwell* (1807) 8 East 308 at 310, per Lord Ellenborough C.J. See too *Armstrong v Sheppard & Short Ltd* [1959] 2 Q.B. 384 at 399 et seq. For the analogy with proprietary estoppel, see *Plimmer v Mayor etc, of Wellington*, above, at 714.

gives B permission to build his house in such a way that it interrupts A's right
to light, A cannot thereafter revoke his licence and require B to demolish his
house.[318] This doctrine differs from proprietary estoppel in that it is a common
law and not an equitable doctrine, and it can operate even where A is unaware
of his proprietary rights when he acquiesces in B's conduct.[319]

---

[318] *Liggins v Inge* (1831) 7 Bing. 682 at 693.
[319] *Armstrong v Sheppard & Short Ltd*, above. In that case, A assented to B building a sewer
on his land, even though he did not appreciate the land was his. B was not guilty of any trespass
in constructing the sewer, but no equity arose in his favour because A was unaware of his
ownership of the land.

CHAPTER 17

THE NATURE AND CREATION OF LEASES

Part 1

INTRODUCTORY

Section 1. Nature and History of Leases

A lease is a bilateral contract[1] which, as a general rule, confers an estate in the land capable of binding third parties.[2] The contract is one "for the exclusive possession and profit of land for some determinate period".[3] The estate so created, whatever its duration, may be referred to as a leasehold, a tenancy or a term of years.[4] In order to comprise a legal estate, the lease must be created by deed, subject to an important exception where the lease does not exceed three years.[5] An informal lease which does not take effect as a legal estate may nevertheless take effect as an equitable lease.[6] A lease may be created even where the grantor has no estate in the land, although such a lease would only be effective between the contracting parties.[7]   **17–001**

1. Leases as interests in land. The relationship of landlord and tenant for years had no place in the old feudal land law. The historical development of   **17–002**

---

[1] Bl. Comm. ii, p.140. See *Hammersmith LBC v Monk* [1992] 1 A.C. 478 at 491.

[2] *Bradshaw v Pawley* [1980] 1 W.L.R. 10 at 14.

[3] *Prudential Assurance Co Ltd v London Residuary Body* [1992] 2 A.C. 386 at 390, per Lord Templeman.

[4] Below, para.17–009.

[5] Below, para.17–040. The lease must be a "term of years absolute", as (widely) defined by LPA 1925 s.205(1)(xxvii); see above, para.6–018.

[6] Below, para.17–047.

[7] It will not create an estate capable of binding third parties if the grantor himself had no estate: see *Bruton v London & Quadrant Housing Trust* [2000] 1 A.C. 406 at 415. See below, paras 17–006, 17–032.

leases from mere personal contracts (rights in personam) into rights of property (rights in rem), which has already been explained,[8] brought the term of
years into the category of estates. At the same time, it brought the term of
years within the principle of tenure[9]; for the theory of tenure requires that all
land which is held for any estate shall be held of a lord. The term of years is
the only form of tenure which retains any practical importance after 1925. It
is owing to the existence of tenure, for example, that the tenant's rent is
properly called rent-service (as opposed to rentcharge)[10] and that the landlord
has traditionally had the remedy of distress for rent owed to him.[11]

17–003   **2. Duration of leases.** Leases therefore came into common use long before
they obtained full protection as interests in land[12]; they appear frequently from
the early 13th century onwards.[13] There is a tradition that in ancient times
leases might not exceed 40 years,[14] but there is no clear evidence that such a
rule ever existed. A lease cannot be granted to endure in perpetuity,[15] but
subject to this the modern law allows the creation of leases of any length. For
example, an ordinary mortgage now takes the form of a lease for 3,000
years[16]; and even a tenant for life, who at common law could not grant a lease
which would continue after his death, may grant a building or forestry lease
of 999 years under the Settled Land Act 1925.[17] Under the system of farming
under agricultural leases, which became widespread in the seventeenth century, farming leases were generally granted for terms up to 21 years.[18] Much
longer terms (e.g. 60 or 99 years) were used for building or mining leases,
which were useful means for the development or exploitation of land. Under
a building lease, for example, the land is let for a long term at a ground rent,
the tenant puts up a building at his own expense, and at the end of the term
this becomes the landlord's property; such a lease is therefore a valuable long-
term investment for the landlord. Leases of anything up to 999 years, or even
more, are sometimes granted for similar purposes; although the reversion is
too remote to have any value, the advantage to the landlord is that he can
control the use of the land by means of covenants in the lease, and a greater
variety of covenants are enforceable under a lease than under an outright
conveyance of the fee simple.[19] Such very long leases may therefore be useful

[8] Above, para.3–009; see also para.4–018.
[9] Above, para.3–015.
[10] Though the modern view is to regard rent as a contractual payment made in consideration of
the grant of the lease: see para.17–005 below.
[11] Below, paras 19–076 et seq., where the pending abolition of the law of distress by the Courts,
Tribunals and Enforcement Act 2007 is explained.
[12] For the history of leaseholders' remedies and the growth of leasehold interests in land, see
above, para.4–019.
[13] P & M. ii, pp.110–112.
[14] Co.Litt. pp.45b, 46a.
[15] *Sevenoaks, Maidstone & Tunbridge Ry v London, Chatham & Dover Ry* (1879) 11 Ch D 625
at 635.
[16] Below, para.24–020.
[17] Below, Appendix para.A–060.
[18] See *Att Gen v Owen* (1805) 10 Ves. 555 at 560.
[19] See generally Ch.20 below.

when a landlord is developing an estate and wishes to keep control over its appearance and character.

The leases that are now most commonly encountered in the residential sector are periodic tenancies, which continue indefinitely from term to term unless and until determined by notice on either side.[20] Agricultural lettings also tend to be periodic tenancies, held from year to year; whereas in the commercial sector, fixed term tenancies of up to and including 21 years are the norm.

3. Leases as conferring a status. As the following chapters will illustrate, the status of tenant carries important rights and obligations, both at common law and by statute. Many of the leading authorities on the distinction between the lease (or tenancy) and the licence are concerned with the issue whether a particular arrangement was subject to protective legislation such as the Rent Acts, and others are concerned with the imposition of other statutory obligations, such as the obligation to repair the premises. This is because the tenant is, in general terms, better protected in terms of security of tenure,[21] as well as in terms of the obligations owed by the landlord.[22]

17–004

4. Leases and rent. In *Street v Mountford*, the leading case on the requirements for the creation of a lease, Lord Templeman appeared to suggest that rent was an essential element.[23] Insofar as this was the view of the court, it was plainly wrong; for, as the Court of Appeal confirmed shortly afterwards,[24] it had long been settled that there can be a valid lease even though no rent is payable.[25] Subsequent decisions have proceeded on the basis, accepted by the parties, that there is no need for rent to be reserved or paid.[26] However, as the lease is a contract, there must be consideration; and it is the acceptance by the tenant of the obligation to pay rent that usually furnishes that consideration.[27] Where no rent is payable, the consideration furnished by the tenant may take any other form, including:

17–005

(i) the payment of a capital sum, called a premium[28];

---

[20] See further paras 17–081 et seq.

[21] See Ch.22 below.

[22] See Ch.19 below.

[23] [1985] A.C. 806 at 816, 825.

[24] *Ashburn Anstalt v Arnold* [1989] Ch. 1 at 9.

[25] *Knight's Case* (1588) 5 Co.Rep. 54b at 55a; LPA 1925 s.205(1)(xxvii).

[26] *Birrell v Carey* (1989) 58 P. & C.R. 184 at 187; *Canadian Imperial Bank of Commerce v Bello* (1991) 64 P. & C.R. 48 at 53, 55; *Wrexham Maelor BC v Macdougall* [1993] 2 E.G.L.R. 23 at 28. In certain circumstances, the proper inference from a rent-free arrangement may be that the parties did not intend to create legal relations: see, e.g. *Vesely v Levy* [2007] EWCA Civ 367; [2008] L. &T.R. 9 at [44] et seq.

[27] See Platt on *Leases*, i, 9; ii, 82. "Rent" is widely defined by LPA 1925 s.205(1)(xxiii) and is taken to include the performance of services: see *Hornsby v Maynard* [1925] 1 K.B. 514 at 525; *Montagu v Browning* [1954] 1 W.L.R. 1039 at 1044, 1045. Thus in *Doe d. Tucker v Morse* (1830) 1 B. & Ad. 365 the tenant was obliged to carry three cart-loads of culm (coal) yearly to the landlord's dwelling-house. See further, on rent, para.19–062 et seq. below.

[28] A premium is one example of a "fine" which is broadly defined by LPA 1925 s.205(1)(xxiii); below, para.19–105.

(ii) the tenant's undertaking to perform the covenants in the lease;

(iii) the remission of interest on a debt owed to him by the landlord[29];

(iv) the right to live rent-free under a sale and lease-back arrangement[30]; or

(v) the mere acceptance of the lease by the tenant.[31]

17–006   **5. Leases as contracts.** In recent years, the fact that leases are contracts has been strongly emphasised, and the application of contractual doctrine has had an important role in the continuing development of this area of the law. A number of examples can be given:

(i) rent is no longer regarded as "a thing issuing from the land",[32] or as a service rendered by the tenant to the landlord, but as a contractual payment for the use of the land[33];

(ii) as a result of the inability of a person to contract with themselves, "a man cannot make himself his own tenant"[34] by granting a lease to himself[35];

(iii) the contractual rules for the implication of terms may be applied by the court to a lease[36];

(iv) a lease may be frustrated, albeit only in exceptional circumstances[37];

(v) a lease may be set aside by the court where it was induced by the fraud of one of the parties[38] or where it amounts to an unconscionable bargain[39];

---

[29] *Canadian Imperial Bank of Commerce v Bello*, above, at 55.

[30] *Skipton BS v Clayton* (1993) 66 P. & C.R. 223.

[31] *Anon* (1698) 2 Freeman 224 at 225. See *Halsbury's* Vol. 27(1), para.1.

[32] H.E.L. vii, p.252.

[33] *Property Holding Co Ltd v Clark* [1948] 1 K.B. 630 at 648 et seq; *C.H. Bailey Ltd v Memorial Enterprises Ltd* [1974] 1 W.L.R. 728 at 732, 735; *United Scientific Holdings Ltd v Burnley BC* [1978] A.C. 904 at 935; *Ingram v IRC* [1995] 4 All E.R. 334 at 340; see further below, para.19–062.

[34] *Rye v Rye* [1962] A.C. 496 at 512, per Lord Radcliffe.

[35] *Rye v Rye*, above; (1962) 78 L.Q.R. 175 (P.V. Baker); *Barratt v Morgan* [2000] 2 A.C. 264 at 271. However, a valid lease may be granted to a nominee: *Ingram v IRC* [2000] 1 A.C. 293 at 305.

[36] *Liverpool CC v Irwin* [1977] A.C. 239; *King v South Northamptonshire DC* (1991) 64 P. & C.R. 35; below, para.19–028.

[37] *National Carriers Ltd v Panalpina (Northern) Ltd* [1981] A.C. 675; below, para.18–102.

[38] *Killick v Roberts* [1991] 1 W.L.R. 1146; [1992] C.L.J. 21 (L. Tee). However, a secure tenancy (for definition, see para.22–162 below) cannot be unilaterally rescinded: *Islington LBC v Uckac* [2006] EWCA Civ 340, [2006] 1 W.L.R. 1303; cf. *Birmingham CC v Qasim* [2009] EWCA Civ 1080, [2010] H.L.R. 19.

[39] *Boustany v Pigott* (1993) 69 P. & C.R. 298 (where the Privy Council set aside a lease on this ground at the landlord's behest); (1993) 109 L.Q.R. 530 (J. Cartwright).

(vi) a breach of covenant may amount to a wrongful repudiation of the lease entitling the other party to terminate it[40];

(vii) one of a number of joint landlords or tenants can unilaterally give an effective notice to terminate a tenancy even though the other landlords or tenants, as the case may be, do not wish to end the lease[41];

(viii) a landlord's right to terminate a lease because of the tenant's denial of his title is now explained in terms of contractual repudiation rather than with regard to the feudal origins of the rule[42];

(ix) a lease is to be interpreted in the same way as any other written contract.[42a]

The right to exclusive possession, which is the hallmark of a lease,[43] is now regarded as a product of the agreement between the parties rather than as a consequence of the ownership of the legal estate.[44] It is clear that this trend to emphasise the contractual nature of leases has potentially far-reaching consequences. However, it should not be over-stated; the English courts remain some distance behind other common law jurisdictions,[45] and they will consider each attempt to invoke contractual doctrine on its merits. For example, the Court of Appeal has refused to hold that a landlord was under an obligation to mitigate his loss, and re-let as soon as reasonably practicable, following the tenant's unilateral abandonment of the premises.[46]

6. Leases as conveyancing devices. Leases are sometimes used as a mere **17–007** conveyancing device, usually in order to provide security for the payment of

[40] *Hussein v Mehlman* [1992] 2 E.G.L.R. 287 (tenant treated the lease as at an end because of landlord's failure to carry out repairing obligations); [1993] Conv. 71 (S. Bright); *Nynehead Developments Ltd v R.H. Fibreboard Containers Ltd* [1999] 1 E.G.L.R. 7 at 12. This application of repudiation to the law of leases has not yet been approved by the Court of Appeal: see *Reichman v Beveridge* [2006] EWCA Civ 1659, [2007] 1 P. & C.R. 20 at [10]. See further below, paras 18–106 et seq.

[41] *Doe d. Aslin v Summersett* (1830) 1 B. & Ad. 135, followed in *Hammersmith LBC v Monk* [1992] 1 A.C. 478 at 492 where the House of Lords explicitly adopted the contractual as opposed to the property approach. The rule has been held to be compliant with ECHR, Art.8: *Harrow LBC v Qazi* [2003] UKHL 43; [2004] 1 A.C. 983; *Wandsworth LBC v Dixon* [2009] EWHC 27 (Admin), [2009] L. & T.R. 28. See further above, para.13–006.

[42] *W.G. Clark (Properties) Ltd v Dupre Properties Ltd* [1992] Ch. 297; *Abidogun v Frolan Health Care Ltd* [2001] EWCA Civ 1821; [2002] L. & T.R. 16.

[42a] *Mexfield Housing Co-operative Ltd v Berrisford* [2011] UKSC 52; [2011] 3 W.L.R. 1091 at [17], [107], [113].

[43] Below, para.17–015.

[44] But see *Bruton v London & Quadrant Housing Trust* [2000] 1 A.C. 406 at 413 et seq.; below, para.17–032. cf. *Ingram v IRC* [1997] 4 All E.R. 395 at 422, where Millett L.J. had suggested otherwise.

[45] See, e.g. *Highway Properties Ltd v Kelly, Douglas & Co Ltd* (1968) 1 D.L.R. (3d) 626 (Supreme Court of Canada); *Progressive Mailing House Pty Ltd v Tabali Pty Ltd* (1985) 157 C.L.R. 17 (High Court of Australia).

[46] *Reichman v Beveridge* [2006] EWCA Civ 1659, [2007] 1 P. & C.R. 20. The tenant's submissions, based on *White & Carter (Councils) Ltd v McGregor* [1962] A.C. 413, required the court to hold that it was unreasonable for the landlord to keep the lease in being and sue for the rent: see *Reichman v Beveridge*, above at [17].

money. For this purpose a long lease is granted, free of rent or other obligations, so that the tenant simply takes a valuable interest in the land which is a good security for money advanced by him. The most important example is one form of legal mortgage by which a lease is granted by a mortgagor to the mortgagee as security for the money lent.[47] It is unusual for the mortgagee to take possession of the land except as a preliminary to exercising his power of sale.[48] This form of lease is not dealt with here.[49] The leases discussed in this chapter are leases where the tenant has the right to occupy the land or to receive the rent from a sub-tenant.

17–008   **7. Leases for lives.** Formerly leases were often granted not for a term of years but for a life or lives. A lease for life or lives[50] had the advantage of giving the tenant a freehold estate, instead of a mere term of years, so that even before the action of ejectment was invented he could recover the land itself.[51] Further, a lease for 21 years or three lives was the longest term which could be granted by a tenant in tail or by an ecclesiastical or charitable corporation (e.g. a college).[52] By the middle of the 19th century wider leasing powers had been given to tenants in tail,[53] ecclesiastical corporations,[54] and certain universities and colleges,[55] and so the practice of granting leases for life had declined. A lease for life, like a lease for years, created tenure between the parties, so that rent or other services could be reserved. Such leases were usually commercial transactions which were quite distinct from tenancies for life under family settlements, where a beneficial interest was granted free of any rent or services. The scheme of the 1925 legislation required life interests to be merely equitable, and this, though suitable for settlements, was unsuitable for leaseholds. Accordingly, most leases for life have been converted by statute into terms of years.[56]

Section 2. Terminology

17–009   It is important to be familiar with the terms used in the law of leases. The person who grants the lease (or tenancy) is known as the lessor; the person to

---

[47] For this form of mortgage, see below, para.24–020. Usually a mortgage is created by means of a charge expressed to be by way of legal mortgage: see below, para.24–025. Indeed where title is registered (as is normally the case today), the charge is presumed to take effect this way: LRA 1925 s.27(1).

[48] Below, para.25–024.

[49] See below for treatment of such leases, para.24–020.

[50] For this phrase, see Challis p.65.

[51] Above, para.3–009.

[52] See above, para.3–077; Platt on *Leases*, i, 66, 67, 247.

[53] See Fines and Recoveries Act 1833; above, para.3–076.

[54] Ecclesiastical Leases Act 1842.

[55] Universities and College Estates Act 1858. The Universities and College Estates Acts, 1925 and 1964, continue the policy of the Universities and College Estates Act 1898 of giving these universities and colleges powers resembling those given to tenants for life under SLA 1882, which are narrower than those given by SLA 1925.

[56] Below, para.17–113.

whom it is granted as the lessee. Traditionally, these expressions have been reserved for the original parties to the lease. However, the owners for the time being of the reversion and the lease are generally referred to as the landlord and the tenant, and these expressions are now commonly used to describe the original parties to the lease as well as their successors in title. On the grant of a lease, the interest which is retained by the landlord (and which he may subsequently assign) is known as the reversion; similarly, the tenant may assign the lease. Instead of assigning the lease (i.e. transferring the property for the whole of the period for which it is held, usually for a consideration), the tenant, as the owner of the lease, may grant a sub-lease (or sub-tenancy or under-lease). A sub-lease must be for a period at least one day shorter than the lease, the parties to this sub-lease being known as the sub-lessor and the sub-lessee respectively. In this book, for purposes of exposition, reference will be made to the landlord and the tenant, rather than the lessor and the lessee, and it will be made clear when the original parties to the lease are being considered.

These expressions may be illustrated as follows:　　　　　　　　**17–010**

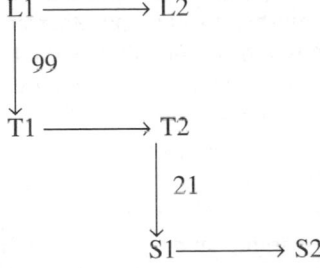

This diagram is the usual way of representing the following events. L1 grants a 99-year lease to T1 and then assigns the reversion to L2. T2 takes an assignment of T1's lease and grants a sub-lease to S1 for 21 years, and S1 in turn assigns his sub-lease to S2. As to the 99-year lease, L1 is the "lessor" (or "original landlord"), L2 is the "assignee of the reversion", and for the time being the "landlord"; and T1 is the "lessee" (or "original tenant"). T2 is in a dual position: as to the 99-year lease, he is the "assignee" or "tenant"; as to the 21-year lease, he is the "sub-lessor" or "landlord". The 99-year lease is called the "head lease", so as to distinguish it from the sub-lease. S1 is the "sub-lessee" or "sub-tenant", and S2, the "assignee" of the sub-lease who becomes a "sub-tenant" by that assignment. By annexing the dates of each transaction to each link in the diagram, the sequence of events may be shown.

"Demise" is the technical term for "let" or "lease"; thus a lease may be　**17–011** referred to as a "demise" and the premises in question as the "demised premises". "Lease" and "term of years" are nearly synonymous terms today[57]; before 1926 a term of years could only be regarded as one kind of

---

[57] But see *Re Land and Premises at Liss, Hants.* [1971] Ch. 986.

lease,[58] since leases for lives were by no means unknown. Today, leases for lives are rarely expressly granted.[59] "Lease" is often used interchangeably, either for the document granting the interest or for the "term of years" or "leasehold interest" granted, although primarily it means the document,[60] and the word "tenancy" is now in common usage to describe the interest enjoyed by the tenant for the time being.

Part 2

CREATION OF LEASES

Section 1. Essentials of a Lease

17–012 It has been explained above that a lease is a bilateral contract.[61] Leases must be distinguished from other contracts concerning the use of land, for there is an infinite variety of such contracts which are not leases. Parties may make any bargain they like between themselves, and enforce it between themselves as a contract. But if one wishes to give the other an estate, that is to say a proprietary interest which will bind not only the grantor but also the rest of the world, then the interest must conform to the requirements by which the law limits the kinds of estates which can be created. For example, if A gives B a mere licence[62] to use A's land, even though for payment, and then A sells the land to P who prevents B from using the land, B can sue A for damages for breach of contract; but he has no rights over the land as against P, for a licence creates no estate or interest in the land.[63] However, if A grants B a lease, then B has a legal estate subject to which P takes, so that B can enforce his rights against P as well as against A. It is therefore of great importance to know what transactions fall within the definition of a lease.

A. The Right to Exclusive Possession must be Given

1. Background

17–013 *(a) The traditional analysis.* It had always been of the essence of a lease that the tenant should be given the right to exclusive possession, that is the right to exclude all other persons, including the landlord, from the premises.[64] A

---

[58] See above, para.17–008.

[59] See below, paras 17–115 et seq.

[60] In the LPA 1925 " lease" includes any tenancy: ss.154, 205(1)(xxiii). Further, the LPA 1925 s.54(2), speaks of parol "leases" (and see s.52(2)(d)), and "oral lease" and its less correct relative "verbal lease" are common expressions.

[61] Above, para.17–001.

[62] See below, Ch.34.

[63] *Street v Mountford* [1985] A.C. 809 at 814; and see below, para.34–019.

[64] If the agreement between the parties confers exclusive possession, the arrangement will constitute a lease, even if it does not confer a legal estate on the tenant (because the landlord had none to grant): *Bruton v London & Quadrant Housing Trust* [2000] 1 A.C. 406 at 413–415; below, para.17–032.

right to occupy premises for a fixed period cannot be a tenancy if the person granting the right remains in general control of the property. It will therefore take effect as a licence. The typical case is where the landlord provides services, such as cleaning, for the occupant.[65]

(b) *The experiment with intention.* These well-established and fundamental **17–014** principles were called into question in a series of decisions[66] between 1951 and 1985 in which the fact of exclusive possession ceased to be conclusive and was given "diminishing weight".[67] Instead, the court examined all the circumstances to determine whether the parties intended the occupier to have a "stake" in the property or merely a personal privilege of occupation.[68] It followed that even where a person was granted exclusive possession the agreement might comprise no more than a licence if that is what the parties actually intended.[69] These developments were principally prompted by the desire of landlords to avoid the security of tenure and the benefit of rent control enjoyed by private sector residential tenants under the Rent Acts,[70] the courts endeavouring to avoid "causing patently unintended injustice to land-lords, whilst guarding against improper avoidance by the latter of the provisions of those Acts".[71] However, this approach was objectionable, not least because it provided a means by which a well-advised landlord could "contract out" of the statutory protection given to residential tenants.[72] As the legal status of an occupier often turned on fine points of construction, the law was rendered both uncertain and difficult to administer.

(c) *The return to exclusive possession.* In *Street v Mountford*,[73] a decision **17–015** that was much welcomed,[74] the House of Lords restored the law to its former more principled position. Where as a matter of fact a person was granted

---

[65] See below, para.17–019.
[66] Beginning with the judgment of Denning L.J. in *Errington v Errington* [1952] 1 K.B. 290.
[67] *Barnes v Barratt* [1970] 2 Q.B. 657 at 669, per Sachs L.J.
[68] See, e.g. *Shell-Mex and B.P. Ltd v Manchester Garages Ltd* [1971] 1 W.L.R. 612 at 615; *Marchant v Charters* [1977] 1 W.L.R. 1181 at 1185.
[69] See, e.g. *Somma v Hazelhurst* [1978] 1 W.L.R. 1014.
[70] See below, paras 22–136 et seq., 22–147 et seq. Lettings of residential accommodation made after January 14, 1989 have been subject to a different regime: see HA 1988, below, paras 22–081 et seq.
[71] *Barnes v Barratt,* above, at 669, per Sachs L.J.
[72] See, e.g. *Somma v Hazelhurst,* above. In reality such agreements were commonly not negotiated by parties at arm's length: *A.G. Securities v Vaughan; Antoniades v Villiers* [1990] 1 A.C. 417 at 458.
[73] [1985] A.C. 809. See too *Eastleigh BC v Walsh* [1985] 1 W.L.R. 525, decided by the House of Lords shortly before *Street v Mountford.*
[74] The House "sought to introduce some order into the law for the better administration of the law and guidance of the learned judges, particularly in the county court, who have to deal with this problem": *Brooker Settled Estates Ltd v Ayers* (1987) 54 P. & C.R. 165 at 167, per O'Connor L.J. See too (1985) 101 L.Q.R. 467 (P. V. Baker); [1985] C.L.J. 351 (S. Tromans); (1985) 48 M.L.R. 712 (J. S. Anderson); [1985] All E.R. Rev. 190 (P. J. Clarke). The one dissentient voice was the unsuccessful claimant: [1985] Conv. 328 (R. Street). For a recent reappraisal, see Bright, "*Street v Mountford* Revisited" in S. Bright (ed.), *Landlord and Tenant Law: Past, Present and Future* (Oxford: Hart Publishing, 2006).

exclusive possession of land "for a term at a rent",[75] that grant created a lease. This was so whatever label the parties might attach to the arrangement.[76] The test was one of substance not of form; the legal consequences of what has been agreed is therefore "a matter of law rather than dependent on what the parties intended".[76a] Although there could be no tenancy in the absence of exclusive possession, an occupier who had exclusive possession would not be a tenant in three circumstances[77]:

(i) if there was no intention to create legal relations[78];

(ii) if the occupier's occupation was referable to some other legal relationship, as where he was a freeholder, a trespasser, a purchaser in possession under a contract of sale, an object of charity or where he occupied under a contract of employment or by reason of some office[79]; or

(iii) where the owner of the land had no power to grant a tenancy.[80]

The House accepted that

"although the Rent Acts must not be allowed to alter or influence the construction of an agreement, the court should . . . be astute[81] to detect and frustrate sham devices and artificial transactions whose only object is to disguise the grant of a tenancy and to evade the Rent Acts".[82]

17–016   It should be noted that, as regards residential accommodation, disputes between the parties as to whether an arrangement has created a lease or

---

[75] *Street v Mountford*, above, at 816, per Lord Templeman. There is in fact no requirement that the agreement be "at a rent", provided that there is consideration of some kind: see para.17–005 above.

[76] "The manufacture of a five-pronged implement for manual digging results in a fork, even if the manufacturer . . . insists that he intended to make and did make a spade"; [1985] A.C. 809 at 819, per Lord Templeman. See also *Addiscombe Garden Estates Ltd v Crabbe* [1958] 1 Q.B. 513 at 522.

[76a] *Mexfield Housing Co-operative Ltd v Berrisford* [2011] UKSC 52; [2011] 3 W.L.R. 1091 at [17] per Lord Neuberger.

[77] See *Dellneed Ltd v Chin* (1986) 53 P. & C.R. 172 at 187; *Camden LBC v Shortlife Community Housing Ltd* (1992) 25 H.L.R. 330 at 340.

[78] *Street v Mountford*, above, at 821 and at 826. See further below paras 17–029 et seq.

[79] *Street v Mountford*, above, at 818 and at 827. Lord Templeman also included in this list the mortgagee in possession: *Street v Mountford*, above, at 818. However such a mortgagee is in fact either a tenant (if the mortgage is by demise or sub-demise) or has all the rights as if he were (if there is a charge by way of legal mortgage): above, para.17–006; below, paras 24–020, 25–025.

[80] *Street v Mountford*, above, at 821.

[81] A word that has been described as "rather emotive": *Stribling v Wickham* (1989) 21 H.L.R. 381 at 390, per Sir Denys Buckley.

[82] *Street v Mountford*, above, at 825, per Lord Templeman. See too *A.G. Securities v Vaughan*; *Antoniades v Villiers* [1990] 1 A.C. 417 at 459; and below, para.17–026 et seq.

licence are now less likely to arise. Since January 15, 1989, the Rent Acts have been gradually phased out, and private sector landlords have in practice been able to grant and to enforce tenancies of dwellings at whatever rent that they may agree with the tenant without the risk of conferring significant security of tenure.[83] However, the distinction between leases and licences remains of fundamental importance whenever third parties are concerned, because only leases can create proprietary rights.[84]

2. Exclusive possession

(a) Meaning. A tenant who has exclusive possession can exercise the rights **17–017** of a landowner.[85] He can exclude both strangers and the landlord[86] save where the landlord is entitled under the terms of the lease to inspect the premises and, e.g. carry out repairs.[87] Exclusive possession must be distinguished from exclusive occupation.[88] Even if the grantee is exclusively entitled to occupy the premises, in the sense that no one else is entitled to live there, he may not have exclusive possession because the grantor may retain control of the premises.[89] Conversely, a grantee may have exclusive possession although he does not occupy the property himself but is in receipt of the rents and profits as a result of subletting it.[90]

(b) Residential property. Persons who lawfully occupy residential accom- **17–018** modation for a term will either be tenants or licensees. Where they have exclusive possession they will be tenants unless they fall within one of the exceptional circumstances explained below.[91] They will not have exclusive possession in at least three instances.

(1) PROVISION OF SERVICES BY LANDLORD. This applies where "the landlord **17–019** provides attendance or services which require the landlord or his servants to

---

[83] See further below, paras 22–081 et seq.
[84] See *Street v Mountford*, above, at 816; *Ashburn Anstalt v Arnold* [1989] Ch. 1 at 13; and see above, para.17–012; below, para.34–019.
[85] *Street v Mountford* [1985] A.C. 809 at 816. The principles applicable to tenants apply equally to subtenants: *Monmouth BC v Marlog* (1994) 27 H.L.R. 30 at 32.
[86] *Heslop v Burns* [1974] 1 W.L.R. 1241 at 1247, 1249.
[87] *Street v Mountford,* above, at 816. The presence of such a term in the agreement between the parties "serves to emphasise the fact" that the grantee has exclusive possession: *Street v Mountford,* above, at 818; *Addiscombe Garden Estates Ltd v Crabbe,* above, at 524; *Dellneed Ltd v Chin,* above, at 184; *Vandersteen v Agius* (1992) 65 P. & C.R. 266 at 273.
[88] Despite the tendency of some judges to use the terms interchangeably: see, e.g. *A.G. Securities v Vaughan; Antoniades v Villiers,* above, at 455, 459 (Lord Templeman).
[89] *Luganda v Service Hotels Ltd* [1969] 2 Ch. 209 at 219. See also *Esso Petroleum Co Ltd v Fumegrange Ltd* [1994] 2 E.G.L.R. 90; *National Car Parks Ltd v Trinity Development Co (Banbury) Ltd* [2001] EWCA Civ 1686, [2002] 2 P. & C.R. 18.
[90] *A.G. Securities v Vaughan; Antoniades v Villiers,* above, at 455. However, if the grantee is *not* entitled to exclusive possession "he cannot acquire it merely by collecting the rents and profits from persons with no greater rights of occupation than he has himself": *Camden LBC v Shortlife Community Housing Ltd,* above, at 381, per Millett J.
[91] Below, para.17–028 et seq.

exercise unrestricted access to and use of the premises",[92] as will usually be the case with rooms in a hotel, hostel or boarding house.[93] The occupier is traditionally referred to in such circumstances as a "lodger", although the term is not a term of art and its use has led to some misunderstanding.[94] In particular, it is not the case that the occupier of residential accommodation is either a tenant or a lodger;[95] while a lodger "is necessarily a licensee, not a tenant, a licensee is not necessarily a lodger."[96] An occupant may have exclusive possession (and so be a tenant) even if the landlord provides some form of attendance or services if it is given under an agreement separate and distinct from the tenancy and it could have been provided instead by some third party.[97]

17–020   (2) NATURE OF ACCOMMODATION. The nature of the accommodation may be such that the landlord retains control of it.[98] In *Westminster City Council v Clarke*,[99] a local authority, in meeting its statutory obligations to house homeless persons, provided and ran a hostel for homeless men. The authority had the right to move any occupant to another room, sharing it if need be with another person.[100] These arrangements did not give the occupant exclusive possession of his room.

17–021   (3) SHARED ACCOMMODATION. Where there is single occupancy of residential accommodation, it is a comparatively straightforward question of fact whether

---

[92] *Street v Mountford*, above, at 818, per Lord Templeman.

[93] *Brillouet v Landless* (1995) 28 H.L.R. 836; *Mehta v Royal Bank of Scotland* (1999) 32 H.L.R. 45. It is not so much the quantum of the services as the need for unrestricted access; *Huwyler v Ruddy* (1996) 28 H.L.R. 550 (twenty minutes each week in order to clean the flat). If the landlord fails to provide services when he is obliged to do so, that failure does not convert the licence into a tenancy. The tenant's entitlement remains, whether or not he chooses to enforce it.

[94] See (1985) 48 M.L.R. 712 at 713 (J. S. Anderson); (1987) 50 M.L.R. 226 (A. J. Waite).

[95] "An occupier of residential accommodation at a rent for a term is either a lodger or a tenant:" *Street v Mountford*, above, at 817, per Lord Templeman; but cf. at 823.

[96] [1989] All E.R. Rev. 184 (P. H. Pettit): see *Brooker Settled Estates Ltd v Ayers* (1987) 54 P. & C.R. 165 at 168; *Hadjiloucas v Crean* [1988] 1 W.L.R. 1006 at 1011, 1012.

[97] *Vandersteen v Agius* (1992) 65 P. & C.R. 266 at 274 (landlady provided cleaning for osteopath's surgery in her house and kept his appointment book).

[98] As where the landlord has the power to relocate the occupant to other accommodation and that power is a genuine one and not a sham. In relation to residential accommodation such cases are likely to be rare. They may be more common in dealings with business or agricultural property: see, e.g. *Dresden Estates Ltd v Collinson* (1987) 55 P. & C.R. 47 (agreement to use a unit for storage under which the landowner could require the occupier to move to other adjoining premises); *McCarthy v Bence* [1990] 1 E.G.L.R. 1 (agricultural share-milking agreement under which the landowner could alter the fields in which the occupier grazed his cattle); [1991] Conv. 58 at 60 (C. Rodgers); Bright [2002] C.L.J. 146.

[99] There was no suggestion in the case that the authority provided attendance or services. The case was not strictly concerned with whether the occupant was a tenant or a licensee (although the cases on the distinction were considered) but with whether he had exclusive possession for the purposes of HA 1985 s.79 (secure tenancies): see [1992] All E.R. Rev. 248 (P. H. Pettit). For a similar case in which an occupant of a hostel was held to be a licensee, see *Brennan v Lambeth LBC* (1997) 30 H.L.R. 481.

[100] There is little doubt that this power was necessary given the character of the occupants: *Westminster CC v Clarke*, above, at 296.

or not the occupier has exclusive possession of the property.[101] Where two or more persons share accommodation, the issues are more complex: "It is not simply that the court has to interpret against their respective backgrounds two or more documents rather than one. It must also take into account the possibility that the documents are linked." [102] There are at least three conclusions at which the court may arrive:

(i) The occupants are joint tenants, being collectively entitled to exclusive possession of the property as a whole. This will only be the case where the requirements for a joint tenancy are satisfied[103] so that there is unity of interest, title, time and possession between the occupants.[104]

(ii) Although the occupants are not joint tenants of the whole property, each occupant is a tenant of a particular part of the property of which they have exclusive possession, such as a bedroom.[105]

(iii) The parties are neither joint tenants of the shared property (because one or more of the four unities is absent) nor do they have exclusive possession of any defined part. In such circumstances, they will be merely licensees.[106] Indeed, the landlord is not excluded from the property because he continues to enjoy possession of it through the other licensees whom he has permitted to occupy the premises.[107] This third construction will often be appropriate "given the informality of many sharing situations, and the obvious contemplation that they may terminate earlier than expected".[108]

Although these three situations are theoretically distinct, it can be difficult **17–022** to distinguish them in practice, particularly where two or more persons

---

[101] In *Street v Mountford*, above, the landlord conceded that the occupier had exclusive possession of the two rooms which were the subject-matter of the parties' agreement.

[102] *Hadjiloucas v Crean*, above, at 1022, per Mustill L.J.; [1988] All E.R. Rev. 171 (P. J. Clarke). For a thought-provoking commentary on the cases on shared accommodation, see R.J. Smith, *Property Law*, 7th edn (2011), 376–381.

[103] Above, para.13–004.

[104] *A.G. Securities v Vaughan; Antoniades v Villiers* [1990] 1 A.C. 417 at 472, 474. The occupants were held to be joint tenants in *Antoniades v Villiers* (the two occupants were cohabitants sharing an attic flat whose agreements were inter-dependent) but not in *A.G. Securities v Vaughan* (the four occupants shared a large four-bedroomed flat pursuant to four agreements which were independent of each other, each being entered into at different times and at different rents).

[105] *A.G. Securities v Vaughan; Antoniades v Villiers*, above, at 460, 466, 471, 473. This contention was not advanced in *A.G. Securities*: see at 471. In such a case, each tenant would presumably have a licence to use the common parts: for the statutory protection conferred on protected tenants and assured tenants in such circumstances, see RA 1977 s.22; HA 1988 ss.3, 10.

[106] This was the case in *A.G. Securities v Vaughan*, above.

[107] *A.G. Securities v Vaughan; Antoniades v Villiers*, above, at 471.

[108] *Hadjiloucas v Crean*, above, at 1023, per Mustill L.J.

simultaneously enter into separate, albeit identical, agreements for the occupation of a flat, and each is severally liable for his share of the rent.[109] In making its determination, the court will have to decide whether any of the terms are to be disregarded because they are a sham[110] and it will be required to construe the relevant written agreements having regard to the surrounding circumstances "including any relationship between the prospective occupiers, the course of negotiations and the nature and extent of the accommodation and the intended and actual mode of occupation of the accommodation".[111]

17–023   Although a tenancy is granted to one or more persons, it may be that a greater number of persons are in occupation of the property. A tenant may, for instance, invite a person with whom he is enjoying an intimate relationship to live with him; or he may come to an informal arrangement with some other person whereby the latter is allowed to occupy one of the rooms in the property. In either of these cases, the third party may pay a weekly or monthly sum to the tenant in consideration for the accommodation being provided. The question may then arise whether the third party has become a tenant of the property. The answer depends upon whether the tenant has granted exclusive possession to the third party. In the first instance above, this is extremely unlikely; the couple are living together, there has been no physical demarcation of the property between them, and it would therefore be difficult if not impossible to say that the third party has exclusive possession of any part of the property. The proper construction of the arrangement will be that the tenant has granted the third party a licence to occupy the property jointly with him for the time being. In the second instance, the case of the third party is stronger; and it will be necessary to consider what rights, if any, the tenant continues to have in relation to the part of the property now occupied by the third party.[112] If the third party can show that he has exclusive possession of a distinct part of the property, the tenant will be held to have granted a sub-tenancy of that part.

17–024   Finally, two persons may have occupied property together as licensees, and one leaves, with the result that there is now only one person left. Normally that occurrence will not affect the status of the remaining occupant,[113] but if the remaining occupant then takes over the entirety of the premises with the landlord's consent, the new arrangement may convert the licence into a tenancy because it gives him exclusive possession. In such circumstances, it will be necessary to decide whether the occupant does have exclusive possession, or whether those factors which had previously rendered the arrangement

---

[109] Compare *Antoniades v Villiers,* above, with *Stribling v Wickham* (1989) 21 H.L.R. 381 and *Mikeover Ltd v Brady* [1989] 3 All E.R. 618. See (1990) 106 L.Q.R. 215 (J. Barton).

[110] This is explained below, paras 17–026 et seq.

[111] *A.G. Securities v Vaughan; Antoniades v Villiers,* above, at 458, per Lord Templeman. See too *Stribling v Wickham,* above, at 386.

[112] *Monmouth BC v Marlog* [1994] 2 E.G.L.R. 68 (defendant who had been allowed by tenant to occupy two rooms of tenant's house held to be a lodger as this was a "contractual house-sharing arrangement" between the tenant and the defendant which did not confer exclusive possession on the latter).

[113] See, e.g. *Mikeover Ltd v Brady,* above.

a licence (in particular what rights the landlord continues to enjoy in relation to the occupant's property) still prevail.[114]

(c) Business or agricultural property. Although *Street v Mountford*[115] con- **17–025** cerns residential property, it is generally accepted that the question whether the landlord has granted exclusive possession for a term, subject to the existence of exceptional circumstances,[116] is similarly decisive in relation to other types of property, such as business premises[117] and agricultural land.[118] The issue in relation to business premises has usually been whether the occupier enjoys the security of tenure conferred by Part II of the Landlord and Tenant Act 1954, which applies only to tenancies and not to licences.[119] In this context, the *Street v Mountford* principles have been applied to the right to use "gallops" for training racehorses,[120] an agreement for the management of a Chinese restaurant,[121] the provision of shop and office accommodation,[122] the use of rooms as an osteopath's surgery,[123] a contract to run a petrol service station,[124] the right to deposit refuse,[125] the management of a car park,[126] and the erection and maintenance of advertising displays.[127] However, where a contract has been negotiated between parties of equal bargaining power, with the benefit of legal advice, the courts are generally reluctant to go behind express provisions clearly indicating the parties' intentions as to the legal effect of the agreement they have executed.[128] As a consequence, it is becoming increasingly clear that, in the business context, the courts are less likely to adopt an interventionist approach, and that it may therefore be more difficult for an occupier of commercial property to establish that a tenancy has been

[114] *Smith v Northside Developments Ltd* (1987) 55 P. & C.R. 164 at 167 (a case concerned with shop premises rather than residential accommodation).

[115] [1985] A.C. 809.

[116] See paras 17–028 et seq. below.

[117] *London & Associated Investment Trust Plc v Calow* (1986) 53 P. & C.R. 340 at 352; [1987] Conv. 137 (S.B.); *Vandersteen v Agius* (1992) 65 P. & C.R. 266; *Mann Aviation Group (Engineering) Ltd (in administration) v Longmint Aviation Ltd* [2011] EWHC 2238 (Ch) at [34]; cf. *Dresden Estates Ltd v Collinson* (1987) 55 P. & C.R. 47 at 52; criticised at (1987) 50 M.L.R. 655 (S.B.); [1987] Conv. 220 (P. F. Smith).

[118] *Colchester BC v Smith* [1991] Ch. 448 at 483 (on appeal [1992] Ch. 421).

[119] See below, para.22–005.

[120] *University of Reading v Johnson–Houghton* [1985] 1 E.G.L.R. 113, [1986] Conv. 275 (C. P. Rodgers).

[121] *Dellneed Ltd v Chin* (1986) 53 P. & C.R. 172; [1987] Conv. 298 (S.B.).

[122] *Smith v Northside Developments Ltd,* above (shop); *London & Associated Investment Trust Plc v Calow,* above (office); *Cameron Ltd v Rolls-Royce Plc* [2007] EWHC 546 (Ch), [2008] L. & T.R. 22 at [17] (office premises and industrial premises).

[123] *Vandersteen v Agius,* above.

[124] *Esso Petroleum Co Ltd v Fumegrange Ltd* [1994] 2 E.G.L.R. 90.

[125] *Hunts Refuse Disposals Ltd v Norfolk Environmental Waste Services Ltd* [1997] 1 E.G.L.R. 16.

[126] *National Car Parks Ltd v Trinity Development Co (Banbury) Ltd* [2001] EWCA Civ 1686; [2002] 2 P. & C.R. 18.

[127] *Clear Channel UK Ltd v Manchester CC* [2005] EWCA Civ 1304; [2006] L. & T.R. 7.

[128] *National Car Parks Ltd v Trinity Development Co (Banbury) Ltd,* above, at [29]; *Clear Channel UK Ltd v Manchester CC,* above, at [29]; *Scottish Widows Plc v Stewart* [2006] EWCA Civ 999 at [63]; *Cameron Ltd v Rolls-Royce Plc,* above.

granted where the terms of the agreement indicate that the parties did not intend the conferment of anything more than a licence.

17–026 **3. Shams or pretences.** "Sham is essentially about saying one thing and doing another."[129] Although the parties will be presumed to mean what they say,[130] the court will be "astute" to detect provisions in their written agreement whose only object is to disguise the grant of a tenancy and so evade the legislation that exists to protect certain tenants.[131] Such provisions have been variously described as "sham devices",[132] "artificial transactions"[133] and "pretences".[134] The court seeks to ascertain whether the parties' true bargain is the same as that which appears on the face of the agreement, for it is the former to which effect will be given and which therefore determines whether the agreement is a lease or licence.[135] It may be evident on the face of the agreement that one or more of its terms is not genuine, such as a requirement that the occupant must vacate the premises between 10.30 a.m. and noon every day, or a provision empowering the landlord to remove furniture from the occupant's room without replacing it.[136] Even if this is not the case, the fact that a term is not genuine may be apparent either from the surrounding circumstances or from the conduct of the parties subsequent to the agreement. Thus a provision by which the landlord could introduce an additional occupant to share the premises with the grantees was held to be a sham where:

    (i) the accommodation consisted respectively of a one-bedroomed flat furnished with a double bed in one case,[137] and a small room just 51 inches wide in another[138];

    (ii) the landlord did not seriously contemplate introducing another occupant[139]; and

---

[129] Bright [2002] C.L.J. 146 at 157.

[130] *Aslan v Murphy (Nos 1 and 2); Duke v Wynne* [1990] 1 W.L.R. 766 at 770.

[131] Other devices have been employed to circumvent this legislation, such as a letting to a company to escape the provisions of the Rent Acts. Such transactions are also subject to scrutiny, often on similar principles, to determine whether they are "expressed in a form which do not truly reflect the parties' intentions": *Kaye v Massbetter Ltd* [1991] 2 E.G.L.R. 97 at 99, per Nicholls L.J. See too *Estavest Investments Ltd v Commercial Express Travel Ltd* [1988] 2 E.G.L.R. 91; *Hilton v Plustitle Ltd* [1989] 1 W.L.R. 149; *Gisborne v Burton* [1989] Q.B. 390; *Eaton Square Properties Ltd v O'Higgins* (2001) 33 H.L.R. 68; *Bankway Properties Ltd v Pensfold-Dunsford* [2001] EWCA Civ 528; [2001] 1 W.L.R. 1369, on which see further below at para.22–090; Bright [2002] C.L.J. 146.

[132] *Street v Mountford* [1985] A.C. 821 at 825, per Lord Templeman.

[133] ibid.

[134] "It would have been more accurate and less liable to give rise to misunderstandings if I had substituted the word "pretence" for the references to "sham devices" and "artificial transactions." *A.G. Securities v Vaughan; Antoniades v Villiers* [1990] 1 A.C. 417 at 462, per Lord Templeman.

[135] *Aslan v Murphy (Nos 1 and 2); Duke v Wynne,* above, at 770.

[136] *Crancour Ltd v Da Silvaesa* [1986] 1 E.G.L.R. 80; *Aslan v Murphy (No.1),* above.

[137] *Antoniades v Villiers,* above.

[138] *Aslan v Murphy (No.1),* above.

[139] *Nicolaou v Pitt* (1989) 21 H.L.R. 487 at 491; *Duke v Wynne,* above, at 775.

(iii) the arrangement was a sale by a couple of their home with a right to live in the property for the rest of their lives.[140]

While the court must "keep a weather eye open for pretences",[141] the onus   **17–027**
of proving that a term is a sham rests on the party asserting that it is.[142] Even if a particular term has never been invoked by the landlord, it is open to him to justify it, e.g. as a matter of commercial practice.[143] The court does not "lean in favour of any particular approach to construction, or any particular inference from the facts of the case".[144] Although the court cannot look at the subsequent conduct of the parties in construing an agreement, it is admissible evidence as to whether the written agreement genuinely reflects their true intentions.[145] Subsequent conduct may occasionally lend support to the landlord's contention that the terms of an agreement were genuine. In one case two cohabitants entered into separate agreements with the landlord for the occupation of a flat by which each was severally liable for half the rent. One of them left and the landlord refused to accept more than half the rent from the occupant remaining. The court held that these agreements were genuinely independent and therefore did not confer exclusive possession of the flat on the two occupants as joint tenants.[146]

4. Exceptional circumstances. In three exceptional circumstances an occu-   **17–028**
pier who has exclusive possession of premises will not be a tenant under a lease.[147] The scope of these exceptions has been narrowly construed and there is no open-ended exception for undefined "special circumstances".[148]

(a) No intention to create legal relations. Where the parties do not intend   **17–029**
to create legal relations no tenancy will arise.[149] Such an agreement appears to create a bare licence rather than a tenancy at will.[150] Cases which fall within this category will commonly come about as a result of some act of kindness

---

[140] *Skipton BS v Clayton* (1993) 66 P. & C.R. 223.
[141] *Aslan v Murphy (Nos 1 and 2); Duke v Wynne* [1990] 1 W.L.R. 766, at 770, per Lord Donaldson M.R.
[142] *Mikeover Ltd v Brady,* above, at 626.
[143] *Esso Petroleum Co Ltd v Fumegrange Ltd* [1994] 2 E.G.L.R. 90 at 93.
[144] *Stribling v Wickham* (1989) 21 H.L.R. 381 at 390, per Sir Denys Buckley.
[145] *A.G. Securities v Vaughan; Antoniades v Villiers,* above, at 469, 475; [1989] Conv. 128 (P. F. Smith); [1989] C.L.J. 19 (C.H.). As to whether a term will be regarded as a sham merely because the landlord chooses not to implement it, see [1988] All E.R. Rev. 175 (P. J. Clarke); and below.
[146] *Mikeover Ltd v Brady* [1989] 3 All E.R. 618.
[147] *Street v Mountford,* above, at 818, 821, 827; above, para.17–015.
[148] *Camden LBC v Shortlife Community Housing Ltd* (1992) 25 H.L.R. 330 at 341, per Millett J. See too *Dellneed Ltd v Chin* (1986) 53 P. & C.R. 172 at 187; *Leadenhall Residential 2 Ltd v Stirling* [2001] EWCA Civ 1011, [2002] 1 W.L.R. 499 at [23].
[149] *Street v Mountford,* above, at 819 et seq.
[150] *Cobb v Lane* [1952] 1 T.L.R. 1037; *Heslop v Burns* [1974] 1 W.L.R. 1241 at 1248, 1250; *Colchester BC v Smith* [1991] Ch. 448 at 485 (on appeal [1992] Ch. 421). For tenancies at will and for the difference between such tenancies and licences, see below, paras 17–102 et seq.

or friendship,[151] typically in the context of some family arrangement,[152] but they are not confined to such circumstances.[153] Thus where a local authority allowed an allotment holder to remain in possession of land rent-free at his own risk because it might wish to utilise the land at short notice, it was held that the arrangement created a licence and not a tenancy.[154] The fact that the occupier is a member of the grantor's family does not of itself preclude the existence of a tenancy.[155] If there is exclusive possession and rent is paid, the transaction is likely to be regarded as a lease.[156] Conversely, although a tenancy can be rent-free,[157] the failure by the landlord to require rent is often held to indicate that the parties did not intend to create legal relations and thereby negates a finding of tenancy.[158] Where a tenancy has come to an end but the former tenant "holds over", continuing to occupy the land and making payments to the former landlord, the court may find that a new tenancy has been created; however, there must be some evidential basis on which the court can impute the parties' intention to create a new tenancy.[159] In the absence of such an evidential basis, no such tenancy will be found.

17–030　　*(b) Occupation referable to some other relationship.* No tenancy will be created if an occupant's exclusive possession is referable to some other legal relationship.[160] Where a person occupied property because of her appointment as an "almsperson", there was no tenancy granted: she was the beneficiary of a charitable trust.[161] A trespasser who, on demand, paid sums to the owner for her unlawful use and occupation of the premises was not a tenant.[162] Nor is a purchaser who enters into possession under either a contract for the sale or letting of land or an option to purchase the premises, because his occupation is "ancillary and referable to" his equitable interest in the property arising from the contract.[163] However occupation was not so referable as regards either a purchaser of the goodwill of

---

[151] See *Booker v Palmer* [1942] 2 All E.R. 674 (evacuee allowed to occupy premises for the duration of the war rent-free); *Heslop v Burns*, above (family permitted to live rent-free in a cottage by former employer); *Sharp v McArthur* (1986) 19 H.L.R. 364 (homeless person permitted to occupy a house pending its sale).

[152] See *Cobb v Lane*, above (brother allowed to live rent-free on premises).

[153] See, e.g. *Holt v Wellington* (1996) 71 P. & C.R. D40 ("sympathetic landlady scheme" for vulnerable persons: D.H.S.S. paid for the occupant's care and there was no contract with her).

[154] *Colchester BC v Smith*, above.

[155] *Ward v Warnke* (1990) 22 H.L.R. 496 at 500.

[156] *Nunn v Dalrymple* (1989) 21 H.L.R. 569; *Ward v Warnke*, above.

[157] Above, para.17–005.

[158] See, e.g. *Booker v Palmer*, above; *Cobb v Lane*, above; *Heslop v Burns*, above; *Sharp v McArthur*, above, *Colchester BC v Smith*, above.

[159] *Burrows v Brent LBC* [1996] 1 W.L.R. 1448 at 1454; *Greenwich LBC v Regan* (1996) 28 H.L.R. 469; *Leadenhall Residential 2 Ltd v Stirling*, above (no new tenancy until the former landlord increased, and obtained, the amount payable for occupation by the former tenant); *Hawkins v Newham LBC* [2005] H.L.R. 42 (no new tenancy where former landlord simply obtained agreement of occupier to make regular payments towards existing arrears of rent). See further para.22–171 et seq. below.

[160] *Street v Mountford* [1985] A.C. 809 at 826, 827.

[161] *Gray v Taylor* [1998] 1 W.L.R. 1093.

[162] *Westminster CC v Basson* (1990) 62 P. & C.R. 57.

[163] *Essex Plan Ltd v Broadminster* (1988) 56 P. & C.R. 353 at 356, per Hoffmann J; *Cameron Ltd v Rolls-Royce Plc* [2007] EWHC 546 (Ch), [2008] L. & T.R. 22. The status of a purchaser

a business conducted on the premises or a person who was merely con-
templating the purchase of the property and who made payments in the
nature of rent. Each was held to be a tenant.[164]

Perhaps the commonest example of this exception is service occupancy.[165] **17–031**
There is no tenancy but only a licence where an employee, such as a
housekeeper or a caretaker, occupies his employer's premises because the
nature of his duties requires it.[166] The test is whether the employee is
genuinely required[167] to occupy the premises for the better performance of his
duties rather than merely for his convenience,[168] and unless it is satisfied, the
exception will not apply.[169]

(c) No power to grant a tenancy. There will be no tenancy where the grantor **17–032**
lacks the legal power or capacity to grant one,[170] as where it is a requisitioning
authority.[171] It had been held that if a grantor had no estate in the land he could
not grant a lease.[172] However, in *Bruton v London and Quadrant Housing
Trust*, the House of Lords rejected this view.[173] Even if the grantor is himself
a mere licensee, if he enters into a contract which gives the grantee the right
to exclusive possession for a term, there will be a lease.[174] It "is the fact that

in possession is usually said to be that of a tenant at will rather than a licensee: see *Wheeler v
Mercer* [1957] A.C. 416 at 425; below, para.17–102. A lease may arise if the purchaser or grantee
makes payments for the use and occupation of the premises.

[164] See *Vandersteen v Agius* (1992) 65 P. & C.R. 266 and *Bretherton v Paton* [1986] 1 E.G.L.R.
172 respectively.

[165] For the effect of termination of service occupancy see below, para.34–008.

[166] See *Dover v Prosser* [1904] 1 K.B. 84 at 85 (school teacher); *Ramsbottom v Snelson* [1948]
1 K.B. 473 (farm labourer); *Glasgow Corporation v Johnstone* [1965] A.C. 609 (church
officer).

[167] It is therefore a question of substance; the fact that the contract of employment states in
terms that the occupation requirement is imposed for the better performance of the employee's
duties is not a weighty consideration: *Wragg v Surrey CC* [2008] EWCA Civ 19, [2008] H.L.R.
30 at [51].

[168] *Norris v Checksfield* [1991] 1 W.L.R. 1241 at 1244 (where there was held to be a licence
and not a tenancy of a bungalow provided so that a coach driver and mechanic would be available
in emergencies); *Wragg v Surrey CC*, above (countryside rangers); cf. *Hughes v Greenwich LBC*
[1994] 1 A.C. 170 (no term could be implied that headmaster was required to occupy house in
school grounds as not essential to carry out duties of employment) applying HA 1985 Sch.1
para.2(1).

[169] See, e.g. *Royal Philanthropic Society v County* [1985] 2 E.G.L.R. 109 (no service occupancy where a teacher occupied a house two miles from the school).

[170] *Street v Mountford*, above, at 821; *Camden LBC v Shortlife Community Housing Ltd* (1992)
25 H.L.R. 330 at 341. In the latter case it was ultra vires the claimant authority to grant a tenancy
without the consent of the Secretary of State.

[171] See, e.g. *Minister of Agriculture and Fisheries v Matthews* [1950] 1 K.B. 148; *Finbow v Air
Ministry* [1963] 1 W.L.R. 697.

[172] *Camden LBC v Shortlife Community Housing Ltd*, above, at 347; *Redbank Schools Ltd v
Abdullahzadeh* (1995) 28 H.L.R. 431; *Bruton v London and Quadrant Housing Trust* [1998] Q.B.
834.

[173] [2000] 1 A.C. 406, approving *Family Housing Association v Jones* [1990] 1 W.L.R. 779; on
which see Rook [1999] Conv. 517; Bright (2000) 116 L.Q.R. 7; Lower [2010] Conv.38. See also
Kay v Lambeth LBC [2006] UKHL 10; [2006] 2 A.C. 465; on which see Bright [2006] Conv. 294;
Hughes and Davis [2006] Conv. 526.

[174] In *Bruton v London & Quadrant Housing Trust*, a licensee was held to have granted a lease
and was therefore liable to the implied obligation of repair under LTA 1985 s.11 (below,
para.19–042).

the agreement is a lease which creates the proprietary interest. It is putting the cart before the horse to say that whether the agreement is a lease depends upon whether it creates a proprietary interest".[175] It follows that although a lease usually creates a proprietary interest, it will not do so if the grantor had no estate out of which to grant one. However where a tenant purports to grant a sublease in breach of a covenant not to assign or sublet the property without the landlord's consent, the sublease is effective to confer a proprietary interest on the subtenant (albeit one that is vulnerable to forfeiture by the landlord).[176]

17–033   **5. Contrast with easements.** The requirement of exclusive possession distinguishes leases not merely from licences but also from easements. An easement is merely a right over land, not a right to its possession.[177] If therefore a right by its nature does not confer exclusive possession on the grantee, such as a right to pass and repass over another's land,[178] it may be a licence or an easement, but it cannot be a tenancy.

B. The Lease must be Created in the Proper Way

I. FORMAL LEASES

17–034   In order to create a legal estate which can rank as a term of years absolute within s.1(1) of the Law of Property Act 1925[179] a lease must be made with the proper formalities. The present formal requirements can only be understood by reference to their historical evolution.[180] This took place in four stages.

17–035   **1. Historical background**

(a) Common law. At common law a lease of corporeal land could be granted in any way, even orally. This illustrates the ancient conception of a lease as a simple contract. But incorporeal rights which are within the definition of real property,[181] such as easements and profits, could be created at common law only by deed: they lay in grant, not in livery.[182] This rule was applied to leases, when they came to be considered estates in land, so that a lease of (for example) shooting or fishing rights had to be made by deed. But if the land to

---

[175] *Bruton v London & Quadrant Housing Trust,* above, at 415, per Lord Hoffmann.
[176] *Dellneed Ltd v Chin* (1986) 53 P. & C.R. 172 at 186, 187.
[177] Below, para.27–020.
[178] *IDC Group Ltd v Clark* [1992] 2 E.G.L.R. 184 at 186 (right to use a fire escape).
[179] Above, para.6–018.
[180] See *Long v Tower Hamlets LBC* [1998] Ch. 197 at 204 et seq; [1992] Conv. 252; 337 (P. Sparkes).
[181] Above, para.6–011, below, para.31–001.
[182] Below, para.27–014.

which such incorporeal rights were appurtenant was itself leased, the appurtenant rights could pass with the land without a deed.

(b) 1677–1845. The common law rule that a lease could be established on **17–036**
oral evidence alone was a fertile source of fraud and perjury. The Court of
Chancery manifested an unwillingness to enforce leases that had been granted
orally. To remedy this, the Statute of Frauds 1677[183] required that every lease
should be in writing (though not necessarily by deed) signed by the party
creating it or his agent authorised in writing. In default of this, only a tenancy
at will was created. An exception was made for a lease for a period not
exceeding three years from its creation at a rent of at least two-thirds of the
full improved value (i.e. the value taking into consideration any improvements
to the property[184]). Such a lease could still be made orally. The rule that leases
of incorporeal rights must be made by deed was not altered by the
statute.[185]

(c) 1845–1926. The Real Property Act 1845 required a deed in all cases in **17–037**
which the existing law required writing. The exception as to leases for three
years or less therefore remained as before, but all other leases had to be made
by deed. The Act provided that "a lease required by law to be in writing . . .
shall be void at law unless also made by deed".[186]

2. The modern law

(a) The statute. The provisions of the two previous Acts were repeated, with **17–038**
certain alterations, by the Law of Property Act 1925, but no attempt was made
to state their combined effect. Section 54 followed the Statute of Frauds 1677
and s.52 was modelled on the Real Property Act 1845. As a result, their
differing provisions continue to stand side by side, presumably because they
had become so familiar that it was thought best to preserve them.

(b) The basic rule. The current law may be stated as follows. A lease cannot **17–039**
create a legal estate unless it is made by deed; for all grants are "void for the
purpose of conveying or creating a legal estate unless made by deed".[187]

(c) The exception. However, no formality is required for a lease which: **17–040**

    (i) takes effect in possession;

    (ii) is for a term not exceeding three years, whether or not the lessee
        is given power to extend the term; and

---

[183] s.1.
[184] s.2.
[185] *Duke of Somerset v Fogwell* (1826) 5 B. & C. 875; *Bird v Higginson* (1837) 6 A. & E.
824.
[186] s.3, replacing the Transfer of Property Act 1844 s.4.
[187] s.52(1); and see ss.54(1), 205(1)(ii).

(iii) is at the best rent which can be reasonably obtained without taking a fine.[188]

Such a lease may be validly created at law either orally or in writing.[189]

17–041   (1) "IN POSSESSION". To fall within the exception, the lease must take effect in possession and not in reversion. Thus a three-month reversionary lease[190] granted today to take effect in 25 days' time will not take effect as a legal lease unless it is made by deed.[191] As many short leases are granted a few days in advance, this restriction may in practice seriously narrow the exception and thereby defeat the whole purpose of exempting short leases from the statutory requirement of a deed.[192] "Possession" is not confined to physical possession, but includes receipt of rents and profits, e.g. from sub-tenants in physical possession.[193]

17–042   (2) "THREE YEARS". The phrase "a term not exceeding three years" includes a monthly or other periodic tenancy,[194] even though such a tenancy will continue indefinitely unless determined by notice,[195] for it cannot be said with certainty it will last for more than three years. The phrase also includes a fixed term for three years or less which contains an option for the tenant to extend it beyond three years,[196] but not a fixed term for more than three years, even though it is determinable within that period.[197] The three years must be computed from the date of the grant.[198]

17–043   *(d) Application.* If all three conditions are complied with, a legal lease can be created either orally or in writing. But the legislation seems to preserve the exception as to incorporeal rights, such as shooting or fishing, which therefore can be leased only by deed.[199] Further, an oral lease is not a "conveyance" within the Law of Property Act 1925,[200] and so it may be less effective than

---

[188] s.54(2); see Brown & Pawlowski [2010] Conv.146 and, for further excluded tenancies, Localism Act 2011 s.156. A "fine", as defined in LPA 1925, s.205(1)(xxiii), is a lump sum payment made in consideration of a reduced rent. It is often called a "premium". Thus premises worth £5,000 per annum may be let for three years at £5,000 per annum (i.e. at a full "rack" rent) or at £500 per annum with a premium of £13,500.

[189] *Long v Tower Hamlets LBC* [1998] Ch. 197 at 210.

[190] Reversionary leases are considered below, para.17–077.

[191] *Long v Tower Hamlets LBC*, above, at 215–219.

[192] For criticism of the restriction, see [1992] Conv. 337 at 340 (P. Sparkes); (1995) 58 M.L.R. 637 at 639 (G. Battersby); [1998] Conv. 229 (S. Bright). If the lease is void for want of formality, it is likely to take effect as a periodic tenancy when the tenant enters and pays rent: see *Long v Tower Hamlets LBC*, above, at 211, 218; below, para.17–070. For the circumstances in which such a tenancy will be inferred, see below, para.17–086.

[193] LPA 1925 s.205(1)(xix); above, para.6–017.

[194] *Ex p. Voisey* (1882) 21 Ch D 442; *Hammond v Farrow* [1904] 2 K.B. 332 at 335.

[195] See below, para.17–090.

[196] See *Hand v Hall* (1877) 2 Ex.D. 355.

[197] *Kushner v Law Society* [1952] 1 K.B. 264.

[198] See *Rawlins v Turner* (1701) 1 Ld.Raym. 736.

[199] *Wood v Leadbitter* (1845) 13 M. & W. 838 at 843; *Swayne v Howells* [1927] 1 K.B. 385; *Mason v Clarke* [1954] 1 Q.B. 460; [1955] A.C. 778; [1954] C.L.J. 189; below, para.28–002.

[200] *Rye v Rye* [1962] A.C. 496.

a lease by deed, e.g. for creating easements.[201] The concession in favour of the grant of an informal lease applies equally to a contract for a lease, i.e. a promise to grant such a lease at a future date.[202] The usual requirement that a contract for the sale or other disposition of land can only be made in writing[203] does not apply to such contracts, which may therefore be made orally.

(e) Assignment. Once a legal lease has been validly granted, a deed is **17–044** required to effect its legal assignment, however short the term may be.[204] Thus the legal assignment of a yearly tenancy can only be made by deed,[205] even if the tenancy was created orally.[206] It follows from this that a contract to assign such a lease must also be made in writing.[207] The result is anomalous and can lead to hardship.[208]

II. INFORMAL LEASES

1. Informal lease void at law. A lease which did not satisfy the above **17–045** requirements was void at law and passed no legal estate. However, independently of the lease, a different tenancy might arise. If a tenant took possession with the landlord's consent, a tenancy at will arose.[209] As the law formerly stood,[210] as soon as rent was paid and accepted, the tenancy at will was automatically converted into a yearly or other periodic tenancy, depending on the way in which the rent was paid.[211] That periodic tenancy was itself a legal estate, for the law implied an oral grant from acceptance of rent by the landlord. Furthermore, it was held subject to any terms which the parties had agreed upon, so far as they were consistent with a periodic tenancy.[212]

An informal lease which was "void at law" under the Real Property Act **17–046** 1845 was thus not entirely ineffective if a yearly tenancy later arose. If, for example, the tenant had covenanted to do repairs, this became one of the terms of the yearly tenancy. Other examples of such terms which are transferable to

---

[201] Below, para.28–027.

[202] LP(MP)A 1989 s.2(5)(a); *Looe Fuels Ltd v Looe Harbour Commissioners* [2008] EWCA Civ 414; [2009] L. & T.R. 29; and see above, para.15–021. Prior to September 27, 1989, such contracts had either to comply with the formal requirements of LPA 1925 s.40, or there had to be sufficient acts of part performance: see the fifth edition of this work at p.638.

[203] LP(MP)A 1989 s.2(1); above, para.15–016.

[204] The grant of a lease out of a registered estate must (with certain exceptions) be completed by registration, and the lease will not take effect as a legal lease until then: LRA 2002 s.27(1), (2); below, para.17–140.

[205] LPA 1925 s.52(1).

[206] *Crago v Julian* [1992] 1 W.L.R. 372. See too *Camden LBC v Alexandrou (No.2)* (1997) 30 H.L.R. 534. cf. FLA 1996 s.53; Sch.7. As to the effect of informal assignment, see below, para.17–139.

[207] To comply with LP(MP)A 1989 s.2(1); above, para.15–018. The exception in s.2(5) is inapplicable.

[208] As it did in *Crago v Julian*, above. See (1995) 58 M.L.R. 637 at 638 (G. Battersby).

[209] Indeed it is provided by statute that an interest in land created without the formality required by law has the force and effect of an interest at will only: LPA 1925 s.54(1); *Goodtitle d. Gallaway v Herbert* (1792) 4 T.R. 680.

[210] The position is now different: below, para.17–086.

[211] *Martin v Smith* (1874) L.R. 9 Ex. 50.

[212] *Doe d. Rigge v Bell* (1793) 5 T.R. 471; *Doe d. Thomson v Amey* (1840) 12 A. & E. 476.

a yearly tenancy are given below.[213] Before 1875, therefore, the position in a court of *common law* of a tenant who had entered and paid rent under a void lease was generally that of a yearly tenant subject to certain of the terms of the lease. The landlord was in a corresponding position. But both parties might have had other rights in equity, as will shortly be explained.

17–047   **2. Effect as contract.** Although such an informal lease failed to create any legal estate, it might be treated as a contract to grant the lease agreed upon. A lease is clearly distinct from a contract to grant a lease: the difference is between "I hereby grant you a lease" and "I hereby agree that I will grant you a lease".[214] Nevertheless both law and equity concurred in treating an imperfect lease as a contract to grant a lease,[215] provided it was made for value and was sufficiently evidenced in writing or, in the case of equity, supported by a sufficient act of part performance.[216] The attitude of equity was particularly important, for under the doctrine of *Parker v Taswell*[217] equity would first treat an imperfect lease of this kind as a contract to grant the lease, and then order specific performance of that contract.[218] Once a proper lease had been granted in pursuance of the decree of specific performance, the position of the parties was the same for the future as if the lease had been granted by deed in the first place.

3. *Walsh v Lonsdale*[219]

17–048   *(a) Effect of right to specific performance.* The rights of the parties under an imperfect lease sufficiently evidenced by writing or part performance were thus clear once specific performance had been decreed. What was not so clear was the position if, as was far more often the case, no decree of specific performance had been granted but the parties were entitled to obtain one. In equity, the parties were treated as if the lease had been granted with proper formalities by application of the principle that "equity looks on that as done

---

[213] Below, para.17–088.

[214] The difference is often not so clear in practice, where the "agreement" made by the parties may be either a contract or a grant, depending on its language. In doubtful cases the court leans towards the interpretation which will give a greater validity to the transaction: *Browne v Warner* (1807) 14 Ves. 156; *Rollason v Leon* (1861) 7 H. & N. 73 ("A agrees to let and B agrees to take"); cf. *Wright v Macadam* [1949] 2 K.B. 744 at 747 ("agreement" held to be a lease).

[215] *Bond v Rosling* (1861) 1 B. & S. 371; *Tiddey v Mollett* (1864) 16 C.B. (N.S.) 298. An imperfect lease is not treated as an agreement for every purpose: see, e.g. *Harte v Williams* [1934] 1 K.B. 201 (unsealed lease prepared by unqualified person).

[216] For the doctrine of part performance, which does not apply to contracts made after September 26, 1989, see above, para.15–015.

[217] (1858) 2 De G. & J. 559; and see *Zimbler v Abrahams* [1903] 1 K.B. 577; *Industrial Properties (Barton Hill) Ltd v Associated Electrical Industries Ltd* [1977] Q.B. 580. As to incorporeal rights, see *Frogley v Earl of Lovelace* (1859) John. 333.

[218] If the lease was void because it exceeded the lessor's power to grant it, it might similarly be treated as a contract for a properly limited lease; cf. LPA 1925 s.152, below, Appendix para.A–062.

[219] (1882) 21 Ch D 9.

which ought to be done." But there was no such principle at law; for at law the transaction was void as a lease, and as a contract for a lease the only remedy was an action for damages.

The difference between law and equity is founded on the difference **17–049** between damages and specific performance. A person entitled merely to damages has no rights in the land; but a person entitled to specific performance has the right to demand the land itself, and so in the eyes of equity such a person is the rightful occupant. Just as a purchaser becomes equitable owner under a contract for sale,[220] so an intended lessee becomes equitable tenant under a contract for a lease. If a proper lease ought already to have been executed, the intended lessee is in the same position as if it had been executed, with one important reservation, namely, that until he has obtained a proper lease his rights are equitable, not legal.

(b) Fusion of courts. A tenant holding under a mere contract for a lease, i.e. **17–050** merely in equity, could, before 1875, always enforce his rights against the landlord by recourse to the Court of Chancery. Here he could obtain a decree of specific performance, and he could meanwhile ask for an injunction to prevent the landlord interfering with the exercise of his equitable rights. After 1875 the tenant no longer needed to rely on the protection of any particular court, for as a result of the Judicature Act 1873–1875 "there is only one Court, and the equity rules prevail in it".[221] This is exemplified by the leading case of *Walsh v Lonsdale*,[222] which laid down that where there is a yearly tenancy at common law but a tenancy for years in equity, the parties' equitable rights prevail over their legal rights.

(c) The decision. In *Walsh v Lonsdale*,[223] L agreed in writing to grant a **17–051** seven year lease of a mill to T at a rent which was to vary with the number of looms run. One of the agreed terms was that on demand T would pay a year's rent in advance. Although no lease was executed, T was let into possession and paid rent in arrears for a year and a half, thereby becoming a yearly tenant at law. L then demanded a year's rent in advance and, on T's refusal to pay, levied distress.[224] T then brought an action for damages for wrongful distress (in effect, for trespass), for an injunction and for specific performance of the agreement, and he applied for an interim injunction restraining the landlord's distress pending trial. It was upon this last application that the case was decided.

T's argument was that distress was a legal, and not an equitable, remedy, **17–052** and that since at law he was only a yearly tenant and no obligation to pay rent in advance could be implied, especially in view of the variable nature of the

---

[220] Above, para.15–052.
[221] *Walsh v Lonsdale* (1882) 21 Ch D 9 at 14, per Jessel M.R., applying JA 1873 s.25(11).
[222] Above.
[223] Above.
[224] For distress, see below, para.19–076.

rent, L could not distrain for the rent.[225] It was held, however, that since the distress would have been legal had the lease agreed upon been granted by deed, and since equity treated the parties as if the deed had been executed, the distress was lawful in equity. In equity's eyes, T was already tenant for seven years subject to all the terms of the agreement, not a yearly tenant subject only to some of its terms. Since 1875 the equitable rule prevailed over the common law rule in all courts, and so T could not complain of the distress.

17–053   The decision was novel and remains controversial,[226] though it has often been applied.[227] Prior to the Judicature Acts, distress was not available in respect of non-payment of rent under an agreement for a lease, because the relationship between the parties was entirely contractual.[228] Furthermore, a court of equity would never have ordered payment of rent or decreed performance of covenants.[229] If appropriate, it would have decreed specific performance of the agreement for a lease and left the parties to their remedy at law. But it was not the general practice to back-date decrees of specific performance except in very limited circumstances.[230]

17–054   *(d) Extent of the principle.* The doctrine of *Walsh v Lonsdale* will operate even where L does not hold the legal estate, provided that he has a specifically enforceable right to obtain it. There can thus be a chain of equitable interests, each in turn potentially effective. This is shown by a case where L was entitled to the legal fee simple under a contract of sale which, though the money had been paid, had never been completed by conveyance, in order to save stamp duty. L granted a "lease" to T which took effect as an agreement for a lease under *Parker v Taswell* and as an effective lease under *Walsh v Lonsdale*, even though L himself was not the legal owner. For either L or T could have enforced the "lease" by bringing in the owner of the outstanding legal estate and obtaining specific performance against him; and accordingly L was entitled to sue T for breach of the covenant to repair contained in the "lease".[231]

17–055   **4. Differences between legal and equitable leases.** The effect of *Walsh v Lonsdale* was often summed up in the words "a contract for a lease is as good

---

[225] See *Manchester Brewery Co v Coombs* [1901] 2 Ch. 608 at 617, 618, per Farwell J.

[226] See (1987) 7 O.J.L.S. 60 (S. Gardner); (1988) 8 O.J.L.S. 350 (P. Sparkes); (1989) 10 J.L.H. 29 (P. Sparkes); R. P. Meagher, W. M. C. Gummow and J. R. F. Lehane, *Equity: Doctrines and Remedies* 3rd edn (Butterworth (Australia), 1992) paras 236–245; *Chan v Cresdon Proprietary Ltd* (1989) 168 C.L.R. 242 at 250 et seq.

[227] See, e.g. *Re a Company Ex p. Tredegar Enterprises Ltd* [1992] 2 E.G.L.R. 39 (surety liable to pay rent under covenant to take a lease in the event of a tenant's insolvency).

[228] *Vincent v Godson* (1853) 1 Sm. & G. 384 at 394.

[229] *Cox v Bishop* (1857) 8 De G.M. & G. 815 at 824.

[230] See *Chan v Cresden Proprietary Ltd*, above at 255; (1989) 10 J.L.H. 29 (P. Sparkes).

[231] *Industrial Properties (Barton Hill) Ltd v Associated Electrical Industries Ltd* [1977] Q.B. 580. As to L's obligation to get in the legal estate, see at 610, per Roskill L.J. T was in any case liable by privity of contract, even if the lease itself was invalid.

as a lease."[232] For many purposes this is true, but as a generalisation it is misleading,[233] for it ignores the vital difference between legal and equitable interests. The difference between the two is in reality substantial. A contract for a lease, as an equitable interest, falls short of a legal lease in the following respects.

(a) Dependence upon specific performance. The effect of *Walsh v Lonsdale*   **17–056**
in equity depends upon the willingness of the court to grant the discretionary remedy of specific performance.[234] If for any reason an agreement for a lease is one of which the court cannot or will not grant specific performance, the parties are under a very different position from that under a legal lease: they can have nothing more than a right to sue for damages under the agreement, although a yearly or other periodic tenancy may arise in the usual way. For example, there can normally be no specific performance in favour of a tenant whose tenancy agreement is subject to a condition precedent (e.g. to repair) which he has not performed,[235] or who is already in breach of one of the terms of the agreement,[236] or whose claim is to an underlease which can be granted to him only in breach of a covenant against sub letting in the head lease.[237] He who comes to equity must come with clean hands, and he who seeks equity must do equity.[238] In such cases the tenant stands by his legal rights and remedies (if any). It is often said that a tenant who is in breach of one of the terms of an agreement for a lease cannot obtain specific performance,[239] but this seems too sweeping, for not every breach of contract will be a bar to specific performance.[240] Although the point is not settled, if the breach is one where the court would have granted relief against forfeiture had the lease been legal, then in principle specific performance should be decreed.[241] Limits to a

---

[232] See *Allhusen v Brooking* (1884) 26 Ch D 559 at 565; *Re Maughan* (1885) 14 QBD 956 at 958; *Furness v Bond* (1888) 4 T.L.R. 457; *Lowther v Heaver* (1889) 41 Ch D 248 at 264.

[233] See *Manchester Brewery Co v Coombs* [1901] 2 Ch. 608 at 617.

[234] *Manchester Brewery Co v Coombs*, above, at 617; and see para.15–115 above. At one time, the court would not decree specific performance of contracts for transient interests: see the fifth edition of this work at p.590. But now such contracts will be specifically enforced, provided that the action is heard before the agreed term has expired. Specific performance has even been decreed of an agreement to grant a licence for two days: *Verrall v Great Yarmouth Borough Council* [1981] Q.B. 202; above, para.9–009.

[235] *Greville v Parker* [1910] A.C. 335; *Cornish v Brook Green Laundry Ltd* [1959] 1 Q.B. 394; *Euston Centre Properties Ltd v H. & J. Wilson Ltd* [1982] 1 E.G.L.R. 57; *Henry Smith's Charity Trustees v Hemmings* [1983] 1 E.G.L.R. 94. See below, para.21–011.

[236] *Coatsworth v Johnson* (1886) 55 L.J.Q.B. 220.

[237] *Warmington v Miller* [1973] Q.B. 877.

[238] See *Snell's Equity*, paras 5–009 to 5–015.

[239] See e.g. Pettit (1960) 24 Conv. (N.S.) 125 at 127.

[240] See, e.g. *Parker v Taswell* (1858) 2 De G. & J. 559; *Zimbler v Abrahams* [1903] 1 K.B. 577 (both cases involving breaches of covenant by tenants under agreements for leases). For the circumstances in which equity will give relief to a party in breach of contract, see *Equity and Contemporary Legal Developments* (ed. S. Goldstein), p. 829 (C.H.).

[241] See (1987) 16 Anglo-American L.R. 160 at 170 (P. Sparkes); *Equity and Contemporary Legal Developments*, above, at pp. 855–859 (C.H.); G. Jones and W. Goodhart, *Specific Performance* (2nd edn), p. 84; and see below, paras 18–079 et seq.

court's jurisdiction may also create difficulties. Thus a claimant's right to specific performance in a county court is limited,[242] whereas a defendant's is not.[243]

17–057   *(b) Third parties.* The effect in relation to third parties is different. The grant of a lease creates a legal estate, good against the world. A contract for a lease creates only an equitable interest, namely the right to the equitable remedy of specific performance. As an equitable interest, the contract for a lease is vulnerable against third parties in both registered and unregistered land, and its proprietary effect will largely depend on whether it has been entered on the appropriate register. In practice, agreements for a lease (especially for short terms) are often not registered, even though this may leave the tenant with no remedy but an action for damages (which is often worthless) if the landlord later grants another lease of the land, or sells or mortgages it. Indeed, as the tenant is under no duty to register, it is in the interest of the landlord to see that the agreement is registered. This obviates any risk of a damages claim against the landlord[244] should he make some subsequent disposition to a third party that was intended to take effect subject to the tenant's interest, but which in fact defeated that interest because it was not registered.[245]

17–058   (1) REGISTERED LAND. Where title to the land is registered, a contract to grant a lease may be protected by the entry of a notice in relation to the landlord's estate, irrespective of the length of the term to be granted.[246] Even if the contract to grant a lease is not registered, it may be protected against third parties as an overriding interest where the tenant is in actual occupation of the property.[247]

17–059   (2) UNREGISTERED LAND. Where title to the land is unregistered, a contract for a lease is registrable as an estate contract. If the contract is not registered it is void against a purchaser for money or money's worth of a legal estate in land.[248] If, therefore, the tenant fails to register the contract against the landlord, he may be defeated by a later purchaser (including a lessee) from the

---

[242] *Foster v Reeves* [1892] 2 Q.B. 255. It is confined to leases the value of which does not exceed £30,000: see CCA 1984 s.23(d); SI 1981/1123, which has effect by reason of Interpretation Act 1978, s.17(2)(b). It is remarkable that this figure has remained unchanged, given that Chancery business can normally be dealt with in either the High Court or the county court: CPR Practice Direction 7A, para.2.5.

[243] *Kingswood Estates Co Ltd v Anderson* [1963] 2 Q.B. 169; and see *Cornish v Brook Green Laundry Ltd*, above; (1959) 75 L.Q.R. 168 (R.E.M.); *Rushton v Smith* [1976] Q.B. 480.

[244] See above, para.8–097.

[245] cf. *Hollington Bros Ltd v Rhodes* [1951] 2 T.L.R. 691; above, para.8–094.

[246] LRA 2002 s.32(1): see above, para.7–070.

[247] LRA 2002 s.29; Sch.3 para.2: see the important qualifications to this general principle explained above, para.7–049. If the tenant does not satisfy the conditions imposed by LRA 2002 Sch.3 para.2, he cannot invoke LRA Sch.3 para.1 even if the lease to be granted does not exceed seven years, as that provision applies only to legal leases: *City Permanent Building Society v Miller* [1952] Ch. 840.

[248] LCA 1972 s.4(6); above, para.8–093.

landlord, even though the tenant is in possession of the land[249] or the purchaser knows of or has notice of the contract.[250] It should be noted that, if the tenant does register his estate contract, his interest will be protected even though he does not take possession. Registration is deemed to be actual notice to all persons for all purposes.[251]

(c) Assignment. A further difference affecting third parties lies in the rules **17–060** concerning assignment where the agreement for a lease was made prior to 1996.[252]

(1) AGREEMENTS MADE PRIOR TO 1996. In relation to a legal lease granted prior **17–061** to 1996, its assignment passes to the assignee not only the tenant's rights but also his obligations to observe all the covenants which touch and concern the land, such as those to pay rent and to repair.[253] By contrast, a contract for a lease made before 1996 creates no legal estate with which the burden of such a covenant can run, i.e. there is no "privity of estate".[254] It is governed by the ordinary rule that the benefit but not the burden of a contract is assignable.[255] The tenant can therefore assign his right to specific performance and all other rights under the agreement, so that the assignee can sue the landlord to enforce them.[256] However for breach of any of the tenant's obligations the landlord can sue only the original tenant and not the assignee,[257] even though the assignee has taken possession.[258]

Where the landlord assigns his reversion, the position has been simplified by statute.[259] The rules are the same whether the tenant holds under a legal lease or a mere contract for a lease.

(2) AGREEMENTS MADE AFTER 1995. The Landlord and Tenant (Covenants) **17–062** Act 1995 has changed the law for leases and agreements for leases made after 1995.[260] It has much simplified the law and has removed the distinction between leases and agreements for leases for the purposes of the transmission

---

[249] LPA 1925 s.14 is not in point: see *Lloyd's Bank Plc v Carrick* [1996] 4 All E.R. 630 at 642; above, para.5–121. Prior to 1926, any purchaser would be bound by the rights of a tenant in possession under an agreement for a lease, because his possession was notice of his rights: above, para.8–020.

[250] *Midland Bank Trust Co Ltd v Green* [1981] A.C. 513; above, para.8–095.

[251] LPA 1925 s.198; above, para.8–085.

[252] For the rules governing assignments, see below, paras 17–138 et seq.

[253] As to the covenants in such leases which run with the land and with the reversion, see below, paras 20–004, 20–107.

[254] For the importance of privity of estate to the running of positive (but not restrictive) covenants in pre–1996 leases, see below, para.20–004.

[255] The assignment takes effect in equity or under LPA 1925 s.136. On the statutory assignment of equitable rights, see *Re Pain* [1919] 1 Ch. 38 at 44–46; Snell's *Equity*, para.3–009.

[256] *Manchester Brewery Co v Coombs* [1901] 2 Ch. 608 at 616. The assignor must usually be made a party.

[257] *Camden v Batterbury* (1860) 7 C.B. (N.S.) 864; *Purchase v Lichfield Brewery Co* [1915] 1 K.B. 184 (mortgagee by assignment held not liable for rent). But see *Boyer v Warbey* [1953] 1 Q.B. 234 at 245; below, para.20–044. The assignee may be liable to forfeiture, or for non-observance of restrictive covenants.

[258] *Cox v Bishop* (1857) 8 De G.M. & G. 815 at 824.

[259] This is explained below, para.20–062.

[260] Below, para.20–085.

of the benefit and burden of covenants. The benefit and burden of all covenants, except those expressed to be personal, pass on an assignment of either a legal lease or an agreement for a lease, or on the assignment of the reversion on such a lease or agreement.[261]

17–063   *(d) Miscellaneous.* Several other differences flow from the fundamental distinction between a grant or contract, or from the wording of statutes. Four examples may be given[262]:

(i) A contract for a lease entitles the landlord to "the usual covenants", which oblige the tenant to repair and make the lease subject to forfeiture for non-payment of rent.[263] An executed legal lease implies no such covenants.

(ii) A mere contract for a lease is not a "conveyance" within s.62 of the Law of Property Act 1925 so as to pass all the appurtenant rights listed in that section.[264]

(iii) Where title is unregistered, it is only under a lease, and not under a contract for a lease, that the tenant can plead purchase without notice against the owner of an unregistrable equitable interest[265] as opposed to a mere equity.[266] It is essential to this plea that the purchaser should obtain the legal estate before he is fixed with notice.[267]

(iv) Some important interests are void against a purchaser of unregistered land unless registered as land charges "before the completion of the purchase".[268] A person who has contracted to take a legal lease, but to whom it has not yet been granted, has not "completed the purchase", and is therefore presumably bound by such interests even though they are not registered.

C. The Requirements as to Duration must be Satisfied

A lease may fail because the estate is not clearly demarcated, e.g. if it purports to be a lease for an indefinite period of time. We shall now deal with the various periods for which leases can validly be granted.

---

[261] See L & TCA 1995 ss.3, 28(1).
[262] These do not exhaust the catalogue of differences. For example, a lease is not affected by the rule against perpetuities, but (depending on when it was made) a contract for a lease may be: see above, paras 9–133 et seq.
[263] Below, para.19–058.
[264] Below, para.28–027.
[265] e.g. a pre-1926 restrictive covenant.
[266] e.g. a right to rescission.
[267] Above, para.8–009; *L. & S. W. Ry v Gomm* (1882) 20 Ch D 562 at 583.
[268] LCA 1972 s.4; above, para.17–059.

Section 2. Types of Leases and Tenancies

The two most commonly encountered leases and tenancies are fixed term **17–064** tenancies and periodic tenancies. A fixed term tenancy lasts until the term specified in the tenancy agreement ends, when it will expire by effluxion of time, without any need for the landlord to serve notice on the tenant. However, the tenancy may terminate before the end of the term by one of the other methods outlined in Chapter 18 below: in particular, the landlord is likely to reserve a right of re-entry in the tenancy agreement so that he may terminate ("forfeit") the tenancy in the event of e.g. breach of covenant by the tenant. A periodic tenancy is a tenancy which does not have a specified term as such but which continues until it is determined by the landlord or the tenant giving notice. It may be a yearly tenancy, a quarterly tenancy, a monthly tenancy or a weekly tenancy, the period being that by reference to which the rent is calculated.

A. Certainty of term

1. Fixed term tenancies

In 1992, the House of Lords held that "principle and precedent dictate that it **17–065** is beyond the power of the landlord and the tenant to create a term which is uncertain."[269] In that case, the landlord's predecessors in title, the London County Council, on purchasing land from an individual N, purported to lease back to him for an annual rent a strip adjacent to the highway from December 19, 1930 until the land was required by the council for the purposes of widening the road (in which event, the landlord could terminate the tenancy by giving two months' notice). Although this arrangement was clearly intended to be of short duration,[270] it became impossible, following an assignment of the landlord's reversion, to satisfy the pre-condition for giving notice to the tenant as the incoming landlord was not a highway authority and had no relevant powers to widen the road. The House of Lords held that the purported lease was void for uncertainty and that the effect of the tenant's continued possession and payment of annual rent was to give rise to a periodic tenancy (specifically a yearly tenancy or a tenancy from year to year) pursuant to which the tenant held on such of the terms of the written agreement as were consistent with a yearly tenancy. The landlord could therefore terminate the tenancy by giving six months' notice although the pre-condition specified in the lease was not, and could no longer be, satisfied.

The principle upon which the House of Lords based this decision was derived from an "ancient and technical rule"[271] which required the maximum

---

[269] *Prudential Assurance Co Ltd v London Residuary Body* [1992] 2 A.C. 386 at 394 per Lord Templeman.

[270] *Prudential Assurance Co Ltd v London Residuary Body*, above at 389.

[271] *Prudential Assurance Co Ltd v London Residuary Body*, above at 396 per Lord Browne-Wilkinson.

duration of a lease to be ascertainable from its commencement.[272] The common law position is underwritten by the Law of Property Act 1925 which, in its definition of "term of years absolute", provides that the term must be "either certain or liable to determination".[273] In 1944 it was settled, after some hesitation, that a lease granted during wartime "for the duration of the war" was void for uncertainty at common law, as it was impossible to say, at the date of its commencement, how long it would last.[274] In that case, as in *Prudential Assurance*, the court gave effect to the parties' arrangement by holding that the tenant's possession and payment of a weekly rent gave rise to a periodic (weekly) tenancy terminable by the landlord giving notice. While later decisions of the Court of Appeal sought to restrict the application of the certainty rule,[275] the orthodox position was restored by the House of Lords in *Prudential Assurance*.

17–066   As regards duration, a lease for 99 years from January 1 next, or a lease for seven years from the determination of an existing tenancy, are examples of terms which are valid under the above rule. A lease to take effect from January 1 next "for so many years as X shall name" will be valid if X names the term before January 1, but not otherwise.[276] The court has sometimes succeeded in construing doubtful transactions as being sufficiently certain. Thus a lease "for years" was interpreted to mean a lease for two years.[277] In certain circumstances, the lease may be saved by an application of principles of proprietary estoppel.[278] Thus where a landlord whose powers of disposition are limited[279] agrees to grant an indefinite tenancy, the court may give effect to the tenant's equity (arising from his reliance upon the grant) by holding him entitled to the longest term which the landlord had power to grant.[280]

It is important to note that the rule invalidating uncertain terms applies only where the maximum duration is uncertain; provided that the maximum extent of the term is fixed, the lease may be made determinable on any uncertain event happening within the term.[281] Thus valid leases may be made "for 90

---

[272] *Say v Smith* (1563) Plowd. 269, 272.

[273] LPA 1925 s.205(1)(xxvii); *Prudential Assurance Co Ltd v London Residuary Body*, above at 391; *Mexfield Housing Co-operative Ltd v Berrisford* [2011] UKSC 52; [2011] 3 W.L.R. 1091 at [36].

[274] *Lace v Chantler* [1944] K.B. 368. The decision would have led to so much inconvenience at the time that such leases were converted retrospectively by the Validity of War-Time Leases Act 1944 into terms of 10 years determinable after the end of the war by one month's notice. The statute applied only to the Second World War and did not rescue tenancies granted for other uncertain periods.

[275] *Re Midland Railway Co's Agreement* [1971] Ch. 725 (periodic tenancy terminable by landlord only when premises were required for their undertaking); *Ashburn Anstalt v Arnold* [1989] Ch. 1 (lease until landlord was ready to develop the property).

[276] *Lace v Chantler*, above, at 371; cf. Co.Litt. p.45b.

[277] *Bishop of Bath's Case* (1605) 6 Co. Rep. 34b.

[278] Above, Ch.16.

[279] e.g. because his own interest was leasehold.

[280] *Siew Soon Wah v Yong Tong Hong* [1973] A.C. 836, applying *Re King's Leasehold Estates* (1873) L.R. 16 Eq. 521; *Kusel v Watson* (1879) 11 Ch D 129.

[281] *Prudential Assurance Co Ltd v London Residuary Body* [1992] 2 A.C. 386 at 390, 395. See too LPA 1925 s.205(1)(xxvii).

years if X shall so long live"[282] or "for 21 years determinable if the tenant ceases to live on the premises". It is therefore perfectly possible to make a lease determinable upon some future uncertain event, provided that the device of a determinable fixed term is employed. Similarly the landlord may (and almost always does) reserve a right of re-entry[283] exercisable if some event happens during the term, e.g. if the tenant commits a breach of covenant. In that case the lease is subject to a condition subsequent and may be determined upon some future event which may be relatively uncertain.

2. Periodic tenancies

It is clear that the certainty rule applies to periodic tenancies as well as to fixed term tenancies. In the case of a periodic tenancy, the tenant's term does not expire as in the case of a fixed term tenancy, but the vice of uncertainty is avoided by the power, exercisable by both parties, to terminate by giving notice in accordance with the provisions of the lease:

17–067

> "A tenancy from year to year is saved from being uncertain because each party has power by notice to determine at the end of any year. The term continues until determined as if both parties made a new agreement at the end of each year for a new term for the ensuing year."[284]

It follows that restrictions upon either party's right to give notice are strictly regulated by the common law. A provision that the landlord shall not give notice:

(i) at all[285]; or

(ii) as long as the tenant observes his undertakings[286]; or

(iii) on the occurrence of some contingency which may never occur[287]

has been held to be void as being repugnant to the nature of a tenancy. On the other hand, a provision that the landlord is not to give notice for a defined period, either at all or subject to some condition being satisfied, has been held to be valid[288]; in effect, the arrangement is treated as a fixed term for the defined period followed by a periodic tenancy terminable by the landlord giving notice.[289]

---

[282] See below, para.17–117.

[283] Below, para.18–012.

[284] *Prudential Assurance Co Ltd v London Residuary Body*, above at 394 per Lord Templeman.

[285] *Centaploy Ltd v Matlodge* [1974] Ch. 1.

[286] *Warner v Browne* (1807) 8 East. 165; *Cheshire Lines Committee v Lewis & Co* (1880) 50 L.J.Q.B. 121 at 124, 128 (landlord not to give notice until premises required for demolition).

[287] *Prudential Assurance Co Ltd v London Residuary Body*, above.

[288] *Breams Property Investment Co Ltd v Stroulger* [1948] 2 K.B. 1.

[289] *Mexfield Housing Co-operative Ltd v Berrisford* [2011] UKSC 52, [2011] 3 W.L.R. 1091 at [88].

3. The certainty rule

17–068   In 2011, in *Mexfield Housing Co-operative Ltd v Berrisford*,[290] the Supreme Court revisited the certainty rule. By a written agreement, the landlord, a fully mutual housing association, let a flat to the tenant in consideration of a weekly rent. The agreement was expressed to be determinable by the tenant giving one month's written notice. However, it could only be terminated by the landlord in certain tightly prescribed circumstances, including the occupier's breach of covenant or the rent being in arrears for 21 days. Despite this provision in the parties' written agreement, the landlord sought to determine the tenancy by giving one month's written notice. The Supreme Court held, applying *Prudential Assurance*, that the tenancy was void for uncertainty as the fetter on notice being given by the landlord was of potentially uncertain duration. Had the tenancy been granted prior to 1926, it would have taken effect as a tenancy for the duration of the tenant's life, determinable by the tenant giving one month's written notice or by the landlord satisfying the conditions set out in the tenancy agreement. As the tenancy was granted after 1925, it was converted by the Law of Property Act 1925 into a 90-year term, determinable by landlord or tenant in accordance with the provisions of the tenancy agreement.

The common law position, as explained above, was succinctly summarised by Lord Neuberger as follows[291]:

(i)   an agreement for a term, whose maximum duration can be identified from the inception can give rise to a valid tenancy;

(ii) an agreement which gives rise to a periodic arrangement determinable by either party can also give rise to a valid tenancy;

(iii) an agreement cannot give rise to a tenancy as a matter of law if it is for a term whose maximum duration is uncertain at the inception;

(iv) (a) a fetter on a right to serve notice to determine a periodic tenancy is ineffective if the fetter is to endure for an uncertain period, but

(b) a fetter for a specified period can be valid.

4. Criticism of the certainty rule

17–069   In *Prudential Assurance*, Lord Browne-Wilkinson was highly critical of the rigidity of the uncertainty rule, noting the "bizarre outcome"[292] it gave rise to:

---

[290] *Mexfield Housing Co-operative Ltd v Berrisford*, above.

[291] *Mexfield Housing Co-operative Ltd v Berrisford*, above at [33].

[292] *Prudential Assurance Co Ltd v London Residuary Body*, above at 396. The tenant's successor in title was left with shop premises without road frontage; the landlord's successor in title was left with a strip of land which, without the road-widening powers vested in the original landlord, was virtually useless to him.

"No one has produced any satisfactory rationale for the genesis of this rule. No one has been able to point to any useful purpose that it serves at the present day. If, by overruling the existing authorities, this House were able to change the law for the future only I would have urged your Lordships to do so. But for this House to depart from a rule relating to land law which has been established for many centuries might upset long established titles. I must therefore confine myself to expressing the hope that the Law Commission might look at the subject to see whether there is in fact any good reason now for maintaining a rule which operates to defeat contractually agreed arrangements between the parties (of which all successors in title are aware) and which is capable of producing such an extraordinary result as that in the present case".[293]

Nearly 20 years later, in *Mexfield*, Lord Neuberger spoke on behalf of all seven members of the Supreme Court in conceding that:

" . . . the law is not in a satisfactory state. There is no apparent practical justification for holding that an agreement for a term of uncertain duration cannot give rise to a tenancy, or that a fetter of uncertain duration on the right to serve a notice to quit is invalid".[294]

However, despite this stated dissatisfaction with the certainty rule, the Supreme Court refused to abolish it, for a number of reasons [295] The rule was fundamental to the concept of the lease and, although a common law principle, it was now enshrined in the property legislation. It had been upheld by the House of Lords in *Prudential Assurance* only 20 years previously, and its removal "might upset long-established titles".[296] Neither counsel in *Mexfield* had set out to challenge the rule itself. As far as the decision in *Mexfield* was concerned, the Supreme Court were able to circumvent the difficulties of the certainty rule by construing the arrangement between the parties as a tenancy for life which was in turn converted by statute into a 90-year term terminable by the tenant or the landlord on compliance with the termination provisions contained in the tenancy agreement. It was not therefore necessary for the decision in the case to overrule past authority such as *Prudential Assurance*.

As a matter of policy, the existence of a certainty rule may have some merit. It serves clearly to distinguish a lease from a fee simple, an essential function in the scheme of the law of property. It avoids the potential injustice that may result from the perpetual continuation of a lease, negotiated without the

---

[293] *Prudential Assurance Co Ltd v London Residuary Body*, above at 396. These comments were supported by Lords Griffiths and Mustill.

[294] *Mexfield Housing Co-operative Ltd v Berrisford*, above at [34]; see also Baroness Hale at [96]; Lord Clarke at [105]; Lord Dyson at [115], recommending reconsideration of the certainty rule by Parliament or the courts as a matter of urgency.

[295] *Mexfield Housing Co-operative Ltd v Berrisford*, above at [35] et seq.

[296] *Prudential Assurance Co Ltd v London Residuary Body*, above at 396, per Lord Browne-Wilkinson.

benefit of legal advice, which the parties had intended to be of a short duration, and where they had made no provision for periodic rent reviews.[297] The law does not recognise a lease in perpetuity.[298] But if a lease were granted at a rent until a particular event were to occur, and it subsequently became impossible for that event ever to happen,[299] the lease would endure perpetually unless a certainty rule prevented it.[300] But while it may remain possible to justify the existence of a certainty rule, there can be little doubt that the rule is "arbitrary and crude" in its current operation and too strict in its current formulation.[301] It is also easy to circumvent by the simple device of creating a fixed term tenancy determinable on the earlier occurrence of a specified contingency.[302]

5. The consequences of uncertainty

17–070   *(a) Periodic tenancy or tenancy at will.* A person, who has entered into possession under a lease that is void because of its uncertain duration, has traditionally been considered to be a tenant at will, at least initially, because he has exclusive possession.[303] Where the tenant has paid rent, however, the court is likely to infer the existence of a periodic tenancy,[304] which may then be determined by either party on the giving of notice in the usual way.[305] It will not be a term of that periodic tenancy that the landlord can give notice to quit only on the occurrence of the specified event that was to bring the void lease to an end.[306] Thus, in *Prudential Assurance*, a yearly tenancy was

[297] *Prudential Assurance Co Ltd v London Residuary Body*, above at 390 (rent agreed in 1930 was £30 p.a.; by time of trial, commercial rent would be £10,000 p.a.); (1993) 109 L.Q.R. 93 at 112 (P. Sparkes); (1993) 13 L.S. 38 at 44 (S. Bright).

[298] *Sevenoaks, Maidstone and Tunbridge Ry Co v London, Chatham and Dover Ry Co* (1879) 11 Ch.D. 625 at 635; *The Raphael Fishing Company Ltd v The State of Mauritius* [2008] UKPC 43 at [68], per Lord Neuberger; see above, para.3–012; para.17–003.

[299] As happened in *Prudential Assurance Co Ltd v London Residuary Body*, above, where the lease was granted until the landlord required the land for road-widening purposes. The reversion subsequently came into the hands of a body that had no power to undertake road works.

[300] cf. *Prudential Assurance Co Ltd v London Residuary Body* [1992] 1 E.G.L.R. 47 at 52, CA; [1992] 2 A.C. 386 at 394, HL. It would closely resemble a fee simple subject to a rent charge, something which can no longer be created: Rentcharges Act 1977 s.2; below, para.31–018. It would however differ significantly from such a fee in that the burden of positive covenants could run with the lease, something which is impossible with a fee simple: *Rhone v Stephens* [1994] 2 A.C. 310; below, para.32–017.

[301] For discussion of the rationale of the rule, see (1993) 109 L.Q.R. 93 (P. Sparkes); (1993) 13 L.S. 38 (S. Bright); [1993] Conv. 461 (P. F. Smith).

[302] *Prudential Assurance Co Ltd v London Residuary Body*, above, at 390; *Mexfield Housing Co-operative Ltd v Berrisford*, above at [89].

[303] *Denn d. Warren v Fearnside* (1747) 1 Wils.K.B. 176; *Wheeler v Mercer* [1957] A.C. 416 at 432. Where a lease is void for non-compliance with the statutory formal requirements, it also takes effect as a tenancy at will: LPA 1925 s.54(1); above, para.17–045.

[304] *Prudential Assurance Co Ltd v London Residuary Body* [1992] 2 A.C. 386 at 392, 393. There is no longer any presumption of a periodic tenancy where a tenant has exclusive possession and pays rent: see below, para.17–086. However, the court is likely to find the necessary intention that there should be such a tenancy in these circumstances because the parties intended there to be a lease.

[305] Below, para.17–090.

[306] *Prudential Assurance Co Ltd v London Residuary Body*, above at 392, reversing on this point [1992] 1 E.G.L.R. 47, CA.

implied in place of the void lease that was granted until the land was required for road-widening, and the landlord could determine the lease by giving six months' notice even though it had no powers to carry out works to widen the road.[307]

(b) *Rent-free arrangements.* It is much more difficult where the tenant paid **17–071** no rent, but a premium or some other consideration for the grant of the void lease.[308] As a mere tenant at will,[309] his interest could be determined whenever the landlord decides.[310] As a lease is a contract as well as an estate,[311] normal contractual principles should apply. Therefore, where a lease is void for uncertainty and the tenant has received no part of what he bargained for (as where he has never entered into possession), there is a total failure of consideration. He is then entitled to restitution of the benefit he has conferred on the landlord.[312] By contrast, where the tenant has received some part of what he had bargained for (as where he had the use of the premises for a period before the lease was held void), the general rule suggests that he can recover nothing.[313] In this latter case, the tenant might sometimes be able to have recourse to the principles of proprietary estoppel.[314] If he had been led to believe that he would have a lease until the occurrence of some event and, in reliance upon that expectation, had acted to his detriment, an equity would arise in his favour.[315] To satisfy that equity, the court might grant the tenant a lease for a term of years determinable on the earlier occurrence of the event.[316]

(c) *Lease for life.* Prior to 1926, the certainty rule did not invalidate leases **17–072** granted for lives, because these, unlike leases for years, conferred a recognised freehold estate. It therefore remained open to the court to construe a doubtful grant in favour of an individual as giving rise to a lease for that individual's life. This occurred where an agreement purported to confer an "option of a lease" (no period being named)[317]; but it was considered impossible to construe a lease for the duration of the war as an agreement for a life

---

[307] *Prudential Assurance Co Ltd v London Residuary Body*, above.

[308] cf. *Canadian Imperial Bank of Commerce v Bello*, above (lease granted because of money owed to tenant).

[309] There can be no periodic tenancy without the payment and acceptance of rent: see *Prudential Assurance Co Ltd v London Residuary Body* [1992] 1 E.G.L.R. 47, CA, at 51.

[310] Below, para.17–104.

[311] Above, para.17–006.

[312] See Goff & Jones, *The Law of Restitution* (7th edn, 2006), para.23–010.

[313] See G.H. Treitel, *The Law of Contract* (12th edn, 2007), para.22–004.

[314] See above, Ch.16.

[315] As in *Siew Soon Wah v Yong Tong Hong* [1973] A.C. 836, where a tenant paid $8,000 premium for a lease granted for as long as he wished to occupy the premises. This created an equity by estoppel in his favour, entitling him to remain there for 30 years. For the doctrine to apply, it will however be necessary to show detriment by the tenant in reliance upon the expectation created. cf. *Canadian Imperial Bank of Commerce v Bello* (1991) 64 P. & C.R. 48, where the lease was granted *after* and because the tenant had incurred detriment; see also *Mexfield Housing Co-operative Ltd v Berrisford* [2010] EWCA Civ 811; [2011] Ch. 244 at [70].

[316] cf. *Griffiths v Williams* [1978] 2 E.G.L.R. 121 at 123, 124.

[317] *Austin v Newman* [1906] 2 K.B. 167; cf. *Buck v Howarth* (1947) 63 T.L.R. 195.

tenancy determinable when the war ended.[318] As is explained below, a lease for life is now almost always converted by statute into a term of 90 years.[319] The statutory provision is premised on the existence of the certainty rule; a tenancy for life, being as from 1926 no longer a legal estate in its own right and outside the definition of "term of years absolute" in view of its uncertain duration, had to be converted into a fixed term tenancy (and thereby a term of years) so that it could retain its status as a legal estate.[320]

It now appears that whenever a landlord grants a tenancy to an individual which falls foul of the certainty rule the tenancy will take effect as a tenancy for the individual's life. While s.149(6) only applies where the tenancy automatically ends on the death of the individual, that will normally be the case on this construction,[321] and it does not matter that the tenancy may, in accordance with its provisions, be terminable for other reasons or in other circumstances.[322] Nor is it necessary for the tenant to establish that the parties actually intended that the tenancy should endure for the duration of the tenant's life.[323] The major limitation of the tenancy for life construction is that it cannot apply where the tenant is not an individual; where, e.g. the tenant is a company or a corporation.[324] In such circumstances, resort must be had to the other possibilities; that a periodic tenancy or tenancy at will can be inferred,[325] or that the court gives effect to the contract between the parties.[326]

17–073   *(d) Contractual licence.* A lease is at one and the same time a contract and an estate.[327] Nevertheless, the courts have been reluctant in the past to infer a contractual licence where the grant of a tenancy fails for uncertainty, and would do so only in exceptional circumstances,[328] on the ground that the grant of exclusive possession is the hallmark of a tenancy.[329] However, it now seems to be the case that this argument carries less weight,[330] and the court is prepared, in circumstances where the estate is void for uncertainty, to enforce the contract between the parties:

> If the Agreement does not create a tenancy for technical reasons, namely because it purports to create an uncertain term, it is hard to see why, as

---

[318] *Lace v Chantler,* above at 371.

[319] LPA 1925 s.149(6); see paras 17–115 et seq. below.

[320] *Mexfield Housing Co-operative Ltd v Berrisford* [2011] UKSC 52 at [36].

[321] *Mexfield Housing Co-operative Ltd v Berrisford*, above at [49].

[322] *Mexfield Housing Co-operative Ltd v Berrisford*, above at [50].

[323] *Mexfield Housing Co-operative Ltd v Berrisford*, above at [43] et seq.

[324] *Mexfield Housing Co-operative Ltd v Berrisford*, above at [94] (Baroness Hale); [105] (Lord Clarke); [119] (Lord Dyson).

[325] See above at para.17–070.

[326] See below at para.17–073.

[327] See para.17–001 above.

[328] *Ashburn Anstalt v Arnold* [1989] Ch. 1 at 13; *Canadian Imperial Bank of Commerce v Bello* (1991) 64 P. & C.R. 48 at 51.

[329] *Lace v Chantler,* above at 372; *Colchester BC v Smith* [1991] Ch. 448 at 483–485 (on appeal [1992] Ch. 421); above, para.17–015.

[330] *Mexfield Housing Co-operative Ltd v Berrisford*, above at [64].

a matter of principle, it should not be capable of taking effect as a contract, enforceable as between the parties personally, albeit not capable of binding their respective successors, as no interest in land or other proprietary interest would subsist.[331]

It is evident that such a construction will be of no avail where the reversion or the term has been assigned by the original parties.

6. The case for reform

The combined effect of the decisions of the House of Lords in *Prudential* **17–074** *Assurance* and the Supreme Court in *Mexfield* has been to leave the law in a highly unsatisfactory state. While the latter decision results in a fair outcome which reflects the initial expectations of the parties, it has serious limitations as a precedent for future cases, in particular that the lease for life construction it adopts will be ineffective unless the tenant is an individual. The concluding words of Lord Dyson make an irresistible case for reform of the certainty rule:

> "There should be no need to have to resort to such reasoning in order to arrive at the result which the parties intended. That is why the radical solution of doing away with the uncertainty rule altogether is so attractive. There is the further point that the section 149(6) route to the right result can only be followed where the purported tenant is an individual and not a corporate entity. To treat an individual and a corporate entity differently in this respect can only be explained on historical grounds. The explanation may lie in the realms of history, but that hardly provides a compelling justification for maintaining the distinction today".[332]

B. Classification

Leases and tenancies may be classified under the four following heads. **17–075**

1. Fixed term tenancies

(a) Length of term. A lease may be granted for any period of certain duration, no matter how long or short. Leases for a week or for 3,000 years are equally valid. A lease may be for discontinuous periods, e.g. for three successive bank holidays.[333] Discontinuous leases are sometimes encountered in the context of time-sharing holiday homes, as where a lump sum is paid for the right to occupy a cottage for one week in each year for 80 years. A lease on these terms has been held not to be "for a term certain exceeding 21 years" since although a single term is expressed to be granted, the interest in it is

---

[331] *Mexfield Housing Co-operative Ltd v Berrisford*, above at [60] per Lord Neuberger. This position is endorsed by Lord Hope at [80], Lord Mance at [102], and Lord Clarke at [108].
[332] *Mexfield Housing Co-operative Ltd v Berrisford*, above at [119].
[333] *Smallwood v Sheppards* [1895] 2 Q.B. 627.

discontinuous.[334] The term cannot begin before the lease itself is granted, but it may be defined by reference to an earlier date. A lease granted "for seven years from this day a year ago" will therefore take effect as a lease for six years.[335]

17-076   If no date for commencement is stated, a grant of a tenancy usually takes effect at once,[336] provided that the date is clear.[337] But if a contract for a lease does not specify the intended date of commencement, it will be void unless the date can be inferred from the parties' language.[338] Where the term of a lease is to run "from" a particular date, there is a presumption that the specified date is not included in the period of the demise,[339] but this is rebuttable by evidence of contrary intention.[340] By contrast, if the term is to commence "on" a specified day, that day is included within the term of the lease.[341]

17-077   *(b) Reversionary leases.* Leases were not subject to the common law rule for freehold estates, based upon the need for livery of seisin in old times, that grants could not be made so as to take effect in the future.[342] The perpetuity rule was not infringed since the lessee took a vested interest forthwith; it was only the vesting in possession that was postponed.[343] It followed that, before 1926, there was no restriction upon the length of time that might elapse before the term began; a lease could thus be granted in 1917 to commence in 1946.[344] Such a lease was known as a reversionary lease.[345]

17-078   However, s.149(3) of the Law of Property Act 1925 provides that any grant of a term at a rent or in consideration of a fine, limited to take effect more than 21 years from the date of the instrument creating it, is void; and the same applies to any contract to create such a term.[346] The provision does not affect contracts for leases which, when eventually granted, will take effect in possession within 21 years of the grant; for these, subject to the perpetuity rule

---

[334] *Cottage Holiday Associates Ltd v Customs and Excise Commissioners* [1983] Q.B. 735 (rating of lease for value added tax).

[335] *Bradshaw v Pawley* [1980] 1 W.L.R. 10.

[336] *Doe d. Phillip v Benjamin* (1839) 9 A. & E. 644 ("agrees to let" construed as grant rather than contract); *Furness v Bond* (1888) 4 T.L.R. 457.

[337] *James v Lock* [1978] 1 E.G.L.R. 1 at 2.

[338] *Harvey v Pratt* [1965] 1 W.L.R. 1025. There is a full review of the authorities by Neuberger J. in *Liverpool CC v Walton Group Plc* [2002] 1 E.G.L.R. 149.

[339] *Whelton Sinclair v Hyland* [1992] 2 E.G.L.R. 158 at 161. The authorities are reviewed in [1993] Conv. 206 (E. Cooke).

[340] *Meadfield Properties Ltd v Secretary of State for the Environment* [1995] 1 E.G.L.R. 39 (where the first and last date of the lease were specified, the term included both). See too *Whelton Sinclair v Hyland,* above (application of presumption would have meant that premises were unlet for one day).

[341] *Sidebotham v Holland* [1895] 1 Q.B. 378 at 382.

[342] Above, para.4–006.

[343] Above, para.9–001.

[344] *Mann, Crossman & Paulin Ltd v Registrar of the Land Registry* [1918] 1 Ch. 202.

[345] Contrast a lease of the reversion: below, para.17–133; and see Preston, *Conveyancing,* ii. pp.145, 146; *Hyde v Warden* (1877) 3 Ex. D. 72 at 83, 84.

[346] The provision does not affect grants or contracts made before 1926 nor does it apply to any term taking effect in equity under a settlement, or created out of an equitable interest under a settlement, or under an equitable power for mortgage, indemnity or other like purposes. The reason for requiring a rent or fine is explained below, para.17–118 et seq.

in certain cases after assignment,[347] are valid even after longer periods, as for example a contract to renew a 50-year lease at the tenant's option. The prohibition applies only to immediate grants the operation of which is suspended for more than 21 years, and to contracts for such grants.[348]

(c) Interesse termini. The Law of Property Act 1925 abolished the common law doctrine of *interesse termini*,[349] whereby a lessee acquired no actual estate in the land until he had taken possession in accordance with the lease, but had a legal proprietary right in the land which carried with it a right of entry.[350]   **17–079**

(d) Determination. As a general rule, a lease for a fixed term automatically determines when the term expires. However, this rule is subject to a number of exceptions contained in legislation enacted to confer a degree of security of tenure on the tenant.[351]   **17–080**

2. Periodic tenancies

(a) Nature. A periodic tenancy (such as a yearly tenancy, a quarterly tenancy, a monthly tenancy or a weekly tenancy) is one which continues from term to term indefinitely until determined by proper notice, notwithstanding the death of either party or the assignment of his interest.[352] Traditionally the law treated each successive term, when it took effect, as part and parcel of the original term, which therefore grew as time elapsed. Thus after 50 years of possession, for example, the yearly tenant's interest was regarded as a 50-year term, but as to the future as a yearly tenancy.[353] However, now that periodic tenancies have been brought unequivocally within the ambit of the certainty rule, this analysis is unlikely to apply,[354] and it is better to regard them as a succession of one-year terms.[355]   **17–081**

(b) Joint tenants. Although a new agreement is implied, a periodic tenancy continues only so long as it is the will of both parties that it should.[356] It   **17–082**

---

[347] Above, para.9–132. The perpetuities rule does not apply to contracts relating to land made after April 5, 2010: see para.9–032 above, and Ch.9 in general.

[348] *Re Strand and Savoy Properties Ltd* [1960] Ch. 582; *Weg Motors Ltd v Hales* [1962] Ch. 49, not following *Northchurch Estates Ltd v Daniels* [1947] Ch. 117; see (1960) 76 L.Q.R. 352 (R.E.M.).

[349] LPA 1925 s.149(1), (2). It was abolished in respect of all leases whenever made.

[350] See generally the fifth edition of this work at p.648.

[351] See Ch.22 below.

[352] A tenancy granted for a term certain of one year, and thereafter from month to month, cannot therefore take effect as a periodic tenancy, as the tenancy that continues after the end of the first year must be for the same duration as the term certain that has expired: *Goodman v Everly* [2001] EWCA Civ 104; [2002] H.L.R. 53;: see para.22–093 below.

[353] Preston, *Conveyancing*, iii, pp.76, 77; *Legg v Strudwick* (1708) 2 Salk. 414; *Oxley v James* (1844) 13 M. & W. 209; *Cattley v Arnold* (1859) 1 J. & H. 651.

[354] But see *A.G. Securities v Vaughan,* above, at 473, where Lord Jauncey spoke of "the continuance of the springing interest". See too (1993) 13 L.S. 38 at 39 (S. Bright).

[355] *Mexfield Housing Co-operative Ltd v Berrisford* [2010] EWCA Civ 811; [2011] Ch. 244 at [82].

[356] *A.G. Securities v Vaughan* [1990] 1 A.C. 417 at 473; *Hammersmith LBC v Monk* [1992] 1 A.C. 478 at 484.

follows that where there are joint tenants, a notice given by one of the tenants is effective to terminate the lease.[357] This perfectly logical principle can give rise to hardship,[358] in particular where a relationship between the joint tenants has broken down and the remaining tenant wishes the tenancy to continue, but a joint tenant is not legally obliged to consult the other joint tenant or tenants prior to giving notice.[359]

17–083   *(c) Creation.* Periodic tenancies can be created as follows:

    (i) by statute;

    (ii) by express agreement;

    (iii) by inference from the conduct of the parties.

17–084   (1) BY STATUTE. On the termination of a fixed-term tenancy which is an assured tenancy pursuant to Part 1 of the Housing Act 1988 (otherwise than by court order or by the tenant's action), a statutory periodic tenancy will arise by force of statute.[360] In certain limited circumstances, a tenancy from year to year of an agricultural holding may be created by statute where land has been let or licensed for agricultural use for an interest less than a tenancy from year to year.[361]

17–085   (2) BY EXPRESS AGREEMENT. Where a periodic tenancy is created by express grant, the precise tenancy created depends upon the true construction of the document.[362] A yearly tenancy will be indicated by a grant to T "from year to year" or "as yearly tenant". A grant "to T for one year and thereafter from year to year" will give T a tenancy for at least two years. T has been given a definite term of one year followed by a yearly tenancy which cannot be determined before the end of its first year.[363] Where a tenancy contains an express provision that it is determinable by some specific period of notice, it will take effect as a periodic tenancy e.g. where the tenancy agreement provides for termination on three months' notice, it will give rise to a quarterly tenancy.[364]

---

[357] *Hammersmith LBC v Monk*, above; *Harrow LBC v Johnstone* [1997] 1 W.L.R. 459 at 471. See above, para.13–006.

[358] The same principle applies in the case of joint landlords.

[359] *Crawley BC v Ure* [1996] Q.B. 13; *Notting Hill Housing Trust v Brackley* [2001] EWCA Civ 601; [2002] H.L.R. 10. A notice that one or more of the tenants does not wish the periodic tenancy to continue when it expires is not regarded as a disposition of property, and it cannot therefore be set aside, e.g. pursuant to MCA 1973 s.37: see *Newlon Housing Trust v Alsulaimen* [1999] 1 A.C. 313.

[360] See further para.22–093 below.

[361] AHA 1986 s.2, on which see para.22–037 below. The Act has very limited application to agreements on or after September 1, 1995: see para.22–035 below.

[362] See further for classification of periodic tenancies para.17–089 below.

[363] *Re Searle* [1912] 1 Ch. 610; *Addis v Burrows* [1948] 1 K.B. 444.

[364] *Kemp v Derrett* (1814) 3 Camp. 510. This is subject to any contrary indication, as in a yearly tenancy with a special period of notice.

(3) BY CONDUCT. A periodic tenancy may be created by inference where a **17–086**
person occupies land with the owner's consent and rent assessed on a periodic
basis is paid and accepted. The issue has always been to determine the likely
intentions of the parties,[365] and it is up to the person asserting that there is a
tenancy to make good his claim.[366] Traditionally the courts applied a presumption that an occupier who pays rent holds as a periodic tenant,[367] the
presumption being rebuttable by contrary evidence of the parties' intentions.[368] However, it is now considered that the presumption "is unsound and
no longer holds good",[369] or at best, will seldom arise.[370] The courts have
taken the view that the expansion of statutory security of tenure has made it
less likely that the parties would intend to create a tenancy and more likely
that they would contemplate a more exiguous relationship, such as a tenancy
at will or a licence.[371] The question is therefore an open one: is it right and
proper in all the circumstances of the case including the payment and acceptance of rent to infer that the parties had reached an agreement for a periodic
tenancy?[372]

The issue commonly arises where a tenant holds over after the termination **17–087**
of a fixed-term lease with the landlord's consent,[373] or a person enters into
possession pending negotiations for a lease,[374] and in each case, pays rent on

---

[365] "The question . . . is, *quo animo* the rent was received, and what the real intention of both
parties was?" *Doe d. Cheny v Batten* (1775) Cowp. 243 at 245, per Lord Mansfield.

[366] *Javad v Aqil* [1991] 1 W.L.R. 1007 at 1017; *London Baggage Company v Railtrack Plc*
[2000] L. & T.R. 439 at 449; *Mann Aviation Group (Engineering) Ltd (in administration) v
Longmint Aviation Ltd* [2011] EWHC 2238 (Ch).

[367] See, e.g. *Dougal v McCarthy* [1893] 1 Q.B. 736; *Lewis v M.T.C. (Cars) Ltd* [1975] 1 W.L.R.
457 at 462.

[368] *Doe d. Bastow v Cox* (1847) 11 Q.B. 122.

[369] *Longrigg Burrough & Trounson v Smith* [1979] 2 E.G.L.R. 42 at 43, per Ormrod L.J.

[370] *Javad v Aqil* [1991] 1 W.L.R. 1007 at 1017; *London Baggage Company v Railtrack Plc*
[2000] L. & T.R. 439 at 445. One situation in which the old presumption still holds good, as
according with the likely intentions of the parties, is where the tenant enters under a void lease
and pays rent on a periodic basis: see *Prudential Assurance Co Ltd v London Residuary Body*
[1992] 2 A.C. 386 at 392; *Inntrepreneur Estates Ltd v Mason* (1993) 68 P. & C.R. 53 at 72.

[371] *Dealex Properties Ltd v Brooks* [1966] 1 Q.B. 542; *Longrigg, Burrough & Trounson v
Smith*, above, at 43; *Sopwith v Stutchbury* (1983) 17 H.L.R. 50. It should be noted that statutory
security is now less pervasive than it was at the time of these decisions: see HA 1988; ATA 1995,
respectively at paras 22–070 and 22–027 below. For tenancies at will, see below at paras 17–102
et seq.

[372] *Longrigg Burrough & Trounson v Smith* [1979] 2 E.G.L.R. 42 at 43, per Ormrod L.J.

[373] Where the holding over is plainly consensual, as where the parties are negotiating a new
lease, it is likely to be regarded as a tenancy at will: see *Dean and Chapter of Canterbury Cathedral
v Whitbread Plc* (1995) 72 P. & C.R. 9 at 13; *London Baggage Company v Railtrack Plc* [2000]
L. & T.R. 439 at 449; below, para.17–102. In some of the modern cases where there was no
intention to create a periodic tenancy, it was unnecessary to characterise the occupant's status:
see, e.g. *Longrigg, Burrough & Trounson v Smith*, above; *Cardiothoracic Institute v Shrewdcrest*
[1986] 1 W.L.R. 368. For the special position of a secure tenant under HA 1985, Pt IV, against
whom an order for possession has been obtained, see *Burrows v Brent LBC* [1996] 1 W.L.R. 1448,
at para.22–171 below.

[374] In some cases, the person has been held to be a tenant at will: see *Javad v Aqil*, above; and
in others a mere licensee; see *P. Dunwell v Hunt* (1996) 72 P. & C.R. D6; see further below
para.17–102.

a periodic basis.[375] While it is accepted that the court is to give effect to the intentions of the parties,[376] having regard to what was agreed and all the surrounding circumstances,[377] it remains unclear whether the parties' intentions are to be subjectively or objectively determined.[378] It is unlikely that a periodic tenancy will arise where the occupant has entered land as a trespasser and the owner has subsequently accepted payment from him for his use and occupation.[379]

17–088   *(d) Terms of yearly tenancy.* In those now unusual cases where a tenant holds over and a yearly tenancy is implied, the tenancy will be subject to such of the terms of the expired or informal lease or agreement as are not inconsistent with a yearly holding.[380] The same applies to a tenant who enters and pays yearly rent under a mere agreement or an informal lease: he is tenant from year to year at law, although he may have other rights in equity.[381] Covenants to repair,[382] to pay rent in advance,[383] to carry on some specified trade on the premises,[384] and provisos for re-entry by the landlord on non-payment of rent or breach of covenant,[385] may all be implied in a yearly tenancy. But a covenant to paint every three years[386] or a provision for two years' notice to quit[387] are inconsistent with a yearly tenancy and cannot be implied in this way.[388]

17–089   *(e) Classification of tenancy.* Where a periodic tenancy is created by inference, the tenancy is classified according to the period by reference to which the parties calculated the rent. An agreement for "£5,200 per annum payable weekly" prima facie creates a yearly tenancy; and the fact that the rent is paid at more frequent intervals than a year will not prevent a yearly

---

[375] Where a tenant holds over and does not pay any rent, the court is likely to infer a tenancy at will: see *Banjo v Brent LBC*, above.

[376] See, e.g. *Vaughan-Armatrading v Sarsah* (1995) 27 H.L.R. 631 at 635; *Greenwich LBC v Regan* (1996) 72 P. & C.R. 507 at 512; *Burrows v Brent LBC*, above, at 1454.

[377] *Longrigg, Burrough & Trounson v Smith*, above, at 43; *Javad v Aqil* [1991] 1 W.L.R. 1007 at 1012.

[378] Compare *Land v Sykes* [1992] 1 E.G.L.R. 1 at 4; *London Baggage Company v Railtrack Plc*, above, at 445 (favouring an objective view) with *Longrigg, Burrough & Trounson v Smith* [1979] 2 E.G.L.R. 42 and 43 (adopting a subjective approach); and see *Dreamgate Properties Ltd v Arnot* (1997) 76 P. & C.R. 25 (where the point was left open).

[379] See, e.g. *Westminster City Council v Basson* (1990) 62 P. & C.R. 57; *Brent LBC v O'Bryan* (1992) 65 P. & C.R. 258; *Vaughan-Armatrading v Sarsah,* above. A landowner is entitled to be compensated for the use of his property, whether the occupier is there lawfully or not: see above, para.4–029.

[380] *Hyatt v Griffiths* (1851) 17 Q.B. 505 (holding over after a term of four years); *Dougal v McCarthy* [1893] 1 Q.B. 736 (holding over after term of one year).

[381] Above, para.17–047.

[382] *Felnex Central Properties Ltd v Montague Burton Properties Ltd* [1981] 2 E.G.L.R. 73.

[383] *Lee v Smith* (1854) 9 Exch. 662.

[384] *Sanders v Karnell* (1858) 1 F. & F. 356.

[385] *Thomas v Packer* (1857) 1 H. & N. 669.

[386] *Pinero v Judson* (1829) 6 Bing. 206; contrast *Martin v Smith* (1874) L.R. 9 Ex. 50 (tenant under unsealed lease held liable on covenant to paint in seventh year, since he had stayed for seven years).

[387] *Tooker v Smith* (1857) 1 H. & N. 732.

[388] cf. *Re Leeds & Batley Breweries Ltd and Bradbury's Lease* [1920] 2 Ch. 548 (option to purchase reversion not implied).

tenancy from arising by implication.[389] However, where the agreement stipulates "£100 per week", a weekly tenancy would be presumed, even though the tenant would make precisely the same payments, namely, £100 every week.[390] The same principle applies in the case of other periods, such as months or quarters.[391] But each case depends upon its own facts. The question is sometimes difficult where a tenant holds over after the expiry of a lease for a term of years at a weekly rent, and continues to pay rent weekly as before.[392] If, in such a case, the court considers that the parties intended there to be a periodic tenancy, it will infer a weekly tenancy unless there is evidence that the weekly payments were instalments of an annual rent.[393]

(f) Determination by notice   **17–090**

(1) THE RULE. A periodic tenancy is determinable by notice.[394] The parties may agree on any period of notice,[395] and the period of notice to be given by the landlord may be different from the tenant's.[396]

A notice to quit "on or before", or "by", the proper date is valid if given by the landlord[397] but void if given by the tenant[398]; for in the former case the tenant knows when he must go, though he can go earlier, whereas in the latter case the landlord is left uncertain when the tenant will go. Notice cannot, it seems, be given before the tenancy begins.[399] But once a valid notice is given, it automatically terminates the tenancy on the date stated, and it cannot be withdrawn or waived; even a purported agreement to withdraw it cannot prevent it operating, though the agreement may create a new tenancy in place of the old.[400]

(2) LENGTH OF NOTICE. The rule at common law is that, subject to contrary   **17–091**
provision in the lease, a periodic tenancy is determinable by notice amounting to at least one full period of the tenancy; thus a monthly tenancy requires notice of one month, and a weekly tenancy notice of one week.[401] There is an

---

[389] *Shirley v Newman* (1795) 1 Esp. 266.

[390] *Ladies Hosiery and Underwear Ltd v Parker* [1930] 1 Ch. 304 at 328.

[391] The statement of Chambre J. in *Richardson v Langridge* (1811) 4 Taunt. 128 at 132 that payment of rent measured by any aliquot part of a year is evidence of a yearly tenancy must not be read as extending Mansfield C.J.'s phrase (at 131) "a yearly rent, though payable half-yearly or quarterly".

[392] See *Ladies Hosiery and Underwear Ltd v Parker,* above; cf. *Richardson v Langridge* (1811) 4 Taunt. 128 at 132.

[393] *Adler v Blackman* [1953] 1 Q.B. 146; cf. where statute provides otherwise: *Church Commissioners for England v Meya* [2006] EWCA Civ 821; [2007] H.L.R. 4, see para.22–093 below.

[394] For notices given by one of two or more joint tenants, see above, para.13–006.

[395] *Re Threlfall* (1880) 16 Ch D 274 at 281; *Allison v Scargall* [1920] 3 K.B. 443.

[396] *Breams Property Investment Co Ltd v Stroulger* [1948] 2 K.B. 1; *Wallis v Semark* [1951] 2 T.L.R. 222. See, for doctrine of repugnancy, para.17–067 above.

[397] *Dagger v Shepherd,* above; *Eastaugh v Macpherson* [1954] 1 W.L.R. 1307.

[398] *Perduzzi v Cohen* [1942] L.J.N.C.C.R. 136; *Dagger v Shepherd,* above, at 224.

[399] *Lower v Sorrell* [1963] 1 Q.B. 959; but the decision on this point may be confined to agricultural holdings. See generally (1963) 79 L.Q.R. 178 (R.E.M.).

[400] *Dagger v Shepherd* [1946] K.B. 215 at 221; *Clarke v Grant* [1950] 1 K.B. 104 (payment and acceptance of rent immaterial); *Lower v Sorrell,* above.

[401] *Lemon v Lardeur* [1946] K.B. 613.

important exception to this rule in that a yearly tenancy is determinable by at least half a year's notice.[402]

17–092   (3) DATE OF EXPIRATION. Notice must expire at the end of a completed period of the tenancy.[403] The notice to quit may specify either the last day of a period of the tenancy (i.e. in the case of a yearly tenancy the day *before* the anniversary of the commencement of the year) or the following day.[404] This is because, in either case, the tenancy actually terminates at the stroke of midnight which ends the period in question.[405] It is possible to employ a general formula in the notice to quit, such as "at the expiration of the year of your tenancy which will expire next after the end of one half year from the service of this notice".[406]

17–093   (4) CONTRARY PROVISION. Both the length of notice and the date of expiration are subject to any contrary agreement.[407] Express words in the lease are required for this purpose.[408]

17–094   (5) FORM OF NOTICE. As a general rule, it is not essential that notice should be in writing,[409] although it is desirable and it is common to find that leases make express provision to such effect. Furthermore, the Protection from Eviction Act 1977 provides that[410] no notice by a landlord or a tenant to quit any premises let as a dwelling[411] shall be valid unless:

---

[402] *Sidebotham v Holland* [1895] 1 Q.B. 378.

[403] *Lemon v Lardeur* [1946] K.B. 613.

[404] *Sidebotham v Holland* [1895] 1 Q.B. 378; *Manorlike Ltd v Le Vitas Travel Agency & Consultancy Services Ltd* [1986] 1 E.G.L.R. 79; *Yeandle v Reigate and Banstead BC* [1996] 1 E.G.L.R. 20. This is a special rule that applies only to periodic tenancies and not to break clauses in fixed-term leases: *Mannai Investment Co Ltd v Eagle Star Life Assurance Co Ltd* [1995] 1 W.L.R. 1508 at 1514 (decision reversed on appeal but expressly affirmed on this point: [1997] A.C. 749).

[405] *Crate v Miller* [1947] K.B. 946 at 948.

[406] *Addis v Burrows* [1948] 1 K.B. 444. Such provision is often made (by way of a "catch-all") as an alternative to the specification of a fixed date for expiration of the notice: see, e.g. *Hussain v Bradford Community Housing Ltd* [2009] EWCA Civ 763; [2010] H.L.R. 16.

[407] *Re Threlfall* (1880) 16 Ch D 274; *H. & G. Simonds Ltd v Haywood* [1948] 1 All E.R. 260.

[408] *Harler v Calder* [1989] 1 E.G.L.R. 88 (notice to comply with statutory requirement but that "no other formality will be required" held insufficient).

[409] *Doe d. Lord Macartney v Crick* (1805) 5 Esp. 196. Notice may be given or received in his own name by an agent of either the landlord or the tenant who has general authority in relation to the property: *Jones v Phipps* (1868) L.R. 3 Q.B. 567; *Townsends Carriers Ltd v Pfizer Ltd* (1977) 33 P. & C.R. 361; *Peel Developments (South) Ltd v Siemens Plc* [1992] 2 E.G.L.R. 85. However, such cases are uncommon because "a general agency is an unusual commercial relationship", and in the absence of express authority, it requires clear evidence to support it: see *Lemmerbell Ltd v Britannia LAS Direct Ltd* [1998] 3 E.G.L.R. 67 at 70 per Peter Gibson L.J.; *Hexstone Holdings Ltd v AHC Westlink Ltd* [2010] EWHC 1280 (Ch); [2010] L. & T.R. 22.

[410] PEA 1977 s.5 (as amended by HA 1988 s.32). These provisions do not apply to "excluded tenancies": see PEA 1977 s.3A (added by HA 1988 s.31); below, para.20–003. The four-week requirement applies to a notice to quit given by either the tenant or the landlord: *Hounslow LBC v Pilling* [1993] 1 W.L.R. 1242 at 1247.

[411] A mere formal tenancy under an attornment clause is excluded (see below, para.25–034): *Alliance BS v Pinwill* [1958] Ch. 788. It has been held that mixed-use premises are not within this provision: *National Trust v Knipe* [1998] 1 W.L.R. 230 (agricultural holding including dwelling-house): cf. more recent interpretation of other provisions in the same Act at para.22–003 below.

(a) it is in writing and contains such information as may be prescribed,[412] and

(b) it is given not less than four weeks before the date on which it is to
take effect.[413]

(6) SERVICE OF NOTICE. In general, a notice to quit must be brought to the **17–095**
attention of the tenant, though in the absence of contrary evidence this will be
presumed if it is delivered to his spouse, employee or agent.[414] The statutory
provisions as to service of notices[415] do not apply to notices to quit unless the
parties have expressly provided that they should.[416]

(g) Application of common law rules as to notice. The above rules apply to **17–096**
particular kinds of periodic tenancy as follows, subject in each case to the
lease making express provision to the contrary and to the possible application
of statute.

(1) YEARLY TENANCIES. If a yearly tenancy began on one of the usual quarter **17–097**
days (Lady Day (March 25), Midsummer Day (June 24), Michaelmas (September 29) or Christmas (December 25)), "half a year" means "two quarters"; otherwise "half a year" means 182 days.[417] Thus the period of the
notice is not necessarily six months,[418] although of course the parties may
agree that such shall be the notice required. There are special statutory rules
for the determination of yearly tenancies of agricultural holdings and farm
business tenancies.[419]

(2) MONTHLY TENANCIES. Similarly, and again subject to contrary provision **17–098**
being made, a monthly tenancy requires a month's notice expiring at the end
of a month of the tenancy.[420] In the case of a lease made by deed or in writing,

---

[412] The information is currently prescribed by SI 1988/2201.

[413] See *Schnabel v Allard* [1967] 1 Q.B. 627 (notice given on Friday to expire on Friday
valid).

[414] See, e.g. *Tanham v Nicolson* (1872) L.R. 5 H.L. 561; *Halsbury's* Vol. 27(1), para.228. There
are certain specific statutory provisions as to service of notices in relation to certain types of
tenancies, see, e.g. AHA 1986 s.93.

[415] See LPA 1925 s.196, (see further para.18–057 below) providing for notices to be left at or
posted to the last known place of abode or business of the person.

[416] *Wandsworth LBC v Attwell* (1995) 27 H.L.R. 536; *Enfield LBC v Devonish* (1996) 29 H.L.R.
691.

[417] *Anon* (1575) 3 Dy. 345a. The odd half-day is ignored.

[418] The phrase "six months" should be avoided, since "half a year" is the proper expression
(*Doe d. Williams v Smith* (1836) 5 A. & E. 350 at 351) although "six months" is sometimes used
in judgments where the point is not material. Six months may be more than two quarters or 182
days, or less, depending on the quarters or months.

[419] Below, paras 22–032, 22–042.

[420] *Precious v Reedie* [1924] 2 K.B. 149. Although there is apparently no authority in point, in
the case of a dwelling, the common law period should prevail over the requirements of PEA 1977
s.5, above where the former period is longer than the latter (as it will be except where notice is
given on January 31).

a month normally means a calendar month[421] ending on the corresponding day of the following month, except that where there is no corresponding day (e.g. under a month's notice is given on March 31), the month naturally ends on its last day.[422]

17–099   (3) QUARTERLY TENANCIES. A quarterly tenancy requires a quarter's notice expiring at the end of one of the quarters of the tenancy.[423] Subject to contrary provision being made, a quarterly tenancy commencing on October 29 could therefore be determined only on January 29, April 29, July 29 or October 29.[424]

17–100   (4) WEEKLY TENANCIES. For a weekly tenancy, unless otherwise agreed,[425] the notice need not be seven *clear* days (reckoned by excluding both the day on which it is given and the day on which it expires, e.g. notice given on Sunday to quit on the following Monday week). Thus a weekly tenancy commencing on a Monday can be determined by notice given on or before one Monday[426] to expire at midnight on the following Sunday. In accordance with the special rule applicable to periodic tenancies,[427] the notice may be given either for "Sunday" or "Monday". Provided no other time is specified, this will be construed as referring to the midnight that divides the two days and the notice will therefore be effective.[428]

17–101   *(h) Jurisdiction to relieve against consequences of non-compliance with rules.* It was formerly the rule that when giving notice to determine a tenancy the requisite period of notice had to be stated accurately. The court would not grant relief against the consequences of forgetfulness or mistake.[429] However, this approach has been rejected by the House of Lords.[430] The courts will now

---

[421] LPA 1925 s.61. At common law, a month meant a lunar month: see *P. Phipps & Co (Northampton and Towcester Breweries) Ltd v Rogers* [1925] 1 K.B. 14 at 23. Query whether the common law rule still applies to *oral* tenancies, which are not within s.61. cf. [1992] Conv. 263 (E. Cooke).

[422] *Dodds v Walker* [1981] 1 W.L.R. 1027. A statutory month is similar: Interpretation Act 1978 Sch.1.

[423] *Kemp v Derrett* (1814) 3 Camp. 510.

[424] *Kemp v Derrett*, above.

[425] *Weston v Fidler* (1903) 88 L.T. 769.

[426] *Newman v Slade* [1926] 2 K.B. 328; *Crate v Miller* [1947] K.B. 946.

[427] *Mannai Investment Co Ltd v Eagle Star Life Assurance Co Ltd* [1995] 1 W.L.R. 1508 at 1514; below, para.17–101.

[428] *Crate v Miller*, above. cf. *Bathavon RDC v Carlile* [1958] 1 Q.B. 461 (notice to quit "by noon on Monday" invalid).

[429] See e.g. *Hankey v Clavering* [1942] 2 K.B. 326 (December 21 stated by mistake for December 25); where the notice was held invalid.

[430] *Mannai Investment Co Ltd v Eagle Star Life Assurance Co Ltd* [1997] A.C. 749, overruling *Hankey v Clavering*, above, and approving the approach in *Carradine Properties Ltd v Aslam* [1976] 1 W.L.R. 442 (notice given in 1974 specified expiry date as in 1973 by mistake for 1975: notice valid) and *Micrografix v Woking 8 Ltd* (1995) 71 P. & C.R. 43 (notice specifying March 23 instead of June 23 held valid). For an application of the "reasonable recipient" principle to a landlord's break clause, see *Trafford MBC v Total Fitness (UK) Ltd* [2002] EWCA Civ 1513; [2003] P. & C.R. 2. The principle applies as much to statutory notices as it does to contractual ones: see paras 22–009 and 22–125 below. However, it cannot be invoked to excuse a failure to comply with specific formal requirements set out in the lease or the statute: *Speedwell Estates Ltd v Dalziel* [2001] EWCA Civ 1277 at [25]; *Burman v Mount Cook Land Ltd* [2001] EWCA Civ

adopt a commercial construction, and the test is an objective one. What would a reasonable person placed in the actual circumstances of the recipient have understood by the notice? If the meaning of the notice was plain, so that the recipient was in no doubt as to its intended effect, it will not be vitiated because it contains a mistake, e.g. as to the date on which it is to operate[431] or the period of notice being given[432] or the description of the property.[433] In this regard, notices to quit and notices under break clauses are not *sui generis*, but "belong to the general class of unilateral notices served under contractual rights reserved, e.g. notices to determine licences and notices to complete".[434]

3. Tenancies at will

(a) Creation. A tenancy at will arises whenever a tenant, with the consent **17–102** of the owner, occupies land as tenant (and not merely as a servant or agent[435]) on the terms that either party may determine the tenancy at any time. This kind of tenancy may be created either expressly[436] or by implication.[437] Common examples are:

(i) where a tenant whose lease has expired holds over with the landlord's permission[438];

(ii) where a person is allowed into possession while the parties negotiate the terms of a lease[439];

1712; [2002] 1 All E.R. 144 at [23], on which see para.22–221 below; *Trafford MBC v Total Fitness (UK) Ltd*, above, at [49].

[431] *Mannai Investment Co Ltd v Eagle Star Life Assurance Co Ltd*, above. A notice by the tenant to terminate the lease one day earlier than authorised was held to be valid and took effect as if it had specified the first moment of the following day. See also *Peer Freeholds Ltd v Clean Wash International Ltd* [2005] EWHC 179 (Ch).

[432] *Trafford MBC v Total Fitness (UK) Ltd*, above. A notice by the landlord to terminate the lease giving 17 days' notice, expressly stating that "for the avoidance of all doubt" the premises would close on October 24, when application of the rule in *Lester v Garland* (1808) 15 Ves. Jun. 248 (that in calculating the notice period the date of giving notice should be excluded) meant that only 16 days' notice had in fact been given.

[433] *Doe d. Cox v Rea* (1803) 4 Esp. 185; *Mannai Investment Co Ltd v Eagle Star Life Assurance Co Ltd*, above, at 775. cf. *Lemmerbell Ltd v Britannia LAS Direct Ltd* [1998] 3 E.G.L.R. 67 at 71 (failure by A to explain how it could give notice on behalf of B vitiated the notice and was not a mere slip).

[434] *Mannai Investment Co Ltd v Eagle Star Life Assurance Co Ltd*, above at 768, per Lord Steyn.

[435] *Mayhew v Suttle* (1854) 4 E. & B. 347.

[436] e.g. *Manfield & Sons Ltd v Botchin* [1970] 2 Q.B. 612.

[437] e.g. *Wheeler v Mercer* [1957] A.C. 416; *Javad v Aqil* [1991] 1 W.L.R. 1007.

[438] See e.g. *Dean and Chapter of Canterbury Cathedral v Whitbread Plc* (1995) 72 P. & C.R. 9 at 13; *Katana v Catalyst Communities Housing Ltd* [2010] EWCA Civ 370; [2010] 2 E.G.L.R. 21. Where the tenant pays rent, it is a question of intention whether or not a periodic tenancy arises: see, e.g. *Cardiothoracic Institute v Shrewdcrest* [1986] 1 W.L.R. 368; above, para.17–086.

[439] See, e.g. *Uzun v Ramadan* [1986] 2 E.G.L.R. 255; *London Baggage Company v Railtrack Plc* [2000] L. & T.R. 439; *Newham LBC v Thomas van-Staden* [2008] EWCA Civ 1414, [2009] L. & T.R. 5. In *Hagee (London) Ltd v A.B. Erikson and Larson* [1976] Q.B. 209 at 217, Scarman L.J. referred to the "classic circumstances" in which a tenancy at will arose of "holding over or holding pending a negotiation".

(iii) where a tenant takes possession under a void lease, or under a mere agreement for lease and no periodic tenancy has arisen from the payment of rent[440]; and

(iv) where a person is allowed to occupy a house rent-free and for an indefinite period.[441]

Another circumstance that often gave rise to a tenancy by will was where a purchaser was let into possession pending completion[442]; but the courts have more recently taken the view that such a purchaser is to be treated as a licensee.[443]

17–103   *(b) Compensation to landlord.* Unless the parties agree that the tenancy shall be rent-free, or the tenant has some other right to rent-free occupation,[444] the landlord is entitled to compensation for the "use and occupation" of the land,[445] which will be the ordinary market value of the premises.[446] If the rent has been agreed upon, it may be distrained for as such in the usual way.[447]

17–104   *(c) Determination.* The essence of the tenancy is that either party can determine it at will, even if it is made determinable at the will of the landlord only, for the law will imply that it is to be determinable at the will of the tenant also.[448] A tenancy at will also comes to an end when either party does any act incompatible with the continuance of the tenancy, as where the tenant commits voluntary waste,[449] or the landlord enters the land and cuts trees or carries away stone,[450] or serves a writ claiming possession of the land,[451] or either party gives notice to the other determining the tenancy.[452] The tenancy is likewise determined if either party dies,[453] or assigns his interest in the

---

[440] Above, para.17–086. In this situation, a periodic tenancy is likely to arise if rent is paid, because it will accord with the probable intentions of the parties: above, para.17–070. cf. where no rent is tendered: *Banjo v Brent LBC* [2005] EWCA Civ 292; [2005] 1 W.L.R. 2520.

[441] *Banjo v Brent LBC*, above.

[442] *Howard v Shaw* (1841) 8 M. & W. 118; *Wheeler v Mercer* [1957] A.C. 416 at 425; Tudor L.C. 16–18.

[443] *Street v Mountford* [1985] A.C. 809 at 827; *Essex Plan Ltd v Broadminster* (1988) 56 P. & C.R. 353 at 355; *Cameron Ltd v Rolls-Royce Plc* [2007] EWHC 546 (Ch), [2008] L. & T.R. 22; above, para.17–030. Furthermore, under the Standard Conditions of Sale (5th edn, 2011), the purchaser occupies expressly as a licensee: condition 5.2.2.

[444] e.g. a purchaser in possession under a contract of sale (if he is indeed still to be regarded as a tenant at will).

[445] *Howard v Shaw*, above; see below, para.19–075.

[446] *Dean and Chapter of Canterbury Cathedral v Whitbread Plc* (1995) 72 P. & C.R. 9.

[447] Litt. p.72; *Anderson v Midland Ry* (1861) 3 E. & E. 614. But note that distress is to be abolished on implementation of the relevant provisions in the Courts, Tribunals and Enforcement Act 2007: see below, para.19–077.

[448] Co.Litt. p.55a.

[449] *Countess of Shrewsbury's Case* (1600) 5 Co. Rep. 13b. But note the doubts expressed in *Halsbury's* Vol. 27(1), para.434.

[450] *Turner v Doe d. Bennett* (1842) 9 M. & W. 643.

[451] *Martinali v Ramuz* [1953] 1 W.L.R. 1196 (a writ is not a notice to quit).

[452] See *Crane v Morris* [1965] 1 W.L.R. 1104 at 1108 (such a notice is not within Protection from Eviction Act 1977 s.5: above, para.11–071).

[453] *James v Dean* (1805) 11 Ves. 383 at 391; *Turner v Barnes* (1862) 2 B. & S. 435.

land.[454] But the tenant may not be ejected until he has knowledge of the act or event which has determined the tenancy.[455]

(d) Conversion to periodic tenancy. Where a person occupies land as a **17–105** tenant at will and rent is paid and accepted on some regular periodic basis, a periodic tenancy may be inferred. However, there is no longer any presumption of a periodic tenancy arising, as there was formerly,[456] and the matter is one of the likely intentions of the parties.[457] While the payment of rent on a periodic basis is one important factor from which the parties' intentions may be inferred, it is not conclusive and a court will consider all the circumstances, not least the statutory protection that the tenant may have if there is a periodic tenancy.[458]

(e) Nature. The precise nature of a tenancy at will has never been defini- **17–106** tively settled.[459] Probably the best analysis of it is that it is a form of tenure but one that confers no estate. Although an estate cannot exist without tenure, there seems no reason why tenure should not exist without any estate. A may therefore hold land of B, but for no fixed period and merely for so long as B may allow. If it is remembered that tenure by itself is a purely personal relationship when unconnected with any estate or interest which can exist as a right in rem, this may explain why a tenancy at will cannot survive death or alienation; and it may also explain why tenancy at will is possible despite the rule which requires every leasehold estate to be for a term certain.

4. Tenancies at sufferance

(a) Creation. A tenancy at sufferance arises where a tenant, having entered **17–107** the land under a valid tenancy, holds over without the landlord's assent or dissent.[460] Such a tenant differs from a trespasser in that his original entry was lawful, and from a tenant at will in that his tenancy exists without the landlord's consent. A tenancy at sufferance can arise only by operation of law,[461] and not by express grant, for it assumes an absence of agreement between landlord and tenant. Indeed, it is strictly incorrect to call it a "tenancy" at all, for there is no "privity", i.e. tenure, between the parties.[462] But since it normally arises between parties who have been landlord and tenant it has acquired the title of tenancy; and the tenant at sufferance is liable

---

[454] *Doe d. Davies v Thomas* (1851) 6 Exch. 854 at 857; *Pinhorn v Souster* (1853) 8 Exch. 763 at 772.

[455] *Doe d. Davies v Thomas,* above.

[456] See above, para.17–086.

[457] *Longrigg, Burrough & Trounson v Smith* [1979] 2 E.G.L.R. 42; *Javad v Aqil* [1991] 1 W.L.R. 1007; *Katana v Catalyst Communities Housing Ltd* [2010] EWCA Civ 370; [2010] 2 E.G.L.R. 21.

[458] *Longrigg, Burrough & Trounson v Smith,* above, at 43; *Javad v Aqil,* above, at 1012.

[459] See the fifth edition of this work at p.655, where the point is more fully considered, and above, para.6–018. The matter is unlikely to have many practical consequences today.

[460] Co.Litt. p.57b; *Remon v City of London Real Property Co Ltd* [1921] 1 K.B. 49 at 58.

[461] Tudor L.C. 8; *Halsbury's* Vol. 27(1), para.206.

[462] Co.Litt. p.270b, Note by Butler, and 271a.

to a claim for "use and occupation",[463] which properly lies against a tenant,[464] rather than to an action for damages for trespass or for mesne profits.[465] There can, of course, be no claim for rent as such, for rent is a *service* which depends upon a proper tenure by consent.[466] The landlord may eject the tenant, or sue for possession, at any time, and the tenant will have no right to emblements.[467]

17–108   *(b) Nature.*[468] A tenant at sufferance is in a position akin to that of a squatter, i.e. an adverse claimant.[469] It has already been explained that a squatter's interest may be a legal estate.[470]

17–109   *(c) Conversion into tenancy at will or periodic tenancy.* A tenancy at sufferance will be converted into a tenancy at will if the landlord assents to the tenant's occupation. The circumstances in which such a tenancy at will may be converted into a yearly or other periodic tenancy have already been explained.[471]

17–110   5. Penalties for wrongfully holding over

There are statutory penalties for tenants who wrongfully hold over after giving or receiving notice to quit.

17–111   (1) DOUBLE VALUE. The Landlord and Tenant Act 1730 provides that if the landlord gives *written* notice to quit to the tenant, and the tenant is a tenant *for life or for years*, the tenant is liable to pay the landlord a sum calculated at twice the annual value of the land in respect of the period for which he wilfully[472] holds over after the notice expires; this can be enforced by court proceedings but not otherwise.[473] This provision applies to tenancies from year to year[474] as well as to tenancies for fixed terms of years or for a year certain,[475] but not to weekly[476] or, it seems, other periodic tenancies.[477]

---

[463] See below, para.19–075.

[464] *Bayley v Bradley* (1848) 5 C.B. 396 at 406; *Leigh v Dickeson* (1884) 15 QBD 60; below, para.19–075.

[465] See above, para.4–029. This may now be a distinction without a difference: *Dean and Chapter of Canterbury Cathedral v Whitbread Plc* (1995) 72 P. & C.R. 9 at 16.

[466] See para.19–062 below.

[467] *Doe d. Bennett v Turner* (1840) 7 M. & W. 226 at 235. But as to ejection, see below, para.22–002. For emblements, see above, para.3–105.

[468] For fuller consideration of this point, see the fifth edition of this work at p.656.

[469] This was not so for the purpose of acquiring title by limitation before 1833; but the doctrine of adverse possession upon which the distinction was founded was abolished by the Real Property Limitation Act 1833; Tudor L.C. 9; below, para.35–016.

[470] Above, para.4–008.

[471] Above, para.17–105.

[472] Which means "as a trespasser": see *Oliver Ashworth (Holdings) Ltd v Ballard (Kent) Ltd* [2000] Ch. 12; below. See, e.g. *French v Elliott* [1960] 1 W.L.R. 40; *Dun & Bradstreet Software Services (England) Ltd v Provident Mutual Life Assurance Association* [1996] E.G.C.S. 62.

[473] Landlord and Tenant Act 1730 s.1.

[474] See *Ryal v Rich* (1808) 10 East. 48.

[475] *Cobb v Stokes* (1807) 8 East 358.

[476] *Lloyd v Rosbee* (1810) 2 Camp. 453.

[477] See *Williamson v Hall* (1837) 3 Bing.N.C. 508.

(2) DOUBLE RENT. If the tenant gives the landlord *written or oral*[478] notice **17–112** to quit, then whatever the type of tenancy (provided it is determinable by notice[479]), the tenant is liable to pay double rent in respect of the period for which he holds over after the notice expires; payment can be enforced by action.[480]

The differing terms of these aged provisions will be noticed. The rent and **17–113** the annual value may be the same, but they often differ, as where premises have been let at a reduced rent in consideration of a fine. However, notwithstanding these differences, it is now clear that the courts will read the two provisions together as a single code. They will apply only where the tenant is a trespasser and is treated as such by the landlord.[481]

B. Statutory Modifications

Although leases can in general be created for such periods as the parties think **17–114** fit, there are special statutory rules for some cases, which sometimes produce surprising results.

1. Leases for lives or until marriage

(a) Conversion to 90-year terms. By the Law of Property Act 1925[482] a **17–115** lease[483] granted at a rent or a fine[484] "for life or lives or for any term of years determinable with life or lives or on the marriage of the lessee, or on the formation of a civil partnership between the lessee and another person", is converted into a term of 90 years. A contract for such a lease is treated in a similar way; but a term "taking effect in equity under a settlement or created out of an equitable interest under a settlement for mortgage, indemnity, or other like purposes" is excluded, even if a rent is reserved.[485] For the statute to apply, the lease must determine automatically on the lessee's death or marriage or the formation of their civil partnership. A lease which may be determined by the giving of notice *after* such death or marriage or civil partnership formation is outside the statute.[486] However, it does not matter that

---

[478] *Timmins v Rowlison* (1764) Wm.Bl. 533.

[479] *Johnstone v Hudlestone* (1825) 4 B. & C. 922.

[480] Distress for Rent Act 1737 s.18. Currently, payment can also be enforced by distress. However, distress will be abolished, and replaced by CRAR (Commercial Rent Arrears Recovery), when the relevant provisions of the Tribunals, Courts and Enforcement Act 2007 are implemented: see below, para.19–077. The provisions of the 1737 Act that permit distress in the circumstances under discussion will be repealed: TC & EA 2007 s.86; Sch.14 para.4.

[481] *Oliver Ashworth (Holdings) Ltd v Ballard*, above.

[482] s.149(6), as amended by Civil Partnership Act 2004 s.81, Sch.8 para.1.

[483] Whether granted before 1926 or after 1925.

[484] A fine has been held to include a discount on the price paid by a purchaser on a sale and leaseback to the vendors for their joint lives: *Skipton BS v Clayton* (1993) P. & C.R. 223 at 231. Where neither rent nor a premium is payable under the lease, the section is inapplicable: *Binions v Evans* [1972] Ch. 359 at 366.

[485] LPA 1925 s.149(6)(a).

[486] *Bass Holdings Ltd v Lewis* [1986] 2 E.G.L.R. 40.

the lease may, in accordance with its provisions, be terminable by either party *before* such death (etc.) for other reasons or in other circumstances.[487]

17–116   When a lease falls within the statute, the lease does not automatically determine on the death, marriage or civil partnership of the original lessee. Instead, following the death (etc.) either party may determine it by serving on the other at least one month's written notice to expire on one of the quarter days applicable to the tenancy, or, if no special quarter days are applicable, on one of the usual quarter days. If the lease is determinable with "the lives of persons other than or besides the lessees", the notice is "capable of being served" on the dropping of their lives, "instead of after the death of the original lessee".

17–117   *(b) Operation of the statute.* For example, leases at a rent or fine granted:

> "to A for life",
> "to B for 10 years if he so long lives", and
> "to C for 99 years if he so long remains a bachelor",

are all converted into terms which will continue for 90 years unless by the proper notice they are determined on a quarter day (not necessarily the first) after the event has occurred. In most cases this position will cause little change in the effective rights of the parties. But it may drastically cut down the lessor's reversion if, in a case like the second of the above examples, he wishes to grant only a short term, conditional upon the lessee remaining alive or unmarried.[488] And the drafting of the statute seems ill-adapted for leases such as "to A during B's life",[489] or "to C for 50 years if D so long remains unmarried", or "to E until he remarries". A tenancy will take effect as a lease for life within the statute whenever a landlord grants to an individual a tenancy which is void for uncertainty.[490]

17–118   *(c) Contrast with life interests.* The general object of these provisions is to bring leases for life within the general scheme of the 1925 legislation,[491] and to distinguish between leases for life which involve the relationship of landlord and tenant[492] and beneficial life tenancies under a settlement.[493] Normally the former are commercial transactions, whereas the latter are family transactions. This distinction is usually marked by whether or not a premium or rent

---

[487] *Mexfield Housing Co-operative Ltd v Berrisford* [2011] UKSC 52; [2011] 3 W.L.R. 1091 at [50].

[488] cf. Wolst. & C. i, 278. The difficulty can be readily overcome by making the lease determinable by the landlord on giving notice after the tenant's death or marriage: see *Bass Holdings Ltd v Lewis,* above.

[489] For it seems that a notice could be served after the death of A even if B is still living.

[490] *Mexfield Housing Co-operative v Berrisford,* above at [38] et seq.; see para.17–072. However, there must be a grant of a tenancy: *Hardy v Havelden* [2011] EWCA Civ 1387; [2011] N.P.C. 122 at [13].

[491] *Mexfield Housing Co-operative v Berrisford,* above at [84].

[492] For these, see above, para.17–008.

[493] For these, see below, Appendix A.

is payable; and this is the test adopted by the statute. Life interests of a family character are subject to the law governing either settled land (if created before 1997) or trusts of land (if created after 1996), but are in either case equitable. Life tenancies of a commercial character are converted into true terms of years, unaffected by the principles of the law of settled land or trusts of land.

The distinction is, however, not always clear-cut. Thus, where a testator **17–119** gives one of his relations the right to be granted a tenancy for life at a nominal rent,[494] or at less than the market rent,[495] the transaction, though at a rent, is also partly of a beneficial or family nature. On the other hand, a commercial transaction in which there is no beneficial or family element may create a tenancy for life which prior to 1997 made the land settled land[496] and will now create a trust of land.[497] Further, the statute itself provides for the exclusion of certain leases even though granted at a rent, e.g. those taking effect in equity under a settlement.[498] Nevertheless, in most cases the distinction is valid.[499]

2. Perpetually renewable leases

(a) Renewability. A perpetually renewable lease is a lease which gives the **17–120** tenant the right to renew it for another period as often as it expires. Such leases are seldom deliberately created today.[500] But they may be created inadvertently by unrestricted renewal clauses, as by an option giving the tenant a right of renewal "on the same terms and conditions, including this clause",[501] or "on identical terms and conditions".[502] The lease is then held to be perpetually renewable even though the parties may have had no such intention: "the courts have manoeuvred themselves into an unhappy position"[503] in these decisions. However the courts lean against perpetual renewals. Thus where a lease contained a covenant to renew on terms which conferred a further right of renewal, that was held to give the tenant a right to renew the lease twice but not perpetually.[504]

(b) Conversion. By the Law of Property Act 1922,[505] perpetually renewable **17–121** leases take effect as terms of 2,000 years from the date fixed for the commencement of the term. Any perpetually renewable sub-lease created out of a

---

[494] *Re Catling* [1931] 2 Ch. 359 (£1 a year).

[495] *Blamires v Bradford Corp* [1964] Ch. 585 (30s. a week).

[496] As in *Binions v Evans* [1972] Ch. 359. In some cases there has, however, been a family relationship of some kind, as in *Bannister v Bannister* [1948] 2 All E.R. 133 (sale of land at reduced price to brother-in-law in return for life interest); *Costello v Costello* (1994) 27 H.L.R. 12 (purchase at discounted price by son but subject to life interest for parents).

[497] See TLATA 1996 ss.1, 2; above, para.12–004.

[498] *Re Catling,* above, seems to be an example of this.

[499] See, e.g. *Kingswood Estate Co Ltd v Anderson* [1963] 2 Q.B. 169 (clearly commercial).

[500] They used to be common in Ireland: see *Swinburne v Milburn* (1884) 9 App.Cas 844 at 855.

[501] *Hare v Burges* (1857) 4 K. & J. 45; *Parkus v Greenwood* [1950] Ch. 644; *Caerphilly Concrete Products Ltd v Owen* [1972] 1 W.L.R. 372.

[502] *Northchurch Estates Ltd v Daniels* [1947] Ch. 117.

[503] *Caerphilly Concrete Products Ltd v Owen,* above, at 376, per Sachs L.J.

[504] *Marjorie Burnett Ltd v Barclay* [1981] 1 E.G.L.R. 41.

[505] s.145 and Sch.15.

perpetually renewable lease is converted into a term of 2,000 years less one day.[506]

17–122   *(c) Terms.* The 2,000-year lease is subject to the same terms as the original lease, with the following modifications:

> (i) The tenant (but not the landlord) may terminate the lease on any date upon which, but for the conversion by the Act, the lease would have expired if it had not been renewed, provided he gives at least 10 days' written notice to the landlord.[507]

> (ii) Every assignment or devolution of the lease must be registered with the landlord or his solicitor or agent within six months, and a fee of one guinea paid.[508]

> (iii) A tenant who assigns the lease is not liable for breaches of covenant committed after the assignment.[509] The general rule for leases granted before 1996 is that the original tenant remains liable for all breaches occurring during the term, even if he parts with the lease.[510] Perpetually renewable leases were made an exception to that rule, because otherwise the original lessee's liability might last for ever.

17–123   *(d) Right to determine.* It should be noted that the landlord has no right to determine the lease at the renewal dates. If the landlord has granted a lease for 21 years with a perpetual right of renewal, the lease therefore continues after the expiry of each 21-year period unless and until the tenant elects to determine it.[511]

17–124   **3. Over-lengthy renewals.** A contract to renew a lease for over 60 years from its termination is void.[512] This is aimed at single renewals, not perpetual renewals.

C. Tenancy by Estoppel

17–125   **1. Estoppel between landlord and tenant.** There is a general rule that a tenant is estopped from denying his landlord's title, and a landlord from

---

[506] LPA 1922 Sch.15 paras 2, 5.

[507] LPA 1922 Sch.15, para.10(1)(i).

[508] LPA 1922 Sch.15, para.10(1)(ii). This operates by way of covenant and is subject to any proviso for forfeiture for breach of covenants of the lease: LPA 1922 Sch.15. As to forfeiture, see below, para.18–006.

[509] LPA 1922 Sch.15 para.11.

[510] See below, para.20–011. The rule has been alleviated by certain provisions of the L & TCA 1995; below, paras 20–021 et seq. For leases granted after 1995, see below, para.20–085.

[511] Prior to 1926, renewal was not automatic: T had to give notice to L.

[512] LPA 1922 Sch.15 para.7(2).

denying his tenant's.[513] Estoppel is a principle of the law of evidence and, in this context, it may arise in one of two ways[514]:

(i) *By deed*. It is an ancient principle that a grantor is precluded from disputing the validity or effect of his grant, often called estoppel by deed.[515]

(ii) *By representation*. A landlord may be estopped by an unambiguous and material representation as to his title (usually in a recital) on the strength of which the tenant takes a lease.[516]

In either case,[517] the landlord cannot question the validity of his own grant, nor can the tenant question it once he is in possession[518] and has the benefit of the lease, "for so long as a lessee enjoys everything which his lease purports to grant, how does it concern him what the title of the lessor, or the heir or assignee of his lessor, really is?"[519] It is otherwise if the tenant is disturbed by title paramount, i.e. if some title superior to the landlord's is made good against him; for then he may be liable for mesne profits to the adverse claimant, and he can reclaim rent paid to the landlord.[520] But in the absence of an adverse title the tenant cannot repudiate his obligations under the lease. He can therefore be sued for breach of a repairing covenant after he has given up possession, even though he can show that the landlord was not the legal owner when the lease was granted.[521] This is an example of the proposition that *jus tertii* cannot be pleaded against a prior possessory title.[522] Even if the landlord was not the true owner when he granted the lease, the tenant may not deny his title to grant it if in fact he has the benefit of it. But the tenant is estopped only from denying the landlord's title to put him into possession: he may always show, if he can, that the landlord's title has

---

[513] *Cooke v Loxley* (1792) 5 T.R. 4; *Cuthbertson v Irving* (1859) 4 H. & N. 742; (1860) 6 H.& N. 135, as explained in *Industrial Properties (Barton Hill) Ltd v Associated Electrical Industries Ltd* [1977] Q.B. 580. See also *Mackley v Nutting* [1949] 2 K.B. 55.

[514] See the leading modern case, *First National Bank Plc v Thompson* [1996] Ch. 231, which follows closely the reasoning in (1964) 80 L.Q.R. 370 (A.M. Prichard). The two types of estoppel have different effects: below, paras 17–129, 17–130.

[515] *Goodtitle v Bailey* (1777) 2 Cowp. 597 at 600, 601; *Bruton v London and Quadrant Housing Trust* [1998] Q.B. 834 at 844, CA. For the circumstances in which an oral lease can found an estoppel, see Co.Litt. p.352a; (1964) 80 L.Q.R. 370 at 395 (A. M. Prichard).

[516] *First National Bank Plc v Thompson*, above, at 237, 243.

[517] It is not confined to cases where there is a recital in the grant of the landlord's legal title: *First National Bank Plc v Thompson*, above.

[518] See *Hall v Butler* (1839) 10 A. & E. 204; *Doe d. Marlow v Wiggins* (1843) 4 Q.B. 367.

[519] *Cuthbertson v Irving* (1859) 4 H. & N. 742 at 758, per Martin B.

[520] See *Industrial Properties (Barton Hill) Ltd v Associated Electrical Industries Ltd*, above, at 596, per Lord Denning M.R.

[521] *Industrial Properties (Barton Hill) Ltd v Associated Electrical Industries Ltd*, above, where the Court of Appeal held that dicta to the contrary in *Harrison v Wells* [1967] 1 Q.B. 263 were made *per incuriam*. See further above, para.17–054.

[522] As explained above, para.4–010. See *Bell v General Accident Fire & Life Assurance Corporation Ltd* [1998] 1 E.G.L.R. 69 at 71.

subsequently come to an end.[523] Thus if the landlord, having conveyed the reversion to X, sues the tenant for rent, the tenant can plead that the rent is now due to X and so deny the landlord's title.[524] Likewise if the landlord's title is a lease which has expired, the tenant can withhold the rent even though no third party is claiming it.[525]

17–126   This estoppel applies to all types of tenancy, including periodic tenancies, tenancies at will and at sufferance,[526] Rent Act statutory tenancies,[527] and business tenancies under the Landlord and Tenant Act 1954.[528] It applies similarly to licences.[529] It operates whether the tenancy was created by deed, in writing or orally.[530] It is a general rule, being part of the doctrine of possessory titles.[531] Subject to one exception, those claiming through the parties are also estopped, so that the estoppel binds the successors in title to both landlord and tenant.[532] The exception is that, where the tenancy by estoppel arises by deed,[533] a bona fide purchaser for value from the grantor without notice of the transaction takes free of it.[534] But where the estoppel is by representation, the grantee's title is good, even against a bona fide purchaser.[535]

17–127   2. Tenancy by estoppel. Where the landlord's title is defective but the parties are bound by the estoppel just described, there is said to be a tenancy by estoppel.[536] It arises out of the relationship of landlord and tenant; in other words, it is "not the estoppel which creates the tenancy, but the tenancy which creates the estoppel."[537] It may occur where, for example, the landlord has

---

[523] *Mountnoy v Collier* (1853) 1 E. & B. 630; *Serjeant v Nash, Field & Co* [1903] 2 K.B. 304; *National Westminster Bank Ltd v Hart* [1983] Q.B. 773; [1984] Conv. 64 (J. W. Price).

[524] *Harmer v Bean* (1853) 3 C. & K. 307.

[525] *National Westminster Bank Ltd v Hart,* above. The authorities indicate, inconsistently, that as against an assignee of the reversion the tenant must be able to show a valid adverse title in a third party.

[526] *Doe d. Bailey v Foster* (1846) 3 C.B. 215 at 229.

[527] See *Stratford v Syrett* [1958] 1 Q.B. 107. For statutory tenancies, see below, para.22–137.

[528] See *Bell v General Accident Fire & Life Assurance Corporation Ltd* [1998] 1 E.G.L.R. 69. For business tenancies, see below, paras 22–004 et seq.

[529] *Doe. d. Johnson v Baytup* (1835) 3 A. & E. 188; *Terunnanse v Terunnanse* [1968] A.C. 1086; *Government of Penang v Bang Hong Oon* [1972] A.C. 425; *Sze To Chun Keung v Kung Kwok Wai David* [1997] 1 W.L.R. 1232; compare *Tadman v Henman* [1893] 2 Q.B. 168 at 171.

[530] *E.H. Lewis & Son Ltd v Morelli* [1948] 2 All E.R. 1021. The limits stated in Co.Litt. p.47b no longer apply: see e.g. *Mackley v Nutting* [1949] 2 K.B. 55.

[531] See above, para.4–012.

[532] *Webb v Austin* (1844) 7 Man. & G. 701; *Cuthbertson v Irving* (1859) 4 H. & N. 742 at 758 (affirmed (1860) 6 H. & N. 135).

[533] For the distinction between estoppel by deed and estoppel by representation, see above, para.17–125.

[534] *General Finance, Mortgage and Discount Co v Liberator Permanent Benefit BS* (1878) 10 Ch D 15; *First National Bank Plc v Thompson* [1996] Ch. 231 at 239, 240, 244. This is a rule of law, not equity; *First National Bank Plc v Thompson,* above, at 240.

[535] *First National Bank Plc v Thompson,* above, at 239.

[536] The doctrine is discussed in (1964) 80 L.Q.R. 370 (A.M. Prichard).

[537] *Bruton v London and Quadrant Housing Trust* [2000] 1 A.C. 406 at 416, per Lord Hoffmann; *Wroe (t/a Telepower) v Exmos Cover Ltd* [2000] 1 E.G.L.R. 66.

contracted to purchase the freehold but where it has not yet been transferred to him. Even though it is apparent to the parties that the landlord's title is defective,[538] then subject to the exception mentioned above, both they and their successors in title will be estopped from denying that the grant was effective to create the tenancy that it purported to create.[539] Thus, in effect, there is brought into being a tenancy under which the parties and their successors in title have (as against one another) most of the rights and liabilities of a legal estate. The tenancy by estoppel will devolve and may be alienated in the same way as any other tenancy.[540] The landlord may distrain for rent in the ordinary way[541]; but, since estoppels do not bind strangers, he cannot exercise his normal right to distrain goods not owned by the tenant.[542]

3. Feeding the estoppel

(a) Where the landlord subsequently acquires a legal estate. If, after creating a tenancy by estoppel, the landlord acquires a legal estate out of which the tenancy could be created (as where he purchases the fee simple), this is said to "feed the estoppel"; and the tenant at once obtains a tenancy based upon the newly acquired estate in place of his tenancy by estoppel.[543] Similarly, if a tenant dies or leaves the premises and another tenant occupies them and pays rent to the landlord, the second tenant has an implied lease by estoppel while the first tenancy remains in existence, and a true tenancy as from its determination[544]; for upon its determination the landlord recovers his immediate legal title, and that feeds the estoppel. **17–128**

(b) Where the landlord has a legal estate at the time of the grant

(1) ESTOPPEL BY DEED. Where the estoppel is by deed and not by representation,[545] the grantor is estopped merely from denying that he has a legal title.[546] No tenancy by estoppel can therefore arise in such circumstances if the lessor **17–129**

---

[538] *Morton v Woods* (1869) L.R. 4 Q.B. 293.

[539] See *Cuthbertson v Irving*, above, at 757, 758.

[540] *Gouldsworth v Knights* (1843) 11 M. & W. 337; *Webb v Austin* (1844) 7 Man. & G. 701; *Cuthbertson v Irving*, above, at 758; *Mackley v Nutting* [1949] 2 K.B. 55.

[541] *Gouldsworth v Knights*, above. That is, until distress is abolished on the implementation of the relevant provisions in the Tribunals, Courts and Enforcement Act 2007: see below, paras 19–077 et seq.

[542] *Tadman v Henman* [1893] 2 Q.B. 168. In principle this seems questionable, since the tenancy by estoppel is probably a possessory legal estate of the kind discussed above, para.4–003.

[543] *Rawlyns's Case* (1587) Jenk. 254; 4 Co.Rep. 52a; *Webb v Austin* (1844) 7 Man. & G. 701 at 724; *Sturgeon v Wingfield* (1846) 15 M. & W. 224; *Rajapakse v Fernando* [1920] A.C. 892 at 897; cf. LPA 1925 s.152(2), below, Appendix para.A–062. The doctrine of feeding the estoppel is not confined to the creation of tenancies, but applies whenever "a grantor has purported to grant an interest in land which he did not at the time possess, but subsequently acquires": *Rajapakse v Fernando*, above, at 897, per Lord Moulton.

[544] *Edward H. Lewis & Son Ltd v Morelli* [1948] 2 AA E.R. 1021; *Mackley v Nutting* [1949] 2 K.B. 55; *Moses v Warsop* (1949) 100 L.J.News. 51.

[545] See above, para.17–125.

[546] *First National Bank Plc v Thompson* [1996] Ch. 231 at 239.

did in fact have any present legal estate (as distinct from a mere equitable interest[547]) in the land when he granted the lease.[548] If the lessor's interest was a freehold, or a leasehold which would outlast the lease which he granted, the lease takes effect in the ordinary way; if it was a leasehold equal to[549] or smaller than[550] the subsequent lease, the grant of that lease operates as an assignment of the lessor's interest.[551] Thus if L grants T a lease for 99 years and subsequently acquires the fee simple (e.g. under his father's will), T will take a lease for 99 years by estoppel if L had no interest in the land when the lease was granted. But if L had a lease for 10 years at the time of grant, the lease for 99 years will operate only as an assignment to T of L's lease for 10 years,[552] and L will not be estopped from recovering the land when the 10-year term expires.

17–130   (2) ESTOPPEL BY REPRESENTATION. Where, by contrast, the estoppel arises from an unequivocal representation of the grantor's title, he is estopped from denying that he has that particular title.[553] Therefore, the estoppel is "not excluded by the ownership of some other and lesser estate".[554]

17–131   *(c) Effect on third parties.* The effect of an estoppel on the grantor's successor in title where the estoppel has been fed by the acquisition of the legal estate is the same as where it has not.[555] The same rules apply whether the title to the land is unregistered or registered.[556] The tenant will of course acquire a legal estate by estoppel. Where the estoppel is by representation, that estate will bind any third party who derives title through or under the grantor regardless of notice.[557] But where the estoppel is by deed, a bona fide purchaser without notice of the earlier transaction takes free of the tenancy.[558] It is at first sight strange both that a purchaser in good faith should take free of a *legal* estate[559] and that questions of notice[560] can arise in relation to registered land.[561] However, this is because the issue is not whether the third

---

[547] *Universal Permanent BS v Cooke* [1952] Ch. 95 at 102 (tenancy by estoppel where the lessor had contracted to buy the property let but had not completed the purchase). A lease by a mortgagor may also take effect by estoppel despite the equity of redemption being still vested in him; below, paras 25–071, 25–080.

[548] Co.Litt. p.47b; *Doe d. Strode v Seaton* (1835) 2 C.M. & R. 728 (lease granted by tenant for life not binding on successors in title); *Cuthbertson v Irving* (1859) 4 H. & N. 742, affirmed (1860) 6 H. & N. 135.

[549] *Beardman v Wilson* (1868) L.R. 4 C.P. 57; *Hallen v Spaeth* [1923] A.C. 684 at 687.

[550] *Wollaston v Hakewill* (1841) 3 Man. & G. 297 at 323 (not a case of estoppel).

[551] For this rule, see below, para.17–142.

[552] See below, para.17–142.

[553] *First National Bank Plc v Thompson* [1996] Ch. 231 at 239.

[554] *First National Bank Plc v Thompson*, above, per Millett L.J.

[555] This has already been explained: above, para.17–129.

[556] For the application of the doctrine of feeding the estoppel to registered land, see *First National Bank Plc v Thompson,* above, at 240 (legal charge); *Woolwich Equitable BS v Marshall* [1952] Ch. 1 (tenancy).

[557] *First National Bank Plc v Thompson,* above, at 239.

[558] *First National Bank Plc v Thompson,* above, at 239, 240, 244.

[559] Above, para.5–011.

[560] At common law in this context, not in equity.

[561] The doctrine of notice is inapplicable to dealings with registered land: above, paras 6–046, 7–064.

party is bound by the estate or interest arising by estoppel, but whether he is bound by the estoppel itself upon which the estate or interest depends. It should be noted, however, that where title is registered, the grantee by estoppel is entitled either to register or to protect by registration his estate or interest.[562] If he does, any purchaser is likely to have notice of his rights.[563]

4. Purchaser in possession before completion. Sometimes a purchaser of **17–132** land is allowed to go into possession before completion. If he then grants a tenancy of the land, and subsequently, on completion, mortgages the land in order to raise the purchase-money, the question arises whether the lease (which, until it was "fed" by completion of the purchase, was a mere lease by estoppel) is binding upon the mortgagee.[564] This is in fact part of a wider question as to whether the mortgage takes effect simultaneously with the conveyance or only subsequent to it. This affects not just tenancies granted by a purchaser who has gone into possession prior to completion, but other rights, e.g. those of a spouse or relative who contributes part of the purchase price and who claims a beneficial interest in the property under a trust.[565] After a period of uncertainty, the Court of Appeal held in 1954 that the purchase and the mortgage were two distinct transactions and that the legal estate had to be vested in the purchaser before any mortgage could become effective.[566] There was considered to be a *scintilla temporis* between the purchaser's acquisition of the legal estate and the creation of the mortgage during which the estoppel could be fed. This doctrine was always controversial[567] because the legal estate could never have been acquired at all without the mortgage. Nor could its reasoning be readily reconciled with the authorities on debentures, where no such *scintilla temporis* was recognised.[568] However, in 1990, the House of Lords dismissed the *scintilla temporis* as "no more than a legal artifice".[569] It held that where the acquisition of the legal estate is dependent upon the provision of funds by a mortgagee, the transfer of legal title to the purchaser

---

[562] *First National Bank Plc v Thompson*, above.

[563] *First National Bank Plc v Thompson*, above, at 244.

[564] Obviously where the mortgage is executed after the conveyance to the purchaser, there can be no doubt that the estoppel will be fed in the interval so as to give priority to the tenant: see *Universal Permanent BS v Cooke* [1952] Ch. 95 (mortgage executed one day after completion).

[565] See above, para.11–016.

[566] *Church of England BS v Piskor* [1954] Ch. 553, following *Woolwich Equitable BS v Marshall* [1952] Ch. 1 and *Universal Permanent BS v Cooke*, above, and overruling on this point *Coventry Permanent Economic BS v Jones* [1951] 1 All E.R. 901. See [1954] C.L.J. 192 (H.W.R.W.).

[567] It was held not to apply where a new mortgage was executed to replace an existing one, but on somewhat different terms: *Walthamstow BS v Davies* (1989) 60 P. & C.R. 99. See too *Equity & Law Home Loans Ltd v Prestidge* [1992] 1 W.L.R. 137 at 144.

[568] In these cases, a purchaser who had contracted to acquire land with the aid of a mortgage, granted a debenture prior to completion of the purchase. The mortgage took priority over the debenture: see *Re Connolly Brothers Ltd (No.2)* [1912] 2 Ch. 25; *Security Trust Co v Royal Bank of Canada* [1976] A.C. 503; and *Lloyds Bank Plc v Rosset* [1989] Ch. 350 at 388–393.

[569] *Abbey National BS v Cann* [1991] 1 A.C. 56 at 93, per Lord Oliver.

and the mortgage occur simultaneously.[570] Strictly speaking, this rule does no more than determine the time at which interests are considered to have been created. However, its effect is to ensure that a mortgagee will always take priority, not only over a tenant by estoppel in possession but even as against some other person who provides a substantial part of the purchase price.[571]

D. Concurrent Leases

17–133 **1. Grant.** If a landlord who has already granted a lease subsequently grants another lease of the same land for some or all of the period of the existing lease, he is said to have granted a lease of the reversion.[572] Where there are concurrent leases, the effect of the second grant depends upon when the first lease was granted. Leases granted before 1996 are governed by rules of common law, whereas those granted after 1995 are subject to the provisions of the Landlord and Tenant (Covenants) Act 1995 which changed the law for new leases.[573] Both sets of rules must be considered.

17–134 *(a) Leases granted before 1996.* Where the first lease was granted before 1996, the second lease is *pro tanto* a disposition of the reversion.[574] This creates the relationship of landlord and tenant between the second and first tenant respectively,[575] whereby the second tenant becomes the landlord of the first tenant, the parties thereafter enjoying all the rights and being subject to all the liabilities (as to rent and other matters) which are capable of running with the tenancy.[576] At the same time, it supplants the relationship of landlord and tenant between the landlord and the first tenant.[577] Thus if L granted a lease of Blackacre to T for 21 years in 1994, and then granted a lease of Blackacre to X for 30 years in 1995, X would become the immediate reversioner upon T's lease, and therefore T's landlord. When T's lease determines in 2015, X will become entitled to possession of Blackacre. The result would be the same if X's lease had been granted for a term shorter than T's,[578] except that X's lease would normally expire before he became entitled

---

[570] *Abbey National BS v Cann,* above. For different views on the case see (1990) 106 L.Q.R. 545 (R. J. Smith); [1990] C.L.J. 397 (A. J. Oakley). See too *Nationwide Anglia BS v Ahmed* (1995) 70 P. & C.R. 381 (unpaid vendor remained in occupation: no *scintilla temporis* in which his lien could gain priority over the mortgagee).

[571] As was the case in *Abbey National BS v Cann,* above.

[572] Contrast a reversionary lease: above, para.17–077.

[573] For the L & TCA 1995, see below, para.20–085. For what constitutes a new lease for these purposes, see below, para.20–010.

[574] Shep. Touch. pp.275, 276; *Neale v Mackenzie* (1836) 1 M. & W. 747; *Harmer v Bean* (1853) 3 C. & K. 307; *Wordsley Brewery Co v Halford* (1903) 90 L.T. 89; *Cole v Kelly* [1920] 2 K.B. 106.

[575] *Birch v Wright* (1786) 1 T.R. 378 at 384. cf. the apparent dictum to the contrary in *Cole v Kelly,* above, at 120, which seems wrong.

[576] *Burton v Barclay* (1831) 7 Bing. 745; *Horn v Beard* [1912] 3 K.B. 181; *Cole v Kelly,* above; Preston, *Conveyancing,* ii, pp.145, 146.

[577] See *Wordsley Brewery Co v Halford,* above (notice to quit by landlord to first lessee bad).

[578] *Neale v Mackenzie,* above; *Re Moore & Hulm's Contract* [1912] 2 Ch. 105.

to take possession. X could collect rent and enforce covenants against T,[579] and if T's lease prematurely determined (e.g. by forfeiture) before X's term expired, X would become entitled to possession of the land.[580] Statute has expressly preserved this rule that a legal term (whether or not a mortgage term) may be created to take effect in reversion expectant upon a longer term.[581]

(b) Leases granted after 1995. Where the first lease has been granted after **17–135** 1995, the second lease no longer operates as a partial disposition of the reversion but as a genuine lease of the reversion. This is because the Landlord and Tenant (Covenants) Act 1995 provides that where L grants a lease to T, and then a lease of the reversion to X, he retains the right to sue T on the covenants of the first lease.[582] It will often be the case that L will be estopped from suing T by his grant of a lease of the reversion to X. He could hardly lease to X the right to receive the rents and profits from T and then claim them himself. However, there may be circumstances in which L may have a good reason for wishing to enforce a covenant directly against T. These are explained more fully later.[583]

2. Effect

(a) Leases granted before 1996. As a lease of the reversion is *pro tanto* an **17–136** assignment of the lease, it must obey the rules governing assignments of reversions explained below.[584] Such a lease can therefore have no effect at law unless it is made by deed. If, in the above example of a lease granted in 1994, X's lease was created orally, it would be wholly void at common law during the full term of T's lease, even if T's lease determined prematurely.[585] And this would be equally true if the term of X's lease did not exceed three years.[586] But once T's term had expired, X's lease (if still in being) could take effect as a lease of the land, not as a disposition of the reversion, and so be valid as a reversionary lease if it conformed to the rules for the creation of such leases.[587] It is not clear, however, whether the relationship between L and X during T's term is that of landlord and tenant or that of assignor and assignee,[588] or whether there is a lease by estoppel between them.[589] Nor is it

---

[579] *Burton v Barclay,* above.
[580] *Stephens v Bridges* (1821) 6 Madd. 66 at 67; *Re Moore & Hulm's Contract* [1912] 2 Ch. 105.
[581] LPA 1925 s.149(5). The statement in Wolst. & C. i, 277, that this and s.149(2) overrule *Neale v Mackenzie,* above, is puzzling.
[582] L & TCA 1995 s.15(1)(a).
[583] Below, para.20–113.
[584] Below, para.17–146.
[585] *Neale v Mackenzie* (1836) 1 M. & W. 747 (where the lease was held void only as to the part of the land already leased).
[586] *Brawley v Wade* (1824) M'Clel. 664 (tenancy from year to year).
[587] *Doe d. Thomas v Jenkins* (1832) 1 L.J.K.B. 190.
[588] The authorities appear to be silent on this point.
[589] Bacon's *Abridgement* (7th edn, 1832), iv, 848; Platt on *Leases,* ii, 59. For tenancy by estoppel, see above, para.17–125.

clear whether the Law of Property Act 1925 has made it possible for X's lease to be created orally if its term does not exceed three years.[590]

17–137   *(b) Leases granted after 1995.* As regards a lease granted after 1995, any subsequent lease of the reversion does not operate as an assignment. If, therefore, L grants a lease to T and then a lease of the reversion to X, the relationship of landlord and tenant and the reciprocal right to enforce the covenants of the relevant lease exists between:

>   (i) L and T;

>   (ii) X and T; and

>   (iii) L and X.[591]

The same doubt mentioned above exists as to whether the lease from L to X could be granted if it were for a term not exceeding three years.

Part 3

ASSIGNMENT OF LEASES AND REVERSIONS

Section 1. Assignment of Leases

17–138   **1. Lease assignable by deed.** A lease, like other forms of property, is freely transferable. Even if, as is common, the lease contains a covenant against assignment, breach of such a covenant will not prevent an assignment from taking effect, though it may expose the assignee to proceedings for forfeiture of the lease or damages.[592]

17–139   Statute provides that a legal lease can only be transferred inter vivos by deed.[593] This applies to all tenancies, even those created orally, e.g. a yearly tenancy.[594] However, on principles similar to those applicable to the creation of leases, an assignment will be effective in equity as between the assignor and the assignee as a contract to assign, provided that it is made in writing and contains all the terms expressly agreed between the parties.[595] Where the lease

---

[590] s.54(2) (above, para.17–040) requires the lease to take effect in possession, but X's lease can take effect only in reversion upon T's lease. By LPA 1925 s.205(1)(xix) "possession" includes the right to receive rents and profits. But presumably this right can pass only under a grant by deed, i.e. as incident to the reversion. See further Woodfall 6.019.

[591] L & TCA 1995 s.15(1)(a); (2); below, paras 20–113 et seq.

[592] See below, para.19–093.

[593] LPA 1925 s.52, above, para.17–044.

[594] *Crago v Julian* [1992] 1 W.L.R. 372 (where this statement was approved at 377); *Camden LBC v Alexandrou* (1997) 30 H.L.R. 534. But see [1992] Conv. 375 (P. Sparkes); (1995) 58 M.L.R. 637 at 638 (G. Battersby); above, para.17–044.

[595] Above, para.17–045; *Parc Battersea Ltd v Hutchinson* [1999] 2 E.G.L.R. 33 at 37. Prior to September 27, 1989, an oral or written assignment was effective in equity if it was evidenced by writing or there were sufficient acts of part performance: see the fifth edition of this work at p.665.

was granted after 1995, the burden of the covenants will pass on such an equitable assignment.[596] However, where such an assignment is made of a lease granted before 1996, the assignee will not be liable to the landlord on the covenants,[597] even if he enters and pays rent, though in special cases he may be estopped from denying liability.[598]

Where, in the case of registered land, the lease assigned is registered with **17–140** its own title, the assignment will not be effective to transfer the legal estate unless it is registered.[599] This may mean that the assignor can exercise a break clause in the lease even after he has executed the transfer of the lease, if it has not then been registered.[600]

2. Contrast with sub-lease. The difference between an assignment of a **17–141** lease and the grant of a sub-lease has already been explained.[601] As will appear later,[602] this is of fundamental importance to the question of liability for breaches of covenant in the event of the original tenant (T1) having made some disposition of the land. If he assigns the lease, he grants his whole estate to the assignee (T2), thus putting the assignee in his shoes as immediate tenant of the landlord. If he grants a sub-lease to S, he does not cease to be tenant, for he retains his estate: he has merely carved out of it a lesser estate in favour of S, in respect of which he owns the immediate reversion. The assignment of a lease transfers an estate but creates no new tenure; the grant of a sub-lease creates a new tenure between sub-lessor and sub-lessee.

3. Sub-lease as assignment. Since the distinction between an assignment **17–142** and a sub-lease is one of substance, not one of form, it follows that if the tenant disposes of the whole residue of his estate, the transaction must operate as an assignment even though the parties intend it to operate as a sub-lease.[603] For example, if three years ago L granted a lease to A for seven years, and A now purports to grant a sub-lease to B for 10 years, the sub-lease operates as an assignment despite the label given by the parties, and any covenants and conditions contained in it (e.g. as to rent, repair or forfeiture) have such operation as they may have under an assignment.[604] As a result, A will cease

---

[596] L & TCA 1995 ss.3(1), (2), 28(1); below, paras 20–086, 20–106.

[597] There was no privity of estate: see above, para.17–061; below, para.20–046.

[598] *Rodenhurst Estates Ltd v W.H. Barnes Ltd* [1936] 2 All E.R. 3, where the landlord had granted a licence for a legal assignment which had been acted upon in all respects except for the execution of a formal assignment. See [1978] C.L.J. 98 at 116 (R. J. Smith). Compare *Official Trustee of Charity Lands v Ferriman Trust Ltd* [1937] 3 All E.R. 85; and see *Richmond v McGann* [1954] 1 W.L.R. 1282.

[599] LRA 2002 s.27(1).

[600] *Brown & Root Technology Ltd v Sun Alliance London Assurance Co Ltd* (1996) 75 P. & C.R. 223 (a case on the construction of the word "assignment" in break clause).

[601] Above, para.17–010.

[602] Below, paras 20–004, 20–006.

[603] *Hicks v Downing* (1696) 1 Ld.Raym. 99; *Palmer v Edwards* (1783) 1 Doug. K.B. 187; *Wollaston v Hakewill* (1841) 3 Man. G. 297; *Milmo v Carreras* [1946] K.B. 306; *Parc Battersea Ltd v Hutchinson*, above. See (1967) 31 Conv.(N.S.) 159 (P. Jackson); below, para.24–041.

[604] As between L and A there is no longer privity to estate (below, para.20–004); but a forfeiture clause may still operate: *Doe d. Freeman v Bateman* (1818) 2 B. Ald. 168.

to be the tenant of L; instead B will become L's tenant, and there will be direct tenure between L and B. A cannot therefore distrain for rent due to him from B under the so-called sub-lease,[605] although it has the legal quality of being rent, and can be sued for.[606] If the so-called sub-lease is followed by a yearly or other periodic tenancy (e.g. to B for 10 years and thereafter from year to year), A cannot give B notice to quit under the periodic tenancy since A is not B's landlord.[607] But if A grants to B a sub-lease for the residue of A's term less one day, this takes effect as a valid sub-lease; the tenant has not disposed of the entirety of his estate but has retained a reversion, albeit for one day only.

17–143   The above rule applies only where the tenant creates an interest which is certain to last as long as, or longer than, his own. Therefore, where a tenant from year to year granted a sub-lease of 34 years, this took effect as a sub-lease, not as an assignment; for the yearly tenancy might have outlasted the sub-lease, and so left a reversion in the sub-lessor.[608] Similarly a tenant from year to year can create a sub-lease from year to year[609]; and it would seem that a tenant for a fixed term may grant a sub-lease of a yearly or other periodic kind, provided that the head lease will outlast at least the initial period of the sub-lease; for there is then always a potential reversion in case the periodic sub-tenancy should be determined by notice.

17–144   **4. Formalities.** Assignments which result from "sub-leases" of the tenant's whole interest are brought about by operation of law, and are excepted from the rule that they must be made by deed.[610] Thus if a tenant with less than three years of his term unexpired purports to grant an informal sub-lease for three years at a rack-rent, this operates as an assignment of the residue of the term. This doctrine produces a paradox in situations such as that just given. If described correctly as an assignment, an informal disposition of a lease is void at law and can operate only in equity; but if described incorrectly as a sub-lease, it takes effect as a valid assignment by operation of law. Assignments of part only of the demised land are dealt with later.[611]

17–145   **5. Covenants and conditions.** An assignment may itself contain covenants by either or both parties, and covenants by the assignee may be enforced by a forfeiture clause entitling the assignor to resume the lease in case of breach. Such a clause creates an equitable right of entry,[612] and where the clause

---

[605] However, distress is being abolished: see below, paras 19–076 et seq.

[606] *Williams v Hayward* (1859) 1 E. E. 1040.

[607] *Milmo v Carreras* [1946] K.B. 306.

[608] *Oxley v James* (1844) 13 M. W. 209. See likewise *William Skelton Son Ltd v Harrison Pinder Ltd* (1974) 29 P. & C.R. 113 (head lease extended indefinitely by Landlord and Tenant Act 1954 Pt II: see below, para.22–008).

[609] *Pike v Eyre* (1829) 9 B. C. 909.

[610] LPA 1925 s.52(2)(g), excepting "conveyances which take effect by operation of law". *Parc Battersea Ltd v Hutchinson* [1999] 2 E.G.L.R. 33. See *Preece v Corrie* (1828) 5 Bing. 24; *Milmo v Carreras* [1946] K.B. 306. But this point has not yet been finally settled.

[611] Below, paras 20–051, 20–118.

[612] Above, para.6–027.

merely provides security for the attainment of a primary purpose which can still be achieved, the court has jurisdiction to grant relief.[613]

Section 2. Assignment of Reversions

1. Need for deed. The landlord's reversion is freely assignable by him, but **17–146** in order to take effect at law the assignment must be made by deed.[614] This was always the rule at common law, since a reversion was regarded as analogous to an incorporeal hereditament which "lay in grant".[615] The rule is now part of the general rule enacted by the Law of Property Act 1925, that legal estates in land can be conveyed or created only by deed.[616]

2. Effect. An absolute assignment of the reversion, if validly made by deed, **17–147** transfers the assignor's fee simple or leasehold legal estate to the assignee, subject to the subsisting lease, so that the assignee becomes the landlord.[617] The effect of the assignment on the enforceability of the covenants in the lease is explained in Chapter 20, as is also the effect of a partial assignment.[618] Assignment for a term of years, often called a lease of the reversion or a concurrent lease, has been discussed above.[619]

---

[613] *Shiloh Spinners Ltd v Harding* [1973] A.C. 691. For relief against forfeiture, see below, paras 18–033, 18–060.

[614] *Brawley v Wade* (1824) M'Clel. 664.

[615] *Brawley v Wade*, above, Challis p.48 (but see also p.53); and see below, para.27–014.

[616] LPA 1925 s.52.

[617] If the property includes a dwelling, it is an offence if the assignee fails to give the tenant written notice of the assignment and his name and address within (usually) two months: L & TA 1985 s.3; below, para.19–072. The landlord who assigns the lease remains liable on the covenants in such circumstances until the tenant is notified of the name and address of the new landlord: L & TA 1985 s.3(3A) (as substituted by L & TA 1987 s.50). Where the assigning landlord had granted the lease, he would remain liable for such breaches of covenant in any event: see below, paras 20–017, 20–096.

[618] Below, paras 20–064, 20–118.

[619] Above, para.17–133.

DETERMINATION OF TENANCIES

18–001 A lease or tenancy may come to an end in the following ways:

    (1) By expiry.

    (2) By notice.

    (3) By forfeiture.

    (4) By surrender.

    (5) By merger.

    (6) By enlargement.

    (7) By disclaimer.

    (8) By frustration.

    (9) By termination for breach.

In this chapter, each of these methods of determination shall be explained. A number of these methods are subject to statutory restrictions on their exercise, as will become apparent. Moreover, in the case of many kinds of tenancy, statute provides the tenant with a security of tenure over and beyond that conferred by the lease itself; in such cases invocation of one of these methods may not be effective to terminate the lease and, even where the lease is terminated, it should not be assumed that the landlord will be able to recover possession as a result.[1]

Section 1. By Expiry

18–002 Expiry is the default method of termination of a fixed term tenancy; at common law, the tenancy ends when the fixed term expires.[2] However, many

[1] See further Ch.22.
[2] Above, para.17–080.

such tenancies (in the commercial, agricultural and residential sectors) will engage statutory provisions conferring a security of tenure on the tenant, and in such circumstances the tenancy may continue beyond the date initially fixed in the lease. It is also possible that a fixed term tenancy may terminate before the date of its expiry. First, it may have been made determinable upon the happening of some event, e.g. if the tenant parts with possession of the property.[3] In that case, the lease will determine automatically, without any action by either party, if it is limited so as to last only until the condition is fulfilled.[4] However, this rule does not apply if the event is a death, for in that case, the tenancy is treated as a lease for life, and is converted by statute into a 90 year term.[5] When the death occurs, the tenancy will not expire, but it becomes terminable by either party giving written notice.[6] Secondly, a lease may be limited to continue until the tenant commits a breach of covenant. This will fall within the provisions of the Law of Property Act 1925 relating to forfeiture and relief in the same way as if the lease were determinable under a proviso for re-entry.[7] Such determinable terms must be distinguished from terms made subject to some proviso or condition subsequent.[8] In the latter case the lease does not end until the landlord re-enters; this is explained below in connection with forfeiture.[9]

Section 2. By Notice

A fixed term tenancy cannot be determined by notice unless this has been expressly agreed. It follows that a lease for a substantial term, such as 21 years, often contains provisions enabling the tenant to determine it, e.g. at the end of the seventh or fourteenth year, in which case the length of the notice required, the time when it is to be given, and other such matters, depend on the terms of the lease.[10] In the absence of any such provision, usually referred to as a "break clause", the tenant will not be able to terminate the tenancy before the end of its term. **18–003**

Periodic tenancies can be determined by notice. Indeed they must be terminable by notice by both landlord and tenant, or the tenancy will fail for **18–004**

---

[3] *Doe d. Lockwood v Clarke* (1807) 8 East 185.
[4] See, however, (1963) 27 Conv.(N.S.) 111 (F. R. Crane).
[5] LPA 1925 s.149(6).
[6] For detail, see paras 17–115 et seq. above.
[7] LPA 1925 s.146(7); for these provisions, see below, para.18–051.
[8] In principle the distinction is similar to that between determinable and conditional fees: above, para.3–056.
[9] Below, para.18–011.
[10] It is commonly provided that the tenant can terminate the tenancy only if he has complied with the covenants of the lease. This will generally be construed as a condition precedent, and while past breaches of covenant that have been remedied will not bar the giving of a valid notice, subsisting breaches will: see *Trane (UK) Ltd v Provident Mutual Life Assurance* [1995] 1 E.G.L.R. 33.

uncertainty.[11] These rules, and those for the determination of tenancies at will and at sufferance, have already been explained.[12]

18–005   In the case of both fixed term tenancies and periodic tenancies, statutory provisions conferring security of tenure upon a tenant may operate to prevent the lease from coming to an end by notice or to permit the tenant to remain in possession even though the lease has been terminated.[13]

Section 3. By Forfeiture

A. *Right to Forfeit*

18–006   The landlord may become entitled to re-take the premises, and so prematurely put an end to the lease. This entitlement must arise under the terms of the lease; its most common manifestation is where a right is expressly reserved to the landlord to terminate the lease following a breach of covenant or condition by the tenant. Much more rarely encountered is forfeiture by denial of title; this used to be explained as arising by operation of law, but it is now generally accepted that such right arises by way of implication from the lease.[14]

18–007   **1. Denial of title.** The rule is that a tenant who denies his landlord's title is liable to forfeit his lease.[15] It is derived from the feudal principle that repudiation of the lord destroys the tenure.[16] In recent times, this "arcane and complex"[17] doctrine has been detached from its feudal foundation; it is now justified on the basis that it is an implied condition of the lease that the tenant will do nothing to prejudice the title of the landlord.[18] The tenant's denial of title is therefore analogous to a repudiation of a contract.[19] The denial must be clear and unambiguous. It must demonstrate an intention by the tenant no longer to be bound by the relationship of landlord and tenant[20]; and it follows that a denial of title as to part only of the property comprised in the lease will

---

[11] Above, para.17–090.

[12] Above, paras 17–090 et seq., 17–104, 17–107.

[13] See generally Ch.22 below.

[14] *Abidogun v Frolan Health Care Ltd* [2001] EWCA Civ 1821; [2002] L. & T.R. 16 at [42].

[15] See Woodfall, 17.302.

[16] *Doe d. Ellerbrock v Flynn* (1834) 1 C.M. & R. 137; *Wisbech St Mary Parish Council v Lilley* [1956] 1 W.L.R. 121. The same applies if a tenant assists another person to deny the landlord's title: *Doe d. Ellerbrock v Flynn*, above.

[17] *Abidogun v Frolan Health Care Ltd*, above, at [14], per Arden L.J. Forfeiture for denial of title has been described as "a largely outdated medieval procedure": *Eastaugh v Crisp* [2007] EWCA Civ 638 at [44], per May L.J.

[18] *W.G. Clarke (Properties) Ltd v Dupre Properties Ltd* [1992] Ch. 297 at 308; see [1993] Conv. 299 (J. Martin).

[19] *W.G. Clarke (Properties) Ltd v Dupre Properties Ltd*, above at 302; *Abidogun v Frolan Health Care Ltd*, above. This is an instance of the increasingly contractual view that is being taken of the relationship of landlord and tenant: see above, para.17–006.

[20] *W.G. Clarke (Properties) Ltd v Dupre Properties Ltd*, above at 303.

not usually suffice.[21] Furthermore, the denial of title, as with any repudiation, must be accepted by the landlord.[22]

The tendency to treat the doctrine in this comparatively narrow way is a **18–008** modern one. At one time it was even held to apply where the tenant inadvertently denied the landlord's title in the pleadings to an action.[23] Subsequently, a general denial which set up no adverse title was held to be innocuous.[24] Although amendment of the pleadings prior to forfeiture being claimed saved the tenant,[25] it would not assist him in the more common case where the landlord had already forfeited the lease by commencing possession proceedings.[26] More recently, in response to the central philosophy of the Civil Procedure Rules, it has been held necessary to enable proper access to justice that a tenant should be able to advance contentions in the course of the pleadings without risking the forfeiture of the tenancy.[27] Denial of title is therefore only likely to be established where the tenant's challenge is clear and unequivocal.[28] If the tenant has acted in good faith, it is unlikely that the doctrine will be satisfied.[29] An oral denial of title will not produce forfeiture in the case of a fixed term tenancy.[30] It will, however, do so in the case of a yearly (or other periodic) tenancy. This is because the tenant, by denying that he has a tenancy, is taken to waive any notice to quit. The landlord can claim possession at once.[31]

The Law Commission has stated the view that forfeiture for denial of title **18–009** is an unnecessary vestige of feudalism.[32] It has recommended that breach of the implied condition that the tenant shall not deny the landlord's title should not be a ground on which a tenancy should be terminable.[33]

---

[21] *W.G. Clarke (Properties) Ltd v Dupre Properties Ltd*, above, at 305. It might be otherwise if the denial related to a physically distinct part of those premises which could be forfeited separately from the rest of the property comprised in the lease: see discussion of *Dumpor's Case* (1603) 4 Co.Rep. 119b in *G.M.S. Syndicate Ltd v Gary Elliott Ltd* [1982] Ch. 1 at 11.

[22] *Abidogun v Frolan Health Care Ltd*, above, at [42] and [54]; *Eastaugh v Crisp* [2007] EWCA Civ 638 at [44].

[23] *Kisch v Hawes Bros Ltd* [1935] Ch. 102; cf. *Barton v Reed* [1932] 1 Ch. 362 at 367. The forfeiture in each case was brought about by a Rule of the Supreme Court that has since been revoked. These decisions were overruled in *Warner v Sampson* [1959] 1 Q.B. 297.

[24] *Warner v Sampson*, above.

[25] *Warner v Sampson*, above.

[26] *W.G. Clarke (Properties) Ltd v Dupre Properties Ltd*, above, at 307. It is now accepted that prior notice must be served on the tenant under LPA 1925 s.146: *W.G. Clarke (Properties) Ltd v Dupre Properties Ltd*, above, at 308, not following *Warner v Sampson*, above; *BT Plc v Department of the Environment*, Unreported, October 9, 1996; *Abidogun v Frolan Health Care Ltd*, above, at [48] and [52].

[27] *Abidogun v Frolan Health Care Ltd*, above, at [35]; *Eastaugh v Crisp* [2007] EWCA Civ 638 at [45] et seq.

[28] *Eastaugh v Crisp*, above, at [39].

[29] *Eastaugh v Crisp*, above, at [38] and [47].

[30] *Doe d. Graves v Wells* (1839) 10 A. & E. 427.

[31] *Wisbech St Mary Parish Council v Lilley* [1956] 1 W.L.R. 121. However, the landlord must first serve a notice on the tenant under LPA 1925 s.146: see fn.26 above.

[32] (1985) Law Com. No.142 paras 5.32–5.35.

[33] (2006) Law Com. No.303 paras 3.39–3.45.

18–010   **2. Covenants.** Nearly every lease contains a list of things which the tenant shall and shall not do, and these may be framed as conditions or covenants. If, as is normally the case, they are framed as covenants (e.g. "The tenant hereby covenants with the landlord as follows . . . "), it was thought until relatively recently that the landlord had no right to determine the lease if they were broken unless the lease contained an express provision for forfeiture on breach of a covenant.[34] There were in fact a number of authorities which established that a lease could be determined by a tenant where there was a repudiatory breach of covenant by the landlord.[35] In the light of these decisions and of the fact that it is now recognised that the doctrine of frustration applies to leases,[36] it has been accepted that leases are subject to the doctrine of repudiatory breach.[37] Both the applicability to leases of the doctrine of repudiatory breach and the extent to which a landlord may thereby circumvent statutory restrictions on the termination of tenancies are considered later in this chapter.[38] Notwithstanding the development of repudiatory breach, it remains the practice to include a forfeiture clause in every lease.

18–011   **3. Conditions.** The tenant's obligations under the lease are usually framed as covenants. However, they may be worded as conditions, as, for example, where the lease is granted "upon condition that" or "provided always that" certain things are done or not done. The continuance of the lease has thereby been made conditional upon the tenant performing his obligations. In such circumstances, the term created by the lease becomes liable to forfeiture if the condition is broken, even if:

  (i) there is no forfeiture clause[39]; or

  (ii) the lease is made in writing and not by deed.[40]

On breach of condition, the lease becomes voidable at the landlord's option. It does not become void automatically, even if the proviso expressly declares that it shall; and so the tenant will not be allowed to set up his breach of condition as determining the lease unless the landlord chooses to determine it by re-entry or by claiming possession.[41] In one case, where it was "stipulated and conditioned that the lessee should not underlet", these words were held to create a condition subsequent, so that the landlord was entitled to re-enter

---

[34] See para.18–106 below.

[35] See para.18–107 below.

[36] *National Carriers Ltd v Panalpina (Northern) Ltd* [1981] A.C. 675; below, para.18–102.

[37] See para.18–106 et seq. below. Denial of title by the tenant is now viewed as a repudiatory breach: see above, para.18–007.

[38] Below, paras 18–052, 18–106.

[39] *Doe d. Lockwood v Clarke* (1807) 8 East 185.

[40] *Doe d. Henniker v Watt* (1828) 8 B. & C. 308 at 315.

[41] For the similar rule governing conditional fees, see above, para.3–058. Formerly this principle did not apply to leases (Co.Litt. p.214b); but the law appears to have changed: *Doe d. Bryan v Bancks* (1821) 4 B. & Ald. 401; *Roberts v Davey* (1833) 4 B. & Ad. 664.

upon breach of the covenant, even though there was no forfeiture clause as such.[42]

4. Forfeiture clauses. A forfeiture clause is a provision which is exercisable only in the event of some default by the tenant and which operates to bring a lease to an end earlier than it would otherwise terminate.[43] Rather than making the lease conditional upon the performance of the tenant's obligations, the usual practice is to set out the tenant's obligations in the form of covenants and then add a forfeiture clause on the following lines:

18–012

> "provided always that if the tenant commits a breach of covenant or becomes bankrupt it shall be lawful for the landlord to re-enter upon the premises and immediately thereupon the term shall absolutely determine".

This has the effect of reserving to the landlord a right of re-entry, which is a proprietary interest capable of binding third parties[44]; and the lease continues unless and until the landlord exercises this right. Even if a forfeiture clause states that the lease shall determine or become void immediately upon the breach, it is settled that the lease remains valid until the landlord re-enters[45] or, perhaps, otherwise indicates his unequivocal intention to determine the lease.[46] It follows that the lease is not void but merely voidable[47] at the instance of the landlord (but not by the tenant[48]).

5. Forfeiture

(a) Peaceable re-entry or possession action. Forfeiture "comprises the ultimate affirmation of the landlord's proprietary power."[49] If a landlord is entitled to re-enter,[50] he can enforce his right either by making peaceable

18–013

---

[42] *Doe d. Henniker v Watt* (1828) 8 B. & C. 308.

[43] *Clays Lane Housing Co-operative Ltd v Patrick* (1984) 49 P. & C.R. 72 (power to give weekly tenant a month's notice to quit if she failed to pay the rent not a forfeiture clause); a similar issue arose, although it was not determined, in *Mexfield Housing Co-operative Ltd v Berrisford* [2010] EWCA Civ 811; [2011] Ch. 244 at [12]. For these purposes, a lease is taken to terminate at the end of the fixed period for which it is granted or, if it is a periodic tenancy, the date on which it could be terminated by a notice to quit.

[44] LPA 1925 s.1(2)(e), above, para.6–027. For its application against third parties, e.g. sub-tenants, see below, para.20–077.

[45] *Arnsby v Woodward* (1827) 6 B. & C. 519; *Davenport v R.* (1877) 3 App.Cas. 115 at 128; *Quesnel Forks Gold Mining Co Ltd v Ward* [1920] A.C. 222; Smith's L.C. i, 45, 46.

[46] *Moore v Ullcoats Mining Co Ltd* [1908] 1 Ch. 575 at 588; *quaere* how far this view can stand with the authorities in fn.45 above.

[47] *Quesnel Forks Gold Mining Co Ltd v Ward*, above, at 227.

[48] *Rede v Farr* (1817) 6 M. & S. 121.

[49] *Inntrepreneur Pub Co (CPC) Ltd v Langton* [2000] 1 E.G.L.R. 34 at 38, per Arden J.

[50] It has been held that a landlord could peaceably re-enter in respect of non-payment of rent, even though he had assigned the right to recover that rent to his predecessor in title: *Kataria v Safeland Plc* [1998] 1 E.G.L.R. 39.

re-entry on the land[51] or by commencing an action for possession.[52] Peaceable re-entry has been described as a "dubious and dangerous method"[53] to determine a lease. Where premises are let as a dwelling, it is unlawful to enforce a right of re-entry or forfeiture otherwise than by court proceedings while any person is lawfully residing in any part of the premises.[54] A landlord who acts precipitously may incur criminal liability under the Criminal Law Act 1977[55] or the Protection from Eviction Act 1977,[56] or liability in damages to the tenant for unlawful eviction.[57] It follows that it is usually inadvisable for a landlord to attempt peaceable re-entry in relation to residential premises save where it is abundantly clear that the tenant has permanently vacated the property. Peaceable re-entry is more commonly encountered in relation to commercial premises. However, a landlord is still at risk of criminal liability under the Criminal Law Act 1977, and it is therefore usual for re-entry to be undertaken outside office hours.[58] If in any doubt, the better course for the landlord is to use the more frequently adopted (and "civilised"[59]) method and to enforce the forfeiture by commencing possession proceedings.

18–014   To constitute peaceable re-entry there must be some unequivocal act or words on the part of the landlord, as where he changes the locks[60] or grants a new tenancy.[61] Where a sub-tenant is in possession, the landlord may peaceably re-enter by making an arrangement by which he holds under a new tenancy from the landlord.[62] There will be no such re-entry if the landlord allows the sub-tenant to remain in possession under the existing tenancy.[63]

[51] *Aglionby v Cohen* [1955] 1 Q.B. 558. Merely re-letting does not suffice: *Parker v Jones* [1910] 2 K.B. 32; but see, contra, *Edward H. Lewis & Son Ltd v Morelli* [1948] 1 All E.R. 433, reversed on other grounds, [1948] 2 All E.R. 1021.

[52] A possession claim must be brought in the county court unless an enactment provides otherwise, or special circumstances apply: see CPR r.55.3. The county court has unlimited jurisdiction in forfeiture cases: cf. CCA 1984 ss.21(1) and 138 (as amended); and see High Court and County Courts Jurisdiction Order 1991 art.2 (SI 1991/724). It should be noted that where the defaulting tenant is bankrupt, the landlord requires the leave of the court to commence forfeiture proceedings: IA 1986 s.285(3). By contrast, he may peaceably re-enter without such leave: see *Razzaq v Pala* [1997] 1 W.L.R. 1336 (where this anomaly is noted); *Re Lomax Leisure Ltd* [2000] Ch. 502.

[53] *Billson v Residential Apartments Ltd* [1992] 1 A.C. 494 at 536, per Lord Templeman.

[54] Protection from Eviction Act 1977 s.2. It has been held that "let as a dwelling" means "let wholly or partly as a dwelling", so that the statutory prohibition on peaceable re-entry applies to "mixed use" premises: *Patel v Pirabakaran* [2006] EWCA Civ 685; [2006] 1 W.L.R. 3112. Where the tenant has ceased to occupy, re-entry may contravene the statute if a sub-tenant is lawfully in occupation: see e.g. *Belgravia Property Investment & Development Co Ltd v Webb* [2001] EWCA Civ 2075; [2002] L. & T.R. 29.

[55] s.6; below, para.22–002. This provision replaced the old Forcible Entry Acts 1381—1623.

[56] s.1; below, para.19–012.

[57] ss.27, 28; below, para.19–009.

[58] As we explain below, para.18–060, a court may grant the tenant relief against forfeiture in such a case. Although this ought to have lessened the attractions of this means of terminating a tenancy, the use of peaceable re-entry has increased in recent years.

[59] *Billson v Residential Apartments Ltd*, above, at 536, per Lord Templeman.

[60] See, e.g. *Billson v Residential Apartments Ltd*, above.

[61] See, e.g. *Re AGB Research Plc* [1995] B.C.C. 1091. Mere acceptance of rent from a third party will not, without more, be sufficient: see *Cromwell Developments Ltd v Godfrey* [1998] 2 E.G.L.R. 62.

[62] *London and County (A. & D.) Ltd v Wilfred Sportsman Ltd* [1971] Ch. 764.

[63] *Ashton v Sobelman* [1987] 1 W.L.R. 177.

In cases where the tenant wishes either to challenge the landlord's right to **18–015** re-enter or to seek relief against forfeiture,[64] he will often seek an interlocutory injunction to restore him to possession pending the outcome of the proceedings.[65] This can ameliorate the often serious consequences for the tenant of peaceable re-entry.[66]

(b) Rights of the parties after commencement of proceedings for possession. **18–016** Where a landlord has commenced proceedings against a tenant[67] which unequivocally claims possession (as distinct from one which includes alternative claims for injunctions based on the continued existence of the lease and its covenants[68]), he is taken to have elected to treat the lease as forfeited.[69] It has been said that "there is room for argument"[70] as to the precise relationship between the landlord and tenant during the "twilight period"[71] after commencement of proceedings but before the court's final decision on whether to order forfeiture of the lease.[72] If the claim is dismissed by the court, or discontinued by the landlord,[73] or the court grants relief against forfeiture,[74] the lease is reinstated retrospectively.[75] It is only when the landlord either obtains an unconditional judgment for possession[76] or the tenant admits the forfeiture[77] that the tenancy is extinguished. Some authorities suggest that the

---

[64] See paras 18–033 et seq., and 18–060 et seq., below.

[65] It has been held that sub-tenants do not have *locus standi* to seek such relief, because they become trespassers on re-entry, and even if they are given relief, it will not be retrospective: *Pellicano v M.E.P.C. Plc* [1994] 1 E.G.L.R. 104. Since that decision, it has been held that retrospective relief *is* available to sub-tenants as well as tenants: see *Escalus Properties Ltd v Robinson* [1996] Q.B. 231; below, para.18–076. The outcome might now be different therefore.

[66] cf. *Kataria v Safeland Plc* [1998] 1 E.G.L.R. 39 (where the tenant did not seek interlocutory relief and was out of possession for nearly a year).

[67] Under the Civil Procedure Rules, proceedings are commenced (whether in the High Court or the county court) when the court issues a claim form at the request of the claimant: CPR r.7.2. The distinction that formerly existed between the issue of a writ and its service no longer obtains. Under the old law, the issue of the writ was not an election to forfeit the lease: it had to be served on the tenant: see *Canas Property Co Ltd v K.L. Television Services Ltd* [1970] 2 Q.B. 433.

[68] See *Calabar Properties Ltd v Seagull Autos Ltd* [1969] 1 Ch. 451; *G.S. Fashions Ltd v B. & Q. Plc* [1995] 1 W.L.R. 1088 at 1095.

[69] See *Jones v Carter* (1846) 15 M. & W. 718; *Moore v Ullcoats Mining Co Ltd* [1908] 1 Ch. 575 at 584; *Associated Deliveries Ltd v Harrison* (1984) 50 P. & C.R. 91; *Hynes v Twinsectra Ltd* (1995) 28 H.L.R. 183; *Ivory Gate Ltd v Spetale* [1998] 2 E.G.L.R. 43 at 46.

[70] *Kingston-upon-Thames Royal LBC v Marlow* [1996] 1 E.G.L.R. 101 at 102, per Simon Brown L.J.

[71] *Meadows v Clerical Medical and General Life Assurance Society* [1981] Ch. 70 at 78, per Megarry V.C.

[72] "The tenancy has a trance-like existence *pendente lite*; none can assert with assurance whether it is alive or dead": *Meadows v Clerical Medical and General Life Assurance Society*, above, at 75, per Megarry V.C. It has been said that the intervening position in this "period of limbo" is "one of very considerable complexity": *Liverpool Properties Ltd v Oldbridge Investments Ltd* [1985] 2 E.G.L.R. 111 at 112, per Parker L.J. See too *Maryland Estates Ltd v Joseph* [1999] 1 W.L.R. 83 at 87.

[73] See *Mount Cook Land Ltd v Media Business Centre Ltd* [2004] EWHC 346; [2004] 2 P. & C.R. 25.

[74] Below, paras 18–033, 18–060.

[75] *Howard v Fanshawe* [1895] 2 Ch. 581; *Dendy v Evans* [1910] 1 K.B. 263.

[76] See, e.g. *Borzak v Ahmed* [1965] 2 Q.B. 320 at 326.

[77] *G.S. Fashions Ltd v B. & Q. Plc* [1995] 1 W.L.R. 1088.

lease is regarded as having been determined during the twilight period, subject to the possibility that it may be restored.[78] The inference from others is that the lease is not finally terminated until there is judgment for possession.[79] In practice, each view may be correct for particular purposes. The tenant has no title to the lease which he can sell under an open contract[80]; but he is a "tenant" for the purposes of both Part II of the Landlord and Tenant Act 1954[81] and the Leasehold Reform Act 1967[82]; and he is a "person interested" in land within s.84 of the Law of Property Act 1925.[83] Similarly, the liability of a surety who has guaranteed the performance of the covenants in the lease does not end when possession proceedings are commenced, but continues until the lease is actually determined.[84]

18–017   Because the commencement of possession proceedings constitutes a decisive election on the part of the landlord to put an end to the lease,[85] he is taken to treat the tenant as a trespasser thereafter.[86] There are a number of consequences of this. First, the tenant is liable to pay mesne profits[87] to the landlord until he obtains possession.[88] This sum will normally be assessed at the ordinary letting value of the premises.[89] Secondly, the landlord can no longer enforce the covenants in the lease pending the outcome of the proceedings.[90]

---

[78] See, e.g. *Dendy v Evans*, above; *Driscoll v Church Commissioners for England* [1957] 1 Q.B. 330.

[79] "The lease is potentially good and the process of forfeiture is not complete until the proceedings are determined:" *Hynes v Twinsectra Ltd*, above, at 195, per Aldous L.J.; [1996] Conv. 55 (M. Pawlowski). See too *Meadows v Clerical Medical and General Life Assurance Society*, above, at 75.

[80] *Pips (Leisure Productions) Ltd v Walton* (1980) 43 P. & C.R. 415. The tenant's right to relief has been described as "an equity": *Fuller v Judy Properties Ltd* (1991) 64 P. & C.R. 176 at 184, per Dillon L.J. See below, para.18–051.

[81] He may therefore be entitled to apply for a new tenancy: *Meadows v Clerical Medical and General Life Assurance Society*, above. For Pt II of the Landlord and Tenant Act 1954, see below, para.22–004 et seq.

[82] He may therefore have the right to acquire the freehold: *Hynes v Twinsectra Ltd*, above. For the Leasehold Reform Act 1967, see below, paras 22–197 et seq.

[83] He may therefore be able to apply for the discharge or modification of a restrictive covenant: *Driscoll v Church Commissioners for England*, above. For LPA 1925 s.84, see below, para.32–085.

[84] *Ivory Gate Ltd v Spetale* [1998] 2 E.G.L.R. 43.

[85] *Peninsular Maritime Ltd v Padseal Ltd* [1981] 2 E.G.L.R. 43 at 45.

[86] *Jones v Carter* (1846) 15 M. & W. 718 at 726; *Billson v Residential Apartments Ltd* [1992] 1 A.C. 494 at 534.

[87] Above, para.4–029.

[88] Pending the outcome of the claim, the court may order the tenant to make interim payments to the landlord on account of mesne profits (if the landlord succeeds) or of rent (if the tenant succeeds), since some payment will be due to the landlord in either event: CPR r.25.7, in particular r.25.7(1)(d); *Old Grovebury Manor Farm Ltd v W. Seymour Plant Sales & Hire Ltd* [1979] 1 W.L.R. 263.

[89] *Swordheath Properties Ltd v Tabet* [1979] 1 W.L.R. 285; *Viscount Chelsea v Hutchinson* [1994] 2 E.G.L.R. 61 (tenant who had sub-let house was liable for the letting value of the whole property from the issue of proceedings because the forfeiture terminated the underleases as well); and see, for exceptions to general rule, para.4–029 above.

[90] *Wheeler v Keeble (1914) Ltd* [1920] 1 Ch. 57; *Associated Deliveries Ltd v Harrison* (1984) 50 P. & C.R. 91.

Thirdly, the lease will be finally determined if the tenant accepts the forfeiture,[91] thereby terminating all future rights and liabilities under the lease and for the property.[92] The landlord cannot thereafter dispute the validity of the forfeiture, e.g. in order to claim rent.[93] By contrast, if the tenant does not treat the lease as determined, he is not, it seems, barred from enforcing the landlord's covenants,[94] which remain "potentially good".[95] There can be a partial forfeiture where the breach affects only part of the premises which can be treated separately from the rest.[96]

Where a landlord has obtained a judgment for possession, he may assert his **18–018** title and eject squatters. This is so, even though his judgment against the tenant is conditional and the tenant will escape forfeiture if he complies with the conditions.[97]

B. Waiver of Breach

1. Waiver. If a landlord waives the tenant's breach of covenant he will be **18–019** unable to proceed with the forfeiture of the lease. This is so whether the waiver takes place before or after he has shown that he is treating the lease as forfeited. Waiver may be express or implied. It will be implied only if two conditions are satisfied.

(a) Landlord's knowledge of the breach. First, the landlord must be aware[98] **18–020** of the acts or omissions of the tenant which make the lease liable for forfeiture. He need not know all the facts, as long as he appreciates enough to put him on inquiry as to the nature of the breach.[99] He must however be put on inquiry, and mere suspicion is not in itself enough.[100] Nor is deemed official notification sufficient for these purposes.[101]

---

[91] *G.S. Fashions Ltd v B. & Q. Plc* [1995] 1 W.L.R. 1088; [1995] Conv. 161 (M. Haley).

[92] *Kingston upon Thames Royal LBC v Marlow* [1996] 1 E.G.L.R. 101 (on vacating the premises, the tenant ceases to be liable to pay rates).

[93] *G.S. Fashions Ltd v B. & Q. Plc,* above.

[94] *G.S. Fashions Ltd v B. & Q. Plc,* above, at 1093; *Peninsular Maritime Ltd v Padseal Ltd* [1981] 1 E.G.L.R. 43. But see *Associated Deliveries Ltd v Harrison,* above, at 101.

[95] *Peninsular Maritime Ltd v Padseal Ltd,* above, at 46, per Stephenson L.J.

[96] *G.M.S. Syndicate Ltd v Gary Elliott Ltd* [1982] Ch.1 (basement used for immoral purposes: forfeiture of basement only; relief refused). cf. *W. G. Clark (Properties) Ltd v Dupre Properties Ltd* [1992] Ch. 297 at 305; above, para.18–007.

[97] *City of Westminster Assurance Co Ltd v Ainis* (1975) 29 P. & C.R. 469. The position where the landlord has commenced proceedings but has not obtained judgment is by no means clear: *City of Westminster Assurance Co Ltd v Ainis,* above, at 471.

[98] Knowledge of an employee or agent may be imputed to the landlord: *David Blackstone Ltd v Burnetts (West End) Ltd* [1973] 1 W.L.R. 1487 (landlord's solicitors knew of breach); *Metropolitan Properties Co Ltd v Cordery* [1979] 2 E.G.L.R. 78 (porters of block of flats knew of unlawful sub-letting).

[99] *Cornillie v Saha* (1996) 72 P. & C.R. 147.

[100] *Van Haarlam v Kasner* (1992) 64 P. & C.R. 214; [1993] Conv. 298 (J. Martin). The tenant, who was arrested for spying, had broken a covenant against using the demised premises for illegal purposes. The landlord, although aware of the circumstances, demanded rent after the tenant's arrest but before his conviction and was held to have waived the breach. cf. *Chrisdell Ltd v Johnson* (1987) 54 P. & C.R. 257; [1988] Conv. 139 (J. Martin) (landlord considered that he had insufficient proof of breach: no waiver).

[101] *Official Custodian for Charities v Parway Estates Developments Ltd* [1985] Ch. 151 at 163 (notification of insolvency through publication in the *London Gazette* not actual knowledge).

18–021   *(b) Unequivocal act recognising existence of lease.* Secondly, the landlord must do some unequivocal act which, objectively considered,[102] "without regard to the motive or intention of the landlord or the actual understanding or belief of the tenant"[103], recognises the continued existence of the lease.[104] There will be no waiver therefore if the landlord, knowing of the breach, adopts a merely passive attitude unaccompanied by any such act.[105] Nor will there be a waiver where the landlord, with knowledge of the breach:

(i)   serves a notice on the tenant, who is in arrears with the rent, calling on him to remedy a breach of another covenant[106];

(ii) sues for rent that fell due prior to peaceable re-entry or the commencement of possession proceedings[107]; or

(iii) sends a letter in the course of negotiations which does not unequivocally indicate that he regards the lease as subsisting.[108]

18–022   A waiver will be implied when a landlord,[109] with knowledge of the tenant's breach, accepts,[110] sues for,[111] or even merely demands,[112] rent

---

[102] *Central Estates (Belgravia) Ltd v Woolgar (No.2)* [1972] 1 W.L.R. 1048 at 1054.

[103] *Expert Clothing Service & Sales Ltd v Hillgate House Ltd* [1986] Ch. 340 at 360, per Slade L.J.

[104] *Matthews v Smallwood* [1910] 1 Ch.777 at 786, approved in *Fuller's Theatre & Vaudeville Co Ltd v Rofe* [1923] A.C. 435. A transaction between the landlord and a third party, not communicated to the tenant, does not imply waiver: below, para.20–069.

[105] *Perry v Davis* (1858) 3 C.B.(N.S.) 769.

[106] *Church Commissioners for England v Nodjoumi* (1985) 51 P. & C.R. 155. Service of such a notice (under LPA 1925 s.146; below, para.18–051), is a statutory prerequisite to forfeiture and cannot therefore unequivocally affirm the existence of the lease.

[107] *Kapur v Houghton* (1995) 70 P. & C.R. D27. See too *Re A Debtor* [1995] 1 W.L.R. 1127 at 1131 (where re-entry was subsequent to the commencement of proceedings for the recovery of rent arrears).

[108] *Expert Clothing Service & Sales Ltd v Hillgate House Ltd*, above, at 360; *Re National Jazz Centre Ltd* [1988] 2 E.G.L.R. 57.

[109] Or his agent, having actual or ostensible authority: see *John Lewis Plc v Viscount Chelsea* (1993) 67 P. & C.R. 120 at 138. In that case receipt by the landlord's bankers of rent that had not been demanded was held not to amount to waiver. On discovering the payment, the landlord had returned it.

[110] *Doe d. Gatehouse v Rees* (1838) 4 Bing. N.C. 384. This will be so even though (as is commonly the case) the landlord's acceptance of the rent is accidental: *Greenwich LBC v Discreet Selling Estates Ltd* (1990) 61 P. & C.R. 405 at 409. However, it may be necessary to distinguish processing a tenant's cheque from acceptance of rent: *Osibanjo v Seahive Investments Ltd* [2008] EWCA Civ 1282; [2009] 2 P. & C.R. 2 (the landlord banked a cheque, tendered by the tenant partly to discharge bankruptcy petition and partly to pay arrears of rent, and then returned a sum representing the rent arrears to the tenant; as the landlord had made clear the basis for the division of the amount, no objective observer would have considered that the amount paid had been accepted as rent by the landlord, and the court held that there was no waiver of forfeiture).

[111] *Dendy v Nicholl* (1854) 4 C.B.(N.S.) 376.

[112] *Segal Securities Ltd v Thoseby* [1963] 1 Q.B. 887. Where a landlord's letter to a tenant made it clear that the tenancy would only be regarded as continuing in the event of the rent being paid, it was not a sufficiently unequivocal act to comprise waiver: *Greenwood Reversions Ltd v World Environment Foundations Ltd* [2008] EWCA Civ 47; [2008] H.L.R. 31.

falling due after the breach.[113] A waiver will also be implied where the landlord levies distress, even in respect of rent due before the breach.[114] Demand or acceptance of rent once proved is in law a waiver, regardless of the intention with which it was demanded or received.[115] This is a "very well-established, if, to some people, a rather archaic rule"[116] which is "quite capable in some instances of operating harshly".[117] The implication of waiver whenever there is a demand for rent falling due after the tenant's breach has been recently questioned by the Court of Appeal but for the time being remains the law.[118]

Although there will be waiver if the landlord demands or accepts rent after **18–023** he has served a notice[119] requiring the tenant to remedy the breach,[120] there will be no waiver if such acts occur *after* the landlord has commenced proceedings for possession (or has peaceably re-entered).[121] The initiation of proceedings is "such a final election by the landlord to determine the tenancy that a subsequent receipt of rent is no waiver of the forfeiture".[122] However, a waiver by demand or acceptance of rent is not ineffective merely because:

(i) the lease provided that any waiver must be in writing[123];

(ii) the rent was accepted "without prejudice"[124]; or

(iii) the demand and acceptance were due to a clerical error[125] or were in some other way "accidental".[126]

---

[113] *Goodright d. Charter v Cordwent* (1795) 6 T.R. 219. The tenant has the unilateral right to appropriate his payment to particular rent due. If the tenant has therefore appropriated the payment to rent due after the breach, acceptance of that rent by the landlord will comprise waiver even if rent due before the breach remains owing: *Thomas v Ken Thomas Ltd* [2006] EWCA Civ 1504; [2007] L. & T.R. 21. It is undecided whether a waiver may be implied where the rent arrears relate to a period after the breach but before the landlord acquired knowledge of the breach: see *Osibanjo v Seahive Investments Ltd*, above at [24] (Mummery L.J.) and at [32] (Rix L.J.)

[114] *Doe d. David v Williams* (1836) 7 C. & P. 322.

[115] *Segal Securities Ltd v Thoseby*, above, at 898; *Central Estates (Belgravia) Ltd v Woolgar (No.2)*, above; *David Blackstone Ltd v Burnetts (West End) Ltd*, above.

[116] *Thomas v Ken Thomas Ltd* [2006] EWCA Civ 1504; [2007] L. & T.R. 21 at [16], per Neuberger L.J.

[117] *Expert Clothing Service & Sales Ltd v Hillgate House Ltd* [1986] Ch. 340 at 360, per Slade L.J.

[118] *Greenwood Reversions Ltd v World Environment Foundations Ltd* [2008] EWCA Civ 47; [2008] H.L.R. 31 at [26] et seq., where the Court of Appeal assumed, without determining, that the two first instance decisions referred to at fn.115 above were correctly decided.

[119] Under LPA 1925 s.146; below, para.18–051.

[120] *Greenwich LBC v Discreet Selling Estates Ltd* (1990) 61 P. & C.R. 405 at 409.

[121] *Evans v Enever* [1920] 2 K.B. 315. The same is true where he distrains after service or re-entry: *Grimwood v Moss* (1872) L.R. 7 C.P. 360.

[122] *Civil Service Co-operative Society Ltd v McGrigor's Trustee* [1923] 2 Ch. 347 at 358, per Russell J.

[123] *R. v Paulson* [1921] 1 A.C. 271.

[124] *Davenport v R.* (1877) 3 App.Cas. 115; *Segal Securities Ltd v Thoseby* [1963] 1 Q.B. 887.

[125] *Central Estates (Belgravia) Ltd v Woolgar (No.2)* [1972] 1 W.L.R. 1048; *John Lewis Plc v Viscount Chelsea* (1993) 67 P. & C.R. 120 at 138.

[126] *Greenwich LBC v Discreet Selling Estates Ltd*, above, at 409 per Staughton L.J..

18–024   It is a question of fact whether money has been tendered and accepted as rent, although it may be necessary to construe the lease in order to see whether a payment demanded or made is a payment by way of rent.[127] It is acknowledged that cases of acceptance of rent "fall into a special category"[128]; in other situations the court is less rigid in its approach, and it is "free to look at *all* the circumstances of the case" to determine whether the act alleged to constitute a waiver was unequivocal.[129] However, waiver has also been implied where a landlord, with the requisite knowledge of breach:

> (i) agreed to grant a lease to the tenant to commence from the normal determination of the existing lease[130];
>
> (ii) offered to purchase the tenant's interest in the property[131]; or
>
> (iii) commenced proceedings to enforce a particular provision of the lease.[132]

18–025   **2. Extent of waiver.** As might be expected, the waiver of a covenant or condition extends only to the particular breach in question and does not operate as a general waiver of all future breaches.[133] The same applies to a licence granted to the tenant to do any act.[134] A waiver of the right to forfeit the tenancy does not preclude the landlord from suing for damages for its breach.[135] Nor does a waiver make lawful *ab initio* an unlawful act done before the waiver.[136] But once the waiver has become effective it is not personal to the tenant but will also benefit any assignee from him.[137]

18–026   **3. Continuing breaches.** Where the breach is of a continuing nature,[138] as, for example, breach of a covenant to repair[139] or of a covenant to use the

---

[127] See, e.g. *Yorkshire Metropolitan Properties Ltd v Co-operative Retail Services Ltd* (1997) [2001] L. & T.R. 26 (sending invoice for insurance payments not a demand for rent).

[128] *Expert Clothing Service & Sales Ltd v Hillgate House Ltd*, above, at 360, per Slade L.J.

[129] *Expert Clothing Service & Sales Ltd v Hillgate House Ltd*, above.

[130] *Ward v Day* (1864) 5 B. & S. 359.

[131] *Bader Properties Ltd v Linley Property Investments Ltd* (1967) 19 P. & C.R. 620 at 641.

[132] *Cardigan Properties Ltd v Consolidated Property Investments Ltd* [1991] 1 E.G.L.R. 64 at 68 (proceedings to compel production of insurance policies); *Cornillie v Saha* (1996) 72 P. & C.R. 147 (proceedings to enforce right to enter and inspect premises under the terms of the lease).

[133] LPA 1925 s.148.

[134] LPA 1925 s.143.

[135] *Stephens v Junior Army and Navy Stores Ltd* [1914] 2 Ch. 516; *Norman v Simpson* [1946] K.B. 158 at 160.

[136] *Muspratt v Johnston* [1963] 2 Q.B. 383.

[137] See *Brikom Investments Ltd v Carr* [1979] Q.B. 467 (not a forfeiture case).

[138] A breach of covenant is not a continuing breach merely because the breach can be remedied. It means the breach of a continuing obligation: *Farimani v Gates* [1984] 2 E.G.L.R. 66 and 68, 69.

[139] *Coward v Gregory* (1866) L.R. 2 C.P. 153; *Spoor v Green* (1874) L.R. 9 Ex. 99 at 111, per Bramwell B. ("the covenant is broken afresh every day the premises are out of repair"); *Greenwich LBC v Discreet Selling Estates Ltd* (1990) 61 P. & C.R. 405 at 412. cf. *Farimani v Gates*, above (breach of covenant to lay out insurance monies on repairs not a continuing breach).

premises in a particular manner,[140] a waiver will extend at most to the time for which the landlord knew that the breaches would continue.[141] Breaches which continue after the date of the waiver will normally give a fresh right of forfeiture.[142] But waiver of the breach of one covenant will extend to a consequential continuing breach of another covenant which the tenant cannot discontinue. Thus where property was sub-let in breach of covenant and used by the sub-tenant for purposes prohibited by the lease, the waiver of the covenant against sub-letting was also a waiver of the breach of the user covenant.[143]

C. Conditions for Forfeiture

The law leans against forfeiture, and a claimant landlord is put to strict proof of his case. Moreover, both equity and statute have intervened so as to allow tenants to rescue themselves from liability to forfeiture in certain cases. There are different sets of rules for forfeiture for non-payment of rent[144] and forfeiture for breaches of other covenants or conditions. This is because equity would commonly relieve a tenant against forfeiture for failure to pay rent, but as a general rule refused relief in all other cases.[145] Accordingly, relief in cases of non-payment of rent is governed by the equitable jurisdiction as amended by statute.[146] In other cases there is a purely statutory jurisdiction, which is quite distinct. The extent to which there is a residual equitable discretion to give relief, where the statutory jurisdiction is for some reason inapplicable, is both controversial and uncertain, though it may now be of little consequence.[147]

18–027

I. FORFEITURE FOR NON-PAYMENT OF RENT

A landlord who according to the lease has the right to re-enter for non-payment of rent may nevertheless be required to make a formal demand for the rent before he may re-enter; and on complying with certain conditions the tenant may be able to have the proceedings for forfeiture terminated, or to obtain relief against the forfeiture. The landlord of a dwelling must ensure that

18–028

---

[140] *Marsden v Edward Heyes Ltd* [1927] 2 K.B. 1; *Creery v Summersell* [1949] Ch. 751.

[141] *Segal Securities Ltd v Thoseby* [1963] 1 Q.B. 887 at 901.

[142] *Doe d. Ambler v Woodbridge* (1829) 9 B. & C. 376; *Cooper v Henderson* [1982] 2 E.G.L.R. 42. The fact that rent is payable in advance is immaterial.

[143] *Downie v Turner* [1951] 2 K.B. 112.

[144] Rent does not for these purposes include the payment of service charges unless, as is common, the lease expressly provides that such charges are deemed to be payable as rent: see *Escalus Properties Ltd v Robinson* [1996] Q.B. 231 at 243; *Khar v Delbounty Ltd* (1998) 75 P. & C.R. 232 at 236; see also *Maryland Estates Ltd v Joseph* [1999] 1 W.L.R. 83; *Mohammadi v Anston Investments Ltd* [2003] EWCA Civ 981; [2004] H.L.R. 8.

[145] For discussion, see *Billson v Residential Apartments Ltd* [1992] 1 A.C. 494 at 512 (Browne-Wilkinson V.C.); *Equity and Contemporary Legal Developments* (ed. S. Goldstein), pp.844–854 (C.H.); [1994] J.B.L. 37 (P. Luxton).

[146] See CLPA 1852 ss.210–212; Supreme Court Act 1981 s.38; *Billson v Residential Apartments Ltd*, above, at 510–512. The county court has no inherent equitable jurisdiction unlike the High Court. It can give relief only where authorised by statute: *Di Palma v Victoria Square Property Co Ltd* [1986] Ch. 150 at 160.

[147] Below, para.18–048.

he provides an address for service, and, in the case of long leases, must serve a statutory notice relating to the payment of rent; failure to comply with these requirements will mean that the rent is not payable, and therefore prevent forfeiture of the lease.[148]

18–029   **1. Landlord's formal demand.** The landlord must either have made a formal demand for the rent, or else be exempted from making such a demand.

(a) Formal demand. To make a formal demand, the landlord or his authorised agent must demand the exact sum due on the day when it falls due at such convenient hour before sunset as will give time to count out the money, the demand being made upon the demised premises and continuing until sunset.[149]

18–030   *(b) Formal demand unnecessary.* In order to avoid the technicalities of a formal demand, every well-drawn lease provides that the lease may be forfeited if the rent is a specified number of days in arrear, "whether formally demanded or not". The words quoted exempt the landlord from making a formal demand. Even if a lease contains no such provision, there is no need for a formal demand in any forfeiture action, whether in the High Court[150] or the county court,[151] if:

> (i) half a year's rent is in arrear, and
>
> (ii) either of two conditions is met in relation to the arrears:
>
>> (a) CRAR is not exercisable to recover the arrears; or
>> (b) there are not sufficient goods on the premises to recover the arrears by CRAR.[152]

2. Tenant's right to stay proceedings

18–031   *(a) Tenant's statutory right.* If the landlord brings an action for possession, the tenant has a statutory right[153] to have the action discontinued (i.e. terminated) by himself[154] paying all arrears of rent and costs:

> (i) at any time before trial in the High Court[155]; or

---

[148] These restrictions, contained in L & TA 1987 s.48 and CLRA 2002 s.166, are dealt with at paras 19–072 and 19–074 below.

[149] See 1 Wms.Saund. (1871) 434 et seq., being notes to *Duppa v Mayo* (1669). 1 Saund. 275.

[150] CLPA 1852 s.210, as amended (by the insertion of s.210A) by T C & EA 2007 s.86; Sch.14 paras 15, 16.

[151] CCA 1984 s.139(1), as amended by TC & EA 2007 s.86; Sch.14 para.40.

[152] For CRAR (commercial rent arrears recovery), replacing the common law of distress, see below, para.19–077.

[153] The court has no discretion in the matter: see *United Dominions Trust Ltd v Shellpoint Trustees Ltd* [1993] 4 All E.R. 310 at 316.

[154] See *Matthews v Dobbins* [1963] 1 W.L.R. 227 (payment by stranger insufficient under CCA 1959 s.191(1) (now CCA 1984 s.138(5)). Payment may, however, be made by sub-tenants or those with derivative interests under the lease: below, para.18–032.

[155] CLPA 1852 s.212.

(ii) not less than five clear days before trial in the county court.[156]

Where proceedings are in the High Court, the ill-drafted provisions of the Common Law Procedure Act 1852 have been held[157] to confine this right to cases where at least half a year's rent is in arrear.[158] Presumably, in other cases, the decision to stay proceedings lies at the discretion of the court[159] and is not automatic.[160] No such restriction applies to proceedings in the county court.[161] Furthermore, in county court proceedings the court cannot require the tenant to give the landlord possession until at least four weeks from the date of its order.[162] That order will not take effect if within that time, or any extension of it,[163] the tenant pays into court or to the landlord all arrears of rent due and the costs of the action.[164] The tenant's automatic right to have proceedings discontinued is therefore greater in the county court than it is in the High Court. Where proceedings are stayed, the tenant holds the land according to the existing lease without the need to grant any new term.[165]

(b) *Rights of sub-tenants and mortgagees.* Where the landlord has begun **18–032** possession proceedings against a tenant, any sub-tenants or mortgagees have the same rights to seek a stay as the tenant, if they pay the arrears of rent and costs due to the landlord from the tenant.[166] This is so whether the action is in the High Court or the county court and even though the sub-tenants or mortgagees are not parties to the proceedings against the tenant.[167] Furthermore, in such circumstances (and "somewhat remarkably"[168]), the lease is

---

[156] CCA 1984 s.138(2).

[157] *Standard Pattern Co Ltd v Ivey* [1962] Ch. 432; but see (1962) 78 L.Q.R. 168 (R.E.M); [1994] J.B.L. 37 at 39 (P. Luxton).

[158] Presumably when proceedings are commenced.

[159] Apart from its inherent jurisdiction, the High Court has a statutory power to grant relief against forfeiture in summary manner in any action for the forfeiture of a lease for non-payment of rent: Senior Courts Act 1981 s.38(1). After judgment for forfeiture s.38 is inapplicable, and recourse must be had instead to the inherent jurisdiction: see, e.g. *Ladup Ltd v Williams & Glyn's Bank Plc* [1985] 1 W.L.R. 851 at 854.

[160] (1962) 78 L.Q.R. 168 (R.E.M.). This produces the absurdity that "a tenant with small arrears may be less well off than one with large arrears".

[161] See CCA 1984 s.138(2). The county court has power to extend the time for payment: CCA 1984 s.138(4). These provisions do not apply where a landlord has obtained a possession order against an assured tenant: *Artesian Residential Investments Ltd v Beck* [2000] Q.B. 541. For assured tenancies under the HA 1988 see below, para.22–081.

[162] CCA 1984 s.138(3).

[163] CCA 1984 s.138(4).

[164] CCA 1984 s.138(5). For these purposes, "the rent in arrear" means the rent due at the time of the summons seeking forfeiture, together with mesne profits for use and occupation due at the time when the court makes its order for possession: *Maryland Estates Ltd v Joseph* [1999] 1 W.L.R. 83.

[165] CLPA 1852 s.212 (High Court); CCA 1984 s.138(5) (as amended by AJA 1985) (county court).

[166] CLPA 1852 s.212; Senior Courts Act 1981 s.38(2); CCA 1984 s.140.

[167] *Doe d. Wyatt v Byron* (1845) 1 C.B. 623; *United Dominions Trust Ltd v Shellpoint Trustees Ltd*, above, at 318; *Escalus Properties Ltd v Robinson* [1996] Q.B. 231 at 244; [1986] Conv. 187 at 190 (S. Tromans).

[168] *Bank of Ireland Home Mortgages v South Lodge Developments* [1996] 1 E.G.L.R. 91 at 93, per Lightman J. Yet the outcome follows naturally from the wording of the statutory provisions.

retrospectively reinstated and is vested in the sub-tenant or mortgagee instead of the tenant.[169] As relief takes the form of the retrospective reinstatement of the lease in the sub-tenant or mortgagee, the landlord cannot claim mesne profits[170] for the period between the service of the proceedings and the date of judgment, but only the rent due.[171]

18–033   **3. Tenant's claim to relief.** Even where the tenant has no other defence, he may still be able to escape forfeiture by claiming relief. The jurisdiction of the court to grant relief is much used. It is of great importance to tenants, and it greatly qualifies the landlord's common law right to forfeit the lease.

18–034   *(a) The claim.* Equity considered that a right of re-entry, in whatever form it was reserved,[172] was merely security for payment of the rent,[173] so that if:

> (i) the tenant paid the rent due; and

> (ii) the tenant paid any expenses to which the landlord had been put; and

> (iii) it was just and equitable to grant relief,

equity would restore the tenant to his position despite the forfeiture of the lease.[174] This equitable jurisdiction to grant relief was of course discretionary.[175] It was not given as of right as is the case where proceedings are stayed as explained above.[176]

18–035   *(b) Time-limit.* Originally there was no limit to the time within which application for relief had to be made,[177] apart from the general principle that equity would give no assistance to stale claims. But this was inconvenient[178] and in 1730 the power to give relief was curtailed.[179]

---

[169] *Escalus Properties Ltd v Robinson*, above.

[170] These will normally be assessed as the ordinary letting value of the premises: above, para.4–029.

[171] Where the property is held on a long lease at a low ground rent, the difference between these sums can be considerable: see, e.g. *Escalus Properties Ltd v Robinson*, above, at 242.

[172] *Richard Clarke & Co Ltd v Widnall* [1976] 1 W.L.R. 845 (right to determine tenancy by giving notice).

[173] *Howard v Fanshawe* [1895] 2 Ch. 581 at 588; *Chandless-Chandless v Nicholson* [1942] 2 K.B. 321 at 323; *Ladup Ltd v Williams & Glyn's Bank Plc* [1985] 1 W.L.R. 851 at 860; *Inntrepreneur Pub Company v Langton* [2000] 1 E.G.L.R. 34 at 38; *Bland v Ingram's Estates Ltd* [2001] Ch. 767 at 788.

[174] See *Howard v Fanshawe* [1895] 2 Ch. 581; *Belgravia Insurance Co Ltd v Meah* [1964] 1 Q.B. 436.

[175] See, e.g. *Silverman v A.F.C.O. (U.K.) Ltd* (1988) 56 P. & C.R. 185; and below, para.18–038.

[176] See para.18–031.

[177] *Hill v Barclay* (1811) 18 Ves. 56 at 59, 60. For the historical background, see [1994] J.B.L. 37 at 38 (P. Luxton).

[178] See *Platt on Leases* (1847), vol.2, p.475.

[179] L & TA 1730 ss.2, 4.

(1) HIGH COURT PROCEEDINGS. The position today as regards proceedings in **18-036** the High Court is that where the landlord has obtained judgment for possession in circumstances which dispense him from making a formal demand for rent,[180] an application for relief must be made within six months of execution of the judgment.[181] In other cases[182] the equitable jurisdiction to grant relief is unimpaired.[183] Although the court may adopt a similar time limit[184] "as a guide",[185] it will not "boggle at a matter of days".[186] Where relief is given, the lease is retrospectively reinstated.[187]

(2) COUNTY COURT PROCEEDINGS. Where a landlord has peaceably re-entered **18-037** for non-payment of rent, the county court has a statutory power to grant relief to the tenant if he applies at any time within six months from the date of re-entry.[188] Formerly, where there were forfeiture proceedings, the court had no power to give relief after its order for possession was effective.[189] Nor could a tenant seek relief in the High Court in such circumstances,[190] because he was "barred from all relief".[191] However, in 1985 the law was changed and the county court may now give relief at any time within six months from the date on which the landlord recovers possession.[192] Where relief is given, the tenant holds under the original lease.[193] A tenant who fails to apply within six months is barred from all relief whether in the county court or the High Court.[194]

(c) Discretion. The discretion to grant relief in cases of non-payment of rent **18-038** "is based on solid principle and not simply to be exercised in a manner which the court considers fair on the particular facts before it."[195] The policy reasons for this approach are clear:

---

[180] For these, see above, para.18–030.

[181] CLPA 1852 ss.210–212 (replacing the provisions of L & TA 1730).

[182] As where forfeiture proceedings are taken where less than six months' rent is in arrears, or the landlord re-enters peaceably.

[183] *Lovelock v Margo* [1963] 2 Q.B. 786; *Di Palma v Victoria Square Property Co Ltd* [1984] Ch. 346 at 366 (on appeal [1986] Ch. 150).

[184] *Howard v Fanshawe* [1895] 2 Ch. 581 at 589.

[185] *Di Palma v Victoria Square Property Co Ltd*, above, per Scott J.

[186] *Thatcher v C.H. Pearce & Sons (Contractors) Ltd* [1968] 1 W.L.R. 748 at 756, per Simon P. (non-contentious re-entry; relief granted on application made six months and four days later).

[187] This is so whether relief is given under the statutory or inherent jurisdiction: see CLPA 1852 s.212; Senior Courts Act 1981 s.38(2); *Howard v Fanshawe* [1895] 2 Ch. 581 at 592.

[188] CCA 1984 s.139(2), (3).

[189] *Di Palma v Victoria Square Property Co Ltd* [1986] Ch. 150.

[190] *Di Palma v Victoria Square Property Co Ltd*, above, overruling *Jones v Barnett* [1984] Ch. 500 (which had held that the High Court could give relief). The tenant's subsequent proceedings before the European Commission of Human Rights, alleging breach of ECHR Art.8 and Art.1 of Protocol 1, were unsuccessful: see *Di Palma v UK* (1988) 10 E.H.R.R. 149.

[191] CCA 1984 s.138(7).

[192] CCA 1984 s.138(9A) (inserted by AJA 1985).

[193] CCA 1984 s.138(9B) (inserted by AJA 1985).

[194] *United Dominions Trust Ltd v Shellpoint Trustees Ltd* [1993] 4 All E.R. 310. For a valuable comment on this important case, see (1994) 110 L.Q.R. 15 (N. Gravells).

[195] *Inntrepreneur Pub Company v Langton* [2000] 1 E.G.L.R. 34 at 38, per Arden J., approved in *Eastaugh v Crisp* [2007] EWCA Civ 638.

"If the courts do not uphold the terms of the lease except in limited situations, there will be a strong disincentive to landlords to invest in property and let it out on lease. By enforcing rights of property, the law promotes the use and availability of this resource within society, and property can be used as in this case for commercial purposes which can serve to increase society's prosperity."[196]

As equity regards the right of re-entry as security for payment of the rent,[197] it is:

"an invariable condition of relief . . . that the arrears, if not already available to the lessor, shall be paid within a time specified by the court."[198]

It is a matter for the court's discretion how long that time is to be in the circumstances of each case, but whether the condition should be imposed is not a discretionary matter; it is "a requirement of law rooted in the principle upon which relief is granted."[199]

18–039   Save in very exceptional circumstances, the court will grant the tenant relief against forfeiture if it is sought within the six-month period, on payment of all arrears of rent and costs.[200] Relief will be granted to the tenant even though he is insolvent,[201] he has been a bad payer in the past,[202] or he has committed other breaches of covenant.[203] There are, however, limits to equity's indulgence, as where the conduct of the tenant has been sufficiently shocking to disqualify him from claiming any relief or assistance whatever,[204] or where no rent has been paid for years and the tenancy has been treated as at an end.[205] Furthermore, the court may refuse relief if the landlord has granted a third party an interest in the property within the six-month period "not unreasonably or precipitately"[206] and the grant of relief would cause either or both of them injustice.[207]

---

[196] *Inntrepreneur Pub Company v Langton*, above, at 38, per Arden J., approved in *Eastaugh v Crisp*, above.

[197] See above, para.18–034.

[198] *Barton Thompson & Co Ltd v Stapling Machines Co* [1966] Ch. 499 at 510, per Pennycuick J; followed in *Bland v Ingrams Estates Ltd (No.2)* [2001] EWCA Civ 1088; [2002] Ch. 177 at [12]; *Eastaugh v Crisp*, above.

[199] *Barton Thompson & Co Ltd v Stapling Machines Co*, above at 510, per Pennycuick J; followed in *Bland v Ingrams Estates Ltd (No.2)*, above at [12]; *Eastaugh v Crisp*, above.

[200] *Gill v Lewis* [1956] 2 Q.B. 1; *Re Brompton Securities (No.2)* [1988] 3 All E.R. 677 at 680.

[201] *Re Brompton Securities (No.2)*, above.

[202] *Gill v Lewis*, above, at 17.

[203] *Gill v Lewis*, above, at 13.

[204] *Gill v Lewis*, above, at 13, where Jenkins L.J. instanced a tenant who was notoriously using the premises "as a disorderly house". But in that case, the court granted relief even though the tenant was in prison for indecently assaulting two boys on the premises.

[205] *Public Trustee v Westbrook* [1965] 1 W.L.R. 1160 (bombed site: no rent paid for 22 years). cf. *Re Brompton Securities (No.2)*, above, at 680.

[206] *Silverman v A.F.C.O. (UK) Ltd* (1988) 56 P. & C.R. 185 at 192, per Slade L.J.

[207] *Silverman v A.F.C.O. (UK) Ltd*, above, at 192.

This situation is most likely to arise where the tenant has in some way led **18–040** the landlord to believe that relief will not be sought but then makes an application towards the end of the six-month period.[208] In such cases two questions arise. First, if the transaction in favour of the purchaser has been completed, was the purchaser bound by the tenant's claim to relief? The circumstances in which that will be so are considered below.[209] Even if the purchaser is not bound, the court may still give relief as between the landlord and the tenant, e.g. by granting the tenant a reversionary lease.[210] Secondly, if the transaction has not been completed, or if the purchaser took subject to the tenant's claim to relief, then the reasonableness of the parties' conduct will largely depend upon their knowledge.[211] For example, where the intending purchaser was (or ought to have been) aware that the six-month period for relief had not expired, but failed to make any enquiries, the court might grant relief to the tenant.[212] In addition to requiring payment of all arrears and costs, in the exercise of its discretion the court may impose further terms on the tenant, e.g. that he should execute outstanding repairs.[213]

(d) Derivative interests. Where a lease is forfeited, any derivative interests **18–041** created out of it, such as mortgages and sub-tenancies, automatically come to an end.[214] This is because "every subordinate interest must perish with the superior interest on which it is dependent".[215] Although sub-tenants, mortgagees and others may apply for relief against forfeiture of the head lease,[216] the existence of a number of overlapping (and not always consistent) jurisdictions means that the law is needlessly complex.

During the course of forfeiture proceedings, whether in the High Court[217] **18–042** or the county court,[218] relief may be given to any "under-lessee" (i.e. sub-tenant) or mortgagee on payment of arrears of rent and costs. In the county court the right to obtain relief is automatic and not discretionary[219] and continues until possession is given, which must be not less than four weeks

---

[208] See *Stanhope v Haworth* (1886) 3 T.L.R. 34; *Silverman v A.F.C.O. (UK) Ltd*, above.

[209] Below, para.18–050.

[210] See *Bank of Ireland Home Mortgages v South Lodge Developments* [1996] 1 E.G.L.R. 91 at 93. cf. *Bhojwani v Kingsley Investment Trust Ltd* [1992] 2 E.G.L.R. 70 and 74.

[211] *Bank of Ireland Home Mortgages v South Lodge Developments*, above, at 94.

[212] *Bank of Ireland Home Mortgages v South Lodge Developments*, above, at 94.

[213] *Newbolt v Bingham* (1895) 72 L.T. 852; *Belgravia Insurance Co Ltd v Meah* [1964] 1 Q.B. 436.

[214] *G.W. Ry v Smith* (1876) 2 Ch D 235 at 253; *Viscount Chelsea v Hutchinson* [1994] 2 E.G.L.R. 61 and 62. There are two statutory exceptions to this rule: see Rent Act 1977 s.137; HA 1988 s.18 (sub-tenancy continues where protected, statutory or assured tenancy terminated).

[215] *Bendall v McWhirter* [1952] 2 Q.B. 466 at 487, per Romer L.J. The position may be different in relation to statutory tenancies that arose under the Rent Acts: *Jessamine Investments Ltd v Schwartz* [1978] Q.B. 64.

[216] For an illuminating analysis, see [1986] Conv. 187 (S. Tromans).

[217] Senior Courts Act 1981 s.38; *Escalus Properties Ltd v Robinson* [1996] Q.B. 231 at 245. The section has no application after judgment has been given: *Ladup Ltd v Williams & Glyn's Bank Plc*, above, at 854.

[218] CCA 1984 ss.138(5), 140; *United Dominions Trust Ltd v Shellpoint Trustees Ltd* [1993] 4 All E.R. 310 at 315.

[219] See *United Dominions Trust Ltd v Shellpoint Trustees Ltd*, above, at 316.

from the court's order.[220] The form of relief in either court will be an order retrospectively vesting the lease in the applicant.[221] It is also the case that where a lessor is proceeding by action or otherwise[222] to enforce a right of re-entry for non-payment of rent, an under-lessee or mortgagee may seek relief under the provisions of the Law of Property Act 1925.[223] On such an application, the court may prospectively[224] grant a new lease of the property or any part of it for the whole term of the lease or for a lesser term. Such relief may be given on such terms and conditions[225] as the court in the circumstances of each case may think fit. In practice the terms of relief will require payment of the outstanding rent, until the date proceedings for forfeiture were commenced, and mesne profits thereafter, together with the landlord's costs.[226]

18–043   Where the landlord has peaceably re-entered, and has not therefore commenced forfeiture proceedings, the under-lessee or mortgagee may within six months of the landlord's re-entry seek an order retrospectively vesting the lease in him.[227] In the High Court relief is given on payment of arrears of rent and costs. In the county court relief may be given on such terms and conditions as the court thinks fit,[228] which in practice is also likely to mean payment of arrears of rent and costs.[229]

18–044   Where the under-lessee or mortgagee applies for relief in the High Court within six months of the landlord executing an order for possession made in forfeiture proceedings, the court may make an order retrospectively vesting the lease in the applicant.[230] In proceedings in the county court the position is the same, except that the court may vest the lease in the applicant either for the remainder of the term or for any lesser term.[231] Relief will not usually be granted where an application is made more than six months after the execution of an order for possession.[232] This is so whether the proceedings are brought in the High Court[233] or the county court.[234]

---

[220] CCA 1984 s.138(3).

[221] Senior Courts Act 1981 s.38(2); CCA 1984 s.138(5).

[222] For the meaning of this expression, see below, para.18–060.

[223] s.146(4); below, para.18–073.

[224] See *Cadogan v Dimovic* [1984] 1 W.L.R. 609 at 613, 616; *Official Custodian for Charities v Mackey* [1985] Ch. 168.

[225] As to "execution of any deed or other document, payment of rent, costs, expenses, damages, compensation, giving security, or otherwise": LPA 1925 s.146(4).

[226] *Escalus Properties Ltd v Robinson*, above, at 242.

[227] As regards the High Court, see CLPA 1852 s.212 (which applies to those with derivative interests: *United Dominions Trust Ltd v Shellpoint Trustees Ltd*, above, at 317, 318); *Howard v Fanshawe* [1895] 2 Ch. 581 at 591. The county court is governed by CCA 1984 s.139(2), (3) (s.139(3) was inserted by AJA 1985).

[228] CCA 1984 s.139(2).

[229] There could be other terms if the justice of the case demanded it.

[230] CLPA 1852 s.210.

[231] CCA 1984 s.138(9C) (inserted by AJA 1985).

[232] But see below.

[233] CLPA 1852 s.210.

[234] CCA 1984 s.138(7); *United Dominions Trust Ltd v Shellpoint Trustees Ltd* [1993] 4 All E.R. 310.

It has been held that the holder of a charging order over a lease is entitled **18–045** to claim relief.[235] Such an equitable chargee[236] may either apply for relief in the county court[237] or invoke the inherent jurisdiction of the High Court.[238] Although the inherent jurisdiction is only available where the applicant is either entitled to possession of the land or has a legal or equitable interest in it, the chargee may enforce the chargor's obligation to take reasonable steps to preserve the security by joining the chargor as defendant to the action and claiming relief indirectly "in his shoes".[239] A person who has no legal interest in the term created by the lease, such as an adverse possessor (a squatter),[240] cannot generally seek relief.[241]

The form of relief sought is likely to depend on who the applicant is. Where **18–046** a mortgagee or chargee[242] applies for relief, he will almost invariably seek to have the defaulting tenant's term vested in him. In the event of relief being granted, the mortgagee will hold the term by way of substituted security[243] and subject therefore both to the tenant's equity of redemption and to his obligations to account to subsequent mortgagees should he realise the security.[244] This could lead to the curious result that the defaulting tenant could redeem the mortgage, and the landlord might find himself once again with an undesirable tenant whose lease he had previously forfeited.[245]

The position is even more difficult where an under-lessee (i.e. a sub-tenant) **18–047** seeks relief. His lease will necessarily be of shorter duration than the defaulting tenant's, and it may be substantially so. It may also comprise only part of

---

[235] In *Croydon (Unique) Ltd v Wright* [2001] Ch. 318 at 336, Butler Sloss L.J. considered it "astonishing that the holder of a charging order over a lease is said to be unable to be heard in forfeiture proceedings and powerless to obtain any relief or protection of the asset which is the object of the charging order." These remarks were supported by Chadwick L.J. in *Bland v Ingram's Estates Ltd* [2001] Ch. 767 at 784.

[236] See Charging Orders Act 1979 s.3(4).

[237] Where landlord is proceeding by action, CCA 1984 s.138(9C): *Croydon (Unique) Ltd v Wright*, above. Where landlord is proceeding by peaceable re-entry, CCA 1984 s.139(2),(3): *Bland v Ingram's Estates Ltd*, above.

[238] Application may not be made under LPA 1925 s.146(4): *Bland v Ingram's Estates Ltd*, above.

[239] *Bland v Ingram's Estates Ltd*, above; cf. *Test Valley BC v Minilec Engineering Ltd (in liquidation)* [2005] 2 E.G.L.R. 113 at 126.

[240] Where a squatter has adversely possessed against a registered leasehold estate, and has acquired the right to be registered as proprietor under LRA 2002 Sch.6 (on which see paras 35–070 et seq., below), he should be entitled to claim relief in the event of forfeiture of the leasehold estate. It is not clear whether a squatter who has made application to be registered as proprietor, but the time available to the proprietor to respond to his application has not elapsed, may claim relief.

[241] *Tickner v Buzzacott* [1965] Ch. 426.

[242] *Bland v Ingram's Estates Ltd*, above; see further *Bland v Ingram's Estates Ltd (No.2)* [2001] EWCA Civ 1088; [2002] Ch. 177 where the Court of Appeal set out terms on which relief was to be granted.

[243] *Chelsea Estates Investment Trust Co Ltd v Marche* [1955] Ch. 328; *Official Custodian for Charities v Parway Estates Developments Ltd* [1985] Ch. 151 at 164.

[244] For the mortgagor's equity of redemption, see below, para.24–017. For the obligations of a mortgagee to account to any subsequent mortgagees for the proceeds of sale of the mortgaged property, see below, paras 25–020, 25–021.

[245] For the anomalies that arise in this situation, see *Chelsea Estates Investment Trust Co Ltd v Marche*, above, at 338; (1955) 18 M.L.R. 301 (L. A. Sheridan).

the property demised by the superior lease. In some cases therefore an under-lessee may seek to have the tenant's lease vested in him. In others, he may seek a new lease that is of lesser duration, of part only of the property, or both. In the former case, if the court grants such relief, the term will be assigned to the under-lessee. In some circumstances this would appear to be excessively generous to him, as where the term is a long lease granted at a premium with a ground rent and the under-lease is for a short term at a rack rent. In such circumstances, the under-lessee should in principle be required to make some payment to the landlord for the value of the lease as well as meeting the outstanding arrears and costs. Yet the court does not have power to impose terms in all cases where relief against forfeiture for non-payment of rent is given.

18–048   (1) DUTY TO NOTIFY. Prior to 1986, a landlord was under no obligation to notify any person having a derivative interest in the lease that he was taking proceedings to forfeit it.[246] There was therefore a real risk that the person with the derivative interest (generally a mortgagee) might not discover the forfeiture until after the time allowed by law for an application for relief[247] had expired.[248] It remains controversial whether in those circumstances the court has any residual jurisdiction to grant relief.[249] In view of subsequent procedural development, however, the existence or otherwise of any such jurisdiction may now be of little practical importance.

18–049   In 1986 the rules of court were amended. Under the current Practice Direction, if the claim relates to residential property, the landlord is required:

(i) to state in the particulars of claim[250] in any forfeiture proceedings, the name and address of any under-lessee or mortgagee entitled to claim relief against forfeiture of whom he knows; and

(ii) to file a copy of the particulars of claim for service by the court on the under-lessee or mortgagee.[251]

---

[246] *Hammersmith and Fulham LBC v Tops Shop Centres Ltd* [1990] Ch. 237 at 252.

[247] Explained at paras 18–035 et seq. above.

[248] See *Abbey National BS v Maybeech* [1985] Ch. 190, where the landlord deliberately did not notify the tenant's mortgagee.

[249] For conflicting views compare *Abbey National BS v Maybeech*, above, and *Billson v Residential Apartments Ltd* [1992] 1 A.C. 494 at 527–531 (Nicholls L.J.), which favour of relief, with *Official Custodian for Charities v Parway Estates Developments Ltd* [1985] Ch. 151 at 164–166; *Smith v Metropolitan City Properties Ltd* [1986] 1 E.G.L.R. 52 (a case where the *tenant* sought to re-open the forfeiture); and *Billson v Residential Apartments Ltd* [1992] 1 A.C. 494 at 516–519 (Browne-Wilkinson V.C.) 520–522 (Parker L.J.), which are against it. See [1992] C.L.J. 216 (S.B.).

[250] Under the Civil Procedure Rules, proceedings in both the High Court and the county court are commenced when the court issues a claim form at the request of the claimant: CPR r.7.2; above, para.18–016. The particulars of claim must either be contained in or served with the claim form or served on the defendant by the claimant within 14 days after service of the claim form: CPR r.7.4.

[251] CPR PD 55A para.2.4. For forms, see PD 55A para.1.4.

If the landlord fails to comply with these rules, any judgment that he obtains against the tenant would be liable to be set aside on the application of the under-lessee or mortgagee as irregular.[252] Even if no copy of the process is served on the under-lessee or mortgagee because the landlord is unaware of his interest, so that any judgment is perfectly regular, an application may be made to set the judgment aside, provided the applicant has a good claim to relief against forfeiture.[253] By contrast, where the landlord does serve a copy of the process on the holder of a derivative interest, who then fails to take any steps to intervene in the judgment,[254] the court will not set aside the judgment in the absence of special circumstances.[255] In the light of these developments, it is of course the normal practice for a mortgagee or under-lessee to inform the head lessor of his interest when it is granted.[256]

(e) The rights of third parties. The possibility that a tenant, sub-tenant or mortgagee may obtain relief after a lease has been forfeited for non-payment of rent[257] creates a potential hazard for any third party who acquires an interest in the land—typically under a new lease—during the period in which relief might be granted. Proceedings for relief which are commenced after forfeiture will be a pending land action[258] and should be protected by the appropriate registration.[259] The right to seek relief against forfeiture has itself been characterised as an equity, even if no proceedings are pending.[260] Where the landlord's title is unregistered, any bona fide purchaser of a legal estate without notice of the equity will take free of it.[261] But where title to the lease is registered,[262] and the registrar is satisfied that the lease has determined, he must close the registered title and cancel any notice in any other registered

18–050

---

[252] *Rexhaven Ltd v Nurse* (1995) 28 H.L.R. 241 at 255, 256. See too *Billson v Residential Apartments Ltd*, above, at 543. For the jurisdiction to set aside, see *Craig v Kanssen* [1943] K.B. 256 at 262; *Fleet Mortgage & Investment Co Ltd v Lower Maisonette 46 Eaton Place Ltd* [1972] 1 W.L.R. 765.

[253] *Rexhaven Ltd v Nurse*, above, at 256.

[254] Or, where relevant, to apply for relief within six months after execution of the judgment under CLPA 1852 s.210; or CCA 1984 s.138(9C); above, para.18–044.

[255] *Rexhaven Ltd v Nurse*, above (copy of proceedings served on mortgagee but inadvertently filed: application to set aside proceedings dismissed).

[256] Actions for negligence against solicitors and licensed conveyancers who have failed to inform the landlord of their client's interest are a regrettable commonplace.

[257] Whether by peaceable re-entry or by legal proceedings.

[258] i.e. any action or proceeding pending in court relating to land or any interest in or charge on land: LCA 1972 s.17(1); above, para.8–064. cf. *Selim Ltd v Bickenhall Engineering Ltd* [1981] 1 W.L.R. 1318 at 1322 (forfeiture proceedings would be a pending land action).

[259] Where title is registered, by entry of a notice: LRA 2002 ss.34(1), 87(1). Where title is unregistered, as a land charge: LCA 1972 s.5. A pending land action cannot take effect as an overriding interest where the lessor's title is registered: LRA 2002 s.87(3). However, where title is unregistered, a purchaser who has express notice of the proceedings will be bound by them even if no pending land action has been registered: LCA 1972 s.5(7).

[260] *Fuller v Judy Properties Ltd* (1991) 64 P. & C.R. 176 at 184. This result seems preferable to the suggestion that a purchaser's knowledge should merely be one factor relevant to the exercise of the court's discretion: cf. [1993] Conv. 297 (J. Martin).

[261] *Fuller v Judy Properties Ltd*, above; *Bank of Ireland Home Mortgages v South Lodge Developments* [1996] 1 E.G.L.R. 91 at 93.

[262] See above, para.7–013.

title relating to that estate.[263] Where the lease is not itself registered, but is noted against the landlord's title, and the registrar is satisfied that the lease has come to an end, he must cancel the notice or make an entry to such effect.[264] If relief is granted once the leasehold title has been closed, application should be made for the title to be restored to the register.[265] Once the register has been altered, any purchaser will take free of any rights that might still exist to claim relief.[266]

II. FORFEITURE FOR BREACH OF OTHER COVENANTS OR CONDITIONS

18–051 The general rule is that the right to re-enter for breach of any covenant or condition[267] other than for payment of rent is subject to:

(i) the landlord's obligation to serve a statutory notice (a "section 146 notice") requiring the tenant to remedy the breach (if possible)[268]; and

(ii) the tenant's right to relief.

It has been explained that relief against forfeiture for non-payment of rent must normally be sought before re-entry or within six months thereafter.[269] Relief in other cases must be sought while the landlord is "proceeding by action or otherwise" to forfeit the lease, though this restriction has been held not to preclude an application for relief after peaceable re-entry.[270] The procedure of serving a preliminary notice gives the tenant an opportunity to apply for relief if he is not otherwise able to comply with its requirements.[271]

18–052 Both the landlord's obligation to serve a section 146 notice and the tenant's right to apply for relief prevail over any contrary stipulation.[272] They cannot be defeated by framing the lease so that it continues only so long as the tenant

---

[263] LRR 2003 r.79(2); Ruoff & Roper, 25–038. The registrar has no discretion. He must amend the register once satisfied by the production of appropriate evidence: *Abbey National BS v Maybeech* [1985] Ch. 190 at 205.

[264] LRR 2003 r.87; Ruoff & Roper, 25–027.

[265] LRA 2002 Sch.4 para.2(1)(b); Ruoff & Roper, 25–044.

[266] *Bank of Ireland Home Mortgages v South Lodge Developments*, above, at 93 (where the title to the forfeited lease was cancelled less than six months after re-entry). This is because a purchaser of registered land takes it free of all interests other than overriding interests and entries on the register: LRA 2002 s.29(1).

[267] Even if involuntary, as on bankruptcy: *Halliard Property Co Ltd v Jack Segal Ltd* [1978] 1 W.L.R. 377; on which see further *Cadogan Estates Ltd v McMahon* [2001] 1 A.C. 378 at 385.

[268] LPA 1925 s.146(1); para.18–053 below.

[269] Above, para.18–037.

[270] Below, para.18–060.

[271] The notice "is intended to give to the person whose interest it is sought to forfeit the opportunity of considering his position before an action is brought against him": *Horsey Estate Ltd v Steiger* [1899] 2 Q.B. 79 at 91 per Lord Russell of Killowen C.J. Although there is a statutory requirement that the landlord must serve a notice on the tenant before he can enforce a right of re-entry, it is unnecessary that the tenant should be aware that re-entry has actually taken place: *Capital and City Holdings Ltd v Dean Warburg Ltd* (1988) 58 P. & C.R. 346 at 354.

[272] LPA 1925 s.146(12).

abstains from committing a breach of covenant[273] or by devices such as an undated surrender executed by the tenant as a guarantee against breach.[274] However, there is some concern that there may be other ways of determining a tenancy for breach without giving either the tenant or those with derivative interests in the lease an opportunity to seek relief against forfeiture. Of these, two deserve specific mention. First, in a case where a tenant, in breach of covenant, sub-let without the landlord's consent, the court granted a mandatory injunction requiring the sub-tenant (who was aware of the breach) to surrender the sub-lease on the grounds that there was a conspiracy between the tenant and the sub-tenant.[275] As there was nothing unusual about the facts, this outcome is surprising.[276] Secondly, the doctrine of repudiatory breach can apply where the tenant is in breach of covenant.[277] It has been held that where the tenant's repudiatory breach comprises a denial of title, it is necessary for the landlord to serve a statutory notice on the tenant.[278] On the basis that the statutory notice is intended to protect the tenant, there are strong policy grounds for requiring its service in all such cases.[279] However, the issue cannot yet be regarded as having been finally decided.

1. General rule

(a) Service of notice

(1) THE NOTICE. Before proceeding to enforce forfeiture either by action or re-entry, the landlord must serve the statutory notice on the tenant under the Law of Property Act 1925 s.146,[280] or else the forfeiture will be void.[281] The notice must:

    (i) specify the particular breach complained of[282]; and

    (ii) require the tenant to remedy the breach if it is capable of remedy; and

18–053

---

[273] LPA 1925 s.146(7).

[274] *Plymouth Corporation v Harvey* [1971] 1 W.L.R. 549. A power to give the tenant notice to quit in the event of a breach of covenant would presumably suffer the same fate: *Richard Clarke & Co Ltd v Widnall* [1976] 1 W.L.R. 845; cf. *Clays Lane Housing Corporation v Patrick* (1984) 17 H.L.R. 188.

[275] *Hemingway Securities Ltd v Dunraven Ltd* [1995] 1 E.G.L.R. 61. There is nothing to suggest that a notice under LPA 1925 s.146 was served. cf. *Old Grovebury Manor Farm Ltd v W. Seymour Plant Sales and Hire Ltd* [1979] 1 W.L.R. 1397 (assignment of lease in breach of covenant effective: landlord required to serve notice under LPA 1925 s.146(1) on assignee).

[276] See the telling criticisms of the case in [1995] Conv. 416 (P. Luxton and M. Wilkie).

[277] Below, para.18–106.

[278] *W. G. Clark (Properties) Ltd v Dupre Properties Ltd* [1992] Ch. 297 at 309; *Abidogun v Frolan Health Care Ltd* [2001] EWCA Civ 1821; [2002] L. & T.R. 16 at [48] and [52]; above, para.18–008.

[279] See *Abidogun v Frolan Health Care Ltd*, above, at [49].

[280] Replacing CA 1881 s.14; CA 1892 ss.2, 4.

[281] *Re Riggs* [1901] 2 K.B. 16.

[282] The notice must specify precisely what breach is alleged: *Akici v Butlin* [2005] EWCA Civ 1296; [2006] 1 W.L.R. 201 (notice which specified breach of covenant by assigning, subletting or parting with possession, but which failed to specify the proven breach by sharing possession, held to be invalid.)

(iii) require the tenant to make compensation in money for the breach
if the landlord requires such compensation.

A landlord who re-enters the premises without complying with these requirements is a trespasser and is liable in damages accordingly.[283] If there is no
breach of covenant or condition, any section 146 notice is of no effect.[284]

18–054   (2) TERMS OF THE NOTICE. Although the provision says that money compensation shall be required "in any case", it has been held that the landlord
need not ask for compensation if he does not want it.[285] It follows that if the
breach is incapable of remedy and no compensation is desired, a notice merely
specifying the breach will suffice.[286] Reasonable details of the breach must be
given, so that the tenant may know what is required of him.[287] A notice is not
invalidated merely because it includes more than the landlord is entitled to
require.[288]

18–055   The requirement that the notice must direct the tenant to remedy the breach
if it is capable of remedy has caused some difficulty. The authorities have not
always distinguished between three quite distinct issues:

(i) whether the covenant is one the breach of which is irremediable as
a matter of law;

(ii) whether the breach of covenant is irremediable on the particular
facts; and

(iii) if the breach is irremediable, whether the case is one where the
court should give relief against forfeiture.

The third issue is considered separately below.[289] There is only one covenant
the breach of which is irremediable as a matter of law, namely the covenant
not to assign or underlet without the landlord's consent[290]; and it must be
doubted whether the authority for this exception would now survive the
scrutiny of the Supreme Court.[291] In the case of any other covenant, whether

---

[283] *Cardigan Properties Ltd v Consolidated Property Investments Ltd* [1991] 1 E.G.L.R. 64.
[284] *Hagee (London) Ltd v Co-operative Insurance Society Ltd* (1991) 63 P. & C.R. 362 (no
breach of covenant where the act in question was carried out by an independent contractor without
instructions from or knowledge of the tenant).
[285] *Lock v Pearce* [1893] 2 Ch. 271.
[286] *Rugby School (Governors) v Tannahill* [1935] 1 K.B. 87.
[287] *Fletcher v Nokes* [1897] 1 Ch. 271; and see *Fox v Jolly* [1916] 1 A.C. 1; *Adagio Properties
Ltd v Ansari* [1998] 2 E.G.L.R. 69.
[288] *Blewett v Blewett* [1936] 2 All E.R. 188; *Silvester v Ostrowska* [1959] 1 W.L.R. 1060.
[289] Below, para.18–060.
[290] *Scala House & District Property Co Ltd v Forbes* [1974] Q.B. 575. The prediction that this
case would lead to the view that the breach of *any* negative covenant was in law incapable of
remedy (see (1973) 89 L.Q.R. 462 (P.V. Baker)) has not been fulfilled.
[291] "Were the point free of authority . . . I would be attracted to the view that a surrender or
assignment back could be a sufficient remedy, at least in most cases, for the purposes of section
146": see *Akici v Butlin*, above, at [66], per Neuberger L.J., where the Court of Appeal refused
to apply *Scala House* to a covenant against parting with, or sharing of, possession. For comment,
see P. F. Smith [2006] Conv. 382.

positive or negative, [292] it is a question of fact and not law whether the breach is remediable.[293] The issue in each case is whether compliance within a reasonable time with a section 146 notice coupled with payment of any appropriate monetary compensation would effectively remedy the harm which the landlord had suffered or was likely to suffer.[294] Because virtually all covenants are in principle remediable, a notice will in practice usually require that the breach be remedied "if it is capable of remedy", so that the landlord can proceed with his action for forfeiture if in fact the breach is not remedied within a reasonable time.[295]

Breaches of a positive covenant will usually be remediable, albeit out of time,[296] though not in all cases.[297] The extent to which breaches of negative covenants against an immoral or illegal user are remediable has been a source of considerable discussion. Normally such a breach of covenant will be irremediable.[298] Mere cessation of the user will not remedy the breach,[299] as the reputation or "stigma" that attaches to the premises does not terminate because the activity ceases even for a reasonable period.[300] In every case the issue must be one of fact. Thus use of premises for immoral purposes by a sub-tenant may not amount to an irremediable breach on the part of the tenant provided that he does not know of it[301] and that he takes prompt steps both to stop the use and to seek forfeiture of the sub-lease.[302]

18–056

(3) MODE OF SERVICE. The section 146 notice may be served under the general provisions governing all notices under the Act,[303] i.e. by a written notice being left at the tenant's last known place of abode or business, or being left on the demised premises.[304] It is sufficient service to despatch the written

18–057

---

[292] *Savva v Houssein* (1996) 73 P. & C.R. 150. In logic "a covenant not to do something, once broken, is broken for ever. As Lady Macbeth, referring to her breach of the sixth (negative) commandment, observed: 'what's done is done.' ": *Bass Holdings Ltd v Morton Music Ltd* [1988] Ch. 493 at 541, per Bingham L.J. However, in practice, the distinction between positive and negative obligations may not be easily drawn.

[293] *Savva v Houssein*, above, disapproving *Billson v Residential Apartments Ltd* (1990) 60 P. & C.R. 392 at 406, and holding that breach of a covenant not to put up signs or make alterations to the property without the landlord's consent was remediable.

[294] *Expert Clothing Service & Sales Ltd v Hillgate House Ltd* [1986] Ch. 340 at 358.

[295] *Glass v Kencakes Ltd* [1966] 1 Q.B. 611 at 629.

[296] *Expert Clothing Service & Sales Ltd v Hillgate House Ltd*, above, at 355.

[297] As where there has been a breach of the covenant to insure the premises which have already burned down: *Expert Clothing Service & Sales Ltd v Hillgate House Ltd*, above, at 355.

[298] Immoral user may not however constitute a breach of a covenant not to cause a nuisance to the neighbours: *Burfort Financial Investments Ltd v Chotard* [1976] 2 E.G.L.R. 53 (brothel in Soho).

[299] *Hoffmann v Fineberg* [1949] Ch. 245 at 257 (gambling); *Van Haarlam v Kasner* (1992) 64 P. & C.R. 214 at 223 (spying).

[300] See *Rugby School (Governors) v Tannahill* [1935] 1 K.B. 87; *Egerton v Esplanade Hotels London Ltd* [1947] 2 All E.R. 88; *Ropemaker Properties Ltd v Noonhaven Ltd* [1989] 2 E.G.L.R. 50. See *Expert Clothing Service & Sales Ltd v Hillgate House Ltd*, above, at 357.

[301] A tenant who deliberately shuts his eyes to the conduct will be taken to know of it: *British Petroleum Pension Trust v Behrendt* (1985) 52 P. & C.R. 117.

[302] *Glass v Kencakes Ltd* [1966] 1 Q.B. 611.

[303] LPA 1925, s.196.

[304] Such service will be good even though the landlord knows that the tenant is not in residence and has made arrangements for all documents to be received by an agent: *Van Haarlam v Kasner* (1992) 64 P. & C.R. 214 at 221.

notice to his last known place of abode or business by registered letter or recorded delivery[305] (but not ordinary post[306]), provided it is not returned as undelivered.[307] But if a repairing covenant is broken, the landlord must prove that the tenant[308] had knowledge of the service of the notice,[309] and service by registered post is only prima facie proof of this[310]; in other cases service by registered post or recorded delivery suffices by itself, and is deemed to have been made when in the ordinary course the letter would have been delivered.[311]

18–058   If there are several tenants, the section 146 notice must be served on all of them.[312] The definition of "lessee" for this purpose includes successors in title[313]; and where the lease has been assigned, even in breach of covenant, the notice must be served on the assignee.[314] But where a notice has been validly served on the tenant, there is no need to serve on a person who subsequently takes an assignment of the lease.[315] There is no need to serve a section 146 notice upon a sub-tenant or a mortgagee.[316] However, in proceedings for forfeiture of residential property,[317] the landlord's particulars of claim must give the name and address of any under-lessee or mortgagee whom he knows to be entitled to claim relief.[318]

18–059   *(b) Time for compliance.* The landlord must then allow the tenant a reasonable time in which to comply with the notice.[319] The Act does not define what is a reasonable time. The issue is one of fact in every case, having regard to the circumstances that actually exist.[320] The nature of the covenant broken and any work that has to be done to remedy it, and the effect of the harm suffered

---

[305] Recorded Delivery Service Act 1962 s.1.

[306] *Holwell Securities Ltd v Hughes* [1973] 1 W.L.R. 757.

[307] LPA 1925 s.196(4).

[308] Or a sub-tenant holding under a sub-lease nearly as long as the lease, or the person who last paid rent.

[309] L & TA 1927 s.18(2).

[310] L & TA 1927 s.18(2).

[311] LPA 1925 s.196(4).

[312] *Blewett v Blewett* [1936] 2 All E.R. 188.

[313] LPA 1925 s.146(5).

[314] *Old Grovebury Manor Farm Ltd v W. Seymour Plant Sales and Hire Ltd (No.2)* [1979] 1 W.LR. 1397. In *Fuller v Judy Properties Ltd* (1991) 64 P. & C.R. 176, a landlord failed to serve a s.146 notice on the assignee, peaceably re-entered and then served a further notice on the assignee. Remarkably, the Court of Appeal upheld the validity of the second notice. But query whether a landlord in possession can serve a valid s.146 notice: see *Fuller v Judy Properties Ltd*, above at 185; [1992] Conv. 343 (J. Martin).

[315] *Kanda v Church Commissioners for England* [1958] 1 Q.B. 323. See also below, para.19–133.

[316] *Egerton v Jones* [1939] 2 K.B. 702; *Church Commissioners for England v Ve-Ri-Best Manufacturing Co Ltd* [1957] 1 Q.B 238; *Smith v Spaul* [2002] EWCA Civ 1830; [2003] Q.B. 983.

[317] Above, para.18–049.

[318] CPR PD 55A para.2.4. Where the lease had been assigned after the service of the notice under LPA 1925 s.146, the particulars would of course have to be served on the assignee as defendant.

[319] LPA 1925 s.146(1).

[320] *Expert Clothing Service & Sales Ltd v Hillgate House Ltd* [1986] Ch. 340 at 356; *Cardigan Properties Ltd v Consolidated Property Investments Ltd* [1991] 1 E.G.L.R. 64 at 67.

by the landlord, are all factors to be taken into account.[321] Even where the breach cannot be remedied, whether in law or in fact (as where the provision is for forfeiture on the bankruptcy of the tenant), reasonable notice must be given so as to enable the tenant to consider his position.[322] In such cases two days' notice has been held inadequate[323] and 14 days' has sufficed.[324]

(c) Relief

(1) CIRCUMSTANCES IN WHICH RELIEF MAY BE SOUGHT. If the tenant fails to **18–060** comply with the s.146 notice within a reasonable time, the landlord may proceed to enforce the forfeiture. This he may do by peaceable re-entry or by commencing court proceedings. While the landlord "is proceeding by action or otherwise" to enforce the forfeiture, the tenant[325] may apply to the court for relief, either in any proceedings of the landlord enforcing the forfeiture or by bringing a separate action of his own.[326] It is now settled that for these purposes a landlord "is proceeding" at any time after he has served a section 146 notice[327] until he has actually entered into possession pursuant to a judgment of the court.[328] It is not enough that judgment for possession has been given, if the landlord has not retaken possession.[329] Furthermore, where he re-enters peaceably, he is still "proceeding"[330] so that the tenant may seek relief at least until lapse of time debars any such claim.[331] Even where judgment has been given against the tenant and the landlord has re-entered,

---

[321] *Expert Clothing Service & Sales Ltd v Hillgate House Ltd* [1986] Ch. 340 at 356; *Cardigan Properties Ltd v Consolidated Property Investments Ltd* [1991] 1 E.G.L.R. 64 at 67. In the case of repairing covenants, "times of up to a year or more have been considered reasonable": *Cardigan Properties Ltd v Consolidated Property Investments Ltd*, above, at 67, per Deputy Judge Cox, Q.C. Giving the tenant four working days in which to deal with nuisances committed by sub-tenants was not a reasonable time: *Courtney Lodge Management Ltd v Blake* [2004] EWCA Civ 975; [2005] 1 P. & C.R. 17. Where the tenant is intransigent, the landlord may take the view that whatever length of time is allowed the tenant will not remedy the breach: *Billson v Residential Apartments Ltd* [1992] 1 A.C. 494 at 508; *Shirayama Shokusan Co Ltd v Danovo Ltd* [2005] EWHC 2589 (Ch) at [51].

[322] *Horsey Estate Ltd v Steiger* [1899] 2 Q.B. 79 at 90.

[323] *Horsey Estate Ltd v Steiger*, above, at 92.

[324] *Civil Service Co-operative Society Ltd v McGrigor's Trustee* [1923] 2 Ch. 347; *Scala House & District Property Co Ltd v Forbes* [1974] Q.B. 575.

[325] Which includes a person deriving title under the tenant, such as an equitable assignee: see LPA 1925 s.146(5); *High Street Investments Ltd v Bellshore Property Investments Ltd* [1996] 2 E.G.L.R. 40; below, para.18–072. If the premises are held by joint tenants, the application must be made by all of them: *Fairclough & Sons Ltd v Berliner* [1931] 1 Ch. 60.

[326] LPA 1925 s.146(2). Prior to the advent of the Civil Procedure Rules, application could be by originating summons: *High Street Investments Ltd v Bellshore Property Investments Ltd*, above (not following on this point *Lock v Pearce* [1893] 2 Ch. 271). Presumably, if there is no substantial dispute of fact the Part 8 procedure (which has replaced originating summonses) is appropriate: CPR Pt 8 r.1.

[327] *Pakwood Transport Ltd v 15 Beauchamp Place Ltd* (1977) 36 P. & C.R. 112.

[328] *Quilter v Mapleson* (1882) 9 Q.B.D. 672; *Rogers v Rice* [1892] 2 Ch. 170; *Billson v Residential Apartments Ltd* [1992] 1 A.C. 494 at 540.

[329] See *West v Rogers* (1888) 4 T.L.R. 229; and see *Egerton v Jones* [1939] 2 K.B. 702.

[330] *Billson v Residential Apartments Ltd*, above: [1992] C.L.J. 216 (S.B.); [1992] Conv. 273 (P. F. Smith). This decision has had a considerable practical impact, and has made peaceable re-entry less attractive for landlords (though it is still widely used).

[331] *Billson v Residential Apartments Ltd*, above, at 543.

relief may be granted to the tenant if the judgment is set aside or successfully appealed.[332]

18–061   (2) FACTORS RELEVANT TO THE GRANTING OF RELIEF. The court may grant relief on such terms as it thinks fit,[333] and on grant of relief the effect is as if the lease had never been forfeited.[334] The statutory discretion is a very wide one and includes the power to order a sale of the lease as a condition of relief.[335] If the breach has been remedied, relief is nearly always granted in the absence of exceptional circumstances.[336] Relief is, however, always discretionary, and it may be refused if, e.g. the tenant's personal qualifications are of importance and he has proved to be an unsatisfactory tenant.[337] The discretion conferred by the section is a wide one and the courts have declined to lay down rigid rules for its exercise.[338] Amongst the factors that the court will consider are the conduct of the tenant,[339] the nature and gravity of the breach, and its relation to the value of the property forfeited.[340] The wilfulness of the breach is relevant to the exercise of discretion but does not of itself bar relief, even in the absence of exceptional circumstances.[341] While the court may give relief in a case of immoral user,[342] it will do so "only in the rarest and most exceptional circumstances".[343] Where the breach consists of a failure to pay a sum of money such as a service charge, the court will apply the same considerations as it does in cases of non-payment of rent, and will generally give relief on payment of the sums due.[344]

---

[332] *Billson v Residential Apartments Ltd*, above, at 540. In such a case, the court "will take into account any consequences of the original order and repossession and the delay of the tenant": *Billson v Residential Apartments Ltd*, above, per Lord Templeman.

[333] LPA 1925 s.146(2). For an example of an elaborate order made on different terms for different parties, see *Duke of Westminster v Swinton* [1948] 1 K.B. 524.

[334] *Dendy v Evans* [1910] 1 K.B. 263; *Driscoll v Church Commissioners for England* [1957] 1 Q.B. 330; *Cadogan v Dimovic* [1984] 1 W.L.R. 609 at 617.

[335] *Khar v Delbounty* (1998) 75 P. & C.R. 232 (sale ordered because tenants had a bad record for paying maintenance charges).

[336] *Cremin v Barjack Properties Ltd* [1985] 1 E.G.L.R. 30 at 31, 32, giving as examples of exceptional circumstances gross and wilful breaches, or where the tenant was unlikely to fulfil his obligations in future.

[337] *Bathurst (Earl) v Fine* [1974] 1 W.L.R. 905.

[338] *Hyman v Rose* [1912] A.C. 623 at 631; *Darlington BC v Denmark Chemists Ltd* [1993] 1 E.G.L.R. 62 at 64.

[339] *Shirayama Shokusan Co Ltd v Danovo Ltd* [2005] EWHC 2589 (Ch) at [55] (tenant acted "in deliberate disregard of the landlord's rights" and made serious and unsubstantiated allegations of misconduct against the landlord: relief refused).

[340] *Cremin v Barjack Properties Ltd*, above, at 31. If the advantage to the landlord of the forfeiture is out of proportion to any damage he has suffered, the court is likely to give relief: *Southern Depot Co Ltd v British Railways Board* [1990] 2 E.G.L.R. 39 at 44. The courts have not so far developed any principle of unjust enrichment by which a tenant may claim compensation in a case where relief against forfeiture has been refused: *Darlington BC v Denmark Chemists Ltd*, above, at 64, 65.

[341] *Southern Depot Co Ltd v British Railways Board*, above, at 43, 44; *Crown Estate Commissioners v Signet Group Plc* [1996] 2 E.G.L.R. 200 at 208–210.

[342] *Central Estates (Belgravia) Ltd v Woolgar (No.2)* [1972] 1 W.L.R. 1048.

[343] *Ropemaker Properties Ltd v Noonhaven Ltd* [1989] 2 E.G.L.R. 50 at 56, per Millett J. (night club used for prostitution: relief granted because activity had ceased, the tenant was in poor health and the lease was very valuable).

[344] *Khar v Delbounty* (1998) 75 P. & C.R. 232; see above, para.18–038.

(3) EFFECT OF RELIEF. Where relief is granted, the lease is retrospectively **18–062** reinstated together with any derivative interests, such as mortgages and under-leases.[345]

2. Exceptional cases. In general, the provisions of s.146 concerning the **18–063** landlord's notice and the tenant's right to apply for relief govern all covenants and conditions (other than those for payment of rent), as well as cases of forfeiture for denial of title.[346] However, there are exceptions to this general rule.

(a) Breach of repairing covenant. In the case of certain leases,[347] a section **18–064** 146 notice served in a case of disrepair must inform the tenant of his right to serve a counter-notice claiming the benefit of the Leasehold Property (Repairs) Act 1938.[348] If such a counter-notice is served, the landlord can take no steps to forfeit the lease by re-entry or action without the leave of the court.[349] This is explained later.[350]

(b) Non-payment of service charge. In relation to leases other than business **18–065** tenancies, tenancies of agricultural holdings or farm business tenancies, the Housing Act 1996 protects tenants from forfeiture for failure to pay service or administration charges. A landlord may not exercise his right to re-enter or forfeit the lease for failure to pay a service charge or administration charge unless:

(i) it has been finally determined, by (or on appeal from) a leasehold valuation tribunal or by a court or by an arbitral tribunal, that the amount of the charge is payable by the tenant; or

(ii) the tenant has admitted that it is so payable.[351]

This will be the case whether the obligation to pay the service charge takes the form of a free-standing covenant or is part of the obligation to pay rent.[352] In

---

[345] *Dendy v Evans* [1910] 1 K.B. 263. But note the court's wide powers to impose conditions on the grant of relief: cf. *Khar v Delbounty*, above.

[346] *W.G. Clark (Properties) Ltd v Dupre Properties Ltd* [1992] Ch. 297 at 308, not following *Warner v Sampson* [1958] 1 Q.B. 404 at 422; *BT Plc v Department of the Environment*, Unreported, October 9, 1996; *Abidogun v Frolan Health Care Ltd* [2001] EWCA Civ 1821; [2002] L. & T.R. 16 at [48] and [52].

[347] For these, see below, para.19–130.

[348] Leasehold Property (Repairs) Act 1938 s.1(1), (4). The notice must not be served on a mortgagee even where the mortgagee has taken possession, and a mortgagee who is wrongly served is not thereby entitled to serve a counter-notice: *Smith v Spaul* [2002] EWCA Civ 1830; [2003] Q.B. 983.

[349] Leasehold Property (Repairs) Act 1938 s.1(3), (5).

[350] Below, para.19–131.

[351] HA 1996 s.81(1), as amended by CLRA 2002 s.170. For the meaning of "service charge", see L & TA 1985 s.18, para.19–082. For the meaning of "administration charge", see CLRA 2002 Sch.11. The "arbitral tribunal" must be acting in proceedings pursuant to a post-dispute arbitration agreement: see further HA 1996 s.81(5)(b) and Arbitration Act 1996 Pt 1.

[352] Whether it is reserved as rent or is merely deemed payable as additional rent. cf. *Escalus Properties Ltd v Robinson* [1996] Q.B. 231 at 243, 244. In such cases, it will not be necessary to serve a s.146 notice as a result of LPA 1925 s.146(11).

cases of dispute, the tenant may have the service charge determined by a leasehold valuation tribunal.[353]

18–066   *(c) Long leases of dwellings.* The Commonhold and Leasehold Reform Act 2002 imposes restrictions on forfeiture of any "long lease of a dwelling".[354] First, a landlord may not exercise a right of re-entry or forfeiture for failure by a tenant to pay an amount consisting of rent, service charges or administration charges (or any combination thereof) unless the sum unpaid exceeds a pre-scribed sum, or consists of or includes an amount which has been payable for more than a prescribed period.[355] Secondly, a landlord may not serve a s.146 notice in respect of any breach by a tenant of a covenant or condition unless either the tenant has admitted the breach or it has been finally determined that the breach has occurred by a leasehold valuation tribunal, a court or an arbitral tribunal.[356]

18–067   *(d) Mining leases.* Section 146 has no application where there has been a breach of a covenant in a mining lease which provides for access to or inspection of the books, accounts, records, weighing machines or other things, or the mine and its workings itself.[357] Since the rent reserved by such a lease usually varies with the quantity of minerals mined, such a covenant is most important to the landlord. There is consequently no restriction upon the landlord forfeiting the lease without serving a notice, and no provision enabling the tenant to obtain relief.

18–068   *(e) Bankruptcy or execution.* Section 146 is in certain circumstances inap-plicable where there has been a breach of a condition against the bankruptcy of the tenant (which includes the winding-up of a corporation[358]) or the taking of the lease in execution.[359] This must be divided into two heads.

18–069   (1) SECTION 146 EXCLUDED. In five specified cases,[360] on breach of such a condition, s.146 has no application at all; the lease can thus be forfeited at

---

[353] L & TA 1985 s.27A, inserted by CLRA 2002 s.155(1).

[354] Defined in CLRA 2002 ss.76, 77 (in outline, terms certain exceeding 21 years and other tenancies of similar duration). Tenancies to which LTA 1954 Pt II applies, tenancies of agri-cultural holdings and farm business tenancies are expressly excluded from these provisions by CLRA 2002 ss.167(4), 169(4).

[355] CLRA 2002 s.167. The currently prescribed sum is £350, and the currently prescribed period is three years: see SI 2004/3086 (England), SI 2005/1352 (Wales). Default charges, that is administration charges levied in respect of the tenant's failure to pay the sum, are to be disregarded in calculating the sum unpaid: CLRA 2002 s.167(3).

[356] CLRA 2002 s.168. The leasehold valuation tribunal may determine whether the tenant is in breach on application by the landlord: CLRA 2002 s.168(4). The court may so determine in any proceedings: CLRA 2002 s.168(2)(c). The arbitral tribunal must be acting in proceedings pursuant to a post-dispute arbitration agreement: CLRA 2002 s.168(2)(c), and see fn.351 above.

[357] LPA 1925 s.146(8)(ii).

[358] LPA 1925 s.205(1)(i).

[359] LPA 1925 s.146(9), (10).

[360] LPA 1925 s.146(9). See *Hockley Engineering Co Ltd v V & P Midlands Ltd* [1993] 1 E.G.L.R. 76.

once without service of notice and without possibility of relief.[361] These cases are those where the lease is of:

(i) agricultural or pastoral land; or

(ii) mines or minerals; or

(iii) a public house or beershop; or

(iv) a furnished house; or

(v) property with respect to which the personal qualifications of the tenant are of importance for the preservation of the value or character of the property, or on the ground of neighbourhood to the landlord or to any person holding under him.[362]

(2) SECTION 146 APPLIES FOR ONE YEAR. In all other cases, on breach of such a condition, the protection of s.146 applies for one year from the bankruptcy[363] or taking in execution. If during that year the landlord wishes to forfeit the lease, he must serve a s.146 notice and the tenant can apply for relief.[364] The period of a year gives the trustee in bankruptcy time to fulfil his obligation to dispose of the bankrupt's assets whilst ensuring that the landlord is not indefinitely saddled with an insolvent tenant.[365] Once the year has elapsed, the tenant is no longer protected. The landlord can enforce the forfeiture of the lease (provided the breach has not been waived) without serving notice and the court has no power to grant relief.[366] Any inherent jurisdiction to do so is ousted by the express legislative provision.[367] **18–070**

In one case under this head, however, the provisions as to notice and relief apply without limit of time. If the tenant's lease is sold during the year, the protection of s.146 continues indefinitely.[368] This allows the trustee in bankruptcy or, in the case of execution, the sheriff, to dispose of the lease to a purchaser at a reasonable price. If the lease were liable to be forfeited after the year without service of the notice or the chance of relief, not only would its value be reduced but it would also be difficult to find a purchaser. **18–071**

---

[361] *Official Custodian for Charities v Parway Estates Developments Ltd* [1985] Ch. 151 at 165.

[362] In determining whether a case falls within this paragraph, the court adopts an objective approach. The importance must arise from the special qualities of the demised premises and be such as to justify the quick eviction of the bankrupt: *Hockley Engineering Co Ltd v V & P Midlands Ltd*, above, at 79.

[363] Probably the date of adjudication.

[364] LPA 1925 s.146(10); *Civil Service Co-operative Society Ltd v McGrigor's Trustees* [1923] 2 Ch. 347 at 355.

[365] *Official Custodian for Charities v Parway Estates Developments Ltd*, above, at 166.

[366] LPA 1925 s.146(10).

[367] *Official Custodian for Charities v Parway Estates Developments Ltd*, above, at 165.

[368] LPA 1925 s.146(10); *Civil Service Co-operative Society Ltd v McGrigor's Trustees*, above, at 355.

18–072   **3. Sub-tenants and mortgagees.** It has been explained that where a lease is forfeited, any derivative interests come to an end with it.[369] It is therefore provided that where the landlord "is proceeding, by action or otherwise"[370] to enforce a right of re-entry or forfeiture against the lessee, any sub-tenant or mortgagee[371] may seek relief against forfeiture in one of two ways, either in the landlord's action against the tenant or in proceedings specifically initiated by the sub-tenant or mortgagee for relief. In outline these two forms of relief, which are explained below, are:

> (i)   the grant of a wholly new lease to the claimant on such terms as the court thinks fit[372]; or

> (ii) the vesting of the tenant's current lease in the claimant.[373]

The circumstances in which the latter form of relief is available are more limited than for the former, but it may be more advantageous for the claimant. Where both forms of relief are available, the court has a discretion as to which it may grant.[374]

(a) Relief under s.146(4)

18–073   (1) WHEN RELIEF MAY BE GRANTED. Under s.146(4) of the Law of Property Act 1925,[375] a sub-tenant (including a mortgagee[376]) may apply for relief against the forfeiture of his landlord's lease on whatever ground that forfeiture is being enforced.[377] A sub-tenant has this right whether the head lease is being forfeited for non-payment of rent,[378] for one of the exceptional matters

---

[369] Above, para.18–041.

[370] For the meaning of this expression, see above, para.18–060.

[371] But not a squatter, at least where title to the lease is unregistered, or, where registered, when the rights of the lessee have not been barred. In such circumstances, an adverse possessor has no interest in the term and has no right to apply for relief: see *Tickner v Buzzacott* [1965] Ch. 426; above, para.18–045. For the limited circumstances in which a squatter may acquire title by adverse possession, see below, Ch.35.

[372] LPA 1925 s.146(4).

[373] LPA 1925 s.146(2).

[374] *Escalus Properties Ltd v Robinson* [1996] Q.B. 231 at 251; *Rexhaven Ltd v Nurse* (1995) 28 H.L.R. 241 at 249; below, para.18–076.

[375] As amended by LP(Am)A 1929 s.1, restoring the law as first enacted by CA 1892 s.4, and inadvertently altered by LPA 1925 s.146(8)–(10).

[376] If the mortgage is by sub-demise or legal charge: *Re Good's Lease* [1954] 1 W.L.R. 309; *Grand Junction Co Ltd v Bates* [1954] 2 Q.B. 160; *Chelsea Estates Investment Trust Co Ltd v Marche* [1955] Ch. 328 (vesting order in favour of mortgagee held not to extinguish right of redemption). An equitable chargee (such as the holder of a charging order over the lease) cannot apply under s.146(4) as he is not a person "claiming as under-lessee any estate or interest in the property comprised in the lease": *Bland v Ingram's Estate Ltd* [2001] Ch. 767.

[377] Before the CA 1892, a sub-tenant could not obtain relief if the tenant's lease was forfeited otherwise than for non-payment of rent: *Burt v Gray* [1891] 2 Q.B. 98.

[378] This jurisdiction is then as described, above, para.18–034: *Belgravia Insurance Co Ltd v Meah* [1964] 1 Q.B. 436.

mentioned above,[379] or for any other reason, even if the tenant himself cannot claim relief.[380] Thus even if a mining lease is forfeited for breach of a covenant for inspection, a sub-tenant can ask for relief although the tenant cannot.

(2) FORM OF RELIEF. An order under s.146(4) vests the whole or any part of **18–074** the demised premises in the sub-tenant "for the whole term of the lease or any less term" on such conditions as it thinks fit, subject to the qualification that the sub-tenant is in no case "entitled to require a lease to be granted to him for any longer term than he had under his original sub-lease".[381] Conditions may be imposed requiring, for example, the sub-tenant to pay a higher rent to the head landlord,[382] to covenant with the landlord to perform the covenants of the forfeited lease,[383] and to make good any subsisting breaches.[384]

(3) THE EFFECT OF RELIEF. When the court grants "relief" by making a **18–075** vesting order under s.146(4),[385] it does not reinstate the former sub-lease, but grants a wholly new lease to the sub-tenant.[386] This has a number of important consequences. First, the new lease need not be on the same terms as the lease that was held prior to the forfeiture of the head lease.[387] Secondly, the grant of the new lease is not retrospective, but takes effect from the date of the order.[388] Thirdly, where the sub-tenant had himself created derivative interests out of his sub-lease, as where he had granted an underlease, such interests are not automatically reinstated on the grant of the new lease under s.146(4).[389] Fourthly, in the period between the forfeiture of the lease[390] and the grant of

---

[379] See para 18–069 above.

[380] See *Imray v Oakshette* [1897] 2 Q.B. 218; *Official Custodian for Charities v Parway Estates Developments Ltd* [1985] Ch. 151 at 164 (where a lease could be forfeited on the insolvency of the tenant, a mortgagee was entitled to seek relief more than a year after the insolvency).

[381] LPA 1925 s.146(4); *Ewart v Fryer* [1901] 1 Ch. 499 at 515, per Romer L.J., obiter (in H.L. [1902] A.C. 187). The conflict within s.146(4) point seems to have been resolved in *Ellerman v Lillywhite* (1923) Unreported: see *Factors (Sundries) Ltd v Miller* [1952] 2 All E.R. 630 at 634. The term of the sub-lease may be extended by statutory security of tenure: *Cadogan v Dimovic* [1984] 1 W.L.R. 609.

[382] *Chatham Empire Theatre (1955) Ltd v Ultrans Ltd* [1961] 1 W.L.R. 817.

[383] *Gray v Bonsall* [1904] 1 K.B. 601 at 608.

[384] *Ewart v Fryer*, above; *Gray v Bonsall*, above.

[385] LPA 1925 s.146(4) does not use the word "relief" ; technically, the remedy is an order for a new lease.

[386] *Official Custodian for Charities v Mackey* [1985] Ch. 168 at 183; *Hammersmith and Fulham LBC v Top Shop Centres Ltd* [1990] Ch. 237 at 250. The fact that it is a new lease may now have a significant effect on the enforceability of covenants if the lease that had been forfeited was granted before 1996: see L & TCA 1995; below, para.20–085.

[387] *Hammersmith and Fulham LBC v Top Shop Centres Ltd*, above, at 250–253.

[388] *Cadogan v Dimovic* [1984] 1 W.L.R. 609 at 617; *Official Custodian for Charities v Mackey*, above; *Viscount Chelsea v Hutchinson* [1994] 2 E.G.L.R. 61 at 62.

[389] "Such reinstatement would require agreement between sub-lessees and the relevant lessor although a measure of reinstatement could be effected by s.146(4) vesting orders made on the application of the sub-lessees"; *Official Custodian for Charities v Mackey*, above, at 188, per Scott J.; *Hammersmith and Fulham LBC v Top Shop Centres Ltd*, above.

[390] i.e. when the landlord either peaceably re-enters or commences proceedings for forfeiture: above, para.18–013.

relief, the sub-tenant is regarded as a trespasser.[391] As such, he is liable to pay mesne profits to the landlord and not rent (which may cause considerable hardship where the lease was granted for a premium and a ground rent).[392] He cannot, however, be compelled to account to the landlord for any sums that he has received by way of rent from any under-lessee,[393] even though he had no right to receive such sums and may therefore be compelled to repay them to the under-lessees as money paid under a mistake of fact.[394]

18–076　　*(b) Relief under s.146(2).* Until the decision of the Court of Appeal in *Escalus Properties Ltd v Robinson*,[395] it had not been appreciated that a sub-tenant could seek relief against forfeiture under s.146(2) of the Law of Property Act 1925. The basis of the decision was that the sub-section provided that relief could be given to a "lessee" and that "lessee" was defined by the statute to include an under-lessee.[396] This conclusion was clearly prompted by the fact that relief under s.146(2) is retrospective to the time of the forfeiture[397] and not merely prospective, as it is when the court makes an order for a new lease under s.146(4).[398] However, the sub-tenant[399] cannot seek relief under s.146(2)—as he can under s.146(4)—where the head lease is forfeited for non-payment of rent or in those other situations where the provisions of s.146 are excluded.[400] The grant of relief under s.146(2) to a mortgagee is unlikely to cause any difficulty. It is settled that the mortgagee will take the lease by way of substituted security and therefore subject to the former tenant's equity of redemption.[401] By contrast, there is a risk that a sub-tenant might be unjustly enriched as against the landlord, for reasons already explained.[402] However, as the court can grant relief on such terms as it thinks fit,[403] the sub-tenant could be required to pay a capital sum for the lease in an appropriate case.

18–077　　*(c) Duty to notify.* The landlord's duty to give the names and addresses of any under-lessees or mortgagees of whom he knows in the particulars of claim

---

[391] *Official Custodian for Charities v Mackey*, above, at 181; *Pellicano v M.E.P.C. Plc* [1994] 1 E.G.L.R. 104 at 106, 107; *Viscount Chelsea v Hutchinson*, above.

[392] *Official Custodian for Charities v Mackey*, above, at 181; *Pellicano v M.E.P.C. Plc* [1994] 1 E.G.L.R. 104 at 106, 107; *Viscount Chelsea v Hutchinson*, above; *Escalus Properties Ltd v Dennis* [1996] Q.B. 231 at 242.

[393] *Official Custodian for Charities v Mackey (No.2)* [1985] 1 W.L.R. 1308. The sums received might not be the same as the mesne profits which the sub-tenant was liable to pay to the landlord: *Official Custodian for Charities v Mackey (No.2)*, above, at 1315.

[394] *Official Custodian for Charities v Mackey (No.2)*, above, at 1315.

[395] [1996] Q.B. 231.

[396] LPA 1925 s.205(1)(xxiii).

[397] Above, para.18–062.

[398] *Escalus Properties Ltd v Robinson*, above, at 242.

[399] Including a mortgagee.

[400] See LPA 1925 s.146(8), (9); above, paras 18–069 et seq.

[401] *Chelsea Estates Investment Trust Co Ltd v Marche* [1955] Ch. 328; *Official Custodian for Charities v Parway Estates Developments Ltd* [1985] Ch. 151 at 164; above, para.18–046.

[402] Above, para.18–047.

[403] LPA 1925 s.146(2). By contrast, in some (but not all) cases of non-payment of rent, the court has no power to impose terms on the grant of relief.

in any proceedings for forfeiture of residential property, and the consequences of any failure to do so, have already been explained.[404]

D. Forfeiture and Equitable Leases

Where the tenant holds under a mere agreement for a lease and breaches its **18–078** terms, the issue will not be whether the court should order the forfeiture of the lease or grant relief to the tenant, but whether it should order specific performance of the agreement in the tenant's favour.[405] The extent to which the principles applicable to the forfeiture of legal leases are relevant to the grant or otherwise of specific performance in such circumstances is in fact remarkably uncertain.[406]

1. The law prior to the Conveyancing Act 1881. Prior to the Convey- **18–079** ancing Act 1881, the position was clear. In the case of a legal lease, the court would grant relief against forfeiture for non-payment of rent but not for breach of any other covenant in the absence of factors justifying equitable intervention, such as fraud, accident or mistake.[407] Where there was a mere agreement for a lease and the tenant was in breach of its terms, specific performance would be refused if the breach would have led to the forfeiture of the lease had it been legal.[408] It followed therefore that where the lease would have contained a forfeiture clause had it been executed, specific performance would not normally be granted except in cases of non-payment of rent.[409] If the court was in doubt, it would decree specific performance retrospectively to the date of the contract, leaving the landlord to his remedy (if any) at law.[410] Where there would have been no forfeiture clause had the lease been executed, the tenant's conduct became relevant to the issue. Specific performance would generally be granted unless the breaches were gross and wilful and could not be compensated by an award of damages at law.[411]

2. The effect of the Conveyancing Act 1881. The present law governing **18–080** forfeiture of a lease for breaches of any covenant other than for payment of

---

[404] Above, para.18–049. See *Rexhaven Ltd v Nurse* (1995) 28 H.L.R. 241.

[405] cf. above, para.17–056. Although where the landlord has peaceably re-entered the issue could arise in trespass proceedings brought by the tenant (as in *Coatsworth v Johnson* (1886) 55 L.J.Q.B. 220), the outcome will depend on whether specific performance would have been granted.

[406] See (1987) 16 Anglo-American L.R. 160 (P. Sparkes); *Equity and Contemporary Legal Developments* (ed. S. Goldstein), 829 at 855 (C.H.).

[407] *Hill v Barclay* (1811) 18 Ves. 56; *Barrow v Isaacs & Son* [1891] 1 Q.B. 417 at 425; and see *Shiloh Spinners Ltd v Harding* [1973] A.C. 691 at 722; *Billson v Residential Apartments Ltd* [1992] 1 A.C. 494 at 512. The point was not uncontroversial: see *Equity and Contemporary Legal Developments*, above, at pp.844 et seq. (C.H.).

[408] *Hare v Burges* (1857) 5 W.R. 585; *Rankin v Lay* (1860) 2 De G.F. & J. 65 at 71.

[409] See e.g. *Gregory v Wilson* (1852) 9 Hare 683 (no specific performance where there were breaches of repairing and insurance covenants).

[410] *Parker v Taswell* (1858) 2 De G. & J. 559 at 573; *Lillie v Legh* (1858) 3 De G. & J. 204.

[411] *Gourlay v Duke of Somerset* (1812) 1 V. & B. 68 at 72; *Parker v Taswell*, above, at 573.

rent was first introduced by the Conveyancing Act 1881,[412] and has already been explained.[413] One effect of that legislation is that the court has power (which it previously lacked) to relieve against forfeiture in relation to any such covenant. In two cases decided shortly after the 1881 Act came into force, the Court of Appeal held that it was inapplicable as a matter of construction to an agreement for a lease, and refused specific performance.[414] The Act was then amended by extending the definition of a lease to include "an agreement for a lease where the lessee has become entitled to have his lease granted".[415] It has been assumed that this provision reversed those earlier decisions, so that agreements for leases are now subject to the provisions of s.146 of the Law of Property Act 1925 as much as are legal leases.[416] Although this seems correct in principle, the point cannot be regarded as finally settled.[417]

18–081 **3. Non-payment of rent.** In cases of non-payment of rent due under an agreement for a lease, a court of equity would normally have granted the tenant specific performance on payment of arrears and costs, because a court would have granted relief against forfeiture had the lease been legal.[418] This practice continued after the Judicature Act 1873.[419] As the jurisdiction of the High Court to decree specific performance is inherent and has not been curtailed, the law should in principle have remained unchanged, though some doubt has been cast upon this.[420] The county court has the same jurisdiction to grant specific performance as the High Court where the value of the property does not exceed the county court limit,[421] and so the same practice should apply there. In any event, the statutory provisions applicable in the county court to the forfeiture of a legal lease for non-payment of rent and the grant of relief in such cases,[422] apply equally to "an agreement for a lease where the lessee has become entitled to have his lease granted".[423] If these words have any meaning,[424] the relief may be given.

---

[412] s.14; re-enacted (with certain amendments) as LPA 1925 s.146.

[413] Above, para.18–051.

[414] *Coatsworth v Johnson* (1886) 55 L.J.Q.B. 220 (breach of husbandry covenant); *Swain v Ayres* (1888) 21 Q.B.D. 289 (breach of repairing covenant). In neither case would specific performance have been decreed prior to CA 1881.

[415] CA 1892 s.5; see now LPA 1925 s.146(5)(a).

[416] *Sport International Bussum BV v Inter-Footwear Ltd* [1984] 1 W.L.R. 777 at 789 (not considered on appeal to the HL: *Sport International Bussum BV v Inter-Footwear Ltd*, above).

[417] It has been suggested that the tenant never becomes entitled to have his lease granted (within LPA 1925 s.146(5)(a)) because of his breach of covenant: (1960) 24 Conv.(N.S.) 125 (P. H. Pettit). But if this is correct, the amendment made in 1892 had no effect.

[418] Above, para.18–079.

[419] See *Zimbler v Abrahams* [1903] 1 K.B. 577, CA.

[420] See *Sport International Bussum BV v Inter-Footwear Ltd*, above, at 790 (CA); criticised (1984) 100 L.Q.R. 369 at 372 (C.H.). The relevant authorities were neither cited nor considered.

[421] CCA 1984 s.23(d). The limit is £30,000.

[422] CCA 1984 ss.138, 139; above, paras 18–031, 18–037.

[423] CCA 1984 s.140.

[424] cf. LPA 1925 s.146(5)(a); above.

E. Reform

It will be apparent from the account that has been given that the law governing **18–082** the forfeiture of tenancies is both exceptionally complex and thoroughly unsatisfactory in its operation. The Law Commission has made recommendations for the replacement of forfeiture with a new statutory scheme providing for the termination of tenancies for tenant default.[425] The essentials of the Law Commission's scheme are as follows:

(i) The present law on forfeiture would be abolished.

(ii) In place of forfeiture, the landlord would be able to terminate a tenancy by taking "termination action" (making a termination claim to the court, or invoking a summary termination procedure) in the event of "tenant default",[426] comprising a breach by the tenant of a covenant or condition of the tenancy. There would be no need, with post-commencement tenancies, to reserve a right of re-entry in the tenancy agreement, although it would be possible for parties expressly to exclude exercise of the statutory termination right.[427]

(iii) The tenancy would continue in existence unless and until it terminates pursuant to a termination order of the court or it terminates pursuant to the summary termination procedure. Initiation of proceedings would not have the same effect on the tenancy as forfeiture currently has.

(iv) Before a landlord could take termination action, he would be required to serve a prescribed notice on the tenant, and holders of certain ("qualifying") derivative interests.[428] The notice would set out details of the tenant default, and would require the tenant to remedy the default if remedy was sought, setting a deadline for completion of any remedial action. Service of a notice would be necessary whatever the nature of the breach of covenant, and it

---

[425] See Law Commission, *Report on Termination of Tenancies for Tenant Default* (HMSO 2006), Law Com. No.303, which includes a draft Landlord and Tenant (Termination of Tenancies) Bill. Earlier Law Commission recommendations, which have now been superseded, were made in the Law Commission, *Report on Forfeiture of Tenancies* (HMSO 1985), Law Com. No.142 and the subsequent Termination of Tenancies Bill (1994) Law Com. No.221. Proposals in the 1985 report for a tenant's termination scheme (to enable tenants to terminate a lease on breach of covenant by a landlord) were not included in the 1994 Bill, and have not been since revived.

[426] Non-payment of rent would constitute tenant default after 21 days, unless the terms of the tenancy provide otherwise: Law Com. No.303 para.3.50.

[427] In the case of pre-commencement tenancies, a breach should not comprise tenant default unless the tenancy contained provision (express or implied) entitling the landlord to forfeit: Law Com. No.303 para.3.27. In the case of post-commencement tenancies, an explanatory statement should be given to the tenant explaining to the tenant what might happen in the event of tenant default: Law Com. No.303 para.3.38.

[428] Law Com. No.303 para.4.10. There is a limited dispensation power: Law Com. No.303 para.4.12.

would have to be effected within a defined period after the tenant default of which complaint was made.[429]

(v) The court would be entitled to make a range of orders once satisfied that a tenant default had occurred, and should make such order as it thinks would be appropriate and proportionate in the circumstances, taking account of a number of considerations set out in the statute.[430] The orders available would include[431]: a termination order (bringing the tenancy to an end on a specified date); a remedial order (requiring the tenant to take specified action to remedy the tenant default); an order for sale (requiring the tenancy to be sold and the proceeds distributed, first to pay costs and any sum owing to the landlord, secondly to pay any third party interests secured over the tenancy, and thirdly to pay any residue to the tenant); a transfer order (requiring transfer of the tenancy to the holder of a derivative interest); a new tenancy order (requiring the grant of a new tenancy of the premises to the holder of a derivative interest); and a joint tenancy adjustment order (providing that one of the current joint tenants should no longer be a tenant from a specified date).

(vi) The doctrine of waiver would be abolished.[432] However, in deciding what, if any, order to make, the court would be required to take account of the conduct of the parties in the course of the dispute.[433]

(vii) Peaceable re-entry would be abolished. However, as an alternative to making a termination claim, a landlord of non-residential premises would be entitled to use a summary termination procedure[434] where the tenant would have no realistic prospect of persuading a court not to make a termination order and there is no other reason why a trial of the claim should take place. It would be particularly useful where the premises have been abandoned by the tenant. Following service of a summary termination notice on the tenant and certain derivative interest holders, the tenancy would automatically terminate within one month. However, pending termination, the tenant and any interest holders may apply for an order from the court discharging the summary termination notice. Should the tenancy be terminated pursuant to this procedure, application may

---

[429] The "default period" within which notice would have to be served would be a period of six months beginning with the first day on which the landlord first knew the tenant default had occurred or any day on which the landlord knew that the tenant default was continuing to occur: Law Com. No.303 para.4.31.

[430] Law Com. No.303 paras 5.109 and 5.113.

[431] Law Com. No.303 Pt 5.

[432] Law Com. No.303 para.3.117.

[433] Law Com. No.303 paras 3.110, 5.116.

[434] Law Com. No.303 Part 7. The recommendations are set out at paras 7.109 to 7.114.

bc made for a post-termination order for a period of six months after the tenancy has been terminated, and the court may make any order that it thinks appropriate and proportionate, save that it may not retrospectively revive the terminated tenancy.

(viii) Special provision would be made in certain cases, dealing (inter alia) with those holding long residential leases,[435] liability for breach of repairing covenants,[436] and the effect of insolvency.[437]

This scheme would be a very considerable improvement on the present law and would remove most of the difficulties to which it has given rise.

Section 4. By Surrender

1. Effect of surrender. "If a tenant surrenders his lease to his immediate landlord, who accepts the surrender, the tenancy is absorbed by the landlord's reversion and is extinguished by operation of law."[438] Surrender is a consensual transaction between the landlord and the tenant, and therefore dependent for its effectiveness on the consent of both parties.[439] In this respect, it is quite different from determination of a tenancy by notice to quit, which is effective whether or not the recipient of the notice gives consent to it.[440] Surrender is a reflection of the principle that a person cannot at the same time be both landlord and tenant of the same premises.[441] The surrender must be to the immediate landlord; the transfer of the lease to a superior landlord does not work a surrender but operates merely as an assignment of the lease. Thus if L leases land to T for 99 years and T sub-leases it to S for 21 years, S's lease will be extinguished by surrender if he transfers it to T but not if he transfers it to L.

18–083

Where, before the surrender, the tenant has granted a sub-lease or created some other incumbrance, the landlord is bound by it for so long as it would have bound the tenant had the lease not been surrendered. Put another way, the sub-tenant holds a derivative title which cannot be prejudiced by the surrender of the head-lease.[442] To return to the above example, if T surrendered his head-lease to L before S's sub-lease expired, L would take subject to S's sub-

18–084

---

[435] Law Com. No.303 para.3.104.
[436] Law Com. No.303 para.5.132.
[437] Law Com. No.303 paras 3.87 and 3.88.
[438] *Barrett v Morgan* [2000] 2 A.C. 264 at 270, per Lord Millett.
[439] *Barrett v Morgan*, above at 270, per Lord Millett; *Kay v Lambeth LBC* [2006] UKHL 10; [2006] 2 A.C. 465 at [141]. Where there are joint tenants, all of them must join in the surrender: *Leek & Moorlands Building Society v Clark* [1952] 2 Q.B. 788.
[440] *Barrett v Morgan*, above, at 270.
[441] *Barrett v Morgan*, above, at 271, following *Rye v Rye* [1962] A.C. 496 at 513.
[442] *Barrett v Morgan*, above, at 272.

lease, for during the residue of the 99-year period L's title is derived from T and is subject to such other interests as T validly created before surrendering his lease to L.[443] However, this principle does not apply where the head-lease is terminated by notice to quit, in which case S's sub-lease determines contemporaneously with T's lease.[444] The sub-tenant's interest having been carved out of T's estate, it is subject to termination in accordance with the terms of T's lease.[445] It is irrelevant whether the notice to quit is served by L or by T, or whether there is collusion between L and T in order to bring about the termination of S's sub-lease.[446] It is not open to L and T to contract out of the rule that termination of T's lease by notice to quit has the effect of terminating S's sub-lease.[447]

Surrender discharges the parties (and their sureties) from all future obligations under the lease but not from liabilities already incurred.[448]

18–085   **2. Express surrender.** Surrender may be either express or by operation of law. For an express surrender, a deed is required by the Law of Property Act 1925,[449] even though the lease was created orally.

3. Surrender by operation of law

18–086   *(a) Act inconsistent with continuation of lease.* Surrender by operation of law requires some act by the parties that is inconsistent with the continuation of the lease, in circumstances such that it would be inequitable for them to rely on the fact that there has been no surrender by deed.[450] The matter is determined objectively, asking whether the parties have acted towards each

---

[443] Co.Litt. p.338a: "having regard to strangers . . . the estate surrendered hath in consideration of law a continuance"; *David v Sabin* [1893] 1 Ch. 523, explained in the sixth edition of this work at para.5–063; *Phipos v Callegari* (1910) 54 S.J. 635; *E.S. Schwab & Co Ltd v McCarthy* (1975) 31 P. & C.R. 196. However, where B has no estate in the land, e.g. B is a so-called *Bruton* tenant, C cannot have a derivative interest capable of surviving the termination of B's lease: see *Kay v Lambeth LBC*, above, at [143].

[444] *Pennell v Payne* [1995] Q.B. 192; [1995] Conv. 263 (P. Luxton and M. Wilkie).

[445] *Barrett v Morgan*, above, at 272; *Kay v Lambeth LBC*, above, at [142].

[446] *Barrett v Morgan*, above, at 274, explaining *Mellor v Watkins* (1874) L.R. 9 Q.B. 400 and overruling *Sparkes v Smart* [1990] 2 E.G.L.R. 245.

[447] *PW & Co v Milton Gate Investments Ltd* [2003] EWHC 1994 (Ch); [2004] Ch. 142. The general rule is that termination of a lease automatically terminates subsidiary estates, such as sub-leases. It is however subject to an exception where the termination of the head lease is by some consensual arrangement, such as surrender, not provided for in the head tenancy: ibid., at [72].

[448] *Torminster Properties Ltd v Green* [1983] 1 W.L.R. 676 (liability for increased rent not yet quantified).

[449] s.52.

[450] *Nickells v Atherstone* (1847) 10 Q.B. 944; *Foster v Robinson* [1951] 1 K.B. 149; *Proudreed Ltd v Microgen Holdings Plc* (1995) 72 P. & C.R. 388. However, there is no need for a separate enquiry into the equity of the matter; an unequivocal acceptance by the landlord that the tenant has given up possession will render it inequitable for the landlord to deny that the tenancy has been surrendered: *Artworld Financial Corporation v Safaryan* [2009] EWCA Civ 303; [2009] L. & T.R. 20 at [28]; *QFS Scaffolding Ltd v Sable* [2010] EWCA Civ 682; [2010] L. & T.R. 30 at [13].

other in a way which is inconsistent with the continuation of the tenancy.[451] Although the conduct of the parties must point unequivocally to the termination of the tenancy, their subjective intentions are irrelevant[452]: "Where both parties act on the basis that the tenancy has ended, the result will be that the tenancy has ended."[453] The basis of this doctrine is the law of estoppel,[454] which operates at the determination of a tenancy much as at the creation of one.[455] It is only the landlord and tenant and those deriving title under them who are bound by the estoppel. It does not bind third parties,[456] though it may affect them.[457] The burden of establishing surrender by operation of law lies on the party making the assertion.[458]

(b) Surrender and re-grant. Surrender by operation of law can occur in a **18–087** number of ways, as where the parties agree that the tenancy shall cease but the tenant shall in future occupy the property rent-free as a licensee,[459] or the landlord grants a lease to a third party with the agreement of the tenant.[460] However, such surrender normally occurs where the tenant accepts a new (and valid[461]) lease of the property from his immediate reversioner. This is so even if the new lease is granted for a shorter term than the original[462] or to take effect at a future date.[463] It is not always easy to distinguish between the grant of a new lease which amounts to a surrender and a mere variation of the terms

---

[451] This is "a high threshold which must be crossed if the tenant is to be held to have surrendered and the landlord is to be held to have accepted the surrender": *Bellcourt Estates Ltd v Adesina* [2005] EWCA Civ 208; [2005] 2 E.G.L.R. 33 at [30], per Peter Gibson L.J.; followed in *Artworld Financial Corporation v Safaryan*, above at [28]; *QFS Scaffolding Ltd v Sable*, above at [12].

[452] *Zionmor v Islington LBC* (1997) 30 H.L.R. 822 at 827; *Mattey Securities Ltd v Ervin* [1998] 2 E.G.L.R. 66 at 68.

[453] *QFS Scaffolding Ltd v Sable* [2010] EWCA Civ 682 at [14] per Morgan J.

[454] *Lyon v Reed* (1844) 13 M. & W. 285; *Wallis v Hands* [1893] 2 Ch. 75; *Foster v Robinson*, above; *Tarjomani v Panther Securities Ltd* (1982) 46 P. & C.R. 32 at 41; *Gibbs Mew Plc v Gemmell* [1999] 1 E.G.L.R. 43 at 45; *Ealing Family Housing Association Ltd v McKenzie* [2003] EWCA Civ 1602; [2004] H.L.R. 21 at [14]. However, "surrender by operation of law is commensurate with what is necessary to give validity to the transaction the surrenderer is estopped from disputing", and, in a particular case, the surrender may operate in relation to part of the property subject to the lease: *Allen v Rochdale B.C.* [2000] Ch. 221 at [24], per Morritt L.J. Where the reversion has been severed, there is some doubt as to whether surrender of part is effective without the consent of all the severed reversioners: *EDF Energy Networks (EPN) Plc v BOH Ltd* [2009] EWHC 3193; [2010] 2 P. & C.R. 3 at [67].

[455] Above, para.17–125.

[456] See, e.g. *Barclays Bank Ltd v Stasek* [1957] Ch. 28 (below, para.25–083). In that case the reversion had been mortgaged. The landlord granted the tenant a new lease which operated as between the landlord and tenant as a surrender by operation of law. The new lease was granted contrary to the terms of the mortgage. As between the mortgagee and the tenant, the new tenancy was ineffective and the original tenancy remained on foot.

[457] Surrender of the tenant's lease will therefore release any surety who had guaranteed performance of the covenants: *Proudreed Ltd v Microgen Holdings Plc* (1995) 72 P. & C.R. 388 at 389.

[458] *Artworld Financial Corporation v Safaryan*, above at [22].

[459] *Foster v Robinson* [1951] 1 K.B. 149; *Scrimgeour v Waller* [1981] 1 E.G.L.R. 68.

[460] *Metcalfe v Boyce* [1927] 1 K.B. 758.

[461] *Corporation of Canterbury v Cooper* (1908) 99 L.T. 612; 100 L.T. 597; *Rhyl UDC v Rhyl Amusements Ltd* [1959] 1 W.L.R. 465.

[462] *Dodd v Acklom* (1843) 6 Man. & G. 672.

[463] *Ive's Case* (1597) 5 Co. Rep. p.11a.

of the existing lease which does not.[464] There will be a surrender by operation of law:

> "if the arrangements made between the landlord and the tenant are such as can only be carried out so as to achieve the result which they have in mind if a new tenancy is in fact created."[465]

The issue is whether what the parties had in mind necessitated a new tenancy on different terms from the old one.[466] A lease has been held to have been surrendered by operation of law where either the length of the term has been increased[467] or the area of the holding has been extended.[468] There was no such surrender and re-grant however where:

  (i) an additional party was added to the lease[469];

  (ii) one rent was fixed for two parcels of land held under different leases on different terms[470];

  (iii) the rent was increased by agreement[471];

  (iv) rent was received from a third party (who was trading on the premises under the same name as the tenant had done) in the mistaken belief that he was the tenant[472]; or

  (v) a new landlord issued the tenant with a rent book containing terms that were inconsistent with the terms under which he held the property.[473]

18–088   *(c) Landlord accepts tenant's giving up possession.* A clear case of surrender by operation of law will arise where:

---

[464] "There must be something in the nature of an agreement and that agreement must amount to more than a mere variation of the terms of an existing tenancy": *Smirk v Lyndale Developments Ltd* [1975] Ch. 317 at 339, per Lawton L.J. For a discussion of whether, in the case of a periodic tenancy, the withdrawal of a notice to quit given by either party amounts to a surrender, see [1994] Conv. 437 (A. Dowling).

[465] *Jenkin R. Lewis & Son Ltd v Kerman* [1971] Ch. 477 at 496 per Russell L.J.

[466] *Take Harvest Ltd v Liu* [1993] A.C. 552 at 565. See, e.g. *Joseph v Joseph* [1967] Ch. 78 (new lease where the parties, rent and term were altered).

[467] *Baker v Merckel* [1960] 1 Q.B. 657; *Jenkin R. Lewis & Son Ltd v Kerman* [1971] Ch. 477 at 496. A landlord may of course grant a tenant a reversionary lease for a further term of years to take effect on the expiry of the existing term, and this does not operate as a surrender.

[468] *Jenkin R. Lewis & Son Ltd v Kerman*, above, at 496.

[469] *Trustees of Saunders dec'd v Ralph* [1993] 1 E.G.L.R. 1.

[470] *J.W. Childers Trustees v Anker* [1996] 1 E.G.L.R. 1.

[471] *Jenkin R. Lewis & Son Ltd v Kerman*, above; *Friends' Provident Life Office v British Railways Board* [1996] 1 All E.R. 336.

[472] *Mattey Securities Ltd v Ervin* [1998] 2 E.G.L.R. 66; *Unicomp Inc v Eurodis Electron Plc* [2004] EWHC 979; [2004] 2 P. & C.R. DG 15.

[473] *Smirk v Lyndale Developments Ltd* [1975] Ch. 317.

(a) the tenant gives up possession of the premises; and

(b) the landlord accepts it.

The landlord's acceptance estops him from asserting that the lease continues even though the tenant's act may be in breach of its terms.[474] His acceptance will not be inferred merely because, to protect his interest, he enters the premises and takes steps to secure them.[475] Abandonment of the premises by the tenant without more (even if rent is unpaid) is not a surrender, because the landlord may wish the tenant's liability to continue.[476] Nor is the delivery of the key of the premises to the landlord enough by itself.[477] Even if he accepts it, it must be shown that he did so with the intention of determining the tenancy[478] and not merely because he had no alternative, e.g. because the tenant has left the country.[479] The test is whether the landlord's conduct is so inconsistent with the continuance of the tenancy "that it can only be justified as lawful on the basis that the landlord has accepted the tenant's implied offer to give back possession and that he has taken possession of the premises beneficially for himself."[480] What is normally required to satisfy this test is evidence that the landlord entered into "profitable occupation",[481] in effect taking the premises over and treating them as his own,[482] typically by re-letting them.[483] Even if there is such a surrender, the tenant may remain liable in damages to the landlord, if the premises are re-let at a lower rent than the tenant was himself paying.[484]

Although giving up possession is the clearest indication by the tenant that **18–089** he no longer intends to be bound by the tenancy, conduct falling short of actually giving up possession may suffice.[485] However, the conduct on the part

---

[474] *Oastler v Henderson* (1877) 2 Q.B.D. 575.

[475] *Bird v Defonvielle* (1846) 2 Car. & K. 415 at 421; *McDougalls Catering Foods Ltd v BSE Trading Ltd* [1997] 2 E.G.L.R. 65 at 69. The onus lies on the tenant to prove that the landlord's conduct went beyond this: *Relvok Properties Ltd v Dixon* (1972) 25 P. & C.R. 1 at 5.

[476] *Preston BC v Fairclough* (1982) 8 H.L.R. 70; aliter if the absence was longer and a substantial sum of rent was owed: ibid. The statement of principle in the text was approved by the Court of Appeal in *Bellcourt Estates Ltd v Adesina* [2005] EWCA Civ 208; [2005] 2 E.G.L.R. 33 at [9].

[477] *Cannan v Hartley* (1850) 9 C.B. 634; *Oastler v Henderson*, above; *Proudreed Ltd v Microgen Holdings Plc* (1995) 72 P. & C.R. 388 at 393; *Laine v Cadwallader* (2000) 33 H.L.R. 36.

[478] *Bolnore Properties Ltd v Cobb* (1996) 75 P. & C.R. 127 (clear evidence of intention to surrender by tenant and acceptance by landlord pursuant to a written agreement).

[479] *Oastler v Henderson* (1877) 2 Q.B.D. 575.

[480] *Artworld Financial Corporation v Safaryan*, above, per H.H. Judge Marshall Q.C. at first instance, and approved by the Court of Appeal at [29].

[481] *Bird v Defonvielle*, above, at 421, per Erle J.

[482] *Artworld Financial Corporation v Safaryan*, above at [25] (trustee landlord allowed a beneficiary to occupy the premises for his own benefit, and not merely as caretaker, in place of the tenant.)

[483] *Hall v Burgess* (1826) 5 B. & C. 332. Merely advertising the premises does not suffice: *Oastler v Henderson*, above.

[484] *Gray v Owen* [1910] 1 K.B. 622.

[485] *Brent LBC v Sharma* (1992) 25 H.L.R. 257 at 260.

of both landlord and tenant must be unequivocal.[486] The court should consider the whole of the parties' conduct before the commencement of proceedings,[487] and where one party's conduct is contradictory it is necessary to evaluate the effect of their conduct as a whole.[488] The service and acceptance of a notice to quit which is invalid may furnish convincing evidence of the parties' intentions to treat the tenancy as at an end.[489] Where a residential tenant gives up her keys to the landlord,[490] takes up occupation elsewhere,[491] or assumes rental obligations in relation to other premises,[492] the landlord being aware of the circumstances, the court may find an implied surrender on the facts.[493] A contract by the tenant to purchase the reversion does not normally bring about a surrender,[494] though the terms of the contract may have this effect.[495]

Section 5. By Merger

18–090   **1. Effect of merger.** Merger is the converse of surrender. A surrender occurs where the landlord acquires the lease; merger occurs where the tenant acquires the reversion (or a third party acquires both lease and reversion). The underlying principle is the same in both: the lease is absorbed by the reversion and destroyed. As with surrender,[496] there may be a merger of part of the demised premises.[497]

18–091   **2. Requirements.** For merger to be effective, the lease and the reversion must be vested in the same person in the same right with no vested estate intervening. If he holds the lease and reversion in different capacities, e.g. if he holds the lease as his own, and the reversion as executor or administrator,

---

[486] *Brent LBC v Sharma*, above; *Bellcourt Estates Ltd v Adesina*, above at [10] (although tenant unequivocally intimated intention by abandoning premises, landlord's failure to submit demands for rent or service charges subsequently could not be said to be unequivocal).

[487] *Brent LBC v Sharma*, above at 259.

[488] *Artworld Financial Corporation v Safaryan*, above at [18].

[489] *Brent LBC v Sharma*, above; *Hackney LBC v Snowden* (2001) 33 H.L.R. 49 (ultimately decided on the basis that the parties could waive the statutory notice requirements of the Protection from Eviction Act 1977 s.5); *Ealing Family Housing Association Ltd v McKenzie* [2003] EWCA Civ 1602; [2004] H.L.R. 21.

[490] *Sanctuary Housing Association v Campbell* [1999] 1 W.L.R. 1279.

[491] *Sanctuary Housing Association v Campbell*, above (tenant re-housed by another landlord); *Ealing Family Housing Association Ltd v McKenzie*, above (tenant re-housed by same social landlord which had policy that no one should have two tenancies of different properties at the same time).

[492] *Ealing Family Housing Association Ltd v McKenzie*, above.

[493] "If both landlord and tenant are unequivocally treating a tenancy as at an end the law has no business to insist on its continuance": *Brent LBC v Sharma*, above, at 260, per Scott L.J.

[494] *Nightingale v Courtney* [1954] 1 Q.B. 399.

[495] See *Turner v Watts* (1928) 97 L.J.Q.B. 403 (interest payable on the balance of the price from the date of contract instead of rent: held to be a surrender). cf. Standard Conditions of Sale (5th edn, 2011), condition 5.2. which obviates this problem.

[496] See fn. 454 above.

[497] *EDF Energy Networks (EPN) Plc v BOH Ltd* [2011] EWCA Civ 19; [2011] L. & T.R. 15.

there is no merger.[498] There was formerly a difference between merger at common law and in equity.[499] At law merger was automatic, whereas in equity merger was a matter of intention. Merger did not occur in equity unless it was intended by the person who acquired the two estates,[500] and there was a presumption against merger if it was against that person's interest.[501] However, "the equitable principles now prevail over the principles applicable at law",[501a] as statute provides that "there is no merger by operation of law only of any estate the beneficial interest in which would not be deemed to be merged or extinguished in equity."[502] It follows that there is no merger either at law or in equity if it is intended that there shall be none.[503] The position of a sub-tenant where the head lease has been surrendered or has become merged is discussed below.[504]

Section 6. By Enlargement

1. The power. Under certain conditions, not often encountered in practice, **18–092** a lease may be enlarged into a fee simple by the tenant executing a deed of enlargement. Under the Law of Property Act 1925[505] this can be done only if:

(i) there is no less than 200 years of the lease unexpired; and

(ii) the lease was originally granted for at least 300 years; and

(iii) no trust or right of redemption[506] exists in favour of the reversioner; and

(iv) the lease is not liable to be determined by re entry for condition broken; and

(v) no rent of any money value is payable. A rent of "one silver penny if lawfully demanded" is rent of no money value,[507] but a rent of three shillings is not.[508] A rent in such a lease which does not

---

[498] *Chambers v Kingham* (1878) 10 Ch D 743.
[499] For a fuller account, see the 5th edition of this work at p.686.
[500] See *Capital and Counties Bank Ltd v Rhodes* [1903] 1 Ch. 631.
[501] *Ingle v Vaughan Jenkins* [1900] 2 Ch. 368.
[501a] *EDF Energy Networks (EPN) Plc v BOH Ltd*, above at [40] per Rimer L.J.
[502] LPA 1925 s.185. The law was first amended by the Judicature Act 1873, s.25(4).
[503] *EDF Energy Networks (EPN) Plc v BOH Ltd* above.
[504] Below, para.20–073.
[505] s.153.
[506] This excludes mortgages: below, paras 24–014 et seq.
[507] *Re Chapman and Hobbs* (1885) 29 Ch D 1007.
[508] *Re Smith and Stott* (1883) 29 Ch D 1009. Similarly, it seems, one shilling a year: see *Blaiberg v Keeves* [1906] 2 Ch. 175.

exceed one pound per annum and which has not been paid for a continuous period of 20 years is deemed to have ceased to be payable[509] and can no longer be recovered.[510]

18–093   For a sub-lease to be capable of enlargement under the section, it must, in addition, be derived out of a lease which is itself capable of enlargement.[511] A tenant of a lease that may be enlarged in this way may acquire an easement against his landlord by prescription,[512] contrary to the normal rule.[513]

18–094   **2. The resulting fee.** A fee simple acquired by enlargement is subject to all the same covenants, provisions and obligations as would have applied to the lease had it not been enlarged.[514] The lessor's reversion, however, presumably disappears, for the existence of a fee simple absolute in possession excludes the possibility of any estate in reversion.

18–095   **3. Effect of enlargement.** This statutory power has been little used, and its possibilities have not yet been worked out. Of these, the one that has been most canvassed is that the power may provide a means of making positive covenants run with freehold land.[515] In principle, if long leases followed by enlargements can be deliberately used as conveyancing devices to bring about such results, the boundaries between freehold and leasehold principles may be liable to break down in important respects. However, there is little evidence of their use for such purposes.[516]

Section 7. By Disclaimer

18–096   **1. The term.** The term *disclaimer* is sometimes used as meaning repudiation of the tenancy in cases where the tenant denies the landlord's title. This type of disclaimer, which can bring about the termination of a lease, has already been explained under the heading of forfeiture.[517]

---

[509] LPA 1925 s.153(4).
[510] LPA 1925 s.153(5).
[511] LPA 1925 s.153(2).
[512] *Bosomworth v Faber* (1992) 69 P. & C.R. 288 at 293; below, para.28–050.
[513] Below, para.28–054.
[514] LPA 1925 s.153(8).
[515] See further, below, para.32–023. For other possibilities, see the fifth edition of this work at p.688 and (1958) 22 Conv.(N.S.) 101 (T. P. D. Taylor).
[516] If commonhold were to become widely used, it may be that the vestigial relevance of enlargement as a means of enforcement of positive covenants would disappear entirely: but see para.33–001 below.
[517] Above, para.18–007. It may be more accurately characterised as an example of termination for breach.

2. Statute. A right to end a lease by disclaimer sometimes arises by statute. **18–097**
Thus tenants whose premises were rendered unfit by war damage were given
a statutory power to disclaim their tenancies; the effect of a valid disclaimer
was the same as if there had been a surrender.[518] Similar rights were given
during war-time to tenants of premises which had been requisitioned.[519]

3. Insolvency. There is a rather different form of disclaimer under the **18–098**
Insolvency Act 1986.[520] This Act authorises a liquidator of a company or a
trustee in bankruptcy to disclaim onerous property belonging to the company
or the bankrupt which has become vested in the trustee under its provisions.
Leaseholds are often onerous. This may be because they are near to expiry and
subject to liabilities, e.g. to repair, or, as is now commonly the case, because
the rental liability in respect of the premises makes the lease uneconomic.[521]
There is no longer any requirement that disclaimer can be made only with the
leave of the court.[522]

Disclaimer, if properly made, brings to an end the rights and liabilities in **18–099**
the lease of the company or of the bankrupt and his trustee,[523] thereby
determining the lease and accelerating the landlord's reversion.[524] It does not,
however, affect the rights or liabilities of any third party except in so far as it
is necessary to release from any liability the company or the bankrupt and his
trustee.[525] Notwithstanding the determination of the lease, the effect of the
statute is to deem the rights and liabilities of third parties to remain as if the
lease had continued.[526] The court may make a vesting order in favour of any
person interested in the property,[527] e.g. a mortgagee. In such a case, there is
a re-creation of the determined lease by statute.[528] If no vesting order is made
and the landlord chooses to re-enter the premises, he will thereby determine
the liability of both the tenant and anyone else to perform the obligations

---

[518] Landlord and Tenant (War Damage) Acts 1939 and 1941.

[519] Landlord and Tenant (Requisitioned Land) Acts 1942 and 1944.

[520] s.178 (liquidator of a company); s.315 (trustee in bankruptcy). For the meaning of disclaimer in this context see *Allied Dunbar Assurance Plc v Fowle* [1994] 1 E.G.L.R. 122 at 126.

[521] This has been the effect of many upwards-only rent review clauses: see, e.g. *Re Park Air Services Plc* [2000] 2 A.C. 172. For rent review clauses, see below, para.19–065.

[522] *Re Hans Place Ltd* [1992] B.C.C. 737. Prior to the Act leave was required in the case of company insolvency: Companies Act 1948, s.323; and in some but not all cases of bankruptcy: Bankruptcy Act 1914 s.54(3); Bankruptcy Rules 1952 r.278.

[523] IA 1986 ss.178(4), 315(3).

[524] *Hindcastle Ltd v Barbara Attenborough Associates Ltd* [1997] A.C. 70.

[525] IA 1986 ss.178(4); 315(3). It should be noted that a trustee in bankruptcy who disclaims a lease is not thereby precluded from claiming any surplus realised on its disposal. The matter then lies in the court's discretion under IA 1986 s.320, below: see *Lee v Lee* [1998] 1 F.L.R. 1018; [1998] Fam. Law 312 (S. Cretney).

[526] *Hindcastle Ltd v Barbara Attenborough Associates Ltd*, above, at 88.

[527] IA 1986 ss.181, 320. The disclaimer of a lease does not take effect unless a copy of it has been served on any person claiming as underlessee or mortgagee of the company or bankrupt, and either no application or no successful application is made by such person for a vesting order: IA 1986, ss.179, 317. For restrictions on the power to make vesting orders see IA 1986 ss.182, 321.

[528] *Hindcastle Ltd v Barbara Attenborough Associates Ltd*, above, at 89.

under the lease thereafter.[529] Any person sustaining loss or damage in consequence of the operation of disclaimer is deemed to be a creditor and may prove for his loss in the winding up or bankruptcy.[530]

18–100   The effect of these provisions, as explained by the House of Lords in *Hindcastle Ltd v Barbara Attenborough Associates Ltd*,[531] is as follows.

(a) Where a surety has guaranteed the performance of the obligations under the lease, disclaimer of the term does not release him from further liability.[532] For nearly a century prior to *Hindcastle*, the contrary rule had applied,[533] thereby depriving the landlord of the benefit of the surety's guarantee in one of the situations in which it was most likely to be required.[534]

(b) Where it is an assignee of the lease who becomes insolvent and the lease is disclaimed, the assignee is released from further liability,[535] but his surety is not.[536] Furthermore, where the lease was granted prior to 1996, the original tenant remains liable on all the covenants in the lease[537] as does any surety of his.[538] Where the lease was granted after 1995, the tenant who assigned the lease may in certain circumstances be liable to the landlord under an authorised guarantee agreement.[539] In either eventuality, the tenant who is called upon to meet the liability may be able to call for an overriding lease of the premises.[540]

---

[529] *Hindcastle Ltd v Barbara Attenborough Associates Ltd*, above, at 89. However, there must be a taking of possession for this to occur: see *Cromwell Developments Ltd v Godfrey* [1998] 2 E.G.L.R. 62. Serving notice on the executors of a deceased tenant requiring them to take a new lease does not amount to a taking of possession, and the old lease will subsist unless and until the executors accept the grant of the new lease: *Basch v Stekel* [2001] L. & T.R. 1.

[530] IA 1986 ss.178(6), 315(5). For the principles upon which a landlord's loss is determined on such a disclaimer, see *Re Park Air Services Plc* [2000] 2 A.C. 172.

[531] [1997] A.C. 70.

[532] *Hindcastle Ltd v Barbara Attenborough Associates Ltd*, above, at 89, overruling *Stacey v Hill* [1901] 1 Q.B. 660.

[533] *Stacey v Hill*, above.

[534] The rule was much criticised: see *W.H. Smith Ltd v Wyndham Investments Ltd* (1994) 70 P. & C.R. 21 at 27. It was not followed in Ireland: see *Maurice Tempany v Royal Liver Trustees Ltd* [1984] B.C.L.C. 568.

[535] *M.E.P.C. Ltd v Scottish Amicable Life Assurance Society* [1993] 2 E.G.L.R. 93. The liquidator or trustee in bankruptcy cannot disclaim liability under the licence to assign unless he also disclaims the lease: ibid.

[536] *Murphy v Sawyer-Hoare* [1993] 2 E.G.L.R. 61, which held to the contrary on the authority of *Stacey v Hill*, above, is no longer good law.

[537] *Hill v East and West India Dock Co* (1884) 9 App.Cas. 448; *Warnford Investments Ltd v Duckworth* [1979] Ch. 127. See too *W.H. Smith Ltd v Wyndham Investments Ltd*, above; and below, para.20–011.

[538] *Hill v East and West India Dock Co*, above; *Hindcastle Ltd v Barbara Attenborough Associates Ltd*, above.

[539] L & TCA 1995 s.16; this is explained below, para.20–089. A former tenant who is a party to an authorised guarantee agreement may remain liable to the landlord following disclaimer of the lease as a result of IA 1986 ss.178(4) and 315(3), although it will depend upon a construction of the agreement: *Shaw v Doleman* [2009] EWCA Civ 279; [2009] 2 P. & C.R. 12.

[540] L & TCA 1995 s.19; below, para.20–025.

(c) Where the lessee is a company which is struck off the register of companies, its property will vest in the Crown as *bona vacantia*.[541] If the Crown disclaims the lease,[542] but the company is then restored to the register, the effect is as if the property had never vested in the Crown at all.[543]

(d) Any sub-lease remains in being[544] and the landlord may distrain on the sub-tenant for rent due under the head lease or re-enter for breach of covenant.[545] Furthermore, if the landlord forfeits the head lease, the sub-tenant may seek relief against forfeiture.[546] However, although the sub-lease subsists, the covenants in the sub-lease are no longer directly enforceable by or against the sub-tenant.[547] It is for that reason that it is provided that if a sub-tenant is not willing to take an order vesting the lease in him,[548] he is thereafter excluded from any interest in the property.[549]

(e) The "notional reversion" of a disclaimed lease may be assigned, with the benefit of such covenants as are annexed to it, as if the lease had not been disclaimed, and the assignee of the reversion may then enforce those covenants.[550]

Section 8. By Frustration

1. General rule. The doctrine of frustration is part of the law of contract, **18–101** and may sometimes be invoked to discharge a party from contractual liability when some unforeseen event has made performance impracticable. As a general rule the doctrine does not apply to executed leases, for a lease creates an estate which vests in the tenant, and cannot be divested except in one or

[541] Companies Act 2006 s.1012, replacing CA 1985 s.654.

[542] CA 2006 s.1013, replacing CA 1985 s.656.

[543] Prior to the decision in *Hindcastle Ltd v Barbara Attenborough Associates Ltd*, above, the liability of any surety would have determined when the company was struck off the register, only to be revived (with retrospective effect from the moment of the company's dissolution) when the company was restored to the register: *Allied Dunbar Assurance Plc v Fowle* [1994] 1 E.G.L.R. 122. The surety's liability would not now determine with the insolvency of the company.

[544] *Re Thompson & Cottrell's Contract* [1943] Ch. 97. See generally *Hindcastle Ltd v Barbara Attenborough Associates Ltd*, above, at 89.

[545] *Ex p. Walton* (1881) 17 Ch D 746; but note pending abolition of distress, below, paras 19–076 et seq.

[546] *Barclays Bank Plc v Prudential Assurance Co Ltd* [1998] 1 E.G.L.R. 44 (relief granted to mortgagee of the head lease, where, after disclaimer, that lease had been forfeited for non-payment of rent and service charge).

[547] *Re A.E. Realisations (1985) Ltd* [1988] 1 W.L.R. 200 at 211.

[548] An application may be made by the landlord to seek such an order: IA 1986 ss.181, 320.

[549] IA 1986 ss.182(4), 321(4); *Re A.E. Realisations Ltd*, above, at 211. Where an underlessee declines to take a vesting order, the freeholder is not entitled to have the head lease vested in him in order to keep the underlease alive: *Sterling Estates v Pickard (UK) Ltd* [1997] 2 E.G.L.R. 33.

[550] *Scottish Widows Plc v Tripipatkul* [2003] EWHC 1874; [2004] 1 P. & C.R. 29 (action by assignee of reversion on surety covenant).

other of the ways enumerated above. In other words, the landlord's principal obligation is executed when he grants the lease and puts the tenant into possession. Normally the doctrine of frustration can apply only to obligations which are executory, and which can therefore be rendered futile or impossible by later events. However, consistent with their emphasis upon the contractual character of the relationship of landlord and tenant, the courts have now accepted that there may occasionally be frustration even of the lease itself on the same basis as frustration of a contract.[551]

18–102   **2. Leases.** The question whether the doctrine of frustration could ever apply to a lease itself, as distinct from the covenants contained in it, was resolved by the House of Lords in 1980 after a period of doubt.[552] The House held that in principle a lease was capable of being frustrated, though cases are likely to be exceedingly rare.[553] On the facts, the House rejected the tenant's plea of frustration and held that the lease continued in existence, and the rent remained payable, where a local authority had closed the only road giving access to the property (a warehouse), thereby rendering it useless for a period likely to last for 20 months in the middle of a 10-year lease. The question was treated as one of degree, so that a longer interruption might have produced frustration.[554] The rival arguments were fully debated, the majority upholding the view that a lease might be frustrated not only by physical catastrophe ("if, for example, some vast convulsion of nature swallowed up the property altogether, or buried it in the depths of the sea"[555]) but also by supervening events so far beyond the contemplation of the parties that it would be unjust to enforce the lease.[556] The primary argument to the contrary is that under settled principles of land law the risk of accidents passes to the purchaser, and that this should apply just as much where he takes a lease (especially if it is a long one) as where he buys the fee simple outright. It is assumed that the effect of frustration of the lease would be the immediate termination of the tenant's estate, and that the land would revert to the landlord free of the

[551] *National Carriers Ltd v Panalpina (Northern) Ltd* [1981] A.C. 675. For the contractual nature of leases, see above, para.17–006. For the historical background to frustration of leases, see (1989) 10 J.Leg.Hist. 90 (J.Price).

[552] *National Carriers Ltd v Panalpina (Northern) Ltd* [1981] A.C. 675. There were conflicting opinions in *Cricklewood Property and Investment Trust Ltd v Leighton's Investment Trust Ltd* [1945] A.C. 221. See further (2001) 52 N.I.L.Q. 82 (W.Barr).

[553] *National Carriers Ltd v Panalpina (Northern) Ltd*, above, holding that it was a matter of "hardly ever" rather than "never".

[554] "Long term speculations and investments are in general less easily frustrated than short term adventures", *National Carriers Ltd v Panalpina (Northern) Ltd*, above, at 691, per Lord Hailsham of St Marylebone, making the point that the longer the lease, the more difficult it would be to establish frustration. See also, e.g. *Prince v Robinson* (1998) 31 H.L.R. 89 at 93 (the doctrine of frustration applied to leases "only in wholly exceptional circumstances", and the court was extremely doubtful that it could apply to a weekly or other periodic tenancy of a flat where fire damage could be repaired in a matter of weeks).

[555] *Cricklewood Property and Investment Trust Ltd v Leighton's Investment Trust Ltd*, above, at 229, per Lord Simon L.C.; and see at 239–241, per Lord Wright.

[556] The doctrine is "an expedient to escape from injustice where such would result from enforcement of a contract in its literal terms after a significant change in circumstances": *National Carriers Ltd v Panalpina (Northern) Ltd*, above, at 701, per Lord Simon.

lease.[557] Termination of an estate, unlike the discharge of a contract, may affect the rights of third parties, such as sub-tenants or mortgagees, whose interests depend upon the lease.[558] Various problems of this kind await solution.[559] Nor is it clear whether frustration depends upon some implied term or upon the fact that the whole basis of the transaction between landlord and tenant has been altered beyond recognition.[560]

3. Destruction of subject-matter. If there is a lease of land and buildings, **18–103** the destruction of the buildings does not affect the continuance of the lease, so that the tenant remains entitled to possession of the land and any buildings that may subsequently be erected on it.[561] But the complete destruction of the whole of the demised premises, as where an upper-floor flat is destroyed by fire, or where the demised land disappears beneath the sea, would raise problems of a different kind.[562] The correct answer may be that the tenancy would come to an end, and with it liability on the covenants,[563] for there would no longer be any physical entity which the tenant could hold of his landlord for any term,[564] and there can hardly be tenure without a tenement.[565] In the case of a flat destroyed by fire it might be contended that the tenancy (and with it liability on the covenants) would endure in the vacant air space[566] and attach to the corresponding flat in any building erected to replace the building destroyed. This would be an equitable solution if the landlord had covenanted to reinstate the building in the case of damage by fire, particularly if the tenant had paid a premium for the lease; but the theoretical difficulties may well be insuperable. Now that the House of Lords has opened the door to the doctrine of frustration, the courts may be able to use it to escape from such problems. It may be noted that a contract to purchase a share in a leasehold block of flats then under construction was held to be frustrated when the building was destroyed by a landslip.[567]

4. Covenants. In accordance with the application of frustration to execu- **18–104** tory obligations, a continuing or future obligation which is imposed by a covenant in a lease may be suspended, or even discharged, by impossibility of

---

[557] See Woodfall, 17.284.

[558] *Cricklewood Property and Investment Trust Ltd v Leighton's Investment Trust Ltd*, above, at 245, per Lord Goddard; similarly Lord Russell of Killowen at 234.

[559] The court has powers to adjust the rights of the parties, within limits, under the Law Reform (Frustrated Contracts) Act 1943.

[560] Both theories are favoured in *National Carriers Ltd v Panalpina (Northern) Ltd*, above.

[561] *Simper v Coombs* [1948] 1 All E.R. 306; *Denman v Brise* [1949] 1 K.B. 22.

[562] Suggestions in Rolle's and Bacon's *Abridgements* that rent abates in case of partial loss or destruction seem to be based on no authority: see Foa L. & T. 111, fn.(g).

[563] See *National Carriers Ltd v Panalpina (Northern) Ltd* [1981] A.C. 675 at 709, per Lord Russell of Killowen, dissenting.

[564] Contrast *Izon v Gorton* (1839) 5 Bing.N.C. 501; but that was a case of partial, not total, destruction.

[565] For the dependence of leases upon tenure, see above, para.17–002.

[566] See *Izon v Gorton*, above, at 507; and see 14 Vin.Abr. 320.

[567] *Wong Lai-ying v Chinachem Investment Co Ltd* [1980] H.K.L.R. 1, 13 B.L.R. 81, PC; above, para.15–057.

performance. If the impossibility ceases before the time for performance is past, the covenant is merely suspended until performance becomes possible.[568] If the impossibility continues until the time for performance is past, the covenant is discharged. For example, under a building lease the landlord lets the site to the tenant for 99 years at a fixed rent, the tenant undertaking to erect a building which at the end of the term will pass to the landlord. If, after the grant of the lease, the erection of the building is prevented by some unforeseen cause, the lease continues and the rent remains payable.[569] However, the landlord will probably have no remedy in damages for failure to build, as the tenant can invoke the doctrine of lawful excuse for his failure to perform the covenant.[570] Even if the landlord has reserved a right to re-enter for breach of the building covenant, he will not be able to exercise it.[571] The supervening impossibility suspends the tenant's obligations for the time being, and there is therefore no breach of covenant.[572] There is no hard-and-fast rule, since every covenant must be construed so as to give effect to the parties' intentions, and it is quite possible to frame the lease in such terms that the landlord may re-enter for failure to perform a covenant in circumstances when its performance is impossible.[573]

18–105   **5. Rent.** An obligation to pay money (e.g. rent) is never regarded as impossible of performance, unless prohibited by statute. Rent remains payable even if the tenant is evicted by armed forces of the Crown,[574] or is prohibited by legislation from occupying the land,[575] or if the property is destroyed by fire[576] or requisitioned during war-time[577]; and the fact that the tenant's intended resource for the payment of rent proves to be unavailable does not

---

[568] *John Lewis Properties Plc v Viscount Chelsea* (1993) 67 P. & C.R. 120 at 133.

[569] *Cricklewood Property and Investment Trust Ltd v Leighton's Investment Trust Ltd* [1945] A.C. 221. These were the facts of the case; the unforeseen cause was the imposition of war-time restrictions on building. See also *John Lewis Properties Plc v Viscount Chelsea*, above. (A 999-year building lease granted in 1934 required the tenant to demolish and develop the site by 1987. The current building was listed in 1969, and, while no application was made for listed building consent, it was thought that such consent would be virtually impossible to obtain. Mummery J. held that the landlords were not entitled to exercise their right of re-entry for breach of covenant as the obligation was suspended for the time being.)

[570] *Cricklewood Property and Investment Trust Ltd v Leighton's Investment Trust Ltd*, above, at 234; *John Lewis Properties Plc v Viscount Chelsea*, above, at 132; [1995] Conv. 74 (J. Morgan).

[571] *Doe d. Marquis of Anglesea v Churchwardens of Rugeley* (1844) 6 Q.B. 107; *John Lewis Properties Plc v Viscount Chelsea*, above.

[572] *Brewster v Kitchell* (1697) 1 Salk. 198; *John Lewis Properties Plc v Viscount Chelsea*, above, at 133.

[573] See, e.g. *Moorgate Estates Ltd v Trower* [1940] Ch. 206 (a case of mortgagor and mortgagee); *Edward H. Lewis & Son Ltd v Morelli* [1948] 1 All E.R. 433, reversed on other grounds [1948] 2 All E.R. 1021.

[574] *Paradine v Jane* (1647) Aleyn 26; and see *Cyprus Cinema & Theatre Co Ltd v Karmiotis* [1967] 1 Cy.L.R. 42.

[575] *London & Northern Estates Co v Schlesinger* [1916] 1 K.B. 20.

[576] *Belfour v Weston* (1786) 1 T.R. 310.

[577] *Whitehall Court Ltd v Ettlinger* [1920] 1 K.B. 680; *Matthey v Curling* [1922] 2 A.C. 180.

render performance of the obligation impossible.[578] For similar reasons tenants are not relieved of liability under a covenant to repair if a building is accidentally destroyed by fire[579] or by enemy action,[580] for it is still possible to repair it, at whatever cost. Even legislation which prohibits the effecting of repairs without a licence does not relieve a tenant who is sued for damages for failure to repair; should a licence be refused, he is not excused by the legislation from paying damages.[581] But all these instances are subject to the reservation that in an exceptional case the court may hold the whole transaction to be frustrated.

Section 9. By Termination for Breach

1. Application to leases. One result of the emphasis on the contractual nature of a lease[582] is the recognition, both in this country[583] and in other jurisdictions in the Commonwealth,[584] that in appropriate circumstances, a party to a lease may terminate it following breach of its terms by the other party.[585] Although there was authority against this view,[586] it was based on the now discredited assumption that a lease could not be frustrated; and there was in any event an earlier body of authority in which it had been accepted that a lease could be terminated for breach.[587] A lease may be terminated for breach if a party to the lease:

18–106

> "evinces an intention not to be bound by the contract or . . . intends to fulfil the contract in a manner substantially inconsistent with his obligations and not in any other way".[588]

[578] "Inability to perform a contract because of impecuniosity does not make performance impossible." *Graves v Graves* [2007] EWCA Civ 660, [2008] H.L.R. 10, at [40], per Thomas L.J. (although the court held that there was an implied condition that if the tenant could not obtain housing benefit the tenancy would come to an end): see further [2008] Conv. 70 (J.Brown).

[579] *Matthey v Curling*, above; and see para.18–103 above.

[580] *Redmond v Dainton* [1920] 2 K.B. 256. But for the possibility of disclaimer under statute, see above, para.18–098.

[581] *Maud v Sandars* [1943] 2 All E.R. 783; *Eyre v Johnson* [1946] K.B. 481. These cases appear to interpret the covenant as imposing an alternative obligation- either to repair or to pay compensation.

[582] Above, paras 17–006 and 18–101.

[583] *Hussein v Mehlman* [1992] 2 E.G.L.R. 87; *Nynehead Developments Ltd v R.H. Fibreboard Containers Ltd* [1999] 1 E.G.L.R. 7 at 12. See too *National Carriers Ltd v Panalpina (Northern) Ltd* [1981] A.C. 675 at 696.

[584] See *Highway Properties Ltd v Kelly, Douglas & Co Ltd* (1971) 17 D.L.R. (3d) 710 (Supreme Court of Canada); *Proprietary Mailing House Pty Ltd v Tabali Pty Ltd* (1985) 157 C.L.R. 17 (High Court of Australia).

[585] Above, para.18–007. See [1993] Conv. 71 (S. Bright); [1993] C.L.J. 212 (C.H.); [1995] Conv. 379 (M. Pawlowski). It should be noted that there is as yet no Court of Appeal decision holding definitively that a lease may end by the tenant's acceptance of the landlord's repudiatory breach: *Reichman v Beveridge* [2006] EWCA Civ 1659 at [10].

[586] *Total Oil Great Britain Ltd v Thompson Garages (Biggin Hill) Ltd* [1972] Ch. 318 at 324.

[587] See below.

[588] *Proprietary Mailing House Pty Ltd v Tabali Pty Ltd*, above, at 33, per Mason J.

To have this result, the breach must probably be one which vitiates "the central purpose of the contract of letting".[589] Clearly both the length and the terms of the lease will be relevant to whether there has been a breach that will justify treating it as terminated. The longer the lease, the more artificial it is to regard it other than as an estate in land. It is therefore only in relation to shorter lettings that an allegation that a breach justifies termination is normally likely to be successful.[590]

18–107 **2. Examples.** The application of the principles of termination for breach to leases has yet to be fully worked out in this country. For instance, the relationship between termination for breach and the analogous doctrines of forfeiture for denial of title and non-derogation from grant is still uncertain. To date, the right to terminate a lease for breach of its terms has been recognised in a range of circumstances,[591] which include the following:

(i) where a landlord let a furnished property in breach of the implied condition that it was fit for human habitation[592]

(ii) where a tenant purported to terminate the lease pursuant to a break clause in circumstances in which he was not entitled to do so[593]

(iii) where a landlord's breach of a repairing covenant rendered the property uninhabitable[594]

(iv) where a tenant denied his landlord's title[595]

(v) where a landlord purported to forfeit a lease for breach of covenant when the tenant was not in breach[596]; and

(vi) where a landlord failed to restrain a nuisance by one tenant of a shopping mall which was seriously impeding the business of another.[597]

---

[589] *Hussein v Mehlman*, above, at 91, per Sedley Q.C. See too *Nynehead Developments Ltd v R.H. Fibreboard Containers Ltd*, above, at 12.

[590] It has therefore been suggested that it would be rare to find that a long lease granted at a small ground rent had been repudiated by the tenant unless he had abandoned the premises: *Proprietary Mailing House Pty Ltd v Tabali Pty Ltd*, above, at 34, 53. See [1993] Conv. 71 at 73 (S. Bright).

[591] Most of the cases concerned short lettings of three years or less.

[592] *Wilson v Finch Hatton* (1877) 2 Ex.D. 336; see below, para.19–030.

[593] *Gray v Owen* [1910] 1 K.B. 622 (landlord entitled to claim damages from tenant for his loss when he re-let at a lower rental); above, para.18–088.

[594] *Hussein v Mehlman* [1992] 2 E.G.L.R. 87 (which contains a valuable analysis of the earlier authorities).

[595] *W. G. Clarke (Properties) Ltd v Dupre Properties Ltd*, above, at 302; *Abidogun v Frolan Health Care Ltd* [2001] EWCA Civ 1821; [2002] L. & T.R. 16. See above, para.18–007.

[596] *G.S. Fashions Ltd v B. & Q. Plc* [1995] 1 W.L.R. 1088, 1093 (*obiter*).

[597] *Chartered Trust Plc v Davies* [1997] 2 E.G.L.R. 83. The case was decided on the basis that the landlord was in breach of its implied covenant not to derogate from its grant: see below, para.19–024.

3. Termination for breach and forfeiture. One particular difficulty about **18–108** the application of the doctrine of repudiation for breach to leases lies in its uncertain relationship with the landlord's right of forfeiture.[598] It has been suggested that the right to terminate may be limited or modified by the express terms of the letting, including in particular any forfeiture clause, so that the landlord could terminate for breach only if he complied with the requirements[599] for forfeiture.[600] Indeed, the right to forfeit a lease under an express right of re-entry and the right to terminate the lease for breach have been equated, so that the latter may in any event be subject to the same statutory requirements as the former.[601] Where a lease is forfeited, the tenant ceases to be liable to pay rent.[602] As part of its proposals for the termination of tenancies,[603] the Law Commission has recommended that it should not be possible for the landlord to circumvent the scheme by having recourse to repudiatory breach.[604]

---

[598] For forfeiture, see above, paras 18–006 et seq.
[599] Including the statutory requirements: see LPA 1925 s.146; above, para.18–051.
[600] *Hussein v Mehlman*, above, at 90.
[601] This is the approach that has been taken in relation to forfeiture for denial of title: *W.G. Clark (Properties) Ltd v Dupre Properties Ltd*, above, at 309; above, paras 18–007, 18–051. cf. *G.S. Fashions Ltd v B. & Q. Plc*, above, at 1093.
[602] Above, para.18–017.
[603] Above, para.18–082.
[604] (2006) Law Com. No.303, draft Bill, cl.1.

COMMON OBLIGATIONS OF LANDLORD AND TENANT

19–001 The rights and obligations of the landlord and tenant under a lease or tenancy fall under four heads. First, the lease may be silent as to everything except the essential terms as to parties, premises, rent and duration. This is not infrequently the case with periodic tenancies. Second, the parties may have agreed to be bound by the "usual covenants". Third, the lease may provide expressly not only for the matters dealt with by the "usual covenants" but also for a number of other matters. Fourth, there are a number of statutory provisions relating to the rights and obligations of the parties to a lease, which can only be summarised in a book of this length.

The question how far covenants in a lease can be enforced between persons other than the original parties is separately considered in Chapter 20 below.

Section 1. Position of the Parties in the Absence of Express Provision

19–002 Except so far as the lease or tenancy agreement otherwise provides, the position of the parties is as set out below.

A. *Position of the Landlord*

1. Implied covenant for quiet enjoyment

19–003 *(a) Implication.* The relationship of landlord and tenant automatically implies a covenant for quiet enjoyment on the part of the landlord.[1] This position was established only after much conflict of judicial opinion, for it was long thought that such a covenant was implied only if the word "demise" was used in the grant.[2] The covenant is thus not linked with any form of words, as it may now be on the grant of a lease.[3]

---

[1] *Budd-Scott v Daniell* [1902] 2 K.B. 351; *Markham v Paget* [1908] 1 Ch. 697.
[2] *Baynes & Co v Lloyd & Sons* [1895] 2 Q.B. 610; cf. *Jones v Lavington* [1903] 1 K.B. 253; *Hart v Windsor* (1843) 12 M. & W. 68 at 85.
[3] Below, para.19–018 ("with full title guarantee" or "with limited title guarantee").

(b) Effect. The covenant gives the tenant the right to be put into possession **19–004**
of the whole of the premises demised.[4] The covenant is broken if the landlord,
or someone claiming under him, does anything that substantially interferes
with the tenant's title to or possession of the demised premises or with his
ordinary and lawful enjoyment of them.[5] It is not necessary that the interference is direct or physical, nor that the acts complained of would support an
action in nuisance.[6] A breach may therefore occur where excessive noise
regularly emanates from adjacent property occupied by tenants of the same
landlord. The tenant:

> "takes the property not only in the physical condition in which he finds
> it but also subject to the uses which the parties must have contemplated
> would be made of the parts retained by the landlord."[7]

This emphasises the important point that the covenant of quiet enjoyment is
prospective in its operation, and therefore relates to the future conduct of the
landlord or others.[8] Where the landlord let inadequately sound-proofed premises to the tenant, the ordinary everyday noise generated by their neighbours
caused them continuous and intolerable disturbance. However, the defect,
inherent in the landlord's building, was present at the date the lease was
granted, and therefore it could not give rise to liability for breach of the
covenant of quiet enjoyment.[9]

Examples of where a landlord has been held to be in breach of the covenant **19–005**
include where:

(i) he causes a subsidence of the land by his mining activities (even
though he had reserved the right to work the minerals under the
land demised)[10];

(ii) he constructs an access way across the tenant's land without his
consent[11];

(iii) he tries to drive out the tenant by persistent threats or violent
behaviour[12];

---

[4] *Ludwell v Newman* (1795) 6 T.R. 458; *Miller v Emcer Products Ltd* [1956] Ch. 304.
[5] *Southwark LBC v Mills* [2001] 1 A.C. 1 at 23.
[6] *Southwark LBC v Mills*, above, at 11 and 23.
[7] *Southwark LBC v Mills*, above, per Lord Hoffmann at 11.
[8] *Southwark LBC v Mills*, above, at 11 and 23. See also *Southwark LBC v Long* [2002] EWCA
Civ 403; [2002] H.L.R. 56 (no breach of covenant arising from design defects in landlord's refuse
collection facilities).
[9] *Southwark LBC v Mills*, above. Nor could the landlord be liable in nuisance, as the neighbours' conduct, being no more than ordinary and reasonable use of the premises, was not itself
an actionable nuisance.
[10] *Markham v Paget* [1908] 1 Ch. 697.
[11] *Branchett v Beaney* [1992] 3 All E.R. 910.
[12] *Kenny v Preen* [1963] 1 Q.B. 499; *Sampson v Floyd* [1989] 2 E.G.L.R. 49.

(iv) he inflicts physical discomfort on the tenant by cutting off his water, gas or electricity or depriving him of proper washing facilities[13];

(v) he causes loss of business to the tenant by obscuring his shop with scaffolding.[14]

There is, however, no breach of the covenant where the landlord re-enters the premises pursuant to an order of the court forfeiting the lease, even if that order is subsequently reversed on appeal.[15]

19–006   *(c) Damages.* An award of damages for breach of the implied covenant is assessed according to normal contractual principles.[16] A court will not therefore award the tenant either aggravated damages for his distress and inconvenience[17] or exemplary damages to punish his landlord.[18] The tenant may of course seek an injunction to restrain the breach of covenant. In many cases these limitations on the damages that the court may award will be of little consequence because the tenant will have other remedies against the landlord in tort for nuisance or trespass, or by statute under the Housing Act 1988.[19] These are commonly sought in the alternative in proceedings on the implied covenant.

(d) Tortious, statutory and criminal liability

19–007   (1) CLAIMS IN TORT. The tenant may be able to bring proceedings for trespass (including trespass to goods), or nuisance against a landlord.[20] Trespass proceedings are commonly brought in cases where the landlord improperly evicts the tenant,[21] or where he undertakes substantial works on the premises in an attempt to encourage the tenant to leave.[22] Proceedings for nuisance

---

[13] *Perera v Vandiyar* [1953] 1 W.L.R. 672; *Guppys (Bridport) Ltd v Brookling* [1984] 1 E.G.L.R. 29.

[14] *Owen v Gadd* [1956] 2 Q.B. 99; *Queensway Marketing Ltd v Associated Restaurants Ltd* [1988] 2 E.G.L.R. 49 (affirming [1984] 2 E.G.L.R. 73, a judgment that contains a valuable statement of the law); *Lawson v Hartley-Brown* (1995) 71 P. & C.R. 242. See too *Mira v Aylmer Square Investments Ltd* [1990] 1 E.G.L.R. 45 (damages awarded for loss of opportunity to sub-let due to construction of penthouses on roof of block of flats).

[15] *Hillgate House Ltd v Expert Clothing Services & Sales Ltd (No.2)* [1987] 1 E.G.L.R. 65.

[16] *Branchett v Beaney* [1992] 3 All E.R. 910 at 917.

[17] *Branchett v Beaney*, above (not following on this point *Sampson v Floyd*, above, because it was decided *per incuriam*).

[18] *Perera v Vandiyar*, above; *Kenny v Preen*, above; *Guppys (Bridport) Ltd v Brookling*, above, at 34. For the distinction between aggravated and exemplary damages, see *Ramdath v Oswald Daley (t/a D. & E. Auto Spares)* [1993] 1 E.G.L.R. 82 at 84.

[19] s.27; explained below, paras 19–009 et seq.

[20] See also the statutory tort of harassment: Protection from Harassment Act 1997 s.3.

[21] Typically, the landlord changes the locks, enters the tenant's room in his absence, and either damages his property or throws it out of the premises: see e.g. *Drane v Evangelou* [1978] 1 W.L.R. 455; *Asghar v Ahmed* (1984) 17 H.L.R. 25; *McMillan v Singh* (1984) 17 H.L.R. 120; *Murray v Aslam* (1994) 27 H.L.R. 284.

[22] e.g. *Branchett v Beaney*, above; *Sampson v Wilson* [1996] Ch. 39.

have been brought where the landlord disconnects essential services such as water or electricity.[23] They may also lie where the tenant suffers discomfort as a result of a nuisance, not deliberately created, which emanates from property in the landlord's possession.[24]

In proceedings in trespass or nuisance, both aggravated damages for dis-   **19–008**
tress and inconvenience[25] and exemplary damages for "monstrous behaviour"[26] may be awarded against the defendant.[27] The latter will be given only where the landlord's conduct is calculated to make him a profit that may exceed any compensation that he has to pay to the tenant.[28] It will not necessarily be a bar to an award of such damages that the landlord has been prosecuted for the conduct in question.[29] Indeed in relation to the statutory offences of unlawful eviction and harassment,[30] any civil liability to which the landlord may be subject is expressly preserved.[31]

(2) STATUTORY TORT. The Housing Act 1988[32] created a new "statutory tort   **19–009**
of unlawful eviction".[33] The tort can only be committed by the landlord[34]—either by his own acts or by a person acting on his behalf—against a "residential occupier", widely defined as a person occupying premises as a residence, whether under a contract or by virtue of some enactment or rule of law giving him the right to remain in occupation or restricting the right of any

---

[23] e.g. *Guppys (Bridport) Ltd v Brookling*, above.

[24] As in *Sharpe v Manchester City Council* (1977) 5 H.L.R. 71 (landlord liable for cockroach infestation via the service ducts from the common parts). cf. *Habinteg Housing Association v James* (1994) 27 H.L.R. 299 (landlord not liable for a cockroach infestation where the source was not under his control).

[25] *Branchett v Beaney* [1992] 3 All E.R. 910 at 914.

[26] *Drane v Evangelou*, above, at 457, per Lord Denning M.R.

[27] For exemplary damages for nuisance, see *Guppys (Bridport) Ltd v Brookling* [1984] 1 E.G.L.R. 29.

[28] *Broome v Cassell & Co Ltd* [1972] A.C. 1027 at 1079; *McMillan v Singh* (1984) 17 H.L.R. 120 at 124; *Ramdath v Oswald Daley (t/a D. & E. Auto Spares)* [1993] 1 E.G.L.R. 82 at 83; *Mehta v Royal Bank of Scotland Plc* (1999) 32 H.L.R. 45 at 66.

[29] See *Asghar v Ahmed* (1984) 17 H.L.R. 25 at 29 (where there was other outrageous conduct by the landlord in addition to the matters that had led to his prosecution); *Sampson v Wilson*, above at 149.

[30] See below, paras 19–012 et seq.

[31] PEA 1977 s.1(5).

[32] ss.27, 28.

[33] *Sampson v Wilson* (1994) 26 H.L.R. 486 at 500, per Judge Roger Cooke (on appeal [1996] Ch. 39). The Act expressly makes the liability tortious: s.27(4)(a). For the retrospective effect of the provisions, see *Jones v Miah* [1992] 2 E.G.L.R. 50.

[34] This includes both the person who, but for the occupier's right to occupy, would be entitled to occupy the premises, and any superior landlord under whom that person derives title: HA 1988 s.27(9)(c). Although a person who has contracted to purchase the reversion may be the landlord for these purposes (see *Jones v Miah*, above), a person who merely expects to enter into such a contract cannot: *Francis v Brown* (1997) 30 H.L.R. 143. A landlord may be vicariously liable for the acts of his agent (i.e. "a person acting on his behalf"), but the agent cannot incur liability himself under the statute: *Sampson v Wilson* [1996] Ch. 39. However, the agent may be liable at common law in trespass or nuisance, and so proceedings may be brought against the landlord and his agents in appropriate circumstances: see, e.g. *Mehta v Royal Bank of Scotland Plc*, above.

other person to recover possession of the premises.[35] The tort may be committed in one of three ways.[36] The first is where the landlord unlawfully deprives the residential occupier of any premises of his occupation of the whole or part of those premises.[37] The second is where the occupier gives up his occupation because the landlord has unlawfully attempted to deprive him of it.[38] The third is where the occupier gives up his occupation because the landlord has interfered with his peace or comfort (or that of members of his household), or has persistently withdrawn or withheld services reasonably required for the occupation of the premises as a residence.[39] To be liable under this third head the landlord must know or have reasonable cause to believe that his conduct is likely to cause the occupier either to give up his occupation of all or part of the premises or to refrain from exercising any right or pursuing any remedy in respect of the premises.[40] It is a defence to any action for the landlord to prove that he believed, and had reasonable cause to believe, that the occupier had ceased to reside in the premises when he did the act complained of, or (where the landlord's conduct fell short of eviction or attempted eviction) that he had reasonable grounds for acting as he did.[41]

19–010   Damages are awarded for the loss of the right to occupy the premises as a residence[42] and are intended to deprive the landlord of any financial gain that may have been obtained from the eviction.[43] The landlord[44] is therefore liable to pay the difference between the value of the premises if the occupier's interest had been determined and their value subject to that interest.[45] This will reflect the period of time for which the tenant would have been entitled to remain on the premises had the eviction not occurred.[46] There will be no

[35] PEA 1977 s.1(1); HA 1988 s.27(9)(a). The definition makes no distinction between tenants and licensees, and those who share accommodation with a resident landlord are within its scope: *Re H* [2008] EWCA Crim 483. Squatters are not: *R. v Phekoo* [1981] 1 W.L.R. 1117 at 1127.

[36] The three forms of the tort are modelled upon the criminal liability of a landlord for unlawful harassment or eviction under PEA 1977 s.1; see below, paras 19–012 et seq.

[37] HA 1988 s.27(1).

[38] HA 1988 s.27(2)(a).

[39] HA 1988 s.27(2)(b). An example would be where a landlord cuts off the tenant's water supply. cf. *Drane v Evangelou* [1978] 1 W.L.R. 455.

[40] HA 1988 s.27(2)(b).

[41] HA 1988 s.27(8); *Kalas v Farmer* [2010] EWCA Civ 108; [2010] H.L.R. 15 at [21]. On whether a mistake of law may comprise a defence, see *Osei-Bonsu v Wandsworth LBC* [1999] 1 W.L.R. 1011.

[42] HA 1988 s.27(5).

[43] *Sampson v Wilson* [1996] Ch. 39 at 49.

[44] Only the landlord can be liable to pay damages under the Act. An agent of the landlord cannot: *Sampson v Wilson*, above.

[45] HA 1988 s.28(1). The damages may be reduced if the conduct of the tenant (or any person living with him) was such that it is reasonable for the court to mitigate them: HA 1988 s.27(7)(a). This is to cover the case where the tenant has "in some measure . . . brought the problem on his head": *Tagro v Cafane* [1991] 1 W.L.R. 378 at 384, per Lord Donaldson M.R. This may include a failure to pay the rent: *Regalgrand Ltd v Dickerson* (1996) 74 P. & C.R. 312. See too *Osei-Bonsu v Wandsworth LBC* [1999] 1 W.L.R. 1011 at 1021.

[46] See *Regalgrand Ltd v Dickerson*, above (tenant would have left a week later); *King v Jackson* (1997) 30 H.L.R. 541 (tenant would have left six days later: no award under the Act, but damages given for breach of the covenant for quiet enjoyment); cf. *Mehta v Royal Bank of Scotland Plc*, above (£45,000 damages award although occupier was not a tenant but a licensee).

liability if the occupier is reinstated in his occupation before the date of proceedings or if the court makes an order which has the effect of reinstating the occupier.[47] The court may reduce the damages payable if, before proceedings[48] were begun, the landlord offered to reinstate the occupier and it was unreasonable for the former residential occupier to refuse that offer, or it would have been had he not obtained alternative accommodation in the meantime.[49] A tenant must elect at trial whether he wishes to claim statutory damages for eviction or a declaration that his tenancy continues. He cannot have both.[50]

Statutory liability for unlawful eviction is in addition to any other liability   **19–011** to which the landlord may be subject, whether in contract, tort or otherwise.[51] Nevertheless, although the occupier can pursue his other remedies, he cannot recover twice over damages for loss of the right to occupy.[52] There has been some uncertainty as to what additional damages may be recovered at common law.[53] It is clear that exemplary damages, being punitive and intended to deprive the landlord of any financial gain from the eviction, cannot be awarded as they duplicate the role of an award of statutory damages.[54] It is less clear whether aggravated damages, compensating for the residential occupier's distress and inconvenience, can be awarded against the landlord in addition to damages under the statute.[55] Damages both for harassment amounting to a breach of the covenant for quiet enjoyment and for trespass to goods have been recovered in addition to statutory damages.[56]

(3) CRIMINAL LIABILITY. In recognition of the "strong public interest in   **19–012** deterring landlords from ejecting tenants unlawfully",[57] the Protection from Eviction Act 1977[58] creates three criminal offences relating to unlawful

---

[47] HA 1988 s.27(6). Reinstatement means allowing the tenant to resume his occupation fully: *Tagro v Cafane*, above, at 385.

[48] i.e. under HA 1988 ss.27, 28: *Tagro v Cafane*, above, at 385.

[49] HA 1988 s.27(7)(b).

[50] *Osei-Bonsu v Wandsworth LBC* [1999] 1 W.L.R. 1011.

[51] HA 1988 s.27(4)(a).

[52] HA 1988 s.27(5).

[53] See [1994] Conv. 411 (S.B.). The suggestion by Hollis J. in *Mason v Nwokorie* [1994] 1 E.G.L.R. 59 at 62, that the occupier can recover either statutory damages or damages at common law but not both, is incorrect: see HA 1988 s.27(5).

[54] *Francis v Brown* (1997) 30 H.L.R. 143. The Court of Appeal further held, at 150 and 152, that exemplary damages cannot be awarded against co-defendants of the landlord, necessarily sued in the tort of trespass rather than under the statute. This is somewhat tenuous; cf. *Mehta v Royal Bank of Scotland Plc*, above, where such damages were awarded.

[55] The question is whether such damages are awarded for the loss of the right to occupy or for something else: HA 1988 s.27(5). In *Francis v Brown*, above, at 150 (Sir Iain Glidewell) and at 152 (Simon Brown L.J.), it was held that aggravated damages could be awarded without the need for set-off; cf. *Mason v Nwokorie*, above, and *Mehta v Royal Bank of Scotland*, above, where aggravated damages were set off against the statutory award. cf. [1994] Conv. 411 (S.B.).

[56] See respectively *Kaur v Gill, The Times*, June 15, 1995; *Tagro v Cafane* [1991] 1 W.L.R. 378.

[57] *Attorney General's Reference (No.1 of 2004)* [2004] EWCA Crim 1025; [2004] 1 W.L.R. 2111 at [114], per Lord Woolf C.J.

[58] s.1, as amended by HA 1988 s.29.

eviction or harassment.[59] These constitute the criminal law analogues of the statutory tort of unlawful eviction. While the first two offences can be committed by any person, the third can only be committed by a landlord or the agent of a landlord. In all three instances, the victim must be a "residential occupier".[60]

19–013   First, it is an offence for any person unlawfully to deprive the residential occupier of his occupation of premises or any part of them unless he proves that he believed, with reasonable cause, that the residential occupier had ceased to reside in them.[61] The deprivation of occupation must have the character of an eviction.[62]

19–014   Secondly, any person commits a criminal offence if he does acts likely to interfere with the peace or comfort of a residential occupier or members of his household or he persistently withdraws or withholds services reasonably required for residential occupation. In addition, he must intend to cause the residential occupier either:

> (i) to give up his occupation of the whole or part of the premises; or

> (ii) to refrain from exercising any right or pursuing any remedy in respect of them.[63]

The offence is not committed where a landlord persuades a tenant to leave temporarily, e.g. to enable the property to be refurbished,[64] but it may be committed where the tenant loses his key and the landlord refuses to replace it.[65] Although a landlord may be guilty of this particular offence even though his acts are not such as to subject him to civil liability,[66] such cases will now be rare since the creation of the statutory tort of unlawful eviction.[67]

19–015   Thirdly, it is an offence for a landlord, or a landlord's agent, to do acts likely to interfere with the peace or comfort of a residential occupier or members of his household or to withdraw or withhold services reasonably

---

[59] The maximum sentence is the same in respect of all three offences: six months' imprisonment on summary conviction, two years' imprisonment on indictment: PEA 1977 s.1(4).

[60] For definition, see para.19–009 above.

[61] PEA 1977 s.1(2). A legal burden is therefore imposed on the defendant to establish his reasonable belief on the balance of probabilities. This has been held to be compatible with ECHR Art 6(2): *Attorney General's Reference (No.1 of 2004)*, above at [112] et seq.

[62] *R. v Yuthiwattana* (1984) 80 Cr.App.Rep. 55 (locking tenant out for a day and a night insufficient).

[63] PEA 1977 s.1(3). The subsection creates one offence which can be committed with one of two possible intentions: *Schon v Camden LBC* (1986) 53 P. & C.R. 361. If the defendant contends that he did not believe that the victim was a residential occupier, it is for the prosecution to prove that he had no such belief: *R. v Phekoo*, above; cf. PEA 1977 s.1(2); *Attorney General's Reference (No.1 of 2004)*, above at [115].

[64] *Schon v Camden LBC*, above.

[65] *R. v Yuthiwattana*, above.

[66] *R. v Burke* [1991] 1 A.C. 135.

[67] HA 1988 s.27; above, paras 19–009 et seq.

required for residential occupation, knowing or having reasonable cause to believe that that conduct is likely to cause the occupier either:

(i) to give up his occupation of the whole or part of the premises; or

(ii) to refrain from exercising any right or pursuing any remedy in respect of them[68];

unless he can prove that he had reasonable grounds for doing the acts or withdrawing or withholding the services in question.[69]

(e) Acts of others and eviction by title paramount

(1) LEASES GRANTED PRIOR TO JULY 1995. In leases granted prior to July 1, 1995, there are no implied covenants for title.[70] The tenant may have remedies against the landlord for the acts of third parties in nuisance, for derogating from his grant, or for breach of the covenant for quiet enjoyment implied in the lease.[71] The covenant for quiet enjoyment extends to the landlord's own acts, whether rightful or wrongful. It also extends to the rightful acts of those claiming under him, such as other tenants, because it is through him that they are able to disturb the tenant. Traditionally, the landlord was not held liable for the wrongful acts of those claiming under him, and the tenant was expected to proceed against them directly.[72] However, this approach has recently been called into question. A landlord who is in a position to control the conduct of other tenants, whether by enforcing covenants in the lease or by proceedings for nuisance, will be expected to do so, and will be held responsible for his failure to do so.[73] For example, where a landlord of a tenant of a shop in a shopping mall failed to control a nuisance caused by other tenants, the

19–016

---

[68] PEA 1977 s.1(3A) (inserted by HA 1988 s.29). The subsection was added because of the difficulties of showing the necessary intent under s.1(3). The defendant must participate himself; there is no "vicarious liability" for this offence: *R. v Quereshi* [2011] EWCA Crim 1584; [2011] H.L.R. 34.

[69] PEA 1977 s.1(3B) (inserted by HA 1988 s.29). The final words impose a legal burden on the defendant to establish the reasonableness of his grounds for withdrawing or withholding services; see fn.61 above.

[70] Above, para.8–047. Even if the landlord purported to grant a lease "as beneficial owner", the covenants for title would not have been implied: LPA 1925 s.76(5).

[71] See *Hilton v James Smith & Sons (Norwood) Ltd* [1979] 2 E.G.L.R. 44. The courts do not attach much significance as to the "label" given to the action in such cases: ibid. For the principle that a landlord must not derogate from his grant, see below, para.19–023.

[72] See *Malzy v Eichholz* [1916] 2 K.B. 308 (no breach of the covenant where other tenants of the lessor caused nuisance without his concurrence); *Mantania v National Provincial Bank Ltd* [1936] 2 All E.R. 633. cf. above, para.19–004.

[73] See *Hilton v James Smith & Sons (Norwood) Ltd*, above (landlord liable for failing to control parking by tenants and their visitors on a private right of way); *Sampson v Hodson-Pressinger* [1981] 3 All E.R. 710 (landlord liable for nuisance caused by the lawful use of an inadequately insulated flat by another of his tenants); *Chartered Trust Plc v Davies* (1998) 76 P. & C.R. 396.

landlord was held to have continued the nuisance and thereby derogated from his grant.[74]

19–017   The covenant for quiet enjoyment gives the tenant no remedy if he is evicted by title paramount, at all events if the word "demise" is not used,[75] and probably even if it is.[76] It follows that, in relation to leases granted before July 1995, the tenant will usually have no remedy against the landlord if his title turns out to be bad.[77]

19–018   (2) LEASES GRANTED AFTER JUNE 1995. For leases granted after June 1995, the provisions of the Law of Property (Miscellaneous Provisions) Act 1994 have changed the law.[78] In consequence of that Act, covenants may be implied into any instrument effecting or purporting to effect a disposition of property.[79] This will be the case in relation to a lease if it is expressed to be granted either "with full title guarantee" or "with limited title guarantee".[80] The covenants that are implied by these words have already been explained[81] and need only be considered to the extent that they relate to the grant of leases.

19–019   Where the lease is granted with full title guarantee, the landlord impliedly covenants that:

(a) he has the right to dispose of the property

(b) he will at his own cost do all that he reasonably can to give the tenant the title which he purports to give

(c) the property is free from all charges, incumbrances and third party rights other than those of which the landlord neither knows nor could reasonably be expected to know; and

(d) where the grant is of a sub-lease, the lease out of which the sub-lease is created is subsisting at the time of the disposition, and that there is no subsisting breach of any term of that lease which would render it liable to forfeiture.[82]

As regards (a), (c) and (d), the landlord is not liable for matters (1) to which the disposition was made expressly subject, (2) of which the tenant had

---

[74] *Chartered Trust Plc v Davies*, above. cf. *Hussain v Lancaster City Council* [2000] Q.B. 1.

[75] *Jones v Lavington* [1903] 1 K.B. 253; *Markham v Paget* [1908] 1 Ch. 697.

[76] See *Baynes & Co v Lloyd & Sons* [1895] 2 Q.B. 610. But contrast an express covenant for quiet enjoyment: *Williams v Burrell* (1845) 1 C.B. 402.

[77] For examples, see *Baynes & Co v Lloyd & Sons*, above (lessee mistakenly granted a sub-lease for longer than his lease: the sub-lessee had no remedy when evicted by the freeholder); *Jones v Lavington*, above (tenant had no remedy against landlord when it transpired that the property was subject to a restrictive covenant against the carrying on of a business on the premises which was enforced against him).

[78] See above, para.7–152.

[79] LP(MP)A 1994 s.1(1). It was expressly intended that covenants for title should apply to leases: see (1991) Law Com. No.199 paras 4.4, 4.5.

[80] Or their Welsh equivalents: LP(MP)A 1994 s.8(4).

[81] Above, para.7–153.

[82] LP(MP)A 1994 ss.2–4.

knowledge or which were patent, or (3) which were entered on the register.[83]

Where the landlord grants the lease with limited guarantee, his obligations are the same except as regards (c). He covenants merely that, since the last disposition of the property for value, he has neither created any subsisting charge, incumbrance or third party right nor suffered the property to be subjected to any such rights.[84]   **19–020**

Because the covenants for title implied under the 1994 Act are absolute and are not confined to the acts of the grantor and certain others through whom he derived title, there will be a breach of the covenant that he has a good right to dispose of the property if the tenant is evicted by title paramount. Similarly, the landlord may find himself liable under the covenant that the property is free from incumbrances because of some undisclosed latent incumbrance affecting the property. The position of the tenant is therefore much strengthened.   **19–021**

(f) Lease not by deed. Where the lease is not granted by deed, there cannot be any covenant in the technical sense, for the essence of a covenant is that it should be entered into by deed; but there will be corresponding contractual obligations.[85]   **19–022**

2. Obligation not to derogate from his grant

(a) The obligation. It is a principle of general application that a grantor must not derogate from his grant[86] as "a man may not give with one hand and take away with the other".[87] This obligation binds not only the grantor himself but persons claiming under him[88]; and the right to enforce it passes to those who claim under the grantee.[89] In the case of leases, the covenant for quiet enjoyment will often extend to conduct which might be construed as a derogation from the landlord's grant; but acts not amounting to a breach of the covenant or to a tort may nevertheless be restrained as being in derogation of the grant. It follows that if land is leased for the express purpose of storing explosives, the landlord and those claiming under him will be restrained from using adjoining land so as to endanger the statutory licence necessary for the storage of explosives.[90] Again, if land is leased to a timber merchant for use   **19–023**

---

[83] LP(MP)A 1994 s.6, as amended by LRA 2002 Sch.11 para.31.

[84] LP(MP)A 1994 s.3(3).

[85] *Baynes & Co v Lloyd & Sons* [1895] 1 Q.B. 820 at 826 (in CA [1895] 2 Q.B. 610).

[86] *Palmer v Fletcher* (1663) 1 Lev. 122; and see below, para.27–046; (1964) 80 L.Q.R. 244 (D.W. Elliott); (1965) 81 L.Q.R. 28 (M.A. Peel).

[87] *Southwark LBC v Mills* [2001] 1 A.C. 1 at 23, per Lord Millett, remarking that there is little, if any difference in scope between the covenant for quiet enjoyment and the obligation not to derogate from grant.

[88] *Aldin v Latimer Clark, Muirhead & Co* [1894] 2 Ch. 437; *Johnston & Sons Ltd v Holland* [1988] 1 E.G.L.R. 264 at 268.

[89] This statement, as expressed in the third edition (1966), was approved in *Molton Builders Ltd v Westminster LBC* (1975) 30 P. & C.R. 182 at 186, per Lord Denning M.R.

[90] *Harmer v Jumbil (Nigeria) Tin Areas Ltd* [1921] 1 Ch. 200. This was an extension of the principle, for the landlord's act had no direct physical effect on the premises: see *Port v Griffith* [1938] 1 All E.R. 295 at 298.

for his business, the landlord and his assigns will be restrained from building on adjoining land so as to interrupt the flow of air to sheds used for drying timber.[91] In neither case would there have been any remedy against such acts by strangers, for they were not torts. However, there will be no derogation from grant if the landlord's activities were clearly contemplated by the parties,[92] unless that permitted activity was carried out in an unreasonable manner that had not been envisaged by them.[93]

19–024   *(b) Extent of the obligation.* To constitute a derogation from grant there must be some act rendering the premises substantially less fit for the purposes for which they were let.[94] The act giving rise to liability will usually be carried out on property in the possession of the grantor at the time of the grant,[95] but in exceptional circumstances, it may take place on land which the grantor had no plans to acquire at that time but which he acquired subsequently.[96] The construction of additional floors on top of a property which had been let without any reservation of the right to do so may amount to a derogation from grant.[97] It is now clear that a failure by the landlord to stop a nuisance by another tenant may itself constitute a derogation.[98]

19–025   No action will lie if the tenant's business is abnormally sensitive to interference and its abnormality was unknown to the landlord when the lease was granted,[99] or if the landlord, having let the premises for some particular trade, e.g. for use as a wool shop only, lets adjoining premises for a trade which competes with it: for the original premises are still fit for use as a wool shop even if the profit will be diminished.[100] Nor, as in the case of the

---

[91] *Aldin v Latimer Clark, Muirhead & Co*, above.

[92] *Lyttelton Times Co Ltd v Warners Ltd* [1907] A.C. 476.

[93] See, e.g. *Yankwood Ltd v Havering LBC* [1998] E.G.C.S. 75 (land adjacent to property let for equestrian pursuits to be used for recreational and social purposes; derogation from grant when those activities were conducted unreasonably).

[94] *Aldin v Latimer Clark, Muirhead & Co*, above.

[95] See e.g. *Lyme Valley Squash Club Ltd v Newcastle-under-Lyme BC* [1985] 2 All E.R. 405 (construction of building so as to interfere with grantee's right to light).

[96] *Johnston & Sons Ltd v Holland* [1988] 1 E.G.L.R. 264 (construction by landlord of hoarding on land acquired after the grant of the lease to obscure wall which tenant used for advertising purposes).

[97] *Lawson v Hartley-Brown* (1995) 71 P. & C.R. 242.

[98] *Chartered Trust Plc v Davies* [1997] 2 E.G.L.R. 83 (landlord of shopping mall in receipt of service charge under obligation to act to prevent nuisance being caused by tenant of one unit to tenant of another); above, para.19–016; cf. *Petra Investments Ltd v Jeffrey Rogers Plc* (2000) 81 P. & C.R. 21 (although landlord's proposal radically to alter character of shopping mall may have derogated from grant, tenant had accepted suspension of service charge in full and final settlement of claim). The landlord may be able to set off any benefits the tenant may have obtained from the landlord's activities against tenant's claim for damages: *Platt v London Underground Ltd* [2001] 2 E.G.L.R. 121 (reduced trade at one kiosk at landlord's underground station was off set by increased trade at another).

[99] *Robinson v Kilvert* (1889) 41 Ch D 88.

[100] *Port v Griffith* [1938] 1 All E.R. 295; *Romulus Trading Co Ltd v Comet Properties Ltd* [1996] 2 E.G.L.R. 70; *Oceanic Village Ltd v Shirayama Shokusan Co Ltd* [2001] L. & T.R. 35; cf. *O'Cedar Ltd v Slough Trading Co* [1927] 2 K.B. 123 (adjoining premises let for purposes increasing fire insurance premiums of the original premises: no derogation); *Molton Builders Ltd v Westminster LBC* (1975) 30 P. & C.R. 183 (Crown Lands Commissioners, as lessors, authorised enforcement of planning control: no derogation).

covenant for quiet enjoyment, will mere invasion of privacy amount to a breach of the obligation, even though the property is let for residential purposes.[101] However, interference with the stability of a house by vibrations caused by powerful engines on adjoining land may be restrained on this ground[102]; and so may excessive noise, such as that caused in altering another flat in the same building,[103] or substantial interference with the light reaching the tenant's windows.[104]

The doctrine of non-derogation from grant may therefore give the tenant a **19–026** wider protection against his landlord than he has against strangers under the ordinary law. However, it is essentially negative in character and cannot be used to compel a grantor to enter into contractual or proprietary relations with another.[105] Nor will it prevent a landlord from barring the tenant's title by adverse possession.[106]

3. Implied condition of safety or fitness in certain cases

(a) General rule: no liability for state and condition of the premises. In **19–027** general, a landlord is under no contractual liability to the tenant for the state of the demised premises in the absence of any express undertaking to repair or maintain them.[107]

> "In the grant of a tenancy it is fundamental to the common understanding of the parties, objectively determined, that the landlord gives no implied warranty as to the condition or fitness of the premises. Caveat lessee."[108]

The landlord gives no implied undertaking that the premises are or will be fit for human habitation, or for any particular use,[109] or that any particular use is lawful,[110] or that he will do any repairs[111] or keep the premises in good condition[112] or rebuild the premises (e.g. if destroyed by fire), even if he has

---

[101] *Browne v Flower* [1911] 1 Ch. 219; *Kelly v Battershell* [1949] 2 All E.R. 830.

[102] *Grosvenor Hotel Co v Hamilton* [1894] 2 Q.B. 836.

[103] *Newman v Real Estate Debenture Corp Ltd* [1940] 1 All E.R. 131.

[104] *Coutts v Gorham* (1829) Moo. & M. 396; *Cable v Bryant* [1908] 1 Ch. 259.

[105] *William Old International Ltd v Arya* [2009] EWHC 599 (Ch); [2009] 2 P. & C.R. 20.

[106] *Sze To Chun Keung v Kung Kwok Wai David* [1997] 1 W.L.R. 1232 at 1235; below, para.35–031.

[107] *Chappell v Gregory* (1864) 34 Beav. 250 at 253.

[108] *Southwark LBC v Mills* [2001] 1 A.C. 1 at 12, per Lord Hoffmann; see also at 17; *Lee v Leeds CC* [2002] EWCA Civ 6; [2002] 1 W.L.R. 1488 at [60] et seq.

[109] *Hart v Windsor* (1843) 12 M. & W. 68; *Cheater v Cater* [1918] 1 K.B. 247; *Stokes v Mixconcrete (Holdings) Ltd* (1978) 38 P. & C.R. 488 (right of way).

[110] *Edler v Auerbach* [1950] 1 K.B. 601 (covenant to carry on profession forbidden by Defence Regulations); *Hill v Harris* [1965] 2 Q.B. 601 (user by sub-tenant in accordance with sub-lease but prohibited by covenant in head lease); *Molton Builders Ltd v Westminster LBC* (1975) 30 P. & C.R. 183.

[111] *Gott v Gandy* (1853) 2 E. & B. 845; *Sleafer v Lambeth BC* [1960] 1 Q.B. 43 (landlord not liable for failure to repair dangerous door, where landlord in practice did repairs and knew of the defect). See too *Tennant Radiant Heat Ltd v Warrington Development Corporation* [1988] 1 E.G.L.R. 41 at 43.

[112] *Lee v Leeds CC*, above.

covenanted for quiet enjoyment.[113] Furthermore the landlord owes no duty of care to the tenant, his family or his lawful visitors[114] except where:

(i) he is under an express or implied obligation to repair or maintain the demised premises or has a right to enter them for that purpose[115]; or

(ii) he was responsible for their design and construction.[116]

These principles are subject to certain qualifications, both common law and statutory.

19–028   *(b) Implied contractual terms.* In certain circumstances, an obligation to repair may be implied as a term of the lease. Whether or not such an implication is to be made "is dependant upon the same considerations that apply to any other contract".[117] However, it will be difficult to imply terms where the lease provides an apparently complete code for the allocation of responsibility between the parties.[118]

19–029   There are two types of term which may be implied into a contract. The first is where a term is implied as an incident of a particular type of contract.[119] In relation to repairing liabilities there are two such categories of contract, furnished lettings and leases of buildings where the landlord retains the essential access to the properties. The second type of implied term is where the implication is necessary to give business efficacy to the agreement.

19–030   (1) FURNISHED LETTINGS. Where a house is let furnished, it is an implied condition of the letting by the landlord that it is fit for human habitation at the time when it is let.[120] If it is not, the tenant may both treat the tenancy as repudiated[121] and recover damages for any loss that he has suffered.[122] The landlord's obligation is satisfied if the premises are fit for human habitation

---

[113] *Brown v Quilter* (1764) Amb. 619; *Southwark LBC v Mills*, above.

[114] *Cavalier v Pope* [1906] A.C. 428; *McNerny v Lambeth LBC* [1989] 1 E.G.L.R. 81. For criticism, see [1989] Conv. 216 (P. F. Smith).

[115] See Defective Premises Act 1972 s.4; below, para.19–046.

[116] *Rimmer v Liverpool CC* [1985] Q.B. 1. In such a case, the landlord owes a duty to take reasonable care to see that the property is free from any defect likely to cause injury: *Targett v Torfaen BC* [1992] 3 All E.R. 27 at 34.

[117] *Hafton Properties Ltd v Camp* [1994] 1 E.G.L.R. 67 at 69, per Judge Fox-Andrews QC. In accordance with normal contractual principles, a court will ignore the conduct of the parties subsequent to the contract in determining whether any repairing obligation is to be implied: *Demetriou v Poolaction Ltd* [1991] 1 E.G.L.R. 100 at 104.

[118] *Duke of Westminster v Guild* [1985] Q.B. 688.

[119] *Liverpool CC v Irwin* [1977] A.C. 239 at 257; *Duke of Westminster v Guild*, above at 698.

[120] *Smith v Marrable* (1843) 11 M. & W. 5 (bugs); *Wilson v Finch Hatton* (1877) 2 Ex.D. 336 (drains); *Bird v Lord Greville* (1884) Cab. & E. 317; (measles); *Collins v Hopkins* [1923] 2 K.B. 617 (tuberculosis).

[121] *Wilson v Finch Hatton*, above. Although this is because the implied covenant is also a condition, the modern approach is to regard covenants as a contractual term, so that a tenant may treat the contract as repudiated if a breach of the covenant by the landlord goes to the root of the contract of letting: see *Hussein v Mehlman* [1992] 2 E.G.L.R. 87 at 90; above, para.17–006.

[122] *Charsley v Jones* (1889) 53 J.P. 280.

when they are let. He is not required to keep them in this condition for the duration of the term.[123] Unfitness in this context appears to be confined to matters which are a danger to health, due to disease or infestation.[124] A landlord who lets a property that is unsafe on grounds of disrepair is not in breach of this condition.[125] The implied undertaking has no application to unfurnished premises.[126] Furthermore, there is no corresponding implied undertaking by the tenant that he is a suitable tenant, e.g. that he is not infected by some contagious disease.[127]

(2) WHERE THE LANDLORD RETAINS ESSENTIAL MEANS OF ACCESS. Where flats   **19–031**
(or other multiple units within a building) are separately let, or individual properties which are let are part of an estate, and the landlord retains either:

  (i) the necessary means of access (such as staircases, lifts or paths); or

  (ii) other facilities essential to the use of the property (such as rubbish ducts);

without the tenants undertaking any liability for them, it may be implied in the lease that the landlord will take reasonable care to keep them in repair.[128] This principle is subject to two qualifications. First, it applies only to rights which are *essential* to the enjoyment of the tenancy. Where the tenant has other rights over property retained by the landlord, such as an easement of drainage, then in the absence of special circumstances, the tenant must bear the cost of keeping the drain in repair,[129] in accordance with the usual rule that the servient owner is not obliged to keep the servient tenement in repair.[130] Secondly, there will only be a breach of the implied obligation if the landlord is negligent. If, for example, the landlord is unable to prevent the means of access from being persistently vandalised even though he has taken reasonable care, he will not be liable.[131]

---

[123] *Sarson v Roberts* [1895] 2 Q.B. 395. It was there suggested that to extend the obligation for the duration of the lease would be "most unreasonable": *Sarson v Roberts*, above, at 398, per A. L. Smith L.J. cf. L & TA 1985 s.8; below, para.19–036.

[124] See the cases cited, above, fn.120.

[125] *Maclean v Currie* (1884) Cab. & E. 361 (no breach where plasterwork was in a dangerous state). cf. L & TA 1985 s.8; below, para.19–036.

[126] *Hart v Windsor* (1843) 12 M. & W. 68, correcting *Smith v Marrable*, above; *Cruse v Mount* [1933] Ch. 278; *Adami v Lincoln Grange Management Ltd* [1998] 1 E.G.L.R. 58 at 60. See (1974) 37 M.L.R. 377 (J. I. Reynolds).

[127] *Humphreys v Miller* [1917] 2 K.B. 122 (leprosy).

[128] *Liverpool CC v Irwin* [1977] A.C. 239 (block of flats); *King v South Northamptonshire DC* (1991) 64 P. & C.R. 35 (housing estate).

[129] *Duke of Westminster v Guild* [1985] Q.B. 688; [1985] Conv. 66 (P. Jackson).

[130] Below, para.27–019, para.30–003; *Liverpool CC v Irwin*, above, at 259; *Stokes v Mixconcrete (Holdings) Ltd* (1978) 38 P. & C.R. 488 (tenant responsible for surfacing of right of way).

[131] *Liverpool CC v Irwin*, above (landlord's vain attempts to keep them in order in a 15-storey tower block).

19–032   (3) TO GIVE BUSINESS EFFICACY TO THE LEASE. A term will be implied into a contract where to do so is necessary to give business efficacy to the agreement, a process that is akin to rectification.[132] Only where it is manifest that the agreement is incomplete will such an implication normally be appropriate.[133] This is because it has never been considered necessary to imply a repairing covenant by the landlord to give business efficacy to a contract of letting.[134] Indeed there may be situations where neither party is under any express or implied obligation to repair all or some part of the premises.[135] The more comprehensive the terms of the agreement therefore, the less likely it is that a term will be implied.[136]

19–033   The cases suggest that a repairing obligation on the part of the landlord may be implied because of a correlative obligation on the part of the tenant,[137] as where he is obliged to pay a specified sum for such service, whether as part of his rental[138] or at fixed intervals.[139] On the same basis, an obligation by the landlord to repair the exterior of the property has been implied where the tenant was required under the lease to repair the interior.[140] Such an implication will not necessarily be made where the tenant's obligation to pay arises only as and when the landlord carries out the work.[141] Nor will an obligation by the landlord be implied merely because he reserves a right to inspect the state of repair of the premises,[142] though in such circumstances he must take reasonable care to ensure that the premises are safe.[143] Where a tenant was obliged to use the demised premises as her only or main home and to keep the inside clean and in a reasonable decorative state, no contractual obligation on the part of the landlord to keep the dwelling in habitable condition was implied.[144] A covenant by a landlord to insure against specific risks implies an obligation by him to lay out any insurance money in making good the damage, but not to undertake repairs not covered by the policies.[145]

---

[132] *Liverpool CC v Irwin*, above, at 258.

[133] *Gordon v Selico Co Ltd* [1986] 1 E.G.L.R. 71 at 77.

[134] *Tennant Radiant Heat Ltd v Warrington Development Corporation* [1988] 1 E.G.L.R. 41 at 43. "Special facts may no doubt justify a departure from the general rule": *Duke of Westminster v Guild*, above, at 697, per Slade L.J. For the right of a tenant holding under a long lease of a flat to apply to a leasehold valuation tribunal for variation of the lease where it fails to make satisfactory provision with respect to repair and maintenance, see L & TA 1987 s.35.

[135] *Demetriou v Poolaction Ltd* [1991] 1 E.G.L.R. 100 at 104; *Lee v Leeds CC* [2002] EWCA Civ 6; [2002] 1 W.L.R. 1488 at [64].

[136] *Gordon v Selico Co Ltd*, above, at 77.

[137] For a useful summary, see *Hafton Properties Ltd v Camp* [1994] 1 E.G.L.R. 67 at 69.

[138] *Barnes v City of London Real Property Co* [1918] 2 Ch. 18 at 32. But not necessarily: see below at para.19–081.

[139] *Edmonton Corp v W.M. Knowles & Son Ltd* (1961) 60 L.G.R. 124.

[140] *Barrett v Lounova (1982) Ltd*, above. However, this decision "must be taken as decided upon the special facts of that case": *Adami v Lincoln Grange Management Ltd* [1998] 1 E.G.L.R. 58 at 61, per Sir John Vinelott.

[141] *Duke of Westminster v Guild* [1985] Q.B. 688 at 697.

[142] *Sleafer v Lambeth BC* [1960] 1 Q.B. 43; *Duke of Westminster v Guild*, above.

[143] Defective Premises Act 1972 s.4(4); below, paras 19–046, 19–119, 19–120.

[144] *Lee v Leeds CC*, above.

[145] *Adami v Lincoln Grange Management Ltd*, above.

(4) HUMAN RIGHTS. Article 8 of the ECHR provides that everyone has the   **19–034**
right to respect for his private and family life, his home and his correspondence, and that there shall be no interference by a public authority with this
right except such as is in accordance with law and is necessary in a democratic
society. In turn, s.6(1) of the Human Rights Act 1998 provides that it is
unlawful for a public authority to act in a way that is incompatible with a
convention right. It has been held that an obligation is therefore imposed on
public authority landlords to take steps to ensure that the housing conditions
of property let for social housing do not infringe Art.8.[146] However, in
determining whether this obligation has been broken, the court must have
regard to the balance to be struck between the individual tenant's needs, the
resources of a local housing authority, and the demands of the community as
a whole.[147] This means that the courts will be reluctant to intervene, as the
"allocation of resources to meet the needs of social housing is very much a
matter for democratically determined priorities".[148] Where local authority
housing was let suffering from condensation and mould, no breach of obligation under Art.8 was therefore established.

(5) REFORM. In 1996, the Law Commission recommended that there should   **19–035**
be implied into many leases[149] a term that the landlord shall keep in repair
both the property let and any other parts of the building under his control.[150]
This implied term would apply unless either:

(a)   an obligation was imposed on a party to the lease (whether by the
      lease or by statute) to keep that property in repair; or

(b)   the parties agreed that it should not.

The proposal would exclude any possibility of an implied repairing obligation
in a lease. It would also mean that a situation in which neither party was under
an obligation to repair could only occur by the parties' deliberate choice and
not by reason of an oversight.

(c) Implied obligation of fitness in houses let at low rent

(1) HUMAN HABITATION. Under the Landlord and Tenant Act 1985,[151] if a   **19–036**
house is let at a very low rent there is an implied condition that the house[152]

---

[146] *Lee v Leeds CC* [2002] EWCA Civ 6; [2002] 1 W.L.R. 1488.

[147] *Lee v Leeds CC*, above, at [49].

[148] *Lee v Leeds CC*, above, at [49] per Chadwick L.J., following *Southwark LBC v Mills* [2001] 1 A.C. 1 at 9.

[149] There are significant exceptions, notably oral leases, leases of agricultural holdings, farm business tenancies and leases of dwellings granted for less than seven years.

[150] (1996) Law Com. No.238 Pt VII.

[151] s.8(1) replacing provisions of the earlier Housing Acts, dating from 1885 onwards. See (1962) 26 Conv. (N.S.) 132 (W.A. West); (1974) 37 M.L.R. 377 (J.I. Reynolds); W.R. Cornish and G. de N. Clark, *Law and Society in England 1750–1950* (London: Sweet & Maxwell, 1989), pp.151–166; 179–184. An equivalent provision applies to certain agricultural workers who are not tenants: L & TA 1985 s.9.

[152] Defined to include both a part of a house and any yard, garden, outhouses and appurtenances belonging to the house or usually enjoyed with it: L & TA 1985 s.8(6).

is fit for human habitation at the commencement of the tenancy, and an implied undertaking that the landlord will keep it in this condition throughout the tenancy. The implied covenant was introduced (by the Housing of the Working Classes Act 1885) to correct the anomaly that on the letting of a furnished dwelling there was an implied condition that it was fit for human habitation,[153] but where the property was unfurnished no equivalent implication was made.[154] This provision, which cannot be excluded by any stipulation to the contrary,[155] applies to houses let on or after July 6, 1957 at an annual rent not exceeding £80 in London and £52 elsewhere.[156] In this context "rent" means the gross rent payable to the landlord, without deduction for any taxes or other outgoings for which the land is liable.[157] The rent limits have remained substantially unaltered since 1957.[158] It was noted by the Court of Appeal in 1985 that, in view of inflation, this provision, which formerly encompassed a very considerable proportion of rented housing,[159] "must now have remarkably little application".[160] More than 25 years later, the rent limits remain the same.

19–037   (2) NOTICE. The undertaking is confined to defects of which the landlord has notice.[161] However this principle is now subject to the qualification that, if the landlord ought to have known of a defect which might make the premises unsafe, he will be in breach of a statutory duty of care if injury to person or property results.[162]

19–038   (3) EXTENT OF DEFECTS. An apparently insignificant defect such as a broken sash-cord may constitute a breach of the statute, for the test is not how difficult it is to repair the defect but whether the state of repair of the house "is such

---

[153] Above, para.19–030. Because of Parliament's unwillingness to change the rent limits, the courts have declined to extend the implied term at common law to unfurnished premises: *McNerny v Lambeth BC* (1988) 21 H.L.R. 188 at 195.

[154] See *Hansard* (HL), July 16, 1885, vol. 299, col. 892 (Marquess of Salisbury, the then Prime Minister).

[155] L & TA 1985 s.8(1).

[156] L & TA 1985 s.8(3), (4). For the meaning of "London", see L & TA 1985 s.8(4) fn.2.

[157] *Rousou v Photi* [1940] 2 K.B. 379. This situation will not often arise now in view of the way in which liability to pay council tax is determined: see Local Government Finance Act 1992 s.6.

[158] A minor amendment was made by the London Government Act 1963 Sch.8 Pt 1 para.2.

[159] From 1885 until at least 1958, the prescribed rental limits were well above average rentals.

[160] *Quick v Taff Ely BC* [1986] Q.B. 809 at 817, per Dillon L.J. See also *McNerny v Lambeth LBC*, above at 194; *Issa v Hackney LBC* [1997] 1 W.L.R. 956 at 964, where Brooke L.J. described the statutory covenant contained in s.8 as a "completely dead letter".

[161] *Morgan v Liverpool Corp* [1927] 2 K.B. 131; *McCarrick v Liverpool Corp* [1947] A.C. 219. For this doctrine, see below, para.19–117.

[162] Defective Premises Act 1972 s.4(1); below, paras 19–046, 19–119. Both *Morgan v Liverpool Corp*, above, and *McCarrick v Liverpool Corp*, above, would probably now be decided differently in consequence, because the landlord ought to have known of the defect which caused the injury to the claimant.

that by ordinary user damage may naturally be caused to the occupier, either in respect of personal injury to life or limb or injury to health".[163] There is a statutory list of the matters to be considered in determining whether a house is unfit for human habitation.[164] However, the landlord's obligation is limited to cases where the house is capable of being made fit for human habitation at reasonable expense.[165]

(4) CONTRACT. Since this statutory duty operates by way of implying a term into the contract,[166] it makes the landlord contractually liable only to the tenant personally.[167] But in certain cases he may be liable to visitors and others for breach of a statutory duty of care.[168]   **19–039**

(5) EXCEPTIONS. There are two principal exceptions to the application of this implied covenant. First, it does not apply to tenancies of houses for less than three years, which are not determinable by option within that period, and which provide that the tenant is to put the house into a condition fit for human habitation.[169] Secondly, it is not binding on the Crown.[170]   **19–040**

(6) REFORM. The Law Commission has recommended that the implied covenant of fitness for human habitation should apply to all leases of houses granted for a period of less than seven years, and that it should cease to be subject to rent limits.[171]   **19–041**

---

[163] *Summers v Salford Corp* [1943] A.C. 283 at 289, per Lord Atkin (citing his own dissenting judgment in *Morgan v Liverpool Corp*, above at 145).

[164] The list comprises repair; stability; freedom from damp; internal arrangement; natural lighting; ventilation; water supply; drainage and sanitary conveniences; facilities for preparation and cooking of food and for the disposal of waste water: L & TA 1985 s.10. Part 1 of the Housing Act 2004 has introduced a new system, the Housing Health and Safety Rating System, for the assessment of housing conditions and the enforcement of housing standards. This system is no longer based on fitness for human habitation, but requires the objective identification of certain hazards as the pre-condition to intervention by the local housing authority. A wide range of orders (e.g. improvement notices, prohibition orders and demolition orders) is available to enforce standards. Although these powers are widely used *by* local authorities, they cannot be used against them by local authority tenants; *R. v Cardiff City Council Ex p. Cross* (1982) 6 H.L.R. 1.

[165] *Buswell v Goodwin* [1971] 1 W.L.R. 92; (1976) 39 M.L.R. 43 (M.J. Robinson).

[166] See *McCarrick v Liverpool Corp*, above, discussed in *O'Brien v Robinson* [1973] A.C. 912.

[167] *Ryall v Kidwell* [1914] 3 K.B. 135.

[168] See below, para.19–046.

[169] L & TA 1985 s.8(5). For the curious omission of building leases from the exceptions, see the fifth edition of this work at p.698.

[170] *Department of Transport v Egoroff* [1986] 1 E.G.L.R. 89.

[171] (1996) Law Com. No.238 Pt VIII. This would make the obligation parallel to the implied obligation on the landlord to keep in repair dwellings let for a term of less than seven years: L & TA 1985 s.11; below at para.19–042; cf. *Issa v Hackney LBC* [1997] 1 W.L.R. 956 at 964–965 (supporting the Commission's proposals). There would be certain exceptions to enable property acquired for development by bodies having powers of compulsory purchase to be used as "short-life" accommodation. For comment see [1996] Conv. 324 (S.B.); [1998] Conv. 189 (P. F. Smith).

(d) Implied repairing obligations in houses let for a short term

19–042   (1) THE OBLIGATION. The Landlord and Tenant Act 1985[172] provides that in any lease of a dwelling-house[173] granted after October 1961[174] for a term of less than seven years[175] there shall be an implied covenant by the landlord:

> (1) to keep in repair[176] the structure and exterior[177] (including drains, gutters and external pipes); and
>
> (2) to keep in repair and proper working order[178] the installations in the dwelling-house[179]:
>
>> (i) for the supply of water, gas and electricity and for sanitation (including basins, sinks, baths and sanitary conveniences[180] but

[172] s.11, replacing HA 1961 s.32. For similar provisions applicable to long leases granted as a result of the exercise by public sector tenants of their right to buy, see HA 1985 s.139; Sch.6 para.14.

[173] Which means a lease by which a building or part of a building is let wholly or mainly as a private residence: L & TA 1985 s.16(b).

[174] L & TA 1985 s.13. Certain leases are excluded from the ambit of s.11, e.g. new business tenancies, tenancies of agricultural holdings and farm business tenancies: L & TA 1985 ss.13(3), 14. The implied obligation is not binding on the Crown: *Department of Transport v Egoroff* [1986] 1 E.G.L.R. 89.

[175] *Brikom Investments Ltd v Seaford* [1981] 1 W.L.R. 863.

[176] The standard of repair is determined by having regard to the age, character and prospective life of the dwelling-house and the locality in which it is situated: L & TA 1985 s.11(3). This is similar to the test applied at common law (see *Proudfoot v Hart* (1890) 25 QBD 42 at 55) except that it requires the prospective life of the property to be taken into account as well: see *Newham LBC v Patel* (1978) 13 H.L.R. 77 at 85. For the meaning of repair, see below, para.19–111.

[177] "The structure of the dwelling-house consists of those elements of the overall dwelling-house which give it its essential appearance, stability and shape." Although it need not be load-bearing, it must be "a material or significant element in the overall construction": *Irvine v Moran* [1991] 1 E.G.L.R. 261 at 262, per Thayne Forbes QC, approved as a "good working definition" in *Marlborough Park Services Ltd v Rowe* [2006] EWCA Civ 436; [2006] H.L.R. 30 at [17], per Neuberger L.J. The structure may therefore include the windows: *Irvine v Moran*, above; *Quick v Taff Ely BC* [1986] Q.B. 809 (but cf. *Holiday Fellowship Ltd v Hereford* [1959] 1 W.L.R. 211 (express covenant)). It has now been held to include internal plasterwork as well: *Grand v Gill* [2011] EWCA Civ 554; [2011] 1 W.L.R. 2253. The exterior may include the means of access to the premises (*Brown v Liverpool Corp* [1969] 3 All E.R. 1345), but not a back yard (*Hopwood v Cannock Chase DC* [1975] 1 W.L.R. 373), steps to a back garden (*McAuley v Bristol CC* [1992] Q.B. 134), or a rear access path not included in the lease (*King v South Northamptonshire DC* (1991) 64 P. & C.R. 35).

[178] This means in good *mechanical* condition. There was therefore no breach where the landlord had failed to lag water pipes: *Wycombe Health Authority v Barnett* (1982) 47 P. & C.R. 394. The installations must be so designed and constructed as to be capable of performing their functions at the commencement of the tenancy: *O'Connor v Old Etonian Housing Association Ltd* [2002] EWCA Civ 150; [2002] Ch. 295 at [16]. In addition, they must be able to function under those future conditions of supply that it is reasonable to anticipate will prevail: *O'Connor v Old Etonian Housing Association Ltd*, above, at [27].

[179] If there is a defect in an installation that is situated in a part of the building in which the landlord does not have an estate or an interest, he is not liable under this covenant: *Niazi Services Ltd v van der Loo* [2004] EWCA Civ 53; [2004] 1 W.L.R. 1254.

[180] The landlord will be in breach of his obligation if the installations are defective in their design: *Liverpool CC v Irwin* [1977] A.C. 239 at 269, 270 (cistern overflowed due to bad design).

not other fixtures, fittings and appliances for making use of
water, gas or electricity); and
(ii) for space heating or heating water.

(2) EXTENSION TO OTHER PARTS OF THE BUILDING. The initial provisions were   **19–043**
restrictively interpreted and were confined to the exterior, structure and
installations comprised within the lease.[181] The obligations did not apply to a
boiler in the basement of a block of flats which provided the hot water for the
whole block, or (except as regards a top floor flat) to the roof. To remedy this
deficiency, the implied repairing covenant was extended in cases where the
dwelling-house forms part only of the building.[182] The obligation to repair the
structure and the exterior therefore applies to any part of the building in which
the landlord has an estate or interest. The obligations in relation to installations apply to those which directly or indirectly serve the dwelling-house and
which either form part of a building in which the landlord has an estate or
interest or are owned by him or under his control.[183] The landlord is under no
liability, however, unless the disrepair or failure to maintain in working order
is such as to affect the tenant's enjoyment of the dwelling-house or of those
common parts which he is entitled to use.[184]

(3) OTHER MATTERS. Contracting out is forbidden except to the extent that   **19–044**
the county court may authorise as reasonable.[185] Furthermore, any covenant
by the tenant to repair or pay money in lieu of repair is modified accordingly.[186] But the tenant remains liable to use the premises in a tenant-like
manner,[187] and the landlord is not required to carry out works within the scope
of the tenant's obligation, or to rebuild or reinstate after fire or other inevitable
accident, or to repair tenant's fixtures.[188] The tenant must allow the landlord
to enter and view the premises at reasonable times after 24 hours' notice in
writing to the occupier.[189]

The landlord's obligation takes effect as a repairing covenant in the   **19–045**
lease.[190] This has three consequences. First, the landlord is liable only for
defects of which he has notice.[191] However, if there is a defect in the premises

---

[181] *Campden Hill Towers Ltd v Gardner* [1977] Q.B. 823; *Douglas-Scott v Scorgie* [1984] 1
W.L.R. 716.
[182] L & TA 1985 s.11(1A) (inserted by HA 1988 s.116).
[183] L & TA 1985 s.11(1A); *Niazi Services Ltd v van der Loo*, above. It is a defence for the
landlord to show that he used all reasonable endeavours to obtain rights enabling him to carry out
the necessary works, but was unable to do so: see L & TA 1985 s.11(3A). This could happen if
he needed access to part of the premises let by him to another tenant. See however Access to
Neighbouring Land Act 1992, below, para.30–035.
[184] L & TA 1985 s.11(1B) (inserted by HA 1988 s.116).
[185] L & TA 1985 s.12.
[186] L & TA 1985 s.11(4), (5). See *Irvine v Moran* [1991] 1 E.G.L.R. 261 at 262.
[187] See below, para.19–051.
[188] L & TA 1985 s.11(2). For tenant's fixtures, see below, paras 23–012 et seq.
[189] L & TA 1985 s.11(6).
[190] *O'Brien v Robinson* [1973] A.C. 912 at 927.
[191] *O'Brien v Robinson*, above, applying the same approach as for the statutory obligation to
keep fit for habitation: above, para.19–037. For the requirement of notice, see below,
para.19–117.

of which he ought to have known and which makes them unsafe, he will be in breach of a statutory duty of care[192] should that defect injure a person or damage their property.[193] Secondly, the obligation is one of repair.[194] The landlord will not therefore be liable if the property is subject to an inherent defect which causes no damage within the scope of the covenant.[195] Thirdly, the tenant has the usual contractual remedies to enforce the covenant. Three points merit particular mention in this regard:

(i) The tenant can seek specific performance of the covenant.[196]

(ii) If the breach of covenant is such as to make the premises uninhabitable, the tenant may treat the lease as repudiated.[197] In such circumstances, not only will the tenant be able to terminate the lease, but the landlord will be liable in damages for the breach.

(iii) The court may award damages for inconvenience and distress.[198]

For the purposes of this implied obligation, "lease" includes an agreement for a lease and a sub-lease,[199] but does not include a mortgage term.[200] If the landlord can[201] determine the lease within seven years it is treated as a lease for less than seven years, but it is not so treated if the tenant can extend it to seven years or more.[202] The rent payable under the lease is irrelevant.

19–046   *(e) Duty of care for safety.* In certain cases a landlord owes to all persons[203] who might reasonably be expected to be affected by defects in the state of the premises a statutory duty to take reasonable care to see that they and their

---

[192] See Defective Premises Act 1972 s.4; below, paras 19–046, 19–119.

[193] See, e.g. *Clarke v Taff Ely BC* (1980) 10 H.L.R. 44.

[194] Below, para.19–111.

[195] "Keeping in repair means remedying disrepair. The landlord is obliged only to restore the house to its previous good condition. He does not have to make it a better house than it originally was." *Southwark LBC v Mills* [2001] 1 A.C. 1 at 8, per Lord Hoffmann, citing *Quick v Taff Ely BC* [1986] Q.B. 809 (premises unfit for human habitation due to condensation caused by the design of the windows: landlord not liable for damage to tenant's property). Being unable to claim for inherent defects is a serious drawback given that the implied covenant of fitness under L & TA 1985 s.8 is virtually redundant: above, paras 19–036 et seq.

[196] See L & TA 1985 s.17; below, para.19–121.

[197] *Hussein v Mehlman* [1992] 2 E.G.L.R. 87; [1993] Conv. 71 (S.B.); [1993] C.L.J. 212 (C.H.).

[198] Breach of a repairing covenant is one of the exceptions to the general rule that damages for inconvenience and distress will not be awarded for a breach of contract: see *Watts v Morrow* [1991] 1 W.L.R. 1421 at 1445. For quantification, see *Wallace v Manchester CC* (1998) 30 H.L.R. 1111; *Shine v English Churches Housing Group* [2004] EWCA Civ 434; [2004] H.L.R. 42; *Earle v Charalambous* [2006] EWCA Civ 1090; [2007] H.L.R. 8.

[199] L & TA 1985 s.36.

[200] L & TA 1985 s.16(a).

[201] A right to do so in certain events is not enough: *Parker v O'Connor* [1974] 1 W.L.R. 1160.

[202] L & TA 1985 s.13(2).

[203] Including the tenant: see *Smith v Bradford Metropolitan Council* (1982) 44 P. & C.R. 171; *Barrett v Lounova (1982) Ltd* [1990] 1 Q.B. 348 at 359.

property are reasonably safe from injury or damage.[204] This duty arises when under the tenancy the landlord is either:

(i) under an obligation to the tenant (whether statutory,[205] express[206] or implied[207]) for the maintenance or repair of the premises[208]; or

(ii) has a right to enter the premises to carry out any description of maintenance or repair of them.[209]

The duty is owed only if the defect falls within the landlord's obligation or right to maintain or repair.[210] However, it is not necessary for the tenant to establish that the landlord knew or ought to have known of the actual defect giving rise to the claimant's injury.[211] The question is whether the landlord failed in his duty to take reasonable care to see that the claimant was reasonably safe from injury.[212] This rule applies to all types of tenancy, including statutory tenancies and tenancies at will or sufferance, but not to mortgage terms or tenancies under attornment clauses in mortgages.[213] It also applies to mere rights of occupation given by contract or statute, which for this purpose are treated as if they were tenancies.[214] No contracting out of the statutory duty is possible.[215]

B. Position of the Tenant

1. Obligation to pay rent. This is discussed below.[216]   **19–047**

2. Obligation to pay rates and taxes. The tenant is under an obligation to   **19–048**
pay all rates and taxes except those for which the landlord is liable. A landlord

---

[204] Defective Premises Act 1972 s.4, replacing Occupiers' Liability Act 1957 s.4. See [1975] C.L.J. 48 at 62 (J.R. Spencer); and below, para.19–119.

[205] Defective Premises Act 1972 s.4(5). An example is the landlord's implied obligation to repair under LTA 1985 s.11; above, para.19–042.

[206] See, e.g. *Smith v Bradford Metropolitan Council*, above.

[207] See, e.g. *McAuley v Bristol City Council* [1992] Q.B. 134.

[208] Defective Premises Act 1972 s.4(1).

[209] Defective Premises Act 1972 s.4(4), not benefiting a tenant who has failed in his own express obligations. The existence of such a right to enter has to be proved: *McAuley v Bristol CC*, above, at 150. See generally, *Hamilton v Martell Securities Ltd* [1984] Ch. 266 at 271.

[210] Defective Premises Act 1972, s.4(3); *McNerny v Lambeth LBC* [1989] 1 E.G.L.R. 81, 83; *McAuley v Bristol City Council*, above, at 145. The fact that there may be a danger in the premises rendering them unsafe does not mean that the landlord is in breach of an obligation to maintain and repair: *Alker v Collingwood Housing Association* [2007] EWCA Civ 343; [2007] 1 W.L.R. 2230 (landlord not liable for tenant's injury caused by putting arm through glass panel in front door.)

[211] *Sykes v Harry* [2001] EWCA Civ 167; [2001] Q.B. 1014; cf. Defective Premises Act 1972, s.4(2); see below, para.19–119.

[212] *Sykes v Harry*, above, at 1025.

[213] Defective Premises Act 1972 s.6(1); see below, para.25–034.

[214] Defective Premises Act 1972 s.4(6).

[215] Defective Premises Act 1972 s.6(3).

[216] Below, para.19–062.

is liable to pay income tax on the profits of a property business carried on by him.[217] By contrast, the tenant is liable to pay:

(i) rates where he is the occupier of non-domestic property[218]; or

(ii) council tax where he is a resident of a dwelling house.[219]

3. Obligation not to commit waste

19–049   *(a) Tenants for years.* The law of voluntary and permissive waste has already been explained in connection with freehold estates.[220] Under the ancient common law it had no application to leaseholds.[221] But since 1267 it has been laid down by statute that, unless there is agreement to the contrary,[222] a tenant for a fixed term of years is liable for both voluntary and permissive waste. This means that if the terms of the tenancy make no provision about repairs,[223] the tenant is liable for them and must maintain the property in the condition in which he took it.[224]

19–050   *(b) Yearly tenancies.* In the case of a tenancy from year to year, the tenant must use the premises in a tenant-like manner.[225] Thus he will be liable for voluntary waste,[226] and he must not alter the character of the property, as by converting premises let as a shop and dwelling into one large shop.[227] As regards permissive waste, a yearly tenant is merely liable to keep the premises wind- and water-tight,[228] fair wear and tear excepted.[229]

---

[217] See Income Tax (Trading and Other Income) Act 2005 Pt 3 (which contains details well beyond the scope of this work).

[218] See Local Government Finance Act 1988 Pt III. The burden of payment falls on the occupier: Local Government Finance Act 1988 s.43. For the definition of "non-domestic property", see Local Government Finance Act 1988 s.66.

[219] See Local Government Finance Act 1992 Pt I. It is the person who resides on the premises who is obliged to pay: Local Government Finance Act 1988 s.6.

[220] Above, para.3–090.

[221] At common law only tenants whose estates arose by operation of law, such as by curtesy or dower, were liable for waste. Tenants whose estates arose by act of parties were not liable unless the grantor had imposed this liability upon them.

[222] Statute of Marlbridge 1267, making lessees for life or years liable for waste; *Yellowly v Gower* (1855) 11 Exch. 274; *Davies v Davies* (1888) 38 Ch D 499 at 504. It has now been determined, after some debate (see Woodfall, 13.124) that this is the effect of the statute: *Dayani v Bromley LBC* [1999] 3 E.G.L.R. 144. The severe penalties imposed by the Statute of Gloucester, 1278, were repealed by the Civil Procedure Acts Repeal Act 1879.

[223] There are conflicting views as to whether, if the tenant covenants to repair, the landlord can sue the tenant in tort for waste rather than on the covenant: see *Mancetter Developments Ltd v Garmanson Ltd* [1986] Q.B. 1212 at 1218 (where Dillon L.J. suggested that he could) and 1223 (where Kerr L.J. took a contrary view). The earlier authorities firmly support the former view: see *Kinlyside v Thornton* (1776) 2 W.Bl. 1111; *Marker v Kenrick* (1853) 13 C.B. 188.

[224] Contrast the statement by Denning L.J. in *Warren v Keen* [1954] 1 Q.B. 15 at 20 that a tenant is prima facie not liable for repair. This branch of the law is strangely uncertain: see (1954) 70 L.Q.R. 9 (R.E.M.); [1954] C.L.J. 71 (H.W.R.W.).

[225] *Marsden v Edward Heyes Ltd* [1927] 2 K.B. 1; *Warren v Keen* [1954] 1 Q.B. 15.

[226] See *Warren v Keen*, above, at 21.

[227] *Marsden v Edward Heyes Ltd*, above.

[228] *Wedd v Porter* [1916] 2 K.B. 91; but the test is doubtful: see *Warren v Keen*, above.

[229] See *Warren v Keen*, above; for fair wear and tear, see below, para.19–116.

(c) Weekly tenancies. A weekly tenant is normally absolved from any **19–051** liability for permissive waste by the implied understanding that "the house will be kept in reasonable and habitable condition . . . by the landlord and not by the tenant".[230] This does not make the landlord liable to repair[231]; it merely absolves the tenant. But the tenant is under a duty to use the premises in a tenant-like manner[232]: he must "take proper care of the place. He must, if he is going away for the winter,[233] turn off the water and empty the boiler. He must clean the chimneys, when necessary, and also the windows. He must mend the electric light when it fuses. He must unstop the sink when it is blocked by his waste . . . . But apart from such things, if the house falls into disrepair through fair wear and tear or lapse of time, or for any reason not caused by him, then the tenant is not liable to repair it".[234] The position of a monthly or quarterly tenant, though uncertain, is probably similar.

(d) Tenancies at will and at sufferance. A tenant at will is not liable for **19–052** permissive waste[235]; but if he commits voluntary waste his tenancy is thereby terminated and he is liable to an action for damages.[236] A tenant at sufferance is liable for voluntary waste[237] but probably not for permissive waste.

(e) Third parties. A person who directs or procures a tenant to commit **19–053** waste may himself be liable in tort for so doing. Thus where a company was a tenant and, on the instruction of its managing director, its employees removed the tenant's fixtures without making good the consequent damage, both the company and the director were held liable in waste.[238]

(f) Reform. The Law Commission has recommended that the tort of waste **19–054** should be abolished to the extent that it applies to tenants for years, tenants at will or at sufferance and to licensees.[239] There would instead be implied covenants by a tenant for years:

(a) to take proper care of the premises as a good tenant;

(b) to make good damage wilfully done by the tenant, any sub-tenant or lawful visitor to the premises; and

(c) not to carry out any alterations or other works which might destroy or alter the character of the premises to the landlord's detriment.

---

[230] *Mint v Good* [1951] 1 K.B. 517 at 522, per Somervell L.J.

[231] *Mint v Good*, above, at 522; *Sleafer v Lambeth BC* [1960] 1 Q.B. 43 (weekly tenancy).

[232] *Warren v Keen*, above.

[233] But not if for two nights: *Wycombe Area Health Authority v Barnett* (1982) 47 P. & C.R. 394.

[234] *Warren v Keen*, above, at 20, per Denning L.J.

[235] *Harnett v Maitland* (1847) 16 M. & W. 257.

[236] *Countess of Shrewsbury's Case* (1600) 5 Co.Rep. 13b.

[237] *Burchell v Hornsby* (1808) 1 Camp. 360.

[238] *Mancetter Developments Ltd v Garmanson Ltd* [1986] Q.B. 1212.

[239] (1996) Law Com. No.238 Pt X. Liability for waste would remain as regards those with limited interests in possession under a trust.

Similar covenants would be implied on the part of a licensee or tenants at will or sufferance.[240]

19–055   **4. Landlord's right to enter and inspect.** The tenant is under an obligation to permit the landlord to enter and view the state of repair of the premises in cases where the landlord is liable to repair them.[241] The landlord may also have a statutory right to enter and view the premises in certain other cases.[242] But apart from these, unless he has reserved a right of entry, he has no right to enter the premises during the term, however good his reason (e.g. to do necessary repairs),[243] for he has given the tenant the right of exclusive possession as long as the tenancy endures.

19–056   **5. Right to estovers.** A tenant for years has the same right to estovers and botes as a tenant for life.[244]

Section 2. Position of the Parties under a Lease containing the Usual Covenants

19–057   **1. Contracts for leases.** The rights and duties set out above are those which arise when a lease is granted and there is no agreement to the contrary. But where, as occasionally happens, the lease is preceded by a contract that such a lease shall be granted,[245] the position of the parties is usually rather different, even where the contract is silent as to the covenants to be included. For the rule is that it is an implied term in a contract for a lease that the lease shall contain "the usual covenants".[246] If nevertheless the lease does not contain them, owing to the mistake of both parties when drawing it up, the lease may be rectified so as to accord with the contract.[247] Where the "usual covenants" are to be included, they do not weaken the ordinary implied obligations of both parties, which have already been explained. In some instances they merely make express provision for what would otherwise be implied; in others they impose rather more extensive liabilities.[248]

19–058   **2. The usual covenants.** The following covenants and conditions are always "usual".[249]

[240] To overcome the problem that such relationships are commonly gratuitous, the tenant or licensee would be deemed to have covenanted for valuable consideration for the purpose of assessing damages for breach of the implied obligations.
[241] *Saner v Bilton* (1878) 7 Ch D 815 (express covenant); *Mint v Good* [1951] 1 K.B. 517 (implied obligation).
[242] See, e.g. L & TA 1927 s.10; L & TA 1985 s.11(6); AHA 1986 s.23.
[243] *Stocker v Planet BS* (1879) 27 W.R. 877; *Regional Properties Ltd v City of London Real Property Co Ltd* [1981] 1 E.G.L.R. 33.
[244] Co.Litt. p.41b: above, para.3–097.
[245] For the distinction between lease and contract, see above, para.17–047.
[246] *Propert v Parker* (1832) 3 My. & K. 280; *Morrall v Krause* [1994] E.G.C.S. 177.
[247] For rectification, see above, para.15–122.
[248] For criticism of the basis on which the usual covenants are implied, see [1992] Conv. 18 (L. Crabb).
[249] See *Hampshire v Wickens* (1878) 7 Ch D 555.

(a) On the part of the landlord, a covenant for quiet enjoyment in the usual qualified form,[250] i.e. extending only to the acts of the lessor or the rightful acts of anyone claiming from or under him.

(b) On the part of the tenant:

    (i) a covenant to pay rent;

    (ii) a covenant to pay tenant's rates and taxes, i.e. all rates and taxes except those which statute requires the landlord to bear[251];

    (iii) a covenant to keep the premises in repair and deliver them up in repair at the end of the term;

    (iv) (if the landlord has undertaken any obligation to repair) a covenant to permit the landlord to enter and view the state of repair;

    (v) a condition of re-entry for non-payment of rent, but not for breach of any other covenant.[252]

3. Other usual covenants. In addition to the above provisions, which are **19–059** always "usual", other covenants may be "usual" in the circumstances of the case, by virtue, for example, of the custom of the neighbourhood or normal commercial usage[253]; in each case this is a question of fact for the court. What is "usual" in this sense means no more than "occurring in ordinary use."[254] "It may very well be that what is usual in Mayfair or Bayswater is not usual at all in other parts of London, such, for instance, as Whitechapel."[255] Under an agreement for a commercial lease of garage workshops in London for 14 years from 1971 it was held that the usual covenants included tenants' covenants not to alter the appearance or user of the building (consent not to be unreasonably withheld), not to obstruct lights or allow encroachments, and not to allow nuisances; and a right of re-entry for breach of any covenant.[256]

4. Covenants commonly inserted. Many covenants which in practice are **19–060** usually inserted in leases and are therefore literally "usual" may nevertheless not be deemed to be "usual" in the technical sense of the word. Examples are

---

[250] *Hampshire v Wickens*, above.

[251] See above, para.19–048.

[252] *Hodgkinson v Crowe* (1875) 10 Ch.App. 662; *Re Anderton & Milner's Contract* (1890) 45 Ch D 476. This is so even in the case of a lease of a public-house: *Re Lander and Bagley's Contract* [1892] 3 Ch. 41.

[253] See *Flexman v Corbett* [1930] 1 Ch. 672 at 678, per Maugham J.: "if it is established that (to put a strong case) in nine cases out of ten the covenant would be found in a lease of premises of that nature for that purpose and in that district, I think the court is bound to hold that the covenant is usual".

[254] *Flexman v Corbett*, above, at 678, per Maugham J.

[255] *Flexman v Corbett*, above, at 678, per Maugham J. See too *Charalambous v Ktori* [1972] 1 W.L.R. 951.

[256] *Chester v Buckingham Travel Ltd* [1981] 1 W.L.R. 96; (1981) 97 L.Q.R. 385 (G. Woodman).

covenants against assignment,[257] covenants against carrying on specified trades,[258] and provision for forfeiture for breaches of any covenant, whether for payment of rent or otherwise.[259] Such provisions are frequently inserted when no contract to take a lease has been made and the terms of the lease are a matter for negotiation between the parties. But if a contract for a lease has been made, no covenant can be inserted in the lease without the concurrence of both parties unless either the contract provides for it or the covenant is technically a "usual" covenant.

Section 3. Position under Certain Covenants Commonly Found in Leases

19–061   In addition to the covenants already considered there are a number of others which are very often agreed upon and need brief explanation.

1. Covenant to pay rent

19–062   *(a) Nature of rent.* Rent has been described as: "(i) a periodical sum, (ii) paid in return for the occupation of land, (iii) issuing out of the land, (iv) for non-payment of which a distress[260] is leviable".[261] This description reflects the fact that, under a normal form of written lease, the landlord has two rights to rent. The first is by reservation of the rent-service in the terms of the grant. The second is under the tenant's express or implied covenant to pay the rent reserved. In practice rent is nowadays normally regarded as a contractual payment.[262] Unless the lease provides otherwise, rent is payable in arrear.[263] Sometimes a service charge is expressed to be payable as rent and will be so treated.[264] However, as already explained, the restrictions on forfeiting a lease for non-payment of service charge will apply to that element of the rent.[265]

19–063   A rent may be made to vary with circumstances (as was done in *Walsh v Lonsdale*[266]) or to "fluctuate according to events",[267] and there is nothing to

---

[257] *Lady De Soysa v De Pless Pol* [1912] A.C. 194.

[258] *Propert v Parker* (1832) 3 My. & K. 280.

[259] *Re Anderton & Milner's Contract* (1890) 45 Ch D 476. Contrast *Chester v Buckingham Travel Ltd*, above; see Woodfall L. & T. 4.031 et seq. for other examples.

[260] Distress for rent is now in the course of being abolished: see below, para.19–076.

[261] *Escalus Properties Ltd v Robinson* [1996] Q.B. 231 at 243, per Nourse L.J. Rent reserved by a lease is properly called rent-*service*, because there is tenure and privity of estate: Litt. pp.113, 214, 215; see above, para.3–015. It is said to be "incident to the reversion" of the landlord: Co.Litt. p.143a. In this way it is distinguished from a rent *charge* (below, para.31–014), which is a rent reserved out of land but not attached to any reversion.

[262] "In modern law rent is no longer thought of as a thing issuing out of land and recoverable by distraint but as a payment which a tenant is bound by his contract to make to his landlord for the use of the land": *Ingram v IRC* [1995] 4 All E.R. 334 at 340, per Ferris J. summarising the effect of the authorities (above, para.17–005).

[263] *Coomber v Howard* (1845) 1 C.B. 440.

[264] *Escalus Properties Ltd v Robinson*, above, at 243; L & TA 1985 s.18(1).

[265] HA 1996 s.81; above, para.18–065.

[266] Above, para.17–051. See also *Selby v Greaves* (1868) L.R. 2 C.P. 594 at 602.

[267] *Smith v Cardiff Corporation (No.2)* [1955] Ch. 159 at 173, per Danckwerts J.; (1957) 21 Conv. (N.S.) 265 (B. Hargrove).

prevent rent being reserved in kind,[268] e.g. bottles of wine,[269] or in services, e.g. the doing of team work[270] or cleaning the parish church.[271] In one case an ill-drafted "gold clause" reserving an annual rent equivalent to £1,900 in gold sterling was held to entitle the landlord only to £1,900 in bank notes, one ground being a variable rent linked to the price of gold was contrary to public policy.[272] But this surprising decision has not been followed.[273]

A provision in a lease entitling the landlord to increase or reduce the rent   **19–064** to any sum that he wishes is not void for uncertainty.[274] What is required is that the rent should be ascertained or ascertainable at the time when payment is due.[275] Once a lease has been granted the court will strive to give meaning to indefinite provisions about rent. Thus it sometimes happens that the lease stipulates the initial rent for a fixed period and then provides that the rent thereafter is to be agreed or determined. If no formula is given for its assessment, the rent will be determined according to what it would be reasonable for the particular parties to the lease to agree.[276] By contrast, where a formula is given, as where the rent was to be "a reasonable rent for the demised premises", the assessment is likely to be an objective one.[277] The difficult case of "a fair and reasonable market rent" has been held to mean an open market rental.[278]

(b) Rent review clauses

(1) NATURE. In the absence of any express provision in the lease or statutory   **19–065** right, the landlord cannot increase the rent except by giving the tenant notice to quit.[279] It has therefore long been the practice for landlords, when granting commercial leases for any length of time, to insert rent review clauses. The general purpose of these provisions "is to enable the landlord to obtain from time to time the market rental which the premises would command if let on

---

[268] Co.Litt. p.142a.

[269] *Pitcher v Tovey* (1692) 4 Mod. 71.

[270] *Duke of Marlborough v Osborn* (1864) 5 B. & S. 67.

[271] *Doe d. Edney v Benham* (1845) 7 Q.B. 976. Contrast *Barnes v Barratt* [1970] 2 Q.B. 657 (services not "rent" for purposes of Rent Acts).

[272] *Treseder-Griffin v Co-operative Insurance Society Ltd* [1956] 2 Q.B. 127 at 145, per Denning L.J.

[273] *Multiservice Bookbinding Ltd v Marden* [1979] Ch. 84, holding that mortgage payments linked to the Swiss franc were enforceable. See too *Nationwide BS v Registry of Friendly Societies* [1983] 1 W.L.R. 1226.

[274] *Greater London Council v Connolly* [1970] 2 Q.B. 100 (increase of council house rent).

[275] *Greater London Council v Connolly*, above.

[276] See *ARC Ltd v Schofield* [1990] 2 E.G.L.R. 52 at 54. For examples, see *Thomas Bates & Son Ltd v Wyndham's (Lingerie) Ltd* [1981] 1 W.L.R. 505; *Central & Metropolitan Estates Ltd v Compusave* [1983] 1 E.G.L.R. 60; *Lear v Blizzard* [1983] 3 All E.R. 662. See too *Beer v Bowden* (1976) [1981] 1 W.L.R. 522 (such rent as was agreed between landlord and tenant but disregarding any tenant's improvements).

[277] *Ponsford v H.M.S. Aerosols Ltd* [1979] A.C. 63 (taken to mean the premises together with the tenant's improvements). cf. *English Exporters (London) Ltd v Eldonwall Ltd* [1973] Ch. 415 ("a rent which would be reasonable for a tenant to pay" may mean that the tenant's improvements are ignored).

[278] *ARC Ltd v Schofield*, above.

[279] *Greater London Council v Connolly*, above, at 108, per Lord Denning M.R. ("He must first determine the tenancy and then get the tenant to agree to pay the increase.")

the same terms on the open market at the review dates", and "to reflect the changes in the value of money and real increases in the value of the property during a long term".[280] In recent years, rent review provisions have become increasingly common in residential leases, in particular where a registered social landlord lets on assured tenancy.[281] Rent review clauses are of the greatest importance in practice, as they often influence the other terms of the lease such as the responsibility for repairs and the ability of the tenant to assign and sublet. However, a full account of them lies beyond the scope of this book.[282]

19–066   (2) CONTENTS. A rent review clause will, typically,[283] make provision for:

> (i) the timing of both the review and the date on which the new rent will become payable;
>
> (ii) the machinery for initiating the review and for agreeing the new rent;
>
> (iii) the method of calculating the new rent[284]; and
>
> (iv) the resolution of disputes.[285]

19–067   (3) TIME. It is settled that as a general rule time is not of the essence for the various steps that have to be taken to initiate the rent review and during the course of it.[286] The presumption is a strong one[287] that will be rebutted only by a compelling contra-indication.[288] Even where the delay is unreasonable or

---

[280] *British Gas Corporation v Universities Superannuation Scheme Ltd* [1986] 1 W.L.R. 398 at 401, per Browne-Wilkinson V.C. See too *M.F.I. Properties Ltd v B.I.C.C. Group Pension Trust Ltd* [1986] 1 All E.R. 974 at 975; *Basingstoke and Deane BC v Host Group Ltd* [1988] 1 W.L.R. 348 at 353.

[281] See, e.g. *Riverside Housing Association Ltd v White* [2007] UKHL 20; [2007] 4 All E.R. 97, in which the House of Lords emphasised the different considerations that may apply to the interpretation of rent review provisions in such circumstances. Although there is a statutory procedure for increase of rent applicable to assured tenancies, the parties may make contrary provision: HA 1988 ss.13, 14; see below, paras 22–121 et seq.

[282] The case law is extensive. Reference should be made to R. Bernstein, K. Reynolds and M. Rodger, *Handbook of Rent Review*; Woodfall, Ch.8.

[283] See Woodfall, 8.002.

[284] Usually some formula for determining an open market rental together with various assumptions and disregards.

[285] Dispute resolution is either by arbitrator or by expert. It is more difficult to challenge an expert's decision than it is an arbitrator's. An arbitrator is subject to the provisions of the Arbitration Act 1996.

[286] *United Scientific Holdings Ltd v Burnley BC* [1978] A.C. 904 (99-year lease provided for rent review in the year preceding each 10-year period of the term: landlord entitled to have the rent reviewed after the stipulated time). If on a true construction of the lease, no notice is required to be served on a particular date, the question whether time is of the essence does not arise: *Riverside Housing Association Ltd v White* [2007] UKHL 20 at [23] to [25]; [2007] 4 All E.R. 97.

[287] *Panavia Air Cargo Ltd v Southend-on-Sea BC* [1988] 1 E.G.L.R. 124.

[288] *Phipps-Faire Ltd v Malbern Construction Ltd* [1987] 1 E.G.L.R. 129 at 131; *Wilderbrook Ltd v Olowu* [2005] EWCA Civ 1361; [2006] 2 P. & C.R. 4; *Secretary of State for Communities & Local Government v Standard Securities Ltd* [2007] EWHC 1808 (Ch); [2008] 1 P. & C.R. 23.

such as will cause hardship to the tenant, the landlord may still claim a rent review which will be retrospective to the relevant date.[289] Time will be of the essence if the agreement makes express or implied provision.[290] For example, the same timetable may be set both for the review and for the tenant's right to determine the tenancy, for which time is of the essence.[291] Where the agreement prescribes the consequences of default, for instance by "deeming provisions", time is very likely to be of the essence.[292] It should not, however, be assumed that because the agreement expressly stipulates that time is of the essence for certain steps in the review process it will necessarily be so for others.[293] Where the tenant has no right to initiate the review, he may serve a notice on the landlord requiring him to do so within a specified time.[294] If the landlord then fails to do so, he will lose his right to a review.[295]

(4) CONSTRUCTION. A rent review clause usually postulates a hypothetical **19–068** letting of the premises at an open market rental between a willing landlord and a willing tenant.[296] In construing a particular clause a court will not generally rely on previous decisions as an aid to construction,[297] though they have accepted some guidelines.[298] The courts will however have regard to the

---

[289] *London & Manchester Assurance Co Ltd v G.A. Dunn & Co* [1983] 1 E.G.L.R. 111 at 118; *Amherst v James Walker Goldsmith & Silversmith Ltd* [1983] Ch. 305. The landlord might be estopped from exercising his right (*Amherst v James Walker Ltd*, above, at 316), as where he represented in some way that he would not activate the clause and the tenant acted to his detriment in reliance upon it, e.g. by not exercising a break clause. Liability for a retrospective rent increase was a relevant consideration when interpreting a rent review clause in an assured tenancy granted by a registered social landlord: *Riverside Housing Association Ltd v White*, above, at [31].

[290] Contrast *Drebbond Ltd v Horsham DC* (1978) 37 P. & C.R. 237 ("and not otherwise") with *Touche Ross & Co v Secretary of State for the Environment* (1982) 46 P. & C.R. 187.

[291] *United Scientific Holdings*, above at 962; *Al Saloom v Shirley James Travel Service Ltd* (1982) 42 P. & C.R. 181; *Coventry City Council v J. Hepworth & Son Ltd* [1983] 1 E.G.L.R. 119; *Legal & General Assurance (Pension Management) Ltd v Cheshire County Council* (1982) 46 P. & C.R. 160. The authorities are reviewed in *Central Estates Ltd v Secretary of State for the Environment* (1995) 72 P. & C.R. 482.

[292] For example, it is common to provide that if the tenant fails to serve a counter-notice in response to the landlord's notice proposing a new rent, the tenant is deemed to agree the rent proposed. The leading authority is *Starmark Enterprises Ltd v CPL Distribution Ltd* [2001] EWCA Civ 1252; [2002] Ch. 306, following *Trustees of Henry Smith's Charity v AWADA, Trading & Promotion Services Ltd* (1984) 47 P. & C.R. 607 and disapproving *Mecca Leisure Ltd v Renown Investments (Holdings) Ltd* (1984) 49 P. & C.R. 12.

[293] *Kings (Estate Agents) Ltd v Anderson* [1992] 1 E.G.L.R. 121; *Lancecrest Ltd v Asiwaju* [2005] EWCA Civ 117; [2005] 1 E.G.L.R. 40.

[294] If the tenant can initiate the review, he cannot serve such a notice: *Factory Holdings Group Ltd v Leboff International Ltd* [1987] 1 E.G.L.R. 135.

[295] See *London & Manchester Assurance Co Ltd v G.A. Dunn & Co* [1983] 1 E.G.L.R. 111 at 118; *Amherst v James Walker Goldsmith & Silversmith Ltd* [1983] Ch. 305 at 318.

[296] There is, however, no assumption as to the state of the market in which these hypothetical parties operate: see *Dennis & Robinson Ltd v Kiossos Establishment* [1987] 1 E.G.L.R. 133 at 135.

[297] See *Equity & Law Life Assurance Society Plc v Bodfield Ltd* [1987] 1 E.G.L.R. 124 at 125; *Prudential Assurance Co Ltd v 99 Bishopsgate Ltd* [1992] 1 E.G.L.R. 119 at 120.

[298] See *British Gas Corporation v Universities Superannuation Scheme Ltd* [1986] 1 W.L.R. 398 at 403.

commercial purpose of a rent review clause.[299] There is therefore a "presumption of reality" by which, in the absence of contrary provision or necessary implication:

> "it is assumed that the hypothetical letting required by the clause is of the premises as they actually were, on the terms of the actual lease and in the circumstances as they actually existed".[300]

If the language employed is capable of more than one meaning, the court will select the one that accords with the commercial purpose of the clause.[301] There is no presumption that a rent review clause is upward only.[302]

19–069 *(c) Payment of rent.* When the tenant tenders the rent to the landlord, the rent ceases to become due.[303] The tenant also ceases to be liable to the landlord for the rent where the amount owing has been paid by a third party under a contract of guarantee,[304] even if the sum is paid by the surety to secure his release from the guarantee.[305] Furthermore, a spouse or civil partner with statutory rights of occupation may pay rent on behalf of the other spouse or partner.[306] However, a tender of rent by a third party without the tenant's prior authority or subsequent ratification will not discharge the tenant from liability.[307] If the landlord refuses to accept rent tendered by the tenant, the tenant may obtain a declaration from the court, at the landlord's expense in costs, that the lease is not liable to forfeiture.[308]

19–070 *(d) Effect of eviction by landlord.* If the tenant is wrongfully evicted from any part of the premises by the landlord[309] or by any person claiming under the landlord,[310] the whole of the rent (but not liability under the other

---

[299] *Basingstoke and Deane BC v Host Group Ltd* [1988] 1 W.L.R. 348 at 353.

[300] *Co-operative Wholesale Society Ltd v National Westminster Bank Plc* [1995] 1 E.G.L.R. 97 at 99, per Hoffmann L.J. See too *Basingstoke and Deane BC v Host Group Ltd*, above at 354; *Ocean Accident & Guarantee Corp v Next Plc* [1996] 2 E.G.L.R. 84 at 86; *Braid v Walsall MBC* (1998) 78 P. & C.R. 94.

[301] *M.F.I. Properties Ltd v B.I.C.C. Group Pension Trust Ltd* [1986] 1 All E.R. 974 at 976.

[302] *Philpots (Woking) Ltd v Surrey Conveyancers Ltd* [1986] 1 E.G.L.R. 97 at 98.

[303] *Bird v Hildage* [1948] 1 K.B. 91 at 99.

[304] *Milverton Group Ltd v Warner World Ltd* [1995] 2 E.G.L.R. 28, applying *Re Hawkins* [1972] Ch. 714 at 728, and holding that remarks to the contrary in *London and County (A. & D.) Ltd v Wilfred Sportsman Ltd* [1971] Ch. 764 at 780 were inconsistent with *P. & A. Swift Investments v Combined English Stores Group Plc* [1989] A.C. 632 at 638, 642.

[305] *Milverton Group Ltd v Warner World Ltd*, above. The landlord is however entitled to appropriate the payments to the sums owed to him and may defer so doing until it becomes necessary: *Milverton Group Ltd v Warner World Ltd*, above, at 31, 32.

[306] FLA 1996 s.30(3), as amended by Civil Partnership Act 2004 s.82; Sch.9 para.1(4), applying also to mortgage payments and other outgoings: see further below, para.34–023.

[307] *Richards v De Freitas* (1974) 29 P. & C.R. 1; *Bessa Plus Plc v Lancaster* (1997) 30 H.L.R. 48.

[308] *Preston v Lindlands Ltd* [1976] 2 E.G.L.R. 50. This may be necessary to allow the tenant to make title to an assignee.

[309] *Morrison v Chadwick* (1849) 7 C.B. 266.

[310] *Neale v Mackenzie* (1836) 1 M. & W. 747. See above, para.19–016.

covenants) is suspended while the eviction lasts. However, where the eviction is by some person lawfully claiming by title paramount, only an apportioned part of the rent is suspended.[311] Where the landlord is the Crown, and the land is requisitioned under statutory powers, there is no unlawful eviction and the tenant will remain liable for the rent.[312]

(e) Illegality. No rent is recoverable if the tenancy was granted for an illegal **19–071** purpose, such as deceiving the rating authorities.[313] There are numerous cases,[314] decided in the 19th and early 20th centuries, where immorality of purpose was successfully invoked as a defence to liability, but it is extremely doubtful what would now comprise a sufficiently immoral purpose to deny recovery of the rent by the landlord. It must surely be inconceivable that a modern court would concern itself with an allegation that a tenant had rented a flat specifically "for the purpose of committing the sin of fornication there."[315] Gone are the days when unmarried cohabitation was considered to be an immoral use of the premises.[316]

(f) Address for notices. Where the premises let consist of or include a **19–072** dwelling,[317] Part VI of the Landlord and Tenant Act 1987 imposes two requirements on the landlord. First, any written demand for rent or other sums payable to the landlord must contain the landlord's name and address.[318] If such a demand fails to comply with this requirement, any part of the amount demanded which comprises a service or administration charge shall be treated as not being due until the necessary information is furnished to the tenant.[319] Secondly, the landlord is required to provide by written notice[320] an address in England and Wales at which notices may be served on him by the tenant.[321] If he fails to do so, any rent (or service or administration charge[322]) otherwise

---

[311] *Neale v Mackenzie*, above, at 758.

[312] *Commissioners of Crown Lands v Page* [1960] 2 Q.B. 274.

[313] *Alexander v Rayson* [1936] 1 K.B. 169.

[314] For example *Smith v White* (1866) L.R. 1 Eq. 626 (brothel); *Pearce v Brooks* (1866) L.R. 1 Ex. 213 (prostitution).

[315] *Upfill v Wright* [1911] 1 K.B. 506 at 510, per Darling J.

[316] *Heglibiston Establishment v Heyman* (1977) 36 P. & C.R. 351.

[317] L & TA 1987 s.46, which specifically excludes business tenancies within L & TA 1954, Part 2. Agricultural holdings which include a dwelling are, however, within s.46: see *Lindsey Trading Properties Inc v Dallhold Estates (UK) Pty Ltd* (1993) 70 P. & C.R. 332; [1994] Conv. 325 (M. Haley).

[318] L & TA 1987 s.47(1). If the landlord's address is outside England and Wales, he must provide an address within the jurisdiction at which notices may be served by the tenant: ibid.

[319] L & TA 1987 s.47(2), as amended by CLRA 2002 s.158, Sch.11, para.10. Unlike s.48 (see below), non-compliance with s.47 does not affect the tenant's liability for rent.

[320] An oral communication will not suffice: see *Rogan v Woodfield Building Services Ltd* (1994) 27 H.L.R. 78; [1995] Conv. 154 (M. Haley).

[321] L & TA 1987 s.48(1). The obligation will be satisfied by a statement of the landlord's name and address in the lease: *Rogan v Woodfield Building Services Ltd*, above. If there is any change of landlord the tenant must be notified in any event: L & TA 1985 s.3. cf. *Lindsey Trading Properties Inc v Dallhold Estates (UK) Pty Ltd*, above. A notice under s.48 is not necessarily invalid because it gives more than one address for service: see *Marath v MacGillivray* (1996) 28 H.L.R. 484 at 495.

[322] CLRA 2002 s.158; Sch.11 para 11.

due is treated as not being due until the landlord does comply with this requirement.[323] Once that happens, however, any arrears of rent are recoverable by him.[324] A letter sent by the landlord's agent to the tenant's solicitors concerning dilapidations and insurance issues and giving an address for correspondence did not comprise notification of an address for service in compliance with the statute.[325]

19–073   *(g) Rent books.* Where a weekly rent is payable for a residence the landlord is required to provide a rent book containing the landlord's name and address and a variety of information in prescribed form.[326] Failure to provide a proper rent book is a criminal offence, but it does not prevent the landlord from recovering rent due.[327]

19–074   *(h) Long leases of dwellings.* Where a dwelling is let on a long lease,[328] the tenant is not liable to make a payment of rent[329] unless the landlord has given him a notice in prescribed form[330] specifying the amount due, the date on which the tenant is liable to pay, and certain other information.[331] The date on which the tenant is liable to pay must not be:

"(a) either less than 30 days or more than 60 days after the day on which the notice is given, or

(b) before that on which he would have been liable to make it in accordance with the lease."[332]

19–075   *(i) Sum for use and occupation.* Where there is no agreement either for a rent or for a rent-free tenancy the landlord may recover from the tenant a reasonable sum, assessed at the ordinary market value,[333] for the use and

---

[323] L & TA 1987 s.48(2). This means that the landlord can neither recover the rent by action, nor succeed in proceedings (e.g. forfeiture) that require proof of arrears of rent or failure to pay rent: *Hussain v Singh* [1993] 2 E.G.L.R. 70 at 71; *Drew-Morgan v Hamid-Zadeh* [1999] L. & T.R. 503.

[324] *Lindsey Trading Properties Inc v Dallhold Estates (UK) Pty Ltd*, above.

[325] *Glen International Ltd v Triplerose Ltd* [2007] EWCA Civ 388; [2007] L. & T.R. 28.

[326] L & TA 1985 s.4(1); SI 1982/1474; SI 1988/ 2198; SI 1990/1067. There is no such obligation if the rent includes a payment in respect of board forming a substantial proportion of the whole rent: L & TA 1985 s.4(2).

[327] *Shaw v Groom* [1970] 2 Q.B. 504.

[328] Defined in CLRA 2002 ss.76, 77. It does not include business tenancies within L & TA 1954 Pt 2, tenancies of agricultural holdings, or farm business tenancies: CLRA 2002 s.166(8).

[329] "Rent" does not include service charges or administration charges: CLRA 2002 s.166(7). Compliance with the statute is a condition precedent to the tenant's liability for the ground rent: *Chasewood Park Residents Ltd v Kim* [2010] EWHC 579 (Ch); [2010] N.P.C. 41 at [41].

[330] For prescribed forms, see SI 2004/3096 (England); SI 2005/1355 (Wales).

[331] CLRA 2002 s.166.

[332] CLRA 2002 s.166(3).

[333] *Dean and Chapter of Canterbury Cathedral v Whitbread Plc* (1995) 72 P. & C.R. 9; *Lewisham LBC v Masterson* (1999) 80 P. & C.R. 117. In assessing this, the court will "look at the actual parties in their actual situation": *Dean and Chapter of Canterbury Cathedral v Whitbread Plc*, above, at 17, per Judge Cooke.

occupation of the land.[334] This right is based upon implied contract and it applies to all forms of tenancy, including tenancies at sufferance.[335] It is to be distinguished from the right of action to recover mesne profits, which lies against a trespasser and has been mentioned above.[336]

(j) Enforcement   19–076

(1) DISTRESS. The landlord may enforce payment of the rent directly, by an action for the money, or indirectly, by threatening to forfeit the lease (assuming that it contains a forfeiture clause) should the tenant fail to pay. An alternative means of direct enforcement is distress for rent, judicially described as a remedy enabling landlords "to recover arrears of rent, without going to court, by taking goods from the demised property and selling them."[337] This ancient feudal remedy, whereby a lord could coerce his tenant into rendering his services,[338] was extended and regulated by statute, and although there were signs that it was falling into disuse,[339] it underwent something of a revival in recent years. In 1991, the Law Commission characterised the law of distress for rent as arcane and obscure,[340] and recommended its abolition, describing it as "wrong in principle".[341] Although this recommendation was accepted in principle, government concluded, following its own consultation process, that distress was an effective remedy for recovering rent arrears, particularly for commercial properties, and that it should not therefore be abolished without replacement in such cases. The Tribunals, Courts and Enforcement Act 2007 obtained Royal assent on July 19, 2007, but Part 3 which contains the relevant provisions outlined below has not, at the time of writing, been brought into force. In March 2009, Government announced that it intended to carry out a further consultation exercise prior to bringing Part 3 into force, and that its projected implementation date was April 2012.[342]

(2) COMMERCIAL RENT ARREARS RECOVERY.[343] Part 3 of the 2007 Act pur-   19–077
ports to abolish the current law on distress for rent,[344] but at the same time introduces a new statutory regime called CRAR ("Commercial Rent Arrears Recovery") enabling landlords of commercial properties to recover rent

---

[334] *Gibson v Kirk* (1841) 1 Q.B. 850; Foa, L. & T. 403.

[335] Above, para.17–107.

[336] Above, para.4–029.

[337] *Rhodes v Allied Dunbar Pension Service* [1989] 1 W.L.R. 800 at 803, per Nicholls L.J. For an account of the common law of distress for rent, see the sixth edition of this work at paras 14–252 et seq.

[338] It might be employed in other situations, e.g. by an owner of a market for tolls.

[339] *Abingdon RDC v O'Gorman* [1968] 2 Q.B. 811 at 819.

[340] See (1991) Law Com. No.194, para.2.17, where the criticisms of the remedy are listed; and [1992] C.L.P. 81 at 111 (A. Clarke). cf. [1991] Conv. 246 (H.W. Wilkinson). See also *Salford Van Hire (Contracts) Ltd v Bocholt Developments Ltd* [1995] 2 E.G.L.R. 50 at 54.

[341] (1991) Law Com. No.194 para.3.1.

[342] *Hansard* HC Vol 489, col 46WS, 17 March 2009.

[343] These provisions are not, at the time of writing, in force: see para.19–076 above. For criticism, see Shea (2008) L. & T.Rev. 126.

[344] TC & EA 2007 s.71.

arrears by using a procedure for taking control of the tenant's goods.[345] The procedure for landlords[346] is identical to the procedure to be followed by enforcement agents when seizing and selling goods pursuant to powers conferred on them by court orders and by other specific statutes.[347] CRAR may only be used where the lease is evidenced in writing[348] (thereby ensuring that its terms are clear to the parties concerned) and where the lease is of commercial premises.[349] A lease will not be of commercial premises if any part of the premises is let as a dwelling (whether under the lease itself or under any sub-lease) or occupied as a dwelling.[350] However, letting the premises as a dwelling in breach of the terms of a superior lease, or occupying them in breach of the lease or any superior lease does not bring them within the exclusion.[351]

19–078   For the purposes of CRAR, "rent" means "the amount payable under a lease (in advance or in arrear) for possession and use of the demised premises", together with any interest payable and any VAT chargeable.[352] However, it does not include any sum in respect of rates, council tax, services, repairs, maintenance, insurance or other ancillary matters, whether or not these items may be referred to as "rent" in the lease.[353] Non-payment of service charges does not therefore entitle the landlord to use the procedure. CRAR can only be exercised in respect of rent that has become due and payable before notice of enforcement is given, and that is certain or capable of being calculated with certainty.[354] The net unpaid rent must not be less than the statutorily prescribed "minimum amount" both at the date of the enforcement notice and at the date that goods are taken control of.[355] The amount recoverable is reduced by "permitted deductions" (i.e. any deduction, recoupment or set-off that the tenant would be entitled to claim in an action by the landlord for the rent).[356]

19–079   The tenant may apply to the court if notice of enforcement is given in exercise of CRAR, and the court may set aside the notice or stay the process, ordering that no further step should be taken under CRAR without further order.[357] In general, CRAR cannot be used once the lease has ended.[358]

[345] TC & EA 2007 s.72; Sch.12. This Schedule prescribes, or enables regulations to prescribe, the process to be followed from serving notice to taking control of goods, including the goods which may be taken, the sale of such goods, and the distribution of proceeds of sale.

[346] For definition of "landlord", see TC & EA 2007 s.73.

[347] There are important, and wide-ranging, anti-avoidance provisions: TC & EA 2007 s.85.

[348] TC & EA 2007 s.74(2). Otherwise, all leases, legal or equitable, and tenancies at will (but not tenancies at sufferance) are included: TC & EA 2007 s.74(1).

[349] TC & EA 2007 s.75.

[350] TC & EA 2007 s.75(1). Agricultural tenancies may qualify as tenancies of commercial premises, but note there are special rules concerning agricultural holdings: TC & EA 2007 s.80.

[351] TC & EA 2007 s.75(4), (5).

[352] TC & EA 2007 s.76(1).

[353] TC & EA 2007 s.76(2).

[354] TC & EA 2007 s.77(1).

[355] TC & EA 2007 s.77(3). For definition of "net unpaid rent", see s.77(5).

[356] TC & EA 2007 s.77(2), (7).

[357] TC & EA 2007 s.78.

[358] TC & EA 2007 s.79(1).

However, there are two exceptions. First, a landlord who has taken control of goods under CRAR may complete the process by selling the goods.[359] Secondly, where the tenant remains in occupation after the lease ends, the landlord may use CRAR for a period of six months thereafter, provided that the lease did not end by forfeiture, the landlord and the tenant remain the same, and any new lease granted to the tenant is of commercial premises.[360]

2. Covenant to pay service charges[361]

(*a*) *Nature of service charges.* A service charge is a sum payable by the   **19–080** tenant on account of costs incurred by the landlord in carrying out repairs, providing insurance, or performing other services in relation to the demised premises. It is common practice for provision for payment of a service charge by the tenant to be included in both commercial and residential leases, in particular, although not exclusively, where there are facilities shared by a number of occupiers of a building or development. Service charges are almost universally calculated by reference to the cost of the services provided, and are therefore variable rather than fixed sums. They may also be encountered in relation to freehold developments, where they take effect as rentcharges,[362] and commonhold, as the "commonhold assessment".[363] However, this section deals only with service charges in relation to leases, first by outlining the common law, and then by summarising the extensive statutory regulation which applies principally to residential leases.[363a]

(*b*) *Common law.* In general, a service charge is payable in respect of   **19–081** obligations undertaken by the landlord pursuant to the covenants contained in the lease. However, it does not necessarily follow that because a service charge is payable the landlord is therefore under an obligation to provide the service.[364] Moreover, the tenant's failure to pay a service charge does not entitle the landlord to withhold services, as payment is not usually a condition precedent to the landlord's obligations arising.[365] A service charge is often expressed as within the definition of "rent" by the terms of the lease. This has important consequences, entitling the landlord to exercise any right of re-entry reserved in the event of non-payment without first serving a notice under s.146

---

[359] TC & EA 2007 s.79(2).

[360] TC & EA 2007 s.79(3), (4).

[361] See generally P. Freedman, E. Shapiro, B. Slater, *Service Charges: Law and Practice*, 4th edn (London: Jordan's Ltd, 2007); G. Sherriff, *Service Charges for Leasehold, Freehold & Commonhold* (Bloomsbury Professional, 2007); Tanfield Chambers, *Service Charges and Management: Law and Practice*, 2nd edn (London: Sweet & Maxwell, 2009).

[362] See paras 31–014 et seq.

[363] See para.33–013 below.

[363a] There is no statutory regulation of service charges in commercial leases: see however, RICS Code of Practice, *Service Charges in Commercial Property* (2011).

[364] *Russell v Laimond Properties Ltd* (1983) 269 E.G. 947.

[365] *Yorkbrook Investments Ltd v Batten* [1985] 2 E.G.L.R. 100. It is a question of construction of the lease in each case: *Bluestorm Ltd v Portvale Holdings Ltd* [2004] EWCA Civ 289; [2004] H.L.R. 49 at [36].

of the Law of Property Act 1925.[366] It is usual for the lease to make express provision for the payment of a service charge, and the court will interpret such provision restrictively, being reluctant to allow recovery for sums which are not clearly included within its terms.[367] There is some authority that, subject to contrary provision in the lease, the charges recoverable may be limited to those that are "fair and reasonable" where residential premises are concerned.[368]

19–082   (c) *Statutory regulation.* Statutory regulation of service charges was first introduced in relation to leases of flats, and gradually extended into a complex regime. Sections 18 to 30 of the Landlord and Tenant Act 1985 are the primary legislative source, but they have been amended and extended by Part V of the Landlord and Tenant Act 1987, Part III of the Housing Act 1996 and Part 2 of the Commonhold and Leasehold Reform Act 2002. For the purposes of the 1985 Act, a service charge is "an amount payable by a tenant[369] of a dwelling[370] as part of or in addition to the rent:

(a) which is payable, directly or indirectly, for services, repairs, maintenance, improvements or insurance or the landlord's costs of management, and

(b) the whole or part of which varies or may vary according to the relevant costs."[371]

Service charges within this definition are regulated as follows.[372]

---

[366] *Escalus Properties Ltd v Robinson* [1996] 2 Q.B. 321; see para.18–065 above.

[367] *Gilje v Charlgrove Securities Ltd* [2001] EWCA Civ 1777; [2002] 1 E.G.L.R. 41; *Earl Cadogan v 27/29 Sloane Gardens Ltd* [2006] 2 E.G.L.R. 89; *McHale v Cadogan* [2010] EWCA Civ 14; [2010] H.L.R. 24 at [16].

[368] *Finchbourne Ltd v Rodrigues* [1976] 3 All E.R. 581; *Holding & Management Ltd v Property Holding & Investment Trust Plc* [1989] 1 W.L.R. 1313. However, it is a matter of construction of each provision, and the Court of Appeal has not extended this principle to commercial leases: *Havenridge v Boston Dyers Ltd* [1994] 2 E.G.L.R. 73.

[369] A sum payable by a tenant in his capacity as shareholder of the landlord company is outside these provisions: *Morshead Mansions Ltd v Di Marco* [2008] EWCA Civ 1371; [2009] H.L.R. 33.

[370] "Dwelling" is defined in L & TA 1985 s.38, and it has been held that the provisions are not restricted in their application to leases of single dwellings: *Oakfern Properties Ltd v Ruddy* [2006] EWCA Civ 1389; [2007] Ch. 335. Holiday chalets have been held to be within the statute: *Phillips v Francis* [2010] L. & T.R. 28; cf. *King v Udlaw* [2008] L. & T.R. 28. Premises with mixed use have not: *Buckley v Bowerbeck Properties Ltd* [2009] 1 E.G.L.R. 43 (consulting rooms with basement flat which could not be separately occupied: Leasehold Valuation Tribunal).

[371] L & TA 1985 s.18(1), as amended by CLRA 2002 s.150; Sch.9 para.7. The "relevant costs" are the costs incurred or to be incurred in any period by or on behalf of the landlord in connection with the matters for which the charge is payable; see L & TA 1985 ss.18(2), (3). They may therefore include costs incurred by a management company: *Cinnamon Ltd v Morgan* [2001] EWCA Civ 1616; [2002] 2 P. & C.R. 10. Courts and tribunals may order that costs of proceedings should not be treated as relevant costs for these purposes: see L & TA 1985 s.20C.

[372] ss.18 to 25 of the 1985 Act do not apply to service charges payable by a tenant to a local authority, a National Park authority or a new town corporation, unless the tenancy is a long tenancy (as defined in L & TA 1985 s.26(2), (3)): L & TA 1985 s.26(1). For the application of the statutory provisions to the Crown, see CLRA 2002 s.172.

(1) REASONABLENESS. The amount payable under a service charge is limited **19–083**
to those costs that are reasonably incurred, and, where they are incurred on the
provision of services or the carrying out of works, costs can only be taken into
account in calculating the amount payable if the services or works are of a
reasonable standard.[373]

(2) CONSULTATION. Insofar as the relevant costs exceed a certain threshold, **19–084**
the landlord must have consulted the tenants before carrying out the works.[374]
Unless the landlord obtains the dispensation of a leasehold valuation tribunal
from these requirements,[375] the excess will not be taken into account in
determining the service charge payable.[376]

(3) CONTENTS OF DEMAND.[377] A demand for a service charge cannot include **19–085**
costs which were incurred more than 18 months previously unless the tenant
was given a written notice, during the 18-month period beginning with the
date that the costs were incurred, warning the tenant that the costs were
incurred and that he would be required to contribute to them.[378] A demand for
a service charge must be accompanied by a summary of the rights and
obligations of tenants of dwellings in relation to service charges.[379]

(4) STATEMENTS OF ACCOUNT. The landlord must supply to the tenant written **19–086**
statements of account for every accounting period.[380] The tenant has the right
to be given reasonable facilities to inspect and copy the accounts, receipts and
other documents relevant to matters dealt with in the statement of
account.[381]

(5) INSURANCE POLICY. Where a service charge includes an amount payable **19–087**
directly or indirectly for insurance, the tenant may require the landlord to
supply a written summary of the insurance being effected in relation to the

---

[373] L & TA 1985 s.19.
[374] L & TA 1985 ss.20, 20ZA, as amended by CLRA 2002 s.151; *Paddington Basin Develop-ments Ltd v West End Quay Estate Management Ltd* [2010] EWHC 833 (Ch); [2010] 1 W.L.R. 2735. The consultation requirements are extremely detailed: see SI 2003/1987 (England), SI 2004/684 (Wales). See also consultation requirements relating to the appointment or employment of managing agents: L & TA 1985 s.30B, inserted by L & TA 1987 s.44.
[375] L & TA 1985 s.20ZA(1), as inserted by CLRA 2002 s.151; *Daejan Investments Ltd v Benson* [2011] EWCA Civ 38; [2011] 1 W.L.R. 2330.
[376] L & TA 1985 ss.20(1), (6), (7), as amended by CLRA 2002 s.151.
[377] See also the requirements of L & TA 1987 s.48; above at para.19–072.
[378] L & TA 1985 s.20B, as inserted by L & TA 1987 Sch.2; *Holding & Management (Solitaire) Ltd v Sherwin* [2010] UKUT 412 (LC); [2011] 9 E.G. 166.
[379] L & TA 1985 s.21B, as inserted by CLRA 2002 s.153. The form and content of the summary to be provided are prescribed: SI 2007/1257 (England); SI 2007/3160 (Wales).
[380] L & TA 1985 s.21, as amended by CLRA 2002 s.152. If the landlord fails to comply, the tenant may withhold payment: L & TA 1985 s.21B, inserted by CLRA 2002 s.152.
[381] L & TA 1985 s.22, as amended by CLRA 2002 s.153.

dwelling.[382] The tenant has a statutory right to challenge the landlord's choice of insurer.[383]

19–088   (6) CONTRIBUTIONS HELD ON TRUST. Any sums paid by contributing tenants by way of service charges,[384] and any investments representing those sums, must be held by the landlord on trust to defray the costs incurred in connection with the matters for which the service charges were payable, any balance being held on trust for the contributing tenants for the time being.[385] On termination of a contributing tenant's lease, the tenant cannot withdraw his share in the fund, which remains held on trust for the remaining contributing tenants.[386] Should all leases terminate, the remaining assets in the fund are held beneficially by the landlord.[387]

19–089   (7) DISPUTES. The leasehold valuation tribunal has jurisdiction to decide whether, when, how, and by and to whom a service charge is payable, as well as to determine how much it should be.[388] However, no application may be made to a leasehold valuation tribunal in respect of anything which the tenant has agreed or admitted, or which has been decided by a court or arbitral tribunal, or which has been, or is to be, referred to arbitration.[389]

19–090   (8) SANCTIONS. In general, where the landlord fails to comply with the statutory requirements, the tenant is entitled to withhold payment of the service charge or part thereof. In addition, the landlord may commit a criminal offence if he without reasonable excuse fails to perform any of the duties imposed by ss.21 to 23 of the 1985 Act.

19–091   *(d) Other provisions.* We have explained above[390] that s.11 of the Landlord and Tenant Act 1985 provides that in leases of dwelling-houses granted after October 1961 for a term of less than seven years there shall be implied a landlord's covenant to keep in repair and working order the structure and exterior and certain installations in the house. This provision, which can only be excluded with the leave of the court, not only imposes repairing obligations on the landlord, it also prohibits the recovery from the tenant of the costs

---

[382] L & TA 1985 s.30A, Sch. as amended by CLRA 2002 ss.157, 165; Sch.10, paras 8–13. For exceptions, see L & TA 1985 Sch. para.9.

[383] L & TA 1985 Sch. para.8, as amended by HA 1996 s.83(2) and by CLRA 2002 s.165. See also the procedure contained in CLRA 2002 s.164.

[384] As defined in L & TA 1985 s.18(1): see para.19–082 above.

[385] L & TA 1987 s.42(2), (3). Tenants of "exempt landlords" (defined in L & TA 1987 s.58(1), as public sector landlords and registered social landlords) are excluded: L & TA 1987 s.42(1). Although not yet in force, provision has been made to require trust funds to be held in "designated accounts" at "relevant financial institutions": L & TA 1987 ss.42A and 42B, inserted by CLRA 2002 s.156(1).

[386] L & TA 1987 s.42(6).

[387] L & TA 1987 s.42(7).

[388] L & TA 1985 s.27A, as inserted by CLRA 2002 s.155(1).

[389] L & TA 1985 s.27A(4).

[390] See para.19–042 above.

incurred.[391] This means that the landlord cannot claim such costs by means of service charge provision in the lease. There are restrictions on forfeiture of leases for non-payment of service charges, which have already been dealt with.[392]

(e) Administration charges. "Administration charges" are defined as **19–092** amounts payable by a tenant of a dwelling either as part of, or in addition to, rent, and which are payable (directly or indirectly) for or in connection with applications for approvals under the lease or the provision of information or documents, or in respect of the tenant's failure to pay sums on their due date, or in connection with an actual or alleged breach of covenant.[393] A require- ment of reasonableness is imposed in respect of any such charges which are variable,[394] any demand must include a statement of the tenant's rights and obligations,[395] and leasehold valuation tribunals have jurisdiction to determine disputes similar to that enjoyed in relation to service charges.[396] Application may be made to vary the lease on the grounds that an administration charge is unreasonable.[397]

3. Covenant against alienation

(a) The right to alienate. If the lease is silent on the matter, the tenant may **19–093** alienate without the landlord's consent.[398] Accordingly a covenant against assignment, underletting, charging or parting with possession of all or any part of the property is often inserted in leases. The tenant's estate is alienable property,[399] and alienation in breach of covenant cannot by itself invalidate the assignment or sub-lease as against the grantee.[400] However, the landlord may sue the assigning tenant for damages, and, in the event of the alienation activating a forfeiture clause in the lease, may forfeit the lease. If, however, the landlord accepts rent from an assignee or sub-tenant, that amounts to an implied consent to the transaction.[401]

---

[391] L & TA 1985 s.11(4),(5).

[392] See para.18–065 above.

[393] CLRA 2002 s.158; Sch.11 para.1.

[394] CLRA 2002 s.158; Sch.11 para.2. An administration charge is variable if it is not specified in the lease nor calculated in accordance with a formula specified in the lease: CLRA 2002 s.158; Sch.11 para.1(3).

[395] CLRA 2002 s.158; Sch.11 para.4.

[396] CLRA 2002 s.158; Sch.11 para.5.

[397] CLRA 2002 s.158; Sch.11 para.3.

[398] See *Doe d. Mitchinson v Carter (No.1)* (1798) 8 T.R. 57 at 60; *Leith Properties Ltd v Byrne* [1983] Q.B. 433 at 439 (sub-letting).

[399] *Parker v Jones* [1910] 2 K.B. 32 at 38; *Property & Bloodstock Ltd v Emerton* [1968] Ch. 94 at 119; *Old Grovebury Manor Farm Ltd v W. Seymour Plant Sales and Hire Ltd (No.2)* [1979] 1 W.L.R. 1397 at 1398; *Peabody Donation Fund (Governors of) v Higgins* [1983] 1 W.L.R. 1091.

[400] Even if the consent is obtained by fraud: *Sanctuary Housing Association v Baker* (1997) 30 H.L.R. 809.

[401] *Hyde v Pimley* [1952] 2 Q.B. 506. For waiver implied from acceptance of rent, see above, para.18–022.

19–094   *(b) Absolute and qualified covenants.* A covenant against alienation may be either absolute or qualified. An absolute covenant prohibits any alienation within its terms. Although the landlord is free to waive breach of such a covenant in any particular instance, he may refuse consent without giving any reasons for doing so, even if his attitude is entirely unreasonable.[402] A qualified covenant prohibits alienation without the landlord's licence or consent.[403] In theory the distinction between the two types of covenant of this kind is one of form, given the landlord's power to waive even an absolute covenant. The reality is otherwise. In practice, few tenants are likely to be willing to take a lease of any length subject to an absolute covenant against assignment. Furthermore, an absolute covenant is likely to have an adverse impact on any rent review.[404] In law, a qualified covenant is subject to significant statutory regulation,[405] whereas an absolute covenant is subject to none.

(c) Statutory restrictions on qualified covenants

19–095   (1) LANDLORD AND TENANT ACT 1927, s.19. The Landlord and Tenant Act 1927[406] requires that, notwithstanding any contrary provision, a qualified covenant[407] condition or agreement "against assigning, underletting, charging or parting with possession of demised premises or any part thereof" shall be deemed to be subject to a proviso that the licence or consent is not to be unreasonably withheld.[408] The effect of the section is to write the words into the covenant in the lease.[409] The section does not affect the form of covenant, still sometimes employed,[410] that the tenant shall offer to surrender his

---

[402] See *Lilley and Skinner v Crump* (1929) 73 S.J. 366; *F.W. Woolworth & Co Ltd v Lambert* [1937] Ch. 37 at 58 (covenant against improvement); but note *Property & Bloodstock Ltd v Emerton*, above, at 119.

[403] There may be occasions where, in the case of such qualified covenant, more than one consent may be needed to an assignment or sub-letting. If the tenant is granted a licence to sub-let on condition that the sub-lessee covenants not to assign without the consent of both the tenant and the head landlord, the tenant impliedly covenants not to approve an assignment without the head landlord's consent: *Drive Yourself Hire Co (London) Ltd v Strutt* [1954] 1 Q.B. 250; or the landlord may be made a covenantee under the LPA 1925 s.56; see below, para.32–006.

[404] For rent reviews, see above, para.19–065.

[405] L & TA 1927 s.19 (as amended, most notably by L & TCA 1995 s.22); L & TA 1988; considered below.

[406] s.19(1). This section does not apply to agricultural holdings or farm business tenancies: s.19(4) (as amended). But it applies to leases whether granted before or after the Act.

[407] Although the point is not wholly free from doubt, the better view is that the subsection has no application to an absolute covenant: see *Bocardo SA v S. & M. Hotels Ltd* [1980] 1 W.L.R. 17 at 21 and at 26; *Vaux Group Plc v Lilley* (1990) 61 & P. & C.R. 446 at 453, 454. cf. *Property & Bloodstock Ltd v Emerton* [1968] Ch. 94 at 119.

[408] For the meaning of reasonableness in this context, see para.19–099 below. The landlord may be entitled to require payment of his reasonable legal and other expenses incurred: s.19(1)(a).

[409] *F. W. Woolworth & Co Ltd v Lambert*, above, at 60; *Vaux Group Plc v Lilley*, above, at 452.

[410] This covenant became common, but intending tenants will not now usually accept it. For the position of such a covenant under L & TA 1954 s.38(1), see *Allnatt London Properties Ltd v Newton* [1981] 2 All E.R. 290 (affirmed [1984] 1 All E.R. 423). For background, see [1983] Conv. 158 (C. Blake).

tenancy to the landlord before alienation.[411] Even where the section does apply, it does not permit the tenant to alienate without seeking the landlord's consent. If the tenant does so, he has committed a breach of covenant even if the landlord could not properly have refused his consent if it had been sought.[412] If the tenant seeks consent and it is unreasonably withheld, he may then go ahead and alienate,[413] claiming (if he wishes) a declaration from the court[414] of his right to do so.[415]

(2) LANDLORD AND TENANT ACT 1988. This Act, which implements recom-   **19–096**
mendations by the Law Commission,[416] is intended to ensure that landlords deal expeditiously with applications for consent to alienate.[417] It applies to any tenancy containing a covenant against assigning, under-letting, charging or parting with possession of the premises (or any part thereof) without the consent of the landlord or any other person where the covenant is subject to the qualification that such consent shall not be unreasonably withheld.[418] Where a tenant serves a written application for permission on the person who under the covenant may consent to a proposed transaction[419]—who will usually be the landlord[420]—he must give his consent within a reasonable

---

[411] *Bocardo SA v S. & M. Hotels Ltd*, above, following *Adler v Upper Grosvenor Street Investment Ltd* [1957] 1 W.L.R. 227, discussed in (1957) 73 L.Q.R. 157 (R.E.M.); see likewise *Creer v P. & O. Lines of Australia Pty Ltd* (1971) 125 C.L.R. 84. If the lease imposes conditions that must be fulfilled before a tenant can apply for consent or sets out circumstances in which an alienation will not be absolutely prohibited, it is likely to be upheld: *Crestfort Ltd v Tesco Stores Ltd* [2005] EWHC 805 (Ch); [2005] 3 E.G.L.R. 25 (requirement that any sub-lease replicate the terms of the head lease); *Level Properties Ltd v Balls Brothers Ltd* [2007] EWHC 744 (Ch); [2008] 1 P. & C.R. 1 (requirement that tenant provide surety in event of any assignment to body with limited liability).
[412] *Eastern Telegraph Co Ltd v Dent* [1899] 1 Q.B. 835.
[413] *Treloar v Bigge* (1874) L.R. 9 Ex. 151.
[414] The county court has jurisdiction to make such a declaration: L & TA 1954 s.53(1) (as amended).
[415] *Young v Ashley Gardens Properties Ltd* [1903] 2 Ch. 112. For the tenant's right to seek damages in such a case, see below.
[416] (1987) Law Com. No.161; [1988] Conv. (H.W. Wilkinson).
[417] For the difficulties that arose prior to the Act, see *29 Equities Ltd v Bank Leumi (UK) Ltd* [1986] 1 W.L.R. 1490 at 1494. For a valuable statement of the law after the Act, see *Kened Ltd v Connie Investments Ltd* (1995) 70 P. & C.R. 370 at 373.
[418] L & TA 1988 s.1(1). The Act does not apply to absolute covenants nor to qualified covenants other than those specified: *Clinton Cards (Essex) Ltd v Sun Alliance & London Assurance Co Ltd* [2002] EWHC 1576; [2003] L. & T.R. 2 (no application to covenant not to underlet at less than the market rent nor to covenant not to change use of premises without landlord's consent). The tenant must fulfil any conditions precedent to seeking consent before landlord's statutory duty will arise: *Allied Dunbar Assurance Plc v Homebase Ltd* [2002] EWCA Civ 666; [2003] 1 P. & C.R. 6.
[419] L & TA 1988 s.1(2)(b). cf. *Dong Bang Minerva (UK) Ltd v Davina Ltd* [1995] 1 E.G.L.R. 41 at 45 (landlord's mortgagee not such a person whose consent was required *under the covenant*: the point did not arise on appeal: [1996] 2 E.G.L.R. 31). The Act has no application to freehold covenants: cf. *Estates Governors of Alleyn's College v Williams* (1994) 70 P. & C.R. 67.
[420] Where the right to manage premises has been acquired by an RTM company (see below, para.19–128), certain functions of the landlord relating to the grant of approval are transferred to the RTM company: CLRA 2002 ss.98, 99.

time⁴²¹ except where it is reasonable for him not to give consent.⁴²² He in turn must serve written notice of his decision on the tenant specifying the reasons for withholding consent⁴²³ or any conditions subject to which it is given.⁴²⁴ The onus of proof is on the landlord to show that he consented within a reasonable time and that any conditions required were reasonable, or, if he withheld consent, that it was reasonable for him to do so.⁴²⁵ Similar obligations are imposed on a head landlord whose consent is required to a disposition by the sub-tenant.⁴²⁶ There may be occasions where, under the covenant, the consent of more than one person (such as a superior landlord or a mortgagee of the reversion) is required to a transaction by a tenant. The Act imposes a duty on the recipient of an application for consent to pass it on within a reasonable time where he believes that the consent of some other person may be required to the transaction.⁴²⁷ An action for damages in tort for breach of statutory duty may be brought against any person who has broken any duty imposed by the Act.⁴²⁸ In appropriate circumstances, an award of exemplary damages may be made.⁴²⁹

19–097   (3) LANDLORD AND TENANT (COVENANTS) ACT 1995. In leases granted prior to 1996, the parties to a lease could not stipulate in advance what was to be regarded as a reasonable ground for the landlord's refusal of consent to an

---

⁴²¹ A reasonable time is usually measured in weeks rather than in months, even in a complicated case: *Go West Ltd v Spigarolo* [2003] EWCA Civ 17; [2003] Q.B. 1140; *NCR Ltd v Riverland Portfolio No.1 Ltd (No.2)* [2005] EWCA Civ 312; [2005] P. & C.R. 27. Once a reasonable time has elapsed, the landlord cannot raise objections to the assignment or sub-letting that he has not hitherto raised: *Norwich Union Life Insurance v Shopmoor Ltd* [1999] 1 W.L.R. 531 at 545; *Footwear Corp Ltd v Amplight Properties Ltd* [1999] 1 W.L.R. 551 at 559; *Go West Ltd v Spigarolo*, above, at [17] et seq.

⁴²² L & TA 1988 s.1(3). It is reasonable for the landlord to require the tenant to undertake to meet the landlord's costs before he will consider the application, but only insofar as the costs are reasonable: *Dong Bang Minerva (UK) Ltd v Davina Ltd* [1996] 2 E.G.L.R. 31. It is not reasonable to refuse to consider the tenant's application to sub-let on the ground that the tenant has failed to specify the proposed rent: *Norwich Union Linked Life Assurance Co Ltd v Mercantile Credit Co Ltd* [2003] EWHC 3064; [2004] 4 E.G. 109 (C.S.).

⁴²³ The Act "requires a landlord to give his reasons for a refusal and limits him to those reasons in justifying his refusal": *Southern Depot Co Ltd v British Railway Board* [1990] 2 E.G.L.R. 39 at 44, per Morritt J.

⁴²⁴ L & TA 1988 s.1(3). Any condition must itself be reasonable: L & TA 1988 s.1(4).

⁴²⁵ L & TA 1988 s.1(6); *Midland Bank Plc v Chart Enterprises Inc* [1990] 2 E.G.L.R. 59; *Air India v Balabel* [1993] 2 E.G.L.R. 66. Prior to the Act, the burden of proving unreasonableness lay on the tenant: *Shanly v Ward* (1913) 29 T.L.R. 714. Where a *freehold* covenant requires the consent of a third party to some act, such consent not to be unreasonably withheld, the burden of proving unreasonableness remains with the covenantor: *Estates Governors of Alleyn's College v Williams*, above.

⁴²⁶ L & TA 1988 s.3.

⁴²⁷ L & TA 1988 s.2(1).

⁴²⁸ L & TA 1988 s.4; see e.g. *CIN Properties Ltd v Gill* [1993] 2 E.G.L.R. 97. The burden is on the tenant to establish loss caused as a result of the breach of duty: *Clinton Cards (Essex) Ltd v Sun Alliance & London Assurance Co Ltd* [2002] EWHC 1576 (Ch); [2003] L. & T.R. 2.

⁴²⁹ *Design Progression Ltd v Thurloe Properties Ltd* [2004] EWHC 324 (Ch); [2005] 1 W.L.R. 1.

assignment. It was said that reasonableness must be determined objectively,[430] for otherwise the purpose of the Landlord and Tenant Act 1927 might be stultified.[431] However, the Landlord and Tenant (Covenants) Act 1995 made important amendments to the 1927 Act in so far as it applies to certain leases granted after 1995.[432] The amendments apply only to a "qualifying lease", which means a "new tenancy" under the 1995 Act[433] of any property, other than a residential lease.[434] The parties to a qualifying lease may enter into an agreement in relation to an assignment,[435] specifying either:

(i) any circumstances in which the landlord may withhold his licence or consent to that assignment; or

(ii) any conditions subject to which any such licence or consent may be granted.[436]

The landlord will not then be regarded as unreasonably withholding his **19–098** licence or consent if he does so on the grounds that such circumstances exist and in fact they do exist.[437] Nor will he be regarded as imposing unreasonable conditions if he gives his consent subject to such conditions.[438] One condition that is likely to be imposed in virtually all cases is that the assignor should guarantee the performance of the covenants by the assignee until the time when the lease is next assigned.[439] It has also become normal practice to prescribe conditions that will have to be satisfied as to the financial standing of any assignee. There are, however, certain limitations on the conditions or circumstances that may be validly specified. They cannot be framed by reference to any matter that falls to be determined by the landlord[440] (or by

---

[430] *Bocardo SA v S. & M. Hotels Ltd* [1980] 1 W.L.R. 17; cf. *Lovelock v Margo* [1963] 2 Q.B. 786 at 789. For the extent to which the test of reasonableness is objective, see below, para.19–099.

[431] *Re Smith's Lease* [1951] 1 All E.R. 346.

[432] s.22, inserting s.19(1A)–(1E) L & TA 1927. For the Landlord and Tenant (Covenants) Act 1995 see Ch.20 below. Its principal purpose was to abolish the rule that the original tenant remains liable on the covenants for the duration of the term notwithstanding the assignment of the lease: see below, para.20–020. The abolition of this rule was made possible by an agreement that had been reached between representatives of the property industry. The amendment of L & TA 1927 s.19 was an important element of that agreement: see below, para.20–085.

[433] See L & TCA 1995 s.1(3)–(7); below, para.20–010.

[434] Defined as "a lease by which a building or part of a building is let wholly or mainly as a single private residence": L & TA 1927 s.19(1E). Note that tenancies of agricultural holdings and farm business tenancies are excluded from L & TA 1927 s.19: fn 406 above. The principal impact of these provisions is on leases of business property.

[435] The provisions apply only on an assignment and not on a sub-letting or a charging of the premises: L & TA 1927 s.19(1A). The agreement need not be contained in the lease and can be made at any time before the application is made for the landlord's consent to the assignment: L & TA 1927 s.19(1B).

[436] L & TA 1927 s.19(1A).

[437] L & TA 1927 s.19(1A).

[438] ibid. In practice this has made L & TA 1988 s.1(4), above, virtually redundant in relation to business leases.

[439] For such "authorised guarantee agreements" see L & TCA 1995 s.16; below, para.20–089.

[440] L & TA 1927 s.19(1C). Thus a condition that the tenant could not assign to any person who, in the landlord's opinion, was not creditworthy, would not be valid.

any other person) unless he has to exercise that determination reasonably or his decision can be reviewed by an independent third party whose identity can be ascertained from the agreement.[441] These provisions are contained in the Landlord and Tenant (Covenants) Act 1995, and are therefore subject to the anti-avoidance provisions of that Act.[442] Any agreement that attempts to restrict or frustrate their operation will in consequence be void.

(d) Reasonableness

19–099   (1) OBJECTIVE OR SUBJECTIVE? It has never been finally determined whether the grounds for a landlord's refusal of consent to an assignment or subletting must be objectively or subjectively reasonable.[443] It has been said that the test is "not a purely objective one".[444] The reasonableness of the decision will be judged according to the circumstances existing and known to the landlord at the time when he withheld his consent.[445] He cannot rely on reasons which did not influence his decision.[446] If he gives a valid reason for refusing consent, that refusal will not be vitiated merely because he gave other reasons which would not have justified his decision.[447] As a landlord must give his reasons for any refusal,[448] he may not rely on a reason which he failed to give in writing within a reasonable time but which nevertheless influenced his decision.[449] However, it is open to the landlord to elaborate upon the reasons given in his initial response to the tenant, and the range of the evidence and argument available to the landlord should not be limited by the relative succinctness of the landlord's statement.[450]

---

[441] L & TA 1927 s.19(1C).

[442] L & T(C)A 1995 s.25; below, para.20–128.

[443] This issue will not arise in the case of qualifying leases granted after 1995 where the parties have specified circumstances in which consent may be withheld or conditions subject to which consent may be granted: see para.19–098 above.

[444] *Bromley Park Garden Estates Ltd v Moss* [1982] 1 W.L.R. 1019 at 1034, per Slade L.J.

[445] *Leeward Securities Ltd v Lilyheath Properties Ltd* (1983) 17 H.L.R. 35; *Rossi v Hestdrive Ltd* [1985] 1 E.G.L.R. 50; *CIN Properties Ltd v Gill* [1993] 2 E.G.L.R. 97 at 98; [1994] Conv. 316 (L. Crabb).

[446] *Bromley Park Garden Estates Ltd v Moss*, above, at 1034; *Blockbuster Entertainment Ltd v Leakcliff Properties Ltd* [1997] 1 E.G.L.R. 28 at 31.

[447] *British Bakeries (Midlands) Ltd v Michael Testler & Co Ltd* [1986] 1 E.G.L.R. 64. This is the position both at common law and under L & TA 1988: *BRS Northern Ltd v Templeheights Ltd* [1998] 2 E.G.L.R. 182.

[448] L & TA 1988 s.1(3); above, para.19–096. It is necessarily implicit in this requirement that he may only rely upon the reasons which he gives for such a refusal: *Norwich Union Life Insurance v Shopmoor Ltd* [1999] 1 W.L.R. 531 at 545.

[449] *Norwich Union Life Insurance v Shopmoor Ltd* [1999] 1 W.L.R. 531 at 545; *Footwear Corp Ltd v Amplight Properties Ltd* [1999] 1 W.L.R. 551 at 559; *Go West Ltd v Spigarolo* [2003] EWCA Civ 17; [2003] Q.B. 1140 at [17]. It was never resolved prior to the 1988 Act whether the landlord could rely on such unarticulated reasons: see (1963) 79 L.Q.R. 479 (REM), where the conflicting authorities are considered. See too *Searle v Burroughs* (1966) 110 S.J. 248; *Bromley Park Gardens Estates Ltd v Moss*, above at 1034.

[450] *Ashworth Frazer Ltd v Gloucester CC* [2001] UKHL 59; [2001] 1 W.L.R. 2180 at [75]; *Royal Bank of Scotland Plc v Victoria Street (No.3) Ltd* [2008] EWHC 3052 (Ch); [2009] L. & T.R. 17 at [37].

(2) PRINCIPLES OF LAW. The principles of law which are applicable in **19–100**
determining whether a landlord has unreasonably refused his consent have
been summarised by the Court of Appeal.[451] The House of Lords has generally approved of these principles, albeit emphasising that (ii), (iii) and (vi)
below should be treated as overriding.[452]

(i)   The purpose of a qualified covenant is to protect a landlord from
having his premises used or occupied either in an undesirable way
or by an undesirable tenant.[453]

(ii) A landlord is not entitled to refuse his consent to an assignment on
grounds which have nothing whatever to do with the relationship
of landlord and tenant in regard to the subject-matter of the
lease,[454] as where a landlord refused consent in order to achieve a
collateral purpose[455] unconnected with the lease.[456] It follows that
refusal of consent is normally reasonable if it is necessary to
protect the landlord's contractual rights from being prejudiced by
the proposed assignment or sub-letting; and it is normally unreasonable for the landlord to seek to impose a condition which is
designed to increase or enhance the rights he enjoys.[457]

(iii) It is not necessary for the landlord to prove that the conclusions
which led him to refuse consent were justified, if they were

---

[451] *International Drilling Fluids Ltd v Louisville Investments (Uxbridge) Ltd* [1986] Ch. 513 at
519–521; [1986] Conv. 287 (L. Crabb); [2006] Conv. 37 (T. Fancourt). These principles, which
have been frequently applied since, are stated as they stand in the light of subsequent
developments.
[452] *Ashworth Frazer Ltd v Gloucester CC*, above.
[453] *Bates v Donaldson* [1896] 2 Q.B. 241 at 247; *Houlder Brothers & Co Ltd v Gibbs* [1925]
Ch. 575. The landlord will not therefore be precluded from refusing consent to an assignment
merely because he is offered a guarantee. A guarantee "is not a satisfactory substitute for a
satisfactory and responsible tenant": *Warren v Marketing Exchange Ltd* [1988] 2 E.G.L.R. 247 at
252, per Judge Finlay QC cf. *Venetian Glass Gallery Ltd v Next Properties Ltd* [1989] 2 E.G.L.R.
42 at 46. Nor does the fact that the landlord may have recourse to the original tenant (in a lease
granted before 1996) disentitle him from refusing consent to assign where he has genuine
concerns about the performance of the covenants by the proposed assignee: *Royal Bank of
Scotland Plc v Victoria Street (No.3) Ltd* [2008] EWHC 3052 (Ch); [2009] L. & T.R. 17 at
[31].
[454] *Houlder Brothers & Co Ltd v Gibbs*, above; *Norwich Union Life Insurance v Shopmoor Ltd*,
above. It is clear that this principle is a corollary to, and must be read together with, (i) above:
see *International Drilling Fluids Ltd v Louisville Investments (Uxbridge) Ltd*, above, at 520. The
landlord's objections must relate to the reasonably anticipated consequences of the proposed
assignment as well as to the matters listed in (ii): see *Jaison Property Development Co Ltd v Roux
Restaurants Ltd* (1996) 74 P. & C.R. 357.
[455] An "uncovenanted advantage": *Bromley Park Garden Estates Ltd v Moss* [1982] 1 W.L.R.
1019 at 1031, per Cumming-Bruce L.J.
[456] *Bromley Park Garden Estates Ltd v Moss*, above (where the landlord told the tenant that it
was not his practice to permit assignments of residential tenancies, but that he would accept a
surrender of the tenancy); [1983] Conv. 140 (L. Crabb).
[457] *Mount Eden Land Ltd v Straudley Investments Ltd* (1996) 74 P. & C.R. 306 at 310; *Landlord
Protect Ltd v St Anselm Development Co Ltd* [2009] EWCA Civ 99; [2009] 2 P. & C.R. 9 at
[17].

conclusions which might be reached by a reasonable person in the circumstances.⁴⁵⁸ It is only if no reasonable landlord could have refused consent for the reasons stated that the decision to withhold consent will be unreasonable. The court is not entitled to substitute its own view for that of the landlord.⁴⁵⁹

(iv) It may be reasonable for the landlord to refuse his consent to an assignment on the ground of the purpose for which the proposed assignee intends to use the premises, even though that purpose is not forbidden by the lease.⁴⁶⁰ However, it will not be reasonable to withhold consent where the terms of the lease contemplate the particular user, and the assignee intends to use them for that purpose.⁴⁶¹

(v) While a landlord need usually only consider his own relevant interests,⁴⁶² there may be cases where there is such a disproportion between the benefit to the landlord and the detriment that the tenant will suffer if the landlord withholds his consent to assignment, that such a refusal of consent will be unreasonable.⁴⁶³ Thus it may be reasonable for a landlord to refuse his consent to an assignment if the assignee would acquire statutory protection under the Rent Acts,⁴⁶⁴ or the right to acquire the freehold under the Leasehold Reform Act 1967,⁴⁶⁵ when in either case the assignor could not claim or did not want such rights. However, there may be circumstances where the refusal of consent may be

---

⁴⁵⁸ *Pimms Ltd v Tallow Chandlers Company* [1964] 2 Q.B. 547 at 564; *Estates Governors of Alleyn's College v Williams* (1994) 70 P. & C.R. 67 at 72; *Kened Ltd v Connie Investments Ltd* (1995) 70 P. & C.R. 370 at 374; *NCR Ltd v Riverland Portfolio No.1 Ltd (No.2)* [2005] EWCA Civ 312; [2005] L. & T.R. 25 at [30] (explaining that the apparent paradox that a decision may be shown to have been reasonable even if it was not justifiable was no more than semantic). The principle is unaffected by L & TA 1988 s.1 (above, para.19–096): *Air India v Balabel* [1993] 2 E.G.L.R. 66 at 69.

⁴⁵⁹ *Kened Ltd v Connie Investments Ltd*, above, at 374.

⁴⁶⁰ *Bates v Donaldson*, above, at 244. This will be so if the purpose is one to which the landlord may reasonably object.

⁴⁶¹ *Rayburn v Wolf* [1985] 2 E.G.L.R. 235 (qualified covenant against assigning or underletting: refusal of consent to assignment on the ground that the assignee intended to sub-let held to be unreasonable).

⁴⁶² *West Layton Ltd v Ford* [1979] Q.B. 593 at 605; *Ponderosa International Development Inc v Pengap Securities (Bristol) Ltd* [1986] 1 E.G.L.R. 66 at 68; *Venetian Glass Gallery Ltd v Next Properties Ltd* [1989] 2 E.G.L.R. 42 at 46; *NCR Ltd v Riverland Portfolio No.1 Ltd (No.2)*, above, at [34].

⁴⁶³ *International Drilling Fluids Ltd v Louisville Investments (Uxbridge) Ltd* [1986] Ch. 513 at 521, attempting to reconcile divergent lines of authority. In that case the diminution in the paper value of the landlord's reversion (which it had no plans to sell) because of the assignee's intended user, was outweighed by the hardship to the tenant, who could find no other assignee.

⁴⁶⁴ *Lee v K. Carter Ltd* [1949] 1 K.B. 85; *Swanson v Forton* [1949] Ch. 143; *West Layton Ltd v Ford*, above; *Leeward Securities Ltd v Lilyheath Properties Ltd*, above.

⁴⁶⁵ *Norfolk Capital Group Ltd v Kitway Ltd* [1977] Q.B. 506; *Bickel v Duke of Westminster* [1977] Q.B. 517.

unreasonable,[466] even though it may lead to the creation of a tenancy that enjoys some form of statutory protection.[467]

(vi) Subject to these propositions, whether or not the landlord has unreasonably withheld his consent is in each case a question of fact depending upon all the circumstances,[468] and the onus of showing that he acted reasonably rests on the landlord.[469]

(3) OPERATION OF THE PRINCIPLES. While the basic principles to be applied **19–101** are the same whether the alienation under consideration is an assignment or a sub-lease,[470] it should be recognised that "the two forms of transaction have different legal and practical implications, which may affect the application of the general principles in any particular case."[471]

The operation of these principles can be illustrated in relation to two **19–102** particular issues. The first is the extent to which it is reasonable for the landlord to take into account the risk that a proposed assignee or sub-tenant may commit a breach of covenant, particularly as to the user of the premises. The landlord is not confined to what will happen in the event of alienation taking place, as in deciding:

"whether to withhold consent to an assignment reasonable landlords need not confine their consideration to what will necessarily happen; like everyone else taking an important decision, they may have regard to what will probably happen".[472]

Each case is dependent on its own facts, but it has been held that a landlord may reasonably refuse his consent to an assignment or underletting where:

---

[466] *Leeward Securities Ltd v Lilyheath Properties Ltd*, above, at 47.

[467] *Deverall v Wyndham* (1988) 58 P. & C.R. 12. The landlord may take into account the likely diminution in value of the reversion where the proposed sub-tenant would be able to claim a new tenancy under Part II of the Landlord and Tenant Act 1954, see *NCR Ltd v Riverland Portfolio No.1 Ltd (No.2)* [2005] EWCA Civ 312; [2005] L. & T.R. 25.

[468] *International Drilling Fluids Ltd v Louisville Investments (Uxbridge) Ltd*, above, at 521. Care must therefore be taken not to elevate a decision made on the facts of a particular case into a principle of law: *Ashworth Frazer Ltd v Gloucester CC* [2001] UKHL 59; [2001] 1 W.L.R. 2180 at [4], [67], approving the general approach of Lord Denning M.R. in *Bickel v Duke of Westminster*, above, at 524. It is "reasonableness in the general sense" that is material: *Viscount Tredegar v Harwood* [1929] A.C. 72 at 78, per Viscount Dunedin, as approved in *Ashworth Frazer Ltd v Gloucester CC*, above, at [5], [67].

[469] L & TA 1988 s.1(6); above, para.19–096.

[470] *Mount Eden Land Ltd v Straudley Investments Ltd* (1996) 74 P. & C.R. 306 at 310.

[471] *NCR Ltd v Riverland Portfolio No.1 Ltd (No.2)* [2005] EWCA Civ 312; [2005] L. & T.R. 25 at [37], per Carnwath L.J., emphasising that on the facts of that case, which concerned a pre-1996 lease, neither transaction would affect the original tenant's continuing liability under the covenants. That would not of course be the position with a post-1995 lease, where an assignment, but not a sub-lease, would normally effect a release of the original tenant: see below para.20–088.

[472] *Ashworth Frazer Ltd v Gloucester CC*, above, at [70], per Lord Rodger of Earlsferry.

(i) under the terms of a proposed underlease, the underlessee was to use the premises in breach of a user covenant in the head lease[473]

(ii) there were long-standing and serious breaches of a repairing covenant and the landlord was not satisfied that the proposed assignee would remedy them[474]

(iii) the tenant was in breach of a positive covenant to keep open a store for retail trade and the proposed assignee was unlikely to take steps to re-open a store.[475]

Where the landlord reasonably believes that the proposed assignee intends to use the demised premises in breach of a user covenant, a refusal of consent to the assignment may be reasonable. It is not therefore essential for the landlord to prove that the proposed assignee would necessarily be in breach of it.[476] The landlord may withhold consent where he genuinely and reasonably believes that the proposed assignment might lead to a breach of the user covenant, and it would be unusual for such refusal to be held to be unreasonable.[477]

19–103   The second issue concerns the degree to which it is reasonable for the landlord to safeguard his own financial position. In general the courts regard such concerns as a reasonable ground for the refusal of consent. It has been held accordingly that a landlord is entitled to refuse his consent to an assignment where:

(i) the proposed assignee's references were unsatisfactory[478];

(ii) the landlord who had developed the site was intending to sell his reversion to an investor (as the tenant knew) and the financial standing of the proposed assignee was not as strong as that of the tenant thereby reducing the value of the reversion[479]; and

---

[473] *Packaging Centre Ltd v Poland Street Estate Ltd* (1961) 178 E.G. 189; *Granada TV Network Ltd v Great Universal Stores Ltd* (1963) 187 E.G. 391.

[474] *Orlando Investments Ltd v Grosvenor Estate Belgravia* [1989] 2 E.G.L.R. 74; [1989] Conv. 371 (P. F. Smith).

[475] *F. W. Woolworth Plc v Charlwood Alliance Properties Ltd* [1987] 1 E.G.L.R. 53. A "keep open" covenant of his kind cannot be enforced by a mandatory injunction: *Co-operative Insurance Society Ltd v Argyll Stores (Holdings) Ltd* [1998] A.C. 1.

[476] *Ashworth Frazer Ltd v Gloucester CC*, above, overruling *Killick v Second Covent Garden Property Co Ltd* [1973] 1 W.L.R. 658.

[477] *Ashworth Frazer Ltd v Gloucester CC*, above.

[478] *Shanly v Ward* (1913) 29 T.L.R. 714. For the evaluation of references, see *British Bakeries (Midlands) Ltd v Michael Testler & Co Ltd* [1986] 1 E.G.L.R. 64; *Ponderosa International Development Inc v Pengap Securities (Bristol) Ltd* [1986] 1 E.G.L.R. 66; *Mount Eden Land Ltd v Towerstone Ltd* [2003] L. & T.R. 4.

[479] *Ponderosa International Development Inc v Pengap Securities (Bristol) Ltd* [1986] 1 E.G.L.R. 66. The landlord would have been willing to consent to a sub-lease to the proposed assignee instead. It is enough if the landlord has genuine concerns on matters relevant to the value of the reversion, even if the prospect of those concerns materialising is relatively small: *NCR Ltd v Riverland Portfolio No.1 Ltd (No.2)* [2005] EWCA Civ 312; [2005] L. & T.R. 25 (refusal of consent to sub-letting held to be reasonable taking into account the relative weakness of the

(iii) the current tenant wished to re-assign the lease to the original tenant to enable the latter to exercise a break clause and terminate the tenancy.[480]

However, where a tenant sought consent to sub-let at a market rent, it was held to be unreasonable for a landlord to refuse consent on the basis that the market was depressed and that the tenant should wait until it improved.[481] And where a tenant company whose covenant was supported by a guarantee of its sole director, it was held to be unreasonable for a landlord to require as a condition of its consent to assign that a guarantor be provided and that such guarantor would not be released from liability, even in the event of a subsequent assignment effected with the landlord's consent, unless and until reasonable alternative security was provided.[482]

(e) Discrimination. The Equality Act 2010[483] renders it unlawful for a **19–104** person whose permission is required for the disposal of premises to discriminate against another person by not giving permission for the disposal of the premises to the other.[484] For these purposes, a disposal includes, in the case of premises subject to a tenancy, assigning, sub-letting or parting with possession of the whole or part of the premises.[485] Discrimination may be on the grounds of disability, gender reassignment, race, religion or belief, sex or sexual orientation.[486] There are exceptions in relation to owner-occupiers and certain small premises.[487]

(f) Fines. Qualified covenants are subject to a further restriction under the **19–105** Law of Property Act 1925,[488] namely a proviso that no "fine" or similar sum shall be payable in respect of any licence or consent unless the lease expressly

---

prospective sub-tenant's covenant and the inability to pursue the current tenant following the grant of a new tenancy under Part II of the Landlord and Tenant Act 1954); cf. *Design Progressions Ltd v Thurloe Properties Ltd* [2004] EWHC 324 (Ch); [2005] 1 W.L.R. 1.

[480] *Olympia & York Canary Wharf Ltd v Oil Property Investment Ltd* (1994) 69 P. & C.R. 43. Had there been a re-assignment to the original tenant, it does not follow that the original tenant would have been able to terminate the lease, as the break clause may have been spent once he had assigned: *Max Factor Ltd v Wesleyan Assurance Society* [1996] 2 E.G.L.R. 210; and see *Aviva Life & Pensions UK Ltd v Linpac Mouldings Ltd* [2010] EWCA Civ 395; [2010] L. & T.R. 10.

[481] *Blockbuster Entertainment Ltd v Leakcliff Properties Ltd* [1997] 1 E.G.L.R. 28.

[482] *Landlord Protect Ltd v St Anselm Development Co Ltd* [2009] EWCA Civ 99; [2009] 2 P. & C.R. 9. The lease was granted before 1996; had it been granted after 1995, the guarantee would have fallen foul of the anti-avoidance provisions in the L & T(C)A 1995: see *Good Harvest Partnership LLP v Centaur Services Ltd* [2010] EWHC 330 (Ch); [2010] Ch. 426.

[483] Replacing the protection formerly to be found in the Sex Discrimination Act 1976 s.31, Race Relations Act 1976 s.24(1) and Disability Discrimination Act 1995 s.23(5).

[484] s.34.

[485] Equality Act 2010 s.38(2),(3).

[486] These are the characteristics protected by the Act; age and marriage and civil partnership are specifically excluded from the relevant Part of the Act: s.32(1).

[487] Sch.5. The exceptions do not render racial discrimination lawful.

[488] s.144. A similar (but not identical) provision exists in relation to covenants against the alteration of the user of the premises without consent: see L & TA 1927 s.19(3). See *Barclays Bank Plc v Daejan Investments (Grove Hall) Ltd* [1995] 1 E.G.L.R. 68.

provides for it. "Fine" is defined in wide terms[489] which include any valuable consideration given in circumstances such that, if it were money, it would be what is commonly known as a fine.[490] It will therefore include a stipulation in a lease of a public-house which makes it a house "tied" to the landlord, a brewer.[491] However the provision preserves the landlord's right to require the payment of a reasonable sum in respect of any legal or other expenses incurred in relation to the licence or consent.[492] If a fine which a tenant need not pay is in fact paid without protest, the tenant cannot recover it, for the payment is not unlawful but merely unnecessary.[493]

19–106   *(g) Building leases.* In one case no consent is required, namely where a building lease (i.e. a lease granted in consideration wholly or partially of the erection, or the substantial improvement, addition or alteration of buildings) is granted for more than 40 years. If that lease contains a covenant against assigning, underletting or parting with possession without the landlord's consent, there is implied a proviso (notwithstanding any contrary provision) that no consent is required to an assignment, underlease or parting with possession made more than seven years before the end of the term, provided that written notice is given to the landlord within six months.[494] This provision does not apply:

> (i) where the lessor is one of certain public and statutory author-
> ities[495]; or
>
> (ii) to a mining lease, a lease of an agricultural holding or a farm
> business tenancy[496]; or
>
> (iii) to a "qualifying lease" within the Landlord and Tenant Act
> 1927.[497]

19–107   *(h) Breaches.* To amount to a breach of a covenant against assignment, underletting, or parting with possession there must in general be some volun-tary dealing with the property *inter vivos.* Thus a bequest of the lease is no

---

[489] LPA 1925 s.205(1)(xxiii).

[490] *Waite v Jennings* [1906] 2 K.B. 11 at 18.

[491] *Gardner & Co Ltd v Cone* [1928] Ch. 955. See also *Comber v Fleet Electrics Ltd* [1955] 1 W.L.R. 566.

[492] LPA 1925 s.144. It has not been finally decided whether the section confers the right to recover such costs even if no licence or consent is in fact granted: see *Goldman v Abbott* [1989] 2 E.G.L.R. 78 at 79, 81.

[493] *Andrew v Bridgman* [1908] 1 K.B. 596.

[494] L & TA 1927 s.19(1)(b).

[495] L & TA 1927 s19(1)(b).

[496] L & TA 1927 s.19(4) (as amended).

[497] L & TA 1927 s.19(1D) (inserted by L & TCA 1995 s.22); above, para.19–080. A "qualify-ing lease" must be a "new tenancy" granted after 1995: see L & TA 1927 s.19(1E); L & TCA 1995 s.1; below, para.20–010. This third exception has removed the practical significance of this provision for most leases granted after 1995. This is because qualified covenants against assign-ment are generally found in business leases, which will be qualifying leases.

breach,[498] nor is the involuntary vesting of the lease in the trustee in bankruptcy upon the tenant's bankruptcy[499] (as distinct from a voluntary sale by the trustee in bankruptcy[500]), or the compulsory sale of the lease under statutory provisions,[501] or the vesting of the lease in new trustees under an order of the court.[502] Loss of the lease by the execution of a judgment is not regarded as a breach, even where the covenant extends to parting with possession,[503] unless the action and judgment were collusive and designed solely to evade the covenant.[504] A mortgage made by the grant of a sub-lease is a breach,[505] but a declaration of trust made by the tenant for the benefit of his creditors is not.[506] It is neither an assignment[507] nor a parting with possession[508] if the tenant merely allows other persons to share in the use of the premises, or grants a licence for the limited use of part of the premises. But allowing a company formed by the tenant to occupy the premises is parting with possession.[509] In a case where the person prima facie entitled to possession is alleged to have parted with possession to a person in occupation, the ultimate question is whether the former has effectively ceded possession to the latter.[510]

A covenant merely against under-letting is perhaps not broken by an **19–108** assignment[511] or by letting lodgings.[512] A covenant against parting with possession is broken by assignment[513]; and it would presumably be broken by allowing a squatter to acquire title by adverse possession. Under-letting or parting with possession of a part of the property is no breach of a general covenant not to underlet or part with possession[514]; but it is of course otherwise if the covenant is worded (as it usually is) so as to extend to the

---

[498] *For v Swann* (1655) Sty. 482; *Doe d. Goodbehere v Bevan* (1815) 3 M. & S. 353; Woodfall, 11,166 (but see *Berry v Taunton* (1594) Cro.Eliz. 331). *Quaere* as to an assent giving effect to a bequest: see Williams on *Assents* 130. *Re Wright* [1949] Ch. 729 suggests that consent is needed; and see (1963) 27 Conv. (N.S.) 159 (D. G. Barnsley).

[499] *Re Riggs* [1901] 2 K.B. 16.

[500] *Re Wright* [1949] Ch. 729.

[501] *Slipper v Tottenham & Hampstead Junction Ry* (1867) L.R. 4 Eq. 112.

[502] *Marsh v Gilbert* [1980] 2 E.G.L.R. 44.

[503] *Doe d. Mitchinson v Carter (No.1)* (1798) 8 T.R. 57.

[504] *Doe d. Mitchinson v Carter (No.2)* (1799) 8 T.R. 300.

[505] *Serjeant v Nash, Field & Co* [1903] 2 K.B. 304; cf. a legal charge (below, para.24–025).

[506] *Gentle v Faulkner* [1900] 2 Q.B. 267.

[507] *Glan Singh & Co v Devraj Nahar* [1965] 1 W.L.R. 412 (premises shared with partners); *Edwardes v Barrington* (1901) 85 L.T. 650 (licence to use refreshment bar, etc., in theatre).

[508] *Chaplin v Smith* [1926] 1 K.B. 198 (company permitted to run demised garage); *Stening v Abrahams* [1931] 1 Ch. 470 (advertisement hoarding); *Akici v LR Butlin Ltd* [2005] EWCA Civ 1296; [2006] 1 W.L.R. 201.

[509] *Lam Kee Ying Snd. Bhd. v Lam Shes Tong* [1975] A.C. 247.

[510] *Akici v LR Butlin Ltd* [2005] EWCA Civ 1296; [2006] 1 W.L.R. 201 at [39].

[511] *Re Doyle & O'Hara's Contract* [1899] I.R. 113 (no breach); *Greenaway v Adams* (1806) 12 Ves. 395 (breach).

[512] *Doe. d. Pitt v Laming* (1814) 4 Camp. 73, doubted in *Greenslade v Tapscott* (1834) 1 Cr.M. & R. 55.

[513] *Marks v Warren* [1979] 1 All E.R. 29.

[514] *Wilson v Rosenthal* (1906) 22 T.L.R. 233; *Cottell v Baker* (1920) 36 T.L.R. 208; *Cook v Shoesmith* [1951] 1 K.B. 752; *Esdaile v Lewis* [1956] 1 W.L.R. 709 (see (1956) 72 L.Q.R. 325: R.E.M.).

property "or any part thereof". A covenant which prohibits the assignment or sub-letting of "any part" of the premises without the landlord's consent, is however broken by a sub-letting of the whole of the property.[515] A covenant against assignment is not broken where the tenant effects a "virtual" assignment which transfers the whole of the economic benefit of the lease but which does not transfer any property interest and does not therefore alter the underlying relationship between landlord and tenant.[516]

19–109   **3. Covenant to use the premises as a private dwelling-house only.** The tenant may covenant not to use the premises other than for the purpose of a private dwelling-house. The issue has arisen whether such a covenant not only restricts what can be done on the premises but also imposes a limitation on the number of households in the premises.[517] In each case, it is a question of construction of the words of the particular covenant in light of the factual matrix.[518] It has been held that such a covenant prohibits more than one household in the premises (and as a result prohibits the sub-letting of part) where the lease contained a covenant not to sub-let the whole of the premises,[519] but not where the lease contained a covenant not to sub-let the whole *or any part of* the premises.[520] Sometimes the covenant may expressly refer to use "as a *single* private dwelling-house",[521] or an inference to that effect may be made.[522] But otherwise the expression "a private dwelling-house" "takes its nature from its context", and it does not "have any fixed connotation of singularity irrespective of whatever the context may indicate."[523] There is a statutory jurisdiction for the county court to authorise the division of a house in certain circumstances.[524]

4. Covenant to repair

19–110   *(a) The covenant.* In longer leases the tenant often covenants to do all repairs. In shorter leases the landlord commonly assumes liability for external and structural repairs and, in some cases, is required to do so by statute.[525] Save where statute imposes an obligation to repair, the matter is one for negotiation. However, the lease may not make either express or implied

---

[515] *Field v Barkworth* [1986] 1 W.L.R. 137; *Troop v Gibson* [1986] 1 E.G.L.R. 1 at 5.

[516] *Clarence House Ltd v National Westminster Bank Plc* [2009] EWCA Civ 1311; [2010] 1 W.L.R. 1216; on which see Turner [2010] Conv. 99.

[517] See in particular *Martin v David Wilson Homes Ltd* [2004] EWCA Civ 1027; [2004] 3 E.G.L.R. 77, dealing with restrictive covenants contained in a freehold conveyance.

[518] *Martin v David Wilson Homes Ltd*, above, at [25] and [49].

[519] *Dobbs v Linford* [1953] 1 Q.B. 48.

[520] *Downie v Turner* [1951] 2 K.B. 112.

[521] *Re Endericks' Conveyance* [1973] 1 All E.R. 843.

[522] *Barton v Keeble* [1928] Ch. 517.

[523] *Martin v David Wilson Homes Ltd*, above, at [44] per Buxton L.J., distinguishing *Crest Nicholson Residential (South) Ltd v McAllister* [2002] EWHC 2443 (Ch); [2003] 1 All E.R. 46.

[524] HA 1985 s.610; below, para.32–092.

[525] See L & TA 1985 s.11; above, para.19–042.

provision for the parties' respective repairing obligations.[526] In such circumstances the tenant may sometimes be liable because of the general law relating to waste,[527] though recourse to this form of liability is now rare.[528]

(1) "REPAIR". "Keeping in repair means remedying disrepair."[529] In turn,   **19–111**
disrepair "connotes the idea of making good damage so as to leave the subject so far as possible as though it had not been damaged."[530] The proof of damage (actual or impending) is therefore a central component of liability to repair, and failure to prove damage to the subject matter of the covenant will be fatal to a claim. Where a tenant complained that his house was uninhabitable owing to condensation dampness, no liability arose as he could not prove that there was any damage to the "structure or exterior" (the subject matter of the relevant statutory covenant) of the premises.[531] There was no disrepair, in that the structure and exterior was in no worse condition than it had ever been.[532]

The extent of the liability of any party under a repairing covenant depends   **19–112**
upon the construction of the particular covenant.[533] Relevant factors in deciding whether work can be regarded as "repair" include the nature of the premises, the terms of the lease, the state when let, the character of the defect, the nature and cost of the remedial work and who is to do it, its effect on the value and lifespan of the building, the comparative cost of alternative remedial works and their impact on the occupants' use and enjoyment of the building. The weight given to each of these factors may vary from case to case.[534]

Where a party is liable to repair the property, he is not required to undertake   **19–113**
the reconstruction of substantially the whole of the subject-matter of the property let, but only the renewal or replacement of subsidiary parts.[535] There is no obligation "to make a new and different thing."[536] However, by virtue of an ancient and anomalous rule, if the premises have been destroyed by a calamity, such as a fire, the whole of the premises must be rebuilt.[537] Nor is

---

[526] *Demetriou v Poolaction Ltd* [1991] 1 E.G.L.R. 100 at 104. See too *Tennant Radiant Heat Ltd v Warrington Development Corp* [1988] 1 E.G.L.R. 41 at 43.

[527] Above, paras 19–049 et seq., where the exceptions are also stated.

[528] See *Mancetter Developments Ltd v Garmanson Ltd* [1986] Q.B. 1212 at 1218.

[529] *Southwark LBC v Mills* [2001] 1 A.C. 1 at 8, per Lord Hoffmann.

[530] *Anstruther-Gough-Calthorpe v McOscar* [1924] 1 K.B. 716 at 734, per Atkin L.J.

[531] *Quick v Taff Ely BC* [1986] Q.B. 809.

[532] *Quick v Taff Ely BC*, above, at 821.

[533] For a useful summary of the tests to be applied in determining whether work falls within the scope of a covenant to repair, see *McDougall v Easington DC* (1989) 58 P. & C.R. 201 at 207.

[534] *Holding and Management Ltd v Property Holding and Investment Trust Plc* [1990] 1 All E.R. 938 at 945 (omitted from the report at [1989] 1 W.L.R. 1313, 1321).

[535] *Lurcott v Wakely* [1911] 1 K.B. 905 at 924 (obligation to rebuild wall); *Minja Properties Ltd v Cussins Property Group Plc* [1998] 2 E.G.L.R. 52 (replacement of window units).

[536] *Lister v Lane* [1893] 2 Q.B. 212 at 217, per Lord Esher M.R. See, e.g. *Halliard Property Co Ltd v Clarke Investments Ltd* [1984] 1 E.G.L.R. 45 (no obligation to replace "jerry-built" structure with properly constructed building).

[537] *Bullock v Dommitt* (1796) 6 T.R. 650. As regards war damage there is now no such liability: see Landlord and Tenant (War Damage) Act 1939 s.1 (reversing the effect of *Redmond v Dainton* [1920] 2 K.B. 256, where there was liability to repair serious bomb damage); above, para.18–097.

an obligation to repair an obligation to improve the premises,[538] though it may be that the repair of a property will necessarily improve it.[539] The question is one of degree.[540] A party who is under an obligation to repair is not absolved from liability because the disrepair has been caused by an inherent defect in the design or construction of the building demised.[541] Indeed, the inherent defect must be corrected if that is the only practicable method of remedying the disrepair.[542] However, there will be no liability to repair if the inherent defect causes no damage within the scope of the covenant.[543] A party who is under an obligation to repair must also make good any consequential damage[544] and pay compensation for any consequential loss.[545]

19–114   Expressions such as "tenantable repair", "sufficient repair", or "good and substantial repair" seem to add little to the meaning of the word "repair",[546] and indicate "such repair as, having regard to the age, character and locality of the house, would make it reasonably fit for the occupation of a reasonably-minded tenant of the class who would be likely to take it".[547] The tenant must keep the premises in substantially the same state as they were at the time of the demise.[548] The standard will not diminish merely because the tenant's failure to repair the premises makes them unattractive,[549] or because of changes in the character of the neighbourhood.[550]

19–115   A covenant to "keep" the premises in good repair imposes an obligation on the covenantor:

---

[538] Neither party is obliged "to provide the other with a better house than there was to start with": *Quick v Taff Ely BC* [1986] Q.B. 809 at 821, per Lawton L.J. See, e.g. *Wainwright v Leeds CC* (1984) 13 H.L.R. 117 (no obligation to install damp course in old house); *Eyre v McCracken* (2000) 80 P. & C.R. 220; cf. *Elmcroft Developments Ltd v Tankersley-Sawyer* [1984] 1 E.G.L.R. 47 (obligation to replace defective slate damp-proof course in flat in a "high-class fashionable residential area" with a silicone injection course was a repair).

[539] *Quick v Taff Ely BC*, above, at 823; *Sutton (Hastoe) Housing Association v Williams* [1988] 1 E.G.L.R. 56 at 58.

[540] *Brew Brothers Ltd v Snax (Ross) Ltd* [1970] 1 Q.B. 612; *Ravenseft Properties Ltd v Davstone (Holdings) Ltd* [1980] Q.B. 12.

[541] *Ravenseft Properties Ltd v Davstone (Holdings) Ltd*, above (tenant liable for inherent defects in walls); *Smedley v Chumley & Hawke Ltd* (1981) 44 P. & C.R. 50 (landlord liable for defective foundations under covenant to keep main walls and roof in good structural repair and condition).

[542] *Ravenseft Properties Ltd v Davstone (Holdings) Ltd*, above, (insertion of expansion joints); *Stent v Monmouth DC* (1987) 54 P. & C.R. 193 (replacement of door); *Creska Ltd v Hammersmith & Fulham LBC* [1998] 3 E.G.L.R. 35 (replacement of underfloor heaters with improved features).

[543] *Quick v Taff Ely BC*, above; *Post Office v Aquarius Properties Ltd* [1987] 1 All E.R. 1055.

[544] Such as damage to the decorative state of the property: *McGreal v Wake* [1984] 1 E.G.L.R. 42; *Bradley v Chorley BC* [1985] 2 E.G.L.R. 49.

[545] Including, where necessary, the cost of temporarily re-housing the tenant: *McGreal v Wake*, above.

[546] *Proudfoot v Hart* (1890) 25 QBD 42 at 50, 51; *Anstruther-Gough-Calthorpe v McOscar* [1924] 1 K.B. 716 at 722, per Bankes L.J.; at 729, per Scrutton L.J. cf. at 731, per Atkin L.J.

[547] *Proudfoot v Hart*, above, at 55, per Lopes L.J.; *Crédit Suisse v Beegas Nominees Ltd* [1994] 4 All E.R. 803 at 821.

[548] *Gutteridge v Munyard* (1834) 7 C. & P. 129 at 133.

[549] *Ladbroke Hotels Ltd v Sandhu* [1995] 2 E.G.L.R. 92 at 95.

[550] *Anstruther-Gough-Calthorpe v McOscar*, above.

(i) to put the premises into repair even if they are in a state of disrepair at the start of the term[551]; and

(ii) to ensure that they do not thereafter fall into a state of disrepair.[552]

The addition of a requirement to keep the premises "in good condition" **19–116** may be significant, and imposes liability on the covenantor to undertake work, such as the correction of an inherent defect, that is not a repair strictly so called.[553] The insertion into the covenant of words such as "fair wear and tear excepted" relieve the tenant from liability for any disrepair which he can show has resulted from the reasonable use of the premises and the ordinary operation of natural forces. However he remains liable for any consequential damage, such as damage to the interior resulting from the tenant's failure to prevent rain entering where tiles have slipped from the roof or a skylight has become defective.[554]

(2) NOTICE OF DISREPAIR. In general, a covenantor is in breach of covenant **19–117** to keep in repair as soon as the disrepair occurs even though he is unaware of it.[555] It is now clear that this is the general rule and not, as was previously thought, the exception to it.[556] It has not been settled whether this rule applies:

(i) where the covenant is merely to repair and not to keep in repair[557]; or

(ii) where the breach is caused by an occurrence wholly outside the covenantor's control.[558]

---

[551] *Payne v Haine* (1847) 16 M. & W. 541 at 545; *Proudfoot v Hart*, above, at 50 and at 55; *Crédit Suisse v Beegas Nominees Ltd*, above, at 821.

[552] *Proudfoot v Hart*, above, at 50.

[553] *Crédit Suisse v Beegas Nominees Ltd*, above, at 821, 822; *Welsh v Greenwich LBC* (2000) 33 H.L.R. 40 (landlord liable for failure to provide thermal insulation causing excessive condensation and black spot mould); *Fluor Daniel Properties Ltd v Shortlands Investments Ltd* [2001] 2 E.G.L.R. 103; *Mason v Totalfinaelf UK Ltd* [2003] EWHC 1604; [2003] 3 E.G.L.R. 91. See too *Norwich Union Life Insurance Society v British Railways Board* [1987] 2 E.G.L.R. 137 (covenant "when necessary to rebuild, reconstruct or replace" in a 150-year lease might require the tenant to rebuild the premises).

[554] *Regis Property Co Ltd v Dudley* [1959] A.C. 370.

[555] *British Telecommunications Plc v Sun Life Assurance Society Plc* [1996] Ch. 69 (breach of landlord's covenant to keep the building in repair broken, when the wall below the demised premises began to bulge) [1997] Conv. 59 (P. F. Smith); *Passley v Wandsworth LBC* (1996) 30 H.L.R. 165 (landlord liable for burst pipe in the roof of a block of flats). See too *Melles & Co v Holme* [1918] 2 K.B. 100; *Bishop v Consolidated London Properties Ltd* (1933) 102 L.J.K.B. 257; *Loria v Hammer* [1989] 1 E.G.L.R. 249; *Ladsky v TSB Bank Plc* (1996) 74 P. & C.R. 372 at 375; cf. *Trane (UK) Ltd v Provident Mutual Life Assurance* [1995] 1 E.G.L.R. 33 at 37.

[556] *British Telecommunications Plc v Sun Life Assurance Society Plc*, above, at 75.

[557] The point was left open in *British Telecommunications Plc v Sun Life Assurance Society Plc*, above, at 79, though in principle, the rule should be equally applicable.

[558] *British Telecommunications Plc v Sun Life Assurance Society Plc*, above, at 79, where it was suggested, *obiter*, that it did not. The contrary is however arguable. The covenantor who has undertaken the obligation might be expected to bear the risk rather than the covenantee, in accordance with normal contractual principles.

However, even where the rule is applicable, the covenantee is well advised to inform the covenantor of the breach in order to mitigate his loss.[559]

19–118   To this general rule, there is an important exception. Where a landlord has covenanted to repair the premises which are the subject matter of the lease (and of which the tenant has therefore been granted exclusive possession), he is not liable for any breach until he has been given notice of the disrepair[560] and has had a reasonable time to remedy it.[561] These conditions are implied into the covenant both because of the unreasonableness of expecting the landlord to respond to something of which he lacks notice and because the tenant is likely to be in a better position than the landlord to know of the defect.[562] However, the rule applies not only to those defects of which the tenant knows, so that he is in a position to give the landlord notice, but also to latent defects where such notice is impossible.[563] It is not necessary that the landlord should be informed by the tenant.[564] It is sufficient if notice of the disrepair comes to the landlord's attention from a responsible source,[565] or if he has information that would place a reasonable landlord on inquiry.[566] The mere fact that the building is visibly out of repair,[567] or that the landlord has reserved a right to enter and view the state of repair,[568] is not however enough.

19–119   The Defective Premises Act 1972[569] has substantially qualified the require-ment that a landlord is not liable for any disrepair to the demised premises until he receives notice. If a landlord is under an obligation to maintain or repair the premises,[570] or has a right to enter them to carry out repairs or maintenance,[571] he owes a duty of care to all persons (including the tenant) who are likely to be affected by defects in the state of the premises. The duty arises when he either knows (from whatever source) or ought in all the circumstances to have known of the relevant defect.[572] It has been emphasised

---

[559] *Minchburn Ltd v Peck* [1988] 1 E.G.L.R. 53 at 55.

[560] *Makin v Watkinson* (1870) L.R. 6 Ex. 25; *Torrens v Walker* [1906] 2 Ch. 166; *McCarrick v Liverpool Corp* [1947] A.C. 219.

[561] *Calabar Properties Ltd v Stitcher* [1984] 1 W.L.R. 287 at 298; *Morris v Liverpool City Council* [1988] 1 E.G.L.R. 47.

[562] *Murphy v Hurly* [1922] 1 A.C. 369 at 375, 376, 383.

[563] *O'Brien v Robinson* [1973] A.C. 912 (tenant injured by collapse of bedroom ceiling). For criticism of this rule, see *McGreal v Wake* [1984] 1 E.G.L.R. 42 at 43; (1974) 37 M.L.R. 377 (J. I. Reynolds).

[564] *Dinefwr BC v Jones* [1987] 2 E.G.L.R. 58 at 59; *Hall v Howard* (1988) 57 P. & C.R. 226 at 230.

[565] *Dinefwr BC v Jones* [1987] 2 E.G.L.R. 58 at 59; *Hall v Howard* (1988) 57 P. & C.R. 226 at 230.

[566] *Griffin v Pillet* [1926] 1 K.B. 17 at 21; *O'Brien v Robinson*, above, at 930; *Hall v Howard*, above, at 230.

[567] *Torrens v Walker*, above.

[568] *Hugall v M'Lean* (1885) 53 L.T. 94; *Torrens v Walker*, above; *McCarrick v Liverpool Corporation* [1947] A.C. 219.

[569] See above, para.19–046; and below.

[570] Defective Premises Act 1972 s.4(1).

[571] Defective Premises Act 1972 s.4(4).

[572] Defective Premises Act 1972 s.4(2); see, e.g. *Clarke v Taff Ely BC* (1980) 10 H.L.R. 44 (reasonably foreseeable that floors might rot due to dampness, but landlord failed to carry out inspections).

that this does not require analysis of concepts of contractual notice, the simple issue being whether the landlord has taken such care as is reasonable in all the circumstances to see that the claimant is reasonably safe from personal injury.[573] The landlord will be liable therefore for any injury to such a person or to their property where:

(i) he was negligent in not discovering the defect that caused the harm, even though he was given no notice of that defect; and

(ii) that defect was one which fell within the scope of his repairing obligations or which he had a right to enter in order to rectify.[574]

(3) EXTENSION OF LIABILITY. The wide duty of care imposed by the Defective Premises Act 1972[575] abrogates the former rule[576] that the landlord's obligation to repair, being contractual, did not cover injury to the tenant's family or visitors.[577] It also extends the landlord's potential liability, in effect converting a mere right to enter to carry out repairs and maintenance into a duty to do such works of repair and maintenance as are necessary to ensure the safety of those who might be injured by reason of the disrepair.[578] That duty is owed to the tenant himself except where the disrepair has arisen because of the tenant's own failure to carry out an express repairing obligation in the tenancy.[579]

19–120

(b) Remedies

(1) WHERE THE LANDLORD IS IN BREACH OF COVENANT. Where it is the landlord who breaks a repairing covenant, damages may not be an adequate remedy for the tenant, particularly if the breach concerns property not comprised in the lease and so is not accessible to the tenant. Specific performance may be and often is[580] decreed against the landlord, either under the court's

19–121

---

[573] *Sykes v Harry* [2001] EWCA Civ 167; [2001] Q.B. 1014 at 1024.

[574] There is no liability if it was outside the scope of those obligations: *McNerny v Lambeth LBC* [1989] 1 E.G.L.R. 81 at 83; *McAuley v Bristol City Council* [1992] Q.B. 134 at 145.

[575] Above. The duty is confined to the premises let and does not include other property of the landlord's over which the tenant is permitted to have access: *King v South Northamptonshire DC* (1991) 64 P. & C.R. 35 at 40. The landlord may however owe the tenant and his visitors a duty of care in respect of such property under the Occupiers' Liability Act 1957 s.2.

[576] See *Cavalier v Pope* [1906] A.C. 428; *Ryall v Kidwell* [1914] 3 K.B. 135.

[577] See *Rimmer v Liverpool City Council* [1985] Q.B. 1 at 11. *Cavalier v Pope* itself would not be decided differently, because the obligation to repair in that case arose under a collateral agreement and not under the tenancy as s.4(1) of the 1972 Act requires. The Act leaves intact the other limb of the decision in *Cavalier v Pope*, above, that in the absence of any relevant repairing obligation, a landlord is under no liability for letting a dangerous house: *Rimmer v Liverpool City Council*, above, at 11; *McNerny v Lambeth LBC* [1989] 1 E.G.L.R. 81.

[578] Defective Premises Act 1972 s.4(4); *Smith v Bradford Metropolitan Council* (1982) 44 P. & C.R. 171; *Hamilton v Martell Securities Ltd* [1984] Ch. 266 at 271; *Barrett v Lounova (1982) Ltd* [1990] 1 Q.B. 348 at 359.

[579] Defective Premises Act 1972 s.4(4).

[580] See *Joyce v Liverpool City Council* [1996] Q.B. 252.

inherent jurisdiction[581] or, in the case of dwellings, by statute.[582] A court may exceptionally even grant a mandatory injunction in interlocutory proceedings to require the performance of a landlord's obligation to repair or maintain.[583]

19–122   In a case where damages are appropriate, the tenant is entitled to those damages which will, so far as possible, put him in the position he would have been if the breach of covenant had not occurred.[584] In turn, its measure will depend upon whether the tenant:

> (i) remains in possession, when it will be the loss of comfort and convenience that results from the disrepair; or

> (ii) disposes of his interest, when it will be the diminution in the value of the lease (if he assigns his interest) or the rental (if he sub-lets) caused by the landlord's breach of covenant.[585]

19–123   If, after giving notice of the default of the landlord, the tenant does the repairs himself, he may deduct his expenditure from his payments of rent, exercising his right of set-off at common law.[586] Even if he does not undertake the repairs, the tenant may withhold any rent payable to the landlord. In proceedings brought by the landlord to forfeit the lease or to recover the rent, the tenant may then claim an equitable set-off in respect of his claim against the landlord for the disrepair.[587] However, the right is a personal, not a proprietary, right,[588] and it is therefore not open to the tenant to assert the set-off against an assignee of the landlord against whom the damages claim is

---

[581] *Jeune v Queens Cross Properties Ltd* [1974] Ch. 97 (landlord ordered to reinstate balcony although not part of demised premises); *Francis v Cowlcliffe Ltd* (1976) 33 P. & C.R. 368 at 374 (lift); *Tustian v Johnston* [1993] 2 All E.R. 673 at 680. For a possible objection, see *Gordon v Selico Co Ltd* [1985] 2 E.G.L.R. 79 at 84; on appeal: [1986] 1 E.G.L.R. 71 at 75.

[582] L & TA 1985 s.17, replacing HA 1974 s.125.

[583] See, e.g. *Peninsular Maritime Ltd v Padseal Ltd* [1981] 2 E.G.L.R. 43; *Parker v Camden LBC* [1986] Ch. 162 at 173.

[584] *Calabar Properties Ltd v Stitcher* [1984] 1 W.L.R. 287.

[585] *Wallace v Manchester City Council* (1998) 30 H.L.R. 1111; *Earle v Charalambous* [2006] EWCA Civ 1090; [2007] H.L.R. 8.

[586] *Lee-Parker v Izzet* [1971] 1 W.L.R. 1688; *Asco Developments Ltd v Gordon* [1978] 2 E.G.L.R. 41 (where the possibility of an equitable set-off for an unliquidated claim was deliberately not explored).

[587] *Melville v Grapelodge Developments Ltd* [1980] 1 E.G.L.R. 42; *British Anzani (Felixstowe) Ltd v International Marine Management (UK) Ltd* [1980] Q.B. 137. Provided that the claim is made in good faith, the landlord's claim for possession will be stayed pending trial: *British Anzani (Felixstowe) Ltd v International Marine Management (UK) Ltd*, above; *Haringey LBC v Stewart* (1991) 23 H.L.R. 557 at 559. Because the right to a set-off is in these circumstances equitable, it is subject to equitable defences, e.g. want of clean hands by the tenant: *Televantos v McCulloch* [1991] 1 E.G.L.R. 123 (where the defence was not established). However, a tenant may not set off a claim against the landlord for damages for disrepair as a defence to an action for service charge brought by a manager appointed by the court or the leasehold valuation tribunal: *Maunder Taylor v Blaquiere* [2002] EWCA Civ 1633; [2003] 1 W.L.R. 379.

[588] *Muscat v Smith* [2003] EWCA Civ 962; [2003] 1 W.L.R. 2853 at [37] et seq., approved in *Edlington Properties Ltd v JH Fenner & Co Ltd* [2006] EWCA Civ 403; [2006] 1 W.L.R. 1583 at [20].

being made.[589] The right to set-off may be excluded by the terms of the lease,[590] but only by a clear and explicit provision.[591]

(2) WHERE THE TENANT IS IN BREACH OF COVENANT. Apart from forfeiture, **19–124** the remedies available to a landlord for breach of a tenant's repairing covenant are damages and, in appropriate cases, a decree of specific performance.[592] Until recently, it was thought that specific performance would not be decreed against a tenant,[593] but the reasons for that limitation was questionable.[594] However, "it will be a rare case in which the remedy of specific performance will be the appropriate one," because the lease will normally have reserved to the landlord the right to forfeit or to enter the premises and do the repairs at the tenant's expense.[595]

The measure of damages recoverable for the breach of a tenant's repairing **19–125** covenant formerly varied according to the time of the breach.[596] If the breach occurred during the term, the damages were calculated on the decrease in the value of the reversion caused by the breach.[597] The longer the lease had to run, the less would be the damages. But if the breach occurred at the end of the term, the full cost of repairing the premises was recoverable by the landlord[598]; and (by way of exception to the ordinary rule that the measure of damages is the loss actually suffered) it was held to make no difference that

[589] *Edlington Properties Ltd v JH Fenner & Co Ltd* [2006] EWCA Civ 403; [2006] 1 W.L.R. 1583, distinguishing *Muscat v Smith* [2003] EWCA Civ 962; [2003] 1 W.L.R. 2853. However, the tenant may claim a set-off against the assignee of the reversion if the lease makes provision to such effect: *Edlington Properties Ltd v JH Fenner & Co Ltd* at [64].

[590] *Electricity Supply Nominees Ltd v I.A.F. Group Ltd* [1993] 1 W.L.R. 1059; *Star Rider Ltd v Inntrepreneur Pub Co* [1998] 1 E.G.L.R. 53; *Unchained Growth III Plc v Granbyvillage (Manchester) Management Co Ltd* [2000] 1 W.L.R. 739. In those cases it was held that such terms are not subject to the provisions of the Unfair Contract Terms Act 1977. It is uncertain whether the Unfair Terms in Consumer Contracts Regulations (SI 1999/2083) apply to such terms: see (1995) 111 L.Q.R. 655 (S. & C. Bright).

[591] *Connaught Restaurants Ltd v Indoor Leisure Ltd* [1994] 1 W.L.R. 501 (landlord's right to payment of rent "without deduction" did not exclude tenant's equitable right of set-off in respect of repairs).

[592] *Rainbow Estates Ltd v Tokenhold Ltd* [1999] Ch. 64; [1998] J.B.L. 564 (P. Luxton); [1999] C.L.J. 283 (S.B.) The trend of modern authority is to decree specific performance if it is appropriate: cf. *Tito v Waddell (No.2)* [1977] Ch. 106 at 321; *Posner v Scott-Lewis* [1987] Ch. 27; [1987] C.L.J. 21 (G. H. Jones).

[593] Based on the authority of *Hill v Barclay* (1810) 16 Ves. 402 at 405.

[594] One of the main justifications was lack of mutuality: *Hill v Barclay*, above, at 405. However, as a tenant can seek specific performance of a landlord's repairing obligations (below), the force of this objection had been "much weakened": *Regional Properties Ltd v City of London Real Property Co Ltd* [1981] 1 E.G.L.R. 33 at 34, per Oliver J. Prior to *Rainbow Estates v Tokenhold Ltd*, above, the Law Commission had recommended that a landlord should be able to obtain specific performance of a tenant's repairing covenants: (1996) Law Com. No.238 Pt IX.

[595] *Rainbow Estates Ltd v Tokenhold Ltd*, above, at 74, per Lawrence Collins, QC. In that case, the lease contained neither a forfeiture clause nor a power for the landlord to enter to execute repairs.

[596] For a useful summary of the principles, see *Crown Estate Commissioners v Town Investments Ltd* [1992] 1 E.G.L.R. 61 at 63.

[597] *Doe d. Worcester Trustees v Rowlands* (1841) 9 C. & P. 734; *Ebbetts v Conquest* [1895] 2 Ch. 377, affirmed, *Conquest v Ebbetts* [1896] A.C. 490. This principle is unaffected by L & TA 1927 s.18 (below): see *Crewe Services & Investment Corporation v Silk* [1998] 2 E.G.L.R. 1.

[598] *Joyner v Weeks* [1891] 2 Q.B. 31.

the landlord did not propose to carry out the repairs but intended to demolish the premises instead.[599]

19–126   However, a statutory cap on damages is imposed by the Landlord and Tenant Act 1927.[600] This provides that damages for breach of a repairing covenant[601] are not to exceed the diminution in the value of the reversion,[602] i.e. the difference between the value of the reversion with the repairs done and its value without.[603] Whether the repairs led to a diminution in value of the reversion depends on the particular facts of each case, and the court may draw inferences from circumstantial evidence.[604] In normal cases when repairs are likely to be done (and in some cases, perhaps even where they are not[605]) the cost of executing them provides the best guide to the diminution in the value of the reversion,[606] at least where the term has come to an end.[607] The landlord's claim is not reduced merely because he has let the premises to a new tenant who has covenanted to repair them,[608] or because his reversion is of very short duration.[609] But no damages at all are recoverable if the premises are to be demolished, or structurally altered in such a way as to make the repairs valueless, at or soon after the end of the term.[610] This is so even if in

---

[599] *Joyner v Weeks*, above, at 44. But this exception does not apply to a covenant to reinstate after alterations: *James v Hutton* [1950] 1 K.B. 9. As to the effects of L & TA 1927 s.19(2), in such a case, *quaere*: *Joyner v Weeks*, above.

[600] s.18.

[601] A covenant to redecorate the premises at the end of the term has been held to comprise a repairing covenant for the purposes of the 1927 Act: *Latimer v Carney* [2006] EWCA Civ 1417; [2007] 1 P. & C.R. 13.

[602] *Smiley v Townshend* [1950] 2 K.B. 311; *Family Management v Gray* [1980] 1 E.G.L.R. 46.

[603] *Hanson v Newman* [1934] Ch. 298; *Shortlands Investments Ltd v Cargill Plc* [1995] 1 E.G.L.R. 51 at 56.

[604] *Latimer v Carney*, above, at [29]. It is not therefore necessary in every case to adduce expert evidence of the diminution in value consequential upon the tenant's breach, as "Parliament certainly did not intend that section 18 should render it impossible for a landlord to obtain proper recompense for breaches of the repair covenant without undue expense or delay": *Latimer v Carney*, above, at [39], per Arden L.J., following *Jones v Herxheimer* [1950] 2 K.B. 106.

[605] See *Shortlands Investments Ltd v Cargill Plc*, above, at 56; but cf. *Haviland v Long* [1952] 2 Q.B. 80 at 84. In the *Shortlands* case, the fact that the landlords had a reversion with a negative value did not deprive them of their claim for dilapidations, because the disrepair increased the amount of the reverse premium that they had to pay to an incoming tenant.

[606] *Jones v Herxheimer*, above; *Culworth Estates Ltd v Society of Licensed Victuallers* [1991] 2 E.G.L.R. 54 at 56; *Latimer v Carney*, above (where the landlord had to carry out repairs before the property could be re-let). If the cost of carrying out the repairs exceeds the diminution in the value of the reversion, it will be reduced accordingly: *Shortlands Investments Ltd v Cargill Plc*, above.

[607] See *Crewe Services & Investment Corporation v Silk* [1998] 2 E.G.L.R. 1, holding that the cost of repairs was not the appropriate measure where the landlord sought damages during the currency of the term. In such a case, if the landlord failed to lead evidence as to the diminution of the value of the reversion caused by the breach, the court would quantify damages by applying a severe discount (75% in *Crewe*) to the cost of repairs: see further on discounting *Latimer v Carney*, above, at [44].

[608] *Haviland v Long*, above.

[609] *Jaquin v Holland* [1960] 1 W.L.R. 258; *Lloyds Bank Ltd v Lake* [1961] 1 W.L.R. 884.

[610] See, e.g. *Cunliffe v Goodman* [1950] 2 K.B. 237; *Mather v Barclays Bank Plc* [1987] 2 E.G.L.R. 254; (1988) 104 L.Q.R. 372 (D. N. Clarke); *Latimer v Carney*, above, at [34] et seq., contrasting circumstances where a purchaser would be likely to upgrade the premises in such a

the event no demolition is carried out.[611] But damages will be recoverable if the reason for the demolition is merely the tenant's breach of his repairing obligations.[612] These rules relate only to repairing covenants. Damages for breach of other covenants (e.g. against making alterations) are recoverable in the usual way.[613] It should be noted, however, that developments in the law of damages mean that the rule embodied in the 1927 Act may do no more than reflect what is now the common law. It appears that a claimant can only recover the cost of remedying a breach of contract if it is reasonable for him to do so, which will not normally be the case unless he intends to do the work (and not always then).[614]

(c) Appointment of a receiver or manager. A problem that has often arisen **19–127** in recent years is that of a landlord of a block of flats who, although in receipt of rent and service charge from the tenants, fails to carry out his repairing obligations under the lease.[615] Part II of the Landlord and Tenant Act 1987 makes provision for a tenant of a flat to apply to a leasehold valuation tribunal for the appointment of a manager.[616] He may be appointed to carry out such functions in connection with the management of the premises and of a receiver as the court thinks fit.[617] The tribunal may appoint a manager only where it is satisfied that it is just and convenient to make an order in all the circumstances of the case and that one of four statutory grounds exist.[618] As regards other forms of leasehold properties, the court has a wide jurisdiction[619] to appoint a receiver and manager if it is just and convenient to do

way that the state of repair was of limited relevance, i.e. only some of the repair works would survive the refurbishment.

[611] *Keats v Graham* [1960] 1 W.L.R. 30.

[612] *Hibernian Property Co Ltd v Liverpool Corp* [1973] 1 W.L.R. 751, also holding that the intention to demolish must be that of the landlord: *sed quaere.*

[613] *Eyre v Rea* [1947] K.B. 567.

[614] *Ruxley Electronics and Construction Ltd v Forsyth* [1996] A.C. 344; *Latimer v Carney,* above at [24]; *PGFSA v Royal & Sun Alliance Insurance Plc* [2010] EWHC 1459 (TCC); [2011] 1 P. & C.R. 11.

[615] See *Clayhope Properties Ltd v Evans* [1986] 1 W.L.R. 1223 at 1231; *Blawdziewicz v Diadon Establishment* [1988] 2 E.G.L.R. 52 at 53.

[616] L & TA 1987 s.21(1). The building must contain two or more flats: L & TA 1987 s.21(2). For the definition of a "flat" for these purposes, see L & TA 1987 s.60(1).

[617] L & TA 1987 s.24(1). The scheme may extend to premises outside the leaseholders' flats provided there is a nexus between the manager's functions and those premises: *Cawsand Fort Management Co Ltd v Stafford* [2007] EWCA Civ 1187; [2008] 1 W.L.R. 371.

[618] L & TA 1987 s.24(2). The grounds are complex: in broad terms, they include breach of an obligation owed to the tenant relating to management, the making of unreasonable service charges or unreasonable variable administration charges and breach of codes of management practice.

[619] Under Senior Courts Act 1981 s.37. This jurisdiction cannot be exercised where application can be made under L & TA 1987 s.24: see L & TA 1987 s.21(6).

so.[620] The receiver, once appointed, collects the payments from the tenants and applies them in carrying out the repairs.[621]

19–128   Part III of the Landlord and Tenant Act 1987 enables tenants of flats to acquire compulsorily their landlord's reversionary interest in certain cases where he is in breach of his obligations of repair, maintenance, insurance or management of the premises.[622] Furthermore, Part 2 of the Commonhold and Leasehold Reform Act 2002[623] confers on certain leaseholders a "right to manage" ("RTM") without proof of fault by, or payment of compensation to, the landlord. The complex statutory provisions apply to property which is predominantly residential, enabling the take-over of the property's management functions through the vehicle of an RTM company without affecting the ownership of the reversion.

19–129   *(d) Internal decorative repairs.* The Law of Property Act 1925[624] enables the court in certain cases to relieve the tenant from liability for internal decorative repairs if the landlord acts unreasonably. There are a number of exceptions,[625] e.g. where the liability arises under an express covenant to decorate which the tenant has never performed. The power of the court to grant relief is not confined to proceedings for forfeiture but extends to actions for damages.

(e) The Leasehold Property (Repairs) Act 1938

19–130   (1) OBJECT AND SCOPE OF ACT. This Act was passed in order to protect tenants of small properties under long leases from having to pay heavy bills for dilapidations under the threat of forfeiture for breach of covenant. The mischief which the Act was designed to remedy was that speculators could buy the reversion of dilapidated dwelling-houses for a low price, enforce forfeiture of the lease on account of non-repair, and thereby get the residue of the term for nothing.[626] As later extended,[627] the Act applies to all types of property (except agricultural holdings and farm business tenancies[628]) where the tenancy was granted for a term certain of not less than seven years, and has at least three years unexpired.[629] However, its applicability is limited to cases where there has been a breach by the tenant of a covenant to keep or put in

---

[620] *Hart v Emelkirk Ltd* [1983] 1 W.L.R. 1289; *Daiches v Bluelake Investments Ltd* (1985) 51 P. & C.R. 51. The court will not appoint a receiver to carry out duties imposed by statute on a particular body (such as a local authority): *Parker v Camden LBC* [1986] Ch. 162.

[621] When such an order is made in interlocutory proceedings, the receiver can only carry out the repairs from receipts. The court will not order the landlord to meet his expenses: *Evans v Clayhope Properties Ltd* [1988] 1 W.L.R. 358.

[622] The pre-conditions for the grant of an acquisition order are strict: see L & TA 1987 s.29.

[623] CLRA 2002 ss.71–113.

[624] s.147.

[625] s.147(2).

[626] See *National Real Estate and Finance Co Ltd v Hassan* [1939] 2 K.B. 61 at 78.

[627] By the Landlord and Tenant Act 1954 s.51, removing (inter alia) the former limits as to rateable value.

[628] See paras 22–028 et seq. and 22–035 below.

[629] Leasehold Property (Repairs) Act 1938 ss.1, 7. The Act applies to leases created before and after the Act (s.5).

repair, and not, e.g. of a covenant to cleanse the premises[630] or to lay out insurance monies in the reinstatement of the premises.[631]

(2) LEAVE OF COURT. Where the Act applies, the landlord may neither sue for **19–131** damages nor enforce forfeiture for failure to repair unless he first serves on the tenant a notice under s.146 of the Law of Property Act 1925,[632] which informs the tenant of his right to serve a counter-notice, and one month elapses thereafter.[633] Within 28 days after service of the notice the tenant may serve a counter-notice claiming the benefit of the Act. The result of this is that the landlord can take no further proceedings without leave of the court. This will be given only if he can prove on the balance of probabilities[634] that the immediate remedying of a breach of the repairing covenant is required in order to save the landlord from substantial loss or damage which he would otherwise sustain.[635] In granting or refusing leave, the court may impose such conditions on either party as it thinks fit.[636] It has been said that "the battle between landlord and tenant must be fought at some stage".[637] It is now fought on the application for leave and not, as was formerly the case, in any subsequent forfeiture proceedings. If the landlord fails, the threat of forfeiture is lifted. If he succeeds, the tenant "will know what steps he must take to avoid forfeiture".[638]

One important feature of the Act is that, where it applies, it shifts the onus **19–132** of applying to the court from the tenant to the landlord. But it does not apply where the landlord is reclaiming from the tenant the cost of tenant's repairs which the landlord has himself carried out under a clause in the lease empowering him to do so, since this is a claim in debt and not in damages.[639]

[630] *Starrokate Ltd v Burry* [1983] 1 E.G.L.R. 56.

[631] *Farimani v Gates* [1984] 1 E.G.L.R. 66.

[632] For this, see above, para.18–053. It has been held that where the landlord executed the repairs himself, he could not then serve a notice under s.146, because the breach had already been remedied: *S.E.D.A.C. Investments Ltd v Tanner* [1982] 1 W.L.R. 1342. The landlord was therefore unable to recover the cost of the repairs from the tenant. Not only is the result unjust, but it is based on a very questionable reading of s.146: see [1986] Conv. 85 (P. F. Smith); and see *Hamilton v Martell Securities Ltd* [1984] Ch. 266 at 281.

[633] Leasehold Property (Repairs) Act 1938 ss.1(2), (4). A notice that does not comply with the requirements of s.1(4) will be invalid: *BL Holdings Ltd v Marcolt Investments Ltd* [1979] 1 E.G.L.R. 97.

[634] *Associated British Ports v C.H. Bailey Plc* [1990] 2 A.C. 703, overruling *Sidnell v Wilson* [1966] 2 Q.B. 67 (where it was held that the landlord had only to show a prima facie case).

[635] Leasehold Property (Repairs) Act 1938 s.1(5), listing five possible grounds on which leave may be given. See *Phillips v Price* [1959] Ch. 181; *Re Metropolitan Film Studio Ltd's Application* [1962] 1 W.L.R. 1315; *Landmaster Properties Ltd v Thackray Property Investments Ltd* [2003] EWHC 959 (QB); [2003] 2 E.G.L.R. 30.

[636] Leasehold Property (Repairs) Act 1938 s.1(6).

[637] *Associated British Ports v C.H. Bailey Plc*, above, at 713, per Lord Templeman.

[638] *Associated British Ports v C.H. Bailey Plc*, above, at 713, per Lord Templeman. The decision has led to a marked change in practice: see [1990] C.L.J. 401 (S.B.).

[639] *Jervis v Harris* [1996] Ch. 195, overruling *Swallow Securities Ltd v Brand* (1981) 45 P. & C.R. 328 (where McNeill J. had held that the Act applied), and approving *Hamilton v Martell Securities Ltd* [1984] Ch. 266; *Colchester Estates (Cardiff) v Carlton Industries Plc* [1986] Ch. 80; and *Elite Investments Ltd v T. I. Bainbridge Silencers Ltd* [1986] 2 E.G.L.R. 43 at 49.

19–133   (3) SERVICE OF NOTICE. There is no need to serve a notice under the Act on a mortgagee of the lease[640]; and if a notice was properly served on the tenant for the time being, no notice need be served on a subsequent assignee, though if the tenant served a counter-notice leave to proceed against the assignee must be obtained.[641] The Act does not protect the original tenant after he has assigned, even where he remains liable on the repairing covenant by privity of contract.[642]

19–134   **5. Covenant to insure.** A covenant to insure against fire is broken if the premises are uninsured for any period, however short, even if no fire occurs.[643] If the covenant is to insure with a named company, or with some other responsible company with the landlord's approval, the landlord may withhold his approval of an alternative company without giving any reasons.[644] A covenant to insure with a named company binds the tenant to take out such policy of the company as is usual at the time, so that if such a policy excepts some specified risks, the tenant is not liable under this covenant if the house is destroyed in one of the excepted ways.[645]

19–135   The respective rights of the landlord and the tenant in relation to the proceeds of any insurance that may have been effected in respect of the leased premises depend upon the terms of both the lease and the policy of insurance.[646] A landlord is entitled to insure the premises demised against destruction to its full reinstatement value. This is so notwithstanding that he has a limited interest in the property and even though the tenant's interest is not noted on the policy.[647] Commonly, the landlord undertakes to insure the premises and the tenant pays him an additional rent to cover that portion of the premiums that is attributable to the leasehold interest. Where in such circumstances the lease contains no obligation on either party to reinstate the premises, the tenant can require the landlord to apply any insurance monies

---

[640] *Church Commissioners for England v Ve-Ri-Best Manufacturing Co Ltd* [1957] 1 Q.B. 238. If leave is given to the landlord to proceed with forfeiture proceedings relating to residential property and he subsequently commences an action for possession, the landlord should furnish the names and addresses of any mortgagee or under-lessee of whom he knows in the particulars of claim to ensure that they are served with copies of those particulars: see above, para.18–049.

[641] *Kanda v Church Commissioners for England* [1958] 1 Q.B. 332.

[642] See *Cusack-Smith v Gold* [1958] 1 W.L.R. 611; but see *Baker v Sims* [1959] 1 Q.B. 114 at 129. A tenant will be liable on grounds of privity only in leases granted prior to 1996: see below, paras 20–020, 20–085.

[643] *Penniall v Harborne* (1848) 11 Q.B. 368.

[644] *Viscount Tredegar v Harwood* [1929] A.C. 72. It may be, for instance, that the landlord wishes to have all his properties insured with one company. In the absence of express provision in the lease, there is no restriction imposed on the landlord's choice of insurers by the common law: *Berrycroft Management Ltd v Sinclair Gardens Investment Co Ltd* (1996) 29 H.L.R. 444; *cf.* statutory regulation, see para.19–136 below.

[645] *Upjohn v Hitchens* [1918] 2 K.B. 48. It is otherwise if no company is named: see *Enlayde Ltd v Roberts* [1917] 1 Ch. 109.

[646] *Beacon Carpets Ltd v Kirby* [1985] Q.B. 755 at 768.

[647] See *Mumford Hotels Ltd v Wheler* [1964] Ch. 117; *Mark Rowlands Ltd v Berni Inns Ltd* [1986] Q.B. 211 at 226. A stranger to the lease has no insurable interest however: see *Sadlers v Clements* [1995] E.G.C.S. 197.

for that purpose.[648] Where the insurance is taken for the benefit of the interests of both landlord and tenant and insurance monies become payable under the policy because of its damage or destruction:

(i) those monies are apportioned between them by reference to the values of their respective interests if through no fault of the parties it becomes impossible to reinstate the premises[649] or if the parties agree that it should not be reinstated[650];

(ii) the landlord cannot sue the tenant for negligence if that was the cause of the damage and was a risk covered by the policy[651]; and

(iii) the tenant may require the insurer to apply the monies in reinstating the premises even though the landlord has sold the reversion and has no claim against the insurer in respect of his own interest.[652]

Where, by contrast, the tenant is required to insure the premises and reinstate them, he will be entitled to the entirety of the proceeds if the premises are destroyed and if without fault on his part it becomes impossible to reinstate them.[653]

The Schedule to the Landlord and Tenant Act 1985,[654] as amended, confers **19-136** important rights on certain tenants with respect to insurance. It is limited in its application to tenants of dwellings,[655] and it does not apply to tenants of a local authority, a National Park authority or a new town corporation unless the tenancy is a long tenancy.[656] Where a service charge[657] is payable by the

---

[648] This is either because the landlord is regarded as insuring for the joint benefit of both parties (see *Mumford Hotels Ltd v Wheler*, above, at 125) or because the court will imply a term that the landlord will exercise the rights conferred by the policy in such a way as to preserve the tenant's interests: *Vural Ltd v Security Archives Ltd* (1989) 60 P. & C.R. 258 at 273. This may include a requirement that the landlord prosecute any claim under the policy with all reasonable speed: *Watermoor Meat Supply Ltd v Walker* [2002] EWHC 3125 (Ch); [2003] L. & T.R. 19.

[649] *Beacon Carpets Ltd v Kirby*, above at 769, distinguishing *Re King* [1963] Ch. 459; considered below.

[650] *Beacon Carpets Ltd v Kirby*, above.

[651] *Mark Rowlands Ltd v Berni Inns Ltd*, above, [1986] C.L.J. 22 (M.A. Clarke). The insurer cannot therefore sue the tenant in exercise of his rights of subrogation. The landlord will be unable to sue the tenant only where the parties intended that the insurance should enure for the benefit of both. This will not be inferred merely because the landlord covenanted to insure the premises: such insurance may be taken for his benefit only. It is not necessary that the lease itself should demonstrate a common intention to insure for the benefit of both parties. Regard may be had, e.g. to correspondence between the parties: see *Lambert v Keymood Ltd* [1997] 1 E.G.L.R. 70 at 74.

[652] Under the Fires Prevention (Metropolis) Act 1774 s.83: *Lonsdale & Thompson Ltd v Black Arrow Group Plc* [1993] Ch. 361; above, para.15–057.

[653] *Re King*, above.

[654] L & TA 1985 s.30A, inserted by L & TA 1987 s.43(1).

[655] For definition, see L & TA 1985 s.38.

[656] L & TA 1985 Sch. para.9, excluding the possibility of criminal liability for breach of the Schedule in such cases. For definition of "long tenancy", see L & TA 1985 s.26(2).

[657] For definition, see para.19–082 above.

tenant which consists of or includes an amount payable directly or indirectly for insurance, the tenant has the following rights:

    (i) to require the landlord to supply him with a written summary of the insurance for the time being effected in relation to the dwelling[658];

    (ii) to require the landlord to afford him reasonable facilities to inspect any relevant policy or associated documents and to take copies or extracts thereof[659];

    (iii) where it appears that damage has been caused to the dwelling in respect of which a claim could be made, and the policy requires a claim to be made within a specified period, to serve on the insurer a notice extending the period for making the claim to six months.[660]

Moreover, whether or not a service charge is payable, the tenant of a dwelling has the right to challenge the landlord's choice of insurer.[661] Where the tenancy requires the tenant to insure the dwelling with an insurer nominated or approved by the landlord, the tenant or landlord may apply to the county court or a leasehold valuation tribunal for a determination whether:

    (i) the insurance is unsatisfactory in any respect; or

    (ii) the premiums payable are excessive.[662]

The court or tribunal may make an order requiring the landlord to nominate or approve such other insurer as it specifies, or requiring him to nominate or approve such other insurer who satisfies such requirements in relation to the insurance as are specified in the order.[663]

19–137 The Commonhold and Leasehold Reform Act 2002, as well as amending the Schedule to the Landlord and Tenant Act 1985 as outlined above, provides that tenants who hold a long lease of a house[664] are not required to insure the house with the landlord's nominated or approved insurer if:

    (i) the house is insured under a policy of insurance issued by an authorised insurer;

---

[658] L & TA 1985 Sch. para.2.

[659] L & TA 1985 Sch. para.3. For position where insurance has been effected by superior landlord, see ibid., para.4; for effect of change of landlord, see L & TA 1985 Sch. para.4A, added by CLRA 2002 Sch.10, para.11. Failure to comply with paras 2 to 4A is a summary offence: L & TA 1985 Sch. para.6.

[660] L & TA 1985 Sch. para.7.

[661] L & TA 1985 Sch. para.8, as amended by CLRA 2002 s.165.

[662] L & TA 1985 Sch. para.8(2).

[663] L & TA 1985 Sch. para.8(4).

[664] "Long lease" is as defined in CLRA 2002 ss.76, 77; "house" is as defined in LRA 1967 Pt I (see para.22–199 below): CLRA 2002 s.164(10).

(ii) the policy covers the interests of both landlord and tenant;

(iii) the policy covers all the risks required to be covered under the lease by the insurance provided by the landlord's insurer; and

(iv) the amount of cover is not less than that which the lease requires to be provided.[665]

In order to exercise this right, the tenant must give notice of cover to the landlord within a 14-day period beginning with the relevant date.[666]

---

[665] CLRA 2002 s.164. For prescribed forms, see SI 2004/3097, as amended by SI 2005/177 (England) and SI 2005/1354 (Wales).

[666] CLRA 2002 s.164(3). If the policy has not been renewed, the relevant date is the day on which it took effect; if it has been renewed, the relevant date is the day from which it was last renewed: CLRA 2002 s.164(4).

LEASEHOLD COVENANTS

20–001 This chapter is concerned with the running of covenants in leases and of guarantees given as security for the performance of such covenants.[1] A fundamental distinction exists between leases granted before and after January 1, 1996. The former are governed largely by common law rules which are of long standing, extended by statute. By contrast, the principles applicable to the latter are found almost exclusively in a code laid down by the Landlord and Tenant (Covenants) Act 1995. This statute, which is of some complexity, creates a new and fundamentally different regime that rests on principles quite distinct from those that apply to leases in existence when it came into force. The rules governing the transmissibility of guarantees continue to be a matter for the common law, whether the obligations guaranteed are found in leases granted before or after January 1, 1996. However, the position of guarantors has been affected in a number of ways by the 1995 Act.

Part 1

GENERAL PRINCIPLES

20–002 A covenant is a promise under seal, i.e. contained in a deed. Such a promise is enforceable, according to the ordinary law of contract, between the persons who are parties to it or their personal representatives. But certain kinds of covenants are so much part of the system of transactions in land that they are enforceable in cases which the law of contract does not cover: they partake, so to speak, of the nature of the estates in connection with which they are made, so that like those estates they may benefit and bind third parties.

---

[1] See generally Fancourt, *Enforceability of Landlord and Tenant Covenants*, 2nd edn (London: Sweet & Maxwell, 2006).

Therefore they belong to the category of interests in land as well as to the law of contract, and two sets of rules have to be considered together. Common examples of these kinds of covenants are covenants in a lease, e.g. to repair, and restrictive covenants taken on a sale so as to bind the purchaser and future occupiers of the land, e.g. not to carry on a business on the property sold.[2] The rules which govern such covenants also apply, in general, to contractual promises not made under seal, such as "covenants" contained in a mere agreement for a lease.[3]

The primary question is how far are covenants made in connection with transactions in land enforceable outside the law of contract. The three fundamental principles, still of general application to leases granted before 1996, are as follows.[4]

1. If there is privity of contract, all covenants are enforceable. There is said to be privity of contract when the parties are in direct contractual relations, i.e. bound to one another by the ordinary law of contract. Clearly, if two people have agreed to do or not to do certain things, their obligations bind them whether their contract has anything to do with land or not. Should a party to a contract die, that party's estate (acting through the deceased's personal representatives) may enforce, and be bound by, the liability conferred by the contract; and in general the benefit, but not the burden, of the contract is assignable, so that assignees of the benefit can sue the original promisor or his personal representatives without resort to the law of property. A covenant can be enforced both at law, by an action for damages, and in equity, by an injunction or specific performance.   **20–003**

2. If there is privity of estate, but not privity of contract, only covenants which touch and concern the land are enforceable. Privity of estate means that the relationship of landlord and tenant exists between the parties or, in other words, that there is a relationship of tenure[5]; cases in this category are thus confined to leases and tenancies.[6] If L1 grants a lease to T1 and then T1 assigns it to T2, there is no privity of contract between L1 and T2 since there is no contract between them. However, there is privity of estate, for T2 has become L1's tenant by acquiring the estate which L1 created and which is   **20–004**

---

[2] The enforceability of such covenants is considered in Ch.32 below.

[3] See, e.g. below, para.20–044.

[4] See *Manchester Brewery Co v Coombs* [1901] 2 Ch. 608 at 614; (1991) 11 L.S. 47 (R. Thornton). For the definition of a lease granted after 1995, see below, para.20–010.

[5] *Milmo v Carreras* [1946] K.B. 306; above, para.17 002. Privity of estate is a legal relationship, not equitable: *Cox v Bishop* (1857) 8 De G. M. & G. 815 at 824. For its meaning in this context, see *Manchester Brewery Co v Coombs*, above, at 613 and 614; *Purchase v Lichfield Brewery Co* [1915] 1 K.B. 184.

[6] "Privity of estate" was, however, also used to describe the relationship of grantor and grantee of the fee simple, where the grantee claimed the *benefit* of a covenant (running with land) as a successor in title to the grantor: see *David v Sabin* [1893] 1 Ch. 523 at 537, 545; *Campbell v Lewis* (1820) 3 B. & Ald. 392; Co.Litt. p.271a.

held of L1 as the immediate landlord. Similarly, if L1 assigns his reversion to L2, there is privity of estate between L2 and T2. In such cases any covenants in the lease which "touch and concern" the land (e.g. repairing covenants) are enforceable both at law and in equity. They have become "imprinted on" the estate.[7]

20–005   Covenants which do not relate to the land are not enforceable under this head, for they have nothing to do with the relationship of landlord and tenant on which this right to enforce covenants against third parties is founded. Nor do all covenants in leases "touch and concern" the land for this purpose, even though they may relate to the land in a general sense. For example, as will be seen shortly, an option to purchase the freehold is not a covenant which "touches and concerns" the land, though it may bind an assignee as an estate contract.[8] Here we are outside the bounds of the law of contract, and the law of property as usual sets limits to the kinds of interests which can be made to bind all comers.

20–006   **3. If there is privity neither of contract nor of estate, then with two exceptions, no covenants are enforceable.** There is privity neither of contract nor of estate[9] between a landlord and a sub-tenant, or between the vendor of freehold land and a person who buys it from the purchaser. In such cases the general rule is that covenants are not enforceable between the parties mentioned. But there are two important exceptions to this rule.

20–007   First, even the common law allowed the *benefit* of a covenant (i.e. the right to sue on it) to be assigned with the land for the benefit of which it was made, provided that the covenant was one which "touched and concerned" that land. One example already mentioned[10] is that of a grantor's covenants for title in a conveyance: the benefit of these covenants runs with the land conveyed so that whoever is entitled to the land is entitled to their benefit. Equity went further, and enforced assignments of the *benefit* of contracts generally, whether or not connected with land; and there is now a statutory procedure for assignment which takes effect at law.[11] Thus it has become the general rule that the benefit of a contract is assignable. But the *burden* of a contract (i.e. the liability to be sued on it) has never been assignable by itself: assignment applies only to rights, not to duties.

20–008   Secondly, equity allows the transmission of both the benefit and the burden of restrictive covenants. A restrictive covenant is a covenant imposing a negative obligation (e.g. not to build) as opposed to a positive covenant (e.g. to build); and the benefit and burden of a restrictive covenant can run in equity

---

[7] *City of London Corporation v Fell* [1993] Q.B. 589 at 604, per Nourse L.J.; approved [1994] 1 A.C. 458 at 465.
[8] Below, para.20–040.
[9] See *Milmo v Carreras*, above.
[10] Above, paras 7–151—7–156.
[11] LPA 1925 s.136.

provided that there is both land which is benefited and land which is burdened. As usual, however, in cases where the doctrine of notice is still relevant, a purchaser of a legal estate without notice takes free from the burden.[12]

The three fundamental principles set out above should always be borne in mind in considering the enforceability of covenants. They should be applied in the following order: **20–009**

    (a) Is there privity of contract? If not, then

    (b) Is there privity of estate? If not, then

    (c) Is the covenant a restrictive covenant?

4. For leases granted after 1995, privity of contract and estate are irrelevant. For leases granted after 1995 the general principles of privity of contract and estate set out above have no application. The Landlord and Tenant (Covenants) Act 1995 provides a discrete statutory code which governs such leases and which supersedes the previous common law and statutory provisions.[13] A number of provisions of the 1995 Act apply both to leases granted before and to leases granted after the Act came into force on January 1, 1996.[14] However, the majority of its provisions apply only to "new tenancies".[15] A new tenancy is for these purposes one that is granted[16] on or after January 1, 1996,[17] unless it is a tenancy granted in pursuance of: **20–010**

    (i) an agreement (including an option or right of pre-emption) entered into before 1996[18]; or

    (ii) an order of the court made before 1996.[19]

---

[12] See above, para.5–011. For the application of the doctrine to covenants in leases and the position where title is registered, see *Oceanic Village Ltd v United Attractions Ltd* [2000] Ch. 234 and below, paras 32–045 and 32–055.

[13] *Oceanic Village Ltd v United Attractions Ltd* [2000] Ch. 234 at 242. The Act expressly provides that the statutory provisions which apply to leases granted prior to January 1, 1996 (sc. LPA 1925 ss.78, 79, 141 and 142) are inapplicable to leases granted thereafter: L & TCA 1995 s.30(4). See below, para.20–085.

[14] See L & TCA 1995 ss.1(2) and 17—20.

[15] L & TCA 1995 ss.1(1), 3–16 and 21.

[16] Although a "grant" may be taken to denote the grant of a *legal* lease (see *City Permanent BS v Miller* [1952] Ch. 840), it is not used in that technical sense here, but includes the creation of an agreement for a lease as well: see fn.20 below. If this were not so, the provisions of the Act could be readily circumvented by the creation of equitable leases.

[17] L & TCA 1995 s.1(3); SI 1995/2963. It includes a tenancy that arises where, as a result of a variation of the lease, there is a deemed surrender and regrant of the lease: L & TCA 1995 s.1(5). For variations which amount to a surrender, see above, para.18–087.

[18] L & TCA 1995 s.1(3)(a), 1(6) and 1(7). A tenancy granted under the statutory right to buy (see HA 1995 s.118) will not fall within the exception, because it is not in the nature of an option.

[19] L & TCA 1995 s.1(3)(b).

A tenancy is defined to mean any lease or other tenancy and includes a sub-tenancy and an agreement for a lease, but not a mortgage term.[20]

Part 2

PRIVITY: COVENANTS IN LEASES GRANTED PRIOR TO 1996

Section 1. Privity of Contract: Liability of the Original Covenantors

1. Liability of the original tenant throughout the term

20–011   *(a) Liability notwithstanding assignment.* Where a lease is granted by L1 (the original landlord) to T1 (the original tenant), there is privity of contract between them. In principle, this means that, where the lease is granted before 1996, L1 may enforce all the covenants in the lease against T1 throughout the term, provided that L1 retains the reversion.[21] Subject to statutory exceptions,[22] T1's liability continues notwithstanding any assignment of the lease by him to T2.[23] T1 cannot divest himself of his personal contractual liability by parting with the land; and L1 may sue T1 for unpaid rent, or for damages if a covenant e.g. to repair is not observed by T2. T1 cannot defend an action by L1 on the basis that T2 is also be liable to L1 (by reason of privity of estate) and that L1 should therefore pursue his remedy against T2.[24] The extent of T1's liability can be onerous. T1 remains liable even if after assignment:

---

[20] L & TCA 1995 s.28(1). Although that definition applies "unless the context otherwise requires", the purpose of the Act would be defeated if it did not apply here. See fn.16, above.

[21] The rule is an ancient one: see *Walker's Case* (1587) 3 Co.Rep. 22a. It applied only to express covenants: *Barnard v Goodscall* (1612) Cro.Jac. 309; *Bachelour v Gage* (1630) Cro.Car. 188. If the obligation to pay rent was merely implied and not express, and T1 assigned the lease to T2 with L1's consent, T1 was not liable for rent unpaid by T2 because the obligation to pay rent depended upon possession of the land: *March v Brace* (1613) 2 Bulst. 151 at 153; *Wadham v Marlowe* (1784) 4 Doug. 54 at 70; *Auriol v Mills* (1790) 4 T.R. 94 at 98; *John Betts & Sons Ltd v Price* (1924) 40 T.L.R. 589 at 590. L1's consent to an assignment was implied if he accepted rent from T2, but not if T1 merely informed L1 of the assignment: *Wadham v Marlowe*, above, at 70; *Mayor of Swansea v Thomas* (1882) 10 QBD 48 at 50. T1 remained liable if L1 did not accept the assignee: *Orgill v Kemshead* (1812) 4 Taunt. 642. These cases on implied covenants to pay rent may be no more than examples of rent service (see above, para.19–062), by which the payment of rent was a condition of tenure. This would explain why it was only the tenant for the time being who was liable for the rent.

[22] See LPA 1922 s.145; Sch.15 para.11 (perpetually renewable leases); above, para.17–120; Family Law Act 1996 Sch.7 para.7(2) (transfer of protected, secure, assured or introductory tenancies or assured agricultural occupancies between spouses, civil partners or cohabitants by court order).

[23] See, e.g. *Walker's Case*, above, at 23a; *Hill v East and West India Dock Co* (1884) 9 App.Cas. 448 at 453.

[24] T1's continuing liability on a covenant does not depend upon his covenanting both for himself and for his assigns, though this is now implied by statute in order to overcome an inconvenient rule at common law: see Law of Property Act 1925 s.79; below.

(i) the rent is increased under a rent review clause[25];

(ii) T2 has become insolvent and his trustee in bankruptcy[26] has disclaimed the lease[27];

(iii) the breach is committed not by T2 but by some subsequent assignee over whose selection T1 had no control[28]; or

(iv) he could not have secured performance of the covenant himself because he had no right of re-entry as against T2.[29]

Two different persons may therefore be liable for a single breach of **20–012** covenant, one by privity of contract and the other by privity of estate. The nature of T1's liability is not that of a surety for T2.[30] He is severally liable with T2 for any breach.[31] It is therefore entirely a matter for L1 whether he sues T1 or T2, or both of them.[32] T1 will be discharged from liability by:

(i) performance of the covenants, whether by T1 or T2,[33] or by any person who has guaranteed the obligations in the lease[34];

(ii) surrender of the whole of the lease[35]; or

---

[25] *Centrovincial Estates Plc v Bulk Storage Ltd* (1983) 46 P. & C.R. 393; *Selous Street Properties Ltd v Oronel Fabrics Ltd* [1984] 1 E.G.L.R. 50. These decisions are supportable on the basis that the tenant's covenant was construed as a promise to pay the reviewed rent: *Friends Provident Life Office v British Railways Board* (1995) 73 P. & C.R. 9 at 20. Where there has been a variation of the rent review clause subsequent to the assignment by T1 to T2, T1 will not be bound by the rent as reviewed: *Beegas Nominees Ltd v Sevington Properties Ltd* (1998) 77 P. & C.R. 14; and see below at para.20–031.

[26] Or, where T2 is a company, its liquidator.

[27] *W. H. Smith Ltd v Wyndham Investments Ltd* (1994) 70 P. & C.R. 21; *Hindcastle Ltd v Barbara Attenborough Associates Ltd* [1997] A.C. 70.

[28] Even though L1's consent is required to the assignment, he owes no duty of care to T1 to assess the creditworthiness of any proposed assignee: *Norwich Union Life Insurance Society v Low Profile Fashions Ltd* (1991) 64 P. & C.R. 187; [1992] C.L.J. 425 (S.B.).

[29] *Thames Manufacturing Co Ltd v Perrotts (Nichol & Peyton) Ltd* (1984) 50 P. & C.R. 1.

[30] *Baynton v Morgan* (1888) 22 QBD 74. He cannot therefore avail himself of the defences that would have been open to a surety.

[31] *Deanplan Ltd v Mahmoud* [1993] Ch. 151 at 159; *Burford Midland Properties Ltd v Marley Extrusions Ltd* [1995] 1 B.C.L.C. 102 at 115.

[32] *Norwich Union Life Insurance Society v Low Profile Fashions Ltd*, above, at 192. L cannot of course have double satisfaction.

[33] *Allied London Investments Ltd v Hambro Life Assurance Ltd* [1984] 1 E.G.L.R. 16 at 19.

[34] See *Milverton Group Ltd v Warner World Ltd* [1995] 2 E.G.L.R. 28; [1995] J.B.L. 181 (M. Haley). In that case T2 failed to pay the rent. It was held that L1 must give T1 credit for any payments received from sureties, even where those sums were paid in consideration for their discharge from their liabilities as guarantors. However, L1 was entitled to appropriate the sums so received against future liabilities that were unquantified at the time when L1 sued T1 for the arrears of rent. L1 could not be compelled to appropriate them to the existing arrears of rent.

[35] *Allied London Investments Ltd v Hambro Life Assurance Ltd*, above, at 46. Surrender of part of the lease will not discharge T1: *Baynton v Morgan*, above (though query whether T1 is discharged *pro tanto*). Surrender may take place by operation of law, as where L1 grants T2 a new lease on different terms from the old tenancy: *Take Harvest Ltd v Liu* [1993] A.C. 552; see above, para.18–087.

(iii) an accord and satisfaction by L1 with T2 under which L1 is precluded from enforcing the debt against T1.[36]

20–013   T1's personal covenant operates independently of the estate granted and is enforceable even though:

(i) the legal term has not yet begun[37]; or

(ii) owing to some defect in L1's title, no legal term is in fact created.[38]

If T1 becomes insolvent,[39] L1 can prove for the loss of his covenant.[40] The measure of that loss is the difference between the market value of the reversion with and without the covenant.[41]

20–014   *(b) Extensions of the term.* The term of a lease may be extended where the tenant exercises an option for renewal contained in the lease, or where the tenant holds over pursuant to a statutory right to do so, e.g. under Part 2 of the Landlord and Tenant Act 1954.[42] Where T1 has assigned the lease before it is extended, he will not be liable for breaches of covenant committed by T2 during any such extension[43] unless and to the extent that he has undertaken that liability.[44] Where T2 exercises an option for renewal, this will normally involve the grant of a new lease under which T1 will not be liable.[45] But T1's liability may continue where the effect of renewal is that the old lease is merely extended under its own terms.[46]

---

[36] This will be determined from the surrounding circumstances and any express or implied terms of that agreement: *Johnson v Davies* [1999] Ch. 117. It is a matter of construction whether or not the agreement is an accord and satisfaction. However, as the liability for rent under the lease of T1 and T2 is a several liability, release of one such debtor does not automatically discharge the others: *Sun Life Assurance Society Plc v Tantofex (Engineers) Ltd* [1999] L. & T.R. 568. The view that T1 would not be discharged merely because T2 came to an arrangement with his creditors (see *R. A. Securities Ltd v Mercantile Credit Co Ltd* [1995] 3 All E.R. 581), was rejected in *Johnson v Davies*. Such an arrangement is treated in the same way as a consensual agreement: *Johnson v Davies*, at 137.

[37] *Bradshaw v Pawley* [1980] 1 W.L.R. 10.

[38] *Industrial Properties (Barton Hill) Ltd v Associated Electrical Industries Ltd* [1977] Q.B. 580. This was a secondary ground of decision, the primary ground being that the tenant was estopped: above, para.17–125.

[39] Or, if T1 is a company, is wound up.

[40] *James Smith & Sons (Norwood) Ltd v Goodman* [1936] Ch. 216.

[41] *Re House Property and Investment Co Ltd* [1954] Ch. 576 at 592; cf. *Stanhope Pension Trust Ltd v Registrar of Companies* [1993] 2 E.G.L.R. 118.

[42] s.24; below, para.22–008.

[43] *City of London Corporation v Fell* [1994] 1 A.C. 458; [1994] C.L.J. 28 (S.B.). It has not been decided whether T1 remains liable on the covenants where the lease is extended *before* he assigns it to T2.

[44] "Everything depends on the contract between the parties": *Herbert Duncan Ltd v Cluttons* [1993] Q.B. 589 at 608, per Nourse L.J.

[45] Generally an alteration to the length of a lease beyond its original term operates as a surrender of the old lease and the grant of a new one: *Re Savile SE* [1931] 2 Ch. 210 at 217; *Jenkin R. Lewis Ltd v Kerman* [1971] Ch. 477 at 496.

[46] *Baker v Merckel* [1960] 1 Q.B. 657 (lease for seven years to be extended to 11 years on notice from the tenant).

(c) Liability to the assignee of the reversion (L2). At common law, the **20–015**
benefit of a covenant did not pass on an assignment of L1's reversion to L2.[47]
Therefore L2 could sue T1 neither for his own breaches nor for those of T2.
The Grantees of Reversions Act 1540[48] changed the law[49] and gave L2 the
same rights to sue T1 for breach of covenants as L1 had had.[50] It was thereby
considered to create privity of contract between those who had privity of
estate.[51] Despite some decisions to the contrary,[52] it became established that
T1 was liable to L2 for breaches of covenant committed by T2, because L1's
privity of contract passed on assignment to L2 under the statute.[53]

Although the Act of 1540 remained in force until the end of 1925,[54] its   **20–016**
provisions were extended (but not superseded) by the Conveyancing Acts
1881—1911.[55] The Conveyancing Acts did not expressly confer on L2 the
same rights of suit for breach of covenant as L1 would have had, but instead
annexed the benefit of covenants touching and concerning the land to the
reversion so that the reversioner for the time being might enforce them.[56]
Those provisions, as amended,[57] were re-enacted by s.141 of the Law of
Property Act 1925, and are now interpreted by the courts without regard to the
law prior to 1881.[58] It is generally assumed that after an assignment of the
reversion L2 (and not L1) can enforce T1's continuing liability[59] and that the
right to do so passes to L2 automatically, without the need for an express
assignment, under s.141 of the Law of Property Act 1925.[60] There is however

---

[47] Below, para.20–060; see *Webb v Russell* (1789) 3 T.R. 393 at 394 *(arguendo)*; *Bickford v Parson* (1848) 5 C.B. 920 at 929 and 931; *Re King* [1963] Ch. 459 at 479.

[48] 32 Hen. 8 c. 34 s.1; below, para.20–061. There were analogous provisions in s.2 of that Act relating to the burden of the covenants in the lease.

[49] *Isherwood v Oldknow* (1815) 3 M. & S. 382 at 394; *P. & A. Swift Investments v Combined English Stores Group Plc* [1989] A.C. 632 at 640.

[50] The right was confined to covenants which touched and concerned the land: below, para.20–061.

[51] *Thursby v Plant* (1670) 1 Wms.Saund. 230 at 240; *Bickford v Parson*, above, at 930.

[52] *Humble v Glover* (1593) Cro.Eliz. 328 *(sub nom. Humble v Oliver* (1594) Poph. 55); *Overton v Sydal* (1594) Cro.Eliz. 555; Platt on *Leases*, ii and 386.

[53] *Brett v Cumberland* (1616) Cro.Jac. 521; *Thursby v Plant*, above; *Edwards v Morgan* (1685) 3 Lev. 229. The statute applied only to leases under seal (below, para.20–062), and in those cases where it was inapplicable, L2 had no remedy against T1: *Allcock v Moorhouse* (1882) 9 QBD 366.

[54] It was repealed by LPA 1925 s.207; Sch.7.

[55] 1881 s.10; 1911 s.2; below, para.20–061. The 1540 Act was still employed: see, e.g. *Stuart v Joy* [1904] 1 K.B. 362 (a case concerned with the transmission of the burden of L's covenants).

[56] CA 1881 s.10.

[57] See CA 1911 s.2.

[58] *Re King* [1963] Ch. 459 at 490 and 494.

[59] See, e.g. *W. H. Smith Ltd v Wyndham Investments Ltd* (1994) 70 P. & C.R. 21; *Milverton Group Ltd v Warner World Ltd* [1995] 2 E.G.L.R. 28 (where, in each case, L2 successfully sued T1 for T2's breach but no argument was addressed as to his right to do so). cf. *Centrovincial Estates Plc v Bulk Storage Ltd* (1983) 46 P. & C.R. 393 at 394, where Harman J. was prepared to assume that it was so in the absence of contrary argument.

[60] See *Burford Midland Properties Ltd v Marley Extrusions Ltd* [1995] B.C.L.C. 102 at 105. Query whether the right might pass under LPA 1925 s.78 (which applies to covenants in leases granted before 1996: *Caerns Motor Services Ltd v Texaco Ltd* [1994] 1 W.L.R. 1249); below, para.32–063.

no decision in which this conclusion has been reached as a matter of construction of the section.[61]

20–017   **2. Liability of the original landlord (L1) throughout the term.** On principles similar to those explained above, L1 remains liable on his covenants for the whole term, notwithstanding any assignment of the reversion to L2.[62] Furthermore L1 is liable not only for his own breaches of covenant, but for those committed by L2.[63] It has been suggested that, in such circumstances, L1's liability can be enforced by T2 if T1 has assigned the lease to him.[64] This is said to be the effect of s.142 of the Law of Property Act 1925,[65] by which the burden of covenants in the lease passes on an assignment of the reversion.[66]

20–018   **3. Liability of an assignee (T2) on a direct covenant.** It is explained below that an assignee of a lease is liable only for breaches of covenant committed while the lease is vested in him.[67] Commonly, however, a lease can be assigned only with the landlord's consent.[68] It is now usual in commercial leases for L1 to require T2 to enter into a direct covenant with him to observe all the terms of the lease as a condition of L1's licence to assign. In the absence of contrary provision, T2's liability to L1 on this direct covenant will not be confined to the period that the lease is vested in him[69] but will continue until it expires.[70] This will be so even though T2's covenant is not made specifically for the residue of the term.[71]

20–019   It has not been settled whether, on an assignment of the reversion, the benefit of L1's direct covenant with T2 automatically passes to L2 or whether an express assignment is necessary for it to do so.[72] As it cannot pass under s.141 of the Law of Property Act 1925,[73] any automatic transmission would

---

[61] Some support is perhaps provided by *Arlesford Trading Co Ltd v Servansingh* [1971] 1 W.L.R. 1080, in which it was held that L2 could sue T1 for a breach of covenant committed before L1 assigned the reversion to L2 (see below, para.20–072). However, there was in that case privity of estate between L2 and T1 at the time of the action (though not at the time of breach). Furthermore, the wording of LPA 1925 s.141(3) implies that rights of action in respect of pre-existing breaches of covenant pass to L2.

[62] *Stuart v Joy* [1904] 1 K.B. 362 (where L1 was liable to T1 for a breach of covenant committed before the assignment of the reversion).

[63] *Wright v Dean* [1948] Ch. 686 (L2 took free of T1's option to purchase the reversion, which T1 had failed to register as a land charge).

[64] *Celsteel Ltd v Alton House Holdings Ltd (No.2)* [1986] 1 W.L.R. 666 at 672; affirmed on this point: [1987] 1 W.L.R. 291 at 296. The remarks were obiter.

[65] Replacing Grantees of Reversions Act 1540 s.2.

[66] Below, para.20–061.

[67] Below, para.20–053.

[68] See above, para.19–093.

[69] An assignee's liability on grounds of privity of estate is so limited: below, para.20–053.

[70] *J. Lyons & Co Ltd v Knowles* [1943] K.B. 366.

[71] *Estates Gazette Ltd v Benjamin Restaurants Ltd* [1994] 1 W.L.R. 1528.

[72] Whether a statutory written assignment under LPA 1925 s.136 or an equitable assignment. In practice, express assignments are widely employed.

[73] Because that section applies only to covenants in the lease itself: s.141(1); *P. & A. Swift Investments v Combined English Stores Group Plc* [1989] A.C. 632 at 639.

either have to be at common law[74] or under some other statutory provision.[75] Analogous situations provide little guidance. Although the benefit of a covenant by a surety guaranteeing the performance of covenants in the lease passes with the reversion at common law,[76] the benefit of a tenant's covenants in a lease did not.[77]

4. Reform: the Landlord and Tenant (Covenants) Act 1995. The con-   **20–020** tinued liability of an original covenantor[78] throughout the term can cause considerable hardship.[79] The widespread use of upward-only rent review clauses[80] may mean that T1 is called upon to discharge obligations substantially more onerous than those he had originally undertaken. Furthermore, although it is reasonable to expect T1 to choose an assignee who is financially responsible, he has no control over subsequent assignments of the term. There was considerable pressure to restrict T1's liability,[81] and in 1988 the Law Commission recommended that:

(i) on an assignment of a lease, a tenant should generally cease to be liable on the covenants and should also cease to have the benefit of the lease; and

(ii) where the landlord's consent to any assignment is necessary, the landlord would be able to require the tenant to guarantee the performance of the covenants by the immediate assignee as a condition for giving his consent (an "authorised guarantee agreement"), but the assigning tenant's liability would cease on a further assignment.[82]

These recommendations were implemented in substantially modified form   **20–021** (as part of a much larger series of measures) by the Landlord and Tenant (Covenants) Act 1995, but only as regards leases granted after 1995.[83] However, that Act also introduced three provisions which apply to leases whenever

---

[74] Below, para.32–056.

[75] See LPA 1925 s.78(1); below, para.32–063.

[76] *Kumar v Dunning* [1989] Q.B. 193; *P. & A. Swift Investments v Combined English Stores Group Plc*, above; see below, paras 20–035 and 20–074.

[77] See *P. & A. Swift Investments v Combined English Stores Group Plc*, above, at 640: and see above, para.20–015.

[78] Who for these purposes also includes an assignee of a lease who enters into a direct covenant with the landlord: see above, para.20–018.

[79] For a summary of the criticisms of the law, see (1988) Law Com. No.174, para.3.1.

[80] For rent review clauses, see above, para.19–065.

[81] Not least because the recession prompted many landlords to have recourse to the original tenant, which came as a surprise to many: see *Mytre Investments Ltd v Reynolds* [1995] 3 All E.R. 588 at 590. For the change in the nature of the relationship of landlord and tenant that made first tenant liability a major issue, see (1996) 59 M.L.R. 78 at 81 (M. Davey).

[82] (1988) Law Com. No.174; [1989] Conv. 145; [1992] Conv. 393 (H. W. Wilkinson).

[83] Below, para.20–085.

granted and which alleviate the position of original tenants.[84] These provisions, which cannot be excluded,[85] are as follows.

20–022   *(a) Restriction on liability.* At common law, L1 was under no obligation to notify T1 that T2 was in arrears with payments of rent, service charge or any other fixed amount. Substantial sums might therefore become due before T1 was aware of his liability. The 1995 Act makes provision "to ensure that original tenants get prior notice of the possibility that they will be looked to for the recovery of rent under a lease which they may have assigned many years before."[86] It follows that where some or all of any "fixed charge" (i.e., rent, any service charge[87] or any sum payable under a liquidated damages clause for breach of covenant)[88] becomes due, and L1 wishes to recover the amount due from T1, L1 must comply with a statutory notice procedure. This requires L1 to serve on T1, within six months of the charge becoming due, a notice informing T1 that the charge is now due and that he intends to recover from T1 the amount specified in the notice with interest (if payable, specifying the basis upon which it has been calculated).[89] If L1 fails to serve such a notice within the statutory time limit, T1 is not liable to pay the sum.[90] The statutory notice procedure operates similarly in relation to those who have guaranteed T1's liability[91]; it is not, however, necessary for L1 to serve a notice on T1 and seek payment from him prior to serving notice on the guarantor.[92]

20–023   The legislation does not deal satisfactorily with the position where a rent review is pending. The rent review process almost always takes time, and there is therefore potential for a sometimes lengthy interval between the review date and the date on which the amount of the revised rent is finally

---

[84] These provisions are the result of proposals made by the property industry: below, para.20–085.

[85] See L & TCA 1995 s.25(1); below, para.20–128.

[86] *Scottish & Newcastle v Raguz (No.3)* [2007] EWCA Civ 150 at [35]; [2007] 2 All E.R. 871, at 882, per Lloyd L.J.

[87] For the meaning of service charge, see L & TA 1985 s.18; above, para.19–082.

[88] L & TCA 1995 s.17(6).

[89] L & TCA 1995 s.17(2). Where a fixed charge had become payable before January 1, 1996, the sum is treated as if it had become due on that date provided that no proceedings for its recovery had been instituted by then: ibid. s.17(5). A notice under s.17 is not invalidated merely because it includes items to which the landlord is not entitled: *Commercial Union Life Assurance Co Ltd v Moustafa* [1999] 2 E.G.L.R. 44; and see *Scottish & Newcastle Plc v Raguz (No.3)* [2008] UKHL 65; [2008] 1 W.L.R. 2494 at [67].

[90] However, if T1 pays the sum claimed, T1 may be able to claim an indemnity from T2 under LRA 2002 Sch.12 para.20 (although not where lease is a "new lease" within L & TCA 1995: see LRA 2002 Sch.12 para.20(5)). Although T1 could not be compelled by L1 to pay the sum in view of L1's failure to serve a notice under s.17, T2 would remain liable to indemnify T1 provided that T1's expenditure was fairly and reasonably incurred: *Scottish & Newcastle Plc v Raguz (No.3)*, above. *Quaere* where the lease is a "new lease" to which LRA 2002 Sch.12 para.20 does not apply. (At common law, in the absence of contrary provision, T2's indemnity is limited to sums T1 can be compelled by L1 to pay: *Moule v Garrett* (1872) L.R. 7 Ex. 101.) There is no need for T1 to serve a s.17 notice on T2 prior to claiming an indemnity: *M.W.Kellogg Ltd v Tobin* [1999] L. & T.R. 513.

[91] L & TCA 1995 s.17(3).

[92] *Cheverell Estates Ltd v Harris* [1998] 1 E.G.L.R. 27.

determined. Problems arise because it is usual for leases to provide that the revised rent is payable from the review date; in other words that the rent review has retrospective effect. The House of Lords has held that in such circumstances rent does not "become due" for the purposes of s.17(2) until the revised rent has been agreed by the parties or determined in accordance with the rent review provisions.[93] It is not therefore necessary for L1 to serve notice on T1, in order to preserve the right to claim the revised rent, until that later date.[94] The effect of this decision, which was arrived at on essentially pragmatic grounds, has been to render s.17(4), which purports to deal with circumstances where subsequent to service of the notice T1's liability is determined to be greater, largely redundant.[95]

Although this statutory notice procedure may be of primary importance as regards leases granted before 1996, it is also of relevance to leases granted after 1995 in two situations which are explained below.[96]   **20–024**

(b) Right to overriding lease

(1) THE NATURE OF AN OVERRIDING LEASE. At common law there is no means   **20–025**
by which T1 can limit his liability for repeated breaches of covenant committed by T2, for although a lease invariably contains a forfeiture clause, T1 cannot compel L1 to exercise it and terminate the tenancy.[97] The 1995 Act gives T1, and also guarantors, a remedy in certain circumstances. Where T1 has paid in full an amount which he has been required to pay in response to a s.17 notice, he is entitled to be granted an overriding lease by L1.[98] An overriding lease is a lease of the reversion.[99] It is granted for a term equal to the remainder of the term of the original tenancy plus three days[100] and contains the same covenants as those in the original tenancy, unless a particular covenant was expressed to be personal between the landlord and the

---

[93] *Scottish & Newcastle Plc v Raguz (No.3)* [2008] UKHL 65; [2008] 1 W.L.R. 2494; and see Stoner [2009] 13 L. & T. Rev.7.
[94] Cf. the decisions of the Court of Appeal at [2007] EWCA Civ 150; [2007] 2 All E.R. 871 and of Hart J at first instance at [2006] EWHC 821 (Ch); [2006] 4 All E.R. 524, holding that the statutory wording captured a debt which although not currently payable would, on subsequently becoming payable, be treated as having fallen due at the earlier date. The majority of the House of Lords held that this reasoning produced "some remarkably silly consequences", per Lord Hoffmann, above, at [10]. For an intermediate view, see Lord Walker of Gestingthorpe, above, at [62] et seq.
[95] This is because "it is hard to think of cases in which a fixed charge within the meaning of the Act will have become actually payable without its amount having been determined." *Scottish & Newcastle Plc v Raguz (No.3)*, above at [13] per Lord Hoffmann.
[96] The first situation is where T1 is liable on an "authorised guarantee agreement": below, para.20–089. The second is where the assignment from T1 to T2 is an "excluded assignment": below, para.20–100.
[97] If T2 is insolvent and there is a disclaimer by the liquidator or trustee in bankruptcy, T1 can seek to have the lease vested in him: IA 1986 ss. 181, 320; above, para.18–099.
[98] L & TCA 1995 s.19(1).
[99] L & TCA 1995 s.19(2). For leases of the reversion, see above, para.17–133.
[100] Or, where L1 is himself a leaseholder, the longest period (less than three days) that will not wholly displace L1's reversion.

tenant,[101] or has ceased to be binding.[102] Once T1 has been granted an overriding lease,[103] he can exercise any right of re-entry and take steps to forfeit T2's tenancy. In the event of that tenancy being terminated, T1's overriding lease will take effect in possession and T1 may occupy the premises, assign the lease or grant a sub-lease.[104] By such means, not only can T1 prevent T2 from committing further breaches of covenant (thereby limiting his own liability), but he may also be able to recoup the amount he has been compelled to pay to L1.[105]

20–026   (2) COMPETING CLAIMS. Where T2 has defaulted under a covenant in the lease to pay one or more fixed sums, L1 may have had recourse not only to T1, but to others who are also liable, such as a guarantor or an intermediate assignee. It is therefore possible that there may be more than one person entitled to an overriding lease. Priority is given to the first person to apply for such a lease.[106] Where L1 receives two applications on the same day, preference is given:

> (i) to a former tenant over a guarantor; and

> (ii) as between former tenants, to the one whose liability commenced earlier.[107]

20–027   (3) GRANT. To seek the grant of an overriding lease, T1 must make a written request to L1 within a year of making the payment that entitles him to the lease, specifying that payment.[108] L1 must then grant and deliver a lease in favour of T1[109] unless:

> (i) L1 has already determined T2's lease[110];

> (ii) L1 has granted an overriding lease to, or received a request for such a lease from, another person[111]; or

---

[101] L & TCA 1995 ss.19(2) and 19(3): see below, para.20–107. If any covenant in the original tenancy operates in some way by reference to its commencement (such as a covenant to repaint the exterior of the premises after three years), the corresponding covenant in the overriding lease also operates by reference to the commencement of the original tenancy: L & TCA s.19(4).

[102] L & TCA 1995 ss.19(2), 19(3) and 19(4).

[103] T can seek an overriding lease, even though he is himself a tenant under an overriding lease: L & TCA 1995 s.19(11).

[104] Subject to any requirement that he first obtains the landlord's consent.

[105] It is uncertain what effect the grant of an overriding lease may have on T1's rights of indemnity against any intermediate assignee. In principle, if T1 is fully recouped from such a grant he should be debarred from such a claim, but not if he is only partially recouped. If he does obtain an indemnity, the intermediate assignee cannot claim an overriding lease. It is only where payment is made to the landlord of the defaulting tenant that such a right arises: L & TCA 1995 s.19(1).

[106] L & TCA 1995 s.19(7).

[107] L & TCA 1995 s.19(8).

[108] L & TCA 1995 s.19(5).

[109] L & TCA 1995 s.19(6). T1 must in turn deliver an executed counterpart of the lease to L1, and meet his reasonable costs: ibid.

[110] L & TCA 1995 s.19(7).

[111] L & TCA 1995 s.19(7).

(iii) T1 has withdrawn his application in writing or abandoned it.[112]

A request by T1 for such a lease may be registered by means of a notice where title is itself registered,[113] or as an estate contract under the Land Charges Act 1972 where it is not.[114] A failure by L1 to grant T1 an overriding lease is a breach of statutory duty for which T1 may recover damages in tort.[115]

(4) MISCELLANEOUS PROVISIONS. To meet the case where L1's reversion is mortgaged on terms that restrict his power to grant further leases,[116] the grant of an overriding lease is deemed to be authorised as against, and binding upon, the mortgagee.[117] Similarly, because the overriding lease contains the same terms as the original tenancy, it may include a covenant against sub-letting or parting with possession. In such a case, T1 is not in breach of the covenant merely because his overriding lease necessarily takes effect subject to T2's lease.[118]   **20–028**

(5) OLD AND NEW TENANCIES. All overriding leases must state that they have been granted under s.19 of the 1995 Act and also whether or not they are new tenancies.[119] Where T1 exercises his right to claim an overriding lease in respect of a tenancy granted before 1996, that overriding lease is not a new tenancy. It is therefore subject to the rules of law applicable to all tenancies granted before 1996,[120] including the rules of privity of contract. Where L1 grants the tenancy after 1995, both that tenancy and any overriding lease that may be granted subsequently will be new tenancies and therefore subject to all the provisions of the 1995 Act. These are explained below.[121]   **20–029**

There are two circumstances in which T1 can seek an overriding lease where the original tenancy to him was granted after 1995. These are also explained below.[122]   **20–030**

(c) *Variations of covenants.* At the time when the 1995 Act was passed, it was thought that T1 was liable on the covenants in the lease even though their terms had been subsequently varied by an agreement between L1 and T2 to   **20–031**

---

[112] L & TCA 1995 s.19(9), providing that T1 is liable for L1's reasonable costs.

[113] L & TCA 1995 s.20(6), as amended by LRA 2002 s.133, Sch.11 para.33. The right cannot be an overriding interest: ibid.

[114] For the registration of estate contracts, see above, para.8–075.

[115] L & TCA 1995 s.20(3).

[116] See below, para.25–079.

[117] L & TCA 1995 s.20(4). L1 is obliged to deliver the counterpart of the overriding lease to the mortgagee within a month, and a failure to do so is deemed to be a breach of the terms of the mortgage. ibid.

[118] L & TCA 1995 s.20(5).

[119] L & TCA 1995 s.20(2). See above, para.20–010.

[120] L & TCA 1995 s.20(1).

[121] Below, para.20–085.

[122] The first situation is where T1 has entered into an authorised guarantee agreement: below, paras 20–089 et seq. The second is where the assignment from T1 to T2 was an excluded assignment so that T1 remains liable on the covenants: below, paras 20–100 et seq.

which T1 was not a party.[123] It was not easy to see any logical basis for a rule so productive of injustice, and the authorities on which it was based have in fact since been disapproved.[124] In any event, the Act places the matter beyond doubt for any variations made after 1995.[125] T is not liable to pay any amount that is referable to any variation of the tenant covenants that is made after T has assigned the lease.[126] The variation must be one which either:

(i) L1 had an absolute right to refuse to allow at the time when it was made[127]; or

(ii) was one L1 would have had an absolute right to refuse if T1 had sought his consent immediately before he assigned the lease to T2.[128]

It follows that T1 cannot object to a variation for which the lease made specific provision and to which he was a party (such as the increase of the rent under a rent review clause).

20–032   The situation which the Act seeks to remedy is of course where the variation makes T2's financial obligations more onerous than were T1's. The application of its provisions should be confined to that situation. If the variation reduces the burden on T2, who subsequently defaults, T1's liability to L1 should therefore be limited to the amount which L1 could have claimed from T2.[129]

Section 2. Privity of Estate: Position of Assignees

A. Covenants Touching and Concerning Land

20–033   **1. The meaning of "touching and concerning".** The rights and liabilities of assignees, either of the lease or of the reversion, depend upon two things: whether there is privity of estate[130] between the claimant and the defendant, and whether the covenant sought to be enforced "touches and concerns the land"[131] or, to use the modern statutory phraseology, "has reference to the

---

[123] See *Centrovincial Estates Plc v Bulk Storage Ltd* (1983) 46 P. & C.R. 393 at 396; *Selous Street Properties Ltd v Oronel Fabrics Ltd* [1984] 1 E.G.L.R. 50; *GUS Property Management Ltd v Texas Homecare Ltd* [1993] 2 E.G.L.R. 63. cf. *Burford Midland Properties Ltd v Marley Extrusions Ltd* [1995] 1 B.C.L.C. 102 at 114 (casting doubt on these decisions).

[124] *Friends' Provident Life Office v British Railways Board* [1996] 1 All E.R. 336 (decided by the Court of Appeal six days after the Act had received the Royal Assent). See too *Beegas Nominees Ltd v Sevington Properties Ltd* (1998) 77 P. & C.R. 14.

[125] L & TCA 1995 s.18. The Act does not apply to variations made before 1996: L & TCA 1995 s.18(6).

[126] L & TCA 1995 s.18(2).

[127] Where L1 has merely a *qualified* right to refuse (as where his consent is required to any such variation), T1 will be bound by the clause as amended. In such circumstances T1 is taken to be aware that the lease may be varied at some future date.

[128] L & TCA 1995 s.18(4).

[129] cf. *Mytre Investments Ltd v Reynolds* [1995] 3 All E.R. 588 at 592. L1 can be regarded as releasing T2 pro tanto from the covenant to the extent that obligation is reduced.

[130] Above, para.20–004.

[131] *Spencer's Case* (1583) 5 Co.Rep. 16a.

subject-matter of the lease".[132] "Generations of conveyancers and law students have been familiar with these phrases and with writers' lists of covenants held by courts to be on or other side of the line."[133] The two phrases are technical expressions which bear the same meaning,[134] and refer to the limited class of covenants which can be made to bind third parties so that the right to enforce them is a proprietary interest as well as a merely contractual right. A covenant which does not "touch and concern" the land cannot run with the land by reason of privity of estate.

2. Uncertainty of the test. The requirement that a covenant must touch and **20–034** concern the land rests upon the idea that obligations that are intended to be personal to the parties to the lease should not run with the lease or reversion. The distinction between personal and proprietary covenants is superficially attractive, but in practice it is one that is not easily drawn. It is impossible to reason by analogy, for the rules concerning it "are purely arbitrary, and the distinctions, for the most part, quite illogical".[135]

An attempt was made to formulate a "satisfactory working test"[136] in a **20–035** series of decisions in which it was held that the benefit of a covenant by a surety to guarantee the performance of a tenant's obligations under the lease touched and concerned the land and passed with the lessor's reversion when it was assigned.[137] A covenant would touch and concern the land if it:

(i) benefited only the owner for the time being of the covenantee's land, and if separated from that land ceased to benefit that covenantee;

(ii) affected the nature, quality, mode of user or value of the land of the covenantee; and

(iii) was not expressed to be personal (neither being given to a specific covenantee nor in respect of the obligations of a specific covenantor).[138]

---

[132] LPA 1925 ss.141 and 142.

[133] *London Diocesan Board v Phithwa* [2005] UKHL 70; [2005] 1 W.L.R. 3956 at [25], per Lord Nicholls of Birkenhead, referring to the list in the sixth edition of this work at paras 15–026—15–027 (and now below at paras 20–039, 20–040.)

[134] *Davis v Town Properties Investment Corp Ltd* [1903] 1 Ch. 797 at 805.

[135] *Grant v Edmondson* [1931] 1 Ch. 1 at 28, per Romer L.J. (giving examples of the illogicalities at 28 and 29); *Cardwell v Walker* [2003] EWHC 3117; [2004] 2 P. & C.R. 9 at [46]; *London Diocesan Board v Phithwa*, above, at [26].

[136] "Without claiming to expound an exhaustive guide": *P. & A. Swift Investments v Combined English Stores Group Plc* [1989] A.C. 632 at 642, per Lord Oliver.

[137] *Kumar v Dunning* [1989] Q.B. 193; *P. & A. Swift Investments v Combined English Stores Group Plc*, above; *Coronation Street Industrial Properties Ltd v Ingall Industries Plc* [1989] 1 W.L.R. 304.

[138] *P. & A. Swift Investments v Combined English Stores Group Plc*, above, at 642. See too *Kumar v Dunning*, above, at 204. A "hybrid" covenant, expressed to be personal to the tenant but assignable on certain conditions being met, may touch and concern the land: *Harbour Estates Ltd v HSBC Bank Plc* [2004] EWHC 1714; [2005] Ch. 194 (benefit of tenant's break clause assignable to permitted assignee), followed in *Aviva Life & Pensions UK Ltd v Linpac Mouldings Ltd* [2010] EWCA Civ 395; [2010] L. & T.R. 10 at [44].

A covenant to pay a sum of money (such as a surety covenant or a covenant to pay rent) could touch and concern the land if it satisfied these three requirements and was "connected with something to be done on to or in relation to the land".[139]

20–036   However, doubts have arisen both as to the applicability of this test and its content. First, it may apply only to the transmission of the benefit of surety covenants. These pass at common law. The benefit of leasehold covenants passes on an assignment of the reversion under s.141 of the Law of Property Act 1925, and it has been suggested that to determine which of them touch and concern the land regard should be had to the authorities on that section rather than to the test devised for surety covenants.[140] By contrast, it has been assumed that the test applies to the passing of the burden of covenants on an assignment of the reversion under s.142 of the Law of Property Act 1925.[141] Secondly, it is clear that the transmission of the benefit of a covenant does not depend on the transmissibility of the burden, and vice versa.[142] Thus a covenant may touch and concern the land even though:

(i) the benefit is personal to the covenantee if the burden is intended to pass[143]; or

(ii) the burden is personal to the covenantor if the benefit is intended to pass.[144]

20–037   Whether or not a covenant touches and concerns the land all too often appears to be purely arbitrary. Thus although a covenant by a surety to guarantee performance of covenants in the lease touches and concerns the land,[145] a covenant by the landlord to repay a security deposit to the tenant does not.[146] This is so, even though the objective of each covenant is to provide the landlord with security for the performance of the obligations in the lease.

---

[139] *P. & A. Swift Investments v Combined English Stores Group Plc*, above, at 642, per Lord Oliver of Aylmerton.

[140] *Caerns Motor Services Ltd v Texaco Ltd* [1994] 1 W.L.R. 1249. The correctness of this suggestion must be open to question. In *Kumar v Dunning*, above, no distinction was drawn in the analysis of the authorities between cases which involved leases and those which did not.

[141] *System Floors Ltd v Ruralpride Ltd* [1995] 1 E.G.L.R. 48. The court did note that it had been formulated in cases in which LPA 1925 ss.141 and 142 were inapplicable: *System Floors Ltd*, at 50.

[142] *System Floors Ltd v Ruralpride Ltd*, above, at 50 and 51.

[143] *System Floors Ltd v Ruralpride Ltd*, above. In that case L1 had granted T1 by side letter a right to surrender the lease after a rent review, and that right was to be personal to T1 alone. When L1 assigned to L2, the burden of L1's undertaking passed to L2.

[144] This is the case where a surety guarantees the performance of the covenants in the lease.

[145] *Kumar v Dunning*, above; *P. & A. Swift Investments v Combined English Stores Group Plc*, above; *Coronation Street Industrial Properties Ltd v Ingall Industries Plc* [1989] 1 W.L.R. 304; [1988] C.L.J. 180 (C.H.).

[146] *Hua Chiao Commercial Bank Ltd v Chiaphua Industries Ltd* [1987] A.C. 99. The decision seems wrong in principle.

3. Examples. The present law can be best understood by examples in   **20–038**
addition to the ones given above. The covenants in the left-hand column
below have been held to touch and concern the land, while those in the right-
hand column have been held not to do so.

(a) Covenants by a tenant   **20–039**

TOUCHING AND CONCERNING | NOT TOUCHING AND CONCERNING

TOUCHING AND CONCERNING

To pay rent.[147]

To repair the property or fixtures on it.[148]

To pay a fixed sum towards redecoration on quitting.[149]

To insure against fire.[150]

To use as a private dwellinghouse only.[151]

Not to assign the lease without the landlord's consent.[152]

Not to let a certain person be concerned in the conduct of the business carried on upon the premises.[153]

To buy beer for a public house[154] or petrol for a filling station[155] only from the landlord.

NOT TOUCHING AND CONCERNING

To pay an annual sum to a third person.[156]

To pay rates in respect of other land.[157]

Not to employ persons living in other parishes to work in the demised mill (the landlord's motive being to benefit his other property in the parish).[158]

To repair and renew the tools of a smithy standing on the land (the tools were movable chattels, not fixtures).[159]

---

[147] *Parker v Webb* (1693) 3 Salk. 5.

[148] *Matures v Westwood* (1597) Cro.Eliz. 599; *Williams v Earle* (1868) L.R. 3 Q.B. 739.

[149] *Boyer v Warbey* [1953] 1 Q.B. 234; and see *Moss' Empires Ltd v Olympia (Liverpool) Ltd* [1939] A.C. 544 (covenant to spend specified sum on repairs annually or pay the sum to the landlord).

[150] *Vernon v Smith* (1821) 5 B. & Ald. 1.

[151] *Wilkinson v Rogers* (1864) 2 De G.J. and S. 62.

[152] *Goldstein v Sanders* [1915] 1 Ch. 549; *Re Robert Stephenson & Co Ltd* [1915] 1 Ch. 802; *Cohen v Popular Restaurants Ltd* [1917] 1 K.B. 480.

[153] *Lewin v American & Colonial Distributors Ltd* [1945] Ch. 225, where there is a useful review of the authorities.

[154] *Clegg v Hands* (1890) 44 Ch D 503; *Manchester Brewery Co v Coombs* [1901] 2 Ch. 608.

[155] *Regent Oil Co Ltd v J. A. Gregory (Hatch End) Ltd* [1966] Ch. 402; *Caerns Motor Services Ltd v Texaco Ltd* [1994] 1 W.L.R. 1249.

[156] *Mayho v Buckhurst* (1617) Cro.Jac. 438.

[157] *Gower v Postmaster General* (1887) 57 L.T. 527.

[158] *Congleton Corporation v Pattison* (1808) 10 East 130.

[159] *Williams v Earle* (1868) L.R. 3 Q.B. 739.

20–040   *(b) Covenants by a landlord*

TOUCHING AND CONCERNING	NOT TOUCHING AND CONCERNING
To renew the lease[160]	To sell the reversion at a stated price, at the tenant's option.[165]
To supply the demised premises with water[161]	To pay at the end of the lease for chattels not amounting to fixtures.[166]
Not to build on a certain part of the adjoining land.[162]	To pay the tenant a sum at the end of the lease unless a new lease is granted.[167]
Not to determine a periodic (quarterly) tenancy during its first three years.[163]	Not to open another public house within half a mile (in a lease of a public house).[168]
To accept a surrender of the lease from the tenant after a rent review.[164]	To allow the tenant to display advertising signs on other premises.[169]

Although it has been held that a covenant does not touch and concern the land merely because its non-performance may cause a lease of the land to be forfeited,[170] this decision is unlikely to be followed. It is inconsistent with the principle that a covenant will touch and concern the land if it affects its value.[171]

20–041   **4. Reform.** The Law Commission recommended the abolition of the requirement that covenants should pass only if they touch and concern the land.[172] These proposals have now been implemented as regards leases

---

[160] *Richardson v Sydenham* (1703) 2 Vern. 447; *Muller v Trafford* [1901] 1 Ch. 54 at 60; *Weg Motors Ltd v Hales* [1962] Ch. 49. This is somewhat anomalous and difficult to justify: *Woodall v Clifton* [1905] 2 Ch. 257 at 279.

[161] *Jourdain v Wilson* [1821] 4 B. & Ald. 266.

[162] *Ricketts v Enfield Churchwardens* [1909] 1 Ch. 544.

[163] *Breams Property Investment Co Ltd v Stroulger* [1948] 2 K.B. 1.

[164] *System Floors Ltd v Ruralpride Ltd* [1995] 1 E.G.L.R. 48.

[165] *Woodall v Clifton*, above; see below, para.20–084, fn.358. Similarly, a right of pre-emption over adjoining land: *Collison v Lettsom* (1815) 6 Taunt. 224.

[166] *Gorton v Gregory* (1862) 3 B. and S. 90.

[167] *Re Hunter's Lease* [1942] Ch. 124.

[168] *Thomas v Hayward* (1869) L.R. 4 Ex. 311. The correctness of this decision has been doubted: *Kumar v Dunning* [1989] Q.B. 193 at 205. In principle a covenant which benefits the business of the lessee should be capable of touching and concerning the land. Not only will a freehold covenant touch and concern the land if it benefits a business conducted on the land (see *Newton Abbot Co-operative Society Ltd v Williamson & Treadgold Ltd* [1952] Ch. 286 at 293), but an easement may accommodate the dominant tenement if it is for the benefit of a business carried on on the premises: *Moody v Steggles* (1879) 12 Ch D 261; below, para.27–008.

[169] *Re No.1, Albemarle Street* [1959] Ch. 531.

[170] *Dewar v Goodman* [1909] A.C. 72 (covenant by sub-lessor to observe covenants in the head lease held not to touch and concern the land).

[171] *Kumar v Dunning* [1989] Q.B. 193 at 205, holding *Dewar v Goodman*, above, to be inconsistent with *Dyson v Foster* [1909] A.C. 98.

[172] (1988) Law Com. No.174.

granted after 1995.[173] In general, the benefit and burden of all covenants passes on an assignment of such a lease or its reversion unless the covenant is expressed to be personal to any person (i.e. usually one or both of the parties to the lease).[174]

B. Principles of Transmission

Having seen which covenants touch and concern the land, we must now examine the rights and liabilities of assignees. As in every other case of enforcing rights of property, two separate points must be considered: **20–042**

    (i) is the defendant liable? and

    (ii) is the claimant entitled to sue?

In the case of the rights and liabilities of assignees under covenants concerning land, it is more usual to put these questions as follows:

    (i) has the burden of the covenant passed? and

    (ii) has the benefit of the covenant passed?

In discussing these questions it will be convenient to deal first with assignments of leases, then with assignments of reversions, then with the transfer of the benefit of surety covenants and the rights of sureties, and finally with forfeiture clauses.[175] The rules which govern the transmissibility of covenants are neither rational nor coherent.[176] For leases granted after 1995, they are replaced with a statutory code that attempts to remove the inconsistencies and anomalies that apply to leases granted before 1996.[177]

I. WHERE THE TENANT ASSIGNS HIS LEASE

If L1 leases land to T1, and T1 assigns the lease to T2, the common law rule laid down in *Spencer's Case*[178] is that T2 is entitled to the benefit, and subject to the burden, of all covenants and conditions touching and concerning the land, because there is privity of estate between L1 and T2. Where there is privity of estate, both the benefit and the burden of the covenants run with the land demised. **20–043**

The details of this fundamental rule must now be studied.

---

[173] L & TCA 1995 s.2(1). This is subject to certain limited exceptions: ibid. s.2(2); see below, para.20–108.

[174] L & TCA 1995 s.3; below, paras 20–107 et seq.

[175] For the transfer of the benefit and burden of covenants with a lease of a right in the nature of an incorporeal hereditament, see the fifth edition of this work at p.756.

[176] For an admirable account of their operation, see (1991) 11 L.S. 47 (R. Thornton).

[177] Below, paras 20–107 et seq.

[178] (1583) 5 Co.Rep. 16a.

20–044   **1. The lease must be in due form.** It used to be held that only a lease made by deed would carry the benefit or burden of special stipulations to an assignee, since they could not otherwise be annexed to the estate.[179] But if the assignee of an informal lease went into possession and paid rent the court would readily infer a new agreement on the same terms as the old, so that the assignee would become bound by privity of contract[180]; and under equitable doctrines, if there was a specifically enforceable agreement for a lease the benefit, but not the burden, of its terms could be assigned.[181] The Court of Appeal has, however, held that the burden (and presumably also the benefit) of a stipulation can pass on the assignment of a lease for three years or less made merely in writing[182]; and dicta in the same case would apparently extend the concession to mere agreements for a lease,[183] thus conflicting with the rule that the burden of a mere agreement is not assignable. The very reasonable decision to hold the assignee bound by the terms of a legal lease not made by deed is rather strangely attributed to "the fusion of law and equity" made by the Judicature Act 1873 which is said to have largely obliterated the distinction between agreements under hand and covenants made by deed.[184] Whether the doctrine extends to tenancies for three years or less which are made merely orally (i.e. without writing) is uncertain.[185]

2. There must be a legal assignment of the whole term

20–045   *(a) Legal assignment.* The benefit and burden of covenants run with the lease only in the case of a legal assignment of the whole of the remainder of the term.[186] Where instead of an assignment there has been a sub-lease, the sub-tenant takes neither the benefit nor the burden of the covenants in the lease,[187] even if his sub-lease is only one day shorter than the head lease. If L1 leases land to T1 for 99 years, T1 assigns the lease to T2, and T2 then sub-lets the land to S for the residue of the term of 99 years less one day, S is a

---

[179] *Elliott v Johnson* (1866) L.R. 2 Q.B. 120 at 127.

[180] *Buckworth v Simpson* (1835) 1 Cr.M. & R. 834; *Cornish v Stubbs* (1870) L.R. 5 C.P. 334 at 338 and 339.

[181] Above, para.17–061.

[182] *Boyer v Warbey* [1953] 1 Q.B. 234 (lease of a flat for three years made in writing and not by deed, with a term that the tenant on quitting would pay £40 towards cost of redecoration: held, this term was binding on an assignee of the lease); cf. *Weg Motors Ltd v Hales* [1962] Ch. 49 (burden of covenant written but not by deed running with the reversion).

[183] *Boyer v Warbey*, above, at 246 (Denning L.J.). Any such agreement would now have to comply with the formal requirements of LP(MP)A 1989 s.2. See above, paras 15–015 and 17–047.

[184] *Boyer v Warbey*, above, at 246. See [1978] C.L.J. 98 at 105 (R. J. Smith).

[185] *Boyer v Warbey*, above, appears to overrule *Elliott v Johnson*, above, where there was a mere oral agreement implied in the case of a tenant who had held over after the expiration of a lease for 14 years. There are obvious difficulties for an assignee in ascertaining the terms of an oral tenancy unless, as in that case, they are contained in an earlier lease.

[186] *West v Dobb* (1869) L.R. 4 Q.B. 634.

[187] *South of England Dairies Ltd v Baker* [1906] 2 Ch. 631; but it is possible that the sub-tenant can take the benefit by virtue of LPA 1925 s.78: see *Smith v River Douglas Catchment Board* [1949] 2 K.B. 500, below, para.32–015. A sub-tenant may be bound by restrictive covenants: below, para.32–045. For the difference between an assignment and a sub-lease, see above, para.17–009.

sub-tenant, not an assignee of the term. There is privity neither of contract nor of estate between L1 and S. T2 is still the tenant under the lease for 99 years and remains liable upon it. Consequently if S does some act which is contrary to a covenant in the 99 years' lease, L1 cannot sue S, but can sue T2. If the lease contains a forfeiture clause, the landlord can take proceedings for forfeiture and so put an end to both head lease and sub-lease together. In practice the covenants inserted in a sub-lease are made at least as stringent as those in the head lease, so that the sub-lessor T2 may have a remedy against the sub-tenant S in case S's acts render T2 liable to the landlord.

(b) Other assignments. Since the covenants run only where there is privity **20–046** of estate, a mere equitable assignment (e.g. under a contract to assign) cannot pass the burden of covenants.[188] But the benefit may itself be assigned as such; and if the covenant creates an interest in land (e.g. a restrictive covenant, or an option), the burden will affect subsequent occupiers in accordance with the ordinary rules governing legal and equitable interests. These cases are explained more fully below.[189]

(c) Squatters. Where title is unregistered, a squatter, i.e. a person who bars **20–047** the lessee's interest by adverse possession for 12 years under the Limitation Act 1980, is not an assignee of the lease, at least where the title to the land is unregistered. He cannot therefore sue or be sued on covenants in the lease which run only where there is privity of estate.[190] But if he claims some advantage under the lease, e.g. a reduction of rent which is conditional on observance of the covenants, he may estop himself from denying that he is bound by the lease.[191] Where the leasehold title is registered the position is quite different. It is no longer possible for a squatter to bar the rights of the lessee by adverse possession alone.[192] However, once the squatter has been in adverse possession for ten years, he may apply to be registered as the proprietor of the registered leasehold estate.[193] Such application is unlikely to succeed,[194] but if it does, the squatter obtains the registered estate, and will become a successor in title to the former tenant. This means that there is privity of estate with the landlord, and that the squatter therefore takes both the benefit and the burden of the covenants in the lease.[195]

(d) Personal representatives. A personal representative of the tenant is an **20–048** assignee by operation of law, for when the tenant dies the lease devolves

---

[188] *Cox v Bishop* (1857) 8 De G.M. & G. 815; *Friary Holroyd & Healey's Breweries Ltd v Singleton* [1899] 1 Ch. 86, reversed on other grounds [1899] 2 Ch. 261. See [1978] C.L.J. 98 (R. J. Smith). There may be facts which estop the assignee from denying liability: see above, paras 17–125 et seq.

[189] See below, paras 20–082 et seq.

[190] *Tichborne v Weir* (1892) 67 L.T. 735; below, para.35–063. The landlord may however be able to forfeit the lease for the breach of covenant in question and thereby recover possession against the squatter: see below, para.20–077.

[191] *Ashe v Hogan* [1920] 1 I.R. 159; below, para.35–063.

[192] LRA 2002 s.96(1).

[193] LRA 2002 s.97 Sch.6.

[194] See below, para.35–070.

[195] LRA 2002 Sch.6 para.9(2).

automatically upon his executor or administrator.[196] But the extent of a personal representative's liability varies. If he takes possession of the land, he is personally liable to the same extent as an ordinary assignee,[197] though by proper pleading he may limit his liability to the annual value of the land.[198] If he does not take possession, he is liable only[199] in his representative capacity, i.e. to the extent of the deceased tenant's assets.[200] The representative liability of an original tenant's estate endures for the whole term of the lease, despite any assignment by him[201] or by his personal representatives.[202]

20–049   This representative liability formerly made it unsafe for a personal representative to distribute the assets to the persons beneficially entitled so long as any liability might arise under the covenants in the lease.[203] However, a personal representative is now protected by statute against his representative liability if he has first satisfied any existing claims, set aside any *fixed* sum agreed to be laid out on the land, and assigned the lease to a beneficiary or purchaser.[204] But this provides no protection if the personal representative or trustee has taken possession and so is liable as an assignee; in such cases he may set aside a fund for his protection,[205] though this will be distributable when all possible claims have been paid or barred by lapse of time.[206]

20–050   *(e) Several assignees.* If the tenancy is vested in two or more assignees, each is liable for the full amount of any damages for breach of covenant and not merely a proportionate share, even if in equity they are not joint tenants but tenants in common.[207]

20–051   **3. Partial assignment.** It is possible for part only of the demised land to be assigned separately from the rest. In that case covenants capable of running with the land will bind the assignee in so far as they relate to the part assigned to him,[208] whether or not that assignment is made with the landlord's consent.[209] In an action for rent the assignee is liable only for the proportion

---

[196] Above, para.14–140.

[197] *Tilny v Norris* (1700) 1 Salk. 309; *Stratford-upon-Avon Corp v Parker* [1914] 2 K.B. 562 at 567.

[198] *Rendall v Andreae* (1892) 61 L.J.Q.B. 630.

[199] *Wollaston v Hakewill* (1841) 3 Man. & G. 297 at 320.

[200] *Helier v Casebert* (1663) 1 Lev. 127; *Youngmin v Heath* [1974] 1 W.L.R. 135 (weekly tenancy).

[201] *Brett v Cumberland* (1616) Cro.Jac. 521; and see *Matthews v Ruggles-Brise* [1911] 1 Ch. 194.

[202] *Pitcher v Tovey* (1691) 4 Mod. 71 at 76.

[203] See *Davis v Blackwell* (1832) 9 Bing. 6; *Collins v Crouch* (1849) 13 Q.B. 542.

[204] TA 1925, s.26; re-enacting legislation first introduced by L.P.(Am.)A. 1859 s.27.

[205] *Re Owers* [1941] Ch. 389; compare *Re Bennett* [1943] 1 All E.R. 467, a curious case.

[206] *Re Lewis* [1939] Ch. 232.

[207] See *United Dairies Ltd v Public Trustee* [1923] 1 K.B. 469 (repair: legal tenancy in common before 1926); Cf. above, paras 13–031—13–034.

[208] *Congham v King* (1630) Cro.Car. 221 (repair), approved in *Stevenson v Lambard* (1802) 2 East 575. For a valuable review of the authorities, see *Lester v Ridd* [1990] 2 Q.B. 430 at 438.

[209] *Lester v Ridd*, above, at 438.

attributable to his part,[210] which in default of agreement,[211] may be determined by the court,[212] or by the appropriate Secretary of State if application is made to him.[213] But although the landlord can sue only for this proportion, the ancient right of distress is available against every part of the demised land for the whole of the rent.[214] If the assignee of part is thus compelled to pay the whole rent, he can claim contribution from the tenant of the other part, on the principle which gives a right of indemnity to persons compelled to pay a debt for which some other person is primarily liable.[215]

4. Covenants relating to things *in posse*. If a covenant made before 1926 **20–052** imposed an obligation upon the tenant to do some entirely new thing, such as to erect a building, the burden of the covenant ran with the land only if the lessee expressly covenanted for himself *and for his assigns* that the covenant would be performed.[216] This rule did not apply to covenants relating to things *in esse* (in existence) nor even to covenants relating only conditionally to something *in posse* (not in existence), such as a covenant to repair a new building if it is erected[217]; in such cases it was immaterial whether or not the covenant mentioned assigns. This unreasonable distinction between covenants relating to things *in posse* and those relating to things *in esse* is still in force as regards all leases granted before 1926; but by the Law of Property Act 1925[218] it does not apply to leases made after 1925.

5. Duration of liability. The original tenant, T1, is liable for all breaches **20–053** of covenant throughout the term of the lease, even after assignment, because there is still privity of contract with the landlord.[219] But, in the absence of a direct covenant with the landlord,[220] an assignee is liable only for breaches of covenant committed while the lease is vested in him,[221] for privity of estate

---

[210] *Curtis v Spitty* (1835) 1 Bing. N.C. 756. Although some doubt was expressed as to this principle in *Whitham v Bullock* [1939] 2 K.B. 81 at 86, "the law has continued to be stated in the text books on the subject as being that an assignee of part of the land cannot be sued for the whole of the rent, but only for a proportionate part thereof": *Lester v Ridd*, above, at 438, per Dillon L.J. cf. Slade L.J. at 442.

[211] Such an agreement will not bind persons not parties to it: *Bliss v Collins* (1822) 5 B. & Ald. 876 (severance of reversion). See LPA 1925 s.190(3) (which is declaratory of the law); and *Lester v Ridd*, above, at 442.

[212] See *Whitham v Bullock*, above, at 86, citing *Bliss v Collins*, above.

[213] L & TA 1927 s.20.

[214] *Whitham v Bullock*, above, at 86; *Lester v Ridd*, above, at 438 and 442. Although see above paras 19–076 et seq., for pending abolition of distress.

[215] *Whitham v Bullock*, above (payment under threat of distress). For another example of this principle, see below, para.20–056.

[216] *Spencer's Case* (1583) 5 Co.Rep. 16a, second resolution; though see *Minshull v Oakes* (1858) 2 H. & N. 793; *Re Robert Stephenson & Co Ltd* [1915] 1 Ch. 802 at 807.

[217] *Minshull v Oakes*, above.

[218] s.79; see *Rhone v Stephens* [1994] 2 A.C. 310 at 322; below, para.32–016.

[219] Above, para.20–011.

[220] Above, para.20–018.

[221] *Eaton v Jaques* (1780) 2 Doug.K.B. 455 at 460; *Chancellor v Poole* (1781) 2 Doug.K.B. 764.

exists only while the assignee holds the estate.[222] An assignee is under no liability for breaches committed before the lease was assigned to him[223] unless they are continuing breaches (as of a covenant to repair),[224] nor is he liable for breaches committed after he has assigned the lease.[225] But if a covenant is broken while the lease is vested in him, his liability for this breach continues despite any assignment.[226] Thus while the original tenant of an onerous lease cannot divest himself of liability for future breaches, a subsequent tenant can do so by assigning the lease.[227] For this reason, it has become the usual practice in business leases to require an incoming assignee to enter into a direct covenant with the landlord, undertaking to observe all the covenants and conditions in the lease for the duration of the term. This has already been explained.[228]

20–054   **6. Right to sue for breach of covenant.** When a lease is assigned, the assignor retains the right to sue for breaches of covenant committed by the landlord prior to that assignment.[229] That right does not pass to the assignee unless it is expressly assigned,[230] though the assignee can enforce any continuing breach of covenant by the landlord.[231] In this respect, an assignment of a lease differs from an assignment of the reversion, where the right to sue for a pre-existing breach of covenant passes with the reversion.[232] For leases granted after 1995, the law has been changed.[233]

20–055   **7. Indemnities by assignee.** If a covenant which runs with the land has been broken, the original tenant and the assignee entitled to the lease at the time of the breach are each liable to be sued by the landlord.[234] But although the landlord may obtain judgment against either or both, he can only have one satisfaction[235]; he has no right to recover twice. The same rule applies to all the other cases in the examples given below where one person may sue more

---

[222] *Johnsey Estates Ltd v Lewis and Manley (Engineering) Ltd* (1987) 54 P. & C.R. 296 at 299.

[223] *Grescot v Green* (1700) 1 Salk. 199. The point has arisen in recent cases concerning unpaid rent: see *Parry v Robinson-Wyllie Ltd* [1987] 2 E.G.L.R. 133 at 134; *Wharfland Ltd v South London Co-operative Building Co Ltd* [1995] 2 E.G.L.R. 21.

[224] *Granada Theatres Ltd v Freehold Investment (Leytonstone) Ltd* [1959] Ch. 592.

[225] *Paul v Nurse* (1828) 8 B. & C. 486.

[226] *Harley v King* (1835) 2 Cr.M. & R. 18.

[227] The assignment will be effective to discharge the assignor's liability even if the assignee is a pauper: *Valliant v Dodemede* (1742) 2 Atk. 546.

[228] Above, para.20–018.

[229] *City and Metropolitan Properties Ltd v Greycroft Ltd* [1987] 1 W.L.R. 1085; [1987] Conv. 374 (P. F. Smith).

[230] The assignment of a right to sue that is ancillary to a property right is not champertous: *Trendtex Trading Corporation v Credit Suisse* [1982] A.C. 679 at 703.

[231] *City and Metropolitan Properties Ltd v Greycroft Ltd*, above, at 1087.

[232] *City and Metropolitan Properties Ltd v Greycroft Ltd*, above; below, para.20–068.

[233] Below, para.20–124.

[234] Unless liability for other persons' acts is expressly restricted, as in *Wilson v Twamley* [1904] 2 K.B. 99 (a covenant not to do or to suffer to be done certain acts was not infringed by the acts of a sub-tenant, who was not the tenant's agent).

[235] See, e.g. *Brett v Cumberland* (1619) Cro.Jac. 521 at 523.

than one defendant in respect of one liability: both may be sued, but the money may be recovered only once. The value of alternative rights of enforcement is that if one defendant is inaccessible or insolvent, satisfaction may be had from the other.

(a) Implied indemnity. The primary liability is that of the assignee, since he   **20–056**
has the exclusive benefit of the lease.[236] If the original tenant, T1, is sued, he may claim indemnity from the assignee in whom the lease was vested at the time of the breach, whether that assignee obtained the lease from T1 directly or from some intermediate assignee.[237] The principle here is a branch of restitution "independent of contract",[238] by which the law implies an obligation between joint debtors to repay money paid by one of them for the exclusive benefit of the other, when both were legally liable to a common creditor.[239] Since the assignee is solely entitled to enjoy the lease, the satisfaction of the landlord's claim by T1 enures to the assignee's benefit alone. T1 has, in fact, paid the assignee's debt for him, and has the same right of indemnity as has a surety.[240] Where performance of the obligations in the lease by the assignee has been guaranteed by a surety, T1 can also seek reimbursement from that surety.[241]

(b) Express indemnity. It is usual practice for an assignor to require a   **20–057**
covenant of indemnity by the assignee against liability for future breaches of covenant, whoever might commit them. The common form of covenant is implied by statute:

    (i) on a conveyance for valuable consideration[242] of the entirety of the land comprised in a lease[243]; and

    (ii) on the transfer of any leasehold interest in registered land otherwise than by way of underlease.[244]

This covenant is purely personal and cannot, of course, run with the land. The assignor can enforce the covenant only against the immediate assignee. He

---

[236] *Moule v Garrett* (1872) L.R. 7 Ex. 101; *Selous Street Properties Ltd v Oronel Fabrics Ltd* [1984] 1 E.G.L.R. 50 at 61.

[237] *Moule v Garrett*, above; *Wolveridge v Steward* (1833) 1 Cr. & M. 644.

[238] *Becton Dickinson UK Ltd v Zwebner* [1989] Q.B. 208 at 217, per McNeill L.J. The decision is criticised by Fancourt, *Enforcement of Landlord and Tenant Covenants*, at p.71.

[239] *Electricity Supply Nominees Ltd v Thorn EMI Ltd* (1991) 63 P. & C.R. 143.

[240] *Moule v Garrett*, above, at 104; cf. above, para.20–051.

[241] *Becton Dickinson UK Ltd v Zwebner*, above.

[242] A conveyance will be for valuable consideration simply by virtue of the assignee assuming the obligation to pay rent and observe the other covenants in the lease, even though the assignment is otherwise for nominal consideration: *Johnsey Estates Ltd v Lewis and Manley (Engineering) Ltd* (1987) 54 P. & C.R. 296 (assignment of lease for £1).

[243] LPA 1925 s.77(1)(C); Sch.2 Pt IX. This covenant includes liability for continuing breaches (e.g. of a repairing covenant) existing when the lease was assigned: *Middlegate Properties Ltd v Bilbao* (1972) 24 P. & C.R. 329. It is not implied where the lease is a new tenancy within L & TCA 1995: L & TCA 1995 Sch.2.

[244] LRA 2002 s.134(2); Sch.12 paras 20(1)(a), (b)(i), (2), (3). However, this covenant is not implied on the transfer of a registered lease which is a new tenancy within L & TCA 1995 (see above, para.20–010): LRA 2002 Sch.12 para.20(5).

cannot compel that assignee (if insolvent) to enforce any rights of indemnity that he might have against a subsequent (solvent) assignee.[245] Where the immediate assignee is in breach, the assignor can still enforce his implied common law right of restitution[246] against the assignee, even if the implied covenant has been expressly excluded in the assignment.[247]

20–058　　*(c) Effect.* The effect of these rights of indemnity may be illustrated thus:

$$L1$$
$$|\ \ 99\ \text{years}$$
$$T1 — T2 — T3 — T4$$
$$|\ \ 21\ \text{years}$$
$$S$$

L1 has leased land to T1 for 99 years; by successive assignments T4 has become entitled to the lease and has granted a sub-lease to S for 21 years. If S does some act contrary to a covenant in the head lease, L1 can sue either T1 (privity of contract) or T4 (privity of estate), but has no right to recover twice.[248] L1 cannot sue T2, T3 or S, for he has no privity of any kind with them. Nor can L1 compel T1 to pursue any claim for indemnity which T1 may have against T2.[249] If L1 sues T1, T1 has an implied restitutionary right of indemnity against T4, but not against S.[250] Alternatively, if on the assignment to T2 a covenant of indemnity was given to T1 (either expressly or by statutory implication), T1 may claim indemnity (pursuant to their contract) from T2. T2 in turn may claim a similar indemnity from T3, and T3 from T4, provided in each case that the covenant for indemnity was given on the assignment.

20–059　　If T1 took a covenant of indemnity from T2, and either:

> (i) T2 failed to take one from T3 as did T3 from T4; or

> (ii) T2 prefers to sue T4 rather than T3,

T2 may claim an indemnity by way of restitution from T4 for anything which he has been compelled to pay. This is because T4 is liable in restitution to T1. He is therefore also similarly liable to T2 if T2 is compelled to discharge this

---

[245] *R.P.H. Ltd v Mirror Group Newspapers Plc* (1992) 65 P. & C.R. 252.

[246] See above.

[247] *Re Healing Research Trustee Co Ltd* [1992] 2 All E.R. 481; [1992] C.L.J. 425 (S.B.). It was assumed in that case that the implication of the covenant *could* be expressly excluded. However, LPA 1925 s.77(6) provides merely that such covenants can be "varied or extended by deed". By contrast, where title is registered, LRA 2002 Sch.12 para.20(1) provides for exclusion of the implication of the covenant.

[248] Above, para.20–055.

[249] Above, para.20–057. If A has taken a direct covenant from C or D as a condition of the licence to assign, he will of course be able to sue them: see above, para.20–018.

[250] *Bonner v Tottenham & Edmonton Permanent Investment BS* [1899] 1 Q.B. 161; this is because F is not jointly liable with B to A, and payment by B to A does not relieve F of any liability. The principle of *Moule v Garrett* (1872) L.R. 7 Ex. 101; above, para.20–056, does not therefore apply.

liability for T4's sole benefit. By parity of reasoning, as T4 is liable to indemnify T2, he is also liable to indemnify T3 if T3 is compelled to pay T2 under a covenant for indemnity. Apart from the rules relating to restrictive covenants,[251] S incurs no liability to anyone except so far as his act was a breach of a covenant in the sub-lease. This makes him liable to T4, because it is only with T4 that S has privity of any kind.

II. WHERE THE LANDLORD ASSIGNS HIS REVERSION

The common law rule was that covenants touching and concerning the land   **20–060** could run with the lease, but not with the reversion.[252] If L1, the fee simple owner, leased his land to T1, and then L1 sold his fee simple, subject to the lease, to L2, L2 was neither able to sue nor liable to be sued on the covenants in the lease. But L2 could sue and be sued on the obligations (often called implied covenants[253]) inherent in the relationship of landlord and tenant, since these arose automatically from the privity of estate (i.e. tenure) between L2 and T1.[254] Thus L2 could sue T1 for the rent, for rent was due not merely under a personal covenant but as a service incident to the tenant's estate.[255] The same applied to any services analogous to rent, e.g. grinding corn at the landlord's mill.[256]

But before *Spencer's Case* laid down the principles upon which covenants   **20–061** could run with leases, statute enabled them to run with reversions. When the monastic lands were seized and distributed it was necessary to enable grantees to enforce the terms of leases, and the Grantees of Reversions Act 1540[257] altered the law generally. The effect of the 1540 Act was that the benefit and burden of all covenants, provisions and conditions contained in a lease which touched and concerned the land[258] passed with the reversion. The meaning of "touching and concerning the land" was here the same as in *Spencer's Case*, discussed above.[259] The subsequent legislative history of these provisions has already been explained.[260] An extended and significantly different version of them, first introduced by the Conveyancing Acts 1881—1911,[261] is now found in the Law of Property Act 1925 ss.141 (benefit) and 142 (burden).

The following points must be observed.

---

[251] Below, paras 32–030 et seq.

[252] Above, para.20–015; *Thursby v Plant* (1670) 1 Wms. Saund. 230 at 240, fn.3. Distinguish the cases where the benefit of a covenant could run with other land belonging to the reversioner (not with the reversion itself): below, para.32–011.

[253] Above, paras 19–002 et seq.

[254] *Wedd v Porter* [1916] 2 K.B. 91 at 100; and see Platt on *Covenants*, 532.

[255] cf. Co.Litt. p.215a (rent payable to lord who took reversion by escheat).

[256] *Vyvyan v Arthur* (1823) 1 B. & C. 410.

[257] 32 Hen. 8 c. 34.

[258] This qualification was added by judicial legislation, by analogy to the principle of *Spencer's Case* (above, paras 20–033 et seq.): see Smith's L.C. i, 59.

[259] Above, para.20–033.

[260] Above, para.20–015.

[261] 1881 ss.10 and 11; 1911 s.2.

20–062　　**1. The lease must be in due form.** The Act of 1540 applied only to leases made by deed,[262] but that of 1881 applied also to leases evidenced in writing,[263] though not to mere oral tenancies.[264] The Act of 1925 applies even to tenancies that are merely oral, as ss.141 and 142 extend to an underlease "or other tenancy"[265]; and "covenant" is not confined to promises made by deed.[266] By a liberal construction it has been held that even a contract for a lease, provided that it satisfies the formal requirements for such a contract[267] and is specifically enforceable, is "a lease", and the intending landlord's interest a "reversionary estate", within the Acts of 1881 and 1925.[268] This implies an extension of the doctrine of *Walsh v Lonsdale*[269] so as to affect third parties: not only the benefit but also the burden of the stipulations becomes assignable by the proposed landlord, although as has been seen only the benefit is assignable by the proposed tenant.[270] The decisions so far given concern only the benefit of the landlord's covenants, but their reasoning applies equally to the burden. This difference between the respective positions of landlord and tenant under a mere contract may perhaps rest in principle on the fact that the burden of an estate contract can run with the landlord's estate as an equitable burden of a proprietary kind, carrying with it the burden of covenants[271]; but the tenant's obligations are purely contractual until a lease is executed, and therefore they cannot be assigned.

20–063　　Sections 141 and 142 of the Law of Property Act apply only to covenants made between landlord and tenant.[272] The benefit and burden of covenants made by strangers to the lease such as sureties[273] or subsequent assignees[274] do not therefore fall within the ambit of the provisions.[275] The benefit of the

---

[262] *Smith v Eggington* (1874) L.R. 9 C.P. 145 (burden); *Standen v Chrismas* (1847) 10 Q.B. 135 (benefit).

[263] *Cole v Kelly* [1920] 2 K.B. 106; *Rye v Purcell* [1926] 1 K.B. 446.

[264] *Blane v Francis* [1917] 1 K.B. 252.

[265] LPA 1925 s.154; see also the dictum of Denning L.J. in *Boyer v Warbey*, above, para. 20–044. That case concerned the assignment of a lease, but the dictum extends to assignment of the reversion.

[266] *Weg Motors Ltd v Hales* [1962] Ch. 49 at 73. It is unclear whether a collateral undertaking not to enforce a particular obligation in the lease is itself an "obligation under a condition or of a covenant", the burden of which will pass with the reversion under LPA 1925 s.142(1): see *System Floors Ltd v Ruralpride Ltd* [1995] 1 E.G.L.R. 48 at 51.

[267] See LP(MP)A 1989 s.2; above, para.15–015.

[268] *Rickett v Green* [1910] 1 K.B. 253; *Rye v Purcell* [1926] 1 K.B. 446; cf. *Manchester Brewery Co v Coombs* [1901] 2 Ch. 608 at 619.

[269] Above, para.17–048.

[270] Above, para.17–061.

[271] Above, para.17–059.

[272] *Kumar v Dunning* [1989] Q.B. 193 at 200; *P. & A. Swift Investments v Combined English Stores Group Plc* [1989] A.C. 632 at 639.

[273] ibid.

[274] For direct covenants by an assignee of the lease with the landlord, see above, para.20–018.

[275] LPA 1925 ss.141 and 142 do not apply, without more, so as to allow covenants contained in a sub-lease to be enforced by a head landlord. However, it has been held, *obiter*, that a wider construction should be adopted in light of HRA 1998 s.3 and Art.1 of the First Protocol ECHR: *PW & Co v Milton Gate Investments Ltd* [2003] EWHC 1994 (Ch); [2004] Ch. 142 at [130] and [134].

tenant's covenants will pass with the reversion only if they are contained in the lease.[276] By contrast, the burden of the landlord's covenants will pass even if they are contained in some other document, such as a collateral option agreement,[277] a collateral contract to execute repairs[278] or a side letter,[279] provided that they were "entered into by a lessor with reference to the subject matter of the lease".[280] There is no obvious reason for this difference.

2. The reversion may have been assigned in whole or in part. The assignee of the entire reversion takes the benefit and burden of the provisions in the lease; and if the reversion is held on trust, it is the trustee, as legal reversioner, and not the beneficiaries, who can enforce the covenants.[281] Where the reversion is not assigned in its entirety, the position is not so simple. Two separate cases must be considered.   **20–064**

(a) Severance as regards the estate. Where the assignee has part of the reversion, e.g. where a fee simple reversioner grants a lease of his reversion to X (whether for a shorter or longer period than the existing lease), the reversion is severed as regards the estate.[282] The benefit and burden of all covenants and conditions touching and concerning the land pass to the assignee under ss.141 and 142 of the Law of Property Act 1925.[283] That is to say, the covenants run with the *immediate* reversion, for it is the person entitled to the next immediate reversion upon the lease who has privity of estate with the tenant.[284] This explains why the benefit and burden of the covenants pass to a tenant of the reversion, but do not pass to a sub-tenant of the lease.   **20–065**

(b) Severance as regards the land. Where the assignee has the reversion of part, e.g. where a fee simple reversioner grants the fee simple of half the land to X, the reversion is severed as regards the land. It has been held that this does not sever the tenancy, so that although there is a severed reversion, there is still a single tenancy.[285] Provision is made by statute for the apportionment of both the benefit and the burden of the covenants in the lease.[286] As regards the benefit of covenants, all conditions and rights of re-entry are apportioned on the severance of the reversion and are annexed to the severed parts of the   **20–066**

---

[276] LPA 1925 s.141(1).

[277] *Weg Motors Ltd v Hales* [1962] Ch. 49 at 73.

[278] *Lotteryking Ltd v AMEC Properties Ltd* [1995] 2 E.G.L.R. 13.

[279] *System Floors Ltd v Ruralpride Ltd* [1995] 1 E.G.L.R. 48.

[280] LPA 1925 s.142(1); *System Floors Ltd v Ruralpride Ltd*, above, at 50.

[281] See *Schalit v Joseph Nadler Ltd* [1933] 2 K.B. 79.

[282] For this see above, para.17–134.

[283] As was also the case under the Grantees of Reversions Act 1540: Co.Litt. pp.215a and 215b, and notes by Butler; *Wright v Burroughes* (1846) 3 C.B. 685. LPA 1925 s.141(2) expressly provides that covenants can be enforced by "the person from time to time entitled, subject to the term, to the income of the whole or any part . . . of the land leased".

[284] Preston, *Conveyancing*, ii, pp.145 and 146; above, para.17–134.

[285] *Jelley v Buckman* [1974] Q.B. 488.

[286] For the law that is applicable in cases where a lease was both made before 1882 and where the reversion was severed before 1926, see the fifth edition of this work at pp.754 and 755.

reversion.[287] The burden of covenants is expressly annexed to "the several parts" of the reversionary estate notwithstanding the severance of that estate.[288] These provisions apply only to a genuine severance of the reversion and not, e.g. to a conveyance to a bare trustee for the assignor.[289]

20–067   There is a statutory rule about a notice to quit which is served after a severance of the reversion and so applies to part of the demised land only. The tenant may elect to terminate the lease of all of the land and thereby quit the whole, provided that within one month he serves on the other reversioner a counter-notice expiring at the same time as the original notice.[290]

3. Effect of assignment of reversion on liability for previous breaches

20–068   *(a) Assignee's right to sue for previous breaches.* An assignee of the reversion acquires the right to sue for breaches of covenant committed before the assignment, and the assignor loses this right.[291] This has been held to be the result of s.141 of the Law of Property Act 1925,[292] which provides that rent and the benefit of leasehold covenants (if they have reference to the subject-matter of the land) and conditions shall be "annexed and incident to *and shall go with*" the reversion.[293] As has been explained,[294] the position of an assignee of the reversion differs in this regard from that of an assignee of the lease, who does not acquire the right to sue for prior breaches of covenant by the landlord.[295] The legislation has in this respect changed the previous law, which was that the assignor of the reversion and not the assignee could sue for rent due and other breaches of covenant committed before the assignment, not being breaches of a continuing character.[296] Thus in a case where, at the time of the assignment of the reversion, there were outstanding breaches of covenants to repair and reinstate the property, the assignee and not the

---

[287] LPA 1925 s.140(1) replacing earlier legislation: LP(Am)A 1859 s.3 (non-payment of rent); CA 1881 s.12 (other conditions). It is not necessary that the right should be *expressly* contained in the lease: *Persey v Bazley* (1983) 47 P. & C.R. 37 at 45 (implied right to serve notice to quit on periodic tenant apportioned on severance).

[288] LPA 1925 s.142(1).

[289] *Persey v Bazley*, above cf. *John v George* [1995] 1 E.G.L.R. 9 (bona fide transfer to trustees to hold for third party a genuine severance).

[290] LPA 1925 s.140(2).

[291] *Re King* [1963] Ch. 459; *London and County (A. & D.) Ltd v Wilfred Sportsman Ltd* [1971] Ch. 764.

[292] For the history of this section, see above, para.20–016.

[293] subs.(1); and see subss.(2) and (3). The words in italics were particularly emphasised in *Re King*, above, at 497 by Diplock L.J. It has not been resolved whether on the termination of a head lease, the head lessor or the lessee can sue the underlessee for breach of covenant committed prior to that termination: *Electricity Supply Nominees Ltd v Thorn EMI Ltd* (1991) 63 P. & C.R. 143. cf. Fox L.J. at 147, suggesting that s.141(3) might be wide enough to allow recovery by the head lessor.

[294] Above, para.20–054.

[295] In *City and Metropolitan Properties Ltd v Greycroft Ltd* [1987] 1 W.L.R. 1085 at 1087, the argument that the right to sue passed under LPA 1925 s.142(1) was rejected. The section "does not say that the right to take advantage of the landlord's covenants is annexed or incident to the term, or 'shall go with' it": ibid., at 1087, per Mowbray, Q.C.

[296] *Flight v Bentley* (1835) 7 Sim. 149 (rent); *Re King*, above (where Lord Denning M.R., dissenting, was of the opinion that the previous law remained unaltered).

assignor is the person entitled to sue.[297] But this rule will, it seems, yield to any contrary intention in the assignment.[298]

(b) Assignee's right to enforce right of re-entry for previous breach. A right **20–069** of re-entry for breach of covenant could not be assigned at common law, so that if a reversion was assigned after a covenant had been broken, the new reversioner could not take advantage of a forfeiture clause.[299] By the Law of Property Act 1925,[300] such rights of re-entry are enforceable by the new reversioner provided they have not been waived.[301] Although the court will often imply waiver,[302] it will not do so merely because the reversion is conveyed to a third party "subject to the lease", since this is *res inter alios acta* and the reference to the lease is a conveyancing formality.[303]

(c) No liability for assignor's breach. Where L1 assigns the reversion to L2, **20–070** L2 is not liable to the tenant for breaches of covenant committed by L1 prior to the assignment.[304] Section 142(1) of the Law of Property Act does not transmit the consequences of past breaches of covenant. Where there is a continuing breach of covenant, the assignee of the reversion is liable for his own breach but not for the damage that has accrued prior to assignment.[305]

This general rule is subject to a statutory exception. Where a landlord of **20–071** premises which consist of or include a dwelling-house assigns the lease, the assignee is required to give notice in writing of the assignment, and of his name and address, to the tenant within two months.[306] If the assignee fails to do so,[307] the assignor remains liable for any breach of covenant that is committed by the assignee after the assignment.[308]

4. Relevance of privity of estate. The benefit of covenants run with the **20–072** reversion by force of the statute, and not because of the doctrine of privity of estate. Thus if T1 assigns the lease to T2 and later L1 assigns the reversion to

---

[297] *Re King*, above.

[298] *Re King*, above, at 488.

[299] *Hunt v Bishop* (1853) 8 Exch. 675; *Hunt v Remnant* (1854) 9 Exch. 635. The Real Property Act 1845 s.6 (above, para.3–068), did not apply: ibid.

[300] s.141(3).

[301] *Rickett v Green* [1910] 1 K.B. 253; *London and County (A. & D.) Ltd v Wilfred Sportsman Ltd* [1971] Ch. 764.

[302] For waiver generally, see above, para.18–019.

[303] *London and County (A. & D.) Ltd v Wilfred Sportsman Ltd*, above, overruling *Davenport v Smith* [1921] 2 Ch. 270, which had treated the phrase as recognising that the lease still existed.

[304] *Duncliffe v Caerfelin Properties Ltd* [1989] 2 E.G.L.R. 38. The tenant cannot set off damages in respect of L1's breaches of covenant against L2's claim for rent falling due after the assignment: *Edlington Properties Ltd v J.H. Fenner & Co Ltd* [2006] EWCA Civ 403; [2006] 1 W.L.R. 1583; [2006] Conv. 460 (M.J.D.). cf. *Muscat v Smith* [2003] EWCA Civ 962; [2003] 1 W.L.R. 2853 (where L2's claim related in part to arrears falling due before the assignment).

[305] *Duncliffe v Caerfelin Properties Ltd*, above, at 39; [1990] Conv. 126 (J. E. Martin).

[306] L & TA 1985 s.3(1).

[307] Such failure, without reasonable excuse, constitutes a criminal offence: L & TA 1985 s.3(3).

[308] L & TA 1985 s.3(3A) and (3B) (inserted by L & TA 1987 s.50), making the assignor jointly and severally liable for the breach with the assignee.

L2, L2 can sue T1 for rent previously due from him, even though there has never been privity of estate between them.[309] By contrast, the burden of covenants passes with the reversion only where there is privity of estate.[310]

20–073   **5. Merger or surrender of the reversion.** At common law, if the reversion disappeared,[311] no covenants could run with it, for privity of estate was destroyed. Thus the surrender of a head lease would:

>   (i) extinguish that lease;

> (ii) leave the sub-lease in existence and binding on the freeholder; but

> (iii) render unenforceable all the covenants in the sub-lease.[312]

By statute however, the benefit and burden of covenants have been preserved from destruction in this way.[313]

III. SURETY COVENANTS AND THE RIGHTS OF SURETIES

20–074   It is common practice in a lease of business premises to require a third party to guarantee the performance of the tenant's obligations in the lease either directly or by undertaking to take a lease in place of the tenant in the event that the tenant becomes insolvent and his trustee in bankruptcy[314] disclaims the lease.[315] After a period of doubt it has been settled that such surety covenants touch and concern the land[316] and pass on an assignment of the reversion at common law.[317]

20–075   A surety who guarantees the performance of the covenants and conditions in the lease has been described as "a quasi tenant who volunteers to be a

---

[309] *Arlesford Trading Co Ltd v Servansingh* [1971] 1 W.L.R. 1080.

[310] *Duncliffe v Caerfelin Properties Ltd* [1989] 2 E.G.L.R. 38 at 39.

[311] For merger and surrender, see above, paras 18–083—18–091.

[312] *Webb v Russell* (1789) 3 T.R. 393. See *Electricity Supply Nominees Ltd v Thorn EMI Ltd* (1991) 63 P. & C.R. 143 at 145, 146.

[313] LPA 1925 s.139, replacing Real Property Act 1845 s.9. For examples see *Phipos v Callegari* (1910) 54 S.J. 635; *Plummer v David* [1920] 1 K.B. 326. The covenants are similarly preserved where the head lease expires and the sub-lease continues under the provisions of L & TA 1954 Pt II: see s.65(2) of that Act. LPA 1925 s.139 does not apply in such circumstances: *Electricity Supply Nominees Ltd v Thorn EMI Ltd*, above, at 146. Nor has it any application where the head lease terminates by notice to quit, as the sub-lease will terminate contemporaneously: see *PW & Co v Milton Gate Investments Ltd* [2003] EWHC 1994 (Ch) at [82] et seq.; [2004] Ch. 142 at 166 et seq.; and see para.18–084 above.

[314] Or, if the tenant is a company, its liquidator.

[315] The reason for this latter form of the covenant was that until recently, on such a disclaimer of the lease, the surety ceased to be liable on his guarantee under the much-criticised rule in *Stacey v Hill* [1901] 1 Q.B. 660: see *Re A.E. Realisations Ltd* [1988] 1 W.L.R. 200 at 203. *Stacey v Hill* has now been overruled by *Hindcastle Ltd v Barbara Attenborough Associates Ltd* [1997] A.C. 70. See above, para.18–100.

[316] Above, para.20–035.

[317] *Kumar v Dunning* [1989] Q.B. 193; *P. & A. Swift Investments v Combined English Stores Group Plc* [1989] A.C. 632 (direct covenant to guarantee performance); *Coronation Street Industrial Properties Ltd v Ingall Industries Plc* [1989] 1 W.L.R. 304 (covenant to take lease).

substitute or twelfth man for the tenant's team and is subject to the same rules and regulations as the player he replaces".[318] His obligations are, at least for some purposes, conterminous with those of the tenant.[319] If the surety pays the tenant's debts to the landlord, he is entitled to have assigned to him "every judgment, specialty, or other security" held by the landlord, and may enforce them to the extent of the payment that he has been compelled to make.[320] This will not entitle the surety to an assignment of the landlord's right to distrain on the tenant's chattels, because a right to distress is not a security for a debt.[321] Nor may a surety enforce the landlord's right to forfeit the lease for non-payment of rent,[322] even though that right has sometimes been regarded for some purposes as a security for payment.[323]

A surety's liability differs from that of the original tenant who, as has been explained, remains liable on the covenants in the lease for the duration of the term.[324] It is apparently the law that any material variation in the terms of the lease will discharge the surety,[325] but not the original tenant.[326]   **20–076**

IV. OPERATION OF FORFEITURE CLAUSES

1. Lack of privity. An occupier of leasehold land (e.g. a sub-tenant, or a squatter) may be in neither privity of contract nor privity of estate with the   **20–077**

---

[318] *P. & A. Swift Investments v Combined English Stores Group Plc*, above, at 638, per Lord Templeman. Pursuing the sporting analogy further, Lord Templeman observed that where the surety was obliged to take a lease due to the tenant's insolvency and the disclaimer of the lease, "the tenant retires mortally wounded and the surety is the substitute": *Coronation Street Industrial Properties Ltd v Ingall Industries Plc*, above, at 309.

[319] "There is a single set of obligations, to pay the rent and perform the covenants, owed by both tenant and guarantor": *Milverton Group Ltd v Warner World Ltd* [1995] 2 E.G.L.R. 28 at 31, per Hoffmann L.J. But cf. *Romain v Scuba T.V. Ltd* [1997] Q.B. 887 at 892–894. One consequence of this is that when the lease is determined by forfeiture, then in the absence of explicit provision, the surety is not liable to the landlord if he claims thereafter for mesne profits in trespass for the tenant's continued possession: *Associated Dairies Ltd v Pierce* (1981) 43 P. & C.R. 208.

[320] Mercantile Law Amendment Act 1856 s.5.

[321] *Re Russell* (1885) 29 Ch D 254.

[322] *BSE Trading Ltd v Hands* [1996] 2 E.G.L.R. 214 at 216. In that case G, one of three co-sureties, was a party to an agreement by which T (who was in arrears with the rent) surrendered the lease to L in consideration of G paying a premium to L. It was held that G could not claim any contribution towards the cost of the premium from the co-sureties. "There is no security in the form of the lease to which the surety and co-surety might have recourse if payment of the rent is made by a surety": *BSE Trading Ltd v Hands* at 216, per Peter Gibson L.J.

[323] *Howard v Fanshawe* [1895] 2 Ch. 581 at 588 ("simply a security for the rent", per Stirling J.). For a full analysis of the extent to which such a right can be regarded as a security; see *Razzaq v Pala* [1997] 1 W.L.R. 1336. The weight of authority is now against treating a right to forfeit as a security: see *Re Lomax Leisure Ltd* [2000] Ch. 502.

[324] Above, para.20–011.

[325] *Holme v Brunskill* (1878) 3 QBD 495. Doubts have been expressed as to the correctness of this decision: *Wardens & Commonalty of the Mystery of Mercers of the City of London v New Hampshire Insurance Co* [1992] 1 W.L.R. 792n.; transcript, p.30 (where Scott L.J. suggested, *obiter*, that discharge might not be absolute but *pro tanto*). However, it continues to be applied: see *Howard de Walden Estates Ltd v Pasta Place Ltd* [1995] 1 E.G.L.R. 79; *Metropolitan Properties Co (Regis) Ltd v Bartholomew* [1996] 1 E.G.L.R. 82. The mere fact that the cost of complying with the terms of the lease, e.g. where the intensity of occupation leads to an increase in service charges, will not discharge the surety: *Metropolitan Properties Co (Regis) Ltd v Bartholomew*, above, at 83.

[326] *Baynton v Morgan* (1888) 22 QBD 74.

head landlord, and so not be bound by the covenants of the head lease; yet he may have to observe them under penalty of forfeiture. This question can arise only where there is an express forfeiture clause.[327] Normally this will be found in the head lease, but it may also be one of the terms of an assignment of a lease[328] or of a grant in fee simple.[329] It creates a conditional right of re-entry that is a proprietary interest[330] and is not merely the benefit of a covenant. Where the right of re-entry is reserved by the landlord in a legal lease, the right will be legal and will therefore bind any occupant of the property.[331] However, where it is reserved by a tenant on an assignment of the lease, it will be equitable.[332] Where title to the lease is registered, an assignee of the lease will take subject to this equitable right only if it is entered on the register.[333] Where title is unregistered, the equitable right will be binding on any assignee with notice of it.[334] The fact that the occupier of the land may not be bound by the covenants themselves is immaterial.[335] It may indeed be just for this reason that a forfeiture clause is employed.

20–078   For example, L demises property to T, T covenanting to repair and L reserving a right of re-entry for breach of this covenant. If T sub-lets to S, and S fails to repair, L can then re-enter and determine both T's and S's estates, subject to the statutory restrictions on enforcing forfeiture and the provisions for relief against forfeiture.[336] T could give S no better rights against L than T had himself, and T's rights were subject to forfeiture. S's failure to repair places T in breach of his covenant.

20–079   **2. Covenants not touching and concerning the land.** The law is less clear where the covenant which precipitates the forfeiture is a covenant of the kind which does not "touch and concern the land". In the first place, s.79 of the Law of Property Act 1925 does not apply to such covenants, so that they only apply to the covenantor personally: he is not liable for the acts of his successors in title unless the covenant expressly so provides. Prior to 1926 a

---

[327] Above, para.18–012.
[328] As in *Shiloh Spinners Ltd v Harding* [1973] A.C. 691 (right of re-entry reserved by assignor of lease to enforce covenants given by assignee).
[329] i.e. a conditional fee: above, para.3–056.
[330] LPA 1925 s.1(2)(e); above, para.6–027.
[331] Where title is registered, the estate vests in the proprietor together with all interests subsisting for its benefit. These will necessarily include any right of re-entry: LRA 2002 ss.11(3), 12(3).
[332] Semble; see [1973] C.L.J. 218 (P. Fairest). The remarks of Lord Wilberforce in *Shiloh Spinners Ltd v Harding*, above, at 719 are ambiguous on this point (in that case, the right of re-entry had been reserved by the assignor for a perpetuity period and not for the residue of the lease). It is uncertain whether a right of entry that was reserved for the unexpired residue of a lease would be one that was "exercisable over or in respect of a term of years absolute" within LPA 1925 s.1(2)(e). cf. above, paras 6–042 et seq.
[333] See above, para.6–008.
[334] LRA 2002 s.29(1).
[335] *Shiloh Spinners Ltd v Harding*, above.
[336] See above, para.18–060.

right of re-entry could not be exercised in respect of such a covenant. At common law, the right of re-entry did not pass on an assignment of the reversion, but it was made to do so by the Grantees of Reversions Act 1540.[337] That Act dealt with covenants and conditions in similar terms, so that when the courts engrafted on to it the qualification that it applied only to covenants which touched and concerned the land,[338] this restriction was applied equally to conditional rights of re-entry. Accordingly, an assignee of the reversion could enforce a forfeiture clause only in respect of a breach of a covenant which touched and concerned the land.[339]

But the statutory provision which has superseded the Act of 1540 (now   **20–080** s.141 of the Law of Property Act 1925) gives to the assignee of a reversion the benefit of "every covenant or provision therein contained, having reference to the subject-matter thereof . . . and every condition of re-entry and other condition therein contained". This wording, it will be noticed, qualifies covenants but not conditions, and appears to intend that the assignee shall be entitled to re-enter even where the condition is something unrelated to the land. This seems reasonable, for now that rights of re-entry are freely assignable[340] there would seem to be no reason why the assignee should not take all the assignable rights of the assignor, and take advantage of a condition that (for example) the lease should be determinable "when X returns from Rome". The House of Lords appears to favour this view.[341]

3. Assignment or sub-lease. There remain the cases where the lease is   **20–081** assigned, or a sub-lease is granted. The latter case presents no difficulty: the sub-lease depends upon the head lease, and shares its fate if it is determined by forfeiture, unless the sub-tenant succeeds in obtaining relief.[342] The more difficult question is whether an assignee of a lease is subject to forfeiture for non-observance of a covenant which does not touch and concern the land. On principle, a right of re-entry for breach of covenant should be exercisable against any assignee of the lease, as well as against any other third party, whether or not the covenant touches and concerns the land; for a right of re-entry is a proprietary interest in its own right,[343] and may be made exercisable on any event, e.g. "when X returns from Rome". In the only direct decision in which the point has been considered, it was suggested that a

---

[337] Above, para.20–060.
[338] Above, para.20–061.
[339] *Stevens v Copp* (1868) L.R. 4 Ex. 20 (proviso for re-entry in case of offence against game laws; breach by sub-tenant of an assignee of the lease; action for possession brought by an assignee of reversion failed).
[340] LPA 1925 s.4(2); above, para.3–068.
[341] See *Shiloh Spinners Ltd v Harding* [1973] A.C. 691 at 717, disparaging *Stevens v Copp*, above.
[342] Above, para.18–072. See, e.g. *Cresswell v Davidson* (1887) 56 L.T. 811; *Westminster (Duke) v Swinton* [1948] 1 K.B. 524.
[343] LPA 1925 s.1(2)(e); above, paras 6–027 and 20–077.

condition of re-entry would run with the lease at law only if the condition touched and concerned the land.[344] However, there must be considerable doubt as to the correctness of this dictum.[345] A right to re-enter for breach of covenant should in principle be exercisable whenever there is a breach of covenant.[346] If an assignee of a lease acts in a manner that is contrary to a covenant in the lease that does not touch and concern the land, he incurs no liability himself on that covenant, but he does nonetheless place the original tenant in breach of it.[347] The landlord should therefore be able to forfeit the lease.

C. Transmission by Other Means

20–082   In certain cases, benefits and burdens which are not transmitted under the rules set out above will nevertheless pass to assignees. This is of special importance in relation to options in a lease to purchase the freehold,[348] which do not touch and concern the land.[349]

20–083   **1. Benefit.** The general principle is that the benefit of any contract is assignable.[350] Accordingly, the benefit of a covenant in a lease is assignable as such, even though it does not touch and concern the land and so run with the land automatically under the rules explained above. For example, a lease may contain an option to purchase the freehold, which will not run automatically[351]; but the benefit of the option will pass to an assignee of the lease if the assignment is construed as extending to the benefit of the option as such. The benefit does not cease to be separately assignable merely because the option is contained in a lease, or because it is assigned along with the lease.[352] Even the conventional definition in the lease of "lessee" as including successors in title has been treated as evidence that an ordinary assignment of the lease was intended to carry also the benefit

---

[344] *Horsey Estate Ltd v Steiger* [1899] 2 Q.B. 79 at 88, where however, the difference between conditions and covenants was not observed, and the condition (against the tenant company's liquidation) in any case touched and concerned the land. The only authority relied on related to assignments of reversions, which are governed by the special construction of the Act of 1540; above, para.20–079.

[345] See the hostile references to *Horsey Estate Ltd v Steiger*, above, in *Shiloh Spinners Ltd v Harding*, above, at 717.

[346] A right of re-entry is normally stated to be exercisable in respect of *any* breach of covenant: see, e.g. *The Encyclopaedia of Forms and Precedents* 5th edn, Vol.22(2)A, para.[1247].

[347] cf. *Wright v Dean* [1948] Ch. 686 at 693–695, dealing with the converse case, where L1 assigned the reversion and L2 acted contrary to a covenant in the lease that did not touch and concern the land. L1 was held liable to the tenant.

[348] On the nature of options, see *Spiro v Glencrown Properties Ltd* [1991] Ch. 537; above, para.15–012.

[349] Above, para.20–040.

[350] Above, para.17–061.

[351] Above, para.15–027.

[352] *Griffith v Pelton* [1958] Ch. 205; *Re Button's Lease* [1964] Ch. 263.

of the option.[353] There must however be some doubt as to the correctness of this conclusion.[354]

2. Burden. Leases may contain covenants of the kind which, under princi- **20–084** ples explained elsewhere, create interests in land, so that the burden will run with the land. Thus restrictive (as opposed to positive) covenants are equitable interests which are capable of binding assignees and others,[355] and their effect is not reduced merely because they occur in a lease.[356] Similarly an equitable interest will normally arise if the owner of land binds himself to sell it or let it, or grants an option for sale or lease.[357] Subject to the rules as to purchase without notice and registration as land charges (where title is unregistered) or protection on the register (where title is registered), such covenants will accordingly bind any assignee or other person interested in the land.[358] Even legal interests can sometimes be created by what in form are mere covenants, for example by covenants creating rentcharges[359] and covenants creating easements, such as rights of way.[360]

Part 3

STATUTORY LIABILITY: COVENANTS IN LEASES GRANTED AFTER 1995

Section 1. The Abolition of Privity of Contract: Position of the Original Parties

1. Introduction

(a) The Landlord and Tenant (Covenants) Act 1995. In leases granted after **20–085** 1995,[361] the Landlord and Tenant (Covenants) Act 1995 governs (1) the

---

[353] ibid. Yet provided the lease does not indicate that the option is purely personal, it should be the terms of the assignment rather than of the lease that are decisive: see [1957] C.L.J. 148 (H.W.R.W.). See also *Re Adams and the Kensington Vestry* (1883) 24 Ch D 199 at 206 (on appeal, (1884) 27 Ch D 394); *Batchelor v Murphy* [1926] A.C. 63; (1957) 73 L.Q.R. 452 (R.E.M.); (1958) 74 L.Q.R. 242 (W. J. Mowbray). *County Hotel and Wine Co Ltd v L.N.W. Ry* [1918] 2 K.B. 251 at 256, 257 (on appeal [1919] 2 K.B. 29; [1921] 1 A.C. 85) seems to show the right approach.

[354] Although *Griffith v Pelton*, above, was applied in *Coastplace Ltd v Hartley* [1987] Q.B. 948 (holding that the benefit of a surety covenant passes on assignment of the reversion), Browne-Wilkinson V.C. subsequently stated that he had "considerable difficulty in understanding what *Griffith v Pelton* did decide": *Kumar v Dunning* [1989] Q.B. 193 at 207 (holding that a surety covenant touched and concerned the land and was thereby annexed to the reversion). See [1988] C.L.J. 180 (C.H.).

[355] Below, para.32–032.

[356] But for a difference as to registration, see above, para.8–079.

[357] Above, paras 5–025, 8–075 and 15–052.

[358] Consider *Woodall v Clifton* [1905] 2 Ch. 257, where the option, had it not been void for perpetuity, would have bound the reversion in equity, even though it did not touch and concern the land and so run at law. The reason why the court decided that it did not run at law was because it had been argued that all covenants capable of running at law were exempt from the perpetuity rule. See the fuller explanation at (1955) 19 Conv. (N.S.) 255 (H.W.R.W.).

[359] Below, paras 31–014 et seq.

[360] Below, para.28–006.

[361] For the meaning of leases granted after 1995, see L & TCA 1995 s.1; above, para.20–010.

liability of the parties under the covenants of the tenancy; and (2) the circumstances in which the benefit and burden of those covenants will pass on an assignment of the lease or of the reversion.[362] The Act had three principal objectives, and it consists of three elements giving effect to each of them.[363] First, it implements in modified form the recommendations of the Law Commission[364] for the abolition of the rule that the original tenant remains liable throughout the duration of the lease for the performance of the covenants of the tenancy.[365] Secondly, it gives effect to unpublished recommendations of the Law Commission for modernising and rationalising the rules on the transmission of the benefit and burden of covenants in tenancies and for integrating the proposals for the abolition of privity of contract into the law on covenants.[366] Thirdly, it incorporates the results of an agreement made between representatives of the property industry which were thought to be necessary to make the abolition of privity of contract acceptable to landlords.[367] The components of this third element, which have already been explained, are:

    (i) the power of a landlord to impose conditions on the giving of consent to an assignment[368];

    (ii) the requirement that the original tenant be notified within six months where an assignee defaults on the payment of some fixed charge[369];

    (iii) the prohibition on increasing the original tenant's liability by variation of the covenants in the lease[370]; and

    (iv) the right of an original tenant in certain circumstances to the grant of an overriding lease.[371]

---

[362] For accounts of the legislative history of the Act and its effect, see (1996) 59 M.L.R. 78 (M. Davey); [1996] C.L.J. 313 (S.B.).

[363] When introduced as a Private Members' Bill under the Ten Minute Rule by Peter Thurnham M.P., it contained only the first of the three elements of the Act. The Bill received government support, but to secure its passage, it was substantially amended in its course through Parliament, and the second and third elements were thereby introduced. For the relevant Parliamentary debates, see *Hansard* (H.L.), June 21, 1995, Vol.565 cols 354–400; July 5, 1995, Vol.565 cols 1104–1109; *Hansard* (H.C.), July 14, 1995, Vol.263 cols 1236–1269.

[364] See (1988) Law Com. No.174; above, para.20–020. See comments of Baroness Hale of Richmond, a former Law Commissioner, in *London Diocesan Fund v Phithwa* [2005] UKHL 70; [2005] 1 W.L.R. 3956 at [37] et seq.

[365] For this rule, based on privity of contract, see above, para.20–011.

[366] The Law Commission had intended to consult on these proposals and had prepared a consultation paper for this purpose. The introduction of the Bill in Parliament precluded its publication. The Commission's proposals would have codified and clarified the law for existing leases as well as making proposals for new leases. It was not thought appropriate to include the former proposals in the Bill, given its curious legislative path.

[367] This agreement, between the British Property Federation and the British Retail Consortium, was the subject of public consultation by the Lord Chancellor's Department.

[368] Above, paras 19–097 et seq.

[369] Above, para.20–022.

[370] Above, para.20–031.

[371] Above, para.20–025.

(b) Applicability of the Act. The provisions of the Act that deal with its first **20–086**
and second elements apply to all tenancies granted after 1995.[372] The general
principle that underlies these two elements is that a party to a lease should
enjoy its benefits, and be subject to its burdens, only for the time that he is the
tenant or the landlord as the case may be.[373] There are three concepts which
are fundamental to the Act, and all are broadly defined. First, the Act applies
to a "tenancy", which means any lease or tenancy, including a sub-tenancy
and an agreement for a lease, but not a mortgage term.[374] Secondly, the Act
is concerned with the rights and liabilities of the parties under a "covenant"
of the tenancy. A covenant is defined to include any term, condition and
obligation, and a covenant of the tenancy includes a covenant contained in a
collateral agreement (whether that agreement is made before or after the
tenancy).[375] A covenant may be express or implied, or one imposed by law.[376]
The Act distinguishes between "landlord" and "tenant" covenants which are
covenants that fall to be complied with by the landlord and by the tenant
respectively.[377] Thirdly, the transaction that is fundamental to the operation of
the Act is an "assignment", whether of the lease or of the reversion. It is
widely defined to include an equitable assignment and an assignment in
breach of covenant or by operation of law.[378] Although the Act refers to
assignments by "the landlord" or "the tenant", those expressions are taken to
include any assignment by which the whole of the party's interest is transferred, even if it is not effected by him but by some third party, e.g. a
mortgagee in exercise of his power of sale.[379] It should be noted that a lease
of the reversion does not operate as a pro tanto assignment of a lease by
operation of law as it does in relation to leases granted before 1996.[380]

The effect of these provisions is that, in relation to leases granted after **20–087**
1995, no distinction is drawn between either legal and equitable leases or legal
and equitable assignments.[381] The reasons for adopting this course were:

(i) to simplify the law by having just one set of rules for the transmission of the benefit and burden of covenants[382]; and

---

[372] L & TCA 1995 ss.1, 31; SI 1995/2963.
[373] See Law Com. No.174, para.4.1; above, para.20–020.
[374] L & TCA 1995 s.28(1).
[375] L & TCA 1985 s.28(1). This could therefore include covenants undertaken by an assignee
in a licence to assign: below, para.20–093.
[376] L & TCA 1995 s.2(1). For an example of a covenant imposed by law, see L & TA 1985 s.11;
above, para.19–042. Note the exclusion of certain covenants imposed in relation to exercise of the
secure tenant's right to buy: L & TCA 1995 s.2(2).
[377] L & TCA 1995 s.28(1).
[378] L & TCA 1995 s.28(1). There are however special provisions applicable to the latter: see
below, para.20–100.
[379] L & TCA 1995 s.28(6).
[380] This is explained below, para.20–114.
[381] Compare the position as regards leases granted prior to 1996: see above, paras 20–046 and
20–062.
[382] This was thought to be desirable not least because of the uncertainty as to the applicable
rules where an equitable lease is assigned or there is an equitable assignment of a legal lease: see
[1978] C.L.J. 98 (R. J. Smith); above, para.20–062. In theory, the effect of treating an equitable
assignment as a completed assignment could mean that a person who had merely contracted to

(ii) to prevent an obvious means of evading the provisions of the Act.[383]

2. Liability of the original tenant

20–088   *(a) Release from liability on assignment.* Subject to exceptions applicable to assignments made in breach of covenant or by operation of law,[384] the Act abolishes the liability of the original tenant for breaches of the covenants in the tenancy committed by any assignee after the lease has been assigned. This is achieved by means of a statutory release of the tenant from liability:

(i) where a tenant assigns the whole of the premises let to him, he is released from the tenant covenants in the tenancy and can no longer enforce the landlord covenants[385];

(ii) where the tenant assigns part only of the premises let, then to the extent that the tenant covenants fall to be complied with in relation to the part assigned, he is released from them and can no longer enforce the landlord covenants.[386]

20–089   *(b) Authorised guarantee agreements.* Although the Act abolishes the privity rule, the tenant may be obliged to guarantee the performance of the tenant covenants by the assignee until the next assignment.[387] This will be the case where:

(i) on an assignment the tenant is to any extent released from a tenant covenant[388]; and

(ii) the tenancy contains a covenant against assignment, whether absolute or qualified.[389]

If the covenant against assignment is absolute, the landlord is entitled to require the tenant to enter into an authorised guarantee agreement as a condition of his consent to any assignment.[390] However, where the covenant

purchase a lease could find himself liable on the covenants of the lease. However, in those circumstances, the purchaser would have a right to indemnity against the vendor and could in many cases terminate the sale on the ground that the vendor had failed to show a good title (because a breach of covenant might lead to a forfeiture of the lease).

[383] For the anti-avoidance provisions of the Act, see s.25; below, para.20–128.
[384] For these, see L & TCA 1995 s.11; below, para.20–100.
[385] L & TCA 1995 s.5(2).
[386] L & TCA 1995 s.5(3).
[387] L & TCA 1995 s.16.
[388] L & TCA 1995 s.16(1).
[389] L & TCA 1995 s.16(3). For meaning of 'absolute' and 'qualified', see above, para.19–094. Covenants against assignment are more likely to be encountered in commercial rather than residential tenancies.
[390] L & TCA 1995 s.16(3). If these pre-conditions for an authorised guarantee agreement are not satisfied, any such agreement entered into by the tenant on an assignment will be void: L & TCA 1995 s.25; below, para.20–128.

is merely qualified, the landlord will be able to do this only if he has stipulated in the lease that entry into such an authorised guarantee agreement will be a condition of the giving of consent to any assignment,[391] or if he has not, if it is reasonable to require the tenant to enter into such an agreement.[392] The application of these provisions in the case of excluded assignments is explained below.[393]

An authorised guarantee agreement may impose on the assigning tenant all or any of the following: **20–090**

    (i) liability as sole or principal debtor for any obligation owed by the assignee under a covenant of the tenancy[394];

    (ii) liability as guarantor in respect of the assignee's performance of the covenants, provided that it is no more onerous than liability under (a) would be[395]; and

    (iii) in the event that the lease is disclaimed,[396] an obligation to take a new lease of no longer duration and with no more onerous covenants than the lease which he had assigned.[397]

An authorised guarantee agreement is subject to the rules of law applicable to guarantees, and in particular those relating to the release of the surety.[398] Furthermore, the former tenant will be liable for any fixed charge under such an agreement only if he is informed of it by notice within six months of the charge falling due.[399] If he makes full payment of any amount which he is required to meet under the guarantee, he is entitled to call for the grant of an overriding lease.[400]   **20–091**

---

[391] L & TA 1927 s.19(1A) (inserted by L & TCA 1995 s.22): above, para.19–097. It is anticipated that this is likely to be the situation in almost every case. However, such a stipulation will not be effective where the lease is a residential lease; see ibid.

[392] L & TA 1988 s.1; above, paras 19–097, 19–098. This requirement is imported because L & TCA 1995 s.16(3)(b) provides that the condition must be one that is lawfully imposed.

[393] Below, para.20–100.

[394] The advantage of this form of guarantee from a landlord's perspective is that the guarantor is not released by any material variation in the terms of the lease, as would otherwise be the case: above, para.20–076.

[395] For an example, see the guarantee agreement in *Prudential Assurance Co Ltd v Ayres* [2008] EWCA Civ 52; [2008] 1 All E.R. 1266.

[396] On the insolvency of the assignee: see above, para.18–100.

[397] L & TCA 1995 s.16(5). The agreement may also make incidental or supplementary provisions: ibid. Where the lease was either granted to the tenant in pursuance of his obligations under an authorised guarantee agreement or had revested in him following disclaimer by an assignee, he may (in the event of an assignment of the lease) nevertheless be required to enter into an authorised guarantee agreement: L & TCA 1995 s.16(7).

[398] L & TCA 1995 s.16(8). Thus a material variation in the terms of the lease will discharge the tenant from his guarantee: see above, para.20–076. Furthermore, if the tenant is required to discharge the assignee's indebtedness, he will have a right of recoupment against that assignee: ibid.

[399] L & TCA 1995 s.17; above, para.20–022.

[400] L & TCA 1995 s.19; above, para.20–025.

20–092   The Act makes provision to ensure that a tenant's liability ceases when the assignee himself assigns. It provides that an agreement will not be an authorised guarantee agreement to the extent that it purports to impose on the tenant:

       (i) any requirement to guarantee performance of any tenant covenant by anybody other than the assignee; or

      (ii) any liability, restriction or requirement after the time when the assignee is released from any tenant covenant under the provisions of the Act.[401]

20–093   **3. Liability of an assignee on a direct covenant.** In the absence of a direct covenant with the landlord, an assignee ceases to be liable on the covenants in the lease after he has further assigned it.[402] He has therefore no need to resort to the provisions of the Act to be released from the tenant covenants, and as a result cannot be required to enter into an authorised guarantee agreement even if the assignment may only be effective with the landlord's consent.[403] However, an assignee of a commercial lease is commonly required, as a condition of the landlord's consent, to enter into a direct covenant with the landlord to observe all the terms of the tenancy for the duration of its term.[404] By this route the assignee becomes subject to the tenant covenants of the tenancy,[405] and but for the Act, his liability would continue despite further assignment of the term. In these circumstances, the provisions of the Acts[406] relating to the release from covenants and to authorised guarantee agreements will apply to the assignee in the same way as they apply to the original tenant.

4. Liability of a guarantor of the tenant

20–094   *(a) Release on assignment.* Section 24(2) of the 1995 Act provides that, where a tenant is released from the tenant covenants, any person who has guaranteed the performance of those covenants will be released to the same extent.[407] It follows that any contractual provision by which a guarantor undertook to remain liable even after the release of the tenant would be rendered void by the anti-avoidance provisions of the Act.[408] Let us assume

---

[401] L & TCA 1995 s.16(4).

[402] Above, para.20–053.

[403] That obligation arises only if the tenant is to any extent released from a tenant covenant by virtue of the Act; above, para.20–089. If the assignee did enter into such an agreement, it would be void under L & TCA 1995 s.25; below, para.20–128.

[404] Above, para.20–018.

[405] Even though these are contained in the licence to assign. That licence is, for the purposes of the Act, a collateral agreement, and the covenants in it are therefore tenant covenants: L & TCA 1995 s.28(1); above, para.20–086.

[406] See above, paras 20–088, 20–089.

[407] L & TCA 1995 s.24(2); *Good Harvest Partnership LLP v Centaur Services Ltd* [2010] EWHC 330 (Ch); [2010] Ch. 426.

[408] L & TCA 1995 s.25(1); below, para.20–128.

that L grants a lease to T1, and G guarantees the obligations of T1 under the lease. When T1 lawfully assigns the lease to T2, T1 will be released from the covenants of the lease, and G will be released at the same time. If G has undertaken, in the lease or elsewhere, to guarantee the obligations of any assignees from T1, that undertaking will be void as it would frustrate the operation of the provision releasing G from liability contemporaneously with T1's release.

> "If it were otherwise, it would mean, for instance, that a landlord, when granting a tenancy, could require a guarantor of the tenant's liabilities, on every assignment of the tenancy, to guarantee the liability of each successive assignee. Such an obligation ... would plainly be wholly contrary to the purpose of s.24(2), as it would enable a well-advised landlord to ensure that any guarantor was in precisely the position in which it would have been before the 1995 Act came into force."[409]

(b) *Authorised guarantee agreements.* Although there is no reference to guarantors in the provisions concerning authorised guarantee agreements,[410] the Court of Appeal has held that it would not frustrate the operation of s.24(2) to require the tenant's guarantor to guarantee the obligations of the assigning tenant under such an agreement, on the basis that there "appears to be nothing inconsistent with s.24(2) if the assignor's guarantor is required to guarantee the assignor's liability under the authorised guarantee agreement: the guarantor is released to precisely the same extent as the assigning tenant."[411] Let us consider again the example given in the preceding paragraph, making the assumption that the lease contains a qualified covenant against assignment whereby L's consent is not be unreasonably withheld. When T1, whose obligations under the lease are guaranteed by G, seeks L's consent to assign to T2, L may require G to continue to guarantee T1's obligations under the authorised guarantee agreement insofar as that is a reasonable condition to impose. Furthermore, the well-advised landlord will no doubt seek to insert into all future commercial leases a clause specifying that consent to assignment will only be granted subject to two conditions: (a) that T1 enter into an authorised guarantee agreement guaranteeing the obligations of T2; and (b) that G guarantees the obligations of T1 under that agreement.[412] Should the landlord attempt to impose a condition that G guarantees the obligations of T2 or any future assignees of the lease, however, that would presumably be struck down as contravening the anti-avoidance provisions of the 1995 Act.

20–095

---

[409] *K/S Victoria Street v House of Fraser (Stores Management) Ltd* [2011] EWCA Civ 904; [2011] 2 P. & C.R. 15 at [21] per Lord Neuberger of Abbotsbury M.R.; and see *Slessenger* [2011] L. & T.Rev. 185.

[410] L & TCA 1995 s.16(1); *Good Harvest Partnership LLP v Centaur Services Ltd*, above at [22](v).

[411] *K/S Victoria Street v House of Fraser (Stores Management) Ltd*, above at [46] per Lord Neuberger of Abbotsbury M.R.

[412] See above, para.19–098.

5. The liability of the original landlord

20–096   *(a) Release on first assignment.* Where a landlord assigns his reversion in whole or part, his position is different from that of the tenant.[413] He not only retains his right to enforce the tenant covenants[414] but he also remains liable on the landlord covenants in the lease. However, except in those cases where the assignment is by operation of law,[415] he may apply to the tenant to be released from the landlord covenants of the tenancy.[416] If the landlord assigns only part of the reversion, any application for release will apply only to the part in question. To secure such a release, the landlord must serve a notice[417] on the tenant either before or within four weeks of the assignment.[418] This must inform the tenant of both the actual or intended assignment and the request that the covenant be released.[419] The covenant will then be released unless the tenant objects by serving a written counter-notice on the landlord within four weeks. In that event there will be no release unless either:

> (i)   the landlord obtains a declaration from the county court that it is reasonable for the covenant to be released; or
>
> (ii) the tenant in writing withdraws his objection.[420]

Any release is effective from the date of the assignment.[421] However, the landlord cannot have his cake and eat it: the corollary of his release from liability is that he loses his right to enforce the tenant covenants from the same date.[422]

20–097   *(b) Effect of express release.* Either party to a tenancy may release the other from any covenant, whether it is a landlord covenant or a tenant covenant.[423] If the tenancy provides that the landlord's liability under a covenant shall be released in the event of assignment of the reversion, such provision will be effective, as it does not contravene the anti-avoidance provisions of the 1995

---

[413] The reason for this difference is that a tenant has no control over an assignment by his landlord, although the landlord may require his consent to the assignment of the lease: see Law Com. No.174, para.4.16.

[414] This is unlikely to be a right of any consequence: see below, para.20–100 and fn.437.

[415] For such excluded assignments, see L & TCA 1995 s.11; below, para.20–100.

[416] L & TCA 1995 s.6(2). The statutory release procedure does not apply to covenants which are expressed to be personal to the covenantor landlord, and not therefore falling to be performed by the person for the time being entitled to the reversion expectant on the term of the tenancy: *BHP Petroleum Ltd v Chesterfield Ltd* [2001] EWCA Civ 1797; [2002] Ch. 194 (landlord could not be released from personal covenant to carry out remedial works); approved in *London Diocesan Board v Phithwa* [2005] UKHL 70; [2005] 1 W.L.R. 3956 at [23].

[417] For the form of notice, see L & TCA 1995 s.27; SI 1995/2964.

[418] It was originally proposed that the notice should pre-date the assignment: see Law Com. No.174, Draft Bill cl. 6. This was changed in the Act because of concerns raised by landlords who often wish to keep negotiations about the assignment of the reversion confidential.

[419] L & TCA 1995 s.8(1).

[420] L & TCA 1995 s.8(2).

[421] L & TCA 1995 s.8(3).

[422] L & TCA 1995 s.6(2).

[423] L & TCA 1995 s.26(1).

Act, and on assignment the landlord will be released.[424] The legislation was not intended to prevent parties from agreeing to a curtailment, release or waiver of their liabilities under the lease.[425] However, any provision in the lease by which a tenant covenants not to object to an application by the landlord for release from a landlord covenant on assignment of the reversion will be void.[426]

(c) *Release on subsequent assignment.* There may be occasions where a **20–098** landlord is not released from the landlord covenants when he assigns the reversion, either because he did not seek or was unable to obtain a release on that occasion, or because the assignment was by operation of law and therefore outside the scope of the release provisions.[427] If this happens, the landlord may apply to be released from the covenants on any subsequent assignment of the reversion.[428] To obtain such a release, the now former landlord must apply to the tenant for the time being[429] in the way that has already been explained.[430]

6. Effect of release. Where any person is released from a covenant by **20–099** virtue of the provisions of the Act, his liability for any breach of covenant committed before the release remains unaffected.[431] Conversely, where under the Act a person ceases to be entitled to the benefit of a covenant, he retains his right to sue for the breach of any covenant that occurred before he ceased to be entitled,[432] though he is free to assign that right.[433]

7. Excluded assignments

(a) *No release until next assignment.* The provisions of the Act by which **20–100** the tenant is automatically released from the tenant covenants on assignment of the lease, and a landlord may be released from the landlord covenants by the tenant or the court on assignment of the reversion, do not apply where the assignment is "excluded".[434] An excluded assignment is one that is either made in breach of covenant or takes effect by operation of law.[435] In practice, an assignment of the reversion will not be in breach of covenant, and so the former is only likely to apply on assignment of the lease.[436] Where a party

---

[424] *London Diocesan Fund v Phithwa* [2005] UKHL 70; [2005] 1 W.L.R. 3956: see [2006] 70 Conv. 79 (M.J.D).
[425] *London Diocesan Fund v Phithwa*, above at [17].
[426] L & TCA 1995 s.25(1)(a); below, para.20–128.
[427] Below, para.20–100.
[428] L & TCA 1995 s.7(1) and (2).
[429] See the definition of "tenant" in L & TCA 1995 s.28(1).
[430] L & TCA 1995 s.8; above.
[431] L & TCA 1995 s.24(1).
[432] L & TCA 1995 s.24(4).
[433] L & TCA 1995 s.23(2); below, para.20–125.
[434] L & TCA 1995 s.11.
[435] L & TCA 1995 s.11(1).
[436] i.e. where the tenant assigns a lease in breach of a qualified or absolute covenant against assignment. For such covenants, see above, para.19–094.

makes an excluded assignment, he remains bound by his covenants of the tenancy but retains his right to enforce those of the other party.[437] However, on the next assignment that is not an excluded assignment the release provisions contained in the Act will be operative.[438] Two examples will demonstrate their effect.

(i) If T1 transfers the lease to T2 in breach of a covenant against assignment, T1 remains liable on the tenant covenants in the lease and can enforce the landlord covenants unless and until T2 lawfully assigns the lease to T3. T1 is then automatically released, and he loses his rights to enforce the landlord covenants save in respect of breaches committed before the assignment to T3.

(ii) Where L1 dies and his reversion passes to L2 under L1's will, L1's estate cannot apply to be released from the landlord covenants. It is only when L2 in turn assigns the reversion that L1's estate can apply to the tenant to be released from the landlord covenants. L1's estate will remain entitled to enforce the tenant covenants unless and until such release occurs.

Where T1 has assigned to T2 in breach of covenant and remains liable on the tenant covenants under the lease, he is entitled to be notified by the landlord of any demand for a fixed charge within six months of it falling due,[439] and, if he is obliged to pay it in full, he may call for an overriding lease.[440]

20–101   *(b) Authorised guarantee agreements.* No authorised guarantee agreement can arise on an excluded assignment of a tenancy, because the assigning tenant remains liable on the tenant covenants.[441] However, on the next assignment of the lease that is not an excluded assignment, that tenant is released. If the tenancy contains an absolute or qualified covenant against assignment the landlord may then be able to require him to enter into an authorised guarantee agreement on that next assignment. This will be so even if the landlord also requires the assignor of the lease to enter into an authorised guarantee agreement as well. Thus if T1 assigns a lease to T2 in breach of a covenant to assign without the landlord's consent, and T2 subsequently assigns the lease to T3 with the landlord's consent, the landlord may then require both T1 and T2 to enter into authorised guarantee agreements. There is no injustice in

---

[437] L & TCA 1995 s.11(2)–(4). The continuing right to enforce the other party's covenants is likely to be of little practical importance. Once a lease or reversion has been assigned, the assignor is unlikely to suffer any loss from any subsequent breach of covenant by the landlord or the tenant (as the case may be). A former landlord will be unable to sue the tenant for arrears of rent falling due after the assignment of the reversion, because he has assigned the right to the rents and profits of the land and will be estopped by his deed from claiming them.

[438] Where the next assignment is only of part of the lease or reversion, it is only in relation to that part that the provisions apply: L & TCA 1995 s.11(7).

[439] L & TCA 1995 s.17; above, para.20–022.

[440] L & TCA 1995 s.19; above, para.20–025.

[441] It is only where the tenant is released that the obligation can arise: see L & TCA 1995 s.16(1); above, para.20–089.

this. The landlord might reasonably have objected to the assignment by T1 to T2, e.g. because of T2's weak financial position, and it would therefore be unreasonable to expect the landlord to have recourse only to T2 as a guarantor of T3's liability. T1 must therefore guarantee the performance of the covenants until T3 assigns the lease with the landlord's consent.

8. Management companies. It is not uncommon for properties which are **20–102** leased to be managed for the landlord by a management company.[442] The management company, which will be a party to the lease, will be obliged to perform certain services. The cost of these is likely to be met by a service charge payable by the tenant or by a management fee payable by the landlord.[443] It was obviously necessary to bring such companies within the scheme of the Act to ensure (in particular) that, after a tenant had assigned his lease, he should be under no liabilities to the management company for any defaults by the assignee. Had provision not been made for such bodies, landlords would have been able to circumvent the provisions of the Act abolishing first tenant liability by the simple expedient of using a management company. The Act therefore makes specific provision in this regard for any third party[444] who is liable as principal under a covenant of the tenancy to discharge any function that has to be carried out in relation to all or any of the premises which have been let.[445]

The Act achieves its objective by employing a fiction. A covenant of the **20–103** tenancy which confers rights that are exercisable by or against the third party is to be treated for the purpose of transmitting the benefit or burden of it as if it were:

(i) a tenant covenant, to the extent that those rights are exercisable by the landlord or against the tenant; and

(ii) a landlord covenant, to the extent that those rights are exercisable by the tenant or against the landlord.[446]

The effect is as follows. First, on an assignment of the lease or the reversion, **20–104** the benefit and burden of any covenant with the third party will pass to the assignee under the provisions of the Act which regulate transmission.[447] Secondly, where a tenant assigns his lease, he is thereby released from the burden, but also loses the benefit, of any covenant with the third party, in the same way as he would as regards the landlord. Thirdly, where the landlord

---

[442] cf. *Hafton Properties Ltd v Camp* [1994] 1 E.G.L.R. 67 (the court would not imply a term in a lease that the landlord would carry out repairs which the management company had failed to execute).
[443] See further paras 19–080 et seq. above.
[444] Other than a guarantor or a person who has undertaken some financial liability referable to the performance or otherwise of a covenant of the tenancy by another party to it: L & TCA 1995 s.12(1)(b).
[445] L & TCA 1995 s.12(1)(a).
[446] L & TCA 1995 s.12(2), (3).
[447] L & TCA 1995 s.3; below, paras 20–106 et seq.

assigns his reversion, he remains liable on any covenant made with, but can continue to enforce any covenant that falls to be performed by, the third party. However he is entitled to apply to the third party for release from the covenant in the same way as he can apply to a tenant for release from a landlord covenant.[448] It was not intended that the Act should make provision for the situation where the management company wishes to transfer its rights and obligations to some other body. Such a transfer would require a novation just as it does in relation to leases granted before 1996.

20–105 **9. Indemnity.** The situations in which an assignor of either a tenancy or a reversion may require an indemnity from the assignee are much more limited than is the case in relation to leases granted before 1996. It is only where the assignor is not released on assignment or where he enters into an authorised guarantee agreement that such an indemnity may be required. The Act abolished the implied statutory indemnity covenant by the assignee[449] as regards leases granted after 1995.[450] In those situations where the assignor remains liable after assignment, he has an implied right to restitution from the assignee should he be called upon to meet the latter's default.[451]

Section 2. Position of Assignees

20–106 **1. A statutory code.** It has been explained that, for leases granted after 1995, the Landlord and Tenant (Covenants) Act 1995 lays down a self-contained code[452] for the transmission of the benefit and burden of landlord and tenant covenants that supersedes the existing law.[453] The concept of privity of estate as traditionally understood[454] has no place in the statutory scheme, for the rules apply even where the lease is equitable or where there has been an equitable assignment of a legal lease.[455]

20–107 **2. Covenants which are transmissible.** The Act abrogates the requirement that the benefit or burden of a leasehold covenant will pass on an assignment of the lease or of the reversion only if it touches and concerns the land.[456] The

---

[448] L & TCA 1995 s.12(3)–(5); see above, para.20–096. The rules governing apportionment (below, para.20–120) also apply: L & TCA 1995 s.12(4).

[449] LPA 1925 s.77(1)(C) and (D); LRA 1925 s.24(1)(b) (see now LRA 2002 Sch.12 para.20); above, para.20–057.

[450] L & TCA 1995 s.14.

[451] See *Moule v Garrett* (1872) L.R. 7 Ex. 101; above, para.20–056.

[452] See *Hansard* (H.C.), July 14, 1995, Vol.263 col. 1241.

[453] Above, para.20–010. Thus LPA 1925 ss.78, 79, 141 and 142 are inapplicable to such leases: L & TCA 1995 s.30(4), though the disapplication of LPA 1925 ss.78 and 79 would appear to be confined to their application to covenants between landlord and tenant, and not, e.g. to a restrictive covenant entered into for the benefit of leasehold land by a neighbour. The common law rules on transmission are also replaced: see below.

[454] Above, para.20–004.

[455] Above, para.20–086.

[456] L & TCA 1995 s.2(1); above, para.20–033.

objective of that requirement, i.e. to prevent purely personal covenants passing on an assignment, is now achieved more simply. The Act lays down a general rule that the benefit and burden of *all* landlord and tenant covenants are transmissible.[457] However, if a covenant is expressed to be personal (in whatever terms) to any person, it will not be enforceable by or against any other person.[458] This does not necessarily mean that such a covenant will be wholly incapable of transmission, for it may be expressed to be personal merely to one of the parties and not to both.[459] The new rule has two advantages over the previous law. First, it allows the parties to make their own bargain and determine for themselves which covenants should pass. Secondly, it leads to certainty, the transmissibility of a covenant no longer depending on the vagaries of the touching and concerning requirement.[460]

There are two exceptions to this general rule:

20–108

(a) The burden of a landlord or tenant covenant will not pass on an assignment of the reversion or lease if it has ceased to be binding on the assignor prior to the assignment,[461] as where it has been released, or being limited to a specific duration, has expired. It often happens that one party to a lease agrees to waive the performance of a particular covenant in the lease by the other, commonly on the understanding that the waiver should be personal to the party to whom it is given. If the latter assigns the lease or reversion, that waiver will not preclude the transmission of the burden of the covenant if the waiver is expressed (in whatever terms) to be personal to the assignor.[462]

(b) The benefit or burden of a landlord or tenant covenant will not pass on an assignment of the reversion or lease if the covenant falls to be complied with in relation to any demised premises not comprised in the assignment.[463] Thus, for example, if there is a partial assignment of property leased, the burden of a tenant covenant to repair a building on the part not transferred would not pass to the assignee. The practical application of the covenant is attributable to the part of the land retained by the assignor.[464]

---

[457] L & TCA 1995 ss.2(1) and 3(1).

[458] L & TCA 1995 s.3(6)(a); *First Penthouse Ltd v Channel Hotels & Properties (UK) Ltd* [2003] EWHC 2713 (Ch); [2004] 1 E.G.L.R. 16.

[459] cf. leases granted before 1996, in which a covenant may touch and concern the land even though it is personal to one of the parties: above, para.20–036.

[460] See above, para.20–034.

[461] L & TCA 1995 ss.3(2) and (3).

[462] L & TCA 1995 s.3(4).

[463] L & TCA 1995 ss.3(2), (3). The Act lays down the circumstances in which a covenant falls to be complied with in relation to a particular part of the premises: L & TCA 1995 ss.28(2) and (3). These include, e.g. where the covenant in its terms applies to that part or, in the case of a money covenant, where the amount payable is determinable specifically by reference to that part.

[464] See L & TCA 1995 s.28(2)(b).

20–109   In relation to leases granted after 1995, the Act abolishes, to the extent that it remains in force, the ancient rule[465] that the burden of a covenant whose subject-matter is not in existence at the time when it is made (such as a covenant to build a wall), does not run with the land unless it is made on behalf of the covenantor and his assigns.[466]

3. Principles of transmission

20–110   *(a) Annexation of covenants and rights of re-entry.* The benefit and burden of all transmissible landlord and tenant covenants are annexed and incident to the whole, and to each and every part, of the premises let by the tenancy and of the reversion in them.[467] They will pass accordingly on an assignment of the whole or any part of those premises or of that reversion.[468] The benefit of a landlord's right of re-entry under a tenancy is similarly annexed so as to pass on an assignment of the whole or any part of the reversion in the premises.[469] By way of an exception, the Act preserves the rule that a purchaser of a lease or reversion takes free of those covenants which are unenforceable against him by reason of non-registration.[470]

20–111   *(b) Right to sue former landlord or tenant who has not been released from his covenants.* It has been explained above that there may be occasions where a landlord or a tenant is not released from a covenant on an assignment of the reversion or the lease respectively and therefore remains liable on the covenants of the lease.[471] Thus, for example, if:

> (i)   L1 assigns his reversion to L2, but does not seek (or cannot obtain) a release of the landlord covenants from T1, the tenant, L1's liability on those covenants continues and he is jointly and severally liable with L2[472] for any breach that L2 may commit; and

---

[465] See *Spencer's Case* (1583) 5 Co.Rep. 16a, second resolution; above, para.20–052. It is circumvented (rather than abolished) in relation to leases granted after 1925 but before 1996, by LPA 1925 s.79.

[466] L & TCA 1995 s.3(7).

[467] The benefit of the landlord's right to receive rent passes under these provisions, reflecting the modern view of rent as a contractual payment for the use of the land: see above, para.19–062. The Act deliberately makes no mention of "rent reserved by the lease", the expression used in LPA 1925 s.141(1) (which governs assignments of reversions on leases granted before 1996).

[468] L & TCA 1995 s.3(1).

[469] L & TCA 1995 s.4. Where, as regards part of the land leased, the lease is surrendered or otherwise terminated, it is thought that the benefit of any right of re-entry and the burden of the tenant covenants will remain annexed to the severed part of the reversion and the lease respectively. Even if L & TCA 1995 ss.3 and 4 do not have this effect, LPA 1925 s.140 (above, para.20–066), expressly does so. That section, unlike LPA 1925 ss.141 and 142, is not repealed for leases granted after 1995.

[470] L & TCA 1995 ss.3(6) and 15(5). The usual case will be an option to renew a lease of unregistered land which is void against an assignee of the reversion for non-registration under LCA 1972, s.4(6): *Phillips v Mobil Oil Co Ltd* [1989] 1 W.L.R. 888; above, paras 8–075, 8–091 and 8–093. An option to renew a lease of registered land will usually bind a purchaser of the reversion as an overriding interest: above, paras 7–089 et seq.

[471] Above, para.20–100.

[472] For joint and several liability in this context, see L & TCA 1995 s.13(1).

(ii) T1 assigns his lease to T2 in breach of a covenant not to assign without the landlord's consent, T1 is similarly liable to L1, the landlord, for any breach of covenant that T2 may commit.

If in (i), T1 subsequently assigns the lease to T2, the right to sue T2 will pass to L2. If in (ii), L1 assigns his reversion to L2, the right to sue L2 will pass to T2. The terms "landlord covenant" and "tenant covenant" include covenants that are binding not just on the landlord or tenant for the time being,[473] but on any former landlord or tenant who has not been released.[474] The right to enforce them must therefore pass on an assignment of the lease or reversion.[475]

(c) Enforcement. The Act lays down detailed rules both as to who can enforce a transmissible covenant[476] that has been annexed to the lease or reversion and as to whom enforcement can be effected against. The rules differ in a number of respects from those applicable to leases granted before 1996.   **20–112**

(1) RIGHT TO ENFORCE ANY TENANT COVENANTS OR RIGHT OF RE-ENTRY. The Act provides that the following persons can enforce the tenant covenants and any right of re-entry in the lease, against both the tenant and any mortgagee in possession of the premises under a mortgage granted by the tenant[477]:   **20–113**

(i) the landlord who granted the lease[478]; and

(ii) a lessee of the reversion[479]; and

(iii) a mortgagee in possession of the reversion.[480]

This marks a departure from the previous law, though the difference may be more apparent than real. In relation to leases granted before 1996, a landlord ceases to be entitled to enforce the tenant covenants if and to the extent that some other person (such as a lessee of the reversion or a mortgagee in possession of the reversion) becomes entitled to the income of all or part of the land leased.[481] Furthermore, as regards any lease granted before 1996, any   **20–114**

---

[473] The Act provides that, unless the context otherwise requires, "landlord" means the person for the time being entitled to the reversion immediately expectant on the term; and "tenant" means the person entitled to the term: L & TCA 1995 s.28(1). Here, the context plainly does require that "landlord" and "tenant" have a different meaning.

[474] This can be deduced from L & TCA 1995 ss.5(2), 7(1) and 11(2).

[475] Under L & TCA 1995 s.3(1); above, para.20–110.

[476] A covenant that is expressed to be personal to any person cannot be enforced by or against any other person: L & TCA 1995 s.15(5)(a). Where a covenant is unenforceable against a person for non-registration, see L & TCA 1995 s.15(5)(b).

[477] L & TCA 1995 s.15(4).

[478] L & TCA 1995 s.15(1), (6).

[479] L & TCA 1995 s.15(1)(a). Leases of the reversion are likely to be more common after 1995, because of the overriding lease provisions of the Act: see L & TCA 1995 s.19; above, para.20–025.

[480] L & TCA 1995 s.15(1)(b).

[481] LPA 1925 s.141(2); above, para.20–065.

subsequent grant of a lease of the reversion operates as a pro tanto assignment of the reversion.[482] By contrast, the grant of a lease of the reversion on a lease granted after 1995 must take effect *as a lease* and not as an assignment,[483] because the landlord retains his right to enforce the tenant covenants in the lease. Subject to any estoppel arising from the grant of the lease of the reversion, both the landlord *and* any lessee of the reversion may in principle enforce the tenant covenants or any right of re-entry in the original lease.[484] While it will almost always be the latter who will wish to exercise these rights, there may be occasions where the tenant's breach of covenant causes loss not only to the interest of the lessee of the reversion but to the landlord's ultimate reversion as well.[485] As each can only recover for the distinct injury to his own reversion, the tenant will not be required to pay damages twice over. If both the landlord and the lessee of the reversion wish to exercise the right of re-entry, the former will have priority.[486] However, he is seldom likely to exercise that right because the effect of terminating the original lease will be that the lessee of the reversion becomes entitled in possession.

The position is similar where a mortgagee of the reversion is in possession. He becomes entitled to enforce the tenant covenants and any right of re-entry and in practice it is he who is likely to do so, rather than the landlord (who retains his rights of enforcement).

20–115   (2) RIGHT TO ENFORCE ANY LANDLORD COVENANTS. Any landlord covenant may be enforced by:

(i) the tenant; or

(ii) any mortgagee in possession of any premises comprised in the lease under a mortgage granted by the tenant[487]

but not by any sub-lessee (as is apparently the case in relation to leases granted before 1996[488]). The covenant is enforceable against:

---

[482] Above, para.17–134.

[483] This was to avoid the possibility that on an assignment of a lease of the reversion the landlord might be able to obtain a release from the landlord covenants of the original lease as a result of L & TCA 1995 ss.7 and 11; above, para.20–098.

[484] "The Act thus creates the spectre of two different persons being entitled to enforce the covenants in a tenancy at the same time": Fancourt, *Enforceability of Landlord and Tenant Covenants*, second edn, 17.18; and see *First Penthouse Ltd v Channel Hotels & Properties (UK) Ltd* [2003] EWHC 2713 (Ch); [2004] 1 E.G.L.R. 16. The landlord will be estopped by his grant from enforcing rights against the tenant that he had leased to the lessee of the reversion, such as the right to claim rent.

[485] As where the tenant is in serious breach of his repairing obligations and the lease of the reversion is about to expire.

[486] The lessee of the reversion necessarily takes subject to the landlord's pre-existing right of re-entry against the tenant.

[487] L & TCA 1995 s.15(3).

[488] This is the apparently fortuitous effect of LPA 1925 s.78; above, para.20–045. There is no good reason why a sub-lessee should be able to enforce covenants against the head lessor when the converse is not the case except as regards restrictive covenants.

(a) the landlord;

(b) any lessee of the reversion; and

(c) any mortgagee in possession of the reversion.[489]

Where, as a result of these provisions, the tenant can sue more than one **20–116** person, the defendants will be jointly and severally liable.[490] However, a landlord who has to pay damages to the tenant for a breach of the landlord covenants by either a lessee of the reversion or a mortgagee in possession, will be entitled to an indemnity from the party in breach.[491]

(3) RESTRICTIVE COVENANTS. Any landlord or tenant covenant that is restric- **20–117** tive of the user of land is capable of being enforced against not only any assignee of the reversion or lease but also any owner or occupier of the premises to which the covenant relates, even though there is no express provision in the tenancy to that effect.[492] This means that any sub-lessee, licensee or even squatter, will be bound automatically by restrictive covenants in the head lease.[493] However, the provision is limited in its application to owners and occupiers of the premises, or any part of the premises, demised by the tenancy. It follows that where a landlord covenanted with a tenant, C, not to permit other property of his to be used in a particular manner, a subsequent tenant of that other property, D, was not bound by the covenant, and C could not enforce the covenant against D.[494] Since October 13, 2003, restrictive covenants made between a lessor and a lessee are registrable insofar as they do not relate to the demised premises.[495] The enforceability of such covenants is therefore dependent on the application of the principles relating to freehold covenants, and not those contained in the 1995 Act.

4. Partial assignments

(a) Attribution of the burden of covenants. Where there has been a partial **20–118** assignment of the lease or of the reversion, then whether and to what extent a particular assignee is subject to the burden of such a covenant depends upon whether it is attributable to a particular part of the property or whether it is applicable to the whole of the premises that are the subject of the lease.[496] No issue of apportionment will arise where a covenant falls to be complied with or performed in relation to either the part retained or the part assigned. The

[489] L & TCA 1995 s.15(2).

[490] L & TCA 1995 s.13(1).

[491] Under the principle that where A is compelled to pay a sum for which B is ultimately liable, A has a right to be indemnified by B: see *Moule v Garrett* (1872) L.R. 7 Ex. 101 at 104; *Brook's Wharf and Bull Wharf Ltd v Goodman Bros* [1937] 1 K.B. 534 at 544.

[492] L & TCA 1995 s.3(5).

[493] In practice this replicates the effect of the law applicable to leases granted before 1996: see below, para.32–054.

[494] *Oceanic Village Ltd v United Attractions Ltd* [2000] Ch. 234.

[495] LRA 2002 s.33(c).

[496] See L & TCA 1995 s.9(6).

burden of the covenant will bind only the part to which it relates.[497] For example, where L1 leases a house and a field to T1, covenanting to keep the exterior of the house in repair, and L1 then assigns the reversion on the house but not the field to L2, T1 can enforce the repairing covenant against L2.[498]

20–119   *(b) Joint and several liability for non-attributable covenants.* A covenant that is not attributable to any premises comprised in the partial assignment of the lease or reversion is charged on the whole of the property. An example is a tenant covenant to pay rent or service charge. In such a case, in the absence of any apportionment, both landlords or (as the case may be) both tenants will be jointly and severally liable for any breach of the covenant.[499] If one of the covenantors is held liable, he may however seek contribution from the other.[500]

20–120   *(c) Apportionment.* Where there is a non-attributable landlord or tenant covenant, its burden may be apportioned on a partial assignment in one of two ways. First, the Act permits apportionment where the relevant parties to the tenancy, namely the landlord, the tenant and the assignee of the lease or the reversion, all agree to it.[501] Secondly, in the absence of any such agreement, the Act creates a means by which the assignor and assignee can agree an apportionment and make it binding upon the landlord or the tenant respectively.[502] Thus, if T assigns to A part of the premises that are leased to him by L, and T and A agree an apportionment of the rent payable in respect of their respective parts,[503] they may apply to L[504] for that apportionment to be made binding on him.[505] That application must be in the form of a notice,[506] served on L before or within four weeks of the assignment.[507] This must inform L of the proposed or actual assignment, provide prescribed particulars of the agreement, and request that the apportionment should become binding on him.[508] The apportionment will then become binding on L unless he serves a written counter-notice on T and A within four weeks of service objecting to

---

[497] See L & TCA 1995 s.3(2) and (3); above, para.20–108.

[498] L1 is not released from his liability under the repairing covenant unless and until he obtains a release from T1 or from the court: see para.20–096 above.

[499] L & TCA 1995 s.13(1).

[500] L & TCA 1995 s.13(3), adapting the provisions of the Civil Liability (Contribution) Act 1978.

[501] L & TCA 1995 s.26(1).

[502] L & TCA 1995 s.9.

[503] The parties may agree that one of them is to be exonerated from all liability under the covenant: L & TCA 1995 s.9(3).

[504] As the "appropriate person": L & TCA 1995 s.9(7). It may be necessary to make the apportionment binding on some other party, e.g. a management company, and the Act makes provision for this: L & TCA 1995 s.9(5).

[505] L & TCA 1995 s.9(1), (4). For the converse case, where an apportionment is made on the assignment of the reversion, see L & TCA 1995 s.9(2) and (4).

[506] See L & TCA 1995 s.27; SI 1995/2964, Form 7.

[507] L & TCA 1995 s.10(1).

[508] L & TCA 1995 s.10(1).

the apportionment. In those circumstances there will be no apportionment unless either:

(i) T and A apply to the county court for, and obtain, a declaration that it is reasonable for the apportionment to become binding; or

(ii) L in writing withdraws his objection.[509]

Any apportionment is effective from the date of the partial assignment.[510] **20–121** Once it has become binding, the apportionment cannot be affected by any subsequent order or decision made under any other statutory power of apportionment.[511]

(d) Excluded assignments. Where the partial assignment is in breach of **20–122** covenant or by operation of law,[512] the parties to it cannot apply for an agreed apportionment to become binding on the landlord or tenant (as the case may be).[513] Such an application can be made only on the next assignment that is not an excluded assignment.[514]

(e) Forfeiture and disclaimer. If a lease containing a right to re-enter for **20–123** breach of covenant is assigned in part, the landlord can forfeit only that part held by the tenant who is in breach and not the whole of the premises to which the right relates.[515] Similarly, where a tenant of part becomes insolvent, the liquidator or trustee in bankruptcy can exercise his power of disclaimer[516] only in respect of that part.[517]

5. Assignee's position in relation to previous breaches of covenant

(a) No liability for breaches by assignor. The Act preserves the rule[518] that **20–124** the assignee of a lease or reversion incurs no liability for breaches of covenant committed by the assignor.[519]

(b) Right to sue for previous breaches does not pass. It has been explained **20–125** that on an assignment of a lease granted before 1996, the right to sue for breaches of covenant committed by the landlord prior to the assignment does not pass on the assignment.[520] By contrast, where the landlord assigns the

---

[509] L & TCA 1995 s.10(2). In the converse case, where L has assigned part of the reversion to R, L and R would of course serve the notice on T, and T would serve any counter-notice on L and R.

[510] L & TCA 1995 s.10(3).

[511] L & TCA 1995 s.26(3). There are many such statutory provisions: see e.g. AHA 1986, s.33.

[512] And therefore an excluded assignment, see above, para.20–100.100

[513] L & TCA 1995 s.11(5)(a).

[514] L & TCA 1995 s.11(5)(b) and (6).

[515] L & TCA 1995 s.21(1).

[516] See above, paras 18–098 et seq.

[517] L & TCA 1995 s.21(2).

[518] Above, para.20–053.

[519] L & TCA 1995 s.23(1).

[520] Above, para.20–054.

reversion on such a lease, the right to sue for pre-existing breaches of covenant does pass to the assignee.[521] As regards leases granted after 1995, the Act lays down one rule which applies equally to the assignment of both the lease and the reversion. Consistently with the underlying principle of the Act that rights and liabilities under the lease should go together,[522] it is provided that:

> (i) the right to sue for any pre-existing breach of covenant does not pass on an assignment of either the lease or the reversion[523]; but
>
> (ii) such a right may be expressly assigned to the assignee.[524]

In practice it is likely that such express assignments will be the norm, particularly on an assignment of a reversion.

20–126   *(c) Right to re-enter for breach prior to assignment.* Although the right to sue for the breach of a covenant committed by the tenant prior to the assignment of the reversion does not pass in the absence of an express assignment, the assignee of the reversion is entitled to exercise any right of re-entry in the lease in respect of such a breach, unless there had been a waiver or release of that breach prior to assignment.[525] If the assignee were not entitled to do this, a tenant who was in breach of covenant might escape the forfeiture of his lease simply because of the fortuitous circumstance that the reversion had been assigned. If, as is likely, the breach occurred shortly before the assignment, the assignor may have had no opportunity to take steps to forfeit the lease.

20–127   The interaction of the principles that, in respect of a breach of covenant committed before the assignment of the reversion, the assignee can forfeit the lease but only the assignor can sue the tenant on the covenant, can be demonstrated by three examples. In each case L1, the landlord of a lease containing a right of re-entry, has assigned the reversion to L2. Prior to that assignment, T, the tenant, has committed a breach of covenant which was not waived or released by L1. L1 has not assigned to L2 his rights of action against T.

> (i) In the simplest case, L2 forfeits the lease and T fails to obtain relief. L1 can still sue T for any loss which he has suffered. This may be for the diminution in the value of the reversion at the time of the sale to L2 (e.g. because of T's failure to repair), or in the case of non-payment of rent or service charge, for the sum unpaid at the time the reversion was assigned to L2.

---

[521] Above, para.20–068.
[522] See Law Com. No.174 paras 4.1 and 4.49; above, para.20–086.
[523] L & TCA 1995 s.23(1).
[524] L & TCA 1995 s.23(2).
[525] L & TCA 1995 s.23(3). For waiver, see above, para.18–019. The commonest example of waiver is where a landlord accepts rent from the tenant in the knowledge that he is in breach of covenant. In many cases therefore, the breach will have been waived before the reversion is assigned.

(ii) In the second case, T has committed a breach of a positive covenant such as a repairing obligation. Under threat of forfeiture, T
remedies the breach. L1 may still sue T for damages for the breach
of the covenant and can recover the loss that he has suffered. That
will be the amount by which the value of his reversion was
diminished by T's breach of covenant at the time of the sale.[526]

(iii) In the third example, T is in arrears of rent at the time when L1
assigns the reversion to L2. If L2 commences forfeiture proceedings against T, T is in practice likely to pay the arrears either to L2
or into court in order to secure relief.[527] In either eventuality, it is
suggested that the payment should discharge T,[528] and that L1 will
be entitled to claim the sum paid by T because L2 has no right to
retain it. L1 may seek restitution either on the basis of the developing law of unjust enrichment,[529] or through the imposition of a
constructive trust on the basis that it is unconscionable for L2 to
retain the sum.[530]

6. Attempts to exclude the operation of the Act. The Act contains **20–128**
sweeping anti-avoidance provisions by which any agreement relating to a
tenancy[531] is void to the extent that it either purports to have certain effects or
places specified obligations upon the tenant.[532]

First, an agreement is void in so far as it would have the effect of excluding, **20–129**
modifying or otherwise frustrating the operation of any provision of the
Act.[533] This is, and was intended by Parliament to be, a provision of considerable breadth.[534] It can reasonably be assumed that the courts will make full use
of this power where it is necessary to defeat sham terms whose principal

---

[526] cf. L & TA 1927 s.18(1); above, para.19–126. The amount will obviously depend on how
much the sale of the reversion had been discounted because of T's breach.

[527] See Common Law Procedure Act 1852 s.212; County Courts Act 1984 s.138(3) (as
amended); above, para.18–031. Each statute requires that, for T to obtain relief, he must pay the
monies either into court or to the *landlord*, who would be L2, not L1.

[528] Because of his compliance with the statutory requirements for obtaining relief against
forfeiture.

[529] See *Lipkin Gorman v Karpnale Ltd* [1991] 2 A.C. 548; *Banque Financière de la Cité v Parc
(Battersea) Ltd* [1999] 1 A.C. 221.

[530] If L2 was aware of the rent arrears and paid less for the reversion because L1 did not assign
to him the benefit of the right to sue for them, the case for imposing a constructive trust would
be strong: cf. *Ashburn Anstalt v Arnold* [1989] Ch. 1; above, para.11–022.

[531] Whether or not the agreement is contained in the tenancy or was made before the creation
of that tenancy: L & TCA 1995 s.25(4).

[532] L & TCA 1995 s.25(1).

[533] For example, a provision in a lease which required a tenant who wished to dispose of his
lease to sub-let for a term exceeding his term, would be void under s.25(1). Such a sub-lease
operates by way of an assignment by operation of law: above, para.17–142. The tenant would not
therefore be released from the covenants: L & TCA 1995 s.11; above, para.20–100. See *Hansard*
(H.C.), July 14, 1995, Vol.263 col. 1266.

[534] See *Hansard* (H.C.), July 14, 1995, Vol.263 cols 1265 and 1266; Law Com. No.174 paras
4.57 and 4.58; *London Diocesan Fund v Phithwa* [2005] UKHL 70; [2005] 1 W.L.R. 3956 at [14],
[18]; *K/S Victoria Street v House of Fraser (Stores Management) Ltd* [2011] EWCA Civ 904;
[2011] 2 P. & C.R. 15 at [23].

objective is to circumvent the Act.[535] It enables a court to examine the purpose of any given term of the lease in the light of the policy of the Act as a whole or of a particular section.[536] However, it is the objective effect of the term in question, rather than the subjective reasons for its existence, which determine its validity or otherwise.[537]

20–130　　　Secondly, an agreement will be void to the extent that it provides for:

　　(i)　the termination or surrender of the tenancy; or

　　(ii)　imposes on the tenant any penalty, disability or liability,

in the event of, in connection with, or in consequence of the operation of any provision of the Act. This is intended to catch obvious devices for circumventing the Act, such as a term which requires a tenant to pay a large premium to the landlord on assignment. Certain transactions, such as absolute or qualified covenants against assignment, and authorised guarantee agreements, are not rendered void by the anti-avoidance provisions.[538]

---

[535] See *Hansard* (H.C.), July 14, 1995, Vol.263 col.1266. For shams, see above, para.17–026.

[536] This was the exercise conducted by the House of Lords in *London Diocesan Fund v Phithwa*, above. A provision in the lease automatically determining the lessor's liability under the covenants in the event of assignment was upheld, on the basis that the mischief at which the statute was aimed was the absence of an "exit route" from future liabilities on a lawful assignment for the parties to the lease. The legislation should not therefore be interpreted so as to close down any existing exit route: in this case, the right of the parties to make provision in the lease bringing an end to the landlord's liability on assignment.

[537] *K/S Victoria Street v House of Fraser (Stores Management) Ltd*, above at [29].

[538] L & TCA 1995 s.25(2), (3).

LEASEHOLD CONVEYANCING

The rules governing contracts for the sale of land have been explained, and **21–001** brief accounts have been given of unregistered and registered conveyancing, though primarily with reference to the sale of a fee simple. Many of the same principles apply to the creation and assignment of leases. For example, it has been explained that a contract to grant or assign a lease must be made in writing in the same way as a contract for sale, and that its operation in equity is similar.[1] On the other hand, the rules as to the formalities necessary when granting (but not assigning) legal leases are in some ways different from the rules for freehold conveyances. The similarities and differences between the rules governing freehold and leasehold dispositions are set out below.

A. Contracts

1. Formality. A contract to grant or assign a lease requires the same **21–002** formalities as any other contract for the disposition of an interest in land.[2] There is however an exception in respect of a contract to grant (but not assign) a lease that may be made orally.[3]

2. Effect in equity. A contract to grant or assign a lease creates an equitable **21–003** interest, analogous to that created by a contract to sell a freehold. It is registrable as an estate contract where title is unregistered and may be protected by means of a notice where title is registered. This has been explained in connection with *Walsh v Lonsdale*.[4]

3. Duty to disclose latent defects in title. Where a person contracts to **21–004** grant or assign a lease, he is under the same obligation to disclose latent defects in title prior to contracting as is a vendor of freehold land.[5] If he fails to do so, the grantee or assignee may terminate the contract at once, even

---

[1] Above, para.15–015.
[2] Above, para.15–015.
[3] Above, paras 15–021; 17–037.
[4] Above, paras 17–047—17–049.
[5] Above, para.15–070.

before the date for the commencement of the term or the completion of the assignment.[6] In the case of a contract to assign a lease, an onerous or unusual covenant is regarded as a defect in title for these purposes, and must be disclosed.[7] The obligation is normally satisfied by giving the purchaser a copy of the lease to inspect prior to contract.[8]

4. Duty to prove good title

21–005   *(a) Unregistered land.* The title which an intending lessee or assignee of unregistered land may require to be deduced under an open contract differs from the title which a purchaser of the freehold is entitled to have shown.[9] The Law of Property Act 1925[10] provides that in default of any express provision to the contrary:

> (i)   under a contract for the grant or assignment of a lease or sub-lease, there is no right to call for the title to the freehold[11];
>
> (ii) under a contract for the assignment of a sub-lease, there is no right to call for the title to the superior lease[12]; and
>
> (iii) under a contract to grant a sub-lease, there is no right to call for the title to the head lease.[13]

These provisions are obscurely worded. It is assumed in practice that the "title to" a lease or sub-lease includes the lease or sub-lease itself.[14] The effect of these rules may then be conveniently summarised by saying that an intending tenant or assignee may always inspect any lease under which the other contracting party holds. There is no right to inspect the title to the freehold.

There is now an important exception to these rules. On a contract to grant a lease in circumstances where that grant will trigger the requirement of compulsory first registration,[15] the principles set out at (i) and (iii) do not apply.[16]

---

[6] See, e.g. *Roper v Coombes* (1827) 9 Dowl. Ry. 562 (lessee contracted to grant sub-lease longer than his term); *Pips (Leisure Productions) Ltd v Walton* (1980) 43 P. & C.R. 415 (lessee contracted to assign its lease after it had been forfeited).

[7] *Reeve v Berridge* (1888) 20 Q.B.D. 523; *Re Haedicke and Lipski's Contract* [1901] 2 Ch. 666; see (1992) 108 L.Q.R. 280 at 325 (C.H.). For the covenants that will not be regarded as "usual", see above, para.19–058.

[8] See, e.g. Standard Conditions of Sale (4th edn), cc. 3.3.2, 8.1.2.

[9] See above, paras 15–076 et seq.

[10] s.44(2)–(4).

[11] s.44(2).

[12] s.44(3).

[13] s.44(4).

[14] The dictum to the contrary in *Gosling v Woolf* [1893] 1 Q.B. 39 at 41 is thought to be wrong, and is not supported by the report in (1892) 68 L.T. 89, indicating that the case concerned the grant (not the assignment) of a sub-lease. See Wolst. & C. i, 111.

[15] For those circumstances, see LRA 2002 s.4; above, para.7–014.

[16] LPA 1925 s.44(4A) (inserted by LRA 2002 s.133 Sch.11 para.2).

Subject to the restrictions set out above, there is an obligation to deduce title in the normal way, with a good root of title that is at least 15 years old.[17] An example might be where L granted a 99-year lease in 1950 to T and that lease was assigned by T to A in 1965, by A to B in 1978 and by B to C in 1989. If C now enters into an open contract to assign it to D, the title which C must deduce will be the lease from L to T; and the assignments from A to B and from B to C. C will not have to deduce L's freehold title, nor the assignment of the lease from T to A.[18]

Since these rules yield to contrary provision in the contract, the intending tenant may stipulate for fuller disclosure, though this is likely to matter less than formerly, because a lease that is to be granted for more than 7 years will be subject to the requirement of compulsory first registration[19] and, as explained above, a contract to grant such a lease is not subject to the restrictions set out in this paragraph.[20] Furthermore, even though an intending tenant or assignee may be precluded from seeing a superior title, he may still object to the title if he discovers from some other source that it is defective.[21]

These statutory limitations on the purchaser's right to inspect the title have **21–006** created a difficulty in relation to those few equitable incumbrances which still bind a purchaser with notice, such as restrictive covenants created before 1926. The lessee or assignee is fixed with notice of everything that he would have discovered had he stipulated for and made a full investigation of title. This has been held to be the case even though he is deprived by statute of the right to make such an investigation.[22] To meet this difficulty, the Law of Property Act 1925 provides that where, by reason of the statutory restrictions, an intending lessee or assignee is unable to make a full investigation of title, "he shall not be deemed to be affected with notice of any matter or thing of which, if he had contracted that such title should be furnished, he might have had notice".[23] The effect of this provision is however merely to shift the hardship from the shoulders of the lessee to the owner of the equitable incumbrance. His interest is void against the lessee as a purchaser of a legal estate for value without notice.[24]

The provision of the Act set out above protects only a purchaser from the consequences of his inability to investigate title fully. It does not protect him if he acquired notice in some other way, e.g. where he actually knew of the incumbrance.[25] This may be important where the equitable incumbrance is

---

[17] LPA 1969 s.23; above paras 8–021, 15–077.
[18] See *Williams v Spargo* [1893] W.N. 100.
[19] LRA 2002 s.4(1)(c).
[20] LPA 1925 s.44(4A), above; and see Standard Conditions of Sale (4th edn), c. 8.2.4.
[21] *Jones v Watts* (1890) 43 Ch D 574.
[22] *Patman v Harland* (1881) 17 Ch D 353; and see above, paras 8–021—8–022.
[23] s.44(5).
[24] As in *Shears v Wells* [1936] 1 All E.R. 832.
[25] The burden of proving notice is on the person seeking to enforce the adverse interest: *Shears v Wells,* above.

registered as a land charge, since registration is deemed to be actual notice.[26] Incumbrances registered as land charges will therefore in any case bind a lessee or sub-lessee or the assignee of a sub-lease.[27] Furthermore, because of the defects of the land charge registration machinery discussed earlier,[28] it may be impossible for a purchaser to discover a registered incumbrance which is binding on him.[29] Unless he either has access to all the title deeds or such deeds as he has include copies of the previous searches of the land charges register,[30] he cannot discover the names of the owners against which he must search, with the exception of the immediate vendor and of persons named in such documents as he is allowed to see.

21–007   *(b) Registered land.* Where the superior title is registered, the difficulties explained above in relation to unregistered land do not arise. First, the statutory restrictions on the title which an intending lessee or assignee may see,[31] do not apply to registered land or to a term of years to be derived out of registered land.[32] Secondly, the register is an open public document which anyone may inspect.[33] If the landlord's title is registered, an intending lessee or assignee can therefore discover any defects in that title which appear on the register. If the superior title is registered with absolute title, any lease granted out of it will normally be registered with an absolute title as well.[34] This is so even where the lease granted is a sub-lease, and the headlease requires the freeholder's consent to any sub-letting.[35]

Where a lease is granted for a term exceeding seven years, or an existing unregistered lease having more than seven years to run is assigned, the lease must be registered with its own title.[36] If the lessee then contracts to assign the lease, he must prove his title in the manner agreed by the parties.[37] By contrast, most leases of registered land granted for seven years or less cannot be registered with their own title,[38] but will take effect as unregistered interests which override first registration or a registered disposition as the case

---

[26] Above, para.8–085.
[27] *White v Bijou Mansions Ltd* [1937] Ch. 610 (in CA [1938] Ch. 351).
[28] Above, para.8–086.
[29] In certain cases the tenant may be entitled to compensation: LPA 1969 s.25; above, para.8–089. It is understood that there have been just two successful claims for compensation under this Act (neither of which involved a lease), suggesting that the problems are more apparent than real.
[30] Which in practice they commonly do.
[31] Set out above: see para.21–005.
[32] LPA 1925 s.44(12) (inserted by LRA 2002 s.133 Sch.11 para.2).
[33] LRA 2002 s.66; above, paras 7–002, 7–120.
[34] See LRA 2002 s.10(2); above, para.7–024.
[35] See Ruoff & Roper, 9.006. For the covenant against assignment or underletting without consent, see above, para.19–093.
[36] LRA 2002 ss.4(1)(c) (lease granted out of unregistered land); 27(2)(b) (lease granted out of registered land); above, paras 7–014, 7–054.
[37] There are no statutory rules under LRA 2002 as to how a disponor of registered land should prove his title: see above, para.7–148. cf. Standard Conditions of Sale (4th edn), c.8.2.4.
[38] Some leases granted for seven years or less are required to be registered: see LRA 2002 s.4(1)(d)—(f) (leases granted out of unregistered land); s.27(2)(b) (leases granted out of registered land); above, paras 7–014, 7–054.

may be.[39] If the lease is granted for more than three years it may, however, be noted on the superior title.[40] Such leases are therefore treated as unregistered land[41] and, on an assignment, title is deduced in accordance with the principles of unregistered conveyancing.[42]

(c) Particular problems. Certain problems arise as to title that are peculiar   **21–008**
to leases, of which two may be mentioned.

(1) VENDOR IN BREACH OF COVENANT. The first is where a tenant, holding   **21–009**
under a lease which contains a proviso for re-entry for breach of covenant, contracts to assign the term at a time when he is in breach of covenant. The courts appear to treat all breaches of covenant as irremovable defects in title, even though most such breaches are in law capable of remedy.[43] It is by statute provided that on a sale of a lease, the purchaser is to assume, unless the contrary appears:

    (i) that the lease was duly granted; and

    (ii) on the production of the receipt for the last payment of rent due under the lease prior to completion, that all the covenants in the lease have been performed and observed up to the actual completion date.[44]

The basis of the second assumption is that, by accepting rent, the landlord waives the breach.[45] However, waiver will not always protect a purchaser because there will normally be a period of time between the rent payment and completion. Where the breach is of a continuing nature[46] it is considered to arise afresh after the waiver,[47] thereby placing the purchaser at risk that the lease will be forfeited. The authorities establish that, if the purchaser is either:

    (i) unaware of the breach of covenant at the time of contracting; or

---

[39] See LRA 2002 Sch.1 para.1; Sch.3 para.1; above, paras 7–030, 7–087.

[40] LRA 2002 s.33(b); above, para.7–070.

[41] e.g. equitable incumbrances affecting such leases are registered as land charges under LCA 1972. For land charges, see paras 8–061 et seq.

[42] Above, para.21–005.

[43] See *Akici v L R Butlin Ltd* [2006] EWCA Civ 1296 at [62] et seq.; [2006] 1 WLR 201 at 213 et seq. If the breaches are remedied, the landlord cannot forfeit the lease: above, paras 18–053— 18–056. Normally a purchaser's knowledge of a removable defect in title at the time of contracting does not affect the vendor's obligation to discharge the incumbrance prior to completion: above, paras 15–082, 15–083. However, this principle is apparently not applied to breaches of leasehold covenants. cf. [1988] Conv. 400 at 408 (C.H.).

[44] LPA 1925 s.45(2). See, e.g. *Clarke v Coleman* [1895] W.N. 114; *Lockharts v Bernard Rosen Co* [1922] 1 Ch. 433. For the analogous provision applicable to the sale of an underlease, see LPA 1925 s.45(3). Both provisions may be ousted if a contrary intention appears from the contract: LPA 1925 s.45(10).

[45] For waiver, see above, para.18–019.

[46] e.g. a breach of a repairing covenant.

[47] Above, para.18–026.

(ii) aware of the breach, but the vendor has expressly contracted to show a good title;

he is not precluded by the statutory assumption from showing the vendor is in breach of covenant.[48] The purchaser may therefore either repudiate the contract or require the vendor to remedy the breach.

21–010   (2) LANDLORD'S CONSENT TO ASSIGNMENT. It has been explained that many leases require the landlord's consent to any assignment.[49] Compliance with the requirement is, anomalously, regarded as a matter of conveyance rather than of title, and the assignor has therefore until completion to obtain it.[50] He will be in breach of contract if consent has not been given by then,[51] unless the landlord withholds it unreasonably. In the latter case, the parties are entitled to proceed with the assignment without it,[52] though a court will not compel the assignee to take an assignment because the vendor's title will be doubtful.[53]

It has long been usual for such contracts to be made conditional upon obtaining the landlord's consent.[54] If consent is not forthcoming:

(i) the purchaser need not complete and may recover any deposit that he has paid; but

(ii) the vendor will not be in breach of contract provided that he has used his best endeavours to secure the consent.[55]

---

[48] See *Re Taunton and West of England Perpetual Benefit B.S. and Roberts' Contract* [1912] 2 Ch. 381; *Re Highett and Bird's Contract* [1903] 1 Ch. 287 as explained in *Re Allen and Driscoll's Contract* [1904] 2 Ch. 226 at 231.

[49] Above, para.19–093. The nature of the consent required will depend upon the terms of the covenant.

[50] Above, para.15–082. All other matters of conveyance involve incumbrances that the vendor can remove as of right, such as mortgages.

[51] *Bain v Fothergill* (1874) L.R. 5 H.L. 158. The measure of damages in such a case would now be different: see LPMPA 1989 s.3; explained in the sixth edition of this work at para.12–103.

[52] *Treloar v Bigge* (1874) L.R. 9 Ex. 151 at 157.

[53] *Re Marshall and Salt's Contract* [1900] 2 Ch. 202. The court would have to determine the issue of the lessor's unreasonableness in proceedings to which he would not be a party and by whose decree he would not therefore be bound.

[54] See, e.g. Standard Conditions of Sale (4th edn), c. 8.3. To satisfy such a condition, the communication from the landlord must (i) record the consent as required by the contract; (ii) be unconditional or subject only to reasonable conditions; and (iii) be unequivocal. Provided those requirements are met, the communication of the landlord's decision *in principle* to consent will satisfy the condition: see *Aubergine Enterprises Ltd v Lakewood International Ltd* [2002] EWCA Civ 177; [2002] 1 W.L.R. 2149. For conditional contracts of this kind, see above, paras 15–007—15–008.

[55] *Lehmann v McArthur* (1868) L.R. 3 Ch.App. 496. The vendor will be liable if he does not use his best endeavours: *Day v Singleton* [1899] 2 Ch. 320. The vendor's obligation under Standard Conditions of Sale, c.8.3, is to obtain a licence to assign to the purchaser. If the purchaser then arranges a sub-sale, he must secure the necessary consent to assign to the sub-purchaser: *Pittack v Naviede* [2010] EWHC 1509 (Ch) at [34]; [2011] 1 W.L.R. 1666 at 1676.

Such conditions, which typically provide a right to rescind if the condition has not been met shortly before the completion date,[56] provide a simple means of escape for a vendor without first having to determine in court proceedings whether or not the landlord had acted unreasonably.[57]

5. Options to renew. A lease will often contain an option for renewal or for **21–011** the purchase of the freehold.[58] It has been the practice for more than two centuries for such options to be subject to the proviso that the tenant has complied with all covenants at a specified date, e.g. the date of the exercise of the option.[59] The general rule in relation to options is that there must be no subsisting actionable breaches of covenant at the specified date,[60] and this is so even though only nominal damages would be awarded for the breach of covenant.[61] However, the fact that there have been breaches in the past is no bar to the enforcement of the option, provided that:

(i) any breach (whether of a positive or a negative covenant) has ceased; and

(ii) there are no subsisting causes of action in respect of it.[62]

It is not uncommon for a proviso of this kind to be qualified, e.g., to require that the tenant should have materially or substantially complied with his obligations under the lease.[63]

6. Remedies. These are generally the same as under contracts for the sale **21–012** of a freehold.[64] It used to be thought that equity would not grant specific

---

[56] As in Standard Conditions of Sale (4th edn), c. 8.3.3. Because such a condition is intended to provide certainty, it must be exercised by the contractual completion date or a day or two thereafter: see *Alchemy Estates Ltd v Astor* [2008] EWHC 2675 (Ch) at [54]; [2009] 1 W.L.R. 940 at 959–960.

[57] See *Bickel v Courtenay Investments (Nominees) Ltd* [1984] 1 W.L.R. 795.

[58] Or a break clause to enable a tenant to terminate the lease prematurely: see above, para.18–003. The principles explained in this section apply to both: see *Reed Personnel Services Plc v American Express Ltd* [1997] 1 E.G.L.R. 229.

[59] *Bass Holdings Ltd v Morton Music Ltd* [1988] Ch. 493 at 517, 528. For the principles applicable where there are preconditions to the exercise of options, see *Little v Courage Ltd* (1994) 70 P. C.R. 469 at 474.

[60] *Bass Holdings Ltd v Morton Music Ltd*, supra (reviewing earlier authorities); (1987) 103 L.Q.R. 504 (P. V. Baker); *West Middlesex Golf Club Ltd v Ealing LBC* (1993) 68 P. & C.R. 461 and 486 (disrepair, but not actionable).

[61] *Bairstow Eves (Securities) Ltd v Ripley* (1992) 65 P. & C.R. 220. See too *Kitney v Greater London Properties Ltd* [1984] 2 E.G.L.R. 83.

[62] *Bass Holdings Ltd v Morton Music Ltd*, above.

[63] Substantial compliance does not require strict compliance with every term and condition of the lease: see *Fitzroy House Epworth Street (No.1) Ltd v Financial Times Ltd* [2006] EWCA Civ 329; [2006] 1 W.L.R. 2207.

[64] Above, para.12–101.

performance of agreements for short leases, e.g. leases of a year or less, but the modern authorities indicate that there is no such rule.[65]

B. Conveyances

21–013   The grant or assignment of a lease by deed is a "conveyance" within the meaning of the Law of Property Act 1925,[66] except where provision is made to the contrary.[67]

21–014   **1. Form.** A specimen of a simple lease that is not required to be registered is given in the next section.

It has been explained that, since June 19, 2006 and subject to minor exceptions, where the grant of a lease out of registered land is a registrable disposition, certain particulars ("required wording") must be included at the beginning of the lease to enable the Land Registry to register the lease correctly.[68] Those particulars include the date of the lease, the title number(s) out of which it is granted, the property demised, the term, any premium, any prohibitions or restrictions on disposing of the lease and any easements for the benefit of the lease or to which it is subject.[69] Registration of a lease is not of itself the registration of separate rights granted under the lease, e.g., the grant to the tenant of an option to renew the lease or to purchase the freehold, which should be separately registered, and noted against any title which they may affect.[70]

The rules governing the creation and assignment of leases have already been explained. The notable difference from freehold conveyancing is, of course, that certain leases may be granted[71] (but not assigned[72]) orally or in writing.

21–015   **2. Covenants for title** The nature of covenants for title has been explained.[73] In relation to a lease granted after June 1995:

>   (i) The tenant has benefit of the landlord's qualified covenant for quiet enjoyment. This is implied not from the use of any particular words or by statute, but from the relationship of landlord and tenant.[74]

---

[65] Above, para.17–056.

[66] s.205(1)(ii).

[67] As in LPA 1925 s.77(3) (a provision concerned with implied covenants on a conveyance of land subject to rentcharge).

[68] LRR 2003 r.58A; Sch.1A; above, paras 7–052, 7–059.

[69] LRR 2003 Sch.1A.

[70] Such rights may be protected against a purchaser of the reversion if the lessee is in actual occupation, because such rights may then be an overriding interest: see LRA 2002 Sch.3 para.2; above, paras 7–089 et seq.

[71] Above, para.17–040.

[72] Above, para.17–138.

[73] See above, para.7–151.

[74] Above, para.19–003.

(ii) Covenants for title will also be implied if the landlord grants the lease with either full or limited title guarantee. This has already been explained.[75]

In relation to leases granted before July 1995, only the covenant for quiet enjoyment was implied.[76]

Where a lease is assigned after June 1995[77] and the disposition is made with either full or limited title guarantee, there will be imported into that assignment: **21–016**

    (i) the covenants for title imported into every disposition by such words[78]; and

    (ii) a covenant that the lease is subsisting at the time of the disposition and that there is no subsisting breach of a condition or tenant's obligation nor anything which at that time would render the lease liable to forfeiture.[79]

3. Indemnity. As regards the assignee's obligations (if any) to indemnify the assignor, it is necessary to distinguish between leases granted before 1996 and those granted thereafter. In relation to the former, the assignee may be required to execute the deed of assignment. He will as a result (and without the need for special words) covenant that he will pay the rent and observe all the covenants in the lease and will indemnify the assignor against the consequences of any breach.[80] The covenant by the assignee is explained more fully below.[81] Where a lease granted after 1995 is assigned, the assignor is released from the covenants in the lease and is not therefore liable for any default by the assignee after the assignment.[82] In consequence no indemnity covenant by the assignee is required and none is implied.[83] If the assignor enters into an authorised guarantee agreement with the landlord at the time of the assignment,[84] he has the usual rights of a surety to be recouped by the assignee (as principal debtor) should he be called upon to discharge that assignee's liability.[85]   **21–017**

---

[75] Above, para.19–018.

[76] See the sixth edition of this work at para.14–305.

[77] For the position of leases assigned before July 1995, see the sixth edition of this work at para.14–305.

[78] For these, see above, paras 7–153; 19–018.

[79] LP(MP)A 1994 s.4.

[80] LPA 1925 s.77(1)(C) and (D), and Sched.2, Pts IX and X (unregistered land); LRA 2002 Sch.12 para.20 (registered land). These provisions do not apply to mortgages.

[81] Above, para.20–043.

[82] LTCA 1995 s.5; below, para.20–088.

[83] LTCA 1995 s.14.

[84] LTCA 1995 s.16; below, para.20–089. The usual rules of suretyship apply to such guarantees: LTCA 1995 s.16(8).

[85] See, e.g. G. M. Andrews & R. Millett, *The Law of Guarantees* 5th edn (London: Sweet & Maxwell, 2008), Ch.10; J. O'Donovan & J. Phillips, *The Modern Contract of Guarantee* 2nd English edn (2008), Ch.12.

C. Precedent of a lease

21–018 Commencement and date. Parties

THIS LEASE made the 2nd day of January, 2011, between William Woodfall of No. 15 Cherry Street Wolstenholme in the County of Sussex solicitor (hereinafter called "the landlord") of the one part and Thomas Platt of No. 4 Stewart Court Brickdale in the County of Gloucester bookseller (hereinafter called "the tenant") of the other part

Testatum

WITNESSETH as follows:—

Demise

1. The landlord hereby demises unto the tenant ALL THAT messuage or dwelling-house with the yard gardens offices and outbuildings thereto belonging known as 32, Lincoln's Inn Fields, London WC2, which premises for purposes of identification and not of limitation are coloured pink on the plan annexed to these presents

Habendum

TO HOLD the same unto the tenant from the 25th day of December, 2010, for the term of five year

Reddendum

PAYING therefor the net yearly rent of £10,000 clear of all deductions (except only such as the tenant may by law be entitled to make notwithstanding any agreement to the contrary) by equal quarterly instalments commencing on the 25th day of March next and thereafter on the usual quarter days.

Tenant's covenants

2. The tenant hereby covenants with the landlord as follows:—

 (i) To pay the rent hereby reserved on the days hereinbefore mentioned.

 (ii) To pay all rates taxes assessments charges and outgoings now or hereafter legally payable in respect of the property hereby demised (save only as aforesaid) whether payable by the owner or occupier thereof.

[*Then follow other covenants by the tenant, e.g. to repair, to insure, not to assign, underlet or part with possession of the premises.*]

Landlord's covenants

3. The landlord hereby covenants with the tenant as follows:—

 (i) That the tenant paying the rent hereby reserved and observing and performing the covenants on his part herein contained shall peaceably hold and enjoy the premises hereby demised during the said term without any interruption or disturbance[86] by the landlord or any person rightfully claiming under or in trust for him.

---

[86] The word "lawful" is often (but inaccurately) inserted before "interruption or disturbance", It does not absolve the landlord from unlawful disturbance of the tenant (*Crosse v Young* (1685) 1 Show.K.B. 425; *Lloyd v Tomkies* (1787) 1 T.R. 671), and it merely duplicates "rightfully claiming" in the case of third parties.

[*Then follow any other covenants by the landlord, e.g. to execute certain classes of repairs or improvements, or to renew the lease at the tenant's request.*]

21–19

Provisos

4. PROVIDED ALWAYS and it is hereby expressly agreed and declared as follows:—

Forfeiture clause

(i) that if the rent hereby reserved or any part thereof shall remain unpaid for twenty-one days after becoming payable (whether formally demanded or not) or if any covenant on the part of the tenant herein contained shall not be performed or observed or if the tenant shall become bankrupt or enter into any composition with his creditors or suffer any distress or execution upon his goods then and in any of the said cases it shall be lawful for the landlord at any time thereafter to re-enter upon the demised premises or any part thereof in the name of the whole and thereupon this demise shall absolutely determine.

[*Then follow any other provisos, e.g. that the tenant may determine the lease by giving notice.*]

SIGNED AS A DEED etc.

(signatures and witnesses)

The PLAN above referred to.

This short form of lease may be compared with the brief precedent of a transfer in fee simple of registered land given earlier.[87]

Subject to any written agreement to the contrary,[88] no party to a lease or tenancy agreement is now liable to pay any legal costs of any other party.[89] Formerly the tenant was usually liable for the costs of both parties, save that the landlord bore the cost of his counterpart (i.e. duplicate) if he had one.[90] The normal practice is for the landlord to take a counterpart executed by the tenant, in order to facilitate the enforcement of the tenant's covenants.

21–021

---

[87] Above, para.7–149.
[88] Which in practice there usually is nowadays.
[89] Costs of Leases Act 1958.
[90] Foa, L.T. 339.

SECURITY OF TENURE

22–001 Chapters 17 to 20 have dealt with the general law of landlord and tenant. It should not be assumed, however, that the general law can be applied indiscriminately across all property sectors. Since the late 19th century, Parliament has made special statutory provision regulating specific kinds of tenancy, e.g. tenancies of houses and flats, tenancies of shops and offices, and tenancies of farms and farmland. The objective of such provisions has been primarily paternalistic, and they have therefore operated to protect tenants from their landlords, on the assumption that their respective bargaining positions give rise to a risk of injustice. The legal matrix that has developed is extremely complex. Its main effect has been to control rents and to restrict the circumstances in which landlords may recover possession of the property let. Statute tends to confer a status upon the parties to a tenancy (or, sometimes, a licence) which satisfies certain conditions and as a result to impose a regulatory regime which may depart very significantly from the actual terms of the tenancy. Not only is the law complicated, it is also highly susceptible to change in what has been viewed (particularly with regard to residential tenancies) as an area that is acutely politically volatile. This chapter gives an overview of the statutory codes that currently operate in relation to the three most important kinds of tenancy: business tenancies, agricultural tenancies, and residential tenancies. To make sense of the current position, it is necessary to understand to some extent the history of statutory regulation in each area. But before we consider the specific provisions dealing with these three main kinds of tenancy, we should deal with certain statutory restrictions on the landlord's common law right to recover possession when a lease or tenancy comes to an end.

Section 1. Statutory restrictions on the recovery of possession

22–002   *(a) Forcible entry.* Under the Criminal Law Act 1977 it is a criminal offence for any person without lawful authority to use or threaten violence for the purpose of securing entry into any premises for himself or any other person, if he knows that someone present on the premises is opposed to the entry.

Having the right to possession or occupation is not lawful authority for this purpose.[1] However, if the person is (or is acting on behalf of) a displaced residential occupier or a protected intending occupier, he shall not be guilty of such an offence.[2] This provision applies to all kinds of property; it is not restricted in its application to dwelling-houses.

(b) Dwellings. The Protection from Eviction Act 1977[3] restricts the recov-   **22–003** ery of possession of premises which have been let as dwellings[4] and which are neither statutorily protected[5] nor excluded tenancies.[6] This protection extends to licences, save those specifically excluded by the Act.[7] When such a tenancy[8] or licence comes to an end but any person lawfully residing in the premises continues to reside in any part of them, it is unlawful for the person entitled to possession to enforce his right of possession otherwise than by proceedings in the county court or, if it has no jurisdiction, the High Court.[9] If the landlord or licensor fails to comply with the requirements of the Act, he may not only be guilty of the offence[10] he may also be liable in the statutory tort of unlawful eviction.[11] The court has some discretion in fixing the date for

---

[1] CLA 1977 ss.6, 12(3). s.13 abolished the common law offences of forcible entry and forcible detainer and repealed the Forcible Entry Acts 1381–1623.

[2] CLA 1977 s.6(1A), inserted by Criminal Justice and Public Order Act 1994 s.72(2). For definitions, see CLA 1977 ss.12, 12A, latter as inserted by Criminal Justice and Public Order Act 1994 s.74.

[3] s.3, as amended by (inter alia) HA 1980 and HA 1988. It has been held to be compatible with Art.8 ECHR: *R (Coombes) v Secretary of State for Communities & Local Government* [2010] EWHC 666 (Admin), [2010] 2 All E.R. 940.

[4] This has been interpreted as meaning "wholly or partly as a dwelling", so that mixed-use premises fall within the protection of the statute: *Patel v Pirabakaran* [2006] EWCA Civ 685; [2006] 1 W.L.R. 3112 (shop with flat above held subject to PEA 1977 s.2), distinguishing *National Trust v Knipe* [1998] 1 W.L.R. 230.

[5] PEA 1977 s.8. The following are "statutorily protected" for these purposes: a protected tenancy under the Rent Act 1977 (but not a statutory tenancy: see *Haniff v Robinson* [1993] Q.B. 419 at 426); an assured tenancy or assured agricultural occupancy under the Housing Act 1988; a protected occupancy or statutory tenancy under the Rent (Agriculture) Act 1976; a tenancy of an agricultural holding under the Agricultural Holdings Act 1986; a farm business tenancy under the Agricultural Tenancies Act 1995; a business tenancy under Part II of the Landlord and Tenant Act 1954; and a long residential tenancy under Part I of the Landlord and Tenant Act 1954 or Schedule 10 to the Local Government and Housing Act 1989. They are excluded because the occupier already enjoys statutory protection, and further protection is therefore unnecessary: see *Patel v Pirabakaran*, above, at [15].

[6] For such tenancies, see PEA 1977 s.3A (inserted by HA 1988 s.31). The long list includes tenancies of accommodation shared with the landlord or a member of his family as his or their only or principal home, holiday lettings and property let otherwise than for money or money's worth. See *West Wiltshire DC v Snelgrove* (1997) 30 H.L.R. 57.

[7] PEA 1977 s.3(2B) (inserted by HA 1988 s.30). Licences are excluded: (i) on the same ground as are tenancies; and (ii) if they confer rights of occupation in hostels provided by certain bodies: PEA 1977 s.3A.

[8] A service occupancy is treated as a tenancy for these purposes: PEA 1977 s.8(2).

[9] PEA 1977 ss.3(1), 9(1). Even if the landlord obtains an order for possession from the court, he cannot peaceably re-enter. The order must be executed by the bailiff: *Haniff v Robinson*, above.

[10] PEA 1977 s.1(2); above, para.19–013.

[11] HA 1988 s.27; above, para.19–009. See e.g. *Haniff v Robinson*, above.

the delivery up of possession.[12] The Act does not, however, affect the jurisdiction of the High Court in proceedings to enforce forfeiture of a lease or a mortgagee's right to possession where the tenancy does not bind him.[13] The Act makes special provision for the court to suspend the execution of any order for possession of an agricultural "tied dwelling", i.e. a dwelling occupied by an agricultural worker under the terms of his employment.[14]

Section 2. Business Tenancies

22–004 Business premises have been protected since the enactment of the Landlord and Tenant Act 1927.[15] This gave the tenant the right to a new lease (or compensation in lieu) provided he could establish that by reason of the carrying on of a business at the premises for not less than five years, goodwill had become attached to them whereby they could be let at a higher rent than they would otherwise have realised.[16] It was essential to show goodwill which remained adherent to the premises after the tenant had gone,[17] a formidably difficult task. Some tenancies of shops were thus protected, but tenancies of professional premises were outside the provisions altogether. These relatively ineffectual provisions were replaced by the much more far-reaching and well-drafted[18] terms of Pt II of the Landlord and Tenant Act 1954, conferring security of tenure on those business tenants to whom it applies.[19] The business tenant has the statutory right to apply for a new tenancy in the event of termination by the landlord. This has been held to comprise a possession for the purposes of Art.1 of the First Protocol to the European Convention on Human Rights; and further that the procedural requirements imposed by Pt II of the 1954 Act on its exercise are not an unjustified deprivation of that right.[20] The business tenant continues to enjoy the closely restricted right to claim compensation for improvements subject to certain conditions, which was introduced by the Landlord and Tenant Act 1927.[21]

---

[12] *McPhail v Persons Unknown* [1973] Ch. 447 at 459, 460.

[13] PEA s.9(3) (reversing the effect of *Borzak v Ahmed* [1965] 2 Q.B. 320, a case on forfeiture); and see *Bolton BS v Cobb* [1966] 1 W.L.R. 1 (tenancy not binding on mortgagee; for such tenancies, see below, para.25–080).

[14] PEA 1977 s.4. See, e.g. *Crane v Morris* [1965] 1 W.L.R. 1104.

[15] They were protected for nearly a year under the Rent Acts: Increase of Rent and Mortgage Interest (Restrictions) Act 1920 s.13. For the history of the statutory regulation of business tenancies, see Haley, (1999) 19 L.S. 207.

[16] Landlord and Tenant Act 1927 ss.4 and 5.

[17] See, e.g. *Whiteman Smith Motor Co Ltd v Chaplin* [1934] 2 K.B. 35.

[18] See *Scholl Mfg Co Ltd v Clifton (Slim-Line) Ltd* [1967] Ch. 41 at 49.

[19] The Act has been substantially amended twice, by the Law of Property Act 1969 and by the Regulatory Reform (Business Tenancies) (England and Wales) Order 2003 (SI 2003/3096). Each of these measures gave effect to recommendations made by the Law Commission (see Law Com No.17 and Law Com No.208 respectively) The amendments made to the 1954 Act by the 2003 Order apply where a landlord gives statutory notice of termination, or the tenant requests a new tenancy, on or after June 1, 2004 (SI 2003/3096 art.29(1)).

[20] *Pennycook v Shaws (EAL) Ltd* [2004] EWCA Civ 100; [2004] Ch. 296.

[21] Below, para.22–026.

1. Tenancies within Pt II of the Landlord and Tenant Act 1954. Part II 22–005
applies to:

> "any tenancy where the property comprised in the tenancy is or includes
> premises which are occupied by the tenant and are so occupied for the
> purposes of a business carried on by him or for those and other
> purposes".[22]

These terms are widely defined. "'Business' includes a trade, profession or
employment, and includes any activity carried on by a body of persons,
whether corporate or unincorporate."[23] Thus shops, offices, factories, clubs,[24]
hospitals,[25] surgeries, laboratories, schools and government offices[26] are all
included, but not a residence where the tenant carries on a voluntary Sunday
school,[27] or takes in a few lodgers,[28] nor a site used for dumping waste
materials from the tenant's shops during reconstruction.[29] "Premises" can
include bare land, such as a public open space,[30] or gallops for training
racehorses,[31] and possibly also an incorporeal hereditament.[32] Occupation
must be "by the tenant". However, occupation by a company which the tenant
controls will suffice; so too, where the tenant is a company, will occupation by
an individual who controls the company.[33] The tenant may occupy premises
by means of those who are genuinely his servants.[34] A tenant of a block of
flats who sub-lets the flats does not thereafter "occupy" the premises for
business purposes, unless the degree of his control and provision of services

---

[22] LTA 1954 s.23(1). On insignificant business use, see *Cheryl Investments Ltd v Saldanha*
[1978] 1 W.L.R. 1329; *Gurton v Parrott* [1991] 1 E.G.L.R. 98; *Wright v Mortimer* (1996) 28
H.L.R. 719; cf. *Broadway Investments Hackney Ltd v Grant* [2006] EWCA Civ 1709; [2007]
H.L.R. 23.

[23] LTA 1954 s.23(2). For business user in breach of a prohibition in the tenancy, see LTA 1954
s.23(4); *Bell v Alfred Franks & Bartlett Co Ltd* [1980] 1 W.L.R. 340; *Trustees of the Methodist
Schools Trust Deed v O'Leary* (1992) 66 P. & C.R. 364.

[24] *Addiscombe Garden Estates Ltd v Crabbe* [1958] 1 Q.B. 513 (lawn tennis club).

[25] *Hills (Patents) Ltd v University College Hospital Board of Governors* [1956] 1 Q.B. 90;
Groveside Properties Ltd v Westminster Medical School (1984) 47 P. & C.R. 507 (flats provided
for hospital's medical students).

[26] *Town Investments Ltd v Department of the Environment* [1978] A.C. 359.

[27] *Abernethie v A, M. & J. Kleiman Ltd* [1970] 1 Q.B. 10.

[28] *Lewis v Weldcrest Ltd* [1978] 1 W.L.R. 1107.

[29] *Hillil Property and Investment Co Ltd v Naraine Pharmacy Ltd* (1979) 39 P. & C.R. 67.

[30] *Wandsworth LBC v Singh* (1991) 62 P. & C.R. 219.

[31] *Bracey v Read* [1963] Ch. 88.

[32] See *Pointon York Group Ltd v Poulton* [2006] EWCA Civ 1001; [2007] 1 P. & C.R. 6; where
the Court of Appeal considered that a right to park could comprise "premises", and suggested that
the test was whether the right in question was capable of occupation. cf. *Land Reclamation Co
Ltd v Basildon District Council* [1979] 1 W.L.R. 767 (distinguished on basis that a right of way
was not "capable of occupation"). The better distinction may be that between a tenancy of land
with an easement ancillary to the grant of the tenancy, and a tenancy of an easement per se.

[33] LTA 1954 ss.23(1A), (1B), inserted by SI 2003/3096 art.13. For test of control, see LTA 1954
s.46(2), inserted by SI 2003/3096 art.17. Where the tenancy is held on trust, occupation by all or
any of the beneficiaries under the trust will be treated as equivalent to that of the tenant: LTA 1954
s.41; *Frish Ltd v Barclays Bank Ltd* [1955] 2 Q.B. 541; *Trustees of the Methodist Schools Trust
Deed v O'Leary* (1992) 66 P. & C.R. 364 at 376.

[34] *Teasdale v Walker* [1958] 1 W.L.R. 1076; cf. *Chapman v Freeman* [1978] 1 W.L.R. 1298.

suffices to constitute occupation.[35] An intention to continue occupying the premises suffices for a tenant who is physically absent owing to events over which he has no control,[36] but not for the tenant who voluntarily absents himself or ceases trading.[37] "Tenancy" is widely defined.[38] It includes any tenancy created by a tenancy agreement,[39] a tenancy by estoppel,[40] but not a tenancy at will.[41] It is immaterial that the tenancy was granted in breach of covenant.[42] In deciding whether a written agreement between commercial parties comprises a tenancy, the courts tend to pay greater regard to the terminology they have used than would be the case in the residential context.[43]

22–006   **2. Exceptions.** Certain tenancies are expressly excluded from Pt II of the Act. Tenancies of licensed premises (i.e. public houses and similar establishment), many of which were initially excluded, were brought within its scope in 1992.[44] The remaining exceptions are as follows.[45]

  (a) Tenancies of agricultural holdings.[46]

  (b) Farm business tenancies.[47]

  (c) Mining leases.[48]

  (d) Service tenancies.[49] These are tenancies granted by reason of the tenant holding an office, appointment or employment, and ending or terminable with it. Unless the tenancy was granted prior to the commencement of the Act, it must have been granted by a written instrument which expressed the purpose for which the tenancy was granted.

---

[35] *Bagettes Ltd v G.P. Estates Ltd* [1956] Ch. 290; cf. *Lee-Verhulst (Investments) Ltd v Harwood Trust* [1973] Q.B. 204. If the sub-tenant is in "occupation" himself, the tenant cannot also be in occupation: *Graysim Holdings Ltd v P. & O. Property Holdings Ltd* [1996] A.C. 329.

[36] *Morrisons Holdings Ltd v Manders Property (Wolverhampton) Ltd* [1976] 1 W.L.R. 533 (severe fire damage); cf. *Demetriou v Robert Andrews (Estate Agencies) Ltd* (1990) 62 P. & C.R. 536 (premises uninhabitable due to tenant's failure to repair).

[37] *Pulleng v Curran* (1980) 44 P. & C.R. 58; *Aspinall Finance Ltd v Viscount Chelsea* [1989] 1 E.G.L.R. 102.

[38] LTA 1954 s.69(1).

[39] ibid.

[40] *Bell v General Accident Fire & Life Assurance Corporation Ltd* [1998] 1 E.G.L.R. 69.

[41] *Wheeler v Mercer* [1957] A.C. 416; *Hagee (London) Ltd v A. B. Erikson and Larsen* [1976] Q.B. 209; *Javad v Aqil* [1991] 1 W.L.R. 1007.

[42] *D'Silva v Lister House Development Ltd* [1971] Ch. 17; *Brimex Ltd v Begum* [2007] EWHC 3498 (Ch); [2009] L. & T.R. 21.

[43] See above, para.17–025.

[44] With effect from July 11, 1992: Landlord and Tenant (Licensed Premises) Act 1990, repealing LTA 1954 s.43(1)(d).

[45] LTA 1954 s.43, as amended (inter alia) by LPA 1969 s.12.

[46] LTA 1954 s.43(1)(a), and see Agricultural Holdings Act 1986: below, para.22–035.

[47] LTA 1954 s.43(1)(aa), added by Agricultural Tenancies Act 1995 s.40, Sch.1 para.10(6): see below, para.22–028.

[48] LTA 1954 s.43(1)(b); as defined in LTA 1927 s.25(1): LTA 1954 s.46(1).

[49] LTA 1954 s.43(2).

(e) Short tenancies. This means any tenancy granted for a term certain not exceeding six months unless it contains provisions for renewing the term or extending it beyond six months from the commencement, or the tenant and any predecessor in his business have been in occupation for more than 12 months in total.[50]

3. Contracting out.[51] The general rule is that the landlord and tenant **22–007** cannot contract out of the security of tenure provisions contained in Pt II of the 1954 Act. Any agreement purporting to preclude the tenant from exercising his statutory rights, or providing for the termination or surrender of the tenancy or for the imposition of any penalty or disability on the tenant in that event, is therefore prima facie void.[52] However, the rule is subject to a major exception where the landlord grants a tenancy for a term of years certain.[53] In such a case, the parties may come to an agreement, before the tenancy is entered into, that security of tenure be excluded in relation to that tenancy.[54] Prior to the 2004 reforms, such an agreement would only be effective if, before the tenancy was entered into, the sanction of the court was obtained.[55] But it is now sufficient for the landlord to serve a statutory notice on the tenant, and to satisfy a number of other statutory requirements regarding acknowledgement of the notice by the tenant.[56] This relatively free availability of contracting out inevitably means that a large number of business tenants no longer enjoy the security provided by Pt II of the 1954 Act.

4. Security of tenure. Security of tenure is conferred by the simple **22–008** provision that a tenancy within Pt II "shall not come to an end unless terminated in accordance with the provisions of this Part of this Act".[57] An

---

[50] LTA 1954 s.43(3); *Cricket Ltd v Shaftesbury Plc* [1999] 3 All E.R. 283.

[51] Haley [2008] Conv. 281.

[52] LTA 1954 s.38; *Joseph v Joseph* [1967] 1 Ch. 78; *Ultimate Leisure Ltd v Tindle* [2007] EWCA Civ 1241; [2008] 1 P. & C.R. DG11.

[53] The presence of a break clause does not prevent the tenancy from being "for a term of years certain": *Receiver for the Metropolitan Police District v Palacegate Properties Ltd* [2001] Ch. 131. However, where a term is defined so as expressly to include any period of holding over or extension (by statute or otherwise), it is not a term of years certain: *Newham LBC v Thomas-van Staden* [2008] EWCA Civ 1414; [2009] L. & T.R. 5; see Colby [2009] L. & T. Rev. 55. An agreement which is not "for a term of years certain" will be ineffective, and the tenancy will therefore be within the security of tenure provisions: see e.g. *Nicholls v Kinsey* [1994] Q.B. 600.

[54] Technically, this does not amount to contracting out of the entirety of Pt II of the 1954 Act, but only out of ss.24 to 28 inclusive. For the implications of this, see Woodfall, 22.039.

[55] LTA 1954 s.38(4), as amended by LPA 1969 s.5. The court invariably approved the agreement to contract out: "when it is made by business people, properly advised by their lawyers. The court has no materials on which to refuse it": *Hagee (London) Ltd v A.B. Erikson and Larsen* [1976] Q.B. 209 at 215, per Lord Denning M.R.

[56] LTA 1954 s.38A(1), as inserted by SI 2003/3096 art.22: for notice and requirements, see SI 2003/3096 Schs 1 and 2; *Chiltern Railway Co Ltd v Patel* [2008] EWCA Civ 178; [2008] 2 P. & C.R. 12. The parties may also agree a surrender: LTA 1954 s.38A(2), as inserted by SI 2003/3096 art.22: and see SI 2003/3096 Schs 3 and 4.

[57] LTA 1954 s.24(1).

ordinary notice to quit given by the landlord thus has no effect, and a tenancy for a fixed term will continue indefinitely after the expiration of the term. A tenancy may still be determined by a notice to quit given by the tenant, or by a surrender or forfeiture, or by the forfeiture of a superior tenancy,[58] but in all other cases the special machinery of the Act must be used. "Landlord" is for these purposes defined as the next immediate reversioner who for the time being has either the fee simple or a tenancy which will not come to an end within 14 months.[59] Where a business tenancy is assigned, the tenancy becomes that of the assignee.[60] The statutory machinery permits an application for a new tenancy to be made to the court in two circumstances:

(i) where the landlord has served a statutory notice determining the current tenancy; or

(ii) where the tenant has made a request for a new tenancy.

22–009   *(a) Determination by landlord.* The landlord may determine the tenancy by giving not less than six[61] nor more than 12 months' notice in the statutory form (universally referred to as a "s.25 notice"),[62] to expire not earlier than the date[63] when, apart from the Act, the tenancy could have been determined by notice to quit, or would have expired.[64] The date of expiration of the s.25 notice thus need not be an anniversary or the end of a complete period of the

---

[58] LTA 1954 s.24(2), as amended by SI 2003/3096 art.28(2), Sch.6 para.1. A tenant's notice to quit is ineffective if given or executed in the first month of occupation by the tenant: LTA 1954 s.27(1). See also *Meadows v Clerical Medical and General Life Assurance Society* [1981] Ch. 70 (no determination while claim for relief against forfeiture subsists); *Cadogan v Dimovic* [1984] 1 W.L.R. 609; *Hill v Griffin* [1987] 1 E.G.L.R. 81.

[59] LTA 1954 s.44; *Bowes-Lyon v Green* [1963] A.C. 420; *Shelley v United Artists Corp* (1989) 60 P. & C.R. 241. For special provisions for joint tenancies, see s.41A, added by LPA 1969 s.9.

[60] *City of London Corp v Fell* [1993] Q.B. 589, CA, at 604. This means that, even if the tenancy pre-dates the L & TCA 1995, the original tenant will not be liable for rent, or under the covenants, into the continuation period unless express contrary provision was made: *City of London Corp v Fell* [1994] 1 A.C. 458, HL. For an example of contrary provision, see consideration of *Herbert Duncan Ltd v Cluttons* appeal in *City of London Corp v Fell* [1993] Q.B. 589 at 605 et seq. If the tenancy was granted on or after January 1, 1996, the L & TCA 1995 will apply to protect the original tenant further: see above, para.20–085.

[61] *Hogg Bullimore & Co v Co-operative Insurance Society Ltd* (1984) 50 P. & C.R. 105.

[62] SI 2004/1005 Sch.1 Forms 1 and 2. The Order provides that forms "substantially to the like effect" as the form prescribed may be used: SI 2004/1005 r.2(2). The name of the landlord must be correctly stated: *Morrow v Nadeem* [1986] 1 W.L.R. 1381; *Pearson v Alyo* [1990] 1 E.G.L.R. 114 (joint landlords). The notice must relate to the whole of the land comprised in the tenancy: *Southport Old Links Ltd v Naylor* [1985] 1 E.G.L.R. 66; *EDF Energy Networks (EPW) Ltd v BOH Ltd* [2009] EWHC 3193 (Ch); [2010] 2 P. & C.R. 3.

[63] Errors of date will be benevolently construed: *Mannai Investment Co Ltd v Eagle Star Life Assurance Co Ltd* [1997] A.C. 749, applied to LTA 1954 Pt II, in *Garston v Scottish Widows Fund & Life Assurance Society* [1998] 1 W.L.R. 1583. For the effect of serving a valid notice following service of an invalid notice, see *Barclays Bank Plc v Bee* [2001] EWCA Civ 1126; [2002] 1 W.L.R. 332.

[64] LTA 1954 s.25; cf. *Lewis v M.T.C. (Cars) Ltd* [1975] 1 W.L.R. 457.

tenancy; it merely must not be too early.[65] On receiving such a notice, the tenant may claim a new tenancy by making an application to the court.[66] Such an application must be made before the end of the period specified in the landlord's notice, subject to the parties agreeing to extend time before that period expires.[67]

(b) Request for new tenancy. If a tenant does not wish to leave the premises, but seeks a new tenancy in place of his existing one, he may serve on the landlord a request for a new tenancy in the statutory form.[68] The tenant may only make such a request where his existing tenancy is either a term certain exceeding a year, or a tenancy for a term certain and thereafter from year to year.[69] A tenant under an ordinary periodic tenancy cannot therefore make a request for a new tenancy, although he may claim a new tenancy if the landlord initiates the process by serving a s.25 notice on him.[70] This must specify a date for the commencement of the new tenancy not less than six nor more than 12 months ahead, and not earlier than the date on which the existing tenancy would expire or could be determined.[71]

22–010

(c) Application to court. When the landlord has served a s.25 notice, or the tenant has made a request for a new tenancy, either party may make application to the court for an order granting a new tenancy.[72] Where the landlord has served a s.25 notice, application to court can be made at once. However, where the tenant has made a request for a new tenancy, the court shall not entertain an application which is made earlier than two months after the request was made.[73] This is to allow the landlord to give formal notice of opposition to the tenant.[74] Once the landlord has given such notice, the court may entertain an application by the tenant for a new tenancy even though it is within two months of the request being made.[75]

22–011

---

[65] *Commercial Properties Ltd v Wood* [1968] 1 Q.B. 15.

[66] LTA 1954 s.24. The tenant is not required to serve a counter-notice on the landlord (as was formerly the case) if the landlord's notice is served on or after June 1, 2004.

[67] LTA 1954 ss.29A and 29B, inserted by SI 2003/3096 art.10.

[68] LTA 1954 s.26(2); SI 2004/1005 Sch.1 Form 3.

[69] LTA 1954 s.26(1).

[70] Indeed, where the landlord has served a notice under s.25, the tenant cannot make a s.26 request. Nor can a tenant make such a request once he has served notice on the landlord under s.27: see below, para.22–013. See generally LTA 1954 s.26(4).

[71] LTA 1954 s.26(2). Where a tenancy is granted for a term of years (and not for a term of years and thereafter from year to year), the tenant cannot seek a new tenancy commencing on a date earlier than the date on which the tenancy expires by effluxion of time: *Garston v Scottish Widows Fund & Life Assurance Society* [1998] 1 W.L.R. 1583.

[72] LTA 1954 s.24(1). The landlord may decide to seek a new tenancy where the terms of the current tenancy (e.g. the rent payable) are less favourable than the terms obtainable on the open market. The tenant may decide to do so for similar reasons, or in order to obtain the relative comfort of a fixed term tenancy in place of a continuation tenancy which is terminable by the landlord (albeit subject to the statutory regime).

[73] LTA 1954 s.29A(3)

[74] LTA 1954 s.26(6).

[75] LTA 1954 s.29A(3).

22–012   *(d) Time limits.* Both parties must ensure that they abide by the strict time limits imposed by statute. The court shall not entertain an application if it is made after the period[76]:

> (i) where a s.25 notice has been served, ending with the date specified in the notice (*sc.* as the date of termination of the tenancy); or

> (ii) where the tenant has made a request for a new tenancy, ending immediately before the date specified in the request (*sc.* as the commencement date of the new tenancy).

22–013   *(e) Determination by the tenant.* A tenant who wishes to leave the premises may determine the tenancy by an ordinary notice to quit, as at common law,[77] or, if the tenancy is for a fixed term, by not less than three months' notice in writing to expire at the end of the term or, where the tenancy is being continued by statute, afterwards.[78] Where the tenant gives up occupation on or before expiry of a fixed term, Pt II of the 1954 Act will cease to apply and no statutory continuation will occur.[79]

22–014   **5. Opposition to a new tenancy.** When application is made under s.24, the court is bound to grant a new tenancy unless the landlord establishes one or more of the statutory grounds of opposition.[80] The landlord may only rely on such grounds as are stated (or indicated[81]) in a notice to determine the tenancy given by him or his predecessor in title,[82] or in a notice opposing the grant of a new tenancy served on the tenant within two months of receiving his request.[83] The seven grounds are as follows.[84]

22–015   *(a) Disrepair.* The tenant ought not to be granted a new tenancy in view of the state of repair of the "holding" (i.e. the premises let, excluding any part not occupied by the tenant or a service tenant of his[85]) due to the tenant's failure to comply with his repairing obligations.

---

[76] LTA 1954 s.29A, inserted by SI 2003/3096 art.10. The time limits are capable of extension by the parties' agreement provided they have not expired: LTA 1954 s.29B, inserted by SI 2003/3096 art.10

[77] LTA 1954 s.24(2); but see above, fn.58.

[78] LTA 1954 s.27.

[79] *Esselte AB v Pearl Assurance plc* [1997] 1 W.L.R. 891, not following *Long Acre Securities Ltd v Electro Acoustic Industries Ltd* (1989) 61 P. & C.R. 177. See further *Surrey v Single Horse Properties Ltd* [2002] EWCA Civ 367; [2002] 1 W.L.R. 2106 (to the same effect even though the tenant had served a counter-notice, and applied for a new tenancy, before going out of occupation.)

[80] LTA 1954 s.29, as substituted by SI 2003/3096 art.5.

[81] *Bolton's (House Furnishers) Ltd v Oppenheim* [1959] 1 W.L.R. 913.

[82] LTA 1954 ss.25(6), (7); *A. D. Wimbush & Son Ltd v Franmills Properties Ltd* [1961] Ch. 419; *Marks v British Waterways Board* [1963] 1 W.L.R. 1008.

[83] LTA 1954 s.26(6).

[84] LTA 1954 s.30(1).

[85] LTA 1954 s.23(3).

(b) Delay in paying rent. The tenant ought not to be granted a new tenancy **22–016** in view of his persistent delay in paying the rent.[86]

(c) Breach of obligation. The tenant ought not to be granted a new tenancy **22–017** in view of other substantial breaches by him of his obligations under the tenancy, or for any other reason connected with his use or management of the holding.[87]

(d) Alternative accommodation. The landlord has offered and is willing to **22–018** provide or secure the provision of suitable alternative accommodation on reasonable terms.

(e) Premises more valuable as a whole. The premises are part of larger **22–019** premises held by the landlord under a tenancy and the tenant ought not to be granted a new tenancy because the landlord could obtain a substantially greater rent for the property as a whole than for the parts separately.

(f) Demolition or reconstruction. "On the termination of the current ten- **22–020** ancy[88] the landlord intends to demolish or reconstruct[89] the premises comprised in the holding or a substantial part[90] of those premises or to carry out substantial work of construction[91] on the holding or part thereof and that he could not reasonably do so without obtaining possession of the holding."[92] The landlord cannot establish this ground if he has a contractual right to enter and do the intended work,[93] or if the tenant is willing to enable the landlord to carry out the intended work[94] (without interfering with the tenant's business to a substantial extent or for a substantial time)[95] by including such right in the new tenancy or by accepting a new tenancy of only part of the holding.[96]

---

[86] The court has a discretion: see, e.g. *Betty's Cafés Ltd v Phillips Furnishing Stores Ltd* [1957] Ch. 67 at 82; *Hurstfell Ltd v Leicester Square Property Co Ltd* [1988] 2 E.G.L.R. 105; *Hazel v Akhtar* [2002] 1 E.G.L.R. 45.

[87] This may include conduct during the tenancy, and also any intention to use the premises illegally in the future: *Eichner v Midland Bank Executor & Trustee Co Ltd* [1970] 1 W.L.R. 1120; *Turner & Bell v Searles (Stanford-le-Hope) Ltd* (1977) 33 P. & C.R. 208; *Fowles v Heathrow Airport Ltd* [2008] EWCA Civ 1270; [2009] 1 P. & C.R. DG8. While breach of covenant is not essential, there must be some element of fault or mismanagement on the part of the tenant: *John Kay Ltd v Kay* [1952] 2 Q.B. 258 at 272.

[88] *Edwards v Thompson* (1990) 60 P. & C.R. 222.

[89] *Percy E. Cadle Ltd v Jacmarch Properties Ltd* [1957] 1 Q.B. 323; *Joel v Swaddle* [1957] 1 W.L.R. 1094; *Romulus Trading Company Ltd v Trustees of Henry Smith's Charity* (1989) 60 P. & C.R. 62; *Pumperninks of Piccadilly Ltd v Land Securities Plc* [2002] EWCA Civ 621; [2002] Ch. 332; *Wessex Reserve Forces & Cadets Association v White* [2005] EWCA Civ 1774; [2006] P. & C.R. 3.

[90] *Bewlay (Tobacconists) Ltd v British Bata Shoe Co Ltd* [1959] 1 W.L.R. 45.

[91] *Botterill v Bedfordshire CC* [1985] 1 E.G.L.R. 82.

[92] i.e. as of right, and not merely by the tenant's permission: *Whittingham v Davies* [1962] 1 W.L.R. 142.

[93] *Heath v Drown* [1973] A.C. 498; *Pumperninks of Piccadilly Ltd v Land Securities Plc* [2002] EWCA Civ 621; [2002] Ch. 332.

[94] *Decca Navigator Co Ltd v G.L.C.* [1974] 1 W.L.R. 748.

[95] These phrases are to be read conjunctively: *Cerex Jewels Ltd v Peachey Property Corporation Plc* [1986] 2 E.G.L.R. 65.

[96] LTA 1954 s.31A, added by LPA 1969 s.7; *Redfern v Reeves* (1978) 37 P. & C.R. 364.

Provided that the landlord retains control of the demolition or reconstruction, it does not matter that it is carried out by some other person, e.g. by employees, independent contractors, or even by a new tenant on his behalf.[97]

22–021   *(g) Own occupation.* "On the termination of the current tenancy the landlord intends to occupy the holding[98] for the purposes, or partly for the purposes, of a business to be carried on by him therein, or as his residence." The landlord may intend to occupy the premises vicariously,[99] or to share occupation with another.[100] Where the landlord controls a company, the intention to occupy may be that of the landlord or of the company; and where the landlord is a company which is controlled by another person, the intention may be that of the landlord or that person.[101] But this ground is not available to a landlord whose interest[102] was purchased[103] or created less than five years before the termination of the current tenancy.[104] Although there is no requirement that the landlord intends to occupy for any particular length of time, there must be some substance in the intended occupation for the purpose of carrying on the landlord's business or as his residence; it follows that the occupation must be "more than short term".[105]

22–022   **6. Intention.** The last two grounds, (f) and (g), both depend on what the landlord "intends". Proof of such intention requires that at the date of the hearing[106] there should be not a mere hope or aspiration, or an exploration of possibilities, but a genuine, firm and settled intention, not likely to be changed,[107] to do something which the landlord has a reasonable prospect of

---

[97] *Gilmour Caterers Ltd v St Bartholomew's Hospital Governors* [1956] 1 Q.B. 387; *Spook Erection Ltd v British Railways Board* [1988] 1 E.G.L.R. 76; *Turner v Wandsworth LBC* (1994) 69 P. & C.R. 433.

[98] *Method Development Ltd v Jones* [1971] 1 W.L.R. 168; *Cam Gears Ltd v Cunningham* [1981] 1 W.L.R. 1011; *Leathwoods v Total Oil Great Britain Ltd* (1985) 51 P. & C.R. 20; *J. W. Thornton Ltd v Blacks Leisure Group Plc* [1986] 2 E.G.L.R. 61; cf. *Nursey v P. Currie (Dartford) Ltd* [1959] 1 W.L.R. 273.

[99] *Teesside Indoor Bowls Ltd v Stockton-on-Tees BC* [1990] 2 E.G.L.R. 87; cf. *Zafiris v Liu* [2005] EWCA Civ 1698; [2006] 1 P. & C.R. 26 (intended business to be carried on by tenant's wife).

[100] *Willis v Association of Universities of the British Commonwealth* [1965] 1 Q.B. 140.

[101] LTA 1954 ss.30(1A), (1B) and (2A), inserted by SI 2003/3096 art.14. For groups of companies, see LTA 1954 s.42(3).

[102] *Artemiou v Procopiou* [1966] 1 Q.B. 878.

[103] *H. L. Bolton (Engineering) Co Ltd v T. J. Graham & Sons Ltd* [1957] 1 Q.B. 159.

[104] LTA 1954 s.30(2); *Diploma Laundry Ltd v Surrey Timber Co Ltd* [1955] 2 Q.B. 604; *VCS Car Park Ltd v Regional Railways Ltd* [2001] Ch. 121.

[105] *Patel v Keles* [2009] EWCA Civ 1187; [2010] Ch. 332 at [36], per Arden L.J. What is "short term" depends on the facts of the particular case: ibid.

[106] *Betty's Cafés Ltd v Phillips Furnishing Stores Ltd* [1959] A.C. 20. Where application for summary judgment, see *Somerfield Stores Ltd v Spring (Sutton Coldfield) Ltd (in administration)* [2010] EWHC 2084 (Ch); [2011] L. & T.R. 8.

[107] *Crossco No.4 Unlimited v Jolan Ltd* [2011] EWHC 803 (Ch); [2011] N.P.C. 38 at [377] et seq. (lengthy judicial consideration of possibility of future changes of mind).

bringing about.[108] Where the intended works require planning permission, the landlord must be able to establish that there is a reasonable prospect that permission will be granted.[109] The intention of a corporate landlord must be ascertained by considering all the relevant circumstances: a formal resolution by the board of directors is neither essential nor conclusive.[110] However, an undertaking to the court to take the requisite steps (e.g. to demolish or reconstruct the premises, or occupy them for business purposes) will, if given by a responsible person or body, normally establish the intention required.[111] A landlord who cannot rely upon ground (g) (own occupation) because of the five years rule may still succeed on the previous ground (demolition or reconstruction) if his intention is genuine and not merely colourable; for the existence of one ground does not exclude all others,[112] and an intention to demolish or reconstruct (or both) is not necessarily inconsistent with an intention to occupy.

7. Terms of new tenancy. When premises are first let to a business tenant there are no restrictions on the rent or other terms of the tenancy which the landlord requires, nor is there any power, except by contract,[113] to revise those terms during the currency of the tenancy. But when a new tenancy is granted under the Act, the rent and other terms are in default of agreement determined by the court. The rent is to be that at which the holding might reasonably be expected to be let in the open market by a willing lessor, disregarding any effect of the occupation of the holding by the tenant or his predecessors, any goodwill due to them, and certain tenant's improvements.[114] In default of agreement,[115] the duration of the new tenancy is whatever the court considers reasonable in all the circumstances, beginning at the date on which the current   **22–023**

---

[108] The matter must have moved "out of the zone of contemplation . . . into the valley of decision": *Cunliffe v Goodman* [1950] 2 K.B. 237 at 254, per Asquith L.J.; *Reohorn v Barry Corporation* [1956] 1 W.L.R. 845; *Gregson v Cyril Lord Ltd* [1963] 1 W.L.R. 41; *Westminster City Council v British Waterways Board* [1985] A.C. 676; *Zarvos v Pradhan* [2003] EWCA Civ 208; [2003] 2 E.G.L.R. 37; *Patel v Keles*, above.

[109] *Westminster City Council v British Waterways Board*, above. It is not necessary to prove the likelihood of grant on the balance of probabilities: *Gatwick Parking Services Ltd v Sargent* [2000] 2 E.G.L.R. 45; *Dogan v Semali Investments Ltd* [2005] EWCA Civ 1036; [2005] 3 E.G.L.R. 51.

[110] *Fleet Electrics Ltd v Jacey Investments Ltd* [1956] 1 W.L.R. 1027; *H. L. Bolton (Engineering) Co Ltd v T. J. Graham & Sons Ltd*, above; *Crossco No.4 Unlimited v Jolan Ltd*, above.

[111] *Espresso Coffee Machine Co Ltd v Guardian Assurance Co Ltd* [1959] 1 W.L.R. 250.

[112] *Fisher v Taylors Furnishing Stores Ltd* [1956] 2 Q.B. 78; *Betty's Cafés Ltd v Phillips Furnishing Stores Ltd* [1959] A.C. 20.

[113] e.g. a rent review clause.

[114] LTA 1954 s.34, as amended by LPA 1969 ss.1 and 2 and by SI 2003/3096 arts 9 and 15. The improvements to be disregarded are those made by any tenant, otherwise than under an obligation to the landlord, within the previous 21 years if the holding has been continuously let under the Act since they were made: LTA 1954 s.34(2). For valuation considerations, see Woodfall, 22.149.

[115] An agreement "subject to contract" or "without prejudice" is not effective: *Derby & Co Ltd v ITC Pension Trust Ltd* [1977] 2 All E.R. 890.

tenancy comes to an end, and not exceeding 15 years[116]; and the other terms of the new tenancy are such as the court may determine having regard to the terms of the current tenancy and to all relevant circumstances,[117] e.g. including a rent review clause,[118] a break clause,[119] a right to display advertisements on neighbouring premises,[120] or a provision requiring a guarantor.[121] In determining the rent and other terms, the court must also take account of the effect of the Landlord and Tenant (Covenants) Act 1995 on rent levels and the standard terms of commercial tenancies.[122] At least in so far as changes in market conditions are not attributable to the operation of that statute, the burden will rest on the party seeking to change the existing terms (usually the landlord).[123] The property to be included in the new tenancy is "the holding",[124] although where the holding is only part of the premises included in the current tenancy the landlord may require the whole of those premises to be included.[125] These provisions give effect to the basic principle of Pt II of the Act, namely, that a business tenant has a prima facie right to continue his business indefinitely in his premises on reasonable terms. There is no limit to the number of times a tenancy may be renewed.

22–024   **8. Interim rent.** Since 1969, a landlord has been able to claim an interim rent pending renewal of the tenancy.[126] The relevant provisions were criticised by the Law Commission and substantially amended with effect from 2003.[127] As a result of those changes, tenants as well as landlords may apply to the court for an interim rent to be determined provided either that a s.25 notice has been served by the landlord or that a s.26 request has been made by the tenant.[128] The interim rent that is duly determined is payable from the earliest

---

[116] LTA 1954 s.33, as amended by SI 2003/3096 art.26: *Upsons Ltd v E. Robins Ltd* [1956] 1 Q.B. 131; *London and Provincial Millinery Stores Ltd v Barclays Bank Ltd* [1962] 1 W.L.R. 510; *Chipperfield v Shell (UK) Ltd* (1980) 42 P. & C.R. 136; *Becker v Hill Street Properties Ltd* [1990] 2 E.G.L.R. 78.

[117] LTA 1954 s.35; *Cardshops Ltd v Davies* [1971] 1 W.L.R. 591. Where the current tenancy includes rights enjoyed by the tenant in connection with the holding, those rights shall be included in the new tenancy: LTA 1954 s.32(3). However, the terms of the new tenancy should not give effect to rights exercised by the tenant outside the lease (on the facts, pursuant to a licence determinable by a third party at any time): *The Picture Warehouse Ltd v Cornhill Investments Ltd* [2008] EWHC 45 (QB).

[118] LTA 1954 s.34(3).

[119] *McCombie v Grand Junction Co Ltd* [1962] 1 W.L.R. 581; *J. H. Edwards & Sons Ltd v Central London Commercial Estates Ltd* [1984] 2 E.G.L.R. 103.

[120] *Re No.1 Albemarle Street* [1959] Ch. 531; cf. *G. Orlik (Meat Products) Ltd v Hastings & Thanet Building Society* (1974) 29 P. & C.R. 126; *Kirkwood v Johnson* (1979) 38 P. & C.R. 392.

[121] *Cairnplace Ltd v C.B.L. (Property Investment) Co Ltd* [1984] 1 W.L.R. 696.

[122] L & TCA 1995 Sch.1 paras 3 and 4, amending LTA 1954 ss.34 and 35.

[123] *O'May v City of London Real Property Co Ltd* [1983] 2 A.C. 726.

[124] See above, para.22–015.

[125] LTA 1954 s.32(2).

[126] LPA 1969 s.3(1), introducing LTA 1954 a.24A.

[127] Law Com No.208 (1992); SI 2003/3096 art 18. The legislative amendments have been cogently criticised: Haley [2008] Conv.114.

[128] LTA 1954 s.24A, as inserted by SI 2003/3096 art.18.

date for renewal which could have been specified in the relevant statutory notice.[129] It is therefore important for applications to be made expeditiously. The 2003 amendments introduced a new method for the calculation of the rent where the landlord does not oppose renewal of the tenancy; in such circumstances, the interim rent is to be determined at the same level as the rent for the new tenancy, subject to adjustment where market conditions, or the terms of the tenancy, change during the interim period.[130] In other circumstances, the old method for the calculation of interim rent is applied. This is broadly based on the rent that is reasonable for the tenant to pay on the hypothesis that there is a tenancy from year to year, having regard to the rent payable under the current tenancy.[131]

9. Compensation following eviction. On quitting the holding, the tenant is **22–025** entitled to compensation from the landlord if the only grounds on which the landlord opposed the grant of a new tenancy were one or more of grounds (e), (f) and (g) listed above,[132] and either the court is thereby precluded from granting a new tenancy or else the tenant does not apply for a new tenancy or withdraws his application.[133] The court may also award compensation to the tenant if the order for termination of the current tenancy is obtained, or a refusal to grant a new tenancy is induced, by misrepresentation or concealment of material facts.[134]

10. Compensation for improvements. Under the Landlord and Tenant Act **22–026** 1927,[135] if a tenant of premises used for a trade, business or profession carries out improvements to the premises which add to their letting value, the tenant may recover compensation from the landlord on leaving. But the tenant must satisfy a number of conditions: in addition to making his claim at the right time and in due form, he must give the landlord three months' notice of his intention to make the improvement. The landlord may then exclude the tenant's right to compensation if he successfully objects to the improvement, or carries it out himself in return for a reasonable increase in rent.

---

[129] LTA 1954 s.24B, as inserted by SI 2003/3096 art.18.
[130] LTA 1954 s.24C, as inserted by SI 2003/3096 art.18.
[131] LTA 1954 s.24D, as inserted by SI 2003/3096 art.18.
[132] These are known as "the compensation grounds": see above, paras 22–019 to 22–021.
[133] For detail of compensation, including formula for calculation, see LTA 1954 s.37, as variously amended by LPA 1969 s.11, Local Government, Planning and Land Act 1980 s.193 and Sch.33, Local Government and Housing Act 1989 s.149 and Sch.7, SI 1990/363 and SI 2003/3096 art.19.
[134] LTA 1954 s.37A, inserted by SI 2003/2036 art.20. The court may also award compensation where the tenant withdraws an application to the court or quits the holding without making any such application if it is shown that he did so by reason of misrepresentation or concealment of material facts: LTA 1954, s.37A(2); see, e.g. *Inclusive Technology v Williamson* [2009] EWCA Civ 718; [2010] 1 P. & C.R. 17.
[135] ss.1–3, as amended by LTA 1954 Pt III. Recommendations for reform were made by the Law Commission in 1989, but have not been implemented: Law Com. No.178.

Section 3. Agricultural Tenancies[136]

22–027 Although agricultural tenancies have been regulated by Parliament for longer than any other form of tenancy, their statutory protection has a history of rise and fall. The Agricultural Holdings (England) Act 1875 gave agricultural tenants a right to compensation for improvements, and, under the Agricultural Holdings Act 1923, for dispossession without good cause. In 1947, statutory security of tenure (and rent protection) was conferred upon many agricultural tenants, the most recent such code being contained in the Agricultural Holdings Act 1986. However, statutory security led to a decline in the use of the lease for agricultural property, as well as to widespread invocation of the various methods of letting outside the legislation which were available and sanctioned by the courts.[137] These methods, essentially short-term arrangements which did not reflect the realities of farming in the late 20th century,[138] resulted in pressure for reform from within the industry, which in turn led to the enactment of the Agricultural Tenancies Act 1995. This important statute has effectively removed statutory security with respect to tenancies entered into after it came into force, and allowed the parties the freedom to contract on their own terms. This legislation, together with fiscal incentives to letting enacted to take effect contemporaneously,[139] was intended to revive the rented sector of agricultural land.[140] The result is that there are two parallel statutory systems. The 1986 Act broadly applies to tenancies which began before September 1, 1995; the 1995 Act to those which have begun subsequently.[141] As the definitional provisions of the two statutes are not identical, it is important in each case to examine closely the statutory terminology.

A. Farm Business Tenancies

I. TENANCIES WITHIN THE AGRICULTURAL TENANCIES ACT 1995[142]

22–028 **1. Definition.** A tenancy[143] is a "farm business tenancy" within the 1995 Act if[144]:

---

[136] See further Muir Watt and Moss, *Agricultural Holdings*, 14th edn (London: Sweet & Maxwell 1998); Scammell & Densham's *Law of Agricultural Holdings* 9th edn (London: Butterworths Law 2007). For a review of the history, see Densham, "Agricultural Tenancies: Past and Present" in S. Bright (ed.), *Landlord and Tenant Law: Past, Present and Future* (2006).

[137] See, e.g. the *Gladstone v Bower* tenancy: below, para.22–037.

[138] See Cardwell [1993] Conv. 138.

[139] Landowners can claim 100% relief from inheritance tax on let agricultural land where it is subject to a new letting after September 1, 1995: Finance Act 1995 s.155, amending Inheritance Tax Act 1984 s.116 (as itself amended by Finance (No.2) Act 1992 Sch.14 paras 4 and 8).

[140] See DEFRA, An Economic Evaluation of the Agricultural Tenancies Act 1995 (2002).

[141] A tenancy "begins" on the date when the tenant is entitled to go into possession: ATA 1995 s.38(4).

[142] This Act (together with the Agricultural Holdings Act 1986) was amended by the Regulatory Reform (Agricultural Tenancies) (England and Wales) Order 2006, SI 2006/2805.

[143] "Tenancy" includes sub-tenancy, and an agreement for a tenancy or sub-tenancy, but not a tenancy at will: ATA 1995 s.38(1).

[144] ATA 1995 s.1(1).

(i) all or part of the land comprised in the tenancy is farmed for the purposes of a trade or business,[145] and has been at all times since the beginning of the tenancy[146]; and

(ii) *either* the character of the tenancy is primarily or wholly agricultural[147] (having regard to the terms of the tenancy, the use of the land, the nature of any commercial activities carried on upon that land, and any other relevant circumstances)[148]
or at the beginning of the tenancy, the character of the tenancy was primarily or wholly agricultural, and on or before that date[149] the landlord and tenant exchanged written notices identifying the land in question and stating their intention that the tenancy was to be (and remain) a farm business tenancy.[150]

2. Exceptions. A tenancy cannot be a farm business tenancy if it began before September 1, 1995, or if it is a tenancy of an agricultural holding within the 1986 Act.[151] Certain tenancies beginning on or after September 1, 1995 will be subject to the earlier legislation.[152]   **22–029**

II. RECOVERY OF POSSESSION

The general effect of the 1995 Act is to require notice of not less than 12 nor more than 24 months in order to determine the farm business tenancy. No prescribed form of notice is required, and no contracting out is permitted.[153] However, where the farm business tenancy is a fixed-term tenancy of two years or less, or a periodic tenancy other than a tenancy from year to year, the 1995 Act allows termination in accordance with the terms of the lease.[154] For example, a landlord will be entitled to recover possession when a farm business tenancy granted for a fixed term of one year expires by effluxion of time.   **22–030**

1. Continuation of tenancies for more than two years. A farm business tenancy may be a fixed-term tenancy or a periodic tenancy.[155] There is no   **22–031**

---

[145] "Farmed" is partially defined as including "the carrying on in relation to land of any agricultural activity": ATA 1995 s.38(2).

[146] The "business conditions": ATA 1995 s.1(2).

[147] Defined as in the Agricultural Holdings Act 1986 (see below, para.22–035): ATA 1995 s.38(1).

[148] The "agricultural condition": ATA 1995 s.1(3).

[149] Or the date, if earlier, on which the written tenancy agreement was entered into.

[150] The "notice conditions": ATA 1995 s.1(4). Compliance with the notice conditions is waived in certain cases of surrender and re-grant: see ATA 1995 s.3(1). For service provisions, see ATA 1995 s.36.

[151] ATA 1995 s.2(1).

[152] ATA 1995 s.4. See further below, paras 22–035 et seq.

[153] ATA 1995 s.5(4).

[154] cf. the so-called *Gladstone v Bower* tenancies in relation to the 1986 Act: below, para.22–037.

[155] For the purposes of the 1995 Act, a "fixed-term tenancy" means any tenancy other than a periodic tenancy: ATA 1995 s.38(1).

minimum or maximum length imposed by statute. If it is a tenancy for a term of more than two years, on expiry of that term it will continue as a tenancy from year to year, in other respects on the same terms as the original fixed-term tenancy, unless, at least 12 months before the term was due to expire, either party gives to the other written notice of his intention to terminate the tenancy.[156]

22–032   **2. Notices to quit.** The "aggregate" of the land comprised in a farm business tenancy is known as the "holding".[157] A notice to quit the holding or part of it will be invalid unless it is in writing, and is given at least 12 months before the date on which it is to take effect. If the tenancy is a tenancy from year to year, the notice must take effect at the end of a year of the tenancy.[158] If the tenancy is for a term of more than two years, any such notice must be given in pursuance of any provision in the tenancy itself.[159] There is no security provided for farm business tenants over and above these requirements.

III. PROTECTION AS TO RENT

22–033   The parties to a farm business tenancy are free to contract concerning rent, and thereby avoid the application of Pt II of the 1995 Act, if the instrument creating the tenancy:

(a) states expressly that the rent is not to be reviewed during the tenancy; or

(b) provides that the rent is to be varied either by or to a specified amount or in accordance with a specified formula which does not preclude reduction or require or permit the exercise of any judgment or discretion in relation to its determination (but otherwise is to remain fixed); or

(c) does not preclude the reduction in rent during the tenancy, expressly stating that Part II is not to apply, and making provision for the reference of rent reviews to an independent expert whose decision is final.[160]

Pt II provides that otherwise, and notwithstanding any agreement to the contrary, either party to a farm business tenancy may, by service of a statutory review notice, refer the rent to be payable to arbitration.[161] Any variation in

---

[156] ATA 1995 s.5(1), as amended by SI 2006/2805 art.13.
[157] ATA 1995 s.38(1).
[158] ATA 1995 s.6(1), as amended by SI 2006/2805 art.13.
[159] ATA 1995 s.7(1), as amended by SI 2006/2805 art.13.
[160] ATA 1995 s.9, as amended by SI 2006/2805 art.14. "Upwards only" rent review clauses will therefore be ineffective. In its amended form (that is, with the inclusion of (c)), s.9 applies only to tenancies created after October 19, 2006.
[161] ATA 1995 s.10(1).

the rent will have effect from the "review date", which must be at least 12, but less than 24, months from the date when the notice is given, and which, in the absence of agreement to the contrary, must be an anniversary of the beginning of the tenancy. The review date must be at least three years from the beginning of the tenancy, or, if later, the date when any previous variation of the rent as a result of arbitration, review, or agreement took effect.[162] On a statutory rent review, the arbitrator has jurisdiction to increase or reduce the rent payable or leave it unchanged. The rent payable is that at which the holding might reasonably be expected to be let on the open market by a willing landlord to a willing tenant, taking account of all relevant circumstances, and disregarding certain tenant's improvements and certain other matters.[163]

IV. COMPENSATION FOR IMPROVEMENTS

Whilst the 1995 Act seriously reduces the security of tenure of agricultural tenants, the recoupment of the tenant's investment on giving up possession remains an important component of legislative policy. Thus there are complex provisions contained in Pt III of the 1995 Act entitling a farm business tenant to be compensated for improvements on quitting the holding. "Improvements" are widely defined so as to include not only physical improvements but also "intangible advantages" (such as milk quotas and planning permissions).[164] The landlord must have consented to the improvements in question[165] (the tenant being entitled to refer a refusal of consent to arbitration),[166] and there are exclusions. The tenant is entitled to be paid an amount equal to the increase attributable to the improvement in the value of the holding at the termination of the tenancy.[167]

22–034

B. Agricultural Holdings

1. AGREEMENTS WITHIN THE 1986 ACT

1. Agreements beginning on or after September 1, 1995. As a general rule, the 1986 Act does not apply to tenancies[168] beginning on or after September 1, 1995. However, there are certain limited exceptions,[169] namely, tenancies of agricultural holdings:

22–035

---

[162] See generally ATA 1995 s.10(2)–(6).
[163] ATA 1995 s.13, as amended by SI 2006/2805 art.15.
[164] For definition of "tenant's improvement", see ATA 1995 s.15.
[165] ATA 1995 s.17.
[166] ATA 1995 s.19.
[167] ATA 1995 s.20. Different principles are applied where the improvement consists of a planning permission: ATA 1995 ss.18, 21. Parties may agree an upper limit to compensation, or that the amount is to be the cost to the tenant of making the improvement: ATA 1995 ss.20(4A) and (4B), added by SI 2006/2805 art.16.
[168] Whilst it is expressly stated that this includes agreements to which AHA 1986 s.2 (see below, paras 22–037 to 22–038) would otherwise apply, it is not clear whether such agreements may come within the exceptional circumstances which are then listed.
[169] ATA 1995 s.4, as amended by SI 2006/2805 art.12.

(i) granted by a written contract of tenancy entered into before that date which indicates that the 1986 Act is to apply to the tenancy; or

(ii) obtained by virtue of certain directions of an Agricultural Land Tribunal on the death or retirement of the previous tenant[170]; or

(iii) granted on an agreed succession[171] by a written contract of tenancy indicating that Pt IV of the 1986 Act is to apply to the tenancy; or

(iv) created by the previous tenant's acceptance of certain compensation provisions[172]; or

(v) granted by a purported variation of a previous tenancy with the tenant of the holding[173] which takes effect as a new tenancy by reason of the operation of the doctrine of "surrender and re-grant".[174] However, an agreement which is expressed to take effect as a new tenancy between the parties will not be subject to the 1986 Act.

2. "Agricultural holding"

22–036   *(a) The definition.* "Agricultural holding" is defined as meaning "the aggregate of the land (whether agricultural land or not) comprised in a contract of tenancy which is a contract for an agricultural tenancy"[175]; and there is a contract for an agricultural tenancy if, having regard to the terms of the tenancy, the actual and contemplated use of the land, and all other relevant circumstances, "the whole of the land" (apart from any insubstantial exceptions) "is let for use as agricultural land".[176] "Agricultural land" is "land used for agriculture which is so used for the purposes of a trade or business"[177]; and "agriculture" has a wide definition which includes horticulture, fruit growing, seed growing, the use of land as grazing land,[178] market gardening,[179] and the use of land as woodlands where that is ancillary to the farming of land or other agricultural purposes.

---

[170] See AHA 1986 ss.39 and 53; below, para.22–053.

[171] Defined in ATA 1995 s.4(2).

[172] The so-called "Evesham custom": AHA 1986 s.80(3)–(5).

[173] Or any agricultural holding which comprised the whole or a substantial part of the land comprised in the holding. Note exception (where holdings have merged on or after September 1, 1995) contained in ATA 1995 s.4(2B).

[174] For this doctrine, see further above, para.18–087.

[175] AHA 1986 s.1(1), which provision excludes service tenancies.

[176] AHA 1986 s.1(2).

[177] AHA 1986 s.1(4). The Minister may designate land as "agricultural land": Agriculture Act 1947 s.109(1).

[178] *Rutherford v Maurer* [1962] 1 Q.B. 16 (grazing the horses of a riding school).

[179] AHA 1986 s.96(1). A letting of a garden centre, at least where a substantial part of the produce is "home-grown", may comprise an agricultural holding: *Short v Greeves* [1988] 1 E.G.L.R. 1.

(b) "Contract of tenancy". The term "contract of tenancy" is restricted to **22–037** "a letting of land, or agreement for letting land, for a term of years or from year to year".[180] However, an agreement for value[181] whereby land is let (or a licence is granted "to occupy" the land[182]) for use as agricultural land for an "interest less than a tenancy from year to year", in circumstances which otherwise would make the land an agricultural holding, takes effect (with the necessary modifications) as if it were an agreement for a tenancy from year to year.[183] The effect of this provision is that most agricultural tenancies, and many licences, appear to fall within the 1986 Act. A fixed-term tenancy for more than one year but less than two is, however, excluded from the security of tenure and succession provisions.[184] A tenancy for one year is within the Act.[185]

The statutory extension to lettings for an interest less than a tenancy from **22–038** year to year does not apply to[186]:

(i) a letting or a grant which had prior Ministerial approval[187];

(ii) an agreement for the letting of the land (or the grant of a licence to occupy it) made "in contemplation[188] of the use of the land only for grazing or mowing during some specified period of the year".[189] Such a period need not be fixed by dates; it will include any period which is so named or described as to be identifiable by persons versed in agricultural matters.[190] Although 364 days may be such a period,[191] one year cannot[192]; or

---

[180] AHA 1986 s.1(5).

[181] *Goldsack v Shore* [1950] 1 K.B. 708; *Collier v Hollinshead* (1984) 272 E.G. 941. The agreement must be made on or after March 1, 1948: AHA 1986 Sch.12 para.1.

[182] Occupation must be exclusive: *Harrison-Broadley v Smith* [1964] 1 W.L.R. 456; *Bahamas International Trust Co Ltd v Threadgold* [1974] 1 W.L.R. 1514; *McCarthy v Bence* [1990] 1 E.G.L.R. 1.

[183] AHA 1986 s.2. For examples, see *Calcott v J. S. Bloor (Measham) Ltd* [1998] 1 W.L.R. 1490; *Well Barn Farming Ltd v Backhouse* [2005] EWHC 1520 (Ch); [2005] 3 E.G.L.R. 109; cf. *Davies v Davies* [2002] EWCA Civ 1791.

[184] *Gladstone v Bower* [1960] 2 Q.B. 384; *E.W.P. Ltd v Moore* [1992] Q.B. 460 (letting for 23 months); cf. *Keen v Holland* [1984] 1 W.L.R. 251 ("back-dating" ineffective). The tenancy is, however, a tenancy of an agricultural holding for other purposes, such as tenant compensation, and the tenancy will therefore be excluded from protection as a business tenancy pursuant to LTA 1954 Pt II: *E.W.P. Ltd v Moore*, above.

[185] *Bernays v Prosser* [1963] 1 Q.B. 592.

[186] See Cardwell [1993] Conv. 138.

[187] AHA 1986, s.2(1). See, e.g. *Finbow v Air Ministry* [1963] 1 W.L.R. 697; *Ashdale Land & Property Co Ltd v Manners* [1992] 2 E.G.L.R. 5.

[188] *Scene Estate Ltd v Amos* [1957] 2 Q.B. 205; cf. *Rutherford v Maurer* [1962] 1 Q.B. 16.

[189] AHA 1986 s.2(3).

[190] *Mackenzie v Laird* 1959 S.C. 266; *Watts v Yeend* [1987] 1 W.L.R. 323 ("seasonal" grazing licences).

[191] *Reid v Dawson* [1955] 1 Q.B. 214; *South West Water Authority v Palmer* (1983) 268 E.G. 357; cf. *Lory v Brent LBC* [1971] 1 W.L.R. 823.

[192] *Rutherford v Maurer*, above; *Brown v Tiernan* (1992) 65 P. & C.R. 324.

            (iii) a sub-tenancy or sub-licence granted by a person having less than
            a tenancy from year to year.[193]

22–039   *(c) Contracting out.*[194] An agreement between landlord and tenant that the
1986 Act is not to apply to their tenancy will be of no effect.[195] However, if
before the grant of a tenancy of not less than two nor more than five years, on
a written application made by both parties jointly, the Minister gave his
approval, no further tenancy will arise on expiry of the fixed term by operation
of law, and the landlord will be entitled to repossession.[196] This provision will
only operate if the contract of tenancy is in writing, contains a statement that
s.3 of the 1986 Act is not to apply to it, and is within the terms of the
ministerial approval.[197]

22–040   *(d) Mixed lettings.* Where agricultural land is let with non-agricultural land,
the Act will either apply to the tenancy as a whole or not at all; there is no
segregation of the agricultural from the non-agricultural.[198]

II. SECURITY OF TENURE

22–041   The general scheme of security contained in the 1986 Act is as follows.[199]
First, a notice to quit of one year in length, such notice expiring at the end of
a year of the tenancy, is required to terminate every agricultural tenancy,
including fixed-term tenancies which have expired. Secondly, the Act prevents any such notice to quit from operating at all except in certain specified
cases. Agricultural tenancies accordingly continue indefinitely until determined on one of the grounds specified in the Act, or until agricultural use is
abandoned.[200]

1. Determination of tenancies

22–042   *(a) Notice to quit.* The 1986 Act makes 12 months' notice to quit requisite
in almost every case. This is effected by the following means. First, as
explained above, certain short tenancies and licences are treated as yearly
tenancies. Secondly, a tenancy for two years or upwards is continued as a
tenancy from year to year[201] from the end of the fixed term unless (not less
than one year nor more than two years before the date fixed for the expiration
of the term) either party has given to the other written notice of his intention

---

[193] AHA 1986 s.2(3).
[194] See Scammell & Densham, 9th edn (2007), Ch.4.
[195] *Johnson v Moreton* [1980] A.C. 37.
[196] AHA 1986 s.5.
[197] AHA 1986 s.5; *Pahl v Trevor* [1992] 1 E.G.L.R. 22.
[198] See AHA 1986 s.1(2); *Howkins v Jardine* [1951] 1 K.B. 614.
[199] Common law methods of termination (notably surrender, forfeiture and disclaimer) remain
available despite the Act.
[200] *Wetherall v Smith* [1980] 1 W.L.R. 1290.
[201] But if the tenant under a tenancy granted after September 12, 1984, dies, the tenancy will
expire at its contractual end, or one year later if he dies in the last year of the term: AHA 1986
s.4(1) and (2).

to terminate the tenancy.[202] Thirdly, and with some exceptions, the Act invalidates a notice to quit[203] an agricultural holding if it purports to terminate the tenancy before the expiration of 12 months from the end of the then current year of the tenancy[204]; and this is so even if the notice is given by the tenant.[205]

(b) Types of notice. A landlord's notice to quit may take one of two forms.[206]   **22–043**

The landlord's notice may refer to one or more of eight "Cases", set out in Sch.3 to the 1986 Act,[207] which the landlord alleges entitles him to enforce the notice to quit. If the tenant wishes to contest a landlord's claim based on Cases A, B, D, or E, he must within one month serve notice on the landlord requiring the question to be determined by arbitration[208] or, where a notice to quit was given under Case D, serve a counter-notice[209]; otherwise he cannot challenge the claim. Cases C, F, G and H cannot be referred to arbitration (which would not in any event be appropriate).

Alternatively, the landlord may serve an ordinary "unqualified" notice to quit which does not specify any of the "Cases". This will enable the tenant to serve a counter-notice claiming security of tenure. On service of such a counter-notice, the landlord will be unable to enforce his notice to quit by repossession unless he obtains the consent of the Agricultural Land Tribunal on proof of certain grounds.[210]

The notice must make it plain which type of notice it is,[211] and which Case,   **22–044** if any, is relied upon.[212] If it specifies a Case which the landlord fails to establish on arbitration, the landlord cannot then argue that the notice was effective as an ordinary "unqualified" notice which the tenant should have met with a counter-notice.[213]

2. Recovery of possession. It can be seen that, in relation to a 1986 Act   **22–045** tenancy, the landlord has two routes to recovering possession, which give rise to a distinction similar to that between the "mandatory" and "discretionary" grounds relevant to residential tenancies.[214] If the landlord can establish one

---

[202] AHA 1986 s.3(1).

[203] Including a notice exercising an option of termination contained in the tenancy agreement: *Edell v Dulieu* [1924] A.C. 38.

[204] AHA 1986 s.25(1). For exceptions, see s.25(2) and (3) and SI 1987/710 arts 7 and 14.

[205] *Flather v Hood* (1928) 44 T.L.R. 698. But the recipient of a shorter notice may agree to treat it as being valid: *Elsden v Pick* [1980] 1 W.L.R. 898.

[206] See generally *Carradine Properties Ltd v Aslam* [1976] 1 W.L.R. 442; *Land v Sykes* [1992] 1 E.G.L.R. 1. For the effect of a fraudulent statement in the notice, see *Rous v Mitchell* [1991] 1 W.L.R. 469.

[207] See below, paras 22–047 to 22–055.

[208] SI 1987/710 art.9, *Att Gen (Duchy of Lancaster) v Simcock* [1966] Ch. 1; *Magdalen College, Oxford v Heritage* [1974] 1 W.L.R. 441.

[209] AHA 1986 s.28.

[210] AHA 1986 ss.26 and 27.

[211] *Cowan v Wrayford* [1953] 1 W.L.R. 1340; *Mills v Edwards* [1971] 1 Q.B. 379.

[212] *Budge v Hicks* [1951] 2 K.B. 335; *Magdalen College, Oxford v Heritage*, above.

[213] *Cowan v Wrayford*, above; *Mills v Edwards*, above.

[214] See below, para.22–096.

of the Cases in Sch.3, he is entitled to recover possession as of right. If, however, the landlord has to rely on the Tribunal consenting to the operation of his notice to quit, he is on much weaker ground, as the recovery of possession depends upon the exercise of discretion in his favour.

22–046   *(a) Schedule 3.* Where the landlord serves a notice to quit specifying one or more of the Cases under Sch.3, the notice will operate unless the tenant refers the landlord's notice to arbitration within one month, a course that is possible only if the notice is based on Cases A, B, D or E. Where the landlord bases his claim on the failure of the tenant to comply with a notice to do work under Case D, the tenant may serve a counter-notice.[215] However, a counter-notice may not be served in any other circumstances, and if the tenant wishes to contest a notice based on any other Case, he must either seek a declaration from the court that the landlord's notice is invalid, or raise his arguments in the course of the landlord's possession proceedings. The Cases in Sch.3 are as follows.

22–047   CASE A: COMPULSORY RETIREMENT OF SMALLHOLDERS.[216] On or after September 12, 1984, a smallholdings authority or the Minister may let a smallholding subject to the provisions of this Case. Such land can be repossessed once the tenant has attained the age of 65, and suitable alternative accommodation[217] is available for him.

22–048   CASE B: PLANNING PERMISSION. The land is required[218] (even if not by the landlord[219]) for some non-agricultural use for which planning permission has been given or (in certain restricted circumstances) is not required.[220]

22–049   CASE C: BAD HUSBANDRY. Not more than six months before the notice to quit was given the Tribunal certified that the tenant was not farming in accordance with the rules of good husbandry.[221]

22–050   CASE D: UNREMEDIED BREACH. The tenant has committed a breach of any term of his tenancy (other than a term inconsistent with good husbandry) and has failed to comply fully[222] with a written notice by the landlord in the prescribed form[223] requiring compliance within two months (in the case of

---

[215] For which, see AHA 1986 s.28.

[216] See further Agriculture Act 1970 Pt III.

[217] AHA 1986 Sch.3 Pt II paras 2–7.

[218] *Jones v Gates* [1954] 1 W.L.R. 222.

[219] *Rugby Joint Water Board v Foottit* [1973] A.C. 202.

[220] In *Bell v McCubbin* [1990] 1 Q.B. 976, a Case B notice to quit was held valid although the landlord, wishing to sub-let for residential purposes, did not seek or require planning permission. Case B was subsequently amended to reverse this ruling, but the amendment applies only to notices served on or after July 29, 1990: Agricultural Holdings (Amendment) Act 1990. See further AHA 1986 Sch.3, Pt II, para.8.

[221] AHA 1986 s.96(3), Sch.3, Pt II, para.9; Agriculture Act 1947 s.11.

[222] *Price v Romilly* [1960] 1 W.L.R. 1360; *Stoneman v Brown* [1973] 1 W.L.R. 459.

[223] SI 1987/711 Sch. Forms 1 and 2. Where the landlord specifies what he requires the tenant to do, he must do so accurately: *Pickard v Bishop* (1975) 31 P. & C.R. 108; *Dickinson v Boucher* (1983) 269 E.G. 1159. But a misdescription of the landlord which is not likely to mislead the tenant may not be critical: *Divall v Harrison* [1990] 1 E.G.L.R. 16.

rent) or (in other cases) a specified reasonable period, being not less than six months if works of repair, maintenance or replacement have to be done.[224]

CASE E: IRREMEDIABLE BREACH. The landlord's interest in the holding has been materially prejudiced by an irremediable breach[225] by the tenant of a valid[226] term of the tenancy (other than a term inconsistent with good husbandry). **22–051**

CASE F: BANKRUPTCY. The tenant is insolvent.[227] **22–052**

CASE G: DEATH. This Case is closely related to the provisions for statutory succession to agricultural holdings[228] which were severely limited by the Agricultural Holdings Act 1984.[229] With certain exceptions,[230] where a tenancy was granted before July 12, 1984, any "eligible person" may within three months of the death[231] apply to the Tribunal for a tenancy.[232] An "eligible person" is any surviving close relative[233] of the deceased who is not himself the occupier of a commercial unit of agricultural land[234] and who, at the death of the tenant and for at least five of the previous seven years, derived his only or principal source of livelihood from agricultural work on the holding.[235] If the Tribunal consider him suitable, he is entitled to a tenancy.[236] However, where the tenancy was granted on or after July 12, 1984,[237] then, with certain exceptions,[238] no statutory succession will take place on the death of the tenant.[239] **22–053**

---

[224] See, e.g. *Lloyds Bank Ltd v Jones* [1955] 2 Q.B. 298; *Sumnall v Statt* (1985) 49 P. & C.R. 367; *Jones v Lewis* (1973) 25 P. & C.R. 375. For procedure and forms, see SI 1987//710 and 711. Case D has been held not to discriminate between those tenants guilty of breaches within the Case (who are given the opportunity to remedy) and those tenants guilty of other breaches (who have no such opportunity) in violation of Arts 1, 6, 8 and 14 of the ECHR: *Lancashire CC v Taylor* [2005] EWCA Civ 284; [2005] 1 P. & C.R. 2.

[225] Although a covenant may have been broken, the landlord may be estopped from relying on it where the parties had acted on the assumption that no such covenant existed (or, presumably, where the landlord has waived it): *Troop v Gibson* [1986] 1 E.G.L.R. 1. See further AHA 1986 Sch.3, Pt II, para.11.

[226] *Johnson v Moreton* [1977] E.G.D. 1, affirmed [1980] A.C. 37.

[227] AHA 1986 s.96(2).

[228] Themselves only introduced eight years earlier: Agriculture (Miscellaneous Provisions) Act 1976. See further on Case G, AHA 1986 Sch.3, Pt II, para.12.

[229] Now see AHA 1986 Pt IV.

[230] AHA 1986 ss.36–38. In particular, there could be only two succession tenancies.

[231] The three month period begins on the day after the death.

[232] AHA 1986 s.39(1). A tenant may retire and nominate an "eligible person" as his successor, thereby occasioning inter vivos statutory succession to pre-1984 Act tenancies: AHA 1986 ss.49–58.

[233] That is, the deceased's husband, wife, civil partner, sibling, child or step-child: see AHA 1986 s.35(2).

[234] AHA 1986 s.36(3)(b) Sch.6, para.3.

[235] AHA 1986 s.36(3)(a); *Welby v Casswell* [1995] 2 E.G.L.R. 1. The Tribunal may treat as an "eligible person" someone who satisfies s.36(3)(a) "to a material extent": AHA 1986 s.41; *Littlewood v Rolfe* [1981] 2 All E.R. 51; *Wilson v Earl Spencer's Settlement Trusts* [1985] 1 E.G.L.R. 3.

[236] AHA 1986 s.39(5). In the event of more than one eligible person, the Tribunal determines who is the most suitable: AHA 1986 s.39(6).

[237] The day the 1984 Act came into force.

[238] AHA 1986 s.34(1)(b).

[239] Although the tenancy will devolve as part of the tenant's estate.

22–054   Case G enables the landlord to give a notice to quit within three months of notice[240] of the death of the sole (or sole surviving) tenant being served on him by the tenant's personal representatives or (if sooner) notice being given to him of an "eligible person" under the above provisions. Such notice to quit, if given "by reason of the tenant's death", will deprive the tenant's estate of security. However, such notice to quit will not have effect unless no application has been made under the statutory succession provisions, or application has been made but the Tribunal has either refused to determine that the applicant is a suitable successor, or consented to the operation of the notice to quit.[241]

22–055   CASE H: MINISTERIAL CERTIFICATE. The notice to quit is given by the Minister, and he certifies that it is given to enable him to effect an amalgamation (within the meaning of the Agriculture Act 1967) or the reshaping of any agricultural unit. This, however, applies only if the tenant agreed, in the tenancy agreement, that it was subject to Case H.

22–056   *(b) Security depending on reasonableness.* There is no security of tenure (and the court cannot grant relief)[242] if the landlord serves an ordinary "unqualified" notice to quit and the tenant[243] fails to serve a counter-notice within one month requiring s.26(1) of the 1986 Act to apply.[244] If the tenant serves a valid counter-notice, the landlord may apply to the Agricultural Land Tribunal within one month[245] for consent to the operation of the notice to quit. However, the discretion of the Tribunal is fettered. They must give consent to the landlord's notice to quit taking effect if (and only if) they are satisfied as to one or more of the "matters" listed in s.27(3). Even if they are so satisfied, they must not give consent if in all the circumstances it appears to them that a fair and reasonable landlord would not insist on possession.[246] The cases in which the tenant's security of tenure depends on the reasonableness of his being evicted (the s.27(3) "matters") are as follows.

22–057   (1) GOOD HUSBANDRY. The landlord proposes to terminate the tenancy for a purpose that is desirable in the interests of good husbandry as respects the land to which the notice relates, treated as a separate unit.

22–058   (2) SOUND MANAGEMENT. The landlord proposes to terminate the tenancy for a purpose that is desirable in the interests of sound management of the land

---

[240] AHA 1986 Sch.3, Pt II, para.12; *B.S.C. Pension Fund Trustees Ltd v Downing* [1990] 1 E.G.L.R. 4; *Lees v Tatchell* [1990] 1 E.G.L.R. 10.

[241] AHA 1986 s.43(1).

[242] *Parrish v Kinsey* (1983) 268 E.G. 1113.

[243] Where there are joint tenants, normally all must concur in the counter-notice: *Featherstone v Staples* [1986] 1 W.L.R. 861; *Cork v Cork* [1997] 1 E.G.L.R. 5.

[244] The counter-notice need not be in prescribed form: it suffices if it evinces a clear intention to invoke the tenant's rights under the Act: *Mountford v Hodkinson* [1956] 1 W.L.R. 422; *Frankland v Capstick* [1959] 1 W.L.R. 204.

[245] SI 2007/3105 Sch.1, r.39.

[246] AHA 1986 s.27(2). As circumstances are likely to change, issue estoppel will not bar the service of successive notices to quit: *Wickington v Bonney* (1982) 47 P. & C.R. 655.

concerned (physically, and not merely financially for the landlord[247] or the tenant[248]) or of the estate of which it forms part.

(3) RESEARCH. Carrying out the purpose for which the landlord proposes to **22–059** terminate the tenancy is desirable for the purposes of agricultural research, education, experiment or demonstration, or for the purposes of the statutes relating to smallholdings or allotments.

(4) GREATER HARDSHIP. Considering all who might be affected,[249] greater **22–060** hardship would be caused by withholding consent than by granting it.

(5) NON-AGRICULTURAL USE. The landlord proposes to terminate the tenancy **22–061** for the purpose of the land being used for some non-agricultural use not falling within Case B.

Where consent is given to the operation of the notice to quit, the Tribunal may impose conditions to secure that the land is used for the purposes stated by the landlord; and the Tribunal may subsequently vary or revoke the conditions.[250]

3. Sub-tenants. These provisions apply as between a tenant and any sub- **22–062** tenant of his,[251] but not as between the sub-tenant and the head landlord. Thus where a landlord's notice to quit takes effect it determines not only the tenancy but also any sub-tenancies; no provision has been made[252] to exclude the common law rule that a sub-tenancy falls with the tenancy out of which it was created.[253] However, the courts will be astute to detect, and to strike down, artificial transactions using nominees as intermediaries which are designed to prevent the effective tenant from exercising his statutory rights.[254] Where the tenant has served a counter-notice on the landlord, the sub-tenant can make representations to the Tribunal, for he may be made a party to the proceedings[255]; and the sub-tenant may be entitled to compensation.[256]

III. PROTECTION AS TO RENT

When a tenancy of an agricultural holding is first granted, the parties are free **22–063** to agree whatever rent they please.[257] However, not more frequently than once

---

[247] *National Coal Board v Naylor* [1972] 1 W.L.R. 908.
[248] *Evans v Roper* [1960] 1 W.L.R. 814.
[249] *Purser v Bailey* [1967] 2 Q.B. 500.
[250] AHA 1986 s.27(4), (5).
[251] See, however, SI 1987/710 art.16.
[252] The Lord Chancellor's power to provide protection for sub-tenants (AHA 1986 s.29 and Sch.4 para.7) has not been exercised; but see below.
[253] *Lord Sherwood v Moody* [1952] 1 All E.R. 389; *Pennell v Payne* [1995] Q.B. 192 (tenant's "upwards" notice to quit).
[254] *Gisborne v Burton* [1989] Q.B. 390; cf. *Barrett v Morgan* [2000] 2 A.C. 264, overruling *Sparkes v Smart* [1990] 2 E.G.L.R. 245.
[255] SI 2007/3105 Sch.1 rr.9, 10.
[256] AHA 1986 s.63.
[257] "Rent" has been held to include any VAT element payable to the landlord by the tenant: *Mason v Boscawen* [2008] EWHC 3100 (Ch); [2009] 1 W.L.R. 2139.

in every three years, either party may demand that the amount of the rent be referred to arbitration by an arbitrator appointed either by agreement or in default by (usually) the President of the RICS, on the basis of the open market rent.[258] Any increase or decrease awarded by the arbitrator takes effect as from the next day on which the tenancy could be determined by a notice to quit given when the reference to arbitration was demanded, provided the arbitrator has been duly appointed before that day.[259] It follows that, unless the tenancy makes contrary provision,[260] no revision of rent is possible during a tenancy for a fixed term which is not determinable by notice to quit. In addition, the landlord may increase the rent in respect of certain improvements carried out by him.[261]

IV. COMPENSATION

22–064　　The tenant's rights to compensation may be put under three heads. None of them can be excluded by any agreement to the contrary[262]; and any provision which would even by implication exclude a claim for compensation (e.g. a provision for determination at such short notice as to leave no time to claim compensation) is void.[263]

22–065　　**1. Compensation for disturbance.** A tenant not in default who quits the holding in consequence of a notice to quit given by the landlord (whether or not the notice is valid)[264] is usually entitled to compensation for disturbance.[265]

22–066　　**2. Compensation for improvements.** When an agricultural tenant quits his holding at the end of his tenancy, he is entitled to compensation for certain improvements carried out by him, provided he has observed the necessary conditions. Such improvements fall into three main categories. First, there are certain long-term improvements (e.g. planting orchards) for which the landlord's consent is required. Secondly, there are other long-term improvements (e.g. the erection of buildings) for which either the landlord's consent or the Tribunal's approval is necessary. Thirdly, there are some short-term improvements (e.g. the chalking or liming of land) for which neither consent nor approval is needed. The measure of compensation is the increase in value of the holding, or, in the case of a short-term improvement, the value of the improvement to an incoming tenant.[266]

---

[258] AHA 1986 s.12, as amended by SI 2006/2805 art.3; for method of calculation together with supplementary provisions (factors, disregards, etc.), see Sch.2.
[259] ibid.; *Sclater v Horton* [1954] Q.B. 1; *University College, Oxford v Durdy* [1982] Ch. 413.
[260] On contracting out, see *Mason v Boscawen*, above; Woodfall, 21.083.
[261] AHA 1986 s.13.
[262] AHA 1986 s.78(1).
[263] *Coates v Diment* [1951] 1 All E.R. 890; *Parry v Million Pigs Ltd* [1981] 2 E.G.L.R. 1.
[264] *Kestell v Langmaid* [1950] 1 K.B. 233.
[265] AHA 1986 ss.60–63.
[266] AHA 1986 ss.64–69 and Schs 7–9.

3. Other compensation. The tenant may claim compensation for any   **22–067**
increase in the value of the holding due to his having adopted a more
beneficial system of farming than that required by his tenancy agreement, or,
if none, than that practised on comparable holdings.[267] He may also be able to
claim compensation in respect of a milk quota.[268] The landlord, on the other
hand, may recover from a tenant who has quitted the holding compensation in
respect of dilapidation or deterioration of the holding, or damage to it caused
by failure to farm in accordance with the rules of good husbandry,[269] having
due regard to the landlord's contractual obligations[270] and the condition of the
property when the tenancy was granted.[271]

4. Fixed equipment. Compensation apart, a tenant may benefit by being   **22–068**
provided with fixed equipment on the holding. In continuation of war-time
regulations, the Agriculture Act 1947 gave the Minister of Agriculture, Fisheries and Food substantial powers to enforce efficient farming by owners and
tenants alike. Most of these powers disappeared with the Agriculture Act
1958, but there is still power (now under the Agricultural Holdings Act
1986[272]) for an Agricultural Lands Tribunal to direct a landlord to provide,
alter or repair fixed equipment on the holding which is needed in order to
avoid contravening statutory requirements, e.g. for producing clean milk. If
the landlord fails to do so, the tenant may do it himself at the landlord's
expense. "Fixed equipment" includes buildings, structures affixed to land,
and works on land.

Section 4. Residential Tenancies

1. Introduction. The protection of private sector residential tenancies   **22–069**
began modestly over 75 years ago. The first "Rent Act", the Increase of Rent
and Mortgage Interest (War Restrictions) Act 1915, was a mere six pages
long; but from it grew a highly complex set of systems laid down in hundreds
of pages of detailed legislation and interpreted in thousands of cases.[273] The
general pattern of the earlier legislation was that rent control was imposed on
the private sector of residential housing, and subsequently expanded in order
to meet war-time shortages; it was gradually attenuated as days of peace
brought relief. Since the Second World War, social and political pressures

---

[267] AHA 1986 s.70.
[268] Agriculture Act 1986 s.13, and Sch.1.
[269] AHA 1986 ss.71–73.
[270] *Barrow Green Estates Co v Walker's Executors* [1954] 1 W.L.R. 231.
[271] *Evans v Jones* [1955] 2 Q.B. 58.
[272] s.11.
[273] The Increase of Rent and Mortgage Interest (War Restrictions) Act 1915. The other "Rent
Acts" were the Increase of Rent and Mortgage Interest (Restrictions) Act 1920; the Rent and
Mortgage Interest Restrictions (Amendment) Act 1933; the Increase of Rent and Mortgage
Interest (Restrictions) Act 1938; the Rent and Mortgage Interest Restrictions Act 1939; the Rent
Act 1957; the Rent Act 1965; and the Rent Act 1977. (The titles shortened as complexity
increased).

have intervened. The Rent Act 1957 released many tenancies from control, and whilst the ensuing years saw a gradual reversal of that policy of deregulation, the Acts being finally consolidated in the Rent Act 1977, legislative developments since then have promoted the freedom of the lettings market.

22–070   Part I of the Housing Act 1988 can be equated to the Rent Act 1957 in that it comprised an attempt to remove rent control from the private sector (to "deregulate"). It sought to phase out the Rent Acts by stipulating that from January 15, 1989 (the date the 1988 Act came into force), new residential lettings would no longer be subject to their control. The Rent Act "regulated" tenancy was replaced as the default mode of letting by the "assured" tenancy, permitting the landlord to charge a commercial rent, whilst at the same time giving the tenant some security in his own home. The Housing Act 1996 confers still greater autonomy on the private sector landlord by providing that, unless the parties agree otherwise, any assured tenancy granted on or after February 28, 1997 will be an assured shorthold tenancy. This form of tenancy, first created in the 1988 Act, enables the landlord to recover possession on giving notice, and thereby denies the tenant any significant security.

22–071   In this field, dates have always been significant, and January 15, 1989 and February 28, 1997 are of central importance. A private sector residential tenancy created before the former date (and a substantial number still exist) will normally be regulated under the Rent Act 1977; one created between the two dates will normally be an assured tenancy (unless the specific criteria for an assured shorthold have been satisfied); and one created on or after the latter date will normally be an assured shorthold tenancy. But these are rules of thumb only. Great care needs to be taken to ensure that the relevant statutory provisions are consulted in each case.

22–072   The residential public sector did not attract legislative protection until the implementation of the Housing Act 1980, which conferred secure tenancy status on the majority of tenants as well as certain licensees, and at the same time gave many such occupiers the right to buy their landlord's interest.

22–073   The six different systems of control we shall consider here may be conveniently listed as follows:

> (1) *Assured tenancies*: private sector tenancies created on or after January 15, 1989, which confer security of tenure and protection as to rent, though only for increases under periodic tenancies.[274]
>
> (2) *Assured shorthold tenancies*: private sector tenancies created on or after January 15, 1989, which confer no security of tenure but protection as to rent.[275]
>
> (3) *Regulated tenancies*: private sector tenancies created before January 15, 1989, which still confer security of tenure and protection as to rent under the Rent Act 1977.[276]

---

[274] Below, para.22–081.
[275] Below, para.22–124.
[276] Below, para.22–131.

(4) *Agricultural occupancies*: tenancies or licences held by agricultural tenants which confer protection similar to that given by assured tenancies and give special rights to alternative accommodation.[277]

(5) *Secure tenancies*: tenancies held from a local authority or other public body which confer protection as to possession (but not rent) and the right to buy the freehold or a long lease at a low rent.[278]

(6) *Residential long tenancies*: long tenancies at a low rent with protection as to possession and the right to buy the freehold or to be granted a new tenancy.[279]

In addition, certain long leases and other tenancies of flats may enjoy a collective statutory right of pre-emption exercisable if the landlord proposes to dispose of the building.[280]

The law that determines the rights and obligations of landlords, tenants and **22–074** other occupiers of dwellings is complex and extremely difficult to ascertain, and as a result the Law Commission has made wide-ranging recommendations for its reform.[281] One problem is that the statutes themselves do not provide a comprehensive code: it may be necessary, when considering whether a landlord is likely to succeed in possession proceedings against a tenant, to have regard to the ECHR, in particular Article 8, and, in certain cases, the possible application of discrimination law.

2. Human rights. Article 8 of the European Convention on Human Rights **22–075** provides that everyone has the right to respect for his home and prohibits interference by a public authority with the enjoyment of this right except interference that is in accordance with the law and that is necessary in a democratic society inter alia for the protection of the rights and freedoms of others.[282] In recent years, there have been many attempts on behalf of residential tenants to invoke Art.8 in the course of possession proceedings by local authorities. It was initially held by the House of Lords that where a court makes an order for possession in accordance with the domestic property law the essence of the right to respect for the home will not be violated, and so there is no need for the court to consider whether the interference is permitted by Art.8(2).[283] It followed that once the court had considered whether "the requirements of the law and the procedural safeguards which it lays down for the protection of the occupier" had been satisfied, it had complied with the

[277] Below, para.22–153.
[278] Below, para.22–161.
[279] Below, para.22–191.
[280] Below, para.22–214.
[281] *Renting Homes: the Final Report*, Law Com. No.297 (2006). At the time of writing, Government had not yet decided whether the recommendations should be implemented.
[282] For Art.1, see above, para.1–024.
[283] *Harrow LBC v Qazi* [2003] UKHL 43; [2004] 1 A.C. 983, as explained in *Kay v Lambeth LBC* [2006] UKHL 10; [2006] 2 A.C. 465 at [72]; Goymour [2006] C.L.J. 696.

ECHR and no further challenge on human rights grounds would be possible.[284]

22–076   However, in two important recent decisions, *Manchester CC v Pinnock*[285] and *Hounslow LBC v Powell*,[286] the Supreme Court has taken a different view. It is now accepted that in order for the law of England and Wales to be compatible with Art.8, the court being asked by a local authority to make a possession order must have the power to assess the proportionality of making the order and, in doing so, to resolve any disputed questions of fact.[287] However, the court will only be expected to conduct such a review where the tenant raises the issue and he is able to satisfy the court that the issue is seriously arguable; this is "a high threshold".[288] Lord Neuberger summarised the correct approach as follows:

> "The question is always whether the eviction is a proportionate means of achieving a legitimate aim. Where a person has no right in domestic law to remain in occupation of his home, the proportionality of making an order for possession at the suit of the local authority will be supported not merely by the fact that it would serve to vindicate the authority's ownership rights. It will also, at least normally, be supported by the fact that it would enable the authority to comply with its duties in relation to the distribution and management of its housing stock, including, for example, the fair allocation of its housing, the redevelopment of the site, the refurbishing of sub-standard accommodation, the need to move people who are in accommodation that now exceeds their needs, and the need to move vulnerable people into sheltered or warden-assisted housing. Furthermore, in many cases (such as this appeal) other cogent reasons, such as the need to remove a source of nuisance to neighbours, may support the proportionality of dispossessing the occupiers."[289]

22–077   It follows that in "the overwhelming majority of cases"[290] there will be no need for the local authority to explain and justify its reasons for seeking a possession order. Instead, the court "need be concerned only with the occupier's personal circumstances and any factual objections she may raise and (in the light only of what view it takes of them) with the question whether making the order for possession would be lawful and proportionate."[291] It is therefore incumbent on the tenant to raise the proportionality issue, and it is not necessary for the landlord (the claimant) to prove anything in addition to its

---

[284] *Kay v Lambeth LBC*, above, at [72] per Lord Hope. For further developments prior to the decisions of the Supreme Court below, see Nield [2010] Conv. 498.

[285] [2010] UKSC 45; [2011] 2 A.C. 104; Loveland [2011] E.H.R.L.R. 151; Goymour [2011] C.L.J. 9.

[286] [2011] UKSC 8; [2011] 2 A.C. 186.

[287] *Manchester CC v Pinnock* at [49].

[288] *Hounslow LBC v Powell* at [33] per Lord Hope.

[289] *Manchester CC v Pinnock*, above at [52].

[290] *Hounslow LBC v Powell*, above at [37] per Lord Hope.

[291] *Hounslow LBC v Powell* at [37] per Lord Hope.

due compliance with the statutory provisions, although there may be cases where the landlord wishes to put forward particular arguments or to adduce evidence in defence of its actions.[292]

It seems that a challenge to the landlord's actions based on Art.8 is viable   **22–078**
in particular where the landlord claims that the court has no discretion, on certain facts being proved, to refuse to make a possession order.[293] This is because the existence of a discretion based on what the court considers to be reasonable will already require the court to confront the issue of the proportionality of the landlord's action in seeking possession; in the words of Lord Neuberger:

> "Reasonableness . . . , like proportionality under article 8(2), requires the court to consider whether to order possession at all, and, if so, whether to make an outright order rather than a suspended order, and, if so, whether to direct that the outright order should not take effect for a significant time."[294]

It remains to be seen whether Art.8 can be invoked by private sector tenants; to date, it has been restricted in its application to those occupying in the public sector.[295]

3. Discrimination. The Disability Discrimination Act 1995 made it unlaw-   **22–079**
ful for a person managing any premises to discriminate against a disabled person occupying those premises whether by eviction or by subjection to any other detriment. It was held that to bring possession proceedings against a disabled tenant was prima facie discriminatory,[296] although it would be open to a landlord to justify the tenant's treatment by contending that it was necessary in order not to endanger the health or safety of any person (including that of the disabled person).[297] It was further held that, if the eviction were unlawful, it would be highly relevant to the court in determining whether it should exercise its discretion to make an order for possession.[298]

---

[292] *Hounslow LBC v Powell* at [43].

[293] *Manchester CC v Pinnock*, above, concerned a demoted tenancy; *Hounslow LBC v Powell*, above, comprised three appeals, two of which concerned introductory tenancies, and one of which concerned a licence to occupy granted to a homeless person. None of these defendants had statutory security.

[294] *Manchester CC v Pinnock*, above at [55].

[295] See *Manchester CC v Pinnock*, above at [50]; see further Loveland [2009] Conv. 396; Luba [2010] L. & T. Rev. 79.

[296] *Manchester CC v Romano* [2004] EWCA Civ 834; [2005] 1 W.L.R. 2775; *Richmond Court (Swansea) Ltd v Williams* [2006] EWCA Civ 1719; [2007] H.L.R. 22; *S v Floyd* [2008] EWCA Civ 201; [2008] 1 W.L.R. 1274; *Malcolm v Lewisham LBC* [2008] UKHL 43; [2008] 1 A.C. 1399.

[297] Disability Discrimination Act 1995 s.24(2), (3); *Manchester CC v Romano*, above.

[298] *North Devon Homes Ltd v Brazier* [2003] EWHC 574; [2003] H.L.R. 59; *Knowsley Housing Trust v McMullen* [2006] EWCA Civ 539; [2006] H.L.R. 43.

22–080   The Equality Act 2010 repealed the 1995 Act with effect from October 1, 2010.[299] Direct or indirect discrimination is now unlawful not only in relation to people with disabilities[300] but also on the ground of certain "protected characteristics", being age, disability, gender reassignment, marriage and civil partnership, pregnancy and maternity, race, religion or belief, sex and sexual orientation.[301] The 2010 Act extends the protection afforded initially by the 1995 Act by making it unlawful for a person managing premises to discriminate against any occupier whether by eviction or by subjection to any other detriment.[302] The 2010 Act also expands the definition of discrimination where disabled persons are concerned. Responding to a decision of the House of Lords on the 1995 Act,[303] it is now discriminatory to treat a disabled person unfavourably because of something arising in consequence of the person's disability, unless the defendant can show that the treatment was a proportionate means of achieving a legitimate aim.[304] It follows from all this that a landlord who seeks to recover possession from a tenant must be careful not to discriminate, as to do so may well lead to the court holding that it would not be reasonable to grant a possession order.[305] Even where the landlord can invoke a mandatory ground for possession, the tenant may be able to defend proceedings on the basis that the landlord is acting unlawfully.[306] In order to discriminate, the landlord must have actual or imputed knowledge of the tenant's protected characteristic; if the landlord neither knows nor has any means of knowing that, for example, the tenant has a certain disability, it will not be possible for the tenant to establish that the treatment of which he complains was related to the disability.[307]

A. Assured Tenancies

I. TENANCIES WITHIN PART I OF THE HOUSING ACT 1988

22–081   **1. Introduction.** An assured tenancy is a contractual tenancy upon which Pt I of the Housing Act 1988 confers additional security of tenure. Although the parties to the tenancy can agree any rent which they wish, there are statutory restrictions on rent increases under assured periodic tenancies. As a result of the Housing Act 1996, and subject to a contrary intention being expressed and certain exceptional circumstances, an assured tenancy entered into on or after February 28, 1997 takes effect as an assured shorthold tenancy. An assured shorthold tenant has, at least in theory, a little more protection as to rent than

---

[299] For a full treatment of the effect of the 2010 Act on landlord and tenant law, see Woodfall, 11.323 et seq.
[300] A disabled person is a person with a disability, that is a physical or mental impairment which has a substantial and long-term adverse effect on their ability to carry out normal day-to-day activities: Equality Act 2010 s.6(1), and for qualifications and exclusions, see Sch.1.
[301] Equality Act 2010 s.4.
[302] Equality Act 2010 s.35(1).
[303] *Malcolm v Lewisham LBC*, above.
[304] Equality Act 2010 s.15(1).
[305] *North Devon Homes Ltd v Brazier*, above.
[306] *Malcolm v Lewisham LBC*, above, at [19], [104], [160].
[307] *Malcolm v Lewisham LBC*.

the "standard" (i.e. non-shorthold) assured tenant, but he has no security of tenure. A large majority of private sector tenancies are now assured short-holds.[308] However, we shall consider first the law that applies to "standard" assured tenancies before examining assured shorthold tenancies in more detail.

2. Definition. Every tenancy under which a dwelling-house is let as a separate dwelling is an assured tenancy if and so long as (a) the tenant (or each of the joint tenants) is an individual[309]; (b) the tenant (or at least one of the joint tenants) occupies the dwelling-house as his only or principal home; and (c) the tenancy is not excluded from assured tenancy status by express statutory provision.[310] In particular, tenancies entered into before, or pursuant to a contract made before, January 15, 1989, cannot be assured tenancies.[311] **22–082**

(a) "Dwelling-house". A dwelling-house may be a house or a part of a house.[312] What is structurally a single dwelling-house often contains many "dwelling-houses" for the purposes of the Act, even if it has not been physically divided into self-contained flats. Thus one or two rooms, with a right to share the bathroom and lavatory, may for this purpose constitute a dwelling-house. **22–083**

(b) "Let as a separate dwelling". The premises must be "let", so that although any form of tenancy suffices (even a tenancy at will or at sufferance), mere licences do not.[313] Whether the premises are let "as" a dwelling depends upon the use provided for or contemplated by the tenancy agreement, or, in default, by the de facto user at the time.[314] The letting must be as "a" (i.e. a single) dwelling, and not for use as two or more dwellings.[315] Although the dwelling must be "separate",[316] the tenant who shares certain living accommodation with other occupiers will be protected by the Act as long as he has **22–084**

---

[308] The latest available figures indicate that in 2008 there were 340,000 assured tenancies and 1,864,000 assured shorthold tenancies: Department for Communities and Local Government *Housing Statistics* Table 731.

[309] Lettings to companies cannot be assured tenancies: see, e.g. *Hiller v United Dairies (London) Ltd* [1934] 1 K.B. 57; *Hilton v Plustitle Ltd* [1989] 1 W.L.R. 149; *Kaye v Massbetter Ltd* (1990) 24 H.L.R. 28.

[310] HA 1988 s.1(1).

[311] HA 1988 Sch.1 para.1. Such tenancies are likely to be regulated under the Rent Acts: see below, paras 22–131 et seq. Note also HA 1988 s.38, as amended by Local Government and Housing Act 1989 s.194(1) and Sch.11.

[312] HA 1988 s.45(1). The house must be part and parcel of the land: *Elitestone v Morris* [1997] 1 W.L.R. 687; *Chelsea Yacht & Boat Co Ltd v Pope* [2000] 1 W.L.R. 1941; *Mew v Tristmire Ltd* [2011] EWCA Civ 912; and see Ch.23 below.

[313] See above, para.17–012.

[314] *Wolfe v Hogan* [1949] 2 K.B. 194; *Russell v Booker* [1982] 2 E.G.L.R. 86.

[315] *Langford Property Co Ltd v Goldrich* [1949] 1 K.B. 511; cf. *Kavanagh v Lyroudias* [1985] 1 All E.R. 560.

[316] Cooking facilities are not an essential feature: *Uratemp Ventures Ltd v Collins* [2001] UKHL 43; [2002] 1 A.C. 301.

exclusive occupation of his own room.[317] If such a tenant shares with the landlord, however, he is likely to be excluded from protection.[318] Finally, the premises must be let as a "dwelling", i.e. for purely residential purposes,[319] and where the premises are let for a mixed use the tenancy cannot therefore be assured.[320] However, premises let partly for business and partly as a residence are treated as being business premises within Pt II of the Landlord and Tenant Act 1954.[321]

22–085   *(c) "Occupation as his only or principal home".* The tenant must occupy the dwelling-house as his only or principal home. It follows that an assured tenant will lose his statutory protection (and no longer be assured) if he ceases to occupy the premises as his home, or, where he has more than one, his principal home. Merely temporary absences are immaterial. However, should the absent tenant lose his *animus revertendi* (intention of returning) or his *corpus possessionis* (a visible indication of his continuing *animus*, such as the presence on the premises of a caretaker, or perhaps furniture), then he will no longer be an assured tenant.[322] A tenant who sub-lets the whole of the premises (even for a relatively short time) is unlikely to preserve continuity of occupation of the premises as his principal home.[323] However, a tenant who departs premises which comprised the home he shared with his spouse or civil partner,[324] leaving his spouse or civil partner in occupation, will remain an assured tenant, as the occupation of the spouse or civil partner will be deemed to be that of the absentee tenant.[325]

22–086   **3. Exceptions.** Certain tenancies which would otherwise be assured tenancies are excluded from the protection of the Act, on a variety of grounds.

22–087   *(a) Personal.* In some cases, the exception is personal to the landlord. Thus, a tenancy cannot be assured if the landlord is the Crown or a government department,[326] or a public body such as local authorities, the Homes and Communities Agency, urban development corporations, and housing action

---

[317] HA 1988 ss.3 and 10.
[318] See below, para.22–091.
[319] It is a matter of construing the contractual purpose: *Andrews v Brewer* (1997) 30 H.L.R. 203.
[320] *Pulleng v Curran* (1980) 44 P. & C.R. 58; *Tan v Sitkowski* [2007] EWCA Civ 30; [2007] 1 W.L.R. 1628.
[321] LTA 1954 s.23(1); HA 1988 Sch.1, para.4; see, e.g. *Cheryl Investments Ltd v Saldanha* [1978] 1 W.L.R. 1329, above, para.22–005.
[322] *Brown v Brash* [1948] 2 K.B. 247; *Tickner v Hearn* [1960] 1 W.L.R. 1406; *Gofor Investments Ltd v Roberts* (1975) 29 P. & C.R. 366; *Hampstead Way Investments Ltd v Lewis-Weare* [1985] 1 W.L.R. 164.
[323] *Ujima Housing Association v Ansah* (1997) 30 H.L.R. 831.
[324] cf. *Hall v King* [1988] 1 F.L.R. 376.
[325] Family Law Act 1996 s.30(4), as amended by Civil Partnership Act 2004 s.82 and Sch.9 para.1; cf. post-divorce, *Metropolitan Properties Co Ltd v Cronan* (1982) 44 P. & C.R. 1.
[326] HA 1988 Sch.1, para.11.

trusts.[327] While tenancies of "fully mutual" housing associations cannot be assured, tenancies of other housing associations can.[328]

(b) Nature of tenancy. Other exceptions depend on the nature of the tenancy. **22–088** Thus, a tenancy is not assured if the letting is rent-free, or the rent payable is £1,000 or less per annum in Greater London or £250 or less elsewhere.[329] Nor is a tenancy assured if it was granted in order to confer on the tenant the right to occupy the dwelling-house for a holiday,[330] or if the tenant is pursuing or intends to pursue a course of study provided by a specified educational institution and the tenancy was granted either by that institution or by another such institution or body of persons.[331] A protected or secure tenancy[332] cannot be an assured tenancy.[333]

(c) Nature of premises. Other exceptions depend upon the nature and status **22–089** of the premises themselves. Thus tenancies of public houses are excluded,[334] and few agricultural lettings will be assured tenancies.[335] Normally, where the main purpose of a letting is the provision of a home for the tenant, any land "let together with" a dwelling-house is treated as being part of it: but the tenancy will not be assured if more than two acres of agricultural land are let together with the house.[336]

(d) High rent or rateable value. The abolition of the domestic rating system **22–090** led to complicated amendments of the exclusion from assured tenancy status of dwelling-houses with high rateable values.[337] Where the tenancy was entered into before April 1, 1990, or subsequently in pursuance of a contract made before that date, then it cannot be assured if the dwelling-house had a rateable value on March 31, 1990 in excess of £1,500 in Greater London or £750 elsewhere.[338] However, where the tenancy commenced on or after April 1, 1990, the test is the level of the rent. If the rent payable exceeds £100,000

---

[327] HA 1988 Sch.1, para.12, as variously amended. Tenancies by such public bodies tend to be "secure tenancies", and subject to a distinct code of protection altogether: see below, para.22–161.

[328] HA 1988 Sch.1, para.12. See also exclusions for accommodation provided for asylum seekers and persons with temporary protection, and exclusions for "family intervention tenancies" (following domestic violence): HA 1988 Sch.1 paras 12A and 12B, inserted by the Immigration and Asylum Act 1999 s.169, Sch.14 para.88; SI 2005/1379 Sch.1 para.6; HA 1988 Sch.1 para.12ZA, inserted by Housing and Regeneration Act 2008 s.297(2).

[329] HA 1988 Sch.1 para.3A, a provision which does not apply if the tenancy was granted before April 1, 1990. For tenancies granted before that date, the rent must be less than two-thirds of the rateable value of the house on March 31, 1990: HA 1988 Sch.1 para.3B.

[330] HA 1988 Sch.1 para.9.

[331] HA 1988 Sch.1 para.8; SI 1998/1967.

[332] On which, see below, paras 22–134 and 22–162 respectively.

[333] HA 1988 Sch.1 para.13.

[334] HA 1988 Sch.1 para.5.

[335] HA 1988 Sch.1 para.7. They will normally be subject to either the Agricultural Holdings Act 1986 or the Agricultural Tenancies Act 1995: see above, paras 22–027 et seq.

[336] HA 1988 s.2; Sch.1 para.6.

[337] References to Rating (Housing) Regulations, SI 1990/434.

[338] HA 1988 Sch.1 para.2A (as amended).

per annum (wherever the premises are situated), the tenancy cannot be assured.[339]

22–091   *(e) Resident landlords.* In order to obviate the "social embarrassment" which may arise out of "close proximity",[340] Pt I of the Housing Act 1988 excludes certain tenancies granted by resident landlords from statutory protection. The term "resident landlord" is used to denote a landlord where the dwelling that is let forms part of a building, and throughout the tenancy, with minor qualifications, the landlord for the time being (or one of two or more joint landlords) has occupied as his only or principal home another dwelling in the same building.[341] The provisions do not apply to a purpose-built block of flats[342] unless the dwelling let is part of a flat in the block and the landlord occupies as his home another dwelling in that flat. Nor does it apply if the tenant was immediately prior to the letting an assured tenant of the dwelling, or of another dwelling in the same building.[343]

II. SECURITY OF TENURE

22–092   The general law sufficiently protects an ordinary tenant against eviction as long as his tenancy exists.[344] But once it has ended, whether by notice to quit, effluxion of time or otherwise, his dwelling-house is liable to repossession by the landlord unless statute otherwise provides. Part I of the Housing Act 1988 gives protection in relation to periodic assured tenancies by rendering service of a notice to quit by the landlord ineffective and in relation to fixed-term assured tenancies by imposing a statutory periodic tenancy on the expiry of the term. Although the tenant can terminate an assured tenancy by exercising such rights as the contract confers (e.g. by giving notice of the appropriate length), the landlord can recover possession only by obtaining an order of the court on proof of one of the statutory grounds for possession. The distinction between fixed-term tenancy and periodic tenancy is central to the machinery of the Act.

22–093   **1. Fixed-term tenancy.** For the purposes of the 1988 Act, a fixed-term tenancy is any tenancy other than a periodic tenancy.[345] The court cannot make an order for possession of a dwelling-house currently being let on a fixed-term assured tenancy unless:

---

[339] HA 1988 Sch.1 para.2 (as amended); the figure was increased from £25,000 with effect from October 1, 2010 in England, and with effect from December 1, 2011 in Wales: SI 2010/908; 2011/1409. See *Bankway Properties Ltd v Penfold-Dunsford* [2001] EWCA Civ 528; [2001] 1 W.L.R. 1369 for an unsuccessful attempt to use this provision to avoid statutory protection.

[340] *Bardrick v Haycock* (1976) 31 P. & C.R. 420 at 424, per Lord Scarman.

[341] HA 1988 Sch.1 para.10 and Pt III.

[342] See, e.g. *Barnes v Gorsuch* (1981) 43 P. & C.R. 294.

[343] HA 1988 Sch.1 para.10(3), an anti-avoidance provision.

[344] See further above, paras 19–007 et seq.

[345] HA 1988 s.45(1). A tenancy granted for a term certain of one year and "thereafter from month to month" is a fixed-term tenancy: *Goodman v Evely* [2001] EWCA Civ 104; [2002] H.L.R. 53.

(a)   the landlord proves one of Grounds 2, 8, 10 to 15, and 17 in Sch.2
      to the Act[346]; and

(b)   "the terms of the tenancy make provision for it to be brought to an
      end on the ground in question (whether that provision takes the form
      of a provision for re-entry, for forfeiture, for determination by notice
      or otherwise)."[347]

The landlord may terminate an assured fixed-term tenancy by exercising a
power reserved in the lease to determine the tenancy in certain circumstances
(as under a break clause, though not a proviso for re-entry for breach of
covenant[348]), but this will not normally entitle the landlord to possession.[349]
On termination of an assured fixed-term tenancy otherwise than by court order
or by the tenant's action, the tenant's right to possession will be preserved
under a periodic tenancy arising by virtue of statute: a statutory periodic
tenancy.[350]

2. Periodic tenancy. An assured periodic tenancy, whether it be contractual   **22–094**
(i.e. where the parties initially agreed upon a periodic tenancy) or statutory,
cannot be brought to an end by the landlord except by obtaining an order of
the court.[351] A court order can only be obtained on proof of one of Grounds
1 to 17 set out in Sch.2 to the Act.[352]

3. Grounds for possession. Proof of a ground for possession is therefore   **22–095**
essential, whether the assured tenancy is fixed-term or periodic. The landlord
and tenant cannot contract out of the protection given by the Act.[353] Unless the
tenant voluntarily gives notice, surrenders his interest, or ceases to be an
assured tenant altogether (e.g. by ceasing to occupy the house as his principal
home), the landlord must seek a court order.[354] However, the assured tenant's
security does not prevent the recovery of possession by local authorities
seeking to exercise their public law powers,[355] or by the tenant's mortgagees
seeking to exercise their contractual or statutory powers.[356]

---

[346] See below, paras 22–099 to 22–117.

[347] HA 1988 s.7(6).

[348] HA 1988 s.45(4).

[349] HA 1988 s.5(1). The court has power to grant demotion orders to certain social landlords
as a response to anti-social behaviour: see further para.22–119 below.

[350] HA 1988 s.5(2) and (3). The periods will be those for which rent was last payable under the
fixed term: *Church Commissioners v Meya* [2006] EWCA Civ 821; [2007] H.L.R. 4. See also s.6,
which contains the machinery whereby the terms of a statutory periodic tenancy other than rent
can be varied.

[351] HA 1988 s.5(1).

[352] HA 1988 s.7(1): see below, paras 22–098 to 22–117. The rights of a mortgagee to bring
possession proceedings are expressly preserved by this provision.

[353] HA 1988 s.5(5).

[354] The court has no jurisdiction to make a possession order by consent unless there is an
express or implied admission of the ground for possession: *Baygreen Properties Ltd v Gil* [2002]
EWCA Civ 1340; [2003] H.L.R. 12.

[355] See, e.g. HA 1985 s.612.

[356] Reserved by HA 1988 s.7(1).

22–096   There are two kinds of ground for possession. On proof of a "mandatory ground" (Grounds 1 to 8), the court must make a possession order, and it has limited flexibility in stipulating the time when the tenant must leave. On proof of a "discretionary ground" (Grounds 9 to 17), the court may make a possession order if it considers it reasonable to do so. Should the court decide to make an order on a discretionary ground, it has a wide discretion to stay or suspend possession, or to postpone the date for delivering up possession.[357] The extent to which a tenant may invoke Art.8 of the ECHR as a defence to possession proceedings by a private sector landlord is currently uncertain.[358]

22–097   It is an implied term of every assured periodic tenancy[359] that the tenant shall not assign, in whole or in part, or sub-let or part with possession of the whole or any part of the dwelling-house without the consent of the landlord.[360] If a dwelling-house is lawfully sub-let[361] by an assured tenant, the head landlord who recovers possession against him will remain bound by the interest of the sub-tenant, the sub-tenant becoming the assured tenant of the head landlord.[362] In such circumstances, the landlord will have to prove a ground for possession as against any other assured tenant.

22–098   *(a) Mandatory grounds.* If the landlord establishes a mandatory ground, the court must order possession, whether or not it is reasonable to do so.[363] The court cannot postpone the date for possession for more than 14 days, or six weeks if "exceptional hardship" would otherwise be caused.[364] The grounds are as follows.[365]

22–099   GROUND 1: OWNER-OCCUPIER. This ground comprises two discrete alternatives:

---

[357] HA 1988 s.9. The assured tenancy will terminate on the date that the order of the court is executed: *Knowsley Housing Trust v White* [2008] UKHL 70; [2009] 1 A.C. 636; HA 1988 s.5(1A), inserted by Housing and Regeneration Act 2008 Sch.11 para.6(2). See further the analogous provisions on secure tenancies at para.22–171 below.

[358] *Manchester CC v Pinnock* [2010] UKSC 45; [2011] 2 A.C. 104 at [50]; see further Loveland [2009] Conv. 396; Luba [2010] L. & T. Rev. 79. However, where possession is sought and granted on a discretionary ground, the exercise required to be conducted by the court is extremely likely to satisfy Art.8; the issue arises with the mandatory grounds: *Manchester CC v Pinnock* at [55] et seq.; see above, paras 22–075 et seq.

[359] Save where express prohibition is made, or a premium is required to be paid on the grant or renewal of the tenancy: HA 1988 s.15(3).

[360] HA 1988 s.15(1). The landlord need not have reasonable grounds for withholding consent, unless the tenancy expressly indicates otherwise: HA 1988 s.15(2).

[361] This will include sub-leases where the head landlord has waived the breach of covenant which they occasioned: see, e.g. *Oak Property Co Ltd v Chapman* [1947] K.B. 886.

[362] Unless the tenancy is precluded from being an assured tenancy by Sch.1 to the HA 1988. See HA 1988 s.18(1) and (2).

[363] HA 1988 s.7(3).

[364] HA 1980 s.89. The compatibility of this provision with Art.8 ECHR was considered, and not entirely resolved, in *Hounslow LBC v Powell* [2011] UKSC 8; [2011] 2 A.C. 186 at [57] et seq.; cf. *Manchester CC v Pinnock*, above at [63].

[365] See generally HA 1988 Sch.2.

(i) the landlord[366] who is now seeking possession occupied the dwelling-house as his only or principal home at some time before the beginning of the tenancy[367]; or

(ii) the landlord[368] who is now seeking possession requires the dwelling-house as his or his spouse or civil partner's only or principal home.[369] In this case, neither the landlord nor any predecessor of his must have become landlord by acquiring the reversion for money or money's worth.[370]

Whenever (i) or (ii) above is relied upon, the landlord must have given written notice to the tenant, not later than the beginning of the tenancy, that possession might be recovered under this ground. The court has power to dispense with this requirement of prior written notice where it is of opinion that it is just and equitable to do so.[371]

GROUND 2: MORTGAGEE SEEKING POSSESSION. The dwelling-house is subject **22–100** to a mortgage granted before the beginning of the tenancy, and the mortgagee, being entitled to exercise a power of sale conferred by the mortgage or by statute, requires possession of the house for the purpose of disposing of it with vacant possession in exercise of that power. As long as notice was given as under Ground 1 (or the court dispenses with such notice), then the court must order possession.

GROUND 3: SHORT LETTING OF HOLIDAY HOME. The tenancy was granted for a **22–101** fixed term not exceeding eight months, and at some time within the 12 months prior to the letting, the dwelling was occupied under a right to occupy it for a holiday. The landlord must have given written notice, not later than the beginning of the tenancy, that possession might be recovered under this ground. The court has no apparent power to dispense with notice.

GROUND 4: SHORT LETTING OF STUDENT RESIDENCE. The tenancy was granted **22–102** for a fixed term not exceeding 12 months, and at some time within the 12 months previous to the letting the dwelling was let to a student by a specified educational institution. The landlord must have given written notice, not later than the beginning of the tenancy, that possession might be recovered under this ground, the court having no power to dispense with this requirement.

GROUND 5: MINISTER OF RELIGION. The dwelling is held for the purpose of **22–103** being available for occupation by a minister of religion as a residence from

---

[366] Or, in the case of joint landlords seeking possession, one of them.
[367] It is not necessary for the landlord to show an intention to resume occupation, so that Ground 1 can be used to obtain vacant possession merely with a view to sale.
[368] See fn.366 above.
[369] As amended by Civil Partnership Act 2004 Sch.8 para.43.
[370] See above, para.22–021.
[371] For guidelines on the use of such a dispensation power, see *Bradshaw v Baldwin-Wiseman* (1985) 49 P. & C.R. 382 at 388. Giving oral notice at the time of grant may be an important factor, but it is not a prerequisite to exercising the power of dispensation: *Boyle v Verrall* [1997] 1 E.G.L.R. 25.

which to perform the duties of his office, and the dwelling is now required for this purpose. As with Grounds 3 and 4, prior written notice must have been given to the tenant.

22–104   GROUND 6: DEMOLITION OR RECONSTRUCTION. The landlord seeking possession[372] intends to demolish or reconstruct the whole or a substantial part of the dwelling-house, or to carry out substantial works on the dwelling-house or any part thereof or any building of which it forms part, and all the following conditions are fulfilled:

> (a) the work cannot reasonably be carried out without the tenant giving up possession, for one of four reasons (the tenant is not willing to agree to a variation of the terms of his tenancy; the nature of the work is such that no such variation is practicable; the tenant is not willing to accept an assured tenancy of a reduced part of the dwelling so that the landlord could then carry out the works; or the nature of the works is such that no such tenancy of a reduced part is practicable); and

> (b) either the landlord seeking possession acquired his interest in the dwelling before the grant of the tenancy, or, if he acquired his interest subsequently, such acquisition was not for money or money's worth; and

> (c) the assured tenancy did not arise by virtue of the succession provisions of the Rent Act 1977[373] or the Rent (Agriculture) Act 1976.[374]

Proof of the landlord's intention will depend on the same factors as the like ground contained in the business tenancy code, on which this provision was modelled.[375]

22–105   GROUND 7: DEATH OF PERIODIC TENANT. Where an assured periodic tenancy devolves by will or on intestacy (and not by statute[376]), the landlord has a 12-month period of grace during which he can decide whether he wishes to recover possession. If in that period (which runs from the date of the death, or, if the court so orders, from the date the landlord became aware of the death) the landlord seeks possession, the court must make the order.

22–106   GROUND 8: NON-PAYMENT OF RENT. At least two months' rent[377] that is lawfully due is unpaid both at the date of the service of the notice seeking

---

[372] Or, if that landlord is a certain type of social landlord (on which see see Ground 6), a superior landlord.
[373] See below, para.22–139.
[374] See below, para.22–155.
[375] LTA 1954 s.30(1)(f); see above, para.22–020.
[376] HA 1988 s.17: see below, para.22–120.
[377] For the precise method of calculating the rent arrears required, see HA 1988 Sch.2 Ground 8, as amended by HA 1996 s.101.

possession[378] and at the date of the hearing.[379] If the landlord is unable to prove Ground 8, he may choose to claim possession on discretionary Grounds 10 or 11 below.

(b) Discretionary grounds. If the overriding requirement of reasonableness **22–107** is satisfied, the court may make an order for possession in the following cases.[380] There is a wide discretion to adjourn the proceedings, or to stay, suspend, or postpone possession, which, when exercised, will often be subject to terms (e.g. as to payment of rent arrears).[381]

GROUND 9: SUITABLE ALTERNATIVE ACCOMMODATION.[382] Suitable alternative **22–108** accommodation is available for the tenant, or will be when the order for possession takes effect. The alternative accommodation must be either on an assured tenancy (neither a shorthold nor a tenancy in respect of which notices under Grounds 1 to 5 have been served) or on terms which afford reasonably equivalent security to the tenant. In addition, it must be reasonably suitable to the needs of the tenant and his family as regards proximity to place of work and either similar as regards rental and extent to houses provided in the neighbourhood by a local housing authority for those with similar needs as regards extent, or else reasonably suitable to the tenant's means and his and his family's needs as regards extent and character. If furniture has been provided, furniture must be provided in the alternative accommodation which either is similar or is reasonably suitable to the needs of the tenant and his family. But the accommodation need not be as good, or as cheap,[383] as the existing accommodation, and it may even consist of part of it[384]: the question is whether it is "reasonably suitable", not "as suitable",[385] and the evaluation of reasonableness is essentially a matter for the court in light of the circumstances of the case.[386] However, a certificate of the local housing authority that it will provide suitable alternative accommodation for the tenant by a specified date is conclusive.[387]

GROUND 10: NON-PAYMENT OF RENT. Some rent lawfully due from the tenant **22–109** is unpaid on the date proceedings are begun, and was also in arrears at the date

---

[378] See below, para.22–118; and for the effect of non-compliance, *Mountain v Hastings* (1993) 25 H.L.R. 427.

[379] The court should not adjourn possession proceedings brought under Ground 8 save in exceptional circumstances. The accumulation of rent arrears owing to delay in the payment of housing benefit is not exceptional for these purposes: *North British Housing Association v Matthews* [2004] EWCA Civ 1736; [2005] 1 W.L.R. 3133.

[380] HA 1988 s.7(4).

[381] HA 1988 s.9.

[382] See further HA 1988 Sch.2, Pt III.

[383] *Cresswell v Hodgson* [1951] 2 K.B. 92.

[384] *Mykolyshyn v Noah* [1970] 1 W.L.R. 1271.

[385] *Warren v Austen* [1947] 2 All E.R. 185 at 188.

[386] *Cresswell v Hodgson*, above; *Whitehouse v Lee* [2009] EWCA Civ 375; [2009] L. & T.R. 29 (on Rent Act 1977 s.98(1) on which see para.22–142 below.)

[387] HA 1988 Sch.2 Pt III para.1.

the landlord served the notice seeking possession[388] (save where the court dispenses with service of such a notice).

22–110   GROUND 11: PERSISTENT DELAY IN PAYMENT OF RENT. The tenant has persistently delayed in paying rent which has become lawfully due. It does not matter that no rent is in arrear at the date proceedings are begun or heard: the object is to give the court power to remove a persistent defaulter.

22–111   GROUND 12: BREACH OF OBLIGATION. Any obligation of the tenancy (other than one related to the payment of rent) has been broken or not performed.

22–112   GROUND 13: DETERIORATION OF DWELLING-HOUSE. The tenant, or any other person residing in the dwelling-house, is responsible, through acts of waste, neglect, or default, for the deterioration of the condition of the dwelling or any of the common parts. Where the waste, neglect or default was that of a lodger or sub-tenant of his, the tenant must have failed to take reasonable steps to remove him.

22–113   GROUND 14[389]: NUISANCE. The tenant or any person residing in or visiting the dwelling-house has been guilty of conduct causing or likely to cause a nuisance or annoyance to a person residing, visiting, or otherwise engaging in a lawful activity in the locality, or has been convicted either of using the dwelling-house, or allowing it to be used, for immoral or illegal purposes[390] or of an indictable offence committed in, or in the locality of, the dwelling-house.[391] In deciding whether it is reasonable to make an order for possession under Ground 14, the court must consider the effect of the nuisance or annoyance on other persons, such as neighbours.[392] Certain social landlords[393] may seek a demotion order from the court where their assured tenant, or another resident of or visitor to the dwelling-house has engaged in, or threatened to engage in, anti-social behaviour.[394]

---

[388] See below, para.22–118.

[389] As amended by HA 1996 s.148.

[390] *S. Schneiders & Sons v Abrahams* [1925] 1 K.B. 301; *Abrahams v Wilson* [1971] Q.B. 88.

[391] This offence may pre-date the commencement of the tenancy: *Raglan Housing Association Ltd v Fairclough* [2007] EWCA Civ 1087; [2008] H.L.R. 21.

[392] HA 1988 s.9A, added by Anti-social Behaviour Act 2003 s.14(6). There is an abundance of case law, across the several statutory regimes, on the courts' appropriate response to anti-social behaviour on the part of tenants and their visitors: see, e.g. *Kensington & Chelsea LBC v Simmonds* (1996) 29 H.L.R. 507; *New Charter Housing (North) Ltd v Ashcroft* [2004] EWCA Civ 310; [2004] H.L.R. 36; *London & Quadrant Housing Association v Root* [2005] EWCA Civ 43; [2005] H.L.R. 28; *Moat Housing Group-South Ltd v Harris* [2005] EWCA Civ 287; [2006] Q.B. 606; *Manchester CC v Higgins* [2005] EWCA Civ 1423; [2006] 1 All E.R. 841; *Knowsley Housing Trust v McMullen* [2006] EWCA Civ 539; [2006] H.L.R. 43; *Brent LBC v Doughan* [2007] EWCA Civ 135; [2007] H.L.R. 28; *Swindon BC v Redpath* [2009] EWCA Civ 943; [2010] 1 All E.R. 1003. See also Bright [2006] Conv. 85.

[393] As defined in HA 1988 s.6A.

[394] HA 1988 s.6A, added by Anti-social Behaviour Act 2003 s.14(4): see further para.22–119 below.

GROUND 14A[395]: DOMESTIC VIOLENCE. The dwelling-house was occupied by **22–114** a married couple, civil partners, or a couple living together as husband and wife or as civil partners, and one partner has left the house, and is unlikely to return because of violence or threats of violence by the other towards that partner or a member of that partner's family residing with that partner. This ground may only be invoked by certain social landlords[396] and charitable housing trusts.[397]

GROUND 15: DETERIORATION OF FURNITURE. The tenant or any other person **22–115** residing with him is responsible, through ill-treatment, for the deterioration of the condition of furniture provided under the tenancy. As with Ground 13 above, the tenant must have failed to take reasonable steps for the removal of such other person who is a lodger or sub-tenant.

GROUND 16: EMPLOYEES' LETTINGS. The dwelling was let to the tenant in **22–116** consequence of his employment by the landlord seeking possession or a previous landlord, and the tenant has ceased to be in that employment.

GROUND 17[398]: FALSE STATEMENT BY TENANT. The landlord was induced to **22–117** grant the tenancy by a false statement made knowingly or recklessly by the tenant (that tenant being the current tenant, or one of them) or a person acting at the tenant's instigation.

4. Possession proceedings[399]

(a) Notice seeking possession. Before beginning proceedings, the landlord **22–118** must serve a notice in prescribed form[400] on the tenant informing him that he intends to bring possession proceedings on one or more grounds specified in the notice, and that those proceedings will not begin earlier than a date specified in the notice. The minimum notice is two weeks (applicable where possession is to be sought on Grounds 3, 4, 8, 10 to 15 inclusive, and 17): otherwise the notice must be no less than two months, and, in the case of a periodic tenancy requiring a longer notice to quit, must be a notice of that length. The court has a discretion to dispense with service of the notice where it considers it just and equitable to do so,[401] but this power cannot be exercised where the landlord seeks to recover possession on Ground 8.

---

[395] Added by HA 1996 s.149, and amended by Civil Partnership Act 2004 Sch.8 para.43; see *Camden LBC v Mallett* (2001) 33 H.L.R. 20. There are additional notice requirements in relation to this ground: see HA 1988 s.8A, inserted by HA 1996 s.150. The ground is not limited in its application to threats or acts of violence while the parties to the relationship were living together: *Metropolitan Housing Trust v Hadjazi* [2010] EWCA Civ 750; [2011] H.L.R. 39.

[396] See Ground 14A, condition (b).

[397] Defined as a housing trust (see Housing Associations Act 1985 s.2) which is a charity (as defined in Charities Act 2006 s.1).

[398] Added by HA 1996 s.102. See also HA 1985 Sch.2 Ground 5.

[399] HA 1988 s.8, as amended by HA 1996 s.151.

[400] SI 1997/194 Form 3; see *Mountain v Hastings* (1993) 25 H.L.R. 427; *Marath v MacGillivray* (1996) 28 H.L.R. 484.

[401] *Kelsey Housing Association v King* (1995) 28 H.L.R. 270; *Knowsley Housing Trust v Revell* [2003] EWCA Civ 496; [2003] H.L.R. 63.

22–119   *(b) Demotion orders.* In order to deal with anti-social behaviour, certain social landlords[402] may seek a demotion order in respect of an assured tenancy.[403] Its effect is to terminate the assured tenancy and to replace it, for the time being, with a "demoted" tenancy under which the tenant's security is diminished to that of an assured shorthold tenant. The landlord must first serve a preliminary notice on the tenant,[404] and then apply to the court for a demotion order. The court must not make such an order unless it is satisfied that it is reasonable to do so, and that the tenant, or a person residing in or visiting the dwelling-house, has engaged, or threatened to engage, in certain conduct.[405] Once a demotion order takes effect, the tenancy becomes an assured shorthold tenancy,[406] and will remain so for a period of one year.[407] If during that period, no notice of possession proceedings is given by the landlord, the tenancy will thereupon cease to be an assured shorthold tenancy and resume its former status as a standard assured tenancy.[407a]

22–120   **5. Succession to assured tenancies.** Where an assured tenant has a fixed-term tenancy, the term will pass on the death of the tenant to the person entitled under the tenant's will or intestacy.[408] Where the assured tenancy is periodic, however, succession provisions in the 1988 Act[409] take precedence over the will or the intestacy rules. By these provisions, an assured periodic tenancy will vest in the tenant's spouse or civil partner (defined so as to include a person living with the tenant as his spouse or civil partner[410]) on his death, provided three conditions are satisfied:

---

[402] The landlord must be a non-profit registered provider of social housing; a profit-making registered provider of social housing (and the dwelling-house let on the tenancy is social housing within Housing and Regeneration Act 2008 Pt. 2); or a registered social landlord: HA 1988 s.6A(1).

[403] HA 1988 ss.6A and 20B, inserted by the Anti-social Behaviour Act 2003 s.14(4). The process of obtaining a demotion order requires the court, following an investigation of the facts, to consider whether it is reasonable to make such an order; it is therefore compatible with Art.8 ECHR: *Manchester CC v Pinnock* [2010] UKSC 45; [2011] 2 A.C. 104 at [66]. See further para.22–178 below.

[404] HA 1988 ss.6A(5) and (6). The court has power to dispense where it is just and equitable to do so.

[405] HA 1988 s.6A(4). The conduct is that to which HA 1996 ss.153A or 153B applies, namely (a) conduct which is capable of causing nuisance or annoyance to any person, and which directly or indirectly relates to or affects the housing management functions of a relevant landlord, or (b) conduct which consists of or involves using or threatening to use housing accommodation owned or managed by a relevant landlord for an unlawful purpose.

[406] HA 1988 s.20B(1).

[407] HA 1988 s.20B(2). The period is extended if the landlord gives notice of proceedings for possession before it expires: HA 1988 s.20B(3).

[407a] In certain circumstances, a landlord who is a private registered provider of social housing will be able to replace the demoted tenancy with a fixed term assured shorthold tenancy: Localism Act 2011 s.163(2), not in force at the time of writing, inserting HA 1988 s.20C.

[408] See Ch.14 above.

[409] HA 1988 s.17, as amended by Civil Partnership Act 2004 s.81; Sch.8 para.41. Amendments in the Localism Act 2011 s.161, not in force at the time of writing, will restrict succession rights where the landlord is a private registered provider of social housing (England only).

[410] The relationship must be one which has been presented to the outside world openly and unequivocally so that society considers it to have the requisite degree of permanence: see *Nutting v Southern Housing Group* [2004] EWHC 2982; [2005] H.L.R. 25; *Baynes v Hedger* [2008] EWHC 1587 (Ch); [2008] 2 F.L.R. 1805. See further para.14–005, fn.21.

(1) the tenant was the sole tenant. If the tenancy was held jointly with another or others, then survivorship will operate;

(2) the spouse or civil partner was occupying the dwelling as his only or principal home immediately before the death of the tenant; and

(3) the tenant was not himself a "successor". He will be a successor for these purposes if the tenancy became vested in him by virtue of the Rent Act 1977 or the Housing Act 1988 under the will or on the intestacy of a previous tenant, or by right of survivorship. It is immaterial that the landlord has granted a new tenancy to him since the succession took place.

6. Protection as to rent. The only jurisdiction enjoyed by rent assessment committees over assured tenancies (with the exception of assured shorthold tenancies)[411] concerns rent increases in periodic tenancies. This jurisdiction is essential for the protection of the landlord as much as the tenant. The landlord is in a weak negotiating position, as he cannot effectively terminate an assured periodic tenancy by service of a notice to quit when faced with a tenant who is unwilling to accept a rent increase. The landlord may have been sufficiently perspicacious to insert a rent review clause into the tenancy agreement: in so far as such a provision is for the time being binding on the tenant, the statutory procedure will not apply.[412] However, it has been held that a rent review clause contained in a fixed-term tenancy is not carried forward into the statutory periodic tenancy that arises on its expiry,[413] and it follows that the procedure provided by the 1988 Act will always be available in the case of a statutory periodic tenancy.   **22–121**

The statutory rent increase procedure[414] requires the landlord to serve notice in prescribed form[415] on the tenant proposing a new rent to take effect at the beginning of a new period of the tenancy. Save where the tenancy is yearly, or based on periods of less than a month (notices of six months and one month are then respectively required), the landlord must give notice no shorter than the length of a period of the tenancy. Where the periodic tenancy is contractual, a landlord cannot attempt to obtain an increased rent in the first year of the tenancy. Where the periodic tenancy is statutory (i.e. taking effect following expiry of a fixed term), there is no such restriction. Where rent has   **22–122**

---

[411] See below, para.22–124.

[412] HA 1988 s.13(1)(b); *Contour Homes Ltd v Rowen* [2007] EWCA Civ 842; [2007] 1 W.L.R. 2982. But sham devices inserted to avoid security of tenure will be struck down: *Bankway Properties Ltd v Penfold-Dunsford* [2001] EWCA 528; [2001] W.L.R. 1369.

[413] The rent review clause is of no effect even if it purports to govern the rent payable once the fixed-term expires: *London District Properties Management Ltd v Goolamy* [2009] EWHC 1367 (Admin); [2010] 1 W.L.R. 307, applying HA 1988 s.5(3).

[414] HA 1988 s.13, as amended by SI 2003/259 art.2.

[415] SI 1997/194, as amended by SI 2003/260: see Form 4B.

previously been increased under the statutory procedures, the usual rule is that it should not be increased for a year after the increase takes effect.[416]

22–123   If the tenant wishes to object to the rent proposed by the landlord, he refers the notice to the rent assessment committee by an application in prescribed form.[417] The committee then determines the rent at which they consider the dwelling-house might reasonably be expected to be let on the open market by a willing landlord under an assured tenancy, disregarding such factors as the tenancy being granted to a sitting tenant, increases in the value of the dwelling attributable to certain tenant's improvements, and reductions in its value attributable to the tenant's failure to comply with the terms of the tenancy.[418] The rent determined will then become the rent payable under the tenancy with effect from the date specified in the landlord's notice, although the committee has a discretion to set a later date where undue hardship would be caused to the tenant.[419] A rent assessment committee has jurisdiction to set a rent above the £100,000 limit for assured tenancies,[420] although the effect of such a determination will be to render the tenancy no longer assured.[421]

B. Assured shorthold tenancies

22–124   In order to encourage the grant of residential tenancies, the Housing Act 1980 permitted landlords to grant, on fulfilling numerous tightly prescribed conditions, a "protected shorthold tenancy". This gave the tenant the same rent control as any other Rent Act regulated tenant, but without the security of tenure. In essence, on termination of the contractual tenancy, the landlord of a protected shorthold tenant could obtain possession as of right. Part I of the Housing Act 1988 phased out the protected shorthold tenancy in much the same way as other regulated tenancies, replacing it in the new regime with the assured shorthold tenancy. Devoid of statutory security of tenure, the assured shorthold tenant has, at least in theory, a little more protection as to rent than the "standard" (i.e. non-shorthold) assured tenant. Until the Housing Act 1996, the landlord had to satisfy relatively strict conditions to create an effective shorthold, in particular requiring him to serve a notice on the tenant informing him of his occupational status. But as a result of the 1996 Act the assured shorthold tenancy became the default tenancy. Unless the parties expressly contract otherwise (or certain exceptions apply) any assured tenancy, whether it is a fixed-term or periodic tenancy, entered into on or after

---

[416] The provisions are complex: see in particular HA 1988 ss.13(3), (3A) and (3B).

[417] HA 1988 s.13(4); SI 1997/194 Form 5. For rent assessment committee regulations, see SI 1971/1065, as amended by, inter alia, SI 1988/2200.

[418] HA 1988 s.14; cf. disrepair for which the tenant's predecessor was responsible: *N. & D. (London) Ltd v Gadson* [1992] 1 E.G.L.R. 112.

[419] HA 1988 s.14(7).

[420] See above, para.22–090.

[421] *R. v London Rent Assessment Panel Ex p. Cadogan Estates Ltd* [1998] Q.B. 398. A similar outcome arose in *Hughes v Borodex Ltd* [2010] EWCA Civ 425; [2010] 1 W.L.R. 2682, on which see below, para.22–196, fn.720.

February 28, 1997 will be an assured shorthold. A large majority of private sector residential tenancies are now assured shortholds.[422]

1. Definition. There are a number of ways whereby an assured shorthold **22–125** tenancy may have been created, much depending on the date of its commencement:

(1) Where any assured tenancy is entered into on or after February 28, 1997 (otherwise than pursuant to a contract made before that date) it will be an assured shorthold tenancy unless it falls within one of a number of statutory exceptions[423]:

(i) the landlord served a notice on the tenant before the tenancy was entered into stating that the tenancy was not to be an assured shorthold[424];

(ii) the landlord served a notice on the tenant after it was entered into stating that the tenancy was no longer to be an assured shorthold[425];

(iii) the tenancy itself contains provision to the effect that the tenancy is not an assured shorthold;

(iv) the assured tenancy has arisen by succession to a Rent Act regulated tenancy (other than a protected shorthold or a tenancy to which Case 19 of the 1977 Act applies);

(v) the tenancy became assured on ceasing to be a secure tenancy;

(vi) the assured tenancy arose by virtue of Sch.10 to the Local Government and Housing Act 1989[426];

(vii) the assured tenancy was granted to an existing standard assured tenant, unless the tenant serves notice in prescribed form[427] on the landlord before the tenancy is entered into stating that the tenancy is to be an assured shorthold. Thus a landlord cannot by the simple expedient of granting a new tenancy to a non-shorthold tenant on or after February 28, 1997, create an assured shorthold tenancy;

(viii) the tenancy comes into being when a non-shorthold tenancy comes to an end (i.e. as a statutory periodic tenancy);

---

[422] See para.22–081 above, fn.308.

[423] HA 1988 s.19A, inserted by HA 1996 s.96(1). The exceptions are listed in HA 1988 Sch.2A, inserted by HA 1996 Sch.7.

[424] See *Andrews v Cunningham* [2007] EWCA Civ 762; [2008] L. & T.R. 1 (giving tenant a rent book with "Assured Tenancy" on the cover does not comprise service of such a notice).

[425] Such a notice cannot prejudice the rights of a tenant who has an application for rent reduction pending before a rent assessment committee: HA 1988 s.22(5A), inserted by HA 1996 Sch.8 para.2(6).

[426] See below, para.22–194.

[427] SI 1997/194 Form 8. A form substantially to the same effect as the prescribed form will suffice; but see *Kahlon v Isherwood* [2011] EWCA Civ 602; [2011] H.L.R. 38 (term in Tomlin order did not set out tenant's understanding and acceptance of change of status).

(ix) former demoted tenancies[428]; and

(x) certain assured agricultural occupancies.

(2) An assured tenancy, entered into before February 28, 1997, created an assured shorthold tenancy if it satisfied the following conditions[429]:

(i) it was a fixed-term tenancy[430] granted for a term certain of not less than six months[431];

(ii) it gave the landlord no power to determine the tenancy at any time earlier than six months from the beginning of the tenancy (otherwise than by means of re-entry or forfeiture for breach of covenant[432]);

(iii) before the tenancy began, a notice in prescribed form[433] was served by the landlord on the tenant[434] stating that the tenancy was to be an assured shorthold tenancy; and

(iv) the grant was not made to an existing standard assured tenant of the dwelling.

The grant of a new tenancy to an existing assured shorthold tenant takes effect as an assured shorthold tenancy, whether or not the above conditions or any of them are satisfied.[435]

(3) A grant of a new tenancy to a *protected* shorthold tenant[436] on or after January 15, 1989 will have conferred an assured shorthold tenancy on the tenant, even though no notice was served on him to that effect.[437]

---

[428] See above, para.22–119.

[429] HA 1988 s.20(1)–(3).

[430] A fixed-term tenancy is "any tenancy other than a periodic tenancy": HA 1988 s.45(1). See above, para.22–093.

[431] Despite the word "shorthold", there was no maximum duration. A tenancy granted on December 18, 1990 expiring on June 17, 1991, is a term of not less than six months: *Bedding v McCarthy* (1993) 27 H.L.R. 103.

[432] See HA 1988 s.45(4).

[433] SI 1988/2203 Form 7, as amended by SI 1990/1532 and SI 1993/654 (all revoked by SI 1997/194 r.4, with savings for notices served before February 28, 1997). A notice substantially to the same effect will suffice. This has been interpreted, in light of *Mannai Investment Co Ltd v Eagle Star Life Assurance Co Ltd* [1997] A.C. 749, that where, notwithstanding an obvious or evident error in the notice, a reasonable recipient would be left in no reasonable doubt as to its terms, the notice will be valid. See *York v Casey* [1998] 2 E.G.L.R. 25 (incorrect termination date); *Ravenseft Properties Ltd v Hall* [2001] EWCA Civ 2034; [2002] H.L.R. 33 (incorrect commencement date); *Osborn & Co Ltd v Dior* [2003] EWCA Civ 281; [2003] H.L.R. 45 (incorrect name and address of landlord); cf. *Manel v Memon* [2001] 33 H.L.R. 24 (advisory notes omitted) *Kahlon v Isherwood*, above at fn.427.

[434] Notice may be served on the tenant's authorised agent: *Yenula Properties Ltd v Naidu* [2002] EWCA Civ 719; [2003] H.L.R. 18.

[435] HA 1988 s.20(4): but not if the landlord serves notice on the tenant that his new tenancy is not a shorthold: s.20(5).

[436] Or a statutory tenant to whom RA 1977 Case 19 applies, i.e. a former protected shorthold tenant holding over following expiry of his fixed term.

[437] HA 1988 s.34(3): unless before the new tenancy began the landlord served notice on the tenant that it was not to be a shorthold.

2. Security of tenure. Where the assured shorthold tenancy is a fixed-term, **22–126** the tenant has no right to terminate by notice save and in so far as the agreement makes provision to such effect. On expiry of the fixed term, the assured shorthold tenant on whom no notice seeking possession has been served will hold over as statutory periodic tenant. This statutory periodic tenancy is itself an assured shorthold tenancy.[438]

The landlord who wishes to recover possession of a dwelling let on assured **22–127** shorthold tenancy may use any of the grounds for possession relevant to assured tenancies. Where the tenancy is a fixed term tenancy, he will be restricted to such grounds.[439] Once the fixed term has expired, and whenever the tenancy is a periodic tenancy, however, the landlord may recover possession as of right provided that he complies with the statutory procedure.[440] This requires the landlord to serve a notice in writing on the tenant stating that, after a date specified in the notice (hereafter "the specified date"), he requires possession of the dwelling.[441] The notice does not have to take any particular form (none is prescribed) nor need it comply with the statutory requirements for a "notice seeking possession".[442] The specified date must not be earlier than two months after the date of service of the notice.[443] Where at the time of service the tenant is a periodic tenant, the specified date must not be earlier than the earliest day on which a periodic tenancy of that length could be terminated under the general law.[444] The specified date must be the last date of a period of the tenancy,[445] although this may be achieved by the use of a formula to the effect that possession is required "at (or after) the end of that period of the tenancy which will end after the expiry of two months from the service of this notice."[446] Landlords seeking to recover possession from most assured shorthold tenants may invoke an accelerated form of proceedings for possession.[447]

There are important differences which arise from the methods of creation of **22–128** assured shorthold tenancies. An assured shorthold tenant created under (1) above[448] has the statutory right to require the landlord to provide him with a

---

[438] HA 1988 ss.5(2) and 20(4).

[439] Only a limited number are available during the currency of the fixed term: HA 1988 s.7(6). See para.22–093 above.

[440] This statutory notice procedure has been held to be compatible with Art.8 of the European Convention on Human Rights: *Poplar Housing & Regeneration Community Association Ltd v Donoghue* [2001] EWCA Civ 595; [2002] Q.B. 48 (defendant was intentionally homeless); *Mullen v Salford CC* [2010] EWCA Civ 336; [2010] H.L.R. 35 at [35].

[441] HA 1988 s.21(1), as amended by HA 1996 s.98. Notice cannot be served under s.21 where the landlord has failed to comply with the statutory requirements concerning tenancy deposits: HA 2004 s.215; see further para.22–130 below.

[442] *Panayi v Roberts* (1993) 25 H.L.R. 421.

[443] HA 1988 s.21(4)(a), as amended by HA 1996 s.98.

[444] HA 1988 s.21(4)(b), as amended by HA 1996 s.98. For the "general law", see above, paras 17–090 et seq.

[445] *McDonald v Fernandez* [2003] EWCA Civ 1219; [2004] 1 W.L.R. 1027.

[446] *Notting Hill Housing Trust v Roomus* [2006] EWCA Civ 407; [2006] 1 W.L.R. 1375, explaining *Lower Street Properties Ltd v Jones* (1996) 28 H.L.R. 877.

[447] CPR rr.55.11–55.19.

[448] That is, a tenancy entered into on or after February 28, 1997: see para.22–125 above.

written statement of certain important terms of the tenancy (the commencement date, the rent, the dates for payment, any rent review, and the length of a fixed term) which are not evidenced in writing.[449] Although such a tenant may hold on periodic tenancy from the outset, the court may not make a possession order to take effect earlier than six months from the beginning of the tenancy. Where the tenancy has come into being when an earlier assured shorthold tenancy has ended (e.g. when a fixed term expires, and the tenant holds over as a statutory periodic tenant), this six-month "moratorium" dates from the commencement of the earlier tenancy.[450]

22–129   **3. Protection as to rent.** Unlike other assured tenants, the assured shorthold tenant can refer (by application in prescribed form)[451] the amount of the rent to a rent assessment committee even though he has agreed that rent with the landlord.[452] The application must be made within six months of the beginning of an assured shorthold tenancy within (1) above[453]; or within the fixed term of an assured shorthold tenancy falling within (2) above.[454] The committee is to determine the rent which the landlord might reasonably be expected to obtain under the assured shorthold tenancy.[455] If the rent agreed by the parties exceeds the rent so determined, the excess is irrecoverable from the tenant.[456] However, the committee must not intervene unless they consider:

(i) that there is a sufficient number of similar dwelling-houses in the locality let on assured tenancies (whether shorthold or not); and

(ii) that the rent payable under the tenancy is significantly higher than the rent which the landlord might reasonably be expected to obtain under the tenancy, having regard to the rents payable by other assured tenants in the locality.[457]

The Secretary of State has power to disapply these rent reduction provisions in such cases, areas or circumstances as he specifies by order.[458]

22–130   **4. Protection of tenancy deposit.** The Housing Act 2004 introduced "tenancy deposit schemes" in an attempt to deal with the "notorious abuse"[459] of tenancy deposits; that is, where landlords require prospective

---

[449] HA 1988 s.20A, inserted by HA 1996 s.97.
[450] HA 1988 s.21(5)–(7), inserted by HA 1996 s.99.
[451] SI 1997/194 Form 6.
[452] HA 1988 s.22.
[453] See above, para.22–125. HA 1988 s.22(2), as amended by HA 1996 s.100.
[454] See above, para.22–125.
[455] HA 1988 s.22(1).
[456] HA 1988 s.22(4).
[457] HA 1988 s.22(3).
[458] HA 1988 s.23.
[459] *UK Housing Alliance (North West) Ltd v Francis* [2010] EWCA Civ 117; [2010] H.L.R. 28 at [7] per Longmore L.J.

tenants to pay deposits by way of security for payment of the rent and compliance with the other tenancy obligations, but then, despite due compliance by the tenant, refuse to repay the deposit back at the end of the tenancy. The Act requires landlords to deal with tenancy deposits[460] received from assured shorthold tenants in accordance with an authorised scheme approved by the Secretary of State.[461] The landlord must, within 14 days of receipt of a tenancy deposit, comply with the "initial requirements" of an authorised scheme[462] and give to the tenant (or any person who paid the deposit on the tenant's behalf) prescribed information regarding the scheme and its implications for the tenant.[463] In the event of non-compliance with these provisions by the landlord,[464] the court must either order the return of the deposit to the tenant or its payment into an authorised custodial scheme.[465] In addition, the court must order the landlord to pay to the tenant, within 14 days of the date of the order, a sum amounting to three times the deposit paid.[466] As a further sanction, the landlord is prohibited from serving a notice

[460] A "tenancy deposit" means any money intended to be held as security for the performance of any of the tenant's obligations or the discharge of any of his liability arising under or in connection with the tenancy: 2004 Act s.212(8). Where no money is paid to the landlord by the tenant, it is unlikely that these provisions will therefore be engaged: see *UK Housing Alliance (North West) Ltd v Francis*, above at [9].

[461] 2004 Act s.212(8). In Wales, authority is vested in the National Assembly: 2004 Act s.261(1). A scheme may be a "custodial scheme" or an "insurance scheme". In the case of the former, the landlord pays the deposit to the scheme administrator who holds it throughout the tenancy, and at its end the administrator decides what should be paid to the parties respectively. In the case of the latter, the landlord retains the deposit but he formally undertakes to the scheme administrator that he will comply with any directions about repaying the deposit to the tenant at the end of the tenancy: see generally 2004 Act Sch.10.

[462] 2004 Act s.213(3). The initial requirements are those requirements imposed by the authorised scheme as fall to be complied with by a landlord on receiving such a deposit: 2004 Act s.213(4); *Draycott v Hannells Letting Ltd* [2010] EWHC 217 (QB); [2011] 1 W.L.R. 1606; see Buckingham [2010] Conv. 261.

[463] 2004 Act s.213(5). For prescribed information, see Housing (Tenancy Deposits) (Prescribed Information) Order 2007, SI 2007/797, art.2. Amendments in Localism Act 2011 s.184, not in force at the time of writing, inter alia extend the period for compliance by the landlord to 30 days.

[464] Or if the tenant is unable to obtain confirmation from the scheme administrator that his deposit is being held in accordance with the authorised scheme notified to him by the landlord: 2004 Act s.214(1)(b).

[465] In either case, within 14 days of the order: 2004 Act s.214(3). For "custodial scheme", see fn.461 above.

[466] 2004 Act s.214(4). Where the landlord fails to comply with the initial requirements, or to give the prescribed information, within 14 days of receipt of the tenancy deposit, but remedies his default before the matter comes before the court, these sanctions do not apply: *Tiensia v Vision Enterprises Ltd* [2010] EWCA Civ 1224; [2011] 1 All E.R. 1059, a decision which, according to Sedley L.J. at [49], dissenting, renders the tenancy deposit provisions "a dead letter"; see Morgan [2010] Conv. 240. The court may however make a costs order adverse to the landlord: *Tiensia v Vision Enterprises Ltd*, above at [44]. The court cannot invoke these sanctions once the tenancy has ended as by then the landlord has no opportunity to remedy his default: *Gladehurst Properties Ltd v Farid Hashemi* [2011] EWCA Civ 604; [2011] 4 All E.R. 556. For the purposes of sanctions, the duty to give prescribed information is to be treated as important as the duty to safeguard the tenant's deposit by complying with the initial requirements: *Suurpere v Nice* [2011] EWHC 2003 (QB); [2011] 39 E.G. 110; cf. *Potts v Denley* [2011] EWHC 1144 (QB), where although the landlord had failed to give the prescribed information by the date of the hearing, the tenant had brought his claim specifically on non-compliance with the initial requirements.

under s.21 of the Housing Act 1988[467] at any time when the deposit is not being held in accordance with an authorised scheme, or the initial requirements have not been complied with in relation to the deposit.[468]

C. Regulated Tenancies

I. TENANCIES WITHIN THE RENT ACTS

22–131   **1. Definition.** Although legislation has considerably reduced the significance of the Rent Acts in recent years, there still remain tenancies which fall within their ambit.[469] The major attributes of a Rent Act regulated tenancy are protection of the tenant as to both rent and possession. In addition, there is a statutory bar on premiums. The residual form of statutory protection pursuant to a "restricted contract" (for certain residential occupiers who did not qualify as regulated tenants) has now been almost entirely phased out.[470]

22–132   There are two categories of "regulated tenancy". The "protected tenancy" is an ordinary contractual tenancy under which the tenancy itself, whilst it continues, protects the tenant's possession, the Rent Act 1977 providing rent control. The "statutory tenancy", on the other hand, is a creature of statute, arising by implication when a protected tenancy ends, and being based upon the tenant's continued occupation of the dwelling as his residence. The 1977 Act prevents a statutory tenant from being evicted save by an order of the court on specified grounds, as well as providing control of the rent.

22–133   As a result of Pt I of the Housing Act 1988, contractual tenancies entered into on or after January 15, 1989 cannot, subject to exceptions, be protected tenancies.[471] However, the 1977 Act continues to apply to those tenancies which remain protected, and on the termination of such a protected tenancy, a statutory tenancy will arise as before. The exceptional circumstances in which tenancies may still be "protected" although entered into on or after the above date are as follows[472]:

> (i) where a contract was made prior to January 15, 1989, for a tenancy beginning on or after that date;
>
> (ii) where a new tenancy is entered into by a landlord with an existing protected or statutory tenant of his.[473] This means that a landlord

---

[467] See above, para.22–127.

[468] 2004 Act s.215(1).

[469] The latest figures indicate that there were 120,000 regulated tenancies, of which 50,000 had a registered rent, in 2008: see Department for Communities and Local Government, *Housing Statistics* Table 731.

[470] HA 1988 s.36. For the effect of restricted contract protection, see the fifth edition of this book, at p.1118.

[471] HA 1988 s.34.

[472] HA 1988 s.34(1). For an unsuccessful attempt to claim a protected tenancy by reference to a chain of tenancy agreements commencing before January 15, 1989, see *Secretarial & Nominee Co Ltd v Thomas* [2005] EWCA Civ 1008; [2006] H.L.R. 5.

[473] Where the tenant held pursuant to an agreement for lease, no formal tenancy having been granted, the new tenancy will not be a regulated tenancy: *Truro Diocesan Board of Finance Ltd v Foley* [2008] EWCA Civ 1162; [2009] 1 W.L.R. 2218.

cannot deprive his Rent Act regulated tenants of protection under the Rent Acts merely by granting them new tenancies;

(iii) if the landlord obtains possession of a dwelling held on a protected or statutory tenancy by virtue of suitable alternative accommodation being provided for the tenant,[474] the court may order, if it decides that an assured tenancy under the 1988 Act would not give the tenant the required security, that the new accommodation is to be held on a protected tenancy; and

(iv) certain tenancies where the landlord was at the time of grant the Commission for the New Towns or a development corporation.[475]

2. Protected tenancies. Every tenancy under which a dwelling-house **22–134** (which may be a house or a part of a house) is let as a separate dwelling is a protected tenancy[476] unless:

(a) subject to the above exceptions, it is entered into on or after January 15, 1989; or

(b) it falls within one of the exceptions listed in the 1977 Act.[477]

The 1977 Act exceptions are similar, although not identical, to those relevant to assured tenancies.[478] Thus lettings by the Crown or government departments, or public bodies such as local authorities, are excluded, as are lettings at a low rent, holiday lets, lettings by resident landlords, and accommodation provided by educational institutions for their students. Tenancies of most housing associations and housing cooperatives are outside Rent Act protection.[479] Further exclusions are agricultural holdings occupied by the farmer, farm business tenancies, public houses and Church of England parsonage houses.[480] A tenancy where the rent includes payments in respect of board or attendance cannot be a protected tenancy, provided that in the case of attendance the amount of rent attributable to it, having regard to its value to the tenant, forms a "substantial part" of the whole rent.[481]

3. Property value. There have been many changes in the levels of rateable **22–135** value which sufficed to exclude a dwelling from Rent Act control,[482] and

---

[474] RA 1977 s.98(1)(a); see below, para.22–144.
[475] See further HA 1988 ss.34(1)(d) and 38(4), as amended by SI 2008/3002, Sch.1 para.37.
[476] RA 1977 s.1. For interpretation of the terminology of this provision, see para.22–084.
[477] RA 1977 ss.4–16.
[478] See above, paras 22–086 et seq.
[479] See RA 1977 ss.15, 16. However, a form of rent control is provided for many such tenancies in RA 1977 Pt VI.
[480] See Woodfall, 23.040.
[481] RA 1977 s.7; *Palser v Grinling* [1948] A.C. 291; *Otter v Norman* [1989] A.C. 129.
[482] See the fourth edition of this book, pp.1130–1132; fifth edition, p.1108.

these, together with the necessary reforms following the abolition of the domestic rating system in 1990, have contrived to make the exercise of determining whether a given dwelling is subject to the protection of the Acts a difficult one. Tenancies entered into on or after April 1, 1990 (unlikely to be protected in any event) will be excluded if the rent payable exceeds £25,000 per annum.[483] Tenancies entered into prior to that date[484] will not be protected if on "the appropriate day" (i.e. the date on which the rateable value for the dwelling was first shown in the valuation list, or, if that was before March 23, 1965, that date[485]) and also on certain subsequent dates, the rateable value exceeded certain amounts.[486]

II. SECURITY OF TENURE

22–136   Unlike the assured tenancy, which the landlord cannot unilaterally terminate without an order of the court, the protected tenancy is terminable by the landlord exercising such rights as are reserved to him under the lease, e.g. notice to quit, or forfeiture for breach of covenant. However, the termination of the protected tenancy will not entitle the landlord to repossess the premises. The Rent Act 1977 provides protection by giving the tenant the right to remain in possession as a "statutory tenant" despite the termination of his contractual tenancy and by prohibiting the court from making an order for possession except on specified grounds.

22–137   **1. Statutory tenancy.** A statutory tenancy is the right of a protected tenant[487] who occupies the dwelling as his residence when the contractual tenancy ends to remain in possession under the Act, despite the termination of his contractual tenancy.[488] He holds on all the terms of the contractual tenancy that are not inconsistent with the Act,[489] unless and until the court makes an order for possession against him. A statutory tenancy is not really a tenancy at all, in the common law sense of the word: the tenant has no estate or interest in the land, but instead a mere personal right of occupation which has been

---

[483] RA 1977 s.4(4)–(7), as inserted by the References to Rating (Housing) Regulations 1990 (SI 1990/434).

[484] Or entered into on or after April 1, 1990 pursuant to a contract made before that date, the dwelling-house having a rateable value on March 31, 1990: see RA 1977 s.4(4).

[485] RA 1977 s.25(3).

[486] RA 1977 s.4(1)–(3), as amended by SI 1990/434. If the appropriate day was before March 22, 1973, the amounts are £200 for the appropriate day, £300 for March 22, 1973, and £750 for April 1, 1973. If the appropriate day was between March 21 and April 1, 1973, the amounts are £300 for the appropriate day and £750 for April 1, 1973. If the appropriate day was after March 31, 1973, the amount is £750 for the appropriate day. In each case these figures are doubled for dwellings in Greater London.

[487] Including one of two or more joint tenants: *Lloyd v Sadler* [1978] Q.B. 774; *Daejan Properties Ltd v Mahoney* (1995) 28 H.L.R. 498 at 510; *De Rothschild v Bell (A Bankrupt)* [2000] Q.B. 33 at 42.

[488] RA 1977 s.2.

[489] RA 1977 s.3.

termed a "status of irremovability".[490] The tenant cannot dispose of his interest by assignment or by will,[491] and it will not vest in his trustee in bankruptcy.[492] However, the tenant has a limited statutory power, exercisable only with the landlord's consent, to substitute another tenant in his place without thereby creating another contractual tenancy,[493] and the court has power to order the transfer of a statutory tenancy in the course of certain family proceedings.[494]

2. Determination. A statutory tenancy will cease to exist[495] if the tenant **22–138** ceases to occupy the premises as his home,[496] or as one of his homes.[497] However, it is not necessary for the dwelling in question to be his principal home if he has more than one.[498] A protected or statutory tenancy may also be determined by a housing authority in the exercise of its public law powers,[499] or by the exercise of a mortgagee's contractual or statutory powers.[500]

3. Succession. If a protected or statutory tenant dies, his spouse or civil **22–139** partner,[501] if residing in the dwelling-house at that time, or otherwise any other member of his family[502] residing with him, becomes statutory tenant in his place.[503] If the tenant died before January 15, 1989, a family member (although not a spouse) must prove six months' residence with the tenant. If the tenant dies on or after that date, the family member must prove two years' residence with the tenant , and he or she becomes entitled to an assured

---

[490] *Keeves v Dean* [1924] 1 K.B. 685 at 686, per Lush J.; and see *Roe v Russell* [1928] 2 K.B. 117 at 131.

[491] *John Lovibond & Sons Ltd v Vincent* [1929] 1 K.B. 687.

[492] *Sutton v Dorf* [1932] 2 K.B. 304.

[493] RA 1977 s.3(5) and Sch.1 paras 13, 14.

[494] Family Law Act 1996 s.53 and Sch.7, as amended.by Civil Partnership Act 2004 s.82 and Sch.9 para.16.

[495] *John M. Brown Ltd v Bestwick* [1951] 1 K.B. 21; *Moreland Properties (UK) Ltd v Dhokia* [2003] EWCA Civ 1639; [2004] L. & T.R. 20.

[496] *Skinner v Geary* [1931] 2 K.B. 546; cf. *Haines v Herbert* [1963] 1 W.L.R. 1401.

[497] *Hallwood Estates Ltd v Flack* (1950) 66(2) T.L.R. 368; *Herbert v Byrne* [1964] 1 W.L.R. 519; *Regalian Securities Ltd v Scheuer* (1982) 47 P. & C.R. 362.

[498] cf. the assured tenancy, see above, para.22–085.

[499] See, e.g. HA 1985 s.612; RA 1977 s.101 (overcrowding).

[500] By virtue of the mortgagee's paramountcy of title: *Dudley & District Building Society v Emerson* [1949] Ch. 707; *Britannia Building Society v Earl* [1990] 1 W.L.R. 422. Where the mortgage post-dates the tenancy, or does not bind the tenant due to non-registration, the tenant will normally have priority over the mortgagee: *Woolwich Building Society v Dickman* [1996] 3 All E.R. 204; *Barclays Bank Plc v Zaroovabli* [1997] Ch. 321.

[501] Where the tenant dies on or after January 15, 1989, these terms include a person living with the tenant as his spouse or civil partner: RA 1977 Sch.1 para.2(2), inserted by HA 1988 Sch.4 para.2, and amended by Civil Partnership Act 2004 s.81, and Sch.8 para.13 to give effect to *Ghaidan v Godin-Mendoza* [2004] UKHL 30; [2004] 2 A.C. 557.

[502] *Carega Properties SA v Sharratt* [1979] 1 W.L.R. 928; *Fitzpatrick v Sterling Housing Association Ltd* [2001] 1 A.C. 27 (same-sex partner could be a member of tenant's family: see amendments to RA 1977 at fn.501 above).

[503] RA 1977 s.2(1)(b); Sch.1 Pt I, as amended by Civil Partnership Act 2004 s.81 and Sch.8 para.13.

tenancy "by succession" rather than a statutory tenancy.[504] Where the deceased tenant was a protected (and so contractual) tenant, that contractual tenancy will devolve under the general law, though it will be suspended while the statutory tenancy lasts.[505] It follows that where a protected tenancy is held by joint tenants, on the death of one, the other or others will take by virtue of the doctrine of survivorship.[506]

22–140 Second successions may occur, although amendments made by the 1988 Act make the criteria difficult to satisfy in the event of a "first successor" dying on or after January 15, 1989.[507] In such circumstances, the second successor must have been a member of the family both of the original tenant and of the first successor, and have been residing in the dwelling-house with the first successor both at the date of his or her death and for the previous two years. A second successor under these provisions becomes an assured tenant by succession.

22–141 **4. Grounds for possession.** The Rent Acts have always been restrictive rather than enabling. If the tenant is a protected tenant, the landlord cannot recover possession unless and until he has terminated the tenancy, e.g. by virtue of a forfeiture clause or by notice to quit. However, on termination of the protected tenancy a statutory tenancy will arise provided that the tenant continues to occupy the dwelling as his residence, and the 1977 Act prevents the court from making an order for possession against a statutory tenant save where the landlord establishes a ground for possession. It follows that proof of a ground is essential if a landlord is to recover possession from a Rent Act regulated tenant. The grounds for possession are either "discretionary" or "mandatory".[508]

22–142 *(a) Discretionary grounds.* An order for possession can only be made if the court considers that in all the circumstances it is reasonable to make such an order.[509] Some of the "Cases" which remain[510] are identical with grounds for possession for assured tenancies, and cross references have accordingly been made in the following text.

22–143 CASE 1: BREACH OF COVENANT. Rent lawfully due has not been paid, or some other obligation of the tenancy which is consistent with the Act has been broken. There is no mandatory ground for non-payment of rent approximating to Ground 8 of the Housing Act 1988.

---

[504] RA 1977 Sch.1 para.3, as amended by HA 1988 s.39(2),(3) and Sch.4 Pt I.
[505] *Moodie v Hosegood* [1952] A.C. 61; cf. the assured tenant: HA 1988 s.17, above, para.22–120.
[506] See *Solihull MBC v Hickin* [2010] EWCA Civ 868; [2010] 1 W.L.R. 2254 (on secure tenancies).
[507] RA 1977 Sch.1 para.6, as substituted by HA 1988 Sch.4 para.6.
[508] RA 1977 s.98(1), (2). See above, para.22–096. The grounds are set out in RA 1977 Sch.15, Pts 1 and 2 respectively.
[509] RA 1977 s.98(1).
[510] Case 7 has been repealed.

CASE 2: NUISANCE.[511]

CASE 3: DETERIORATION OF DWELLING-HOUSE.[512]

CASE 4: DETERIORATION OF FURNITURE.[513]

CASE 5: TENANT'S NOTICE TO QUIT. The tenant has given notice to quit, and the landlord has acted on it so as to be seriously prejudiced if he cannot obtain possession.

CASE 6: ASSIGNMENT OR SUB-LETTING. The tenant, without the landlord's consent,[514] has assigned or sub-let the whole of the dwelling-house, or has sub-let part, the remainder being already sub-let.[515]

CASE 8: REQUIRED FOR LANDLORD'S EMPLOYEE. The dwelling-house is reasonably required as a residence for a person engaged (or with whom a conditional contract has been made) in the whole-time employment of the landlord or some tenant of his, and it was let to the tenant in consequence of[516] his employment[517] by the landlord (or a former landlord), which has come to an end.

CASE 9: REQUIRED FOR LANDLORD OR FAMILY. The landlord reasonably requires the dwelling-house for occupation as a residence for himself,[518] a child of his over 18 years old, or one of his parents or parents-in-law. This Case is not available:

(i) to a landlord who became landlord by purchasing[519] any interest in the dwelling-house after March 23, 1965 or certain other specified dates; or

(ii) if the tenant satisfies the court that in all the circumstances "greater hardship" would be caused by granting the order for possession than by refusing to grant it.[520]

CASE 10: EXCESSIVE RENT. The tenant has sub-let part of the premises at a rent in excess of that recoverable having regard to the 1977 Act.

SUITABLE ALTERNATIVE ACCOMMODATION.[521] Suitable alternative accommodation is available for the tenant, or will be when the order for possession   **22–144**

---

[511] See HA 1988 Ground 14, above, para.22–113.
[512] See HA 1988 Ground 13, above, para.22–112.
[513] See HA 1988 Ground 15, above, para.22–115.
[514] *Hyde v Pimley* [1952] 2 Q.B. 506.
[515] *Leith Properties Ltd v Byrne* [1983] Q.B. 433. The assignment or sub-letting must be after certain dates set out in the statute.
[516] *Braithwaite & Co Ltd v Elliot* [1947] K.B. 177.
[517] *Duncan v Hay* [1956] 1 W.L.R. 1329.
[518] *Richter v Wilson* [1963] 2 Q.B. 426.
[519] *Powell v Cleland* [1948] 1 K.B. 262; *Thomas v Fryer* [1970] 1 W.L.R. 845.
[520] RA 1977 Sch.15, Pt III; *Harte v Frampton* [1948] 1 K.B. 73.
[521] RA 1977 s.98(1) and Sch.15 Pt IV.

takes effect. The first element of "suitability" requires the alternative accommodation to be let on a protected tenancy (other than one which would permit the landlord to invoke a mandatory ground for possession), or let as a separate dwelling on terms affording a reasonably equivalent security of tenure. The court has jurisdiction to order that the alternative accommodation is to be held on a protected tenancy, even though the tenancy is entered into on or after January 15, 1989, where it is satisfied that an assured tenancy would not afford the required security.[522] Otherwise, this ground for possession is practically identical to Ground 9 of the 1988 Act, to which reference should be made.[523]

22–145 *(b) Mandatory grounds.* Upon the landlord establishing a mandatory ground, the court must order possession, and has as little scope for giving the protected or statutory tenant time as it has in relation to assured tenants when a mandatory ground is proved under the 1988 Act.[524] For each of the mandatory grounds which follow, the landlord must have given the tenant written notice, normally before the tenancy began, that possession might be recovered under the particular Case. In Cases 11, 12 and 20, however, if the court considers it just and equitable to make an order for possession, it may dispense with this requirement, and also with the further requirement of these Cases that there should have been no previous letting of the dwelling on a protected tenancy after certain dates without such a notice.[525]

22–146 CASE 11: OWNER-OCCUPIER. The owner, having at any time previously occupied the dwelling-house as his residence, let it on a regulated tenancy, and one of the following conditions is satisfied[526]:

    (i) the dwelling is genuinely required[527] as a residence for the owner[528] or any member of his family who resided with him when he last lived in it;

    (ii) the owner has died, and the dwelling is required as a residence for a member of his family who was residing with him when he died;

    (iii) the owner has died, and the dwelling is required by a successor in title as his residence or for disposal with vacant possession;

    (iv) the dwelling is subject to a mortgage granted by deed before the tenancy, and the mortgagee requires to sell the dwelling with vacant possession under a contractual or statutory power; or

---

[522] HA 1988 s.34(1)(c).
[523] See above, para.22–108.
[524] See above, para.22–098.
[525] RA 1977 Sch.15 Pt II; *Bradshaw v Baldwin-Wiseman* (1985) 49 P. & C.R. 382.
[526] RA 1977 Sch.15, Pt II; HA 1980 s.66 and Sch.7.
[527] Reasonableness is not needed: *Kennealy v Dunne* [1977] Q.B. 837.
[528] One of two or more joint owners will do: *Tilling v Whiteman* [1980] A.C. 1.

(v) the dwelling is not reasonably suitable to the owner's needs in relation to his place of work, and he requires it for sale with vacant possession in order to use the proceeds to acquire a dwelling more suitable to those needs.

CASE 12: RETIREMENT HOME. The landlord, although intending to occupy the dwelling as his residence on his retirement from regular employment, has let it on protected tenancy before such retirement, and either now has retired and requires the dwelling as a residence, or one of the conditions set out in paragraphs (ii) to (iv) above is satisfied.

CASE 13: SHORT LETTING OF HOLIDAY HOME.[529]

CASE 14: SHORT LETTING OF STUDENT RESIDENCE.[530]

CASE 15: MINISTER OF RELIGION.[531]

CASE 16: AGRICULTURAL WORKER.

CASE 17: FARMHOUSE REDUNDANT ON AMALGAMATION.

CASE 18: OTHER REDUNDANT FARMHOUSES. The general purpose of the complex provisions of Cases 16–18 is to enable a landlord to obtain possession of an agricultural holding for a farm worker of his from a tenant who lacks sufficient agricultural justification for retaining it.

CASE 19: PROTECTED SHORTHOLD TENANCY. This category of protected tenancy has now been superseded by the assured shorthold tenancy of Pt I of the Housing Act 1988.[532]

CASE 20: SERVICEMEN.[533] The landlord was a member of the regular armed forces both at the time when he acquired the dwelling and when he let it, and either he requires the dwelling as his residence or one of the conditions set out in paras (ii) to (v) above is satisfied.

III. PROTECTION AS TO RENT

The great advantage traditionally enjoyed by regulated tenants over assured tenants is rent control. Not only is there a system which imposes and enforces a maximum rent, but there are also prohibitions on premiums. **22–147**

1. No registered rent. The control of rents is based on the determination and registration of a "fair rent" for the dwelling. Until this has been done, there is generally no restriction on the rent that may be charged. But if a **22–148**

---

[529] See HA 1988 Ground 3, above, para.22–101.
[530] See HA 1988 Ground 4, above, para.22–102.
[531] See HA 1988 Ground 5, above, para.22–103.
[532] See above, para.22–124.
[533] Added by Housing Act 1980 s.67 and Sch.7.

protected tenancy is granted to an existing tenant, or to someone who could succeed him as a statutory tenant, the rent must not exceed the existing rent unless the parties have signed a special form of "rent agreement", which states, inter alia, that the tenant can apply for registration of a fair rent; and the same applies to any increase of rent under an existing tenancy.[534] Further, the rent payable by a statutory tenant is limited to the rent recoverable at the end of the previous protected tenancy.[535] There are provisions for adjusting the rent for changes in the landlord's provision of services or furniture.[536]

22–149   **2. Registered rent.** Once a rent for a dwelling is registered, it will govern every subsequent regulated tenancy, provided that the dwelling is substantially the same dwelling. The registered rent for an unfurnished tenancy will therefore continue to apply if the premises are subsequently let furnished unless and until a new rent is registered.[537] No rent may exceed the registered rent, and if it does, any excess paid is recoverable by the tenant within two years.[538] If the rent is less than the registered rent, the landlord may by notice increase it up to the registered rent.[539]

3. Registration of fair rent

22–150   *(a) Applications.* Under a regulated tenancy, either the landlord or the tenant may apply to the rent officer for the area for the registration of a rent, and each is entitled to be heard.[540] The rent officer registers the rent, if he thinks it fair, or, if not, determines the fair rent and registers it; and within 28 days of receiving notice of this, either landlord or tenant may make an objection requiring the matter to be referred to a rent assessment committee.[541] After giving the parties an opportunity of being heard, the committee must either confirm the rent, or determine a fair rent which will be registered. Unless otherwise ordered, all registrations take effect from the date of application for registration; and for two years neither party can apply for the registration of a different rent unless there has been a change in the condition of the dwelling or in other circumstances which make the registered rent no longer a fair rent.[542] The registered rent constitutes the rent limit which must not be exceeded.[543]

---

[534] RA 1977 ss.51 and 54.
[535] RA 1977 s.45(1).
[536] RA 1977 s.47.
[537] *Rakhit v Carty* [1990] 2 Q.B. 315.
[538] RA 1977 ss.44 and 57.
[539] RA 1977 s.45(2).
[540] RA 1977 s.67(1) and Sch.11; SI 1980/1696 and 1697; *Druid Development Co (Bingley) Ltd v Kay* (1982) 44 P. & C.R. 76.
[541] RA 1977 Sch.11 para.6; SI 1971/1065, as amended.
[542] RA 1977 s.67(2); *London Housing and Commercial Properties Ltd v Cowan* [1977] Q.B. 148.
[543] RA 1977 ss.44 and 45. For cancellation of registration, see s.73; SI 1980/1698.

(b) Fair rent. In determining a fair rent, regard must be had "to all the **22–151** circumstances (other than personal circumstances[544]) and in particular to the age, character, locality and state of repair of the dwelling-house", and the quantity, quality and condition of any furniture that is provided.[545] But the effect of local shortages of housing accommodation (the "scarcity" element) must be disregarded.[546] So too must voluntary improvements carried out by the tenant or his predecessors in title; any disrepair or other defects due to his or their failure to comply with the terms of the tenancy; any improvement to the furniture by the tenant or his predecessor in title; and any deterioration in its condition due to ill-treatment by the tenant, persons residing with him, or his sub-tenants.[547] It is important to realise that the determination of a fair rent will usually involve the committee considering rents of comparable properties in the locality. Some such properties will be let on regulated, and some on assured, tenancies. Assured tenancy rents should not be discounted on the ground that such rents might be higher, as a "fair rent" must not be interpreted as a "reasonable rent".[548] However, there is a maximum fair rent limit in respect of applications for rent registration made after January 1999 which effectively provides for an index-linked ceiling of rent increases.[549] The limit applies only where there is an existing registered rent, and does not therefore affect applications for registration of a fair rent where there is no rent currently registered.[550]

4. Premiums. There have long been wide provisions which prohibit any **22–152** person[551] from requiring a premium as a condition of the grant, renewal, continuance or assignment of any protected tenancy,[552] or in connection therewith; and these prevent a statutory tenant (who has no assignable interest) from asking for or receiving any consideration from anyone except the landlord as a condition of giving up possession, or in connection therewith. Rent payable before the relevant rental period begins, and excessive prices for furniture, are treated as being premiums. It is an offence to require a premium; and, if paid, the money is recoverable.[553]

---

[544] *Mason v Skilling* [1974] 1 W.L.R. 1437; *Palmer v Peabody Trust* [1975] Q.B. 604; *Spath Holme Ltd v Greater Manchester & Lancashire Rent Assessment Committee* [1995] 2 E.G.L.R. 80.

[545] RA 1977 s.70(1); *Black v Oliver* [1978] Q.B. 870.

[546] RA 1977 s.70(2); *Metropolitan Property Holdings Ltd v Finegold* [1975] 1 W.L.R. 349; *Western Heritable Investment Co Ltd v Husband* [1983] 2 A.C. 849.

[547] RA 1977 s.70(3). See generally *Metropolitan Properties Co (F.G.C.) Ltd v Lannon* [1968] 1 W.L.R. 815 (reversed on the issue of bias at [1969] 1 Q.B. 577).

[548] *Spath Holme Ltd v Greater Manchester & Lancashire Rent Assessment Committee* [1995] 2 E.G.L.R. 80; *Curtis v London Rent Assessment Committee* [1999] Q.B. 92.

[549] SI 1999/6, made pursuant to LTA 1985 s.31, and upheld as *intra vires*: *R (Spath Holme Ltd) v Secretary of State for the Environment, Transport and the Regions* [2001] 2 A.C. 349.

[550] SI 1999/6 art.2(6).

[551] *Farrell v Alexander* [1977] A.C. 59 (not confined to landlord).

[552] There are no restrictions on premiums in connection with assured tenancies.

[553] RA 1977 Pt IX and Sch.1 Pt II.

D. Agricultural occupancies

22–153   Many agricultural workers who are housed by their employers, usually on or close to a farm (traditionally in a "tied cottage"), were for long outside the Rent Acts because even if they were tenants and not licensees, they paid little or no rent: the cottage or other dwellings "went with the job". In such cases, the loss of the job meant the loss of the home, for it would be needed for a new farm worker. The general scheme of the Rent (Agriculture) Act 1976[554] was to give such workers much of the protection of regulated tenancies, and yet to protect the farmer by imposing a special obligation on housing authorities to provide alternative accommodation for the occupier when agricultural efficiency required it. Part I of the Housing Act 1988 phased out the "protected occupier" status created in the 1976 Act, replacing it by assured agricultural occupancies, which have similar security to assured tenancies.

1. Rent (Agriculture) Act 1976: protected occupiers

22–154   *(a) Definition.* A person is a "protected occupier" if he is a "qualifying worker", or is incapable of whole-time work in agriculture in consequence of a qualifying injury or disease, and under a "relevant licence or tenancy" is in occupation of a dwelling in "qualifying ownership".[555] A person is a qualifying worker if he has worked whole-time in agriculture[556] for at least 91 out of the previous 104 weeks.[557] A relevant licence is one that gives exclusive occupation of a separate dwelling and would, if a tenancy, have been a protected tenancy under the Rent Act 1977 but for the low rent or certain other matters; and a relevant tenancy is correspondingly defined.[558] It follows that a licence or tenancy entered into on or after January 15, 1989 cannot be a relevant licence or tenancy under the 1976 Act, unless it is entered into pursuant to a contract made before that date, or it is granted to an existing protected occupier or statutory tenant (within the 1976 Act) of the landlord.[559]

22–155   *(b) Security of tenure.* Even if he has only a licence, the occupier becomes a statutory tenant after his protected occupancy has determined, unless the landlord is the Crown or one of a specified number of public or housing bodies.[560] When a protected occupier dies, his spouse or civil partner,[561] or

[554] Amended by, although not consolidated in, the Rent Act 1977; further amendments were made by the Housing Acts of 1980 and 1988.

[555] RAA 1976 s.2. A dwelling is in qualifying ownership if the occupier is employed in agriculture and his employer either owns the dwelling or has arranged for his agricultural workers to live in it. RAA 1976 Sch.3, para.3.

[556] Very widely defined: RAA 1976 s.1; but see *Earl of Normanton v Giles* [1980] 1 W.L.R. 28.

[557] RAA 1976 Sch.3, para.1.

[558] RAA 1976 Sch.2, as amended by RA 1977 Sch.23.

[559] HA 1988 s.34(4).

[560] RAA 1976 ss.4 and 5. For the terms of the statutory tenancy, see RAA 1976 Sch.5.

[561] Including a person living with the occupier as his spouse or civil partner: RAA 1976 s.4(5A), inserted by HA 1988 Sch.4 and amended by Civil Partnership Act 2004 s.81 and Sch.8, para.10.

any member of his family, if residing in the dwelling-house, can succeed the occupier (the spouse or civil partner as statutory tenant, any other family member as assured tenant by succession).[562] No order for possession can be made against a protected occupier or statutory tenant except on certain specified grounds which closely resemble the discretionary and mandatory grounds for regulated tenancies, save that the mandatory grounds are limited to lettings by owner-occupiers, retirement homes, and cases of over-crowding.[563]

(c) Rents. With some modifications, the system of registered rents applies **22–156** to a protected occupier.[564] But if he becomes a statutory tenant, no rent is payable until the parties agree upon one or the landlord serves a notice of increase on the tenant.[565] The rent must not then in either case exceed the registered rent, or, if none is registered, an amount calculated in accordance with a statutory formula.[566]

2. Assured agricultural occupancies

(a) Definition. Where a licence or tenancy is entered into on or after January **22–157** 15, 1989, it cannot, subject to exceptions, be protected by the 1976 Act.[567] However, a tenancy or licence conferring exclusive occupation of a separate dwelling which would, if a tenancy, have been an assured tenancy under the Housing Act 1988 but for the low rent or certain other matters,[568] will be an "assured agricultural occupancy" provided that the "agricultural worker condition" is for the time being fulfilled. This requires the tenant or licensee to be either a "qualifying worker" as defined in the 1976 Act,[569] or a person incapable of whole-time work in agriculture in consequence of a qualifying injury or disease.[570] The dwelling must also be in "qualifying ownership".[571] A tenancy will not be an assured agricultural occupancy if it is an assured shorthold tenancy.[572] However, where the agricultural worker condition is fulfilled with respect to a dwelling-house which is subject to an assured tenancy entered into on or after February 28, 1997, that tenancy will only be a shorthold if a notice in prescribed form has been served on the tenant prior

---

[562] RAA 1976 ss.3 and 4, as amended by Civil Partnership Act 2004 s.81 and Sch.8 para.9. A member of the occupier's family must have resided with him in the dwelling for two years before his death in order to qualify: RAA 1976 s.4(4), as amended by HA 1988 Sch.4.

[563] RAA 1976 ss.6 and 7 and Sch.4; and see above, para.22–146.

[564] RAA 1976 s.13; above, para.22–150.

[565] RAA 1976 s.10.

[566] RAA 1976 ss.11 and 12, as amended by SI 1990/434.

[567] HA 1988 s.34(4).

[568] The tenancy is comprised in an agricultural holding, or the holding is held under a farm business tenancy, and is occupied by the person responsible for the control or management of the holding. However, if the tenancy is itself a tenancy of an agricultural holding, or a farm business tenancy, it will be excluded: HA 1988 s.24, as amended by HA 1996 s.103.

[569] See above, para.22–154.

[570] HA 1988 Sch.3.

[571] RAA 1976 Sch.3, applied by HA 1988 Sch.3.

[572] HA 1988 s.24(2)(a).

to the tenancy.[573] Thus, the adoption of the assured shorthold tenancy as the default method of tenure by the Housing Act 1996[574] does not apply in the context of agricultural occupancies.

22–158   *(b) Security of tenure.* The assured agricultural occupancy confers a security of tenure identical to that enjoyed by the assured tenant in all respects but one: the discretionary ground available where an assured tenant's employment has ceased (Ground 16) may not be used.[575] The worker's spouse or civil partner,[576] or other members of the worker's family, may succeed on his death to the occupancy.[577]

22–159   *(c) Rents.* The rent payable under an assured agricultural occupancy will be determined by the agreement of the parties. The system of registered rents does not apply. A landlord who wishes to increase rent under a periodic occupancy may serve notice as for any other assured periodic tenancy,[578] and the occupant may refer the notice to a rent assessment committee for a determination of the market rent.[579]

22–160   **3. Re-housing.** A local housing authority must use its "best endeavours" to provide suitable alternative accommodation for assured agricultural occupants, protected occupiers and statutory tenants (or similarly protected or statutory agricultural tenants under the Rent Act 1977) if the owner satisfies the authority on three matters, namely:

> (1) he requires vacant possession of the dwelling for an agricultural worker of his
>
> (2) he cannot himself by any reasonable means provide suitable alternative accommodation for the person occupying the dwelling; and
>
> (3) in the interests of efficient agriculture the authority ought to provide such accommodation.[580]

This obligation does not apply if, when the alternative accommodation is available, the owner is still employing the person for whom it is to be provided

---

[573] See further HA 1996 Sch.7 para.9; SI 1997/194 Form 9.

[574] See above, para.22–124.

[575] HA 1988 ss.24(3) and 25(2).

[576] HA 1988 Sch.3 para.3(1),(2). This term includes a person living with the occupier as his spouse or civil partner: HA 1988 Sch.3 para.3(5), as amended by Civil Partnership Act 2004 s.81 and Sch.8 para.44.

[577] Subject to conditions of prior residence: HA 1988 Sch.3 para.3(3), as amended by Civil Partnership Act 2004 s.81 and Sch.8 para.44.

[578] See above, para.22–122.

[579] HA 1988 ss.13, 14, and 24(4).

[580] RAA 1976 ss.27 and 28, as amended by HA 1988 s.26 and Sch.17.

in the same capacity, and will continue to do so if that accommodation is provided.[581]

E. Secure Tenancies

Until Pt I of the Housing Act 1980 came into force on October 3, 1980, a **22–161** tenant had virtually no statutory protection if his landlord was a local authority or one of various other public bodies, as the Rent Acts had long been excluded in such cases.[582] Since 1945, the number of tenants who for this reason were unprotected had greatly increased, and so the changes made by the 1980 Act were highly significant. Public sector tenants were given the right to buy their dwellings or take a long lease of them on advantageous terms, together with a security of tenure that resembled the protection conferred upon Rent Act regulated tenants. In subsequent years, further measures have promoted the transfer of housing away from the public sector. There has been a resultant decline in the public housing stock, and the number of secure tenancies has fallen significantly.[583]

I. TENANCIES WITHIN PART IV OF THE 1985 ACT

1. Secure tenancies

(a) *Definition.* Subject to exceptions, a secure tenancy is a tenancy[584] under **22–162** which a dwelling-house is let as a separate dwelling[585] at any time when the "landlord condition" and the "tenant condition" are both satisfied.[586] The landlord condition is satisfied[587] if the landlord's interest belongs to one of a number of public bodies, including local authorities, development corporations, and certain housing associations[588] and housing co-operatives.[589] The tenant condition is satisfied if the tenant is an individual who occupies the dwelling as his only or principal home; for joint tenants, it suffices if they are

---

[581] RAA 1976 s.28(9).

[582] Rent Act 1977 s.14.

[583] In 2010, there were 155,000 tenancies of local authorities in England; only 25% of new tenancies were secure tenancies, largely attributable to the popularity among local authority landlords of the introductory tenancy (see para.22–177 below): Department for Communities and Local Government, *Housing Statistics*, Table 601.

[584] A tenancy at will is probably not a tenancy for these purposes: *Banjo v Brent LBC* [2005] EWCA Civ 292; [2005] 1 W.L.R. 2520.

[585] See above, para.22–084; *Central YMCA Housing Association Ltd v Saunders* (1990) 23 H.L.R. 212; *Tyler v Royal Borough of Kensington & Chelsea* (1991) 23 H.L.R. 380; *Amoah v LB Barking & Dagenham* (2001) 82 P. & C.R. DG6.

[586] HA 1985 s.79(1).

[587] HA 1985 s.80, as amended by HA 1988 ss.83 and 140, Sch.17 para.106 and Sch.18.

[588] A housing association satisfies the landlord condition if it is (i) a housing association which is a private registered provider of social housing or a registered social landlord, but which is not a co-operative housing association; or (ii) a co-operative housing association which is neither a private registered provider of social housing nor a registered social landlord: HA 1985 s.80(2), as amended by SI 2010/866 Sch.2 para.19.

[589] The housing co-operatives that satisfy the landlord condition are housing co-operatives within HA 1985 s.27B where the dwelling-house is comprised in a housing co-operative agreement within s.27B: HA 1985 s.80(4), added by Housing and Planning Act 1986 s.24(2), and Sch.5 Pt II para.26.

all individuals and at least one occupies the dwelling as his home.[590] Part IV also applies to a licence which, had it been a tenancy, would have been a secure tenancy.[591]

22–163   *(b) Exceptions.* There is a long list of exceptions.[592] Some of these corre- spond to exceptions for protected tenancies under the Rent Act 1977 or assured tenancies under the Housing Act 1988, such as long tenancies, agricultural holdings, farm business tenancies, licensed premises, student lettings and business tenancies. Others meet the special needs of the public sector, such as the tenancies of certain employees whose employment is linked to the dwelling (including the police and fire services), various forms of short-term accommodation, e.g. for homeless persons, asylum-seekers and those provided accommodation for temporary protection, those who come to the area seeking employment and permanent accommodation, those holding "introductory tenancies"[593] or "demoted tenancies",[594] and certain licences granted by almshouse charities.

22–164   *(c) Cessation.* A tenancy may cease to be a secure tenancy, as where the landlord condition or the tenant condition is no longer satisfied.[595] Assignment of secure tenancies is generally prohibited.[596] The exceptions to this general rule are "assignments by way of exchange", property adjustment orders made in connection with certain family proceedings, and assignments to potential successors.[597] Where a tenant sub-lets the whole of the dwelling, or, having sub-let part, sub-lets the remainder, the tenancy will cease to be secure.[598]

22–165   **2. Succession on death.** The Housing Act 1985 makes provision for the succession to a secure tenancy on the death of the tenant.[598a] It is therefore necessary to consider whether there is a person who "qualifies to succeed" the deceased tenant, i.e. a person who at the death was occupying the dwelling as his only or principal home, and was either (i) the tenant's spouse or civil

---

[590] HA 1985 s.81; e.g. *Crawley BC v Sawyer* (1987) 20 H.L.R. 98.

[591] HA 1985 s.79(3). The licence must confer exclusive possession: *City of Westminster v Clarke* [1992] 2 A.C. 288. Licences granted as a "temporary expedient" to those who entered as trespassers are excluded: Housing Act 1985 s.79(4). An express term in the licence agreement stating that it did not confer a secure tenancy is of no effect: *Mansfield DC v Langridge* [2008] EWCA Civ 264; [2008] H.L.R. 34.

[592] HA 1985 Sch.1, as amended.

[593] See below, para.22–177.

[594] See below, para.22–178.

[595] HA 1985 ss.80 and 81.

[596] HA 1985 s.91. Secure tenancies for a term certain granted before November 5, 1982, may be assigned, but this will normally lead to the tenancy ceasing to be secure.

[597] HA 1985 ss.91(3) and 92, as amended by HA 1996 s.222 and Sch.18 Pt III para.12 and by Civil Partnership Act 2004 s.81 and Sch.8 para.24.

[598] HA 1985 s.93.

[598a] Amendments in Localism Act 2011 s.160, not in force at the time of writing, restrict succession rights to secure tenancies in England but will only apply to secure tenancies granted on or after the day on which the provision comes into force.

partner, or (ii) another member of the tenant's family,[599] who had resided with him throughout the 12 months ending with his death.[600] If there are two or more qualified persons, the spouse or civil partner is to be preferred to the others, and as between the others, the selection, in default of agreement, is made by the landlord.[601] If the secure tenancy is a periodic tenancy, it vests in the qualified person and remains a secure tenancy.[602] If it is a tenancy for a fixed term it vests in the tenant's personal representatives; it then remains a secure tenancy if it is vested in a qualified person, but ceases to be a secure tenancy when it is vested in somebody else (or when it is known that on vesting it will not be a secure tenancy).[603] There can be only one such succession: these provisions do not apply where the deceased tenant was himself a successor.[604] Where the secure tenancy is held jointly, and one of the tenants dies, survivorship will operate, and (in the event of two joint tenants) the survivor will take the tenancy as of right and without reference to the above statutory provisions.[605]

II. SECURITY OF TENURE

1. Termination of secure tenancy

(a) Termination by tenant. A secure tenancy can be terminated by the tenant **22–166** according to its terms, e.g. by giving notice to quit,[606] or by surrendering the lease.[607]

---

[599] This term is defined widely in Housing Act 1985 s.113, as amended by Civil Partnership Act 2004 s.81 and Sch.8 para.27, so as to include most of those who would take on an intestacy (see above, para.14–104), as well as those who live with the tenant as his spouse or civil partner. This statutory definition of relatives is exhaustive, and no challenge is tenable under arts 8 and 14 ECHR: *Wandsworth LBC v Michalak* [2002] EWCA Civ 271; [2003] 1 W.L.R. 617; *Sheffield CC v Wall's Personal Representative* [2010] EWCA Civ 922; [2010] H.L.R. 47.

[600] HA 1985 s.87. Residence need not have been in the premises to which succession is claimed: *Waltham Forest LBC v Thomas* [1992] 2 A.C. 198. However, the requirement that the successor has "resided with" the tenant means that the successor must be able to show, as well as living in the same property as the tenant, an intention to make a home with him: *Freeman v Islington LBC* [2009] EWCA Civ 536; [2010] H.L.R. 6.

[601] HA 1985 s.89(2).

[602] HA 1985 s.89.

[603] HA 1985 s.90 (see amendments, not in force at the time of writing, in Localism Act 2011 s.162(1)). Compare Rent Act regulated tenancies, above, para.22–131.

[604] HA 1985 s.88. "Successor" is widely defined so as to include succession to a tenancy by survivorship. However, if the succession occurred at a time when the tenancy was not yet a secure tenancy (e.g. it pre-dated the coming into force of the Housing Act 1980), the surviving tenant will not be a successor: *Walker v Birmingham CC* [2007] UKHL 22; [2007] 2 A.C. 262. The single successor rule, which is less generous than the equivalent provisions contained in the Rent Act 1977, has been held to be compatible with Arts 8 and 14 ECHR: *R. v Hounslow LBC Ex p. Gangera* [2003] EWHC 794; [2003] H.L.R. 68.

[605] *Solihull MBC v Hickin* [2010] EWCA Civ 868; [2010] 1 W.L.R. 2254. However, the survivor will be a successor (see above), and so no statutory succession will be possible on the survivor's death.

[606] *Greenwich LBC v McGready* (1982) 6 H.L.R. 36; *Hammersmith & Fulham LBC v Monk* [1992] 1 A.C. 478 (notice to quit by one joint tenant terminates the tenancy); *Harrow LBC v Qazi* [2003] UKHL 43; [2004] 1 A.C. 983.

[607] *R. v Croydon LBC Ex p. Toth* (1986) 20 H.L.R. 576; *Sanctuary Housing Association v Campbell* (1999) 32 H.L.R. 641. Surrender may be express or by operation of law: see above, paras 18–085 et seq.

22–167   *(b) Termination by landlord.* Termination of a secure tenancy by the landlord is heavily proscribed by the 1985 Act, the provisions of which have caused considerable difficulties in their practical operation. The general rule is that the landlord may only recover possession of a dwelling let on a secure tenancy by obtaining an order for possession from the court on one of the grounds specified in Pt IV of the 1985 Act.[608] Even where the parties consent to the recovery of possession by the landlord, the court has no jurisdiction to make a possession order unless the tenant admits a ground of possession, either expressly or by necessary implication.[609] Provisions in the Localism Act 2011 will, when they come into force, permit landlords in England to grant "flexible tenancies", that is secure tenancies which would enable the landlord to recover possession as of right at the end of the tenancy.[609a]

22–168   *(c) Orders of the court.* Short of obtaining a possession order,[610] the 1985 Act provides two additional ways by which a secure tenancy may be terminated:

   (i)   in relation to a fixed-term tenancy, by obtaining an order from the court which terminates the fixed-term and causes a periodic tenancy to arise in its place[611];

   (ii) in relation to a fixed-term tenancy or a periodic tenancy, by obtaining a demotion order which terminates the secure tenancy and causes a demoted tenancy to arise in its place.[612]

However, neither of these two methods will usually result in the recovery of possession by the landlord. The first method enables landlords to bring the tenant's fixed-term tenancy to an end, and thereby to reduce the level of the tenant's security. It is only available where the tenancy contains provision for forfeiture or re-entry (for breach of covenant), and the court may only terminate the fixed-term tenancy where it would have made an order for possession on an application by the landlord to forfeit.[613] The effect of such an order will usually be that the tenant will continue in possession as a secure tenant, by virtue of a periodic tenancy arising by statute.[614] The second

---

[608] HA 1985 s.82(1).

[609] *R. v Bloomsbury & Marylebone County Court Ex p. Blackburne* (1984) 14 H.L.R. 56; *R. v Worthing BC Ex p. Bruce* (1993) 26 H.L.R. 223. See, for similar position regarding assured tenancies and regulated tenancies, para.22–095, fn.354 and para.22–137, above.

[609a] Tenants will have the right to demand a review by the landlord of its decision to offer a flexible tenancy in the first place or to seek an order for possession. In general, the flexible tenancy must be granted for a fixed term of not less than two years: see Localism Act 2011 ss.154, 155.

[610] HA 1985 s.82(1A)(i), inserted by HRA 2008 Sch.11 para.2(3).

[611] HA 1985 s.82(1A)(ii), inserted by HRA 2008 Sch.11 para.2(3); s.82(3).

[612] HA 1985 ss.82(1A)(iii), inserted by HRA 2008 Sch.11 para.2(3); s.82A, inserted by Anti-social Behaviour Act 2003 s.14(2).

[613] HA 1985 s.82(3). The landlord must comply with the provisions of LPA 1925 s.146: HA 1985 s.82(4).

[614] HA 1985 s.86.

method enables landlords to respond to anti-social behaviour by removing the tenant's statutory security while permitting the tenant to continue in occupation for the time being. It is more fully explained below.[615]

(d) Notice seeking possession. Prior to seeking a possession order, or an **22–169** order terminating a fixed-term tenancy, the landlord must serve a notice in prescribed form[616] on the tenant particularising the grounds for the application. If the tenancy is periodic, the notice must also specify the date after which proceedings may be begun; and this must not be earlier than the date when the notice, if a notice to quit, could have determined the tenancy, apart from the Act.[617] The notice ceases to be effective 12 months after the specified date.[618] No order can be made on any grounds not specified in the landlord's notice, although with the leave of the court those grounds may be added to or altered.[619]

(e) Powers of the court. Unless the possession order is made on Grounds 9 **22–170** to 11,[620] the court has wide powers to adjourn the proceedings, or to stay or suspend execution of the order, or to postpone the date for possession; but on doing this the court must impose terms as to making payments for occupation and paying any arrears of rent, unless this would cause "exceptional hardship" to the tenant or would otherwise be unreasonable.[621] Where Grounds 9 to 11 are relied upon, however, the court cannot postpone the date for possession for more than 14 days, or six weeks if "exceptional hardship" would otherwise be caused.[622]

(f) Date of termination of tenancy. One of the most difficult issues affecting **22–171** the termination of secure tenancies has concerned the date upon which a tenancy ends following the grant of a possession order. In a decision shortly

---

[615] See para.22–178.

[616] SI 1987/755, as amended by SI 1997/71 and 377, SI 2004/1627 and SI 2005/1226. There are separate notices for periodic tenancies, fixed-term tenancies and for applications for a demoted tenancy; and in each case a form substantially to the same effect as that prescribed will suffice: see *Torridge DC v Jones* (1985) 18 H.L.R. 107; *Dudley Metropolitan Council v Bailey* (1990) 22 H.L.R. 424; *City of London Corporation v Devlin* (1995) 29 H.L.R. 58; *Camden LBC v Oppong* (1996) 28 H.L.R. 701. The court has power to dispense with the notice where it is just and equitable to do so: HA 1985 s.83, as amended by HA 1996 s.147.

[617] There are modifications where the landlord is invoking Grounds 2 or 2A: see HA 1996 s.147, amending HA 1985 s.83, and adding HA 1985 s.83A. For the date to specify, see decisions on HA 1988 s.21(4) at para.22–127 above.

[618] HA 1985 s.83, as amended. There is no need to serve an additional notice in relation to the "automatic" periodic tenancy which arises on termination of a secure term certain: HA 1985 s.83(6).

[619] HA 1985 s.84(3).

[620] See below, para.22–175.

[621] HA 1985 s.85. The court may be faced with an application to adjourn the possession proceedings so that the tenant can exercise the right to buy: *Bristol CC v Lovell* [1998] 1 W.L.R. 446; *Basildon CC v Wahlen* [2006] EWCA Civ 326; [2006] 1 W.L.R. 2744, and see para.22–181 below.

[622] HA 1980 s.89(1); and see above, para.22–098, in particular fn.364.

after the 1985 Act came into force,[623] the Court of Appeal held that a secure tenancy terminated on the date on which the court specified that possession was to be given up. It followed that where the court made an order for possession, but suspended its execution on certain conditions (e.g. that the tenant paid the rent arrears at a particular rate), the tenancy would automatically terminate in the event of the condition being broken.[624] As a result, a large number of dwellings in the public sector were occupied by persons who were ostensibly secure tenants but who on closer examination of the circumstances had no right to be there as a result of the termination of their tenancy following breach of a suspended possession order. These persons became known as "tolerated trespassers".[625] The precise nature of this "conceptually peculiar, even oxymoronic, status",[626] and its legal consequences, was somewhat dubious,[627] and imaginative attempts were made to formulate the terms of possession orders in such a way as to keep the secure tenancy in existence for as long as possible.[628]

22–172   *(g) The demise of the tolerated trespasser.* Following consultation,[629] Parliament enacted Schedule 11 to the Housing and Regeneration Act 2008 which amended the 1985 Act with effect from May 20, 2009. It is now provided that where the landlord obtains an order for possession in relation to a dwelling held on secure tenancy the tenancy will terminate when the order is executed and not before.[630] This provision, which is not retrospective, has the effect that a secure tenant will remain so until he is evicted by order of the court. The problem of tolerated trespassers is further dealt with by providing that such persons who have been in occupation throughout the period from the termination of their secure tenancy to the commencement date of the legislation shall regain their former status (and in most cases, become secure tenants[631]) with effect from May 20, 2009. By the time this legislation came into force, the House of Lords had enjoyed a further opportunity to revisit the problem,[632] but in view of the impending legislative changes decided that it was inappropriate to overrule the earlier authorities affecting the termination

---

[623] *Thompson v Elmbridge BC* [1987] 1 W.L.R. 1425.

[624] *Marshall v Bradford MBC* [2001] EWCA Civ 594; [2002] H.L.R. 22 at [29]; *Lambeth LBC v O'Kane* [2005] EWCA Civ 1010; [2006] H.L.R. 2 at [58].

[625] *Burrows v Brent LBC* [1996] 1 W.L.R. 1448. In 2007, Government estimated that there were over 250,000 tolerated trespassers: see DCLG, *Tolerated Trespassers: a Consultation*, p.8.

[626] *Knowsley Housing Trust v White* [2008] UKHL 70; [2009] 1 A.C. 636, per Lord Neuberger at [79].

[627] See Bright (2003) 119 L.Q.R. 495; Loveland (2007) 123 L.Q.R. 455.

[628] See, e.g. *Bristol CC v Hassan* [2006] EWCA Civ 656; [2006] 1 W.L.R. 2582, ameliorating the problems caused by the earlier decision in *Harlow DC v Hall* [2006] EWCA Civ 156; [2006] 1 W.L.R. 2116.

[629] DCLG, *Tolerated Trespassers: a Consultation* (2007).

[630] HA 1985 s.82(2), amended by HRA 2008 Sch.11, para.2(3).

[631] Where, for instance, the occupiers were introductory tenants or demoted tenants (on which see below), that would the status to which they would revert.

[632] *Knowsley Housing Trust v White*, above; on which see [2009] Conv. 268 (S.B.); [2009] C.L.J. 515 (Thornton).

of secure tenancies, although certain steps were taken to alleviate the transition back from tolerated trespasser to secure tenant.[633] A further, and probably now final, attempt before the Supreme Court to challenge those earlier authorities foundered on the basis that to do so in light of the legislative amendments that had been introduced would be to "contradict the will of Parliament."[634]

2. Grounds for possession. Part IV of the Act specifies 18 grounds for   **22–173**
possession.[635] Many of these are closely similar to the grounds for possession for assured and regulated tenancies considered above, and so are not detailed here. There are three categories. The court cannot make an order:

   (i) on Grounds 1 to 8 unless the court considers it reasonable to make the order

   (ii) on Grounds 9 to 11, unless the court is satisfied that suitable alternative accommodation[636] will be available for the tenant when the order takes effect; or

   (iii) on Grounds 12 to 16, unless both these requirements are satisfied.[637]

(a) Reasonableness.

GROUND 1: RENT UNPAID OR BREACH OF COVENANT.[638]   **22–174**

GROUND 2: NUISANCE.[639]

GROUND 2A: DOMESTIC VIOLENCE.[640]

GROUND 3: DETERIORATION OF DWELLING-HOUSE.

GROUND 4: DETERIORATION OF FURNITURE.

GROUND 5: FALSE STATEMENT.[641]

GROUND 6: PREMIUM. The tenancy has been assigned for a premium.

GROUND 7: MISCONDUCT. A service tenant is guilty of misconduct.

---

[633] In particular, by holding (1) that a court could make a "proleptic" suspended possession order whereby payment of all arrears and costs would effect an automatic discharge without need to return to court (overruling *Marshall v Bradford MBC*, above); and (2) that a tenant could apply to the court for variation and discharge of the suspended possession order even though the terms of the order had not been fully complied with (overruling *Swindon BC v Aston* [2002] EWCA Civ 1850, [2003] H.L.R. 610).

[634] *Austin v Southwark LBC* [2010] UKSC 28; [2011] 1 A.C. 355 at [30] per Lord Hope.

[635] HA 1985 s.84 and Sch.2.

[636] Although this is similar to "suitable alternative accommodation" for assured and regulated tenancies, the 1985 Act is rather more detailed: see Sch.2 Pt IV thereof.

[637] HA 1985 s.84(2).

[638] Note importance of compliance with pre-action protocol in such cases: *Civil Procedure 2011*, Vol.1 para.C11–001, p.2607.

[639] Amended by HA 1996 s.144.

[640] Added by HA 1996 s.145.

[641] Amended by HA 1996 s.146.

GROUND 8: TEMPORARY ACCOMMODATION. The tenant became a temporary tenant of the dwelling while works were being carried out on another dwelling which he occupied as his only or principal home on a secure tenancy, and after completion of the works that other dwelling is again available for him on a secure tenancy.

(b) Suitable alternative accommodation available.

22–175 GROUND 9: OVERCROWDING. The dwelling is over-crowded in circumstances that render the occupier guilty of an offence.[642]

GROUND 10: DEMOLITION OR RECONSTRUCTION. The landlord intends, within a reasonable time of obtaining possession of the dwelling, to demolish or reconstruct some or all of the premises comprising the dwelling, or to do other works on it, and he cannot reasonably do this without obtaining possession of the dwelling.

GROUND 10A: REDEVELOPMENT.[643] The landlord wishes to dispose of the dwelling in accordance with an approved redevelopment scheme.[644]

GROUND 11: CHARITY. The landlord is a charity and the tenant's continued occupation of the dwelling conflicts with the charity's objects.

GROUND 12: SERVICE TENANT. In certain cases either the dwelling is reasonably required for an employee or the tenant is a service tenant whose employment has ended.

(c) Reasonableness, and suitable alternative accommodation available.

22–176 GROUND 13: DISABLED PERSON'S HOME. Features of the dwelling designed to make it suitable for occupation by a physically disabled person differ substantially from those of ordinary dwellings, but no such person lives there, and the landlord requires it for occupation by such a person.

GROUND 14: SPECIAL NEEDS. The landlord is a housing association or housing trust which lets dwellings only to those whose circumstances (other than merely financial) make it especially difficult for them to satisfy their housing needs, but no such person lives in the dwelling (or else a local authority has offered the tenant a separate dwelling on a secure tenancy), and the landlord requires it for occupation by such a person.

GROUND 15: SPECIAL FACILITIES.[644a] The dwelling is one of a group of dwellings which the landlord habitually lets to those with special needs, and some social service or special facility is provided nearby in order to assist

---

[642] Under HA 1985 Pt X.
[643] Added by the Housing and Planning Act 1986 s.9(1).
[644] See further HA 1985 Sch.2 Pt V, added by the Housing and Planning Act 1986 s.9(2).
[644a] Localism Act 2011 s.162(2), not in force at the time of writing, introduces a new Ground 15A in relation to dwelling houses in England where the tenant succeeded to the tenancy on death, although not as the deceased tenant's spouse or civil partner, and the accommodation is more extensive than the tenant reasonably requires.

such persons, but no such person lives in the dwelling any more, and the landlord requires it for occupation by such a person.

GROUND 16: OVER-EXTENSIVE ACCOMMODATION.[644b] The dwelling provides more extensive accommodation than the tenant normally requires, and not only did the tenant succeed to the tenancy when the previous tenant died (as a member of the family, but not as his spouse or civil partner), but also notice of the proceedings for possession was given more than six but less than 12 months after the death.[645]

III. INTRODUCTORY TENANCIES

Part V of the Housing Act 1996, titled "Conduct of Tenants", permits local housing authorities and housing action trusts to operate, by election, an "introductory tenancy regime". Such a scheme enables the landlord to give new tenants a trial or "probationary" period, during which recovery of possession may be effected expeditiously, without proof of a ground for possession. Where a landlord elects to operate an introductory tenancy scheme, every periodic tenancy[646] entered into or adopted[647] by the landlord which would otherwise have been a secure tenancy will, subject to limited exceptions,[648] be an introductory tenancy for a 12-month period from the date the tenancy was entered into or adopted.[649] While the tenancy is introductory, the landlord has an absolute right to a possession order from the court, provided that proper notice is given to the tenant, together with the reasons for the landlord's decision to claim possession.[650] The tenant has the right to have the decision reviewed by the landlord.[651] Although there is no statutory right to an independent review, the Supreme Court has held that, in defending possession proceedings, an introductory tenant may challenge the landlord's decision to bring those proceedings on the ground that to grant possession

22–177

[644b] See amendments, not in force at the time of writing, in Localism Act 2011 s.162(3).

[645] Where no notice is served, and the court dispenses with service, the possession proceedings must be begun within this time: HA 1996 s.147(3). In determining the tenant's reasonable requirements, the court must consider the circumstances at the date of the hearing: *Wandsworth LBC v Randall* [2007] EWCA Civ 1126; [2008] 1 W.L.R. 359. For relationship of Ground 16 with estoppel, see *Newport CC v Charles* [2008] EWCA Civ 1541; [2009] 1 W.L.R. 1884.

[646] "Tenancy" includes most licences to occupy: see HA 1996 s.126.

[647] A periodic tenancy is adopted by a person if that person becomes the landlord under the tenancy, whether on a disposal or surrender of the interest of the former landlord: HA 1996 s.124(4).

[648] In particular where, immediately before the tenancy was entered into or adopted, the tenant (or one of joint tenants) was a secure tenant or a "relevant" assured (but not assured shorthold) tenant of the same or another dwelling-house: HA 1996 s.124(2), as amended by SI 2010/866, Sch.2, para.96(2). An assured tenancy is relevant if the landlord is a private registered provider of social housing (and this is social housing) or a registered social landlord: HA 1996 s.124(2A), inserted by SI 2010/866, Sch.2 para.96(2).

[649] For calculation of period, and counting of earlier time as a tenant, see HA 1996 s.125.

[650] HA 1996 ss.127 and 128. The court has a duty to satisfy itself that the statutory procedure has been complied with: *Merton LBC v Williams* [2002] EWCA Civ 980; [2003] H.L.R. 20.

[651] HA 1996 s.129; and see further SI 2006/1077 (in Wales, SI 2006/2983).

would be disproportionate and therefore contrary to the tenant's article 8 rights.[652]

If no proceedings are brought within the 12-month period, and the landlord does not have the period extended,[653] the tenancy will automatically become secure within Part IV of the Housing Act 1985. Provision is made for succession to an introductory tenancy on death.[654] An introductory tenancy cannot be assigned, save by virtue of certain orders in family proceedings, or by an inter vivos assignment to the prospective successor.[655]

IV. DEMOTED TENANCIES

22–178   As part of its statutory powers to deal with anti-social behaviour, the court may make a demotion order in relation to a secure tenancy.[656] The court must not make such an order unless it is satisfied that the tenant, or a person residing in or visiting the dwelling-house, has engaged or threatened to engage in certain conduct[657] and that it is reasonable to make the order.[658] The effect of the demotion order is to reduce the tenant's security, by replacing the secure tenancy with a demoted tenancy.[659] Provision is made for succession to a demoted tenancy on death.[660] A demoted tenancy cannot be assigned, save by virtue of certain orders in family proceedings, or by an inter vivos assignment to the prospective successor.[661] The tenancy remains a demoted tenancy for a period of one year,[662] during which time the court is obliged to grant an order for possession to the landlord provided a statutory procedure is followed.[663] The status of the demoted tenant is similar to that of the introductory tenant. In making application for a possession order, the landlord must state its reasons for doing so,[664] and the tenant is entitled to request the landlord to

---

[652] *Hounslow LBC v Powell* [2011] UKSC 45; [2011] 2 A.C. 186, in particular at [50] et seq. The court read into HA 1996 ss.127 and 128 a requirement that the landlord was acting lawfully and in compliance with Art.8.

[653] The period may be extended by six months by service of notice at least eight weeks before the period expires: HA 1996 s.125A, added by HA 2004 ss.179(1) and (3).

[654] HA 1996 ss.131–133.

[655] HA 1996 s.134. See also provisions requiring publication of information, and for consultation with tenants: HA 1996 ss.136 and 137.

[656] See similar powers in relation to assured tenancies, above at para.22–119.

[657] The conduct must be conduct to which HA 1996 s.153A or s.153B applies (housing-related anti-social behaviour or using the premises for unlawful purposes): see above, para.22–119.

[658] HA 1985 s.82A(4), added by Anti-social Behaviour Act 2003 s.14(2). The requirement of reasonableness has led the Supreme Court to rule that the requirements of Art 8 ECHR are met by the statute: *Manchester CC v Pinnock* [2010] UKSC 45; [2011] 2 A.C. 104 at [66].

[659] HA 1985 s.82A(3), added by Anti-social Behaviour Act 2003 s.14(2). The demoted tenancy regime has been held to be compatible with Art.6 ECHR: *R (Gilboy) v Liverpool CC* [2008] EWCA Civ 751; [2009] Q.B. 699.

[660] HA 1996 s.143H, added by Anti-social Behaviour Act 2003 s.14(5) and Sch.1 para.1.

[661] HA 1996 s.143I, Anti-social Behaviour Act 2003 s.14(5) and Sch.1 para.1.

[662] HA 1996 s.143B(1), added by Anti-social Behaviour Act 2003 s.14(5) and Sch.1 para.1.

[663] HA 1996 s.143D(1), added by Anti-social Behaviour Act 2003 s.14(5) and Sch.1 para.1.

[664] HA 1996 s.143F(1), added by Anti-social Behaviour Act 2003 s.14(5), and Sch.1 para.1. For regulations, see SI 2004/1679 (England); SI 2005/1228 (Wales).

review its decision to take possession proceedings.[665] However, before making a possession order, the court is required to resolve any relevant disputes of fact between the parties and to assess the proportionality of the order that is being sought.[666]

Part IV of the Housing Act 1985 provides security of tenure, but imposes no system of rent control. When dwellings are owned by local authorities, they may make "such reasonable charges as they may determine for the tenancy or occupation of their houses".[667] A tenant may challenge the rent set by his local authority landlord by judicial review, although the courts have proved to be somewhat reluctant to intervene.[668] **22–179**

Part V of the Housing Act 1985[669] confers on many secure tenants the right to buy, at discounted prices, either the freehold of the dwelling or a long lease of it at a low rent. The practical result is that tenants who exercise this statutory right will become owners, and although they will normally continue to make regular payments much as they did while they were tenants, these can go towards discharging a mortgage instead of being mere rent. However, the tenant's rights to a mortgage from the landlord, to defer completion and to a shared ownership lease, all part of the original statutory bundle, were abolished in 1993,[670] and the tenant's right to acquire on "rent to mortgage terms", itself introduced in 1993,[671] was similarly removed in 2004.[672] **22–180**

1. Conditions

(a) The tenant.[673] A secure tenant has the right to buy only if he has been a "public sector tenant" for a total of at least five years.[674] Such a tenant is **22–181**

---

[665] HA 1996 s.143E(5), added by Anti-social Behaviour Act 2003 s.14(5) and Sch.1 para.1.

[666] *Manchester CC v Pinnock*, above, at [77], applying Art.8 ECHR; see further paras 22–075 et seq. above.

[667] HA 1985 s.24(1). It is no longer required that, in setting rents, local authorities in England (cf. Wales) must have particular regard to the principle that the rents of houses of any class or description should bear broadly the same proportion to private sector rents as the rents of houses of any other class or description: HA 1985 s.24(3), as amended by Local Government Act 1993 s.92(1).

[668] *Luby v Newcastle under Lyme Corp* [1965] 1 Q.B. 214; *Wandsworth LBC v Winder (No.2)* (1988) 20 H.L.R. 400.

[669] Consolidating, inter alia, Pt I of the Housing Act 1980.

[670] LRHUDA 1993 s.107.

[671] LRHUDA 1993 s.108 et seq.

[672] For explanation, see sixth edition of this work at para.22–299. Abolition was effected by HA 1985 s.142A, added by HA 2004 s.190.

[673] HA 1985 ss.118 and 119 and Sch.4.

[674] HA 1985 s.119, as amended by HA 2004 s.180(1). The five year period only applies to secure tenancies created after January 18, 2005: HA 2004 ss.180(5), and 270(3). Prior to this amendment, the qualifying period was two years, which period still applies to tenancies existing at that date.

closely similar to a secure tenant, although the list of landlords who satisfy the "landlord condition" is longer. Different periods can be added together to make up the five years, and so may periods when the tenant would have been a public sector tenant if Pt V or its predecessor had been in force, together with any periods of a public sector tenancy of his deceased spouse or civil partner if they occupied the same dwelling as their only or principal home.[675] Neither the landlord nor the dwelling need have been the same throughout, though any period when the landlord was exempt from the tenant's right to buy is excluded. The tenant cannot exercise the right if during the course of his application he ceases to be a secure tenant, if a possession order has been made against him,[676] or if he is the subject of bankruptcy proceedings.[677] As part of its powers to deal with anti-social behaviour, the court may, on application of the landlord, make a suspension order to the effect that the right to buy may not be exercised in relation to the dwelling-house for a specified period.[678]

22–182   *(b) The landlord.*[679] There is no right to buy if the landlord is a charitable housing trust or a housing association that is charitable, co-operative or unsubsidised.[680] Moreover, the right to buy does not arise unless the landlord owns the freehold or has an interest sufficient to grant a lease for a term exceeding 21 years (in the case of a house) or a term of not less than 50 years (in the case of a flat).[681]

22–183   *(c) The dwelling-house.*[682] Certain types of dwelling are exempt. These include certain sheltered or adapted accommodation for physically disabled, mentally disordered or elderly persons, and dwelling-houses which are subject to a final demolition notice. Dwellings let to service tenants by local authorities, development corporations and certain other public bodies are also exempt if they are held mainly for non-housing purposes.

---

[675] No period during which the tenancy is a demoted tenancy (see para.22–178 above) may be counted for these purposes: HA 1985 Sch.4 para.9A, added by Anti-social Behaviour Act 2003 s.14 and Sch.1 para.2.

[676] On the effect of a concurrent application for a possession order and initiation of the right to buy procedure, see *Bristol City Council v Lovell* [1998] 1 W.L.R. 446. A possession order has the effect of suspending, for the duration that it is operative, the exercise of the right to buy, but in the event of discharge of the order, the tenant's right will retrospectively revive: *Knowsley Housing Trust v White* [2008] UKHL 70; [2009] 1 A.C. 636 at [114] et seq.

[677] HA 1985 s.121; *Sutton LBC v Swann* (1985) 18 H.L.R. 140; *Muir Group Housing Association Ltd v Thornley* (1992) 25 H.L.R. 89. For effect of applications under HA 1985 Sch 2 Ground 16, see *Basildon DC v Wahlen* [2006] EWCA Civ 326; [2006] 1 W.L.R. 2744; *Manchester CC v Benjamin* [2008] EWCA Civ 189; [2009] 1 W.L.R. 2202.

[678] HA 1985 s.121A, added by HA 2004 s.192.

[679] HA 1985 Sch.4 paras 7 to 8.

[680] HA 1985 s.120 and Sch.5 paras 1–3.

[681] HA 1985 Sch.5 para.4, the lease commencing, in either case, with the date on which the tenant's notice claiming to exercise the right to buy is served. For definition of "house" and "flat", see para.22–184 below.

[682] HA 1985 s.120 and Sch.5 paras 5—13, as amended by HA 1988 s.123 and LRHUDA 1993 s.106.

2. Freehold or long lease.[683] If the dwelling is a "house" and the landlord **22–184**
is the freeholder, the right is to buy the freehold. If the dwelling is a "flat",
the right is to buy a long lease. If the dwelling is a house, and the landlord is
not the freeholder, the right is to buy a long lease, but the tenant may still have
the right to buy the freehold if those who hold interests superior to those of the
landlord are themselves public sector bodies.[684] For these purposes, a dwelling is a "house" if it is "a structure reasonably so called"; and every dwelling
that is not a "house" is a "flat".[685] If a building is divided horizontally, the
flats or other units are not "houses", but if it is divided vertically the units may
be houses, though no unit can be a house if a material part of it lies above or
below the rest of the structure. The tenant may require any land used with the
dwelling to be included, if this is reasonable.[686]

3. The price. The price payable is the value of the dwelling when the right **22–185**
to buy is exercised, less the discount.[687]

(a) Value.[688] The value of the dwelling is the price that it would fetch if sold **22–186**
with vacant possession by a willing seller on the open market, on the assumption that neither the tenant nor any member of his family living with him
wants to buy it. For these purposes, any improvements made by the tenant or
certain predecessors of his are to be disregarded, and so is any failure by them
to keep the dwelling in good internal repair. What is valued is the interest
obtained by the tenant, namely, the fee simple, or, if he buys a lease, a lease
at a ground rent not exceeding £10 a year for not less than 125 years, or for
the whole of the landlord's term (less five days) if the landlord has only a
shorter leasehold. In each case there are various specified terms as to easements, covenants, and so on.

(b) Discount.[689] From the value so ascertained, a discount based on the **22–187**
length of the qualifying period is deducted. In broad terms, the qualifying
period is the total of the periods for which the tenant (or his spouse or civil
partner or deceased spouse or civil partner) has been a public sector tenant or
has been occupying service accommodation as a member of the regular armed
forces of the Crown. In the case of a house,[690] the discount is 35 per cent of
the value plus 1 per cent for each year by which the qualifying period exceeds
five years. But the discount may not exceed either 60 per cent of the value, nor
may it reduce the price below an amount determined by the Secretary of State

---

[683] HA 1985 s.118.
[684] See SI 1993/2240.
[685] HA 1985 s.183.
[686] HA 1985 s.184. (Land let together with the dwelling, in so far as it is not agricultural land
exceeding two acres, is automatically treated as part of the dwelling).
[687] HA 1985 s.126.
[688] HA 1985 ss.127 and 139 and Sch.6.
[689] HA 1985 ss.129–131 and Sch.4, as amended by HA 1988 s.122; Civil Partnership Act 2004
s.81 and Sch.8 para.34; HA 2004 ss.180(2) and (3); SI 1998/2997.
[690] In the case of a flat, the discount is 50%, plus 2% for each year over the five years, with a
ceiling of 70%.

as being the costs incurred in respect of the dwelling over the last eight years; and the discount will be reduced by the amount of certain previous discounts given.

22–188　　　*(c) Repayment of discount.*[691] If, within five years of the conveyance or grant pursuant to the right to buy, the freehold or lease is disposed of, the tenant or his successors in title must pay the landlord such sum as the landlord considers appropriate, subject to a maximum of the discount, less one-fifth for each year that has elapsed since the conveyance or grant. The conveyance or lease must contain a covenant to this effect, and the liability will be a registrable charge on the dwelling. But certain disposals are exempted, e.g. disposals within the family or under a will or intestacy.

22–189　　　**4. Procedure.** The tenant claims his right to buy by serving a notice in the prescribed form[692] on the landlord.[693] Within four weeks the landlord must serve on the tenant a notice in the prescribed form either admitting the tenant's right to buy, or denying it and stating the reasons.[694] When the right has been admitted or established, the landlord must within eight weeks (or 12, if a lease is being bought) serve a notice on the tenant, describing the dwelling (including structural defects known to the landlord), stating the price and how it was computed, estimating service charges or improvement contributions, and stating the terms to be contained in the conveyance or lease, with certain other matters.[695] If the value or the discount are disputed, the tenant may then have them determined by the district valuer or the county court respectively.[696] When all matters relating to the grant have been agreed or determined, the landlord is bound to convey the fee simple or grant the lease to the tenant, unless his rent is four weeks in arrear; and this duty is enforceable by injunction.[697] If the tenant defaults after receiving successive notices to complete, his notice to buy is deemed to be withdrawn.[698] The county court has a general jurisdiction in these matters[699]; and if one or more tenants have

---

[691] HA 1985 ss.155, 156, 159, and 160, as amended by Housing and Planning Act 1986 s.2 and Sch.5 and by HA 2004 ss.185 and 186.

[692] Forms prescribed for the right to buy procedure are to be found in SI 1986/2194, as amended by SI 1993/2246.

[693] HA 1985 s.122. The tenant may elect to "share" the right to buy with any members of his family (up to a maximum of three) who are occupying the dwelling-house as their only or principal home. Such persons are then treated as joint tenants for the purposes of the application, and can, in the event of the death of the tenant, insist on completion of the acquisition: HA 1985 s.123; *Harrow LBC v Tonge* (1992) 25 H.L.R. 99.

[694] HA 1985 s.124.

[695] HA 1985 ss.125 and 125A–C, added by Housing and Planning Act 1986 s.4(2).

[696] HA 1985 ss.128 and 181.

[697] HA 1985 s.138; *Dance v Welwyn Hatfield DC* [1990] 1 W.L.R. 1097; *Taylor v Newham LBC* [1993] 1 W.L.R. 444. For further sanctions, see HA 1985 ss.153A, 153B, added by HA 1988 s.124; *Hanoman v Southwark LBC* [2009] UKHL 29; [2009] 1 W.L.R. 1367.

[698] HA 1985 ss.140 and 141. The burden is on the landlord to establish the validity of notices to complete: *Milne-Berry v Tower Hamlets LBC* (1995) 28 H.L.R. 225. For abandonment by tenant of right to buy generally, see *Martin v Medina Housing Association Ltd* [2006] EWCA Civ 367; [2007] 1 W.L.R. 1965.

[699] HA 1985 s.181.

difficulty in exercising their right to buy effectively and expeditiously, the Secretary of State may carry out the landlord's duties, with power to make vesting orders.[700]

5. Preserved right to buy. In the event of an assignment of the reversion   **22–190** to a private sector landlord, the tenant's right to buy will, subject to exceptions, be "preserved" in favour of the tenant and certain successors.[701] The tenant should register this right, as it cannot be treated as an overriding interest even though the tenant may be in actual occupation.[702]

F. Residential Long Tenancies

The long lease is a widely used device for holding land in English law. It is   **22–191** a property interest of considerable value, and on the assignment of a long lease the price paid by the purchaser may not be significantly less than the price which would be paid on a disposal of the freehold. The origin of many long leases lies in the building lease. The lessee takes an interest, commonly for 99 years, at a mere ground rent representing the undeveloped value of the land, and builds a house upon it at his own expense. He and his successors then have a long period of enjoyment at this low rent; but at the expiry of the lease, the house, being part of the land, reverts to the landlord or his successors, whose object in the bargain, long-term capital gain, is thereby achieved. Moreover, the disposition of property on a long lease carries advantages in the imposition and enforceability of obligations on the tenant which the alienation of freeholds does not: thus positive obligations to pay service charges and observe repairing covenants, which pose serious difficulties in relation to freeholders, can be enforced by virtue of the doctrine of privity of estate.[703]

However, the long lease poses problems for the tenant. It is a depreciating   **22–192** asset, and as the fixed term comes towards its end the leasehold interest will prove difficult to alienate, not least because lending institutions will be reluctant to take it as security. Long leaseholders have also experienced difficulties with landlords who fail to comply with repairing or service obligations expeditiously or at all. The last 40 years have seen considerable statutory intervention designed to improve the leaseholder's lot.

The legislation can be summarised as follows.[704] By Part I of the Landlord   **22–193** and Tenant Act 1954, long leaseholders were given security of tenure. The Leasehold Reform Act 1967 conferred on long leaseholders of lower value houses the right to "enfranchise", i.e. the opportunity to buy the freehold, or

---

[700] HA 1985 s.164; *R. v Secretary of State for the Environment Ex p. Norwich CC* [1982] Q.B. 808.

[701] HA 1985 ss.171A–171H, added by Housing and Planning Act 1986 s.8(1), and subsequently amended by Housing Act 1988 s.127. For details of the present law, see SI 1993/2241.

[702] HA 1985 Sch.9A, added by Housing and Planning Act 1986 s.8(2) and Sch.2, and as amended by LRA 2002 Sch.11, para.18.

[703] See Ch.20 above.

[704] See further Davey, "Long Residential Leases: Past and Present" in S. Bright (ed.) *Landlord and Tenant Law: Past, Present and Future* (2006).

the right to extend their leases. The Landlord and Tenant Act 1987, a statute which is not confined to long leaseholders, gave certain tenants of flats the right of first refusal on the landlord's disposal of his interest, and provided remedies for tenants dissatisfied with their landlord's failure to comply with his obligations under the lease. The Leasehold Reform, Housing and Urban Development Act 1993 extended enfranchisement rights to houses of higher value, and conferred both collective and individual enfranchisement rights on long leaseholders of flats. Finally, Pt 2 of the Commonhold and Leasehold Reform Act 2002 not only introduced commonhold as an alternative form of land tenure,[705] but also made significant further extensions to the existing statutory regimes.

There are four heads:

(1) security of tenure;

(2) individual enfranchisement of houses;

(3) collective enfranchisement of flats; and

(4) individual lease extension of flats.

I. SECURITY OF TENURE

22–194 **1. Introduction: the two regimes.** Since 1954, a statutory security of tenure has been conferred on those tenants who but for the lowness of the rent would have been entitled to retain possession of the premises under the Rent Acts.[706] This analogy ceased to be effective on January 15, 1989, as a tenancy entered into on or after that date could not, save in exceptional circumstances, be a protected tenancy.[707] As a result, a new code, contained in Sch.10 to the Local Government and Housing Act 1989, was enacted (some time after the Housing Act 1988 came into force) so as to apply to any long tenancy at a low rent which but for the low rent would have been an assured tenancy under Pt I of the Housing Act 1988.[708] The 1989 Act has had the effect of phasing out the operation of the 1954 Act. Not only are all qualifying long tenancies granted on or after January 15, 1989 subject to the 1989 Act, but all qualifying long tenancies granted before that date become subject to the 1989 Act if they expire on or after January 15, 1999.[709]

22–195 **2. " Long tenancy at a low rent".** The 1989 Act applies to a "long tenancy at a low rent". A tenancy is "long" if it is granted for a term of years certain

---

[705] See Ch.33 below.
[706] Landlord and Tenant Act 1954 Pt I (see in particular s.2); RA 1977 s.5.
[707] HA 1988 s.34(1).
[708] See HA 1988 Sch.1, paras 3 to 3C.
[709] LGHA 1989 Sch.10, para.3. Where a long tenancy was granted between January 15, 1989 and March 30, 1990, it is arguable that the 1989 Act has no application, an unfortunate result of Parliament's apparent failure, when enacting the Housing Act 1988, to appreciate its effect on the security of long tenancies at a low rent.

exceeding 21 years[710] whether or not subsequently extended by act of the parties or by any enactment; but any tenancy which is, or may become, terminable before the end of the term by notice given to the tenant is excluded.[711] Such a tenancy is at a "low rent" if either no rent is payable or the rent payable does not exceed certain limits equivalent to those set by Pt I of the Housing Act 1988.[712]

3. Protection. The tenancy continues by operation of law after the date on **22–196** which the fixed term expires ("the term date").[713] While during the fixed term the tenant can rely on his rights under the lease, after its expiry he is protected by statute. However, on or after the term date, the landlord can (following service of certain notices)[714] either, on proof of statutory grounds, obtain a court order entitling him to possession, or transform the tenancy into an assured tenancy. The landlord must give not less than six nor more than 12 months' notice,[715] and such notice must take one of two forms. A "landlord's notice to resume possession" states that if the tenant is not willing to give up possession by the specified date, the landlord proposes to apply to the court for possession on one or more specified grounds.[716] The landlord then has four months in which to apply to the court for possession on statutorily prescribed grounds.[717] If the tenant formally intimates his intention to retain possession by notice, the landlord's application must be made within two months of the "election to retain possession".[718] Alternatively, the landlord may serve a notice proposing an assured tenancy.[719] The terms of the tenancy are at the outset those of the long tenancy from which it derives, with obvious differences such as the length of the term, but the Act contains provision for subsequent variation by agreement with reference to a rent assessment committee[720] in case of dispute. The tenant may terminate a tenancy which is continuing by virtue of the protective code by one month's written notice.[721]

---

[710] "Back-dating" the tenancy will be ineffective: see *Roberts v Church Commissioners for England* [1972] 1 Q.B. 278. However, where there has been a term exceeding 21 years, subsequent grants for a shorter term at a low rent will be deemed to be long tenancies: see LGHA 1989 Sch.10 para.16.

[711] LGHA 1989 Sch.10 para.2(3).

[712] LGHA 1989 Sch.10 para.2(4) and (5), as amended by the References to Rating (Housing) Regulations 1990 (SI 1990/434).

[713] LGHA 1989 Sch.10 para.3.

[714] On the tenant, on which see *Galinski v McHugh* [1989] 1 E.G.L.R. 109.

[715] LGHA 1989 Sch.10, para.4. For forms, see SI 1997/3005 and 3008.

[716] LGHA 1989 Sch.10 para.4(5)(b).

[717] For the grounds, see LGHA 1989 Sch.10 para.5.

[718] LGHA 1989 Sch.10 paras 4(7), 13(1) and (2).

[719] LGHA 1989 Sch.10 para.4(5)(a).

[720] See Sch.10 paras 9—12. Once the rent of the assured periodic tenancy has been fixed pursuant to these provisions, further applications by the landlord to increase the rent payable are to be made under HA 1988 ss.13, 14 (and, unlike under LGHA 1989 Sch.10, tenants' improvements are to be taken into account): *Hughes v Borodex Ltd* [2010] EWCA Civ 425; [2010] 1 W.L.R. 2682.

[721] LGHA 1989 Sch.10 para.8.

II. INDIVIDUAL ENFRANCHISEMENT FOR TENANTS OF HOUSES: THE LEASEHOLD
REFORM ACT 1967

22–197   **1. Introduction.** The Leasehold Reform Act 1967 conferred on certain tenants occupying houses under long leases at a low rent the right to enfranchisement (i.e. to purchase the freehold) or to extend the lease (for 50 years) on paying a price or rent based on the value of the land alone, ignoring the house itself. It never applied to flats. The Act of 1967 has survived challenge before the European Court of Human Rights based on its allegedly confiscatory nature,[722] and recent statutes have widened the availability of enfranchisement (but not extension of the lease).

22–198   **2. Qualifying tenancies.** The 1967 Act initially conferred on a tenant, who occupied the house as his residence, the right to acquire the freehold, or an extended lease, of the house provided that the tenancy was a "long tenancy" at a "low rent" and that, at the time of giving notice to acquire, the tenant had been occupying the house for the last three years (or for three out of the last ten years).[723] In addition, the rateable value of the house and premises had to be below certain limits.[724] As a result of amendments made by a series of statutes,[725] the tenant's right to acquire the freehold has been significantly enhanced. With effect from July 26, 2002, the residence requirement (with very limited exceptions) and the low rent test (for freehold enfranchisement only) have been abolished, and the qualifying period of occupation has been reduced to two years.[726] These developments have been questioned. The purpose of the 1967 Act was to assist residential tenants to obtain the freehold of their only or main residence. Yet it is now the case that the 1967 Act may apply to "empty and substantially commercial buildings, even if nobody recently lived there or is even intending to live there", provided that the building can reasonably be called a house, and that tenants, who may be companies rather than individuals, may "enfranchise many properties at the same time, even though they do not live in any of those properties".[727]

The conditions that must now be satisfied in order for the right to arise are:

    (i) the tenancy must be of a house

    (ii) the tenancy must be a long tenancy

---

[722] See the fifth edition of this work at p.1127. The Act does not breach Art.1 of the First Protocol to the European Convention on Human Rights: *James v United Kingdom* [1986] 8 E.H.R.R. 123; and see *Pitts v Earl Cadogan* [2008] UKHL 71; [2010] 1 A.C. 226 at [48].

[723] LRA 1967 s.1(1).

[724] These limits were abolished by LRHUDA 1993 s.63, inserting LRA 1967 s.1A.

[725] The Rent Acts 1968 and 1977, the Housing Acts 1974, 1980 and 1985, the Leasehold Reform Act 1979, the Housing and Planning Act 1986, the References to Rating (Housing) Regulations 1990, the Leasehold Reform, Housing and Urban Development Act 1993, the Housing Act 1996 and the Commonhold and Leasehold Reform Act 2002.

[726] Commonhold and Leasehold Reform Act 2002 ss.137–149; SI 2002/1912.

[727] *Day v Hosebay Ltd* [2010] EWCA Civ 748; [2010] 1 W.L.R. 2317 at [56], per Lord Neuberger M.R.; and see Morgan [2010] Conv. 444.

(iii) at the time of giving notice the tenant must have been the tenant of the house for the last two years.

(a) House. The premises must consist of a house, as defined.[728] This **22–199** includes semi-detached and terrace houses, but not individual flats or maisonettes. If the premises are part of a larger building, the division must in effect be vertical.[729] It suffices if the premises can reasonably be called a house (e.g. where part is a shop and the rest a dwelling) even though they can reasonably be described as something else. The question is one of law, not fact.[730]

(b) Long tenancy. A long tenancy is a tenancy granted for a term of years **22–200** certain exceeding 21 years, even if determinable during the term.[731] Business tenancies (that is, tenancies to which Pt 2 of the Landlord and Tenant Act 1954 applies) are excluded save where they are granted for a term exceeding 35 years or in other limited circumstances,[732] or where the tenant has been occupying the house as his only or main residence[733] for the last two years (or for two of the last ten years).[734] Certain shared ownership leases are also excluded.[735] If the house is let with other land or premises to which it is ancillary, or if the house is comprised in an agricultural holding or a holding held under a farm business tenancy, the tenancy is excluded from the Act.[736]

The Act applies equally to sub-tenancies. To avoid conflicting claims being **22–201** made, where a house is let under two or more tenancies, the tenant under any

---

[728] LRA 1967 s.2(1): "'house' includes any building designed or adapted for living in . . . ", requiring the court to consider the purpose for which the building was initially designed or has subsequently been adapted: *Boss Holdings Ltd v Grosvenor Properties Ltd* [2008] UKHL 5; [2008] 1 W.L.R. 289 (building not fit for immediate residential occupation nevertheless a house for the purposes of the 1967 Act). If a building is initially designed as a house, it may cease to be a house as a result of being subsequently adapted to non-residential uses: *Day v Hosebay Ltd*, above, at [31] et seq.

[729] The Act does not apply to a house "which is not structurally detached and of which a material part lies above or below a part of the structure not comprised in the house": s.2(2). See *Parsons v Viscount Gage* [1974] 1 W.L.R. 435; *Malekshad v Howard de Walden Estates Ltd* [2002] UKHL 49; [2003] 1 A.C. 1013, disapproving *Duke of Westminster v Birrane* [1995] Q.B. 262.

[730] LRA 1967 s.2(1); *Lake v Bennett* [1970] 1 Q.B. 663; *Tandon v Trustees of Spurgeon's Homes* [1982] A.C. 755. It is a question that is "to be determined essentially by reference to its external and internal physical character and appearance": *Day v Hosebay Ltd*, above, at [46], per Lord Neuberger M.R., following *Boss Holdings Ltd v Grosvenor Properties Ltd*, above; cf. *Grosvenor Estates Ltd v Prospect Estates Ltd* [2008] EWCA Civ 1281; [2009] 1 W.L.R. 1313 (very limited living accommodation ancillary to the preponderant use of the premises as an office).

[731] LRA 1967 s.3; *Roberts v Church Commissioners for England* [1972] 1 Q.B. 278; *Eton College v Bard* [1983] Ch. 321. Specific provision is made for perpetually renewable leases, leases terminable by notice on death, marriage or formation of a civil partnership, and tenants holding over after expiry of the term of years certain.

[732] LRA 1967 s.1(1ZC), inserted by CLRA 2002 s.140. The other circumstances are those mentioned in fn.537 above.

[733] *Poland v Earl Cadogan* [1980] 3 All E.R. 544 is the leading authority.

[734] LRA 1967 s.1(1B), inserted by CLRA 2002 s.139(2).

[735] LRA 1967 s.1(1A), s.33A and Sch.4A, inserted by Housing and Planning Act 1986 s.18 and Sch.4.

[736] LRA 1967 s.1(3)(b); see *Lester v Ridd* [1990] 2 Q.B. 430.

tenancy which is superior to that held by a tenant on whom the Act confers rights does not himself have any rights under the Act.[737]

22–202   *(c) Qualifying period.* The general requirement that the tenant must have occupied the house as his residence was abolished with effect from July 26, 2002. Instead, it is now required that the tenant must, at the relevant time,[738] have been tenant of the house under a long tenancy at a low rent for the last two years.[739]

22–203   *(d) Low rent.* It is no longer generally necessary, for the purposes of a claim to enfranchisement, that the tenancy is at a low rent.[740] The one case where a low rent remains relevant to an enfranchisement claim is where the tenancy is an "excluded tenancy".[741] However, the low rent restriction remains relevant for the purposes of all claims to lease extension. The definition of "low rent" is very complicated.[742]

22–204   *(e) Property value.* The 1967 Act imposed certain limits on the value of property which could be the subject of a claim. In effect, the rateable value of the premises had to be less than a certain amount on "the appropriate day".[743] Following the abolition of domestic rates, a statutory formula was introduced, to be used where tenancies were entered into on or after April 1, 1990.[744] Then by the 1993 Act, the requirement that the house be of a certain value for the purposes of enfranchisement (but not for the purposes of lease extension) was effectively neutralised by extending the right to enfranchise to houses exceeding the value limits.[745] However, the distinction between tenancies which were eligible for enfranchisement before the 1993 Act reforms and those which only became eligible thereafter remains of some significance for the purposes of establishing the price, and compensation, payable to the landlord.

22–205   **3. Claim.** A tenant who wishes to claim either enfranchisement or extension must do so by serving on his landlord a written notice to this effect in the prescribed form.[746] He may do this at any time while his long tenancy exists under the lease itself or while it is being automatically continued on the

---

[737] LRA 1967 s.1(1ZA), inserted by CLRA 2002 s.138(2).

[738] That is, the time when the tenant gives notice of his desire to enfranchise or extend the lease: LRA 1967 s.1(1)(b), inserted by CLRA 2002 s.139(1).

[739] LRA 1967 s.1(1)(b).

[740] LRA 1967 s.1AA, inserted by HA 1996 s.106 and Sch.9. For a recent decision where the court had to consider whether a long tenancy (granted in 1965) was at a low rent, see *Neville v Cowdray Trust Ltd* [2006] EWCA Civ 709; [2006] 1 W.L.R. 2097.

[741] Excluded tenancies are those granted on or before April 1, 1997, or subsequently but before July 26, 2002 for a term not exceeding 35 years, where the house is in an designated rural area and the freehold is owned together with adjoining non-residential land: see LRA 1967 s.1AA(3).

[742] LRA 1967 ss.4 and 4A. inserted by LRHUDA 1993 s.65.

[743] LRA 1967 s.1(1)(a).

[744] SI 1990/434.

[745] LRA 1967 s.1A, inserted by LRHUDA 1993 s.63.

[746] LRA 1967 s.22 and Sch.3 para.6; SI 1997/640.

original terms under Sch.10 to the Local Government and Housing Act 1989.[747] But if under these statutes the landlord serves a notice seeking to terminate the tenancy, the tenant will lose his rights under the 1967 Act unless he serves his notice within two months.[748] When served, the tenant's notice takes effect as a contract "freely entered into" for the landlord to convey the freehold of the "house and premises" (i.e. the house and any premises let and used with it), or to grant the new tenancy of them, as the case may be.[749] It can be protected by the entry of a notice in the landlord's register of title,[750] or by registration as an estate contract in the case of unregistered land.[751] In default of agreement on the price or rent, these and the other terms will be determined by a leasehold valuation tribunal[752]; otherwise the terms are a matter for the county court, which has general jurisdiction over claims under the Act.[753] For enfranchisement (but not for extension) there is a right for the tenant to withdraw within a month of the price being agreed or determined[754]; and there is also a special procedure where the landlord is unknown or cannot be found.[755]

4. Completion

(a) *Extension.* If the tenant's notice seeks an extension of his tenancy, he is entitled to the grant of a tenancy for 50 years from the expiry of his existing lease, on corresponding terms.[756] The rent is to be a ground rent representing the letting value of the site when the new tenancy begins, disregarding the value of the buildings on it, though after 25 years the landlord may require the rent to be raised to the then current letting value of the site[757]; and the tenant must pay the landlord's reasonable costs of the transaction.[758] The tenant can claim enfranchisement, but no further extension, during a term thus extended.[759] The extended tenancy will be protected under Sch.10 to the Local Government and Housing Act 1989, but other statutory rights to security of tenure are excluded.[760]

22–206

---

[747] LRA 1967 s.3(2). For the relationship with forfeiture proceedings, see *Twinsectra Ltd v Hynes* (1995) 28 H.L.R. 183.

[748] LRA 1967 Sch.3 para.2.

[749] LRA 1967 s.5.

[750] The tenant's rights following service of statutory notice on the landlord cannot comprise an overriding interest: LRA 1967 s.5(5), as amended by LRA 2002 s.133 and Sch.11 para.8.

[751] LRA 1967 s.5(5).

[752] LRA 1967 s.21; Housing Act 1980 s.142.

[753] LRA 1967 s.20.

[754] LRA 1967 s.9(3), as substituted by CLRA 2002 s.139(3). No new notice may be given for 12 months, and the tenant must compensate the landlord for his reasonable costs: LRA 1967 ss.9(3),(4).

[755] LRA 1967 s.27, as amended by CLRA 2002 s.149; *Re Robertson's Application* [1969] 1 W.L.R. 109.

[756] LRA 1967 ss.14 and 15.

[757] LRA 1967 s.15(2).

[758] LRA 1967 s.14(2).

[759] LRA 1967 s.16, as amended by CLRA 2002 s.143.

[760] LRA 1967 s.16.

22–207   *(b) Enfranchisement.* If the tenant's notice seeks enfranchisement, he is entitled to a conveyance in fee simple subject to his tenancy and any incumbrances on it, but otherwise free from most incumbrances on the freehold such as mortgages.[761] There are two bases of assessment of the purchase price, depending on whether the value of the house and premises exceeds certain limits.[762]

> (1) If the value does not exceed these limits, the price is the value of the freehold of the house and premises on the open market (excluding from that market the tenant and members of his family), on the assumption that the tenancy will be extended under the Act.[763] The price will thus be based on the capitalised value of the ground rents payable during the existing and extended terms, with the right to possession of the house and premises deferred until those terms have expired.[764]

> (2) If the value exceeds these limits, the price is the value of the freehold of the house and premises on the open market (including the tenant and his family), subject to the tenancy and the right of the tenant to remain in possession pursuant to Sch.10 to the Local Government and Housing Act 1989, but on the assumption that the tenant has no right to enfranchisement or extension under the 1967 Act.[765] A reduction is made for any tenant's improvements,[766] and it is assumed that the tenant has no liability to carry out repairs, maintenance or redecorations during any statutory continuation.[767] In this case, the price will reflect more of the value of the house.[768]

---

[761] LRA 1967 s.8(1). But not redeemable rentcharges: LRA 1967 s.11, as amended by the Rentcharges Act 1977 Sch.2. For ancillary rights and obligations, see LRA 1967 s.10. The rule in *Wheeldon v Burrows* (see para.28–020 below) does not apply: *Kent v Kavanagh* [2006] EWCA Civ 162; [2007] Ch. 1.

[762] LRA 1967 s.9. Where the house and premises had a rateable value on March 31, 1990, the limit (adjusted to take account of tenant's improvements) is a rateable value of £1,000 in Greater London, and £500 elsewhere, on that date. Where the property had no rateable value on that date, a statutory formula is applied.

[763] LRA 1967 s.9(1).

[764] *Farr v Millersons Investments Ltd* (1971) 22 P. & C.R. 1055. "Hope value" is not to be taken into account: *Pitts v Earl Cadogan* [2008] UKHL 71; [2010] 1 A.C. 226 at [81] to [84].

[765] LRA 1967 s.9(1A), added by Housing Act 1974 s.118(4), and subsequently amended by Housing and Planning Act 1986 s.23 and LGHA 1989 s.194(1) and Sch.11 para.9. "Hope value" is excluded: *Pitts v Earl Cadogan*, above at [85] to [93].

[766] For what comprises an improvement, see *Shalson v Keepers & Governors of the Free Grammar School of John Lyon* [2003] UKHL 32; [2004] 1 A.C. 802; *Fattal v Keepers & Governors of the Free Grammar School of John Lyon* [2004] EWCA Civ 1530; [2005] 1 W.L.R. 803.

[767] LRA 1967 s.9(1A), (1B), added by Housing Act 1974, s.118(4), and subsequently amended as above; *Norfolk v Trinity College, Cambridge* (1976) 32 P. & C.R. 147.

[768] Where the right to acquire the freehold arises by virtue of certain amendments to the 1967 Act (ss.1A, 1AA and 1B, and see also CLRA 2002 s.147(1)), the valuation rules set out in this paragraph are modified: see LRA 1967 s.9(1C), inserted by LRHUDA 1993 s.66(1).

Under either head, the tenant must pay the landlord's reasonable costs of the transaction.[769]

5. Modifications. No contract can exclude or modify the tenant's right to   **22–208**
enfranchisement or extension, or to compensation as mentioned below[770]; but
the Act itself limits the provisions for enfranchisement or extension in certain
cases.

(a) Required for residence by landlord. A tenant's right to enfranchisement   **22–209**
or extension will be defeated if, after he has given notice claiming it, the
landlord obtains an order for possession of the house for occupation as the
only or main residence for himself or for an adult member of his family; but
no order will be made if to make it would cause greater hardship than to refuse
it.[771] A tenant whose claim is defeated in this way is entitled to compensation
(determined by a leasehold valuation tribunal in default of agreement) equal
to the open market value of a tenancy of the house as extended under the Act,
though with nothing for losing the right of enfranchisement.[772]

(b) Redevelopment. If an extension has been granted, or application for an   **22–210**
extension has been made, and it is not more than a year before the contractual
term expires, the landlord may apply for an order for possession on the ground
that for purposes of redevelopment he proposes to demolish or reconstruct the
house or a substantial part of it.[773] If this ground is established, the court must
declare that the landlord is entitled to possession and the tenant to compensation. Such a declaration will determine any extended tenancy that has already
been granted and defeat any claim to an extension, though the tenant will be
entitled to compensation as above.[774] A claim for enfranchisement cannot
normally be defeated on this ground.[775]

(c) Development by public bodies.[776] If a Minister certifies that the landlord,   **22–211**
a public body, will require the property within 10 years for development for
the purposes of that body, a tenant cannot effectively claim either enfranchisement or extension under the Act. But if before the certificate is served, or
within two months thereafter, the tenant claims enfranchisement or extension,
the tenancy is treated as having been extended; and if the public body wishes
to obtain possession, it must apply to the court as under the provisions for

---

[769] LRA 1967 ss.9(4) and (4A), inserted by CLRA 2002 s.176 and Sch.13 para.2.
[770] LRA 1967 s.23. An agreement between the landlord and a third party may be affected by
this provision: see *Rennie & Rennie v Proma Ltd* (1989) 22 H.L.R. 129. However, an agreement
which has the effect of making enfranchisement more expensive to the tenant is not, although
certain agreements of this kind are invalidated by the Leasehold Reform Act 1979 s.1: see further
Jones v Wrotham Park Settled Estates [1980] A.C. 74.
[771] LRA 1967 s.18.
[772] LRA 1967 s.21(1)(c) and Sch.2 para.5.
[773] LRA 1967 s.17.
[774] LRA 1967 s.21(1)(c) and Sch.2 para.5.
[775] LRA 1967 s.17.
[776] LRA 1967 s.28.

redevelopment in the last paragraph.[777] On such an application, the Minister's certificate is conclusive as to the required purposes. The term "public body" includes local authorities, universities, certain health authorities and nationalised industries.[778]

22–212   *(d) The Crown.*[779] A tenant holding directly from the Crown cannot claim either enfranchisement or extension under the Act; but usually the Crown will, as of grace, agree to grant one or the other on the terms of the Act.

22–213   *(e) Management.* Where there was an area occupied by tenants under one landlord, the appropriate Minister could certify, on application made to him before 1970,[780] that in order to maintain standards it was in the general interest that the landlord should retain powers of management and control over the development and use of houses in the area. A scheme for this purpose (e.g. regulating the redevelopment or use of enfranchised property, and providing for repairs) could then subsequently be submitted to the High Court and, if approved, take effect.[781] Provision was also made by the 1993 Act for landlords to retain powers of management under estate management schemes by making application to a leasehold valuation tribunal before November 2, 1995, or subsequently, with the consent of the Secretary of State.[782] Although schemes of management may regulate enfranchised property in many matters of detail, they do not prevent enfranchisement or extension.

III. COLLECTIVE ENFRANCHISEMENT FOR TENANTS OF FLATS: THE LEASEHOLD REFORM, HOUSING AND URBAN DEVELOPMENT ACT 1993[783]

22–214   **1. Introduction.** The 1993 Act conferred on "qualifying tenants" a right of collective enfranchisement in respect of certain premises.[784] The premises must consist of a self-contained[785] building or part of a building, and contain two or more flats[786] held by qualifying tenants. The total number of flats held by qualifying tenants must be not less than two-thirds of the total number of

---

[777] If the landlord succeeds under LRA 1967 s.17, he is liable to compensate the tenant: see para.22–210 above.

[778] LRA 1967 s.28(5).

[779] LRA 1967 s.33. For other exclusions, see LRA 1967 ss.31, 32 and 32A (added by LRHUDA 1993 s.68) and 33A.

[780] Before July 31, 1976, for tenancies brought within the Act solely by the higher rateable values of the Housing Act 1974: see HA 1974 s.118.

[781] LRA 1967 s.19. See e.g. *Re Sherwood Close (Barnes) Management Co Ltd* [1972] Ch. 208; *Eton College v Nassar* [1991] 2 E.G.L.R. 271.

[782] LRHUDA 1993 ss.69–75.

[783] See Bright [1994] Conv. 211; Clarke [1994] Conv. 223; Davey (1994) 57 M.L.R. 773.

[784] LRHUDA 1993 s.1.

[785] A building, or part of a building, may be self-contained even though it may be capable of further sub-division into smaller self-contained parts: *41–60 Albert Place Mansions Ltd v Craftrule Ltd* [2011] EWCA Civ 185; [2011] 1 W.L.R. 2425.

[786] "Flat" means a separate set of premises (whether or not on the same floor) which forms part of a building, and is constructed or adapted for use as a dwelling, and either the whole or a material part of it lies above or below some other part of the building: LRHUDA 1993 s.101(1).

flats contained in the premises.[787] Where part of the premises is neither occupied (nor intended to be occupied) for residential purposes nor comprised in common parts, and that part comprises more than 25 per cent of the internal floor area of the premises as a whole, the premises are excluded from the right of enfranchisement.[788] Also excluded are premises which contain no more than four units and have a resident landlord[789]; as are premises where different persons own the freehold of different parts of the premises, provided that any of those parts is a self-contained part of a building.[790] Important amendments were made to the 1993 Act by Part 2 of the Commonhold and Leasehold Reform Act 2002. The former requirements that tenancies are at a low rent and that certain flats are occupied by qualifying tenants have been removed, and acquisition may now be made by an "RTE" ("right to enfranchise") company.

2. Qualifying tenants. A "qualifying tenant" is a tenant of a flat under a **22–215** "long lease".[791] A "long lease" is a lease granted for a term exceeding 21 years, even if determinable during the term.[792] There are three important exclusions:

(1) business leases

(2) flats let by charitable housing trusts as housing accommodation in pursuit of their charitable purposes; and

(3) "unlawful" sub leases unless the superior lease was itself a long lease.[793]

If a tenant qualifies in respect of three or more flats in the premises, there is taken to be no qualifying tenant of any of those flats.[794]

3. The right to collective enfranchisement. The right to collective enfran- **22–216** chisement conferred on qualifying tenants is the right to have the freehold of the premises in which their flats are contained acquired on their behalf by a person or persons (usually a company formed for this purpose)[795] appointed by them, at a price determined in accordance with the statute.[796] They are also entitled to acquire the freehold of appurtenant property and "common

---

[787] LRHUDA 1993 s.3, which further defines "building".

[788] LRHUDA 1993 s.4(1), as amended by CLRA 2002 s.115.

[789] LRHUDA 1993 s.4(4). "Resident landlord" is widely defined in s.10 (as amended by CLRA 2002 s.118) so as to include members of the landlord's family: see also *Slamon v Planchon* [2004] EWCA Civ 799; [2005] Ch. 142.

[790] LRHUDA 1993 s.4(3A), added by HA 1996 s.107.

[791] LRHUDA 1993 s.5(1). The requirement that the long tenancy be at a low rent (LRHUDA 1993 s.8) was abolished by CLRA 2002 s.117.

[792] See further LRHUDA 1993 s.7, a lengthy provision which contains a complex definition.

[793] LRHUDA 1993 s.5(2).

[794] LRHUDA 1993 s.5(5).

[795] In time, the company may be an RTE company: see CLRA 2002 s.122, inserting LRHUDA 1993 ss.4A, 4B and 4C. To date, the provisions have only been brought in force so that regulations may be made: SI 2002/1912 art.2(c).

[796] LRHUDA 1993 s.1(1).

parts",[797] whether or not contained in the premises as such.[798] However, the freeholder may require the purchaser to grant a leaseback of such flats in the premises as are not let to qualifying tenants (and of such parts of the premises as are not flats); and in the case of flats let on secure tenancies and certain lettings by housing associations such leaseback is mandatory, and not therefore dependent on the freeholder serving a notice of his claim.[799] The leaseback to the freeholder is for a term of 999 years at a peppercorn rent.[800] The freeholder may prevent the acquisition of his property altogether if the court is satisfied that not less than two-thirds of the long leases of the flats in the premises are due to terminate within five years, that for the purposes of redevelopment the freeholder intends on termination of the leases to demolish, reconstruct, or carry out substantial works of construction of the whole or a substantial part of the premises, and that he could not reasonably do so without obtaining possession of the premises demised by those leases.[801]

22–217   **4. The price.** The price to be paid by the purchaser to the freeholder is calculated by adding three elements.[802]

> (1) *The value of the freeholder's interest in the premises.*[803] This is the amount that might be expected to be obtained for the interest by a willing seller on the open market, with neither the nominee purchaser nor any tenant in the premises nor any owner of an interest which the purchaser is to acquire, buying or seeking to buy. In other words, this element is based on the capitalised value of the ground rents during the existing (and any extended) term, and the value of the reversion on expiry of the term. Various assumptions are made. In valuing the freeholder's interest, account may be taken of the possibility that tenants who were not participating in the current purchase might subsequently wish to obtain new leases of their flats in the open market.[804]
>
> (2) *The freeholder's share of the "marriage value".*[805] The "marriage value" is the difference between:

---

[797] *Earl Cadogan v Panagopoulos* [2010] EWCA Civ 1259; [2011] Ch.177 (caretaker's flat held to be common parts).

[798] LRHUDA 1993 s.1(2), (3), as amended by HA 1996 s.105(3). By granting "permanent rights" over the common parts the purchaser may acquit his obligation to transfer the freehold of such property: s.1(4). Leasehold interests superior to those of the qualifying tenants may also be acquired: LRHUDA 1993 s.2.

[799] LRHUDA 1993 s.36 and Sch.9 Pts II and III. The landlord must state his desire for a leaseback in the counter-notice to the tenant's claim notice: *Cawthorne v Hamdan* [2007] EWCA Civ 4; [2007] Ch. 187.

[800] LRHUDA 1993 s.36 and Sch.9, para.8. For other terms of lease, see LRHUDA 1993 Sch.9, Pt IV.

[801] LRHUDA 1993 s.23.

[802] LRHUDA 1993 s.32 and Sch.6, as amended by HA 1996 s.107.

[803] LRHUDA 1993 Sch.6 para.3, as amended by HA 1996 s.109.

[804] The so-called "hope value": *Pitts v Earl Cadogan* [2008] UKHL 71; [2010] 1 A.C. 226, on appeal from *Earl Cadogan v Sportelli* [2007] EWCA Civ 1042; [2008] 1 W.L.R. 2142.

[805] LRHUDA 1993 Sch.6 para.4, as amended by CLRA 2002 s.127.

(i) the aggregate value of the freehold and intermediate leasehold interests in the premises prior to the acquisition; and

(ii) the aggregate value of those interests after acquisition.

The marriage value is thus the increase in value attributable to the participating tenants' potential ability, subsequent to acquisition, to grant themselves new leases without payment of premiums and without restrictions as to the length of the term. The freeholder's share of the marriage value is 50 per cent of this.

(3) *Compensation for loss resulting from enfranchisement.*[806] The freeholder is entitled to reasonable compensation for loss or damage suffered by virtue of any diminution in the value of any interest he has in other property resulting from the acquisition, and also any loss of development value in the property being acquired.

The reasonable costs of acquisition (as listed in the statute) are to be met by the nominee purchaser.[807] The purchaser may also have to pay for any intermediate leasehold interests, and indeed other interests, which are acquired.[808]

5. Claim. A claim is initiated by notice to "the reversioner", who will **22–218** normally be the freeholder of the premises.[809] This "initial notice" must be given by a number of qualifying tenants of flats contained in the premises which is not less than one-half of the total number of such flats.[810] The notice must designate the nominee purchaser, and contain detailed particulars of the claim.[811] The reversioner then has a period of not less than two months in which to give a counter-notice to the nominee purchaser admitting or denying the right claimed, or claiming an intention to redevelop.[812] Where the reversioner contests entitlement to enfranchise in a counter-notice, and the nominee purchaser wishes to proceed, he should apply to the court within two months,

---

[806] LRHUDA 1993 Sch.6 para.5.
[807] LRHUDA 1993 s.33.
[808] LRHUDA 1993 Sch.6 Pts III and IV.
[809] LRHUDA 1993 s.9.
[810] LRHUDA 1993 s.13(2), as amended by CLRA 2002 s.119.
[811] LRHUDA 1993 s.13. The notice must be properly signed by all the tenants: *Cascades & Quayside Ltd v Cascades Freehold Ltd* [2007] EWCA Civ 1555; [2008] L.& T.R. 23. A failure to comply by one of the tenants will render the notice invalid: *Hilmi & Associates Ltd v 20 Pembridge Villas Freehold Ltd* [2010] EWCA Civ 314; [2010] 1 W.L.R. 2750 (corporate tenant failing to comply with provisions of Companies Act 1986). Where the tenants serve an invalid s.13 notice, there is nothing to prevent them from serving another notice: *Sinclair Gardens Investments (Kensington) Ltd v Poets Chase Freehold Co Ltd* [2007] EWHC 1776 (Ch); [2008] 2 All E.R. 187.
[812] LRHUDA 1993 s.21. For whether counter-notice valid, see *7 Strathray Gardens Ltd v Pointstar Shipping & Finance Ltd* [2004] EWCA Civ 1669; [2005] H.L.R. 20 (failure to state that premises not within estate management scheme); *9 Cornwall Crescent London Ltd v Kensington & Chelsea RLBC* [2005] EWCA Civ 324; [2006] 1 W.L.R. 1186 (landlord specifies inflated price for freehold). For intention to redevelop, see LRHUDA 1993 s.23, above, para.22–210. In the event of a failure to give a counter-notice within the requisite period, the court has power to determine the terms of acquisition: s.25.

and seek a declaration of entitlement.[813] Where an intention to redevelop is claimed, any appropriate landlord should apply to the court within the same period for a declaration that the right to collective enfranchisement is not exercisable in relation to those premises.[814] Where the counter-notice accepts that the right exists and is exercisable, any remaining disputes as to the terms of acquisition (including the price payable by the nominee purchaser) should be referred to a leasehold valuation tribunal.[815]

22–219 **6. Estate management schemes.** The 1993 Act contains provisions analogous to those in the Leasehold Reform Act 1967 enabling landlords to apply to leasehold valuation tribunals (within a period of two years from the provisions coming into force[816]) for approval of an estate management scheme.[817] On such approval being given, the landlord will retain powers of management in respect of the house or premises, and have rights against the property in question arising from the exercise elsewhere of his powers of management.[818]

IV. INDIVIDUAL LEASE EXTENSION FOR TENANTS OF FLATS: LEASEHOLD REFORM HOUSING AND URBAN DEVELOPMENT ACT 1993

22–220 **1. Extended leases.** A tenant who is a "qualifying tenant" within the Act of 1993[819] may not wish to, or may not be able to, benefit from collective enfranchisement. He may, however, choose to assert his individual right to a new lease of 90 years on payment of a premium. To do so, he must have been a qualifying tenant of the flat for the last two years.[820] There is no exclusion relating to user of the premises, or occupation by a resident landlord. Since 2003, it has not been necessary that the tenant satisfy a residence requirement,[821] and the House of Lords has held that it is therefore sufficient that the premises include a flat, irrespective of the nature and extent of the other property which may be included in the demise.[822] It follows that this statutory right is not restricted to resident occupiers, and a person who is the head lessee of a block of flats may be able to claim, as a qualifying tenant, a lease extension in relation to each of the flats within the block.

---

[813] LRHUDA 1993 s.22.

[814] LRHUDA 1993 s.23.

[815] LRHUDA 1993 s.24; for procedure, see *Goldeagle Properties Ltd v Thornbury Court Ltd* [2008] EWCA Civ 864; [2009] H.L.R. 13; *Pledream Properties v 5 Felix Avenue London Ltd* [2010] EWHC 3048 (Ch); [2011] L. & T.R. 20.

[816] Where the right to collective enfranchisement arose by virtue of the amendments in the HA 1996 Sch.9 para.1, the period of two years runs from April 1, 1997. HA 1996 s.118; SI 1997/618.

[817] LRHUDA 1993 ss.69–75, as amended by HA 1996 s.118.

[818] LRHUDA 1993 s.69(1).

[819] See above, para.22–215.

[820] LRHUDA 1993 s.39, as amended by CLRA 2002 ss.130 and 131 (abolishing former residence and low rent requirements).

[821] CLRA 2002 s.130.

[822] *Howard de Walden Estates Ltd v Aggio* [2008] UKHL 44; [2009] 1 A.C. 39.

2. The claim. The tenant's claim is made by notice to his landlord,[823]   **22–221**
particularising the property, the lease, and the premium which the tenant
proposes to pay.[824] The landlord replies by counter-notice, admitting or
denying the tenant's claim, and the court has power to determine whether the
tenant has the right to acquire a new lease of his flat.[825] In cases of dispute
over terms, leasehold valuation tribunals have jurisdiction, and there are
provisions for vesting orders if the landlord proves uncooperative or untraceable.[826] If the landlord establishes an intention to redevelop any premises in
which the flat is contained[827] and the tenant's lease is due to terminate within
five years, the court may make an order declaring that the tenant's right to
acquire a new lease should not be exercisable.[828]

3. The lease. The tenant who establishes his claim is entitled to be granted,   **22–222**
in substitution for the existing lease, a new lease of the flat[829] for a peppercorn
rent for a term expiring 90 years after the term date of the existing lease.[830]
The tenant must pay a premium comprising[831]:

(1) *The diminution in value of the landlord's interest in the flat,* being
    the difference between the value of the landlord's interest in the
    tenant's flat prior to the grant of the new lease and the value of his
    interest once the new lease is granted, various assumptions being
    made[832];

(2) *The landlord's share of the marriage value.*[833] The marriage value
    is the difference between:

[823] Defined in LRHUDA 1993 s.40.

[824] LRHUDA 1993 s.42. Provision is made for the continuation of the lease pending the trial: LRHUDA 1993 Sch.12 para.5; *Ackerman v Lay* [2008] EWCA Civ 1428; [2009] 1 W.L.R. 1556.

[825] LRHUDA 1993 ss.45, 46. The statutory requirement that the counter-notice admit, or not admit, the tenant's claim, is mandatory, and the court should not waive it by application of the "reasonable recipient" principle in *Mannai Investments Co Ltd v Eagle Star Life Assurance Co Ltd* [1997] A.C. 749: *Burman v Mount Cook Land Ltd* [2001] EWCA Civ 1712; [2002] Ch. 256. However, the court may apply that principle where the counter-notice merely misstated the landlord's name: *Lay v Ackerman* [2004] EWCA Civ 184; [2004] H.L.R. 40.

[826] LRHUDA 1993 ss.48–51.

[827] What comprises "premises" is to be determined objectively by examining the existing state of the building in which the flat is situated: *Majorstake Ltd v Curtis* [2008] UKHL 10; [2008] 1 A.C. 787 (the landlord's intention to combine the tenant's flat with the flat below in order to form a single duplex apartment held not to comprise an intention to redevelop the relevant premises, which on the facts comprised the block containing the flat).

[828] LRHUDA 1993 s.47.

[829] "Flat" includes any garage, outhouse, garden, yard and appurtenances belonging to or usually enjoyed with the flat and let with it to the tenant: LRHUDA 1993 s.62(2); *Cadogan Viscount Chelsea v McGirk* (1996) 29 H.L.R. 294.

[830] LRHUDA 1993 s.56.

[831] See generally LRHUDA 1993 Sch.13, as amended by HA 1996 s.110 and by CLRA 2002 ss.134–136.

[832] LRHUDA 1993 Sch.13 para.3. It is assumed that the tenant and members of his family are not in the market, and it has been held that the "hope value" (that such persons may subsequently join the market) cannot be taken into account in valuing the landlord's interest under Sch.13: *Pitts v Earl Cadogan* [2008] UKHL 71; [2010] 1 A.C. 226, in particular at [94] and [95].

[833] LRHUDA 1993 Sch.13 para.4.

(i) the aggregate value, prior to the grant of the new lease, of the tenant's interest under his existing lease, the landlord's interest in the tenant's flat, and all intermediate leasehold interests (if any); and

(ii) the aggregate value, once the new lease is granted, of the tenant's interest under his new lease, the landlord's interest in the tenant's flat, and all intermediate leasehold interests (if any).

The landlord's share of the marriage value is 50 per cent of this difference. However, where the unexpired term of the tenant's interest exceeds 80 years, the marriage value is deemed to be nil.[834]

(3) *Such compensation as is payable to the landlord* in relation to loss suffered by any resultant diminution in value in any other property or resulting from the landlord's ownership of such interest (including loss of development value).[835]

22–223   The landlord is not obliged to execute the lease until the premium, together with any sums payable to owners of intermediate leasehold interests,[836] and any other sums and costs then payable, including rent arrears, have been tendered.[837] Where a lease has been granted pursuant to the 1993 Act, any future tenant may claim a further statutory extension, but none of the statutory provisions conferring security of tenure will apply to the lease or to derivative sub-leases.[838]

F. Tenancies of Flats within the Landlord and Tenant Act 1987, Part I

22–224   **1. Introduction.** Prior to the introduction of the more radical measures of collective and individual enfranchisement conferred on long leaseholders occupying flats under the Leasehold Reform, Housing and Urban Development Act 1993, Pt I of the Landlord and Tenant Act 1987 had granted to certain tenants, not necessarily long leaseholders, rights of first refusal on a disposal of the landlord's interest in the property.[839] The Act remains of importance, as it is in some respects wider in ambit than the more recent provisions. However, the right of first refusal which it confers is only activated

---

[834] LRHUDA 1993 Sch.13 para.4(2A), inserted by CLRA 2002 s.136.
[835] LRHUDA 1993 Sch.13 para.5.
[836] LRHUDA 1993 s.56(2); Sch.13 Pt III.
[837] LRHUDA 1993 s.56(3).
[838] LRHUDA 1993 s.59.
[839] The Landlord and Tenant Act 1987 was enacted in response to the Report of the Nugee Committee, *The Management of Privately Owned Blocks of Flats*. See further Percival (1988) 51 M.L.R. 97; Rodgers [1988] Conv. 122. Following trenchant judicial criticism of the drafting, which, per Hobhouse L.J. in *Belvedere Court Management Ltd v Frogmore Developments Ltd* [1997] Q.B. 858 at 882, "does not disclose a clear and consistent policy and . . . falls between the two stools of being both excessively and inadequately detailed", it was significantly amended by the Housing Act 1996.

by the landlord's decision to dispose of the property, and the tenants can only buy at the price which he has agreed with the third party purchaser. The Act applies to premises which consist of the whole or part of a building, and which contain two or more flats held by qualifying tenants. The number of flats held by qualifying tenants must exceed 50 per cent of the total number of flats contained in the premises.[840] However, the Act does not apply where more than 50 per cent of the internal floor area of the premises is occupied otherwise than for residential purposes (disregarding the common parts), or the landlord's interest is held by an "exempt landlord" or a "resident landlord".[841]

2. Qualifying tenants. A qualifying tenant is a tenant of a flat under a   **22–225**
tenancy *other than* an assured tenancy[842] (or assured agricultural occupancy), a business tenancy, a tenancy terminable on the cessation of his employment, or a protected shorthold tenancy.[843] Thus, most long leaseholders will qualify,[844] as will Rent Act protected or statutory tenants. There is no residence requirement, but a person is not a qualifying tenant of any flat contained in any particular premises consisting of the whole or part of a building if by virtue of one or more tenancies (none of which is excluded as above) he is the tenant not only of the flat in question but also of at least two other flats contained in the premises.[845]

3. Machinery. When the landlord proposes to make a "relevant disposal"   **22–226**
(i.e. a disposal of any legal or equitable interest in the premises,[846] subject to a lengthy list of exceptions),[847] he must serve an "offer notice" to this effect on the qualifying tenants of the flats contained in the premises.[848] The tenants are given a minimum period of two months in which to decide whether to accept or reject the offer, or to make a counter-offer of their own. If the parties reach agreement, then a binding contract will arise.[849] If the landlord does not inform the qualifying tenants of his disposal (or otherwise contravenes the provisions as to notice), then the tenants can enforce their rights against the

---

[840] LTA 1987 s.1(2).

[841] LTA 1987 s.1(3), and (4). For the definition of "exempt landlord" (mainly public bodies) and "resident landlord", see LTA 1987 s.58.

[842] Which expression includes assured shorthold tenancies: see Housing Act 1988 s.20(1).

[843] LTA 1987 s.3(1), as amended by HA 1988 Sch.13.

[844] As the rent is low, it is unlikely that they will be assured tenants: HA 1988 Sch.1 para.3.

[845] LTA 1987 s.3(2), as amended by HA 1988 s.119 (with savings: see SI 1988/2152).

[846] Disposals of part of the premises, or of appurtenances to the premises, may suffice: *Denetower Ltd v Toop* [1991] 1 W.L.R. 945; *Dartmouth Court Blackheath Ltd v Berisworth Ltd* [2008] EWHC 350 (Ch); [2008] 2 P. & C.R. 3.

[847] LTA 1987 s.4, as amended by (inter alia) HA 1996 s.90. A disposal takes place on completion of the transfer of the reversion: *Mainwaring v Trustees of Henry Smith's Charity* [1998] Q.B. 1.

[848] LTA 1987 ss.1(1) and 5(1). Failure to serve a notice without reasonable excuse is a criminal offence: LTA 1987 s.10A, added by HA 1996 s.91.

[849] See, for the detailed procedure, LTA 1987 ss.5–10, as amended by HA 1996 s.92 and Sch.6.

transferee ("the new landlord") by serving a purchase notice on him[850]; and similar provisions operate against subsequent purchasers of the landlord's interest.[851] The new landlord is obliged to give notice not only of the assignment of the landlord's interest[852] but also of the rights to which it has given rise.[853] The qualifying tenants are entitled to a transfer of the landlord's reversionary interest to them although the building may be comprised in separate titles, and although the statute does not expressly say that the tenants have this right against the new landlord.[854]

22–227   **4. Price.** The price to be paid by the qualifying tenants on their acquisition of the landlord's interest is the price at which the disposal which had been proposed would have been made. Leasehold valuation tribunals are given jurisdiction to determine questions relating to purchase notices,[855] but this does not entitle the tribunal to determine the amount of consideration *de novo* as between landlord and tenants.[856]

---

[850] LTA 1987 s.12B, inserted by HA 1996 Sch.6, Pt.II. On time limits for service of a purchase notice, see *Savva v Galway-Cooper* [2005] EWCA Civ 1068; [2005] 3 E.G.L.R. 40. It is important that the correct form of purchase notice is served: see *Kensington Heights Commercial Co Ltd v Campden Hill Developments Ltd* [2007] EWCA Civ 245; [2007] Ch. 318.

[851] LTA 1987 s.16, inserted by HA 1996 Sch.6, Pt.III.

[852] LTA 1985 s.3.

[853] LTA 1985 s.3A, added by HA 1996 s.93. Failure to give such notice is a criminal offence.

[854] *Belvedere Court Management Ltd v Frogmore Developments Ltd* [1997] Q.B. 858; *Kay Green v Twinsectra Ltd* [1996] 1 W.L.R. 1587.

[855] LTA 1987 s.13, inserted by HA 1996 Sch.6, Pt.II.

[856] *Cousins v Metropolitan Guarantee Ltd* [1989] 2 E.G.L.R. 223; *Gregory v Saddiq* [1991] 1 E.G.L.R. 237.

FIXTURES

The meaning of "real property" in law extends to a great deal more than **23–001** "land" in everyday speech.[1] It comprises, for instance, incorporeal hereditaments; and it includes certain physical objects which are treated as part of the land itself. The general rule is *"quicquid planatur solo, solo cedit"*[2] ("whatever is attached to the soil becomes part of it"). Thus if a building is erected on land and objects are permanently attached to the building, then the soil, the building and the objects affixed to it are all in law "land," i.e. they are real property, not chattels. They will become the property of the owner of the land, unless otherwise granted or conveyed.[3] This is so, notwithstanding that it was the common intention of the parties that there should be no merger of ownership.[4] "The subjective intention of the parties cannot affect the question whether the chattel has, in law, become part of the freehold ."[5]

The traditional approach has been to refer to objects treated as part of the **23–002** land as "fixtures", and to distinguish such objects, which may include buildings, from chattels. However, it is now thought preferable to apply a three-fold classification.[6] An object which is brought onto land may therefore be:

(a) a chattel;

(b) a fixture; or

(c) part and parcel of the land itself.

---

[1] Above, para.6–011; below, paras 27–001 et seq.

[2] *Minshall v Lloyd* (1837) 2 M. & W. 450 at 459.

[3] *Royco Homes Ltd v Eatonwill Construction Ltd* [1979] Ch. 276 at 289; *Melluish v B.M.I. (No.3) Ltd* [1996] A.C. 454 at 473.

[4] *Melluish v B.M.I. (No.3) Ltd*, above, overruling in part *Simmons v Midford* [1969] 2 Ch. 415.

[5] *Elitestone Ltd v Morris* [1997] 1 W.L.R. 687 at 693, per Lord Lloyd; applied in *Wessex Reserve Forces & Cadets Association v White* [2005] EWHC 983 (QB); [2006] 1 P. & C.R. 22; cf. *National Australia Bank Ltd v Blacker* (2000) 179 A.L.R. 97.

[6] *Elitestone Ltd v Morris*, above at 691, citing Woodfall, 13.131. This classification has since been applied in *Chelsea Yacht & Boat Co Ltd v Pope* [2000] 1 W.L.R. 1941 and in *Wessex Reserve Forces & Cadets Association v White*, above.

Categories (b) and (c) are treated as being part of the land; category (a) is not. This classification is intended to ensure that "fixtures" bears the same limited meaning in law as it does in everyday life:

> "In ordinary language one thinks of a fixture as being something fixed to a building. One would not ordinarily think of the building itself as a fixture."[7]

In relation to buildings, the question is not therefore whether the building is a fixture, but whether the building has become part and parcel of the land.

23–003   Whether an object is treated as part of the land is relevant to a number of circumstances[8]:

(i) whether on a sale of land, the object is to pass to the purchaser or to remain the property of the vendor;

(ii) whether on a devise of land by will, the object is to pass to the devisee or to remain part of the testator's estate;

(iii) whether on a mortgage of land, the object is to be part of the mortgagee's security or to remain the unencumbered property of the mortgagor;

(iv) whether, where land is held in trust for A for life, with remainder to B, the object is to pass to A's estate on A's death or to be left for B on the land; and

(v) whether on a lease of land, the object is or is not part of the demise to the tenant.

23–004   In the context of landlord and tenant (that is (v) above,)[9] there is a further important distinction between "landlord's fixtures", which must be left on the premises on the expiry of the lease, and "tenant's fixtures", which may be removed by the tenant. This distinction generally applies in relation to "fixtures" in its traditional legal meaning as anything which has become so attached to land as to form in law part of the land.[10] However, the meaning of "fixtures" may be restricted by the context. Thus, if part of a house is leased,

---

[7] *Elitestone Ltd v Morris*, above at 690, per Lord Lloyd.

[8] Whether an object has become part of the land or remains a chattel can be important in many other contexts as well, e.g. for the purposes of listed building consent (see *Kennedy v Secretary of State for Wales* [1996] 1 P.L.R. 97; [1996] E.G.C.S. 17); in a claim for capital allowances against corporation tax (see *Melluish v B.M.I. (No.3) Ltd*, above); in a claim for a grant relating to construction operations (see *Gibson Lea Retail Interiors Ltd v Makro Self Service Wholesalers Ltd* [2001] B.L.R. 407); whether a tenancy is of a dwelling house for the purposes of the RA 1977 (*Elitestone Ltd v Morris*, above) or the HA 1988 (*Chelsea Yacht & Boat Co Ltd v Pope*, above; *Mew v Tristmire Ltd* [2011] EWCA Civ 912); and whether a landlord intends to demolish a substantial part of the demised premises for the purposes of the LTA 1954 s.30(1)(f) (*Wessex Reserve Forces & Cadets Association v White*, above).

[9] The distinction is also of some significance in case (iv): see below, para.23–019.

[10] *Elitestone Ltd v Morris*, above at 691, explaining *Webb v Frank Bevis Ltd* [1940] 1 All E.R. 247.

a covenant to repair the interior "including all landlord's fixtures" does not extend to the windows which, in relation to what was demised, are not fixtures but part of the original structure.[11]

A. *Distinction between Chattels and Land*

A physical object will usually be either land or a chattel, but its nature may change according to the use made of it. The materials used for building a house are thereby converted from chattels into land, and so automatically pass out of the ownership of the person who owned them as chattels and become the property of the owner of the land to which they are attached; and it makes no difference whether the person who attached them had a right to do so or not.[12] Conversely, when a house is pulled down, the person who severs the materials from the building converts them from land into chattels. The question whether an object has become part of the land will therefore often determine the question of ownership as between competing claimants. A tenant, for example, who attaches objects to the demised premises may thereby make them the property of his landlord; and a purchaser of land may claim all objects which were part of the land at the date of the contract. The first need, therefore, is to be able to decide what is to be treated as part of the land, whether as a "fixture" or as "part and parcel of the land". In borderline cases this is often difficult; but in principle it depends upon two tests, namely:

23–005

(1) the degree of annexation, and

(2) the purpose of annexation.

1. Degree of annexation. An article is prima facie a fixture if it has some substantial connection with the land or a building on it. An article which merely rests on the ground by its own weight, such as a cistern[13] or a free-standing greenhouse,[14] is prima facie not a fixture. On the other hand a chattel attached to the land or a building on it in some substantial manner, e.g. by nails or screws, will prima facie be a fixture even if it would not be difficult to remove it. Examples in this category are fireplaces, panelling, wainscot, and a conservatory on a brick foundation.[15] It has been said that:

23–006

"if an object cannot be removed without serious damage to, or destruction of, some part of the realty, the case for its having become a fixture is a strong one".[16]

---

[11] *Boswell v Crucible Steel Co* [1925] 1 K.B. 119, discussed in *Holiday Fellowship Ltd v Hereford* [1959] 1 W.L.R. 211 and in *Elitestone Ltd v Morris*, above at 690–691; see also *Pole-Carew v Western Counties and General Manure Co Ltd* [1920] 2 Ch. 97.

[12] See below, para.23–023.

[13] *Mather v Fraser* (1856) 2 K. & J. 536.

[14] *H.E. Dibble Ltd v Moore* [1970] 2 Q.B. 181; *Deen v Andrews* (1985) 52 P. & C.R. 17 (where the facts were similar); *Hynes v Vaughan* (1985) 50 P. & C.R. 444 at 450 (chrysanthemum growing frame held to be a chattel).

[15] *Buckland v Butterfield* (1820) 2 Brod. & B. 54.

[16] *Berkley v Poulett* [1977] 1 E.G.L.R. 86 at 88, per Scarman L.J.

Although the degree of annexation was formerly the primary test, "today so great are the technical skills of affixing and removing objects to land or buildings", that it has become subordinate to the test of purpose.[17] However, buildings will generally be regarded as part and parcel of the land unless they are constructed in such a way as to be removable.[18] A building that can be removed as a unit or in sections may remain a chattel, but this will not be the case if it can be removed only by destroying it.[19]

23–007   **2. Purpose of annexation.** The original common law rule was that everything substantially attached to the land became the property of the landowner. The severity of this rule was ameliorated by two exceptions. First, certain kinds of chattels were held to remain chattels even after annexation, if the purpose of the annexation was for the better enjoyment of the object as a chattel rather than to improve the land permanently.[20] Secondly, even though an object was clearly a fixture, and therefore part of the land, a tenant for years or for life was allowed to sever and remove it if he had annexed it to the land for certain purposes.

23–008   In principle the distinction is plain. Objects of the first class are removable because they never cease to be the property of the person who annexed them. By contrast, objects of the second class are fixtures properly so called, and become the property of the owner of the land, but the law confers a special power of removal on the person who was the owner of the object while it was a chattel. In practice, although the distinction between these two exceptions can have important consequences,[21] it is often blurred.[22] This confusion has been criticised by the House of Lords, and was one reason why it chose to restrict the term "fixture" to situations which the word more literally described.[23] In determining whether an object is to be treated as a chattel or

[17] *Berkley v Poulett*, above, at 89. See too *Hamp v Bygrave* [1983] 1 E.G.L.R. 174 at 177 ("the purpose of the annexation is now of first importance": per Boreham J.); *TSB Bank Plc v Botham* (1996) 73 P. & C.R. D1 at D2.

[18] *Elitestone Ltd v Morris* [1997] 1 W.L.R. 687 at 692 et seq.

[19] *Elitestone Ltd v Morris*, above, at 693; see also *Wessex Reserve Forces & Cadets Association v White* [2005] EWHC 983 (QB); [2006] 1 P. & C.R. 22 (portacabin, garden shed, and easily removable sectional concrete building all chattels; huts fixed to the ground and not easily removable were prima facie part of the land, albeit tenant's fixtures; stone shed pre-dating the lease was part of the land).

[20] In this context, the "purpose" is determined objectively from the evidence. It does not mean the subjective purpose of the person who annexed the chattel: see above, para.23–001 and *Deen v Andrews*, above, at 22.

[21] See *Crossley Brothers Ltd v Lee* [1908] 1 K.B. 86; below, para.23–012.

[22] Compare the treatment of certain tapestries in *Re De Falbe* [1901] 1 Ch. 523 in the Court of Appeal and on appeal to the House of Lords, sub nom. *Leigh v Taylor* [1902] A.C. 157. A life tenant displayed certain tapestries by fixing them to a framework of wood and canvas nailed to the walls. Each tapestry was then surrounded with a moulding which was also fastened firmly to the wall. When the life tenant died, the issue was whether the tapestries passed with the settled land or with the life tenant's personal estate. The Court of Appeal appears to have regarded them as tenant's fixtures which could therefore be removed by the life tenant and those entitled to her estate after her death. The House of Lords, by contrast, appears to have considered that the tapestries had never lost their character as chattels. There was no other way that the tapestries could be enjoyed except by fixing them to the walls.

[23] *Elitestone Ltd v Morris*, above, at 691; above, para.23–002.

as part of the land, it is "the purpose which the object is serving which has to be regarded, not the purpose of the person who put it there."[24]

The distinction between chattels on the one hand and fixtures and other objects that have become part and parcel of the land was authoritatively stated in a leading case[25]: **23–009**

> "Perhaps the true rule is, that articles not otherwise attached to the land than by their own weight are not to be considered as part of the land, unless the circumstances are such as to show that they were intended to be part of the land, the onus of showing that they were so intended lying on those who assert that they have ceased to be chattels, and that, on the contrary, an article which is affixed to the land even slightly is to be considered as part of the land, unless the circumstances are such as to show that it was intended all along to continue a chattel, the onus lying on those who contend that it is a chattel."[26]

> "Thus blocks of stone placed one on top of another without any mortar or cement for the purpose of forming a dry stone wall would become part of the land, though the same stones, if deposited in a builder's yard and for convenience sake stacked on top of each other in the form of a wall, would remain chattels."[27]

Again, "the anchor of a large ship must be very firmly fixed in the ground . . . yet no one could suppose that it became part of the land".[28] However, material such as piles of abandoned spoil from a slate quarry may become a permanent accretion to the land.[29]

These examples are clear, but others are less so. Looms in a worsted mill, fixed by nails to wooden beams and plugs in the floor, have been held to be part of the land,[30] although they were easily removable without damage to the building, and on application of the test "is there any more fixing than was necessary for the enjoyment of the chattel as such?"[31] they might have been thought to be chattels. But machinery standing merely by its own weight **23–010**

---

[24] ibid., at 698, per Lord Clyde.

[25] See (2004) 24 O.J.L.S. 597 (P. Luther).

[26] *Holland v Hodgson* (1872) L.R. 7 C.P. 328 at 335, per Blackburn J. (cited with approval in *Elitestone Ltd v Morris* [1997] 1 W.L.R. 687 at 692). In *Bradshaw v Davey* [1952] 1 All E.R. 350 this dictum was applied to a yacht's mooring (a movable arrangement of anchors and chains) which was held to be a chattel and not a hereditament for rating purposes.

[27] *Holland v Hodgson*, above, at 335, per Blackburn J. (cited with approval in *Elitestone Ltd v Morris*, above, at 693 and 698).

[28] ibid. This passage was cited with approval in *Chelsea Yacht & Boat Co Ltd v Pope* [2000] 1 W.L.R. 1941 at 1944.

[29] *Mills v Stokman* (1967) 116 C.L.R. 61.

[30] *Holland v Hodgson*, above (as between mortgagor and mortgagee); cf. *Reynolds v Ashby & Son* [1904] A.C. 466 (machinery fixed by bolts passed to mortgagee with land); *Jordan v May* [1947] K.B. 427 (electric light generating engine fixed by bolts held a fixture, but batteries held to be chattels).

[31] *Re De Falbe* [1901] 1 Ch. 523 at 536, per Vaughan Williams L.J.

remains personalty,[32] unless (perhaps) it can be shown to be installed for the permanent improvement of the premises. Statues, figures, vases and stone garden seats have been held to become part of the land on the basis that they were essentially part of the design of a house and grounds, even though standing merely by their own weight.[33] But the contrary has been held in the case of a statue standing on a plinth and a sundial resting on a pedestal.[34] Movable dog grates, substituted for fixed grates, have been held to be fixtures,[35] and so have some temporary structures, such as a corrugated iron shed bolted to metal straps fixed in concrete foundations.[36] House-boats have been held to be chattels in two recent cases, both of which were concerned with the question whether a letting comprised an assured tenancy under the Housing Act 1988.[37] In the first, the boat was attached by ropes to the river wall and by an anchor to the river bed, and temporarily connected to pontoons for the provision of services.[38] In the second, the boats, all of which were converted landing craft, rested on wooden platforms in a harbour which supported them clear of the tide, and at the time of their placement on these platforms could be removed without being dismantled or destroyed.[39]

B. Right to Remove Fixtures

23–011 If according to the above rules an object is not part of the land, it can be removed by the person who brought it onto the land or by his successors in title, though not by a subsequent tenant who is granted a new tenancy by the landlord.[40] But if the object is part of the land, prima facie it cannot be removed from the land and must be left for the fee simple owner. Nevertheless, as already mentioned, there are some exceptional cases where something which is undeniably part of the land may be removed by the person who affixed it: the object is a fixture, but the person who affixed it has a power to sever and remove it. This power arises in certain cases if the object has been

---

[32] *Hulme v Brigham* [1943] K.B. 152 (mortgagor and mortgagee).

[33] *D'Eyncourt v Gregory* (1866) L.R. 3 Eq. 382. Although the correctness of part of the decision in this case has been doubted on its facts (see *Re De Falbe* [1901] 1 Ch. 523 at 531), the principle that an object resting on its own weight can be a fixture if it is part of the overall design of the property has been approved: *Berkley v Poulett* [1977] 1 E.G.L.R. 86 at 89. See too *Kennedy v Secretary of State for Wales* [1996] E.G.C.S. 17 (carillon clock which rested on its own weight a fixture, as it was part of the design of a historic house). "White goods" (oven, refrigerator, dishwasher, etc.) are not fixtures, even if they are part of the overall design of the kitchen, because they do not permanently improve it: *TSB Bank Plc v Botham* (1996) 73 P. & C.R. D1.

[34] *Berkley v Poulett*, above (purchaser's claim failed). Contrast *Hamp v Bygrave* [1983] 1 E.G.L.R. 174, where *Berkley v Poulett*, above, was not cited.

[35] *Monti v Barnes* [1901] 1 Q.B. 205 (they were the only means of heating the house). cf. *TSB Bank Plc v Botham*, above (mock coal gas fires held not to be fixtures).

[36] *Webb v Frank Bevis Ltd* [1940] 1 All E.R. 247 (tenant's fixture), not cited in *Billing v Pill* [1954] 1 Q.B. 70 (army hut similarly attached held a mere chattel and so the subject of larceny); *Wessex Reserve Forces & Cadets Association v White* [2005] EWHC 983 (QB); [2006] 1 P. & C.R. 22 (cf. *LCC v Wilkins* [1957] A.C. 362.)

[37] See above, paras 22–081 et seq.

[38] *Chelsea Yacht & Boat Co Ltd v Pope* [2000] 1 W.L.R. 1941.

[39] *Mew v Tristmire Ltd* [2011] EWCA Civ 912.

[40] *Re Thomas* (1881) 44 L.T. 781; and see *Leschallas v Woolf* [1908] 1 Ch. 641; *Smith v City Petroleum Co Ltd* [1940] 1 All E.R. 260.

affixed for certain purposes. The test of "purpose of annexation" therefore applies again here, although in a different way. It is best to consider separately the classes of cases in which the power of removal can and cannot arise.

1. Landlord and tenant. Prima facie, all fixtures attached by the tenant are **23–012** "landlord's fixtures", i.e. must be left for the landlord at the end of the lease.[41] But important exceptions to this rule have arisen, and fixtures which can be removed under these exceptions are known as "tenant's fixtures". This expression must not be allowed to obscure the fact that the legal title to the fixture is in the landlord until the tenant chooses to exercise his power and sever it.[42] The tenant may do so only during the tenancy or (except in cases of forfeiture or surrender)[43] within such reasonable time thereafter as may properly be attributed to his lawful possession *qua* tenant.[44]

Where the tenancy is determinable by a week's notice, for example, and the **23–013** fixtures cannot reasonably be removed within a week,[45] the tenant will be allowed a reasonable time after the notice has expired. Once that time has elapsed, the tenant loses his right of removal and the landlord's title to the fixture is absolute[46]; any extension of time that he grants to the tenant binds only him and not, e.g. a mortgagee who has taken possession.[47] But a tenant retains his right of removal if, when his tenancy ends, he remains in possession as tenant, whether under some statutory right[48] or because he has been granted a new tenancy.[49] In general, a tenant is under no obligation to remove anything that he has lawfully affixed to the land.[50] A tenant who fails to make good any damage when tenants' fixtures are removed may be liable for voluntary waste, even though that failure is in the nature of an omission.[51]

The following are tenants' fixtures.

(a) Trade fixtures. Fixtures attached by the tenant for the purpose of his **23–014** trade or business have long been removable by the tenant at any time during

[41] See, e.g. *Stokes v Costain Property Investments Ltd* [1984] 1 W.L.R. 763 (lifts and other plant installed by tenant were landlord's fixtures).

[42] A neat illustration of the position is *Crossley Brothers Ltd v Lee* [1908] 1 K.B. 86 at 90 (tenant's fixtures may not be taken on a distress (above, para.19–076), since they are not chattels but part of the demised premises).

[43] *Pugh v Arton* (1869) L.R. 8 Eq. 626; *Ex p. Brook* (1878) 10 Ch D 100. But contrast surrender by operation of law: fn.49 below.

[44] See *Ex p. Stephens* (1877) 7 Ch D 127 at 130. The exact limits of the rule are rather obscure: see *Ex p. Brook*, above, at 109; [1987] Conv. 253 (G. Kodilinye).

[45] *Smith v City Petroleum Co Ltd*, above.

[46] *Lyde v Russell* (1830) 1 B. & Ad. 394; *Smith v City Petroleum Co Ltd*, above.

[47] *Thomas v Jennings* (1896) 66 L.J.Q.B. 5.

[48] For example, where the tenant is a regulated tenant under the RA 1977: see paras 22–131 et seq. above.

[49] *New Zealand Government Property Cpn. v H.M. & S. Ltd* [1982] Q.B. 1145, overruling earlier authority that the right of removal was lost if there was a surrender by operation of law when an existing tenancy was replaced by a new tenancy: see above, para.18–086.

[50] See *Never-Stop Railway (Wembley) Ltd v British Empire Exhibition (1924) Incorporated* [1926] Ch. 877 (licensee).

[51] *Mancetter Developments Ltd v Garmanson Ltd* [1986] Q.B. 1212. In that case, the director of the company which committed the tort was held personally liable for waste as well because he instructed its commission: see above, para.19–049.

the term, but not after it has come to an end.[52] Vats, fixed steam engines and boilers,[53] a shed for making varnish,[54] shrubs planted by a market gardener,[55] the fittings of a public house,[56] floor coverings and light fittings[57] and petrol pumps affixed to tanks embedded in the ground[58] have all been held to come within this category.

23–015   *(b) Ornamental and domestic fixtures.* This exception appears to be rather more limited than the previous one, and seems to extend only to chattels perfect in themselves which can be removed without substantial injury to the building.[59] An article which can be moved entire is more likely to fall within this exception than one which cannot.[60] Thus a conservatory on brick foundations has been held not to be removable[61]; but looking glasses,[62] ornamental chimney pieces,[63] panelling,[64] window blinds,[65] stoves, grates and kitchen ranges,[66] pumps and coppers,[67] and bells,[68] have all been held to be removable during the tenancy.

23–016   *(c) Agricultural fixtures.* At common law agricultural fixtures were not regarded as falling within the exception of trade fixtures.[69] Market gardeners were regarded as being engaged primarily in trade, not agriculture, and so could remove their fixtures[70]; but farmers were liable in damages if they removed sheds, sties and the like erected by them, even if they removed them before the end of the term and did no damage.[71] The matter has however been regulated by statute for many years.[72] There are different rules for:

> (i) tenancies of agricultural holdings under the Agricultural Holdings Act 1986; and

---

[52] *Poole's Case* (1703) 1 Salk. 368.

[53] *Climie v Wood* (1869) L.R. 4 Ex. 328.

[54] *Penton v Robart* (1801) 2 East 88.

[55] *Wardell v Usher* (1841) 3 Scott N.R. 508.

[56] *Elliott v Bishop* (1854) 10 Exch. 496.

[57] *Young v Dalgety Plc* [1987] 1 E.G.L.R. 116 (these items were installed by the tenant under a contractual obligation, and were to be disregarded in determining an open market rent under a rent review clause). This is open to doubt, because such items lack the necessary quality of permanence to be fixtures: see *TSB Bank Plc v Botham* (1996) 73 P. & C.R. D1.

[58] *Smith v City Petroleum Co Ltd* [1940] 1 All E.R. 260.

[59] See *Martin v Roe* (1857) 7 E. & B. 237 at 244; *Spyer v Phillipson* [1931] 2 Ch. 183; *Young v Dalgety Plc*, above, at 119.

[60] *Grymes v Boweren* (1830) 6 Bing. 437.

[61] *Buckland v Butterfield* (1820) 2 Brod. & B. 54.

[62] *Beck v Rebow* (1706) 1 P. Wms. 94.

[63] *Leach v Thomas* (1835) 7 C. & P. 327.

[64] *Spyer v Phillipson* [1931] 2 Ch. 183.

[65] *Colegrave v Dias Santos* (1823) 2 B. & C. 76 at 77.

[66] *Darby v Harris* (1841) 1 Q.B. 895.

[67] *Grymes v Boweren* (1830) 6 Bing. 437 at 439.

[68] *Lyde v Russell* (1830) 1 B. & Ad. 394.

[69] *Elwes v Maw* (1802) 3 East 38.

[70] *Wardell v Usher* (1841) 3 Scott N.R. 508 (shrubs and young trees); *Mears v Callender* [1901] 2 Ch. 388 (glass-houses).

[71] *Elwes v Maw*, above.

[72] For earlier legislation see, e.g. L & TA 1851 s.3; AHA 1923 s.22; and AHA 1948 s.13.

(ii) farm business tenancies under the Agricultural Tenancies Act 1995.[73]

In each case, the tenant is given a qualified right to remove any fixture that he has attached to the land or any building that he has erected, whether or not it would otherwise be characterised as a tenant's fixture.

(1) TENANCIES OF AGRICULTURAL HOLDINGS. A tenant of an agricultural **23–017** holding may remove any engine, machinery, fencing or other fixture (whether agricultural or not) that he has affixed to the land, or any building that he has erected on the holding, at any time before, or within two months of, the termination of the tenancy.[74] Contrary to the general rule that has already been explained, the fixture or building remains his property for as long as he has a right to remove it.[75] Certain fixtures and buildings may not be removed.[76] Prior to removal, the tenant must have paid all rent owing and satisfied all his other obligations as tenant, and served a written notice of his intention to remove at least one month before both the exercise of the right and the termination of the tenancy.[77] No avoidable damage may be done in the removal and any damage done must be immediately made good.[78] The landlord has the right to retain the fixtures if he serves a written counter-notice and pays the tenant their fair value to an incoming tenant.[79] However, the landlord has no right to retain any trade, ornamental or domestic fixtures if the tenant is unwilling to sell them. This is because the tenant's common law right to remove such fixtures is expressly preserved and overrides the landlord's right to purchase them.[80]

(2) FARM BUSINESS TENANCIES. A farm business tenant has a similar statutory **23–018** right to remove a fixture or building as does a tenant of an agricultural holding,[81] but any common law rights to remove tenant's fixtures are abrogated.[82] Fixtures or buildings may not be removed where they comprise an improvement for which the landlord gave his consent on condition that the tenant agreed not to remove them.[83] Thus instead of giving the landlord a right to purchase a tenant's fixtures, the Act provides for a system of compensation for tenant's improvements.[84]

---

[73] For these tenancies, see above paras 22–027 et seq.
[74] AHA 1986 s.10(1).
[75] ibid.
[76] Fixtures affixed or buildings erected either in pursuance of some obligation or instead of some fixture or building belonging to the landlord, and buildings in respect of which the tenant is entitled to compensation: AHA 1986 s.10(2).
[77] AHA 1986 s.10(3).
[78] AHA 1986 s.10(5).
[79] AHA 1986 s.10(4).
[80] ibid., s.10(8).
[81] ATA 1995 s.8(1).
[82] ibid., s.8(7).
[83] ibid., s.8(2).
[84] See above, para.22–034.

23–019   **2. Tenant for life and remainderman.** If land is held in trust for A for life with remainder to B, the question arises whether fixtures which A has attached to the land can be removed on the death of A and treated as part of A's estate or whether they must be left for B. The position here is similar, but not identical, to that between landlord and tenant. Prima facie all the fixtures must be left for B, with the common law exception of trade, ornamental and domestic fixtures, which applies to a tenant for life in the same way as to a tenant for years.[85] However the statutory exception of agricultural fixtures does not apply.

23–020   **3. Devisee and personal representative.** If land is given by will the rule is that all fixtures pass under the devise; the testator's personal representatives are not entitled to remove them for the benefit of the testator's estate, whether they are ornamental, trade or any other kind of fixture.[86] For the devise naturally carries with it everything which can fairly be said to be part of the land[87]; and there is no question of hardship upon a limited owner, as in the case of a lessee or life tenant. The same rule applied to descent to the heir on intestacy.[88]

23–021   **4. Vendor and purchaser.** Without exception, all fixtures attached to the land at the time of a contract of sale must be left for the purchaser unless otherwise agreed.[89] The conveyance will be effective to pass the fixtures to the purchaser without express mention.[90] The statutory "general words" operate to convey all buildings, erections and fixtures along with the land, in default of contrary intention[91]; but they will not convey structures which are not fixtures, such as greenhouses merely resting on the land and not attached to it.[92]

23–022   **5. Mortgagor and mortgagee.** If land is mortgaged, all fixtures on it are included in the mortgage without special mention[93]; the exceptions as between

---

[85] *Lawton v Lawton* (1743) 3 Atk. 13; *Re Hulse* [1905] 1 Ch. 406 at 410; but it has been said that a tenant for life is less favoured than a tenant for years: see *Norton v Dashwood* [1896] 2 Ch. 497 at 500.

[86] *Bain v Brand* (1876) 1 App.Cas. 762 (machinery); *Re Whaley* [1908] 1 Ch. 615 (tapestry so fixed as to improve the premises as such held not to be removable even though ornamental); *Re Lord Chesterfield's SE* [1911] 1 Ch. 237 (wood carvings).

[87] See *Re Hulse* [1905] 1 Ch. 406 at 410.

[88] See *Norton v Dashwood* [1896] 2 Ch. 497 at 500.

[89] *Colegrave v Dias Santos* (1823) 2 B. & C. 76; *Phillips v Lamdin* [1949] 2 K.B. 33; *Berkley v Poulett* [1977] 1 E.G.L.R. 86; *Hamp v Bygrave* [1983] 1 E.G.L.R. 174; *Taylor v Hamer* [2002] EWCA Civ 1130; [2003] 1 E.G.L.R. 103; *Wickens v Cheval Property Developments Ltd* [2010] EWHC 2249 (Ch); [2011] 1 P. & C.R. DG9.

[90] *Colegrave v Dias Santos*, above.

[91] LPA 1925 s.62: see above, para.8–045.

[92] *H.E. Dibble Ltd v Moore* [1970] 2 Q.B. 181; *Deen v Andrews* (1985) 52 P. & C.R. 17.

[93] LPA 1925 ss.62(1) and 205(1)(ii).

landlord and tenant do not apply.[94] The mortgagor is not even entitled to remove fixtures which he has attached after the date of the mortgage.[95]

C. Rights of Third Parties

It has already been seen that the primary rule governing fixtures, namely, that they become the property of the owner of the land, applies irrespective of the title of the person who affixed them: "the title to chattels may clearly be lost by being affixed to real property by a person who is not the owner of the chattels".[96] If, for example, X steals Y's bricks and builds them into a house on Z's land, the owner of the bricks is not Y but Z; there is no room for the principle that a man cannot give a better title than he has (*nemo dat quod non habet*), since the title to the object as a chattel is extinguished entirely when it is turned into land.[97]

23–023

A person who lets out goods on hire may be able to protect himself to some extent against the consequences of the law of fixtures if he reserves a right of entry against the owners of the land on which the goods are to be used. If A hires machinery from B and fixes it to the floor of A's factory, and the factory is mortgaged (whether before or after the machinery is fixed), the machinery will become subject to the mortgage as against B.[98] But if the agreement between A and B entitles B to enter and retake the machinery if A fails to pay the hire instalments, this creates an equitable interest in A's land (apparently a right of entry.[99]) Where title to A's land is registered, this equitable right of entry can be protected by B's registration of a notice.[100] Where title to A's land is not registered, the equitable right of entry, which does not appear to be registrable as a land charge, will bind all later takers except a bona fide purchaser of a legal estate for value without notice.[101]

23–024

---

[94] *Monti v Barnes* [1901] 1 Q.B. 205; *Climie v Wood* (1869) L.R. 4 Ex. 328 at 330 (trade fixtures); cf. *Lyon & Co v London City & Midland Bank* [1903] 2 K.B. 135.

[95] *Reynolds v Ashby & Son* [1904] A.C. 466.

[96] *Reynolds v Ashby & Son*, above, at 475, per Lord Lindley; see also *Gough v Wood* [1894] 1 Q.B. 713 at 718; *Crossley Brothers Ltd v Lee* [1908] 1 K.B. 86.

[97] But, of course, Y may have a personal remedy against X in tort (conversion).

[98] *Hobson v Gorringe* [1897] 1 Ch. 182 (before); *Reynolds v Ashby & Son* [1904] A.C. 466 (after).

[99] *Re Morrison, Jones & Taylor Ltd* [1914] 1 Ch. 50 at 58; above, para.6–027.

[100] LRA 2002 s.32(1).

[101] *Poster v Slough Estates Ltd* [1969] 1 Ch. 495; *Shiloh Spinners Ltd v Harding* [1973] A.C. 691. See also (1963) 27 Conv. (N.S.) 30 (A. G. Guest and J. Lever).

CHAPTER 24

THE NATURE AND CREATION OF MORTGAGES AND CHARGES

Part 1

NATURE OF MORTGAGES

24–001　**1. General nature of a mortgage.** When one person lends money to another, he may be content to make the loan without security for the debt, or he may demand some security for the repayment of the money. In the former case, the lender has a right to sue for the money if it is not duly paid, but that is all, and if the borrower becomes insolvent, the lender may lose part or all of his money. However, if some security of adequate value is given for the loan, the lender is protected even if the borrower becomes insolvent because the lender has a claim to the security which takes precedence over any other creditors.

The most important kind of security for a debt is the mortgage and the borrower is known as the "mortgagor", the lender as the "mortgagee". The essential nature of a mortgage in its original form was that it was a conveyance of a legal or equitable interest in property, with a provision for redemption, i.e. that upon repayment of a loan or the performance of some other obligation stipulated in the mortgagee, the conveyance became void or the interest had to be reconveyed. Modern mortgages of registered estates are executed by a charge by deed by way of legal mortgage which does not operate as a conveyance, although this has no practical consequences for the parties.[1]

A mortgage must be distinguished from a lien, a pledge and a charge.[2]

24–002　**2. Lien.** A lien may arise at common law, in equity or under certain statutes. A common law lien is the right to retain possession of the property of another

---

[1] Santley v Wilde [1899] 2 Ch. 474, per Lindley M.R., approved in Noakes & Co Ltd v Rice [1902] A.C. 24 at 28; and see Swiss Bank Corp v Lloyds Bank Ltd [1982] A.C. 584 at 595, per Buckley L.J. For the nature of the modern charge, see below para. 24–026 and 24–032 et seq.

[2] See Holiday v Holgate (1868) L.R. 3 Ex. 299 at 302.

until a debt is paid; thus a garage proprietor has a common law lien upon a motor-car repaired by him.[3] This lien is a mere passive right of retention, giving no right to sell[4] or otherwise deal with the property, and is extinguished if the creditor parts with possession to the debtor or his agent.[5] It is therefore merely a means of coercing the debtor into payment, rather than a security against payment not being made.

An equitable lien is not dependent upon continued possession of the property[6] and in this respect resembles a mortgage. It is also within the definition of "mortgage" in the Law of Property Act 1925.[7] However, it differs from a mortgage (inter alia) in that a mortgage is intentionally created by contract[8] whereas an equitable lien arises automatically under some doctrine of equity.[9] Thus a vendor of land has an equitable lien on it until the full purchase price is paid, even if he has conveyed the land to the purchaser and put him into possession.[10] This lien gives him no right to possession of the land, but enables him to apply to the court for a declaration of charge and for an order for sale of the land, under which he will be paid the money due.[11] If he is paid off by a third party, the third party can claim the benefit of the lien by subrogation.[12] An equitable lien is therefore a species of equitable charge arising by implication of law.[13]

24–003

A statutory lien is the creature of the statute under which it arises, and the rights which it confers depend on the terms of that statute. For example, railway companies,[14] solicitors[15] and airports[16] have been given such rights.

3. Pledge. A pledge (or pawn) is a loan of money secured by the possession of chattels delivered to the lender. Although the lender has certain powers of sale, the general property in the goods remains in the borrower and the lender has their possession.[17] In a mortgage, on the other hand, the lender acquires

24–004

---

[3] *Green v All Motors Ltd* [1917] 1 K.B. 625.

[4] *Mulliner v Florence* (1878) 3 QBD 484.

[5] *Pennington v Reliance Motor Works Ltd* [1923] 1 K.B. 127.

[6] *Wrout v Dawes* (i858) 25 Beav 369.

[7] s.205(i)(xvi).

[8] Although it may arise by reason of proprietary estoppel in exceptional circumstances, *Kinane v Alimamy Mackie-Conteh* [2005] EWCA Civ 45, (2005) 6 E.G. 140 (CS).

[9] See *Mackreth v Symmons* (1808) 15 Ves. 329 at 340; *Re Beirnstein* [1925] Ch. 12 at 17.

[10] Above, para.15–055. There is also a purchaser's lien: above, paras 15–056, 15–108.

[11] V. & P. 988.

[12] *Coptic Ltd v Bailey* [1972] Ch. 446; *Orakpo v Manson Investments Ltd* [1978] A.C. 95 (subrogation displaced by specific charge; contrast *Bank of Ireland Finance Ltd v D. J. Daly Ltd* [1978] I.R. 83); *UCB Group Ltd v Hedworth* [2003] EWCA Civ 1717 (sub-subrogation applied to give a lien over property). For a novel use of subrogation in a mortgage context see *Halifax Plc v Omar* [2002] EWCA Civ 121, (2002) 16 EG 180 (CS) (subrogation available to an innocent lender against an innocent *third party* purchaser of an equitable interest in the property).

[13] *Re Birmingham* [1959] Ch. 523.

[14] Railways Clauses Consolidation Act 1845 s.97.

[15] Solicitors Act 1974 s.73. This does not exclude a lien arising under common law, *Withers LLP v Mariusz Rybak* [2011] EWHC 1151 (Ch); [2011] 3 All E.R. 842.

[16] Civil Aviation Act 1982 s.88. The imposition of such a lien does not amount to a breach of the European Convention on Human Rights, Article 1, Protocol 1, *Global Knafaim Leasing Ltd v Civil Aviation Authority*, [2010] EWHC 1348 (Admin); (2011) 1 Lloyd's Rep 324.

[17] See *Re Morritt* (1886) 18 QBD 222.

rights of ownership and the borrower usually retains possession. The great advantage of a mortgage, as opposed to a pledge, is that the borrower can thus keep possession of his property for the time being. Land, being immovable, is naturally mortgaged, not pledged; chattels may be either pledged or mortgaged.[18]

24–005   **4. Charge.** For most practical purposes a charge should be regarded as a species of mortgage and it is so dealt with in this chapter. Nevertheless there is an essential difference between a mortgage and a charge. A mortgage is properly a conveyance of property subject to a right of redemption, whereas a charge conveys nothing and instead gives the chargee certain rights over the property as security for the loan. However, although the modern method of creating a mortgage of a registered title is to use a "charge", this is treated for all purposes as a mortgage proper.[19]

Part 2

CREATION OF MORTGAGES

Section 1. Methods of Creating Legal Mortgages and Charges

24–006   The methods of creating a legal mortgage have changed over the years as both lending practices and Parliamentary intervention have sought to make the process more efficient and simpler. Much also depends on whether the land is registered or unregistered and whether the mortgaged estate is freehold or leasehold. It remains necessary to understand the way in which mortgages developed prior to the 1925 property law legislation and the Land Registration Act 2002 for this explains many of the attributes of the modern mortgage.

A. Freeholds

I. HISTORY BEFORE 1926

24–007   **1. 12th and 13th centuries.** In the 12th and 13th centuries the forms of mortgage were influenced by the laws against usury, which was both a crime and a sin.[20] Since lending money at a fixed rate of interest was prohibited, other transactions were resorted to which escaped the usury laws but which were sufficiently profitable to the lender. Most commonly, the mortgagor leased the land to the mortgagee, who went into possession.[21] This therefore resembled a pledge rather than a mortgage. If the income from the land was used to discharge the mortgage debt, the transaction was known as *vivum*

---

[18] Mortgages of chattels are effected by bills of sale, which are outside the scope of this book.
[19] See below, para.24–032 and 24–042.
[20] H.E.L. viii, p.102; Glanvil, Bk. 7, 16.
[21] H.E.L. iii, p.130.

vadium (a live pledge), since it was self-redeeming. If the mortgagee kept the income, it was known as *mortuum vadium* (a dead pledge).[22] This latter form was not unlawful, but the Church regarded it as sinful, for the income was taken by way of interest. In either case, if the money was not repaid by the time the lease expired, the mortgagee's lease was enlarged into a fee simple by a condition subsequent expressed in the mortgage.

2. 15th century. By the middle of the 15th century, the common form of **24–008** mortgage had changed. Even in the 13th century a form of mortgage by conveyance of the fee simple had been known, and this form gradually ousted the others, for it gave seisin, and therefore impregnable security, to the mortgagee.[23] The mortgagor conveyed the land to the mortgagee in fee simple, subject to a condition that the mortgagor might re-enter and determine the mortgagee's estate if the money lent was repaid on a named date.[24] The mortgagee still took possession forthwith. The condition was construed strictly so that if the mortgagor was a single day late in offering to repay the money, he lost the land for ever and yet remained liable for the debt.[25]

3. 17th century onwards

(a) Form of mortgage. By the beginning of the 17th century two changes **24–009** had taken place. First, the form of a mortgage was usually a conveyance in fee simple with a covenant to reconvey the property if the money was paid on the fixed date. This was the modern form before 1926, and it simplified proof of title. Whether the fee simple was vested in the mortgagor or not no longer depended merely upon whether the money had been paid within the fixed time, but depended upon whether a reconveyance had been executed by the mortgagee.[26] Mortgages made by granting leases of the property were, however, equally possible,[27] and were employed where there were special reasons for preferring them.[28]

(b) Intervention of equity. Secondly, a far more important change had been **24–010** made by the intervention of equity. By this time loans at interest were no longer illegal, but a maximum rate of interest was from time to time fixed by

---

[22] H.E.L. iii, p.128; Glanvil, Bk. 10, pp.6, 8. Hence the name "mortgage"; mort (dead) gage (pledge).

[23] H.E.L. iii, pp.129, 130; (1967) 83 L.Q.R. 229 (J. L. Barton). Doubts had also arisen as to the validity of the idea that a term of years could swell into a fee simple.

[24] H.E.L. iii, pp.129, 130. A variant of this form was a conveyance of the fee simple subject to a condition that the conveyance should be void if the money was paid on the named date.

[25] *Kreglinger v New Patagonia Meat and Cold Storage Co Ltd* [1914] A.C. 25 at 35.

[26] See *Durham Brothers v Robertson* [1898] 1 Q.B. 765 at 772.

[27] See e.g. *Home v Darbyshire* (1619) Ritchies's BA.C.CA.C. 188; *Aldrige v Duke* (1679) Rep.t.Finch 439.

[28] e.g. for raising portions in family settlements. For portions, see the fifth edition of this work at pp.412 et seq. where a leasehold interest left the other limitations of the settlement undisturbed.

statute.[29] This greatly altered the function of a mortgage, for instead of providing both security for capital and a source of profit in lieu of interest, the mortgage ought henceforth to be a security only, and should not yield profit to the mortgagee over and above the interest permitted by law. The Court of Chancery, at this time expanding its jurisdiction and concerned as always to prevent unconscionable dealing, now undertook to enforce this policy. No longer might the mortgagee reap any benefit from his fee simple. If he took possession, equity held him liable to account for a full rent to the mortgagor.[30] Thus it was no longer an advantage to the mortgagee to occupy the land and there emerged the modern type of mortgage where the mortgagor remains in possession and conveys the fee simple to the mortgagee merely by way of security.[31]

24–011   *(c) Mortgages as securities.* Another facet of equity's intervention was that it was repugnant to every idea of equity that the mortgagor should lose his property merely because he was late in repaying the loan. At first equity intervened in cases of accident, mistake, special hardship and the like, but soon relief was given in all cases.[32] Even if the date fixed for repayment had long passed, equity compelled the mortgagee to reconvey the property to the mortgagor on payment of the principal with interest and costs. The mortgagor was thus given an equitable right to redeem at a time when the agreement between the parties provided that the mortgagee was to be the absolute owner of the land.[33] No longer, therefore, did the mortgagee stand to gain by obtaining a property which might be worth much more than the debt. Equity compelled him to treat the property as no more than a security for the money actually owed to him. This equity of redemption became a valuable interest vested in the mortgagor: the measure of its value was the difference between the amount of the debt and the value of the mortgaged property. Since it was an equitable interest in the land,[34] the mortgagor could enforce it not only against the mortgagee personally but against anyone to whom the mortgagee transmitted his fee simple, save only a bona fide purchaser without notice of the mortgage.[35]

24–012   *(d) Foreclosure.* There had, of course, to be some limit to the equitable right to redeem, for otherwise the security would not have fulfilled its purpose of enabling the mortgagee to recover his capital when required. Equity therefore

---

[29] The Usury Acts of 1545 (37 Hen. 8, c. 9) and 1571 (13 Eliz. 1, c. 8) allowed 10%; this was reduced to 8% in 1623 (21 JA.C. 1, c. 17) and to 5% in 1714 (13 Ann. c. 15; Ruff., 12 Ann., St. 2, c. 16). The usury laws were finally repealed by the Usury Laws Repeal Act 1854. For their history, see H.E.L. viii, p.100. The court now has wide powers to modify or set aside extortionate transactions or those based on unfair relationships: see below, para.25–117.

[30] *Holman v Vaux* (c. 1616) Tot. 133; *Pell v Blewet* (1630) Tot. 133; H.E.L. v. p.331.

[31] But as to "Welsh mortgages", see Coote, *Mortgages*, Ch.III.

[32] H.E.L. v. pp.330–332. This may have been due to "the piety" or else to the "love of fees of those who administered equity": *Salt v Marquess of Northampton* [1892] A.C. at 19, per Lord Bramwell.

[33] See *Salt v Marquess of Northampton* [1892] A.C. 1 at 18.

[34] See e.g. *Casborne v Scarfe* (1738) 1 Atk. 603 at 605.

[35] Above, paras 5–011, 5–012.

devised the decree of foreclosure, which was an order of the court, made on the mortgagee's application, declaring that the equitable right to redeem was at an end, and thus leaving the mortgagee with an unhampered fee simple.[36] However, if the property was much more valuable than the debt, the court would order a sale of the property, out of which the mortgagee would receive only the balance due to him, and the mortgagor would take the rest. Foreclosure could not therefore be used oppressively, and in any case a mortgagee who sought it had to come before the court.

(e) Date for redemption. These revolutionary changes made mortgages into **24–013** fair and convenient commercial transactions instead of instruments of extortion. The day fixed for repayment by the mortgage deed (the legal date for redemption) became unimportant, because the equitable right of redemption extended far beyond it. It therefore became customary to fix the initial legal redemption date very early, commonly six months after the mortgage, so that the mortgagee might have the right to call in his loan, and if necessary start foreclosure proceedings, at any time thereafter. This was no hardship to the mortgagor, who had his equity of redemption, and was convenient to the mortgagee, for his investment was then easily realisable.

(f) The two rights to redeem. The result was to make the legal effect of a **24–014** mortgage much less intimidating than its appearance. An ordinary mortgage deed at this time would recite the loan, and then convey the fee simple to the mortgagee subject only to a proviso for redemption in six months' time (a date when neither party, probably, would have the least wish for redemption). This legal redemption date would soon pass and according to the terms of the deed the property would belong absolutely to the mortgagee, but the mortgagor would be fully protected by equity, which would enforce his rights in defiance of the terms of the deed.[37] As is apparent, this means that the two rights to redeem are quite distinct.

(1) LEGAL RIGHT TO REDEEM. This is a contractual right at law to redeem on **24–015** the precise day fixed by the mortgage, neither before nor after. This is exercisable as of right, irrespective of any equitable considerations.

(2) EQUITABLE RIGHT TO REDEEM. This is a right conferred by equity to **24–016** redeem at any time after[38] the stipulated day; but this is exercisable only on terms considered proper by equity, for "he who seeks equity must do equity".[39]

---

[36] *How v Vigures* (1628) 1 Ch.Rep. 32; H.E.L. v. pp.331, 332.

[37] This now defunct form of mortgage drew many unfavourable comments: "No one . . . by the light of nature ever understood an English mortgage of real estate", per Lord Macnaghten, *Samuel v Jarrah Timber and Wood Paving Corporation Ltd* [1904] A.C. 323 at 326. Maitland called a mortgage "one long *suppressio yeri* and *suggestio falsi*": *Equity*, 2nd edn, 182.

[38] Or before if the mortgagee has demanded payment, e.g. by taking possession: below para.25–024.

[39] The doctrine of consolidation is an example: see below, para.25–055.

24–017   *(g) The equity of redemption.* The equitable right to redeem must be distinguished from the "equity of redemption",[40] in its wider sense, although sometimes the terms are used interchangeably. First, the equitable right to redeem does not arise until the contractual date for redemption has passed,[41] whereas the equity of redemption arises as soon as the mortgage is made.[42] Secondly, and more important, the equitable right to redeem is a particular and singular right,[43] whereas the equity of redemption is an equitable interest in the land consisting of the sum total of the mortgagor's rights in the property. Although at law the mortgagor has parted with his land and has only a limited right to recover it, in equity he is the owner of the land, though subject to the mortgage[44]; the mortgagee, on the other hand, is at law the owner but in equity a mere incumbrancer.

24–018   The mortgagor's equity of redemption, in the wider sense of the term, is thus an interest in the land[45] which includes his right to redeem it, but is much more than a mere right of redemption. It is an interest in the land which the mortgagor can convey, devise, settle, lease or mortgage, just like any other interest in land.[46] If, for example, a property worth £50,000 is mortgaged to secure a debt of £10,000, the value of the equity of redemption is obvious; and the mortgagor must clearly be at liberty to deal with it like any other property which is subject to incumbrances. He may wish to sell the property (which subject to the mortgage would be worth about £40,000) or to raise a further loan on it by a second mortgage. Of course, before 1926 the mortgagee usually held the legal fee simple, and so any such dealings must necessarily have been equitable. Consequently, before 1926, a second mortgage was therefore usually an equitable mortgage, i.e. a mortgage of the equity of redemption.

II. AFTER 1925 TO THE LAND REGISTRATION ACT 2002

24–019   By the Law of Property Act 1925, freeholds could no longer be mortgaged by conveyance of the fee simple. Two methods only were permitted by the Act for effecting legal mortgages of freeholds.[47] These methods may still be used for unregistered land[48] and could be used in respect of registered title until the entry into force of the Land Registration Act 2002 on October 13, 2003. For mortgages of registered title executed after October 12, 2003, the Land

---

[40] See *Kreglinger v New Patagonia Meat & Cold Storage Co Ltd* [1914] A.C. 25 at 48.

[41] *Brown v Cole* (1845) 14 Sim. 427.

[42] *Kreglinger v New Patagonia Meat & Cold Storage Co Ltd*, above, at 48.

[43] Perhaps a "mere equity", for which see above, para.8–012.

[44] *Re Wells* [1933] Ch. 29 at 52.

[45] He has "an equitable right inherent in the land": *Pawlett v Att Gen* (1667) Hardres 465 at 469, per Hale C.B.

[46] *Casborne v Scarfe* (1738) 1 Atk. 603 at 605; and see *Fawcett v Lowther* (1751) 2 Ves. Sen.300 at 303 (descent of equity of redemption according to custom of gavelkind).

[47] s.85(1) LPA 1925. For criticism of the variety of forms of mortgage under the 1925 legislation see (1978) 94 L.Q.R. 571 (P. Jackson).

[48] In reality, a mortgage of unregistered land will be effected by the second of these methods: the legal charge. A mortgage of unregistered land triggers compulsory first registration of title and mortgages of registered title take effect as registered charges, see para.7–014.

Registration Act 2002 essentially prescribes only one method for creating a mortgage, being the second of the two methods considered below.[49] The methods available for unregistered land and for registered land *prior* to the entry into force of Land Registration Act 2002 are:

(i) a demise for a term of years absolute, subject to a provision for cesser on redemption; or

(ii) a charge by deed expressed to be by way of legal mortgage.

A legal mortgage could therefore be created only by deed: a demise or a charge by deed.

1. Demise for a term of years absolute

(a) *Form of mortgage.* The term of years granted to the mortgagee was usually a long term, e.g. 3,000 years. The provision for cesser on redemption, being a clause providing that the term of years should cease when the loan was repaid, strictly was unnecessary, for on repayment the term became a satisfied term and automatically ceased.[50] In other respects, however, the position was much as it was before 1926. A fixed redemption date was still named, and was usually six months after the date of the mortgage; thereafter the mortgagor had an equitable right to redeem in lieu of his legal right. The difficulty that a mortgagee by demise had no right to the title deeds was obviated by an express provision giving a first mortgagee the same right to the deeds as if he had the fee simple.[51]   **24–020**

(b) *Retention of fee simple.* The principal change brought about by the 1925 legislation was that the mortgagor retained the legal fee simple. This brought the legal position rather more into accord with reality, for the mortgagor remained owner at law as well as in equity (he already had the equity of redemption), and the mortgagee had an incumbrance only. In fact, the change was one of form rather than of substance, for it did not alter the rights of mortgagor and mortgagee; it merely made the conveyancing machinery more logical.[52]   **24–021**

(c) *Equity of redemption.* In particular, the equity of redemption in no way lost its importance. A fee simple giving the right to possession of land only when a lease for 3,000 years has expired is of little value compared with the right to insist that the fee simple shall forthwith be freed from the term of 3,000 years on payment of the money due. Indeed, the term "equity of   **24–022**

---

[49] See below para.24–034. Strictly, there are two methods of creating a legal mortgage by charge of a registered title, see ss.23(1)(a) and 23(1)(b) LRA 2002, but these are similar in form and by virtue of the LRA 2002 s.51 take effect identically.

[50] See *Knightsbridge Estates Trust Ltd v Byrne* [1939] Ch. 441 at 461 (in HL [1940] A.C. 613); and below, para.24–031.

[51] See below, para.24–037.

[52] Save that on a sale by the mortgagee the estate that he conveys is no longer one that is vested in him but one vested in the mortgagor that the mortgagee conveys by virtue of a statutory power; see below, para.25–013.

redemption" is sometimes used as including the mortgagor's legal estate, for it was the equity of redemption which was the substantial interest, and the legal estate which was the shadow. Little has changed in this regard even for mortgages of registered titles taking effect under the Land Registration Act 2002.

24–023   *(d) Successive legal mortgages.* As the mortgagor retained the legal fee simple, he could grant further legal terms of years. Consequently second, third and subsequent mortgages could all be legal after 1925. Thus A, the fee simple owner of Blackacre, could create successive legal mortgages in favour of X, Y and Z. The term he granted to each mortgagee was usually[53] at least one day longer than the previous mortgage. Thus X could be given 2,000 years, Y 2,000 years and a day, and Z 2,000 years and two days, so that each mortgagee had a reversion upon the prior mortgage term. Here again the change was purely formal.[54] The rights of Y and Z at law were quite nebulous: no one would lend money on the security of one day's reversion at 2,000 years' distance! What was valuable security to Y and Z was their interest in the equity of redemption. Subject to X's mortgage, they had the next prior claims to the property in equity.[55]

24–024   *(e) Purported conveyance.* A purported conveyance of a fee simple which in fact[56] was made by way of mortgage operated as a grant of a term of 3,000 years without impeachment of waste but subject to cesser on redemption.[57] An attempt to create a second or subsequent mortgage in the same way took effect as the grant of a term one day longer than the preceding term.[58] The system was thus foolproof.

24–025   **2. Charge by deed expressed to be by way of legal mortgage.** As noted below, this is the only permissible method of creating a mortgage of a registered title after October 12, 2003. However, in fact the method was introduced first by the Law of Property Act 1925 and was already in common use before 2003.[59] Indeed, even in 1925 the effect of this innovation was mainly formal. It is sometimes for brevity called a "legal charge". The "legal charge" is a statutory form of legal mortgage which is shorter and simpler than the historic form by demise. The deed states merely that the property has been charged with the debt by way of legal mortgage. There is no conveyance of any estate to the mortgagee. This legal charge must be:

---

[53] This is not essential: below para.24–031.

[54] Perhaps there is this substantial difference, that the mortgagor's covenants which touch and concern the land (e.g. his covenants to repair, insure, etc., but not his covenant to repay the loan) will run with the reversion if the mortgagor assigns his interest: see above; below, para.25–143.

[55] See below.

[56] See *Grangeside Properties Ltd v Collingwoods Securities Ltd* [1964] 1 W.L.R. 139 (on the similar wording of LPA 1925 s.86(2): below, para.25–100).

[57] LPA 1925 s.85(2).

[58] LPA 1925 s.85(1).

[59] LPA 1925 s.87(1). See also LPA 1925 s.87(4) (inserted by LRA 2002 Sch.11 para.8) managing the effect of the inability now to create a mortgage of registered land by demise or sub-demise. See below para.24–034.

(i) made by deed[60]; a charge simply in writing will have no effect at law[61]; and

(ii) expressed to be by way of legal mortgage[62]; the deed must contain a statement that the charge is made by way of legal mortgage; and

(iii) in relation to a registered estate, be properly registered in accordance with the provisions of Sch.2 to the Land Registration Act 2002.[63] Note, however, that even a charge under an unregistered deed still enjoys all those powers of a mortgage created by deed.[64] Although only equitable,[65] such a charge is still by deed within ss.85 and 88 LPA 1925.

The effect of such a charge of freeholds is that the chargee (whether first or subsequent) gets "the same protection, powers and remedies" as if he had a term of 3,000 years without impeachment of waste.[66] Thus, although he gets no actual legal term of years, he is as fully protected as if he had one,[67] so that he is as able to create tenancies and enforce covenants relating to the land (whether or not they are connected with the charge) as if he had an actual term vested in him.[68] The name "charge" is thus a little misleading, because although a legal charge is by nature a "charge" and not a "mortgage",[69] for all practical purposes it takes effect as a mortgage.   **24–026**

The advantages of a legal charge are considered below,[70] and a precedent of such a charge is also given.[71]

B. Leaseholds

I. BEFORE 1926

The intervention of equity in the case of mortgages of leaseholds produced the same results in matters of substance as in the case of freeholds.[72] As to form, a legal mortgage of leaseholds could be made before 1926 in either of two ways: **24–027**

---

[60] LPA 1925 s.87(1).

[61] But it may sometimes take effect in equity as a contract to grant a mortgage and hence an equitable mortgage: see below, para.24–041.

[62] LPA 1925 s.87(1).

[63] LRA 2002 s.27 and Sch.2 para.8. See Ruoff & Roper 27–004. Of course, usually this will be done routinely, and eventually electronically.

[64] *Swift 1st Ltd v Colin* [2011] EWHC 2410 (Ch)

[65] LRA 2002 ss.27(1) and 27(2)(f).

[66] LPA 1925 s.87(1).

[67] See *Grand Junction Co Ltd v Bates* [1954] 2 Q.B. 160; *Weg Motors Ltd v Hales* [1962] Ch. 49 at 74; *Cumberland Court (Brighton) Ltd v Taylor* [1964] Ch. 29.

[68] *Oil Co Ltd v J. A. Gregory (Hatch End) Ltd* [1966] Ch. 402.

[69] Above, para.24–005.

[70] Below, para.24–036.

[71] Below, para.24–043.

[72] Above, para.24–010.

(i) by assignment of the lease to the mortgagee with a covenant for reassignment on redemption; or

(ii) by the grant to the mortgagee of a sub-lease at least one day shorter than the lease, with a proviso for cesser on redemption.

24–028   **1. Liability under the lease.** The first method was rarely employed, for it brought the mortgagee into privity of estate with the landlord, and so made the mortgagee liable for the rent and for the performance of such other covenants in the lease as ran with the land.[73] This was not so under the second method, for then the mortgagee was only an underlessee and there was privity neither of contract nor of estate between him and the lessor.[74] In either case, the mortgage normally contained the usual provision for redemption on a fixed date six months ahead, and thereafter the mortgagor had an equitable right to redeem.

24–029   **2. Subsequent mortgages.** Where a mortgage had been made by assignment, second and subsequent mortgages were made by a mortgage of the mortgagor's equity of redemption. Where the prior mortgage had been made by a sub-lease, subsequent mortgages were made by the grant of other sub-leases, each normally being longer than the previous one but shorter than the borrower's own term. By the second, and also usual, method it was therefore possible to create several legal mortgages of a leasehold property. It was desirable to leave a space of, say, 10 days between the end of the first sub-lease and the end of the lease itself, so as to leave room for further mortgage terms, each longer by one day than the preceding sublease.[75]

II. AFTER THE LAW OF PROPERTY ACT 1925 TO THE LAND REGISTRATION ACT 2002

24–030   By the Law of Property Act 1925[76] leaseholds could no longer be mortgaged by assignment. Two methods only were possible at law and, for registered titles, this remained the case until the entry into force of the Land Registration Act 2002. Both methods remain available in theory for unregistered leasehold estates, but again the second is the practical and near universal form. They are:

(i) by a subdemise for a term of years absolute, subject to a provision for cesser on redemption, the term being at least one day shorter than the term vested in the mortgagor; or

(ii) by a charge by deed expressed to be by way of legal mortgage.

---

[73] Above, para.20–003.
[74] Above, para.20–006.
[75] The extra day was not essential to the creation of a legal estate (above, para.17–003), but it made it clear beyond doubt that the second or later mortgagee was the immediate reversioner.
[76] s.86(1).

1. Subdemise for a term of years absolute. The term of the sub-lease had   **24–031**
to be at least one day shorter than the term of the lease which was being
mortgaged, otherwise it would have operated as an assignment.[77] If the lease
required the tenant to obtain the landlord's licence before a subdemise by way
of mortgage could be made, the licence could not be unreasonably refused.[78]
It was usual to make the sub-term 10 days shorter than the lease, so as to allow
room for second and subsequent mortgages. Thus if T's 50 years' lease was
mortgaged, a first mortgage would be secured by a lease for 50 years less 10
days, a second by 50 years less nine days and so on. But this was not essential,
for the old rule that a lease may take effect in reversion upon another lease of
the same or greater length[79] was confirmed by the Law of Property Act
1925.[80] Thus if the first mortgage was made by a sub-term of 50 years less one
day, the second mortgage could be secured by a sub-term of the same length
and so on; each mortgage would then take effect in its proper order.

Since 1925, a purported assignment of a lease which in fact is made as a   **24–032**
mortgage[81] operates as a subdemise for a term of years absolute subject to
cesser on redemption.[82] A first or only mortgagee takes a term 10 days shorter
than the lease mortgaged. Second and subsequent mortgagees take terms one
day longer than the previous mortgagee if this is possible; in every case,
however, the sub-term must be at least one day shorter than the term mortgaged.[83] If the mortgaged lease is subject to forfeiture, a mortgagee by
subdemise (or indeed by legal charge) has the same right to relief as any other
subtenant.[84]

2. Charge by way of legal mortgage. A charge by deed expressed to be by   **24–033**
way of legal mortgage gives the mortgagee (whether first or subsequent) the
same rights and remedies as if he had a sub term one day shorter than the term
vested in the mortgagor.[85] As in the case of freeholds, he gets no actual term
of years but is as fully protected as if he had one.

III. MORTGAGES OF REGISTERED TITLES UNDER THE LAND REGISTRATION ACT

2002

Section 23 of the Land Registration Act 2002 provides that an owner's powers   **24–034**
in relation to a registered estate, whether freehold or leasehold, do not include

---

[77] *Beardman v Wilson* (1868) L.R. 4 C.P. 57 above, paras 17–129, 17–142.
[78] LPA 1925 s.86(1); cf. above, para.19–076.
[79] *Re Moore & Hulm's Contract* [1912] 2 Ch. 105; above, para.17–133.
[80] LPA 1925 s.149(5).
[81] It is a question of substance, not form. See *Grangeside Properties Ltd v Collingwoods Securities Ltd* [1964] 1 W.L.R. 139, where it was held that the assignment need not be expressed to be by way of mortgage for it to be treated as such and hence be converted into a mortgage by sub-demise.
[82] LPA 1925 s.86(2).
[83] LPA 1925 s.86(2). Thus if more mortgages are made than spare days are available, the last mortgagees each take a term of one day less than the term mortgaged.
[84] Above para.18–073.
[85] LPA 1925 ss.87(1), 87(4).

the power to mortgage by sub-demise.[86] Instead, the proprietor may mortgage the estate either by the common method of executing a charge by deed by way of legal mortgage (as before) or simply by charging the estate with payment of money. The effect is the same in either case: on completion of registration, the charge takes effect as a charge by deed by way of legal mortgage.[87] It is thus impossible to create an effective legal charge of a registered estate in any manner other than by executing a legal charge and registering it.[88] The creation of a charge in this manner amounts to a registrable disposition and enjoys the benefit of the priority rules found in ss.28 and 29 of the Land Registration Act 2002.[89]

24–035   **Sub-mortgages.** A sub-mortgage is effectively a mortgage of a mortgage and is parasitic on the principal debt. Under the Land Registration Act 2002, a sub-mortgage of a registered estate must take the form of a charge on the indebtedness of the primary charge, rather than a charge on the estate itself.[90] It is not possible to create a legal sub-mortgage by transfer of the mortgage, by sub-demise or even a charge by way of legal mortgage. However, a sub-chargee, being a person who holds a charge on the indebtedness of the primary charge, has all the powers of the sub-chargor (i.e. the primary chargee) in relation to the *property* subject to the primary charge.[91]

C. Advantages of a Legal Charge

24–036   Although there was nothing in the Law of Property Act 1925 which suggested any reason why a legal charge, either of freeholds or leaseholds, should be preferred to a traditional mortgage by demise, that preference has been made explicit in relation to mortgages of registered estates after October 12, 2003. Although the mortgage by demise remains available in relation to unregistered estates, it is clear that there are practical advantages in using a legal charge even when another method is available.[92]

> (i) It is a convenient way of mortgaging freeholds and leaseholds together; the deed states simply that all the properties specified in the Schedule are charged by way of legal mortgage, instead of setting out the length of the various mortgage terms in each case.

---

[86] There was considerable support for this proposal during the consultation period prior to the LRA 2002. See Law Commission Report No.271, *Land Registration for the Twenty-First Century*, para.4.7.

[87] LRA 2002 s.51.

[88] Above para.24–025.

[89] Above para.7–053.

[90] See the combined effect of LRA 2002 s.23(2)(a), s.23(2)(b) and s.23(3).

[91] LRA 2002 s.53.

[92] See Law Commission Report No.271, *Land Registration for the Twenty-First Century*, para.7.2, adopting the following analysis.

(ii) It is probable that the grant of a legal charge on a lease does not amount to a breach of any covenant in that lease against subletting, for the charge creates no actual sub-lease in favour of the mortgagee but merely gives him the same rights as if he had a sublease.[93]

(iii) The form of a legal charge is short and simple.

Even before the method became mandatory in relation to registered estates, the charge by way of legal mortgage was employed almost invariably.[94] It was for some time prior to the 2002 Act "difficult to justify the continued existence of the mortgage by demise, given that it is no longer used in practice".[95]

D. Custody of Title Deeds

In the case of land with unregistered title, it has always been to the mort-   **24–037** gagee's advantage to take into his custody the title deeds of the property,[96] for then any person to whom the mortgagor might try to convey or re-mortgage it would soon discover from the absence of the deeds that there was a prior mortgage. This precaution was of particular importance in the case of equitable mortgages (discussed below), in order to prevent a purchase of the legal estate without notice of the mortgagee's rights. But a legal mortgagee of an unregistered estate would also wish to have the deeds deposited with him, for the same reasons. When mortgages were made by a grant of the fee simple, this automatically entitled the mortgagee to take the deeds, but now that legal mortgages are made by legal charge,[97] the first mortgagee has been given a statutory right to possession of the documents of title,[98] for he would not otherwise be entitled to demand them.[99]

In the rare case of a legal mortgage of a leasehold by assignment before   **24–038** 1926, the mortgagee was automatically entitled to possession of the lease. In the more common case of mortgage by subdemise, he was not so entitled, but he would usually stipulate expressly for it to be handed over. This stipulation is no longer necessary, for a first mortgagee of leaseholds has now, by statute,

---

[93] See Wolst. & C. i, 178; *Gentle v Faulkner* [1900] 2 Q.B. 267; *Matthews v Smallwood* [1910] 1 Ch. 777; *Grand Junction Co Ltd v Bates* [1954] 2 Q.B. 160 at 168. However, where the covenant in question also prohibits the tenant from parting with possession of the property (as it usually will), there will be a breach if the mortgagee enforces his right to possession.

[94] Under the LRA 1925, there was, in effect, a rebuttable presumption that a registered charge took effect as a charge by way of legal mortgage: see the now defunct LRA 1925 s.27(1). Section 51 of the LRA 2002 effectively mirrors this position.

[95] (1991) Law Com. No.204 para.2.13.

[96] "Title deeds" is used in a wide sense, so as to include all documents necessary to prove the mortgagor's title, e.g. assents by personal representatives made in writing but not by deed: above para.14–127. For limits on what amount to title deeds, see *Clayton v Clayton* [1930] 2 Ch. 12 at 21.

[97] And for unregistered title may (at least in theory) be made by demise/subdemise.

[98] LPA 1925 s.85(1).

[99] Above, para.24–020.

the same right to possession of documents as if he were mortgagee by assignment.[100]

Necessarily, however, these rules must be seen in the light of the requirement that dealings with unregistered estates will usually trigger compulsory first registration of title. Thus, a first legal mortgage of unregistered freehold land or of a lease with more than seven years to run triggers the requirement of compulsory registration.[101] The underlying legal estate must be registered and the mortgage will then be registered as a registered charge over that estate.

Where the title to be mortgaged is already registered, there are of course no title deeds of which any registered chargee can have custody. Moreover, under the Land Registration Act 2002, the Land Registry no longer issues land or charge certificates and existing ones have ceased to have legal significance. Instead, on completion of an application to register a charge, the Land Registry will issue an official copy of the register and a Title Information Document giving basic information and which serves as confirmation that the application has been completed. If the charge was effected using an approved form of charge, or a certified copy of the charge has been provided by the lender, the Land Registry also will issue the original charge.[102] In essence, the chargee is protected by the fact of his registration and, if further protection is required, should seek the entry of a Restriction precluding the proprietor of the estate from making any further disposition of the land without the chargee's consent.[103]

Section 2. Methods of Creating Equitable Mortgages and Charges

24-039   The fundamental difference between a mortgage and a charge is that a mortgage is a conveyance of property (legal or equitable), subject to a right of redemption, whereas a charge conveys nothing but merely gives the chargee certain rights over the property charged.[104] Only mortgages could be created at common law; but in equity both mortgages and charges were possible. Equitable charges are still occasionally created, but the remedies of an equitable chargee are inferior to those of an equitable mortgagee.[105]

A. Equitable Mortgages

24-040   **1. Mortgage of an equitable interest.** If the mortgagor has no legal estate but only an equitable interest, any mortgage he effects must necessarily be

---

[100] LPA 1925 s.86(1).
[101] LRA 2002 ss.4(1)(g), 4(2)(b).
[102] See Ruoff & Roper para.27–004.
[103] See Ruoff & Roper para.27–005.
[104] *Jones v Woodward* (1917) 116 L.T. 378 at 379; *London County and Westminster Bank Ltd v Tompkins* [1918] 1 KB. 515 (esp. at 528). But note that a charge by way of *legal* mortgage is in substance a mortgage, not merely a simple charge, since the chargee has all the rights of a mortgagee.
[105] See below, para.25–050.

equitable. Thus the beneficiaries under a trust of land have only equitable interests and can create only equitable mortgages.[106] The 1925 legislation did not affect the form of equitable mortgages of equitable interests.[107] Such mortgages are still made by a conveyance of the whole equitable interest with a proviso for reconveyance. The actual form of words employed is immaterial, provided the meaning is plain.[108] Nor need the mortgage be made by deed, as is essential for a legal mortgage; but it must be made (and not merely evidenced[109]) in writing signed by the mortgagor or his agent authorised in writing.[110] It is wise, though not essential, for the mortgagee to give notice of his mortgage to the trustees in whom the legal estate is vested, both to prevent the trustees from paying any income to the mortgagor instead of the chargee, and to preserve priority.[111]

2. Contract to create a mortgage. A contract to create a legal mortgage,   **24–041** like other contracts to create legal estates, gives an equitable interest to any party entitled to specific performance.[112] However, an equitable mortgage of this type is more than a mere preliminary to a legal mortgage because equity treats it as an actual mortgage[113] given that, in the great majority of cases, the execution of a legal mortgage is never intended and never carried out. In theory the mortgagee may call for a legal mortgage, but in practice he is content to rest upon his equitable rights.

A contract for a mortgage must comply with the formal requirements of s.2 of the Law of Property (Miscellaneous Provisions) Act 1989. It must be made in writing, signed by both parties and incorporate all the terms agreed.[114] This has had a very significant consequence which has already been explained.[115] For two centuries before the 1989 Act came into force on September 27, 1989, it had been possible to create a mortgage informally, without even a written memorandum, by depositing the title deeds to a property as security for a loan.[116] Although the basis of such mortgages was contractual, they were enforceable on the basis of the doctrine of part performance.[117] Such mortgages were in common commercial use, and lenders purported to create them even after the passing of the 1989 Act. However, it has now been decided that a mortgage supported by a deposit of title deeds is ineffective unless it

---

[106] Assuming of course, a beneficiary could find someone prepared to lend on such security.
[107] It is true that LPA 1925 ss.85(2), 86(2), unlike ss.85(1), 86(1), are not in terms confined to mortgages effected "at law"; yet such a restriction would probably be implied.
[108] *William Brandt's Sons & Co v Dunlop Rubber Co Ltd* [1905] A.C. 454 at 462.
[109] See above, para.11–044.
[110] LPA 1925 s.53(1)(c).
[111] See below, paras 26–015, 26–040.
[112] See above, para.5–025.
[113] See *Ex p. Wright* (1812) 19 Ves. 255 at 258.
[114] Above, para.15–015.
[115] Above, paras 15–016 et seq.
[116] See *Russel v Russel* (1783) 1 Bro. CC. 269. For an account of such mortgages, see the fifth edition of this work at p.927.
[117] See *Re Alton Corp* [1985] B.C.L.C. 27 at 33. For the doctrine of part performance see above, para.15–015.

complies with the requirements of s.2 of that Act.[118] This is because the doctrine of part performance has been abrogated by the 1989 Act.[119]

Where the title to the land is registered, the mortgagee should protect the priority of his equitable interest by the entry of a notice.[120] It is no longer possible to enter a notice of deposit.[121]

B. Equitable Charges

24–042   An equitable charge is created by appropriating specific property to the discharge of some debt or other obligation without there being any change in ownership either at law or in equity.[122] No special form of words is required: it is sufficient if the parties have made plain their intention that the property should constitute a security.[123] Thus, if A signs a written contract agreeing that he thereby charges his land with the payment of £500 to B, an equitable charge is created.[124] The same applies where a will or voluntary settlement charges land with the payment of a sum of money.[125]

Section 3. Form of Legal Charge

24–043   "THIS LEGAL CHARGE[126] is made the first day of January 2007 between William Fisher of etc. ('the borrower') of the one part and Lightwood Finance Plc. of etc. ('the lender') of the other part
WHEREAS—

> (1) The borrower is the estate owner in respect of the fee simple absolute in possession of the property described in the Schedule ("the mortgaged property")
>
> (2) The lender has agreed to lend the borrower the sum of £180,000 upon having the repayment thereof with interest thereon secured in the manner hereinafter appearing

---

[118] *United Bank of Kuwait Plc v Sahib* [1997] Ch. 107.

[119] It is possible that a mortgage might arise from the operation of proprietary estoppel, based on oral dealings: see *Kinane v Alimamy Mackie-Conteh* [2005] EWCA Civ 45, (2005) 6 E.G. 140 (C.S.).

[120] See Ruoff & Roper, 27–013.

[121] See Ruoff & Roper, 27–013.

[122] *Carreras Rothmans Ltd v Freeman Mathews Treasure Ltd* [1985] Ch. 207 at 227; *Re Cosslett (Contractors) Ltd* [1998] Ch. 495 at 508; and see above, para.24–005.

[123] *Cradock v Scottish Provident Institution* (1893) 69 L.T. 380, affirmed 70 L.T. 718; *National Provincial and Union Bank of England v Charnley* [1924] 1 K.B. 431 at 440, 445, 459.

[124] *Matthews v Goodday* (1861) 31 L.J.Ch. 282 at 282, 283.

[125] *Re Owen* [18941 3 Ch. 220; *Matthews v Goodday*, above.

[126] In the fifth edition of this work at p.929, a precedent was given of a legal mortgage by demise. As such mortgages were seldom, if ever, used, and now may not be used in relation to a registered estate, this was omitted from previous editions and has not been included in the present edition. In practice, charges by way of legal mortgage are now usually made on the lender's standard form (a form likely to be approved by the Land Registry for ease of electronic conveyancing), and by reference to its mortgage conditions, rather than in the form given in the text.

NOW THIS DEED made in pursuance of the said agreement and in consideration of the sum of £180,000 now paid to the borrower by the lender (the receipt of which the borrower hereby acknowledges) WIT-NESSETH as follows:—

1. The borrower hereby covenants with the lender to pay the lender on the first day of July next the said sum of £180,000 with interest thereon from the date of this deed at the rate of 8 per cent per annum and further if the said moneys shall not be so paid to pay the lender interest at the rate aforesaid by equal monthly payments on the first day of every month in each year on the moneys for the time being remaining due on this security.

2. The borrower charges ALL THAT the mortgaged property by way of legal mortgage with full title guarantee with the payment to the lender of the principal money, interest, and other money hereby covenanted to be paid by the borrower under this deed.

3. The borrower hereby covenants with the lender:

[There will then be set out covenants by the mortgagor to repair, insure, etc., and any other terms agreed upon]

SIGNED AS A DEED etc."

C. Statutory Regulation

1. Consumer Credit Acts 1974 and 2006. The Consumer Credit Act 1974, **24–044** as amended by the Consumer Credit Act 2006, contains an elaborate scheme of safeguards for the purpose of consumer protection in credit transactions of widely varying kinds. In principle it applies to certain mortgages, but only where none of the exemptions apply.[127] The exemptions include transactions where the creditor is a building society, an institution authorised under the Banking Act 1987 or a local authority and numerous other cases specified by ministerial order.[128] In fact, mortgages for residential purposes are likely to regulated instead under the Financial Services and Markets Act 2000.[129] The combined effect of these provisions is that most ordinary mortgages for house purchase or commercial finance are exempt and in reality the Acts are aimed

---

[127] As discussed below, up until April 2008, even if a mortgage was not exempt per se, the Act applied only to those where the credit provided did not exceed £25,000, see SI 1983/1878, as amended by SI 1998/996. Section 2 of the Consumer Credit Act 2006 removes this upper limit. Note also that persons of certified high net worth can be exempt from the operation of the Acts and the financial limit will continue to apply where the loan is for an individual's business purposes: CCA 2006 ss.3, 4.

[128] s.16; SI 1989/869.

[129] Being "regulated mortgage contracts": that is, those where a first legal charge is taken, the borrower is an individual or trustee and at least 40% of the property is occupied by the borrower or his family: see the Financial Services and Markets Act 2000 (Regulated Activities) (Amendment) (No.1) Order 2003 (SI 2003/1475).

at second mortgages by which house-owners may be tempted to borrow improvidently for personal needs. The 1974 Act also contained a financial limit for credit agreements (£25,000) over which the Act would not apply,[130] but the abolition of this by the 2006 Act[131] is likely to mean that there will be a marginal increase in the number of mortgages brought within the updated scheme for regulating consumer credit.

24–045   Where the 1974 Act (as amended) applies, the agreement must be in the form prescribed by regulations so as to make the mortgagor aware of his rights and duties, the amount of the total charge for credit and the rate of interest, and the protection and remedies provided by the Act.[132] It must contain all the agreed terms, except implied terms, and must be signed by both parties.[133] In addition, the mortgagee must supply the mortgagor with a copy of the proposed agreement seven days in advance and refrain from approaching him in the meantime, in order to give him an opportunity to withdraw.[134] An agreement which fails to comply with these requirements is improperly executed and enforceable only on an order of the court.[135] A mortgage within the Act is in any case enforceable only on a court order,[136] but the court may take account of improper execution in assessing any prejudice caused and the degree of culpability for it.[137]

24–046   As noted, the Consumer Credit Act 2006 modifies and amends the 1974 Act in significant ways. The 1974 Act is not repealed, and the structural provisions discussed above remain, but consumer protection is enhanced by modifications and additions to the original scheme. Among many other matters, from April 2008 the Act replaces the "extortionate credit bargain" test[138] with a test of "unfair relationships" between a creditor and debtor.[139] This new test applies to *all* credit agreements (including agreements already in existence and regulated by the CCA 1974), except a first legal mortgage over residential land that is an exempt agreement under CCA 1974 s.16(6C), being a mortgage that is regulated under the Financial Services and Markets Act 2000. A

---

[130] Existing mortgages not caught by the 1974 Act will not, in general, be caught by the 2006 Act simply by reason of the abolition of the financial limit. However, it was suggested that problems might arise in relation to some loans previously unregulated by the CCA 1974 if they are varied after April 2008. By reason of the CCA 1974 s.82(2), variations of existing agreements could have beeen regarded as "new" agreements and thus potentially within the CCA 2006. However, the Consumer Credit Act 2006 (Commencement No.4 and Transitional Provisions) Order 2008, SI 2008/831 has done much to solve this problem, see reg.4.

[131] CCA 2006 s.2. Note also that persons of certified high net worth can be exempt from the operation of the Acts and the financial limit will continue to apply where the loan is for an individual's business purposes: CCA 2006 ss.3, 4.

[132] ss.60, 61. See the Consumer Credit (Agreements) Regulations 1983 (SI 1983/1553) (as amended).

[133] s.61.

[134] ss.58, 61(2).

[135] ss.6l, 65.

[136] s.126. No order is necessary if the mortgagor consents: s.173(3).

[137] s.127, as amended by s.15 Consumer Credit Act 2006 (repealing ss.127(3) to (5)).

[138] CCA 2006 ss.19–22.

[139] CCA 2006 s.19, inserting a new s.140A and s.140B in to the CCA 1974.

relationship arising out of the agreement[140] may be unfair by reference to any one of a number of factors: viz. any of its terms or those of a related agreement; the way in which the creditor has exercised or enforced any of his rights under the agreement or a related agreement; or any other thing done, or not done by, or on behalf of the creditor.[141] If an agreement falls within this provision, a court has broad powers to deal with the unfair relationship, including the making of an order concerning repayment, return of property, alteration of the terms, or setting aside in whole or in part the agreement.[142] Although many standard "purchase mortgages" will be outside of this provision because they are regulated by the Financial Services and Markets Act 2000, it should be noted that the test of "unfair relationships" and the court's broad powers apply to *all* other credit agreements whether or not they are otherwise regulated by the Consumer Credit Acts.[143]

---

[140] The unfairness must be generated by the agreement, not by reason of some pre-existing situation or relationship.

[141] CCA 1974 s.140A(1).

[142] CCA 2006 s.20, inserting s.140B in to the CCA 1974.

[143] As was the case with the provisions of the CCA 1974 concerning "extortionate credit bargains".

CHAPTER 25

THE RIGHTS OF THE PARTIES UNDER A MORTGAGE OR CHARGE

25–001 The rights of the parties under a mortgage or charge will be considered under three heads:

    (i) the rights of the mortgagee or chargee;

    (ii) rights common to both parties; and

    (iii) the rights of the mortgagor or chargor.

Section 1. Rights of the Mortgagee or Chargee

A. Remedies for Enforcing his Security

25–002 Unless the parties have otherwise agreed, a mortgagee or chargee has certain standard remedies. First of all, he may of course sue for the money due, as soon as the date fixed for repayment has arrived, though not before.[1] But mortgages and charges are much more than mere contracts for a loan and they encompass special remedies for enforcing the security. These additional remedies may be, and nowadays often are, sought in addition to a money judgment for the sums due under the mortgage.[2] These remedies may be classified as follows:

---

[1] See, e.g. *Bolton v Buckenham* [1891] 1 Q.B. 278. A mortgagor's obligation to repay is presumed in the absence of express provision from the receipt of the loan: see *Sutton v Sutton* (1882) 22 Ch D 511 at 515. For the rebuttal of the presumption where the mortgagor's property was security for a loan to a third party, see *Fairmile Portfolio Management Ltd v Davies Arnold Cooper* [1998] E.G.C.S. 149.

[2] See *Cheltenham and Gloucester BS v Grattidge* (1993) 25 H.L.R. 454; *Cheltenham and Gloucester BS v Grant* (1994) 26 H.L.R. 703 at 708; *Cheltenham and Gloucester BS v Johnson* (1996) 73 P. & C.R. 293 (money judgment sought in addition to order for possession); below, para.25–031.

(a) Remedies primarily for recovery of capital:

   (i) foreclosure;
   (ii) sale.

(b) Remedies primarily for recovery of interest:

   (i) taking possession;
   (ii) appointment of receiver.

The first two remedies are necessarily final remedies, since they put an end **25–003** to the entire transaction. The other two remedies are useful if the mortgagee wishes to keep the mortgage alive, as where there is a favourable rate of interest, and to enforce punctual payment of the interest. The rights to foreclose and to take possession arise from the very nature of the security. The powers to sell and to appoint a receiver are improvements designed originally by conveyancers and now incorporated by statute in virtually all mortgages. They may usually be exercised out of court, whereas in most cases the mortgagee can enforce payment of the money due, foreclose or obtain possession only by proceedings in court. The jurisdictional position in relation to such proceedings is as follows:

(a) in claims for the payment of moneys secured by a mortgage:

   (i) the jurisdiction of the county court is confined to cases where the amount owing is less than £30,000, except where possession is also sought where its jurisdiction is unlimited[3]; and
   (ii) in other cases the matter must be heard by the Chancery Division of the High Court[4]

(b) in claims for foreclosure,[5] the jurisdiction of the county court is confined to cases where the amount owing is less than £30,000[6]: in other cases the matter must be heard by the Chancery Division of the High Court[7];

(c) all claims for possession, for all types of property, must be *started* in the county court save for exceptional cases where there is justification for commencing the claim in the Chancery Division of the High Court.[8] Moreover, save in respect of foreclosure, the county

---

[3] CCA 1984 ss.21 (as amended), 23(c). £30,000 is the present county court limit.

[4] See generally CPR part 7.

[5] The mortgagee must genuinely seek foreclosure, and must not have added it "as a mere colourable claim": *Trustees of Manchester Unity Life Insurance Collecting Society v Sadler* [1974] 1 W.L.R. 770 at 773, per Walton J. (a decision on earlier legislation).

[6] CCA 1984 s.23(c). The parties may agree to proceedings in the county court where the sum is greater than £30,000: CCA 1984, s.24(1), (2)(g).

[7] Senior Courts Act 1981 s.61(1); Sch.1 para.1.

[8] CPR Part 55.3, PD 55. The Practice Direction makes it clear that claims for possession in the High Court will be exceptional. Justification for commencing claims in the High Court include those cases where the County Court does not have jurisdiction, where there are complicated disputes of fact, there are points of law of general importance or the claim is against trespassers and there is a substantial risk of public disturbance, PD 55.3 1.3.

court now has exclusive jurisdiction in relation to dwelling-houses outside London, and concurrent jurisdiction with the Chancery Division of the High Court as regards all other types of property.[9] Further, in respect of residential property, both parties are expected to comply with the Pre-Action Protocol for Possession Claims in order to maximise the possibility of the borrower keeping their home despite falling into arrears.[10]

25–004   It is no longer possible for a mortgagee to obtain a judgment in default of defence.[11] Prior to the introduction of the Civil Procedure Rules 1998, such a judgment was possible, but only with the leave of the court. However, this restriction was narrowly interpreted and did not apply:

(i) if the mortgaged property had already been sold by a prior mortgagee, so that the money was no longer secured on any property[12]; or

(ii) to an action brought for the repayment of a loan that happened to be secured by a mortgage, but without reference to or reliance upon it.[13]

All the above remedies are available to a legal mortgagee or chargee, and his position will be considered first. An equitable mortgagee or chargee has more restricted remedies, which are considered later.

Where the mortgage is regulated by the Consumer Credit Act 1974 (as amended by the Consumer Credit Act 2006),[14] it is enforceable only on an order of the court, which has wide discretion to extend time limits or impose conditions or suspend the operation of the order[15]; and it may not be enforced so as to give the creditor a benefit greater than the debt.[16]

I. LEGAL MORTGAGE OR LEGAL CHARGE

25–005   A legal mortgagee or legal chargee has the following remedies for enforcing his security.

---

[9] CCA 1984 s.21(1), (3). Where a claim for possession of a dwelling-house outside London has been commenced in the county court, there is no jurisdiction to transfer it to the High Court: see *Yorkshire Bank Plc v Hall* [1999] 1 W.L.R. 1713.

[10] *Pre-Action Protocol for Possession Claims based on Mortgage or Home Purchase Plan Arrears in Respect of Residential Property*, in force November 19, 2008. The Protocol applies if the claim for possession includes a money claim, and seeks to make possession a matter of last resort. It does not alter the rights of the parties under the mortgage or charge, but failure to comply with the Protocol may result in a sanction in terms of case management and costs.

[11] CPR 12.2(c); 12PD para.1.3(5).

[12] *Newnham v Brown* [1966] 1 W.L.R. 875.

[13] *National Westminster Bank Plc v Kitch* [1996] 1 W.L.R. 1316 (judgment in default of defence validly obtained in the Queen's Bench Division of the High Court).

[14] Above para.24–044.

[15] See below para.25–031.

[16] s.113. This may rule out foreclosure unless the court orders the mortgagee to account for any surplus value.

1. To foreclose

(a) The right of foreclosure

(1) EQUITY'S INTERVENTION. By giving the mortgagor an equitable right to redeem after he had lost his legal right of redemption, equity interfered with the bargain made between the parties. But equity prescribed limits to the equitable right to redeem which it created. Thus, before 1926, a legal first mortgagee of freeholds had the fee simple vested in him, and once the legal date for redemption had passed, the mortgagor's right to redeem was merely equitable. "Foreclosure" was the name given to the process whereby the mortgagor's equitable right to redeem was declared by the court to be extinguished and the mortgagee was left owner of the property, both at law and in equity. Equity had interfered to prevent the conveyance by way of mortgage from having its full effect; but there had to be some final point at which the mortgagee could enforce his security, and therefore by foreclosure "the court simply removes the stop it has itself put on".[17] The mortgagee was from the first entitled to the property at law; and when he obtained the necessary order of the court, foreclosure made him an absolute owner in equity as well.[18]

25–006

(2) ORDER OF COURT. An order of the court is essential for foreclosure. "Foreclosure is done by the order of the court, not by any person."[19] Since 1925 a mortgagee does not have the whole legal estate of the mortgagor vested in him.[20] Consequently it is no longer sufficient for a decree of foreclosure merely to destroy the mortgagor's equity of redemption; and the Law of Property Act 1925 provides that a foreclosure decree absolute shall vest the mortgagor's fee simple[21] or term of years[22] in the mortgagee.

25–007

In practice, "foreclosure actions are almost unheard of today and have been for many years".[23] This is both because of the lack of finality of a foreclosure decree,[24] and because mortgagees prefer to exercise other remedies, such as sale or the appointment of a receiver.[25]

(3) RIGHT TO FORECLOSE. The right to foreclose does not arise until repayment has become due at law,[26] for until the equitable right to redeem has arisen, it cannot be extinguished by foreclosure. Repayment is due at law when the legal date for redemption has passed, or, if the mortgage has made the money fall due on breach of any term of the mortgage, on the occurrence

25–008

---

[17] *Carter v Wake* (1877) 4 Ch D 605 at 606, per Jessel M.R.
[18] *Heath v Pugh* (1881) 6 QBD 345 at 360.
[19] *Re Farnol Eades Irvine & Co Ltd* [1915] 1 Ch. 22 at 24, per Warrington J.
[20] But see above, para.24–040, as to equitable mortgages of equitable interests.
[21] s.88(2).
[22] s.89(2).
[23] *Palk v Mortgage Services Funding Plc* [1993] Ch. 330 at 336, per Nicholls V.C.
[24] Below para.25–012.
[25] *Palk v Mortgage Services Funding Plc*, above, at 336. See too *Halifax BS v Thomas* [1996] Ch. 217 at 226.
[26] *Williams v Morgan* [1906] 1 Ch. 804.

of any such breach, such as failure to make due payment of interest[27] or of an instalment of principal.[28] Once this has occurred, the mortgagee may begin foreclosure proceedings unless he has agreed not to do so[29]; and the mere acceptance of a late payment will not by itself waive the right to foreclose for a breach.[30] In practice the mortgagee sometimes contracts not to enforce the security by foreclosure or other means until he has given some specified notice or until the mortgagor has broken one of his covenants in the mortgage.[31] If no redemption date is fixed[32] or if the loan is repayable on demand,[33] the right to foreclose arises when a demand for repayment has been made and a reasonable time thereafter has elapsed.[34]

25–009   *(b) Parties to a foreclosure action.* An action for foreclosure can be brought by any mortgagee of property, whether he is the original mortgagee or an assignee,[35] and whether he is a first or subsequent mortgagee.[36] The effect of a foreclosure order absolute in an action brought by the first mortgagee is to make him the sole owner both at law and in equity, free from any subsequent mortgages; if the action is brought by a second or subsequent mortgagee, he will hold the property subject to prior incumbrances[37] but free from all subsequent incumbrances. These are the natural results of extinguishing the equity of redemption.

As will be seen shortly,[38] a foreclosure action gives the mortgagor and all others interested in the equity of redemption an opportunity of redeeming the mortgage or of applying for a sale in lieu of foreclosure. Consequently all persons interested in the equity of redemption must be made parties to the action.[39] Thus if X has made successive mortgages of his property to A, B and C, and B starts foreclosure proceedings,[40] A will not be affected by them and so need not be made a party to the action.[41] But if the action is successful, C will lose his mortgage and X his equity of redemption, and so both must be made parties to the action.[42] The same may apply to X's spouse and to certain other "connected persons".[43]

---

[27] *Keene v Biscoe* (1878) 8 Ch D 201; *Twentieth Century Banking Corp Ltd v Wilkinson* [1977] Ch. 99; contrast *Burrowes v Molloy* (1845) 2 Jo. & Lat. 521.
[28] *Kidderminster Mutual Benefit BS v Haddock* [1936] W.N. 158.
[29] *Ramsbottom v Wallis* (1835) 5 L.J. Ch. 92.
[30] See *Keene v Biscoe*, above, and contrast *Re Taaffe's Estate* (1864)14 Ir.Ch.R. 347.
[31] See *Seaton v Twyford* (1870) L.R. 11 Eq. 591.
[32] *Fitgerald's Trustee v Mellersh* [1892] 1 Ch. 385.
[33] *Balfe v Lord* (1842) 2 Dr. & War. 480.
[34] *Brighty v Norton* (1862) 3 B. & 5. 305; *Toms v Wilson* (1862) 4 B. & 5. 442. But see Coote, *Mortgages*, Ch.III, for "Welsh mortgages".
[35] *Platt v Mendel* (1884) 27 Ch D 246 at 247.
[36] *Rose v Page* (1829) 2 Sim. 471.
[37] See *Slade v Rigg* (1843) 3 Hare 35 at 38.
[38] See below, para.25–011.
[39] *Brisco v Kenrick* (1832) 1 Coop.t.Cott. 371; *Westminster Bank Ltd v Residential Properties Improvement Co Ltd* [1938] Ch. 639 (need to join debenture holders of company).
[40] As in *Rose v Page* (1829) 2 Sim. 471.
[41] *Richards v Cooper* (1842) 5 Beav. 304.
[42] *Tylee v Webb* (1843) 6 Beav. 552 at 557.
[43] Below, para.25–099.

(c) Procedure. Foreclosure proceedings may be commenced under the Civil **25–010**
Procedure Rules Part 8 procedure (which is akin to the old originating
summons[44]). The court then makes a foreclosure order nisi.[45] This directs the
taking of the necessary accounts and provides that if the mortgagor pays the
money due by a fixed day (usually six months from the accounts being settled
by the master), the mortgage shall be discharged; but that if this is not done
the mortgage shall be foreclosed. If there are several mortgagees and the first
mortgagee is foreclosing, each mortgagee is given the alternative of either
losing his security or else redeeming the first mortgage, i.e. buying it up.
Sometimes the court will give the mortgagees successive periods (e.g. of six
months) to effect this redemption,[46] but usually there will be only one period
between them.[47]

In the special case of instalment mortgages of dwelling houses the court has
wide discretionary power to adjourn the proceedings or to suspend its order,
as explained below.[48]

(d) Sale in lieu of foreclosure. At the request of the mortgagee or of any **25–011**
person interested (e.g. a later mortgagee or the mortgagor) the court may order
a sale of the property instead of foreclosure. It may do so notwithstanding that
any person dissents. This jurisdiction[49] has always existed, but it is now
statutory.[50] It is an important safeguard where the property mortgaged is (as
can be the case) worth substantially more than the mortgage debt. If, for
example, X borrows £20,000 from A on a first mortgage of a property worth
£50,000, and then borrows £10,000 from B on a second mortgage, foreclosure
by A will be manifestly unjust. For A will obtain far more than is due to him,
X will lose far more than he owes, and B will lose his security altogether. X
or B will therefore apply for a sale by order of the court (a "judicial sale"),
and though the court has a free discretion, an order for sale will almost
certainly be made in such a case.[51] When the sale has taken place, each
incumbrancer is paid what is due to him according to his priority, and the
balance belongs to the mortgagor.[52]

(e) Opening the foreclosure. If no order for sale is made and the property **25–012**
is not duly redeemed, a foreclosure order absolute is made. This destroys the
mortgagor's equity of redemption and transfers his fee simple[53] or term of

[44] CPR Pt 8, Practice Direction 8, para.3.3.
[45] i.e. the mortgage will be foreclosed unless (nisi) the mortgagor redeems.
[46] *Smithett v Hesketh* (1890) 44 Ch D 161.
[47] *Platt v Mendel* (1884) 27 Ch D 246.
[48] Below, para.25–031.
[49] Which may now be exercised by the county court where the amount owing at the commencement of proceedings does not exceed £30,000: LPA 1925 s.91(8) (as inserted).
[50] LPA 1925 s.91(2). See *Twentieth Century Banking Corp Ltd v Wilkinson* [1977] Ch. 99, not deciding whether the applicant, if the mortgagee, need show that he is entitled to foreclose. It would seem not, since any person interested may apply for sale under the wide terms of the subsection.
[51] In *Silsby v Holliman* [1955] Ch. 552 special circumstances made a sale inequitable.
[52] Waldock, *Mortgages*, 366, 367.
[53] LPA 1925 s.88(2).

years[54] to the mortgagee, who thus becomes sole owner at law and in equity, subject only to prior incumbrances. But even the order of foreclosure absolute is not necessarily final, for the court will sometimes "open[55] the foreclosure".[56] Circumstances which may influence the court to do this are an accident at the last moment preventing the mortgagor from raising the money, any special value which the property had to the mortgagor (e.g. if it was an old family estate), a marked disparity between the value of the property and the amount lent, and the promptness of the application.[57] Even if the mortgagee has sold the property after foreclosure absolute, the court may still open the foreclosure. This is unlikely, however, if the purchaser bought the property some time after foreclosure and without notice of circumstances which might induce the court to interfere.[58] It is the lack of finality in foreclosure proceedings which sometimes leads mortgagees, as well as mortgagors, to apply for judicial sale instead.

2. To sell

25–013   *(a) History.* There is no right, either at common law or in equity, for a mortgagee to sell the mortgaged property free from the equity of redemption. He can freely transfer the estate which is vested in him subject to the equity of redemption, that is to say, he can transfer or assign the mortgage. But he cannot rely upon being able to realise his security in this way, for it may be difficult to find a willing transferee. Yet he desires a better remedy than foreclosure, for foreclosure requires elaborate proceedings before the court and is in many ways an unsatisfactory remedy.

The solution was found by inserting an express power in mortgage deeds enabling the mortgagee to sell the property out of court and free from the equity of redemption.[59] This power was carefully drafted so as to allow the mortgagee to take only what was due to him out of the proceeds of sale, and only to exercise the power in proper circumstances, for otherwise equity would have intervened. The power has long enjoyed statutory approval, and need no longer be inserted expressly.[60] The power is now contained in the Law of Property Act 1925,[61] though a limited power was first granted by Lord Cranworth's Act 1860.[62]

---

[54] LPA 1925 s.89(2).

[55] Or "reopen".

[56] See *Campbell v Holyland* (1877) 7 Ch D 166 at 172–175.

[57] *Campbell v Holyland*, above, per Jessel M.R.; and see *Lancashire & Yorkshire Reversionary Interest Co Ltd v Crowe* (1970) 114 S.J. 435.

[58] See *Campbell v Holyland*, above.

[59] This did not become the usual practice until about 1820 or 1830: see *Stevens v Theatres Ltd* [1903] 1 Ch. 857 at 860; *Clarke v Royal Panopticon* (1857) 4 Drew. 26 at 30.

[60] Although they often are, see *Horsham Properties v Clark* [2009] 1 WLR 1255 at 1260.

[61] LPA 1925 ss.101–107. These provisions have no application to ship mortgages: see *The Maule* [1997] 1 W.L.R. 528 at 532, 533; [1997] L.M.C.L.Q. 329 at 333, 334 (A. Clarke).

[62] & 24 Vict. c.145 ss.11–16. See Sugden, *Powers*, p.877–883. The power was extended by both CA 1881 s.19 and CA 1911.

(b) The power

(1) POWER ARISING. In the absence of an expression of contrary intention in **25–014** the mortgage,[63] every mortgagee has a power of sale, provided that:

>   (i) the mortgage was made by deed[64] (and all legal mortgages must be made in this way); and

>   (ii) the mortgage money is due,[65] i.e. the legal date for redemption has passed. If the mortgage money is payable by instalments, the power of sale arises as soon as any instalment is in arrear.[66]

(2) POWER EXERCISABLE. When the foregoing conditions have been fulfilled, **25–015** the statutory power of sale arises; nevertheless, the power does not become exercisable unless one of the three following conditions has been satisfied:

>   (i) notice requiring payment of the mortgage money has been served on the mortgagor and default has been made in payment of part or all of it for three months thereafter[67]; or

>   (ii) some interest under the mortgage is two months or more in arrear[68]; or

>   (iii) there has been a breach of some provision contained in the Act[69] or in the mortgage deed[70] (other than the covenant for payment of the mortgage money or interest) which should have been observed or performed by the mortgagor or by someone who concurred in making the mortgage.[71]

A mortgagee's power to sell is unaffected by any disclaimer of the estate mortgaged by the mortgagor's liquidator or trustee in bankruptcy. This is so, even though, if the estate is a fee simple, it is terminated when it escheats to the Crown on such disclaimer.[72]

---

[63] LPA 1925 s.101(4).

[64] LPA 1925 s.101(1). So also even if the mortgage by deed is not registered under LRA 2002 s.27(1) and defaults to an equitable mortgage, *Swift 1st Ltd v Colin* 2011] EWHC 2410 (Ch).

[65] LPA 1925 s.101(1).

[66] *Payne v Cardiff RDC* [1932] 1 K.B. 241. Contrast *Twentieth Century Banking Corporation Ltd v Wilkinson* [1977] Ch. 99 (interest in arrear but principal not yet due: no power of sale).

[67] LPA 1925 s.103(i). Alternatively the notice may demand payment in three months' time, and the mortgagee, if unpaid, may then sell at once: *Barker v Illingworth* [1908] 2 Ch. 20.

[68] LPA 1925 s.103(ii).

[69] See *Public Trustee v Lawrence* [1912] 1 Ch. 789 (failure to deliver counterpart of lease as required by s.99(11); see below para.25–074.

[70] e.g. breach of covenant to repair or insure.

[71] LPA 1925 s.103(iii).

[72] *Scmlla Properties Ltd v Gesso Properties (BVI) Ltd* [1995] BCC 793 at 799, 810. For escheat of freeholds, see above, para.2–023.

25–016   *(c) Protection of purchaser.* The difference between the power of sale arising and becoming exercisable is that if the power has not arisen, the mortgagee has no statutory power of sale at all; he can only transfer his mortgage. But if the power of sale has arisen, he can make a good title to a purchaser free from the equity of redemption even if the power has not become exercisable. The purchaser's title is not impeachable merely because none of the three specified events has occurred or the power of sale has in some way been irregularly or improperly exercised.[73] Any person injured by an unauthorised, improper or irregular exercise of the power has a remedy in damages against the person exercising it.[74] Thus while a purchaser from a mortgagee must satisfy himself that the power of sale has arisen, he need not inquire whether it has become exercisable.[75] Proof of title is thereby simplified, for the existence of the power of sale is proved by the form of the mortgage and the redemption date specified in it. The purchaser's title does not depend on the fact of some later default by the mortgagor.

If, however, the purchaser in fact "becomes aware . . . of any facts showing that the power of sale is not exercisable,[76] or that there is some impropriety in the sale" (as there would be if the mortgagee is selling even though the mortgagor has tendered principal and interest[77]), then notwithstanding the statutory provision that the purchaser's title is not to be impeachable "he gets no good title on taking the conveyance".[78] To hold otherwise, it has been said, would be to convert the provisions of the statute into an instrument of fraud.[79] Yet the purchaser need not make the inquiries which a suspicious man would make, though he should not shut his eyes to suspicious circumstances.[80] It is clear that the sale can be set aside on this ground by the mortgagor only if the purchaser is aware of the *mortgagee's* impropriety: any impropriety by the purchaser alone does not entitle the mortgagor to impeach the sale by the mortgagee because the impropriety of the purchaser is irrelevant to the mortgagor.[81]

---

[73] LPA 1925 s.104(2). It is unnecessary to state that the sale is made in exercise of the statutory power, for that is presumed: s.104(3).

[74] LPA 1925 s.104(2).

[75] *Bailey v Barnes* [1894] 1 Ch. 25 at 35.

[76] See *Selwyn v Garfit* (1888) 38 Ch D 273 (decided on an express power of sale).

[77] *Jenkins v Jones* (1860) 2 Giff. 99 (decided on an express power of sale). But simply selling at an undervalue does not necessarily connote impropriety, *Corbett v Halifax Building Society* [2003] 1 W.L.R. 964.

[78] *Lord Waring v London and Manchester Assurance Co Ltd* [1935] Ch. 310 at 318, per Crossman J.

[79] *Bailey v Barnes* [1894] 1 Ch. 25 at 30, per Stirling J., impliedly confirmed by the Court of Appeal. For an analogous construction of a different statute, see *Le Neve v La Neve* (1747) Amb. 436.

[80] See *Bailey v Barnes* [1894] 1 Ch. 25 at 30, 34. This seems to lay down a somewhat different standard from that usually applied under the doctrine of notice: see above para.8–018.

[81] *Corbett v Halifax Building Society* above, where the purchaser deceived the mortgagee into selling to him when such was prohibited by the mortgagee's standard agency terms (being a relative of an employee of the mortgagee). The sale was in fact at an undervalue which sounded against the mortgagee in damages.

(d) Mode of sale

(1) THE MORTGAGEE'S RIGHTS. In general, the statutory power of sale is **25–017** exercisable without any order of the court[82] and without first taking possession.[83] This is its principal advantage over foreclosure. The mortgagee may sell by public auction or private contract and has a wide discretion as to the terms and conditions upon which the sale is made,[84] and as to making the sale subject to restrictions.[85] The power is exercised as soon as a contract for sale is made, even if it is merely conditional; thereafter the mortgagor's equity of redemption is suspended while the contract subsists, and he cannot stop the sale by tendering the money due.[86] Before entering into such a contract, the mortgagee usually first obtains and executes an order for possession (if he is not already in possession).[87] If he does not, he may be unable to give the purchaser vacant possession on completion, and is therefore likely to be in breach of contract[88] unless the purchaser has agreed to take the property with the borrower still in possession. In such cases, the borrower becomes a trespasser and the purchaser may pursue the normal remedies for recovery of the land.[89] The risk of unintentionally leaving the borrower in possession is particularly acute where the mortgage is of a dwelling house. If the mortgagee seeks an order for possession only after contracting to sell with vacant possession, he runs the risk that the court will exercise its power to suspend or adjourn the order[90] and place the lender in breach of contract.

A disposition or contract to sell made by the mortgagor has no effect on the mortgagee's power of sale.[91]

(2) NO TRUSTEESHIP. Despite some earlier uncertainty, it now seems clear **25–018** that a mortgagee's conduct in relation to his power of sale is governed exclusively by principles of equity and does not encompass a duty of care in tort either to the mortgagor or other persons who may have an interest in the

---

[82] An exceptional case arises under LPA 1925 s.110, in cases where a mortgage provides that a power of sale shall be exercisable in case of bankruptcy. Leave of the court is there required, but a purchaser is not concerned: LPA 1925 s.104(2). Where a mortgagee does not have priority over an equitable owner of the property, so that its statutory power of sale is in effect useless, it may apply to the court for an order for sale under s.14 Trusts of Land and Appointment of Trustees Act, see above paras 13–064, 13–069.

[83] *Horsham Properties v Clark* [2009] 1 WLR 1255. This would circumvent the statutory restrictions on seeking possession of a dwelling house, below para.25–031, but does not contravene the borrower's human rights, at p.1266.

[84] LPA 1925 s.101(1)(i).

[85] LPA 1925 s.101(2). The mortgagee may remain totally passive, *Silven Properties v Royal Bank of Scotland* [2004] 1 W.L.R. 997.

[86] *Lord Waring v London & Manchester Assurance Co Ltd* [1935] Ch. 310; *Property & Bloodstock Ltd v Emerton* [1968] Ch. 94.

[87] For possession proceedings, see below, para.25–024.

[88] For a vendor's obligation to give vacant possession on completion, see above, para.15–089.

[89] *Horsham Properties* above.

[90] Under AJA 1970 s.36; below, para.25–031. The hope when the court exercises its discretion is that the mortgagor will retain possession, pay off any arrears (or remedy any other default), and ultimately redeem the mortgage.

[91] *Duke v Robson* [1973] 1 W.L.R. 267.

mortgaged property.[92] The duties arise in equity from the relationship between the mortgagor and mortgagee.[93] However, although this now seems settled, the content of any obligations in equity are flexible and will be adjusted to "fit the requirements of the time".[94] The mortgagee is under a general duty, both to the mortgagor and to any others interested in the equity of redemption (such as subsequent encumbrancers or guarantors), to act in good faith and to use his powers only for proper purposes,[95] but he is not a trustee for the mortgagor of his power of sale.[96] That power is given to the mortgagee for his own benefit to enable him to realise his security more effectively,[97] and his interest in the property has priority over the mortgagor's.[98] However, the mortgagor is both interested in the proceeds of sale in so far as they exceed the debt, and liable for any shortfall if they are insufficient to discharge his indebtedness. His interests must not be sacrificed.[99] In all matters relating to the power, the mortgagee must therefore act in good faith and behave fairly towards the mortgagor,[100] and it would be an improper exercise of the power if no part of his motive for exercising the power was to recover the debt secured.[101] But the mortgagee is not under any general duty of care to the mortgagor.[102] He is therefore free to choose the time at which he sells,[103] even though this (or any of the terms of the sale) may be disadvantageous to the mortgagor.[104] He is under no obligation to postpone sale even if delay might increase the value of

[92] *Silven Properties v Royal Bank of Scotland*, above; *Bishop v Blake* (2006) 17 E.G. 113 (CS). For argument see [1990] Conv. 431 (L. Bently); (1995) 46 N.I.L.Q. 182 (P. Devonshire). Note, however, in *Raja v Lloyds TSB*, TLR 16/5/2000, decided before *Silven*, it was held that being closely allied to the duty of care in negligence, the limitation period in respect of an alleged breach in equity was six years.

[93] See *China and South Sea Bank Ltd v Tan* [1990] 1 A.C. 536 at 543; *Parker-Tweedale v Dunbar Bank Plc* [1991] Ch. 12 at 18, 19; *Downsview Nominees Ltd v First City Corp Ltd* [1993] A.C. 295 at 315; *AIB Finance Ltd v Debtors* [1998] 2 All E.R. 929; *Yorkshire Bank Plc v Hall* [1999] 1 W.L.R. 1713 at 1728.

[94] *Medforth v Blake* [1999] 3 All E.R. 97 at 111, per Scott V.C.

[95] *Burgess v Auger* [1998] 2 B.C.L.C. 478 at 482; *Yorkshire Bank Plc v Hall*, above, at 1728.

[96] *Colson v Williams* (1889) 58 L.J.Ch. 539 at 540; *Kennedy v De Trafford* [1897] A.C. 180; *Cuckmere Brick Co Ltd v Mutual Finance Ltd* [1971] Ch. 949 at 965; *Bishop v Bonham* [1988] 1 W.L.R. 742 at 749; *Silven v Royal Bank of Scotland* above.

[97] *Warner v Jacob* (1882) 20 Ch D 220 at 224; *Raja v Austin Gray* [2002] EWCA Civ 1965.

[98] *Palk v Mortgage Services Funding Plc* [1993] Ch. 330 at 337. Such duties as the mortgagee owes are "qualified by being subordinated to the protection of his own interests": *Re Potters Oils Ltd* [1986] 1 W.L.R. 201 at 206, per Hoffmann J.

[99] *Cuckmere Brick Co Ltd v Mutual Finance Ltd*, above, at 969.

[100] *Kennedy v De Trafford*, above, at 185, 192; *Palk v Mortgage Services Funding Plc*, above, at 337.

[101] *Meretz Investments NV v ACP Ltd* [2007] 2 W.L.R. 403; but the mortgagee need not have purity of purpose, *Nash v Eads* (1880) 25 Sol. J. 95.

[102] *Downsview Nominees Ltd v First City Corporation Ltd* [1993] A.C. 295 at 315. This decision has been criticised in relation to receivers under a floating charge: see G. Lightman and G. Moss, *The Law of Receivers of Companies* 2nd edn (London: Sweet & Maxwell) pp.7–13; (1994) 45 N.I.L.Q. 61 (M. Fealy); [1996] J.B.L. 113 at 119 (Lightman J.).

[103] *Parker-Tweedale v Dunbar Bank Plc*, above, at 18.

[104] *Cuckmere Brick Co Ltd v Mutual Finance Ltd*, above, at 965; *Downsview Nominees Ltd v First City Corporation Ltd*, above, at 315. See too *Tse Kwong Lam v Wong Chit Sen* [1983] 1 W.L.R. 1349 at 1355.

the land.[105] Indeed, he is not obliged to exercise the power at all.[106] If he does not, and the value of the security declines, he incurs no liability to the mortgagor,[107] and he still has his remedy on the personal covenant against the mortgagor and any surety.[108]

Although his general duty is to act in good faith, the mortgagee is, in certain circumstances, under a specific duty of care.[109] If he decides to sell, he must take reasonable care to obtain what has variously been described as "the true market value",[110] the "proper price"[111] and "the best price reasonably obtainable at the time".[112] Where the mortgage security includes a business conducted on the premises charged, the mortgagee must "ensure that the value of the combined asset is maximised".[113] However, his obligation to do so arises only if he takes possession of those premises.[114] As noted above, although this duty of care has been treated as tortious in a number of cases,[115] the better view is that it arises in equity as an incident of the relationship between mortgagor and mortgagee.[116] A similar duty is owed by the mortgagee to a guarantor[117] and to a subsequent mortgagee,[118] but not to a beneficiary under a trust of which the mortgagor is trustee,[119] nor to a tenant at will of the

---

[105] *Silven Properties v Royal Bank of Scotland* above (no obligation to apply for planning permission or wait for the grant of leases which might increase the value of the land).

[106] *Palk v Mortgage Services Funding Plc*, above, at 337.

[107] *China and South Sea Bank Ltd v Tan*, above, at 545. This is the case even if he is professionally advised to do so: *Lloyds Bank Plc v Bryant* (1996, Lightman J., unreported).

[108] *China and South Sea Bank Ltd v Tan*, above, at 545. This is the case even if he is professionally advised to do so: *Lloyds Bank Plc v Bryant* Unreported 1996, Lightman J.

[109] *Yorkshire Bank Plc v Hall* [1999] 1 W.L.R. 1713 at 1728; *Medforth v Blake* [1999] 3 All E.R. 97 at 107, 108.

[110] *Cuckmere Brick Co Ltd v Mutual Finance Ltd*, above, at 966, per Salmon L.J. See too *Palk v Mortgage Services Funding Plc*, above, at 338.

[111] *Silven Properties v Royal Bank of Scotland* above at para.19.

[112] *Tse Kwong Lam v Wong Chit Sen* above, at 1355; per Lord Templeman. A building society is, by statute, under a similar duty to ensure that the price is the best reasonably obtainable: Building Societies Act 1986 Sch.4 para.1(a), replacing earlier legislation: see *Reliance Permanent BS v Harwood-Stamper* [1944] Ch. 362.

[113] *AIB Finance Ltd v Debtors* [1997] 4 All E.R. 677 at 687, per Carnwath J.

[114] *AIB Finance Ltd v Debtors* [1998] 2 All E.R. 929 (CA) (no liability where business had closed down before the mortgagee took possession).

[115] See, e.g. *Knight v Lawrence* [1993] B.C.L.C. 215 at 221.

[116] *Silven Properties v Royal Bank of Scotland*, above. See also, e.g. *AIB Finance Ltd v Debtors* [1998] 2 All E.R. 929. The duty is closely analogous to the mortgagee's equitable duty when in possession to maximise his return from the property: see *Palk v Mortgage Services Funding Plc*, above, at 338; *Downsview Nominees Ltd v First City Corporation Ltd* [1993] A.C. 295 at 315; *Bishop v Blake* above.

[117] *Standard Chartered Bank Ltd v Walker* [1982] 1 W.L.R. 1410; followed in *American Express International Banking Corporation v Hurley* [1985] 3 All E.R. 564. The duty was in each case treated as tortious. However, "equity intervenes to protect a surety": *China and South Sea Bank Ltd v Tan* [1990] 1 A.C. 536 at 544, per Lord Templeman. A surety may be required by a mortgagee to pay the debt, and if that is so, will be subrogated to the mortgage. In principle, the equitable duty to sell at the market price should therefore be owed to a surety as well as to the mortgagor: cf. *China and South Sea Bank Ltd v Tan*, above, at 545. See too *Medforth v Blake* [1999] 3 All E.R. 97 at 109.

[118] By virtue of his interest in the equity of redemption: see *Tomlin v Luce* (1889) 43 Ch D 191.

[119] *Parker-Tweedale v Dunbar Bank Plc* [1991] Ch. 12. cf. *Hayim v Citibank NA* [1987] A.C. 730 at 748.

property.[120] Likewise, suggestions that a mortgagee's selling agent owes a duty of care in tort to the mortgagor must now be doubted.[121] Although a mortgagee may exclude liability for loss caused to the mortgagor on any sale, such clauses are narrowly construed.[122]

25–019   The authorities provide some indication of the circumstances in which a mortgagee will be liable for breach of his duty.[123] Examples include:

(i) where the mortgagee advertised the property without mentioning that the land had valuable planning permission[124];

(ii) where the mortgagee sold at a "crash sale valuation" to obtain an immediate sale rather than exposing the property properly to the open market[125];

(iii) where the mortgagee's receiver failed to serve notices on tenants of the mortgaged property to trigger a rent review, thereby making the reversion less valuable when sold[126]; and

(iv) where the mortgagee sold to tenants of the mortgagor, with whom she had been in prior discussions, and where the property had not been properly advertised for sale.[127]

It has not been finally settled whether a mortgagee discharges his duty simply by employing a competent agent. However, the tenor of the authorities is against it.[128] Some of the earlier cases suggested that the mortgagee's duties

---

[120] *Jarrett v Barclays Bank Ltd* [1947] Ch. 187. Such a person has no interest in the property charged.

[121] See *Cuckmere Brick Co Ltd v Mutual Finance Ltd* [1971] Ch. 949 at 973; *Garland v Ralph Pay & Ransom* [1984] 2 E.G.L.R. 147 at 151. cf. *Routestone Ltd v Minories Finance Ltd* [1997] 1 E.G.L.R. 123 at 124.

[122] *Bishop v Bonham* [1988] 1 W.L.R. 742 (authority to the mortgagee to sell on such terms as he saw fit, meant in accordance with the duty to take reasonable care imposed by law).

[123] The burden lies on the mortgagor or guarantor to prove lack of proper care: *Haddington Island Quarry Co Ltd v Huson* [1911] A.C. 722.

[124] *Cuckmere Brick Co Ltd v Mutual Finance Ltd*, above. See too *American Express International Banking Corp v Hurley* [1985] 3 All E.R. 564 (receiver liable when he failed either to take specialist advice or to advertise in specialist journals when selling lighting and sound equipment for pop concerts).

[125] *Predeth v Castle Phillips Finance Co Ltd* [1986] 2 E.G.L.R. 144; [1986] Cony. 442 (M. P. Thompson). It was accepted in that case that the mortgagee could sell at such time as he saw fit and was not obliged to wait for the market to pick up. However, the decision inevitably casts some doubt on the extent to which a mortgagee can proceed with a "forced sale", despite previous recognition of the legitimacy of such sales: see *Farrar v Farrars Ltd* (1888) 40 Ch D 395 at 398.

[126] *Knight v Lawrence* [1993] B.C.L.C. 215. For rent review clauses, see above, para.19–065. For receivers, see below, para.25–036.

[127] *Bishop v Blake*, above.

[128] *Tomlin v Luce* (1889) 43 Ch D 191; *Cuckmere Brick Co Ltd v Mutual Finance Ltd*, above, at 969, 973, 980. cf. *Routestone Ltd v Minories Finance Ltd*, above, at 124; See also *Corbett v Halifax Building Society* [2003] 1 W.L.R. 964.

in relation to any sale were not onerous because he was at liberty to decide when (if at all) he would exercise his power of sale. However, these may no longer be good law.[129]

In any case the sale must be a true sale; a "sale" by the mortgagee to himself, either directly[130] or through an agent,[131] is no true sale and may be set aside[132] or ignored.[133] Thus if the mortgagee sells to himself and later purports to sell as absolute owner, the first sale will be disregarded and so the second will operate as a sale by a mortgagee as such.[134] But there is nothing to prevent a sale to one of two mortgagors being a true sale, and not a mere redemption of the mortgage, even if the price is the exact sum due under the mortgage.[135] Nor is a sale to a company in which the mortgagee holds shares necessarily irregular, provided that it is proper in other respects.[136]

(e) Proceeds of sale. Although the mortgagee is not a trustee of his power of sale,[137] he is a trustee of the proceeds of sale.[138] These must be employed in the following order[139]:   **25–020**

(i) in discharge of any prior incumbrances free from which the property was sold;

(ii) in discharge of the expenses of the sale or any attempted sale;

(iii) in discharge of the money due[140] to the mortgagee under the mortgage[141]; and

---

[129] See the fifth edition of this work at p.939.

[130] *Farrar v Farrars Ltd* (1888) 40 Ch D 395 at 409.

[131] *Downes v Grazebrook* (1817) 3 Mer. 200.

[132] And see *Hodson v Deans* [1903] 2 Ch. 647 (sale by auction by mortgagee Friendly Society to one of its trustees who had been concerned with conduct of sale: sale set aside). But note, a sale by a mortgagee to an employee who had deceived it into agreeing the sale sounds only in damages for any undervalue, *Corbett v Halifax Building Society* above.

[133] *Henderson v Asiwood* [1894] A.C. 150; *Williams v Wellingborough Borough Council* [1975] 1 W.L.R. 1327 (council house sold to tenant with purchase money left on mortgage; purported sale by council to itself held void). But councils are now empowered to take back such houses with leave of the county court and with due adjustment of accounts: HA 1985 s.452; Sch.17, para.1 (as amended by the Housing and Planning Act 1986).

[134] *Henderson v Astwood*, above.

[135] *Kennedy v De Trafford* [1896] 1 Ch. 762 at 776; [1897] A.C. 180.

[136] *Tse Kwong Lam v Wong Chit Sen* [1983] 1 W.L.R. 1349. Where the sale is to an associated company, the burden of proof lies on the mortgagee to show that it had taken all reasonable steps to obtain the best price reasonably obtainable, *Mortgage Express v Mardner* [2004] EWCA Civ 1859; *Bradford and Bingley v Ross* LTL 14/3/2005.

[137] Above, para.25–018.

[138] LPA 1925 s.105, and See *Banner v Berridge* (1881) 18 Ch D 254 at 269; *Thorne v Heard* [1895] A.C. 495.

[139] LPA 1925 s.105. See *Re Thompson's Mortgage Trusts* [1920] 1 Ch. 508. Including statute-barred arrears of interest: below, para.35–068.

[140] Both principal and interest.

[141] Despite any cross-claim against him by the mortgagor: *Samuel Keller (Holdings) Ltd v Martins Bank Ltd* [1971] 1 W.L.R. 43; *Inglis v Commonwealth Trading Bank of Australia Ltd* (1972) 126 C.L.R. 161 (no injunction to restrain sale).

(iv) by paying the balance to the next subsequent incumbrancer or, if none, to the mortgagor.[142]

25–021   If the balance is paid to a subsequent incumbrancer, he in turn will hold it on trust to pay his own claim, and pass on the balance, if any. Where title is unregistered, a mortgagee who has a surplus should therefore search the Land Charges Register[143] to discover the existence of any subsequent mortgagees because registration is equivalent to notice.[144] If the mortgagee pays the money to the mortgagor he will be liable to any subsequent mortgagee who is thereby prejudiced.[145] The same is now true of registered title, where it is provided specifically in reference to a mortgagee's power of sale that "in its application to the proceeds of sale of registered land, a person shall be taken to have notice of anything in the register immediately before the disposition on sale".[146] A selling mortgagee should therefore conduct a search of the register[147] for else he will be liable in the same way as a mortgagee of unregistered land. If the rights of all subsequent incumbrancers and the mortgagor have become barred by lapse of time,[148] the mortgagee may retain the money himself.[149] In cases of difficulty the money may be paid into court.[150]

The rules explained above apply even in the case where the mortgage was obtained by fraud. A mortgagee who, in such circumstances decides to affirm the mortgage (rather than seeking to avoid it) and exercise his power of sale, must account for any surplus to the mortgagor notwithstanding the latter's fraud.[151]

25–022   *(f) Effect of sale.* A sale by a mortgagee under his statutory powers vests the whole estate of the mortgagor, whether it is a fee simple[152] or a term of

---

[142] s.105 makes the surplus payable "to the person entitled to the mortgaged property". Literally this means the purchaser, but plainly the phrase must be read as "to the person who immediately before the sale was entitled to the mortgaged property", i.e. the next mortgagee or the mortgagor: see *British General Insurance Co Ltd v Att Gen* [1945] L.J.N.C.C.R. 113 at 115.

[143] Below, para.26–027.

[144] LPA 1925 s.198(1). cf. *Rignall Developments Ltd v Halil* [1988] Ch. 190 at 202.

[145] *West London Commercial Bank v Reliance Permanent BS* (1885) 29 Ch D 954.

[146] LRA 2002 s.54.

[147] Above, para.7–105.

[148] See below, paras 35–035, 35–036.

[149] *Young v Clarey* [1948] Ch. 191.

[150] TA 1925 s.63.

[151] *Halifax BS v Thomas* [1996] Ch. 217; [1996] R.L.R. 92 (P. Jaffey). Because the mortgagee affirms the mortgage, there is no constructive trust in his favour: [1996] Ch. 217 at 228. If, instead, the mortgagee avoided the mortgage for fraud, the mortgagor might be a constructive trustee of the property acquired with the money advanced on account of his fraud. The mortgagee might then be able to trace the fund into the proceeds and assert a proprietary claim to the property: ibid. Some of the remarks in *Halifax BS v Thomas*, above, as to the availability of a constructive trust may be too narrow: cf. *Lonrho Plc v Fayed (No.2)* [1992] 1 W.L.R. 1 at 11, 12; *Westdeutsche Landesbank Girozentrale v Islington LBC* [1996] A.C. 669 at 716.

[152] LPA 1925 ss.88(1), 104(1). But see below, para.25–042.

years,[153] in the purchaser, subject to any prior mortgages, but free from the mortgage of the vendor and all subsequent mortgages, and free from the mortgagor's equity of redemption, which is extinguished. If the mortgagee had not obtained vacant possession before sale, the mortgagor becomes a trespasser and may be evicted by the purchaser.[154] For example, if X has mortgaged his freehold property successively to A, B and C, and B sells, the purchaser will take the fee simple subject to A's mortgage but free from the claims of B, C and X, which are overreached,[155] i.e. transferred to the purchase-money. The mortgagee now conveys a fee simple or leasehold that is vested in the mortgagor by virtue of his statutory power.[156] Where the property is a leasehold and the landlord's licence is required for any assignment, it must not be unreasonably refused.[157]

(g) Order for sale. Quite apart from the mortgagee's power of sale, the **25–023** court has jurisdiction to order a sale of the mortgaged property on the application of anyone interested either in the mortgage money or in the equity of redemption.[158] Something has already been said about this provision in the context of foreclosure,[159] but it has been employed in two very different situations in recent years.

First, the court has sanctioned a sale by a mortgagee even though the statutory power of sale had become exercisable.[160] The purchaser's title could not therefore be impeached by the mortgagor. An order of this kind is exceptional. It will be justified only where the mortgagee reasonably fears that the sale may be lost, because the mortgagor is likely to threaten proceedings in an attempt to spoil the transaction, even though there is little prospect of his successfully impeaching it.[161]

Secondly, the court has exercised the jurisdiction, on the application of a mortgagor, to order a sale of the mortgaged property, even though the proceeds would be insufficient to discharge the mortgage debt.[162] The circumstances were, however, exceptional. The mortgagee was seeking possession in order to let the property until there was a sufficient upturn in the property market to justify a sale. Any rental income was likely to fall far short of the interest that would accrue on the debt. A sale would, by contrast, substantially reduce the mortgagor's indebtedness. The mortgagee intended to reserve its right to sue the mortgagor on the personal covenant should an upturn in the

---

[153] LPA 1925 ss.89(1), 104(1). See s.89(6) as to a sale where the mortgage includes only part of the land which has been leased.

[154] *Horsham Properties v Clark* [2009] 1 WLR 1255; above para.25–017.

[155] LPA 1925 s.2(1)(iii).

[156] On a sale before 1926, a first mortgagee conveyed the fee simple that was vested in him.

[157] LPA 1925 s.89(1).

[158] LPA 1925 s.91.

[159] Above, para.25–011.

[160] *Arab Bank Plc v Mercantile Holdings Ltd* [1994] Ch. 71.

[161] *Arab Bank Plc v Mercantile Holdings Ltd*, above, at 90.

[162] *Palk v Mortgage Services Funding Plc* [1993] Ch. 330. See also *Polonski v Lloyds Bank Mortgages Ltd* (1998) 1 F.L.R. 896 (sale justified by pressing social need to protect self and children from violent neighbourhood).

market not occur. A major factor in the court's decision to order a sale was that the mortgagee was gambling on the possibility of a rise in property prices at the mortgagor's expense.[163]

It should be noted, however, that a court will seldom order a sale under this power where the proceeds will not pay off the mortgage debt.[164] In particular, it will not do so if the mortgagee can show that there is a real possibility that a postponement of sale may be beneficial,[165] or if the mortgagee is himself seeking possession with a view to sale.[166] Furthermore, even though the mortgagee will be seeking possession in the county court,[167] the mortgagor will often have to apply to the High Court to obtain such an order for sale.[168] However, he will be unable in nearly all cases to seek a suspension of the court's order for possession to enable him to make such an application if the sale is unlikely to meet the sums due under the mortgage.[169]

3. To take possession

25–024   *(a) The right.* Since a legal mortgage gives the mortgagee a legal estate in possession, he is entitled, subject to any agreement to the contrary, to take possession of the mortgaged property as soon as the mortgage is made, even if the mortgagor is guilty of no default.[170] A legal chargee has a corresponding statutory right.[171] The mortgagee "may go into possession before the ink is dry on the mortgage".[172] He may do so without a court order, even in those cases where the mortgaged property includes a dwelling-house and a court could have granted relief to a mortgagor.[173] If the property was already let to

---

[163] Although such a sale would deprive the mortgagee of its security, it was open to it to purchase the property and then take advantage of any increase in value that might subsequently occur: *Palk v Mortgage Services Funding Plc*, above, at 340, 345.

[164] But see *Polonski v Lloyds Bank Mortgages Ltd* above

[165] e.g. because of a likely rise in property prices or because of the revenue that the property may generate. The court will give the mortgagee the benefit of the doubt: *Palk v Mortgage Services Funding Plc*, above, at 343.

[166] *Cheltenham and Gloucester Plc v Krausz* [1997] 1 W.L.R. 1558, disapproving *Barrett v Halifax BS* (1995) 28 H.L.R. 634 (which had suggested that, in all cases of so-called "negative equity", the mortgagor could resist possession proceedings and seek an order under LPA 1925 s.91, that he and not the mortgagee should be able to sell the property).

[167] See below, para.25–024.

[168] The county court can only make an order under LPA 1925 s.91, where the amount due under the mortgage does not exceed £30,000: LPA 1925 s.91(8); above, para.25–011.

[169] *Cheltenham and Gloucester Plc v Krausz*, above, at 1567; below, para.25–032. But cf. (1998) 18 L.S. 279 (M.J.D).

[170] *Birch v Wright* (1786) 1 T.R. 378 at 383; *Four-Maids Ltd v Dudley Marshall (Properties) Ltd* [1957] Ch. 317. The mortgagor thereupon becomes entitled to redeem forthwith without notice: below, para.19–148. The mortgagee must be sure of his right, since unlawful eviction of a residential occupier is a criminal offence: PEA 1977 s.1. His right may also be restricted by AJA 1970 s.36; below, para.25–031: cf. *Ropaigealach v Barclays Bank Plc* [2000] QB 263, below; and below, para.25–031.

[171] LPA 1925 s.87(1).

[172] *Four-Maids Ltd v Dudley Marshall (Properties) Ltd*, above, at 320, per Harman J.; and see *Westminster City Council v Haymarket Publishing Ltd* [1980] 1 W.L.R. 683 at 686 ("the well-established rule": per Dillon J.).

[173] *Ropaigealach v Barclays Bank Plc*, above; reluctantly rejecting the contrary view advanced in [1983] Conv. 293 (A. Clarke). For the statutory jurisdiction to grant relief, see AJA 1970 s.36; below, para.25–031. cf. PEA 1977 s.1, above.

a tenant before the mortgage was made, or if a subsequent lease is binding on the mortgagee,[174] the mortgagee cannot take physical possession; but he may take possession by directing the tenants to pay their rents to him instead of to the mortgagor.[175] If the property is let to a tenant and the lease is not binding on the mortgagee (for example it is subsequent to the mortgage and not authorised by the mortgagee as required by the terms of the mortgage), then the mortgagee is entitled to possession. However, in respect of a dwelling house, the unauthorised tenant may apply to the court for an order postponing the date for delivery of possession for two months, in order that they may find alternative accommodation.[176]

After entry by a mortgagee his right to possession dates back to the time at which his legal right to enter accrued. He can therefore bring an action for trespass committed before the entry.[177]

An agreement restricting the mortgagee's right to take possession may be either express or implied. It will more readily be implied where the principal is repayable by instalments, as is common in building society mortgages[178]; but that fact by itself is not sufficient, and the court will not lightly restrict the mortgagee's right.[179] A mortgagee must exercise his right to possession in good faith and for the purpose of enforcing the security.[180] In consequence, a mortgagee will not normally be granted possession against just one of two joint mortgagors where that is of no benefit to the mortgagee.[181] Nor will a mortgagee be allowed to exercise this right collusively for purposes other than the protection or enforcement of his security. Thus where a mortgagor arranged for his wife to pay off the mortgage and so become the mortgagee, she was held to be acting as his agent so that she could not assert the paramount rights of the original mortgagee and evict tenants of the mortgagor.[182] It was said that "equity has ample power to restrain any unjust use of the right to possession"[183] and that a mortgagee's rights are only vested in him

25–025

---

[174] See below, para.25–071.

[175] *Horlock v Smith* (1842) 6 Jur. 478; and see *Heales v M'Murray* (1856) 23 Beav. 401; cf. *Kitchen's Trustee v Madders* [1949] Ch. 588, affirmed [1950] Ch. 134.

[176] The Mortgage Repossessions (Protection of Tenants etc.) Act 2010. See [2011] 75 Conv. 380 (Charles O'Neill).

[177] *Ocean Accident and Guarantee Corporation Ltd v Ilford Gas Co* [1905] 2 K.B. 493.

[178] See *Birmingham Citizens Permanent BS v Caunt* [1962] Ch. 883, where a term entitling the mortgagees to take possession if any instalment was one month in arrear implied that they could not do so otherwise.

[179] *Esso Petroleum Co Ltd v Alstonbridge Properties Ltd* [1975] 1 W.L.R. 1474; *Western Bank Ltd v Schindler* [1977] Ch. 1. See [1979] Conv. 266 (R. J. Smith).

[180] *Quennell v Maltby* [1979] 1 W.L.R. 318 at 322; *Albany Home Loans Ltd v Massey* [1997] 2 All E.R. 609 at 612, 613. See too *Palk v Mortgage Services Funding Plc* [1993] Ch. 330 at 337, 338. For the power of sale, see above, para.25–013. For the power to appoint a receiver, see below, para.25–036.

[181] *Albany Home Loans Ltd v Massey*, above. This is especially the case where the mortgagors are spouses.

[182] *Quennell v Maltby*, above. For the rules about transfer and "keeping alive", see below, para.25–102.

[183] *Quennell v Maltby*, above, at 323, per Lord Denning M.R., who relied upon equity, not agency.

to protect his position as a mortgagee and to enable him to obtain repayment.[184]

25–026   *(b) Mortgagee's liability to account strictly.* A mortgagee's object in taking possession may be to protect his security by carrying out repairs or preventing waste or vandalism.[185] But his usual object is to enforce the security by either selling or intercepting the net rents and profits and so securing punctual payment of interest. The mortgagee may, if he wishes, apply any surplus to paying off the principal debt; but he may, if he prefers, hand it over to the mortgagor, for he cannot be compelled to accept repayment in parts.[186] What he may not do is to reap any personal advantage beyond what is due to him under the mortgage; for he is liable to account in equity for any such advantage.[187] He is liable to account strictly, "on the footing of wilful default". This means that he must account not only for all that he receives but also for all that he ought to have received, had he managed the property with due diligence.[188] Indeed, he "must take reasonable care to maximise his return from the property".[189] However, this does not mean that he is bound or allowed to enter into speculation and adventure,[190] but merely that he will be liable for negligence amounting to wilful default.[191]

For example, where the mortgagee was a brewer and the mortgaged property a "free" house, a mortgagee who took possession and let the property as a "tied" house was held liable for the additional rent he would have obtained if he had let the property as a "free" house.[192] If the mortgagee occupies the property himself instead of letting it, he is liable for a fair occupation rent.[193] More usually he will wish to let it; his power to grant binding leases is explained below.[194] The most convenient situation for the mortgagee is where the property is already let, so that he has no responsibility for the amount of the existing rents.

25–027   *(c) Powers of mortgagee in possession.* While in possession, a mortgagee whose mortgage was made by deed has a statutory power to cut and sell timber and other trees ripe for cutting which were not planted or left standing

---

[184] *Quennell v Maltby*, above, at 324, per Templeman L.J.
[185] See *Western Bank Ltd v Schindler*, above.
[186] *Nelson v Booth* (1858) 3 De G. & J. 119; *Wrigley v Gill* [1905] 1 Ch. 241.
[187] Above, para.24–010.
[188] *Chaplin v Young (No.1)* (1863) 33 Beav. 330 at 337, 338. See (1979) 129 N.L.J. 334 (H. E. Markson). cf. *Medforth v Blake* [1999] 3 All E.R. 97 at 108.
[189] *Palk v Mortgage Services Funding Plc* [1993] Ch. 330 at 338, per Nicholls V.C. See too *Downsview Nominees Ltd v First City Corp Ltd* [1993] A.C. 295 at 315.
[190] *Hughes v Williams* (1806) 12 Ves. 493.
[191] *Hughes v Williams*, above at 495.
[192] *White v City of London Brewery Co* (1889) 42 Ch D 237. The "tie" was to the mortgagee, but he was held not accountable for the profit on beer sold to the tenant.
[193] *Marriou v Anchor Reversionary Co* (1861) 3 De G.E. & J. 177 at 193; thus he need pay no rent if the property is too ruinous to be capable of beneficial occupation: *Marshall v Cave* (1824) 3 L.J. (os.) Ch. 57.
[194] Below, para.25–103.

for shelter or ornament, or contract for this to be done within 12 months of the contract.[195] Although he is not liable for waste,[196] he will be liable if he improperly cuts timber[197]; and despite his right to work mines already opened,[198] he may not open new mines.[199] But if the property becomes insufficient security for the money due, the court will not interfere if he cuts timber and opens mines, provided he is not guilty of wanton destruction.[200] He must effect reasonable repairs[201] and may without the mortgagor's consent effect reasonable improvements,[202] though not excessive improvements which might cripple the mortgagor's power to redeem[203]; for the cost of the repairs and improvements will be charged to the mortgagor in the accounts.

(d) *Irrelevance of any counterclaim.* The mortgagee's right to possession is **25–028** unaffected by the existence of a cross-claim, even if it exceeds the amount of the mortgage debt.[204] This will be so whether the claim is liquidated or unliquidated.[205] Although the results can be harsh,[206] the principle is sound. The mortgagor has no right to appropriate the amount of the cross-claim unilaterally,[207] because the mortgagee might have good reasons for keeping the mortgage alive, however large that cross-claim might be.[208] Furthermore, there is an obvious risk that specious cross-claims could be brought to impede the mortgagee's rights.[209] The only possible exception to this principle may be where there is a right of equitable set-off in respect of a sum that is equal to or greater than the mortgage debt. In that situation, the claim might discharge the mortgage.[210] However, the point remains undecided.[211]

---

[195] LPA 1925 s.101(1).

[196] LPA 1925 ss.85(2), 86(2), 87(1).

[197] *Withrington v Banks* (1725) Ca.t.King 30.

[198] *Elias v Snowden Slate Quarries Co* (1879) 4 App.Cas. 454.

[199] *Millett v Davey* (1863) 31 Beav. 470 at 475.

[200] *Millett v Davey*, above at 476.

[201] *Richards v Morgan* (1753) 4 Y. & C. Ex. 570.

[202] *Shepard v Jones* (1882) 21 Ch D 469 at 479.

[203] *Sandon v Hooper* (1843) 6 Beav. 246; affirmed 14 L.J. Ch. 120.

[204] *Mobil Oil Co Ltd v Rawlinson* (1981) 43 P. & C.R. 221 (cross-claim for breach of supply and loan agreements); *Citibank Trust Ltd v Ayivor* [1987] 1 W.L.R. 1157 (cross-claim for negligence and breach of warranty); *National Westminster Bank Plc v Skelton* (1989) [1993] 1 W.L.R. 72n (cross-claim for breach of banker's duty of confidence); *Ashley Guarantee Plc v Zacaria* [1993] 1 W.L.R. 62 (cross-claim for passing off etc.); *Midland Bank Plc v McGrath* [1996] E.G.C.S. 61 (cross-claim for breach of contract, negligence and conspiracy); *Albany Home Loans Ltd v Massey* [1997] 2 All E.R. 609 (cross-claim for unfair dismissal). See [1993] Conv. 459 (J. E. Martin).

[205] *Mobil Oil Co Ltd v Rawlinson*, above, at 226.

[206] See *Ashley Guarantee Plc v Zacaria*, above, at 70.

[207] *Mobil Oil Co Ltd v Rawlinson*, above, at 226.

[208] e.g. an attractive rate of interest or fiscal considerations: *Samuel Keller (Holdings) Ltd v Martins Bank Ltd* [1971] 1 W.L.R. 43 at 48, 51.

[209] *Samuel Keller (Holdings) Ltd v Martins Bank Ltd*, above, at 51; *National Westminster Bank Plc v Skelton*, above, at 78.

[210] *National Westminster Bank Plc v Skelton*, above, at 78; *Ashley Guarantee Plc v Zacaria*, above, at 66.

[211] *National Westminster Bank Plc v Skelton*, above, at 78.

(e) Relief of mortgagor

25–029   (1) THE POSITION AT COMMON LAW. Formerly a mortgagee could obtain summarily an order for possession in the Queen's Bench Division of the High Court without the matter coming before a judicial officer.[212] But since 1936, when the jurisdiction to hear mortgagees' claims for possession was transferred from the King's Bench to the Chancery Division,[213] the High Court has assumed a limited discretionary jurisdiction to refuse an immediate order for possession, whether the proceedings were commenced by writ (or now, a claim form) or originating summons (or now Part 8 procedure under the Civil Procedure Rules).[214] Although the point has not been explicitly decided, it appears that the county court has a similar power,[215] especially as all possession actions normally must start in the county court.[216] Under this jurisdiction, a short adjournment may be granted in order to give the mortgagor a chance of paying off the mortgagee in full or otherwise satisfying him. If there is no reasonable prospect of this, an adjournment will be refused.[217] Nor will the courts extend this jurisdiction to allow an adjournment in other situations.[218] The precise limits of the court's inherent jurisdiction have not been fully clarified,[219] though it retains a residual role.[220]

25–030   (2) STATUTORY RELIEF. There are two situations in which the court has statutory powers to postpone or suspend the mortgagee's right to possession in some way.

(i) Agreements regulated under the Consumer Credit Act 1974, as amended by the Consumer Credit Act 2006. In those cases where the mortgage is

---

[212] *Redditch Benefit BS v Roberts* [1940] Ch. 415 at 420.

[213] For the reasons behind this change, see *National Westminster Bank Plc v Kitch* [1996] 1 W.L.R. 1316.

[214] For a survey of the inherent and statutory powers to grant relief, see (1997) 17 L.S. 483 (M. Haley).

[215] See *Cheltenham and Gloucester Plc v Booker* (1996) 73 P. & C.R. 412. It would be anomalous if the county court lacked such a power, given its exclusive jurisdiction in a significant class of mortgage possession actions: see above, para.25–003.

[216] CPR Part 55 and PD55 and PD 55A.

[217] *Hinckley and South Leicestershire Permanent Benefit BS v Freeman* [1941] Ch. 32; *Robinson v Cilia* [1956] 1 W.L.R. 1502; *Braithwaite v Winwood* [1960] 1 W.L.R. 1257; *Birmingham Citizens Permanent BS v Caunt* [1962] Ch. 883 (reviewing the authorities). See (1962) 78 L.Q.R. 171 (R.E.M.).

[218] *Cheltenham and Gloucester Plc v Krausz* [1997] 1 W.L.R. 1558 at 1566, 1567 (no power for the High Court to adjourn proceedings where a mortgagor, defending an action for possession in the county court, wished to apply to the High Court for an order for sale under LPA 1925 s.91). See above, para.25–023.

[219] In particular, it has been suggested that such adjournments can be granted only in cases where the capital is repayable by instalments concurrently with interest, and the mortgagee undertakes not to go into possession so long as the payments are punctually made: *Four Maids Ltd v Dudley Marshall (Properties) Ltd* [1957] Ch. 317; (1957) 73 L.Q.R. 300 (R.E.M.); cf. above, para.25–023. Later decisions have thrown doubt on this notion: see *Braithwaite v Winwood*, above; *Birmingham Citizens Permanent BS v Caunt*, above. There is no general jurisdiction to stay execution of a possession order pending the outcome of an appeal in separate proceedings, *State Bank of New South Wales v Carey* [2002] EWCA Civ 363.

[220] Below, para.25–032. See *Cheltenham & Gloucester Plc v Booker* [1997] 1 F.L.R. 311.

subject to the Consumer Credit Act 1974 (as amended),[221] if it appears just to the court to do so, it may:

(1) suspend an order for possession[222]; and/or

(2) make a "time order" providing for payment of any sums owed by such instalments, payable at such times as it considers reasonable, having regard to the means of the debtor.[223]

It is not a prerequisite to the exercise of (1) that the mortgagor should be able to repay the instalments within a reasonable time. However, in deciding whether it is just to make an order under either of these provisions, the court will consider the creditor's position as well as the debtor's,[224] and it might refuse to exercise its powers, therefore, if there was no prospect of repayment within a reasonable time.

    (ii) Dwelling-houses. In cases where the mortgagee of property, which **25–031** consists of or includes a dwelling-house,[225] brings proceedings for possession[226] against the mortgagor,[227] the court has a wide statutory discretion under the Administration of Justice Act 1970 to adjourn those proceedings, suspend the execution of any order it makes for possession, or postpone the date for delivery of possession for such period[228] as it thinks fit.[229] This discretion may be exercised whether or not the mortgagor is in default.[230] There are two major restrictions on the statutory discretion. First, if the

---

[221] See above, para.24–044.

[222] CCA 2006 s.135.

[223] CCA 2006 s.129. The court is empowered to amend any agreement or security in consequence of any term of the order that it makes: CCA 2006 s.136.

[224] *First National Bank Plc v Syed* [1991] 2 All E.R. 250 at 256 ("time order" refused where there was a history of default and where the instalments that the debtor could afford did not even meet the interest falling due); (1994) 110 L.Q.R. 221 (N. Hickman).

[225] See, e.g. *Lord Marples of Wallasey v Holmes* (1975) 31 P. & C.R. 94 (hotel containing a residential flat). See too AJA 1970 s.39(2) (a property will be a dwelling-house for the purposes of s.36, even if part of it is used as a shop or for business, trade or professional purposes). The relevant time for determining whether the premises are a dwelling house is the time when the mortgagee claims possession, not when the mortgage was granted, *Royal Bank of Scotland v Miller* [2001] EWCA Civ 344; [2001] 3 W.L.R. 523.

[226] Other than a foreclosure action. But see AJA 1973 s.8(3); below.

[227] For these purposes, "mortgagor" and "mortgagee" include any person deriving title under the original mortgagor or mortgagee: AJA 1970 s.39. However, a statutory tenant under the Rent Act 1977 does not derive title under the mortgagor and cannot invoke s.36: *Britannia BS v Earl* [1990] 1 W.L.R. 422. Nor could any tenant whose lease was a breach of the mortgage agreement, and so not binding on the mortgagor: *Britannia BS v Earl*, above, at 430. See [1990] Conv. 450 (S.B). *Quaere* whether a purchaser who purchased from a mortgagee would be bound, or whether the mortgagor's rights would have been overreached by the sale: cf. *Ropaigealach v Barclays Bank Plc* [1999] 2 W.L.R. 17 at 36, 37; [1999] C.L.J. 281 at 282, 283 (M.J.D).

[228] Which must be "a stretch of time ending with some specified or ascertainable date": *Royal Trust Co of Canada v Markham* [1975] 1 W.L.R. 1416 at 1421, per Sir John Pennycuick. For the difficulties in determining such a period where the mortgagor is not in default, see *Western Bank Ltd v Schindler* [1977] Ch. 1.

[229] AJA 1970 s.36.

[230] *Western Bank Ltd v Schindler*, above (but the contrary opinion of Goff L.J. is preferable). See (1977) 40 M.L.R. 356 (C.H.).

mortgagee takes possession without a court order, it is inapplicable.[231] Second, if the mortgagee has sold to a purchaser deliberately without first obtaining possession, the purchaser is not subject to the statutory discretion, not being a "mortgagee" seeking a possession order.[232] Where it is exercisable, the court's statutory power applies to all types of mortgage[233] except one which secures a regulated agreement under the Consumer Credit Act 1974 (as amended),[234] where the court has the powers conferred by that Act.[235] Where an order for possession has been suspended under the 1970 Act, the court may entertain an application by the mortgagee at any time for leave to enforce that order.[236] There are limits on the court's discretion. Once an order for possession has been executed, there is no jurisdiction either:

(1) to order its suspension; or

(2) to set it aside, make a new order for possession, and then suspend that order.[237]

The court may only exercise its powers where it appears that "the mortgagor is likely to be able within a reasonable period to pay any sums due under the mortgage"[238] or to remedy any default. To resolve a difficulty that arose soon after the statutory power was first conferred, it is now provided by the Administration of Justice Act 1973 that, in the case of an instalment mortgage, or of a mortgage which otherwise permits deferred repayment,[239] the "sums due" are merely any instalments or payments in arrear and not the whole

---

[231] *Ropaigealach v Barclays Bank Plc*, above; [1999] C.L.J. 281 (M.J.D.); above, para.25–022. In that case, Clarke L.J. commented that it was "very curious that mortgagors should only have protection in the case where the mortgagee chooses to take legal proceedings and not in the case where he chooses simply to enter the property": above, at 35.

[232] *Horsham Properties v Clark* above; above 25–017.

[233] *Royal Trust Co of Canada v Markham*, above, at 1421.

[234] AJA 1970 s.38A. This limitation was overlooked in *First National Bank Plc v Syed* [1991] 2 All E.R. 250. The decision is therefore *per incuriam*: see (1994) 110 L.Q.R. 221 (N. Hickman).

[235] Above.

[236] *Abbey National Mortgages Plc v Bernard* (1995) 71 P. & C.R. 257 at 261.

[237] *National and Provincial BS v Ahmed* [1995] 2 E.G.L.R. 127. Once such an order has been executed, the mortgagee can safely contract to sell the property without any risk that the sale might be defeated by an application under AJA 1970 s.36. See too *Mortgage Agency Services Number Two Ltd v Bal* (1998) 77 P. & C.R. D7.

[238] The payment must be one which the mortgagor can afford and which will be sufficient to pay off the arrears within the period: *First National Bank Plc v Syed* [1991] 2 All E.R. 250 at 255.

[239] This has been held to include a traditional mortgage which could be kept alive indefinitely: *Centrax Trustees Ltd v Ross* [1979] 2 All E.R. 952; and an interest-only endowment mortgage where the capital was repayable at the end of a specified number of years: *Governor and Company of the Bank of Scotland v Grimes* [1985] Q.B. 1179; *Citibank Trust Ltd v Ayivor* [1987] 1 W.L.R. 1157. It did not include a mortgage to secure a bank overdraft repayable on demand in writing, because the mortgagor was not permitted to defer payment: *Habib Bank Ltd v Taylor* [1982] 1 W.L.R. 1218; [1982] All E.R. Rev. 177 (P. J. Clarke). See [1984] Conv. 91 (S. Tromans).

capital sum.[240] This is so, even if (as is usual) the mortgage makes this payable on any default by the mortgagor.[241] But the court's powers under the 1970 Act are then exercisable only if there is a likelihood that, at the end of the "reasonable period", the mortgagor will be able to pay any further amounts then due under the mortgage.[242] Where the mortgage falls within the 1973 Act the court's discretionary powers extend also to foreclosure actions,[243] whether or not possession is sought in the same proceedings.[244]

In determining what amounts to a "reasonable period" under both the 1970 and 1973 Acts, the court will take into account the interests of both mortgagor and mortgagee.[245] The starting point will normally be the full term of the mortgage, and the court will consider the mortgagor's ability to pay off all the arrears over that time.[246] However, a shorter period is likely to be imposed where the mortgagor cannot discharge the arrears by periodical payments but only by a sale of the property,[247] or where there has been a breach of some term other than that for payment.[248]

The county court has a statutory power to suspend on terms any money judgment against a debtor who is unable to pay it, until such time as his inability ceases.[249] In a case in which the 1970 Act is applicable, and a mortgagee seeks both possession and a judgment for the moneys due under the mortgage, the court may (and usually will) suspend any money judgment on the same terms as any order which it makes for possession.[250] The court

---

[240] AJA 1973 s.8(1). The courts will not lay down rigid guidelines as to how the discretion under this section and AJA 1970 s.36, should be exercised: see *Cheltenham and Gloucester BS v Grant* (1994) 26 H.L.R. 703. cf. [1995] Conv. 51 (M. P. Thompson).

[241] This was the difficulty that was brought to light in *Halifax BS v Clark* [1973] Ch. 307 and which prompted the enactment of AJA 1973 s.8. It was assumed in that case that a "reasonable period" was a short one, and that there was no likelihood that the mortgagor could repay the whole capital sum within that time. However, it was subsequently held in *First Middlesborough Trading and Mortgage Co Ltd v Cunningham* (1973) 28 P. & C.R. 69 that a reasonable period might be the whole term of the mortgage.

[242] AJA 1973 s.8(2).

[243] Which is not the case in respect of mortgages which fall exclusively within AJA 1970 s.36; above.

[244] AJA 1973 s.8(3). There is no discretion in other cases: see *Lord Marples of Wallasey v Holmes* (1975) 31 P. & C.R. 94.

[245] *Cheltenham and Gloucester BS v Norgan* [1996] 1 W.L.R. 343 at 356.

[246] *Cheltenham and Gloucester BS v Norgan*, above; (1996) 112 L.Q.R. 553 (J. Morgan). On this basis a number of earlier cases might now be decided differently: see, e.g. *Citibank Trust Ltd v Ayivor* [1987] 1 W.L.R. 1157 (24-year mortgage term: no relief where proposed repayment of arrears would take 812 years).

[247] *Bristol and West BS v Ellis* (1996) 73 P. & C.R. 158. That case makes clear that although a period of six months to a year is likely to be the maximum in such a case (see *National and Provincial BS v Lloyd* [1996] 1 All E.R. 630), there is no fixed rule to that effect: see (1996) 73 P. & C.R. at 162, 163, where the relevant criteria for selecting the length of the period are set out. A short suspension is probable if there is likely to be a considerable delay in selling or if the value of the property is close to the total of the mortgage debt.

[248] e.g. if the mortgagor had let the premises to a tenant in breach of covenant.

[249] CCA 1984 s.71(2).

[250] *Cheltenham and Gloucester BS v Grattidge* (1993) 25 H.L.R. 454; *Cheltenham and Gloucester BS v Grant* (1994) 26 H.L.R. 703 at 708; *Cheltenham and Gloucester BS v Johnson* (1996) 73 P. & C.R. 293.

may however depart from this practice in special circumstances.[251] There is no equivalent power for the High Court to suspend a money judgment: the most that the court can do is to stay its execution.[252]

25–032   (3) EXERCISE OF DISCRETION WHERE A SALE IS CONTEMPLATED. One situation in which the court is often asked to exercise its discretion to suspend an order for possession (whether under its common law or statutory powers) is where it is proposed to sell the property to discharge the mortgagor's liabilities. The real issue in such a case is whether the mortgagor or mortgagee should have the conduct of the sale. Where the mortgagee's power of sale has become exercisable,[253] the mortgagee has a right to sell the property if and when he chooses.[254] But a repossession sale by a mortgagee with vacant possession is likely to yield a lower price than a sale by a mortgagor in possession.[255] However, if an order for possession is adjourned to enable the mortgagor to sell, there is an obvious danger that he will prevaricate.[256] The court undoubtedly has power to suspend an order for possession, under either its inherent jurisdiction or the 1970 Act (if applicable), to enable the mortgagor to sell the property, provided that the value is likely to be sufficient to discharge his indebtedness.[257] It may even exercise its powers so as to allow the mortgagor to remain in possession where the property is to be sold by the mortgagee.[258] However, that will seldom be appropriate, and possession will normally be given to the party having the conduct of the sale.[259]

There is no power, under either the 1970 Act or the court's inherent jurisdiction, to suspend an order for possession to enable a sale to take place at a price that will not discharge the mortgagor's indebtedness.[260]

25–033   *(f) Procedure.* A claim for possession need be served only on the mortgagor and any other person in possession who claims a right to possession against the mortgagee,[261] although in some circumstances notice must be given before

---

[251] *Cheltenham and Gloucester BS v Grattidge*, above, at 458; *Cheltenham and Gloucester BS v Johnson*, above, at 302.

[252] By writ of fieri facias. There is as yet no authority as to what the High Court would do in such a case.

[253] Which will almost always be the case.

[254] *China and South Sea Bank Ltd v Tan* [1990] 1 A.C. 536; above, para.25–018.

[255] cf. *Target Homes Ltd v Clothier* [1994] 1 All E.R. 439 at 448.

[256] See *Cheltenham and Gloucester Plc v Krausz* [1997] 1 W.L.R. 1558 at 1564.

[257] Inherent jurisdiction: *Cheltenham and Gloucester Plc v Booker* (1996)73 P. & C.R. 412 at 415; *Royal Trust Co of Canada v Markham* [1975] 1 W.L.R. 1416 at 1420; AJA 1970 s.36: *Royal Trust Co of Canada v Markham*, above, at 1422; *Bristol and West BS v Ellis* (1996) 73 P. & C.R. 158 at 162. For the factors that will influence the court in selecting the length of any suspension under s.36, see *Bristol and West BS v Ellis*, above, at 162, 163; above, para.25–031.

[258] *Cheltenham and Gloucester Plc v Booker*, above, at 415.

[259] *Cheltenham and Gloucester Plc v Booker*, above, at 416.

[260] See AJA 1970 s.36(1); *Cheltenham and Gloucester Plc v Krausz*, above, at 1567. See above, para.25–023. Note the argument, above, that there may be such a power under LPA s.91.

[261] See now CPR Pt 55. Despite the repeal of RSC 1883 Ord.55 r.55A, *Alliance BS v Yap* [1962] 1 W.L.R. 857 and *Brighton and Shoreham BS v Hollingdale* [1965] 1 W.L.R. 376 (deserted wife) are probably still good law.

execution to an unauthorised tenant in possession.[262] There is also a statutory duty to serve notice of the action on persons who have registered their matrimonial home rights under the Family Law Act 1996 (or earlier equivalent legislation).[263]

(g) Attornment clause. At one time, many mortgages contained an attornment clause by which the mortgagor attorned, or acknowledged himself to be, a tenant at will or from year to year of the mortgagee, usually at a nominal rent such as a peppercorn or five pence.[264] This practice grew up to enable mortgagees to take advantage of a speedy procedure for recovering possession that was available to landlords but not at that time to mortgagees.[265] However, as mortgagees have in their own right enjoyed a similar speedy procedure for more than 60 years, there is now no substantial advantage in an attornment clause and they are no longer much used.[266]

25–034

Despite earlier doubts, it is established that an attornment clause still effectually creates the relationship of landlord and tenant.[267] Nevertheless, the substance of the transaction is a mortgage to which the attornment clause is merely ancillary. The resultant tenancy has therefore been held to be outside a number of statutes which are intended to protect those who in substance are tenants.[268] But in other respects the general law of landlord and tenant applies. Thus if the mortgagee wishes to take possession, he must first determine the tenancy by proper notice,[269] unless (as is often the case) the attornment clause creates a mere tenancy at will, or makes the tenancy determinable without notice, e.g. upon default being made by the mortgagor.[270] Similarly a mere tenancy at will determines automatically as soon as the mortgagor assigns his interest.[271] But in other cases the assignee will be bound by the tenancy and by covenants which run with it under the ordinary rules.[272] There is, in fact, a duality of positions: under the tenancy arising from the mortgage or charge the mortgagor is the landlord and the mortgagee the tenant, whereas under the sub tenancy created by the attornment clause their positions are reversed. Nevertheless, any covenants by the mortgagor in the mortgage are enforceable against the assignee from the mortgagor if they relate to the premises (e.g.

---

[262] The Mortgage Repossessions (Protection of Tenants etc.) Act 2010; above para.25–024.

[263] FLA 1996 s.56; below, para.25–099.

[264] See *Woolwich Equitable BS v Preston* [1938] Ch. 129.

[265] See the fifth edition of this work at p.946.

[266] See *Ingram v IRC* [1997] 4 All E.R. 395 at 422.

[267] *Regent Oil Co Ltd v JA Gregory (Hatch End) Ltd* [1966] Ch. 402.

[268] See, e.g. *Portman BS v Young* [1951] 1 All E.R. 191 (Rent Acts); *Peckham Mutual BS v Registe* (1980) 42 P. & C.R. 186 (PEA 1977); *Steyning and Littlehampton BS v Wilson* [1951] Ch. 1018 (AHA 1948).

[269] *Hinckley and Country BS v Henny* [1953] 1 W.L.R. 352.

[270] See, e.g. *Woolwich Equitable BS v Preston* [1938] Ch. 129, where it is said that the issue of a summons for possession takes effect as a re-entry and turns the tenancy into a tenancy at will, and the service of the summons terminates the tenancy at will.

[271] *Regent Oil Co Ltd v J. A. Gregory (Hatch End) Ltd* [1966] Ch. 402 at 429, 438; above, para.17–104.

[272] *Regent Oil Co Ltd v J. A. Gregory (Hatch End) Ltd*, above.

covenants to repair them, or not to use them for certain purposes).[273] They will therefore bind the assignee, whether the mortgagee is enforcing them *qua* tenant or *qua* sub-landlord.[274]

25–035   *(h) Limitation.* If a mortgagee remains in possession of unregistered mortgaged land for 12 years, or has completed 12 years possession in respect of registered land before October 13, 2003, without acknowledging the mortgagor's title or receiving any payment of principal or interest from him, the right to redeem the land is extinguished[275] and the mortgagee acquires a title to the land. If the mortgagee remains in possession of registered land but has not completed 12 years before the entry into force of the Land Registration Act 2002, then no period of limitation will run,[276] but the provisions of Sch.6 to the Land Registration Act 2002 will apply.[277]

4. To appoint a receiver

25–036   *(a) History.* In order to avoid the responsibilities of taking possession and yet achieve substantially the same result, well-drawn mortgages used to provide for the appointment of a receiver with extensive powers of management of the mortgaged property. Thus the mortgagee, without taking possession himself, could ensure that the property was efficiently managed and that his claim for interest was made a first charge on the net rents and profits. At first the appointment was made by the mortgagor at the request of the mortgagee; but subsequently mortgagees began to reserve a power for themselves, acting in theory as agents for the mortgagor, to appoint a receiver.[278] In such circumstances the receiver was, by the terms of the power, deemed the agent of the mortgagor,[279] and the mortgagee was not liable to account strictly in the same way as would have been the case if he had taken possession or the receiver had been his agent.[280] Lord Cranworth's Act 1860[281] gave a somewhat unsatisfactory statutory power to appoint a receiver, but the Conveyancing Act 1881[282] (replaced by the Law of Property Act 1925[283]) conferred a power which satisfies most mortgagees.

---

[273] This is so whether the mortgage was made before 1996 or after 1995. The rules laid down in L&TCA 1995 for the transmission of covenants (above, Ch.20) do not apply to mortgage terms: see the definition of "tenancy" in L&TCA 1995 s.28(1).

[274] *Regent Oil Co Ltd v J. A. Gregory (Hatch End) Ltd*, above.

[275] Limitation Act 1980 s.16 (and see s.29(4) as to the date from which time runs); *Young v Clarey* [1948] Ch. 191: see below, para.35–035.

[276] LRA 2002 s.96(2).

[277] See para.35–070.

[278] *Gaskell v Gosling* [1896] 1 Q.B. 669 at 692. See too *Medforth v Blake* [1999] 3 All E.R. 97 at 103.

[279] *Jefferys v Dickson* (1866) 1 Ch.App. 183 at 190; and see *Lever Finance Ltd v Needlemans' Trustee* [1956] Ch. 375 at 382.

[280] Above para.25–026. See *Saffron Walden Herts & Essex BS v Bunbury* (1998) 77 P. & C.R. D22 at D23.

[281] 23 & 24 Vict. c.145, ss.17–23.

[282] s.19.

[283] s.101(1)(iii).

Compared with taking possession, the appointment of a receiver has one minor disadvantage: lapse of time may confer a title to the land upon a mortgagee in possession of unregistered land (or registered land where the mortgagee's possession was completed before October 13, 2003)[284] but not upon a mortgagee who has appointed a receiver.

(b) The power. The statutory power to appoint a receiver arises and becomes **25–037** exercisable in the same circumstances as the power of sale.[285] A mortgagee has power to appoint a receiver provided:

(i) his mortgage was made by deed; and

(ii) the mortgage money is due.[286]

But this power is not exercisable until one of the three events set out earlier[287] has occurred,[288] although persons paying money to the receiver are not bound to see that his appointment has been thereby justified.[289] A mortgagee who is in possession is not thereby debarred from appointing a receiver.[290] In deciding whether or not to exercise the power, the mortgagee must act in good faith, but owes no duty of care to the mortgagor (or to any guarantor).[291] However, where he does appoint a receiver, he may owe a duty to select one who is competent.[292] The statutory power to appoint a receiver usually makes it unnecessary to apply to the court for a receiver, although the court has long had jurisdiction to make the appointment on such terms as it thinks just in all cases in which it appears to be just and convenient to do so.[293]

(c) Procedure. The mortgagee must make the appointment by writing,[294] **25–038** and may remove or replace the receiver in the same way.[295] Though appointed by, and for the benefit of the mortgagee,[296] the receiver is deemed to be the agent of the mortgagor, who is solely responsible for his acts.[297] This will not be the case if the mortgage otherwise provides[298]; or if the mortgagee either represents the receiver as being his agent,[299] or directs or interferes with his

---

[284] Above.
[285] Above, paras 25–014, 25–015.
[286] LPA 1925 s.101(1)(iii).
[287] Above, para.25–015.
[288] LPA 1925 s.109(1).
[289] LPA 1925 s.109(4).
[290] *Refuge Assurance Co Ltd v Pearlberg* [1938] Ch. 687.
[291] *Shamji v Johnson Matthey Bankers Ltd* [1991] B.C.L.C. 36.
[292] *Shamji v Johnson Matthey Bankers Ltd*, above, at 42.
[293] Senior Courts Act 1981 s.37 (replacing legislation dating back to 1873).
[294] LPA 1925 s.109(1).
[295] LPA 1925 s.109(5).
[296] See *Re B. Johnson & Co (Builders) Ltd* [1955] Ch. 634 at 644.
[297] LPA 1925 s.109(2), confirming the general rule: see *Jeffreys v Dickson* (1866) L.R; 1 Ch.App. 183 at 190.
[298] LPA 1925 s.109(2).
[299] *Chatsworth Properties Ltd v Effiom* [1971] 1 W.L.R. 144.

activities.[300] The agency also ceases if the mortgagor becomes insolvent.[301] If the receiver continues to act thereafter, he does so as principal,[302] unless the mortgagee by his conduct constitutes him as his agent.[303] Where a receiver is the mortgagee's agent, the latter will be liable for his conduct, as where he sells the mortgaged property and fails to obtain the true market price.[304]

Although a receiver is under a general duty to act in good faith and to exercise his powers for proper purposes,[305] he is under specific duties to take reasonable care and act with due diligence in conducting any sale of, or in managing any business on, the mortgaged property.[306] A receiver does not have to take additional steps in order to increase or maximise the value of the property and in this respect is in the same position as a selling mortgagee.[307] The receiver has power to recover the income of the property by action, distress or otherwise, and to give valid receipts for it.[308] If the mortgagee so directs in writing, the receiver must insure the property against fire to the same extent as the mortgagee might have insured,[309] and the mortgagee may by writing delegate his powers of leasing[310] and accepting surrenders of leases.[311]

25–039   *(d) Application of receipts.* The money received by the receiver must be applied in the following order[312]:

(i) In discharge of rents, rates and taxes.

(ii) In keeping down annual sums and the interest on principal sums having priority to the mortgage.

(iii) In payment of his commission and insurance premiums and, if so directed in writing by the mortgagee, the cost of repairs. His commission is 5 per cent on the gross sum received unless his appointment specifies less or the court otherwise directs.[313]

(iv) In payment of the interest under the mortgage.

---

[300] *American Express International Banking Corp v Hurley* [1985] 3 All E.R. 564 at 571.
[301] *Gosling v Gaskell* [1897] A.C. 575.
[302] See R. P. Meagher, W. M. C. Gummow and J. R. F. Lehane, *Equity: Doctrines and Remedies* 3rd edn, para.2842. cf. *Sowman v David Samuel Trust Ltd* [1978] 1 W.L.R. 22 at 27–30.
[303] *American Express International Banking Corp v Hurley*, above, at 568.
[304] *American Express International Banking Corp v Hurley*, above. See too *Circuit Systems Ltd v Zuken-Redac (UK) Ltd* [1997] 1 W.L.R. 721 at 739.
[305] *Downsview Nominees Ltd v First City Corp Ltd* [1993] A.C. 295 at 315; *Silven Properties v Royal Bank of Scotland*, above.
[306] *Medforth v Blake* [1999] 3 All E.R. 97. cf. above, para.25–018. "The receiver must be active in the protection and preservation of the charged property over which he is appointed": *Silven Properties v Royal Bank of Scotland* at para.23 (per Lightman J.).
[307] *Silven Properties v Royal Bank of Scotland*, above.
[308] LPA 1925 s.109(3).
[309] LPA 1925 s.109(7).
[310] LPA 1925 s.99(19).
[311] LPA 1925 s.100(13). For these powers, see below, paras 25–071, 25–081.
[312] LPA 1925 s.109(8).
[313] LPA 1925 s.109(6).

(v) If the mortgagee so directs in writing, towards the discharge of the principal money lent; otherwise it must be paid to the person who would have received it if the receiver had not been appointed, i.e. normally the mortgagor.

The mortgagee's remedies are cumulative. A mortgagee is not bound to **25-040** select any one of his remedies and pursue that exclusively. Subject to his not recovering more than is due to him, he may employ any or all of the remedies to enforce payment.[314] If he sells the property for less than the mortgage debt, he may still sue the mortgagor upon the personal covenant for payment of the balance,[315] and the same applies on a sale by the court, even if the mortgagee, with the leave of the court, has bought the property at the sale and later resold it at an increased price.[316] If he takes possession, he is not thereby prevented from appointing a receiver.[317]

Foreclosure, however, puts an end to other remedies, since if the mortgagee takes the whole security he cannot also claim payment. He may therefore sue on the personal covenant only if he opens the foreclosure, so that the mortgagor, if he can pay, may also redeem.[318] The mortgagor thus has the option of either paying the whole of the mortgage debt and recovering his property, or paying the difference between the mortgage debt and the value of the property and losing the property. If by disposing of the property after foreclosure (e.g. by selling it) the mortgagee has put it out of his power to reopen the foreclosure, he can no longer sue the mortgagor[319] (or a guarantor[320]) upon the personal covenant,[321] even though the proceeds of sale are less than the amount of the debt.[322] Further, a foreclosure order nisi suspends the power of sale, and the mortgagee must obtain the leave of the court if he wishes to sell.[323] Unless the proceedings have been registered as a pending land action,[324] the order will not bind a purchaser of unregistered land without express notice.[325] Where the title is registered, a purchaser acquiring title under a registered disposition would take free of the order regardless of the doctrine of notice, unless the proceedings had been protected by entering a unilateral Notice against the title.[326]

---

[314] *Palmer v Hendrie* (1859) 27 Beav. 349 at 351; *Alliance & Leicester Plc v Slayford* [2001] 33 H.L.R. 743.

[315] *Rudge v Richens* (1873) L.R. 8 C.P. 358. The limitation period for the recovery of capital is twelve years, *West Bromwich Building Society v Wilkinson* [2005] UKHL 44, [2005] 1 W.L.R. 2303; *Bristol and West Plc v Bartlett* [2002] EWCA Civ 1181, [2003] 1 W.L.R. 284.

[316] *Gordon Grant & Co Ltd v Boos* [1926] A.C. 781.

[317] *Refuge Assurance Co Ltd v Pearlberg* [1938] Ch. 687.

[318] *Perry v Barker* (1806) 13 Ves. 198.

[319] *Palmer v Hendrie* (1859) 27 Beav. 349.

[320] *Lloyds & Scottish Trust Ltd v Britten* (1982) 44 P. & C.R. 249.

[321] *Palmer v Hendrie*, above.

[322] *Lockhart v Hardy* (1846) 9 Beav. 349.

[323] *Stevens v Theatres Ltd* [1903] 1 Ch. 857.

[324] *Stevens v Theatres Ltd*, at 863.

[325] LCA 1972 s.5(7); above, para.8-088.

[326] LRA 2002 s.87(1)(a). An agreed notice is possible, but unlikely in the circumstances.

II. EQUITABLE MORTGAGEE

25–041   The extent to which the foregoing remedies are exercisable by an equitable mortgagee is as follows.

25–042   **1. To foreclose.** Foreclosure is the primary remedy of an equitable mortgagee. Since he has no legal estate the court's order absolute will direct the mortgagor to convey the land to the mortgagee unconditionally, i.e. free from any right to redeem.[327]

25–043   **2. To sell.** The statutory power of sale[328] applies only where the mortgage was made by deed[329]; other mortgagees have no power of sale. For this reason, as already mentioned, many equitable mortgages are made by deed.[330] But even then there may be a difficulty, for it has been held that the statutory power to sell "the mortgaged property"[331] enables the mortgagee to sell only the interest which he has, i.e. the equitable interest.[332] In other words, the power is a power over the equity of redemption and not a power over the legal estate if vested in some other person. But this narrow interpretation has been doubted.[333] Since of course the power of sale is of little value unless it extends to the legal estate, it is often so extended by either or both of two conveyancing devices.

25–044   *(a) Power of attorney.* A power of attorney[334] is inserted in the deed empowering the mortgagee or his assigns[335] to convey the legal estate.[336] This power, being given for value, may be made irrevocable in perpetuity in favour of a purchaser, and so will not be affected by any act of the mortgagor, or by his death.[337]

25–045   *(b) Declaration of trust.* A clause is inserted in the deed whereby the mortgagor declares that he holds the legal estate on trust for the mortgagee and empowers the mortgagee to appoint himself or his nominee as trustee in

---

[327] *James v James* (1873) L.R. 16 Eq. 153.

[328] Above, para.25–013.

[329] LPA 1925 s.101(1).

[330] Thus, a charge by deed by way of legal mortgage over a registered title which is not registered as required by LRA 2002 s.27 is an equitable mortgage, but the power of sale remains because it was made by deed, *Swift 1st v Colin*, above.

[331] LPA 1925 s.101(1)(i).

[332] *Re Hodson & Howes' Contract* (1887) 35 Ch D 668.

[333] *Re White Rose Cottage* [1965] Ch. 940 at 951 per Lord Denning M.R., invoking the contrast in wording between CA 1881 s.21(1) and LPA 1925 s.104(1). Yet the phrase relied on ("the subject of the mortgage") is the same in each subsection. This apparent doubt not raised in *Swift 1st v Colin*, where the purchaser from the equitable mortgagee was registered with absolute title; i.e. the equitable mortgagee had sold the legal title.

[334] These powers are now regulated by the Powers of Attorney Act 1971, as amended by the Senior Courts Act 1981 s.152(4) and Sch.7.

[335] LPA 1925 s.128.

[336] In *Re White Rose Cottage*, above, the property was in fact sold by the mortgagor, with a release of the mortgage by the mortgagee; the conveyance was validly executed by the mortgagee but as attorney for the mortgagor.

[337] LPA 1925 s.126.

place of the mortgagor.[338] The mortgagee can in this way vest the legal estate in himself or a purchaser.[339]

In the case of an equitable mortgage not made by deed (for example, a written contract for a mortgage) there is no power of sale out of court. But the court has the power to order a sale[340] on the application of either party, and to vest a legal term of years in the mortgagee, so that he can sell as if he were a legal mortgagee.[341]

3. To take possession

(a) *The right*. It is generally said that an equitable mortgagee has no right **25–046** to take possession.[342] Certainly he has none at law, for he has no legal estate. But in equity he should be entitled to the same rights as if he had a legal mortgage, and there would seem to be no reason why he should not take possession under the doctrine of *Walsh v Lonsdale*,[343] for the basis of an equitable mortgage is the creation of the relationship of mortgagor and mortgagee forthwith, rather than a mere contract for a future mortgage.[344] The court may, in any case, award him possession[345]; and there is some authority which indicates that he may take possession in his own right,[346] as in principle one would expect. He may certainly do so if the agreement so provides.[347]

(b) *Collection of rents*. What the equitable mortgagee cannot do without an **25–047** order of the court[348] is to collect the rents if the land is let[349]; but the true reason for this disability is that rent is payable to the legal reversioner and

---

[338] See *London & County Banking Co v Goddard* [1897] 1 Ch. 642.

[339] Under TA 1925 s.40; see above, para.11 068.

[340] LPA 1925 s.91(2); above, para.25–011; *Oldham v Stringer* (1884) 51 L.T. 895.

[341] LPA 1925 ss.90, 91(7).

[342] Coote, *Mortgages*, 832; Waldock, *Mortgages*, 235; Halsb. vol.32, para.673; and see *Barclays Bank Ltd v Bird* [1954] Ch. 274 at 280. But no satisfactory authority is cited; see (1954) 70 L.Q.R. 161 (R.E.M.) *Garfitt v Allen* (1887) 37 Ch D 48 is a case of charge, not mortgage, and a chargee plainly has no right to take possession. Since the Judicature Acts 1873–1875, an action for the recovery of land will not be defeated merely for want of the legal estate: *General Finance Mortgage and Discount Co v Liberator Permanent Benefit BS* (1878) 10 Ch D 15 at 24; *Re O'Neill* [1967] NI. 129. For fuller discussion, see (1955) 71 L.Q.R. 204 (H.W.R.W.).

[343] (1882) 21 Ch D 9; above, para.17–048.

[344] See above, para.24–041.

[345] *Barclays Bank Ltd v Bird*, above; *Re O'Neill*, above.

[346] *Ex p. Bignold* (1834) 4 Deac. & Ch. 259, per Erskine C.J. (contra the opinion of Sir G. Rose); *Re Gordon* (1889) 61 L.T. 299; *Tichborne v Weir* (1892) 67 L.T. 735; *Antrim County Land Building and Investment Co Ltd v Stewart* [1904] 2 I.R. 357 (the judgment of Palles C.B. is particularly helpful); *Spencer v Mason* (1931) 75 S.J. 295. See (1955) 71 L.Q.R. 204 (H.W.R.W.).

[347] *Ocean Accident & Guarantee Corporation Ltd v Ilford Gas Co* [1905] 2 K.B. 493.

[348] The court's order is for the appointment of a receiver by way of equitable execution: *Vacuum Oil Co Ltd v Ellis* [1914] 1 K.B. 693 at 703. For the appointment of a receiver, see below, para.25–049.

[349] *Re Pearson* (1838) 3 Mont. & A. 592; *Finck v Trabover* [1905] 1 K.B. 427; *Vacuum Oil Co Ltd v Ellis* [1914] K.B. 693, where the dicta should probably be limited to the points which were before the court, i.e. that there was no right to possession as against a prior tenant in possession, and no legal title to the rents.

that—at least where the lease was granted prior to 1996—an equitable assignment of the reversion does not create the legal relationship of landlord and tenant (i.e. privity of estate, or tenure) upon which the right to receive rent depends.[350] It does not follow that because an equitable mortgagee is not entitled to demand rent as against a tenant, he is not entitled to possession as against the mortgagor. For the effect of the contract in equity, as between the contracting parties, is something quite different from its effect upon third parties such as tenants.[351]

25–048   *(c) Possible implied term.* The only possible basis for the rule, as commonly stated, that an equitable mortgagee has no right to possession would seem to be an implied term in the contract. It might be said that a contract for a mortgage does not contemplate giving possession to the mortgagee, as contrasted with a contract for a lease, which contemplates possession by the tenant. But there seems to be no authority, and no evident necessity, for implying such a term, nor would it accord with the decisions.[352]

25–049   **4. To appoint a receiver.** An equitable mortgagee has always had the right to have a receiver appointed by the court in a proper case,[353] e.g. when interest is in arrear.[354] If his mortgage is by deed he has also the statutory power,[355] which is more convenient since there is no need to apply to the court.

III. EQUITABLE CHARGEE

25–050   The primary remedies of an equitable chargee are to apply to the court for an order for sale[356] or for the appointment of a receiver.[357] But since the statutory definition of a mortgage extends to a charge,[358] an equitable chargee by deed is in the same position as an equitable mortgagee as regards sale or the appointment of a receiver out of court. An equitable chargee can neither foreclose[359] nor take possession,[360] since he has neither a legal estate nor the benefit of a contract to create one.[361]

---

[350] *Cox v Bishop* (1857) 8 De G.M. & G. 815; *Friary Holroyd & Healey's Breweries Ltd v Singleton* [1899] 1 Ch. 86 at 90 (reversed on the facts [1899] 2 Ch. 261); and see above, para.20–033. Where a lease has been granted after 1995, the benefit of a covenant passes on both a legal and an equitable assignment of the reversion: see L&TCA 1995 ss.3, 28(1); above, paras 20–065, 20–080.

[351] Above para.17–057.

[352] See fn.335, above.

[353] Senior Courts Act 1981 s.37.

[354] *Shakel v Duke of Marlborough* (1819) 4 Madd. 463.

[355] LPA 1925 s.101(1)(iii); above, para.25–037.

[356] The court has power under LPA 1925 s.90 (above para.25–043) to vest in the chargee a legal term of years so that he can sell as if he were a legal mortgagee; *Ladup Ltd v Williams & Glyn's Bank Plc* [1985] 1 W.L.R. 851 at 855.

[357] *Tennant v Trenchard* (1869) 4 Ch.App. 537; *Re Owen* [1894] 3 Ch. 220.

[358] LPA 1925 s.205(1)(xvi).

[359] *Tennant v Trenchard*, above, at 542; *Re Lloyd* [1903] 1 Ch. 385 at 404.

[360] *Garfitt v Allen* (1887) 37 Ch D 48 at 50.

[361] See *Carreras Rothmans Ltd v Freeman Mathews Treasure Ltd* [1985] Ch. 207 at 227; *Ladup Ltd v Williams & Glyn's Bank Plc*, above, at 855.

B. Other Rights of a Mortgagee

Certain other rights of a mortgagee must now be considered. The law is in **25–051**
general the same for both mortgages and charges, whether legal or equitable,
and "mortgage" will accordingly be used hereafter to include all such incumbrances unless the contrary is indicated.

1. Right to fixtures. It is a question of construction to decide what property **25–052**
is included in a mortgage. Subject to any contrary intention, a mortgage
includes all fixtures attached to the land either at the date of the mortgage or
thereafter.[362] A mortgagor does not have the same power to remove certain
fixtures that is enjoyed by tenants.[363]

2. Right to possession of the title deeds. As already mentioned, where title **25–053**
to the land is unregistered, a first mortgagee has the same right to the title
deeds as if he had the fee simple or an assignment of the lease which has been
mortgaged, as the case may be.[364] The introduction of new triggers for
compulsory registration of title in March 1998 meant that this right seldom
arose thereafter,[365] and this will continue under the triggers found in the Land
Registration Act 2002.[366] Where it did apply, then notwithstanding any contrary agreement, the mortgagor was entitled to inspect and make copies of the
deeds at reasonable times and on payment of the mortgagee's costs.[367] For
cases where title remains unregistered and the mortgagee retains the title
deeds, as long as the mortgage exists the mortgagee is not liable for negligent
loss of the deeds.[368] But if at redemption he fails to deliver them to the
mortgagor he may be ordered to pay him compensation.[369] Upon redemption
the mortgagee must deliver the deeds to the mortgagor,[370] unless he has notice
of some subsequent incumbrance, in which case the deeds should be delivered
to the incumbrancer next in order of priority of whom the mortgagee has
notice.[371]

---

[362] Above, para.23–022.

[363] Above, para.23–012.

[364] Above, paras 24–037, 24–038.

[365] Above, para.24–038. After March 1998, any first legal mortgage of an unregistered freehold
or of a lease having more than 21 years to run, which was supported by documents of title,
triggered the requirement to register the underlying freehold or lease: LRA 1925 s.123(2) (as
substituted by LRA 1997).

[366] See above para.7–013, where the triggers remain substantially the same as those existing in
March 1998 save for the reduction in the qualifying period for leases to first mortgages of
unregistered leases of over seven years: LRA 2002 s.4(1)(g).

[367] LPA 1925 s.96(1).

[368] *Browning v Handiland Group Ltd* (1976) 35 P. & C.R. 345. LPA 1925 s.13, preserves the
(questionable) principle of the pre-1926 law, which was that the mortgagee, being owner of the
land, was also owner of the deeds and could not be liable for losing his own property.

[369] *Browning v Handiland Group Ltd* (1976) 35 P. & C.R. 345. LPA 1925 s.13, preserves the
(questionable) principle of the pre-1926 law, which was that the mortgagee, being owner of the
land, was also owner of the deeds and could not be liable for losing his own property.

[370] See *James v Rumsey* (1879) 11 Ch D 398.

[371] See *Corbett v National Provident Institution* (1900) 17 T.L.R. 5.

Contrary to the general rule that registration is notice, registration under the Land Charges Act 1972 or in a local register is not deemed to be notice for this purpose.[372] The mortgagee accordingly need not make a search before returning the deeds, although, as has been seen, a mortgagee is bound to search before he distributes any surplus after a sale.[373] If a mortgage becomes statute-barred by lapse of time,[374] the mortgagee must return the deeds even if no part of the mortgage debt has been or will be paid.[375]

25–054   **3. Right to insure against fire at the mortgagor's expense.** This enables the mortgagee to protect the value of his security. It used to be incorporated expressly, but is now imported[376] by the Law of Property Act 1925[377] into every mortgage made by deed. The mortgagee is empowered to insure the mortgaged property against fire and charge the premiums on the property in the same way as the money lent.[378] The power is exercisable as soon as the mortgage is made.[379] The amount of the insurance must not exceed the amount specified in the deed, or, if none, two-thirds of the amount required to restore the property in case of total destruction.[380] But the mortgagee cannot exercise his power if:

(i) the mortgage deed declares that no insurance is required; or

(ii) the mortgagor keeps up an insurance in accordance with the mortgage deed (as is very often stipulated); or

(iii) the mortgage deed is silent as to insurance and the mortgagor keeps up an insurance to the amount authorised by the Act with the mortgagee's consent.[381]

If the mortgagor insures on his own account and not under these provisions, the mortgagee has no right to the policy money.[382] Where, however, the mortgagor insures pursuant to a covenant in the mortgage, that covenant operates to give the mortgagee a charge over the proceeds, and this is so even if the insurance is in the name of the mortgagor.[383] Because the charge operates by way of a partial equitable assignment, the mortgagee should notify the insurer accordingly.[384]

---

[372] LPA 1925 s.96(2), added by LP(Am)A 1926 Sch. For another case where registration does not constitute notice, see below, para.26–067.

[373] Above, para.25–021.

[374] See below, para.25–036.

[375] *Lewis v Plunket* [1937] Ch. 306.

[376] Subject to the provisions of the mortgage: LPA 1925 s.101(3), (4).

[377] LPA 1925 ss.101(1)(ii), 108.

[378] The premiums are only a charge on the property; they cannot be recovered from the mortgagor as a debt: Halsbury Vol.25, para.560.

[379] LPA 1925 s.101(1)(ii).

[380] LPA 1925 s.108(1).

[381] LPA 1925 s.108(2).

[382] *Halifax BS v Keighley* [1931] 2 K.B. 248.

[383] *Colonial Mutual General Insurance Co Ltd v ANZ Banking Group (New Zealand) Ltd* [1995] 1 W.L.R. 1140.

[384] The rule in *Dearle v Hall* (1828) 3 Russ. 1; below, para.26–016.

4. Right to consolidate

(a) The right. Consolidation may be described as the right of a person in **25–055**
whom two or more mortgages are vested to refuse to allow one mortgage to
be redeemed unless the other or others are also redeemed. If A has mortgaged
both Blackacre and Whiteacre to X, each property being worth £15,000 and
each loan being £10,000, it would be unfair, if the value of Blackacre
subsequently sinks to £5,000 and the value of Whiteacre doubles, to allow A
to redeem Whiteacre and leave Blackacre unredeemed. In such a case equity
permits X to consolidate, and so oblige A to redeem both mortgages or
neither. In seeking redemption after the legal date for redemption has passed,
A is asking for the assistance of equity, and equity puts its own price upon its
interference[385]: he who seeks equity must do equity.[386] This is a notable case
of equity restricting rather than extending the right to redeem. Even more
remarkably, the mortgagee is allowed to consolidate even though each property is still sufficient security for its debt. What was originally a principle of
equity is now an automatic right. Even a mortgagee who is foreclosing may
insist upon it.[387]

(b) Conditions of exercise. The principle of consolidation has been elabo- **25–056**
rated to some extent, particularly with regard to third parties, e.g. where one
of the properties is sold subject to its mortgage, or one of the mortgages is
transferred. The rules on the subject are now that there can be no consolidation
unless each of the following four conditions is satisfied.

(1) RESERVATION OF RIGHT. One or both of the mortgage deeds must show an **25–057**
intent[388] to allow consolidation.[389] The Law of Property Act 1925 excludes
consolidation unless a contrary intention is expressed in "the mortgage deeds
or one of them".[390] These words may confine consolidation to cases where
each mortgage (or possibly one of them) is by deed.

Where the title to the land is registered, there was once doubt as to whether
it is possible to exclude the provision of the Law of Property Act 1925
explained above, and thereby reserve the right to consolidate.[391] However, the
Land Registration Rules 2003, make express provision for consolidation,[392]
and there is no doubt that it is permissible under the Land Registration Act
2002.[393]

---

[385] *Cummins v Fletcher* (1880) 14 Ch D 699 at 708.
[386] *Willic v Lugg* (1761) 2 Eden 78 at 80.
[387] *Cummins v Fletcher* (1880) 14 Ch D 699.
[388] See *Hughes v Britannia Permanent Benefit BS* [1906] 2 Ch. 607.
[389] LPA 1925 s.93(i) (re-enacting in substance CA 1881 s.17); *Re Salmon* [1903] 1 K.B.
147.
[390] s.93(1).
[391] This was because of the wording of an obscure provision in the now repealed LRA 1925
s.25(3)(ii).
[392] r.110.
[393] Land Registry Form CC is both necessary and sufficient. See Ruoff & Roper, 27–016, where
the procedure is explained. See below, para.25–066.

25–058   (2) REDEMPTION DATES PASSED. In the case of both mortgages, the legal dates for redemption must have passed.[394] Consolidation is an equitable doctrine and does not override the legal right to redeem on the date agreed.

25–059   (3) SAME MORTGAGOR. Both mortgages must have been made by the same mortgagor.[395] Mortgages made by different mortgagors can never be consolidated, even if both properties later come into the same hands. This is so even if X makes one mortgage and Y, as trustee for X, makes the other,[396] or if A makes one mortgage and A and B jointly make the other.[397] But it is immaterial whether or not the mortgages were made to the same mortgagees.

25–060   (4) SIMULTANEOUS UNIONS OF MORTGAGES AND EQUITIES. There must have been a time when both the mortgages were vested in one person and simultaneously both the equities of redemption were vested in another.[398] If this state of affairs once existed, it is immaterial that the equities of redemption have subsequently become vested in different persons. The one exception is where consolidation is based on an express contractual right to consolidate, and not merely on the equitable doctrine. In such a case, a purchaser of the equity of redemption takes subject to the risk of the consolidation of mortgages subsequently created by the mortgagor,[399] except where the mortgagee had notice of the purchase before making the subsequent loans.[400] As for the mortgagee, both mortgages must be vested in him when he seeks to consolidate, so that there can be no consolidation if one is vested in him solely and the other jointly.[401]

25–061   *(c) Examples.* There is no need to illustrate (1) and (2), but the following examples may be given of the operation of (3) and (4).
(i)

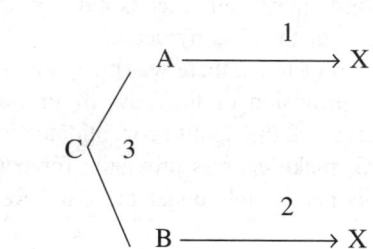

This represents the following steps:

---

[394] *Cummins v Fletcher*, above.
[395] *Sharp v Richards* [1909] 1 Ch. 109.
[396] *Re Raggett* (1880) 16 Ch D 117 at 119.
[397] *Thorneycroft v Crockett* (1848) 2 H.L.C. 239; *Cummins v Fletcher* (1880) 14 Ch D 699 at 710.
[398] See *Pledge v White* [1896] A.C. 187 at 198.
[399] *Andrew v City Permanent Benefit BS* (1881) 44 L.T. 641; *sed quaere.*
[400] *Hughes v Britannia Permanent Benefit BS* [1906] 2 Ch. 607, borrowing from the law of tacking (below, para.26–053).
[401] *Riley v Hall* (1898) 79 L.T. 244.

(a) A mortgages one property to X.

(b) B mortgages another property to X.

(c) C purchases the equities of redemption of both properties.

There can be no consolidation here, even though condition (4) is satisfied, for the mortgages were made by different mortgagors.

(ii)   25–062

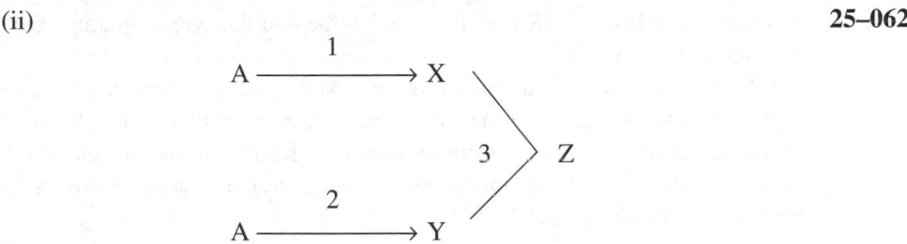

(a) A mortgages one property to X.

(b) A mortgages another property to Y.

(c) Z purchases both mortgages.

Here Z can consolidate, provided conditions (1) and (2) are satisfied. Condition (3) is satisfied, and so is condition (4). Similarly X could consolidate if he acquired Y's mortgage, or Y if he acquired X's.

(iii)   25 063

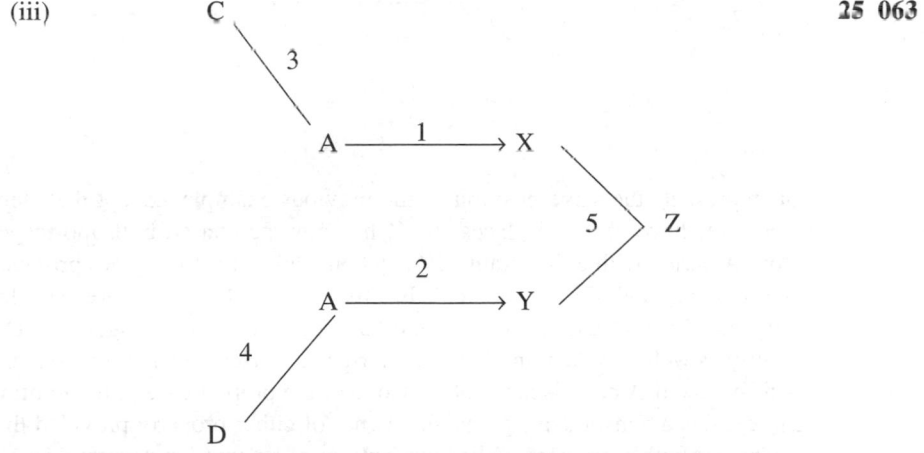

(a) A mortgages one property to X.

(b) A mortgages another property to Y.

(c) C purchases the first property.

(d) D purchases the second property.

(e) Z purchases both mortgages.

There can be no consolidation here, for condition (4) is not satisfied. It is true that at one stage (after step (b)), both equities were in one person's hands, and that at another stage (step (e)) both mortgages were in another person's hands; but at no one moment have both these conditions obtained. The equities of redemption separated before the mortgages came together.[402] The result would be the same if only one of the properties had been sold (e.g. if step (d) were omitted), since it would be equally true that the equities were separated before the mortgages were united.

If C instead of D had purchased the second property, Z could have consolidated, even though at the time of C's purchase no right to consolidate had arisen; the purchaser of two or more properties from a single mortgagor takes subject to the risk of the mortgages coming into the same hands and so permitting consolidation.[403]

25–064   (iv)

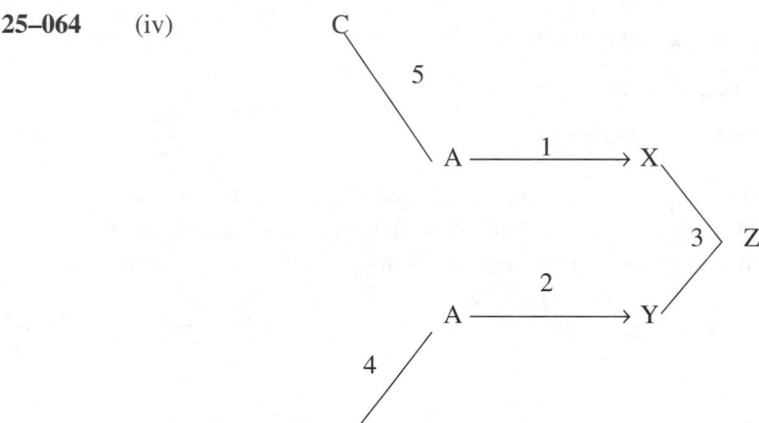

This represents the same position as the previous example, except that steps (c) and (e) have changed places. As Z has now purchased both mortgages before A parted with either equity, Z may consolidate the mortgages provided conditions (1) and (2) are satisfied. In this event, if C seeks to redeem his mortgage, Z can refuse redemption unless C purchases the mortgage on D's property as well as redeeming his own mortgage.[404] Here again it would make no difference if A had disposed of only one of the properties, e.g. by omitting step (e): Z can consolidate against the owner of either property provided that he acquired both mortgages while both equities of redemption were still in A's hands.[405]

---

[402] *Harter v Coleman* (1882) 19 Ch D 630; *Minter v Carr* [1894] 3 Ch. 498. *Beevor v Luck* (1867) L.R. 4 Eq. 537 is no longer law.
[403] *Vint v Padget* (1858) 2 De G. & J. 611 at 613; *Pledge v White* [1896] A.C. 187.
[404] *Jennings v Jordan* (1880) 6 App.Cas 698 at 701.
[405] *Jennings v Jordan* (1880) 6 App.Cas. 698 at 701.

(d) Three or more mortgages. These rules of consolidation apply equally **25–065** when it is sought to consolidate more than two mortgages. Sometimes it will be found that while mortgage I can be consolidated with mortgages II and III, there is no right to consolidate mortgages II and III with each other, e.g. if only mortgage I contains a consolidation clause. Examples containing more than two mortgages are best worked out by taking the mortgages in pairs and applying the rules to each pair in turn.

(e) Application of doctrine. The nature of the mortgages or of the property **25–066** mortgaged is immaterial. There can be consolidation even if one mortgage is legal and one equitable,[406] or if both are equitable,[407] or if one mortgage is of personalty and the other of realty,[408] or if both are mortgages of personalty.[409] The doctrine has even been applied, though probably wrongly, to two mortgages on the same property.[410] It is immaterial whether the equity of redemption has been conveyed outright or whether it has merely been mortgaged,[411] or has devolved under a will or intestacy, or under the bankruptcy law.[412] Thus if a mortgagee has a right of consolidation, it is effective against all the mortgagor's successors in title.

(f) Danger to purchaser

(1) UNREGISTERED LAND. It will be seen that the doctrine of consolidation **25–067** makes it dangerous to buy property subject to a mortgage without careful inquiry, for it may be that the mortgagor may also have mortgaged other property and both mortgages may be held by the same mortgagee. The difficulty is that the purchaser has no means of finding out about this if the two properties are held by different titles; and it is no defence that he bought without notice of the other mortgage,[413] for the right to redeem which he must assert against the mortgagee is an equitable right, and therefore subject to prior equitable interests, irrespective of notice.[414] Even if his own mortgage reserves no right to consolidate, the other mortgage may well do so and that will suffice.[415] If he redeems the other mortgage he of course becomes a transferee and takes the benefit of it.[416] But, unreasonable as it seems, he may

---

[406] *Cracknall v Janson* (1879) 11 Ch D 1 at 18.

[407] *Tweedale v Tweedale* (1857) 23 Beav. 341.

[408] *Tassel v Smith* (1858) 2 De G. & J. 713.

[409] See *Watts v Symes* (1851) 1 De G.M. & G. 240.

[410] *Re Salmon* [1903] 1 K.B. 147. *Pace* Waldock, *Mortgages*, 285, this is not a question of tacking, i.e. of priority, but of the right to redeem. But *Re Salmon* is not a convincing case. A mortgagor who redeems cannot keep the mortgage alive to the prejudice of a mortgagee (below, para.25–101), and if he redeems the earlier mortgage (i.e. that which is the better secured) he improves the mortgagee's security for the later mortgage. How the principle of consolidation (that redemption of one property alone may impair the security given by the other) can then fit the case is inexplicable.

[411] *Beevor v Luck* (1867) L.R. 4 Eq. 537 at 546.

[412] *Selby v Pomfret* (1861) 3 De G.F. & J. 595.

[413] *Ireson v Denn* (1796) 2 Cox Eq. 425.

[414] The legal estate obtained from the mortgagor is of no avail, since it is subject to the mortgage term and that can only be cleared off by exercising the equitable right to redeem.

[415] Above, para.25–057.

[416] Below, para.25–102.

then have to pay the penalty of the mortgagee's imprudence as a lender, since consolidation is most likely to be enforced where the security for the other mortgage is insufficient.

25–068   (2) REGISTERED LAND. The potential danger to a purchaser of registered land subject to a registered charge is less than it is where the title is unregistered. This is because where the right to consolidate relates to a specified charge, the registrar will require the production of the charge in which the right is reserved (unless already registered) and details of the charges to be consolidated. Form CC must be used for this purpose. The result will be a note on the register that the specified charges are consolidated.[417]

25–069   *(g) Value of doctrine.* In practice, the right to consolidate causes less trouble than might be supposed. But as a source of risk to an innocent purchaser it is a freak of equity; it is "not one of those doctrines of the Court of Chancery which has met with general approbation".[418] There may well be doubts as to the wisdom of equity in allowing a mortgagee who has made two distinct bargains, one good and one bad, to use the success of one to rescue him from the failure of the other. But the doctrine has existed almost as long as the equity of redemption itself,[419] and is too well settled to be questioned.[420]

25–070   **5. Right to tack.** This is considered below,[421] since it is part of the subject of priorities.

Section 2. Rights Common to Both Parties

A. Power of Leasing

25–071   **1. The mortgagor.** The most important right common to both parties is the right of leasing the mortgaged property. Apart from any statutory or contractual provisions, the position of the mortgagor as soon as he has executed a mortgage is that he has (or, in the normal case of a charge by way of legal mortgage, is deemed to have) granted a long term of years to the mortgagee and retains merely the reversion on the lease together with an equity of redemption. But since the mortgagor is usually left in possession of the land he needs an owner's usual powers of management. Any lease which he purports to grant will at least be binding as between him and his tenant, as a lease by estoppel,[422] and so the mortgagor may sue or distrain for the rent.[423]

---

[417] See Ruoff & Roper, 27.016.
[418] *Pledge v White* [1896] A.C. 187 at 192, per Lord Davey.
[419] It first appeared in *Bovey v Skipwith* (1671) 1 Ch.Cas. 201.
[420] *Pledge v White*, above.
[421] Below. para.26–056.
[422] *Webb v Austin* (1844) 7 Man. & G. 701; *Cuthbertson v Irving* (1859) 4 H. & N. 742 at 754 (affirmed (1860) 6 H. & N. 135); presumably also it is a good lease in equity. For leases by estoppel, see above, para.17–102.
[423] *Trent v Hunt* (1853) 9 Exch. 14.

But this is subject to the paramount rights of the mortgagee.[424] The mortgagee is always entitled to take possession or to require the rent (including even arrears[425]) to be paid to himself,[426] though in the latter case he must make an effective demand for payment in order to defeat the claim of the mortgagor.[427] The mortgagor cannot, of course, fetter the mortgagee's right to take possession[428]; against the mortgagee therefore the tenant has no defence.[429] Similarly the statutory provisions about protection from eviction after a tenancy has ended do not fetter the mortgagee.[430]

2. The mortgagee. The mortgagee always has the legal right to possession and the power to grant leases; but such leases, like the mortgage itself, will usually be subject to the equity of redemption.[431] Again, therefore, the tenant from the mortgagee will have no security against the other party to the mortgage. **25–072**

3. The statutory power. It will be seen from this that once property has been mortgaged, a satisfactory lease could be made only with the concurrence of both mortgagor and mortgagee. The mortgagee's concurrence might be implied from some later act[432]; but it would not be implied from his mere knowledge of the lease, even though the mortgagor was in default at the time.[433] The only satisfactory solution was for the mortgage to confer upon either or both of the parties a power to grant binding leases.[434] The Law of Property Act 1925[435] confers such a power, though subject to contrary agreement.[436] It provides as follows. **25–073**

(a) Power to lease. A power to grant leases and to make agreements for leases[437] which will be binding on both mortgagor and mortgagee is exercisable: **25–074**

---

[424] LPA 1925 s.98. The difficulties arising from the language of this provision, discussed in *Fairclough v Marshall* (1878) 4 Ex.D. 37 and *Matthews v Usher* [1900] 2 Q.B. 535, are perhaps best explained by Farwell L.J. in *Turner v Walsh* [1909] 2 K.B. 484 at 495.

[425] *Moss v Gallimore* (1779) 1 Doug.K.B. 279.

[426] *Pope v Biggs* (1829) 9 B. & C. 245; *Underhay v Read* (1887) 20 QBD 209.

[427] See *Kitchen's Trustee v Madders* [1950] Ch. 134, below, para.25–114.

[428] See *Thunder d. Weaver v Beicher* (1803) 3 East 449.

[429] *Rogers v Humphreys* (1835) 4 A. & E. 299 at 313; *Dudley & District Benefit BS v Emerson* [1949] Ch. 707; *Rust v Goodale* [1957] Ch. 33.

[430] *Bolton BS v Cobb* [1966] 1 W.L.R. 1. For these provisions, see above, para.19–034.

[431] See *Franklinski v Ball* (1864) 33 Beav. 560 at 563, 564; *Chapman v Smith* [1907] 2 Ch. 97 at 102.

[432] See *Parker v Braithwaite* [1952] 2 All E.R. 837; *Stroud BS v Delamont* [1960] 1 W.L.R. 431, approved in *Chatsworth Properties Ltd v Effiom* [1971] 1 W.L.R. 144. For a more recent example, see *Mann v Nijar* [1998] E.G.C.S. 188.

[433] *Taylor v Ellis* [1960] Ch. 368; and see *Barclays Bank Ltd v Kiley* [1961] 1 W.L.R. 1050; *Mann v Nijar*, above.

[434] See e.g. *Carpenter v Parker* (1857) 3 C.B. (N.S.) 206.

[435] LPA 1925 s.99.

[436] For registered title, the mortgagee and mortgagor have power to make a disposition of any kind permitted by the general law in relation to an interest of that description, other than a legal sub-mortgage, s.23(1), (2) LRA 2002 confirms.

[437] LPA 1925 s.99(17); see below, para.25–075.

(1) by the mortgagee if he is in possession[438] or has appointed a receiver who is still acting[439] (in which case the mortgagee may by writing delegate his powers of leasing to the receiver[440]); otherwise,

(2) by the mortgagor, being in possession.[441]

In fact, when a mortgagee grants a lease, he thereby takes possession of the land.[442] It follows therefore that a lease granted by a first mortgagee will be binding on any subsequent mortgagee, even if, under the terms of a subsequent mortgage, no lease may be granted without that mortgagee's consent.[443] Were this not so, the priority enjoyed by the first mortgagee would be meaningless.[444]

25–075   *(b) Term of lease.* If the mortgage was made after 1925, a lease may be granted for not more than:

(i) 50 years for agricultural or occupation purposes;

(ii) 999 years for building.[445]

25–076   *(c) Conditions of lease.* To fall within the statutory powers, any lease granted must comply with the following conditions:

(1) It must be limited to take effect in possession not later than 12 months after its date.[446]

(2) It must reserve the best rent reasonably obtainable, and with certain qualifications, no fine may be taken.[447] But in a building lease the rent may be nominal for not more than the first five years,[448] although the lessee must (whether the rent is nominal or not) agree to erect, improve or repair buildings within five years if he has not done so already.[449]

(3) It must contain a covenant by the lessee for payment of rent and a condition of re-entry on the rent not being paid for a specified period not exceeding 30 days.[450]

---

[438] LPA 1925 s.99(2).
[439] LPA 1925 s.99(19).
[440] LPA 1925 above, para.25–038.
[441] LPA 1925 s.99(1).
[442] *Mexborough UDC v Harrison* [1964] 1 W.L.R. 733 at 736.
[443] *Berkshire Capital Funding Ltd v Street* [1999] 25 E.G. 191.
[444] *Berkshire Capital Funding Ltd v Street*, above at 193.
[445] LPA 1925 s.99(3). The subsection lays down different periods in respect of mortgages granted before 1926.
[446] LPA 1925 s.99(5).
[447] LPA 1925 s.99(6).
[448] LPA 1925 s.99(10).
[449] LPA 1925 s.99(9).
[450] LPA 1925 s.99(7).

(4) A counterpart of the lease must be executed by the lessee and delivered to the lessor.[451] A counterpart of any lease granted by the mortgagor must be delivered within one month to the mortgagee; but the lessee is not concerned to see that this is done,[452] and non-compliance does not invalidate the lease, although it makes the power of sale exercisable.[453]

These regulations, however, do not prevent informal transactions, since the definition of "lease" here extends, "as far as circumstances admit ... to an agreement, whether in writing or not, for leasing or letting".[454] An oral lease or agreement may thus be a valid exercise of the power. However, it is not certain whether the conditions, mentioned above, as to covenants and conditions of re-entry apply in such a case.[455] A lease by the mortgagor is not invalidated merely because it includes furniture and sporting rights not comprised in the mortgage[456]; but it will not bind the mortgagee if it includes other land at a single inclusive rent.[457]   **25–077**

(d) Non-compliance. By statute,[458] if a lease does not comply with the statutory requirements but is made in good faith, and the tenant has entered under it, it may nevertheless take effect in equity as a contract for a lease, varied so as to comply with the requirements. This provision for assisting defective leases made under powers has already been encountered elsewhere.[459]   **25–078**

(e) Contrary agreement. The statutory power may be either excluded[460] or extended[461] by agreement of the parties expressed in the mortgage or otherwise in writing. It could not, however, be excluded in any mortgage of agricultural land that was made after March 1, 1948 but before September 1, 1995.[462] Nor can its exclusion hamper the power of the court to order the grant of a new lease of business premises under the Landlord and Tenant Act   **25–079**

---

[451] LPA 1925 s.99(8).

[452] LPA 1925 s.99(11).

[453] *Trustee v Lawrence* [1912] 1 Ch. 789 (above, para.25–015); and see *Rhodes v Dalby* [1971] 1 W.L.R. 1325.

[454] LPA 1925 s.99(17).

[455] *Pawson v Revell* [1958] 2 Q.B. 360. Wolst. & C. i, p.200, retains unchanged the passage doubted in the case at p.370 and *Rhodes v Dalby* [1971] 1 W.L.R. 1325 now supports the book in saying that the conditions do not apply.

[456] *Brown v Peto* [1900] 1 Q.B. 346 at 354 (aff'd [1900] 2 Q.B. 653).

[457] *King v Bird* [1909] 1 K.B. 837.

[458] LPA 1925 s.152. See *Pawson v Revell* [1958] 2 Q.B. 360 (omission of condition of re-entry).

[459] Below, Appendix para.A–062.

[460] LPA 1925 s.99(13) ("as far as a contrary intention is not expressed"). Where title is registered, any exclusion of the powers must be noted on the register to be effective against a disponee: see LRA 2002 s.26(2). For comment on the operation of this rule under the LRA 1925 see (1998) 114 L.Q.R. 354 (M. Robinson).

[461] LPA 1925 s.99(14).

[462] LPA 1925 s.99(13A) (inserted by ATA 1995 s.31). Mortgages of agricultural land made after August 1995 may therefore exclude the statutory power.

1954.[463] In practice, most mortgages expressly exclude the power, and in addition the mortgagor is often required to covenant not to make any letting without the mortgagee's consent.

25–080   **4. Leases not under the statutory power.** If the power is excluded and the mortgagor nevertheless grants an unauthorised lease, the lease is void as against the mortgagee and his successors in title[464] (unless they are estopped from asserting this[465]), but valid as between the parties to it. The statutory powers of leasing do not deprive the parties of their common law rights to create leases not binding upon each other. For example, if a mortgage contains a covenant by the mortgagor not to exercise the statutory power of leasing without the mortgagee's written consent, the mortgagor may nevertheless grant a yearly tenancy which binds the mortgagor under the principle of estoppel but which does not bind the mortgagee.[466]

Where a lease has been granted prior to the mortgage, the mortgagee will of course take subject to it[467] even if the mortgage prohibits any further letting.[468] In some cases, the tenant may agree to waive his priority,[469] but this cannot be validly done where the tenancy is protected under the Rent Act 1977.[470]

B. Power of Accepting Surrenders of Leases

25–081   If the parties have not expressed a contrary intention, either in the mortgage or otherwise in writing,[471] the Law of Property Act 1925[472] enables a surrender of any lease or tenancy to be effected, binding the parties to the mortgage, on the following terms.

---

[463] LTA 1954 s.36(4). For the Act, see above, para.22–003.

[464] *Rust v Goodale* [19571 Ch. 33; *Quennell v Maltby* [1979] 1 W.L.R. 318 at 323; *Britannia BS v Earl* [1990] 1 W.L.R. 422.

[465] *Lever Finance Ltd v Needlemans' Trustee* [1956] Ch. 375. See (1978) 128 N.L.J. 773 (A. Walker).

[466] See *Iron Trades Employers Insurance Association Ltd v Union Land and House Investors Ltd* [1937] Ch. 313. But note the requirement that the mortgagee may be subject to the unauthorised tenant's rights under the Mortgage Repossessions (Protection of Tenants etc.) Act 2010, above para.25–024.

[467] Provided, in registered land, that the tenancy achieves priority within LRA 2002 s.29. This is most likely as the tenancy is likely to amount to an unregistered interest which overrides within LRA 2002 Sch.3.

[468] *Barclays Bank Plc v Zaroovabli* [1997] Ch. 321 (tenancy granted after the charge was executed but before it was registered held binding on the mortgagee); see [1997] C.L.J. 496 (D. G. Barnsley). For a survey of the rights of such tenants as against a mortgagee who seeks possession, see [1991] J.S.W.L. 220 (D. G. Bamsley).

[469] There is no direct authority on this point, but it seems correct in principle. cf. *Skipton BS v Clayton* (1993) 66 P. & C.R. 223 at 228, 229.

[470] *Woolwich BS v Dickman* [1996] 3 All E.R. 204; [1997] Conv. 402 (J. Morgan). This conclusion follows from RA 1977 s.98(1) (restricting the grounds on which possession can be given against a protected or statutory tenant). cf. *Appleton v Aspin* [1988] 1 W.L.R. 410.

[471] LPA 1925 s.100(7).

[472] s.100.

1. Power to accept. The surrender may be accepted: 25–082

    (i) by the mortgagee, if he is in possession[473] or has appointed a receiver who still acts[474] (in which case the mortgagee may by writing delegate his powers of accepting surrenders to the receiver[475]); or

    (ii) by the mortgagor, if he is in possession.[476]

2. Conditions of surrender. For the surrender to be valid: 25–083

    (i) an authorised lease of the property must be granted to take effect in possession within one month of the surrender;

    (ii) the term of the new lease must not be shorter than the unexpired residue of the surrendered lease; and

    (iii) the rent reserved by the new lease must not be less than the rent reserved by the surrendered lease.[477]

The statutory power of accepting a surrender is thus exercisable only for the purpose of replacing one lease by another; and a surrender which does not comply with these conditions is void.[478] But the power may be extended by an agreement in writing, whether in the mortgage or not.[479]

Section 3. Rights of the Mortgagor

A. Right of Redemption

I. PROTECTION OF THE MORTGAGOR

The distinction between the mortgagor's legal right to redeem and his equita-   25–084
ble right to redeem has already been considered.[480] The latter right, being the creature of equity, must be protected by equity; for otherwise the mortgagee, who often can bring pressure to bear on a prospective mortgagor by threatening to withhold the loan,[481] might be able to defeat the whole purpose of a

---

[473] LPA 1925 s.100(2).
[474] LPA 1925 s.100(13).
[475] LPA 1925 s.100(13).
[476] LPA 1925 s.100(1).
[477] LPA 1925 s.100(5).
[478] See, e.g. *Barclays Bank Ltd v Stasek* [1957] Ch. 28; (1957) 73 L.Q.R. 14 (R.E.M.).
[479] LPA 1925 s.100(10).
[480] Above, para.24–014.
[481] "For necessitous men are not, truly speaking, free men, but, to answer a present exigency, will submit to any terms that the crafty may impose upon them": *Vernon v Bethell* (1762) 2 Eden 110 at 113, per Lord Henley L.C.

mortgage, i.e. that it should provide security and nothing more. The mortgagor's equity of redemption is inviolable; the maxim is "once a mortgage, always a mortgage".[482] The principle is applied in two ways.

25–085   **1. The test of a mortgage is in substance, not form.** If a transaction is in substance a mortgage, equity will treat it as such, even if it is dressed up in some other guise,[483] as by the documents being cast in the form of an absolute conveyance.[484] Thus if a mortgage is expressed in the form of a conveyance with an option for the mortgagor to repurchase the property in a year's time, the mortgagor is entitled to redeem it even after the year has expired.[485] "In all these cases the question is what was the real intention of the parties?",[486] and parol evidence is admissible to show what it was.[487]

25–086   **2. No clogs on the equity.** There must be no clog or fetter on the equity of redemption. This means both that the mortgagor cannot be prevented from eventually redeeming his property on repayment of the sum advanced together with interest due and the mortgagee's proper costs, and also that, after redemption, he is free from all the conditions of the mortgage. This will be considered under the two heads.

(a) No irredeemability[488]

25–087   (1) REDEMPTION. "Redemption is of the very nature and essence of a mortgage, as mortgages are regarded in equity."[489] The right exists whether or not it has been expressly reserved in the mortgage.[490] It is inconsistent with the very nature of a mortgage that it shall be totally irredeemable[491] or that the right of redemption shall be confined to certain persons (such as the mortgagor and the heirs male of his body[492]) or to a limited period (such as the joint lives of the mortgagor and mortgagee[493] or the life of the mortgagor alone[494]), or to

---

[482] *Seton v Slade* (1802) 7 Ves. 265 at 273, per Lord Eldon L.C.

[483] See *Williams v Owen* (1840) 5 My. & Cr. 303 at 306; *Re Watson* (1890) 25 QBD 27.

[484] *England v Codrington* (1758) 1 Eden 169; *Barnhart v Greenshields* (1853) 9 Moo.P.C. 18.

[485] See *Danby v Read* (1675) Rep.t.Finch 226; *Muttylol Seal v Annundochunder Sandle* (1849) 5 Moo.Ind.App. 72; *Croft v Powel* (1738) 2 Com. 603; *Waters v Mynn* (1850) 15 L.T. (OS) 157; cf. *Salt v Marquess of Northampton* [1892] A.C. 1 (Lord Bramwell's attack on the equity of redemption as an interference with freedom of contract is entertaining). The test works in reverse, so an apparent mortgage may be regarded as a sale-purchase agreement which does enable the "mortgagee" to purchase the property, *Warnborough Ltd v Garmite Ltd* [2006] EWHC 10 (Ch) (2006) 3 E.G. 120 (CS).

[486] *Manchester Sheffield and Lincolnshire Ry v North Central Wagon Co* (1888) 13 App.Cas. 554 at 568, per Lord Macnaghten.

[487] *Lincoln v Wright* (1859) 4 De G. & J. 16; *Barton v Bank of New South Wales* (1890) 15 App.Cas. 379.

[488] *Fairclough v Swan Brewery Co Ltd* [1912] A.C. 565 at 570.

[489] *Noakes & Co Ltd v Rice* [1902] A.C. 24 at 30, per Lord Macnaghten.

[490] *National Westminster Bank Plc v Powney* (1989) 60 P. & C.R. 420 at 438 (omitted from the report in [1991] Ch. 339).

[491] *Re Wells* [1933] Ch. 29 at 52.

[492] *Howard v Harris* (1683) 1 Vern. 190.

[493] *Spurgeon v Collier* (1758) 1 Eden 55.

[494] *Newcomb v Bonham* (1681) 1 Vern. 7; *Salt v Marquess of Northampton* [1892] A.C. 1.

part only of the mortgaged property.[495] Thus if the property mortgaged is a lease together with an option to renew it, or to purchase the freehold, and the mortgagee exercises the option, the mortgagor is entitled on redemption not only to the lease but also, on paying the cost of acquisition, to the fruits of exercising the option.[496]

(2) EXCLUSION OF REDEMPTION. Any express stipulation which is incon-   **25–088**
sistent with the right of redemption will be ineffective. No mortgagee can secure, as a condition of the mortgage, that the property shall become his absolutely when some specified event occurs.[497] In all such cases the owner of the equity of redemption may redeem as if there had been no such restriction. If, for example, a term of the mortgage agreement gives the mortgagee an option to purchase the mortgaged property, that term is void, as repugnant to the equity of redemption, even though the transaction is not in itself oppressive to the mortgagor.[498] In so far as the term gives such a right before the equitable right to redeem has arisen or preserves such a right after the exercise of the contractual right, it is also inconsistent with the mortgage contract and may be held invalid at law.[499] But a mere right of pre-emption (i.e. of first refusal) is probably unobjectionable if its terms are fair, since the mortgagor cannot be compelled to sell.[500]

Once the mortgage has been made, equity will not intervene if the mortgagor, by a separate and independent transaction, gives the mortgagee an interest in the property, even if it may wholly or partly destroy the equity of redemption, such as an option to purchase[501] or a long lease.[502] Equity will protect the mortgagor while he is in the defenceless position of one seeking a loan; once he has obtained his loan, this protection is not needed. But where a mortgagor seeks to escape from his mortgagee by procuring a transfer of the mortgage to a new mortgagee, there is in effect a new loan, and any option obtained by the new mortgagee will be subject to the rules stated above.[503]

---

[495] See *Re Wells*, above; *Salt v Marquess of Northampton*, above.

[496] *Nelson v Hannam* [1943] Ch. 59.

[497] *Toomes v Conset* (1745) 3 Atk. 261.

[498] *Samuel v Jarrah Timber and Wood Paving Corporation Ltd* [1904] A.C. 323, where the House of Lords expressed a distaste for the rule in the case of a fair commercial bargain, but felt bound to apply it. cf. *J. A. Pye (Oxford) Estates Ltd v Ambrose* [1994] N.P.C. 53 (21-year option to purchase granted in return for £8,000, secured by a mortgage. The loan was only repayable if the option was not exercised. There was no clog on the equity, because the mortgage was only enforceable if the option was spent).

[499] *Jones v Morgan* [2001] EWCA Civ 995, (2001) Lloyd's Rep Bank 323, relying on Lord Parker in *G and C Kregliner v New Patagonia Meat and Cold Storage Company Ltd*, above at 50, 55–56.

[500] See *Orby v Trigg* (1722) 9 Mod. 2, where the only objection to a right of pre-emption was that the mortgagee exercised it too late and misled the mortgagor.

[501] *Reeve v Lisle* [1902] A.C. 461. In *Jones v Morgan*, above, Pill L.J. dissented on the ground that the option was contained in a later agreement that could be regarded as a genuinely separate contract, rather than part of the mortgage transaction. He was in full agreement with the majority's analysis of the law.

[502] *Alex Lobb (Garages) Ltd v Total Oil Great Britain Ltd* [1983] 1 W.L.R. 87 at 98, 99 (51-year lease of part of property). This point was not considered on appeal: [1985] 1 W.L.R. 173.

[503] *Lewis v Frank Love Ltd* [1961] 1 W.L.R. 261. For transfer of mortgages, see below.

25–089   (3) POSTPONEMENT OF REDEMPTION. A provision postponing the date of redemption until some future period longer than the customary six months may be valid, provided the mortgage as a whole is not so oppressive and unconscionable that equity would not enforce it,[504] and provided it does not make the equitable right to redeem illusory.[505] The question here is one of degree. An excessive postponement of the redemption date may in itself be oppressive and thus a clog on the equity of redemption. In one case a lease for 20 years was mortgaged on conditions which prevented its redemption until six weeks before the end of the term. Such a provision rendered the equitable right to redeem illusory; for it prohibited redemption until the lease was nearly valueless and redemption was not worth having. The mortgagor was accordingly allowed to redeem after only three years.[506]

25–090   In the case of a wasting security, therefore, any long postponement of the right to redeem is likely to be objectionable. But in other cases it is often not so. In *Knightsbridge Estate Trust Ltd v Byrne*,[507] the Knightsbridge company had mortgaged a large number of properties to an insurance company on terms that repayment should be made by half-yearly instalments over a period of 40 years. The mortgagees, for their part, agreed not to call in the money in advance of the due dates. Six years later the Knightsbridge company sought a declaration that the company was entitled to redeem the mortgage, claiming, inter alia, that it was oppressive that they should be unable to redeem their properties for 40 years. However, on this ground their action failed, for it was held that in the circumstances the agreement was a perfectly fair one and the contractual right of redemption was in no way illusory. The court is concerned to see that the essential requirements of a mortgage are observed, and that oppressive or unconscionable terms are not enforced,[508] but it is naturally reluctant to interfere with a contract made as a matter of business by parties well able to look after themselves. "The directors of a trading company in search of financial assistance are certainly in a very different position from that of an impecunious landowner in the toils of a crafty money-lender."[509] Even though a business contract is unlikely to be struck down as being

---

[504] *Knightsbridge Estates Trust Ltd v Byrne* [1939] Ch. 441 at 463 (affirmed on other grounds [1940] A.C. 613).

[505] *Knightsbridge Estates Trust Ltd v Byrne*, above at 456.

[506] *Fairclough v Swan Brewery Co Ltd* [1912] A.C. 565; cf. *Davis v Symons* [1934] Ch. 442, as explained in the Knightsbridge case, above, at 460–462 (same principle applied to mortgage of insurance policies due to mature before redemption date 20 years distant). *Contrast Santley v Wilde* [1899] 2 Ch. 474, where it was held by the Court of Appeal that a 10-year lease of a theatre was irredeemable because part of the mortgagee's security was a covenant by the mortgagor to pay one-third of the profits to the mortgagee during the whole remainder of the lease. The decision proceeded on the ground that without the covenant there would have been insufficient security. It has been criticised in the House of Lords: *Noakes & Co Ltd v Rice* [1902] A.C. 24 at 31, 34.

[507] [1939] Ch. 441; affirmed on other grounds [1940] A.C. 613.

[508] *Knightsbridge Estates Trust Ltd v Byrne* [1939] Ch. 441 at 457.

[509] *Samuel v Jarrah Timber and Wood Paving Corp Ltd* [1904] A.C. 323 at 327, per Lord Macnaghten.

oppressive or unconscionable, it may, however, be in unlawful restraint of trade.[510] The test in such cases is whether the restraint is:

(i) reasonable between the parties; and

(ii) not contrary to the public interest.[511]

If one element in the transaction is a mortgage which is to be irredeemable during the period of unlawful restraint, the fetter on redemption may be held inoperative.[512] A significant factor in determining whether the tie is unlawful is, in practice, its length.[513] It is possible that the validity of such tied-house arrangements may be challenged under Article 85 of the Treaty of Rome rather than on grounds of restraint of trade.[514]

(4) DEBENTURES. The decision of the Court of Appeal in *Knightsbridge* **25–091** *Estates Trust Ltd v Byrne*[515] is now the leading case on postponement of redemption. It was affirmed by the House of Lords,[516] but on the ground that the security was a debenture. A debenture is a written acknowledgment of indebtedness made by a company, and it is usually secured by a mortgage or charge on some property of the company. A factory building may, for example, be mortgaged to trustees for the debenture holders; and even an ordinary mortgage by a company appears to be a debenture. Mortgages created to secure debentures form a statutory exception to the general rule prohibiting irredeemability,[517] since it is provided by the Companies Act 2006[518] that debentures may be made irredeemable, or redeemable only on the happening of a contingency or the expiration of a period of time.

(5) REGULATED MORTGAGES. In the relatively few cases where the mortgage **25–092** is regulated by the Consumer Credit Act 1974 (as amended by the Consumer Credit Act 2006),[519] the mortgagor is entitled to repay the loan at any time,

---

[510] It should be emphasised that this is a distinct ground of invalidity that is unconnected with the equitable doctrine of clogs and fetters.

[511] See, e.g. *Esso Petroleum Co Ltd v Harper's Garage (Stourport) Ltd* [1968] A.C. 269 at 300.

[512] *Esso Petroleum Co Ltd v Harper's Garage (Stourport) Ltd*, above, (mortgagor to sell only mortgagee's brand of petrol for 21 years and to redeem only by instalments over 21 years: restraint held excessive and mortgage held redeemable; a similar agreement in relation to another garage for less than five years was, by contrast, upheld as valid).

[513] See *Alec Lobb (Garages) Ltd v Total Oil (Great Britain) Ltd* [1985] 1 W.L.R. 173 at 178, where Dillon L.J. accepted that the Esso case had laid down a "rule of thumb" that an agreement was not in restraint of trade if it lasted no longer than five years (but the court there upheld a tie that would last for at least seven years). See, e.g. *Texaco Ltd v Mulberry Filling Station Ltd* [1972] 1 W.L.R. 814. cf. [1985] Conv. 141 (P. Todd).

[514] See [1994] Conv. 150 (T. Frazer); (1998) 49 N.I.L.Q. 202 (N. Hopkins); above, para.16–032. It should be noted that the European Commission often gives exemptions from Art.85 in respect of such solus agreements.

[515] [1939] Ch. 441.

[516] [1940] A.C. 613.

[517] Strictly, however, an irredeemable debenture "is not a mortgage at all": *Samuel v Jarrah Timber and Wood Paving Corp Ltd* [1904] A.C. 323 at 330, per Lord Lindley.

[518] s.739, replacing earlier legislation.

[519] Above, para.24–044.

even before the due date; and any term of the mortgage is void to the extent that it is inconsistent with this right.[520] Thus the mortgagor has an overriding right of redemption exercisable at any time.

25–093   *(b) Redemption free from conditions in the mortgage.* The mortgagor cannot be prevented from redeeming the property free from all the conditions of the mortgage. Redemption must be complete redemption, so that the mortgagor is restored to his original position and all the liabilities of the mortgage transaction are ended.

25–094   (1) COLLATERAL ADVANTAGES. The essence of a mortgage is a loan of a certain sum of money upon security. Sometimes terms are inserted in a mortgage which give the mortgagee some other advantage in addition to his security and interest. For example, in the case of a mortgage of a public house to a brewery company the mortgagee will usually stipulate that the mortgagor shall sell only the mortgagee's beer. And in business transactions, which include an investment of money secured by mortgage, there may be other provisions giving some commercial advantage to the mortgagee. These "collateral advantages" were at one time held void,[521] for before the repeal of the usury laws in 1854[522] any such advantage was an evasion of the law limiting the rate of interest. But since 1854 the attitude has changed,[523] and it is clear that collateral advantages are objectionable only if they are unconscionable[524] or clog the equity of redemption.

An example of an unconscionable advantage is an excessive premium imposed unfairly. In one case a property company sold a house to one of its tenants, advancing £2,900 under a mortgage which made no provision for interest but which required repayment of £4,553. This premium of £1,653 was held to be an unreasonable and unconscionable collateral advantage, since it was far more than a fair rate of interest and, by making the charge exceed the value of the house, it rendered the equity of redemption worthless. The mortgagor was therefore entitled to redeem by paying £2,900 with reasonable interest fixed by the court.[525]

25–095   The court declined to intervene, on the other hand, where a company had mortgaged its business premises upon terms which deferred redemption for 10 years and indexed both principal and interest to the Swiss franc.[526] At the end of the 10 years the pound sterling had fallen to a third of its original value against the Swiss franc, so that in terms of sterling the mortgagee obtained a very large premium. But this was held in the circumstances to be neither unfair nor oppressive, even though it might be unreasonable by the standard

---

[520] ss.94, 173.

[521] *Jennings v Ward* (1705) 2 Vern. 520 at 521.

[522] Above, para.24–010.

[523] *Biggs v Hoddinott* [1898] 2 Ch. 307 at 316; *Kreglinger v New Patagonia Meat & Cold Storage Co Ltd* [1914] A.C. 25 at 54, 55; and see at 46, per Lord Mersey ("an unruly dog").

[524] See *Barrett v Hartley* (1866) L.R. 2 Eq. 789 at 795; *James v Kerr* (1889) 40 Ch D 449.

[525] *Cityland and Property (Holdings) Ltd v Dabrah* [1968] Ch. 166.

[526] *Multiservice Bookbinding Ltd v Marden* [1979] Ch. 84. As to obligations linked to foreign currencies, see above, para.19–053.

which the court would adopt if it had to settle the terms itself.[527] The court resolved the ambiguity in the earlier decisions by holding that a collateral advantage was not objectionable merely because it was unreasonable. It would be condemned only if it was unfair and unconscionable, being imposed in a morally reprehensible manner; and that could not be said of such a transaction between businessmen acting with their eyes open, even though it was a hard bargain. It is where there is some inequality of bargaining power or undue influence that the court is most disposed to grant relief. The Court of Appeal has subsequently endorsed this view.[528]

(2) INVALIDITY AFTER REDEMPTION. A collateral advantage which is not unconscionable is valid until redemption but not afterwards. The principle is illustrated by a mortgage of a public house under which the mortgagor covenants to sell only the mortgagee's beer. While the mortgage is still on foot the mortgagor is bound by the covenant.[529] But so soon as he redeems he is free from it,[530] even though it was intended to bind him for a fixed period, for otherwise he could not redeem his property completely; he mortgaged a "free house", and if he could redeem only a "tied house" he would still be fettered by the terms of the mortgage after redemption. The same principle appears in *Bradley v Carritt*,[531] where the mortgagor mortgaged to a tea broker the shares which gave him a controlling interest in a tea company. As a condition of the loan he guaranteed that the mortgagee should always remain broker to the company thereafter. The mortgagor, having paid off the mortgage, was held to be free from this apparently unlimited guarantee. Had it been otherwise he could never have disposed of his shares after redemption, for he would have been compelled to keep control of the company.

25–096

(3) VALIDITY AFTER REDEMPTION. In some cases the courts, in their desire not to unsettle commercial contracts for doctrinal reasons, have allowed collateral stipulations in mortgages to remain binding even after redemption. The leading case is *Kreglinger v New Patagonia Meat and Cold Storage Co Ltd*,[532] where the meat company had raised a loan from a firm of woolbrokers on a mortgage by way of a floating charge[533] on the company's undertaking. It was made a condition that for five years the company should not sell any sheepskins to any other person without first offering them to the woolbrokers

25–097

---

[527] Certain other onerous terms were taken into account.

[528] *Alec Lobb (Garages) Ltd v Total Oil (Great Britain) Ltd* [1985] 1 W.L.R. 173 at 183. The case involved a lease-back agreement rather than a mortgage. Dillon L.J. there explained that "the courts would only interfere in exceptional cases where as a matter of common fairness it was not right that the strong should be allowed to push the weak to the wall".

[529] *Biggs v Hoddinott* [1898] 2 Ch. 307.

[530] *Noakes & Co Ltd v Rice* [1902] A.C. 24 (covenant to buy mortgagee's beer during whole residue of mortgagor's lease: House of Lords unanimous).

[531] [1903] A.C. 253 (House of Lords divided 3–2).

[532] [1914] A.C. 25 (House of Lords unanimous); applied in *Re Cuban Land & Development Co* (1911) Ltd [1921] 2 Ch. 147; and cf. *De Beers Consolidated Mines Ltd v British South Africa Co* [1912] A.C. 52; below, para.25–097.

[533] i.e. a charge on such assets as the company had from time to time, which would "crystallise" on certain specified events occurring, and attach to the company's then assets.

at the best price obtainable elsewhere, and that the woolbrokers should have a commission on all sheepskins sold by the company to other persons. The company redeemed the property after two years and claimed to be freed from the option[534] and commission clauses. But the House of Lords held that they remained bound, on the ground that these clauses were in truth a separate agreement, part of the consideration for the mortgage but not part of the mortgage itself, and therefore no impediment to complete redemption. These principles have been applied to an exclusive sale agreement and mortgage between a garage and its supplier, on the basis that it was a commercial transaction of which the mortgage was merely a part, and therefore outside the clogs and fetters doctrine.[535]

25–098   (4) DISTINCTIONS. The reasons given for these decisions are, as a matter of logic, not entirely easy to reconcile. There is clearly a distinction between a case where the parties negotiate a loan, and the mortgagee then succeeds in getting the mortgagor to agree to a stipulation giving the mortgagee some additional advantage, and a case where from the outset the bargain is for some advantage in return for a loan.[536] In the former situation there is likely to be equality of bargaining power, whereas in the latter there is not. A condition which restricts the alienability of the mortgaged property after redemption, as in *Bradley v Carritt*, is also clearly distinguishable. It may in addition be important whether, as in *Bradley v Carritt*, specific property is bound, or whether, as in the Kreglinger case, there is merely a floating charge.[537]

A distinction that is perhaps even more important—though it is less clearly stated—is whether the borrower is a private individual or a person or company engaged in commerce. The former may require the protection of the law, the latter may not. A collateral advantage that is a term of a personal loan, is more difficult to regard as an independent transaction than one which forms part of an elaborate commercial agreement. In the former case the advantage can generally be terminated on redemption without hardship to the mortgagee. In the latter case, if the court interferes with a commercial contract, it may deprive the mortgagee of the valuable fruits of a careful investment. The test of "severability", which *Kreglinger's Case* introduced, provides a convenient but indefinable rule for dealing with such cases on their merits.

"The question is one not of form but of substance, and it can be answered in each case only by looking at all the circumstances, and not by mere

---

[534] *Quaere* whether the right was not merely a right of pre-emption; and see above, para.25–088.

[535] *Re Petrol Filling Station, Vauxhall Bridge Road, London* (1968) 20 P. & C.R. 1. The possibility that the agreement might have been in unlawful restraint of trade was held over for subsequent proceedings.

[536] See, e.g. *Biggs v Hoddinott* [1898] 2 Ch. 307 at 316, 317; *Kreglinger v New Patagonia Meat & Cold Storage Co Ltd*, above, at 39, 45, 61.

[537] See *Kreglinger's Case*, above, at 41, 42.

reliance on some abstract principle, or upon the dicta which have fallen obiter from judges in other and different cases."[538]

It is also important to consider what has been included in the mortgage. **25–099** Thus where a company agreed to grant a perpetual licence for mining on its land, and later mortgaged the land to the licensee, it was held that after redemption the agreement to grant the licence still bound the company. This was so even though the agreement for the licence expressly contemplated the subsequent mortgage, for the two transactions were substantially independent of each other.[539] When the property was mortgaged, it had already been "burdened and encumbered with the prior obligation, superior to the mortgage security, to grant the licence",[540] and so there was no clog on the equity; for on redemption "everything which had been charged was restored to the mortgagor".[541]

It should perhaps be noted that recourse to the technical doctrines of clogs and fetters has become increasingly rare, and the most recent case attracted adverse criticism from the court, despite holding for the mortgagor.[542] In part at least, this may be due to their uncertain application, but also to the institutionalised nature of mortgages and the large number of mortgage providers, few of whom are interested in anything other than a good security and regular payment of interest.[543]

II. WHO CAN REDEEM

1. Persons interested. Redemption is usually sought by the mortgagor; but **25–100** the right to redeem is not confined to him and may be exercised by any person interested in the equity of redemption,[544] however small his interest.[545] Once the mortgagor has parted with his whole interest in the property he ceases to be able to redeem[546]; but if he is subsequently sued on the covenant for payment he acquires a fresh right of redemption.[547] The right to redeem extends to assignees of the equity of redemption (even if the assignment was voluntary[548]), subsequent mortgagees,[549] unless they are statute-barred,[550] and

---

[538] *Kreglinger's Case*, above, at 39 per Lord Haldane: his speech is analysed in *Re Petrol Filling Station, Vauxhall Bridge Road, London* (1968) 20 P. & C.R. 1.

[539] *De Beers Consolidated Mines Ltd v British South Africa Co* [1912] A.C. 52. Compare the principle explained in connection with options: above, para.25–088.

[540] *De Beers Consolidated Mines Ltd v British South Africa Co*, at 66, per Lord Atkinson.

[541] *De Beers Consolidated Mines Ltd v British South Africa Co*, at 73, per Earl Loreburn L.C.

[542] *Jones v Morgan*, above, Lord Phillips M.R. noting that "the doctrine of a clog on the equity of redemption is, so it seems to me, an appendix to our law which no longer serves a useful purpose and would be better excised" at p.86.

[543] It may be material that both parties in *Jones v Morgan* were private individuals.

[544] *Pearce v Morris* (1869) 5 Ch.App. 227 at 229.

[545] *Hunter v Macklew* (1846) 5 Hare 238.

[546] Consider *Moore v Morton* [1886] W.N. 196.

[547] *Kinnaird v Trollope* (1888) 39 Ch D 636.

[548] *Howard v Harris* (1683) 1 Vern. 190.

[549] *Fell v Brown* (1787) 2 Bro CC 276.

[550] *Cotterell v Price* [1960] 1 W.L.R. 1097.

even a lessee under a lease granted by the mortgagor but not binding on the mortgagee.[551]

If several persons simultaneously seek to redeem a mortgage the first in order of priority has the first claim.[552]

25–101   **2. Spouses and "connected persons".** A spouse or civil partner who has statutory matrimonial home rights under the Family Law Act 1996,[553] will be entitled to redeem a mortgage of the matrimonial home as being a person interested in the equity of redemption, as explained above.[554] In addition, the spouse or civil partner is expressly empowered to make mortgage payments due from the other spouse or civil partner in respect of the home.[555] The spouse or civil partner is also entitled to be made a party to any action brought by the mortgagee to enforce his security[556] and if a Class F land charge has been registered, to be served with notice of the action.[557]

The Family Law Act 1996 has extended some of these rights to certain "connected persons", namely former spouses or civil partners, cohabitants and former cohabitants,[558] but only in the circumstances prescribed by the Act.[559] These are the rights to make mortgage payments due from the mortgagor,[560] and to be made a party to any action brought by the mortgagee to enforce his security.[561]

III. EFFECT OF REDEMPTION

25–102   **1. Discharge or transfer.** Where redemption is effected by the only person interested in the equity of redemption, and the mortgage redeemed is the only incumbrance on the property, the effect of redemption is to discharge the mortgage and leave the property free from incumbrances. But in other cases, as where a second mortgagee redeems the first mortgage, the effect of redemption will normally be that the person paying the money takes a transfer of the mortgage[562]; for, of course, the redemption enures to the benefit of the person redeeming, and the second mortgagee must be able to maintain the first mortgage as against the mortgagor.

25–103   **2. Redemption by mortgagor.** By contrast, if the mortgagor himself redeems a mortgage which has priority over one or more subsequent mortgages, this discharges the mortgage, and the mortgagor cannot claim to have

---

[551] *Tarn v Turner* (1888) 39 Ch D 456.
[552] *Teevan v Smith* (1882) 20 Ch D 724 at 730.
[553] Below, para.34–023.
[554] See *Hastings and Thanet BS v Goddard* [1970] 1 W.L.R. 1544.
[555] FLA 1996 s.30(3).
[556] Subject to the court being satisfied that this may affect the outcome: FLA 1996 s.55.
[557] FLA 1996 s.56; see above, para.25–023.
[558] See FLA 1996 s.54(5).
[559] For those conditions, see FLA 1996 ss.35, 36.
[560] FLA 1996 ss.35(13), 36(15).
[561] FLA 1996 s.55.
[562] cf. LPA 1925 s.115(2).

it kept alive to the prejudice of the subsequent mortgagees.[563] He "cannot derogate from his own bargain by setting up the mortgage so purchased against a second mortgagee".[564] This is so even if some third party provided him with the money.[565] Thus if the property proves insufficient to satisfy all the claims the mortgagor cannot claim priority for the amount due on the first mortgage. If the mortgagor redeems a first mortgage he therefore improves the security for any later mortgagees.

3. Subsequent purchaser. The above rule applies only to the mortgagor, **25–104** and not to later purchasers of the equity of redemption. Thus if Blackacre has been mortgaged first to A and then to B, and is then sold or mortgaged (subject to the mortgages) to X, X may pay off A's mortgage but keep it alive against B.[566] Similarly, if the sale is made not to X but to A, A can keep his mortgage alive against B. It will be presumed in such cases, in the absence of contrary evidence, that there is no intention of a merger of the two interests if it is to the advantage of the purchaser that merger should not take place.[567]

4. Right to compel transfer. Instead of redeeming, a person who is entitled **25–105** to redeem a mortgage may usually insist upon the mortgagee transferring the mortgage to a nominee of the person paying the money.[568] This right exists notwithstanding any stipulation to the contrary, and applies irrespective of the date of the mortgage,[569] though it is exercisable only upon the same terms as the right of redemption.[570] If there are competing claims they take effect in order of priority,[571] as in the case of redemption. The right is excluded, however, if the mortgagee is or has been in possession,[572] for he thereby became liable to account strictly[573] despite any transfer of the mortgage and is liable for any defaults of the transferee[574] unless he transferred under an order of the court.[575] It would thus be unfair if the mortgagor could compel him to make a transfer.[576]

---

[563] *Otter v Lord Vaux* (1856) 6 De G.M. & G. 638 (purported sale by mortgagee to mortgagor under power of sale, intended to give mortgagor a title free from claims of later mortgagees, held ineffective for this purpose); and see LPA 1925 s.115(3), recognising the rule.
[564] *Whiteley v Delaney* [1914] A.C. 132 at 145, per Lord Haldane L.C.
[565] *Parkash v Irani Finance Ltd* [1970] Ch. 101.
[566] *Adams v Angell* (1877) 5 Ch D 634; *Thorne v Cann* [1895] A.C. 11; *Whiteley v Delaney* [1914] A.C. 132.
[567] Above, para.18–072; LPA 1925 s.185. The decision in *Toulmin v Steere* (1817) 3 Mer. 210, to the effect that merger will not be presumed if the purchaser has notice of later mortgages at the time he redeems, is of doubtful authority: see *Whiteley v Delaney*, above, at 144, 145.
[568] LPA 1925 s.95(1), (2); and see Hood and Challis, pp.190, 191.
[569] LPA 1925 s.95(5).
[570] LPA 1925 s.95(1). Thus it may be subject to a right of consolidation.
[571] LPA 1925 s.95(2); see *Teevan v Smith* (1882) 20 Ch D 724.
[572] LPA 1925 s.95(3).
[573] See above, para.25–026.
[574] *Hinde v Blake* (1841) 11 L.J. Ch. 26; and see 1 Eq.Ca.Abr. 328, pl. 2.
[575] *Hall v Heward* (1886) 32 Ch D 430.
[576] But see Hood and Challis, pp.190, 191.

IV. TERMS OF REDEMPTION

25–106   **1. Method.** A mortgage may be redeemed either in court or out of court; the latter is the more usual except in complicated cases. The mortgage remains in being until the money due has actually been paid and accepted.[577] The mortgagor remains liable for interest under it until either he duly tenders repayment and, if it is not accepted, sets the money aside,[578] or else the mortgagee waives tender, e.g. by unequivocally refusing a proposed repayment.[579] If a mortgagee unreasonably refuses to accept a proper tender of the money due and so makes an action for redemption necessary, he may be penalised in costs.[580]

25–107   **2. Notice.** The mortgagor may redeem on the legal date for redemption (or before, if the mortgagee has sought payment, e.g. by taking possession[581]) without giving notice of his intention to do so.[582] After that date,[583] when (as is usual) he is forced to rely upon his equitable right to redeem, it is a rule of practice[584] that he must either:

> (i) give the mortgagee reasonable[585] notice (i.e. normally, or, in the absence of express provision, perhaps always,[586] six months) of his intention to redeem[587]; or
>
> (ii) pay him six months' interest instead.[588]

It is only fair that the mortgagee should have a reasonable opportunity to find investment for his money.[589] But the mortgagee is not entitled to any notices or interest instead:

> (i) if the mortgage is merely of a temporary nature[590]; or

---

[577] *Samuel Keller (Holdings) Ltd v Martins Bank Ltd* [1971] 1 W.L.R. 43.
[578] *Barratt v Gough-Thomas (No.3)* [1951] 2 All E.R. 48.
[579] *Chalikani Venkatarayanim v Zamindar of Tuni* (1922) L.R. 50 Ind.App. 41.
[580] *Graham v Seal* (1918) 88 L.J. Ch. 31.
[581] *Bovill v Endle* [1896] 1 Ch. 648; 65 L.J. Ch. 542.
[582] See *Crickmore v Freeton* (1870) 40 L.J. Ch. 137.
[583] Which is usually six months after the execution of the mortgage: see above, para.24–013.
[584] *Smith v Smith* [1891] 3 Ch. 550; *Centrax Trustees Ltd v Ross* [1979] 2 All E.R. 952 at 955. Nowadays mortgages normally contain express provisions to deal with redemption.
[585] *Browne v Lockhart* (1840) 10 Sim. 420 at 424.
[586] See *Cromwell Property Investment Co Ltd v Western & Toovey* [1934] Ch. 322, where, at 332, Maugham J. calls the rule "harsh".
[587] *Shrapnell v Blake* (1737) West.t.Hard. 166.
[588] *Johnson v Evans* (1889) 61 L.T. 18.
[589] *Browne v Lockhart*, above, at 424.
[590] *Fitzgerald's Trustee v Mellersh* [1892] 1 Ch. 385. That case was concerned with an equitable mortgage by deposit of title deeds. Such mortgages must now take the form of a contract to grant a mortgage that complies with LP(MP)A 1989 s.2: see above, para.24–041.

(ii) if he has taken steps to enforce his security,[591] as by taking possession,[592] or starting foreclosure proceedings,[593] or giving the mortgagor notice to repay the loan so as to entitle the mortgagee to sell on default being made,[594] "It is said, 'You have demanded payment by your proceedings, and here is payment: you cannot decline what you have demanded'."[595]

If the mortgagor gives six months' notice and fails to pay on the proper day, he must usually give a further six months' notice or pay six months' interest instead,[596] unless he can give a reasonable explanation of his failure to pay. If he can, it is enough if he gives reasonable notice, e.g. three months.[597]

3. Interest and costs. Even if the mortgage makes no provision for interest, **25–108** the mortgagor, on redeeming, must pay interest on the loan, and the rate will, if necessary, be fixed by the court.[598] If a redemption action is brought the mortgagor must also pay the mortgagee's proper costs, including any expenses incurred for protecting his security.[599]

V. SALE IN LIEU OF REDEMPTION

Any person entitled to redeem may apply to the court for an order for sale, and **25–109** is apparently entitled to such an order as of right.[600]

VI. "REDEEM UP, FORECLOSE DOWN"

1. Parties to action. The maxim "Redeem up, foreclose down" applies **25–110** where there are several incumbrancers and one of them seeks by action to redeem a superior mortgage. The effect is best shown by an example. X has mortgaged his property successively to A, B, C, D and E, the mortgages ranking in that order; X thus ranks last, e.g. in claiming any surplus if the property is sold. Suppose that D wishes to redeem B, and owing to the complexity of the accounts or some other circumstance an action for redemption is begun. Before B can be redeemed, the exact amount due to him must be settled by the court. This amount, however, does not affect only B and D, for C, E and X are all concerned with the amount which has priority to their interests. Thus if the property were to be sold, C, E and X would all wish to

---

[591] *Re Alcock* (1883) 23 Ch D 372 at 376.
[592] *Bovill v Endle* [1896] 1 Ch. 648.
[593] *Hill v Rowlands* [1897] 2 Ch. 361 at 363.
[594] *Edmonson v Copland* [1911] 2 Ch. 301.
[595] *Bovill v Endle*, above, at 651, per Kekewich J.
[596] *Re Moss* (1885) 31 Ch D 90 at 94.
[597] *Cromwell Property Investment Co Ltd v Western & Toovey* [1934] Ch. 322.
[598] See *Cityland and Property (Holdings) Ltd v Dabrah* [1968] Ch. 166. Even statute-barred interest must be paid: below, para.35–018.
[599] See *Sinfield v Sweet* [1967] 1 W.L.R. 1489. Though a charge on the property, the mortgagor is not personally liable for these expenses.
[600] LPA 1925 s.91(1). See *Clarke v Pannell* (1884) 29 S.J. 147; and see above, paras 25–011, 25–044.

know whether what B was entitled to was, say, £6,000 or £16,000, for upon that figure might depend their chances of receiving anything from the proceeds of sale. Consequently the court will insist upon their being made parties to D's action for redemption, so that they can be represented in the taking of the accounts between B and D and thus be bound by the final result.[601]

25–111   **2. Rights of the parties.** It would, however, be unfair to give C, E and X the trouble and expense of taking part in the action merely to watch accounts being taken,[602] with the risk of a similar event taking place in the future. The court therefore insists that the rights of all parties concerned in the action shall be settled once and for all. A is not concerned[603]; it is immaterial to him what is due to B, for A's mortgage has priority to B's. A, therefore, need not be joined in the action,[604] and will be left undisturbed in his position of first mortgagee.[605] But all the other parties are concerned, and the order of the court will be that D shall redeem not only B, but also C, for both their mortgages have priority to D's. E and X must also be disposed of, and that can be done only by foreclosure: that is, each of them will have the opportunity of saving his rights by paying off the prior mortgages concerned in the action, or of asking for a sale, but if he does neither, he will be foreclosed.[606] "The natural decree is, that the second mortgagee shall redeem the first mortgagee, and that the mortgagor shall redeem him or stand foreclosed."[607] Thus if E and X fail to redeem and are foreclosed, the final result will be that D, at the price of redeeming B and C, now holds the equity of redemption subject only to the first mortgage in favour of A.

25–112   **3. The principle.** The principle may be stated thus: a mortgagee who seeks to redeem a prior mortgage by action must not only redeem any mortgages standing between him and that prior mortgage,[608] but must also foreclose all subsequent mortgagees and the mortgagor.[609] In short, "redeem up, foreclose down".

25–113   **4. Limits to the principle.** It is important to notice that this principle has no application to redemptions made out of court.[610] And there is no converse rule "foreclose down; redeem up": a mortgagee who forecloses is under no obligation to redeem any prior mortgages,[611] although he must foreclose all

---

[601] This also protects B against a further taking of his account if a later incumbrancer should offer to redeem both B and D: *Johnson v Holdsworth* (1850) 1 Sim. (N.S.) 106 at 109.
[602] *Ramsbottom v Wallis* (1835) 5 L.J. Ch. 92.
[603] *Slade v Rigg* (1843) 3 Hare 35 at 38.
[604] *Rose v Page* (1829) 2 Sim. 471; *Slade v Rigg*, above.
[605] *Brisco v Kenrick* (1832) 1 L.J. Ch. 116; 1 Coop.t.Cott. 371.
[606] *Fell v Brown* (1787) 2 Bro.C.C. 276 at 278.
[607] *Fell v Brown*, above, at 278, per Lord Thurlow L.C.
[608] *Teevan v Smith* (1882) 20 Ch D 724 at 729.
[609] *Farmer v Curtis* (1829) 2 Sim. 466.
[610] See *Smith v Green* (1844) 1 Coll. CC 555.
[611] *Richards v Cooper* (1842) 5 Beav. 304.

subsequent mortgagees as well as the mortgagor.[612] In other words, for foreclosure the rule is simply "foreclose down": a mortgagee cannot foreclose a subsequent mortgagee or the mortgagor unless he forecloses everyone beneath him.[613]

VII. TERMINATION OF EQUITY OF REDEMPTION

An equity of redemption may be extinguished *against* the mortgagor's will: **25–114**

(i) by foreclosure[614];

(ii) by sale[615]; or

(iii) by lapse of time.[616]

In addition, the mortgagor may himself extinguish it by releasing it to the mortgagee,[617] or by redeeming.

B. Right to Bring Actions

1. Mortgagor's right to sue. A mortgagor's right to bring actions of   **25–115** various kinds needs special consideration, since he is normally left in possession of the property but has not immediate legal title to possession as against the mortgagee. As against third parties, e.g. trespassers or neighbours committing nuisances, the mortgagor, like any other person lawfully in possession of land, could sue at common law to protect that possession,[618] and thus, e.g. recover the land from anyone other than the mortgagee or someone claiming through him. In equity, he was regarded as owner of the land, subject to the mortgage, and so could obtain equitable remedies (such as an injunction[619]) against any person, e.g. to prevent injury to the property,[620] or to enforce a restrictive covenant.[621]

2. Action as landlord. Difficulties arose, however, when the right of action   **25–116** depended on the legal relationship of landlord and tenant, for example in the case of actions for rent or to enforce covenants against tenants to whom the

---

[612] *Bishop of Winchester v Beavor* (1797) 3 Ves. 314; *Anderson v Stather* (1845) 2 Coll. CC209.

[613] *Cockes v Sherman* (1676) Free.Ch. 13. In this context note *Anfield (UK) Ltd v Bank of Scotland* [2011] 1 W.L.R. 2414 which permits a mortgagee to be subrogated to, and registered as proprietor of, an intermediate lender's charge and thereby to gain priority.

[614] Above, para.25–006.

[615] Above, para.25–013.

[616] Below, para.35–035, and subject to the scheme established by the Land Registration Act 2002 for registered interests.

[617] e.g. *Knight v Marjoribanks* (1849) 2 Mac. & G. 10; *Reeve v Lisle* [1902] A.C. 461, see above, para.25–088.

[618] See below, Ch.35, where the possessory nature of title to land is explained.

[619] *Van Gelder, Apsimon & Co v Sowerby Bridge United District Flour Society* (1890) 44 Ch D 374.

[620] *Matthews v Usher* [1900] 2 Q.B. 535 at 538; *Turner v Walsh* [1909] 2 K.B. 484 at 487.

[621] *Fairclough v Marshall* (1878) 4 Ex.D. 37.

land had been let before the date of the mortgage.[622] In such cases the mortgage was of course an assignment of the reversion, and thereafter the covenants became enforceable by the mortgagee only.[623] Moreover the court would only allow the mortgagor to sue in the mortgagee's name if the mortgagor offered to redeem,[624] though without doing this he could distrain for rent as agent of the mortgagee.[625]

This difficulty is now remedied by statute.[626] Provided that the mortgagee has not given effective notice of his intention to take possession or enter into receipt of the rents and profits,[627] the mortgagor in possession may:

(i)   sue in his own name for possession or for the rent and profits;

(ii) bring an action to prevent, or recover damages for, any trespass or other wrong[628]; and

(iii) enforce all covenants and conditions in leases of the property.[629]

C. Rights to Relief and Other Rights

25–117   **1. Extortionate credit bargains under the Consumer Credit Act 1974.** Until April 2008, the mortgagor had the right to seek relief from an extortionate credit bargain,[630] and although this jurisdiction no longer exists, it is important to appreciate the origins of consumer credit control and how it impacted on the enforcement of mortgages. This helps explain the current law. This right was conferred by the Consumer Credit Act 1974, which defined an extortionate credit bargain as one which required the debtor or a relative of his to make payments which were "grossly exorbitant", or which otherwise "grossly contravenes ordinary principles of fair dealing".[631] The court had to have regard to all relevant considerations, including prevailing rates of interest,[632] the mortgagor's age, experience, state of health and business capacity

---

[622] If the mortgage was made before the lease the mortgagor could of course sue: *Turner v Walsh*, above, at 495. As to the nature and effect of such leases, which operate by estoppel, see above, paras 17–132, 25–071.

[623] *Turner v Walsh*, above, at 495; *Matthews v Usher* [1900] 2 Q.B. 535. For the general law, see above, paras 20–004, 20–010.

[624] *Turner v Walsh*, above, at 495, 496.

[625] *Trent v Hunt* (1853) 9 Exch. 14.

[626] LPA 1925 ss.98, 141 (where the lease was granted prior to 1996), L&TCA 1995 s.15 (where the lease was granted after 1995).

[627] Proceedings for possession which by a technical defect are a nullity do not suffice: *Kitchen's Trustee v Madders* [1949] Ch. 588, affirmed [1950] Ch. 134.

[628] LPA 1925 s.98(1). For the limits of this, see *Turner v Walsh*, above.

[629] LPA 1925 s.141(2) (leases granted prior to 1996); L&TCA 1995 s.15 (leases granted after 1995).

[630] See [1989] Conv. 164; 234 (L. Bently and G. G. Howells).

[631] s.138. For the jurisdiction to set aside an extortionate credit bargain entered into within three years of the commencement of: (i) a corporation's winding up; and (ii) an individual's bankruptcy, see respectively IA 1986 ss.244, 343.

[632] See *Davies v Directloans Ltd* [1986] 1 W.L.R. 823 at 834–836. In examining the rate of interest, the court will have regard to the credit record of the debtor and the risk to the lender: see, e.g. *Woodstead Finance Ltd v Petrou* (sub nom. *Petrou v Woodstead Finance Ltd*) 1986 F.L.R. 158 (42 per cent not extortionate given the debtor's "appalling record").

and any financial pressure upon him.[633] This definition was a comprehensive one, and in determining whether a bargain was extortionate, the courts would not look outside the Act to the equitable jurisdiction to relieve against unconscionable bargains.[634] A transaction will not be set aside merely because it is unwise. "The jurisdiction seems to . . . contemplate at least a substantial imbalance in bargaining power of which one party has taken advantage."[635] In contrast, the mortgagee had an entirely legitimate interest in conducting its business in its best commercial interest, even if this meant serious hardship to the mortgagor.[636] Thus, while a power to vary interest rates did not itself amount to an extortionate credit bargain, the varying of those rates dishonestly, capriciously or unreasonably might well have caused that result.[637] If found extortionate, the agreement could be reopened by the court at the instance of the debtor or a surety,[638] and the court could relieve either of them from any payment in excess of what was fairly due and reasonable[639] and could alter the terms of the agreement or the security.[640] These provisions were not restricted by any financial limit such as the Act imposes for other purposes.[641] The only exemption was where the debtor is a corporation.[642] The burden of proof was on the creditor.[643]

2. Unfair relationships under the Consumer Credit Act 2006. With **25–118** effect from April 2008, ss.137–140 of the Consumer Credit Act 1974 are repealed.[644] The Consumer Credit Act 2006 introduces a new provision into the 1974 Act concerning "unfair relationships" between creditors and debtors. Statutory control thus focuses on the nature of the parties' relationship, rather

---

[633] Consumer Credit Act 1974 s.138.

[634] *Davies v Directloans Ltd*, above, at 831. For this equitable jurisdiction, see below, para.25–137.

[635] *Wills v Wood* [1984] C.C.L.R. 7 at 15, per Donaldson M.R. If the lender has been implicated in any fraudulent conduct, this may constitute a gross contravention of the principles of fair dealing: *Coldunell Ltd v Gallon* [1986] Q.B. 1184 at 1211.

[636] *Paragon Finance v Pender* [2005] EWCA Civ 760, [2005] 1 W.L.R. 3412. See also *Broadwick Financial Services Ltd v Spencer* [2002] EWCA Civ 35, [2002] 1 All E.R. (Comm) 446.

[637] *Nash v Paragon Finance* [2001] EWCA Civ 1466, [2002] 1 W.L.R. 685.

[638] In *Castle Phillips Finance Co Ltd v Williams* [1986] C.C.L.R. 13, the debtor failed to plead an extortionate credit bargain, but the court referred the papers to the Director General of Fair Trading for him to consider whether any action was required against the lender under the Consumer Credit Act 1974 (including revocation of its licence).

[639] The court has no power under this provision to relieve a person from an obligation to convey property: *JA Pye (Oxford) Estates Ltd v Ambrose* [1994] N.P.C. 53 (transcript, p.41).

[640] Consumer Credit Act 1974, ss.137, 139. In *A. Ketley Ltd v Scott* [1981] I.C.R. 241, the court refused relief where the debtor was an experienced businessman, legally advised, who wanted to complete a house purchase the same day and agreed to pay interest at 12 per cent for three months, equivalent to 48 per cent. The debtor's application for the loan had in fact been deceitful. A credit bargain may be extortionate even if the rate of interest does not exceed 48 per cent: *Castle Phillips Finance Co Ltd v Williams*, above, at 20.

[641] Above, para.24–044.

[642] Consumer Credit Act 1974 s.137(2). However, where a corporation was in receipt of credit under an extortionate credit bargain within three years of its being wound up, the court has similar powers to those conferred by the 1974 Act: see IA 1986 s.244.

[643] Consumer Credit Act 1974, s.171(7). See *Coldunell Ltd v Gallon* [1986] Q.B. 1184.

[644] CCA 2006, Sch.4.

than the nature of the bargain itself.[645] This new test applies to all credit agreements (including agreements already in existence and regulated by the CCA 1974), except a first legal mortgage over residential land that is an exempt agreement under CCA 1974 s.16(6C), being a mortgage that is regulated under the Financial Services and Markets Act 2000. A relationship arising out of the agreement[646] is unfair because of either any of its terms or those of a related agreement, the way in which the creditor has exercised or enforced any of his rights under the agreement or a related agreement, or any other thing done, or not done by, or on behalf of the creditor.[647] If an agreement falls within this provision, the court has broad powers[648] in relation to an unfair relationship, including the making or an order concerning repayment, return of property, alteration of the terms, or set aside in whole or in part of the agreement. Although many standard "purchase mortgages" will be outside of this provision because they will fall within the FSMA 2000, it should be noted that the test of "unfair relationships" applies to all other credit agreements whether or not they are otherwise regulated by the Consumer Credit Acts.[649]

25–119   Because a mortgage involves the provision of financial services, certain terms may not be enforceable against the mortgagor if they are "unfair" for the purposes of the Unfair Terms in Consumer Contracts Regulations 1994.[650] A detailed consideration of these Regulations lies outside the scope of this book.[651] However, it may be noted here that they will apply to terms in a mortgage which have not been individually negotiated[652] where:

> (i) the mortgagee supplies financial services whilst acting for purposes relating to his business; and

> (ii) the mortgagor, in making the contract, is acting for purposes which are outside his business.[653]

25–120   Mortgages vitiated by notice of fraud, misrepresentation or undue influence. A mortgagor may have a right to have the mortgage set aside because it was induced by fraud or undue influence. The issue arises nowadays in a case where the mortgagor (or person whose consent is necessary to

---

[645] CCA 2006 ss.19–22, inserting a new s.140A and s.140B into the CCA 1974.

[646] The unfairness must be generated by the agreement, not by reason of some pre-existing situation or relationship.

[647] CCA 1974 s.140A(1).

[648] CCA 2006 s.20, inserting s.140B into the CCA 1974.

[649] As was the case with the provisions of the CCA 1974 concerning "extortionate credit bargains".

[650] SI 1994/3159, implementing EC Council Directive 93/13. It is now clear that mortgages are within the scope of the Regulations: see (1999) 115 L.Q.R. 360 (S. Bright). See too (1995) 111 L.Q.R. 655 (S. and C. Bright). For what constitutes unfairness, see reg.4.

[651] For a detailed consideration, see John Hunt, *Unfair Terms in Consumer Contracts Regulations 1994.*

[652] reg.3(1).

[653] reg.2(1).

give the mortgagee priority[654]) has been induced to agree to its execution by the fraud, misrepresentation or undue influence of the debtor whose liability is secured by the mortgage. The same problem arises where a person either guarantees a debt, or cedes priority to a mortgagee over his rights in the property charged, having been similarly induced to act. The typical situation is where the matrimonial home (or similar) is jointly owned, the man seeks to mortgage it as security for his business debts, and induces his wife or partner to agree to the charge.[655] When the mortgagee comes to enforce its security, the question arises as to whether the wife or partner is bound by the charge. The legal principles governing this situation were in some confusion until two decisions of the House of Lords, delivered at the same time, *Barclays Bank Plc v O'Brien*[656] and *C.I.B.C. Mortgages Plc v Pitt*[657] in which the earlier authorities were largely rejected and the law was restated according to first principles.[658] This has been followed by a third House of Lord's decision in *Royal Bank of Scotland v Etridge*,[659] which clarifies areas of remaining uncertainty but principally advises lenders on how to avoid claims of undue influence in the future.

1. The basis of liability. In the first two cases, the House of Lords **25–121** established that a mortgage[660] or guarantee could not be enforced against the surety if it had been procured by the fraud, misrepresentation or undue influence of the principal debtor[661] and either:

> (i) the principal debtor was acting as agent for the creditor in securing the agreement of the surety; or

---

[654] For example, *Alliance & Leicester Building Society v Slayford.*

[655] These cases are, in a sense, a sequel to the decision in *Williams & Glyn's Bank Ltd v Boland* [1981] A.C. 487. It has been the practice of mortgagees since that case to require that any person who has (or may have) a beneficial interest in the property should either be a party to the mortgage or agree to subordinate their rights to the lender.

[656] [1994] 1 A.C. 180.

[657] [1994] 1 A.C. 200. The cases are noted at (1994) 110 L.Q.R. 167 (J. R. F. Lehane); [1994] C.L.J. 21 (M.J.D); (1995) 15 O.J.L.S. 119 (S. H. Goo). There is an important summary of the law and practice as it has since developed in *Royal Bank of Scotland Plc v Etridge (No.2)* [1998] 4 All E.R. 705 at 710 et seq.

[658] There is a considerable literature on this subject: see especially (1995) 15 L.S. 35 (G. Battersby); [1995] L.M.C.L.Q. 346 (R. Hooley); (1995) 7 C.F.L.Q. 104 (M. Oldham); [1995] C.L.J. 280 (A. Lawson); [1997] C.L.J. 60 (M. Chen-Wishart); and [1998] J.B.L. 355 (M. Haley).

[659] [2001] UKHL 44, [2002] 2 A.C. 773. In fact, there were eight appeals. There is much literature: e.g. M. Oldham. (2002), 61 C.L.J. 29; G. Andrews [2002] Conv. 456; 2002; P. Kenny [2002] Conv. 91; M. Briggs (2002) 13 Fam. L.J. 9; S Wong [2002] J.B.L. 439–456.

[660] Or a waiver of prior proprietary rights in favour of the mortgagee, to which the same principles apply: see *Banco Exterior Internacional v Mann* [1995] 1 All E.R. 936 at 942; *Halifax BS v Brown* [1996] 1 F.L.R. 103 at 112–115.

[661] It is not necessary that the principal debtor who is responsible for the wrongdoing should be a party to the transaction between the surety and the creditor: see *Banco Exterior internacional SA v Thomas* [1997] 1 W.L.R. 221 at 229. It is therefore immaterial whether the mortgage is of property owned by the surety alone or concurrently with the principal debtor.

(ii) the facts were such as to put the creditor on notice of the risk of such wrongdoing, and it failed to take adequate steps to ensure that the surety received independent legal advice as to the risks that he was running.[662]

In a number of cases prior to *O'Brien* and *Pitt*, it had been held that a creditor was liable if the principal debtor had been acting in some sense as its agent when he improperly obtained the surety's consent.[663] Such a finding of agency was contrary to the true position, namely that the creditor required the principal debtor to provide a surety, and the principal debtor acted for himself in procuring the concurrence of that surety.[664] It is clear from *O'Brien* that although there may be situations where the principal debtor was indeed acting for the creditor in procuring the surety's assent, "such cases will be of very rare occurrence".[665] The security will usually be impugned because the creditor had notice of the principal debtor's improper conduct in securing it.

25–122   **2. Undue influence, fraud or misrepresentation.** The first element that must be established is that the surety was induced to execute the mortgage (or to agree to subordinate his rights in favour of the mortgagee) by undue influence, fraud or misrepresentation.[666] In a number of cases, the principal debtor has either failed to disclose or has misrepresented to the surety the extent of his liability.[667] In most, however, the surety's consent has been obtained by undue influence. There are two types of undue influence, presumed and actual.

25–123   *(a) Presumed undue influence.* According to *O'Brien*, undue influence will be presumed in two types of case, although in *Etridge*, Lord Nicholls reminds us that two different types of "presumption" are in play[668]:

(i) as a matter of law from certain relationships such as doctor and patient, solicitor and client,[669] guardian and ward, religious superior and inferior. This "presumption" is really a reflection of "a sternly protective attitude towards certain types of relationship in

---

[662] For a clear summary of the principles, see *National Bank of Abu Dhabi v Mohamed* (1997) 30 H.L.R. 383 at 391. For a refreshing re-examination which challenges orthodox analysis see Sir Kim Lewinson, *Under the Influence* [2011] 19 R.L.R.

[663] See *B.C.C.I. International SA v Aboody* [1990] 1 Q.B. 923, where the authorities are reviewed.

[664] *O'Brien* [1994] 1 A.C. 180 at 194.

[665] *O'Brien*, above, at 195, per Lord Browne-Wilkinson. See too *Bradford & Bingley BS v Chandock* (1996) 72 P. & C.R. D28 at D29.

[666] *O'Brien*, above, at 198. It is largely immaterial whether the facts are analysed as undue influence or misrepresentation, *Annulment Funding Lo Ltd v Cowey* [2010] EWCA Civ 711.

[667] See, e.g. *O'Brien*, above; *T.S.B. Bank Plc v Camfield* [1995] 1 W.L.R. 430; *Bank Melli Iran v Samadi-Rad* [1995] 2 F.L.R. 367.

[668] *Etridge*, paras 17–18.

[669] See *Pathania v Adedeji* [2010] EWHC 3085 (QB) where the presumption was re-butted.

which one party acquires influence over another person who is vulnerable and dependant"[670]; and

(ii) as a matter of fact where one person reposed trust and confidence in another and the impugned transaction called for an explanation.[671] This is effectively a rebuttable evidentiary presumption which shifts the burden of proof to the person trying to uphold the impugned transaction.[672]

However, in either case, the party alleging undue influence must also show that the transaction was to his manifest disadvantage.[673] Although this last requirement has attracted criticism,[674] Lord Nicholls in *Etridge*[675] explains that it would not be right to depart from the House of Lords decision in *National Westminster Bank Plc v Morgan*[676] because the requirement served to emphasise that a transaction may be impugned only if it calls for an explanation. Many transactions do not call for an explanation, as evidenced by the lack of disadvantage for the alleged victim of the undue influence, and so raise no presumption of undue influence. As such, the need for "manifest disadvantage" in cases of presumed undue influence reflects the fact that the burden of proof may fall on the party seeking to uphold the transaction because there is "something which calls for an explanation".[677] Of course, the presumption of undue influence can be rebutted by showing that the party alleged to have been influenced had entered into the transaction freely and as an exercise of independent will.[678]

(b) Actual undue influence. In cases where there is no presumption of undue   **25–124** influence, the party influenced will have to prove actual undue influence by showing that:

---

[670] *Etridge*, para.17.

[671] See *Steeples v Lea* [1998] 1 F.L.R. 138 at 141.

[672] *Etridge*, para.14.

[673] *National Westminster Bank Plc v Morgan* [1985] A.C. 686 at 706. cf. *Goldsworthy v Brickell* [1987] Ch. 378 at 401; *Petrou v Woodstead Finance Ltd* 1986 F.L.R. 158.

[674] See (1985) 48 M.L.R. 579 (D. Tiplady). See *B.C.C.I. International SA v Aboody* [1990] 1 Q.B. 923 at 962–964; *Pitt* [1994] 1 A.C. 200 at 209 for the difficulties of reconciling the requirement of manifest disadvantage with the authorities on abuse of confidence. See too *Royal Bank of Scotland Plc v Etridge (No.2)* [1998] 4 All E.R. 705 at 713.

[675] *Etridge*, para.24.

[676] Above.

[677] *Etridge*, para.24. The transaction in *Pathania v Adedeji* above was to the claimant's advantage (when it took place) and this was a significant factor in rebutting the presumption of undue influence.

[678] Commonly this will be shown by proving that the complainant received independent advice: see *Inche Noriah v Shaik Allie Bin Omar* [1929] A.C. 127 at 135, especially if the lender follows the *Etridge* guidelines (see below paras 25–130, 25–131). Also *Pathania v Adedeji* above. However, "taking independent advice is neither always necessary nor always sufficient to rebut the presumption of undue influence": *Claughton v Price* (1997) 30 H.L.R. 396 at 408, per Nourse L.J. The presumption may be rebutted simply by weighing the facts as alleged by the claimant, *Wallbank v Price*, [2007] EWHC 3001 (Ch).

(i) the party who induced the transaction had the capacity to influence him;

(ii) influence was exercised;

(iii) it was undue; and

(iv) its exercise brought about the transaction.[679]

Actual undue influence is a species of fraud. If, therefore, these four elements are established, the party influenced is entitled to have the transaction set aside. He does not have to show additionally that the transaction was manifestly disadvantageous to him[680] because the transaction by its nature is bad. Neither does he have to show that he made no conscious decision of his own or that his will was completely overborne: a conscious exercise of will can be vitiated by undue influence.[681]

25–125   **3. Notice of the wrongdoing.** The second element that must be shown to make the creditor liable is that he had notice of the fraud, misrepresentation or undue influence. This will depend upon three closely interconnected factors.

25–126   *(a) The nature of the transaction.* In general, the creditor will not be put on inquiry unless, by the transaction, the surety makes himself responsible in some way to the creditor for the debts of the principal debtor.[682] By contrast, where a lender makes a joint advance to A and B on the security of their co-owned property, the transaction is not usually of a kind to put him on notice that A may have acted improperly to induce B to agree to it.[683] However, even in the case of a joint advance, the circumstances may be such as to put the lender on inquiry.[684] In *Etridge*, Lord Nicholls considered this point at length, and favoured a less technical approach than that adopted by the Court of Appeal in *Etridge* itself. In his view, the "test should be simple and clear and easy to apply in a wide range of circumstances".[685] Consequently, the lender would be put on notice whenever a wife, husband,[686] lover or similar partner stood surety for the other's debts and cohabitation was not essential.[687]

25–127   *(b) Whether the transaction was to the financial disadvantage of the surety.* In addition to the "family"-type situations covered by Lord Nicholls' simple

---

[679] *B.C.C.I. International SA v Aboody*, above, at 967.

[680] *Pitt*, above, at 208, 209, overruling (on this point) *B.C.C.I. International SA v Aboody*, above. There cannot be both actual and presumed undue influence: the situations in which they arise are mutually exclusive: *Bank of Scotland v Bennett* (1998) 77 P. & C.R. 447 at 465.

[681] *Hewett v First Plus Financial Group plc* (2010) 2 FLR 177.

[682] *Pitt*, above, at 211.

[683] *Pitt*, above. Confirmed by *Etridge*, above, para.48.

[684] Below.

[685] *Etridge*, para.46.

[686] *Barclays Bank Plc v Rivett* (1997) 29 H.L.R. 893, husband standing surety for his wife's debts.

[687] *Etridge* para.47. See *Massey v Midland Bank Plc* [1995] 1 All E.R. 929, where a woman charged her house as surety for her (male) lover with whom she did not cohabit.

test, the creditor will also be put on inquiry if "the transaction is on its face not to the financial advantage" of the surety,[688] as where the surety guarantees the debts of the principal debtor[689] or subordinates his rights in the property to those of the creditor.[690] As noted, where, by contrast, the transaction is a joint loan for a purpose that is apparently for the benefit of both the borrowers, the creditor will not usually be put on inquiry.[691] In a number of cases, a wife has made herself liable in some way for a loan made to a family company in which she has a shareholding. Where the family income is derived from the company, the provision of security by the wife "cannot be said to be extravagantly or even necessarily improvident".[692] However, the transaction may, nonetheless, be to her financial disadvantage if it is a particularly hazardous one,[693] or if her liability is disproportionate to her interest in the company.[694] In such circumstances, the creditor will not be exonerated from inquiry.[695] In *Etridge*, Lord Nicholls regarded such cases as particularly difficult, but could not equate them with "joint-loan" cases where both parties took sufficient advantage to rebut a presumption of undue influence. In his view, the bank should normally be regarded as being put on inquiry because the "shareholding interests, and the identity of the directors, are not a reliable guide to the identity of the persons who actually have the conduct of the company's business".[696] However, the creditor will not be under any liability if the transaction is not in fact to the surety's financial disadvantage even if on its face it appeared to be, and so should have put the creditor on inquiry.[697]

---

[688] *O'Brien* [1994] 1 A.C. 180 at 196, per Lord Browne-Wilkinson. In determining whether this is so, the court must necessarily look at the transaction through the eyes of the creditor, having regard to the facts known to it: see *Bank of Scotland v Bennett*, above, at 469. In other words, the transaction must in fact be manifestly disadvantageous (which, according to *Bank of Cyprus (London) Ltd v Markou* [1999] 2 All E.R. 707 at 717, is determined by reference to the positions of the debtor and the surety) and must also appear to the creditor to be so on its face. Only then will a creditor be put on inquiry: see *Bank of Scotland v Bennett*, above, at 470.

[689] See, e.g. *Bank of Baroda v Rayarel* [1995] 2 F.L.R. 376.

[690] See, e.g. *Banco Exterior Internacional v Mann* [1995] 1 All E.R. 936; *Halifax BS v Brown* [1996] 1 F.L.R. 103.

[691] *Pitt* [1994] 1 A.C. 200 at 211; *Britannia BS v Pugh* (1996) 29 H.L.R. 423; *Birmingham Midshires Mortgage Services v Mahal* (1996) 73 P. & C.R. D7; *Dunbar Bank Plc v Nadeem* [1998] 3 All E.R. 876; *Davies v Norwich Union Life Insurance Society* (1998) 78 P. & C.R. 119. See too *Society of Lloyd's v Khan* [1999] 1 F.L.R. 246 (wife became a name at Lloyd's on her husband's direction: transaction not manifestly disadvantageous).

[692] *Bank of Scotland v Bennett*, above, at 469, per Chadwick L.J.

[693] *Nightingale Finance Ltd v Scott* [1997] E.G.C.S. 161 (the creditor also knew that the wife relied entirely on her husband).

[694] Compare *Goode Durrant Administration v Biddulph* (1994) 26 H.L.R. 625 (wife had 2.5 per cent interest in the company, but was potentially liable for more than £300,000: transaction not for her financial benefit) with *Barclays Bank Plc v Sumner* [1996] E.G.C.S. 65 (wife had 50 per cent interest in the company, and was jointly liable on an unlimited guarantee: transaction not disadvantageous). cf. [1994] Fam. Law 675 (S. Cretney) and see *Bank of Scotland v Bennett*, above.

[695] *Bank of Scotland v Bennett* [1997] 1 F.L.R. 801 at 832. The decision in that case was, however, reversed on appeal on its facts: see (1998) 77 P. & C.R. 447.

[696] *Etridge* para.49.

[697] *Scotlife Home Loans (No.2) Ltd v Hedworth* (1995) 28 H.L.R. 771 (loan granted for husband's "business purposes" in fact used to discharge existing mortgages on the family home).

25–128   *(c) The relationship between the principal debtor and the surety.* The creditor will also be put on inquiry if the character of the transaction is such that there is a substantial risk that the principal debtor has committed a legal or equitable wrong in procuring a person to act as surety, and that wrong is one that entitles the surety to set aside the transaction.[698] If the two preceding factors are present, it will be the nature of the relationship that will determine whether or not that risk exists. In *O'Brien*, the House of Lords was concerned with the position of a wife who acted as surety for her husband's debts and this is now covered by Lord Nicholls' blanket approach in *Etridge*. However, authorities subsequent to *O'Brien* indicate that the principles can be applied where there was no cohabitation and where the relationship between the parties was one of trust rather than an emotional one. Other relationships which have been either held or alleged to put a creditor on inquiry include the following:

    (i) where a woman charged her house as surety for the borrowings of a close (male) friend[699];

    (ii) where a junior employee mortgaged her house as security for her employer's indebtedness[700];

    (iii) where a father charged his property to secure a loan to his son[701];

    (iv) where a sister mortgaged her home as principal debtor to secure a loan for her brother[702]; and

    (v) where a mother had agreed to charge her property by way of second mortgage to secure a loan for her son, her joint registered proprietor.[703]

It is clear from these cases that a creditor will now be put upon inquiry whenever he knows that the surety had such trust and confidence in the principal debtor that undue influence would be presumed between them.[704] The creditor's obligation to make inquiry is not confined to cases where he

---

[698] *O'Brien* [1994] 1 A.C. 180 at 196. This will be judged according to the circumstances known to the creditor at the time of the transaction: *Scottish Equitable Life Plc v Virdee* [1999] 1 F.L.R. 863 at 866.

[699] *Banco Exterior Internacional SA v Thomas* [1997] 1 W.L.R. 221 (the relationship "was neither a romantic nor a sexual one": *Banco Exterior Internacional SA v Thomas*, above, at 224, per Scott V.C.).

[700] *Credit Lyonnais Bank Nederland N.V. v Burch* [1997] 1 All E.R. 144; *Steeples v Lea* [1998] 1 F.L.R. 138.

[701] *UCB Bank Plc v Sharif* [1997] E.G.C.S. 52 (creditor not fixed with notice of any undue influence on the facts). See too *Avon Finance Co Ltd v Bridger* (1979) [1985] 2 All E.R. 281 (elderly parents induced by misrepresentation to stand surety for their son); approved in *O'Brien* [1994] 1 A.C. 180 at 198.

[702] *Northern Rock BS v Archer* (1998) 78 P. & C.R. 65.

[703] *Abbey National Bank v Stringer* [2006] EWCA Civ 338.

[704] See above, para.25–123.

knows that the relationship between surety and principal debtor is a sexual one.[705]

4. The effect of notice

(a) Ensuring informed consent to the transaction

(1) WHERE THERE IS A POSSIBILITY OF FRAUD OR UNDUE INFLUENCE. Where **25–129** the creditor has notice that the surety's consent to the proposed transaction may be obtained by fraud or undue influence, he is not expected to inquire of the surety whether he has in fact been unduly influenced or misled by the principal debtor.[706] He must instead seek to neutralise the effect of any such fraud or undue influence by taking reasonable steps to ensure that the surety enters into the transaction freely and with full knowledge of the true facts.[707] If he does not do this, he will be unable to enforce his security against the surety.[708] As regards any transaction entered into after the decision in *O'Brien*, the House of Lords has made it clear what is expected of a creditor. He must:

(i) warn the surety (at a meeting not attended by the principal creditor) of the amount of his potential liability and of the risks involved, and

(ii) advise him to obtain independent legal advice.[709]

The House was mindful of the need to balance the protection of the vulnerable against the danger of making the matrimonial home unacceptable as security for financial institutions.[710]

As regards transactions that had taken place prior to the *O'Brien* decision, their validity is judged according to whether the creditor had taken reasonable steps to bring home to the surety the risks that he was running, and had advised him to take independent advice.[711]

(2) WHERE THERE IS A PROBABILITY OF UNDUE INFLUENCE. Whether the **25–130** transaction took place before or after *O'Brien*, the House accepted that there might be exceptional cases where the creditor knew that undue influence was probable rather than merely possible. In such a case, the creditor would have

---

[705] *Credit Lyonnais Bank Nederland N.V. v Burch*, above, at 155.

[706] *O'Brien* [1994] 1 A.C. 180 at 196. To make such an inquiry would be "plainly impossible": per Lord Browne-Wilkinson.

[707] See [1995] L.M.C.L.Q. 346 at 356 (R. Hooley); [1995] C.L.J. 536 (J. Mee).

[708] *O'Brien*, above, at 196, 198.

[709] *O'Brien*, above, at 196, 197, 199. In fact, creditors do not hold a private meeting with the surety, but insist that he obtains independent legal advice and that this is confirmed in writing. See below, para.25–131.

[710] *O'Brien* above, at 188. See too *Pitt* [1994] 1 A.C. 200 at 21 1; *Scotlife Home Loans (No.2) Ltd v Hedworth* (1995) 28 H.L.R. 771 at 782.

[711] *O'Brien*, above, at 196.

to insist that the surety took separate advice.[712] This may be the best explanation of two cases in each of which a junior employee guaranteed the debts of her employer without independent legal advice, and the mortgage was set aside.[713] Indeed there may be some cases so extreme that even where the surety receives independent legal advice, the creditor will still be regarded as having constructive notice of the undue influence.[714] This will be the case if the transaction is one into which no competent solicitor could advise the surety to enter.[715]

25–131   *(b) Independent legal advice.* In the transactions which pre-dated the *O'Brien* decision (that is, before lenders adopted procedures to minimise their risk), the issue was whether, on the facts as they appeared to the creditor,[716] he had taken sufficient steps to warn the surety and to encourage him to take independent advice.[717] He would have done so if he had ensured that the surety received independent legal advice,[718] but a creditor was not absolved from liability even if the surety did take independent legal advice if he was in possession of material information not available to the solicitor advising the surety.[719] However, the creditor was not required either to inquire into the relationship between the principal debtor and the surety and the latter's motives for agreeing to guarantee the debt[720]; or to ensure that the surety actually took independent advice even though urged to do so,[721] except in those rare cases where there was a probability of undue influence.[722]

Where the surety did take legal advice, it was regarded as independent even when it was given by the solicitor acting for the creditor or the principal debtor[723] and the creditor was entitled to assume that appropriate advice had

---

[712] *O'Brien*, above, at 197.

[713] *Credit Lyonnais Bank Nederland N.V. v Burch* [1997] 1 All E.R. 144; *Steeples v Lea* [1998] 1 EL.R. 138.

[714] See *Credit Lyonnais Bank Nederland N. V v Burch*, above, at 156; *Barclays Bank Plc v Caplan* [1998] 1 F.L.R. 532 at 545 (where Deputy Judge Sumption Q.C. characterised such cases as those where "no chargor who understood the transaction could possibly enter into it").

[715] *Royal Bank of Scotland Plc v Etridge (No.2)* [1998] 4 All E.R. 705 at 722.

[716] This is the test: see *Banco Exterior Internacional v Mann* [1995] 1 All E.R. 936 at 944.

[717] The absence of a private meeting between the surety and creditor, although not good practice, was held not to be fatal where the surety obtained independent legal advice: see *Massey v Midland Bank Plc* [1995] 1 All E.R. 929 at 934. In transactions after *O'Brien*, such a meeting is in practice unusual. The creditor insists instead that the surety obtain independent legal advice: *Royal Bank of Scotland Plc v Etridge (No.2)*, above, at 720; above, para.25–131.

[718] *National Bank of Abu Dhabi v Mohamed* (1997) 30 H.L.R. 383. Independent advice means advice in relation to the surety's own position vis-à-vis both the creditor and the debtor: see *Northern Rock BS v Archer* (1998) 78 P. & C.R. at 76.

[719] See the Court of Appeal decision in *Royal Bank of Scotland Plc v Etridge (No.2)* [1998] 4 All E.R. 705 at 722.

[720] *Banco Exterior Internacional SA v Thomas* [1997] 1 W.L.R. 221 at 230.

[721] *Massey v Midland Bank Plc*, above, at 934, 935; *Birmingham Midshires Mortgage Services v Mahal* (1996) 73 P. & C.R. D7; *Turner v Barclays Bank Plc* [1997] 2 F.C.R. 151.

[722] Above.

[723] See *Midland Bank Plc v Serter* (1995) 71 P. & C.R. 264; *Bradford & Bingley BS v Chandock* (1996) 72 P. & C.R. D28; *Barclays Bank Plc v Thomson* [1997] 4 All E.R. 816. cf. [1997] Conv. 216 (M. P. Thompson). Confirmed by *Etridge*, para.74.

been properly given.[724] The courts rejected the view that, in such cases, the solicitor could still be regarded as the creditor's agent[725] and the creditor was not therefore fixed with notice of anything that the solicitor discovered while advising the surety, because the matter did not come to the solicitor's notice while he was acting as the creditor's agent.[726]

In *Etridge*, the House of Lords revisited the matter and issued detailed guidance as to the steps that should be taken to ensure that the risks are brought home to the surety so that the lender can lend in safety. In general terms, for cases arising after *Etridge*:

> "a bank satisfies these requirements if it insists that the wife attend a private meeting with a representative of the bank at which she is told of the extent of her liability as surety, warned of the risk she is running and urged to take independent legal advice. In exceptional cases the bank, to be safe, has to insist that the wife is separately advised."[727]

In practical terms, a bank placed on notice should adopt the following steps[728]:

(1) "[s]ince the bank is looking for its protection to legal advice given to the wife by a solicitor who, in this respect, is acting solely for her . . . the bank should take steps to check *directly with the wife* the name of the solicitor she wishes to act for her. To this end, in future the bank should communicate directly with the wife, informing her that for its own protection it will require written confirmation from a solicitor, acting for her, to the effect that the solicitor has fully explained to her the nature of the documents and the practical implications they will have for her. She should be told that the purpose of this requirement is that thereafter she should not be able to dispute she is legally bound by the documents once she has signed them. She should be asked to nominate a solicitor whom she

---

[724] Bank of *Baroda v Shah* [1988] 3 All E.R. 24 at 29, 31; *Massey v Midland Bank Plc*, above, at 935; *Bank of Baroda v Rayarel* [1995] 2 F.L.R. 376; *Bank of Scotland v Bennett* [1997] 1 F.L.R. 801 at 833, 834. This is so even if the confirmation that independent advice has been given comes from the creditor's solicitor rather then directly from the surety's: see *Scottish Equitable Life Plc v Virdee* [1999] 1 F.L.R. 863 at 866.

[725] *Barclays Bank Plc v Thomson*, above; *National Westminster Bank Plc v Beaton* (1997) 30 H.L.R. 99. [1997] J.B.L. 220 (M. Haley).

[726] See LPA 1925 s.199(1)(ii)(b) (above, para.8–023); *Halifax Mortgage Services Ltd v Stepsky* [1996] Ch. 207; *Birmingham Midshires Mortgage Services v Mahal*, above; *Barclays Bank Plc v Thomson*, above, at 828, 829; *National Westminster Bank Plc v Beaton*, above; *Leamington Spa BS v Verdi* (1997) 75 P. & C.R. D16. This approach is preferable to but not easy to reconcile with earlier authority: see *Dryden v Frost* (1838) 3 My. & Cr. 670; *Kennedy v Green* (1834) 3 My. & K. 699; *Lloyds Bank Ltd v Marcan* [1973] 1 W.L.R. 339 at 348; above, para.8–023. This approach was criticised, It has been said that creditor's assumption that the surety has received adequate legal advice is one which the creditor "almost always knows to be false": (1998) 114 L.Q.R. 214 at 220 (Sir Peter Millett).

[727] *Etridge*, para.50.

[728] *Etridge*, para.79.

is willing to instruct to advise her, separately from her husband, and act for her in giving the necessary confirmation to the bank. She should be told that, if she wishes, the solicitor may be the same solicitor as is acting for her husband in the transaction. If a solicitor is already acting for the husband and the wife, she should be asked whether she would prefer that a different solicitor should act for her regarding the bank's requirement for confirmation from a solicitor. The bank should not proceed with the transaction until it has received an appropriate response directly from the wife."

(2) "It should become routine practice for banks, if relying on confirmation from a solicitor for their protection, to send to the solicitor the necessary financial information . . . Ordinarily this will include information on the purpose for which the proposed new facility has been requested, the current amount of the husband's indebtedness, the amount of his current overdraft facility, and the amount and terms of any new facility. If the bank's request for security arose from a written application by the husband for a facility, a copy of the application should be sent to the solicitor. The bank will, of course, need first to obtain the consent of its customer to this circulation of confidential information. If this consent is not forthcoming the transaction will not be able to proceed."

(3) "Exceptionally there may be a case where the bank believes or suspects that the wife has been misled by her husband or is not entering into the transaction of her own free will. If such a case occurs the bank must inform the wife's solicitors of the facts giving rise to its belief or suspicion."

(4) The bank should in every case obtain from the wife's solicitor a written confirmation to the effect mentioned above.[729]

This guidance highlights the difficult position that now faces any solicitor who is asked to give independent advice to an intending surety. For example, if the solicitor considers that the transaction is one into which the surety should not enter, he should so advise the client. He should then inform the creditor that he has given "certain advice" and has declined to act further for the surety.[730] The creditor is unlikely to proceed with the transaction in those circumstances.

25–132   5. The function of notice. It is the creditor's actual or constructive notice "of the facts on which the equity to set aside the transaction is founded" that

---

[729] This will normally protect the bank, but not if it knows, or should have known, that the independent advice was defective, *National Westminster Bank v Amin* (2002) 1 F.L.R. 735; M. Haley [2002] Conv. 499.

[730] This notionally respects the confidentiality of the advice while in fact telling the creditor that he has advised against the transaction.

will vitiate the mortgage or waiver of rights in his favour.[731] Such notice implicates him in the principal debtor's undue influence or other wrongdoing.[732] In other words, where C (the creditor) enters into a transaction[733] with B (the surety) where he has notice that B was induced to do so by the wrongdoing of A (the principal debtor), the transaction will be voidable by B.[734] That is, of course, very different from the situation where A transfers property to C who claims to take free of B's rights in the property as a purchaser without notice.[735] The distinction is an important one but it was not appreciated by some commentators. It was initially suggested that the principle in the O'Brien case could not apply to registered land, where the doctrine of the purchaser for value without notice has no application.[736] However, it has now been settled that the analysis given above is the correct one, and "it is irrelevant whether the land is registered or unregistered".[737]

6. Pleading and burden of proof. The surety must adequately plead, and **25–133** bears the burden of proving, that the creditor had notice of the undue influence or other wrongdoing.[738] The onus of proof will be discharged by the surety showing that the creditor knew of the relationship between the surety and the debtor, that the transaction was to the surety's financial disadvantage, and that there was, therefore, a risk that the surety's consent had been obtained improperly.[739]

7. Relief

(a) Rescission ab initio where the surety receives no benefit. Where a **25–134** creditor is held to have notice of the principal debtor's fraud or undue influence, then subject to the usual discretionary bars (such as delay or acquiescence), a surety who has gained no benefit from the transaction is entitled to rescind it.[740] Thus where a wife agreed to a mortgage of the matrimonial home on the basis of a misrepresentation by her husband that the maximum liability would be £15,000, when it was in fact unlimited, the wife

---

[731] *Barclays Bank Plc v Boulter* [1998] 1 W.L.R. 1 at 11, per Mummery L.J. As explained above, para.25–129, the effect of such notice can be neutralised if the creditor takes reasonable steps to ensure that the surety seeks independent advice.

[732] *O'Sullivan v Management Agency and Music Ltd* [1985] Q.B. 428 at 464.

[733] Whether a mortgage or a waiver of rights.

[734] Below, para.25–134.

[735] This distinction was made in [1994] Conv. 421 (C.H. and M.J.D.); (1995) 15 L.S. 35 (G. Battersby). See too *Barclays Bank Plc v Boulter*, above, at 8, 9.

[736] See [1994] Conv. 140 (M. P. Thompson). For the inapplicability of the doctrine of notice to registered land, see above, paras 6–046, 8–006. cf. [1995] Conv. 250 (P. Sparkes).

[737] *Barclays Bank Plc v Boulter*, above, at 11, per Mummery L.J., preferring the view expressed in [1994] Conv. 421.

[738] *Barclays Bank Plc v Boulter* Unreported, October 21, 1999, (HL) affirming the Court of Appeal ([1998] 1 W.L.R. 1) on the facts but reversing it on the law.

[739] *Barclays Bank Plc v Boulter*, above, where Lord Hoffmann illustrated the point by reference to the common case where a wife acts as surety for her husband's indebtedness.

[740] *T.S.B. Bank Plc v Camfield* [1995] 1 W.L.R. 430 (resolving conflicting decisions at first instance); (1995) 111 L.Q.R. 555 (P. Ferguson).

was able to rescind the mortgage and was not liable even for £15,000.[741] Because this principle applies only where the surety has received no benefits from the transaction, there are none which he has to restore to the creditor to achieve *restitutio in integrum*.[742]

There may, however, be exceptional cases where it is possible to sever one part of an agreement that is not vitiated by fraud or undue influence from another part that is, so that only the latter is struck down.[743] This could happen where an existing and valid charge is subsequently extended to cover further indebtedness and where that extension is vitiated by fraud or undue influence of which the creditor has notice.[744]

25–135   *(b) Rescission on terms where the surety has received some benefit.* Where the surety has received some benefit from the transaction, rescission will be given on the usual basis that the surety makes counter restitution.[745] Thus, where a husband applied part of a loan from the creditor to discharge an earlier mortgage of the matrimonial home to which his wife had been a willing party, the creditor was subrogated to that earlier mortgage, notwithstanding the husband's misrepresentation of which the creditor had notice.[746]

25–136   *(c) Where rescission is impossible.* Circumstances could arise in which rescission might be impossible, as where the surety raised the issue of fraud or undue influence by the principal debtor only after the creditor had enforced his security by selling the property charged by the surety.[747] There are two possible answers to this problem. First, the courts may no longer regard the sale of property as a bar to rescission,[748] not least because of their willingness to make elaborate financial adjustments on rescission to effect *restitutio in integrum*.[749] Secondly, even if this is not the case, the court might order the creditor to make a monetary payment to the surety. There are two possible bases for this. First, there is an equitable jurisdiction to award compensation

---

[741] *T.S.B. Bank Plc v Camfield*, above. See too *O'Brien* [1994] 1 A.C. 180 (husband misrepresented to wife that liability on the mortgage was limited to £60,000, whereas it was unlimited).

[742] cf. *T.S.B. Bank Plc v Camfield*, above, at 434; *MacKenzie v Royal Bank of Canada* [1934] A.C. 468 at 476 (a case in which there had been a misrepresentation by the creditor to the surety).

[743] But not if all parts of the transaction are tainted by the undue influence, *Annulment Funding Co ltd v Cowey* above.

[744] *Barclays Bank Plc v Caplan* [1998] 1 F.L.R. 532.

[745] *Dunbar Bank Plc v Nadeem* [1998] 3 All E.R. 876 at 884. The case demonstrates the necessity to determine what benefit the surety received and which he must restore.

[746] *Castle Phillips Finance v Piddington* [1995] 1 F.L.R. 783. The case was in fact one of double subrogation. The first mortgage was valid. The second mortgage (which discharged the first) was tainted by misrepresentation. The third mortgage (which discharged the second) was obtained by the husband forging his wife's signature. The third mortgagee was, by double subrogation, able to enforce the first mortgage against the wife.

[747] For a mortgagee's power of sale, see above, para.25–014.

[748] See *Smith New Court Securities Ltd v Citibank NA* [1997] A.C. 254 at 262. cf. [1994] 1 W.L.R. 1271 at 1280 (CA, sub nom. *Smith New Court Securities Ltd v Scrimgeour Vickers (Asset Management) Ltd*).

[749] See, e.g. *O'Sullivan v Management Agency and Music Ltd* [1985] Q.B. 428.

for breach of duty arising out of a confidential relationship,[750] and it has been exercised against a person who acquired property from another through the exercise of undue influence.[751] However, not every case of undue influence will involve a breach of fiduciary duty, and in any event, it seems unlikely that the jurisdiction could be extended so that compensation could be awarded against a creditor who merely had notice of the principal debtor's undue influence. The second (and better) approach would be to treat the surety's claim as one in restitution to prevent the creditor's unjust enrichment.[752]

8. Unconscionable bargains. There may be situations where the surety can set aside the charge directly as against the creditor because it constitutes an unconscionable bargain,[753] rather than indirectly, on the ground that the creditor is implicated by notice in the principal debtor's undue influence. Although unconscionable conduct is well-recognised as a vitiating factor,[754] the principles governing its operation are not yet firmly settled.[755] The adoption of this alternative approach has been seen by some to be preferable to the principles laid down in the *O'Brien* and *Etridge* cases because the latter has "substituted an inappropriate bright line rule for proper investigation of the facts" and has "failed the vulnerable in the process".[756] However, it is likely that a transaction will be set aside on grounds of unconscionability only in extreme cases. In most situations, the *O'Brien* principles may be the only applicable ones.[757]

25–137

9. *O'Brien* in Scotland. The principles laid down in the *O'Brien* case have been imported into Scottish law by the House of Lords, but on a different basis.[758] There was some unease about imposing liability on a creditor on the basis that he had constructive notice of the principal debtor's fraud or undue

25–138

---

[750] See *Nocton v Lord Ashburton* [1914] A.C. 932.

[751] *Mahoney v Purnell* [1996] 3 All E.R. 61 at 86–91. See (1997) 113 L.Q.R. 8 (J. D. Heydon).

[752] See [1997] R.L.R. 72 (P. Birks). The amount of the surety's claim would presumably be determined by the value of the property when it was sold, even though the property had declined in value since the date of the charge: cf. *Cheese v Thomas* [1994] 1 W.L.R. 129.

[753] See *Credit Lyonnais Bank Nederland NV v Burch* [1997] 1 All E.R. 144. In that case, Millett L.J. described the transaction (by which a junior employee entered into an unlimited guarantee charged on her house as surety for her employer) as one that "shocks the conscience of the court": *Credit Lyonnais Bank Nederland NV v Burch*, above at 152. See (1997) 113 L.Q.R. 10 (H. Tjio); [1997] L.M.C.L.Q. 17 (R. Hooley and J. O'Sullivan).

[754] See *Hart v O'Conner* [1985] A.C. 1000 at 1018. For the circumstances in which relief may be given in respect of a collateral advantage in a mortgage that is unconscionable, see above, paras 25–094, 25–095.

[755] The fullest statement is to be found in *Boustany v Pigott* (1993) 69 P. & C.R. 198 at 303. For a valuable review of the authorities, see [1995] L.M.C.L.Q. 538 (N. Bamforth). See too (1998) 114 L.Q.R. (D. Capper).

[756] (1998) 114 L.Q.R. 214, 220 (Sir Peter Millett). cf. *Credit Lyonnais Bank Nederland NV v Burch*, above, at 152–157.

[757] For a valuable analysis of the extent to which principles of unconscionability underlie the *O'Brien* decision, see [1997] C.L.J. 60 (M. Chen-Wishart).

[758] *Smith v Bank of Scotland* 1997 S.L.T. 1061. See (1998) 114 L.Q.R. 17 (C. E. F. Rickett).

influence. Although a creditor could be regarded as having constructive notice of undue influence between a husband and wife, it had never been suggested that "any particular class of persons is more likely to misrepresent in relation to a contract than any other class".[759] The House therefore based its decision not on notice (or indeed any other concept of equity) but on the duty of good faith that was required of a creditor in a contract of cautionry (suretyship). It held that a creditor owed a duty to give advice to a potential cautioner (surety) "where the creditor should reasonably suspect that there may be factors bearing on the participation of the cautioner which might undermine the validity of the contract through his or her intimate relationship with the debtor".[760] If the creditor wished to enforce the contract, he should warn the cautioner of the consequences of entering into the transaction and advise him to take independent advice.[761]

The Scottish approach is both simpler and more direct than the English one. A creditor is under an explicit duty to warn a surety where there is a risk that the surety may have been induced to act by some impropriety on the part of the principal debtor. English law reaches the same conclusion but by the much more circuitous (and potentially misleading) route of constructive notice,[762] although the decision in *Etridge* goes some way to bringing the two approaches into line in practice.

III. OTHER RIGHTS

25–139   The mortgagor's rights to have the property sold under an order of the court,[763] to inspect the title deeds,[764] and to compel a transfer of the mortgage,[765] have been explained in an earlier section.

Part 1

TRANSFER OF RIGHTS

Section 1. Death of Mortgagor

25–140   In relation to all deaths after 1925,[766] the Administration of Estates Act 1925, replacing an earlier patchwork of provisions, provides that property (whether

---

[759] 1997 S.L.T. 1061, at 1064, per Lord Jauncey.
[760] *Smith v Bank of Scotland*, above at 1068, per Lord Clyde.
[761] *Smith v Bank of Scotland*.
[762] English law was for some time equivocal as to whether contracts of guarantee were contracts uberrimae fidei. However, it was eventually held that they were not, and that only a nondisclosure that amounted to implied misrepresentation entitled the surety to avoid the guarantee: see *North British Insurance Co v Lloyd* (1854) 10 Exch. 523; *Seaton v Heath* [1899] 1 Q.B. 782 at 792. The principles laid down in *O'Brien* have effectively created an exception to this in cases where there is a risk of fraud or undue influence: above, para.25–120.
[763] Above para.25–011.
[764] Above para.25–053.
[765] Above para.25–105.
[766] For the position prior to 1926, see the fifth edition of this work at p.979.

real or personal) mortgaged or charged shall, as between the different persons claiming through a deceased person, be primarily liable to answer the debt, unless the deceased has signified a contrary intention in some document.[767] A general direction to pay debts out of personal estate or out of residue is not by itself to be deemed to show contrary intention.[768] Such an intention may be shown in any document (e.g. a letter[769]), and it may be partial, e.g. applying to mortgages but not to liens.[770] A direction to pay mortgages out of a special fund suffices,[771] though only to the extent of that fund[772]; but it is not enough merely to make a specific devise of part of the mortgaged land, as distinct from the whole.[773]

These provisions do not affect any rights the mortgagee may have against the estate of the mortgagor; they merely ensure that as between the person taking the mortgaged property and the other beneficiaries, the burden of the mortgage should fall primarily upon the former. They do not apply to a person who is given by a will the right to purchase part of the estate, even at a favourable price; for he is a purchaser and not a devisee or legatee.[774]

Section 2. Death of Mortgagee

A. Death of Sole Mortgagee

When a sole legal mortgagee dies, the mortgage vests in his personal representatives in the usual way.[775] Prior to the Conveyancing Act 1881,[776] the legal estate (which was realty) and the right to the money lent (which was personalty) had devolved in different ways.[777]   **25–141**

B. Death of One of Several Mortgagees

Where two or more persons lend money on mortgage and one of them dies the legal title to the mortgage vests in those surviving by virtue of the right of survivorship.[778] In equity there is a presumption of a tenancy in common where two or more together lend on mortgage.[779] Formerly, in the absence of any provision to the contrary, when one of the mortgagees died his equitable   **25–142**

---

[767] AEA 1925 ss.35, 55(1)(xvii). See, e.g. *Re Turner* [1938] Ch. 593 (bequest of shares subject to lien of company).

[768] s.35(2).This slightly modifies the earlier provisions.

[769] See, e.g. *Re Wakefield* [1943] 2 All E.R. 29 (letter to solicitors directing them to complete a purchase held to show no intention that the devisee should take the property free from the vendor's lien for unpaid purchase-money); and see *Re Birmingham* [1958] Ch. 523.

[770] *Re Beirnstein* [1925] Ch. 12.

[771] *Allie v Katah* [1963] 1 W.L.R. 202.

[772] *Re Fegan* [1928] Ch. 45.

[773] *Re Neeld* [1962] Ch. 643, overruling *Re Biss* [1956] Ch. 243.

[774] *Re Fison's W.T.* [1950] Ch. 394.

[775] AEA 1925 ss.1(1), 3(1); above, para.14–140.

[776] s.30.

[777] See the fifth edition of this work at p.981.

[778] Above, para.13–003.

[779] *Rigden v Vallier* (1751) 2 Ves.Sen. 252 at 258: above, para.13–028.

share passed to his personal representatives. If the mortgagor redeemed they would have to join in the transaction.[780] If they did not the mortgagor would not obtain a good receipt for the money from the persons entitled to receive it, and the reconveyance would not give him a good title.[781] To overcome this difficulty, it is provided by statute[782] that as between the mortgagor and the mortgagees, the mortgagees are deemed to have advanced the money on a joint account unless a contrary intention appears from the mortgage. As a result, the survivor or survivors can give a complete discharge for all monies due notwithstanding any notice of severance which the mortgagor may have.[783]

This is, of course, mere conveyancing machinery, enabling the surviving mortgagees to overreach the beneficial interests in the mortgaged property. It does not affect the rights of the mortgagees inter se; if they are beneficially entitled and not trustees, the survivors must account to the personal representatives of the deceased mortgagee for his share. The joint account clause by itself does not alter the presumption as to a tenancy in common.[784]

Section 3. Transfer of Equity of Redemption Inter Vivos

25–143   A mortgagor may at any time without the mortgagee's consent make a conveyance of his property subject to the mortgage. Notwithstanding any such conveyance, and even if the transferee undertakes personal liability to the mortgagee,[785] the mortgagor remains personally liable on the covenant to pay the money.[786] He therefore usually takes an express covenant for indemnity from the transferee, but even if he does not[787] a transferee for value[788] will be under an implied obligation to indemnify him.[789]

A mortgagor who wishes to sell free from the mortgage may do so:

> (i) if he redeems; or
>
> (ii) if the mortgagee consents (as he may well do if the security is adequate or if some other property is substituted for the property in question); or

---

[780] *Vickery v Cowell* (1839) 1 Beav. 529.

[781] A similar problem arose where the mortgagees were trustees investing trust money; see the fifth edition of this work at pp.981–982, where these points are more fully considered.

[782] LPA 1925 s.111. By s.112, a purchaser is absolved from notice of trusts merely because a transfer of the mortgage is stamped SOp instead of ad valorem. By s.113, trusts of the mortgage money do not concern a person dealing in good faith with the mortgagee, or with the mortgagor after discharge.

[783] LPA 1925 s.111(1).

[784] *Re Jackson* (1887) 34 Ch D 732.

[785] *West Bromwich BS v Bullock* [1936] 1 All E.R. 887.

[786] *Kinnaird v Trollope* (1888) 39 Ch D 636.

[787] *Mills v United Counties Bank Ltd* [1912] 1 Ch. 231 (implied obligation excluded by express but limited obligation).

[788] But not a volunteer: see *Re Best* [1924] 1 Ch. 42.

[789] *Bridgman v Daw* (1891) 40 W.R. 253.

(iii) if the mortgagor takes advantage of the statutory provision enabling the court to declare property free from an incumbrance upon
sufficient money being paid into court.[790]

An assignee of the equity of redemption in general steps into the shoes of the
mortgagor; but he does not merely by the assignment become personally
liable to the mortgagee to pay the mortgage debt to him.[791]

Section 4. Transfer of Mortgage Inter Vivos

A. In General

1. Mortgages of unregistered land. A mortgagee may transfer his mort-   **25–144**
gage at any time.[792] He may do so by a simple form of transfer. Since 1925
a deed executed by a mortgagee purporting to transfer his mortgage, or the
benefit of it, transfers to the transferee the estate in the land together with the
right to the money and the benefit of all covenants, powers and securities
therefore, unless a contrary intention appears.[793] The transfer can be made
without the concurrence of the mortgagor, but he should always be made a
party if possible, for then he admits the state of accounts, i.e. he acknowledges
that some specified sum is still due under the mortgage. If he does not join in
the transfer, the transferee gets the benefit only of that sum which is actually
due,[794] even if the transferor represents that more is owing.[795]

Once the transfer has been made, the transferee should give notice of it to
the mortgagor, unless the mortgagor has notice already, e.g. because he was a
party to the transfer. If the mortgagor has no actual or constructive notice, the
transferee cannot complain if the mortgagor pays to the transferor money due
under the mortgage.[796]

2. Registered charges. Where registered land is subject to a registered   **25–145**
charge, the proprietor of that charge has a right as owner to transfer it in the
prescribed manner, unless there is an entry to the contrary on the register.[797]
The transfer is completed only when it is registered and, until then, the
transferor remains proprietor.[798] A registered transferee takes the charge free

---

[790] LPA 1925 s.50(1), (2). This provision is particularly useful if the legal right to redeem has
not arisen.
[791] *Re Errington* [1894] 1 Q.B. 11.
[792] See, e.g. *Turner v Smith* [1901] 1 Ch. 213.
[793] LPA 1925 s.114.
[794] *Bickerton v Walker* (1885) 31 Ch D 151 at 158. He cannot add the costs of the transfer to
the mortgage debt: *Re Radcliffe* (1856) 22 Beav. 201.
[795] *Turner v Smith*, above.
[796] *Dixon v Winch* [190011 Ch. 736 at 742.
[797] LRA 2002 ss.23, 26. See Ruoff & Roper, 27.001.
[798] LRA 2002 s.25 and Sch.2, and s.27(1). See Ruoff & Roper, 28.003.

of any irregularity or invalidity unless this is noted on the register or such limitation is imposed by the Act itself.[799]

B. Sub-mortgages

25–146   **1. Meaning.** A sub-mortgage is a mortgage of a mortgage. A mortgagee may, instead of transferring his mortgage outright, borrow money upon the security of it. A well-secured debt is in itself a good security for another loan. Thus if X has lent £100,000 upon a mortgage made by B, and X then wishes to raise a temporary loan of £10,000 himself, it would clearly be inadvisable for X to call in the whole of his loan. Consequently, X would raise the money by mortgaging his mortgage, i.e. by making a sub-mortgage.

2. Creation

25–147   *(a) Unregistered land.* Where unregistered land has been mortgaged, a submortgage may be created:

> (i) in the case of an equitable mortgage or a legal charge, by assigning the mortgage debt to the sub-mortgagee subject to a proviso for redemption[800];
>
> (ii) in the case of a legal mortgage by demise or sub-demise, by grant of a sub-term or by a legal charge[801]; or
>
> (iii) in the case of a legal charge or a legal mortgage by demise or sub-demise, by an equitable contract to sub-mortgage.

25–148   *(b) Registered land.*[802] Where registered land is subject to a registered charge, the proprietor of that charge may create a sub-charge only by charging the indebtedness secured by the primary mortgage.This rationalisation was introduced by the Land Registration Act 2002 and it makes it clear that it is the indebtedness of the primary charge that is charged as security.[803] Thus, it is no longer possible to create a sub-charge by transfer of the mortgage, demise or even a charge by deed by way of legal mortgage. There is, however, no loss of rights or powers for the sub-chargee, for these are expressly preserved.[804] The sub-charge is a registered disposition and must be completed by registration.[805] If so registered, it will be protected in the event of a registered disposition for value of the registered estate over which it operates and also will enjoy the benefit of the priority rule in relation to earlier, unprotected interests.[806]

---

[799] LRA 2002 s.26.
[800] Fisher & Lightwood, *Mortgage*, p.272.
[801] See LPA 1925 s.86(1), (3).
[802] See Ruoff & Roper, 27.002.
[803] LRA 2002 ss.23(2)(a) and (b) and 23(3).
[804] LRA 2002 s.53.
[805] LRA 2002 s.27(1), (3).
[806] LRA 2002 s.29.

3. Powers. In general, where title is unregistered, the sub-mortgagee takes **25–149**
over the mortgagee's rights of enforcing payment under the original mortgage.
He may, for example, sell the property under a power of sale. Alternatively he
may exercise his remedies against the mortgage. If the sub-mortgage confers
a power of sale, he may sell the mortgage or charge itself.

Where title is registered, the proprietor of the sub-charge has the same
powers as the proprietor of the principal charge.[807]

Section 5. Discharge of Mortgage

A. Unregistered Land

1. Indorsed receipt. In the case of any mortgage of unregistered land **25–150**
discharged after 1925,[808] a receipt indorsed on or annexed to the mortgage
deed, signed[809] by the mortgagee and stating the name of the person paying
the money, normally operates as a surrender of the mortgage term or a
reconveyance, as the case may be, and discharges the mortgage.[810] The
mortgagor may, if he prefers, have a reassignment, surrender, release or
transfer executed instead.[811] This is necessary if only part of the debt is being
paid and part of the property redeemed.[812]

2. Transfer. If the receipt shows that the person paying the money was not **25–151**
entitled to the immediate equity of redemption and makes no provision to the
contrary, it operates as a transfer of the mortgage to him.[813] Thus where a third
mortgagee pays off the first mortgage, the statutory receipt will transfer the
mortgage to him. But this does not enable the mortgagor, on paying off a
mortgage, to keep it alive against a subsequent mortgagee.[814]

3. Building societies. A building society may use either a reconveyance or **25–152**
else a special form of statutory receipt. This receipt does not state who paid
the money and cannot operate as a transfer of the mortgage; but otherwise it
takes effect under these provisions.[815]

4. Satisfied term. Apart from these provisions, once a mortgage by sub- **25–153**
demise has been redeemed, the sub-term becomes a satisfied term and ceases

---

[807] LRA 2002 s.53.
[808] See LPA 1925 s.115(8), (10).
[809] *Simpson v Geoghegan* [1934] W.N. 232.
[810] LPA 1925 s.115(1).
[811] LPA 1925 s.115(4).
[812] Fisher & Lightwood, *Mortgage*, p.572.
[813] LPA 1925 s.115(2).
[814] *Otter v Lord Vaux* (1856) 6 De G.M. & G. 638; LPA 1925 s.115(3); see *Cumberland Court (Brighton) Ltd v Taylor* [1964] Ch. 29.
[815] Building Societies Act 1986 s.13(7); Sch.4 para.2, replacing earlier legislation.

forthwith.[816] Under this provision an ordinary receipt (i.e. one not complying with the conditions relating to indorsed receipts) might be thought to operate as a sufficient discharge. However, conveyancers do not in practice rely upon such a receipt, because it is only prima facie proof of payment.[817]

B. Registered Land

25–154 The provisions governing the discharge of mortgages of unregistered land are inapplicable where title is registered.[818] Discharge of a registered charge (whether in whole or part) is made by vacation of the relevant entry on the register, and this may be done in either documentary form or electronically.[819] An application to discharge in documentary form must be made by on the correct Land Registry form[820] and should be executed as a deed.[821] The actual discharge of the mortgage is achieved by a change to the register on receipt of the appropriate additional form requesting such a change, rather than by the discharge itself.[822] The special form of discharge where the registered proprietor of the charge is a building society does not apply to registered titles.[823]

Electronic discharge of charges is possible under the "ED" system. This is a computer-to computer system wherein there is no intervention by Land Registry staff.[824] The result in most cases is removal of the charge automatically.

Where a mortgage is not registered as a charge but is noted on the register by means of an agreed or unilateral notice, that notice may be cancelled or withdrawn in accordance with the provisions concerning the cancelation or withdrawal of notices.[825] The charge is discharged when the notice is cancelled or withdrawn. Satisfactory evidence that the mortgage has been discharged will of course be required and this will vary according to the type of charge.[826]

---

[816] LPA 1925 ss.5, 116; cf. above. This now applies to terms created out of leaseholds as well as those created out of freeholds.

[817] Woist. & C. i, p.225.

[818] LPA 1925 s.115(10).

[819] See Ruoff & Roper, 28.012.

[820] LRR 2003 r.114. Form DS1 (whole) or DS3 (part).

[821] The Land Registry may approve other arrangements, so enabling effective agreements with individual lenders, LRR 2003 r.114.

[822] Form AP1 or Form DS2, as circumstances require.

[823] Above, para.25–150. See Building Societies Act 1986 s.13(7); Sch.4 para.2(4) (which restricts the statutory receipt to unregistered land).

[824] See Ruoff & Roper 28.014.01.

[825] See above paras 7–069 et seq. and Ruoff & Roper, Ch.42. Form AP1 is used to effect the change to the register.

[826] Forms DS1 or DS3 may be used, as well as an endorsed receipt for equitable charges. Company charges may be discharged by use of Companies Registry Form 403A, or by written evidence of discharge.

CHAPTER 26

PRIORITY OF MORTGAGES

Where there is more than one mortgage on the same property, it is some- **26–001**
times necessary to determine the priority of the mortgages; for example, if the
property is sold by one mortgagee and there is not enough money to satisfy all
mortgages. There is no question of the various mortgagees sharing the loss.
Each mortgagee takes his full claim in order of priority, because it is for a later
mortgagee to satisfy himself as to viability of the security before he takes his
mortgage. Cases of dispute as to priority are most likely to arise where,
perhaps because of the fraud of the mortgagor, a later mortgagee advances his
money in ignorance of an earlier mortgage.

> "It happens with unfortunate frequency that a man having title to land
> contrives by means of fraudulent concealment to get money from a
> number of different persons on the security of the land—then
> disappears—and the lenders are left to dispute among themselves as to
> the order in which they are to be paid out of the value of the land which
> is insufficient to pay all of them."[1]

This particular malpractice, however, seems to have been commoner in the
past than it is today.[2]

Fundamentally the rules which govern priority are general rules about the **26–002**
relationship of estates, both legal and equitable, as modified where relevant by
principles of land registration. Thus the question whether a first equitable
mortgage takes priority over a second legal mortgage is essentially the same
as the question whether an equitable mortgage binds a later purchaser of the
fee simple. The rules are not peculiar to mortgages, but it is in connection with
mortgages that they are most likely to present problems. The question whether
a mortgage takes priority over a lease in a case where a purchaser of land lets
it before completing the purchase and the mortgage that funds it, has been

---

[1] Maitland, *Equity*, 125.
[2] No doubt, this is due in large measure to the modern system of land registration. However,
even with registered title, such fraud is possible, *Halifax plc v Curry Popeck (A Firm)* [2008]
EWHC 1692 (Ch), [2009] 1 P. & C.R. DG3. See (2009) 129 L.Q.R. 401 (M.J.D.).

considered elsewhere.[3] It has also been explained that some statutory charges may have an overriding priority of their own, regardless of the ordinary rules.[4]

The general rules for determining priority in unregistered land will be discussed first, followed by the rules relating to tacking, which is a method of altering the priorities that is settled by general rules. In each case, it is first necessary to explain the rules as they stood before 1926. Those rules remain the essential foundation, but their operation in relation to unregistered land is radically affected by the system of registration of land charges introduced in 1925 and by other amendments. The position where the title is registered, which has already been explained,[5] is then briefly summarised.

It should also be noted that where there are two mortgages of the same property, the mortgagees can agree to alter the priority of those charges without the mortgagor's consent. If a mortgagor wishes to prevent this happening, he must ensure that the mortgage contains a specific contractual provision precluding such alteration.[6]

Section 1. Unregistered Land: General Rules

A. Priority Before 1926

26–003 Before 1926, there was one set of rules for determining priorities where the property mortgaged was an interest in land and a separate set of rules for cases where the property mortgaged was an interest in pure personalty, i.e. personalty other than leaseholds.[7] Since the rules about personalty affected interests under trusts for sale of land, both sets of rules require explanation.

I. MORTGAGES OF AN INTEREST IN LAND

26–004 Two main rules applied to mortgages of land, including sub-mortgages, that is, mortgages of a mortgage of land.[8] These rules applied whether the interest was legal or equitable[9] and whether the land was freehold or leasehold.[10]

(i) "He who is first in time is stronger in law" (*Qui prior est tempore, potior est jure*). Thus, mortgages primarily ranked in the order of their creation, or "first made, first paid"; but

---

[3] It is now settled that the mortgage takes priority, *Abbey National BS v Cann* [1991] 1 A.C. 56. See above, para.17–132.

[4] Above para.7–068. The possibility of such charges being incurred by the mortgagor can impair the mortgagee's security: see *Westminster City Council v Haymarket Publishing Ltd* [1980] 1 W.L.R. 683 (rating surcharge takes priority over earlier legal mortgage).

[5] Above, paras 7–050, 7–102.

[6] *Cheah v Equiticorp Finance Group Ltd* [1992] 1 A.C. 472.

[7] See below, para.26–004.

[8] *Taylor v London & County Banking Co* [1901] 2 Ch. 231.

[9] *Wilmot v Pike* (1845) 5 Hare 14; *Wiltshire v Rabbits* (1844) 14 Sim. 76.

[10] *Rooper v Harrison* (1855) 2 K. & J. 86; *Union Bank of London v Kent* (1888) 39 Ch D 238.

(ii) "Where the equities are equal, the law prevails". Thus if, apart from the order of their creation, a legal and an equitable mortgage had equal claims to be preferred, the legal mortgage would have priority.[11]

Bearing those rules in mind, in practice a conflict between two mortgages accordingly fell into one of four types and these will be considered in turn. **26–005**

(i) Where both mortgages were legal.

(ii) Where the first mortgage was legal and the second equitable.

(iii) Where the first mortgage was equitable and the second legal.

(iv) Where both mortgages were equitable.

1. Both mortgages legal. Conflicts where both mortgages were legal rarely **26–006** came before the courts, since most mortgages of freeholds were effected by a conveyance of the fee simple, which made the creation of subsequent legal mortgages impossible. Successive legal mortgages could, however, be created by the grant of successive terms of years,[12] and a lease might be mortgaged by the grant of two successive subleases.[13] In any such cases, where two or more legal mortgages were created in succession, priority normally depended on the order of creation,[14] for after the grant of one lease, the second lease must take effect in reversion upon the first, and a legal estate in reversion was postponed to one in possession.[15]

2. Legal mortgage followed by equitable mortgage. Where a legal mort- **26–007** gage was followed by an equitable mortgage, the legal mortgagee had a double claim to priority, both as being prior in point of time and as being a legal mortgagee in competition with a mere equitable mortgagee. But this natural priority might be displaced in a number of ways.

(a) By fraud. If the legal mortgagee was party to some fraud whereby the **26–008** equitable mortgagee was deceived into believing that there was no legal mortgage on the property, the legal mortgagee was postponed to the equitable mortgagee.[16]

---

[11] *Bailey v Barnes* [1894] 1 Ch. 25 at 36. "Equality means the non-existence of any circumstance which affects the conduct of one of the rival claimants, and makes it less meritorious than that of the other": *Bailey v Barnes*, per Lindley L.J.

[12] *Aldridge v Duke* (1697) Rep.t.Finch 439.

[13] *Jones v Rhind* (1869) 17 W.R. 1091.

[14] As explained later (see below), a legal mortgagee could lose priority by negligently parting with the title deeds (see *Jones v Rhind*, above), and no doubt also by failure to obtain them, or by fraud.

[15] Coote, *Mortgages*, p.1240. See *Ex p. Knott* (1806) 11 Yes. 609; *Hurst v Hurst* (1852) 16 Beav. 372. See also *Re Russell Road Purchase-Moneys* (1871) L.R. 12 Eq. 78 (lease mortgaged first by the grant of a legal sub-term and then by legal assignment; the mortgagee by assignment claimed priority over an intervening equitable mortgage of which he had no notice, but the case was compromised before the Court of Appeal could give judgment).

[16] *Peter v Russet* (1716) 1 Eq.Ca.Abr. 321.

26–009   *(b) By estoppel.* If the legal mortgagee either expressly or by implication made some misrepresentation by which the equitable mortgagee was deceived, the legal mortgagee might be estopped from asserting his priority.[17] Thus if the legal mortgagee indorsed a receipt for his money on the mortgage and somebody was thereby induced to lend money on an equitable mortgage of the property, the legal mortgagee could not afterwards claim priority for his loan even if in fact it had not been discharged.[18] Again, if the legal mortgagee returned the deeds to the mortgagor in order to enable him to raise a further loan, he was postponed to any subsequent mortgagee who lent money without notice of the first mortgage, even if the mortgagor had agreed to inform the second mortgagee of the first mortgage,[19] or had agreed to borrow only a limited amount which in fact he exceeded.[20] Once the legal mortgagee had clothed the mortgagor with apparent authority to deal with the property freely, he could not afterwards claim the protection of any undisclosed limits set to this authority.[21]

26–010   *(c) By gross negligence in relation to the title deeds.* It was held in one case that an earlier legal mortgagee could never lose his priority by mere carelessness or want of prudence in relation to the title deeds, falling short of fraud.[22] However, the law appears rather to have been that a legal mortgagee could lose priority as against a later conscientious equitable mortgagee[23] if by gross negligence he fails to obtain the title deeds,[24] or, perhaps, to retain them.[25] "Gross negligence" is an indefinable expression, but it was used to indicate a degree of negligence which made it unjust to enforce the natural

---

[17] *Dixon v Muckleston* (1872) 8 Ch.App. 155 at 160. This may continue to operate in the modern law, as where one legal mortgagee is estopped from denying that another legal mortgage had priority, even though under land registration rules it should not: *Scottish & Newcastle plc v Lancashire Mortgage Corp Ltd* [2007] EWCA Civ 684; (2007) NPC 84.

[18] *Rimmer v Webster* [1902] 2 Ch. 163; cf. *Rice v Rice* (1853) 2 Drew. 73 (two equitable incumbrances).

[19] *Briggs v Jones* (1870) L.R. 10 Eq. 92; and see *Martinez v Cooper* (1826) 2 Russ. 198.

[20] *Perry Herrick v Attwood* (1857) 2 De G. & J. 21.

[21] *Brocklesby v Temperance Permanent BS* [1895] A.C. 173; *Rimmer v Webster*, above, at 173; *Abigail v Lapin* [1934] A.C. 491.

[22] *Northern Counties of England Fire Insurance Co v Whipp* (1884) 26 Ch D 482.

[23] Being one who exercised due diligence: *Hunt v Elmes* (1860) 2 De G.F. & J. 578 at 586, 587. See *Walker v Linom* [1907] 2 Ch. 104 at 114.

[24] *Colyer v Finch* (1856) 5 H.L.C. 905; *Clarke v Palmer* (1882) 21 Ch D 124; *Walker v Linom* [1907] 2 Ch. 104. In the last case W conveyed land to trustees, handing over a bundle of title deeds but keeping the last previous deed, a conveyance to himself. Later he made, or purported to make, a mortgage with the help of this deed. It was held that the mortgagee took priority over the trustees, and that a beneficiary under the trust was in no better position than the trustees. It might have been thought that the mortgagee, who saw only one deed (seven years old) and cannot have investigated the title properly, had little claim in equity against the legal owner. But this point does not appear to have arisen. For this case, see further below, para.26–011.

[25] This is less certain. In *Northern Counties of England Fire Insurance Co v Whipp*, above, the manager of a company mortgaged his property to the company. Later he took back the deeds, which had been placed in a safe to which he had a key, and gave them to X under a mortgage. Held, that the company had priority over X. A distinction between failure to obtain deeds and failure to retain them is difficult to justify, and the Court of Appeal's decision is probably open to question in the light of *Derry v Peek* (1889) 14 App.Cas. 337: see Waldock, *Mortgages*, p.397.

order of priority.[26] A legal mortgagee who failed to ask for the deeds at all[27] would certainly be postponed. But a legal mortgagee might claim the benefit of the doctrine, explained below,[28] which preserves priority for mortgagees who ask for the deeds and are given a reasonable excuse for their non-production.[29] Further, in a case where the mortgagee knew that the deeds were in the hands of a prior equitable mortgagee but gave him no notice, so that when the mortgagor paid off the equitable mortgage the mortgagor recovered the deeds and was enabled to create a later equitable mortgage, he was held not guilty of such gross negligence as would postpone him.[30] Nor was the legal mortgagee postponed merely because he failed to obtain all the title deeds: if he obtained some of them reasonably believing them to be all, he was not postponed.[31]

The postponement of an earlier legal to a later equitable mortgagee for any **26–011** of the above three reasons is explicable only as an intervention by equity against the ordinary rules governing estates, in particular against the rule that no one can convey what he has not got. The later equitable mortgagee could obtain from the mortgagor only a mortgage of the equity of redemption: the legal estate was with the first mortgagee, and could be obtained only by redeeming. Nevertheless, if the conduct of the first mortgagee raised a case of fraud, estoppel or gross negligence, the second mortgagee could enforce a prior equitable right to the legal estate, and so ultimately obtain it without redemption of the apparently prior mortgage. In such a case, for example, if the later mortgage gave the mortgagee a power of sale, he could give a good title to a purchaser, free from the earlier mortgage which in law stood first but which in equity stood second.[32] Conversely, it seems probable that if the earlier legal mortgagee transferred his mortgage to a transferee for value who took without notice of the circumstances (e.g. of fraud), the transferee would take free from the legal mortgagee's liability to postponement in equity.

---

[26] See *Oliver v Hinton* [1899] 2 Ch. 264 at para.26–013.

[27] *Clarke v Palmer* (1882) 21 Ch D 124; *Walker v Linom*, above.

[28] Below, para.26–012.

[29] *Manners v Mew* (1885) 29 Ch D 725. *Quaere* whether the excuse given there would be treated as reasonable today; but the case can perhaps be supported on the relationship between the parties: see, e.g. *Hewitt v Loosemore* (1851) 9 Hare 449; below, para.26–011.

[30] *Grierson v National Provincial Bank of England Ltd* [1913] 2 Ch. 18.

[31] *Cottey v The National Provincial Bank of England Ltd* (1904) 20 T.L.R. 607. See *Walker v Linom*, above.

[32] *Walker v Linom* [1907] 2 Ch. 104; above, para.26–010. In a note to Maitland, *Equity*, 138, the editor (J. W. Brunyate) draws attention to the second incumbrancer's lack of title in that case. The facts were striking, since the prior disposition was an outright conveyance, not a mere mortgage. But a mere mortgage would have had the same effect before 1926, as regards the legal estate. In fact the peculiarity seems to apply equally to all the cases in this class. The legal estate remains vested in the person to whom it was first conveyed (*Walker v Linom*, at 110), but presumably the person entitled to priority in equity can compel a transfer of it. He is said to have "a subsequent equitable estate" (at 114), but this seems to arise from an intervention of the court rather than from any interest which the mortgagor had power to create.

3. Equitable mortgage followed by legal mortgage

26–012   (*a*) *Purchaser without notice*. Where an equitable mortgage was followed by a legal mortgage, the primary rule that the mortgages rank in the order of creation might be displaced by the superiority of a legal estate. For this to occur, the legal mortgagee had to show that he was a bona fide purchaser[33] for value of a legal estate without notice[34] of the prior equitable mortgage.[35] In general, a failure to inquire for the deeds at all,[36] or the inability of the mortgagor to produce the title deeds, would amount to constructive notice to the legal mortgagee that some prior mortgage or conveyance had already been made.[37] But there might be good reason for the absence of the deeds (e.g. that they had been destroyed in a fire), and if the later legal mortgagee accepted a "reasonable excuse" for the non-production of the deeds, he was held to have no notice of the prior mortgage.

26–013   (*b*) *Excuses for not producing deeds*. The courts have, however, been satisfied by surprisingly frail excuses, imperfectly investigated, in order to hold that the later legal mortgagee had no notice of the prior equitable mortgage. The excuse that the deeds also related to other property has been held insufficient[38]; but prior equitable mortgagees, in possession of the deeds, have lost priority in favour of later legal mortgagees who have been told by the mortgagor that he was busy, but would produce the deeds later,[39] or that the deeds were in Ireland, where the property was.[40] Such cases appear to deviate from the ordinary principle of notice, which gives priority to a purchaser of a legal estate only if he has taken all the steps which a prudent man of business, properly advised, would be expected to take.[41] A mere story invented by the mortgagor to explain lack of deeds, and not investigated by the later legal mortgagee, may deprive that mortgagee of his anticipated priority over an earlier equitable mortgage.

---

[33] "Purchaser" includes a mortgagee: *Brace v Duchess of Marlborough* (1728) 2 P. Wms. 491; *Pilcher v Rawlins* (1872) 7 Ch.App. 259.

[34] It was only when the equities were equal that the law prevailed, and "he that has Notice has no Equity at all"; *Oxwith v Plummer* (1708) Gilb.Ch. 13 at 15, per Lord Cowper L.C.

[35] Above, para.8–011. As there mentioned, a better equitable right to an outstanding legal estate would do; see the case put in *Wilmot v Pike* (1845) 5 Hare 14 at 21, 22, which may be paraphrased thus: successive mortgages are made to A (legal), B (equitable) and C (equitable); A joins in the mortgage to C and (neither A nor C then knowing of B's mortgage) declares himself trustee for C subject to A's own mortgage. C then takes priority to B because of his better title to the legal estate; but not if either A or C knew of B's mortgage at the time of the declaration of trust. This shows the importance of B giving notice to A. C could not secure priority merely by giving notice to A before B did so, for the rule in *Dearle v Hall* (1828) 3 Russ. 1 (see below, para.26–015) did not apply to realty; therefore a declaration of trust was essential to C's claim.

[36] *Berwick & Co v Price* [1905] 1 Ch. 632.

[37] That, indeed, is a primary object in depositing the deeds: see above, para.24–037.

[38] *Oliver v Hinton* [1899] 2 Ch. 264.

[39] *Hewitt v Loosemore* (1851) 9 Hare 449, and earlier cases there cited; cf. *Ratcliffe v Barnard* (1871) 6 Ch.App. 652 (receipt by legal mortgagee of some only of the deeds, in reasonable belief that they were all).

[40] *Agra Bank Ltd v Barry* (1874) L.R. 7 HL 135.

[41] Above, para.8–017.

This rule (that the later legal mortgagee generously may not be held to have notice) probably owes its origin to a doctrine about "gross negligence" which has caused some confusion. It has often been said that the later legal mortgagee is entitled to priority if he has not been fraudulent or grossly negligent.[42] But in this type of case, unlike the type previously discussed, the generous approach to "notice" (or rather lack of it) contradicts the principle that an equitable interest should bind a purchaser who does not investigate the title. It is, however, firmly established.

4. Both mortgages equitable. Where both mortgages were equitable, the **26–014** primary rule was that priority depended upon the order in which the mortgages were created.[43] This, however, was subject to the equities being in other respects equal,[44] so that although the vested interest of the prior mortgagee would not lightly be displaced,[45] the order might be altered by the inequitable behaviour of the prior mortgagee.[46] Accordingly, a first mortgagee who failed to ask for the title deeds,[47] or who, having obtained them, redelivered them to the mortgagor without pressing for their early return,[48] might be postponed to a second mortgagee who took all proper precautions but who was nevertheless deceived. But a first mortgagee who accepted some only of the title deeds, on the mortgagor's written assurance that he had received all of them, did not lose his priority.[49]

II. MORTGAGES OF AN EQUITABLE INTEREST IN PURE PERSONALTY

1. The rule in *Dearle v Hall.* Legal mortgages of chattels fall under the **26–015** head of bills of sale and are outside the scope of this book. So also are mortgages of choses in action. However, prior to 1997, equitable interests in pure personalty included the rights of those interested under a trust for sale of

---

[42] See *Hewitt v Loosemore*, above; *Oliver v Hinton* [1899] 2 Ch. 264; *Hudston v Viney* [1921] 1 Ch. 98. In *Oliver v Hinton* there was first an equitable mortgage by deposit, followed by an outright sale of the legal estate to a purchaser who had no actual notice of the mortgage but who accepted an inadequate excuse for non-production of the deeds (namely that they related also to other property). It was held that the purchaser took subject to the mortgage. On general grounds it should have sufficed to say that the purchaser had constructive notice, and the case was so decided by Romer J. at first instance, at 268 (this was also the view of Parker J. in *Walker v Linom* [1907] 2 Ch. 104 at 114). But the Court of Appeal held the purchaser liable not because of notice but because of his "gross negligence": see Lindley M.R.'s judgment at 273, 274. Why this doctrine was needed, or how, if at all, it differs from the doctrine of notice, is not explained.

[43] *Rice v Rice* (1853) 2 Drew. 73 at 78.

[44] *Rice v Rice*, above.

[45] *Cory v Eyre* (1863) 1 De G.J. & S. 149 at 167.

[46] Whether priority will be lost only by the same degree of gross negligence as will displace a legal mortgagee is doubtful: see *Taylor v Russell* [1891] 1 Ch. 8, at 14–20, where the authorities are reviewed. See also the decision of the House of Lords in that case ([1892] A.C. 244 at 262) and *National Provincial Bank of England v Jackson* (1886) 33 Ch D 1, for the view that a smaller degree of negligence may suffice to displace an equitable mortgagee. See R. P. Meagher, W. M. C. Gummow and J. R. F Lehane, *Equity: Doctrines and Remedies* 4th edn, paras 806–818.

[47] *Farrand v Yorkshire Banking Co* (1888) 40 Ch D 182.

[48] *Waldron v Sloper* (1852) 1 Drew. 193; *Dowle v Saunders* (1864) 2 H. & M. 242.

[49] *Dixon v Muckleston* (1872) 8 Ch.App. 155.

land,[50] and so must be dealt with here. Mortgages of such interests were governed by the rule in *Dearle v Hall*.[51] This laid down that priority depended upon the order in which notice of the mortgages or other dealings was received by the owner of the legal estate or interest (the trustees, in the case of a trust for sale), but also that a mortgagee who, when he lent his money, had actual or constructive notice of a prior mortgage could not gain priority over it by giving notice to the legal owner first.

26–016   **2. Basis of the rule.** The rule in *Dearle v Hall* is a general principle of equity governing dealings with equitable interests in pure personalty. Various explanations of the basis of the rule have been given.[52] The "leading consideration" is that as between two equally innocent incumbrancers, priority should be given to the one who, by giving notice, had prevented the mortgagor from representing himself to be the unincumbered owner of the property and so defrauding third parties.[53] The rule may also be based on an analogy with chattels, where title passes by delivery of possession. An assignee of an equitable interest in personalty must, it was held, take steps to obtain the equivalent to possession by giving notice to the trustee, and so perfecting his title.[54] An imperfect title would not prevail over a later assignee's perfected title; and the earlier assignee's equity was all the weaker for his own negligence in allowing the trustees to suppose that the later assignee was the first. Although the rule was founded on equitable principles, it soon crystallised into a rigid rule[55] and by the beginning of the 20th century it was settled that it would not be extended.[56]

26–017   **3. Loan without notice.** It is clear that for a second mortgagee to claim priority over a first mortgagee by giving notice, first he must be able to show that at the time of lending his money he had no notice of the first mortgage.[57] If at that time he had notice, and yet he lent his money, it would be inequitable for him subsequently to claim priority merely because he gave notice to the legal owner first, for the failure of the first mortgagee to give notice had in no

---

[50] *Lee v Howlett* (1856) 2 K. & J. 531. This was because of the doctrine of conversion, explained, above, para.10–029. Since TLATA 1996 came into force on January 1, 1997, trusts for sale have become trusts of land and the doctrine of conversion has been abolished: see above, paras 12–006, 12–007. Interests under a trust of land necessarily are an interest in land and not governed by the rule considered here.

[51] (1828) 3 Russ. 1, approved by the House of Lords in *Foster v Cockerell* (1835) 3 Cl. & F. 456; and see *Ward v Duncombe* [1893] A.C. 369.

[52] See. e.g. *Ward v Duncombe*, above, at 392.

[53] *Ward v Duncombe*, above, at 378.

[54] But see Lord Macnaghten's criticisms in Ward v Duncombe, above; cf. Lord Herschell's speech at 378. The House of Lords discussed the rule in *BS Lyle Ltd v Rosher* [1959] 1 W.L.R. 8.

[55] See, e.g. *Re Dallas* [1904] 2 Ch. 385 (X charged a legacy he was expecting under the will of a living testator, who had become insane, first to A and then to B: the testator then died and A and B each gave notice to the administrator as soon as they knew of his appointment, B's notice being received first: held B had priority).

[56] *Ward v Duncombe*, above, at 394; *Hill v Peters* [1918] 2 Ch. 273.

[57] *Re Holmes* (1885) 29 Ch D 786.

way prejudiced him; he lent his money knowing of the first mortgage. But if he lent his money without notice of the first mortgage, it was immaterial that he had notice of the first mortgage *at the time* when he gave notice to the trustees.[58] Indeed, such knowledge is just what would impel him to give his own notice, so as to obtain priority.[59]

4. Details of the rule. The details of the rule were worked out in a series **26–018** of cases, which may be summarised under three main heads.

(a) Priority depended upon notice being received, not given. Although it **26–019** was both usual and advisable for a mortgagee to give express notice, the test was not whether the mortgagee had taken active steps to give notice but whether the trustees had received knowledge of the mortgage from any reliable source. For example, where one chargee left written notice with the legal owner, a bank, after closing hours, and other chargees gave notice the next day, as soon as the bank opened, it was held that the bank must be treated as having received all notices simultaneously, and consequently that the charges ranked in the order of creation.[60] Clear and distinct oral notice sufficed,[61] but a statement made in a casual conversation with a trustee did not.[62] Knowledge received through reading a notice in a paper,[63] and knowledge acquired by a trustee before his appointment which continued to operate on his mind after his appointment,[64] have both been held sufficient to protect a prior mortgagee against a later mortgagee who gave express notice, although neither would obtain priority for a later mortgagee over a prior mortgagee.[65] Stronger measures are needed to upset the natural order of the mortgages than are needed to maintain it.

(b) It was advisable to give notice to all the trustees. This was because of **26–020** the following:

(i) Notice given to all the existing trustees remained effective even though they all retired or died without communicating the notice to their successors.[66]

---

[58] *Mutual Life Assurance Society v Langley* (1886) 32 Ch D 460.

[59] cf. *Wortley v Birkhead* (1754) 2 Ves.Sen. 571 at 574. cf. below, para.26–053, for a somewhat similar situation in the old law of tacking.

[60] *Calisher v Forbes* (1871) 7 Ch.App. 109; and see *Johnstone v Cox* (1880) 16 Ch D 571 (affirmed 19 Ch D 17). *Re Dallas* [1904] 2 Ch. 385 at 405 must, it seems, be taken to refer to simultaneous notices.

[61] *Browne v Savage* (1859) 4 Drew. 635 at 640; *Re Worcester* (1868) 3 Ch.App. 555 (statement at directors' meeting); compare the simultaneous notices in *Calisher v Forbes*, above.

[62] *Re Tichener* (1865) 35 Beav. 317.

[63] *Lloyd v Banks* (1868) 3 Ch.App. 488.

[64] *Ipswich Permanent Money Club Ltd v Arthy* [1920] 2 Ch. 257.

[65] *Ipswich Permanent Money Club Ltd v Arthy*, above, at 271; *Arden v Arden* (1885) 29 Ch D 702.

[66] *Re Wasdale* [1899] 1 Ch. 163.

(ii) Notice given to one of several trustees was effective against all incumbrances created during his trusteeship, and for this purpose remained effective after his death or retirement.[67]

(iii) But notice given to one of several trustees was not effective against incumbrancers who advanced money after the death or retirement of that trustee, unless he had communicated the notice to one or more of the continuing trustees.[68]

(iv) If the mortgagor was a trustee, the mere fact that he knew of the transaction would not affect priorities because such notice afforded no protection to those intending to lend on subsequent mortgages.[69] But if the mortgagee was a trustee, his knowledge of the transaction did affect priorities; for to protect his mortgage he would readily disclose its existence to any prospective subsequent incumbrancers.[70]

26–021   *(c) A mortgagee who lent his money with notice of a prior mortgage could not gain priority over it by giving notice first.* This has been discussed above.[71]

26–022   **5. Protection on distribution.** In addition to securing priority, notice to the trustees, though not essential to the validity of the mortgage,[72] safeguarded the mortgagee by ensuring that his claims would not be disregarded when the funds were distributed. Trustees were bound to give effect to all claims of which they knew,[73] but were not liable if they distributed the trust funds to the prejudice of a mortgagee of whom they did not know.[74] Nor were they bound to answer inquiries either by the beneficiary or a prospective mortgagee as to the extent to which the beneficiary's share was incumbered: "it is no part of the duty of a trustee to assist his cestui que trust in selling or mortgaging his beneficial interest and in squandering or anticipating his fortune."[75]

B. Priority After 1925

26–023   The general scheme of the 1925 legislation called for some amendment of the rules relating to priority. In particular, the old rule of the superiority of the

---

[67] *Ward v Duncombe* [1893] A.C. 369.
[68] *Timson v Ramsbottom* (1836) 2 Keen 35, criticised by Lord Macnaghten in *Ward v Duncombe*, above, at 394, but accepted by Lord Herschell at 381, 382, and followed in *Re Phillips' Trusts* [1903] 1 Ch. 183.
[69] *Lloyds Bank v Pearson* [1901] 1 Ch. 865. To hold otherwise would make the rule in *Dearle v Hall* "a mere trap": *Lloyds Bank v Pearson*, at 873, per Cozens-Hardy J.
[70] *Browne v Savage* (1859) 4 Drew. 635 at 641.
[71] Above, para.26–017.
[72] *Burn v Carvalho* (1839) 4 My. & Cr. 690; *Gorringe v Irwell India Rubber & Gutta Percha Works* (1886) 34 Ch D 128.
[73] *Hodgson v Hodgson* (1837) 2 Keen 704.
[74] *Phipps v Lovegrove* (1873) L.R. 16 Eq. 80.
[75] *Low v Bouverie* [1891] 3 Ch. 82 at 99, per Lindley L.J.

legal estate was clearly inappropriate to a system which encouraged the creation of more than one legal mortgage of the same property; and since the interests of beneficiaries under strict settlements could no longer be legal, for the purposes of priority they could conveniently be classed with interests arising under a trust for sale.

Before 1926 the bright line distinction was the line between interests in land and interests in pure personalty: if the former, the matter was governed by the rules relating to the order of creation and the superiority of the legal estate; if the latter, by the rule in *Dearle v Hall*. However, since 1925, the question is whether the interest mortgaged is legal or equitable. A mortgage of a legal estate in land now depends for its priority upon possession of the title deeds or upon registration (as the case may be); a mortgage of an equitable interest in realty or personalty depends upon the rule in *Dearle v Hall*. Thus if an equitable interest in settled land was mortgaged before 1926, priority depended on the order in which the mortgages were created; if it is mortgaged after 1925, priority is governed by the rule in *Dearle v Hall*.

I. MORTGAGES OF A LEGAL ESTATE IN UNREGISTERED LAND

This category includes all mortgages *of a legal estate*, whether the mortgage **26–024** itself is legal or equitable. The question is "Has a legal estate been mortgaged?", not "Is the mortgage legal or equitable?" Legal and equitable mortgages need no longer be separated, since the legislation of 1925 treats them both on the same lines.[76]

1. Categories of mortgages: unregistered land

(a) The scheme. The scheme of the legislation is to divide all mortgages of **26–025** a legal estate in unregistered land into two groups:

(i) mortgages protected by deposit of deeds; and

(ii) mortgages not so protected;

and to make group (ii) registrable as land charges under the Land Charges Act 1972 (replacing the Land Charges Act 1925).[77] The aim is to make all mortgages readily ascertainable. If a mortgagee has possession of the deeds, their absence will proclaim his mortgage to all other persons seeking to deal with the land. If does not have the title deeds, he can proclaim his interest to the world by land charge registration. Indeed, protection by deposit of deeds is in practice so effective that there is no need to require the registration of mortgages belonging to class (i).[78] However, there is some risk that this

---

[76] There is a general survey of priorities of such mortgages at (1940) 7 C.L.J. 243 (R.E.M.).
[77] For the rules where the title to the land is registered, see above, paras 7–050; 7–102 and 26–071.
[78] But see below, para.26–038, for the risk of "reasonable excuse".

scheme may have been unsettled because of the manner in which informal mortgages by deposit of title deeds have been held to operate.[79]

26–026 *(b) Mortgages not registrable as land charges.* If the risk just mentioned is disregarded for the moment, it is clear that mortgages protected by deposit of title deeds (group (i) above) are intended to be outside the registration machinery and are governed, as regards priority, by the same rules as applied before 1926. They are defined as mortgages "protected" (or "secured") by a "deposit of documents relating to the legal estate affected". There is no positive enactment about them; they are simply excluded (as will shortly be seen) from the classes of land charges among which unprotected mortgages are intended to be registered. Although it is not clear, probably "protected" (or "secured") means originally protected or secured, rather than continuously protected or secured, for otherwise the mortgage would fluctuate between being registrable and unregistrable as often as the mortgagee parted with the deeds and regained them.[80]

26–027 *(c) Mortgages registrable as a land charge.* Mortgages not protected by deposit of title deeds (group (ii) above), if made after 1925, are registrable in the following classes.

(i) IF LEGAL, AS "PUISNE MORTGAGES". A puisne mortgage is defined as a legal mortgage not "protected by a deposit of documents relating to the legal estate affected".[81]

(ii) IF EQUITABLE, AS "GENERAL EQUITABLE CHARGES". A general equitable charge is any equitable charge which, not being "secured by a deposit of documents relating to the legal estate affected", does not arise under a trust of land or a settlement; and is not included in any other class of land charge.[82]

As will shortly be explained, there is a possibility that a contract to grant a mortgage may have to be registered as an "estate contract", even if it is supported by a deposit of title deeds.[83]

26–028 *(d) Failure to register as a land charge when required.* The penalty for failing to register a registrable mortgage as a land charge is loss of priority over a later purchaser *or* incumbrancer. The mortgage remains valid as between mortgagor and mortgagee, but as against a later purchaser from the mortgagor (including a later mortgagee) it is void. There are two provisions to be applied:

(i) s.97 of the Law of Property Act 1925, which provides that every such mortgage "shall rank according to its date of registration as

---

[79] Below, para.26–029.
[80] See (1940) 7 C.L.J. 249 (R.E.M.).
[81] LCA 1972 s.2(4).
[82] LCA 1972 s.2(4); above, para.8–072.
[83] LCA 1972 s.2(4); above, para.8–074.

a land charge pursuant to the Land Charges Act, 1925 or 1972"[84]; and

(ii) s.4(5) of the Land Charges Act 1972, which provides that a puisne mortgage or general equitable charge created after 1925 shall "be void as against a purchaser of the land charged therewith, or of any interest in such land, unless the land charge is registered in the appropriate register before the completion of the purchase". In the Act, unless the context otherwise requires, "purchaser" means "any person (including a mortgagee or lessee) who, for valuable consideration, takes any interest in land or in a charge on land".[85] Thus a registrable but unregistered mortgage is void against a later mortgagee, even if he had actual knowledge if it; for when an interest is void for non-registration as against a purchaser, he is not prejudicially affected by notice of it.[86]

(e) Equitable mortgages as estate contracts. Before the operation of these **26–029** rules is illustrated, one problem must be faced. It is plain that the design of the Land Charges Acts is to exempt all protected mortgages (i.e. those supported by deposit) from registration.[87] However, it has been held that an equitable mortgage by deposit of title deeds takes effect as a contract to grant a mortgage and not as something sui generis.[88] It would therefore appear to fall within the definition of an "estate contract" (any contract "to convey or create a legal estate"[89]), which contains nothing to exclude equitable mortgages by deposit.[90] The difficulty with this view—that such equitable mortgages would have to be registered as an "estate contract"—is that it "was plainly not envisaged"[91] when the Land Charges Act was drafted, and would upset the scheme of the Act. It would also destroy the security of many equitable mortgages, not being registered.[92] The point remains unresolved[93] and, for the future, the only safe course is to register such a mortgage as an estate contract even though it has been acknowledged judicially that in the scheme of the Land Charges Act 1972, "all mortgages must be registered unless protected

---

[84] LCA 1972 s.18(6) in effect inserts the last two words.

[85] LCA 1972 s.17(1).

[86] LPA 1925 s.199(1); above, paras 6–058, 8–093.

[87] The usual view is that they are not registrable: Waldock, *Mortgages*, p.410.

[88] *United Bank of Kuwait Plc v Sahib* [1997] Ch. 107; above, paras 15–042, 24–041. The decision was in the context of the formal requirements of LP(MP)A 1989 s.2. It should be noted that since the LP(MP)A 1989 s.2 an equitable mortgage by deposit which is unsupported by signed writing is invalid, below.

[89] LCA 1972 s.2(4)(iv); above, para.8–075.

[90] See (1930) 69 L.J. News 227 (J.M.L.); (1940) 7 C.L.J. 250, 251 (R.E.M.); (1949) 10 C.L.J. 245 (S. J. Bailey); (1962) 26 Conv. (N.S.) 445 (R. F Rowley).

[91] *United Bank of Kuwait Plc v Sahib*, above, at 139, per Peter Gibson L.J.

[92] Many such informal mortgages created since LP(MP)A 1989 s.2 was brought into force may, in fact, have been invalidated by the absence of writing, see *United Bank of Kuwait Plc v Sahib*, above. See above, paras 15–042; 24–041.

[93] *United Bank of Kuwait Plc v Sahib*, above, at 139.

by deposit of title deeds".[94] It remains to be seen whether this point will now be settled, given the diminishing role of unregistered land.[95]

The examples that follow are given on the assumption that equitable mortgages by deposit of title deeds are *not* registrable, and they must be read subject to the caveat that this may prove not to be the case.[96]

2. Operation of the rules. The rules can operate in four possible combinations of mortgages.

26–030   *(a) Both mortgages protected by a deposit of deeds.* There is nothing to require the deposit of all the deeds; therefore it may be possible for two or more mortgages of the same property to be exempted from registration provided that the deeds deposited do in fact "protect" or "secure" the mortgage. For example, A may make a mortgage to X and hand over all the existing deeds; A may then sell the property to B, subject to the mortgage; and B may then mortgage it to Y and deposit with Y the conveyance from A to B. In such a case registration is inapplicable and the old law applies. The 1925 legislation has not altered the basic principle that prima facie mortgages rank in the order of their creation,[97] subject to the rules as to loss of priority, e.g. by fraud, gross negligence, or the plea of purchaser without notice.[98] In this class of case it may therefore still matter whether the mortgages are legal or equitable.

(b) Neither mortgage protected by a deposit of deeds

26–031   (1) BOTH MORTGAGES REGISTRABLE. In this instance, both mortgages are registrable. No difficulty arises if the first mortgage is duly registered before the second is made. Even if the first is equitable and the second legal, the first prevails, for the provision that registration as a land charge amounts to notice prevents the legal mortgagee from claiming to be a purchaser "without notice".[99] Nor is there any difficulty if neither mortgage is registered. Even if the first mortgage is legal and the second equitable, under s.4(5) LCA 1972, the first is void against the second for want of registration and so the second has priority. Indeed, if there are several successive registrable mortgages, none of which has been registered, the maxim "qui prior est tempore, potior estjure" is now reversed, for the last will rank first and so on.

---

[94] *United Bank of Kuwait Plc v Sahib*, above, at 138, per Peter Gibson L.J.

[95] The suggestion in the fifth edition of this work (at pp.998, 999) that even if a mortgage by deposit of title deeds were invalid as an unwritten estate contract, it could be valid as a mere charge is precluded by the decision in *United Bank of Kuwait Plc v Sahib*, above, at 128.

[96] It should be noted that, by LCA 1972 s.4(6), an unregistered estate contract is void "as against a purchaser for money or money's worth . . . of a legal estate in the land charged with it". An unregistered estate contract enjoys greater protection than an unregistered puisne mortgage or general equitable charge. See above, para.8–093.

[97] See *Roberts v Croft* (1857) 2 De G. & J. 1; *Beddoes v Shaw* [1937] Ch. 81; [1936] 2 All E.R. 1108.

[98] See *Dixon v Muckleston* (1872) 8 Ch.App. 155; above, paras 26–007 et seq.

[99] Above, para.8–085.

(2) CONFLICT OF STATUTES. The more difficult case is where the first mort-   **26–032**
gage was registered *after* the creation of the second mortgage. For
example:

January 1	A grants a registrable mortgage to X
February 2	A grants a registrable mortgage to Y
March 3	X registers
March 4	Y registers

Here the provisions of the Law of Property Act 1925 (s.97) and the Land
Charges Act 1972 (s.4(5)) are in apparent conflict. According to s.4(5), the
order of priority is plainly Y, X, for X's mortgage is void against Y. But,
according to a simple reading of s.97, the order should be X, Y, for the section
requires every such mortgage to "rank according to its date of registration".[100]
How this conflict would be resolved (were it ever now to arise) is uncertain,
but it might well be that s.4(5) would be held to prevail, despite the argument
(not a strong one[101]) that s.97 would then be meaningless. If X's mortgage is
void as against Y, it is difficult to see how the subsequent registration of X's
mortgage can give priority to something which, *ex hypothesi*, has no existence
as regards Y.[102] Against that, s.4(5) is a general provision that applies to
mortgages only by reason of the statutory definition of "purchaser", which
itself is applicable only unless the context otherwise requires,[103] whereas s.97
is patently intended to regulate the priority of mortgages per se; and *generalia
specialibus non derogant.*[104]

(3) AVOIDANCE OF CONFLICT. A possible interpretation of s.97 which avoids   **26–033**
any conflict is that it merely refers to the machinery of the Land Charges Act
and is intended to operate in accordance with it. The section says that an
unprotected mortgage "shall rank according to its date of registration as a land
charge pursuant to the Land Charges Act", 1925 or 1972. But it does not
necessarily follow that this means that the first mortgage when registered
(being after the second mortgage is executed) stands first in priority. Section
97 does not say, to quote the language of another Act of 1925,[105] that

---

[100] An argument for this solution, and for the rejection of s.4(5), is put forward in (1950) 13
M.L.R. at pp.534–535 (A. D. Hargreaves). It depends on a distinction between mortgages and
other purchases which is not convincing.
[101] This could equally well be said of s.199(1)(i) for the same reason. Overlapping provisions
are by no means rare.
[102] See (1926) 61 L.J.News. 398 (J.M.L.); (1940) 7 C.L.J. 255 (R.E.M.); *Hollington Bros Ltd
v Rhodes* [1951] 2 T.L.R. 691 at 696. And technically LCA 1925 (the predecessor of LCA 1972),
was a later statute than LPA 1925, and should prevail in the case of irreconcilable conflict. Of two
conflicting provisions in the same Act, the later prevails: *Eastbourne Corporation v Fortes Ice
Cream Parlour (1955) Ltd* [1959] 2 Q.B. 92 at 107.
[103] LCA 1972 s.17(1).
[104] General provisions do not derogate from special provisions.
[105] The now repealed LRA 1925 s.29. See now LRA 2002 s.48 where mortgages rank between
themselves in the order *shown* in the register. This may not be, but usually is, the order in which
they were actually registered. It may not be the order in which they were created, LRR 2003
r.101.

registrable charges shall "rank according to the order in which they are entered on the register"; and it might have been more natural to say this had it been intended.[106] On this interpretation s.97 merely provides that registrable mortgages shall rank for priority according to the provisions of the Land Charges Act, i.e. according to s.4(5), which assumes proper registration in proper order.

To conclude, the argument that the two sections really are in conflict draws its strength from the evident intention of s.97 to deal with the question of priority. Precedents can be found for similar forms of words in Acts requiring registration,[107] and s.97 may have been modelled upon them. If s.97 really was intended as a mere reference to the Land Charges Act, it seems both redundant and contradictory. The argument against conflict, on the other hand, has the merit that this type of argument (that statutes do not conflict) should always prevail in case of doubt. The presumption against Parliament simultaneously enacting two contradictory systems is strong, especially where one of the two supposedly conflicting Acts expressly makes reference to the other.[108]

26–034   (4) THREE OR MORE MORTGAGES. Where there are three or more registrable mortgages it is possible to construct insoluble problems. For example:

January 1   A grants a registrable mortgage to X
February 2   A grants a registrable mortgage to Y
March 3   X registers
April 4   A grants a registrable mortgage to Z

Here Y has priority to X and Z has priority to Y; but X has priority to Z, so that the priorities run not in a series but in a circle. There is some authority for solving such problems by recourse to the doctrine of subrogation, by which one creditor is allowed to stand in the shoes of another on equitable grounds.[109] The court's order then might be to pay Z to the extent of Y's claim against X; then to pay X in full; then to pay any balance due to Z on his own claim; and finally to pay any balance to Y. It is easy to find fault with any such solution, for the problem of the circulus inextricabilis is in fact insoluble. Here

---

[106] cf. Bills of Sale Act 1878 s.10: "shall have priority in the order of the date of their registration".

[107] cf. Merchant Shipping (Registration etc.) Act 1993 s.8(1) (the priority of mortgages of ships is to be determined "by the order in which the mortgages were registered"); and see the repealed Yorkshire Registries Act 1884 s.14 ("shall have priority according to the date of registration thereof"). The Middlesex Registry Act 1708 (also repealed) provided with exemplary clarity that an unregistered assurance was void against a subsequent purchaser unless registered before the registration of the subsequent purchaser's assurance.

[108] "All this property legislation must be construed together; and obviously a result which would make the sections . . . mutually conflict must be avoided, unless there is no escape": *Northchurch Estates Ltd v Daniels* [1947] Ch. 117 at 123, per Evershed J. in another context.

[109] See *Benham v Keane* (1861) 1 J. & H. 685; 3 De G.F. & J. 318; and see *Re Wyatt* [1892] 1 Ch.188 at 209 (a puzzle suggested by the rule in *Dearle v Hall*, above, para.26–015); *Re Armstrong* [1895] 1 I.R. 87; *Re Weniger's Policy* [1910] 2 Ch. 291. For discussion, see (1968) 32 Conv. (N.S.) 325 (W. A. Lee).

Y is sacrificed to X, whereas Y should be paid before X. Subrogation produces an arbitrary result, for there is no logical point at which to break the circle and begin the process; and if begun at a different point it gives a different solution. The reported cases, of which there are unlikely to be any further, suggest that the court would elect to take the mortgages in order of date of creation and begin by subrogating the latest mortgagee to the earliest, as in the above example.[110]

(5) PRIORITY NOTICES AND OFFICIAL SEARCHES. Since it was physically **26–035** impossible to register a land charge the instant after it had been created, there was at first a dangerous gap between the creation of a mortgage and its registration under the Land Charges Act. Further, even if a search for prior incumbrances was made, the mortgagee could not be sure that no incumbrance had been registered between the time of his search and the completion of the mortgage. These difficulties have been met by the devices of the priority notice and the official search which have been dealt with in the chapter on land charge registration[111]

(c) First but not second mortgage protected by a deposit of deeds. In this **26–036** case the first mortgage, by taking its priority from the date of its creation, will normally have priority over the second mortgage, subject to the established rules as to loss of priority, e.g. by fraud or gross negligence.[112]

(d) Second but not first mortgage protected by a deposit of deeds. Here **26–037** s.4(5) and s.97 must work in harmony, whichever way s.97 is interpreted. If the first mortgage is registered before the second is made, the first ranks for priority "according to its date of registration" (s.97), i.e. prior to the second mortgage, and s.4(5) has no application. If the first mortgage is not registered when the second mortgage is made, the first mortgage is void against the second for want of registration; and even if it is subsequently registered, it takes priority from the date of registration and therefore ranks second.

3. Summary

(a) Deposit of deeds. A mortgage protected by a deposit of deeds ranks **26–038** according to the date on which it was created. The mortgagee may lose this priority:

  (i) by conduct which before 1926 would have had this effect; or

  (ii) if his mortgage is equitable, by a legal mortgage being made to a mortgagee for value without notice, or to a mortgagee who accepts a "reasonable excuse" for non-production of the deeds.[113]

---

[110] See generally (1961) 71 Yale L.J. 53 (G. Gilmore).
[111] Above, paras 8–102, 8–105.
[112] Above, paras 26–008, 26–111.
[113] Above, para.26–013.

26–039   *(b) No deposit of deeds.* A mortgage not protected by deposit of deeds should be protected by registration as a land charge. If the mortgagee fails to do this, he will not be protected against a subsequent mortgagee (s.4(5)), even if (as it seems) he registers before him (s.97 notwithstanding). If he does register, he will be protected against all mortgages made thereafter.

Since an equitable mortgagee who has custody of the title deeds may through no fault of his own lose priority to a later legal mortgagee to whom the mortgagor makes some excuse for non-production of the deeds,[114] it seems in theory to be safer for the first mortgagee to refuse to take the title deeds, and to register a general equitable charge under the Land Charges Act. But in fact mortgagees of unregistered land preferred the practical security of having the title deeds to the theoretical advantage of refusing them.

II. MORTGAGES OF AN EQUITABLE INTEREST

26–040   A mortgage of an equitable interest under a trust of any property, whether land or pure personalty, now takes priority according to the rule in *Dearle v Hall*,[115] as amended by the Law of Property Act 1925.[116] That is to say, the rule in *Dearle v Hall* has now been amended, and extended from the realm of personalty to that of land; but as regards land it applies only to dealings with an equitable interest under a trust, e.g. mortgages of the beneficial interest of a tenant for life under a settlement, whether in the land itself or in the capital money representing it. Mortgages of such interests are therefore now governed by the principle that priority depends upon the order in which notice of the mortgages is received by the appropriate trustee or trustees.

This principle "does not apply until a trust has been created".[117] The meaning of this restriction is not entirely clear, but it appears to be designed to exclude equitable interests which fall outside the ordinary categories of trusts, such as the interest of a purchaser under a contract of sale or lease.[118] The amendments made by the Law of Property Act 1925 to the rule in *Dearle v Hall* are as follows.

26–041   **1. Notice in writing.** No notice given or received can affect priority unless it is in writing.[119] Apart from this, no alteration has been made in the rules relating to notice.[120]

---

[114] Above, para.26–013.

[115] Above, para.26–015.

[116] ss.137, 138. See [1993] Conv. 22 (J. Howell).

[117] LPA 1925 s.137(10).

[118] As, for example, in *Property Discount Corp Ltd v Lyon Group Ltd* [1981] 1 W.L.R. 300, where an equitable charge of a building contractor's rights to obtain leases took priority under different rules: above, para.8–098.

[119] LPA 1925 s.137(3). *Quaere* whether the notice in *Lloyd v Banks* (1868) 3 Ch.App. 488 (above, para.26–019) would not still be sufficient, for it was "received" by the trustee in printed form. Yet LPA 1925 s.137(2) speaks of the persons "to be served with notice".

[120] Above, paras 26–117 to 26–021.

2. Persons to be served. The persons to be served with notice are: **26–042**

    (i) in the case of settled land,[121] the trustees of the settlement;

    (ii) in the case of a trust of land, the trustees; and

    (iii) in the case of any other land, the estate owner[122] of the land affected.[123]

Thus the person to be served is normally the owner of the legal estate, except in the case of settled land, where notice to the tenant for life might well not secure protection, e.g. if it was his life interest which had been mortgaged. In cases other than the three mentioned above, no special provision has been made, so that notice must be given to the legal owner as before 1926. Nor has any alteration been made to the law relating to notice received by one of several trustees.[124]

3. Indorsement of notice. If for any reason a valid notice cannot be served   **26–043**
(e.g. where there are no trustees), or can be served only at unreasonable cost or delay, a purchaser[125] may require that a memorandum be indorsed on or permanently annexed to the instrument creating the trust, and this has the same effect as notice to the trustees.[126] He may also require the instrument to be produced in order to prove proper indorsement.[127] The document to be used for this purpose is:

    (i) in the case of settled land, the trust instrument; and

    (ii) the case of a trust of land, the instrument creating the equitable interest.[128]

If the trust is created by statute or by operation of law, or there is no instrument creating the trust, the document to be used is that under which the equitable interest is acquired or which evidences its devolution, e.g. in the case of an intestacy, the probate or letters of administration in force when the dealing was effected.[129]

4. Notice to trust corporation. The instrument creating the trust, the   **26–044**
trustees, or the court, may nominate a trust corporation to receive notices instead of the trustees.[130] In such cases, only notice to the trust corporation

---

[121] Including capital money or securities representing capital money.
[122] i.e. the owner of a legal estate: LPA 1925 s.205(1)(v); above, para.6–012.
[123] LPA 1925 s.137(2) (as amended by TLATA 1996 Sch.3 para.15).
[124] Above, paras 26–017 to 26–021.
[125] Including, of course, a mortgagee.
[126] LPA 1925 s.137(4).
[127] LPA 1925 s.137(4).
[128] LPA 1925 s.137(5) (as amended by TLATA 1996 Sch.3 para.15).
[129] LPA 1925 s.137(6).
[130] LPA 1925 s.138(1).

affects priority; notice to the trustees has no effect until they deliver it to the trust corporation, which they are bound to do forthwith.[131] Provision is made for:

(i) the indorsement of notice of the appointment on the instrument upon which notices may be indorsed[132];

(ii) the keeping of a register of notices[133];

(iii) the inspection of the register[134];

(iv) the answering of inquiries[135]; and

(v) the payment of fees for performing these functions.[136]

This is in effect machinery for setting up a private register of charges. In practice, little use has been made of these provisions.

26–045   **5. Production of notices.** On the application of any person interested in the equitable interest, the trustees or estate owner must now produce any notices served on them or their predecessors.[137] This reverses what had previously been the law.[138]

C. Summary

A summary of the principal divisions of the rules relating to the priority of mortgages in unregistered land may be useful.

1. Before 1926

26–046   *(a) Legal or equitable interests in land.* Priority was governed by the order of creation, subject to the doctrine of purchaser without notice, and to special rules as to fraud, estoppel, gross negligence, and "reasonable excuse" for non-production of title deeds.

26–047   *(b) Equitable interests in pure personalty. Dearle v Hall* applied.

2. After 1925

26–048   *(a) Legal estates in land.* Priority is governed by the same rules as before 1926, subject to the rules requiring land charge registration of mortgages not protected by deposit of documents.

---

[131] LPA 1925 s.138(3), (4).
[132] LPA 1925 s.138(2).
[133] LPA 1925 s.138(7).
[134] LPA 1925 s.138(9).
[135] LPA 1925 s.138(10).
[136] LPA 1925 s.138(9), (10), (11).
[137] LPA 1925 s.137(8), (9).
[138] See *Low v Bouverie* [1891] 3 Ch. 82; above, para.26–022. In that case, it had been held that the trustees were under no duty to disclose notices to third parties, so that a prospective mortgagee might not be able to discover previous incumbrances.

(b) Equitable interests in any property. Dearle v Hall applies. **26–049**

Section 2. Unregistered Land: Tacking

Tacking is a special way of obtaining priority for a secured loan by amalga- **26–050**
mating it with another secured loan of higher priority. It may apply both to
realty and to personalty.[139] Before 1926 there were two forms of tacking:

(i) what was called the tabula in naufragio ("the plank in the ship
wreck"); and

(ii) the tacking of further advances.

The 1925 legislation abolished the first kind of tacking and amended the law
as to the second. The first will be briefly explained for the sake of its intrinsic
interest,[140] and the second as the necessary prologue to the amendments of
1925.

A. Before 1926

I. THE *TABULA IN NAUFRAGIO*

1. The doctrine. In a contest between two equitable mortgagees, the later **26–051**
could sometimes gain priority over the earlier by acquiring a legal mortgage
which had priority to both.[141] The insufficiency of the security was the
"shipwreck", and the legal estate was the "plank" which any equitable
mortgagee might seize without concern for the others.[142] The metaphor
implies a disaster where someone must lose, and each party may save himself
as best he can. There is no moral equity in the doctrine, which has often been
criticised,[143] and "could not happen in any other country but this".[144] It is a
curious example of the deference paid by equity to the legal estate.[145] Where,
apart from the order of creation, the equities between the mortgagees were
equal, the holder of the legal estate had priority[146]; "where the equities are
equal, the law prevails", and so upsets the natural equitable order of
priority.

The opportunity for this master-stroke occurred when there was first a legal **26–052**
and then two equitable mortgages, all made to different mortgagees, and the
mortgagor managed to conceal the second mortgage at the time when he

[139] Coote, *Mortgages*, p.1245.
[140] For a recent case in which the doctrine had to be considered, see *Macmillan Inc v
Bishopsgate Investment Trust Plc* [1995] 1 W.L.R. 978 at 1002, 1003.
[141] *Marsh v Lee* (1671) 2 Vent. 337, *Peacock v Burt* (1834) 4 Li. Ch. 33.
[142] The phrase is Hale L.J.'s: see *Brace v Duchess of Marlborough* (1728) 2 P.Wms. 491, per
Jekyll M.R.
[143] See Waldock, *Mortgages*, p.391.
[144] *Wortley v Birkhead* (1754) 2 Ves.Sen. 571 at 574, per Lord Hardwicke L.C.
[145] *Bailey v Barnes* [1894] 1 Ch. 25 at 36.
[146] *Wortley v Birkhead* (1754) 2 Ves.Sen. 571 at 574.

created the third.[147] Thus if A mortgaged his property to X by a legal mortgage and then to Y and Z by successive equitable mortgages, Z's mortgage could be given priority over Y's if Z bought X's mortgage, provided Z had no notice of Y's mortgage when he advanced his money.[148] X's legal mortgage was the plank in the shipwreck, and if Z could secure it before Y, he could throw onto Y the loss which would otherwise have fallen upon himself. Since Z knew nothing of Y's mortgage when he took his own mortgage, he might naturally have lent more than the security would satisfy. A property worth £100,000 might for example have been mortgaged first to X for £20,000, then to Y for £60,000, and then again to Z for £60,000, Z knowing nothing of Y's mortgage. Thus when the mortgagor defaulted a shipwreck was inevitable.

26–053   **2. No notice.** The mortgagee seeking to tack must have had no notice of the prior equitable mortgage when he advanced his money[149]; if he had notice, he could not tack, for obviously his equity was then not equal to Y's.[150] But if he had no notice at that time, it was immaterial that he obtained notice later, before he acquired the legal estate.[151] Indeed, on a principle similar to the rule in *Dearle v Hall*[152] notice of the prior equitable mortgage before the later mortgagee acquired the legal estate was "the very occasion, that shews the necessity of it".[153] The natural time for tacking was when the third mortgagee, who when he made his loan imagined that he was taking a second mortgage, discovered later that there was an intervening mortgage, and then took a transfer of the first legal mortgage in order to secure priority. Notice to the first mortgagee (who held the legal estate) was immaterial, so that the second mortgagee could not protect himself against tacking by giving him notice.[154] Such circumstances "look very like a conspiracy between the first and third mortgagees to cheat the second, which cannot be right".[155] But such was the law.

26–054   A legal estate which was already held on trust for the intervening mortgagee would not be used against him by a later mortgagee who took it with notice of the trust,[156] for the trust would then bind the later mortgagee.[157] He "must not, to get a plank to save himself, be guilty of a breach of trust".[158] Thus if a third mortgagee took the legal estate from the first mortgagee with

---

[147] See *Phillips v Phillips* (1862) 4 De G.E. & J. 208 at 216.

[148] *Brace v Duchess of Marlborough*, above.

[149] *Bates v Johnson* (1859) Johns. 304 at 313.

[150] *Lacey v Ingle* (1847) 2 Ph. 413.

[151] *Taylor v Russell* [1892] A.C. 244 at 259.

[152] Above, para.26–015.

[153] *Wortley v Birkhead* (1754) 2 Ves.Sen. 571 at 574, per Lord Hardwicke L.C.

[154] *Peacock v Burt* (1834) 4 Li. Ch. 33.

[155] *West London Commercial Bank v Reliance Permanent BS* (1885) 29 Ch D 954 at 963, per Lindley L.J.; and see *Bates v Johnson*, above, at 314.

[156] *Sharples v Adams* (1863) 32 Beav. 213; *Mumford v Stohwasser* (1874) L.R. 18 Eq. 556 at 562; cf. *Taylor v London & County Banking Co* [1901] 2 Ch. 231 at 256.

[157] *Saunders v Dehew* (1692) 2 Vern. 271.

[158] *Saunders v Dehew*, above per Lords Commissioners.

notice that the first mortgage had already been paid off (so that the legal estate was held by the first mortgagee merely as trustee for those entitled to it, including the second mortgagee), tacking was impossible.[159] But while the first mortgage was still unredeemed, notice that the second mortgagee wished to redeem did not, it seems, make it a breach of trust for the first mortgagee to give priority to the third mortgagee by transferring the legal estate to him,[160] although he might thus have been able to sell it to the highest bidder.

3. Legal estate. It was of the essence of tacking that the mortgagee should secure a legal estate. Any prior[161] legal estate would do, e.g. an outstanding term of years,[162] or even a judgment giving legal rights against the land[163]; but an equitable interest would not suffice.[164] Nevertheless, in accordance with the doctrine that the better right to the legal estate may rank as possession of it,[165] an express declaration of trust by the owner of the legal estate in favour of the mortgagee seeking to tack, or a transfer of the legal estate to a trustee for him, might be sufficient.[166] In all cases the mortgage and the legal estate had to be held in the same right, and not one on trust and the other beneficially.[167] Further, if the mortgagee parted with the legal estate he thereupon lost his right to tack.[168] Although tacking usually took place when a later mortgagee acquired the legal estate, the principle extended also to a legal incumbrancer who acquired a later mortgage without notice of an intervening incumbrance, e.g. where a first legal mortgagee took a transfer of a third mortgage without notice of the second.[169]

26–055

II. TACKING OF FURTHER ADVANCES

1. The doctrine. The "tacking of further advances" was the more important branch of the doctrine of tacking. It often happened that a mortgagee would be content to lend more money on an existing security at some later date. If, then, the borrower had mortgaged the property to another mortgagee between

26–056

---

[159] See *Bates v Johnson* (1859) Johns 304 at 315–3 17; *Prosser v Rice* (1859) 28 Beav. 68 at 74; *Harpham v Shacklock* (1881) 19 Ch D 207; *Macmillan Inc v Bishopsgate Investment Trust Plc* [1995] 1 W.L.R. 978 at 1003.

[160] *Bates v Johnson*, above, at 313, 314, criticised in *West London Commercial Bank v Reliance Permanent BS* (1885) 29 Ch D 954 at 960; the point is reserved at 961.

[161] In *Cooke v Wilton* (1860) 29 Beav. 100 the first (equitable) mortgagee had a right to a legal mortgage, which was in fact executed after the intervening mortgage; this was held to relate back to the date of the original mortgage, and so to be effective for tacking.

[162] *Willoughby v Willoughby* (1756) 1 T.R. 763; and see *Maundrell v Maundrell* (1804) 10 Ves. 246.

[163] *Morret v Paske* (1740) 2 Atk. 52.

[164] *Brace v Duchess of Marlborough* (1728) 2 P.Wms. 491 at 495, 496.

[165] See above, para.8–011.

[166] See *Wilkes v Bodington* (1707) 2 Vern. 599 at 600; *Earl of Pomfret v Lord Windsor* (1752) 2 Ves.Sen. 472 at 486; *Pease v Jackson* (1868) 3 Ch.App. 576; *Crosbie-Hill v Sayer* [1908] 1 Ch. 866 at 875, 876.

[167] *Morret v Paske*, above, at 53; *Harnett v Weston* (1806) 12 Ves. 130.

[168] *Rooper v Harrison* (1855) 2 K. & J. 86.

[169] *Morret v Paske*, above, at 53.

the dates of the first and second loans from the original mortgagee, the question was whether the last loan could be "tacked" to the first so as to take priority over the second. This question arose very commonly in banking, where a mortgage was made to secure an overdraft which might be increased as further cheques were cashed.

26–057	**2. Forms of tacking.** Before 1926 there were two cases where tacking of this kind was allowed.

26–058	*(a) Agreement of intervening incumbrancer.* The mortgagee could tack if the intervening incumbrancer agreed; here it was immaterial whether the first mortgage was legal or equitable. Building estates sometimes provided examples of this, when the owner required more money to build on his estate and thus make it a better security. The second mortgagee, not wishing to lend any more money, might agree to the first mortgagee making a further advance to be expended on further building and to rank in priority to the second mortgage. In this case priority was secured simply by contract between the mortgagees.

26–059	*(b) No notice of intervening incumbrance.* If a further advance was made without notice of the intervening mortgage, it might be tacked if either of the following conditions was satisfied.

26–060	(1) LEGAL ESTATE. The further advance was made either by a legal mortgagee,[170] or by an equitable mortgagee with the best right to the legal estate (as where A advanced money and had the legal estate conveyed to a trustee).[171] Priority here resulted from the strength of the legal estate.

26–061	(2) CONTRACT. The prior mortgage expressly provided that the security should extend to any further advances, whether or not it was obligatory for the mortgagee to make them. A bank, for example, might take a mortgage to secure an overdraft, with a clause stating that the security should cover any further overdraft which the bank might allow. Such tacking was said to be available to any mortgagee, legal or equitable; for it was tacking not by virtue of a legal estate but by virtue of the contract whereby the equity of redemption was potentially charged with any further advances, so that an intervening mortgagee took it subject to this right.[172]

26–062	**3. Effect of notice.** It was an invariable rule that a further advance could not be tacked if at the time of making it the mortgagee had notice of the intervening mortgage.[173] This was a suitable rule for tacking in class (1), for

---

[170] *Wyllie v Pollen* (1863) 3 De G.J. & S. 596.

[171] See above, paras 8–011, 26–055; and see *Wilmot v Pike* (1945) 5 Hare 14, explained above, para.26–012. See also *Wormald v Maitland* (1866) 35 L.J. Ch. 69, where this point received perfunctory treatment.

[172] See Fisher and Lightwood, *Mortgage*, p.486 citing *Calisher v Forbes* (1871) 7 Ch.App. 109 and *Re Weniger's Policy* [1910] 2 Ch. 291 at 295; but see above, fn.64.

[173] *Hopkinson v Rolt* (1861) 9 H.L.C. 514, explained in *Bradford Banking Co Ltd v Henry Briggs, Son & Co Ltd* (1886) 12 App.Cas. 29, and *Union Bank of Scotland v National Bank of Scotland* (1886) 12 App.Cas. 53.

the law should prevail only where the equities are equal. But, after some hesitation, the courts extended it to class (2),[174] whereas it might have been thought that if a paramount right to tack was secured by the terms of the first mortgage, it could not be taken away by a later mortgagee giving notice of his charge. The rule was applied even to the case where the first mortgage obliged the mortgagee to make further advances,[175] though the mortgagee was protected by the rule that he was released from the obligation to make the further advances as soon as the mortgagor, by creating a later incumbrance, prevented any further advance from having the priority of the original mortgage.[176]

The effect of these rules was that a mortgagee with notice of a subsequent incumbrance could never tack further advances against it, and an equitable mortgagee without notice could tack only if his mortgage made provision for further advances, or if he was one of the rare examples of an equitable mortgagee who had some prior claim on the legal estate.[177]

B. After 1925

The law as to tacking is now to be found in s.94 of the Law of Property Act **26–063** 1925. The position is as follows.

I. THE *TABULA IN NAUFRAGIO*

Without prejudice to any priority gained before 1926, this right to tack, except **26–064** in respect of further advances, was abolished at the end of 1925.[178] That was the end of the *tabula in naufragio*.

II. TACKING OF FURTHER ADVANCES

The tacking of further advances has been modified so as to make it immaterial **26–065** whether any of the mortgages concerned are legal or equitable,[179] and so as to make the rules more reasonable where the first mortgage expressly contemplates further advances. After 1925 a prior mortgagee may tack further advances so as "to rank in priority to subsequent mortgagee"[180] in the three cases set out below. As this exemption from the general abolition of tacking is confined to mortgages, it seems that further advances cannot be tacked so as to take priority over other intervening interests such as estate contracts.[181] The three cases are as follows.

---

[174] *Hopkinson v Rolt*, above, where opinions in the House of Lords were divided.

[175] *West v Williams* [1899] 1 Ch. 132. Having reached this point, the authorities had become inconsistent with the notion that an equitable mortgagee could tack at all. The doctrine that an agreement for further advances created a potential charge was denied in *West v Williams* at 143, 146, and this struck at the root of an equitable mortgagee's power to tack.

[176] See *West v Williams*, above, at 143, 146.

[177] See above, para.26–055.

[178] LPA 1925 s.94(3).

[179] LPA 1925 s.94(1).

[180] LPA 1925 s.94(1).

[181] See Maitland, *Equity*, 214 (I. W. Brunyate); (1958) 22 Conv. (N.S.) 44 at 56 (R. G. Rowley); this is probably a failure in drafting.

26–066   **1. Agreement of intervening incumbrancer.** The position is unchanged.[182]

26–067   **2. No notice of intervening incumbrance.** A further advance can be tacked if it was made without notice of the intervening mortgage.[183] Where the intervening mortgage is protected by a deposit of deeds and is thus not registrable as a land charge, the normal rules as to notice operate.[184] If the mortgage is not protected in this way and is accordingly registrable (as will usually be the case), the rule that registration amounts to notice[185] will normally apply and so protect it if it is registered. But, by a special exception, if the prior mortgage was made expressly for securing further advances (e.g. in the case of an overdraft at a bank, where the debt is increased or decreased as sums are drawn out or paid in), mere registration of a later mortgage as a land charge is not deemed to be notice, unless that mortgage was registered when the last search was made by the prior mortgagee.[186] The same applies to a spouse's matrimonial home rights under the Family Law Act 1996 which are registered after a mortgage has been made. Even if the spouse's charge arose before the mortgage, the charge is deemed for this purpose to be a subsequent mortgage.[187]

26–068   An example may make this clearer. Mortgages have been made to A (who took the deeds) and B, in that order, and A has made further advances. If when A made his further advances he had actual, constructive or imputed notice of B's mortgage, he cannot tack under this head even if his mortgage, without obliging him to make further advances, was stated to be security for any further advances he might choose to make.[188] If he had no such notice of B's mortgage when he made his further advances, but B's mortgage was registered at that time, then if A's mortgage is silent as to further advances, the registration amounts to notice and prevents A from tacking. But if A's mortgage was expressed to be security for any further advances he might make, the registration will not prevent him from tacking, and thus he need not search before making each further advance. It would be unreasonable, in particular, to require banks to make a search before cashing each cheque on a secured overdraft.

This highlights a practical point. Even if a second mortgage has been duly registered, the mortgagee should still give express notice of his mortgage to the first mortgagee, for this:

(i) prevents tacking under this head; and

---

[182] LPA 1925 s.94(1)(a).
[183] LPA 1925 s.94(1)(b).
[184] Above, para.8–015.
[185] LPA 1925 s.198(1).
[186] LPA 1925 s.94(2), as amended by LP(Am)A 1926. The amendment safeguards a mortgage registered (presumably by priority notice: above, para.8–104 before the principal mortgage was created.
[187] s.3l(12), replacing earlier legislation. See below, para.34–023.
[188] This confirms *Hopkinson v Rolt* (1861) 9 H.L.C. 514; above, para.26–062.

(ii) compels the first mortgagee to hand over the deeds to him when the first mortgage is discharged.[189]

In these two respects land charge registration by itself is not notice.

3. Obligation to make further advances. A further advance may be tacked **26–069** if the prior mortgage imposes an obligation on the mortgagee to make it.[190] In this case, not even express notice will prevent tacking.[191] If in return for a mortgage a bank binds itself to honour a customer's cheques up to an overdraft of £100,000, there is no question of the bank losing priority, for not even express notice will prevent the bank from tacking each further advance.[192] The principle of this is, of course, that the later mortgagee has clear warning that the prior mortgagee has further claims on the security.

Section 3. Registered Land: Priority

The priority of mortgages and charges where title is registered has already **26–070** been explained.[193] It may be summarised as follows.

1. Priority of registered charges. Save for special provisions relation to **26–071** certain statutory charges,[194] registered charges rank in priority according to the order shown on the register and not according to the order of their creation.[195] The priority that would result from first registration can, however, be altered by agreement between the registered chargees[196] and this is why priority is determined by the "order shown" rather than "the date of registration" per se. The same principle applies to the priority of sub-charges.

2. Priority of mortgages which are not registered charges. The priority **26–072** of mortgages which are not registered charges is determined by the rules which govern the priority of property interests generally. Thus, as against a later registered disposition, which may include a registered charge, an unprotected mortgage loses its priority.[197] This is simply another example of the priority rules of registered land in operation. As between each other, the

---

[189] Above, para.25–051.

[190] LPA 1925 s.94(1)(c).

[191] This reverses *West v Williams*, above, para.26–062.

[192] *Quaere* whether this affects *Deeley v Lloyds Bank Ltd* [1912] A.C. 756 (payments into the account prima facie go in reduction of the bank's prior charge, thus improying the later mortgagee's position).

[193] Above, paras 7–050, 7–102.

[194] See Ruoff & Roper 27.017.

[195] LRA 2002 s.48 above, paras 7–050, 7–102.

[196] LRR 2003 r.102. The changed priority would be noted on the register. Note the possibility that a later lender might be subrogated to, and therefore registered as proprietor of, an earlier charge, so as to gain priority: *Anfield (UK) Ltd v Bank of Scotland* [2011] 1 W.L.R. 2414.

[197] LRA 2002 s.29. The mortgage should generally be protected by the registration of a notice.

priority of mortgages which are not registered charges is as follows. First, where an interest under a trust is mortgaged, priority is preserved by giving notice to the trustees under the rule in *Dearle v Hall*[198] as it has been applied by the Law of Property Act 1925.[199] Secondly, in other cases, because such mortgages take effect in equity, the priority of competing mortgages is determined by the date on which such rights are created.[200] Such priority is unaffected by the fact that one or other mortgage is protected by the entry on the register of a notice.[201] However, where a mortgage which has taken effect in equity is subsequently registered as a registered charge, that may affect priorities. For example:

January 1	A executes a charge in favour of X: the charge is not registered, but takes effect in equity and is not protected by notice on the register.
February 2	A executes a charge in favour of Y: Y does not initially register the charge, which therefore takes effect subject to X's under s.28 LRA 2002.
March 3	Y registers his charge as a registered charge. A registered charge takes effect as a registered disposition and, as such, the chargee takes free of unprotected interests.[202] Y therefore ceases to be bound by X's charge.

26–073   **3. Tacking.** It has already been explained that the provisions of the Law of Property Act 1925 which relate to the tacking of further advances[203] are inapplicable to registered land,[204] and that where title is registered, the Land Registration Act 2002 establishes the circumstances in which further advances may be tacked.[205]

---

[198] (1828) 3 Russ. 1.
[199] s.137; above, para.26–040.
[200] LRA 2002 s.28. Above para.7–060. See also *Halifax Plc v Curry Popeck* (A Firm) [2008] EWHC 1692 (Ch); (2009) 125 L.Q.R. 401 (M.J.D.).
[201] Above para.7–060.
[202] LRA 2002 s.29.
[203] s.94; above, para.26–065.
[204] LPA 1925 s.94(4).
[205] LRA 2002 s.49. See Ruoff & Roper 27–014.

THE NATURE OF EASEMENTS AND PROFITS

Section 1. Nature of Easements

The common law recognised a limited number of rights which one landowner   **27–001**
could acquire over the land of another; and these rights were called easements
and profits à prendre (hereafter profits). Examples of easements are rights of
way, rights of light and rights of water. Examples of profits are rights to dig
gravel, or cut turf, or to take game or fish. Nowadays both easements and
profits are classified as incorporeal hereditaments.[1] But before the 18th century, easements were not properly so described, because an easement could
exist only if it was "appurtenant" (i.e. annexed) to some piece of land (the
dominant tenement) so as to benefit it. It was therefore said that easements
were not incorporeal hereditaments, but rights appurtenant to corporeal hereditaments[2]; in other words, that an easement was not an object of property in
itself, but was a privilege which could be obtained for the benefit of corporeal
land. The same could be said of a profit when it was attached to and passed
with some particular parcel of land. However, unlike easements, profits could
also exist "in gross", that is to say without any dominant tenement. For
example, rights of mining or of shooting are often held by persons who are not
adjacent landowners. Rights held in gross were clearly incorporeal
hereditaments.

In modern times the attempt to distinguish rights which are merely appurte-   **27–002**
nances has been abandoned, and easements and profits are now classed
together as incorporeal hereditaments. This is convenient, for they have many
common points and both should fall within the definition of land. Logically,
no doubt, restrictive covenants[3] should also be included. But they are a
relatively recent innovation and, being purely equitable, have many different
characteristics; and they therefore stand apart from the older interests which

---

[1] *Hewlins v Shippam* (1826) 5 B. & C. 221 at 229; *Hill v Midland Ry* (1882) 21 Ch D 143;
Great Western Ry v Swindon & Cheltenham Extension Ry (1882) 22 Ch D 677, (1884) 9 App.Cas.
787; *Jones v Watts* (1890) 43 Ch D 574 at 585; cf. *Re Brotherton's and Markham's SE* (1907) 97
L.T. 880 at 882, on appeal 98 L.T. 547; Sweet's note to Challis pp.55, 56.
[2] Challis pp.51, 52, 55.
[3] See below, Ch.32.

are hereditaments in themselves.[4] The Law Commission has recently made recommendations for the reform of a number of discrete areas of the law of easements and profits, as well as the law of covenants, and has published a draft Bill to give effect to them.[5] Reference will be made to these recommendations in the text that follows.

27–003　　An easement is "either a right to do something or a right to prevent something".[6] In order to explain what rights can and cannot exist as easements we must examine:

(a) the essentials of an easement; and

(b) the distinction between easements and certain analogous rights.

A. Essentials of an Easement

27–004　Four requirements must be satisfied before there can be an easement.[7] First, there must be a dominant tenement and a servient tenement. Secondly, the easement must confer a benefit on (or "accommodate") the dominant tenement. Thirdly, the dominant and servient tenements must not be owned and occupied by the same person. Fourthly, the easement must be capable of forming the subject-matter of a grant. Each of these requirements must now be examined.

27–005　　**1. There must be a dominant and a servient tenement.** If X owns Blackacre and grants a right to use a path across Blackacre to the owner for the time being of the neighbouring plot Whiteacre, Blackacre is the servient tenement and Whiteacre the dominant tenement. Had X granted the right to A who owned no land at all, A would have acquired a licence to walk over Blackacre, but his right could not exist as an easement, for there would be no dominant tenement. According to the distinction already explained, an easement cannot exist in gross[8] but only as appurtenant to a dominant tenement; indeed, technically, the easement is appurtenant to an estate in the dominant

---

[4] For general accounts of the law of easements, see *Gale on Easements*, 18th edn (2008); C. Sara, *Boundaries and Easements*, 4th edn (2008).

[5] Law Com. No.327, Making Land Work: Easements, Covenants and profits à prendre (2011); see also prior Consultation Paper, Law Com CP No.186 (2008). For previous Law Commission publications, see Law Commission Working Paper No.36, Transfer of Land: Appurtenant Rights (1971) and (on covenants) Law Com. No.127, Transfer of Land: The Law of Positive and Restrictive Covenants; Law Com. No.201, Transfer of Land: Obsolete Restrictive Covenants (1991).

[6] Gale, 1–78.

[7] *Re Ellenborough Park* [1956] Ch. 131 at 163; *London & Blenheim Estates Ltd v Ladbroke Retail Parks Ltd* [1994] 1 W.L.R. 31 at 36; *Polo Woods Foundation v Shelton-Agar* [2009] EWHC 1361 (Ch); [2010] 1 P. & C.R. 12 at p.241 (applying same test in relation to profit à prendre).

[8] *Rangeley v Midland Ry* (1868) 3 Ch.App. 306 at 310; *Hawkins v Rutter* [1892] 1 Q.B. 668; *London & Blenheim Estates Ltd v Ladbroke Retail Parks Ltd*, above, at 36 (where Peter Gibson L.J. described the proposition as "trite law").

land.[9] The reason for this requirement is said to lie in the policy of the law against encumbering land with burdens of uncertain extent.[10]

On any transfer of the dominant tenement, the easement will pass with the **27–006** land, so that the occupier for the time being can enjoy it,[11] even if he is a mere tenant.[12] Where the dominant tenement is severed, the benefit of the easement will pass with each and every part of it,[13] subject to two restrictions.[14] First, the severed part of the dominant tenement must itself be accommodated by the easement. Secondly, the burden on the servient tenement must not be increased as a result of the severance. A dominant tenement may be wholly incorporeal,[15] or partly corporeal and partly incorporeal, as where it consists of the whole undertaking of a waterworks company and thus comprises both physical land and rights over the land of others, such as the right to lay pipes.[16]

Where an easement is created by an express grant there is no legal necessity **27–007** for it to specify or refer to the dominant tenement.[17] The court will consider all the relevant facts known to the grantor and the grantee at the time of the grant[18] to see whether there was in fact a dominant tenement for the benefit of which the easement was granted,[19] and what its extent and identity were.[20] Documentary evidence to identify the dominant tenement will assist the person claiming the benefit of the easement and is therefore desirable in practice,[21] but it is not required as a matter of law. It is however essential that there should be an identifiable dominant tenement in existence at the time that the easement is granted.[22]

---

[9] Law Com. No.327 para. 2.21; cf. *Wall v Collins* [2007] EWCA Civ 444; [2007] Ch. 390 at [15], per Carnwath L.J. (holding that where the 999-year lease held by the dominant owner merged into the freehold reversion, the easement was not thereby extinguished) and see also Lyall [2010] Conv. 300. See further Law Com. CP No.186, paras 5.72 et seq. at 306; Law Com. No.327, para.3.232.

[10] *London & Blenheim Estates Ltd v Ladbroke Retail Parks Ltd*, above, at 37; but see (1980) 96 L.Q.R. 557 at 564–567, where M. F. Sturley questions the rationale, and criticises the rule. See too (1982) 98 L.Q.R. 279 at 305, 306 (S. Gardner); Challis pp.54, 55. cf. Gale, 1–87. See further Law Com. CP No.186 paras 3.3 et seq.; Law Com No.327 paras 2.24 et seq.

[11] *Leech v Schweder* (1874) 9 App.Cas. 463 at 474; LPA 1925 s.187(1).

[12] *Thorpe v Brumfitt* (1873) 8 Ch.App. 650.

[13] *Newcomen v Coulson* (1877) 5 Ch D 133 at 141.

[14] See *Gallagher v Rainbow* (1994) 68 A.L.J.R. 512 at 516 (High Court of Australia). There is a remarkable dearth of English authority on the severance of the dominant tenement.

[15] *Hanbury v Jenkins* [1901] 2 Ch. 401 at 422 (several profit of piscary).

[16] *Re Salvin's Indenture* [1938] 2 All E.R. 498.

[17] The express grant or reservation of a legal easement over a registered estate is a disposition which is required to be completed by registration: LRA 2002 s.27(2)(d); below, para.28–002.

[18] *Johnstone v Holdway* [1963] 1 Q.B. 601 at 611; *Hamble PC v Haggard* [1992] 1 W.L.R. 122 at 130.

[19] *Thorpe v Brumfitt* (1873) 8 Ch.App. 650; *Johnstone v Holdway*, above; *London & Blenheim Estates Ltd v Ladbroke Retail Parks Ltd* [1992] 1 W.L.R. 1278 at 1283 (on appeal [1994] 1 W.L.R. 31). cf. *Callard v Beeney* [1930] 1 K.B. 353.

[20] *The Shannon Ltd v Venner Ltd* [1965] Ch. 682 (easement held appurtenant not only to land acquired when it was granted but also to land previously acquired).

[21] For the position in the parallel case of restrictive covenants, see below, paras 32–061 and 32–064.

[22] *London & Blenheim Estates Ltd v Ladbroke Retail Parks Ltd* [1994] 1 W.L.R. 31; *Voice v Bell* (1993) 68 P. & C.R. 441 (in each case a right had been granted or reserved for a dominant

2. The easement must accommodate the dominant tenement

27–008   *(a) Benefit to land.* A right cannot exist as an easement unless it confers a benefit on the dominant tenement as such.[23] It is not sufficient that the right should give the owner for the time being some personal advantage; the test is whether the right makes the dominant tenement a better and more convenient property. This may be done not only by improving its general utility, as by giving means of access or light, but also by benefiting some trade which is conducted on the dominant tenement, at least if the trade is long established. For example, a public house may have an easement to fix a signboard to the house next door,[24] or a shop may have an easement to put out a stall in the street on market day.[25] However, the requirement of benefit is subsumed within the larger question whether the easement accommodates and serves the dominant tenement; a right may accommodate although the benefit is not by any means substantial, and it may not be helpful to treat benefit as an element independent from that of accommodation.[26]

27–009   *(b) Propinquity.* The servient tenement must be close enough to the dominant tenement to confer a practical benefit on it. Thus if X owns land in Northumberland, he cannot burden it with an easement of way in favour of land in Kent, for although it may be very convenient for the owner of the Kentish land to walk across X's Northumberland estate when he goes north, the right of way does not improve the Kentish land.[27] This does not mean that the dominant and servient tenements must be adjacent; even if they are separated by other land, an easement can still exist, provided that they are near enough for the dominant tenement to receive some benefit as such.[28] For example, a right to use a cart track may be appurtenant to a farm even though the track crosses properties lying at some little distance from the farm and does not lead directly to it. And the use of a pew in a church may belong to the owners of a house in the parish.[29] Nor will a right be any less an easement merely because it benefits other land as well as the dominant tenement.[30]

tenement that had neither been acquired nor identified at the time of the grant or reservation). The Law Commission has rejected a proposal that it should be possible to create easements in order to benefit land not yet owned, e.g. by a developer: Law Com. No.327, para. 2.27.

[23] See *Mason v Shrewsbury & Hereford Ry* (1871) L.R. 6 Q.B. 578 at 587.

[24] *Moody v Steggles* (1879) 12 Ch D 261 (and see the examples given by Fry J. at 266); *William Hill (Southern) Ltd v Cabras Ltd* (1986) 54 P. & C.R. 42 at 46.

[25] *Ellis v Mayor, etc., of Bridgnorth* (1863) 15 C.B. (N.S.) 52.

[26] See discussion in *Polo Woods Foundation v Shelton-Agar*, above, at p.241 et seq.

[27] The example is given in *Bailey v Stephens* (1862) 12 C.B. (N.S.) 91 at 115.

[28] *Todrick v Western National Omnibus Co Ltd* [1934] Ch. 561; *Pugh v Savage* [1970] 2 Q.B. 373.

[29] *Philipps v Halliday* [1891] A.C. 228. This easement is of an exceptional kind.

[30] *Simpson v Mayor, etc., of Godmanchester* [1897] A.C. 696 (right to open sluice gates to protect dominant tenement from flooding: held, this could be an easement even though it protected other land as well).

(c) Personal advantage. In *Hill v Tupper*[31] the owner of a canal leased land **27–010** on the bank of the canal to Hill and granted him the sole and exclusive right of putting pleasure boats on the canal. Tupper, without any authority, put rival pleasure boats on the canal. The question was whether Hill could successfully sue Tupper. If Hill's right amounted to an easement, he could sue anyone who interfered with it, for it was a right of property enforceable against all the world. If it was not an easement, then it could only be a licence,[32] i.e. a mere personal permission given to Hill by the canal owner, and not a proprietary interest which Hill could defend against third parties in his own right. It was held that the right to put out pleasure boats was not an interest in property which the law could recognise as being appurtenant to land. The monopoly which Hill had obtained was therefore a merely personal advantage, not connected with the use of his land as such. The result would have been different if the right granted had been to cross and re-cross the canal to get to and from Hill's land, and Tupper's boats had been so numerous as to interfere with it. If Hill had taken a lease of the canal itself he could, of course, have sued Tupper for trespassing on it.[33] Similarly Tupper could have been sued for trespass, on the facts as they were, by the owner of the canal.

3. The dominant and servient tenements must not be both owned and **27–011** **occupied by the same person.** An easement is essentially a right *in alieno solo* (in the soil of another). It follows that a person cannot have an easement over his own land.[34] "When the owner of Whiteacre and Blackacre passes over the former to Blackacre, he is not exercising a right of way in respect of Blackacre; he is merely making use of his own land to get from one part of it to another."[35] As this observation implies, an easement cannot exist only where the same person both owns and occupies both tenements; there is no difficulty about the existence of an easement in favour of a tenant against his own landlord, or against another tenant of his landlord, although the landlord owns the freehold of both dominant and servient tenements.[36]

The rule is therefore really no more than the self-evident proposition that a **27–012** man cannot have rights against himself. When an easement has come into existence as between two different landowners, and both their properties later

---

[31] (1863) 2 H. & C. 121. cf. *Manchester Airport Plc v Dutton* [2000] Q.B. 133 (licensee with contractual right to possession able to bring possession proceedings against squatters); see above, para.4–026.

[32] For licences see Ch.34 below.

[33] *Lord Chesterfield v Harris* [1908] 2 Ch. 397 at 412 (a river or canal is treated as land covered with water, and the trespass is to the land underlying the water).

[34] *Metropolitan Ry v Fowler* [1892] 1 Q.B. 165 at 171; *Sovmots Investments Ltd v Secretary of State for the Environment* [1979] A.C. 144 at 169; *London & Blenheim Estates Ltd v Ladbroke Retail Parks Ltd* [1992] 1 W.L.R. 1278 at 1283 (on appeal [1994] 1 W.L.R. 31). The Law Commission has recommended reform in this area: see below, para.29–016.

[35] *Roe v Siddons* (1888) 22 Q.B.D. 224 at 236, per Fry L.J.

[36] See, e.g. *Borman v Griffith* [1930] 1 Ch. 493, below, para.28–039. See also *Buckby v Coles* (1814) 5 Taunt. 311 at 315; *Richardson v Graham* [1908] 1 K.B. 39. There are difficulties about acquiring such easements by prescription: see below, para.28–056.

come into the hands of a single person, e.g. under a lease,[37] the question arises whether the easement is extinguished or merely suspended while the two properties are in one hand. This question is dealt with later in connection with the extinguishment of easements.[38]

27–013   Rights habitually exercised by a man over part of his own land which, if the part in question were owned and occupied by another would be easements, are often called quasi-easements.[39] The term is sometimes used to include other rights similar to easements, such as customary rights of way[40]; but in this book it is used only in the stricter sense. Quasi-easements are of some importance, for they may sometimes become true easements if the land is subsequently sold in separate parcels.[41]

27–014   **4. The easement must be capable of forming the subject-matter of a grant.** All easements "lie in grant"; that is to say, no right can exist as an easement unless it could have been granted by deed. The principles underlying this rule are that only certain kinds of rights are capable of being rights of property which one person can convey to another,[42] and that every easement in theory owes its existence to a grant by deed. Although in practice many easements are established by long user, this is always based upon the presumption that a grant was once made.[43] This assumption that an easement must have been created by deed leads to the following rules.

(a) The right must be within the general nature of rights capable of being created as easements

27–015   (1) THE LIST IS NOT CLOSED. Although most easements fall under one of the well-known heads of easements, such as way, light, support or water, the list of easements is not closed.[44] "The category of servitudes and easements must alter and expand with the changes that take place in the circumstances of mankind."[45] An example of this might be a right for a house to have telephone lines running across a neighbour's land. There has as yet been no decision that this can be an easement.[46] But a right to use a clothes line is probably capable of being one,[47] and the analogy may be close enough for the purpose. New

---

[37] See, e.g. *Thomas v Thomas* (1835) 2 Cr.M. & R. 34.

[38] See below, para.29–014.

[39] See, e.g. *Wheeldon v Burrows* (1879) 12 Ch D 31 at 49.

[40] *Brocklebank v Thompson* [1903] 2 Ch. 344 at 348.

[41] See below, para.28–020.

[42] cf. above, para.20–005.

[43] For prescription, see below, para.28–043. Exceptions to the presumption of a lost grant occur under the Prescription Act 1832: para.28–100 below.

[44] See the list of easements recorded in Gale, 1–73 et seq.

[45] *Dyce v Lady James Hay* (1852) 1 Macq. 305 at 312, 313, per Lord St Leonards.

[46] Although see *Lancashire & Cheshire Telephone Exchange Co v Manchester Overseers* (1884) 14 Q.B.D. 267, referred to in Cheshire & Burn, 17th edn, p.594.

[47] *Drewell v Towler* (1832) 3 B. & Ad. 735; *cf.* the right to run a timber "traveller" (aerial tramway) over other land: *Harris v De Pinna* (1886) 33 Ch D 238 at 251, 260.

rights have, therefore, from time to time been recognised as easements. Thus in 1896 the courts recognised as an easement the right to go upon the land of another to open sluice gates,[48] in 1915 the right to store casks and trade produce on land,[49] in 1955 the right to use a neighbour's lavatory,[50] in 1973 the right to use an airfield,[51] and in 1982 the right to park cars anywhere in a defined area, e.g. round a block of flats.[52]

(2) LIMITS. There are, however, limits. "It must not therefore be supposed **27–016** that incidents of a novel kind can be devised and attached to property at the fancy or caprice of any owner."[53] This expresses the overriding principle that the various kinds of proprietary interests are fixed by the law, and finite in number.[54] But even though the list of easements is not closed, it is not open to interests which do not conform to the rules about the general nature of easements.[55] For example, a right to an unspoilt view cannot exist as an easement.[56] Nor can a right to drain rainwater falling on A's land into B's ditches.[57] Nor can a right to receive radio or telephone signals over B's land.[58] Nor can a right to have the wall of a house protected from the weather by an adjoining house.[59] Such a right is too uncertain in its ambit to be an easement,[60] and might in any event require expenditure by the servient owner,[61] something which is generally fatal to the acceptance of a right as an easement.[62] However the right of support which often exists in favour of semi-

[48] *Simpson v Mayor, etc., of Godmanchester* [1896] 1 Ch. 214; [1897] A.C. 696.
[49] *Att Gen of Southern Nigeria v John Holt & Co (Liverpool) Ltd* [1915] A.C. 599 at 617 (see below, para.27–045). See too *Smith v Gates* [1952] C.P.L. 814.
[50] *Miller v Emcer Products Ltd* [1956] Ch. 304 at 316.
[51] *Dowty Boulton Paul Ltd v Wolverhampton Corporation (No.2)* [1976] Ch. 13.
[52] *Newman v Jones* (Unreported, March 22, 1982, Megarry V.C.); see below, para.27–021.
[53] *Keppell v Bailey* (1834) 2 My. & K. 517 at 535, per Lord Brougham L.C.
[54] See above, para.27–014.
[55] *London & Blenheim Estates Ltd v Ladbroke Retail Parks Ltd* [1994] 1 W.L.R. 31 at 37 (a right intended to be an easement and attached to a servient tenement before the dominant tenement was acquired could not exist as an easement).
[56] See below, para.27–022.
[57] *Palmer v Bowman* [2000] 1 All E.R. 22 (as a natural right, it is an essential incident of the ownership of land, and cannot therefore form the subject-matter of a grant); cf. *Green v Lord Somerleyton* [2003] EWCA Civ 198; [2004] 1 P. & C.R. 33 at [121].
[58] *Hunter v Canary Wharf Ltd* [1997] A.C. 655 at 709.
[59] *Phipps v Pears* [1965] 1 Q.B. 76. The reason for the decision was that "the law has been very chary of creating any new negative easements" because they unduly restrict what the servient owner may do on his land: *Phipps v Pears*, at 83, per Lord Denning M.R. This reasoning has been criticised: (1964) 80 L.Q.R. 318 (REM); (1964) 28 Conv. (N.S.) 450 at 451 (M. A. Peel). A right to protection from the weather has been held to exist as between owners of a party wall: *Upjohn v Seymour Estates Ltd* [1938] 1 All E.R. 614.
[60] See (1964) 80 L.Q.R. 318 at 320 (REM).
[61] This would certainly have been the case in *Phipps v Pears*, above. The defendant had been compelled to demolish his property by the local authority. He would necessarily have had to expend money to weatherproof the wall thereby exposed.
[62] See below, para.27–019. The possibility that a right to protection in the horizontal plane by means of a roof might be an easement has been canvassed: see *Sedgwick Forbes Bland Payne Group Ltd v Regional Properties Ltd* [1981] 1 E.G.L.R. 33 at 36.

detached or terraced houses is well-recognised as an easement, and this may indirectly confer some right to protection from the elements.[63]

27–017   In general, the courts are reluctant to extend the categories of negative easements, on the basis that they may operate unduly to restrict what the servient owner may do on his own land.[64] Such restrictions should be "limited and precise".[65] "As they represent an anomaly in the law because they restrict the owners' freedom, the law takes care not to extend them beyond the categories which are well known to the law."[66] One particular area of difficulty is the right to carry on a state of affairs which would otherwise be a nuisance; it has recently been doubted whether there can be a valid easement to create a noise.[67]

27–018   It used to be said that a right to use a garden or a park merely for recreational purposes, being a mere *jus spatiandi*, is incapable of being an easement[68]; but this right, which is of value to many houses adjacent to parks and gardens, has since been admitted into the company of easements,[69] and the same may apply to a right to boat on a neighbouring lake.[70] The law of easements may protect projecting buildings, or even the projecting bowsprits of ships using a dock[71]; but it will not extend to overhanging trees.[72] More examples of the various species of easements are given below.[73]

27–019   (3) EXPENDITURE. "A right to have something done is not an easement."[74] It is therefore most unlikely that a right would be accepted as an easement if it involved the servient owner in the expenditure of money.[75] None of the

---

[63] *Rees v Skerrett* [2001] 1 W.L.R. 1541 (right of support held to confer protection from damage caused by wind suction as opposed to rain penetration). For rights of support generally, see below, para.30–021.

[64] *Phipps v Pears* [1965] 1 Q.B. 76 at 83, criticised in (1964) 80 L.Q.R. 318 (REM); (1964) 28 Conv. (N.S.) 450 at 451 (M. A. Peel); *Hunter v Canary Wharf Ltd* [1997] A.C. 655.

[65] *Hunter v Canary Wharf Ltd* [1997] A.C. 655 at 709, per Lord Hoffmann.

[66] *Hunter v Canary Wharf Ltd*, above, at 726, per Lord Hope. The Law Commission has considered but rejected a proposal that negative easements should be prospectively abolished: Law Com. No.327, paras 5.97 et seq.

[67] *Lawrence v Fen Tigers Ltd* [2011] EWHC 360 (Ch); and see below para 30–023.

[68] *International Tea Stores Co v Hobbs* [1903] 2 Ch. 165 at 172, per Farwell J; see also *Att Gen v Antrobus* [1905] 2 Ch. 188.

[69] *Re Ellenborough Park* [1956] Ch. 131; *Mulvaney v Gough* [2002] EWCA Civ 1078; [2003] 1 W.L.R. 360 (upholding a prescriptive claim to enjoyment of a communal garden); Thompson [2002] Conv. 571. For the position of a *jus spatiandi* as a public right, see *R. v Doncaster BC, Ex p. Braim* (1986) 57 P. & C.R. 1; [1988] Conv. 369 at 371 (J. Hill).

[70] *Re Ellenborough Park* above, at 175. Contrast a mere commercial right to hire out boats on the water: above, para.27–010.

[71] *Suffield v Brown* (1864) 4 De G.J. & S. 185.

[72] *Lemmon v Webb* [1895] A.C. 1.

[73] See Ch.30.

[74] Gale, 1–78.

[75] *Regis Property Co Ltd v Redman* [1956] 2 Q.B. 612 (covenant to supply hot water creates no easement, being a right to services); *Rance v Elvin* (1985) 50 P. & C.R. 9 at 13 (servient owner could not be obliged to pay for supply of water to his own land so that it could pass to the dominant land); *Cardwell v Walker* [2003] EWHC 3117; [2004] 2 P. & C.R. 9 (quaere whether servient owner could be obliged to provide access to electricity supply by providing tokens for dominant owners: decided on other grounds); *William Old International Ltd v Arya* [2009] EWHC 599 (Ch); [2009] 2 P. & C.R. 20. See [1985] C.L.J. 458 (A. J. Waite), where the generality of the rule is questioned.

recognised easements does so,[76] with the anomalous exception of the obligation to fence land in order to keep out cattle[77] and, perhaps, certain obligations to repair sea-walls, river banks and gutters (though the status of such rights as easements is questionable).[78] It follows that a right of way to cross a bridge, for example, imposes no obligation on the servient owner to keep the bridge in repair.[79] Where positive action is needed to maintain an easement, the general principle is that the dominant owner may enter and execute repairs upon the servient land, e.g. to a pipe or pump which he is entitled to use; all this is implicit in the concept of grant.[80] The servient owner's only obligation is to refrain from doing anything which impedes the enjoyment of the easement. In the case of an easement of support, the servient owner may allow the supporting structure to fall into decay and collapse,[81] but he may not himself pull it down[82]; and the dominant owner is entitled to enter and repair it as soon as this is necessary to protect his own building.[83] Nor may the servient owner do anything which might prevent the dominant owner from executing repairs.[84]

(4) THE RIGHT MUST NOT BE TOO EXTENSIVE. An easement is no more than a **27-020** right over land, and not a right to either possession or joint user of it.[85] It follows that if "what the dominant owner can do on the servient land actually amounts to an ownership right—regardless of the words used—then it cannot be an easement."[86] This restriction has been in issue in a number of cases where A has claimed the right to store goods or to park vehicles on B's land.[87] In this context, the courts have developed an analogous "ouster" principle which focuses on the effect of exercising the right on the use that can be made of the land by the servient owner; if its exercise will "leave the servient owner without any reasonable use of his land, whether for parking or anything else, it could not be an easement though it might be some larger or different

---

[76] See *Pomfret v Ricroft* (1669) 1 Wms.Saund. 321.

[77] *Lawrence v Jenkins* (1873) L.R. 8 Q.B. 274 at 279, per Archibald J., citing Gale; below, para.30–022. The Law Commission has recommended that such an obligation should for the future take effect as a land obligation and not as an easement: Law Com. No.327, para. 5.93. There are certain statutory duties to fence: e.g. under the Railways Clauses Consolidation Act 1845; see *R. Walker & Sons v British Railways Board* [1984] 1 W.L.R. 805.

[78] See e.g. *Hudson v Tabor* (1876) 2 Q.B.D. 290; *R. v Commissioners for Sewers for Essex* (1885) 14 Q.B.D. 561; (1964) 28 Conv. (N.S.) 450 at 451 (M. A. Peel); [1985] C.L.J. 458 at 461 (A. J. Waite).

[79] *Jones v Pritchard* [1908] 1 Ch. 630 at 637.

[80] Gale 1–91 et seq.; *Goodhart v Hyett* (1883) 25 Ch D 182; *Jones v Pritchard*, above.

[81] *Bond v Nottingham Corp* [1940] Ch. 429 at 438. He may be liable independently in nuisance: *Bradburn v Lindsay* [1983] 2 All E.R. 408. See [1984] Conv. 54 (P. Jackson). cf. [1987] Conv. 47 (A. J. Waite).

[82] See below, para.30–021.

[83] *Bond v Nottingham Corp*, above.

[84] *Goodhart v Hyett*, above (injunction against servient owner building over water pipe).

[85] *Copeland v Greenhalf* [1952] Ch. 488 at 498.

[86] Law Com. No.327, para.3.191. "There is no easement known to law which gives exclusive and unrestricted use of a piece of land": *Reilly v Booth* (1890) 44 Ch D 12 at 26, per Lopes L.J.

[87] [2007] Conv. 223 (A. Hill-Smith).

grant."[88] Application of the ouster principle involves the court asking a question of degree.[89] It is the area of land over which the right is being exercised, not the entirety of the servient owner's estate, which must be considered.[90] On this basis, the claim by a wheelwright to park an unlimited number of vehicles on a strip of his neighbour's land adjacent to the highway failed because it went "wholly outside any normal idea of an easement".[91] However, the ouster principle should not be pushed too far; the fact that the exercise of a right may detract from the servient owner's enjoyment of his land, or even that it may involve the servient owner's temporary exclusion from the land, is not incompatible with its status as an easement.[92]

27–021   It is now generally accepted by the Court of Appeal that certain rights to park vehicles may exist in law as an easement.[93] Indeed, the House of Lords has questioned, albeit *obiter* in an appeal on the Scots law of servitudes, the rationale for the current distinction between a right to park a vehicle in an area that can hold as many as twenty or as few as two vehicles (capable of taking effect as an easement) and a right to park a vehicle in a defined space, bay or garage that is large enough only for that vehicle (not capable of taking effect as an easement).[94] This distinction has been judicially criticised as "somewhat contrary to common sense".[95] Both the House of Lords and the Law Commission have criticised the ouster principle. The House of Lords would prefer to ask whether, the servient owner has retained "possession and, subject to the reasonable exercise of the right in question, control of the servient land."[96] The Law Commission, considering the ouster principle "unclear", and having

[88] *London & Blenheim Estates Ltd v Ladbroke Retail Parks Ltd* [1992] 1 W.L.R. 1278 at 1288 per Judge Baker QC; *Batchelor v Marlow* [2001] EWCA Civ 1051; [2003] 1 W.L.R. 764 (prescriptive claim to park six cars on servient land during working hours from Monday to Friday held to be incapable of comprising an easement as it would leave servient owner without any reasonable use of his land).

[89] ibid., and see also *Grigsby v Melville* [1972] 1 W.L.R. 1355 at 1364 (on appeal [1974] 1 W.L.R. 80); *P & S Platt v Crouch* [2003] EWCA Civ 1110; [2004] 1 P. & C.R. 18 at [45].

[90] *Moncrieff v Jamieson*, above, at 2641.

[91] *Copeland v Greenhalf*, above, at 498, per Upjohn J.

[92] *Miller v Emcer Products Ltd* [1956] Ch. 304 at 316 (right to use a lavatory held to be an easement); *P & S Platt Ltd v Crouch*, above, at [46] (right to moor boats along whole of defendants' river frontage and ancillary rights of access held not to deprive them of any reasonable user of land); *Polo Woods Foundation v Shelton-Agar* [2009] EWHC 1361 (Ch); [2010] 1 P. & C.R 12 (right to graze 10 ponies on less than one acre of land for twelve hours a day during eight months a year held not to preclude reasonable use by the servient owners).

[93] *Newman v Jones* (Unreported March 22, 1982, Megarry V.C.); *London & Blenheim Estates Ltd v Ladbroke Retail Parks Ltd*, above, at 1288, per H.H. Judge Paul Baker QC (on appeal [1994] 1 W.L.R. 31); *Handel v St Stephens Close Ltd* [1994] 1 E.G.L.R. 70 at 71, 72; *Hair v Gillman* (2000) 80 P. & C.R. 108 at 112; *Saeed v Plustrade Ltd* [2001] EWCA Civ 2011; [2002] 2 P. & C.R. 19; *Montrose Court Holdings Ltd v Shamash* [2006] EWCA Civ 251. However, it should be noted that in none of these cases was the Court of Appeal required to decide whether the right to park claimed could, as a matter of law, comprise an easement.

[94] *Moncrieff v Jamieson* [2007] UKHL 42; [2007] 1 W.L.R. 2620.

[95] *Moncrieff v Jamieson*, above, at 2663 per Lord Neuberger.

[96] *Moncrieff v Jamieson*, above, at 2643 per Lord Scott. The appeal was one from the Court of Session on a point of Scots law; it has been held, at first instance, that the ouster principle is still to be applied in the English courts: *Virdi v Chana* [2008] EWHC 2901 (Ch) (H.H. Judge Purle QC sitting as a High Court judge.) See further Goymour [2008] C.L.J. 20; Haley [2008] Conv. 244.

the undesirable effect of putting valuable parking rights at risk, has recommended its abolition, at the same time recognising that the grant of exclusive
possession to the dominant owner cannot, and should not, be effected by
means of an easement.[97]

(b) The right must be sufficiently definite. The extent of the right claimed **27–022**
must be capable of reasonably exact definition, for otherwise it could not be
granted at all. This rule is really a corollary of the preceding one, but it helps
to explain the exclusion of certain kinds of rights. Thus, although there can be
an easement of light where a defined window receives a defined amount of
light,[98] there can be no easement of indefinite privacy[99] or prospect (i.e. the
right to a view).[100] Again, an easement may exist for the passage of air
through a defined channel[101]; but there can be no easement for the general
flow of air over land to a windmill,[102] chimney,[103] drying shed for timber,[104]
or otherwise.[105] A catalogue of recognised species of easements and profits
will be found in Chapter 30.

Of course, it is often possible to secure by way of contract rights which are **27–023**
too indefinite to be easements; and a restrictive covenant properly framed may
be used to confer what is in substance a right of amenity, e.g. an unspoilt view,
upon one piece of land as against another.[106] Another doctrine which may
sometimes circumvent the limits of the easement definition is the rule against
"derogation from grant".[107]

(c) There must be a capable grantor. There can be no claim to an easement **27–024**
if at the relevant time the servient tenement was owned by someone incapable
of granting an easement, e.g. a statutory corporation with no power to grant
easements,[108] an incumbent who has not obtained a faculty to grant a right of
way over a churchyard,[109] or a tenant under a lease who has no power to bind
the reversion.[110] Where the claim is based on an express grant, the grantor
must, of course, have been capable of granting the easement: thus an easement
over a common cannot be granted by some only of the commoners.[111]

---

[97] Law Com. No.327, paras 3.205 et seq.
[98] See below, para.30–011.
[99] *Browne v Flower* [1911] 1 Ch. 219 at 225.
[100] *William Aldred's Case* (1610) 9 Co.Rep. 57b at 58b, per Wray C.J.: "for prospect, which is
a matter only of delight, and not of necessity, no action lies for stopping thereof . . . the law does
not give an action for such things of delight".
[101] *Bass v Gregory* (1890) 25 Q.B.D. 481 (ventilation shaft for cellar); *Cable v Bryant* [1908]
1 Ch. 259 (aperture in stable).
[102] *Webb v Bird* (1863) 13 C.B. (N.S.) 841.
[103] *Bryant v Lefever* (1879) 4 C.P.D. 172.
[104] *Harris v De Pinna* (1886) 33 Ch D 238.
[105] *Chastey v Ackland* [1895] 2 Ch. 389.
[106] See below, para.32–030; below, para.27–043.
[107] See below, para.27 046.
[108] *Mulliner v Midland Ry* (1879) 11 Ch D 611.
[109] *Re St Clement's, Leigh-on-Sea* [1988] 1 W.L.R. 720 at 728.
[110] *Derry v Sanders* [1919] 1 K.B. 223 at 231.
[111] *Paine & Co Ltd v St Neots Gas & Coke Co* [1939] 3 All E.R. 812.

27–025   *(d) There must be a capable grantee.* An easement can be claimed only by a legal person capable of receiving a grant.[112] Thus a claim by a company with no power to acquire easements must fail.[113] A fluctuating body of persons, such as "the inhabitants for the time being of the village of X", cannot claim an easement, for no grant can be made to them. But they may have similar rights if there is a valid custom to that effect,[114] such as a customary right of way across land to reach the parish church,[115] or a customary right to take water from a spout,[116] or to water cattle at a pond,[117] or for recreation on a common,[118] or to play games[119] or dry nets[120] on certain land.

B. Distinctions between Easements and Certain Analogous Rights

27–026   It will have been gathered that the attempt to define an easement leads to a list of miscellaneous examples rather than to a precise definition. Some further help may be had from contrasting easements with certain other rights which are distinct from them.

I. NATURAL RIGHTS

27–027   **1. Support.** A "natural right" is a right protected by the law of tort, breach of which may lead to liability in nuisance. Every landowner has a natural right to support for his land from his neighbour's land.[121] It exists automatically, and unlike an easement does not require a grant in order to be acquired. But due to developments in the law of tort, the current extent of the right of support and the consequences of its breach are no longer easy to summarise.

27–028   It is clear that where a neighbour deliberately removes support by quarrying,[122] or removes the subjacent strata of minerals by pumping brine,[123] an action in nuisance will lie. More difficult is where the neighbour fails to take steps to abate a "natural nuisance".[124] "It is only in comparatively recent times that the law has recognised an occupier's duty as one of a more positive character than merely to abstain from creating, or adding to, a source of danger or annoyance."[125] The occupier, confronted with a nuisance not of his own creation, may nevertheless be under a "measured duty" to act: "based

---

[112] *Re Salvin's Indenture* [1938] 2 All E.R. 498.
[113] *National Guaranteed Manure Co Ltd v Donald* (1859) 4 H. & N. 8.
[114] For custom see below, para.27–049.
[115] *Brocklebank v Thompson* [1903] 2 Ch. 344.
[116] *Harrop v Hirst* (1868) L.R. 4 Ex. 43.
[117] *Manning v Wasdale* (1836) 5 A. & E. 758.
[118] *R. v Doncaster BC, Ex p. Braim* (1986) 57 P. & C.R. 1.
[119] *New Windsor Corporation v Mellor* [1975] Ch. 380.
[120] *Mercer v Denne* [1905] 2 Ch. 538.
[121] *Backhouse v Bonomi* (1861) 9 H.L.C. 503; *Dalton v Angus & Co Ltd* (1881) 6 App.Cas. 740 at 791.
[122] *Redland Bricks Ltd v Morris* [1970] A.C. 652 (damages awarded but mandatory injunction refused).
[123] *Lotus Ltd v British Soda Co Ltd* [1972] Ch. 123 (damages and an injunction awarded).
[124] W.V.H. Rogers, *Winfield & Jolowicz on Tort*, 18th edn (London: Sweet & Maxwell 2010), para.14–21.
[125] *Goldman v Hargrave* [1967] 1 A.C. 645 at 657 per Lord Wilberforce.

upon knowledge of the hazard, ability to foresee the consequences of not checking or removing it, and the ability to abate it . . . . The standard ought to be to require of the occupier what is reasonable to expect of him in his individual circumstances."[126] An occupier may therefore be liable in nuisance for failing to take reasonable steps to prevent movement of his land onto the adjoining land below it. [127]

There is a similar right of support where the surface of the land and the soil underneath are owned by different persons. The owner of the surface has a natural right to have it supported by the subjacent soil, and even if he has let or sold minerals lying below the surface he can sue if the mining causes subsidence,[128] provided of course that he has not agreed to the surface being let down.[129] By contrast, no action lies when the support is removed by the neighbour's abstraction of water.[130] It is traditionally thought that the natural right of support extends only to land "in its natural state",[131] and that it does not apply to buildings or to the additional burden on land which they cause.[132] "The owner of the adjacent soil may with perfect legality dig that soil away, and allow his neighbour's house, if supported by it, to fall in ruins to the ground."[133] Similarly it is generally considered that there is no natural right to have buildings supported by neighbouring buildings.[134] If no more damage is done than is necessary, a man may pull down his house without having to provide support for his neighbour's house.[135]   **27–029**

But these bold statements asserting the apparent autonomy of the land-owner must be read subject to certain reservations. First, there is the "meas-ured duty of care" recognised above, which may be broken "if a neighbour does something which would foreseeably cause damage to a neighbouring owner or fails to take action to avoid such damage."[136] Secondly, it has long been accepted that if it can be shown that withdrawing support would have caused actionable damage even if nothing had been built, the damages recov-erable will include any damage to the buildings.[137] Thirdly, there is the   **27–030**

---

[126] *Goldman v Hargrave*, above, at 663 per Lord Wilberforce.

[127] *Leakey v National Trust* [1980] Q.B. 485; cf. *Lambert v Barratt Homes Ltd* [2010] EWCA Civ 681; [2011] H.L.R. 1.

[128] *L. & N.W. Ry v Evans* [1893] 1 Ch. 16 at 30.

[129] See, e.g. *Butterknowle Colliery Co Ltd v Bishop Auckland Industrial Co-operative Co Ltd* [1906] A.C. 305 at 309.

[130] *Stephens v Anglian Water Authority* [1987] 1 W.L.R. 1381 (there is a useful summary of the law at 1384). See too *Brace v SE Regional Housing Association Ltd* [1984] 1 E.G.L.R. 144 at 145; [1988] Conv. 175 (M. Harwood). cf. *Home Brewery Co Ltd v William Davis & Co (Leicester) Ltd* [1987] Q.B. 339; [1987] C.L.J. 205 (J. R. Spencer).

[131] *Hunt v Peake* (1860) Johns. 705.

[132] *Wyatt v Harrison* (1832) 3 B. & Ad. 871.

[133] *Dalton v Angus & Co* (1881) 6 App.Cas. 740 at 804, per Lord Penzance.

[134] *Peyton v The Mayor & Commonalty of London* (1829) 9 B. & C. 725.

[135] *Southwark & Vauxhall Water Co v Wandsworth District Board of Works* [1898] 2 Ch. 603 at 612.

[136] Gale, 10–38, discussing *Holbeck Hall Hotel Ltd v Scarborough BC* [2000] Q.B. 836; Thompson [2001] Conv. 177; *Rees v Skerrett* [2001] 1 W.L.R. 1541.

[137] *Stroyan v Knowles* (1861) 6 H. & N. 454; *Lotus Ltd v British Soda Co Ltd* [1972] Ch. 123 (where, however, the real injury was abstraction of the plaintiff's own subsoil); *Ray v Fairway Motors (Barnstaple) Ltd* (1968) 20 P. & C.R. 261.

possibility that a right of support has been acquired as an easement.[138] The cause of action for the tort of interference with a natural right of support does not arise until damage has been suffered, though the court may grant a quia timet injunction if damage is anticipated. If remedial work is carried out by the landowner in anticipation of subsidence, that expenditure will therefore be irrecoverable.[139]

27–031   **2. Light and water.** "No natural right exists to a single ray of light."[140] This is, no doubt, because land in its natural state must always receive light through the air-space above it, which is protected by the law of trespass.[141] There are no natural rights in respect of buildings. But there is a natural right to water, where it flows naturally in a definite channel.[142] Therefore if the stream is dammed or diverted the riparian owners can sue.[143] The right to dam or divert it, on the other hand, may be acquired as an easement.[144] There is no natural right to water percolating underground, for there is then no definite channel.[145]

II. PUBLIC RIGHTS

27–032   An easement must always be appurtenant to land; it is a right exercisable by the owner for the time being by virtue of his estate in the land.[146] A public right, on the other hand, is a right exercisable by anyone, whether he owns land or not, merely by virtue of the general law.[147] Thus there is a public right to fish and navigate over the foreshore (the area between the ordinary high and

---

[138] See below, para.30–021. The provision of statutory rights of support has been suggested from time to time: Law Reform Committee, 14th Report, Cmnd. 3100 (1966), paras 89, 90; Law Commission Working Paper No.36 (1971), para.82.

[139] *Midland Bank Plc v Bardgrove Property Services Ltd* (1992) 65 P. & C.R. 153. But where a person reasonably carries out necessary works to eliminate a nuisance, the cost may be recovered from the neighbour responsible for the nuisance: *Delaware Mansions Ltd v Westminster City Council* [2001] UKHL 55; [2002] 1 A.C. 321.

[140] Gale, 12th edn, 6. An easement of light can be acquired for a building, however: see below, para.30–010 et seq.

[141] See above, para.3–043.

[142] *Palmer v Bowman* [2000] 1 All E.R. 22. However, it has been recognised that "naturally flowing water" is capable of meaning not simply water flowing in its natural direction (i.e. downhill) but water flowing downhill in "natural" surroundings, or over a "natural" surface, and that "in the English landscape . . . the distinction between 'natural' features and those which are 'artificial' in the sense that they owe something to human agency may not be an easy one to draw." *Green v Lord Somerleyton* [2003] EWCA Civ 198; [2004] 1 P. & C.R. 33 at [81], per Jonathan Parker L.J.

[143] *Swindon Waterworks Co Ltd v Wilts and Berks Canal Navigation Co* (1875) L.R. 7 H.L. 697; and see above, para.3–049.

[144] Gale, 6–41.

[145] *Acton v Blundell* (1843) 12 M. & W. 324; *Chasemore v Richards* (1859) 7 H.L.C. 349; *Bradford Corp v Pickles* [1895] A.C. 587. See too *Stephens v Anglian Water Authority* [1987] 1 W.L.R. 1381.

[146] See above, para.27–005.

[147] This definition was approved by the Court of Appeal in *Overseas Investment Services Ltd v Simcobuild Construction Ltd* (1995) 70 P. & C.R. 322 at 328, 330.

low water marks) when it is covered with water, but no right of bathing, walking or beachcombing on it.[148]

The public rights which most closely resemble easements are public rights of way.[149] The land over which a public right of way exists is known as a highway[150]; and although most highways have been made up into roads, and most easements of way exist over footpaths, the presence or absence of a made road has nothing to do with the distinction. There may be a highway over a footpath, while a well-made road may be subject only to an easement of way, or may exist only for the landowner's benefit and be subject to no easement at all. A highway may exist as such even if it does not lead to another highway or any public place.[151] If the highway is maintainable at public expense, it vests in the statutory highway authority.[152] That authority then holds the surface of the land affected, together with so much of the land below and the air-space above as is required by their statutory duties, for a statutory fee simple interest determinable on the land ceasing to be used as a highway.[153]

27–033

1. Creation. A public right of way may be created in the following ways.

27–034

(a) By statute. A highway may be created by the exercise of statutory powers, in which case no further act of the land owner, or user by the public, is required to complete the process of creation.[154] The Highways Act 1980, for example, makes provision for the adoption of an existing highway and for the adoption and dedication of one that is to be constructed.[155] But where a statute simply authorises the setting out of a public road, no highway will come into existence until the road has been set out in substantial compliance with the statutory requirements.[156]

(b) By dedication and acceptance.

(1) AT COMMON LAW. To establish a highway at common law by dedication and acceptance it must be shown:

27–035

---

[148] *Brinckman v Matley* [1904] 2 Ch. 313; *Alfred F. Beckett Ltd v Lyons* [1967] Ch. 449. Such activities are enjoyed not as of right, but by tolerance.

[149] See [1993] Conv. 129 (M. Welstead).

[150] At common law highways are of three kinds: (i) a full highway or cartway (right of passage on foot, with beasts of burden, or with vehicles and cattle); (ii) a bridleway (right of passage on foot and with beasts of burden); and (iii) a footpath (right of passage on foot only): *Suffolk CC v Mason* [1979] A.C. 705 at 709, 710.

[151] *Williams-Ellis v Cobb* [1935] 1 K.B. 310.

[152] Highways Act 1980 s.263.

[153] *Foley's Charity Trustees v Dudley Corp* [1910] 1 K.B. 317 at 322; *Tithe Redemption Commission v Runcorn UDC* [1954] Ch. 383; *Wiltshire CC v Frazer* (1983) 47 P. & C.R. 69 at 72.

[154] *R. v Inhabitants of Leake* (1833) 5 B. & Ad. 469.

[155] s.38.

[156] *Cubitt v Lady Caroline Maxse* (1873) L.R. 8 C.P. 704; *Hale v Norfolk CC* [2001] Ch. 717 (where the Court of Appeal held that the Public Health Act 1925 s.30, did not confer powers to create public rights of way over private land). However, there may subsequently be adoption by user.

(i) that the owner of the land dedicated the way to the public, and

(ii) that the public accepted that dedication, the acceptance normally being shown by user by the public.[157]

Dedication may be formal, although this is comparatively infrequent.[158] It is usually inferred from long user by the public,[159] so that user is thus effective to prove both dedication and acceptance.[160] But in order to raise a presumption of dedication there must have been open user as of right[161] for so long a time and in such a way that the landowner must have known that the public were claiming a right.[162] User with the landowner's permission or tolerance is not user as of right,[163] and the court is slow to find a claim of right where the user is attributable to the landowner's indulgence.[164] The user must also have been without interruption by the owner. A practice frequently adopted to disprove any intention to dedicate is to close the way for one day in each year, for this asserts the landowner's right to exclude the public at will.[165]

27–036   The length of the enjoyment to be shown depends on the circumstances of the case. Where the circumstances have pointed to an intention to dedicate, 18 months has been held to be enough[166]; where the circumstances are against dedication, a substantially greater period may be insufficient,[167] especially if in recent years there has been no occupier capable of dedicating a highway in perpetuity.[168] Evidence of objections having been made at a public inquiry by someone who may have been the landowner 20 years previously may be relevant to the question whether there has been acquiescence giving rise to an inference of dedication.[169]

27–037   At common law it is possible for an occupier of adjoining land to be liable for repair of the highway under the conditions of tenure of the land, *ratione tenurae*.[170] This liability is in effect a burden running with land,[171] since it falls on successive owners and occupiers, though it seems that they bear only

---

[157] See *Cubitt v Lady Caroline Maxse* (1873) L.R. 8 C.P. 704 at 715.

[158] *Simpson v Att Gen* [1904] A.C. 476 at 494.

[159] The inference of dedication is very difficult to draw in the absence of public use: see, e.g. *Sinclair v Kearsley* [2010] EWCA Civ 112; [2010] N.P.C. 24.

[160] *Cubitt v Lady Caroline Maxse*, above.

[161] See *Hue v Whiteley* [1929] 1 Ch. 440 at 445; and see below, para.28–048.

[162] *Greenwich District Board of Works v Maudslay* (1870) L.R. 5 Q.B. 397 at 404.

[163] *R. v Broke* (1859) 1 F. & F. 514; cf. below, para.28–052.

[164] *Att Gen v Antrobus* [1905] 2 Ch. 188 (no public right of access to Stonehenge).

[165] *British Museum Trustees v Finnis* (1833) 5 C. & P. 460.

[166] *North London Ry v Vestry of St Mary's, Islington* (1872) 27 L.T. 672.

[167] *R. v Hudson* (1732) 2 Stra. 909 (4 years).

[168] See *Williams-Ellis v Cobb* [1935] 1 K.B. 310.

[169] *Wild v Secretary of State for the Environment, Food and Rural Affairs* [2009] EWCA Civ 1406.

[170] See *Pratt & Mackenzie on Highways*, 21st edn (London: Butterworth, Shaw & Sons, 1967), p.76.

[171] Where the title is registered it is an interest which overrides first registration or a registered disposition: LRA 2002 Sch.1 para.5 Sch.3 para.5.

personal liability. In theory, the tenure must have been created before 1290,[172] but in practice liability is proved by showing that the occupier and his predecessors have repaired the highway over a long period of time.

(2) UNDER THE HIGHWAYS ACT 1980. Section 31 of the Highways Act **27–038** 1980,[173] which was modelled upon the Prescription Act 1832,[174] facilitates proof of dedication by laying down a definite period of use which will suffice to show that a right of way exists. However, the Act of 1980 "supplemented the common law rather than replaced it."[175] The public can therefore claim a right of way based on a shorter period of use than that laid down by the Act if an intent to dedicate can be inferred.[176]

The Act provides[177] that a right of way can be established by 20 years' **27–039** enjoyment of a way over land[178] by the public as of right[179] and without interruption, unless there is sufficient evidence[180] that there was no intention during that period to dedicate it.[181] Where user of a way is merely incidental to some other activity, such as recreation, it will not give rise to a presumption

---

[172] See above, para.2–015.

[173] Which replaced the Rights of Way Act 1932 and later legislation.

[174] See below, para.28–066 et seq.; and see *R (Godmanchester Town Council) v Secretary of State for the Environment, Food and Rural Affairs* [2007] UKHL 28; [2008] 1 A.C. 221 at 245 et seq.

[175] *Wild v Secretary of State for the Environment, Food and Rural Affairs* [2009] EWCA Civ 1406 at [26] per Scott Baker L.J.

[176] s.31(9), preserving the common law rule: see *Wild v Secretary of State for the Environment, Food and Rural Affairs*, above, at [16].

[177] Highways Act 1980 s.31(1).

[178] Although "land" is defined to include "land covered with water" (Highways Act 1980 s.31(11)), the section does not apply to rights of navigation over a river or canal: *Att Gen ex rel. Yorkshire Derwent Trust Ltd v Brotherton* [1992] 1 A.C. 425. The definition is included *ex abundanti cautela* to cover cases where the way passes through a ford or is subjected to flooding: *Att Gen ex rel. Yorkshire Derwent Trust Ltd v Brotherton*, above, at 437, 442. "I cannot . . . think that any reader of Alfred Lord Tennyson would have regarded the Lady of Shalott, as she floated down to Camelot through the noises of the night, as exercising a right of way over the subjacent soil": *Att Gen ex rel. Yorkshire Derwent Trust Ltd v Brotherton*, above, at 435, per Lord Oliver.

[179] This has the same meaning as in the case of easements, namely user which is *nec vi, nec clam, nec precario*: see *R. v Oxfordshire CC Ex p. Sunningwell PC* [2000] 1 A.C. 335, reviewing the authorities; and see below, paras 28–048 et seq. User under a licence will not therefore suffice: *R. v Secretary of State for the Environment Ex p. Billson* [1999] Q.B. 374.

[180] The onus is upon the landowner to adduce this evidence in order to rebut the presumption of intention to dedicate: *Ward v Durham CC* (1994) 70 P. & C.R. 585 at 589.

[181] The statement of Lord Denning MR in *Fairey v Southampton CC* [1956] 2 Q.B. 439 at 458 ("In order for there to be 'sufficient evidence that there was no intention' to dedicate the way, there must be evidence of some overt acts on the part of the landowner such as to show the public at large—the public who used the path, in this case the villagers—that he had no intention to dedicate") has been approved by the House of Lords: *R (Godmanchester Town Council) v Secretary of State for the Environment, Food and Rural Affairs* [2007] UKHL 28; [2008] 1 A.C. 221 at 249 et seq. The test is therefore objective, addressing neither what the landowner may have subjectively intended nor what users of the way may have subjectively assumed but rather whether a reasonable user would have understood that the landowner was intending to disabuse him of the notion that the way was a public highway: *R (Godmanchester Town Council) v Secretary of State for the Environment, Food and Rural Affairs*, above, at 252.

of dedication as a highway.[182] "Without interruption" means "without physical obstruction", and not merely "not contentious"[183]; and even a physical obstruction at times when nobody was likely to use the way is no interruption.[184] A mere restriction on the user of the way may not amount to an interruption.[185] The absence of any intention to dedicate can be shown either in one of the usual means, as by closing the way for one day in each year,[186] or in one of the special statutory methods namely, by exhibiting a notice visible to those using the way,[187] or by depositing a map with the local authority with a statement of what ways the landowner admits to be highways, and lodging statutory declarations at intervals of not more than six years stating whether any other ways have been dedicated.[188] The 20-year period is to be calculated as that next before the time when the right to use the way was brought into question by a notice exhibited to the public negativing the intention to dedicate the way as a highway.[189] Enjoyment prior to the date of the Act suffices.[190]

27–040   A reversioner or a remainderman is at risk that a public right of way may be acquired by 20 years' user against the tenant for life or years. The Highways Act 1980 therefore provides that:

  (i) where the land is let on lease, the reversioner may exhibit a notice rebutting dedication[191]; and

  (ii) where it is held by a tenant for life, the reversioner or remainderman may take proceedings for trespass as if he were already in possession.[192]

27–041   Local authorities are required to maintain definitive maps and statements, subject to the determination of objections, of public footpaths and bridleways in their areas.[193] These maps are conclusive as to the rights shown.[194] How-

---

[182] *Dyfed CC v Secretary of State for Wales* (1989) 59 P. & C.R. 275 at 279 (where user of a path may have been merely ancillary to the use of a lake for fishing, swimming, sunbathing and picnicking).

[183] See *Merstham Manor Ltd v Coulsdon and Purley UDC* [1937] 2 K.B. 77.

[184] *Lewis v Thomas* [1950] 1 K.B. 438.

[185] *Gloucestershire CC v Farrow* [1985] 1 W.L.R. 741 at 747 (right of way subject to restriction twice a year due to the holding of a fair).

[186] *Merstham Manor Ltd v Coulsdon and Purley UDC*, above, at 85.

[187] Highways Act 1980 s.31(3). If this is torn down or defaced, a written notice to the local council will be effective: s.31(5); on which see *Paterson v Secretary of State for the Environment, Food and Rural Affairs* [2010] EWHC 394 (Admin); [2010] N.P.C. 26. If the land is leased, the landlord is entitled to enter and erect a notice: s.31(4).

[188] Highways Act 1980 s.31(6).

[189] Highways Act 1980 s.31(2); cf. below, paras 28–069 et seq.

[190] *Att Gen and Newton Abbot RDC v Dyer* [1947] Ch. 67; *Fairey v Southampton CC* [1956] 2 Q.B. 439. See [1956] C.L.J. 172 (R. N. Gooderson).

[191] s.31(4).

[192] s.33.

[193] Wildlife and Countryside Act 1981 Pt III, replacing (with amendments) earlier legislation. This duty was introduced by the National Parks and Access to the Countryside Act 1949 Pt IV.

[194] Wildlife and Countryside Act 1981 s.56(1).

ever, the local authority is under a duty to keep them under continuous review and to amend them accordingly; and it therefore follows that the definitive map is always subject to modification.[195] The conclusiveness of the maps is therefore without prejudice to the question of whether greater rights exist.[196] Moreover, rights erroneously included may be either deleted or reclassified as a lesser form of right, e.g. where a bridleway is reclassified as a mere footpath.[197]

2. Extinguishment. Once a highway has been established, it can be extin-   **27–042** guished only:

(i) by natural causes, such as inroads of the sea or landslips[198]; or

(ii) if it is closed or diverted by an order made under certain statutory provisions[199]; or

(iii) if closing orders have extinguished all ways leading to it.[200]

The mere obstruction of the highway or the failure of the public to use it will not destroy the rights of the public, for "once a highway always a highway".[201] A mere closing order for a highway leaves unaffected any easement over the route of the highway,[202] while the statutory extinguishment of an easement may not affect a highway over the route.[203] Nor is it possible to obtain title to a highway by means of adverse possession.[204]

III. RESTRICTIVE COVENANTS

Easements and restrictive covenants[205] are similar in that they each may   **27–043** entitle a landowner to restrict the use that his neighbour makes of his land; for example, the owner of an easement of light may prevent his neighbour from obstructing his light by erecting a building on the servient land. There are other similarities, such as the need for both dominant and servient tenements.

---

[195] Wildlife and Countryside Act 1981 s.53; *R. v Secretary of State for the Environment Ex p. Burrows and Simms* [1991] 2 Q.B. 354 at 385; *R. (Norfolk C.C.) v Secretary of State for the Environment, Food and Rural Affairs* [2005] EWHC 119 (Admin); *Kotarski v Secretary of State for the Environment, Food and Rural Affairs* [2010] EWHC 1036 (Admin).

[196] Wildlife and Countryside Act 1981 s.56. Amendment of the definitive map (in this case by reclassifying a road used as a public path as a bridleway) does not operate to extinguish existing public rights: *R. (Kind) v Secretary of State for the Environment, Food and Rural Affairs* [2005] EWHC 1324 (Admin); [2006] Q.B. 113.

[197] Wildlife and Countryside Act 1981 s.53; *R. v Secretary of State for the Environment Ex p. Burrows and Simms* [1991] 2 Q.B. 354.

[198] *R. v Secretary of State for the Environment Ex p. Burrows and Simms*, above, at 363.

[199] e.g. Highways Act 1980 s.116; Town and Country Planning Act 1990 Pt X.

[200] See *Bailey v Jamieson* (1876) 1 C.P.D. 329.

[201] *Dawes v Hawkins* (1860) 8 C.B. (N.S.) 848 at 858, per Byles J.; *R (Smith) v Land Registry* [2010] EWCA Civ 200; [2011] Q.B. 413.

[202] *Walsh v Oates* [1953] 1 Q.B. 578.

[203] *Att Gen v Shonleigh Nominees Ltd* [1974] 1 W.L.R. 305.

[204] *R (Smith) v Land Registry*, above.

[205] For restrictive covenants generally, see Ch.32 below.

In general it is possible to say that the law of restrictive covenants is an equitable extension of the law of easements.[206] But, historically, this was not a case of equity following the law. The enforcement of restrictive covenants against purchasers with notice was really a new departure, founded on equitable principles. Moreover, although restrictive covenants have some elements in common with easements, it will be seen below[207] that they are a fundamentally different kind of interest. Easements may exist at law as well as in equity, and they may be acquired by prescription (i.e. long enjoyment). Neither of these characteristics apply to restrictive covenants.

27–044   There is some overlap, nevertheless. Certain rights of a negative kind, such as rights to light, air, support, or water, may be either acquired as easements or secured by restrictive covenants. But more often restrictive covenants are used for some purpose outside the scope of easements, such as preserving the amenity of a neighbourhood. And a restrictive covenant cannot confer a positive right like a right of way.

IV. LICENCES

27–045   Here again there is some overlap. If A permits B to use a path across A's land, this may simply be a licence[208] given by A to B. But if the relevant requirements are satisfied, B may acquire an easement (a right of way). Yet not all licences have their counterparts in the law of easements. In general the categories of easements are old and restricted, whereas the categories of licences are new and flexible. In particular, there are the following differences:

(i)   An easement requires a dominant tenement, whereas a licence does not.

(ii) There are rules of formality for the creation of easements,[209] but not for licences.[210]

(iii) An easement cannot give a general right to occupy land.[211] A licence may do so.[212] For example, the right to occupy a room as lodgings is a licence, but cannot be an easement.

Whether or not a particular grant creates an easement or a licence is a matter of construction.[213] However, the use of the term "licence" and not the words

---

[206] See below, para.32–035.
[207] Ch.32.
[208] For licences see Ch.34 below.
[209] See below, para.28–001 et seq.
[210] But see below, paras 34–005 et seq.
[211] See above, para.27–020.
[212] See above, para.17–018. In *Att Gen of Southern Nigeria v John Holt & Co (Liverpool) Ltd* [1915] A.C. 599, above, para.27–015, a claim to occupy foreshore failed as an easement but succeeded as a licence.
[213] *IDC Group Ltd v Clark* [1992] 2 E.G.L.R. 184. Contrast the position where the issue is whether a right of occupation creates a lease or a licence: above, para.17–015. There is no logical reason why the distinction between a licence and an easement should be one of construction while that between a lease and a licence is a matter of law.

usually employed to grant an easement, in a professionally drafted deed will strongly suggest that a licence was intended.[214]

1. Derogation. A person who sells or lets land, knowing that the purchaser **27–046** intends to use it for a particular purpose, may not do anything which hampers the use of the purchaser's land for the purpose which both parties contemplated at the time of the transaction. A grantor may not derogate from his grant.[215] Although this principle "conjures up images of parchment and sealing wax, of copperplate handwriting and fusty title deeds",[216] it "merely embodies in a legal maxim a rule of common honesty".[217] "A grantor having given a thing with one hand is not to take away the means of enjoying it with the other."[218] "If A lets a plot to B, he may not act so as to frustrate the purpose for which in the contemplation of both parties the land was hired."[219]

2. A right of property. In so far as this doctrine restricts the grantor's **27–047** freedom to use any of his neighbouring land which he may have retained, it is really part of the law of property, since the rights which it creates bind not only the grantor but also all who claim title through him; so that, in effect, the grantee and his successors in title have a proprietary interest of a special kind against the grantor's land, into whosesoever hands it may pass.[220] For example, where a lease was granted to a timber merchant who required a free flow of air to his stacks of drying timber, it was held that a purchaser of the landlord's adjoining land could not build upon it so as to obstruct the ventilation required by the tenant.[221] The right claimed was one which could not exist as an easement since the air did not flow through any definable channel or aperture.[222] "The implications usually explained by the maxim . . . do not stop short with easements."[223] It is in this that the importance of the doctrine lies. Paradoxically, the law will allow a grant made for a particular purpose to create rights which are really proprietary and which yet, according to the rules for easements, do not lie in grant. Where land was purchased subject to a right of way for all purposes, and specifically to enable lorries to

---

[214] *IDC Group Ltd v Clark*, above.

[215] cf. above, paras 19–023 et seq., where examples are given. See generally (1964) 80 L.Q.R. 244 (D. W. Elliott).

[216] *Johnston & Sons Ltd v Holland* [1988] 1 E.G.L.R. 264 at 267, per Nicholls L.J. The case contains an important discussion of the principle.

[217] *Harmer v Jumbil (Nigeria) Tin Areas Ltd* [1921] 1 Ch. 200 at 225, per Younger L.J.

[218] *Birmingham Dudley & District Banking Co v Ross* (1888) 38 Ch D 295 at 313, per Bowen L.J; *Carter v Cole* [2009] EWCA Civ 410; [2009] 2 E.G.L.R. 15 at [8].

[219] *Lyttelton Times Co Ltd v Warners Ltd* [1907] A.C. 476 at 481, per Lord Loreburn L.C.

[220] *Johnston & Sons Ltd v Holland*, above, at 268.

[221] *Aldin v Latimer Clark, Muirhead & Co* [1894] 2 Ch. 437; cf. *Thomas v Owen* (1887) 20 Q.B.D. 225.

[222] See above, para.27–022.

[223] *Browne v Flower* [1911] 1 Ch. 219 at 225, per Parker J. See too *Johnston & Sons Ltd v Holland*, above, at 267.

gain access to a water bottling factory, the purchasers were held to have derogated from their grant when they interfered with the visibility splay which was necessary so that the lorries could safely enter the public road.[224]

27–048   **3. Application.** The doctrine is not confined to cases of landlord and tenant: it may apply as well to a sale as to a lease.[225] Indeed it applies to all forms of grant[226] and is not confined to real property.[227] It is sometimes said to rest upon an implied promise[228]; but it is in truth an independent rule of law, and has nothing to do with restrictive covenants or the equitable doctrine of notice.[229]

VI. CUSTOMARY RIGHTS OF FLUCTUATING BODIES

27–049   We have already seen examples of customary rights, e.g. for parishioners to use a path to the church, or to water cattle at a pond.[230] Such rights differ from easements in that they are exercisable by all who are included within the custom, independently of ownership of a dominant tenement and independently of any grant. They differ from public rights in that they are exercisable only by members of some local community,[231] not by members of the public generally.

27–050   A custom really amounts to a special local law, a local variation of the common law. The common law recognises such variations only if they are ancient, certain, reasonable and continuous.[232] To be "ancient" a custom must date back to the year 1189, the beginning of legal memory; but ancient origin may be presumed if there has been long enjoyment and there is no proof of a later origin.[233] Nor is it a fatal objection that the nature of the custom has changed with the times. For example, an ancient custom to play games has been held to cover cricket, "although it is reasonably certain that cricket was unknown until long after the time of Richard I".[234] Customs have been proved

---

[224] *Carter v Cole* [2009] EWCA Civ 410; [2009] 2 E.G.L.R. 15.

[225] *Cable v Bryant* [1908] 1 Ch. 259, where the maxim was resorted to because the adjoining land was in lease at the time of the sale, and it was said that a reversionary easement could not be granted; *Woodhouse & Co Ltd v Kirkland (Derby) Ltd* [1970] 1 W.L.R. 1185.

[226] *Johnston & Sons Ltd v Holland*, above, at 267.

[227] It has been applied to the sale of a car by the manufacturer: *British Leyland Motor Corp Ltd v Armstrong Patents Ltd* [1986] A.C. 577 at 641.

[228] *North Eastern Ry v Elliot* (1860) 1 J. & H. 145 at 153.

[229] *Cable v Bryant*, above, at 264. This statement was approved by Lord Denning M.R. in *Molton Builders Ltd v City of Westminster LBC* (1975) 30 P. & C.R. 182 at 186. See too *Johnston & Sons Ltd v Holland*, above, at 267.

[230] See above, para.27–025.

[231] *Manning v Wasdale* (1836) 5 A. & E. 758 (parish); *Race v Ward* (1855) 4 E. & B. 702 (town).

[232] *Lockwood v Wood* (1844) 6 Q.B. 50 at 64; and see the discussion of such rights in *Mercer v Denne* [1904] 2 Ch. 534 at 552 et seq.; [1905] 2 Ch. 538.

[233] See *Simpson v Wells* (1872) L.R. 7 Q.B. 214 (custom to have stalls in statutory hiring fair held bad because origin of fair was statute of Edward III or later); *Mercer v Denne*, above.

[234] *Mercer v Denne* [1904] 2 Ch. 534 at 553, per Farwell J. (aff'd [1905] 2 Ch. 538); *R. v Oxfordshire CC Ex p. Sunningwell PC* [2000] 1 A.C. 335 at 357.

for the holding of a fair or wake[235]; for the fishermen of a parish to dry their nets on private land[236]; and for inhabitants of a parish "to enter upon certain land in the parish, and erect a maypole thereon, and dance round and about it, and otherwise enjoy on the land any lawful and innocent recreation at any times in the year".[237] Such rights are not lost by disuse or waiver.[238] They may have led to the registration of the land over which they have been enjoyed as a town or village green.

VII. TOWN OR VILLAGE GREENS

Legislation has recognised the significance of town or village greens since **27–051** 1845.[239] That significance was however considerably enhanced by registration requirements imposed by the Commons Registration Act 1965.[240] The Act required the registration, in a register of town or village greens, of land which is a town or village green.[241] It provided for three classes of greens[242]:

   (i) Class A: land which has been allotted by or under any Act for the exercise or recreation of the inhabitants of any locality;

   (ii) Class B: land on which the inhabitants of any locality have a customary right to indulge in lawful sports and pastimes; and

   (iii) Class C: land on which for not less than 20 years a significant number of the inhabitants of any locality,[243] or any neighbourhood (or neighbourhoods[244]) within a locality, have indulged in lawful sports and pastimes as of right, and either continue to do so, or have ceased to do so for not more than such period as may be prescribed or determined in accordance with prescribed provisions.[245]

[235] *Wyld v Silver* [1963] Ch. 243 (discussing the mode of enforcement of such rights).

[236] *Mercer v Denne* [1905] 2 Ch. 538.

[237] *Hall v Nottingham* (1875) 1 Ex.D. 1, headnote.

[238] *Wyld v Silver*, above; *New Windsor Corp v Mellor*, above (right of inhabitants to use town green for sports and pastimes).

[239] Inclosure Act 1845 s.15: see *Oxfordshire CC v Oxford CC* [2006] UKHL 25; [2006] 2 A.C. 674 at [7].

[240] Ubhi & Denyer-Green, *Law of Commons and of Town and Village Greens*, 2nd edn (London: Jordans, 2006), Ch.9.

[241] CRA 1965 s.1(1).

[242] CRA 1965 s.22(1). The classification does not appear on the face of the statute but has been judicially accepted: see *R. v Suffolk CC Ex p. Steed* [1995] Q.B. 487 at 491; *R. v Oxfordshire CC Ex p. Sunningwell PC* [2000] 1 A.C. 335 at 347.

[243] For definition of "locality", see *Paddico (267) Ltd v Kirklees Metropolitan Council* [2011] EWHC 1606 (Ch); [2011] N.P.C. 66. It is immaterial that "many or even most" of the users come from elsewhere, as long as a significant number of the users are inhabitants of the locality or neighbourhood as the case may be: *R (Oxfordshire & Buckinghamshire Mental Health NHS Foundation Trust) v Oxfordshire CC* [2010] EWHC 530 (Admin); [2010] 2 E.G.L.R. 171 at [71].

[244] *Leeds Group plc v Leeds CC* [2010] EWCA Civ 1438; [2011] 2 W.L.R. 1010.

[245] As amended by the Countryside and Rights of Way Act 2000 s.98, with effect from January 30, 2001. The amendment does not apply retrospectively to applications for registration made before its implementation: *Betterment Properties (Weymouth) Ltd v Dorset CC* [2008] EWCA Civ 22; [2009] 1 W.L.R. 334.

Land capable of being registered as a town or village green had to be registered before August 1970,[246] and applications for registration had to be made before January 3, 1970.[247] Failure to register was conclusive, and it extinguished such rights of recreation as were registrable at that date.[248] However, there remains the possibility that land may have become a town or village green after January 2, 1970, that is where a claim is made to a new Class C green based on 20 years' user as of right.[249]

27–052   The Commons Registration Act 1965 is in the course of being repealed by the Commons Act 2006.[250] However, commons registration authorities will continue to be required to keep registers of town or village greens,[251] and they will have the power (denied under the 1965 Act[252]) to correct the register in certain circumstances.[253] Furthermore, it remains possible for application to be made for registration of a town or village green where a significant number of the inhabitants of any locality, or of any neighbourhood within a locality, have indulged as of right in lawful sports and pastimes on the land for a period of at least 20 years.[254] That period may be the period up to the date of the application being made, or a period expiring two years after cessation of the use.[255] Provision is made for applications to de-register land as town or village green in certain restricted circumstances.[256]

27–053   In recent years, registration of new town and village greens has become "an area of unusually vigorous legal activity," as attempts are made to restrict residential or commercial development of open land.[257] Claims have been made in relation to land which is certainly not within the "traditional" understanding of what a green connotes.[258] It has been established that it is

[246] CRA 1965 s.1(2); SI 1970/383.

[247] CRA 1965 s.4(6); SI 1966/1470.

[248] *Oxfordshire CC v Oxford CC*, above, at [18].

[249] It appears that claims to Class A and B greens which were not registered ceased to become tenable after January 2, 1970: *R. v Oxfordshire CC Ex p. Sunningwell PC*, above, at 348.

[250] Commons Act 2006 s.53 Sch.6. The 2006 Act is being implemented, and the 1965 Act being repealed, incrementally: see further para 27–058 below and SI 2007/456 and SI 2008/1960 which implement certain provisions in "pilot areas" specified in the Schedule to the instrument (and listed at fn.290 below).

[251] Commons Act 2006 s.1.

[252] Pending implementation of the Commons Act 2006 (see above, fn.250), any application for rectification of the register has to be to the High Court: CRA 1965 s.14; see, e.g. *Betterment Properties (Weymouth) Ltd v Dorset CC* [2010] EWHC 3045 (Ch); [2010] N.P.C. 115; *Paddico (267) Ltd v Kirklees Metropolitan Council* [2011] EWHC 1606 (Ch).

[253] Commons Act 2006 s.19, and see also s.22 Sch.2.

[254] Commons Act 2006 s.15.

[255] Commons Act 2006 s.15(2), (3), and see also transitional provisions in s.15(4), (5). Section 15 came into force on April 6, 2007: SI 2007/456.

[256] The de-registration provisions (see below, para.27–062) apply both to town and village greens and to commons.

[257] *Oxfordshire CC v Oxford CC* [2006] Ch. 43 at 61, per Carnwath L.J; and see *R (Lewis) v Redcar & Cleveland BC* [2010] UKSC 11; [2010] 2 A.C. 70 at [47] and [84].

[258] That is not however a relevant factor. "To say that the registration authority will recognise a village green when it sees one seems inadequate": *Oxfordshire CC v Oxford CC* [2006] UKHL 25; [2006] 2 A.C. 674 at [39], per Lord Hoffmann. In another leading decision, the town green registered was "really just an open space that formed part of a golf course": *R (Lewis) v Redcar & Cleveland BC* [2010] UKSC 11; [2010] 2 A.C. 70 at [97], per Lord Hope; Meager [2010] C.L.J. 238.

unnecessary for the claimant to prove a subjective belief in the existence of the right to recreation on the part of the users[259]; and that a claim to use of the land as of right cannot be defeated by proof of implied permission on the part of the owner of the green[260] or by deference being paid by the users towards the owner.[261] Land does not become a green until it has been registered.[262] Once it has been registered, the town or village green can be used generally for sports and pastimes on the part of the relevant inhabitants, not merely for those activities carried out in the prescriptive period.[263] Although there is some resistance to the idea that the inhabitants will have unrestricted rights of recreation following registration of the green,[264] the extent to which the owner will be able to police inhabitants' activities remains unclear.[265] As a consequence of registration, the green is accorded statutory protection.[266] However, exercise of compulsory purchase powers may override the rights of the inhabitants.[267]

The House of Lords has taken the view that the prescriptive acquisition of **27–054** Class C greens does not amount to a deprivation of property which cannot be justified and that it is therefore consistent with the owner's rights under Art.1 of the First Protocol to the ECHR.[268] First, the owner is not entirely excluded from the land and still has the right to use it in any way which does not interfere with the recreational rights of the inhabitants.[269] Secondly, the registration of town and village greens in the 1965 Act was introduced to give effect to the public interest in the preservation of open spaces.[270] However, the issue cannot be regarded as having been finally decided.[271]

Section 2. Nature of Profits à Prendre

A profit à prendre has been described as "a right to take something off another **27–055** person's land".[272] This it is, but not all such rights are profits. If the right is to be a profit, the thing taken must be either part of the land (e.g. minerals or

---

[259] *R. v Oxfordshire CC Ex p. Sunningwell PC*, above.
[260] *R. (Beresford) v Sunderland City Council* [2003] UKHL 60; [2004] 1 A.C. 889.
[261] *R (Lewis) v Redcar & Cleveland BC*, above.
[262] *Oxfordshire CC v Oxford CC*, above, at [43].
[263] *Oxfordshire CC v Oxford CC*, above, at [50].
[264] *Oxfordshire CC v Oxford CC* at [51] and [105] et seq.
[265] *R (Lewis) v Redcar & Cleveland BC*, above, at [47], [84] and [115].
[266] Inclosure Act 1857 s.12; Commons Act 1876 s.29: and see *Oxfordshire CC v Oxford CC*, above, at [54]–[57].
[267] See Town and Country Planning Act 1990 s.241; *BDW Trading Ltd (t/a Barratt Homes) v Spooner* [2011] EWHC 1486 (Q.B.).
[268] *Oxfordshire CC v Oxford CC*, above, at [58]–[59] and [86]–[90].
[269] "There has to be give and take on both sides": *Oxfordshire CC v Oxford CC*, above, at [59] per Lord Hoffmann; *R (Lewis) v Redcar & Cleveland BC*, above.
[270] *Oxfordshire CC v Oxford CC*, above, at [59].
[271] Goymour [2007] 18 K.L.J. 145 at 153.
[272] *Duke of Sutherland v Heathcote* [1892] 1 Ch. 475 at 484, per Lindley L.J.; *Polo Woods Foundation v Shelton-Agar* [2009] EWHC 1361 (Ch); [2010] 1 P. & C.R. 12 at p.238.

crops)[273] or the wild animals existing on it[274]; and the thing taken must at the time of taking be susceptible of ownership.[275] A right to "hawk, hunt, fish and fowl" may thus exist as a profit,[276] for this gives the right to take creatures living on the soil which, when killed, are capable of being owned.[277] But a right to take water from a spring or a pump,[278] or the right to water cattle at a pond,[279] may be an easement but cannot be a profit; for the water, when taken, was not owned by anyone[280] nor was it part of the soil.[281] Rights exercised by a person over part of his own land which, if that part were owned and occupied by another, would be profits, are sometimes called quasi-profits; and similar principles apply to them as apply to quasi-easements.[282]

A. Classification of Profits à Prendre

I. AS TO OWNERSHIP

27–056   A profit à prendre may be enjoyed:

>   (i) by one person to the exclusion of all others: this is known as a several profit; or

>   (ii) by one person in common with others: this is known as a profit in common, or a right of common.

27–057   **1. Several profits.** "Every right of common is . . . a profit à prendre, but not every profit à prendre is a right of common."[283] This is because a profit à prendre may be a several profit, or, as it is sometimes referred to, "a profit sole". In such circumstances, only one person has been granted, and currently enjoys, the right over the servient land.[284]

---

[273] *Manning v Wasdale* (1836) 5 A. & E. 758 at 764.

[274] *Halsbury* Vol.14, para.242.

[275] *Race v Ward* (1855) 4 E. & B. 702 at 709; *Lowe v J.W. Ashmore Ltd* [1971] Ch. 545 at 557.

[276] *Wickham v Hawker* (1840) 7 M. & W. 63.

[277] *Case of Swans* (1592) 7 Co.Rep. 15b at 17b; *Blades v Higgs* (1865) 11 H.L.C. 621; *Lord Fitzhardinge v Purcell* [1908] 2 Ch. 139 at 168. There is no established meaning to the word "game". The scope of a grant or reservation of a right to take game is therefore a matter of construction: *Inglewood Investment Co Ltd v Forestry Commissioners* [1988] 1 W.L.R. 1278 (reservation of "all game woodcocks snipe and other wild fowl hares rabbits and fish" did not include deer); *Pole v Peake* [1998] E.G.C.S. 125.

[278] See *Polden v Bastard* (1865) L.R. 1 Q.B. 156.

[279] *Manning v Wasdale*, above. As to water stored in a tank, see (1938) 2 Conv. (N.S.) 203 (J. S. Fiennes); but the authorities seem unsatisfactory.

[280] *Embrey v Owen* (1851) 6 Exch. 353 at 369. Game becomes the subject of ownership as soon as killed (see fn.277, above), i.e. sometimes before being taken; water is reduced into ownership only at the time of taking. Yet the difference between taking fish in a net and taking water in a bucket seems slight.

[281] *Manning v Wasdale*, above, at 764; *Race v Ward*, above, at 709.

[282] See above, para.27–013.

[283] Gale, para.1–129.

[284] See, e.g. *Barton v Church Commissioners for England* [2008] EWHC 3091 (Ch); and see further para.30–033 below.

2. Rights of common[285]

27–058

(a) Regulation of rights of common. Legislative regulation of rights of common has existed since the 19th century, and the Law of Property Act 1925 introduced rights of public access to certain commons as well as a requirement for ministerial consent for works preventing or impeding access on all commons which remained subject to rights of common at that time. With the passage of time and changed social and economic conditions, there were many uncertainties about what lands were subject to rights of common, and what rights of common existed over these lands.[286] In order to lay a foundation for further legislation to govern the management and improvement of common land (which currently amounts to around 550,000 hectares, that is about 4 per cent of the total area of England and Wales), the Commons Registration Act 1965 enacted a scheme for ascertaining what rights were claimed to be still in existence, registering them and for extinguishing the others.[287] The 1965 Act is generally acknowledged to have been deficient in a number of respects,[288] and its reform has been actively discussed for many years. In 2002, the Government published its Common Land Policy Statement.[289] The recommendations contained within that Statement were implemented in the Commons Act 2006, which received Royal Assent on July 19, 2006. The 2006 Act is being introduced gradually; on 1 October 2008, its registration provisions were brought into force in a number of pilot areas,[290] but they do not yet apply elsewhere. Once the 2006 Act is fully in force, the 1965 Act will be repealed. However, as the 2006 Act requires commons registration authorities to maintain the registers of common land that were initially compiled under the 1965 Act,[291] it remains necessary to understand how that legislation operated.

(b) Registrable rights. The 1965 Act made registrable:

27–059

(i) land in England or Wales which is common land or a town or village green;

(ii) rights of common over such land; and

(iii) persons claiming to be, or found to be, owners of such land.[292]

---

[285] See generally N. Ubhi & B. Denyer-Green, *Law of Commons and of Town and Village Greens*, 2nd edn (2006). For a valuable summary of the legal history of common land, see *Hampshire CC v Milburn* [1991] 1 A.C. 325 at 338 et seq., per Lord Templeman.

[286] See Report of Royal Commission on Common Land, 1955–1958 (Cmnd. 462).

[287] For a survey of the working of the Act, see [1985] Conv. 24 (A. Samuels).

[288] For a powerful commentary on the "deficiencies of the 1965 commons legislation", see *R. v Suffolk CC Ex p. Steed* (1995) 70 P. & C.R. 487 at 489–494, per Carnwath J. (on appeal [1997] 1 E.G.L.R. 131).

[289] DEFRA, July 2002.

[290] SI 2008/1960. The pilot areas are the registration areas of the commons registration authorities for Blackburn with Darwen BC, Cornwall CC, Devon CC, Herefordshire DC, Hertfordshire CC, Kent CC and Lancashire CC.

[291] Commons Act 2006 s.1.

[292] s.1(1). For town or village greens, see above, paras 27–051 et seq.

"Common land" means land that is subject to rights of common, as well as waste land of a manor which is not subject to rights of common.[293] After considerable controversy it was settled that waste land of the manor means "waste land now or formerly of a manor" or "waste land of manorial origin".[294] To be waste, land must be open, uncultivated and unoccupied.[295] Rights of common cannot be registered if they are merely held for a term of years or from year to year.[296]

27–060 *(c) Mode of registration.* The 1965 Act and the regulations made under it required registration to be made with county and county borough councils. Any person might apply for registration of any land as common land.[297] Registration had to be effected before August 1970[298]; and all applications for registration had to be made before January 3, 1970.[299] Registration was merely provisional,[300] pending the determination of any objection, which had to be lodged before August 1972[301]; and provisional registration was of itself no evidence of the existence of the right registered.[302] If an objection was made, the validity of the registration was decided by a Commons Commissioner, the burden of proof being on the person making the registration.[303] There was a right of appeal to the High Court on a point of law[304]; and after the Commissioners were appointed, their jurisdiction excluded that of the courts in all save cases of bad faith.[305] Registration became final if no objection was duly lodged, or if after determining the objection the Commissioner or the court ordered confirmation.[306] Such registration was conclusive evidence as to the land being common land and as to the registered rights of common over it as at the date of registration,[307] even where an entry was

---

[293] s.22(1).

[294] *Hampshire CC v Milburn* [1991] 1 A.C. 325, where the House of Lords approved *Re Chewton Common* [1977] 1 W.L.R. 1242, at 1249, in which Slade J. defined waste land of the manor as land "which was once waste land of a manor in the days when copyhold tenure still existed" and held that land does not cease to be common land merely because the owner conveys the lordship of the manor to a third party while retaining the land (or vice versa).

[295] *Re Britford Common* [1977] 1 W.L.R. 39.

[296] CRA 1965 s.22(1). This restriction is retained in the definition of "right of common" contained in the Commons Act 2006 s.61(1).

[297] CRA 1965 s.4(2).

[298] CRA 1965 ss.1–4; SI 1970/383.

[299] CRA 1965 s.4(6); SI 1966/1470; but see below, para.27–061.

[300] CRA 1965 s.4(5). See *Cooke v Amey Gravel Co Ltd* [1972] 1 W.L.R. 1310.

[301] SI 1968/989; SI 1970/384.

[302] *Cooke v Amey Gravel Co Ltd*, above. Such provisional registration is not without effect however: see *Dynevor (Lord) v Richardson* [1995] Ch. 173 (provisional registration of an expressly granted grazing right precluded any further claim to an equivalent right arising by lost modern grant in the period pending determination of the claim).

[303] *Re Sutton Common, Wimborne* [1982] 1 W.L.R. 647; *Re Ilkley and Burley Moors* (1983) 47 P. & C.R. 324 at 328. An objection to the registration of part only of the land in a registered unit put in issue the registration of the whole: *Re West Anstey Common* [1985] Ch. 330.

[304] CRA 1965 ss.6, 17, 18.

[305] *Thorne RDC v Bunting* [1972] Ch. 470 (court's jurisdiction before any commissioners were appointed); *Wilkes v Gee* [1973] 1 W.L.R. 742.

[306] CRA 1965 ss.6, 7, 10.

[307] CRA 1965 s.10.

clearly wrong.[308] The effect of the 1965 Act was that no land capable of being registered was to be deemed to be common land unless so registered; and no rights of common were exercisable over any such land unless they were either registered under the Act or had been registered previously[309] in the register of title.[310] These provisions operated to extinguish all existing unregistered rights,[311] including statutory rights of common derived from enclosure awards,[312] and public rights of access.[313]

(d) *New rights of common.* By themselves, the provisions explained above **27–061** would have prevented any new rights from arising as from its date of commencement. However, the 1965 Act provided for the registration of land becoming common land after January 2, 1970, as well as for the registration of rights of common over such land, and rights of ownership.[314] The Commons Act 2006 has, however, restricted the circumstances in which a right of common can be created in the future. As from the date of commencement of the 2006 Act,[315] a right of common will no longer be capable of creation by virtue of prescription.[316] Such a right may only be created by way of express grant (and then only if the right is attached to land, and the land is not registered as town or village green)[317] or by statute.[318] When created by express grant, the right will not comprise a legal interest until it is registered in a register of common land.[319] The register is conclusive[320] subject to such constraints as there may be on the exercise of the right of common that do not appear on the register.[320a]

(e) *Extinguishment and release.* The 2006 Act makes important amend- **27–062** ments to the circumstances in which rights of common may be extinguished.

---

[308] *Corpus Christi College Oxford v Gloucestershire CC* [1983] Q.B. 360; *Dance v Savery* [2011] EWCA Civ 1250; [2011] N.P.C. 114 at [63]. The register may be rectified or amended in case of fraud or change of circumstances, such as where land ceases to be common land, or becomes common land, or where registered rights are extinguished, varied or transferred: CRA 1965, ss.13, 14. See also Common Land (Rectification of Registers) Act 1989, summarised in the previous edition of this book at para.27–051.

[309] See CRA 1965 s.1(1).

[310] CRA 1965 s.1(2), as amended by LRA 2002 Sch.11 para.7(2); SI 1970/383. In this context, "registered" includes both provisional and final registration: *Dynevor (Lord) v Richardson* [1995] Ch. 173.

[311] *Central Electricity Generating Board v Clwyd CC* [1976] 1 W.L.R. 151.

[312] *Re Turnworth Down, Dorset* [1978] Ch. 251.

[313] *R. v Doncaster MBC Ex p. Braim* (1986) 57 P. & C.R. 1 at 7, 8; [1988] Conv. 369 at 370 (J. Hill). For public rights over common land, see LPA 1925 s.193.

[314] SI 1969/1843. See *R. v Suffolk CC Ex p. Steed* [1997] 1 E.G.L.R. 131.

[315] October 1, 2008 in relation to the pilot areas (see fn.290 above); otherwise, on a date to be appointed.

[316] 2006 Act s.6(1). See also Law Com. No. 327 (2011), paras 3.3 et seq., recommending that profits à prendre should only be capable of express creation in the future.

[317] 2006 Act s.6(2)(a), (3).

[318] 2006 Act s.6(2)(b).

[319] 2006 Act s.6(5).

[320] 2006 Act s.18.

[320a] A right to graze livestock on a register unit may therefore be subject to a constraint (that does not appear on the register) to the effect that the right is exercisable for a specified number of animals over land comprised in more than one register unit: *Dance v Savery*, above.

The common law right of the lord of a manor to "approve" the manorial waste over which the tenants exercised rights of pasture (by taking part of the waste for his separate enjoyment) is finally abolished.[321] Various statutory powers to inclose land are also repealed.[322] Although the procedure contained in the Commons Act 1876 is retained,[323] it is expected that owners of land who wish to have it released from the rights of common will do so by formal application to the appropriate national authority[324] to have the land deregistered.[325] If the land to be released exceeds 200 square metres in area, the owner must propose other land to replace it as common land.[326]

27–063   *(f) Exemptions.* Certain land is outside the provisions of the 1965 Act, such as the New Forest and Epping Forest, and any other land exempted by ministerial order[327]; and provision is also made for the vesting and protection of land which has been registered as common land but which has no registered owner.[328] Part 1 of the 2006 Act does not apply to the New Forest or Epping Forest, and shall not be taken to apply to the Forest of Dean.[329]

II. IN RELATION TO LAND

27–064   Unlike an easement, a profit is not necessarily appurtenant to land. It may exist in the following forms.

27–065   **1. A profit appurtenant.** This is a profit, whether several or in common, which by act of parties, actual or presumed,[330] is annexed to some nearby dominant tenement and runs with it. In general there must be compliance with the four conditions necessary for the existence of an easement,[331] which is always appurtenant.[332] Thus a profit of piscary appurtenant cannot be exploited for commercial purposes; the number of fish taken must be limited to the needs of the dominant tenement.[333] With effect from June 28, 2005, a right of common which is registered as attached to any land, and would be

---

[321] 2006 Act s.47, which repeals the Commons Act 1285. See previous edition of this book at para.18–177 for the right of approvement.

[322] 2006 Act Sch.6 Pt 3.

[323] See further the sixth edition of this book at para.18–178.

[324] That is, in relation to England, the Secretary of State, and in relation to Wales, the National Assembly for Wales: 2006 Act s.61(1).

[325] 2006 Act ss.16, 17.

[326] 2006 Act s.16(2).

[327] CRA 1965 s.11. See SI 1965/2000, 1965/2001.

[328] CRA 1965 ss.8, 9.

[329] 2006 Act s.5.

[330] "It is a creature of grant, either an express grant or a grant presumed under prescription": *White v Taylor* [1969] 1 Ch. 150 at 158 per Buckley J.

[331] See para.27–004 above.

[332] *Polo Woods Foundation v Shelton-Agar* [2009] EWHC 1361 (Ch); [2010] 1 P. & C.R. 12 at p.241.

[333] *Harris v Earl of Chesterfield* [1911] A.C. 623; *Polo Woods Foundation v Shelton-Agar*, above at p.246 et seq.; and see below, para.30–033.

capable of being severed from that land and thereupon converted into a profit in gross, can no longer be severed.[334]

2. A profit appendant. This is a profit annexed to land by operation of law; **27–066** it probably exists only in the form of a common of pasture.[335] If before the Statute *Quia Emptores* 1290[336] the lord of a manor subinfeudated arable land to a freeholder, the freeholder obtained as appendant to the arable land the right to pasture, on the waste land of the manor, animals to plough and manure the land granted to him[337]; for "he must have some place to keep such cattle in whilst the corn is growing on his own arable land".[338] This right was known as a common of pasture appendant and was limited both as to the kind and number of animals which could be depastured. It extended only to horses and oxen (to plough the land) and cows and sheep (to manure it),[339] and only to the number of these "levant and couchant" on the land to which the right was appendant, i.e. the number which the dominant tenement was capable of maintaining by its produce during the winter, including the hay and other crops obtained from it in the other seasons of the year.[340] It was immaterial that the land was at any particular time used for purposes temporarily rendering the maintenance of cattle impossible, for the test was not the number actually supported but the number which the land could be made to support.[341] Where rights of pasture are registered under the Commons Registration Act,[342] levancy and couchancy are abolished. Instead the registration must be for a fixed number of animals.[343]

No common appendant could be created after 1290, for a conveyance of freehold land in a manor after that date resulted in the feoffee holding of the feoffor's lord, and the land passed out of the manor altogether.[344]

3. A profit pur cause de vicinage. This exists only in the form of a **27–067** common of pasture. It is a true right of common and not merely a defence to

---

[334] Commons Act 2006 s.9. This provision was introduced to reverse the effect of the decision of the House of Lords in *Bettison v Langton* [2002] 1 A.C. 27, which held that following quantification of the number of animals for the purposes of registering a right of grazing, the commoner could dispose of the right independently from the land. This had the disadvantage of removing the local link between the commoners and the land over which their rights were being exercised.

[335] See *Halsbury*, Vol.13, para.433. Tudor L.C.R.P. states that other profits appendant exist, e.g. piscary (713), estovers (714) and turbary (716), but authority for this seems to be lacking.

[336] See above, para.2–015.

[337] *Earl of Dunraven v Llewellyn* (1850) 15 Q.B. 791 at 810.

[338] *Bennett v Reeve* (1740) Willes 227 at 231, per Willes C.J.

[339] *Tyrringham's Case* (1584) 4 Co.Rep. 36b at 37a.

[340] *Robertson v Hartopp* (1889) 43 Ch D 484 at 516; *Re Ilkley and Burley Moors* (1983) 47 P. & C.R. 324 at 329.

[341] *Robertson v Hartopp*, above, at 516, 517.

[342] s.15; see below, para.30–030. For the registration of commons, see above, paras 27–058 et seq.

[343] *Bettison v Langton*, above.

[344] *Baring v Abingdon* [1892] 2 Ch. 374 at 378; see above, para.2–015.

an action of trespass.³⁴⁵ If two adjoining commons are open to each other, there is a common *pur cause de vicinage* if the cattle put on one common by the commoners have always been allowed to stray to the other common and vice versa.³⁴⁶ The claim fails if in the past the cattle have been driven off one common by the commoners thereof,³⁴⁷ or if the commons have been fenced off (as may be done from either side at any time),³⁴⁸ or if the two commons are not contiguous to each other, even if they are separated only by a third common.³⁴⁹

27–068   **4. A profit in gross.** This is a profit, whether several or in common, exercisable by the owner independently of his ownership of land; there is no dominant tenement.³⁵⁰ Thus a right to take fish from a canal without stint (i.e. without limit) can exist as a profit in gross,³⁵¹ but not, as already seen,³⁵² as a profit appurtenant. A profit in gross is an interest in land which will pass under a will or intestacy or can be sold or dealt with in any of the usual ways,³⁵³ being an incorporeal hereditament.³⁵⁴

B. Distinctions between Profits à Prendre and Certain Analogous Rights

I. PUBLIC RIGHTS

27–069   The public right which most closely resembles a profit is the right of the public to fish in the sea and all tidal waters.³⁵⁵ In theory the right is the Crown's, and it was formerly possible for the Crown to grant to an individual the exclusive right to fish in a specified part of the sea or tidal waters. Such a franchise³⁵⁶ was known as a free fishery.³⁵⁷ The public may therefore fish in all tidal waters except a free fishery. But it has been held that the effect of Magna Carta 1215 was to prevent the Crown from creating any new free fisheries,³⁵⁸ although any already existing remain valid and transferable to this

---

³⁴⁵ *Newman v Bennett* [1981] Q.B. 726.
³⁴⁶ *Prichard v Powell* (1845) 10 Q.B. 589 at 603; *Newman v Bennett*, above. For a modern example, see *Dance v Savery* [2011] EWCA Civ 1250; [2011] N.P.C. 114.
³⁴⁷ *Heath v Elliott* (1838) 4 Bing.N.C. 388.
³⁴⁸ *Tyrringham's Case* (1584) 4 Co.Rep. 36b.
³⁴⁹ *Commissioners of Sewers of the City of London v Glasse* (1874) L.R. 19 Eq. 134.
³⁵⁰ *Lord Chesterfield v Harris* [1908] 2 Ch. 397 at 421 (in HL [1911] A.C. 623).
³⁵¹ *Staffordshire and Worcestershire Canal Navigation v Bradley* [1912] 1 Ch. 91.
³⁵² See above, para.27–065.
³⁵³ e.g. leased *Staffordshire and Worcestershire Canal Navigation v Bradley*, above.
³⁵⁴ *Webber v Lee* (1882) 9 QBD 315; *Lovett v Fairclough* (1990) 61 P. & C.R. 385 at 396.
³⁵⁵ The right to fish includes the ancillary rights to cross the foreshore in order to fish and to take worms from the foreshore to be used as bait for that fishing: *Anderson v Alnwick DC* [1993] 1 W.L.R. 1156; *Adair v National Trust* [1998] N.I. 33.
³⁵⁶ A franchise is an incorporeal hereditament: see below, para.31–013.
³⁵⁷ Cru.Dig. iii, p.261. A free fishery is sometimes referred to as a several fishery: see *Malcomson v O'Dea* (1863) 10 H.L.C. 593 at 618; *Isle of Anglesey v Welsh Ministers* [2009] EWCA Civ 94; [2010] Q.B. 163 at [80].
³⁵⁸ *Malcomson v O'Dea*, above at 618, criticised in Theobald, *Law of Land*, 2nd edn (Saint Catherine Press, 1929), pp.58 et seq.

day[359]; and a lawful origin may be inferred from long-continued enjoyment.[360]

The right of fishery in non-tidal waters is dealt with below.[361]

II. RIGHTS OF FLUCTUATING BODIES

There can be no custom for a fluctuating body of persons to take a profit.[362] **27–070** The reason is said to be that otherwise the subject-matter would be destroyed, "and such a claim, which might leave nothing for the owner of the soil, is wholly inconsistent with the right of property in the soil".[363] Neither can such rights exist as profits, for a profit lies in grant just like an easement[364] and a fluctuating body is not a capable grantee. Yet if such a right has in fact been enjoyed for a long time, as of right[365] and not merely by toleration,[366] the courts will strive to find a legal origin for it. "The first thing the court looks at as the criterion of property is usage and enjoyment . . . . Very high judges have said they would presume any thing in favour of a long enjoyment and uninterrupted possession."[367] Upon this principle two methods have been evolved for circumventing the rule against these customs, which in modern times finds little favour with the courts.

1. Presumed incorporation by Crown grant. The Crown is able to **27–071** incorporate any body of persons and so endow them, as a corporation, with a single legal personality. Thus the Crown could grant a charter to a village making it a city or borough. Consequently there is nothing to prevent the Crown from making a grant of a profit to the inhabitants of a district and providing therein that for the purposes of the grant they should be treated as a corporation, though for other purposes they remain unincorporated. The obstacle that there is no definite person or persons in whose favour a grant could be presumed[368] is thus surmounted by presuming the existence of a corporation created ad hoc in a grant from the Crown. In fact such grants have been made but rarely.[369] Their chief importance is that the court will presume such a grant to have been made,[370] provided that:

(i) long enjoyment is proved; and

---

[359] *Neill v Duke of Devonshire* (1882) 8 App.Cas. 135 at 180.

[360] *Malcomson v O'Dea*, above; *Loose v Castleton* (1978) 41 P. & C.R. 19.

[361] See below, para.30–033.

[362] *Gateward's Case* (1607) 6 Co.Rep. 59b; *Commissioners of Sewers of the City of London v Glasse* (1872) 7 Ch.App. 456 at 465; *Alfred F. Beckett Ltd v Lyons* [1967] Ch. 449.

[363] *Race v Ward* (1855) 4 E. & B. 702 at 709, per Lord Campbell C.J.; and see *Chesterfield v Fountaine* (1895) [1908] 1 Ch. 243n.

[364] See above, para.27–014.

[365] See below, para.28–048.

[366] *Alfred F. Beckett Ltd v Lyons*, above.

[367] *Att Gen v Lord Hotham* (1823) T. & R. 209 at 217 et seq., per Plumer M.R.

[368] *Fowler v Dale* (1593) Cro.Eliz. 362.

[369] See, e.g. *Willingale v Maitland* (1866) L.R. 3 Eq. 103, explained in *Chilton v Corp of London (No.2)* (1878) 7 Ch D 735.

[370] *Re Free Fishermen of Faversham* (1887) 36 Ch D 329.

(ii) the right claimed derives from the Crown; and

(iii) those claiming the grant and their predecessors have always regarded themselves as a corporation and acted as such as regards the right, as by holding meetings or appointing some officer to supervise the right.[371]

27–072 **2. Presumed charitable trust.** Even when the claimants are destitute of any sign of corporate capacity,[372] the difficulty may not be insuperable. If long enjoyment[373] is shown the court may succeed in finding a legal origin for the right by presuming a grant of the profit to some existing corporation, subject to a trust or condition that the corporation should allow the claimants to exercise the right claimed. Thus in *Goodman v Mayor of Saltash*[374] the free inhabitants of certain ancient tenements had for 200 years enjoyed an oyster fishery from Candlemas (February 2) to Easter Eve each year. This right had been shared by the local corporation, which had enjoyed the right all the year round from time immemorial. The House of Lords refused to presume a grant incorporating the inhabitants for the purpose of the grant, but by "a splendid effort of equitable imagination in furtherance of justice"[375] held that the corporation was entitled to a profit subject to a trust or condition in favour of the free inhabitants. More recently, a court applying these principles has been prepared to presume that a right of recreation over Doncaster Common, in favour of the general public, had a lawful origin.[376] Such a trust is charitable, since it exists to benefit the inhabitants of a particular place, as a section of the public, and so it is not subject to the rule against trusts of perpetual duration.[377] But enjoyment as of right is essential. Local inhabitants claiming to be entitled to collect coal on the foreshore therefore failed when they could show only a practice sufficiently explained by mere toleration.[378] A trust is not normally presumed against a landowner who can show a documentary title bearing no trace of it.[379] This is not an absolute rule, however, and the facts may be such that the court can presume the express creation of a trust by the landowner by a document since lost.[380]

---

[371] See *Lord Rivers v Adams* (1878) 3 Ex.D. 361 at 366 (where the claim failed for want of corporate acts).

[372] See e.g. *Harris v Earl of Chesterfield* [1911] A.C. 623 at 639.

[373] e.g. *Haigh v West* [1893] 2 Q.B. 19 (claim to pasturage by roadside succeeded on proof of 115 years' user). Examples of unsuccessful claims under this doctrine are *Lord Fitzhardinge v Purcell* [1908] 2 Ch. 139; *Harris v Earl of Chesterfield* [1911] A.C. 623.

[374] (1882) 7 App.Cas. 633. For a discussion of the problems of reconciling the *Goodman* case with general principles of the law of charity, see *Peggs v Lamb* [1994] Ch. 172 at 193 et seq.

[375] *Harris v Earl of Chesterfield* [1911] A.C. 623 at 633, per Lord Ashbourne, dissenting.

[376] *R. v Doncaster BC Ex p. Braim* (1986) 57 P. & C.R. 1; [1988] Conv. 369 (J. Hill). Doncaster Common is used (*inter alia*) as the venue of the St Leger.

[377] See above, para.9–051.

[378] *Alfred F. Beckett Ltd v Lyons* [1967] Ch. 449. See similarly *Mahoney v Neenan* [1966] I.R. 559 (seaweed).

[379] *Goodman v Mayor of Saltash* (1882) 7 App.Cas. 633 at 647; *Att Gen v Antrobus* [1905] 2 Ch. 188.

[380] *R. v Doncaster BC Ex p. Braim*, above, at 11 (court prepared to presume grant where land had been acquired by Doncaster Corporation in 1505).

THE CREATION OF EASEMENTS AND PROFITS

An easement or a profit à prendre may take effect at law, as a legal interest, **28–001** or in equity, as an equitable interest. It is important to be able to identify whether an easement or profit is legal or equitable, as this will determine its proprietary consequences, in particular whether and when it will bind successors in title to the servient land.

An easement or profit can exist as a legal interest in land only if it is: **28–002**

(i) held for an interest equivalent to a fee simple absolute in possession or term of years absolute[1]; and

(ii) created either by statute, deed or prescription.

If such an easement or profit is created by express grant or reservation over a registered estate, there is an additional condition that must be satisfied before it can operate as a legal interest: it must be completed by registration.[2] This requires a notice of the easement or profit to be entered on the title register of the servient estate and, if the dominant estate is also registered, the proprietor of that estate to be entered in the register as the proprietor of the interest.[3] However, the registration requirement does not apply to easements or profits

---

[1] LPA 1925 s.1(2); see above, para.6–020. Although the subsection does not mention profits expressly, it is almost beyond argument that they are covered by the words "easement, right, or privilege". In any case, a profit would fall within the definition of "land" in s.205(1)(ix), and would thus come within s.1(1). LPA 1925 s.62, which is manifestly intended to include profits, also does not mention them expressly, but is content to use words similar to those in s.1(2).

[2] LRA 2002 ss.27(1) and (2)(d). The registration requirement does not apply to rights which are capable of being registered under Pt 1 of the Commons Act 2006: LRA 2002 s.27(2)(d). See above, para.7–054.

[3] LRA 2002 Sch.2 para.7. The benefit of a profit in gross created for more than seven years is, however, not to be registered as appurtenant to another registered estate but instead with its own title: LRA 2002 Sch.2 para.6.

which are created over a registered estate by implied grant or reservation, or by prescription, or by the operation of s.62 of the Law of Property Act 1925.[4] Where an easement is implied into a conveyance, it takes its character from the nature of the conveyance, so that an easement which is implied into the grant or reservation of a legal estate by any of these methods is capable of existing as a legal easement.[5]

28–003   Easements which do not meet the above conditions for existing at law may nevertheless take effect in equity. For example, a document that is not a deed cannot create a legal[6] easement or profit, not even (it seems) for a term of three years or less.[7] But if made for value it may create a valid equitable easement[8] or profit[9] provided that it complies with the formal requirements for a contract for the sale of land, or the circumstances merit the imposition of a constructive trust.[10] An equitable easement may also arise where the servient estate is registered and where all the conditions for the express creation of a legal easement are satisfied except the requirement of registration. This will be the case even if the grant which created the easement was not specifically enforceable, e.g. where the easement was created gratuitously by deed.[11]

28–004   The effect of the Land Registration Act 2002 was to restrict the circumstances in which an easement or profit which is not entered on the register (either as required or voluntarily) may take effect as an overriding interest; in particular, by providing that equitable easements could no longer override in the event of their non-registration.[12] However, legal easements and profits à prendre remain an important class of overriding interest. All legal easements and profits override first registration.[13] They will also override a registered disposition in most circumstances.[14] It follows that any purchaser of a registered estate must realise that there is a substantial risk that easements or

---

[4] Rights arising by implication or by prescription are necessarily excluded as they are not created by express grant or reservation. Rights created by the operation of s.62, although sometimes treated as a species of express grant, are expressly excluded from the requirement of registration: LRA 2002 s.27(7); Law Com. No.271, para.4.25.

[5] To this effect, see *R (Beresford) v Sunderland CC* [2003] UKHL 60; [2004] 1 A.C. 889 at [36].

[6] LPA 1925 s.52; *Hewlins v Shippam* (1826) 5 B. & C. 221 (easement); *Duke of Somerset v Fogwell* (1826) 5 B. & C. 875 (profit); *Armstrong v Sheppard and Short Ltd* [1959] 2 Q.B. 384.

[7] *Hewlins v Shippam*, above, at 229; *Wood v Leadbitter* (1845) 13 M. & W. 838 at 843; *Mason v Clarke* [1954] 1 Q.B. 460 at 468, 471, reversed on other grounds, [1955] A.C. 778. LPA 1925 s.54(2), will not assist interests which could not validly be created by parol at common law: *Rye v Rye* [1962] A.C. 496, see above, para.17–043.

[8] *May v Belleville* [1905] 2 Ch. 605. For a valuable analysis of the circumstances in which an equitable easement may now arise, see (1999) 115 L.Q.R. 89 (D. G. Barnsley). cf. above, paras 8–080 and 8–081.

[9] *Frogley v Earl of Lovelace* (1859) John 333. But if for any reason the court would refuse specific performance of the contract (e.g. because it is tainted with fraud) there is no such equitable right: see *Mason v Clarke*, above. For this principle, see above, para.15–061.

[10] See LP (MP)A 1989 s.2(1)–(3), (5); above, para.15–042.

[11] This is the effect of LRA 2002 s.27; above, para.7–053.

[12] See LRA 1925 s.70(1)(a), repealed by LRA 2002 Sch.13 para.1.

[13] LRA Sch.1 para.3.

[14] LRA Sch.3 para.3; above, paras 7–098 et seq.

profits, although created informally and not easily discoverable, may never-theless be effective and enforceable against him.[15]

The various methods of acquisition must now be considered.

A. By Statute

Easements and profits created by statute are most frequently found in the case 28–005 of local Acts of Parliament, e.g. an Act giving a right of support to a canal constructed under statutory powers,[16] or an Inclosure Act giving the lord of the manor shooting rights over land allotted to the commoners.[17] But statutory rights analogous to easements are also often created by general Acts, e.g. Acts giving rights to public utility undertakings in respect of such things as electric cables, gas pipes, water pipes and sewers.[18]

B. By Express Grant or Reservation

1. Grant. The simplest way to create an easement or profit is by an express 28–006 grant by deed. No special words are needed for a grant, so that a covenant or agreement, if contained in a deed, will have the same effect.[19] A grant of an easement without words of limitation, made after 1925, seems to give the grantee an easement in fee simple under the ordinary rule,[20] provided that the grantor is able to create such an interest, and that no contrary intention appears.[21] The provisions of s.62 of the Law of Property Act 1925, discussed below,[22] often cause a conveyance to operate as an express grant of easements and profits which are not expressly mentioned in the conveyance.

Since a grant requires a grantee, a developer selling off plots of land cannot 28–007 create easements in advance of each sale. This rule has proved extremely inconvenient to conveyancers and to Land Registry, and as a result the Law Commission has recommended that, once title to the dominant and servient estates is registered, the fact that they are in common ownership and posses-sion should no longer prevent the creation of easements or profits.[23]

It has been argued, but not decided, that an easement cannot be granted in 28–008 reversion, i.e. to take effect at some future time.[24] Easements have been held

---

[15] See Law Com. CP No.186 (2008), para.4.6.
[16] See, e.g. *London & North Western Ry v Evans* [1893] 1 Ch. 16.
[17] Halsbury 4th edn., Vol.14, p.122; 5th edn., Vol.13, para.419.
[18] See (1956) 20 Conv. (N.S.) 208 (J. F. Garner).
[19] *Russell v Watts* (1885) 10 App.Cas. 590 at 611; *Dowty Boulton Paul Ltd v Wolverhampton Corp (No.2)* [1976] Ch. 13.
[20] See above, para.3–026.
[21] LPA 1925 s.60(1), as read with s.205(1)(ii), (ix) defining "conveyance" and "land". The wording of s.60(1) is not wholly appropriate to the creation of new interests as distinct from the transfer of existing interests (see above, para.3–026), but it would be inconvenient to hold it inapplicable to grants de novo.
[22] See below, para.28–027.
[23] Law Com. No. 327 (2011), paras 4.19 to 4.41; see further para.29–016 below.
[24] *Cable v Bryant* [1908] 1 Ch. 259; above, para.27–048.

to be subject to the common law rule against perpetuities,[25] but as a result of the Perpetuities and Accumulations Act 2009 easements granted on or after April 6 2010 are no longer subject to the rule.[26]

28–009   **2. Reservation.** Reservation is the converse of grant. When a landowner disposes of part of his land and retains the rest, he may wish to reserve easements or profits over the part sold. Although this can now be achieved quite simply, there were formerly difficulties. Before 1926 a legal easement or profit could not be created by a simple reservation in favour of the grantor. Any part of the land, or any pre-existing right over it, could be *excepted* from the grant, as, for example, minerals[27]; and some new right could be *reserved* if it was to issue out of the land granted, as did a rentcharge.[28] But an easement or profit created on a sale fell outside both these rules. It was not a pre-existing right, and it lay only in grant. Before 1926 a person could not grant to himself.[29] Although devices were employed to overcome this obstacle,[30] the problem was finally solved by the Law of Property Act 1925. It provides[31] that the reservation of a legal estate or interest "shall operate at law without execution of the conveyance by the grantee ... or any regrant by him".

28–010   **3. Effect of grant.** The effect of a grant is a question of construction.[32] The document must be construed according to the natural meaning of the words contained in the document as a whole, read in the light of the surrounding circumstances at the time of its execution.[33] Two rules have an important influence upon construction: that where the court cannot ascertain the meaning of the grant, it should in general be construed against the grantor[34]; and

---

[25] *Dunn v Blackdown Properties Ltd* [1961] Ch. 433; *Shrewsbury v Adam* [2005] EWCA Civ 1006; [2006] 1 P. & C.R. 27 at [43]; *Magrath v Parkside Hotels Ltd* [2011] EWHC 143 (Ch); see above, para.9–024.

[26] See para 9–032 above.

[27] See Co.Litt. p.47a; *Durham & Sunderland Ry v Walker* (1842) 2 Q.B. 940 at 967.

[28] Co.Litt. p.143a.

[29] *Durham & Sunderland Ry v Walker*, above, at 967.

[30] For an explanation of these, see the fifth edition of this work at p.857.

[31] s.65(1). The Act also provides that a conveyance of a legal estate expressed to be made subject to another legal estate not in existence immediately before the date of the conveyance, shall operate as a reservation, unless a contrary intention appears: s.65(2). A conveyance of land subject to an easement not yet in existence falls within this subsection, and takes effect as a reservation: see *Wiles v Banks* (1984) 50 P. & C.R. 80.

[32] For the general principles of construction, see *Investors Compensation Scheme v West Bromwich Building Society* [1998] 1 W.L.R. 896 at 912, applied in *Mobil Oil Company Ltd v Birmingham City Council* [2001] EWCA Civ 1608; [2002] 2 P. & C.R. 14 at [24] and [62]; *Partridge v Lawrence* [2003] EWCA Civ 1121; [2004] 1 P. & C.R. 14 at [28]; *Shrewsbury v Adam* [2005] EWCA Civ 1006; [2006] 1 P. & C.R. 27 at [29] et seq; *Alford v Hannaford* [2011] EWCA Civ 1099 at [11] et seq.

[33] *St Edmundsbury & Ipswich Diocesan Board of Finance v Clark (No.2)* [1975] 1 W.L.R. 468 at 476.

[34] *Williams v James* (1867) L.R. 2 C.P. 577 at 581; *Neill v Duke of Devonshire* (1882) 8 App.Cas. 135 at 149; *Partridge v Lawrence*, above at [28]; cf. *Alford v Hannaford*, above at [15], where Patten L.J. doubted whether this rule "still retains any intellectual respectability".

that a person may not derogate from his grant.[35] Examples of the latter rule have already been given,[36] and examples of the former are given below.[37]

4. Effect of reservation. The above rules governing grants ought equally to **28–011** govern reservations. The principle is that in case of doubt a man's legal acts should be construed against him, since the person who dictates the terms of the transaction cannot complain of not being given the benefit of any doubt.[38] But it has several times been said that the creation of easements by reservation under the Law of Property Act 1925 (explained above) represents a mere change of machinery, and that a reservation is to be construed as if it were a regrant.[39] These statements conflict not only with the principle but also with express words in the Act ("shall operate at law without . . . any regrant . . . "), which do not seem to have been given their full effect.[40] The Court of Appeal has conceded that there is "much force in this reasoning"[41]; but it has held itself bound (though only obiter) by its earlier decision that a vendor's reservation is to be construed against the purchaser, contrary to the general rule for other reservations and exceptions.[42] The Law Commission, having criticised the current state of the law as "quite illogical",[43] has decided, with the benefit of consultation, not to recommend reform.[44]

However, the judicial addiction to the anomaly of the pre-1926 law has been carried beyond questions of construction. Where land held upon trust was sold and conveyed by a deed which both the legal and the equitable owners executed, and in which the equitable owner reserved a right of way, it was held that this took effect in law as a regrant by the purchaser (to the equitable owner) of a legal easement, so that it did not create a mere equitable easement requiring registration as a land charge.[45]

C. By Implied Reservation or Grant

1. Implied reservation. The general rule, as explained above, is that a grant **28–012** is construed in favour of the grantee. This is because any implied reservation

---

[35] Above, para.27–046.

[36] Above, para.27–047.

[37] Below, paras 28–012, 30–005.

[38] Thus at common law reservations (e.g. of rent or other services) and exceptions are construed against the person making them: *Lofield's Case* (1612) 10 Co.Rep. 106a; *Savill Bros Ltd v Bethell* [1902] 2 Ch. 523; Shep. Touch. 100.

[39] *Bulstrode v Lambert* [1953] 1 W.L.R. 1064; *Mason v Clarke* [1954] 1 Q.B. 460, reversed on other grounds, [1955] A.C. 778; *Johnstone v Holdway* [1963] 1 Q.B. 601. See [1954] C.L.J. 191 (H.W.R.W.).

[40] *Cordell v Second Clanfield Properties Ltd* [1969] 2 Ch. 9, holding that the reservation should be construed against the vendor.

[41] See *St Edmundsbury and Ipswich Diocesan Board of Finance v Clark (No.2)* [1975] 1 W.L.R. 468 at 479.

[42] *St Edmundsbury and Ipswich Diocesan Board of Finance v Clark (No.2)* above, treating the point as concluded by *Johnstone v Holdway*, above. See too *Trailfinders Ltd v Razuki* [1988] 2 E.G.L.R. 46 at 48.

[43] Law Com. CP No.186 (2008), paras 4.13 et seq.

[44] Law Com. No. 327 (2011), para.2.53.

[45] *Johnstone v Holdway*, above.

will run counter to the express terms of the instrument[46] and will therefore be, on the face of it, a derogation from the grant.[47] Therefore no easements will normally be implied in favour of a grantor. If he wishes to reserve any easements he must do so expressly.[48] As will be seen, the law is readier to imply a grant than a reservation.[49] This position has been criticised as giving rise to the potential for injustice; once successors in title are involved, it is a matter of chance whether the claim being made is based on implied grant or implied reservation.[50] The Law Commission has accordingly recommended that in determining whether an easement should be implied, it should not be material whether the easement would take effect by grant or by reservation.[51]

To the general rule as explained above there are two exceptions which will now be considered. In either case, a grantor alleging an intended reservation of an easement bears a heavy burden of proof.[52]

(a) Easements of necessity

28–013   (1) NECESSITY. If a grantor grants a plot of land in such circumstances as to cut himself off completely from some other part of his own land (e.g. if a plot retained in the middle is completely surrounded by the part granted) there may be implied in favour of the part retained a way of necessity over the part granted; for otherwise there would be no means of access to the land retained.[53] This rule is one of construction of the relevant grant, depending upon the intention of the parties as implied from the circumstances, and not upon public policy.[54] Whether the former owner of both plots of land retains or parts with the landlocked close, he may select the particular way to be enjoyed,[55] provided it is a convenient way.[56] Once selected, the route cannot subsequently be changed.[57] It is essential that the necessity should exist at the

---

[46] *Chaffe v Kingsley* (1999) 79 P. & C.R. 404 at 417.

[47] *Holaw (470) Ltd v Stockton Estates Ltd* (2001) 81 P. & C.R. 29 at [82].

[48] *Wheeldon v Burrows* (1879) 12 Ch D 31 at 49 (a leading case on reservation of easements, reviewing the authorities); *Liddiard v Waldron* [1934] 1 K.B. 435; *Re Webb's Lease* [1951] 1 Ch. 808 at 828; *Holaw (470) Ltd v Stockton Estates Ltd*, above at [81] et seq. For a neat illustration of the different positions of grantor and grantee, see Williams, V. & P. 661, 662.

[49] Law Com. No. 327 (2011), para.3.28.

[50] Law Com. CP No.186 (2008), para.4.49.

[51] Law Com. No. 327, para.3.30.

[52] *Re Webb's Lease*, above.

[53] *Pinnington v Galland* (1853) 9 Exch. 1; *Manjang v Drammeh* (1990) 61 P. & C.R. 194 at 197 (where Lord Oliver lists the essentials for the implication of such an easement of necessity). See (1981) 34 C.L.P. 133 (P. Jackson).

[54] *Nickerson v Barraclough* [1981] Ch. 426; *Manjang v Drammeh*, above, at 197; *Adealon International Proprietary Ltd v Merton LBC* [2007] EWCA Civ 362; [2007] 1 W.L.R. 1898 at [11]. Consequently there could be no such easement where land was acquired by escheat (*Proctor v Hodgson* (1855) 10 Exch. 824) or by adverse possession (*Wilkes v Greenway* (1890) 6 T.L.R. 449).

[55] *Bolton v Bolton* (1879) 11 Ch D 968 at 972. On a simultaneous grant of both plots (e.g. by devise) it seems that in the absence of any indication from the terms of the grant, any existing way which is used at the time will constitute the way of necessity: *Pearson v Spencer* (1861) 1 B. & S. 571 at 585; aff'd. (1863) 3 B. & S. 761; Braithwaite [2009] Conv. 93.

[56] *Pearson v Spencer*, above.

[57] *Deacon v South Eastern Ry* (1889) 61 L.T. 377.

time of the grant and not merely arise subsequently.[58] A way of necessity may be implied even if some of the surrounding land belongs to third parties,[59] but if there were other realistic possibilities of access to the retained land at the time of the grant, it will be particularly difficult for the claimant to discharge the burden of establishing that a way of necessity was intended to be reserved.[60]

If some other way exists, even if it is by water rather than over land,[61] no way of necessity will be implied unless that other way is merely precarious and not as of right,[62] or unless, perhaps, it would be a breach of the law to use that other way for the purpose in question.[63] Nor will there be a way of necessity if the other way is merely inconvenient,[64] and so where there is pedestrian but not vehicular access to a house, no vehicular right of way is to be implied[65]; for the principle is that an easement of necessity is one "without which the property retained cannot be used at all, and not one merely necessary to the reasonable enjoyment of that property".[66] Thus if a person grants land and retains an adjoining house, no easement of light is implied in his favour, for the house is not unusable without the easement.[67] Yet where a landowner grants away the subsoil of his land (e.g. for mining), but retains the surface, an easement of support is implied in his favour.[68]

28–014

(2) CESSATION OF NECESSITY. It has not been conclusively settled whether an easement of necessity, once acquired, ceases when the necessity ceases.[69] Although there is some authority which suggests that it does,[70] the weight of English authority is now against it.[71] This seems correct in principle. A grant once implied should not be "affected by the chance subsequent acquisition of other property" by the grantee.[72]

28–015

(b) *Easements giving effect to intended use.* Where the parties intended that the retained land should be used for a particular purpose, those easements that

28–016

---

[58] *Midland Ry v Miles* (1886) 33 Ch D 632.

[59] *Barry v Hasseldine* [1952] Ch. 835.

[60] *Adealon International Proprietary Ltd v Merton LBC*, above, at [16].

[61] *Manjang v Drammeh* (1990) 61 P. & C.R. 194 (no easement of necessity where there was water-borne access to premises over the River Gambia); [1992] C.L.J. 220 (C.H.).

[62] *Barry v Hasseldine*, above.

[63] See *Hansford v Jago* [1921] 1 Ch. 322 at 342, where it was suggested but not decided that a way of necessity might arise when the only alternative way of emptying earth closets was by carrying the contents through cottages in breach of a bye-law.

[64] *Dodd v Burchell* (1862) 1 H. & C. 113.

[65] *M.R.A. Engineering Ltd v Trimster Co Ltd* (1987) 56 P. & C.R. 1; cf. [1989] Conv. 355 at 356 (J. E. Martin).

[66] *Union Lighterage Co v London Graving Dock Co* [1902] 2 Ch. 557 at 573, per Stirling L.J.; *M.R.A. Engineering Ltd v Trimster Co Ltd*, above, at 6.

[67] *Ray v Hazeldine* [1904] 2 Ch. 17.

[68] *Richards v Jenkins* (1868) 18 L.T. 437.

[69] See [1981] C.L.P. 133 at 145 (P. Jackson); [1990] Conv. 292 at 294 (G. Kodilinye).

[70] *Holmes v Goring* (1824) 2 Bing. 76; better reported on this point at 9 Moo.C.P. 166. The remarks were *obiter*, but were followed in *Donaldson v Smith* [2007] W.T.L.R. 421 at [44] per David Donaldson QC.

[71] See *Proctor v Hodgson* (1855) 10 Exch. 824; *Barkshire v Grubb* (1881) 18 Ch D 616 at 620; *Huckvale v Aegean Hotels Ltd* (1989) 58 P. & C.R. 163 at 168.

[72] *Maude v Thornton* [1929] I.R. 454 at 458, per Meredith J.

are necessary to give effect to that intended use will be implied in favour of the grantor even though they are not expressed in the conveyance. It is essential for such implication that the parties should intend that the land retained should be used in a definite and particular way,[73] and that the easement claimed is necessary to give effect to that intended use.[74] An intent that there should be user which might or might not involve the user claimed as an easement is not enough.[75] In one case,[76] the defendant constructed a building for the purpose of sharing it with the plaintiff. It was intended that the plaintiff should use the upper floors as a hotel, and that the defendant should use the lower floors for its printing works. The defendant's printing machinery caused more noise and vibrations than expected. Nevertheless, the plaintiff's claim in nuisance failed. The court held that there was an implied reservation in favour of the defendant of such easements as were necessary to give effect to the intended use of the retained land as printing works. The disturbance caused was not more than was necessary for that purpose.

28–017   **2. Implied grant.** Easements are implied much more readily in favour of a grantee, on the principle that a grant must be construed in the amplest rather than in the narrowest way. An express grant of the land is therefore often accompanied by the implied grant of easements.[77] Rights which will arise by implied grant are as follows.

28–018   *(a) Easements of necessity,*[78] and

(b) Easements giving effect to intended use. The rules which apply in these two cases are similar to those in the case of implied reservation, except that the court is readier to imply easements in favour of the grantee than in favour of the grantor.[79] The grantee must show that at the date of the grant, the parties had a common intention that the property should be used in some definite and particular manner, and that the easement claimed was necessary to give effect to this purpose.[80] This rule, and the rule in *Wheeldon v Burrows,*[81] have been considered to be:

> "no more than examples of the application of a general and well established principle which applies to contracts, whether relating to grants of

---

[73] *Pwllbach Colliery Co Ltd v Woodman* [1915] A.C. 634 at 647; *Stafford v Lee* (1992) 65 P. & C.R. 172 at 175.

[74] *Pwllbach Colliery Co Ltd v Woodman*, above, at 643; *Stafford v Lee*, above, at 175.

[75] *Pwllbach Colliery Co Ltd v Woodman*, above, at 647.

[76] *Lyttelton Times Co Ltd v Warners Ltd* [1907] A.C. 476.

[77] *Phillips v Low* [1892] 1 Ch. 47 at 50.

[78] *Pinnington v Galland* (1853) 9 Exch. 1 at 12.

[79] *Richards v Rose* (1853) 9 Exch. 218; *Pwllbach Colliery Co Ltd v Woodman*, above, at 646; *Stafford v Lee*, above, at 175; *Adealon International Proprietary Ltd v Merton LBC* [2007] EWCA Civ 362; [2007] 1 W.L.R. 1898 at [14]; and see *Wheeldon v Burrows* (1879) 12 Ch D 31 at 49 et seq.

[80] *Stafford v Lee*, above. In the absence of extrinsic evidence of the parties' intentions at that time, the court will construe the grant in the light of surrounding circumstances.

[81] See para.28–019 below.

land or other arrangements. That principle is that the law will imply a term into a contract where, in the light of the terms of the contract and the facts known to the parties at the time of the contract, such a term would have been regarded as reasonably necessary or reasonably obvious to the parties."[82]

The parties' common intention need not be express, but may be ascertained from the terms of the conveyance, the position on the ground, and any communications passing between the parties before the conveyance was executed.[83] In one case a landlord let cellars to a tenant who covenanted to use them as a restaurant, to eliminate smells and to comply with health regulations. In fact, unknown to the parties, this could not lawfully be done without installing a proper ventilation system. It was held that the tenant had an easement of necessity to construct such a system (partly on the landlord's part of the premises) and use it.[84] Similarly, easements necessary for the enjoyment of some right expressly granted will be implied, e.g. a right to use stairs, lifts and rubbish chutes on the letting of a maisonette in a tower block,[85] or a right of way to a spring, on the grant of an easement to draw water from it.[86] If, however, the common intention is incapable of immediate realisation, but is dependent on circumstances which have not yet arisen, e.g. development of the servient land, no immediately enforceable easement can be implied until those circumstances arise.[87] A squatter can claim no way of necessity.[88]

(c) Easements within the rule in Wheeldon v Burrows

(1) SCOPE OF THE RULE. *Wheeldon v Burrows*[89] determines what easements **28–019** are implied in favour of the grantee of one part of a holding against the owner of the remainder. It is really a branch of the general rule against derogation from grant.[90] It relates not to the transmission of existing easements over the land of third parties (these, being already appurtenant to the land granted, naturally pass with it) but to the translation into easements of rights over the

---

[82] *Moncrieff v Jamieson* [2007] UKHL 42; [2007] 1 W.L.R. 2620 at 2657 per Lord Neuberger.

[83] *Shrewsbury v Adam* [2005] EWCA Civ 1006; [2006] 1 P. & C.R. 27 at [28]; *Davies v Bramwell* [2007] EWCA Civ 821; [2008] 1 P. & C.R. DG2.

[84] *Wong v Beaumont Property Trust Ltd* [1965] 1 Q.B. 173, CA.

[85] *Liverpool City Council v Irwin* [1977] A.C. 239.

[86] *Pwllbach Colliery Co Ltd v Woodman*, above, at 646.

[87] *Shrewsbury v Adam*, above (CA held that the right comprised either (1) a contractual entitlement to claim a right of way once the road over which it was to be exercised was completed or (2) an immediate right of way which could only be enjoyed on completion of the road. If (1) it failed for perpetuity, if (2) it failed either for perpetuity or for non-registration as a Class D(iii) land charge).

[88] *Wilkes v Greenway* (1890) 6 T.L.R. 449; see above, para.4–103.

[89] (1879) 12 Ch D 31.

[90] *Wheeldon v Burrows*, above, at 49; *M.R.A. Engineering Ltd v Trimster Co Ltd* (1987) 56 P. & C.R. 1 at 7. For that rule, see above, para.27–046. Consequently no such easements arise on a compulsory purchase: *Sovmots Investments Ltd v Secretary of State for the Environment* [1979] A.C. 144. Nor do they arise on leasehold enfranchisement, albeit for different reasons: see *Kent v Kavanagh* [2006] EWCA Civ 162; [2007] Ch. 1.

grantor's retained land which are necessary to the proper enjoyment of the land granted. It is natural for this purpose to look at the grantor's previous use of the land, and to allow the grantee to take easements corresponding to the facilities which the grantor himself found necessary.[91] Before the grant they cannot have been easements because of the common ownership. They are therefore called "quasi-easements", i.e. rights which are potential easements in case of a division of the land.[92] But where the two parts of the grantor's holding, although in common ownership, have not been in common occupation prior to that division, *Wheeldon v Burrows* may be of limited application.[93]

28–020   (2) THE RULE. *Wheeldon v Burrows*[94] was a case where a long line of earlier authorities was summed up in a general rule.[95] It laid down that upon the grant of part of a tenement, there would pass to the grantee as easements all quasi-easements over the land retained which:

(i) were continuous and apparent;

(ii) were necessary for the reasonable enjoyment of the land granted[96]; and

(iii) had been, and were at the time of the grant,[97] used by the grantor for the benefit of the part granted.

Although it is by no means clear how far requirements (i) and (ii) are distinct,[98] recent authority has tended to treat them as separate requirements, both of which must be met.[99] The distinction between "continuous and

---

[91] Regard may be had to issues such as safety in determining what is necessary: see *Millman v Ellis* (1995) 71 P. & C.R. 158 at 163 (egress on to main road unsafe without right of way).

[92] See above, para.27–013.

[93] "It seems to me an unnecessary and artificial construct to hold that the grantor, as common owner and the landlord of the land conveyed, is himself using the rights over the retained land which his tenant enjoys under the lease." *Kent v Kavanagh* [2006] EWCA Civ 162 at [45]; [2007] Ch. 1 at 22, per Chadwick L.J. In such circumstances, LPA 1925 s.62 is likely to operate to convey rights over the retained land which are at the time of the conveyance enjoyed by a tenant in occupation of the land being conveyed.

[94] (1879) 12 Ch D 31.

[95] The decision itself, however, was concerned with implied reservation rather than with implied grant. The rules for implied grant were set out by way of contrast.

[96] This does not mean that it must be an easement of necessity, i.e. an easement without which the property cannot be enjoyed *at all*, but merely that *reasonable* enjoyment of the property cannot be had without the easement: see *Wheeler v J.J. Saunders Ltd* [1996] Ch. 19 at 25, 31. The easement must of course do more than merely accommodate the dominant tenement: see [1995] Conv. 239 at 240 (M. P. Thompson).

[97] See *Re St. Clement's, Leigh-on-Sea* [1988] 1 W.L.R. 720 at 729 (no implied grant where use of way had ceased long before the relevant conveyance).

[98] In *Wheeldon v Burrows* (1879) 12 Ch D 31 they are treated in one place as synonymous (at 49) and in another as alternative (at 58). See *Squarey v Harris-Smith* (1981) 42 P. & C.R. 118; (1967) 83 L.Q.R. 240 at 245 (A. W. B. Simpson); (1977) 41 Conv. (N.S.) 415 (C.H.).

[99] *Millman v Ellis* (1995) 71 P. & C.R. 158; [1995] Conv. 346 (J. West); *Robinson Webster (Holdings) Ltd v Agombar* [2002] 1 P. & C.R. 20; *Donaldson v Smith* [2007] W.T.L.R. 421; cf. *Wheeler v J.J. Saunders Ltd*, above, at 31; and [1995] Conv. 239 at 240 (M. P. Thompson).

apparent" easements and others was unknown to English law until 1839, when it seems to have been imported by a text-writer from the French law of prescription.[100] It then became a source of confusion, since it did not fit easily into the older and wider English rule against derogation from grant[101]; nor was it always insisted upon, or correctly understood. However, the history of the rule provides justification for the view that the Court of Appeal has now taken, as it tends to suggest that the two requirements were intended to have distinct functions.[102]

Because the rule rests on the principle of non-derogation from grant, it can apply even though the conveyance of the dominant tenement includes the express grant of a more limited easement.[103] But the implication of an easement will not be made if it is inconsistent with the terms of the express grant.[104]

28–021

(3) "CONTINUOUS AND APPARENT". A "continuous" easement is one which is enjoyed passively, such as a right to use drains or a right to light, as opposed to one requiring personal activity for its enjoyment, such as a right of way.[105] An "apparent" easement is one which is evidenced by some sign on the dominant tenement[106] (or perhaps the servient tenement[107]) discoverable on "a careful inspection by a person ordinarily conversant with the subject".[108] Thus an underground drain into which water from the eaves of a house runs may be both continuous and apparent. Other examples are a watercourse running through visible pipes,[109] windows enjoying light[110] and a building enjoying support. On the other hand, a right to take water from a neighbour's

28–022

---

[100] *Gale on Easements*, 1st edn (1839) p.53; see *Dalton v Angus & Co* (1881) 6 App.Cas. 740 at 821, where Lord Blackburn explains the origins of this expression. In *Suffield v Brown* (1864) 4 De G.J. & S. 185 at 195 Lord Westbury criticises it as "a mere fanciful analogy, from which rules of law ought not to be derived"; and see further at 199 (though at 194 he appears to accept the doctrine for grants as distinct from reservations). In *Wheeldon v Burrows*, above, the Court of Appeal applied his distinction between grants and reservations, thus rejecting the principle of the French law which applied to both equally. Why the French terminology was nevertheless preserved is a mystery.

[101] The English rule goes back at least to 1663: *Palmer v Fletcher* (1663) 1 Lev. 122.

[102] See *Watts v Kelson* (1870) 6 Ch.App. 166 at 172; [1979] Conv. 113 at 117 (C.H.).

[103] *Millman v Ellis*, above, at 165. cf. *Gregg v Richards* [1926] Ch. 521.

[104] *Millman v Ellis*, above, at 164.

[105] Code Civil, Art.688. See (1967) 83 L.Q.R. 240 (A. W. B. Simpson). *Suffield v Brown*, above, at 199, holding that "continuous" requires incessant use, is evidently erroneous. Gale in his first edition, 1839, at 53, confined his doctrine to "those easements only which are attended by some alteration which is in its nature obvious and permanent; or, in technical language, to those easements only which are apparent and continuous". It seems that he equated "continuous" with "permanent".

[106] Code Civil, Art.689; *Schwann v Cotton* [1916] 2 Ch. 120 at 141 (aff'd at 459); *Ward v Kirkland* [1967] Ch. 194 at 225 (right to go on neighbour's land to maintain wall on edge of dominant land held not continuous and apparent).

[107] See *Ward v Kirkland*, above, at 225.

[108] *Pyer v Carter* (1857) 1 H. & N. 916 at 922, per Watson B. In so far as this case applied the same rule to implied reservation it cannot now be good law: *Wheeldon v Burrows* (1879) 12 Ch D 31.

[109] *Watts v Kelson* (1870) 6 Ch.App. 166.

[110] *Phillips v Low* [1892] 1 Ch. 47 at 53.

pump from time to time[111] or a right to project the bowsprits of ships when in dock over the land of another[112] have been held to be outside the meaning of "continuous and apparent" easements.

28–023   Despite their adoption of these unsuitable terms, the courts have not applied them rigidly. Thus a right of way over a made road,[113] or one which betrays its presence by some indication such as a worn track[114] or its obvious use in connection with the land granted,[115] will pass under the rule in *Wheeldon v Burrows*; and the court will, it seems, turn a blind eye to the requirement that a right of way is not "continuous".[116] The rule against derogation from grant is a flexible doctrine, capable, indeed, of creating rights which cannot be easements at all.[117]

28–024   (4) SIMULTANEOUS GRANTS. The rules relating to implied grant apply also to cases where the grantor, instead of retaining any land himself, makes simultaneous grants to two or more grantees. Each grantee obtains the same easements over the land of the other as he would have obtained if the grantor had retained it.[118]

28–025   (5) WILLS. Gifts by will are treated no differently from grants by deed for the purposes of implied easements.[119] Thus on a devise of adjoining houses to different devisees, mutual rights of way over a connecting passage running behind the houses have been implied.[120] The rules are rules of common law and do not depend upon the grantee giving valuable consideration.

28–026   (6) LAW REFORM. The Law Commission has criticised the complexity of the existing rules for the implication of easements and is of the view that a single statutory test for implication is required to replace the existing methods.[121] It recommends that an easement should be implied as a term of a disposition where it is necessary for the reasonable use of the land at the date of that disposition.[122] In determining what is necessary, consideration should be given to the use of the land at the time of the grant; the presence on the land of any relevant physical features; any intention for the future use of the land known to both parties at the time; the available routes for the easement in question (depending on the type of easement claimed); and the potential

---

[111] *Polden v Bastard* (1865) L.R. 1 Q.B. 156; and see *Ward v Kirkland*, above.
[112] *Suffield v Brown*, above.
[113] *Brown v Alabaster* (1887) 37 Ch D 490.
[114] *Hansford v Jago* [1921] 1 Ch. 322; *Borman v Griffith* [1930] 1 Ch. 493; *Millman v Ellis*, above.
[115] *Borman v Griffith*, above.
[116] *Borman v Griffith*, above, at 499.
[117] See above, para.27–047.
[118] *Swansborough v Coventry* (1832) 2 Moo. & Sc. 362 (a better report than that in 9 Bing. 305: see *Broomfield v Williams* [1897] 1 Ch. 602 at 616); *Hansford v Jago*, above.
[119] *Phillips v Low* [1892] 1 Ch. 47.
[120] *Milner's Safe Co Ltd v Great Northern & City Ry* [1907] 1 Ch. 208.
[121] Law Com. No. 327 (2011), para 3.31.
[122] Law Com. No. 327 (2011), para 3.45.

interference with the servient land or inconvenience to the servient owner.[123]

D. By s.62 of the Law of Property Act 1925

1. Section 62. The operation of the rules relating to implied grant has been considerably modified by the Law of Property Act 1925 s.62. This provision dates from 1881[124] and it applies to all conveyances executed since then.[125] It was designed to make it unnecessary to set out the full effect of every conveyance by "general words" extending it to all kinds of particulars. If no contrary intention is expressed, every conveyance of land passes (inter alia) "all . . . liberties, privileges, easements, rights, and advantages whatsoever, appertaining or reputed to appertain to the land, or any part thereof, or, at the time of conveyance, . . . enjoyed with . . . the land or any part thereof."[126] "Conveyance" includes, inter alia, mortgages, leases, and assents,[127] but not a mere contract, e.g. for a lease for over three years[128] or for the sale of the fee simple.[129] But a contract for sale may be relevant in providing some evidence of what rights exist which can fall within the statutory language when the conveyance is made.[130] Section 62 applies to both registered and unregistered land.

28–027

2. Creation of easements and profits

(a) No application to existing appurtenances. Section 62 has no effect on existing easements or profits appurtenant to the land conveyed, which pass with it automatically and without express mention.[131] Indeed where a person is registered as proprietor of registered land (whether as first or subsequent proprietor), such appurtenances vest in him by statute.[132]

28–028

(b) Creation of easements and profits

(1) APPLIES TO ALL QUASI-EASEMENTS AND QUASI-PROFITS. Section 62 has the important effect of creating new easements and profits, by way of express grant,[133] out of all kinds of quasi-easements and quasi-profits.[134] It therefore

28–029

---

[123] Ibid.
[124] It replaces CA 1881 s.6.
[125] LPA 1925 s.62(6).
[126] LPA 1925 s.62(1); and see subs.(2) for conveyances of land with buildings on it. A right enjoyed with part of the land conveyed may benefit the whole: *Graham v Philcox* [1984] Q.B. 747.
[127] LPA 1925 s.205(1)(ii).
[128] *Borman v Griffith* [1930] 1 Ch. 493.
[129] *Re Peck and the School Board for London's Contract* [1893] 2 Ch. 315.
[130] See *White v Taylor (No.2)* [1969] 1 Ch. 160.
[131] *Godwin v Schweppes Ltd* [1902] 1 Ch. 926 at 932.
[132] LRA 2002 ss.11, 12.
[133] *Gregg v Richards* [1926] Ch. 521 at 534.
[134] *White v Williams* [1922] 1 K.B. 727 (quasi-profit of sheepwalk); *Crow v Wood* [1971] 1 Q.B. 77 (quasi-easement).

goes beyond the rule in *Wheeldon v Burrows*, which applies only to continuous and apparent quasi-easements and may not apply at all to quasi-
profits. A quasi-easement which is not reasonably necessary to the enjoyment
of the property granted but merely convenient (e.g. an alternative way of
access through another person's house) can become an easement under s.62,
although it cannot under *Wheeldon v Burrows*.[135]

28–030   (2) NATURE OF RIGHTS CONVERTED. Section 62 will convert into full easements or profits (inter alia) the following rights:

>   (i) a licence[136];

>   (ii) a right that was accustomed to be exercised but the origin of which
>   was perhaps unknown[137];

>   (iii) a right that was reputed to be exercised with a particular prop-
>   erty[138]; and

>   (iv) a continuous and apparent quasi-easement[139]

provided that such right was enjoyed at the time when the conveyance was
made.[140] "It matters not . . . whether the user is continuous and permanent or
permissive and precarious."[141] In other words, it is the fact that the right has
been enjoyed, not the legal basis upon which the right has been asserted,
which is material,[142] for "the key to the operation of the section is enjoyment
in fact, not title."[143]

28–031   **3. Operation of the section.** Illustrations of the wide operation of s.62 are
to be found in cases where the grantee has previously been tenant of the quasi-
dominant tenement and has enjoyed certain additional rights by permission of
the landlord.[144] In one case, the tenant of a house had been allowed to use a
roadway leading into a yard belonging to his landlord. When the tenant

---

[135] *Goldberg v Edwards* [1950] Ch. 247.

[136] *International Tea Stores Co v Hobbs* [1903] 2 Ch. 165.

[137] *White v Williams*, above. In the case of a quasi-easement of fencing, "it is immaterial that
a party has voluntarily fenced his premises simply for . . . his own protection": *Crow v Wood*,
above, at 87, per Edmund Davies L.J.

[138] *Newman v Jones*, Unreported, March 22, 1982, Megarry V.C.; applied in *Handel v St.
Stephens Close Ltd* [1994] 1 E.G.L.R. 70 at 71 (where tenants in a block of flats habitually parked
their cars within the curtilage, the right was reputed to appertain to the flats and it was irrelevant
that a previous tenant of a particular flat had not in fact had a car); *Pretoria Warehousing Co Ltd
v Shelton* [1993] E.G.C.S. 120.

[139] *Bayley v Great Western Railway* (1884) 26 Ch D 434; below, para.28–033.

[140] See below, para.28–032.

[141] *White v Williams*, above, at 740, per Younger L.J.

[142] *International Tea Stores Co v Hobbs*, above, at 172; *Lewis v Meredith* [1913] 1 Ch. 571 at
579; *Graham v Philcox* [1984] Q.B. 747.

[143] *Wall v Collins* [2007] EWCA Civ 444; [2007] Ch. 390 at [24], per Carnwath L.J.

[144] Section 62 may operate where a tenant acquires the reversion of his landlord by "leasehold
enfranchisement" under the Leasehold Reform Act 1967: *Kent v Kavanagh* [2006] EWCA Civ
162; [2007] Ch. 1.

purchased the reversion of the house, he acquired an easement to use the roadway, even though his previous user was purely precarious.[145] A renewal of the tenant's lease would have had the same result, for a lease is equally a "conveyance" within the meaning of s.62; and no less so because it was made informally,[146] provided that it was made in writing and not merely by word of mouth.[147] A landlord about to renew a lease should therefore ensure that he first revoke any licences which he has given to the tenant and prevent any further enjoyment of them, or else insert some provision in the new lease to exclude the application of s.62; otherwise s.62 may turn them into easements and give the tenant a right to enjoy them for the full duration of the lease.[148] Again, if a landlord lets a tenant into possession before granting a lease, and permits him to use a passage through the landlord's other property, the subsequent grant of the lease will turn this revocable licence into an irrevocable easement; for s.62 operates at the date of conveyance, and not at the date appointed by the conveyance for the beginning of the tenant's term.[149]

4. Limits of the section

(a) Right must be capable of existing as an easement. Section 62 cannot **28–032** create as an easement or profit a right which is incapable of being an easement or profit.[150] The object of the provision is to shorten conveyances, not to extend the categories of interests known to the law. Thus s.62 cannot confer an easement for the protection of one house by another against weather.[151] Nor can it create a precarious right to take water from an artificial watercourse and pond if and when the landowner chooses to let water into them,[152] or a right to use a particular way if and when it was not inconvenient to the landowner[153]; for such rights cannot exist as easements. Since s.62 operates by way of express grant, it will not create a right which the grantor had no power to grant,[154] as where he did not own the servient tenement.[155] Nor will it create a right out of some facility which was not being enjoyed at the time of the

---

[145] *International Tea Stores Co v Hobbs*, above; *Handel v St Stephens Close Ltd*, above (easement to park cars claimed by tenants following the renewal of their leases).

[146] *Wright v Macadam* [1949] 2 K.B. 744.

[147] *Rye v Rye* [1962] A.C. 496. For informal leases, see above, para.17–045.

[148] The automatic continuance of a weekly or other periodic tenancy for each new period would not be a "conveyance", but merely a continuance of the original grant: see above para.17–081; *Cattley v Arnold* (1859) 1 J. & H. 651. See also (1962) 106 S.J. 483.

[149] *Goldberg v Edwards* [1950] Ch. 247.

[150] *International Tea Stores Co v Hobbs*, above, at 172; *Bartlett v Tottenham* [1932] 1 Ch. 114; *Regis Property Co Ltd v Redman* [1956] 2 Q.B. 612; *Anderson v Bostock* [1976] Ch. 312.

[151] *Phipps v Pears* [1965] 1 Q.B. 76; cf. *Rees v Skerrett* [2001] EWCA Civ 760; [2001] 1 W.L.R. 1541; above, para.27–016, and see also above, para.3–042.

[152] *Burrows v Lang* [1901] 2 Ch. 502.

[153] *Green v Ashco Horticulturist Ltd*, above.

[154] *Quicke v Chapman* [1903] 1 Ch. 659; *Re St Clement's, Leigh-on-Sea* [1988] 1 W.L.R. 720 at 728. See too LPA 1925 s.62(5).

[155] *M.R.A. Engineering Ltd v Trimster Co Ltd* (1987) 56 P. & C.R. 1.

grant,[156] or was being enjoyed with land other than the land granted.[157] "Section 62 is apt for conveying existing rights, but it does not resurrect mere memories of past rights."[158] However, a right may be "reputed to appertain" within s.62 even if it was not being enjoyed at the time of the grant, but had been shortly before the conveyance.[159] It is therefore necessary to look at a reasonable period of time before the grant in question in order to see whether there was "anything over that period which could be called a pattern of regular user in any particular way or ways".[160]

28–033   *(b) Diversity of occupation or continuous and apparent.* Section 62 does not apply unless at the time of the grant there was either:

> (i) prior diversity of occupation of the dominant and servient tenements; or

> (ii) the "right" was continuous and apparent.[161]

The section applies only to "easements, rights and advantages" which appertain to or are enjoyed with the land. Therefore "when land is under one ownership one cannot speak in any intelligible sense of rights, or privileges, or easements being exercised over one part for the benefit of another. Whatever the owner does, he does as owner and, until a separation occurs, of ownership or at least of occupation, the condition for the existence of rights, etc., does not exist".[162] It follows that if A conveys to B part of his land which B has previously occupied (whether as a tenant or as a licensee),[163] then any right which B had enjoyed over A's land prior to the conveyance which is capable of being an easement will become one. If however A owns and occupies all of his land and sells part of it to B, the section will not operate to pass to B as an easement any quasi-easements enjoyed by A.[164]

---

[156] *Payne v Inwood* (1996) 74 P. & C.R. 42 at 47; *Campbell v Banks* [2011] EWCA Civ 61 at [37] et seq.

[157] *Nickerson v Barraclough* [1981] Ch. 426 at 445. A right may be "enjoyed with" the land even if there is no actual user at the time of the conveyance: *Re Yateley Common, Hampshire* [1977] 1 W.L.R. 840 at 850; *Re Broxhead Common, Whitehill, Hampshire* (1977) 33 P. & C.R. 451.

[158] *Penn v Wilkins* (1974) 236 E.G. 203, per Megarry J.

[159] *Castagliola v English* (1969) 210 E.G. 1425 at 1429, 1431; approved in *Pretoria Warehousing Co Ltd v Shelton* [1993] E.G.C.S. 120 (right to free use of shopping-centre concourse which terminated six months before conveyance held to pass under the section); [1994] Conv. 238 (A. Dowling).

[160] *Green v Ashco Horticulturist Ltd*, above, at 898, per Cross J.

[161] *Long v Gowlett* [1923] 2 Ch. 177; [1979] Conv. 113 (C.H.).

[162] *Sovmots Investments Ltd v Secretary of State for the Environment* [1979] A.C. 144 at 169, per Lord Wilberforce. See also *Bolton v Bolton* (1879) 11 Ch D 968 at 970, 971; *Roe v Siddons* (1888) 22 QBD 224 at 236; *Metropolitan Ry v Fowler* [1892] 2 Q.B. 165 at 171.

[163] Such as a purchaser who is allowed into possession prior to completion: *Lyme Valley Squash Club Ltd v Newcastle under Lyme BC* [1985] 2 All E.R. 405; cf. the grantee of a grazing licence for limited periods of the year: *Alford v Hannaford* [2011] EWCA Civ 1099 at [37].

[164] *Sovmots Investments Ltd v Secretary of State for Environment*, above; *Payne v Inwood*, above.

This principle is not however unqualified. It is settled by Court of Appeal **28–034** authority that both quasi-easements of light[165] and continuous and apparent quasi-easements[166] (such as a watercourse which runs through a man-made culvert,[167] or a made-up road[168]) will pass under the general words. The easement of light is an exception to many rules.[169] The reasons for the exception of continuous and apparent quasi-easements are largely historical. Although it was always acknowledged that a person could not have an easement over his own land, continuous and apparent quasi-easements were regarded as an exception to this.[170] Such "rights" are considered to pass under the general words either because they are enjoyed with the land or because they appertain or are reputed to appertain to it.[171]

The existence of this exception to the general rule requiring prior diversity **28–035** of occupation has now been acknowledged by the Court of Appeal.[172] If therefore A conveys part of his land to B, there will pass to B, by s.62, all those continuous and apparent quasi-easements that were enjoyed by A at the time of the conveyance. This will be so even if the rights were merely convenient and not necessary for the reasonable enjoyment of the land granted. In such cases, it will be unnecessary to have recourse to the rule in *Wheeldon v Burrows*.[173] Where s.62 does not apply, as where it is expressly excluded,[174] there may nevertheless be an implied grant under that rule, provided that the criteria for its application are satisfied.

5. Contrary intention. Section 62 applies "only if and as far as a contrary **28–036** intention is not expressed in the conveyance".[175] An express grant of a more limited right of way than s.62 would carry does not by itself amount to a contrary intention for this purpose.[176] But s.62 is also subject to any contrary intention which may be implied from those circumstances existing at the time

---

[165] *Broomfield v Williams* [1897] 1 Ch. 602; *Sovmots Investments Ltd v Secretary of State for Environment*, above, at 176.

[166] *Watts v Kelson* (1870) 6 Ch.App. 166; *Bayley v Great Western Railway* (1884) 26 Ch D 434 at 456. See too *Barkshire v Grubb* (1881) 18 Ch D 616.

[167] *Watts v Kelson*, above.

[168] *Barkshire v Grubb*, above.

[169] *Sovmots Investments Ltd v Secretary of State for Environment*, above, at 176. However quasi-easements of light may be merely one example of continuous and apparent quasi-easements and so fall within the second exception rather than being a distinct exception in themselves: see *Broomfield v Williams*, above, at 615, 617.

[170] See [1979] Conv. 113 at 114 et seq. (C.H.); [1995] Conv. 239 at 241 (M. P. Thompson).

[171] *P. & S. Platt Ltd v Crouch* [2003] EWCA Civ 1110; [2004] 1 P. & C.R. 18 at [42]; *Alford v Hannaford* [2011] EWCA Civ 1099 at [36]; cf. *Bayley v Great Western Railway*, above, at 457.

[172] *P. & S. Platt Ltd v Crouch*, above; *Alford v Hannaford*, above.

[173] There is a suggestion in *M.R.A. Engineering Ltd v Trimster Co Ltd* (1987) 57 P. & C.R. 1 by Nourse L.J. (at 7) that s.62 has superseded the rule in *Wheeldon v Burrows* and applies to quasi-easements; but cf. Dillon L.J. (at 5).

[174] See below.

[175] LPA 1925 s.62(4).

[176] *Gregg v Richards* [1926] Ch. 521; *Snell & Prideaux Ltd v Dutton Mirrors Ltd* [1995] 1 E.G.L.R. 259 at 264; *Alford v Hannaford*, above at [39].

of the grant.[176a] If, for example, the plot sold and the plot retained are both subject to a building scheme, the purchaser of a house standing on the plot sold will not be able to prevent the plot retained from being built upon so as to diminish his light; for the light was enjoyed "under such circumstances as to show that there could be no expectation of its continuance".[177] But the mere fact that the parties to the conveyance may have believed that the right being previously enjoyed was "precarious" (in the sense of being revocable at the will of the servient owner) is not enough to preclude the operation of s.62. It must have been within the parties' common knowledge that the right must come to an end at some future date because of the nature of the property over which it was being enjoyed (e.g. if both parties to a lease realised that the landlord intended to demolish the shed in which the tenant stored his coal).[178]

28–037   **6. Reform of section 62.** The transformative effect of the provision has not escaped adverse criticism.[179] It is a "trap for the unwary",[180] and while on occasion it may prevent the loss of important rights:

> "it does so only when the facts fit a particular pattern, and it may equally preserve unimportant arrangements, converting a friendly permission into a valuable property right, contrary to the intention of the "grantor"."[181]

The Law Commission has recently recommended that it should no longer operate to transform precarious benefits into legal easements or profits on a conveyance of land.[182]

E. Difference between Effects of Contract and of Grant

28–038   **1. Comparing contract and grant.** In the great majority of cases, conveyances of a freehold are intended to give effect to some previous contract for a sale. It is important to realise that the rules which determine the operation of a conveyance do not in any way affect the interpretation of a contract.[183]

[176a] See, e.g. *Alford v Hannaford*, above at [38] et seq.

[177] *Birmingham, Dudley & District Banking Co v Ross* (1888) 38 Ch D 295 at 307, per Cotton L.J.; *Selby DC v Samuel Smith Old Brewery (Tadcaster) Ltd* (2000) 80 P. & C.R. 466.

[178] *Wright v Macadam* [1949] 2 K.B. 744 at 751; *Hair v Gillman* (2000) 80 P. & C.R. 108; *P. & S. Platt v Crouch* [2003] EWCA Civ 1110; [2004] 1 P. & C.R. 18 at [29] et seq.

[179] *Wright v Macadam* [1949] 2 K.B. 744 at 755; *Green v Ashco Horticulturist Ltd* [1966] 1 W.L.R. 889 at 897; *Hair v Gillman* (2000) 80 P. & C.R. 108 at 116; *Commission for the New Towns v Gallagher* [2002] EWHC 2668 (Ch); [2003] 2 P. & C.R. 3 at [61]; [1998] Conv. 115 (L. Tee).

[180] Law Com. CP No.186 (2008), para. 4.74.

[181] Law Com. No.327 (2011), para. 3.59.

[182] Law Com. No.327 (2011), para. 3.59 et seq. However, the Commission recommends that the provision should continue to be able to convert easements, but not profits à prendre, from leasehold to freehold interests: Law Com. No.327, para. 3.66 et seq.

[183] *Re Peck and the School Board for London's Contract* [1893] 2 Ch. 315 at 318.

The rule in *Wheeldon v Burrows*[184] presupposes a grant and proceeds on the principle that a person who has made a grant may not derogate from it. Section 62 of the Law of Property Act 1925 applies only to a "conveyance", which, although widely defined,[185] does not include a contract.[186] The rules which govern the operation of conveyances merely say what the result will be if the conveyance is made without reservations. But a vendor of land, even under an open contract, is not necessarily under any obligation to make such a conveyance: his obligation is to convey what he has contracted to sell; and while he may not convey less, he need not convey more.

2. Scope of contract. A purchaser of land is ordinarily entitled by the contract to existing easements or profits which are appendant or appurtenant to the land sold.[187] As regards quasi-easements, he is entitled to such rights as may fairly be implied into the contract.[188]

28–039

> "When a property with a particular mode of access apparently and actually constructed as a means of access to it is contracted to be sold the strong presumption is that the means of access is included in the sale."[189]

Thus in *Borman v Griffith*[190] there was an agreement to let a house in a large park which stood close to a driveway leading to a larger house, and it was held that the agreement included the right to use the driveway for general purposes. This was plainly within the scope of the contract, since the lease stated that the house was let to the tenant for his trade of poultry and rabbit farming, and he proved that the only other way of access existing at the time of the contract was quite impracticable for many purposes of this trade. In another case, where there was a contract to sell house property in London which was approached by made-up private roads both from the east and west, the purchaser was held entitled to the use of one of them only, as a way of necessity, and not to the use of the other.[191] In such a case, subject to allowing for the reasonable convenience of the purchaser, the vendor is entitled to select the way.[192]

---

[184] See above, para.28–019.
[185] LPA 1925 s.205(1)(ii); see above, para.28–027.
[186] *Borman v Griffith* [1930] 1 Ch. 493.
[187] *Re Walmsley & Shaw's Contract* [1917] 1 Ch. 93.
[188] This statement was adopted by Forbes J. in *Sovmots Investments Ltd v Secretary of State for the Environment* [1977] Q.B. 411 at 441 (on appeal [1979] A.C. 144).
[189] *Re Walmsley & Shaw's Contract*, above, at 98, per Eve J.
[190] [1930] 1 Ch. 493.
[191] *Bolton v Bolton* (1879) 11 Ch D 968.
[192] See *Re Peck and the School Board for London's Contract*, above; *Re Walmsley and Shaw's Contract*, above. The words "and the appurtenances" do not narrow the scope of a contract but may enlarge the scope of a conveyance: *Hansford v Jago* [1921] 1 Ch. 322.

28–040   **3. Scope of grant.** It therefore seems that there is no general rule that a contract entitles the purchaser to all the rights which an unrestricted conveyance would pass to him.[193] He is entitled only to existing easements, and such quasi-easements as are necessary or intended[194]; and by an action for specific performance he cannot compel the vendor to convey more. The vendor may therefore insert limitations into the conveyance so as to make it accord with the contract.[195] In *Borman v Griffith*[196] it was held that the tenant was entitled by the contract to such rights as would have passed to him under a conveyance executed before 1882, i.e. including quasi-easements within the rule in *Wheeldon v Burrows*[197]; for he was held to be entitled to the same rights as if specific performance had been decreed in his favour before 1882 and the conveyance had made no mention of rights of way.

28–041   The reasoning (though not the result) of this case is somewhat difficult. As explained above, a contract to grant land will prima facie comprise only such quasi-easements as are necessary or intended; and it should make no difference to assume specific performance, for a vendor need never convey more than he has contracted to sell. But since the rule governing contracts is so similar in its scope to the rule which governed grants without special words made before 1882, it is not always perceived that they are really two distinct rules. The first rule, for contracts, is still unaltered. The second rule, for grants, has been widened by statute, so that a conveyance may easily transfer more extensive rights than the purchaser is entitled to demand, unless the vendor takes care to make the proper reservations. A way of convenience over the vendor's other land is an example of a quasi-easement which may fall outside a contract for sale but within the wide general words of s.62.[198]

28–042   **4. Rectification.** Even if the vendor mistakenly makes an unrestricted conveyance, and so conveys more rights than he has agreed to sell, there is the possibility of rectification.[199] The court has an equitable jurisdiction to rectify the conveyance, and so make it accord with the contract, if by the common mistake of both parties it has been wrongly worded. The common intention of the parties appears from the contract, so that a mistake in the conveyance is a common mistake. For example, where a conveyance of a plot of land operated by reason of s.62 to create (unintentionally, as regards the vendor) a right of way over a track across the vendor's other land, because the track had

---

[193] *Sovmots Investments Ltd v Secretary of State for the Environment* [1977] Q.B. 411 at 441.

[194] See Williams, V. & P. 658.

[195] *Re Peck and the School Board for London's Contract,* above (the object and limitations of the statutory formula are well explained by Chitty J. at 318); *Re Hughes and Ashley's Contract* [1900] 2 Ch. 595; *Re Walmsley and Shaw's Contract,* above.

[196] [1930] 1 Ch. 493; see the text, above, para.28–039.

[197] See above, para.28–020.

[198] *Bolton v Bolton* (1879) 11 Ch D 968; *Re Peck and the School Board for London's Contract,* above; *Re Walmsley and Shaw's Contract,* above; *Clark v Barnes* [1929] 2 Ch. 368 at 380 (purchaser under open contract (but subject to an express oral agreement excluding the right of way in question: see at 382) held not entitled to a reputed way which fell within s.62).

[199] See above, para.15–021.

in fact been used in connection with the land sold, the court rectified the conveyance by expressly excluding this right of way, even though the purchaser alleged that he agreed to buy the land on the assumption that he would get the right of way.[200] But there are limits to the use of rectification, and it by no means nullifies the operation of s.62. Since it is an equitable remedy, it will not be awarded to a vendor who has misled the purchaser, or who has unduly delayed claiming it; nor will it be awarded against a bona fide purchaser for value who had no notice of the discrepancy between the contract and the conveyance.[201]

F. By Presumed Grant, or Prescription

Rules of prescription perform the important function of preventing "the disturbance of long-established de facto enjoyment."[202] English law: **28–043**

> "has never had a consistent theory of prescription. It did not treat long enjoyment as being a method of acquiring title. Instead, it approached the question from the other end by treating the lapse of time as either barring the remedy of the former owner or giving rise to a presumption that he had done some act which conferred a lawful title upon the person in de facto possession or enjoyment."[203]

In the context of the prescriptive acquisition of easements and profits, lapse of time gives rise to a presumption that the enjoyment was pursuant to a right having a lawful origin.[204] Thus the court may presume, on proof of the fact of long enjoyment, that there once was an actual grant of the right, even though it is impossible to produce any direct evidence of such a grant.[205] It is then "the habit, and in my view, the duty, of the court, so far as it lawfully can, to clothe the fact with right".[206] "The court is endowed with a great power of imagination for the purpose of supporting ancient user."[207] This policy extinguishes stale claims, quiets titles, and preserves established property, while at the same time paying lip service to the doctrine that every easement must owe its origin to a grant.

Today it may be questioned whether this policy should be preserved. There is no doubt that it has produced far too complex a body of law. There are no less than three methods of prescription, namely, at common law, by lost modern grant, and under the Prescription Act 1832. Whichever route is   **28–044**

---

[200] *Clark v Barnes*, above; cf. *Barkshire v Grubb* (1881) 18 Ch D 616 (rectification in favour of purchaser).

[201] For this purpose the right to rectification is a "mere equity": above, para.8–012.

[202] *R. v Oxfordshire CC Ex p. Sunningwell PC* [2000] 1 A.C. 335 at 349, per Lord Hoffmann. For the evolution of prescription, see J. Getzler (ed.), "Roman and English Prescription for Incorporeal Property", in *Rationalising Property, Equity and Trusts*, (2003).

[203] *R. v Oxfordshire CC Ex p. Sunningwell PC*, above at 349, per Lord Hoffmann.

[204] *R. v Oxfordshire CC Ex p. Sunningwell PC*, above at 350.

[205] *Gardner v Hodgson's Kingston Brewery Co Ltd* [1903] A.C. 228 at 239.

[206] *Moody v Steggles* (1879) 12 Ch D 261 at 265, per Fry J.

[207] *Neaverson v Peterborough RDC* [1902] 1 Ch. 557 at 573, per Collins M.R.

chosen, it is not enough to show long user by itself; there must have been continuous user "as of right" before the court will go so far as to presume a grant, and even then the court will not presume a grant except in fee simple. It may therefore be contended that there is little justification in acceding to claims for an easement or profit simply on the basis of long use. In 1966, the Law Reform Committee reported "that the law of prescription is unsatisfactory, uncertain and out of date, and that it needs extensive reform". A majority of the committee recommended its total abolition; but a strong minority recommended that in lieu of all existing forms of prescription there should be an improved Prescription Act for easements, though not for profits, based on a 12-year period of user.[208]

28–045   As a result of concerns about the compatibility of the acquisition of title to land by adverse possession[209] with Art.1 of the First Protocol of the European Convention on Human Rights,[210] the law has now been reformed by statute so as to make it much more difficult for squatters to obtain title to registered land by adverse possession.[211] There is an obvious analogy to be drawn between the acquisition of title by adverse possession and the prescriptive acquisition of rights over land such as easements and profits, although there are significant differences in terms of the extent of the rights in issue.[212] These differences may provide ample justification for retention of a law of prescription.[213] The Law Commission has recently revisited the issue of reform, considering whether prescriptive acquisition should be abolished or reformed, and it has recommended that the current law should be replaced with a new statutory scheme for the prescriptive acquisition of easements, but not profits which should no longer be capable of prescriptive acquisition.[214] A similar approach has been implemented by legislation in the Republic of Ireland.[215]

28–046   **1. Presumption of grant.** Prescription and limitation are in many ways similar principles, but as the law has developed they have become quite distinct.[216] By *limitation* one person may acquire the land of another by adverse possession for a period which is now generally 12 years. By *prescription* one person may acquire rights such as easements and profits over the land

---

[208] 14th Report, Cmnd. 3100 (1966). The "strong minority" included Mr R.E. Megarry QC.
[209] See para.28–046 below.
[210] *Pye v United Kingdom* (2006) 43 E.H.R.R. 3; (2008) 46 E.H.R.R. 45; Goymour [2006] C.L.J. 696.
[211] LRA 2002 s.97; Sch.6; see below paras 35–070 et seq.
[212] See further Clarke, "Use, Time and Entitlement" (2004) 57 C.L.P. 238; Bridge, "Prescriptive Acquisition of Easements: Abolition or Reform?" in E. Cooke (ed.), *Modern Studies in Property Law*, Vol.III (Oxford: Hart Publishing, 2005).
[213] *Oxfordshire CC v Oxford CC* [2006] UKHL 25; [2006] 2 A.C. 674 at [58]–[59] and at [86]–[90].
[214] Law Com. No. 327 (2011), paras 3.71 et seq.
[215] Land and Conveyancing Law Reform Act 2009, Part 8, implementing recommendations of the Irish Law Reform Commission in *The Acquisition of Easements and Profits a Prendre by Prescription*, LRC 66–2002.
[216] For limitation, see below, Ch.35. For discussion of the historical development of prescription, see *R. v Oxfordshire CC Ex p. Sunningwell PC* [2000] 1 A.C. 335 at 349 et seq.

of another. One important difference is that limitation is extinctive but prescription is acquisitive: that is to say, adverse possession of land for 12 years extinguishes the previous owner's title, leaving the adverse possessor with a title based on his own actual possession[217]; but prescription creates a new right, an incorporeal hereditament, which no one possessed previously. Prescription therefore must have positive operation, so as to create a new title. This is brought about by presuming a grant, as "all prescription presupposes a grant."[218]

While the conduct giving rise to a prescriptive claim is always likely to have been unlawful in the sense of tortious, the extent to which the claimant's contravention of the criminal law may prevent the acquisition of an easement or profit by long use is more contentious. It had been asserted judicially that the court "will not recognise an easement established by illegal activity."[219] This principle was, however, considered to have been too widely stated in a case involving the vehicular access to domestic properties over privately owned common land.[220] By s.193 of the Law of Property Act 1925,[221] it is an offence, punishable by a fine, to drive a vehicle upon common land "without lawful authority". For over 50 years, owners of properties adjoining a common had gained access to their homes by driving from the highway along tracks and roads on the common, although the owner of the common had never consented to such use. The House of Lords held that the unlawfulness of the owners' actions did not prevent the prescriptive acquisition of private rights of way over the common, because it would have been possible for the owner of the common to make a grant of such easements, and by doing so to confer dispensation from criminal liability.

28–047

2. User as of right. The claimant must show that he has used the right as if he were entitled to it, for otherwise there is no ground for presuming that he enjoys it under a grant. "User as of right" does not therefore mean "user of right"; its meaning is closer to "user as if of right".[222] From early times English authorities have followed the definition of Roman law[223]: the user

28–048

---

[217] See above, para.4–003. For the application of the Statutes of Limitation to incorporeal hereditaments, see Co.Litt. p.115a and notes by Hargrave.

[218] Bl.Comm. ii, p.265; *Gardner v Hodgson's Kingston Brewery Co Ltd* [1903] A.C. 229 at 239, per Lord Lindley; *Bakewell Management Ltd v Brandwood* [2004] UKHL 14; [2004] 2 A.C. 519 at [49].

[219] *Cargill v Gotts* [1981] 1 W.L.R. 441 at 446, per Templeman L.J.

[220] *Bakewell Management Ltd v Brandwood*, above, overruling *Hanning v Top Deck Travel Group Ltd* (1993) 68 P. & C.R. 14 and disapproving *Massey v Boulden* [2002] EWCA Civ 1634; [2003] 1 W.L.R. 1792 (decided on a similar statutory provision, Road Traffic Act 1988 s.34). See Fox [2004] Conv. 173, McNall [2004] Conv. 67, 517.

[221] For scope of application, see *ADM Milling v Tewkesbury Town Council* [2011] EWHC 595 (Ch); [2011] 3 W.L.R. 674.

[222] *R. (Beresford) v Sunderland CC* [2003] UKHL 60; [2004] 1 A.C. 889 at [72], per Lord Walker of Gestingthorpe; see also at [3], per Lord Bingham.

[223] Dig. 8.5.10; 43.17.1; Bracton lib. 2 fo. 51b, 52a, 222b; Co.Litt. p.114a. For modern authorities, see Gale, 4–77 et seq., and the paragraphs below.

which will support a prescriptive claim must be user *nec vi, nec clam, nec precario* (without force, without secrecy, without permission).[224]

> "The unifying element in these three vitiating circumstances was that each constituted a reason why it would not be reasonable to expect the owner to resist the exercise of the right—in the first case, because rights should not be acquired by the use of force, in the second, because the owner would not have known of the user and in the third, because he had consented to the user, but for a limited period."[225]

Since the necessary conditions are negative, it is usually the servient owner who alleges that the user was either forcible, secret or permissive. The burden of proof on these matters nevertheless rests on the claimant.[226]

28-049   The essence of the rule is that the claimant must prove not only his own user but also circumstances which show that the servient owner acquiesced in it as in an established right[227]:

> "The whole law of prescription ... [rests] upon acquiescence ... I cannot imagine any case of acquiescence in which there is not shown to be in the servient owner: 1, a knowledge of the acts done; 2, a power in him to stop the acts or to sue in respect of them; and 3, an abstinence on his part from the exercise of such power."[228]

The message for a landowner who wishes to ensure that prescriptive rights are not acquired over his land is that a failure to act can be fatal and that he must not therefore "suffer in silence"[229]: "Consent is not a synonym for acquiescence, but almost its antithesis: the former negatives user as of right, whereas the latter is an essential ingredient of prescription by user as of right."[230]

28-050   *(a) Nec vi (not by force).* Forcible user extends not only to user by violence, as where a claimant to a right of way breaks open a locked gate, but also to

---

[224] *Solomon v Mystery of Vintners* (1859) 4 H. & N. 585 at 602 (common law prescription); *Sturges v Bridgman* (1879) 11 Ch D 852 at 863 (lost modern grant); *Tickle v Brown* (1836) 4 A. & E. 369 at 382 (prescription under the Prescription Act 1832; and see ss.1, 2).

[225] *R. v Oxfordshire CC Ex p. Sunningwell PC* [2000] 1 A.C. 335 at 350, per Lord Hoffmann.

[226] *Gardner v Hodgson's Kingston Brewery Co Ltd* [1903] A.C. 229; *Patel v W.H. Smith (Eziot) Ltd* [1987] 1 W.L.R. 853.

[227] *Sturges v Bridgman*, above, at 863.

[228] *Dalton v Angus & Co* (1881) 6 App.Cas. 740 at 773, 774, per Fry J.; and see at 803, per Lord Penzance. See also *Oakley v Boston* [1976] Q.B. 270, discussing the problem of establishing acquiescence by persons in a fiduciary position whose consent to any grant is requisite.

[229] *R. (Beresford) v Sunderland CC* [2003] UKHL 60 at [77]; [2004] 1 A.C. 889 at 913, per Lord Walker of Gestingthorpe.

[230] *R. (Beresford) v Sunderland CC*, above, at [81], per Lord Walker of Gestingthorpe, explaining the decision in *Mills v Silver* [1991] Ch. 271.

user which is contentious or allowed only under protest.[231] User is considered to be forcible "once there is knowledge on the part of the person seeking to establish prescription that his user is being objected to and that the use which he claims has become contentious".[232] If there is a state of "perpetual warfare" between the parties there can obviously be no user as of right.[233] Similarly, if the servient owner chooses to resist not by physical means but by seeking legal redress, such as making unequivocal protests or taking legal action, the claimant's user can no longer form the basis for a prescriptive claim.[234] "A user is contentious when the servient owner is doing everything, consistently with his means and proportionately to the user, to contest and to endeavour to interrupt the user."[235] It is important to appreciate that user may become contentious even though the servient owner's actions do not comprise an interruption within the Prescription Act 1832.[236]

(b) Nec clam (not secretly). As the basis of a prescriptive claim is acquies-   **28–051** cence by the owner of the servient tenement,[237] he "must have knowledge or the means of knowledge that the act is done".[238] Secret user will not therefore found a prescriptive claim. It is illustrated by cases where the right claimed is exercised underground, e.g. by discharging waste fluid from a factory intermittently and secretly (though without active concealment) into a local authority's sewers,[239] or by fixing the sides of a dock to the adjacent land by underground rods.[240] The same objection may be made to a claim for support of one building by another if the degree of support required for the dominant building is abnormally great because of some peculiarity not apparent to the servient owner.[241] But the servient owner cannot make the user secret by shutting his own eyes: it must be:

> "of such a character that an ordinary owner of the land, diligent in the protection of his interests, would have, or must be taken to have, a reasonable opportunity of becoming aware of that enjoyment".[242]

---

[231] *Eaton v Swansea Waterworks Co* (1851) 17 Q.B. 267; *Dalton v Angus & Co* (1881) 6 App.Cas. 740 at 786. For recent claims which have failed as user has been held to be *vi*, see *Dennis v Ministry of Defence* [2003] 2 E.G.L.R. 121 (protests to continued noise caused by Harrier jump-jets); *Field Common Ltd v Elmbridge BC* [2005] EWHC 2933 (Ch) (threat of legal action resulted in claimant disavowing any intention to claim prescriptive rights).

[232] *Newnham v Willison* (1987) 56 P. & C.R. 8 at 19, per Kerr L.J.

[233] *Eaton v Swansea Waterworks Co*, above, at 273.

[234] *Eaton v Swansea Waterworks Co*, above; *Dalton v Angus & Co*, above.

[235] *Smith v Brudenell-Bruce* [2002] 2 P. & C.R. 4 at [12], per Pumfrey J.

[236] *Smith v Brudenell-Bruce*, above at [18], referring in particular to *Newnham v Willison*, above. For further discussion, see Gale, 4–86 et seq.

[237] *Dalton v Angus* (1881) 6 App.Cas. 740 at 773.

[238] *Diment v N.H. Foot Ltd* [1974] 1 W.L.R. 1427 at 1433, per Pennycuick V.-C., discussing the circumstances in which an agent's knowledge or means of knowledge might suffice.

[239] *Liverpool Corporation v H. Coghill & Sons Ltd* [1918] 1 Ch. 307.

[240] *Union Lighterage Co v London Graving Dock Co* [1902] 2 Ch. 557.

[241] *Dalton v Angus & Co* (1881) 6 App.Cas. 740.

[242] *Union Lighterage Co v London Graving Dock Co*, above, at 571, per Romer L.J.

Thus a plea of *clam* failed where an outbuilding in a yard had for many years been supported by the wall of a dye-works, even though the outbuilding could not be seen from the servient tenement, for the servient owner should have had sufficient opportunity to discover its existence.[243]

28–052   *(c) Nec precario (not by permission).* Permissive user is the most common kind of enjoyment which will vitiate a claim by prescription. Prescriptive rights are necessarily established because of the acquiescence or tolerance of the landowner over whose property they are exercised.[244] If a reasonable person would appreciate that A was asserting a continuous right of enjoyment over B's land, and B did nothing to resist it, B would be taken to have assented to A's conduct, and his acquiescence or tolerance would not make the exercise of that right permissive.[245] User under licence is of course permissive, whether or not there is a contract or some periodic payment being made.[246] The advantage of a periodic payment is that it shows that permission is regularly sought and renewed; otherwise user which was at first permissive may in time become user as of right if the circumstances indicate that the original permission is no longer relied upon.[247] Where permission is granted, it does not matter that it is not solicited.[248] Licence may be implied from the circumstances surrounding the use, although some overt conduct of the servient owner demonstrating that the use is with his permission may be necessary.[249] Passive inactivity cannot however lead to the inference of a licence.[250]

The right to receive an artificial flow of water is often permissive by its very nature, since it frequently depends upon the servient owner being willing to continue it. Thus although waste water pumped from mines had flowed to the claimant's land for over 60 years he had no right to its continuance, since he had enjoyed it only because the servient owner chose to supply it.[251]

---

[243] *Lloyds Bank Ltd v Dalton* [1942] Ch. 466; contrast *Davies v Du Paver* [1953] 1 Q.B. 184, where the plaintiff claimed a profit of sheepwalk over part of a hill farm in Wales in country where there had been little fencing; the owner lived some distance away and had only recently bought the farm: held, despite some evidence that the enjoyment was "common knowledge" in the district, the plaintiff had failed to show user with the owner's knowledge and his claim failed. This decision creates difficulties: see below, para.28–088, fn.397.

[244] *Sturges v Bridgman* (1879) 11 Ch D 852 at 863.

[245] *Mills v Silver* [1991] Ch. 271, rejecting earlier dicta which had suggested otherwise; [1992] C.L.J. 220 at 221 (C.H.). See too *R. v Oxfordshire CC Ex p. Sunningwell PC* [2000] 1 A.C. 335 at 358; *R. (Beresford) v Sunderland CC* [2003] UKHL 60; [2004] 1 A.C. 889 at [6].

[246] *Monmouthshire Canal Co v Harford* (1834) 1 Cr.M. & R. 614; *Tickle v Brown* (1836) 4 Ad. & E. 369 at 382; *Mills v Colchester Corp* (1867) L.R. 2 C.P. 476 at 486; *Gardner v Hodgson's Kingston Brewery Co Ltd* [1903] A.C. 229.

[247] This is a question of fact: *Gaved v Martyn* (1865) 19 C.B. (N.S.) 732. See further *London Tara Hotel Ltd v Kensington Close Hotel Ltd* [2010] EWHC 2749 (Ch); [2011] 1 P. & C.R. DG16 (personal licence granted to defendant's predecessor in title held not to lead to necessary inference that defendant's use was by permission).

[248] *Odey v Barber* [2006] EWHC 3109 (Ch); [2008] Ch. 175, not following text in the 6th edn. of this work at para.18–126, fnn.19–20.

[249] *R. (Beresford) v Sunderland CC*, above, in particular at [83].

[250] *R. (Beresford) v Sunderland CC*, above, at [79].

[251] *Arkwright v Gell* (1839) 5 M. & W. 203; cf. *Wood v Waud* (1849) 3 Ex. 748; *Bartlett v Tottenham* [1932] 1 Ch. 114; and see above, para.28–032.

(d) User qua easement or profit. User during unity of possession, i.e. while   **28–053**
the claimant was in possession of both dominant and servient tenements,
cannot be user as of right.[252] Proof that the claimant exercised his right in the
mistaken belief that a valid easement or profit had already been granted to him
will not prevent the user from being as of right.[253] In general, the subjective
belief of the claimant is irrelevant.[254] The principle is that the right must have
been exercised qua easement or profit and not, for example, under any actual
or supposed right of an occupant of both tenements.

3. User in fee simple

(a) User by and against the fee. The user must be by or on behalf of a fee   **28–054**
simple owner against a fee simple owner.[255] "The whole theory of prescription at common law is against presuming any grant or covenant not to
interrupt, by or with anyone except an owner in fee."[256] As prescription
presumes that a permanent right has been duly created at some unspecified
time in the past, it follows that an easement or profit for life or for years cannot
be acquired by long use.[257] The rule that the user must be by, and against, a
freeholder, has been criticised,[258] and there is little doubt that the theory of
prescription does not deal properly with cases where the servient land is in the
hands of a limited owner.[259] It seems irrational to allow prescription against
land if occupied by an owner in fee simple but not if occupied under a long
lease, even one for 999 years.[260] Lord Millett, sitting in the Hong Kong Court
of Final Appeal, has characterised the rule as being:

[252] *Bright v Walker* (1834) 1 Cr.M. & R. 211 at 219; *Outram v Maude* (1881) 17 Ch D 391
(dominant owner holding servient land under lease); and see *Clayton v Corby* (1842) 2 Q.B. 813
(profit); *Damper v Bassett* [1901] 2 Ch. 350 (easements), both decided under the Prescription Act
1832.
[253] *Earl de la Warr v Miles* (1881) 17 Ch D 535 (profit); *Bridle v Ruby* [1989] Q.B. 169
(easement). cf. [1989] Conv. 261 (G. Kodilinye).
[254] *R. v Oxfordshire CC v Sunningwell PC* [2000] 1 A.C. 335. See further *Chamber Colliery Co
v Hopwood* (1886) 32 Ch D 549, and discussion in Gale at 4–103.
[255] *Bright v Walker* (1834) 1 Cr.M. & R. 211 at 221 (prescription at common law); *Simmons
v Dobson* [1991] 1 W.L.R. 720 at 724 (lost modern grant); *Kilgour v Gaddes* [1904] 1 K.B. 457
at 460 (Prescription Act 1832). It might have been expected that this rule would not apply to cases
of lost modern grant, although it is now clear that it does. For lost modern grant, see below,
para.28–062.
[256] *Wheaton v Maple & Co* [1893] 3 Ch. 48 at 63, per Lindley L.J.
[257] *Wheaton v Maple & Co*, above, at 63; *Kilgour v Gaddes*, above, at 460 (Prescription Act
1832); *Simmons v Dobson*, above, at 724. These decisions of the Court of Appeal appear to be
decisive. For contrary views, see *Bright v Walker* (1834) 1 Cr.M. & R. 211 at 221 (suggestion that
before the Prescription Act 1832, a grant by a termor could be presumed from long user); *East
Stonehouse UDC v Willoughby Bros Ltd* [1902] 2 K.B. 318 at 332.
[258] Law Com. CP No. 186 (2008), paras 4.238 et seq.
[259] Compare the position in Ireland, where prescription against limited owners is permitted:
Flynn v Harte [1913] 2 I.R. 326; *Tallon v Ennis* [1937] I.R. 549; and see (1958) 74 L.Q.R. 82
(V.T.H. Delany); Irish Law Reform Commission, *The Acquisition of Easements and Profits à
Prendre by Prescription*, LRC 66–2002, paras 1.28 et seq. and 3.28 et seq.
[260] Although this was acknowledged in *Simmons v Dobson* [1991] 1 W.L.R. 720 at 724, the
Court of Appeal extended the rule against prescription by tenants to cases of lost modern grant.
For criticism, see [1992] Conv. 167 (P. Sparkes). However, for the case of a long lease which may
be enlarged into a freehold under LPA 1925 s.153 (above, paras 18–092 et seq.), see now
Bosomworth v Faber (1992) 69 P. & C.R. 288 at 293; below, para.28–065.

"counter-intuitive and contrary to the policy of the law. It is counter-intuitive because it is difficult to see why it should be impossible to presume a lost grant of an easement by or to a lessee for the term of his lease when such a grant may be made expressly... It is contrary to the policy of the law, for if the disturbance of long established de facto enjoyment of a right is contrary to legal policy, then this is equally the case whether the enjoyment is by or against a freeholder of a leaseholder."[261]

Lord Millett was of the view that the rule would be unlikely to withstand the scrutiny of the House of Lords.[262] However, following consultation, the Law Commission has decided not to recommend reform of this rule in England and Wales, on the ground that to do so would both complicate the law and expand the scope of prescription to an unknown extent.[263]

28–055   Where the servient land is let, the question to be asked is whether the freehold owner of that land (the servient owner) acquiesced in the relevant user.[264] This in turn requires consideration of whether the servient owner had knowledge, actual or imputed, of that user and, if so, whether the servient owner could have taken steps to prevent it.[265] The fact that the servient owner was out of possession when the user began and then throughout its duration is likely to lead to the conclusion that knowledge of the user should not be imputed.[266] It follows that, where the tenancy pre-dates the commencement of user, it is more difficult, although not impossible, for the claimant to show acquiescence on the part of the freehold owner of the servient land.[267] But if it can be shown that the tenancy post-dates the commencement of user (i.e. that user as of right began against the servient owner), it will not be less effective because the land was later let[268]; and in such circumstances user against the fee simple will be presumed, unless the servient owner can show the contrary.[269]

---

[261] *China Field Ltd v Appeal Tribunal (Buildings)* [2009] HKCU 1650 at [54]; Merry [2010] Conv. 176.

[262] [2009] HKCU 1650 at [86].

[263] Law Com. No. 327 (2011), paras 3.144 et seq.; see also Law Com. CP No. 186 (2008), paras 4.238 et seq.

[264] *Pugh v Savage* [1970] 2 Q.B. 373; *Williams v Sandy Lane (Chester) Ltd* [2006] EWCA Civ 1738; [2007] 1 P. & C.R. 27; *Llewellyn (deceased) v Lorey* [2011] EWCA Civ 37; [2011] N.P.C. 14.

[265] The answer to this question is likely to depend on the terms of the tenancy: see *Williams v Sandy Lane (Chester) Ltd*, above at [24].

[266] *Williams v Sandy Lane (Chester) Ltd*, above at [24].

[267] *Pugh v Savage*, above; *Williams v Sandy Lane (Chester) Ltd*, above; *Llewellyn (deceased) v Lorey*, above. The same principles apply where the land is subject to a life tenancy: see *Llewellyn (deceased) v Lorey*, above at [34].

[268] *Palk v Shinner* (1852) 18 Q.B. 568; *Pugh v Savage*, above, in effect approving this passage, and suggesting that it remains correct even if the tenancy, though granted after the user commenced, began before the 20 years' period next before action under the Prescription Act 1832 began to run.

[269] *Davis v Whitby* [1973] 1 W.L.R. 629, aff'd [1974] Ch. 186; contrast *Diment v N.H. Foot Ltd* [1974] 1 W.L.R. 1427 (onus discharged). See also *Williams v Sandy Lane (Chester) Ltd*, above.

(b) User by tenant. Where it is the dominant land that is let, a tenant cannot **28–056** make a claim by prescription to an easement as annexed to his limited estate. If a tenant claims an easement on the strength of his own user, he must necessarily claim it for his landlord as well as for himself. If follows that a tenant cannot prescribe for an easement over his landlord's adjacent land, for the landlord can have no right against himself.[270] For the same reason, if A leases two plots of his land to two tenants, one tenant cannot prescribe for an easement against the other, for otherwise the result would be that A would acquire an easement over his own land.[271]

(c) Exceptions. There are certain modifications of this rule. First, profits in **28–057** gross may be acquired by prescription at common law[272] (though not under the Prescription Act 1832).[273] In this case the right is not claimed in respect of any dominant tenement but on behalf of the claimant personally. The claimant must show enjoyment by himself and his predecessors in title to the profit,[274] instead of by himself and his predecessors in title to the dominant tenement. Secondly, certain exceptions arise under the Prescription Act 1832, as is explained below.[275]

4. Continuous user. The claimant must show continuity of enjoyment.[276] **28–058** This is interpreted reasonably. In the case of rights of way it is clearly not necessary to show ceaseless user by day and night.[277] User whenever circumstances require it is normally sufficient,[278] provided the intervals are not excessive. However, merely casual or occasional user does not suffice.[279] A claim which clearly fell on the wrong side of the line was where a right of way

---

[270] *Gayford v Moffat* (1868) 4 Ch.App. 133.

[271] *Kilgour v Gaddes* [1904] 1 K.B. 457. Here again the law is different in Ireland: *Flynn v Harte* [1913] 2 I.R. 326; *Tallon v Ennis* [1937] I.R. 549.

[272] *Johnson v Barnes* (1873) L.R. 8 C.P. 527; *Lovett v Fairclough* (1990) 61 P. & C.R. 385 at 396. This is known as "prescription in gross". The Law Commission has recommended that, in future, profits should no longer be capable of creation by prescription, but only by express grant or reservation or by statute: Law Com. No. 327 (2011), paras 3.3 et seq.

[273] *Shuttleworth v Le Fleming* (1865) 19 C.B. (N.S.) 687.

[274] *Welcome v Upton* (1840) 6 M. & W. 536. There can therefore be no prescriptive claim to a profit in gross unless the claimant can show that either he or those through whom he derived title by inheritance or by assignment had exercised the right for the requisite period. The claimant cannot add his period of user to that of some stranger who happened to have exercised the same right before him: *Lovett v Fairclough*, above, at 399.

[275] See below, para.28–094 et seq.

[276] *Dare v Heathcote* (1856) 25 L.J.Ex. 245 (common law); *Att Gen v Simpson* [1901] 2 Ch. 671 at 698 (lost modern grant); *Hollins v Verney* (1884) 13 QBD 304 at 314 et seq. (Prescription Act 1832).

[277] *Hollins v Verney*, above, at 308.

[278] *Dare v Heathcote*, above (easement); see *Earl de la Warr v Miles* (1881) 17 Ch D 535 at 600 (profit). Compare *Parker v Mitchell* (1840) 11 A. & E. 788 (easement: user shown from 50 years before action down to four years before action, but no user shown during the last four years: claim failed) with *Carr v Foster* (1842) 3 Q.B. 581 (profit: 30 years' user shown, except for two years near the middle of the 30, when the claimant had no commonable cattle: claim succeeded).

[279] *Ironside v Cook* (1978) 41 P. & C.R. 326 (intermittent encroachments on verge of track merely for enabling two vehicles to pass: claim failed).

had been exercised only on three occasions at intervals of 12 years.[280] But continuity is not broken merely by some agreed variation in the user, as by the parties altering the line of a right of way for convenience.[281] The requirement of continuity of user must be distinguished both from the special rule under the Prescription Act 1832 as to user "without interruption", and from the degree of disuse that may extinguish an easement or profit after it has been acquired.[282]

The three methods of prescription must now be described.

I. PRESCRIPTION AT COMMON LAW

28–059   **1. Time immemorial.** At common law a grant would be presumed only where user as of right had continued from time immemorial, "from time whereof the memory of men runneth not to the contrary".[283] For this purpose the year 1189 was fixed as the limit of legal memory, so that any right enjoyed at that date was unchallengeable. This date was first fixed by statute in 1275,[284] and applied primarily to limitation; but it was also adopted for prescription. Although the law of limitation was changed by later statutes,[285] they were held not to alter the limit of legal memory for the purposes of prescription. A claimant to prescription at common law must therefore have the boldness to assert that he and his predecessors have enjoyed the right since 1189.[286]

28–060   **2. Twenty years' user.** As time went on, proof of lawful origin by establishing continuous user since 1189 became for practical purposes impossible.[287] The courts therefore "filled the gap"[288] with a presumption that if user as of right for 20 years or more were shown, they would presume continuity of use since 1189.[289] The period of 20 years was probably adopted by analogy with the limitation period laid down by the Limitation Act 1623.[290] Such user for less than 20 years requires supporting circumstances to raise the presumption[291]; and if there is evidence of user as far back as the period of living memory, it is immaterial that no continuous period of 20 years is covered.[292] This rule reduced to reasonable proportions a burden of proof which in theory was absurdly onerous.

---

[280] *Hollins v Verney* (1884) 13 QBD 304.
[281] *Davis v Whitby* [1974] Ch. 186.
[282] *Smith v Baxter* [1900] 2 Ch. 138 at 143, 146; below, paras 28–071, 29–009.
[283] Litt. p.170.
[284] Statute of Westminster I, 1275, c.39; below, para.35–003.
[285] See below, para.35–003.
[286] See the account of this rule given by Cockburn C.J. in *Bryant v Foot* (1867) L.R. 2 Q.B. 161 at 180.
[287] *R. v Oxfordshire CC Ex p. Sunningwell PC* [2000] 1 A.C. 335 at 350.
[288] *R. v Oxfordshire CC Ex p. Sunningwell PC*, above, per Lord Hoffmann.
[289] *Darling v Clue* (1864) 4 F. & F. 329 at 334.
[290] *Bright v Walker* (1834) 1 Cr.M. & R. 211 at 217; below, para.35–003.
[291] *Bealey v Shaw* (1805) 6 East 208 at 215.
[292] *R.P.C. Holdings Ltd v Rogers* [1953] 1 All E.R. 1029.

3. Defects. Serious obstacles remained, however. The worst was that the **28–061** presumption of user from time immemorial could be rebutted by showing that at some time since 1189 the right could not or did not exist.[293] Thus an easement of light cannot be claimed by common law prescription for a building which is shown to have been erected since 1189.[294] Consequently it was very difficult to establish a claim to light at common law. Again, if it could be shown that at any time since 1189 the dominant and servient tenements had been in the same ownership and occupation, any easement or profit would have been extinguished[295] and so any claim at common law would fail. Yet again, a person could not prescribe for a right contrary to custom.[296] To remedy these defects the courts invented the "revolting fiction"[297] of the lost modern grant.

II. LOST MODERN GRANT

1. Nature of doctrine. The weakness of common law prescription was the **28–062** inevitable failure of a claim if it was shown that user had begun after 1189. The doctrine of lost modern grant avoided this by presuming from long user that an easement or profit had been actually granted after 1189 but prior to the user supporting the claim,[298] and that the deed of grant had been lost. The doctrine was an entirely judge-made fiction.[299] It is therefore really a variety of prescription at common law, but it was a fairly late and distinct development[300] and is always classified separately. It has been described as "in the nature of an estoppel by conduct".[301]

2. Presumption of grant.

> "Juries were first told that from user, during living memory, or even **28–063** during 20 years, they might presume a lost grant or deed; next they were recommended to make such presumption; and lastly, as the final consummation of judicial legislation, it was held that a jury should be told, not only that they might, but also that they were bound to presume the existence of such a lost grant, although neither judge nor jury, nor anyone else, had the shadow of belief that any such instrument had ever really existed".[302]

In their anxiety to find a legal origin for a right of which there had been open and uninterrupted enjoyment for a long period, unexplained in any other

---

[293] *Hulbert v Dale* [1909] 2 Ch. 570 at 577.
[294] *Bury v Pope* (1586) Cro.Eliz. 118; *Duke of Norfolk v Arbuthnot* (1880) 5 C.P.D. 390.
[295] See below, para.29–014; *Keymer v Summers* (1769) Bull.N.P. 74.
[296] *Perry v Eames* [1891] 1 Ch. 658 at 667.
[297] *Angus & Co v Dalton* (1877) 3 QBD 85 at 94, per Lush J.
[298] See, e.g. *Dalton v Angus & Co* (1881) 6 App.Cas. 740 at 813.
[299] *Bridle v Ruby* [1989] Q.B. 169 at 173.
[300] The earliest case in the reports is said to be *Lewis v Price* (1761), noted in 2 Wms.Saund., 16th edn, 175; 85 E.R. 926: see *Dalton v Angus & Co*, above, at 812.
[301] *Angus & Co v Dalton* (1878) 4 Ch D 162 at 173, per Thesiger L.J.
[302] *Bryant v Foot* (1867) L.R. 2 Q.B. 161 at 181, per Cockburn C.J.

way,[303] the courts presumed that a grant had been made. It was immaterial that enjoyment had not continued since 1189. "Grant" is not confined to dispositions nor to the creation of easements and profits, but to other rights such as licences[304] or franchises.[305] Thus the court may be willing to presume a lost faculty from an ecclesiastical authority,[306] a lost Crown charter, a lost ministerial consent,[307] and even a lost port authority's regulation,[308] though it is very difficult to presume a lost statute.[309] 20 years' user will normally raise such presumptions,[310] but that is perhaps the minimum period.[311]

28–064   **3. Improbability of grant.** Presuming the existence of grants which had probably never been made was frequently felt to be objectionable, particularly when it fell to juries who were required to find it as a fact upon oath. But the doctrine was elaborately considered and approved by the House of Lords in *Dalton v Angus & Co*,[312] and is now unquestionable. Certain rules survive as relics of judicial reluctance to strain the consciences of juries more than necessary. In the first place, rather stronger evidence of user is required to induce the court to presume a lost modern grant than is required for prescription at common law.[313] Although it is said that the doctrine can be invoked only if something excludes common law prescription,[314] in practice the common law claim is regarded as adding nothing in most cases to the claim based on lost modern grant: "they stand or fall together".[315] Since the doctrine is admittedly a fiction, the claimant will not be ordered to furnish particulars of the fictitious grant, e.g. as to the parties,[316] though he must plead whether the grant is alleged to have been made before or after a particular date.[317]

28–065   **4. Impossibility of grant.** It is now settled that the presumption cannot be rebutted by evidence that no grant was in fact made.[318] But it is a good

---

[303] *Att Gen v Simpson* [1901] 2 Ch. 671 at 698.

[304] *Re St Martin le Grand, York* [1990] P. 63 (no easement could be created over consecrated ground, but the court found an indefinite licence).

[305] *Dysart (Earl of) v Hammerton* [1914] 1 Ch. 822; *General Estates Co v Beaver* [1914] 3 K.B. 918 (franchise of ferry). See Gale, 4–16.

[306] *Phillips v Halliday* [1891] A.C. 228; *Re St Martin le Grand, York*, above.

[307] *Re Edis's Declaration of Trust* [1972] 1 W.L.R. 1135.

[308] *Att Gen v Wright* [1897] 2 Q.B. 318.

[309] *Harper v Hedges* [1924] 1 K.B. 151.

[310] *Penwarden v Ching* (1829) Moo. & M. 400; *Dalton v Angus & Co* (1881) 6 App.Cas. 740, e.g. at 812.

[311] *Mann v R.C. Eayrs Ltd* (1973) 231 E.G. 843.

[312] Above.

[313] *Tilbury v Silva* (1890) 45 Ch D 98 at 123.

[314] *Bryant v Lefever* (1879) 4 C.P.D. 172 at 177.

[315] *Mills v Silver* [1991] Ch. 271 at 278, per Dillon L.J.

[316] *Palmer v Guadagni* [1906] 2 Ch. 494.

[317] *Tremayne v English Clays Lovering Pochin & Co Ltd* [1972] 1 W.L.R. 657; contrast *Gabriel Wade & English Ltd v Dixon & Cardus Ltd* [1937] 3 All E.R. 900.

[318] *Tehidy Minerals Ltd v Norman* [1971] 2 Q.B. 528; *Bridle v Ruby* [1989] Q.B. 169 (party acting under a mistaken belief that an easement had been reserved, when in fact the reservation had been deleted from the conveyance). This proposition was for long controversial: see the fifth edition of this work at p.878.

defence that during the entire period when the grant could have been made, there was nobody who could lawfully have made it.[319] Thus the court has refused to presume a lost grant of a way where the land had been in strict settlement (under which there was no power to grant in fee simple) from the time when the user began, down to the time of action.[320] When no grant could be made without some authority's consent, the court has refused to presume that consent without evidence of the authority's acquiescence in the user.[321] The court has refused to presume a lost grant which would be contrary to statute[322] or custom.[323] However, although the law in England is now firmly settled to the contrary,[324] there seems nothing in principle that necessarily excludes a lost modern grant by or to a person owning less than a fee simple.[325] It has at least been held that a lessee, who has a unilateral right by statute to enlarge his leasehold interest into a fee simple,[326] may acquire an easement by lost modern grant over other land belonging to his landlord.[327]

III. UNDER THE PRESCRIPTION ACT 1832

In due course, the legislature intervened "to save the consciences of judges and juries."[328] The Prescription Act 1832 was designed to reduce the difficulties and uncertainties of prescription, and in particular the difficulty of persuading juries to presume grants to have been made when they knew this was not true.[329] Although in many cases it has substituted certainty for uncertainty and thus simplified a claimant's position, the Act of 1832 is notorious as "one of the worst drafted Acts on the Statute Book".[330] "No doubt it is remarkable   **28–066**

---

[319] *Neaverson v Peterborough RDC* [1902] 1 Ch. 557; *Tehidy Minerals Ltd v Norman*, above, at 552.

[320] *Roberts v James* (1903) 89 L.T. 282, where it was also held that an intervening resettlement made no difference; this leaves little, if anything, of *Williams v Ducat* (1901) 65 J.P. 40. The question whether the court could presume a grant under the Settled Land Act (below, Appendix para.A–058) was not raised and may still be open. Similar cases where lost grants were not presumed are *Barket v Richardson* (1821) 4 B. & Ald. 579 (user against glebe land over which the rector could not grant an easement); *Rochdale Canal Co v Radcliffe* (1852) 18 Q.B. 287 (corporation with limited power of grant); *Daniel v North* (1809) 11 East 372 (user against leaseholder).

[321] *Oakley v Boston* [1976] Q.B. 270 (grant of right of way over glebe land required consent of Ecclesiastical Commissioners). *Sed quaere.* cf. *Re St Martin le Grand, York* [1990] P. 63.

[322] *Neaverson v Peterborough RDC*, above; *Hulley v Silversprings Bleaching and Dyeing Co Ltd* [1922] 2 Ch. 268; but see now *Bakewell Management Ltd v Brandwood* [2004] UKHL 14; [2004] 2 A.C. 519 as explained above at para.28–047.

[323] *Wynstanley v Lee* (1818) 2 Swans. 333; *Perry v Eames* [1891] 1 Ch. 658 at 667 (City of London custom against prescription for light, except under s.3 of the Prescription Act 1832; below, para.28–095); *Bowring Services Ltd v Scottish Widows' Fund & Life Assurance Society* [1995] 1 E.G.L.R. 158 at 160.

[324] *Simmons v Dobson* [1991] 1 W.L.R. 720; above, para.28–054.

[325] See (1958) 74 L.Q.R. 82 (V. T. H. Delaney); [1992] Conv. 167 (P. Sparkes).

[326] Under LPA 1925 s.153 (or earlier legislation having like effect); see above, para.18–092.

[327] *Bosomworth v Faber* (1992) 69 P. & C.R. 288 at 293.

[328] *R. v Oxfordshire CC Ex p. Sunningwell PC* [2000] 1 A.C. 335 at 350, per Lord Hoffmann.

[329] *Mounsey v Ismay* (1865) 3 H. & C. 486 at 496.

[330] Law Reform Committee, 14th Report, Cmnd. 3100 (1966), para.40; see further Law Com. CP, No.186 (2008), paras 4.159 et seq.

that in the twenty-first century a central part of the law relating to real property is still to be found in a statute of 1832 whose drafting has been criticised repeatedly."[331] The Law Commission for England and Wales has recommended its repeal, and the replacement of the current law of prescription with a new statutory scheme.[332] The Act has already been repealed in the Republic of Ireland following recommendations of its Law Reform Commission.[333]

Easements of light are treated separately from other easements, both in the 1832 Act and by the Rights of Light Act 1959. In this exposition of the 1832 Act, other easements will be covered first, together with profits, and then rights of light will be dealt with. The elements of the Act are as follows.

1. Easements (other than light) and profits

(a) The statutory periods

28–067
    (i) An easement enjoyed for 20 years as of right and without interruption cannot be defeated by proof that user began after 1189.[334]

    (ii) An easement enjoyed for 40 years as of right and without interruption is deemed "absolute and indefeasible" unless enjoyed by written consent.[335]

    (iii) The same rules apply to profits, except that the periods are 30 and 60 years respectively.[336]

    (iv) All periods of enjoyment under the Act are those periods next before some suit or action in which the claim is brought into question.[337]

    (v) No act is to be deemed an interruption until it has been submitted to or acquiesced in for one year after the party interrupted had notice both of the interruption and of the person making it.[338]

28–068
    (b) Shorter and longer periods. The shorter periods (20 and 30 years for easements and profits respectively) operate negatively, i.e. they assist prescription at common law by prohibiting one kind of defence. The longer periods (40 and 60 years) operate positively, for then the Act declares the right

---

[331] *Smith v Brudenell-Bruce* [2002] 2 P. & C.R. 4 at [20], per Pumfrey J.
[332] Law Com. No. 327 (2011), paras 3.71 et seq.
[333] Land & Conveyancing Law Reform Act 2009; and see Irish Law Reform Commission, *The Acquisition of Easements and Profits à Prendre by Prescription*, LRC 66–2002.
[334] s.2.
[335] s.2.
[336] s.1. The Act does not apply to profits in gross: see above, para.28–057.
[337] s.4.
[338] s.4.

to be "absolute and indefeasible". This important distinction is further discussed below, in the light of other provisions of the Act.[339]

(c) "Next before some suit or action". The Act does not say that an **28–069** easement or profit comes into existence after 20, 30, 40 or 60 years' user in the abstract; all periods under the Act are those next before some action in which the right is questioned. Thus until some action is brought, there is no right to any easement or profit under the Act, however long the user.[340] It is sometimes said that the right remains merely inchoate until action is brought.[341] The important point is that the fruits of the Act can be reaped only by a litigant. Any person who wishes to consolidate an inchoate right under the Act can commence proceedings against the servient owner claiming a declaration that he is entitled to an easement or profit.[342] He need not wait for some interference with it by the servient owner.

Even if there has been user for longer than the statutory periods, the vital **28–070** period remains the period next before action. Thus if user commenced 50 years ago but ceased five years ago, a claim to an easement will fail if the action is commenced today, for during the 20 or 40 years next before the action there has not been continuous user.[343] Similarly a claim under the Act will fail if there has been unity of possession for a substantial time during the period immediately before the action, for then there has not been user as an *easement* during the whole of the vital period.[344]

(d) "Without interruption"

(1) ONE YEAR'S ACQUIESCENCE. The user must be "without interruption". In **28–071** this context, "interruption" has a special meaning.[345] If D has used a way over S's land for over 20 years, and then a gate is locked or a barrier erected barring his way, D can still succeed in establishing an easement provided that, at the time an action is brought, he has not acquiesced in or submitted to the obstruction for one year after he has known both of the obstruction and of the person responsible for it.[346] Acquiescence occurs where D is eventually satisfied to submit to the interruption. Submission occurs when D is not willing to submit, but fails to make his opposition apparent directly to S.[347]

> "In other words, in order to disprove "submission," a plaintiff must prove both unwillingness on his part to accept the interruption and some

---

[339] See below, paras 28–086, 28–087.

[340] *Colls v Home and Colonial Stores Ltd* [1904] A.C. 179 at 190; *Hyman v Van den Bergh* [1908] 1 Ch. 167.

[341] *Colls v Home and Colonial Stores Ltd*, above, at 190; *Newnham v Willison* (1987) 56 P. & C.R. 8 at 12, 17.

[342] If the case is plain the servient owner will not defend and the plaintiff will obtain judgment on satisfying the court of his claim.

[343] *Parker v Mitchell* (1840) 11 Ad. & El. 788.

[344] *Damper v Bassett* [1901] 2 Ch. 350, discussing earlier authorities.

[345] See para.28–072 below.

[346] Both elements are essential: *Seddon v Bank of Bolton* (1882) 19 Ch D 462.

[347] *Dance v Triplow* (1991) 64 P. & C.R. 1 at 5; [1992] Conv. 197 (J.E. Martin).

words or act by which his opposition is made clear to the person who is responsible for the interruption."[348]

While the best way for D to prove that he did not acquiesce in or submit to the interruption is by commencing an action, protests will do as well if they can be proved[349]; and protests may continue to have effect for some while after they are made. It follows that protests prior to the year may negative acquiescence during the year.[350]

28–072   (2) "INTERRUPTION". "Interruption" means some hostile obstruction[351] (even though by a stranger). Mere non-user,[352] or natural occurrences, such as the drying-up of a stream,[353] do not suffice. Prolonged non-user, however, may mean that there has been insufficient enjoyment to support a claim[354]; and, conversely, an interruption may be too intermittent to be effective.[355] It is important to realise that "interruption" does not mean user by permission, which is to be contrasted with user "as of right" rather than with user "without interruption".[356] Interruption means some interference with enjoyment or cessation of enjoyment.[357] Enjoyment by permission, or subject to protest,[358] is not interrupted, but rather continuing.

28–073   (3) 19 YEARS AND A DAY. The special meaning of "interruption" can be illustrated by the case of a claimant who has used an easement for 19 years and a day, and is then interrupted. For the remainder of the 20th year he has no right to contest the interruption, for he cannot show 20 years' enjoyment.[359] But there will come a time (the first day of the 21st year) when, if he issues his writ on that day, he will succeed. He can then show 20 years' enjoyment before action brought, and the interruption is disregarded since it is for one day less than a year. A writ issued on the following day will be too

---

[348] *Dance v Triplow*, above, at 5, per Glidewell L.J.
[349] *Bennison v Cartwright* (1864) 5 B. & S. 1; *Glover v Coleman* (1874) L.R. 10 C.P. 108; *Newnham v Willison* (1987) 56 P. & C.R. 8.
[350] The question is one of fact: *Davies v Du Paver* [1953] 1 Q.B. 184 (claim to a profit of sheepwalk).
[351] *Davies v Williams* (1851) 16 Q.B. 546.
[352] *Smith v Baxter* [1900] 2 Ch. 138 at 143; *Carr v Foster* (1842) 3 Q.B. 581 (non-user of right of pasture for two years owing to lack of cattle: claim upheld); *Smith v Brudenell-Bruce* [2002] 2 P. & C.R. 4 at [21] (claimant refrained from use during mediation of dispute).
[353] *Hall v Swift* (1838) 4 Bing.N.C. 381.
[354] For examples of this, see *Parker v Mitchell* (1840) 11 A. & E. 788 (non-user for four or five years next before action); *Hollins v Verney* (1884) 13 QBD 304 (intervals of 12 years between each act of user).
[355] *Presland v Bingham* (1889) 41 Ch D 268 (piles of packing cases obstructing light to varying extents from time to time).
[356] *Plasterers' Co v Parish Clerks' Co* (1851) 6 Exch. 630.
[357] *Plasterers' Co v Parish Clerks' Co*, above.
[358] *Reilly v Orange* [1955] 2 Q.B. 112.
[359] *Lord Battersea v Commissioners of Sewers for the City of London* [1895] 2 Ch. 708; *Barff v Mann, Crossman & Paulin Ltd* (1905) 49 S.J. 794 (writ issued after 19 years and 352 days held premature).

late, for the interruption will then have lasted a full year.[360] But if instead the servient owner starts proceedings disputing the right, he can effectively defeat the claim to the easement; for his action is not an "interruption",[361] as defined, and the dominant owner cannot complete 20 years' enjoyment as of right.[362]

(e) User "as of right"

(1) MEANING. Sections 1 and 2 provide that the enjoyment must be by a "person claiming the right thereto", and s.5 provides that it is sufficient to plead enjoyment "as of right". Claims under the Act must be based on user of the same character as is required at common law.[363] Under the Act, the requisite user "as of right" means not only user *nec vi, nec clam, nec precario*, but also user by or on behalf of one fee simple owner against another.[364]   **28–074**

(2) NEC PRECARIO. At common law any consent or agreement by the servient owner, whether oral or written, rendered the user *precario*. It made no difference how long ago the permission was given provided that user was in fact enjoyed under it and not under a claim to use as of right. Under the Act this rule applies to the shorter periods (20 years for easements, 30 years for profits). But a dilemma arises in the case of the longer periods (40 years for easements, 60 years for profits) because of the provision that the right shall be absolute unless enjoyed by written consent or agreement.[365] This clearly implies that enjoyment by oral consent shall be effective; but what then becomes of the rule that enjoyment must be as of right?   **28–075**

The House of Lords partially solved this dilemma by deciding that a right enjoyed by oral permission renewed every year cannot give rise to the prescriptive acquisition of an easement as the right is not enjoyed "as of right" in any sense.[366] Indeed, even a single oral consent given during the period will vitiate the user, since there is no difference in principle between permission   **28–076**

---

[360] See *Flight v Thomas* (1840) 11 Ad. & E. 688 at 701; 8 Cl. & F. 231. Perhaps the claimant could save himself by proving that he had contested the interruption, and so had not "submitted to or acquiesced in" it for a full year; see above, para.28–071. But non-acquiescence is presumably effective only in the period after the 20 years have expired. Before the expiration of the 20 years the claimant has no right to contest the interruption: therefore he can be compelled to submit to it, and whether he protests or not can hardly matter. As soon as he acquired an enforceable right to contest the interruption, his acquiescence or non-acquiescence becomes important, as in *Glover v Coleman* (1874) L.R.10 C.P. 108.

[361] *Reilly v Orange*, above.

[362] This reasoning may not apply to rights of light, where user as of right is not a necessary ingredient of the claim: see further Barnes & Bignell [2009] Conv. 474 at 479 et seq.

[363] *Tickle v Brown* (1836) 4 Ad. & E. 369 at 382; *Gardner v Hodgson's Kingston Brewery Co Ltd* [1903] A.C. 229 at 238, 239.

[364] *Kilgour v Gaddes* [1904] 1 K.B. 457; and see above, para.28–054.

[365] ss.1 and 2.

[366] *Gardner v Hodgson's Kingston Brewery Co Ltd* [1903] A.C. 229 (no easement by prescription where way was used for at least 70 years, 15 shillings being paid annually for the user. Payment was evidence of the servient owner's consent; the result would have been the same if no money had been paid, but annual consents had been given orally); and see further *Monmouthshire Canal Co v Harford* (1834) 1 Cr.M. & R. 614 at 630 (20 years' period).

given once or more often.[367] But if the only oral permission was given before the period began to run, and was not later renewed, it is probable that the claim under the Act will succeed because the original licence was not made in writing[368]; if it were otherwise the provision about written permission would be redundant. The position can be summarised as follows.

(i) Any consents, whether oral or written, which have been given from time to time during the period render the user *precario* and defeat a claim based on either the shorter or longer periods.[369]

(ii) A written consent given at the beginning of the user (and extending throughout) defeats a claim based on either the shorter or longer periods.

(iii) An oral consent given at the beginning of the user (and extending throughout) defeats a claim based on the shorter periods but not a claim based on the longer periods.[370]

If user commences by consent, the question whether it continues by consent is one of fact.[371]

28–077   (3) POWER TO CONSENT. The person competent to give consent is the occupier of the servient tenement, for it is by his sufferance that the claimant's enjoyment continues.[372] Similarly, the occupier of the dominant tenement, who in fact enjoys the right, may make that enjoyment precarious by acknowledging that he has no indefeasible right.[373] It is a question of fact who is an occupier: he may be the fee simple owner, or a tenant for life or years, or even a squatter; but a mere lodger or servant is not an occupier. A tenant may frustrate his landlord's claim to an easement under the Act by acknowledging that his user is permissive; for then the period immediately before action brought is not a period of continuous user as of right.[374] But if the landlord can

---

[367] *Tickle v Brown* (1836) 4 Ad. & E. 369; and see *Ward v Kirkland* [1967] Ch. 194 (period of permissive user).

[368] *Tickle v Brown*, above, at 383; cf. *Gardner v Hodgson's Kingston Brewery Co Ltd* [1901] 2 Ch. 198 at 215; [1903] A.C. 229 at 236.

[369] This will include the case where user continues on a common understanding that it is to be permissive: *Jones v Price* (1992) 64 P. & C.R. 404.

[370] *Healey v Hawkins* [1968] 1 W.L.R. 1967 (approving this sentence). As to the shorter period, see *Tickle v Brown*, above, at 383. The better view may be that the question is one of fact, but that it is difficult to draw the inference that user in such a case is user as of right: see *Gaved v Martyn* (1865) 19 C.B. (N.S.) 732 at 744; (1968) 32 Conv. (N.S.) 40 (P. S. Langan); *London Tara Hotel Ltd v Kensington Close Hotel Ltd* [2010] EWHC 2749 (Ch); [2011] 1 P. & C.R. DG16 at [64].

[371] *Gaved v Martyn* (1865) 19 C.B. (N.S.) 732; *Healey v Hawkins*, above; *London Tara Hotel Ltd v Kensington Close Hotel Ltd*, above.

[372] See, e.g. *Lowry v Crothers* (1871) I.R. 5 C.L. 98 (tenant for life).

[373] *Bewley v Atkinson* (1879) 13 Ch D 283; *Hyman v Van den Bergh* [1908] 1 Ch. 167.

[374] See the discussion of these points in *Hyman v Van den Bergh* [1907] 2 Ch. 516 at 531 (Parker J.) and [1908] 1 Ch. 167 at 179 (Farwell L.J.). This decision concerned the easement of light, but its principle seems applicable to all claims made under the Act. Lost modern grant was not pleaded in the alternative, and conflicting opinions were expressed as to the possibility of pleading it successfully in a case where a defence provided by the Act had been made out. As to pleading claims in the alternative, see below, para.28–090.

make out a case by prescription at common law or lost modern grant, his rights so acquired cannot be given away by a tenant or other occupier of the dominant land, for they are vested rights in fee simple which a tenant has no power to dispose of.[375]

(f) Calculation of the periods. No presumption arises in support of a claim on proof of enjoyment for less than the statutory periods.[376] However, there is a distinction between a presumption and an inference, and inferences may be drawn from such enjoyment.[377] Thus user for less than the statutory periods may be taken into account with other circumstances in establishing an easement.[378]

28–078

Section 7 applies to both easements and profits, but is limited in its effect to the shorter periods. It provides that any period during which the servient tenant has been a minor, mental patient or tenant for life shall automatically be deducted from those periods.[379] Further, any period during which an action is pending or being actively prosecuted is also to be deducted.[380]

28–079

Section 8 applies only to easements, and not to profits. It provides that if the servient tenement has been held under a "term of life, or any term of years exceeding three years from the granting thereof", that term shall be excluded in computing the 40 years' period in the case of a "way or other convenient [*sic*] watercourse or use of water", provided that the claim is resisted by a reversioner upon the term within three years of its determination. The word "convenient" is "not unreasonably supposed to be a misprint for 'easement' ",[381] so that the phrase should read "or other easement, watercourse or use of water", thus corresponding with the phrase used in s.2. If so, s.8 may apply to all easements; but the point is unsettled.[382]

28–080

(g) Effect of deductions. Where either s.7 or s.8 applies, the period deducted is excluded altogether when calculating the period next before action. Thus if there has been enjoyment of a profit for 45 years in all, consisting of 25 years' user against the fee simple owner, then 19 years against a life tenant, and then a further year against the fee simple owner, the claim fails; this is because s.7 provides that the period of the life tenancy is deducted when calculating the period next before action brought, and so less than 30 years' user would remain. But if the user continues for another four years, the claim will then succeed, for there would then be 30 years' user (consisting of 25 years before

28–081

---

[375] *Hyman v Van den Bergh* [1907] 2 Ch. 516 at 531; [1908] 1 Ch. 167 at 179.

[376] s.6.

[377] *Hollins v Verney* (1884) 13 QBD 304 at 308.

[378] *Hanmer v Chance* (1865) 4 De G.J. & S. 626 at 631.

[379] Despite the changes made by the 1925 legislation, it seems that the periods of minorities and life tenancies will still be deducted: see LPA 1925 s.12.

[380] The same deduction would probably be allowed in the case of the longer periods; but the Act makes no provision for it.

[381] *Laird v Briggs* (1880) 50 L.J.Ch. 260 at 261, per Fry J. (omitted from the report in 16 Ch D 440 at 447); and see *Wright v Williams* (1836) Tyr. & G. 375 at 390, by counsel in argument.

[382] In *Laird v Briggs*, above, the point was reserved on appeal: see (1881) 19 Ch D 22 at 33, 36, 37.

and five years after the life tenancy). Since the period of the life tenancy is disregarded, the 30-year period is, for the purposes of the Act, that next before action.[383] Sections 7 and 8 have the effect of connecting the periods immediately before and after the period deducted, but they will not connect two periods separated in any other way, e.g. by a period of unity of possession.[384] Nor will events that have occurred during the life tenancy, such as an interruption, be disregarded. The provisions are for the benefit not of the claimant but of those resisting the claim,[385] and they appear to operate merely mathematically, not as a cloak of oblivion.

(h) Disabilities within sections 7 and 8.

28–082   (1) THE DISABILITIES. Section 7 applies if the servient owner is a minor, mental patient or tenant for life. Section 8 applies where the servient tenement has been held under a term for over three years, or for life. Thus a life tenancy is the only disability which applies to both the longer and the shorter periods. Infancy and mental illness affect only the shorter periods, and leases affect only the longer periods for the claims mentioned in s.8. Thus if D enjoys a way over S's land for 25 years, but S has been mentally ill for the last 15 of those years, s.7 defeats D's claim. If D continues his user for another 15 years, however, his claim succeeds, even though S remains mentally ill throughout.

28–083   (2) LEASES FOR YEARS. It is curious that leases for years, unlike life tenancies, may be deducted only under s.8 and not under s.7. Thus where there had been user of a way for 20 years, the servient land being under lease for 15 of the 20 years, but free from any lease at the beginning of the period, an easement was established.[386] Such user began against a fee simple owner who, by leasing the land, voluntarily put it out of his power to resist the user. Had the lease been granted before the user began and continued throughout, the position would have been different, for in such circumstances (unlike the case when the servient owner had granted a number of successive tenancies)[387] no user as against a fee simple owner able to resist it could have been shown.[388] It will also be seen that even if there had been user for 40 years, the claim would have succeeded only on the last 20 years' user; a claim based on 40 years' user would make the lease deductible, leaving a period of 25 years' user only. In such a case, therefore, a claim based on the shorter period may succeed where one based on the longer period will fail.

28–084   (3) EFFECT OF LEASE. A lease may therefore affect a claim in two ways:

> (i) by showing that there has been no user against a fee simple owner
> who knows of it and can resist it; and

[383] s.4; *Clayton v Corby* (1842) 2 Q.B. 813.
[384] *Onley v Gardiner* (1838) 4 M. & W. 496.
[385] *Clayton v Corby*, above, at 825.
[386] *Palk v Shinner* (1852) 18 Q.B. 568.
[387] See *Bishop v Springett* (1831) 1 L.J.K.B. 13.
[388] *Daniel v North* (1809) 11 East 372; *Bright v Walker* (1834) 1 Cr.M. & R. 211.

(ii) by falling within the provisions of section 8 allowing deduction.

The first of these is a common law rule not affected by the Act[389]; the second is a creature of the statute and can apply only to claims under the Act.

(i) Right to deduct. In s.7 the provision for deduction is absolute; in s.8 it **28–085** is subject to the condition that the reversioner resists the claim within three years of the determination of the term of years or life.[390] Thus if the reversioner fails to resist the claim within the three years, he has no right of deduction at all. Another peculiarity of s.8 is that it extends only to a reversioner and not to a remainderman,[391] so that it will rarely apply to land held by a tenant for life under the usual kind of settlement. It can be seen that s.7 is wide in its scope, giving an absolute right of deduction from the shorter periods for both easements and profits. Section 8, on the other hand, is very narrow, giving only a reversioner a conditional right of deduction from the 40 years' period in the case of (possibly) only two classes of easements.

(j) Difference between shorter and longer periods

(1) SHORTER PERIODS. In the case of the shorter periods, the only benefits **28–086** which the Act of 1832 confers upon a claimant are that the period for which he must show user is clearly laid down, and that he cannot be defeated by proof that his enjoyment began after 1189. The nature of the user required is still substantially the same as it was prior to the Act, so that the claimant must show continuous uninterrupted user as of right by or on behalf of a fee simple owner against a fee simple owner who both knew of the user and could resist it, at least at the time when user began.[392] The effect of the Act was therefore merely to facilitate prescription at common law, by eliminating the objection to user which is not of immemorial antiquity. Apart from that, the Act provides that a claim based on the shorter period "may be defeated in any other way by which the same is now liable to be defeated".[393] "The Act was an Act 'for shortening the time of prescription in certain cases'. And really it did nothing more."[394]

(2) LONGER PERIODS. User as of right is equally necessary in the case of the **28–087** longer periods. But here the language of the Act is positive: the right becomes "absolute and indefeasible". This is held not to alter the fundamental rule that prescription must operate for and against a fee simple estate.

---

[389] Unless it is unnecessary to presume a grant in the case of the longer period: see below, para.28–086.

[390] *Wright v Williams* (1836) 1 M. & W. 77 at 100.

[391] *Symons v Leaker* (1885) 15 QBD 629 (remainderman held unable to deduct life tenancy of 55 years). But see *Holman v Exton* (1692) Carth. 246 (remainderman held to be "within the equity" of a statute applicable to reversioners).

[392] See above, paras 28–048 et seq.

[393] Prescription Act 1832 ss.1, 2.

[394] *Gardner v Hodgson's Kingston Brewery Co Ltd* [1903] A.C. 229 at 236, per Lord Macnaghten.

"An easement for a term of years may, or course, be created by grant; but such an easement cannot be gained by prescription [*sc.* at common law], and, not being capable of being so acquired, it does not fall within the scope of the statute."[395]

A tenant cannot therefore prescribe against his own landlord, or against another tenant of his own landlord.[396]

28–088   One difference, however, arises from the positive words of the Act. It is no defence that user began against a mere tenant or other occupier. Thus by 40 years' user against a tenant for years or for life the claimant can acquire an easement against the fee simple, even though the fee simple owner was in no position to contest the user, provided that a defence is not available under s.8.[397] In principle it should also be possible under the longer periods to prescribe against corporations which have no power of grant, for the positive right conferred by the Act should require no presumption of a grant by the servient owner. However, the Court of Appeal has now held (albeit *obiter*) that, where the servient owner does not have power to grant, a prescriptive right cannot be acquired.[398]

28–089   *(k) Limitations.* The Prescription Act 1832 does not create easements or profits which could not exist as such at common law.[399] Thus a claim by the freemen and citizens of a town to enter land and hold races thereon on Ascension Day cannot be established under the Act.[400] Nor does it apply to the acquisition of profits in gross, which can therefore be prescribed for only at common law or by lost modern grant.[401]

28–090   *(l) Alternative claims.* One of the many uncertainties raised by the Act of 1832 was whether it had abolished the other methods of prescription. It is now clearly settled that it did not.[402] The doctrine of lost modern grant is therefore still available, even in the case of light.[403] Consequently all three methods of

---

[395] *Wheaton v Maple* [1893] 3 Ch. 48 at 64, per Lindley L.J. Although a case about rights of light, its principle was applied to other easements in *Kilgour v Gaddes* [1904] 1 K.B. 457.

[396] *Kilgour v Gaddes*, above (unsuccessful claim to use of a pump, habitually used for over 40 years, by one tenant against another tenant of the same landlord).

[397] *Wright v Williams* (1836) 1 M. & W. 77, not cited in *Davies v Du Paver* [1953] 1 Q.B. 184, where the contrary was held: see (1956) 72 L.Q.R. 32 (R.E.M.).

[398] *Housden v Conservators of Wimbledon & Putney Commons* [2008] EWCA Civ 200; [2008] 1 W.L.R. 1172, disapproving of text in the sixth edition of this work at para.18–160, and holding "with considerable reluctance" (per Mummery LJ at [66]) that the Court was bound by the decision in *Proprietors of the Staffordshire & Worcestershire Canal Navigation v Proprietors of the Birmingham Canal Navigations* (1866) L.R. 1 H.L. 254. See [2009] C.L.J. 40 (S.B.); [2009] Conv. 349 (N. Piska).

[399] *Wheaton v Maple & Co* [1893] 3 Ch. 48 at 65.

[400] *Mounsey v Ismay* (1865) 3 H. & C. 486.

[401] See above, para.27–068.

[402] *Aynsley v Glover* (1875) 10 Ch.App. 283; *Healey v Hawkins* [1968] 1 W.L.R. 1967. See also (1958) 74 L.Q.R. at 86, 87 (V.T.H. Delany) and cases cited below.

[403] *Tisdall v McArthur & Co (Steel & Metal) Ltd* [1951] I.R. 228; *Marine & General Mutual Life Assurance v St James' Real Estate Co Ltd* [1991] 2 E.G.L.R. 178; *Marlborough (West End) Ltd v Wilks Head & Eve* Unreported December 20, 1996, Lightman J.). This seems the better view. Although in *Tapling v Jones* (1865) 11 H.L.C. 290 at 304, Lord Westbury suggested that the right to ancient lights rested on the provisions of the Prescription Act 1832 and "ought not to

prescription may be relied upon in the alternative,[404] without pleading them individually.[405]

Claims at common law or (in particular) by lost modern grant therefore **28–091** remain of great importance, since in many cases a claim under the Act may be defeated by some technicality, e.g. an interruption, or a consent by a tenant of the dominant land, or unity of possession.[406] The principle that the period under the Act is that next before action marks an important distinction between statutory prescription and prescription by lost modern grant which has no such requirement. Where it is possible to establish user as of right over a 20 year period which ended some time before the current litigation, a claim under the Act is doomed to fail; however, the claimant may be able to succeed on lost modern grant.[407] In one case[408] a claim by lost modern grant succeeded where a right of way of modern origin had been subject to unity of possession for 16 out of the last 20 years, so that neither common law nor the Act were of any help. In a comparable case the court presumed a lost modern grant of a right of grazing although the servient land had been under requisition, thus preventing user, for 19 of the 30 years next before action.[409] In relation to profits, lost modern grant has the substantial advantage that 20 years' user suffices, whereas the Act requires at least 30.[410] It should be noted that, for all its shortcomings, prescription under the Prescription Act 1832 is, from a conveyancing point of view, preferable to prescription by lost modern grant. Because it has to be exercised without interruption "next before some suit or action", it may be easier for any purchaser of the servient tenement to discover.[411]

---

be rested on any presumption of grant or fiction of a licence", those remarks, properly understood, do not contradict the view in the text: see *Tisdall v McArthur & Co (Steel & Metal) Ltd*, above, at 235–242. For the potential advantages of a claim to a right of light based on lost modern grant, see Barnes & Bignell [2009] Conv. 474 at 481.

[404] See *Bass v Gregory* (1890) 25 QBD 481; *Aynsley v Glover*, above, at 284.

[405] *Pugh v Savage* [1970] 2 Q.B. 373 (claim to right of way "by prescription": lost modern grant presumed). The comments in that case were specifically in the context of the county court, "where ideal pleadings are not to be expected": per Harman L.J. (at 386), but it is thought that the same would now apply in the High Court as well: cf. CPR Pt 7.

[406] See *Healey v Hawkins*, above (lost modern grant where user not continuous to time of action brought). In *Hyman v Van den Bergh* [1908] 1 Ch. 167 at 176–178, Farwell L.J. expressed the opinion that a plea of lost modern grant would not succeed in a case where one of the defences provided by the Prescription Act had been made out; but later decisions impose no such restriction.

[407] See, e.g., *Smith v Brudenell-Bruce* [2002] 2 P. & C.R. 4; *Llewellyn (deceased) v Lorey* [2011] EWCA Civ 37; [2011] N.P.C. 14 at [31].

[408] *Hulbert v Dale* [1909] 2 Ch. 570.

[409] *Tehidy Minerals Ltd v Norman* [1971] 2 Q.B. 528 (user as of right, 1920–1941; requisition, 1941–1960; user by consent, 1960–1966). See too *Mills v Silver* [1991] Ch. 271 at 278.

[410] *Tehidy Minerals Ltd v Norman*, above.

[411] If an easement has been acquired by lost modern grant, it will not be lost by mere non-user (below, para.29–009), and a purchaser may be bound by such an easement even though he could not have discovered its existence. For this reason, the Law Commission and Land Registry provisionally recommended in 1998 that, pending a full review of the law of easements and profits, the only form of prescription applicable to registered land should be that under the Prescription Act 1832: Law Com. No.254, para.10.91. This recommendation was not however carried forward in the final recommendations: Law Com No.271 (2002), para 1.19. The conveyancing problem was addressed in a different way: see Law Com No.271, paras 8.68–8.71; and see

28–092   The Court of Appeal has commented on the "unnecessary complication and confusion" caused by the co-existence of three separate methods of prescription,[412] but a much better Act will be required before the judge-made methods can be eliminated. The recent Report of the Law Commission gives practical effect to its recommendation for a new statutory scheme for prescriptive acquisition of easements (but not profits) in the form of a draft Bill which has much to commend it.[413]

28–093   **2. The easement of light.** There are special provisions for facilitating claims to light, both under the Prescription Act 1832 and the Rights of Light Act 1959.

(a) Under the Prescription Act 1832

28–094   (1) THE STATUTE. The easement of light, having been perhaps the most difficult easement to acquire by prescription before the Act of 1832,[414] then became the easiest. Section 3 provides that the actual enjoyment of the access of light to a "dwelling-house, workshop, or other building" for 20 years without interruption shall make the right absolute and indefeasible unless it was enjoyed by written consent or agreement. "Building" here includes a church,[415] a greenhouse,[416] and a cowshed,[417] but not a structure for storing timber.[418] A right acquired under the section is an easement for the access of light to a building, not to a particular room within it.[419]

28–095   (2) EFFECT. The general effect of s.3, therefore, is that 20 years' enjoyment of light is equivalent to 40 years' enjoyment of any other easement.[420] But there are three important differences:

   (i) Section 3 says nothing of user as of right. Enjoyment by itself suffices, even though precarious,[421] unless the consent is in writing.

   (ii) Sections 7 and 8 are inapplicable, so that there are no disabilities which can be pleaded against a claim to light.

---

above, paras 7–098—7–100. The Law Commission's recent Report on the law of easements, profits and covenants does not recommend that the "next before action" requirement should be carried forward into its new statutory scheme: see Law Com No.327 (2011), paras 3.131 et seq.

[412] *Tehidy Minerals Ltd v Norman*, above, at 543, per Buckley L.J. See the recommendations of the Law Commission in Law Com No.327 (2011), paras 3.110 et seq.; see also Law Reform Committee, above, para.28–044.

[413] Law Com. No. 237 (2011); see above para 28–045.

[414] See above, para.28–061.

[415] *Ecclesiastical Commissioners for England v Kino* (1880) 14 Ch D 213.

[416] *Clifford v Holt* [1899] 1 Ch. 698: *Allen v Greenwood* [1980] Ch. 119.

[417] *Hyman v Van den Bergh* [1908] 1 Ch. 167.

[418] *Harris v De Pinna* (1886) 33 Ch D 238.

[419] *Carr-Saunders v Dick McNeil Associates Ltd* [1986] 1 W.L.R. 922 at 928.

[420] *Dalton v Angus & Co* (1881) 6 App.Cas. 740 at 800.

[421] *Colls v Home and Colonial Stores Ltd* [1904] A.C. 179 at 205.

(iii) No easement of light can be acquired over Crown land, for unlike ss.1 and 2, s.3 is not expressed to bind the Crown.[422]

In other respects, rights of light are governed by the same rules as other easements: the 20 years' period is that next before action,[423] and, subject to the Rights of Light Act 1959,[424] "interruption" has the same special meaning as in other cases.[425]

(3) USER AS OF RIGHT UNNECESSARY. The fact that user as of right is unnecessary in claims to light under the Act has far-reaching implications, for the whole basis of prescription is thus changed. For instance, the proviso that written consent defeats the claim is the only fragment of *nec vi, nec clam, nec precario* which is left in claims to light under the Act; oral consent is no bar,[426] even though evidenced by periodic payments.[427] From this there arises a crop of peculiarities connected with tenants. A tenant can acquire a right to light against his own landlord,[428] or against another tenant of his own landlord,[429] though in each case the landlord's reservation in the lease of a right to rebuild the adjoining property may amount to a consent in writing that will defeat the claim.[430] Where the easement is acquired against another tenant, and the lease of the servient land expires first, the easement binds the landlord and all subsequent occupiers.[431]

28–096

(4) WRITTEN CONSENT OR AGREEMENT. Whether an agreement satisfies the proviso to s.3, and thereby prevents the prescriptive acquisition of a right to light, is a matter of construction of the particular agreement in its legal context.[432] Where the terms of the claimant's lease, although not expressly referring to light, have the effect of rendering the enjoyment of light permissive or consensual or capable of being terminated or interfered with by the adjoining owner, that will suffice to preclude prescriptive acquisition.[433] However, where the servient owner merely undertook not to enforce his rights of light to the extent that they might be adversely affected by a particular

28–097

---

[422] *Wheaton v Maple & Co* [1893] 3 Ch. 48. This includes land held under Crown Leases. The wording also makes s.3 prevail against any custom to the contrary, e.g. against prescriptive rights of light in the City of London: *Perry v Eames* [1891] 1 Ch. 658 at 667; above, para.28–065.

[423] *Hyman v Van den Bergh* [1908] 1 Ch. 167.

[424] See below, paras 28–101 et seq.

[425] *Smith v Baxter* [1900] 2 Ch. 138.

[426] *London Corporation v Pewterers' Co* (1842) 2 Moo. & R. 409.

[427] *Plasterers' Co v Parish Clerks' Co* (1851) 6 Exch. 630.

[428] *Foster v Lyons & Co Ltd* [1927] 1 Ch. 219 at 227.

[429] *Morgan v Fear* [1907] A.C. 425. The older authorities were discussed in the Court of Appeal: see [1906] 2 Ch. 406.

[430] *Willoughby v Eckstein* [1937] Ch. 167 (landlord and tenant); *Blake & Lyons Ltd v Lewis Berger & Sons Ltd* [1951] 2 T.L.R. 605 (tenant and tenant).

[431] *Morgan v Fear*, above.

[432] *Marlborough (West End) Ltd v Wilks Head & Eve* Unreported December 20, 1996 (Lightman J.); *RHJ Ltd v FT Patten (Holdings) Ltd* [2007] 4 All E.R. 744 at [34]; on appeal [2008] EWCA Civ 151; [2008] Ch. 341 at [48]; *Salvage Wharf Ltd v G & S Brough Ltd* [2009] EWCA Civ 21; [2010] Ch. 11.

[433] *RHJ Ltd v FT Patten (Holdings) Ltd*, above.

development, whereby any diminution then contemplated would not be so substantial as to give rise to legitimate complaint, that did not amount to an abandonment of those rights engaging the proviso to s.3.[434]

28–098   (5) EASEMENTS ONLY IN FEE. Nevertheless, an easement for a term of years cannot be acquired by prescription even in the case of light. Thus where there was 20 years' enjoyment against a tenant of the Crown it was held that since the Crown could not be bound, so neither could the tenant.[435] It therefore seems that light must be acquired, if at all, in fee simple, even though user is against a tenant. Thus a common landlord will not only be bound if the lease of the servient land expires first: he will also benefit if the lease of the dominant land expires first. It is of course paradoxical that easements can arise both for and against the same fee simple reversion, but that is attributable to the strength of the words "absolute and indefeasible" when freed from the requirement of user as of right.

28–099   (6) UNITY OF POSSESSION. Another divergence appears, though somewhat darkly, in cases where there is unity of possession during the statutory period. In the case of easements other than light we have seen that this vitiates any claim under the Act.[436] In the case of light it has been said that unity of possession merely suspends the running of the period, so that enjoyment for 25 years can be successfully pleaded even though during that time there was five years' unity of possession.[437] The principle on which this distinction rests is obscure[438]; and it is difficult to see how it can be reconciled with s.4, requiring all periods to be those next before action.

28–100   (7) NO GRANT. It is clear that there is no presumption of a grant in the case of light.[439] Thus a right of light may be acquired under the 1832 Act against a corporation having no power of grant.[440] But it seems unlikely that the Act has by implication abolished claims to light under the doctrine of lost modern grant.[441]

28–101   *(b) Under the Rights of Light Act 1959.* This Act changed the law in a number of respects.[442] It extends to Crown land, though it preserves the Crown's immunity against claims to light under the Prescription Act 1832.[443]

---

[434] *Salvage Wharf Ltd v G & S Brough Ltd,* above.
[435] *Wheaton v Maple & Co* [1893] 3 Ch. 48.
[436] See above, para.28–070.
[437] *Ladyman v Grave* (1871) 6 Ch.App. 763.
[438] According to *Ladyman v Grave,* above, the same rule applies to all easements; but according to *Damper v Bassett* [1901] 2 Ch. 350 it is confined to light.
[439] *Tapling v Jones* (1865) 11 H.L.C. 290 at 304, 318.
[440] *Jordeson v Sutton, Southcoates & Drypool Gas Co* [1898] 2 Ch. 614 at 626 (aff'd [1899] 2 Ch. 217).
[441] *Marine & General Mutual Life Assurance v St James' Real Estate Co Ltd* [1991] 2 E.G.L.R. 178; Barnes & Bignell [2009] Conv. 474 at 481; above, para.28–090.
[442] It was enacted in response to the *Report of the Committee on Rights of Light,* 1958, Cmnd. 473. For a clear explanation of the origin and scheme of the Act, see *Bowring Services Ltd v Scottish Widows' Fund and Life Assurance Society* [1995] 1 E.G.L.R. 158 at 159.
[443] Rights of Light Act 1959 s.4; and see above, para.28–095.

In order to comprise an interruption for the purposes of the Act of 1832, there had to be a physical obstruction, lasting for at least a year, which was acquiesced in by the dominant owner.[444] Traditionally, those concerned at the acquisition of rights of light over their land by reason of prescription sought to interrupt the claimant's user by erecting screens and hoardings. Not only was this expensive, unsightly and cumbersome, it was also potentially subject to planning controls. The Act of 1959 provides for a surrogate obstruction in the form of the registration by the servient owner of a notice as a local land charge. The Upper Tribunal must first certify either that due notice has been given to those likely to be affected or that a temporary notice should be registered on grounds of exceptional urgency.[445] The notice, which must be in prescribed form,[446] must identify the servient land and the dominant building, and specify the position and size of an obstruction on the servient land to which the notice is intended to be equivalent.[447] It then takes effect, both under the Act of 1832 and otherwise, as if the access of light had in fact been so obstructed, and as if the obstruction had been both known to and acquiesced in by all concerned.[448]

The notice remains effective for one year unless before then it is cancelled **28–102** or, being temporary, expires.[449] While it is in force the dominant owner may sue for a declaration as if his light had actually been obstructed, and may claim cancellation or variation of the registration. For this purpose the dominant owner may treat his enjoyment as having begun one year earlier than it did, thus avoiding the problem of interruption during the final year of the period.[450] This provision may have the effect, for the claimant who plays his cards correctly, of reducing the prescriptive period from 20 years to 19[451]; and it has been forcefully contended that it is based on "an erroneous, or at least highly questionable, understanding" of the pre-existing law.[452]

---

[444] Prescription Act 1832 s.4; "The consequence of a sufficient and effective interruption is that the clock is turned back to zero": Barnes & Bignell [2009] Conv. 474 at 476.

[445] Rights of Light Act 1959 s.2(3). See Tribunal Procedure (Upper Tribunal) (Lands Chamber) Rules 2010 (SI 2010/2600) Pt 7.

[446] Local Land Charges Rules 1977 (SI 1977/985) r.10, Form A; and see above, para.8–107.

[447] Rights of Light Act 1959 s.2(2).

[448] Rights of Light Act 1959 s.3; and see above, para.28–071.

[449] Rights of Light Act 1959 s.3. See *Bowring Services Ltd v Scottish Widows' Fund and Life Assurance Society*, above at 161.

[450] Rights of Light Act 1959, s.3(4).

[451] See [1959] C.L.J. 184 (H.R.H.W.) This means that the servient owner who uses the notional obstruction process of the Act of 1959 is in a stronger position than one who erects a physical obstruction: see further Barnes & Bignell [2009] Conv. 474.

[452] Barnes & Bignell [2009] Conv. 474.

CHAPTER 29

ENFORCEMENT AND EXTINGUISHMENT OF EASEMENTS AND
PROFITS

A. Remedies for Infringement of Easements and Profits

29–001 Where an easement or profit is infringed, the claimant may commence legal proceedings, or, less commonly, seek to abate the nuisance that has arisen.

1. Easements

29–002 *(a) Action.* The claimant may seek damages, an injunction,[1] a declaration,[2] or any combination of these.[3] Trivial or temporary infringements will not justify an injunction.[4] But in other cases an injunction is a valuable remedy, for otherwise the servient owner could in effect make a compulsory purchase of the easement.[5] If damages are sought, some substantial interference with the enjoyment of the easement must be shown, and not merely injury to the servient land[6]; but proof of actual damage is not essential.[7] It is a defence to a claim for infringement that the defendant was acting in order to discharge a statutory obligation.[8]

29–003 Since the owner of an easement does not occupy the servient tenement in any sense, he has not the occupier's right of protection against third parties

---

[1] An injunction may be mandatory, requiring the defendant to demolish a building that he has erected: *Pugh v Howells* (1984) 48 P. & C.R. 298.

[2] *Litchfield-Speer v Queen Anne's Gate Syndicate (No.2) Ltd* [1919] 1 Ch. 407.

[3] *Leeds Industrial Co-operative Society Ltd v Slack* [1924] A.C. 851 at 857. See further, for remedies where a right of light is infringed, below, para.30–018.

[4] *Cowper v Laidler* [1903] 2 Ch. 337 at 341; *Pettey v Parsons* [1914] 1 Ch. 704 (reversed on another point [1914] 2 Ch. 653), where an injunction was refused, but £5 damages awarded for a "petty" infringement.

[5] *Dent v Auction Mart Co* (1866) L.R. 2 Eq. 238 at 246; *Pugh v Howells*, above, at 304.

[6] *Weston v Lawrence Weaver Ltd* [1961] 1 Q.B. 402; *Saint v Jenner* [1973] Ch. 275.

[7] *Nicholls v Ely Beet Sugar Factory Ltd (No.2)* [1936] Ch. 343 at 349.

[8] *Jones v Cleanthi* [2006] EWCA Civ 1712; [2007] 1 W.L.R. 1604 (servient owner obliged to build wall in order to comply with notice requiring works under Housing Act 1985 s.352), applying *Department of Transport v North West Water Authority* [1984] 1 A.C. 336.

without proof of title. In other words, in an action for infringement he must be prepared to prove his title even against a third party. If, for example, an artificial watercourse is polluted by someone other than the servient owner, it is a defence that there was no capable grantor of the right.[9] This is a case where title rests upon the concept of absolute ownership, not possessory rights, and where therefore the defendant may plead *jus tertii*.[10] This applies to the title to the easement, not to the title to the dominant tenement. Any occupier of the land to which an easement (already duly acquired) is appurtenant (e.g. a tenant for life[11] or years[12]) may sue for disturbance of his right without having to prove his title to the land,[13] unless the defendant himself claims title to that land. A reversioner may also sue if the interference is such as to injure the reversion, e.g. by withdrawal of support to a building, or obstruction of light.[14]

(b) Abatement. Provided that no more force is used than is reasonably **29–004** necessary,[15] that there is no injury to innocent third parties or the public,[16] and that the circumstances are not likely to lead to a breach of the peace,[17] the owner of the easement may abate any obstruction to its exercise without notice to the servient owner,[18] e.g. by breaking open a locked gate or removing boards interfering with his light. But the law does not favour abatement.[19]

2. Profits

(a) Action. The rules are the same as in the case of easements,[20] with one **29–005** notable exception. This is that a profit, by conferring a right to take something from the servient land, is held to give a sufficient degree of possession to enable the possessor to sue a third party for infringement without proving his title to the profit. Thus where a "several fishery" was injured by the discharge from a factory some miles upstream, it was held that the defendant could not

---

[9] *Paine & Co Ltd v St Neots Gas & Coke Co* [1939] 3 All E.R. 812. But see cases noted above, para.4–008, fn.39, which were not cited.

[10] For the rule against this defence in other cases, see above, para.4–010 and contrast the rule as to profits given below.

[11] *Simper v Foley* (1862) 2 J. & H. 555.

[12] *Fishenden v Higgs & Hill Ltd* (1935) 153 L.T. 128.

[13] Gale 14–15; cf. *William Aldred's Case* (1610) 9 Co.Rep. 57b. fn. A.

[14] Gale 14–17 et seq.

[15] *Hill v Cock* (1872) 26 L.T. 185 at 186.

[16] *Roberts v Rose* (1865) L.R. 1 Ex. 82 at 89.

[17] *Davies v Williams* (1851) 16 Q.B. 546 (e.g. demolition of an occupied dwelling house).

[18] See *Perry v Fitzhowe* (1846) 8 Q.B. 757. This and the previous case were cases on profits, but in this respect the same law applies to easements: see *Lane v Capsey* [1891] 3 Ch. 411. In practice it will always be prudent to give notice first.

[19] *Lagan Navigation Co v Lambeg Bleaching, Dyeing and Finishing Co Ltd* [1927] A.C. 226 at 244.

[20] See e.g. *Fitzgerald v Firbank* [1897] 2 Ch. 96 at 102 (damages); *Peech v Best* [1931] 1 K.B. 1 (declaration).

dispute the plaintiff's title and so plead *jus tertii*.[21] This exception is connected with the doctrine that a profit, unlike an easement, may exist in gross.[22] Had the action been against the servient owner, it would have been open to him to contest the title; but a mere stranger cannot contest the title of a person in possession.[23]

29–006   *(b) Abatement.* This remedy (e.g. pulling down a fence or house which has been erected to the detriment of a profit of pasture) is governed by the same principles as in the case of easements.[24]

B. *Extinguishment of Easements and Profits à Prendre*

29–007   **1. By statute.** There is no statutory procedure for the discharge or modification of obsolete or obstructive easements or profits, although the Law Commission has now recommended that the jurisdiction of the Lands Chamber of the Upper Tribunal in relation to restrictive covenants[25] should be extended to bring easements and profits within its scope.[26] Until recently, there were statutory methods of extinguishment peculiar to commons (namely approvement, inclosure or under the Commons Registration Act 1965)[27] but these methods have now been abolished by the Commons Act 2006.[28] Certain statutory powers permit the extinguishment of easements and similar rights.[29] In the event of compulsory purchase of the servient land, such rights which are not extinguished (by statute or by agreement) may be overridden by statute.[30] As a result of legislative amendment promoted by the Law Commission,[31] the statutory immunity conferred on the acquiring authority from liability for interference is effective in relation both to the carrying out of the intended works and to the subsequent use of the land.[32]

29–008   **2. By express release.** At law a deed is required for an express release of an easement or profit.[33] In equity, however, an informal release will be

---

[21] *Nicholls v Ely Beet Sugar Factory Ltd (No.1)* [1931] 2 Ch. 84. For *jus tertii*, see above, para.4–010.

[22] See *Paine & Co Ltd v St Neots Gas & Coke Co* [1939] 3 All E.R. 812 at 823, per Luxmoore L.J. In *Mason v Clarke* [1954] 1 Q.B. 460 at 470, Denning L.J. appears to deny that a claim to a profit may be based on a possessory title, but the decision was reversed by the House of Lords: [1955] A.C. 778, esp. at 794, per Viscount Simonds.

[23] See above, para.4–008, for discussion of this principle.

[24] *Arlett v Ellis* (1827) 7 B. & C. 346, (1829) 9 B. & C. 671; *Davies v Williams* (1851) 16 Q.B. 546.

[25] LPA 1925 s.84, on which see below, para.32–085.

[26] Law Com. No.327 (2011), paras 7.27 et seq.

[27] See the sixth edition of this work at paras 18–177 et seq.

[28] See above, para.27–058 et seq.

[29] See Housing Act 1985 s.295; Town and Country Planning Act 1990 s.236; Regional Development Agencies Act 1998 ss.19, 20 and Sch.6.

[30] Town and Country Planning Act 1990 s.237, as amended by Planning Act 2008 Sch.9 para.4.

[31] Law Com. No.291 (2004), paras 8.2–8.39.

[32] *Thames Water Utilities Ltd v Oxford City Council* [1999] 1 E.G.L.R. 167 has been prospectively overruled; see further Law Com. CP No.186 (2008), paras 5.4 et seq.

[33] Co.Litt. p.264b; *Lovell v Smith* (1857) 3 C.B. (N.S.) 120 at 127; but see *Norbury v Meade* (1821) 3 Bli. 211 at 241, 242 (easement).

effective provided it would be inequitable for the dominant owner to claim that the right still exists,[34] as where he has orally consented to his light being obstructed and the servient owner has spent money on erecting the obstruction.[35] A release of a portion of a common appurtenant extinguishes the whole common,[36] but this does not apply to a several profit appurtenant.[37]

3. By implied release

(a) *Abandonment.* Abandonment of an easement or profit will not be lightly **29–009** inferred.[38] An owner of property does not normally wish to divest himself of it even though he may have no present use for it.[39] Mere non-user will not of itself suffice therefore,[40] even if accompanied by a mistaken belief that the right has been extinguished.[41] It must be proved[42] that the person having the right intends to abandon it,[43] that is, that neither he nor any of his successors in title intends thereafter to exercise it.[44] "It is one thing not to assert an intention to use a way, and another thing to assert an intention to abandon it."[45] While it was once thought that non-user for a continuous period of 20 years gave rise to a presumption of abandonment,[46] this is no longer the law[47]; although the Law Commission has recommended that there should be a rebuttable presumption in such circumstances.[48]

---

[34] *Davies v Marshall* (1861) 10 C.B. (N.S.) 697 at 710.

[35] *Waterlow v Bacon* (1866) L.R. 2 Eq. 514.

[36] *Miles v Etteridge* (1690) 1 Show.K.B. 349.

[37] *Johnson v Barnes* (1873) L.R. 8 C.P. 527.

[38] *Huckvale v Aegean Hotels Ltd* (1989) 58 P. & C.R. 163 at 171, 173; *Snell & Prideaux Ltd v Dutton Mirrors Ltd* [1995] 1 E.G.L.R. 259 at 261. Abandonment, where it is established, may be partial and not total (semble): *Snell & Prideaux Ltd v Dutton Mirrors Ltd*, at 261. For the view that the true basis of abandonment is a form of estoppel, see [1995] Conv. 291 (C. J. Davis).

[39] *Gotobed v Pridmore* (1971) 217 E.G. 759 at 760; *Benn v Hardinge* (1992) 66 P. & C.R. 246 at 257, 262; *Bosomworth v Faber* (1992) 69 P. & C.R. 288 at 294; *CDC 2020 Plc v Ferreira* [2005] EWCA Civ 611; [2005] 3 E.G.L.R. 15 at [24].

[40] *Ward v Ward* (1852) 7 Exch. 838 at 839; *Re Yateley Common* [1977] 1 W.L.R. 840 at 845; *Llewellyn (deceased) v Lorey* [2011] EWCA Civ 37; [2011] N.P.C. 14 at [31]. For an extreme case, see *Treweeke v 36 Wolseley Road Pty Ltd* (1973) 128 C.L.R. 274 (way survives despite vertical rock faces, impenetrable bamboo plantations, swimming pool and fence).

[41] *Obadia v Morris* (1974) 232 E.G. 333.

[42] The onus lies on the party asserting abandonment: *Re Yateley Common*, above, at 845.

[43] *Swan v Sinclair* [1924] 1 Ch. 254, aff'd [1925] A.C. 227; but see below, para.29–013, fn.62.

[44] *Gotobed v Pridmore*, above, at 760; *Tehidy Minerals Ltd v Norman* [1971] 2 Q.B. 528 at 553; *Williams v Usherwood* (1981) 45 P. & C.R. 235 at 256; *Lovett v Fairclough* (1990) 61 P. & C.R. 385 at 400; *Snell & Prideaux Ltd v Dutton Mirrors Ltd*, above; *CDC 2020 Plc v Ferreira*, above, at [37].

[45] *James v Stevenson* [1893] A.C. 162 at 168, per Sir Edward Fry.

[46] *Crossley & Sons Ltd v Lightowler* (1867) 2 Ch.App. 478 at 482.

[47] *Benn v Hardinge*, above, rejecting a statement to the contrary in the fifth edition of this work at p.898. In that case, 175 years' non-user was held not to amount to abandonment when there was no substantial physical change to the servient tenement and no obstacle to the exercise of the right. See too *Gotobed v Pridmore*, above (abandonment not inferred from 65 years' non-user).

[48] Law Com. No.327 (2011), paras 3.212 et seq; and see further discussion in Law Com. CP No.186 (2008), paras 5.14 et seq.

29–010   It is a question of fact whether an act was intended as an abandonment.[49] Grazing rights have been held not to be abandoned merely by the commoners making temporary arrangements for regulating their rights, even if this is accompanied by payments to the servient owner[50]; and the bricking-up of a door for over 30 years was held no abandonment of a right of way.[51] On the other hand, replacing a wall containing windows by a blank wall was held to be an abandonment of light after 17 years.[52] However, in that case the servient owner had meanwhile erected buildings which would have obstructed the former lights, and the presumption of abandonment is naturally stronger where the dominant owner has allowed the servient owner to incur expense without any protest.[53] The court will be reluctant to find such an intention unless there has been some fundamental change to the dominant tenement.[54]

29–011   Alterations to the dominant tenement which make the enjoyment of an easement or profit impossible or unnecessary may show an intent to abandon the right. Thus, if a mill to which an easement of water is appurtenant is demolished without any intent to replace it, the easement is released[55]; and a profit of pasture appurtenant will be extinguished if the dominant land becomes part of a town, or a reservoir, but not if the altered land could easily be turned to the purpose of feeding cattle.[56] The demolition of a house to which an easement of light is appurtenant may amount to an implied release, but not if it is intended to replace the house by another building.[57] It is not essential that the new windows should occupy exactly the same positions as the old, provided they receive substantially the same light[58]; the test is identity of light, not identity of aperture.[59]

29–012   An alteration to the servient tenement may bring about an extinguishment if it is acquiesced in by the dominant owner[60] or if it is made to give effect to an agreement between the dominant and servient owners to replace the existing right with a new one.[61]

---

[49] *Cook v Mayor and Corporation of Bath* (1868) L.R. 6 Eq. 177 at 179.

[50] *Tehidy Minerals Ltd v Norman* [1971] 2 Q.B. 528.

[51] *Cook v Mayor and Corporation of Bath* (1868) L.R. 6 Eq. 177. See too *Carder v Davies* (1998) 76 P. & C.R. D33 (right to use roadway with no limit as to point of access not abandoned when one entry point was built over).

[52] *Moore v Rawson* (1824) 3 B. & C. 332.

[53] *Cook v Mayor and Corporation of Bath*, above, at 179; cf. *Waterlow v Bacon* (1866) L.R. 2 Eq. 514.

[54] *Re Yateley Common* [1977] 1 W.L.R. 840 at 848.

[55] *Liggins v Inge* (1831) 7 Bing. 682 at 693; and see *National Guaranteed Manure Co Ltd v Donald* (1859) 4 H. & N. 8 (canal converted into railway: right to water for canal extinguished).

[56] *Carr v Lambert* (1866) L.R. 1 Ex. 168.

[57] *Ecclesiastical Commissioners for England v Kino* (1880) 14 Ch D 213.

[58] *Scott v Pape* (1886) 31 Ch D 554.

[59] *Andrews v Waite* [1907] 2 Ch. 500 at 510. These rules apply equally to alterations made while the light is being acquired: *Andrews v Waite* at 509.

[60] *Scrutton v Stone* (1893) 9 T.L.R. 478 (pasture claimed over land which had become covered with buildings).

[61] *Bosomworth v Faber* (1992) 69 P. & C.R. 288 (new tank and pipes for taking water from the plaintiff's land pursuant to a written licence held to extinguish existing easement).

(b) Effect of excessive user. It has been suggested that if the burden of the **29–013** easement is substantially increased, the right may thereupon be extinguished altogether,[62] but it is thought that this is only the case where continuous easements, such as rights of light or support, are concerned.[63] Excessive use of an easement will render the dominant owner liable in nuisance.[64] The servient owner is then entitled to an injunction to restrain the excessive use.[65] The grant of an injunction does not extinguish or suspend the easement itself,[66] and once the dominant owner reverts to a lawful use, the prior excessive use will become irrelevant.[67] The servient owner may obstruct the exercise of an easement where it is being used excessively, and where "it is impossible to sever the good user from the excessive user."[68] An increase in the intensity of use of the dominant land, even if it is substantial, resulting in a concomitant increase in the use of the easement, does not in itself render the use excessive.[69] Nor will a change in the use of, or the erection of new buildings upon, the dominant land affect the dominant owner's right to use the easement unless it affects the nature or extent of the use of the easement to the prejudice of the servient owner.[70]

C. By Unity of Ownership and Possession

If the dominant and servient tenements come into the ownership and posses- **29–014** sion of the same person, any easement or profit is extinguished.[71] Unity of possession without unity of ownership is not enough[72]; and unity of ownership means acquisition of both tenements for a fee simple absolute.[73] If there is only unity of possession the right is merely suspended until the unity of

---

[62] "An easement is extinguished when its mode of user is so altered as to cause prejudice to the servient tenement": *Ray v Fairway Motors (Barnstaple) Ltd* (1968) 20 P. & C.R. 261 at 266, per Willmer L.J. (easement of support extinguishable, irrespective of intention, by greatly increasing weight on dominant land—though this was not proved on the facts). See too *Ankerson v Connelly* [1906] 2 Ch. 544, aff'd [1907] 1 Ch. 678 (easement of light for aperture in partly-open shed extinguished by enclosing shed and shutting out all other light).

[63] But see *Woodhouse v Consolidated Property Corporation Ltd* (1992) 66 P. & C.R. 234 at 243 (material alteration to the nature of use required to extinguish easement of support).

[64] Gale 6–94, as approved in *McAdams Homes Ltd v Robinson* [2004] EWCA Civ 214; [2005] 1 P. & C.R. 30 at [27].

[65] *Jelbert v Davis* [1968] 1 W.L.R. 589; *Hamble PC v Haggard* [1992] 1 W.L.R. 122 at 134.

[66] *Graham v Philcox* [1984] Q.B. 747.

[67] *Graham v Philcox*, above, at 756.

[68] *Hamble PC v Haggard*, above, at 134, per Millett J.

[69] *McAdams Homes Ltd v Robinson* [2004] EWCA Civ 214; [2005] 1 P. & C.R. 30 at [24] (the court was considering the effect of change of use upon an easement granted by implication.)

[70] *McAdams Homes Ltd v Robinson*, above, at [29]; see Law Com. CP No.186 (2008), paras 5.32–5.63.

[71] *Tyrringham's Case* (1584) 4 Co. Rep. 36b at 38a (profit); *Buckby v Coles* (1814) 5 Taunt. 311 (easement). See (1977) 41 Conv. (N.S.) 107 (J. D. A. Brooke-Taylor). cf. *Re Tiltwood, Sussex* [1978] Ch. 269 (restrictive covenants), below, para.32–084.

[72] *Canham v Fisk* (1831) 2 Cr. & J. 126; and see *Thomas v Thomas* (1835) 2 Cr.M. & R. 34 at 40.

[73] Gale 12–02; *R. v Inhabitants of Hermitage* (1692) Carth. 239 at 241 (union of base fee with fee simple absolute works no extinguishment).

possession ceases.[74] If there is only unity of ownership the right continues until there is also unity of possession.[75] Thus if both dominant and servient tenements are under lease, the easement or profit will not be extinguished merely because both leases are assigned to X,[76] or both reversions to Y[77]; but if both leases and both reversions become vested in Z, the right is gone. Similarly, if the fee simple owner of one tenement takes a lease of the other, the right is merely suspended during the lease.[78]

29–015   A common appurtenant has been held to be wholly extinguished if the dominant owner acquires any part of the servient tenement, since otherwise the remainder of the servient tenement would be unduly burdened.[79] But in the case of a common appendant the burden was apportioned,[80] and much may be said for extending this more liberal rule to commons appurtenant.[81]

29–016   In its recent Report, the Law Commission has considered two practical difficulties that arise as a result of the rule that the dominant and servient tenements must not be owned and occupied by the same person.[82] The first problem is that the owner of a plot who wishes to sell part cannot, prior to the sale, create an easement that benefits one part and burdens the other. This causes particular difficulties for developments of large residential estates where it is intended to sell off the individual plots as and when they are completed.[83] The second problem is that if the dominant tenement is purchased by the servient owner, in circumstances where he then becomes entitled to possession of both plots, the easement will cease to exist. Where both plots are registered, although the easement will be extinguished, it will usually remain on the register, and guaranteed by Land Registry, thereby giving rise to potential liability for Land Registry's indemnity fund. In order to resolve these difficulties, the Law Commission has recommended that where title to the dominant and servient tenements are registered, the fact that they are in common ownership and possession should no longer prevent the creation, or continued existence, of easements or profits.[84]

---

[74] *Canham v Fisk*, above.
[75] *Richardson v Graham* [1908] 1 K.B. 39. For this reason "unity of seisin" is not a satisfactory term for the unity of both ownership and possession which is required.
[76] *Thomas v Thomas*, above.
[77] *Richardson v Graham*, above. This was a case on light, and it is not clear whether the decision was founded on the peculiar nature of the easement of light, or the doctrine of non-derogation from grant (above, para.27–046). In principle the rule should be the same for all easements. cf. *Buckby v Coles* (1814) 5 Taunt. 311 at 315, 316.
[78] *Simper v Foley* (1862) 2 J. & H. 555 at 563.
[79] *White v Taylor* [1969] 1 Ch. 150.
[80] *Wyat Wyld's Case* (1609) 8 Co.Rep. 78b.
[81] Consider *Benson v Chester* (1799) 8 T.R. 396 at 401.
[82] Law Com. No.327 (2011), paras 4.19 et seq.
[83] For practical illustration, see Law Com. No.327 (2011), paras 4.25 et seq. There is an additional problem in relation to mortgages of part: see ibid., paras 4.34 et seq.
[84] Law Com. No.327 (2011), para.4.44.

CHAPTER 30

SPECIES OF EASEMENTS AND PROFITS

A. Rights of Way

1. Extent of easements of way

(a) General or limited. An easement of way may be either general or **30–001** limited. A general right of way is one which may be used by the owner of the dominant tenement and his visitors[1] at any time and in any way. A limited right of way is one which is restricted in some respect. The restriction may be as to time, e.g. it can be used only in the daytime[2]; or it may be as to the mode in which the way can be used, e.g. a way limited to pedestrians,[3] or to cattle and other animals in charge of a drover,[4] or to wheeled traffic,[5] and the like.

(b) Other land. A right of way can normally be used only as a means of **30–002** access to the dominant tenement. The rule in *Harris v Flower* states that "if a right of way be granted for the enjoyment of close A, the grantee, because he owns or acquires close B, cannot use the way in substance for passing over close A to close B."[6] If, however, Plot A is used as a means of access to Plot B at the time of the grant, the grant would normally be construed, subject to contrary intention being expressed, so as to permit access to Plot B.[7] The mere

---

[1] *Jalnarne Ltd v Ridewood* (1989) 61 P. & C.R. 143 at 160; *Re St Martin le Grand, York* [1990] Fam. 63 at 78 et seq.; *Moncrieff v Jamieson* [2007] UKHL 42; [2007] 1 W.L.R. 2620 at 2632.
[2] *Collins v Slade* (1874) 23 W.R. 199; cf. *Hollins v Verney* (1884) 13 QBD 304 (right of way to remove timber cut every 12 years).
[3] *Cousens v Rose* (1871) L.R. 12 Eq. 366 ("foot-passengers").
[4] *Brunton v Hall* (1841) 1 Q.B. 792.
[5] *Ballard v Dyson* (1808) 1 Taunt. 279.
[6] *Harris v Flower* (1904) 74 L.J. Ch. 127 at 132 per Romer L.J.; *Colchester v Roberts* (1839) 4 M. & W. 769 at 774; *Skull v Glenister* (1864) 16 C.B. (N.S.) 81. See further *Bracewell v Appleby* [1975] Ch. 408; *Alvis v Harrison* (1990) 62 P. & C.R. 10 at 15; *Jobson v Record* [1998] 1 E.G.L.R. 113. cf. *Britel Developments (Thatcham) Ltd v Nightfreight (G.B.) Ltd* [1998] 4 All E.R. 432.
[7] *Nickerson v Barraclough* [1980] Ch. 325 at 336, not affected on appeal [1981] Ch. 426 (implied grant under LPA 1925 s.62).

fact that Plot B is added to Plot A, so that the dominant tenement is enlarged, will not necessarily destroy a right of way previously appurtenant to Plot A.[8] This depends on whether the user for the purposes of Plot B is merely "ancillary" to the user for the purposes of Plot A.[9] Use of the right of way to go on to Plot B can be ancillary where it is insubstantial (e.g. going on to Plot B for a picnic[10]) or where it does not benefit Plot B (i.e. it does not enlarge the dominant tenement).[11] However, using the right of way for access to farm two fields only one of which had the benefit of the easement could not be described as ancillary, as one or two more annual visits were involved than would otherwise have been necessary.[12] In another case, a right of way conferring access to a dwelling-house on Plot A could not be used in order to reach a parking area on Plot B, as this would be a substantial use of the way for the benefit of land outside the dominant tenement.[13] The rule in *Harris v Flower* does not preclude the grant of a right of way to part of the dominant tenement being construed as a grant for the benefit of the whole of that tenement.[14]

30–003   *(c) Construction and repair.* Liability to construct or to repair the way once constructed primarily depends upon the terms of the grant or reservation. In the absence of express stipulation,[15] or special circumstances,[16] the following rules apply.[17] There is no obligation on the grantor to construct the way, and the grantee may enter the servient land for purposes of construction if necessary to make the grant effective.[18] Once the way exists, neither the servient owner nor the dominant owner is liable to maintain or repair it, but either owner is entitled to maintain and repair should they choose to do so.[19]

---

[8] *Graham v Philcox* [1984] Q.B. 747; but see *National Trust v White* [1987] 1 W.L.R. 907 at 913, treating *Graham v Philcox* as an authority only on LPA 1925 s.62(2) (by which a conveyance includes all easements appertaining to the land "or any part thereof"); [1987] Conv. 363 (J. E. Martin); Gale 9–37.

[9] *Harris v Flower* (1904) 74 L.J. Ch. 127 at 132; *National Trust v White*, above (car park merely ancillary to right of way to iron age hill fort); *Massey v Boulden* [2002] EWCA Civ 1634; [2003] 1 W.L.R. 1792 at [45]; *Wall v Collins* [2007] EWCA Civ 444; [2007] Ch. 390 at [50] et seq.; and see Law Com. CP No.186, paras 5.64 et seq.

[10] *Peacock v Custins* [2002] 1 W.L.R. 1815 at [22].

[11] *Macepark (Whittlebury) Ltd v Sargeant* [2003] EWHC 427 (Ch); [2003] 1 W.L.R. 2284 at 2289.

[12] *Peacock v Custins*, above.

[13] *Das v Linden Mews Ltd* [2002] EWCA Civ 590; [2003] 2 P. & C.R. 4.

[14] *Callard v Beeney* [1930] 1 K.B. 353.

[15] *Taylor v Whitehead* (1781) 2 Doug.K.B. 745 at 749. The contrary agreement may be implied rather than express: *Liverpool City Council v Irwin* [1977] A.C. 239; *King v South North-amptonshire DC* (1991) 64 P. & C.R. 35.

[16] *Miller v Hancock* [1893] 2 Q.B. 177, not affected on this point by *Fairman v Perpetual Investment BS* [1923] A.C. 74.

[17] *Carter v Cole* [2006] EWCA Civ 398; [2006] N.P.C. 46 at [8].

[18] *Newcomen v Coulson* (1877) 5 Ch D 133; *Stokes v Mixconcrete (Holdings) Ltd* (1978) 38 P. & C.R. 488. Lord Upjohn's denial of this right in *Redland Bricks Ltd v Morris* [1970] A.C. 652 at 665 seems to have been *per incuriam*.

[19] *Transco Plc v Stockport Metropolitan Borough Council* [2003] UKHL 61 at [80]; [2004] 2 A.C. 1 at 30. For an unusual case where the parties were contesting entitlement to repair (as opposed to liability to repair), see *Carter v Cole*, above.

The dominant owner has the right to enter the servient land in order to carry out necessary repairs in a reasonable manner.[20] The benefit of a covenant to repair the way may run with the easement,[21] but as such a covenant is positive, the burden cannot run with the servient land.[22] If the way becomes impassable, there is no right to deviate from it[23] unless the servient owner has obstructed it.[24] A limited right of way cannot be converted into a general right of way by improving it.[25]

(d) *Interference.* Although any obstruction of a public way is actionable per **30–004** se, no action will lie in respect of a private right of way unless the interference with its exercise is substantial.[26] This will be the case only where the act or conduct interferes with the reasonable use of the right of way.[27] The test of an actionable interference is not whether what the dominant owner is left with is reasonable, but whether his insistence on being able to continue to use the whole of what was contracted for is reasonable.[28] The dominant owner may prefer to use the way in a particular manner and, provided such preference is neither unreasonable nor perverse, such preference should be respected.[29] It follows that the servient owner has no right to alter the route of a right of way unless such a right has been expressly or impliedly conferred on him either by the grant or reservation of the easement or by subsequent agreement.[30] Such an alteration would normally be an actionable interference, even if it is equally convenient to the servient owner, but the existence of such an alternative route may be reflected in the remedy awarded by the court.[31] In highly exceptional

[20] *Taylor v Whitehead* (1781) 2 Doug. K.B. 745; *Jones v Pritchard* [1908] 1 Ch. 630 at 638.

[21] *Gaw v Coras Iompair Eireann* [1953] I.R. 232; contrast *Grant v Edmondson* [1931] 1 Ch. 1 (rentcharge: below, para.31–029).

[22] See below, para.32–017. If, as a matter of construction, use of the right of way is conditional on the payment of the costs of maintenance and repair, the dominant owner may not exercise the right until payment is made: *Carter v Cole* [2006] EWCA Civ 398 at [16] and [30], applying the principle in *Halsall v Brizell* (see further below, para.32–025).

[23] *Bullard v Harrison* (1815) 4 M. & S. 387.

[24] *Selby v Nettlefold* (1873) 9 Ch.App. 111.

[25] *Mills v Silver* [1991] Ch. 271. Although the dominant owner may improve the land, in doing so he may "not substantially alter the nature of the road nor otherwise prejudice the servient tenement": *Alvis v Harrison* (1990) 62 P. & C.R. 10 at 15, per Lord Jauncey.

[26] *Pettey v Parsons* [1914] 2 Ch. 653 at 662; *Siggery v Bell* [2007] EWHC 2167 (Ch). "The plaintiff cannot complain, unless he can prove an obstruction which injures him": *Thorpe v Brumfitt* (1873) 8 Ch.App. 650 at 656, per James L.J. Whether the servient owner may maintain a locked gate and provide a key to the dominant owner as and when use of the way is required is a question of construction of the grant: *Guest Estates Ltd v Milner's Safes Ltd* [1911] 28 T.L.R. 59; *Dawes v Adela Estates Ltd* (1970) 216 E.G. 1405; *Siggery v Bell*, above.

[27] *Keefe v Amor* [1965] 1 Q.B. 334 at 347, per Russell L.J.; *Celsteel Ltd v Alton House Holdings Ltd* [1985] 1 W.L.R. 204 at 216; *West v Sharp* (2000) 79 P. & C.R. 327 at 332.

[28] *B & Q Plc v Liverpool and Lancashire Properties Ltd* (2001) 81 P. & C.R. 20 at [45].

[29] *B & Q Plc v Liverpool and Lancashire Properties Ltd*, above.

[30] *Greenwich Healthcare NHS Trust v London and Quadrant Housing Trust* [1998] 1 W.L.R. 1749.

[31] *Greenwich Healthcare NHS Trust v London and Quadrant Housing Trust*, above; *Heslop v Bishton* [2009] EWHC 607 (Ch); [2009] 2 E.G.L.R. 11.

circumstances, there may be an actionable interference as a result of an act on land adjacent to the servient tenement such as the erection of a structure which substantially affects the exercise of the right of way.[32]

30–005 **2. Effect of mode of acquisition.** The extent of an easement of way depends upon the manner of its acquisition.

(a) Express grant or reservation. Here the question is primarily one of determining the intention of the parties as a matter of construction from the words of the grant read in the light of the surrounding circumstances at the time that the grant was made.[33] The rules of construction, as already explained,[34] are that in case of doubt:

(i) the grant of an easement is construed against the person making it in accordance with the general rule[35]; but

(ii) the reservation of an easement is treated as if it were still made by means of a grant and regrant and is construed against the owner of the servient tenement.[36]

30–006 Rights of way are often granted in very wide terms, e.g. "at all times and for all purposes". Even without such words the right, if granted in general terms, is not confined to the purpose for which the land is used at the time of the grant, but may be used for any other lawful purpose.[37] Nor is it to be confined to use only when other available routes are not reasonably practicable.[38] A right of way for general purposes granted as appurtenant to a house can be used for the business of a hotel (though not enlarged[39]) if that house is subsequently converted into a hotel.[40] A right of way over a strip of land 20 feet wide approached by a narrow gap may be exercisable over the whole width when later the gap is widened.[41] A right of way expressed to be

---

[32] *Waterman v Boyle* [2009] EWCA Civ 115; [2009] 2 E.G.L.R. 7 at [20] et seq.

[33] *St. Edmundsbury & Ipswich Diocesan Board of Finance v Clark (No.2)* [1975] 1 W.L.R. 468 at 477; *Investors Compensation Scheme Ltd v West Bromwich Building Society* [1998] 1 W.L.R. 896 at 912; *Mobil Oil Co Ltd v Birmingham CC* [2001] EWCA Civ 1608; [2002] 2 P. & C.R. 14 at [24] and [62]; *Brooks v Young* [2008] EWCA Civ 816; [2008] 3 E.G.L.R. 27 at [12]; *Davill v Pull* [2009] EWCA Civ 1309; [2010] 1 P. & C.R. 23 at p.448; *Carpenter v Calico Quays Ltd* [2011] EWHC 96 (Ch) at [23]; *Alford v Hannaford* [2011] EWCA Civ 1099 at [11] et seq.

[34] See above, para.28–010.

[35] *Williams v James* (1867) L.R. 2 C.P. 577 at 581.

[36] See above, paras 28–010 and 28–011.

[37] *South Eastern Ry v Cooper* [1924] 1 Ch. 211; *Jalnarne Ltd v Ridewood* (1989) 61 P. & C.R. 143 at 157; *Alvis v Harrison*, above, at 15; *Davill v Pull*, above, at p.449 et seq.

[38] *Brooks v Young*, above, at [14].

[39] *White v Grand Hotel, Eastbourne, Ltd* [1913] 1 Ch. 113 at 116.

[40] *White v Grand Hotel, Eastbourne, Ltd*, above (aff'd 84 L.J.Ch. 938). See also *Robinson v Bailey* [1948] 2 All E.R. 791 (way to building plot held to cover business user).

[41] *Keefe v Amor* [1965] 1 Q.B. 334.

exercisable over a "roadway" could be enjoyed over the roadside verges as well as the tarmac surface of the road.[42] A vehicular right of way may include an ancillary right to halt and load or unload,[43] and even a right to park,[44] but only where it would be reasonably necessary (and not merely desirable) to do so for the duration of the user's visit to the property.[45] A right of way "with or without vehicles" granted in a conveyance which expressly reserved to the grantor a right of way "with or without vehicles *or animals*" did not confer the right to drive livestock along the track.[45a] A right to cross a railway line "with all manner of cattle" may be a right of way for all purposes and not confined to agricultural purposes.[46] But where the servient owner is liable to repair the way, user may not be increased so as to add to that liability.[47] A way granted as appurtenant to an open space *as such* cannot be used as a means of access to a cottage subsequently built on it.[48] Nor, of course, can a way be used so as to infringe the rights of others entitled to use it.[49] Where a right of way is granted "for all purposes" in common with other persons, the exercise of that right must not interfere unreasonably with the use by the others so entitled.[50]

If a way is granted "as at present enjoyed", prima facie these words refer **30–007** to the quality of the user (e.g. on foot or with vehicles) and do not limit the quantity of the user to that existing at the time of the grant.[51] In case of difficulty, as where there is a simple grant or reservation of "a right of way", the surrounding circumstances must be considered.[52] Thus both the condition of the way (e.g. whether it is a footpath or a metalled road) and the nature of the dominant tenement (e.g. whether it is a dwelling-house or a factory) may

[42] *Carpenter v Calico Quays Ltd* [2011] EWHC 96 (Ch) (in light of the circumstances, as the express words of the grant were not themselves conclusive).

[43] *Bulstrode v Lambert* [1953] 1 W.L.R. 1064; *McIlraith v Grady* [1968] 1 Q.B. 468. Each case depends upon the true construction of the grant: see *Todrick v Western National Omnibus Co Ltd* [1934] Ch. 561; *London and Suburban Land and Building Co (Holdings) Ltd v Carey* (1991) 62 P. & C.R. 480; *B & Q plc v Liverpool and Lancashire Properties Ltd* (2001) 81 P. & C.R. 20. The right to unload may include the right to adequate "swing space" overhead and alongside: see *V.T. Engineering Ltd v Richard Barland & Co Ltd* (1968) 19 P. & C.R. 890.

[44] *Moncrieff v Jamieson* [2007] 1 W.L.R. 2620. This was, however, a case which "turned on its special facts": see *Waterman v Boyle* [2009] EWCA Civ 115; [2009] 2 E.G.L.R. 7 at [34] per Arden L.J.

[45] *Waterman v Boyle*, above at [24] et seq (as transfer of dominant land contained express grant of parking rights on dedicated spaces, parking elsewhere could not satisfy test of reasonable necessity).

[45a] *Alford v Hannaford* [2011] EWCA Civ 1099.

[46] *British Railways Board v Glass* [1965] Ch. 538; cf. *White v Richards* [1993] R.T.R. 318.

[47] *T.R.H. Sampson Associates Ltd v British Railways Board* [1983] 1 W.L.R. 170 (Board liable for repair of bridge).

[48] *Allan v Gomme* (1840) 11 A. & E. 759; cf. *Graham v Philcox* [1984] Q.B. 747.

[49] *Jelbert v Davis* [1968] 1 W.L.R. 589 (user of way for 200-caravan site).

[50] *Rosling v Pinnegar* (1986) 54 P. & C.R. 124 (user of way by coaches bringing visitors to see mansion excessive).

[51] *Hurt v Bowmer* [1937] 1 All E.R. 797.

[52] *St Edmundsbury & Ipswich Diocesan Board of Finance v Clark (No.2)* [1975] 1 W.L.R. 468; *Russell v Finn* [2003] EWCA Civ 399 at [20] et seq.

be of assistance in determining whether any vehicles, and if so, which, may use the way.[53]

30–008 *(b) Implied grant or reservation.* A way of necessity is limited to the necessity existing at the time the right arose. Thus if an encircled plot is used for agricultural purposes at the time of the grant, the way of necessity over the surrounding land is limited to agricultural purposes and cannot be used for transporting building materials.[54]

In other cases of implied grant the circumstances of the case must be considered. Where a testator devised adjoining plots of land to different persons, and one plot was bought by a railway company for conversion into a railway station, it was held that a way which had been used in the testator's lifetime for domestic purposes and for the purposes of warehouses on the land could not be used as a public approach to the station.[55]

30–009 *(c) Prescription.* Where an easement of way is acquired by long user, "the right acquired must be measured by the extent of the enjoyment which is proved".[56] Thus a way acquired by long user for farming purposes cannot be used for mineral purposes,[57] or for a camping ground,[58] or for the cartage of building materials.[59] It has been held that user during the prescriptive period as a carriageway does not authorise the driving of cattle[60]; but it covers user as a footway[61] (since prima facie the greater includes the less[62]) and it extends to user for motor traffic even if the user proved was for horse-drawn vehicles alone, for the right is essentially a right for vehicles, and the mode of propulsion is immaterial.[63] Apart from any radical change in the dominant tenement, the user of the way is not limited by reference to numbers or frequency during the prescriptive period, so that a way acquired for a sparsely occupied caravan site may still be used when the site holds more caravans,[64] and user of a way acquired for business purposes may increase with the expansion of the business.[65]

---

[53] *Cannon v Villars* (1878) 8 Ch D 415 at 420; *Att Gen v Hodgson* [1922] 1 Ch. 429 (carriageway granted in 1861 held to extend to motor cars); *Kain v Norfolk* [1949] Ch. 163 (grant for use by "carts" held to cover use by motor-lorries). There is a general discussion of this issue in *St Edmundsbury & Ipswich Diocesan Board of Finance v Clark (No.2)*, above.

[54] *Corp of London v Riggs* (1880) 13 Ch D 798.

[55] *Milner's Safe Co Ltd v Great Northern & City Ry* [1907] 1 Ch. 208.

[56] *Williams v James* (1867) L.R. 2 C.P. 577 at 580, per Bovill C.J. See also *United Land Co v Great Eastern Ry* (1875) 10 Ch.App. 586 at 590; *Ironside v Cook* (1978) 41 P. & C.R. 326 at 336; *Mills v Silver* [1991] Ch. 271 at 287; *Property Point Ltd v Kirri* [2009] EWHC 2958 (Ch) at [33] et seq.; *Dewan v Lewis* [2010] EWCA Civ 1382; [2010] N.P.C. 123 at [24].

[57] *Bradburn v Morris* (1876) 3 Ch D 812.

[58] *R.P.C. Holdings Ltd v Rogers* [1953] 1 All E.R. 1029.

[59] *Wimbledon & Putney Commons Conservators v Dixon* (1875) 1 Ch D 362: the fact that there has been occasional user for the cartage of materials to enlarge the farm house and rebuild a cottage on the farm does not enable the dominant owner to cart materials to build new houses.

[60] *Ballard v Dyson* (1808) 1 Taunt. 279; *Dewan v Lewis*, above.

[61] *Davies v Stephens* (1836) 7 C. & P. 570.

[62] See Gale 9–02.

[63] *Lock v Abercester Ltd* [1939] Ch. 861.

[64] *British Railways Board v Glass* [1965] Ch. 538.

[65] *Woodhouse & Co Ltd v Kirkland (Derby) Ltd* [1970] 1 W.L.R. 1185.

B. Rights of Light[66]

1. No natural right. There is no natural right to light.[67] An owner is **30–010**
therefore entitled to build on his land so as to prevent any light from reaching
his neighbour's windows,[68] unless his neighbour has an easement of light or
some other right such as a restrictive covenant against building. Indeed, the
access of light to windows is sometimes deliberately obstructed to prevent an
easement of light being acquired by prescription.[69] Long established rights to
light are sometimes called "ancient lights".

2. Quantum of light. An easement of light can exist only in respect of a **30–011**
building which receives it through a window[70] or other aperture such as a
skylight,[71] or through transparent panels as in the case of a greenhouse.[72] The
amount of light to which the dominant owner is entitled was determined by
the House of Lords in *Colls v Home and Colonial Stores Ltd*.[73] This amount
is enough light according to the ordinary notions of mankind for the comfort-
able use of the premises as a dwelling, or, in the case of business premises, for
the beneficial use of the premises as a warehouse, shop or other place of
business. The same test applies, *mutatis mutandis*, to any other premises, e.g.
a church,[74] a greenhouse,[75] or a photographic studio.[76] The measure is thus
"ordinary user"; the dominant owner is not entitled to object even to a
substantial diminution in his light, provided enough is left for ordinary
purposes. The test is not "How much light has been taken away?", but "How
much light is left?"[77] However, the light needed for ordinary user depends
upon the nature of the building. The high level of light required for a
greenhouse can be acquired as an easement either by grant or by
prescription.[78]

An easement of a greater amount of light than that required for ordinary **30–012**
purposes can, it seems, be granted, and also be acquired by prescription if for

---

[66] See generally S. Bickford-Smith & A. Francis, *Rights of Light: The Modern Law*, 2nd edn
(London: Jordans, 2007).

[67] See above, para.27–031.

[68] *Tapling v Jones* (1865) 11 H.L.C. 290.

[69] See e.g. *Mayor, etc., of Paddington v Att Gen* [1906] A.C. 1. Since 1959, it has been possible
to interrupt prescriptive use by registering a notice as a local land charge: see above,
para.28–101.

[70] *Levet v Gas Light & Coke Co* [1919] 1 Ch. 24.

[71] *Easton v Isted* [1903] 1 Ch. 405.

[72] *Allen v Greenwood* [1980] Ch. 119.

[73] [1904] A.C. 179.

[74] *Newham v Lawson* (1971) 22 P. & C.R. 852.

[75] *Allen v Greenwood*, above.

[76] *Colls v Home and Colonial Stores Ltd*, above at 203; *Allen v Greenwood*, above at 133.

[77] See *Higgins v Betts* [1905] 2 Ch. 210 at 215, per Farwell J.; *Carr-Saunders v Dick McNeil
Associates Ltd* [1986] 1 W.L.R. 922 at 928. This rule is not affected by the Prescription Act 1832:
Kelk v Pearson (1871) 6 Ch.App. 809.

[78] *Allen v Greenwood*, above (claim under Prescription Act 1832 succeeded). The Court of
Appeal left open the question of claims involving heat only, e.g. for solar heating. For the
problems which can arise where a room is so badly lit that any deprivation of light will render it
unfit for ordinary use, see [1984] Conv. 408 (A. H. Hudson).

20 years the dominant owner has both needed and enjoyed it to the knowledge of the servient owner.[79] On the other hand, the quantum of light to which the dominant owner is entitled is not affected by the fact that he has used the room for purposes which only require a little light.[80] A right of light is a right to have access of light for all ordinary purposes to which the room may be put,[81] which may include a subdivision of the space into smaller units if this is an ordinary and reasonable use of it.[82]

30–013　　**3. Alteration.** If the dominant owner alters the user of his premises, or the size or position of the windows,[83] the burden on the servient tenement is not increased, for "the actual user will neither increase nor diminish the right."[84] An obstruction which would not have been actionable before the alteration will therefore not be actionable even if it deprives the altered window of most of its light[85]; the test is "identity of light, not identity of aperture."[86] If the alterations to the dominant tenement render it impossible for the court to determine the extent to which the light received by the old windows is received by the new, the easement is lost.[87] Yet if an easement of light for one set of windows is infringed, and another set of windows (for which no easement exists) is deprived of light by the same obstruction, the dominant owner can recover damages in respect of both sets of windows, for the obstruction is illegal and the damage to both sets of windows is the direct and foreseeable consequence of it.[88] But such "parasitic damages" may be recoverable only in respect of windows which would necessarily benefit from an injunction protecting the dominant windows.[89]

30–014　　**4. Standard of light.** The standard of light varies to some extent from neighbourhood to neighbourhood,[90] the test being that laid down in *Colls'* case. There is no "45 degrees" rule, i.e. no rule that an interference with light is actionable only if the obstruction arises above a line drawn upwards and outwards from the centre of the window at an angle of 45 degrees,[91] at the

---

[79] *Allen v Greenwood*, above, as the secondary ground of decision, following *Lanfranchi v Mackenzie* (1867) L.R. 4 Eq. 421 in preference to *Ambler v Gordon* [1905] 1 K.B. 417. The requirement of acquiescence seems to be a gloss on the Act.

[80] *Price v Hilditch* [1930] 1 Ch. 500 (scullery).

[81] *Yates v Jack* (1866) 1 Ch.App. 295.

[82] *Carr-Saunders v Dick McNeil Associates Ltd*, above; [1987] C.L.J. 26 (S.B.).

[83] *Smith v Evangelization Society (Incorporated) Trust* [1933] Ch. 515.

[84] *Colls v Home and Colonial Stores Ltd* [1904] A.C. 179 at 204, per Lord Davey.

[85] *Ankerson v Connelly* [1907] 1 Ch. 678.

[86] *Andrews v Waite* [1907] 2 Ch. 500 at 510, per Neville J; above, para.29–011.

[87] *Ankerson v Connelly* [1906] 2 Ch. 544 at 548 (aff'd [1907] 1 Ch. 678); *News of the World Ltd v Allen Fairhead & Sons Ltd* [1931] 2 Ch. 402 at 407.

[88] *Re London, Tilbury & Southend Ry and the Trustees of the Gower's Walk Schools* (1889) 24 QBD 326; *Griffith v Richard Clay & Sons Ltd* [1912] 2 Ch. 291. Contrast *Scott v Goulding Properties Ltd* [1973] I.R. 200.

[89] See (1975) 39 Conv. (N.S.) 116 (A. H. Hudson).

[90] *Fishenden v Higgs & Hill Ltd* (1935) 153 L.T. 128; *Ough v King* [1967] 1 W.L.R. 1547. But see *Horton's Estate Ltd v James Beattie Ltd* [1927] 1 Ch. 75.

[91] *Colls v Home and Colonial Stores Ltd* [1904] A.C. 179 at 210; *Fishenden v Higgs & Hill Ltd*, above.

most, this test provides a very slight presumption.[92] Scientific methods today permit accurate measurement of light, and tests which have been propounded are whether the whole room, or half of it,[93] receives light not below a factor called the "grumble point".[94] But these are not reliable guides, since the court may take account not only of the locality but of the higher standard which may reasonably be required in present times.[95]

5. Other sources of light. In considering whether an easement of light has   **30–015** been obstructed, other sources of light of which the dominant owner cannot be deprived must be taken into account, such as vertical light through a sky-light[96]; and if this has been blocked up by the dominant owner during the prescriptive period, his rights will be assessed on the footing of it being unobstructed.[97] In one case[98] a room was lit through two sets of windows, one set facing A's land and the other facing B's land. It was held that the light received by both sets of windows had to be considered, but that A could not obscure the greater part of the light passing over his land in reliance upon B supplying a larger quantity of light. Neither servient owner could build to a greater extent than, assuming a building of like height on the other servient tenement, would still leave the dominant tenement with sufficient light according to the test in *Colls'* case.

6. Precarious light. Light which the dominant tenement receives from   **30–016** other sources but of which it may be deprived at any time must be ignored.[99] Nor is it a sufficient answer for the servient owner to offer to provide glazed tiles or mirrors to reflect the light,[100] for no provision can be made which will effectively bind future owners of the servient tenement to keep the tiles or mirrors clean.[101] An easement to receive reflected light apparently cannot exist[102]; but in considering whether an easement of light has been infringed, reflected or diffused light entering from ordinary sources cannot be disregarded.[103]

7. Artificial light. In determining whether there has been actionable inter-   **30–017** ference with an easement of light, the fact that the occupiers of the dominant tenement (such as a modern office block) habitually use artificial lighting is

---

[92] *Ecclesiastical Commissioners for England v Kino* (1880) 14 Ch D 213 at 220.
[93] *Fishenden v Higgs & Hill Ltd*, above.
[94] See *Charles Semon & Co Ltd v Bradford Corp* [1922] 2 Ch. 737 at 747, 748.
[95] *Ough v King*, above; *Deakins v Hookings* [1994] 1 E.G.L.R. 190; and see the criticisms in *McGrath v Munster & Leinster Bank Ltd* [1959] I.R. 313.
[96] *Smith v Evangelization Society (Incorporated) Trust* [1933] Ch. 515.
[97] *Smith v Evangelization Society (Incorporated) Trust*, above.
[98] *Sheffield Masonic Hall Co Ltd v Sheffield Corp* [1932] 2 Ch. 17.
[99] *Colls v Home and Colonial Stores, Ltd*, above, at 211.
[100] *Black v Scottish Temperance Life Assurance Co* [1908] 1 I.R. 541, HL.
[101] *Dent v Auction Mart Co* (1866) L.R. 2 Eq. 238 at 251.
[102] *Goldberg v Waite* [1930] E.G.D. 154.
[103] *Sheffield Masonic Hall Co Ltd v Sheffield Corpn*, above, at 24.

immaterial.[104] The question to be asked is whether there has been a substantial diminution of the natural light. However, the likely resort to artificial light may weigh in determining the appropriate relief.[105]

8. Remedies.

30–018   *(a) Injunction.* A claimant is prima facie entitled to an injunction against the defendant who has committed nuisance by interfering with his right of light and who has thereby invaded his legal right.[106] Although the court may award damages in lieu, it should exercise its discretion to do so in accordance with principle and even then only in very exceptional circumstances.[107] The factors which are relevant may include: whether the injury to the claimant's rights was small; whether that injury could be estimated in money; whether it could be adequately compensated by a small money payment; whether it would be oppressive to the defendant to grant an injunction; whether the claimant had shown that he only wanted money; and whether the claimant's conduct rendered it unjust to give him more than pecuniary relief.[108] However, recent authorities indicate a judicial reluctance to award injunctive relief where the successful claimant habitually used artificial lighting to illuminate office premises, in which case the court will award damages in lieu.[109]

(b) Damages. Where damages are awarded, assessment is broadly based upon the sum that would have been agreed by reasonable and willing negotiating parties as the price for release of the claimant's right of light.[110] This involves the court deciding upon the likely fair result of a hypothetical negotiation between the parties, taking account of the context, including such matters as the nature and seriousness of the breach, the significant bargaining position that may be assumed by a claimant who has the right to prevent development, and the fact that such a claimant would normally be expected to receive some part of the likely profit from the development.[111] The size of the award should not be so large that the development would not have taken place had such a sum been payable, but if there is evidence of the likely size of the profit to be made by the defendant, the court should normally award a sum which reflects a fair percentage of that profit.[112] If there is no evidence of the

[104] *Midtown Ltd v City of London Real Property Co Ltd* [2005] EWHC 33; [2005] 1 E.G.L.R. 65 at [55] et seq.; *Tamares (Vincent Square) Ltd v Fairpoint Properties (Vincent Square) Ltd* [2006] EWHC 3589; [2007] 1 W.L.R. 2148 at [30].

[105] *Midtown Ltd v City of London Real Property Co Ltd*, above at [63]; *Tamares (Vincent Square) Ltd v Fairpoint Properties (Vincent Square)* Ltd, above at [30].

[106] *Shelfer v City of London Electric Lighting Company* [1895] 1 Ch. 287 at 322; *Slack v Leeds Industrial Co-operative Society Ltd* [1924] 2 Ch. 475 at 492.

[107] See sources cited above.

[108] See sources cited above, as approved in *Regan v Paul Properties Ltd* [2006] EWCA Civ 1319 at [36].

[109] *Midtown Ltd v City of London Real Property Co Ltd*, above; *Tamares (Vincent Square) Ltd v Fairpoint Properties (Vincent Square) Ltd*, above.

[110] See generally Gale 14–124 et seq.

[111] *Tamares (Vincent Square) Ltd v Fairpoint Properties (Vincent Square) Ltd* [2007] EWHC 212 (Ch); [2007] 1 W.L.R. 2167.

[112] ibid. The court will not however order an account of profits save in exceptional circumstances: *Forsyth-Grant v Allen* [2008] EWCA Civ 505; [2008] 2 E.G.L.R. 16.

likely profit, the court should do the best it can by awarding a sum to represent the claimant's loss of amenity.[113]

9. Law Reform. The Law Commission has included a project on rights to **30–019** light in its Eleventh Programme of Law Reform.[114] The project is intended to examine the current balance between those benefiting from rights of light and those seeking to develop land that may be affected by them, as well as the relationship between the planning system and rights of light.[115] A Consultation Paper is expected in early 2013.[116]

C. Rights of Water

A variety of easements may exist in connection with water,[117] such as **30–020** rights:

(i) to take water from a river,[118] a spring[119] or a pump[120];

(ii) to water cattle at a pond[121];

(iii) to take water from a stream running through the dominant tenement for purposes which the natural rights of ownership[122] do not permit[123];

(iv) to receive water through a pipe on the servient land[124];

(v) to pollute the waters of a stream or river[125];

(vi) to discharge water on to the land of another[126];

(vii) to receive the discharge of water from the land of another[127];

---

[113] *Tamares (Vincent Square) Ltd v Fairpoint Properties (Vincent Square) Ltd* [2007] EWHC 212 (Ch); [2007] 1 W.L.R. 2167.

[114] Law Com. No. 330 (2011).

[115] ibid., para.2.70.

[116] ibid., para.2.71.

[117] See Gale 6–37.

[118] *Cargill v Gotts* [1981] 1 W.L.R. 441 (right to take water from mill pond for ordinary farming purposes allows increased abstraction for crop-spraying).

[119] *Race v Ward* (1855) 4 E. & B. 702.

[120] *Polden v Bastard* (1865) L.R. 1 Q.B. 156.

[121] *Manning v Wasdale* (1836) 5 A. & E. 758.

[122] For these, see above, para.27–027 et seq.

[123] *McCartney v Londonderry & Lough Swilly Ry* [1904] A.C. 301 at 313.

[124] *Goodhart v Hyett* (1883) 25 Ch D 182; *Rance v Elvin* (1985) 50 P. & C.R. 9. See too *Duffy v Lamb* (1997) 75 P. & C.R. 364 (right to receive electricity via a cable).

[125] *Baxendale v McMurray* (1867) 2 Ch.App. 790.

[126] *Mason v Shrewsbury & Hereford Ry* (1871) L.R. 6 Q.B. 578 at 587.

[127] *Ivimey v Stocker* (1866) 1 Ch.App. 396. It is harder to obtain this by prescription than the previous right, which is complementary to it; for it is difficult to contend that because a man's pump had dripped onto the land of another for 20 years, the latter had a right to say that the pump must go on leaking· *Chamber Colliery Co v Hopwood* (1886) 32 Ch D 549 at 558. See also *Arkwright v Gell* (1839) 5 M. & W. 203 and *Burrows v Lang* [1901] 2 Ch. 502 for the difficulties which may lie in the way of a claim to continue to receive water temporarily flowing from another person's land.

(viii) to enter the land of another to open sluice gates[128];

(ix) to permit rainwater to drop from a roof onto a neighbour's land ("easement of eavesdrop").[129]

These rights must be distinguished from the natural rights which a landowner may have in respect of water,[130] which have already been mentioned.[131] There is no easement of natural drainage (that is, the right to permit naturally occurring water to drain from higher land to lower land) known to law, as it is an incident of the ownership of the higher land.[132]

D. *Rights of Support*

30–021 As already mentioned,[133] a landowner's natural right of support for his land extends only to his land in its natural state; it does not include buildings. But a right of support for buildings may be acquired as an easement. Thus where one of two adjoining houses was converted into a coach factory which threw more pressure upon the other house, and was so used for over 20 years, the House of Lords held that an action lay for demolishing the other house and so causing part of the factory to collapse.[134] Where adjoining buildings support one another it is therefore difficult for their owners to preserve their liberty to demolish them for more than 20 years. Probably their only course is to issue a writ claiming a declaration that no easement as yet subsists, so preventing user as of right. Although there is no natural right for a landowner to have the surface of his land supported by water but only by subjacent strata of minerals,[135] there is no such limitation as regards an easement of support. Removal of support is actionable even if it is caused by the draining of water from the subsoil.[136]

Where an easement of support exists, it entitles the dominant owner to enter and execute repairs to the servient tenement; but it does not put the servient owner under any obligation to keep the supporting building in repair, since the easement cannot entail a positive obligation.[137]

---

[128] *Simpson v Mayor, etc. of Godmanchester* [1897] A.C. 696.

[129] *Harvey v Walters* (1873) L.R. 8 C.P. 162.

[130] See Gale 6–01 et seq.

[131] See above, para.27–031.

[132] *Home Brewery Co Ltd v William Davis & Co (Leicester) Ltd* [1987] Q.B. 339; *Palmer v Bowman* [2000] 1 W.L.R. 842. cf. *Green v Lord Somerleyton* [2003] EWCA Civ 198; [2004] 1 P. & C.R. 33.

[133] See above, para.27–029.

[134] *Dalton v Angus & Co* (1881) 6 App.Cas. 740. This is the leading case on easements of support, and contains a great many important observations about easements generally. A local authority cannot exercise compulsory powers to demolish the servient house without providing equivalent support: *Bond v Nottingham Corporation* [1940] Ch. 429.

[135] *Stephens v Anglia Water Authority* [1987] 1 W.L.R. 1381; above, para.27–029.

[136] *Brace v SE Regional Housing Association Ltd* [1984] 1 E.G.L.R. 144.

[137] See above, para.27–029.

E. Right of Fencing

The right to require a neighbouring landowner to repair his fences has been **30–022**
called a "spurious easement",[138] and even a "quasi-easement".[139] In fact it
appears to be an easement,[140] though exceptional in requiring positive action
by the servient owner. It lies in grant[141]; it will pass under s.62 of the Law of
Property Act 1925[142]; and it can be acquired by prescription.[143] In order to
establish the right it must be shown that the servient owner repaired his fence
not merely to keep his cattle in or the dominant owner's out, but as a matter
of obligation to the dominant owner, e.g. by habitually repairing the fence on
his demand.[144] The servient owner cannot be required to repair fences on the
dominant owner's land.[145] A corresponding right may also be acquired by
custom.[146] There are certain statutory obligations which require a landowner
to fence his property.[147]

F. Miscellaneous Easements

There are many miscellaneous easements, such as rights: **30–023**

(i) to create a nuisance by the discharge of gases, fluids or smoke,[148]
   or perhaps even by making noises[149] or vibrations[150];

(ii) to hang clothes on a line passing over another's land[151];

---

[138] *Coaker v Willcocks* [1911] 2 K.B. 124 at 131, per Farwell L.J.; and see above, para.27–019.
The obligation binds the landowner "to put up such fence that a pig not of a peculiarly wandering
disposition, nor under any excessive temptation, will not get through it" (*Child v Hearn* (1874)
L.R. 9 Ex. 176 at 182, per Bramwell B.); but the fence need not be sufficient to exclude sheep of
a "peculiarly wandering and saltative disposition" (*Coaker v Willcocks* [1911] 1 K.B. 649 at 654,
per Darling J.), nor need it to be "so close and strong that no pig could push through it, or so high
that no horse or bullock could leap it" (*Child v Hearn*, above, at 181, per Bramwell B.). For a
discussion of this obligation, see (1971) 87 L.Q.R. 13 (P. V. Baker).

[139] *Jones v Price* [1965] 2 Q.B. 618; for the normal meaning of this term, see above, paras
27–013, 28–019.

[140] *Crow v Wood* [1971] 1 Q.B. 77.

[141] *Crow v Wood*, above. However, it is impossible to draft an express grant of such a right. It
could only be created expressly by means of a covenant.

[142] See above, para.28–027.

[143] *Lawrence v Jenkins* (1873) L.R. 8 Q.B. 274; *Jones v Price*, above.

[144] *Hilton v Ankesson* (1872) 27 L.T. 519.

[145] *Jones v Price*, above; *Egerton v Harding* [1975] Q.B. 62.

[146] *Egerton v Harding*, above, not following *Crow v Wood*, above.

[147] See Halsbury, Vol.4(1), p.432.

[148] *Crump v Lambert* (1867) L.R. 3 Eq. 409 at 413 (dictum by Romilly M.R.); but see fn.150,
below.

[149] *Elliotson v Feetham* (1835) 2 Bing.N.C. 134; *Ball v Ray* (1873) 8 Ch.App. 467 at 471
(neither finding such an easement on the facts); and see now *Lawrence v Fen Tigers Ltd* [2011]
EWHC 360 (QB) where H.H. Judge Seymour QC, sitting as a High Court judge, challenges the
concept of a prescriptive right to create a noise (at [214]) and at one point states that the law does
not recognise an easement of noise (sc. at all, at [223]).

[150] *Sturges v Bridgman* (1879) 11 Ch D 852. As with the cases mentioned at fn.149 above, the
claim did not succeed. If 20 years' user as of right could have been shown, the question would
have arisen whether such rights can lie in grant. This seems highly questionable: there is no direct
authority; *contra*, *Lemmon v Webb* [1895] A.C. 1, and see above, para.27–017.

[151] *Drewell v Towler* (1832) 3 B. & Ad. 735.

    (iii) to fix a signboard on a neighbouring house[152];

    (iv) to mix manure on the servient tenement for the benefit of the adjoining farm[153];

    (v) to place stones on the servient tenement to prevent sand or earth from being washed away by the sea[154];

    (vi) to use a wall for nailing trees to it[155] or for supporting a creeper[156];

    (vii) to extend the bowsprits of ships over a wharf[157];

    (viii) to store casks and trade products on the servient tenement[158];

    (ix) to use a coal shed on the servient tenement[159];

    (x) to park a car[160];

    (xi) to use an airfield[161];

    (xii) to let down the surface of land by mining operations under it[162];

    (xiii) to use a kitchen[163] or a lavatory[164];

    (xiv) to use a letter-box[165];

    (xv) to use a pew in a church.[166]

G. Species of Profits à Prendre

30–024 The following are the main types of profits à prendre. They are more often met with as commons than as several profits.

---

[152] *Moody v Steggles* (1879) 12 Ch D 261.

[153] *Pye v Mumford* (1848) 11 Q.B. 666 (the right was claimed as a profit à prendre).

[154] *Philpot v Bath* (1905) 21 T.L.R. 634.

[155] *Hawkins v Wallis* (1763) 2 Wils.K.B. 173.

[156] *Simpson v Weber* (1925) 133 L.T. 46.

[157] *Suffield v Brown* (1864) 4 De. G.J. & S. 185.

[158] *Att Gen of Southern Nigeria v John Holt & Co (Liverpool) Ltd* [1915] A.C. 599; above, para.27–020.

[159] *Wright v Macadam* [1949] 2 K.B. 744.

[160] See above, para.27–021.

[161] *Dowty Boulton Paul Ltd v Wolverhampton Corporation (No.2)* [1976] Ch. 13.

[162] *Rowbotham v Wilson* (1860) 8 H.L.C. 348 at 362. But see *Newcastle-under-Lyme BC v Wolstanton Ltd* [1939] 3 All E.R. 597 (aff'd [1940] A.C. 860) as to the acquisition of such a right by prescription; and see (1940) 56 L.Q.R. 438 (R.E.M.).

[163] See *Heywood v Mallalieu* (1883) 25 Ch D 357.

[164] *Miller v Emcer Products Ltd* [1956] Ch. 304; and see *Simmons v Midford* [1969] 2 Ch. 415 (exclusive right to use a drain).

[165] *Goldberg v Edwards* [1950] Ch. 247.

[166] *Philipps v Halliday* [1891] A.C. 228. But see *Brumfitt v Roberts* (1870) L.R. 5 C.P. 224 at 233.

1. Profit of pasture. A profit of pasture is a true profit; the taking and **30–025** carrying away is effected by means of the mouths and stomachs of the cattle in question.[167] A profit of pasture may exist in the following forms.

(a) Appendant. A profit of pasture appendant is limited to horses, oxen, **30–026** cows and sheep. The numerical test is that of levancy and couchancy.[168]

(b) Appurtenant. A profit of pasture appurtenant is not confined to any **30–027** particular animals, but depends on the terms of the grant or, in the case of prescription, the animals habitually turned out to pasture.[169] Thus it may extend to sheep, when it is known as a "foldcourse"[170] or "sheepwalk".[171] The number of animals may either be limited by levancy and couchancy, or be fixed; it cannot be unlimited.[172]

(c) Pur cause de vicinage. Under a common of pasture *pur cause de* **30–028** *vicinage*,[173] the commoners of one common may not put more cattle upon it than it will maintain; thus, if Common A is 50 acres in extent and Common B 100 acres, the commoners of A must not put more cattle on A than 50 acres will support in reliance upon their cattle straying to B.[174]

(d) In gross. A profit of pasture in gross[175] may exist for a fixed number of **30–029** animals or *sans nombre*. The last phrase means literally "without number" (an alternative form is "without stint"), but such a right is limited to not more cattle than the servient tenement will maintain in addition to any existing burdens.[176]

For the purpose of registration under the Commons Registration Act **30–030** 1965[177] rights of common which consist of or include a right, not limited by number, to graze animals must be registered for a definite number of animals. When such registration has become final, the right is exercisable only in relation to the number so registered.[178] Where these provisions apply, they replace levancy and couchancy as a test,[179] as well as the test for a profit *sans*

---

[167] See Preston, *Estates*, i, p.15.

[168] See above, para.27–066.

[169] Hall, Profits à Prendre, (1871) 263.

[170] *Robinson v Duleep Singh* (1878) 11 Ch D 798. For the distinction between this and a grant of herbage, see *Robinson v Duleep Singh* at 820.

[171] *White v Williams* [1922] 1 K.B. 727.

[172] *Benson v Chester* (1799) 8 T.R. 396 at 401; *Anderson v Bostock* [1976] Ch. 312. A profit of pasture "without stint" or "*sans nombre*" means a profit for animals *levant et couchant*: Halsbury Vol.13, para.441, fn.2; 1 Wm. Saund., 6th edn, 28, fn.(4).

[173] See above, para.27–067.

[174] *Sir Miles Corbet's Case* (1585) 7 Co.Rep. 5a.

[175] See above, para.27–068.

[176] Halsbury Vol.13, para.447; and see Commons Act 2006 s.7(5).

[177] For registration, see above, paras 27–058 et seq.

[178] Commons Registration Act 1965, s.15. See above, para.27–066. The number specified represents the upper limit for the register unit and is not determinative of whether the right is separate (i.e. applicable only to the unit) or split (i.e. applicable to more than one unit): *Dance v Savery* [2011] EWCA Civ 1250; [2011] N.P.C. 114 at [65].

[179] *Bettison v Langton* [2001] UKHL 24 at [60]; [2002] 1 A.C. 27 at [60].

nombre; and commoners may license others to graze their beasts up to the registered number.[180]

30–031   **2. Profit of turbary.** A profit of turbary is the right to dig and take from the servient tenement peat or turf for use as fuel in a house on the dominant tenement. It may exist as appurtenant, or, where it is limited to some specified quantity, in gross.[181] Where it is appurtenant, the turves can be used only for the benefit of the dominant tenement and not, e.g. for sale,[182] even if the dominant owner is entitled to a fixed quantity.[183]

30–032   **3. Profit of estovers.** A profit of estovers is the right to take wood from the land of another as hay-bote, house-bote, or plough-bote.[184] It may exist as appurtenant, or, if limited to a specified quantity, in gross.[185] If it is appurtenant to a house, the right will not be increased if the house is enlarged.[186] It sometimes includes the right to cut timber,[187] but may be limited to trees of small value.[188] It may extend to furze, gorse, heather, fern or long grass for fuel, manure or litter.[189] In every case the profit must be limited in some way as to quantity, either by reference to some defined quantity or by reference to the needs of the dominant tenement.[190] Similar rights to profits of estovers are rights of lopwood, i.e. to lop wood for fuel at certain periods of the year,[191] and pannage, i.e. to send pigs onto the servient tenement in order to eat acorns or beech-mast which have fallen to the ground.[192]

30–033   **4. Profit of piscary and other sporting rights.** A profit of piscary is a right to catch and take away fish. It can exist in gross (when it may be unlimited)[193] or as appurtenant (when it must be limited to the needs of the dominant tenement).[194] Other sporting rights, such as a right of hunting (venery), shooting, fowling (auceptary), and the like, may also exist as profits à

---

[180] *Davies v Davies* [1975] Q.B. 172.
[181] *Mellor v Spateman* (1668) 1 Wms.Saund. 339.
[182] *Valentine v Penny* (1604) Noy 145.
[183] *Hayward v Cunnington* (1666) 1 Lev. 231.
[184] See above, para.3–097. This must be distinguished from the similar rights a tenant for life has over the land of which he is tenant, for a profit of estovers is exercised over the land of another.
[185] Halsbury Vol.13, para.459.
[186] *Brown & Tucker's Case* (1610) 4 Leon. 241.
[187] *Russel & Broker's Case* (1586) 2 Leon. 209.
[188] *Anon* (1572) 3 Leon. 16.
[189] *Warrick v Queen's College, Oxford* (1871) 6 Ch.App. 716; *Earl de la Warr v Miles* (1881) 17 Ch D 535.
[190] *Clayton v Corby* (1843) 5 Q.B. 415 at 419.
[191] *Chilton v Corporation of London (No.2)* (1878) 7 Ch D 735.
[192] *Chilton v Corporation of London (No.1)* (1878) 7 Ch D 562. The servient owner may nevertheless lop the trees in the ordinary course of management, and fell the trees when ripe.
[193] *Staffordshire and Worcestershire Canal Navigation v Bradley* [1912] 1 Ch. 91; *Lovett v Fairclough* (1990) 61 P. & C.R. 385 at 396: above, para.27–068.
[194] *Harris v Earl of Chesterfield* [1911] A.C. 623; *Barton v Church Commissioners for England* [2008] EWHC 3091 (Ch); [2008] N.P.C. 141 at [30]; see above, para.27–066.

prendre.[195] Rights of fishing may be exclusive (and the fishery is referred to as a several fishery),[196] but other sporting rights are not.[197] It is no infringement of a right to take game if the servient owner merely cuts timber in the ordinary way, even if he thereby drives away game[198]; but it is otherwise if fundamental changes in the land are made, as where the whole or a substantial part of the land is built upon or converted into racing stables.[199] Such a right imposes no obligation to keep down the numbers of birds or animals.[200]

5. Profit in the soil. A profit in the soil is the right to enter the servient tenement and take sand,[201] stone,[202] gravel,[203] brick-earth,[204] coal,[205] minerals[206] and the like.[207] It may exist as appurtenant or in gross.   **30–034**

H. Rights of Access to Neighbouring Land

1. No right of access at common law. It is often the case that one landowner, A, cannot carry out works of repair or improvement to his own property without going onto the land of his neighbour, B, to execute them. There is however no right at common law[208] for A to enter B's land unless: **30–035**

(i) he has an easement to go onto B's property to carry out the works[209]; or

(ii) B has consented to his so doing.

Any unauthorised entry by A is a trespass which may be restrained by injunction, and this is so even though A is required to carry out the works by

---

[195] *Ewart v Graham* (1859) 7 HLC 331 at 345. See the extensive rights claimed in *Thorne RDC v Bunting* [1972] Ch. 470.

[196] Where a fishery is exclusive, it means that no other person has a co-extensive right with the owner. "The fact that some other person has a right to a particular class of fish in the fishery or has a right to fish in common with the owner of the several fishery does not destroy the severalty of the fishery": *Barton v Church Commissioners for England*, above, at [30] per Morgan J. There may be some difficulty about the rules of construction: see *Lady Dunsany v Bedworth* (1979) 38 P. & C.R. 546 at 548.

[197] *Duke of Sutherland v Heathcote* [1892] 1 Ch. 475.

[198] *Gearns v Baker* (1875) 10 Ch.App. 355.

[199] *Peech v Best* [1931] 1 K.B. 1.

[200] *Seligman v Docker* [1949] Ch. 53.

[201] *Blewett v Tregonning* (1835) 3 A. & E. 544 at 575.

[202] *Heath v Deane* [1905] 2 Ch. 86.

[203] *Constable v Nicholson* (1863) 14 C.B. (N.S.) 230 at 239.

[204] *Church v The Inclosure Commissioners* (1862) 11 C.B. (N.S.) 664.

[205] See *Duke of Portland v Hill* (1866) L.R. 2 Eq. 765.

[206] *Duke of Sutherland v Heathcote* [1892] 1 Ch. 475 at 483.

[207] Co.Litt. p.122a. As to a right to take ice from a canal, see *Newby v Harrison* (1861) 1 J & H. 393; (1938) 2 Conv. (N.S.) 203 at 204 (J. S. Fiennes).

[208] There is a statutory right to enter a neighbour's land to repair a party wall under the Party Walls, etc., Act 1996, s.2: see below, para.30–047.

[209] Such an easement is known to the law: *Ward v Kirkland* [1967] Ch. 194.

the local authority because the premises are in a dangerous condition.[210] In such a case, A is caught between "the Scylla of the dangerous building" and "the Charybdis of trespassing on the plaintiff's land".[211] To provide a partial solution to this problem, Parliament enacted the Access to Neighbouring Land Act 1992,[212] which came into force on January 31, 1993.[213] The provisions of this Act, which are of limited effect, must now be considered.

2. Access orders under the Access to Neighbouring Land Act 1992

(a) Access orders

30–036 (1) GROUNDS ON WHICH AN ORDER MAY BE MADE. If A wishes to carry out works that are reasonably necessary for the preservation of the whole or any part of his land,[214] and it is either impossible or substantially more difficult[215] for him to do so without access to B's adjacent or adjoining land, A may apply to the court for an access order, should B's consent be needed but not forthcoming.[216] Although the Act does not attempt to define comprehensively what works will be reasonably necessary for the preservation of the land, it does provide that (without prejudice to the generality of that requirement) certain works will be so. These are as follows:

(a) Specified "basic preservation works" (broadly involving maintenance, repair or renewal of existing buildings, structures, drains, sewers, pipes, cables, hedges, trees, shrubs or ditches in or on A's land).[217]

(b) If the court considers it fair and reasonable in the circumstances of the case, works which are reasonably necessary for the preservation of the land or which would comprise "basic preservation works" but which incidentally involve:

(i) the making of some alteration, adjustment or improvement to A's land; or

---

[210] *John Trenberth Ltd v National Westminster Bank Ltd* (1979) 39 P. & C.R. 104; [1980] Conv. 308 (H. Street). For the powers of the local authority in relation to dangerous buildings, see the Building Act 1984 s.77.

[211] *John Trenberth Ltd v National Westminster Bank Ltd*, above, at 106, per Walton J.

[212] The Act was based upon (but does not in all respects follow) the recommendations of the Law Commission: (1985) Law Com. No.151. See [1992] Conv. 225 (H. W. Wilkinson).

[213] SI 1992/3349.

[214] For these purposes, "land" includes a party wall: *Dean v Walker* (1996) 73 P. & C.R. 366. For party walls, see below, paras 30–041 et seq. It is no longer necessary to rely on the Access to Neighbouring Land Act 1992 in relation to the repair of party walls because of the Party Walls, etc., Act 1996: see below, para.30–047.

[215] In many cases it may be more expensive for A to carry out the works without access to B's land. Query whether this makes it "more difficult" within the meaning of the Act.

[216] s.1(1), (2). All actions must be commenced in the county court but may be transferred to the High Court: s.7.

[217] s.1(4).

>   (ii) the demolition of the whole or part of some building or struc-
>   ture upon it.[218]

> (c) Anything that is a necessary incident of carrying out the works,[219]
> including the right to enter B's land for certain purposes of
> inspection.[220]

The court shall not make an access order if it is satisfied that to do so would
either:

>   (i) interfere with or disturb the enjoyment of B's land by the occu-
>   pant; or

>   (ii) cause that person hardship,

to such a degree (by reason of A's entry) that it would be unreasonable.[221]

(2) TERMS AND EFFECT OF THE ORDER. An access order made by the court **30–037**
must define certain matters (such as the works to be carried out, the area of B's
land that may be entered, and the date or period when entry will be permitted),[222] and may be made subject to such terms and conditions as the court
considers reasonably necessary to avoid or restrict any loss, damage, injury,
inconvenience or loss of privacy that might otherwise be caused to B (or any
other person).[223] If the works which A undertakes on B's land lead to an
increase in the value of A's land, the court may require him to make a
payment to B unless A's land is residential land.[224]

The access order will authorise A or any or his "associates"[225] to enter the **30–038**
land and to bring onto it (and, before the permitted period ends, remove) such
materials, plant and equipment as are reasonably necessary for the specified
works or waste from carrying them out.[226] It will require him to remove waste,
to make good B's land, and to indemnify B for any damage caused in the
execution of the order.[227] B is required (so far as he has power to do so) to
permit A or any of his associates to do anything which the order authorises or
requires A to do.[228] The court may order any person who contravenes or fails
to comply with any requirement imposed upon him by or under the Act to pay

---

[218] s.1(5).
[219] s.1(6).
[220] s.1(7).
[221] s.1(3).
[222] s.2(1).
[223] s.2(2), (3). A may be required to pay compensation for any such loss, damage or inconvenience: s.2(4).
[224] s.2(5), (6). "Residential land" is widely defined: s.2(7).
[225] Defined by the Act to include any persons whom A may reasonably authorise to enter the
land to carry out the works (whether or not they are his servants or agents): s.3(7).
[226] s.3(2).
[227] s.3(3).
[228] s.3(1).

damages to any other person affected by that breach.[229] The court also has wide powers to suspend the order or to vary the terms and conditions upon which it was given.[230]

30–039   *(b) Effect on third parties.* The benefit of an access order is apparently personal to the applicant, A.[231] There is nothing in the Act which makes the right appurtenant to his land so that it can be enforced by a successor in title.[232] By contrast, an access order will both bind and be enforceable by any person:

> (i) who is a successor in title to B; or

> (ii) who has acquired an estate, interest or right in or over B's land subsequent to the making of the access order;

provided that the order has been registered as provided by the Act.[233] Where the title to B's land is unregistered, the order is registrable as a land charge in the register of writs and orders affecting land.[234] Where the title is registered, a notice should be entered on the register protecting the rights conferred by the order.[235] They are not capable of constituting an overriding interest.[236]

30–040   *(c) Limited effect of access orders.* The Access to Neighbouring Land Act 1992 provides no mechanism for A to go onto B's land to improve or redevelop his own property. An access order can be granted only in respect of works that are reasonably necessary for the preservation of A's property, and only incidental improvements or demolition works may be sanctioned. Even where the works are reasonably necessary for the preservation of A's property, no order can be made unless it is substantially more difficult for A to carry them out without entry onto B's land. All that the Act provides therefore is "a very restricted and temporary form of compulsory acquisition of an easement".[237]

I. Party Walls

30–041   Boundary walls dividing one property from another may be in the sole ownership of one owner, free from any rights of the other. But often each of

---

[229] s.6(2). The right to seek damages is not confined to A or B. If the breach affected a neighbour, he could seek damages. The statutory power to award damages is without prejudice to any other remedy available, such as an injunction.

[230] s.6(1).

[231] The Act throughout refers to the "applicant", which is never defined to include successors in title.

[232] It is understood that Land Registry will not therefore register the benefit of an access order as appurtenant to registered land and this appears correct in principle.

[233] s.4(1), (2). The application for an access order is treated as a pending land action: s.5(6).

[234] s.5(1), amending LCA 1972 s.6(1).

[235] LRA 2002 s.32.

[236] s.5(5), as amended by LRA 2002 Sch.11 para.26(4).

[237] [1992] Conv. 225 at 230 (H. W. Wilkinson). Contrast the sweeping powers enjoyed in relation to party walls under the Party Walls, etc., Act 1996; below, para.30–047.

the adjoining owners has certain rights over the walls. Such walls are known as party walls, and need special treatment. This is because although party walls used to be subject to the ordinary law as to co-ownership or easements of support, they obviously had to be excepted from the statutory trust for sale that was imposed in cases of co-ownership after 1925. Brief mention must also be made of the provisions of the Party Wall etc. Act 1996, which is concerned to regulate the construction and repair of party walls and not with their ownership.

1. "Party wall". There is no precise definition of the expression "party wall".[238] Since 1925 it may mean any one of the following[239]:   **30–042**

   (i) a wall divided longitudinally into strips, one belonging to each of the neighbouring owners[240]; or

  (ii) a wall divided as in (i), but each half being subject to an easement of support in favour of the owner of the other half[241];

 (iii) a wall belonging entirely to one of the adjoining owners, but subject to an easement or right in the other to have it maintained as a dividing wall.[242]

Prior to 1926 there was a fourth category. There could be a party wall of which the two adjoining owners were tenants in common. The disadvantage of such a wall was that either owner could insist upon partition.[243] Had special provision not been made by statute, all party walls in this category would have become subject to a trust for sale after 1925. It was consequently provided that after 1925 all party walls of this kind, whether created before 1926[244] or after 1925,[245] should be deemed to be severed vertically, and that the owner of each part should have such rights of support and user over the rest of the wall as were requisite for giving the parties rights similar to those which they would have enjoyed had they been tenants in common of the wall.[246] The practical effect of this provision was to translate all party walls of this kind into the second category listed above.

The characteristics of each of these categories must now be explained.

---

[238] *Kempston v Butler* (1861) 12 Ir.C.L.R. 516 at 526. For the meaning of "party wall" in the context of the Party Wall etc. Act 1996, see below, para.30–047.

[239] *Watson v Gray* (1880) 14 Ch D 192 at 194, as modified by LPA 1925 s.38.

[240] *Matts v Hawkins* (1813) 5 Taunt. 20.

[241] See *Wiltshire v Sidford* (1827) 1 Man. & Ry. 404 at 408; *Jones v Pritchard* [1908] 1 Ch. 630.

[242] See *Sheffield Improved Industrial and Provident Society v Jarvis* [1871] W.N. 208; [1872] W.N. 47.

[243] *Mayfair Property Co v Johnston* [1894] 1 Ch. 508. The alternative of a sale (introduced by the Partition Act 1868) was normally unsuitable.

[244] LPA 1925 Sch.1, Pt V, para.1.

[245] LPA 1925 s.38(1).

[246] LPA 1925 s.38, Sch.1, Pt V, para.1. In case of dispute the court may make an order declaratory of the rights of the parties: ibid.

2. Characteristics

30–043   *(a) Longitudinal division into two strips.* As a general rule, ownership of a party wall follows the ownership of the land upon which it is built.[247] There is therefore a presumption that, where a wall between adjacent properties is constructed so that the median line follows the boundary,[248] ownership of the wall is split longitudinally between the two landowners.[249] The presumption is not a strong one and cases of longitudinal division of this kind are in fact rare.[250] An inconvenient characteristic of this type of party wall is that neither owner has any right of lateral support from the other.[251] Either owner, acting with reasonable care,[252] can remove his half of the wall and leave a structure which may be incapable of standing alone.[253]

30–044   *(b) Longitudinal division with mutual easements of support.* At common law there was a presumption that adjoining owners were tenants in common of a party wall, at all events if evidence was given that each owner had exercised dominion over the entire wall[254] provided that:

> (i) the exact boundary could not be shown; or

> (ii) the site of the wall could be shown to have been owned in common.[255]

This presumption still applies, but its effect is qualified by the provisions of the Law of Property Act 1925.[256] The party wall is no longer owned in common but longitudinally, with each party having an easement of support over the property of the other.

30–045   Neither party is under any positive obligation to repair his half of the wall (though he may if he wishes repair his neighbour's half).[257] However neither owner is entitled to pull down the wall[258] (except for the purpose of rebuilding

---

[247] *Jones v Read* (1876) 10 I.R.C.L. 315 at 320. It should be noted however that a wall may be in sole ownership for part of its height and a party wall for the rest: *Weston v Arnold* (1873) 8 Ch.App. 1084.

[248] This presumption applies even if the middle of the wall is not precisely on the boundary: *Reading v Barnard* (1827) Moo. & M. 71 at 73, 74.

[249] *Matts v Hawkins*, above, at 23; *Kempston v Butler* (1861) 12 Ir.C.L.R. 516 at 526.

[250] cf. *Cubitt v Porter* (1828) 8 B. & C. 257 at 263; *Mason v Fulham Corp* [1910] 1 K.B. 631 at 637.

[251] *Wigford v Gill* (1592) Cro. Eliz. 269.

[252] See *Bradbee v Governors of Christ's Hospital* (1842) 4 Man. & G. 714 at 760; *Kempston v Buller* (1861) 12 Ir.C.L.R. 516. It is desirable (see *Massey v Goyder* (1829) 4 C. & P. 161) but not essential (*Chadwick v Trower* (1839) 6 Bing. N.C. 1) to give warning of the intention to pull down the wall.

[253] *Wigford v Gill*, above, *Wiltshire v Sidford*, above, at 408; *Cubitt v Porter*, above, at 264. See however the Building Act 1984 ss.80–82.

[254] *Wiltshire v Sidford*, above, at 407; *Cubitt v Porter*, above, *Jones v Read*, above, *Standard Bank of British South America v Stokes* (1878) 9 Ch D 68 at 71; *Watson v Gray*, above, at 194.

[255] *Wiltshire v Sidford*, above, at 407, 409.

[256] s.38; above, para.30–042.

[257] *Jones v Pritchard*, above, at 637; *Sack v Jones* [1925] Ch. 235.

[258] *Jones v Read*, above.

it with reasonable dispatch[259]), or to demolish his half of it, thereby removing his neighbour's support.[260] Nor can either owner prevent the other from enjoying any part of the wall, as by covering the top with broken glass or replacing it with part of a shed.[261] For these purposes the two owners still enjoy the same rights as if they were tenants in common,[262] and therefore neither can oust the other.[263]

(c) *Wall in single ownership subject to easement.* Where the party wall is **30–046** built entirely on the land of one owner, there is a presumption that the wall belongs to that landowner.[264] This category of party wall can be established only on proof that an appropriate easement has either been expressly granted or has been acquired by prescription.[265] The servient owner is under no obligation to repair the wall, though the other party may enter his land to do so.[266]

3. The Party Wall, etc., Act 1996. The Party Wall etc. Act 1996 extends **30–047** to the whole of England and Wales certain provisions that have existed in some form or another in inner London and other parts of the country for many years.[267] The definition of party wall in the Act is not in terms of the ownership but of the function of the wall. A wall will be a party wall in two circumstances:

(a) where a wall forms part of a building, and the wall itself (and not merely its foundations) projects beyond the boundary into the land of the adjoining owner; or

(b) where the wall is built on the land of one owner but separates buildings belonging to different owners.[268]

---

[259] *Cubitt v Porter*, above, *Standard Bank of British South America v Stokes*, above, at 71; *Joliffe v Woodhouse* (1894) 38 S.J. 578.

[260] *Upjohn v Seymour Estates Ltd* [1938] 1 All E.R. 614; *Brace v SE Regional Housing Association Ltd* [1984] 1 E.G.L.R. 144. See too *Bradburn v Lindsay* [1983] 2 All E.R. 408 (owner liable in negligence where local authority demolished his side of a party wall because the property was unsafe due to his neglect).

[261] *Stedman v Smith* (1857) 8 E. & B. 1 at 6 (construction of wash house roof across the entire width of the party wall).

[262] LPA 1925 s.38.

[263] Above, para.30–042.

[264] *Hutchinson v Mains* (1832) Alc. & N. 155. Similarly if one landowner makes an addition to his neighbour's wall, the addition prima facie belongs to the neighbour: *Waddington v Naylor* (1889) 60 L.T. 480.

[265] For the creation of easements, see Ch.28 above.

[266] *Jones v Pritchard*, above, at 637, 638.

[267] See e.g. London Building Acts (Amendment) Act 1939 and Bristol Improvements Act 1847. The relevant parts of this local legislation were repealed under the Party Wall, etc., Act 1996 s.21: see SI 1997/671. The Party Wall, etc., Act 1996, which came into force on July 1, 1997, was promoted by the Pyramus and Thisbe Club, a body of surveyors who specialise in party wall matters. See generally S. Bickford Smith, C. Sydenham, A. Redler, *Party Walls: Law and Practice*, 3rd edn (London: Jordans, 2009).

[268] Described as the "line of junction": Party Wall, etc., Act 1996 s.20. cf. *Knight v Pursell* (1879) 11 Ch D 412.

The legislation makes provision for the following:

(i) the construction of a new party wall[269];

(ii) the repair of and a wide variety of other works[270] to an existing party wall[271]; and

(iii) any excavation work within a certain distance of any building or structure on the adjacent owner's land.[272]

30–048 The Act requires a building owner who intends to carry out any of those works to serve a notice of a specified kind on the adjoining owner.[273] It provides for the resolution of disputes by a form of arbitration by "surveyors"[274] who are required to make an "award".[275] This may determine the right of the building owner to execute any work and the time and manner in which it may be done, together with any incidental matters.[276] There is, surprisingly, no mechanism for the registration of such an award.[277]

30–049 Sweeping rights are conferred on a person who is carrying out works under the Act.[278] These include the right to enter any land, remove any furniture or fittings, and even (if accompanied by a police officer) to break open doors or fences to enter the premises.[279] There is a correlative obligation to compensate the adjoining owner or occupier for any loss or damage caused in execution of the works.[280] If a building owner fails to comply with the requirements of the Act in carrying out works that fall within it, he commits a nuisance and is

---

[269] Party Wall, etc., Act 1996 s.1.

[270] Such as underpinning, thickening, raising, demolition and replacement of the wall.

[271] Party Wall, etc., Act 1996 s.2.

[272] Party Wall, etc., Act 1996 s.6 (for some purposes the distance is 3 metres, for others, 6).

[273] For the adjoining owner's right to serve a counter-notice and the effect of his failure to do so, see ibid., ss.4, 5.

[274] Such persons need not be surveyors at all (though in practice they will be): see ibid., s.20.

[275] Party Wall, etc., Act 1996 s.10(10).

[276] Party Wall, etc., Act 1996 s.10(12). An award authorises the claimant to carry out the work. It does not operate to extinguish easements, although extinguishment will occur once the works that have been authorised prevent the easement from being exercised: *Arena Property Services Ltd v Europa 2000 Ltd* [2003] EWCA Civ 1943. An award may include provision for the payment of costs, but only with respect to the statutory dispute resolution procedure: *Reeves v Blake* [2009] EWCA Civ 611; [2010] 1 W.L.R. 1.

[277] See *Observatory Hill Ltd v Camtel Investments S.A.* [1997] 1 E.G.L.R. 140 (party wall award in respect of registered land could not be protected by a caution). cf. Access of Neighbouring Land Act 1992 s.4; see para.30–039 above.

[278] Party Wall, etc., Act 1996 s.8. An exercise of rights under s.8 might contravene Art.8 of the European Convention on Human Rights, which confers (inter alia) a right to peaceful enjoyment of the home.

[279] A person may not enter under s.8 unless he serves a notice of his intention to enter on the owner or occupier of the land at least 14 days in advance of such entry (except in cases of emergency, when he must give such notice as is reasonably practicable): s.8(3), (4). It is a criminal offence to obstruct a person who is entitled to enter: s.16.

[280] s.7. However, the claimant must show that the loss or damage is by reason of the works executed. Where A, having served notice of intention to carry out works, removed a pipe serving B's premises, B could only obtain compensation on proof that he had an easement to use the pipe: *Arena Property Services Ltd v Europa 2000 Ltd* [2003] EWCA Civ 1943.

liable as such.[281] In exceptional circumstances, a court may even grant a mandatory injunction requiring the removal or reversal of any unauthorised works.[282]

The rights conferred under the Party Wall etc. Act 1996 are considerably **30–050** more extensive than those enjoyed by a landowner who needs to enter his neighbour's property in order to carry out works which are reasonably necessary for the preservation of all or part of his own land. These rights, which are given by the Access to Neighbouring Land Act 1992, are explained above.[283] A landowner will therefore rely upon the Act of 1992 only if he cannot bring himself within the provisions of the Act of 1996.[284]

[281] See *Louis v Sadiq* [1997] 1 E.G.L.R. 136, a case on the London Building Acts (Amendment) Act 1939.

[282] cf. *London & Manchester Assurance Co Ltd v O & H Construction Ltd* [1989] 2 E.G.L.R. 185 (also a case on the London Buildings Acts (Amendment) Act 1939).

[283] See para.30–036 above.

[284] The Access to Neighbouring Land Act 1992 applies to party walls: see *Dean v Walker* (1996) 73 P. & C.R. 366; see para.30–036 above.

CHAPTER 31

OTHER INCORPOREAL HEREDITAMENTS

Part 1

INCORPOREAL HEREDITAMENTS

31–001   **1. Meaning of term.** Incorporeal hereditaments are rights of property. Their distinguishing feature is that the law of real property applies to them, just as it applies to corporeal land,[1] but since the property owned is a right and not a physical object, the property is called incorporeal. The list of incorporeal hereditaments is a varied one and, as well as easements and profits,[2] it includes several anomalous matters. This is because it was for historical rather than logical reasons that certain rights were treated as real property instead of personal property. However, most of them are closely connected with land.

31–002   **2. Rules governing realty.** There are a number of consequences of designating a particular right as a hereditament and therefore real property, of which two may be given as examples.[3] First, such a right can be conveyed only by deed because it "lies in grant".[4] Second, a will leaving "all my real property to X and all my personal property to Y" will pass a rentcharge to X but money and goods to Y. Although some incorporeal hereditaments are now of little general significance (e.g. tithes), others, such as easements and profits, are among the most important property rights. This chapter will consider the nature of incorporeal hereditaments generally and a number of specific examples other than easements and profits. In particular, there is a fuller analysis of rentcharges.

---

[1] Above, para.1–011; cf. LPA 1925 s.205(1)(ix).
[2] Above, Ch.27.
[3] The distinction was formerly of some importance when land devolved on intestacy in a different manner from personalty: see the fifth edition of this work at p.813.
[4] Above, para.27–014.

3. Contrast with corporeal hereditaments. Corporeal and incorporeal   **31–003**
hereditaments together make up what is "real property".[5] Corporeal hereditaments are physical objects, not rights, and they are of only one type: land,
including buildings and other fixtures.[6] Incorporeal hereditaments are rights,
not physical objects, and are of many types. This treatment of *rights* (incorporeal) and *things* (corporeal) as if they were similar has been criticised,[7] but it
is the inevitable outcome of having two separate ways of dealing with
"property". A line has to be drawn between "real" and "personal" property
in terms of the matters which are governed by each set of rules. But there are
many species of property which are not physical things but yet must be
governed by real property law. Personal property must include, for example,
choses in action, e.g. debts, money in a bank, stocks and shares; real property
must equally necessarily include certain special interests of an intangible kind.
The illogicality does not lie in the inclusion of rights as well as physical land
within the realm of real property, but rather in the kinds of rights which have
been allotted to realty and personalty respectively. The early tendency to treat
all rights as proprietary if that was at all possible made our law "rich with
incorporeal things": this is "the most medieval part of medieval law".[8]

The distinction between corporeal and incorporeal hereditaments is not
always easily drawn in practice. Thus the right to graze beasts on a piece of
land, known as "cattlegate"[9] can exist either as an incorporeal grazing right
or as a form of corporeal co-ownership of the land in common with other
"stint-holders".[10] It can be difficult to distinguish between these two forms of
the right.[11]

4. Principal incorporeal hereditaments. The following are the most   **31–004**
important incorporeal hereditaments to be found nowadays.[12]

(a) Rentcharges. A rentcharge is an annuity secured on some specified   **31–005**
land.[13] Although the circumstances in which rentcharges can now be created
are circumscribed by statute, and most will be abolished in due course,[14] they
remain of some importance and are considered below.[15]

(b) Annuities. An annuity differs from a rentcharge in not being secured   **31–006**
upon or connected with land. An annuity, e.g. £10,000 a year, could be granted

---

[5] Above, para.1–011. But "real property" and "hereditaments" were not exactly coterminous.
An annuity of inheritance was a hereditament but not real property, since real property was
property recoverable by a real action: cf. Woist. & C. i, 337.
[6] For fixtures, see above, para.23–001.
[7] Cheshire and Burn, *Modern Law of Real Property*, 17th edn (Oxford: OUP) p.154 (142).
[8] P. & M. ii, 124, 149.
[9] Also known as "stint", "beastgate" and "pasturegate". For "shackage" (the right to graze after
the taking of arable crops), see *R. v Suffolk CC, Ex p. Steed* (1995) 70 P. & C.R. 487 at 496.
[10] *Brackenbank Lodge Ltd v Peart* (1993) 67 P. & C.R. 249 at 255.
[11] See *Brackenbank Lodge Ltd v Peart*, above.
[12] For a fuller account, see the previous edition of this work at pp.814 et seq.
[13] Litt. p.218.
[14] Under the provisions of the Rentcharges Act 1977, considered below.
[15] Below, para.31–018. For a recent example see *Orchard Trading Estate Management Ltd v
Johnson Security Ltd* [2002] EWCA Civ 406, (2002) 18 E.G. 155.

or devised to a person and his heirs and would then devolve as a hereditament, like land.[16]

31–007   *(c) Advowsons.* An advowson is the perpetual right of presentation to an ecclesiastical living.[17] The owner of an advowson is known as the patron and has the right, when the living becomes vacant, to nominate the clergyman who shall next hold it. However, the exercise of this right is now much restricted.[18] An advowson is an incorporeal hereditament and therefore, somewhat curiously, real property. However, although the patron has an estate in land, an advowson cannot be sold,[19] and it cannot be registered under the Land Registration Act 2002.[20] The functions of a patron cannot be exercised unless the advowson was registered with the registrar of the diocese by the beginning of 1989.[21]

31–008   *(d) Tithes and chancel repair liability.*[22] A tithe was the right of a rector to a tenth part of the produce of all the land in his parish. The right to tithes has been almost entirely dismantled by a series of statutes,[23] and little vestige remains of it today, except the liability of certain landowners ("lay rectors") to repair chancels. This remains a potential conveyancing trap and must be explained.

31–009   (1) THE BASIS OF LIABILITY.[24] On the dissolution of the monasteries in the reign of Henry VIII many rectories passed into royal hands and were granted to lay landowners. The right to tithes thus passed into lay hands in many cases and was said to be "impropriated" by the lay rector. This carried with it (inter alia) the rector's common law liability to repair the chancel of the church.[25] In some circumstances that liability became attached to the ownership of certain land.[26] The liability is a legal right which can bind all transferees and purchasers, and where the title is registered, it takes effect as an unregistered

---

[16] H.E.L. iii, p.152; Wolst. & C. v, 79; Challis p.46. Such a "personal hereditament" could not be entailed; it was enforceable only against the grantor or his estate.
[17] Co.Litt. p.17b.
[18] By the Patronage (Benefices) Measure 1986.
[19] Patronage (Benefices) Measure 1986 s.3.
[20] s.3. Under the LRA 1925, an advowson was not classed as "land" and ceased to be registrable: Patronage (Benefices) Measure 1986 ss.6(1), 6(2).
[21] Patronage (Benefices) Measure 1986 s.1(1).
[22] See the fifth edition of this work at p.830.
[23] See, e.g. Tithe Acts 1836, 1918, 1925, 1936, 1951; Statute Law (Repeals) Act 1998.
[24] For a full account of the history of this form of liability, see (1985) Law Com. No.152, App. B. See too the fifth edition of this work at pp.830–833.
[25] See *Parochial Church Council of Aston Cantlow & Wilmcote with Billesley, Warwickshire* v *Wallbank* [2003] UKHL, [2004] 1 A.C. 546, where Lord Scott gives a full account of the origins and development of the liability; (2005) 113 Fam. Law 17; (2004) 63 C.L.J. 7 (Leslie Turano); (2004) 120 L.Q.R. 41 (Peter Cane); (2008) Conv. 140 (Mark Reading). See also *Wickhambrook Parochial Church Council v Croxford* [1935] 2 K.B. 417; *Chivers & Sons Ltd v Air Ministry* [1955] Ch. 585; Millard, *Tithes*, pp.143–145; Chancel Repairs Act 1932. For an admirable summary of the law, see (1984) 100 L.Q.R. 181 (J. H. Baker).
[26] See (1984) 100 L.Q.R. 181 at 183; Law Com. No.152, paras 2.2–2.7 and App. B; *Tithe Records in the Public Record Office* (PRO Leaflet 13, 1981), para.14.

interest which overrides.[27] Liability is not capped at the amount equivalent to the profits of the land, and where more than one impropriator is liable, it is several and not joint.[28] When an impropriator sells the land in question, he ceases to be liable for repairs which arise thereafter.[29]

(2) PROPOSALS FOR REFORM. The chances of a landowner being fixed with **31–010** liability for chancel repairs is entirely capricious and depends upon factors such as whether the church was founded before the dissolution of the monasteries[30] and whether any particular land became burdened by it, e.g. because of an inclosure award.[31] Not only can the liability prove to be heavy,[32] but because records are incomplete, its existence and extent may be virtually impossible for a purchaser to discover.[33] Chancel repair liability is therefore precisely the kind of encumbrance that a system of conveyancing should seek to avoid and the unamended version of the Land Registration Act 2002 pursued that goal by omitting the liability from the list of overriding interests. However, as noted above,[34] following the House of Lords decision in *Parochial Church Council of Aston Cantlow & Wilmcote with Billesley, Warwickshire v Wallbank*,[35] the liability was reintroduced in to the Land Registration Act 2002 and now will override until October 13, 2013.[36]

(e) Easements. It is only in modern times that easements have been recog- **31–011** nised as incorporeal hereditaments,[37] though they are now the most important of such rights. Examples include private rights of way and rights of light. Easements have been considered in detail above.[38]

---

[27] LRA 2002 Sch.1 para.16 (against a first registration) and LRA 2002 Sch.3 para 16 (against a registered disposition). This was added to the LRA 2002 by the Land Registration Act 2002 (Transitional Provisions) (No.2) Order 2003, having been omitted from the list of interests which override on the basis that such liability was unenforceable as violation of the European Convention on Human Rights. That view became untenable when the House of Lords overturned the Court of Appeal on this point, *Parochial Church Council of Aston Cantlow & Wilmcote with Billesley, Warwickshire v Wallbank* above. The liability will cease to override on October 12, 2013, LRA s.117(1), see above paras 7–031, 7–088.

[28] *Wickhambrook Parochial Church Council v Croxford*, above. See also *Aston Cantlow & Wilmcote with Billesley, Parochial Church Council v Wallbank, The Times*, February 21, 2007, where it was decided additionally that the liability is to repair; it is not limited merely to making the chancel wind and watertight.

[29] *Chivers & Sons Ltd v Air Ministry*, above.

[30] It cannot apply to those which were founded thereafter: Law Com. No.152, para.12. One estimate is that 3,785,000 acres of land may be subject to this form of liability.

[31] See Law Com. No.152, App. B, paras 2.11, 2.12.

[32] See the case cited in Law Com. No.152, para.1.3, of a landowner, who although unaware of his liability, had to pay over £10,000. Estimates of the liability for the chancel in Aston Cantlow vary, but the latest figure was £186,969.50, with a potential for VAT on top, *Aston Cantlow & Wilmcote with Billesley, Parochial Church Council v Wallbank*, above. In 2009, Mr and Mrs Wallbank sold the property in order to settle the liability and meet legal costs.

[33] See Law Com. No.152, Pt III.

[34] Above, fn.27.

[35] Above, fn.25.

[36] Above, fn.27.

[37] See generally Ch.27.

[38] Above, Chs 27–30.

31–012   *(f) Profits à prendre.* A profit is a right to take something off another's land, such as a right of common or of shooting or fishing. Such rights are of considerable importance and have been considered together with easements.

31–013   *(g) Franchises.* A franchise is "a royal privilege or branch of the royal prerogative subsisting in the hands of a subject, by grant from the King".[39] In the early Middle Ages they were of many kinds, such as fairs, markets, the right to wrecks and treasure trove,[40] and free fisheries.[41] Today, the most important franchise is that of market.[42] Where such a franchise exists, no rival market[43] may be set up within six and two-thirds miles.[44] Breach of the franchise is actionable in tort as a nuisance,[45] and damages are awarded without proof of loss.[46] Under the Land Registration Act 2002, it is possible to register certain franchises with their own title.[47]

Part 2

RENTCHARGES

Section 1. Nature of Rentcharges

31–014   **1. Rentcharges and rent services.** Periodical payments in respect of land fall under the two main heads of rentcharges and rent services. Where the relationship of lord and tenant exists between the parties, any rent payable by virtue of that relationship by the tenant to the lord is a rent service.[48] If there is no relationship of lord and tenant, the rent is a rentcharge. Thus if L grants a lease to T at £100 per annum and X charges his fee simple estate with the payment of £200 per annum to Y, L has a rent service and Y a rentcharge. Since the Statute *Quia Emptores* 1290 it has been impossible for a grantor to reserve any services on a conveyance of freehold land in fee simple, for the grantee holds of the grantor's lord, and not of the grantor.[49] Consequently no

---

[39] *Spook Erection Ltd v Secretary of State for the Environment* [1989] Q.B. 300 at 305, per Nourse L.J. See P. & M. i, p.571; H.E.L. i, p.87; iii, p.169; Bl.Comm. i, p.302.

[40] For details of treasure trove at common law, see the fifth edition of this work at p.65. For the Treasure Act 1996, which now governs treasure trove, see above, para.3–045.

[41] See below, para.26–062.

[42] For the regime of rights affecting a franchise market, see *Gloucester CC v Williams* (1990) 88 L.G.R. 853 at 857, 858.

[43] Which may include a "car boot sale": *Newcastle-upon-Tyne CC v Noble* (1990) 89 L.G.R. 618. On what constitutes a rival market, see *Kingston upon Hull CC v Greenwood* (1984) 82 L.G.R. 586.

[44] See *Birmingham CC v Anvil Fairs* [1989] 1 W.L.R. 312. The same rule applies to a statutory market: *Manchester CC v Walsh (1985)* 84 L.G.R. 1.

[45] *Sevenoaks DC v Pattullo & Vinson Ltd* [1984] Ch. 211.

[46] *Stoke-on-Trent CC v W & J. Wass Ltd* (1989) 87 L.G.R. 129 (discussing the measure of damages).

[47] LRA 2002 s.3(1)(c). Registration is voluntary and the compulsory triggers do not apply. The franchise must constitute a legal estate and be, either, perpetual or for a term of years with more than seven years unexpired.

[48] Above, para.19–062.

[49] Above, para.2–015.

rent reserved on a conveyance of *freehold* land in fee simple after 1290 can be a rent service.

The only rent service met with in practice is thus the rent reserved upon the grant of a lease. A rent reserved by a lease is annexed to a reversion in land, while a rentcharge stands on its own as an incorporeal hereditament.

2. Legal and equitable rentcharges. As we have seen, a rentcharge is real   **31–015** property. Prior to 1926, both at law and in equity it could be held for any of the usual estates or interests.[50] However, since 1925, an interest in a rentcharge can be legal only if it is:

(a)   in possession,[51] and

(b)   either perpetual or for a term of years absolute.[52]

Further, a legal rentcharge cannot be created at law without certain formalities.[53] A mere contract for a rentcharge may however create an equitable interest in the usual way.[54]

3. Rentcharge on a rentcharge. At common law a rentcharge could be   **31–016** charged only upon a corporeal hereditament. There could be no rentcharge charged upon another rentcharge[55] or other incorporeal hereditament,[56] since obviously there could then be no right of distress. But this technical obstacle was removed both for the past and for the future by the Law of Property Act 1925,[57] which validates rentcharges charged on other rentcharges and provides special machinery for enforcing payment.

4. Rentcharges in conveyancing. In certain parts of the country, especially   **31–017** in the areas of Manchester, Bristol and Bath, rentcharges were long used as a substitute for capital payments on the sale of land.[58] Instead of a capital sum the vendor either took a perpetual rentcharge charged on the land, or he took the purchase price in the form partly of a capital sum and partly of a rentcharge. These freehold rentcharges were known as chief rents or fee farm rents. These rentcharges complicated conveyancing, particularly where they were of long standing and the land in question had been subdivided, and were unpopular with land owners because they were "repugnant to the concept of

---

[50] Such as an estate tail: *Chaplin v Chaplin* (1733) 3 P.Wms. 229; or a term of years: *Re Fraser* [1904] 1 Ch. 726.
[51] As to when a rentcharge is deemed to be in possession, see above, para.6–017.
[52] LPA 1925 s.1(2)(b); above, para.6–008.
[53] See below.
[54] *Jackson v Lever* (1792) 3 Bro.C.C. 605; cf. above, para.17–047.
[55] Co.Litt. p.47a; *Earl of Stafford v Buckley* (1750) 2 Ves.Sen. 170 at 178.
[56] *Re The Alms Corn Charity* [1901] 2 Ch. 750 at 759.
[57] s.122; below, para.31–032.
[58] For a full survey, see (1975) Law Com. No.68, on which the Rentcharges Act 1977 was based.

freehold ownership".[59] Since they had ceased to play any useful part in the financing of the purchase of property, they were abolished for the future by the Rentcharges Act 1977, as explained below.

Rentcharges are more suitably employed in connection with schemes of development, particularly where plots or flats are sold freehold and the purchasers contribute to the cost of maintaining the common parts of the buildings or grounds, or where there is a need to provide for management of common areas and facilities of a commercial development. In this context they have proved useful as a device for circumventing the rule that the burden of positive covenants cannot run with freehold land.[60] Consequently such rentcharges have not been abolished by the Rentcharges Act 1977.

Section 2. Abolition of Rentcharges

31–018   **1. Rentcharges abolished.** In accordance with recommendations of the Law Commission, the Rentcharges Act 1977 made provision for the abolition of those rentcharges which were inconvenient and unpopular, while exempting those which were useful. It defines a rentcharge as "any annual or other periodic sum charged on or issuing out of land, except rent reserved by a lease or tenancy, or any sum payable by way of interest".[61] It then provides as follows[62]:

> (i) No rentcharge, whether legal or equitable, may be created after August 21, 1977.

> (ii) A pre-existing rentcharge shall be extinguished at the end of 60 years from July 22, 1977 or 60 years from the date when it first became payable, whichever is the later; but in the case of a variable rentcharge the period of 60 years runs only from the date, if any, on which it ceases to be variable.

> (iii) Certain rentcharges are exempted from the above provisions.

31–019   **2. Rentcharges exempted.** The rentcharges which are exempted from the Rentcharges Act 1977, and therefore permitted, are the following.[63]

> (i) Those which give effect to family charges under Schedule 1 to the Trusts of Land and Appointment of Trustees Act 1996.[64] These charges, which are imposed voluntarily or in consideration of

---

[59] Law Com. No.68, para.26.
[60] For example, *Orchard Trading Estate Management Ltd v Johnson Security Ltd* [2002] EWCA Civ 406, (2002) 18 E.G. 155 and see below, para.32–021.
[61] s.1.
[62] ss.2, 3, 18(2).
[63] s.2(3) (as amended by TLATA 1996 Sch.3 para.15); s.2(4).
[64] para.3.

marriage or by way of family arrangement, have been explained in connection with settled land and trusts of land.[65]

(ii) "Estate rentcharges", meaning those created for the purpose of:

(a) making covenants enforceable (by the device mentioned earlier),[66] or

(b) meeting expenses incurred by the rent owner in performing covenants for services, maintenance, repairs or insurance, or for any payment for the benefit of the burdened land.

If created for purpose (a), the rentcharge must be of a nominal amount only, and if created for purpose (b), its amount, if not nominal, must be reasonable in relation to the covenanted services, etc.[67] The object of this limitation in the extent of allowable rentcharges is to prevent the exemptions being used to create substantial rentcharges which ought to be abolished. However, the exemptions should not be interpreted narrowly if it is clear that the rentcharge is intended, and can be construed to operate, within the exemption. So, in *Orchard Trading Estate Management Ltd v Johnson Security Ltd*, a rentcharge which was intended to ensure that the management company could meet the costs associated with running the trading estate (such as sewerage costs) was for the "benefit" of the burdened land (the individual units), even though the rentcharge enabled recovery of the costs of ownership of the common parts owned by the management company. Further, the costs were presumptively "reasonable" within the exemption if they were no more than the actual costs incurred by the management company in providing the services for the burdened land.[68]

(iii) Rentcharges payable in lieu of tithes.[69]

(iv) Statutory rentcharges created in connection with the execution of works on land or the commutation of any obligation to do them.

(v) Rentcharges created under an order of the court.

The last two heads can be illustrated from the provisions of the Settled Land Act 1925 for the repayment by instalments of capital money expended on improvements to settled land, under which a rentcharge may be created by the tenant for life or by a court order.[70]

---

[65] Above, para.12–004.
[66] Below, para.32–021.
[67] s.2(5). But pre-existing rentcharges created for these purposes are exempt from extinguishment regardless of their amount s.3(3)(b).
[68] [2002] EWCA Civ 406 at para.23 et seq. There does not need to be an express limitation to "reasonableness" in the deed creating the rentcharge, ibid. at para.29.
[69] s.3(3)(a), applying for purposes of extinguishment only. Tithe redemption annuities were extinguished in 1977, but corn rents do still exist (and continue to be collected): see (1998) Law Com. No.254, para.5.40, and the fifth edition of this work at p.833.
[70] s.85; and see fn.71, below.

Section 3. Creation and Transfer of Rentcharges

31–020   **1. Creation.** When permitted by the Rentcharges Act 1977, a rentcharge may be created by statute, by an instrument inter vivos, or by will.

31–021   *(a) By statute.* A rentcharge may be created by statute, or by virtue of powers conferred thereby.[71]

31–022   *(b) By instrument inter vivos.* Apart from statute, a legal rentcharge can be created inter vivos only by a deed,[72] although it has always been possible for a person disposing of land to reserve a rentcharge to himself, without the grantee of the land executing the deed.[73]

An equitable rentcharge may be created by enforceable contract[74] or by signed writing.[75]

31–023   *(c) By will.* A will operates only in equity[76]; therefore, if a rentcharge is created or devised by will, the beneficiary gets no legal interest until the personal representatives have assented to the gift. The assent must be in writing, but need not be by deed.[77]

2. Words of limitation

31–024   *(a) Transfer.* The words of limitation required for the transfer of an existing rentcharge are governed by the ordinary rules for dispositions of land,[78] so that a will made after 1837 or a deed executed since 1925 will pass the whole interest in the rentcharge unless a contrary intention is shown.[79]

31–025   *(b) Creation.* On the creation of a new rentcharge the Wills Act 1837 s.28, has been held not to apply for it is confined to the transfer of an existing interest.[80] Accordingly the devisee of a rentcharge created by the will can take it only for life unless a contrary intention appears.[81]

It is not so clear whether the Law of Property Act 1925 s.60[82] applies to the creation of rentcharges by deed, though the better view is that it does.[83] If that

---

[71] See, e.g. Improvement of Land Acts, 1864 and 1899, which empowered a landowner (e.g. a tenant for life) to obtain an order from the Ministry of Agriculture, Fisheries and Food charging the land with repayment of money borrowed to finance improvements. These Acts were in general superseded by the Settled Land Acts 1882 and 1925 (above, Ch.10), but the Act of 1864 is still occasionally resorted to because (by s.59) it may give the rentcharge priority over other incumbrances.
[72] *Hewlins v Shippam* (1826) 5 B. & C. 221 at 229. The usual exceptions apply: see LPA 1925 s.52.
[73] Co.Litt. p.143a.
[74] Above, fn.54.
[75] LPA 1925 s.53.
[76] LP(Am)A 1924 Sch.IX.
[77] AEA 1925 s.36; above, para.14–127.
[78] Above paras 3–023 et seq.
[79] Wills Act 1837 s.28; LPA 1925 s.60(1).
[80] *Nichols v Hawkes* (1853) 10 Hare 342.
[81] Above, para.3–032.
[82] Above, para.3–030; cf. above, para.28–006, fn.19.
[83] For a fuller treatment of this point, see the fifth edition of this work at p.823.

is correct, a perpetual rentcharge will need no special words of limitation when created by deed.

(c) Rentcharges charged upon registered land.[84] In those circumstances in **31–026** which a rentcharge may still be created after the Rentcharges Act 1977,[85] a registered freehold proprietor has the power to make a disposition of any kind permitted by the general law.[86] He may either:

(i) grant; or

(ii) transfer the registered land subject to the reservation of,[87]

a rentcharge in possession that is either perpetual or for a term of years. A registered leasehold proprietor has the same power, save that he may only grant a rentcharge to the extent of his estate.[88] The grant or reservation of a rentcharge out of a registered estate is a registrable disposition.[89] A legal rentcharge should be registered with its own title,[90] and also noted against the title affected.[91]

Section 4. Means of Enforcing Payment of Rentcharges

A. Rentcharge Charged on Land

There are four remedies available to the owner of a rentcharge if it is not paid. **31–027** The first is the common law action for the money. The other three are implied into every rentcharge by statute,[92] subject to any expression of contrary intention in the instrument creating the rentcharge.[93] These statutory remedies do not extend the law, because they confer no greater powers than would an express stipulation to the same effect.[94]

1. Action for the money. A personal action for the rent (as for a debt) will **31–028** lie against the "terre tenant" (the freehold tenant for the time being of the land upon which the rent is charged), even if the rent was not created by him[95] and even if it exceeds the value of the land.[96] If the land charged has been divided,

---

[84] See Ruoff & Roper, Ch.29.
[85] Above, para.31–018.
[86] LRA 2002 ss.23, 24.
[87] LRA 2002 ss.23, 24.
[88] LRA 2002 ss.23, 24.
[89] LRA 2002 s.27(2)(e) Above, para.7–053.
[90] LRR 2003 r.2(2).
[91] LRA 2002 Sch.2 para.6; Ruoff & Roper, 29–014.
[92] LPA 1925 s.121. Section 121(2) LPA 1925 would be repealed on entry into force of the relevant provisions of the Tribunals, Courts and Enforcement Act 2007 s.71. See below, para.31–029, fn.102.
[93] LPA 1925 s.121(5), (7).
[94] LPA 1925 s.121(1).
[95] *Thomas v Sylvester* (1873) L.R. 8 Q.B. 368.
[96] *Pertwee v Townsend* [1896] 2 Q.B. 129.

the terre tenant of any part is liable for the full amount.[97] A mere lessee for a term of years is not liable,[98] for the action is the modern successor of one of the ancient real actions,[99] which lay only against the person seised of the land, i.e. the freeholder in possession. Its "real" nature is attested by the fact that though nominally a personal action it lies against assignees of the land. In truth, "the land is the debtor",[100] and the action asserts title to an incorporeal hereditament.

Although the right to sue and the liability to be sued run with the rentcharge and the land respectively, the benefit of an express covenant for payment does not run with the rentcharge without express assignment.[101] Thus if a rentcharge created by A in favour of X is conveyed to Y and the land to B, Y cannot sue A on his covenant for payment if B fails to pay: A's liability to Y exists only while A is entitled in possession, unless Y is an express assignee of X's rights under the covenant to pay. This is another illustration of the medieval view of a rent as a thing rather than a promise.

31–029   **2. Distress.** If an express power of distress is given by the instrument creating the rentcharge, the extent of the right is a question of construction. If there is no such express power, the rentcharge owner can distrain as soon as the rent or any part of it is 21 days in arrear.[102]

31–030   **3. Entry into possession.** In the absence of any expression of contrary intention in the instrument creating the rentcharge, the rentcharge owner may, when the rent or any part of it is 40 days in arrear, enter and take possession of the land without impeachment of waste and take the income until he has paid himself all rent due with costs.[103]

31–031   **4. Demise to a trustee.** If the rentcharge shows no contrary intention, the rentcharge owner may, if the rent or any part of it is 40 days in arrear, demise the land to a trustee for a term of years, with or without impeachment of waste, on trust to raise the money due, with all costs and expenses, by creating

---

[97] *Christie v Barker* (1884) 53 L.J.Q.B. 537.
[98] *Re Herbage Rents* [1896] 2 Ch. 811. A mortgagee is therefore not liable since 1925, for he holds a mere term of years; previously he was liable if he took a freehold estate: *Cundiff v Fitzsimmons* [1911] 1 K.B. 513.
[99] Below, Appendix.
[100] *Thomas v Sylvester*, above, at 372, per Quain J.
[101] *Grant v Edmondson* [1931] 1 Ch. 1, where the rentcharge was created before 1926; for rentcharges created after 1925, see Halsbury Vol.39(2), para.876. For criticism of *Grant v Edmondson* see (1931) 47 L.Q.R. 380 (W. Strachan).
[102] LPA 1925 s.121(2), (5), (7). If the relevant provisions of the Tribunals, Courts and Enforcement Act 2007 ever come into force, they appear to abolish the remedy of distress even for rentcharges. Distress in respect of a rentcharge is likely to be abrogated because of the potential repeal of s.121(2) LPA 1925, rather than directly by s.71 TCE Act 2007. Note, that distress would be replaced for a "landlord under a lease of commercial premises" by the commercial rent recovery scheme, s.71, 72. This implies that the commercial rent recovery scheme would not be available to enforce a rentcharge.
[103] LPA 1925 s.121(3), (5), (7).

a mortgage, receiving the income or any other reasonable means.[104] If a rentcharge owner has only an equitable interest, he can grant only an equitable lease to the trustee,[105] but the estate owner can be compelled to clothe the equitable lease with the legal estate.[106]

As regards rentcharges created before July 16, 1964, the rule against perpetuities was disapplied in relation to these last three remedies and to any like powers conferred by any instrument for enforcing payment of a rent-charge.[107] Where a rentcharge was created after July 15, 1964 but before April 6, 2010, the rule does not apply to any powers or remedies for recovery or enforcing payment, whether statutory or otherwise.[108] The rule against perpetuities does not apply to rentcharges created after April 5, 2010, so that these exceptions are no longer needed.[109]

B. Rentcharge Charged on Another Rentcharge[110]

Instead of the statutory remedies of distress, entry into possession, and demise **31–032** to a trustee, the owner of a rentcharge charged upon another rentcharge may appoint a receiver if the rent or any part of it is 21 days in arrear.[111] The receiver has all the powers of a receiver appointed by a mortgagee.[112] Thus if Blackacre is charged with a rent of £1,000 per annum and that rentcharge is charged with a rent of £250 per annum in favour of X, a receiver of the £1,000 can be appointed by X if the £250 is unpaid for 21 days.

There is no provision for any personal action against an assignee of the rentcharge upon which the second rentcharge is charged; but since the latter can be created "in like manner as" the same could have been made to issue out of land[113] it may be that the right to such a rentcharge is implicitly accompanied by the usual common law remedy.[114]

Section 5. Apportionment of Rentcharges

1. Voluntary appointment. If land which is subject to a rentcharge is **31–033** divided, the owner of each part of it is liable for the full amount, as already explained. The owner of the rentcharge may, however, agree to an apportion-ment, in which case the liability of each part will be limited accordingly. If the landowners make an apportionment among themselves without the agreement of the owner of the rentcharge, the owner will not be bound by it, and it will

---

[104] LPA 1925 s.121(4), (5), (7).
[105] LPA 1925 s.121(4).
[106] LPA 1925 ss.3(1), 8(2); SIA 1925 s.16.
[107] LPA 1925, s.121(6) (amended by PAA 1964, s.11(2)). See the previous edition of this work at para.31–031.
[108] PAA 1964 ss.11(1), 15(5); above, para.9–142.
[109] See above, para.9–142.
[110] Above para.31–016.
[111] LPA 1925 s.122.
[112] LPA 1925; and see below, para.25–036, for such a receiver's powers.
[113] LPA 1925 s.122(1).
[114] Above, para.31–028.

merely entitle one landowner to reclaim from the others if compelled to pay more than his agreed proportion. Apportionments which do and do not bind the owner are known as legal and equitable apportionments respectively,[115] though the latter are not technically based on principles of equity. Equitable apportionments are given statutory force by the Law of Property Act 1925 so as to bind and benefit successors in title and to give remedies of distress and appropriation of income which are exempt from the perpetuity rule.[116]

31–034 **2. Compulsory apportionment.** Under the Rentcharges Act 1977 the Secretary of State[117] may authorise compulsory legal apportionment so as to bind the owner of the rentcharge.[118] An owner of part or all of the burdened land may apply for an apportionment order, so that an owner about to divide his land may apply as well as an owner of a part already divided. But no application may be made in respect of statutory rentcharges or rentcharges in lieu of titles,[119] or where a part already divided has been charged with the whole liability to the exoneration of the remaining land. A draft of the order must be served on the owner of the rentcharge who may object on the ground that it will be inadequately secured; but unless the Secretary of State modifies the order in the light of the objection, he must apportion the rentcharge in the way proposed by the owner or owners of the burdened land, or as he thinks fit if there are several such owners who have not agreed. Where an apportioned amount is £5 or less per annum, it may be ordered to take effect only for the purpose of being redeemed. An apportionment order is subject to appeal to the Lands Chamber.

Section 6. Extinguishment of Rentcharges

31–035 A rentcharge may be extinguished by release, merger, lapse of time or statutory redemption.

31–036 **1. Release.** The owner of a rentcharge may by deed release the land from the rent, either wholly or in part. A partial release may take the form of releasing all of the land from part of the rent,[120] or releasing part of the land from the whole of the rent.[121] An informal release may be valid in equity.

A limited owner, e.g. a life tenant, of a rentcharge cannot release more than his own interest, except under the powers conferred by the Settled Land Act 1925.[122] Nor can the owner of a rentcharge charged upon several different

---

[115] See Rentcharges Act 1977 s.13(1).
[116] s.190.
[117] For the Environment, or for Wales.
[118] ss.4–7.
[119] i.e. those exempted from the Act (above para.31–019), classes (iii) and (iv)).
[120] Co.Litt. p.148a.
[121] LPA 1925 s.70.
[122] Below, Appendix para.A–026.

properties increase the liability on one of them by releasing another, unless the owner of the property to be burdened concurs in the release.[123] Thus if a rent of £1,000 is charged on five plots of land owned by five different people, and one plot is released, the rentcharge owner can recover £1,000 in respect of the four remaining plots if the owners concurred in the release,[124] but only £800 if they did not concur.[125]

2. Merger. At common law, if a rentcharge became vested in the same person as the land upon which it was charged, the rentcharge became extinguished by merger, even if this was not the intention.[126] For this to occur, both the rent and the land must have been vested in the same person at the same time and in the same right.[127] This automatic rule of the common law no longer applies, for by the Law of Property Act 1925[128] there is to be no merger at law except in cases where there would have been a merger in equity, and the equitable rule is that merger depends upon the intention of the parties.[129] Even if an intention that there should be no merger cannot be shown, there will be a presumption against merger if it is to the interest of the person concerned to prevent it.[130]

31–037

3. Lapse of time. If a rentcharge is not paid for 12 years and no sufficient acknowledgment of the owner's title is made, it is extinguished.[131] It is also extinguished, unless exempt, on the expiry of the 60-year period under the Rentcharges Act 1977, as explained above.[132]

31–038

4. Statutory redemption. Under the Rentcharges Act 1977,[133] replacing the Law of Property Act 1925,[134] the owner of land which is subject to a rentcharge is entitled to redeem it by paying an equivalent capital sum to the owner of the rentcharge or into court. The Act of 1977 grants this right only in respect of rentcharges which are subject to the provisions for extinguishment in 60 years, already explained[135]; thus it strengthens the position of "estate rentcharges" and the other exempted classes, which formerly were liable to redemption under the Act of 1925. The capital sum is computed according to a statutory formula which takes account of the fact that the rentcharge is now a wasting asset. When this sum has been duly paid under the statutory procedure the Secretary of State issues a redemption certificate which discharges the land from the rentcharge, but without prejudice to the recovery of arrears.

31–039

[123] LPA 1925 s.70.
[124] *Price v John* [1905] 1 Ch. 774.
[125] *Booth v Smith* (1884) 14 QBD 318.
[126] *Capital and Counties Bank Ltd v Rhodes* [1903] 1 Ch. 631 at 652, 653.
[127] *Re Radcliffe* [1892] 1 Ch. 227 at 231.
[128] s.185.
[129] *Ingle v Vaughan Jenkins* [1900] 2 Ch. 368.
[130] *Re Fletcher* [1917] 1 Ch. 339; but see *Re Attkins* [1913] 2 Ch. 619.
[131] LA 1980 ss.15, 38; *Shaw v Crompton* [1910] 2 K.B. 370; below, para.35–034.
[132] Above, paras 31–018, 31–019.
[133] ss.8–10. Payment into court may be authorised in case of difficulty, e.g. if the owner of the rentcharge cannot be found.
[134] s.191.
[135] Above, para.31–019.

CHAPTER 32

FREEHOLD COVENANTS

32–001 This chapter is concerned with the running of covenants with freehold land. Much of this topic consists of the law of restrictive covenants, being covenants that limit the use of land or activities on it. The transformation of these once merely contractual obligations in to proprietary obligations in the 19th century is a remarkable example of the contribution of equity to the development of the law of real property.

32–002 **1. Classification.** A freehold covenant resembles an incumbrance and is a burden on land. The covenant creates a right over land in favour of someone who is a stranger to it, and the occupier is bound by the covenant just as by any other third party right such as an easement or mortgage. There is necessarily some overlap with the law on leasehold covenants as explained in Chapter 20. First, the principles governing covenants made by third parties guaranteeing the performance of obligations in leases are subject to the rules relating to freehold rather than leasehold covenants.[1] Second, a landlord may be able to sue a sub-tenant on a covenant in the head lease if it qualifies as a "restrictive covenant" and is binding on the sub-tenant under the rules explained in this chapter.

32–003 **2. Divergence of law and equity.** At common law it has always been possible for the benefit, as opposed to the burden, of a covenant to run with the land automatically, even where the parties to the covenant do not stand in the relationship of landlord and tenant. If P, on buying a plot of land from V, enters into a covenant with V for the benefit of V's other land (e.g. if P covenants to clean annually the ditches on V's side of the boundary), the benefit of this covenant may pass at law to successors in title to V.[2] By

---

[1] Above, para.20–056.
[2] Below, para.32–009.

contrast, the burden of P's covenant cannot not run with his land at law so as to bind his successors in title.[3] The covenant binds only P himself and (after his death) his estate.[4]

In equity the rules are of relatively more recent origin, and have a wider effect on the land. First, equity allowed the benefit of a contract or covenant to be assigned as a chose in action,[5] whether or not it concerned land, although it is now clear that express assignments may have legal as well as equitable effect if they comply with the Law of Property Act 1925.[6] Second, equity followed the law in allowing the benefit of certain covenants to be annexed to the land so as to run with the land without express assignment. Third, however, the revolutionary contribution of equity was to recognise that, subject to certain conditions, the burden of restrictive covenants (i.e. those being negative or prohibitory in effect), such as covenants not to build or not to carry on a particular activity on the land, could run with the land that was subject to them.[7] This transformed the law of covenants in cases where there was neither privity of contract nor privity of estate. It meant that the effectiveness of a covenant concerning the covenantor's land was no longer confined to the period for which the original covenantor retained his land, but might continue indefinitely to affect the land irrespective of who came to own or occupy it. Once it could be shown that the necessary conditions had been satisfied, a restrictive covenant might continue to burden one plot of land for the benefit of another irrespective of the number of times each plot changed hands. The web of possibilities created by these developments must now be examined in some detail and for the sake of completeness, the position of the original parties to the covenant will be considered as well, even though that is simply a matter of privity of contract.

Section 1. The Position At Law

A. *The Benefit of the Covenant*

I. THE ORIGINAL COVANANTEE

1. Enforcement. The original covenantee can always enforce any express[8] **32–004** covenant against the original covenantor, provided that the covenantee has not expressly assigned the benefit to some other person. But if the covenant was made for the benefit of land belonging to the covenantee, and the covenantee

---

[3] *Austerberry v Corp of Oldham* (1885) 29 Ch D 750 at 781–785; *Smith v Colbourne* [1914] 2 Ch. 533 at 542; *E. & G.C. Ltd v Bate* (1935) 97 L.J. News 203 (covenant to build road; assignee of benefit failed against devisee of covenantor); *Cator v Newton* [1940] 1 K.B. 415; *Jones v Price* [1965] 2 Q.B. 618; *Rhone v Stephens* [1994] 2 A.C. 310; below, para.32–017.

[4] See, e.g. *Hall v National Provincial Bank Ltd* [1939] L.J.N.C.C.R. 185.

[5] For this reason a right to specific performance is assignable: above, para.17–061.

[6] s.136.

[7] *Tulk v Moxhay* (1848) 2 Ph. 774; below, para.32–003.

[8] Implied covenants arise out of the grant of a lease and so may be sued upon only where there is a present relationship of landlord and tenant. See above, para.19–003.

has parted with the land before the breach occurred, he may only recover nominal damages, for the real loss is likely to fall not on him but on the assignee of the land. The assignee himself may or may not be able to sue, as is explained below.

32–005   **2. Parties to the deed.** Normally the original covenantee will be a party to the deed containing the covenant. At common law it was a strict rule that no one could sue on a deed made *inter partes* unless they were a party to it.[9] However, this rule was never applied to a deed poll, i.e. a deed executed by one party alone as a unilateral act, so that any person with whom he purported to contract could enforce the contract.[10]

32–006   **3. Non-parties.** The rule for deeds *inter partes* has been qualified by the Law of Property Act 1925 s.56, under which a person may take an interest in "land or other property" or the benefit of any condition, covenant or agreement respecting land or other property, "although he may not be named as a party to the conveyance or other instrument". "Land or other property" may mean "land or other real property" or it may extend to personal property[11]; but on any footing the section appears to apply only to agreements which relate to some pre-existing property and not, for example, to contracts for personal services.[12] To this extent, s.56 has abolished the common law rule requiring anyone claiming any benefit under a deed to be named as a party to it, and so it extends in an important way the class of persons who can be brought within the benefit of a covenant as original covenantees. For example, if V sells land to P, and P enters into a covenant with V "and also with the owners for the time being" of certain adjacent plots of land, the persons who are the adjacent owners at the time of the covenant can sue as original covenantees, for although they are not named as parties to the conveyance, they are covenantees just as much as is V.[13] Thus, if the benefit of the covenant is capable of running with land (as explained below), it can benefit the successors in title of the adjacent owners as well as the successors in title of V.

32–007   **4. Ambit of section 56.** The true aim of s.56 seems to be not to allow a third party to sue on a contract merely because it is made for his benefit, but only

---

[9] *Lord Southampton v Brown* (1827) 6 B. & C. 718.
[10] *Chelsea & Walham Green BS v Armstrong* [1951] Ch. 853: a registered transfer (see above, para.7–053) held equivalent to deed poll, so that a covenant therein could be enforced by the covenantee, even though not a party to the transfer.
[11] See the differing views in *Beswick v Beswick* [1968] A.C. 58, where the majority took the former view and the minority took the latter (and preferable) view: see at 76, 81, 87, 94, 105.
[12] But see *Beswick v Beswick*, above, at 76.
[13] *Westhoughton UDC v Wigan Coal & Iron Co Ltd* [1919] 1 Ch. 159; *Re Ecclesiastical Commissioners for England's Conveyance* [1936] Ch. 430. The suggestion that the section is confined to covenants running with the land is denied at 438; but there is Court of Appeal authority for it in *Forster v Elvet Colliery Co Ltd* [1908] 1 K.B. 629 (affirmed sub nom. *Dyson v Forster* [1909] A.C. 98) and *Grant v Edmondson* [1931] 1 Ch. 1. Since s.56 may now extend to property other than land the suggestion seems difficult to justify.

where the contract purports to be made *with* him.[14] Just as, under the first part of the section, a person cannot benefit by a conveyance unless it purports to be made to him (as grantee), so he cannot benefit by a covenant which does not purport to be made with him (as covenantee).[15] On this view, if A covenants with B that A will convey land to C, B can enforce the covenant but C cannot; for B is a covenantee, but C is merely a third party. But if A's covenant is expressed to be made with B and with C, C can enforce it as well as B, even though B was a party to the deed and C was not.[16] This interpretation follows the sound principle that a promisor should be liable only to those to whom he chooses to engage himself.

Contrary to this approach, however, the Court of Appeal has asserted that s.56 enables a mere third party, not being an intended promisee, to enforce a contract made for his benefit.[17] Although the House of Lords rejected the application of s.56 on appeal in the same case, the opinion of the majority was that s.56 was inapplicable because it was confined to real property,[18] not specifically because it could not benefit a mere third party. On this footing, it is conceivable that the Court of Appeal's generous and unorthodox approach may still be operative as regards real property.[19] However, two opinions were given to the contrary,[20] after a review of the history and true purpose of the section, and these are altogether more convincing. These opinions, limiting

[14] *Beswick v Beswick*, above, at 106 per Lord Upjohn, Lord Pearce concurring. Though said (at 105) to be "obiter and tentative", this judgment confirms what has long been the better opinion: see *White v Bijou Mansions Ltd* [1937] Ch. 610 at 624 (in CA [1938] Ch. 351); *Re Sinclair's Life Policy* [1938] Ch. 799; *Re Foster* [1938] 3 All E.R. 357 at 365; *Re Miller's Agreement* [1947] Ch. 615. For Lord Denning's opinions to the contrary see *Drive Yourself Hire Co (London) Ltd v Strutt* [1954] 1 Q.B. 250 (cf. *Smith v River Douglas Catchment Board* [1949] 2 K.B. 500); *Beswick v Beswick* [1966] Ch. 538. These cases were criticised (see [1954] C.L.J. 66 (H.W.R.W.), and have not been followed because they are inconsistent with *Beswick v Beswick*, above: see *Amsprop Trading Ltd v Harris Distribution Ltd* [1997] 1 W.L.R. 1025, also disapproving *Re Shaw's Application* (1994) 68 P. & C.R. 591 at 598.

[15] s.56 of the LPA 1925 "can be called in aid only by a person who, although not a party to the conveyance or other instrument in question, is yet a person to whom that conveyance or other instrument purports to grant something or with whom some agreement or covenant is thereby purported to be made": *Re Foster*, above, at 365, per Crossman J., summarising earlier cases; and similarly *White v Bijou Mansions Ltd*, above, at 625, per Simonds J.; *Lyus v Prowsa Developments Ltd* [1982] 1 W.L.R. 1044 at 1049, per Dillon J.

[16] *Stromdale & Ball Ltd v Burden* [1952] Ch. 223 is a borderline case.

[17] *Beswick v Beswick* [1966] Ch. 538, CA; [1968] A.C. 58, HL. A coal merchant transferred his business to his nephew, the nephew promising to pay an annuity of £5 a week to the merchant's widow; held (by the Court of Appeal), the widow could enforce the promise under s.56. The House of Lords upheld her claim, but only *qua* the merchant's administratrix, representing the promisee personally. The House surmounted the difficulty that the merchant's estate suffered no loss by granting specific performance. Of course, under the Contracts (Rights of Third Parties) Act 1999 s.1, a person who is not a party to a contract will usually be able to enforce it if there is either a term to that effect or if the contract purports to confer a benefit on him: see above, para.11–022.

[18] See *Beswick v Beswick* [1968] A.C. 58; above, para.32–006 and fn.11; *Southern Water Authority v Carey* [1985] 2 All E.R. 1077 at 1083.

[19] Lords Hodson and Guest seem to support this: *Beswick v Beswick*, above, at 80, 85, 87.

[20] Per Lords Pearce and Upjohn: *Beswick v Beswick*, above, at 94, 106; above, para.32–007. The scope of s.56 after *Beswick v Beswick* remains uncertain.

the effect of s.56 to cases where the intention is to make another person a true promisee under the covenant, have been followed at first instance.[21]

32–008   **5. Non-existent persons.** It seems to be clear that a person cannot be a covenantee within the scope of s.56 unless he is in existence and identifiable at the time the covenant is made.[22] Thus in the example given above[23] the covenant cannot be made to benefit any *future* purchaser of a plot *directly*. However, such a person may obtain the benefit of the covenant under the rules relating to assignees, as either a successor in title to V or as a successor to one of the adjacent plot-owners who *was* in existence and identifiable at the time the covenant was made. This is simply an example of the rule that if a covenant is expressed to be made with an owner of land and his successors in title, the present owner is the only *original* covenantee (like the present owners of adjacent plots). Thus, successors in title can claim the benefit only under the rules concerning assignees.

II. ASSIGNEES OF THE LAND

32–009   Where a covenantee disposes of his land, the benefit of the covenant may pass at law to the transferee in one of two ways. First, it may be expressly assigned as a chose in action. Secondly, in certain circumstances it may run automatically with the land.

32–010   **1. Express assignment as a chose in action.** The benefit of a covenant may be expressly assigned as a chose in action. This will usually be by means of a statutory assignment under s.136 of the Law of Property Act 1925.[24] As such it must be made in writing with written notice to the covenantor. There are two relevant limitations on this statutory power to assign. First, the covenant must not be of a purely personal nature.[25] Secondly, the assignment must, by the section, be absolute: in other words, it can only be assigned once, for no rights may be left with the assignor. If therefore the covenantee were to sell part of his land and to assign the benefit of the covenant as a chose in action under s.136, he would no longer be able to enforce the covenant himself and would be unable to assign the benefit to any purchaser of the remainder.

2. The benefit of the covenant may run with the land

32–011   *(a) Introduction.* The benefit of a covenant may run with the covenantee's land at law in certain circumstances. When it does, the person entitled to the

---

[21] *Amsprop Trading Ltd v Harris Distribution Ltd* [1997] 1 W.L.R. 1025. Dicta of Lord Denning to the contrary in *Drive Yourself Hire Co (London) LD v Strutt and Another* [1954] 1 Q.B. 250 is expressly not followed in *Amsprop*, at p.1029 per Neuberger J.

[22] *Re Ecclesiastical Commissioners for England's Conveyance* [1936] Ch. 430 at 437; *Lyus v Prowsa Developments Ltd* [1982] 1 W.L.R. 1044 at 1049; *Pinemain Ltd v Welbeck International Ltd* [1984] 2 E.G.L.R. 91 at 93, 94; *Re Distributors & Warehousing Ltd* [1986] 1 E.G.L.R. 90 at 94.

[23] Above, para.32–006.

[24] See Snell, *Equity*, Ch.3. The benefit of the chose could also be transferred by means of an equitable assignment: Snell, Id.

[25] Edwin Peel, *Treitel on the Law of Contract*, 13th edn (2011) Ch.15.

benefit of covenant may sue for damages for its breach or otherwise enforce it[26] in the same way as the original covenantee could have done. However, before examining the circumstances in which the benefit will run, it is important to appreciate two matters. Although neither of them affects the transmissibility of a covenant at law, each is important in relation to aspects of the enforceability of restrictive covenants in equity and may be noted here for ease of reference.[27]

(i) It is immaterial whether the covenant is negative (not to do something) or positive (to do something). Thus the common law doctrine applies equally to a covenant not to build on the land purchased by P or a covenant to supply pure water to the land retained by V.[28]

(ii) There is no requirement that the covenant should have any relevance to land belonging to the covenantor, or indeed that he should have any land at all. Three examples may be taken to illustrate this. First, in an ancient case a Prior covenanted with the lord of the manor that he and his convent would sing divine service in the chapel of the manor. It was held that the lord's successors in title could sue the Prior for non-performance.[29] Second, in a more recent decision, a river catchment Board entered into a covenant with a farmer to repair and maintain the banks of a river that abutted his property. The Board was held liable in damages to the farmer's successors in title when, due to the inadequacy of the work, a field was flooded.[30] Third, the benefit of the covenants for title implied in a conveyance ran with land conveyed at common law.[31]

(b) Requirements for the benefit to run. For the benefit of a covenant to run **32–012** at common law, two conditions must be satisfied.[32] First, the covenant must "touch and concern" the land. Second, the covenantee must have had, and the

---

[26] e.g. by injunction.

[27] Below, paras 32–040, 32–044.

[28] *Sharp v Waterhouse* (1857) 7 E. & B. 816; *Shayler v Woolf* [1946] 1 All E.R. 464 at 467 (affirmed [1946] Ch. 320).

[29] *The Prior's Case* (also known as *Pakenham's Case*) Y.B. 42 Edw. 3, Hil., pl. 14 (1368); Co.Litt. p.385a; Smith's L.C. i, p.55; below, para.32–014.

[30] *Smith v River Douglas Catchment Board* [1949] 2 K.B. 500. See too *Williams v United Construction Co Ltd* (1951) 19 Conv. (N.S.) 262.

[31] Smith's L.C. i, p.73; above, para.8–047. These covenants now run by force of LPA 1925 s.76(6) (if entered into prior to July 1, 1995); and LP(MP)A 1994 s.7 (if entered into after June 30, 1995). Each of these provisions applies to transfers of registered land: LRR 2003 r.67.

[32] *Rogers v Hosegood* [1900] 2 Ch. 388 at 395; *P. & A. Swift Investments v Combined English Stores Group Plc* [1989] A.C. 632 at 639, 640. See too (1984) Law Com. No.127, paras 3.17–3.19.

assignee must now have, a legal estate in the land benefited. There is a suggestion in some cases that there may be a third condition, namely that the parties must have intended that the benefit should run with the land.[33] However, it is far from certain that there ever was such a requirement,[34] and the House of Lords has restated the requirements for a covenant to run at common law without reference to this supposed requirement.[35] In any event, as regards covenants entered into after 1925, annexation both at law and in equity is effected automatically without proof of intention to annex under the provisions of s.78 of the Law of Property Act 1925.[36] This is explained fully later.[37]

32–013   (1) THE COVENANT MUST TOUCH AND CONCERN THE LAND OF THE CONVENANTEE. The traditional words "touch and concern" are adopted from the rules for covenants in leases.[38] In the present context they signify that the covenant must be made for the benefit of land owned by the covenantee (i.e. V in the above examples) at the time of the covenant, in the sense that it is designed to benefit both V and his successors in title, and not V alone.[39] This sense will readily be inferred if the circumstances indicate that the covenant will be of importance to successive owners and will enhance the value of the land. A covenant by a catchment Board to keep river banks in repair will touch and concern the covenantee's adjacent farmland which is liable to be flooded if repair is neglected,[40] and a covenant to keep a road in repair will touch and concern the covenantee's land reached by the road, if the land will be more valuable on that account.[41] Where the covenant is to keep something in repair, or to do other recurrent acts, the benefit to the land and the identity of that land are usually obvious from the circumstances in which the covenant was taken,

---

[33] "Every covenant which has those characteristics does not necessarily run with the land. That is a question of intention in each case"; *Rogers v Hosegood*, above, at 396, per Farwell J. See too *Smith v River Douglas Catchment Board*, above, at 506, 511; *Williams v Unit Construction Co Ltd*, above, at 265. cf. (1982) 2 L.S. 53 at 57 (D. J. Hurst).

[34] There is no reference to it in either *Dyson v Forster* [1909] A.C. 98 (on appeal from *Forster v Elvet Colliery Co Ltd* [1908] 1 K.B. 629) or *Westhoughton UDC v Wigan Coal & Iron Co Ltd* [1919] 1 Ch. 159.

[35] *P. & A. Swift Investments v Combined English Stores Group Plc*, above, at 639, 640.

[36] *Federated Homes Ltd v Mill Lodge Properties Ltd* [1980] 1 W.L.R. 594. It is clear from that case that statutory annexation applies as much to the transmission of covenants at law as in equity, because at 605, the Court of Appeal relied on two cases on assignment at law, *Smith v River Douglas Catchment Board*, above, and *Williams v Unit Construction Co Ltd*, above.

[37] Below, para.32–063.

[38] Above, paras 20–022, 20–024, *Rogers v Hosegood*, above; *Kumar v Dunning* [1989] Q.B. 193; *P. & A. Swift Investments v Combined English Stores Group Plc*, above.

[39] Co.Litt. p.385a; *Rogers v Hosegood*, above, at 395; *Formby v Barker* [1903] 2 Ch. 539 at 554; *Dyson v Forster*, above, at 102; *Smith v River Douglas Catchment Board*, above, at 506; *Williams v Unit Construction Co Ltd*, above, at 264, 265; *Re Gadd's Land Transfer* [1966] Ch. 56 at 66; *P. & A. Swift Investments v Combined English Stores Group Plc*, above, at 640–642.

[40] As in *Smith v River Douglas Catchment Board*, above.

[41] As in *Williams v Unit Construction Co Ltd*, above (company covenanted with lessee of building land to make up and maintain roads and footpaths; sub-lessee of one plot who was injured by disrepair of footpath recovered damages from company).

so that no special words to this effect need be included in it.[42] The facts themselves show that the benefit is annexed to the land.[43]

Where the covenant is made between landlord and tenant, the lessor's reversion alone will not rank as "land" for this purpose, for it will be recalled that the benefit of covenants could not run with the reversion at common law, before the Grantees of Reversion Act 1540.[44] But some incorporeal hereditaments rank as "land". Thus the benefit of a covenant to repair a footpath may run with an easement of way over the path.[45]

It is now clear that where the covenant runs with the land, there is a rebuttable presumption that it is annexed both to the whole and to each and every part of the land.[46] This applies to annexation of covenants at law as much as it does in equity.[47]

(2) THE COVENANTEE MUST HAVE HAD, AND THE ASSIGNEE MUST NOW HAVE, A **32-014** LEGAL ESTATE IN THE LAND BENEFITED. A common law court could take no cognisance of an equitable interest before 1875,[48] and if the covenantee was merely an equitable owner (e.g. a mortgagor, prior to 1926) the benefit of a covenant could not run at law with his interest.[49] In addition, until the Law of Property Act 1925, there were even uncertainties as to the precise circumstances in which an assignee with a legal estate could enforce a covenant.

During the medieval period the circumstances in which some person other than the original covenantee might sue at law on a covenant were obscure.[50] Some covenants could be enforced only by the covenantee's heirs,[51] whilst others were enforceable by whoever had the land.[52] It was not until the 16th century that it was finally settled that a covenant might run with the land at law so that it could be enforced by a stranger to whom the land had been

---

[42] *Smith v River Douglas Catchment Board*, above.

[43] *Westhoughton UDC v Wigan Coal & Iron Co Ltd* [1919] 1 Ch. 159 at 170 where Swinfen Eady M.R. said: " . . . the covenant touches and concerns the land. The covenant is, therefore, to be deemed to be annexed to the land; the benefit of it runs at law with the land; and the assignee can sue upon it".

[44] Above, para.20–060.

[45] *Gaw v Coras Impair Eireann* [1953] I.R. 232. However *Grant v Edmondson* [1931] 1 Ch. 1 (holding that a covenant to pay a rentcharge will not run with the rentcharge) was not cited. See above, para.31–028.

[46] *Federated Homes Ltd v Mill Lodge Properties Ltd* [1980] 1 W.L.R. 594 at 606. The same is true for covenants granted before January 1, 1926, *Hugh Small v Oliver & Saunders (Developments) Limited* [2006] EWCH 1293 (Ch), para.30, provided that an express or implied intention to annex is found.

[47] *Williams v Unit Construction Co Ltd* (1951) 19 Conv. (N.S.) 262; *Federated Homes Ltd v Mill Lodge Properties Ltd*, above, at 606.

[48] Above, paras 5–016, 5–017.

[49] *Webb v Russell* (1789) 3 T.R. 393; *Rogers v Hosegood* [1900] 2 Ch. 388 at 404.

[50] See A.W.B. Simpson, *A History of the Common Law of Contract*, pp.37–40.

[51] Who might not have the same estate as the covenantee. Thus the plaintiff in *The Prior's Case*, YB. 42 Edw. 3, Hil., pl. 14 (1368), was a tenant in tail but the covenantee had been the owner in fee simple.

[52] *The Prior's Case*, above; quoted in Holmes, *The Common Law*, p.397. "Precisely what was decided in the case is not at all clear"; A. W. B. Simpson, op. cit., at p.38.

conveyed.[53] It also appears to have become customary for covenants to be made with the covenantee, his heirs and assigns, even though those additional words strictly were not necessary in order that the benefit should run.[54] However, in fact, these words may have limited the range of persons who might enforce the covenant and there was some authority to the effect that an assignee who sought to enforce the covenant had to have the *same* estate as the original covenantee.[55] Thus, by the Conveyancing Act 1881,[56] a covenant relating to land was deemed to be made "with the covenantee, his heirs and assigns" and was to take effect as if those persons were expressed, thereby shortening the wording of covenants.[57] It was held that those who derived title under but did not take the same estate as the covenantee (such as his lessees) were not his "assigns" and could not therefore enforce the covenant.[58] However, doubts were expressed as to the correctness of this conclusion.[59]

32–015   As regards covenants entered into after 1925, the provisions of the Act of 1881 have been replaced by the Law of Property Act 1925, s.78. It provides that:

> "a covenant relating to any land of the covenantee shall be deemed to be made with the covenantee and his successors in title and the persons deriving title under him or them,[60] and shall have effect as if such successors and other persons were expressed".

The change in the wording is explained in part because the term "heirs" became obsolete under the 1925 legislation.[61] However, it is likely that it was also intended to resolve the doubts as to who could enforce a covenant which

---

[53] *Spencer's Case* (1583) 5 Co.Rep. l6a at 17b, 18a; A. W. B. Simpson op cit., at p.39.

[54] *Lougher v Williams* (1673) 2 Lev. 92. The rule derived from the principles applicable to covenants in leases. These would run with the landlord's reversion even though the word "assigns" was not used: *Kitchen v Buckly* (1663) 1 Lev. 109.

[55] *Webb v Russell* (1789) 3 T.R. 393 at 402, 403; *Rogers v Hosegood* [1900] 2 Ch. 388 at 404.

[56] s.58.

[57] It appears to have been erroneously thought that such words were necessary to make the benefit of a covenant run: see Wolstenholme's *Conveyancing and Settled Land Acts* 10th edn 1913, p.129.

[58] *Westhoughton UDC v Wigan Coal & Iron Co Ltd* [1919] 1 Ch. 159 (lessee could not enforce covenant made with the freeholder); *South of England Dairies Ltd v Baker* [1906] 2 Ch. 631 (underlessee unable to enforce covenant made with the lessee).

[59] See *Westhoughton UDC v Wigan Coal & Iron Co Ltd*, above, at 176 (Duke L.J.); (1980) 43 M.L.R. 445 at 449 (D. J. Hayton). In *Taite v Gosling* (1879) 11 Old. 273, Fry J. held that a lessee was an "assign" for the purposes of enforcing a restrictive covenant that had been granted to a freeholder. In so doing he relied on *Wright v Burroughes* (1846) 3 C.B. 685, a decision at law, which held that a lessee of the reversion was an "assignee" for the purposes of the Grantees of Reversions Act 1540.

[60] Subject to what is said in relation to registered land, (below, para.32–063, fn.282), in relation to positive covenants, these words will not include squatters and licensees. The former are not "successors in title" and the latter have no "title". By contrast, squatters and licensees will be able to enforce *restrictive* covenants because, as regards such covenants, the owners and occupiers for the time being are deemed to be successors in title by the section: see fn.62, below.

[61] Above, para.14–104. Two amendments were made to CA 1881, by LPA 1922 s.96(2)–(4), and by LP(Am)A 1924 Sch.3 Pt I cl.11. The words "his successors in title and the persons deriving title under him or them" appeared for the first time in LPA 1925 s.78. The Act of 1925

ran with the land in order to make it clear that it included lessees, sub-lessees and mortgagees.[62] The courts have certainly interpreted it in this way[63] and it means that an assignee does not have to have the *same* legal estate as the covenantee in order to enforce the covenant. Thus, in a case where a catchment board covenanted to maintain the banks of a river, and the land was later sold to a purchaser who let it to a tenant, both the purchaser and the tenant were able to recover damages for injury to their respective interests (the reversion and the tenancy) after the land had been inundated due to breach of covenant.[64] The result of this change is welcome even though the reasoning behind it has been questioned by some.[65] The provisions of the 1881 Act, with the attendant doubts as to their precise scope, will continue to apply to covenants entered into before 1926.[66]

(c) Relationship between ss.78 and 79. Doubts have been expressed about **32–016** this interpretation of s.78 of the Law of Property Act 1925[67] because it is worded in similar terms to its partner s.79, which has been held to have a more limited effect. Section 79(1) provides that:

> "a covenant relating to any land of the covenantor or capable of being bound by him, shall, unless a contrary intention is expressed, be deemed to be made by the covenantor on behalf of himself, his successors in title and the persons deriving title under him or them, and, subject as aforesaid, shall have effect as if such successors and other persons were expressed".

The subsection expressly encompasses "a covenant to do some act relating to the land, notwithstanding that the subject-matter may not be in existence when the covenant is made". It has been held by the House of Lords that this provision "has always been regarded as intended to remove conveyancing difficulties with regard to the form of covenants and to make it unnecessary to

---

was a consolidating Act, and while there is a presumption that such an Act is not intended to change the law, "this prima facie view must yield to plain words to the contrary": *Grey v IRC* [1960] A.C. 1 at 13, per Viscount Simonds. Whether the clarification of a point of doubt should be regarded as a change in the law is debatable. cf. (1981) 97 L.Q.R. 32 at 40 (G. H. Newsom, Q.C.).

[62] The view that LPA 1925 s.78 was intended to clarify who could enforce covenants which ran with the land gains further support from the fact that, for the purposes of enforcing restrictive covenants, the section deems to be "successors in title" the owners and occupiers of the land for the time being of the land of the covenantee intended to be benefited. This extension of the section was clearly intended: see LP(Am)A 1924 Sch.3 Pt I cl.11. See below, para.32–063.

[63] *Smith v River Douglas Catchment Board* [1949] 2 K.B. 500, especially at 516. See similarly *Williams v Unit Construction Co Ltd* (1951) 19 Conv. (N.S.) 262 at 265–267.

[64] *Smith v River Douglas Catchment Board*, above.

[65] See (1956) 20 Conv. (N.S.) 43 at 53 (D. W. Elliott).

[66] cf. *J. Sainsbury Plc v Enfield LBC* [1989] 1 W.L.R. 590.

[67] See, e.g. (1981) 97 L.Q.R. 32 at 34, 47 (G. H. Newsom QC).

refer to successors in title".[68] The principal "conveyancing difficulties" are as follows.

(i) The burden of a *restrictive* covenant will run with the covenantor's land only if the parties so intend.[69] The effect of s.79 is that such an intention will be presumed unless the contrary is expressed.[70]

(ii) By an old rule (if and in so far as it existed), the burden of a covenant in a lease obliging the tenant to do some entirely new thing (such as building a wall) did not run unless the covenant was made expressly with the lessee and his assigns.[71] The section overcomes that difficulty.[72]

In the same case, the House of Lords also held that s.79 does not cause the burden of a *positive* covenant to run with the land.[73] The House reached this conclusion "without casting any doubt" on the decisions, explained above,[74] by which s.78 has been held to annex the benefit of a covenant to the land and to be enforceable not only by successors in title, but also by those with derivative interests.[75] There is therefore no support for a limited interpretation of s.78 by comparison with s.79.

B. The Burden of the Covenant

32–017   **1. The general rule: the burden does not run.** The rule at law is that the burden of a covenant will not pass with freehold land.[76] This is of particular relevance to positive covenants, for the burden of restrictive covenants may run in equity. The rationale for the distinction between positive and restrictive covenants was explained by the House of Lords in *Rhone v Stephens*.[77]

---

[68] *Rhone v Stephens* [1994] 2 A.C. 310 at 322, per Lord Templeman.
[69] Below, para.32–049. The burden of a positive covenant will not run at all.
[70] See *Tophams Ltd v Earl of Sefton* [1967] 1 A.C. 50 at 81. The contrary expression need not take the form of an express provision but may be "sufficiently contained in the wording and context of the instrument": *Re Royal Victoria Pavilion, Ramsgate* [1961] Ch. 581 at 589, per Pennycuick J.
[71] *Spencer's Case* (1583) 5 Co. Rep. 16a, second resolution. See above, para.20–052.
[72] For another possible function of s.79, see below, para.32–038. For the abolition of this rule for leases granted after 1995, see L & TCA 1995 s.3(7); above, para.20–107.
[73] *Rhone v Stephens*, above, at 322. See too *Tophams Ltd v Earl of Sefton*, above, at 81.
[74] *Smith v River Douglas Catchment Board* [1949] 2 K.B. 500; *Williams v Unit Construction Co Ltd* (1951) 19 Conv. (N.S.) 262; *Federated Homes Ltd v Mill Lodge Properties Ltd* [1980] 1 W.L.R. 594.
[75] *Rhone v Stephens*, above, at 322, per Lord Templeman. The House noted that in *Federated Homes Ltd v Mill Lodge Properties*, above, at 606, Brightman L.J. had considered that s.79 involved "quite different considerations" and did not provide "a helpful analogy".
[76] *Austerberry v Corporation of Oldham* (1885) 29 Ch D 750; above, paras 20–006, 32–003.
[77] [1994] 2 A.C. 310; noted (1994) 110 L.Q.R. 346 (N. P. Gravells); [1994] Conv. 477 (J. Snape). See too *Thamesmead Town Ltd v Allotey* [1998] 3 E.G.L.R. 97.

"Equity cannot compel an owner to comply with a positive covenant entered into by his predecessors in title without flatly contradicting the common law rule that a person cannot be made liable upon a contract unless he is a party to it. Enforcement of a positive covenant lies in contract; a positive covenant compels an owner to exercise his rights. Enforcement of a negative covenant lies in property; a negative covenant deprives the owner of a right over property."[78]

In that case, the common owner of a house and cottage sold the cottage and covenanted "for himself and his successors in title" with the purchaser to maintain part of the roof of the house which also covered part of the cottage. The House of Lords held that the purchaser's successor in title could not enforce the covenant against the vendor's successor in title, and declined to overrule the earlier authority which held that the burden of positive covenants would not run with the land. To have done so would have retrospectively imposed liabilities on many property owners who had entered into positive covenants on the basis of a clearly settled rule of law. Any solution lay in the hands of Parliament.[79]

The rule that the burden of positive covenants does not run with freehold   **32–018** land is in sharp contrast to the position in relation to leasehold property where such covenants are enforceable if, in the case of leases granted before 1996, they touch and concern the land and there is privity of estate, or, in leases granted after 1995, the covenants are not expressed to be personal.[80] The "ill-consequences" of the rule have often been noted.[81] Two of the most obvious are as follows.

(i) Two neighbours cannot enter into agreements for such everyday matters as the maintenance of a wall or the pruning of trees in such a way that the burden will run with the land.

(ii) Flying freeholds[82] cannot in practice be granted because of the difficulties of ensuring rights of support for the upper floors and for the maintenance of the roof. Flats are therefore granted by means of a lease so that the necessary covenants can be both imposed and enforced.

---

[78] [1994] 2 A.C. 310 at 318, per Lord Templeman. For criticism of this reasoning (but not of the actual decision in the case), see [1995] C.L.J. 60 at 63 (S. Gardner).

[79] [1994] 2 A.C. 310 at 321. The Law Commission have now proposed such a reform, see *Making Land Work: Easements Covenants and Profits Prendre* (2011), Law Com. No.327.

[80] Above, paras 20–004, 20–106.

[81] See, e.g. (2011) Law Com. No.327, para.5.4 and 5.21 et seq. Also, (1984) Law Com. No.127, para.4.4 (from which the two examples below are drawn) [1972B] C.L.J. 157 (H.W.R.W.); (1995) 58 M.L.R. 486 (D.N. Clarke). In *Rhone v Stephens* (1993) 67 P. & C.R. 9 at 14, CA, Nourse L.J. commented that the discovery of this rule had "shocked more than one eminent judge unversed in the subtleties of English real property law".

[82] Above, para.3–035.

Although there have been a number of proposals for reform[83] to date "nothing has been done".[84] Note, however, that there are already certain important statutory exceptions to the rule that the burden of positive covenants do not run with the land. For example, under the Town and Country Planning Act 1990 (as amended),[85] any person interested in land may, by agreement or otherwise, enter into a planning obligation with the local authority, enforceable by injunction,[86] requiring specified operations or activities to be carried out in, on, under or over the land.[87] This obligation, which is registrable as local land charge,[88] is enforceable against both the person entering into the obligation and any person deriving title from him.[89]

32–019   2. Indirect methods of transmitting the burden. Although the burden of a positive covenant does not run with the land, it is possible to circumvent this rule to some extent by the use of certain devices.[90] None of them provides an effective general solution to the problem however.[91]

32–020   *(a) Chain of covenants.* If V sells land to P, and P covenants, for example, to erect and maintain a fence, P will remain liable to V on the covenant by virtue of privity of contract even if P sells the land to Q. P will accordingly protect himself by extracting from Q a covenant of indemnity against future breaches of the covenant to fence. If Q then fails to maintain the fence, V cannot sue Q, but he can sue P, and P can then sue Q on the covenant for indemnity.[92] Similarly if P dies without having parted with the land, P's

---

[83] Below, para.32–027. See *The Report on the Committee on Positive Covenants Affecting Land* (1965) Cmnd. 2719; *The Law of Positive and Restrictive Covenants* (1984) Law Com. No.127; *Commonhold: A Consultation Paper* (1990) Cm. 1345 and more recently, a comprehensive set of proposals recommended in *Making Land Work: Easements Covenants and Profits Prendre* (2011), Law Com. No.327.

[84] *Rhone v Stephens* [1994] 2 A.C. 310 at 321, per Lord Templeman. See too *TRW Steering Systems Ltd v North Cape Properties Ltd* (1993) 69 P. & C.R. 265 at 266. It is unclear whether the 2011 proposal stands any greater chance of enactment than its predecessor. But see [2011] Conv. 191 (P. O'Connor) for a note of caution.

[85] s.106 (substituted by Planning and Compensation Act 1991 s.12); below, para.32–094. This replaces and considerably extends earlier legislation: see T & CPA 1971 s.52. It does not have retrospective effect: *Good v Epping Forest DC* [1994] 1 W.L.R. 376 at 380. For another example, see the Local Government (Miscellaneous Provisions) Act 1982 s.33 (as amended).

[86] T & CPA 1990 s.106(5).

[87] T & CPA 1990 s.106(1). Other planning obligations may restrict the development or use of land, require the land to be used in any specified way, or pay a sum or sums to the local authority.

[88] T & CPA 1990 s.106(11).

[89] T & CPA 1990 s.106(3). The local authority has power in certain circumstances to enter the land to carry out the operations if the landowner defaults: T & CPA 1990 s.106(6).

[90] See Law Com. No.327 at paras 5.23–5.5.26 and Law Com. No.127 paras 3.3 1–3.42; (1973) 37 Conv. (N.S.) 194 (A. Prichard); (1995) 58 M.L.R. 486 (D. N. Clarke).

[91] Law Com. No.127 para.3.42 and Law Com. CP No.186 (2008), p.136.

[92] Although in practice such an express covenant of indemnity is invariably taken (see *Rhone v Stephens* (1993) 67 P. & C.R. 9 at 14, CA), there is in fact an implied right to indemnity: *TRW Steering Systems Ltd v North Cape Properties Ltd* (1993) 69 P. & C.R. 265 at 272. All actions may be heard together by bringing in indemnifiers as third parties: in accordance with CPR Pt 20. This makes no difference to the substantive law.

personal representatives remain liable in damages, and may require an indemnity from anyone to whom P may have left the land by his will.[93] But a chain of purely personal covenants is unsatisfactory for many reasons. The longer it grows, the more liable it is to be broken by the insolvency or disappearance of one of the parties, or by the neglect of one of them to take a covenant of indemnity from his successor; and the remedy can only be in damages, whereas a mandatory injunction is the remedy usually desired.[94]

(b) *Right of entry annexed to rentcharge.*[95] Since a right of entry annexed **32–021** "for any purpose" to a legal rentcharge is a legal interest in land,[96] it will be enforceable against successors in title to the land charged even though its primary purpose is to secure the performance of a positive covenant rather than the payment of money.[97] It had the further advantages that the enforcement of the rentcharge was exempt from the perpetuity rule[98] and that it avoided complications under the Settled Land Act 1925.[99] Consequently a device commonly used in practice for securing the performance of covenants to build, repair, and so on, is to reserve a rentcharge, and to annex to it a right of entry allowing its proprietor to enter and make good any default in the observance of the covenants, charging the cost to the owner in possession.[100] Such covenants will usually relate to the rentcharge since they will improve the security, but the words "for any purpose" suggest that no particular connection is necessary; and in practice the rentcharge may be of a nominal amount and may serve merely as a peg on which to hang enforcement of the covenants.[101] This device, though untested judicially,[102] has received the implied blessing of Parliament in the Rentcharges Act 1977, which permits the continued use of rentcharges imposed for the purpose of making covenants enforceable against successive owners.[103]

---

[93] AEA 1925 s.36(10).

[94] Note also the increasing practice of substituting damages for an injunction even for breach of a negative covenant, *Hugh Small v Oliver & Saunders (Developments) Ltd* [2006] EWHC 1293 (Ch).

[95] See [1988] Conv. 99 (S.B.).

[96] Above, para.6–008.

[97] It is immaterial that the covenant does not itself bind successors: *Shiloh Spinners Ltd v Harding* [1973] A.C. 691 at 717. The court may grant relief: LPA 1925 s.146(5); above, para.3–059.

[98] LPA 1925 s.4(3); Perpetuities and Accumulations Act 1964 s.11. Rentcharges are not listed in PAA 2009 s.1 and therefore are not caught by perpetuity at all. Consequently, for rentcharges created after 5 April 2010, the statutory exception just noted is not needed. Above para. 9.141.

[99] Above, paras 6–014, 6–015, below, Appendix para.A–037.

[100] For a description see (1975) Law Com. No.68 para.49. For a precedent see Prideaux, i,719.

[101] Law. Com. No.68, as above.

[102] But Lindley L.J. described it as "means known to conveyancers" whereby the result could be achieved "with comparative ease": *Austerberry v Corporation of Oldham* (1885) 29 Ch D 750 at 783.

[103] Below, para.31–019.

32–022   *(c) Rights of re-entry.* It would appear to be possible for the vendor of a freehold to reserve a right of re-entry as a means of enforcing a positive covenant without creating a rentcharge. This device has been employed by a lessee who assigned a lease[104] and should in principle be available to a freeholder as well. Such rights if created before April 6, 2010 are subject to the rule against perpetuities, although if created after April 5, 2010 generally they are not.[105] This means that it will now be possible to create a right of re-entry in order to enforce a positive obligation that may exist in perpetuity. Note, however, that there is clear authority that such rights of entry, when not annexed to a rentcharge, must be equitable. [106] Consequently, although such equitable rights of entry are not registrable as land charges where title is unregistered, and hence fall within the doctrine of notice,[107] they need to be protected by the entry of a notice in the more usual case of registered title.[108]

32–023   *(d) Enlarged long lease.* A more artificial device, of untested validity and subject to difficulties, is to insert the covenant in a long lease which can be enlarged into a fee simple under the statutory power.[109] If the lease is enlarged, the resultant fee simple is, by statute, made subject to all the same covenants, provisions and obligations as the lease would have been subject to had it not been enlarged.[110] It seems that a fee simple may by these means be made subject to any covenant which touches and concerns the land, e.g. a covenant to repair.[111] It should, however, be noted that a lease which can be enlarged is not necessarily governed by all the same rules as a lease which cannot.[112]

32–024   *(e) Condition of taking benefits.* Since it is the general rule that the benefit but not the burden of a contract is assignable, it is normal for the burden to remain with the assignor although the benefit passes to the assignee.[113] But it is possible for acceptance of the burden to be made a condition of enjoyment of the benefit, and thus effectively for the burden to pass. If A conveys land to B reserving to himself the mining rights but "so that compensation in money be made" for any damage done while mining, the liability to pay compensation is a condition of the exercise of the mining rights and will run

---

[104] See *Shiloh Spinners Ltd v Harding* [1973] A.C. 691.

[105] Unless they are created under trust. See above, para.9–029. A royal lives clause was employed in *Shiloh Spinners Ltd v Harding*, above.

[106] *Shiloh Spinners Ltd v Harding*, above, arising from

[107] *Shiloh Spinners Ltd v Harding*, above.

[108] Above, para.7–069.

[109] LPA 1925 s.153, for which see above and see *Re M'Naul's Estate* [1902] 1 L.R. 114. See generally (1958) 22 Conv. (N.S.) 101 (T. P. D. Taylor).

[110] LPA 1925 s.153(8).

[111] Challis pp.334, 335; Hood & Challis, p.282.

[112] See *Bosomworth v Faber* (1992) 69 P. & C.R. 288 at 292, 293, where it was held that the rule that a tenant cannot acquire a lease by prescription against his own landlord (or another tenant of his landlord, below, para.28–040) does not apply to a tenant under a lease which he could at any time unilaterally enlarge into the fee simple.

[113] As illustrated above, paras 6–024, 20–045, 20–047.

with them so as to bind A's successors in title.[114] This gives B or his successors the right to claim both compensation under the condition and an injunction to forbid future mining unless compensation is paid.[115] If the provision for compensation is expressed as a covenant separately from the grant or reservation of the covenantor's rights, it may still operate as a condition if it is held, as a matter of construction, that "the benefit and the burden have been annexed to each other *ab initio*".[116]

Even if the burden is imposed by a separate covenant, as distinct from a **32–025** condition, it may still bind successors in title under a doctrine which evolved with the aid of an old rule relating to deeds: "it is ancient law that a man cannot take benefit under a deed without subscribing to the obligations thereunder".[117] This proposition was invoked in a case where purchasers of plots on a building estate were entitled under a trust deed to use private roads and other amenities, and each on purchasing his plot covenanted to pay a just proportion of the cost of their maintenance. It was held that the purchasers' successors were liable for their due contribution while they made use of the roads.[118] That decision was approved by the Court of Appeal in enforcing an informal agreement between neighbours under which one was to have a right of way across the other's yard in exchange for withdrawing objection to a small encroachment on his land by the foundations of the other's building: so long as the encroachment was permitted, the right of way could not be withdrawn.[119]

However, there must now be some doubt both as to the correctness of the **32–026** Court of Appeal decision and as to the precise extent of the principle of mutual benefit and burden. The House of Lords has rejected any "pure" principle of benefit and burden,[120] by which "any party deriving any benefit from a conveyance must accept any burden in the same conveyance".[121]

---

[114] *Aspden v Seddon (No.2)* (1876) 1 Ex.D. 496; *Chamber Colliery Co v Twyerould* (1893) reported in [1915] 1 Ch. 268n., HL.

[115] *Westhoughton UDC v Wigan Coal & Iron Co Ltd* [1919] 1 Ch. 159 at 171, 172.

[116] *Tito v Waddell (No.2)* [1977] Ch. 106 at 290, per Megarry V.C., discussing in detail the cases here cited.

[117] *Halsall v Brizell* [1957] Ch. 169 at 172, per Upjohn J. The decision was approved in *Rhone v Stephens* [1994] 2 A.C. 310 at 322.

[118] *Halsall v Brizell*, above. It was unnecessary in that case for Upjohn J. to explain how the obligation to pay might be enforced. It has been suggested that it could not be enforced by action as such, but only by withholding from the purchasers' successors the right to use the road unless and until they paid the charges due: *IDC Group Ltd v Clark* [1992] 1 E.G.L.R. 187 at 190 (affirmed [1992] 2 E.G.L.R. 184). See too *Four Oaks Estates Ltd v Hadley* (1986) 83 L.S.Gaz. 2326 (estate management company could not apportion cost of maintaining the roads over the whole estate when house owners had only covenanted to contribute to the maintenance of roads adjacent to their houses).

[119] *E.R. Ives Investment Ltd v High* [1967] 2 Q.B. 379. There were other grounds for this decision for which see above, para.32–006. See similarly *Hopgood v Brown* [1955] 1 W.L.R. 213 (reciprocal licences to use drains); above, paras 32–014, 32–031. In *Parkinson v Reid* (1966) 56 D.L.R. (2d) 315 the Supreme Court of Canada held that when the benefit (use of a party wall) ceased to be enjoyed, the covenantor's successor was freed from the burden (to maintain a staircase), even assuming that such a burden could run.

[120] Such a principle had been distilled from the authorities in *Tito v Waddell (No.2)*, above, at 302. See the fifth edition of this work at p.769.

[121] *Rhone v Stephens*, above, at 322, per Lord Templeman.

Although the House accepted that conditions could be attached expressly or impliedly to the exercise of a power, this was so only where the condition was "relevant to the exercise of the right".[122] The party must, "at least in theory", be able to elect between enjoying the right and performing his obligation or renouncing the right and freeing himself of the burden.[123] On that basis, the House held that the fact that A's roof was supported by B's property did not mean that B could enforce against A a positive covenant made by A's predecessor in title with B's to repair the roof. However, the approach taken by the House provides little guidance as to when a party will be regarded as having a genuine choice whether or not to renounce the benefits in order to be relieved of the burdens.[124] In the case mentioned above,[125] it seems improbable that the neighbour who enjoyed the benefit of the right of way could in reality give it up so as to require the removal of the foundations of his neighbour's building from his land.[126] Perhaps the real difficulty for the person seeking to enforce the positive covenant was that there was no "mutuality" in the benefit and burden: they were not in fact connected in the way that the right to use a road is connected to the cost of its upkeep.

The policy underlying the decision of the House in *Rhone* seems to be to restrict the ambit of the doctrine of benefit and burden as a means of circumventing the rule that the burden of positive covenants cannot run. The intention would seem to be to prompt the abolition of the rule by legislation that had taken full account of all the consequences, rather than by slight of judicial hand.[127]

32–027   **3. Proposals for reform.** The issues with the current law have been considered on more than one occasion, and proposals made for reform.[128] One of these proposals—the re-casting of any new covenants as land obligations (which could be positive or negative) is under active consideration following the final recommendations of the Law Commission and their publication of a draft Bill. One partial reform is encompassed within the system of commonhold and is noted below and dealt with in more detail later.[129]

32–028   *(a) Covenants as land obligations.* In 2011, the Law Commission recommended a scheme whereby covenants would operate as "land obligations".

---

[122] *Rhone v Stephens*, above.

[123] *Rhone v Stephens*, above. See too *Thamesmead Town Ltd v Allotey* [1998] 3 E.G.L.R. 97 (emphasising that the doctrine was only applicable where the successor in title had a choice whether or not to take the benefit.

[124] See (1994) 110 L.Q.R. 346 at 348 et seq. (N. P. Gravells); [1994] Conv. 477 at 480 et seq. (J. Snape). cf. *Amsprop Trading Ltd v Harris Distribution Ltd* [1997] 1 W.L.R. 1025 at 1034.

[125] *E.R. Ives Investment Ltd v High*, above; para.32–025.

[126] See *Rhone v Stephens*, above, at 323. *E.R. Ives Investment Ltd v High* was not cited to the House.

[127] Lord Templeman warned that "social injustice can be caused by logic", citing the difficulties that the enforcement of positive covenants had given rise to in relation to leases: *Rhone v Stephens*, above, at 321.

[128] Above, para.32–018.

[129] Ch.33.

This followed earlier reports in 1984 and an extensive consultation paper in 2008.[130] The covenant (i.e. land obligation), the details of which are explained below,[131] would generally be a new *legal* interest in land (although it could default to an equitable interest in the normal way if formality requirements for legal interests were not met), operating in respect of a dominant and servient tenement, and capable only of express creation. It could operate in both registered and unregistered land, although likely to be rare in the latter. Such an obligation would be akin to an easement, but there would be no requirement for the benefited and burdened estates to be owned and possessed by different persons provided that the titles are registered.[132]

Under the new proposals, it would no longer be possible to create new covenants under the rule in *Tulk v Moxhay*, although the definition of a land obligation would be functional, so nearly all obligations have the effect of a *Tulk*-style covenant would amount to a land obligation, however named.[133] Remedies for breach of a land obligation would be an injunction, an order for performance of the obligation, damages or an order requiring the defendant to pay the amount due under the obligation.[134]

(b) Commonhold. A system of "commonhold" has been introduced by Part **32–029** I of the Commonhold and Leasehold Reform Act 2002.[135] This establishes a version of freehold strata titles,[136] which, for reasons explained above,[137] was nearly impossible to achieve within the conventional structure of real property. Commonhold was devised against the background of the earlier proposals on land obligations and it is intended that the two systems will complement each other, when and if the proposals on land obligations reach the statute book. The scheme for Commonhold under the Act and as detailed

---

[130] (2011) Law Com. No.327, *Making Land Work: Easements Covenants and Profits a Prendre*; (1984) Law Com. No.127, (2008) Law Com. CP No.186. Note that some of the objectives of the 1984 proposal have been achieved by the commonhold legislation: see *Commonhold: A Consultation Paper* (1990) Cm. 1345, para.3.49.30. For Commonhold, see Ch.33. The 2011 Report also proposes changes to the law of easements and profits.

[131] Below para.32–081.

[132] This is because the register brings clarity to the benefits and burdens affecting each plot, including whether the intention is to maintain the obligation when the titles come into common ownership. In those cases where the new obligation was to be created over land of unregistered title (not itself being a transaction that triggers first registration of title), unity of seisin would defeat the obligation.

[133] Even if called a "covenant". See Law Com. No.237 para.5.82 et seq. Existing covenants would remain unaffected and continue to be enforceable under *Tulk*.

[134] Law Com. No.237 para.6.165. Damages would be assessed on a contractual basis.

[135] For the history of the legislation see *Commonhold, Freehold Flats and Freehold Ownership of Other Interdependent Buildings* (1987), Cm. 179 (report of a working group chaired by T. Aldridge); *Commonhold: A Consultation Paper* (1990) Cm. 1345; [1991] Conv. 170 (H. W. Wilkinson). For a detailed examination of the commonhold proposals and its relationship with leasehold enfranchisement, see (1995) 58 M.L.R. 486 (D. N. Clarke); [1998] Conv. 283 (T. Crabb). See also Ch.33 and *Commonhold: The New Law* (D. N. Clarke).

[136] Other countries have made statutory provision for this, including elaborate schemes of management which can be adopted for blocks of flats and similar developments. This is known in North America as the law of condominium, and in Australasia as that of strata titles.

[137] Above, paras 32–017, 32–018.

in various Statutory Instruments is necessarily very elaborate but its main features may be summarised as follows.[138]

(i) A commonhold consists of two or more units (such as a block of flats or offices) which because of their shared facilities and services require a system of communal management.

(ii) The units making up the commonhold have to be structurally independent of any building outside the scheme, but buildings within the same scheme may be independent of each other (such as flats with a detached garage block).

(iii) Each unit owner is registered as the freehold owner of his unit and that ownership automatically carries with it the right to essential facilities and any communal services.

(iv) Ownership of the common parts is vested in a commonhold association who are registered with a freehold in the common parts. The association is a corporate body limited by guarantee and run exclusively by the unit owners. The common parts, facilities and services are managed by the association.

(v) A commonhold can be wound up. The freehold in the individual units then vests automatically in the commonhold association and the rights of unit owners are converted into a share in the net assets of the association.

(vi) The title to all commonholds are registered at the Land Registry because commonhold can be created only out of registered freehold land.[139]

Section 2. In Equity: Restrictive Covenants

32–030   **1. Law and equity.** The relationship between the divergent rules of common law and of equity is best understood by imagining the two separate jurisdictions which existed before 1875.[140] Equity's jurisdiction had, furthermore, two distinct aspects of its own. First, equity followed the law but provided better remedies than damages. Secondly, equity broke away from the rule that the burden of a covenant affecting land can only run with a lease, and allowed *restrictive* covenants to be enforced against successors in title to a freeholder.

[138] See Pt I of the 2002 Act and Explanatory Note. See also *Commonhold: A Consultation Paper* (1990) Cm. 1345, pp.1–18, and *Commonhold—The Way Ahead* (Lord Chancellor's Department, 1993).
[139] For the possible limits on the powers of commonholders to lease and mortgage their units, see (1995) 58 M.L.R. 486 at 500, 501 (D. N. Clarke).
[140] Above, paras 5–015, 5–016.

2. Equitable remedies. The special equitable remedies may be disposed of **32–031** shortly. The value of a covenant affecting land is generally of a "real" character; that is to say, it lies in continued observance rather than in monetary compensation for a breach. Therefore an injunction, an equitable remedy, is usually more valuable than damages, at any rate where the obligation is merely negative. An injunction would normally be awarded[141] in a court of equity (and since 1875 in any Division of the High Court[142]) in any case where a covenant was enforceable at law.[143]

·**3. Restrictive covenants.** In developing special rules about restrictive **32–032** covenants, equity added a new chapter to the canon of the law of property. The essentials of a restrictive covenant are that it is negative, and made for the benefit of land belonging to the covenantee. An example is where V, having two adjacent houses, sells one of them to P, and P covenants not to carry on any trade or business in the house he has bought, in order to preserve the residential value of V's other house.[144] The real starting point, after some doubts[145] and precursors[146] was the decision in *Tulk v Moxhay*[147] in 1848, a time when the full effect of the vast expansion in industrial and building activities was being felt. It was held that a restrictive covenant could be enforced against a later purchaser of the burdened land unless (as always, in equity) he bought without notice of the covenant. A corpus of detailed rules evolved around this equitable doctrine. First, the circumstances in which the burden of a covenant would pass were defined. Subsequently, rules were

[141] *Doherty v Allman* (1878) 3 App.Cas. 709 at 719.
[142] Above, para.5–016.
[143] But see *Hugh Small v Oliver & Saunders (Developments) Limited*, above, on the suitability of awarding damages in lieu of an injunction.
[144] Such covenants are not in unlawful restraint of trade when given on the acquisition of new property. It may be otherwise when the property already belonged to the covenantor: *Esso Petroleum Co Ltd v Harper's Garage (Stourport) Ltd* [1968] A.C. 269; *Cleveland Petroleum Co Ltd v Dartstone Ltd* [1969] 1 W.L.R. 116. The remarkable operation of this distinction, suggested for the first time during the argument in the *Esso* case in the House of Lords, is illustrated by the example put in argument at p.289 of that case. It is perhaps significant that, in a subsequent sale and leaseback case, the Court of Appeal upheld a tying covenant: *Alec Lobb (Garages) Ltd v Total Oil (Great Britain) Ltd* [1985] 1 W.L.R. 173. Such tying covenants may now be vulnerable under Art.85 of the Treaty of Rome, which prohibits certain anti-competitive agreements and which can apply to such covenants even though both parties are within, and performance is to take place in, the same Member State of the European Union. See *Inntrepreneur Estates Ltd v Mason* (1993) 68 P. & C.R. 53; *Inntrepreneur Estates (G.L.) Ltd v Boyes* (1993) 68 P. & C.R. 77; *Star Rider Ltd v Inntrepreneur Pub Co* [1998] 1 E.G.L.R. 53; and for a valuable commentary, [1994] Conv. 150 (T. Frazer). cf. *Gibbs Mew Plc v Gemmell* [1999] 1 E.G.L.R. 43. It should be noted that even if a covenant is void under Art.85 against the landlord who granted it, it may be valid and enforceable by an assignee of the reversion: see *Passmore v Morland Plc* [1999] 1 E.G.L.R. 51 (tying covenant could be enforced by assignee of the reversion, which was a small regional brewer, even though it might have been void as regards the assignor, a major brewery group).
[145] The doctrine was denied in *Keppell v Bailey* (1834) 2 My. & K. 517 at 546, 547 (on which see Challis p.185) and treated as still unsettled in *Bristow v Wood* (1844) 1 Coll.C.C. 480.
[146] *Whatinan v Gibson* (1838) 9 Sim. 196; *Mann v Stephens* (1846) 15 Sim. 377.
[147] 2 Ph. 774.

developed as to when the benefit might be transmitted. Somewhat surprisingly, the latter caused greater difficulties than the former, but these problems have now been overcome. Each must be examined in turn.

A. The Burden of the Covenant

32–033   **1. The decision.** *Tulk v Moxhay*,[148] decided in 1848, laid the first foundations of the modern doctrine of restrictive covenants. Previously the burden of a covenant (not made in a lease) would no more run in equity than it would at law. But in that case it was held by Lord Cottenham L.C., affirming Lord Langdale M.R.,[149] that a covenant to maintain the garden at Leicester Square uncovered with any buildings would be enforced by injunction against a purchaser of the land who bought with notice of the covenant. Thus was invented a new interest in land, purely equitable in nature.[150] No longer was a negative covenant enforceable only against the covenantor (or his personal representatives) as a mere contract: it was now enforceable against his successors in title as an incumbrance, a right in some other person's favour over the land itself.

32–034   **2. Original basis.** For some while the question was thought to depend on two things only: the character of the covenant, and the fact of notice. A person who took land with notice that it was bound by some restriction could not, it was thought, disregard that restriction. On this footing it was immaterial whether the restriction had been imposed to benefit other land or merely the covenantee personally.[151] In fact, the suit in *Tulk v Moxhay* had been brought by the original covenantee, who had other property in Leicester Square, and Lord Cottenham had relied on the argument that if the covenant did not run "it would be impossible for an owner of land to sell part of it without incurring the risk of rendering what he retains worthless".[152]

32–035   **3. Dominant tenement.** The argument relied upon by Lord Cottenham in fact became the foundation of the doctrine; and since 1903 it has been settled that equity will enforce a restrictive covenant against a purchaser only if it was made for the protection (i.e. benefit) of other land.[153] Restrictive covenants came to resemble easements as being rights over one plot of land ("the servient tenement") existing for the benefit of another plot of land ("the

---

[148] (1848) 2 Ph. 774. For a sequel see *Tulk v Metropolitan Board of Works* (1868) 16 W.R. 212.

[149] (1848) 11 Beav 571. The appeal was decided a mere 16 days after the decision below.

[150] cf. above, para.5–026. See the survey at (1971) 87 L.Q.R. 539 (D. J. Hayton).

[151] *Catt v Tourle* (1869) 4 Ch.App. 654 and *Luker v Dennis* (1877) 7 Ch D 227 are two examples which are no longer good law.

[152] *Tulk v Moxhay*, above, 2 Ph. at 777. For more recent litigation concerning another covenant entered into in 1874 on a sale of land in Leicester Square by a member of the Tulk family, see *R. v Westminster City Council Ex p. Leicester Square Coventry Street Association* (1989) 87 L.G.R. 675.

[153] *Formby v Barker* [1903] 2 Ch. 539; *LCC v Allen* [1914] 3 K.B. 642 at 659, 660. There are certain exceptions to this rule; below, para.32–045.

dominant tenement"). It was said that the new principle was "either an extension in equity of the doctrine of *Spencer's Case* to another line of cases, or else an extension in equity of the doctrine of negative easements; such, for instance, as a right to the access of light, which prevents the owner of the servient tenement from building so as to obstruct the light".[154] But in reality the rule was a new departure, and eventually it was recognised that a new type of equitable interest had been created.[155]

4. Essentials. It was accordingly established that this new liability could run with land only where: **32–036**

    (i) the covenant was restrictive, i.e. negative, in nature;
    (ii) two plots of land were concerned, one bearing the burden and the other receiving the benefit; and
    (iii) the defendant could not set up the overriding defence in equity of purchase of the legal estate for value without notice.

We consider first the special position of the person who originally entered into the covenant, and then deal with these three conditions in order, bearing in mind that the doctrine of notice has been replaced largely by principles of registration.

1. THE ORIGINAL COVENANTOR

The original covenantor normally remains liable on the covenant, even if there is no dominant tenement, and even if he has parted with the servient tenement.[156] This is because his liability is purely contractual and exists quite apart from the law of property, just as in the case of an original tenant under a lease granted before 1996 who has assigned his lease.[157] Indeed, in the absence of an expression of contrary intention, a person is, by statute, deemed to covenant on behalf of himself, his successors in title and those deriving title under him.[158] There is some dispute as to the significance of these words. There appear to be two possible interpretations of them. **32–037**

---

[154] *London and South Western Ry v Gomm* (1882) 20 Ch D 562 at 583, per Jessel M.R. For discussion and criticism of the principles evolved in the decisions of this period, see (1982) 98 L.Q.R. 279 at 293 (S. Gardner). See also [1978] Conv. 24 (J. D. A. Brooke-Taylor).

[155] *Re Nisbet and Potts' Contract* [1905] 1 Ch. 391 at 396 (on appeal, [1906] 1 Ch. 386).

[156] Unless, of course, the covenant is limited by express words to that period that he is in possession of the land. See the analogous argument in respect of leases in *Avonridge Property Co Ltd v London Diocesan Fund & Ors* [2005] UKHL 70; (2005) 1 W.L.R. 3956.

[157] Above, para.20–052. For leases granted after 1995, see above, paras 20–085, 20–087.

[158] LPA 1925 s.79(1); above, para.32–016. As regards restrictive covenants, "successors in title" is deemed to include the owners for the time being of the land: LPA 1925 s.79(2). Prior to 1926, a person would commonly covenant expressly "for himself, his heirs and assigns, and other persons claiming under him".

32–038

    (i) The words are included merely to show an intention that the burden of the covenant should run with the land and not to make the covenantor personally liable for the acts of his successors in title.[159] This view must be open to serious doubt. In the analogous case of leaseholds granted before 1996, it is clear that the original lessee cannot escape from liability on his covenants simply by assigning the lease, and it seems to be immaterial whether he has covenanted on behalf of his successors in title or not.[160]

    (ii) That the covenantor is in effect taken to give a personal warranty that neither he nor any of his successors in title will infringe the terms of the covenant.[161] If that is so, the words are, in one sense, mere surplusage. The original covenantor is liable for the acts of his successors in title simply by virtue of privity of contract, and this has always been perceived to be the reason why the first tenant under a lease granted before 1996 remains liable on the covenants throughout the duration of the term.[162] However, the words implied by the statute do preclude any ambiguity as to the extent of the original covenantor's liability. By covenanting on behalf of his successors in title, he makes it apparent that he will remain liable on the basis of privity of contract for the acts of his successors in title notwithstanding that he may have parted with the land.[163] If he wishes to limit his liability to his own acts, he must covenant expressly to that effect.

In practice there is little authority on the liability of the original covenantor for breach of a restrictive covenant *after* he has disposed of the burdened land. This is not surprising given that the owner of the land benefited by the restrictive covenant is likely to wish to restrain by injunction any act that contravenes the covenant, rather than merely seeking damages for its breach.[164] The appropriate defendant will therefore be the person who presently owns or occupies the land and not the original covenantor.

---

[159] *Powell v Hemsley* [1909] 1 Ch. 680 at 688 (Eve J.); cf. [1909] 2 Ch. 252 at 256, 258, CA.

[160] cf. *Walker's Case* (1587) 3 Co.Rep. 22a at 23a. In the case of a lease, the natural inference is that parties intended to contract for the duration of the term. In relation to a freehold covenant the inference that a covenantor intends to bind himself in perpetuity is perhaps less obvious.

[161] cf. *Baily v De Crespigny* (1869) L.R. 4 Q.B. 180 at 186.

[162] Above, para.20–011.

[163] A covenantor could in principle limit his liability by covenanting only on behalf of successors in title and not on behalf of all owners and occupiers for the time being of the land (as he is deemed to do under LPA 1925 s.79(2) in relation to restrictive covenants). cf. *Baily v De Crespigny*, above, at 186, 187.

[164] Below, para.32–051. The court may award damages in lieu of an injunction under the Supreme Court Act 1981, s.50. The original covenantor should (and usually will) take an indemnity covenant from any transferee of the land burdened: see Standard Conditions of Sale, 5th edition (2011) c.4.6.4.

II. ASSIGNEES

An assignee of the original covenantor's land is bound by the covenant if, but only if, four conditions are fulfilled.   **32–039**

1. The covenant must be negative in nature

(a) Negativity. After a few cases in which the court was prepared to enforce a positive covenant,[165] the rule was settled in 1881 that only a negative covenant would be enforced by equity.[166] The equitable interest created by the covenant is one primarily enforceable by injunction, and whereas a negative injunction restraining the commission or continuance of specified acts normally presents no difficulties of enforcement, equity has long been chary of making orders to perform a series of acts requiring supervision,[167] even though it has the necessary jurisdiction to decree specific performance or grant a mandatory injunction,[168] ordering specified acts to be done. The *Tulk* doctrine is confined to negative covenants because effect can be given to these "by means of the land itself".[169]   **32–040**

(b) Substance. The question is whether the covenant is negative in substance: it is immaterial whether the wording is positive or negative. Thus the covenant in *Tulk v Moxhay*[170] was positive in wording (to maintain the Leicester Square garden "in an open state, uncovered with any buildings") but negative in nature, for it merely bound the covenantor to refrain from building, without requiring him to do any positive act. A test which is often applied is whether the covenant requires expenditure of money for its performance; if the covenant requires the covenantor "to put his hand into his pocket", it is not negative in nature.[171] But the converse does not necessarily follow; a covenant that can be performed without expense may still require some positive act and so not be restrictive. A covenant to use the premises as a private dwelling-house only is negative in nature, for really it is a prohibition   **32–041**

---

[165] *Morland v Cook* (1868) L.R. 6 Eq. 252; *Cooke v Chilcott* (1876) 3 Ch D 694. For differing interpretations of these cases see [1981] Conv. 55 (C. D. Bell); [1983] Conv. 29 (R. Griffith); 327 (C. D. Bell). For the enforcement of positive covenants today, see above, paras 32–017 et seq.

[166] *Haywood v Brunswick Permanent Benefit BS* (1881) 8 QBD 403. This principle has been reaffirmed by the House of Lords: *Rhone v Stephens* [1994] 2 A.C. 310.

[167] But this is less so than formerly: cf. above, paras 19–121, 19–122.

[168] See *Jackson v Normandy Brick Co* [1899] 1 Ch. 438 (order to demolish buildings erected in breach of covenant).

[169] *Re Nisbet & Potts' Contract* [1905] 1 Ch. 391 at 397, per Farwell J. "To enforce a positive covenant would be to enforce a personal obligation against a person who has not covenanted. To enforce negative covenants is only to treat the land as subject to a restriction": *Rhone v Stephens*, above, at 321, per Lord Templeman.

[170] (1848) 2 Ph. 774; above, para.32–033.

[171] *Haywood v Brunswick Permanent Benefit BS*, above, at 409, 410. See too *Bedwell Park Quarry Co Ltd v Hertfordshire County Council* [1993] J.P.L. 349 (obligation by quarry company to restore quarry to agriculture: "it was hard to think of an obligation that was more positive in substance as well as form": per Sir Christopher Slade at 352).

against use for other purposes[172] and the same applies to a covenant to give the first refusal of a plot of land,[173] for in effect it is a covenant not to sell to anyone else until the covenantee has had an opportunity of buying. But a covenant "not to let the premises fall into disrepair", despite its apparently negative form, is in substance positive, for it can be performed only by the expenditure of money on repairs.

32–042   *(c) Severance.* If a covenant has both positive and negative elements in it, the negative element may bind the land even though the positive cannot.[174] Even a positive obligation may be binding if it is no more than a condition of a negative one; thus a covenant to submit plans before building may be enforceable against a purchaser as a covenant not to build without first submitting plans.[175]

32–043   *(d) Common covenants.* Some examples may be given of the restrictive covenants that are most frequently encountered in practice, particularly in transfers or leases of urban property. They include covenants against:

> (i) building on land[176];
>
> (ii) carrying on any trade or business (or certain specified trades or businesses) on the premises[177];
>
> (iii) carrying on any activity that constitutes a nuisance, or is offensive or dangerous[178]; and

---

[172] e.g. *German v Chapman* (1877) 7 Ch D 271; *Crest Nicholson Residential (South) Limited v McAllister* [2004] EWCA Civ 410 [2004] 1 W.L.R. 2409.

[173] See *Manchester Ship Canal Co v Manchester Racecourse Co* [1901] 2 Ch. 37; *Lange v Lange* [1966] N.Z.L.R. 1057.

[174] *Shepherd Homes Ltd v Sandham (No.2)* [1971] 1 W.L.R. 1062 (approved in *Bedwell Park Quarry Co Ltd v Hertfordshire County Council*, above, at 351); *Crest Nicholson Residential (South) Limited v McAllister* above. Thus in *Tulk v Moxhay* (above, para.32–033) the covenant was to maintain the garden as well as not to build upon it.

[175] *Powell v Hemsley* [1909] 1 Ch. 680; 2 Ch. 252; and see *Westhoughton UDC v Wigan Coal & Iron Co Ltd* [1919] 1 Ch. 159 (not to let down surface without paying compensation).

[176] *Wrotham Park Estate Co Ltd v Parkside Homes Ltd* [1974] 1 W.L.R. 798; *R. v Westminster City Council Ex p. Leicester Square Coventry Street Association* (1989) 87 L.G.R. 675 (covenant not infringed by the mere sale of the property to a third party who intended to build); *Rees v Peters* [2011] EWCA Civ 836 (not to build or place any moveable structure without consent).

[177] See, however, *Petrofina (Gt Britain) Ltd v Martin* [1966] Ch. 146. It has now been held that a covenant restraining alienation is within the doctrine: see *Hemingway Securities Ltd v Dunraven Ltd* [1995] 1 E.G.L.R. 61 at 62. cf. above, para.3–063. The covenant is breached only if the trade or business is undertaken on the land burdened by it and not if the property is used merely as a means of access to other land on which such trade or business is carried on: *Elliott v Safeway Stores Plc* [1995] 1 W.L.R. 1396.

[178] *Hall v Ewin* (1887) 37 Ch D 74 (covenant infringed by user of house in Edgware Road to display lions); *Tod-Heatley v Benham* (1888) 40 Ch D 80 (covenant infringed by user of house as hospital treating over 50 persons each day). cf. *National Schizophrenia Fellowship v Ribble Estates SA* [1994] 1 E.G.L.R. 181 (covenant not infringed by acquisition of house to accommodate elderly mental patients).

(iv) using the premises for any purpose other than as a private dwelling-house.[179]

2. The covenant must be made for the protection of land retained by the covenantee.[180] It is axiomatic that the justification for converting a personal covenant into an equitable incumbrance is to enable the covenantee to preserve the value of other land of his in the neighbourhood.[181] As with easements,[182] therefore, there must be two plots of land in the case: the doctrine depends on a relation of "dominancy" and "serviency" of lands.[183] Whether this relationship exists is a question of fact in each case, and proof of the facts may make the relationship plain.[184] Proximity is essential: covenants allegedly binding land in Hampstead will be too remote to benefit land in Clapham.[185] A covenantee similarly ceases to be able to enforce a covenant (except as against the original covenantor) if he parts with all the land for the benefit of which the covenant was taken,[186] or if it ceases to be reasonably possible to regard the covenant as being for the benefit of the land.[187] It might be thought, by parity of reasoning, that a covenant made for the protection of a leasehold interest should ceases to be enforceable when the lease determines, e.g. by merger in the freehold and there is authority to this effect.[188] However, the Court of Appeal has held that the merger of a leasehold estate with a freehold estate did not have the effect that easements attached to the leasehold interest were thereby extinguished on the ground that the benefit of an easement might be annexed to the land itself, rather than any particular estate in it.[189] Although

32–044

---

[179] *C. & G. Homes Ltd v Secretary of State for Health* [1991] Ch. 365 (covenant infringed by use of house to provide supervised housing for a group of mental patients). See too *Brown v Heathlands Mental Health NHS Trust* [1996] 1 All E.R. 133 at 135. The covenant is breached by using premises as short-term holiday lets, *Caradon District Council v Paton* (2000) 3 E.G.L.R. 57. This form of covenant is narrower than a covenant against carrying on a trade or business: see [1991] Conv. 388 (P. Devonshire). See too *Jaggard v Sawyer* [1995] 1 W.L.R. 269 (covenant not to use land except as a private garden contravened by construction of a driveway). In rural areas there may be a covenant against using the premises for any save agricultural purposes: *Holdom v Kidd* (1990) 61 P. & C.R. 456 (covenant infringed by user of land to accommodate gypsy caravans: it was irrelevant that many of the gypsies worked on local farms).

[180] *Millbourn v Lyons* [1914] 2 Ch. 231 (the relevant date is that of the covenant, not the contract therefore); *LCC v Allen* [1914] 3 K.B. 642.

[181] Above, para.32–032.

[182] Below, para.27–008.

[183] *Formby v Barker* [1903] 2 Ch. 539 at 552 (Vaughan Williams L.J.). For a detailed account of the evolution of this rule, see *LCC v Allen*, above, at 664 et seq. For comment see (1982) 98 L.Q.R. 279 at 306 (S. Gardner).

[184] In other words, it need not appear from the covenant itself: *Tulk v Moxhay* (1848) 2 Ph. 774; *Marten v Flight Refuelling Ltd* [1962] Ch. 115.

[185] *Kelly v Barrett* [1924] 2 Ch. 379 at 404.

[186] *Chambers v Randall* [1923] 1 Ch. 149 at 157, 158.

[187] *Wrotham Park Estate Co Ltd v Parkside Homes Ltd* [1974] 1 W.L.R. 798; *Hugh Small v Oliver & Saunders (Developments) Limited* [2006] EWHC 1293 (Ch) above.

[188] *Golden Lion Hotel (Hunstanton) Ltd v Carter* [1965] 1 W.L.R. 1189. LPA 1925 s.139 (above, para.20–073) does not cover this situation.

[189] *Wall v Collins* [2007] EWCA 44.

concerned with easements, the reasoning, were it to prove persuasive,[190] would apply with equal force to covenants, save in so far as the decision turned on the fact that an easement could exist as a legal interest in land.[191]

There are the following exceptions and qualifications to the rule requiring the covenantee to hold land capable of benefiting from the covenant.

32–045   *(a) Leases and mortgages.* The doctrine of *Tulk v Moxhay* applies equally to covenants contained in leases, although it is not always needed because of the special rules about the enforceability of leasehold covenants. Moreover, the landlord enjoys an important dispensation: his reversion is apparently a sufficient interest to enable him to sue a sub-lessee in equity on a restrictive covenant contained in the lease. There is therefore no need for any other land which could be called a dominant tenement.[192] In relation to leases granted before 1996, this is an important extension of the reversioner's rights, for where the covenant is negative he may have a remedy against someone, such as a sub-tenant, with whom he has neither privity of contract nor privity of estate.[193] A similar dispensation appears to apply to mortgages, so that the mortgagee's interest in the mortgaged land likewise suffices.[194]

32–046   *(b) Scheme of development.* The meaning of "scheme of development" will be explained shortly.[195] When, under such a scheme, the common vendor disposes of the last of the plots laid out for development, often he may retain no land capable of benefiting. But even if the owners of the other plots are not expressly made covenantees under the covenants made when the last plot is sold,[196] the last purchaser's covenants are enforceable by the owners of the other plots against both the last purchaser himself and his successors in title. The rule in *Tulk v Moxhay* applies.

32–047   *(c) Statutory exceptions.* The rules applied to private landowners have been modified by numerous statutes for the benefit of public bodies. These statutes enable such bodies to enforce covenants in gross, that is, when they are not owners of adjacent land or indeed any land.[197] For example, under the Town

---

[190] There must be some doubt whether it is possible to maintain that an incumbrance attaches to the land, rather than the claimant's estate in it. There would be no difficulty if the easement or covenant can be construed as being granted originally for the benefit of any estate in the land, not merely the estate of the original grantee. In Law Com. No. 327, the Law Commission recommend that *Wall* be reversed but that a mechanism be provided to enable the person entitled to the benefit of an easement to preserve it on merger and surrender, at para.3.255.

[191] *Wall v Collins* above at para.15.

[192] *Hall v Ewin* (1887) 37 Ch D 74, decided before the requirement of benefited land was firmly settled, but approved by Harman L.J. in *Regent Oil Co Ltd v JA Gregory (Hatch End) Ltd* [1966] Ch. 402 at 433; and see *Teape v Douse* (1905) 92 L.T. 319.

[193] cf. above, para.20–006. For leases granted after 1995, see above, para.20–117.

[194] *John Brothers Abergarw Brewery Co v Holmes* [1900] 1 Ch. 188; *Regent Oil Co Ltd v JA Gregory (Hatch End) Ltd*, above, per Harman L.J.

[195] Below, para.32–075.

[196] Above, para.32–006.

[197] Such statutes have been employed for many years: see *Governors of Peabody Donation Fund v London Residuary Body* (1987) 55 P. & C.R. 355 (Artisans and Labourers Dwellings Improvement Act 1875).

and Country Planning Act 1990 (as amended) any person interested in land may (by agreement or otherwise) enter into a planning obligation with a local authority restricting the land in any specified way.[198] Such an agreement is enforceable against both the person entering into the obligation and his successor in title.[199] Where, in carrying out its obligations in relation to housing under the Housing Act 1985, a local authority enters into a covenant on the disposal of land held by it for housing purposes, or with any landowner, that covenant is enforceable against the covenantor and his successors in title even though it was not taken for the benefit of any land owned by the authority.[200] The National Trust may enforce a covenant made with it against the successor in title of the covenantor as if it had been made for the benefit of the Trust's land.[201] Likewise local authorities can enforce agreements made with landowners against their successors under the Ancient Monuments Act 1979[202] and the Wildlife and Countryside Act 1981.[203]

(d) Remedies in contract and tort. It has been held[204] that where there is a **32–048** covenant not to "cause or permit" land to be used otherwise than for specified purposes, it will be no breach of the covenant for the covenantor to agree to sell the land to a purchaser whom he knows to intend to use it for other purposes, and to assist him in obtaining planning permission for that use. For the vendor, on selling, loses control of the property, and "one cannot permit that which one does not control".[205] But if the covenant had been framed so as to prohibit parting with control in such circumstances, it appears that both the vendor and the purchaser could have been restrained by injunction from completing the sale, and that the covenantee, if he suffered damage, could have sued the purchaser in tort for wrongfully inducing a breach of contract,[206] and perhaps also for conspiracy.[207] In one case where the covenantor and the purchaser were companies controlled by a third company and the land was transferred in conspiracy with the object of breaking the covenant, the court granted a mandatory injunction requiring the land to be reconveyed to

---

[198] s.106(1) (substituted by the Planning and Compensation Act 1991 s.12); above, para. 32–018. This section replaces with a different and much more extensive regime, so-called "s.52 agreements": see the now repealed T & CPA 1971 s.52.

[199] T & CPA 1990 s.106(3).

[200] HA 1985 s.609.

[201] National Trust Act 1938 s.8. See, e.g. *Gee v National Trust* [1966] 1 W.L.R. 170; *Re Whitting's Application* (1988) 58 P. & C.R. 321.

[202] s.17(5).

[203] s.39(3).

[204] *Tophams Ltd v Earl of Sefton* [1967] 1 A.C. 50 (proposal to build houses on Aintree Racecourse).

[205] *Tophams Ltd v Earl of Sefton*, above, at 65, per Lord Hodson.

[206] *Sefton v Tophams Ltd* [1965] Ch. 1140, CA; reversed, above, fn.98. But there was no appeal against this part of the decision. See (1977) 41 Conv. (N.S.) 318 (R. J. Smith); (1982) 45 M.L.R. 241 (N. Cohen-Grabeisky). cf. above, para.6–067.

[207] *Midland Bank Trust Co Ltd v Green (No.3)* [1982] Ch. 529. This tort requires concerted action with the dominant purpose of causing injury, and can be committed by husband and wife.

the covenantor.[208] A purchaser must therefore remember that even when a covenant will not bind him as a successor in title,[209] he may yet become implicated in a breach of contract by the vendor.

32–049   **3. The burden of the covenant must have been intended to run with the covenantor's land.** A covenant may be so worded as to bind the covenantor alone, and of course, in such a case, assignees of the covenantor's land will not be bound by the covenant.[210] But if the covenant is made by the covenantor for himself, his heirs and assigns, the burden will normally run with his land. Covenants relating to the covenantor's land which are made after 1925 are deemed to have been made by the covenantor on behalf of himself, his successors in title, and the persons deriving title under him or them, unless a contrary intention appears.[211] The burden of a covenant restricting the use of land and made since 1925 will therefore prima facie run with the land.[212]

32–050   **4. The burden of the covenant runs only in equity.** There are two principal consequences of the rule that the burden of the covenant runs only in equity.

(a) Only equitable remedies are available

32–051   (1) INJUNCTION. Only equitable remedies are available and this means in practice that the case must be remediable by injunction, which is the only equitable remedy appropriate to a negative covenant. This is in keeping with the nature of a restrictive covenant as an equitable interest: it is not intended as a subject for monetary compensation, but as a means of preserving the value of land specifically. A mandatory injunction may be granted if necessary, e.g. for the removal of a building erected in breach of covenant,[213] or to order the surrender of a sub-lease granted in breach of a covenant in the head lease.[214]

---

[208] *Esso Petroleum Co Ltd v Kingswood Motors (Addlestone) Ltd* [1974] Q.B. 142 (covenant to buy all motor fuel from plaintiffs and to procure similar covenant from any transferee; damages held inadequate remedy).

[209] In the *Sefton* case, above, the vendor retained no land benefited by the covenant.

[210] *Re Fawcett and Holmes' Contract* (1889) 42 Ch D 150; *Re Royal Victoria Pavilion, Ramsgate* [1961] Ch. 581. This principle, which is contractual in origin has been confirmed by the House of Lords in the context of leases, including post-1995 leases falling under the Landlord and Tenant (Covenants) Act 1995, *Avonridge Property Co Ltd v London Diocesan Fund & Ors* [2005] UKHL 70; (2005) 1 W.L.R. 3956.

[211] LPA 1925 s.79, explained above, para.32–038. See also *Morrells of Oxford Ltd v Oxford United Football Club Ltd* [2001] Ch. 459 where it is made clear that the s.79 presumption is rebuttable (so that the burden may not run) either expressly or where the meaning of the covenant in its commercial context makes it clear that there was no intention that the burden should run.

[212] The burden of positive covenants cannot run with the land, irrespective of the intentions of the parties, and s.79 has not altered this rule: above, para.32–016.

[213] As in *Wakeham v Wood* (1981) 43 P. & C.R. 40 (building obstructed plaintiff's sea view), where the Court of Appeal explained the practice in granting such orders.

[214] *Hemingway Securities Ltd v Dunraven Ltd* [1995] 1 E.G.L.R. 61.

Like other equitable remedies, an injunction lies in the discretion of the court. This does not mean that it will not be granted as a matter of course in an ordinary case. But it will be refused if it would be inequitable to grant it, as it may be where, for example, the claimant has known of the breach for five years and taken no action[215]; and in an increasing number of cases the court may award damages in lieu while refusing an injunction.[216] Although failure to enforce a covenant against one person does not necessarily waive it as against others,[217] an injunction may be refused if the claimant has exhibited such inactivity in the face of open breaches of covenant as to justify a reasonable belief that he no longer intends to enforce the covenant.[218] It is also possible for an injunction to be refused because the character of the neighbourhood has been so completely changed that the covenant has become valueless.[219] But otherwise a restrictive covenant remains enforceable indefinitely, even after the perpetuity period has run.[220]

(2) DAMAGES IN LIEU OF AN INJUNCTION. Since the Chancery Amendment **32-052** Act 1858[221] the court has been empowered to award damages in any case where an injunction or specific performance could have been awarded. Such damages are not awarded as of right to a claimant who makes out his case, unlike damages at common law.[222] Nor will they be awarded if no injunction could have been granted.[223] An award of damages in lieu of an injunction is intended as a substitute for loss arising from future wrongs, a situation for which no remedy exists at common law.[224] Where a claimant seeks damages

---

[215] *Gaskin v Balls* (1879) 13 Ch D 324.

[216] As in *Shaw v Applegate* [1977] 1 W.L.R. 970 and *Hugh Small v Oliver & Saunders (Developments) Limited* [2006] EWHC 1293 (Ch). See also *Amec Developments Ltd v Jury's Hotel Management (UK) Ltd* (2001) 1 E.G.L.R. 81.

[217] *German v Chapman* (1877)7 Ch D 271.

[218] See *Chatsworth Estates Co v Fewell* [1931] 1 Ch. 224. But not where the delay was not unconscionable in the sense of producing an effect on the covenantor, as where the owner of the burdened land did not believe he was bound by the covenant and that belief was not engendered by the covenantee, *Harris v Williams-Wynne* [2005] EWHC 151 (Ch).

[219] *Chatsworth Estates Co v Fewell*, above; and see *Westripp v Baldock* [1939] 1 All E.R. 279. In the former case (at 227, 228), it was doubted whether it was legitimate to consider (as was done in *Sober v Sainsbury* [1913] 2 Ch. 513) changes in property outside the district. For the discharge of obsolete covenants, see below, para.32–086.

[220] *Mackenzie v Childers* (1889) 43 Ch D 265 at 279.

[221] s.2. See now Supreme Court Act 1981 s.50.

[222] See *Kelly v Barrett* [1924] 2 Ch. 379.

[223] As where the defendant had sold the houses it had built in breach of covenant and the purchasers had not been joined as parties to the action: *Surrey County Council v Bredero Homes Ltd* [1993] 1 W.L.R. 1361. The question, which is "effectively one of jurisdiction", is "whether at the date of the writ the court could have granted an injunction, not whether it would have done": *Jaggard v Sawyer* [1995] 1 W.L.R. 269 at 285, per Millett L.J. But note, damages can be awarded even though an injunction would have been refused on the ground of waiver, *Harris v Williams-Wynne* [2005] EWHC 151 (Ch), above. In this case, the jurisdiction to grant an injunction existed and the reasons for refusing injunctive discretionary relief did not also preclude the claim in damages. It seems however, that as claimant and defendant were the original parties to the covenant, the claim for damages should been seen as a claim at law on the contract, and as of right, and not as being in lieu of the discretionary equitable remedy.

[224] *Jaggard v Sawyer*, above, at 290. Damages may of course be awarded in addition for any loss that has already been suffered before the matter is adjudicated.

in lieu of an injunction for breach of a restrictive covenant,[225] then even if the breach would cause no diminution in the value of his land,[226] the court may award him damages measured by the amount which he could have obtained for the release of the covenant.[227]

32–053 *(b) Effect on third parties.* Because a restrictive covenant is only equitable it must usually be protected by the appropriate form of registration if it is to bind third parties who purchase a legal estate. A restrictive covenant will always be enforceable against a donee, a devisee or a squatter because none of them is a purchaser.[228]

32–054 (1) UNREGISTERED LAND. Where title to the land is unregistered, any restrictive covenants will be registrable as land charges under the Land Charges Act 1972 except those entered into before 1926 or made between a lessor and lessee.[229] A covenant which is registrable but not registered will be void against a subsequent purchaser for money or money's worth of a legal estate in the land charged with it.[230] Registration of a covenant constitutes actual notice of it to all persons and for all purposes.[231] As regards covenants that are within the two classes which are not registrable, the position is as follows.

> (i) Covenants entered into before 1926 or made between lessor and lessee where the lease was granted before 1996 still depend upon the doctrine of notice. They will not therefore be binding on a bona fide purchaser for value of a legal estate[232] without notice of the covenant, or someone claiming through such a person.[233] In a lease

[225] The typical case is where the defendant has constructed a building in contravention of a restrictive covenant and the claimant took no steps to seek an interlocutory injunction to restrain him: see, e.g. *Jaggard v Sawyer*, above. For an analogous situation where damages may be awarded in lieu of an injunction where a person builds so as to obstruct an easement, see *Snell & Prideaux Ltd v Dutton Mirrors Ltd* [1995] 1 E.G.L.R. 259.

[226] So that if the court could not have awarded an injunction any damages that might have been awarded at common law against the original covenantor would have been nominal: *Surrey County Council v Bredero Homes Ltd*, above.

[227] *Wrotham Park Estate Co Ltd v Parkside Homes Ltd* [1974] 1 W.L.R. 798. Although doubts have been expressed as to the correctness of this decision (see e.g. *Surrey County Council v Bredero Homes Ltd*, above, at 1386), it has now been approved: see *Jaggard v Sawyer*, above and *Hugh Small v Oliver & Saunders (Developments) Limited* [2006] EWHC 1293 (Ch), above. Although there has been considerable debate as to whether in *Wrotham Park Estate Co Ltd v Parkside Homes Ltd*, above, the court was awarding the plaintiff compensation for his loss (i.e. the right to extract payment for the release of the covenant) or granting him in part at least the defendant's gain, the former has now been established: *Jaggard v Sawyer*, above; cf. *Wrotham Park SE v Hertsmere BC* [1993] 2 E.G.L.R. 15 at 18.

[228] *Re Nisbet and Potts' Contract* [1906] 1 Ch. 386 (squatter).

[229] LCA 1972 s.2(5)(ii); above, para.8–079.

[230] LCA 1972 s.4(6); above, para.8–092.

[231] LPA 1925 s.198(1) above, para.8–085. For the difficulties which arise for a tenant who cannot investigate the freehold title, but who will nevertheless be bound by any covenant registered against a previous owner of the reversion, see above, para.21–006.

[232] Not a mere equitable interest: *London & South Western Ry v Gomm* (1882) 20 Ch D 562 at 583; *Osborne v Bradley* [1903] 2 Ch. 446 at 451.

[233] Not a mere equitable interest: *London & South Western Ry v Gomm* (1882) 20 Ch D 562 at 583; *Osborne v Bradley* [1903] 2 Ch. 446 at 451.

granted prior to 1996, a restrictive covenant in a head lease will be binding on a sub-lessee who took with notice of it.[234] As the sub-lessee will have the right to see the head lease, he will in practice be fixed with notice of any restrictive covenant in it.[235]

(ii) In a lease granted after 1995,[236] a restrictive covenant is enforceable against the assignee and any other person who is the owner or occupier of any demised premises to which the covenant relates.[237] A sub-lessee will be bound by the covenant therefore even though there is no express provision in the sub-lease to that effect.[238]

(2) REGISTERED LAND. Where title is registered, a restrictive covenant[239] requires protection by means of a notice against the burdened title.[240] Where sufficient evidence has been produced to the Registrar or there is consent from the registered proprietor of the burdened land,[241] an agreed notice may be used. In other cases, a unilateral notice may be used.[242] Where a notice is entered—of either type—this preserves the priority of the covenant over all future purchasers of the land taking under a registered disposition.[243] A covenant between a lessor and lessee relating to the demised premises is not registrable by means of a notice.[244] However, any restrictive covenant in a lease will bind a sub-lessee because he takes the land subject to all implied and express covenants, obligations, and liabilities incident to the estate created.[245] In any event, a restrictive covenant in a lease granted after 1995 is binding on any sub-lessee under the provisions of the Landlord and Tenant (Covenants) Act 1995.[246]

32–055

B. The Benefit of the Covenant

In order to enforce a covenant, the plaintiff must show that he is entitled to the benefit of it. The original covenantee can of course sue the original covenantor, and he can also sue a successor in title of the original covenantor, if the burden has passed to him. However, the original covenantee cannot sue a successor in title if he has parted with all the land for the benefit of which the covenant was taken,[247] for equity would not allow the doctrine of *Tulk v*

32–056

---

[234] *Hall v Ewin* (1887) 37 Ch D 74 at 79 (the remarks were obiter as the injunction was sought against the tenant rather than the sub-tenant).

[235] Above, para.21–005.

[236] For the leases in question, see L & TCA 1995 s.1; above, para.20–010.

[237] L & TCA 1995 s.3(5).

[238] L & TCA 1995 ss.3(5), 28(1).

[239] For the powers of a registered proprietor to create or discharge a restrictive covenant, see LRA 2002 s.23.

[240] LRA 2002 s.32(1).

[241] LRA 2002 34(3). Above, paras 7–069, 7–070.

[242] LRA 2002 s.35 paras 7–073, 7–074.

[243] LRA 2002 s.29.

[244] LRA 2002 s.33(c).

[245] LRA 2002 s.29(2)(b).

[246] ss.3(5), 28(1); above.

[247] *Chambers v Randall* [1923] 1 Ch. 149.

Moxhay to operate where the covenant was divorced from the land it was intended to protect.[248]

As for successors in title of the original covenantee, it should be remembered that the benefit of a restrictive covenant could, and still can, run with the covenantee's land at common law, without the help of equity, under the rules already stated.[249] Of course, in order to succeed at law the plaintiff must be legal owner of the land to which the covenant relates, but in equity he can succeed if he has some lesser estate,[250] or is merely an equitable owner, such as a successor under the covenantee's will or intestacy who has not yet obtained a legal title,[251] or a person for whom the benefit of the covenant is otherwise held upon trust.[252] The benefit is regarded as an interest in property which devolves on death in the ordinary way.[253]

32–057 Since 1875 it ought to make no practical difference whether the benefit passes under the rules of law or of equity, since the same court can enforce both. In one leading case the court was prepared to allow the benefit to run with the benefited land at law even where the defendant, being a successor of the covenantor, was liable only in equity.[254] Equity here merely followed the law. But more complicated rules developed which were assumed to apply in all actions against such defendants, so making the law follow equity.[255] However, since the end of 1979, many of these rules have become irrelevant because of the effect of the decision of the Court of Appeal in *Federated Homes Ltd v Mill Lodge Properties Ltd*,[256] which has greatly simplified the rules governing the transmission of the benefit of restrictive covenants entered into since 1925.[257] The rules for transmission of the benefit in equity may be stated as follows.

32–058 **1. The covenant must touch and concern land of the covenantee.** This is the same as the rule at common law.[258] The benefit of a covenant can run only with land to which the covenant in fact relates; and in the case of a restrictive covenant the essential object, on which the doctrine of *Tulk v Moxhay* depends,[259] is to preserve the value of the covenantee's other land. A covenant will satisfy this requirement if it benefits a business conducted on the

---

[248] See *Chambers v Randall* above, at 157, 158; below, para.32–066.

[249] Above, para.32–004.

[250] *Taite v Gosling* (1879) 11 Ch D 273 (tenant of purchaser from covenantee).

[251] *Lord Northbourne v Johnston* [1922] 2 Ch. 309; *Newton Abbot Co-operative Society Ltd v Williamson & Treadgold Ltd* [1952] Ch. 286; *Earl of Leicester v Wells-next-the-Sea UDC* [1973] Ch. 110.

[252] *Lord Northbourne v Johnston*, above; *Marten v Flight Refuelling Ltd* [1962] Ch. 115.

[253] *Ives v Brown* [1919] 2 Ch. 314.

[254] *Rogers v Hosegood* [1900] 2 Ch. 388 at 394, 404.

[255] See *Re Union of London and Smith's Bank Ltd's Conveyance* [1933] Ch. 611 at 630, saying that equity prescribed special rules.

[256] [1980] 1 W.L.R. 594; below, para.32–063.

[257] The decision does not affect covenants entered into prior to 1926: below, para.32–064.

[258] *Rogers v Hosegood* [1900] 2 Ch. 388; *Re Union of London & Smith's Bank Ltd's Conveyance* [1933] Ch. 611; *Re Ballard's Conveyance* [1937] Ch. 473; see above, para.32–013.

[259] Above, para.32–031.

dominant land.[260] Whether that land is in fact benefited must be established by extrinsic evidence.[261]

2. The benefit of the covenant must have passed to the plaintiff in one of three ways: by annexation; by assignment; or under a scheme of development. In principle this rule is the same as the preceding one.[262] Under that rule the benefit of a covenant could run at law, and equity needed only to follow the law. But in the case of negative covenants, which assumed a new importance when the burden of them was allowed to run in equity, the rule was held to require further elaboration.[263] The examples of the benefit running at law were mostly cases of positive covenants where it was obvious from the facts that identifiable land of the covenantee was to be benefited, as explained earlier.[264] But a restrictive covenant, which merely prohibits the covenantor from some kind of activity on his own land, does not ordinarily indicate that it is intended to benefit any land, still less any particular land, of the covenantee.[265] It was considered that if the benefit of a restrictive covenant was to run with the covenantee's land, something further was required to identify the land. This could be done in one of three ways:

32–059

(i) by showing that the benefit was annexed to that land; or

(ii) by expressly assigning the benefit; or

(iii) by showing that the land lay within a scheme of development.

In fact, most restrictive covenants entered into after 1925 will be automatically annexed by statute to the covenantee's land benefited by them. Other forms of annexation are now relevant only to restrictive covenants entered into before 1926 and are therefore treated only in outline.[266] The circumstances in which the benefit of a covenant will require assignment are now very limited. Schemes of development remain of considerable importance for reasons that are explained later.[267] Details of the three alternative methods of transmitting the benefit are as follows.

---

[260] *Newton Abbot Co-operative Society Ltd v Williamson & Treadgold Ltd* [1952] Ch. 286 at 293; *Re Quaffers Ltd's Application* (1988) 56 P. & C.R. 142 at 152. *cf.* the requirement that an easement must accommodate the dominant tenement, where the same rule applies: below, para.27–006.

[261] See, e.g. *Re Ballard's Conveyance*, above.

[262] In *Rogers v Hosegood*, above, Farwell J. spoke (at 395) of the covenant touching and concerning the land, while the Court of Appeal spoke (at 407) of the benefit being annexed to it. The meaning appears to be the same, although the former decision was based on the rules of common law and the latter on the rules of equity, it having transpired in the Court of Appeal that the legal estate was outstanding in a mortgagee.

[263] For criticism of this exposition, see (1982) 2 L.S. 53 (D. J. Hurst). But the difference here stressed is not that between the rules of law and of equity, but that between positive and negative covenants.

[264] Above, para.32–013.

[265] Though sometimes the covenant itself may make it plain, as in *Westhoughton UDC v Wigan Coal & Iron Co Ltd* [1919] 1 Ch. 159 (covenant not to let down surface of land).

[266] For a fuller exposition, see the fifth edition of this work at pp.782—785.

[267] Below, para.32–075.

I. ANNEXATION

32–060   *(a) Annexation in equity.* A covenant may be made for the benefit of the covenantee personally or for the benefit of land which he owns. It might have been thought that if a covenant touched and concerned the land so that it was not merely personal to the covenantee, it could be regarded as having been taken for the benefit of the covenantee's land.[268] However this is not so. It has long been established that it is necessary to show in addition that it was the intention of the parties that the covenant should be annexed to the covenantee's land.[269] This may be established either from the express words of the covenant or from a construction of the instrument creating it, having regard to the surrounding circumstances.[270]

32–061   (1) EXPRESS ANNEXATION.[271] The benefit will be effectively annexed to the land so as to run with it if in the instrument the land is sufficiently indicated and the covenant is either stated to be made for the benefit of the land, or stated to be made with the covenantee in his capacity as owner of the land[272]; for then in either case it is obvious that future owners of that land are intended to benefit. A classic formula is:

> "with intent that the covenant may enure to the benefit of the vendors their successors and assigns and others claiming under them to all or any of their lands adjoining".[273]

It will be noted that this formula indicates the benefited land only in general terms,[274] so that precise definition is not required. On the other hand, to covenant merely with "the vendors their heirs executors administrators and assigns" is insufficient, for no reference is made to any land, and the reference to executors and others is so wide that it indicates no particular purpose.[275]

---

[268] Compare the position in relation to leases granted prior to 1996 where, if the covenant touches and concerns the land, it is annexed to the estate of the covenantee: see above, para.20–022.

[269] *Renals v Cowlishaw* (1878) 9 Ch D 125 at 129; affirmed (1879) 11 Ch D 866; *Rogers v Hosegood* [1900] 2 Ch. 388 at 396; *Sainsbury Plc v Enfield LBC* [1989] 1 W.L.R. 590 at 595. The test is whether the covenant was intended to enure for the benefit of the particular land of the covenantee: *Re Union of London and Smith's Bank Ltd's Conveyance* [1933] Ch. 611 at 628.

[270] *Renals v Cowlishaw* (1878) 9 Ch D 125 at 129; *Shropshire County Council v Edwards* (1982) 46 P. & C.R. 270 at 276; *Sainsbury Plc v Enfield LBC*, above, at 597.

[271] See *R. v Westminster City Council Ex p. Leicester Square Coventry Street Association* (1989) 87 L.G.R. 675 at 681.

[272] See *Osborne v Bradley* [1903] 2 Ch. 446 at 450; *Drake v Gray* [1936] Ch. 451 at 466.

[273] *Rogers v Hosegood* [1900] 2 Ch. 388.

[274] Reliance should not be placed on unduly strict statements in *Renals v Cowlishaw* (1879) 11 Ch D 866 at 868; *Re Union of London and Smith's Bank Ltd's Conveyance* [1933] Ch. 611 at 625; *Newton Abbot Co-operative Society Ltd v Williamson & Treadgold* [1952] Ch. 286 at 289. See [1972B] C.L.J. 157 at 166 (H.W.R.W.).

[275] *Renals v Cowlishaw* (1878) 9 Ch D 125; affirmed (1879) 11 Ch D 866. "Assigns" has been said to be ambiguous, for it may mean assigns of the benefit of the covenant as well as assigns of the land benefited: see *Rogers v Hosegood* [1900] 2 Ch. 388 at 396. "Heirs and assigns" sufficed in *Mann v Stephens* (1846) 15 Sim. 377, though this was before it had been settled that there must be dominant land (above, para.32–044).

(2) IMPLIED ANNEXATION.[276] It has now been clearly recognised that annexa- **32–062**
tion may be implied rather than express.[277] Although express words of
annexation are highly desirable, they are not necessary.[278]

> "If, on the construction of the instrument creating the restrictive cove-
> nant, both the land which is intended to be benefited and an intention to
> benefit that land, as distinct from benefiting the covenantee personally,
> can be clearly established, then the benefit of the covenant will be
> annexed to that land and run with it, notwithstanding the absence of
> express words of annexation."[279]

However, an intention to annex will not be implied merely from the surrounding circumstances. It must be manifested in the instrument containing the
covenant when construed in the light of those attendant circumstances.[280]

(b) Statutory annexation

(1) SECTION 78. These rules on express and implied annexation are now **32–063**
crucial only to covenants made prior to 1926. While conveyancers may still
employ express annexation, as regards any covenants made since 1925,
usually they will be annexed by statute. In relation to such covenants it is no
longer necessary to show an intention to annex per se. By s.78(1) of the Law
of Property Act 1925:

> "a covenant relating to any land of the covenantee shall be deemed to be
> made with the covenantee and his successors in title and the persons
> deriving title under him or them, and shall have effect as if such
> successors and other persons were expressed".[281]

As regards restrictive (but not positive) covenants, the words "successors in
title" are given a wider meaning than they would normally have, and are
deemed to include the owners and occupiers for the time being of the

---

[276] For a fuller treatment of this subject, see the fifth edition of this work at p.784; and [1972B]
C.L.J. 157 at 169 (H.W.R.W.). The doubts raised in (1968) 84 L.Q.R. 22 at 30 (P.V. Baker) as to
the existence of implied annexation as a distinct category, have now been dispelled by
authority.

[277] *Shropshire County Council v Edwards* (1982) 46 P. & C.R. 270 at 277; *Sainsbury Plc v
Enfield LBC* [1989] 1 W.L.R. 590 at 597; *Re W & S. (Long Eaton) Ltd (1989)* [1994] J.P.L. 840.
cf. *Jamaica Mutual Life Assurance Society v Hillsborough Ltd* [1989] 1 W.L.R. 1101 at 1105,
1106.

[278] Where the connection with the benefited land is obvious, to insist upon express words would
involve "not only an injustice but a departure from common sense": *Marten v Flight Refuelling
Ltd* [1962] Ch. 115 at 133, per Wilberforce J.

[279] *Shropshire County Council v Edwards*, above, at 277, per Judge Rubin.

[280] *Sainsbury Plc v Enfield LBC*, above, at 595–597; *Jamaica Mutual Life Assurance Society v
Hillsborough Ltd*, above, at 1105; [1991] Conv. 52 (S. Goulding).

[281] For an interesting illustration of the operation of the section, see *Caerns Motor Services Ltd
v Texaco Ltd* [1994] 1 W.L.R. 1249 at 1267.

covenantee's land.[282] The wording of s.78 is "significantly different"[283] from that of its predecessor, s.58 of the Conveyancing Act 1881. This has already been explained.[284]

The wording of s.78 strongly suggests that it was intended to annex to the land of the covenantee the benefit of any covenant which touched and concerned it. If the words of the section were used expressly in a covenant,[285] there seems little doubt that they would be effective to annex it.[286] The reference in it to successors in title, to derivative owners and to owners and occupiers for the time being of the land, could not more clearly show that the covenant was intended to be for the benefit of the covenantee's land and not for the covenantee personally. However, the possibility that the section might have this effect remained unconsidered until the decision of the Court of Appeal in *Federated Homes Ltd v Mill Lodge Properties Ltd*[287] in 1979.

In that case it was held that a covenant against erecting more than 300 dwellings on the covenantor's land was enforceable by successors in title of the covenantee. The lack of any express words of annexation was made good by s.78 since it was clear from the facts that the covenant related to the covenantee's adjoining land. The court pointed out, approving suggestions in a previous edition of this book and elsewhere,[288] that it was deciding consistently with the cases on the running of the benefit of positive covenants, in which s.78 had played some part.[289]

---

[282] LPA 1925 s.78(2). The words will therefore embrace squatters (other than a squatter who has been registered as the proprietor of registered land which he has adversely possessed, who is a successor in title: see below, para.35–087) and licensees, who may in consequence enforce an annexed restrictive covenant even though they could not enforce an annexed positive covenant: see above, para.32–015. This is logical because a restrictive covenant may be described as "an extension in equity of the doctrine of negative easements": *London & South Western Ry v Gomm* (1882) 20 Ch D 562 at 583, per Jessel M.R. The owner or occupier for the time being of land would be entitled to enjoy the benefit of any easement which was appurtenant to land therefore part of it.

[283] *Federated Homes Ltd v Mill Lodge Properties Ltd* [1980] 1 W.L.R. 594 at 604, per Brightman L.J.

[284] Above, para.32–015.

[285] By the section they are of course deemed to be.

[286] See above, para.32–016.

[287] [1980] 1 W.L.R. 594; (1980) 43 M.L.R. 445 (D. J. Hayton); [1980] Conv. 216 (A. Sydenham). There were no words of annexation; the benefit had been expressly assigned to the first successor in title but not by that successor to the plaintiff. The judgment of Brightman L.J., unlike so many in this area, is clear and straightforward, and firmly based on realities. For comment, criticism and legislative history see (1981) 97 L.Q.R. 32; (1982) 98 L.Q.R. 202; [1982] J.P.L. 295 (G. H. Newsom QC); (1982) 2 L.S. 53 (D. J. Hurst). The articles by G. H. Newsom QC attack the decision from the orthodox conveyancer's standpoint, but do not consider the opposing arguments. The strongest argument against the interpretation of s.78 adopted in *Federated Homes* is that there are a number of provisions in the Act by which the benefit of a covenant is annexed by the words, "shall be annexed and incident to and shall go with" a particular estate and which do not feature in s.78: see LPA 1925 ss.76(6), 77(5), 141(1). However, each of those provisions (unlike s.78) was carried forward from CA 1881, and the words "shall go with" appear to have an effect that is additional to the annexation of the covenant: see *Re King* [1963] Ch. 459 at 497.

[288] (1941) 57 L.Q.R. 203 at 205 (G. R.Y. Radcliffe); [1972B] C.L.J. 157 at 173 (H.W.R.W.); this book, fourth edition p.765.

[289] For these cases see above, para.32–015.

(2) LIMITS ON STATUTORY ANNEXATION. Although some commentators have **32–064** suggested that the decision in *Federated Homes* can be interpreted narrowly,[290] it was decided on the basis of the broad principle that:

"if the condition precedent of section 78 is satisfied—that is to say, there exists a covenant which touches and concerns the land of the covenantee—that covenant runs with the land for the benefit of his successors in title, persons deriving title under him or them and other owners and occupiers".[291]

On this basis, in respect of the benefit, the rules for positive and negative covenants are largely assimilated[292] and simplified,[293] and much of the unnecessary mystique and semantics which had accumulated round negative covenants is swept away. The law has in consequence become altogether simpler and more reasonable.[294]

However, it. is clear that there are a number of limitations on annexation under s.78. First, it remains the case that the land benefited by the covenant must be identifiable in the appropriate manner. In *Federated Homes Ltd v Mill Lodge Properties Ltd* itself, Brightman L.J. left it open whether the benefited land had to be identified by the deed of covenant or whether it sufficed if it was identifiable from the surrounding circumstances, perhaps even from evidence wholly outside the document.[295] This issue became critical in the later case of *Crest Nicholson Residential (South) Limited v McAllister*.[296] In that case, Chadwick L.J. reviewed the authorities, in particular *Marquess of Zetland v Driver*,[297] and decided that statutory annexation via the decision in *Federated Homes* could occur only if the covenant or conveyance itself identified the land to be benefited, either explicitly or by necessary implication.[298] Thus, while it was possible to utilise evidence outside the document fully to identify the land—for example, where the conveyance described the land in terms that enabled it to be identified from other evidence[299]—statutory

---

[290] See particularly [1985] Conv. 177 (P. N. Todd).

[291] [1980] 1 W.L.R. 594 at 605, per Brightman L.J. See too *Sainsbury Plc v Enfield LBC* [1989] 1 W.L.R. 590 at 598.

[292] But the assimilation is not complete. The range of persons who can enforce an annexed restrictive covenant includes the owners and occupiers for the time being of the land of the covenantee: LPA 1925 s.78(2); fn.62, above. Only successors in title (in the strict sense) and derivative owners can enforce positive covenants: above, para.32–015.

[293] cf. *Rhone v Stephens* [1994] 2 A.C. 310 at 327, where Lord Templeman was careful not to cast doubt on the decisions, considered above, para.32–015, in which "it was held by the Court of Appeal that section 78 . . . had the effect of making the benefit of a positive covenant run with the land".

[294] The decision has been applied in *Jalarne Ltd v Ridewood* (1989) 61 P. & C.R. 143 at 152; *Robins v Berkeley Homes (Kent) Ltd* [1996] E.G.C.S. 75. It was referred to without any suggestion of doubt by Lord Templeman in *Rhone v Stephens* [1994] 2 A.C. 310 at 322.

[295] *Federated Homes Ltd v Mill Lodge Properties Ltd*, above, at 604.

[296] [2004] EWCA Civ 410; [2004] 1 W.L.R. 2409; [2004] Conv. 507 (Jean Howell); (2004) 133 P.L.J. 10 (Gerald Moran).

[297] [1939] Ch. 1.

[298] *Crest Nicholson* above at 2421.

[299] *Rogers v Hosegood* [1900] 2 Ch. 388.

annexation was not achieved where the benefited land could be identified *only* by reference to the surrounding circumstances or other evidence wholly outside the document. Although his seems contrary to the position operating in relation to express annexation,[300] Chadwick L.J. was bolstered in his view by the desire to ensure that a person inspecting the register of title should be able to determine the benefited land by inspection of the register rather than having to engage in a wider search for the person entitled to enforce the covenant.[301] Although this does not seem an overpowering argument, and one might argue that Chadwick L.J. is wrong to equate the need for land to be easily identifiable with a requirement that this can be done only by words in the conveyance, this more limited interpretation must be regarded as definitive. Statutory annexation occurs only if the conveyance itself identifies the land expressly or by necessary implication.

Second, statutory annexation applies only to covenants made since 1925. It has been held that the predecessor of s.78, the differently worded s.58 of the Conveyancing Act 1881,[302] did not annex the benefit of a covenant without proof of intention that the covenant should run.[303]

Third, annexation under s.78 will occur only where the covenant is unqualified. Although the section makes no provision for exclusion of its operation by an expression of contrary intention,[304] a covenant will not be annexed by it if it is clear that it is only to pass by express assignment.[305] Indeed this is implicit in the *Federated Homes* decision itself, for Brightman L.J. acknowledged that "a covenantee may expressly or by necessary implication retain the benefit of a covenant wholly under his own control, so that the benefit will not pass unless the covenantee chooses to assign".[306]

In the light of these limitations, the effect of statutory annexation may be summarised as follows.

> (i) A restrictive covenant entered into after 1925 which touches and concerns the land will be annexed by statute to the covenantee's land, unless either expressly or by necessary implication the covenant is intended to pass only by express assignment, provided the

[300] See above, para.32–061.

[301] *Crest Nicholson* above at 2421. See also *Mohammadzadeh v Joseph* [2008] 1 P. & C.R. 6.

[302] Above, para.32–014.

[303] *Sainsbury Plc v Enfield LBC*, above, at 601. See too *Federated Homes Ltd v Mill Lodge Properties Ltd*, above, at 604. Compare however [1972B] C.L.J. 157 at 173 (H.W.R.W.). It should also be noted that LPA 1925 s.78 does not apply to new tenancies granted after 1995 under L & TCA 1995: see LPA 1925 s.30(4); above, para.20–079. However, this disapplication is restricted to covenants in the lease. Thus a tenant under a lease granted after 1995 could take advantage of a covenant that was annexed to the freehold under LPA 1925 s.78 (as in *Smith v River Douglas Catchment Board* [1949] 2 K.B. 500; above, para.32–015). The section would also apply to a covenant entered into with the tenant for the benefit of his leasehold estate by a neighbour.

[304] Unlike LPA 1925 s.79: see above, para.32–016. That section has been said to involve "quite different considerations" from s.78: *Federated Homes Ltd v Mill Lodge Properties Ltd*, above, at 606, per Brightman L.J.

[305] *Roake v Chadha* [1984] 1 W.L.R. 40; [1984] Conv. 68 (P. N. Todd).

[306] [1980] 1 W.L.R. 594 at 606.

benefited land is ascertainable from the conveyance or covenant itself.

(ii) A restrictive covenant entered into prior to 1926 will pass only if it has been expressly or impliedly annexed to the covenantee's land or if it is expressly assigned by a landowner who has the benefit of it.

It will be apparent from this that the benefit of restrictive covenants will nowadays seldom need to be expressly assigned if on grant they have been drafted in such a way that the benefited land is identifiable from the covenant.

(3) SECTION 62. It has been suggested that the benefit of a restrictive **32–065** covenant might pass on any conveyance of the benefited land under the general words implied by s.62 of the Law of Property Act 1925.[307] Although this was the basis of the decision at first instance in the *Federated Homes* case,[308] it has since been held by the Court of Appeal that:

"a right under covenant cannot appertain to the land[309] unless the benefit is in some way annexed to the land. If the benefit of a covenant passes under s.62 even if not annexed to the land, the whole modern law of restrictive covenants would have been established on an erroneous basis".[310]

This seems unlikely.

(c) Area. If the benefit of a covenant is annexed to the covenantee's land, **32–066** then prima facie it is taken to be annexed both to the whole of the land and to each and every part of it, unless the contrary clearly appears.[311] This means that anyone who subsequently acquires some part of the benefited land can enforce the covenant, as can the person who retains the remainder. It is

---

[307] See (1971) 87 L.Q.R. 539 at 570 (D. J. Hayton). For LPA 1925 s.62, see below, para.31–018.

[308] The decision is unreported, but see [1980] 1 W.L.R. 594 at 601. cf. *Shropshire County Council v Edwards* (1982) 46 P. & C.R. 270 at 279.

[309] As the section requires.

[310] *Kumar v Dunning* [1989] Q.B. 193 at 198, per Browne-Wilkinson V.C. See too *Roake v Chadha*, above, at 47.

[311] *Federated Homes Ltd v Mill Lodge Properties Ltd* [1980] 1 W.L.R. 594 at 606. Prior to this decision, it appears to have been thought that a covenant was annexed to the whole of the land only, in the absence of evidence to the contrary, and that on a sale of part of the property the benefit could pass only if it was expressly assigned: see, e.g. *Re Jeff's Transfer (No.2)* [1966] 1 W.L.R. 841 (a case that would probably now be decided differently). The reversal of the presumption has brought about a welcome simplification of the law. See now *Hugh Small v Oliver & Saunders (Developments) Limited* [2006] EWHC 1293 (Ch), where the presumption of annexation to each and every part of the benefited land was applied to a pre-1925 covenant.

possible that a covenant may be annexed to the whole of the land only and not to every part of it,[312] but this will now have to be clearly shown.[313]

A covenant will be annexed only if, at the time when it is imposed, it benefits the land for which it is taken.[314] However, such benefit will be presumed in the absence of either exceptional circumstances[315] or contrary evidence.[316] Furthermore, even if the covenant purports to be taken for an area that is greater than can reasonably be benefited by it, the owner of any part of that land which is in fact so benefited may be able to enforce it.[317] This will be so where the covenant is annexed to each and every part of the land (which is now presumed) and not to the whole only.[318]

32–067   *(d) Transmission.* Once the benefit of the covenant is annexed to land, it passes with the land to each successive owner, tenant or occupier,[319] even if he knew nothing of it when he acquired the land.[320] It is "a hidden treasure which may be discovered in the hour of need".[321]

II. ASSIGNMENT

32–068   Even if the benefit of the covenant has not been annexed to the land to be benefited, an assignee of the land may nevertheless succeed in enforcing the covenant if the benefit of the covenant has also been assigned to him. However, since the *Federated Homes* decision,[322] the circumstances in which it will be necessary to have recourse to assignment are likely to be rare.[323] It will be necessary to do so in four cases:

> (i)   where the covenant was entered into prior to 1926, the benefit was not expressly or impliedly annexed to the covenantee's land, and

---

[312] See *Re Union of London and Smith's Bank Ltd's Conveyance* [1933] Ch. 611 at 628; *Re Ballard's Conveyance* [1937] Ch. 473. Likewise, and conversely, it is possible to provide expressly that the benefit be annexed only if parts are sold, and not if the whole is assigned, but this is not something to be lightly presumed, *Rees v Peters* [2011] EWCA Civ 836.

[313] "I find the idea of the annexation of a covenant to the whole of the land but not to part of it a difficult conception fully to grasp": *Federated Homes Ltd v Mill Lodge Properties Ltd*, above, at 606, per Brightman L.J. Applied in *Hugh Small v Oliver & Saunders (Developments) Limited* [2006] EWHC 1293 (Ch).

[314] *Marquess of Zetland v Driver* [1939] Ch. 1 at 8.

[315] As "where the covenant was on the face of it taken capriciously or not bona fide": *Marten v Flight Refuelling Ltd* [1962] Ch. 115 at 136, per Wilberforce J.

[316] *Earl of Leicester v Wells-next-the-Sea UDC* [1973] Ch. 110 at 124, 125.

[317] *Marquess of Zetland v Driver*, above, at 10.

[318] cf. *Re Ballard's Conveyance*, above (a case which on its facts might now be decided differently).

[319] LPA 1925 s.78, above, para.32–063; *Taite v Gosling* (1879) 11 Ch D 273.

[320] *Rogers v Hosegood* [1900] 2 Ch. 388; *R. v Westminster City Council Ex p. Leicester Square Coventry Street Association* (1989) 87 L.G.R. 675 at 682.

[321] *Lawrence v South County Freeholds Ltd* [1939] Ch. 656 at 680, per Simonds J.

[322] [1980] 1 W.L.R. 594; above, para.32–063.

[323] See above, para.32–064. For a recent example see *Rees v Peters* (2011), above, although it is not clear that assignment was necessary rather than merely conventional for the conveyancers involved. For a fuller treatment of assignment see the fifth edition of this work at p.787.

the intending assignor is either the original covenantee[324] or has
acquired the benefit by an unbroken chain of assignments[325];

(ii) where the covenant, at whatever date it was entered into, was
expressly taken for the benefit of and annexed to the whole of the
covenantee's land only, and where the covenantee wished to dispose of some part of that land with the benefit of the covenant;

(iii) where by the terms of the covenant (at whatever date it was entered
into), the benefit was to pass only by express assignment; and

(iv) where statutory annexation fails because the benefited land is not
ascertainable from the covenant or conveyance itself.

(*a*) *Form of assignment.* Although the assignment must ordinarily be made   **32–069**
expressly, the assignment will be effective provided that there is a distinct
agreement between the vendor and the purchaser that the covenant shall pass
to the assignee.[326] The benefit will not run with the land in the absence of such
an agreement unless the covenant is annexed.[327]

(*b*) *Assignment with land.* It has already been explained that if the assignee   **32–070**
is suing the original covenantor or his personal representative (who are liable
at law), he has only to prove that the benefit of the covenant has been properly
assigned to him as a chose in action.[328] He may then seek either damages or
an injunction. However, if he is suing some successor in title to the covenantor's land (who can be liable only in equity under the rule in *Tulk v Moxhay*),
he must also prove that the benefit was assigned to him with the land benefited
as part of the same transaction. It appears to be the case that the covenant must
be assigned together with all or part of the land as the case may be.[329] The
primary purpose of the covenant is to preserve the value of the land retained
by the vendor, and:

"if he has been able to sell any particular part of his property without
assigning to the purchaser the benefit of the covenant, there seems no
reason why he should at a later date and as an independent transaction be
at liberty to confer upon the purchaser such benefit".[330]

---

[324] Which is unlikely to be the case nowadays unless the covenantee is a corporation.
[325] For a doubt as to whether an unbroken chain of assignments is in fact necessary or whether
the first express assignment annexes the benefit of the covenant, see below, para.32–073.
[326] *Renals v Cowlishaw* (1878) 9 Ch D 125 at 129–131; affirmed (1879) 11 Ch D 866; *Re Union
of London and Smith's Bank Ltd's Conveyance* [1933] Ch. 611 at 628; *Drake v Gray* [1936] Ch.
451 at 455.
[327] *Renals v Cowlishaw*, above.
[328] Above, para.32–010.
[329] A vendor who already has disposed of whole of the benefited land can no longer assign the
benefit of the covenant in equity: *Chambers v Randall* [1923] 1 Ch. 149; *Re Union of London and
Smith's Bank Ltd's Conveyance*, above.
[330] *Re Union of London and Smith's Bank Ltd's Conveyance*, above, at 632, per Romer L.J. See
too *Re Rutherford's Conveyance* [1938] Ch. 396.

This special rule of equity applies only for the purposes of an action brought against a successor in title to the covenantor's land. There is no objection to a later assignment which merely gives effect to an existing equitable right to the benefit of the covenant, as where the benefited land is conveyed by trustees to a beneficiary and they later assign the benefit of the covenant to him.[331]

32–071   *(c) Assignment with part.* In those rare cases in which annexation of the covenant was only to the benefited land as a whole, the benefit may nevertheless be assigned with part only of the land. Although at law the benefit cannot be assigned in pieces, equity allows the benefit to be assigned with any part or parts of the benefited land.[332]

32–072   *(d) Intention to benefit.* Where there has been an express assignment of the benefit of a covenant, the purchaser will be able to sue on it only if he can show that the covenant was intended to benefit the land which he has purchased. However, it is unnecessary to prove the connection from the deed of covenant. It may be proved instead from the surrounding circumstances.[333]

32–073   *(e) Chain of assignments.* It has been held that where the benefit of a covenant has not been annexed to the land, the benefit will pass to subsequent owners of it only if there is an unbroken chain of assignments.[334] However, the older authorities had suggested that when the benefit was once assigned it became annexed to the land,[335] because the assignment demonstrated that the benefit of the covenant was intended to pass with the land and not remain a separate right.[336] Although on principle the view taken in these older cases is to be preferred, it may not apply in all situations, as where the covenant was on its face to pass only by express assignment.[337]

32–074   *(f) Assignor.* It is not always necessary that the assignment should be made by the original covenantee: it may be made by anyone in whom the land and the benefit of the covenant are both vested. If, for example, the original covenantee dies, and under his will or intestacy his son becomes entitled both

---

[331] *Lord Northbourne v Johnston* [1922] 2 Ch. 309 (assignment to devisee of beneficiary). This decision appears to assume that the benefit ran in equity without either annexation or assignment.

[332] *Re Union of London and Smith's Bank Ltd's Conveyance*, above, at 630.

[333] *Newton Abbot Co-operative Society Ltd v Williamson & Treadgold Ltd* [1952] Ch. 286 at 297. See too *Marten v Flight Refuelling Ltd* [1962] Ch. 115 at 130–133.

[334] *Re Pinewood Estate, Farnborough* [1958] Ch. 280, where the authorities to the contrary were not cited: see [1957] C.L.J. 146 (H.W.R.W.); (1968) 84 L.Q.R. 22 at 31 (P. V. Baker). See also *Federated Homes Ltd v Mill Lodge Properties Ltd* [1980] 1 W.L.R. 594 at 603 ("delayed annexation by assignment" not accepted at first instance).

[335] It has been suggested that "express assignment is delayed annexation": (1968) 84 L.Q.R. 22 at 29 (P. V. Baker).

[336] *Renals v Cowlishaw* (1878) 9 Ch D 125 at 130, 131 (affirmed (1879) 11 Ch D 866); *Rogers v Hosegood* [1900] 2 Ch. 388 at 408; *Reid v Bickerstaff* [1909] 2 Ch. 305 at 320, 326, 328.

[337] As in *Roake v Chadha* [1984] 1 W.L.R. 40.

to the benefited land and to the benefit of the covenant (two separate assets of the deceased), the son can effectively assign the benefit of the covenant if he subsequently sells the land.[338] The benefit of the covenant will pass to him automatically with the benefited land if it is clear from the facts that the covenant was intended to protect the land.[339]

III. SCHEMES OF DEVELOPMENT

(a) *An independent equity*. Building and other development schemes have special rules of their own, which derive from the wider principle that the benefit of covenants runs in equity according to the common intention and common interest of the original parties.[340] Where land is to be sold or let in lots according to a plan, restrictions are often imposed on the purchasers of each lot for the benefit of the estate generally, such as covenants restraining trading on the estate, or prohibiting the erection of cheap buildings. Much of the purpose of the covenants given by a purchaser of one lot would be lost if they could not be enforced: **32–075**

    (i) by those who have previously bought lots, and

    (ii) by those who subsequently buy the unsold lots.

Both these results could be achieved without any special rules for schemes of development. The first could be achieved if the purchaser's covenants were expressed to be made with the owners of the lots previously sold as well as with the vendor.[341] The second could be achieved by framing the covenants expressly for the benefit of the whole or any part of the land retained by the vendor, and so annexing the benefit of them to each lot to be sold in the future, or by express assignment to the later purchasers, as already described.

The special character of schemes of development makes it possible to dispense with these cumbersome methods. If such a scheme exists, the covenants given on the sale of each plot are enforceable by the owner for the time being of any plot on the estate. "Community of interest necessarily . . . requires and imports reciprocity of obligation."[342] The covenants in effect form a sort of local law for the estate.[343] They give rise to "an equity which **32–076**

---

[338] *Newton Abbot Co-operative Society Ltd v Williamson & Treadgold Ltd*, above.

[339] *Earl of Leicester v Wells-next-the-Sea UDC* [1973] Ch. 110. The personal representatives hold the benefit of the covenant upon trust for him, so that he can sue in equity. Alternatively they themselves can sue: *Ives v Brown* [1919] 2 Ch. 314.

[340] *Re Dolphin's Conveyance* [1970] Ch. 654. The doctrine can be traced back to *Whatman v Gibson* (1838) 9 Sim. 196, thus antedating *Tulk v Moxhay* (1848) 2 Ph. 774. It was approved by the House of Lords in *Spicer v Martin* (1888) 14 App.Cas. 12; see *Lawrence v South County Freeholds Ltd* [1939] Ch. 656 at 675. And see (1938) 6 C.L.J. 363, 364 (5. J. Bailey).

[341] LPA 1925 s.56, replacing RPA 1845 s.5, discussed above, para.32–006. But the possibility of this was not fully understood until *Forster v Elvet Colliery Co Ltd* [1908] 1 K.B. 629 (affirmed sub nom. *Dyson v Forster* [1909] A.C. 98), and the rules relating to schemes had by then been settled.

[342] *Spicer v Martin* (1888) 14 App.Cas. 12 at 25, per Lord Macnaghten.

[343] *Reid v Bickerstaff* [1900] 2 Ch. 305 at 319; *Brunner v Greenslade* [1971] Ch. 993 at 1004.

is created by circumstances and is independent of contractual obligation",[344] thus transcending ordinary restrictions. In particular:

> (i) the annexation of the benefit of the covenants to every plot still unsold proves itself from the surrounding facts,[345] so that no special formula for annexation need be used;

> (ii) the owners of plots sold previously are shown by the facts to be within the benefit of the covenants, even though not expressly mentioned as covenantees[346];

> (iii) no unsold plot may later be disposed of by the vendor without his requiring the purchaser to enter into the covenants of the scheme; and

> (iv) the vendor is himself bound by the covenants of the scheme, even if he has not himself entered into them.

As soon as the first disposition under the scheme has been made, the scheme crystallises, and all the land within the scheme is bound.[347] The vendor himself is in the position of a trustee, and is not at liberty to authorise breaches of the covenants.[348]

Whether or not a scheme of development exists is a question of fact which may depend upon extraneous circumstances as well as upon the terms of the conveyances.[349]

(b) Elements of a scheme

32–077   (1) INTENTION. The classic statement of the facts to be proved required that there should have been a common vendor who first laid out the property for sale in lots subject to restrictions consistent only with a scheme of development; that the common vendor should have intended the restrictions to benefit all the lots to be sold; and that the purchasers from the common vendor should have purchased on the footing that the restrictions were for the benefit of the other lots.[350] Although this statement of the requirements is still accepted as a starting point,[351] it has never been treated as a comprehensive statement of

---

[344] *Lawrence v South County Freeholds Ltd* [1939] Ch. 656 at 682 (Simonds J.); *Brunner v Greenslade* [1971] Ch. 993.

[345] Above, paras 32–061, 32–064.

[346] *Spicer v Martin* (1888) 14 App.Cas. 12.

[347] *Brunner v Greenslade*, above, at 1003, summarising the first principles of schemes; and see below, para.32–079.

[348] *Brunner v Greenslade*, above, at 1003.

[349] *Texaco Antilles Ltd v Kernochan* [1973] A.C. 609; *Whitgift Homes v Stocks* [2001] EWCA Civ 1732, (2001) 48 E.G. 130 (CS).

[350] *Elliston v Reacher* [1908] 2 Ch. 374 at 384 (Parker J.); affirmed [1908] 2 Ch. 655.

[351] See *Page v Kings Parade Properties Ltd* (1967) 20 P. & C.R. 710 at 716; *Emile Elias & Co Ltd v Pine Groves Ltd* [1993] 1 W.L.R. 305 at 309.

the law nor has it inhibited further development. Later decisions have emphasised two pre-requisites of a building scheme.[352] The first is that there must be reciprocity of obligation between the purchasers of the various lots.[353] There must be an intention to impose a scheme of mutually enforceable restrictions in the interest of all the purchasers and their successors,[354] which must be known to them.[355] The second is that the area affected by the scheme should be clearly defined.[356] It is not sufficient that the common vendor has himself defined the area. It must also be known to the purchasers.[357] Neither is it sufficient that the particular claimant and defendant are within an area affected by an alleged scheme if there is uncertainty as to the full geographical reach of the scheme, as it must be certain which purchasers of which plots are entitled to enjoy mutual enforcement.[358] However, if these two requirements are satisfied, neither a common vendor nor laying out in lots is indispensable.[359] The present tendency is to relax formal requirements and to give effect to the manifest intention of the transaction.

(2) EVIDENCE. It is not necessary to prove an express undertaking by each **32–078** purchaser that the covenants given by him are to be enforceable by the owners of all the other lots, provided the circumstances show that he must have realised it.[360] This will be so if before his purchase he saw some plan of the estate with the restrictions indorsed on it. But the absence of a proper plan may prove fatal,[361] if the intention to impose a scheme of mutually enforceable restrictions does not otherwise appear.[362] The evidence must, of course, show that the vendor intended to do more than merely benefit himself.[363] A building scheme will not be implied merely from "a common vendor and the existence of common covenants".[364]

[352] *Jamaica Mutual Life Assurance Society v Hillsborough Ltd* [1989] 1 W.L.R. 1101 at 1106.
[353] *Kingsbury v L.W. Anderson Ltd* (1979) 40 P. & C.R. 136 at 142, 143; *Jamaica Mutual Life Assurance Society v Hillsborough Ltd*, above, at 1106; *Emile Elias & Co Ltd v Pine Groves Ltd*, above, at 311, 312.
[354] This is lacking, for example, if the covenants on one side are merely for indemnifying the vendor: *Kingsbury v L.W. Anderson Ltd*, above.
[355] *White v Bijou Mansions Ltd* [1938] Ch. 351 at 362; *Re Shaw's Application* (1994) 68 P. & C.R. 591 at 597. See *Hugh Small v Oliver & Saunders (Developments) Limited* [2006] EWHC 1293 (Ch) paras 45–47 where an alleged scheme failed on this ground.
[356] *Reid v Bickerstaff* [1909] 2 Ch. 305; *Jamaica Mutual Life Assurance Society v Hillsborough Ltd* [1989] 1 W.L.R. 1101 at 1106, 1107; *Whitgift Homes v Stocks*, above.
[357] *Lund v Taylor* (1975) 31 P. & C.R. 167; *Emile Elias & Co Ltd v Pine Groves Ltd*, above, at 310.
[358] *Whitgift Homes v Stocks* [2001] EWCA Civ 1732, (2001) 48 E.G. 130 (CS).
[359] *Baxter v Four Oaks Properties Ltd* [1965] Ch. 816 (no lotting: size of plots variable); *Re Dolphin's Conveyance* [1970] Ch. 654 (two successive vendors; no lotting; no plan).
[360] As where this was made clear in the advertisements for the sale of the properties: cf. *Jamaica Mutual Life Assurance Society v Hillsborough Ltd*, above, at 1108.
[361] e.g. *Osborne v Bradley* [1903] 2 Ch. 446; *Kelly v Barrett* [1924] 2 Ch. 379; *Re Wembley Park Estate Co Ltd's Transfer* [1968] Ch. 491; cf. *Hodges v Jones* [1935] Ch. 657 (plan with no restrictions on it not enough).
[362] As in *Re Dolphin's Conveyance*, above; *Lund v Taylor*, above.
[363] *Tucker v Vowles* [1893] 1 Ch. 195; *Willé v St. John* [1910] 1 Ch. 325.
[364] *Re Wembley Park Estate Co Ltd's Transfer*, above, at 503, per Goff J.; *Jamaica Mutual Life Assurance Society v Hillsborough Ltd*, above, at 1108.

Although "a common code of covenants" is "one of the badges of an enforceable building scheme",[365] the following matters will not negative the existence of such a scheme:

(i) the reservation of a power by the vendor either to release all or part of the land from the restrictions,[366] or to vary the details of the scheme or the restrictions imposed on later purchasers[367];

(ii) the employment of an express formula of annexation in the conveyances or transfers[368]; or

(iii) the fact that the restrictions imposed on each plot are not identical.[369]

But, if the agreement provides for the covenants to be enforced by the vendor on behalf of all parties, that is inconsistent with mutual enforceability.[370]

32–079   (3) SUB-SCHEMES. If one of the plots is later subdivided, the covenants of the scheme will be mutually enforceable between the sub-purchasers inter se, so far as they are applicable, as well as between them and the occupiers of the other plots, even though none of the sub-purchasers themselves gave covenants.[371] If the sub-purchasers themselves entered into "scheme of development" covenants differing from those of the main scheme, they can enforce only their own sub-scheme inter se, but can still enforce the head scheme against others.[372] The covenants of the head scheme thus remain operative unless some contrary intention appears.[373] This illustrates the special operation of such covenants as "a local law for the area of the scheme".[374] Another illustration is that if two plots come into common ownership but are later separated, the covenants are not discharged by unity of ownership but will continue to operate.[375]

[365] *Emile Elias & Co Ltd v Pine Groves Ltd* [1993] 1 W.L.R. 305 at 311, per Lord BrowneWilkinson.
[366] *Elliston v Reacher* [1908] 2 Ch. 665 at 672; *Pearce v Maryon-Wilson* [1935] Ch. 188 (leaseholds); *Newman v Real Estate Debenture Corp Ltd* [1940] 1 All E.R. 131; *Re Wembley Park Estate Co Ltd's Transfer*, above.
[367] *Re 6, 8, 10 and 12 Elm Avenue, New Milton* [1984] 1 W.L.R. 1398 at 1406. The inclusion of such a power points to the existence of a building scheme because it would be unnecessary in the absence of such a scheme: ibid. See too *Re Beechwood Homes Ltd's Application* [1994] 2 E.G.L.R. 178 (power to vary layout of estate).
[368] *Texaco Antilles Ltd v Kernochan* [1973] A.C. 609.
[369] *Collins v Castle* (1887) 36 Ch D 243 at 253, 254; *Reid v Bickerstaff* [1909] 2 Ch. 305 at 319; *Emile Elias & Co Ltd v Pine Groves Ltd* [19931 1 W.L.R. 305 at 311; *Hugh Small v Oliver & Saunders (Developments) Limited* [2006] EWHC 1293 (Ch).
[370] *White v Bijou Mansions Ltd* [1938] Ch. 351 at 363.
[371] *Brunner v Greenslade* [1971] Ch. 993.
[372] On sub-schemes see *Knight v Simmonds* [1896] 1 Ch. 653; *Lawrence v South County Freeholds Ltd* [1939] Ch. 656; *Brunner v Greenslade*, above.
[373] *Brunner v Greenslade*, above, at 1006.
[374] *Brunner v Greenslade*, above at 1004.
[375] *Brunner v Greenslade*, above; *Texaco Antilles Ltd v Kernochan*, above. See (1977) 41 Conv. (N.S.) 107 at 115 (J. D. A. Brooke-Taylor).

(c) Extent of principle. The law for schemes of development originated with **32–080** building schemes, but the principle applies to numerous other types of schemes of development involving uniform covenants; the term "scheme of development" is the genus and "building scheme" is merely a species.[376] If an estate already fully built upon is disposed of in sections, whether freehold or leasehold, and the appropriate conditions for schemes of development are satisfied, the covenants will be enforceable as they are in building schemes.[377] The principle of such schemes can apply to a block of residential flats let on similar leases,[378] so that the landlord will be restrained from letting[379] or using[380] any of them otherwise than for residential purposes, even though it was only the tenants, and not the landlord, who entered into any express covenant as to user.

If the parties to a scheme modify it by releasing the covenants and substituting new covenants, it seems that the new covenants will not have the benefit of the rules as to schemes.[381]

Covenants under a scheme of development enjoy no dispensation from the requirement of registration, so that the "local law" principle depends upon due registration against all the purchasers if the land is freehold and developed after 1925.[382] Registration governs the running of the burden of the covenant, whereas the development scheme rules govern the running of the benefit.

C. Reform

1. Covenants as land obligations. The present law of restrictive covenants **32–081** has been criticised on the grounds of both its complexity and its uncertainty.[383] In 2011, the Law Commission proposed the replacement of the present system for the future with a scheme whereby covenants would be regarded as land obligations.[384] This followed earlier proposals, with some changes of detail.[385] The Commission originally had proposed the creation of two types

---

[376] *Brunner v Greenslade*, above, at 999.

[377] *Nottingham Patent Brick & Tile Co v Butler* (1886) 16 QBD 778; *Spicer v Martin* (1888) 14 App.Cas. 12 (leasehold); *Torbay Hotel Ltd v Jenkins* [1927] 2 Ch. 225.

[378] *Hudson v Cripps* [1896] 1 Ch. 265; *Alexander v Mansions Proprietary* (1900) 16 T.L.R. 431; *Gedge v Bartlett* (1900) 17 T.L.R. 43; *Jaegar v Mansions Consolidated Ltd* (1903) 87 L.T. 690; cf. *Kelly v Battershell* [1949] 2 All E.R. 830 (no scheme found).

[379] *Gedge v Barlett*, above.

[380] *Newman v Real Estate Debenture Corp Ltd* [1940] 1 All E.R. 131 ("the high watermark of cases where a scheme can be inferred": *Kelly v Battershell*, above, at 841, per Cohen L.J.).

[381] *Re Pinewood Estate Farnborough* [1985] Ch. 280. This seems questionable: see [1957] C.L.J. 146 (H.W.R.W.).

[382] Above, paras 32–053—32–055.

[383] (1984) Law Com. No.127, para.4.8; (2008) Law Com. CP No.186 paras 7.39 et seq. (2011) Law Com/. No.327, para. 5.4.

[384] (2011) Law Com. No.327, *Making Land Work: Easements Covenants and Profits a Prendre*.

[385] (1984) Law Com. No.127; (2008) Law Com. CP No.186. Note that some of the objectives of the 1984 proposal have been achieved by the commonhold legislation: see *Commonhold: A Consultation Paper* (1990) Cm. 1345, para.3.49.30. For Commonhold, see Ch.33. The 2011 Report proposes that it should be possible to create land obligations over unregistered land, a view not taken in the Consultation Paper.

of land obligation on the model of easements, neighbour obligations and development obligations.[386] However, in the light of the introduction of commonhold,[387] the need for "development obligations" is obviated and the 2011 proposals and Draft Bill suggest the creation of a single class of land obligation, albeit one that could involve a positive or restrictive obligation.[388]

32–082   **2. Assimilation of positive and restrictive covenants.** A land obligation would be created between two neighbouring landowners, and it would be a requirement that there had to be both land benefited by the obligation and land burdened by it. The obligation might be restrictive or positive, or it might involve a reciprocal payment obligation. The proposals as to positive obligations and those involving reciprocal payment have already been noted.[389] A restrictive obligation would in essence be equivalent to what we know currently as a restrictive covenant.[390] A land obligation (of any type) could only be created expressly and it would have to be proprietary in substance, in the sense that it would have to touch and concern the benefited estate. Once created validly, the benefit would be appurtenant to the benefited estate and would always pass with it. A land obligation could be created over land of registered and unregistered title, but would be a legal interest only if created by deed and appropriately registered.[391] In this sense, the creation of a land obligation would have to be completed by registration and should not operate at law until such requirements were met.[392]

In registered land, the benefit of a land obligation would be entered in the register of the benefitted estate and a notice of interest entered on the register of the burdened estate. A land obligation could never constitute an unregistered interest which overrides.[393] A restrictive obligation so created and registered would be binding on all estates and interests derived from the burdened estate except those that have priority under normal rules and a mortgagee *not* in possession; a positive obligation so created and registered would be binding on all estates and interests derived out of a burdened estate which confer a right to immediate possession of the burdened land, in accordance with the normal priority rules (save a lease for seven years or less) and binding on a mortgagee *when* they come into possession of the burdened

---

[386] Law Com. No.127, para.6.2.

[387] The test of whether something amounted to a "land obligation" would be substantive, and hence obligations could continue to be called "covenants" (and probably would be) but would be within the new scheme, see Cl. 1 and 2, Draft Bill.

[388] Law Com. CP No.186 paras 8.13 et seq. See also *Commonhold: A Consultation Paper* (1990) Cm. 1345, para.3.49.

[389] Above para.32–028.

[390] Law Com. No.327 para.6.88. See also Law Com. No.127, para.6.6.

[391] The Draft Bill ensures that the new obligation does not fall foul of s.1 of the Law of Property Act 1925, see Law Com. No.327 para.6. Equitable land obligations could exist under normal principles—e.g. specifically enforceable contracts—but would be rare.

[392] Failure to comply would default the obligation to an equitable interest.

[393] Law Com. No.327 para.6.67

estate.[394] In unregistered land, the burden of a land obligation should be registrable as a land charge under the Land Charges Act 1972, and if not registered should be void against a purchaser of the burdened land or of any interest in that land. [395]

Section 3. Declaration as to Restrictive Covenants

In the case of freehold land (or certain long leaseholds[396]) it is now possible to apply to the court for a declaration stating whether the land is or would be affected by any restriction, and if so, the nature, extent and enforceability of it.[397] If the court declares that the land is not subject to restrictive covenants, the effect would operate in rem and the court will therefore only make such a declaration if it is clear from the evidence that the property is not burdened by restrictions.[398] This provision is a convenience to intending purchasers or lessees who wish to find out whether some long-standing restriction is really operative or not. It is often used to test the many 19th-century covenants which may today be unenforceable in practice through non-compliance with the rules governing the transfer of the benefit. In such cases, although the land appears burdened by a restriction, the lack of any person entitled to enforce the covenant renders it otiose and the restriction should be removed to reflect the reality of the situation and to ensure that the register of title remains accurate.

32–083

Section 4. Discharge of Restrictive Covenants

1. Unity of ownership. If the land benefited and the land burdened come into common ownership the covenant can no longer have effect and is therefore permanently discharged.[399] But this may not be the case where there is a scheme of development, as already mentioned, in case the merged land reverts to its former status as distinct plots.

32–084

2. Statutory modification or discharge

(a) The power. Restrictive covenants, being free from any perpetuity rule, may last indefinitely, but changes in the social and economic environment

32–085

---

[394] Law Com. No. 327 para.6.104 and para.6.115.

[395] Law Com. No. 327 para.6.57.

[396] LPA 1925 s.84(12).

[397] LPA 1925 s.84(2), as amended by LPA 1969 s.28(4). See e.g. *Re Freeman-Thomas Indenture* [1957] 1 W.L.R. 560; *Re Gadd's Land Transfer* [1966] Ch. 56; *Griffiths v Band* (1974) 29 P. & C.R. 243.

[398] *Re 6, 8, 10 and 12 Elm Avenue, New Milton* [1984] 1 W.L.R. 1398 at 1407.

[399] *Texaco Antilles Ltd v Kernochan* [1973] A.C. 609 at 626; *Re Tiltwood, Sussex* [1978] Ch. 269. This would change in respect of registered titles if the Law Commission's proposals were enacted and the covenant was appropriately registered.

may render them obsolete or may make their enforcement anti-social. As the court has no inherent power to declare that a covenant is obsolete and thereby unenforceable,[400] a discretionary[401] power has been given to what is now the Lands Chamber of the Upper Tribunal (subject to appeal on a point of law to the Court of Appeal)[402] to modify or discharge the restrictive covenant[403] with or without the payment of compensation.[404] The applicant must satisfy the Upper Tribunal that one of the following four grounds exists.

32–086   (1) OBSOLETE. That by reason of changes in the character of the property or the neighbourhood or other material circumstances the restriction ought to be deemed obsolete.[405] This requirement is not satisfied if the covenant still provides real protection to persons entitled to enforce it.[406]

32–087   (2) OBSTRUCTIVE. That its continued existence would impede some reasonable use of the land for public or private purposes, in a case where either it confers no practical benefit of substantial value or is contrary to the public interest and (in either case) any loss can be adequately compensated in money.[407] The "practical benefit" may include the enjoyment of a fine view,[408] or the preservation of the peaceful character of a neighbourhood.[409] It need not necessarily be enjoyed on the land benefited by the covenant. It may be, for example, a beautiful view enjoyed from land nearby.[410] However,

---

[400] *Westminster City Council v Duke of Westminster* [1991] 4 All E.R. 138 at 142.

[401] *Driscoll v Church Commissioners for England* [1957] 1 Q.B. 330.

[402] The Lands Chamber is successor to the Lands Tribunal and operates the same jurisdiction, The Transfer of Tribunal Functions (Lands Tribunal and Miscellaneous Amendments) Order 2009. See also TribunalProcedure (Upper Tribunal) (Lands Chamber) Rules 2010, SI 2010/2600, in force November 2010.

[403] The Lands Tribunal had no jurisdiction to modify positive covenants: *Westminster City Council v Duke of Westminster*, above, at 147. This remains true for the Lands Chamber, above fn.402.

[404] LPA 1925 s.84(1) as extended by LPA 1969 s.28. Procedure is now prescribed by SI 1996/1022 (consolidating earlier orders). See Preston and Newsom, *Restrictive Covenants* 10th edn (London: Sweet & Maxwell 2011), Ch.15.

[405] LPA 1925 s.84(1)(a). See, e.g. *Re Quaffers Ltd's Application* (1988) 56 P. & C.R. 142 (amenity diminished due to motorway construction); *Re Wards Construction (Medway) Ltd's Application* (1994) 67 P. & C.R. 379 (change in neighbourhood and need for some redevelopment of the site in any event).

[406] The typical case is where the covenants made under a building scheme still preserve the character of the estate: see, e.g. *Re Truman, Hanbury, Buxton & Co Ltd's Application* [1956] 1 Q.B. 261; *Re Sheehy's Application* (1991) 63 P. & C.R. 95.

[407] LPA 1925 ss.84(1)(aa); 84(1A). Compare *Re Lloyd's Application* (1993) 66 P. & C.R. 112 (contrary to public interest to impede user of a residential house as rehabilitation centre for mental patients for which there was a "desperate" local need) with *Re Solaifilms (Sales) Ltd's Application* (1993) 67 P. & C.R. 110 (no similar pressing need for the "Puddleduck's Children's Nursery" in a residential estate).

[408] *Re Bushell's Application* (1987) 54 P. & C.R. 386.

[409] *Stannard v Issa* [1987] A.C. 175 at 188 (covenant restricting the number of dwellings in the neighbourhood).

[410] *Gilbert v Spoor* [1983] Ch. 27 (view enjoyed by a number of owners within development scheme).

the mere loss of a bargaining position is not regarded as a practical benefit.[411]

(3) AGREEMENT: That the persons of full age and capacity entitled to the benefit of the restrictions have agreed, either expressly or by implication by their acts and omissions, to the discharge or modification sought.[412]   **32–088**

(4) NO INJURY. That the discharge or modification will not injure the persons entitled to the benefit of the covenant.[413]   **32–089**

The Lands Chamber must take into account the development plan and any declared or ascertainable planning policy for the area[414] and any other material circumstances, e.g. permissions granted by those entitled to enforce the covenant.[415] There is no increased presumption that a restriction would be maintained if it arose originally under a building scheme, although this would inform the weight of objections to its discharge or modification.[416] As a condition of modification or discharge the Tribunal may require the applicant to compensate those persons in money either for any loss on their part or for any reduction in the price of the land due to the imposition of the covenant. They may also require him to accept reasonable alternative restrictions. The respective jurisdictions to discharge or modify a restriction are not always co-extensive. Thus, if the Lands Chamber finds that the reasonable user of the land will be impeded unless the restriction is discharged, it has no power to order its modification as a reasonable compromise.[417]

(b) Covenants within the power. These provisions as to discharge, and the provisions mentioned above as to declarations, apply to restrictions whenever made and of whatever kind, even if they are not capable of running with land[418] and even if made under statutory authority and not benefiting any land[419]; but they do not apply to restrictions imposed on a disposition made either gratuitously or for a nominal consideration for public purposes.[420] They   **32–090**

---

[411] *Stockport MBC v Alwiyah Developments* (1983) 52 P. & C.R. 278; *Re Bennett's and Tamarind Ltd's Application* (1987) 54 P. & C.R. 378; *Re Hyde shire Ltd's Application* (1993) 67 P. & C.R. 93.

[412] LPA 1925 s.84(1)(b).

[413] See *Re Freeman-Thomas Indenture* [1957] 1 W.L.R. 560 (estate broken up and no one entitled to benefit); *Ridley v Taylor* [1965] 1 W.L.R. 611 at 622 (discouragement of frivolous objections); contrast *Gee v The National Trust* [1966] 1 W.L.R. 170.

[414] LPA 1925 s.84(1B). However, the grant of planning permission is merely a circumstance that will be taken into account by the Lands Chamber. It has no wider effect: *Re Martins' Application* (1988) 57 P. & C.R. 119 at 125; *Re Beech's Application* (1990) 59 P. & C.R. 502; [1990] Conv. 455 (N. D. M. Parry).

[415] See *Re Ghey and Gallon's Application* [1957] 2 Q.B. 650.

[416] *Dobbin v Redpath* [2007] EWCA Civ 570.

[417] See *Re University of Westminster* [1998] 3 All E.R. 1014 at 1023, 1024.

[418] *Shepherd Homes Ltd v Sandham (No.2)* [1971] 1 W.L.R. 1062; *Gilbert v Spoor*, above.

[419] *Gee v The National Trust*, above; see e.g. *Re Beecham Group Ltd's Application* (1980) 41 P. & C.R. 369 (agreement with local planning authority).

[420] LPA 1925 s.84(7).

apply as between the original contracting parties as well as between successors in title,[421] though discretion may be exercised against an original covenantor who himself accepted the restriction not long previously.[422] They apply to restrictions on freehold land, and to restrictions on leasehold land if the lease was made for more than 40 years and at least 25 years have expired; but they do not apply to mining leases.[423] The court may be less willing to modify or discharge covenants affecting leaseholds than covenants affecting freeholds, because of the landlord's interest in the future of the property.[424]

32–091   *(c) Stay of proceedings.* A defendant in an action to enforce a restrictive covenant may apply for a stay of proceedings in order that he may apply to the Lands Chamber for an order of discharge or modification[425]; but there is no similar power to stay proceedings for forfeiture of a lease for breach of a restrictive covenant.[426]

32–092   *(d) Conversion of houses.* There is also provision for the county court, on such terms as the court thinks fit, to authorise the conversion of a house into two or more tenements in contravention of a restrictive covenant or a provision in a lease if owing to changes in the neighbourhood the house cannot readily be let as a whole, or if planning permission for the conversion has been granted.[427]

32–093   *(e) Reform.* As part of its work in preparing a scheme of land obligations to replace for the future the existing law of positive and restrictive covenants,[428] the Law Commission also considered the position of existing covenants. Not all of the original proposals made by the Law Commission have been carried through to the final Report. In particular, while the Lands Chamber would have jurisdiction to modify or discharge a land obligation (and would continue to have such in relation to existing covenants), there would be no change to the grounds on which such an order could be made. The grounds for discharge or modification would not be extended or re-cast in respective of restrictive land obligations (i.e. it would be as is current for restrictive covenants), but necessarily new grounds would be formulated for positive land obligations. Nor would there be a change to the basis of compensation payable to the

[421] *Ridley v Taylor* [1965] 1 W.L.R. 611.
[422] *Cresswell v Proctor* [1968] 1 W.L.R. 906 (two years). But the time factor is not necessarily decisive, even where only a few months have elapsed: *Jones v Rhys-Jones* (1974) 30 P. & C.R. 451.
[423] LPA 1925 s.84(12) as amended by LTA 1954 s.52. For an application in respect of a lease (refused) see *Re Holiday Chalets at Point Curlew* [2011] UKUT 346 (LC).
[424] *Ridley v Taylor*, above.
[425] See LPA 1925 s.84(9); *Fielden v Byrne* [1926] Ch. 620; *Richardson v Jackson* [1954] 1 W.L.R. 447; *Shepherd Homes Ltd v Sandham (No.2)*, above.
[426] *Iveagh v Harris* [1929] 2 Ch. 281.
[427] HA 1985 s.610 (replacing earlier legislation). See Preston and Newsom, *Restrictive Covenants*, App. VI. For the limits of this, see *Josephine Trust Ltd v Champagne* [1963] 2 Q.B. 160.
[428] Above, para.32–081.

owner of the burdened estate in the event of a discharge or modification and persons benefitted by the obligation would (as now) not be able to apply for modification or discharge.[429] However, the jurisdiction of the Lands Chamber would be extended to cover easements and profits and the Chamber would be given the power to make declarations under s.84(2) LPA 1925 alongside the court. The current limitation on the Chamber's jurisdiction whereby it can make an order only in respect of certain types of lease would be removed.[430]

Section 5. Restrictive Covenants and Planning

The extension of planning control has somewhat reduced the importance of **32–094** restrictive covenants. The effect of this control[431] is to impose restrictions throughout England and Wales on any change in the use of any land, subject to various exceptions. Restrictive covenants need no longer be employed so widely and their scope can be more limited. Nevertheless, restrictive covenants have not been superseded by planning control. A landowner must see that what he proposes to do will contravene neither the private system of restrictive covenants nor the public system of planning control. Restrictive covenants sometimes extend to matters not covered by the planning legislation, as for example a change of the business carried on on the premises. Not only may it be better to be able to enforce a restrictive covenant as of right than to be dependent on the local planning authority enforcing planning control,[432] but the covenant may enable the covenantee or his successor in title to achieve greater control over the use of the servient land.[433]

The grant of planning permission does not by itself authorise the breach of a restrictive covenant.[434] But there are special provisions where a local authority has acquired land, or appropriated its own land,[435] for planning purposes. The erection, construction or carrying out, or maintenance, of any building or work on land in accordance with planning permission is then authorised by statute even though this involves a breach of restrictive covenants or interference with easements and similar rights of third parties.[436] This provision extends both to the local authority and to their successors in title, but

---

[429] (2011) Law Com. No.237 para 7.6 et seq. Compare (2008) Law Com. CP No.186 Part 13. There was widespread agreement that the basis for the payment of compensation should be reformed, but no consensus on what might replace the current provision, see s.84(1) LPA 1925. Note also that a person who has parted with the benefitted land cannot object to an application by the burdened owner, even if they later re-acquire ownership of part, *Re Hutchinson sub nom 1 Captains Gorse, Upper Basildon, Reading, Berkshire, RG8 8SZ* [2009] UKUT 182 (LC).

[430] (2011) Law Com. No.327 para.7.24 et seq.

[431] See Ch.22.

[432] For further discussion see (1964) 28 Conv. (N.S.) 190 (A. R. Mellows).

[433] *Re Jones' and White & Co's Application* (1989) 58 P. & C.R. 512 at 516 (a case concerned with a planning agreement under T & CPA 1971 s.52).

[434] *Re Martins' Application* (1988) 57 P. & C.R. 119 at 124.

[435] cf. *Sutton LBC v Bolton* [1993] 2 E.G.L.R. 181.

[436] T & CPA 1990 s.237(1).

statutory undertakers are excepted from its effect.[437] Where any such expropriation occurs, the owners of such rights may claim compensation.[438]

Planning authorities make much use of their statutory power to enter into planning obligations[439] with landowners for the purpose of restricting or regulating the development or use of land.[440] It has already been explained that such authorities do not need to possess adjacent land in order to enforce restrictions taken for this purpose.[441]

Section 6. Restrictive Covenants and Compulsory Acquisition

32–095 Where land which is subject to a restrictive covenant is acquired compulsorily by a public authority under statutory powers,[442] no action lies for breach of the covenant if what is done on the land is validly done in the exercise of those statutory powers.[443] The authority of Parliament then overrides the contractual restriction, and the covenantee's only remedy is to claim compensation for the injury to his own land which was previously benefited by the covenant.[444] "The remedy is given because Parliament, by authorising the works, has prevented damages caused by them from being actionable, and the compensation is given as a substitute for damages at law."[445] Such an award of compensation does not extinguish the covenant, which continues to bind the acquired land as regards any use not authorised by statute. Thus where the Air Ministry compulsorily purchased agricultural land for use as an aerodrome and later let it to a firm for use for commercial flying, an injunction was granted to prevent the firm from so using the land in breach of a covenant restricting it to agricultural use; but an injunction to prevent them for using it for Air Ministry work was refused.[446]

---

[437] T & CPA 1990 s.237(3).

[438] T & CPA 1990 s.237(4). See below.

[439] Formerly there was a system of planning agreements under T & CPA 1971 s.52, re-enacted as T & CPA 1990 s.106. Since October 25, 1991, it has not been possible to enter into such agreements. Instead a new and very different system of planning obligations has applied: Planning and Compensation Act 1991 s.12, substituting a new T & CPA 1990 s.106, and inserting new ss.106A, 106B. Although planning agreements were consensual, this is not always true of planning obligations which may be imposed on a local authority, e.g. on an appeal against a refusal to grant planning permission to a planning inspector or to the Secretary of State. To modify or discharge planning agreements application was made to the Lands Chamber under LPA 1925 s.84 (above, para.32–085). A planning obligation can be modified or discharged either by agreement with the local authority or at a determination made by the authority on application to it: T & CPA 1990 s.106A. Appeal lies to the Secretary of State: T & CPA 1990 s.106B.

[440] T & CPA 1990 s.106 (as substituted). Planning obligations may also impose positive obligations: above, para.32–018.

[441] Above, para.32–047.

[442] As to purchase by agreement under statutory powers, see *Kirby v Harrogate School Board* [1896] 1 Ch. 437.

[443] *Kirby v Harrogate School Board*, above; *Marten v Flight Refuelling Ltd* [1962] Ch. 115.

[444] *Long Eaton Recreation Grounds Co Ltd v Midland Ry* [1902] 2 K.B. 574. *cf. Hawley v Steele* (1877) 6 Ch D 521.

[445] *Horn v Sunderland Corporation* [1941] 2 K.B. 26 at 43, per Scott L.J. On the measure of compensation in such a case, see *Wrotham Park SE v Hertsmere BC* [1993] 2 E.G.L.R. 15.

[446] *Marten v Flight Refuelling Ltd*, above. 36 ss.1–3, 21.

Section 7. Restrictive Covenants and Race Relations

Under the Race Relations Act 1976 it is unlawful for a person disposing of or **32–096** managing any premises to discriminate against another person on grounds of colour, race, nationality or ethnic or national origins.[447] There is an exception for the provision of accommodation in, or the disposal of "small premises" in which the proprietor or manager (or a near relative) resides and which are shared with other persons not members of his household.[448]

The Act does not directly prohibit restrictive covenants *requiring* racial discrimination (for example segregation) although plainly such covenants are void in so far as they require discrimination prohibited by the Act. But, it seems that they may be effective in requiring discrimination that is permitted by the exception for "small premises".

[447] ss.1—3, 21.
[448] s.22. For "small premises" see above, para.19–104.

CHAPTER 33

COMMONHOLD

33–001   **1. Establishment.** Part 1 of the Commonhold and Leasehold Reform Act 2002 (CLRA 2002) came into force on September 27, 2004[1] together with the Commonhold Regulations 2004 (as amended by the Commonhold (Amendment) Regulations 2009) and the Commonhold (Land Registration) Rules 2004.[2] Together this primary and secondary legislation established a form of land holding in England and Wales previously unknown to the law of real property. But commonhold is neither a new estate nor a new form of tenure, for a "commonhold" may exist only in respect of a registered freehold estate. It is thus a hybrid of the freehold estate, operating only in respect of land with registered title,[3] and created by statute and governed by extensive Regulations. In April 2011, the Land Registry reported that there were 17 registered commonholds, very considerably less than was anticipated.

33–002   **2. Origins of commonhold.** Commonhold is designed to meet the perceived shortcomings of the leasehold estate, particularly as viewed from the perspective of the tenant. A lease is a wasting asset and the tenant by definition quits the land at the end of the lease with no property interest or capital gain. For many this is unfair, although for others it is precisely why a leasehold reversion is a useful financial tool and a valuable asset in its own right. Likewise, ultimate legal power in a leasehold lies with the landlord (subject of course to the terms of the lease) and the potential for abuse of this position—for example, in relation to unreasonable service charges or avoidance of repairing obligations is well known. The tenant, having no permanent stake in the land, is all too often a bystander in matters of consequence. On the other hand, the freehold estate cannot achieve all that a leasehold does. As well as the fact that a leasehold allows two or more persons to exploit the value of land at the same time (in the economic exchange of possession for

---

[1] Part 1 of CLRA 2002 has been amended by the Companies Act 2006 in order to reflect changes to general company law. See Companies Act 2006 (Consequential Amendments, Transitional Provisions and Savings) Order 2009, SI 2009/1941.

[2] s.21(5), relating to part-unit interests is not yet in force. See generally CLRA 2002 (Commencement No.3) Order 2003, SI 2003/2377; CLRA 2002 (Commencement No.5 and Saving and Transitional Provisions) Order 2004, SI 2004/1832; CLRA 2002 Commonhold (Amendment) Regulations 2009, SI 2009/2363. Commonhold (Land Registration) Rules 2004, SI 2004/1830.

[3] Consequently, if it is desired to establish a commonhold over unregistered land—which may well be the case if the land is previously undeveloped—it will be necessary to apply for first registration of title.

income), positive obligations generally do not run with freehold land.[4] This makes the freehold unsuitable for communal developments (whether a residential block of flats or commercial units on an industrial estate, or a mixture thereof) because it is difficult to ensure the mutual enforcement of common obligations—such as those concerning repair of the roof or dividing walls, or relating to maintenance of the estate's private roads, sewers and perimeter fence. Thus, where communal developments are concerned, be they residential, commercial or mixed use, the leasehold is believed to be structurally unfair to tenants and the freehold cannot easily serve the purpose.

The development of commonhold as a solution to these problems—be they real or imagined—was the result of a collaboration between the (then) Office of the Deputy Prime Minister and the (then) Lord Chancellor's Department. Following extensive consultation,[5] a draft Bill was published in August 2000 and introduced into Parliament shortly thereafter, but this fell with the general election of May 2001. An amended Bill was re-introduced to Parliament in June 2001 and gained Royal Assent on May 1, 2002.

3. The essence of commonhold. The purpose of commonhold is to provide an alternative to the two established forms of landholding in England and Wales in cases where land, or a building, or buildings, is divided into separate units owned by different persons (e.g. flats, industrial premises on an estate, detached dwellings in an enclosed community), and where it is necessary or desirable to have a legal person owning the common parts and being responsible for the overall management of the development (e.g. lifts, roofs, stairwells, fences, private drainage, leisure facilities). Individuals will own a *unit*, but the common parts will be owned and managed by a *commonhold association*, whose members are the unit holders. Thus the unit holders will have the security of a freehold, but the common parts will be managed for the benefit of all unit holders by an association (limited by guarantee) in which they all participate and which they effectively own. There is no external third party whose interest might be opposed to that of the unit holders. Detailed Regulations exist concerning the legal framework within which the commonhold association must operate and which specify in general terms its rights and responsibilities.[6] The precise powers etc. of the commonhold association in relation to the particular land that falls within the commonhold will be specified in its articles of association, but these must conform to the scheme of the Regulations both in terms of minimum and maximum responsibilities. In addition, all commonholds must operate under a *commonhold community statement* which deals in depth with the relationship between the commonhold association and the unit holders and the rights of the unit holders *inter se*.

33–003

---

[4] Save by various unsatisfactory devices, see Ch.32. This will change if the Law Commission's proposals for the reform of freehold covenants is enacted, above para.32–081.

[5] Department for constitutional Affairs, *Commonhold and Leasehold Reform: Draft Bill and Consultation Paper* August 21, 2000.

[6] See generally Sch.3 CLRA 2002, the Commonhold Regulations 2004 and the Commonhold (Amendment) Regulations 2009.

Consideration of the detail of the workings of commonhold is outside the scope of this Chapter and what follows is an explanation of the broad nature of a commonhold.[7]

33–004 **4. General structure of commonhold land.** A commonhold will comprise the unit holders having freehold title to their individual units and the commonhold association, having freehold title to the common parts. The commonhold association will be limited by guarantee and its powers will be specified in its articles of association, subject to certain mandatory requirements established by the Regulations. There will be a commonhold community statement dealing in detail with the rights of the unit holders and their relationship to the commonhold association.

33–005 **5. Land in respect of which a commonhold may be registered.** Not all land may be subject to commonhold. Commonhold may exist only in relation to registered land and only in respect of land registered with absolute title,[8] although it is possible to apply for first registration of title and apply for its registration as commonhold land at the same time.[9] Successful registration of a commonhold will result in the land (both units and common parts) being registered as land subject to a "freehold estate in commonhold". In addition, s.4 CLRA 2002 and Sch.2 provide that certain types of land may not be commonhold land, even if held as a registered freehold with absolute title.

33–006 **6. Land which may not be held commonhold.** This is land which wholly or partly comprises:

(a) flying freeholds, being freehold land above ground where all of the land between the freehold and the ground is not itself freehold[10]

(b) agricultural land within the meaning of the Agriculture Act 1947, or an agricultural holding within the meaning of the Agricultural Holdings Act 1986, or a farm business tenancy within the meaning of the Agricultural Tenancies Act 1995[11]

(c) land held of a contingent title in the sense that the land might revert or vest in a person other than the current registered proprietor by reason of a right of reverter existing under specified statutes.[12]

---

[7] See generally Featherstonehaugh, Peters and Sefton, *Commonhold:* (Oxford, OUP, 2004); T. Aldridge, *Commonhold Law* (London: Sweet & Maxwell); D. Clarke, *Clarke on Commonhold* (London: Jordans).

[8] CLRA 2002 s.2.

[9] Thus, only a proprietor registered with absolute title, or a person entitled to be registered as such, may apply to have land registered as a commonhold, CLRA 2002 s.2(3)(a) and (b).

[10] CLRA 2002 Sch.2 para.1.

[11] CLRA 2002 Sch.2 para.2.

[12] CLRA 2002 Sch.2 para.3. The specified statutes are the School Sites Act 1841; the Lands Clauses Acts; the Literary and Scientific Institutions Act 1854; and the Places of Worship Sites Act 1873.

7. Statutory definition of commonhold land. As a consequence of these   **33–007**
provisions, land is commonhold land if[13]:

(i) the freehold estate in the land is registered as a freehold estate in commonhold land; and

(ii) the articles of association of the commonhold association specifies this land as land in respect of which the association will exercise its functions; and

(iii) a commonhold community statement makes provision for the rights and duties of the commonhold association and the unit holders.

8. The circumstances in which a commonhold may arise. A common-   **33–008**
hold may arise either:

(i) on the application of a person who is the registered freehold proprietor of a new development (or a person entitled to be registered as such: e.g. at first registration of title) and who wishes to establish a commonhold as the preferred method of utilising the site; or

(ii) by conversion of an existing development (e.g. a leasehold block of flats) into a commonhold.

However, given that only a proprietor registered with absolute title, or a person entitled to be registered as such, may apply to have land registered as a commonhold,[14] all applications must be accompanied by the consent of those persons specified in s.3 of the CLRA 2002.[15] This is to ensure that other persons interested in the land are in agreement with the establishment of the commonhold, especially as this is likely to modify or even terminate their existing interests in the land.[16] These might be existing leaseholders or chargees holding a mortgage over the whole or part of the land. Without the required consents, the application to register cannot proceed and the commonhold cannot be established.[17] The number of consents required will of course vary according to each case, but in the case of conversions from an existing leasehold, all existing leaseholders must consent. The requirement of unanimity among existing leaseholders, and the absence of a general power in the

---

[13] See CLRA 2002 s.1(1).
[14] Above, fn.8.
[15] Or in addition, such persons as Regulations may prescribe, CLRA 2002 s.3(1d).
[16] For example, on conversion from an existing leasehold, the long leases are, of necessity, extinguished, albeit that they may be replaced with a freehold of a unit. Short leases may be extinguished altogether.
[17] Land Registry Form CON1 must be used to give consent.

court to dispense with the consents that are required,[18] means that it is unlikely that many commonholds will arise from conversions. It will be simpler, easier and less expensive to establish a commonhold de novo in respect of a development in which the developer only has interests.

33–009 **9. Consents.** The persons whose consent is required[19] are:

(i) the registered proprietor of the freehold estate in the whole or part of the land[20]; and

(ii) the registered proprietor of a leasehold estate in the whole or part of the land granted for a term of more than 21 years; and

(iii) the registered proprietor of a charge over the whole or part of the land; and

(iv) any other person prescribed by Regulations. This currently includes: the estate owner of any unregistered freehold estate in the whole or part of the land; the estate owner of any unregistered leasehold estate in the whole or part of the land granted for a term of more than 21 years; the owner of any mortgage, charge or lien for securing money or money's worth over the whole or part of any unregistered land included in the application; and the holder of a lease granted for a term of not more than 21 years which will be extinguished by virtue of s.7(3)(d) or 9(3)(f) (being extinguishment as a result of a successful application to register a commonhold).[21]

33–010 **10. The application to register a commonhold.** Provided that the land is capable of being commonhold land,[22] and that the application is made by a person entitled to apply,[23] and that all required consents are obtained,[24] there are two types of registration that may be applied for. A commonhold may be created by registration without unit holders, or with unit holders and both types of application must be accompanied by a site plan of sufficient detail to

---

[18] CLRA 2002 s.3(e) and (f) provides that consent may be deemed or dispensed with in specified circumstances. Reg.5 of the Commonhold Regulations 2004 provides that the power to deem consent, or to dispense with consent exists where the person whose consent is required cannot be identified, traced or when they do not respond to a request for consent. However, there is no power to override a refusal to give consent.

[19] CLRA 2002 s.3(1).

[20] Usually, this will be the applicant for commonhold registration and, as such, their consent will be deemed, Commonhold regulations 2004, reg.4(5)(b).

[21] Commonhold Regulations 2004 reg.3. In some circumstances, consent of leaseholders of leases for 21 years or less whose leases face extinguishment under s.7(3)(d) or 9(3)(f), may not be required, principally where they are entitled to a new lease (out of the commonhold) on the same terms and such entitlement has been protected by an entry of a notice in the title register or land charges register as they case may be, see reg.3(2)(a) and (b).

[22] Above paras 33–006, 33–007.

[23] Above para.33–008.

[24] Above para.33–009.

identify the common parts, the (proposed or actual) individual units and the full extent of the commonhold land.[25] The first type of registration is suitable for persons developing land de novo for commonhold and who expect the individual units to be sold off in due course. The second type of registration is suitable for land converting from other forms of ownership (e.g. an existing development subject to leasehold or from a merger of freehold estates) or where there are already persons interested in individual units (for example a new development where purchasers buy units "off plan" as a way of financing the development).

11. Registration without unit holders.[26] Registration without unit holders **33–011** is governed by s.7 of CLRA 2002.[27] The common parts are registered as one title in the name of the applicant and the individual units are each given a separate title but are also registered in the name of the applicant. Usually, this will be the developer. Thus, after this initial registration as commonhold, all titles comprising the commonhold are registered in the name of the applicant and each title is identified on the register as a freehold estate in commonhold. Following this initial registration, the commonhold is said to be in a transitional period, being the period between the initial registration of the freehold estate in commonhold and the registration of another person as a unit holder.[28] During this period, which is effectively the period before any unit is sold or transferred, certain provisions of the CLRA 2002 and the Regulations will not be in force. In particular, the commonhold community statement will not be operative.[29]

The registration of another person as the registered proprietor of a freehold estate in commonhold of one or more (but not all) of the units brings the transitional period to an end: for example, when the developer sells the first unit. Such registration triggers the full implementation of the commonhold scheme and the commonhold community statement comes into force. In addition, the common parts are now registered in the name of the commonhold association. The original applicant retains title to the unsold units but these are, of course, registered in the names of their new owners as and when they are transferred. Eventually, the original applicant will have no registered titles: the common parts will have been registered in the name of the commonhold association since the transfer of the first unit, and the units will be registered in the names of the individual owners.[30]

---

[25] Commonhold (Land Registration) Rules 2004 r.8 gives the Registrar power to reject applications if the plan is not sufficiently clear.

[26] Unless the application for registration specifies that it is to be treated under CLRA 2002 s.9 (registration with unit holders), all applications are treated on this basis.

[27] Using Land Registry Form CM1.

[28] CLRA 2002 s.8(1), referring to s.7(3). Registration of another person with *all* of the units does not bring the transitional period to an end, CLRA 2002 s.7(3).

[29] CLRA 2002 s.7(2)(b).

[30] Other consequential changes are made to the register entries, including cancellation of entries in relation to interests that have been extinguished by the creation of the commonhold. See Ruoff & Roper para.22–009.

33–012   **12. Registration with unit holders.** Registration with unit holders operates under CLRA 2002 s.9, but an applicant must specify that he wishes the application to be treated under this section, else it will be treated as an application for registration without unit holders.[31] With an application of this type, the commonhold community statement will come in to force at the moment of registration of the titles. The commonhold association will be registered as proprietor of the common parts,[32] and the existing unit holders will be registered as proprietors of their individual units.[33] The registered titles of the land prior to registration as a commonhold (e.g. long leasehold titles in a block of flats) will be closed.

33–013   **13. The commonhold community statement (CCS).** The commonhold community statement will describe the physical attributes of the land subject to the commonhold and will contain the rules and regulations under which the commonhold will operate.[34] The statement must contain certain core provisions,[35] and must be in a prescribed form. It will identify the number of units and their location; identify the rights of unit holders over the common parts as well as the obligations affecting the units for the benefit of the commonhold. It will regulate the financial obligations of unit holders to contribute to the costs of the commonhold and the maintenance of the common parts (the commonhold assessment) and will establish the rules of the commonhold (e.g. as to repairs, maintenance, insurance) There will be provision for the transfer or lease of a unit, in whole or in part, provision for the amendment of the statement as required and a procedure for dispute resolution. It is, in effect, the constitution of the commonhold and will be a substantial document.[36]

33–014   **14. The commonhold association.** The commonhold association will be the registered proprietor of the common parts and is the vehicle through which the common parts are managed.[37] All unit holders are entitled to be members of the association[38] (but need not be), and membership is not open to any other person. The association will be a company limited by guarantee.[39] As a company, the association will be required to conform to the general requirements of the Companies Acts (e.g. as to the filing of accounts, directors, audits etc.), but it is also subject to special rules found in the Act and the Regulations.[40] The Articles of Association of the commonhold association will

---

[31] CLRA 2002 s.9(1)(b).

[32] CLRA 2002 s.9(3)(a).

[33] The unit holders are indentified on the application for registration by completion of Land Registry Form COV.

[34] CLRA 2002 ss.31–33.

[35] CLRA 2002 s.31.

[36] See an archived draft provided by the Department of Constitutional Affairs at *http://www.dca.gov.uk/legist/commonhold/schedule3.pdf*.

[37] CLRA 2002 ss.34–36 and Sch.3. Commonhold Regulations 2004 as amended by the Commonhold Regulations 2009.

[38] If a unit is jointly owned, only one may be a member of the association.

[39] CLRA 2002 s.34(1).

[40] The name of the company must be in the form XYZ Commonhold Association Limited.

stipulate its powers and obligations in the normal way, but generally these are prescribed by Regulations and may not be departed from.[41] The directors of the association are under a duty to exercise their powers to facilitate the exercise of rights and enjoyment of land by the unit holders.[42] In essence, the association exists for the benefit of its members, the unit holders, and there is no external influence with a countervailing interest.

15. The unit holders and the commonhold unit. A person is a "unit holder" of a commonhold unit for the purposes of the commonhold scheme if he is registered as proprietor of a unit or is entitled to be so registered.[43] A unit holder is entitled to be a member of the commonhold association. A commonhold unit is held freehold and while it may be a flat or industrial unit, it might equally be a house, a parking space or undeveloped land. The commonhold community statement will define the units, and there is no requirement that all the units must be of the same type. In other words, a single commonhold might comprise residential and commercial units, houses, flats and undeveloped land. Commonhold units may be transferred, leased or charged in the normal way,[44] and the commonhold community statement must not prevent or restrict the exercise of these rights of alienation.[45] However, a unit may well be subject to obligations for the benefit of the commonhold and other unit owners—for example, in relation to shared walls, ceilings, services. A commonhold unit is freely transferable and the transferee will be registered as the new proprietor of the freehold estate in commonhold of the unit. The commonhold community statement may not prevent or restrict such a transfer.[46] However, the leasing of residential commonhold units is restricted in order to prevent a repetition of the problems that occur with leaseholds proper.[47] In essence, leasing is restricted to a term of seven years, which must be non-renewable, save that a lease of no-longer than 21 years may be granted to a person whose lease over the land was extinguished on the creation of the commonhold.[48] Leasing of commercial units is possible, but only as provided for in the commonhold community statement.[49] The commonhold community statement may not prevent or restrict a unit holder's right to charge the unit as security, or to borrower by way of mortgage.[50]

16. The common parts. The common parts are registered in the name of the commonhold association and comprise all that land within the commonhold that is not defined by the commonhold community statement as a unit.[51]

33–015

33–016

---

[41] Commonhold Regulations 2004 Schedule 2 (substituted by Commonhold Regulations 2009).
[42] CLRA 2002 s.35(1).
[43] CLRA 2002 s.12 and s.13(1) (joint unit holders).
[44] CLRA 2002 ss.15, 17, 20.
[45] CLRA 2002 s.20.
[46] CLRA 2002 s.15(2).
[47] CLRA 2002 s.17.
[48] Commonhold Regulations 2004 r.11.
[49] CLRA 2002 s.18.
[50] CLRA 2002 s.20.
[51] CLRA 2002 s.25.

Typically it will include stairways, lifts, gardens, pathways, utilities ducting and similar. The commonhold community statement will make provision for the use of the common parts, including maters such as repair, insurance and costs.[52]

33–017   **17. De-registration.** If an application is made to register land as commonhold without unit holders, a transitional period will be in operation which comes to an end when the first unit is registered in the name of a new proprietor.[53] Before the end of the transitional period, the developer may apply to de-register the land as commonhold land.[54] Technically, this is not a termination of the commonhold—for the commonhold community statement never came into operation—but the application to de-register must be accompanied by the consent of all those persons whose consent was required for the initial application to register.[55]

33–018   **18. Termination of the commonhold.**[56] A commonhold may come to an end in one of three ways. First, the unit holders may determine to wind up the commonhold association voluntarily.[57] This may be because the land itself is being disposed of (e.g. for its development value) or because the unit holders wish to operate under some other legal structure. A liquidator will be appointed who will apply to the Land Registry for a termination and a *termination statement* will indicate how the assets of the commonhold association are to be dealt with and what will happen to the titles of the unit holders. Secondly, termination may result from a court order winding up the commonhold association on the grounds of insolvency.[58] The court will usually make a succession order[59] substituting a new commonhold association who will be duly registered as proprietor of the common parts. However, where this is not possible, the commonhold may cease to exist and the land dealt with according to the terms of a termination statement. Thirdly, a court can make an order that all land subject to the commonhold cease to be commonhold land, and this is likely to be used when there has been some error in the registration process or some defect in the legal structure of the commonhold association.[60] Such termination by court order may result in a re-application for registration under a new commonhold scheme or a liquidator may be appointed in the normal way.

---

[52] CLRA 2002 s.26.
[53] Above para.33–011.
[54] CLRA 2002 s.8(4) and Commonhold Regulations 2004 r.14 (as amended by Commonhold Regulations 2009)
[55] CLRA 2002 s.8(5). It is possible to de-register part of the land intended to be subject to commonhold and the commonhold community statement must be amended and lodged with the Land Registry, CLRA 2002 s.33.
[56] See Ruoff & Roper 22–025 et seq.
[57] CLRA 2002 ss.43–49.
[58] CLRA 2002 ss.50–54.
[59] CLRA 2002 s.51(4).
[60] CLRA 2002 s.55.

CHAPTER 34

LICENCES

Section 1. Nature of a Licence

A licence is a mere permission which makes it lawful for the licensee to do **34–001** what would otherwise be a trespass.[1] Such rights are commonplace, and examples include lodging in a person's house,[2] going onto his land to play cricket,[3] storing goods on his premises,[4] or advertising on a hoarding on his wall.[5] Such a licence is merely a defence to an action in tort and confers no estate or interest in land.[6] "A licence in connection with land while entitling the licensee to use the land for the purposes authorised by the licence does not create an estate in land."[7] A licence cannot therefore bind a successor in title of the licensor as a matter of property law. Furthermore, at common law, a licensor might always revoke his licence,[8] though he might have to pay damages for breach of contract if the licence arose under a contract.

The boundary of the law of property is drawn between licences and leases,[9] and to a lesser extent in practice between licences and easements. Where the requirements for a tenancy are not satisfied, the interest can be no more than a licence,[10] and if a person crosses my land and has no easement, they will be

[1] See *Thomas v Sorrell* (1673) Vaugh. 330 at 351.
[2] Above, para.17–018.
[3] *Frank Warr & Co Ltd v LCC* [1904] 1 K.B. 713 at 723.
[4] *Morris-Thomas v Petticoat Lane Rentals* (1986) 53 P. & C.R. 238 (storage of antiques in a former bacon curing oven).
[5] *Kewal Investments Ltd v Arthur Maiden Ltd* [1990] 1 E.G.L.R. 193; *Arthur Maiden Ltd v Patel* [1990] 1 E.G.L.R. 269.
[6] *Ashburn Anstalt v Arnold* [1989] Ch. 1 at 22. In *IDC Group Ltd v Clark* [1992] 2 E.G.L.R. 184 at 186, Nourse L.J. stated that "a licence properly so called is a permission to do something on or over land which creates no interest in it".
[7] *Street v Mountford* [1985] A.C. 809 at 814, per Lord Templeman. See too *Wettern Electric Ltd v Welsh Development Agency* [1983] Q.B. 796 at 805; *Camden LBC v Shortlife Community Housing Ltd* (1992) 90 L.G.R. 358 at 373.
[8] For the position in equity, see below, para.34–009.
[9] And to a lesser extent in practice between licences and easements. See below for a discussion of the so-called "*Bruton* tenancy" stemming from the House of Lords judgment in *Bruton v London & Quadrant Housing Trust* [2000] 1 A.C. 406.
[10] Above, para.17–012.

either a licensee or a trespasser. If A owns a lodging house and sells it, B, the purchaser, can recover possession from the lodgers,[11] who are in law mere licensees, notwithstanding their agreements,[12] unless in the circumstances B's conduct is sufficiently unconscionable to warrant the intervention of equity.[13] In the usual case, the lodger's only remedy is to sue A for damages.[14] Although there was an attempt to elevate licences into interests in land, the traditional nature of licences has since been reasserted.[15]

Section 2. Types of Licences

34-002 Licences can be granted in a wide variety of forms. At one end of the scale is an occupational licence which confers a right of occupation but not of exclusive possession,[16] such as the licence of a lodger in a lodging-house[17] or permission to use land and a farmyard for the extraction and storage of peat.[18] At the other end of the scale are all kinds of miscellaneous licences for temporary purposes, such as the hire of a concert hall for a few days,[19] permission to erect an advertisement hoarding[20] or electric sign,[21] permission to use pleasure boats on a canal,[22] the grant of the right to use refreshment rooms in a theatre[23] and permission to view a race on a racecourse[24] or a film in a cinema.[25] There is no limit to the possible circumstances in which a licence to use land might arise, although three main varieties require consideration.

---

[11] B will have to obtain a court order: see PEA 1977 s.3(1), (2B) (inserted by HA 1988 s.30). There is however an exception from this requirement in the case of certain "excluded licences" (which are licences of accommodation shared in some way with the landlord or which fall within certain other specified categories): see PEA 1977 s.3A (added by HA 1988 s.31).

[12] *Clore v Theatrical Properties Ltd* [1936] 3 All E.R. 483.

[13] Below, para.34–019. In such a case, the licence may be held effective against the purchaser, but not in virtue of any proprietary status.

[14] *King v David Allen & Sons (Billposting) Ltd* [1916] 2 A.C. 54.

[15] Below, paras 34–016, 34–019.

[16] Above, para.17–018. A person may be in exclusive possession but not in actual occupation, as where a tenant sub-lets the premises leased to him: *Camden LBC v Shortlife Community Housing Ltd* (1992) 90 L.G.R. 358 at 381.

[17] *Allen v Liverpool Overseers* (1874) L.R. 9 Q.B. 180 at 190, 191. An occupier is a lodger "if the landlord provides attendance or services which require the landlord or his servants to exercise unrestricted access to and use of the premises": *Street v Mountford* [1985] A.C. 809 at 818, per Lord Templeman.

[18] *Crow v Waters*, Chancery Division May 15, 2007.

[19] *Taylor v Caldwell* (1863) 3 B. & S. 826.

[20] *Wilson v Tavener* [1901] 1 Ch. 578.

[21] *Walton Harvey Ltd v Walker and Homfrays Ltd* [1931] 1 Ch. 274.

[22] *Hill v Tupper* (1863) 2 H. & C. 121.

[23] *Frank Warr & Co Ltd v LCC* [190411 K.B. 713; *Clore v Theatrical Properties Ltd* [1936] 3 All E.R. 483. Similarly in *Isaac v Hotel de Paris Ltd* [1960] 1 W.L.R. 239 the right to use one floor of a hotel as a night bar at a monthly rent was held to be a licence.

[24] *Wood v Leadbitter* (1845) 13 M. & W. 838.

[25] *Hurst v Picture Theatres Ltd* [1915] 1 K.B. 1.

1. Bare licence. This is the simplest form of licence. A bare licence is a **34–003** licence which is not supported by any contract, and includes a gratuitous permission to enter a house or to cross a field. Such a licence may be expressly given or it may be implied. Thus a person with lawful business may enter a householder's gate and proceed to the door of the house,[26] or he may go into a shop that is open.[27] A bare licence can be revoked at any time[28] on reasonable notice without rendering the licensor liable in damages,[29] but the licensee will not be a trespasser until he has had reasonable time to withdraw.[30] Even a licence granted by deed may be revocable,[31] provided that there is no covenant not to revoke it. A revocable licence is automatically determined by the death of the licensor or the assignment of the land.[32]

Under the rule already explained,[33] a licensee in possession is estopped from denying the title of the licensor, so that he cannot resist making any agreed payment by pleading that the licensor is not the true owner[34] but under the same rule the estoppel ceases to operate when he gives up possession.[35]

2. Contractual licence. A licence will often be granted under the terms of **34–004** some contract which restricts the licensor's right to revoke it. The contract is normally express but it may sometimes be implied.[36] Examples include a lodger in a lodging-house and a ticket-holder at a cricket match, at a concert or travelling on the railway.

Contractual licences are subject to the same rules which govern all contracts, as three examples will demonstrate. First, in appropriate circumstances a court will imply terms into a licence to give it business efficacy,[37] such as

---

[26] *Robson v Hallett* [1967] 2 Q.B. 939 at 953, 954.

[27] *Davis v Lisle* [1936] 2 K.B. 434 at 440.

[28] There is an ancient common law doctrine that a licence is irrevocable after being acted upon: see, e.g. *Webb v Paternoster* (1619) 2 Roll. 152, Palm. 71 at 74; *Feltsam v Cartwright* (1839) 5 Bing. NC. 569; *Hounslow LBC v Twickenham Garden Developments Ltd* [1971] Ch. 233 at 255; above, para.16–037; below, para.34–012.

[29] *Aldin v Latimer Clark, Muirhead & Co* [1894] 2 Ch. 437 (where the licensor gave no reasonable notice and so was liable in damages); *Armstrong v Sheppard and Short Ltd* [1959] 2 Q.B. 384.

[30] *Cornish v Stubbs* (1870) L.R. 5 C.P. 334; *Mellor v Watkins* (1874) L.R. 9 Q.B. 400; *Aldin v Latimer Clark, Muirhead & Co*, above (damages awarded but injunction refused); *Canadian Pacific Ry v The King* [1931] A.C. 414; *Minister of Health v Bellotti* [1944] K.B. 298; *Australian Blue Metal Ltd v Hughes* [1963] A.C. 74.

[31] *Wood v Leadbitter* (1845) 13 M. & W. 838 at 845. A licence by deed acquires no proprietary status simply by reason of the formality of its creation.

[32] *Terunnanse v Terunnanse* [1968] A.C. 1086.

[33] Above, para.17–125.

[34] *Terunnanse v Terunnanse*, above; *Sze To Csun Keung v Kung Kwok Wai David* [1997] 1 W.L.R. 1232 at 1235.

[35] *Government of Penang v Beng Hong Oon* [1972] A.C. 425.

[36] *Tanner v Tanner* [1975] 1 W.L.R. 1346; *Chandler v Kerley* [1978] 1 W.L.R. 693. See too *Horrocks v Forray* [1976] 1 W.L.R. 230 at 239.

[37] *Winter Garden Theatre (London) Ltd v Millennium Productions Ltd* [1948] A.C. 173; *Smith v Nottinghamshire CC*, The Times, November 13, 1981; *Wettern Electric Ltd v Welsh Development Agency* [1983] Q.B. 796.

a term that the licensor will not disturb the quiet enjoyment of a residential licensee[38] or will permit access so as to enable effective use of a licence to park.[39] Such terms are not necessarily the same as those which would be implied into a lease even where the licence is for the use and occupation of land.[40] Second, a person who knowingly induces the breach of a contractual licence may commit the tort of inducing breach of contract.[41] Third, the licensor or licensee may commit a breach of the terms of a contractual licence that will entitle the other to treat it as at an end. If, however, a licensee elects to affirm the contract, he will remain liable to pay the licence fee as long as he occupies the premises.[42]

34–005   **3. Licence coupled with an interest.** The one form of licence which caused no problems at common law was a licence coupled with a recognised interest in property. A right to enter another man's land to hunt and take away the deer killed, or to enter and cut down a tree and take it away, involves two things, namely, a licence to enter the land and the grant of an interest (a profit à prendre[43]) in the deer or tree.[44] At common law such a licence is both irrevocable[45] and assignable,[46] but only as an adjunct of the interest with which it is coupled. It therefore has no independent existence merely as a licence. It may be reinforced by the principle that a person may not derogate from his grant,[47] which is explained further above.[48] In any case, such a licence is not only irrevocable but is enforceable by and against successors in

---

[38] *Smith v Nottinghamshire CC*, above (injunction granted to restrain building work during examination period at a students' hall of residence).

[39] *Donington Park Leisure Ltd v Wheatcroft & Son*, Chancery Division, Lawtel 19/4/2006. The term was implied on the ground of non-derogation from grant, but this property law principle seems out of place in relation to this licence where there was no "coupling" with a property interest, see below para.34–005.

[40] *Wettern Electric Ltd v Welsh Development Agency*, above (obligation implied that newly constructed factory premises were fit for the purposes of the licensee, even though no such obligation would have been implied into a lease: see above, para.19–017). cf. *Morris-Thomas v Petticoat Lane Rentals* (1986) 53 P. & C.R. 238 at 249, 255 (no such implied term where the licensee knew the state of the property when she took the licence).

[41] *Binions v Evans* [1972] Ch. 359 at 371; *Arthur Maiden Ltd v Patel* [1990] 1 E.G.L.R. 269. See above, para.6–067.

[42] *Dudley Port Warehousing Co Ltd v Gardner Transport & Distribution Ltd* [1995] E.G.C.S. 5.

[43] For such interests see above, paras 27–055, 30–024.

[44] See *Thomas v Sorrell* (1673) Vaugh. 330 at 351; *Wood v Leadbitter* (1845) 13 M. & W. 838 at 845.

[45] *James Jones & Sons Ltd v Earl of Tankerville* [1909] 2 Ch. 440 at 442 (sale of timber); *Doe d. Hanley v Wood* (1819) 2 B. & Aid. 724 at 738 (sale of hay); *Wood v Manley* (1839) 11 A. & E. 34; *Wood v Leadbitter* (1845) 13 M. & W. 838 at 845.

[46] *Muskett v Hill* (1839) 5 Bing. NC. 694 at 707, 708.

[47] cf. *Wood v Manley* (1839) 11 A. & E. 34 at 37, 38. See also *Donington Park Leisure Ltd v Wheatcroft & Son* Lawtel 19/4/2006 where there was no profit à prendre to which the licence could be attached. If, as the judge said in that case, the "interest" to which the licence was attached was a tenancy, then the so-called licence was in reality a term of the lease and had no independent existence.

[48] Para.27–046; and see also, para.19–023.

title of the grantee and grantor respectively, as part and parcel of the interest granted.

The interest to which the licence is "coupled" must, of course, have been **34–006** validly created. Similarly, the licence is only effective against a third party if the interest to which it is attached is enforceable against the third party under the normal rules of registered and unregistered conveyancing. If the licence was to go upon land to take game or dig for materials, these rights, being profits à prendre, must have been duly granted by deed[49] or acquired by prescription.[50] An interest in chattels, however, can be created with less formality, as where there is a sale of hay or timber already cut, coupled with a licence to the purchaser to cart them away.[51] An interest in standing timber or growing crops can be created, it seems, only by the formalities appropriate for land.[52] In equity, as usual, effect will be given to a specifically enforceable agreement to grant such an interest; and thus a licence coupled with a profit à prendre granted for value but merely in writing[53] can be enforced by injunction.[54]

Licences have occasionally been held to be coupled with an interest, and so irrevocable, even though no recognisable interest was involved.[55] But the better view must be that some kind of proprietary interest is necessary.[56]

Licences of this class may be contrasted with rights of entry, which are recognised interests in land in their own right.[57]

Section 3. Revocability of Licences

At common law, a licence, unless coupled with an interest, was always **34–007** revocable, for the licencee had no estate or interest in the land that would entitle him to remain there. However, this simple position has been modified in important respects.

---

[49] *Duke of Somerset v Fogwell* (1826) 5 B. & C. 875 at 886 (fishing lease). And be appropriately registered, see LRA 2002 s.27(2).

[50] Above, para.28–043.

[51] See para.34–005 above.

[52] Although a sale of timber to be cut forthwith is not a contract for the sale of an interest in land (*semble*, see above, para.15–026), the property in the timber cannot pass until it is cut, i.e. no proprietary interest can be created informally so long as the timber is in fact part of the land: *Morison v Lockhart*, 1912 S.C. 1017, followed in *Kursell v Timber Operators and Contractors Ltd* [1927] 1 KB 298. "Timber trees cannot be felled with a goose quill": *Liford's Case* (1614) 11 Co Rep. 46b at 50a.

[53] A contract to grant such an interest is void unless it is made in writing, contains all the terms agreed, and is signed by each party to it: above, para.15–018.

[54] *Frogley v Earl of Lovelace* (1859) John 333: cf. *Duke of Devonshire v Eglin* (1851) 14 Beav. 530; *McManus v Cooke* (1887) 35 Ch D 681; cf. above, para.17–047.

[55] As in *Vaughan v Hampson* (1875) 33 L.T. 15 (successful action for assault by licensee ejected from meeting); *Hurst v Picture Theatres Ltd*, below. Or, as in *Donington Park Leisure Ltd v Wheatcroft & Son* above, with an interest that did not need a licence to support it.

[56] *Hounslow LBC v Twickenham Garden Developments Ltd* [1971] Ch. 233.

[57] Above, para.6–027.

1. Revocation restricted by contract

34–008   *(a) Revocability a matter of construction.* Except in those cases which are governed by statute,[58] then whether or not a contractual licence is revocable is a question of construction of the contract.[59] If the contract makes no express provision for determination, the court will imply a term that is appropriate in the circumstances.[60] Thus in cases of service occupancy,[61] the licence will normally be granted for the duration of the licensee's employment.[62] It is implicit therefore that it will terminate when that employment ceases,[63] even if the licensee has been wrongfully dismissed.[64] With most contractual licences the court usually implies a term that reasonable notice shall be given.[65] If the licensor purports to terminate the licence without giving reasonable notice, that notice will be effective, but only after a reasonable time has elapsed.[66] However, if the contract specifies the period of notice, any purported determination that is not in accordance with the contract is a nullity.[67] On the termination of the licence, the licensee is permitted a reasonable time to vacate the premises.[68]

Under the Protection from Eviction Act 1977, the licensor must give the licensee not less than four weeks' written notice to quit in the case of certain "periodic licences"[69] of a dwelling.[70] This requirement does not however apply to "excluded licences" where the period of notice will be that specified

---

[58] Such as those falling within the PEA 1977. Below.

[59] *Millennium Productions Ltd v Winter Garden Theatre (London) Ltd* [1946] 1 All E.R. 678 at 680; [1948] A.C. 173 at 196, 198 (sub nom. *Winter Garden Theatre (London) Ltd v Millennium Productions Ltd*). In construing the contract the court has regard to the circumstances existing when the contract is made: *Australian Blue Metal Ltd v Hughes* [1963] A.C. 74 at 99.

[60] *Winter Garden Theatre (London) Ltd v Millennium Productions Ltd*, above.

[61] A service occupancy will exist where the licensee's occupation of the premises is either necessary for the performance of his duties, or is required by his employer for the better performance of those duties: *Norris v Checksfield* [1991] 1 W.L.R. 1241 at 1244. cf. *Hughes v Greenwich LBC* [1994] 1 A.C. 170 at 178.

[62] *Ivory v Palmer* [1975] I.C.R. 340; *Burgoyne v Griffiths* [1991] 1 E.G.L.R. 14 at 16.

[63] *Norris v Checksfield* [1991] 1 W.L.R. 1241 at 1248.

[64] *Ivory v Palmer*, above.

[65] *Winter Garden Theatre (London) Ltd v Millennium Productions Ltd*, above; *Greater London Council v Jenkins* [1978] 1 W.L.R. 155 at 158; *Smith v Northside Developments Ltd* [1987] 2 E.G.L.R. 151 at 152. What is reasonable is determined in the light of circumstances existing at the time when the notice is given: *Australian Blue Metal Ltd v Hughes*, above, at 99. See too *Governing Body of Henrietta Barnett School v Hampstead Garden Suburb* [1995] B.G.C.S. 55.

[66] *Minister of Health v Bellotti* [1944] Q.B. 298. This has been criticised: see [1996] C.L.J. 229 (T. Kerbel), where it is suggested that a notice that fails to specify a period that is in fact reasonable ought to be invalid. cf. *Canadian Pacific Ry v The King* [1931] A.C. 414.

[67] *Wallshire Ltd v Advertising Sites Ltd* [1988] 2 E.G.L.R. 167.

[68] The "packing-up period": *Winter Garden Theatre (London) Ltd v Millennium Productions Ltd*, above, at 206, per Lord MacDermott; *Minister of Health v Bellotti*, above, at 305, 306.

[69] A term not defined by PEA 1977 and described by Woolf L.J. in *Norris v Checksfield* [1991] 1 W.L.R. 1241 at 1246 as "a new animal". It is apparently a licence granted on a periodic basis in a similar manner to a periodic tenancy: *Norris v Checksfield*, above.

[70] PEA 1977 s.5(1A) (added by HA 1988 s.23). For the prescribed information that the notice to quit must contain, see SI 1988/2201.

in the licence agreement or, in the absence of such, what is reasonable in the circumstances.[71]

(b) Remedies for improper revocation. In *Wood v Leadbitter*[72] a ticket **34-009** holder was wrongfully removed from Doncaster racecourse, but failed in an action for assault, even though he would have succeeded in an action for breach of contract. The defect of the common law remedy in contract is that the plaintiff can merely recover the price of the ticket; he cannot insist on his right to remain on the land. However, if the contract is specifically enforceable in equity, e.g. by an injunction against wrongful interference with the licensee, the licensee has then a specific equitable right to remain on the land because an injunction will be granted to restrain a threatened revocation of the licence and also to restrain a wrongful revocation from being enforced.[73] Specific performance may also be granted before the licensee has entered on the land, as it was where a local authority, after a change of political control, repudiated an agreement for the hire of a hall for a two-day conference of the National Front.[74] Equity may thus protect the licensee effectively, at least before and during the period of the licence. Even if the licensee cannot seek an equitable remedy until afterwards, the fact that it was due to him at the time of the wrongful revocation may entitle him to sue for assault if ejected.[75]

However, what is the position if equity will not assist the licensee so that **34-010** the matter falls to be dealt with at common law? In one case, the owners of two schools agreed to share premises owned by one of them, and after revocation of the licence the licensee re-entered forcibly. The Court of Appeal held that he was a trespasser, even if the revocation was a breach of contract.[76] Equity would not assist him, since "the court cannot specifically enforce an agreement for two people to live peaceably under the same roof".[77] This affirmed the old doctrine that at common law a licensor had a power to eject his licensee even if it transpired that he had no right to do so. Shortly afterwards this doctrine was repudiated in the House of Lords, but only in a

---

[71] PEA 1977 s.5(1B) (added by HA 1988 s.32). For "excluded licences", see PEA 1977 s.3A; above, para.34-001.

[72] (1845) 13 M. & W. 838. Contrast *Feltham v Cartwright* (1829) 5 Bing.N.C. 569, where a contractual licence was held irrevocable after being acted upon (above, para.34-003, fn.28 and below para.34-012), and *Butler v Manchester-Sheffield & Lincolnshire Ry* (1888) 21 QBD 207, where the Court of Appeal allowed an action for assault to a ticket-holder who was wrongfully turned off a railway train.

[73] *Winter Garden Theatre (London) Ltd v Millennium Productions Ltd* [1946] 1 All E.R. 678 at 684 (reversed on other grounds, below) per Lord Greene M.R.; and see *Errington v Errington* [1952] 1 K.B. 290; *Hounslow LBC v Twickenham Garden Developments Ltd* [1971] Ch. 233. This is an equitable right to *remain*, not an equitable interest in the land.

[74] *Verrall v Great Yarmouth Borough Council* [1981] Q.B. 202, rejecting the contention that specific performance is not granted for short lettings. It is not clear why an injunction was not the more suitable remedy.

[75] This appears to be the explanation of *Hurst v Picture Theatres Ltd* [1915] 1 K.B. 1 (successful action for assault by ticket-holder ejected from cinema).

[76] *Thompson v Park* [1944] K.B. 408; (interlocutory injunction against licensee granted).

[77] *Thompson v Park*, above, at 409, per Goddard L.J.

case where the question did not really arise, for it was held that the contract impliedly permitted revocation of the licence.[78]

Since then the Court of Appeal has adopted the views of the House of Lords, though again in a case where the question did not arise since the licensee was entitled to the assistance of equity and was granted an order of specific performance when the licensor purported to revoke the licence.[79] The judicial consensus is now to the effect that a licensor has no right to eject a licensee in breach of contract, even where equity will not assist the licensee, and that if he does so forcibly the licensee can sue for assault.[80] It seems to follow that the licensor is equally liable for assault if he forcibly and in breach of contract resists the licensee's entry, though in most cases the licensee's natural remedy will be an injunction against the breach of contract. A licensor acting in breach of contract is himself unlikely to be awarded equitable remedies.[81]

34-011   *(c) Informal family arrangements.* In a number of cases of informal family arrangements the court has found an implied contract which prevented or restricted the revocation of a licence.[82] Where a man bought a house and installed his mistress and their children in it, the mistress having given up her rent-controlled flat, a contractual licence was inferred under which the mistress and children were entitled to retain the house so long as the children were of school age and reasonably required it.[83] Where a mother bought a house for her son and his wife, asking them to pay £7 per week, and the son deserted the wife, the court imputed a contractual licence under which the mother could not evict the wife provided that she made the stipulated payments and that nothing occurred to justify revocation of the licence, a proviso which the court did not further explain.[84] It was admitted that the parties never in fact formed the intention imputed to them: the contractual licence was employed as a flexible device for achieving an equitable result. But the mere fact that a man

---

[78] *Winter Garden Theatre (London) Ltd v Millennium Productions Ltd* [1948] A.C. 173, per Lord Simon, holding that the mere contract gives the licensee a right to remain. The licence was for the use of a theatre for the production of plays. Lord Simon's explanation of *Wood v Leadbitter*, above, was not accepted by Lord Porter. Lord Porter and Lord Uthwatt, however, speak only of cases where equity is available to assist the licensee.

[79] *Verrall v Great Yarmouth Borough Council*, above, disapproving *Thompson v Park*, above, and approving the comment on that case in the *Hounslow* case, above.

[80] As suggested in (1948) 64 L.Q.R. 57 (H.W.R.W.).

[81] *Hounslow LBC v Twickenham Garden Developments Ltd*, above (injunction against contractor remaining on building site refused). Contrast *Thompson v Park*, above (injunction granted to expel violent intruder). In each case the decision preserved the status quo: see the *Hounslow* case at 250.

[82] These cases date from the late 1970s. In a more recent decision, the court was reluctant to find such an implied contract: see *Coombes v Smith* [1986] 1 W.L.R. 808 at 814, 815.

[83] *Tanner v Tanner* [1975] 1 W.L.R. 1346. In fact, the plaintiff had been rehoused, and so was awarded damages. cf. *Chandler v Kerley* [1978] 1 W.L.R. 693 (mistress held to have contractual licence revocable on 12 months' notice). See also *Parker v Parker* [2002] EWCH 1846 (Ch), a dispute as to the occupation of the family home of the Earls of Macclesfield, where a term was implied that the licence could not be revoked save on giving two years' notice.

[84] *Hardwick v Johnson* [1978] 1 W.L.R. 683. See similarly *Re Sharpe* [1980] 1 W.L.R. 219, below, para.34-018.

installs his mistress and their child in a house will not give her an irrevocable licence if the court sees no reason for inferring that the arrangement was contractual.[85]

An irrevocable licence does not become revocable merely because the licensee harasses or obstructs the licensor or his successors in title, since the licensor should pursue his ordinary remedies in trespass or nuisance.[86] But grave misconduct may amount to a breach of an implied term in a contractual licence and so prevent the licensee from relying on equity to restrain revocation.[87]

2. No revocation of a licence acted upon. It has already been explained **34-012** that it is a long-established rule of the common law that a licence once acted upon (in the sense that the licensee has completed their use) cannot usually be revoked.[88]

> "If A gives authority to B for the doing of an act on A's land, and the act is done and completed, then, whatever be the strict description of the authority . . . it is, generally speaking at any rate, too late for A, who gave the authority, to complain of it."[89]

The principle which underlies this rule is similar to the equitable doctrine of proprietary estoppel.[90] It is unreasonable for B to incur expense in reliance upon A's licence, and for A then to revoke that licence and treat B as a trespasser.[91] Thus where A, with B's permission, lowers a river bank and diverts part of the flow of a river over a weir which he has constructed, that licence cannot be revoked so as to make A's conduct tortious.[92] Similarly, if B has an easement of light and permits A to build a wall against B's window, B cannot complain of the infringement of his right to light.[93] The doctrine may apply even where A has merely started to perform the act authorised by B and has not completed it.[94] The doctrine has been overlooked on occasions,[95] and

---

[85] *Horrocks v Forray* [1976] 1 W.L.R. 230 (gift of house intended but not effected because of conveyancing costs).

[86] *Williams v Staite* [1979] Ch. 291.

[87] *Brynowen Estates Ltd v Bairne* (1981) 131 N.L.J. 1212; and see *Williams v Staite*, above, at 298; *Hardwick v Johnson*, above, at 689, per Lord Denning M.R.

[88] Above, para.16–037."A licence executed is not countermandable, but only when it is executory": *Winter v Brockwell* (1807) 8 East 308 at 310, per Lord Ellenborough C.J.

[89] *Armstrong v Sheppard & Short Ltd* [1959] 2 Q.B. 384 at 399, per Lord Evershed M.R.

[90] For the differences between the two doctrines, see above, para.16–037.

[91] *Winter v Brockwell*, above, at 310.

[92] *Liggins v Inge* (1831) 7 Bing. 682.

[93] *Liggins v Inge*, above, at 693; *Armstrong v Sheppard & Short Ltd*, above, at 399, 400.

[94] *Winter Garden Theatre (London) Ltd v Millennium Productions Ltd* [1948] A.C. 173 at 194; *Hounslow LBC v Twickenham Garden Developments Ltd* [1971] Ch. 233 at 255.

[95] See the criticism of *Wood v Leadbitter* (1845) 13 M. & W. 838 in *Hounslow LBC v Twickenham Garden Developments Ltd* above, at 255.

instances are now more likely to be regarded as examples of the equitable doctrine of proprietary estoppel.

34–013   **3. Revocation restricted by estoppel.** The doctrine of proprietary estoppel has already been explained.[96] It has no necessary connection with the law of licences, though the converse was once thought to be true.[97] If A has a licence over B's land, and B encourages him to act to his detriment in the belief that he will acquire certain rights over B's property, an equity may arise in A's favour. One way in which the court may satisfy that equity arising by estoppel is by declaring A's licence to be irrevocable, either in perpetuity[98] or only on the occurrence of certain events[99] or only by giving an extended period of notice.[100]

Section 4. Licences and Third Parties

A. Transmission of the Benefit

34–014   Whether or not the benefit of a licence is assignable must depend upon the circumstances of its grant. If the licence was intended to be personal to the licensor it will not be assignable. This is clearly settled in relation to contractual licences: it is a matter of construction of the contract.[101] Even if the benefit is assignable, this may be subject to terms or limited to certain circumstances.[102] It is more difficult to see how a bare licence is capable of assignment. It is neither a contractual nor a proprietary right but only bare permission. In practice, any "assignment" of a bare licence may be better explained either as a renewal to the assignee of the licence,[103] or as a case where the permission given by the licensor was intended to include not only the original licensee but also his assigns.[104]

---

[96] Above, Ch.16.

[97] Above, paras 16–006, 16–037. Much of the confusion arose because many cases of proprietary estoppel grew out of situations where the claimant was already using the land as licensee and then events occurred which resulted in an equitable estoppel.

[98] *Plimmer v Mayor etc., of Wellington* (1884) 9 App.Cas. 699.

[99] *Inwards v Baker* [1965] 2 Q.B. 29 (licence for A to remain as long as he wished).

[100] *Parker v Parker*, above.

[101] See, e.g. *Clapman v Edwards* [1938] 2 All E.R. 507; *Shayler v Woolf* [1946] Ch. 320. An assignment of a contractual licence must be made in writing with notice to the licensor: see LPA 1925 s.136.

[102] *Donington Park Leisure Ltd v Wheatcroft & Son*, above, where the benefit of the licence was assignable only if respect of use of the whole of the burdened land.

[103] *E.R. Ives Investment Ltd v High* [1967] 2 Q.B. 379 at 404.

[104] Under the Contracts (Rights of Third Parties) Act 1999 s.1, it would be possible to ensure that the benefit of a contractual licence extended to a third party. On a related matter, it seems likely, but controversial, than a licensee (and hence an assignee of the benefit) can maintain a possession action against a trespasser—even though the licencee has no estate in the land, *Manchester Airport Plc v Dutton* [2000] Q.B. 133. Note the reservations expressed in *Mayor of London v Hall* [2010] EWCA Civ 817; [2011] 1 W.L.R. 504, per Lord Neuberger at 515–516.

B. Transmission of the Burden

1. General. In principle, the burden of a licence should not be transmissible   **34–015**
because it creates no interest in land.[105] This is certainly true of a bare licence
which, as has been explained, is "automatically determined by the death of the
licensor or by the assignment of the land over which the licence is exercised".[106] However the position of contractual licences historically has been
uncertain and calls for fuller explanation.

2. Contractual licences

(a) The orthodox position. The law for long set its face firmly against the   **34–016**
notion that a contractual licence could be binding upon the licensor's successors in title, on the principle that licences were personal transactions which
created no proprietary interests in land. A purchaser of the licensor's land
therefore had no concern with any mere licence, even when he bought with
express notice of it.[107] Thus, where a licence had been granted to sellers of
refreshments giving them the exclusive use of the refreshment rooms of a
theatre, a purchaser of the theatre was able to prevent an assignee of the
licensee from enforcing his rights, and the Court of Appeal held that the
proper remedy was in damages against the licensor.[108]

(b) Contractual licences as possible equitable interests. The first sign of a   **34–017**
different attitude appeared in *Errington v Errington*.[109] The Court of Appeal
held that a contractual licence for the occupation of a dwelling-house would
bind a person to whom the licensor left the house by will, and it was said that
a contractual licence could create an equitable interest in land which would
bind all persons except a purchaser without notice. Not only was this view
contrary to earlier House of Lords and Court of Appeal authority,[110] but the
creation of new equitable interests appears to have been prohibited by the Law

---

[105] Above, para.34–001. Licences coupled with an interest are of course a special case. The
licence is no more than ancillary to the proprietary interest. If the proprietary interest binds a
transferee of the land then so too does the licence.
[106] *Terunnanse v Terunnanse* [1968] A.C. 1086 at 1095, per Lord Devlin; above, para.34–003.
See too *Wallis v Harrison* (1838) 4 M. & W. 528 at 543, 544.
[107] *King v David Allen & Sons, Billposting Ltd* [1916] 2 A.C. 54 (agreement for licence to
display advertisements on a building held not binding on tenant to whom licensor later demised
the land); *Clore v Theatrical Properties Ltd*, below; cf. *Plimmer v Mayor etc., of Wellington*
(1884) 9 App.Cas. 699 at 714; contrast *Webb v Paternoster* (1619) Poph. 151, per Montague
C.J.
[108] *Clore v Theatrical Properties Ltd* [1936] 3 All E.R. 483.
[109] [1952] 1 K.B. 290; amplified in *Bendall v McWhirter* [1952] 2 Q.B. 466 at 474 et seq. and
repeated by Lord Denning M.R. in *Binions v Evans* [1972] Ch. 359; criticised in (1952) 68 L.Q.R.
337 (H.W.R.W.) and (1953) 69 L.Q.R. 466 (A.D. Hargreaves); approved in (1953) 16 M.L.R. 1
(G.C. Cheshire). cf. *Kelaghan v Daly* [1913] 2 I.R. 328, and contrast *Wallace v Simmers*, 1960
S.C. 225.
[110] *Daly v Edwardes* (1900) 83 L.T. 548; *King v David Allen & Sons, Billposting Ltd*, above;
Clore v Theatrical Properties Ltd, above. See too *Millennium Productions Ltd v Winter Garden
Theatre (London) Ltd* [1946] 1 All E.R. 678 at 680 ("a licence created by contract is not an
interest": per Lord Greene M.R.).

of Property Act 1925.[111] In *Errington*, a father bought a house, raising part of the money on mortgage, and allowed his son and daughter-in-law to live in it, saying that if they paid all the mortgage instalments the house would become theirs. Before the instalments had all been paid the father died, having by his will left the house to his widow. The widow failed in an action to recover the house, on the ground that it was occupied under a licence which was binding upon her. For reasons which are hard to understand, the court rejected the more orthodox argument that the transaction was actually a contract to convey the house on completion of the payments, which would have created an equitable proprietary interest (an estate contract) of a familiar type.[112]

34–018   (c) *Contractual licences and constructive trusts.* The next development arose from a Court of Appeal decision that a contractual licence could give rise to a constructive trust. The case in question concerned the purchaser of a cottage who had agreed in the contract to take it subject to a contractual licence previously granted by the vendor to an employee's widow, entitling her to live in it for life, the purchaser having paid a reduced price on that account. On those facts, it was relatively straightforward to hold on conventional principles that the purchaser had made himself a constructive trustee for the licensee.[113] However, this later developed into a broader proposition, one that was both innovative and unorthodox: namely, that "a contractual licence (under which a person has the right to occupy premises indefinitely) gives rise to a constructive trust, under which the legal owner is not allowed to turn out the licensee".[114] This second case did not itself involve successors in title, but it designated contractual licences as equitable interests which would necessarily bind successors according to the ordinary rules of registered and unregistered conveyancing. Consequently, this occurred in a third case where a man had bought a house with the aid of a loan from his aunt and had told her that she could live in it for so long as she liked. It was held that the aunt had an irrevocable licence until the loan was repaid and that this was binding upon the nephew's trustee in bankruptcy, "whether it be called a contractual licence or an equitable licence or an interest under a constructive trust".[115]

[111] s.4(1) (proviso); above, para.6–064. cf. (1988) 51 M.L.R. 226 at 229 (J. Hill).

[112] Above, para.15–052. A written contract would not have been necessary, since the taking of possession would at that time have amounted to part performance: see the fifth edition of this work at p.594. Nor would non-registration have mattered, for the plaintiff was not a purchaser. The court rejected this interpretation on the ground that there is no equitable interest where there is no obligation to complete the transaction. But this is contrary to well-recognised authority, e.g. in the case of options: see above, paras 15–062, 15–064. See the criticism of *Errington* in *National Provincial Bank Ltd v Ainsworth* [1965] A.C. 1175 at 1239, per Lord Upjohn and at 1251, per Lord Wilberforce; *Re Solomon* [1967] Ch. 573 at 585, per Goff J.

[113] *Binions v Evans* [1972] Ch. 359. Compare *Lyus v Prowsa Development Ltd* [19821 1 W.L.R. 1044, above, para.11–022, where this type of constructive trust is discussed.

[114] *D.H.N. Food Distributors Ltd v Tower Hamlets LBC* [1976] 1 W.L.R. 852 at 859 per Lord Denning M.R. (company occupying premises under irrevocable licence held entitled to full compensation for disturbance on compulsory acquisition by local authority on the ground (among others) that it owned an equitable interest).

[115] *Re Sharpe* [1980] 1 W.L.R. 219 at 224, per Browne-Wilkinson J.

The judge observed, with some understatement, that the law was "very confused and difficult to fit in with established equitable principles".[116]

(d) *Return to orthodoxy.* Fortunately, the Court of Appeal restored the law **34–019** to some semblance of principle. In *Ashburn Anstalt v Arnold*,[117] it held that a contractual licence did not create an interest in land. Although the court did not doubt the correctness of the actual decision in *Errington v Errington*,[118] it considered that the reasoning conflicted with earlier decisions of the House of Lords[119] and should not therefore be followed. The court also held that although a constructive trust might be imposed on a transferee of land in respect of an interest affecting that land which would not otherwise bind him, it would do so only where the transferee's conscience was affected.[120] The mere fact that land was conveyed "subject to" a right such as a contractual licence was not sufficient.[121] This has already been explained.[122] Although the comments in the *Ashburn* case were obiter,[123] they have been widely endorsed.[124] It has been said that the case "finally repudiated the heretical view that a contractual licence creates an interest in land capable of binding third parties"[125] and that it "put the quietus to the heresy that parties to a contractual licence necessarily become constructive trustees".[126]

3. Licences irrevocable by estoppel. If a contractual licence is a purely **34–020** personal right, then in principle the same should be true of a licence held to be irrevocable in satisfaction of an equity arising by proprietary estoppel.[127] It

---

[116] *Re Sharpe*, above, at 226, per Browne-Wilkinson J.

[117] [1989] Ch. 1 at 13 et seq. See [1988] C.L.J. 353 (A.J. Oakley); (1988) 104 L.Q.R. 175 (P. Sparkes); (1988) 51 M.L.R. 226 (J. Hill); [1988] Conv. 201 (MP. Thompson).

[118] [1952] 1 K.B. 290. The court offered three explanations of the case: [1989] Ch. 1 at 17.

[119] *Edwardes v Barrington* (1901) 85 L.T. 650; *King v David Allen & Sons, Billposting Ltd* [1916] 2 A.C. 54.

[120] [1989] Ch. 1 at 25.

[121] *Ashburn Anstalt v Arnold*, above. There will have to be "very special circumstances showing that the transferee of the property undertook a new liability to give effect to provisions for the benefit of third parties": *IDC Group Ltd v Clark* [1992] 1 E.G.L.R. 187 at 190, per Browne-Wilkinson V.C. (on appeal [1992] 2 E.G.L.R. 184). See too *Kewal Investments Ltd v Arthur Maiden Ltd* [1990] 1 E.G.L.R. 193 at 194; *Sparkes v Smart* [1990] 2 E.G.L.R. 245 at 249, 250; *Lloyd v Dugdale* [2001] EWCA Civ 1754 at para.52; (2001) 48 E.G. 129 (CS); *Chaudhary v Yavuz* [2011] EWCA Civ 1314.

[122] Above, paras 6–068, 11–022.

[123] The actual decision in the case (that a lease might exist in some circumstances without a term certain) has now been overruled: *Prudential Assurance Co Ltd v London Residuary Body* [1992] 2 A.C. 386; above, para.17–065. But see the impact of *Mexfield Housing Co-operative Ltd v Berrisford* [2011] UKSC 52, discussed at paras 17–068 et seq.

[124] See *Kewal Investments Ltd v Arthur Maiden Ltd*, above, at 194; *Canadian Imperial Bank of Commerce v Bello* (1991) 64 P. & C.R. 48 at 51, 52; *IDC Group Ltd v Clark*, above, at 189, 190; *Camden LBC v Shortlife Community Housing Ltd* (1992) 90 L.G.R. 358 at 373; *Nationwide Anglia BS v Ahmed* (1995) 70 P. & C.R. 381 at 387–389; *Lloyd v Dugdale*, above.

[125] *Camden LBC v Shortlife Community Housing Ltd*, above, at 373, per Millett J. See too *Nationwide Anglia BS v Ahmed*, above, at 389.

[126] *IDC Group Ltd v Clark*, above, at 189, per Browne-Wilkinson V.C. However, in eliminating one heresy, the courts may have created another: see (1997) 1 E.L.R. 437 at 451 (C.H.).

[127] Above, para.16–006. See [1991] Conv. 36 (G. Battersby). cf. *Habermann v Koehler* (1996) 73 P. & C.R. 515 at 520.

has already been explained that there has in the past been some confusion between the equity which arises by estoppel[128] and the right eventually conferred by the court in giving effect to that equity.[129] If the right so conferred is a property right, it will bind third parties if appropriately protected.[130] If however the right is merely a licence, it does not cease to be personal merely because the licensor loses his power to revoke it through the operation of proprietary estoppel.[131]

Section 5. Matrimonial Homes

34–021   **1. The short-lived "deserted wife's equity".** Another short-lived revolution in the law of licences was the appearance of the "deserted wife's equity". This was based around the notion of a "matrimonial" rather than a contractual licence.[132] Despite authority to the contrary,[133] it was held that a wife who had been deserted by her husband enjoyed an irrevocable licence to occupy the matrimonial home and that this was enforceable in equity against third parties, such as her husband's trustee in bankruptcy[134] or a purchaser with notice of her situation.[135] This right was held to be a "mere equity",[136] and not an equitable interest,[137] and to be determinable at the discretion of the court.[138] Unless otherwise agreed, it became revocable on divorce[139] or, apparently, on commission of a matrimonial offence by the wife.[140]

All this law, which was the subject of much criticism,[141] was summarily swept away by the House of Lords in 1965. The case was one where the

---

[128] That equity itself may bind third parties: above, paras 16–030, 16–032.

[129] Above, para.16–006.

[130] In registered land, this is likely to be, if at all, on the basis of discoverable actual occupation within the LRA 2002 Sch.3 para.2. See *Lloyd v Dugdale*, above, where the estoppel did not bind because of the absence of actual occupation under the old LRA 1925 s.70(1)(g). It is unlikely that the claimant will have had the forethought to have entered a Notice, although that would be advisable if the parties were in dispute and there was a danger that the landowner would transfer the estate before the estoppel claim was resolved.

[131] "Once the interest has come into existence, the fact that it arose by estoppel becomes irrelevant": [1991] Conv. 36 at 39 (G. Battersby). There is, however, scope for confusion, see *Parker v Parker*, above.

[132] See *Re Solomon* [1967] Ch. 573 at 581–586 (husband's undertaking to court not contractual).

[133] See *Thompson v Earthy* [1951] 2 K.B. 596; *Bradley-Hole v Cusen* [1953] 1 Q.B. 300 at 306.

[134] *Bendall v McWhirter* [1952] 2 Q.B. 466, per Denning L.J.

[135] *Ferris v Weaven* [1952] 2 All E.R. 233; *Street v Denham* [1954] 1 W.L.R. 624.

[136] See above, paras 8–012, 8–013.

[137] *Westminster Bank Ltd v Lee* [1956] Ch. 7; see (1955) 71 L.Q.R. 481 (R.E.M.); [1955] C.L.J. 158 (H.W.R.W.).

[138] *Jess B. Woodcock and Sons Ltd v Hobbs* [1955] 1 W.L.R. 152; *Churcher v Street* [1959] Ch. 251.

[139] *Vaughan v Vaughan* [1953] 1 Q.B. 762.

[140] *Wabe v Taylor* [1952] 2 Q.B. 735; but contrast *Short v Short* [1960] 1 W.L.R. 833.

[141] See (1952) 68 L.Q.R. 379 (REM.). See generally (1953) 16 M.L.R. 215 (O. Kahn-Freund); (1952) 16 Conv. (N.S.) 323 (F. R. Crane); (1953) 17 Conv. (N.S.) 440 (L. A. Sheridan); see also *Brennan v Thomas* [1953] V.L.R. 111; *Dickson v McWhinnie* [1958] S.R.(N.S.W.) 179 (a full survey); (1956) 72 L.Q.R. 477 (R.E.M.).

husband had deserted his wife and then conveyed the matrimonial home to a company, whereupon the company charged it to a bank as security for money owed. The House of Lords held that the bank could enforce its security and take possession of the property, and that the wife must vacate it.[142] It was made clear that a wife was not a licensee in her husband's house, and that if it was his sole property she had no sort of proprietary interest in it, even if she had been deserted. She had rights against her husband personally which flowed from her status as wife, and she might be able to obtain an injunction restraining him from dealing with the matrimonial home in a way which infringed these rights.[143] But she could enforce them against her husband alone, and not against his successors in title or other third parties.[144]

2. Statutory rights to occupy the matrimonial home. The collapse of the **34–022** "deserted wife's equity" admittedly left an unsatisfactory situation. The solution was to give statutory "matrimonial home rights"[145] to husbands and wives alike,[146] and now to civil partners.[147] These rights are more properly described as matrimonial rights than as licences, but arise automatically[148] from the fact of marriage[149] or civil partnership in cases where one spouse or civil partner is entitled[150] to the home and the other is not. This far-reaching change was effected by the Matrimonial Homes Act 1967. The legislation has now been recast in amended form in the Family Law Act 1996 as part of a statutory code that deals with the family home and domestic violence.[151] The

[142] *National Provincial Bank Ltd v Ainsworth* [1965] A.C. 1175, approving *Thompson v Earthy*, above, and overruling *Bendall v McWhirter*, above, *Street v Denham*, above, and *Jess B. Woodcock & Sons Ltd v Hobbs*, above.

[143] *Lee v Lee* [1952] 2 Q.B. 489. cf. *Short v Short* [1960] 1 W.L.R. 833.

[144] Of course, the wife might be entitled to a genuine proprietary interest in the property were she able to rely on the law of constructive and resulting trusts. But the deserted wife cases pre-dated *Pettitt v Pettitt* [1970] A.C. 777.

[145] This term was introduced by FLA 1996 s.30(2) instead of "rights of occupation" which had been used in the legislation which that Act replaced: see MHA 1983 s.1(1). See too FLA 1996 Sch.9 paras 11–15.

[146] It should be noted that although the legislation applies to both spouses, "its primary purpose was . . . to protect the occupational rights of the deserted wife, as the so-called equity of the deserted wife had done until that doctrine was disapproved": *Kashmir Kaur v Gill* [1988] Fam. 110 at 117, per Bingham L.J.

[147] Civil Partnership Act 2004.

[148] But they can be released: FLA 1996 Sch.4 para.5(1).

[149] Even if polygamous: FLA 1996 s.63(5).

[150] i.e. is entitled to occupy by virtue of a beneficial interest, contract or statute: FLA 1996 s.30(1). It will therefore include a right to occupy under either the Rent Acts or HA 1988 (see *Penn v Dunn* [1970] 2 Q.B. 686 at 692). Property held by the spouse or civil partner on trust is excluded unless he is also beneficially interested in it. In determining whether a spouse or civil partner is entitled to occupy a property, a right to possession which he has as mortgagee is disregarded: FLA 1996 s.54(1).

[151] For a discussion of the legislation, which is not without its difficulties, see *Wroth v Tyler* [1974] Ch. 30. In 1978 the Law Commission considered MHA 1967 and made recommendations for its amendment: Law Com. No.86, Book 2. These were enacted in the Matrimonial Homes and Property Act 1981. The legislation was consolidated by MHA 1983. The Law Commission recommended further changes in 1992: see Law Com. No.207, Pt IV. These were enacted in FLA 1996 Pt IV. These changes include the extension of occupation rights to cohabitants and former spouses, and former civil partners. However, such rights are not capable of binding a purchaser, unlike those of a spouse or civil partner.

purpose of the legislation is to confer on the spouse or civil partner "a judicially protected right of occupation".[152] The courts will not countenance its use for any ulterior purpose (e.g. to apply financial pressure to the other spouse or civil partner).[153]

34–023   *(a) Matrimonial home rights.* The statutory "matrimonial home rights" are given to a spouse or civil partner who either has no right to occupy the home by virtue of any estate, interest, contract or statute, or has only an equitable interest in it,[154] and does not have the legal fee simple or a legal term of years in it, either solely or jointly.[155] Thus if the husband is the sole owner, or if he holds the legal estate in trust for himself and his wife (or civil partner) jointly or in common, the wife (or civil partner) but not the husband has the statutory matrimonial home rights.

The statutory matrimonial home rights are the right:

> (i) not to be evicted or excluded from occupation; and

> (ii) to enter and occupy with leave of the court.[156]

These rights will be brought to an end only by:

> (i) the death of the other spouse or civil partner;

> (ii) the termination (otherwise than by death) of the marriage or civil partnership; or

> (iii) the determination of the spouse or civil partner's entitlement to occupy the property.[157]

34–024   However, the court has power to extend the statutory matrimonial home rights even after the termination of the marriage or civil partnership by death or otherwise,[158] in any case where it considers that in all circumstances it is just and reasonable to do so.[159] On the application of either spouse or civil partner,[160] the court has power to enforce those rights as against the other spouse or civil partner and may also in some way restrict or terminate that

---

[152] *Richards v Richards* [1984] A.C. 174 at 211, per Lord Scarman.

[153] *Barnett v Hassett* [1981] 1 W.L.R. 1385.

[154] FLA 1996 s.30(9) adds "or in its proceeds of sale". However, following the abolition of the doctrine of conversion by TLATA 1996 s.3(1), these words will be otiose except in relation to the two transitional situations excepted from that abolition: TLATA 1996 ss.3(2); 18(3). See above, para.12–006.

[155] FLA 1996 s.30(1), (9). Until MHA 1967 was amended by MPPA 1970 s.38, it protected only what Lord Denning M.R. memorably described as a "bare" wife, having no proprietary, contractual or statutory right in the home: *Gurasz v Gurasz* [1970] P. 11 at 17.

[156] FLA 1996 s.30(2).

[157] FLA 1996 ss.30(8), 3 1(8).

[158] FLA 1996 s.33(5).

[159] FLA 1996 s.33(8).

[160] See FLA 1996 s.33(1)(a).

other spouse or civil partner's rights of occupation.[161] In deciding whether to exercise its discretion, the court is required to have regard to all the circumstances including the housing needs and resources of each party and any relevant child,[162] the financial resources of each spouse or civil partner, and the likely effect of any order (or decision not to make an order) on the health and well-being of the parties and on any relevant child.[163]

The provisions of the Family Law Act 1996 may apply to any dwelling house which either is or at any time has been the home of the person having the matrimonial home rights and the other spouse or civil partner, or was intended by them to be their home.[164] Where the matrimonial home is leasehold and one of the spouses or civil partners is the tenant, the extent to which he can determine the tenancy so as to deprive the other spouse or civil partner of her occupation is not finally settled. Thus one spouse or civil partner's occupation is treated as that of the other for the purposes of the Rent Act 1977 and the Housing Act 1988,[165] and it has been held that a tenant cannot validly surrender a tenancy protected under the Rent Act so as to defeat the rights of the other spouse or civil partner.[166] By contrast, a surrender by a tenant of a contractual tenancy under the Housing Act 1985 was effective as against her spouse.[167]

(b) Successors in title. Successors in title may be bound by these matrimonial home rights, but only where the owning spouse or civil partner's rights are founded on an estate or interest, as opposed to a contract or statute.[168] In that case, the non-owning spouse or civil partner's rights are a charge on the estate or interest and have "the same priority as if it were an equitable interest" created on January 1, 1968, on marriage or civil partnership, or on

34–025

---

[161] FLA 1996 s.33(3).

[162] For the meaning of "relevant child", see FLA 1996 s.62(2).

[163] FLA 1996 s.33(6). The court must make an order if it appears that the applicant or any relevant child is likely to suffer significant harm attributable to the conduct of the other spouse or civil partner if such an order is not made: FLA 1996 s.33(7).

[164] FLA 1996 s.33(1)(b). A person may therefore have matrimonial home rights in more than one property, including a property that was acquired as a common home even though the parties never lived there, e.g. because the relationship terminated before they could move in. This is a change in the law (cf. MHA 1983 s.1(10)) and implements a recommendation in (1992) Law Com. No.207 para.4.4. The Act does not apply to a property that never was nor was ever intended to be a matrimonial home: FLA 1996 s.30(7).

[165] See FLA 1996 s.30(4). For the protection conferred by RA 1977 and HA 1988, see below, paras 22–069 et seq.

[166] This was a common law rule: see *Old Gate Estates Ltd v Alexander* [1950] 1 K.B. 311; *Penn v Dunn* [1970] 2 Q.B. 686 at 691; *Hoggett v Hoggett* (1979) 39 P. & C.R. 121. The authorities are reviewed in *Hall v King* (1987) 55 P. & C.R. 307 at 309, 310; *Griffiths v Renfree* [1989] 2 E.G.L.R. 46 at 48, 49.

[167] *Sanctuary Housing Association v Campbell* [1999] 1 W.L.R. 1279, distinguishing *Hoggett v Hoggett*, above, and casting doubt on the common law authorities cited in the previous note on which it was based. For secure tenancies under HA 1985, see below, paras 22–207 et seq.

[168] FLA 1996 s.31(1). Rights under a contract for sale or lease, which creates an equitable interest, ought in principle to count as an interest rather than as a contract, but the position is not clear.

the acquisition of the estate or interest, whichever is the latest.[169] The charge is registrable, but may not amount to an interest which overrides in registered land.[170] It follows that, so long as the owning spouse or civil partner is alive, the marriage or civil partnership lasts or the rights are extended by court notwithstanding the termination of the marriage or civil partnership by death or otherwise,[171] the non-owning spouse or civil partner can enforce the charge against third parties,[172] provided that, in the case of a purchaser, it has been duly registered.[173] However in exercising its discretion, the court is entitled to take into account the circumstances of the purchaser,[174] and may decline to make an order against him.[175] Successors in title may in any event apply to the court to have the spouse or civil partner's rights of occupation restricted or terminated in the same manner as may the owning spouse or civil partner.[176] Where the spouse or civil partner's rights extend to two or more dwelling-houses, they are registrable as a charge against only one of them at any one time. If they have been registered against more than one property, only the last registration may stand.[177]

34–026   *(c) Bankruptcy of the owning spouse or civil partner.* Where a spouse or civil partner's matrimonial home rights exist prior to the bankruptcy of the owning spouse or civil partner,[178] they will bind his trustee in bankruptcy,[179] and any application for an order under the Family Law Act 1996 must be made to the bankruptcy court.[180] On such an application,[181] the court is

---

[169] FLA 1996 s.31(2), (3). "The charge seems to be neither legal nor equitable, but a pure creature of statute, with a priority (though not a nature) defined by reference to equity": *Wroth v Tyler* [1974] Ch. 30 at 43, per Megarry J.

[170] Where title is unregistered, it is registrable as a Class F land charge: above, para.8–107. Where title is registered, it is registrable as an agreed notice: FLA 1996 s.31(10)(a) and LRR 2003 r.80; above para.7–070. As noted, the charge cannot take effect as an overriding interest, FLA 1996 s.31(10)(b) (as amended by LRA 2002 Sch.11 para.33(4)).

[171] FLA 1996 ss.31(8), 33(5).

[172] FLA 1996 s.3 1(9) also protects it against merger, e.g. where the owning spouse or civil partner acquires the freehold of a leasehold home.

[173] A spouse or civil partner not in occupation may register effectively: *Watts v Waller* [1973] Q.B. 153. The right of one spouse or civil partner to enforce a right of occupation against *the other* is not dependent on registration: *Hoggett v Hoggett* (1979) 39 P. & C.R. 121 at 127.

[174] FLA 1996 ss.33(6), 34. The court has power to make an order under s.33 against a successor in title of the owning spouse or civil partner if it considers that it is just and reasonable to do so: FLA 1996 s.34(2).

[175] *Kashmir Kaur v Gill* [1988] Fam. 110; [1988] C.L.J. 355 (C.H.). cf. [1988] Conv. 295 (M. Welstead). The decision is in effect codified by FLA 1996 s.34(2).

[176] FLA 1996 s.34; *Kashmir Kaur v Gill*, above.

[177] FLA 1996 Sch.4 para.2.

[178] Matrimonial home rights cannot be acquired in the period between the presentation of a bankruptcy petition against an owning spouse or civil partner until the time when his estate vests in his trustee in bankruptcy, if the matrimonial home is part of the bankrupt's estate: IA 1986 s.336(1) (as amended by FLA 1996 Sch.8 para.57).

[179] Formerly the charge was void against the trustee: MHA 1983 s.2(7) (repealed by IA 1985 s.235(3); Sch.10).

[180] IA 1986 s.336(2) (as amended by FLA 1996 Sch.8 para.57).

[181] Which may be made by the other spouse or civil partner, or by the owning spouse or civil partner's trustee in bankruptcy. The trustee has the right to apply because he derives title under the owning spouse or civil partner: FLA 1996 s.34.

required to make such order as it thinks just and equitable having regard to a number of factors including "all the circumstances of the case other than the needs of the bankruptcy".[182] Once a year has elapsed since the vesting of the bankrupt's estate, the court is required to assume, unless the circumstances of the case are exceptional, that the interests of the bankrupt's creditors outweigh all other considerations.[183] The trustee in bankruptcy is therefore likely to apply to have any rights of occupation terminated so that the matrimonial home can be sold.[184]

(d) *Conveyancing implications.* The power to register a charge naturally **34–027** makes it possible for the non-owning spouse or civil partner to impede the owning spouse or civil partner should they wish to deal with the property, even if the non-owner is in no danger of being left homeless and merely objects to moving. However, notice of the registration of a charge is always served on the registered proprietor[185] and thus there is now considerably less risk of the non-owner registering a charge without the knowledge of the owner and so rendering the owner liable in damages by frustrating a prior contract of sale.[186] In fact, the vast majority of these charges are in practice left unregistered, so that the conveyancing goes forward on the curious basis of the mass invalidation of the charges for want of registration.[187] It appears that the registration of adverse interests in relation to the matrimonial home is regarded as inappropriate and, consequently, in the words of a former Master of the Rolls, "precious little use".[188]

[182] IA 1986 s.336(4) (as amended by FLA 1996 Sch.8 para.57).

[183] IA 1986 s.336(5). See, e.g. *Re Bremner* [1999] 1 F.L.R. 912. cf. above, para.13–072. The interpretation of "exceptional circumstances" in this provision is regarded as the same as that in IA 1986 s 335(A) and s 337, *Hosking v Michaelides* [2006] B.P.I.R. 1192. *Everitt v Budhram* [2009] EWHC 1219 (Ch), [2010] Ch. 170. See also *Martin-Sklan v White* [2006] EWHC 3313 (Ch). Note the criticisms made in *Barca v Mears* [2005] 2 F.L.R. 1 of the mechanical application of this rule, especially in relation to potential transgression of rights protected under the Human Rights Act 1998. But such criticism has been dismissed, *Nicholls v Lan* [2006] EWHC 1255 (Ch), [2007] 1 F.L.R. 744; *Foyle v Turner* [2007] B.P.I.R. 24; *Turner v Avis* [2009] 1 F.L.R. 74. See also para.13–072.

[184] Note the effect of the Enterprise Act 2000 s.261, inserting s.283A into the IA 1986, and providing that the trustee's interest in a dwelling house which at the date of bankruptcy was occupied by the bankrupt, bankrupt's spouse or former spouse as the principal residence, shall terminate (subject to exceptions specified in s.283A(3)) at the end of three years beginning with the date of bankruptcy. The point is to ensure that assets are realised quickly so that the bankruptcy can be brought to an end.

[185] This was not the case under the LRA 1925, see Ruoff & Roper, release 24 at 39–11.

[186] See under the LRA 1925, *Watts v Waller*, above; *Wroth v Tyler* [1974] Ch. 30. Where rights of occupation have been registered and the owning spouse or civil partner then contracts to sell the house with vacant possession, it is an implied term of the contract that he will procure the cancellation of that charge prior to completion: FLA 1996 Sch.4 para.3.

[187] See *Wroth v Tyler*, above, at 46. For the conveyancing implications of the decision, see (1974) 38 Conv. (N.S.) 110 (D.J. Hayton). In practice most spouses or civil partners will rely for their protection on the beneficial interest that they will commonly have in the home. It is not unknown for spouses or civil partners in that position also to frustrate a contract of sale by virtue of their interests: see *Watts v Spence* [1976] Ch. 165.

[188] *Williams & Glyn's Bank Ltd v Boland* [1979] Ch. 312 at 328, per Lord Denning M.R. See too at 339, per Ormrod L.J., pointing out that registration is an essentially hostile proceeding, not well suited to married couples living on good terms.

CHAPTER 35

ADVERSE POSSESSION AND LIMITATION

Part 1

GENERAL PRINCIPLES

35–001   **1. Limitation and prescription.** "Limitation" means the extinction of stale claims and obsolete titles. Rights of action are limited in point of time, and are lost if not pursued within due time. Some principle of this kind is necessary to every system of law. In English law it depends wholly on statute, because limitation was unknown to the common law. Different periods of limitation have been laid down for different kinds of action. In relation to unregistered land (for which the period is now in general 12 years) it is in the public interest that a person who has long been in undisputed possession should be able to deal with the land as owner.[1] It is more important that an established and peaceable possession should be protected than that the law should assist the agitation of old claims.[2] A statute which effects this purpose is "an act of peace. Long dormant claims have often more cruelty than of justice in them".[3]

Limitation also fulfils another important function. It facilitates the investigation of title to unregistered land.[4] Possession is the root of unregistered title, such title is relative, and the owner is the person who has the best right to possess the land.[5] Adverse possession extinguishes earlier rights to possess

[1] cf. *Harrow LBC v Qazi* [2003] UKHL 43 at [124]; [2004] 1 A.C. 983 at 1024. The position in relation to registered land is different, see below, paras 35–070—35–071.
[2] *Cholmondeley v Lord Clinton* (1820) 2 Jac. & W. 1 at 140; (1821) 4 Bli. 1 at 106; *Manby v Berwicke* (1857) 3 K. & J. 342 at 352.
[3] *A'Court v Cross* (1825) 3 Bing. 329 at 332, per Best C.J. See too *Cave v Robinson Jarvis & Rolf* [2002] UKHL 18 at [6]; [2003] 1 A.C. 384 at 390.
[4] See [1985] Conv. 272 (M. Dockray).
[5] See above, paras 4–007, 4–008.

and thereby reduces the period of title which an intending purchaser must investigate. That period of title, at present 15 years,[6] is directly related to the limitation period and this has long been the case.[7] The statutes of limitation have therefore provided "a kind of qualified guarantee that any possible outstanding claims to ownership by third parties are time-barred".[8]

It should be noted at the outset that a person who has been in adverse possession of unregistered land for the limitation period does not just bar the right of action for its recovery. He extinguishes the landowner's title.[9]

There is far less justification for permitting the acquisition of rights by adverse possession where the title to land is registered.[10] The register, and not possession, is the basis of title to registered land.[11] The identity of the owner appears from the register and there is generally no need to quiet titles. Adverse possession runs counter to the principle of the indefeasibility of a registered title[12] and can only be justified in limited circumstances.[13] Although it has been held by the Grand Chamber of the Court of Human Rights that the application to registered land of the same principles of adverse possession as apply to unregistered land does not contravene the European Convention on Human Rights,[14] the law has now been changed. The Land Registration Act 2002 introduced a completely new system of adverse possession in relation to registered land, which was intended to reflect the differences between registered and unregistered land.[15]

Limitation must be distinguished from prescription, because although similar in result they are fundamentally different in principle. Prescription is primarily a common law doctrine, though extended by statute, by which certain incorporeal rights (such as easements and profits) can be acquired over the land of others.[16] Fundamentally it is a rule of evidence, leading to a presumption of a grant from the owner of the land and therefore of a title derived through him. Limitation is the antithesis of prescription and rests on

35–002

---

[6] LPA 1969 s.23, above, para.8–021.

[7] [1985] Conv. 272 at pp.278 et seq. (M. Dockray). See too S. Jourdan and O. Radley-Gardner, *Adverse Possession*, 2nd edn (London, Bloomsbury Professional, 2011), paras 3–21 et seq.

[8] [1985] Conv. 272 at 278.

[9] LA 1980 s.17; below, para.35–055. The same rule applies in relation to actions for the recovery of chattels: see LA 1980 s.3(2).

[10] A registered proprietor can only be divested of his legal title by an alteration of the register. Accordingly, the only right that a squatter can acquire in relation to registered land is a right to be registered as proprietor.

[11] See above, paras 7–025, 7–053, 7–115—7–117.

[12] See above, paras 7–001, 7–113 et seq.

[13] See (1998) Law Com. No.254, paras 10.11 et seq.

[14] See *J A Pye (Oxford) Ltd v UK* No.44302/02; (2007) 46 E.H.R.R. 1083 reversing the decision of the Court of Human Rights ([2005] 3 E.G.L.R. 1). The claim was made under Art.1 of Protocol 1 of the ECHR. The Grand Chamber held that the principles of adverse possession constituted a control of user of property but not a deprivation of possessions. The decision was applied by the Court of Appeal in *Ofulue v Bossart* [200] EWCA Civ 7; [2009] Ch. 1. See too, on appeal, [2009] UKHL 16 at [68]; [2009] A.C. 990 at 1016.

[15] See below, paras 35–070 et seq.

[16] Above, paras 28–032 et seq.

wrongful possession rather than on any presumption of right.[17] It is wholly statutory, and is concerned with the title to the land itself.

Where the title to the land is unregistered, limitation simply extinguishes a former owner's right to recover possession of the land, leaving some other person with a title based on adverse possession of the land. Prescription operates positively like a conveyance, whereas limitation operates negatively, by eliminating the claim of a person having a superior title, without any "parliamentary conveyance" or transfer from that person.[18] It has already been explained how this negative operation helps to reveal the possessory character of title to land at common law.[19]

Where title is registered, the contrast is less marked. In the limited circumstances in which a person in adverse possession may now be registered, he is substituted as registered proprietor in place of the previous registered proprietor.[20] There is, therefore, a parliamentary conveyance. This was equally true under the law prior to the Land Registration Act 2002.[21]

35–003   **2. Statutes of limitation.** Statutes of limitation have a long history. At first, periods of limitation were fixed from time to time in relation to particular events or dates of public knowledge, such as the death of Henry I, or the last voyage of Henry II into Normandy.[22] Ultimately the Statute of Westminster I 1275[23] laid down a prohibition against disputing rights enjoyed in 1189, a date that is still of significance in relation to prescription.[24] For two-and-a-half centuries this remained the law, so that there gradually ceased to be any effective system of limitation.

The modern type of limitation, which, instead of selecting fixed dates, sets a preclusive period to rights of action as from the time they arise, was introduced by a statute of 1540,[25] which fixed periods of 60 years or less for the various real actions.[26] In 1623 rights of entry were limited to 20 years,[27] and this period therefore governed the action of ejectment. A 20-year limitation period for actions for land generally was fixed by the Real Property Limitation Act 1833.[28] However, the period was reduced to 12 years by the Real Property Limitation Act 1874.[29] The earlier statutes were repealed by the

[17] *Buckinghamshire County Council v Moran* [1990] Ch. 623 at 644; *Sze To Chun Keung v Kung Kwok Wai David* [1997] 1 W.L.R. 1232 at 1235.
[18] Above, para.4–003.
[19] Above, Ch.4.
[20] LRA 2002 Sch.6, para.9; see below, para.35–087.
[21] See *Central London Commercial Estates Ltd v Kato Kagaku Ltd* [1998] 4 All E.R. 948; and para.21–058 of the sixth edition of this work.
[22] See, e.g. *Glanvill*, XIII, 32; ed. G.D.G. Hall, p.167.
[23] Chapter 39 forbade writs of right based on seisin obtained prior to 1189, and fixed 1216 and 1242 as the corresponding dates for other real actions.
[24] See above, para.28–044.
[25] 32 Hen. 8, c.2 (periods of 60, 50 and 30 years).
[26] See the historical sketch in *Bryant v Foot* (1867) L.R. 2 Q.B. 161 at 179–181, per Cockburn C.J.; and see P. & M. ii, 81.
[27] LA 1623.
[28] s.2.
[29] s.1.

Limitation Act 1939.[30] That Act was in turn amended by the Limitation Amendment Act 1980[31] and the law was then consolidated in the Limitation Act 1980.[32] As regards registered land, adverse possession of registered land is now dealt with by the Land Registration Act 2002 and certain provisions of the Limitation Act 1980 no longer apply to registered land.

The provisions of the Limitation Act 1980 will be treated in three sections:

(1) the length of the limitation period or the period of adverse possession;

(2) when time starts to run; and

(3) the effect of lapse of time.

The position of registered land under the Land Registration Act 2002 is dealt with separately at the end of the chapter. Although, in practice, most cases of adverse possession will be of registered land, the principles applicable are built on the traditional principles that continue to apply where the Land Registration Act 2002 is inapplicable, and which it is therefore more convenient to explain first. Furthermore, a number of the principles set out below apply equally where the title is registered. A summary is provided below as to which matters affect registered land.[33]

Part 2

THE LENGTH OF THE LIMITATION PERIOD OR PERIOD OF ADVERSE POSSESSION

1. Three main periods of limitation. The Limitation Act 1980 lays down three main periods of limitation which are relevant to the law of real property, except to the extent that they are disapplied by the Land Registration Act 2002.   **35–004**

(a) Six years. A period of six years applies for actions on simple contracts,[34] for arrears of rent[35] and on any judgment.[36] The same period applies to actions in tort,[37] except that a three-year period, subject to special provisions for extension, has been imposed for actions for personal injuries.[38]   **35–005**

---

[30] Based on the recommendations in Cmd. 5334 (1936).

[31] Based upon a report of the Law Reform Committee, Cmnd. 6923 (1977).

[32] Repealing the earlier Acts. It came into force on May 1, 1981: LA 1980 s.41(2). For the history of the history of limitation in England and Wales, see S. Jourdan and O. Radley-Gardner, *Adverse Possession*, 2nd edn, Ch.2.

[33] See para.35–072.

[34] LA 1980 s.5.

[35] LA 1980 s.19.

[36] LA 1980 s.24; see below, para.35–054.

[37] LA 1980 s.2.

[38] LA 1980 ss.11, 12, 33.

35–006   *(b) Specialties.* A period of 12 years applies for actions on a specialty.[39] A specialty includes a deed, such as a covenant contained in a conveyance or in a lease.[40] Although a specialty includes a statute,[41] an action to recover any sum recoverable by virtue of any enactment is barred after a period of six years.[42]

35–007   *(c) Land.* A period of 12 years applies in relation to an action brought to recover any unregistered land.[43] The same period is prescribed for the recovery of money charged on land, e.g. by a mortgage, or the proceeds of sale of land, as where trustees of land have exercised their power of sale.[44] "Land" for this purpose includes rentcharges and tithes, but not other incorporeal hereditaments such as profits à prendre.[45] It also includes any legal or equitable interest in land.[46]

In general, once time begins to run for the purposes of limitation, it will continue to do so unless the true owner brings an action to recover the disputed land.[47] For these purposes, an "action" refers to court proceedings[48] and does not include, for example, an application to the land registrar to cancel a caution against dealings.[49] Furthermore, the action must be brought to recover the disputed land.[50] It must therefore either seek possession or specifically raise the claimant's right to possession.[51] In principle it should include proceedings brought for a declaration that the claimant has a good title to the disputed land,[52] but it does not include court proceedings brought to

---

[39] LA 1980 s.8. The obligation must be created or secured by the specialty, not merely acknowledged or evidenced by it: *Re Compania de Electricidad de la Provincia de Buenos Aires Ltd* [1980] Ch. 146.

[40] Any contract made by deed will be a specialty for the purposes of s.8: see *Aiken v Stewart Wrightson Members Agency Ltd* [1995] 1 W.L.R. 1281 at 1291–1293. The duty of care imposed upon a mortgagee when exercising his power of sale (see above, para.25–018) is a duty implied by law and does not arise as a term implied into the mortgage deed. Accordingly, an action for breach of that duty is not an action on a specialty: see *Raja v Lloyds TSB Bank Plc* (2001) 82 P. & C.R. 191.

[41] *Cork & Brandon Ry v Goode* (1853) 13 C.B. 826.

[42] LA 1980 s.9(1). See, e.g. *Swansea CC v Glass* [1992] Q.B. 844.

[43] LA 1980 s.15. This does not apply to registered land: see LRA 2002 s.96(1).

[44] LA 1980 s.20(1). This section applies to charges over both registered and unregistered land.

[45] LA 1980 s.38(1).

[46] LA 1980 s.38(1).

[47] *Re Benzon* [1914] 2 Ch. 68 at 76; S. Jourdan and O. Radley-Gardner, *Adverse Possession*, 2nd edn, para.15–03.

[48] This includes proceedings before the Lands Tribunal: see *Hillingdon LBC v A.R.C. Ltd* [1999] Ch. 139 at 156. The implication from the remarks in that case is that it would include, e.g., proceedings before the Adjudicator to the Land Registry (for the Adjudicator, see above, para.7–130). This view is supported by *Chief Land Registrar v Tatnall* [2011] EWCA Civ 801 at [37]; [2011] 41 E.G. 116 at 121.

[49] *J A Pye (Oxford) Ltd v Graham* [2000] Ch. 676 at 699. Cautions against dealings were prospectively abolished by LRA 2002: see above, paras 7–007, 7–069.

[50] References in LA 1980 to a right of action to recover land are taken to include references to a right of entry (as where there is right of re-entry in relation to a conditional fee simple: see above, para.3–058): LA 1980 s.38(7).

[51] *J A Pye (Oxford) Ltd v Graham*, above, at 702.

[52] S. Jourdan and O. Radley-Gardner, *Adverse Possession*, 2nd edn, para.1–20.

remove a caution against dealings in the register of title.[53] The commencement of possession proceedings, in which, for whatever reason, no final judgment is given, has no effect on the running of time for the purposes of limitation.[54]

2. Registered land. Subject to transitional provisions,[55] no period of limitation applies to actions for the recovery of registered land.[56] A squatter may, however, apply to be registered as proprietor after a period of 10 years' adverse possession.[57] This is explained later.[58]   **35–008**

3. Limitation: special cases. Longer periods of limitation are provided in the following special cases.[59]   **35–009**

(a) Crown lands. For actions for the recovery of Crown lands the period is 30 years.[60] Before the Limitation Act 1939, it was 60 years,[61] a period which has been retained in the one case of foreshore owned by the Crown.[62] Claims by subjects to recover lands from the Crown are barred after the ordinary period of 12 years.[63]   **35–010**

(b) Corporations sole. The title of a spiritual or eleemosynary (*i.e.* charitable) corporation sole, such as a bishop, or the master of a hospital, is barred after 30 years.[64]   **35–011**

4. Reform. The Law Commission has recommended that the limitation period in actions for the recovery of unregistered land should be 10 years (in place of the present 12).[65] As regards such actions, it has recommended that the special periods that presently apply to Crown lands and corporations sole should cease to do so.[66]   **35–012**

---

[53] *J A Pye (Oxford) Ltd v Graham*, above, at 700–702. The same must be true of proceedings brought to cancel a caution against first registration under LRA 2002 s.18 (above, para.7–047).

[54] *Markfield Investments Ltd v Evans* [2001] 1 W.L.R. 1321 (where the first action for possession had been struck out for want of prosecution).

[55] See LRA 2002 Sch.12 para.18.

[56] LRA 2002 s.96(1).

[57] LRA 2002 Sch.6 para.1(1).

[58] See para.35–073.

[59] As regards the Provinces of Canterbury and York, there were formerly special periods of limitation for advowsons: see LA 1980 s.25, but these have ceased to have effect: Patronage (Benefices) Measure 1986 ss.1(2), 4(3), 42(2).

[60] LA 1980 Sch.1 para.10.

[61] Crown Suits Acts 1769, 1861, called the "Nullum Tempus Acts", from the maxim *nullum tempus occurrit regi*. LA 1623 had fixed 1564 as the limitation date for Crown actions.

[62] LA 1980 Sch.1 para.11.

[63] The Crown can acquire title to land by adverse possession, see *Roberts v Swangrove Estates Ltd* [2008] EWCA Civ 98; [2008] Ch. 439.

[64] LA 1980 Sch.1 para.10. For successors in title the rule is the same as for successors to Crown land: LA 1980 Sch.1. para.12.

[65] (2001) Law Com. No.270, para.4.135.

[66] (2001) Law Com. No.270, para.4.144.

Part 3

THE RUNNING OF TIME

35–013   In relation to limitation, which will now generally apply only to unregistered land (but with some exceptions), in order to find the moment when a right of action becomes barred, three questions must be considered: first, when time begins to run; secondly, what will postpone this date; and thirdly, what will start time running afresh.[67]

Section 1. When Time Begins to Run

35–014   In the case of actions for the recovery of either unregistered land or capital sums charged on land (whether registered or unregistered), time begins to run in accordance with the following rules.

1. Owner entitled in possession

35–015   *(a) Dispossession, discontinuance and adverse possession.*[68] When the owner of land is entitled in possession, time begins to run as soon as both:

> (i) the owner has been dispossessed, or has discontinued his possession[69]; and

> (ii) adverse possession has been taken by some other person.[70]

There will be a dispossession of the true owner in any case where, there being no discontinuance, a squatter assumes possession in the ordinary sense of the word.[71] Dispossession does not therefore require an ouster of the true owner.[72] Discontinuance occurs where the true owner abandons possession of the land.[73] It is thus not necessary that the owner should have been driven out of possession. If the owner abandons possession,[74] or if he dies and the person

---

[67] In general, once time has begun to run, it runs continuously: *Prideaux v Webber* (1661) 1 Lev. 31; *Rhodes v Smethurst* (1840) 6 M. & W. 351; but see *Bowring-Hanbury's Trustee v Bowring-Hanbury* [1943] Ch. 104, discussed at (1943) 59 L.Q.R. 117 (R.E.M.). Disability or fraud may postpone the date when time begins to run, and an acknowledgment or part payment may start time running afresh. There has been, however, one instance in which statutory provision was made for the running of time to be suspended for a period and then resumed: Limitation (Enemies and War Prisoners) Act 1945.

[68] S. Jourdan and O. Radley-Gardner, *Adverse Possession*, 2nd edn, paras 5–08—5–17.

[69] LA 1980 Sch.1 para.1.

[70] LA 1980 Sch.1 para.8.

[71] *J A Pye (Oxford) Ltd v Graham* [2002] UKHL 30 at [38]; [2003] 1 A.C. 419 at 434–5.

[72] *J A Pye (Oxford) Ltd v Graham* [2002] UKHL 30 at [38]; [2003] 1 A.C. 419 at 434–5.

[73] *Rimington v Cannon* (1853) 12 C.B. 18 at 33; *McDonnell v McKiniy* (1847) 10 Ir.L.R. 514 at 526; *Smith v Lloyd* (1854) 9 Exch. 526 at 572. Mere non-user is not enough: *Tecbild Ltd v Chamberlain* (1969) 20 P. & CR. 633.

[74] Abandonment will not however be lightly presumed, and the slightest acts done by the owner will negative discontinuance: *Powell v McFarlane* (1977) 38 P. & C.R. 452 at 472. Cases of abandonment are therefore uncommon. For a modern example, see *Red House Farms (Thorndon) Ltd v Catchpole* [1977] 2 E.G.L.R. 125.

next entitled (e.g., as devisee or remainderman) does not take possession, time will begin to run as soon as adverse possession is taken by another. What matters is not how the paper ceased to be in possession, but that some other person has taken possession that is adverse to his title. Until there is nobody against whom the owner is failing to assert his rights. Accordingly, nothing is likely to turn in practice on the distinction between dispossession and discontinuance.[75]

In the absence of concealed fraud, it is irrelevant that the owner is ignorant that he has been dispossessed.[76] Nor is there any requirement that adverse possession must be objectively apparent.[77] However, "it is hard to imagine cases where legal possession could be established without it being apparent to a properly-informed owner visiting the property at appropriate times in the 12-year period".[78]

(b) Adverse possession. Before 1833, "adverse possession" bore a highly **35–016** technical meaning.[79] Today it merely means possession inconsistent with and in denial of the title of the true owner,[80] and not, e.g. possession under a licence from him[81] or under some contract or trust.[82] There is a presumption that the owner of the land with the paper title is in possession of the land.[83] To establish adverse possession, a squatter must prove[84] that he had both factual possession of the land and the requisite intention to possess (*animus possidendi*).[85] If a person is in possession of land with the permission of the

[75] See *Buckinghamshire CC v Moran* [1990] Ch. 623 at 644; S. Jourdan and O. Radley-Gardner, *Adverse Possession*, 2nd edn, paras 5–19– 5–21.

[76] *Powell v McFarlane* (1977) 38 P. & C.R. 452 at 480.

[77] See *Prudential Assurance Co Ltd v Waterloo Real Estate Inc* [1999] 2 E.G.L.R. 85 at 87; *Purbrick v Hackney LBC* [2003] EWHC 1871 (Ch) at [27], [28]; [2004] 1 P. & C.R. 553 at 561; *Wretham v Ross* [2005] EWHC 1259 (Ch) at [23]–[33].

[78] *Wretham v Ross* [2005] EWHC 1259 (Ch) at [31], per David Richards J. cf. *Roberts v Swangrove Estates Ltd* [2007] EWHC 513 (Ch) at [40]; [2007] 2 P. & C.R. 326 at 339, where Lindsay J. suggested that the squatter's possession should be such that, "if the owner were present on the land, he would appreciate that the squatter was dispossessing him".

[79] See Lightwood, *Time Limit on Actions*, p.6; Lightwood, *Possession*, p.180; *J A Pye (Oxford) Ltd v Graham* [2002] UKHL 30 at [33]–[36]; [2003] 1 A.C. 419 at 433–4. Thus before RPLA 1833 possession by a younger brother was deemed possession by the heir (Co.Litt. 242a); possession by one co-owner was deemed possession by all; possession by a tenant at will or at sufferance was deemed possession by the lessor.

[80] *Wilson v Martin's Exors* [1993] 1 E.G.L.R. 178 at 179, 180; *Ramnarace v Lutchman* [2001] UKPC 25 at [10]; [2001] 1 W.L.R. 1651 at 1654; *Ashe v National Westminster Bank Plc* [2008] EWCA Civ 55 at [54]–[58]; [2008] 1 W.L.R. 710, at 720. LA 1980 Sch.1 para.8(1) requires merely possession by "some person in whose favour the period of limitation can run". Adverse possession is not further defined by the Act.

[81] *Hughes v Griffin* [1969] 1 W.L.R. 23; *Buckinghamshire County Council v Moran* [1990] Ch. 623 at 636. Contrast the position of a tenant at will, below, para.35–032.

[82] *Hyde v Pearce* [1982] 1 W.L.R. 560 (purchaser in possession under contract of sale for 14 years: possession not adverse since referable to the contract).

[83] *Powell v McFarlane* (1977) 38 P. & C.R. 452 at 470. This includes the strata below the surface of the land: *Bocardo SA v Star Energy UK Onshore Ltd* [2010] UKSC 35; at [31]; [2011] 1 A.C. 380 at 399.

[84] The burden of proof is on him: see *Powell v McFarlane*, above at pp.470, 472.

[85] *Buckinghamshire County Council v Moran*, above, at 636; *Marsden v Miller* (1992) 64 P. & C.R. 239 at 242, 243; *J A Pye (Oxford) Ltd v Graham* [2002] UKHL 30 at [40], [74]; [2003] 1 A.C. 419 at 435, 447.

true owner, his possession cannot be adverse.[86] That permission may be expressly given or it may be implied. The circumstances in which it will be implied have not yet been finally determined.[87] There is a line of authority in which it has been held that:

(i) For there to be such an implication, there had to be some overt act by the landowner or some demonstrable circumstance from which it can be inferred that permission was given.

(ii) It was immaterial whether the squatter was aware of these matters but they must be probative of and not merely consistent with the giving of permission.

(iii) They had also to be such that a reasonable person would have appreciated that the user was with the permission of the landowner.[88]

However, these cases rested upon a dictum in a decision on a prescriptive claim,[89] subsequently discredited on appeal to the House of Lords,[90] which had equated passive acquiescence with permission. Accordingly, it has been contended (but not decided) that permission requires a communication to the licensee, whether by writing, spoken words or conduct, that was intended to be and was understood as permission to do what would otherwise be trespass.[91] Nevertheless, the propositions set out above have been accepted as a correct statement of the law.[91a]

Possession with permission, which can never be adverse, is quite different from possession in which the landowner acquiesces, which may be adverse.[92] Whether or not permission once given has been revoked is a factual question. If a licence is given for a fixed period or until the occurrence of an event, possession may become adverse after that period has passed or the event has occurred.[93] If permission is given indefinitely, but subject to conditions,

---

[86] See, e.g. *Moses v Lovegrove* [1952] 2 Q.B. 533 at 540, 544; *Smith v Lawson* (1997) 74 P. & C.R. D34.

[87] See S. Jourdan and O. Radley-Gardner, *Adverse Possession*, 2nd edn, paras 35–20 et seq.

[88] *London Borough of Lambeth v Rumbelow* Unreported, January 25, 2001, per Etherton J.; applied in *Colin Dawson Windows Ltd v King's Lynn & West Norfolk Borough Council* [2005] EWCA Civ 9; at [34] [2005] 2 P. & C.R. 333 at 343; and *Batsford Estates (1983) Co Ltd v Taylor* [2005] EWCA Civ 489 at [22], [23]; [2005] 2 E.G.L.R. 12 at 15; *Hicks Developments Ltd v Chaplin* [2007] EWHC 141 (Ch) at [33]; [2007] 1 E.G.L.R. 1.

[89] *R. (Beresford) v Sunderland City Council* [2001] 1 W.L.R. 1327 at 1340, [43] (claim that land was a town or village green).

[90] [2003] UKHL 60; [2004] 1 A.C. 889; above, para.27–053.

[91] See *J Alston & Sons Ltd v BOCM Pauls Ltd* [2008] EWHC 3310 (Ch) at [121]–[133]; [2009] 1 E.G.L.R. 93 at 103, 104.

[91a] *Zarb v Parry* [2011] EWCA Civ 1306 at [26] and [65].

[92] *Hicks Developments Ltd v Chaplin*, above, at [33].

[93] See, e.g. *J A Pye (Oxford) Ltd v Graham* [2002] UKHL 30; [2003] 1 A.C. 419; *Sandhu v Farooqui* [2003] EWCA Civ 531 at [20]; [2004] 1 P. & C.R. 19 at 25; *Topplan Estates Ltd v Townley* [2004] EWCA Civ 1369; [2005] 1 E.G.L.R. 89.

possession remains permissive while those conditions continue to be met.[94] Where the terms of the licence have to be implied, it may be an implied term that the licence continues until one party gives notice of its termination.[95]

The principles which determine whether conduct amounts to adverse possession were affirmed by the House of Lords in *J A Pye (Oxford) Ltd v Graham*,[96] largely in accordance with "a remarkable judgment"[97] given in *Powell v McFarlane*.[98] In *Pye*, the House held that, where licensees remained in possession of grazing land for more than 12 years after the expiry of their licence, they had acquired title to the land by adverse possession, because they were in factual possession and shown the requisite intention.

Once adverse possession is established, the true owner's cause of action accrues and continues to be treated as accrued unless the land ceases to be in adverse possession.[99] Adverse possession will cease where:

   (i) the squatter vacates the property;

   (ii) the squatter gives a written acknowledgment of the owner's title (which causes time to run afresh)[100];

   (iii) the true owner grants the squatter a licence or tenancy (as explained above);

   (iv) the paper brings an action for possession against the squatter[101]; or

   (v) the true owner re-takes possession of the property.[102]

(1) FACTUAL POSSESSION. "Possession is a legal concept which depends on **35–017** the performance of overt acts",[103] For a squatter to prove that he has factual possession he must show that:

   (i) he had an appropriate degree of physical control of the land;

   (ii) his possession was a single possession: there can be a single possession by several squatters jointly, but not severally[104];

---

[94] See, e.g. *Trustees of Grantham Christian Fellowship v The Scout Association Trust Corporation* [2005] EWHC 209 (Ch); [2005] P.L.S.C.S. 63 (indefinite permission to use land on condition that the licensee cut the grass and kept the land tidy).

[95] *Sandhu v Farooqui* [2003] EWCA Civ 531; [2004] 1 P. & C.R. 19 (entry into possession under a contract of sale that was never completed was not adverse as no notice of termination of the licence was given, even though it was clear that the sale would never be completed).

[96] [2002] UKHL 30; [2003] 1 A.C. 419.

[97] *J A Pye (Oxford) Ltd v Graham*, above, at [31]; p.432, per Lord Browne-Wilkinson.

[98] (1977) 38 P. & C.R. 452, Slade J. The principles can be traced to Pollock & Wright, *Possession*, pp.28–35.

[99] *Markfield Investments Ltd v Evans* [2001] 1 W.L.R. 1321 at 1324.

[100] See below, para.35–051.

[101] See above, para.35–007.

[102] *Markfield Investments Ltd v Evans*, above, at 1324.

[103] *Simpson v Fergus* (1999) 79 P. & C.R. 398 at 402, per Robert Walker L.J.

[104] See, e.g., *Brazil v Brazil* [2005] EWHC 584 (Ch).

(iii) his possession was exclusive[105]: a squatter cannot be in possession at the same time as the true owner[106]; and

(iv) he dealt with the land in question as an occupying owner might have been expected to deal with it and no-one else has done.[107]

35–018   Whether the squatter has taken a sufficient degree of control is a matter of fact, depending on all the circumstances, in particular the nature of the land and the manner in which such land is commonly enjoyed.[108] "The type of conduct which indicates possession must vary with the type of land."[109] In the case of open land, absolute physical control is normally impracticable.[110] There are obvious difficulties in establishing a squatter's title to part of a swamp[111]; but where marshy land is virtually useless except for shooting, shooting over it may amount to adverse possession.[112] In many cases adverse possession cannot in the nature of things be continuous from day to day.[113] "Enclosure is the strongest possible evidence of adverse possession, but is not indispensable",[114] nor is it necessarily conclusive.[115] But where the adverse possessor performs clear acts of ownership, he does not have to show that they

---

[105] If a squatter deliberately exclude himself from part of the land which he claims because of a dispute with some person other than the true owner, that interruption may defeat his claim to adverse possession of that part: *Generay Ltd v The Containerised Storage Ltd* [2005] EWCA Civ 478; [2005] 2 E.G.L.R. 7. Time would run afresh from the resumption of possession.

[106] Accordingly, the squatter must do some act to exclude the true owner: *Sava v SS Global Ltd* [2008] EWCA Civ 1308 at [72]–[75].

[107] *Powell v McFarlane*, above at 470, 471; *J A Pye (Oxford) Ltd v Graham* [2002] UKHL 30 at [41]; [2003] 1 A.C. 419 at 436.

[108] *Powell v McFarlane*, above, at 471. For a detailed treatment, see S. Jourdan and O. Radley-Gardner, *Adverse Possession*, 2nd edn, Chs.12, 13. Trivial acts will rarely suffice to establish adverse possession: see, e.g. *Boosey v Davis* (1987) 55 P. & C.R. 83 (occasional grazing of goats and clearance of scrub); *Pavledes v Ryesbridge Properties Ltd* (1989) 58 P. & C.R. 459 (parking of cars on a small scale on a large site); *Wilson v Martin's Exors* [1993] 1 E.G.L.R. 178 (cutting timber and repairing fences).

[109] *Wuta-Ofei v Danquah* [1961] 1 W.L.R. 1238 at 1243, per Lord Guest. See too *Lord Advocate v Lord Lovat* (1880) 5 App.Cas. 273 at 288; *West Bank Estates Ltd v Arthur* [1967] 1 A.C. 665 at 678; *Powell v McFarlane*, above, at 470, 471.

[110] *Powell v McFarlane*, above, at 471. Acts of possession undertaken on parts of a piece of land to which possessory title is claimed, may be evidence of possession of the whole: *Higgs v Nassauvian Ltd* [1975] A.C. 464 at 474.

[111] *West Bank Estates Ltd v Arthur*, above; and see *Higgs v Nassauvian Ltd*, above (rotational farming).

[112] *Red House Farms (Thorndon) Ltd v Catchpole* [1977] 2 E.G.L.R. 125. For acts which may constitute adverse possession of an area of water, see S. Jourdan and O. Radley-Gardner, *Adverse Possession*, 2nd edn, para.12–27; and *Roberts v Swangrove Estates Ltd* [2007] EWHC 513 (Ch); [2007] 2 P. & C.R. 326 (dredging).

[113] *Bligh v Martin* [1968] 1 W.L.R. 804.

[114] *Seddon v Smith* (1877) 36 L.T. 168 at 169, per Cockburn C.J.; *Simpson v Fergus* (1999) 79 P. & C.R. 398 at 402. See, e.g. *Hughes v Cork* [1994] E.G.C.S. 25.

[115] See *Littledale v Liverpool College* [1900] 1 Ch. 19; *George Wimpey & Co Ltd v Sohn* [1967] Ch. 487 (fencing of gardens equivocal as excluding public as well as owner); *Marsden v Miller* (1992) 64 P. & C.R. 239 (fence erected but removed by true owner within 24 hours); *Batt v Adams* [2001] 2 E.G.L.R. 92 at 95; *The Inglewood Investment Co Ltd v Baker* [2002] EWCA Civ 1733; [2003] 2 P. & C.R. 319 (fencing to keep stock in rather than people out); [1982] Conv. 256, 345 (M. Dockray).

inconvenienced or otherwise affected the owner.[116] The adverse possessor need not himself be in physical possession of the land. If he grants a tenancy or licence, the tenant or licensee possesses on his behalf and is estopped from denying the licence or tenancy.[117]

Both because exclusive control is essential to establish adverse possession and because of the presumption that the true owner remains in possession of the land, trivial acts will rarely suffice to establish adverse possession.[118] Once factual possession has been established, it will not be terminated merely because the true owner sends a letter to the squatter requiring him to vacate the premises. Time will continue to run in favour of the squatter unless and until he vacates the premises or acknowledges the true owner's title.[119]

(2) *ANIMUS POSSIDENDI*. The squatter must have "an intention for the time being to possess the land to the exclusion of all other persons, including the owner with the paper title".[120] As regards that intention: **35–019**

(i) It is an intention to possess and not an intention to own.[121]

(ii) It an intention to exclude the world in the squatter's own name and on his own behalf.[122]

(iii) It is an intention to possess and not an intention to dispossess.[123] Accordingly, the animus can be sufficiently established even if both the true owner and the squatter mistakenly believe that the land belongs to the latter,[124] or where a squatter did not realise that he was trespassing on another's land.[125]

(iv) It is an intention *for the time being* to possess the land. The intention does not have to be to exclude the owner with the paper title in all future circumstances.[126] As regards the true owner, the

---

[116] *Treloar v Nute* [1976] 1 W.L.R. 1295 (land fenced off and levelled for building); see similarly *Williams v Usherwood* (1981) 45 P. & C.R. 235 (land fenced, driveway paved and cars parked).

[117] *Sze To Chun Keung v Kung Kwok Wai David* [1997] 1 W.L.R. 1232 at 1235. See too *Des Barres v Shey* (1873) 29 L.T. (N.S.) 592. For tenancies and licences by estoppel, see above, paras 17–125; 34–003.

[118] See *Boosey v Davis* (1987) 55 P. & C.R. 83 (occasional grazing of goats and clearance of scrub); *Pavledes v Ryesbridge Properties Ltd* (1989) 58 P. & C.R. 459 (parking of cars on a small scale on a large site); *Wilson v Martin's Exors* [1993] 1 E.G.L.R. 178 (cutting timber and repairing fences).

[119] *Mount Carmel Investments Ltd v Peter Thurlow Ltd* [1988] 1 W.L.R. 1078. See too *Ramnarace v Lutchman* [2001] UKPC 25 at [3], [20]; [2001] 1 W.L.R. 1651 at 1653, 1657.

[120] *Buckinghamshire County Council v Moran* [1990] Ch. 623 at 643, per Slade L.J.

[121] *Buckinghamshire County Council v Moran*, above, at p.643; *J A Pye (Oxford) Ltd v Graham* [2002] UKHL 30 at [42], [43]; [2003] 1 A.C. 419 at 436, 437.

[122] *Powell v McFarlane* (1977) 38 P. & C.R. 452 at 471, 472.

[123] *Hughes v Cork* [1994] E.G.C.S. 25; *J Alston & Sons Ltd v BOCM Pauls Ltd* [2008] EWHC 3310 (Ch) at [99]; [2009] 1 E.G.L.R. 93 at 101.

[124] *Pulleyn v Hall Aggregates (Thames Valley) Ltd* (1992) 65 P. & C.R. 276 at 282; *Hughes v Cork*, above.

[125] *Prudential Assurance Co Ltd v Waterloo Real Estate Inc* [1999] 2 E.G.L.R. 85.

[126] *Buckinghamshire County Council v Moran* [1990] Ch. 623 at 642, 643.

intention can only be to exclude him "so far as is reasonably practicable and so far as the processes of the law will allow".[127] Accordingly, it is not fatal to a squatter's claim that he would have been willing to pay for his occupation had he been asked to do so by the true owner.[128]

(v) The intention to possess must be manifested clearly, so that it is apparent that the squatter was not merely a persistent trespasser, but was seeking to dispossess the true owner.[129] If the squatter's acts are equivocal then he will not be treated as having the requisite *animus possidendi*.[130] A request to the true owner to exclude trespassers is inconsistent with an intention to possess.[131] However, an acknowledgement of the true owner's title, although it will cause time to start to run afresh,[132] will not necessarily be inconsistent with the squatter having the necessary intention to possess.[133]

The true owner's intention is, in contrast to that of the squatter, "irrelevant in practice",[134] and the contrary view "heretical and wrong".[135] It follows that a squatter may be in adverse possession even though his acts do not substantially interfere with the true owner's future plans.[136] There will be no

[127] *Powell v McFarlane* (1977) 38 P. & C.R. 452 at 471, 472; *J A Pye (Oxford) Ltd v Graham*, above, at [43], [77]; pp.437, 448.

[128] *Ocean Estates Ltd v Pinder* [1969] 2 A.C. 19, 24; *Lambeth LBC v Blackburn* [2001] EWCA Civ 912; (2001) 82 P. & C.R. 494; *J A Pye (Oxford) Ltd v Graham*, above, at [45]; pp.436, 438. A person who is in fact in adverse possession, but mistakenly believes that he has the owner's consent to be there, will still have the necessary animus if he intended to remain in possession so long as the true owner continued to permit him to do so: see *Wretham v Ross* [2005] EWHC (Ch) 1259 at [41]; *J Alston & Sons Ltd v BOCM Pauls Ltd* [2008] EWHC 3310 (Ch) at [90]–[98]; [2009] 1 E.G.L.R. 93 at 100, 101 (not following *Clowes Developments (UK) Ltd v Walters* [2005] EWHC 669 (Ch) at [40]).

[129] *Powell v McFarlane* (1977) 38 P. & C.R. 452, at 480; *Prudential Assurance Co Ltd v Waterloo Real Estate Inc*, above, at 87 (the squatter's conduct "must be unequivocal in the sense that his intention to possess has been made plain to the world", per Peter Gibson L.J.); *Smith v Waterman* [2003] EWHC 1266 (Ch) at [81]. The intention must, in practice, be determined objectively, because evidence of the squatter's subjective intention is likely to be self-serving: *Bolton Metropolitan BC v Musa* (1998) 77 P. & C.R. D36.

[130] *Tecbild Ltd v Chamberlain* (1969) 20 P. & C.R. 633 at 642 (grazing ponies and allowing children to play on the land insufficient); *Powell v McFarlane*, above, at 472 (grazing a cow, shooting, and taking pasturage by a 14-year-old boy regarded as a taking of profits from the land rather than as evidence of an intention to dispossess); *Buckinghamshire County Council v Moran*, above, at p.642.

[131] *Pavledes v Ryesbridge Properties Ltd* (1989) 58 P. &C.R. 459 at 480.

[132] See below, para.35–051.

[133] As where a squatter acknowledges the true owner's title but makes it clear that he will not give up possession.

[134] *Buckinghamshire County Council v Moran* [1990] Ch. 623 at 645, per Nourse L.J.

[135] *J A Pye (Oxford) Ltd v Graham* [2002] UKHL 30 at [45]; [2003] 1 A.C. 419 at 438, per Lord Browne-Wilkinson. See too *Wills v Wills* [2003] UKPC 84 at [18]–[21].

[136] *Buckinghamshire County Council v Moran*, above, rejecting the existence of such a supposed rule (said to derive from remarks attributed to Bramwell L.J. in *Leigh v Jack* (1879) 5 Ex.D 264 at 273, but which are omitted from all other reports of the case); *J A Pye (Oxford) Ltd v Graham*, above, at [44], [45]; pp.437, 438.

presumption in such circumstances that he is a licensee unless the actual facts of the case warrant it.[137] The squatter's knowledge that the true owner uses or intends to use the land for some special purpose may perhaps place a heavier onus upon him to prove by unequivocal conduct the necessary intention to possess, but such cases will be rare.[138] Although, the "heresy" that had been rightly extirpated has since been resurrected under guise of supposed compliance with the Human Rights Act 1998,[139] that view is now untenable, because the law of adverse possession does not contravene the European Convention on Human Rights.[140]

(3) PROPERTY WHICH MAY BE ADVERSELY POSSESSED. There can be adverse **35–020** possession of a subterranean building or of sub-soil even though the true owner remains in possession of the surface.[141] There may also be adverse possession of a party wall.[142] A squatter's title may be subject to rights similar to easements in favour of the dispossessed owner if they have been exercised by the latter during the period of dispossession, such as a right to trim a hedge and clean a drain[143] or a right of entry for repairing an adjacent house.[144] Although it is clear that it is possible to acquire by adverse possession land that is subject to a public highway,[145] a person cannot acquire title by adverse possession to land which comprises only the public highway because the highway authority's statutory title[146] cannot be extinguished by adverse possession so long as the highway is maintainable at public expense.[147] Land can be acquired by adverse possession against a person or body that had itself acquired title by statute.[148]

---

[137] LA 1980 Sch.1 para.8(4) controverting the opinion of Lord Denning M.R. in *Wallis's Cayton Bay Holiday Camp Ltd v Shell-Mex and BP Ltd* [1975] Q.B. 94, at 103 and of the Court of Appeal in *Gray v Wykeham-Martin* [1977] C.L.Y. (Unreported Cases) §537: see *Powell v McFarlane*, above, at 484; *J A Pye (Oxford) Ltd v Graham*, above, at [32], [45]; pp.433, 438. For an example where the facts warranted the finding of an implied licence, see *Batsford Estates (1983) Co Ltd v Taylor* [2005] EWCA Civ 489; [2005] 2 E.G.L.R. 12.

[138] *J A Pye (Oxford) Ltd v Graham*, above, at [45]; p.438.

[139] See *Beaulane Properties Ltd v Palmer* [2005] EWHC 817 (Ch); [2006] Ch. 79.

[140] *J A Pye (Oxford) Ltd v UK* No.44302/02 (2007) (Grand Chamber, Court of Human Rights); *Ofulue v Bossart* [2008] EWCA Civ 7 at [49]; [2009] Ch 1 at 20, applying the decision of the Grand Chamber, and disapproving of the decision in *Beaulane Properties Ltd v Palmer*, above.

[141] *Rains v Buxton* (1880) 14 Ch D 537 (cellar).

[142] *Prudential Assurance Co Ltd v Waterloo Real Estate Inc* [1999] 2 E.G.L.R. 85; *Palfrey v Wilson* [2007] EWCA Civ 94.

[143] *Marshall v Taylor* [1895] 1 Ch. 641.

[144] *Williams v Usherwood* (1981) 45 P. & C.R. 235, holding that such rights are implied by law where necessary.

[145] See, e.g. *J A Pye (Oxford) Ltd v Graham* [2002] UKHL 30 at [8]; [2003] 1 A.C. 419 at 427, where the land claimed by the squatter was subject to a public footpath. No argument was advanced that this precluded adverse possession. See S. Jourdan and O. Radley-Gardner, *Adverse Possession*, 2nd edn, paras 12–02—12–08.

[146] Under Highways Act 1980 s.263; above, para.27–034.

[147] *R. (Smith) v Land Registry (Peterborough)* [2010] EWCA Civ 200; [2011] Q.B. 413. The case left open the difficult question as to whether the illegality of a squatter's conduct precluded his claim of adverse possession: see S. Jourdan and O. Radley-Gardner, *Adverse Possession*, 2nd edn, paras 7–130—7–140.

[148] *Rhondda Cynon Taff County BC v Watkins* [2003] EWCA Civ 129; [2003] 1 W.L.R. 1864 (a local authority that had acquired land under compulsory purchase powers).

2. Successive squatters

35–021   *(a) Dispositions by squatter.* As already explained, a squatter has a title based on his own possession, and this title is good against everyone except the true owner.[149] Accordingly, if a squatter who has not barred the true owner sells the land he can give the purchaser a right to the land which is as good as his own. The same applies to devises, gifts or other dispositions by the squatter, and to devolution on his intestacy; in each case the person taking the squatter's interest can add the squatter's period of possession to his own.[150] Thus if X, who has occupied A's land for eight years, sells the land to Y, A will be barred after Y has held the land for a further four years.

35–022   *(b) Squatter dispossessed by squatter.* If a squatter is himself dispossessed the second squatter can add the former period of occupation to his own as against the true owner.[151] This is because time runs against the true owner from the time when adverse possession began,[152] and so long as adverse possession continues unbroken, it makes no difference who continues it.[153] But as against the first squatter, the second squatter must himself occupy for the full period before his title becomes unassailable. This has already been explained,[154] but a simple example may be useful here. If land owned by A has been occupied by X for eight years and Y dispossesses X, A will be barred when 12 years have elapsed from X first taking possession. But although at the end of that time A is barred, X will not be barred until 12 years from Y's first taking possession; for Y cannot claim to be absolutely entitled until he can show that everybody with any claim to the land has been barred by the lapse of the full period.

35–023   *(c) Possession abandoned.* There is no right to add together two periods of adverse possession if a squatter abandons possession before the full period has run and some time passes before either someone else takes adverse possession or he retakes adverse possession of the land.[155] During the gap between the two squatters, the owner has possession in law, and there is no person whom he can sue. The land therefore ceases to be in adverse possession; and when adverse possession is taken by the second squatter a fresh right of action accrues to the true owner, who has the full period within which to enforce it.[156]

---

[149] Above, para.4–004.

[150] Above, para.4–008; *Asher v Whitlock* (1865) L.R. 1 Q.B. 1; *Mount Carmel Investments Ltd v Peter Thurlow Ltd* [1988] 1 W.L.R. 1078.

[151] *Site Developments (Ferndown) Ltd v Cuthbury Ltd* [2010] EWHC 10 (Ch); [2011] Ch. 226.

[152] LA 1980 Sch.1 para.8(1), governing para.1.

[153] See *Willis v Earl Howe* [1893] 2 Ch. 545. *Site Developments (Ferndown) Ltd v Cuthbury Ltd* [2010] EWHC 10 (Ch) at [175]; [2011] Ch. 226 at 240.

[154] Above, para.4–008.

[155] For a case where a squatter resumed possession after a period of non-occupation, see *King (t/a Oakland Services UK) v Job* [2002] EWCA Civ 181; [2002] 2 P. & C.R. D13. The electoral roll was held admissible to show that the defendant had lived at another address for several years.

[156] LA 1980 Sch.1 para.8(2) (making statutory the decision in *Trustees, Executors and Agency Co Ltd v Short* (1883) 13 App.Cas. 793).

3. Future interests. Future interests are governed by two rules.

(a) Alternative periods. If adverse possession began before the reversion or remainder fell into possession, the 12-year period runs against the reversioner or remainderman from the beginning of the adverse possession; but he has an alternative period of six years from the falling into possession of his interest. In other words, he must sue within 12 years of the previous owner's dispossession, or within six years of his own interest vesting in possession, whichever is the longer period.[157] Thus, if land is held by A for life with remainder to B in fee simple, and X dispossesses A 20 years before A's death, B still has six years from A's death in which to recover the land. If X had dispossessed A three years before A's death, B would have 12 years from the dispossession of A, i.e. nine years from A's death. But if X had not taken adverse possession until after A's death, the ordinary period of 12 years from the taking of possession would apply, for B's interest would have ceased to be a future interest before time began to run.[158]

(b) Entails. A reversioner or remainderman expectant upon an entail in possession is not entitled to the alternative six-year period if his interest could have been barred by the tenant in tail.[159] Thus if B has granted land to A in tail,[160] retaining the fee simple reversion, and X dispossesses A or the heirs of his body, B's reversion is barred 12 years after the dispossession, even though B himself had no right to the land during the period. This rule emphasises again the precarious nature of an interest expectant upon an entail: it may be barred by limitation, as well as by disentailment, and the owner is powerless to intervene.

4. Leaseholds

(a) Reversioner on a lease. The above provisions do not apply to a reversioner on a lease when the tenant has been ousted. No matter when the dispossession occurred, time does not run against the reversioner until the lease expires.[161] Thus, if L grants T a lease for 99 years and T is dispossessed by X, the 12-year period runs against T from the dispossession but against L only from the determination of the lease. X can therefore retain the land as against T during the rest of the term, but L can recover it from X at the end of the term, provided L takes proceedings within 12 years of that date.[162] If, at the end of the term, L, instead of evicting X, grants a new lease, the new

35–024

35–025

35–026

---

[157] LA 1980 s.15(2). His trustees may also sue on his behalf: s.18(4).

[158] See LA 1980 Sch.1 paras 4, 8.

[159] This is the combined effect of LA 1980 ss.5(1), (3) and 38(5), requiring the reversioner or remainderman to be treated as a person claiming through the tenant in tail in such cases, and so to be barred together with him.

[160] No new entails can be created after 1996: see TLATA 1996 Sch.1, para.5; above, para.3–031.

[161] LA 1980 s.15(2); the words "not being a term of years absolute" confirm *Walter v Yalden* [1902] 2 K.B. 304 on this point. See *Chung Ping Kwan v Lam Island Development Co Ltd* [1997] A.C. 38 at 46.

[162] See further below, para.35–059.

tenant can recover the land from X because he claims through L. This is so even if that new tenant is T, whose title X had barred.[163] Where, however, that new lease was granted pursuant to an option in the lease, T will be unable to recover the land from X because his rights under the original lease are barred.[164]

35–027   *(b) Title acquired by tenant.* A tenant cannot acquire a title against his landlord during the currency of the lease. Occupation by a tenant is never adverse to the landlord's title, which the tenant is estopped from denying.[165] There are two situations which may arise.

First, any encroachments by the tenant on land belonging to third parties will, anomalously,[166] enure for the landlord's benefit,[167] provided that:

>   (i) The land "is very close to the demised land and occupied by the tenant together with the demised land"[168]; and
>
>   (ii) No different intention is shown by the conduct of the landlord or tenant within the 12 years of adverse possession.[169] The parties' acts subsequent to the expiry of the 12-year period are relevant only in so far as they cast light on what the parties believed or intended at the end of that period.[170]

Although this principle is anomalous, it can be explained as part of the law of adverse possession.[171]

Secondly, if the tenant occupies other land belonging to the landlord but not included in the demise, after the expiry of the limitation period that land is presumed to be an addition to the land demised to the tenant ("a mere extension of the locus of his tenancy"[172]), so that it becomes subject to the

---

[163] *Chung Ping Kwan v Lam Island Development Co Ltd*, above, at 46, 47. See (1998) 28 H.K.L.J. 329 (C.H.).

[164] *Chung Ping Kwan v Lam Island Development Co Ltd*, above, at 48, 49. This outcome has been described as "a little incongruous": (1997) 71 A.L.J. 98 at 99 (P. Butt). A tenant who finds himself in this position, is likely to seek the grant of a new lease from the landlord instead of exercising the option.

[165] Above, paras 4–011, 17–125.

[166] For criticism, see *Batt v Adams* [2001] 2 E.G.L.R. 92 at 96, [38]. The basis of the doctrine is difficult to discern: *Tower Hamlets LBC v Barrett* [2005] EWCA Civ 923 at [28]; [2006] 1 P. & C.R. 132 at 139, 140. See [2007] C.L.J. 16 (D.M. Fox).

[167] *Whitmore v Humphries* (1871) L.R. 7 C.P. 1; *Att Gen v Tomline* (1880) 5 Ch D 150; *East Stonehouse UDC v Willoughby Bros Ltd* [1902] 2 K.B. 318; *King v Smith* [1950] 1 All E.R. 553; above, para.4–008, fn.43.

[168] *Tower Hamlets LBC v Barrett* [2005] EWCA Civ 923 at [31]; [2006] 1 P. & C.R. 132 at 140, per Neuberger L.J.

[169] *Kingsmill v Millard* (1855) 11 Exch. 313; *Smirk v Lyndale Developments Ltd* [1975] Ch. 317, approving (at 337) the analysis of the law made by Pennycuick V.C.; *Long v Tower Hamlets LBC* [1998] Ch. 197 at 203.

[170] *Tower Hamlets LBC v Barrett*, above, at [91]; p.151.

[171] See [2007] C.L.J. 16 (D.M. Fox).

[172] *Lord Hastings v Saddler* (1898) 79 L.T. 355 at 356, per Lord Russell C.J.

terms of the tenancy.[173] Although the tenant may acquire a title to it against the landlord for the remainder of the term, he must give it up to him when the tenancy ends.[174] However, the presumption may be rebutted, e.g. by the tenant conveying the land to a third party and informing the landlord of this while the tenancy is still running.[175] This doctrine is well-established,[176] but it cannot rest upon limitation for two reasons:

(i) a squatter acquires a freehold estate even if he adversely possesses against a leasehold estate,[177] whereas under this doctrine the tenant merely acquires an accretion to his lease; and

(ii) adverse possession for the limitation period extinguishes the true owner's title.[178]

The doctrine has been explained as being akin to estoppel.[179]

(c) Non-payment of rent. Failure to pay rent merely bars the landlord's claim to recover any particular instalment of rent after six years from its falling due.[180] It has no effect on the landlord's title to the land. **35–028**

(d) Right of re-entry. A right of re-entry under a forfeiture clause (e.g. for non-payment of rent) is a right to recover land,[181] and is therefore barred if not exercised for 12 years. But this does not affect the landlord's title to the reversion, for he will have a fresh right of action when the lease expires.[182] A fresh right of entry arises every time the forfeiture clause is brought into play, e.g. by non-payment of rent falling due subsequently. In the case of continuing breaches of covenant,[183] such as failure to repair or user for a prohibited purpose, time continually begins running afresh, and forfeiture can be claimed at any time. **35–029**

(e) Adverse receipt of rent. A landlord's title may, indeed, be barred if adverse possession is taken not of the land but of the rent from it. The rule is that if a tenant who holds under a written lease pays a rent of at least £10 per **35–030**

---

[173] *J F Perrott & Co Ltd v Cohen* [1951] 1 K.B. 705 (repairing covenant). The doctrine is well-established: see *Batsford Estates (1983) Co Ltd v Taylor* [2005] EWCA Civ 489 at [30]; [2005] 2 E.G.L.R. 12 at 15. However, it cannot rest upon limitation, because a squatter acquires a freehold estate even if he adversely possesses against a leasehold estate: see para.35–057. Furthermore, adverse possession for the limitation extinguishes the true owner's title: see LA 1980 s.17; below, para.35–055. The doctrine is probably best regarded as one of estoppel.

[174] *Tabor v Godfrey* (1895) 64 L.J.Q.B. 245; *Smirk v Lyndale Developments Ltd*, above.

[175] *Kingsmill v Millard*, above; *Smirk v Lyndale Developments Ltd*, above, not following *Lord Hastings v Saddler*, above.

[176] See *Batsford Estates (1983) Co Ltd v Taylor* [2005] EWCA Civ 489 at [30]; [2005] 2 E.G.L.R. 12 at 15.

[177] See below, para.35–057.

[178] LA 1980 s.17; below, para.35–055.

[179] See *J F Perrott & Co Ltd v Cohen* [1951] 1 K.B. 705 at 710. See S. Jourdan and O. Radley-Gardner, *Adverse Possession*, 2nd edn, paras 25–07—25–11.

[180] See below para.35–067.

[181] LA 1980 s.38(7).

[182] LA 1980 Sch.1 para.7(2).

[183] See above para.18–026.

annum for 12 years to some person who wrongfully claims the reversion, this bars the landlord's rights altogether.[184] Adverse receipt of rent by a third party is equivalent to adverse possession of the reversion by him,[185] and after 12 years it will extinguish the reversion, even if the true owner of it is also the tenant who paid the rent.[186]

35–031 *(f) Adverse possession by landlord.* Although a tenant cannot acquire title against his landlord during the term of his lease because he is in possession with the landlord's consent,[187] there is no similar constraint on the landlord. He can therefore bar the leasehold title of his own tenant by adverse possession, notwithstanding the rule that he must not derogate from his grant. This is because adverse possession is "possession as of wrong".[188]

35–032 **5. Tenants at will and at sufferance.** Time begins to run in favour of a tenant at will only from the determination of the tenancy.[189] In the case of a tenancy at sufferance, time begins to run from the commencement of the tenancy. This is because a tenancy at sufferance is really not a tenancy at all, but is adverse possession.[190]

35–033 **6. Yearly or periodic tenants.** A tenant under a yearly or other periodic tenancy who does not hold under a lease in writing[191] is in a stronger position than other tenants. Time runs from the end of the first year or other period of the tenancy,[192] subject to extension by payment of rent[193] or written acknowledgment. An oral tenancy will thus in time ripen into ownership if the rent is not paid.[194] If there is a lease in writing, time runs from the determination of the tenancy.

---

[184] LA 1980 Sch.1 para.6. Payment of rent to the true reversioner will stop time running: LA 1980 Sch.1 para.6; *Nicholson v England* [1926] 2 K.B. 93. These rules do not apply to any lease granted by the Crown: para.6(2).

[185] LA 1980 Sch.1 para.8(3).

[186] *Bligh v Martin* [1968] 1 W.L.R. 804.

[187] Above paras 35–016, 35–027.

[188] *Sze To Chun Keung v Kung Kwok Wai David* [1997] 1 W.L.R. 1232 at 1235, per Lord Hoffmann (Crown in adverse possession to its lessee). See above, paras 35–002, 35–018. For non-derogation from grant, see above, para.19–023.

[189] This follows because LA 1980 (unlike LA 1939) contains no provision deeming a tenancy at will to terminate after a specified period: *Colchester BC v Smith* [1991] Ch. 448 at 481 (in CA [1992] Ch. 421). The old law applies elsewhere in the Commonwealth: see *Ramnarace v Lutchman* [2001] UKPC 25; [2001] 1 W.L.R. 1651 (Trinidad and Tobago).

[190] Above, para.17–107.

[191] A document that merely evidences the terms of an agreement for a lease is not a lease in writing for these purposes because it does not create the term: see *Long v Tower Hamlets LBC* [1998] Ch. 197.

[192] LA 1980 Sch.1 para.5.

[193] Time then runs from the last receipt of rent: LA 1980 Sch.1 para.5(2); see *Price v Hartley* [1995] E.G.C.S. 74.

[194] *Moses v Lovegrove* [1952] 2 Q.B. 533, holding that the Rent Acts did not prevent time from running, and that a rent book is not a "lease in writing"; *Hayward v Chaloner* [1968] 1 Q.B. 107, where there was disagreement whether there was adverse possession; *Jessamine Investment Co v Schwartz* [1978] Q.B. 264, following *Moses v Lovegrove*, above. Time will run in favour of the tenant even though he thinks he is paying rent when this is not in fact the case: *Lodge v Wakefield Metropolitan CC* [1995] 2 E.G.L.R. 124.

A tenant, who holds over and remains in possession after the determination of his tenancy for the requisite limitation period, thereby satisfies the requirements for adverse possession.[195]

7. Rentcharges. In the case of a rentcharge[196] in possession, time runs from the last payment of rent to the owner of the rentcharge.[197] Thus the owner's rights are barred: **35–034**

(i) if no rent is paid for 12 years, in which case the rentcharge is extinguished; or

(ii) if the rent is paid to a stranger for 12 years, in which case the rentcharge remains enforceable against the land but the former owner's claim to it is extinguished in favour of the stranger.

The definition of rentcharge excludes rent service.[198] Rent due under a lease (which is rent service) is dealt with elsewhere.[199]

8. Mortgages

(a) The mortgagor's right to redeem. As regards unregistered land,[200] the right to redeem, whether legal or equitable, is barred if the mortgagee remains in possession of the mortgaged land for 12 years without giving any written acknowledgment of the title of the mortgagor or of his equity of redemption and without receiving any payment on account of principal or interest[201] made by or on behalf of the mortgagor. The mere receipt of rents and profits while in possession does not count for this purpose,[202] although the mortgagee is accountable to the mortgagor for them.[203] The rule that a mortgagee in possession can bar the mortgagor's title is an exception to the general rules that time runs only where there is adverse possession, and that a lessee (here, a mortgagee having a long term of years in the rare cases where there is a mortgage by demise[204]) may not bar his lessor's title.[205] The position is anomalous and has nothing to commend it. **35–035**

When a second mortgagee's rights against the mortgagor are barred, he can no longer exercise his right to redeem the first mortgagee,[206] because his interest in the property is at an end.[207]

---

[195] *Williams v Jones* [2002] EWCA Civ 1097; [2002] 3 E.G.L.R. 69.

[196] Defined as "land": LA 1980 s.38(1).

[197] LA 1980 s.38(8).

[198] LA 1980 s.38(1), also excluding mortgage interest.

[199] Mentioned above, and discussed below, para.35–067.

[200] For the position as regards registered land, see below, para.35–072.

[201] LA 1980 ss.16, 29(4); *Young v Clarey* [1948] Ch. 191 (mortgagor and second mortgagee barred by mortgagee in possession); and see below, para.35–051.

[202] *Harlock v Ashberry* (1882) 19 Ch D 539; and see *Re Lord Clifden* [1900] 1 Ch. 774.

[203] Above, para.25–026.

[204] See above, para.24–020.

[205] Above, para.35–027.

[206] See above, para.25–111.

[207] *Cotterell v Price* [1960] 1 W.L.R. 1097.

35–036   (b) *Mortgagee's right to enforce the mortgage.* Whether the land is registered or unregistered,[208] the mortgagee's rights to foreclose,[209] to sue for possession,[210] and to sue for the principal[211] all become barred after 12 years from the date when repayment became due under the mortgage.[212] His title is then extinguished.[213] For the purposes of the Limitation Act 1980,[214] the mortgagor's possession is adverse as against the mortgagee.[215] But time begins to run afresh if during the period the mortgagor makes any written acknowledgment or if he or the person in possession of the land makes any payment of interest or of capital which complies with the Act.[216]

Where the mortgagee enforces his security and there is a shortfall, the right to sue for that shortfall is subject to the period of 12 years mentioned above.[217] The period runs from the date when repayment became due and is unaffected by the sale.[218]

As regards charging orders under the Charging Orders Act 1979,[219] these have the same effect and are enforceable in the same manner as an equitable charge created by a debtor under hand.[220] There are no provisions in the Limitation Act 1980 which apply to such orders, and they remain enforceable regardless of the lapse of time.[221]

35–037   **9. Claims through Crown or corporation sole.** It has been seen that the Crown is entitled to a period of 30 years instead of the usual 12.[222] If a person against whom time has started to run conveys his land to the Crown, the only change is that the limitation period becomes 30 years from the dispossession instead of 12.[223] But in the converse case where time has started to run against

---

[208] See LRA 2002 s.96(1).

[209] LA 1980 s.20(4), treating this as an action to recover land.

[210] LA 1980 ss.15, 17; *Cotterell v Price*, above.

[211] LA 1980 s.20(1). For interest, see below, para.35–068.

[212] See *Lloyds Bank Ltd v Margolis* [1954] 1 W.L.R. 644 (charge to secure bank overdraft with covenant to pay "on demand": time runs from demand); *Gotham v Doodes* [2006] EWCA Civ 1080; [2007] 1 W.L.R. 86 (charge under IA 1986 s.313: time runs from date of order for sale of the property).

[213] See *Lewis v Plunket* [1937] 1 All E.R. 530 at 534 (omitted from [1937] Ch. 306); *Cotterell v Price*, above.

[214] See Sch.1 para.8

[215] *Ashe v National Westminster Bank Plc* [2008] EWCA Civ 55 at [54]–[58]; [2008] 1 W.L.R. 710 at 720.

[216] LA 1980 s.29; and *Ashe v National Westminster Bank Plc* [2008] EWCA Civ 55 at [44], [45]; [2008] 1 W.L.R. 710 at 729. For the details of acknowledgments, see below, para.35–052.

[217] i.e., under LA 1980 s.20(1). It is neither a claim for a simple contract debt under LA 1980 s.5, nor an action on a specialty, under LA 1980 s.8: see *Bristol and West Plc v Bartlett* [2002] EWCA 1181; [2003] 1 W.L.R. 284.

[218] *West Bromwich BS v Wilkinson* [2005] UKHL 44; [2005] 1 W.L.R. 2303 (rejecting the contention that the sale stopped time running).

[219] For charging orders, see above, para.13–074.

[220] Charging Orders Act 1979 s.3(4); above, para.13–075.

[221] *Yorkshire Bank Finance Ltd v Mulhall* [2008] EWCA Civ 1156; [2009] 1 P. & C.R. 345. See too *Ezekial v Orakpo* [1997] 1 W.L.R. 340; and see below, para.35–068.

[222] Above, para.35–010.

[223] LA 1980 Sch.1 para.10.

the Crown and the Crown then conveys the land to X, the rule is that X is barred at the expiration of 30 years from the original dispossession or 12 years from the conveyance to him, whichever is the shorter.[224] Thus X is entitled to 12 years from the date of the conveyance unless at that time there were less than 12 years of the Crown period unexpired, in which case X merely has the residue of that period. The same is true where time begins to run against W, W then conveys the land to the Crown, and the Crown then sells the land to X. X will be barred 30 years after the original dispossession or 12 years from the conveyance to him by the Crown.[225]

Similar rules apply to the longer periods for a spiritual or eleemosynary corporation sole.[226]

10. Equitable titles, trusts and remedies

(a) Adverse possession by a stranger. In general, the 12-year period for the recovery of unregistered land applies as much to equitable interests in such land as to legal estates.[227] But adverse possession of trust property by a stranger does not bar the trustee's title to the property until all the beneficiaries have been barred.[228] Thus if land is held on trust for the benefit of A for life with remainder to B, 12 years' adverse possession of the land by X bars A's equitable interest and, but for the provision just mentioned, would bar the trustees' legal estate. But time will not start to run against B's equitable interest until A's death,[229] and the same accordingly applies to the trustees' legal estate. Consequently, after the 12 years have run, the trustees will hold the legal estate on a future trust for B as from A's death.[230] This is so even if A is the trustee, as will normally be the case if the land is settled land.

35–038

(b) Adverse possession by a trustee. It is a general principle that a trustee can never obtain a title by adverse possession against his beneficiaries. There is, indeed, a limitation period of six years for actions to recover trust property or in respect of breach of trust, in cases where no other period of limitation is prescribed.[231] However, it does not apply to a beneficiary's action against a trustee:

35 039

(i) for any fraud or fraudulent breach of trust to which the trustee was a party or privy; or

---

[224] LA 1980 Sch.1 para.12.

[225] *Hill v Transport for London* [2005] EWHC 856 (Ch); [2005] Ch. 379.

[226] LA 1980 Sch.1 paras 10, 12.

[227] LA 1980 ss.18(1) (as amended by TLATA 1996 Sch.4), 20(1).

[228] LA 1980 s.18(2), (3), (4).

[229] Above, para.35–024.

[230] As to X's interest, see below, paras 35–056.

[231] LA 1980 s.21(3). This subsection applies only "an action by a beneficiary". An action brought by the Attorney-General in respect of a charitable trust is not within the subsection and is subject to no limitation period: *Att Gen v Cocke* [1988] Ch. 414. However, the subsection applies "at least by analogy" to a claim brought exclusively on behalf of beneficiaries by the trustees: *Cattley v Pollard* [2006] EWHC 3130 (Ch) at [102]; [2007] Ch. 353 at 377, per Sheldon QC.

(ii) for recovery of the trust property or its proceeds in the possession of the trustee, or previously received by him and converted to his own use.[232]

In these cases, the trustee can never bar the claims of his beneficiaries. As regards this principle:

(a) It is subject to one exception, namely, where the trustee is also a beneficiary and acted honestly and reasonably in distributing the property. In that case, once the appropriate period has expired, his liability to restore either the property or its proceeds is limited to the excess over his own proper share.[233]

(b) Persons are "trustees" if their trusteeship precedes the breach of trust complained of, namely where they are either expressly appointed or they take it upon themselves to act as trustees.[234] It had been thought that persons whose trusteeship did not precede but was a direct consequence of the unlawful transaction which is impeached by the claimant, did not fall within these provisions.[235] This would mean, for example, that claims against a person who dishonestly assisted the commission of a breach of trust were barred six years after the cause of action accrued.[236] However, it has recently been suggested that this is not the case and the claim against such an intermeddler is never barred by mere lapse of time.[237]

(c) Personal representatives may be trustees for the purposes of the principle.[238] The limitation period for claims to a deceased person's estate is 12 years,[239] even where the claim is made against a third party, e.g. someone to whom the estate has been wrongly distributed.[240] But personal representatives are often expressly given the duties of trustees, and claims against them in the latter capacity are governed by the rules as to trustees, explained above.[241]

---

[232] LA 1980 s.21(1).

[233] LA 1980 s.21(2).

[234] Such as an executor de son tort: see *James v Williams* [2000] Ch. 1.

[235] See *Paragon Finance Plc v D.B. Thakerar & Co* [1999] 1 All E.R. 400 at 407–414; *Cattley v Pollard* [2006] EWHC 3130 (Ch) at [102]; [2007] Ch. 353 at 377.

[236] This is either under LA 1980 s.21(3) (above), or by analogy: see *Cattley v Pollard*, above, at [92]; at p.375. On this form of constructive trust, see above, para.11–019.

[237] *Statek Corpn v Alford* [2008] EWHC 32 (Ch) at [115]–[125]; [2008] BCC 266 at 292, 293; not following on this point *Cattley v Pollard* [2006] EWHC 3130 (Ch) at [80]–[91]; [2007] Ch. 353 at 373–375. Given the wording of the statute this seems wrong in principle: see *Paragon Finance Plc v D.B. Thakerar & Co* [1999] 1 All E.R. 400 at 413.

[238] LA 1980 s.38(1); TA 1925 s.68(17). And see above, para.14–126.

[239] Above, para.35–007 (land); LA 1980 s.22(a) (personalty). Time does not begin to run until the personal representative has paid the expenses and liabilities of the estate and any pecuniary legacies, because it is only then that he is in a position to distribute the estate: *Re Loftus* [2006] EWCA Civ 1124; [2007] 1 W.L.R. 591. LA 1980 s.22, has no application to an action to remove a personal representative.

[240] *Ministry of Health v Simpson* [1951] A.C. 251.

[241] See *Re Oliver* [1927] 2 Ch. 323.

(c) Adverse possession by a beneficiary. Under the Limitation Act 1980 **35–040**
time will not run against a trustee in favour of a beneficiary in possession,
except where the beneficiary in possession is solely and absolutely entitled,
and it will not run against a co-beneficiary.[242] Where a purchaser is in
possession under an uncompleted contract of sale and the vendor has been
paid, it has been held that time will run against the vendor,[243] who is in effect
a bare trustee.[244] However, if the vendor has not been paid, it seems that time
does not run against him, at least if the purchaser acknowledges that he is in
possession under the contract and not as a trespasser, since his possession is
not then adverse.[245]

(d) Equitable remedies. Except where, as explained above, the Limitation **35–041**
Act specifically imposes periods of limitation, there are no statutory time
limits for claims for specific performance or for an injunction or for other
equitable relief.[246] These remedies are expressly exempted from the time
limits applicable in actions based on tort or simple contract or on a specialty.[247] If beneficial interests are not affected, such remedies may be
awarded after long intervals of time, for example for the purpose of getting in
an outstanding legal estate.[248] But other cases are subject to the long established doctrine that equity, following the law, adopts a time limit by analogy
with any comparable statutory period.[249] Before fixed periods were imposed
upon claims based on equitable titles and trusts, equitable claims to recover
land were dismissed if not brought within the 20-year period then prescribed
for similar actions at law[250]; and equitable money claims, if analogous to
claims at law for money had and received, were limited by the same six-year
period.[251] As there are now fixed periods for many equitable claims, there is
little scope left for the doctrine of analogy. It will, of course, not apply where
the Limitation Act deliberately excludes some particular case, such as liability
for fraudulent breach of trust. The six-year limitation period applicable to
actions founded on a simple contract[252] does not apply by analogy to specific
performance proceedings.[253]

---

[242] LA 1980 Sch.1 para.9; see *Earnshaw v Hartley* [2000] Ch. 155.

[243] *Bridges v Mees* [1957] Ch. 457, where Harman J. rejected the argument that the vendor had no right of action which could be barred. See also fn.241, below.

[244] Above, para.15–056. See S. Jourdan and O. Radley-Gardner, *Adverse Possession*, 2nd edn, paras 28–25 et seq.

[245] *Hyde v Pearce* [1982] 1 W.L.R. 560.

[246] e.g. rectification (above, para.15–122) or relief from mistake (below, para.35–050).

[247] LA 1980 s.36(1). The same applies in actions for statutory debts and actions to enforce judgments and certain arbitration awards.

[248] *Shepheard v Walker* (1875) L.R. 20 Eq. 659; (1876) 34 L.T. 230 (specific performance awarded after 18 years); *Williams v Greatrex* [1957] 1 W.L.R. 31 (specific performance awarded after 10 years).

[249] *Smith v Clay* (1763) 3 Bro.C.C. 639n. See generally Brunyate, *Limitation of Actions in Equity*, Ch. 1.

[250] *Cholmondely v Clinton* (1821) 4 Bli. 1.

[251] *Re Robinson* [1911] 1 Ch. 502.

[252] LA 1980 s.5.

[253] *P & O Nedlloyd BV v Arab Metals Co (No.2)* [2006] EWCA Civ 1717; [2007] 1 WLR 2288.

On the other hand, there is the equitable doctrine of laches, which requires that remedies be sought without unreasonable delay.[254] In cases governed specifically by the Act the court will not refuse relief within the statutory period on the ground of delay alone.[255] However, it may do so where the delay is coupled with circumstances indicating acquiescence or abandonment, so making it inequitable to prosecute the claim.[256] Mere delay by itself may be fatal where the case is omitted from the Act,[257] and probably also where the Act is followed by analogy.[258] The Act expressly preserves the equitable jurisdiction to refuse relief "on the ground of acquiescence or otherwise".[259]

An action for an account leads to an equitable remedy, since the corresponding action at common law has long been obsolete.[260] It is now subject to the same time limit as applies to the claim which is the basis of the duty to account.[261]

11. Co-ownership

35–042   (a) *Ouster.* At common law, the unity of possession between co-owners meant that if one joint tenant or tenant in common occupied the whole of the land, or took the whole of the rents and profits, this by itself was not adverse possession which would start time running. Some further act, such as ouster of the co-owners was needed.[262] However, a presumption of ouster might arise from long exclusive enjoyment by one co-owner.[263] After 1833, by statute,[264] time normally began to run as between co-owners as soon as one enjoyed more than his share of the land or of the rents and profits, to the exclusion of the other.[265]

35–043   (b) *After 1925.* Since 1925 the law has been changed, perhaps unintentionally, by the imposition of what is now the statutory trust of land which

---

[254] See Brunyate, op. cit., Ch.7; Snell, *Equity*, para.5–019.

[255] *Re Pauling's S.T (No.1)* [1964] Ch. 303.

[256] *Re Loftus, decd.*, [2006] EWCA Civ 1124 at [40]; [2007] 1 W.L.R. 591 at 605. The test is whether, in the circumstances, it has become unconscionable for the plaintiff to rely upon his legal right": *Shaw v Applegate* [1977] 1 W.L.R. 970 at 980, per Goff L.J.; *Frawley v Neill* [1999] 5 C.L. §531 (CA); *Re Loftus, decd.*, above, at [42], p.605. cf. above, Ch.16; and see Brunyate, op. cit. Ch.7; Lightwood, *The Time Limit on Actions*, p.252.

[257] Thus insufficiently explained delays of one year (*Watson v Reid* (1830) 1 Russ. & M. 236), or three-and-a half years (*Eads v Williams* (1854) 4 De G.M. & G. 674) have been held to bar specific performance. Contrast *Wroth v Tyler* [1974] Ch. 30 at 53.

[258] Brunyate, op. cit., 258; contrast Lightwood, op. cit., 254.

[259] s.36(2).

[260] See *Tito v Waddell (No.2)* [1977] Ch. 106 at 250, discussing the problems of LA 1939 s.2(2), (7) before the amendments made by Limitation Amendment Act 1980 Sch.1 paras 2, 8.

[261] LA 1980 s.23. As the obligation to account in equity arises not from the breach of any duty but simply from the existence of a fiduciary relationship, s.23 may have very little application: *Att Gen v Cocke* [1988] Ch. 414.

[262] See Carson's *Real Property Statutes* 2nd edn, p.149.

[263] See *Doe d. Fishar v Taylor* (1774) 1 Cowp. 217. cf. *Doe d. Hellings v Bird* (1809) 11 East 49.

[264] RPLA 1833 s.12.

[265] See *Paradise Beach Co Ltd v Price-Robinson* [1968] A.C. 1072.

operates in all cases of tenancy in common and beneficial joint tenancy.[266] This brings into play the rules relating to trusts, mentioned above,[267] in particular the rules that a trustee cannot bar his beneficiary, and that one beneficiary cannot bar another beneficiary. Thus in a case[268] where one of two tenants in common took all the rents and profits from 1925 for over 12 years, the other tenant's claim failed in respect of the years 1923–1925, when the old law applied. However, it succeeded in respect of the later years, for after 1925 the legal estate was vested in the two tenants as trustees for sale[269] on their own behalf, and so neither could plead the Limitation Act against the other. Since 1940, moreover, the position would be the same even if other persons were trustees,[270] because of the provision that one beneficiary cannot bar another.[271]

Section 2. Postponement of the Period

The date from which time begins to run may be postponed on account of disability, fraud, deliberate concealment, or (in certain special cases) mistake.   **35–044**

A. Disability

1. Alternative periods. If the owner of an interest in unregistered land is under a disability when the right of action accrues, he is allowed an alternative period of six years from the time when he ceases to be under a disability or dies, whichever happens first, with a maximum period in the case of land of 30 years from the date when the right of action first accrued.[272] Thus if X takes possession of A's land at a time when A is a mental patient, A will have 12 years from the dispossession or six years from his recovery from mental disability in which to bring his action, whichever is longer. However, in no case can A sue after 30 years from the dispossession. The following rules should be noted.   **35–045**

---

[266] Above, para.9–051.

[267] Above 35–038 et seq. See too *Earnshaw v Hartley* [2000] Ch. 155, where (at 160), Nourse L.J. noted "the reintroduction of the doctrine of non-adverse possession among beneficial co-owners of land".

[268] *Re Landi* [1939] Ch. 828, rejecting the argument that the old law is preserved by LPA 1925 s.12 (a saving clause for the operation of statutes and the general law of limitation). cf. *Re Milking Pail Farm Trusts* [1940] Ch. 996; and see (1941) 57 L.Q.R. 26 (R.E.M.); (1971) 35 Conv. (N.S.) 6 (G. Battersby).

[269] They would now be trustees of land.

[270] For example if the legal estate were vested in personal representatives under LPA 1925 s.34(3); above, para.13–051.

[271] LA 1980 Sch.1 para.9 (as amended by TLATA 1996 Sch.3, para.18, and Sch.4); above, para.35–040.

[272] LA 1980 s.28.

35–046   **2. Disability.** A person is under a disability for this purpose if he is a minor or of unsound mind.[273] A disability is immaterial unless it existed at the time when the cause of action accrued.[274] Thus if A becomes insane the day before he is dispossessed, the provisions for disability apply, whereas if he becomes insane the day after he has been dispossessed, they do not.[275]

35–047   **3. Successive disabilities.** In the case of successive disabilities, if a person is under one disability and before that ceases another disability begins, the period is extended until both disabilities cease, subject to the 30 years' maximum.[276] But if one disability comes to an end before another starts, or if the person under disability is succeeded by another person under disability, time runs from the ceasing of the first disability. For example, A is a minor when the cause of action accrues. If later, during his minority, he becomes mentally ill, the six-year period does not start to run until he ceases to be ill and is also of full age.[277] But if he reaches full age before he becomes mentally ill, or if he dies a minor and B, a mental patient becomes entitled to the land, the six-year period runs from A's majority in the first case and his death in the second. In no case can the right of action survive for more than 30 years after it accrued.

B. Fraud, Concealment and Mistake

35–048   **1. Fraud or deliberate concealment.** Where:

> (i) an action is based on the fraud of the defendant or his agent (or any person through whom he claims, or his agent); or
>
> (ii) a fact relevant to the right of action has been deliberately concealed by the fraud of any such person,

time does not begin to run until the claimant discovers the fraud or concealment or could with reasonable diligence have discovered it.[278] A person will have shown reasonable diligence if he takes those steps which a prudent person would have taken in the circumstances. He is not required to do everything possible.[279] Deliberate concealment extends to a deliberate breach of duty in circumstances which make it unlikely to be discovered for some time.[280] The relevant concealment may occur after the cause of action has accrued and time had therefore begun to run. In such a case, in accordance

---

[273] LA 1980 s.38(2)–(4).
[274] LA 1980 s.28(1); see, e.g. *Gamer v Wingrove* [1905] 2 Ch. 233.
[275] *Goodhall v Skerratt* (1855) 3 Drew. 216.
[276] LA 1980 s.28(1).
[277] See, e.g. *Borrows v Ellison* (1871) L.R. 6 Ex. 128 (infancy and coverture).
[278] LA 1980 s.32(1).
[279] *Peco Arts Inc v Hazlitt Gallery Ltd* [1983] 1 W.L.R. 1315 at 1323.
[280] LA 1980 s.32(2).

with the wording of the Limitation Act 1980, time does not run until the fact is discovered by the claimant.[281]

These rules are a restatement of the previous law, substituting "deliberately **35–049** concealed" for the former words "concealed by fraud".[282] The latter term had become misleading, since in contrast to "fraud", which here as elsewhere necessarily implies dishonesty,[283] "fraudulent concealment" has been carried far beyond its natural meaning, and dishonesty or moral turpitude were not indispensable elements.[284] Following the change in the law, there will be deliberate concealment so as to deprive a defendant of a defence of limitation in the two circumstances set out in the statute, namely:

> (i) where he takes active steps to conceal his own breach of duty after he becomes aware of it; or
>
> (ii) where he is guilty of deliberate wrongdoing and conceals or fails to disclose it in circumstances where it is unlikely to be discovered for some time.[285]

A person does not, however, lose the defence of limitation where he commits a breach of duty but is unaware of that breach (as where he gives negligent advice).[286] There is no fraudulent concealment in the open occupation of land, even if it was subterranean and the owner had no knowledge of the occupation.[287]

The plea of fraud or concealment will not postpone the beginning of the ordinary period of limitation if the defendant is or claims through a purchaser for value who was not a party to the fraud or concealment and at the time of his purchase neither knew nor had reason to believe that it had been committed.[288]

2. Relief from mistake. Similar provisions apply to an action "for relief **35–050** from the consequences of a mistake".[289] This rule has a narrow scope, and applies only where the mistake is the gist of the action, i.e. where it is the mistake itself that gives a right to apply to the court for relief. An example is

---

[281] *Sheldon v R.H.M. Outhwaite (Underwriting Agencies) Ltd* [1996] A.C. 102. As Lord Nicholls explained in that case, although time has started to run, "in the case of subsequent concealment the clock is turned back to zero": see at 152.

[282] The change was made by the Limitation Amendment Act 1980 s.7. Although deliberate concealment will almost always involve unconscionable conduct by the defendant, it is not an additional factor that must be proved by the claimant under LA 1980 s.32: see *Cave v Robinson Jarvis & Rolf* [2002] UKHL 18 at [65]; [2003] 1 A.C. 384 at 404.

[283] See *Beaman v ARTS Ltd* [1949] 1 K.B. 550 at 558.

[284] *Kitchen v RAF Association* [1958] 1 W.L.R. 563; *Clark v Woor* [1965] 1 W.L.R. 650; *Tito v Waddell (No.2)* [1977] Ch. 106 at 204; and see *Bartlett v Barclays Bank Trust Co Ltd (No.1)* [1980] Ch. 515 at 537 ("unconscionable").

[285] *Cave v Robinson Jarvis & Rolf* [2002] UKHL 18 at [25]; [2003] 1 A.C. 384 at 394.

[286] *Cave v Robinson Jarvis & Rolf*, above, at [26]; at p.394.

[287] *Rains v Buxton* (1880) 14 Ch D 537.

[288] LA 1980 s.32(3), (4).

[289] LA 1980 s.32(1), (3), (4).

an action for the recovery of money paid under a mistake,[290] whether of fact or law.[291] In the case of land, most claims for relief against mistake are based on equitable grounds, e.g. to set aside a conveyance executed under a misapprehension,[292] or by way of rectification,[293] or rescission.[294] These are not subject to any period of limitation,[295] and so nothing would be gained by providing that the period shall not begin to run until some later date. There is no general rule that mistake stops time from running,[296] e.g. where a landowner allows his neighbour to take adverse possession of a strip of land owing to a mistake about his boundary. Nor does mere ignorance stop time from running.[297]

Section 3. Starting Time Running Afresh

35–051   **1. Acknowledgment or payment.** Time may be started running afresh:

> (i) by a written and signed acknowledgment of the claimant's title[298]; or

> (ii) by payment of part of the principal or interest due in respect of a debt.[299]

The acknowledgment or payment must be:

[290] See *Phillips-Higgins v Harper* [1954] 1 Q.B. 411. A person who has mistakenly paid too much has an extension of time, whereas one who has mistakenly received too little has not. In an action to recover money paid by mistake, the mistake is the gist of the action, whereas the remedy for an underpayment is merely to sue for the balance, and mistake has nothing to do with that.

[291] Money paid under a mistake of law is recoverable: see *Kleinwort Benson Ltd v Lincoln CC* [1999] 1 A.C. 153; *Nurdin & Peacock Plc v D.B. Ramsden & Co Ltd (No.2)* [1999] 1 W.L.R. 1249.

[292] *Cooper v Phibbs* (1867) L.R. 2 H.L. 149; cf. above, para.15–123.

[293] Above, para.15–122.

[294] Above, para.15–112.

[295] Above, para.35–041.

[296] See *Phillips-Higgins v Harper*, above.

[297] See *Cartledge v E. Jopling & Sons Ltd* [1963] A.C. 758. LA 1980 (as amended by the Latent Damage Act 1986 and the Consumer Protection Act 1987) s.11, 11A, 12, 14, 14A, 14B, allows (under certain conditions) an extension of time for ignorance in actions for damages for personal injuries and in respect of defective products and other cases of latent damage. See *Haward v Fawcetts (a firm)* [2006] UKHL 9; [2006] 1 W.L.R. 682; *3M United Kingdom Plc v Linklaters & Paines* [2006] EWCA Civ 530; [2006] 2 E.G.L.R. 53.

[298] LA 1980 ss.29(1), (2), 30. The requirement of writing provides certainty and rules out fraud, mistake or failure of memory: see *Browne v Perry* [1991] 1 W.L.R. 1297. Although the writing must acknowledge the claimant's title, it does not have to admit his immediate right to possession: *Ofulue v Bossert* [2009] UKHL 16 at [74], [75]; [2009] 1 A.C. 990 at 1017.

[299] LA 1980 s.29(3)–(6). Although "part payment can be intelligibly regarded as a sub-species of acknowledgment, it is explicitly separated from acknowledgment and given equal status to it by s.29(5)": *Ashcroft v Bradford & Bingley Plc* [2010] EWCA Civ 223 at [14]; [2010] 2 P. & C.R. 193 at 196, per Sedley L.J. Although an acknowledgment may be clearly referable to an admitted part of a debt, if (i) that is not the case; (ii) the payment was in respect of a debt; and (iii) there was no other debt to which it could relate except the debt claimed, it will satisfy the requirements of s.29: see *Ashcroft v Bradford & Bingley Plc*, above.

(a) made by or on behalf of the person in whose favour time is running[300];

(b) to or for the account of the person whose title is being barred[301]; and

(c) signed by the person making it.[302]

An acknowledgment signed by a solicitor authorised by a mortgagor to "clear up" his affairs binds the mortgagor.[303] However, an acknowledgment to some third party, such as the Inland Revenue, will not satisfy the Act,[304] and interrogatories cannot be used so as to wring an acknowledgment out of a litigant.[305]

2. Sufficiency of acknowledgment.

"For a document to constitute an acknowledgment of title all that is required is that, as between himself and the owner of the paper title, the person in possession acknowledges that the paper title owner has better title to the land. Whether or not such a particular writing amounts to an acknowledgment depends on the true construction of the document in all the surrounding circumstances."[306]   **35–052**

The acknowledgment must be of an existing liability, and not merely of a possible liability[307]; but any statement recognising the claimant's right to sue is enough.[308] Accordingly, statements in a company's balance sheets which relate to past periods will not suffice[309] unless they are put forward as showing the existing position.[310] No special form is required, nor need there be any intention to make an acknowledgment. Thus the following have sufficed as acknowledgements of an owner's title:

(i) a letter by a squatter to the owner offering, subject to contract, to buy the land, because it recognised that the owner has the better title[311];

---

[300] An acknowledgment made on behalf a company that had been dissolved was therefore ineffective: *Allen v Matthews* [2007] EWCA Civ 216; [2007] 2 P. & C.R. 441.

[301] LA 1980 s.30(2); *Re Compania de Electricidad de la Provincia de Buenos Aires Ltd* [1980] Ch.146 (balance sheet effective acknowledgement if received by creditor).

[302] LA 1980 s.30(1).

[303] *Wright v Pepin* [1954] 1 W.L.R. 635.

[304] *Bowring-Hanbury's Trustees v Bowring-Hanbury* [1943] Ch. 104.

[305] *Lovell v Lovell* [1970] 1 W.L.R. 1451.

[306] *Allen v Matthews* [2007] EWCA Civ 216 at [75]; [2007] 2 P. & C.R. 441, 454, per Lawrence Collins L.J.

[307] *Re Flynn (No.2)* [1969] 2 Ch. 403; *Kamouh v Associated Electrical Industries International Ltd* [1980] Q.B. 199.

[308] *Moodie v Bannister* (1859) 4 Drew. 432.

[309] *Consolidated Agencies Ltd v Bertram Ltd* [1965] A.C. 470.

[310] *Jones v Beligrove Properties Ltd* [1949] 2 K.B. 700; *Re Overmark Smith Warden Ltd* [1982] 1 W.L.R. 1195.

[311] *Edginton v Clark* [1964] 1 Q.B. 367; *Ofulue v Bossert* [2009] UKHL 16; [2009] 1 A.C. 990.

(ii) a letter by the squatter to the owner informing him that he had been applying for funds to be used in refurbishing the owner's property[312];

(iii) a petition to the owner not to sell the land to a third party[313]; and

(iv) recitals in a signed counterpart of a lease that was in fact void.[314]

An acknowledgment of unquantified indebtedness (e.g. the "amount I owe you") is sufficient because extrinsic evidence is admissible to quantify it.[315] However, the statement must acknowledge that there is a debt and not merely that there may be a claim. It is not therefore enough to state that, "the question of outstanding rent can be settled as a separate agreement as soon as you present your account".[316]

In the absence of impropriety, an acknowledgment in a "without prejudice" communication is not admissible and cannot therefore satisfy the requirements of the 1980 Act.[317]

35–053   **3. Expiration of period.** A current period of limitation may be repeatedly extended by further acknowledgments or payments.[318] Furthermore, where a landowner's claim for possession has been compromised, the squatter will be estopped by the agreement from subsequently asserting title by adverse possession.[319] But when once the full period has run, no payment or acknowledgment can revive any right to recover land,[320] for the lapse of time will have extinguished not only the owner's remedies for recovering the land but also his right to it.[321]

35–054   **4. Judgment for possession.** Where a judgment has been given, the successful party may either enforce that judgment or bring an action upon it, though the latter is unusual in relation to domestic judgments.[322] However, there are time limits upon each of these alternatives.

---

[312] *Lambeth LBC v Archangel* (2001) 33 H.L.R. 490.
[313] *Lambeth LBC v Bigden* (2001) 33 H.L.R. 478.
[314] *Rehman v Benfield* [2006] EWCA Civ 1392; [2007] 2 P. & C.R. 317.
[315] *Dungate v Dungate* [1965] 1 W.L.R. 1477; *Bradford & Bingley Plc v Rashid* [2006] UKHL 37; [2006] 1 W.L.R. 2066; and see *Wright v Pepin*, above.
[316] *Good v Parry* [1963] 2 Q.B. 418, as construed in *Dungate v Dungate*, above.
[317] *Ofulue v Bossert* [2009] UKHL 16; [2009] 1 A.C. 990.
[318] LA 1980 s.29(7).
[319] *Colchester BC v Smith* [1992] Ch. 421. Such compromises are in a wholly different position from the subsequent acknowledgments or payments caught by s.29(7): *Colchester BC v Smith* [1992] Ch. 421 at 435.
[320] LA 1980 s.29(7); *Sanders v Sanders* (1881) 19 Ch D 373; *Nicholson v England* [1926] 2 K.B. 93.
[321] Below, para.35–055.
[322] See *Bennett v Governor and Company of the Bank of Scotland* [2004] EWCA Civ 988 at [4], [18].

(i) The true owner cannot enforce any judgment for possession against a squatter without the leave of the court if more than six years has elapsed since it was entered.[323] Normally, the court will refuse to exercise its discretion after that time, save where it is demonstrably just to do so.[324] It should be noted that the squatter remains in adverse possession until the judgment is executed.[325] Accordingly, the squatter may have been in adverse possession for more than 12 years by the time that the judgment is actually enforced.[326] If a squatter has been in adverse possession for more than 12 years and the court refuses leave to enforce the judgment, the true owner's title will be extinguished.[327]

(ii) Instead of enforcing the judgment, the true owner may bring an action on judgment, but must do so within six years of the date of that judgment.[328]

Part 4

THE EFFECT OF THE LAPSE OF TIME

Section 1. Title to Land

A. Effect on Owner's Title

The effect of adverse possession upon the title of the true owner of unregistered land is as follows.[329]

Before 1833 the effect of the Statutes of Limitation was merely to bar rights **35–055** of action. They extinguished remedies not rights.[330] Thus a person whose right to recover land had been barred might, if he could recover it peaceably, reassert his old title.[331] This principle still applies to pure personalty, other than chattels[332]; but as regards land it was abolished by the Real Property Limitation Act 1833.[333] The rule now is that, at the end of the limitation period, both the right of action to recover the land and the claimant's title to

---

[323] CPR Sch.1 RSC Ord.46.2(a); Sch.2 CCR Ord.26.5(a). LA 1980 s.24(1) (above, para. 35–005) only bars a subsequent action brought on the judgment: see *Lowsley v Forbes* [1999] 1 A.C. 329.

[324] *National Westminster Bank Plc v Powney* [1991] Ch. 339 at 363; *Duer v Frazer* [2001] 1 W.L.R. 919.

[325] See S. Jourdan and O. Radley-Gardner, *Adverse Possession*, 2nd edn, para.15–21.

[326] *BR Properties Ltd v Buckler* (1987) 55 P. & C.R. 337 (decided under LA 1939).

[327] S. Jourdan and O. Radley-Gardner, *Adverse Possession*, 2nd edn, para.15–21.

[328] See LA 1980 s.24(1); above, para.35–005.

[329] For adverse possession of registered land under LRA 1925, see the sixth edition of this work at para.21–056.

[330] See *Wainford v Barker* (1697) 1 Ld.Raym. 232; *Hunt v Burn* (1703) 2 Salk. 422.

[331] See *Doe d. Burrough v Reade* (1807) 8 East 353 (possession peaceably taken when the land was vacant after a death).

[332] See LA 1980 s.3(2).

[333] s.34.

it are extinguished.[334] This applies equally to redemption and foreclosure actions.

When title to land has been extinguished by adverse possession, the rights which that title carried are also extinguished. The former owner cannot thereafter sue the squatter either for rent that fell due before title was extinguished or for damages for trespass.[335]

B. The Squatter's Title

35–056   **1. Rights of third parties.** The general character of a title to unregistered land acquired by limitation has already been discussed.[336] The squatter[337] holds a new estate of his own, founded on his adverse possession and the absence of any better title, but he holds it subject to any third party rights which run with the land and have not themselves been extinguished. Thus a squatter will be bound by easements or restrictive covenants affecting the land. It makes no difference whether such incumbrances are legal or equitable, or whether (if registrable as land charges) they are registered. If they are legal, they bind all corners, including squatters. If they are equitable (and even if they are registrable as land charges but unregistered[338]) they bind all persons who are not purchasers for value, and a squatter gives no value.[339]

As regards any mortgage affecting the property, the squatter will be bound by a mortgage created prior to the commencement of his adverse possession.[340] The squatter will not be bound by a charge that was created after he commenced his adverse possession,[341] because once adverse possession has commenced, it is unaffected by any disposition which the true owner may make.[342]

35–057   **2. Progressive improvement.** A squatter's estate is normally a fee simple absolute,[343] though it may be cut down by the unextinguished rights of other

---

[334] LA 1980 s.17. Notwithstanding these provisions, a squatter may be estopped from asserting that he has acquired title by his adverse possession: see *St Pancras and Humanist Housing Association v Leonard* [2008] EWCA Civ 1442.

[335] *Re Jolly* [1900] 2 Ch. 616; *Mount Carmel Investments Ltd v Peter Thurlow Ltd* [1988] 1 W.L.R. 1078.

[336] Above paras 4–003 et seq. For the position in relation to registered land under LRA 1925, see the sixth edition of this work at para.21–058.

[337] Meaning a true adverse possessor and not a mere trespasser, as explained above, para.35–016.

[338] See above, para.8–093.

[339] *Re Nisbet & Potts' Contract* [1906] 1 Ch. 386 (squatter bound by restrictive covenant: above para.4–013); *Scott v Scott* (1854) 4 H.L.C. 1065 (squatter bound by trusts of a settlement). Contrast *Bolling v Hobday* (1882) 31 W.R. 9, above, para.5–013; and an equitable title to possession may be barred: above, para.35–038.

[340] See *Ludbrook v Ludbrook* [1901] 2 K.B. 96; *Carroll v Manek* (1999) 79 P. & C.R. 173.

[341] *Thornton v France* [1897] 2 Q.B. 143; S. Jourdan and O. Radley-Gardner, *Adverse Possession*, 2nd edn, paras 26–53—26–58.

[342] LA 1980 s.15(4); S. Jourdan and O. Radley-Gardner, *Adverse Possession*, 2nd edn, para.15–06.

[343] See, e.g. *Leach v Jay* (1878) 9 Ch D 42 at 44, 45; *Rosenberg v Cook* (1881) 8 Q.B.D. 162 at 165; *Central London Commercial Estates Ltd v Kato Kagaku Ltd* [1998] 4 All E.R. 948 at 951; S. Jourdan and O. Radley-Gardner, *Adverse Possession*, 2nd edn, paras 20–23 et seq.

persons.[344] If, for example, land is held by trustees of land on trust for A for life with remainder to B in fee simple, and S occupies it for 12 years during A's lifetime, A's life interest is extinguished, but B will have at least six years from A's death in which to assert his rights.[345] Meanwhile S, who has extinguished A's equitable life interest but not the legal estate which is held on trust,[346] has an independent legal estate based on his own occupation, but subject to B's future right when it accrues. S's estate is in effect an estate *pur autre vie*. However, it is more correct to call it a fee simple subject to an adverse title, and therefore a legal estate.[347] This is because, unless B sues within the time allowed, his title will also be barred. In other words, S's title is not one which comes to a sudden stop at A's death. It continues indefinitely, until someone having a superior title contests it. The interest gained by S is therefore not necessarily commensurate with the interest lost by A.[348] The principle is that S's title may progressively improve as each successive adverse claimant becomes barred.

3. Effect on third parties. Time runs in favour of the adverse possessor throughout successive ownerships of the paper title. Any action is barred after the expiry of the limitation period, whether it accrued to the claimant himself or to some predecessor in title.[349]   **35–058**

4. Leases

(a) *Landlord not barred.* Interesting questions can arise where a squatter bars a leasehold tenant. If L leases land to T for 99 years and S occupies the land adversely to T for 12 years, S has extinguished T's title. But this has no effect on L's title.[350] L has disposed of his right to possession for the term of the lease, and nothing done by third parties in the meantime will give it back to him. L cannot therefore eject S, since apart from any right of forfeiture,[351] no right of action to recover the land will accrue to L until the expiry of the term of T's lease[352]; and S being in possession, has the best immediate title.[353]   **35–059**

---

[344] See above, para.35–024.

[345] Above para.4–008.

[346] Above, para.35–038.

[347] Above, para.4–009.

[348] See *Taylor v Twinberrow* [1930] 2 K.B. 16 at 23. Earlier dicta to the contrary are attributable to the "parliamentary conveyance" heresy: see above, para.35–002.

[349] LA 1980 s.15(1).

[350] See *Chung Ping Kwan v Lam Island Development Co Ltd* [1997] A.C. 38 at 47.

[351] e.g. for breach of covenant against parting with possession (see below), or if T denies L's title: see above, paras 18–006, 20–077.

[352] See *Jessamine Investment Co v Schwartz* [1978] Q.B. 264, where the tenant's title was barred by a sub-tenant but when the head lease expired the sub-tenant was protected by the Rent Act 1968; *Spectrum Investment Co v Holmes* [1981] 1 W.L.R. 221, where the landlord was unable to eject the squatter who had barred the tenant during a 99-year lease.

[353] Above, para 4–008. This can perhaps be made clear by comparison with the barring of a fee simple. If A is fee simple owner and sells to B, and B's title is extinguished by S (a squatter), A can assert no title against S. The same is true in the case of a reversioner as regards any time before the reversion is due to fall into possession.

35–060   *(b) Surrender of lease.* Where the title to land is unregistered,[354] if T surrenders his lease to L after time has run in S's favour, it has been held by the House of Lords that L is then entitled to eject S.[355] Thus T, whose title against S is bad, can nevertheless confer upon L a good title against S, and thus accelerate L's right to possession. This is said to follow from the fact that the lease remains valid as between L and T. But this reasoning seems unsound,[356] since it ignores the fact that T has lost all power to eject S and cannot therefore confer any such power upon L. As against S, T's lease is no longer a good title, whether pleaded by T or by L, and to allow it to be so pleaded violates the fundamental principle that no one can confer a better title than he has himself (*nemo dat quod non habet*).[357] It would be different if L had a present right to determine T's lease, for he could then assert an immediate paramount title of his own without relying upon any right derived through T.[358] The House of Lords' decision gravely impairs the squatter's statutory title, by putting it into the power of the person barred (T) to enable a third party (1) to eject the squatter. The operation of the Limitation Act 1980 in respect of leaseholds is thus substantially curtailed. It is otherwise in the case of registered land, as explained below.

35–061   *(c) Acquisition of the reversion.* If T acquires L's reversion after S has taken adverse possession, T has the same rights as L. Thus in one case, where the reversion was purchased by T, a yearly tenant whose title as such had already been barred by another person, it was held that T acquired a fresh right of action at once by stepping into the landlord's shoes. The lease merged in the freehold forthwith, for it was determined by notice and T could not give notice to himself.[359] The result is held to be the same even if the lease is for a fixed term of years which L could not determine, so that L could not eject S.[360] L's

[354] The same rules apply where the title is registered, but where the lease is granted for a term of seven years or less and so takes effect as an overriding interest under LRA 2002 Sch.3 para.1. Such leases are dealt with in the same way as unregistered land: above, para.8–001.

[355] *St Marylebone Property Co Ltd v Fairweather* [1963] A.C. 510, overruling *Walter v Yalden* [1902] 2 K.B. 304, and approving *Taylor v Twinberrow* [1930] 2 K.B. 16; and applied (though without violation of principle) in *Jessamine Investment Co v Schwartz*, above. For further criticism, see (1962) 78 L.Q.R. 541 (H.W.R.W.). The *St Marylebone* case has not been followed in Ireland: *Perry v Woodfarm Homes Ltd* [1975] I.R. 104, and the Privy Council has left open its correctness in the light of the "powerful critique" mentioned above: see *Chung Ping Kwan v Lam Island Development Co Ltd* [1997] A.C. 38 at 47, per Lord Nicholls. For a defence of the *St Marylebone* case, see (1994) 14 L.S. 1 at 7 (E. Cooke), where it is suggested that, "the tenant no longer has a key to the door, but he can stand out of the way so that the landlord can use his own key". As the tenant's interest has been extinguished, it is not clear how he can do this.

[356] See (1998) Law Com. No.254, at para.10.25, where it is pointed out: (i) that, as a contract, the lease remains on foot between L and T and T can therefore surrender his contractual liabilities (see below, para.35–062); but (ii) that this cannot affect the leasehold estate which continues to exist, even though nobody actually owns it or can deal with it.

[357] A principle to which there have been no exceptions (apart from statute) since the abolition of the old tortious conveyances: above, para.4–001.

[358] *Taylor v Twinberrow*, above.

[359] *Taylor v Twinberrow*, above. For merger, see above, para.18–090.

[360] See dicta in *St Marylebone Property Co Ltd v Fairweather* [1963] A.C. 510 at 541, 555. The House of Lords treated *Taylor v Twinberrow*, above, as inconsistent with *Walter v Yalden* [1902] 2 K.B. 304, despite the significance of the landlord's power in the former case to determine the tenancy by notice and so eject the squatter.

conveyance of the reversion thus gives T a power which L does not possess, against violating the principle *nemo dat quod non habet.*

(d) Continuing liability of tenant. Where, in relation to a lease the title to **35–062** which is not registered, a tenant has lost his title to an interloper by adverse possession, he may still remain liable to the landlord on the covenants in the lease (e.g. for rent) because of the continuing privity of contract. It has been held that, since the leasehold estate is extinguished, there is no longer any privity of estate, so that if the tenant were an assignee of the lease rather than the original tenant he would cease to be liable on the covenants when his title became barred.[361] But the better view is that the leasehold estate is extinguished only as against the squatter, and that privity of estate remains as between the landlord and the tenant.[362]

(e) Liability of squatter. The position of S, in our example, is that he has a **35–063** legal fee simple,[363] subject to a right of entry at the end of the period of the original term. Having no privity of estate with L, S is not liable on the covenants in T's lease,[364] except so far as they may be enforceable in equity as restrictive covenants.[365] But if T's lease was determinable by notice, or contained a forfeiture clause, L can enforce these terms against S,[366] and so by threat of notice or forfeiture compel S to perform the covenants. In such case, S has no right to apply for relief against forfeiture.[367] The reason why such a clause is enforceable against S, even where the covenant itself is not, is that a covenant creates a purely personal obligation unless it is a restrictive covenant or there is privity of estate. However, a clause which reserves to the lessor a conditional right of entry gives him a proprietary right (a right of entry for condition broken)[368] and therefore binds a squatter just like any other successor in title. Furthermore, although a squatter might not be liable to be sued on the covenant for the rent, he might be liable to distress if he did not pay it.[369] This is because distress was a tenurial remedy enforceable against all occupiers of the land if the rent-service was not paid.[370]

---

[361] *Re Field* [1918] 1 I.R. 140.

[362] *Spectrum Investment Co v Holmes* [1981] 1 W.L.R. 221 at 226; *Taylor v Twinberrow* [1930] 2 K.B. 16.

[363] See *Central London Commercial Estates Ltd v Kato Kagaku Ltd* [1998] 4 All E.R. 948 at 951.

[364] *Tichborne v Weir* (1892) 67 L.T. 735 (unsuccessful action for damages on repairing covenant against assignee of a mortgage of a lease who had taken possession and barred the tenant's equity of redemption; the action was brought after the term had expired). Nor will a squatter be bound by "implied covenants", for they arise from the relationship of landlord and tenant, i.e. from privity of estate; above, para.19–002.

[365] *Re Nisbet & Potts' Contract* [1906] 1 Ch. 386; above para.35–056.

[366] *Humfrey v Damion* (1612) Cro.Jac. 300 (forfeiture); and cf. *Taylor v Twinberrow* above.

[367] *Tickner v Buzzacott* [1965] Ch. 426. For the question whether T can deliberately bring about a forfeiture, e.g. by not paying rent, and so enable L to eject S, see *St Marylebone Property Co Ltd v Fairweather* [1963] A.C. 510 at 547; and (1962) 78 L.Q.R. 541 at 555 (H.W.R.W.).

[368] LPA 1925 ss.1(2)(e), 4(2)(b); above, para.6–027. For the operation of forfeiture clauses against third parties, see above, paras 20–077, 20–078.

[369] *Humfrey v Damion*, above.

[370] Distress is to be abolished, subject to the introduction of a new system of commercial rent arrears recovery: see above, paras 19–076, 19–077.

It follows that an adverse occupant of unregistered leasehold land will almost always have to pay the rent. Although the matter depends on the intentions of the parties in any case, the trend of modern authority is, however, to treat those who have entered as trespassers but from whom the landlord has accepted rent, as tenants at will rather than periodic tenants.[371] However, if the squatter takes advantage of the previous tenant's lease he may estop himself from denying that he holds under it. In this way—but only in this way—he may become bound by the covenants. The principle here is that a person who claims the benefit of a deed is estopped from denying that he has accepted all its terms.[372] Mere payment of the rent reserved by the former lease raises no estoppel against a squatter,[373] for he is not claiming any benefit from the lease but merely performing one of the conditions of tenure. But it was held that an estoppel arose where the squatter took advantage of a clause in the lease that the rent should be halved so long as the covenants were observed. Having paid rent at the half rate, he was said to be precluded from denying that he was bound by the covenants.[374]

C. Proof of Title

35–064   **1. Long possession not enough.** As between vendor and purchaser of unregistered land, a good title cannot be shown under open contract[375] merely by proving adverse possession of land, however long the period.[376] If A and his predecessors in title have been in possession for 20, 50 or 100 years, that does not prove that A is entitled to it, for the true owner:

(i)   might have been under disability at the time of dispossession; or

(ii) might have been the Crown; or

(iii) might have been the reversioner or remainderman under a settlement; or

(iv) might be the reversioner on a long lease.

35–065   **2. Proving owner barred.** Consequently, in order to establish a good title to unregistered land by operation of the Limitation Act, the vendor must prove:

---

[371] See above, para.17–084.

[372] Litt. 374, and authorities cited in *Norton on Deeds*, 26, 27. However, this principle is a limited one: see [1998] C.L.J. 522 at 523–525 (C. Davies); and above, paras 32–024—32–025.

[373] *Tichborne v Weir* (1892) 67 L.T. 735.

[374] *Ashe v Hogan* [1920] 1 I.R. 159 (999-year lease at rent of £8 reducible to £4 so long as covenants observed); and see *O'Connor v Foley* [1906] 1 I.R. 20. Yet it is not easy to see what other course is open to the squatter than to pay such rent as is legally due, or why by paying the one and only correct amount he makes any representation which estops him.

[375] See above, para.15–001.

[376] *Moulton v Edmonds* (1859) 1 De G.F. & J. 246 at 250; *Jacobs v Revell* [1900] 2 Ch. 858.

(i) the title of the former owner of the interest in land in question; and

(ii) the extinction of that title in the vendor's favour.

This is a heavy burden of proof, particularly since, if the title is unregistered, the vendor will often not have access to the title deeds of the land acquired by limitation.[377] But if the vendor can discharge the burden of proof, he can force the purchaser to accept his title.[378]

D. Exclusion of Limitation

In specified cases statute precludes the acquisition of a title by limitation. Thus no right adverse to the title of the Coal Authority to any coal or mine of coal can be acquired by limitation.[379]

    There may be circumstances in which a person is estopped from relying upon a defence under the Limitation Act 1980. This will only be the case where there is a shared and communicated assumption that there was a valid claim and the party who could have taken the defence would not do so.[380]

35–066

Section 2. Arrears of Income

1. Rent. The recovery of arrears of income is a matter distinct from the recovery of the land or capital money which produces it. The arrears of rent which a landlord or the owner of a rentcharge may recover, whether by action or distress, are limited to the arrears accrued due during the preceding six years,[381] whether or not the rent is payable under a deed.[382] Each time a gale of rent falls due, a new cause of action accrues,[383] and so the six years' period begins to run in respect of it. Even if the rent has not been paid for, say, 20 years, a landlord whose title has not become barred[384] may at any time enforce payment of the last six years' arrears of rent, and future rent as it falls due. With the exception of a nominal rent payable under a lease capable of

35–067

---

[377] But he may be able to demand them under the rule that the deeds belong to the owner of the land: above, para.8–034.

[378] *Scott v Nixon* (1843) 3 Dr. & War. 388; *Games v Bonnor* (1884) 54 L.J.Ch. 517; *Re Atkinson & Horsell's Contract* [1912] 2 Ch. 1. Contrast *George Wimpey & Co Ltd v Sohn* [1967] Ch. 87. Unless he has been registered with an absolute title, a vendor will in practice always sell such land subject to a special condition of sale.

[379] Coal Industry Act 1994 s.10(2). For earlier legislation, see Coal Act 1938 s.17(2); Coal Industry Nationalisation Act 1946 s.49(3); Coal Industry Act 1987 s.1.

[380] See *Hillingdon London Borough Council v ARC Ltd (No.2)* [2000] 3 E.G.L.R. 97 at 104; *Llanelec Precision Engineering Co Ltd v Neath Port Talbot County Borough Council* [2000] 3 E.G.L.R. 158, at 163.

[381] LA 1980 s.19. This rule applies not only to the tenant but also to any guarantor who has expressly undertaken the same obligations as the tenant: *Romain v Scuba TV Ltd* [1997] Q.B. 887.

[382] LA 1980 s.8(2).

[383] *Re Jolly* [1900] 2 Ch. 616.

[384] See above, para.35–026. It is otherwise if the title of the landlord has been barred: see *Re Jolly*, above; *Mount Carmel Investments Ltd v Peter Thurlow Ltd* [1988] 1 W.L.R. 1078 at 1088; above, para.35–055.

enlargement into a fee simple,[385] mere non-payment of rent never extinguishes the liability for future rent[386]; but it is otherwise with rentcharges.[387] However, in the case of agricultural holdings, the landlord's right of distress is restricted to rent which fell due, or would normally have been paid, in the year preceding the distress[388]; and there are special rules for bankruptcy.[389]

35–068   **2. Mortgage interest.** There is also a six years' period for any action for arrears of mortgage interest.[390] But a mortgagee who exercises his power of sale may retain all arrears of interest, however old, out of the proceeds of sale, for this is not recovery by action.[391] If the first mortgagee sells, the second mortgagee is similarly entitled to all his arrears of interest out of the surplus proceeds of sale.[392] A secured creditor, who has obtained a charging order, may recover more than six years' interest out of the proceeds of enforcing his security.[393] Further, a mortgagor who seeks to redeem can do so only on the equitable terms of paying all arrears of interest.[394]

35–069   **3. Part payment.** Though payment of part of any arrears of rent or interest may start time running again in respect of the land or the capital,[395] it does not extend the period for claiming the rest of the arrears.[396]

Part 5

ADVERSE POSSESSION OF REGISTERED LAND

Section 1. General Principles

35–070   **1. Introduction.** A squatter in possession of unregistered land has a title that is good against all the world except the rightful owner.[397] By reason of the

---

[385] LPA 1925 s.153; see above, para.14–178. In such cases a rent of £1 a year or less becomes irrecoverable if unpaid for a continuous period of 20 years, of which at least five have elapsed since 1925: LPA 1925 s.153.

[386] Above, para.35–028.

[387] Above, para.35–034.

[388] AHA 1986 s.16 (replacing earlier legislation). It does not affect an action for the rent, as distinct from distress. There is no equivalent provision in relation to farm business tenancies under ATA 1995.

[389] IA 1986 s.347 (six months' rent due before commencement of bankruptcy).

[390] LA 1980 s.20(5); but see subs.(6) for the position where a prior incumbrancer has been in possession; and see subs.(7) as regards capitalisation of arrears of interest.

[391] *Re Marshfield* (1887) 34 Ch D 721; *Re Lloyd* [1903] 1 Ch. 385. *Secus* if the mortgage itself is barred: *Re Hazeldine's Trusts* [1908] 1 Ch. 34.

[392] *Thomson's Mortgage Trusts* [1920] 1 Ch. 508; compare *Young v Clarey* [1948] Ch. 191, where the right of redemption was barred.

[393] *Ezekial v Orakpo* [1997] 1 W.L.R. 340. See too *Yorkshire Bank Finance Ltd v Mulhall* [2008] EWCA Civ 1156; [2009] 1 P. & C.R. 345.

[394] *Elvy v Norwood* (1852) 5 De G. & Sm. 240; *Dingle v Coppen* [1899] 1 Ch. 726; *Holmes v Cowcher* [1970] 1 W.L.R. 834 (approving this statement); *Ezekial v Orakpo* [1997] 1 W.L.R. 340 at 347.

[395] Above para.35–051.

[396] LA 1980 s.29(6).

[397] See above, paras 4–003, 4–004.

principles of adverse possession that have been explained in this chapter, the squatter will acquire an indefeasible title once the true owner's title is extinguished.[398] Although title to unregistered land is normally derivative,[399] it rests ultimately upon possession. A vendor of unregistered land proves his title by showing that the property has been enjoyed according to a paper title for at least 15 years.[400] The basis of title to registered land is registration and the register proves a vendor's title.[401] The registration of a person as proprietor vests in him the legal and beneficial ownership,[402] and this is so even if the title would not otherwise have vested in him, as where registration is induced by a forged conveyance or transfer.[403] In most states within the Commonwealth which have a system of registered title, the principles of adverse possession that apply to unregistered land in this country have either been abolished or modified.[404] For a period between 1875 and 1898 adverse possession of registered land in England and Wales was impossible.[405] However, that position was abandoned, and the law of adverse possession was applied to registered land in a similar (but not identical) manner to unregistered land.[406] The Land Registration Act 2002 introduced a completely new system for dealing with adverse possession of registered land, which was intended to reflect the indefeasible nature of the title conferred by registration.[407]

Under the new system, adverse possession of a registered estate has no effect as such upon the title of the registered proprietor however long that period of adverse possession may have been. However, after 10 years, the squatter may apply to be registered as proprietor.[408] If the registered proprietor objects to the application, it will be rejected except in very limited circumstances. If, before any application to register is made, the registered proprietor takes proceedings to establish his right to possession, those proceedings will be successful except where the squatter would have been entitled to be registered had he applied. Where a squatter's application to be registered is rejected, the registered proprietor must take takes steps either to evict the squatter or to legitimise his possession within two years of that rejection, or the squatter may re-apply and, provided that he has remained in adverse possession for that two-year period, his application will be successful.[409]

---

[398] See *Perry v Clissold* [1907] A.C. 73 at 76.

[399] See above, para.4–003.

[400] See above, paras 15–076, 15–077.

[401] See above, para.15–086.

[402] See above, paras 7–116 (first registration), 7–117 (registration as proprietor of a registered estate).

[403] See LRA 2002 s.58.

[404] See (1998) Law Com. No.254, para.10.17.

[405] (1998) Law Com. No.254, para.10.20.

[406] See LRA 1925 s.75. For the principles of adverse possession under LRA 1925, see the sixth edition of this work at paras 21–056, 21–058, 21–060, 21–064, 21–066, 21–068, 21–069.

[407] See (2001) Law Com. No.271, Pt.XIV.

[408] See LRA 2002 s.97; Sch.6.

[409] The relevant provisions are LRA 2002 ss.96–98 and Sch.6; and see LRPG 4.

35–071   **2. Disapplication of limitation periods.** Under the Land Registration Act 2002, the time limits applicable under the Limitation Act 1980 to:

> (i) actions for the recovery of land[410]; and
>
> (ii) actions for redemption[411];

are disapplied in relation to an estate in land or a rentcharge the title to which is registered.[412]

The reason why the Limitation Act 1980 does not apply to actions for the recovery of the registered estate or rentcharge is because the register is conclusive as to the ownership of that registered estate or rentcharge.[413] The conclusive nature of such registration protects that registered proprietor.[414] Time does not run in favour of registered chargee because such possession is not adverse and the rule applicable to unregistered land is anomalous.[415] Where time does not run, it is further provided that the title of the person against whom there has been adverse possession will not be extinguished either.[416] In consequence of these provisions, a registered proprietor's title can never be barred by adverse possession.

This rule is subject to one exception: actions brought for the recovery of land by chargees remain subject to the time limits in the Limitation Act 1980.[417] This is because the chargee's rights to recover possession or fore-close[418] are directly linked to, and are a form of security for, his rights to recover the monies secured by the charge. If the chargee can no longer sue for those monies, his other remedies should also be barred.[419]

35–072   Accordingly, the provisions of the Limitation Act 1980 will not apply in any of the following situations:

> (i) where a squatter has taken adverse possession of a registered freehold or leasehold estate;
>
> (ii) where no rent has been paid under a registered rentcharge or has been paid to a third party; or

---

[410] Under LA 1980 s.15; above, paras 35–007, 35–034.

[411] Under LA 1980 s.16; above, para.35–035.

[412] LRA 2002 s.96(1), (2).

[413] See (2001) Law Com. No.271, at para.14.10.

[414] And those who derive title under him in the case of lessees holding under leases granted by the registered proprietor that, by reason of their duration are not registrable with their own titles. For the lease which must be registered, which includes all leases granted after October 12, 2003 for more than 7 years, see above, para.7–054.

[415] See (2001) Law Com. No.271 at paras 14.15–14.18, where the reasons are set out in detail.

[416] LRA 2002 s.96(3). cf. LA 1980 s.17; above, para.35–055.

[417] LRA 2002 s.96(1).

[418] Which is treated as an action for possession for these purposes: see LA 1980 s.20(4); above, para.35–036.

[419] See (2001) Law Com. No.271, paras 14.12–14.14.

(iii) where a registered chargee has taken possession of a registered estate subject to the charge.

Conversely, in the following cases involving registered land, the provisions of the Limitation Act 1980 will apply in the usual way to:

(i) a registered chargee's right to enforce its charge by proceedings for possession or foreclosure[420];

(ii) an action for possession brought against a lessee under a lease, which, by reason of its duration, is not registered[421];

(iii) an action for possession brought by a licensee or a tenant at will who is ousted by a squatter;

(iv) an action for possession brought by squatter A against squatter B, where squatter B has ousted squatter A[422];

(v) proceedings brought to enforce a right of re-entry in relation to a lease (as where there has been a breach of covenant)[423]; and

(vi) proceedings brought to enforce a right of re-entry in relation to a fee simple that is subject to a condition subsequent, where the conditional event has occurred.[424]

Situations (iii) and (iv) are cases where proceedings are brought by an occupant of registered land who is not a registered proprietor, but who has a better right to possession than the person who ousts him unless and until his rights are barred by adverse possession. In situations (v) and (vi), what is barred by limitation is not a registered estate, but the right of re-entry.

3. Applications for registration

(a) *The general rule.* As a general rule,[425] a person may apply to the **35–073** registrar to be registered as proprietor of a registered estate in land if he has been in adverse possession of the estate for a period of 10 years ending on the date of the application.[426] Although the estate must be registered at the date of the application, it need not have been registered throughout the period of

---

[420] See above, para.35–036.

[421] In practice this will be limited to leases granted for 21 years or less prior to October 13, 2003, when LRA 2002 was brought into force. Such leases were not registrable and took effect as overriding interests under LRA 1925 s.70(1)(k). Under LRA 2002, the only leases that are not required to be registered are those granted for a term of seven years or less (but even this is subject to exceptions): see above, para.7–054.

[422] cf. above, para.4–008.

[423] See above, para.35–029.

[424] See above, 35–007.

[425] For certain special cases, see below, paras 35–093 (rentcharges) and 35–094 (trusts).

[426] LRA 2002 Sch.6, para.1(1). In relation to the foreshore, were the estate is registered in the name of the Crown or Royal Duchy, the relevant period of adverse possession is 60 years rather than 10: LRA 2002 Sch.6 para.13. cf. para.35–010, above.

adverse possession.[427] For these purposes, subject to technical exceptions,[428] adverse possession has the same meaning as it does in the context of actions for the recovery of unregistered land.[429] Accordingly, the squatter must prove both factual possession and the necessary *animus possidendi*.[430] The 10-year period of adverse possession must necessarily be continuous, just as it must be in relation to adverse possession of unregistered land.[431] If squatter A abandons possession and subsequently squatter B takes possession, B cannot count the period of A's adverse possession, because there has been a time when no person was in adverse possession. Where there have been successive squatters, A and B, B can take advantage of squatter A's prior period of adverse possession if:

(i) B is A's successor in title[432]; or

(ii) A had evicted B, and B has then recovered possession from A.[433]

However, if B has dispossessed A without any prior claim to possess, B cannot add A's period of adverse possession to his own, because he is not A's successor in title. This is different from the position where title is unregistered.[434] The purpose of the rule is to ensure that if the applicant for registration is successful, there can be no challenge to his title by some prior squatter.[435]

The mere fact that, within the period when the squatter claims to have been in adverse possession, he has made a written acknowledgment of the registered proprietor's title, does not cause time to run afresh. A registered proprietor does not need that additional protection because adverse possession for however long a period has no effect as such on the registered proprietor's title.[436] A written acknowledgment by a squatter may still be relevant, because it may demonstrate that the squatter lacked the necessary *animus possidendi* to be in adverse possession.[437]

If a person, who had not in fact been in adverse possession for 10 years, applied to be registered as proprietor under the provisions of the Act that are explained below, and he was registered, that registration would be a mistake.

---

[427] LRA 2002 Sch.6 para.1(4).
[428] See LRA 2002 Sch.6 para.11(3): see (2001) Law Com. No.271, para.14.23.
[429] Above, para.35–016. By LRA 2002 Sch.6 para.11(1), a person will be in adverse possession if a period of limitation under the provisions of LA 1980 s.15 (above, para.35–007), would run in his favour but for LRA 2002 s.96. For LRA 2002 s.96, see above, para.35–071.
[430] See above, paras 35–016—35–019.
[431] See above, para.35–023.
[432] As where B acquired the land by a conveyance on sale from A.
[433] LRA 2002 Sch.6 para.11(2).
[434] See above, para.35–022.
[435] See (2001) Law Com. No.271, para.14.26
[436] See above, para.35–071.
[437] cf. above, para.35–019.

The registrar or court could therefore order the alteration of the register to reinstate the true owner.[438]

If a squatter has been in adverse possession of a registered estate for 10 **35–074** years or more, he will not lose his right to apply to be registered if he is evicted by the registered proprietor or a person claiming under the registered proprietor provided that:

(i) his application for registration is made within six months of his eviction;

(ii) he was entitled to apply to be registered on the day before his eviction; and

(iii) his eviction was not pursuant to a judgment for possession.[439]

(b) Where no application can be made. A squatter may not apply to be **35–075** registered in four circumstances:

(i) If he is a defendant in proceedings which involve asserting a right to possession of the land.[440]

(ii) Where a judgment for possession has been given against him in the last two years.[441]

(iii) During any period in which the existing registered proprietor is, for the purposes of the Limitation (Enemies and War Prisoners) Act 1945[442] an enemy or detained in enemy territory and within 12 months thereafter.[443]

(iv) During any period in which the existing registered proprietor is either unable because of mental disability[444] to make decisions about issues of the kind to which such an application would give rise, or unable to communicate such a decision because of mental disability or physical impairment.[445]

Where it appears to the registrar that either situation (iii) or (iv) applies in relation to a registered estate in land, he may include a note to that effect in the register.[446] That is seldom likely to be the case.

---

[438] *Baxter v Mannion* [2011] EWCA Civ 120; [2011] 1 W.L.R. 1594. For alteration of the register, see LRA 2002 Sch.4; above, paras 7–132 et seq.

[439] LRA 2002 Sch.6 para.1(2).

[440] LRA 2002 Sch.6 para.1(3)(a).This would include not just possession proceedings as such, but also proceedings for declaratory or injunctive relief. cf. para.35–007 above, in the context of LA 1980 s.15.

[441] LRA 2002 Sch.6 para.1(3)(b).

[442] See above, para.35–013.

[443] LRA 2002 Sch.6 para.8(1).

[444] That is, a disability or disorder of the mind or brain, whether permanent or temporary, which results in an impairment or disturbance of mental functioning: LRA 2002 Sch.6 para.8(3).

[445] LRA 2002 Sch.6 para.8(2).

[446] LRA 2002 Sch.6 para.8(4).

35–076   *(c) Application for registration.* The application by the squatter to be registered must be made in prescribed form[447] and must be supported by a statutory declaration or statement of truth[448] that:

> (i) sets out the evidence of adverse possession upon which the applicant relies;
>
> (ii) contains certain other specified information; and
>
> (iii) exhibits a plan of the land claimed that enables it to be identified either from the Ordnance Survey map or from the relevant title plan.[449]

35–077   The registrar must give notice of the application to the following persons[450]:

> (i) the proprietor of the estate to which the application relates[451];
>
> (ii) the proprietor of any charge on the estate[452];
>
> (iii) where the estate is leasehold, the proprietor of any superior registered estate[453]; and
>
> (iv) any person who can satisfy the registrar that he has an interest in a registered estate in land or in a registered rentcharge which would be prejudiced by the registration of any other person as proprietor of that estate or rentcharge under the adverse possession provisions of Schedule 6 of the Land Registration Act 2002.[454]

The notice given by the registrar will inform the recipient:

> (a) of the squatter's application[455];
>
> (b) that the recipient can serve a counter-notice on the registrar requiring the registrar to reject the application unless the squatter can satisfy one of the conditions which entitle him to be registered[456]; and

---

[447] Application is made on Form ADV1: LRR 2003 r.188(1).

[448] The statement of truth may be made in Form ST1: see LRR 2002 r.188(4).

[449] LRR 2003 r.188(1), (2).

[450] Although the registrar may (and does) notify other persons of the application (see LRPG 4, para.6.3), only the persons set out in (i)–(iv) are given the right to object to the application that is explained in para.35–078 below.

[451] LRA 2002 Sch.6 para.2(1)(a).

[452] LRA 2002 Sch.6 para.2(1)(b).

[453] LRA 2002 Sch.6 para.2(1)(c).

[454] This states the effect of LRA 2002 Sch.6 paras 2(1)(d), (e); LRR 2003 r.194(1). A person must apply to the registrar using Form ADV2 to establish his entitlement: see LRR 2003 r.194(2). It is not enough that a person has an interest in the land in adverse possession. It must be one that will be prejudiced by the registration of the squatter.

[455] LRA 2002 Sch.6 para.2(1).

[456] See para.35–078.

(c)   that if such a counter-notice is not served, the registrar must enter the applicant as the new proprietor of the estate.[457]

Because of the importance of the registrar's notice of an application by a squatter, it is essential that all registered proprietors ensure that their address for service with the Land Registry is kept up-to-date.[458]

On receipt of the notice of the application from the registrar, the recipient may: **35–078**

(i)   consent to the application; or

(ii)   object to the application because the applicant should not have made it,[459] e.g. because he has not been in adverse possession for 10 years or at all, or because no valid application could be made[460]; and/or

(iii)   serve a counter-notice requiring the registrar to deal with the squatter's application in the manner explained below.[461]

Although only the recipient of the notice can consent to the registration or serve a counter-notice, anyone may object to the application for registration,[462] so that someone with no direct interest in the land claimed might object to the application. Commonly, the recipient of the registrar's notice will both object to the application and serve a counter-notice,[463] and the prescribed form of counter-notice has provision for an objection to be made within it.[464]

If the recipient of the registrar's notice consents to the application, or fails **35–079** to serve a counter-notice, the squatter must be registered as proprietor.[465] The reason for this is that, in cases where the registered proprietor has, e.g., disappeared, or chooses not to contest the application because the land is of little value to him, it is desirable that the title should follow possession and that the squatter should therefore be registered. This is because it ensures that the land remains marketable.[466]

---

[457] LRA 2002 Sch.6 paras 2(2), 4.

[458] For the address for service of notice, see LRR 2003 r.198.

[459] An objection must be made in accordance with LRR 2003 r.19.

[460] See above, para.35–075.

[461] At paras 35–079—35–080; see LRA 2002 Sch.6 para.3(1). The counter-notice must be in Form NAP (LRR 2003 r.190) and must be served within 65 business days of the registrar's notice: LRA 2002 Sch.6 para.3(2); LRR 2003 r.189. If, by mistake, the recipient fails to tick the box in Form NAP which states that he requires the registrar to deal with the matter pursuant to LRA 2002 Sch.6 para.5, but a reasonable recipient of the counter-notice would realise his mistake, the matter can be dealt with under para.5: *Hopkins v Beacon* [2011] EWHC 2899 (Ch).

[462] LRA 2002 s.73(1); above, para.7–129.

[463] See LRPG 4, para.6.3.

[464] See Form NAP. The grounds of objection must be specified.

[465] LRA 2002 Sch.6 para.4.

[466] See (2001) Law Com. No.271, para.14.6(2).

By contrast, if a counter-notice is served, the registrar must reject the squatter's application, unless the squatter can show that he satisfies one of the three conditions[467] which are explained below.[468] In the statutory declaration accompanying the application for registration, the squatter must state whether he intends to rely upon any of the three grounds should a counter-notice be served, and if he does, the facts that support his reliance.[469] If he fails to state such grounds, his application will be rejected on receipt of a counter-notice.[470] If he does rely upon such grounds, the registrar will consider whether the squatter has shown an arguable ground for his reliance. If the registrar considers that there are such arguable grounds, he will contact the persons who served a counter-notice.[471] If they dispute the grounds or have already objected to them in the counter-notice, then unless the registrar considers that their objection is groundless, he must refer the matter to the adjudicator to be resolved.[472]

Where there has been an objection to the application whether or not there has also been a counter-notice, the registrar must also refer the matter to the adjudicator provided that he does not consider that the objection is groundless.[473]

35–080   *(d) The three grounds on which a squatter may be registered.* If a counter-notice is served, a squatter is only entitled to be registered if one of three conditions is satisfied. Only the third condition is based solely upon adverse possession. In the other two cases, it would be open to the squatter to seek registration on other grounds. It will necessarily be incumbent on the squatter to show that he satisfies the condition or conditions upon which he relies.

35–081   (1) ESTOPPEL. The first condition is that it would be unconscionable because of an equity by estoppel for the registered proprietor to seek to dispossess the applicant and the circumstances are such that the applicant ought to be registered as proprietor.[474] The situation is therefore one where the squatter seeks to be registered according to the principles of proprietary estoppel, so as to give effect to an equity that has arisen in his favour. Those principles have been explained.[475] Situations in which it would be unconscionable for an owner to dispossess a squatter by reason of such an equity are likely to be rare, because the squatter is a trespasser, but they might occur, as where a squatter mistakenly builds on a neighbour's land, thinking it to be his own, and the neighbour, realising the squatter's mistake, acquiesces in it.[476]

---

[467] LRA 2002 Sch.6 para.5(1).
[468] Paras 35–080—35–083.
[469] See LRR 2003 r.188(2)(g).
[470] See LRPG 4, para.8.
[471] LRPG 4, para.8.
[472] LRA 2002 s.73(7); above, para.7–129. For the adjudicator, see above, para.7–130.
[473] See LRPG 4, para.7.
[474] LRA 2002 Sch.6 para.5(2).
[475] See above, Ch.16.
[476] See (2001) Law Com. No.271, para.14.40.

There may be cases which come before the court or the adjudicator in which an equity may have arisen in favour of a squatter, where the judge or the adjudicator considers that the squatter is entitled to some relief, but not to the extent that he should be registered as proprietor of the land which he has adversely possessed. In such circumstances, both the court, under its equitable jurisdiction, and the adjudicator, by statute,[477] have power to give effect to the equity by giving some less extensive relief.

A squatter who considers that he is entitled to the land in question because of an equity arising by estoppel does not have to apply to the registrar to be registered under the procedures under the Land Registration Act 2002 that have been explained above. He may, of course, take court proceedings in the usual way to establish his equity and to ask the court to give effect to it.

(2) OTHER REASON ENTITLING THE APPLICANT TO BE REGISTERED. The second condition is that the applicant is for some other reason entitled to be registered.[478] There are no limitations on what this other reason might be.[479] It is irrelevant that the applicant could have established his right to be registered in some other way, whether by way of an application to alter the register or in court proceedings. If the applicant can demonstrate that he has been in adverse possession for 10 years, he is entitled to apply under the adverse possession provisions of the Land Registration Act 2002. It may be more convenient to do so, as where the applicant is relying on two or more of the three conditions in the alternative. **35–082**

(3) MISTAKE AS TO BOUNDARY. Although the register is conclusive as to title,[480] it is not normally conclusive as to boundaries because, except in the rare cases where the boundary has been determined,[481] the register does not determine the exact line of the boundary.[482] In relation to boundaries, therefore, acquisition of title by adverse possession can be justified for much the same reasons as it can in relation to unregistered land, and, in particular, it quiets titles.[483] The Land Registration Act 2002 permits a squatter to acquire title solely on the ground of adverse possession in one tightly drawn situation.[484] **35–083**

---

[477] LRA 2002 s.110(4).

[478] LRA 2002 Sch.6 para.5(3).

[479] Examples might include where the squatter is entitled to a conveyance of the land, e.g. under a will or an intestacy, or because he has purchased and paid for the land, but where, in either case, there had been no transfer in his favour: see (2001) Law Com. No.271, para.14.43. Although the wording of LRA 2002 Sch.6 para.5(3) would appear to be wide enough to include the case where the applicant claimed to have been in adverse possession for more than 12 years before LRA 2002 came into force, which would give him a right to be registered (see below, para. 35–095), the practice of the Land Registry is to require such an application for registration to be made by Form AP1: see LRPG 5, para.5.2. For Form AP1, see above, para.7–059.

[480] LRA 2002 s.58; above, para.7–117.

[481] Under LRA 2002 s.60(3), (4); LRR 2003 rr.118–122; above, para.7–118.

[482] The so-called "general boundaries rule": see LRA 2002 s.60(1); above, para.7–118.

[483] See above, para.35–001.

[484] LRA 2002 Sch.6, para.5(4). See *Zarb v Parry* [2011] EWCA Civ 1306.

To establish this third condition, the squatter must show each of the following:

(i) The land to which the application relates is adjacent to land belonging to the applicant.[485] This requirement restricts the condition to boundary disputes.

(ii) The exact line of the boundary between the two properties has not been determined under the procedure provided for in the Act and the Rules.[486] In other words, the condition applies only to a general boundary. Once a boundary has been determined in accordance with the statutory procedure,[487] the register is conclusive and the justification for the third condition no longer exists.

(iii) That the squatter or a predecessor in title has not only been in adverse possession for at least 10 years ending on the date of the application,[488] but that for at least 10 years of that period, the applicant or his predecessor in title reasonably believed that the land to which the application related belonged to him.[489] This mental element is the most important requirement of this condition and it means that the period of adverse possession necessary to support the condition will in fact have to be longer than 10 years.[490] The period of reasonable belief as to ownership must last for 10 years. That period of reasonable belief will come to an end once the squatter becomes aware that he does not own the land. Only then will he realise that an application for registration must be made. He must remain in adverse possession until he makes that application, unless he is evicted by the registered proprietor otherwise than pursuant to a judgment for possession, and on the day before his eviction, he satisfied this mental element.[491]

(iv) The estate to which the application relates must have been registered more than one year prior to the date of the application.[492] This requirement is intended to meet the situation which would arise where the title to unregistered land was first registered at a time when a squatter had been in adverse possession of that land

---

[485] LRA 2002 Sch.6 para.5(4)(a).

[486] LRA 2002 Sch.6 para.5(4)(b).

[487] Under LRA 2002 s.60(3), (4); LRR 2003 rr.118–122.

[488] Or 60 years in the case of Crown foreshore: see above, para.35–073.

[489] LRA 2002 Sch.6 para.5(4)(c). The period for which this belief must be held is 10 years even in the case of Crown foreshore, where there must have been 60 years of adverse possession before an application for registration can be made: see LRA 2002 Sch.6 para.13; above, para.35–073.

[490] If the squatter can satisfy this requirement, he is likely thereby to satisfy the requirement of *animus possidendi* for adverse possession, because he believed that he was the owner of the land: see *Prudential Assurance Co Ltd v Waterloo Real Estate Inc* [1999] 2 E.G.L.R. 85; above, para.35–019. See too (2001) Law Com. No.271, para.14.51.

[491] See LRA 2002 Sch.6 para.5(5). See LRA 2002 Sch.6 para.1(2); above, para.35–074.

[492] LRA 2002 Sch.6 para.5(5).

for more than 10 years but less than 12 years.[493] But for this provision, the squatter could apply to be registered as proprietor as soon as the title was registered even though he had not extinguished the unregistered title by adverse possession prior to first registration. In that situation, by reason of this requirement, the registered proprietor has a period of one year after first registration to terminate a squatter's adverse possession, whether by seeking possession or by granting the squatter a lease or licence.

The third condition will commonly apply in cases where the legal and **35–084** physical boundaries of land do not coincide.[494] Sometimes this happens because, e.g., on the construction of a new estate, the fences or walls between the different lots are constructed in the wrong place. It can also happen, where the legal boundary does not follow the natural features on the land. Another case where the third condition might apply is where the registered proprietor leads the squatter to believe that the parcel of land is his. If the squatter acts to his detriment in reliance upon this representation (express or implied), he can rely upon the first condition (estoppel).[495] But where there is no such reliance, the squatter will have to rely on this third condition.[496]

(e) The squatter's right to make a further application. If a squatter's **35–085** application to be registered is rejected, the effect of the Act is to require the registered proprietor to take steps within two years of that rejection to terminate the squatter's adverse possession, whether by taking possession proceedings or by granting the squatter a lease or licence to remain on the land. Under the Act, where:

(i) a squatter has been in adverse possession for 10 years or more and has applied to be registered as proprietor;

(ii) the registered proprietor has objected to that application;

(iii) the squatter cannot bring himself within one of the three conditions explained above;

(iv) the squatter's application has therefore been rejected; but

(v) the squatter remains in adverse possession for two years beginning on the date of the rejection of his application

---

[493] See (2001) Law Com. No.271, para.14.45.

[494] See (2001) Law Com. No.271, para.14.46; *Zarb v Parry* [2011] EWCA Civ 1306. Where this is the case, and the squatter can show 10 years of adverse possession, there will in practice be a presumption that he has satisfied the requirement of reasonable belief. In those circumstances, the registered proprietor would have to show that the squatter or his predecessor in title did in fact know that the disputed land was not his, e.g., because he had been told.

[495] See above, para.35–081.

[496] See (2001) Law Com. No.271, para.14.46.

the squatter is entitled to make a further application to be registered[497] and, if he does, he is entitled to be registered as proprietor.[498]

Rules have made provision as to the form of application[499] and the contents of the supporting statutory declaration.[500] The categories of persons to whom the registrar will give notice of the squatter's application are the same as in the case of the squatter's initial application.[501] The squatter will be registered if no objection is made to the application[502] or if the recipients of the notice consent to it.[503] The only grounds on which an objection can be made are that:

> (i) the squatter was not in adverse possession for all or part of the two year period following the rejection of his application to be registered; or
>
> (ii) the squatter was not entitled to make the application for the reasons explained in the next paragraph, and that the statements in the statutory declaration supporting the application are therefore incorrect.[504]

35–086   A squatter cannot make an application to be registered two years after the rejection of his initial application in three circumstances:

> (i) if he is at that time a defendant in proceedings which involve asserting a right to possession of the land in dispute, as where the registered proprietor has commenced possession proceedings against him[505];
>
> (ii) if judgment for possession of the land has been given against him in the last two years; or
>
> (iii) he has been evicted from the land pursuant to a judgment for possession.[506]

If the registered proprietor (or any chargee of the land affected) obtained a judgment for possession against the squatter within the two-year period, but took no steps to enforce it for two years, that judgment would cease to be enforceable.[507] The squatter would then be able to apply to be registered,

---

[497] LRA 2002 Sch.6 para.6(1).

[498] LRA 2002 Sch.6 para.7.

[499] Application is on Form ADV1: see LRR 2003 r.188(1).

[500] LRR 2003 r.188(3).

[501] See above, para.35–077; and see LRPG 4, para.10.2.

[502] The registrar allows 15 business days for the response: see LRR 2003 r.197(2); and LRPG 4, para.10.2.There is no prescribed form of counter-notice. The recipient makes an objection in writing in the usual way: see LRR 2003 r.19.

[503] LRA 2002 Sch.6 para.7.

[504] See LRPG 4, para.10.3.

[505] If proceedings for possession have been commenced by the registered proprietor, but have been discontinued or struck out, that will not prevent the squatter making an application.

[506] LRA 2002 Sch.6 para.6(2).

[507] LRA 2002 s.98(4): see below, para.35–091.

provided that he had been in adverse possession for two years after the date when his initial application to be registered was rejected.

(f) The effect of registering a squatter as proprietor. Where a squatter is **35–087** registered under the provisions explained above, he is registered as the proprietor of the existing registered estate in place of the previous proprietor.[508] He is therefore the successor in title of the former registered proprietor and will be registered with the same class of title as the previous registered proprietor (which will usually be an absolute or a good leasehold title).[509] The squatter's fee simple estate, which he had by virtue of his adverse possession,[510] is extinguished.[511] Subject to one significant exception, the registration of the squatter has no effect on the priority of any interest affecting the registered estate.[512] The squatter therefore holds the land subject to the same estates, rights and interests as the previous registered proprietor.

The one exception concerns registered charges.[513] Where a squatter applies **35–088** to be registered under the provisions explained above, notice of his application will be served on, amongst others, the proprietor of any charge on the estate.[514] The chargee, like the registered proprietor, can therefore serve a counter-notice requiring the registrar to reject the application unless the squatter can satisfy one of the conditions that entitle him to be registered.[515] The Land Registration Act 2002 provides that if the squatter is registered, he will take free of the registered charge,[516] unless he was registered because he satisfied one of the three conditions explained above.[517] In such circumstances, a counter-notice will necessarily have been served.[518]

The effect of these provisions is that a chargee must ensure that:

(i) a counter-notice is always served when a squatter applies to be registered; and

(ii) the squatter is evicted or his position is regularised if his application to be registered is rejected.

A registered chargee, like the registered proprietor, can take steps to stop the registration of the squatter. The chargee will lose his charge if he fails to do so, just as the registered proprietor will lose his registered estate.[519]

It follows from the previous paragraph that, where the squatter is registered **35–089** as proprietor because he satisfies one of the three conditions explained

---

[508] See LRA 2002 Sch.6, paras 4 and 7 ("the new proprietor of the estate").

[509] For the classes of title, see above, paras 7–023 et seq.

[510] See above, para.35–057.

[511] LRA 2002 Sch.6 para.9(1).

[512] LRA 2002 Sch.6 para.9(2).

[513] Equitable charges are subject to the general rule stated in the previous paragraph.

[514] LRA 2002 Sch.6 para.2(1)(b); above, para.35–077.

[515] LRA 2002 Sch.6 para.3(1); above, para.35–078.

[516] LRA 2002 Sch.6 para.9(3).

[517] LRA 2002 Sch.6 para.9(4). For the three conditions, see above, paras 35–080 et seq.

[518] Above, para.35–079.

[519] See (2001) Law Com. No.271, paras 14.74, 14.75.

above,[520] he will take subject to any charge that affects the registered estate. It sometimes happens that there will be a charge over a number of parcels of land, including the one acquired by the squatter. In relation to unregistered land, where several parcels of land are subject to one charge, a person entitled to redeem the charge[521] must pay the full amount secured by the charge, even if he only owns part of the property.[522] If this rule were to apply to a squatter who acquired land subject to a charge, the squatter might, in practice, be unable to pay off the charge in full and would therefore be unable to sell the land which he had acquired by adverse possession. To meet this difficulty, and to further the policy of the Land Registration Act 2002 of keeping land in commerce,[523] where a registered estate continues to be subject to a charge notwithstanding the registration of the squatter under the provisions explained above, and that charge affects other property as well, the proprietor of the estate acquired by adverse possession[524] may require the chargee to apportion the amount secured by the charge at that time between the registered estate acquired by adverse possession and the other property subject to the charge on the basis of their respective values.[525] The registered proprietor who requires the apportionment is entitled to a discharge of his estate from the charge on payment of the amount apportioned to the registered estate and the costs incurred by the chargee as a result of the apportionment.[526] On such discharge, the liability of the chargor to the chargee is reduced by the amount apportioned to the registered estate.[527]

35–090   **4. Possession proceedings.** In general, because proceedings against a squatter are never barred by lapse of time,[528] a registered proprietor who brings such proceedings will be entitled to judgment. However, the Land Registration Act 2002 provides a number of defences to such proceedings. Their effect is that where a squatter would be entitled to be registered as proprietor under the provisions explained above, that entitlement is a good defence to any possession proceedings brought against him, where no application for registration has been made. The rules in more detail are as follows.

First, a squatter has a defence to an action for possession if, on the day before the action was brought, he was entitled to make an application to be

---

[520] See paras 35–080 et seq.

[521] Which will include any person whose land is subject to the charge.

[522] "A person who has any right to redeem has a right to redeem the whole of the mortgaged property, and not a part of it, unless there is a special bargain": *Hall v Heward* (1886) 32 Ch D 430 at 436, per Lindley L.J. See too *Carroll v Manek* (1999) 79 P. & C.R. 173 at 188, [62]. The owner of part of the property charged who repays the whole of the debt will be subrogated to the chargee's charge in relation to those parts which he does not own.

[523] See (2001) Law Com. No.271, para.14.78.

[524] Which may be the squatter himself or a successor in title.

[525] LRA 2002 Sch.6 para.10(1).

[526] LRA 2002 Sch.6 para.10(2). There is a power to make provision about apportionment by rules (see LRA 2002 Sch.6 para.10(4)), but do date no rules have been made.

[527] LRA 2002 Sch.6 para.10(3).

[528] See above para.35–071.

registered as proprietor under the provisions explained above,[529] and had such an application been made, the third condition, mistake as to boundary,[530] would have been satisfied.[531]

Secondly, a squatter has a defence to an action for possession if on the day before such proceedings were brought, the following facts can be shown[532]:

(i) the squatter or his predecessor in title had been in adverse possession for 10 years or more;

(ii) the squatter had made an application to be registered under the provisions of the Land Registration Act 2002, explained above[533];

(iii) that application had been rejected; and

(iv) the squatter had remained in adverse possession for a further two years after that rejection, so that he would have been entitled to make a further application to be registered.[534]

In each of these two cases, it the defence is made out, the court must order the registrar to register the squatter as proprietor of the estate in relation to which he could have made an application to be registered.[535]

It will be noted that the Land Registration Act 2002 provides no express defence in the cases where, if the squatter had applied to be registered, he could have established either the first or second conditions that would have entitled him to be registered, namely, estoppel[536] or some other right to the land.[537] However, such matters are already good defences to an action for possession and the defences given by the Land Registration Act 2002 are additional to any other defences which a person may have.[538]

There are two other situations where the court must order the registrar to **35–091** register a squatter as the proprietor of the estate in relation to which he could have applied to be registered. The purpose of the provisions is to ensure that adverse possession disputes are resolved expeditiously.[539]

The first situation is where, in any proceedings, it is established that:

(i) a registered proprietor has obtained a judgment for possession against a squatter;

---

[529] LRA 2002 Sch.6 para.1.
[530] LRA 2002 Sch.6 para.5(4); above, para.35–083.
[531] LRA 2002 s.98(1).
[532] See LRA 2002 s.98(3).
[533] See paras 35–073 et seq.
[534] For such applications, see LRA 2002 Sch.6 para.6(1); above, paras 35–085 et seq.
[535] LRA 2002 s.98(5)(a).
[536] Above, para.35–081.
[537] Above, para.35–082.
[538] LRA 2002 s.98(6).
[539] See (2001) Law Com. No.271, para.14.60.

(ii) that squatter could have applied to be registered as proprietor under provisions of the Land Registration Act 2002 explained above,[540] because he had been in adverse possession of the land for a period of 10 years at the time when those possession proceedings were commenced; and

(iii) the registered proprietor has failed to enforce that judgment for possession for a period of two years after it was obtained.

In those circumstances, the judgment for possession ceases to be enforceable,[541] and the court must order the registrar to register the squatter as proprietor.[542] This is a departure from the normal rule under which a judgment for possession can be enforced without the leave of the court for a period of six years.[543]

The second situation is where, in any proceedings, it is established that:

(i) a squatter had been in adverse possession of a registered estate for 10 years and had applied to be registered;

(ii) his application was rejected;

(iii) the registered proprietor then obtained a judgment for possession against him; and

(iv) two years have elapsed since that judgment was given and it has not been enforced against the squatter.

Once again, the judgment for possession becomes unenforceable after two years have expired, and the court must direct the registrar to register the squatter as proprietor of the land in question.[544]

35–092 **5. Special cases.** The Land Registration Act 2002 makes provision for two special cases. There are also transitional provisions that will continue to be important for some time.[545]

35–093 *(a) Rentcharges.* It has been explained above that there are two forms of adverse possession of a rentcharge[546]:

(i) a rentcharge will be extinguished if it has not be paid for 12 years; and

---

[540] See paras 35–073 et seq.
[541] LRA 2002 s.98(2).
[542] LRA 2002 s.98(5)(b).
[543] See above, para.35–054.
[544] LRA 2002 s.98(3), (5)(b).
[545] A number of transitional provisions in LRA 2002 relating to adverse possession are already spent and are not, therefore, discussed.
[546] See above, para.35–034.

(ii) if the rent is paid to a third party for 12 years, the rentcharge owner's title is extinguished in favour of that third party.

The detailed provisions on the adverse possession of rentcharges issuing out of registered land are found in rules and not in the Land Registration Act 2002.[547] Those rules prescribe a modified form of the procedure that applies to applications in relation to registered estates.[548] Under the provisions, a person may apply to be registered as proprietor of a registered rentcharge if he has been in adverse possession of that rentcharge (in either of the two ways mentioned above) for a period of 10 years ending on the date of the application.[549] In the usual case of adverse possession by non-payment of the rentcharge, the application to be registered as proprietor of the rentcharge is in fact an application for the closure of the title of the rentcharge, and that will be the consequence of a successful application.[550] The system of application for registration necessarily differs from that which applies in relation to a registered estate in a number of respects. For example, there are only two (rather than three) grounds upon which the person in adverse possession of the rentcharge is entitled to be registered as proprietor, namely, where the rentcharge owner is estopped from claiming the rentcharge, and where the applicant is for some other reason entitled to be registered as proprietor of the rentcharge.[551] The third ground—mistake as to boundary[552]—cannot arise in relation to a rentcharge. There is a right for the adverse possessor to make a further application to be registered after two years if his first application to be registered is rejected but his adverse possession continues for that two-year period.[553]

(*b*) *Trusts.* The Land Registration Act 2002 protects beneficiaries with **35–094** future interests under trusts of land and settlements. It provides that a person is not to be regarded as being in adverse possession of an estate for the purposes of the provisions on applications for registration by squatters, unless the interest of each of the beneficiaries in the estate is an interest in possession.[554] Accordingly, if registered land was held in trust for W for life, thereafter for X for life, thereafter for Y and Z in equal shares absolutely, and a squatter went into adverse possession of the land during W's lifetime and remained there until X's death, that adverse possession would not give the squatter any right to apply to be registered under the provisions explained above, because it would not be "adverse" for the purposes of those provisions.[555] The squatter could apply to be registered as proprietor after he had been in adverse possession for 10 years against Y and Z.

---

[547] See LRA 2002 Sch.6 para.14; LRR 2003 rr.191, 192; Sch.8.
[548] See LRR 2003 Sch.8.
[549] LRR 2003 Sch.8 para.1(1).
[550] LRR 2003 r.192.
[551] LRR 2003 Sch.8 para.5. For those two grounds, see above, paras 35–081, 35–082.
[552] See above, para.35–083.
[553] LRR 2003 Sch.8 para.6.
[554] LRA 2002 Sch.6 para.12.
[555] See paras 35–073 et seq.

Neither a trustee nor a beneficiary under a trust of registered land can apply to be registered on the basis of adverse possession, because neither can be an adverse possessor for the purposes of the Land Registration Act 2002.[556]

35–095   *(c) Transitional.* Where a squatter was in adverse possession for 12 years or more of registered land[557] prior to the coming into force of the Land Registration Act 2002, that squatter is entitled to be registered as proprietor of that land,[558] and that entitlement is a defence to any action for possession brought against him.[559] If a court decides that the squatter is entitled to a defence under this provision, it must order the registrar to register the squatter as the proprietor of the registered estate in question.[560]

---

[556] See the definition of "adverse possession" in LRA 2002 Sch.6 para.11(1), which is by reference to limitation under LA 1980: see above, para.35–073. No period of limitation under LA 1980 s.15 will run in favour of either trustee of beneficiary: see LA 1980 Sch.1, para.9; above, paras 35–040, 35–043.

[557] Which includes land that was unregistered when the squatter commenced his adverse possession but had been registered at the end of the 12-year period.

[558] LRA 2002 Sch.12 para.18(1).

[559] LRA 2002 Sch.12 para.18(2).

[560] LRA 2002 Sch.12 para.18(3).

DISABILITIES

Certain types of person are subject to disabilities as to the interests in land that **36–001**
they can hold, create or alienate. Formerly the range of persons subject to
disability was much greater than it is now,[1] and once included married
women,[2] traitors and felons,[3] aliens[4] and corporations.[5] However, this is
generally no longer the case and the three principal categories of persons still
subject to some form of disability, and which are considered in this chapter,
are minors, mental patients and charities. The last of these—charities—are in
fact now largely free of restrictions on their capacity, and are therefore treated
briefly.

Section 1. Minors

A minor is a person who has not attained full age.[6] A person attains the age **36–002**
of majority (and is therefore no longer a minor) at the first moment of the 18th
anniversary of his birth.[7] The following are the main principles governing a
minor's rights in land.

1. Ownership of land. Before 1926 a minor was capable of holding both **36–003**
legal estates and equitable interests in land. After 1925 a minor cannot hold a
legal estate in land,[8] whether registered or unregistered, though he may still
hold an equitable interest.[9]

---

[1] Reference should be made to the fifth edition of this work for an account of the former
law.

[2] See the fifth edition of this work at p.1020.

[3] See the fifth edition of this work at p.1026.

[4] See the fifth edition of this work at p.1027.

[5] See the fifth edition of this work at p.1027.

[6] The term "minor" is now generally employed instead of "infant" in legal usage.

[7] Family Law Reform Act 1969 s.9. This has been the law since January 1, 1970: Family Law
Reform Act 1969 s.1. Prior to that date a person attained majority at the first moment of the day
preceding the 21st anniversary of his birth. For an explanation of this, see the fifth edition of this
work at p.1015.

[8] LPA 1925 s.1(6).

[9] See SLA 1925 s.26(6); TLATA 1996 s.2(6); Sch.1 para.1.

36–004   **2. Attempted conveyance to a minor.** The effect of an attempted conveyance of a legal estate to a minor after 1925 depends upon whether it was made
before 1997 or after 1996.[10]

36–005   *(a) Attempted conveyance prior to 1997.* An attempt made prior to 1997 to
convey a legal estate to a minor either alone or jointly with other minors
operated as a contract for value by the intending transferor to make a proper
settlement under the Settled Land Act 1925 by means of a vesting deed and
trust instrument. In the meantime, the party making the conveyance held the
land on trust for the minor or minors.[11] Any such contract that was still in
existence when the Trusts of Land and Appointment of Trustees Act came into
force at the beginning of 1997 ceased to have effect. Instead the conveyance
operated as a declaration that the land was held in trust for the minors.[12] An
attempted conveyance of a legal estate to a minor jointly with a person of full
age vested the legal estate in the person of full age on a statutory trust for sale
for himself and the minor.[13] Any such trust that was subsisting on January 1,
1997 became a trust of land.[14] These rules did not apply to a conveyance to
a minor as mortgagee or trustee, for which special provision was made.[15]

36–006   *(b) Attempted conveyance after 1996.* After 1996, an attempted conveyance
to one or more minors does not pass the legal estate but operates as a
declaration that the transferor holds the property in trust for those minors.[16]
An attempted conveyance to one or more minors together with another person
or persons of full age, vests the land in the adult transferees in trust for both
the minors and adults.[17] These rules apply as much to any purported attempt
to create a mortgage of a legal estate as they do to an attempted outright
conveyance of a freehold or leasehold or the grant of a lease.[18]

36–007   **3. Mortgages.** A minor cannot be a legal mortgagee or chargee. Prior to
1997, an attempt to grant or transfer a legal mortgage to one or more minors
operated as an agreement for value to execute a proper mortgage or transfer
when the minor or minors came of age. In the meantime the grantor or
transferor held any beneficial interest in the mortgage debt in trust for the
persons intended to benefit.[19] But a mortgage to a minor and other persons of
full age operated, so far as the legal estate was concerned, as if the minor were

---

[10] The Trusts of Land and Appointment of Trustees Act 1996 entered into force on January 1,
1997.
[11] LPA 1925 s.19(1); SLA 1925 s.27(i). Both provisions have now been repealed.
[12] TLATA 1996 Sch.1 para.1(3).
[13] LPA 1925 s.19(2) (now repealed).
[14] TLATA 1996 s.1(2).
[15] LPA 1925 s.19(3) (now repealed). For mortgages, see below.
[16] See TLATA 1996 s.2(6); Sch.1 para.1(1). In registered land, the interests of the minors
should be protected by the entry of a restriction, LRR 2003 Sch.4 Form B.
[17] TLATA 1996 Sch.1 para.1(2).
[18] This follows from the definition of "conveyance": see TLATA 1996 s.23(2); LPA 1925
s.205(1)(ii).
[19] LPA 1925 s.19(6) (now repealed).

not named, although any beneficial interest of his in the mortgage debt was not affected.[20]

It has been explained above that, after 1996, any purported grant or transfer of a mortgage or charge to one or more minors either alone or jointly with adult transferees operates in the same way as an attempted conveyance of the legal estate.

4. Personal representatives. A minor can be neither an executor[21] nor an   **36–008**
administrator.[22] If a minor would be entitled to be an administrator but for his minority, or is appointed sole executor, he cannot take a grant until he is of full age. In the meantime a grant may be taken by someone on his behalf, e.g. his guardian. In the case of administration, the grant must normally be made to at least two persons or a trust corporation on the minor's behalf, since a minor is interested in the estate.[23] If a minor is appointed one of several executors, the remainder of whom are of full age, he must wait until he attains his majority, when he can join in the grant of probate previously made to the others.

5. Trustees. No minor can be appointed a trustee after 1925.[24] This applies   **36–009**
to trusts of any property, real or personal. The effect of a purported convey-ance of a legal estate in land to a minor as trustee, although governed by different (and not identically worded) statutory provisions, is in substance the same whether it was made before 1997 or after 1996.

    (i) If the minor is a sole trustee, the conveyance operates as a declara-tion of trust by the grantor in favour of the intended beneficiaries and no legal estate passes. The effect is the same if the conveyance is to two or more trustees, all of whom are minors.[25]

    (ii) If the minor is one of two or more trustees, at least one of whom is of full age, the conveyance operates to vest the land in the adult transferee (or transferees) in trust for the intended beneficiaries.[26]

These provisions do not prevent a minor from becoming a trustee of property other than a legal estate in land[27] in other ways, e.g. under a constructive trust.[28]

---

[20] LPA 1925 s.19(6) (now repealed).
[21] Senior Courts Act 1981 s.118.
[22] *In b. Manuel* (1849) 13 Jur. 664.
[23] Senior Courts Act 1981 s.114(2).
[24] LPA 1925 s.20.
[25] Pre-1997: LPA 1925 s.19(4) (now repealed); post-1996: TLATA 1996 s.2(6); Sch.1 para.1(1).
[26] Pre-1997: LPA 1925 s.19(5) (now repealed); post-1996: TLATA 1996 Sch.1 para.1(2).
[27] See above, para.36–003.
[28] Above, para.11–017.

6. Beneficial ownership of land

36–010   *(a) Land acquired prior to 1997.* Land to which a minor became entitled in possession prior to 1997 was deemed to be settled land.[29] This was so even if the minor was absolutely entitled. The purpose of applying the Settled Land Act 1925 machinery to minors was to make the land freely alienable.[30] The legal estate and statutory powers were, in such a case, vested in the statutory owners.[31]

36–011   *(b) Land acquired after 1996.* After 1996, no settlement may be created under the Settled Land Act 1925.[32] If a minor now becomes entitled to a legal estate in land[33] other than by a purported conveyance, e.g. under a will or intestacy, it is held in trust for him until he comes of age.[34] In practice the trustees are likely to be the personal representatives, at least initially.[35]

7. Dispositions by minors

36–012   *(a) Voidable.* Any disposition by a minor of an interest in land is voidable at the option of the minor (but not of the grantee[36]) on the minor attaining his majority,[37] or within a reasonable time thereafter.[38] If the minor dies under age, his personal representatives may avoid the disposition within a reasonable time.[39] This is a long established rule of common law. As the disposition is voidable and not void, it is binding if the minor fails to repudiate it within a reasonable time after attaining his majority.[40]

36–013   *(b) Statutory owner.* It has been explained that where a minor became entitled in possession to a fee simple absolute or term of years in land prior to 1997, the land became settled land.[41] Under the Settled Land Act 1925 the statutory owner has power to make a binding disposition of the minor's land and is not handicapped by his privilege of revocation.[42] The Act permits sales, exchanges, leases and mortgages on certain terms; but in general it does not permit gifts or marriage settlements.

[29] SLA 1925 s.1(1); below, Appendix para.A–035.
[30] See the fifth edition of this work at p.318.
[31] SLA 1925 s.26; above.
[32] TLATA 1996 s.2(1); above, Appendix para.A–001, para.10–034.
[33] Including the benefit of a legal charge.
[34] TLATA 1996 Sch.1 para.2.
[35] Where title to the land is registered, the personal representatives cannot transfer the title to the minor until he comes of age see Ruoff & Roper 13–005.01. They could of course transfer it to other trustees to hold on trust for the minor. cf. TA 1925 s.36.
[36] *Zouch d. Abbot v Parsons* (1765) 3 Burr. 1794.
[37] *Ashfeild v Ashfeild* (1628) W.Jo. 157 (lease). See *Chaplin v Leslie Frewin (Publishers) Ltd* [1966] Ch. 71.
[38] *Carnell v Harrison* [1916] 1 Ch. 328.
[39] Cru.Dig. iv, p.69.
[40] *Edwards v Carter* [1893] A.C. 360.
[41] SLA 1925 s.1(1); above, Appendix para.A–035.
[42] See the fifth edition of this work at p.318.

(c) Trustees of land. In a case where a minor becomes entitled to an estate **36–014** in land after 1996, so that the land is held by trustees on a trust of land,[43] the trustees have in relation to the land all the powers of an absolute owner.[44] Those powers are conferred for the purposes of exercising their functions as trustees.[45] If, under the express terms of a trust of land, the consent of a person who is a minor is required to the exercise of any function relating to the land:

(i) in favour of a purchaser, his consent is not required; but

(ii) the trustees are required to obtain the consent of either a parent who has parental responsibility for him[46] or a guardian.[47]

8. Transfer on death. A minor cannot make a will,[48] except if he is **36–015** privileged as a soldier or mariner, as already explained.[49]

Normally, therefore, any interest vested in a minor will pass on his death by intestacy. But there is one statutory complication. The relevant provision[50] has been altered as regards any minor who dies after 1996.[51] The law is therefore stated as it applies both to deaths before 1997 and after 1996. It can be most readily understood in tabular form.

(a) Deemed entail or life estate   **36–016**

DATE OF DEATH OF THE MINOR:	PRIOR TO 1997	AFTER 1996
PROVISION APPLIES:	(i) Where the minor died without having been married; and	(i) Where the minor dies without having been married *and* without issue; and

---

[43] Above, paras 12–004, 36–011.
[44] TLATA 1996 s.6(i); above, para.12–016.
[45] TLATA 1996 s.6(i); above, para.12–015.
[46] For the meaning of this expression, see Children Act 1989 s.3.
[47] TLATA 1996 s.10(3). In the absence of any express requirement of consent, trustees of land, when exercising their powers, are obliged to consult (so far as practicable) only the beneficiaries of full age who are beneficially entitled to an interest in possession in the land: TLATA 1996 s.11(1).
[48] Wills Act 1837 s.7.
[49] Above, para.14–048.
[50] AEA 1925 s.51(3).
[51] By TLATA 1996 Sch.3 para.4.

DATE OF DEATH OF THE MINOR:	PRIOR TO 1997	AFTER 1996
PROVISION APPLIES:	(ii) where he would, but for the provision, have been entitled at his death under a settlement[52] (including a will or intestacy[53]) to a vested estate in fee simple,[54] or an absolute interest in property settled to devolve with such land as freehold land.	(ii) he would, but for the provision, have been entitled at his death under a trust or settlement (including a will or intestacy) to a vested estate in fee simple in freehold land or in any property to devolve with that estate as freehold land.
EFFECT:	The minor was deemed to have an *entailed interest* and the settlement was construed accordingly.	The minor is deemed to have a *life interest* and the trust or settlement is construed accordingly.

The reason for the change after 1996 is that an entail can no longer be created.[55] A life estate is therefore substituted.

36–017   *(b) Purpose.* The objects of this somewhat strange provision appear to be:

(i) to make it unnecessary always to take out a grant of administration to the infant's estate; and

(ii) to make the land revert to the donor.

That was certainly the way in which the provision operated before April 4, 1988 and how it operates after 1996, though in the intervening period, the effect could be different as an example will demonstrate. If D settled land on A for life with remainder to B (a minor) in fee simple, and B died a minor without having married, the position may be summarised as follows.

---

[52] As defined by SLA 1925 ss.1(1), 117(1)(xxiv); AEA 1925 s.55(1)(xxiv); above, para.36–010.
[53] *Re Taylor* [1931] 2 Ch. 242; but see (1932) 76 S.J. 227.
[54] Including perhaps, a fee simple in remainder: see (1932) 76 S.J. 227.
[55] TLATA 1996 Sch.1 para.5; above, para.3–031.

WHERE B DIED BEFORE APRIL 4, 1988:	WHERE B DIED AFTER APRIL 3, 1988 BUT BEFORE 1997:	WHERE B DIES AFTER 1996:
(i) B was deemed to have an entail. Since he could have no legitimate children, the notional entail came to an end. (ii) D was entitled in fee simple subject to A's life estate.[57]	(i) B was deemed to have an entail. If B had any issue the entail would take effect and devolve on the relevant child.[56] (ii) If B had issue, there was an entail in remainder, subject to A's life interest. In the absence of issue D was entitled in fee simple subject to A's life estate.	(i) B is deemed to have a life interest in the absence of any issue. If B has issue the provision is inapplicable. (ii) In the absence of issue D is entitled in fee simple subject to A's life estate.

It is not apparent why in 1925 the draftsman adopted the device of an entail **36–018** rather than a life estate to achieve his purpose. The entail would never take effect because B, who would only fall within the provision if he died unmarried, could never leave legitimate issue who could take in tail.[58] Once it became possible to create an entail in favour of an illegitimate child in 1988,[59] the result could be different (as the above example demonstrates). The changes that were made in 1996 restrict the rule to cases where the minor dies both unmarried and childless, and achieve with greater simplicity the apparent objectives of the provision.

9. Leases. The effect of an attempted grant of a legal term of years to a **36–019** minor depends on whether it was made prior to 1997 or after 1996. In the former case it operated merely as a covenant by the lessor to make a settlement on the minor, and in the meantime to hold the term in trust for him.[60] If the grant is made after 1996, it operates as a declaration that the transferor holds the property in trust for the minor.[61] In either case, the minor can only take an equitable interest. He may disclaim this interest within a

[56] After April 3, 1988, an entail could arise in favour of an illegitimate child: Family Law Reform Act 1987 ss.1(1); 19(1), (2); see above, para.14–132.

[57] If B was solely entitled on D's intestacy, a perpetual oscillation of the land between B's estate and D's estate was avoided by carrying the land from D's estate to the person who, after B, would be entitled on D's intestacy: *Re Taylor* [1931] 2 Ch. 242.

[58] The consequences of this (including the grotesque result of a conveyance for value) are more fully explored in the fifth edition of this work at p.1019. The difficulties canvassed there are now unlikely ever to be in issue.

[59] Above, para.14–026.

[60] Above, para.36–005; *Davies v Beynon-Harris* (1931) 47 T.L.R. 424.

[61] Above, para.36–006.

reasonable time after attaining full age.[62] If he does so, this will discharge him from liability for future rent but not from liability in respect of his past use and occupation of the premises.[63] Nor will disclaimer enable him to recover rent that he has already paid.[64] If he does not then disclaim, he is bound by the terms of the tenancy even though he was a minor when he entered into it.[65] Although there is some authority that during his minority a minor is liable to pay for the use and occupation of property of the premises only if they can be said to be "necessary",[66] this may not represent the law. The preferable view is that an infant is liable to pay for use and occupation even if the lease is disadvantageous to him, unless he disclaims it on coming of age.[67] If the lease is set aside by the landlord because the minor obtained it by fraudulently representing himself to be of full age, he cannot also make the infant liable for use and occupation.[68]

Section 2. Mental Incapacity

36–020   Where a person is suffering from a mental disorder someone must be appointed to manage his property, because he is himself incapacitated.

1. Control over property

36–021   *(a) The jurisdiction.* Under statutes dating from the 14th-century De Prerogativa Regis[69] and later the Lunacy Act 1890, the Crown had jurisdiction over the property of persons then called "lunatics". This was exercised by the Lord Chancellor and certain judges and, until October 1, 2007, the jurisdiction was governed by Part VII of the Mental Health Act 1983.[70] In practice, this jurisdiction usually was exercised by the Master, Deputy Master or a nominated judge of the Court of Protection, which was an office of the Senior Courts[71] and it arose when it was established that "a person is incapable, by reason of mental disorder, of managing and administering his property and affairs".[72] With effect from October 1, 2007, Part VII of the Mental Health Act 1983 is repealed and replaced by the provisions of the Mental Capacity

---

[62] *Ketsey's Case* (1613) CroJac. 320; and see *Edwards v Carter* [1893] A.C. 360 (settlement).

[63] *Blake v Concannon* (1870) I.R. 4 CL. 323.

[64] *Valentini v Canali* (1889) 24 QBD 166.

[65] *Davies v Beynon-Harris*, above.

[66] *Lowe v Griffith* (1835) 4 L.J.C.P. 94.

[67] *North Western Ry v M'Michael* (1850) 5 Ex. 114 at 128.

[68] *Lemprière v Lange* (1879) 12 Ch D 675.

[69] Of uncertain date, printed as 17 Ed. II, St. 1, cc. 9, 10; 1324 (Ruff).

[70] ss.93–113. The system was introduced by the Mental Health Act 1959 and consolidated in the Mental Health Act 1983. The ancient prerogative of the Crown to act as parens patriae in relation to the person and property of those of unsound mind no longer exists: *Re F (Mental Patient: Sterilisation)* [1990] 2 A.C. 1 at 57, 58.

[71] Mental Health Act 1983 ss.93, 105. The Chancery Division may also exercise jurisdiction in certain cases of small trusts: see Re *K's S T* [1969] 2 Ch. 1.

[72] Mental Health Act 1983 s.94(2).

Act 2005.[73] Under the new system, a new Court of Protection is established with more comprehensive powers,[74] along with a new statutory office of Public Guardian.[75]

(b) *Powers.* Under Part VII of the Mental Health Act 1983, there were wide   **36–022** powers of ordering or authorising dispositions and other transactions concerning the patient's property, whether for the benefit of the patient himself or his family or other persons for whom he might have been expected to provide.[76] In cases of emergency these powers could have been exercised before the question of incapacity had been determined.[77] The powers extended, for example, to the making of settlements[78] and wills,[79] the management of a business, and the conduct of litigation, and included the power, commonly exercised, to appoint a receiver[80] who may have exercised any of the powers under the court's directions.[81] There was no power to make a disposition which the patient could not himself have made if of sound mind.[82] Where property of the patient had been disposed of, those who would have taken it under the patient's will or intestacy could have claimed corresponding interests in the property which represented it.[83]

The Mental Capacity Act 2005 replaces and expands these powers with effect from October 1, 2007. As well as providing powers to do acts in connection with the care and treatment of another person,[84] the Act contains wide powers authorising payment for goods and services[85] and general expenditure[86] for the person lacking capacity.[87] There is also a general power to make decisions for the person incapable,[88] including decisions about personal

[73] Its origins lay in Law Commission Report No.231 on Mental Incapacity published in 1995 and was refined by a Government Policy Statement, *Making Decisions*, in October 1999.

[74] Mental Capacity Act 2005 Pt 2. The court is a superior court of record and not merely an office of the Senior Courts.

[75] MCA 2005 s.57.

[76] Mental Health Act 1983 ss.95, 96. The powers conferred under these sections applied only to "business matters, legal transactions and other dealings of a similar kind" and not to wider issues, such as medical treatment: *Re F (Mental Patient: Sterilisation)*, above, at 59, per Lord Brandon. Where the patient has never enjoyed a rational mind, the court will assume that he "would have been a normal decent person, acting in accordance with contemporary standards of morality": *Re C (a patient)* [1991] 3 All E.R. 866 at 870, per Hoffmann J. What the court does will be determined according to the circumstances of the individual patient: see *Re S (Gifts by Mental Patient)* [1997] 1 F.L.R. 96.

[77] Mental Health Act 1983 s.98.

[78] See e.g. *Re D.M.L.* [1965] Ch. 1133; *Re L. (W.J.G.)* [1966] Ch. 135.

[79] Mental Health Act 1983 ss.96, 97, not applying to patients who are minors, and substituting special formalities for those of the Wills Act 1837 s.9. See *Re Davey* [1981] 1 W.L.R. 164. *Re D. (J.)* [1982] Ch. 237 and *Re C (a patient)*, above, examine the principles for making such wills.

[80] Or some named person.

[81] Mental Health Act 1983 s.99. See, e.g. *Re E.* [1985] 1 W.L.R. 245.

[82] *Pritchard v Briggs* [1980] Ch. 339 at 409.

[83] Mental Health Act 1983 s.101.

[84] MCA 2005 s.5.

[85] MCA 2005 s.7.

[86] MCA 2005 s.8.

[87] See MCA 2005 ss.2, 3.

[88] MCA 2005 s.16.

welfare[89] and property and affairs.[90] The latter includes, inter alia, the control and management of the person incapable's (P's) property, the acquisition of property in P's name or on P's behalf, the settlement of any of P's property, the execution for P of a will and the exercise of any power (including a power to consent) vested in P whether beneficially or as trustee or otherwise.[91]

36–023   **2. Patient's incapacity.** The principles that govern a person's capacity differ according to whether or not the court has taken control of his affairs.[92]

36–024   *(a) Where the court has taken control of the patient's affairs under the Mental Health Act 1983.* Once a patient has been placed under the jurisdiction of the Court of Protection, he cannot make any valid disposition of his property inter vivos, even in a lucid interval.[93] Any other rule "would raise a conflict with the court's control of his affairs",[94] and would mean that his affairs would be under both his own control and the receiver's.[95] By contrast, a will made by a patient in a lucid interval would be valid, because "a will does not take effect until death, at which time the Court of Protection has no further concern for his affairs".[96] Where the patient is a proprietor of registered land, the receiver (or other person authorised to manage his property and affairs) may exercise all of the powers that the patient could have done if he had been free from disability.[97] No restriction will be entered on the register unless the receiver either so requests or is himself registered as proprietor.[98]

(b) Under the Mental Capacity Act 2005, the Court may by order make decisions on behalf of the person incapable or may appoint a "deputy" to make decisions on his behalf.[99] The deputy will have such powers as the court determines, including power in relation to real property.[100] It is anticipated that the role of the deputy in relation to the land of the person incapable will be similar to that formerly of a receiver under the Mental Health Act and that there will be no substantive change in land registry practice.

36–025   *(c) Where the court has not intervened.* Where either:

(i) the court has not intervened; or

---

[89] MCA 2005 s.17.
[90] MCA 2005 s.18.
[91] MCA 2005. See also Sch.2.
[92] The general principles have not been affected by the Mental Health Acts 1959 and 1983 nor the Mental Capacity Act 2005.
[93] *Re Beaney* [1978] 1 W.L.R. 770 at 772, summarising the effect of *Re Walker* [1905] 1 Ch. 160 and *Re Marshall* [1920] 1 Ch. 284.
[94] *Re Beaney*, above, at 772, per Nourse, QC.
[95] *Re Marshall*, above, at 289.
[96] *Re Beaney*, above, at 772, per Nourse, QC. See too *In b. Walker* (1912) 28 T.L.R. 466.
[97] A copy of the court order must be filed with the registrar, see Ruoff & Roper 13–005.02.
[98] See Ruoff & Roper 13–005.02.
[99] MCA 2005 s.16 and see s.19 on the appointment of deputies generally.
[100] MCA 2005 s.18.

(ii) the validity of a will is in issue after a patient's death

any disposition or any will made during mental incapacity is voidable at the instance of those who would otherwise be entitled.[101] However it cannot be set aside either where the incapacity was unknown to the other party,[102] or at the instance of the person making it, unless he can prove that the other party knew of the incapacity.[103]

It has been held that "capacity to perform a juristic act exists when the person who purported to do the act had at the time the mental capacity, with the assistance of such explanation as he may have been given, to understand the nature and effect of that particular transaction".[104] The degree of understanding required to uphold the disposition is therefore relative to the particular transaction.[105] In the case of a will the degree required is always high.[106] In the case of a contract or a gift the degree varies with the circumstances, and it will be as high as it is for a will if a patient is disposing of all or most of his assets.[107]

3. Enduring powers of attorney under the Enduring Powers of Attorney Act 1985. It is possible to avoid the necessity of court proceedings in many cases by employing a power of attorney. From October 1, 2007 no new enduring power of attorney can be made and the Enduring Powers of Attorney Act 1985 is repealed.[108] But existing enduring powers remain valid and have the same legal effect as they had at the time they were made.[109] The Enduring Powers of Attorney Act 1985: 36–026

"was intended to provide an inexpensive method by which a person could confer power to manage his affairs on a person of his own choice which would remain effective notwithstanding any change in his mental capacity".[110]

---

[101] *Re Beaney*, above (inter vivos gift of house); *Hart v O'Connor* [1985] A.C. 1000 at 1018, 1019 (contract); *Simpson v Simpson* [1992] 1 F.L.R. 601 (inter vivos transfers of shares and bank deposits).

[102] *Hart v O'Connor*, above. A transaction will of course be voidable if there are other distinct grounds for setting the transaction aside as unconscionable: *Hart v O'Connor*, at 1021. For the relevant principles, see *Boustany v Pigott* (1993) 69 P. & C.R. 298 at 303. The plea that the other party knew of the incapacity appears only in cases where the patient is sued on a contract. But since its basis is that the other party fraudulently took advantage of the patient (*Browne v Joddrell* (1827) Moo. & M. 105), it should in principle be equally applicable to dispositions.

[103] See *Imperial Loan Co v Stone* [1892] 1 Q.B. 599.

[104] *Re K (Enduring Power of Attorney)* [1988] Ch. 310 at 313, per Hoffmann J.

[105] *Re Beaney* [1978] 1 W.L.R. 770 at 774; *Simpson v Simpson*, above, at 613.

[106] For the matters which must be understood by the testator, see *Banks v Goodfellow* (1870) L.R. 5 Q.B. 549 at 565.

[107] *Re Beaney*, above, at 774 (gift of house to daughter declared void since donor did not appreciate claims of her other children and had no other assets).

[108] MCA 2005 s.67 and Sch.7.

[109] MCA 2005 Sch.4.

[110] *Re K (Enduring Power of Attorney)*, above, at 311, per Hoffmann J. See too *Re R (Enduring Power of Attorney)* [1990] Ch. 647 at 650. The Trustee Delegation Act 1999, which came into force on January 1, 2000, made some amendments to the Enduring Powers of Attorney Act 1985.

Prior to the Act this was not possible because the authority of a donee acting under a power of attorney was revoked by the donor's loss of mental capacity.[111] A person had capacity to create such a power provided that he understood its nature and effect, even though he was no longer able to manage his property and affairs.[112] Such a power was therefore valid in the common case where it was created by the donor after he had shown the first signs of mental incapacity.[113] The enduring power had to be executed in the prescribed form and manner by both the donor of the power and the attorney.[114] It could either have conferred a general authority on the attorney or have been confined to specified matters.[115] There could have been more than one attorney.[116] An enduring power could only be granted in relation to "the property and affairs" of the donor,[117] which did not extend to matters such as healthcare or welfare.[118]

An enduring power cannot be exercised once the donor becomes incapable (except by order of the court[119]) until the attorney registers the power with the Court of Protection.[120] If, therefore, the attorney has reason to believe that the donor is becoming mentally incapable, he should register the power.

36–027 **4. Lasting powers of attorney under the Mental Capacity Act 2005.** From October 1, 2007, it will not be possible to create an enduring power of attorney. They are replaced by lasting powers of attorney.[121] A donor of an enduring power may, if they have capacity, revoke the enduring power and replace it with a lasting power. A lasting power will allow a donor to nominate one or more attorneys. They may be of two types: a power in relation to property and affairs[122] and these are similar to enduring powers; and a power in relation to personal welfare, which may include the giving or refusing of consent to medical treatment.[123] Detailed provisions concerning the making

---

[111] *Re K (Enduring Power of Attorney)*, above, at 312, 313; *Yonge v Toynbee* [1910] 1 K.B. 215 at 228. If, after the donor becomes incapable, the attorney enters into a transaction which is invalid as a result, he may be liable for breach of his warranty of authority, even though he did not know of the incapacity: *Yonge v Toynbee*, above.

[112] *Re K (Enduring Power of Attorney)*, above, particularly at 316, where the requirements are explained in detail.

[113] *Re K (Enduring Power of Attorney)*, above, at 315.

[114] Enduring Powers of Attorney Act 1985 s.2(1)–(3). See now MCA 2005 Sch.4 para.2.

[115] Enduring Powers of Attorney Act 1985 s.3(1). See now MCA 2005 Sch.4 para.3.

[116] For the power to be an enduring power of attorney, the attorneys must be appointed either jointly, or jointly and severally: Enduring Powers of Attorney Act 1985 s.11(1).

[117] Enduring Powers of Attorney Act 1985 s.3(1).

[118] cf. *Re F (Mental Patient: Sterilisation)* [1990] 2 A.C. 1 at 59; above, para.36–022. An enduring power cannot therefore be employed to empower the donee to make decisions as to the medical treatment which the donor is to receive, or where he should live. But contrast with the lasting power of attorney under the MCA 2005, below.

[119] Enduring Powers of Attorney Act 1985 s.1(1).

[120] Enduring Powers of Attorney Act 1985 s.6. It has been said that an enduring power of attorney "has very limited effect until it is registered. When registered, it takes effect according to its terms": *Re R (Enduring Power of Attorney)* [1990] Ch. 647 at 651, per Vinelott J. See now MCA 2005 Sch.4 para.1.

[121] MCA 2005 s.9.

[122] MCA 2005 s.9(1)(b).

[123] MCA 2005 s.9(1)(a).

and registration of the power are set out in Sch.1 to the Act. If the lasting power relates only to property and affairs, the donee may be an individual or a trust corporation[124] and if two or more person are appointed they may be required to act jointly or jointly and severally.[125]

Section 3. Charities

Charities were formerly subject to restrictions both as to the gifts of land that they might receive[126] and as to their powers to dispose of lands which they held.[127] The former were abolished by the Charities Act 1960,[128] and nothing further need be said about them. The latter restrictions have been largely removed by the Charities Act 1992 (the relevant provisions of which are now consolidated in the Charities Act 1993, with some amendment by the Charities Act 2006 both of which are consolidated in the Charities Act 2011, in force anticipated March 2012-01-16) and the Trusts of Land and Appointment of Trustees Act 1996. These changes require some explanation.

36–028

1. Powers of disposition of charity trustees. Prior to 1997 land held upon charitable trusts was deemed for some but not all purposes to be settled land, and in consequence charity trustees had the powers conferred on the life tenant and the trustees of a settlement by the Settled Land Act 1925.[129] After 1996, charity trustees hold any land upon a trust of land.[130] As such they have in relation to the land and for the purposes of exercising their functions as trustees, all the powers of an absolute owner,[131] subject only to the restrictions on their exercise laid down in the Charities Act 2011.[132]

Certain university and college lands are dealt with separately by the Universities and College Estates Acts 1925 and 1964.[133]

36–029

2. Restrictions on disposition. Prior to 1993, there were restrictions on the powers of most charities to make dispositions of land which formed part of their permanent endowment or which were or had been occupied for the purposes of the charity. No such dispositions could be made without the order of the court or the Charity Commissioners,[134] except by an exempt charity.[135]

36–030

---

[124] MCA 2005 s10(1).

[125] MCA 2005 s.10(4).

[126] See the fifth edition of this work at p.1028.

[127] See the fifth edition of this work at pp.1028, 1029.

[128] ss.38, 48, Sch.7.

[129] SLA 1925 s.29(1) (repealed by TLATA 1996 s.25(2); Sch.4; there is a limited exemption from this repeal in respect of the Chequers and Chevening Estates: TLATA 1996 s.25(3)).

[130] TLATA 1996 ss.1(1), 2(5).

[131] TLATA 1996 s.6(1). See above, para.12–016.

[132] Pt 7. Formerly Pt V Charities Act 1993. The powers conferred by TLATA 1996 s.6(1) are made subject to restrictions imposed by other statutes: TLATA 1996 s.6(6).

[133] TLATA 1996 does not apply to such lands: TLATA 1996 s.1(3).

[134] Charities Act 1960 s.29 (repealed by Charities Act 1992 s.78(2); Sch.7).

[135] For exempt charities, see below.

In practice such consent was given on conditions that were intended to ensure that the trustees acted in the best interests of the charity. Under the Charities Act 2011,[136] these rules no longer apply,[137] and charity trustees may sell or lease land held by the charity subject to certain conditions.[138] Those conditions are generally[139] that the trustees obtain a written report from qualified independent surveyor, advertise the proposed disposition to the extent that he advises, and decide that they are satisfied that the terms on which the disposition is to be made are the best that can reasonably be obtained by the charity.[140] There are also restrictions on the mortgaging powers of charity trustees.[141] There are supplementary provisions which are intended to ensure that the restrictions on a charity's powers of disposition are brought to the attention of:

(i) any purchaser or mortgagee of the charity's land; and

(ii) recorded on the title or, as will now usually be the case, the register of title, of any land acquired by the charity.[142]

These restrictions do not apply to dispositions by exempt charities. The charities designated as exempt include many universities and a number of other bodies such as the Boards of Trustees of the principal London museums.[143] There are also certain other exceptions, e.g. dispositions under statutory authority.[144]

---

[136] Pt 7, consolidating Pt V Charities Act 1993.

[137] Except in relation to dispositions to a connected person or a trustee for a connected person (generally a relative or an associate of the donor or trustee): Charities Act 2011 ss.117(2), 118.

[138] Charities Act 2011 s.121. The conditions are similar to those which were formerly imposed by the court or by the Charity Commissioners when consenting to a disposition.

[139] Less stringent requirements apply to leases granted for seven years or less except where the lease is granted wholly or partly for a fine: Charities Act 1993 s.36(5).

[140] Charities Act 2011 s.119(1).

[141] Charities Act 2011 s.124. The charity trustees are required to obtain and consider proper advice on the necessity for the mortgage to enable them to pursue the course of action for which the loan is sought, the reasonableness of the terms of the mortgage and the ability of the charity to repay the loan: Charities Act 1993 s.38(2), (3).

[142] See Charities Act 2011 ss.123, 126, Ruoff & Roper, Ch.38.

[143] The list of exempt charities is to be found in the Charities Act 2011 Sch.3, see Ruoff & Roper, para.38–008.

[144] Charities Act 2011 s.117(3).

SUCCESSIVE INTERESTS: SETTLED LAND

This Appendix explains the law which governs successive interests in land as **A–001** regulated by the Settled Land Act 1925. However, the law which governs successive interests underwent a fundamental reform through the Trusts of Land and Appointment of Trustees Act 1996. This made a significant break with the past by introducing a unitary system of trusts of land, which applies whatever form the beneficial interests may take. Although existing settlements remain subject to the Settled Land Act 1925, any new ones are governed by the Trusts of Land and Appointment of Trustees Act 1996.[1] Subject to certain minor exceptions,[2] it ceased to be possible to create any new settlements governed by the Settled Land Act 1925 after 1996. The 1996 Act is explained in the main text.[3]

Consequently, this Appendix is confined to an account of the traditional method of settling land by means of a strict settlement under the Settled Land Act 1925, bearing in mind its limited application in the modern law of real property. Its inclusion in an Appendix, rather than the main body of the text, reflects the fact that much of the material concerning settlements is now of largely historical interest, although specialist practitioners are likely to face issues concerning settlements from time to time.

The Appendix contains a discussion of the manner in which a settlement under the Settled Land Act 1925 would have arisen, its legal attributes and the powers and duties of the parties to the settlement: the trustees of the settlement and the tenant for life. The alternative method of creating successive interests in land *prior* to 1997—the trust for sale of land[4]—is explained in the main text as it was the forerunner of the trust of land established by the Trusts of Land and Appointment of Trustees Act 1996.[5]

---

[1] See TLATA 1996 s.2. There are two exceptions to this: see TLATA 1996 s.2(2); below, Appendix para.A–054.

[2] See TLATA 1996 s.2(2); above, para.12–002.

[3] Ch.12.

[4] For a detailed treatment of trusts for sale reference should be made to the fifth edition of this work at p.385.

[5] Above, para.10–020.

A–002   **1. Settlements of unregistered land made after 1925 and before 1997**

(a) Settlements made inter vivos. Any settlement of a legal estate in unregistered land made inter vivos after 1925 and before 1997,[6] had to be made by two deeds: a principal vesting deed and a trust instrument.[7] The contents of those two documents were as follows.

A–003   (1) TRUST INSTRUMENT. The trust instrument[8]:

>   (i) declared the trusts affecting the settled land;

>   (ii) bore any *ad valorem* stamp duty payable in respect of the settlement;

>   (iii) appointed trustees of the settlement;

>   (iv) contained the power, if any, to appoint new trustees of the settlement; and

>   (v) set out, either expressly or by reference, any powers intended to be conferred by the settlement in extension of those conferred by the Act.

A–004   (2) PRINCIPAL VESTING DEED. The principal vesting deed[9]:

>   (i) described the settled land, either specifically or generally[10];

>   (ii) declared that the settled land was vested in the person or persons to whom it was conveyed or in whom it was declared to be vested upon the trusts from time to time affecting the settled land;

>   (iii) stated the names of the trustees of the settlement;

>   (iv) stated the names of any persons empowered to appoint new trustees of the settlement; and

>   (v) stated any additional or larger powers conferred by the trust instrument.

The last three particulars of both documents were similar. The vesting deed acted as a précis of those parts of the trust instrument which are of concern to a purchaser, so that he need inquire no further. The first and second parts of the vesting deed were the operative parts, and vested the legal estate in the tenant for life. The second part was worded so as to cover two cases:

>   (1) where the vesting deed acted as a conveyance from the settlor to the tenant for life or statutory owner, as where X settled property on A for life with remainders over; and

---

[6] It has not been possible to create new settlements after 1996: above, para.12–002.
[7] SLA 1925 s.4(1).
[8] SLA 1925 s.4(3).
[9] SLA 1925 s.5(1).
[10] See SLA 1925 s.5(2).

(2) where the same person was both settlor and tenant for life, so that there was no transfer of the legal estate, as where Z on his marriage settled property on himself for life with remainders over.

A vesting deed was not invalidated merely because of some mistake in the statutory particulars.[11] It was, however, inoperative if it had some fundamental defect, e.g. if the wrong person executed it.[12]

(b) Settlements made by will. Where land was settled by the will of a **A–005** testator dying after 1925 and before 1997, the will was treated as the trust instrument.[13] The legal estate, by the ordinary law, vested immediately in the testator's personal representatives.[14] They were subject to a trust under the Act to transfer the legal estate to the tenant for life by means of a proper vesting instrument.[15] Since personal representatives can convey land by means of a simple assent in writing,[16] a vesting assent could be employed instead of a vesting deed. A vesting assent had to contain the same particulars as a vesting deed.

2. Settlements of registered land made after 1925 and before 1997.[17] **A–006** The provisions of the Settled Land Act 1925 apply as much to registered land as to unregistered. To create a settlement of registered land, there had to be a trust instrument in the usual way. It was the duty of the registered proprietor (or if he was dead, his personal representatives) to execute an appropriate vesting transfer in statutory form[18] in favour of the tenant for life or statutory owner,[19] and to procure the registration of the necessary restrictions on the register.[20] Where the proprietor was himself the life tenant, the vesting transfer was merely declaratory.

The interests of the beneficiaries under the settlement cannot be overriding interests.[21] They should therefore be protected by the entry of a restriction on the register.[22] When the tenant for life is registered as proprietor, the restriction will provide in substance that[23]:

---

[11] SLA 1925 s.5(3).
[12] *Re Cayley and Evans' Contract* [1930] 2 Ch. 1 43; *cf. Re Curwen* [1931] 2 Ch. 341.
[13] SLA 1925 s.6(a).
[14] Above, para.14–140.
[15] SLA 1925 ss.6(b), 8(4).
[16] Above, para.14–141.
[17] The creation of a settlement of unregistered land was not, as the law then stood, an occasion on which the title to the land was required to be registered (though it could be registered voluntarily). However, now a vesting deed or assent triggers compulsory registration: see LRA 2002 s.4. Although this is irrelevant as regards the creation of settlements (as none can now be created), it is relevant to dispositions of the settled land during the life of the settlement.
[18] Which took the place of and contained the same information as a vesting instrument.
[19] See now LRR 2003 Sch.7 para.1.
[20] LRR 2003 Sch.7 para.1.
[21] LRA 2002 Sch.1 para.2; Sch.3 para.2; above, para.7–091.
[22] LRR 2003 Sch.7; Ruoff & Roper 37–016.
[23] See Standard from Restrictions G, H, I, LRR 2003 Sch.7 para.3; Sch.4.

(i) except under an order of the registrar, no disposition will be registered unless it is authorised either by the Settled Land Act 1925 or under any additional powers conferred by the settlement; and

(ii) no disposition under which capital money arises is to be registered unless the money is paid to the trustees of the settlement (of which there must be two and not more than four, or a trust corporation), or into court.

It follows that the registrar cannot register any transaction that is on its face outside the powers of the tenant for life.[24] The restrictions entered on the register, although binding on the tenant for life, do not restrain or in any other way affect a disposition made by his personal representatives.[25]

A–007   **3. Section 13.** Some provision had to be made to prevent evasion of the requirement that there should be a vesting instrument. The policy of the Act was therefore to make it impossible to deal with the land in any case where a vesting instrument ought to have existed but did not. First, a settlement of a legal estate in land made by a single document could not transfer or create a legal estate.[26] The tenant for life or statutory owner could require the trustees of the settlement (not the settlor) to remedy matters by executing a vesting deed.[27] Secondly, s.13 of the Settled Land Act 1925[28] (sometimes called the "paralysing section") in effect provides that where a tenant for life or statutory owner has become entitled to have a vesting instrument executed in his favour, no disposition of a legal estate can be made until a vesting instrument has been executed in accordance with the Act. Until this has been done, any purported disposition of the land inter vivos by any person operates only as a contract for valuable consideration[29] to carry out the transaction after the necessary vesting deed has been executed. In effect this forced the tenant for life to obtain a proper vesting instrument before he could exercise his dispositive powers under the Act. The section does not appear to affect any disposition not made under the Act.[30] Nor does it prevent the tenant for life from disposing of his equitable interest or exercising any equitable powers given to him by the trust instrument.[31] Although it has not been possible to

[24] See Ruoff & Roper, 37–013 *et seq.*
[25] LRR 2003 Sch.7 para.3(3).
[26] SLA 1925 ss.4(1), (6).
[27] SLA 1925 ss.4, 9.
[28] As amended by LP(Am)A 1926 s.6 and Sch.
[29] Registrable (where the title was unregistered) as an estate contract, and, if not registered, void against a purchaser of a legal estate for money or money's worth: above, para.8–075. Where the title was registered, the estate contract should have been protected by registration (above, paras 7–069, 7–070). It could, however, take effect as an overriding interest if the purchaser were in actual occupation: above, para.7–089.
[30] SLA 1925 s.112(2); *Re Ale founder's WT* [1927] 1 Ch. 360; but consider Wolst. & C. ii, 55; *Weston v Henshaw* [1950] Ch. (on s.18; see below, Appendix para.A–027).
[31] SLA 1925 s.13.

create new settlements after 1996,[32] it is conceivable that s.13 may not yet be spent. There could still be situations where a settlement was made prior to 1997 but where a vesting instrument has still to be executed.

To this rule against premature disposal of a legal estate there are certain exceptions which may be briefly considered.

(a) Dispositions by personal representatives. The section does not apply **A–008** where the disposition was made by a personal representative.[33] This preserves the usual powers of personal representatives to deal freely with the land in the due course of administering the estate and to make title to a purchaser by virtue of their office.[34]

(b) Purchaser without notice of the settlement. The section does not apply **A–009** where the disposition is made to a purchaser of a legal estate without notice of the tenant for life or statutory owner having become entitled to a vesting instrument.[35] This might happen if, e.g. a settlor declared himself trustee of land for A for life with remainders over, and then sold the land to B, apparently as beneficial owner.

(c) Settlement at an end. The section does not apply where the settlement **A–010** has come to an end before a vesting instrument has been executed.[36] The settlement ends when one person becomes solely and absolutely entitled, and the trusts of the trust instrument are otherwise exhausted. When the land ceases to be settled, the fetters of s.13 fall away.[37]

The operation of these provisions may be illustrated by the example of a case where, prior to 1997, a settlor attempted to make a settlement inter vivos in favour of his son and family by means of a single document. This was an imperfect settlement, and:

(i) the document was ineffective to transfer or create any legal estate, which therefore remained vested in the settlor[38];

(ii) the document was treated as the trust instrument[39];

(iii) the trustees of the settlement might either have executed a principal deed on their own initiative, or have been required to execute

---

[32] Above, para.12–002.
[33] SLA 1925 s.13.
[34] See above, para.14–143.
[35] SLA 1925 s.13, as amended by LP(Am)A 1926 Sch. If title to the land is registered, the interests under the settlement will not be binding on any purchaser, regardless of notice. They cannot now be made the subject of a notice on the register, LRA 2002 s.33 and should be protected by registration of a restriction: above, para.7–077.
[36] *Re Ale founder's WT* [1927] 1 Ch. 360, applying SLA 1925 s.112(2).
[37] See, e.g. *Re Ale founder's WT,* above (tenant in tail in possession barred his entail thereby causing the settlement to end: no vesting instrument was required).
[38] SLA 1925 s.4(1).
[39] SLA 1925 s.9(1)(iii).

one by the tenant for life. This would have transferred the legal estate from the settlor to the tenant for life[40];

(iv) until the trustees had duly executed the vesting deed, s.13 would operate to prevent any disposition of the land being made. It was only the trustees of the settlement who could execute a vesting deed[41];

(v) even after a vesting deed had been executed the settlement would not have been as convenient as one made in the proper manner. This was because the document which created the settlement, although treated as the trust instrument, was not behind the curtain.[42] This is the most important exception to the rule that a purchaser is not concerned with the trust instrument.[43] A settlement inter vivos which was wrongly made in the first place must be investigated by any purchaser to make sure that the vesting deed, executed at a later date, really contained the true particulars about the land, the tenant for life, and the trustees.

A–011   **4. Subsidiary vesting deed.** Where unregistered land is brought into an existing settlement, it must be conveyed to the tenant for life or statutory owner by a vesting deed.[44] This requires a subsidiary vesting deed.[45] This must be done in the following cases:

(i) Where land is acquired with capital money or in exchange for settled land.[46]

(ii) Where capital money has been lent on mortgage and the mortgagor's right to redeem has become barred (e.g. by limitation or foreclosure). In this case the trustees at first hold the land on a trust of land, but at the request of the tenant for life or statutory owner they must execute a subsidiary vesting deed.[47]

Since April 1998, a subsidiary vesting deed of unregistered land is a disposition that triggers the requirement of compulsory registration. The tenant for

---

[40] SLA 1925 s.9(2). If the legal estate was already vested in the life tenant (e.g. because he was the settlor), the vesting deed would have been merely declaratory.

[41] If there were no trustees and no person able and willing to appoint them, it would have been necessary to make an application to the court for the appointment of trustees: SLA 1925 s.9(3).

[42] SLA 1925 s.110(2).

[43] For the other (less important) exceptions, see s.110(2) and below, Appendix para.A–014.

[44] SLA 1925 s.10(1). It should be noted that if there ceases to be any land or heirlooms subject to the settlement, but merely capital money, the settlement comes to an end: see TLATA 1996 s.2(4): below, Appendix para.A–025.

[45] SLA 1925 s.10(1) proviso.

[46] SLA 1925 s.10(1). Another case is the reservation of a rentcharge on the sale of settled land; but after the Rentcharges Act 1977 (see above, para.31–018), such cases can only rarely arise.

[47] LPA 1925 s.31 (as amended by TLATA 1996 s.5(1); Sch.2 para.1).

life must therefore be registered as proprietor of the land subject to the entry of the usual restrictions.[48]

A subsidiary vesting deed, in addition to conveying the land to the tenant for life or statutory owner (if it is not already vested in him), must contain the following particulars[49]:

(i) particulars of the last or only principal vesting deed affecting the land subject to the settlement;

(ii) a statement that the land conveyed is to be held upon and subject to the same trusts and powers as the land comprised in the principal vesting deed;

(iii) the names of the trustees of the settlement;

(iv) the name of any person entitled to appoint new trustees of the settlement.

It is unnecessary to refer to the trust instrument or to any additional powers which it confers.[50]

Where registered land is brought into the settlement, the transfer to the life tenant must be made by a specially prescribed form of transfer.[51] This is deemed to fulfil the requirements of the Settled Land Act 1925 for vesting deeds.[52]

A. A Purchaser May Not Go Behind the Vesting Deed

1. The curtain. The objects of having a separate vesting deed (where the title is unregistered) or a vesting transfer and the entry on the register of appropriate restrictions (where the title is registered) may be summarised as follows: **A–012**

(i) to vest the fee simple in the tenant for life, or declare it to be vested in him;

(ii) to indicate on the face of the title that the legal owner is a tenant for life;

(iii) to define his powers of disposition; and

(iv) to ensure that the trusts of the settlement are overreached by payment of any capital monies to the trustees of the settlement.[53]

---

[48] See above, Appendix para.A–006.
[49] SLA 1925 s.10(2).
[50] Wolst. & C. ii, 51.
[51] LRR 2003 Sch.7 para.6. see Ruoff & Roper, 37–015. The application must both state the names of the trustees of the settlement and seek the entry of restrictions in the form usual for settled land: above, Appendix para.A–006.
[52] Ruoff & Roper para.37–015.
[53] For the overreaching provisions, see, below, Appendix paras A–094 *et seq.*

In this way the trust instrument is kept off the title: indeed it is a document which no purchaser is entitled to see.[54] Furthermore, the disposition of settled land is facilitated, and the interests of the beneficiaries are protected.

A–013   **2. Errors.** A vesting deed or transfer is not invalidated by any mistake in the particulars required to be contained in it,[55] and it is provided by s.110(2) of the Act[56] that a purchaser of a legal estate in settled land is bound and entitled to assume that those particulars are correct as to the persons who are the tenant for life and the trustees.[57] There is no statutory provision to indicate what is to happen if any of the matters is wrongly stated in the vesting instrument. An example is where, prior to 1997, land was settled on W for life or until remarriage, with remainder to X in fee simple. If W is widowed and secretly remarries, she will cease to be a tenant for life, the land would no longer be settled, and she would hold the property on a bare trust for X; yet this would not be apparent to any person dealing with the land. If W purported as tenant for life to exercise some power of disposition, would P, a purchaser of a legal estate, obtain a good title if he both dealt with W on the assumption that she was a tenant for life and paid any capital monies to the trustees? One view is that because P is not a purchaser of a legal estate in settled land, he is not entitled to treat the vesting deed as conclusive that W is the tenant for life. P purchases the land with notice that the land is held on trust and therefore, it is said, takes the land subject to X's interest. A number of solutions to this problem have been offered.[58] First, both from the wording of s.110(2) itself[59] and from other provisions of the Act,[60] there is reason to think that P would in fact be regarded as a purchaser of a legal estate in settled land and could therefore claim the protection of the section. Secondly, although P would have notice that the property was held on trust, there would be nothing to put him on inquiry that the settlement had terminated so that the conveyance to him was in breach of trust.[61]

The spread of registration of title has done much to eliminate such slight risk as there may be that this problem could arise. If the title to the land is registered and the settlement is protected by the usual restriction,[62] W will

---

[54] SLA s.110(2); nor may he see any deed appointing trustees, if curtained off by a deed of declaration: below, Appendix para.A–091.

[55] SLA 1925 s.5(3). But a vesting deed executed by the wrong person is inoperative: above, Appendix para.A–004.

[56] Subject to certain exceptions considered below.

[57] Where the title is registered, a purchaser will not see the vesting transfer. There is no statutory provision to indicate whether he is bound and entitled to make the same assumptions about the restrictions on the register.

[58] See [1984] Conv. 354 (P. A. Stone); and the fifth edition of this work at p.335. *cf.* [1985] Conv. 377 (R. Warrington).

[59] See s.110(2)(e), which provides that a purchaser of a legal estate in settled land is bound and entitled to assume that any statements contained in any deed of discharge are correct. If there is a deed of discharge, the land cannot be settled land: below, Appendix para.A–020.

[60] See s.36(1), where "settled land" includes land which is notionally treated as if it were settled: see the previous edition of this work at p.452. *cf.* above, para.13–091.

[61] [1984] Conv. 354 at 360 (P. A. Stone).

[62] Above, Appendix para.A–006.

have all the powers of disposition conferred by the Settled Land Act 1925. Any transaction made by W in exercise of those powers will necessarily confer a good title on P.[63]

3. Exceptions. In four situations, a purchaser is entitled to inspect the trust instrument and should do so.[64] They are: **A–014**

(i) pre–1926 settlements, whether made by will or deed[65];

(ii) imperfect settlements made inter vivos after 1925[66];

(iii) instruments which by the Act are for special reasons "deemed to be settlements"[67]; and

(iv) settlements which are "deemed to have been made by any person".[68]

All four cases are abnormal in that no proper vesting instrument was drawn up in the course of constituting the settlement. The accuracy of a vesting deed executed at a later stage should therefore be checked by reference to the trust instrument.

B. The Legal Estate Must be Transferred in Due Form

Because the title to the legal estate is independent of the trust instrument, it remains in the tenant for life until he disposes of it or dies. **A–015**

1. Transfer of the legal estate during the lifetime of the tenant for life. **A–016**
A tenant for life may transfer the legal estate during the course of his life for one of two reasons. First, he may of course sell the land under his statutory power. The legal estate will then pass to the purchaser upon conveyance or registration.[69] Secondly, his interest under the settlement may come to an end because it is determinable upon an event which occurs. If that occurs, he must forthwith convey the land to the new owner in the appropriate manner.[70] The method of conveyance will depend upon whether the land remains settled or

---

[63] LRA 2002 ss.23, 26 above, paras 7–049, 7–051.

[64] SLA 1925 s.110(2).

[65] SLA 1925 Sch.2.

[66] Above, Appendix paras A–007, A–010.

[67] The principal example of this—SLA 1925 s.29—which deemed land held on trust for charitable, ecclesiastical or public purposes to be settled land, and the instruments creating such trusts to be settlements, has been repealed (except for a limited saving in relation to the Chequers and Chevening Estates: see TLATA 1996 s.25(3)). Such trusts now take effect as trusts of land: see TLATA 1996 s.2(5); above, para.36–029.

[68] e.g. under SLA 1925 ss.1(2) (minor entitled under intestacy), 1(3) (dower assigned by metes and bounds), 20(3) (curtesy).

[69] The method will depend upon whether the title is already registered or not. If it is not, the purchaser will have to complete his title by registration: LRA 2002 s.4.

[70] SLA 1925 s.7(4). If a paramount right to the legal estate arises (e.g. by condition broken and re-entry) the tenant for life must convey accordingly: SLA 1925 s.16(1)(ii).

not and whether the title to it is registered or unregistered. For example, land is settled on A for life or until she remarries, remainder to B for life, remainder to C in fee simple.

(i) If A remarries during B's lifetime, A is bound to convey the legal estate to B. If the title is unregistered this must be done by a further vesting deed because the land remains settled.[71] If the title is registered, A is required to transfer the land to B. It is then the duty of the trustees of the settlement to apply for such alteration, if any, in the restrictions as may be required for the protection of the interests under the settlement.[72]

(ii) If B dies and then A remarries, A must convey the land to C. If the title is unregistered, this should be done by means of an ordinary conveyance, for C is absolutely entitled and the settlement is at an end.[73] Should the title be registered, A must transfer the land to C. The trustees of the settlement should execute a deed declaring that they are discharged from the trust[74] and that deed should be lodged at the Land Registry together with an application to cancel the Settled Land Act restrictions.[75]

If any necessary document is not executed, the court may make a vesting order instead of it.[76]

A–017   **2. Death of tenant for life.** Similar principles apply where the tenant for life dies, though they are complicated by special rules for devolution on death. Two possible situations may arise.

A–018   *(a) Land ceases to be settled.* On the death of the tenant for life, the land may cease to be settled, either because the remainderman becomes absolutely entitled to the property or because the land becomes subject to a trust of land. In such circumstances, the legal estate vests in the general personal representatives of the tenant for life in the usual way. They must transmit it to the remainderman or to the trustees of land by means of an ordinary assent or conveyance.[77] Where the title is registered, the personal representatives should lodge an assent in the usual way.[78] If the land is to vest in the remainderman, it is probably not necessary either to seek the removal of the

---

[71] SLA 1925 s.8(4)(a). That vesting deed will now trigger the requirement to register the title: see LRA 2002 s.4.

[72] LRR 2003 Sch.7 para.7.

[73] SLA 1925 s.7(5). That conveyance will trigger the requirement to register the title: see LRA 2002 s.4.

[74] SLA 1925 s.17.

[75] Ruoff & Roper, 37–018.

[76] SLA 1925 s.12. See, e.g. *Re Shawdon Estates Settlement* [1930] 2 Ch. 1.

[77] *Re Bridgett and Hayes' Contract* [1928] Ch. 163. Where title is unregistered, this assent or conveyance will, once again, trigger the requirement to register the title: LRA 2002 s.4. If the life tenant dies intestate his administrator succeeds to the legal estate: see Wolst. & C. v. 26.

[78] LRR 2003 Sch.7 para.11.

restrictions that had hitherto applied to the tenant for life (because these will be removed) or to execute a deed of discharge.[79] If the land is to vest in trustees of land, this should be made apparent on the application for registration, to ensure that the proper restriction is entered on the register.[80]

(b) Land remains settled. If the land remains settled on the death of the **A–019** tenant for life, it vests in the trustees of the settlement[81] in the capacity of special personal representatives.[82] They should:

(i) take out a grant of probate or letters of administration limited to the settled land;

(ii) execute a vesting assent in favour of the next life tenant; and

(iii) whether or not the title is already registered, secure both his registration as registered proprietor and entry on the register of the appropriate restrictions.[83]

The special and general personal representatives can each deal with the land under their control independently of each other.[84] Accordingly, if the land remains settled, it follows a different course of devolution through special personal representatives.

C. Deed of Discharge as Evidence of End of Settlement

1. Need for deed of discharge. A deed of discharge is the instrument **A–020** designed by the Act to cancel the effect of the vesting deed when its work has been done. If the land eventually devolves upon someone who is absolutely entitled, he must have some means of proving this to a purchaser without showing him the trust instrument. The Act therefore requires that, when the legal estate is held free from all limitations of a trust instrument, the trustees of the settlement must execute a deed declaring that they are discharged from their duties.[85] In case of difficulty, the court may make an order to the same

---

[79] See Ruoff & Roper, 37–017. Once the restrictions have been removed, a deed of discharge fulfils no practical purpose.

[80] See Ruoff & Roper, 37–016.02.

[81] AEA 1925 s.22(1) (will); Supreme Court Act 1981 s.116 (intestacy), under which the court will presumably be guided by the repealed provisions of IA 1925 s.162, as amended by the Administration of Justice Act 1928 s.9.

[82] "Special executors" in the case of a will: AEA 1925 s.22. In the case of the intestacy no statutory title is now prescribed (see preceding note). And see *Re Rawlinson* (1934) 78 S.J. 602 (special personal representatives held beneficially entitled); *Re Mortifee* [1948] P. 274.

[83] Where title is already registered, see LRR 2003 Sch.7. Ruoff & Roper, 37–017. Where title is unregistered, the assent triggers compulsory registration: LRA 2002 s.4. On registration the appropriate restrictions will then be entered on the register.

[84] AEA 1925 s.24.

[85] SLA 1925 s.17 (as amended by TLATA 1996 s.25(1); Sch.3). There is a proviso for securing interests created by any derivative settlement, e.g. where a beneficial interest has itself been settled.

effect.[86] The deed or order of discharge entitles (and compels[87]) a purchaser to assume that the trusts mentioned in the vesting deed no longer exist. He may then safely pay the money to the vendor, for his notice of the trusts is cancelled by the deed of discharge.

A–021 **2. Deed of discharge not required.** There are two cases where no deed of discharge is required.

A–022 *(a) No vesting instrument executed.* The object of a deed of discharge is to neutralise the vesting deed, and so no deed of discharge is needed if the land ceases to be settled before any vesting instrument has been executed. In such circumstances there is no tenant for life or statutory owner, and the land must be dealt with outside the Settled Land Act 1925.[88]

A–023 *(b) Disposition of unregistered land under ordinary conveyance or assent on the title.* In relation to unregistered land, no deed of discharge is required if, after a vesting assent has been executed, there appears on the title a simple assent or conveyance not referring to the trustees of the settlement. This follows from a provision that if a vesting instrument has been executed, but there is a subsequent conveyance or assent on the title which does not contain a statement of the names of the Settled Land Act trustees, a bona fide purchaser of a legal estate for value[89] is both entitled and bound to assume that every statement in the assent or conveyance is correct and that the person in whom the land was thereby vested holds it free from all rights under the settlement.[90] For the future, this provision will be of little importance. since April 1998, any conveyance or assent on the termination of the settlement is now required to be completed by registration.[91] The person entitled to the land will be registered as proprietor without the entry of any restriction, and can therefore transfer a good title.

A–024 **3. Registered land.** We have already seen that where the title is registered, the interests under the settlement are protected by restrictions.[92] Once those restrictions are removed, the registered proprietor is free to deal with the land as absolute owner.

D. Duration of Settlements

A–025 A settlement created prior to 1997 is deemed to continue for the purposes of the Settled Land Act so long as there is still "relevant property" which is subject to the settlement[93] and:

---

[86] SLA 1925 s.17(2).
[87] SLA 1925 s.110(2)(e).
[88] *cf. Re Ale founder's WT* [1927] 1 Ch. 360.
[89] SLA 1925 ss.110(5), 117(1)(xxi): as usual, this includes a lessee or mortgagee: SLA 1925.
[90] SLA 1925 s.110(5).
[91] LRA 2002 s.4.
[92] See above, Appendix para.A–006.
[93] TLATA 1996 s.2(4).

(i) any limitation, charge or power of charging under the settlement still subsists or is capable of being exercised; or

(ii) the person beneficially entitled in possession is a minor.[94]

For these purposes "relevant property" means land and personal chattels included within the settlement.[95] It follows that, if all the settled property is sold, the settlement ceases, and this is so even if (as they are empowered to do) the trustees subsequently purchase more land with the proceeds of sale. Such new land will be held by the trustees on a trust of land.[96] By contrast, if at a time when there is still relevant property, the trustees of the settlement apply capital money in the purchase of more land, that land will be brought within the settlement, and will be settled land.[97]

A settlement will no longer be deemed to continue when the only subsisting limitation is an absolute interest vested in a person of full age. Even if there is still a trust in favour of such a person,[98] it is generally assumed that the settlement is nevertheless at an end.[99]

E. While Settlement Continues, No Dealings Except Under Act

1. Unauthorised dealings. We have already seen how s.13 paralyses dealings in the land until there is a vesting instrument.[100] After the vesting instrument has been executed, and for so long as the settlement continues, although the tenant for life or statutory owner has the legal estate, he cannot deal with it freely, but only as allowed by the Act, or any other Act,[101] or by any additional powers conferred by the settlement.[102] By s.18 any disposition by the tenant for life or statutory owner which is not authorised by the Act is void,[103] except for the purpose of binding the tenant for life's own beneficial interest while it continues. In one case,[104] a father sold land to his son and later bought it back again. On his death he settled the land by will upon his son for life with remainder to a grandson. The son mortgaged the land, not under his

A–026

---

[94] SLA 1925 s.3 (as amended by TLATA 1996 s.25(1); Sch.3).

[95] TLATA 1996 s.2(4). For settled chattels, see SLA 1925 s.67; below, Appendix para.A–070.

[96] See TLATA 1996 ss.2(6), 6(3), (4), 17; Sch.1 para.6.

[97] Above, Appendix para.A–011.

[98] As where the land is still vested in the personal representatives of the last tenant for life on a bare trust for the absolute owner under the final limitation of the final settlement.

[99] Wolst. & C. ii, 34; and see *Re Bridgett and Hayes' Contract* [1928] Ch. 163; above, Appendix para.A–018.

[100] Above, Appendix para.A–007.

[101] e.g. LP(Am)A 1926.

[102] He can of course dispose of his beneficial interest, if any.

[103] s.18 ceases to apply when the settlement ends, even though no deed of discharge has been executed: see s.18(1)(a), (b), (c) (once the settlement is at an end no "tenant for life" or "capital money" can exist: ss.19, 20).

[104] *Weston Henshaw* [1950] Ch. 510. See too *Bevan v Johnston* [1990] 2 E.G.L.R. 33, where a tenant for life of registered land granted an oral lease not authorised by the Act. The lease was held to be void even though the purchaser could not at that time have inspected the register and discovered the restrictions on the proprietor's powers: see (1991) 107 L.Q.R. 596 at 601 (J. Hill). But now the register is open to all: see above, para.7–002.

Settled Land Act powers, but for his own personal needs, showing to the mortgagee only his original title by purchase from his father. Since he was in fact tenant for life and his father's executors had made a vesting assent in his favour, his improper mortgages were held void against the grandson so that the mortgagee lost his security.

A–027   **2. Scheme of the Act.** A sharp contrast is therefore revealed between s.13 and s.18. While the settlement is still incipient and there is no vesting instrument, s.13 allows a purchaser of a legal estate without notice of the settlement to obtain a good title.[105] But once there is a vesting instrument, s.18 operates in its full rigour, without any exception in favour of innocent purchasers. The scheme of the Act is that once the legal estate has been vested in the tenant for life as such, he can deal with it only in accordance with the powers conferred upon him by the Act or by the settlement. Although he has a legal estate, he is treated as if he were the mere donee of a power.[106] Any disposition that is ultra vires will be void and will not pass the legal estate.[107] To this extent he remains in the position of a tenant for life at common law, who could give no better title than he had himself.

A–028   **3. Registered land.** Where the title to settled land is registered, a purchaser will be better protected than if it is not. Provided that the usual restriction has been entered, no transaction will be registered unless it is authorised by either the Act or the settlement.[108] It is only in transactions that are not required to be completed by registration that s.18 can operate to defeat the purchaser's title.[109] If the tenant for life were to forge a deed of discharge so that any restrictions on the register were removed, any ultra vires disposition would confer on the purchaser a good title,[110] subject only to the possibility that the register might be rectified against him.[111]

A–029   **4. Protection of purchasers.** A certain (or perhaps uncertain) measure of protection is nevertheless given to purchasers by s.110(1). This provides that a purchaser dealing in good faith with a tenant for life or statutory owner shall, as against all parties entitled under the settlement, be conclusively taken:

> (i) to have given the best consideration reasonably obtainable[112]; and

> (ii) "to have complied with all the requisitions of this Act".

---

[105] Above, Appendix para.A–007.
[106] For powers, see the sixth edition of this work para.10–077.
[107] See (1971) 87 L.Q.R. 338 at 341 (D. W. Elliott); [1990] C.L.J. 277 at 280 (C.H.).
[108] Above, Appendix para.A–006.
[109] See *Bevan v Johnston*, above.
[110] *cf. Hounslow LBC v Hare* (1990) 24 H.L.R. 9.
[111] See above, paras 7–132, 7–136.
[112] See, e.g. *Hurrell v Littlejohn* [1904] 1 Ch. 689 (where a purchaser who had bought property from a tenant for life for £2,000 and promptly resold it for £3,000 was held to be protected by the section).

This provision which, unlike s.18, derives from the 1882 Act,[113] applies to all kinds of dispositions, including sales, leases, mortgages and contracts to enter into such dispositions.[114] However, it applies only to "transactions under this Act".[115] In a case concerning a lease it was explained that it "confirms the view that in the case of a lessee dealing in good faith the remedy, if any, of the persons entitled under the settlement for any neglect of the provisions of the Act is to be against the tenant for life in his fiduciary character, not against the lessee, and is not to affect the validity of the lease".[116] For this reason, it is difficult to see how s.110 can temper the rigour of s.18. It would appear to protect a purchaser only where the transaction is authorised by the Act or settlement,[117] but where there is some peripheral irregularity, such as where a lease was granted at a time when there were no trustees of the settlement,[118] or where the tenant for life exercised a power of disposition for some improper motive.[119] It will have no application where the transaction is wholly outside the powers of the tenant for life.[120] Even in those circumstances, when the transaction is one of leasing, the lease may be validated under the Law of Property Act 1925, provided that the irregularities are of an insubstantial character.[121] However these provisions have sometimes been overlooked.[122]

5. No knowledge of life tenancy. There is a conflict of authority as to   A–030
whether a purchaser who does not know that he is dealing with a tenant for life can rely upon the protection of s.110(1). Although there is a decision to the contrary,[123] the better view is that he can,[124] because he may have no means of discovering the status of the vendor.[125] Thus in one case, a tenant for life granted a lessee an option to renew a lease at a rent alleged by the remaindermen to be inadequate and therefore a contravention of the Act. He was able to rely upon s.110(1), even though he did not know that the lease had been

---

[113] SLA 1882 s.54. This explains the uncertain relationship of the section with SLA 1925 s.18.

[114] *Re Morgan's Lease* [1972] Ch. 1 (contract to grant a lease).

[115] SLA 1925 s.112(2).

[116] *Mogridge v Clapp* [1892] 3 Ch. 382 at 400, per Kay L.J. (on SLA 1882 s.54, the precursor to SLA 1925 s.110(1)).

[117] *cf. Gilbey v Rush* (1905) 75 L.J.Ch. 32 at 34 (not included in the report in [1906] 1 Ch. 11).

[118] *Mogridge v Clapp,* above.

[119] Wolst. & C. iii, 224. This was evidently the draftsman's intention: *cf. Wolstenholme's Conveyancing Statutes* (10th edn), p.456 (commenting on SLA 1882 s.54).

[120] In this way *Weston v Henshaw* [1950] Ch. 510 (where a mortgage was outside the tenant for life's powers) can be reconciled with *Re Morgan's Lease,* above (where a contract to grant a lease that was within the tenant for life's powers was upheld).

[121] s.152; below, Appendix para.A–062; *Re Morgan's Lease,* above, at 4; (1971) 87 L.Q.R. 338 (D. W. Elliott).

[122] *cf. Bevan v Johnston,* above, where a lease within the tenant for life's powers was held to be void because it had been granted orally instead of by deed. Neither SLA 1925 s.110 nor LPA 1925 s.152 was considered by the court.

[123] *Weston v Henshaw,* above.

[124] *Mogridge v Clapp,* above; *Re Morgan's Lease,* above.

[125] e.g. a lessee has no right to see his landlord's title: LPA 1925 s.44; above, para.21–005.

granted by a tenant for life.[126] If, however, the purchaser knows that the transaction is improper, or if its impropriety is apparent on its face, the purchaser will lose the protection of s.110 since he will not be acting in good faith.[127]

Section 1. Other Provisions Relating to Settled Land

A. *Essentials of Settled Land*

A–031   **1. Land is settled land if "it is or is deemed to be the subject of a settlement".**[128] There are three questions of primary importance:

(1) whether the land is the subject of a settlement;

(2) who is the tenant for life; and

(3) who are the trustees.

I. DEFINITION OF SETTLEMENT

A–032   **1. "Settlement".** The policy of the Settled Land Act 1925 was to give full powers of management to all limited owners. In general, therefore, any limited interest (e.g. for life, or for a determinable fee) created prior to 1997 indicated a settlement. But the statutory definition of "settlement" extended to various other situations and its precise limits were not always clear.

For the purposes of the Act a "settlement" meant either the actual document or documents creating the settlement,[129] or more usually, the state of affairs in relation to certain land brought about by one or more documents.[130] Without a document there could be no "settlement" within the Act.[131] By s.1(1), a settlement was created by any deed, will, agreement, Act of Parliament[132] or other instrument, or any other number of instruments,[133] by which one of the following conditions was satisfied.

A–033   *(a) Succession:* where land stood "for the time being limited in trust for any persons by way of succession". In addition to cases such as limitations "to A for life, remainder to B in fee simple", this definition seemed to be wide

---

[126] *Re Morgan's Lease*, above.

[127] *Re Handman and Wilcox's Contract* [1902] 1 Ch. 599; *Gilbey v Rush*, above; *Kisch v Hawes Bros Ltd* [1935] Ch. 102; *Davies v Hall* [1954] 1 W.L.R. 855.

[128] SLA 1925 s.2.

[129] See, e.g. SLA 1925 ss.1(1), 47, 64.

[130] *Re Ogle's SE* [1927] 1 Ch. 229 at 232.

[131] See *Griffiths v Williams* [1978] 2 E.G.L.R. 121 at 123, revealing an earlier judicial oversight in relation to proprietary estoppel: below, Appendix para.A–041.

[132] SLA 1925 s.1(1); see, e.g. *Vine v Raleigh* [1896] 1 Ch. 37 (settlement composed of a will and a public Act of Parliament, the Accumulations Act 1800). *cf. Talbot v Scarisbrick* [1908] 1 Ch. 812, where a private Act merely conferred powers and did not directly or indirectly create or incorporate any of the limitations.

[133] e.g. *Re Lord Hereford's SE* [1932] W.N. 34 (one private Act of Parliament and three conveyances).

enough to cover the following cases, which were somewhat superfluously set out in the section as independent heads. These were where land was limited in trust for any person in possession:

    (i) for an entailed interest, whether or not capable of being barred or defeated;

    (ii) for an estate in fee simple or for a term of years absolute subject to an executory gift over (e.g. a devise to trustees in trust for "A in fee simple but for B in fee simple when B marries");

    (iii) for a base or determinable fee, including a fee determinable by condition,[134] (other than a fee which is a fee simple absolute by virtue of s.7 of the Law of Property Act 1925)[135] or any corresponding interest in leasehold land.

In all of these cases there was an element of succession sufficient to satisfy the definition in (a). Furthermore, all of the interests which were so created are to be treated as subsisting under the settlement,[136] so that they can be overreached by a sale under the statutory power.[137]

(b) Springing interests: where land was limited in trust for an estate in fee   **A–034** simple or a term of years absolutely contingently on the happening of any event (e.g. a devise to trustees on trust for X in fee simple if his brothers died under the age of 21 years[138]). Here too there would usually be an element of succession, although sometimes there might not. It was (and remains) possible for a settlor to direct that the rents and profits should meanwhile be accumulated for the eventual beneficiary,[139] within the limits allowed by the rule against accumulations.[140]

(c) Minors: where land stood limited in trust for a minor in possession for   **A–035** an estate in fee simple or for a term of years absolute.[141]

(d) Family charges: where land stood charged, whether voluntarily or in   **A–036** consideration of marriage or by way of family arrangement, with the payment of any sums for the benefit of any persons.[142]

---

[134] SLA 1925 s.117(i)(iv).

[135] See SLA 1925 s.1(1)(ii)(c) (as amended by TLATA 1996 s.25(1); Sch.3 para.2). The amendment was intended to be no more than declaratory: see (1989) Law Com. No.181 para.17.1.

[136] SLA 1925 s.1(4). See *Re Hunter & Hewlett's Contract* [1907] 1 Ch. 46 (on the corresponding provision in SLA 1882 s.2(2)).

[137] For overreaching, see below, Appendix para.A–093.

[138] See *Re Bird* [1927] 1 Ch. 210; *Re Walmsley's SE* (1911) 105 L.T. 332.

[139] Under a will, this happens in any case, in default of other directions: LPA 1925 s.175.

[140] Above, para.9–152.

[141] For the position where land is held in trust for a minor after 1996, see above, para.36–011.

[142] For a full discussion of this case, and also of married women subject to restraint upon anticipation, see the fifth edition of this work at p.346. For the effect of family charges created after 1996, see TLATA 1996 s.2(6); Sch.1 para.3; above, para.12–002.

A–037   **2. "Limited in trust".** It will be noted that under heads (a) (succession), (b) (springing interests) and (c) (minors), but not (d) (family charges), it was necessary for the land to be "limited in trust" if it was to fall within the definition. However, this requirement was automatically satisfied, since none of the beneficial interests mentioned under heads (a), (b) and (c) could exist as a legal estate.[143] Either the interest was a limited one (i.e. less than a fee simple absolute), or it was not yet in possession, or it was held by a minor who since 1925 cannot hold a legal estate.[144] Consequently, on the principle that there is usually a trust if the legal estate is in one person and the equitable interest in another,[145] the land would be held upon trust in these cases.[146]

One exception was possible. A fee simple defeasible by condition subsequent might, if so limited, still exist as a legal estate. The reason for this was to ensure that certain types of conditional fees did not fall within the Settled Land Act 1925.[147] It is now clear from an amendment to that Act, which was intended to be no more than declaratory, that there was no settlement, where there was a fee simple which was subject to a legal or equitable right of entry or re-entry.[148] If, however, a trust were employed, the land would have been settled land, as for example where there was, prior to 1997, a devise "to A in fee simple, but if A succeeds to Blackacre then to B" (for wills automatically create a trust[149]) or a grant by deed "to T in fee simple upon trust for A . . . "[150] for a similar interest.

Under head (d) no limitation by way of trust was required. Whether the estate which was made subject to the family charges was conveyed directly to the beneficiary or whether it was held in trust for the beneficiary, the land was nevertheless settled land.

A–038   **3. Sale subject to family charges.** There were a number of situations where land which was not settled land before 1926 became so after 1925.[151] One of these caused some difficulty. This was where land was vested in fee simple in a person absolutely entitled, but subject to family charges under the

---

[143] LPA 1925 s.1(1), (2); above, paras 6–013 *et seq.* and as to wills, see LP(Am)A 1924 Sch.9 para.3.

[144] LPA 1925 s.1(6); above, para.36–003.

[145] See *Rayner v Preston* (1881) 18 Ch D 1 at 13; *Hardoon v Belilos* [1901] A.C. 118 at 123. This will not always be the case: see *Westdeutsche Landesbank Girozentrale v Islington LBC* [1996] A.C. 669 at 706 at 707.

[146] In *Ungurian v Lesnoff* [1990] Ch. 206 at 225, Vinelott J. held that land was "limited" in trust if the trust arose by operation of law and not by express limitation (as where land is devised "to A in tail"), notwithstanding earlier remarks to the contrary by Lord Denning M.R. in *Binions v Evans* [1972] Ch. 359 at 366.

[147] Above, para.6–015.

[148] See SLA 1925 s.1(i)(ii)(c) (as amended by TLATA 1996 s.25(1); Sch.3 para.2); (1989) Law Com. No.181, para.17.1.

[149] Above, para.14–140.

[150] A devise in fee simple absolute by the owner of land subject to a fee farm rent (above, para.6–013) presumably created no settlement (or were it to occur now, a trust of land), since the condition was a legal right attaching to the legal estate itself and was not part of the trusts upon which it was held: *cf.* Wolst. & C. 11, 24.

[151] For a full treatment, see the fifth edition of this work at pp.345–349.

settlement.[152] The owner of such land found that he could only sell it by complying with the troublesome Settled Land Act procedure. To meet this difficulty, it was enacted that a person of full age, who was beneficially entitled to land in fee simple or for a term of years absolute which was settled land solely because it was subject to family charges, might nevertheless create or convey a legal estate subject to the charges in the same way as if the land were not settled land.[153]

4. Borderline cases. Prior to the Settled Land Act 1882, a person who was   **A–039** given a right to reside in a property for his lifetime or for some lesser determinable period was usually regarded as a mere licensee.[154] However in most cases after 1882 and before 1997, a person with such a right was held to be a tenant for life under the relevant Settled Land Act.[155] This was so, even though the settlor never intended that the person should have the extensive powers which were conferred by statute on a tenant for life.[156] This reflected the policy of the Acts which was "to render land a marketable article notwithstanding the settlement".[157] The fact that a settlement arose in such circumstances gave rise to difficulties in two situations.

(a) Where a settlement inadvertently arose under an order of the court. This   **A–040** occurred:

> (i) where a court either sanctioned an agreement made between the parties on divorce by which the wife was allowed to live in a particular house rent free for her lifetime or made such an order itself under the Matrimonial Causes Act 1973[158];
>
> (ii) where an equity arose by estoppel and the court gave effect to it by granting the claimant a licence to reside on the premises for life or as long as he desired.[159]

---

[152] See above, Appendix para.A–036.

[153] LP(Am)A 1926. For a fuller treatment, see the fifth edition of this work at pp.346–348.

[154] See, e.g. *Parker v Parker* (1863) 1 New Rep. 508; *May v May* (1881) 44 L.T. 412. The right was usually given by will. See generally, B.W. Harvey, *Settlements of Land*, Ch.6.

[155] *Ungurian v Lesnoff* [1990] Ch. 206 at 226, per Vinelott J.; below, Appendix para.A–046. See, e.g. *Costello v Costello* (1994) 27 H.L.R. 12 (where the authorities are reviewed). *cf. Dent v Dent* [1996] 1 W.L.R. 683, where an undertaking (professionally drawn) that a person could reside on property for her lifetime created a licence. It merely formalised an existing family arrangement and did not involve the creation of any trust or make any disposition of the estate.

[156] *Re Came's SE* [1899] 1 Ch. 324 at 330; *Re Baroness Llanover's Will* [1902] 2 Ch. 679 at 683. *cf. Ayer v Benton* (1967) 204 E.G. 359, where Buckley J. "found" a trust for sale, quite unwarranted by the facts, to avoid the consequences of an application of the Act.

[157] *Re Mundy & Roper's Contract* [1899] 1 Ch. 275 at 288, per Chitty L.J. See too *Lord Henry Bruce v Marquess of Ailesbury* [1892] A.C. 356 at 361; *Ungurian v Lesnoff*, above, at 226.

[158] *Morss v Morss* [1972] Fam. 264 (but *cf.* Stamp L.J. at 279), *Martin v Martin* [1978] Fam. 12; and see [1978] Conv. 229 (P. W. Smith).

[159] See, e.g. *Inwards v Baker* [1965] 2 Q.B. 29; *Williams v Staite* [1979] Ch. 291. For rights arising by proprietary estoppel, see Ch.16.

In each situation, it would have been open to the court to have made some other order.[160] Thus, in other cases where an equity arising by estoppel might have been satisfied by granting the claimant a right to reside on the property for life, the court has in its discretion granted him some lesser right to ensure that he did not obtain the extensive powers of tenant for life.[161]

A claimant who became a tenant for life without appreciating that fact was vulnerable because he was unlikely to ensure that a vesting deed or transfer was executed in his favour. There is a risk therefore that his interest might at some stage be defeated by a disposition by the legal owner in favour of a purchaser.[162]

A–041   *(b) Where the court held that an informal settlement had arisen by estoppel or constructive trust.* In some cases it was held that a settlement had arisen either by proprietary estoppel[163] or under a constructive trust.[164] This appears to be at variance with the requirement of s.1(1) of the Act that the settlement should arise from some document or instrument.[165] Where the interest arose by estoppel, the order of the court giving effect to the equity might itself have been the "instrument".[166] However this reasoning could not apply where a settlement came into being through the imposition of a constructive trust. Such a trust arises either from the common intention of the parties or because it would be inequitable for a landowner to deny a claimant an interest in the property.[167] In such circumstances the claimant's beneficial interest in the property crystallises at the time of his detrimental reliance, not when he seeks to vindicate his rights before a court.[168] It was assumed in such cases that there was a settlement,[169] and that it fell within s.1(1) of the Act because it arose as a result of an "agreement".[170] But this view could not be reconciled with the wording of the Act in cases where the agreement was informal and was not contained in any document.

---

[160] For the wide powers of the court on divorce, see MCA 1973 ss.24, 24A, 25. The court has a discretion when satisfying an equity arising by estoppel and may ensure that the claimant does not obtain a greater interest than the parties intended. See above, para.16–021.

[161] *Dodsworth v Dodsworth* (1973) 228 E.G. 1115; *Griffiths v Williams* [1978] 2 E.G.L.R. 121. *cf. Costello v Costello* (1994) 27 H.L.R. 12 at 19.

[162] Above, Appendix para.A–009.

[163] For proprietary estoppel, see Ch.16.

[164] For constructive trusts, see above, para.11–017.

[165] See *Griffiths v Williams*, above, at 123; above, Appendix para.A–032.

[166] *Griffiths v Williams,* above, at 123.

[167] Above, paras 11–022, 11–023.

[168] Above, paras 11–032, 11–033.

[169] *Bannister v Bannister* [1948] 2 All E.R. 133; *Binions v Evans* [1972] Ch. 359 (Lord Denning dissenting on this point); *Ungurian v Lesnoff* [1990] Ch. 206. For criticism of these decisions see (1977) 93 L.Q.R. 561 (J. A. Hornby); (1991) 107 L.Q.R. 596 (J. Hill). *cf. Ivory v Palmer* [1975] I.C.R. 340 (right of occupation granted for the term of the claimant's employment, which was said to be "for life", conferred only a contractual licence); and *Chandler v Kerley* [1978] 1 W.L.R. 693 at 698.

[170] *Ungurian v Lesnoff*, above, at 226. Where A claimed an interest under a constructive trust in land owned by B, the "settlement" could not have been the conveyance of the land to B, because A might have acquired his interest only subsequently: above, para.11–027. *cf.* (1991) 107 L.Q.R. 596 at 599 (J. Hill).

1. Tenant for life

(a) Definition. The primary definition of "tenant for life" in the Settled   **A–042**
Land Act 1925 is "the person of full age who is for the time being entitled
under a settlement to possession of settled land for his life".[171] But the
definition also includes any person (other than a statutory owner[172]) who has
the statutory powers.[173] As those powers are conferred not only on those who
have life interests (by s.19), but also on many other persons (under s.20),
"tenant for life" has for this purpose an artificially extended meaning. Generally speaking, every limited owner who is of full age and beneficially
entitled in possession under the settlement[174] is thus a "tenant for life", so that
the definition of tenant for life is complementary to the definition of settled
land. A "tenant for life" may thus be a person entitled to a life interest, a
tenant in tail,[175] a tenant in fee simple subject to a gift over or to family
charges, a tenant for years not at a rent terminable on life,[176] a tenant *pur autre
vie*, a person entitled to the income of land for his own or any other life, and
others. As explained earlier,[177] two or more persons entitled jointly may also
constitute the tenant for life.

(b) Special cases. Although it is essential that the person claiming to have   **A–043**
the powers of tenant for life should fit precisely into one or other of the
specified classes, there is usually little difficulty in ascertaining him. The
following cases do however require special mention.[178]

(1) TENANTS FOR YEARS. The Settled Land Act 1925 is only concerned with   **A–044**
"family" and not "commercial" leases. The definition of tenant for life
extends to tenants for years determinable on life,[179] and tenants *pur autre vie*,
provided in both cases that they do not hold "merely under a lease at a
rent".[180]

(2) PERSONS ENTITLED TO THE INCOME OF THE LAND. If the settlement gave   **A–045**
the land to trustees upon trust to pay the income to A for life, all the statutory
powers are vested in A and not in the trustees.[181] A can therefore call for a

---

[171] SLA 1925 s.19(1).

[172] Below, Appendix para.A–048.

[173] SLA 1925 s.117(1)(xxvii).

[174] See below, Apendix para.A–046.

[175] Even if unable to bar his entail, unless the property was purchased with money provided by
Parliament and statute prohibits barring the entail: SLA 1925 s.20(1)(i). But see *Re Duke of
Marlborough's Parliamentary Estates* (1891) 8 T.L.R. 179; *Re Duke of Marlborough's Blenheim
Estates* (1892) 8 T.L.R. 582; and see SLA 1925 s.23(2).

[176] SLA 1925 s.20(1)(iv). See too SLA 1925 s.20(1)(vi) (determinable interests); *Re Boyer's SE*
[1916] 2 Ch. 404.

[177] Above, para.13–090.

[178] For fuller treatment, see the fifth edition of this work at pp.350–352.

[179] *Re Mundy & Ropers Contract* [1899] 1 Ch. 275 at 298.

[180] s.20(1)(iv), (v). A person who paid a rent of £1 per annum was held not to be the tenant for
life: *Re Catling* [1931] 2 Ch. 359.

[181] SLA 1925 s.20(1)(viii): below, Appendix para.A–080.

vesting deed in his own favour, and so obtain the right to occupy the land.[182] To fall within this category:

(i) the person must be entitled to the whole of the net income of the land,[183] and not merely to some part of it[184]; and

(ii) the right must be for his lifetime, for the life of some other person, or until sale of the land or the determination of his interest.[185]

A–046   *(c) Beneficially entitled in possession.* A tenant for life must, as an additional requirement, be of full age (i.e. not a minor[186]) and beneficially entitled in possession under the settlement.[187] A future interest in remainder or reversion will not suffice.[188] However, a right to occupy will suffice, as where, in the will of a testator who died before 1997, the trustees of his settlement are instructed to permit his widow to reside in a specific house for as long as she might wish.[189]

Although the terms "beneficially entitled" and "under the settlement" appear only in s.19 (in relation to a tenant with an actual life interest) and not in s.20 (as regards those with other interests such as a tenant in tail), it is thought that the requirement that the tenant for life should have a beneficial interest is implied in all cases.[190] An executor of a person beneficially entitled is also, exceptionally, regarded as satisfying the words "beneficially entitled"[191] Although he is not entitled for his own benefit, he can represent the deceased's beneficial interest as against others. Where the tenant for life assigns his interest, he remains tenant for life for the purposes of the Act.[192] This is because the assignee is entitled under the assignment and not "under the settlement".[193]

---

[182] There was no such right to possession prior to 1926, unless the court thought it proper to give it to him: see *Re Bagot's Settlement* [1894] 1 Ch. 177.

[183] It is not enough that he is an object of a power of appointment in respect of such income: *Re Atkinson* (1886) 31 Ch D 577; *Re Gallenga WT* [1938] 1 All E.R. 106; Wolst. & C. ii, 78, 79.

[184] *Re Frewen* [1926] Ch. 580.

[185] *Re Astor* [1922] 1 Ch. 364.

[186] A corporation may therefore be a life tenant: *Re Earl of Carnarvon's Chesterfield SE* [1927] 1 Ch. 138 (limited company).

[187] SLA 1925 ss.19(1), 20(1).

[188] *Re Morgan* (1883) 24 Ch D 114 at 116; and see *Re Strangeways* (1886) 34 Ch D 423; *Re Martyn* (1900) 69 L.J.Ch. 733; *Re Beauchamp's WT* [1914] 1 Ch. 676.

[189] *Re Came's SE* [1899] 1 Ch. 324. See similarly *Re Baroness Llanover's Will* [1903] 2 Ch. 16; *Re Boyer's SE* [1916] 2 Ch. 404; *Re Anderson* [1920] 1 Ch. 175; *Re Gibbons* [1920] 1 Ch. 372. A mere right to occupy such one of 14 houses as the beneficiary might choose was not enough: *Re Bond* (1904) 48 S.J. 192.

[190] This was so prior to 1926: see *Re Jemmett & Guest's Contract* [1907] 1 Ch. 629. It is not thought that the comparatively minor changes in drafting made in 1925 have affected this conclusion.

[191] See *Vine v Raleigh* [1896] 1 Ch. 37; *Re Johnson* [1914] 2 Ch. 134.

[192] *Re Earl of Carnarvon's Chesterfield SE* [1927] 1 Ch. 138.

[193] *Re Earl of Carnarvon's Chesterfield SE* [1927] 1 Ch. 138. This is also the result of SLA 1925 s.104, explained below, Appendix para.A–086.

(d) Effect of definition. The practical effect of the definition is that where **A–047** there is some person of full age beneficially entitled to possess or occupy some specific land or to receive the whole of the income from it, that person will have the statutory powers.

The position where two or more persons are entitled jointly or in common in this way has been explained earlier.[194]

2. Cases where there is no tenant for life. In some cases there may be a **A–048** settlement, but no person entitled as tenant for life. Examples include the following[195]:

(i) Where the person beneficially entitled is a minor.[196]

(ii) Where no person is entitled to the whole of the net income, as where there is a trust to pay a fixed annuity to X, with a direction to accumulate the balance.[197]

(iii) Where no person is entitled to the income at all, as where there is a discretionary trust for the trustees to pay the income to such person or persons as they think fit.

(iv) Where trustees are directed to accumulate the income for a future contingent beneficiary, without any other limitations which create successive interests.[198]

In any case where there is no tenant for life, the legal estate and statutory powers are vested in the statutory owner.[199] A statutory owner is not subject to all the duties and restrictions imposed upon tenants for life, unless they are expressed to apply. The definition of "tenant for life" specifically excludes statutory owners.[200]

III. DEFINITION OF TRUSTEES OF THE SETTLEMENT

1. The definition. The trustees of the settlement are defined by section 30 **A–049** of the Settled Land Act 1925. There are five heads, which must be applied in turn. If there are trustees under one head, they will exclude any trustees under a subsequent head.[201] The definition is as follows.

---

[194] Above, paras 13–090, 13–091.

[195] *cf. Wolst.* & C. iii, 86.

[196] Above, Appendix para.A–048. For the special powers of the statutory owners in such a case, see SLA 1925 s.102.

[197] *Re Jeffreys* [1939] Ch. 205.

[198] In this case too special powers of interim management are conferred by SLA 1925 s.102.

[199] Above, Appendix para A–048.

[200] SLA 1925 s.117(1)(xxviii); *Re Craven's SE* [1926] Ch. 985.

[201] For a list of the trustees' duties and an explanation of the documents used in case of a change of trustees, see below, Appendix paras A–091, A–092.

(i) The persons who, under the settlement, are trustees with power to sell the land (even if this power is subject to the consent of anyone, e.g. the tenant for life[202]) or with power to consent to or to approve the exercise of a power of sale.[203]

For example, if in a settlement on A for life, with remainders over, there was provision giving X and Y power to sell the land, this made them trustees of the settlement, in preference even to any other persons expressly appointed Settled Land Act trustees. X and Y would in fact have no power to sell, for as will be seen,[204] this power is given to A, the tenant for life.[205] Nevertheless, the attempt to give them the power sufficed to make them trustees of the settlement.[206]

(ii) The persons declared by the settlement to be trustees thereof for the purposes of the Settled Land Acts 1882 to 1890, or 1925, or any of them.[207]

This is the head under which the trustees of the settlement were usually to be found. To satisfy this head, it was necessary to specify in the settlement that X and Y were appointed not merely trustees or trustees of the settlement, but "for the purposes of the Settled Land Act 1925".[208]

(iii) Persons who, under the settlement, are trustees with:

(a) a power or duty to sell; or
(b) a power to consent to or approve the exercise of the power of sale of, *other* land held under the same settlement and upon the same trusts.[209]

(iv) Persons who, under the settlement, are trustees with:

(a) a *future* power or duty to sell; or
(b) a power of consenting to or approving the exercise of such a future power of sale, even if the power or duty does not take effect in all events.[210]

A–050   Thus if there was a settlement of Blackacre and Whiteacre which attempted to give the trustees (albeit ineffectively) a power of sale over Blackacre alone, clause (iii) made those trustees Settled Land Act trustees of both properties.[211]

---

[202] *Constable v Constable* (1886) 32 Ch D 233.
[203] SLA 1925 s.30(1)(i).
[204] Below, Appendix para.A–080.
[205] SLA 1925 s.108(2).
[206] SLA 1925 s.30(2).
[207] SLA 1925 s.30(1)(ii).
[208] See, e.g. *Re Bentley* (1885) 54 L.J.Ch. 782 ("trustees").
[209] SLA 1925 s.30(1)(iii) (as amended by TLATA 1996 s.25(i); Sch.3 para.2).
[210] SLA 1925 s.30(1)(iv) (as amended by TLATA 1996 s.25(i); Sch.2 para.2).
[211] *Re Moore* [1906] 1 Ch. 789.

Again, if Greenacre is settled on A for life with remainder to X and Y upon trust to sell the land,[212] clause (iv) made X and Y Settled Land Act trustees.[213]

Under both (iii) and (iv), it is immaterial that the powers given by the settlement are, under the Act, not exercisable by the trustees.[214]

> (v) The persons appointed by deed by those able to dispose of the whole equitable interest in the settled land.[215]

For example, if land is settled on A for life, remainder to B in tail, A and B can appoint trustees of the settlement. B could bar the entail with A's consent, and thus between them they could dispose of the whole interest in the land.[216]

There is nothing in the Act which prevents the tenant for life himself from being one of the trustees, or even two or more joint tenants for life from being the sole trustees.[217] It is of course the primary duty of the trustees to protect the interests of future beneficiaries against abuse of the tenant for life's powers.

2. Personal representatives. Where a settlement arose under a will or **A–051** intestacy and there were no trustees under any other provisions, the personal representatives were trustees of the settlement until other trustees were appointed.[218] This provision dealt with the most frequent cause of a lack of trustees, namely a will made without proper legal advice. Where even this provision failed (e.g. where there was a home-made settlement created inter vivos) the court was empowered to appoint trustees on the application of any person interested under the settlement.[219] Once persons have become trustees, whether by order of the court or otherwise, they or their successors in office remain trustees as long as the settlement subsists.[220]

---

[212] Which will now take effect as a trust of land. For the effect of any such duty to sell, see TLATA 1996 s.4; above, para.12–005.

[213] *Re Johnson's SE* [1913] W.N. 222. This would not be the case if the trust to sell was void for perpetuity: *Re Davies and Kent's Contract* [1910] 2 Ch. 35 at 45. For the perpetuity rule, see above, para.4–018.

[214] SLA 1925 s.30(2); below, Appendix para.A–080.

[215] SLA 1925 s.30(1)(v).

[216] *Re Spearman SE* [1906] 2 Ch. 502, *cf. Re Spencer's SE* [1903] 1 Ch. 75 (appointment executed by some only of the beneficiaries held invalid).

[217] See *Re Jackson's SE* [1902] 1 Ch. 258; *Re Davies and Kent's Contract*, above, at 50, 51; *Re Pennant's WT* [1970] Ch. 75; and see SLA 1925 s.68(3).

[218] SLA 1925 s.30(3). If there was only one personal representative, and he was not a trust corporation, he was bound to appoint another trustee to act with him: SLA 1925 s.30(3). The section does not empower the personal representatives to retire and appoint new trustees, but they may do so under TA 1925 ss.64(i), 68(5); *Re Dark* [1954] Ch. 291.

[219] SLA 1925 s.34.

[220] SLA 1925 s.33. See the example in Wolst. & C. iii, 101. As to appointment, replacement and removal of trustees, see above, paras 11–050, 11–054, 11–057, 11–065.

A–052   **3. Referential settlements.** Special provision was made[221] for referential settlements, that is to say, settlements which referred to earlier settlements, e.g. directing Blackacre to be held on the same trusts as Whiteacre, which was already settled.[222] Unless trustees were separately appointed under head (ii) above, the trustees of the earlier settlement became trustees of the later settlement which referred to it.[223]

B. Compound Settlements[224]

A–053   "Compound settlement" is the term used to describe the situation when the trusts affecting the land were created by two or more instruments, as where a settlement was followed by a resettlement. Occasionally it is used to describe a referential settlement.[225] However, it is best confined to two or more sets of trusts applying to one parcel of land rather than two or more parcels of land governed by similar trusts.[226] For example, suppose that land had been settled on A for life with remainder to his son in tail, and that on the son attaining his majority, A and the son barred the entail and resettled the property on A for life, with remainder to the son for life and remainders over. Since a settlement might consist of a single instrument or any number of instruments,[227] there would then be three distinct settlements to consider:

   (i) the original settlement;

   (ii) the resettlement; and

   (iii) the compound settlement, which is a separate entity.[228]

A–054   It should be noted in this context that, although the Trusts of Land and Appointment of Trustees Act 1996 precludes the creation of any new settlements after 1996,[229] that is subject to two exceptions,[230] namely where a settlement is created on the occasion of an alteration in any interest in, or of a person becoming entitled under, a settlement which:

   (i) was in existence on January 1, 1997 (when the Act came into force); or

   (ii) derived from a settlement within (i), or a derivative settlement within (ii).

---

[221] SLA 1925 s.32.
[222] See, e.g. *Re Shelton's SE* [1928] W.N. 27.
[223] SLA 1925 s.32(1); see, e.g. *Re Adair* (1927) 71 S.J. 844. For the difficulties to which referential settlements could give rise, see the fifth edition of this work at pp.356, 357.
[224] For a fuller account, and for the difficulties that sometimes arose before 1926, see the fifth edition of this work, p.357.
[225] See, e.g. *Re Byng's SE* [1892] 2 Ch. 219; for such settlements, see the text above.
[226] See *Re Adair*, above.
[227] SLA 1925 s.1(1).
[228] See *Re Coull's SE* [1905] 1 Ch. 712 at 720.
[229] TLATA 1996 s.2(1); above, paras 12–002, 10–013.
[230] TLATA 1996 s.2(2).

The effect of (i) is that any resettlement will itself take effect as a settlement under the Settled Land Act 1925, and not as a trust of land. The effect of (ii) is that where a sub-settlement is created under a power of appointment that is contained in a settlement, resettlement or previous sub-settlement, it too will be governed by the Settled Land Act 1925. The reason for these exceptions was to prevent management conflicts that might otherwise have arisen, if the settlement had been governed by the 1925 Act, but any resettlement or sub-settlement had taken effect as a trust of land. Under a trust of land, the legal estate and powers of disposition are vested in the trustees and not in the person beneficially entitled in possession,[231] subject to a power for them to delegate their functions to such person.[232] If the parties to any resettlement or sub-settlement wish it to take effect as a trust for land, they may so provide in the instrument or instruments by which it is created.[233]

Under a compound settlement, the tenant for life can exercise any additional powers conferred by either settlement, and also overreach the rights of the beneficiaries under both the settlement and the resettlement.[234] The trustees of the original settlement (provided it is still subsisting[235]) or, in default,[236] the trustees of the resettlement, will be the trustees of the compound settlement.[237]

C. Powers and Position of a Tenant for Life

I. POWERS OF A TENANT FOR LIFE

A tenant for life can of course deal with his limited interest in the land as he likes, subject only to the law of waste.[238] Therefore he may lease it rent-free, or give away valuable rights over it such as easements. However, these transactions will not bind his successors since they can take effect only out of his interest.[239] His successors will be bound only by transactions authorised by the Act or by any additional powers given by the settlement.[240] For this reason an account of those powers must be given. It should be noted that although the legal estate is vested in the tenant for life, he cannot dispose of any legal estate or interest except as provided by the Act.[241]

A–055

---

[231] TLATA 1996 s.6; above, para.12–015.

[232] TLATA 1996 s.9; above, para.12 024.

[233] TLATA 1996 s.2(3).

[234] See *Re Cowley SE* [1926] Ch. 725.

[235] *Re Gordon and Adams' Contract* [1914] 1 Ch 110; compare *Re Lord Alington and the LCC's Contract* [1927] 2 Ch. 253; SLA 1925 ss.3, 33.

[236] *Re Cayley and Evans' Contract* [1930] 2 Ch. 143.

[237] SLA 1925 s.31(1), as amended by LP(Am)A 1926 Sch. See, e.g. *Re Symons* [1927] 1 Ch. 344.

[238] Above, para.3–090.

[239] SLA 1925 s.18(1).

[240] Above, para.10–016.

[241] SLA 1925 s.18; above, Appendix para.A–026. But if the disposition complies with the Act, it need not be intended to be an exercise of the statutory power: *Re Pennant's WT* [1970] Ch. 75.

A tenant for life is normally subject to no control in the exercise of his statutory powers.[242] The chief safeguards against abuse are:

(1) his position as trustee for the beneficiaries;

(2) the provision that in the case of the most important powers he must give notice to the trustees of his intention to exercise them; and

(3) the provision that in a few exceptional cases he must not exercise his powers without the leave of the trustees or an order of the court.

The treatment which is given to the powers of a tenant for life (and those of the trustees of the settlement) is, in this edition, considerably more abbreviated than in the previous ones.[243] This reflects the diminishing importance of settlements under the Settled Land Act 1925, which were not very common even before their prospective abolition by the Trusts of Land and Appointment of Trustees Act 1996. Furthermore, prior to 1997, both trustees for sale[244] and trustees of charitable and ecclesiastical trusts[245] had, in relation to any land held in trust, the same powers as a tenant for life and the trustees of the settlement under the Settled Land Act 1925. By contrast, after 1996, for the purposes of exercising their functions as trustees, trustees of land[246] have in relation to the land, all the powers of an absolute owner.[247]

A–056   **1. The tenant for life's position as trustee.** This fundamental safeguard is explained below.[248]

A–057   **2. Powers exercisable upon giving notice.** If the tenant for life intends to make a sale, exchange, lease, mortgage or charge, or to grant an option, he must give notice to the trustees of the settlement and, if known, to the solicitor for the trustees.[249] Trustees who are also the statutory owner are not required to give notice to themselves.[250] The notice must be given by a registered or recorded delivery letter *post*ed at least one calendar[251] month before the transaction or the contract to enter into it.[252] The notice is invalid unless when

---

[242] One joint tenant for life cannot force the other to sell: *Re 90 Thornhill Road, Tolworth* [1970] Ch. 261.

[243] See, for example, sixth edition Ch.8.

[244] LPA 1925 s.28(1) (repealed by TLATA 1996 s.25(2); Sch.4).

[245] SLA 1925 s.29 (repealed by TLATA 1996 s.25(2); Sch.4).

[246] Who include trustees of charitable and ecclesiastical trusts: TLATA 1996 ss.1, 2(5); above, para.36–029.

[247] TLATA 1996 s.6(1); above, para.10–034.

[248] Below, Appendix paras A–078, A–080. See also above, paras 10–014, 10–015.

[249] SLA 1925 s.101(1).

[250] See *Re Countess of Dudley's Contract* (1887) 35 Ch D 338 at 342.

[251] Interpretation Act 1978, Sch.

[252] SLA 1925 s.101(1); Recorded Delivery Service Act 1962, S.J. Sch.1. This provision is cast in an alternative form which seems to be satisfied by a notice given at least a month before the transaction, even if less than a month before the contract: *Duke of Marlborough v Sartoris* (1886) 32 Ch D 616; *sed quaere*.

it is given the trustees consist of two or more persons or a trust corporation.[253] Thus if there are no trustees, a tenant for life is not entitled to exercise these powers,[254] and an injunction may be granted to restrain him from doing so.[255]

The object of this provision for giving notice seems to be to enable the trustees to prevent any improper dealing[256] by applying to the court for an injunction.[257] Furthermore, if the tenant for life fails to give notice, he may be refused the equitable remedy of specific performance against a purchaser.[258] But for general purposes the requirement of notice gives little protection, for:

(i) although the trustees may bring an improper transaction before the court,[259] they are not apparently obliged to do so[260];

(ii) except in the case of a mortgage or charge, a notice in general terms suffices.[261] However, the tenant for life must, at the request of a trustee of the settlement, give reasonable information as to any sales, exchanges or leases effected, in progress or immediately intended[262];

(iii) any trustee may by writing accept less than one month's notice or waive it altogether,[263] even if the contract was made before any trustees had been appointed[264]; and

(iv) a person dealing in good faith with the tenant for life is not concerned to inquire whether notice has been given.[265] Even if there are no trustees, a purchaser in good faith for value of a legal estate gets a good title if the transaction is one on which no capital money is payable,[266] e.g. the grant of a lease without a premium.[267]

Each of the powers in respect of which notice is normally required must be explained in outline.[268]

[253] SLA 1925 s.101(1).

[254] *Re Bentley* (1885) 54 L.J.Ch. 782.

[255] *Wheelwright v Walker (No.1)* (1883) 23 Ch D 752.

[256] See *Lord Monson's SE* [1898] 1 Ch. 427 at 432.

[257] See *Hampden v Earl of Buckinghainshire* [1893] 2 Ch. 531, where some of the beneficiaries obtained an injunction.

[258] Wolst. & C. iii, 204. For a vendor's right to specific performance, see above, para.15–115.

[259] SLA 1925 s.93.

[260] SLA 1925 s.97.

[261] SLA 1925 s.101(2). See *Re Ray's SE* (1884) 25 Ch D 464.

[262] SLA 1925 s.101(3).

[263] SLA 1925 s.101(4).

[264] *Hatten v Russell* (1888) 38 Ch D 334.

[265] SLA 1925 s.101(5).

[266] SLA 1925 ss.104(4), 117(1)(xxi).

[267] See *Mogridge v Clapp* [1892] 3 Ch. 382.

[268] For a fuller account, see the fifth edition of this work at pp.360–377.

A–058   *(a) Power to sell.* A tenant for life may sell all or part of the settled land, or any easement, right or privilege of any kind over the land.[269] The general rule is that he must obtain the best consideration in money that can reasonably be obtained.[270] It follows that, subject to certain exceptions, he cannot give away the land or any rights over it.[271] The sale may be by auction or by private treaty. It may be made in one lot or several lots and free from or subject to stipulations as to title or otherwise.[272] If the land is sold at auction, the tenant for life may fix a reserve and buy it in.[273]

A–059   *(b) Power to exchange.* Settled land, or any part of it, or any easement, right or privilege over it, may be exchanged for other land or any easement, right or privilege.[274] For "equality of exchange" (i.e. to adjust any difference in value) capital money may be paid or received[275] and every exchange must be for the best consideration obtainable.[276] But settled land in England and Wales may not be given in exchange for land outside England and Wales.[277]

   (c) Power to lease

A–060   (1) THE POWER. The settled land, or any part of it, or any easement, right or privilege over it (e.g. for shooting or fishing, or to let down the surface by mining[278]) may be leased for any period not exceeding:

   (i) 999 years for building or forestry;

   (ii) 100 years for mining;

   (iii) 50 years for any other purpose.[279]

The Act provides definitions and lays down specific requirements in respect of building, mining and forestry leases.[280] Where land is to be leased in lots there are certain restrictions to ensure an even apportionment of the rent.[281] The tenant for life has no power to lease settled land together with his own land unless the rent is apportioned between the two.[282]

---

[269] SLA 1925 s.38(i).
[270] SLA 1925 s.39(1). See *Wheelwright v Walker (No.2)* (1883) 31 W.R. 912. *cf. Buttle v Saunders* [1950] 2 All E.R. 193; (1975) 39 Conv. (N.S.) 177 (A. Samuels).
[271] For these exceptions, see SLA 1925 ss.54 (water rights), 55 (public or charitable purposes— see too SLA 1925 s.57(2)), 56 (dedication of highways and open spaces). Even in these cases, the disposition must be for the general benefit of the settled land.
[272] SLA 1925 s.39(6).
[273] SLA 1925 s.39(7).
[274] SLA 1925 s.38(iii).
[275] SLA 1925 ss.38(iii), 73(1)(v).
[276] SLA 1925 s.40(1).
[277] SLA 1925 s.40(3).
[278] *Sitwell v Earl of Londesborough* [1905] 1 Ch. 460.
[279] SLA 1925 s.41. The court may extend the periods (below, Appendix para.A–061) and the limits do not apply to mortgage terms: see below, Appendix para.A–064.
[280] See SLA 1925 ss.44–48, 117(1)(x). For further details, see the fifth edition of this work at p.362.
[281] SLA 1925 s.44(3); *Re Rycroft's Settlement* [1962] Ch. 263.
[282] *Re Rycroft's Settlement,* above.

"Lease" includes an agreement for a lease (as it does throughout the Act[283]), but in this context it has been held to include only such tenancy agreements as take effect either in law or in equity as demises.[284] Contracts for the grant of future leases are the subject of different provisions.[285]

(2) CONDITIONS OF LEASE. Every lease of settled land must comply with the following conditions. **A–061**

    (i) It must be made by deed.[286]

    (ii) It must be made to take effect in possession not more than one year after its date, or in reversion after an existing lease with not more than seven years to run at the date of the new lease.[287] Thus if a tenant for life grants a lease to commence in 14 months' time it is invalid[288] unless it is to commence on the determination of an existing lease.[289] But a contract to grant a lease in, say, 10 years' time is valid.[290]

    (iii) It must reserve the best rent reasonably obtainable in the circumstances, regard being had to any fine taken, and to any money laid out or to be laid out for the benefit of the land.[291] "Fine" is widely defined as including any premium or fore-gift, and any payment, condition or benefit in the nature of a fine, premium or fore-gift,[292] so that although it usually means a lump sum paid for the grant of the lease, it is not confined to such payments.[293] Any fine is capital money.[294]

    (iv) It must contain a covenant by the lessee for payment of rent and a condition of re-entry (i.e. a provision for forfeiture of the lease) on rent not being paid within a specified time not exceeding 30 days.[295]

---

[283] SLA 1925 s.117(1)(x).

[284] *Re Rycroft's Settlement,* above; but see *Re Morgan's Lease* [1972] Ch. 1, holding that an executory contract is included. For this distinction, see above, para.17–040. Below, Appendix para.A–076.

[285] Below, Appendix para.A–076.

[286] SLA 1925 s.42(1)(i). cf. *Bevan v Johnston* [1990] 2 E.G.L.R. 33.

[287] SLA 1925 s.42(1)(i).

[288] See *Kisch v Hawes Bros Ltd* [1935] Ch. 102; but see also LPA 1925 s.152, explained below, Appendix para.A–062.

[289] For the general rules about reversionary leases, see above, para.17–061.

[290] See the preceding paragraph.

[291] SLA 1925 s.42(1)(ii).

[292] SLA 1925 s.117(1)(xxii).

[293] *Lloyd-Jones v Clark-Lloyd* [1919] 1 Ch. 424 at 438; and see *Waite v Jennings* [1906] 2 K.B. 11; *Comber v Fleet Electrics Ltd* [1955] 1 W.L.R. 566.

[294] SLA 1925 s.42(4); see *Pumford v W Butler & Co Ltd* [1914] 2 Ch. 353; for certain special rules applicable to building, forestry and mining leases, see the fifth edition of this work at p.363.

[295] SLA 1925 s.42(1)(iii).

(v) A counterpart (i.e. a copy) of the lease must be executed by the lessee and delivered to the tenant for life. It is sufficient evidence that this has been done if the tenant for life duly executes the lease.[296]

The normal rules that a lease must be made by deed and that notice must be given to the trustees is relaxed in certain cases. No notice is required if the lease is not for more than 21 years, but otherwise satisfies the conditions set out above.[297] Furthermore, if the lease is not for more than three years,[298] it may also be made merely in writing and not by deed, with an agreement, instead of a covenant to pay the rent.[299] In the case of building and mining leases, the court may relax the statutory requirements, including the maximum term, if these conflict with what is customary in the district or make it difficult to grant such leases.[300]

A–062   (3) DEFECTIVE LEASES. A lease which does not comply with the require-ments of the Act is void, except so far as it binds the beneficial interest of the tenant for life.[301] But under statutory provisions now contained in the Law of Property Act 1925,[302] leases which are invalid because they fail to comply with the terms of a power may nevertheless be effective in equity at the lessee's option as contracts for leases,[303] subject to such variations as are necessary in order to comply with the power. This saving enactment applies only if the lease was made in good faith and the lessee has taken possession,[304] so that only sitting tenants are benefited. By judicial construction its operation is confined, it seems, to the curing of minor irregularities only, such as the omission of some restriction or condition, or a mistake in form.[305]

Furthermore, the Settled Land Act 1925[306] gives special protection to a purchaser (including a tenant) who deals in good faith with the tenant for life.[307] He is conclusively presumed, as against those entitled under the

[296] SLA 1925 s.42(2).

[297] SLA 1925 s.42(5).

[298] And this appears to include a weekly or other periodic tenancy, even though it may last more than three years: see *Davies v Hall* [1954] 1 W.L.R. 855.

[299] SLA 1925 s.42(5). *cf. Bevan v Johnston* [1990] 2 E.G.L.R. 33.

[300] SLA 1925 s.46.

[301] SLA 1925 s.18(1) (above, Appendix para.A–026); *Bevan v Johnston,* above.

[302] s.152. The provisions date back to the Leases Acts 1849, 1850.

[303] Registrable as estate contracts (Wolst. & C. i, 281); but in any case remaindermen or reversioners will be bound since they are not purchasers: LCA 1972 s.4, above para.8–091. But it is arguable that registration is not required, since LPA 1925 s.152(1), provides that the contract "shall take effect" against successors in title. Where title is registered, the lessee will be protected as he will be in actual occupation, even if registration were otherwise required: see LRA 2002 Sch.3 para.2: above, para.7–089.

[304] See LPA 1925 s.152(1).

[305] *Hallett v Martin* (1883) 24 Ch D 624; *Brown v Peto* [1900] 1 Q.B. 346; *Re Newell* [1900] 1 Ch. 30; Halsb. vol. 27(1), para.120. This provision appears to have been overlooked in *Bevan v Johnston* [1990] 2 E.G.L.R. 33, where a weekly tenancy that had been g*ranted orally* (rather than in writing as required by SLA 1925 s.42(5)) was held to be void.

[306] s.110(1).

[307] See above, Appendix para.A–029.

settlement, to have given the best consideration reasonably obtainable and to have complied with the other requirements of the Act. If the consideration is insufficient, therefore, the title of such tenant is none the worse, and the point can only be disputed as between the beneficiaries under the settlement. If, however, the lease on its face violates the requirements of the Act, the tenant will not be taken to have dealt in good faith and he may have to be prepared to prove that he gave the best consideration reasonably obtainable, or complied with any of the other statutory conditions which are alleged to have been violated.[308]

As a corollary to his power to grant leases, a tenant for life has wide powers of accepting surrenders of leases[309] and of varying or waiving the terms of any lease.[310] These powers are exercisable without notice to the trustees.

(4) RENT FROM LEASES. The normal rule is that the tenant for life is entitled to the whole of the rent from leases of the settled land.[311] It has already been noted that this rule does not apply to mining leases, which are subject to special rules.[312]

(d) *Power to mortgage.* In the absence of a contrary provision in the settlement,[313] a tenant for life has no power to mortgage or charge the legal estate for his own benefit. If he wishes to raise money for his own use, he can of course do so by mortgaging his beneficial interest. The legal estate, on the other hand, can be mortgaged or charged for the following purposes only. **A–063**

    (i) To provide money which is required to be raised under the provisions of the settlement,[314] e.g. portions.[315] **A–064**

    (ii) To provide money where it is reasonably required[316] for certain specified purposes.[317] These are all cases connected with the well being of the land, and include:

---

[308] *Davies v Hall* [1954] 1 W.L.R. 855, explaining the dictum of Farwell J. in *Kisch v Hawes Bros Ltd* [1935] Ch. 102 at 109, 110; and see *Re Morgan's Lease* [1972] Ch. 1, holding that the protection extends to an option to renew a lease. See generally (1971) 87 L.Q.R. 338 (D. W. Elliott).

[309] SLA 1925 s.52.

[310] SLA 1925 s.59. See *Re Saville SE* [1931] 2 Ch. 210 (mining lease for 60 years extended to 100 years).

[311] See, e.g. *Re Wix* [1916] 1 Ch. 279.

[312] Above, para.3–104. See SLA 1925 s.47; and the sixth edition of this work at pp.365, 366. The rules applicable to a tenant for life who works the minerals himself are different from those which are applicable where he leases the land: see above, para.3–103.

[313] See *Re Egertons' SE* [1926] Ch. 357.

[314] SLA 1925 s.16(1): if such sums have already been raised by means of an equitable charge affecting the whole of the land, the tenant for life can replace this charge by a legal mortgage or charge: SLA 1925. Whether the money has already been raised or not, on being requested in writing the tenant for life is bound to create the requisite legal mortgage or charge: SLA 1925.

[315] For these, see above, para.9–173.

[316] *Re Clifford* [1902] 1 Ch. 87; *Re Bruce* [1905] 2 Ch. 372 at 376.

[317] SLA 1925 s.71(1).

(a) discharging an incumbrance of a permanent nature (and not, e.g. annual sums payable for a life or term of years[318]) on all or part of the land, including such matters as charges for making up streets.[319] Thus it may be possible to pay off two or more mortgages by raising money on a new mortgage at a lower rate of interest,[320] and the whole of the land may be mortgaged in order to pay off a mortgage on part[321];

(b) paying for authorised improvements[322];

(c) equality of exchange[323];

(d) extinguishing manorial incidents; and

(e) paying the costs of the above and certain other transactions, e.g. the costs of discharging mortgages.[324]

Since a mortgage overrides the beneficiaries' interests under the settlement,[325] and they do not automatically attach to the money raised by the mortgage, the court will intervene to prevent the power of mortgaging being used to prejudice beneficiaries. It will treat any such inequitable mortgage as a breach of trust.[326] However a mortgagee is not concerned to see:

(i) that any money advanced by him is wanted for any purpose under the Act; nor

(ii) that no more than is wanted is raised, provided that the mortgage monies were received by the trustees of the settlement or paid at their direction.[327]

A mortgage of the legal estate is required to be a legal mortgage or a charge by way of legal mortgage.[328] But since an equitable mortgage is really a contract to create a legal mortgage,[329] and a tenant for life can make such a contract,[330] it seems that an equitable mortgage would be effective, provided that it was made for one of the permitted purposes.

---

[318] SLA 1925 s.71(2).

[319] *Re Smith's SE* [1901] 1 Ch. 689; and see *Re Pizzi* [1907] 1 Ch. 67.

[320] *More v More* (1889) 37 W.R. 414.

[321] *Lord Monson's SE* [1898] 1 Ch. 427.

[322] See below, Appendix para.A–072.

[323] Above, Appendix para.A–059.

[324] *More v More,* above; and see *Re Maryon-Wilson's SE* [1915] 1 Ch. 29.

[325] See below, Appendix para.A–094.

[326] *Hampden v Earl of Buckinghamshire* [1893] 2 Ch. 531: this is the case "in which the court has gone the furthest in controlling the discretion of the tenant for life": *Re Richardson* [1900] 2 Ch. 778 at 790, per Stirling J.

[327] SLA 1925 s.95. This position is the same where title to the land is registered: Ruoff & Roper, 37–016.01.

[328] SLA 1925 ss.16(1), 17(1), 117(1)(xi). s.71(3) expressly empowers the tenant for life to grant the long term of years (e.g. 3,000 years) by which legal mortgages are made in unregistered land (above, para.24–020), despite the restrictions on the length of leases imposed in other cases by the Act (above, Appendix para.A–061). For mortgages of registered land, see above, para.7–102.

[329] Below, para.24–039.

[330] SLA 1925 s.90(1)(i).

(e) Power to grant options. A tenant for life may grant an option in writing **A–065**
to purchase or take a lease of all or any part of the settled land or any
easement, right or privilege over it.[331] But:

    (i) the price or rent must be the best reasonably obtainable[332] and
        must be fixed at the time of granting the option[333];

    (ii) the option must be made exercisable within an agreed number of
        years not exceeding 10[334]; and

    (iii) the option may be granted with or without any consideration being
        paid,[335] but if any is paid, it is capital money.[336]

3. Powers exercisable with consent of the trustees or under an order of **A–066**
the court. In the following cases the tenant for life can exercise his powers
only with the consent of the trustees of the settlement or under an order of the
court.

(a) Power to dispose of the principal mansion house. If the tenant for life **A–067**
wishes to make a disposition[337] of the principal mansion house,[338] if any, and
the pleasure grounds and park (whether or not usually occupied therewith),
and land, if any, usually occupied therewith, the consent of the trustees or an
order of the court is required if the settlement expressly so requires.[339] In other
cases, no consent is required, but the usual notice must be given.

(b) Power to cut and sell timber. This has already been explained.[340] **A–068**

(c) Power to compromise claims. Subject to the consent in writing of the **A–069**
trustees, the tenant for life has a wide power to compromise and settle disputes
relating to all or any part of the settled land.[341] He has a similar power by deed
or writing to release, waive or modify rights over other land which benefit the
settled land, e.g. easements and restrictive covenants, whether or not consideration is given.[342]

---

[331] SLA 1925 s.51(1).
[332] SLA 1925 s.51(3).
[333] SLA 1925 s.51(1). This is an unfortunate limitation, as it precludes a sale at a market
valuation at the time when the option is exercised. It may be based on the view that a trustee has
no power to sell at a valuation, because to do so would be a delegation of his discretion to
determine the price: *cf. Re Earl of Wilton's SE* [1907] 1 Ch. 50 at 55. That view cannot be
reconciled with more modern authorities which make it clear that valuation involves no element
of discretion: see *Sudbrook Trading Estate Ltd v Eggleton* [1983] 1 A.C. 444 at 483; [1985] Conv.
44 (G. Lightman).
[334] SLA 1925 s.51(2).
[335] SLA 1925 s.51(1).
[336] SLA 1925 s.51(5).
[337] See SLA 1925 s.117(1)(v).
[338] For what does and does not constitute a principal mansion house, see SLA 1925 s.65(2), and
the fifth edition of this work at pp.368, 369.
[339] SLA 1925 s.65(1).
[340] Above, para.3–101.
[341] SLA 1925 s.58(1).
[342] SLA 1925 s.58(2).

A–070   *(d) Power to sell settled chattels.* Special provision was made in the Settled
Land Act for personal chattels settled so as to devolve with (or as nearly
possible with) settled land.[343] The tenant for life is empowered to sell[344] (but
not lease[345]) such chattels, provided that he first obtains an order of the
court.[346]

A–071   *(e) Power to do anything proper with the court's consent.* The court has a
statutory jurisdiction to authorise the tenant for life to effect any transaction
not otherwise authorised by the Act or the settlement[347] if it affects the settled
land, is for the benefit of the land or the beneficiaries,[348] and is a transaction
which an absolute owner could validly effect.[349] "Transaction" is widely
defined, and includes the application of capital money.[350] The court has, for
example, authorised a tenant for life to mortgage the land, and to save himself
from bankruptcy, where his debts arose from the expenses of maintaining the
land.[351] It has also sanctioned the following schemes:

> (i) a transfer of property (made for tax reasons) from one settlement
>   to another in order to establish a maintenance fund[352]; and

> (ii) a transfer to trustees to hold the property on trust for sale (and no
>   longer as a settlement).[353]

Furthermore, this jurisdiction allows the court to authorise a scheme which
alters the beneficial interests under the settlement, not only on behalf of those
who cannot consent (such as minors and unborn persons),[354] but also those of
beneficiaries of full age and capacity who did not consent.[355]

4. Other powers of a tenant for life

A–072   *(a) Power to effect improvements.* Improvements have to be distinguished
in principle from current repairs. The former are special operations of a capital

---

[343] SLA 1925 s.67(1). For a fuller account, see the fifth edition of this work at pp.370–371.
[344] SLA 1925 s.67(1).
[345] See *Re Lacon's Settlement* [1911] 1 Ch. 351 at 353, 354; [1911] 2 Ch. 17 at 19.
[346] SLA 1925 s.67(3). There is no provision enabling him to sell with the consent of the
trustees.
[347] See *Re Symons* [1927] 1 Ch. 344 at 345.
[348] See, e.g. *Re Cleveland Literary and Philosophical Society's Land* [1931] 2 Ch. 247.
[349] SLA 1925 s.64, as amended by the Settled Land and Trustee Acts (Court's General Powers)
Acts 1943 s.2. See also s.1 of the latter Act, giving power to authorise expenses of management
to be treated as capital outgoings.
[350] SLA 1925 s.64(2) (as amended). See *Hambro v Duke of Marlborough* [1994] Ch. 158 at
164–166. "Capital money" includes capital assets that could be turned into capital money: *Raikes
v Lygon* [1988] 1 W.L.R. 281 at 289.
[351] *Re White-Popham SE* [1936] Ch. 725.
[352] *Raikes v Lygon,* above.
[353] *Hambro v Duke of Marlborough,* above (transfer of the Parliamentary Estates to trustees for
sale because of concerns about the heir apparent's "unbusinesslike habits and lack of
responsibility").
[354] *Re Simmons* [1956] Ch. 125. Prior to the Variation of Trusts Act 1958, this could not
normally be done under the general law: *cf. Chapman v Chapman* [1954] A.C. 429.
[355] *Hambro v Duke of Marlborough,* above. This is now the leading case on SLA 1925 s.64. See
[1994] Conv. 492 (E. Cooke); (1996) 47 N.I.L.Q. 63 (J. Howell).

nature, the latter are ordinary outgoings and must be paid for out of income. A tenant for life may of course make both improvements and repairs at his own expense. Indeed, in the case of repairs, he may have to pay for them himself. In the case of improvements he may be entitled to have the costs borne either temporarily or permanently by capital money, or raised by a mortgage or charge of the settled land.

The Settled Land Act provides that capital money may be applied by the tenant for life in or towards payment for an improvement only if the payment is authorised by that Act and certain specified requirements are satisfied.[356] The tenant for life can be required to repay the cost of carrying out certain improvements.[357]

(b) Power to require investments for capital money. Capital money may be **A–073** applied according to the general power of investment contained in section 3 of the Trustee Act 2000, or otherwise as specified in section 73 of the SLA 1925.[358] This includes investments in Government securities,[359] discharge of incumbrances,[360] paying for authorised improvements, the purchase of land held in fee simple or on a lease with 60 or more years unexpired,[361] and any other method authorised by the settlement. The trustees may exercise discretion as to investments and shall consult the tenant for life.[362] The tenant for life's beneficial interest shall not be altered by such investment without his consent.[363]

(c) Power to dedicate highways and open spaces. For the general benefit of **A–074** the residents on the settled land or any part of it, the tenant for life has wide powers of dedicating land for use as streets, paths, squares, gardens or other open spaces.[364]

(d) Power to take a lease of other land. There may be practical advantages **A–075** to the settled land in taking on lease other land, mines, easements, rights or privileges which can conveniently be held or worked with it, and in such cases the lease should devolve with the settled land after the tenant for life's death. A tenant for life is therefore empowered to take such leases.[365] The lease is deemed to be a subsidiary vesting deed and the requisite particulars may be

---

[356] SLA 1925 s.84. These are explained in detail in the fifth edition of this work at pp.373–376, to which reference should be made.

[357] See SLA 1925 Sch.3 Pts II and III. The tenant for life may be required to repay the cost of improvements in Pt II, and must do so as regards those listed in Pt III.

[358] SLA 1925 s.73(1) as amended by TA 2000 Sch.2, para.9.

[359] Including those authorised by the settlement, s.73(i)(i) SLA 1925.

[360] Ch.24.

[361] See *Re Wellsted's WT* [1949] Ch. 296. Compare the position where land is held on a trust of land: above, para.12–018.

[362] SLA 1925 s.75(2).

[363] SLA s.73(4A).

[364] SLA 1925 s.56; and see above, Appendix para.A–058, fn.52.

[365] SLA 1925 s.53(1).

either inserted in it or indorsed on it.[366] No fine may be paid out of capital money.[367]

A–076 *(e) Power to contract.* Detailed powers are conferred on tenants for life to enter into contracts for sales, leases, mortgages and other dispositions authorised by the Act.[368] Such contracts are enforceable by and against the tenant for life's successors in title,[369] and are subject to any directions by the court.[370] The transaction must be authorised by the Act at the time when the contract comes to be performed, so that in the case of a contract for a lease the rent must be the best rent reasonably obtainable when the lease is finally granted, and the other statutory conditions must also be satisfied then.[371] The powers extend to the variation and rescission of contracts.

II. POSITION OF TENANT FOR LIFE

A–077 **1. The tenant for life is trustee both of the land and of his powers.** This has already been explained in general terms.[372] However, two special aspects of this trusteeship require discussion here.

A–078 *(a) Capital money.* All receipts of a capital nature must be treated as capital money and paid to the trustees of the settlement or into court.[373] The term "capital money" has a broad meaning[374] and includes:

    (i) the proceeds of sale or mortgage;

    (ii) fines upon the grant of leases;

    (iii) part of the proceeds of mining and timber transactions;

    (iv) money (not being rent) paid by a tenant either as compensation for breach of covenant,[375] or payable as the price of being allowed to surrender his lease[376] (unless in either case the court otherwise directs);

    (v) insurance money receivable under a policy of insurance kept up under a requirement of the settlement or of the Act, or by a tenant for life impeachable for waste[377];

    (vi) any money arising outside the Act "which ought to be capital money"[378]; and

[366] SLA 1925 s.53(2).
[367] SLA 1925 s.53(1).
[368] SLA 1925 s.90.
[369] SLA 1925 s.90(2).
[370] SLA 1925 s.90(3).
[371] *Re Rycroft's Settlement* [1962] Ch. 263. For these conditions, see above.
[372] Above, paras 10–014, 10–015.
[373] Above, Appendix para.A–098.
[374] *cf.* SLA 1925 s.117(1)(ii).
[375] SLA 1925 s.80(1).
[376] SLA 1925 s.52(7).
[377] TA 1925 s.20. See, e.g. *Re Scholfield's Trusts* [1949] Ch. 341.
[378] SLA 1925 s.81; see Woist. & C. iii, 180, giving examples.

(vii) various other specified receipts.[379]

Despite the wide meaning of capital money, tenants for life have been held to be entitled to retain compensation for damage done to property while under requisition,[380] and also income tax allowances resulting from improvements that were carried out with capital money.[381]

(b) Acquisition by tenant for life. The tenant for life is given a special power **A–079** to acquire any or all of the settled land for himself. It is a long-established rule of equity that no trustee may acquire the trust property for himself either directly or indirectly, no matter how fair the transaction may be.[382] The "court will not permit a party to place himself in a situation in which his interest conflicts with his duty".[383] To avoid this difficulty, the Settled Land Act 1925[384] authorises the trustees of the settlement to exercise all the powers of a tenant for life in carrying out any transaction whereby the tenant for life acquires any interest in the settled land. The trustees are empowered to act in the name and on behalf of the tenant for life even if he is one of them, in which case he should join in the transaction with them as a trustee.[385] (not being the tenant for life) unless the court approves the transaction.[386] There is a similar power to carry out certain other transactions, such as a purchase from the tenant for life of land to be brought into the settlement.[387]

2. No powers can be given to anyone except the tenant for life. Any **A–080** power, other than a power of revocation or appointment, which the settlement purports to give to anyone except the tenant for life, is exercisable not by that person but by the tenant for life as if it were an additional power conferred by the settlement.[388] This is so whether or not the tenant for life already has such a power under the Act.[389] Thus if in a will of a person dying before 1997, land had been devised "to X and Y in fee simple with power to sell, on trust for A for life and then for B absolutely", X and Y would not have had the power of sale. It would have been given to A, notwithstanding that he already had such a power of sale by statute. However, the abortive attempt to give a power

---

[379] For a list, see Wolst. & C. iii, 156.
[380] *Re Pomfret's Settlement* [1952] Ch. 48; contrast *Re Thompson* [1949] Ch. 1.
[381] *Re Pelly's WT* [1957] Ch. 1.
[382] *Fox v Mackreth* (1791) 2 Cox Eq. 320; *Ex p. Hughes* (1802) 6 Ves. 617; *Ex p. Lacey* (1802) 6 Ves. 625; *Ex p. James* (1803) 8 Ves. 337; *Sanderson v Walker* (1807) 13 Ves. 601; *Whitcomb v Minchin* (1820) 5 Madd. 91.
[383] *Re Bloye's Trusts* (1849) 1 Mac. & G. 488 at 495, per Lord Cottenham L.C.; affirmed *sub nom. Lewis v Hillman* (1852) 3 H.L.C. 607. *cf. Swain v The Law Society* [1982] 1 W.L.R. 17 at 36; and see *Sargeant v National Westminster Bank Plc* (1990) 61 P. & C.R. 518.
[384] s.68.
[385] *Re Pennant's WT* [1970] Ch. 75; and see above, Appendix para.A–050.
[386] SLA 1925 s.68(3).
[387] SLA 1925 s.68(1).
[388] SLA 1925 s.108(2).
[389] SLA 1925.

of sale to X and Y might not be wholly without effect. It may have made them Settled Land Act trustees.[390]

A–081 **3. The statutory powers cannot be ousted, curtailed or hampered**

(a) The Act prevails. The settlor may confer additional powers on the tenant for life, and such powers are exercisable in the same way as if they were conferred by the Act.[391] Further, nothing in the Act in any way restricts powers which the settlement gives to the tenant for life or purports to give to the trustees to be exercised with the approval of the tenant for life.[392] The powers given by the Act and the settlement are cumulative.[393] But in other respects, so far as the settlement and the Act conflict in relation to powers exercisable under the Act, the Act prevails.[394] For example, if the settlement provides that no sale shall be made without the consent of some specified person, this provision is inconsistent with the unfettered power of sale given by the Act and the latter prevails.[395]

A–082 *(b) Void provisions.* There is a sweeping section[396] which makes void any provision in any document (e.g. another settlement[397]) "as far as it purports, or attempts, or tends, or is intended to have, or would or might have" the effect of preventing or discouraging the tenant for life from exercising his statutory powers or from requiring the land to be vested in him.[398] This applies even when the attempt to restrain the exercise of the powers is made by way of a determinable limitation.[399] A settlement on "Y for life until he attempts to alienate the land" gave Y a life interest which would continue despite any alienation by him.[400] Nevertheless, for the section to operate, there must be someone who, but for the restriction that is in issue, would be the tenant for life under the Act.[401] The section does nothing to enlarge the beneficiary's estate.[402] Finally, it is provided that notwithstanding anything in a settlement, the exercise of a statutory power can never cause a forfeiture.[403]

A–083 *(c) Extent of invalidity.* Provisions for the curtailment or forfeiture of the interest of a tenant for life are not automatically invalidated by these rules. They are affected only so far as they in fact tend to fetter the statutory powers of the tenant for life or statutory owner. This may be illustrated by a condition

[390] Above Appendix para.A–050.
[391] SLA 1925 s.109: see, e.g. *Re The Earl of Egmont's SE* (1900)16 T.L.R. 360; *Re Duke of Westminster's SE (No.2)* [1921] 1 Cb. 585; *Re Cowley's SE* [1926] Ch. 725.
[392] Such powers are exercisable by the tenant for life: see above.
[393] SLA 1925 s.108(1); see *Re Jeffreys* [1939] Ch. 205.
[394] SLA 1925 s.108(2).
[395] *Re Jeffreys*, above.
[396] SLA 1925 s.106(1).
[397] *Re Smith* [1899] 1 Ch. 331; *Re Burden* [1948] Ch. 160.
[398] See *Ungurian v Lesnoff* [1990] Ch. 206 at 226.
[399] SLA 1925 s.106(2).
[400] SLA 1925.
[401] *Re Atkinson* (1886) 31 Ch D 577 at 581.
[402] *Re Hazle's SE* (1885) 29 Ch D 78 at 84.
[403] SLA 1925 s.106(3).

of residence, e.g. a provision in the settlement that the tenant for life shall forfeit his interest on ceasing to reside on the settled land. In such cases, if the tenant for life ceases to reside there for some reason other than the exercise of his statutory powers (as where he prefers to live elsewhere) the proviso for forfeiture is operative and he loses his interest.[404] But if the reason for his ceasing to reside there is that he has exercised his statutory powers, as by leasing[405] or selling[406] the land, or both,[407] there is no forfeiture.[408] He continues to be entitled as tenant for life, receiving the rent from the lease[409] or the income from the purchase-money.[410] Another example to which the same distinction applies is a condition that the tenant for life should provide a home for X on the settled land.[411]

(d) Inoperative fetters. One result of these rules is that a provision which **A–084** attempts to fetter the powers may actually encourage their exercise. If the tenant for life is subject to a condition of residence but wishes to reside elsewhere, he can protect his life interest from the condition by first selling or letting the land. Furthermore, quite apart from these rules:

    (i) provisions of this nature are sometimes void under the doctrine that conditions subsequent will be construed strictly and held to be ineffective unless it can be seen precisely upon what grounds a forfeiture will be incurred[412]; and

    (ii) a minor who cannot control his place of residence cannot be said to "refuse or neglect" to reside on the property so as to incur a forfeiture.[413]

(e) Upkeep of the property. Difficulty sometimes arises over funds provided **A–085** by the settlor for the payment of taxes and other such outgoings during the tenant for life's personal occupation. Here the settlor's object is to enable the tenant for life to live on the property free from the expenses of its upkeep. It has been held that the tenant for life can still claim such payments after letting the land,[414] but not after selling it.[415] There has been some difference of

---

[404] *Haynes* (1887) 37 Ch D 306; *Re Trenchard* [1902] 1 Ch. 378. As to what constitutes "residence", contrast *Re Moir (1884)* 25 Ch D 605 (residence) with *Re Wright* [1907] 1 Ch. 231 (non-residence).

[405] *Re Gibbons* [1920] 1 Ch. 372.

[406] *Re Paget's SE* (1885) 30 Ch D 161.

[407] *Re Acklom* [1929] 1 Ch. 195.

[408] *Re Orlebar* [1936] Ch. 147; *cf. Re Ames* [1893] 2 Ch. 479.

[409] *Re T J. Freme* (1912) 56 S.J. 362.

[410] *Sarah Dalrymple* (1901) 49 W.R. 627.

[411] *Re Richardson* [1904] 2 Ch. 777 (condition that the life tenant X provide a home for Y void so far as it prevented X from exercising her Settled Land Act powers).

[412] Above, para.3–058. Contrast *Sifton v Sifton* [1938] A.C. 656 ("so long as she shall continue to reside in Canada" held too vague) with *Re Gape* [1952] Ch. 743 (condition requiring "permanent residence" in England held effective).

[413] *Partridge v Partridge* [1894] 1 Ch. 351.

[414] *Re Patten* [1929] 2 Ch. 276.

[415] *Re Simpson* [1913] 1 Ch. 277, not following *Re Trenchard* (1900)16 T.L.R. 525; *Re Burden* [1948] Ch. 160; *Re Aberconway's S.T* [1953] Ch. 647. Contrast *Re Ames* [1893] 2 Ch. 479; and *cf. Re Eastman's SE* (1898) 68 L.J.Ch. 122 (provision for reduction of annuity).

judicial opinion on this difficult subject, which has been fully reviewed by the Court of Appeal.[416] Further, where the Act gives special powers to the trustees (for example, the powers of management during a minority[417]), the powers are made subject to any contrary intention and are not, therefore, protected like the powers of the tenant for life.

A–086   **4. The tenant for life cannot assign, release or contract not to exercise his powers**[418]

(a) Exercise of powers. A statutory owner can release his powers,[419] but a tenant for life cannot. Once a person has become a tenant for life, he is incapable of divesting himself of his powers, even if he parts with his entire beneficial interest,[420] as he is entitled to do.[421] It is he, and not the assignee of his beneficial interest, who alone can exercise the statutory powers,[422] and this is so whether the disposition was voluntary or involuntary (e.g. on bankruptcy), and even if it was made while the life interest was still in remainder.[423] But in three exceptional cases[424] the statutory powers may become exercisable by someone other than the tenant for life.

A–087   (1) EXTINGUISHMENT OF INTEREST. Where the interest of the tenant for life has been assured, with intent to extinguish it, to the person next entitled under the settlement, the statutory powers cease to be exercisable by the tenant for life and become exercisable as if he were dead.[425] For this purpose, an "assurance" is any surrender, conveyance, assignment or appointment which operates in equity to extinguish the interest.[426] A partial surrender is insufficient,[427] and so is a surrender to a later remainderman where some intermediate gift remains capable of taking effect, even though contingently.[428] But it is immaterial that a term of years or charge intervenes between the interest surrendered and that of the person next entitled, or that the latter interest is defeasible, or that the interest surrendered was in remainder at the time.[429]

The provision may be illustrated by a settlement of land on A for life, remainder to B for life, remainder to C in fee simple. If A surrenders his life interest to B, the statutory powers become exercisable by B instead of A, and

---

[416] *Re Aberconway's ST* above; see [1954] C.L.J. 60 (R. N. Gooderson); and *Raikes v Ly*gon [1988] 1 W.L.R. 281 at 288.

[417] SLA 1925 s.102; above, para.10–018.

[418] SLA 1925 s.104(1), (2); and see s.19(4).

[419] *Re Craven's SE* [1926] Ch. 985.

[420] *Re Mundy and Roper's Contract* [1899] 1 Ch. 275; *Re Cope and Wadland's Contract* [1919] 2 Ch. 376.

[421] *Re Trenchard* [1902] 1 Ch. 378 at 384, 385.

[422] *Re Earl of Carnarvon's Chesterfield SE* [1927] 1 Ch. 138 at 145, 146; see, e.g. *Earl of Lonsdale v Lowther* [1900] 2 Ch. 687.

[423] SLA 1925 s.104(1).

[424] See also above, Appendix para.A–079 (acquisition of the settled land).

[425] SLA 1925 s.105(1).

[426] SLA 1925 s.105(2).

[427] *Re Barlow's Contract* [1903] 1 Ch. 382.

[428] *Re Maryon-Wilson's Instrument* [1971] Ch. 789.

[429] SLA 1925 s.105(1).

A must at once convey the legal estate to B by a vesting deed.[430] If A is bankrupt, his trustee in bankruptcy can surrender A's interest with the same effect.[431] If A refuses to execute the necessary vesting deed, the court can instead make a vesting order.[432] If after the surrender of A's interest, B then surrenders his life interest to C, he must convey the legal estate to C.[433] This will be by an ordinary conveyance as the land ceases to be settled land.[434]

(2) ORDER OF COURT. If the tenant for life: **A–088**

(i) has ceased to have a substantial interest in the land, whether by bankruptcy, assignment or otherwise; and

(ii) either consents to an order being made or else has unreasonably refused to exercise his statutory powers,[435]

any person interested in the land may apply to the court for an order authoris-ing the trustees to exercise any or all of the statutory powers in the name and on behalf of the tenant for life.[436] Such an order prevents the tenant for life from exercising any of the powers affected by the order, but until it has been registered[437] the order does not affect persons dealing with the tenant for life.[438] It should be noted that such an order vests neither the legal estate nor the statutory powers in the trustees, who do not become the statutory owners. The order merely authorises the trustees to exercise the powers on behalf of the tenant for life and in his name. Furthermore, the provision is confined to tenants for life, and does not apply to statutory owners.[439] Where the title to the settled land is registered, the trustees of the settlement must file an office copy of the court's order with the Land Registry before they exercise any of the powers that it confers upon them.[440]

(3) MENTAL PATIENT. Where the tenant for life is a mental patient, his   **A–089** statutory powers may be exercised under an order of the judge or Court of Protection, e.g. by his receiver.[441] They may also be exercised by a donee of an enduring or lasting power of attorney made by the tenant for life prior to his mental incapacity.[442]

(b) *Position of assignees.* Usually neither a voluntary assignee of the   **A–090** beneficial interest of a tenant for life, nor his trustee in bankruptcy, who is an

---

[430] SLA 1925 ss.7(4), 8(4).
[431] *Shawdon Estates Settlement* [1930] 2 Ch. 1.
[432] SLA 1925 s.12(1); see, e.g. *Re Shawdon Estates Settlement*, above.
[433] SLA 1925 s.7(5).
[434] Wolst. & C. iii, 43; *cf.* above, para.8–032.
[435] See *Re Thornhill's Settlement* [1941] Ch. 24 (neglect or failure to exercise powers by a tenant for life is not a ground for making an order under s.24: there must be a refusal to act).
[436] SLA 1925 s.24(1) see, e.g. *Re Cecil's SE* [1926] W.N. 262.
[437] As an "order affecting land": see LCA 1972 s.6 (above, para.8–066); LRA 2002 s.87(1)(b) (above, para.7–085).
[438] SLA 1925 s.24(2).
[439] *Re Craven's SE* [1926] Ch. 985.
[440] Ruoff & Roper Ch.37.
[441] Mental Health Act 1983, Mental Capacity Act 2005 Pt VII. See above, para.36–021.
[442] Mental Health Act 1983, Mental Capacity Act 2005 Pt VII. See above, para.36–021.

assignee by operation of law, has control over the exercise of the tenant for life's powers.[443] Whether or not the assignment was made for money or money's worth, the assignee's consent is not required for the exercise of the statutory powers.[444] However such an assignee does have certain rights of control. For the application of capital money affected by the assignment for any purpose other than for investment in trustee securities, his consent is required if the assignment so provides or if it takes effect by operation of the law of bankruptcy, and the trustees have notice of this.[445] Further, unless the assignment otherwise provides, notice of any intended transaction must be given to the assignee.[446] No period of notice is specified, and a purchaser is not concerned to see or inquire whether notice has been given.[447]

If the land is sold, the rights of the assignee are transferred to the capital money which represents the land,[448] and provision is made for obtaining consents in any cases of difficulty.[449]

D. The Appointment and Functions of Settled Land Act Trustees

A–091   **1. Their appointment.** It has already been explained how the initial trustees of the settlement were to be found.[450] The usual rules for the retirement of existing trustees and the appointment of new ones are then applicable.[451] The number of such trustees should not rise above four or fall below two, or one, if it is a trust corporation.[452]

The curtain principle extends to the appointment and discharge of Settled Land Act trustees, so that a purchaser does not have to investigate such matters. The Settled Land Act 1925 provides for the execution of a "deed of declaration" stating who are the trustees of the settlement after any appointment or discharge.[453] In favour of a purchaser this is conclusive evidence of the matters stated in it.[454] This deed is made supplemental to the principal vesting deed, on which the names of the new trustees are also indorsed.[455] The actual deed of appointment or discharge is kept by the trustees and is not seen by the purchaser. The deed of declaration provides the necessary link in his title between the old and the new trustees.

A–092   **2. Their functions.** Trustees of the settlement under the Settled Land Act 1925 are unusual in that they do not normally hold any property on trust

---

[443] See SLA 1925 s.104(4), (10).
[444] SLA 1925 s.104(4); and see subss.(10), (11).
[445] SLA 1925 s.104(4).
[446] SLA 1925.
[447] SLA 1925.
[448] Below, Appendix para.A–094.
[449] Above, Appendix para.A–088.
[450] Above, Appendix para.A–049.
[451] Above, paras 11–053 *et seq.*, 11–064.
[452] TA 1925 ss.34, 39. These rules are applicable to both registered and unregistered land.
[453] SLA 1925 s.35(1). Where the title is registered, it is unnecessary to produce this deed to the Registrar: Ruoff & Roper, 37–016.02.
[454] SLA 1925 s.35(3).
[455] SLA 1925 s.35(1); TA 1925 s.35(2).

unless and until the settled land is sold. Their principal functions may be summarised as follows:

(i) To receive and hold capital money.[456]

(ii) To receive notice from the tenant for life of his intention to effect certain transactions.[457]

(iii) To give consent to certain transactions.[458]

(iv) To act as special personal representatives on the death of a tenant for life.[459]

(v) To act as statutory owner if the tenant for life is a minor or there is no tenant for life.[460]

(vi) To execute the principal vesting deed in cases where it is not provided in the ordinary case.[461]

(vii) To execute a deed of discharge, when it is necessary, on the determination of the settlement.[462]

(viii) To exercise the powers of the tenant for life if he wishes to acquire the settled land for his own benefit.[463]

(ix) To exercise the powers of the tenant for life where he has no substantial beneficial interest and either consents to such exercise or unreasonably refuses to exercise his powers.[464]

(x) To exercise a general supervision over the well-being of the settled land.[465] They will have to be parties to all litigation concerning the land. If they are not opposed to a transaction for which the tenant for life is seeking the authority of the court, their duty is "to hold an even hand" and refrain from supporting the application.[466]

Section 2. Overreaching Effect of Dispositions

Overreaching occurs when a disposition is made pursuant to a trust or power.[467] A sale or other disposition by trustees of land (who have the   **A–093**

---

[456] SLA 1925 ss.18(1)(b), 75(1); above, Appendix para.A–078.

[457] Above, Appendix para.A–057.

[458] Above, Appendix para.A–066.

[459] Above, Appendix para.A–019.

[460] Above, para.10–017.

[461] Above, Appendix para.A–007.

[462] Above, Appendix para.A–020.

[463] Above, Appendix para.A–079.

[464] Above, Appendix para.A–088.

[465] Above paras 10–014, 10–015; and see *Re Boston's WT* [1956] Ch. 395 at 405.

[466] See *Re Hotchkin's SE* (1887) 35 Ch D 41 at 43; *cf. Re Marquis of Aylesbury's SE* [1892] 1 Ch. 506 at 526.

[467] *State Bank of India v Sood* [1997] Ch. 276 at 281.

dispositive powers of an absolute owner[468]) will therefore automatically overreach the interests under the trust.[469] However, dispositions by a life tenant or statutory owner under the Settled Land Act 1925, will overreach the interest under the trust or settlement only if they are made under powers conferred either by statute[470] or by the settlement itself. In relation to both settled land and trusts for sale, the legislation of 1925 extended the device of overreaching and modified its application to provide greater protection for the beneficiaries under the settlement or trust.[471] This Appendix considers the law relating to settled land.[472]

A–094   **1. Under the Settled Land Act 1925.** Section 72 of the Settled Land Act 1925 authorises a tenant for life to effect a sale or other transaction by deed. It then goes on to state the overreaching effect of such a deed (a term which here includes any lease authorised by the Act to be made merely in writing[473]). In its policy the section distinguishes between the beneficial interests of the family, which ought to be overreached on sale, and commercial interests which ought not to be overreached. For example, the beneficial interest of a tenant for life is overreachable. However, a lease or easement created by the tenant for life is not. If the land is sold, it must (like any other land) be sold subject to such leases and other interests as have been validly created.

Interests (both family and commercial) which arise under the settlement must be distinguished from interests which affected the land before it was settled, and which therefore have priority to the settlement. The overreaching principle has been extended to some of these prior interests, but only to those of a family character.

Three specific interests which are registrable as land charges under what is now the Land Charges Act 1972[474] may also be overreached under the express terms of s.72. As will be explained,[475] these are all claims to money, and are not prejudiced by being transferred to the proceeds of sale.

Section 72 applies as much where the title to the settled land is registered as it does where it is not. Where the title is registered, the overreaching effect of s.72 is achieved by the entry on the register of appropriate restrictions which are framed to ensure that only family interests under the trust will be overreached.[476] It should be noted that, where title is unregistered, most dispositions by a tenant for life of the legal estate will now trigger the requirement of compulsory registration.[477]

---

[468] TLATA 1996 s.6(i); above, para.10–034.
[469] Provided that the purchaser complies with the requirements as to the payment of capital money: below, Appendix para.A–098.
[470] Below, Appendix para.A–098.
[471] See [1990] C.L.J. 277 at 287 *et seq.* (C.H.).
[472] Trusts of land are considered in Ch.12.
[473] SLA 1925 s.72(4); see above, Appendix para.A–061.
[474] Namely an annuity, a limited owner's charge and a general equitable charge.
[475] Below, Appendix para.A–097.
[476] LRR 2003 Sch.7; above, Appendix para.A–006.
[477] LRA 2002 s.4; see Ch.7 above.

2. Rights under the settlement

(a) Rights overreached. The rights and interests overreached by the deed **A–095**
are:

    (i) all the limitations, powers, and provisions of the settlement; and

    (ii) all estates, interests, and charges subsisting or to arise under the
    settlement.[478]

It is immaterial whether or not the purchaser has notice of these rights.[479] He
therefore takes the land free from interests under the settlement,[480] and from
all other rights created out of them, such as mortgages of beneficial
interests.[481]

(b) Exceptions. This general principle, if it stood unqualified, would be too **A–096**
sweeping and would mean that commercial as well as family interests could
be overreached. It is therefore subject to a number of qualifications. Certain
rights which are prior to the settlement, and numerous commercial interests
which have been created under the settlement by the exercise of the Settled
Land Act powers, are excepted. These exceptions fall into three categories.

First, a purchaser takes subject to "all legal estates and charges by way of
legal mortgage having priority to the settlement"[482] This exception is largely
redundant, as there is no power to overreach rights prior to the
settlement.[483]

Secondly, a purchaser will be bound by "all legal estates and charges by
way of legal mortgage[484] which have been conveyed or created for securing
money actually raised at the date of the deed"[485] This is a true exception, for
it excludes a commercial interest arising under the settlement which otherwise
would have been included in the overreaching provision.[486]

Thirdly, a purchaser will be bound by all leases and grants of other rights
which at the date of the deed were:

    (i) created for money or money's worth (or agreed so to be) under the
    settlement or any statutory power, or otherwise made binding on
    the successors in title of the tenant for life; and

---

[478] SLA 1925 s.72(2).

[479] LPA 1925 s.2(1).

[480] The interests of assignees of the equitable interests are overreached, together with those of
the beneficiaries.

[481] *Re Dickin and Kelsall's Contract* [1908] 1 Ch. 213; *Re Davies and Kent's Contract* [1910]
2 Ch. 35.

[482] SLA 1925 s.72(2)(i).

[483] *Davies and Kent's Contract,* above, at 54, 57. *cf.* 77 L.J. News 39 (J. M. Lightwood).

[484] *cf.* above, Appendix para.A–064.

[485] SLA 1925 s.72(2)(ii). An example would be where the tenant for life had created a legal
mortgage of the settled land to pay for improvements.

[486] *Re Dickin and Kelsall's Contract,* above, at 221.

1574 *Appendix*

(ii) duly registered, if capable of registration.[487]

This is also a true exception. It means that commercial interests created under the settlement, either in accordance with the directions of the settlor or under the Settled Land Act powers, are not overreached. These include legal estates, rights and interests, such as leases and easements, properly granted by the tenant for life, and equitable rights of a commercial sort, such as options and restrictive covenants.[488] Also protected under this exception are those dispositions which a tenant for life is allowed to make voluntarily, such as gifts of land for public purposes.[489]

A–097   **3. Rights prior to the settlement.** Section 72 provides that certain rights will always be overreached, even though they were created prior to the settlement. These rights will therefore be overreachable whether they exist under the settlement or take priority to it. The Act provides that:

(i) an annuity[490];

(ii) a limited owner's charge[491]; and

(iii) a general equitable charge[492]

shall be overreached on a disposition under the Settled Land Act even if they have been duly protected by registration as a land charge.[493] These rights are treated as if they had been created by the settlement even if in fact they arose before it came into existence.[494] Although not exclusively family rights, these are all rights which represent merely claims to money. They will not therefore suffer if they are transferred to the purchase-money. It is therefore convenient to take the opportunity to clear them off the title when an overreaching disposition is made.

4. Payment of capital money

A–098   *(a) Payment.* There is one important condition which must be observed if a conveyance or transfer is to take effect under the Act and so have an overreaching effect.[495] This is the rule that any capital money[496] payable in respect of the transaction must be paid either:

---

[487] SLA 1925 s.72(2)(iii).
[488] Though these must be protected by registration, whether as land charges (if title is unregistered) or as registered interests (where title is registered).
[489] See SLA 1925 ss.54–57; above, Appendix para.A–074.
[490] See the fifth edition of this work at p.172.
[491] Above, para.8–073.
[492] Above, para.8–074. A general equitable charge must be prior to the settlement, for, by definition, it cannot exist under the settlement.
[493] Where the title is registered, the annuity, limited owner's charge or general equitable charge cannot be protected by notice, but only by a restriction, so as to ensure that it can be overreached, LRA 2002 s.33.
[494] SLA 1925 s.72(3).
[495] SLA 1925 s.18(1)(b); LPA 1925 s.2(1)(i).
[496] As to what is capital money, see above, Appendix para.A–078.

(i) to, or by the direction of, all the trustees of the settlement,[497] who must be either two or more in number or a trust corporation[498]; or

(ii) into court.[499]

This rule applies notwithstanding anything to the contrary in the settlement,[500] so that a provision authorising the tenant for life as sole trustee to give a receipt for capital money is ineffective. A "trust corporation" is elaborately defined, and includes the Public Trustee, Treasury Solicitor, the Official Solicitor, and companies incorporated in the United Kingdom or under the law of any Member State of the European Union to undertake trust business if they have:

(i) a place of business in the United Kingdom; and

(ii) an issued capital of at least £250,000 of which not less than £100,000 has been paid up in cash.[501]

(b) Failure. If a purchaser fails to pay his money in accordance with these provisions and pays it, for example, to the tenant for life:

A–099

(i) he will not get a good discharge;

(ii) he will not take the land free from beneficial interests[502]; and

(iii) he will be unable to make a good title to a subsequent purchaser.[503]

The tenant for life may choose whether payment should be to the trustees or into court.[504] However, if there are no trustees, he cannot direct payment into court,[505] but if he does so, a purchaser who is unaware that there are no trustees will get a good discharge.[506] Where no capital money arises on a transaction (as where a lease is granted without taking a premium), a disposition in favour of a bona fide purchaser for value of a legal estate[507] takes effect

---

[497] SLA 1925 s.18(l)(b).
[498] SLA 1925 s.18(l)(c).
[499] SLA 1925 s.18(l)(b).
[500] SLA 1925 s.18(l)(c).
[501] Public Trustee Rules (SI 1975/1189; SI 1976/836; SI 1981/109; SI 1985/132; SI 1987/1891); LP(Am)A 1926 s.3; LPA 1925 s.205(l)(xxviii); SLA 1925 s.117(1)(xxx); Charities Act 1993 s.35. For details, see Snell, *Equity*, 199.
[502] SLA 1925 s.18(l)(b); above, Appendix para.A–094.
[503] *Re Norton & Las Casas' Contract* [1909] 2 Ch. 59.
[504] SLA 1925 s.75(1).
[505] *Hatten v Russell* (1888) 38 Ch D 334 at 345.
[506] *Fisher & Grazebrook's Contract* [1898] 2 Ch. 660 at 662.
[507] SLA 1925 s.117(i)(xxi).

under the Act and thus has an overreaching effect even though there are no trustees.[508]

A–100   *(c) Capital money as land.* The capital money and any investments representing it are for all purposes of disposition, transmission and devolution treated as land. They are held for, and go to, the same persons, in the same manner and for the same estates, interests and trusts, as the land from which they arise would have been held and would have gone under the settlement.[509] The object of this provision is "to preserve the legal character of settled land notwithstanding its conversion into capital money . . . Where you are dealing with a settled freehold which is sold, the capital money would be treated as freehold, and where you have a settled leasehold which is sold, the capital money would be treated as leasehold".[510] Thus an absolute interest in the capital money representing settled freeholds cannot be disposed of by a will that only disposes of personalty.[511] However, for fiscal purposes, the money is not treated as land.[512] In general, the state in which the settled property happens to be at any given moment, whether it is in land, investments or money, cannot affect the rights of the beneficiaries or those claiming under them.

---

[508] SLA 1925 s.110(4). This provision applies to both registered and unregistered land. It is irrelevant that the purchaser knows or has notice that there are no trustees: SLA 1925 s.110(2).

[509] SLA 1925 s.75(5).

[510] *Re Cartwright* [1939] Ch. 90 at 103, 104, per Greene M.R.

[511] *Re Cartwright,* above.

[512] *Earl of Midleton v Baron Cottesloe* [1949] A.C. 418.

INDEX

LEGAL TAXONOMY
FROM SWEET & MAXWELL

This index has been prepared using Sweet & Maxwell's Legal Taxonomy. Main index entries conform to keywords provided by the Legal Taxonomy except where references to specific documents or non-standard terms (denoted by quotation marks) have been included. These keywords provide a means of identifying similar concepts in other Sweet & Maxwell publications and online services to which keywords from the Legal Taxonomy have been applied. Readers may find some minor differences between terms used in the text and those which appear in the index. Suggestions to *sweet&maxwell.taxonomy@thomson.com*.

Abandonment
easements, 29–009—29 012
profits a prendre, 29–009—29–012
Abatement
easements, 29–004
profits a prendre, 29–006
Absolute title
See also **First registration**
covenants, obligations and liabilities
incident to estate, 7–033—7–034
generally, 7–024—7–026
interests acquired under Limitation Act
with notice, 7–032
interests subject to entry in register as to
the estate, 7–027
overriding interests, 7–028—7–031
Abstract of title
consideration, 8–029
delivery, 8–028
Abstraction of water
fee simple, 3–050
Access to neighbouring land
access orders
effect, 30–037—30–038
grounds, 30–036
limited effect, 30–040
terms, 30–037—30–038
third parties, and, 30–039
common law, and, 30–035
Accretion
land registration, 7–118
right to everything in, over and on the
land, 3–037
Accumulations
See also **Rule against accumulations**
exceptions, 9–182—9–188
excessive accumulation, 9–172—9–176
generally, 9–162
overview, 1–004
rule in *Saunders v Vautier*, 9–180—9–181
statutory periods, 9–163—9–171
surplus income, 9–177—9–179
Acknowledgment
limitation periods, 35–051—35–052
Acquiescence
prescription, 28–049

Action of ejectment
See **Ejectment**
Actual occupation
See **Occupation**
Adjudicators
appointment, 7–130
Administration charges
generally, 19–092
Administration de bonis non
generally, 14–139
Administrators
vesting of legal estate, 14–139
Adopted children
intestacy, and, 14–127
wills, 14–073
Adverse possession
applications for registration
content, 35–076
effect of registration, 35–087—35–089
estoppel, 35–081
excluded applications, 35–075
form, 35–076
further applications, 35–085—35–086
general rule, 35 073—35–074
grounds for registration,
35–080—35–084
notices, 35–077
response to notices, 35 078—35–079
boundaries, 35–083—35–084
effect of registration, 35–087—35–089
estoppel, 35–081
first registration, 7–032
further applications, 35–085—35–086
grounds for registration
estoppel, 35–081
introduction, 35–080
mistake as to boundary,
35–083—35–084
other reasons entitling applicant, 35–082
unconscionable, 35–081
introduction, 35–070
limitation periods
animus possidendi, 35 019
beneficiary, by, 35–040
disapplication, 35–071—35 072
effect of lapse of time, 35–054

1577